THE EDINBURGH EDITION OF THE WAVERLEY NOVELS

VOLUME TWENTY-FIVE [B]

THE MAGNUM OPUS

EDINBURGH EDITION OF THE WAVERLEY NOVELS

in thirty volumes

Each novel is published separately but original conjoint publication of certain works is indicated in the EEWN volume numbering [4a, b; 7a, b, etc.].

1 Waverley [1814] P. D. Garside
2 Guy Mannering [1815] P. D. Garside
3 The Antiquary [1816] David Hewitt
4a The Black Dwarf [1816] P. D. Garside
4b The Tale of Old Mortality [1816] Douglas Mack
5 Rob Roy [1818] David Hewitt
6 The Heart of Mid-Lothian [1818] David Hewitt and Alison Lumsden
7a The Bride of Lammermoor [1819] J. H. Alexander
7b A Legend of the Wars of Montrose [1819] J. H. Alexander
8 Ivanhoe [1820] Graham Tulloch
9 The Monastery [1820] Penny Fielding
10 The Abbot [1820] Christopher Johnson
11 Kenilworth [1821] J. H. Alexander
12 The Pirate [1822] Mark Weinstein and Alison Lumsden
13 The Fortunes of Nigel [1822] Frank Jordan
14 Peveril of the Peak [1822] Alison Lumsden
15 Quentin Durward [1823] J. H. Alexander and G. A. M. Wood
16 Saint Ronan's Well [1824] Mark Weinstein
17 Redgauntlet [1824] G. A. M. Wood with David Hewitt
18a The Betrothed [1825] J. B. Ellis with others
18b The Talisman [1825] J. B. Ellis with others
19 Woodstock [1826] Tony Inglis with others
20 Chronicles of the Canongate [1827] Claire Lamont
21 The Fair Maid of Perth [1828] A. D. Hook and D. Mackenzie
22 Anne of Geierstein [1829] J. H. Alexander
23a Count Robert of Paris [1831] J. H. Alexander
23b Castle Dangerous [1831] J. H. Alexander
24 The Shorter Fiction Graham Tulloch and Judy King
25a Introductions and Notes from the Magnum Opus: Waverley to A Legend of the Wars of Montrose [1829–30] J. H. Alexander with others
25b Introductions and Notes from the Magnum Opus: Ivanhoe to Castle Dangerous [1830–33] J. H. Alexander with others

WALTER SCOTT

INTRODUCTIONS AND NOTES FROM

THE MAGNUM OPUS

IVANHOE
TO
CASTLE DANGEROUS

Edited by
J. H. Alexander
with
P. D. Garside and Claire Lamont

EDINBURGH
University
Press

Edinburgh University Press
22 George Square, Edinburgh

Typeset in Linotronic Ehrhardt
by Speedspools, Edinburgh
and printed and bound in Great Britain by
TJ Books Limited, Padstow, Cornwall

ISBN 978 0 7486 1491 2

A CIP record for this book is available from the British Library

MIX
Paper from responsible sources
FSC® C013056
FSC
www.fsc.org

CONTENTS

IVANHOE

Editorial Note

Ivanhoe fills Volume 1 and part of Volume 2 of the 1822 octavo *Historical Romances*, MSS 23013 and 23014 in the Interleaved Set. An entry in Scott's *Journal* suggests he began annotating the novel on 18 June 1829: 'At home I set to correct *Ivanhoe*. I had twenty other things more pressing but after all these novels deserve a preference' (*Journal*, 576). He was still working on the annotation on 3 December when he returned a copy of Richard Bannatyne's *Journal of the Transactions in Scotland* and requested a transcription of two passages from it for inclusion in a long note providing a Scottish parallel to the threatened torture of Isaac in Torquilstone (*Letters*, 11.268). On 18 December he told Cadell to 'send for the Volumes containing Ivanhoe which were ready' (MS 21043, f. 9v), but on 14 January 1830 Cadell sent him 'a Copy of Ivanhoe for the addition you wish to make to it' (MS 3912, f. 49r). However after Cadell asked him on 23 January for the additional material promised the day before, he recorded that Scott 'could not find the book from which he wished to make an extract', a problem resolved on 2 February when Cadell again 'asked him about a Note to Ivanhoe about Coningsburgh Castle about which there is some difficulty', and which Scott put right 'by cancelling part of what he wrote for it' (MS 21043, ff. 13v, 14r, 18v). Material in the Interleaved Set shows Scott had intended to end his disquisition on the relationship between Coningsburgh and the 'duns' and 'burghs' of Scotland by relating a story from 'the historian of the Orcades' of the attack and defence of one of these in a quarrel over a woman. Evidently he was later able to find his source, the Icelander Torfaeus, for he used the information in a note to *The Pirate* (see 155–56 below). But for the Magnum he changed the end of the note so that it concludes with Gough's description of the castle, supplied in a copy by John Buchanan. One strange consequence of this uncertainty was that Scott, in his confusion, produced another version of the note which had the Gough termination in view from the outset. It is shorter than the original version that was adopted:

> I could have wishd that leisure had permitted me to take a nearer view ⟨of this celebrated Castle⟩ and afford the reader a more accurate description of this very curious fabrick whis is so interesting both to the admirer of romantic scenery and the professd antiquary. But I was deprived of the opportunity by the circumstances under which I was travelling at the time. I was induced however to form an opinion which better antiquaries with ⟨more⟩ time for more minute research may be ⟨af⟩ able to refute or to confirm. The round Keep or principal ⟨p⟩ tower seems to me especially curious as the connecting step between the Duns or Burgs as ⟨those⟩ the ⟨?rug⟩ rude remains of those fortresses are calld which are to be found in numbers in the Zetland islands and Hebrides and also on the Scottish continent. The ruins of that in Glenelg calld Dun-Dornadilla is engraved by ⟨?sp⟩ Pennant but a far more perfect specimen exists in the Castle or Burg on the Island of Mousa in Zetland which is almost entire. ↑NL↓ These buildings the most ancient probably of a defensive character that exist are obviously executed by a people who did not know the use of cement in building who could not throw an arch or raise a stair & had not or could not use wood for the purpose of rafters. Yet they have a species of architecture belonging to themselves and indicate ⟨st⟩ som share of skill and contrivance. NL They have a circular form of various diameter in the shape of an old fashiond pigeon-house. The walls are composed loose stones built ⟨with⟩ compactly and with much neatness. They have no windows to the exterior. But to the inner circle inclosed by the walls there are four regular⟨ly⟩ ⟨apertures⟩ ↑sets of openings↓ looking to the four points of the compass & rising ⟨f⟩ ⟨the one above the⟩ each above the other from the bottom of the area to the top of the building These served to give light and air to a series ⟨rin⟩ of concentric rings or galleries within the thickness of the wall which are placed one above the other rising on the same scale with the windows to the top of the burgh. The construction of these galleries is of the most simple description. The wall being double the inner and outer walls are connected regularly by layers of long flat stones each course of which forms the floor of one of these galleries and the roof of ⟨the one⟩ ↑that↓

which is beneath. Undoubtedly the garrison had their lodging in these galleries and a fire kindled in the centrical area would dispense to them some share of heat.

The mode of access is as primitive as the rest of the construction a slopin ascent or inclined ↑plain↓ winds round the internal part of the wall like a cork-screw cutting each gallery as it ascend [end of line] ascends and thus gaining the top of the incosure.

Some acquaintance with these very original buildings induced me to think that I saw particulars about Coningsburgh Castle which seemd to it belonged to class of fortresses which though far advanced before the Burghs or Duns in as much as the builders understood the art of the arch and the roof together with that of using cement still shows the source in which its originated by its round shape its excavation in the walls and the rude mode of access from one storey to another.

That some better antiquary may have the means of following out the train of ideas suggested by the resemblance of this Saxon castle to the species of architecture used by the Scandinavians in their earlier stage I add Goughs description of ⟨Con⟩ [eol] Coningsburgh

In the meantime Cadell had been revising Scott's introduction and notes, recording the activity in his diary between 6 January and 8 February 1830 (MS 21020, ff. 3v–8v). However Scott was not finished with *Ivanhoe*, and on 20 April he sent a short letter with 'an additional note to Ivanhoe which is I presume in time to be inserted' (both are now bound into the Interleaved Set). Scott had been criticised for a heraldic solecism in placing an azure (blue) device against a sable (black) background—that is, colour on colour. Obviously upset by the imputation that he was ignorant of a fundamental rule of heraldry, he had already added a note defending himself on the grounds that he was depicting an early stage of heraldry which 'had only its first rude origin during the crusades'. Now he inserted a further corroboration of this, discussing the arms granted to Godfrey of Boulogne in the First Crusade. At this late stage in the setting of the text the extra material was not added to the existing note but printed rather awkwardly at the end of the chapter where Scott had directed it should be placed (perhaps because he no longer had the relevant volume of the Interleaved Set to show him where the earlier note had been inserted).

The Magnum Introduction provides a supplement to the first edition's 'Dedicatory Epistle'. Written in the voice of the supposed author of the novel, Laurence Templeton, the 'Epistle' reflects on Scott's radical change of geographical and historical setting as he moved from the seventeenth- and eighteenth-century Scottish settings of his previous novels to twelfth-century England, offering some information about the historical sources he was planning to use. In the Magnum introduction, writing now in his own voice and using new images to convey his ideas, Scott again addresses the issue of his major change of direction. This time, however, he dwells on the literary sources of the novel, and in particular the ballad 'The King and the Hermit', on which he had modelled two early chapters of the first edition's second volume. He also reveals the source of the hero's name in an 'old rhyme' and suggests that it was John Logan's play *Runnamede* which gave him the idea of contrasting the Saxons and Normans.

Like the Introduction, the notes to *Ivanhoe* supplement existing material from the first edition. From the beginning *Ivanhoe* had had an unusually large number of footnotes, intended to help Scott's readers with his move to a more remote period of history. Over the initials 'L.T.', they mostly explained unfamiliar terms either with simple glosses or with longer commentary. In the Magnum Scott adds further glosses and short explanations as footnotes, but slips up in glossing 'rotes', having missed the fact that it was already glossed on the previous page as part of a note on 'crowths'. There are also some seventeen longer notes, presented either as footnotes or endnotes: the two longest (on Scottish torture and on Coningsburgh) have already been mentioned. In notes on negro slaves in the Middle Ages, on Richard as a minstrel and his singing of an English song, and on the heathen nature of Ulrica's death-song, Scott defends himself against possible charges of anachronism, but he also takes the opportunity to correct a 'great geographical blunder', his confusion of Stamford and Stamford Bridge as the site of the battle between King Harold and his brother in 1066 which had been pointed out to him by Robert Belt of Yorkshire: this entails rewriting part of the text. Scott's final and most revealing note explains that it was James Ballantyne's 'vehement entreaties' that led him to the improbable resuscitation of Athelstane after his apparent death in battle.

There are four Magnum illustrations for this title. The frontispiece to Volume 16 (MAG0031 / TB348.16) was designed by John Martin and engraved by Edward J. Portbury. It depicts Rebecca rebuffing the advances of Bois-Guilbert as both stand on the ramparts of Torquilstone Castle (EEWN 8, 200.2–5: ' "Here," she said, "I take my stand . . . to the Templar" '). The title-page vignette

(MAG0032 / TB348.16) was designed by John Cawse and engraved by W. James Taylor. It depicts Gurth and Wamba in conversation in the forest, with accompanying mongrel hound (EEWN 8, 21.43–22.9 (abridged): ' "Gurth," said the Jester . . . a wise man:'). The frontispiece to Volume 17 (MAG0033 / TB348.17) was designed by William Boxall and engraved by Robert Graves. It depicts Rebecca saying farewell to Rowena, and declining to convert to Christianity (EEWN 8, 400.39–42: ' "No, lady" . . . in which I seek to dwell." '). The title-page vignette (MAG0034 / TB348.17) was designed by Solomon Alexander Hart and engraved by Samuel Davenport. It depicts Isaac delivering a letter to Beaumanoir in the garden at the Preceptory of Templestowe (EEWN 8, 309.20–22: ' "Back, dog!" . . . and give it to me.').

John Martin. E. Portbury.

IVANHOE.

'Here,' she said, "I take my stand. Remain where thou art; and if thou shalt attempt to diminish by one step the distance now between us, thou shalt see that the Jewish maiden will rather trust her soul with God, than her honour to the Templar"

PUBLISHED 1830. BY R. CADELL EDINBURGH. & WHITTAKER &Cº LONDON.

WAVERLEY NOVELS.

VOL. XVI.

IVANHOE.

"Gurth", said the Jester, "I know thou thinkest me a fool, or thou would'st not be so rash in putting thy head into my mouth.
"Dog, thou would'st not betray me," said Gurth.
Betray thee!" answered the Jester" no that were the trick of a wise man:

PRINTED FOR ROBERT CADELL EDINBURGH.
AND WHITTAKER & Co. LONDON.
1830.

W. Boxall. R. Graves.

IVANHOE.

"No, lady," answered Rebecca, the same calm melancholy reigning in her soft voice and beautiful features— "that may not be. I may not change the faith of my fathers like a garment unsuited to the climate in which I seek to dwell."

PUBLISHED 1830, BY R. CADELL, EDINBURGH & WHITTAKER & Cº LONDON.

WAVERLEY NOVELS.

VOL. XVII.

IVANHOE.

"Back dog!" said the Grand Master; "I touch not misbe-lievers, save with the sword.—Conrade, take thou the letter from the Jew, and give it to me.

PRINTED FOR ROBERT CADELL EDINBURGH.
AND WHITTAKER & Co LONDON.
1830.

Introduction to Ivanhoe

THE Author of the Waverley Novels had hitherto proceeded in an unabated course of popularity, and might, in his peculiar district of literature, have been termed *L'Enfant Gâté* of success. It was plain, however, that frequent publication must finally wear out the public favour, unless some mode could be devised to give an appearance of novelty to subsequent productions. Scottish manners, Scottish dialect, and Scottish characters of note, being those with which the author was most intimately and familiarly acquainted, were the groundwork upon which he had hitherto relied for giving effect to his narrative. It was, however, obvious, that this kind of interest must in the end occasion a degree of sameness and repetition, if exclusively resorted to, and that the reader was likely at length to adopt the language of Edwin, in Parnell's Tale:—

——"Reverse the spell," he cries,
"And let it fairly now suffice,
The gambol has been shown."

Nothing can be more dangerous for the fame of a professor of the fine arts, than to permit (if he can possibly prevent it) the character of a mannerist to be attached to him, or that he should be supposed capable of success only in a particular and limited style. The public are, in general, very ready to adopt the opinion, that he who has pleased them in one peculiar mode of composition, is, by means of that very talent, rendered incapable of venturing upon other subjects. The effect of this disinclination, on the part of the public, towards the artificers of their pleasures, when they attempt to enlarge their means of amusing, may be seen in the censures usually passed by vulgar criticism upon actors or artists who venture to change the character of their efforts, that, in so doing, they may enlarge the scale of their art.

There is some justice in this opinion, as there always is in such as attain general currency. It may often happen on the stage, that an actor, by possessing in a pre-eminent degree the external qualities necessary to give effect to comedy, may be deprived of the right to aspire to tragic excellence; and in painting or literary composition, an artist or poet may be master exclusively of modes of thought, and powers of expression, which confine him to a single course of subjects. But much more frequently the same capacity which carries a man to popularity in one department will obtain for him success in another, and that must be more particularly the case in literary composition, than either in acting or painting, because the adventurer in that department is not impeded in his exertions by any peculiarity of features, or conformation of person, proper for particular parts, or, by any peculiar mechanical habits of using the pencil, limited to a particular class of subjects.

Whether this reasoning be correct or otherwise, the present author felt, that, in confining himself to subjects purely Scottish, he was not only like to weary out the indulgence of his readers, but also greatly to limit his own power of affording them pleasure. In a highly polished country, where so much genius is monthly employed in catering for public amusement, a fresh topic, such as he had himself had the happiness to light upon, is the untasted spring of the desert;—

> Men bless their stars and call it luxury.

But when men and horses, cattle, camels, and dromedaries, have poached the spring into mud, it becomes loathsome to those who at first drank of it with rapture; and he who had the merit of discovering it, if he would preserve his reputation with the tribe, must display his talent by a fresh discovery of untasted fountains.

If the author, who finds himself limited to a particular class of subjects, endeavours to sustain his reputation by striving to add a novelty of attraction to themes of the same character which have been formerly successful under his management, there are manifest reasons why, after a certain point, he is likely to fail. If the mine be not wrought out, the strength and capacity of the miner become necessarily exhausted. If he closely imitates the narratives which he has before rendered successful, he is doomed to "wonder that they please no more." If he struggles to take a different view of the same class of subjects, he speedily discovers that what is obvious, graceful, and natural, has been exhausted; and, in order to obtain the indispensable charm of novelty, he is forced upon caricature, and, to avoid being trite, must become extravagant.

It is not, perhaps, necessary to enumerate so many reasons why the author of the Scottish Novels, as they were then exclusively termed, should be desirous to make an experiment on a subject purely English. It was his purpose, at the same time, to have rendered the experiment as complete as possible, by bringing the intended work before the public as the effort of a new candidate for their favour, in order that no degree of prejudice, whether favourable or the reverse, might attach to it, as a new production of the Author of Waverley; but this purpose was afterwards departed from, for reasons to be hereafter mentioned.

The period of the narrative adopted was the reign of Richard I., not only as abounding with characters whose very names were sure to attract attention in every bosom, but as affording a striking contrast betwixt the Saxons, by whom the soil was cultivated, and the Normans, who still reigned in it as conquerors, reluctant to mix themselves with the vanquished, or acknowledge themselves of the same stock. The idea of this contrast was taken from the ingenious and unfortunate Logan's tragedy of Runnamede, in which, about the same period of history, the author had seen the Saxon and Norman barons opposed to each other on different sides of the stage. He does not recollect that there was any attempt to contrast the two races in their habits and sentiments; and indeed it was obvious, that history was violated by introducing the Saxons still existing as a high-minded and martial race of nobles.

They did, however, survive as a people, and some of the ancient Saxon families possessed wealth and power, although they were exceptions to the humble condition of the race in general. It seemed to the author, that the existence of the two races in the same country, the vanquished distinguished by their plain, homely, blunt manners, and the free spirit infused by their ancient institutions and laws; the victors, by the high spirit of military fame, personal adventure, and whatever could distinguish them as the Flower of Chivalry, might, intermixed with other characters belonging to the same time and country, interest the reader by the contrast, if the author should not fail on his part.

Scotland, however, had been of late used so exclusively as the scene of what is called Historical Romance, that the preliminary letter of Mr Laurence Templeton became in some measure necessary. To this, as to an Introduction, the reader is referred, as expressing the author's purpose and opinions in undertaking this species of composition, under the necessary reservation, that he is far from thinking he has attained the point at which he aimed.

It is scarce necessary to add, that there was no idea or wish to pass off the supposed Mr Templeton as a real person. But a species of continuation of the Tales of my Landlord had been recently attempted by a stranger, and it was supposed this Dedicatory Epistle might pass for some imitation of the same kind, and thus putting enquirers upon a false scent, induce them to believe they had before them the work of some new candidate for their favour.

After a considerable part of the work had been finished and printed, the Publishers, who pretended to discern in it a germ of popularity, remonstrated strenuously against its appearing as an absolutely anonymous production, and contended that it should have the advantage of being announced as by the Author of Waverley. The author did not make any obstinate opposition, for he began to be of opinion with Dr Wheeler, in Miss Edgeworth's excellent tale of "Manœuvring," that "Trick upon Trick" might be too much for the patience of an indulgent public, and might be reasonably considered as trifling with their favour.

The book, therefore, appeared as an avowed continuation of the Waverley Novels; and it would be ungrateful not to acknowledge, that it met with the same favourable reception as its predecessors.

Such annotations as may be useful to assist the reader in comprehending the characters of the Jew, the Templar, the Captain of the mercenaries, or Free Companions, as they were called, and others proper to the period, are added, but with a sparing hand, since sufficient information on these subjects is to be found in general history.

An incident in the tale, which had the good fortune to find favour in the eyes of many readers, is more directly borrowed from the stores of old romance. I mean the meeting of the King with Friar Tuck at the cell of that buxom hermit. The general tone of the story belongs to all ranks and all countries, which emulate each other in describing the rambles of a disguised sovereign, who, going in search of information or amusement, into the lower ranks of life, meets with adventures diverting to the reader or hearer, from the contrast betwixt the monarch's outward appearance, and his real character. Thus the Eastern tale-teller has for his theme the disguised expeditions of Haroun Alraschid with his faithful attendants, Mesrour and Giafar, through the midnight streets of Bagdad; and Scottish tradition dwells upon the similar exploits of James V., distinguished during such excursions by the travelling name of the Goodman of Ballengeigh, as the Commander of the Faithful, when he desired to be incognito, was known by that of Il Bondocani. The French minstrels are not silent on so popular a theme. There must have been a Norman original of the Scottish metrical romance of Rauf Colziar, in which Charlemagne is introduced as the unknown guest of a charcoal-man.* It seems to have been the original of other poems of the kind.

In merry England there is no end of popular ballads on this theme. The poem of John the Reeve, or Steward, mentioned by Bishop Percy, in the Reliques of English Poetry,† is said to have

* This very curious poem, long a *desideratum* in Scottish literature, and given up as irrecoverably lost, was lately brought to light by the researches of Dr Irvine of the Advocates' Library, and has been reprinted by Mr David Laing, Edinburgh.

† Vol. ii. p. 167.

turned on such an incident; and we have besides, the King and the Tanner of Tamworth, the King and the Miller of Mansfield, and others on the same topic. But the peculiar tale of this nature to which the author of Ivanhoe has to acknowledge an obligation, is more ancient by two centuries than any of these last mentioned.

It was first communicated to the public in that curious record of ancient literature, which has been accumulated by the combined exertions of Sir Egerton Brydges and Mr Hazlewood, in the periodical work entitled the British Bibliographer. From thence it has been transferred by the Reverend Charles Henry Hartshorne, M.A., editor of a very curious volume, entitled "Ancient Metrical Tales, printed chiefly from original sources, 1829." Mr Hartshorne gives no other authority for the present fragment, except the article in the Bibliographer, where it is entitled the Kyng and the Hermite. A short abstract of its contents will show its similarity to the meeting of King Richard and Friar Tuck.

King Edward (we are not told which among the monarchs of that name, but, from his temper and habits, we may suppose Edward IV.) sets forth with his court to a gallant hunting-match in Sherwood Forest, in which, as is not unusual for princes in romance, he falls in with a deer of extraordinary size and swiftness, and pursues it closely, till he has outstripped his whole retinue, tired out hounds and horse, and finds himself alone under the gloom of an extensive forest, upon which night is descending. Under the apprehensions natural to a situation so uncomfortable, the king recollects that he has heard how poor men, when apprehensive of a bad night's lodging, pray to Saint Julian, who, in the Romish calendar, stands Quarter-Master-General to all forlorn travellers that render him due homage. Edward puts up his orisons accordingly, and by the guidance, doubtless, of the good Saint, reaches a small path, conducting him to a chapel in the forest, having a hermit's cell in its close vicinity. The King hears the reverend man, with a companion of his solitude, telling his beads within, and meekly requests of him quarters for the night. "I have no accommodation for such a lord as ye be," said the Hermit. "I live here in the wilderness upon roots and rinds, and may not receive into my dwelling even the poorest wretch that lives, unless it were to save his life." The King enquires the way to the next town, and, understanding it is by a road which he cannot find without difficulty, even if he had daylight to befriend him, he declares, that with or without the Hermit's consent, he is determined to be his guest that night. He is admitted accordingly, not without a hint from the Recluse, that were he himself out of his priestly weeds, he would care little for his threats of using violence, and that he gives way to him not out of intimidation, but simply to avoid scandal.

The King is admitted into the cell—two bundles of straw are shaken down for his accommodation, and he comforts himself that he is now under shelter, and that

A night will soon be gone.

Other wants, however, arise. The guest becomes clamorous for supper, observing,

"For certainly, as I you say,
I ne had never so sorry a day,
  That I ne had a merry night."

But this indication of his taste for good cheer, joined to the annunciation of his being a follower of the Court, who had lost himself at the great hunting-match, cannot induce the niggard Hermit to produce better fare than bread and cheese, for which his guest showed little appetite; and "thin drink," which was even less acceptable. At length the King presses his host on a point to which he had more than once alluded, without obtaining a satisfactory reply:

Then said the King, "by Godys grace,
Thou wones in a merry place,
  To shoot thou should lere;
When the foresters go to rest,
Sometyme thou might have of the best,
  All of the wild deer;
I wold hold it for no scathe,
Though thou hadst bow and arrows baith,
  Althoff thou best a Frere."

The Hermit, in return, expresses his apprehension that his guest means to drag him into some confession of offence against the forest laws, which, being betrayed to the King, might cost him his life. Edward answers by fresh assurances of secrecy, and again urges on him the necessity of producing some venison. The Hermit replies, by once more insisting on the duties incumbent upon him as a churchman, and continues to affirm himself free from all such breaches of order:—

"Many day I have here been,
And flesh-meat I eat never,
  But milk of the kye;
Warm thee well, and go to sleep,
And I will lap thee with my cope,
  Softly to lye."

It would seem that the manuscript is here imperfect, for we do not find the reasons which finally induce the curtal Friar to amend the King's cheer. But acknowledging his guest to be such a "good fellow" as has seldom graced his board, the holy man at length produces the best his cell affords. Two candles are placed on a table, white bread and baked pasties are displayed by the light, besides choice of venison, both salt and fresh, from which they select collops. "I might have eat my bread dry," said the King, "had I not pressed thee on the score of archery, but now have I dined like a prince—if we had but drink enow."

This too is afforded by the hospitable anchorite, who dispatches an assistant to fetch a pot of four gallons from a secret corner near his bed, and the whole three set in to serious drinking. This amusement is superintended by the Friar, according to the recurrence of certain fustian words, to be repeated by every compotator in turn before he drank—a species of High Jinks, as it were, by which they regulated their potations, as toasts were given in latter times. The one toper says *fusty bandias*, to which the other is obliged to reply, *strike pantnere*, and the Friar passes many jests on the King's want of memory, who sometimes forgets the words of action. The night is spent in this jolly pastime. Before his departure in the morning, the King invites his reverend host to Court, promises to requite his hospitality at least, and expresses himself much pleased with his entertainment. The jolly Hermit at length consents to venture thither, and to enquire for Jack Fletcher, which is the name assumed by the King. After the Hermit has shown Edward some feats of archery, the joyous pair separate. The King rides home, and rejoins his retinue. As the romance is imperfect, we are not acquainted how the discovery takes place; but it is probably much in the same manner as in other narratives turning on the same subject, where the host, apprehensive of death for having trespassed on the respect due to his Sovereign, while incognito, is agreeably surprised by receiving honours and reward.

In Mr Hartshorne's collection, there is a romance on the same foundation, called King Edward and the Shepherd,* which, considered as illustrating manners, is still more curious than the King and the Hermit; but it is foreign to the present purpose. The reader has here the original legend from which the incident in the romance is derived; and the identifying the irregular Eremite with the Friar Tuck of Robin Hood's story, was an obvious expedient.

The name of Ivanhoe was suggested by an old rhyme. All novelists have had occasion at some time or other to wish with Falstaff, that

* Like the Hermit, the Shepherd makes havock amongst the King's game; but by means of a sling, not of a bow; like the Hermit, too, he has his peculiar phrases of compotation, the sign and countersign being Passilodion and Berafriend. One can scarce conceive what humour our ancestors found in this species of gibberish; but

I warrant it proved an excuse for the glass.

they knew where a commodity of good names was to be had. On such an occasion the author chanced to call to memory a rhyme recording three names of the manors forfeited by the ancestor of the celebrated Hampden, for striking the Black Prince a blow with his racket, when they quarrelled at tennis;—

> Tring, Wing, and Ivanhoe,
> For striking of a blow,
> Hampden did forego,
> And glad he could escape so.

The word suited the author's purpose in two material respects, —for, first, it had an ancient English sound; and secondly, it conveyed no indication whatever of the nature of the story. He presumes to hold this last quality to be of no small importance. What is called a *taking* title, serves the direct interest of the bookseller or publisher, who by this means sometimes sells an edition while it is yet passing the press. But if the author permits an over degree of attention to be drawn to his work ere it has appeared, he places himself in the embarrassing condition of having excited a degree of expectation which he proves unable to satisfy, an error fatal to his literary reputation. Besides, when we meet such a title as the Gunpowder Plot, or any other connected with general history, each reader, before he has even seen the book, has formed to himself some particular idea of the sort of manner in which the story is to be conducted, and the nature of the amusement which he is to derive from it. In this he is probably disappointed, and in that case may be naturally disposed to visit upon the author or the work, the unpleasant feelings thus excited. In such a case the literary adventurer is censured, not for having missed the mark at which he himself aimed, but for not having shot off his shaft in a direction he never thought of.

On the footing of unreserved communication which the Author has established with the reader, he may here add the trifling circumstance, that a roll of Norman warriors, occurring in the Auchinleck Manuscript, gave him the formidable name of Front-de-Bœuf.

Ivanhoe was highly successful upon its appearance, and may be said to have procured for its author the freedom of the Rules, since he has ever since been permitted to exercise his powers of fictitious composition in England, as well as Scotland.

The character of the fair Jewess found so much favour in the eyes of some fair readers, that the writer was censured, because, when arranging the fates of the characters of the drama, he had not assigned the hand of Wilfred to Rebecca, rather than the less interesting Rowena. But, not to mention that the prejudices of the age rendered such an union almost impossible, the author may, in passing, observe, that he thinks a character of a highly virtuous and lofty stamp, is degraded rather than exalted by an attempt to reward virtue with temporal prosperity. Such is not the recompense which Providence has deemed worthy of suffering merit, and it is a dangerous and fatal doctrine to teach young persons, the most common readers of romance, that rectitude of conduct and of principle is either naturally allied with, or adequately rewarded by, the gratification of our passions, or attainment of our wishes. In a word, if a virtuous and self-denied character is dismissed with temporal wealth, greatness, rank, or the indulgence of such a rashly formed or ill assorted passion as that of Rebecca for Ivanhoe, the reader will be apt to say, verily Virtue has had its reward. But a glance on the great picture of life will show, that the duties of self-denial, and the sacrifice of passion to principle, are seldom thus remunerated; and that the internal consciousness of their high-minded discharge of duty, produces on their own reflections a more adequate recompense, in the form of that peace which the world cannot give or take away.

ABBOTSFORD, *1st September*, 1830.

Notes to Ivanhoe

1.6 (title-page) loth to depart The motto alludes to the Author returning to the stage repeatedly after having taken leave.

9.33 (Dedicatory Epistle) Queen-Hoo-Hall The author had revised this posthumous work of Mr Strutt. See General Preface to the present edition, Vol. 25a. pp. 34–36.

13.29 (Dedicatory Epistle) Secretary to the Antiquarian Society Mr Skene of Rubislaw is here intimated, to whose taste and skill the author is indebted for a series of etchings, exhibiting the various localities alluded to in these novels.

20.33 (Ch. 1) unfit for their trade

THE RANGER OF THE FOREST, THAT CUTS THE FORE-CLAWS OFF OUR DOGS. A most sensible grievance of these aggrieved times were the Forest Laws. These oppressive enactments were all the produce of the Norman Conquest, for the Saxon laws of the chase were mild and humane; while those of William, enthusiastically attached to the exercise and its rights, were to the last degree tyrannical. The formation of the New Forest bears evidence to his passion for hunting, where he reduced many a happy village to the condition of that one commemorated by my friend, Mr William Stewart Rose,

> Amongst the ruins of the church
> The midnight raven found a perch,
>   A melancholy place;
> The ruthless Conqueror cast down,
> Woe worth the deed, that little town,
>   To lengthen out his chase.

The disabling dogs, which might be necessary for keeping flocks and herds, from running at the deer, was called *lawing*, and was in general use. The Charter of the Forest, designed to lessen those evils, declares that inquisition, or view, for lawing dogs, shall be made every third year, and shall be then done by the view and testimony of lawful men, not otherwise; and they whose dogs shall be then found unlawed, shall give three shillings for mercy; and for the future, no man's ox shall be taken for lawing. Such lawing also shall be done by the assize commonly used, and which is, that three claws shall be cut off without the ball of the right foot. See on this subject the Historical Essay on the Magna Charta of King John, (a most beautiful volume,) by Richard Thomson.

25.17 (Ch. 2) some distant eastern country

NEGRO SLAVES. The severe accuracy of some critics has objected to the complexion of the slaves of Brian de Bois-Guilbert, as being totally out of costume and propriety. I remember the same objection being made to a set of sable functionaries, whom my friend, Mat Lewis, introduced as the guards and mischief-doing satellites of the wicked Baron, in his Castle Spectre. Mat treated the objection with great contempt, and averred in reply, that he made the slaves black, in order to obtain a striking effect of contrast, and that, could he have derived a similar advantage from making his heroine blue, blue she should have been.

I do not pretend to plead the immunities of my order so highly as this; but neither will I allow that the author of a modern antique romance is obliged to confine himself to the introduction of those manners only which can be proved to have absolutely existed in the times he is depicting, so that he restrain himself to such as are plausible and natural, and contain no obvious anachronism. In this point of view, what can be more natural, than that the Templars, who, we know, copied closely the luxuries of the Asiatic warriors with whom they fought, should use the service of the enslaved Africans, whom the fate of war transferred to new masters? I am sure, if there are no precise proofs of their having done so, there is nothing, on the other hand, that can entitle us positively to conclude that they never did. Besides, there is an instance in romance.

John of Rampayne, an excellent juggler and minstrel, undertook to effect the escape of one Audulf de Bracy, by presenting himself in disguise at the court of the king, where he was confined. For this purpose, "he stained his hair and his whole body entirely as black as jet, so that nothing was white but his teeth," and succeeded in imposing himself on the king, as an Ethiopian minstrel. He effected, by stratagem, the escape of the prisoner. Negroes, therefore, must have been known in England in the dark ages.*

37.38 (Ch. 3) hership Pillage.

49.9 (Ch. 5) Sir Tristrem There was no language which the Normans more formally separated from that of common life than the terms of the chase. The objects of their pursuit, whether bird or animal, changed their name each year, and there were a hundred conventional terms, to be ignorant of which was to be without one of the distinguishing marks of a gentleman. The reader may consult Dame Juliana Berners' book on the subject. The origin of this science was imputed to the celebrated Sir Tristrem, famous for his tragic intrigue with the beautiful Ysolte. As the Normans reserved the amusement of hunting strictly to themselves, the terms of this formal jargon were all taken from the French language.

67.26 (Ch. 7) during the game This species of masquerade is supposed to have occasioned the introduction of supporters into the science of heraldry.

79.4 (Ch. 8) we trust These lines are part of an unpublished poem by Coleridge, whose muse so often tantalizes with fragments which indicate her powers, while the manner in which she flings them from her betrays her caprice, yet whose unfinished sketches display more talent than the laboured masterpieces of others.

80.31 (Ch. 8) the attaint This term of chivalry transferred to the law, gives the phrase of being attainted of treason.

92.21 (Ch. 9) outrecuidance Presumption, insolence.

147.43 (Ch. 16) make the harp-strings tinkle

THE JOLLY HERMIT.—All readers, however slightly acquainted with black letter, must recognise in the Clerk of Copmanhurst, Friar Tuck, the buxom Confessor of Robin Hood's gang, the Curtal Friar of Fountain's Abbey.

148.30 (Ch. 17) a ballat in the vulgar English

MINSTRELSY. The realm of France, it is well known, was divided betwixt the Norman and Teutonic race, who spoke the language in which the word Yes is pronounced as *oui*, and the inhabitants of the southern regions, whose speech bearing some affinity to the

* Dissertation on Romance and Minstrelsy, prefixed to Ritson's Ancient Metrical Romances, p. clxxxvii.

Italian, pronounced the same word *oc*. The poets of the former race were called *Minstrels*, and their poems *Lays:* those of the latter were termed *Troubadours*, and their compositions called *sirventes*, and other names. Richard, a professed admirer of the joyous science in all its branches, could imitate either the minstrel or troubadour. It is less likely that he should have been able to compose or sing an English ballad; yet so much do we wish to assimilate Him of the Lion Heart to the land of the warriors whom he led, that the anachronism, if there be one, may readily be forgiven.

176.10 (Ch. 21) (Magnum variant) [For Ed1 'the walls of Stamford, and the fatal Welland renowned in prophecy,*' the Magnum text has 'the distant towers of York, and the bloody streams of the Derwent,*'. The present chapter endnote replaces the footnote in Ed1.]

BATTLE OF STAMFORD. A great topographical blunder occurred here in former editions. The bloody battle alluded to in the text, fought and won by King Harold, over his brother the rebellious Tosti, and an auxiliary force of Danes or Norsemen, was said, in the text, and a corresponding note, to have taken place at Stamford, in Leicestershire, and upon the river Welland. This is a mistake, into which the author has been led by trusting to his memory, and so confounding two places of the same name. The Stamford, Strangford, or Staneford, at which the battle really was fought, is a ford upon the river Derwent, at the distance of about seven miles from York, and situated in that large and opulent county. A long wooden bridge over the Derwent, the site of which, with one remaining buttress, is still shown to the curious traveller, was furiously contested. One Norwegian long defended it by his single arm, and was at length pierced with a spear thrust through the planks from a boat beneath.

The neighbourhood of Stamford, on the Derwent, contains some memorials of the battle. Horseshoes, swords, and the heads of halberds, or bills, are often found there; one place is called the "Danes' well," another the "Battle flats." From a tradition that the weapon with which the Norwegian champion was slain, resembled a pear, or, as others say, that the trough or boat in which the soldier floated under the bridge to strike the blow, had such a shape, the country people usually begin a great market, which is held at Stamford, with an entertainment called the Pear-pie feast, which after all may be a corruption of the Spear-pie feast. For more particulars, Drake's History of York may be referred to. The author's mistake was pointed out to him, in the most obliging manner, by Robert Belt, Esq. of Bossal House. The battle was fought in 1066.

182.26 (Ch. 22) that glowing charcoal

THE RANGE OF IRON BARS ABOVE THAT GLOWING CHARCOAL. This horrid species of torture may remind the reader of that to which the Spaniards subjected Guatimozin, in order to extort a discovery of his concealed wealth. But, in fact, an instance of similar barbarity is to be found nearer home, and occurs in the annals of Queen Mary's time, containing so many other examples of atrocity. Every reader must recollect, that after the fall of the Catholic Church, and the Presbyterian Church Government had been established by law, the rank, and especially the wealth, of the Bishops, Abbots, Priors, and so forth, were no longer vested in ecclesiastics, but in lay impropriators of the church revenues, or, as the Scottish lawyers called them, *titulars* of the temporalities of the benefice, though having no claim to the spiritual character of their predecessors in office.

If these laymen, who were thus invested with ecclesiastical revenues, were men of high birth and rank, like the famous Lord James Stewart, the Prior of St Andrews, they did not fail to keep for their own use the rents, lands, and revenues of the church. If, on the other hand, the titulars were men of inferior importance, who had been inducted into the office by the interest of some powerful person, it was generally understood that the new Abbot should grant for his patron's benefit such leases and conveyances of the church lands and tithes as might afford their protector the lion's share of the booty. This was the origin of those who were wittily termed Tulchan* Bishops, being a sort of imaginary prelate, whose image was set up to enable his patron and principal to plunder the benefice under his name.

There were other cases, however, in which men who had got grants of these secularised benefices, were desirous of retaining them for their own use, without having the influence sufficient to establish their purpose; and these became frequently unable to protect themselves, however unwilling to submit to the exactions of the feudal tyrant of the district.

Bannatyne, secretary to John Knox, recounts a singular course of oppression practised on one of those titular abbots, by the Earl of Cassilis in Ayrshire, whose extent of feudal influence was so wide that he was usually termed the King of Carrick. We give the fact as it occurs in Bannatyne's Journal, only premising that the

* A *Tulchan* is a calf's skin stuffed, and placed before a cow who has lost its calf, to induce the animal to part with her milk. The resemblance between such a Tulchan and a Bishop named to transmit the temporalities of a benefice to some powerful patron, is easily understood.

Journalist held his master's opinions, both with respect to the Earl of Cassilis as an opposer of the king's party, and as being a detester of the practice of granting church revenues to titulars, instead of their being devoted to pious uses, such as the support of the clergy, expense of schools, and the relief of the national poor. He mingles in the narrative, therefore, a well deserved feeling of execration against the tyrant who employed the torture, with a tone of ridicule towards the patient, as if, after all, it had not been ill bestowed on such an equivocal and amphibious character as a titular abbot. He entitles his narrative,

THE EARL OF CASSILIS' TYRANNY AGAINST A QUICK (*i.e.* LIVING) MAN.

"Master Allan Stewart, friend to Captain James Stewart of Cardonall, by means of the Queen's corrupted court, obtained the abbacy of Crossraguel. The said Earl thinking himself greater than any king in those quarters, determined to have that whole benefice (as he hath divers others) to pay at his pleasure; and because he could not find sic security as his insatiable appetite required, this shift was devised. The said Mr Allan being in company with the Laird of Bargany, (also a Kennedy,) was, by the Earl and his friends, enticed to leave the safeguard which he had with the Laird, and come to make good cheer with the said Earl. The simplicity of the imprudent man was suddenly abused; and so he passed his time with them certain days, which he did in Maybole with Thomas Kennedie, uncle to the said Earl: after which the said Mr Allan passed, with quiet company, to visit the place and bounds of Crossraguel, [his abbacy,] of which the said Earl being surely advertised, determined to put in practice the tyranny which long before he had conceaved. And so, as king of the country, apprehended the said Mr Allan, and carried him to the house of Dunure, where for a season he was honourably treated, (gif a prisoner can think any entertainment pleasing;) but after that certain days were spent, and that the Earl could not obtain the feus of Crossraguel according to his awin appetite, he determined to prove gif a collation could work that which neither dinner nor supper could do for a long time. And so the said Mr Allan was carried to a secret chamber: with him passed the honourable Earl, his worshipful brother, and such as were appointed to be servants at that banquet. In the chamber there was a grit iron chimlay, under it a fire; other grit provision was not seen. The first course was,—'My Lord Abbot,' (said the Earl,) 'it will please you confess here, that with your own consent you remain in my company, because ye durst not commit yourself to the hands of others.' The Abbot answered, 'Would you, my lord, that I should make a manifest leasing for your pleasure? The truth is, my lord, it is against my will that I am here; neither yet have I any pleasure in your company.' 'But ye shall remain with me, nevertheless, at this time,' said the Earl. 'I am not able to resist your will and pleasure,' said the Abbot, 'in this place.' 'Ye man then obey me,' said the Earl,—and with that were presented unto him certain letters to subscribe, amongst which there was a five years' tack, and a nineteen years' tack, and a charter of feu of all the lands of Crossraguel, with all the clauses necessary for the Earl to haste him to hell. For gif adultery, sacrilege, oppression, barbarous cruelty, and theft heaped upon theft, deserve hell, the great King of Carrick can no more escape hell for ever, than the imprudent Abbot escaped the fire for a season as follows.

"After that the Earl spied repugnance, and saw that he could not come to his purpose by fair means, he commanded his cooks to prepare the banquet: and so first they flayed the sheep, that is, they took off the Abbot's cloathes even to his skin, and next they bound him to the chimney—his legs to the one end, and his arms to the other; and so they began to beet [*i.e.* feed] the fire sometimes to his buttocks, sometimes to his legs, sometimes to his shoulders and arms; and that the roast might not burn, but that it might rest in soppe, they spared not flambing with oil, (basting as a cook bastes roasted meat); Lord, look thou to sic cruelty! And that the crying of the miserable man should not be heard, they closed his mouth that the voice might be stopped. It may be suspected that some practisian of the King's [Darnley's] murder was there. In that torment they held the poor man, till that often he cried for God's sake to dispatch him; for he had as meikle gold in his awin purse as would buy powder enough to shorten his pain. The famous King of Carrick and his cooks perceiving the roast to be aneuch, commanded it to be tane fra the fire, and the Earl himself began the grace in this manner:—'*Benedicite, Jesus Maria*, you are the most obstinate man that ever I saw; gif I had known that ye had been so stubborn, I would not for a thousand crowns have handled you so; I never did so to man before you.' And yet he returned to the same practice within two days, and ceased not till that he obtained his formost purpose, that is, that he had got all his pieces subscryvit alsweill as ane half-roasted hand could do it. The Earl thinking himself sure enough so long as he had the half-roasted Abbot in his awin keeping, and yet being ashamed of his presence by reason of his former cruelty, left the place of Dunure in the hands of certain of his servants, and the half-roasted Abbot to be kept there as prisoner. The Laird of Bargany, out of whose company the said Abbot had been enticed, understanding, (not the extremity,) but the retaining of the man, sent to the court, and raised letters of deliverance of the person of the man according to the order, which being disobeyed, the said Earl for his contempt was denounced rebel, and put to the horne. But yet hope was there none, neither to the afflicted to be delivered, neither yet to the purchaser [*i.e.* procurer] of the letters to obtain any comfort thereby; for in that time God was despised, and the lawful authority was contemned in Scotland, in hope of the sudden return and regiment of that cruel murderer of her awin husband, of whose lords the said Earl was called one; and yet, oftener than once, he was solemnly sworn to the King and to his Regent."

The Journalist then recites the complaint of the injured Allan Stewart, Commendator of Crossraguel, to the Regent and Privy Council, averring his having been carried, partly by flattery, partly by force, to the Black Vault of Dunure, a strong fortalice, built on a rock overhanging the Irish channel, where its ruins are still visible. Here he stated he had been required to execute leases and conveyances of the whole churches and parsonages belonging to the Abbey of Crossraguel, which he utterly refused as an unreasonable demand, and the more so that he had already conveyed them to John Stewart of Cardonall, by whose interest he had been made Commendator. The complainant proceeds to state, that he was, after many menaces, stript, bound, and his limbs exposed to fire in the manner already described, till, compelled by excess of agony, he subscribed the charter and leases presented to him, of the contents of which he was totally ignorant. A few days afterwards, being again required to execute a ratification of these deeds before a notary and witnesses, and refusing to do so, he was once more subjected to the same torture, until his agony was so excessive that he exclaimed, "Fye on you, why do you not strike your whingers into me, or blow me up with a barrel of powder, rather than torture me thus unmercifully?" upon which the Earl commanded Alexander Richard, one of his attendants, to stop the patient's mouth with a napkin, which was done accordingly. Thus he was once more compelled to submit to their tyranny. The petition concluded with stating, that the Earl, under pretence of the deeds thus iniquitously obtained, had taken possession of the whole place and living of Crossraguel, and enjoyed the profits thereof for three years.

The doom of the Regent and Council shows singularly the total interruption of justice at this calamitous period, even in the most clamant cases of oppression. The Council declined interference with the course of the ordinary justice of the county, (which was completely under the said Earl of Cassilis' control,) and only enacted, that he should forbear molestation of the unfortunate Commendator, under the surety of two thousand pounds Scots. The Earl was appointed also to keep the peace towards the celebrated George Buchanan, who had a pension out of the same Abbacy, to a similar extent, and under the like penalty.

The consequences are thus described by the Journalist already quoted.

"The said Laird of Bargany perceiving that the ordiner justice (the oppressed as said is) could neither help him, nor yet the afflicted, applied his mind to the next remedy, and in the end, by his servants, took the house of Dunure, where the poor Abbot was kept prisoner. The bruit flew fra Carrick to Galloway, and so suddenly assembled herd and hyre-man that pertained to the band of the Kennedies; and so within a few hours was the house of Dunure environed again. The master of Cassilis was the frackast [*i.e.* the readiest or boldest] and would not stay, but in his heat would lay fire to the dungeon, with no small boasting that all enemies within the house should die.

"He was required and admonished by those that were within to be more moderate, and not to hazard himself so foolishly. But no admonition would help, till that the wind of an hacquebute blasted his shoulder, and then ceased he from further pursuit in fury. The Laird of Bargany had before purchest [obtained] of the authorities, letters, charging all faithfull subjects to the King's Majesty, to assist him against that cruel tyrant and mansworn traitor, the Earl of Cassilis; which letters, with his private writings, he published, and shortly found sic concurrence of Kyle and Cunynghame with his other friends, that the Carrick company drew back fra the house: and so the other approached, furnished the house with mea men, delivered the said Mr Allan, and carried him to Ayr, where, publicly at the market cross of the said town, he declared how cruelly he was entreated, and how the murdered King suffered not sic torment as he did, excepting only he escaped the death: and, therefore, publickly did revoke all things that were done in that extremity, and especially he revoked the subscription of the three writings, to wit, of a fyve yeir tack and nineteen year tack, and of a charter of feu. And so the house remained, and remains (till this day, the 7th of February, 1571,) in the custody of the said Laird of Bargany and of his servants. And so cruelty was disappointed of proffeit present, and shall be eternallie punished, unless he earnestly repent. And this far for the cruelty committed, to give occasion unto others, and to such as hate the monstrous dealing of degenerate nobility, to look more diligently upon their behaviours, and to paint them forth unto the world, that they themselves may be ashamed of their own beastliness, and that the world may be advertised and admonished to abhor, detest, and avoid the company of all sic tyrants, who are not worthy of the society of men, but ought to be sent suddenly to the devil, with whom they must burn without end, for their contempt of God, and cruelty committed against his creatures. Let Cassilis and his brother be the first to be the example unto others. Amen. Amen."*

This extract has been somewhat amended or modernized in orthography, to render it more intelligible to the general reader. I have to add, that the Kennedies of Bargany, who interfered in behalf of the oppressed Abbot, were themselves a younger branch of the Cassilis family, but held different politics, and were powerful enough in this, and other instances, to bid them defiance.

The ultimate issue of this affair does not appear; but as the house of Cassilis are still in possession of the greater part of the feus and leases which belonged to Crossraguel Abbey, it is probable the talons of the King of Carrick were strong enough, in those disorderly times, to retain what they had so mercilessly fixed upon.

I may also add, that it appears by some papers in my possession, that the officers or Country Keepers on the border, were accustomed to torment their prisoners by binding them to the iron bars of their chimneys, to extort confession.

244.36 (Ch. 29) blue on the black shield The author has been here upbraided with false heraldry, as having charged metal upon metal. It should be remembered, however, that heraldry had only its first rude origin during the crusades, and that all the minutiæ of its fantastic science were the work of time, and introduced at a much later period. Those who think otherwise must suppose that the Goddess of *Armoiries*, like the Goddess of Arms, sprung into the world completely equipped in all the gaudy trappings of the department she presides over.

Addition to Note.

In corroboration of what is above stated, it may be observed, that the arms, which were assumed by Godfrey of Boulogne himself, after the conquest of Jerusalem, was a cross counter potent cantoned with four little crosses or, upon a field azure, displaying thus metal upon metal. The heralds have tried to explain this undeniable fact in different modes—but Ferne gallantly contends, that a prince of

* Bannatyne's Journal.

Godfrey's qualities should not be bound by the ordinary rules. The Scottish Nisbet, and the same Ferne, insist that the chiefs of the Crusade must have assigned to Godfrey this extraordinary and unwonted coat-of-arms, in order to induce those who should behold them to make enquiries, and hence the name of *arma inquirenda*. But with reverence to these grave authorities, it seems unlikely that the assembled princes of Europe should have adjudged to Godfrey a coat armorial so much contrary to the general rule, if such rule had then existed; at any rate, it proves that metal upon metal, now accounted a solecism in heraldry, was admitted in other cases similar to that in the text. See Ferne's *Blazon of Gentrie*, p. 238. Edition 1586. Nisbet's *Heraldry*, vol. i. p. 113. Second Edition.

265.39 (Ch. 31) instantly follow me The author has some idea that this passage is imitated from the appearance of Philidaspes, before the divine Mandane, when the city of Babylon is on fire, and he proposes to convey her from the flames. But the theft, if there be one, would be rather too severely punished by the penance of searching for the original passage through the interminable volumes of the Grand Cyrus.

270.41 (Ch. 31) I also must perish

ULRICA'S DEATH SONG. It will readily occur to the antiquary, that these verses are intended to imitate the antique poetry of the Scalds—the minstrels of the old Scandinavians—the race, as the Laureate so happily terms them,

> Stern to inflict, and stubborn to endure,
> Who smiled in death.

The poetry of the Anglo-Saxons, after their civilisation and conversion, was of a different and softer character; but in the circumstances of Ulrica, she may be not unnaturally supposed to return to the wilder strains which animated her forefathers during their times of Paganism and untamed ferocity.

273.30 (Ch. 32) Theow and Esne Thrall and bondsman.

273.31 (Ch. 32) Folk-free and sacless A lawful freeman.

281.17 (Ch. 32) (Magnum addition) [For EdI '"I will repay thee' the Magnum text has '"I am content to take thy cuff* as a loan, but I will repay thee'.]

RICHARD CŒUR-DE-LION. The interchange of a cuff with the jolly priest is not entirely out of character with Richard I., if romancers read him aright. In the very curious romance on the subject of his adventures in the Holy Land, and his return from thence, it is recorded how he exchanged a pugilistic favour of this nature, while a prisoner in Germany. His opponent was the son of his principal warder, and was so imprudent as to give the challenge to this barter of buffets. The King stood forth like a true man, and received a blow which staggered him. In requital, having previously waxed his hand, a practice unknown, I believe, to the gentlemen of the modern Fancy, he returned the box on the ear with such interest as to kill his antagonist on the spot.—*See, in Ellis's Specimens of English Romance, that of Cœur-de-Lion.*

283.30 (Ch. 33) he has so pledged it A commissary is said to have received similar consolation from a certain Commander-in-chief, to whom he complained that a general officer had used some such threat towards him as that in the text.

292.4 (Ch. 33) (Magnum variant) [For EdI 'Thou liest, Jack Priest,"' the Magnum text has 'Thou be'st a hedge-priest,"*']

HEDGE-PRIESTS. It is curious to observe, that in every state of society, some sort of ghostly consolation is provided for the members of the community, though assembled for purposes diametrically opposite to religion. A gang of beggars have their Patrico, and the banditti of the Apennines have among them persons acting as monks and priests, by whom they are confessed, and who perform mass before them. Unquestionably, such reverend persons, in such a society, must accommodate their manners and their morals to the community in which they live; and if they can occasionally obtain a degree of reverence for their supposed spiritual gifts, are, on most occasions, loaded with unmerciful ridicule, as possessing a character inconsistent with all around them.

Hence the fighting parson in the old play of Sir John Oldcastle, and the famous friar of Robin Hood's band. Nor were such characters ideal. There exists a monition of the Bishop of Durham against irregular churchmen of this class, who associated themselves with the clans of Border robbers, and desecrated the holiest offices of the priestly function, by celebrating them for the benefit of thieves, robbers, and murtherers, amongst ruins or in caverns of the earth, without regard to canonical form, and with torn and dirty attire, and maimed rites, altogether improper for the occasion.

305.36 (Ch. 35) Ut Leo semper feriatur In the ordinances of the Knights of the Temple, this phrase is repeated in a variety of forms, and occurs in almost every chapter, as if it were the signal-word of the Order; which may account for its being so frequently put in the Grand Master's mouth.

313.12 (Ch. 36) propter oblectationem carnis The edict which he quotes, is against communion with women of light character.

334.16 (Ch. 38) capul *Capul*, i.e. horse; in a more limited sense, work-horse.

360.18 (Ch. 40) Sherwood Forest From the ballads of Robin

Hood, we learn that this celebrated outlaw, when in disguise, sometimes assumed the name of Locksley, from a village where he was born, but where situated we are not distinctly told.

368.36 (Ch. 41) the neighbouring church-yard

CASTLE OF CONINGSBURGH. When I last saw this interesting ruin of ancient days, one of the very few remaining examples of Saxon fortification, I was strongly impressed with the desire of tracing out a species of theory on the subject, which, from some recent acquaintance with the architecture of the ancient Scandinavians, seemed to me peculiarly interesting. I was, however, obliged by circumstances to proceed on my journey, without leisure to do more than take a transient view of Coningsburgh. Yet the idea dwells so strongly in my mind, that I feel irresistibly tempted to waste a page or two in detailing at least the outline of my hypothesis, leaving better antiquaries to correct or refute conclusions which are perhaps too hastily drawn.

Those who have visited the Zetland Islands, are familiar with the description of castles called by the inhabitants Burghs; and by the Highlanders—for they are also to be found both in the Western Isles and on the mainland—Duns. Pennant has engraved a view of the famous Dun-Dornadilla in Glenelg; and there are many others, all of them built after a peculiar mode of architecture, which argues a people in the most primitive state of society. The most perfect specimen is that upon the island of Mousa, near to the mainland of Zetland, which is probably in the same state as when inhabited.

It is a single round tower, the wall curving in slightly, and then curving outward again in the form of a dice-box, so that the defenders on the top might the better protect the base. It is formed of rough stones, selected with care, and laid in courses or circles, with much compactness, but without cement of any kind. The tower has never, to appearance, had roofing of any sort; a fire was made in the centre of the space which it encloses, and originally the building was probably little more than a wall drawn as a sort of screen around the great council fire of the tribe. But, although the means or ingenuity of the builders did not extend so far as to provide a roof, they supplied the want by constructing apartments in the interior of the walls of the tower itself. The circumvallation formed a double enclosure, the inner side of which was, in fact, two feet or three feet distant from the other, and connected by a concentric range of long flat stones, thus forming a series of concentric rings or stories of various heights, rising to the top of the tower. Each of these stories or galleries has four windows, facing directly to the points of the compass, and rising of course regularly above each other. These four perpendicular ranges of windows admitted air, and, the fire being kindled, heat, or smoke at least, to each of the galleries. The access from gallery to gallery is equally primitive. A path, on the principle of an inclined plane, turns round and round the building like a screw, and gives access to the different stories, intersecting each of them in its turn, and thus gradually rising to the top of the wall of the tower. On the outside there are no windows; and I may add, that an enclosure of a square, or sometimes a round form, gave the inhabitants of the Burgh an opportunity to secure any sheep or cattle which they might possess.

Such is the general architecture of that very early period when the Northmen, yet heathen, swept the seas, and brought back to their rude houses, such as I have described them, the plunder of more polished nations. In Zetland there are several scores of these Burghs, occupying in every case, capes, headlands, islets, and similar places of advantage singularly well chosen. I remember the remains of one upon an island in a small lake near Lerwick, which at high tide communicates with the sea, the access to which is very ingenious, by means of a causeway or dike, about three or four inches under the surface of the water. This causeway makes a sharp angle in its approach to the Burgh. The inhabitants, doubtless, were well acquainted with this, but strangers, who might approach in a hostile force, and were ignorant of the direction of the causeway where it suddenly changes its course, would probably plunge into the lake, which is six or seven feet in depth at the least. This must have been the device of some Vauban or Coehorn of those early times.

The style of these buildings evinces that the architect possessed neither the art of using lime or cement of any kind, nor the skill to throw an arch, construct a roof, or erect a stair; and yet, with all this ignorance, showed great ingenuity in selecting the situation of Burghs, and regulating the access to them, as well as neatness and regularity of execution in the erection, since the buildings themselves show a style of advance in the arts scarce consistent with the ignorance of so many of the principal branches of architectural knowledge.

I have always thought, that one of the most curious and valuable objects of antiquaries has been to trace the progress of society, by the efforts made in early ages to improve the rudeness of their first expedients, until they either approach excellence, or, as is most frequently the case, are supplied by new and fundamental discoveries, which supersede both the earlier and ruder system, and the improvements which have been ingrafted upon it. For example, if we conceive the recent discovery of gas to be so much improved and adapted to domestic use, as to supersede all other modes of producing domestic light; we can already suppose, some centuries afterward, the heads of a whole Society of Antiquaries half turned by the discovery of a pair of patent snuffers, and by the learned theories which would be brought forward to account for the form and purpose of so singular an implement.

Following some such principle, I am inclined to regard the singular Castle of Coningsburgh—I mean the Saxon part of it—as a step in advance from the rude architecture, if it deserves the name, which must have been common to the Saxons as to other Northmen. The builders had attained the art of using cement, and of roofing a building,—great improvements on the original Burgh. But in the round keep, a shape only seen in the most ancient castles—the chambers excavated in the thickness of the walls and buttresses—the difficulty by which access is gained from one story to those above it, Coningsburgh still retains the simplicity of its origin, and shows by what slow degrees man proceeded from occupying such rude and inconvenient lodgings, as were afforded by the galleries of the Castle of Mousa, to the more splendid accommodations of the Norman castles, with all their stern and Gothic graces.

I am ignorant if these remarks are new, or if they will be confirmed by closer examination; but I think, that, on a hasty observation, Coningsburgh offers means of curious study to those who may wish to trace the history of architecture back to the times preceding the Norman Conquest.

It would be highly desirable that a cork model should be taken of the Castle of Mousa, as it cannot be well understood by a plan.

The Castle of Coningsburgh is thus described by Gough:—

"The castle is large, the outer walls standing on a pleasant ascent from the river, but much overtopt by a high hill, on which the town stands, situate at the head of a rich and magnificent vale, formed by an amphitheatre of woody hills, in which flows the gentle Don. Near the castle is a barrow, said to be Hengist's tomb. The entrance is flanked to the left by a round tower, with a sloping base, and there are several similar in the outer wall; the entrance has piers of a gate, and on the east side the ditch and bank is double and very steep. On the top of the churchyard wall is a tombstone, on which are cut in high relief, two ravens, or such-like birds. On the south side of the churchyard lies an ancient stone, ridged like a coffin, on which is carved a man on horseback; and another man with a shield encountering a vast winged serpent, and a man bearing a shield behind him. It was probably one of the rude crosses not uncommon in churchyards in this county. See it engraved on the plate of crosses for this volume, plate 14. fig. 1. The name of Coningsburgh, by which this castle goes in the old editions of the Britannia, would lead one to suppose it the residence of the Saxon kings. It afterwards belonged to King Harold. The Conqueror bestowed it on William de Warren, with all its privileges and jurisdiction, which are said to have been over twenty-eight towns. At the corner of the area, which is of an irregular form, stands the great tower, or keep, placed on a small hill of its own dimensions, on which lie six vast projecting buttresses, ascending in a steep direction to prop and support the building, and continued upwards up the sides as turrets. The tower within forms a complete circle, twenty-one feet in diameter, the walls fourteen feet thick. The ascent into the tower is by an exceeding deep flight of steep steps, four feet and a half wide, on the south side leading to a low doorway, over which is a circular arch crossed by a great transom stone. Within this door is the staircase which ascends straight through the thickness of the wall, not communicating with the room on the first floor, in whose centre is the opening to the dungeon. Neither of these lower rooms is lighted except from a hole in the floor of the third story; the room in which, as well as in that above it, is finished with compact smooth stonework, both having chimney-pieces, with an arch resting on triple clustered pillars. In the third story, or guard-chamber, is a small recess with a loop-hole, probably a bedchamber, and in that floor above a niche for a saint or holy-water pot. Mr King imagines this a Saxon castle of the first ages of the Heptarchy. Mr Watson thus describes it. From the first floor to the second story, (third from the ground,) is a way by a stair in the wall five feet wide. The next staircase is approached by a ladder, and ends at the fourth story from the ground. Two yards from the door, at the head of this stair, is an opening nearly east, accessible by treading on the ledge of the wall, which diminishes eight inches each story; and this last opening leads into a room or chapel ten feet by twelve, and fifteen or sixteen high, arched with freestone, and supported by small circular columns of the same, the capitals and arches Saxon. It has an east window, and on each side in the wall, about four feet from the ground, a stone basin, with a hole and iron pipe to convey the water into or through the wall. This chapel is one of the buttresses, but no sign of it without, for even the window, though large within, is only a long narrow loop-hole, scarcely to be seen without. On the left side of this chapel is a small oratory, eight by six in the thickness of the wall, with a niche in the wall, and enlightened by a like loop-hole. The fourth stair from the ground, ten feet west from the chapel door, leads to the top of the tower through the thickness of the wall, which at top is but three yards. Each story is about fifteen feet high, so that the tower will be seventy-five feet from the ground. The inside forms a circle, whose diameter may be about twelve feet. The well at the bottom of the dungeon is filled with stones."—GOUGH's *Edition of Camden's Britannia*. Second Edition, vol. iii. p. 267.

369.37 (Ch. 41) crowds The crowth, or crowd, was a species of violin. The rote a sort of guitar, or rather hurdy-gurdy, the strings of which were managed by a wheel, from which the instrument took its name.

376.17 (Ch. 42) like something arisen from the dead The resuscitation of Athelstane has been much criticised, as too violent a breach of probability, even for a work of such fantastic character. It was a *tour-de-force*, to which the author was compelled to have recourse, by the vehement entreaties of his friend and printer, who was inconsolable upon the Saxon being conveyed to the tomb.

THE MONASTERY

Editorial Note

The Monastery occupies the second part of Volume 2 and all of Volume 3 of the 1822 octavo *Historical Romances*, MSS 23014 and 23015 in the Interleaved Set. Scott was working on the annotation of *The Monastery* in December 1829: on the 14th of that month he showed Cadell 'the Monastery with very copious additions' (MS 21043, f. 8r). He continued work on it together with *The Abbot* in January 1830, when he asked Cadell to return the relevant Interleaved Set volumes, 'my notes & all having a good deal to do to complete them' (*Letters*, 11.286): presumably he had passed them temporarily to the publisher so that he could estimate lengths. Cadell carried out his work on the novel between 27 January and 11 May (MS 21020, ff. 6v–21v). *The Monastery* was published as Volumes 18 and 19 of the Magnum on 1 November and 1 December 1830. With 365 and 356 pages in all respectively, these volumes are at the lower end of the acceptable length: Scott has chosen to add a twenty-eight-page Introduction, 19 pages of endnotes (6 in the first volume, and 13 in the second), and some mostly very short footnotes.

The Introduction is an elaborate performance, mainly concerned to make the best case for a work that had been unfavourably received. Scott begins with an extended justification of the Border setting for his Reformation story. Cunningly, he stresses the prevalence of superstitious beliefs in the region: the real point of this emphasis becomes clear only later in the Introduction. He displays his grasp of local Border topography and history in order to demonstrate that his setting is deliberately fictionalised, and goes on to reject the identification of Clutterbuck with a supposed original, stressing rather his typical qualities. Scott then addresses three main issues raised by the novel's critics. He presents the White Lady as prompted by a desire to give a new slant to an over-familiar Border setting, and does his best to justify her as having distinguished literary forbears and supported by attested local superstitions: the reason for the emphasis at the beginning of the Introduction is now clear. Sir Percie Shafton is similarly justified as typical, and his failure attributed to the general difficulty in making transient fashions interesting to the readers of a later age. Finally, Scott concedes that his plotting in this work is both tame and loose.

The only noteworthy feature in the remarkably fluent manuscript of the Introduction is that the paragraph beginning 'The extravagance of Euphuism' (50.3) starts a new leaf, most of the preceding leaf being blank (it is a short one, probably trimmed), but there is no other internal or external evidence to suggest a break in composition. The Chaucer quotation at 43.10–12 was probably inserted in proof.

The first-edition *Monastery* has a considerable number of glossarial footnotes, and only four further such glosses are added for the Magnum. One of them is a sort of gloss in reverse at 60.3–5, where the term 'Blind-road' is in the note rather than the text. The remaining six, more substantial, footnotes produced for the Magnum are mostly concerned to elucidate specific relations between the fiction and non-fictional reality. The literary tourist might be misled by a castle in a different location (60.6–14), or conceivably by an imaginary tree (67.4–6). But the peculiar bridge is founded on a clear original, for which Scott is able to draw on oral information and personal observation (57.26–58.15). Two of the footnotes and two of the dozen endnotes expand on existing 'pegs' in the text (names or terms crying out for explanation), though they had had to wait for a decade before the notes were provided (58.16–19; 58.20–31; 59.8–60.2; 64.33–67.2). The last of these with the Latin charter quoted is aimed at the antiquarian reader, but it keeps the non-specialist on board with a summary in English. Scott is in antiquarian mode again when he engages in debate on two family trees (67.7–68.27). Two endnotes take up themes from the Introduction: one with an anecdote illustrating the survival of superstitious beliefs to the present (56.30–57.24), and one drawing primarily on Ben Jonson to support the euphuistic speech and flamboyant costume displayed in the novel (62.2–64.11). On occasion Scott is concerned to provide mini-essays demonstrating that specific actions of thought-patterns in the novel may be seen as typical of a more general human trait or custom (56.8–29; 60.28–33; 64.15–31): the last of these supports the 'Good Faith of the Borderers' evident in the action with an anecdote from a contemporaneous source which Scott had been involved in editing.

The last sentence of the note at 57.23–24 is apparently a proof addition, avoiding the baldness of the manuscript ending. At 62.13–15 the short Jonson quotation also seems to have come in at proof stage, enriching the note.

In addition to notes on the novel proper there are several new footnotes to the first-edition Introductory Epistle. Among them are two filling in details concerning Scott's contemporaries Lord Somerville and Thomas Thomson, and one identifying the host of the George Inn at Melrose as David Kyle. Three explain points of the publishing history of *The Monastery* in 1820 to readers a decade later.

There are four Magnum illustrations for this title. The frontispiece to Volume 18 (MAG0035 / TB348.18) was designed by Gilbert Stuart Newton and engraved by Edward Frances Finden. It depicts Abbot Boniface seated after his evening meal in the palace of the Monastery of Saint Mary's (EEWN 9, 69.17–25 (abridged): 'Abbot Boniface was seated . . . towers and steeples in the red embers.'). The title-page vignette (MAG0036 / TB348.18) was designed by Alexander Chisholm and engraved by Timothy Stansfeld Engleheart. It depicts the Lady of Avenel and her daughter Mary, with the pony Shagram, being guided over open country to seek refuge at Glendearg (EEWN 9, 46.4–8 (abridged): 'The exiled family . . . to explore the way.'). The frontispiece to Volume 19 (MAG0037 / TB348.19) was designed by David Wilkie and engraved by Charles Fox. It depicts Henry Warden as a prisoner before Father Eustace in the Monastery of Saint Mary's, with Christie of Clinthill as guard (EEWN 9, 287.18–25 (abridged): 'Henry Warden was led in . . . the character of centinel'). The title-page vignette (MAG0038 / TB348.19) was designed by Alexander Fraser, the elder, and engraved by Francis Engleheart. It depicts Halbert and his pedlar guide sharing a meal by the wayside (EEWN 9, 319.17–21: 'He was courteous . . . completed the feast.').

G. S. Newton. A.R.A. E. Finden.

THE MONASTERY.

"Abbot Boniface was seated in his highbacked chair,
He was gazing indolently on the fire, partly engaged in meditation on his past and present fortunes,
partly occupied by endeavouring to trace towers
and steeples in the red embers."

EDINBURGH; PUBLISHED 1830, BY CADELL & Co. and WHITTAKER & Co. LONDON.

WAVERLEY NOVELS.

VOL. XVIII.

THE MONASTERY.

The exiled family then set forward. Mary Avenel riding gipsy fashion upon Shagram, the Lady of Avenel walking by the animal's side; Tibb leading the bridle, and old Martin walking a little before, looking anxiously around him to explore the way.

PRINTED FOR R. CADELL & COMPANY, EDINBURGH,
AND WHITTAKER & Co. LONDON.
1830.

D. Wilkie R.A. C. Fox.

THE MONASTERY.

Henry Warden was led in, his hands still bound, but his feet at liberty. "Clear the apartment," said the Sub-Prior. All retired excepting Christie of the Clinthill, who unsheathed his sword, and placed himself beside the door, as if taking upon him the character of centinel.

EDINBURGH, PUBLISHED 1830. BY R. CADELL & Co and WHITTAKER & Co LONDON.

WAVERLEY NOVELS.

VOL. XIX.

THE MONASTERY.

"He was courteous, however, and offered Halbert a share of the provisions which he carried about him for refreshment. They were of the coarsest kind—oat-bread baked into cakes, oat-meal slaked with cold water, an onion or two, and a morsel of smoked ham, completed the feast."

PRINTED FOR R. CADELL & COMPANY, EDINBURGH.
AND WHITTAKER & Co LONDON.
1830.

Introduction to The Monastery

It would be difficult to assign any good reason why the author of Ivanhoe, after using, in that work, all the art he possessed to remove the personages, action, and manners of the tale, to a distance from his own country, should choose for the scene of his next attempt the celebrated ruins of Melrose, in the immediate neighbourhood of his own residence. But the reason, or caprice, which dictated his change of system, has entirely escaped his recollection, nor is it worth while to attempt recalling what must be a matter of very little consequence.

The general plan of the story was, to conjoin two characters in that bustling and contentious age, who, thrown into situations which gave them different views on the subject of the Reformation, should, with the same sincerity and purity of intention, dedicate themselves, the one to the support of the sinking fabric of the Catholic Church, the other to the establishment of the Reformed doctrines. It was supposed that some interesting subjects for narrative might be derived from opposing two such enthusiasts to each other in the path of life, and contrasting the real worth of both to their passions and prejudices. The localities of Melrose suited the scenery of the proposed story well; the ruins themselves form a splendid theatre for any tragic incident which might be brought forward; joined to the vicinity of the fine river, with all its tributary streams, flowing through a country which has been the scene of so much fierce fighting, and is rich with so many recollections of former times, and lying almost under the immediate eye of the author, by whom they were to be used.

The situation had yet further recommendations. On the opposite bank of the Tweed might be seen the remains of ancient enclosures, surrounded by sycamores and ash-trees of considerable size. These had once formed the crofts or arable ground of a village, now reduced to a single hut, the abode of a fisherman, who also manages a ferry. The cottages, even the church which once existed there, have sunk into vestiges hardly to be traced without visiting the spot, the inhabitants having gradually withdrawn to the more prosperous town of Galashiels, which has risen into consideration, within two miles of their neighbourhood. Superstitious eld, however, has tenanted the deserted groves with aerial beings, to supply the want of the mortal tenants who have deserted it. The ruined and abandoned churchyard of Boldside has been long believed to be haunted by the Fairies, and the deep broad current of the Tweed, wheeling in moonlight round the foot of the steep bank, with the number of trees originally planted for shelter round the fields of the cottagers, but now producing the effect of scattered and detached groves, fill up the idea which one would form in imagination for a scene that Oberon and Queen Mab might love to revel in. There are evenings when the spectator might believe, with Father Chaucer, that the

> ———Queen of Faery,
> With harp, and pipe, and symphony,
> Were dwelling in the place.

Another, and even a more familiar refuge of the elfin race, (if tradition is to be trusted,) is the glen of the river, or rather brook, named the Allen, which falls into the Tweed from the northward, about a quarter of a mile above the present bridge. As the streamlet finds its way behind Lord Somerville's hunting-seat, called the Pavilion, its valley has been popularly termed the Fairy Dean, or rather the Nameless Dean, because of the supposed ill luck attached by the popular faith of ancient times, to naming or alluding to the irritable race, whom our fathers distinguished as the Good Neighbours, and the Highlanders called Daoine Shie, or Men of Peace; rather by way of compliment, than on account of any particular idea of friendship or pacific relation which either Highlander or Borderer entertained towards the beings whom they thus distinguished, or supposed them to bear to humanity.*

In evidence of the actual operations of the fairy people even at this time, little pieces of calcareous matter are found in the glen after a flood, which either the labours of those tiny artists, or the eddies of the brook among the stones, have formed into a fantastic resemblance of cups, saucers, basins, and the like, in which children who gather them pretend to discern fairy utensils.

Besides these circumstances of romantic locality, *mea paupera regna* (as Captain Dalgetty denominates his territory of Drumthwacket) are bounded by a small but deep lake, from which eyes that yet look on the light are said to have seen the water-bull ascend, and shake the hills with his roar.

Indeed, the country around Melrose, if possessing less romantic beauty than some other scenes in Scotland, is connected with so many associations of a fanciful nature, in which the imagination takes delight, as might well induce even one less attached to the spot than the author, to accommodate, after a general manner, the

* See Rob Roy, Vol. 25a. pp. 275–76.

imaginary scenes he was framing to the localities to which he was partial. But it would be a misapprehension to suppose, that, because Melrose may in general pass for Kennaquhair, or because it agrees with it in the circumstances of the drawbridge, the mill-dam, and other points of resemblance, that therefore an accurate or perfect local similitude is to be found in all particulars of the picture. It was not the purpose of the author to present a landscape copied from nature, but a piece of composition, in which a real scene, with which he is familiar, had afforded him some leading outlines. Thus the resemblance of the imaginary Glendearg with the real vale of the Allen, is far from being minute, nor did the author aim at identifying them. This must appear plain to all who know the actual character of the Glen of Allen, and have taken the trouble to read the account of the imaginary Glendearg. The stream in the latter case is described as wandering down a romantic little valley, shifting itself, after the fashion of such a brook, from one side to the other, as it can most easily find its passage, and touching nothing in its progress that gives token of cultivation. It rises near a solitary tower, the abode of a supposed church vassal, and the scene of several incidents in the Romance.

The real Allen, on the contrary, after traversing the romantic ravine called the Nameless Dean, thrown off from side to side alternately, like a billiard ball repelled by the sides of the table on which it has been played, and in that part of its course resembling the stream which pours down Glendearg, may be traced upwards into a more open country, where the banks retreat farther from each other, and the vale exhibits a good deal of dry ground, which has not been neglected by the active cultivators of the district. It arrives, too, at a sort of termination, striking in itself, but totally irreconcilable with the narrative of the Romance. Instead of a single peel-house, or border tower of defence, such as Dame Glendinning is supposed to have inhabited, the head of the Allen, about five miles above its junction with the Tweed, shows three ruins of Border houses, belonging to different proprietors, and each, from the desire of mutual support so natural to troublesome times, situated at the extremity of the property of which it is the principal messuage. One of these is the ruinous mansion-house of Hillslap, formerly the property of the Cairncrosses, and now of Mr Innes of Stow; a second the tower of Colmslie, an ancient inheritance of the Borthwick family, as is testified by their crest, the Goat's Head, which exists on the ruin; a third, the house of Langshaw, also ruinous, but near which the proprietor, Mr Baillie of Jerviswood and Mellerstain, has built a small shooting box.

All these ruins, so strangely huddled together in a very solitary spot, have recollections and traditions of their own, but none of them bear the most distant resemblance to the descriptions in the Romance of the Monastery; and as the author could hardly have erred so grossly regarding a spot within a morning's ride of his own house, the inference is, that no resemblance was intended. Hillslap is remembered by the humours of the last inhabitants, two or three elderly ladies, of the class of Miss Raylands, in the Old Manor House, though less important by birth and fortune. Colmslie is commemorated in song:—

Colmslie stands on Colmslie hill,
The water it flows round Colmslie mill;
The mill and the kiln gang bonnily,
And it's up with the whippers of Colmslie!

Langshaw, though larger than the other mansions assembled at the head of the supposed Glendearg, has nothing about it more remarkable than the inscription of the present proprietor over his shooting lodge—*Utinam hanc etiam viris impleam amicis*—a modest wish, which I know no one more capable of attaining upon an extended scale, than the gentleman who has expressed it upon a limited one.

Having thus shown that I could say something of these desolated towers, which the desire of social intercourse, or the facility of mutual defence, had drawn together at the head of this Glen, I need not add any further reason to show, that there is no resemblance between them and the solitary habitation of Dame Elspeth Glendinning. Beyond these dwellings are some remains of natural wood, and a considerable portion of morass and bog; but I would not advise any who may be curious in localities, to spend time in looking for the fountain and holly-tree of the White Lady.

While I am on this subject I may add, that Captain Clutterbuck, the imaginary editor of the Monastery, has no real prototype in the village of Melrose or neighbourhood, that ever I saw or heard of. To give some individuality to this personage, he is described as a character which sometimes occurs in actual society—a person who has spent his life within the necessary duties of a technical profession, and when at length emancipated from these, finds himself without any occupation whatever, and is apt to become the prey of ennui, until he discovers some petty subject of investigation commensurate to his talents, the study of which gives him employment in solitude; while the conscious possession of information peculiar to himself, adds to his consequence in society. I have often observed, that the lighter and trivial branches of antiquarian study are singularly useful in relieving the vacuity of such a mind, and have known them serve many a Captain Clutterbuck to retreat upon; I was therefore a good deal surprised, when I found the antiquarian Captain identified with a neighbour and friend of my own, who could never have been confounded with him by any who had read the book, and seen the party alluded to. This erroneous identification occurs in a work entitled, "Illustrations of the Author of Waverley, being Notices and Anecdotes of real Characters, Scenes, and Incidents, supposed to be described in his works, by Robert Chambers." The work was, of course, liable to many errors, as any one of the kind must be, whatever the ingenuity of the author, which takes the task of explaining what can be only known to another person. Mistakes of place or inanimate things referred to, are of very little moment; but the ingenious author ought to have been cautious of attaching real names to fictitious characters. I think it is in the Spectator we read of a rustic wag, who, in a copy of "The Whole Duty of Man," wrote opposite to every vice the name of some individual in the neighbourhood, and thus converted that excellent work into a libel on a whole parish.

The scenery being thus ready at the author's hand, the reminiscences of the country were equally favourable. In a land where the horses remained almost constantly saddled, and the sword seldom quitted the warrior's side—where war was the natural and constant state of the inhabitants, and peace only existed in the shape of brief and feverish truces—there could be no want of the means to complicate and extricate the incidents of his narrative at pleasure. There was a disadvantage, notwithstanding, in treading this Border district, for it had been already ransacked by the author himself, as well as others; and unless presented under a new light, was like to afford ground to the objection of *Crambe bis cocta*.

To attain the indispensable quality of novelty, something, it was thought, might be gained by contrasting the character of the vassals of the church with those of the dependants of the lay barons, by whom they were surrounded. But much advantage could not be derived from this. There were, indeed, differences betwixt the two classes, but, like tribes in the mineral and vegetable world, which, resembling each other to common eyes, can be sufficiently well discriminated by naturalists, they were yet too similar, upon the whole, to be placed in marked contrast with each other.

Machinery remained—the introduction of the supernatural and marvellous; the resort of distressed authors since the days of Horace, but whose privileges as a sanctuary have been disputed in the present age, and wellnigh exploded. The popular belief no longer allows the possibility of existence to the race of mysterious beings which hovered betwixt this world and that which is invisible. The fairies have abandoned their moonlight turf; the witch no longer holds her black orgies in the hemlock dell; and

> Even the last lingering phantom of the brain,
> The churchyard ghost, is now at rest again.

From the discredit attached to the vulgar and more common modes in which the Scottish superstition displays itself, the author was induced to have recourse to the beautiful, though almost forgotten, theory of astral spirits, or creatures of the elements, surpassing human beings in knowledge and power, but inferior to them, as subject, after a certain space of years, to a death which is to them annihilation, as they have no share in the promise made to the sons of Adam. These sprites are supposed to be of four distinct kinds, as the elements from which they have their origin, and are known, to those who have studied the cabalistical philosophy, by the names of Sylphs, Gnomes, Salamanders, and Naiads, as they belong to the elements of Air, Earth, Fire, or Water. The general reader will find an entertaining account of these elementary spirits in the French book, entitled, "Entretiens du Compte de Gabalis." The ingenious Compte de la Motte Fouqué composed, in German, one of the most successful productions of his fertile brain, where a beautiful and even an afflicting effect is produced by the introduction of a water-nymph, who loses the privilege of immortality, by consenting to become accessible to human feelings, and unite her lot with that of a mortal, who treats her with ingratitude.

In imitation of an example so successful, the White Lady of Avenel was introduced into the following sheets. She is represented as connected with the family of Avenel by one of those mystic ties, which, in ancient times, were supposed to exist, in certain circumstances, between the creatures of the elements and the children of men. Such instances of mysterious union are recognised in Ireland, in the real Milesian families, who are possessed of a Banshie; and they are known among the traditions of the Highlanders, which, in many cases, attached an immortal being or spirit to the service of particular families or tribes. These demons, if they are to be called so, announced good or evil fortune to the families connected with them; and though some only condescended to meddle with matters of importance, others, like the May Mollach, or Maid of the Hairy Arms, condescended to mingle in ordinary sports, and even to direct the Chief how to play at draughts.

There was, therefore, no great violence in supposing such a being as this to have existed, while the elementary spirits were believed in; but it was more difficult to describe or imagine its attributes and principles of action. Shakspeare, the first of authorities in such a case, has painted Ariel, that beautiful creature of his fancy, as only approaching so near to humanity as to know the nature of that sympathy which the creatures of clay felt for each other, as we learn from the expression—"Mine would if I were human." The inferences from this are singular, but seem capable of regular deduction. A being, however superior to man in length of life—in power over the elements—in certain perceptions respecting the present, the past, and even the future, yet still incapable of human passions, of sentiments of moral good and evil, of meriting future rewards or punishments, belongs rather to the class of animals than of human creatures, and must therefore be presumed to act more from temporary benevolence or caprice, than from any thing approaching to feeling or reasoning. Such a being's superiority in power can only be compared to that of the elephant or lion, who are greater in strength than man, though inferior in the scale of creation. The partialities which we suppose such spirits to entertain must be like those of the dog; their sudden starts of passion, or the indulgence of a love of frolic, or mischief, may be compared to those of the numerous varieties of the cat. All these propensities are, however, controlled by the laws which render the elementary race subordinate to the command of man—liable to be subjected by his science, (so the sect of Gnostics believed, and on this turned the Rosicrucian philosophy,) or to be overpowered by his superior courage and daring, when it set their illusions at defiance.

It is with reference to this idea of the supposed spirits of the elements, that the White Lady of Avenel is represented as acting a varying, capricious, and inconsistent part in the pages assigned to her in the narrative; manifesting interest and attachment to the family with whom her destinies are associated, but evincing whim, and even a species of malevolence, towards other mortals, as the Sacristan and the Border robber, whose incorrect life subjected them to receive petty mortifications at her hand. She is scarce supposed, however, to have possessed either the power or inclination to do more than inflict terror or create embarrassment, and is always subjected by those mortals, who, by virtuous resolution, and mental energy, could assert authority over her. In these particulars she seems to constitute a being of a middle class, between the *esprit follet* who places its pleasure in misleading and tormenting mortals, and the benevolent Fairy of the East, who uniformly guides, aids, and supports them.

Either, however, the author executed his purpose indifferently, or the public did not approve of it; for the White Lady of Avenel was far from being popular. He does not now make the present statement, in the view of arguing readers into a more favourable opinion on the subject, but merely to exculpate himself from the charge of having wantonly intruded into the narrative a being of inconsistent powers and propensities.

In the delineation of another character, the author of the Monastery failed, where he hoped for some success. As nothing is so successful a subject of ridicule as the fashionable follies of our own time, it occurred to him that the more serious scenes of his narrative might be relieved by the humours of a cavaliero of the age of Queen Elizabeth. In every period, the attempt to gain and maintain the highest rank of society, has depended on the power of assuming and supporting a certain fashionable kind of affectation, usually connected with some vivacity of talent and energy of character, but distinguished at the same time by a transcendental flight, beyond sound reason and common sense; both faculties too vulgar to be admitted into the estimate of one who claims to be esteemed a "choice spirit of the age." These, in their different phases, constitute the gallants of the day, whose boast it is to drive the whims of fashion to extremity.

On all occasions, the manners of the sovereign, the court, and the time, must give the tone to the peculiar species of qualities by which those who would attain the height of fashion must seek to distinguish themselves. The reign of Elizabeth, being that of a maiden queen, was distinguished by the decorum of the courtiers, and especially the affectation of the deepest deference to the sovereign. After acknowledgment of the Queen's matchless perfections, the same devotion was extended to beauty as it existed among the lesser stars in her court, who sparkled, as it was the mode to say, by her reflected lustre. It is true, that gallant knights no longer vowed to Heaven, the peacock, and the ladies, to perform some feat of extravagant chivalry, in which they endangered the lives of others as well as their own. But although their chivalrous displays of personal gallantry seldom went further in Elizabeth's days than the tiltyard, where barricades, called barriers, prevented the shock of the horses, and limited the display of the cavaliers' skill to the comparatively safe encounter of their lances, the language of the lovers to their ladies was still in the exalted terms which Amadis would have addressed to Oriana, before encountering a dragon for her sake. This tone of romantic gallantry found a clever but conceited author, to reduce it to a species of constitution and form, and lay down the courtly manner of conversation, in a pedantic book, called Euphues and his England. Of this, a brief account is given in the text, to which it may now be proper to make some additions.

The extravagance of Euphuism, or a symbolical jargon of the same class, predominates in the romances of Calprenade and Scuderi, which were read as the amusement of the fair sex in France during the long reign of Louis XIV., and were supposed to contain the only legitimate language of love and gallantry. In this reign they encountered the satire of Molière and Boileau. A similar disorder, spreading into private society, formed the ground of the affected dialogue of the *Précieuses*, as they were styled, who formed the coterie of the Hotel de Rambouillet, and afforded Molière matter for his admirable comedy, *Les Précieuses Ridicules*. In England, the humour does not seem to have long survived the accession of James I.

The author had the vanity to think that a character, whose peculiarities should turn on extravagances which were once universally fashionable, might be read in a fictitious story with a good chance of affording amusement to the existing generation, who, fond as they are of looking back on the actions and manners of their ancestors, may be also supposed to be sensible of their absurdities. He must fairly acknowledge that he was disappointed, and that the Euphuist, far from being accounted a well drawn and humorous character of the period, was condemned as unnatural and absurd.

It would be easy to account for this failure, by supposing the defect to arise from the author's want of skill, and, probably, many readers may not be inclined to look further. But, as the author himself can scarce be supposed willing to acquiesce in this final cause, if any other can be alleged, he has been led to suspect, that, contrary to what he originally supposed, his subject was injudiciously chosen, in which, and not in his mode of treating it, lay the source of the want of success.

The manners of a rude people are always founded on nature, and the feelings of a more polished generation immediately sympathize with them. We need no numerous notes, no antiquarian dissertations, to enable the most ignorant to recognise the sentiments and diction of the characters of Homer; we have but, as Lear says, to strip off our lendings—to set aside the factitious principles and adornments which we have received from our comparatively artificial system of society, and our natural feelings are in unison with those of the bard of Chios and the heroes who live in his verses. It is the same with great part of the narratives of my friend Mr Cooper. We sympathize with his Indian chiefs and backwoodsmen, and acknowledge, in the characters which he presents to us, the same human nature by which we should feel ourselves influenced if placed in the same condition. So much is this the case, that though it is difficult, or almost impossible, to reclaim a savage, bred from his youth to war and the chase, to the restraints and the duties of civilized life, nothing is more easy or common, than to find men who have been educated in all the habits and comforts of improved society, willing to exchange them for the wild labours of the hunter and the fisher. The very amusements most pursued and relished by men of almost all ranks, whose constitution permits active exercise, are hunting, fishing, and in some instances, war, the natural and necessary business of the savage of Dryden, where his hero talks of being

——As free as nature first made man,
When wild in woods the noble savage ran.

But although the occupations, and even the sentiments, of primitive human beings, find access and interest in the minds of the more civilized part of the species, it does not therefore follow, that the national tastes, opinions, and follies, of one civilized period, should afford either the same interest or the same amusement to those of another. These generally, when driven to extravagance, are founded not upon any natural taste proper to the species, but upon the growth of some peculiar cast of affectation, with which mankind in general, and succeeding generations in particular, feel no common interest or sympathy. The extravagances of coxcombry in manners and apparel are indeed the legitimate, and often the successful objects of satire, during the time when they exist. In evidence of this, theatrical critics may observe how many dramatic *jeux d'esprit* are well received every season, because the satirist levels at some well-known or fashionable absurdity; or, in the dramatic phrase, "shoots folly as it flies." But when that folly keeps the wing no longer, it is reckoned but waste of powder to pour a discharge on what has no longer an existence; and the pieces in which such forgotten absurdities are made the subject of ridicule, fall quietly into oblivion with the follies which gave them fashion, or only continue on the scene, because they contain upon the whole a more permanent interest than that which connects them with manners and follies of a temporary character.

This, perhaps, affords a reason why the comedies of Ben Jonson, founded upon system, on what the age termed humours,—by which was meant factitious and affected characters, superinduced over that which was common to the rest of their race,—in spite of acute satire, deep scholarship, and strong sense, do not now afford general pleasure, but are confined to the closet of the antiquary, whose studies have assured him that the personages of the dramatist were once, though they are now no longer, portraits of existing nature.

Let us take another example of our hypothesis from Shakspeare himself, who, of all authors, drew his portraits for all ages. With the whole sum of the idolatry which affects us at his name, the mass of readers peruse, without amusement, the characters formed on the extravagances of temporary fashion; and the Euphuist Don Armado, the pedant Holofernes, even Nym and Pistol, are read with little pleasure by the mass of the public, as portraits of which we cannot recognise the humour, because the originals no longer exist. In like manner, while the distresses of Romeo and Juliet continue to interest every bosom, Mercutio, drawn as an accurate representation of the finished fine gentleman of the period, and as such received by the unanimous approbation of contemporaries, has so little to interest the present age, that, stripped of all his puns and quirks of verbal wit, he only retains his place in the scene, in virtue of his fine and fanciful speech upon dreaming, which belongs to no particular age, and as a personage whose presence is indispensable to the plot.

We have already prosecuted perhaps too far an argument, the tendency of which is to prove, that the introduction of an humorist, acting, like Sir Piercie Shafton, upon some forgotten and obsolete model of folly, once fashionable, is rather likely to awake the disgust of the reader, as unnatural, than find him food for mirth. Whether owing to this theory, or whether to the more simple and probable cause of the author's failure to delineate the subject he had proposed to himself, the formidable objection of *incredulus odi* was applied to the Euphuist, as well as to the White Lady of Avenel; and the one was denounced as unnatural, while the other was rejected as impossible.

There was little in the story to atone for these failures in two principal points. The incidents were inartificially huddled together. There was no part of the intrigue to which deep interest was found to apply; and the conclusion was brought about, not by incidents arising out of the story itself, but in consequence of public transactions, with which the narrative had little connexion, and which the reader had little opportunity to become acquainted with.

This, if not a positive fault, was yet a great defect in the Romance. It is true, that not only the practice of some great authors in this department, but even the general course of human life itself, may be quoted in favour of the more obvious, and less artificial practice, of arranging a narrative. It is seldom that the same circle of personages who have surrounded an individual at his first outset in life, continue to have an interest in his career till his fate comes to a crisis. On the contrary, and more especially if the events of his life be of a varied character, and worth communicating to others, or to the world, the hero's later connexions are usually totally separated from those with whom he began the voyage, but whom the individual has outsailed, or who have drifted astray, or foundered on the passage. This hackneyed comparison holds good in another point. The numerous vessels of so many different sorts, and destined for such different purposes, which are launched on the same mighty ocean, although each endeavours to preserve its own course, are every one more influenced by the winds and tides, that are common to the element which they all navigate, than by their own separate exertions. And it is thus in the world, that, when human prudence has done its best, some general, perhaps national event, destroys the schemes of the individual, as the casual touch of a more powerful being sweeps away the web of the spider.

Many excellent romances have been composed in this view of human life, where the hero is conducted through a variety of detached scenes, in which various agents appear and disappear, without, perhaps, having any permanent influence on the progress of the story. Such is the structure of Gil Blas, Roderick Random, and the Lives and Adventures of many other heroes, who run through different stations of life, and incur various adventures, only connected with each other by having happened to, or been witnessed by, the same individual, whose identity unites them together, as the string of a necklace links beads, which are otherwise detached.

But though such an unconnected course of adventures is what most frequently occurs in nature, yet the province of the romance writer being artificial, there is more required from him than a mere compliance with the simplicity of reality,—just as we demand from the scientific gardener, that he shall arrange, in curious knots and artificial parterres, the flowers which "nature boon" distributes freely on hill and dale. Fielding, accordingly, in most of his novels, but especially in Tom Jones, his *chef-dœuvre*, has set the distinguished example of a story regularly built and consistent in all its parts, in which nothing occurs, and scarce a personage is introduced, that has not some share in tending to advance the catastrophe.

To demand equal correctness and felicity in those who may follow in the track of that illustrious novelist, would be to fetter too much the power of giving pleasure, by surrounding it with formal rules; since of this species of light literature it may be said—*tout genre est permis, hors le genre ennuyeux*. Still, however, the more closely and happily the story is combined, and the more natural and felicitous the catastrophe, the nearer such a composition will approach the perfection of the novelist's art; nor can an author neglect this branch of his profession, without incurring proportional censure.

For such censure the Monastery gave but too much occasion. The intrigue of the Romance, neither very interesting in itself, nor very happily detailed, is at length finally disentangled by the breaking out of national hostilities between England and Scotland, and the as sudden renewal of the truce. Instances of this kind, it is true, cannot in reality have been uncommon, but the resorting to such, in order to accomplish the catastrophe, as by a *tour de force*, was objected to as inartificial, and not perfectly intelligible to the general reader.

Still the Monastery, though exposed to severe and just criticism, did not fail, judging from the extent of its circulation, to have some interest for the public. And this, too, was according to the ordinary course of such matters; for it very seldom happens that literary reputation is gained by a single effort, and still more rarely is it lost by a solitary miscarriage.

The author, therefore, had his days of grace allowed him, and time if he pleased, to comfort himself with the burthen of the old Scots song,

> If it isna weel bobbit,
> We'll bob it again.

ABBOTSFORD, 1*st November*, 1830.

Notes to The Monastery

8.25 (Introductory Epistle) heard vociferating The George was, and is, the principal inn in the village of Kennaquhair, or Melrose. But the landlord of the period was not the same civil and quiet person by whom the inn is now kept. David Kyle, a Melrose proprietor of no little importance, a first-rate person of consequence in whatever belonged to the business of the town, was the original owner and landlord of the inn. Poor David! Like many other busy men, he took so much care of public affairs, as in some degree to neglect his own. There are persons still alive at Kennaquhair who can recognise him and his peculiarities in the following sketch of mine Host of the George.

9.14 (Introductory Epistle) unless he were a virtuoso There is more to be said about this old bridge hereafter. See Note at 57.26–58.15.

10.18 (Introductory Epistle) relish your ale at e'en The nobleman whose boats are mentioned in the text, is the late kind and amiable Lord Somerville, an intimate friend of the author. David Kyle was a constant and privileged attendant when Lord Somerville had a party for spearing salmon; on such occasions, eighty or a hundred fish were often killed between Glenmayne and Leaderfoot.
11.16 (Introductory Epistle) Mr Deputy Register of Scotland Thomas Thomson, Esq., whose well-deserved panegyric ought to be found on another page than one written by an intimate friend of thirty years' standing.
11.42 (Introductory Epistle) their ancient barony The family of De Haga, modernized into Haig, of Bemerside, is of the highest antiquity, and is the subject of one of the prophecies of Thomas the Rhymer:—

> Betide, betide, whate'er betide,
> Haig shall be Haig of Bemerside.

12.26 (Introductory Epistle) some ancient fabliau It is curious to remark at how little expense of invention successive ages are content to receive amusement. The same story which Ramsay and Dunbar have successively handled, forms also the subject of the modern farce, No Song, no Supper.
18.37 (Introductory Epistle) de trop in the groupe This is one of those passages which must now read awkwardly, since every one knows that the Novelist and the author of the Lay of the Minstrel, is the same person. But before the avowal was made, the author was forced into this and similar offences against good taste, to meet an argument, often repeated, that there was something very mysterious in the Author of Waverley's reserve concerning Sir Walter Scott, an author sufficiently voluminous at least. I had a great mind to remove the passages from this edition, but the more candid way is to explain how they came there.
29.22 (Answer) disputes about his identity I am since more correctly informed, that Mr Cleishbotham died some months since at Gandercleugh, and that the person assuming his name is an impostor. The real Jedidiah made a most Christian and edifying end; and, as I am credibly informed, having sent for a Cameronian clergyman when he was *in extremis*, was so fortunate as to convince the good man, that, after all, he had no wish to bring down on the scattered remnant of Mountain folks, "the bonnets of Bonny Dundee." Hard that the speculators in print and paper will not allow a good man to rest quiet in his grave!

This note, and the passages in the text, were occasioned by a London bookseller having printed, as a speculation, an additional collection of Tales of My Landlord, which was not so fortunate as to succeed in passing on the world as genuine.

30.20 (Answer) a brother publisher In consequence of the pseudo Tales of My Landlord printed in London, as already mentioned, the late Mr John Ballantyne, the author's publisher, had a controversy with the interloping bibliopolist, each insisting that his Jedidiah Cleishbotham was the real Simon Pure.

40.28 (Ch. 2) our foragers As gallantry of all times and nations has the same mode of thinking and acting, so it often expresses itself by the same symbols. In the civil war 1745–6, a party of Highlanders, under a Chieftain of rank, came to Rose Castle, the seat of the Bishop of Carlisle, but then occupied by the family of Squire Dacre of Cumberland. They demanded quarters, which of course were not to be refused to armed men of a strange attire and unknown language. But the domestics represented to the captain of the mountaineers, that the lady of the mansion had been just delivered of a daughter, and expressed her hope, that, under these circumstances, his party would give as little trouble as possible. "God forbid," said the gallant chief, "that I or mine should be the means of adding to a lady's inconvenience in such a case. May I request to see the infant?" The child was brought, and the Highlander, taking his cockade out of his bonnet, and pinning it on the child's breast, "That will be a token," he said, "to any of our people who may come hither, that Donald M'Donald of Kinloch-Moidart, has taken the family at Rose Castle under his protection." The lady who received in infancy this gage of Highland protection, is now Mary, Lady Clerk of Pennycuick; and on the 10th of June still wears the cockade which was pinned on her breast, with a white rose as a kindred decoration.

45.41 (Ch. 3) supposed to haunt This superstition continues to prevail, though one would suppose it must now be antiquated. It is only a year or two since an itinerant puppet show-man, who, disdaining to acknowledge the profession of Gines de Passamonté, called himself an artist from Vauxhall, brought a complaint of a singular nature before the author, as Sheriff of Selkirkshire. The remarkable dexterity with which the show-man had exhibited the machinery of his little stage, had, upon a Selkirk fair-day, excited the eager curiosity of some mechanics of Galashiels. These men, from no worse motive that could be discerned than a thirst after knowledge beyond their sphere, committed a burglary upon the barn in which the puppets had been consigned to repose, and carried them off in the nook of their plaids, when returning from Selkirk to their own village.

But with the morning cool reflection came.

The party found they could not make Punch dance, and that the whole troop were equally intractable; they had also, perhaps, some apprehension of the Rhadamanth of the district; and, willing to be quit of their booty, they left the puppets seated in a grove by the side of the Ettrick, where they were sure to be touched by the first beams of the rising sun. Here a shepherd, who was on foot with sunrise to pen his master's sheep on a field of turnips, to his utter astonishment, saw this train, profusely gay, sitting in the little grotto. His examination proceeded thus:—

Sheriff. You saw these gay-looking things? what did you think they were?

Shepherd. Ou, I am no that free to say what I might think they were.

Sheriff. Come, lad, I must have a direct answer—who did you think they were?

Shepherd. Ou, sir, troth I am no that free to say that I mind wha I might think they were.

Sheriff. Come, come, sir! I ask you directly, did you think they were the fairies you saw?

Shepherd. Indeed, sir, and I winna say but I might think it was the Good Neighbours.

Thus unwillingly was he brought to allude to the irritable and captious inhabitants of fairy land.

63.23 (Ch. 5) the rate of pontage

DRAWBRIDGE AT BRIDGE-END. A bridge of the very peculiar construction described in the text, actually existed at a small hamlet about a mile and a half above Melrose, called from the circumstance Bridge-End. It is thus noticed in Gordon's *Itinerarium Septentrionale:—*

"In another journey through the south parts of Scotland, about a mile and a half from Melrose, in the shire of Teviotdale, I saw the remains of a curious bridge over the river Tweed, consisting of three octangular pillars, or rather towers, standing within the water, without any arches to join them. The middle one, which is the most entire, has a door towards the north, and, I suppose, another opposite one towards the south, which I could not see without crossing the water. In the middle of this tower is a projection or cornice surrounding it: the whole is hollow from the door upwards, and now open at the top, near which is a small window. I was informed that not long ago a countryman and his family lived in this tower—and got his livelihood by laying out planks from pillar to pillar, and conveying passengers over the river. Whether this be ancient or modern, I know not; but as it is singular in its kind, I have thought fit to exhibit it."

The vestiges of this uncommon species of bridge still exist, and the author has often seen the foundations of the columns when drifting down the Tweed at night, for the purpose of killing salmon by torch-light. Mr John Mercer of Bridge-end recollects, that about fifty years ago the pillars were visible above water; and the late Mr David Kyle of the George Inn, Melrose, told the author that he saw a stone taken from the ruins bearing this inscription:—

I, Sir John Pringle of Palmer stede,
Give an hundred markis of gowd sae reid,
To help to bigg my brigg ower Tweed.

Pringle of Galashiels, afterwards of Whytbank, was the Baron to whom the bridge belonged.

97.21 (Ch. 9) double ale It was one of the few reminiscences of Old Parr, or Henry Jenkins, I forget which, that, at some convent in the veteran's neighbourhood, the community, before the dissolution, used to dole out roast-beef by the measure of feet and yards.

127.37 (Ch. 13) convenient to hear A brood of wild-geese, which long frequented one of the uppermost islands in Loch-Lomond, called Inch-Tavoe, were supposed to have some mysterious connexion with the ancient family of MacFarlane of that ilk, and it is said were never seen after the ruin and extinction of that house. The MacFarlanes had a house and garden upon that same island of Inch-Tavoe. Here James VI. was, on one occasion, regaled by the chieftain. His majesty had been previously much amused by the geese pursuing each other on the Loch. But, when one which was brought to table, was found to be tough and ill fed, James observed—"that MacFarlane's geese minded their play more than their meat," a proverb which has been current ever since.

145.20 (Ch. 15) most lovely Protection There are many instances to be met with in the ancient dramas of this whimsical and conceited custom of persons who formed an intimacy, distinguishing each other by some quaint epithet. In *Every Man out of his Humour*, there is a humorous debate upon names most fit to bind the relation betwixt Sogliardo and Cavaliero Shift, which ends by adopting those of Countenance and Resolution. What is more to the point is in the speech of Hedon, a voluptuary and a courtier in *Cynthia's Revels*. "You know that I call Madam Philantia my HONOUR, and she calls me her AMBITION. Now, when I meet her in the presence, anon, I will come to her and say, 'Sweet Honour, I have hitherto contented my sense with the lilies of your hand, but now I will taste the roses of your lip.' To which she cannot but blushing answer, 'Nay, now you are too ambitious;' and then do I reply, 'I cannot be too ambitious of Honour, sweet lady. Wilt not be good?'" —I think there is some remnant of this foppery preserved in masonic lodges, where each brother is distinguished by a name in the Lodge, signifying some abstract quality, as Discretion, or the like. See the poems of Gavin Wilson.

159.31 (Ch. 16) Rowland Yorke, Stukely

ROWLAND YORKE, AND STUKELY. "Yorke," says Camden, "was a Londoner, a man of a loose and dissolute behaviour, and desperately audacious—famous in his time amongst the common bullies and swaggerers, as being the first that, to the great admiration of many at his boldness, brought into England the bold and dangerous way of fencing with the rapier in duelling. Whereas, till that time, the English used to fight with long swords and bucklers, striking with the edge, and thought it no part of man either to push or strike beneath the girdle."

Having a command in the Low Countries, Yorke revolted to the Spaniards, and died miserably, poisoned, as was supposed, by his new allies. Three years afterwards, his bones were dug up and gibbeted by the command of the States of Holland.

Thomas Stukely, another distinguished gallant of the time, was bred a merchant, being the son of a rich clothier in the west. He wedded the daughter and heiress of a wealthy alderman of London, named Curtis, after whose death he squandered the riches he thus acquired in all manner of extravagance. His wife, whose fortune supplied his waste, represented to him that he ought to make more of her. Stukely replied, "I will make as much of thee, believe me, as it is possible for any to do;" and he kept his word in one sense, having stripped her even of her wearing apparel, before he finally ran away from her.

Having fled to Italy, he contrived to impose upon the Pope, with a plan of invading Ireland, for which he levied soldiers, and made some preparations; but ended by engaging himself and his troops in the service of King Sebastian of Portugal. He sailed with that prince on his fatal voyage to Barbary, and fell with him at the battle of Alcazar.

Stukely, as one of the first gallants of the time, has had the honour to be chronicled in song, in Evans' Old Ballads, vol. iii. edition 1810. His fate is also introduced in a tragedy, by George Peel, as has been supposed, called the Battle of Alcazar, from which play Dryden is alleged to have taken the idea of Don Sebastian; if so, it is surprising he omitted a character so congenial to King

Charles the Second's time, as the witty, brave, and profligate Thomas Stukely.

212.39 (Ch. 23) walking on it This species of path, visible when looked at from a distance, but not to be seen when you are upon it, is called on the Border by the significant name of a Blind-road.

214.6 (Ch. 23) lifted at night It is in vain to seek near Melrose for any such castle as is here described. The lakes at the head of the Yarrow, and those at the rise of the water of Ale, present no object of the kind. But in Yetholm Loch, (a romantic sheet of water, in the dry march, as it is called,) there are the remains of a fortress called Lochside Tower, which, like the supposed Castle of Avenel, is built upon an island, and connected with the land by a causeway. It is much smaller than the Castle of Avenel is described, consisting only of a single ruinous tower.

215.7 (Ch. 24) a thief in his heart It was of Lochwood, the hereditary fortress of the Johnstones of Annandale, a strong castle situated in the centre of a quaking bog, that James V. made this remark.

216.26 (Ch. 24) the buist *Buist*—The brand, or mark, set upon sheep or cattle by their owners.

217.15 (Ch. 24) the White Lady of Avenel There is an ancient English family, I believe, which bears, or did bear, a ghost or spirit passant sable in a field argent. This seems to have been a device of a punning or *canting* herald.

221.24 (Ch. 24) the old miser Miser, used in the sense in which it often occurs in Spenser, and which is indeed its literal import,—"wretched old man."

226.35 (Ch. 25) handfasting This custom of handfasting actually prevailed in the upland days. It arose partly from the want of priests. While the convents subsisted, monks were detached on regular circuits through the wilder districts, to marry those who had lived in this species of connexion. A practice of the same kind existed in the Isle of Portland.

229.32 (Ch. 25) be without them

JULIAN AVENEL. If it were necessary to name a prototype for this brutal, licentious, and cruel Border chief, in an age which showed but too many such, the Laird of Black Ormiston might be selected for that purpose. He was a friend and confidant of Bothwell, and an agent in Henry Darnley's murder. At his last stage, he was, like other great offenders, a seeming penitent; and, as his confession bears, divers gentlemen and servants being in the chamber, he said, "For God's sake, sit down and pray for me, for I have been a great sinner otherwise," (that is, besides his share in Darnley's death,) "for the which God is this day punishing me; for of all men on the earth, I have been one of the proudest, and most high-minded, and most unclean of my body. But specially I have shed the innocent blood of one Michael Hunter with my own hands. Alas! therefore, because the said Michael, having me lying on my back, having a fork in his hand, might have slain me if he had pleased, and did it not, which of all things grieves me most in conscience. Also, in a rage, I hanged a poor man for a horse;—with many other wicked deeds, for whilk I ask my God mercy. It is not marvel I have been wicked, for the wicked company that ever I have been in, but specially within the seven years by-past, in which I never saw two good men or one good deed, but all kind of wickedness, and yet God would not suffer me to be lost."—See the whole confession in the State Trials.

Another worthy of the Borders, called Geordy Bourne, of somewhat subordinate rank, was a similar picture of profligacy. He had fallen into the hands of Sir Robert Carey, then Warden of the English East Marches, who gives the following account of his prisoner's confession:—

"When all things were quiet, and the watch set at night, after supper, about ten of the clock, I took one of my men's liveries and put it about me, and took two other of my servants with me in their liveries; and we three, as the Warden's men, came to the Provost Marshal's, where Bourne was, and were let into his chamber. We sate down by him, and told him that we were desirous to see him, because we heard he was stout and valiant, and true to his friend, and that we were sorry our master could not be moved to save his life. He voluntarily of himself said, that he had lived long enough to do so many villainies as he had done; and withal told us, that he had lain with above forty men's wives, what in England what in Scotland; and that he had killed seven Englishmen with his own hands, cruelly murdering them; and that he had spent his whole time in whoring, drinking, stealing, and taking deep revenge for slight offences. He seemed to be very penitent, and much desired a minister for the comfort of his soul. We promised him to let our master know his desire, who, we knew, would presently grant it. We took leave of him; and presently I took order that Mr Selby, a very honest preacher, should go to him, and not stir from him till his execution the next morning; for after I had heard his own confession, I was resolved no conditions should save his life, and so took order, that at the gates opening the next morning, he should be carried to execution, which accordingly was performed."—*Memoirs of Sir Robert Carey, Earl of Monmouth.*

254.10 (Ch. 27) some alteration in his apparel

FOPPERY OF THE SIXTEENTH CENTURY. Sir Piercie Shafton's extreme love of dress was an attribute of the coxcombs of this period. The display made by their forefathers was in the numbers of their retinue; but as the actual influence of the nobility began to be restrained both in France and England by the increasing power of the crown, the indulgence of vanity in personal display became more inordinate. There are many allusions to this change of custom in Shakspeare and other dramatic writers, where the reader may find mention made of

Bonds enter'd into
For gay apparel against the triumph day.

Jonson informs us, that for the first entrance of a gallant, "'twere good you turned four or five hundred acres of your best land into two or three trunks of apparel."—*Every Man out of his Humour.*

In the Memorie of the Somerville family, a curious instance occurs of this fashionable species of extravagance. In the year 1537, when James V. brought over his shortlived bride from France, the Lord Somerville of the day was so profuse in expense of apparel, that the money which he borrowed on the occasion was compensated by a perpetual annuity of threescore pounds Scottish, payable out of the barony of Carnwath till doomsday, which was assigned by the creditor to Saint Magdalen's Chapel. At this deep expense the Lord Somerville had rendered himself so glorious in apparel, that the King, who saw so brave a gallant enter the Park at Holyrood, followed by only two pages, called upon several of the courtiers to ascertain who it could be who was so richly dressed and so slightly attended, and he was not recognised until he entered the presence-chamber. "You are very brave, my lord," said the King, as he received his homage; "but where are all your men and attendants?" The Lord Somerville readily answered, "If it please your Majesty, here they are," pointing to the lace that was on his own and his pages' clothes; whereat the King laughed heartily, and having surveyed the finery more nearly, bade away with it all, and let him have his stout band of spears again.

There is a scene in Jonson's "Every Man out of his Humour," (Act IV. Scene 6,) in which a Euphuist of the time gives an account of the effects of a duel on the clothes of himself and his opponent, and never departs a syllable from the catalogue of his wardrobe. We shall insert it in evidence that the foppery of our ancestors was not inferior to that of our own time.

"*Fastidius.* Good faith, signior, now you speak of a quarrel, I'll acquaint you with a difference that happened between a gallant and myself, Sir Puntarvolo. You know him if I should name him—Signior Luculento.

"*Punt.* Luculento! What inauspicious chance interposed itself to your two loves?

"*Fast.* Faith, sir, the same that sundered Agamemnon and great Thetis' son; but let the cause escape, sir. He sent me a challenge, mixt with some few braves, which I restored; and, in fine, we met. Now indeed, sir, I must tell you, he did offer at first very desperately, but without judgment; for look you, sir, I cast myself into this figure; now he came violently on, and withal advancing his rapier to strike, I thought to have took his arm, for he had left his body to my election, and I was sure he could not recover his guard. Sir, I mist my purpose in his arm, rashed his doublet sleeves, ran him close by the left cheek and through his hair. He, again, light me here—I had on a gold cable hat-band, then new come up, about a murrey French hat I had; cuts my hat-band, and yet it was massy goldsmith's work, cuts my brim, which, by good fortune, being thick embroidered with gold twist and spangles, disappointed the force of the blow; nevertheless, it grazed on my shoulder, takes me away six purls of an Italian cut-work band I wore, cost me three pounds in the Exchange but three days before——

"*Punt.* This was a strange encounter.

"*Fast.* Nay, you shall hear, sir. With this, we both fell out and breathed. Now, upon the second sign of his assault, I betook me to my former manner of defence; he, on the other side, abandoned his body to the same danger as before, and follows me still with blows; but I, being loth to take the deadly advantage that lay before me of his left side, made a kind of stramazoun, ran him up to the hilt through the doublet, through the shirt, and yet missed the skin. He, making a reverse blow, falls upon my embossed girdle,—I had thrown off the hangers a little before,—strikes off a skirt of a thick-laced satin doublet I had, lined with four taffatas, cuts off two panes embroidered with pearl, rends through the drawings-out of tissue, enters the linings, and skips the flesh.

"*Car.* I wonder he speaks not of his wrought shirt.

"*Fast.* Here, in the opinion of mutual damage, we paused. But, ere I proceed, I must tell you, signior, that in the last encounter, not having leisure to put off my silver spurs, one of the rowels catched hold of the ruffles of my boot, and, being Spanish leather and subject to tear, overthrows me, rends me two pair of silk stockings that I put on, being somewhat of a raw morning, a peach colour and another, and strikes me some half-inch deep into the side of the calf: He seeing the blood come, presently takes horse and away: I having bound up my wound with a piece of my wrought shirt——

"*Car.* O, comes it in there?

"*Fast.* Ride after him, and, lighting at the court-gate both together, embraced, and marched hand in hand up into the presence. Was not this business well carried?

"*Maci.* Well! yes; and by this we can guess what apparel the gentleman wore.

"*Punt.* 'Fore valour! it was a designment begun with much resolution, maintained with as much prowess, and ended with more humanity."

306.11 (Ch. 33) the Lord James Lord James Stewart, afterwards the Regent Murray.

308.2 (Ch. 33) a mailed glove on that

GOOD FAITH OF THE BORDERERS. As some atonement for their laxity of morals on most occasions, the Borderers were severe observers of the faith which they had pledged, even to an enemy. If any person broke his word so plighted, the individual to whom faith had not been observed, used to bring to the next Border-meeting a glove hung on the point of a spear, and proclaim to Scots and English the name of the defaulter. This was accounted so great a disgrace to all connected with him, that his own clansmen sometimes destroyed him, to escape the infamy he had brought on them.

Constable, a spy engaged by Sir Ralph Sadler, talks of two Border thieves, whom he used as his guides,—"That they would not care to steal, and yet that they would not betray any man that trusts in them, for all the gold in Scotland or in France. They are my guides and outlaws. If they would betray me they might get their pardons, and cause me to be hanged; but I have tried them ere this."—*Sadler's Letters during the Northern Insurrection.*

310.27 (Ch. 34) boiled almonds

INDULGENCES OF THE MONKS. The *biberes*, *caritas*, and boiled almonds, of which Abbot Boniface speaks, were special occasions for enjoying luxuries, afforded to the monks by grants from different sovereigns, or from other benefactors to the convent. There is one of these charters called *De Pitancia Centum Librarum*. By this charter, which is very curious, our Robert Bruce, on the 10th January, and in the twelfth year of his reign, assigns, out of the customs of Berwick, and failing those, out of the customs of Edinburgh or Haddington, the sum of one hundred pounds, at the half-yearly terms of Pentecost and Saint Martin's in winter, to the abbot and community of the monks of Melrose. The precise purpose of this annuity is to furnish to each of the monks of the said monastery, while placed at food in the refectory, an extra mess of rice boiled with milk, or of almonds, or peas, or other pulse of that kind which could be procured in the country. This addition to their commons is to be entitled the King's Mess. And it is declared, that although any monk should, from some honest apology, want appetite or inclination to eat of the king's mess, his share should, nevertheless, be placed on the table with those of his brethren, and afterwards carried to the gate and given to the poor. "Neither is it our pleasure," continues the bountiful sovereign, "that the dinner, which is or ought to be served up to the said monks according to their ancient rule, should be diminished in quantity, or rendered inferior in quality, on account of this our mess, so furnished as aforesaid." It is, moreover, provided, that the abbot, with the consent of the most prudent of his brethren, shall name a provident and discreet monk for receiving, directing, and expending, all matters concerning this annuity for the benefit of the community, agreeably to the royal desire and intention, rendering a faithful accompt thereof to the abbot and superiors of the same convent. And the same charter declares the king's farther pleasure, that the said men of religion should be bound yearly and for ever, in acknowledgment of the above donation, to clothe fifteen poor men at the feast of Saint Martin in winter, and to feed them on the same day, delivering to each of them four ells of large or broad, or six ells of narrow cloth, and to each also a new pair of shoes or sandals, according to their order; and if the said monks shall fail in their engagements, or any of them, it is the king's will that the fault shall be redeemed by a double performance of what has been omitted, to be executed at the sight of the chief forester of Ettrick for the time being, and before the return of Saint Martin's day succeeding that on which the omission has taken place.

Of this charter, respecting the pittance of L.100 assigned to furnish the monks of Melrose with a daily mess of boiled rice, almonds, or other pulse, to mend their commons, the antiquarian reader will be pleased, doubtless, to see the original.

Carta Regis Roberti I. Abbati et Conventui de Melross.

Carta de Pitancia Centum Librarum.

"Robertus Dei gracia Rex Scottorum omnibus probis hominibus tocius terre sue Salutem. Sciatis nos pro salute anime nostre et pro salute animarum antecessorum et successorum nostrorum Regum Scocie Dedisse Concessisse et hac presenti Carta nostra confirmasse

Deo et Beate Marie virgini et Religiosis viris Abbati et Conventui de Melross et eorum successoribus in perpetuum Centum Libras Sterlingorum Annui Redditus singulis annis percipiendas de firmis nostris Burgi Berwici super Twedam ad terminos Pentecostis et Sancti Martini in hyeme pro equali portione vel de nova Custuma nostra Burgi predicti si firme nostre predicte ad dictam summam pecunie sufficere non poterunt vel de nova Custuma nostra Burgorum nostrorum de Edenburg et de Hadington Si firme nostre et Custuma nostra ville Berwici aliquo casu contingente ad hoc forte non sufficiant. Ita quod dicta summa pecunie Centum Librarum eis annuatim integre et absque contradictione aliqua plenarie persolvatur pre cunctis aliis quibuscunque assignacionibus per nos factis seu faciendis ad inveniendum in perpetuum singulis diebus cuilibet monacho monasterii predicti comedenti in Refectorio unum sufficiens ferculum risarum factarum cum lacte, amigdalarum vel pisarum sive aliorum ciborum consimilis condicionis inventorum in patria et illud ferculum ferculum Regis vocabitur in eternum. Et si aliquis monachus ex aliqua causa honesta de dicto ferculo comedere noluerit vel refici non poterit non minus attamen sibi de dicto ferculo ministretur et ad portam pro pauperibus deportetur. Nec volumus quod occasione ferculi nostri predicti prandium dicti Conventus de quo antiquitus communiter eis deserviri sive ministrari solebat in aliquo pejoretur seu diminuatur. Volumus insuper et ordinamus quod Abbas ejusdem monasterii qui pro tempore fuerit de consensu saniorum de Conventu specialiter constituat unum monachum providum et discretum ad recipiendum ordinandum et expendendum totam summam pecunie memorate pro utilitate conventus secundum votum et intencionem mentis nostre superius annotatum et ad reddendum fidele compotum coram Abbate et Maioribus de Conventu singulis annis de pecunia sic recepta. Et volumus quod dicti religiosi teneantur annuatim in perpetuum pro predicta donacione nostra ad perpetuam nostri memoriam vestire quindecim pauperes ad festum Sancti Martini in hieme et eosdem cibare eodem die liberando eorum cuilibet quatuor ulnas panni grossi et lati vel sex ulnas panni stricti et eorum cuilibet unum novum par sotularium de ordine suo. Et si dicti religiosi in premissis vel aliquo premissorum aliquo anno defecerint volumus quod illud quod minus perimpletum fuerit dupplicetur diebus magis necessariis per visum capitalis forestarii nostri de Selkirk, qui pro tempore fuerit. Et quod dicta dupplicatio fiat ante natale domini proximo sequens festum Sancti Martini predictum. In cujus rei testimonium presenti Carte nostre sigillum nostrum precipimus apponi. Testibus venerabilibus in Christo patribus Willielmo, Johanne, Willielmo et David Sancti Andree, Glasguensis, Dunkeldensis et Moraviensis ecclesiarum dei gracia episcopis Bernardo Abbate de Abirbrothock Cancellario, Duncano, Malisio, et Hugone de Fyf de Strathin et de Ross, Comitibus Waltero Senescallo Scocie. Jacobo domini de Duglas et Alexandro Fraser Camerarionostro Scocie militibus. Apud Abirbrothock, decimo die Januarij. Anno Regni nostri vicesimo.

327.22 (Ch. 36) spur-whang *Spur-whang*—Spur-leather.

344.10 (Ch. 37) the oak at Mamre It is scarce necessary to say, that in Melrose, the prototype of Kennaquhair, no such oak ever existed.

346.10 (Ch. 37) never in the fountain

PEDIGREE OF THE DOUGLAS FAMILY. The late excellent and laborious antiquary, Mr George Chalmers, has rebuked the vaunt of the House of Douglas, or rather of Hume of Godscroft, their historian, but with less than his wonted accuracy. In the first volume of his Caledonia, he quotes the passage in Godscroft for the purpose of confuting it.

The historian (of the Douglasses) cries out, "We do not know them in the fountain, but in the stream; not in the root, but in the stem; for we know not which is the mean man that did rise above the vulgar." This assumption Mr Chalmers censures as ill-timed, and alleges, that if the historian had attended more to research than to declamation, he might easily have seen the first mean man of this renowned family. This he alleges to have been one Theobaldus Flammaticus, or Theobald the Fleming, to whom Arnold, Abbot of Kelso, between the year 1147 and 1160, granted certain lands on Douglas water, by a deed which Mr Chalmers conceives to be the first link of the chain of title-deeds to Douglasdale. Hence, he says, the family must renounce their family domain, or acknowledge this obscure Fleming as their ancestor. Theobald the Fleming, it is acknowledged, did not himself assume the name of Douglas; "but," says the antiquary, "his son William, who inherited his estate, called himself, and was named by others, De Duglas;" and he refers to the deeds in which he is so designed. Mr Chalmers's full argument may be found in the first volume of his Caledonia, p. 579.

This proposition is one which a Scottish man will admit unwillingly, and only upon undeniable testimony; and as it is liable to strong grounds of challenge, the present author, with all the respect to Mr Chalmers which his zealous and effectual researches merit, is not unwilling to take this opportunity to state some plausible grounds for doubting that Theobaldus Flammaticus was either the father of the first William de Douglas, or in the slightest degree connected with the Douglas family.

It must first be observed, that there is no reason whatever for concluding Theobaldus Flammaticus to be the father of William de Douglas, excepting that they had both lands upon the small river of Douglas; and that there are two strong presumptions to the contrary. For, first, the father being named Fleming, there seems no good reason why the son should have assumed a different designation; secondly, there does not occur a single instance of the name of Theobald during the long line of the Douglas pedigree—an omission very unlikely to take place, had the original father of the race been so called. These are secondary considerations indeed; but they are important, in so far as they exclude any support of Mr Chalmers's system, except from the point which he has rather assumed than proved, namely, that the lands granted to Theobald the Fleming were the same which were granted to William de Douglas, and which constituted the original domain of which we find this powerful family lords.

Now, it happens, singularly enough, that the lands granted by the Abbot of Kelso to Theobaldus Flammaticus are not the same with those of which William de Douglas was in possession. Nay, it would appear, from comparing the charter granted to Theobaldus Flammaticus, that, though situated on the water of Douglas, they never made a part of the barony of that name, and therefore cannot be the same with those held by William de Douglas in the succeeding generation. But if William de Douglas did not succeed Theobaldus Flammaticus, there is no more reason for holding these two persons to be father and son than if they had lived in different provinces; and we are still as far from having discovered the first mean man of the Douglas family as Hume of Godscroft was in the 16th century. We leave the question to antiquaries and genealogists.

346.17 (Ch. 37) Alanus Dapifer

PEDIGREE OF THE STEWART FAMILY. To atone to the memory of the learned and indefatigable Chalmers for having ventured to impeach his genealogical proposition concerning the descent of the Douglasses, we are bound to render him our grateful thanks for the felicitous light which he has thrown on that of the House of Stewart, still more important to Scottish history.

The acute pen of Lord Hailes, which, like the spear of Ithuriel, conjured so many shadows from Scottish history, had dismissed among the rest those of Banquo and Fleance, the rejection of which fables left the illustrious family of Stewart without an ancestor beyond Walter the son of Allan, who is alluded to in the text. The researches of our late learned antiquary detected in this Walter, the descendant of Allan, the son of Flaald, who obtained from William the Conqueror the Castle of Oswestry in Shropshire, and was the father of an illustrious line of English nobles, by his first son, William, and by his second son, Walter, the progenitor of the royal family of Stewart.

350.18 (Ch. 37) till this moment

THE WHITE SPIRIT. The contrivance of provoking the irritable vanity of Sir Piercie Shafton, by presenting him with a bodkin, indicative of his descent from a tailor, is borrowed from a German romance by the celebrated Tieck, called Das Peter Manchen, *i.e.* The Dwarf Peter. The being who gives name to the tale, is the Burg-geist, or castle spectre, of a German family, whom he aids with his counsel, as he defends their castle by his supernatural power. But the Dwarf Peter is so unfortunate an adviser, that all his counsels, though producing success in the immediate result, are in the issue attended with mishap and with guilt. The youthful baron, the owner of the haunted castle, falls in love with a maiden, the daughter of a neighbouring count, a man of great pride, who refuses him the hand of the young lady, on account of his own superiority of descent. The lover, repulsed and affronted, returns to take counsel with the Dwarf Peter, how he may silence the count and obtain the victory in the argument, the next time they enter on the topic of pedigree. The dwarf gives his patron or pupil a horse-shoe, instructing him to present it to the count when he is next giving himself superior airs on the subject of his family. It has the effect accordingly; the count, understanding it as an allusion to a misalliance of one of his ancestors with the daughter of a black-smith, is thrown into a dreadful passion with the young lover, the consequences of which are the seduction of the young lady, and the slaughter of her father.

If we suppose the dwarf to represent the corrupt part of human nature,—that "law in our members which wars against the law of our minds"—the work forms an ingenious allegory.

THE ABBOT

Editorial Note

The Abbot occupies the whole of Volume 4 and the first part of Volume 5 of the 1822 octavo *Historical Romances*, MSS 23016 and 23017 in the Interleaved Set. Scott was working on the annotation of *The Abbot* by 2 January 1830, when he asked Cadell to arrange for a quotation from the *Provincial Antiquities* to be copied for a note on the Abbot of Unreason (87.8–35: *Letters*, 11.283). He had finished his work by 26 January 1830 when Cadell 'received The Abbot & Kenilworth with Introductions & Notes' (MS 21043, f. 16r). Cadell's revision was carried out between 8 March and 23 April when he 'revised the conclusion', with some further work on 10 May when he 'revised proof of Introduction' (MS 21020, ff. 12r, 19r, 21v). The novel appeared as Volumes 20 and 21 of the Magnum on 1 January and 1 February 1831 (EEWN 10, 397).

The Introduction is, appropriately, a companion to that for *The Monastery*. It is a shorter, bravura essay drawing on a wide range of images, quotations, and allusions to explain how Scott decided, after the comparative failure of the previous novel, to trust to his ability as a prolific author to put disappointment behind him. As Christopher Johnson has shown (EEWN 10, 378–79), this opening of the Introduction is at least as fictional as the novel, but that may be felt to enhance rather than diminish its appeal. Scott goes on to refer the reader to the brief first-edition Introductory Epistle for the exclusion of the White Lady from the present novel. Intriguingly he offers justifications of two omissions from that Epistle: any explanation of the abortive nature of the matter of the casket with the Bruce's heart which had occupied so much space in the Introduction to the first edition of *The Monastery* only to disappear from view; and any mention of Mary Queen of Scots, the popular high-profile subject on which (Scott here resumes the unacknowledged fictional autobiographical mode of the opening of the Introduction) he had decided to risk all.

For the most part, the Introduction seems to have been written consecutively, without any evident signs of interruption. There is one major exception, though. Originally the passage at 81.18–43 read 'at last very imperfectly explaind. [new paragraph] Neither would it have been prudent'. The whole passage at 18–42 was an afterthought, though it may have been written in the same session. Inserted in the fluently written manuscript on the verso (except for the sentence with a favourite reference to 'Mungo in the Padlock', presumably added in proof), it develops significantly Scott's ideas on why some things are best left unexplained. A sentence inserted on the verso facing the end of the second paragraph of the Introduction may have been omitted accidentally by the copyist, but it reads more like the author talking to himself rather than to his readers: 'But I need not dilate upon my opinions in this matter since I have detaild them with nearly the sam[e] illustrations in Introductory Epistle to The fortunes of Nigel'. Another significant deletion was certainly made at a subsequent stage at 80.25, where the beginning of the paragraph runs thus in manuscript: 'It must be added that his incognito gave him the greater courage to ?renew his attempts on ⟨publick favour⟩ the public. While a⟨n⟩ repeated annoyance can be traced to the intrusion of a single recognized individual it requires unusual audacity on the part of the individual to stand the genral volley of criticism by which he is assaild in return for his pertinacity. But the ⟨authors⟩ uncertainty concerning the author⟨s⟩ of the Waverley novels gave him the same advantage which Jack the Giant Killer received from his coat of darkness.' At 83.4 an intriguing final sentence was cut from the end of the paragraph which concludes in manuscript: '. . . I naturally paid attention to principles of composition as I conceived were best suited to the historical novel. What these are I will take occasion in the course of thes[e] annotations to detail at some length.' The second sentence may have been deleted at a later stage because it was felt (with some justice) that the annotations do not fulfil this promise in any sustained manner. Contrariwise the quotation from *1 Henry IV* at 79.29 is part of an enriching later insertion (26–31).

Scott annotates this novel heavily for the Magnum. There are numerous footnotes, mostly glossarial or offering brief explanations or identifications of sources, sometimes of 'peg'-like references in the original text. The endnotes include several virtual essays on topics touched on in the text, drawing on Scott's wide range of reading. Pre-eminent among them are a trio on the Abbot of

Unreason, the hobby-horse, and the Robin Hood game (86–92). Several other footnotes and endnotes deal with the shifting relationship of the fictitious events to recorded history. Among the most notable of these is one of those very brief endnotes, demonstrating how 'A romance . . . wants but a hair to make a tether of' (96.9–17). Different emphases can be observed in two further endnotes: in one the details of Mary's resignation are 'imaginary; but the outline of the events is historical' (94.31–33); in the other the author has been 'tolerably strict in adhering to the incidents' of the Battle of Langside though the traditional location adopted in the novel is erroneous (100.6–8). In the latter case it is also worth observing, firstly that Scott is prompted into a discussion of the reliability of tradition in general, and secondly that he leaves it to the reader to compare a long extract from *The Memoirs of Sir James Melvil of Halhill* with the account of the battle given in the novel. Another endnote, teasing out the relationship between the fiction and the various accounts of Mary's escape from Lochleven, ends with a suggestion that such a note is particularly important in a novel such as this: 'In another case, it would be tedious to point out in a work of amusement such minute points of historical fact; but the general interest taken in the fate of Queen Mary, renders every thing of consequence which connects itself with her misfortunes' (99.9–13). Not all the endnotes are likely to be helpful in elucidating the novel: the succinct and varied biographical sketch of George, Lord Seyton (93–94) is really for separate reading. Perhaps the most loosely attached of the endnotes is the final item, evidently prompted by a 'very curious letter' of Robert the Bruce and relating to Scott's earliest plans for the fiction represented by this novel and its predecessor, rather than to the work as it stands.

There are four Magnum illustrations for this title. The frontispiece to Volume 20 (MAG0039 / TB348.20) was designed by Alfred Edward Chalon and engraved by Charles Heath. It depicts Mary with ladies-in-waiting and Roland as page, in her apartments at Loch Leven Castle (EEWN 10, 191.16–25 (abridged): '"But it is over . . . of a Grecian prophetess.'). The title-page vignette (MAG0040 / B348.20) was designed by Edwin Landseer and engraved by William Henry Watt. It depicts Roland as a boy being rescued by the greyhound Wolf from the loch of Avenel (EEWN 10, 9–16 (abridged): 'Wolf marked the object . . . towards the causeway.'). The frontispiece to Volume 21 (MAG0041 / TB348.21) was designed by John Burnet and engraved by William Finden. It depicts Mary abdicating in favour of her son, with Lord Ruthven, Sir Robert Melville, and Lord Lindesay looking on (EEWN 10, 210: the caption reads simply 'THE ABBOT.'). The title-page vignette (MAG0042 / TB348.21) was designed by David Octavius Hill and engraved by William Miller. It depicts Mary and her rescuers landing on the shore of Loch Leven, with the island and Castle behind them (EEWN 10, 341.40–43: 'They landed and while . . . house of the gardener.').

A.E. Chalon R.A.   Charles Heath.

THE ABBOT.

"But it is over -- and I am Mary Stuart once more. She snatched from her head the curch or cap, shook down the thick clustered tresses, and, drawing her slender fingers across the labyrinth which they formed, she arose from the chair, and stood like the inspired image of a Grecian prophetess.

EDINBURGH, PUBLISHED 1831, BY ROBERT CADELL and WHITTAKER & C[o] LON

WAVERLEY NOVELS.

VOL. XX.

THE ABBOT.

Wolf marked the object of her anxiety, he swam straight to the spot where his assistance was so much wanted, and, seizing the childs under-dress in his mouth, he not only kept him afloat, but towed him towards the causeway.

PRINTED FOR R. CADELL & COMPANY, EDINBURGH;
AND WHITTAKER, TREACHER & C°. LONDON.
1831.

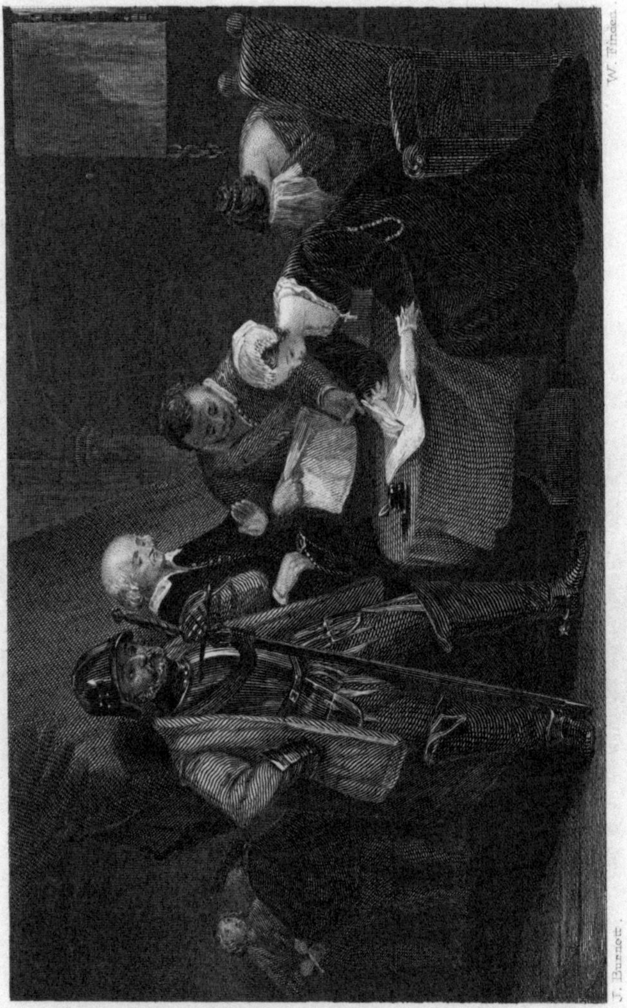

THE ABBOT.

WAVERLEY NOVELS.

VOL. XXI.

THE ABBOT.

"They landed, and while the abbot returned thanks aloud to Heaven, which had thus far favoured their enterprise, Douglas enjoyed the best reward of his desperate undertaking, in conducting the queen to the house of the gardener."

PRINTED FOR ROBERT CADELL, EDINBURGH.
AND WHITTAKER & C? LONDON.
1831.

Introduction to The Abbot

FROM what is said in the Introduction to the Monastery, it must necessarily be inferred, that the Author considered that romance as something very like a failure. It is true, the booksellers did not complain of the sale, because, unless upon very felicitous occasions, or on those which are equally the reverse, literary popularity is not gained or lost by a single publication. Leisure must be allowed for the tide both to flow and ebb. But I was conscious that, in my situation, not to advance was in some degree to recede, and being naturally unwilling to think that the principle of decay lay in myself, I was at least desirous to know of a certainty, whether the degree of discountenance which I had incurred, was now owing to an ill-managed story, or an ill-chosen subject.

I was never, I confess, one of those who are willing to suppose the brains of an author to be a kind of milk, which will not stand above a single creaming, and who are eternally harping to young authors to husband their efforts, and to be chary of their reputation, lest it grow hackneyed in the eyes of men. Perhaps I was, and have always been, the more indifferent to the degree of estimation in which I might be held as an author, because I did not put so high a value as many others upon what is termed literary reputation in the abstract, or at least upon the species of popularity which had fallen to my share; for though it were worse than affectation to deny that my vanity was satisfied at my success in the department in which chance had in some measure enlisted me, I was, nevertheless, far from thinking that the novelist or romance-writer stands high in the ranks of literature. But I spare the reader farther egotism on this subject, as I have expressed my opinion very fully in the Introductory Epistle to the Fortunes of Nigel, first edition; and, although it be composed in an imaginary character, it is as sincere and candid as if it had been written "without my gown and band."

In a word, when I considered myself as having been unsuccessful in the Monastery, I was tempted to try whether I could not restore, even at the risk of totally losing, my so called reputation, by a new hazard—I looked round my library and could not but observe, that, from the time of Chaucer to that of Byron, the most popular authors had been the most prolific. Even the Aristarch Johnson allowed that the quality of readiness and profusion had a merit in itself, independent of the intrinsic value of the composition. Talking of Churchill, I believe, who had little merit in his prejudiced eyes, he allowed him that of fertility, with some such qualification as this, "A crab apple can bear but crabs after all; but there is a great difference in favour of that which bears a large quantity of fruit, however indifferent, and that which produces only a few."

Looking more attentively at the patriarchs of literature, whose career was as long as it was brilliant, I thought I perceived that in the busy and prolonged course of exertion, there were no doubt occasional failures, but that still those who were favourites of their age triumphed over these miscarriages. By the new efforts which they made, their errors were obliterated, they became identified with the literature of their country, and after having long received law from the critics, came in some degree to impose it. And when such a writer was at length called from the scene, his death first made the public sensible what a large share he had occupied in their attention. I recollected a passage in Grimm's Correspondence, that while the unexhausted Voltaire sent forth tract after tract to the very close of a long life, the first impression made by each as it appeared, was, that it was inferior to its predecessor; an opinion adopted from the general idea that the Patriarch of Ferney must at last find the point from which he was to decline. But the opinion of the public finally ranked in succession the last of Voltaire's *essais* on the same footing with those which had formerly charmed the French nation. The inference from this and similar facts seemed to me to be, that new works were often judged of by the public, not so much from their own intrinsic merit, as from extrinsic ideas which readers had previously formed with regard to them, and over which a writer might hope to triumph by patience and by exertion. There is a risk in the attempt;

> If he fall in, good night, or sink or swim.

But this is a chance incident to every literary attempt, and by which men of a sanguine temper are little moved.

I may illustrate what I mean, by the feelings of most men in travelling. If we have found any stage particularly tedious, or in an especial degree interesting, particularly short, or much longer than we expected, our imaginations are so apt to exaggerate the original impression, that, on repeating the journey, we usually find that we have considerably over-rated the predominating quality, and the road appears to be duller or more pleasant, shorter or more tedious, than what we expected, and, consequently, than what is the actual case. It requires a third or fourth journey to enable us to form an accurate judgment of its beauty, its length, or its other attributes.

In the same manner, the public, judging of a new work, which it receives perhaps with little expectation, if surprised into applause, becomes very often ecstatic, gives a great deal more approbation than is due, and elevates the child of its immediate favour to a rank which, as it affects the author, it is equally difficult to keep, and painful to lose. If, on this occasion, the author trembles at the height to which he is raised, and becomes afraid of the shadow of his own renown, he may indeed retire from the lottery with the prize which he has drawn, but, in future ages, his honour will be only in proportion to his labours. If, on the contrary, he rushes again into the lists, he is sure to be judged with severity proportioned to the former favour of the public. If he be daunted by a bad reception on this second occasion, he may again become a stranger to the arena. If, on the contrary, he can keep his ground, and stand the shuttlecock's fate, of being struck up and down, he will probably, at length, hold with some certainty the level in public opinion which he may be found to deserve; and he may perhaps boast of arresting the general attention, in the same manner as the Bachelor Samson Carrasco, of fixing the weathercock La Giralda of Seville for weeks, months, or years, that is, for as long as the wind shall uniformly blow from one quarter. To this degree of popularity the author had the hardihood to aspire, while, in order to attain it, he assumed the daring resolution to keep himself in the view of the public by frequent appearances before them.

It must be added, that the author's incognito gave him the greater courage to renew his attempts on the public, and an advantage similar to that which Jack the Giant-killer received from his coat of darkness. In sending the Abbot out so soon after the Monastery, he had used the well-known practice recommended by Bassanio:—

> In my school days, when I had lost one shaft,
> I shot another of the self same flight,
> The self same way, with more advised watch,
> To find the other forth.

And, to continue the simile, his shafts, like those of the lesser Ajax, were discharged more readily that the archer was as inaccessible to criticism, personally speaking, as the Grecian archer under his brother's sevenfold shield.

Should the reader desire to know upon what principles the Abbot was expected to amend the fortune of the Monastery, I have first to request his attention to the Introductory Epistle addressed to the imaginary Captain Clutterbuck; a mode by which, like his predecessors in this walk of fiction, the real author makes one of his *dramatis personæ* the means of communicating his own sentiments to the public, somewhat more artificially than by a direct address to the readers. A pleasing French writer of fairy tales, Monsieur Pajon, author of the History of Prince Soly, has set a diverting example of the same machinery, where he introduces the presiding Genius of the land of Romance conversing with one of the personages of the tale.

In this Introductory Epistle, the author communicates, in confidence, to Captain Clutterbuck, his sense that the White Lady had not met the taste of the times, and his reason for withdrawing her from the scene. I did not deem it equally necessary to be candid respecting another alteration. The Monastery was designed, at first, to have contained some supernatural agency, arising out of the fact, that Melrose had been the place of deposit of the great Robert Bruce's heart. I flinched, however, from filling up, in this particular, the sketch as it was originally traced; nor did I venture to resume, in the continuation, the subject which I had left unattempted in the original work. Thus, the incident of the discovery of the heart, which occupies the greater part of the Introduction to the Monastery, is a mystery unnecessarily introduced, and which remains at last very imperfectly explained. In this particular, I am happy to shroud myself by the example of the author of "Caleb Williams," who never condescends to inform us of the actual contents of that Iron Chest which makes such a figure in his interesting work, and gives the name to Mr Colman's drama.

The public had some claim to enquire into this matter, but it seemed indifferent policy in the author to give the explanation. For, whatever praise may be due to the ingenuity which brings to a general combination all the loose threads of a narrative, like the knitter at the finishing of her stocking, I am greatly deceived if in many cases a superior advantage is not attained, by the air of reality which the deficiency of explanation attaches to a work written on a different system. In life itself, many things befall every mortal, of which the individual never knows the real cause or object; and were we to point out the most marked distinction between a real and a fictitious narrative, we would say, that the former, in reference to the remote causes of the events it relates, is obscure, doubtful, and mysterious; whereas, in the latter case, it is a part of the author's duty to afford satisfactory details upon the causes of the separate events he has recorded, and, in a word, to account for every thing. The reader, like Mungo in the Padlock, will not be satisfied with hearing what he is not made fully to comprehend.

I omitted, therefore, in the Introduction to the Abbot, any attempt to explain the previous story, or to apologize for unintelligibility.

Neither would it have been prudent to have endeavoured to proclaim, in the Introduction to the Abbot, the real spring, by which I hoped it might attract a greater degree of interest than its immediate predecessor. A taking title, or the announcement of a popular subject, is a recipe for success much in favour with booksellers, but which authors will not always find efficacious. The cause is worth a moment's examination.

There occur in every country some peculiar historical characters, which are, like a spell or charm, sovereign to excite curiosity and attract attention, since every one in the slightest degree interested in the land which they belong to, has heard much of them, and longs to hear more. A tale turning on the fortunes of Alfred or Elizabeth in England, or of Wallace or Bruce in Scotland, is sure by the very announcement to excite public curiosity to a considerable degree, and ensure the publisher's being relieved of the greater part of an impression, even before the contents of the work are known. This is of the last importance to the bookseller, who is at once, to use a technical phrase, "brought home," all his outlay being repaid. But it is a different case with the author, since it cannot be denied that we are apt to feel least satisfied with the works of which we have been induced, by titles and laudatory advertisements, to entertain exaggerated expectations. The intention of the work has been anticipated, and misconceived or misrepresented, and although the difficulty of executing the work again reminds us of Hotspur's task of "o'erwalking a current roaring loud," yet the adventurer must look for more ridicule if he fails, than applause if he executes, his undertaking.

Notwithstanding a risk, which should make authors pause ere they adopt a theme which, exciting general interest and curiosity, is often the preparative for disappointment, yet it would be an injudicious regulation which should deter the poet or painter from attempting to introduce historical portraits, merely from the difficulty of executing the task in a satisfactory manner. Something must be trusted to the generous impulse, which often thrusts an artist upon feats of which he knows the difficulty, while he trusts courage and exertion may afford the means of surmounting it.

It is especially when he is sensible of losing ground with the public, that an author may be justified in using with address, such selection of subject or title as is most likely to procure a rehearing. It was with these feelings of hope and apprehension, that I ventured to awaken, in a work of fiction, the memory of Queen Mary, so interesting by her wit, her beauty, her misfortunes, and the mystery which still does, and probably always will, overhang her history. In doing so, I was aware that failure would be a conclusive disaster, so that my task was something like that of an enchanter who raises a spirit over whom he is uncertain of possessing an effectual control; and I naturally paid attention to such principles of composition, as I conceived were best suited to the historical novel.

Enough has been already said to explain the purpose of composing the Abbot. The historical references are, as usual, explained in the notes. That which relates to Queen Mary's escape from Lochleven Castle, is a more minute account of that romantic adventure, than is to be found in the histories of the period.

ABBOTSFORD, 1st *January*, 1831.

Notes to The Abbot

7.15 (Ch. 1) in the eyes of bibliographers The tracts which appeared in the Disputation between the Scottish Reformer and Quentin Kennedy, Abbot of Crosraguel, are among the scarcest in Scottish Bibliography. See M'Crie's *Life of Knox*, p. 258.

15.24 (Ch. 2) Nicol-forest A district of Cumberland, lying close to the Scottish Border.

26.32 (Ch. 3) their baronage

GLENDONWYNE OF GLENDONWYNE. This was a house of ancient descent and superior consequence, including persons who fought at Bannockburn and Otterburn, and were closely connected by alliance and friendship with the great Earls of Douglas. The Knight in the story argues as most Scotsmen would do in his situation, for all of the same clan are popularly considered as descended from the same stock, and as having a right to the ancestral honour of the chief branch. This opinion, though sometimes ideal, is so strong, even at this day of innovation, that it may be observed as a national difference between my countrymen and the English. If you ask an Englishman of good birth, whether a person of the same name be connected with him, he answers, (if *in dubio*,) "No—he is a mere namesake." Ask a similar question of a Scot, (I mean a Scotsman,) he replies—"He is one of our clan; I daresay there is a relationship, though I do not know how distant." The Englishman thinks of discountenancing a species of rivalry in society; the Scotsman's answer is grounded on the ancient idea of strengthening the clan.

35.16 (Ch. 4) a Jeddart staff A species of battle-axe, so called as being in especial use in that ancient burgh, whose armorial bearings still represent an armed horseman brandishing such a weapon.

58.35 (Ch. 7) a pouch for my hawks' meat This same bag, like every thing belonging to falconry, was esteemed an honourable distinction, and worn often by the nobility and gentry themselves. One of the Somervilles of Camnethan was called *Sir John with the red bag*, because it was his wont to wear his hawking pouch covered with satin of that colour.

62.32 (Ch. 8) intended to represent

CELL OF SAINT CUTHBERT. I may here observe, that this is entirely an ideal scene. Saint Cuthbert, a person of established sanctity, had, no doubt, several places of worship on the Border, where he flourished whilst living; but Tillmouth Chapel is the only one which bears some resemblance to the hermitage described in the text. It has, indeed, a well, famous for gratifying three wishes for every worshipper who shall quaff the fountain with sufficient belief in its efficacy. At this spot the Saint is said to have landed in his stone coffin, in which he sailed down the Tweed from Melrose, and here the stone coffin long lay, in evidence of the fact. The late Sir Francis Blake Delaval is said to have taken the exact measure of the coffin, and to have ascertained, by hydrostatic principles, that it might have actually swum. A profane farmer in the neighbourhood announced his intention of converting the last bed of the Saint into a trough for his swine; but the profanation was rendered impossible, either by the Saint, or some pious votary on his behalf, for next morning the stone sarcophagus was found broken in two fragments.

Tillmouth Chapel, with these points of resemblance, lies, however, in exactly the opposite direction as regards Melrose, which the supposed cell of Saint Cuthbert is said to have borne towards Kennaquhair.

63.19 (Ch. 8) the bird in thy bosom An expression used by Sir Ralph Percy, slain in the battle of Hedgely-moor in 1464, when dying, to express his having preserved unstained his fidelity to the House of Lancaster.

73.25 (Ch. 9) my gay goss-hawk

GOSS-HAWK. The comparison is taken from some beautiful verses in an old ballad, entitled Fause Foodrage, published in the "Minstrelsy of the Scottish Border." A deposed queen, to preserve her infant son from the traitors who have slain his father, exchanges him with the female offspring of a faithful friend, and goes on to direct the education of the children, and the private signals by which the parents are to hear news each of her own offspring.

And you shall learn my gay goss-hawk
  Right well to breast a steed;

And so will I your turtle dow,
  As well to write and read.

And ye shall learn my gay goss-hawk
  To wield both bow and brand;
And so will I your turtle dow,
  To lay gowd with her hand.

At kirk or market when we meet,
  We'll dare make no avow,
But, "Dame, how does my gay goss-hawk?"
  "Madame, how does my dow?"

85.18 (Ch. 11) arles *Anglicé*—Earnest-money.

91.13 (Ch. 12) for her food
NUNNERY OF SAINT BRIDGET. This, like the Cell of Saint Cuthbert, is an imaginary scene, but I took one or two ideas of the desolation of the interior from a story my father told me. In his youth—it might be near eighty years since, as he was born in 1729—he had occasion to visit an old lady who resided in a Border castle of considerable renown. Only one very limited portion of the extensive ruins sufficed for the inhabitants' accommodation, and my father amused himself by wandering through the rest. In a dining apartment, having a roof richly adorned with arches and drops, there was pitched down a large stack of hay, and two calves were helping themselves from opposite sides. As my father was scaling a dark ruinous turnpike staircase, his greyhound ran up before him, and probably was the means of saving his life, for it fell through some trap-door, or breach in the stair, warning the owner of the danger of the ascent. As the dog continued howling from a great depth, my father got the ancient butler, who alone knew most of the localities about the castle, to unlock a sort of stable, in which Kill-buck was found safe and sound, the place being filled with the same commodity which littered the stalls of Augeas, and which had rendered the dog's fall an easy one.

94.39 (Ch. 13) the Nun of Kent A fanatic nun, called the Holy Maid of Kent, who pretended to the gift of prophecy and power of miracles. Having denounced the doom of speedy death against Henry VIII. for his marriage with Anne Boleyn, the prophetess was attainted in Parliament, and executed, with her accomplices. Her imposture was for a time so successful, that even Sir Thomas More was disposed to be a believer.

102.8 (Ch. 13) yet more abridged In Catholic countries, in order to reconcile the pleasures of the great with the observances of religion, it was common, when a party was bent for the chase, to celebrate a mass, abridged and maimed of its rites, called a hunting-mass, the brevity of which was designed to correspond with the impatience of the audience.

103.29 (Ch. 14) Lord Abbot [The Magnum text has 'Lord Abbot of Unreason'.]

ABBOT OF UNREASON. We learn from no less authority than that of Napoleon Bonaparte, that there is but a single step between the sublime and ridiculous; and it is a transition from one extreme to another, so very easy, that the vulgar of every degree are peculiarly captivated with it. Thus the inclination to laugh becomes uncontrollable, when the solemnity and gravity of time, place, and circumstance, render it peculiarly improper. Some species of general license, like that which inspired the ancient Saturnalia, or the modern Carnival, has been commonly indulged to the people at all times, and in almost all countries. But it was, I think, peculiar to the Roman Catholic Church, that while they studied how to render their church rites imposing and magnificent, by all that pomp, music, architecture, and external display could add to them, they nevertheless connived, upon special occasions, at the frolics of the rude vulgar, who, in almost all Catholic countries, enjoyed, or at least assumed, the privilege of making some Lord of the revels, who, under the name of the Abbot of Unreason, the Boy Bishop, or the President of Fools, occupied the churches, profaned the holy places by a mock imitation of the sacred rites, and sung indecent parodies on hymns of the church. The indifference of the clergy, even when their power was greatest, to these indecent exhibitions which they always tolerated, and sometimes encouraged, forms a strong contrast to the sensitiveness with which they regarded any serious attempt, by preaching or writing, to impeach any of the doctrines of the church. It could only be compared to the singular apathy with which they endured, and often listened to, the gross novels which Chaucer, Dunbar, Boccacio, Bandello, and others, composed upon the bad morals of the clergy. It seems as if the churchmen in both instances had endeavoured to compromise with the laity, and allowed them occasionally to gratify their coarse humour by indecent satire, providing they would abstain from any grave question concerning the foundation of the doctrines on which was erected such an immense fabric of ecclesiastical power.

But the sports thus licensed assumed a very different appearance, so soon as the Protestant doctrines began to prevail; and the license which their forefathers had exercised in mere gaiety of heart, and without the least intention of dishonouring religion by their frolics, was now persevered in by the common people as a mode of testifying their utter disregard for the Roman priesthood and its ceremonies.

I may observe, for example, the case of an apparitor sent to Borthwick from the Primate of Saint Andrews, to cite the lord of that castle, who was opposed by an Abbot of Unreason, at whose command the officer of the spiritual court was appointed to be ducked in a mill-dam, and obliged to eat up his parchment citation.

The reader may be amused with the following whimsical details of this incident, which took place in the castle of Borthwick, in the year 1547. It appears, that in consequence of a process betwixt Master George Hay de Minzeane and the Lord Borthwick, letters of excommunication had passed against the latter, on account of the contumacy of certain witnesses. William Langlands, an apparitor or macer *(bacularius)* of the See of St Andrews, presented these letters to the curate of the church of Borthwick, requiring him to publish the same at the service of high mass. It seems that the inhabitants of the castle were at this time engaged in the favourite sport of enacting the Abbot of Unreason, a species of high-jinks, in which a mimic prelate was elected, who, like the Lord of Misrule in England, turned all sort of lawful authority, and particularly the church ritual, into ridicule. This frolicsome person with his retinue, notwithstanding of the apparitor's character, entered the church, seized upon the primate's officer without hesitation, and, dragging him to the mill-dam on the south side of the castle, compelled him to leap into the water. Not contented with this partial immersion, the Abbot of Unreason pronounced, that Mr William Langlands was not yet sufficiently bathed, and therefore caused his assistants to lay him on his back in the stream, and duck him in the most satisfactory and perfect manner. The unfortunate apparitor was then conducted back to the church, where, for his refreshment after his bath, the letters of excommunication were torn to pieces, and steeped in a bowl of wine; the mock abbot being probably of opinion that a tough parchment was but dry eating, Langlands was compelled to eat the letters, and swallow the wine, and dismissed by the Abbot of Unreason, with the comfortable assurance, that if any more such letters should arrive during the continuance of his office, "they should a' gang the same gate," *i. e.* go the same road.

A similar scene occurs betwixt a sumner of the Bishop of Rochester, and Harpool, the servant of Lord Cobham, in the old play of Sir John Oldcastle, when the former compels the church-officer to eat his citation. The dialogue, which may be found in the note, contains most of the jests which may be supposed appropriate to such an extraordinary occasion.*

* *Harpool.* Marry, sir, is this process parchment?
Sumner. Yes, marry is it.

[P.T.O.

104.38 (Ch. 14) the hobbie-horse

THE HOBBY-HORSE. This exhibition, the play-mare of Scotland, stood high among holytide gambols. It must be carefully separated from the wooden chargers which furnish out our nurseries. It gives rise to Hamlet's ejaculation,—

> But oh, but oh, the hobby-horse is forgot!

There is a very comic scene in Beaumont and Fletcher's play of "Women Pleased," where Hope-on-high Bombye, a puritan cobbler, refuses to dance with the hobby-horse. There was much difficulty and great variety in the motions which the hobby-horse was expected to exhibit.

The learned Mr Douce, who has contributed so much to the illustration of our theatrical antiquities, has given us a full account of this pageant, and the burlesque horsemanship which it practised.

"The hobby-horse," says Mr Douce, "was represented by a man equipped with as much pasteboard as was sufficient to form the head and hinder parts of a horse, the quadrupedal defects being concealed by a long mantle or footcloth that nearly touched the

---

Harpool. And this seal wax?

Sumner. It is so.

Harpool. If this be parchment, and this be wax, eat you this parchment and wax, or I will make parchment of your skin, and beat your brains into wax. Sirrah Sumner, dispatch—devour, sirrah, devour.

Sumner. I am my Lord of Rochester's sumner; I came to do my office, and thou shalt answer it.

Harpool. Sirrah, no railing, but betake thyself to thy teeth. Thou shalt eat no worse than thou bringest with thee. Thou bringest it for my lord; and wilt thou bring my lord worse than thou wilt eat thyself?

Sumner. Sir, I brought it not my lord to eat.

Harpool. O, do you *Sir* me now? All's one for that; I'll make you eat it for bringing it.

Sumner. I cannot eat it.

Harpool. Can you not? 'Sblood, I'll beat you till you have a stomach!

(Beats him.)

Sumner. Oh, hold, hold, good Mr Servingman; I will eat it.

Harpool. Be champing, be chewing, sir, or I will chew you, you rogue. Tough wax is the purest of the honey.

Sumner. The purest of the honey!—O Lord, sir! oh! oh!

Harpool. Feed, feed; 'tis wholesome, rogue, wholesome. Cannot you, like an honest sumner, walk with the devil your brother, to fetch in your bailiff's rents, but you must come to a nobleman's house with process? If the seal were broad as the lead which covers Rochester Church, thou shouldst eat it.

Sumner. Oh, I am almost choked—I am almost choked!

Harpool. Who's within there? will you shame my lord? is there no beer in the house? Butler, I say.

Enter BUTLER.

Butler. Here, here.

Harpool. Give him beer. Tough old sheep-skin 's but dry meat.

First Part of Sir John Oldcastle, Act II. Scene 1.

ground. The performer, on this occasion, exerted all his skill in burlesque horsemanship. In Sampson's play of the Vow-breaker, 1636, a miller personates the hobby-horse, and being angry that the mayor of the city is put in competition with him, exclaims, 'Let the mayor play the hobby-horse among his brethren, an he will; I hope our town-lads cannot want a hobby-horse. Have I practised my reins, my careers, my pranckers, my ambles, my false trots, my smooth ambles, and Canterbury paces, and shall master mayor put me besides the hobby-horse? Have I borrowed the forehorse bells, his plumes, and braveries; nay, had his mane new shorn and frizzled, and shall the mayor put me besides the hobby-horse?' "—DOUCE's *Illustrations*, vol. II., p. 468.

105.10 (Ch. 14) Little John at their head

REPRESENTATION OF ROBIN HOOD AND LITTLE JOHN. The representation of Robin Hood was the darling May-game both in England and Scotland, and doubtless the favourite personification was often revived, when the Abbot of Unreason, or other pretences of frolic, gave an unusual degree of license.

The Protestant clergy, who had formerly reaped advantage from the opportunities which these sports afforded them of directing their own satire and the ridicule of the lower orders against the Catholic church, began to find that, when these purposes were served, their favourite pastimes deprived them of the wish to attend divine worship, and disturbed the frame of mind in which it can be attended to advantage. The celebrated Bishop Latimer gives a very *naïve* account of the manner in which, bishop as he was, he found himself compelled to give place to Robin Hood and his followers.

"I came once myselfe riding on a journey homeward from London, and I sent word over night into the towne that I would preach there in the morning, because it was holiday, and me thought it was a holidayes worke. The church stood in my way, and I tooke my horse and my company, and went thither, (I thought I should have found a great company in the church,) and when I came there the church doore was fast locked. I tarryed there halfe an houre and more. At last the key was found, and one of the parish comes to me, and said,—'Sir, this is a busie day with us, we cannot hear you; it is Robin Hood's day. The parish are gone abroad to gather for Robin Hood. I pray you let them not.' I was faine there to give place to Robin Hood. I thought my rochet should have been regarded, though I were not: but it would not serve, it was faine to give place to Robin Hood's men. It is no laughing matter, my friends, it is a weeping matter, a heavie matter, a heavie matter. Under the pretence for gathering for Robin Hood, a traytour, and a theif, to put out a preacher; to have his office lesse esteemed; to preferre Robin Hood before the ministration of God's word; and all this hath come of unpreaching prelates. This realme hath been ill provided for, that it hath had such corrupt judgements in it, to prefer Robin Hood to God's word."—*Bishop Latimer's sixth Sermon before King Edward.*

While the English Protestants thus preferred the outlaw's pageant to the preaching of their excellent Bishop, the Scottish calvinistic clergy, with the celebrated John Knox at their head, and backed by the authority of the magistrates of Edinburgh, who had of late been chosen exclusively from this party, found it impossible to control the rage of the populace, when they attempted to deprive them of the privilege of presenting their pageant of Robin Hood.

(1561.) "Vpon the xxi day of Junij, Archibalde Dowglas of Kilspindie, Provest of Ed$^{r.}$, David Symmer and Adame Fullartoun, baillies of the samyne, causit ane cordinare servant, callit James Gillon, takin of befoir, for playing in Ed$^{r.}$ with Robene Hude, to wnderly the law, and put him to the knawlege of ane assyize, qlk yaij haid electit of yair favoraris, quha with schort deliberatioun condemnit him to be hangit for ye said cryme. And the deaconis of ye craftismen, fearing vproare, maid great solistatnis at ye handis of ye said provost and baillies, and als requirit John Knox, minister, for eschewing of tumult, to superceid ye executioun of him, vnto ye tyme yai suld adverteis my Lord Duke yairof. And yan, if it wes his mynd and will yat he should be disponit vpoun, ye said deaconis and craftismen sould convey him yaire; quha answerit, yat yai culd na way stope ye executioun of justice. Quhan ye time of ye said pouer mans hanging approchit, and yat ye hangman wes cumand to ye jibbat with ye ledder, vpoune ye qlk ye said cordinare should have bene hangit, ane certaine and remanent craftischilder, quha wes put to ye horne with ye said Gillione, ffor ye said Robene Hude's *playes*, and vyris yair assistaris and favoraris, past to wappinis, and yai brak down ye said jibbat, and yan chacit ye said provest, baillies, and Alexr. Guthrie, in ye said Alexander's writing buith, and held yame yairin; and yairefter past to ye tolbuyt, and becaus the samyne was steikit, and onnawayes culd get the keyes thairof, thai brake the said tolbuith dore with foure hamberis, per force, (the said provest and baillies luckand thairon,) and not onlie put thar the said Gillione to fredome and libertie, and brocht him furth of the said tolbuit, bot alsua the remanent personaris being thairintill; and this done, the said craftismen's servands, with the said condempnit cordonar, past doun to the Netherbow, to have past furth thairat; bot becaus the samyne on their coming thairto wes closet, thai past vp agane the Hie streit of the said bourghe to the Castellhill, and in this menetyme the saidis provest and baillies and thair assistaris being in the writting buith of the said Alexr. Guthrie, past and enterit in the said tolbuyt, and in the said servandes passage vp the Hie streit, then schote furth thairof at thame ane dog, and hurt ane servand of the said childer. This being done, thair wes nathing vthir but the one partie schuteand out and castand stanes furth of the said tolbuyt, and the vther pairtie schuteand hagbuttis in the same agane. And sua the craftismen's servandis, aboue written, held and inclosit the said provest and baillies continewallie in the said tolbuyth, frae three houris efternone, quhill aught houris at even, and na man of the said town preassit to relieve thair said provest and baillies. And than thai send to the maisters of the Castell, to caus tham if thai mycht stay the said servandis, quha maid ane maner to do the same, bot thai could not bring the same to ane finall end, ffor the said servands wold on nowayes stay fra thair said purpois, quhill thai had revengit the hurting of ane of them; and thairefter the constable of the castell come down thairfra, and he with the said maisters treatet betwix the said pties in this maner:—That the said provost and baillies sall remit to the said craftischilder, all actioun, cryme, and offens that thai had committit aganes thame in any tyme bygane; and band and oblast thame never to pursew them thairfor; and als commandit their maisters to resaue them agane in thair services, as thai did befoir. And this being proclamit at the mercat cross, thai scalit, and the said provest and baillies come furth of the same tolbouyth," &c. &c. &c.

John Knox, who writes at large upon this tumult, informs us it was inflamed by the deacons of crafts, who, resenting the superiority assumed over them by the magistrates, would yield no assistance to put down the tumult. "They will be magistrates alone," said the recusant deacons, "e'en let them rule the populace alone;" and accordingly they passed quietly to take *their four-hours penny*, and left the magistrates to help themselves as they could. Many persons were excommunicated for this outrage, and not admitted to church ordinances till they had made satisfaction.

114.30 (Ch. 15) Under the greenwood tree These rude rhymes are taken, with trifling alterations, from a ballad called Trim-go-trix. It occurs in a singular collection, entitled, "A Compendious Book of Godly and Spiritual Songs, collected out of sundrie parts of the Scripture, with sundry of other ballatis changed out of prophane sanges, for avoyding of sin and harlotrie, with Augmentation of sundrie Gude and Godly Ballates. Edinburgh, printed by Andro Hart." This curious collection has been reprinted in Mr John Grahame

Dalyell's Scottish Poems of the 16th Century. Edin. 1801, 2 vols.

116.35 (Ch. 15) my father's old fox *Fox*, an old-fashioned broad-sword was often so called.

117.8 (Ch. 15) Saint Martin of Bullions The Saint Swithin, or weeping Saint of Scotland. If his festival (fourth July) prove wet, forty days of rain are expected.

124.5 (Ch. 15) dragged over the threshold

INABILITY OF EVIL SPIRITS TO ENTER A HOUSE UNINVITED. There is a popular belief respecting evil spirits, that they cannot enter an inhabited house unless invited, nay, dragged over the threshold. There is an instance of the same superstition in the Tales of the Genii, where an enchanter is supposed to have intruded himself into the Divan of the Sultan.

"'Thus,' said the illustrious Misnar, 'let the enemies of Mahomet be dismayed! but inform me, O ye sages! under the semblance of which of your brethren did that foul enchanter gain admittance here?'—'May the lord of my heart,' answered Balihu, the hermit of the faithful from Queda, 'triumph over all his foes! As I travelled on the mountains from Queda, and saw neither the footsteps of beasts, nor the flight of birds, behold, I chanced to pass through a cavern, in whose hollow sides I found this accursed sage, to whom I unfolded the invitation of the Sultan of India, and we, joining, journeyed toward the Divan; but ere we entered, he said unto me, "Put thy hand forth, and pull me toward thee into the Divan, calling on the name of Mahomet, for the evil spirits are on me, and vex me."'"

I have understood that many parts of these fine tales, and in particular that of the Sultan Misnar, were taken from genuine Oriental sources by the editor, Mr James Ridley.

But the most picturesque use of this popular belief occurs in Coleridge's beautiful and tantalizing fragment of Christabel. Has not our own imaginative poet cause to fear that future ages will desire to summon him from his place of rest, as Milton longed

> To call him up, who left half told
> The story of Cambuscan bold?

The verses I refer to are when Christabel conducts into her father's castle a mysterious and malevolent being, under the guise of a distressed female stranger.

> They cross'd the moat, and Christabel
> Took the key that fitted well;
> A little door she open'd straight,
> All in the middle of the gate;
> The gate that was iron'd within and without,
> Where an army in battle array had march'd out.

The lady sank, belike thro' pain,
And Christabel with might and main
Lifted her up, a weary weight,
Over the threshold of the gate:
Then the lady rose again,
And moved as she were not in pain.

So free from danger, free from fear,
They cross'd the court:—right glad they were,
And Christabel devoutly cried
To the lady by her side:
"Praise we the Virgin, all divine,
Who hath rescued thee from this distress."
"Alas, alas!" said Geraldine,
"I cannot speak from weariness."
So free from danger, free from fear,
They cross'd the court:—right glad they were.

144.23 (Ch. 17) Lord Seyton

SEYTEN, OR SEYTON. George, fifth Lord Seyton, was immovably faithful to Queen Mary during all the mutabilities of her fortune. He was grand master of the household, in which capacity he had a picture painted of himself with his official baton, and the following motto:—

In adversitate, patiens;
In prosperitate, benevolus.
Hazard yet forward.

On various parts of his castle he inscribed, as expressing his religious and political creed, the legend,

UN DIEU, UN FOY, UN ROY, UN LOY.

He declined to be promoted to an earldom, which Queen Mary offered him at the same time when she advanced her natural brother to be Earl of Mar, and afterwards of Murray.

On his refusing this honour, Mary wrote, or caused to be written, the following lines in Latin and French:—

Sunt comites, ducesque alii; sunt denique reges;
Sethoni dominum sit satis esse mihi.

Il ya des comptes, des roys, des ducs; ainsi
C'est assez pour moy d'estre Seigneur de Seton.

Which may be thus rendered:—

Earl, duke, or king, be thou that list to be;
Seton, thy lordship is enough for me.

This distich reminds us of the "pride which aped humility," in the motto of the house of Couci:

Je suis ni roy, ni prince aussi;
Je suis le Seigneur de Coucy.

After the battle of Langside, Lord Seton was obliged to retire abroad for safety, and was an exile for two years, during which he was reduced to the necessity of driving a waggon in Flanders for his subsistence. He rose to favour in James VI.'s reign, and resuming his paternal property, had himself painted in his waggoner's dress, and in the act of driving a wain with four horses, on the north end of a stately gallery at Seton Castle. He appears to have been fond of the arts; for there exists a beautiful family-piece of him in the centre of his family. Mr Pinkerton, in his Scottish Iconographia, published an engraving of this curious picture. The original is the property of Lord Somerville, nearly connected with the Seton family, and is at present at his lordship's fishing villa of the Pavilion, near Melrose.

148.29 (Ch. 18) Fernieherst Both these Border chieftains were great friends of Queen Mary.

149.41 (Ch. 18) Maiden of Morton *Maiden of Morton*—a species of guillotine which the Regent Morton brought down from Halifax, certainly at a period considerably later than intimated in the tale. He was himself the first who suffered by the engine.

209.34 (Ch. 22) imprinted on mine arm

THE RESIGNATION OF QUEEN MARY. The details of this remarkable event are, as given in the preceding chapter, imaginary; but the outline of the events is historical. Sir Robert Lindesay, brother to the author of the Memoirs, was at first intrusted with the delicate commission of persuading the imprisoned Queen to resign her crown. As he flatly refused to interfere, they determined to send the Lord Lindesay, one of the rudest and most violent of their own faction, with instructions, first to use fair persuasions, and if these did not succeed, to enter into harder terms. Knox associates Lord Ruthven with Lindesay in this alarming commission. He was the son of that Lord Ruthven who was prime agent in the murder of Rizzio; and little mercy was to be expected from his conjunction with Lindesay.

The employment of such rude tools argued a resolution on the part of those who had the Queen's person in their power, to proceed to the utmost extremities, should they find Mary obstinate. To avoid this pressing danger, Sir Robert Melville was dispatched by them to Lochleven, carrying with him, concealed in the scabbard of his sword, letters to the Queen from the Earl of Athole, Maitland of Lethington, and even from Throgmorton, the English ambassador, who was then favourable to the unfortunate Mary, conjuring her to yield to the necessity of the times, and to subscribe such deeds as Lindesay should lay before her, without being startled by their tenor; and assuring her that her doing so, in the state of captivity under which she was placed, would neither, in law, honour, or conscience, be binding upon her when she should obtain her liberty. Submitting, by the advice of one part of her subjects, to the menace of the others, and learning that Lindesay was arrived in a boasting, that is, threatening humour, the Queen, "with some reluctancy, and with tears," saith Knox, subscribed one deed resigning her crown to her infant son, and another establishing the Earl of Murray regent. It seems agreed by historians, that Lindesay behaved with great brutality upon the occasion. The deeds were signed 24th July, 1567.

229.12 (Ch. 24) Ganelon Gan, Gano, or Ganelon of Mayence, is, in the Romances on the subject of Charlemagne and his Paladins, always represented as the traitor by whom the Christian champions are betrayed.

240.32 (Ch. 26) his chamberlain At Scottish fairs, the bailie, or magistrate, deputed by the lord in whose name the meeting is held, attends the fair with his guard, decides trifling disputes, and punishes on the spot any petty delinquencies. His attendants are usually armed with halberds, and, sometimes at least, escorted by music. Thus, in the "Life and Death of Habbie Simpson," we are told of that famous minstrel,—

> At fairs he play'd before the spear-men,
> And gaily graithed in their gear-men;—
> Steel bonnets, jacks, and swords shone clear then,
> Like ony bead;
> Now wha shall play before sic weir-men,
> Since Habbie's dead!

246.41 (Ch. 26) Mother Nicneven This was the name given to the grand Mother Witch, the very Hecate of Scottish popular superstition. Her name was bestowed, in one or two instances, upon sorceresses, who were held to resemble her by their superior skill in "Hell's black grammar."

267.25 (Ch. 28) the Dark Grey Man By an ancient, though improbable tradition, the Douglasses are said to have derived their name from a champion who had greatly distinguished himself in an action. When the king demanded by whom the battle had been won, the attendants are said to have answered, "Sholto Douglas, sir;" which is said to mean, "Yonder dark grey man." But the name is undoubtedly territorial, and taken from Douglas river and dale.

314.29 (Ch. 32) the summer wind

SUPPOSED CONSPIRACY AGAINST THE LIFE OF MARY. A romancer, to use a Scottish phrase, wants but a hair to make a tether of. The whole detail of the steward's supposed conspiracy against the life of Mary, is grounded upon an expression in one of her letters, which affirms, that James Drysdale, one of the Laird of Lochleven's servants, had threatened to murder William Douglas, (for his share in the Queen's escape,) and avowed that he would

plant a dagger in Mary's own heart.—CHALMERS'S *Life of Queen Mary*, vol. i. p. 278.
315.26 (Ch. 33) flaunes Pancakes.
321.13 (Ch. 33) muffled man
MUFFLED MAN. Generally a disguised man; originally one who wears his cloak or mantle muffled round the lower part of the face to conceal his countenance. I have on an ancient piece of iron the representation of a robber thus accoutred, endeavouring to make his way into a house, and opposed by a mastiff, to whom he in vain offers food. The motto is *Spernit dona fides*. It is part of a fire-grate said to have belonged to Archbishop Sharpe.
324.6 (Ch. 34) quarrel-pane Diamond-shaped; literally, formed like the head of a *quarrel*, or arrow for the crossbow.
325.18 (Ch. 34) cart-avers Cart-horses.
329.3 (Ch. 34) broken clan A broken clan was one which had no chief able to find security for their good behaviour—a clan of outlaws; and the Græmes of the Debateable Land were in that condition.
330.26 (Ch. 34) Oliver Sinclair A favourite, and said to be an unworthy one, of James V.
330.29 (Ch. 34) the Ladies Sandilands and Olifaunt The names of these ladies, and a third frail favourite of James, are preserved in an epigram too *gaillard* for quotation.
335.30 (Ch. 35) Sir John Holland Sir John Holland's poem of The Howlet is known to collectors by the beautiful edition presented to the Bannatyne Club by Mr David Laing.
338.36 (Ch. 35) noble and royal courage
DEMEANOUR OF QUEEN MARY. In the dangerous expedition to Aberdeenshire, Randolph, the English ambassador, gives Cecil the following account of Queen Mary's demeanour:—

"In all these garbulles, I assure your honour, I never saw the Queen merrier, never dismayed; nor never thought I that stomache to be in her that I find. She repented nothing but, when the Lords and others, at Inverness, came in the morning from the watches, that she was not a man to know what life it was to lye all night in the fields, or to walk upon the causeway with a jack and a knapscap, a Glasgow buckler, and a broadsword."—RANDOLPH *to* CECIL, *September* 18, 1562.

The writer of the above letter seems to have felt the same impression which Catherine Seyton, in the text, considered as proper to the Queen's presence among her armed subjects.

"Though we neither thought nor looked for other than on that day to have fought or never—what desperate blows would not have been given, when every man should have fought in the sight of so noble a Queen, and so many fair ladies, our enemies to have taken them from us, and we to save our honours, not to be bereft of them, your honour can easily judge!"—*The same to the same, September* 24, 1562.

341.21 (Ch. 35) puts shame on us all

ESCAPE OF QUEEN MARY FROM LOCHLEVEN. It is well known that the escape of Queen Mary from Lochleven was effected by George Douglas, the youngest brother of Sir William Douglas, the lord of the castle. But the minute circumstances of the event have been a good deal confused, owing to two agents having been concerned in it who bore the same name. It has been always supposed that George Douglas was induced to abet Mary's escape by the ambitious hope that, by such service, he might merit her hand. But his purpose was discovered by his brother Sir William, and he was expelled from the castle. He continued, notwithstanding, to hover in the neighbourhood, and maintain a correspondence with the royal prisoner and others in the fortress.

If we believe the English ambassador Drury, the Queen was grateful to George Douglas, and even proposed a marriage with him; a scheme which could hardly be serious, since she was still the wife of Bothwell, but which, if suggested at all, might be with a purpose of gratifying the Regent Murray's ambition, and propitiating his favour. He was, it must be remembered, the brother uterine of George Douglas, for whom such high honour was said to be designed.

The proposal, if seriously made, was treated as inadmissible, and Mary again resumed her purpose of escape. Her failure in her first attempt has some picturesque particulars, which might have been advantageously introduced in fictitious narrative. Drury sends Cecil the following account of the matter:—

"But after, upon the 25th of the last, (April 1567,) she interprised an escape, and was the rather nearer effect, through her accustomed long lying in bed all the morning. The manner of it was thus: there cometh in to her the laundress early as other times before she was wonted, and the Queen according to such a secret practice putteth on her the weed of the laundress, and so with the fardel of clothes and the muffler upon her face, passeth out and entreth the boat to pass the Loch; which, after some space, one of them that rowed said merrily, 'Let us see what manner of dame this is,' and therewith offered to pull down her muffler, which, to defend, she put up her hands, which they espied to be very fair and white; wherewith they entered into suspicion whom she was, beginning to wonder at her enterprise. Whereat she was little dismayed, but charged them, upon danger of their lives, to row her over to the shore, which they nothing regarded, but eftsoons rowed her back again, promising her it should be secreted, and especially from the lord of the house, under whose guard she lyeth. It seemed she knew her refuge, and where to have found it if she had once landed; for there did, and yet do linger, at a little village called Kinross, hard at the Loch side, the same George Douglas, one Sempil, and one Beton, the which two were sometime her trusty servants, and, as yet appeareth, they mind her no less affection."—BISHOP KEITH'S *History of the Affairs of Church and State in Scotland*, p. 470.

Notwithstanding this disappointment, little spoke of by historians, Mary renewed her attempts to escape. There was in the Castle of Lochleven a lad, named William Douglas, some relation probably of the baron, and about eighteen years old. This youth proved as accessible to Queen Mary's prayers and promises, as was the brother of his patron, George Douglas, from whom this William must be carefully kept distinct. It was young William who played the part commonly assigned to his superior, George, stealing the keys of the castle from the table on which they lay, while his lord was at supper. He let the Queen and a waiting woman out of the apartment where they were secured, and out of the tower itself, embarked with them in a small skiff, and rowed them to the shore. To prevent instant pursuit, he, for precaution's sake, locked the iron grated door of the tower, and threw the keys into the lake. They found George Douglas and the Queen's servant, Beton, waiting for them, and Lord Seyton and James Hamilton of Orbieston in attendance, at the head of a party of faithful followers, with whom they fled to Niddrie Castle, and from thence to Hamilton.

In narrating this romantic story, both history and tradition confuse the two Douglasses together, and confer on George the successful execution of the escape from the castle, the merit of which belongs, in reality, to the boy called William, or, more frequently, the Little Douglas, either from his youth or his slight stature. The reader will observe, that in the romance, the part of the Little Douglas has been assigned to Roland Græme. In another case, it would be tedious to point out in a work of amusement such minute points of historical fact; but the general interest taken in the fate of Queen Mary, renders every thing of consequence which connects itself with her misfortunes.

366.34 (Ch. 37) set forward

BATTLE OF LANGSIDE. I am informed in the most polite manner, by D. MacVean, Esq. of Glasgow, that I have been incorrect in my locality, in giving an account of the battle of Langside. Crookstone Castle, he observes, lies four miles west from the field of battle, and rather in the rear of Murray's army. The real place from which Mary saw the rout of her last army, was Cathcart Castle, which, being a mile and a half east from Langside, was situated in the rear of the Queen's own army. I was led astray in the present case, by the authority of my deceased friend, James Grahame, the excellent and amiable author of the Sabbath, in his drama on the subject of Queen Mary; and by a traditionary report of Mary having seen the battle from the Castle of Crookstone, which seemed so much to increase the interest of the scene, that I have been unwilling to make, in this particular instance, the fiction give way to the fact, which last is undoubtedly in favour of Mr MacVean's system.

It is singular how tradition, which is sometimes a sure guide to truth, is, in other cases, prone to mislead us. In the celebrated field of battle at Killiecrankie, the traveller is struck with one of those rugged pillars of rough stone, which indicate the scenes of ancient conflict. A friend of the author, well acquainted with the circumstances of the battle, was standing near this large stone, and looking on the scene around, when a Highland shepherd hurried down from the hill to offer his services as Cicerone, and proceeded to inform him, that Dundee was slain at that stone, which was raised to his memory. "Fie, Donald," answered my friend, "how can you tell such a story to a stranger? I am sure you know well enough that Dundee was killed at considerable distance from this place, near the house of Fascally, and that this stone was here long before the battle, in 1688."—"Oich ! oich !" said Donald, no way abashed, "and your honour's in the right, and I see you ken a' about it. And he wasna killed on the spot neither, but lived till the next morning; but a' the Saxon gentlemen like best to hear he was killed at the great stane." It is on the same principle of pleasing my readers, that I retain Crookstone Castle instead of Cathcart.

If, however, the author has taken a liberty in removing the actual field of battle somewhat to the eastward, he has been tolerably strict in adhering to the incidents of the engagement, as will appear from a comparison of events in the novel, with the following account from an old writer.

"The Regent was out on foot and all his company, except the Laird of Grange, Alexander Hume of Manderston, and some Borderers to the number of two hundred. The Laird of Grange had already viewed the ground, and with all imaginable diligence caused every horseman to take behind him a footman of the Regent's, to guard behind them, and rode with speed to the head of the Langside-hill, and set down the said footmen with their culverings at the head of a straight lane, where there were some cottage houses and yards of great advantage. Which soldiers with their continual shot killed divers of the vaunt guard, led by the Hamiltons, who, courageously and fiercely ascending up the hill, were already out of breath, when the Regent's vaunt guard joined with them. Where the worthy Lord Hume fought on foot with his pike in his hand very manfully, assisted by the Laird of Cessford, his brother-in-law, who helped him up again when he was strucken to the ground with many strokes upon his face, by the throwing pistols at him after they had been discharged. He was also wounded with staves, and had many strokes of spears through his legs; for he and Grange, at the joining, cried to let their adversaries first lay down their spears, to bear up theirs; which spears were so thick fixed in others' jacks, that some of the pistols and great staves that were thrown by them which were behind, might be seen lying upon the spears.

"Upon the Queen's side the Earl of Argyle commanded the battle, and the Lord of Arbroath the vaunt guard. On the other part the Regent led the battle, and the Earl of Morton the vaunt guard. But the Regent committed to the Laird of Grange the special care, as being an experimented captain, to oversee every danger, and to ride to every wing, to encourage and make help where greatest need was. He perceived, at the first joining, the right wing of the Regent's vaunt guard put back, and like to fly, whereof the greatest part were commons of the barony of Renfrew; whereupon he rode to them, and told them that their enemy was already turning their backs, requesting them to stay and debate till he should bring them fresh men forth of the battle. Whither at full speed he did ride alone, and told the Regent that the enemy were shaken and flying away behind the little village, and desired a few number of fresh men to go with him. Where he found enough willing, as the Lord Lindesay, the Laird of Lochleven, Sir James Balfour, and all the Regent's servants, who followed him with diligence, and reinforced that wing which was beginning to fly; which fresh men with their loose weapons struck the enemies in their flanks and faces, which forced them incontinent to give place and turn back after long fighting and pushing others to and fro with their spears. There were not many horsemen to pursue after them, and the Regent cried to save and not to kill, and Grange was never cruel, so that there were few slain and taken. And the only slaughter was at the first rencounter by the shot of the soldiers, which Grange had planted at the lane-head behind some dikes."

It is remarkable that, while passing through the small town of Renfrew, some partisans, adherents of the House of Lennox, attempting to arrest Queen Mary and her attendants, were obliged to make way for her, not without slaughter.

374.32 (Ch. 38) sleep among its ruins

BURIAL OF THE ABBOT'S HEART IN THE AVENEL AISLE. This was not the explanation of the incident of searching for the heart, mentioned in the introduction to the tale, which the author originally intended. It was designed to refer to the heart of Robert Bruce. It is generally known that that great monarch, being on his death-bed, bequeathed to the good Lord James of Douglas, the task of carrying his heart to the Holy Land, to fulfil in a certain degree his own desire to perform a crusade. Upon Douglas's death, fighting against the Moors in Spain, a sort of military *hors d'œuvre* to which he could have pleaded no regular call of duty, his followers brought back the Bruce's heart, and deposited it in the Abbey church of Melrose, the Kennaquhair of the tale.

This Abbey had been always particularly favoured by the Bruce. We have already seen his extreme anxiety that each of the reverend brethren should be daily supplied with a service of boiled almonds, rice and milk, pease, or the like, to be called the King's mess, and that without the ordinary service of their table being either disturbed in quantity or quality. But this was not the only mark of the benignity of good King Robert towards the monks of Melrose, since, by a charter of the date, 29th May, 1326, he conferred on the Abbot of Melrose the sum of two thousand pounds sterling, for rebuilding the church of St Mary's, ruined by the English; and there is little or no doubt that the principal part of the remains which now display such exquisite specimens of Gothic architecture, at its very purest period, had their origin in this munificent donation. The money was to be paid out of crown lands, estates forfeited to the King, and other property or demesnes of the crown.

A very curious letter written to his son about three weeks before his death, has been pointed out to me by my friend Mr Thomas Thomson, Deputy-Register for Scotland. It enlarges so much on the love of the royal writer to the community of Melrose, that it is well worthy of being inserted in a work connected in some degree with Scottish History.

LITERA DOMINI REGIS ROBERTI AD FILIUM SUUM DAVID.

"Robertus dei gratia Rex Scottorum, David precordialissimo filio suo, ac ceteris successoribus suis; Salutem, et sic ejus precepta tenere, ut cum sua benedictione possint regnare. Fili carissime, digne censeri videtur filius, qui, paternos in bonis mores imitans, piam ejus nititur exequi voluntatem; nec proprie sibi sumit nomen heredis, qui salubribus predecessoris affectibus non adherit: Cupientes igitur, ut piam affectionem et scinceram dilectionem, quam erga monasterium de Melros, ubi cor nostrum ex speciali devotione disposuimus tumulandum, et erga Religiosos ibidem Deo servientes, ipsorum vita sanctissima nos ad hoc excitante, concepimus; Tu ceterique successores nostri pia scinceritate prosequamini, ut, ex vestre dilectionis affectu dictis Religiosis nostri causa post mortem nostram ostenso, ipsi pro nobis ad orandum fervencius et forcius animentur: Vobis precipimus quantum possumus, instanter supplicamus, et ex toto corde injungimus, Quatinus assignacionibus quas eisdem viris Religiosis pro fabrica Ecclesie sue de novo fecimus ac eciam omnibus aliis donacionibus nostris, ipsos libere gaudere permittatis, Easdem potius si necesse fuerit augmentantes quam diminuentes, ipsorum peticiones auribus benevolis admittentes, ac ipsos contra suos invasores et emulos pia defensione protegentes. Hanc autem exhortacionem supplicacionem et preceptum tu, fili ceterique successores nostri, prestanti animo complere curetis, si nostram benedictionem habere velitis, una cum benedictione filii summi Regis, qui filios docuit patrum voluntates in bono perficere, asserens in mundum se venisse non ut suam voluntatem faceret sed paternam. In testimonium autem nostre devotionis erga locum predictum sic a nobis dilectum et electum concepte, presentem literam Religiosis predictis dimittimus, nostris successoribus in posterum ostendendam. Data apud Cardros, undecimo die Maij, Anno Regni nostri vicesimo quarto."

If this charter be altogether genuine, and there is no appearance of forgery, it gives rise to a curious doubt in Scottish history. The letter announces that the King had already destined his heart to be deposited at Melrose. The resolution to send it to Palestine, under the charge of Douglas, must have been adopted betwixt 11th May 1329, the date of the letter, and 7th June of the same year, when the Bruce died; or else we must suppose that the commission of Douglas extended not only to taking the Bruce's heart to Palestine, but to bring it safe back to its final place of deposit in the Abbey of Melrose.

It would not be worth enquiring by what caprice the author was induced to throw the incident of the Bruce's heart entirely out of the story, save merely to say, that he found himself unable to fill up the canvass he had sketched, and indisposed to prosecute the management of the supernatural machinery with which his plan, when it was first rough-hewn, was concerted and combined.

KENILWORTH

Editorial Note

Kenilworth occupies the second part of Volume 5 and the whole of Volume 6 of the 1822 octavo *Historical Romances*, MSS 23017 and 23018 in the Interleaved Set. Scott's main annotatory work on the novel was completed by 26 January 1830 when Cadell 'received The Abbot & Kenilworth with Introductions and Notes' (MS 21043, f. 16r). Scott made two further additions before Cadell executed his revision between 26 April and 19 May (MS 21020, ff. 19v, 22v). The novel appeared as Volumes 22 and 23 of the Magnum on 1 March and 1 April 1831 (EEWN 11, 412).

The Introduction is short and simple, amounting to little more than long quotations of Scott's principal sources for the story of Amy Robsart in Ashmole and Mickle. Little is offered by way of commentary, and Scott leaves it to the reader to deduce just how much he owed to the two documents. It is impossible to test adequately his opening suggestion that the 'real or supposed' success of his treatment of Mary in *The Abbot* prompted him to 'attempt something similar respecting . . . the celebrated Elizabeth', but the scanty surviving evidence would seem to broadly support it (EEWN 11, 395–96).

Kenilworth is not heavily annotated, but several of the notes are of considerable interest. Scott comments on characters in their historical manifestation. One footnote runs: 'Sir Francis Drake, Morgan, and many a bold Buccanier of those days, were, in fact, little better than pirates' (119.4–6). The tone here is quite different from anything in the dialogue to which it is attached, recalling the ironical modern notes which accompanied Scott's long narrative poems from their first appearance. There is a similar gap, though perhaps not so pronounced, between the Robert Laneham of the narrative and the 'small man in office' and 'coxcomb' of an endnote and footnote (121.23–24; 123.6). Two notes on the historical Sir Walter Ralegh may be seen as offering a more ambiguous picture than the fictional presentation (120–21).

More than once, Scott seeks to justify his handling of historical characters. He seems rather uneasy with his toning-down of Leicester's reputed villainy: 'It is unnecessary to state the numerous reasons why the Earl is represented in the tale as being rather the dupe of villains, than the unprincipled author of their atrocities' (122.33–35) In fact, he goes on to make just one point: 'In the latter capacity, which a part at least of his contemporaries imputed to him, he would have made a character too disgustingly wicked, to be useful for the purposes of fiction.' That, one might conjecture, was a character reserved for Varney. An endnote quoting Anthony Forster's epitaph is more uneasy. It begins 'If faith is to be put in epitaphs, Anthony Forster was something the very reverse of the character represented in the novel', but by the end of the note Scott rather implausibly suggests a narrative which would bring the historical character closer to his fictitious representation (117–18). Justification of a different sort is involved when material is adduced to head off accusations of exaggeration in the narrative: Elizabeth's flirtatious behaviour towards Leicester (125.25–36), or the splendours of the furnishings at Kenilworth (127.30–33).

For certain novels Scott depended on one or more of his correspondents for local information. In the case of *Kenilworth* his informants about Berkshire matters were Mary Ann Hughes and her husband. On 9 or 10 October 1828 he had written to Mrs Hughes asking for any Berkshire material relevant to the novel (*Letters*, 11.5–8), which the couple duly provided at length in a series of letters between 13 October that year and 2 January 1830. Scott actually used only a few details, as indicated in the explanatory notes: the Anthony Forster note mentioned above ends with material derived from the Hugheses, and he added information concerning Wayland's Smithy, noted in Mrs Hughes's letter of 7 June [1829] (MS 3909, f. 86v), at a subsequent stage as the last two sentences in the relevant note (119.34–37). On the other hand, the inventory of the Kenilworth furnishings was communicated on a one-off basis by William Hamper, and, unusually, part of it found its way into the Magnum text itself (see 124–27, note to 307.42 below).

The final brief endnote to *Kenilworth* is so placed as almost to form part of the text. The epitaph on Leicester may serve to bring readers' attention back to that character as they close the volume.

There are four Magnum illustrations for this title. The frontispiece to Volume 22 (MAG0043 / TB348.22) was designed by Charles

Robert Leslie and engraved by Joseph Goodyear. It depicts Leicester and Amy together in a room at Cumnor Place, with Amy examining a chivalric collar worn by the Earl (EEWN 11, 58.18–20: 'But this other fair collar . . . does that emblem signify?'). The title-page vignette (MAG0044 / TB348.22) was designed by Charles Robert Leslie and engraved by William Henry Watt. It depicts Wayland Smith, as a pedlar, displaying clothing to Amy and Janet at Cumnor Place (EEWN 11, 203.31–34: 'Is it not of an absolute fancy . . . for a graceful habit.'). The frontispiece to Volume 23 (MAG0045 / TB348.23) was designed by Abraham Cooper and engraved by Alfred William Warren. It depicts Wayland leading Amy on horseback away from Cumnor Place (EEWN 11, 237.7–10 (with 'Janet' for 'She'): 'Janet re-entered the postern-door . . . dubious and moonlight journey.'). The title-page vignette (MAG0046 / TB348.23) was designed by Alexander Fraser, the elder, and engraved by Timothy Stansfeld Engleheart. It depicts Doboobie (Alasco) in his laboratory, with distilling equipment for alchemical experiments, Forster looking on, and Varney leaving with a flask (EEWN 11, 226.37–227.17 (abridged): ' "I swear it," . . . he left the room.').

The ground-plan of Kenilworth Castle (110) originally appeared at the end of Volume 23 of the Magnum in most copies. Scott acknowledges its receipt in a note at 123.17–24.

C. R. Leslie. J. Goodyear.

KENILWORTH.

"But this other fair collar, so richly wrought, with some jewel like a sheep hung by the middle attached to it, what", said the young Countess, "does that emblem signify?"

EDINBURGH. PUBLISHED 1831. BY ROBERT CADELL and WHITTAKER & Cº LONDON

WAVERLEY NOVELS.

VOL. XXII.

KENILWORTH.

C. R. Leslie, R.A. W. H. Watt.

"Is it not of an absolute fancy Janet?
"Nay my lady", replied Janet, if you consult my poor judgment, it is, methinks, over gawdy for a graceful habit."

PRINTED FOR ROBERT CADELL, EDINBURGH.
AND WHITTAKER & C° LONDON.
1831.

A. Cooper, R.A. A.W. Warren.

KENILWORTH.

Janet re-entered the postern-door, and locked it behind her, while Wayland, taking the horse's bridle in his hand, and walking close by its head, they began in silence their dubious and moonlight journey.

EDINBURGH, PUBLISHED 1831, BY ROBERT CADELL, and WHITTAKER & Cº LONDON.

WAVERLEY NOVELS.

VOL. XXIII.

KENILWORTH.

"I swear it," said Alasco,"that the elixir thou hast there in the flask will not prejudice life! Foster, thou wert worse than a pagan to disbelieve it", said Varney, "debate the matter with him, Doctor Alasco; I will be with you anon". So speaking, Varney arose, and taking the flask from the table he left the room.

PRINTED FOR ROBERT CADELL, EDINBURGH,
AND WHITTAKER & Cº LONDON.
1831.

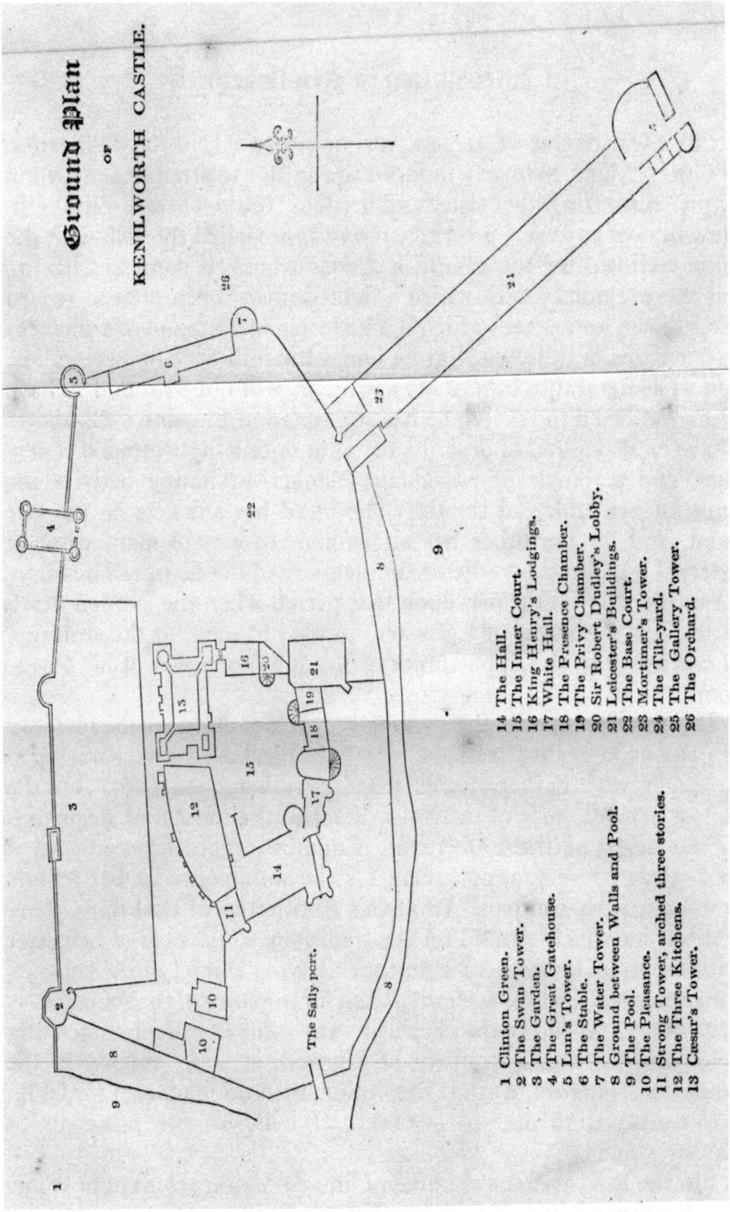
Ground Plan
OF
KENILWORTH CASTLE.
The Sally port.
1 Clinton Green.
2 The Swan Tower.
3 The Garden.
4 The Great Gatehouse.
5 Lun's Tower.
6 The Stable.
7 The Water Tower.
8 Ground between Walls and Pool.
9 The Pool.
10 The Pleasance.
11 Strong Tower, arched three stories.
12 The Three Kitchens.
13 Cæsar's Tower.
14 The Hall.
15 The Inner Court.
16 King Henry's Lodgings.
17 White Hall.
18 The Presence Chamber.
19 The Privy Chamber.
20 Sir Robert Dudley's Lobby.
21 Leicester's Buildings.
22 The Base Court.
23 Mortimer's Tower.
24 The Tilt-yard.
25 The Gallery Tower.
26 The Orchard.

Introduction to Kenilworth

A CERTAIN degree of success, real or supposed, in the delineation of Queen Mary, naturally induced the author to attempt something similar respecting "her sister and her foe," the celebrated Elizabeth. He will not, however, pretend to have approached the task with the same feelings; for the candid Robertson himself confesses having felt the prejudices with which a Scottishman is tempted to regard the subject; and what so liberal a historian avows, a poor romance-writer dares not disown. But he hopes the influence of a prejudice, almost as natural to him as his native air, will not be found to have greatly affected the sketch he has attempted of England's Elizabeth. I have endeavoured to describe her as at once a high-minded sovereign, and a female of passionate feelings, hesitating betwixt the sense of her rank and the duty she owed her subjects on the one hand, and on the other her attachment to a nobleman, who, in external qualifications at least, amply merited her favour. The interest of the story is thrown upon that period when the sudden death of the first Countess of Leicester, seemed to open to the ambition of her husband the opportunity of sharing the crown of his sovereign.

It is possible that slander, which very seldom favours the memory of persons in exalted stations, may have blackened the character of Leicester with darker shades than really belonged to it. But the almost general voice of the times attached the most foul suspicions to the death of the unfortunate Countess, more especially as it took place so very opportunely for the indulgence of her lover's ambition. If we can trust Ashmole's Antiquities of Berkshire, there was but too much ground for the traditions which charge Leicester with the murder of his wife. In the following extract of the passage, the reader will find the authority I had for the story of the romance:—

"At the west end of the church are the ruins of a manor, anciently belonging (as a cell, or place of removal, as some report) to the monks of Abington. At the Dissolution, the said manor, or lordship, was conveyed to one —— Owen, (I believe,) the possessor of Godstow then.

"In the hall, over the chimney, I find Abington arms cut in stone, viz. a patonce between four martletts; and also another escutcheon, viz. a lion rampant, and several mitres cut in stone about the house. There is also in the said house, a chamber called Dudley's chamber, where the Earl of Leicester's wife was murdered; of which this is the story following:

"Robert Dudley, Earl of Leicester, a very goodly personage, and singularly well featured, being a great favourite to Queen Elizabeth, it was thought, and commonly reported, that had he been a batchelor or widower, the Queen would have made him her husband; to this end, to free himself of all obstacles, he commands, or perhaps, with fair flattering intreaties, desires his wife to repose herself here at his servant Anthony Forster's house, who then lived in the aforesaid manor-house; and also prescribed to Sir Richard Varney, (a prompter to this design,) at his coming hither, that he should first attempt to poison her, and if that did not take effect, then by any other way whatsoever to dispatch her. This, it seems, was proved by the report of Dr Walter Bayly, sometime fellow of New College, then living in Oxford, and professor of physic in that university; who, because he would not consent to take away her life by poison, the Earl endeavoured to displace him from the court. This man, it seems, reported for most certain, that there was a practice in Cumnor among the conspirators, to have poisoned this poor innocent lady, a little before she was killed, which was attempted after this manner:—They seeing the good lady sad and heavy, (as one that well knew by her other handling, that her death was not far off,) began to persuade her that her present disease was abundance of melancholy and other humours, &c., and therefore would needs counsel her to take some potion, which she absolutely refusing to do, as still suspecting the worst; whereupon they sent a messenger on a day (unawares to her) for Dr Bayly, and entreated him to persuade her to take some little potion by his direction, and they would fetch the same at Oxford; meaning to have added something of their own for her comfort, as the doctor upon just cause and consideration did suspect, seeing their great importunity, and the small need the lady had of physic, and therefore he premptorily denied their request; misdoubting, (as he afterwards reported,) lest, if they had poisoned her under the name of his potion, he might after have been hanged for a colour of their sin, and the doctor remained still well assured, that this way taking no effect, she would not long escape their violence, which afterwards happened thus. For Sir Richard Varney above-said, (the chief projector in this design,) who, by the Earl's order, remained that day of her death alone with her, with one man only and Forster, who had that day forcibly sent away all her servants from her to Abington market, about three miles distant from this place; they (I say, whether first stifling her, or else strangling her) afterwards flung her down a pair of stairs and broke her neck, using much violence upon her; but, however, though it was vulgarly reported that she by chance fell down stairs, (but still without hurting her hood that was upon her head,) yet the inhabitants will tell you there, that she was conveyed from her usual chamber where she lay, to another where the bed's head of the chamber stood close to a privy postern door, where they in the night came and stifled her in her bed, bruised her head very much, broke her neck, and at length flung her down stairs, thereby believing the world would have thought it a mischance, and so have blinded their villainy. But behold the mercy and justice of God in revenging and discovering this lady's murder, for one of the persons that was a coadjutor in this murder, was afterwards taken for a felony in the marches of Wales, and offering to publish the manner of the aforesaid murder, was privately made away in the prison by the Earl's appointment; and Sir Richard Varney the other, dying about the same time in London, cried miserably, and blasphemed God, and said to a person of note, (who hath related the same to others since,) not long before his death, that all the devils in hell did tear him in pieces. Forster, likewise, after this fact, being a man formerly addicted to hospitality, company, mirth, and music, was afterwards observed to forsake all this, and with much melancholy and pensiveness, (some say with madness,) pined and drooped away. The wife also of Bald Butler, kinsman to the Earl, gave out the whole fact a little before her death. Neither are these following passages to be forgotten, that as soon as ever she was murdered, they made great haste to bury her before the coroner had given in his inquest, (which the Earl himself condemned as not done advisedly,) which her father, or Sir John Robertsett, (as I suppose,) hearing of, came with all speed hither, caused her corpse to be taken up, the coroner to sit upon her, and further enquiry to be made concerning this business to the full; but it was generally thought that the Earl stopped his mouth, and made up the business betwixt them; and the good Earl, to make plain to the world the great love he bare to her while alive, and what a grief the loss of so virtuous a lady was to his tender heart, caused (though the thing, by these and other means, was beaten into the heads of the principal men of the University of Oxford) her body to be re-buried in St Mary's church in Oxford, with great pomp and solemnity. It is remarkable, when Dr Babington, the Earl's chaplain, did preach the funeral sermon, he tript once or twice in his speech, by recommending to their memories that virtuous lady so pitifully *murdered*, instead of saying pitifully slain. This Earl, after all his murders and poisonings, was himself poisoned by that which was prepared for others, (some say by his wife at Cornbury Lodge before mentioned,) though Baker in his Chronicle would have it at Killingworth, anno 1588."*

The same accusation had been adopted and circulated by the author of Leicester's Commonwealth, a satire written directly against the Earl of Leicester, which loaded him with the most horrid crimes, and, among the rest, with the murder of his first wife. It was alluded to in the Yorkshire Tragedy, a play erroneously ascribed to Shakspeare, where a Rake, who determines to destroy all his family, throws his wife down stairs, with this allusion to the supposed murder of Leicester's lady,—

The only way to charm a woman's tongue
Is, break her neck—a politician did it.

The reader will find I have borrowed several incidents as well as names from Ashmole, and the more early authorities; but my first acquaintance with the history was through the more pleasing medium of verse. There is a period in youth when the mere power of numbers has a more strong effect on ear and imagination, than in more advanced life. At this season of immature taste the author was greatly delighted with the poems of Mickle and Langhorne, poets who, though by no means deficient in the higher branches of their art, were eminent for their powers of verbal melody above most who have practised this department of poetry. One of those pieces of Mickle, which the author was particularly pleased with, is a ballad, or rather a species of elegy, on the subject of Cumnor Hall, which, with others by the same author, were to be found in Evans's Old Ballads, (volume iv., page 130,) to which work Mickle made liberal contributions. The first stanza especially had a peculiar species of enchantment for the youthful ear of the author, the force of which is not even now entirely spent; some others are sufficiently prosaic.

CUMNOR HALL.

The dews of summer night did fall;
  The moon, sweet regent of the sky,
Silver'd the walls of Cumnor Hall,
  And many an oak that grew thereby.

Now nought was heard beneath the skies,
  The sounds of busy life were still,

* Ashmole's Antiquities of Berkshire, vol. i. p. 149. The tradition as to Leicester's death was thus communicated by Ben Jonson to Drummond of Hawthornden:—"The Earl of Leicester gave a bottle of liquor to his Lady, which he willed her to use in any faintness, which she, after his returne from court, not knowing it was poison, gave him, and so he died."—BEN JONSON'S *Information to* DRUMMOND *of Hawthornden, MS.*—SIR ROBERT SIBBALD'S *Copy.*

Save an unhappy lady's sighs,
That issued from that lonely pile.

"Leicester," she cried, "is this thy love
That thou so oft has sworn to me,
To leave me in this lonely grove,
Immured in shameful privity?

"No more thou com'st with lover's speed,
Thy once beloved bride to see;
But be she alive, or be she dead,
I fear, stern Earl, 's the same to thee.

"Not so the usage I received
When happy in my father's hall;
No faithless husband then me grieved,
No chilling fears did me appal.

"I rose up with the cheerful morn,
No lark more blithe, no flower more gay;
And like the bird that haunts the thorn,
So merrily sung the livelong day.

"If that my beauty is but small,
Among court ladies all despised,
Why didst thou rend it from that hall,
Where, scornful Earl, it well was prized?

"And when you first to me made suit,
How fair I was you oft would say!
And proud of conquest, pluck'd the fruit,
Then left the blossom to decay.

"Yes! now neglected and despised,
The rose is pale, the lily's dead;
But he that once their charms so prized,
Is sure the cause those charms are fled.

"For know, when sick'ning grief doth prey,
And tender love's repaid with scorn,
The sweetest beauty will decay,—
What floweret can endure the storm?

"At court, I'm told, is beauty's throne,
Where every lady's passing rare,
That Eastern flowers, that shame the sun,
Are not so glowing, not so fair.

"Then, Earl, why didst thou leave the beds
Where roses and where lilies vie,
To seek a primrose, whose pale shades
Must sicken when those gauds are by?

"'Mong rural beauties I was one,
Among the fields wild flowers are fair;
Some country swain might me have won,
And thought my beauty passing rare.

"But, Leicester, (or I much am wrong,)
  Or 'tis not beauty lures thy vows;
Rather ambition's gilded crown
  Makes thee forget thy humble spouse.

"Then, Leicester, why, again I plead,
  (The injured surely may repine,)—
Why didst thou wed a country maid,
  When some fair princess might be thine?

"Why didst thou praise my humble charms,
  And, oh! then leave them to decay?
Why didst thou win me to thy arms,
  Then leave me to mourn the livelong day?

"The village maidens of the plain
  Salute me lowly as they go;
Envious they mark my silken train,
  Nor think a Countess can have woe.

"The simple nymphs! they little know
  How far more happy's their estate;
To smile for joy—than sigh for woe—
  To be content—than to be great.

"How far less blest am I than them?
  Daily to pine and waste with care!
Like the poor plant, that, from its stem
  Divided, feels the chilling air.

"Nor, cruel Earl! can I enjoy
  The humble charms of solitude;
Your minions proud my peace destroy,
  By sullen frowns or pratings rude.

"Last night, as sad I chanced to stray,
  The village death-bell smote my ear;
They wink'd aside, and seemed to say,
  'Countess, prepare, thy end is near!'

"And now, while happy peasants sleep,
  Here I sit lonely and forlorn;
No one to soothe me as I weep,
  Save Philomel on yonder thorn.

"My spirits flag—my hopes decay—
  Still that dread death-bell smites my ear;
And many a boding seems to say,
  'Countess, prepare, thy end is near!'"

Thus sore and sad that lady grieved,
  In Cumnor Hall, so lone and drear;
And many a heartfelt sigh she heaved,
  And let fall many a bitter tear.

And ere the dawn of day appear'd,
  In Cumnor Hall, so lone and drear,
Full many a piercing scream was heard,
  And many a cry of mortal fear.

The death-bell thrice was heard to ring,
  An aerial voice was heard to call,
And thrice the raven flapp'd its wing
  Around the towers of Cumnor Hall.

The mastiff howl'd at village door,
  The oaks were shatter'd on the green;
Woe was the hour—for never more
  That hapless Countess e'er was seen!

And in that Manor now no more
  Is cheerful feast and sprightly ball;
For ever since that dreary hour
  Have spirits haunted Cumnor Hall.

The village maids, with fearful glance,
  Avoid the ancient moss-grown wall;
Nor ever lead the merry dance,
  Among the groves of Cumnor Hall.

Full many a traveller oft hath sigh'd,
  And pensive wept the Countess' fall,
As wand'ring onwards they've espied
  The haunted towers of Cumnor Hall.

ABBOTSFORD, 1*st March*, 1831.

Notes to Kenilworth

27.23 (Ch. 3) to await their return

FORSTER, LAMBOURNE, AND THE BLACK BEAR. If faith is to be put in epitaphs, Anthony Forster was something the very reverse of the character represented in the novel. Ashmole gives this description of his tomb. I copy from the Antiquities of Berkshire, vol. i., p.143.

"In the north wall of the chancel at Cumnor church, is a monument of grey marble, whereon, in brass plates, are engraved a man in armour, and his wife in the habit of her times, both kneeling before a fald-stoole, together with the figures of three sons kneeling behind their mother. Under the figure of the man is this inscription:

ANTONIUS FORSTER, generis generosa propago,
  Cumneræ Dominus, Bercheriensis erat.
Armiger, Armigero prognatus patre Ricardo,
  Qui quondam Iphlethæ Salopiensis erat.
Quatuor ex isto fluxerunt stemmate nati,
  Ex isto Antonius stemmate quartus erat.
Mente sagax, animo precellens, corpore promptus;
  Eloquii dulcis, ore disertus erat.
In factis probitas; fuit in sermone venustas,
  In vultu gravitas, relligione fides,

In patriam pietas, in egenos grata voluntas,
  Accedunt reliquis annumeranda bonis.
Si quod cuncta rapit, rapuit non omnia Lethum,
  Si quod Mors rapuit, vivida fama dedit.

* * * *

"These verses following are writ at length, two by two, in praise of him:

Argute resonas Cithare pretendere chordas
  Novit, et Aonia concrepuisse Lyra.
Gaudebat terre teneras defigere plantas;
  Et mira pulchras construere arte domos,
Composita varias lingua formare loquelas
  Doctus, et edocta scribere multa manu.

"The arms over it thus:

Quart. { I. 3 *Hunter's Horns* stringed.
II. 3 *Pinions* with their points upwards.

"The crest is a *Stag* Couchant, vulnerated throngh the neck by a broad arrow; on his side is a *Martlett* for a difference."

From this monumental inscription it appears, that Anthony Forster, instead of being a vulgar, low-bred, puritanical churl, was in fact a gentleman of birth and consideration, distinguished for his skill in the arts of music and horticulture, as also in languages. In so far, therefore, the Anthony Forster of the romance has nothing but the name in common with the real individual. But notwithstanding the charity, benevolence, and religious faith imputed by the monument of grey marble to its tenant, tradition, as well as secret history, name him as the active agent in the death of the Countess; and it is added, that from being a jovial and convivial gallant, as we may infer from some expressions in the epitaph, he sunk, after the fatal deed, into a man of gloomy and retired habits, whose looks and manners indicated that he suffered under the pressure of some atrocious secret.

The name of Lambourne is still known in the vicinity, and it is said some of the clan partake the habits, as well as name, of the Michael Lambourne of the romance. A man of this name lately murdered his wife, outdoing Michael in this respect, who only was concerned in the murder of the wife of another man.

I have only to add, that the jolly Black Bear has been restored to his predominance over bowl and bottle, in the village of Cumnor.

34.6 (Ch. 4) before Dudman and Ramhead meet Two headlands on the Cornish coast. The expressions are proverbial.

45.35 (Ch. 6) many an oak that grew thereby This verse is the commencement of the ballad already quoted, as what suggested the novel.

67.4 (Ch. 7) The Bear The Leicester cognizance was the ancient device adopted by his father, when Earl of Warwick, the bear and ragged staff.

71.15 (Ch. 7) no peace beyond the Line Sir Francis Drake, Morgan, and many a bold Buccanier of those days, were, in fact, little better than pirates.

79.40 (Ch. 8) did firm remain This verse, or something similar, occurs in a long ballad, or poem, on Flodden-Field, reprinted by the late Henry Weber.

80.7 (Ch. 8) Saddle them well This verse of an old song *actually* occurs in an old play, where the singer boasts,—

> "Courteously I can both counter and knack
> Of Martin Swart and all his merry-men."

126.32 (Ch. 13) Wayland Smith

LEGEND OF WAYLAND SMITH. The great defeat, given by Alfred to the Danish invaders, is said, by Mr Gough, to have taken place near Ashdown, in Berkshire. "The burial place of Bacseg, the Danish chief, who was slain in this fight, is distinguished by a parcel of stones, less than a mile from the hill, set on edge, enclosing a piece of ground somewhat raised. On the east side of the southern extremity, stand three squarish flat stones, of about four or five feet over either way, supporting a fourth, and now called by the vulgar WAYLAND SMITH, from an idle tradition about an invisible smith replacing lost horse-shoes there."—GOUGH'S *edition of* CAMDEN'S *Britannia*, vol. i., p. 221.

The popular belief still retains memory of this wild legend, which, connected as it is with the site of a Danish sepulchre, may have arisen from some legend concerning the northern Duergar, who resided in the rocks, and were cunning workers in steel and iron. It was believed that Wayland Smith's fee was sixpence, and that, unlike other workmen, he was offended if more was offered. Of late his offices have again been called to memory; but fiction has in this, as in other cases, taken the liberty to pillage the stores of oral tradition. This monument must be very ancient, for it has been kindly pointed out to me that it is referred to in an ancient Saxon charter, as a landmark. The monument has been of late cleared out, and made considerably more conspicuous.

131.3 (Ch. 13) from Yoglan Orvietan, or Venice treacle, as it was sometimes called, was understood to be a sovereign remedy against poison; and the reader must be contented, for the time he peruses these pages, to hold the same opinion, which was once universally received by the learned as well as the vulgar.

133.5 (Ch. 14) intelligible to the reader

Leicester and Sussex. Naunton gives us numerous and curious particulars of the jealous struggle which took place between Ratcliffe, Earl of Sussex, and the rising favourite Leicester. The former, when on his deathbed, predicted to his followers, that, after his death, the gipsy (so he called Leicester, from his dark complexion) would prove too many for them.

135.17 (Ch. 14) hexameters

Sir Walter Raleigh. Among the attendants and adherents of Sussex, we have ventured to introduce the celebrated Raleigh, in the dawn of his court favour.

In Aubrey's correspondence there are some curious particulars of Sir Walter Raleigh. "He was a tall, handsome, bold man; but his næve was that he was damnably proud. Old Sir Robert Harley of Brampton Brian Castle, who knew him, would say, 'twas a great question who was the proudest, Sir Walter, or Sir Thomas Overbury; but the difference that was, was judged in Sir Thomas's side. In the great parlour at Downton, at Mr Raleigh's, is a good piece, an original of Sir Walter, in a white satin doublet, all embroidered with rich pearls, and a mighty rich chain of great pearls about his neck. The old servants have told me that the real pearls were near as big as the painted ones. He had a most remarkable aspect, an exceeding high forehead, long-faced, and sour-eyelidded." A rebus is added, to this purpose:

> The enemy to the stomach, and the word of disgrace,
> Is the name of the gentleman with the bold face.

Sir Walter Raleigh's beard turned up naturally, which gave him an advantage over the gallants of the time, whose mustaches received a touch of the barber's art to give them the air then most admired. —*See* Aubrey's *Correspondence*, vol. ii., part ii., pp. 509–12.

147.26 (Ch. 15) love of power

Court favour of Sir Walter Raleigh. The gallant incident of the cloak is the traditional account of this celebrated statesman's rise at court. None of Elizabeth's courtiers knew better than he how to make his court to her personal vanity, or could more justly estimate the quantity of flattery which she could condescend to swallow. Being confined in the Tower for some offence, and understanding the Queen was about to pass to Greenwich in her barge, he insisted on approaching the window, that he might see, at whatever distance, the Queen of his Affections, the most beautiful object which the earth bore on its surface. The Lieutenant of the Tower (his own particular friend) threw himself between his prisoner and the window; while Sir Walter, apparently influenced by a fit of unrestrainable passion, swore he would not be debarred from seeing his light, his life, his goddess! A scuffle ensued, *got up* for effect's sake, in which the Lieutenant and his captive grappled and struggled with fury—tore each other's hair,—and at length drew daggers, and were only separated by force. The Queen being informed of this scene exhibited by her frantic adorer, it wrought, as was to be expected, much in favour of the captive Paladin. There is little doubt that his quarrel with the Lieutenant was entirely contrived for the purpose which it produced.

170.28 (Ch. 17) finger them tightly

ROBERT LANEHAM. Little is known of Robert Laneham, save in his curious letter to a friend in London, giving an account of Queen Elizabeth's entertainments at Kenilworth, written in a style of the most intolerable affectation, both in point of composition and orthography. He describes himself as a *bon vivant*, who was wont to be jolly and dry in the morning, and by his good-will would be chiefly in the company of the ladies. He was, by the interest of Lord Leicester, Clerk of the Council Chamber door, and also keeper of the same. "When council sits," says he, "I am at hand. If any makes a babbling, *Peace*, say I. If I see a listener or a pryer in at the chinks or lockhole, I am presently on the bones of him. If a friend comes, I make him sit down by me on a form or chest. The rest may walk, a God's name!" There has been seldom a better portrait of the pragmatic conceit and self-importance of a small man in office.

182.22 (Ch. 17) the Scotch wild cattle A remnant of the wild cattle of Scotland are preserved at Chillingham Castle, near Wooler, in Northumberland, the seat of Lord Tankerville. They fly before strangers; but if disturbed and followed, they turn with fury on those who persist in annoying them.

193.26 (Ch. 18) your destination

DR JULIO. The Earl of Leicester's Italian physician, Julio, was affirmed by his contemporaries to be a skilful compounder of poisons, which he applied with such frequency, that the Jesuit Parsons extols ironically the marvellous good luck of this great favourite in the opportune deaths of those who stood in the way of his wishes. There is a curious passage on the subject:

"Long after this, he fell in love with the Lady Sheffield, whom I signified before, and then also had he the same fortune to have her husband dye quickly, with an extreme rheume in his head, (as it was given out,) but as others say, of an artificiall catarre, that stopped his breath.

"The like good chance had he in the death of my Lord of Essex, (as I have said before,) and that at a time most fortunate for his purpose; for when he was coming home from Ireland, with intent to revenge himselfe upon my Lord of Leicester for begetting his wife with childe in his absence, (the childe was a daughter, and brought up by the Lady Shandoes, W. Knooles his wife,) my Lord of Leicester hearing thereof, wanted not a friend or two to accompany the deputy, as among other a couple of the Earles own servants, Crompton, (if I misse not his name,) yeoman of his bottles, and Lloid his secretary, entertained afterward by my Lord of Leicester, and so he dyed in the way, of an extreme fluxe, caused by an Italian receipe, as all his friends are well assured, the maker whereof was a chyrurgeon (as is beleeved) that then was newly come to my Lord from Italy,—a cunning man and sure in operation, with whom, if the good Lady had been sooner acquainted, and used his help, she should not have needed to sitten so pensive at home, and fearefull of her husband's former returne out of the same country. - - - - - - - - Neither must you marvaile though all these died in divers manners of outward diseases, for this is the excellency of the Italian art, for which this chyrurgian and Dr Julio were entertained so carefully, who can make a man dye in what manner or show of sicknesse you will: by whose instructions no doubt but his lordship is now cunning, especially adding also to these the counsell of his Doctor Bayly, a man also not a little studied (as he seemeth) in his art; for I heard him once myselfe, in a publique act in Oxford, and that in presence of my Lord of Leicester, (if I be not deceived,) maintain, that poyson might be so tempered and given as it should not appear presently, and yet should kill the party afterward, at what time should be appointed; which argument belike pleased well his lordship, and therefore was chosen to be discussed in his audience, if I be not deceived of his being that day present. So, though one dye of a flux, and another of a catarre, yet this importeth little to the matter, but showeth rather the great cunning and skill of the artificer."—PARSONS'S *Leicester's Commonwealth*, p. 23.

It is unnecessary to state the numerous reasons why the Earl is represented in the tale as being rather the dupe of villains, than the unprincipled author of their atrocities. In the latter capacity, which a part at least of his contemporaries imputed to him, he would have made a character too disgustingly wicked, to be useful for the purposes of fiction.

I have only to add, that the union of the poisoner, the quacksalver, the alchymist, and the astrologer, in the same person, was familiar to the pretenders to the mystic sciences.

289.2 (Ch. 30) such a sight as this This is an imitation of Gascoigne's verses spoken by the Herculean porter, as mentioned in the text. The original may be found in the republication of the Princely Pleasures of Kenilworth, by the same author, in the History of Kenilworth, already quoted. Chiswick, 1821.

291.9 (Ch. 30) vengeably afraid See Laneham's Account of the Queen's Entertainment at Killingworth Castle, in 1575, a very diverting tract, written by as great a coxcomb as ever blotted paper. (See p. 121 above.) The original is extremely rare, but it has been twice reprinted; once in Mr Nichols's very curious and interesting collection of the Progresses and Public Processions of Queen Elizabeth, vol. i.; and more lately in a beautiful antiquarian publication termed *Kenilworth Illustrated*, printed at Chiswick, for Meridew of Coventry, and Radcliffe of Birmingham. It contains reprints of Laneham's Letter, Gascoigne's Princely Progress, and other scarce pieces, annotated with accuracy and ability. The author takes the liberty to refer to this work as his authority for the account of the festivities.

I am indebted for a curious ground-plan of the Castle of Kenilworth, as it existed in Queen Elizabeth's time, to the voluntary kindness of Richard Badnall, Esq. of Olivebank, near Liverpool. From his obliging communication, I learn that the original sketch was found among the manuscripts of the celebrated J. J. Rousseau, when he left England. These were intrusted by the philosopher to the care of his friend Mr Davenport, and passed from his legatee into the possession of Mr Badnall.—See Plan, p. 110 above.

292.9 (Ch. 31) a slight caress To justify what may be considered as a high-coloured picture, the author quotes the original of the courtly and shrewd Sir James Melville, being then Queen Mary's envoy at the Court of London.

"I was required," says Sir James, "to stay till I had seen him made Earle of Leicester, and Baron of Denbigh, with great solemnity; herself (Elizabeth) helping to put on his ceremonial, he sitting on his knees before her, keeping a great gravity and a discreet behaviour; but she could not refrain from putting her hand to his neck to kittle (*i.e.* tickle) him, smilingly, the French Ambassador and I standing beside her."—MELVILLE'S *Memoirs, Bannatyne Edition*, p. 120.

299.40 (Ch. 32) the passage The incident alluded to occurs in the poem of Orlando Innamorato of Boiardo, libro ii. canto 4, stanza 26.

> Non era per ventura, &c.

It may be rendered thus:—

> As then, perchance, unguarded was the tower,
> So enter'd free Anglanté's dauntless knight.

No monster and no giant guard the bower
  In whose recess reclined the fairy light,
Robed in a loose cymar of lily white,
  And on her lap a sword of breadth and might,
In whose broad blade, as in a mirror bright,
  Like maid that trims her for a festal night,
The fairy deck'd her hair, and placed her coronet aright.

Elizabeth's attachment to the Italian school of poetry was singularly manifested on a well-known occasion. Her godson, Sir John Harrington, having offended her delicacy by translating some of the licentious passages of the Orlando Furioso, she imposed on him, as a penance, the task of rendering the *whole* poem into English.

307.42 (Ch. 32) he withdrew

FURNITURE OF KENILWORTH. In revising this work for the present edition, I have had the means of making some accurate additions to my attempt to describe the princely pleasures of Kenilworth, by the kindness of my friend William Hamper, Esq., who has had the goodness to communicate to me an inventory of the furniture of Kenilworth in the days of the magnificent Earl of Leicester. I have adorned the text with some of the splendid articles mentioned in the inventory, but antiquaries, especially, will be desirous to see a more full specimen than the story leaves room for.

EXTRACTS FROM KENILWORTH INVENTORY, A. D. 1584.

A Salte, ship-fashion, of the mother of perle, garnished with silver and divers workes, warlike-ensignes, and ornaments, with xvj peeces of ordinance, whereof ij on wheles, two anckers on the foreparte, and on the stearne the image of Dame Fortune standing on a globe with a flag in her hand. Pois xxxij oz.

A gilt salte like a swann, mother of perle. Pois xxx oz. iij quarters.

A George on horseback, of wood, painted and gilt, with a case for knives in the tayle of the horse, and a case for oyster knives in the brest of the Dragon.

A green barge-cloth, embrother'd with white lions and beares.

A perfuming pann, of silver. Pois xix oz.

In the halle. Tabells, long and short, vj. Forms, long and short, xiiij.

HANGINGS.

(These are minutely specified, and consisted of the following subjects, in tapestry, and gilt and red leather.)

Flowers, beasts, and pillars arched. Forest worke. Historie. Storie of Susanna, the Prodigall Childe, Saule, Tobie, Hercules, Lady Fame, Hawking and Hunting, Jezabell, Judith and Holofernes,

David, Abraham, Sampson, Hippolitus, Alexander the Great, Naaman the Assyrian, Jacob, &c.

Bedsteds, with their Furniture.

(These are magnificent and numerous. I shall copy, *verbatim*, the description of what appears to have been one of the best.)

A bedsted of wallnut-tree, toppe fashion, the pillers redd and varnished, the ceelor, tester, and single vallance of crimson sattin, paned with a broad border of bone lace of golde and silver. The tester richlie embrothered with my Lo. armes in a garland of hoppes, roses, and pomegranetts, and lyned with buckerom. Fyve curteins of crimson sattin to the same bedsted, striped downe with a bone lace of gold and silver, garnished with buttons and loops of crimson silk and golde, containing xiiij bredths of sattin, and one yarde iij quarters deepe. The celor, vallance, and curteins lyned with crymson taffata sarsenet.

A crymson sattin counterpointe, quilted and embr. with a golde twiste, and lyned with redd sarsenet, being in length iij yards good, and in breadth iij scant.

A chaise of crymson sattin, suteable.

A fayre quilte of crymson sattin, vj breadths, iij yardes 3 quarters naile deepe, all lozenged over with silver twiste, in the midst a cinquefoile within a garland of ragged staves, fringed round aboute with a small fringe of crymson silke, lyned throughe with white fustian.

Fyve plumes of coolered feathers, garnished with bone lace and spangells of goulde and silver, standing in cups* knitt all over with goulde, silver, and crymson silk.

A carpett for a cupboarde of crymson sattin, embrothered with a border of goulde twiste, aboute iij parts of it fringed with silk and goulde, lyned with bridges† sattin, in length ij yards, and ij bredths of sattin.

(There were eleven down beds and ninety feather beds, besides thirty-seven mattresses.)

Chayres, Stooles, and Cushens.

(These were equally splendid with the beds, &c. I shall here copy that which stands at the head of the list.)

A chaier of crimson velvet, the seate and backe partlie embrothered, with R. L. in cloth of goulde, the beare and ragged staffe in

* Probably on the centre and four corners of the bedstead. Four bears and ragged staves occupied a similar position on another of these sumptuous pieces of furniture.

† *i.e.* Bruges.

clothe of silver, garnished with lace and fringe of goulde, silver, and crimson silck. The frame covered with velvet, bounde aboute the edge with goulde lace, and studded with gilt nailes.

A square stoole and a foote stoole, of crimson velvet, fringed and garnished suteable.

A long cushen of crimson velvet, embr. with the ragged staffe in a wreathe of goulde, with my Lo. posie "*Droyte et Loyall*" written in the same, and the letters R. L. in clothe of goulde, being garnished with lace, fringe, buttons, and tassels, of gold, silver, and crimson silck, lyned with crimson taff., being in length 1 yard quarter.

A square cushen, of the like velvet, embr. suteable to the long cushen.

Carpets.

(There were 10 velvet carpets for tables and windows, 49 Turkey carpets for floors, and 32 cloth carpets. One of each I will now specify.)

A carpett of crimson velvet, richlie embr. with my Lo. posie, beares and ragged staves, &c., of clothe of goulde and silver, garnished upon the seames and aboute with golde lace, fringed accordinglie, lyned with crimson taffata sarsenett, being 3 breadths of velvet, one yard 3 quarters long.

A great Turquoy carpett, the grounde blew, with a list of yelloe at each end, being in length x yards, in bredthe iiij yards and quarter.

A long carpett of blew clothe, lyned with bridges sattin, fringed with blew silck and goulde, in length vj yards lack a quarter, the whole bredth of the clothe.

Pictures.

(Chiefly described as having curtains.)

The Queene's Majestie, (2 great tables.) 3 of my Lord. St Jerome. Lo. of Arundell. Lord Mathevers. Lord of Pembroke. Counte Egmondt. The Queene of Scotts. King Philip. The Baker's Daughters. The Duke of Feria. Alexander Magnus. Two Yonge Ladies. Pompæa Sabina. Fred. D. of Saxony. Emp. Charles. K. Philip's Wife. Prince of Orange and his Wife. Marq. of Berges and his Wife. Counte de Horne. Count Holstrate. Monsr. Brederode. Duke Alva. Cardinal Grandville. Duches of Parma. Henrie E. of Pembrooke and his young Countess. Countis of Essex. Occacion and Repentance. Lord Mowntacute. Sir Jas. Crofts. Sir Wr. Mildmay. Sr. Wm. Pickering. Edwin Abp. of York.

A tabell of an historie of men, women, and children, molden in wax.

A little foulding table of ebanie, garnished with white bone, wherein are written verses with lres. of goulde.

A table of my Lord's armes.

Fyve of the plannetts, painted in frames.

Twentie-three cardes,* or maps of countries.

INSTRUMENTS.

(I shall give two specimens.)

An instrument of organs, regalls, and virginalls, covered with crimson velvet, and garnished with goulde lace.

A fair pair of double virginalls.

CABONETTS.

A cabonett of crimson sattin, richlie embr. with a device of hunting the stagg, in goulde, silver, and silck, with iiij glasses in the topp thereof, and xvj cupps of flowers made of goulde, silver, and silck, in a case of leather, lyned with greene sattin of bridges.

(Another of purple velvet. A desk of red leather.)

A CHESS BOARDE of ebanie, with checkars of christall and other stones, layed with silver, garnished with beares and ragged staves, and cinquefoiles of silver. The xxxij men likewyse of christall and other stones sett, the one sort in silver white, the other gilte, in a case gilded and lyned with green cotton.

(Another of bone and ebanie. A pair of tabells of bone.)

A GREAT BRASON CANDLESTICK to hang in the roofe of the howse, verie fayer and curiouslye wrought, with xxiiij branches, xij greate and xij of lesser size, 6 rowlers and ij wings for the spreade eagle, xxiiij socketts for candells, xij greater and xij of a lesser sorte, xxiiij sawcers, or candle-cupps, of like proporcion to putt under the socketts, iij images of men and iij of weomen, of brass, verie finely and artificiallie done.

These specimens of Leicester's magnificence may serve to assure the reader that it scarce lay in the power of a modern author to exaggerate the lavish style of expense displayed in the princely pleasures of Kenilworth.

391.40 (Ch. 41) another person

DEATH OF THE EARL OF LEICESTER. In a curious manuscript copy of the information given by Ben Jonson to Drummond of Hawthornden, as abridged by Sir Robert Sibbald, Leicester's death is ascribed to poison administered as a cordial by his countess, to whom he had given it, representing it to be a restorative in any

* *i.e.* Charts.

faintness, in the hope that she herself might be cut off by using it. We have already quoted Jonson's account of this merited stroke of retribution in a note, p. 114 of Introduction to the present work. It may be here added, that the following satirical epitaph on Leicester occurs in Drummond's Collections, but is evidently not of his composition:

EPITAPH ON THE ERLE OF LEISTER.

Here lies a valiant warriour,
  Who never drew a sword;
Here lies a noble courtier,
  Who never kept his word;
Here lies the Earle of Leister,
  Who govern'd the estates,
Whom the earth could never living love,
  And the just Heaven now hates.

THE PIRATE

Editorial Note

On 24 March 1830 Scott informed Cadell that *The Pirate*, together with *The Fortunes of Nigel*, was 'nearly quite notified': optimistically, he thought that he might have all his work for the Magnum 'well nigh finishd in May' (*Letters*, 11.311). Two weeks later Cadell endorsed a further letter from the author 'Pirate with Notes' (*Letters*, 11.324). On 8 June Cadell noted in his diary that he had 'revised 100 pages' (MS 21020, f. 25v). As usual, his use of 'revision' is difficult to interpret precisely. He would have started by transferring Scott's textual revisions into a clean copy of the printed text, and copying out the additional notes: this stage was probably completed by 26 June when he 'brought author's copy of the Pirate with me & sent it to Sir Walter' (MS 21020, f. 28r). On 5 July he 'had a spell at the Pirate' and the following day 'concluded first revise' (MS 20120, ff. 25v, 29v). A further stage of revision occupied his attention between 14 July and 11 August (MS 21020, ff. 30v, 34v): this probably involved correcting the Magnum proofs, and on 30 August Cadell revised the Introduction (MS 21020, f. 37v).

In mid-August there was something of a crisis. It was feared that both *Peveril* and *The Pirate* were of insufficient length to make three and two normal Magnum volumes respectively (Jane Millgate, *Scott's Last Edition* (Edinburgh, 1987), 24–25). On 21 August Scott wrote to Cadell: 'I can stick in more bombast & binding into the Pirate. But I will need the Copy and also will require to know what quantity you will still need. I believe I had better put in a chapter or two at once into the main body of the work instead of more notes I can easily do this & it will have a better effect than cramming the notes. I suppose an addition of of twenty five pages to each volume would be about the mark' (MS 745, f. 197r–v: he also noted, though, 'that the Black Dwarf only runs to 340 pages'). In the event this drastic course of action was not adopted. There was indeed no need for it. The Introduction to *The Pirate* is quite brief; the accumulated length of the notes is similar to that in several other novels; and the volumes are both of normal length. It seems, though, that some of the notes were added at a late stage, since in March 1831 there was a temporary panic when printed volumes (probably the Magnum proofs) containing additional notes presumably in manuscript seemed to have gone missing (MS 15980, ff. 37v–38r, 39v: Scott to Cadell 2 and 5 March).

The volumes containing *The Pirate* (24 and 25) appeared on 1 May and 1 June 1831 respectively.

The modest Introduction consists largely of a short account of the northern voyage of 1814 in search of scenery for *The Lord of the Isles*, with an intriguing suggestion (which was added subsequent to the original manuscript) that Scott was already contemplating the possibility of a future work of fiction set in the northern isles. There is also a partial defence of Norna from the charge that she is merely a re-hash of Meg Merrilies from *Guy Mannering*.

The footnotes are largely glosses or brief explanations, either very brief or running to a few lines. Two references are inserted in the text, presumably as pegs to hang footnotes on (156.27–157.11). The procedures adopted in most of the endnotes are typified in an attractive essay on 'Monsters of the Northern Seas' (141.40–142.37). It begins with an expansion of a bibliographical reference in the text, proceeds with a quotation from Felicia Hemans, and concludes with a series of modern instances of conjectural sea monsters. The next endnote, on 'Sale of Winds' (143.34–144.25), similarly moves from a 1555 book in Scott's library to a modern supporting anecdote from Orkney; and the longest of the endnotes, on 'The Sword-Dance' (146.23–151.8), sets a passage from the same book alongside an extended quotation of a play involving such a dance sent by an acquaintance of the author in Shetland. This combination of library and oral communications is characteristic of these endnotes, and there is also sometimes an element of personal observation, presumably recollected from sixteen years since. A persistent theme is the survival of very old customs and ways of thinking into modern times. Unusually one endnote, on the Dwarfie Stone (151.13–152.11), replaces a first-edition footnote with a more elaborate account.

There are four Magnum illustrations for this title. The frontispiece to Volume 24 (MAG0047 / TB348.24) was designed by James Inskipp and engraved by Charles Rolls. It depicts Brenda Troil tacking the bodice of her sister Minna in their room (EEWN 12, 189.12–15: 'That error shall be presently mended . . . a difficult matter.'). The title-page vignette (MAG0048 / TB348.24) was designed by William Fraser and engraved by Samuel Sangster. It depicts Mertoun attending to the shipwrecked Cleveland, with Norna rebuking Bryce the Pedlar for attempting to remove Cleveland's rings (EEWN 12, 73.6–11 (abridged): 'So saying, the pedlar . . . through the Isles.'). The frontispiece to Volume 25 (MAG0049 / TB348.25) was designed by Clarkson Stanfield and engraved by James Mitchell. It depicts Cleveland confronting Captain Goffe on his return to the pirate vessel, with other crew members on either side (EEWN 12, 313: the caption reads simply 'THE PIRATE.'). The title-page vignette (MAG0050 / TB348.25) was designed by Abraham Cooper and engraved by Alfred Robert Freebairn. It depicts Minna on horseback at the edge of a cliff, with arms outstretched and with her sister Brenda riding in the background (EEWN 12, 255.1–7 (abridged): 'She could not help . . . when balancing itself.').

J. Inskipp. C. Rolls.

THE PIRATE.

"That error shall be presently mended", said Brenda; "and then, as one of our friends might say, I will haul tight and belay—but you draw your breath so deeply, that it will be a difficult matter".

EDINBURGH, PUBLISHED 1831, BY ROBERT CADELL & WHITTAKER & C° LONDON.

WAVERLEY NOVELS.

VOL. XXIV.

THE PIRATE.

"So saying, the pedlar seized one of the man's cold hands, and began his charitable work of removing the rings, which seemed to be of some value. 'As you love your life, forbear," said Norna sternly, 'or I will lay that on you which shall spoil your travels through the Isles.

PRINTED FOR ROBERT CADELL, EDINBURGH,
AND WHITTAKER & Co. LONDON.
1831.

C. Stanfield. J. Mitchell.

THE PIRATE.

WAVERLEY NOVELS,

VOL. XXV.

THE PIRATE.

She could not help looking back to see how Minna should pass the point of peril, which she herself had just rounded; Minna, with an eager look dropped the bridle, and stretched forward her arms, and even her body, over the precipice in the attitude of a wild swan, when balancing itself.

PRINTED FOR ROBERT CADELL, EDINBURGH,
AND WHITTAKER & Co LONDON.
1831.

Introduction to The Pirate

Quoth he, there was a ship.

THIS brief preface may begin like the tale of the Ancient Mariner, since it was on shipboard that the author acquired the very moderate degree of local knowledge and information, both about people and scenery, which he has endeavoured to embody in the romance of the Pirate.

In the summer and autumn of 1814, the author was invited to join a party of Commissioners for the Northern Light-House Service, who proposed making a voyage round the coast of Scotland, and through its various groups of islands, chiefly for the purpose of seeing the condition of the many lighthouses under their direction, —edifices so important, whether regarding them as benevolent or political institutions. Among the commissioners who manage this important public concern, the sheriff of each county of Scotland which touches on the sea, holds ex-officio a place at their board. These gentlemen act in every respect gratuitously, but have the use of an armed yacht, well found and fitted up, when they choose to visit the lighthouses. An excellent engineer, Mr Robert Stevenson, is attached to the Board, to afford the benefit of his professional advice. The author accompanied this frolic as a guest; for Selkirkshire, though it calls him Sheriff, has not, like the kingdom of Bohemia in Corporal Trim's story, a seaport in its circuit, nor its magistrate, of course, any place at the Board of Commissioners,—a circumstance of little consequence where all were old and intimate friends, bred to the same profession, and disposed to accommodate each other in every possible manner.

The nature of the important business which was the principal purpose of the voyage, was connected with the amusement of visiting the leading objects of a traveller's curiosity; for the wild cape, or formidable shelve, which requires to be marked out by a lighthouse, is generally at no great distance from the most magnificent scenery of rocks, caves, and billows. Our time, too, was at our own disposal, and, as most of us were freshwater sailors, we could at any time make a fair wind out of a foul one, and run before the gale in quest of some object of curiosity which lay under our lee.

With these purposes of public utility and some personal amusement in view, we left the port of Leith on the 26th July, 1814, ran along the east coast of Scotland, viewing its different curiosities, stood over to Zetland and Orkney, where we were some time detained by the wonders of a country which displayed so much that was new to us; and having seen what was curious in the Ultima Thule of the ancients, where the sun hardly thought it worth while to go to bed, since his rising was at this season so early, we doubled the extreme northern termination of Scotland, and took a rapid survey of the Hebrides, where we found many kind friends. There, that our little expedition might not want the dignity of danger, we were favoured with a distant glimpse of what was said to be an American cruiser, and had opportunity to consider what a pretty figure we should have made had the voyage ended in our being carried captive to the United States. After visiting the romantic shores of Morven, and the vicinity of Oban, we ran over to the coast of Ireland, and visited the Giant's Causeway, that we might compare it with Staffa, which we had surveyed in our course. At length, about the middle of September, we ended our voyage in the Clyde, at the port of Greenock.

And thus terminated our pleasant tour, to which our equipment gave unusual facilities, as the ship's company could form a strong boat's crew, independent of those who might be left on board the vessel, which permitted us the freedom to land wherever our curiosity carried us. Let me add, while reviewing for a moment a sunny portion of my life, that among the six or seven friends who performed this voyage together, some of them doubtless of different tastes and pursuits, and remaining for several weeks on board a small vessel, there never occurred the slightest dispute or disagreement, each seeming anxious to submit his own particular wishes to those of his friends. By this mutual accommodation all the purposes of our little expedition were attained, while for a time we might have adopted the lines of Allan Cunningham's fine sea-song,

> The world of waters was our home,
> And merry men were we!

But sorrow mixes her memorials with the purest remembrances of pleasure. On returning from the voyage which had proved so satisfactory, I found fate had deprived her country most unexpectedly of a lady, qualified to adorn the high rank which she held, and who had long admitted me into a share of her friendship. The subsequent loss of one of those comrades who made up the party, he the most intimate friend I had in the world, casts also its shade on recollections which would be otherwise so satisfactory.

I may here briefly observe, that my business in this voyage, so far as I could be said to have any, was to endeavour to discover some localities which might be useful in the "Lord of the Isles," a poem which I then was threatening the public with, and was afterwards printed without attaining much success. But as at the same time the nameless novel of "Waverley" was making way on the public, I already augured the possibility of a second effort in this department of literature, and I saw much in the wild islands of the Orkneys and Zetland, which I judged might be made in the highest degree interesting, should these islands ever become the scene of a narrative of fictitious character. I learned the history of Gow the pirate from an old sibyl, (the subject of a note, p. 144 of this volume,) whose principal subsistence was by a trade in favourable winds, which she sold to mariners at Stromness. Nothing could be more interesting than the kindness and hospitality of the gentlemen of Zetland, which was to me the more affecting, as several of them had been friends and correspondents of my father.

I was indeed to go a generation or two further back, to find materials from which I might trace the features of the old Norwegian Udaller, the Scottish gentry having in general occupied the place of that primitive race, and their language and peculiarities of manner having entirely disappeared. The only difference now to be observed betwixt the gentry of these islands, and those of Scotland in general, is, that the wealth and property is more equally divided among our more northern countrymen, and that there exists among the resident proprietors no men of very great wealth, whose display of its luxuries might render the others discontented with their own lot. From the same cause of general equality of fortunes, and the cheapness of living, which is its natural consequence, I found the officers of a veteran regiment who had maintained the garrison at Fort Charlotte, in Lerwick, discomposed at the idea of being recalled from a country where their pay was so adequate to their wants, and it was singular to hear natives of merry England herself regretting their departure from the melancholy isles of the Ultima Thule.

Such are the trivial particulars attending the origin of that publication, which took place several years later than the agreeable journey in which it took its rise.

The state of manners which I have introduced in the romance, was necessarily in a great degree imaginary, though founded in some measure upon slight hints, which, showing what was, seemed to give reasonable indication of what must once have been.

In one respect I was judged somewhat hastily, perhaps, when the character of Norna was pronounced by the critics a mere copy of Meg Merrilies. That I had fallen short of what I wished and desired to express is unquestionable, otherwise my object could not have been so widely mistaken; nor can I yet think that any person who shall take the trouble of reading the Pirate with some attention, can fail to trace in Norna,—the victim of remorse and insanity, and the dupe of her own imposture, her mind, too, flooded with all the wild literature and extravagant superstitions of the north,—something distinct from the Dumfries-shire gipsy, whose pretensions to supernatural powers are not beyond those of a Norwood prophetess. The foundations of such a character may be perhaps traced, though it be too true that the necessary superstructure cannot have been raised upon them, otherwise these remarks would have been unnecessary. There is also great improbability in the statement of Norna possessing power and opportunity to impress on others that belief in her supernatural gifts which distracted her own mind. Yet, amid a very credulous and ignorant population, it is astonishing what success may be attained by an impostor, who is, at the same time, an enthusiast. It is such as to remind us of the couplet which assures us that

> The pleasure is as great
> In being cheated as to cheat.

Indeed, as I have observed elsewhere, the professed explanation of a tale, where appearances or incidents of a supernatural character are referred to natural causes, has often, in the winding up of the story, a degree of improbability almost equal to an absolute goblin narrative. Even the genius of Mrs Radcliffe could not always surmount this difficulty.

ABBOTSFORD, 1st *May*, 1831.

Notes to The Pirate

12.3 (Ch. 1) plantie-cruive Patch of ground for vegetables. The liberal custom of the country permits any person, who has occasion for such a convenience, to select out of the unenclosed moorland a small patch, which he surrounds with a drystone wall, and cultivates as a kail-yard, till he exhausts the soil with cropping, and then he deserts it, and encloses another. This liberty is so far from inferring an invasion of the right of proprietor and tenant, that the last degree of contempt is inferred of an avaricious man, when a Zetlander says he would not hold a *plantie cruive* of him.

12.5 (Ch. 1) lispunds A lipsund is about thirty pounds English, and the value is averaged by Dr Edmonston at ten shillings sterling.

15.20 (Ch. 2) finner *Finner*, small whale.

15.21 (Ch. 2) as weak and unstable as water The sagas of the

Scalds are full of descriptions of these champions, and do not permit us to doubt that the Berserkar, so called from fighting without armour, used some physical means of working themselves into a frenzy, during which they possessed the strength and energy of madness. The Indian warriors are well known to do the same by dint of opium and bang.

17.23 (Ch. 2) the oldest fowlers Fatal accidents, however, sometimes occur. When I visited the Fair Isle in 1814, a poor lad of fourteen had been killed by a fall from the rocks about a fortnight before our arrival. The accident happened almost within sight of his mother, who was casting peats at no great distance. The body fell into the sea, and was seen no more. But the islanders account this an honourable mode of death; and as the children begin the practice of climbing very early, fewer accidents occur than might be expected.

18.3 (Ch. 2) some dreaded sorceress

NORSE FRAGMENTS. Near the conclusion of this chapter it is noticed that the old Norwegian sagas were preserved and often repeated by the fishermen of Orkney and Zetland, while that language was not yet quite forgotten. Mr Baikie of Tankerness, a most respectable inhabitant of Kirkwall, and an Orkney proprietor, assured me of the following curious fact.

A clergyman, who was not long deceased, remembered well when some remnants of the Norse were still spoken in the island called North Ronaldshaw. When Gray's Ode, entitled the "Fatal Sisters," was first published, or at least first reached this remote island, the reverend gentleman had the well-judged curiosity to read it to some of the old persons of the isle, as a poem which regarded the history of their own country. They listened with great attention to the preliminary stanzas:—

"Now the storm begins to lour,
  Haste the loom of hell prepare,
Iron sleet of arrowy shower
  Hurtles in the darken'd air."

But when they had heard a verse or two, they interrupted the reader, telling him they knew the song well in the Norse language, and had often sung it to him when he asked them for an old song. They called it the Magicians, or the Enchantresses. It would have been singular news to the elegant translator, when executing his version from the text of Bartholine, to have learned that the Norse original was still preserved by tradition in a remote corner of the British dominions. The circumstances will probably justify what is said in the text concerning the traditions of the inhabitants of those remote isles, at the beginning of the eighteenth century.

Even yet, though the Norse language is entirely disused, except in so far as particular words and phrases are still retained, those fishers of the Ultima Thule are a generation much attached to these ancient legends. Of this the author learned a singular instance.

About twenty years ago, a missionary clergyman had taken the resolution of traversing those wild islands, where he supposed there might be a lack of religious instruction, which he believed himself capable of supplying. After being some days at sea in an open boat, he arrived at North Ronaldshaw, where his appearance excited great speculation. He was a very little man, dark-complexioned, and from the fatigue he had sustained in removing from one island to another, appeared before them ill-dressed and unshaved, so that the inhabitants set him down as one of the Ancient Picts, or, as they call them with the usual strong guttural, Peghts. How they might have received the poor preacher in this character, was at least dubious; and the schoolmaster of the parish, who had given quarters to the fatigued traveller, set off to consult with Mr S—, the able and ingenious engineer of the Scottish Light-House Service, who chanced to be on the island. As his skill and knowledge were in the highest repute, it was conceived that Mr S— could decide at once whether the stranger was a Peght, or ought to be treated as such. Mr S— was so good-natured as to attend the summons, with the view of rendering the poor man some service. The stranger, who had waked for three nights, was now fast asleep, little dreaming what odious suspicions were current respecting him. The inhabitants were assembled round the doors. Mr S—, understanding the traveller's condition, declined disturbing him, upon which the islanders produced a pair of very little uncouth-looking boots, with prodigiously thick soles, and appealed to him whether it was possible such articles of raiment could belong to any one but a Peght. Mr S—, finding the prejudices of the natives so strong, was induced to enter the sleeping apartment of the traveller, and was surprised to recognise in the supposed Peght a person whom he had known in his worldly profession of an Edinburgh shopkeeper, before he had assumed his present vocation. Of course he was enabled to dispel all suspicions of Peghtism.

18.28 (Ch. 2) abandoned faith in them

Monsters of the Northern Seas. I have said, in the text, that the wondrous tales told by Pontoppidan, the Archbishop of Upsal, still find believers in the Northern Archipelago. It is in vain they are cancelled even in the later editions of Guthrie's Grammar, of which instructive work they used to form the chapter far most attractive to juvenile readers. But the same causes which probably gave birth to the legends concerning mermaids, sea-snakes, krakens, and other marvellous inhabitants of the Northern Ocean, are still afloat in those climates where they took their rise. They had their origin probably from the eagerness of curiosity manifested by our elegant poetess, Mrs Hemans:

What hidest thou in thy treasure-caves and cells,
Thou ever-sounding and mysterious Sea?

The additional mystic gloom which rests on these northern billows for half the year, joined to the imperfect glance obtained of occasional objects, encourage the timid or the fanciful to give way to imagination, and frequently to shape out a distinct story from some object half seen and imperfectly examined. Thus, some years since, a large object was observed in the beautiful Bay of Scalloway in Zetland, so much in vulgar opinion resembling the kraken, that though it might be distinguished for several days, if the exchange of darkness to twilight can be termed so, yet the hardy boatmen shunned to approach it, for fear of being drawn down by the suction attending its sinking. It was probably the hull of some vessel which had foundered at sea.

The belief in mermaids, so fanciful and pleasing in itself, is ever and anon refreshed by a strange tale from the remote shores of some solitary islet.

The author heard a mariner of some reputation in his class vouch for having seen the celebrated sea-serpent. It appeared, so far as could be guessed, to be about a hundred feet long, with the wild mane and fiery eyes which old writers ascribe to the monster; but it is not unlikely the spectator might, in the doubtful light, be deceived by the appearance of a good Norway log floating on the waves. I have only to add, that the remains of an animal, supposed to belong to this latter species, were driven on shore in the Zetland Isles, within the recollection of man. Part of the bones were sent to London, and pronounced by Sir Joseph Banks to be those of a basking shark; yet it would seem that an animal so well known, ought to have been immediately distinguished by the northern fishermen.

26.30 (Ch. 4) the scarf [The Magnum text has 'the scart'.] The cormorant; which may be seen frequently dashing in wild flight along the roosts and tides of Zetland, and yet more often drawn up in ranks on some ledge of rock, like a body of the Black Brunswickers in 1815.

31.11 (Ch. 4) cummers *i.e.* Gossips.

36.22 (Ch. 4) worth as many pennies This is admitted by the English agriculturist:—

> My music since hath been the plough,
>   Entangled with some care among;
> The gain not great, the pain enough,
>   Hath made me sing another song.

37.37 (Ch. 4) a fanciful and scheming man
GOVERNMENT OF ZETLAND.—At the period supposed, the Earls of Morton held the islands of Orkney and Zetland, originally granted in 1643, confirmed in 1707, and rendered absolute in 1742. This gave the family much property and influence, which they usually exercised by factors, named chamberlains. In 1766 this property was sold by the then Earl of Morton to Sir Lawrence Dundas, by whose son, Lord Dundas, it is now held.

45.35 (Ch. 5) a jagger A pedlar.

53.22 (Ch. 6) the beetle The beetle with which the Scottish housewives used to perform the office of the modern mangle, by beating newly-washed linen on a smooth stone for the purpose, called the beetling-stone.

58.27 (Ch. 6) the chapman's drouth The chapman's drouth, that is, the pedlar's thirst, is proverbial in Scotland, because these pedestrian traders were in the use of modestly asking only for a drink of water, when, in fact, they were desirous of food.

59.9 (Ch. 6) I will test Test upon it, *i.e.* leave it in my will; a mode of bestowing charity, to which many are partial as well as the good dame in the text.

59.14 (Ch. 6) said Tronda Although the Zetlanders were early reconciled to the reformed faith, some ancient practices of Catholic superstition survived long amongst them. In very stormy weather a fisher would vow an *oremus* to Saint Ronald, and acquitted himself of the obligation by throwing a small piece of money in at the window of a ruinous chapel.

65.20 (Ch. 7) those who are port-bound
SALE OF WINDS. The King of Sweden, the same Eric quoted by Mordaunt, "was," says Olaus Magnus, "in his time held second to none in the magical art; and he was so familiar with the evil spirits whom he worshipped, that what way soever he turned his cap, the wind would presently blow that way. For this he was called Windy-cap." *Historia de Gentibus Septentrionalibus. Romæ*, 1555. It is well known that the Laplanders derive a profitable trade in selling *winds*, but it is perhaps less notorious, that within these few years such a commodity might be purchased on British ground, where it was like to be in great request. At the village of Stromness, on the

Orkney main island, called Pomona, lived, in 1814, an aged dame, called Bessie Millie, who helped out her subsistence by selling favourable winds to mariners. He was a venturous master of a vessel who left the roadstead of Stromness without paying his offering to propitiate Bessie Millie. Her fee was extremely moderate, being exactly sixpence, for which, as she explained herself, she boiled her kettle and gave the bark advantage of her prayer, for she disclaimed all unlawful arts. The wind thus petitioned for was sure, she said, to arrive, though occasionally the mariner had to wait some time for it. The woman's dwelling and appearance were not unbecoming her pretensions. Her house, which was on the brow of the steep hill on which Stromness is founded, was only accessible by a series of dirty and precipitous lanes, and for exposure might have been the abode of Eolus himself, in whose commodities she dealt. She herself was, as she told us, near one hundred years old, withered and dried up like a mummy. A clay-coloured kerchief, folded round her head, corresponded in colour to her corpse-like complexion. Two light-blue eyes that gleamed with a lustre like that of insanity, an utterance of astonishing rapidity, a nose and chin that almost met together, and a ghastly expression of cunning, gave her the effect of Hecaté. She remembered Gow the pirate, who had been a native of these islands, in which he closed his career, as mentioned in the preface. Such was Bessie Millie, to whom the mariners paid a sort of tribute, with a feeling betwixt jest and earnest.

70.35 (Ch. 7) do you some capital injury

Reluctance to Save a Drowning Man. It is remarkable, that in an archipelago where so many persons must be necessarily endangered by the waves, so strange and inhuman a maxim should have ingrafted itself upon the minds of a people otherwise kind, moral, and hospitable. But all with whom I have spoken agree, that it was almost general in the beginning of the eighteenth century, and was with difficulty weeded out by the sedulous instructions of the clergy, and the rigorous injunctions of the proprietors. There is little doubt it had been originally introduced as an excellent excuse for suffering those who attempted to escape from the wreck to perish unassisted, that, no person belonging to the vessel surviving, she might be considered as lawful plunder. A story was told me, I hope an untrue one, that a vessel having got ashore among the breakers on one of the remote Zetland islands, five or six men, the whole or greater part of the unfortunate crew, endeavoured to land by assistance of a hawser, which they had secured to a rock; the inhabitants were assembled, and looked on with some uncertainty, till an old man said, "Sirs, if these men come ashore, the additional mouths will eat all the meal we have in store for winter; and how are we to get more?" A young fellow, moved with this argument, struck the rope asunder with his axe, and all the poor wretches were immersed among the breakers, and perished.

75.18 (Ch. 7) mair wrecks ere winter

MAIR WRECKS ERE WINTER. The ancient Zetlander looked upon the sea as the provider of his living, not only by the plenty produced by the fishings, but by the spoil of wrecks. Some particular islands have fallen off very considerably in their rent, since the commissioners for the lighthouses have ordered lights on the Isle of Sanda and the Pentland Skerries. A gentleman, familiar with those seas, expressed surprise at seeing the farmer of one of the isles in a boat with a very old pair of sails. "Had it been His will" —said the man, with an affected deference to Providence, very inconsistent with the sentiment of his speech—"Had it been *His* will that light had not been placed yonder, I would have had enough of new sails last winter."

88.7 (Ch. 9) trock Barter.

105.23 (Ch. 11) call a corn-mill

ZETLAND CORN-MILLS. There is certainly something very extraordinary to a stranger in Zetland corn-mills. They are of the smallest possible size; the wheel which drives them is horizontal, and the cogs are turned diagonally to the water. The beam itself stands upright, and is inserted in a stone quern of the old-fashioned construction, which it turns round, and thus performs its duty. Had Robinson Crusoe been in Zetland, he would have had no difficulty in contriving a machine for grinding corn in his desert island. These mills are thatched over in a little hovel, which has much the air of a pig-sty. There may be five hundred such mills on the islands, not capable any one of them of grinding above a sackful of corn at a time.

107.26 (Ch. 11) seek better kitchen What is eat by way of relish to dry bread is called *kitchen* in Scotland, as cheese, dried fish, or the like relishing morsels.

127.42 (Ch. 13) (Magnum addition) [The Magnum adds the following passage after 'through the company' at 127.42:

The good old toasts dedicated to the prosperity of Zetland, were then honoured with flowing bumpers. "Death to the head that never wears hair!" was a sentiment quaffed to the success of the fishing, as proposed by the sonorous voice of the Udaller. Claud Halcro proposed with general applause, "The health of their worthy landmaster, the sweet sister meat-mistresses; health to man, death to fish, and growth to the produce of the ground." The same recurring sentiment was proposed more concisely by a whiteheaded compeer of Magnus Troil, in the words, "God open the mouth of the grey fish, and keep his hand about the corn!"]

See Hibbert's Description of the Zetland Islands, p. 470.

137.28 (Ch. 15) a Norse ditty See note to Chapter II., p. 140. Norse Fragments.

140.31 (Ch. 15) the wilds of Strathnavern Montrose, in his last and ill-advised attempt at invading Scotland, augmented his small army of Danes and Scottish Royalists, with some bands of raw troops, hastily levied, or rather pressed into his service, in the Orkney and Zetland Isles, who, having little heart either to the cause or manner of service, behaved but indifferently when they came to action.

140.41 (Ch. 15) old John Urry, or Hurry Here, as afterwards remarked in the text, the Zetlander's memory deceived him grossly. Sir John Urry, a brave soldier of fortune, was at that time in Montrose's army, and made prisoner along with him. He had changed so often that the mistake is pardonable. After the action, he was executed by the Covenanters; and

> Wind-changing Warwick then could change no more.

Strachan commanded the body by which Montrose was routed.

141.36 (Ch. 15) the sword-dance

THE SWORD-DANCE. The Sword-Dance is celebrated in general terms by Olaus Magnus. He seems to have considered it as peculiar to the Norwegians, from whom it may have passed to the Orkneymen and Zetlanders, with other northern customs.

"OF THEIR DANCING IN ARMS.

"Moreover, the northern Goths and Swedes had another sport to exercise youth withall, that they will dance and skip amongst naked swords and dangerous weapons: And this they do after the manner of masters of defence, as they are taught from their youth by skilful teachers, that dance before them, and sing to it. And this play is showed especially about Shrovetide, called in Italian *Maschararum.* For, before carnivals, all the youth dance for eight days together, holding their swords up, but within the scabbards, for three times turning about; and then they do it with their naked swords lifted up. After this, turning more moderately, taking the points and pummels one of the other, they change ranks, and place themselves in an hexagonal figure, and this they call *Rosam;* and presently they dissolve it by drawing back their swords and lifting them up, that upon every one's head there may be made a square Rosa, and then by a most nimble whisking their swords about collaterally, they quickly leap back, and end the sport, which they guide with pipes or songs, or both together; first by a more heavy, then by a more vehement, and lastly, by a most vehement dancing. But this speculation is scarce to be understood but by those who look on, how comely and decent it is, when at one word, or one commanding, the whole armed multitude is directed to fall to fight, and clergymen may exercise themselves, and mingle themselves amongst others at this sport, because it is all guided by most wise reason."

To the Primate's account of the sword-dance, I am able to add the words sung or chanted, on occasion of this dance, as it is still performed in Papa Stour, a remote island of Zetland, where alone the custom keeps its ground. It is, it will be observed by antiquaries, a species of play or mystery, in which the Seven Champions of Christendom make their appearance, as in the interlude presented in "All's Well that Ends Well." This dramatic curiosity was most kindly procured for my use by Dr Scott of Hazlar Hospital, son of my friend Mr Scott of Mewbie, Zetland. Mr Hibbert has, in his Description of the Zetland Islands, given an account of the sword-dance, but somewhat less full than the following:

"WORDS USED AS A PRELUDE TO THE SWORD-DANCE, A DANISH OR NORWEGIAN BALLET, COMPOSED SOME CENTURIES AGO, AND PRESERVED IN PAPA STOUR, ZETLAND.

PERSONAE DRAMATIS.*

(*Enter* MASTER, *in the character of* ST GEORGE.)

Brave gentles all within this boor,†
If ye delight in any sport,
Come see me dance upon this floor,
Which to you all shall yield comfort.
Then shall I dance in such a sort,
As possible I may or can;
You, minstrel man, play me a Porte,‡
That I on this floor may prove a man.

(*He bows, and dances in a line.*)

Now have I danced with heart and hand,
Brave gentles all, as you may see,
For I have been tried in many a land,

* So placed in the old MS.

† *Boor*—so spelt, to accord with the vulgar pronunciation of the word *bower*.

‡ *Porte*—so spelt in the original. The word is known as indicating a piece of music on the bagpipe, to which ancient instrument, which is of Scandinavian origin, the sword-dance may have been originally composed.

As yet the truth can testify;
In England, Scotland, Ireland, France, Italy, and Spain,
Have I been tried with that good sword of steel.
(*Draws, and flourishes.*)
Yet, I deny that ever a man did make me yield;
For in my body there is strength,
As by my manhood may be seen;
And I, with that good sword of length,
Have oftentimes in perils been,
And over champions I was king.
And by the strength of this right hand,
Once on a day I kill'd fifteen,
And left them dead upon the land.
Therefore, brave minstrel, do not care,
But play to me a Porte most light,
That I no longer do forbear,
But dance in all these gentles' sight;
Although my strength makes you abased,
Brave gentles all, be not afraid,
For here are six champions, with me, staid,
All by my manhood I have raised.
(*He dances.*)
Since I have danced, I think it best
To call my brethren in your sight,
That I may have a little rest,
And they may dance with all their might;
With heart and hand as they are knights,
And shake their swords of steel so bright,
And show their main strength on this floor,
For we shall have another bout
Before we pass out of this boor.
Therefore, brave minstrel, do not care
To play to me a Porte most light,
That I no longer do forbear,
But dance in all these gentles' sight.
(*He dances, and then introduces his knights, as under.*)
Stout James of Spain, both tried and stour,*
Thine acts are known full well indeed;
And champion Dennis, a French knight,
Who stout and bold is to be seen;
And David, a Welshman born,
Who is come of noble blood;
And Patrick also, who blew the horn,
An Irish knight, amongst the wood.
Of Italy, brave Anthony the good,
And Andrew of Scotland King;
St George of England, brave indeed,
Who to the Jews wrought muckle tinte.†
Away with this!—Let us come to sport,
Since that ye have a mind to war,
Since that ye have this bargain sought,
Come let us fight and do not fear.

* *Stour*, great.
† *Muckle tinte*, much loss or harm; so in MS.

Therefore, brave minstrel, do not care
To play to me a Porte most light,
That I no longer do forbear,
But dance in all these gentles' sight.

(*He dances, and advances to* JAMES *of Spain.*)

Stout James of Spain, both tried and stour,
Thine acts are known full well indeed,
Present thyself within our sight,
Without either fear or dread.
Count not for favour or for feid,
Since of thy acts thou hast been sure;
Brave James of Spain, I will thee lead,
To prove thy manhood on this floor.

(JAMES *dances.*)

Brave champion Dennis, a French knight,
Who stout and bold is to be seen,
Present thyself here in our sight,
Thou brave French knight,
Who bold hast been;
Since thou such valiant acts hast done,
Come let us see some of them now
With courtesy, thou brave French knight,
Draw out thy sword of noble hue.

(DENNIS *dances, while the others retire to a side.*)

Brave David a bow must string, and with awe
Set up a wand upon a stand,
And that brave David will cleave in twa.*

(DAVID *dances solus.*)

Here is, I think, an Irish knight,
Who does not fear, or does not fright,
To prove thyself a valiant man,
As thou hast done full often bright;
Brave Patrick, dance, if that thou can.

(*He dances.*)

Thou stout Italian, come thou here;
Thy name is Anthony, most stout;
Draw out thy sword that is most clear,
And do thou fight without any doubt;
Thy leg thou shake, thy neck thou lout,†
And show some courtesy on this floor,
For we shall have another bout,
Before we pass out of this boor.
Thou kindly Scotsman, come thou here;
Thy name is Andrew of Fair Scotland;
Draw out thy sword that is most clear,
Fight for thy king with thy right hand;
And aye as long as thou can stand,
Fight for thy king with all thy heart;
And then, for to confirm his band,
Make all his enemies for to smart.—(*He dances.*)

(*Music begins.*)

* Something is evidently amiss or omitted here. David probably exhibited some feat of archery.

† *Lout*—to bend or bow down, pronounced *loot,* as *doubt* is *doot* in Scotland.

FIGUIR.*

"The six stand in rank with their swords reclining on their shoulders. The master (St George) dances, and then strikes the sword of James of Spain, who follows George, then dances, strikes the sword of Dennis, who follows behind James. In like manner the rest—the music playing—swords as before. After the six are brought out of rank, they and the master form a circle, and hold the swords point and hilt. This circle is danced round twice. The whole, headed by the master, pass under the swords held in a vaulted manner. They jump over the swords. This naturally places the swords across, which they disentangle by passing under their right sword. They take up the seven swords, and form a circle, in which they dance round.

"The master runs under the sword opposite, which he jumps over backwards. The others do the same. He then passes under the right-hand sword, which the others follow, in which position they dance, until commanded by the master, when they form into a circle, and dance round as before. They then jump over the right-hand sword, by which means their backs are to the circle, and their hands across their backs. They dance round in that form until the master calls 'Loose,' when they pass under the right sword, and are in a perfect circle.

"The master lays down his sword, and lays hold of the point of James's sword. He then turns himself, James, and the others, into a clew. When so formed, he passes under out of the midst of the circle; the others follow; they vault as before. After several other evolutions, they throw themselves into a circle, with their arms across the breast. They afterwards form such figures as to form a shield of their swords, and the shield is so compact that the master and his knights dance alternately with this shield upon their heads. It is then laid down upon the floor. Each knight lays hold of their former points and hilts with their hands across, which disentangle by figuirs directly contrary to those that formed the shield. This finishes the Ballet.

"EPILOGUE.

Mars does rule, he bends his brows,
He makes us all agast;†
After the few hours that we stay here,
Venus will rule at last.

Farewell, farewell, brave gentles all,
That herein do remain,

* *Figuir*—so spelt in MS.
† *Agast*—so spelt in MS.

I wish you health and happiness
Till we return again.

[*Exeunt*."

The manuscript from which the above was copied was transcribed from *a very old one* by Mr William Henderson, Jun., of Papa Stour, in Zetland. Mr Henderson's copy is not dated, but bears his own signature, and, from various circumstances, it is known to have been written about the year 1788.

164.7 (Ch. 17) to fish flounders The contest about the whale will remind a poetical reader of Waller's Battle of the Summer Islands.

180.27 (Ch.19) sitting by the Dwarfie Stone

THE DWARFIE STONE. This is one of the wonders of the Orkney Islands, though it has been somewhat undervalued by their late historian, Mr Barry. The island of Hoy rises abruptly, starting as it were out of the sea, which is contrary to the gentle and flat character of the other Isles of Orkney. It consists of a mountain, having different eminences or peaks. It is very steep, furrowed with ravines, and placed so as to catch the mists of the Western Ocean, and has a noble and picturesque effect from all points of view. The highest peak is divided from another eminence, called the Ward-hill, by a long swampy valley full of peat-bogs. Upon the slope of this last hill, and just where the principal mountain of Hoy opens in a hollow swamp, or corrie, lies what is called the Dwarfie Stone. It is a great fragment of sandstone, composing one solid mass, which has long since been detached from a belt of the same materials, cresting the eminence above the spot where it now lies, and which has slid down till it reached its present situation. The rock is about seven feet high, twenty-two feet long, and seventeen feet broad. The upper end of it is hollowed by iron tools, of which the marks are evident, into a sort of apartment, containing two beds of stone, with a passage between them. The uppermost and largest bed is five feet eight inches long, by two feet broad, which was supposed to be used by the dwarf himself; the lower couch is shorter, and rounded off, instead of being squared at the corners. There is an entrance of about three feet and a half square, and a stone lies before it calculated to fit the opening. A sort of skylight window gives light to the apartment. We can only guess at the purpose of this monument, and different ideas have been suggested. Some have supposed it the frolic of some travelling mason; but the *cui bono* would remain to be accounted for. The Rev. Mr Barry conjectures it to have been a hermit's cell. But it displays no symbol of Christianity, and the door opens to the westward. The Orcadian traditions allege the work to have been that of a dwarf, to whom they ascribe supernatural powers, and a malevolent disposition, the attributes of that race in Norse mythology. Whoever inhabited this singular den certainly enjoyed

> Pillow cold, and sheets not warm.

I observed, that commencing just opposite to the Dwarfie Stone, and extending in a line to the sea-beach, there are a number of small barrows, or cairns, which seem to connect the stone with a very large cairn where we landed. This curious monument may therefore have been intended as a temple of some kind to the Northern Dii Manes, to which the cairns might direct worshippers.

186.17 (Ch. 19) blindness and agony This cruelty is practised by some fishers, out of a vindictive hatred to these ravenous fishes.

201.20 (Ch. 21) 1588 The Admiral of the Spanish Armada was wrecked on the Fair Isle, half-way betwixt the Orkney and Zetland Archipelagos. The Duke of Medina Sidonia came ashore, with some of his people, and pillaged the islanders of their winter stores. They remained in the island by force, and on bad terms with the inhabitants, till spring returned, and then effected their departure.

203.29 (Ch. 21) galdragon *Galdra-Kinna*—the Norse for a sorceress.

204.30 (Ch. 21) respectful observance

FORTUNE-TELLING RHYMES. The author has in the preceding chapter supposed that a very ancient northern custom, used by those who were accounted soothsaying women, might have survived, though in jest rather than earnest, among the Zetlanders, their descendants. The following original account of such a scene will show the ancient importance and consequence of such a prophetic character as was assumed by Norna:—

"There lived in the same territory (Greenland) a woman named Thorbiorga, who was a prophetess, and called the little Vola, (or fatal sister,) the only one of nine sisters who survived. Thorbiorga during the winter used to frequent the festivities of the season, invited by those who were desirous of learning their own fortune, and the future events which impended. Torquil being a man of consequence in the country, it fell to his lot to enquire how long the dearth was to endure with which the country was then afflicted; he therefore invited the prophetess to his house, having made liberal preparation, as was the custom, for receiving a guest of such consequence. The seat of the soothsayer was placed in an eminent situation, and covered with pillows filled with the softest eider down. In the evening she arrived, together with a person who had been sent to meet her, and show her the way to Torquil's habitation. She was attired as follows: She had a sky-blue tunick, having the front ornamented with gems from the top to the bottom, and wore around her throat a necklace of glass beads.* Her head-gear was of black lambskin, the lining being the fur of a white wild-cat. She leant on a staff, having a ball at the top.† The staff was ornamented with brass, and the ball or globe with gems or pebbles. She wore a Hunland (or Hungarian) girdle, to which was attached a large pouch, in which she kept her magical implements. Her shoes were of sealskin, dressed with the hair outside, and secured by long and thick straps, fastened by brazen clasps. She wore gloves of the wild-cat's skin, with the fur inmost. As this venerable person entered the hall, all saluted her with due respect; but she only returned the compliments of such as were agreeable to her. Torquil conducted her with reverence to the seat prepared for her, and requested she would purify the apartment and company assembled, by casting her eyes over them. She was by no means sparing of her words. The table being at length covered, such viands were placed before Thorbiorga as suited her character of a soothsayer. There was a preparation of goat's milk, and a mess composed of the hearts of various animals. The prophetess made use of a brazen spoon, and a pointless knife, the handle of which was composed of a whale's tooth, and ornamented with two rings of brass. The table being removed, Torquil addressed Thorbiorga, requesting her opinion of his house and guests, at the same time intimating the subjects on which he and the company were desirous to consult her.

"Thorbiorga replied, it was impossible for her to answer their enquiries until she had slept a night under his roof. The next morning, therefore, the magical apparatus necessary for her purpose was prepared, and she then enquired, as a necessary part of the ceremony, whether there was any female present who could sing a magical song called '*Vardlokur*.' When none such as she desired could be found, Gudrida, the daughter of Torquil, replied, 'I am no sorceress or soothsayer; but my nurse, Haldisa, taught me, when in Iceland, a song called *Vardlokur*.'—'Then thou knowst more than I was aware of,' said Torquil. 'But as I am a Christian,' continued Gudrida, 'I consider these rites and the song itself as matters which it is unlawful to promote.'—'Nevertheless,' answered the soothsayer, 'thou mayst help us in this matter without any harm to thy

* We may suppose the beads to have been of the potent adderstone, to which so many virtues were ascribed.

† Like those anciently borne by porters at the gates of distinguished persons, as a badge of office.

religion, since the task will remain with Torquil to provide every thing necessary for the present purpose.' Torquil also earnestly entreated Gudrida, till she consented to grant his request. The females then surrounded Thorbiorga, who took her place on a species of elevated stage; Gudrida then sung the magic song, with a voice so sweet and powerful, as to excel any thing that had been heard by any present. The soothsayer, delighted with the melody, returned thanks to the singer, and then said, 'Much I have now learned of dearth and disease approaching the country, and many things are now clear to me which before were hidden as well from me as others. Our present dearth of substance shall not long endure for the present, and plenty will in spring succeed to scarcity. The contagious diseases also, with which the country has been for some time afflicted, will in a short time take their departure. To thee, Gudrida, I can, in recompense for thy assistance on this occasion, announce a fortune of higher import than any one could have conjectured. You shall be married to a man of great name here in Greenland; but you shall not long enjoy that union, for your fate recalls you to Iceland, where you shall become the mother of a numerous and honourable family, which shall be enlightened by a luminous ray of good fortune. So, my daughter, wishing thee health, I bid thee farewell.' The prophetess, having afterwards given answers to all queries which were put to her, either by Torquil or his guests, departed to show her skill at another festival, to which she had been invited for that purpose. But all which she had presaged, either concerning the public or individuals, came truly to pass."

The above narrative is taken from the Saga of Erick Randa, as quoted by the learned Bartholine in his curious work. He mentions similar instances, particularly of one Heida, celebrated for her predictions, who attended festivals for the purpose, as a modern Scotsman might say, of *spaeing* fortunes, with a gallant *tail*, or retinue, of thirty male and fifteen female attendants.—See *De Causis Contemptæ a Danis adhuc gentilibus Mortis, lib. III., cap.* 4.

213.14 (Ch. 22) the promise of Odin

PROMISE OF ODIN. Although the Father of Scandinavian mythology has been as a deity long forgotten in the archipelago, which was once a very small part of his realm, yet even at this day his name continues to be occasionally attested as security for a promise.

It is curious to observe, that the rites with which such attestations are still made in Orkney, correspond to those of the ancient Northmen. It appears from several authorities, that in the Norse ritual, when an oath was imposed, he by whom it was given, passed his hand through a massive ring of silver kept for that purpose.* In like manner, two persons, generally lovers, desirous to take the promise of Odin, which they considered as peculiarly binding, joined hands through a circular hole in a sacrificial stone, which lies in the Orcadian Stonehenge, called the Circle of Stennis, of which we shall speak more hereafter. The ceremony is now confined to the troth-plighting of the lower classes, but at an earlier period may be supposed to have influenced a character like Minna.

215.10 (Ch. 22) implicit faith An elder brother, now no more, who was educated in the navy, and had been a midshipman in Rodney's squadron in the West Indies, used to astonish the author's boyhood with tales of those haunted islets. On one of them, called, I believe, Coffin-key, the seamen positively refused to pass the night, and came off every evening while they were engaged in completing the watering of the vessel, returning the following sunrise.

222.12 (Ch. 23) save memory of you I cannot suppress the pride of saying, that these lines have been beautifully set to original music, by Mrs Arkwright, of Derbyshire.

224.7 (Ch. 23) the court of England The celebrated Sortes Virgilianæ were resorted to by Charles I. and his courtiers, as a mode of prying into futurity.

245.6 (Ch. 26) Continuation of Auld Robin Gray It is worth while saying, that this motto, and the ascription of the beautiful ballad from which it is taken to the Right Honourable Lady Ann Lindsay, occasioned the ingenious authoress's acknowledgment of the ballad, of which the Editor, by her permission, published a small impression, inscribed to the Bannatyne Club.

254.9 (Ch. 27) their shivering inhabitants

THE PICTISH BURGH. The Pictish Burgh, a fort which Norna is supposed to have converted into her dwelling-house, has been fully described in the Notes upon Ivanhoe, pp. 30–31 of this volume. An account of the celebrated Castle of Mousa is there given, to afford an opportunity of comparing it with the Saxon Castle of Coningsburgh. It should, however, have been mentioned, that the Castle of Mousa underwent considerable repairs at a comparatively recent period. Accordingly, Torfæus assures us, that even this ancient pigeon-house, composed of dry stones, was fortification enough, not indeed to hold out a ten years' siege, like Troy in similar circumstances, but to wear out the patience of the besiegers. Erland, the son of Harold the Fair-spoken, had carried off a beautiful woman, the mother of a Norwegian earl, also called Harold, and sheltered himself with his fair prize in the Castle of Mousa. Earl Harold followed with an army,

* See the Eyrbiggia Saga.

and, finding the place too strong for assault, endeavoured to reduce it by famine; but such was the length of the siege, that the offended Earl found it necessary to listen to a treaty of accommodation, and agreed that his mother's honour should be restored by marriage. This transaction took place in the beginning of the thirteenth century, in the reign of William the Lion of Scotland.* It is probable that the improvements adopted by Erland on this occasion, were those which finished the parapets of the castle, by making them project outwards, so that the tower of Mousa rather resembles the figure of a dice-box, whereas others of the same kind have the form of a truncated cone. It is easy to see how the projection of the highest parapet would render the defence more easy and effectual.

260.35 (Ch. 28) no other whatsoever The MacRaws were followers of the MacKenzies, whose chief has the name of Caberfae, or Buckshead, from the cognisance borne on his standards. Unquestionably the worthy piper trained the seal on the same principle of respect to the clan-tune which I have heard has been taught to dogs, who, unused to any other air, dance after their fashion to that of Caberfae.

261.24 (Ch. 28) spae-women Sorceresses and fortune-tellers.

268.1 (Ch. 28) Scottish antiquities The spells described in this chapter are not altogether imaginary. By this mode of pouring lead into water, and selecting the part which chances to assume a resemblance to the human heart, which must be worn by the patient around her or his neck, the sage persons of Zetland pretend to cure the fatal disorder called the loss of a heart.

277.8 (Ch. 30) (Magnum addition) [The Magnum text reads:

"*Jokul, jokul!** was Laurence's joyful answer; and he hastened for the basket.

"By the bicker of Saint Magnus,"† said Halcro, "and the burliest bishop that ever quaffed it for luck's sake, there is no finding your locker empty, Magnus! I believe sincerely that ere a friend wanted, you could, like old Luggie the warlock, fish up boiled and roasted out of the pool of Kibster."‡

You are wrong there, Jarto Claud," said Magnus Troil, "for far from helping me to a supper, the foul fiend, I believe, has carried off great part of mine this blessed evening; but you are welcome to share and share of what is left." This was said while the party entered the hut.

Here, in a cabin . . .]

* *Jokul*, yes, sir; a Norse expression, still in common use.

† The Bicker of Saint Magnus, a vessel of enormous dimen-

* See Torfæi Orcadus, p. 131.

sions, was preserved at Kirkwall, and presented to each bishop of the Orkneys. If the new incumbent was able to quaff it out at one draught, which was a task for Hercules or Rorie Mhor of Dunvegan, the omen boded a crop of unusual fertility.

‡ Luggie, a famous conjurer, was wont, when storm prevented him from going to his usual employment of fishing, to angle over a steep rock, at a place called, from his name, Luggie's Knoll. At other times he drew up dressed food while they were out at sea, of which his comrades partook boldly from natural courage, without caring who stood cook. The poor man was finally condemned and burnt at Scalloway.

279.15 (Ch. 30) gold amang them too

ANTIQUE COINS FOUND IN ZETLAND. While these sheets were passing through the press, I received a letter from an honourable and learned friend, containing the following passage, relating to a discovery in Zetland:—"Within a few weeks, the workmen taking up the foundation of an old wall, came on a hearth-stone, under which they found a horn, surrounded with massive silver rings, like bracelets, and filled with coins of the Heptarchy, in perfect preservation. The place of finding is within a very short distance of the [supposed] residence of Norna of the Fitful-head."—Thus one of the very improbable fictions of the tale is verified by a singular coincidence.

280.14 (Ch. 30) staig Young unbroken horse.

283.38 (Ch. 30) Shogh In Gaelic, *there*.

291.4 (Ch. 31) went off before them It is very curious that the grouse, plenty in Orkney as the text declares, should be totally unknown in the neighbouring archipelago of Zetland, which is only about sixty miles distance, with the Fair Isle as a step between.

308.33 (Ch. 33) within the circle of Odin See an explanation of this promise, Note to Chapter 10, pp. 154–55, of this volume.

311.2 (Ch. 33) the most miserable of beings

CHARACTER OF NORNA. The character of Norna is meant to be an instance of that singular species of insanity, during which the patient, while she or he retains much subtlety and address for the power of imposing upon others, is still more ingenious in endeavouring to impose upon themselves. Indeed, maniacs of this kind may be often observed to possess a sort of double character, in one of which they are the being whom their distempered imagination shapes out, and in the other, their own natural self, as seen to exist by other people. This species of double consciousness makes wild work with the patient's imagination, and, judiciously used, is perhaps a frequent means of restoring sanity of intellect. Exterior circumstances striking the senses, often have a powerful effect in undermining or battering the airy castles which the disorder has excited.

A late medical gentleman, my particular friend, told me the case of a lunatic patient confined in the Edinburgh Infirmary. He was so far happy that his mental alienation was of a gay and pleasant character, giving a hint of joyous indulgence to all that came in contact with him. He considered the large house, numerous servants, &c., of the hospital, as all matters of state and consequence belonging to his own personal establishment, and had no doubt of his own wealth and grandeur. One thing alone puzzled the man of wealth. Although he was provided with a first-rate cook and proper assistants, although his table was regularly supplied with every delicacy of the season, yet he confessed to my friend, that by some uncommon depravity of the palate, every thing which he ate *tasted of porridge*. This peculiarity, of course, arose from the poor man being fed upon nothing else, and because his stomach was not so easily deceived as his other senses.

312.1 (Ch. 33) birds of prey

BIRDS OF PREY. So favourable a retreat does the Island of Hoy afford for birds of prey, that instances of their ravages, which seldom occur in other parts of the country, are not unusual there. An individual was living in Orkney not long since, whom, while a child in its swaddling clothes, an eagle actually transported to its nest in the hill of Hoy. Happily the eyry being known, and the bird instantly pursued, the child was found uninjured, playing with the young eaglets. A story of a more ludicrous transportation was told me by the reverend clergyman who is minister of the island. Hearing one day a strange grunting, he suspected his servants had permitted a sow and pigs, which were tenants of his farm-yard, to escape into his barley crop. Having in vain looked for the transgressors upon solid earth, he at length cast his eyes upward, when he discovered one of the litter in the talons of a large eagle, which was soaring away with the unfortunate pig (squeaking all the while with terror) towards her nest in the crest of Hoy.

316.12 (Ch. 34) his pleasantry This was really an exploit of the celebrated Avery the pirate, who suddenly, and without provocation, fired his pistols under the table where he sate drinking with his messmates, wounded one man severely, and thought the matter a good jest. What was still more extraordinary, his crew regarded it in the same light.

335.28 (Ch. 36) the best bummock that ever was brewed Liquor brewed for a Christmas treat.

359.21 (Ch. 38) long-suffering Heaven

THE STANDING STONES OF STENNIS. The Standing Stones of Stennis, as by a little pleonasm this remarkable monument is termed, furnishes an irresistible refutation of the opinion of such antiquaries as hold that the circles usually called Druidical, were peculiar to that race of priests. There is every reason to believe, that the custom was as prevalent in Scandinavia as in Gaul or Britain, and as common to the mythology of Odin as to Druidical superstition. There is even reason to think, that the Druids never occupied any part of the Orkneys, and tradition, as well as history, ascribes the Stones of Stennis to the Scandinavians. Two large sheets of water, communicating with the sea, are connected by a causeway, with openings permitting the tide to rise and recede, which is called the Bridge of Broisgar. Upon the eastern tongue of land appear the Standing Stones, arranged in the form of a half circle, or rather a horse-shoe, the height of the pillars being fifteen feet and upwards. Within this circuit lies a stone, probably sacrificial. One of the pillars, a little to the westward, is perforated with a circular hole, through which loving couples are wont to join hands when they take the *Promise of Odin*, as has been repeatedly mentioned in the text. The enclosure is surrounded by barrows, and on the opposite isthmus, advancing towards the Bridge of Broisgar, there is another monument of Standing Stones, which, in this case, is completely circular. They are less in size than those on the eastern side of the lakes, their height running only from ten or twelve to fourteen feet. This western circle is surrounded by a deep trench drawn on the outside of the pillars; and I remarked four tumuli, or mounds of earth, regularly disposed around it. Stonehenge excels this Orcadian monument; but that of Stennis is, I conceive, the only one in Britain which can be said to approach it in consequence. All the northern nations marked by those huge enclosures the places of popular meeting, either for religious worship or the transaction of public business of a temporal nature. The *Northern Popular Antiquities* contain, in an abstract of the Eyrbiggia Saga, a particular account of the manner in which the Helga Fels, or Holy Rock, was set apart by the Pontiff Thorolf for solemn occasions.

I need only add, that, different from the monument on Salisbury Plain, the stones which were used in the Orcadian circle seem to have been raised from a quarry upon the spot, of which the marks are visible.

THE FORTUNES OF NIGEL

Editorial Note

The Fortunes of Nigel occupies the second part of Volume 2, the whole of Volume 3, and the first part of Volume 4 of the 1824 octavo *Novels and Romances*, MSS 23020 and 23022 in the Interleaved Set. On 19 February 1830 Cadell noted that Scott 'mentioned that he now found it more for his ease to go over all the Novels attentively and mark during his progress where notes ought to be—he was doing it with Nigel' (MS 21043, f. 27r). The list of points requiring annotation at the beginning of the Interleaved Set volumes containing *Nigel* contains 23 items, all except 8 of which resulted in notes at the points specified. The first item in the list comes some way into the novel: 'Lord Henry Howard' (see 182 below). Scott's main annotatory work on the novel was nearly complete by 24 March 1830, on which date he informed Cadell that 'The pirate and Nigel are nearly quite notified', and on the 30th both *The Pirate* and *Nigel* were 'tolerably *notified*' (*Letters*, 11.311). Cadell revised *Nigel* between 13 August and 6 October. The epitaph on Alison Primrose (176) was transmitted to Scott by way of William Blackwood on 24 January 1831 (MS 3916, f. 80r) and duly incorporated into the proofs. Cadell took the 'beginning of Nigel' to the printing house together with the conclusion to *Saint Ronan's Well* on 22 March 1831 (MS 21021, f. 14v), and the novel appeared as Volumes 26 and 27 of the Magnum on 1 July and 1 August 1831 (EEWN 13, 438).

The Introduction (which is fluently written) begins with a somewhat curious linking of Jeanie Deans and George Heriot, in order to suggest that Scott was moved to his new narrative by the possibility of finding in Heriot a successor to the untypical romance heroine of its predecessor, distinguished by 'worth of character, goodness of heart, and rectitude of principle' in 'one who laid no claim to high birth, romantic sensibility, or any of the usual accomplishments of those who strut through the pages of this sort of composition'. This suggestion cannot be tested, and it may be suspected that it is another example of Scott's construction of a coherent literary autobiography in the Magnum introductions. Thereafter the Introduction centres on two of Scott's favourite themes: the conjunction of old and new manners, here exemplified in the Jacobean period; and the historical justification of what might seem overstrained in the fiction. It is clear from the final paragraphs that Scott sees in this novel unusual rewards for those who are not reading for the (exiguous) plot, but, as Sir Walter Scott rather than the anonymous Author of Waverley, he finds the Introductory Epistle embarrassing in tone.

The Magnum notes for *Nigel* are among the richest in the series, demonstrating Scott's intimate familiarity with the period. The footnotes are mostly of the usual glossarial, explanatory, and source-indicating sort. The endnotes draw on a variety of printed material to provide historical details about the characters and events appearing in or alluded to in the novel: most entertainingly in the lightly censored account of James's demeanour (177–78); most surprisingly in the emphasis on David Ramsay's penchant for the occult (173–75); and most outrageously in the printing of the long Latin epitaph on George Heriot's young wife, on the optimistic grounds that 'every thing concerning George Heriot is interesting' (175–76). Frequently these notes are attached to 'pegs' already in the first-edition text, the effect here being to confirm the reader's sense of a well-stocked authorial library able to furnish at will vivid details for the narrative. The David Ramsay note excepted, the biographical details relating to characters tend to support rather than undermine their manifestations in the novel.

The EEWN reader is encouraged to look at the explanatory note at 186–87 for the intriguing and only partly solved mystery surrounding an alleged source for the scene in Greenwich Park in a painting attributed to Federico Zucchero. This has some claims to be the strangest thing in all the notes provided for the Magnum series.

There are four Magnum illustrations for this title. The frontispiece to Volume 26 (MAG0051 / TB348.26) was designed by Abraham Cooper and engraved by Charles Rolls. It depicts Moniplies presenting his master's supplication to the mounted King James (EEWN 13, 47.14–20 (abridged): 'I cram'd the sifflication . . . a clean coup.'). The title-page vignette (MAG0052 / TB348.26) was designed by William Boxall and engraved by Augustus Fox. It depicts Jenkin, disconsolate in a chair, drinking with Dame Ursula Suddlechop in the back room of her husband's Fleet Street barber's shop (EEWN 13, 230.31–34 (with 'Jin Vin' for 'he'): 'Jin Vin, threw . . . sound of Bow-bell.'). The frontispiece to Volume 27 (MAG0053 / TB348.27) was designed by Robert Smirke and engraved by Samuel Davenport. It depicts Margaret addressing the seated Lady Hermione in her apartment (EEWN 13, 208.42–209.3: 'Metaphors are no arguments . . . from one's betters.'). The title-page vignette (MAG0054 / TB348.27) was designed by John William Wright and engraved by Samuel Sangster. It depicts a kneeling Heriot presenting Glenvarloch's supplication to the seated King James (EEWN 13, 71.17–20: 'The goldsmith who had complied . . . the Lord of Glenvarloch.').

A. Cooper, R.A. C. Rolls

THE FORTUNES OF NIGEL.

"I cram'd the sifflication into his hand, and just as he saw the first line, I was minded to make a reverence, and I had the ill luck to hit his jaud o'a beast on the nose with my hat, she swarved aside, and the King, that sits na muckle better than a draff-pock on the saddle, was like to have gotten a clean coup."

EDINBURGH. PUBLISHED 1831, BY ROBERT CADELL, and WHITTAKER & Co. LONDON.

WAVERLEY NOVELS.

VOL. XXVI.

THE FORTUNES OF NIGEL.

"Jin Vin, threw himself into the great leathern chair, in which Dame Ursley was went to solace herself of an evening, he declared "himself the most miserable dog within the sound of Bow-bell."

PRINTED FOR ROBERT CADELL, EDINBURGH.
AND WHITTAKER & C° LONDON.
1831.

R. Smirk. R.A. S. Davenport.

THE FORTUNES OF NIGEL.

Metaphors are no arguments, my pretty maiden" said the Lady Hermione, smiling. "I am sorry for that, madam", answered Margaret; "for they are such a pretty indirect way of telling one's mind when it differs from one's betters."

EDINBURGH, PUBLISHED 1831, BY ROBERT CADELL, & WHITTAKER & C° LONDON.

WAVERLEY NOVELS.

VOL. XXVII.

THE FORTUNES OF NIGEL.

"The goldsmith, who had complied with great accuracy with all the prescribed points of the ceremonial, here completed it, to James's no small astonishment, by placing in his hand the petition of the Lord of Glenvarloch."

PRINTED FOR ROBERT CADELL, EDINBURGH,
AND WHITTAKER & C° LONDON.
1831.

Introduction to The Fortunes of Nigel

But why should lordlings all our praise engross?
Rise, honest Muse, and sing the Man of Ross.
POPE.

HAVING, in the tale of the Heart of Mid-Lothian, succeeded in some degree in awakening an interest in behalf of one devoid of those accomplishments which belong to a heroine almost by right, I was next tempted to choose a hero upon the same unpromising plan; and as worth of character, goodness of heart, and rectitude of principle, were necessary to one who laid no claim to high birth, romantic sensibility, or any of the usual accomplishments of those who strut through the pages of this sort of composition, I made free with the name of a person who has left the most magnificent proofs of his benevolence and charity that the capital of Scotland has to display.

To the Scottish reader little more need be said than that the man alluded to is George Heriot. But for those south of the Tweed, it may be necessary to add, that the person so named was a wealthy citizen of Edinburgh, and the King's goldsmith, who followed James to the English capital, and was so successful in his profession, as to die, in 1624, extremely wealthy for that period. He had no children; and after a full provision to such as might have claims on him, he left the residue of his fortune to establish an hospital, in which the sons of Edinburgh freemen are gratuitously brought up and educated for the station to which their talents may recommend them, and are finally enabled to enter life under respectable auspices. The Hospital in which this charity is maintained is a noble quadrangle of the Gothic order, and as ornamental to the city as a building, as the manner in which the youths are provided for and educated, renders it useful to the community as an institution. To the honour of those who have the management, (the Magistrates and Clergy of Edinburgh,) the funds of the Hospital have increased so much under their care, that it now sustains and educates one hundred and thirty youths annually, many of whom have done honour to their country in different departments.

The author of such a charity as this may be reasonably supposed to have walked through life with a steady pace, and an observant eye, neglecting no occasion of assisting those who were not possessed of the experience necessary for their own guidance. In supposing his efforts directed to the benefit of a young nobleman, misguided by the aristocratic haughtiness of his own time, and the prevailing tone of selfish luxury which seems more peculiar to ours, as well as the seductions of pleasure which are predominant in all, some amusement, or even some advantage, might, I thought, be derived from the manner in which I might bring the exertions of this civic Mentor to bear in his pupil's behalf. I am, I own, no great believer in the moral utility to be derived from fictitious compositions; yet, if in any case a word spoken in season may be of advantage to a young person, it must surely be when it calls upon them to attend to the voice of principle and self-denial, in place of that of precipitate passion. I could not, indeed, hope or expect to represent my prudent and benevolent citizen in a point of view so interesting as that of the peasant girl, who nobly sacrificed her family affections to the steadiness of her moral character. Still, however, something I hoped might be done not altogether unworthy the fame which George Heriot has secured by the lasting benefits he has bestowed on his country.

It appeared likely, that out of this simple plot I might weave something attractive for the public; because the reign of James I., in which George Heriot flourished, was of a character which gave unbounded scope to invention in the fable, while at the same time it admitted of much greater variety and discrimination of character than could, with historical consistency, have been introduced, if the scene had been laid a century earlier. Lady Mary Wortley Montague has said, with equal truth and taste, that the most romantic region of every country is that where the mountains unite themselves with the plains or lowlands. For similar reasons, it may be in like manner said, that the most picturesque period of history is that where the ancient rough and wild manners of a barbarous age are just becoming innovated upon, and contrasted, by the illumination of increased or revived learning, and the instructions of renewed or reformed religion. The strong contrast produced by the opposition of ancient manners to those which are gradually subduing them, affords the lights and shadows demanded for the effect of a fictitious narrative; and while such a period entitles the author to introduce incidents of a marvellous and improbable character, as arising out of the turbulent independence and ferocity, belonging to old habits of violence, still influencing the manners of a people who had been so lately in a barbarous state; yet, on the other hand, the character and sentiments of many of the actors may, with the utmost probability, be described with great variety of shading and delineation, as belonging to the newer and more improved period, of which the world has but lately received the light.

The reign of James I. of England possessed this advantage in a peculiar degree. Some beams of chivalry, although its planet had been for some time set, continued to animate and gild the horizon, and although probably no one acted precisely on its Quixotic dictates, men and women still talked the chivalrous language of Sir Philip Sydney's Arcadia; and the ceremonial of the tilt-yard was yet exhibited, though it now only flourished as a *Place de Carrousel.* Here and there a high-spirited Knight of the Bath, witness the too scrupulous Lord Herbert of Cherbury, was found devoted enough to the vows he had taken, to imagine himself obliged to compel, by the sword's-point, a felon-knight or squire to restore the top-knot of ribbon which he had stolen from a fair damsel.* And yet, while men were taking each other's lives on such punctilios of honour, the hour was already arrived when Bacon was to teach the world that they were no longer to reason from authority to fact, but to establish truth by advancing from fact to fact, till they fixed an indisputable authority, not from hypothesis, but from experiment.

The state of society in the reign of James I. was also strangely disturbed, and the license of a part of the community was perpetually giving rise to acts of blood and violence. The bravo of the Queen's day, of whom Shakspeare has given us so many varieties, as Bardolph, Nym, Pistol, Peto, and the other companions of Falstaff, men who had their *humours*, or their particular turn of extravaganza, had, since the commencement of the Low Country wars, given way to a race of sworders, who used the rapier and dagger, instead of the far less dangerous sword and buckler; so that a historian says on this subject, "that private quarrels were nourished, but especially between the Scots and English; and duels in every street maintained; divers sects and particular titles passed unpunished and unregarded, as the sect of the Roaring Boys, Bonaventors, Bravadors, Quarterors, and such like, being persons prodigal, and of great expense, who, having run themselves into debt, were constrained to run into factions, to defend themselves from danger of the law. These received countenance from divers of the nobility; and the citizens through lasciviousness consuming their estates, it was like that the number [of these desperadoes] would rather increase than diminish; and under these pretences they entered into many desperate enterprises, and scarce any durst walk in the street after nine at night."†

* See Lord Herbert of Cherbury's Memoirs.

† History of the First Fourteen Years of King James's Reign. See Somers's Tracts, edited by Scott, vol. ii. p. 266.

The same authority assures us farther, that "ancient gentlemen, who had left their inheritance whole and well furnished with goods and chattels (having thereupon kept good houses) unto their sons, lived to see part consumed in riot and excess, and the rest in possibility to be utterly lost; the holy state of matrimony made but a May-game, by which divers families had been subverted; brothel houses much frequented, and even great persons, prostituting their bodies to the intent to satisfy their lusts, consumed their substance in lascivious appetites. And of all sorts, such knights and gentlemen, as either through pride or prodigality had consumed their substance, repairing to the city, and to the intent to consume their virtues also, lived dissolute lives; many of their ladies and daughters, to the intent to maintain themselves according to their dignity, prostituting their bodies in shameful manner. Alehouses, dicing-houses, taverns, and places of iniquity, beyond measure abounding in most places."

Nor is it only in the pages of a puritanical, perhaps a satirical writer, that we find so shocking and disgusting a picture of the coarseness of the beginning of the seventeenth century. On the contrary, in all the comedies of the age, the principal character for gaiety and wit is a young heir, who has totally altered the establishment of the father to whom he has succeeded, and, to use the old simile, who resembles a fountain, which plays off in idleness and extravagance the wealth which its careful parents painfully had assembled in hidden reservoirs.

And yet, while that spirit of general extravagance seemed to be at work over a whole kingdom, another and very different sort of men were gradually forming the staid and resolved characters, which afterwards displayed themselves during the civil wars, and powerfully regulated and affected the character of the whole English nation, until, rushing from one extreme to another, they sunk in a gloomy fanaticism the splendid traces of the reviving fine arts.

From the quotations which I have produced, the selfish and disgusting conduct of Lord Dalgarno will not perhaps appear overstrained; nor will the scenes in Whitefriars and places of similar resort seem too highly coloured. This indeed is far from being the case. It was in James I.'s reign that Vice first appeared affecting the better classes with gross and undisguised depravity. The entertainments and amusements of Elizabeth's time had an air of that decent restraint which became the court of a maiden sovereign; and, in that earlier period, to use the words of Burke, Vice lost half its evil by being deprived of all its grossness. In James's reign, on the contrary, the coarsest pleasures were publicly and unlimitedly indulged, since, according to Sir John Harrington, the men wallowed in beastly delights; and even ladies abandoned their delicacy, and rolled about in intoxication. After a ludicrous account of a mask, in which the actors had got drunk, and behaved themselves accordingly, he adds, "I have much marvelled at these strange pageantries, and they do bring to my recollection what passed of this sort in our Queen's days, in which I was sometime an assistant and partaker: but never did I see such lack of good order and sobriety as I have now done. — — — The gunpowder fright is got out of all our heads, and we are going on hereabouts as if the devil was contriving every man should blow up himself by wild riot, excess, and devastation of time and temperance. The great ladies do go well masqued; and indeed, it be the only show of their modesty to conceal their countenance; but alack, they meet with such countenance to uphold their strange doings, that I marvel not at aught that happens."*

Such being the state of the court, coarse sensuality brought along with it its ordinary companion, a brutal degree of undisguised selfishness, destructive alike of philanthropy and good breeding; both of which, in their several spheres, depend upon the regard paid to the interest as well as the feelings of others. It is in such a time that the heartless and shameless man of wealth and power may, like the supposed Lord Dalgarno, brazen out the shame of his villainies, and affect to triumph in their consequences, so long as they were personally advantageous to his own pleasures or profit.

Alsatia is elsewhere explained as a cant name for Whitefriars, which, possessing certain privileges of sanctuary, became for that reason a nest of those mischievous characters who were generally obnoxious to the law. These privileges were derived from its having been an establishment of the Carmelites, or White Friars, founded, says Stow, in his Survey of London, by Sir Richard Grey, in 1241. Edward I. gave them a plot of ground in Fleet Street, to build their church upon. The edifice then erected was rebuilt by Courtney, Earl of Devonshire, in the reign of Edward III. In the time of the Reformation the place retained its immunities as a sanctuary, and

* Harrington's Nugæ Antiquæ, vol. i., p. 352. For the gross debauchery of the period, too much encouraged by the example of the monarch, who was, in other respects, neither without talents or a good-natured disposition, see Winwood's Memorials, Howel's Letters, and other Memorials of the time; but particularly, consult the Private Letters and Correspondence of Steenie, *alias* Buckingham, with his reverend Dad and Gossip, King James, which abound with the grossest as well as the most childish language. The learned Mr D'Israeli, in an attempt to vindicate the character of James, has only succeeded in obtaining for himself the character of a skilful and ingenious advocate, without much advantage to his royal client.

James I. confirmed and added to them by a charter in 1608. Shadwell was the first author who made some literary use of Whitefriars, in his play of the Squire of Alsatia, which turns upon the plot of the Adelphi of Terence.

In this old play, two brothers of fortune educate two young men, (sons to the one and nephews to the other,) each under his own separate system of rigour and indulgence. The elder of the subjects of this experiment, who has been very rigidly brought up, falls at once into all the vices of the town, is debauched by the cheats and bullies of Whitefriars, and, in a word, becomes the Squire of Alsatia. The poet gives, as the natural and congenial inhabitants of the place, such characters as the reader will find in the note.* The play, as we learn from the dedication to the Earl of Dorset and Middlesex, was successful above the author's expectations, "no comedy these many years having filled the theatre so long together. And I had the great honour," continues Shadwell, "to find so many friends, that the house was never so full since it was built as upon the third day of this play, and vast numbers went away that could not be admitted."† From the Squire of Alsatia the author derived some few hints, and learned the footing on which the bullies and thieves of the Sanctuary stood with their neighbours, the fiery young students of the Temple, of which some intimation is given in the dramatic piece.

Such are the materials to which the author stands indebted for the composition of the Fortunes of Nigel, a novel which may be perhaps one of those that are more amusing on a second perusal, than when read for the sake of the story, the incidents of which are few and meagre.

The Introductory Epistle is written, in Lucio's phrase, "according to the trick," and would never have appeared had the writer medit-

* "*Cheatly*, a rascal, who by reason of debts dares not stir out of Whitefriars, but there inveigles young heirs of entail, and helps them to goods and money upon great disadvantages, is bound for them, and shares with them till he undoes them. A lewd, impudent, debauched fellow, very expert in the cant about town.

"*Shamwell*, cousin to the Belfonds, who, being ruined by Cheatly, is made a decoy-duck for others, not daring to stir out of Alsatia, where he lives. Is bound with Cheatly for heirs, and lives upon them a dissolute debauched life.

"*Captain Hackum*, a blockheaded bully of Alsatia, a cowardly, impudent, blustering fellow, formerly a sergeant in Flanders, who has run from his colours, and retreated into Whitefriars for a very small debt, where by the Alsatians he is dubb'd a captain, marries one that lets lodgings, sells cherry-brandy, and is a bawd.

"*Scrapeall*, a hypocritical, repeating, praying, psalm-singing, precise fellow, pretending to great piety; a godly knave, who joins with Cheatly, and supplies young heirs with goods and money."—*Dramatis Personæ to the Squire of Alsatia*, SHADWELL'S *Works*, vol. iv.

† Dedication to the Squire of Alsatia, Shadwell's Works, vol. iv.

ated making his avowal of the work. As it is the privilege of a masque or incognito to speak in a feigned voice and assumed character, the author attempted, while in disguise, some liberties of the same sort; and while he continues to plead upon the various excuses which the introduction contains, the present acknowledgment must serve as an apology for a species of "hoity toity, whisky frisky" pertness of manner, which, in his avowed character, the author should have considered as a departure from the rules of civility and good taste.

ABBOTSFORD, 1*st July*, 1831.

Notes to The Fortunes of Nigel

4.42 (Introductory Epistle) revise The uninitiated must be informed, that a second proof-sheet is so called.

28.38 (Ch. 1) David Ramsay

DAVID RAMSAY. David Ramsay, watchmaker and horologer to James I., was a real person, though the author has taken the liberty of pressing him into the service of fiction. Although his profession led him to cultivate the exact sciences, like many at this period he mingled them with pursuits which were mystical and fantastic. The truth was, that the boundaries between truth and falsehood in mathematics, astronomy, and similar pursuits, were not exactly known, and there existed a sort of *terra incognita* between them, in which the wisest men bewildered themselves. David Ramsay risked his money on the success of the vaticinations which his researches led him to form, since he sold clocks and watches under condition, that their value should not become payable till King James was crowned in the Pope's chair at Rome. Such wagers were common in that day, as may be seen by looking at Jonson's Every Man out of his Humour.

David Ramsay was also an actor in another singular scene, in which the notorious astrologer Lilly was a performer, and had no small expectation on the occasion, since he brought with him a half-quartern sack to put the treasure in.

"David Ramsay, his Majesty's clock-maker, had been informed that there was a great quantity of treasure buried in the cloister of Westminster Abbey. He acquaints Dean Williams therewith, who was also then Bishop of Lincoln. The Dean gave him liberty to search after it, with this proviso, that if any was discovered, his church should have a share of it. Davy Ramsay finds out one John

Scott, who pretended the use of the Mosaical rods, to assist him herein.* I was desired to join with him, unto which I consented. One winter's night, Davy Ramsay, with several gentlemen, myself, and Scott, entered the cloisters. We played the hazel rods round about the cloisters. Upon the west end of the cloisters the rods turned one over another, an argument that the treasure was there. The labourers digged at least six feet deep, and then we met with a coffin; but which, in regard it was not heavy, we did not open, which we afterwards much repented.

"From the cloisters we went into the abbey church, where, upon a sudden, (there being no wind when we began,) so fierce and so high, so blustering and loud a wind did rise, that we verily believed the west end of the church would have fallen upon us. Our rods would not move at all; the candles and torches, also, but one were extinguished, or burned very dimly. John Scott, my partner, was amazed, looked pale, knew not what to think or do, until I gave directions and command to dismiss the demons; which, when done, all was quiet again, and each man returned unto his lodging late, about twelve o'clock at night. I could never since be induced to join with any such like actions.

"The true miscarriage of the business was by reason of so many people being present at the operation; for there was above thirty, some laughing, others deriding us; so that, it we had not dismissed the demons, I believe most part of the abbey church would have been blown down. Secrecy and intelligent operators, with a strong confidence and knowledge of what they are doing, are best for the work."—LILLY'S *Life and Times*, p. 46.

David Ramsay had a son called William Ramsay, who appears to have possessed all his father's credulity. He became an astrologer, and in 1651–2 published "*Vox Stellarum*, an Introduction to the Judgment of Eclipses and the Annual Revolutions of the World." The edition of 1652 is inscribed to his father. It would appear, as indeed might be argued from his mode of disposing of his goods, the old horologer had omitted to make hay while the sun shone; for his son, in his dedication, has this exception to the paternal virtues, "It's true your carelessness in laying up while the sun shone for the tempests of a stormy day, hath given occasion to some inferior spirited people not to value you according to what you are by nature and in yourself, for such look not to a man longer than he is in prosperity, esteeming none but for their wealth, not wisdom, power, nor virtue." From these expressions, it is to be apprehended

* The same now called, I believe, the Divining Rod, and applied to the discovery of water not obvious to the eye.

that while old David Ramsay, a follower of the Stewarts, sunk under the Parliamentary government, his son, William, had advanced from being a dupe to astrology to the dignity of being himself a cheat.

39.17 (Ch. 2) the passengers

GEORGE HERIOT. This excellent person was but little known by his actions when alive, but we may well use, in this particular, the striking phrase of Scripture, "that being dead he yet speaketh." We have already mentioned, in the Introduction, the splendid charity of which he was the founder; the few notices of his personal history are slight and meagre.

George Heriot was born at Trabroun, in the parish of Gladsmuir; he was the eldest son of a goldsmith in Edinburgh, descended from a family of some consequence in East Lothian. His father enjoyed the confidence of his fellow-citizens, and was their representative in Parliament. He was, besides, one of the deputies sent by the inhabitants of the city to propitiate the King, when he had left Edinburgh abruptly, after the riot of 17th December, 1596.

George Heriot, the son, pursued his father's occupation of a goldsmith, then peculiarly lucrative, and much connected with that of a money-broker. He enjoyed the favour and protection of James, and of his consort, Anne of Denmark. He married, for his first wife, a maiden of his own rank, named Christian Marjoribanks, daughter of a respectable burgess. This was in 1586. He was afterwards named jeweller to the Queen, whose account to him for a space of ten years amounted to nearly L.40,000. George Heriot, having lost his wife, connected himself with the distinguished house of Rosebery, by marrying a daughter of James Primrose, Clerk to the Privy Council. Of this lady he was deprived by her dying in child-birth in 1612 before attaining her twenty-first year. After a life spent in honourable and successful industry, George Heriot died in London, to which city he had followed his royal master, on the 12th February, 1624, at the age of sixty-one years. His picture, (copied by Scougal from a lost original,) in which he is represented in the prime of life, is thus described: "His fair hair, which overshades the thoughtful brow and calm calculating eye, with the cast of humour on the lower part of the countenance, are all indicative of the genuine Scottish character, and well distinguish a person fitted to move steadily and wisely through the world, with a strength of resolution to ensure success, and a disposition to enjoy it."—*Historical and Descriptive Account of Heriot's Hospital, with a Memoir of the Founder, by Messrs James and John Johnstone*. Edinburgh, 1827.

I may add, as every thing concerning George Heriot is interesting, that his second wife, Alison Primrose, was interred in Saint

Gregory's church, from the register of which parish the Rev. Mr Barham, Rector, has, in the kindest manner, sent me the following extract:—"Mrs Alison, the wife of Mr George Heriot, gentleman, 20th April, 1612." Saint Gregory's, before the Great Fire of London which consumed the cathedral, formed one of the towers of old Saint Paul's, and occupied the space of ground now filled by Queen Anne's statue. In the south aisle of the choir Mrs Heriot reposed under a handsome monument, bearing the following inscription:—

"Sanctissimæ et charissimæ conjugi ALISONÆ HERIOT, *Jacobi Primrosii, Regiæ Majestatis in Sanctiori Concilio Regni Scotiæ Amanuensis, filiæ, feminæ omnibus tum animi tum corporis dotibus, ac pio cultu instructissimæ, mæstissimus ipsius maritus* GEORGIUS HERIOT, ARMIGER, *Regis, Reginæ, Principum Henrici et Caroli Gemmarius, bene merenti, non sine lachrymis, hoc Monumentum pie posuit.*

"Obiit Mensis Aprilis die 16, *anno salutis* 1612, *ætatis* 20, *in ipso flore juventæ, et mihi, parentibus, et amicis tristissimum sui desiderium reliquit.*

Hic Alicis Primrosa
Jacet crudo obruta fato,
Intempestivas
Ut rosa passa manus.
Nondum bisdenos
Annorum impleverat orbes,
Pulchra, pudica,
Patris delicium atque viri:
Quum gravida, heu! nunquam
Mater, decessit, et inde
Cura dolorq: patri,
Cura dolorq: viro.
Non sublata tamen
Tantum translata recessit;
Nunc Rosa prima Poli
Quæ fuit ante soli."

The loss of a young, beautiful, and amiable partner, at a period so interesting, was the probable reason of her husband devoting his fortune to a charitable institution. The epitaph occurs in Strype's edition of Stowe's Survey of London, Book iii, page 228.

47.41 (Ch. 3) guts to a bear I am certain this prudential advice is not original on Mr Linklater's part, but I am not at present able to produce my authority. I think it amounted to this, that James flung down a petition presented by some supplicant who paid no compliments to his horse, and expressed no wonder at the splendour of his furniture, saying, "Shall a king cumber himself about the petition of a beggar, while the beggar disregards the king's splendour?" It is, I think, Sir John Harrington who recommends, as a sure mode to the king's favour, to praise the paces of the royal palfrey.

49.33 (Ch. 3) to his Majesty

PROCLAMATION AGAINST THE SCOTS COMING TO ENGLAND. The English agreed in nothing more unanimously than in censuring James for the beggarly rabble which not only attended the King at his coming first out of Scotland, "but," says Osborne, "through his whole reign, like a fluent spring, were found still crossing the Tweed." Yet it is certain, from the number of proclamations published by the Privy Council in Scotland, and bearing marks of the King's own diction, that he was sensible of the whole inconveniences and unpopularity of this importunate crowd of disrespectable suitors, and as desirous to get rid of them as his Southern subjects could be. But it was in vain that his Majesty argued with his Scottish subjects on the disrespect they were bringing on their native country and sovereign, by causing the English to suppose there were no well-nurtured or independent gentry in Scotland, they who presented themselves being, in the opinion and conceit of all beholders, "but idle rascals, and poor miserable bodies." It was even in vain that the vessels which brought up this unwelcome cargo of petitioners were threatened with fine and confiscation; the undaunted suitors continued to press forwards, and, as one of the proclamations says, many of them under pretence of requiring payment of "auld debts due to them by the King," which, it is observed with great *naïveté*, "is, of all kinds of importunity, most unpleasing to his Majesty." The expressions in the text are selected from these curious proclamations.

51.19 (Ch. 4) plots of the piece Meaning, probably, playbills.

60.1 (Ch. 4) becking Curtsying.

64.20 (Ch. 5) with one quill A biblical commentary by Gill, which (if the author's memory serves him) occupies between five and six hundred printed quarto pages, and must therefore have filled more pages of manuscript than the number mentioned in the text, has this quatrain at the end of the volume—

> With one good pen I wrote this book,
> Made of a grey goose quill;
> A pen it was when it I took,
> And a pen I leave it still.

67.33 (Ch. 5) civil war

KING JAMES. The dress of this monarch, together with his personal appearance, is thus described by a contemporary:—

"He was of a middle stature, more corpulent through [*i. e.* by means of] his clothes than in his body, yet fat enough. His legs were very weak, having had, as was thought, some foul play in his youth, or rather before he was born, that he was not able to stand at seven years of age. That weakness made him ever leaning on other men's shoulders. His walk was ever circular; his hands ever in that walk fiddling about his [a part of dress now laid aside.] He would make a great deal too bold with God in his passion, both with cursing and swearing, and a strain higher verging on blasphemy; but would, in his better temper, say, he hoped God would not impute them as sins, and lay them to his charge, seeing they proceeded from passion. He had need of great assistance, rather than hope, that would daily make thus bold with God."—DALZELL'S *Fragments of Scottish History*, pp. 85, 87.

84.41 (Ch. 6) had interrupted

SIR MUNGO MALAGROWTHER. It will perhaps be recognised by some of my countrymen, that the caustic Scottish knight, as described in the preceding chapter, borrowed some of his attributes from a most worthy and respectable baronet, who was to be met with in Edinburgh society about twenty-five or thirty years since. It is not by any means to be inferred, that the living person resembled the imaginary one in the course of life ascribed to him, or in his personal attributes. But his fortune was far inadequate to his rank and the antiquity of his family; and, to avenge himself of this disparity, the worthy baronet lost no opportunity of making the more avowed sons of fortune feel the edge of his satire. This he had the art of disguising under the personal infirmity of deafness, and usually introduced his more severe things by an affected mistake of what was said around him. For example, at a public meeting of a certain county, this worthy gentleman had chosen to display a laced coat, of such a pattern as had not been seen in society for the better part of a century. The young men who were in company amused themselves with rallying him on his taste, when he suddenly singled out one of the party:—"Auld d'ye think my coat?—indeed it canna be new; but it was the wark of a braw tailor, and that was your grandfather, who was at the head of the trade in Edinburgh about the beginning of last century." Upon another occasion, when this type of Sir Mungo Malagrowther heard a nobleman, the high chief of one of those Border clans who were accused in ancient times of very little attention to the distinctions of *Meum* and *Tuum*, addressing a gentleman of the same name as if there should be some relationship between them, he volunteered to ascertain the nature of the connexion by saying, that the "Chief's ancestors had *stolen* the cows, and the other gentleman's ancestors had *killed* them,"—

fame ascribing the origin of the latter family to a butcher. It may be well imagined, that among a people that have been always punctilious about genealogy, such a person, who had a general acquaintance with all the flaws and specks in the shields of the proud, the pretending, and the *nouveaux riches*, must have had the same scope for amusement as a monkey in a china shop.

101.22 (Ch. 8) Earls of Dalwolsey The head of the ancient and distinguished house of Ramsay, and to whom, as their chief, the individuals of that name look as their origin and source of gentry. Allan Ramsay, the pastoral poet, in the same manner, invokes

> Dalhousie of an auld descent,
> My chief, my stoup, my ornament.

102.14 (Ch. 8) Mistress Turner

MRS ANNE TURNER. Mrs Anne Turner was a dame somewhat of the occupation of Mrs Suddlechop in the text; that is, half milliner half procuress, and secret agent in all manner of proceedings. She was a trafficker in the poisoning of Sir Thomas Overbury, for which so many subordinate agents lost their lives, while, to the great scandal of justice, the Earl of Somerset and his Countess were suffered to escape, upon a threat of Somerset to betray something which nearly affected his master, King James. Mrs Turner introduced into England a French custom of using yellow starch in *getting up* bands and cuffs, and, by Lord Coke's orders, she appeared in that fashion at the place of execution. She was the widow of a physician, and had been eminently beautiful, as appears from her description in the poem called Overbury's Vision. There were produced in court a parcel of dolls or puppets belonging to this lady, some naked, some dressed, and which she used for exhibiting fashions upon. But, greatly to the horror of the spectators, who accounted these figures to be magical devices, there was, on their being shown, "heard a crack from the scaffolds, which caused great fear, tumult, and confusion, among the spectators and throughout the hall, every one fearing hurt, as if the devil had been present, and grown angry to have his workmanship showed to such as were not his own scholars." Compare this curious passage in the History of King James for the First Fourteen Years, 1651, with the Aulicus Coquinarius of Dr Heylin. Both works are published in the Secret History of King James.

113.10 (Ch. 9) sacred life

LORD HUNTINGLEN. The credit of having rescued James I. from the dagger of Alexander Ruthven, is here fictitiously ascribed to an imaginary Lord Huntinglen. In reality, as may be read in every history, it was John Ramsay, afterwards created Earl of Holderness, who stabbed the younger Ruthven with his dagger while he was struggling with the King. Sir Anthony Weldon informs us, that, upon the annual return of the day, the King's deliverance was commemorated by an anniversary feast. The time was the fifth of August, "upon which," proceeds the satirical historian, "Sir John Ramsay, for his good service in that preservation, was the principal guest, and so did the King grant him any boon he would ask that day. But he had such limitations set to his asking, as made his suit as unprofitable, as that he asked it for was unserviceable to the King."

113.34 (Ch. 9) your enemy

BUCKINGHAM. Buckingham, who had a frankness in his high and irascible ambition, was always ready to bid defiance to those by whom he was thwarted or opposed. He aspired to be created Prince of Tipperary in Ireland, and Lord High Constable of England. Coventry, then Lord Keeper, opposed what seemed such an unreasonable extent of power as was annexed to the office of Constable. On this opposition, according to Sir Anthony Weldon, "the Duke peremptorily accosted Coventry, 'Who made you, Coventry, Lord Keeper?' He replied, 'The King.' Buckingham sur-replied, 'It's false; 'twas I did make you, and you shall know that I, who made you, can, and will, unmake you.' Coventry thus answered him, 'Did I conceive that I held my place by your favour, I would presently unmake myself, by rendering up the seals to his Majesty.' Then Buckingham, in a scorn and fury, flung from him, saying, 'You shall not keep it long;' and surely, had not Felton prevented him, he had made good his word."—WELDON'S *Court of King James and Charles.*

127.34 (Ch. 10) the Douglas' wars The cruel civil wars waged by the Scottish barons during the minority of James VI., had this name from the figure made in them by the celebrated James Douglas Earl of Morton. Both sides executed their prisoners without mercy or favour.

129.34 (Ch. 10) for such redemption As each covenant in those days of accuracy had a special place nominated for execution, the tomb of the Regent Earl of Murray in Saint Giles's Church was frequently assigned for the purpose.

134.14 (Ch. 11) Kings and Kesars

PAGES IN THE SEVENTEENTH CENTURY. About this time the ancient customs arising from the long prevalence of chivalry, began to be grossly varied from the original purposes of the institution. None was more remarkable than the change which took place in the breeding and occupation of *pages*. This peculiar species of menial originally consisted of youths of noble birth, who, that they might be trained to the exercise of arms, were early removed from their paternal house, where too much indulgence might have been expected, to the family of some prince or man of rank and military renown, where they served, as it were, an apprenticeship to the duties of chivalry and courtesy. Their education was severely moral, and strictly pursued respecting useful exercises, and what were deemed elegant accomplishments. From being pages, they were advanced to the second gradation of squires; from squires, these candidates for the honours of knighthood were frequently made knights.

But in the sixteenth century the page had become, in many instances, a mere domestic, who sometimes, by the splendour of his address and appearance, was expected to make up in show for the absence of a whole band of retainers with swords and bucklers. We have Sir John's authority when he cashiers part of his train.

> Falstaff will learn the humour of the age,
> French thrift, you rogues, myself and skirted page.

Jonson, in a high tone of moral indignation, thus reprobated the change. The Host of the New Inn replies to Lord Lovel, who asks to have his son for a page, that he would, with his own hands, hang him, sooner

> Than damn him to this desperate course of life.
> *Lovel.* Call you that desperate, which, by a line
> Of institution, from our ancestors
> Hath been derived down to us, and received
> In a succession, for the noblest way
> Of brushing up our youth, in letters, arms,
> Fair mien, discourses civil, exercise,
> And all the blazon of a gentleman?
> Where can he learn to vault, to ride, to fence,
> To move his body gracefully, to speak
> The language purer, or to turn his mind
> Or manners more to the harmony of nature,
> Than in these nurseries of nobility?
> *Host.* Ay, that was when the nursery's self was noble,
> And only virtue made it, not the market,
> That titles were not vented at the drum
> And common outcry; goodness gave the greatness,
> And greatness worship: every house became
> An academy of honour, and those parts
> We see departed in the practice now
> Quite from the institution.
> *Lovel.* Why do you say so,
> Or think so enviously? do they not still
> Learn there the Centaur's skill, the art of Thrace,
> To ride? or Pollux' mystery, to fence?
> The Pyrrhick gestures, both to stand and spring
> In armour; to be active for the wars;
> To study figures, numbers, and proportions,

May yield them great in counsels and the arts;
To make their English sweet upon their tongue,
As reverend Chaucer says?
Host. Sir, you mistake;
To play Sir Pandarus, my copy hath it,
And carry messages to Madam Cressid;
Instead of backing the brave steed o' mornings,
To kiss the chambermaid, and for a leap
O' the vaulting horse, to ply the vaulting house;
For exercise of arms a bale of dice,
And two or three packs of cards to show the cheat
And nimbleness of hand; mis-take a cloak
From my lord's back, and pawn it; ease his pockets
Of a superfluous watch, or geld a jewel
Of an odd stone or so; twinge three or four buttons
From off my lady's gown: These are the arts,
Or seven liberal deadly sciences,
Of pagery, or rather paganism,
As the tides run; to which, if he apply him,
He may, perhaps, take a degree at Tyburn,
A year the earlier come to read a lecture
Upon Aquinas, at Saint Thomas-a-Watering's,
And so go forth a laureate in hemp circle."

The New Inn, Act I.

135.29 (Ch. 11) Lord Henry Howard

LORD HENRY HOWARD. Lord Henry Howard was the second son of the poetical Earl of Surrey, and possessed considerable parts and learning. He wrote, in the year 1583, a book called, "A Defensative against the Poison of supposed Prophecies." He gained the favour of Queen Elizabeth, having, he says, directed his battery against a sort of prophets and pretended soothsayers, whom he accounted *infesti regibus*, as he expresses it. In the last years of the Queen, he became James's most ardent partisan, and conducted with great pedantry, but much intrigue, the correspondence betwixt the Scottish King and the younger Cecil. Upon James's accession, he was created Earl of Northampton, and Lord Privy Seal. According to De Beaumont the French Ambassador, Lord Henry Howard was one of the greatest flatterers and calumniators who ever lived.

136.38 (Ch. 11) endangering his life thrice

SKIRMISHES IN THE PUBLIC STREETS. Edinburgh appears to have been one of the most disorderly towns in Europe, during the sixteenth and beginning of the seventeenth century. The Diary of the honest citizen Birrel, repeatedly records such incidents as the following: "The 24 of November [1567], at two afternoon, the Laird of Airth and the Laird of Weems met on the High Gate of Edinburgh, and they and their followers fought a very bloody skirmish, where there were many hurt on both sides with shot of pistol." These skirmishes also took place in London itself. In Shadwell's play of the Scowrers, an old rake thus boasts of his early exploits: —"I knew the Hectors, and before them the Muns, and the Tity-retu's; they were brave fellows indeed! In these days a man could not go from the Rose Garden to the Piazza once, but he must venture his life twice, my dear Sir Willie." But it appears that the affrays, which, in the Scottish capital, arose out of hereditary quarrels and ancient feuds, were in London the growth of the licentiousness and arrogance of young debauchees.

144.36 (Ch. 12) made upon at all

FRENCH COOKERY. The exertion of French ingenuity mentioned in the text is noticed by some authorities of the period; the siege of Leith was also distinguished by the protracted obstinacy of the besieged, in which was displayed all that the age possessed of defensive war, so that Brantome records that those who witnessed this siege, had, from that very circumstance, a degree of consequence yielded to their persons and opinions. He tells a story of Strozzi himself, from which it appears that his jests lay a good deal in the line of the *cuisine*. He caused a mule to be stolen from one Brusquet, on whom he wished to play a trick, and served the flesh up so well disguised, that it passed with Brusquet for venison.

145.41 (Ch. 12) hear that repeated

CUCKOO'S NEST. The quarrel in this chapter between the pretended captain and the citizen of London, is taken from a burlesque poem called The Counter Scuffle, that is, the Scuffle in the Prison at Wood street, so called. It is a piece of low humour, which had at the time very considerable vogue. The prisoners, it seems, had fallen into a dispute amongst themselves "which calling was of most repute," and a lawyer put in his claim to be most highly considered. The man of war repels his pretence with much arrogance.

"Wer't not for us, thou swad," quoth he,
"Where wouldst thou fay to get a fee?
But to defend such things as thee
'Tis pity;
For such as you esteem us least,
Who ever have been ready prest
To guard you and your cuckoo's nest,
The City."

The offence is no sooner given than it is caught up by a gallant citizen, a goldsmith, named Ellis.

"Of London city I am free,
And there I first my wife did see,
And for that very cause," said he,
"I love it.
And he that calls it cuckoo's nest,
Except he say he speaks in jest,

He is a villain and a beast,—
        I'll prove it!

For though I am a man of trade,
And free of London city made,
Yet can I use gun, bill, and blade,
        In battle.
And citizens, if need require,
Themselves can force the foe retire,
Whatever this low country squire
        May prattle."

The dispute terminates in the scuffle, which is the subject of the poem. The whole may be found in the second edition of Dryden's Miscellany, 12mo, vol. iii. 1716.

150.28 (Ch. 12) Burbage

BURBAGE. Burbage, whom Camden terms another Roscius, was probably the original representative of Richard III., and seems to have been early almost identified with his prototype. Bishop Corbet, in his Iter Boreale, tells us that mine host of Market Bosworth was full of ale and history.

Hear him, See you yon wood? there Richard lay
With his whole army; look the other way,
And lo, where Richmond, in a field of gorse,
Encamp'd himself o'er night and all his force.
Upon this hill they met. Why, he could tell
The inch where Richmond stood, where Richard fell;
Besides, what of his knowledge he could say,
He had authentic notice from the play,
Which I might guess by's mustering up the ghosts
And policies not incident to hosts;
But chiefly by that one perspicuous thing,
Where he mistook a player for a king,
For when he would have said, that Richard died,
And call'd, a horse! a horse! he Burbage cried.

RICHARD CORBET'S *Poems, Edition* 1815, p. 193.

152.7 (Ch. 13) to feed them The condition of men of wit and talents was never more melancholy than about this period. Their lives were so irregular, and their means of living so precarious, that they were alternately rioting in debauchery, or encountering and struggling with the meanest necessities. Two or three lost their lives by a surfeit brought on by that fatal banquet of Rhenish wine and pickled herrings, which is familiar to those who study the lighter literature of that age. The whole history is a most melancholy picture of genius, degraded at once by its own debaucheries, and the patronage of heartless rakes and profligates.

191.42 (Ch. 17) the gentry cove Look sharp. See how the girl is coquetting with the strange gallants!

198.25 (Ch. 17) the donor Of the cant words used in this inauguratory oration, some are obvious in their meaning, others, as Harman Beck (constable), and the like, derive their source from that ancient piece of lexicography, the Slang Dictionary.

267.19 (Ch. 24) weight in gold Only three copies are known to exist; one in the library at Kennaquhair, and two—one foxed and cropped, the other tall and in good condition—both in the possession of an eminent member of the Roxburghe Club.—*Note by* CAPTAIN CLUTTERBUCK.

297.35 (Ch. 27) most Sacred Majesty The Scots, till within the last generation, disliked swine's flesh as an article of food as much as the Highlanders do at present. It was remarked as extraordinary rapacity, when the Border depredators condescended to make prey of the accursed race, whom the fiend made his habitation. Ben Jonson, in drawing James's character, says, he loved "no part of a swine."

306.34 (Ch. 27) sinister purpose
MHIC-ALLASTAR-MORE. This is the Highland patronymic of the late gallant Chief of Glengarry. The allusion in the text is to an unnecessary alarm taken by some lady, at the ceremonial of the coronation of George IV., at the sight of the pistols which the Chief wore as a part of his Highland dress. The circumstance produced some confusion, which was talked of at the time. All who knew Glengarry (and the author knew him well) were aware his principles were of devoted loyalty to the person of the sovereign.

307.17 (Ch. 27) cup of comfort
KING JAMES'S HUNTING BOTTLE. Roger Coke, in his detection of the Court and State of England, London, 1697, p. 71, observes of James I., "The king was excessively addicted to hunting, and drinking, not ordinary French and Spanish wines, but strong Greek wines, and thought he would compound his hunting with these wines; and to that purpose, he was attended by a special officer, who was, as much as he could be, always at hand to fill the King's cup in hunting when he called for it. I have heard my father say, that, hunting with the King, after the King had drank of the wine, he also drank of it; and though he was young, and of a healthful disposition, it so deranged his head that it spoiled his pleasure and disordered him for three days after. Whether it were from drinking these wines, or from some other cause, the King became so lazy and so unwieldy, that he was trussed on horseback, and as he was set, so would he ride, without stirring himself in the saddle; nay, when his hat was set upon his head he would not take the trouble to alter it, but it sate as it was put on."

The trussing, for which the demipique saddle of the day afforded particular facility, is alluded to in the text; and the author, among other nicknacks of antiquity, possesses a leathern flask, like those carried by sportsmen, which is labelled, "King James's Hunting Bottle," with what authenticity is uncertain. Coke seems to have exaggerated the King's taste for the bottle. Welldon says James was not intemperate in his drinking; "However, in his old age, Buckingham's jovial suppers, when he had any turn to do with him, made him sometimes overtaken, which he would the next day remember, and repent with tears. It is true he drank very often, which was rather out of a custom than any delight; and his drinks were of that kind for strength, as Frontiniack, Canary, high country wine, tent wine, and Scottish ale, that had he not had a very strong brain, he might have been daily overtaken, though he seldom drank at any one time above four spoonfuls, many times not above one or two."—*Secret History of King James*, vol. ii., p. 3. Edin. 1811.

309.5 (Ch. 27) fallen to the ground

SCENE IN GREENWICH PARK. I cannot here omit mentioning, that a painting of the old school is in existence, having a remarkable resemblance to the scene described in the foregoing chapter, although it be nevertheless true that the similarity is in all respects casual, and that the author knew not of the existence of the painting till it was sold, amongst others, with the following description attached to it in a well-drawn-up catalogue.

"FREDERIGO ZUCCHERO.

"*Scene as represented in the Fortunes of Nigel, by Frederigo Zucchero, the King's painter.*

"This extraordinary picture, which, independent of its pictorial merit, has been esteemed a great literary curiosity, represents most faithfully the meeting, in Greenwich Park, between King James and Nigel Oliphaunt, as described in the Fortunes of Nigel, showing that the author must have taken the anecdote from authenticated facts. In the centre of the picture sits King James on horseback, very erect and stiffly. Between the King and Prince Charles, who is on the left of the picture, the Duke of Buckingham is represented riding a black horse, and pointing eagerly towards the culprit, Nigel Olifaunt, who is standing on the right side of the picture. He grasps with his right hand a gun, or crossbow, and looks angrily towards the King, who seems somewhat confused and alarmed. Behind Nigel, his servant is restraining two dogs which are barking fiercely. Nigel and his servant are both clothed in red, the livery of the Oliphaunt family in which, to this day, the town-officers of Perth are clothed, there being an old charter, granting to the Oliphaunt family, the privilege of dressing the public officers of Perth in their livery. The Duke of Buckingham is in all respects equal in magnificence of dress to the King or the Prince. The only difference that is marked between him and royalty is, that his head is uncovered. The King and the Prince wear their hats. In Lucy Aikin's Memoirs of the Reign of King James, will be found a letter from Sir Thomas Howard to Lord J. Harrington, in which he recommends the latter to come to court, mentioning that his Majesty has spoken favourably of him. He then proceeds to give him some advice, by which he is likely to find favour in the King's eyes. He tells him to wear a bushy ruff, well starched; and after various other directions as to his dress, he concludes, 'but above all things fail not to praise the roan jennet whereon the King doth daily ride.' In this picture King James is represented on the identical roan jennet. In the background of the picture are seen two or three suspicious-looking figures, as if watching the success of some plot. These may have been put in by the painter, to flatter the King, by making it be supposed that he had actually escaped, or successfully combated, some serious plot. The King is attended by a numerous band of courtiers and attendants, all of whom seem moving forward to arrest the defaulter. The painting of this picture is extremely good, but the drawing is very Gothic, and there is no attempt at the keeping of perspective. The picture is very dark and obscure, which considerably adds to the interest of the scene."

309.14 (Ch. 27) personal damage from him

KING JAMES'S TIMIDITY. The fears of James for his personal safety were often excited without serious grounds. On one occasion, having been induced to visit a coal-pit on the coast of Fife, he was conducted a little way under the sea, and brought to daylight again on a small island, or what was such at full tide, down which a shaft had been sunk. James, who conceived his life or liberty aimed at, when he found himself on an islet surrounded by the sea, instead of admiring, as his cicerone hoped, the unexpected change of scene, cried *Treason* with all his might, and could not be pacified till he was rowed ashore. At Lochmaben he took an equally causeless alarm from a still slighter circumstance. Some *vendisses*, a fish peculiar to the Loch, were presented to the royal table as a delicacy; but the King, who was not familiar with their appearance, concluded they were poisoned, and broke up the banquet "with most admired disorder."

311.24 (Ch. 27) that of Nigel

TRAITOR'S GATE. Traitor's Gate, which opens from the Tower of London to the Thames, was, as its name implies, that by which persons accused of state offences were conveyed to their prison. When the tide is making, and the ancient gate is beheld from within the buildings, it used to be a most striking part of the old fortress; but it is now much injured in appearance, being half built up with masonry to support a steam-engine, or something of that sort.

313.3 (Ch. 28) the firmest resolution These memorials of illustrious criminals, or of innocent persons who had the fate of such, are still preserved, though at one time, in the course of repairing the rooms, they were in some danger of being whitewashed. They are preserved at present with becoming respect, and have most of them been engraved.—*See* BAYLEY'S *History and Antiquities of the Tower of London.*

336.41 (Ch. 30) Archie Armstrong The celebrated Court Jester.

339.1 (Ch. 30) an end of that matter Wilson informs us that when Colonel Grey, a Scotsman who affected the buff dress even in the time of peace, appeared in that military garb at Court, the King, seeing him with a case of pistols at his girdle, which he never greatly liked, told him, merrily, "he was now so fortified, that, if he were but well victualled, he would be impregnable."—WILSON'S *Life and Reign of James VI., apud* KENNET'S *History of England*, vol. ii. p. 789. In 1612, the tenth year of James's reign, there was a rumour abroad that a shipload of pocket-pistols had been exported from Spain, with a view to a general massacre of the Protestants. Proclamations were of consequence sent forth, prohibiting all persons from carrying pistols under a foot long in the barrel. *Ibid.* p. 690.

340.17 (Ch. 30) the same magnanimity

PUNISHMENT OF STUBBS BY MUTILATION. This execution, which so captivated the imagination of Sir Mungo Malagrowther, was really a striking one. The criminal, a furious and bigoted Puritan, had published a book in very violent terms against the match of Elizabeth with the Duke of Alençon, which he termed an union of a daughter of God with a son of antichrist. Queen Elizabeth was greatly incensed at the freedom assumed in this work, and caused the author Stubbs, with Page the publisher, and one Singleton the printer, to be tried on an act passed by Philip and Mary against the writers and dispersers of seditious publications. They were convicted, and although there was an opinion strongly entertained by lawyers, that the act was only temporary, and expired with Queen Mary, Stubbs and Page received sentence to have their right hands struck off. They accordingly suffered the punishment, the wrist being divided by a cleaver driven through the joint by force of a mallet. The printer was pardoned. "I remember," says the historian Camden, "being then present, that Stubbs, when his right hand was cut off, plucked off his hat with the left, and said, with a loud voice, 'God save the Queen!' The multitude standing about was deeply silent, either out of horror of this new and unwonted kind of punishment, or out of commiseration towards the man, as being of an honest and unblamable repute, or else out of hatred to the marriage, which most men presaged would be the overthrow of religion."—CAMDEN'S *Annals for the Year* 1581.

353.13 (Ch. 31) emphatic clamour

RICHIE MONIPLIES BEHIND THE ARRAS. The practical jest of Richie Moniplies going behind the arras to get an opportunity of teasing Heriot, was a pleasantry such as James might be supposed to approve of. It was customary for those who knew his humour to contrive jests of this kind for his amusement. The celebrated Archie Armstrong, and another jester called Drummond, mounted on other people's backs, used to charge each other like knights in the tilt-yard, to the monarch's great amusement. The following is an instance of the same kind, taken from Webster upon Witchcraft. The author is speaking of the faculty called ventriloquism.

"But to make this more plain and certain, we shall add a story of a notable impostor, or ventriloquist, from the testimony of Mr Ady, which we have had confirmed from the mouth of some courtiers, that both saw and knew him, and is this:—It hath been (saith he) credibly reported, that there was a man in the court in King James his days, that could act this imposture so lively, that he could call the King by name, and cause the King to look round about him, wondering who it was that called him, whereas he that called him stood before him in his presence, with his face towards him. But after this imposture was known, the King, in his merriment, would sometimes take occasion by this impostor to make sport upon some of his courtiers, as, for instance:—

"There was a knight belonging to the court, whom the King caused to come before him in his private room, (where no man was but the King, and this knight and the impostor,) and feigned some occasion of serious discourse with the knight; but when the King began to speak, and the knight bending his attention to the King, suddenly there came a voice as out of another room, calling the knight by name, 'Sir John, Sir John; come away, Sir John;' at which the knight began to frown that any man should be so unmannerly as to molest the King and him; and still listening to the King's discourse, the voice came again, 'Sir John, Sir John; come away and drink off your sack.' At that Sir John began to swell with anger, and looked into the next rooms to see who it was that dared to call him so importunately, and could not find out who it was, and having chid with whomsoever he found, he returned again to the King. The King had no sooner begun to speak as formerly, but the voice came again, 'Sir John, come away, your sack stayeth for you.' At that Sir John began to stamp with madness, and looked out and returned several times to the King, but could not be quiet in his discourse with the King, because of the voice that so often troubled him, till the King had sported enough."—WEBSTER on *Witchcraft*, p. 124.

361.5 (Ch. 32) a leglen-girth A leglen-girth is the lowest hoop upon a *leglen*, or milk-pail. Allan Ramsay applies the phrase in the same metaphorical sense.

> Or bairns can read, they first maun spell,
> I learn'd this frae my mammy,
> And cast a leggen-girth mysell,
> Lang ere I married Tammy.
>
> *Christ's Kirk on the Green.*

368.17 (Ch. 33) Jeddart staves The old-fashioned weapon called the Jeddart staff was a species of battle-axe. Of a very great tempest, it is said, in the south of Scotland, that it rains Jeddart staffs, as in England the common people talk of its raining cats and dogs.

368.31 (Ch. 33) behind the arras

LADY LAKE. Whether out of a meddling propensity common to all who have a gossiping disposition, or from the love of justice, which ought to make part of a prince's character, James was very fond of enquiring personally into the *causes célébres* which occurred during his reign. In the imposture of the Boy of Bilson, who pretended to be possessed, and of one Richard Haydock, a poor scholar, who pretended to preach during his sleep, the King, to use the historian Wilson's expression, took delight in sounding with the line of his understanding, the depth of these brutish impositions, and in doing so, showed the acuteness with which he was endowed by Nature. Lady Lake's story consisted in a clamorous complaint against the Countess of Exeter, whom she accused of a purpose to put to death Lady Lake herself, and her daughter, Lady Ross, the wife of the Countess's own son-in-law, Lord Ross; and a forged letter was produced, in which Lady Exeter was made to acknowledge such a purpose. The account given of the occasion of obtaining this letter, was, that it had been written by the Countess at Wimbledon, in presence of Lady Lake and her daughter, Lady Ross, being designed to procure their forgiveness for her mischievous intention. The King remained still unsatisfied, the writing, in his opinion, bearing strong marks of forgery. Lady Lake and her daughter then alleged, that, besides their own attestation, and that of a confidential domestic, named Diego, in whose presence Lady Exeter had written the confession, their story might also be supported by the oath of their waiting-maid, who had been placed behind the hangings at the time the letter was written, and heard the Countess of Exeter read over the confession after she had signed it. Determined to be at the bottom of this accusation, James, while hunting one day near Wimbledon, the scene of the alleged confession, suddenly left his sport, and, galloping hastily to Wimbledon, in order to examine personally the room, discovered, from the size of the apartment, that the alleged conversation could not have taken place in the manner sworn to; and that the tapestry of the chamber, which had remained on the walls for thirty years, was too short by two feet, and, therefore, could not have concealed any one behind it. This matter was accounted an exclusive discovery of the King by his own spirit of shrewd investigation. The parties were punished in the Star Chamber by fine and imprisonment.

385.3 (Ch. 35) I trow Clarendon remarks, that the importance of the military exercise of the citizens was severely felt by the cavaliers during the civil war, notwithstanding the ridicule that had been showered upon it by the dramatic poets of the day. Nothing less than habitual practice could, at the battle of Newbury and elsewhere, have enabled the Londoners to keep their ranks as pikemen, in spite of the repeated charge of the fiery Prince Rupert and his gallant cavaliers.

385.30 (Ch. 35) the Duke of Exeter's daughter A particular species of rack, used at the Tower of London, was so called.

387.24 (Ch. 35) his breeks This elegant speech was made by the Earl of Douglas, called Tineman, after being wounded and made prisoner at the battle of Shrewsbury, where

His well labouring sword
Had three times slain the semblance of the King.

400.15 (Ch. 37) money is in question The penny-wedding of the Scots, now disused even among the lowest rank, was a peculiar species of merry-making, at which, when the wedded pair were popular, the guests who convened, contributed considerable sums under pretence of paying for the bridal festivity, but in reality to set the married folk afloat in the world.

405.25 (Ch. 37) grew Thrill, or curdle.

PEVERIL OF THE PEAK

Editorial Note

Peveril of the Peak occupies the second part of Volume 4, the whole of Volume 5, and the first part of Volume 6 in the 1824 octavo *Novels and Romances*, MSS 23022, 23023, and 23024 in the Interleaved Set. Cadell received the 'Notes & Introductions' from the author on 12 April 1830 (MS 21020, f. 17v), but substantial new Manx material came to hand in June and July, so that on 5 August Scott was still anxious to 'finish Peveril of the Peak' (MS 745, f. 190v). On 10 August he wrote to the publisher: 'I have mad[e] such additions to Peveril of the peak as I think will serve your turn & give some curious particulars of the Isle of Man I send the volumes and will be obliged to you to look whether the[y] will run to the length you wish as more buckram can easily be added' (MS 745, f. 193r). Cadell responded on the 18th: 'If you could conveniently aid me a little farther with ⟨Nigel⟩ ↑Peveril↓, it might be safer, all the matter received will make three Volumes of 356 pages each, which is under our mark a little, but if you find you cannot manage it quite to your mind I can easily make up the different by an advertisement, only when these Volumes come to be found with the others the advertisement will come out & they will look thin.' Scott apparently offered to insert an additional chapter or two, but Cadell was firmly of the view that additional notes would be more appropriate (MS 3919, f. 303r: 23 August 1830). On 25 August Scott tells Cadell: 'It is as easy to add the new matter to the notes of Pevril as to the text easier indeed But I should [wish] to know the precise amount wanted of additional matter over and above that formerly added[.] I had the calculation but fear I have mislaid it' (MS 745, f. 205r). On 2 September he writes that he is 'making up Peveril of the Peak who wands about half a volume', and on 30 September he declares that 'Peveril shall be stuffd out to your satisfaction without loss of time and also the measure of the cushion' (MS 745, ff. 276r, 221r). It is difficult to know how much material Scott added to the Interleaved Set at this late stage. It may not have been very much, for when *Peveril* appeared as Volumes 28–30 of the Magnum on 1 September, 1 October, and 1 November 1831 they contained 369, 349, and 352 pages respectively, the last two shorter than Cadell's optimum length.

On 9 October Cadell 'revised part of Peveril for the press' (MS 21020, f. 43r). He worked on it intensively for the rest of the month, and more sporadically during November and December. As late as 8 January 1831 he 'revised long note for conclusion of Peveril' and three days later 'revised notes for Peveril' (MS 21021, f. 4r–v). During these months several of Scott's letters express anxiety about possible confusion in the Magnum material. In October 1830 the first five leaves of the six-page Introduction went missing, so that Scott had to re-constitute them (MS 3914, ff. 129r, 167r; MS 745, f. 227r). A particularly anguished letter, endorsed by Cadell 'Abbotsford 19 Nov 1830', is inserted immediately before the first leaf of the Introduction in the Interleaved Set:

> The printer & publisher must be aware that Peveril of the Peak is under very particular circumstances which unless attended to will occasion great and peculiar errors in printing the effect of which may extend very far. The author therefore calls upon them thus formal[ly] to be kind enough to remember that this novel & its notes preface &c has been written rewritten lost and supplied till the whole is a confused in the authors [mind.] It is unavoidably that there must be repeated passages. The author therefore while he desires to see the proofs as usual will be greatly obliged to the printer to send *running copy* that he may see what has been done when settling what we are to day[.] It will be also extremely necessary that this work is carried on without delay and not after long intervals so that the whole may be kept in view at the same time

In spite of what Scott says above, the surviving manuscript, bound into the Interleaved Set, extends only to five leaves, is fluently written and shows no signs of the apparent confusion surrounding its composition. But the problems were real: Scott struggled to provide enough material for three decent-sized Magnum volumes in consequence of the fact that although *Peveril* was a four-volume novel it was not part of a series like *The Tale of Old Mortality* and *The Heart of Mid-Lothian*, so that it had to be expanded to fill three Magnum volumes on its own. For illuminating accounts of the making of the Magnum *Peveril* the reader is referred to two articles by Jane Millgate: 'Adding More Buckram: Scott and the Amplification of *Peveril of the Peak*', *English Studies in Canada*, 13 (1987), 174–81; and 'Proofing *Peveril*', *The Bibliotheck*, 17:1–3 (1990–91), 1–18.)

Some of Scott's notes are of types familiar from earlier volumes in the Magnum: many of the liberally supplied short footnotes in the Magnum *Peveril* are like those which a modern editor would provide, explaining some of the incidental references to personages and incidents of the Restoration period (e.g. 278–79; 294). But there are also a number of unusual features. No fewer than five of the notes are attached to 'pegs' inserted into the text for the purpose (237; 244; 264; 274).

Whether or not Scott drew anything specific from the lost papers of his late brother Tom (206) cannot be determined. He did, though, make use of two assiduous later informants, of very different sorts. One was Joseph Train, who acted as a self-appointed research assistant. Train turned out to be a specially valuable source of information for *Peveril*. In a document prepared for J. G. Lockhart when he was working on the biography of his late father-in-law Train notes: 'The peculiarities of the Manks and their Island having attracted my attention, and as they appeared to me very remarkable I resolved if time should ever permit me to write a History of the Isle of Man' (MS 3277, p. 199). On 1 December 1829 Train sent Scott a compilation of 'the Ancient Laws of the Isle of Man' (MS 3911, f. 104r). Scott does not seem to have made use of this, but he did draw on information about Cutlar McCulloch, sent by Train in a letter of 16 July 1830 (MS 874, ff. 232r–234Br). This material, which Train proudly indicated to Lockhart after Scott's death 'had been overlooked by all our Historians' (MS 3277, p. 199), results in the 'pegged' note at 264. (This is one of several notes which give the impression of wider authorial research than was actually the case, with a tell-tale reproduction of an enigmatic source which puzzles the present editors.)

Scott's other main informant was John Christian of Unrigg (or Ewanrigg) in Cumberland, a descendant of the family which plays a major part in *Peveril*. On 5 June 1830 Wordsworth wrote to Scott passing on John Christian's unhappiness with the presentation of William in the novel and offering to send supporting documents (*The Letters of William and Dorothy Wordsworth*, 2nd edn, 5:2, ed. Ernest de Selincourt, rev. Alan G. Hill (Oxford, 1979), 276–78). Scott replied on 16 July, indicating that although he considered Christian's concerns 'a little fantastic' he would nevertheless use any remarks that might be sent in a way which might be 'agreeable to him and fair to the memory of his ancestry' (*Letters*, 11.371–72). It is amusing that, although Scott maintained his right as a romancer to modify historical figures for the purposes of fiction (whether deliberately or out of ignorance: 206–08), he reproduces the pamphlet by Mark Wilks, *Historical Notices of Edward and William Christian* (including its voluminous footnotes), which Christian sent him on 16 July 1830, in the first Appendix to the Introduction, and that part relating to the historical Edward Christian is essentially repeated in the endnote on 'Richard Ganlesse' (263–64). The second half of the pamphlet survives bound into the Interleaved Set, showing printers' marks which indicate that they were simply directed to reproduce Wilks's work. It is also amusing to observe Scott changing the description of William in the text and drawing attention to the change (245): one might suspect a degree of irony in the note, but there is a similar change in the next novel, *Quentin Durward*. On 16 July Christian also sent some remarks on the novel by the Manx surgeon J. R. Oswald, probably those preserved in duplicate at MS 874, ff. 249–54 and 255–60, and 'a Translation of the Manx Song or Lament in memory of "Illiam Dhone"' (MS 3919, f. 231r). A fortnight later Christian transmitted 'a Copy of the proceedings had before the King in Council on the 5th and 14th Augt. 1663' (MS 3919, f. 262r: 2 August 1830), and these form the second and third Appendices (the copies sent by Christian have apparently not survived). In the same letter Christian expressed himself entirely satisfied with the 'explanation, which you so handsomely propose to give in your new Edition' (f. 262v). It should be noted that Train also transmitted material collected by Oswald, and by James M'Crone of Castle Mona. It is not always possible to determine which material came to Scott by way of Train, and which by way of Christian: MS 874 is nominally devoted to Train material, but some of the documents sent by Christian may well be included in it.

The amount of material supplied for *Peveril* overall is very considerable, but the Introduction proper is a modest 12 pages: the self-confessed compulsive 'romancer' tells how his brother Tom's papers first turned his imagination towards the Isle of Man, defends his modifications of historical characters, and explains how a family tradition contributed to the story of Fenella. The Appendices already mentioned add 47 pages.

The only noteworthy feature in the manuscript of the Introduction is the absence of the rather curious reference to Virgil's treatment of Dido at 208.7–9: this came in at a subsequent stage. (The items reproduced in Appendix II and Appendix III are not preserved in the Interleaved Set.)

It is not possible to determine precisely which of the notes were produced at what stage. Scott's checklist at the beginning of the relevant Interleaved Set volumes contains 23 items, seven of which are not taken up at the place indicated. At the other end of the process all except the first paragraph of the note on 'Popular Pastimes in the Isle of Man' (242–45) was added in proof, notably the egregious reproduction of the rules governing Manx horse-racing. The handful of other additions at a subsequent stage are on a much small scale.

There are 26 endnotes in all, occupying 70 pages: 6 (14 pages) in the first volume, 13 (28 pages) in the second, and 7 (23 pages) in the third. Several of these endnotes are very long—the faithful and accurate transcriber John Buchanan has been unusually hard at work—and there are moments when one is conscious that Scott is not entirely happy with the book-making he is engaged in. The most egregious of the long notes is probably the fifteen-page biographical sketch of Colonel Blood which concludes the final volume. Scott protests its appropriateness rather too much. Near the beginning (276.23–30) he says: 'The arrangement of the present volume admitting of a lengthened digression, we cannot, perhaps, enter upon a subject more extraordinary or entertaining, than the history of this notorious desperado, who exhibited all the elements of a most accomplished ruffian. As the account of these adventures is scattered in various and scarce publications, it will probably be a service to the reader to bring the most remarkable of them under his eye, in a simultaneous point of view.' The 'perhaps' and 'probably' there are significant. In the final paragraph (289.13–16) he tries again, asserting that the adventures of such a person 'cannot . . . be deemed foreign to a work dedicated, like the present to the preservation of extraordinary occurrences, whether real or fictitious.' The author's discomfort with this gargantuan note is further emphasised by his reference to 'various and scarce publications': in fact most of the material in the note comes from two publications.

Signs of Scott's unease in his book-making role can be detected elsewhere in the Magnum *Peveril*. One of the 'peg' notes already referred to, on the 'Trial and Execution of Christian' (237–38), suggests that the author has received information directly from the Vicar of Malew, whereas it is part of the rich store of information sent by the ever-obliging Joseph Train, who in turn, as noted above, received material from the Manxman James M'Crone. Another of the 'peg' notes (241–45) quotes, with acknowledgment, a description of Manx entertainments from George Waldron's *Description of the Isle of Man* and Magnus Olaus, and adds as a 'curiosity' the rules relating to horse-racing, transmitted by Thomas Frognall Dibdin. Waldron is again used for material 'fascinating to the antiquary' in the note on 'Sodor' (246–50), repeating (presumably inadvertently) the passage quoted in a footnote a few pages earlier (see entry for 246.12 at 622 below). Still more extensive is the note on 'Manx Superstitions' (250–60) from the same source ('a huge mine, in which I have attempted to discover some specimens of spar, if I cannot find treasure'), which ends with the justification that this 'extremely curious' quotation touches on the similarity of superstitions in different cultures. A further moment of unease is apparent in the odd opening sentence of the 'peg' note on 'The Sheriff of London' (274.35–37): 'It can hardly be forgotten that one of the great difficulties of Charles II.'s reign was to obtain for the crown the power of choosing the sheriffs of London.'

The Magnum *Peveril* is a distinctly different work from the first-edition narrative. Much of the material is of considerable interest, but it moves the volumes in the direction of an entertaining anthology, and the novel indeed becomes to a certain extent a work 'dedicated . . . to the preservation of extraordinary occurrences, whether real or fictitious'. It may be charitably suggested that this is not so much an imposition on the reader as an emphasising, even an enhancing, of the freak-show element in the novel.

There are six Magnum illustrations for this title. The frontispiece to Volume 28 (MAG0055 / TB348.28) was designed by Richard Parkes Bonington and engraved by William Ensom. It depicts Alice and Julian seated together in a parlour at Black Fort, disturbed by the figure of Bridgenorth in the doorway (EEWN 14, 133.19–24 (abridged): 'Then, by Heaven . . . Ralph Bridgenorth.'). The title-page vignette (MAG0056 / TB348.28) was designed by J. Webster and engraved by Frederick Bacon. It depicts Peveril and Alice as children in the gilded parlour at Martindale Castle (EEWN 14, 49.4–7: 'Yet naturally bold . . . an Abencerrage of Grenada.'). The frontispiece to Volume 29 (MAG0057 / TB348.29) was designed by Richard Parkes Bonington and engraved by William Henry Watt. It depicts Buckingham in an apartment at his town mansion leaning over and attempting to seduce Fenella, disguised as Zarah the sorceress (EEWN 14, 399.30–43 (abridged): 'A slender foot . . . simplicity of his niece.'). The title-page vignette (MAG0058 / TB348.29) was designed by Alexander Fraser, the elder, and engraved by Robert Graves. It depicts Peveril and Christian leaving the Cat and Fiddle Inn, with Peveril on horseback embracing the landlady after receiving a stirrup-cup (EEWN 14, 216.14–19 (abridged): 'The landlady offered . . . saluting her at parting.'). The frontispiece to Volume 30 (MAG0059 / TB348.30) was designed by Charles Robert Leslie and engraved by Joseph Goodyear. It depicts Peveril seated at a window, in the Castle of Holm-peel, with Fenella at his feet (EEWN 14, 184.4–8 (abridged): 'Peveril unclasped his arms … elfin Fenella.'). The title-page vignette (MAG0060 / TB348.30) was designed by David Wilkie and engraved by Charles Fox. It depicts Peveril in his cell at Newgate being shown a book containing Madamoiselle Scudéry's romances by Sir Geoffrey Hudson (EEWN 14, 364.5–8 (abridged): 'The dwarf imparted . . . a great admirer.').

R. P. Bonington. W. Ensom.

PEVERIL OF THE PEAK.

"Then, by Heaven," answered Julian, "I will watch his arrival in this Island, and ere he has locked thee in his arms, he shall answer to me on the subject of my suit." "Then demand that answer now" said a voice from without the door which was at the same time slowly opened, "for here stands Ralph Bridgenorth."

EDINBURGH, PUBLISHED 1831. BY ROBERT CADELL and WHITTAKER & Cº LONDON.

WAVERLEY NOVELS.

VOL. XXVIII.

PEVERIL OF THE PEAK.

"Yet naturally bold and high-spirited, the little champion placed himself beside his defenceless sister, continuing to brandish his weapon in her defence as boldly as he had himself been an Abencerrage of Grenada".

PRINTED FOR ROBERT CADELL, EDINBURGH.
AND WHITTAKER & Co. LONDON.
1831.

PEVERIL OF THE PEAK.

"A slender foot and ankle, was the only part of her person distinctly seen; the rest was enveloped in a long veil of silver gauze, the whole attire argued at least coquetry on the part of a fair one, and induced Buckingham to smile internally at Christian's account of the extreme simplicity of his niece."

WAVERLEY NOVELS.

VOL. XXIX.

PEVERIL OF THE PEAK.

The landlady offered Peveril a glass from her own peculiar bottle. For this purpose, she mounted on the horse-block, he returned the courtesy in the most approved manner, namely, by throwing his arm over his landlady's shoulder, and saluting her at parting.

PRINTED FOR ROBERT CADELL, EDINBURGH.
AND WHITTAKER & Cº LONDON.
1831.

C. R. Leslie. J. Goodyear.

PEVERIL OF THE PEAK.

"Peveril unclasped his arms, which, in meditation, had been folded on his bosom; and withdrawing his eyes from the vacant prospect of the sea-coast, without much consciousness upon what they rested, he beheld beside him the little dumb maiden, elfin Fenella."

WAVERLEY NOVELS.

VOL. XXX.

PEVERIL OF THE PEAK.

D. Wilkie. Chas Fox.

'The dwarf imparted to Peveril a volume similar to that which formed his own studies, one of Scuderi's now forgotten romances, of which Geoffrey Hudson was a great admirer'

PRINTED FOR ROBERT CADELL, EDINBURGH.
AND WHITTAKER & Co LONDON.
1831.

Introduction to Peveril of the Peak

If I had valued my own reputation, as it is said I ought in prudence to have done, I might have now drawn a line, and remained for life, or (who knows?) perhaps for some years after death, the "ingenious author of Waverley." I was not, however, more desirous of this species of immortality, which might have lasted some twenty or thirty years, than Falstaff was of the embowelling which was promised him after the field of Shrewsbury, by his patron the Prince of Wales. "Embowel'd? If you embowel me to-day, you may powder and eat me to-morrow!"

If my occupation as a romancer were taken from me, I felt I should have at a late hour in life to find me out another; when I could hardly expect to acquire those new tricks, which are proverbially said not to be learned by those dogs who are getting old. Besides, I had yet to learn from the public, that my intrusions were disagreeable; and while I was endured with some patience, I felt I had all the reputation which I greatly coveted. My memory was well stocked, both with historical, local, and traditional notices, and I had become almost as licensed a plague to the public as the well-remembered beggar of the ward, whom men distinguish by their favour, perhaps for no better reason than that they had been in the habit of giving him alms, as a part of the business of the daily promenade. The general fact is undeniable,—all men grow old, all men must wear out; but men of ordinary wisdom, however aware of the general fact, are unwilling to admit in their own case any special instances of failure. Indeed, they can hardly be expected themselves to distinguish the effects of the Archbishop of Granada's apoplexy, and are not unwilling to pass over in their composition, as instances of mere carelessness or bad luck, what others may consider as symptoms of mortal decay. I had no choice save that of absolutely laying aside the pen, the use of which at my time of life was become a habit, or to continue its vagaries, until the public should let me plainly understand they would no more of me; a hint which I was not unlikely to meet with, and which I was determined to take without waiting for a repetition. This hint, that the reader may plainly understand me, I was determined to take, when the publication of a new Waverley novel should not be the subject of some attention in the literary world.

An accidental circumstance decided my choice of a subject for the present work. It was now several years since my immediate younger brother, Thomas Scott, already mentioned in these notes, had resided for two or three seasons in the Isle of Man, and, having access to the registers of that singular territory, had copied many of them, which he subjected to my perusal. These papers were put into my hands while my brother had thoughts of making some literary use of them, I do not well remember what; but he never came to any decision on that head, and grew tired of the task of transcription. The papers, I suppose, were lost in the course of a military man's life. The tenor of them, that is, of the most remarkable, remained engraved on the memory of the author.

The interesting and romantic story of William Christian especially struck my fancy. I found the same individual, as well as his father, particularly noticed in some memorials of the island, preserved by the Earl of Derby, and published in Dr Peck's Desiderata Curiosa. This gentleman was the son of Edward, formerly governor of the island; and William himself was afterwards one of its two Dempsters, or supreme judges. Both father and son embraced the party of the islanders, and contested some feudal rights claimed by the Earl of Derby as King of the Island. When the Earl had suffered death at Bolton-le-Moors, Captain Christian placed himself at the head of the Roundheads, if they might be so called, and found the means of holding communication with a fleet sent by the Parliament. The island was surrendered to the Parliament by the insurgent Manxmen. The high-spirited Countess and her son were arrested, and cast into prison, where they were long detained, and very indifferently treated. When the restoration took place, the Countess, or by title the Queen-dowager of the Island, seized upon William Dhône, or Fair-haired William, as William Christian was termed, and caused him to be tried and executed, according to the laws of the island, for having dethroned his liege mistress, and imprisoned her and her family. Romancers, and readers of romance, will generally allow, that the fate of Christian, and the contrast of his character with that of the high-minded, but vindictive Countess of Derby, famous during the civil wars for her valiant defence of Latham House, contained the essence of an interesting tale. I have, however, dwelt little either on the death of William Christian, or on the manner in which Charles II. viewed that stretch of feudal power, and the heavy fine which he imposed upon the Derby estates, for that extent of jurisdiction of which the Countess had been guilty. Far less have I given any opinion on the justice or guilt of that action, which is to this day judged of by the people of the island as they happen to be connected with the sufferer, or perhaps as they may look back with the eyes of favour upon the Cavaliers or Roundheads of those contentious days. I do not conceive that I have done injury to the memory of this gentleman, or any of his descendants in his person; at the same time I have most willingly given his representative an opportunity of stating in this edition of the Novel what he thinks necessary for the vindication of his ancestor, and the reader will find the exposition in the Notices, for which Mr Christian desires admission.* I could do no less, considering the polite and gentlemanlike manner in which he stated feelings concerning his ancestry, to which a Scotsman can hardly be supposed to be indifferent.

In another respect, Mr Christian with justice complains, that Edward Christian, described in the romance as the brother of the gentleman executed in consequence of the Countess's arbitrary act of authority, is pourtrayed as a wretch of unbounded depravity, having only ingenuity and courage to rescue him from abhorrence, as well as hatred. Any personal allusion was entirely undesigned on the part of the author. The Edward Christian of the tale is a mere creature of the imagination. Commentators have naturally enough identified him with a brother of William Christian, named Edward, who died in prison after being confined seven or eight years in Peel Castle, in the year 1650. Of him I had no access to know any thing; and as I was not aware that such a person had existed, I could hardly be said to have traduced his character. It is sufficient for my justification, that there lived at the period of my story a person named Edward Christian, "with whom connected, or by whom begot," I am a perfect stranger, but who we know to have been engaged in such actions as may imply his having been guilty of any thing bad. The fact is, that upon the 5th June, 1680, Thomas Blood, (the famous crown-stealer,) *Edward Christian*, Arthur O'Brien, and others, were found guilty of being concerned in a conspiracy for taking away the life and character of the celebrated Duke of Buckingham; but that this Edward was the same with the brother of William Christian, is impossible, since that brother died in 1650; nor would I have used his christened name of Edward, had I supposed there was a chance of its being connected with any existing family. These genealogical matters are fully illustrated in the notes to the Appendix.

I ought to have mentioned in the former editions of this romance, that Charlotte de la Tremouille, Countess of Derby, represented as a Catholic, was, in fact, a French Protestant. For misrepresenting the noble dame in this manner, I have only Lucio's excuse—"I spoke according to the trick." In a story, where the greater part is

* See Appendix, No. I.

avowedly fiction, the author is at liberty to introduce such variations from actual fact as his plot requires, or which are calculated to enhance it; in which predicament the religion of the Countess of Derby, during the Popish Plot, appeared to fall. If I have overestimated a romancer's privileges and immunities, I am afraid this is not the only, nor most important, case in which I have done so. To speak big words, the heroic Countess has far less grounds for an action of scandal, than the memory of Virgil might be liable to for his posthumous scandal of Dido.

The character of Fenella, which, from its peculiarity, made a favourable impression on the public, was far from being original. The fine sketch of Mignon, in Wilhelm Meister's Lehrjahre, a celebrated work from the pen of Goethe, gave the idea of such a being. But the copy will be found greatly different from my great prototype; nor can I be accused of borrowing any thing, save the general idea, from an author, the honour of his own country, and an example to the authors of other kingdoms, to whom all must be proud to own an obligation.

Family tradition supplied me with two circumstances, which are somewhat analogous to that in question. The first is an account of a lawsuit, taken from a Scottish report of adjudged cases, quoted in note to Chapter 20, p. 260.

The other—of which the editor has no reason to doubt, having often heard it from those who were witnesses of the fact—relates to the power of a female in keeping a secret, (sarcastically said to be impossible,) even when that secret refers to the exercise of her tongue.

In the middle of the eighteenth century, a female wanderer came to the door of Mr Robert Scott, grandfather of the present author, an opulent farmer in Roxburghshire, and made signs that she desired shelter for the night, which, according to the custom of the times, was readily granted. The next day the country was covered with snow, and the departure of the wanderer was rendered impossible. She remained for many days, her maintenance adding little to the expense of a considerable household; and by the time that the weather grew milder, she had learned to hold intercourse by signs with the household around her, and could intimate to them that she was desirous of staying where she was, and working at the wheel and other employment, to compensate for her food. This was a not unfrequent compact at that time, and the dumb woman entered upon her thrift, and proved a useful member of the patriarchal household. She was a good spinner, knitter, carder, and so forth, but her excellence lay in attending to the feeding and bringing up the domestic poultry. Her mode of whistling to call them together was so peculiarly elfish and shrill, that it was thought, by those who heard it, more like that of a fairy than a human being.

In this manner she lived three or four years, nor was there the slightest idea entertained in the family that she was other than the mute and deprived person she had always appeared. But in a moment of surprise, she dropped the mask which she had worn so long.

It chanced upon a Sunday that the whole inhabitants of the household were at church excepting Dumb Lizzie, whose infirmity was supposed to render her incapable of profiting by divine service, and who therefore stayed at home to take charge of the house. It happened that, as she was sitting in the kitchen, a mischievous shepherd boy, instead of looking after his flock on the lea, as was his duty, slunk into the house to see what he could pick up, or perhaps out of mere curiosity. Being tempted by something which was in his eyes a nicety, he put forth his hand, unseen, as he conceived, to appropriate it. The dumb woman came suddenly upon him, and in the surprise, forgot her part, and exclaimed, in broad Scottish, and with distinct articulation, "Ah, you little deevil's limb!" The boy, terrified more by the character of the person who rebuked him, than by the mere circumstance of having been taken in the insignificant offence, fled in great dismay to the church, to carry the miraculous news that the dumb woman had found her tongue.

The family returned home in great surprise, but found their inmate had relapsed into her usual mute condition, would communicate with them only by signs, and in that manner denied positively what the boy affirmed.

From this time confidence was broken betwixt the other inmates of the family and their dumb, or rather silent, guest. Traps were laid for the supposed impostor, all of which she skilfully eluded; firearms were often suddenly discharged near her, but never on such occasions was she seen to start. It seems probable, however, that Lizzie grew tired of all this mistrust, for she one morning disappeared as she came, without any ceremony of leave-taking.

She was seen, it is said, upon the other side of the English border, in perfect possession of her speech. Whether this was exactly the case or not, my informers were no way anxious in enquiring, nor am I able to authenticate the fact. The shepherd boy lived to be a man, and always averred that she had spoken distinctly to him. What could be the woman's reason for persevering so long in a disguise as unnecessary as it was severe, could never be guessed, and was perhaps the consequence of a certain aberration of the mind. I can only add, that I have every reason to believe the tale to be perfectly authentic, so far as it is here given, and it may serve to parallel the supposed case of Fenella.

ABBOTSFORD, 1*st July*, 1831.

APPENDIX No. I

THE following Notices were recommended to my attention, in the politest manner possible, by John Christian, Esq. of Milntown, in the Isle of Man, and Unrigg, in Cumberland, Dempster at present of the Isle of Man. This gentleman is naturally interested in the facts which are stated, as representative of the respectable family of Christian, and lineally descended from William Dhône, put to death by the Countess of Derby. I can be no way interested in refusing Mr Christian this justice, and willingly lend my aid to extend the exculpation of the family.

HISTORICAL NOTICES

OF EDWARD AND WILLIAM CHRISTIAN; TWO CHARACTERS IN "PEVERIL OF THE PEAK."

THE venerable Dr Dryasdust, in a preparatory dialogue, apprizes the Eidolon, or apparition of the author, that he stood "much accused for adulterating the pure sources of historical knowledge;" and is answered by that emanation of genius, "that he has done some service to the public if he can present to them a lively fictitious picture, for which the original anecdote or circumstance which he made free to press into his service, only furnished a slight sketch;" "that by introducing to the busy and the youthful,

> Truths severe in fairy fiction dress'd,

and by creating an interest in fictitious adventures ascribed to a historical period and characters, the reader begins next to be anxious *to learn what the facts really were*, and how far the novelist has justly represented them."

The adventures ascribed to "historical characters" would, however, fail in their moral aim, if fiction were placed at variance with truth; if Hampden, or Sydney, for example, were painted as swindlers; or Lady Jane Grey, or Rachel Russel, as abandoned women.

"Odzooks! must one swear to the truth of a song?" although an excellent joke, were a bad palliation in such a case. Fancy may be fairly indulged in the illustration, but not in the perversion of fact;

and if the fictitious picture should have no general resemblance to the original, the flourish of

> Truths severe in fairy fiction dress'd,

were but an aggravation of the wrong.

The family of CHRISTIAN is indebted to this splendid luminary of the North for abundant notoriety.

The William Christian represented on one part as an ungrateful traitor, on the other as the victim of a judicial murder, and his brother (or relative) Edward, one of the suite of *a* Duke* of Buckingham, were so far real historical persons. Whether the talents and skill of Edward in imposing on Fenella a feigned silence of several years, be among the legitimate or supernatural wonders of this fertile genius, his fair readers do not seem to be agreed. Whether the residue of the canvass, filled up with a masterly picture of the most consummate hypocrite and satanic villain ever presented to the imagination, be consistent with the historical character of this individual, is among the subjects of research to which the novelist has given a direct invitation in his prefatory chapter.

English history furnishes few materials to aid the investigation of transactions chiefly confined to the Isle of Man. Circumstances led me, many years ago, to visit this ancient Lilliput; whether as one of those "smart fellows worth talking to," "in consequence of a tumble from my barouche," "as a ruined miner," or as "a disappointed speculator," is of no material import. It may be that temporary embarrassment drove me into seclusion, without any of the irresistible inducements alluded to; and want of employment, added to the acquaintance and aid of a zealous local antiquary, gradually led to an examination of all accessible authorities on this very subject among others. So it happened, that I had not landed many hours before I found the mournful ditty of "William Dhône" (*brown* or *fair-haired William*, this very identical William Christian) twanged through the demi-nasal, demi-guttural trumpet of the carman, and warbled by the landlady's pretty daughter; in short, making as great a figure in its little sphere as did once the more important ballad of Chevy Chace in its wider range; the burden of the song purporting that William Dhône was the mirror of virtue and patriotism, and that envy, hatred, and malice, and all uncharitableness, operate the destruction of the wisest and the best.

Themes of popular feeling naturally attract the earliest notice of a stranger; and I found the story of this individual, though abundantly garbled and discoloured on the insular records, full of circumstances

* Not the Duke described in Peveril, but the companion of Charles I. in his Spanish romance.

to excite the deepest interest, but which, to be rendered intelligible, must be approached by a circuitous route, in which neither elfin page, nor maiden fair, can be the companion of our walk.

The loyal and celebrated James, seventh Earl of Derby, was induced, by the circumstances of the times, to fix his chief residence in the Isle of Man from 1643 to 1651.* During this period he composed, in the form of a letter† to his son Charles, (Lord Strange,) an historical account of that island, with a statement of his own proceedings there; interspersed with much political advice for the guidance of his successor; full of acute observation, and evincing an intimate acquaintance with the works of Machiavelli, which it appears, by a quotation,‡ that he had studied in a Latin edition. The work, although formally divided into chapters and numbered paragraphs, is professedly desultory,§ and furnishes few means of determining the relative dates of his facts, which must accordingly be supplied by internal evidence, and in some cases by conjecture.

He appears to have been drawn thither, in 1643, by letters|| intimating the danger of a revolt: the "people had begun the fashion of England in murmuring;" "assembled in a tumultuous manner; desiring new laws, they would have no bishops, pay no tithes to the clergie, despised authority, rescued people committed by the Governor," &c. &c.

The Earl's first care was to apply himself to the consideration of these insurrectionary movements; and as he found some interruption to his proceedings in the conduct of *Edward Christian*,¶ an attempt shall be made, so far as our limits will admit, to extract the

* His countess resided at Latham House (her heroic defence of which is well known) until 1644 or 5, when she also retired to the Isle of Man. A contemporary publication, the *Mercurius Aulicus*, by John Birkenhead, says, "the Countesse, it seems, stole the Earl's breeches, when he fled long since into the Isle of Man, and hath in his absence played the Man at Latham." This insinuation is certainly unjust; but the Earl seems to consider some explanation necessary, "why he left the land, when every gallant spirit had engaged himself for king and country." Danger of revolt and invasion of the island constitute the substance of this explanation. There is reason, however, to conjecture, that he had been disappointed of the command he had a right to expect, when he brought a considerable levy to join the King at York. Any explanation, in short, might be listened to, except a doubt of his loyalty and ardent military spirit, which were above all impeachment.

† Published in Peck's Desiderata Curiosa, in 1779.

‡ Peck, p. 446,—fortiter calumniari aliquid adhærebit.

§ Peck, p. 446. "Loath to dwell too long on one subject," skip over to some other matter.

|| Peck, p. 434.

¶ For a history of this family, established in the Isle of Man so early as 1422, see Hutchinson's History of Cumberland, vol. ii. p. 146. They had previously been established in Wigtonshire.

Earl's own account of this person. "I was newly* got acquainted with Captain Christian, whom I perceived to have abilities enough to do me service. I was told he had made a good fortune in the Indies; that he was a Mankesman born." - - "He is excellent good companie; as rude as a sea captain should be; but refined as one that had civilized himself half a year at Court, where he served the Duke of Buckingham." - - - "While he governed here some few years he pleased me very well," &c. &c. "But such is the condition of man, that most will have some fault or other to blurr all their best vertues; and his was of that condition which is reckoned with drunkenness, viz. *covetousness*, both marked *with age* to increase and grow in man." - - "When a Prince has given all, and the favourite can desire no more, they both grow weary of one another."†

An account of the Earl's successive public meetings, short, from the limits of our sketch, is extracted in a note‡ from the headings of the chapters (apparently composed by Peck.) In the last of these

* This is an example of the difficulty of arranging the relative dates; the word *newly*, thus employed at the earliest in 1643, refers to 1628, the date of the appointment of E. Christian to be governor of the Isle of Man, which office he had till 1635, (Sacheverill's Account of the Isle of Man, published in 1702, p. 100,) the Earl being then Lord Strange, but apparently taking the lead in public business during his father's lifetime.

† Peck, p. 444. There is apparently some error in Hutchinson's genealogy of the family in his History of Cumberland: 1st brother, John, born 1602; 2d, died young; 3d, William, born 1608; 4th, Edward, Lieut.-Governor of the Isle of Man, 1629, (according to Sacheverill, p. 100, 1628.) This Edward's birth cannot be placed earlier than 1609, and he could not well have made a fortune in the Indies, have frequented the Court of Charles I., and be selected as a fit person to be a governor, at the age of 19 or 20. The person mentioned in the text was obviously of *mature age;* and *Edward the governor* appears to have been the younger brother of *William Christian*, a branch of the same family, possessing the estate of Knockrushen, near Castle Rushen, who, as well as Edward, was imprisoned in Peel Castle in 1643.

‡ Peck, p. 438, et seq. "Chap. viii. The Earl appoints a meeting of the natives, every man to give in his grievances; upon which some think to outwit him, which he winks at, being not ready for them, therefore cajoles and divides them; on the appointed day he appears with a good guard; the people give in their complaints quietly and retire. Chap. ix. Another meeting appointed, when he also appears with a good guard. Many busy men speak only Mankes, which a more designing person (probably Captain Christian, a late governor) would hinder, but the Earl forbids it; advice about it appearing in public; the Mankesmen great talkers and wranglers; the Earl's spies get in with them and wheedle them. Chap. x. The night before the meeting the Earl consults with his officers what to answer; but tells them nothing of his spies; compares both reports, and keeps back his own opinion; sends some of the officers, who he knew would be troublesome, out of the way, about other matters; the (present) governor afresh commended; what counsellors the properest. Chap. xi. The Earl's carriage to the people at his first going over; his carriage at the meeting to modest petitioners, to impudent, to the most confident, and to the most dangerous, *viz.* them who stood behind and prompted others. All things being agreed, Captain Christian cunningly begins disturbance; the Earl's reply and speech to the people; Christian is stroke blank; several people committed to prison and fined, which quiets them."

meetings it appears that Edward Christian attempted at its close to recapitulate the business of the day: "Asked if we did not agree thus and thus," mentioning some things (says the Earl) "he had instructed the people to aske; which happily they had forgot." The Earl accordingly rose in wrath, and, after a short speech, "bade the court to rise, and no man to speak more."—"Some," he adds, "were *committed to prison*, and there abided, until, upon *submission* and assurance of *being very good* and *quiet*, they were released, and others were put into their rooms.—I thought fit to make them be *deeply fined;* since this they all come in most submisse and *loving manner*."* Pretty efficient means of producing *quiet*, if the despot be strong enough, and with it such *love* as suits a despot's fancy! Among the prisoners were *Edward Christian* and his brother William of Knockrushen; the latter was released in 1644, on giving bond, among other conditions, *not to depart the island without license*.

Of Edward, the Earl says, "I will return unto Captain Christian, whose business must be heard next week" (either in 1644 or early in 1645.) "*He is still in prison*, and I believe many wonder thereat, as savouring of injustice, and that his trial should be deferred so long." "Also his business is of that condition that it *concerns not himself alone*." "If a Jurie of the people do passe upon him, (being he had so cajoled them to believe he suffers for their sakes,) it is likely they should quit him, and then might he laugh at us, whom I had rather he had betrayed." "I remember one said it was much safer to take men's lives than their estates: for their children will sooner much forget the death of their father than the loss of their patrimonie."† Edward *died in custody* in Peel Castle in 1650,‡ after an imprisonment of between seven and eight years; and so far, at least, no ground can be discovered for that gratitude which is afterwards said to have been violated by this family, unless indeed we transplant ourselves to those countries where it is the fashion to flog a public officer one day and replace him in authority the next.

The insular records detail with minuteness the complaints of the people relative to the exactions of the church, and their adjustment by a sort of public arbitration in October 1643. But it is singular, that neither in these records, nor in the Earl's very studied narrative of the modes of discussion, the offences, and the punishments, is

* Peck, 442.

† Peck, 448–9.

‡ Feltham's Tour, p. 161, places this event, (while a prisoner in Peel Castle,) on the authority of a tombstone, in 1660, "John Greenhalgh being governor." Now John Greenhalgh ceased to be governor in 1651; the date is probably an error in the press for 1650.

one word to be found regarding the more important points actually at issue between himself and the people. The fact, however, is fully developed, as if by accident, in one of the chapters (xvi.) of this very desultory but sagacious performance. "There comes this very instant an occasion to me to acquaint you with a special matter, which, if by reason of these troublesome and dangerous times, I cannot bring to passe my intents therein, you may in your better leisure consider thereof, and make some use hereafter of my present labors, in the matter of a certain holding in this country, called the tenure of the straw;* whereby *men thinke their dwellings are their own auntient inheritances*, and that they may passe the same to any, and dispose thereof *without license* from the Lord, but paying him a bare small rent like unto a fee-farme in England: wherein they are much deceived."

William the Conqueror, among his plans *for the benefit of his English subjects*, adopted that of inducing or compelling them to surrender their allodial lands, and receive them back to hold by feudal tenure. The Earl of Derby projected the surrender of a similar right, in order to create tenures more profitable to himself—a simple lease for three lives, or twenty-one years. The measure was entirely novel, although the attempt to prevent† alienation without license from the lord, for purposes of a less profitable exaction, may be traced, together with the scenes of violence it produced, through many passages in the ancient records, which would be inexplicable without this clue.

The Earl proceeded, certainly with sufficient energy and considerable skill, to the accomplishment of his object. In the very year of his arrival, Dec. 1643, he appointed commissioners‡ to compound for leases, consisting of some of his principal officers, (members of

* In the transfer of real estates both parties came into the common law court, and the grantor, in the face of the court, transferred his title to the purchaser by the delivery of a straw; which being recorded, was his title. The same practice prevailed in the transfer of personal property. Sir Edward Coke, iv. 69, when speaking of the Isle of Man, says, "upon the sale of a horse, or any contract for any other thing, they make the stipulation perfect per *traditionem stipulæ*," (by the delivery of a straw.) Perhaps a more feasible etymology of *stipulation*, than the usual derivation from stipes (a stake or land-mark), or stips (a piece of money or wages).

† Among those instances in which "the commands of the lord proprietor have" (in the emphatic words of the commissioners of 1791, p. 67) "been *obtruded* on the people as laws," we find, in 1583, the prohibition to dispose of lands without license of the lord, is prefaced by the broad admission, that, "contrary to good and laudable order, and divers and sundry general restraints made, the inhabitants *have*, and *daily do*, notwithstanding the said restrainte, *buy*, *sell*, *give*, *grant*, *chop* and *exchange* their farms, *lands*, *tenements*, &c., *at their liberties and pleasures*." Alienation fines were first exacted in 1643. Report of Commissioners of 1791. App. A., No. 71, Rep. of Law Officers.

‡ The governor-comptroller, receiver; and John Cannel, deemster.

council,) who had themselves been prevailed on by adequate considerations to surrender their estates, and are by general tradition accused of having conspired to delude their simple countrymen into the persuasion, that having no title-deeds, their estates were insecure; that leases were title-deeds; and although nominally for limited terms, declared the lands to be descendible to their eldest sons. It is remarkable that the names of *Ewan* and *William Christian*, two of the council, are alone excluded from this commission.

We have already seen two of the name committed to prison. The following notices, which abundantly unfold the ground of the Earl's hostility to the name of Christian, relate to Ewan Christian, the father of William Dhône, and one of the Deemsters excluded from the commission. "One presented me a petition against Deemster* Christian, on the behalf of an infant who is conceived to have a right unto his Farme Rainsway (Ronaldsway), one of the principal holdings in this country, who, by reason of his eminencie here, and that he holdeth much of the same tenure of the straw in other places, he is soe observed, that certainly as I temper the matter with him in this, soe shall I prevail with others."† - - - "By policie‡ they (the Christians) are crept into the principal places of power, and they be seated round about the country, and in the heart of it; they are matched with the best families," &c.

"The prayer of the petition§ formerly mentioned was to this effect, that there might be a fair tryal, and *when the right was recovered*, that *I would graunt them a lease thereof—this being in the tenure of the straw*." - - - "Upon some conference with the petitioner, I find a motion heretofore was made by my commissioners, that the Deemster should give this fellow a summe of money. But he would part with none, neverthelesse now it may be he will, and I hope be so wise as to assure unto himself his holding, by compounding with me for the lease of the same, to which, if they two agree, I shall grant it him on easy terms. For if he break the ice, I may haply catch some fish."||

* Deemster, evidently Anglicized, the person who deems the law; a designation anciently unknown among the natives, who continue to call this officer *Brehon*, identical with the name of those judges and laws so often mentioned in the Histories of Ireland.

† Peck, 447. ‡ Ib. 448. § I have ascertained the date of this petition to be 1643.

|| *Covetousness* is not attributed to the head of this family; but the Earl makes himself merry with his gallantry—natural children, it seems, took the name of their father, and not of their mother, as elsewhere, and "the deemster did not get soe many for lust's sake, as to make the name of Christian flourish." Of him, or a successor of the same name, it is related, that he "won L.500 at play from the Bishop of Sodor and Man, with which he purchased the manor of *Ewanrigg* in Cumberland, still possessed by that family."

The issue of this piscatory project was but too successful. Ewan bent to the *reign of terror*, and gave up Ronaldsway to his son William, who accepted the lease, and named his own descendants for the lives. Still the objects attained were unsubstantial, as being contrary to all law, written or oral; and the system was incomplete, until sanctioned by the semblance of legislative confirmation.

We have seen that the Earl had in the island a considerable military force, and we know from other sources* that they lived in a great measure at free quarters. We have his own testimony for stating, that he achieved his objects by imprisoning, until his prisoners "*promised to be good;*" and successively filling their places with others, until they also *conformed to his theory of public virtue.* And the reader will be prepared to hear, without surprise, that the same means enabled him, in 1645, to arrange a legislature† capable of yielding a forced assent to this notable system of submission and loving kindness.

This is perhaps the most convenient place for stating, that, in the subsequent surrender of the Island to the troops of the Parliament, the only stipulation made by the Islanders was, "that they might enjoy their lands and liberties as they formerly had." In what manner this stipulation was performed, my notes do not enable me to state. The restoration of Charles II., propitious in other respects, inflicted on the Isle of Man the revival of its feudal government; and the affair of the tenures continued to be a theme of perpetual contest and unavailing complaint, until finally adjusted in 1703, through the mediation of the excellent Bishop Wilson in a legislative compromise, known by the name of the Act of Settlement, whereby the people obtained a full recognition of their ancient rights, on condition of doubling the actual quit rents, and consenting to alienation fines, first exacted by the Earl James in 1643.‡

In 1648, William Dhône was appointed Receiver General; and in the same year we find his elder brother, John, (assistant Deemster to his father Ewan,) committed to Peel Castle on one of these occasions, which strongly marks the character of the person and the times, and affords also a glimpse at the feeling of the people, and at the condition of the devoted family of Christian. The inquisitive

* Evidence on the mock trial of William Dhône.

† We shall see, by and by, a very simple method of packing a judicial and legislative body, by removing and replacing *seven individuals* by one and the same mandate.

‡ Report of 1791. App. A. No. 71.

will find it in a note;* other readers will pass on.

The circumstances are familiarly known, to the reader of English history, of the march of the Earl of Derby, in 1651, with a corps from the Isle of Man for the service of the King; his joining the royal army on the eve of the battle of Worcester; his flight and imprisonment at Chester, after that signal defeat; and his trial and execution at Bolton in Lancashire, by the officers of the Parliament, on the 15th October of that year.

Immediately afterwards, Colonel Duckenfield, who commanded at Chester on behalf of the Parliament, proceeded with an armament of ten ships, and a considerable military force, for the reduction of the Isle of Man.

William Christian was condemned and executed in 1662–3, for acts connected with its surrender, twelve years before, which are still involved in obscurity; and it will be most acceptable to the general reader that we should pass over the intermediate period,† and leave the facts regarding this individual, all of them extraordinary, and some of peculiar interest, to be developed by the record of the trial, and documents derived from other sources.

* A person named Charles Vaughan is brought to lodge an information, that being in England, he fell into company with a young man named Christian, who said he had lately left the Isle of Man, and was in search of a brother, who was clerk to a Parliament Officer; that in answer to some questions, he said, "The Earl did use the inhabitants of that Isle very hardly; had estreated great fines from the inhabitants; had changed the ancient tenures, and *forced* them to take leases. That he had taken away one hundred pounds a-year from his father, and had kept his uncle in prison four or five years. But if ever the Earl came to England, he had used the inhabitants so hardly, that he was sure they would never suffer him to land in that island again." An order is given to imprison John Christian (probably the reputed head of the family, his father being advanced in years) in Peel Castle, until he entered into bonds to be of good behaviour, and *not to depart the Isle without license.*—(Insular Records.) The young man in question is said to have been the son of William Christian of Knockrushen.

† Some readers may desire an outline of this period. The lordship of the Island was given to Lord Fairfax, who deputed commissioners to regulate its affairs; one of them (Chaloner) published an account of the Island in 1656. He puts down William Christian as Receiver General in 1653. We find his name as Governor, from 1656 to 1658, (Sacheverill, p. 101,) in which year he was succeeded by Chaloner himself. Among the anomalies of those times, it would seem that he had retained the office of Receiver while officiating as Governor; and episcopacy having been abolished, and the receipts of the see added to those of the exchequer, he had large accounts to settle, for which Chaloner sequestered his estates in his absence, and imprisoned and held to bail his brother John, for aiding what he calls his escape; his son George returned from England, by permission of Lord Fairfax, to settle his father's accounts. Chaloner informs us, that the revenues of the suppressed see were *not appropriated* to the private use of Lord Fairfax, who, "for the better encouragement and support of the ministers of the Gospel and for the promoting of learning, hath conferred all this revenue upon the ministers, and also for maintaining free schools, *i.e.* at Castletown, Peel, Douglass, and Ramsay." Chaloner pays a liberal tribute to the talents of the clergy, and the learning and piety of the late bishops.

A mandate by Charles, 8th Earl of Derby, dated at Latham in September 1662, after descanting on the heinous sin of rebellion, "aggravated by its being instrumental* in the death of the Lord; and stating that he is himself concerned to revenge a father's blood," orders William Christian to be proceeded against forthwith, for all his illegal actions at, before, or after, the year 1651, (a pretty sweeping range.) The indictment charges him with "being the head of an insurrection against the Countess of Derby in 1651, assuming the power unto himself, and depriving her Ladyship, his Lordship, and heirs thereof."

A series of depositions appear on record from the 3d to the 13th October, and a reference by the precious depositaries of justice of that day, to the twenty-four Keys,† "Whether upon the examination taken and read before, you find Mr W. Christian of Ronaldsway, within compass of the statute of the year 1422,—that is, to receive a sentence *without quest*, or to be tried in the ordinary course of law." This body, designated on the record "so many of the Keys as were then present," were in number seventeen; but not being yet sufficiently select to approve of *sentence without trial*, made their return, To be tried by course of law.

On the 26th November, it is recorded, that the Governor and Attorney-General having proceeded to the jail "with a guard of soldiers, to require him (Christian) to the bar to receive his trial, he refused, and denied to come, and abide the same"—(admirable courtesy to invite, instead of bringing him to the bar!) Whereupon the Governor demanded the law of Deemster Norris, who then sat in judication. Deemster John Christian having not appeared, and Mr Edward Christian,‡ his son, and assistant, having also *forborne to sit* in this Court, he the said Deemster Norris craved the advice and assistance of the twenty-four Keys; and the said Deemster and Keys deemed the law therein, to wit, that he is at the mercy of the Lord for life and goods.

It will be observed, that seven of the Keys were formerly absent, on what account we shall presently see. All this was very cleverly

* See the remark in Christian's dying speech, that the late Earl had been executed eight days before the insurrection.

† The court for criminal trials was composed of the governor and council (including the deemsters) and the keys, who also, with the lord, composed the three branches of the legislative body; and it was the practice in cases of doubt to refer points of customary law to the deemsters and keys.

‡ The grandson of *Evan*. It appears by the proceedings of the King in council, 1663, that "*he did, when the court refused to admit of the deceased William Christian's plea* of the Act of Indemnity, *make his protestation* against their *illegal proceedings*, and did withdraw himself, and came to England to solicit his Majesty, and implore his justice."

arranged by the following recorded order, 29th December—"*These of the twenty-four Keys are removed of that Company, in reference to my Honourable Lord's order in that behalf;*" enumerating seven names, not of the seventeen before mentioned, and naming seven others who "are sworn* in their places." The judicature is farther improved by transferring an eighth individual of the first seventeen to the council, and filling his place with another proper person. These facts have been related with some minuteness of detail for two reasons; 1st, Although nearly equalled by some of the subsequent proceedings, they would not be credited on common authority; and 2d, They render all comment unnecessary, and prepare the reader for any judgment, however extraordinary, to be expected from such a tribunal.

Then come the proceedings of the 29th December—The Proposals, as they are named, to the Deemsters,† and twenty-four Keys now assembled, "to be answered in point of law." 1st, Any malefactor, &c. being indicted, &c. and denying to abide the law of his country in that course, (notwithstanding any argument or plea he may offer for himself,) and thereupon deemed to forfeit body and goods, &c. whether he may afterwards obtain the same benefit, &c. &c.; to which, on the same day, they answered in the negative. It was found practicable, on the 31st, to *bring* the prisoner to the bar, to hear his sentence of being "*shot to death, that thereupon his life may depart from his body;*" which sentence was executed on the 2d of January, 1663.

That he made "an excellent speech" at the place of execution, is recorded, where we should little expect to find it, in the Parochial Register; the accuracy of that which has been preserved as such in the family of a clergyman, (and appears to have been printed on or before 1776,‡) rests chiefly on internal evidence; and on its accordance, in some material points, with facts suppressed or distorted in the Records, but established in the proceedings of the Privy Council. It is therefore given without abbreviation, and the material points of evidence in the voluminous depositions on both trials§

* The Commissioners of 1791 are in doubt regarding the time when, and the manner in which, the keys were first elected; this notable precedent had perhaps not fallen under their observation.

† Hugh Cannel was now added as a second Deemster.

‡ One of the copies in my possession is stated to be transcribed in that year from the printed speech, the other as stated in the text.

§ Both trials: the first is for the same purposes as the English grand jury, with this most especial difference, that evidence is admitted *for the prisoner*, and it thus becomes what it is frequently called, the first trial; the second, if the indictment be found, is in all respects like that by petty jury in England.

are extracted for reference in a note.*

The last speech of William Christian, Esq., who was executed 2d January 1662–3:

"Gentlemen, and the rest of you who have accompanied me this day to the gate of death, I know you expect I should say something at my departure; and indeed I am in some measure willing to satisfy

* This testimony will of course be received with due suspicion, and confronted with the only defence known, that of his dying speech. It goes to establish that Christian had placed himself at the head of an association, bound by a secret oath, to "withstand the Lady of Derby in her designs until she had yielded or condescended to their aggrievances;" among which grievances, during the Earl's residence, we find incidentally noticed, "the troop that was in the Isle and their free quarterage;" that he had represented her ladyship to have deceived him, by entering into negotiations with the Parliament, contrary to her promise to communicate with him in such a case; that Christian and his associates declared that she was about to sell them for twopence or threepence a-piece; that he told his associates, that he had entered into correspondence with Major Fox and the Parliament, and received their authority to raise the country; that in consequence of this insurrection her ladyship appointed commissioners to treat with others "*on the part of the country*," and articles of agreement were concluded (see the speech) which nowhere now appear; that on the appearance of Duckenfield's ships, standing for Ramsay Bay, one of the insurgents boarded them off Douglas, "to give intelligence of the condition of the country;" the disposable troops marched under the governor, Sir Philip Musgrave, for Ramsay; that when the shipping had anchored, a deputation of three persons, *viz.* John Christian, Ewan Curphey, and William Standish, proceeded on board, to negotiate for the surrender of the Island (where William was does not appear.) The destruction of the articles of agreement, and the silence of the records regarding the relative strength of the forces, leave us without the means of determining the degree of merit or demerit to be ascribed to these negotiators, or the precise authority under which they acted; but the grievances to be redressed, are cleared from every obscurity by the all-sufficient testimony of the terms demanded from the victors, "*that they might enjoy their lands and liberties as formerly they had;* and that it was demanded whether they asked any more, but nothing else was demanded that this examinant heard of." The taking of Loyal Fort near Ramsay, (commanded by a Major Duckenfield, who was made prisoner,) and of Peel Castle, appear on record; but nothing could be found regarding the *surrender of Castle Rushen, or of the Countess of Derby's subsequent imprisonment.* Had the often repeated tale, of William Christian having "treacherously seized upon the lady and her children, with the governors of both castles, in the middle of the night"—(Rolt's History of the Isle of Man, published in 1773, p. 89)—rested on the slightest semblance of truth, we should inevitably have found an attempt to prove it in the proceedings of this mock trial. In the absence of authentic details, the tradition may be adverted to, that her ladyship, on learning the proceedings at Ramsay, hastened to embark in a vessel she had prepared, but was intercepted before she could reach it. The same uncertainty exists with regard to any negotiations on her part, with the officers of the Parliament, as affirmed by the insurgents; the Earl's first letter, after his capture and before his trial, says, "Truly, as matters go, it will be best for you to make conditions for yourself, children, and friends, in the manner as we have proposed, or as you can farther agree with Col. Duckenfield; who being so much a gentleman born, will doubtless, for his own honor, deal fairly with you." He seems also to have hoped at that time that it might influence his own fate: and the eloquent and affecting letter written immediately before his execution, repeats the same admonitions *to treat*. Rolt, pp. 74 and 84.

you, having not had the least liberty, since my imprisonment, to acquaint any with the sadness of my sufferings, which flesh and blood could not have endured, without the power and assistance of my most gracious and good God, into whose hands I do now commit my poor soul, not doubting but that I shall very quickly be in the arms of his mercy.

"I am, as you now see, hurried hither by the power of *a pretended court of justice*, the members whereof, or at least the greatest part of them, are by no means qualified, but very ill befitting their new places. The reasons you may give yourselves.

"The cause for which I am brought hither, as the *prompted* and *threatened* jury has delivered, is high treason against the Countess Dowager of Derby, for that I did, as they say, in the year fifty-one, raise a force against her for the suppressing and rooting out that family. How unjust the accusation is, very few of you that hear me this day but can witness; and *that the then rising of the people*, in which afterwards I came to be engaged, did not at all, or in the least degree, intend the prejudice or ruin of that family; *the chief whereof being, as you well remember, dead eight days, or thereabout, before that action happened.* But the true cause of that rising, as* *the jury did twice bring in*, was to present grievances to our Honourable Lady; which was done by me, and afterwards approved by her Ladyship, under the hand of her then secretary, M. Trevach, who is yet living, *which agreement hath since, to my own ruin and my poor family's endless sorrow, been forced from me.* The Lord God forgive them the injustice of their dealings with me, and I wish from my heart it may not be laid to their charge another day!

"You now see me here *a sacrifice ready to be offered up for that which was the preservation of your lives and fortunes which were then in hazard, but that I stood between you and your* (then in all appearance) *utter ruin*. I wish you still may, as hitherto, enjoy the sweet benefit and blessing of peace, though from that minute until now I have still been prosecuted and persecuted, nor have I ever since found a place to rest myself in. But my God be for ever blessed and praised, who hath given me so large a measure of patience!

"What services I have done for that Noble Family, by whose power I am now to take my latest breath, I dare appeal to themselves, whether I have not deserved better things from some of them, than the sentence of my bodily destruction, and seizure of the poor estate my son ought to enjoy, being purchased and left him by his grandfather. It might have been much better had I not spent it in the service of my Honourable Lord of Derby and his family; these

* This fact, as might be expected, is not to be traced on the record of the trial.

things I need not mention to you, for that most of you are witnesses to it. I shall now beg your patience while I tell you here, in the presence of God, that I never in all my life acted any thing with intention to prejudice my Sovereign Lord the King, nor the late Earl of Derby, nor the now Earl; yet notwithstanding, *being in England at the time* of his sacred Majesty's happy restoration, I went to London, with many others, to have a sight of my gracious King, whom God preserve, and whom until then, I never had seen. But I was not long there when I was arrested upon an action of twenty thousand pounds, and clapped up in the Fleet; unto which action, I being a stranger, could give no bail, but was there kept nearly a whole year. How I suffered God he knows; but at last, having gained my liberty, I thought good to advise with several gentlemen concerning his Majesty's gracious Act of Indemnity that was then set forth, in which I thought myself concerned; unto which they told me, there was no doubt to be made but that all actions committed in the Isle of Man, relating in any kind to the war, were pardoned by the Act of Indemnity, and all other places within his Majesty's dominions and countries. Whereupon, and having been forced to absent myself from my poor wife and children near three years, being all that time under persecution, I did with great content and satisfaction return into this Island, hoping then to receive the comfort and sweet enjoyment of my friends and poor family. But alas! I have fallen into the snare of the fowler; but my God shall ever be praised,—though he kill me, yet will I trust in him.

"I may justly say no man in this Island knows better than myself the power the Lord Derby hath in this Island, subordinate to his sacred Majesty, of which *I have given a full account in my declaration presented to my judges, which I much fear will never see light,* which is no small trouble to me.*

"It was his Majesty's most gracious Act of Indemnity gave me the confidence and assurance of my safety; on which, and an appeal I made to his sacred Majesty and Privy Council, from the unjustness of the proceedings had against me, I did much rely, being his Majesty's subject here, and a denizen of England both by birth and fortune. And *in regard I have disobeyed the power of my Lord of Derby's Act of Indemnity, which you now look upon, and his Majesty's Act cast out as being of no force*, I have with greater violence been persecuted; yet nevertheless I do declare, that no subject whatever can or ought to take upon them acts of indemnity but his sacred Majesty only, with the confirmation of Parliament.

"It is very fit I should say something as to my education and

* The apprehension was but too correct.

religion. I think I need not inform you, for you all know, I was brought up a son of the Church of England, which was at that time in her splendour and glory; and to my endless comfort I have ever since continued a faithful member, witness several of my actions in the late times of liberty. And as for government, I never was against monarchy, which now, to my soul's great satisfaction, I have lived to see is settled and established. I am well assured that men of upright life and conversation may have the favourable countenance of our gracious King, under whose happy government, God of his infinite mercy long continue these his kingdoms and dominions. And now I do most heartily thank my good God that I have had so much liberty and time to disburden myself of several things that have laid heavy upon me all the time of my imprisonment, in which I have not had *time or liberty to speak or write* any of my thoughts; and from my soul I wish all animosity may after my death be quite laid aside, and my death by none be called in question, for I do freely forgive all that have had any hand in my persecution; and may our good God preserve you all in peace and quiet the remainder of your days!

"Be ye all of you his Majesty's liege people, loyal and faithful to his sacred Majesty; and, according to your oath of faith and fealty to my Honourable Lord of Derby, *do you likewise, in all just and lawful ways, observe* his commands; and know that you must one day give an account of all your deeds. And now the blessing of Almighty God be with you all, and preserve you from violent death, and keep you in peace of conscience all your days!

"I will now hasten, for my flesh is willing to be dissolved, and my spirit to be with God, who hath given me full assurance of his mercy and pardon for all my sins, of which his unspeakable goodness and loving kindness my poor soul is exceedingly satisfied."

*Note.** Here he fell upon his knees, and passed some time in prayer; then rising exceedingly cheerful, he addressed the soldiers appointed for his execution, saying—"Now for you, who are appointed by lot my executioners, I do freely forgive you." He requested them and all present to pray for him, adding, "There is but a thin veil betwixt me and death; once more I request your prayers, for now I take my last farewell."

The soldiers wished to bind him to the spot on which he stood. He said, "Trouble not yourselves or me; for I that dare face death in whatever form he comes, will not start at your fire and bullets; nor can the power you have deprive me of my courage." At his desire a piece of white paper was given him, which with the utmost

* This note is annexed to all the copies of the speech.

composure he pinned to his breast, to direct them where to aim; and after a short prayer addressed the soldiers thus—"Hit this, and you do your own and my work." And presently after, stretching forth his arms, which was the signal he gave them, he was shot through the heart and fell.

Edward Christian, the nephew, and George, the son of the deceased, lost no time in appealing to his Majesty in Council against this judicial murder; and George was furnished with an order "to pass and repass," &c. "and bring with him such records and persons as he should desire, to make out the truth of his complaint." Edward returned with him to the Island for that purpose; for we find him, in April 1663, compelled, in the true spirit of the day, to give bond "that he would at all times appear and answer to such charges as might be preferred against him, and *not depart the Isle without license*." George was prevented, by various contrivances, from serving the King's order; but on presenting a second petition, the Governor, Deemster, and Members of Council, were brought up to London by a Sergeant-at-Arms; and these six persons, together with the Earl of Derby, being compelled to appear, a full hearing took place before the King in person, the Chancellor, the Lord Chief Justice, Lord Chief Baron, and other Members of Council; judgment was extended on the 5th August, and that judgment was on the 14th of the same month ordered "to be printed in folio, in such manner as Acts of Parliament are usually printed, and his Majesty's Arms prefixed."

This *authentic document* designates the persons brought up as "*Members of the pretended Court of Justice;*" declares "that the general Act of Pardon and Amnesty did extend to the Isle of Man, and ought to have been taken notice of by the Judges in that Island, *although it had not been pleaded;* that the Court *refused to admit* the deceased William Christian's *plea* of the Act of Indemnity," &c. "Full restitution is ordered to be made to his heirs of all his estates, real and personal." Three* other persons "who were by the same Court of Justice imprisoned, and their estates *seized and confiscated without any legal trial*," are ordered, together with the Christians, "to be restored to all their estates, real and personal, and to be fully repaired in all the charges and expenses which they have been at since their first imprisonment, as well in the prosecution of this business, as in their journey hither, or in any other way thereunto relating." The mode of raising funds for the purposes of this restitution is equally peculiar and instructive; these "sums of money are ordered to be furnished by the Deemsters, Members, and Assistants

* Ewan Curphey, Samuel Ratcliffe, and John Cæsar, men of considerable landed property.

of the said Court of Justice," who are directed "to raise and make due payment thereof to the parties."

"And to the end that the blood that has been unjustly spilt may in some sort be expiated," &c., the Deemsters are ordered to be committed to the King's Bench to be proceeded against, &c. &c., and receive condign punishment. [It is believed that this part of the order was afterwards relaxed or rendered nugatory.] The three Members of Council were released on giving security to appear, if required, and to make the restitution ordered. "And in regard that Edward Christian, being one of the Deemsters or Judges in the Isle of Man, *did, when the Court refused to admit of the deceased W. Christian's plea of the Act of Indemnity, make his protestation against their illegal proceedings, and did withdraw himself, and come to England to solicit his Majesty and implore his justice*, it is ordered that the Earl of Derby do forthwith, by commission, &c., restore and appoint him as Deemster, so to remain and continue," &c. [which order was disobeyed.] And lastly, that Henry Nowell, Deputy Governor, whose fault hath been *the not complying with*, and *yielding due obedience to, the order* of his Majesty and this Board sent into the Island*, [O most lame and impotent conclusion!] be permitted to return to the Isle, and enforce the present Order of the King in Council."

Of the Earl of Derby no farther mention occurs in this document. The sacrifices made by this noble family in support of the royal cause, drew a large share of indulgence over the exceptionable parts of their conduct; but the mortification necessarily consequent on this appeal, the incessant complaints of the people, and the difficulty subsequently experienced by them in obtaining access to a superior tribunal, receive a curious illustration in an order of the King in council, dated 20th August, 1670, on a petition of the Earl of Derby, "that the clerk of the council in waiting receive no petition, appeal, or complaint, *against the lord or government of the Isle of Man*, without having first good security from the complainant to answer costs, damages and charges."

The historical notices of this kingdom† of Lilliput are curious and instructive with reference to other times and different circumstances, and they have seemed to require little comment or antiquarian remark; but to condense what may be collected with regard to

* Tradition, in accordance with the dirge of William Dhône, says that the order to stop proceedings and suspend the sentence arrived on the day preceding that of his execution.

† Earl James, although studious of kingcraft, assigns good reasons for having never pretended to assume that title, and among others, "Nor doth it please a king that any of his subjects should too much love that name, were it but to act it in a play."—Peck, 436.

Edward Christian, the accomplished villain of Peveril, the insinuations of his accuser* constitute in themselves an abundant defence. When so little can be imputed by such an adversary, the character must indeed be invulnerable. Tradition ascribes to him nothing but what is amiable, patriotic, honourable, and good, in all the relations of public and private life. He died, after an imprisonment of seven or eight years, the victim of incorrigible obstinacy, according to one, of ruthless tyranny, according to another vocabulary; but resembling the character of the Novel in nothing but unconquerable courage.

Treachery and ingratitude have been heaped on the memory of William Christian with sufficient profusion. Regarding the first of these crimes: if all that has been affirmed or insinuated in the mock trial, rested on a less questionable basis, posterity would scarcely pronounce an unanimous verdict of moral and political guilt, against an association to subvert such a government as is described by its own author. The *peculiar* favours for which he or his family were ungrateful, are not to be discovered in these proceedings; except, indeed, in the form of "chastisements of the Almighty—blessings in disguise." But if credit be given to the dying words of William Christian, his efforts were strictly limited to a redress of grievances,—a purpose always criminal in the eye of the oppressor. If he had lived and died on a larger scene, his memory would probably have survived among the patriots and the heroes. In some of the manuscript narratives he is designated as a *martyr* for the rights and liberties of his countrymen; who add, in their homely manner, that he was condemned without trial, and murdered without remorse.

We have purposely abstained from all attempt to enlist the passions in favour of the sufferings of a people, or in detestation of oppressions, which ought, perhaps, to be ascribed as much to the character of the times as to that of individuals. The naked facts of the case (unaided by the wild and plaintive notes in which the maidens of the isle were wont to bewail "*the† heart-rending death of fair-haired William*") are sufficient of themselves to awaken the sympathy of every generous mind; and it were a more worthy exercise of that despotic power over the imagination, so eminently possessed by the Great Unknown, to embalm the remembrance of two such men in his immortal pages, than to load their memories with crimes, such as no human being ever committed.

---

* Peck, passim.

† The literal translation given to me by a young lady.

I AM enabled to add the translation of the lament over the fair-haired William Christian. It is originally composed in the Manx language, and consists of a series of imprecations of evil upon the enemies of Christian, and prophecies to the same purpose:—

On the Death and Murder of Receiver-General William Christian of Ronaldsway, who was shot near Hango Hill, January 2, 1662.

1.

In so shifting a scene, who would confidence place
In family power, youth, or in personal grace?
No character's proof against enmity foul;
And thy fate, William Dhône, sickens our soul.

2.

You are Derby's receiver of patriot zeal,
Replete with good sense, and reputed genteel,
Your justice applauded by the young and the old;
And thy fate, &c.

3.

A kind, able patron both to church and to state—
What roused their resentment but talents so great?
No character's proof against enmity foul;
And thy fate, &c.

4.

Thy pardon, 'tis rumour'd, came over the main,
Nor late, but conceal'd by a villain* in grain;
'Twas fear forced the jury to a sentence so foul;
And thy fate, &c.

5.

Triumphant stood Colcott, he wish'd for no more,
When the pride of the Christians lay welt'ring in gore,
To malice a victim, though steady and bold;
And thy fate, &c.

6.

With adultery stain'd, and polluted with gore,
He Ronaldsway eyed, as Loghuecolly before,
'Twas the land sought the culprit, as Ahab before;
And thy fate, &c.

7.

Proceed to the once famed abode of the Nuns,
Call the Colcotts aloud, till you torture your lungs,
Their short triumph's ended, extinct is the whole;
And thy fate, &c.

* A person named in the next stanza is said to have intercepted a pardon sent from England for William Christian, found, it is said, in the foot of an old woman's stocking. The tradition is highly improbable. If Christian had been executed against the tenor of a pardon actually granted, it would not have failed to be charged as a high aggravation in the subsequent proceedings of the Privy Council.

8.
For years could Robert lay crippled in bed,
Nor knew the world peace while he held up his head,
The neighbourhood's scourge in iniquity bold;
And thy fate, &c.

9.
Not one's heard to grieve, seek the country all through,
Nor lament for the name that Bemacan once knew;
The poor rather load it with curses untold;
And thy fate, &c.

10.
Ballaclogh and the Criggans mark strongly their sin,
Not a soul of the name's there to welcome you in;
In the power of the strangers is centred the whole;
And thy fate, &c.

11.
The opulent Scarlett on which the sea flows,
Is piecemeal disposed of to whom the Lord knows;
It is here without bread or defence from the cold;
And thy fate, &c.

12.
They assert then in vain, that the law sought thy blood,
For all aiding the massacre never did good;
Like the rooted-up golding deprived of its gold,
They languish'd, were blasted, grew wither'd and old.

13.
When the shoots of a tree so corrupted remain,
Like the brier or thistle, they goad us with pain;
Deep, dark, undermining, they mimic the mole;
And thy fate, &c.

14.
Round the infamous wretches who spilt Cæsar's blood,
Dead spectres and conscience in sad array stood,
Not a man of the gang reach'd life's utmost goal;
And thy fate, &c.

15.
Perdition, too, seized them who caused *thee* to bleed,
To decay fell their houses, their lands and their seed
Disappear'd like the vapour when morn's tinged with gold;
And thy fate, &c.

16.
From grief all corroding, to hope I'll repair,
That a branch of the Christians will soon grace the chair,
With royal instructions his foes to console;
And thy fate, &c.

17.

With a book for my pillow, I dreamt as I lay,
That a branch of the Christians would hold Ronaldsway;
His conquests his topic with friends o'er a bowl;
And thy fate, &c.

18.

And now for a wish at concluding my song,—
May th' Almighty withhold me from doing what's wrong;
Protect every mortal from enmity foul,
For thy fate, William Dhône, sickens our soul!*

APPENDIX No. II

At the Court of Whitehall, the 5th August, 1663.

GEORGE CHRISTIAN, son and heir of William Christian, deceased, having exhibited his complaint to his Majesty in Council, that his father, being at a house of his in his Majesty's Isle of Man, was imprisoned by certain persons of that island, pretending themselves to be a Court of Justice; that he was by them accused of high treason, pretended to be committed against the Countess Dowager of Derby, in the year 1651; and that they thereupon proceeded to judgment, and caused him to be put to death, notwithstanding the act of General Pardon and Indemnity, whereof he claimed the benefit: and his appeal to his Majesty, and humbly imploring his Majesty's princely compassion towards the distressed widow and seven fatherless children of the deceased: His Majesty was graciously pleased, with the advice of his Council, to order that Thomas Noris and Hugh Cannell, the two judges, (by them in that island called Deemsters,) and Richard Stevenson, Robert Calcot, and Richard Tyldesley, three of the members of the pretended Court of Justice, and Henry Howell, deputy of the said island, should be forthwith sent for, and brought up by a sergeant-at-arms here, before his Majesty in Council, to appear and answer to such accusations as should be exhibited against them; which said six persons being accordingly brought hither the fifteenth day of July last appointed for a full hearing of the whole business, the Earl of Derby then also summoned to appear, and the Lord Chief Justice of the King's Bench, and the Lord Chief-Baron of his Majesty's Exchequer, with the King's Council, learned in the laws, required to be present, and all the parties called in with their counsel and witnesses, after full hearing of the matter on both sides, and the parties withdrawn, the said judges being desired to deliver their

* It may be recollected, that these verses are given through the medium of a meagre translation, and are deprived of the aid of the music, otherwise we should certainly think the memory of William Dhône little honoured by his native bard.

opinion, did, in presence of the King's Council, learned in the laws, declare that the Act of General Pardon and Indemnity did, and ought to be understood to, extend to the Isle of Mann, as well as into any other of his Majesty's dominions and plantations beyond the seas; and that, being a publique General Act of Parliament, it ought to have been taken notice of by the Judges in the Isle of Mann, although it had not been pleaded, and although there were no proclamations made thereof. His Majesty being therefore deeply sensible of this violation of his Act of General Pardon, whereof his Majesty hath always been very tender, and doth expect and require that all his subjects in all his dominions and plantations shall enjoy the full benefit and advantage of the same; and having this day taken the business into further consideration, and all parties called in and heard, did, by and with the advice of the Council, order, and it is hereby ordered, that all persons any way concerned in the seizure of the estate of the said William Christian, deceased, or instrumental in the ejection of the widow and children out of their houses and fortune, do take care that entire restitution is to be made of all the said estate, as well real or personal, as also all damages sustained, with full satisfaction for all profits by them received since the said estate hath been in their hands; and that, whereas the said William Christian, deceased, was one of the two lives remaining in an estate in Lancashire, that the detriment accruing by the untimely death of the said William Christian therein, or in like cases, shall be estimated, and in like manner fully repaired. That in regard of the great trouble and charges the complainants have been at in pursuit of this business, ordered, that they do exhibit to this Board a true account, upon oath, of all expences and damages by them sustained in the journies of themselves and witnesses, and of all other their charges in the following of this business.

And whereas Ewan Curghey, Sammual Radcliffe, and John Casar, were by the same Court of Justice imprisoned, and had their estates seized and confiscated, without any legal trial, it is ordered, that the said Ewan Curghey, Sammual Radcliffe, and John Casar, be likewise reinstated to all their estates, real and personall, and fully repaired in all the charges and expences which they have been at since their first imprisonment, as well in the prosecution of this business, as in their journey thither, or any other way whatsoever thereunto relating. The which satisfaction, expences, and all the sums of money to be raised by virtue of this order, are to be furnished by the Deemsters, Members, and Assistants of the said Court of Justice, who are hereby ordered to raise all such the said sums, and thereof to make due payment, and give full satisfaction unto the parties respectively hereby appointed to receive it.

And to the end, the guilt of blood which hath been unjustly spilt, may in some sort be expiated, and his Majesty receive some kind of satisfaction for the untimely loss of a subject, it is ordered, that the said Thomas Norris and Hugh Cannell, who decreed this violent death, be committed, and remain prisoners in the King's Bench, to be proceeded against in the ordinary course of justice, so to receive condign punishment according to the merit of so heinous a fact.

That Richard Stevenson, Robert Calcot, and Richard Tyldesley, be discharged from farther restraint, giving good security to appear at this Board whensoever summoned, and not depart this city until full satisfaction be given, and all orders of this Board whatsoever relating to this business fully executed in the island. And in regard, that upon the examination of this business, it doth appear, that Edward Christian, being one of the Deemsters or Judges in the Isle of Mann, did, when the Court refused to admit of the deceased William Christian's plea of the Act of Indemnity, make his protestation against their illegal proceedings, and did withdraw himself, and come into England to solicit his Majesty, and implore his justice, it is ordered, that the Earl of Derby do forthwith, by commission, in due and accustomed manner, restore, constitute, and appoint the said Edward Christian, one of the Deemsters or Judges of the said island so to remain and continue in the due execution of the said place.

And lastly, it is ordered that the said Henry Howell, Deputy-Governour, whose charge hath been the not complying with, and yielding due obedience to, the orders of his Majesty, and this Board sent into this island, giving good security to appear at this Board whensoever summoned, be forthwith discharged from all further restraint, and permitted to return into the island; and he is hereby strictly commanded to employ the power and authority he hath, which by virtue of his commission he hath in that island, in performance of, and obedience to, all commands and orders of his Majesty and this Board in this whole business, or any way relating thereunto.

(Signed by)

LORD CHANCELLOR.	EARL OF CARBERRY.
LORD TREASURER.	LORD BISHOP OF LONDON.
LORD PRIVY SEAL.	LORD WENTWORTH.
DUKE OF ALBEMARLE.	LORD BERKELEY.
LORD CHAMBERLAIN.	LORD ASHLEY.

EARL OF BERKSHIRE.
EARL OF ST ALBAN.
EARL OF ANGLESEY.
EARL OF SANDWICH.
EARL OF BATH.
EARL OF MIDDLETON.
SIR WILLIAM CROMPTON.
MR TREASURER.
MR VICE CHAMBERLAIN.
MR SECRETARY MORICE.
MR SECRETARY BENNETT.

RICHARD BROWNE,
Clerk of the Council.

APPENDIX No. III

At the Court at Whitehall, August 14th, 1663.

Present.

THE KING'S MOST EXCELLENT MAJESTY.

LORD CHANCELLOR.
LORD TREASURER.
LORD PRIVY SEAL.
DUKE OF BUCKINGHAM.
DUKE OF ALBEMARLE.
LORD CHAMBERLAIN.
EARL OF BERKSHIRE.
EARL OF ST ALBAN.
EARL OF SANDWICH.
EARL OF ANGLESEY.
EARL OF BATH.
EARL OF MDDLETON.
EARL OF CARBERRY.
LORD BISHOP OF LONDON.
LORD WENTWORTH.
LORD BERKELEY.
LORD ASHLEY.
SIR WILLIAM CROMPTON.
MR TREASURER.
MR VICE CHAMBERLAIN.
MR SECRETARY MORICE.
MR SECRETARY BENNETT.

TO the end the world may the better take notice of his Majesty's royal intention, to observe the Act of Indemnity and General Pardon inviolably for the publique good and satisfaction of his subjects —it was this day ordered, that a copy of the order of this Board of the 5th inst., touching the illegal proceedings in the Isle of Mann against William Christian, and putting him to death contrary to the said Act of General Pardon, be sent unto his Majesty's printer, who is commanded forthwith to print the same in the English letters, in folio, in such manner as Acts of Parliament are usually printed, and his Majesty's Arms prefixed.

RICHARD BROWNE.

Notes to Peveril of the Peak

7.24 (Prefatory Letter) select bibliomaniacs The author has pride in recording, that he had the honour to be elected a member of this distinguished association, merely as the Author of Waverley, without any other designation; and it was an additional inducement to throw off the mask of an anonymous author, that it gives him the right to occupy the vacant chair at that festive board.

10.39 (Prefatory Letter) in fairy fiction dressed The Doctor has denied the author's title to shelter himself under this quotation: but the author continues to think himself entitled to all the shelter, which, threadbare as it is it may yet be able to afford him. The *truth severe* applies not to the narrative itself, but to the moral it conveys, in which the author has not been thought deficient. The "fairy fiction" is the conduct of the story which the tale is invented to elucidate.

31.24 (Ch. 3) Eldon-hole A chasm in the earth supposed to be unfathomable, one of the wonders of the Peak.

47.28 (Ch. 4) silvered by the planet

CAVALIERS AND ROUNDHEADS. The attempt at contrasting the manners of the jovial Cavaliers, and enthusiastic, yet firm and courageous, Puritans, was partly taken from a hint of Shadwell, who sketched several scenes of humour with great force, although they hung heavy on his pencil when he attempted to finish them for the stage.

In a dull play named the Volunteers, or the Stock-Jobbers, the *dramatis personæ* present "Major-General Blunt, an old cavalier officer, somewhat rough in speech, but very brave and honest, and of good understanding, and a good patriot." A contrast to the General is "Colonel Hackwell, senior, an old Anabaptist Colonel of Cromwell's, very stout and godly, but somewhat immoral."

These worthies, so characterised, hold a dialogue together, which will form a good example of Shadwell's power of dramatizing. The stage is filled by Major-General Blunt and some of his old acquaintance cavaliers, and Hackwell, the ancient parliamentarian.

"*Major-General Blunt*. Fear not, my old cavaliers. According to your laudable customs, you shall be drunk, swagger, and fight over all your battles, from Edgehill to Brentford. You have not forgotten how this gentleman (*points to Colonel Hackwell*) and his demure psalm-singing fellows used to drub us?

"*1st Cavalier*. No, 'gad! I felt 'em once to purpose.

"*M.-G. Blunt*. Ah! a-dod, in high-crowned hats, collared bands, great loose coats, long tucks under 'em, and calves-leather boots, they used to sing a psalm, fall on, and beat us to the devil!

"*Hackwell, senior*. In that day we stood up to the cause; and the cause, the spiritual cause, did not suffer under our carnal weapons, but the enemy was discomfited, and lo! they used to flee before us.

"*1st Cavalier.* Who would think such a snivelling, psalm-singing puppy, would fight? But these godly fellows would lay about 'em as if the devil were in 'em.

"*Sir Nicholas.* What a filthy slovenly army was this! I warrant you not a well-dressed man among the Roundheads.

"*M.-G. Blunt.* But these plain fellows would so thrash your swearing, drinking, fine fellows in laced coats—just such as you of the drawing-room and Locket's fellows are now—and so strip them, by the Lord Harry, that after a battle those saints looked like the Israelites loaden with the Egyptian baggage.

"*Hackwell.* Verily, we did take the spoil; and it served us to turn the penny, and advanced the cause thereby; we fought upon a principle that carried us through.

"*M.-G. Blunt.* Prithee, Colonel, we know thy principle—'twas not right: thou foughtest against children's baptism, and not for liberty, but who should be your tyrant; none so zealous for Cromwell as thou wert then, nor such a furious agitator and test-man as thou hast been lately.

"*Hackwell, senior.* Look you, Colonel, we but proceeded in the way of liberty of worship.

"*M.-G. Blunt.* A-dod, there is something more in it. This was thy principle, Colonel—*Dominion is founded in grace, and the righteous shall inherit the earth.* And, by the Lord Harry, thou didst so; thou gottest three thousand pounds a-year by fighting against the Court, and I lost a thousand by fighting for it."—See *The Volunteers, or Stock-Jobbers*, SHADWELL'S *Works*, vol. iv., p. 437.

In a former scene, Hackwell, the old fanatic officer, conceiving himself offended by one of the *dramatis personæ*, says, with great *naïveté*—" I prithee, friend, put me not to use the carnal weapon in my own defence." Such are the traits of phraseology with which Shadwell painted the old Puritan officers, many of whom he—no mean observer of human nature—must have known familiarly.

49.21 (Ch. 5) a delusion

CONCEALMENT OF THE COUNTESS OF DERBY. The concealment and discovery of the Countess of Derby, is taken from a picturesque account of a similar event, described to me by the person by whom it was witnessed in childhood. This lady, by name Mrs Margaret Swinton, and a daughter of that ancient house, was a sister of my maternal grandmother, and of course my grandaunt. She was, as often happens on such occasions, our constant resource in sickness, or when we tired of noisy play, and closed around her to listen to her tales. As she might be supposed to look back to the beginning of the last century, the fund which supplied us with amusement often related to events of that period. I may here notice that she told me the unhappy story of the Bride of Lammermoor, being nearly related to the Lord President, whose daughter was the heroine of that melancholy tragedy.

The present tale, though of a different character, was also sufficiently striking, when told by an eyewitness. Aunt Margaret was, I suppose, seven or eight years old, when residing in the old mansion-house of Swinton, and already displayed the firmness and sagacity which distinguished her through life. Being one of a large family, she was, owing to slight indisposition, left at home one day when the rest of the family went to church, with Sir John and Lady Swinton, their parents. Before leaving the little invalid, she was strictly enjoined not to go into the parlour where the elder party had breakfasted. But when she found herself alone in the upper part of the house, the spirit of her great ancestress Eve took possession of my Aunt Margaret, and forth she went to examine the parlour in question. She was struck with admiration and fear at what she saw there. A lady, "beautiful exceedingly," was seated by the breakfast table, and employed in washing the dishes which had been used. Little Margaret would have had no doubt in accounting this singular vision an emanation from the angelical world, but for her employment, which she could not so easily reconcile to her ideas of angels.

The lady with great presence of mind, called the astonished child to her, fondled her with much tenderness, and judiciously avoiding to render the necessity of secrecy too severe, she told the girl she must not let any one know that she had seen her except her mother. Having allowed this escape-valve for the benefit of her curiosity, the mysterious stranger desired the little girl to look from the window of the parlour to see if her mother was returning from church. When she turned her head again, the fair vision had vanished, but by what means Miss Margaret was unable to form a conjecture.

Long watched, and eagerly wished for, the Lady Swinton at last returned from church, and her daughter lost no time in telling her extraordinary tale. "You were a very sensible girl, Peggy," answered her mother, "for if you had spoken of that poor lady to any one but me, it might have cost her her life. But now I will not be afraid of trusting you with any secret, and I will show you where the poor lady lives." In fact she introduced her to a concealed apartment opening by a sliding panel from the parlour, and showed her the lady in the hiding place, which she inhabited. It may be said, in passing, that there were few Scottish houses belonging to families of rank which had not such contrivances, the political incidents of the time often calling them into occupation.

The history of the lady of the closet was both melancholy and bloody, and though I have seen various accounts of the story, I do not pretend to distinguish the right edition. She was a young woman of extreme beauty, who had been married to an old man, a writer, named MacFarlane. Her situation, and perhaps her manners, gave courage to some who desired to be accounted her suitors. Among these was a young Englishman, named Cayley, who was a commissioner of Government upon the estates forfeited in the rebellion of 1715. In 1716, Mr Cayley visited this lady in her lodgings, when they quarrelled, either on account of his having offered her some violence, or, as another account said, because she reproached him with having boasted of former favours. It ended in her seizing upon a pair of pistols, which lay loaded in a closet, her husband intending to take them with him on a journey. The gallant commissioner approached with an air of drollery, saying, "What, madam, do you intend to perform a comedy?"—"You shall find it a tragedy," answered the lady; and fired both pistols, by which Commissioner Cayley fell dead.

She fled, and remained concealed for a certain time. Her claim of refuge in Swinton House, I do not know—it arose probably from some of the indescribable genealogical filaments which connect Scottish families. A very small cause would even at any time have been a reason for interfering between an individual and the law.

Whatever were the circumstances of Mrs MacFarlane's case, it is certain she returned, and lived and died in Edinburgh, without being brought to trial. Indeed, considering the times, there was no great wonder; for, to one strong party, the death of an English commissioner was not a circumstance to require much apology. The Swintons, however, could not be of that opinion, the family being of Presbyterian and Whig principles.

54.8 (Ch. 5) devotion to his king The Earl of Derby and King in Man was beheaded at Bolton-on-the-Moors, after having been made prisoner in a previous skirmish in Wiggan Lane.

58.12 (Ch. 5) a file of musketeers [The Magnum text reads: 'a file of musketeers in the common place of execution, called Hango-hill'.]

TRIAL AND EXECUTION OF CHRISTIAN. The reader will find, in an Appendix to the Introduction, an account of this tragedy, as related by one who may be said to favour the sufferer. It must be admitted, on the other hand, that Captain Christian's trial and execution were conducted according to the laws of the island. He was tried in all due form, by the Dempster, or chief judge, then named Norris, the Keys of the island, and other constituted authorities, making what is called a Tinwald court. This word, yet retained in many parts of Scotland, signifies *Vallis Negotii*, and is applied to those artificial mounds which were in ancient times assigned to the meeting of the inhabitants for holding their *Comitia*. It was pleaded that the articles of accusation against Christian were found fully relevant, and as he refused to plead at the bar, that he was, according to the Laws of Man, most justly sentenced to death. It was also stated that full time was left for appeal to England, as he was apprehended about the end of September, and not executed until the 2d January, 1662. These defences were made for the various officers of the Isle of Man called before the Privy Council, on account of Christian's death, and supported with many quotations from the Laws of the Island, and appear to have been received as a sufficient defence for their share in those proceedings.

I am obliged to the present reverend Vicar of Malew, for a certified extract to the following effect:—"Malew Burials, A.D. 1662. Mr William Christian of Ronalds-way, late receiver, was shot to death at Hango Hill, the 2d January. He died most penitently and couradgeously, made a good end, prayed earnestly, made an excellent speech, and the next day was buried in the chancell of kirk Malew."

It is certain that the death of William Christian made a very deep impression upon the minds of the islanders, and a Mr Calcell or Colquit was much blamed on the occasion. Two lesser incidents are worth preservation as occurring at his execution. The place on which he stood was covered with white blankets, that his blood might not fall on the ground; and, secondly, the precaution proved unnecessary, for, the musket wounds bleeding internally, there was no outward effusion of blood.

Many on the island deny Christian's guilt altogether, like his respectable descendant, the present Dempster; but there are others, and those men of judgment and respectability, who are so far of a different opinion, that they only allow the execution to have been wrong in so far as the culprit died by a military rather than a civil death. I willingly drop the veil over a transaction, which took place *flagrantibus odiis* at the conclusion of a civil war, when Revenge at least was awake if Justice slept.

63.32 (Ch. 6) directing eye This peculiar collocation of apartments may be seen at Haddon Hall, Derbyshire, once a seat of the Vernons, where, in the lady's pew in the chapel, there is a sort of scuttle, which opens into the kitchen, so that the good lady could ever and anon, without much interruption of her religious duties, give an eye that the roast-meat was not permitted to burn, and that the turn-broche did his duty.

66.39 (Ch. 6) more fortunate times Even down to a later period than that in which the tale is laid, the ladies of distinction had for their pages young gentlemen of distinguished rank, whose education proceeded within the family of their patroness. Anne, Duchess of Buccleuch and Monmouth, who in several respects laid claim to the honour due to royal blood, was, I believe, the last person of rank who kept up this old custom. A general officer distinguished in the American war was bred up as a page in her family. At present the youths whom we sometimes see in the capacity of pages of great ladies, are, I believe, mere lackeys.

87.41 (Ch. 8) the usurpation The ejection of the Presbyterian clergy took place on Saint Bartholomew's day, thence called Black Bartholomew. Two thousand Presbyterian pastors were on that day displaced and silenced throughout England. The preachers indeed had only the alternative to renounce their principles, or subscribe certain articles of uniformity. And to their great honour, Calamy, Baxter, and Reynolds, refused bishoprics, and many other Presbyterian ministers declined deaneries and other preferments, and submitted to deprivation in preference.

101.10 (Ch. 10) the Dobby's Walk Dobby is an old English name for a goblin.

107.12 (Ch. 10) a Catholic I have elsewhere noticed that this is a deviation from the truth—Charlotte, Countess of Derby, was a Huguenot.

108.34 (Ch. 10) a butt's length The celebrated insurrection of the Anabaptists and Fifth Monarchy men in London, in the year 1661.

109.18 (Ch. 10) circumstances of suspicion

PERSECUTION OF THE PURITANS. It is naturally to be supposed, that the twenty years' triumph of the puritans, and the violences towards the malignants, as they were wont to call the cavaliers, had generated many grudges and feuds in almost every neighbourhood, which the victorious royalists failed not to act upon, so soon as the Restoration gave them a superiority. Captain Hodgson, a parliamentary officer who wrote his own memoirs, gives us many instances of this. I shall somewhat compress his long-winded account of his sufferings.

"It was after the King's return to London, one night a parcel of armed men comes to my house at Coalley Hall, near Halifax, and in an unseasonable hour in the night demands entrance, and my servants having some discourse with them on the outside, they gave threatening language, and put their pistols in at the windows. My wife being with child, I ordered the doors to be opened, and they came in. After they had presented a pistol to my breast, they showed me their authority to apprehend me, under the hands and seals of two knights and deputy-lieutenants, 'for speaking treasonable words against the King.'" The ci-devant captain was conveyed to prison at Bradford, and bail refused. His prosecutor proved to be one Daniel Lyster, brother to the peace-officer who headed the troop for his apprehension. It seems that the prisoner Hodgson had once in former days bound over to his good behaviour this Daniel Lyster, then accused of adultery and other debauched habits. "After the King came in," says Hodgson, "this man meets me, and demands the names of those that informed against him, and a copy of their information. I told him that the business was over, and that it was not reasonable to rip up old troubles, on which he threatened me, and said he would have them. 'The sun,' he said, 'now shines on our side of the hedge.'" Such being his accuser, Hodgson was tried for having said, "There is a crown provided, but the King will never wear it;" to which was added, that he alleged he had "never been a turncoat,—never took the oath of allegiance, and never would do." Little or no part of the charge was proved, while on the contrary it was shown that the prosecutor had been heard to say, that if times ever changed, he would sit on Hodgson's skirts. In fine, Hodgson escaped for five months' imprisonment, about thirty pounds expenses, and the necessity of swallowing the oath of allegiance, which seems to have been a bitter pill.

About the middle of June 1662, Captain Hodgson was again arrested in a summary manner by one Peebles an attorney, quarter-master to Sir John Armytage's troop of horse-militia, with about twelve other cavaliers, who used him rudely, called him rebel and traitor, and seemed to wish to pick a quarrel with him, upon which he demanded to see their authority. Peebles laid his hand on his sword, and told him it was better authority than any ever granted by Cromwell. They suffered him, however, to depart, which he partly owed to the valour of his landlady, who sate down at the table-end betwixt him and danger, and kept his antagonists at some distance.

He was afterwards accused of having assembled some troopers, from his having been accidentally seen riding with a soldier, from which accusation he also escaped. Finally, he fell under suspicion of being concerned in a plot, of which the scene is called Sowerby.

On this charge he is not explicit, but the grand jury found the bill ignoramus.

After this the poor Roundhead was again repeatedly accused and arrested; and the last occasion we shall notice occurred on 11th September, 1662, when he was disarmed by his old friend Mr Peebles, at the head of a party. He demanded to see the warrant; on which he was answered as formerly, by the quartermaster laying his hand on his sword-hilt, saying it was a better order than Oliver used to give. At length a warrant was produced, and Hodgson submitting to the search, they took from his dwelling house better than L.20 value in fowling-pieces, pistols, muskets, carbines, and such like. A quarrel ensued about his buff coat, which Hodgson refused to deliver, alleging they had no authority to take his wearing apparel. To this he remained constant, even upon the personal threats of Sir John Armytage, who called him rebel and traitor, and said, "If I did not send the buff coat with all speed, he would commit me to jail. I told him," says Hodgson, "I was no rebel, and he did not well to call me so before these soldiers and gentlemen, to make me the mark for every one to shoot at." The buff coat was then peremptorily demanded, and at length seized by open force. One of Sir John Armytage's brethren wore it for many years after, making good Prince Henry's observation, that a buff jerkin is a most sweet robe of durance. An agent of Sir John's came to compound for this garment of proof. Hodgson says he would not have taken ten pounds for it. Sir John would have given about four, but insisting on the owner's receipt for the money, which its former possessor was unwilling to grant, the tory magistrate kept both sides, and Hodgson never received satisfaction.

We will not prosecute Mr Hodgson's tale of petty grievances any farther. Enough has been said to display the melancholy picture of the country after the civil war, and to show the state of irritability and oppression which must have extended itself over the face of England, since there was scarce a county in which battles had not been fought, and deep injuries sustained, during the ascendency of the roundheads, which were not afterwards retaliated by the vengeance of the cavaliers.

110.29 (Ch. 11) (Magnum addition) [The Magnum adds several sentences to the first-edition paragraph: 'The islanders also, become too wise for happiness, had lost relish for the harmless and somewhat childish sports in which their simple ancestors had indulged themselves. May was no longer ushered in by the imaginary contest between the Queen of returning winter and advancing spring; the listeners no longer sympathized with the lively music of the followers of the one, or the discordant sounds with which the other asserted a more noisy claim to attention. Christmas, too, closed, and the steeples no longer jangled forth a dissonant peal. The wren, to seek for which used to be the sport dedicated to the holytide, was left unpursued and unslain. Party spirit had come among these simple people, and destroyed their good-humour, while it left them their ignorance. Even the races, a sport generally interesting to people of all ranks, were no longer performed, because they were no longer attractive. The gentlemen were divided by feuds hitherto unknown, and each seemed to hold it scorn to be pleased with the same diversions that amused those of the opposite faction. The hearts of both parties revolted from the recollection of former days, when all was peace among them, when the Earl of Derby, now slaughtered, used to bestow the prize, and Christian, since so vindictively executed, started horses to add to the amusement.*']

POPULAR PASTIMES IN THE ISLE OF MAN. Waldron mentions the two popular festivities in the Isle of Man which are alluded to in the text, and vestiges of them are, I believe, still to be traced in this singular island. The Contest of Winter and Summer seems directly derived from the Scandinavians, long the masters in Man, as Olaus Magnus mentions a similar festival among the northern nations. On the first of May, he says, the country is divided into two bands, the captain of one of which hath the name and appearance of Winter, is clothed in skins of beasts, and he and his band armed with fire forks. They fling about ashes, by way of prolonging the reign of Winter; while another band, whose captain is called Florro, represent Spring, with green boughs, such as the season offers. These parties skirmish in sport, and the mimic contest concludes with a general feast.—*History of the Northern Nations by* OLAUS, Book xv. Chap. 2.

Waldron gives an account of a festival in Man, exactly similar:

"In almost all the great parishes, they choose from among the daughters of the most wealthy farmers, a young maid, for the Queen of May. She is drest in the gayest and best manner they can, and is attended by about twenty others, who are called maids of honour. She has also a young man, who is her captain, and has under his command a good number of inferior officers. In opposition to her, is the Queen of Winter, who is a man drest in woman's clothes, with woollen hoods, fur tippets, and loaded with the warmest and heaviest habits, one upon another; in the same manner are those, who represent her attendants, drest; nor is she without a captain and troop for her defence. Both being equipt as proper emblems of the beauty of the spring, and the deformity of the winter, they set forth from their respective quarters; the one preceded by violins and flutes, the other with the rough music of the tongs and cleavers. Both companies march till they meet on a common, and then their trains engage in a mock battle. If the Queen of Winter's forces get the better, so far as to take the Queen of May prisoner, she is ransomed for as much as pays the expenses of the day. After this ceremony, Winter and her company retire, and divert themselves in a barn, and the others remain on the green, where having danced a considerable time, they conclude the evening with a feast; the queen at one table with her maids, the captain with his troop at another. There are seldom less than fifty or sixty persons at each board, but not more than three or four knives. Christmas is ushered in with a form much less meaning, and infinitely more fatiguing. On the 24th of December, towards evening, all the servants in general have a holiday; they go not to bed all night, but ramble about till the bells ring in all the churches, which is at twelve o'clock; prayers being over, they go to hunt the wren, and after having found one of these poor birds, they kill her, and lay her on a bier with the utmost solemnity, bringing her to the parish church, and burying her with a whimsical kind of solemnity, singing dirges over her in the Manx language, which they call her knell; after which Christmas begins. There is not a barn unoccupied the whole twelve days, every parish hiring fiddlers at the public charge; and all the youth, nay, sometimes people well advanced in years, making no scruple to be among these nocturnal dancers."—WALDRON'S *Description of the Isle of Man, folio*, 1731.

With regard to horse-racing in the Isle of Man, I am furnished with a certified copy of the rules on which that sport was conducted, under the permission of the Earl of Derby, in which the curious may see that a descendant of the unfortunate Christian entered a horse for the prize. I am indebted for this curiosity to my kind friend, the learned Dr Dibdin.

INSULA MONÆ. *Articles for the plate which is to be run for in the said island, being of the value of five pounds sterling, (the fashion included,) given by the Right Honourable William Earl of Derby, Lord of the said Isle, &c.*

"*1st.* The said plate is to be run for upon the 28th day of July, in euery year, whiles his honour is pleased to allow the same, (being the day of the nativity of the Honourable James Lord Strange,) except it happen upon a Sunday, and if soe, the said plate is to be run for upon the day following.

"*2d.* That noe horse, gelding, or mair, shall be admitted to run for the said plate, but such as was foaled within the said island, or in the Calfe of Mann.

"3*d.* That euery horse, gelding, or mair, that is designed to run, shall be entred at or before the viiijth day of July, with his masters name and his owne, if he be generally knowne by any, or els his collour, and whether horse, mair, or gelding, and that to be done at the x comprs. office, by the cleark of the rolls for the time being.

"4*th.* That euery person that puts in either horse, mair, or gelding, shall, at the time of their entring, depositt the sume of fiue shill. apiece into the hands of the said clerk of the rolls, which is to goe towards the augmenting of the plate for the year following, besides one shill. apiece to be giuen by them to the said clerk of the rolls, for entering their names, and engrossing these articles.

"5*th.* That euery horse, mair, or gelding, shall carry horseman's weight, that is to say, ten stone weight, at fourteen pounds to each stone, besides sadle and bridle.

"6*th.* That euery horse, mair, or gelding, shall haue a person for its tryer, to be named by the owner of the said horse, mair, or gelding, which tryers are to have the command of the scales and weights, and to see that euery rider doe carry full weight, according as is mentioned in the foregoing article, and especially that the winning rider be soe with the usual allowance of one pound for.

"7*th.* That a person be assigned by the tryers to start the runinge horses, who are to run for the said plate, betwixt the howers of one and three of the clock in the afternoon.

"8*th.* That euery rider shall leave the two first powles which are sett upp in Macybraes close, in this manner following, that is to say, the first of the said two powles upon his right hand, and the other upon his left hand; and the two powles by the rockes are to be left upon the left hand likewise; and the fifth powle, which is sett up at the lower end of the Conney-warren, to be left alsoe upon the left hand, and soe the turning powle next to Wm. Looreyes house to be left in like maner upon the left hand, and the other two powles, leading to the ending powle, to be left upon the right hand; all which powles are to be left by the riders as aforesaid, excepting only the distance-powle, which may be rid on either hand, at the discretion of the rider," &c. &c. &c.

"*July* 14*th*, 1687.

"The names of the persons who have entered their horses to run for the within plate for this present year, 1687.

"Ro. Heywood, Esq., Governor of this Isle, hath entered ane bay-gelding, called by the name of Loggerhead, and hath deposited towards the augmenting of the plate for the next year, L.00 05 00
"Captain Tho. Hudlston hath entered one white gelding, called Snowball, and hath depositted, 00 05 00
"Mr William Faigler bath entred his gray gelding, called the Gray-Carraine, and depositted, 00 05 00
"Mr Nicho. Williams hath entred one gray stone horse, called the Yorkshire gray, and depositted, 00 05 00
"Mr Demster Christian hath entred one gelding, called the Dapplegray, and hath depositted, 00 05 00

"*28th July*, 1687.

"MEMORANDUM,

"That this day the above plate was run for by the foremencioned horse, and the same was fairly won by the right worshipful governor's horse at the two first heates.

"*17th August*, 1688.

"Received this day the above , which I am to pay to my master to augment ye plate, by me,

"JOHN WOOD.

"It is my good-will and pleasure y^t ye 2 prizes formerly granted (by me) for hors runing and shouting, shall continue as they did, to be run, or shot for, and soe to continue dureing my good-will and pleasure. Given under my hand at Lathom, ye 12th of July, 1669.

DERBY.

"To my governor's deputy-governor, and ye rest of my officers in my Isle of Man."

114.31 (Ch.11) misfortune I am told that a portrait of the unfortunate William Christian is still preserved in the family of Waterson of Ballnahow of Kirk Church, Rushin. William Dhône is dressed in a green coat without collar or cape, after the fashion of those puritanic times, with the head in a close-cropt wig, resembling the bishop's peruke of the present day. The countenance is youthful and well looking, very unlike the expression of foreboding melancholy. I have so far taken advantage of this criticism, as to bring my ideal portrait in the present edition nearer to the complexion at least of the fair-haired William Dhône.

148.38 (Ch. 14) one of her noblest hearts

WHALLEY THE REGICIDE. There is a constant tradition in America, that this person, who was never heard of after the Restoration, fled to Massachusetts, and, living for some years concealed in that province, finally closed his days there. The remarkable and beautiful story of his having suddenly emerged from his place of concealment, and, placing himself at the head of a party of settlers, shown them the mode of acquiring a victory, which they were on the point of yielding to the Indians, is also told; and in all probability truly. I have seen the whole tradition commented upon at large in a late North American publication, which goes so far as to ascertain the obscure grave to which the remains of Whalley were secretly committed. This singular story has lately afforded the justly celebrated American novelist, Mr Cooper, the material from which he has compiled one of those impressive narratives with the aboriginal inhabitants of the Transatlantic woods and the hardy Europeans by whom they were invaded and dispossessed.

151.10 (Ch. 15) Sodor, or Holm-peel

SODOR, OR HOLM-PEEL, IN THE ISLE OF MAN. The author has never seen this ancient fortress, which has in its circuit so much that is fascinating to the antiquary. Waldron has given the following description, which is perhaps somewhat exaggerated:—

"Peel, or Pile-Town, is so called from its garrison and castle: though in effect the castle cannot properly be said to be in the town, an arm of the sea running between them, which in high tides would be deep enough to bear a ship of forty or fifty ton, though sometimes quite drained of salt water; but then it is supplied with fresh by a river which runs from Kirk Jarmyn Mountains, and empties itself into the sea. This castle, for its situation, antiquity, strength, and beauty, might justly come in for one of the wonders of the world. Art and nature seem to have vied with each other in the model, nor ought the most minute particular to escape observation. As to its situation, it is built upon the top of a huge rock, which rears itself a stupendous height above the sea, with which, as I said before, it is surrounded. And also by natural fortifications of other lesser rocks, which render it unaccessible but by passing that little arm of the sea which divides it from the town; this you may do in a small boat; and the natives, tucking up their clothes under their arms, and plucking off their shoes and stockings, frequently wade it in low tides. When you arrive at the foot of the rock, you ascend about some threescore steps, which are cut out of it to the first wall, which is immensely thick and high, and built of a very durable and bright stone, though not of the same sort with that of Castle Russin in Castle Town; and has on it four little houses, or watch-towers, which overlook the sea. The gates are wood, but most curiously arched, carved, and adorned with pilasters. Having passed the first, you have other stairs of near half the number with the former to mount, before you come at the second wall, which, as well as the other, is full of port-holes for cannon, which are planted on stone crosses on a third wall. Being entered, you find yourself in a wide plain, in the midst of which stands the castle, encompassed by four churches, three of which time has so much decayed, that there is little remaining, besides the walls, and some few tombs, which seem to have been erected with so much care, as to perpetuate the memory of those buried in them till the final dissolution of all things. The fourth is kept a little better in repair; but not so much for its own sake, though it has been the most magnificent of them all, as for a chapel within it; which is appropriated to the use of the bishop, and has under it a prison, or rather dungeon, for those offenders who are so miserable as to incur the spiritual censure. This is certainly one of the most dreadful places that imagination can form. The sea runs under it through the hollows of the rock with such a continual roar, that you would think it were every moment breaking in upon you, and over it are the vaults for burying the dead. The stairs descending to this place of terrors are not above thirty, but so steep and narrow, that they are very difficult to go down, a child of eight or nine years old not being able to pass them but sideways. Within it are thirteen pillars, on which the whole chapel is supported. They have a superstition, that whatsoever stranger goes to see this cavern out of curiosity, and omits to count the pillars, shall do something to occasion being confined there. There are places for penance also under all the other churches, containing several very dark and horrid cells; some have nothing in them either to sit or lie down on, others a small piece of brick work; some are lower and more dark than others, but all of them, in my opinion, dreadful enough for almost any crime humanity is capable of being guilty of; though 'tis supposed they were built with different degrees of horror, that the punishment might be proportionate to the faults of those wretches who were to be confined in them. These have never been made use of since the times of popery; but that under the bishop's chapel is the common and only prison for all offences in the spiritual court, and to that the delinquents are sentenced. But the soldiers of the garrison permit them to suffer their confinement in the castle, it being morally impossible for the strongest constitution to sustain the damps and noisomeness of the cavern even for a few hours, much less for months and years, as is the punishment sometimes allotted. But I shall speak hereafter more fully of the severity of the ecclesiastical jurisdiction. 'Tis certain that here have been very great architects in this island; for the noble monuments in this church, which is kept in repair, and indeed in the ruins of the others also, show the builders to be masters of all the orders in that art, though the great number of Doric pillars prove them to be chiefly admirers of that. Nor are the epitaphs and inscriptions on the tombstones less worthy of remark; the various languages in which they are engraved, testify by what a diversity of nations this little spot of earth has been possessed. Though time has defaced too many of the letters to render the remainder intelligible, yet you may easily perceive fragments of the Hebrew, Greek, Latin, Arabian, Saxon, Scotch and Irish characters; some dates yet visibly declare they were written before the coming of Christ; and, indeed, if one considers the walls, the thickness of them, and the durableness of the stone of which they are composed, one must be sensible that a great number of centuries must pass before such strong workmanship could be reduced to the condition it now is. These churches, therefore, were doubtless once the temples of Pagan deities, though since consecrated to the worship of the true divinity; and what confirms me more strongly in this conjecture, is, that there is still a part of one remaining, where stands a large stone directly in form and manner like the Triposes, which in those days of ignorance, the priests stood upon, to deliver their fabulous oracles. Through one of these old churches, there was formerly a passage to the apartment belonging to the captain of the guard, but is now closed up. The reason they give you for it, is a pretty odd one; but as I think it not sufficient satisfaction to my curious reader, to acquaint him with what sort of buildings this island affords, without letting him know also what traditions are concerning them, I shall have little regard to the censure of those critics, who find fault with every thing out of the common road; and in this, as well as in all other places, where it falls in my way, shall make it my endeavour to lead him into the humours and very souls of the Manx people. They say, that an apparition, called in their language the Mauthe Doog, in the shape of a large black spaniel with curled shaggy hair, was used to haunt Peel Castle, and has been frequently seen in every room, but particularly in the guard-chamber, where, as soon as candles were lighted, it came and lay down before the fire, in presence of all the soldiers, who at length, by being so much accustomed to the sight of it, lost great part of the terror they were seized with at its first appearance. They still, however, retained a certain awe, as believing it was an evil spirit which only waited permission to do them hurt, and for that reason forbore swearing and all profane discourse while in its company. But though they endured the shock of such a guest when all together in a body, none cared to be left alone with it; it being the custom, therefore, for one of the soldiers to lock the gates of the castle at a certain hour, and carry the keys to the captain, to whose apartment, as I said before, the way led through a church, they agreed among themselves, that whoever was to succeed the ensuing night, his fellow in this errand should accompany him that went first, and by this means, no man would be exposed singly to the danger; for I forgot to mention that the Mauthe Doog was always seen to come out from that passage at the close of day, and return to it again as soon as the morning dawned, which made them look on this place as its peculiar residence. One night a fellow being drunk, and by the strength of his liquor rendered more daring than ordinary, laughed at the simplicity of his companions, and though it was not his turn to go with the keys, would needs take that office upon him, to testify his courage. All the soldiers endeavoured to dissuade him, but the more they said, the more resolute he seemed, and swore that he desired nothing more than that Mauthe Doog would follow him, as it had done the others, for he would try if it were dog or devil. After having talked in a very reprobate manner for some time, he snatched up the keys, and went out of the guard-room; in some time after his departure a great noise was heard, but nobody had the boldness to see what occasioned it, till the adventurer returning, they demanded the knowledge of him; but as loud and noisy as he had been at leaving them, he was now become sober and silent enough, for he was never heard to speak more; and though all the time he lived, which was three days, he was entreated by all who came near him, either to speak, or, if he could not do that, to make some signs, by which they might understand what had happened to him, yet nothing intelligible could be got from him, only, that by the distortion of his limbs and features, it might be guessed that he died in agonies more than is common in a natural death. The Mauthe Doog was, however, never seen after in the castle, nor would any one attempt to go through that passage, for which reason it was closed up, and another way made. This accident happened about threescore years since, and I heard it attested by several, but especially by an old soldier, who assured me he had seen it oftener than he had then hairs on his head. Having taken notice of every thing remarkable in the churches, I believe my reader will be impatient to come to the castle itself, which, in spite of the magnificence the pride of modern ages has adorned the palaces of princes with, exceeds not only every thing I have seen, but also read of, in nobleness of structure. Though now no more than a garrison for soldiers, you cannot enter it without being struck with a veneration, which the most beautiful buildings of later years cannot inspire you with;

the largeness and loftiness of the rooms, the vast echo resounding through them, the many winding galleries, the prospect of the sea, and the ships, which, by reason of the height of the place, seem but like buoys floating on the waves, make you fancy yourself in a superior orb to what the rest of mankind inhabit, and fill you with contemplations the most refined and pure that the soul is capable of conceiving."—WALDRON'S *Description of the Isle of Man, folio*, 1731, p. 103.

In this description, the account of the inscriptions in so many Oriental languages, and bearing date before the Christian era, is certainly as much exaggerated as the story of the *Mauthe Doog* itself. It would be very desirable to find out the meaning of the word *Mauthe* in the Manx language, which is a dialect of the Gaelic. I observe, that Maithe in Gaelic, amongst other significations, has that of *active* or *speedy;* and also, that a dog of Richard II., mentioned by Froissart, and supposed to intimate the fall of his master's authority, by leaving him and fawning on Bolingbroke, was termed Mauthe; but neither of these particulars tends to explain the very impressive story of the fiendish hound of Peel Castle.

164.22 (Ch. 16) what is supernatural

MANX SUPERSTITIONS. The story often alludes to the various superstitions which are, or at least were, received by the inhabitants of the Isle of Man, an ancient Celtic race, still speaking the language of their fathers. They retained a plentiful stock of those wild legends which overawed the reason of a dark age, and in our own time annoy the imagination of those who listen to the fascination of the tale, while they despise its claims to belief. The following curious legendary traditions are extracted from Waldron, a huge mine, in which I have attempted to discover some specimens of spar, if I cannot find treasure.

"'Tis this ignorance," meaning that of the islanders, "which is the occasion of the excessive superstition which reigns among them. I have already given some hints of it, but not enough to show the world what a Manksman truly is, and what power the prejudice of education has over weak minds. If books were of any use among them, one would swear the Count of Gabalis had been not only translated into the Manks tongue, but that it was a sort of rule of faith to them, since there is no fictitious being mentioned by him, in his book of absurdities, which they would not readily give credit to. I know not, idolizers as they are of the clergy, whether they would not be even refractory to them, were they to preach against the existence of fairies, or even against their being commonly seen; for though the priesthood are a kind of gods among them, yet still tradition is a greater god than they; and as they confidently assert that the first inhabitants of their island were fairies, so do they maintain that these little people have still their residence among them. They call them the Good People, and say they live in wilds and forests, and on mountains, and shun great cities because of the wickedness acted therein; all the houses are blest where they visit, for they fly vice. A person would be thought impudently prophane, who should suffer his family to go to bed without having first set a tub, or pail, full of clean water, for these guests to bathe themselves in, which the natives aver they constantly do, as soon as ever the eyes of the family are closed, wherever they vouchsafe to come. If any thing happen to be mislaid, and found again in some place where it was not expected, they presently tell you a fairy took it and returned it; if you chance to get a fall and hurt yourself, a fairy laid something in your way to throw you down, as a punishment for some sin you have committed. I have heard many of them protest they have been carried insensibly great distances from home, and, without knowing how they came there, found themselves on the top of a mountain. One story in particular was told me of a man who had been led by invisible musicians for several miles together; and not being able to resist the harmony, followed till it conducted him to a large common, where were a great number of little people sitting round a table, and eating and drinking in a very jovial manner. Among them were some faces whom he thought he had formerly seen, but forbore taking any notice, or they of him, till the little people, offering him drink, one of them, whose features seemed not unknown to him, plucked him by the coat, and forbade him, whatever he did, to taste any thing he saw before him; for if you do, added he, you will be as I am, and return no more to your family. The poor man was much affrighted, but resolved to obey the injunction; accordingly a large silver cup, filled with some sort of liquor, being put into his hand, he found an opportunity to throw what it contained on the ground. Soon after the music ceasing, all the company disappeared, leaving the cup in his hand, and he returned home, though much wearied and fatigued. He went the next day and communicated to the minister of the parish all that had happened, and asked his advice how he should dispose of the cup; to which the parson replied, he could not do better than devote it to the service of the church; and this very cup, they tell me, is that which is now used for the consecrated wine in Kirk-Merlugh.

"Another instance they gave me to prove the reality of fairies, was of a fiddler, who, having agreed with a person, who was a stranger, for so much money, to play to some company he should bring him to, all the twelve days of Christmas, and received earnest for it, saw his new master vanish into the earth the moment he had made the bargain. Nothing could be more terrified than was the poor fiddler; he found he had entered himself into the devil's service, and looked on himself as already damned; but having recourse also to a clergyman, he received some hope; he ordered him, however, as he had taken earnest, to go when he should be called; but that whatever tunes should be called for, to play none but psalms. On the day appointed, the same person appeared, with whom he went, though with what inward reluctance 'tis easy to guess; but punctually obeying the minister's directions, the company to whom he played were so angry, that they all vanished at once, leaving him at the top of a high hill, and so bruised and hurt, though he was not sensible when, or from what hand he received the blows, that he got not home without the utmost difficulty. The old story of infants being changed in their cradles, is here in such credit, that mothers are in continual terror at the thoughts of it. I was prevailed upon myself to go and see a child, who they told me was one of these changelings; and, indeed, must own was not a little surprised, as well as shocked, at the sight: nothing under heaven could have a more beautiful face; but though between five and six years old, and seemingly healthy, he was so far from being able to walk or stand, that he could not so much as move any one joint; his limbs were vastly long for his age, but smaller than an infant's of six months; his complexion was perfectly delicate, and he had the finest hair in the world; he never spoke nor cried, eat scarce any thing, and was very seldom seen to smile; but if any one called him a fairy-elf, he would frown and fix his eyes so earnestly on those who said it, as if he would look them through. His mother, or at least his supposed mother, being very poor, frequently went out a-chairing, and left him a whole day together; the neighbours, out of curiosity, have often looked in at the window to see how he behaved when alone; which, whenever they did, they were sure to find him laughing, and in the utmost delight. This made them judge that he was not without company more pleasing to him than any mortals could be; and what made this conjecture seem the more reasonable, was, that, if he were left ever so dirty, the woman, at her return, saw him with a clean face, and his hair combed with the utmost exactness and nicety.

"A second account of this nature I had from a woman to whose offspring the fairies seemed to have taken a particular fancy. The fourth or fifth night after she was delivered of her first child, the family were alarmed with a most terrible cry of fire, on which every body ran out of the house to see whence it proceeded, not excepting the nurse, who, being as much frighted as the others, made one of the number. The poor woman lay trembling in her bed alone, unable to help herself, and her back being turned to the infant, saw not that it was taken away by an invisible hand. Those who had left her having enquired about the neighbourhood, and finding there was no cause for the outcry they had heard, laughed at each other for the mistake; but as they were going to re-enter the house, the poor babe lay on the threshold, and by its cries preserved itself from being trod upon. This exceedingly amazed all that saw it, and the mother being still in bed, they could ascribe no reason for finding it there, but having been removed by fairies, who, by their sudden return, had been prevented from carrying it any farther. About a year after, the same woman was brought to bed of a second child, which had not been born many nights before a great noise was heard in the house where they kept their cattle; (for in this island, where there is no shelter in the fields from the excessive cold and damps, they put all their milch-kine into a barn, which they call a cattle-house.) Every body that was stirring ran to see what was the matter, believing that the cows had got loose; the nurse was as ready as the rest, but, finding all safe, and the barn door close, immediately returned, but not so suddenly but that the new-born babe was taken out of the bed, as the former had been, and dropt on their coming, in the middle of the entry. This was enough to prove the fairies had made a second attempt; and the parents sending for a minister, joined with him in thanksgiving to God, who had twice delivered their children from being taken from them. But in the time of her third lying-in, every body seemed to have forgot what had happened in the first and second, and on a noise in the cattle-house, ran out to know what had occasioned it. The nurse was the only person, excepting the woman in the straw, who stay'd in the house, nor was she detained through care or want of curiosity, but by the bonds of sleep, having drank a little too plentifully the preceding day. The mother, who was broad awake, saw her child lifted out of the bed, and carried out of the chamber, though she could not see any person touch it; on which she cried out as loud as she could, Nurse, nurse! my child, my child is taken away! but the old woman was too fast to be awakened by the noise she made, and the infant was irretrievably gone. When her husband, and those who had accompanied him, returned, they found her wringing her hands, and uttering the most piteous lamentations for the loss of her child; on which, said the husband, looking into the bed, The woman is mad, do not you see the child lies by you? On which she turned, and saw indeed something like a child, but far different from her own, who was a very beautiful, fat, well-featured babe; whereas, what was now in the room of it, was a poor, lean, withered, deformed creature. It lay quite naked, but the clothes belonging to the child that was exchanged for it, lay wrapt up altogether on the bed. This creature lived with them near the space of nine years, in all which time it eat nothing except a few herbs, nor was ever seen to void any other excrement than water. It neither spoke, nor could stand or go, but seemed enervate in every joint, like the changeling I mentioned before, and in all its actions showed itself to be of the same nature.

"A woman, who lived about two miles distant from Ballasalli, and used to serve my family with butter, made me once very merry with a story she told me of her danghter, a girl of about ten years old, who being sent over the fields to the town, for a pennyworth of tobacco for her father, was on the top of a mountain surrounded by a great number of little men, who would not suffer her to pass any farther. Some of them said she should go with them, and accordingly laid hold of her; but one seeming more pitiful, desired they would let her alone; which they refusing, there ensued a quarrel, and the person who took her part fought bravely in her defence. This so incensed the others, that to be revenged on her for being the cause, two or three of them seized her, and pulling up her clothes, whipped her heartily; after which, it seems, they had no further power over her, and she run home directly, telling what had befallen her, and showing her buttocks, on which were the prints of several small hands. Several of the townspeople went with her to the mountain, and she conducting them to the spot, the little antagonists were gone, but had left behind them proofs (as the good woman said) that what the girl had informed them was true, for there was a great deal of blood to be seen on the stones. This did she aver with all the solemnity imaginable.

"Another woman, equally superstitious and fanciful as the former, told me, that being great with child, and expecting every moment the good hour, as she lay awake one night in her bed, she saw seven or eight little women come into her chamber, one of whom had an infant in her arms; they were followed by a man of the same size with themselves, but in the habit of a minister. One of them went to the pail, and finding no water in it, cried out to the others, what must they do to christen the child? On which they replied, it should be done in beer. With that the seeming parson took the child in his arms, and performed the ceremony of baptism, dipping his hand into a great tub of strong beer, which the woman had brewed the day before to be ready for her lying-in. She told me that they baptized the infant by the name of Joan, which made her know she was pregnant of a girl, as it proved a few days after, when she was delivered. She added also, that it was common for the fairies to make a mock christening when any person was near her time, and that according to what child, male or female, they brought, such should the woman bring into the world.

"But I cannot give over this subject without mentioning what they say befell a young sailor, who, coming off a long voyage, though it was late at night, chose to land rather than be another night in the vessel; being permitted to do so, he was set on shore at Douglas. It happened to be a fine moonlight night, and very dry, being a small frost; he therefore forbore going into any house to refresh himself, but made the best of his way to the house of a sister he had at Kirk-Merlugh. As he was going over a pretty high mountain, he heard the noise of horses, the hollow of a huntsman, and the finest horn in the world. He was a little surprised that any body pursued those kinds of sports in the night, but he had not time for much reflection before they all passed by him, so near, that he was able to count what number there was of them, which, he said, was thirteen, and that they were all dressed in green, and gallantly mounted. He was so well pleased with the sight, that he would gladly have followed, could he have kept pace with them; he crossed the footway, however, that he might see them again, which he did more than once, and lost not the sound of the horn for some miles. At length, being arrived at his sister's, he tells her the story, who presently clapped her hands for joy that he was come home safe; for, said she, those you saw were fairies, and 'tis well they did not take you away with them. There is no persuading them but that these huntings are frequent in the island, and that these little gentry, being too proud to ride on Manks horses, which they might find in the field, make use of the English and Irish ones, which are brought over and kept by gentlemen. They say that nothing is more common than to find these poor beasts, in a morning, all over in a sweat and foam, and tired almost to death, when their owners have believed they have never been out of the stable. A gentleman of Ballafletcher assured me he had three or four of his best horses killed with these nocturnal journeys.

"At my first coming into the island, and hearing these sort of stories, I imputed the giving credit to them merely to the simplicity of the poor creatures who related them; but was strangely surprised when I heard other narratives of this kind, and altogether as absurd, attested by men who passed for persons of sound judgment. Among this number, was a gentleman, my near neighbour, who affirmed with the most solemn asseverations, that being of my opinion, and entirely averse to the belief that any such beings were permitted to wander for the purposes related of them, he had been at last convinced by the appearance of several little figures playing and leaping over some stones in a field, whom at a few yards' distance he imagined were schoolboys, and intended, when he came near enough, to reprimand for being absent from their exercises at that time of the day, it being then, he said, between three and four of the clock; but when he approached, as near as he could guess, within twenty paces, they all immediately disappeared, though he had never taken his eye off them from the first moment he beheld them; nor was there any place where they could so suddenly retreat, it being an open field without hedge or bush, and, as I said before, broad day.

"Another instance, which might serve to strengthen the credit of the other, was told me by a person who had the reputation of the utmost integrity. This man being desirous of disposing of a horse he had at that time no great occasion for, and riding him to market for that purpose, was accosted, in passing over the mountains, by a little man in a plain dress, who asked him if he would sell his horse. 'Tis the design I am going on, replied the person who told me the story. On which the other desired to know the price. Eight pounds, said he. No, resumed the purchaser, I will give no more than seven; which, if you will take, here is your money. The owner, thinking he had bid pretty fair, agreed with him; and the money being told out, the one dismounted, and the other got on the back of the horse, which he had no sooner done, than both beast and rider sunk into the earth immediately, leaving the person who had made the bargain in the utmost terror and consternation. As soon as he had a little recovered himself, he went directly to the parson of the parish, and related what had passed, desiring he would give his opinion whether he ought to make use of the money he had received or not. To which he replied, that as he had made a fair bargain, and no way circumvented, nor endeavoured to circumvent, the buyer, he saw no reason to believe, in case it was an evil spirit, it could have any power over him. On this assurance, he went home well satisfied, and nothing afterward happened to give him any disquiet concerning this affair.

"A second account of the same nature I had from a clergyman, and a person of more sanctity than the generality of his function in this island. It was his custom to pass some hours every evening in a field near his house, indulging meditation, and calling himself to an account for the transactions of the past day. As he was in this place one night, more than ordinarily wrapt in contemplation, he wandered, without thinking where he was, a considerable way farther than it was usual for him to do; and, as he told me, he knew not how far the deep musing he was in might have carried him, if it had not been suddenly interrupted by a noise, which, at first, he took to be the distant bellowing of a bull; but as he listened more heedfully to it, found there was something more terrible in the sound than could proceed from that creature. He confessed to me, that he was no less affrighted than surprised, especially when the noise coming still nearer, he imagined, whatever it was that it proceeded from, it must pass him. He had, however, presence enough of mind to place himself with his back to a hedge, where he fell on his knees, and began to pray to God with all the vehemence so dreadful an occasion required. He had not been long in that position, before he beheld something in the form of a bull, but infinitely larger than ever he had seen in England, much less in Man, where the cattle are very small in general. The eyes, he said, seemed to shoot forth flames, and the running of it was with such a force, that the ground shook under it as an earthquake. It made directly toward a little cottage, and thereafter most horribly roaring, disappeared. The moon being then at the full, and shining in her utmost splendour, all these passages were visible to our amazed divine, who, having finished his ejaculation, and given thanks to God for his preservation, went to the cottage, the owner of which, they told him, was that moment dead. The good old gentleman was loath to pass a censure which might be judged an uncharitable one; but the deceased having the character of a very ill liver, most people who heard the story, were apt to imagine this terrible apparition came to attend his last moments.

"A mighty bustle they also make of an apparition, which, they say, haunts Castle Russin, in the form of a woman, who was some years since executed for the murder of her child. I have heard not only persons who have been confined there for debt, but also the soldiers of the garrison, affirm they have seen it various times; but what I took most notice of, was the report of a gentleman, of whose good understanding, as well as veracity, I have a very great opinion. He told me, that happening to be abroad late one night, and catched in an excessive storm of wind and rain, he saw a woman stand before the castle gate, where, being not the least shelter, it something surprised him that any body, much less one of that sex, should not rather run to some little porch, or shed, of which there are several in Castle Town, than chuse to stand still, exposed and alone, to such a dreadful tempest. His curiosity exciting him to draw nearer, that he might discover who it was that seemed so little to regard the fury of the elements, he perceived she retreated on his approach, and at last, he thought, went into the Castle, though the gates were shut. This obliging him to think he had seen a spirit, sent him home very much terrified; but the next day, relating his adventure to some people who lived in the Castle, and describing, as near as he could, the garb and stature of the apparition, they told him it was that of the woman abovementioned, who had been frequently seen, by the soldiers on guard, to pass in and out of the gates, as well as to walk through the rooms, though there was no visible means to enter. Though so familiar to the eye, no person has yet, however, had the courage to speak to it, and, as they say a spirit has no power to reveal its mind without being conjured to do so in a proper manner, the reason of its being permitted to wander is unknown.

"Another story of the like nature I have heard concerning an apparition, which has frequently been seen on a wild common near Kirk Jarmyn mountains, which, they say, assumes the shape of a wolf, and fills the air with most terrible howlings. But having run on so far in the account of supernatural appearances, I cannot forget what was told me by an English gentleman, and my particular friend. He was about passing over Douglas Bridge before it was broken down, but the tide being high, he was obliged to take the river, having an excellent horse under him, and one accustomed to swim. As he was in the middle of it, he heard, or imagined he heard, the finest symphony, I will not say in the world, for nothing human ever came up to it. The horse was no less sensible of the harmony than himself, and kept in an immovable posture all the time it lasted; which, he said, could not be less than three quarters of an hour, according to the most exact calculation he could make, when he arrived at the end of his little journey, and found how long he had been coming. He, who before laughed at all the stories told of fairies, now became a convert, and believed as much as ever a Manksman of them all. As to circles in the grass, and the impression of small feet among the snow, I cannot deny but I have seen them frequently, and once thought I heard a whistle, as though in my ear, when nobody that could make it was near me. For my part, I shall not pretend to determine if such appearances have any reality, or are only the effect of the imagination; but as I had much rather give credit to them, than be convinced by ocular demonstration, I shall leave the point to be discussed by those who have made it more their study, and only say, that whatever belief we ought to give to some accounts of this kind, there are others, and those much more numerous, which merit only to be laughed at—it not being at all consonant to reason, or the idea religion gives us of the fallen angels, to suppose spirits, so eminent in wisdom and knowledge, as to be exceeded by nothing but their Creator, should visit the earth for such trifling purposes as to throw bottles and glasses about a room, and a thousand other as ridiculous gambols mentioned in those voluminous treatises of apparitions.

"The natives of this island tell you also, that before any person dies, the procession of the funeral is acted by a sort of beings, which for that end render themselves visible. I know several that have offered to make oath, that as they have been passing the road, one of these funerals has come behind them, and even laid the bier on their shoulders, as though to assist the bearers. One person, who assured me he had been served so, told me that the flesh of his shoulder had been very much bruised, and was black for many weeks after. There are few or none of them who pretend not to have seen or heard these imaginary obsequies, (for I must not omit that they sing psalms in the same manner as those do who accompany the corpse of a dead friend,) which so little differ from real ones, that they are not to be known till both coffin and mourners are seen to vanish at the church doors. These they take to be a sort of friendly demons, and their business, they say, is to warn people of what is to befall them; accordingly, they give notice of any stranger's approach, by the trampling of horses at the gate of the house where they are to arrive. As difficult as I found it to bring myself to give any faith to this, I have frequently been very much surprised, when, on visiting a friend, I have found the table ready spread, and every thing in order to receive me, and been told by the person to whom I went, that he had knowledge of my coming, or some other guest, by these good-natured intelligencers; nay, when obliged to be absent some time from home, my own servants have assured me they were informed by these means of my return, and expected me the very hour I came, though perhaps it was some days before I hoped it myself at my going abroad. That this is fact, I am positively convinced by many proofs; but how or wherefore it should be so, has frequently given me much matter of reflection, yet left me in the same uncertainty as before. Here, therefore, I will quit the subject, and proceed to things much easier to be accounted for."—WALDRON'S *Description of the Isle of Man*, folio, 1731, p. 125.

This long quotation is extremely curious, as containing an

account of those very superstitions in the Isle of Man, which are frequently collected both in Ireland and in the Highlands of Scotland, and which have employed the attention of Mr Crofton Croker, and of the author of the Fairy Mythology. The superstitions are in every respect so like each other, that they may be referred to one common source; unless we conclude that they are natural to the human mind, and, like the common orders of vegetables, which naturally spring up in every climate, these naturally arise in every bosom; as the best philologists are of opinion, that fragments of an original speech are to be discovered in almost all languages in the globe.

186.32 (Ch. 18) command it in mine The reader cannot have forgotten that the Earl of Derby was head of the great house of Stanley.

197.36 (Ch. 19) entirely abandoned This curious legend, and many others, in which the Isle of Man is perhaps richer than even Ireland, Wales, or the Highlands of Scotland, will be found in a note at the end of Chapter 15, page 246 of this volume.

203.16 (Ch. 20) all her retinue

SALE OF A DANCING GIRL. An instance of such a sale of an unfortunate dancing girl occurred in Edinburgh in the end of the seventeenth century.

"13th January, 1687.—Reid, the mountebank, pursues Scott of Harden and his lady, for stealing away from him a little girl called *The tumbling lassie*, that danced upon a stage, and he claimed damages, and produced a contract, by which he bought her from her mother for thirty pounds Scots, [L.2, 10s. sterling]. But we have no slaves in Scotland," continues the liberal reporter, "and mothers cannot sell their bairns: and physicians attested that the employment of tumbling would kill her, and her joints were now grown stiff, and she declined to return, though she was at least a prentice, and could not run away from her master. Yet some cited Moses's Law, that if a servant shelter himself with thee, against his master's cruelty, thou shalt surely not deliver him up. The Lords, *renitente cancellario*, assoilzied [*i.e.* acquitted] Harden."—FOUNTAINHALL'S *Decisions*, vol. i. p. 441.

A man may entertain some vanity in being connected with a patron of the cause of humanity; so the author may be pardoned mentioning, that he derives his own direct descent from the father of this champion of humanity.

Reid the mountebank apparently knew well how to set the sails of his own interest to whatever wind proved most likely to turn them. He failed not to avail himself of King James's rage for the conversion of heretics, on which subject Fountainhall has this sarcastic memorandum:—

"Reid the mountebank is received into the Popish church, and one of his blackamoors was persuaded to accept of baptism from the Popish priests, and to turn Christian Papist, which was a great trophy. He was christened James after the King, and Chancellor, and the Apostle James!"—*Ibid.* p. 440.

209.5 (Ch. 20) pay the fees

WITNESSES OF THE POPISH PLOT. The infamous character of those who contrived and carried on the pretended Popish Plot, may be best estimated by the account given in North's Examen, who describes Oates himself with considerable power of colouring. "He was now in his trine exaltation, his plot in full force, efficacy, and virtue; he walked about with his guards [assigned for fear of the Papists murdering him.] He had lodgings in Whitehall, and L.1200 per annum pension: And no wonder, after he had the impudence to say to the House of Lords, in plain terms, that, if they would not help him to more money, he must be forced to help himself. He put on an Episcopal garb, (except the lawn sleeves,) silk-gown and cassock, great hat, satin hatband and rose, long scarf, and was called, or most blasphemously called himself, the Saviour of the nation; whoever he pointed at, was taken up and committed: so that many people got out of his way, as from a blast, and glad they could prove their two last years' conversation. The very breath of him was pestilential, and, if it brought not imprisonment, or death, over such on whom it fell, it surely poisoned reputation, and left good Protestants arrant Papists, and something worse than that —in danger of being put in the plot as traitors. Upon his examination before the Commons, the Lord-Chief-Justice Scroggs was sent for to the House, and there signed warrants for the imprisonment of five Roman Catholic peers, upon which they were laid up in the Tower. The votes of the Houses seemed to confirm the whole. A solemn form of prayer was desired upon the subject of the plot, and when one was prepared, it was found faulty, because the Papists were not named as authors of it: God surely knew whether it were so or not: however, it was yielded to, that omniscience might not want information. The Queen herself was accused at the Commons' bar. The city, for fear of the Papists, put up their posts and chains: and the chamberlain, Sir Thomas Player, in the Court of Aldermen, gave his reason for the city's using that caution, which was, that he did not know but the next morning they might all rise with their throats cut. The trials, convictions, and executions of the priests, Jesuits, and others, were had, and attended with vast mob and noise. Nothing ordinary or moderate was to be heard in people's communication; but every debate and action was high-flown and tumultuous. All freedom of speech was taken away; and not to believe the plot, was worse than being Turk, Jew, or infidel. For this fact of Godfrey's murder, the three poor men of Somerset-house were, as was said, convicted. The most pitiful circumstance was that of their trial, under the popular prejudice against them. The Lord-Chief-Justice Scroggs took in with the tide, and ranted for the plot, hewing down Popery, as Scanderbeg hewed the Turk; which was but little propitious to them. The other judges were passive, and meddled little, except some that were takers in also; and particularly the good Recorder Treby, who eased the Attorney-General, for he seldom asked a question, but one might guess he foresaw the answer. Some may blame the (at best) passive behaviour of the judges; but really, considering it was impossible to stem such a current, the appearing to do it in vain had been more unprofitable, because it had inflamed the great and small rout, drawn scandal on themselves, and disabled them from taking in when opportunity should be more favourable. The prisoners, under these hardships, had enough to do to make any defence; for where the testimony was positive, it was conclusive; for no reasoning *ab improbabili* would serve the turn; it must be *ab impossibili*, or not at all. Whoever doth not well observe the power of judging, may think many things, in the course of justice, very strange. If one side is held to demonstration, and the other allowed presumptions for proofs, any cause may be carried. In a word, anger, policy, inhumanity, and prejudice, had, at this time, a planetary possession of the minds of most men, and destroyed in them that golden rule, of doing as they would be done unto."

In another passage Oates's personal appearance is thus described.—"He was a low man, of an ill cut, very short neck, and his visage and features were most particular. His mouth was the centre of his face; and a compass there would sweep his nose, forehead, and chin, within the perimeter. *Cave quos ipse Deus notavit.* In a word, he was a most consummate cheat, blasphemer, vicious, perjured, impudent, and saucy, foul-mouth'd wretch; and were it not for the truth of history, and the great emotions in the public he was the cause of, not fit (so little deserving) to be remembered."

221.24 (Ch. 21) carrying on the same

NARRATIVES OF THE PLOT. There is no more odious feature of this detestable plot than that the forsworn witnesses by whose oath the fraud was supported, claimed a species of literary interest in their own fabrications by publications under such titles as the following: "A narrative and impartial discovery of the horrid Popish Plot, carried on for burning and destroying the cities of London and Westminster, with their suburbs, setting forth the several consults, orders, and resolutions of the Jesuits concerning the same, by (a person so and so named), lately engaged in that horrid design, and one of the Popish committee for carrying on such fires."

At any other period, it would have appeared equally unjust and illegal to poison the public mind with stuff of this kind, before the witnesses had made their depositions in open court. But in this moment of frenzy, every thing which could confirm the existence of these senseless delusions, was eagerly listened to; and whatever seemed to infer doubt of the witnesses, or hesitation concerning the existence of the plot, was a stifling, strangling, or undervaluing the discovery of the grand conspiracy. In short, as expressed by Dryden,

> 'Twas worse than plotting, to suspect the plot.

224.13 (Ch 21) from within the house

RICHARD GANLESSE. It will be afterwards found, that in the supposed Richard Ganlesse, is first introduced into the story the detestable Edward Christian, a character with as few redeeming good qualities as the author's too prolific pencil has ever attempted to draw. He is a mere creature of the imagination; and although he may receive some dignity of character from his talents, courage, and influence over others, he is, in other respects, a moral monster, since even his affection for his brother, and resentment of his death, are grounded on vindictive feelings, which scruple at no means, even the foulest, for their gratification. The author will be readily believed when he affirms, that no original of the present times, or those which preceded them, has given the outline for a character so odious. The personage is a mere fancy piece. In particular the author disclaims all allusion to a gentleman named Edward Christian, who actually existed during those troublesome times, was brother of William Christian, the Dempster, and died in prison in the Isle of Man. With this unfortunate gentleman the character in the novel has not the slightest connexion, nor do the incidents of their lives in any respect agree. There existed, as already stated, an Edward Christian of the period, who was capable of very bad things, since he was a companion and associate of the robber Thomas Blood, and convicted along with him of a conspiracy against the celebrated Duke of Buckingham. This character was probably not unlike that of his namesake in the novel, at least the feats ascribed to him are *haud aliena a Scævolæ studiis*. But Mr Christian of Unrigg, if there existed a rogue of his name during that period of general corruption, has the more right to have him distinguished from his unfortunate relative, who died in prison before the period mentioned.

227.34 (Ch. 22) (Magnum addition) [The Magnum adds two sentences to the Ed1 paragraph: 'Smith accordingly treated him as a mere novice in epicurism, cautioning him to eat his soup before the bouilli, and to forget the Manx custom of bolting the boiled meat before the broth, as if Cutlar MacCullloch* and all his whingers were at the door. Peveril took the hint in good part, and the entertainment proceeded with animation.']

CUTLAR MACCULLOCH. This alludes to a singular custom of the inhabitants of the northern coast of the Isle of Man, who used of old to eat the sodden meat before they supped the broth, lest, it is said, they should be deprived of the more substantial part of the meal, if they waited to eat it at the second course.

They account for this anomaly in the following manner:—About the commencement of the sixteenth century, the Earl of Derby, being a fiery young chief, fond of war and honour, made a furious inroad, with all his forces, into the Stewartry of Kirkcudbright, and committed great ravages still remembered in Manx song. Mr Train, with his usual kindness, sent me the following literal translation of the verses:

There came Thomas Derby, born king,
He it was who wore the golden crupper;
There was not one Lord in wide England itself,
With so many vassals as he had.

On Scottishmen he avenged himself;
He went over to Kirkcudbright,
And there made such havoc of houses,
That some are uninhabitable to this day.

Was not that fair in a youth,
To avenge himself on his foe while he was so young;
Before his beard had grown around his mouth,
And to bring home his men in safety?

This incursion of the Earl with the golden crupper was severely revenged. The gentlemen of the name of MacCulloch, a clan then and now powerful in Galloway, had at their head, at the time, a chief of courage and activity, named Cutlar MacCulloch. He was an excellent seaman, and speedily equipped a predatory flotilla, with which he made repeated descents on the northern shores of the Isle of Man, the dominions of the Earl of Derby, carrying off all that was not, in the Border phrase, too hot or too heavy.

The following is the deposition of John Machariotic concerning the losses he had suffered by this sea-king and his Galloway men.

It is dated at Peel Castle.—"Taken by Collard MacCulloch and his men by wrongous spoliation, Twa box beddes and aykin burdes, i c lathe, a feder bouster, a cote of Mailzie, a mete burde, two kystis, five barrels, a gyle-fat, xx pipes, twa gunys, three bolls of malt, a querne of rosate of vi stane, certain petes [peats], extending to i c load, viii bolls of threschit corn, xii unthraschin, and xl knowte."—CHALLONER, p. 47, edit. London, 1653.

This active rover rendered his name so formidable, that the custom of eating the meat before the broth was introduced by the islanders whose festivals he often interrupted. They also remembered him in their prayers and graces; as,

God keep the house and all within,
From Cut MacCulloch and his kin;

or, as I have heard it recited,

God keep the good corn, and the sheep, and the bullock,
From Satan, from sin, and from Cutlar MacCulloch.

It is said to have chanced, as the master of the house had uttered one of these popular benisons, that Cutlar in person entered the habitation with this reply:

Gudeman, gudeman, ye pray too late,
MacCulloch's ships are at the Yaite.

The *Yaite* is a well-known landing-place on the north side of the Isle of Man.

This redoubted corsair is, I believe, now represented by the chief of the name, James MacCulloch, Esq. of Ardwell, the author's friend and near connexion.

230.8 (Ch. 22) the French King

CORRESPONDENCE OF COLEMAN. The unfortunate Coleman, executed for the Popish Plot, was secretary to the late Duchess of York, and had been a correspondent of the French King's confessor, Pere la Chaise. Their correspondence was seized, and although the papers contained nothing to confirm the monstrous fictions of the accusers, yet there was a great deal to show that he and other zealous Catholics anxiously sought for and desired to find the means to bring back England to the faith of Rome. "It is certain," says Hume, "that the restless and enterprising spirit of the Catholic Church, particularly of the Jesuits, merits attention, and is in some degree dangerous to every other communion. Such zeal of proselytism actuates that sect, that its missionaries have penetrated into every region of the globe, and in one sense there is a Popish plot continually carrying on against all states, Protestant, Pagan, and Mahometan."—*History of England*, vol. viii., p. 72, edit. 1797.

230.17 (Ch. 22) such a prodigy

Funeral Service of Sir Edmondsbury Godfrey. This solemnity is especially mentioned by North. "The crowd was prodigious, both at the procession and in and about the church, and so heated, that any thing called Papist, were it a cat or a dog, had probably gone to pieces in a moment. The Catholics all kept close in their houses and lodgings, thinking it a good composition to be safe there, so far were they from acting violently at that time. But there was all this while upheld among the common people an artificial fright, so that every one almost fancied a Popish knife just at his throat; and at the sermon, beside the preacher, two thumping divines stood upright in the pulpit, to guard him from being killed while he was preaching, by the Papists. I did not see this spectre, but was credibly told by some that affirmed that they did see it, and I never met with any that did contradict it. A most portentous spectacle, sure, three parsons in one pulpit! Enough of itself, on a less occasion, to excite terror in the audience. The like, I guess, was never seen before, and probably will never be seen again; and it had not been so now, as is most evident, but for some stratagem founded upon the impetuosity of the mob."—*Examen*, p. 104.

It may be here remarked, that the singular circumstance of Sir Edmondsbury Godfrey, the justice before whom Oates had made his deposition, being found murdered, was the incident upon which most men relied as complete proof of the existence of the plot. As he was believed to have lost his life by the Papists, for having taken Oates's deposition, the panic spread with inconceivable rapidity, and every species of horror was apprehended—every report, the more absurd the better, eagerly listened to and believed. Whether this unfortunate gentleman lost his life by Papist or Protestant, by private enemies, or by his own hand, (for he was a low-spirited and melancholy man,) will probably never be discovered.

231.10 (Ch. 22) Dun Dun was the hangman of the day at Tyburn. He was successor of Gregory Brunden, who was by many believed to be the same who dropped the axe upon Charles I., though others were suspected of being the actual regicide.

253.27 (Ch. 24) he had assumed A Scottish gentleman *in hiding*, as it was emphatically termed, for some concern in a Jacobite insurrection or plot, was discovered among a number of ordinary persons, by the use of his toothpick.

278.30 (Ch. 27) Sir George Wakeman acquitted

First Check to the Plot. The first check received by Doctor Oates and his colleagues in the task of supporting the Plot by their testimony, was in this manner:—After a good deal of prevarication, the prime witness at length made a direct charge against

Sir George Wakeman, the Queen's physician, of an attempt to poison the King, and even connected the Queen with this accusation, whom he represented as Wakeman's accomplice. This last piece of effrontery recalled the King to some generous sentiments. "The villains," said Charles, "think I am tired of my wife; but they shall find I will not permit an innocent woman to be persecuted." Scroggs, the Lord Chief-Justice, received accordingly instructions to be favourable to the accused; and, for the first time, he was so. Wakeman was acquitted, but thought it more for his safety to retire abroad. His acquittal, however, indicated a turn of the tide, which had so long set in favour of the Plot, and of the witnesses by whom it had hitherto been supported.

278.40 (Ch. 27) That's over—the epitaph The epitaph alluded to is the celebrated epigram made by Rochester on Charles II. It was composed at the King's request, who nevertheless resented its poignancy.

The lines are well known:—

> Here lies our sovereign lord the King,
> Whose word no man relies on;
> Who never said a foolish thing,
> And never did a wise one.

279.22 (Ch. 27) the great Madam The Duchess of Portsmouth, Charles II.'s favourite mistress; very unpopular at the time of the Popish Plot, as well from her religion as her country, being a Frenchwoman and a Catholic.

279.23 (Ch. 27) Little Anthony Anthony Ashley Cooper, Earl of Shaftesbury, the politician and intriguer of the period.

280.43 (Ch. 27) mew about the King Such was the extravagance of Shaftesbury's eloquence.

281.28 (Ch. 27) Louise de Querouaille Charles's principal mistress *en titre*. She was created Duchess of Portsmouth.

281.33 (Ch. 27) begot it himself Shaftesbury himself is supposed to have said that he knew not who was the inventor of the Plot, but that he himself had all the advantage of the discovery.

292.23 (Ch. 28) with the doctors Doctor, a cant name for false dice.

294.16 (Ch. 28) this Settle Elkana Settle, the unworthy scribbler whom the envy of Rochester and others tried to raise to public estimation, as a rival to Dryden; a circumstance which has been the means of elevating him to a very painful species of immortality.

294.33 (Ch. 28) exercise of late

Employment of Assassins in England. It was the unworthy distinction of men of wit and honour about town, to revenge their own quarrels with inferior persons by the hands of bravoes. Even in the days of chivalry, the knights, as may be learned from Don Quixote, turned over to the chastisement of their squires such adversaries as were not dubb'd; and thus it was not unusual for men of quality in Charles II.'s time, to avenge their wrongs by means of private assassination. Rochester writes composedly concerning a satire imputed to Dryden, but in reality composed by Mulgrave, "If he falls upon me with the blunt, which is his very good weapon in wit, I will forgive him, if you please, and leave the repartee to Black Will with a cudgel." And, in conformity with this cowardly and brutal intimation, that distinguished poet was waylaid and beaten severely in Rose Street, Covent Garden, by ruffians who could not be discovered, but whom all concluded to be the agents of Rochester's mean revenge.

296.15 (Ch. 28) Harry Bennet

EARL OF ARLINGTON. Bennet, Earl of Arlington, was one of Charles's most attached courtiers during his exile. After the Restoration, he was employed in the ministry, and the name of Bennet supplies its initial B to the celebrated word Cabal. But the King was supposed to have lost respect for him; and several persons at court took the liberty to mimic his person and behaviour, which was stiff and formal. Thus it was a common jest for some courtier to put a black patch on his nose, and strut about with a white staff in his hand, to make the King merry. But, notwithstanding, he retained his office of Lord Chamberlain and his seat in the Privy Council, till his death in 1685.

296.41 (Ch. 28) his father-in-law Mary, daughter of Thomas Lord Fairfax, was wedded to the Duke of Buckingham, whose versatility made him capable of rendering himself for a time as agreeable to his father-in-law, though a rigid Presbyterian, as to the gay Charles II.

299.41 (Ch.28) Jerningham

LETTER FROM THE DEAD TO THE LIVING. The application of the very respectable old English name of Jerningham to the valet-de-chambre of the Duke of Buckingham, has proved of force sufficient to wake the resentment of the dead, who had in early days worn that illustrious surname,—for the author received by post the following expostulation on the subject:—

"*To the learned Clerk and worshipful Knight, Sir Walter Scott, give these:*

"Mye mortal frame has long since mouldered into dust, and the young saplinge that was planted on the daye of mye funeral, is now a doddered oak, standinge hard bye the mansion of the familie. The windes doe whistle thro' its leaves, moaninge among its moss-covered branches, and awakening in the soules of my descendants, that pensive melancholy which leads back to the contemplating those that are gone!—I, who was once the courtly dame, that held high revelry in these gaye bowers, am now light as the blast!

"If I essaye, from vain affection, to make my name be thought of by producing the noise of rustlinge silkes, or the slow tread of a midnight foot along the chapel floor, alas! I only scare the simple maidens, and my wearie efforts (how wearie none alive can tell) are derided and jeered at, by my knightlie descendants. Once indeed —but it boots not to burthen your ear with this particular, nor why I am still sad and aching, between earth and heaven! Know only, that I still walk this place (as mye playmate, your great-grandmother, does here.) I sit in my wonted chair, tho' now it stands in a dusty garret. I frequent my lady's room, and I have hushed her wailing babes, when all the cunning of the nurse has failed. I sit at the window where so long a succession of honorable dames have presided their daye, and are passed away! But in the change that centuries brought, honor and truth have remained; and, as adherents to King Harry's eldest daughter, as true subjects to her successors, as faithful followers of the unfortunate Charles and his posteritie, and as loyal and attached servauntes of the present royal stock, the name of *Jerningham* has ever remained unsullied in honour, and uncontaminated in aught unfitting its ancient knightlie origin. You, noble and learned sir, whose quill is as the trumpet arousinge the slumberinge soule to feelings of loftie chivalrie,—you, Sir Knight, who feel and doe honour to your noble lineage, wherefore did you say, in your chronicle or historie of the brave knight, Peveril of the Peake, that my lord of Buckingham's servaunte was a Jerningham!!! a vile varlet to a viler noble! Many honourable families have, indeed, shot and spread from the parent stock into wilde entangled mazes, and reached perchance beyond the confines of gentle blood; but it so pleased Providence, that mye worshipful husband, good Sir Harry's line, has flowed in one confined, but clear deep stream, down to mye well-beloued son, the present Sir George Jerningham (by just claim Lorde Stafforde;) and if any of your courtly ancestors that hover round your bed, could speak, they would tell you that the Duke's valet was not Jerningham, but Sayer or Sims.—Act as you shall think mete hereon, but defend the honoured names of those whose champion you so well deserve to be.

J. JERNINGHAM."

Having no mode of knowing how to reply to this ancient dignitary, I am compelled to lay the blame of my error upon wicked example, which has misled me; and to plead that I should never have been guilty of so great a misnomer, but for the authority of one Oliver Goldsmith, who, in an elegant dialogue between the Lady Blarney and Miss Carolina Wilhelmina Amelia Skeggs, makes the former assure Miss Skeggs as a fact, that the next morning my lord called out three times to his valet-de-chambre, "Jernigan, Jernigan, Jernigan! bring me my garters!" Some inaccurate recollection of this passage has occasioned the offence rendered, for which I make this imperfect, yet respectful apology.

342.21 (Ch. 32) silk armour

SILK ARMOUR. Roger North gives us a ridiculous description of these warlike habiliments, when talking of the Whig Club in Fuller's Rents. "The conversation and ordinary discourse of the club was chiefly on the subject of bravery in defending the cause of liberty and property, and what every Protestant Englishman ought to venture and do, rather than be overrun with Popery and slavery. There was much recommendation of silk armour, and the prudence of being provided with it, against the time that Protestants were to be massacred; and accordingly there were abundance of these silken backs, breasts, and pots, (*i.e.* head-pieces) made and sold, which were pretended to be pistol proof, in which any man dressed up was as safe as in a house; for it was impossible any one could go to strike him for laughing, so ridiculous was the figure, as they say, of hogs in armour—an image of derision insensible but to the view, as I have had it, (viz. that none can imagine without seeing it, as I have.) This was armour of defence, but our sparks were not altogether so tame as to carry their provisions no farther; for truly they intended to be assailants upon fair occasion, and had for that end recommended to them a certain pocket weapon, which, for its design and efficacy, had the honour to be called a Protestant flail. It was for street and crowd work, and the instrument lurking *perdue* in a coat-pocket, might readily sally out to execution, and by clearing a great hall, or piazza, or so, carry an election, by a choice way of polling, called 'knocking down.' The handle resembled a farrier's blood-stick, and the fall was joined to the end by a strong nervous ligature, that in its swing fell just short of the hand, and was made of *lignum-vitæ*, or rather, as the poet termed it, *mortis*."—*Examen*, p. 573.

This last weapon will remind the reader of the blood-stick so cruelly used, as was alleged, in a murder committed in England some years ago, and for a participation in which two persons were tried and acquitted at the assizes of autumn 1830.

355.38 (Ch. 34) I could think of

GEOFFREY HUDSON. Geoffrey or Jeffrey Hudson is often mentioned in anecdotes of Charles I.'s time. His first appearance at court was his being presented, as mentioned in the text, in a pie, at an entertainment given by the Duke of Buckingham to Charles I. and Henrietta Maria. Upon the same occasion, the Duke presented the tenant of the pasty to the Queen, who retained him as her page. When about eight years of age, he was but eighteen or twenty inches high; and remained stationary at that stature till he was thirty years old, when he grew to the height of three feet nine inches, and there stopped.

This singular *lusus naturæ* was trusted in some negotiations of consequence. He went to France to fetch over a midwife to his mistress, Henrietta Maria. On his return, he was taken by Dunkirk privateers, when he lost many valuable presents sent to the Queen from France, and about L.2500 of his own. Sir William Davenant makes a real or supposed combat between the dwarf and a turkey-cock, the subject of a poem called Jeffreidos. The scene is laid at Dunkirk, where, as the satire concludes—

> Jeffrey strait was thrown, when, faint and weak,
> The cruel fowl assaults him with his beak.
> A lady midwife now he there by chance
> Espied, that came along with him from France.
> "A heart brought up in war, that ne'er before
> This time could bow," he said, "doth now implore
> Thou, that *delivered* hast so many, be
> So kind of nature as deliver me."

We are not acquainted how far Jeffrey resented this lampoon. But we are assured he was a consequential personage, and endured with little temper the teasing of the domestics and courtiers, and had many squabbles with the King's gigantic porter.

The fatal duel with Mr Crofts actually took place, as mentioned in the text. It happened in France. The poor dwarf had also the misfortune to be taken prisoner by a Turkish pirate. He was, however, probably soon set at liberty, for Hudson was a captain for the King during the civil war. In 1644, the dwarf attended his royal mistress to France. The Restoration recalled him, with other royalists, to England. But this poor being, who received, it would seem, hard measure both from nature and fortune, was not doomed to close his days in peace. Poor Jeffrey, upon some suspicion respecting the Popish Plot, was taken up in 1682, and confined in the Gatehouse prison, Westminster, where he ended his life in the sixty-third year of his age.

Jeffrey Hudson has been immortalized by the brush of Vandyke, and his clothes are said to be preserved as articles of curiosity in Sir Hans Sloan's Museum.

375.38 (Ch. 36) tour at you The smart girls, who turn out to look at you.

378.21 (Ch. 36) Traitors' gate See Fortunes of Nigel, 187–88 above.

384.42 (Ch. 37) as wide as Coventry's The ill usage of Sir John Coventry by some of the Life Guardsmen, in revenge of something said in Parliament concerning the King's theatrical amours, gave rise to what was called Coventry's Act, against cutting and maiming the person.

389.35 (Ch. 38) Mohun Then a noted actor.

391.37 (Ch. 38) war-caper A Privateer.

392.38 (Ch. 38) a Narrative concerning the Plot

COLONEL BLOOD'S NARRATIVE. Of Blood's Narrative, Roger North takes the following notice,—"There was another sham plot of one Netterville. - - - - - And here the good Colonel Blood, that stole the Duke of Ormond, and, if a timely rescue had not come in, had hanged him at Tyburn, and afterwards stole the crown, though he was not so happy as to carry it off; no player at small games, he, even he, the virtuous Colonel, as this sham plot says, was to have been destroyed by the Papists. It seems these Papists would let no eminent Protestant be safe. But some amends were made to the Colonel by sale of the narrative, licensed Thomas Blood. It would have been strange if so much mischief were stirring, and he had not come in for a snack."—*Examen*, edit. 1711, p. 311.

395.21 (Ch. 38) for thy life! Stock-jobbing, as it is called, that is, dealing in shares of monopolies, patents, and joint-stock companies of every description, was at least as common in Charles II.'s time as our own; and as the exercise of ingenuity in this way promised a road to wealth without the necessity of industry, it was then much pursued by dissolute courtiers.

400.36 (Ch. 39) riding boots This case is not without precedent. Among the jealousies and fears expressed by the Long Parliament, they insisted much upon an agent for the King departing for the continent so abruptly, that he had not time to change his court dress—white buskins, to wit, and black silk pantaloons—for an equipment more suitable to travel with.

408.17 (Ch. 40) a prince's chamber In Evelyn's Memoirs is the following curious passage respecting Nell Gwyn, who is hinted at in the text:—" I walked with him [King Charles II.] through Saint James's Park to the garden, where I both saw and heard a very familiar discourse between . . . [*the King*] and Mrs Nelly, as they called her, an impudent comedian, she looking out of her garden on a terrace at the top of the wall, and [*the King*] standing on the green walk under it. I was heartily sorry at this scene."—EVELYN'S *Memoirs*, vol. i. p. 413.

412.24 (Ch. 40) the Chapel of the Tower A story of this nature is current in the legends of the Tower. The affecting circumstances are, I believe, recorded in one of the little manuals which are put into the hands of visitors, but are not to be found in the later editions.

414.2 (Ch. 40) the King's attention

COLONEL BLOOD. The conspirator Blood even fought or made his way into good society, and sat at good men's feasts. Evelyn's Diary bears, 10th May, 1671,—"Dined at Mr Treasurer's, where dined Monsieur de Grammont and several French noblemen, and one Blood, that impudent, bold fellow, that had not long ago attempted to steal the Imperial crown itself out of the Tower, pretending curiosity of seeing the Regalia, when, stabbing the keeper, though not mortally, he boldly went away with it through all the guards, taken only by the accident of his horse falling down. How he came to be pardoned, and even received into favour, not only after this, but several other exploits almost as daring, both in Ireland and here, I could never come to understand. Some believed he became a spy of several parties, being well with the sectaries and enthusiasts, and did his Majesty service that way, which none alive could do so well as he. But it was certainly, as the boldest attempt, so the only treason of the sort that was ever pardoned. The man had not only a daring, but a villainous unmerciful look, a false countenance, but very well spoken and dangerously insinuating."—EVELYN'S *Memoirs*, vol. i. p. 413.

This is one of the many occasions on which we might make curious remarks on the disregard of our forefathers for appearances, even in the regulation of society. What should we think of a Lord of the Treasury, who, to make up a party of French nobles and English gentlemen of condition, should invite as a guest Barrington or Major Semple, or any well-known *chevalier d'industrie?* Yet Evelyn does not seem to have been shocked at the man being brought into society, but only at his remaining unhanged.

424.9 (Ch. 41) advised me otherwise It was on such terms that Dr Oates was pleased to claim the extraordinary privilege of dealing out the information which he chose to communicate to a court of justice. The only sense in which his story of the fox, stone, and goose, could be applicable, is by supposing, that he was determined to ascertain the extent of his countrymen's credulity before supplying it with a full meal.

439.20 (Ch. 43) Charles's reign This insurrection took place in 1660. Those engaged in it believed themselves invulnerable and invincible. They proclaimed the Millennium, and disturbed London greatly. The day after their mad rebellion, they were put down and subdued; and their leaders not having the good fortune to be considered as madmen, were tried and punished as traitors.

448.27 (Ch. 44) Bully Tom Armstrong Thomas, or Sir Thomas Armstrong, a person who had distinguished himself in youth by duels and drunken exploits. He was particularly connected with the Duke of Monmouth, and was said to be concerned in the Rye-House Plot, for which he suffered capital punishment, 20th June, 1684.

449.29 (Ch. 44) his black periwig Charles, to suit his dark complexion, always wore a black peruke. He used to say of the players, that if they wished to represent a villain on the stage, "Odds-fish, they always clapp'd on him a black periwig, whereas the greatest rogue in England [meaning, probably, Dr Oates] wears a white one."—*See* CIBBER'S *Apology*.

450.41 (Ch. 44) (Magnum addition) [The Magnum text reads: 'and care not for expense; you will find most of them at the Club-House in Fuller's Rents."*']

The place of meeting of the Green Ribbon Club. "Their place of meeting," says Roger North, "was in a sort of Carrefour at Chancery Lane, in a centre of business and company most proper for such anglers of fools. The house was double balconied in the front, as may yet be seen, for the clubbers to issue forth *in fresco*, with hats and no perukes, pipes in their mouths, merry faces, and dilated throats for vocal encouragement of the canaglia below on usual and unusual occasions."

462.39 (Ch. 46) the High Bailiff [The Magnum text reads: 'let the High Bailiff collect his civil officers, and command the Sheriffs to summon their worshipful attendants, from javelin-men to hangmen,* and have them in readiness . . . '.]

THE SHERIFF OF LONDON. It can hardly be forgotten that one of the great difficulties of Charles II.'s reign was to obtain for the crown the power of choosing the sheriffs of London. Roger North gives a lively account of his brother, Sir Dudley North, who agreed to serve for the court. "I omit the share he had in composing the tumults about burning the Pope, because that is accounted for in the Examen, and the life of the Lord Keeper North. Neither is there occasion to say any thing of the rise and discovery of the Rye Plot, for the same reason. Nor is my subject much concerned with this latter, farther than that the conspirators had taken especial care of Sir Dudley North. For he was one of those who, if they had succeeded, was to have been knocked on the head, and his skin to be stuffed, and hung up in Guildhall. But, all that apart, he reckoned it a great unhappiness, that so many trials for high treason, and executions, should happen in his year. However, in these affairs, the sheriffs were passive; for all returns of panels, and other dispatches of the law, were issued and done by under-officers; which was a fair screen for them. They attended at the trials and executions, to coerce the crowds, and keep order, which was enough for them to do. I have heard Sir Dudley North say, that, striking with his cane, he wondered to see what blows his countrymen would take upon their bare heads, and never look up at it. And indeed, nothing can match the zeal of the common people to see executions. The worst grievance was the executioner coming to him for orders, touching the abscinded members, and to know where to dispose of them. Once, while he was abroad, a cart, with some of them, came into the court-yard of his house, and frighted his lady almost out of her wits; and she could never be reconciled to the dog hangman's saying he came to speak with his master. These are inconveniences that attend the stations of public magistracy, and are necessary to be borne with, as magistracy itself is necessary. I have now no more to say of any incidents during the shrievalty; but that, at the year's end, he delivered up his charges to his successors in like manner as he had received them from his predecessor; and, having reinstated his family, he lived well and easy at his own house, as he did before these disturbances put him out of order."

469.6 (Ch. 47) Bei Got Brantome tells us of a court lady who chose to have this tune played when she was dying, and at the end of the burden repeated, "Oui, tout verlore et à bon escient," and therewith expired.

493.1 (Ch. 49) the exercise of her faculties This little piece of superstition was suggested by the following incident. The Author of Waverley happened to be standing by with other gentlemen, while the captain of the Selkirk Yeomanry was purchasing a horse for the use of his trumpeter. The animal offered was a handsome one, and neither the officer, who was an excellent jockey, nor any one present, could see any imperfection in wind or limb. But a person happened to pass, who was asked to give an opinion. This man was called Blind Willie, who drove a small trade in cattle and horses, and what seemed as extraordinary, in watches, notwithstanding his having been born blind. He was accounted to possess a rare judgment in these subjects of traffic. So soon as he had examined the horse in question, he immediately pronounced it to have something of his own complaint, and in plain words, stated it to be blind, or verging upon that imperfection, which was found to be the case on close examination. None present had suspected this fault in the animal; which is not wonderful, considering that it may frequently exist, without any appearance in the organ affected. Blind Willie, being asked how he made a discovery imperceptible to so many gentlemen who had their eyesight, explained, that after feeling the horse's limbs, he laid one hand on its heart, and drew the other briskly across the animal's eyes, when finding no increase of pulsation, in consequence of the latter motion, he had come to the conclusion that the horse must be blind.

494.12 (Ch. 49) to make the inquiry It was said that very unfair means were used to compel the prisoners, committed on account of the Popish Plot, to make disclosures, and that several of them were privately put to the torture.

495.9 (Ch. 49) its gleam

HISTORY OF COLONEL THOMAS BLOOD. This person, who was capable of framing and carrying into execution the most desperate enterprises, was one of those extraordinary characters, who can only arise amid the bloodshed, confusion, destruction of morality, and wide-spreading violence which take place during civil war. The arrangement of the present volume admitting of a lengthened digression, we cannot, perhaps, enter upon a subject more extraordinary or entertaining, than the history of this notorious desperado, who exhibited all the elements of a most accomplished ruffian. As the account of these adventures is scattered in various and scarce publications, it will probably be a service to the reader to bring the most remarkable of them under his eye, in a simultaneous point of view.

Blood's father is reported to have been a blacksmith; but this was only a disparaging mode of describing a person who had a concern in iron-works, and had thus acquired independence. He entered early in life into the Civil War, served as a lieutenant in the Parliament forces, and was put by Henry Cromwell, Lord Deputy of Ireland, into the commission of the peace, when he was scarcely two-and-twenty. This outset in life decided his political party for ever; and however unfit the principles of such a man rendered him for the society of those who professed a rigidity of religion and morals, so useful was Blood's rapidity of invention, and so well was he known, that he was held capable of framing with sagacity, and conducting with skill, the most desperate undertakings, and in a turbulent time, was allowed to associate with the non-jurors, who affected a peculiar austerity of conduct and sentiments. In 1663, the Act of Settlement in Ireland, and the proceedings thereupon, affected Blood deeply in his fortune, and from that moment he appears to have nourished the most inveterate hatred to the Duke of Ormond, the Lord Lieutenant of Ireland, whom he considered as the author of the measures under which he suffered. There were at this time many malecontents of the same party with himself, so that Lieutenant Blood, as the most daring among them, was able to put himself at the head of a conspiracy which had for its purpose the exciting a general insurrection, and, as a preliminary step, the surprising of the castle of Dublin. The means proposed for the last purpose, which was to be the prelude to the rising, augured the desperation of the person by whom it was contrived, and yet might probably have succeeded, from its very boldness. A declaration was drawn up by the hand of Blood himself, calling upon all persons to take arms for the liberty of the subject, and the restoration of the Solemn League and Covenant. For the surprise of the castle, it was provided, that several persons with petitions in their hands, were to wait within the walls, as if they staid to present them to the Lord Lieutenant, while about fourscore of the old daring disbanded soldiers were to remain on the outside, dressed like carpenters, smiths, shoemakers, and other ordinary mechanics. As soon as the Lord Lieutenant went in, a baker was to pass by the main guard with a large basket of white bread on his back. By making a false step, he was to throw down his burden, which might create a scramble among the soldiers, and offer the fourscore men before mentioned an opportunity of disarming them, while the others with petitions in their hands secured all within; and being once master of the castle and the Duke of Ormond's person, they were to publish their declaration. But some of the principal conspirators were apprehended about twelve hours before the time appointed for the execution of the design, in which no less than seven members of the House of Commons (for the Parliament of Ireland was then sitting) were concerned. Leckie, a minister, the brother-in-law of Blood, was with several others tried, condemned, and executed. Blood effected his escape, but was still so much the object of public apprehension, that a rumour having arisen during Leckie's execution, that Major Blood was at hand with a party to rescue the prisoner, every one of the guards, and the executioner himself, shifted for themselves, leaving Leckie, with the halter about his neck, standing alone under the gallows; but as no rescue appeared, the sheriff-officers returned to their duty, and the criminal was executed. Meantime Blood retired among the mountains of Ireland, where he herded alternately with fanatics and Papists, provided only they were discontented with the government. There were few persons better acquainted with the intrigues of the time than this active partisan, who was alternately Quaker, Anabaptist, or Catholic, but always a rebel, and revolutionist; he shifted from place to place, and from kingdom to kingdom; became known to the Admiral de Ruyter, and was the soul of every desperate plot.

In particular, about 1665, Mr Blood was one of a revolutionary committee, or secret council, which continued its sittings, notwithstanding that government knew of its meetings. For their security, they had about thirty stout fellows posted around the place where they met, in the nature of a *corps de garde*. It fell out, that two of the members of the council, to save themselves, and perhaps for the sake of a reward, betrayed all their transactions to the ministry, which Mr Blood soon suspected, and in a short time got to the bottom of the whole affair. He appointed these two persons to meet him at a tavern in the city, where he had his guard ready, who secured them without any noise, and carried them to a private place provided for the purpose, where he called a kind of court-martial, before whom they were tried, found guilty, and sentenced to be shot two days after in the same place. When the time appointed came, they were brought out, and all the necessary preparations made for putting the sentence in execution; and the poor men, seeing no hopes of escape, disposed themselves to suffer as well as they could. At this critical juncture, Mr Blood was graciously pleased to grant them his pardon, and at the same time advised them to go to their new master, tell him all that had happened, and request him, in the name of their old confederates, to be as favourable to such of them as should at any time stand in need of his mercy. Whether these unfortunate people carried Mr Blood's message to the king, does not anywhere appear. It is however certain, that not long after the whole conspiracy was discovered; in consequence of which, on the 26th of April, 1666, Col. John Rathbone, and some other officers of the late disbanded army, were tried and convicted at the Old Bailey for a plot to surprise the Tower, and to kill General Monk.

After his concern with this desperate conclave, who were chiefly fanatics and Fifth-Monarchy men, Blood exchanged the scene for Scotland, where he mingled among the Cameronians, and must have been a most acceptable associate to John Balfour of Burley, or any other who joined the insurgents more out of spleen or desire of plunder, than from religious motives. The writers of the sect seem to have thought his name a discredit, or perhaps did not know it; nevertheless it is affirmed in a pamphlet written by a person who seems to have been well acquainted with the incidents of his life, that he shared the dangers of the defeat at Pentland Hills, 27th November, 1666, in which the Cameronians were totally routed. After the engagement, he found his way again to Ireland, but was hunted out of Ulster by Lord Dungannon, who pursued him very closely. On his return to England, he made himself again notorious by an exploit, of which the very singular particulars are contained in the pamphlet already mentioned.* The narrative runs as follows:—"Among the persons apprehended for the late fanatic conspiracy, was one Captain Mason, a person for whom Mr Blood had a particular affection and friendship. This person was to be removed from London to one of the northern counties, in order to his trial at the assizes; and to that intent was sent down with eight of the Duke's troop to guard him, being reckoned to be a person bold and courageous. Mr Blood having notice of this journey, resolves by the way to rescue his friend. The prisoner and his guard went away in the morning, and Mr Blood having made choice of three more of his acquaintance, set forward the same day at night, without boots, upon small horses, and their pistols in their trowsers, to prevent suspicion. But opportunities are not so easily had, neither were all places convenient, so that the convoy and their prisoner were gone a good way beyond Newark, before Mr Blood and his friends had any scent of their prisoner. At one place, they set a sentinel to watch his coming by; but whether it was out of fear, or that the person was tired with a tedious expectation, the sentinel brought them no tidings either of the prisoner or his guard, insomuch that Mr Blood and his companions began to think their friend so far before them upon the road, that it would be in vain to follow him. Yet not willing to give over an enterprise so generously undertaken, upon Mr Blood's encouragement, they rode on, though despairing of success, till finding it grow towards evening, and meeting with a convenient inn upon the road, in a small village not far from Doncaster, they resolved to lie there all night, and return for London the next morning. In that inn they had not sat long in a room next the street, condoling among themselves the ill success of such a tedious journey, and the misfortune of their friend, before the convoy came thundering up to the door of the said inn with their prisoner, Captain Mason having made choice of that inn, as being best known to him, to give his guardians the refreshment of a dozen of drink. There Mr Blood, unseen, had a full view of his friend, and of the persons he had to deal with. He had bespoke a

* Remarks on the Life of the famed Mr Blood. London, 1680. Folio.

small supper, which was at the fire, so that he had but very little time for consultation, finding that Captain Mason's party did not intend to alight. On this account he only gave general directions to his associates to follow his example in whatever they saw him do. In haste, therefore, they called for their horses, and threw down their money for their reckoning, telling the woman of the house, that since they had met with such good company, they were resolved to go forward. Captain Mason went off first upon a sorry beast, and with him the commander of the party, and four more; the rest staid behind to make an end of their liquor. Then away marched one more single, and in a very small time after the last two. By this time, Mr Blood and one of his friends being horsed, followed the two that were hindmost, and soon overtook them. These four rode some little time together, Mr Blood on the right hand of the two soldiers, and his friend on the left. But upon a sudden, Mr Blood laid hold of the reins of the horse next him, while his friend, in observation to his directions, did the same on the other hand; and having presently by surprise dismounted the soldiers, pulled off their bridles, and sent their horses to pick their grass where they pleased. These two being thus made sure of, Mr Blood pursues his game, intending to have reached the single trooper; but he being got to the rest of his fellows, now reduced to six, and a barber of York, that travelled in their company, Mr Blood made up, heads the whole party, and stops them; of which some of the foremost, looking upon him to be either drunk or mad, thought the rebuke of a switch to be a sufficient chastisement of such a rash presumption, which they exercised with more contempt than fury, till, by the rudeness of his compliments in return, he gave them to understand he was not in jest, but in very good earnest. He was soon seconded by his friend that was with him in his first exploit; but there had been several rough blows dealt between the unequal number of six to two, before Mr Blood's two other friends came up to their assistance; nay, I may safely say seven to two; for the barber of York, whether out of his natural propensity to the sport, or that his pot-valiantness had made him so generous as to help his fellow-travellers, would needs show his valour at the beginning of the fray; but better he had been at the latter end of a feast; for though he showed his prudence to take the stronger side, as he guessed by the number, yet because he would take no warning, which was often given him, not to put himself to the hazard of losing a guitar-finger by meddling in a business that nothing concerned him, he lost his life, as they were forced to dispatch him, in the first place, for giving them a needless trouble. The barber, being become an useless instrument, and the other of Mr Blood's friends being come up, the skirmish began to be very smart, the four assailants having singled out their champions as fairly and equally as they could. All this while, Captain Mason, being rode before upon his thirty-shilling steed, wondering his guard came not with him, looked back, and observing a combustion, and that they were altogether by the ears, knew not what to think. He conjectured it at first to have been some intrigue upon him, as if the troopers had a design to tempt him to an escape, which might afterwards prove more to his prejudice; just like cats, that, with regardless scorn, seem to give the distressed mouse all the liberty in the world to get away out of their paws, but soon recover their prey again at one jump. Thereupon, unwilling to undergo the hazard of such a trial, he comes back, at which time Mr Blood cried out to him, Horse, horse, quickly! an alarm so amazing at first, that he could not believe it to be his friend's voice when he heard it; but as the thoughts of military men are soon summoned together, and never hold Spanish councils, the Captain presently settled his resolution, mounts the next horse that wanted a rider, and puts in for a share of his own self-preservation. In this bloody conflict, Mr Blood was three times unhorsed, occasioned by his forgetfulness, as having omitted to new girt his saddle, which the ostler had unloosed upon the wadding his horse at his first coming into the inn. Being then so often dismounted, and not knowing the reason, which the occasion would not give him leave to consider, he resolved to fight it out on foot; of which two of the soldiers taking the advantage, singled him out, and drove him into a court-yard, where he made a stand with a full body, his sword in one hand, and his pistol in the other. One of the soldiers taking that advantage of his open body, shot him near the shoulder-blade of his pistol arm, at what time he had four other bullets in his body, that he had received before; which the soldier observing, flung his discharged pistol at him with that good aim and violence, that he hit him a stunning blow just under the forehead, upon the upper part of the nose between the eyes, which for the present so amazed him, that he gave himself over for a dead man; yet resolving to give one sparring blow before he expired, such is the strange provocation and success of despair, with one vigorous stroke of his sword, he brought his adversary with a vengeance from his horse, and laid him in a far worse condition than himself at his horse's feet. At that time, full of anger and revenge, he was just going to make an end of his conquest, by giving him the fatal stab, but that in the very nick of time, Captain Mason, having, by the help of his friends, done his business where they had fought, by the death of some, and the disabling of others that opposed them, came in, and bid him hold and spare the life of one that had been the civilest person to him upon the road, a fortunate piece of kindness in the one, and of gratitude in the other; which Mr Blood easily condescending to, by the joint assistance of the Captain, the other soldier was soon mastered, and the victory, after a sharp fight, that lasted above two hours, was at length completed. You may be sure the fight was well maintained on both sides, while two of the soldiers, besides the barber, were slain upon the place, three unhorsed, and the rest wounded. And it was observable, that though the encounter happened in a village, where a great number of people were spectators of the combat, yet none would adventure the rescue of either party, as not knowing which was in the wrong, or which in the right, and were therefore wary of being arbitrators in such a desperate contest, where they saw the reward of assistance to be nothing but present death. After the combat was over, Mr Blood and his friends divided themselves, and parted several ways."

Before he had engaged in this adventure, Blood had placed his wife and son in an apothecary's shop at Rumford, under the name of Weston. He himself afterwards affected to practise as a physician under that of Ayliffe, under which guise he remained concealed until his wounds were cured, and the hue and cry against him and his accomplices was somewhat abated.

In the meantime this extraordinary man, whose spirits toiled in framing the most daring enterprises, had devised a plot, which, as it respected the person at whom it was aimed, was of a much more ambitious character than that for the delivery of Mason. It had for its object the seizure of the person of the Duke of Ormond, his ancient enemy, in the streets of London. In this some have thought he only meant to gratify his resentment, while others suppose that he might hope to extort some important advantages by detaining his Grace in his hands as a prisoner. The Duke's historian, Carte, gives the following account of this extraordinary enterprise:—" The Prince of Orange came this year (1670) into England, and being invited on Dec. 6, to an entertainment in the city of London, his Grace attended him thither. As he was returning homewards in a dark night, and going up St James's Street, at the end of which, facing the palace, stood Clarendon House, where he then lived, he was attacked by Blood and five of his accomplices. The Duke always used to go attended with six footmen; but as they were too heavy a load to ride upon a coach, he always had iron spikes behind it to keep them from getting up; and continued this practice to his dying day, even after this attempt of assassination. These six footmen used to walk on both sides of the street over against the coach; but by some contrivance or other, they were all stopped and out of the way, when the Duke was taken out of his coach by Blood and his son, and mounted on horseback behind one of the horsemen in his company. The coachman drove on to Clarendon House, and told the porter that the duke had been seized by two men, who had carried him down Pickadilly. The porter immediately ran that way, and Mr James Clarke chancing to be at that time in the court of the house, followed with all possible haste, having first alarmed the family, and ordered the servants to come after him as fast as they could. Blood, it seems, either to gratify the humour of his patron, who had set him upon this work, or to glut his own revenge by putting his Grace to the same ignominious death, which his accomplices in the treasonable design upon Dublin Castle had suffered, had taken a strong fancy into his head to hang the Duke at Tyburn. Nothing could have saved his Grace's life, but that extravagant imagination and passion of the villain, who, leaving the Duke mounted and buckled to one of his comrades, rode on before, and (as is said) actually tied a rope to the gallows, and then rode back to see what was become of his accomplices, whom he met riding off in a great hurry. The horseman to whom the Duke was tied, was a person of great strength, but being embarrassed by his Grace's struggling, could not advance as fast as he desired. He was, however, got a good way beyond Berkeley (now Devonshire) House, towards Knightsbridge, when the Duke having got his foot under the man's, unhorsed him, and they both fell down together in the mud, where they were struggling, when the porter and Mr Clarke came up. The villain then disengaged himself, and seeing the neighbourhood alarmed, and numbers of people running towards them, got on horseback, and having with one of his comrades, fired their pistols at the Duke, (but missed him, as taking their aim in the dark, and in a hurry,) rode off as fast as they could to save themselves. The Duke (now sixty years of age) was quite spent with struggling, so that when Mr Clarke and the porter came up, they knew him rather by feeling his star, than by any sound of voice he could utter; and they were forced to carry him home, and lay him on a bed to recover his spirits. He received some wounds and bruises in the struggle, which confined him within doors for some days. The King, when he heard of this intended assassination of the Duke of Ormond, expressed a great resentment on that occasion, and issued out a proclamation for the discovery and apprehension of the miscreants concerned in the attempt."

Blood, however, lay concealed, and with his usual success, escaped apprehension. While thus lurking, he entertained and digested an exploit, evincing the same atrocity which had characterised the undertakings he had formerly been engaged in; there was also to be traced in his new device something of that peculiar disposition which inclined him to be desirous of adding to the murder of the Duke of Ormond, the singular infamy of putting him to death at Tyburn. With something of the same spirit he now resolved to show his contempt of monarchy, and all its symbols, by stealing the crown, sceptre, and other articles of the regalia out of the office in which they were deposited, and enriching himself and his needy associates with the produce of the spoils. This feat, by which Blood is now chiefly remembered, is, like all his transactions, marked with a daring strain of courage and duplicity, and like most of his undertakings, was very likely to have proved successful. John Bayley, Esq. in his History and Antiquities of the Tower of London, gives the following distinct account of this curious exploit. At this period, Sir Gilbert Talbot was Keeper, as it was called, of the Jewel House.

"It was soon after the appointment of Sir Gilbert Talbot, that the Regalia in the Tower first became objects of public inspection, which King Charles allowed in consequence of the reduction in the emoluments of the master's office. The profits which arose from showing the jewels to strangers, Sir Gilbert assigned in lieu of a salary, to the person whom he had appointed to the care of them. This was an old confidential servant of his father's, one Talbot Edwards, whose name is handed down to posterity as keeper of the regalia, when the notorious attempt to steal the crown was made in the year 1673; the following account of which is chiefly derived from a relation which Mr Edwards himself made of the transaction.

"About three weeks before this audacious villain Blood made his attempt upon the crown, he came to the Tower in the habit of a parson, with a long cloak, cassock, and canonical girdle, accompanied by a woman, whom he called his wife. They desired to see the regalia, and, just as their wishes had been gratified, the lady feigned sudden indisposition; this called forth the kind offices of Mrs Edwards, the keeper's wife, who, having courteously invited her into their house to repose herself, she soon recovered, and, on their departure, professed themselves thankful for this civility. A few days after, Blood came again, bringing a present to Mrs Edwards, of four pairs of white gloves from his pretended wife; and having thus begun the acquaintance, they made frequent visits to improve it. After a short respite of their compliments, the disguised ruffian returned again; and in conversation with Mrs Edwards, said that his wife could discourse of nothing but the kindness of those good people in the Tower—that she had long studied, and at length bethought herself of a handsome way of requital. You have, quoth he, a pretty young gentlewoman for your daughter, and I have a young nephew, who has two or three hundred a-year in land, and is at my disposal. If your daughter be free, and you approve it, I'll bring him here to see her, and we will endeavour to make it a match. This was easily assented to by old Mr Edwards, who invited the parson to dine with him on that day; he readily accepted the invitation; and taking upon him to say grace, performed it with great seeming devotion, and casting up his eyes, concluded it with a prayer for the King, Queen, and royal family. After dinner, he went up to see the rooms, and observing a handsome case of pistols hang there, expressed a great desire to buy them, to present to a young lord, who was his neighbour; a pretence by which he thought of disarming the house against the period intended for the execution of his design. At his departure, which was a canonical benediction of the good company, he appointed a day and hour to bring his young nephew to see his mistress, which was the very day that he made his daring attempt. The good old gentleman had got up ready to receive his guest, and the daughter was in her best dress to entertain her expected lover; when, behold, Parson Blood, with three more, came to the jewel-house, all armed with rapier-blades in their canes, and every one a dagger, and a brace of pocket-pistols. Two of his companions entered in with him, on pretence of seeing the crown, and the third staid at the door, as if to look after the young lady, a jewel of a more charming description, but in reality as a watch. The daughter, who thought it not modest to come down till she was called, sent the maid to take a view of the company, and bring a description of her gallant; and the servant, conceiving that he was the intended bridegroom who staid at the door, being the youngest of the party, returned to soothe the anxiety of her young mistress with the idea she had formed of his person. Blood told Mr Edwards that they would not go up stairs till his wife came, and desired him to show his friends the crown to pass the time till then; and they had no sooner entered the room, and the door, as usual, shut, than a cloak was thrown over the old man's head, and a gag put in his mouth. Thus secured, they told him that their resolution was to have the crown, globe, and sceptre; and, if he would quietly submit to it, they would spare his life; otherwise he was to expect no mercy. He thereupon endeavoured to make all the noise he possibly could, to be heard above; they then knocked him down with a wooden mallet, and told him, that, if yet he would lie quietly, they would spare his life; but if not, upon his next attempt to discover them, they would kill him. Mr Edwards, however, according to his own account, was not intimidated by this threat, but strained himself to make the greater noise, and in consequence, received several more blows on the head with the mallet, and was stabbed in the belly; this again brought the poor old man to the ground, where he lay for some time in so senseless a state, that one of the villains pronounced him dead. Edwards had come a little to himself, and hearing this, lay quietly, conceiving it best to be thought so. The booty was now to be disposed of, and one of them, named Parrot, secreted the orb. Blood held the crown under his cloak; and the third was about to file the sceptre in two, in order that it might be placed in a bag, brought for that purpose; but, fortunately, the son of Mr Edwards, who had been in Flanders with Sir John Talbot, and on his landing in England, had obtained leave to come away post to visit his father, happened to arrive whilst this scene was acting; and on coming to the door, the person that stood sentinel, asked with whom he would speak; to which he answered, that he belonged to the house; and, perceiving the person to be a stranger, told him that if he had any business with his father that he would acquaint him with it, and so hastened up stairs to salute his friends. This unexpected accident spread confusion amongst the party, and they instantly decamped with the crown and orb, leaving the sceptre yet unfiled. The aged keeper now raised himself upon his legs, forced the gag from his mouth, and cried, Treason! murder! which being heard by his daughter, who was, perhaps, anxiously expecting far other sounds, ran out and reiterated the cry. The alarm now became general, and young Edwards and his brother-in-law, Captain Beckman, ran after the conspirators, whom a warder put himself in a position to stop, but Blood discharged a pistol at him, and he fell, although unhurt, and the thieves proceeded safely to the next post, where one Sill, who had been a soldier under Cromwell, stood sentinel; but he offered no opposition, and they accordingly passed the drawbridge. Horses were waiting for them at St Catherine's gate; and as they ran that way along the Tower wharf, they themselves cried out, Stop the rogues! by which they passed on unsuspected, till Captain Beckman overtook them. At his head Blood fired another pistol, but missed him, and was seized. Under the cloak of this daring villain was found the crown, and, although he saw himself a prisoner, he had yet the impudence to struggle for his prey; and when it was finally wrested from him, said, It was a gallant attempt, however unsuccessful; it was for a crown! Parrot, who had formerly served under General Harrison, was also taken; but Hunt, Blood's son-in-law, reached his horse and rode off, as did two other of the thieves; but he was soon afterwards stopped, and likewise committed to custody. In this struggle and confusion, the great pearl, a large diamond, and several smaller stones, were lost from the crown; but the two former, and some of the latter, were afterwards found and restored; and the Ballas ruby, broken off the sceptre, being found in Parrot's pocket, nothing considerable was eventually missing.

"As soon as the prisoners were secured, young Edwards hastened to Sir Gilbert Talbot, who was then master and treasurer of the Jewel House, and gave him an account of the transaction. Sir Gilbert instantly went to the King, and acquainted his majesty with it; and his majesty commanded him to proceed forthwith to the Tower, to see how matters stood; to take the examination of Blood and the others; and to return and report it to him. Sir Gilbert accordingly went; but the King in the meantime was persuaded by some about him, to hear the examination himself, and the prisoners were in consequence sent for to Whitehall; a circumstance which is supposed to have saved these daring wretches from the gallows."

On his examination under such an atrocious charge, Blood audaciously replied, "that he would never betray an associate, or defend himself at the expense of uttering a falsehood." He even averred, perhaps, more than was true against himself, when he confessed that he had lain concealed among the reeds for the purpose of killing the King with a carabine, while Charles was bathing; but he pretended that on this occasion his purpose was disconcerted by a secret awe,—appearing to verify the allegation in Shakspeare, "There's such divinity doth hedge a king, that treason can but peep to what it would, acts little of its will." To this story, true or false, Blood added a declaration that he was at the head of a numerous following, disbanded soldiers and others, who, from motives of religion, were determined to take the life of the King, as the only obstacle to their obtaining freedom of worship and liberty of conscience. These men, he said, would be determined, by his execution, to persist in the resolution of putting Charles to death; whereas, he averred that, by sparing his life, the King might disarm a hundred poniards directed against his own. This view of the case made a strong impression on Charles, whose selfishness was uncommonly acute: yet he felt the impropriety of pardoning the attempt upon the life of the Duke of Ormond, and condescended to ask that faithful servant's permission, before he would exert his authority, to spare the assassin. Ormond answered, that if the King chose to pardon the attempt to steal his crown, he himself might easily consent that the attempt upon his own life, as a crime of much less importance, should also be forgiven. Charles, accordingly, not only gave Blood a pardon, but endowed him with a pension of L.500 a-year; which led many persons to infer, not only that the King wished to preserve himself from the future attempts of this desperate man, but that he had it also in view to secure the services of so determined a ruffian, in case he should have an opportunity of employing him in his own line of business. There is a striking contrast between the fate of Blood, pensioned and rewarded for this audacious attempt, and that of the faithful Edwards, who may be safely said to have sacrificed his life in defence of the property intrusted to him! In remuneration for his fidelity and his sufferings, Edwards only obtained a grant of L.200 from the Exchequer, with L.100 to his son; but so little pains were taken about the regular discharge of these donatives, that the parties entitled to them were glad to sell them for half the sum. After this wonderful escape from justice, Blood seems to have affected the airs of a person in favour, and was known to solicit the suits of many of the old republican party, for whom he is said to have gained considerable indulgences, when the old cavaliers, who had ruined themselves in the cause of Charles the First, could obtain neither countenance nor restitution. During the ministry called the Cabal, he was high in favour with the Duke of Buckingham; till upon their declension his favour began also to fail, and we find him again engaged in opposition to the Court. Blood was not likely to lie idle amid the busy intrigues and factions which succeeded the celebrated discovery of Oates. He appears to have passed again into violent opposition to the Court, but his steps were no longer so sounding as to be heard above his contemporaries. North hints at his being involved in a plot against his former friend and patron the Duke of Buckingham. The passage is quoted at length in a note in this volume, page 272.

The Plot, it appears, consisted in an attempt to throw some scandalous imputation upon the Duke of Buckingham, for a conspiracy to effect which Edward Christian, Arthur O'Brien, and Thomas Blood, were indicted in the King's Bench, and found guilty, 25th June, 1680. The damages sued for were laid as high as ten thousand pounds, for which Colonel Blood found bail. But he appears to have been severely affected in health, as, 24th August, 1680, he departed this life in a species of lethargy. It is remarkable enough that the story of his death and funeral was generally regarded as fabricated, preparative to some exploit of his own; nay, so general was this report, that the coroner caused his body to be raised, and a jury to sit upon it, for the purpose of ensuring that the celebrated Blood had at length undergone the common fate of mankind. There was found unexpected difficulty in proving that the miserable corpse before the jury was that of the celebrated conspirator. It was at length recognised by some of his acquaintances, who swore to the preternatural size of the thumb, so that the coroner, convinced of the identity, remanded this once active, and now quiet person, to his final rest in Tothill-fields.

Such were the adventures of an individual, whose real exploits, whether the motive, the danger, or the character of the enterprises be considered, equal, or rather surpass, those fictions of violence and peril which we love to peruse in romance. They cannot, therefore, be deemed foreign to a work dedicated, like the present, to the preservation of extraordinary occurrences, whether real or fictitious.

QUENTIN DURWARD

Editorial Note

Quentin Durward occupies the second part of Volume 6 and the whole of Volume 7 of the 1824 octavo *Novels and Romances*, MSS 23024 and 23025 in the Interleaved Set. Scott annotated the work during April 1830, and Cadell revised it between 21 December that year and 15 January 1831, dealing with proofs of the new material from 27 January to 16 February (EEWN 15, 425). The novel appeared as Volumes 31 and 32 of the Magnum on 1 December 1831 and 1 January 1832.

The Introduction is perhaps the least satisfactory of the series. Scott presents an overview of the decline of chivalry, which is familiar territory for his readers, linked with a much more one-sided view of Louis XI as a Mephistolean Machiavel than appears in the novel. This demonisation of Louis persisted to proof stage, when Scott added the sentence at 297.24–27: 'Nor is it to be forgotten that Louis possessed to a great extent that caustic wit which can turn into ridicule all that a man does for any other person's advantage but his own, and was, therefore, peculiarly qualified to play the part of a cold-hearted and sneering fiend.' The last two paragraphs are by far the most interesting. Scott may well be reading intentions into the compositional process, as he often does, but his assertion that 'Amidst so great an abundance of materials, it was difficult to select such as should be most intelligible and interesting to the reader' is of value, and his defence of the essential probability of the plot centring on Isabelle de Croye is not implausible. Also worthy of consideration is his perception that the novel's popularity on the Continent was because 'the historical allusions awakened more familiar ideas' than in Britain.

The manuscript of the Introduction shows no major changes of mind in the course of composition. The reference to Fénelon comes in on the verso ('Fenelon also has left . . . remarkable passage': 302.15–17) and Scott has noted on the title-page of the Interleaved volume 'Wanting passage from Fenelon Introduction p. 6 to Quentin Durward'. Probably at proof stage Scott inserted (in addition to the sentence already noted) the images of Durindarte and Louis as an athlete running a race (299.17–24; 300.42–301.3).

The text is provided with a host of footnotes, a few of them glossarial, but mostly explanatory of particular points or filling in historical details, often in the manner of a modern editor. The historicising tendency of the notes is reinforced by one suggesting that if the author had had the information at the time of writing Petit-André would have been called Petit-Jean (306.26–33). Scott retains the first-edition name, but on another occasion he explains in a note that he has changed the description of the historian Comines to conform with recently discovered historical information (315.8–41): he had made a similar change to William Christian in the previous novel *Peveril of the Peak*. To counterbalance this historicising tendency, though, there are occasional reminders that this is a work of fiction where partial and even complete romancing is entirely in order (313.40–314.29; 323.30–34; 325.5–17). In one fascinating footnote (316.27–38) Scott indicates that the arrival at Péronne of the romance writer Seigneur d'Urfé with his two brothers, all imprisoned by Louis, 'might have been happily enough introduced into the present work'. In a phrase introduced probably at proof stage he explains (it may or may not have been an afterthought) that 'the fate of the Euphuist [Sir Piercie Shafton in *The Monastery*] was a warning to the author'. Of the endnotes, three amount to short essays, two on gipsies and one on heralds (306–09; 312–13; 321–23). In the former the final paragraph, based on personal observation, is probably a proof addition. Seven of the notes continue the Introduction's denigration of Louis, either as their central point, or in the last three cases rather in the by-going (311.1–11, 36–39; 317.34–43; 318.2–40; 319–21; 321.11–39; 321–23).

Finally, it may be noted that on two occasions Scott takes advantage of footnotes to explain his intention in seeking 'to give the odious Tristan a species of dogged and brutal fidelity to Louis, similar to the attachment of a dull-dog to his master' (319.3–5), and to indicate that in his toning down of an anecdote relating to Comines he has 'endeavoured to give the anecdote a turn more consistent with the sense and prudence of the great author concerned' (321.8–10).

There are four Magnum illustrations for this title. The frontispiece to Volume 31 (MAG0061 / TB348.31) was designed by Richard

Parkes Bonington and engraved by Edward Goodall. It depicts Quentin at the ford confronting Louis and Tristan L'Hermite, both disguised, the former as Maitre Pierre (EEWN 32.12–17 (abridged): 'His opponent seeing . . . in the swollen ford.'). The title-page vignette (MAG0062 / TB348.31) was designed by John William Wright and engraved by James Mitchell. It depicts Louis, seated, being served by Jacqueline (the Countess of Croye) in the inn, with Quentin offering assistance (EEWN 15, 50.29–31: 'The mountain chivalry . . . resigned to him.'). The frontispiece to Volume 32 (MAG0063 / TB348.32) was designed by Robert Scott Lauder and engraved by John Horsburgh. It depicts Quentin attending to the prostrate figure of Isabelle in Schonwaldt Castle, with the Syndic Herman Pavillon looking on in the background (EEWN 15, 230.23–25 (with 'Quentin' for 'He'): 'Quentin hastily raised her . . . the Countesss Isabelle.'). The title-page vignette (MAG0064 / TB348.32) was designed by Edwin Landseer and engraved by Robert Graves. It depicts Hayraddin, disguised as the herald Rouge Sanglier, being pulled down by pursuing boar-hounds (EEWN 15, 365.30–32: 'At length the speed . . . soon have throttled him.').

QUENTIN DURWARD.

"His opponent, seeing himself thus menaced, laid hand upon his sword, but his more considerate comrade, who came up, commanded him to forbear, and, turning to the young man, accused him in turn of precipitation in plunging in the swollen ford".

EDINBURGH, PUBLISHED 1831, BY ROBERT CADELL & WHITTAKER & C° LONDON.

WAVERLEY NOVELS.

VOL. XXXI.

QUENTIN DURWARD.

J. W. Wright. J. Mitchell.

The mountain chivalry of Quentin Durward was instantly awakened, and he hastened to approach Jacqueline, and relieve her of the burthen she bore, and which she passively resigned to him.

PRINTED FOR ROBERT CADELL, EDINBURGH,
AND WHITTAKER & C° LONDON.
1831.

R. Lauder. J. Horsburgh.

QUENTIN DURWARD.

"Quentin hastily raised her from the ground, and, joy of joys! it was she whom he sought to save—the Countess Isabelle."

EDINBURGH, PUBLISHED 1831, BY ROBERT CADELL & WHITTAKER & C° LONDON.

WAVERLEY NOVELS.

VOL. XXXII.

QUENTIN DURWARD.

"At length the speed of the pseudo herald, could save him no longer from the fangs of his pursuers, they seized him, pulled him down, and would probably, soon have throttled him."

PRINTED FOR ROBERT CADELL, EDINBURGH,
AND WHITTAKER & C? LONDON.
1831.

Introduction to Quentin Durward

THE scene of this romance is laid in the fifteenth century, when the feudal system, which had been the sinews and nerves of national defence, and the spirit of chivalry, by which, as by a vivifying soul, that system was animated, began to be innovated upon and abandoned by those grosser characters, who centred their sum of happiness in procuring the personal objects on which they had fixed their own exclusive attachment. The same egotism had indeed displayed itself even in more primitive ages; but it was now for the first time openly avowed as a professed principle of action. The spirit of chivalry, however overstrained and fantastic many of its doctrines may appear to us, had in it this point of excellence, that it founded on generosity and self-denial, of which if the earth was deprived, it is difficult to conceive the existence of virtue among the human race.

Amongst those who were the first to ridicule and abandon the self-denying principles in which the young Knight was instructed, and to which he was so carefully trained up, Louis the XIth of France was the chief. That Sovereign was of a character so purely selfish—so guiltless of entertaining any purpose unconnected with his ambition, covetousness, and desire of selfish enjoyment, that he almost seems an incarnation of the devil himself, permitted to do his utmost for corrupting our ideas of honour in its very source. Nor is it to be forgotten that Louis possessed to a great extent that caustic wit which can turn into ridicule all that a man does for any other person's advantage but his own, and was, therefore, peculiarly qualified to play the part of a cold-hearted and sneering fiend.

In this point of view, Goethe's conception of the character and reasoning of Mephistophiles, the tempting spirit in the singular play of Faust, appears to me more happy than that which has been formed by Byron, and even than the Satan of Milton. These last great authors have given to the Evil Principle something which elevates and dignifies his wickedness; a sustained and unconquerable resistance against Omnipotence itself—a lofty scorn of suffering compared with submission, and all those points of attraction in the Author of Evil, which have induced Burns and others to claim him as the Hero of the Paradise Lost. The great German poet has, on the contrary, rendered his seducing spirit a being who, otherwise totally unimpassioned, seems only to have existed for the purpose of increasing, by his persuasions and temptations, the mass of moral evil, and who calls forth by his seductions those slumbering passions which otherwise might have allowed the human being who was the object of the Evil Spirit's operations to pass the tenor of his life in tranquillity. For this purpose Mephistophiles is, like Louis XI., endowed with an acute and depreciating spirit of caustic wit, which is employed incessantly in undervaluing and vilifying all actions, the consequences of which do not lead certainly and directly to self-gratification.

Even an author of works of mere amusement may be permitted to be serious for a moment, in order to reprobate all policy, whether of a public or private character, which rests its basis upon the principles of Machiavel, or the practice of Louis XI.

The cruelties, the perjuries, the suspicions of this prince, were rendered more detestable, rather than amended, by the gross and debasing superstition which he constantly practised. The devotion to the heavenly saints, of which he made such a parade, was upon the miserable principle of some petty deputy in office, who endeavours to hide or atone for the malversations of which he is conscious, by liberal gifts to those whose duty it is to observe his conduct, and endeavours to support a system of fraud, by an attempt to corrupt the incorruptible. In no other light can we regard his creating the Virgin Mary a countess and colonel of his guards, or the cunning that admitted to one or two peculiar forms of oath the force of a binding obligation, which he denied to all others, strictly preserving the secret, which mode of swearing he really accounted obligatory, as one of the most valuable of state mysteries.

To a total want of scruple, or, it would appear, of any sense whatever of moral obligation, Louis XI. added great natural firmness and sagacity of character, with a system of policy so highly refined, considering the times he lived in, that he sometimes overreached himself by giving way to its dictates.

Probably there is no portrait so dark as to be without its softer shades. He understood the interests of France, and faithfully pursued them so long as he could identify them with his own. He carried the country safe through the dangerous crisis of the war termed "for the public good;" in thus disuniting and dispersing this grand and dangerous alliance of the great crown vassals of France against the Sovereign, a King of a less cautious and temporizing character, and of a more bold and less crafty disposition than Louis XI., would, in all probability, have failed. Louis had also some personal accomplishments not inconsistent with his public character. He was cheerful and witty in society; caressed his victim like the cat, which can fawn when about to deal the most bitter wound; and none was better able to sustain and extol the superiority of the coarse and selfish reasons by which he endeavoured to supply those nobler motives for exertion, which his predecessors had derived from the high spirit of chivalry.

In fact that system was now becoming ancient, and had, even while in its perfection, something so overstrained and fantastic in its principles, as rendered it peculiarly the object of ridicule, whenever, like other old fashions, it began to fall out of repute, and the weapons of raillery could be employed against it, without exciting the disgust and horror with which they would have been rejected at an early period, as a species of blasphemy. In the fourteenth century a tribe of scoffers had arisen, who pretended to supply what was naturally useful in chivalry by other resources, and threw ridicule upon the extravagant and exclusive principles of honour and virtue, which were openly treated as absurd, because, in fact, they were cast in a mould of perfection too lofty for the practice of fallible beings. If an ingenuous and high-spirited youth proposed to frame himself on his father's principles of honour, he was vulgarly derided as if he had brought to the field the good old knight's Durindarte or two-handed sword, ridiculous from its antique make and fashion, although its blade might be the Ebro's temper, and its ornaments of pure gold.

In like manner, the principles of chivalry were cast aside, and their aid supplied by baser stimulants. Instead of the high spirit which pressed every man forwards in defence of his country, Louis XI. substituted the sword of the ever ready mercenary soldier, and persuaded his subjects, among whom the mercantile class began to make a figure, that it was better to leave to mercenaries the risks and labours of war, and supply the Crown with means of paying them, than to peril themselves in defence of their own substance. The merchants were easily persuaded by this reasoning. The hour did not arrive, in the days of Louis XI., when the landed gentry or nobles could be in like manner excluded from the ranks of war; but the wily monarch commenced that system, which, acted upon by his successors, at length threw the whole military defences of the state into the hands of the Crown.

He was equally forward in altering the principles which were wont to regulate the intercourse of the sexes. The doctrines of chivalry had established in theory at least, a system in which Beauty was the governing and remunerating divinity—Valour her slave, who caught his courage from her eye, and gave his life for her slightest service. It is true, the system here, as in other branches, was stretched to fantastic extravagance, and cases of scandal not unfrequently arose. Still they were generally such as those mentioned by Burke, where frailty was deprived of half its guilt, by being purified from all its grossness. In Louis XIth's practice, it was far otherwise. He was a low voluptuary, seeking pleasure without sentiment, and despising the sex from whom he desired to obtain it; his mistresses were of inferior rank, as little to be compared with the elevated though faulty character of Agnes Sorel, as Louis was to his heroic father, who freed France from the impending yoke of England. In like manner, by selecting his favourites and ministers from among the dregs of the people, Louis showed the slight regard which he paid to eminent station and high birth; and although this might be not only excusable but even meritorious, where his fiat promoted obscure talent, or called forth modest worth, it was very different when the King made his favourite associates of such men as Tristan l'Hermite, the Chief of his Marshalsea, or police; and it was evident such a prince could no longer be, as his descendant Francis elegantly designed himself, "the first gentleman in his dominions."

Nor were Louis's sayings and actions in private or public, of a kind which could redeem such gross offences against the character of a man of honour. His word, generally accounted the most sacred test of a man's character, and the least impeachment of which is a capital offence by the code of honour, was forfeited without scruple on the slightest occasion, and often by the perpetration of the most enormous crimes. If he broke his own personal and plighted faith, he did not treat that of the public with more ceremony. His sending an inferior person disguised as a herald to Edward IV., was in those days, where heralds were esteemed the sacred depositaries of public and national faith, a daring imposition, of which few save this unscrupulous prince would have been guilty.*

In short, the manners, sentiments, and actions of Louis XI. were such as were inconsistent with the principles of chivalry, and his caustic wit was sufficiently disposed to ridicule a system adopted on what he considered as the most absurd of all bases, since it was founded upon the principle of devoting toil, talents, and time, to the accomplishment of objects, from which no personal advantage could, in the nature of things, be obtained.

It is more than probable that, in thus renouncing almost openly the ties of religion, honour, and morality, by which mankind at large feel themselves influenced, Louis sought to obtain great advantages in his negotiations with parties who might esteem themselves bound, while he himself enjoyed liberty. He started from the

* See note, Disguised Herald, 321–23 below.

goal, he might suppose, like the racer who has got rid of the weights with which his competitors are still encumbered, and expects to succeed of course. But Providence seems always to unite the existence of peculiar danger, with some circumstance which may put those exposed to the peril upon their guard. The constant suspicion attached to any public person who becomes badly eminent for breach of faith, is to him what the rattle is to the poisonous serpent; and men come at last to calculate, not so much on what their antagonist says, as upon that which he is like to do; a degree of mistrust which tends to counteract the intrigues of such a faithless character, more than his freedom from the scruples of conscientious men can afford him advantage. The example of Louis XI. raised disgust and suspicion rather than a desire of imitation among other nations in Europe, and the circumstance of his outwitting more than one of his contemporaries, operated to put others on their guard. Even the system of chivalry, though much less generally extended than heretofore, survived this profligate monarch's reign, who did so much to sully its lustre, and long after the death of Louis XI. it inspired the Knight without Fear and Reproach, and the gallant Francis I.

Indeed, although the reign of Louis had been as successful in a political point of view as he himself could have desired, the spectacle of his deathbed might of itself be a warning-piece against the seduction of his example. Jealous of every one, but chiefly of his own son, he immured himself in his Castle of Plessis, intrusting his person exclusively to the doubtful faith of his Scottish mercenaries. He never stirred from his chamber; he admitted no one into it, and wearied Heaven and every saint with prayers, not for forgiveness of his sins, but for prolongation of his life. With a poverty of spirit totally inconsistent with his shrewd worldly sagacity, he importuned his physicians, until they insulted as well as plundered him. In his extreme desire of life, he sent to Italy for some choice relics, and the yet more extraordinary importation of an ignorant crack-brained peasant, who, from laziness probably, had shut himself up in a cave, and renounced flesh, fish, eggs, or the produce of the dairy. This man, who did not possess the slightest tincture of letters, Louis reverenced as if he had been the Pope himself, and to gain his goodwill founded two cloisters.

It was not the least singular circumstance of this course of superstition, that bodily health and terrestrial felicity seemed to be his only objects. Making any mention of his sins when talking on the state of his health, was strictly prohibited; and when at his command a priest recited a prayer to Saint Eutropius, in which he recommended the

King's welfare both in body and soul, Louis caused the two last words to be omitted, saying it was not prudent to importune the blessed saint by too many requests at once. Perhaps he thought by being silent on his crimes, he might suffer them to pass out of the recollection of the celestial patrons, whose aid he invoked for his body.

So great were the well-merited tortures of this tyrant's deathbed, that Philip des Comines enters into a regular comparison between them and the numerous cruelties inflicted on others by his order; and, considering both, comes to express an opinion, that the worldly pangs and agony suffered by Louis were such as might compensate the crimes he had committed, and that, after a reasonable quarantine in purgatory, he might in mercy be found duly qualified for the superior regions.

Fénélon also has left his testimony against this prince, whose mode of living and governing he has described in the following remarkable passage:—

"Pygmalion, tourmenté par une soif insatiable des richesses, se rend de plus en plus misérable et odieux à ses sujets. C'est un crime à Tyr que d'avoir de grands biens; l'avarice le rend défiant, soupçonneux, cruel; il persécute les riches, et il craint les pauvres.

"C'est un crime encore plus grand à Tyr d'avoir de la vertu; car Pygmalion suppose que les bons ne peuvent souffrir ses injustices et ses infamies; la vertu le condamne, il s'aigrit et s'irrite contre elle. Tout l'agite, l'inquiète, le ronge; il a peur de son ombre; il ne dort ni nuit ni jour; les Dieux, pour le confondre, l'accablent de trésors dont il n'ose jouir. Ce qu'il cherche pour être heureux est précisément ce qui l'empêche de l'être. Il regrette tout ce qu'il donne, et craint toujours de perdre; il se tourmente pour gagner.

"On ne le voit presque jamais; il est seul, triste, abattu, au fond de son palais; ses amis mêmes n'osent l'aborder, de peur de lui devenir suspects. Une garde terrible tient toujours des épées nues et des piques levées autour de sa maison. Trente chambres qui communiquent les unes aux autres, et dont chacune a une porte de fer avec six gros verroux, sont le lieu où il se renferme; on ne sait jamais dans laquelle de ces chambres il couche; et on assure qu'il ne couche jamais deux nuits de suite dans la même, de peur d'y être égorgé. Il ne connoît ni les doux plaisirs, ni l'amitié encore plus douce. Si on lui parle de chercher la joie, il sent qu'elle fuit loin de lui, et qu'elle refuse d'entrer dans son cœur. Ses yeux creux sont pleins d'un feu âpre et farouche; ils sont sans cesse errans de tous cotés; il prête l'oreille au moindre bruit, et se sent tout ému; il est pâle, défait, et les noirs soucis sont peints sur son visage toujours ridé. Il se tait, il soupire, il tire de son cœur de profonds gémissemens, il ne peut cacher les remords qui déchirent ses entrailles. Les mets les plus exquis le dégoûtent. Ses enfans, loin d'être son espérance, sont le sujet de sa terreur: il en a fait ses plus dangereux ennemis. Il n'a eu toute sa vie aucun moment d'assuré: il ne se conserve qu'à force de répandre le sang de tous ceux qu'il craint. Insensé, qui ne voit pas que sa cruauté, à laquelle il se confie, le fera périr! Quelqu'un de ses domestiques, aussi défiant que lui, se hâtera de délivrer le monde de ce monstre."

The instructive, but appalling scene of this tyrant's sufferings, was at length closed by death, 30th August, 1483.

The selection of this remarkable person as the principal character in the romance—for it will be easily comprehended, that the little love intrigue of Quentin is only employed as the means of bringing out the story—afforded considerable facilities to the author. The whole of Europe was, during the fifteenth century, convulsed with dissensions from such various causes, that it would have required almost a dissertation to have brought the English reader with a mind perfectly alive and prepared to admit the possibility of the strange scenes to which he was introduced.

In Louis XIth's time, extraordinary commotions existed throughout all Europe. England's civil wars were ended rather in appearance than reality, by the short-lived ascendency of the House of York. Switzerland was asserting that freedom which was afterwards so bravely defended. In the Empire, and in France, the great vassals of the crown were endeavouring to emancipate themselves from its control, while Charles of Burgundy by main force, and Louis more artfully by indirect means, laboured to subject them to subservience to their respective sovereignties. Louis, while with one hand he circumvented and subdued his own rebellious vassals, laboured secretly with the other to aid and encourage the large trading towns of Flanders to rebel against the Duke of Burgundy, to which their wealth and irritability naturally disposed them. In the more woodland districts of Flanders, the Duke of Gueldres, and William de la Marck, called from his ferocity the Wild Boar of Ardennes, were throwing off the habits of knights and gentlemen, to practise the violences and brutalities of common bandits.

A hundred secret combinations existed in the different provinces of France and Flanders: numerous private emissaries of the restless Louis, Bohemians, pilgrims, beggars, or agents disguised as such, were everywhere spreading the discontent which it was his policy to maintain in the dominions of Burgundy.

Amidst so great an abundance of materials, it was difficult to select such as should be most intelligible and interesting to the reader; and the author had to regret, that though he made liberal use of the power of departing from the reality of history, he felt by no means confident of having brought his story into a pleasing, compact, and sufficiently intelligible form. The mainspring of the plot is that which all who know the least of the feudal system can easily understand, though the facts are absolutely fictitious. The right of the feudal superior was in nothing more universally acknowledged than in his power to interfere in the marriage of a female vassal. This may appear contradictory of both the civil and canon law, which declare that marriage shall be free, while the feudal or municipal jurisprudence, in case of a fief passing to a female, acknowledges an interest in the superior of the fief to dictate the choice of her companion in marriage. This is accounted for on the principle that the superior was, by his bounty, the original grantor of the fief, and is still interested that the marriage of the vassal shall place there no one who may be inimical to his liege lord. On the other hand, it might be reasonably pleaded that this right of dictating to the vassal to a certain degree in the choice of a husband, is only competent to the superior, from whom the fief is originally derived. There is therefore no violent improbability in a vassal of Burgundy flying to the protection of the King of France, to whom Burgundy himself was vassal; nor is it a great stretch of probability to affirm, that Louis, unscrupulous as he was, should have formed the design of betraying the fugitive into some alliance which might prove inconvenient, if not dangerous, to his formidable kinsman and vassal of Burgundy.

I may add, that this romance of QUENTIN DURWARD, which acquired a popularity at home more extensive than some of its predecessors, found also unusual success on the continent, where the historical allusions awakened more familiar ideas.

ABBOTSFORD, 1*st December*, 1831.

Notes to Quentin Durward

3.1 (Introduction) Introduction It is scarcely necessary to say, that all which follows is imaginary.

11.2 (Introduction) le Chevalier Scott It is scarce necessary to remind the reader that this passage was published during the author's incognito; and, as Lucio expresses it, spoken "according to the trick."

26.23 (Ch. 1) very precious This *editio princeps* which, when in good preservation, is much sought after by connoisseurs, is entitled, *Les Cent Nouvelles Nouvelles, contenant Cent Histoires Nouveaux, qui sont moult plaisans à raconter en toutes bonnes compagnies par manière de joyeuxeté. Paris, Antoine Verard. Sans date d'année d'impression; in-folio gotique*. See DE BURE.

37.13 (Ch. 2) peculiarly appropriate Every vocation had, in the middle ages, its protecting saint. The chase, with its fortunes and hazards, the business of so many, and the amusement of all, was placed under the direction of Saint Hubert.

This silvan saint was the son of Bertrand, Duke of Acquitaine, and, while in the secular state, was a courtier of King Pepin. He was passionately fond of the chase, and used to neglect the attendance on divine worship for this amusement. While he was once engaged in this pastime, a stag appeared before him, having a crucifix bound betwixt his horns, and he heard a voice which menaced him with eternal punishment if he did not repent of his sins. He retired from the world and took orders, his wife having also retreated into the cloister. Hubert afterwards became Bishop of Maestrecht and Liege; and from his zeal in destroying remnants of idolatry, is called the Apostle of Ardennes and of Brabant. Those who were descended of his race were supposed to possess the power of curing persons bitten by mad dogs.

43.11 (Ch. 3) covin-tree The large tree in front of a Scottish castle, was sometimes called so. It is difficult to trace the derivation; but at that distance from the castle, the laird received guests of rank, and thither he conveyed them on their departure.

48.11 (Ch. 4) the young Duke of Gueldres This was Adolphus, son of Arnold and of Catherine de Bourbon. The present story has little to do with him, though one of the most atrocious characters of his time. He made war against his own father; in which unnatural strife he made the old man prisoner, and used him with the most brutal violence, proceeding, it is said, even to the length of striking him with his hand. Arnold, in resentment of this usage, disinherited the unprincipled wretch, and sold to Charles of Burgundy whatever rights he had over the duchy of Gueldres and earldom of Zutphen. Mary of Burgundy, daughter of Charles, restored these dominions to the unnatural Adolphus, who was slain in 1477.

49.6 (Ch. 4) opposite ends This part of Louis XIth's reign was much embarrassed by the intrigues of the Constable Saint Paul, who affected independence, and carried on intrigues with England, France, and Burgundy, at the same time. According to the usual fate of such versatile politicians, the Constable ended by drawing upon himself the animosity of all the powerful neighbours whom he had in their turn amused and deceived. He was delivered up by the Duke of Burgundy to the King of France, tried, and hastily executed for treason, A.D. 1475.

49.18 (Ch. 4) Saint Quentin It was by his possession of this town of Saint Quentin that the Constable was able to carry on those political intrigues, which finally cost him so dear.

50.40 (Ch. 4) know you all It was a part of Louis's very unamiable character, and not the best of it, that he entertained a great contempt for the understanding, and prejudice against the character, of the fair sex.

61.10 (Ch. 5) a pair of stilts The crutches or stilts, which in Scotland are used to pass rivers, are employed by the peasantry of the country near Bourdeaux, to traverse those deserts of loose sand called Landes.

70.36 (Ch. 6) fremit kindred *Better kind strangers than estranged kindred.* The motto is engraved on a dirk, belonging to a person who had but too much reason to choose such a device. It was left by him to my father, and is connected with a strange course of adventures, which may one day be told. The weapon is now in my possession.

72.36 (Ch. 6) skene dhu Black knife; a species of knife without a clasp or hinge, formerly much used by the Highlanders, who seldom travelled without such an ugly weapon, though it is now rarely used.

77.26 (Ch.6) Louis XI. One of these two persons, I learned from the Chronique de Jean de Troyes, but too late to avail myself of the information, might with more accuracy have been called Petit-Jean, than Petit-André. This was actually the name of the son of Henry de Cousin, master executioner of the High Court of Justice. The Constable Saint Paul was executed by him with such dexterity, that the head, when struck off, struck the ground at the same time with the body. This was in 1475.

82.32 (Ch. 6) Crawford and Oliver

GIPSIES OR BOHEMIANS. In a former volume of this edition of the Waverley Novels, (Guy Mannering,) the reader will find some remarks upon the gipsies as they are found in Scotland. But it is well known that this extraordinary variety of the human race exists in nearly the same primitive state, speaking the same language, in almost all the kingdoms of Europe, and conforming in certain respects to the manners of the people around them, but yet remaining separated from them by certain material distinctions, in which they correspond with each other, and ascertain their pretensions to be considered as a distinct race. Their first appearance in Europe took place in the beginning of the fifteenth century, when various bands of this singular people appeared in the different countries of Europe. They claimed an Egyptian descent, and their features attested that they were of Eastern origin. The account given by these singular people was, that it was appointed to them, as a penance, to travel for a certain number of years. This apology was probably selected as being most congenial to the superstitions of the countries which they visited. Their appearance, however, and manners, strongly contradicted the allegation that they travelled from any religious motive.

Their dress and accoutrements were at once showy and squalid; those who acted as captains and leaders of any horde, and such always appeared as their commanders, were arrayed in dresses of the most showy colours, such as scarlet or light green; were well mounted; assumed the title of dukes and counts, and affected considerable consequence. The rest of the tribe were most miserable in their diet and apparel, fed without hesitation on animals which had died of disease, and were clad in filthy and scanty rags, which hardly sufficed for the ordinary purposes of common decency. Their complexion was positively Eastern, approaching to that of the Hindoos.

Their manners were as depraved as their appearance was poor and beggarly. The men were in general thieves, and the women of the most abandoned character. The few arts which they studied with success, were of a slight and idle, though ingenious description. They practised working in iron, but never upon any great scale. Many were good sportsmen, good musicians, and masters, in a word, of all those trivial arts, the practice of which is little better than mere indolence. But their ingenuity never ascended into industry. Two or three other peculiarities seem to have distinguished them in all countries. Their pretensions to read fortunes, by palmistry and by astrology, acquired them sometimes respect, but oftener drew them under suspicion as sorcerers; and lastly, the universal accusation that they augmented their horde by stealing children, subjected them to doubt and execration. From this it happened, that the pretension set up by these wanderers, of being pilgrims in act of penance, although it was at first admitted, and in many instances obtained them protection from the governments of the countries through which they travelled, was afterwards totally disbelieved, and they were considered as incorrigible rogues and vagrants; they incurred almost everywhere sentence of banishment, and, where suffered to remain, were more objects of persecution than of protection to the Law.

There is a curious and accurate account of their arrival in France in the Journal of a Doctor of Theology, which is preserved and published by the learned Pasquier. The following is an extract:—"On August 27th, 1427, came to Paris twelve penitents, *Penanciers*, (penance doers,) as they called themselves, viz. a duke, an earl, and ten men, all on horseback, and calling themselves good Christians. They were of Lower Egypt, and gave out that, not long before, the Christians had subdued their country, and obliged them to embrace Christianity on pain of being put to death. Those who were baptized were great lords in their own country, and had a king and queen there. Soon after their conversion, the Saracens overran the country, and obliged them to renounce Christianity. When the Emperor of Germany, the King of Poland, and other Christian princes, heard of this, they fell upon them, and obliged the whole of them, both great and small, to quit the country, and go to the Pope at Rome, who enjoined them seven years' penance to wander over the world, without lying in a bed.

"They had been wandering five years when they came to Paris first; the principal people, and soon after the commonalty, about 100 or 120, reduced (according to their own account) from 1000 or 1200, when they went from home, the rest being dead, with their king and queen. They were lodged by the police at some distance from the city, at Chapel St. Denis.

"Nearly all of them had their ears bored, and wore two silver rings in each, which they said were esteemed ornaments in their country. The men were black, their hair curled; the women remarkably black, their only clothes a large old duffle garment, tied over the shoulders with a cloth or cord, and under it a miserable rocket. In short, they were the most poor miserable creatures that had ever been seen in France; and, notwithstanding their poverty, there were among them women who, by looking into people's hands, told their fortunes, and what was worse, they picked people's pockets of their money, and got it into their own, by telling these things through airy magic, et cætera."

Notwithstanding the ingenious account of themselves rendered by these gipsies, the Bishop of Paris ordered a friar, called Le Petit Jacobin, to preach a sermon, excommunicating all the men and women who had had recourse to consult these Bohemians on the subject of the future, and shown their hands for that purpose. They departed from Paris for Pontoise in the month of September.

Pasquier remarks upon this singular journal, that however the story of a penance savours of a trick, these people wandered up and down France, under the eye, and with the knowledge, of the magistrates, for more than a hundred years; and it was not till 1561, that a sentence of banishment was passed against them in that kingdom.

The arrival of the Egyptians (as these singular people were called) in various parts of Europe, corresponds with the period in which Timur or Tamerlane invaded Hindostan, affording its natives the choice between the Koran and death. There can be little doubt that these wanderers consisted originally of the Hindostanee tribes, who were displaced, and, flying from the sabres of the Mahommedans, undertook this species of wandering life, without well knowing whither they were going. It is natural to suppose the band, as it now exists, is much mingled with Europeans, but most of these have been brought up from childhood among them, and learned all their practices.

It is strong evidence of this, that where they are in closest contact with the ordinary peasants around them, they still keep their language a mystery. There is little doubt, however, that it is a dialect of the Hindostanee, from the specimens produced by Grellmann, Hoyland, and others, who have written on the subject. But the author has, besides their authority, personal occasion to know that an individual, out of mere curiosity, and availing himself with patience and assiduity of such opportunities as offered, has made himself capable of conversing with any gipsy whom he meets, or can, like the royal Hal, drink with any tinker in his own language. The astonishment excited among these vagrants on finding a stranger participant of their mystery, occasions very ludicrous scenes. It is to be hoped this gentleman will publish the knowledge he possesses on so singular a topic.

There are prudential reasons for postponing this disclosure at present; for although much more reconciled to society since they have been less the objects of legal persecution, the gipsies are still a ferocious and vindictive people.

But notwithstanding this is certainly the case, I cannot but add, from my own observation of nearly fifty years, that the manners of these vagrant tribes are much ameliorated;—that I have known individuals amongst them who have united themselves to civilized society, and maintain respectable characters, and that great alteration has been wrought in their cleanliness and general mode of life.

83.37 (Ch. 7) locusts might do See Note on the Gipsies or Bohemians, end of preceding Chapter.

86.16 (Ch. 7) the Provost-Marshal's guard Such disputes between the Scots Guards, and the other constituted authorities of the ordinary military corps, often occurred. In 1474, two Scottish men had been concerned in robbing John Pensart, a fishmonger, of a large sum of money. They were accordingly apprehended by Philip du Four, Provost, with some of his followers. But ere they could lodge one of them, called Mortimer, in the prison of the Chastellet, they were attacked by two Archers of the King's Scottish Guard, who rescued the prisoner.—See Chronique de Jean de Troyes, at the said year, 1474.

86.22 (Ch. 7) a bargain A quarrel, videlicet.

87.1 (Ch. 7) that is up-come That is, if your courage corresponds with your personal appearance.

87.37 (Ch. 7) Vernoil and Beaugé In both these battles, the Scottish auxiliaries of France, under Stewart, Earl of Buchan, were distinguished. At Beaugé they were victorious, killing the Duke of Clarence, Henry Vth's brother, and cutting off his army. At Vernoil they were defeated, and nearly extirpated.

91.6 (Ch. 7) Skeoch doch nan skial "Cut a tale with a drink;" an expression used when a man preaches over his liquor, as *bon vivants* say in England.

96.20 (Ch. 8) Oliver Dain Oliver's name, or nickname, was Le Diable, which was bestowed on him by public hatred, in exchange for Le Daim, or Le Dain. He was originally the King's barber, but afterwards a favourite counsellor.

102.37 (Ch. 8) a stronger one Dr Dryasdust here remarks, that cards, said to have been invented in a preceding reign, for the amusement of Charles V. during the intervals of his mental disorder, seem speedily to have become common among the courtiers, since they already furnished Louis XI. with a metaphor. The same proverb was quoted by Durandarte, in the enchanted cave of Montesinos. The alleged origin of the invention of cards, produced one of the shrewdest replies I have ever heard made in evidence. It was returned by the late Dr Gregory of Edinburgh to a counsel of great eminence at the Scottish bar. The Doctor's testimony went to prove the insanity of the party whose mental capacity was the point at issue. On a cross-interrogation, he admitted that the person in question played admirably at whist. "And do you seriously say, doctor," said the learned counsel, "that a person having a superior capacity for a game so difficult, and which requires in a pre-eminent degree, memory, judgment, and combination, can be at the same time deranged in his understanding?"—"I am no card player," said the doctor, with great address, "but I have read in history that cards were invented for the amusement of an insane king." The consequences of this reply were decisive.

111.23 (Ch. 9) I should augur Here the King touches upon the very purpose for which he pressed on the match with such tyrannic severity, which was, that as the Princess's personal deformity admitted little chance of its being fruitful, the branch of Orleans, which was next in succession to the crown, might be, by the want of heirs, weakened or extinguished. In a letter to the Compte de Dammartin, Louis, speaking of his daughter's match, says, "Qu'ils n'auroient pas beaucoup d'embarras à nourrir les enfans que naitroient de leur union; mais cependant elle aura lieu, quelque chose qu'on en puisse dire."—WRAXALL'S *History of France*, vol. i. p. 143, note.

112.31 (Ch. 9) anxious to learn A friendly, though unknown correspondent, has pointed out to me that I have been mistaken in alleging that the Cardinal was a bad rider. If so, I owe his memory an apology; for there are few men who, until my latter days, have loved that exercise better than myself. But the Cardinal may have been an indifferent horseman, though he wished to be looked upon as equal to the dangers of the chase. He was a man of assumption and ostentation, as he showed at the siege of Paris in 1465, where, contrary to the custom and usage of war, he mounted guard during the night with an unusual sound of clarions, trumpets, and other instruments. In imputing to the Cardinal a want of skill in horsemanship, I recollected his adventure in Paris when attacked by assassins, on which occasion his mule, being scared by the crowd, ran away with the rider, and taking her course to a monastery, to the abbot of which she formerly belonged, was the means of saving her master's life.—See JEAN DE TROYES' *Chronicle*.

121.38 (Ch. 10) Roland's Gallery Charlemagne, I suppose on account of his unsparing rigour to the Saxons and other heathens, was accounted a saint during the dark ages; and Louis XI., as one of his successors, honoured his shrine with peculiar observance.

125.25 (Ch. 10) Ecosse, en avant Forward, Scotland.

127.36 (Ch. 10) the Castle of Genappes During his residence in Burgundy, in his father's lifetime, Genappes was the usual abode of Louis. This period of exile is often alluded to in the novel.

129.5 (Ch. 10) his place of concealment The nature of Louis XIth's coarse humour may be guessed at by those who have perused the "Cent Nouvelles Nouvelles," which are grosser than most similar collections of the age.

159.14 (Ch. 13) the means of filling it

GALEOTTI. Martius Galeotti was a native of Narni, in Umbria. He was secretary to Matthias Corvinus, King of Hungary, and tutor to his son, John Corvinus. While at his court, he composed a work,

De jocose dictis et factis Regis Matthiæ Corvini. He left Hungary in 1477, and was made prisoner at Venice on a charge of having propagated heterodox opinions in a treatise entitled, *De homine interiore et corpore ejus.* He was obliged to recant some of these doctrines, and might have suffered seriously but for the protection of Sextus IV., then Pope, who had been one of his scholars. He went to France, attached himself to Louis XI., and died in his service.

172.41 (Ch. 15) the Cardinal Balue Who himself tenanted one of these dens for more than eleven years.

178.9 (Ch. 16) I have no religion

RELIGION OF THE BOHEMIANS. It was a remarkable part of the character of these wanderers, that they did not, like the Jews, whom otherwise they resembled in some particulars, possess or profess any particular religion, whether in forms or principles. They readily conformed, as far as might be required, with the religion of any country in which they happened to sojourn, nor did they ever practise it more than was demanded of them. It is certain that in India they embraced neither the tenets of the religion of Bramah nor of Mahomet. They have hence been considered as belonging to the outcast East Indian tribes of Nuts or Parias. Their want of religion is supplied by a good deal of superstition. Such of their ritual as can be discovered, for example that belonging to marriage, is savage in the extreme, and resembles the customs of the Hottentots more than of any civilized people. They adopt various observances, picked up from the religion of the country in which they live. It is, or rather was, the custom of the tribes on the Borders of England and Scotland, to annex success to those journeys which are commenced by passing through the parish church; and they usually try to obtain permission from the beadle to do so when the church is empty, for the performance of divine service is not considered as essential to the omen. They are, therefore, totally devoid of any effectual sense of religion; and the higher, or more instructed class, may be considered as acknowledging no deity save those of Epicurus, and such is described as the faith, or no faith, of Hayraddin Maugrabin.

I may here take notice, that nothing is more disagreeable to this indolent and voluptuous people, than being forced to adopt any regular profession. When Paris was garrisoned by the Allied troops in the year 1815, the author was walking with a British officer, near a post held by the Prussian troops. He happened at the time to smoke a cigar, and was about, while passing the sentinel, to take it out of his mouth, in compliance with a general regulation to that effect, when, greatly to the astonishment of the passengers, the soldier addressed them in these words; "*Rauchen sie immerfort; verdamt sey der Preussiche dienst!*" that is, "Smoke away! May the Prussian service be d—d!" Upon looking closely at the man, he seemed plainly to be a *Zigeuner*, or gipsy, who took this method of expressing his detestation of the duty imposed on him. When the risk he ran by doing so is considered, it will be found to argue a deep degree of dislike which could make him commit himself so unwarily. If he had been overheard by a sergeant or corporal, the *prugel* would have been the slightest instrument of punishment employed.

185.22 (Ch. 16) monasterium vestrum A similar story is told of the Duke of Vendome, who answered in this species of macaronic Latin the classical expostulations of a German convent against the imposition of a contribution.

198.38 (Ch. 18) in consequence

> Vox quoque Mœrim
> Jam fugit ipsa; lupi Mœrim videre priores.
> VIRGILII, ix. ecloga.

The commentators add, in explanation of this passage, the opinion of Pliny: "The being beheld by a wolf in Italy is accounted noxious, and is supposed to take away the speech of a man, if these animals behold him ere he sees them."

214.42 (Ch. 19) the bourgeoisie of Liege The adventure of Quentin at Liege may be thought overstrained, yet it is extraordinary what slight circumstances will influence the public mind in a moment of doubt and uncertainty. Most readers must remember, that, when the Dutch were on the point of rising against the French yoke, their zeal for liberation received a strong impulse from the landing of a person in a British volunteer-uniform, whose presence, though that of a private individual, was received as a guarantee of succours from England.

216.1 (Ch. 19) an unpalatable one "A sooth bourd [true joke] is no bourd," says the Scot.

231.10 (Ch. 21) Saint Tron Fought by the insurgents of Liege against the Duke of Burgundy, Charles the Bold, when Count of Charolois, in which the people of Liege were defeated with much slaughter.

242.23 (Ch. 22) his own episcopal throne

MURDER OF THE BISHOP OF LIEGE. In assigning the present date to the murder of the Bishop of Liege, Louis de Bourbon, history has been violated. It is true that the Bishop was made prisoner by the insurgents of that city. It is also true that the report of the insurrection came to Charles with a rumour that the Bishop was slain, which excited his indignation against Louis, who was then in his power. But these things happened in 1468, and the Bishop's murder did not take place till 1482. In the months of August and September of that year, William de la Marck, called the Wild Boar of Ardennes, entered into a conspiracy with the discontented citizens of Liege against their Bishop, Louis of Bourbon, being aided with considerable sums of money by the King of France. By this means, and the assistance of many murderers and banditti, who thronged to him as to a leader befitting them, De la Marck assembled a body of troops, whom he dressed in scarlet as a uniform, with a boar's head on the left sleeve. With this little army he approached the city of Liege. Upon this the citizens, who were engaged in the conspiracy, came to their Bishop, and, offering to stand by him to the death, exhorted him to march out against these robbers. The Bishop, therefore, put himself at the head of a few troops of his own, trusting to the assistance of the people of Liege. But so soon as they came in sight of the enemy, the citizens, as before agreed, fled from the Bishop's banner, and he was left with his own handful of adherents. At this moment De la Marck charged at the head of his banditti with the expected success. The Bishop was brought before the profligate Knight, who first cut him over the face, then murthered him with his own hand, and caused his body to be exposed naked in the great square of Liege before Saint Lambert's cathedral.

Such is the actual narrative of a tragedy which struck with horror the people of the time. The murder of the Bishop has been fourteen years antedated in the text, for reasons which the reader of romances will easily appreciate.

258.28 (Ch. 23) the Lanzknechts
SCHWARZ-REITERS. Fynes Morrison describes this species of soldiery as follows: "He that at this day looks upon their *Schwarz-reiters*, (that is, black horsemen,) must confess, that, to make their horses and boots shine, they make themselves as black as colliers. These horsemen wear black clothes, and poor though they be, yet spend no small time in brushing them. The most of them have black horses, which, while they painfully dress, and (as I have said) delight to have their boots and shoes shine with blacking-stuff, their hands and faces become black, and thereof they have their foresaid name. Yet I have heard Germans say, that they do thus make themselves black to seem more terrible to their enemies."—FYNES MORRISON'S *Itinerary*. Edition 1617, p. 165.

258.41 (Ch. 23) das geht nichts "No, no! that must not be."

273.34 (Ch. 25) an unhappy death D'Hymbercourt, or Imbercourt, was put to death by the inhabitants of Ghent with the Chancellor of Burgundy, in the year 1477. Mary of Burgundy, daughter of Charles the Bold, appeared in mourning in the market-place, and with tears besought the life of her servants from her insurgent subjects, but in vain.

274.10 (Ch. 25) Duke Charles the Bold

PHILIP DES COMINES. Philip des Comines was described in the former editions of this work as a little man, fitted rather for counsel than action. This was a description made at a venture, to vary the military portraits with which the age and work abound. Sleidan the historian, upon the authority of Matthieu d'Arras, who knew Philip des Comines, and had served in his household, says he was a man of tall stature, and a noble presence. The learned Monsieur Petitot, editor of the edition of Memoirs relative to the History of France, a work of immense value, intimates that Philip des Comines made a figure at the games of chivalry and pageants exhibited on the wedding of Charles of Burgundy with Margaret of England in 1468.—See the Chronicle of Jean de Troyes, in Petitot's edition of the *Memoirs Relatifs à l'Histoire de France*, vol. xiii. p. 375. Note. I have looked into Oliver de la Marche, who, in lib. ii., chapter iv., of his Memoirs, gives an ample account of these "fierce vanities," containing as many miscellaneous articles as the reticule of the old merchant of Peter Schleml, who bought shadows, and carried with him in his bag whatever any one could wish or demand in return. There are in that splendid description, knights, dames, pages, and archers, good store besides of castles, fiery dragons, and dromedaries; there are leopards riding upon lions; there are rocks, orchards, fountains, spears broken and whole, and the twelve labours of Hercules. In such a brilliant medley I had some trouble in finding Philip des Comines. He is the first named, however, of a gallant band of assailants, knights and noblemen, to the number of twenty, who, with the Prince of Orange as their leader, encountered, in a general tourney, with a party of the same number under the profligate Adolf of Cleves, who acted as challenger, by the romantic title of *Arbre d'or*. The encounter, though with arms of courtesy, was very fierce, and separated by main force, not without difficulty. Philip des Comines has, therefore, a title to be accounted *tam Marte quam Mercurio*, though, when we consider the obscurity which has settled on the rest of this *troupe dorée*, we are at no loss to estimate the most valuable of his qualifications.

275.29 (Ch. 25) Montl'hery

MEETING OF LOUIS AND CHARLES AFTER THE BATTLE OF

MONTL'HERY. After the battle of Montl'hery, in 1465, Charles, then Compte de Charolois, had an interview with Louis under the walls of Paris, each at the head of a small party. The two princes dismounted, and walked together so deeply engaged in discussing the business of their meeting, that Charles forgot the peculiarity of his situation; and when Louis turned back towards the town of Paris, from which he came, the Count of Charolois kept him company so far as to pass the line of outworks with which Paris was surrounded, and enter a field-work which communicated with the town by a trench. At this period he had only five or six persons in company with him. His escort caught an alarm for his safety, and his principal followers rode forward from where he had left them, remembering that his grandfather had been assassinated at Montereau in a similar parley, on 10th September, 1419. To their great joy the Count returned uninjured, accompanied with a guard belonging to Louis. The Burgundians taxed him with rashness in no measured terms. "Say no more of it," said Charles; "I acknowledge the extent of my folly, but I was not aware what I was doing till I entered the redoubt."—*Memoires de* PHILIPPE DES COMINES, chap. xiii.

Louis was much praised for his good faith on this occasion; and it was natural that the Duke should call it to recollection when his enemy so unexpectedly put himself in his power by his visit to Peronne.

276.41 (Ch. 25) Le Glorieux The jester of Charles of Burgundy, of whom more hereafter.

282.4 (Ch. 26) in the town itself The arrival of three brothers, Princes of the House of Savoy, of Monseigneur de Lau, whom the King had long detained in prison, of Sire Poncet de Rivière, and the Seigneur d'Urfé,—who, by the way, as a romance writer of a peculiar turn, might have been happily enough introduced into the present work, but the fate of the Euphuist was a warning to the author —all of these nobles bearing the emblem of Burgundy, the cross, namely, of Saint Andrew, inspired Louis with so much suspicion, seeing so many of his enemies were assembled, that he very impolitically demanded to be lodged in the old Castle of Peronne, and thus rendered himself an absolute captive.—See COMINES' *Memoirs for the Year* 1468.

282.16 (Ch. 26) to the sheath This gesture, very indicative of a fierce character, is also by stage-tradition a distinction of Shakspeare's Richard III.

286.32 (Ch. 26) Earl Tineman An Earl of Douglas, so called.

297.25 (Ch. 27) the Wild Huntsman The famous apparition, sometimes called le Grand Veneur. Sully gives some account of this hunting spectre.

304.24 (Ch. 27) his new apartment The historical facts attending this celebrated interview, are expounded and enlarged upon in the foregoing chapter. Agents sent by Louis had tempted the people of Liege to rebel against their superior, Duke Charles, and persecute and murder their Bishop. But Louis was not prepared for their acting with such promptitude. They flew to arms with the temerity of a fickle rabble, took the Bishop prisoner, menaced and insulted him, and tore to pieces one or two of his canons. This news was sent to the Duke of Burgundy at the moment when Louis had so unguardedly placed himself in his power; and the consequence was, that Charles placed guards on the Castle of Peronne, and, deeply resenting the treachery of the King in exciting sedition in his dominions, while he pretended the most intimate friendship, he deliberated whether he should not put Louis to death.

Three days Louis was detained in this very precarious situation; and it was only his profuse liberality amongst Charles's favourites and courtiers which finally ensured him from death or deposition. Comines, who was the Duke of Burgundy's chamberlain at the time, and slept in his apartment, says, Charles neither undressed or slept, but flung himself from time to time on the bed, and, at other times, wildly traversed the apartment. It was long before his violent temper became in any degree tractable. At length he only agreed to give Louis his liberty, on condition of his accompanying him in person against, and assisting to subdue with his arms, the mutineers whom his intrigues had instigated to arms.

This was a bitter and degrading alternative. But Louis, seeing no other mode of compounding for the effects of his rashness, not only submitted to this discreditable condition, but swore to it upon a crucifix said to have belonged to Charlemagne. These particulars are from Comines. There is a succinct epitome of them in Sir Nathaniel Wraxall's History of France, vol. i.

309.39 (Ch. 28) the detestable Balue Louis kept his promise of vengeance against Cardinal La Balue, whom he always blamed as having betrayed him to Burgundy. After he was returned to his own kingdom, he caused his late favourite to be immured in one of the iron cages at Loches. These were contrived with horrible ingenuity, so that a person of ordinary size could neither stand up at his full height nor lie lengthwise in them. Some ascribe this horrid device to Balue himself. At any rate, he was confined in one of these dens for eleven years, nor did Louis permit him to be liberated till his last illness.

311.20 (Ch. 28) in this respect
PRAYER OF LOUIS XI. While I perused these passages in the old manuscript chronicle, I could not help feeling astonished that an intellect acute as that of Louis XI. certainly was, could so delude itself by a sort of superstition, of which one would think the stupidest savages incapable; but the terms of the King's prayer, on a similar occasion, as preserved by Brantome, are of a tenor fully as extraordinary. It is that which, being overheard by a fool or jester, was by him made public, and let in light on an act of fratricide, which might never have been suspected. The way in which the story is narrated by the corrupted courtier, who could jest with all that is criminal as well as with all that is profligate, is worthy the reader's notice; for such actions are seldom done where there are not men with hearts of the nether millstone, capable and willing to make them matters of laughter.

"Among the numerous good tricks of dissimulation, feints, and finesses of gallantry, which the good King (Louis XI.) did in his time, he put to death his brother, the Duke de Guyenne, at the moment when the Duke least thought of such a thing, and while the King was making the greatest show of love to him during his life, and of affliction for him at his death, managing the whole concern with so much art, that it would never have been known had not the King taken into his own service a fool who had belonged to his deceased brother. But it chanced that Louis, being engaged in his devout prayers and orisons at the high altar of our Lady of Clery, whom he called his good patroness, and no person nigh except this fool, who, without his knowledge, was within earshot, he thus gave vent to his pious homilies:—

"'Ah, my good Lady, my gentle mistress, my only friend, in whom alone I have resource, I pray you to supplicate God in my behalf, and to be my advocate with him that he may pardon me the death of my brother whom I caused to be poisoned by that wicked Abbot of Saint John. I confess my guilt to thee as to my good patroness and mistress. But then what could I do? he was perpetually causing disorder in my kingdom. Cause me then to be pardoned, my good Lady, and I know what a reward I will give thee.'"

This singular confession did not escape the jester, who upbraided the King with the fratricide in face of the whole company at dinner, which Louis was fain to let pass without observation, in case of increasing the slander.

314.34 (Ch. 28) over-dispatch Varillas, in a history of Louis XI., observes, that his Provost-Marshal was often so precipitate in execution as to slay another person instead of him whom the King had indicated. This always occasioned a double execution, for the wrath or revenge of Louis was never satisfied with a vicarious punishment.

316.43 (Ch. 28) in one way or other The author has endeavoured to give the odious Tristan l'Hermite a species of dogged and brutal fidelity to Louis, similar to the attachment of a bull-dog to his master. With all the atrocity of his execrable character, he was certainly a man of courage, and was, in his youth, made knight on the breach of Fronsac, with a great number of other young nobles, by the honour-giving hand of the elder Dunois, the celebrated hero of Charles the VIIth's reign.

321.26 (Ch. 29) that of your Majesty

MARTIUS GALEOTTI. The death of Martius Galeotti was in some degree connected with Louis XI. The astrologer was at Lyons, and hearing that the King was approaching the city, got on horse-back in order to meet him. As he threw himself hastily from his horse to pay his respects to the King, he fell with violence which, joined to his extreme corpulence, was the cause of his death in 1478.

But the acute and ready-witted expedient to escape instant death, had no reference to the history of this philosopher. The same, or nearly the same story, is told of Tiberius, who demanded of a soothsayer, Thrasullus, if he knew the day of his own death, and received for answer, it would take place just three days before that of the Emperor. On this reply, instead of being thrown over the rocks into the sea, as had been the tyrant's first intention, he was taken great care of for the rest of his life.—*Taciti Annal.* lib. vi. cap. 22.

The circumstances in which Louis XI. received a similar reply from an astrologer are as follow:—The soothsayer in question had presaged that a female favourite, to whom the King was very much attached, should die in a week. As he proved a true prophet, the King was as much incensed as if the astrologer could have prevented the evil he predicted. He sent for the philosopher, and had a party stationed to assassinate him as he retired from the royal presence. Being asked by the King concerning his own fortunes, he confessed that he perceived signs of some imminent danger. Being farther questioned concerning the day of his own death, he was shrewd enough to answer with composure, that it would be exactly three days before that of his Majesty. There was, of course, care taken that he should escape the destined fate; and he was ever after much protected by the King, as a man of real science, and intimately connected with the royal destinies.

Although almost all the historians of Louis represent him as a dupe to the common but splendid imposture of judicial astrology, yet his credulity could not be deep-rooted, if the following anecdote, reported by Bayle, be correct.

Upon one occasion, Louis intending to hunt, and doubtful of the weather, enquired of an astrologer near his person whether it would be fine. The sage, having recourse to his astrolabe, answered with confidence in the affirmative. At the entrance of the forest the royal cortège was met by a charcoalman, who expressed to some menials of the train his surprise that the King should have thought of hunting in a day which threatened tempest. The collier's prediction proved true. The King and his court were driven from their sport well drenched; and Louis, having heard what the collier had said, ordered the man before him. "How were you more accurate in foreseeing the weather, my friend," said he, "than this learned man?"—"I am an ignorant man, Sire," answered the collier, "was never at school, and cannot write or read. But I have an astrologer of my own, who shall foretell weather with any of them. It is, with reverence, the ass who carries my charcoal, who always, when bad weather is approaching, points forwards his ears, walks more slowly than usual, and tries to rub himself against walls; and it was from these signs that I foretold yesterday's storm." The King burst into a fit of laughing, dismissed the astrological biped, and assigned the collier a small pension to maintain the quadruped, swearing he would never in future trust to any other astrologer than the charcoal-man's ass.

But if there is any truth in this story, the credulity of Louis was not of a nature to be removed by the failure there mentioned. He is said to have believed in the prediction of Angelo Cattho, his physician, and the friend of Comines, who foretold the death of Charles of Burgundy in the very time and hour when it took place at the battle of Nancy. Upon this assurance, Louis vowed a silver screen to the shrine of Saint Martin, which he afterwards fulfilled at the expense of one hundred thousand francs. It is well known, besides, that he was the abject and devoted slave of his physicians. Coctier, or Cottier, one of their number, besides the retaining fee of ten thousand crowns, extorted from his royal patient great sums in lands and money, and, in addition to all, the Bishopric of Amiens for his nephew. He maintained over Louis unbounded influence, by using to him the most disrespectful harshness and insolence. "I know," he said to the suffering King, "that one morning you will turn me adrift like so many others. But, by Heaven, you had better beware, for you will not live eight days after you have done so!" It is unnecessary to dwell longer on the fears and superstitions of a prince, whom the wretched love of life induced to submit to such indignities.

334.21 (Ch. 30) subjects of pleasantry The story is told more bluntly, and less probably, in the French memoirs of the period, which affirm that Comines, out of a presumption inconsistent with his excellent good sense, had asked of Charles of Burgundy to draw off his boots, without having been treated with any previous familiarity to lead to such a freedom. I have endeavoured to give the anecdote a turn more consistent with the sense and prudence of the great author concerned.

340.7 (Ch. 30) into his entrails There is little doubt that, during the interesting scene at Peronne, Philip des Comines first learned intimately to know the great powers of mind of Louis XI., by which he was so much dazzled that it is impossible, in reading his Memoirs, not to be sensible he was blinded by them to the more odious shades of his character. He entertained from this time forwards a partiality to France. The historian passed into France about 1472, and rose high in the good graces of Louis XI. He afterwards became the proprietor of the Lordship of Argenton and others, a title which was given him by anticipation in the former editions of this work. He did not obtain it till he was in the French service. After the death of Louis, Philip des Comines fell under the suspicion of the daughter of Louis, called our Lady of Beaujeu, as too zealous a partisan of the rival House of Orleans. The historian himself was imprisoned for eight months in one of the iron cages which he has so forcibly described. It was there that he regretted the fate of a court life. "I have ventured on the great ocean," he said, in his affliction, "and the waves have devoured me." He was subjected to a trial, and exiled from court for some years by the Parliament of Paris, being found guilty of holding intercourse with disaffected persons. He survived this cloud, however, and was afterwards employed by Charles VIII. in one or two important missions, where talents were required. Louis XII. also transferred his favour to the historian, but did not employ him. He died at his Castle of Argenton, in 1509, and was regretted as one of the most profound statesmen, and certainly the best historian of his age. In a poem to his memory by the poet Ronsard, he received the distinguished praise that he was the first to show the lustre which valour and noble blood derived from being united with learning.

359.16 and 364.24 (Ch. 33) trumpery / disguised as a herald Disguised Herald. The heralds of the middle ages, like the *feciales* of the Romans, were invested with a character which was held almost sacred. To strike a herald was a crime which inferred a capital punishment; and to counterfeit the character of such an august official was a degree of treason towards those men who were accounted the depositaries of the secrets of monarchs and the honour of nobles. Yet a prince so unscrupulous as Louis XI. did not hesitate to practise such an imposition, when he wished to enter into communication with Edward IV. of England.

Exercising that knowledge of mankind for which he was so eminent, he selected, as an agent fit for his purpose, a simple valet. This man, whose address had been known to him, he disguised as a herald, with all the insignia of his office, and sent him in that capacity to open a communication with the English army. Two things are remarkable in this transaction. First, that the stratagem, though of so fraudulent a nature, does not seem to have been necessarily called for, since all that King Louis could gain by it would be, that he did not commit himself by sending a more responsible messenger. The other circumstance worthy of notice, is, that Comines, though he mentions the affair at great length, is so pleased with the King's shrewdness in selecting, and dexterity at indoctrinating, his pseudo-herald, that he forgets all remark on the impudence and fraud of the imposition, as well as the great risk of discovery. From both which circumstances, we are led to the conclusion, that the solemn character which the heralds endeavoured to arrogate to themselves, had already begun to lose regard among statesmen and men of the great world.

Even Ferne, zealous enough for the dignity of the herald, seems to impute this intrusion on their rights in some degree to necessity. "I have heard some," he says, "but with shame enough, allow of the action of Louis XI. of the kingdom of France, who had so unknightly a regard both of his own honour, and also of armes, that he seldom had about his court any officer-at-armes. And therefore, at such time as Edward IV., King of England, had entered France with a hostile power, and lay before the town of Saint Quentin, the same French King, for want of a herald to carry his mind to the English King, was constrained to suborn a vadelict, or common serving-man, with a trumpet-banner, having a hole made through the middest for this preposterous herauld to put his head through, and to cast it over his shoulders instead of a better coat-armour of France. And thus came this hastily-arrayed courier as a counterfeit officer-at-armes, with instructions from his sovereign's mouth to offer peace to our King. 'Well,' replies Torquatus, the other interlocutor in the dialogue, 'that fault was never yet to be seen in any of our English Kings, nor ever shall be, I hope.'"—FERNE'S *Blazen of Gentry*, 1586, p. 161.

In this curious book, the author, besides some assertions in favour of coat-armour, too nearly approaching blasphemy to be quoted, informs us, that the Apostles were gentlemen of blood, and many of them descended from that worthy conqueror, Judas Maccabæus; but through the tract of time and persecution of wars, poverty oppressed the kindred, and they were constrained to servile works. So were the four doctors and fathers of the church (Ambrose, Augustine, Hierome, and Gregorie) gentlemen both of blood and arms, p. 98. The author's copy of this rare work (memorial of a hopeful young friend, now no more) exhibits a curious sally of the national and professional irritability of a Scottish herald.

This person appears to have been named Thomas Drysdale, Islay Herald, who purchased the volume in 1619, and seems to have perused it with patience and profit till he came to the following passage in Ferne, which enters into the distinction between sovereign and feodary crowns. "There is also a King, and he a homager, or fœdatorie to the estate and majestie of another King, as to his superior lord, as that of Scotland to our English empire." This assertion set on fire the Scottish blood of Islay Herald, who, forgetting the book had been printed nearly forty years before, and that the author was probably dead, writes on the margin in great wrath, and in a half text hand, "*He is a traitor and lyar in his throat, and I offer him the combat, that says Scotland's Kings were ever feudatorie to England.*"

380.8 (Ch.35) dwelt upon it The perilling the hand of an heiress upon the event of a battle, was not so likely to take place in the fifteenth century as when the laws of chivalry were in more perfect observance. Yet it was not unlikely to occur to so absolute a Prince as Duke Charles, in circumstances like those supposed.

382.21 (Ch. 36) could be aware of It is almost unnecessary to add, that the marriage of William de la Marck with the Lady Hameline, is as apocryphal as the lady herself. The real bride of the Wild Boar of Ardennes was Joan D'Arschel, Baroness of Schoonhoven.

388.20 (Ch. 36) my slumbers

ATTACK UPON LIEGE. The Duke of Burgundy, full of resentment for the usage which the Bishop had received from the people of Liege, (whose death, as already noticed, did not take place for some years after,) and knowing that the walls of the town had not been repaired since they were breached by himself after the battle of Saint Tron, advanced recklessly to their chastisement. His commanders shared his presumptuous confidence; for the advanced guard of his army, under the Maréchal of Burgundy and Seigneur

D'Hymbercourt, rushed upon one of the suburbs, without waiting for the rest of their army, which, commanded by the Duke in person, remained about seven or eight leagues in the rear. The night was closing, and, as the Burgundian troops observed no discipline, they were exposed to a sudden attack from a party of the citizens commanded by Jean de Vilde, who, assaulting them in front and rear, threw them into great disorder, and killed more than eight hundred men, of whom one hundred were men-at-arms.

When Charles and the King of France came up, they took up their quarters in two villas situated near to the wall of the city. In the two or three days which followed, Louis was distinguished for the quiet and regulated composure with which he pressed the siege, and provided for defence in case of sallies; while the Duke of Burgundy, no way deficient in courage, and who showed the rashness and want of order which was his principal characteristic, seemed also extremely suspicious that the King would desert him and join with the Liegeois.

They lay before the town for five or six days, and at length fixed the 30th of October, 1468, for a general storm. The citizens, who had probably information of their intent, resolved to prevent their purpose, and determined on anticipating it by a desperate sally through the breaches in their walls. They placed at their head six hundred of the men of the little territory of Franchemont, belonging to the Bishopric of Liege, and reckoned the most valiant of their troops. They burst out of the town on a sudden, surprised the Duke of Burgundy's quarters ere his guards could put on their armour, which they had laid off to enjoy some repose before the assault. The King of France's lodgings were also attacked and endangered. A great confusion ensued, augmented incalculably by the mutual jealousy and suspicions of the French and Burgundians. The people of Liege were, however, unable to maintain their hardy enterprise, when the men-at-arms of the King and Duke began to recover from their confusion, and were finally forced to retire within their walls, after narrowly missing the chance of surprising both King Louis and the Duke of Burgundy, the most powerful Princes of their time. At daybreak the storm took place, as had been originally intended, and the citizens, disheartened and fatigued by the nocturnal sally, did not make so much resistance as was expected. Liege was taken, and miserably pillaged, without regard to sex or age, things sacred or things profane. These particulars are fully related by Comines in his Memoirs, liv. ii. chap. 11, 12, 13, and do not differ much from the account of the same events in this and the preceding chapter.

390.8 (Ch. 37) two and a plack An homely Scottish expression for something you value.

397.17 (Ch. 37) old Small-Back A cant expression in Scotland for Death, usually delineated as a skeleton.

398.15 (Ch. 37) all who had seen him We have already noticed the anachronism respecting the crime of this atrocious baron; and it is scarce necessary to repeat, that if he in reality murdered the Bishop of Liege in 1482, the Count of La Marck could not be slain in the defence of Liege fourteen years earlier. In fact, the Wild Boar of Ardennes, as he was usually termed, was of high birth, being the fourth son of John I., Count of La Marck and Aremberg, and ancestor of the branch called Barons of Lumain. He did not escape the punishment due to his atrocity, though it did not take place at the time, or in the manner, narrated in the text. Maximilian, Emperor of Austria, caused him to be arrested at Utrecht, where he was beheaded in the year 1485, three years after the Bishop of Liege's death.

398.28 (Ch. 37) the Less-lee An old rhyme, by which the Leslies vindicate their descent from an ancient knight, who is said to have slain a gigantic Hungarian champion, and to have formed a proper name for himself by a play of words upon the place where he fought his adversary.

SAINT RONAN'S WELL

Editorial Note

Saint Ronan's Well occupies Volumes 33 and 34 of the Magnum series, published in February and March 1832 when Scott was in Italy. An interleaved copy of the novel had been prepared for him using the octavo edition of *Tales and Romances of the Author of Waverley* published in 7 volumes in 1827. *Saint Ronan's Well* occupies the first and part of the second volumes in this series. These interleaved volumes are now in the National Library of Scotland, MSS 23026 and 23027. The new material for the Magnum is written in Scott's hand, mostly on the interleaves but also on the printed pages. The manuscript of the Introduction is on four folded leaves inserted in MS 23026 between pp. 376 and 377; it does not include the final two paragraphs of the text as printed.

It is not known exactly when Scott prepared the Magnum material for *Saint Ronan's Well*. On 9 October 1830 Cadell assured him that 'St. Ronans Well and all after, there is no hurry about, six months ↑hence↓ will do quite well' (MS 3914, f. 129r). Clearly Scott turned to the task considerably earlier than that, since Cadell's diary records that he 'revised' parts of the novel between 18 and 31 January 1831 (MS 21021, ff. 5v–7v). Presumably he was transcribing Scott's new material for the printer and correcting as he did so. He was engaged with *Saint Ronan's Well* again in the second half of February. On 24 February he 'revised during the evening the conclusion of St Ronans Well', and the next day he was 'busy during the evening revising St Ronans Well emendations which I got completed' (MS 21021, f. 11r). That was not all, however, as on 25 March he revised the Notes to the novel, and on 2 April he revised its Introduction (MS 21021, ff. 15r, 16r).

Saint Ronan's Well in its Magnum volumes occupies 340 and

359 pages, which is shorter than the normal length of these volumes. Scott did not, however, take the opportunity of extending Volume 33 by adding a long Introduction. Indeed, its eight-page Introduction is one of the shortest in the series, and for the reader one of the least satisfying, because it does not give the sources of the tragic plot of the novel. Scott acknowledges the brevity of the Introduction: 'The story, being entirely modern, cannot require much explanation, after what has been here given, either in the shape of notes, or a more prolix introduction.' What this hides is that it is precisely because the novel is 'entirely modern' that the issue of its sources was sensitive. (See EEWN 16, 443–45 and articles by Richard D. Jackson in *The Scott Newsletter*, 36 and 37 (Aberdeen University, 2000).) The most likely reason for Scott's silence on the subject is that his sources were contemporary, and any attempt at tracing the story's origins would be likely to uncover the family or families in which the tragic circumstances described in the novel had taken place. Instead the Introduction concentrates on the issue of the novel's contemporary and domestic setting, explaining the usefulness to a novelist of a watering-place for an assemblage of different characters. The final two paragraphs outline the response of English and Scottish critics to the novel.

Scott did not think this novel required 'much explanation', and the introduction and notes are shorter than for any other title: Volume 33 has seventeen footnotes (in addition to the two first-edition footnotes) and three endnotes; Volume 34 has seven footnotes (in addition to the two first-edition footnotes) and three endnotes. The notes to *Saint Ronan's Well* add to the novel's concern with details of Scottish social culture, relishing Scottish verbal expressions. Many of them are short and simply explain a verbal usage in the text. Others explain Scottish ways and customs, for instance the charges in a Scottish inn in the eighteenth century (336–37), and recommended ways of cooking salmon (338.21–33). Of the six endnotes, one explains the law relating to building-feus in Scotland (337) and another explains the unsatisfactory outcome of 'compulsory charity by poor's rates' (341). Two others recount anecdotes which are amplificatory, telling a story which adds a further example or illustration to an episode in the text. The story of Magopico illustrates the case of Mr Cargill's batchelor household (338–39); the story of Yarrow, the dog trained by its owners to steal sheep, is analogous to Lord Etherington's use of his servant Solmes (340). Of course the subject of this note had been used before by Scott, as the basis of his Blackwood's story, 'Alarming Increase of Depravity among Animals' (EEWN 24, 29–37, 178–81).

From the point of view of the novel's plot the most interesting, and tantalising, note is that on Coleridge's 'The Dark Ladye' (338.7–14), suggesting as it does a source for the character of Clara Mowbray in a novel where sources are steadfastly hidden. Since, however, 'The Dark Ladye' was not published until 1834 the allusion invites comparison with other occasions on which Scott recalled lines of Coleridge which he had received orally before publication (see Seamus Perry, 'Coleridge's Literary Influence', in *The Oxford Handbook of Samuel Taylor Coleridge*, ed. Frederick Burwick (Oxford, 2009), 661–76).

The final endnote comes at the very end of Volume 34 and describes the celebrity enjoyed by St Ronan's and Meg Dods after the end of the novel. In so doing it returns the reader to the place and character introduced at the opening of the novel, and entirely reverses the mood of desertion and failure with which the novel ends.

There are four Magnum illustrations for this title. The frontispiece to Volume 33 (MAG0065 / TB348.33) was designed by John Watson Gordon and engraved by John Horsburgh. It depicts Scott seated with cane in hand, with his dog Bran in the bottom right corner; a view of the Eildon Hills to the left. The caption is 'SIR WALTER SCOTT BART.' Disliking a recent portrait by David Wilkie, Robert Cadell commissioned this portrait in March 1830, planning to have it engraved to accompany a volume of the Magnum: see Francis Russell, *Portraits of Sir Walter Scott* (London, 1987), Item 55. The title-page vignette (MAG0066 / TB348.33) was designed by Charles Robert Leslie and engraved by Joseph Goodyear. It depicts Winterblossom exhibiting pieces of artwork to others assembled in the public room at Saint Ronan's Well (EEWN 16, 30.2–4: 'Mr Winterblossom . . . at the public room.'). The frontispiece to Volume 34 (MAG0067 / TB348.34) was designed by William Mulready and engraved by Robert Graves. It depicts Touchwood, cane in hand, disturbing the Rev. Joseph Cargill, the latter studying a large folio book (EEWN 16, 154.19–23 (abridged): 'The minister of St. Ronan's . . . to announce the presence.'). The title-page vignette (MAG0068 / TB348.34) was designed by John Wood and engraved by William Chevalier. It depicts the dying Hannah Irwin, attended by Cargill, with the appearance of Clara Mowbray (EEWN 16, 365.3–7 (abridged): 'Slowly and with a feeble hand . . . by the bedside.').

John Watson Gordon. 1830. John Horsburgh.

SIR WALTER SCOTT, BAR^T.

EDINBURGH, PUBLISHED 1833, BY ROBERT CADELL, and WHITTAKER & C^O LONDON.

WAVERLEY NOVELS.

VOL. XXXIII.

ST. RONAN'S WELL.

'Mr Winterblossom was also distinguished for possessing a few curious engravings, and other specimens of art, with the exhibition of which he occasionally beguiled a wet morning at the public room.'

PRINTED FOR ROBERT CADELL, EDINBURGH,
AND WHITTAKER & Co LONDON.
1832.

W. Mulready R. A. R. Graves.

ST. RONAN'S WELL.

"The minister of St. Ronan's was so intently engaged in studying the book before him, that he totally disregarded the noise which Mr Touchwood made in entering the room, as well as the coughs and hems with which he thought proper to announce his presence."

WAVERLEY NOVELS.

VOL. XXXIV.

ST. RONAN'S WELL.

"Slowly and with a feeble hand, the curtains of the bed opposite to the side at which Cargill was, were opened, and the figure of Clara Mowbray, stood by the bedside."

PRINTED FOR ROBERT CADELL, EDINBURGH,
AND WHITTAKER & C° LONDON.
1832.

Introduction to Saint Ronan's Well

THE novel which follows is upon a plan different from any other that the author has ever written, although it is perhaps the most legitimate which relates to this kind of light literature.

It is intended, in a word—*celebrare domestica facta*—to give an imitation of the shifting manners of our own time, and paint scenes, the originals of which are daily passing round us, so that a minute's observation may compare the copies with the originals. It must be confessed that this style of composition was adopted by the author rather from the tempting circumstance of its offering some novelty in his compositions, and avoiding worn-out characters and positions, than from the hope of rivalling the many formidable competitors who have already won deserved honours in this department. The ladies, in particular, gifted by nature with keen powers of observation and light satire, have been so distinguished by these works of talent, that, reckoning from the authoress of Evelina to her of Marriage, a catalogue might be made, including the brilliant and talented names of Edgeworth, Austin, Charlotte Smith, and others, whose success seems to have appropriated this province of the novel as exclusively their own. It was therefore with a sense of temerity that the author intruded upon a species of composition which had been of late practised with such distinguished success. This consciousness was lost, however, under the necessity of seeking for novelty, without which, it was much to be apprehended, such repeated incursions on his part would nauseate the long indulgent public at the last.

The scene chosen for the author's little drama of modern life was a mineral spring, such as are to be found in both divisions of Britain, and which are supplied with the usual materials for restoring health, or driving away care. The invalid often finds relief from his complaints, less from the healing virtues of the Spaw itself, than because his system of ordinary life undergoes an entire change, in his being removed from his ledger and accompt-books—from his legal folios and progresses of title-deeds—from his counters and shelves,—from whatever else forms the main source of his constant anxiety at home, destroys his appetite, mars the custom of his exercise, deranges the digestive powers, and clogs up the springs of life. Thither, too, comes the saunterer, anxious to get rid of that wearisome attendant *himself*, and thither come both males and females, who, upon a different principle, desire to make themselves double.

The society of such places is regulated, by their very nature, upon a scheme much more indulgent than that which rules the world of fashion, and the narrow circles of rank in the metropolis. The titles of rank, birth, and fortune, are received at a watering-place without any very strict investigation, as adequate to the purpose for which they are preferred; and as the situation infers a certain degree of intimacy and sociability for the time, so to whatever heights it may have been carried, it is not understood to imply any duration beyond the length of the season. No intimacy can be supposed more close for the time, and more transitory in its endurance, than that which is attached to a watering-place acquaintance. The novelist, therefore, who fixes upon such a scene for his tale, endeavours to display a species of society, where the strongest contrast of humorous characters and manners may be brought to bear on and illustrate each other with less violation of probability, than could be supposed to attend the same miscellaneous assemblage in any other situation.

In such scenes, too, are frequently mingled characters, not merely ridiculous, but dangerous and hateful. The unprincipled gamester, the heartless fortune-hunter, all those who eke out their means of subsistence by pandering to the vices and follies of the rich and gay, who drive, by their various arts, foibles into crimes, and imprudence into acts of ruinous madness, are to be found where their victims naturally resort, with the same certainty that eagles are gathered together at the place of slaughter. By this the author takes a great advantage for the management of his story, particularly in its darker and more melancholy passages. The impostor, the gambler, all who live loose upon the skirts of society, or, like vermin, thrive by its corruptions, are to be found at such retreats, when they easily, and as a matter of course, mingle with those dupes, who might otherwise have escaped their snares. But besides those characters who are actually dangerous to society, a well frequented watering-place generally exhibits for the amusement of the company, and the perplexity and amazement of the more inexperienced, a sprinkling of persons called by the newspapers eccentric characters—individuals, namely, who, either from some real derangement of their understanding, or, much more frequently, from an excess of vanity, are ambitious of distinguishing themselves by some striking peculiarity in dress or address, conversation or manners, and perhaps in all. These affectations are usually adopted, like Drawcansir's extravagances, to show *they dare;* and I must needs say, those who profess them are more frequently to be found among the English, than among the natives of either of the other two divisions of the united kingdoms. The reason probably is, that the consciousness of wealth, and a sturdy feeling of independence, which generally pervade the English nation, are, in a few individuals, perverted into absurdity, or at least peculiarity. The witty Irishman, on the contrary, adapts his general behaviour to that of the best society, or that which he thinks such; nor is it any part of the shrewd Scot's national character unnecessarily to draw upon himself public attention. These rules, however, are not without their exceptions; for we find men of every country playing the eccentric at these independent resorts of the gay and the wealthy, where every one enjoys the license of doing what is good in his own eyes.

It scarce needed these obvious remarks to justify a novelist's choice of a watering-place as the scene of a fictitious narrative. Unquestionably, it affords every variety of character, mixed together in a manner which cannot, without a breach of probability, be supposed to exist elsewhere; neither can it be denied that in the concourse which such miscellaneous collections of persons afford, events extremely different from those of the quiet routine of ordinary life may, and often do, take place.

It is not, however, sufficient that a mine be in itself rich and easily accessible; it is necessary that the engineer who explores it should himself, in mining phrase, have an accurate knowledge of the *country*, and possess the skill necessary to work it to advantage. In this respect, the author of Saint Ronan's Well could not be termed fortunate. His habits of life had not led him much, of late years at least, into its general or bustling scenes, nor had he mingled often in the society which enables the observer to "shoot folly as it flies." The consequence perhaps was, that the characters wanted that force and precision which can only be given by a writer who is familiarly acquainted with his subject. The author, however, had the satisfaction to chronicle his testimony against the practice of gambling, a vice which the devil has contrived to render all his own, since it is deprived of whatever pleads an apology for other vices, and is founded entirely on the cold-blooded calculation of the most exclusive selfishness. The character of the traveller, meddling, self-important, and what the ladies call fussing, but yet generous and benevolent in his purposes, was partly taken from nature. The story, being entirely modern, cannot require much explanation, after what has been here given, either in the shape of notes, or a more prolix introduction.

It may be remarked, that the English critics, in many instances, though none of great influence, pursued Saint Ronan's Well with hue and cry, many of the fraternity giving it as their opinion that the author had exhausted himself, or, as the technical phrase expresses it, written himself out; and as an unusual tract of success too often provokes many persons to mark and exaggerate a slip when it does occur, the author was publicly accused, in prose and verse, of having committed a literary suicide in this unhappy attempt. The voices, therefore, were, for a time, against Saint Ronan's on the southern side of the Tweed.

In the author's own country, it was otherwise. Many of the characters were recognised as genuine Scottish portraits, and the good fortune which had hitherto attended the productions of the Author of Waverley, did not desert, notwithstanding the ominous vaticinations of its censurers, this new attempt, although out of his ordinary style.

1st *February*, 1832.

Notes to Saint Ronan's Well

6.28 (Ch. 1) Quære aliud hospitium In a colloquy of Erasmus, called *Diversoria*, there is a very unsavoury description of a German inn of the period, where an objection of the guest is answered in the manner expressed in the text—a great sign of want of competition on the road.

7.11 (Ch. 1) a favourite one This circumstance shows of itself, that the Meg Dods of the tale cannot be identified with her namesake Jenny Dods, who kept the inn at Howgate, on the Peebles road; for Jenny, far different from our heroine, was unmatched as a slattern.

7.21 (Ch. 1) make the lawing less This was universally the case in Scotland forty or fifty years ago; and so little was charged for a domestic's living when the author became first acquainted with the road, that a shilling or eighteenpence was sufficient board wages for a man-servant, when a crown would not now answer the purpose. It is true the cause of these reasonable charges rested upon a principle equally unjust to the landlord, and inconvenient to the guest. The landlord did not expect to make any thing upon the charge for eating which his bill contained; in consideration of which, the guest was expected to drink more wine than might be convenient or agreeable to him, "*for the good*," as it was called, "*of the house*." The landlord indeed was willing and ready to assist, in this species of duty, every stranger who came within his gates. Other things were in proportion. A charge for lodging, fire, and candle, was long a thing unheard of in Scotland. A shilling to the housemaid settled all such considerations. I see, from memorandums of 1790, that a young man, with two ponies and a serving-lad, might travel from the house of one Meg Dods to another, through most part of Scotland, for about five or six shillings a-day.

8.30 (Ch. 1) the desertion of Meg Dods became general BUILDING-FEUS IN SCOTLAND. In Scotland a village is erected upon a species of landright, very different from the copyhold so frequent in England. Every alienation or sale of landed property must be made in the shape of a feudal conveyance, and the party who acquires it holds thereby an absolute and perfect right of property in the fief, while he discharges the stipulations of the vassal, and, above all, pays the feu-duties. The vassal or tenant of the site of the smallest cottage holds his possession as absolutely as the proprietor, of whose large estate it is perhaps scarce a perceptible portion. By dint of excellent laws, the sasines, or deeds of delivery of such fiefs, are placed on record in such order, that every burden affecting the property can be seen for payment of a very moderate fee; so that a person proposing to lend money upon it, knows exactly the nature and extent of his security.

From the nature of their landrights being so explicit and secure, the Scottish people have been led to entertain a jealousy of building-leases, of however long duration. Not long ago, a great landed proprietor took the latter mode of disposing of some ground near a thriving town in the west country. The number of years in the lease was settled at nine hundred and ninety-nine. All was agreed to, and the deeds were ordered to be drawn. But the tenant, as he walked down the avenue, began to reflect that the lease, though so very long as to be almost perpetual, nevertheless had a termination; and that after the lapse of a thousand years, lacking one, the connexion of his family and representatives with the estate would cease. He took a qualm at the thought of the loss to be sustained by his posterity a thousand years hence; and going back to the house of the gentleman who feued the ground, he demanded, and readily obtained, the additional term of fifty years to be added to the lease.

8.39 (Ch. 1) they maun hae a hottle This Gallic word (hôtel) was first introduced in Scotland during the author's childhood, and was so pronounced by the lower class.

19.30 (Ch. 2) Luckie Buchan in the west The foundress of a sect called Buchanites; a species of Joanna Southcote, who long after death was expected to return and head her disciples on the road to Jerusalem.

20.16 (Ch. 2) the cruells *Escrouelles*, King's Evil.

24.21 (Ch. 3) taking a start and an owerloup The usual expression for a slight encroachment on a neighbour's property.
24.34 (Ch. 3) the piper of Peebles The said piper was famous at the mystery.
26.16 (Ch. 3) sketchers Skates are called sketchers in Scotland.
53.27 (Ch. 6) 'the Dark Ladye'
DARK LADYE. The Dark Ladye is one of those tantalizing fragments, in which Mr Coleridge has shown us what exquisite powers of poetry he has suffered to remain uncultivated. Let us be thankful for what we have received, however. The unfashioned ore, drawn from so rich a mine, is worth all that art can add its highest decorations to from less abundant sources. The verses beginning the poem which are published separately by the Poet, are said to have soothed the last hours of Mr Fox. They are the stanzas entitled LOVE.
60.32 (Ch. 7) fo'k come far and near to see him The late Dr Gregory is probably intimated, as one of the celebrated Dr Cullen's personal habits is previously mentioned. Dr Gregory was distinguished for putting his patients on a severe regimen.
63.2 (Ch. 7) spleuchan A fur pouch for keeping tobacco.
103.5 (Ch. 11) bogle Bogle—in English, Goblin.
110.31 (Ch. 12) a kettle of fish A kettle of fish is a *fête-champêtre* of a particular kind, which is to other *fêtes-champêtres* what the piscatory eclogues of Brown or Sannazario are to pastoral poetry. A large caldron is boiled by the side of a salmon river, containing a quantity of water, thickened with salt to the consistence of brine. In this the fish is plunged when taken, and eaten by the company *fronde super viridi*. This is accounted the best way of eating salmon, by those who desire to taste the fish in a state of extreme freshness. Others prefer it after being kept a day or two, when the curd melts into oil, and the fish becomes richer and more luscious. The more judicious gastronomes eat no other sauce than a spoonful of the water in which the salmon is boiled, together with a little pepper and vinegar.
132.5 (Ch. 14) a crime has been committed For example, a man cannot be tried for a murder merely in the case of the non-appearance of an individual; there must be proof that the party has been murdered.
134.22 (Ch. 15) a very small needle This was a peculiarity in the countenance of the celebrated Cossack leader, Platoff.
134.39 (Ch. 15) I last heard of a soft An epithet which expresses, in Scotland, what the barometer calls rainy.
150.32 (Ch. 16) his state of celibacy
MAGO-PICO. This satire, once very popular even in Scotland, at

least with one party, was composed at the expense of a reverend presbyterian divine, of whom many stories are preserved, being Mr Pyet, the Mago-Pico of the Tale, minister of Dunbar. The work is now little known in Scotland, and not at all in England, though written with much strong and coarse humour, resembling the style of Arbuthnot. It was composed by Mr Haliburton, a military chaplain. The distresses attending Mago-Pico's bachelor life, are thus stated:—

"At the same time I desire you will only figure out to yourself his situation during his celibacy in the ministerial charge—a house lying all heaps upon heaps; his bed ill-made, swarming with fleas, and very cold on the winter nights; his sheep's-head not to be eaten for wool and hair, his broth singed, his bread mouldy, his lamb and pig all scouthered, his house neither washed nor plastered; his black stockings darned with white worsted above the shoes; his butter made into cat's harns; his cheese one heap of mites and maggots, and full of large avenues for rats and mice to play at hide-and-seek and make their nests in. Frequent were the admonitions he had given his maid-servants on this score, and every now and then was turning them off; but still the last was the worst, and in the meanwhile the poor man was the sufferer. At any rate, therefore, matrimony must turn to his account, though his wife should prove to be nothing but a creature of the feminine gender, with a tongue in her head, and ten fingers on her hands, to clear the papers of the housemaid, not to mention the convenience of a man's having it in his power to beget sons and daughters in his own house."—*Memoirs of Mago-Pico. Second edition. Edinburgh,* 1761, p. 19.

152.27 "rained in" *Scotticé*, for "admitted the rain."

181.38 (Ch. 20) the proposed theatricals At Kilruddery, the noble seat of Lord Meath, in the county of Wicklow, there is a situation for private theatrical exhibitions in the open air, planted out with the evergreens which arise there in the most luxuriant magnificence. It has a wild and romantic effect, reminding one of the scene in which Bottom rehearsed his pageant, with a green plot for a stage, and a hawthorn brake for a tiringroom.

184.22 (Ch. 20) the Highland and Grecian costume "The Arnaouts or Albanese," (says Lord Byron,) "struck me forcibly by their resemblance to the Highlanders of Scotland, in dress, figure, and manner of living. Their very mountains seem Caledonian, with a kinder climate. The kilt, though white; the spare, active form; their dialect Celtic, in the sound, and their hardy habits, all carried me back to Morven."—*Notes to the Second Chapter of Childe Harold's Pilgrimage.*

222.15 (Ch. 23) the motto of our cousins, the McIntoshes The well-known crest of this ancient race, is a cat rampant, with a motto bearing the caution—"Touch not the cat, but [*i.e. be out*, or without] the glove."

282.36 (Ch. 30) ein kleine wenig Forgive me, sir, I was bred in the Imperial service, and must smoke a little.

282.40 (Ch. 30) den lieben topf Smoke as much as you please; I have got my pipe, too.—See what a beautiful head!

289.9 (Ch. 31) bing folks on the low toby "Rob as a footpad."

304.13 (Ch. 32) if they met accidentally There were several instances of this dexterity, but especially those which occurred in the celebrated case of Murdison and Millar in 1773. These persons, a sheep-farmer and his shepherd, settled in the vale of Tweed, commenced and carried on for some time an extensive system of devastation on the flocks of their neighbours. A dog belonging to Millar was so well trained, that he had only to show him during the day the parcel of sheep which he desired to have; and when dismissed at night for the purpose, Yarrow went right to the pasture where the flock had fed, and carried off the quantity shown him. He then drove them before him by the most secret paths to Murdison's farm, where the dishonest master and servant were in readiness to receive the booty. Two things were remarkable. In the first place, that if the dog, when thus dishonestly employed, actually met his master, he observed great caution in recognising him, as if he had been afraid of bringing him under suspicion; secondly, that he showed a distinct sense that the illegal transactions in which he was engaged were not of a nature to endure daylight. The sheep which he was directed to drive, were often reluctant to leave their own pastures, and sometimes the intervention of rivers or other obstacles made their progress peculiarly difficult. On such occasions, Yarrow continued his efforts to drive his plunder forward, until the day began to dawn, a signal which, he conceived, rendered it necessary for him to desert his spoil, and slink homeward by a circuitous road. It is generally said this accomplished dog was hanged along with his master; but the truth is, he survived him long, in the service of a man in Leithen, yet was said afterwards to have shown little of the wonderful instinct exhibited in the employment of Millar.

Another instance of similar sagacity, a friend of mine discovered in a beautiful little spaniel, which he had purchased from a dealer in the canine race. When he entered a shop, he was not long in observing that his little companion made it a rule to follow at some interval, and to estrange himself from his master so much as to appear totally unconnected with him. And when he left the shop, it was the dog's custom to remain behind him till he could find an opportunity of seizing a pair of gloves, or silk stockings, or some similar property, which he brought to his master. The poor fellow probably saved his life by falling into the hands of an honest man.

311.12 (Ch. 32) their sossings and their swoopings The author has made an attempt in this character to draw a picture of what is too often seen, a wretched being whose heart becomes hardened and spited at the world, in which she is doomed to experience much misery and little sympathy. The system of compulsory charity by poor's rates, of which the absolute necessity can hardly be questioned, has connected with it on both sides some of the most odious and malevolent feelings that can agitate humanity. The quality of true charity is not strained. Like that of mercy, of which, in a large sense, it may be accounted a sister virtue, it blesses him that gives and him that takes. It awakens kindly feelings both in the mind of the donor and in that of the relieved object. The giver and receiver are recommended to each other by mutual feelings of good-will, and the pleasurable emotions connected with the consciousness of a good action fix the deed in recollection of the one, while a sense of gratitude renders it holy to the other. In the legal and compulsory assessment for the proclaimed parish pauper, there is nothing of all this. The alms are extorted from an unwilling hand, and a heart which desires the annihilation, rather than the relief, of the distressed object. The object of charity, sensible of the ill-will with which the pittance is bestowed, seizes on it as his right, not as a favour. The manner of conferring it being directly calculated to hurt and disgust his feelings, he revenges himself by becoming impudent and clamorous. A more odious picture, or more likely to deprave the feelings of those exposed to its influence, can hardly be imagined; and yet to such a point have we been brought by an artificial system of society, that we must either deny altogether the right of the poor to their just proportion of the fruits of the earth, or afford them some means of subsistence out of them by the institution of positive law.

372.42 (Ch. 13) Saint Ronan's Well

MEG DODS. *Non omnis moriar.* Saint Ronan's, since this veracious history was given to the public, has revived as a sort of *alias*, or second title, to the very pleasant village of Inverleithen upon Tweed, where there is a medicinal spring much frequented by visitors. Prizes for some of the manly and athletic sports, common in the pastoral districts around, are competed for under the title of the Saint Ronan's Games. Nay, Meg Dods has produced herself of late from obscurity as authoress of a work on Cookery, of which, in justice to a lady who makes so distinguished a figure as this excellent dame, we insert the title-page:

"The Cook and Housewife's Manual: A Practical System of Modern Domestic Cookery and Family Management.

'——Cook, see all your sawces
Be sharp and poynant in the palate, that they may
Commend you: look to your roast and baked meats handsomely,
And what new kickshaws and delicate made things.'

BEAUMONT AND FLETCHER.

By Mistress Margaret Dods, of the Cleikum Inn, St Ronan's."

Though it is rather unconnected with our immediate subject, we cannot help adding, that Mrs Dods has preserved the recipes of certain excellent old dishes which we would be loath should fall into oblivion in our day; and in bearing this testimony, we protest that we are no way biassed by the receipt of two bottles of excellent sauce for cold meat, which were sent to us by the said Mrs Dods, as a mark of her respect and regard, for which we return her our unfeigned thanks, having found them capital.

REDGAUNTLET

Editorial Note

Redgauntlet occupies part of Volume 2 and the whole of Volume 3 of the 1827 octavo *Tales and Romances*, MSS 23027 and 23028 in the Interleaved Set. Scott worked on the annotation in January and February 1831, sending Cadell the first Interleaved Set volume on 28 January and the second on 21 February (MS 15980, f. 16r; *Journal*, 634). On 11 and 17 March Cadell 'wrote out some of the notes' and 'copied Sundry notes' to the novel (MS 21021, ff. 13r, 14r). He continued his work during the second part of March, and on 19 April he 'compared [presumably 'proof-read'] Part of Redgauntlet' (MS 21021, f. 18r). On the 23rd of that month James Ballantyne sent Scott proofs of the Introduction 'which you will find to require somewhat of your correcting hand' (MS 3917, f. 288r). On 16 May he was revising the notes, and on the following two days the Introduction (MS 21021, f. 22v). He put a final touch to the novel the following year. On 1 March he was 'busy after tea with part of Redgauntlet at a Note—the part I allude to was struck of out of text when book was at Press', and the next day he 'wrote to James Ballantyne as to Redgauntlet Note' (MS 21022, f. 12r). The note in question is presumably that on the 'Coronation of George III', discussed below. *Redgauntlet* appeared as Volumes 35 and 36 of the Magnum on 1 April and 1 May 1832. The Introduction occupies 20 pages. There are only 10 endnotes, most of them filling only part of the page dedicated to them (there are 12 pages in all), and pretty well equally divided between the two volumes; but there are numerous footnotes, some of them longer than the shorter endnotes.

The Introduction consists almost entirely of an elegant essay sketching the decline in the Young Pretender's fortunes. It is strange that such a lucid performance should end with a paragraph whose import is less than obvious: 'It was while reflecting on these things that the novel of Redgauntlet was undertaken. But various circumstances in the composition induced the author to alter its purport considerably, as it passed through his hands, and to carry the action to that point in time when the Chevalier Charles Edward, though fallen into the sere and yellow leaf, was yet meditating a second attempt, which could scarcely have been more hopeless than his first'. It would appear from this that, according to Scott's recollection, he had originally intended the novel to be set nearer to 1745 than 1765. This is perhaps why he begins the Introduction with another enigmatic statement: 'The Jacobite enthusiasm of the eighteenth century, particularly during the rebellion of 1745, afforded a theme, perhaps the finest that could be selected, for fictitious composition, founded upon real or probable incident.' That is how it appears in print. In manuscript the dating is less clear-cut (even ignoring the erroneous 'seventeenth' there): 'The Jacobitism enthusiasm of the seventeenth century afforded about the middle of the century a theme perhaps the finest that could be selected for fictitious composition founded ⟨upon the⟩ upon real incident.' The change of plan must have preceded the commencement of actual composition, since the opening chapters are clearly set in the Edinburgh of the 1760s: if Scott's recollection is correct the expression 'as it passed through his hands' is misleading.

The manuscript of the Introduction begins as usual in Scott's hand, but from 352.9 ('In one instance') William Laidlaw acts as amanuensis. The writing in both hands is fluent throughout.

Scott's annotation of *Redgauntlet* is in his most relaxed manner. The time of the action is just within living memory, and many of the brief footnotes hover between explanation and general recollection, with phrases such as 'It is well known and remembered', 'all Scotsmen know', 'The simile is obvious, from the old manufacture of Scotland', and 'Every one must remember' (360.7, 15–16; 365.20–21; 366.42). Both footnotes and endnotes often draw on personal memory, albeit hazy at times, and anecdotes and traditions handed down orally, to suggest sources or parallels for aspects of the narrative. The tone is sometimes nostalgic or elegiac. At proof stage the note on the 'Coronation of George III' (369–70) was revised. It acquired a general introduction on persisting Jacobite expectations and lost the anecdote which ended the original manuscript note in the Interleaved Set illustrating George's 'goodness of heart and soundness of policy'. The reasons for this change are not evident.

There are four Magnum illustrations for this title. The frontispiece to Volume 35 (MAG0069 / TB348.35) was designed by Alexander Fraser, the elder, and engraved by James Mitchell. It depicts Redgauntlet at supper alongside Darsie, with Cristal Nixon and Mabel Moffat also at the table, and Greenmantle (Lilias Redgauntlet) saying grace (EEWN 17, 29: the caption is simply 'REDGAUNTLET.'). The title-page vignette (MAG0070 / TB348.35) was designed by James Inskipp and engraved by Robert Graves. It depicts Darsie, having handed over his fishing-rod to Benjie (EEWN 17, 18.31–34: 'I was induced . . . with my own hand.'). The frontispiece to Volume 36 (MAG0071 / TB348.36) was designed by David Octavius Hill and engraved by Augustus Fox. It depicts Steenie Steenson, bagpipes under his arm, presenting a bag of money as rent to Sir Robert Redgauntlet, with Dougal MacCallum in attendance (EEWN 17, 90.1–5 (abridged): 'Are ye come light-handed . . . that does something clever.'). The title-page vignette (MAG0072 / TB348.36) was designed by William Kidd and engraved by John Hursburgh. It depicts Peter Peebles in Parliament Close, with the equestrian statute of Charles II prominent in the square (EEWN 17, 118.33–43 (abridged): 'The identical Peter . . . an immense cocked hat.').

A. Fraser. J. Mitchell.

REDGAUNTLET.

WAVERLEY NOVELS.

VOL. XXXV.

REDGAUNTLET.

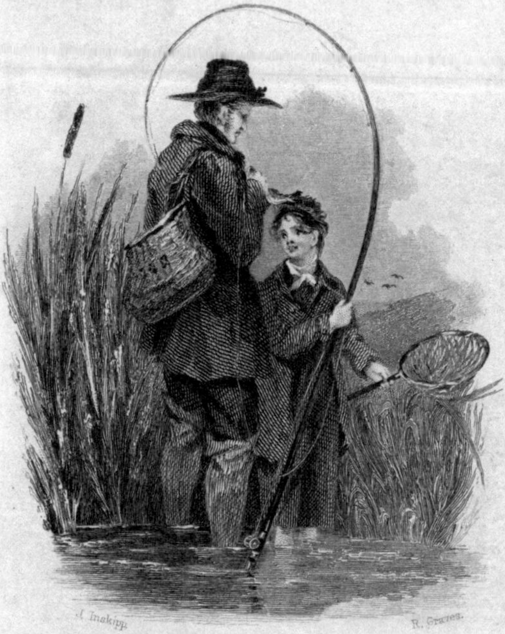

"I was induced at last to lend the rod to the sneering scoundrel, to see what he would make of it; and he not only half filled my basket in an hour, but literally taught me to kill two trouts with my own hand."

PRINTED FOR ROBERT CADELL, EDINBURGH,
AND WHITTAKER & C° LONDON.
1832.

D. O. Hill. Agus. Fox.

REDGAUNTLET.

"Are ye come light-handed, ye son of a toom whistle?" said Sir Robert.—My gudesire, placed the bag of money on the Table wi' a dash, like a man that does something clever.

EDINBURGH, PUBLISHED 1832, BY ROBERT CADELL, and WHITTAKER & C° LONDON

Introduction to Redgauntlet

THE Jacobite enthusiasm of the eighteenth century, particularly during the rebellion of 1745, afforded a theme, perhaps the finest that could be selected, for fictitious composition, founded upon real or probable incident. This civil war, and its remarkable events, were remembered by the existing generation without any degree of the bitterness of spirit which seldom fails to attend internal dissension. The Highlanders, who formed the principal strength of Charles Edward's army, were an ancient and high-spirited race, peculiar in their habits of war and of peace, brave to romance, and exhibiting a character turning upon points better adapted to poetry than to the prose of real life. Their Prince, young, valiant, patient of fatigue, and despising danger, heading his army on foot in the most toilsome marches, and defeating a regular force in three battles,—all these were circumstances fascinating to the imagination, and might well be supposed to seduce young and enthusiastic minds to the cause in which they were found united, although wisdom and reason frowned upon the enterprise.

The adventurous Prince, as is well known, proved to be one of those personages who distinguish themselves during some single and extraordinarily brilliant period of their lives, like the course of a shooting star, at which men wonder, as well on account of the briefness, as the brilliancy of its splendour. A long trace of darkness overshadowed the subsequent life of a man, who, in his youth, showed himself so capable of great undertakings; and, without the painful task of tracing his course further, we may say the latter pursuits and habits of this unhappy Prince, are those painfully evincing a broken heart, which seeks refuge from its own thoughts in sordid enjoyments.

Still, however, it was long ere Charles Edward appeared to be, perhaps it was long ere he altogether became, so much degraded from his original self; as he enjoyed for a time the lustre attending the progress and termination of his enterprise. Those who thought they discerned in his subsequent conduct an insensibility to the distresses of his followers, coupled with that egotistical attention to his own interests, which has been often attributed to the Stewart Family, and which is the natural effect of the principles of divine right in which they were brought up, were now generally considered as dissatisfied and splenetic persons, who, displeased with the issue of their adventure, and finding themselves involved in the ruins of a failing cause, indulged themselves in undeserved reproaches against their leader. Indeed, such censures were by no means frequent among those of his followers, who, if what was alleged had been just, had the best right to complain. Far the greater number of those unfortunate gentlemen suffered with the most dignified patience, and were either too proud to take notice of ill treatment on the part of their Prince, or so prudent as to be aware their complaints would meet with little sympathy from the world. It may be added, that the greater part of the banished Jacobites, and those of high rank and consequence, were not much within reach of the influence of the Prince's character and conduct, whether well regulated or otherwise.

In the meantime, that great Jacobite conspiracy, of which the insurrection of 1745–6 was but a small part, precipitated into action on the failure of a far more general scheme, was resumed and again put into motion by the Jacobites of England, whose force had never been broken, as they had prudently avoided bringing it into the field. The surprising effect which had been produced by small means, in 1745–6, animated their hopes for more important successes, when the whole nonjuring interest of Britain, identified as it then was with great part of the landed gentlemen, should come forwards to finish what had been gallantly attempted by a few Highland chiefs.

It is probable, indeed, that the Jacobites of the day were incapable of considering that the very small scale on which the effort was made, was in one great measure the cause of its unexpected success. The remarkable speed with which the insurgents marched, the singular good discipline which they preserved, the union and unanimity which for some time animated their councils, were all in a considerable degree produced by the smallness of their numbers. Notwithstanding the discomfiture of Charles Edward, the nonjurors of the period long continued to nurse unlawful schemes, and to drink treasonable toasts, until age stole upon them. Another generation arose, who did not share the sentiments which they cherished; and at length the sparkles of disaffection, which had long smouldered, but had never been heated enough to burst into actual flame, became entirely extinguished. But in proportion as the political enthusiasm died gradually away among men of ordinary temperament, it influenced those of warm imaginations and weak understandings, and hence wild schemes were formed, as desperate as they were adventurous.

Thus a young Scottishman of rank is said to have stooped so low as to plot the surprisal of St James's palace, and the assassination of the royal family. While these ill-digested and desperate conspiracies were agitated among the few Jacobites who still adhered with more obstinacy to their purpose, there is no question but that other plots might have been brought to an open explosion, had it not suited the policy of Sir Robert Walpole, rather to prevent or disable the conspirators in their projects, than to promulgate the tale of danger, which might thus have been believed to be more widely diffused than was really the case.

In one instance alone this very prudential and humane line of conduct was departed from, and the event seemed to confirm the policy of the general course. Doctor Archibald Cameron, brother of the celebrated Donald Cameron of Lochiel, and attainted for the rebellion of 1745, was found by a party of soldiers lurking with a comrade in the wilds of Loch Katrine, five or six years after the battle of Culloden, and was there seized. There were circumstances in his case, so far as was made known to the public, which attracted much compassion, and gave to the judicial proceedings against him an appearance of cold-blooded revenge on the part of government; and the following argument of a zealous Jacobite in his favour was received as conclusive by Dr Johnson, and other persons who might pretend to impartiality. Dr Cameron had never borne arms, although engaged in the Rebellion, but used his medical skill for the service, indifferently, of the wounded of both parties. His return to Scotland was ascribed exclusively to family affairs. His behaviour at the bar was decent, firm, and respectful. His wife threw herself, on three different occasions, before George II. and the members of his family, was rudely repulsed from their presence, and at length placed, it was said, in the same prison with her husband, and confined with unmanly severity.

Dr Cameron was finally executed, with all the severities of the law of treason; and his death remains in popular estimation a dark blot upon the memory of George II., being almost publicly imputed to a mean and personal hatred of Donald Cameron of Lochiel, the sufferer's heroic brother.

Yet the fact was, that whether the execution of Archibald Cameron was political or otherwise, it might certainly have been justified, had the King's ministers so pleased, upon reasons of a public nature. The unfortunate sufferer had not come to the Highlands solely upon private affairs, as was the general belief; but it was not judged prudent by the English ministry to let it be generally known that he came to enquire about a considerable sum of money which had been remitted from France to the friends of the exiled family. He had also a commission to hold intercourse with the well known

M'Pherson of Cluny, chief of the clan Vourich, whom the Chevalier had left behind at his departure from Scotland in 1746, and who remained during ten years of proscription and danger, skulking from place to place in the Highlands, and maintaining an uninterrupted correspondence between Charles and his friends. That Dr Cameron should have held a commission to assist this chief in raking together the dispersed embers of disaffection, is in itself sufficiently natural, and, considering his political principles, in no respect dishonourable to his memory. But neither ought it to be imputed to George II., that he suffered the laws to be enforced against a person taken in the act of breaking them. When he lost his hazardous game, Dr Cameron only paid the forfeit which he must have calculated upon. The ministers, however, thought it proper to leave Dr Cameron's new schemes in concealment, lest by divulging them they had indicated the channel of communication which, it is now well known, they possessed to all the plots of Charles Edward. But it was equally ill advised and ungenerous to sacrifice the character of the King to the policy of the administration. Both points might have been gained by sparing the life of Dr Cameron after conviction, and limiting his punishment to perpetual exile.

These repeated and successive Jacobite plots rose and burst like bubbles on a fountain; and one of them, at least, the Chevalier judged of importance enough to induce him to risk himself within the dangerous precincts of the British capital. This appears from Dr King's Anecdotes of his Own Times.

"September, 1750.—I received a note from my Lady Primrose, who desired to see me immediately. As soon as I waited on her, she led me into her dressing-room, and presented me to ——," [the Chevalier, doubtless.] "If I was surprised to find him there, I was still more astonished when he acquainted me with the motives which had induced him to hazard a journey to England at this juncture. The impatience of his friends who were in exile, had formed a scheme which was impracticable; but although it had been as feasible as they had represented it to him, yet no preparation had been made, nor was any thing ready to carry it into execution. He was soon convinced that he had been deceived; and, therefore, after a stay in London of five days only, he returned to the place from whence he came." Dr King was in 1750 a keen Jacobite, as may be inferred from the visit made by him to the Prince under such circumstances, and from his being one of that unfortunate person's chosen correspondents. He, as well as other men of sense and observation, began to despair of making their fortune in the party which they had chosen. It was indeed sufficiently dangerous; for, during the short visit just described, one of Dr King's servants remarked the stranger's likeness to Prince Charles, whom he recognised from the common busts.

The occasion taken for breaking up the Stewart interest, we shall tell in Dr King's own words:—"When he (Charles Edward) was in Scotland, he had a mistress whose name was Walkinshaw, and whose sister was at that time, and is still, housekeeper at Leicester House. Some years after he was released from his prison, and conducted out of France, he sent for this girl, who soon acquired such a dominion over him, that she was acquainted with all his schemes, and trusted with his most secret correspondence. As soon as this was known in England, all those persons of distinction who were attached to him were greatly alarmed: they imagined that this wench had been placed in his family by the English ministers; and, considering her sister's situation, they seemed to have some ground for their suspicion; wherefore, they dispatched a gentleman to Paris, where the Prince then was, who had instructions to insist that Mrs Walkinshaw should be removed to a convent for a certain term; but her gallant absolutely refused to comply with this demand; and although Mr M'Namara, the gentleman who was sent to him, who has a natural eloquence, and an excellent understanding, urged the most cogent reasons, and used all the arts of persuasion, to induce him to part with his mistress, and even proceeded so far as to assure him, according to his instructions, that an immediate interruption of all correspondence with his most powerful friends in England, and, in short, that the ruin of his interest, which was now daily increasing, would be the infallible consequence of his refusal; yet he continued inflexible, and all M'Namara's entreaties and remonstrances were ineffectual. M'Namara staid in Paris some days beyond the time prescribed to him, endeavouring to reason the Prince into a better temper; but finding him obstinately persevere in his first answer, he took his leave with concern and indignation, saying, as he passed out, 'What has your family done, sir, thus to draw down the vengeance of Heaven on every branch of it, through so many ages?' It is worthy of remark, that in all the conferences which M'Namara had with the Prince on this occasion, the latter declared that it was not a violent passion, or indeed any particular regard, which attached him to Mrs Walkinshaw, and that he could see her removed from him without any concern; but he would not receive directions, in respect to his private conduct, from any man alive. When M'Namara returned to London, and reported the Prince's answer to the gentlemen who had employed him, they were astonished and confounded. However, they soon resolved on the measures which they were to pursue for the future, and determined no longer to serve a man who could not be persuaded to serve himself, and chose rather to endanger the lives of his best and most faithful friends, than part with an harlot, whom, as he often declared, he neither loved nor esteemed."

From this anecdote, the general truth of which is indubitable, the principal fault of Charles Edward's temper is sufficiently obvious. It was a high sense of his own importance, and an obstinate adherence to what he had once determined on—qualities which, if he had succeeded in his bold attempt, gave the nation little room to hope that he would have been found free from the love of prerogative and desire of arbitrary power, which characterised his unhappy grandfather. He gave a notable instance how far this was the leading feature of his character, when, for no reasonable cause that can be assigned, he placed his own single will in opposition to the necessities of France, which, in order to purchase a peace become necessary to the kingdom, was reduced to gratify Britain by prohibiting the residence of Charles within any part of the French dominions. It was in vain that France endeavoured to lessen the disgrace of this step by making the most flattering offers, in hopes to induce the Prince of himself to anticipate this disagreeable alternative, which, if seriously enforced, as it was like to be, he had no means whatever of resisting, by leaving the kingdom as of his own free-will. Inspired, however, by the spirit of hereditary obstinacy, Charles preferred a useless resistance to a dignified submission, and by a series of idle bravadoes, laid the French court under the necessity of arresting their late ally, and sending him to close confinement in the Bastile, from which he was afterwards sent out of the French dominions, much in the manner in which a convict is transported to the place of his destination.

In addition to these repeated instances of a rash and inflexible temper, Dr King also adds faults alleged to belong to the Prince's character, of a kind less consonant with his noble birth and high pretensions. He is said by this author to have been avaricious, or parsimonious at least, to such a degree of meanness, as to fail, even when he had ample means, in relieving the sufferers who had lost their fortune, and sacrificed all in his ill-fated attempt.* We

* The reproach is thus expressed by Dr King, who brings the charge:—"But the most odious part of his character is his love of money, a vice which I do not remember to have been imputed by our historians to any of his ancestors, and is the certain index of a base and little mind. I know it may be urged in his vindication, that a Prince in exile ought to be an economist. And so he ought; but, nevertheless, his purse should be always open as long as there is any thing in it, to relieve the necessities

must receive, however, with some degree of jealousy what is said by Dr King on this subject, recollecting that he had left at least, if he did not desert, the standard of the unfortunate Prince, and was not therefore a person who was likely to form the fairest estimate of his virtues and faults. We must also remember, that if the exiled Prince gave little, he had but little to give, especially considering how late he nourished the scheme of another expedition to Scotland, for which he was long endeavouring to hoard money.

The case, also, of Charles Edward must be allowed to have been a difficult one. He had to satisfy numerous persons, who, having lost their all in his cause, had, with that all, seen the extinction of hopes which they accounted nearly as good as certainties; some of these were perhaps clamorous in their applications, and certainly ill pleased with their want of success. Other parts of the Chevalier's conduct may have afforded grounds for charging him with coldness to the sufferings of his devoted followers. One of these was a sentiment which has nothing in it that is generous, but it was certainly a principle in which the young Prince was trained, and which may be too probably denominated peculiar to his family, educated in all the high notions of passive obedience and non-resistance. If the unhappy Prince gave implicit faith to the professions of statesmen holding such notions, which is implied by his whole conduct, it must have led to the natural, though ungracious inference, that the services of a subject could not, to whatever degree of ruin they might bring the individual, create a debt against his sovereign. Such a person could only boast that he had done his duty; nor was he entitled to be claimant for a greater reward than it was convenient for the Prince to bestow, or to hold his sovereign his debtor for losses which he had sustained through his loyalty. To a certain extent the Jacobite principles inevitably led to this cold and egotistic mode of reasoning on the part of the sovereign; nor, with all our natural pity for the situation of royalty in distress, do we feel entitled to affirm that Charles did not use this opiate to his feelings, on viewing the misery of his followers, while he certainly possessed, though in no great degree, the means of affording them more relief than he practised. His own history, after leaving France, is brief and melancholy. For a time he seems to have held the firm belief that

---

of his friends and adherents. King Charles II., during his banishment, would have shared the last pistole in his pocket with his little family. But I have known this gentleman with two thousand louis-d'ors in his strong-box, pretend he was in great distress, and borrow money from a lady in Paris who was not in affluent circumstances. His most faithful servants, who had closely attended him in all his difficulties, were ill rewarded."—KING'S *Memoirs*.

Providence, which had borne him through so many hazards, still reserved him for some distant occasion, in which he should be empowered to vindicate the honours of his birth. But opportunity after opportunity slipt by unimproved, and the death of his father gave him the fatal proof that none of the principal powers of Europe were hereafter likely to interest themselves in his quarrel. They refused to acknowledge him under the title of the King of England, and, on his part, he declined to be then recognised as the Prince of Wales.

Family discord came to add its stings to those of disappointed ambition; and, though a humiliating circumstance, it is generally acknowledged, that Charles Edward, the adventurous, the gallant, and the handsome, the leader of a race of pristine valour, whose romantic qualities may be said to have died alongst with him, had, in his latter days, yielded to those humiliating habits of intoxication, in which the meanest mortals seek to drown the recollection of their disappointments and miseries. Under such circumstances, the unhappy Prince lost the friendship even of those faithful followers who had most devoted themselves to his misfortunes, and was surrounded, with some honourable exceptions, by men of a lower description, regardless of the character which he was himself no longer able to protect.

It is a fact consistent with the author's knowledge, that persons totally unentitled to, and unfitted for, such a distinction, were presented to the unfortunate Prince in moments unfit for presentation of any kind. Amid these clouds was at length extinguished the torch which once shook itself over Britain with such terrific glare, and at last sunk in its own ashes, scarce remembered and scarce noted.

Meantime, while the life of Charles Edward was gradually wasting in disappointed solitude, the number of those who had shared his misfortunes and dangers had shrunk into a small handful of veterans, the heroes of a tale which had been told. Most Scottish readers who can count the number of sixty years, must recollect many respected acquaintances of their youth, who, as the established phrase gently worded it, had been *out in the Forty-five.* It may be said, that their political principles and plans no longer either gained proselytes or attracted terror,—those who held them had ceased to be the subjects either of fear or opposition. Jacobites were looked upon in society as men who had proved their sincerity by sacrificing their interest to their principles; and in well-regulated companies, it was held a piece of ill-breeding to injure their feelings or ridicule the compromises by which they endeavoured to keep themselves abreast of the current of the day. Such, for example, was the evasion of a gentleman of fortune in Perthshire, who, in having the newspapers read to him, caused the King and the Queen to be designated by the initial letters of K. and Q., as if, by naming the full word, he might imply an acquiescence in usurpation. George III., having heard of this gentleman's custom in the above and other particulars, commissioned the member for Perthshire to carry his compliments to the steady Jacobite—"that is," said the excellent old King, "not the compliments of the King of England, but of the Elector of Hanover, and tell him how much I respect him for the steadiness of his principles."

Those who remember such old men, will probably agree that the progress of time, which has withdrawn all of them from the field, has removed, at the same time, a peculiar and striking feature of ancient manners. Their love of past times, their tales of bloody battles fought against romantic odds, were all dear to the imagination, and their little idolatry of locks of hair, pictures, rings, ribbons, and other memorials of the time in which they still seemed to live, was an interesting enthusiasm; and although their political principles, had they existed in the relation of fathers, might have rendered them dangerous to the existing dynasty, yet, as we now recollect them, there could not be on the earth supposed to exist persons better qualified to sustain the capacity of innocuous and respectable grandsires.

It was while reflecting on these things that the novel of Redgauntlet was undertaken. But various circumstances in the composition induced the author to alter its purport considerably, as it passed through his hands, and to carry the action to that point of time when the Chevalier Charles Edward, though fallen into the sere and yellow leaf, was yet meditating a second attempt, which could scarcely have been more hopeless than his first; although one, to which, as we have seen, the unfortunate Prince, at least as late as seventeen hundred and fifty-three, still looked with hope and expectation.

1*st April*, 1832.

Notes to Redgauntlet

1.9 Noble-House The first stage on the road from Edinburgh to Dumfries *via* Moffat.

2.38 (Lett. 1) hold the bannets Break a window, head a skirmish with stones, and hold the bonnet or handkerchief, which used to divide high-school boys when fighting.

2.42 (Lett. 1) the Kittle nine-steps A pass on the very brink of the Castle-rock to the north, by which it is just possible for a goat, or a high-school boy, to turn the corner of the building where it rises from the edge of the precipice. This was so favourite a feat with the "hell and neck boys" of the higher classes, that at one time sentinels were posted to prevent its repetition. One of the nine-steps was rendered more secure because the climber could take hold of the root of a nettle, so precarious were the means of passing this celebrated spot. The manning the Cowgate Port, especially in snow-ball time, was also a choice amusement, as it offered an inaccessible station for the boys who used these missiles to the annoyance of the passengers. The gateway is now demolished; and probably most of its garrison lie as low as the fortress. To recollect that the author himself, however naturally disqualified, was one of those juvenile dreadnoughts, is a sad reflection to one who cannot now step over a brook without assistance.

3.20 (Lett. 1) brocards of law The Hall of the Parliament House of Edinburgh was, in former days, divided into two unequal portions by a partition, the inner side of which was consecrated to the use of the Courts of Justice and the gentlemen of the law; while the outer division was occupied by the stalls of stationers, toymen, and the like, as in a modern bazaar. From the old play of the Plain Dealer, it seems such was formerly the case with Westminster-Hall. Minos has now purified his courts in both cities from all traffic but his own.

4.9 (Lett. 1) doubting with Dirleton, and resolving these doubts with Stewart "Sir John Nisbett of Dirleton's Doubts and Questions upon the Law, especially of Scotland;" and, "Sir James Stewart's Dirleton's Doubts and Questions on the Law of Scotland resolved and answered," are works of authority in Scottish jurisprudence. As is generally the case, the Doubts are held more in respect than the solution.

4.10 (Lett. 1) the cramp speech Till of late years, every advocate who entered at the Scottish bar made a Latin address to the Court, faculty, and audience, in set terms, and said a few words upon a text of the civil law, to show his Latinity and jurisprudence. He also wore his hat for a minute, in order to vindicate his right of being covered before the court, which is said to have originated from the celebrated lawyer, Sir Thomas Hope, having two sons on the Bench while he himself remained at the bar. Of late this ceremony has been dispensed with, as occupying unnecessarily the time of the court. The entrant lawyer merely takes the oaths to government, and swears to maintain the rules and privileges of his order.

4.41 (Lett. 1) Sinning my mercies A peculiar Scottish phrase, expressive of ingratitude for the favours of Providence.

5.14 (Lett. 1) old M—— Probably Mathieson, the predecessor of Dr Adams, to whose memory the author and his contemporaries owe a deep debt of gratitude.

5.40 (Lett. 1) my Lord Stair Celebrated as a Scottish lawyer.

6.37 (Lett. 1) my proposed tour It is well known and remembered, that when Members of Parliament enjoyed the unlimited privilege of franking by the mere writing the name on the cover, it was extended to the most extraordinary occasions. One noble lord, to express his regard for a particular regiment, franked a letter for every rank and file. It was customary also to save the covers and return them, in order that the correspondence might be carried on as long as the envelopes could hold together.

7.15 (Lett. 2) A mile aboon Dundee Alluding, as all Scotsmen know, to the humorous old song:—

> The old man's mare's dead,
> The puir man's mare's dead,
> The auld man's mare's dead,
> A mile aboon Dundee.

11.33 (Lett. 2) the society of mere boys The diminutive and obscure *place* called Brown's Square, was hailed about the time of its erection as an extremely elegant improvement upon the style of designing and erecting Edinburgh residences. Each house was, in the phrase used by appraisers, "finished within itself," or, in the still newer phraseology, "self-contained." It was built about the year 1763–4; and the old part of the city being near and accessible, this square soon received many inhabitants, who ventured to remove to so moderate a distance from the High Street.

16.16 (Lett. 3) Rob Roy MacGregor, and Sergeant Alan Mhor Cameron Of Rob Roy we have had more than enough. Alan Cameron, commonly called Sergeant Mhor, a freebooter of the same period, was equally remarkable for strength, courage, and generosity.

25.1 (Lett. 4) the hallan The partition which divides a Scottish cottage.

27.7 (Lett. 4) The bink The frame of wooden shelves placed in a Scottish kitchen for holding plates.

35.13 (Lett. 5) the Old Assembly Close Of old this almost deserted alley formed the most common access betwixt the High Street and the southern suburbs.

48.28 (Lett. 6) the saumon raun The bait made of salmon-row salted and preserved. In a swelled river, and about the month of October, it is a most deadly bait.

64.12 (Lett. 7) more days than one In explanation of this circumstance, I cannot help adding a note not very necessary for the reader, which yet I record with pleasure, from recollection of the kindness which it evinces. In early youth I resided for a considerable time in the vicinity of the beautiful village of Kelso, where my life passed in a very solitary manner. I had few acquaintances, scarce any companions, and books, which were at the time almost essential to my happiness, were difficult to come by. It was then that I was particularly indebted to the liberality and friendship of an old lady of the Society of Friends, eminent for her benevolence and charity. Her deceased husband had been a medical man of eminence, and left her, with other valuable property, a small and well-selected library. This the kind old lady permitted me to rummage at pleasure, and carry home what volumes I chose, on condition that I should take, at the same time, some of the tracts printed for encouraging and extending the doctrines of her own sect. She did not even exact any assurance that I would read these performances, being too justly afraid of involving me in a breach of promise, but was merely desirous that I should have the chance of instruction within my reach, in case whim, curiosity, or accident, might induce me to have recourse to it.
72.6 (Lett. 8) Eppie of Buckhaven Well known in the Chap-Book, called the History of Buckhaven.
78.22 (Lett. 10) all our men were drinking. The original of this catch is to be found in Cowley's witty comedy of the Guardian, the first edition. It does not exist in the second and revised edition, called the Cutter of Coleman Street.

CAPTAIN BLADE. Ha, ha, boys, another catch i'faith.

And all our men were very very merry,
And all our men were drinking.

CUTTER. *One man of mine.*
DOGREL. *Two men of mine.*
BLADE. *Three men of mine.*
CUTTER. *And one man of mine.*
OMNES. *As we went by the way we were drunk, drunk, damnably drunk.*
And all our men were very very merry, &c.

Such are the words, which are somewhat altered and amplified in the text. The play was acted in presence of Charles II., then Prince of Wales, in 1641. The catch in the text has been happily set to music.

83.28 (Lett. 10) Rory Dall Blind Rorie, a famous performer, according to tradition.
84.23 (Lett. 10) our society separated It is certain that in many cases the blind have, by constant exercise of their other organs, learned to overcome a defect which one would think incapable of being supplied. Every reader must remember the celebrated Blind Jack of Knaresborough, who lived by laying out roads.
87.26 (Lett. 11) Carrifra-gawns A precipitous side of a mountain in Moffatdale.
88.31 (Lett. 11) a deevil incarnate The caution and moderation of King William III., and his principles of unlimited toleration, deprived the Cameronians of the opportunity they ardently desired, to retaliate the injuries which they had received during the reign of prelacy, and purify the land, as they called it, from the pollution of blood. They esteemed the Revolution, therefore, only a half measure, which neither comprehended the rebuilding the Kirk in its full splendour, nor the revenge of the death of the Saints on their persecutors.
89.17 (Lett. 11) the warlock that was burnt A celebrated wizard, executed at Edinburgh for sorcery and other crimes.
96.34 (Lett. 11) the silver bullet had made The personages here mentioned are most of them characters of historical fame; but those less known and remembered may be found in the tract entitled, "The Judgment and Justice of God Exemplified, or, a Brief Historical Account of some of the Wicked Lives and Miserable Deaths of some of the most remarkable Apostates and Bloody Persecutors, from the Reformation till after the Revolution." This constitutes a sort of postscript or appendix to John Howie of Lochgoin's "Account of the Lives of the most eminent Scots Worthies." The author has, with considerable ingenuity, reversed his reasoning upon the inference to be drawn from the prosperity or misfortunes which befall individuals in this world, either in the course of their lives or in the hour of death. In the account of the martyrs' sufferings, such inflictions are mentioned only as trials permitted by Providence, for the better and brighter display of their faith, and constancy of principle. But when similar afflictions befall the opposite party, they are imputed to the direct vengeance of Heaven upon their impiety. If, indeed, the life of any person obnoxious to the historian's censures happened to have passed in unusual prosperity, the mere fact of its being finally concluded by death, is assumed as an undeniable token of the judgment of Heaven, and, to render the conclusion inevitable, his last scene is generally garnished with some singular circumstances. Thus the Duke of Lauderdale is said, through old

age but immense corpulence, to have become so sunk in spirits, "that his heart was not the bigness of a walnut."

97.42 (Lett. 11) the Threave Castle The reader is referred for particulars to Pitscottie's History of Scotland.

101.20 (Lett. 11) charged for a warlock I have heard in my youth some such wild tale as that placed in the mouth of the blind fiddler, of which, I think, the hero was Sir Robert Grierson of Lagg, the famous persecutor. But the belief was general throughout Scotland, that the excessive lamentation over the loss of friends disturbed the repose of the dead, and broke even the rest of the grave. There are several instances of this in tradition, but one struck me particularly, as I heard it from the lips of one who professed receiving it from those of a ghost-seer. This was a Highland lady, named Mrs C—— of B——, who probably believed firmly in the truth of an apparition, which seems to have originated in the weakness of her nerves and strength of her imagination. She had been lately left a widow by her husband, with the office of guardian to their only child. The young man added to the difficulties of his charge by an extreme propensity for a military life, which his mother was unwilling to give way to, while she found it impossible to repress it. About this time the Independent Companies, formed for preservation of the peace of the Highlands, were in the course of being levied; and as a gentleman named Campbell, nearly connected with Mrs C——, commanded one of those companies, she was at length persuaded to compromise the matter with her son, by permitting him to enter this company in the capacity of a cadet; thus gratifying his love of a military life without the dangers of foreign service, to which no one then thought these troops were at all liable to be exposed, while even their active service at home was not like to be attended with much danger. She readily obtained a promise from her relative that he would be particular in his attention to her son, and therefore concluded she had accommodated matters between her son's wishes and his safety in a way sufficiently attentive to both. She set off to Edinburgh to get what was awanting for his outfit, and shortly after received melancholy news from the Highlands. The Independent Company into which her son was to enter had a skirmish with a party of catherans engaged in some act of spoil, and her friend the Captain being wounded, and out of the reach of medical assistance, died in consequence. This news was a thunderbolt to the poor mother, who was at once deprived of her kinsman's advice and assistance, and instructed by his fate of the unexpected danger to which her son's new calling exposed him. She remained also in great sorrow for her relative, whom she loved with sisterly affection. These conflicting causes of anxiety, together with her uncertainty whether to continue or change her son's destination, were terminated in the following manner:—

The house in which Mrs C—— resided in the old town of Edinburgh, was a flat or story of a land, accessible, as was then universal, by a common stair. The family who occupied the story beneath were her acquaintances, and she was in the habit of drinking tea with them every evening. It was accordingly about six o'clock, when, recovering herself from a deep fit of anxious reflection, she was about to leave the parlour in which she sate in order to attend this engagement. The door through which she was to pass opened, as was very common in Edinburgh, into a dark passage. In this passage, and within a yard of her when she opened the door, stood the apparition of her kinsman, the deceased officer, in his full tartans, and wearing his bonnet. Terrified at what she saw, or thought she saw, she closed the door hastily, and, sinking on her knees by a chair, prayed to be delivered from the horrors of the vision. She remained in that posture till her friends below tapped on the floor to intimate that tea was ready. Recalled to herself by the signal, she arose, and, on opening the apartment door, again was confronted by the visionary Highlander, whose bloody brow bore token, on this second appearance, to the death he had died. Unable to endure this repetition of her terrors, Mrs C—— sunk on the floor in a swoon. Her friends below, startled with the noise, came up stairs, and, alarmed at the situation in which they found her, insisted on her going to bed and taking some medicine, in order to compose what they took for a nervous attack. They had no sooner left her in quiet, than the apparition of the soldier was once more visible in the apartment. This time she took courage and said, "In the name of God, Donald, why do you haunt one who respected and loved you living?" To which he answered readily, in Gaelic, "Cousin, why did you not speak sooner? My rest is disturbed by your unnecessary lamentation—your tears scald me in my shroud. I come to tell you that my untimely death should make no difference in your views for your son; God will raise patrons to supply my place, and he will live to the fulness of years, and die honoured and at peace." The lady of course followed her kinsman's advice; and as she was accounted a person of strict veracity, we may conclude the first apparition an illusion of the fancy, the final one a lively dream suggested by the other two.

116.27 (Lett. 13) Peter Peebles.

Peter Peebles. This unfortunate litigant (for a person named Peter Peebles actually flourished) frequented the courts of justice in Scotland about the year 1792, and the sketch of his appearance is given from recollection. The author is of opinion he himself had at one time the honour to be counsel for Peter Peebles, whose voluminous course of litigation served as a sort of assay-pieces to most young men who were called to the bar. The scene of the consultation is entirely imaginary.

117.5 (Lett. 13) pokes Process-bags.

121.9 (Lett. 13) by warrant of a judge Multiplepoinding is, I believe, equivalent to what is called in England a case of Double Distress.

126.34 (Ch. 1) at a certain period

OLD-FASHIONED SCOTTISH CIVILITY.—Such were literally the points of politeness observed in general society during the author's youth, where it was by no means unusual in a company assembled by chance, to find individuals who had borne arms on one side or other in the civil broils of 1745. Nothing, according to my recollection, could be more gentle and decorous than the respect these old enemies paid to each other's prejudices. But in this I speak generally. I have witnessed one or two explosions.

131.3 (Ch. 1) hanks of yarn The simile is obvious, from the old manufacture of Scotland, when the guidwife's thrift, as the yarn wrought in the winter was called, when laid down to bleach by the burn-side, was peculiarly exposed to the inroads of the pigs, seldom well-regulated about a Scottish farm-house.

131.24 (Ch. 1) John's Coffee-house This small dark coffee-house, now burnt down, was the resort of such writers and clerks belonging to the Parliament House above thirty years ago, as retained the ancient Scottish custom of a meridian, as it was called, or noontide dram. If their proceedings were watched, they might be seen to turn fidgety about the hour of noon, and exchange looks with each other from their separate desks, till at length some one of formal and dignified presence assumed the honour of leading the band, when away they went, threading the crowd like a string of wild-fowl, crossed the square or close, and following each other into the coffeehouse, received in turn from the hand of the waiter, the meridian, which was placed ready at the bar. This they did, day by day: and though they did not speak to each other, they seemed to attach a certain degree of sociability to their performing the ceremony in company.

134.22 (Ch. 1) spoil a horn Said of an adventurous gipsy, who resolves at all risks to convert a sheep's horn into a spoon.

135.41 (Ch. 1) the auld bitch next Tradition ascribes this whimsical style of language to the ingenious and philosophical Lord Kaimes.

138.16 (Ch. 2) (Magnum addition) [The Magnum text has, for 'manner.' 'manner, or, as he termed it, as summing up the duties of a solicitor, to *agé as accords*.'] A Scots law phrase of no very determinate import, meaning, generally, to do what is fitting.

142.15 (Ch. 2) their masters' titles The Scottish Judges are distinguished by the title of Lord prefixed to their own temporal designation. As the ladies of these official dignitaries do not bear any share in their husbands' honours, they remain plain Mistresses distinguished only by their Lords' family name. They were not always contented with this species of Salique law, which certainly is somewhat inconsistent. But their pretensions to title are said to have been long since repelled by James V., the Sovereign who founded the College of Justice. "I," said he, "made the carles Lords, but who the devil made the carlines Ladies?"

162.6 (Ch. 4) had been exposed

RIOTOUS ATTACK UPON THE DAM-DIKE OF SIR JAMES GRAHAM OF NETHERBY. It may be here mentioned, that a violent and popular attack upon what the country people of this district considered as an invasion of their fishing right, is by no means an improbable fiction. Shortly after the close of the American war, Sir James Graham of Netherby constructed a dam-dike, or cauld, across the Esk, at a place where it flowed through his estate, though it has its origin, and the principal part of its course, in Scotland. The new barrier at Netherby was considered as an encroachment calculated to prevent the salmon from ascending into Scotland; and the right of erecting it being an international question of law betwixt the sister kingdoms, there was no court in either competent to its decision. In this dilemma, the Scots people assembled in numbers by signal of rocket lights, and, rudely armed with fowling-pieces, fishspears, and such rustic weapons, marched to the banks of the river for the purpose of pulling down the dam-dike objected to. Sir James Graham armed many of his own people to protect his property, and had some military from Carlisle for the same purpose. A renewal of the Border wars had nearly taken place in the eighteenth century, when prudence and moderation on both sides saved much tumult, and perhaps some bloodshed. The English proprietor consented that a breach should be made in his dam-dike sufficient for the passage of the fish, and thus removed the Scottish grievance. I believe the river has since that time taken the matter into its own disposal, and entirely swept away the dam-dike in question.

186.4 (Ch. 7) Slaint an Rey The King's health.

201.7 (Ch. 9) sometimes of satire Every one must remember instances of this festive custom, in which the adaptation of the tune to the toast was remarkably felicitous. Old Niel Gow, and his son Nathaniel, were peculiarly happy on such occasions.

206.42 (Ch. 10) have ever qualified By taking the oaths to Government.

215.7 (Ch. 10) have been expected Scotland, in its half civilized state, exhibited too many examples of the exertion of arbitrary force and violence, rendered easy by the dominion which lairds exerted over their tenants, and chiefs over their clans. The captivity of Lady Grange, in the desolate cliffs of Saint Kilda, is in the recollection of every one. At the supposed date of the novel also, a man of the name of Merrilees, a tanner in Leith, absconded from his country to escape his creditors; and after having slain his own mastiff dog, and put a bit of red cloth in its mouth, as if it had died in a contest with soldiers, and involved his own existence in as much mystery as possible, made his escape into Yorkshire. Here he was detected by persons sent in search of him, to whom he gave a portentous account of his having been carried off and concealed in various places. Mr Merrilees was, in short, a kind of male Elizabeth Canning, but did not trespass on the public credulity quite so long.

215.23 (Ch. 11) London correspondents Not much in those days, for within my recollection the London post was brought north in a small mail-cart; and men are yet alive who recollect when it came down with only one single letter for Edinburgh, addressed to the manager of the British Linen Company.

216.1 (Ch. 11) the Assembly-Room I remember hearing this identical answer given by an old Highland gentleman of the Forty-Five, when he heard of the opening of the New Assembly-Rooms in George Street.

222.34 (Ch. 11) such a venture again

ESCAPE OF PATE-IN-PERIL. The escape of a Jacobite gentleman while on the road to Carlisle to take his trial for his share in the affair of 1745, took place at Errickstane-brae, in the singular manner ascribed to the Laird of Summertrees in the text. The author has seen in his youth the gentleman to whom the adventure actually happened. The distance of time makes some indistinctness of recollection, but it is believed the real name was MacEwen, or Macmillan.

222.36 (Ch. 11) another opportunity An old gentleman of the author's name was engaged in the affair of 1715, and with some difficulty saved from the gallows, by the intercession of the Duchess of Buccleuch and Monmouth. Her Grace, who maintained a good deal of authority over her clan, sent for the object of her intercession, and warning him of the risk which he had run, and the trouble she had taken on his account, wound up her lecture by intimating, that in case of such disloyalty again, he was not to expect her interest in his favour. "An it please your Grace," said the stout old Tory, "I fear I am too old to see another opportunity."

223.9 (Ch. 11) braxy mutton BRAXY MUTTON.—The flesh of sheep that has died by the visitation of providence, not by the hand of the butcher. In pastoral countries it is used as food with little scruple.

244.21 (Ch. 13) peremptory pint-stoup The Scottish pint of liquid measure comprehends four English measures of the same denomination. The jest is well-known of my poor countryman, who, driven to extremity by the raillery of the Southron, on the small denomination of the Scottish coin, at length answered, "Ay, ay! But the deil tak them that has the *least pint-stoup.*"

251.6 (Ch. 13) a single glass of brandy

CONCEALMENTS FOR THEFT AND SMUGGLING. I am sorry to say, that the modes of concealment described in the imaginary premises of Mr Trumbull, are of a kind which have been common on the frontiers of late years. The neighbourhood of two nations having different laws, though united in government, still leads to a multitude of transgressions on the Border, and extreme difficulty in apprehending delinquents. About twenty years since, as far as my recollection serves, there was along the frontier an organized gang of coiners, forgers, smugglers, and other malefactors, whose operations were conducted on a scale not inferior to what is here described. The chief of the party was one Richard Mendham, a carpenter, who rose to opulence, although ignorant even of the arts of reading and writing. But he had found a short road to wealth, and had taken singular measures for conducting his operations. Amongst these, he found means to build, in a suburb of Berwick called Spittal, a street of small houses, as if for the investment of property. He himself inhabited one of these; another, a species of public-house, was open to his confederates, who held secret and unsuspected communication with him by crossing the roofs of the intervening houses, and descending by a trap-stair, which admitted them into the alcove of the diningroom of Dick Mendham's private mansion. A vault, too, beneath Mendham's stable, was accessible in the manner mentioned in the novel. The post of one of the stalls turned round on a bolt being withdrawn, and gave admittance to a subterranean place of concealment for contraband and stolen goods, to a great extent. Richard Mendham, the head of this very formidable conspiracy, which involved malefactors of every kind, was tried and executed at Jedburgh, where the author was present as Sheriff of Selkirkshire. Mendham had previously been tried, but escaped by want of proof and the ingenuity of his counsel.

264.16 (Ch. 15) a statesman A small landed proprietor.

299.39 (Ch. 18) its mother's miseries Several persons have brought down to these days the impressions which Nature had thus recorded, when they were yet babes unborn. One lady of quality, whose father was long under sentence of death, previous to the rebellion, was marked on the back of the neck by the sign of a broad axe. Another, whose kinsmen had been slain in battle, and died on the scaffold to the number of seven, bore a child spattered on the right shoulder, and down the arm, with scarlet drops, as if of blood. Many other instances might be quoted.

308.14 (Ch. 18) go through with it

CORONATION OF GEORGE III. The particulars here given are of course entirely imaginary; that is, they have no other foundation than what might be supposed probable, had such a circumstance actually taken place. Yet a report to such an effect was long and generally current, though now having wholly lost its lingering credit; those who gave it currency, if they did not originate it, being, with the tradition itself, now mouldered in the dust. The attachment to the unfortunate house of Stewart among its adherents, continued to exist and to be fondly cherished, longer perhaps than in any similar case in any other country; and when reason was baffled, and all hope destroyed, by repeated frustration, the mere dreams of imagination were summoned in to fill up the dreary blank, left in so many hearts. Of the many reports set on foot and circulated from this cause, the tradition in question, though amongst the least authenticated, is not the least striking; and, in excuse of what may be considered as a violent infraction of probability in the foregoing chapter, the author is under the necessity of quoting it. It was always said, though with very little appearance of truth, that upon the coronation of George III., when the Champion of England, Dymock, or his representative, appeared in Westminster Hall, and, in the language of chivalry, solemnly wagered his body to defend in single combat the right of the young King to the crown of these realms, at the moment when he flung down his gauntlet as the gage of battle, an unknown female stepped from the crowd and lifted the pledge, leaving another gage in room of it, with a paper expressing, that if a fair field of combat should be allowed, a champion of rank and birth would appear with equal arms to dispute the claim of King George to the British kingdoms. The story, as we have said, is probably one of the numerous fictions which were circulated to keep up the spirits of a sinking faction. The incident was, however, possible, if it could be supposed to be attended by any motive adequate to the risk, and might be imagined to occur to a person of Redgauntlet's enthusiastic character. George III., it is said, had a police of his own, whose agency was so efficient, that the Sovereign was able to tell his prime minister that the Pretender was in London. The prime minister began immediately to talk of measures to be taken, warrants to be procured, messengers and guards to be got in readiness. "Pooh, pooh," said the good-natured Sovereign, "since I have found him out, leave me alone to deal with him."—"And what," said the minister, "is your Majesty's purpose in so important a case?"—"To leave the young man to himself," said George III.; "and when he tires he will go back again." The truth of this story does not depend on that of the lifting of the gauntlet; and while the latter could be but an idle bravado, the former expresses George III.'s goodness of heart and soundness of policy.

317.12 (Ch. 19) over the Rikargate The northern gate of Carlisle was long garnished with the heads of the Scottish rebels executed in 1746.

317.35 (Ch. 19) the existing dynasty The Highland regiments were first employed by the celebrated Earl of Chatham, who assumed to himself no small degree of praise for having called forth to the support of the country and the government, the valour which had been too often directed against both.

326.12 (Ch. 19) the King's keys In common parlance, a crowbar and hatchet.

334.12 (Ch. 20) a sticket stibbler A student of divinity who has not been able to complete his studies in theology.

339.36 (Ch. 21) a collier or a salter

COLLIER AND SALTER. The persons engaged in these occupations were at this time bondsmen; and in case they left the ground of the farm to which they belonged, and as pertaining to which their services were bought or sold, they were liable to be brought back by a summary process. The existence of this species of slavery being thought irreconcilable with the spirit of liberty, colliers and salters were declared free, and put upon the same footing with other servants, by the Act 15 Geo. III. chapter 28th. They were so far from desiring or prizing the blessing conferred on them, that they esteemed the interest taken in their freedom to be a mere device on the part of the proprietors to get rid of what they called head and harigald money, payable to them when a female of their number, by bearing a child, made an addition to the live stock of their master's property.

THE BETROTHED

Editorial Note

The Betrothed was published in 1825 as the first of two novels which appeared under the heading *Tales of the Crusaders*, the other being *The Talisman*. In the Magnum it occupies Volume 37, published in June 1832, the month in which Scott returned to London after his journey to the Mediterranean in search of health. An interleaved copy of the novel had been prepared for him using the octavo edition of *Tales and Romances of the Author of Waverley* published in 7 volumes in 1827. *The Betrothed* occupies the fourth and part of the fifth volumes in this series. The interleaved volumes are now in the National Library of Scotland MSS 23029 and 23030. The manuscript of the Introduction to the novel, mostly in the hand of William Laidlaw, is written on ten folded and mostly unnumbered leaves mounted on stubbs between the title-page and the beginning of the novel in MS 23029. It is complete except for the last sentence which is not in the manuscript. The holograph material in the interleaved volumes is in the hands of Scott and three amanuenses: William Laidlaw as already mentioned, John Buchanan, and an unidentified helper.

Preparation of *The Betrothed* for its appearance in the Magnum started in January 1831. First, how many volumes it would occupy had to be decided. It was established at the outset of the series that three first-edition volumes would occupy two volumes in the Magnum; in consequence difficulties arose in the case of works originally published in four volumes. The most recent case was *Peveril of the Peak*, still in preparation, whose four volumes appeared in the Magnum in three, requiring Scott to be generous with notes and appendices in order to fill out the volumes. *Tales of the Crusaders* had also first appeared in four volumes, and Cadell's initial view, communicated to Scott on 3 January 1831, was to proceed 'upon the same principle as Peveril' (MS 3916, f. 14v). Scott assumed from this suggestion that generous notes would be required, and was confident that he could supply them (MS 15980, f. 3r–v: 4 January 1831). On 13 January Cadell wrote again: '*Tales of the Crusaders* I am glad to say are 100 pages longer than Peveril, and will cost you so much less trouble' (MS 3916, f. 43r). Cadell's confidence that what was required for publication in three volumes 'will not be much' makes it puzzling to know why in the end the decision was made to publish in two volumes, one for each novel. A possible explanation is that it was connected with the decision that, instead of the proposed 50 volumes, the Magnum series should finish at 48 volumes. As a result of publishing the original four volumes in two, those containing *Tales of the Crusaders* are the longest in the series, *The Betrothed* being 485 pages and *The Talisman* 494 pages.

Scott did not start on material for *The Betrothed* in the Magnum until the end of February 1831. On 21 February he had completed *Redgauntlet* and noted in his *Journal* (364), '*The Tales of the Crusaders* come next'. The following day he 'Read Littelton's *History of England* to get some notes for *Crusaders* vol. I. After dinner Mr. Laidlaw from six to eight: sent off six pages.' A passage taken from Lyttelton occupies the last three pages of the Magnum Introduction to the novel. William Laidlaw, the factor at Abbotsford and a friend and neighbour of Scott's, had recently taken on the task of writing to Scott's dictation, a procedure made necessary by the author's increased difficulty in writing legibly. On 24 February Scott wrote to Cadell asking for a copy of the *Memoirs of Lady Fanshawe* which was used in the note on the 'Bahr-Geist' (*Letters*, 11.475). On 29 March he sent Cadell, 'the next v[o]lume of Magnum being the 1st of the ⟨cru⟩ Crusades' (MS 15980, f. 54r). Cadell set to work, and on 20 May he was able to assure Scott that 'the Printer had got the Crusaders from me' (MS 3918, f. 63r). On 1 July he was presumably working on proofs when he recorded revising 'Introduction to Betrothed' (MS 21021, f. 29r).

The Introduction starts with a self-conscious passage about novel writing, and the novelist's view of the act of publishing and the response of readers. It moves on to the main source of the plot of the novel, the 'returning crusader' theme which had long interested Scott. He gives three examples: that of the son fathered by the River Tweed, the ballad of 'The Noble Moringer', and the story of Sir William Bradshaigh and his wife. Most of the Introduction is in the hand of William Laidlaw, and it is probable that the 'six pages' which Scott referred to on 22 February are the first six leaves of the Introduction. Laidlaw's writing breaks off at the top of f. 7r with the injunction '(NB. what follows must be printed with the utmost accuracy and ⟨pr⟩ in Anglo-Saxon type)'. There follows a passage giving the story of Sir William Bradshaigh and his wife, Mabel, transcribed in the hand of John Buchanan. At the foot of f. 7r is a pencil drawing of the tomb of Sir William and his wife. Beside it Scott has written 'This may be drawn in wood it it can be neatly & without'. Scott's presence is more substantial on f. 7v, the only leaf on which there is material on a verso. The passage in his hand starts at 'Mab's Cross' (382.17) and ends at 'on the tomb' (382.23), plus the footnote. The rest of the 'Introduction' from that point is in Laidlaw's hand.

The volume contains twenty-one new footnotes (in addition to three first-edition footnotes). It has no endnotes, although several of the footnotes, in view of their length, could well have been presented as endnotes. In some cases there has plainly been some doubt as to which part of the text some of the longer notes should be attached. All the new notes are in Scott's hand in the Interleaved Copy, with the exception of two. In the first, headed 'Eudorchawg, or Gold Chains of the Welsh' (386–87), the first two lines are in Scott's hand on an interleaf before p. 183 in the Interleaved Copy; the remainder of the note is in Laidlaw's hand on another interleaf after p. 182. In a similar manner the beginning of the note headed 'Bahr-Geist' (387–88) is in Scott's hand at the foot of page 253 and on the interleaf after page 252 in the Interleaved Copy, but Laidlaw takes over after 'tells her story thus'.

The notes added to *The Betrothed* reflect particularly the Welsh setting of the novel. Of the twenty-one notes, nine are given to Welsh topics, for instance, the Welsh language, Welsh ale, Welsh houses, and features associated with the military theme, Welsh archers and page-boys, Welsh courage and Welsh cruelties. There are short footnotes which simply explain a verbal usage in the text, and longer ones drawn out by quotations from historical or literary sources. Although the setting is Welsh Scott cannot resist bringing in both Ireland and the Highlands of Scotland for comparison in several notes. In a similar way he does not remain exclusively in the middle ages and occasionally brings in analogous material from more recent periods, for instance a supposed feudal memory circulating during the French Revolution in the note at 385.33–39.

There are two Magnum illustrations for this title. The frontispiece to Volume 37 (MAG0073 / TB348.37) was designed by Edwin Landseer and engraved by Robert Graves. It depicts Eveline with attendants on a hunting expedition by the Red Pool, with a falcon in pursuit of a heron (EEWN 18a, Ch. 23: the caption is simply 'THE BETROTHED.'). The title-page vignette (MAG0074 / TB348.37) was designed by Alexander Fraser, the elder, and engraved by Joseph Goodyear. It depicts Eveline, with spear in hand, and Rose standing guard on the ramparts of the besieged Garde Doloureuse, over the sleeping sentinel Peterkin, with Wilkin Flammock entering from below (EEWN 18a, 70.41–71.5 (abridged): 'Once more . . . the rest which I envied.').

E. Landseer, R.A. R. Graves

THE BETROTHED.

WAVERLEY NOVELS.

VOL. XXXVII.

THE BETROTHED.

"Once more, where is Peterkin Vorst, who should have kept this post? He was overcome with toil, said Eveline, and when I saw him sleep, I would not disturb the rest which I envied."

PRINTED FOR ROBERT CADELL, EDINBURGH,
AND WHITTAKER & Co. LONDON.
1832.

Introduction to The Betrothed

THE Tales of the Crusaders was determined upon as the title of the following series of these novels, rather by the advice of the few friends whom death has now rendered still fewer, than by the author's own taste. Not but that he saw plainly enough the interest which might be excited by the very name of the Crusades, but he was conscious at the same time that that interest was of a character which it might be more easy to create than to satisfy, and that by the mention of so magnificent a subject each reader might be induced to call up to his imagination a sketch so extensive and so grand that it might not be in the power of the author to fill it up, who would thus stand in the predicament of the dwarf bringing with him a standard to measure his own stature, and showing himself, therefore, says Sterne, "a dwarf more ways than one."

It is a fact, if it were worth while to examine it, that the publisher and author, however much their general interests are the same, may be said to differ so far as titlepages are concerned; and it is a secret of the tale-telling art, if it could be termed a secret worth knowing, that a taking title, as it is called, best answers the purpose of the bookseller, since it often goes far to cover his risk, and sells an edition not unfrequently before the public have well seen it. But the author ought to seek more permanent fame, and wish that his work, when its leaves are first cut open, should be at least fairly judged of. Thus many of the best novelists have been anxious to give their works such titles as render it out of the reader's power to conjecture their contents, until they should have an opportunity of reading them.

All this did not prevent the Tales of the Crusaders from being the title fixed on; and the celebrated year of projects (eighteen hundred and twenty-five) being the time of publication, an introduction was prefixed according to the humour of the day.

The first tale of the series was influenced in its structure, rather by the wish to avoid those general expectations which might be formed from the title, than to comply with any one of them, and so disappoint the rest. The story was, therefore, less an incident belonging to the Crusades, than one which was occasioned by the singular cast of mind introduced and spread wide by those memorable undertakings. The confusion among families was not the least concomitant evil of the extraordinary preponderance of this superstition. It was no unusual thing for a Crusader, returning from his long toils of war and pilgrimage, to find his family augmented by some young off-shoot, of whom the deserted matron could give no very accurate account, or perhaps to find his marriage-bed filled, and that, instead of becoming nurse to an old man, his household dame had preferred being the lady-love of a young one. Numerous are the stories of this kind told in different parts of Europe; and the returned knight or baron, according to his temper, sat down good-naturedly contented with the account which his lady gave of a doubtful matter, or called in blood and fire to vindicate his honour, which, after all, had been endangered chiefly by his forsaking his household gods to seek adventures in Palestine.

Scottish tradition, quoted, I think, in some part of the Border Minstrelsy, ascribes to the clan of Tweedie, a family once stout and warlike, a descent which would not have misbecome a hero of antiquity. A baron, somewhat elderly we may suppose, had wedded a buxom young lady, and some months after their union he left her to ply the distaff alone in his old tower, among the mountains of the county of Peebles, near the sources of the Tweed. He returned after seven or eight years, no uncommon space for a pilgrimage to Palestine, and found his family had not been lonely in his absence, the lady having been cheered by the arrival of a stranger, (of whose approach she could give the best account of any one,) who hung on her skirts, and called her mammy, and was just such as the baron would have longed to call his son, but that he could by no means make his age correspond, according to the doctrine of civilians, with his own departure for Palestine. He applied to his wife, therefore, for the solution of this dilemma. The lady, after many floods of tears, which she had reserved for the occasion, informed the honest gentleman, that, walking one day alone by the banks of the infant river, a human form arose from a deep eddy, still known and termed Tweed-pool, who deigned to inform her that he was the tutelar genius of the stream, and, *bongré, malgré*, became the father of the sturdy fellow, whose appearance had so much surprised her husband. This story, however suitable to Pagan times, would have met with full credence from few of the baron's coevals, but the wife was young and beautiful, the husband old and in his dotage; her family (the Frasers, it is believed) were powerful and warlike, and the baron had had fighting enough in the holy wars. The event was, that he believed, or seemed to believe, the tale, and remained contented with the child with whom his wife and the Tweed had generously presented him. The only circumstance which preserved the memory of the incident was, that the youth retained the name of Tweed, or Tweedie. The baron, meanwhile, could not, as the old Scotch song says, "Keep the cradle rowing," and the Tweed apparently thought one natural son was family enough for a decent *Presbyterian* lover; and so little gall had the baron in his composition, that having bred up the young Tweed as his heir while he lived, he left him in that capacity when he died, and the son of the river-god founded the family of Drummelzier and others, from whom have flowed, in the phrase of the Ettrick Shepherd, "many a brave fellow, and many a bauld feat."

The tale of the Noble Moringer is somewhat of the same nature —it exists in a collection of German popular songs, entitled, Sammlung Deutscher Volkslieder, Berlin, 1807; published by Messrs Busching and Von der Hagen. The song is supposed to be extracted from a manuscript chronicle of Nicolas Thomann, chaplain to St Leonard in Weissenhorn, and dated 1533. The ballad, which is popular in Germany, is supposed, from the language, to have been composed in the fifteenth century. The Noble Moringer, a powerful baron of Germany, about to set out on a pilgrimage to the land of St Thomas, with the geography of which we are not made acquainted, resolves to commit his castle, dominions, and lady, to the vassal who should pledge him to keep watch over them till the seven years of his pilgrimage were accomplished. His chamberlain, an elderly and a cautious man, declines the trust, observing, that seven days, instead of seven years, would be the utmost space to which he would consent to pledge himself for the fidelity of any woman. The esquire of the Noble Moringer confidently accepts the trust refused by the chamberlain, and the baron departs on his pilgrimage. The seven years are now elapsed, all save a single day and night, when, behold, a vision descends on the noble pilgrim as he sleeps in the land of the stranger.

It was the noble Moringer within an orchard slept,
When on the Baron's slumbering sense a boding vision crept,
And whispered in his ear a voice, "'Tis time, Sir Knight, to wake—
Thy lady and thy heritage another master take.

"Thy tower another banner knows, thy steeds another rein,
And stoop them to another's will thy gallant vassal train;
And she, the lady of thy love, so faithful once and fair,
This night, within thy father's hall, she weds Marstetten's heir."

The Moringer starts up and prays to his patron St Thomas, to rescue him from the impending shame, which his devotion to his patron had placed him in danger of incurring. St Thomas, who must have felt the justice of the imputation, performs a miracle. The Moringer's senses were drenched in oblivion, and when he waked he lay in a well-known spot of his own domain; on his right the Castle of his fathers, and on his left the mill, which, as usual, was built not far distant from the Castle.

He leaned upon his pilgrim's staff, and to the mill he drew—
So altered was his goodly form that none their master knew.
The baron to the miller said, "Good friend, for charity,
Tell a poor pilgrim, in your land, what tidings may there be?"

The miller answered him again—"He knew of little news,
Save that the lady of the land did a new bridegroom choose;
Her husband died in distant land, such is the constant word,
His death sits heavy on our souls, he was a worthy lord.

"Of him I held the little mill, which wins me living free—
God rest the baron in his grave, he aye was kind to me!
And when St Martin's tide comes round, and millers take their toll,
The priest that prays for Moringer shall have both cope and stole."

The baron proceeds to the Castle gate, which is bolted to prevent intrusion, while the inside of the mansion rung with preparations for the marriage of the lady. The pilgrim prayed the porter for entrance, conjuring him by his own sufferings, and for the sake of the late Moringer; by the orders of his lady, the warder gave him admittance.

Then up the hall paced Moringer, his step was sad and slow;
It sat full heavy on his heart, none seemed their lord to know.
He sat him on a lowly bench, oppressed with woe and wrong;
Short while he sat, but ne'er to him seemed little space so long.

Now spent was day, and feasting o'er, and come was evening hour,
The time was nigh when new made brides retire to nuptial bower.
"Our Castle's wont," a bride's man said, "hath been both firm and long—
No guest to harbour in our halls till he shall chant a song."

When thus called upon, the disguised baron sung the following melancholy ditty:—

"Chill flows the lay of frozen age," 'twas thus the pilgrim sung,
"Nor golden meed, nor garment gay, unlocks his heavy tongue.
Once did I sit, thou bridegroom gay, at board as rich as thine,
And by my side as fair a bride, with all her charms, was mine.

"But time traced furrows on my face, and I grew silver-haired,
For locks of brown and cheeks of youth, she left this brow and beard;
Once rich, but now a palmer poor, I tread life's latest stage,
And mingle with your bridal mirth the lay of frozen age."

The lady, moved at the doleful recollections which the palmer's song recalled, sent to him a cup of wine. The palmer, having exhausted the goblet, returned it, and having first dropped in the cup his nuptial ring, requested the lady to pledge her venerable guest.

The ring hath caught the lady's eye, she views it close and near,
Then might you hear her shriek aloud, "The Moringer is here!"
Then might you see her start from seat, while tears in torrents fell,
But if she wept for joy or woe, the ladies best can tell.

Full loud she uttered thanks to Heaven, and every saintly power,
That had restored the Moringer before the midnight hour;
And loud she uttered vow on vow, that never was there bride,
That had like her preserved her troth, or been so sorely tried.

"Yes, here I claim the praise," she said, "to constant matrons due,
Who keep the troth that they have plight so steadfastly and true;
For count the term howe'er you will, so that you count aright,
Seven twelvemonths and a day are out when bells toll twelve to-night."

It was Marstetten then rose up, his falchion there he drew,
He kneeled before the Moringer, and down his weapon threw;
"My oath and knightly faith are broke," these were the words he said;
"Then take, my liege, thy vassal's sword, and take thy vassal's head."

The noble Moringer he smiled, and then aloud did say,
"He gathers wisdom that hath roamed seven twelvemonths and a day;
My daughter now hath fifteen years, fame speaks her sweet and fair;
I give her for the bride you lose, and name her for my heir.

"The young bridegroom hath youthful bride, the old bridegroom the old,
Whose faith was kept till term and tide so punctually were told;
But blessings on the warder kind that oped my castle gate,
For had I come at morrow tide, I came a day too late."

There is also, in the rich field of German romance, another edition of this story, which has been converted by M. Tieck (whose labours of that kind have been so remarkable) into the subject of one of his romantic dramas. It is, however, unnecessary to detail it, as the present author adopted his idea of the tale chiefly from the edition preserved in the mansion of Haighhall, of old the mansion-house of the family of Bradshaigh, now possessed by their descendants on the female side, the Earls of Balcarras. The story greatly resembles that of the Noble Moringer, only there is no miracle of St Thomas to shock the belief of good Protestants. I am permitted, by my noble friends, the lord and lady of Haighhall, to print the following extract from the family genealogy.

Sir William Bradshaghe 2d Sone to Sr iohn was A great traueller and A Souldyer and married To	Mabell daughter and Sole heire of Hugh Noris de Haghe and Blackrode and had issue †N. 8. E 2.

of this Mabel is a story by tradition of undouted
verity that in Sr William Bradshage's absence
(being 10 yeares away in the wares) she
married a welch k^t. Sr William retorninge
from the wares came in a Palmers habit amongst the Poore to haghe. Who when she saw &
congetringe that he favoured her former

husband wept, for which the k[t] chasticed her
at wich S[r] William went and made him selfe
Knawne to his Tennants in wch space the k[t]
fled. but neare to Newton Parke Sr William ouer-
tooke him and slue him. The said Dame
Mabell was enioyned by her confessor to
doe Pennances by going onest euery week
barefout and bare legg'd to a Crosse ner Wigan
from the haghe wilest she liued & is called
Mabb † to this day; & ther monument Lyes
in wigan Church as you see ther Portfd

An: Dom: 1315

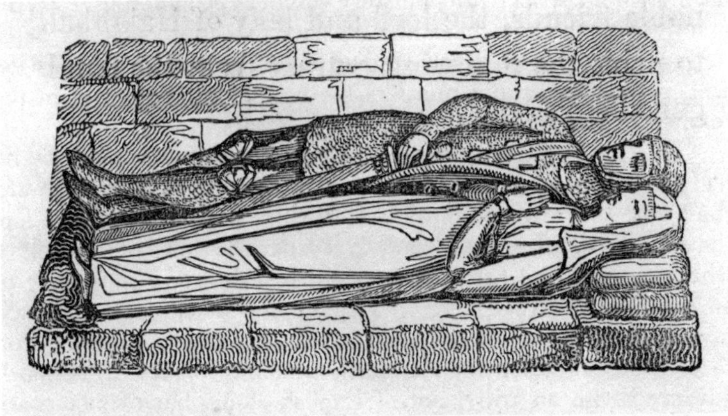

There were many vestiges around Haighhall, both of the Catholic penances of the Lady Mabel, and of this melancholy transaction in particular; the whole history was within the memory of man portrayed upon a glass window in the hall, where unfortunately it has not been preserved. Mab's Cross is still extant. An old decayed building is said to have been the place where the Lady Mabel was condemned to render penance, by walking hither from Haighhall barefooted and barelegged for the performance of her devotions. This relic, to which an anecdote so curious is annexed, is now unfortunately ruinous. Time and whitewash, says Mr Roby, have altogether defaced the effigies of the knight and lady on the tomb. The particulars are preserved in Mr Roby's Traditions of Lancashire,* to which the reader is referred for further particulars. It does not appear that Sir William Bradshaigh was irreparably offended against the too hasty Lady Mabel, although he certainly showed himself of a more fiery mould than the Scottish and German

* A very elegant work, 2 vols. 1829. By J. Roby, M.R.S.L.

barons who were heroes of the former tales. The tradition, which the author knew very early in life, was told to him by the late Lady Balcarras. He was so much struck with it, that being at that time profuse of legendary lore, he inserted it in the shape of a note to Waverley,* the first of his romantic offences. Had he then known, as he now does, the value of such a story, it is likely that, as directed in the inimitable receipt for making an epic poem, preserved in the Guardian, he would have set it by for some future opportunity.

As, however, the tale had not been completely told, and was a very interesting one, and as it was sufficiently woven in with the Crusades, the wars between the Welsh and the Norman lords of the Marches were selected as a period when all freedoms might be taken with the strict truth of history without encountering any well-known fact, which might render the narrative improbable. Perhaps, however, the period which vindicates the probability of the tale, will, with its wars and murders, be best found described in the following passage of Gryffyth Ap Edwin's wars.

"This prince in conjunction with Algar, Earl of Chester, who had been banished from England as a traitor, in the reign of Edward the Confessor, marched into Herefordshire and wasted all that fertile country with fire and sword, to revenge the death of his brother Rhees, whose head had been brought to Edward in pursuance of an order sent by that King on account of the depredations which he had committed against the English on the borders. To stop these ravages the Earl of Hereford, who was nephew to Edward, advanced with an army, not of English alone, but of mercenary Normans and French, whom he had entertained in his service, against Gryffyth and Algar. He met them near Hereford, and offered them battle, which the Welsh monarch, who had won five pitched battles before, and never had fought without conquering, joyfully accepted. The earl had commanded his English forces to fight on horseback, in imitation of the Normans, against their usual custom; but the Welsh making a furious and desperate charge, that nobleman himself, and the foreign cavalry led by him, were so daunted at the view of them, that they shamefully fled without fighting; which being seen by the English, they also turned their backs on the enemy, who, having killed or wounded as many of them as they could come up with in their flight, entered triumphantly into Hereford, spoiled and fired the city, razed the walls to the ground, slaughtered some of the citizens, led many of them captive, and (to use the words of the Welsh Chronicle) left nothing in the town but blood and ashes. After this exploit they immediately

* Waverley, present edition, vol. 25a, 65 (note to 17.30).

returned into Wales, undoubtedly from a desire of securing their prisoners, and the rich plunder they had gained. The King of England hereupon commanded Earl Harold to collect a great army from all parts of the kingdom, and assembling them at Gloucester, advanced from thence to invade the dominions of Gryffyth in North Wales. He performed his orders, and penetrated into that country without resistance from the Welsh; Gryffyth and Algar retiring into some parts of South Wales. What were their reasons for this conduct we are not well informed; nor why Harold did not pursue his advantage against them; but it appears that he thought it more advisable at this time to treat with, than subdue, them; for he left North Wales, and employed himself in rebuilding the walls of Hereford, while negotiations were carrying on with Gryffyth, which soon after produced the restoration of Algar, and a peace with that king, not very honourable to England, as he made no satisfaction for the mischief he had done in the war, nor any submissions to Edward. Harold must doubtless have had some private and forcible motives to conclude such a treaty. The very next year the Welsh monarch, upon what quarrel we know not, made a new incursion into England, and killed the Bishop of Hereford, the sheriff of the county, and many more of the English, both ecclesiastics and laymen. Edward was counselled by Harold, and Leofrick, Earl of Mercia, to make peace with him again; which he again broke: nor could he be restrained by any means, from these barbarous inroads, before the year one thousand and sixty-three; when Edward, whose patience and pacific disposition had been too much abused, commissioned Harold to assemble the whole strength of the kingdom, and make war upon him in his own country, till he had subdued or destroyed him. That general acted so vigorously, and with so much celerity, that he had like to have surprised him in his palace: but just before the English forces arrived at his gate, having notice of the danger that threatened him, and seeing no other means of safety, he threw himself with a few of his household into one of his ships which happened at the instant to be ready to sail, and put to sea."— LYTTLETON'S *Hist. of England*, vol. ii. p. 338.

This passage will be found to bear a general resemblance to the fictitious tale told in the Romance.

ABBOTSFORD, 1st *June*, 1832.

Notes to The Betrothed

6.4 (Introduction) by the help of the steam-engine A Romance, by the Author of Waverley, having been expected about this time at the great commercial mart of literature, the Fair of Leipsic, an ingenious gentleman of Germany, finding that none such appeared, was so kind as to supply its place with a work, in three volumes, called Walladmor, to which he prefixed the Christian and surname at full length. The character of this work is given with tolerable fairness in the text.

6.10 (Introduction) back-speer Scottish for cross-examine him.

6.13 (Introduction) crw The ale of the ancient British is called *crw* in their native language.

6.27 (Introduction) goes more trippingly off This was an opinion universally entertained among the friends of the author.

18.40 (Ch. 2) the morsel which I hold in my hand It is said in Highland tradition, that one of the Macdonalds of the Isles, who had suffered his broadsword to remain sheathed for some months after his marriage with a beautiful woman, was stirred to a sudden and furious expedition against the mainland, by hearing conversation to the above purpose among his body-guard.

19.32 (Ch.2) to avoid its stifling fumes The Welsh houses, like those of the cognate tribes in Ireland and in the Highlands of Scotland, were very imperfectly supplied with chimneys. Hence, in the History of the Gwydir Family, the striking expression of a Welsh chieftain, who, the house being assaulted and set on fire by his enemies, exhorted his friends to stand to their defence, saying he had seen as much smoke in the hall upon a Christmas even.

20.11 (Ch. 2) in his lap or bosom See Madoc for this literal *foot page's* office and duties. Mr Southey's notes inform us: "The foot-bearer shall hold the feet of the King in his lap, from the time he reclines at the board till he goes to rest, and he shall chafe them with a towel; and during all that time shall watch that no harm befalls the King. He shall eat of the same dish from which the King takes his food: he shall light the first candle before the King." Such are the instructions given for this part of royal ceremonial in the laws of Howell Dha. It may be added, that probably upon this Celtic custom was founded one of those absurd and incredible representations which were propagated at the time of the French Revolution, to stir up the peasants against their feudal superiors. It was pretended that some feudal seigneurs asserted their right to kill and disembowel a peasant, in order to put their own feet within the expiring body, and so recover them from the chill.

42.11 (Ch. 4) so vengeful an enemy

COURAGE OF THE WELSH.—This is by no means exaggerated in the chapter we have just closed. A very honourable testimony was given to their valour by King Henry II., in a letter to the

Greek Emperor, Emanuel Comnenus. This prince having desired that an account might be sent him of all that was remarkable in the island of Great Britain, Henry, in answer to that request, was pleased to take notice, among other particulars, of the extraordinary courage and fierceness of the Welsh, who were not afraid to fight unarmed with enemies armed at all points, valiantly shedding their blood in the cause of their country, and purchasing glory at the expense of their lives.

47.28 (Ch. 5) Crogan This is a somewhat contumelious epithet, applied by the Welsh to the English.

60.9 (Ch. 7) the western battlements Old Henry Jenkins, in his recollections of the abbacies before their dissolution, has preserved the fact, that roast-beef was delivered out to the guests, not by weight, but by measure.

68.12 (Ch. 8) more secure deliberation ARCHERS OF WALES.—The Welsh were excellent bowmen; but, under favour of Lord Lyttleton, they probably did not use the long-bow, the formidable weapon of the Normans, and afterwards of the English yeomen. That of the Welsh most likely rather resembled the bow of the cognate Celtic tribes of Ireland, and of the Highlands of Scotland. It was shorter than the Norman long-bow, as being drawn to the breast, not to the ear, more loosely strung, and the arrow having a heavy iron head; altogether, in short, a less effective weapon. It appears from the following anecdote, that there was a difference between the Welsh arrows and those of the English.

In 1122, Henry the II., marching into Powys-Land to chastise Meredyth ap Blethyn and certain rebels, in passing a defile was struck by an arrow on the breast. Repelled by the excellence of his breastplate, the shaft fell to the ground. When the King felt the blow and saw the shaft, he swore his usual oath, by the death of our Lord, that the arrow came not from a Welsh, but an English bow; and, influenced by this belief, hastily put an end to the war.

76.5 (Ch. 9) very strong bodies of horse Even the sharp and angry clang made by the iron scabbards of modern cavalry ringing against the steel-tipp'd saddles and stirrup, betrays their approach from a distance. The clash of the armour of knights, armed *cap-à-piè*, must have been much more easily discernible.

81.12 (Ch. 10) the rank of the Welch Prince EUDORCHAWG, OR GOLD CHAINS OF THE WELSH.—These were the distinguished marks of rank and valour among the numerous tribes of Celtic extraction. Manlius, the Roman Champion, gained the name of Torquatus, or he of the chain, on account of an ornament of this kind, won, in single combat, from a gigantic Gaul. Aneurin, the Welsh bard, mentions, in his poem on the battle of Catterath, that no less than three hundred of the British, who fell there, had their necks wreathed with the Eudorchawg. This seems to infer that the chain was a badge of distinction, and valour perhaps, but not of royalty; otherwise there would scarce have been so many kings present in one battle. This chain has been found accordingly in Ireland and Wales, and sometimes, though more rarely, in Scotland. Doubtless it was of too precious materials not to be usually converted into money by the enemy into whose hands it fell.

87.8 (Ch. 10) the honours of a separate funeral

CRUELTIES OF THE WELSH.—The Welsh, a fierce and barbarous people, were often accused of mangling the bodies of their slain antagonists. Every one must remember Shakspeare's account, how

—the noble Mortimer,
Leading the men of Herefordshire to fight
Against the irregular and wild Glendower—
Was, by the rude hands of that Welshman, taken,
And a thousand of his people butcher'd:
Upon whose dead corpse there was such misuse,
Such beastly shameless transformation,
By these Welshwomen done, as may not be,
Without much shame, retold or spoken of.

121.7 (Ch. 14) To-morrow you shall know all

BAHR-GEIST.—The idea of the Bahr-Geist was taken from a passage in the Memoirs of Lady Fanshaw, which have since been given to the public, and received with deserved approbation.

The original runs as follows. Lady Fanshaw, shifting among her friends in Ireland, like other sound loyalists of the period, tells her story thus:—

"From thence we went to the Lady Honor O'Brien's, a lady that went for a maid, but few believed it. She was the youngest daughter of the Earl of Thomond. There we staid three nights—the first of which I was surprised at being laid in a chamber, where, when about one o'clock, I heard a voice that awakened me. I drew the curtain, and in the casement of the window I saw, by the light of the moon, a woman leaning through the casement into the room, in white, with red hair and pale and ghastly complexion. She spoke loud, and in a tone I had never heard, thrice, "A horse;" and then, with a sigh more like the wind than breath, she vanished, and to me her body looked more like a thick cloud than substance. I was so much frightened that my hair stood on end, and my night clothes fell off. I pulled and pinched your father, who never awoke during the disorder I was in, but at last was much surprised to see me in this fright, and more so when I related the story and showed him the window opened. Neither of us slept any more that night; but he entertained me by telling me how much more these apparitions were common in this country than in England; and we concluded the cause to be the great superstition of the Irish, and the want of that knowing faith which should defend them from the power of the devil, which he exercises among them very much. About five o'clock the lady of the house came to see us, saying she had not been in bed all night, because a cousin O'Brien of hers, whose ancestors had owned that house, had desired her to stay with him in his chamber, and that he died at two o'clock; and she said, I wish you to have had no disturbance, for 'tis the custom of the place, that, when any of the family are dying, the shape of a woman appears every night in the window until they be dead. This woman was many ages ago got with child by the owner of this place, who murdered her in his garden, and flung her into the river under the window; but truly I thought not of it when I lodged you here, it being the best room in the house. We made little reply to her speech, but disposed ourselves to be gone suddenly."

158.34 (Ch. 18) surquedry Self-importance, or assumption.

202.17 (Ch. 24) the Cymry Cymbri, or Welsh.

225.8 (Ch. 27) this old swallow's tail The pennon of a knight was, in shape, a long streamer, and forked like a swallow's tail; the banner of a Banneret was square, and was formed into the other by cutting the ends from the pennon. It was thus the ceremony was performed on the pennon of John Chandos, by the Black Prince, before the battle of Nejara.

250.35 (Ch. 30) those which follow are little felt Such an expression is said to have been used by Mandrin the celebrated smuggler, while in the act of being broken upon the wheel. This dreadful punishment consists in the executioner, with a bar of iron, breaking the shoulder bones, arms, thigh-bones, and legs of the criminal, taking his alternate sides. The punishment is concluded by a blow across the breast, called the *coup de grace*, because it removes the sufferer from his agony. When Mandrin received the second blow over the left shoulder bone, he laughed. His confessor enquired the reason of demeanour so unbecoming his situation. "I only laugh at my own folly, my father," answered Mandrin, "who could suppose that sensibility of pain should continue after the nervous system had been completely deranged by the first blow."

THE TALISMAN

Editorial Note

The Talisman occupies much of Volume 5 and the first half of Volume 6 in the 1827 octavo *Tales and Romances*, MS 23030 and 23031 in the Interleaved Set. It is difficult to know exactly when Scott worked on the annotation of *The Talisman*, but it would appear to have been between 29 March and 12 April 1831 (EEWN 18b, 310). On 25 and 26 April Cadell 'revised part of Tales of the Crusaders' (MS 21021, f. 19v): this was presumably *The Betrothed*, but it is likely that some of the subsequent reference to 'Crusaders' cover a progression to *The Talisman*. The first specific reference to Cadell's revising that novel is on 20 May, when he 'revised part of the Talisman' (MS 20121, f. 23r). Three days later he 'recd from Sir Walter during the [morning the] missing volume of the Conclusion of the Talisman & Woodstock' (MS 20121, f. 23v), that is MS 23031, which Scott had confusedly taken to be entirely occupied by *Woodstock*, leading him to believe that the conclusion of *The Talisman* had gone missing. Cadell completed his work on the novel on 16 July (EEWN 18b, 311). *The Talisman* appeared as Volume 38 of the Magnum on 1 July 1832. Like *The Betrothed* this was a substantial book, with 494 pages. Given the amount of material to be squeezed in, Scott kept his Introduction very short (10 pages, but with a further 10 pages of Appendix), and provided only three endnotes and a handful of glossarial or explanatory footnotes.

The main argument of the Introduction is somewhat tenuous. Scott asserts that he had been wary of undertaking a novel set in the Middle East because of fears that his lack of acquaintance with the region would make the work appear inferior when set beside recent oriental novels and poems. He decided that he could avoid 'entering into competition with them' by centring *The Talisman* on the contrasting characters of Richard and Saladin. The logic is strained, but Scott seems to be relying, apart from his well-tried technique of contrasts, on his familiarity with sources relating to Richard and on the device of the talisman suggested by the Lee Penny. Scott's adaptation of the Penny 'to his own purposes' prompts a final defence of his modification of Conrade of Montserrat as being essentially in line with tradition as far as his relation with Richard is concerned. This rather desultory Introduction is followed by an Appendix with liberal quotations from the medieval romance *Richard Cœur de Lion*.

The manuscript of the main Introduction is mostly in Scott's own hand, but Laidlaw takes over at the end of the third leaf (295.31: 'A principal incident') and continues to the end of the Appendix. Everything is fluently written.

The only matter worthy of comment in the handful of notes is that the final endnote on 'The Lee Penny' was added at a very late stage and does not appear in the state printed from unrevised plates.

There are two Magnum illustrations for this title. The frontispiece to Volume 38 (MAG0075 / TB348.38) was designed by John Watson Gordon and engraved by Charles Rolls. It depicts Conrade of Montserrat being unhorsed by the hound Roswal, in front of King Richard and the Christian princes as they file past the English banner (EEWN 18b, 222.36–39 (abridged): 'The Nubian slipped the leash . . . down from the saddle.'). The title-page vignette (MAG0076 / TB348.38) was designed by John Watson Gordon and engraved by Samuel Sangster. It depicts Sir Kenneth and (the as yet unidentified) Saladin seated together, with weapons on the ground, by a spring with palm trees behind, enjoying refreshments, in the wake of their inconclusive combat (EEWN 18b, 12.42–13.1 (omitting 'next' before 'sat'): 'Christian and Saracen . . . for their own refreshment.').

Watson Gordon. Charles Rolls.

THE TALISMAN.

"The Nubian slipped the leash, and the hound rushing on, leapt upon Conrade's noble charger, and seizing the Marquis by the throat, pulled him down from the saddle."

EDINBURGH, PUBLISHED 1832, BY ROBERT CADELL, & WHITTAKER & C° LONDON.

WAVERLEY NOVELS.

VOL. XXXVIII.

THE TALISMAN.

'Christian and Saracen, sat down together on the turf, and produced each the small allowance of store which they carried for their own refreshment.'

PRINTED FOR ROBERT CADELL, EDINBURGH.
AND WHITTAKER & C° LONDON.
1832.

Introduction to The Talisman

THE "Betrothed" did not greatly please one or two friends, who thought that it did not well correspond to the general title of "The Crusaders." They urged, therefore, that, without direct allusion to the manners of the Eastern tribes, and to the romantic conflicts of the period, the title of a "Tale of the Crusaders" would resemble the playbill, which is said to have announced the tragedy of Hamlet, the character of the Prince of Denmark being left out. On the other hand, I felt the difficulty of giving a vivid picture of a part of the world with which I was well nigh totally unacquainted, unless by early recollections of the Arabian Nights' Entertainments; and not only did I labour under the incapacity of ignorance, in which, as far as regards Eastern manners, I was as thickly wrapped as an Egyptian in his fog; but my contemporaries were, many of them, as much enlightened upon the subject, as if they had been inhabitants of the favoured land of Goshen. The love of travelling had pervaded all ranks, and carried the subjects of Britain into all quarters of the world. Greece, so attractive by its remains of art, by its struggles for freedom against a Mohamedan tyrant, by its very name, where every fountain had its classical legend;—Palestine, endeared to the imagination by yet more sacred remembrances, had been of late surveyed by British eyes, and described by recent travellers. Had I, therefore, attempted the difficult task of substituting manners of my own invention, instead of the genuine costume of the East, almost every traveller I met, who had extended his route beyond what was anciently called "The Grand Tour," had acquired a right, by ocular inspection, to chastise me for my presumption. Every member of the Travellers' Club, who could pretend to have thrown his shoe over Edom, was, by having done so, constituted my lawful critic and corrector, a situation in which I had not hitherto stood, and was not ever willing to place myself. It occurred, therefore, that where the author of Anastasius, as well as he of Hadji Baba, had described the manners and vices of the Eastern nations, not only with fidelity, but with the humour of Le Sage and the ludicrous power of Fielding himself, one who was a perfect stranger to the subject must necessarily produce an unfavourable contrast. The Poet Laureate also, in the charming tale of "Thalaba," had shown how extensive might be the researches of a person of acquirements and talent, by dint of investigation alone, into the ancient doctrines, history, and manners of the Eastern countries, in which we are probably to look for the cradle of mankind; Moore, in his "Lalla Rookh," had successfully trod the same path; in which, too, Byron, joining ocular experience to extensive reading, had written some of his most attractive poems. In a word, the Eastern themes had been already so sufficiently handled by those who were acknowledged masters of their craft, that I was diffident of making the attempt.

These were powerful objections, nor did they lose force when they became the subject of anxious reflection, although they did not finally prevail. The arguments on the other side were, that though I had no hope of rivalling the contemporaries whom I have mentioned, yet it occurred to me as possible to acquit myself of the task I was engaged in, without entering into competition with them. At the utmost, European manners and those of the middle ages, in which I was allowed to be in some degree at home, should occupy the larger part of a tale on the subject of the Crusades. With regard to the other or smaller portion, which was necessarily the least important, I imagined that it was possible by keeping in generals to avoid any remarkable errors or anachronisms. The extreme simplicity as well as unchanging character of eastern manners, are taught us early in the enchanting terms which our infancy learns, and our manhood and age recall to mind, often without the exertion even of the faculty of volition. So that in some degree every person of a lively imagination is supplied with a stock of articles, to use the shopkeeper's phrase, upon a true oriental pattern. Books of travels are numerous, and for history and events the Bibliotheque Orientale was at hand to supply them.

If an author, therefore, is not disposed to venture out of his depth, he is in no great danger of drowning, and methought this species of general acquaintance might very well serve the turn of an ignorant scribbler like myself.

The period relating more immediately to the Crusades which I at last fixed upon, was that at which the warlike character of Richard I., wild and generous, a pattern of chivalry, with all its extravagant virtues, and its no less absurd errors, was opposed in the scales to that of Saladin, in which the Christian and English monarch showed all the cruelty and violence of an Eastern sultan; and Saladin, on the other hand, displayed the deep policy and prudence of a European sovereign, whilst they contended which should excel the other in the knightly qualities of bravery and generosity. This singular contrast afforded, as the author conceived, materials for a work of fiction, possessing peculiar interest. One of the inferior characters introduced, was a supposed relation of Richard Cœur de Lion; a violation of the truth of history, which gave offence to Mr Mills, the Author of the History of Chivalry and the Crusades, who was not, it may be presumed, aware that romantic fiction naturally includes the power of such invention, which is indeed one of the requisites of the art.

Prince David of Scotland, who was actually in the host, and was the hero of some very romantic adventures on his way home, was also pressed into my service, and constitutes one of my *dramatis personæ*.

It is true I had already brought upon the field Him of the lion heart. But it was in a more private capacity than he was here to be exhibited in the Talisman; then as a disguised knight, now in the avowed character of a conquering monarch; so that I doubted not a name so dear to Englishmen as that of King Richard I. might contribute to their amusement for more than once.

I had access to all which antiquity believed, whether of reality or fable, on the subject of that magnificent warrior, who was the proudest boast of Europe and their chivalry, and with whose dreadful name the Saracens, according to a historian of their own country, were wont to rebuke their startled horses. "Do you think," said they, "that King Richard is on the track, that you stray so wildly from it?" The most curious register of the history of King Richard, is an ancient romance, translated originally from the Norman; and at first certainly having a pretence to be termed a work of chivalry, but latterly becoming stuffed with the most astonishing and monstrous fables. There is perhaps no metrical romance upon record, where, along with curious and genuine history, are mingled more absurd and exaggerated incidents. We have placed in the Appendix to this Introduction, the passage of the romance in which Richard figures as an Ogre, or literal cannibal.—(Appendix, p. 397.)

A principal incident in the story, is that from which the title is derived. Of all people who ever lived, the Persians were perhaps most remarkable for their unshaken credulity in amulets, spells, periapts, and similar charms, framed, it was said, under the influence of particular planets, and bestowing high medical powers, as well as the means of advancing men's fortunes in various manners. A story of this kind, relating to a Crusader of eminence, is often told in the west of Scotland, and the relic alluded to is still in existence, and even yet held in veneration.

Sir Simon Lockhart of Lee and Cartland made a considerable figure in the reigns of Robert the Bruce and of his son David. He was one of the chief of that band of Scottish chivalry, who accompanied James, the Good Lord Douglas, on his expedition to the

Holy Land, with the heart of King Robert Bruce. Douglas, too impatient to get at the Saracens, entered into war with those of Spain, and was killed there. Lockhart proceeded to the Holy Land with such Scottish knights as had escaped the fate of their leader, and assisted for some time in the wars against the Saracens.

The following adventure is said by tradition to have befallen him:—

He made prisoner in battle an Emir of considerable wealth and consequence. The antient mother of the captive came to the Christian camp, to redeem her son from his state of captivity. Lockhart is said to have fixed the price at which his prisoner should ransom himself; and the lady, pulling out a large embroidered purse, proceeded to tell down the ransom, like a mother who pays little respect to gold in comparison of her son's liberty. In this operation, a pebble inserted in a coin, some say of the Lower Empire, fell out of the purse, and the Saracen matron testified so much haste to recover it, as gave the Scottish knight a high idea of its value, when compared with gold or silver. "I will not consent," he said, "to grant your son's liberty, unless that amulet be added to his ransom." The lady not only consented to this, but explained to Sir Simon Lockhart the mode in which the Talisman was to be used, and the uses to which it might be put. The water in which it was dipt operated as a styptic, as a febrifuge, and possessed several other properties as a medical talisman.

Sir Simon Lockhart, after many experiences of the wonders which it wrought, brought it to his own country, and left it to his heirs, by whom, and by Clydesdale in general, it was, and is still, distinguished by the name of the Lee-penny, from the name of his native seat of Lee.

The most remarkable part of its history, perhaps, was, that it so especially escaped condemnation when the Church of Scotland chose to impeach many other cures which savoured of the miraculous, as occasioned by sorcery, and censured the appeal to them, excepting only that to the amulet, called the Lee-penny, to which it had pleased God to annex certain healing virtues which the Church did not presume to condemn. It still, as has been said, exists, and its powers are sometimes resorted to. Of late, they have been chiefly restricted to the cure of persons bitten by a mad dog; and as the illness in such cases frequently arises from imagination, there can be no reason for doubting that water which has been poured on the Lee-penny furnishes a congenial cure.

Such is the tradition concerning the Talisman, which the author has taken the liberty to vary in applying it to his own purposes.

Considerable liberties have also been taken with the truth of history, both with respect to Conrade of Montserrat's life, as well as his death. That Conrade, however, was reckoned the enemy of Richard, is agreed both in history and romance. The general opinion of the terms upon which they stood, may be guessed from the proposal of the Saracens, that the Marquis of Montserrat should be invested with certain parts of Syria, which they were to yield to the Christians. Richard, according to the romance which bears his name, "could no longer repress his fury. The Marquis, he said, was a traitor, who had robbed the Knights Hospitallers of sixty thousand pounds, the present of his father, Henry; that he was a renegade, whose treachery had occasioned the loss of Acre; and he concluded by a solemn oath, that he would cause him to be drawn to pieces by wild horses, if he should ever venture to pollute the Christian camp by his presence. Philip attempted to intercede in favour of the Marquis, and throwing down his glove, offered to become a pledge for his fidelity to the Christians; but his offer was rejected, and he was obliged to give way to Richard's impetuosity." —*Specimens of Early English Metrical Romances*.

Conrade of Montserrat makes a considerable figure in those wars, and was at length put to death by one of the followers of the Scheik, or Old Man of the Mountain: nor did Richard remain free of the suspicion of having instigated his death.

It may be said, in general, that most of the incidents introduced in the following tale are fictitious; and that reality, where it exists, is only retained in the characters of the piece.

ABBOTSFORD, 1st *July*, 1832.

APPENDIX TO INTRODUCTION

WHILE warring in the Holy Land, Richard was seized with an ague.

The best leeches of the camp were unable to effect the cure of the King's disease; but the prayers of the army were more successful. He became convalescent, and the first symptom of his recovery was a violent longing for pork. But pork was not likely to be plentiful in a country whose inhabitants had an abhorrence for swine's flesh; and

—though his men should be hanged,
They ne might, in that countrèy,
For gold, ne silver, ne no monèy,
No pork find, take, ne get,
That King Richard might aught of eat.

An old knight with Richard biding,
When he heard of that tiding,
That the kingis wants were swyche,
To the steward he spake privyliche—
"Our lord the king sore is sick, I wis,
After porck he alonged is;
Ye may none find to selle;
No man be hardy him so to telle!
If he did he might die.
Now behoves to done as I shall say,
That he wete nought of that.
Take a Saracen, young and fat;
In haste let the thief be slain,
Opened, and his skin off flayn;
And sodden full hastily,
With powder and with spicery,
And with saffron of good coloùr.
When the king feels thereof savoùr,
Out of ague if he be went,
He shall have thereto good talènt.
When he has a good taste,
And eaten well a good repast,
And supped of the *brewis** a sup,
Slept after and swet a drop,
Through Goddis help and my counsail,
Soon he shall be fresh and hail."
The sooth to say, at wordes few,
Slain and sodden was the heathen shrew.
Before the king it was forth brought:
Quod his men, "Lord, we have pork sought;
Eates and sups of the brewis *soote*,†
Thorough grace of God it shall be your boot."
Before King Richard carff a knight,
He ate faster than he carve might.
The king ate the flesh and *gnew*‡ the bones,
And drank well after for the nonce.
And when he had eaten enough,
His folk hem turned away, and *lough*.§
He lay still and drew in his arm;
His chamberlain him wrapped warm.
He lay and slept, and swet a stound,
And became whole and sound.
King Richard clad him and arose,
And walked abouten in the close.

An attack of the Saracens was repelled by Richard in person, the consequence of which is told in the following lines.

When King Richard had rested a whyle,
A knight his arms 'gan unlace,
Him to comfort and solàce.
Him was brought a sop in wine.
"The head of that ilke swine,
That I of ate!" (the cook he bade,)

* Broth. † Sweet. ‡ Gnawed. § Laughed.

"For feeble I am, and faint and mad.
Of mine evil now I am fear;
Serve me therewith at my soupere!"
Quod the cook, "That head I ne have."
Then said the king, "So God me save,
But I see the head of that swine,
For sooth, thou shalt lesen thine!"
The cook saw none other might be;
He fet the head and let him see.
He fell on knees, and made a cry—
"Lo, here the head! my Lord, mercỳ!"

The cook had certainly some reason to fear that his master would be struck with horror at the recollection of the dreadful banquet to which he owed his recovery, but his fears were soon dissipated.

The swarte *vis** when the king seeth,
His black beard and white teeth,
How his lippes grinned wide,
"What devil is this?" the king cried,
And gan to laugh as he were wode.
"What! is Saracen's flesh thus good?
That, never erst I nought wist!
By God's death and his uprist,
Shall we never die for default,
While we may in any assault,
Slee Saracens, the flesh may take,
And seethen and roasten and do hem bake,
[And] Gnawen her flesh to the bones!
Now I have it proved once,
For hunger ere I be wo,
I and my folk shall eat mo!"

The besieged now offered to surrender, upon conditions of safety to the inhabitants; while all the public treasure, military machines, and arms, were delivered to the victors, together with the further ransom of one hundred thousand bezants. After this capitulation, the following extraordinary scene took place. We shall give it in the words of the humorous and amiable George Ellis, the collector and the editor of these Romances.

"Though the garrison had faithfully performed the other articles of their contract, they were unable to restore the cross, which was not in their possession, and were therefore treated by the Christians with great cruelty. Daily reports of their sufferings were carried to Saladin; and as many of them were persons of the highest distinction, that monarch, at the solicitation of their friends, dispatched an embassy to King Richard with magnificent presents, which he offered for the ransom of the captives. The ambassadors were persons the most respectable from their age, their rank, and their eloquence. They delivered their message in terms of the utmost

* Black face.

humility, and, without arraigning the justice of the conqueror in his severe treatment of their countrymen, only solicited a period to that severity, laying at his feet the treasures with which they were intrusted, and pledging themselves and their master for the payment of any further sums which he might demand as the price of mercy.

"King Richard spake with wordes mild,
'The gold to take, God me shield!
Among you *partes** every charge.
I brought in shippes and in barge,
More gold and silver with me,
Than has your lord, and swilke three.
To his treasure have I no need!
But for my love I you bid,
To meat with me that ye dwell;
And afterward I shall you tell.
Thorough counsel I shall you answèr,
What *bode*† ye shall to your lord bear.'

"The invitation was gratefully accepted. Richard, in the meantime, gave secret orders to his marshal that he should repair to the prison, select a certain number of the most distinguished captives, and, after carefully noting their names on a roll of parchment, cause their heads to be instantly struck off; that these heads should be delivered to the cook with instructions to clear away the hair, and, after boiling them in a caldron, to distribute them on several platters, one to each guest, observing to fasten on the forehead of each the piece of parchment expressing the name and family of the victim.

"'An hot head bring me beforn,
As I were well apayed withall,
Eat thereof fast I shall;
As it were a tender chick,
To see how the others will like.'

"This horrible order was punctually executed. At noon the guests were summoned to wash by the music of the waits; the King took his seat, attended by the principal officers of his court, at the high table, and the rest of the company were marshalled at a long table below him. On the cloth were placed portions of salt at the usual distances, but neither bread, wine, nor water. The ambassadors, rather surprised at this omission, but still free from apprehension, awaited in silence the arrival of the dinner, which was announced by the sound of pipes, trumpets, and tabours; and beheld, with horror and dismay, the unnatural banquet introduced by the steward and his officers. Yet their sentiments of disgust and abhorrence, and even their fears, were for a time suspended by their curiosity. Their eyes were fixed on the King, who, without the slightest change

* Divide. † Message.

of countenance, swallowed the morsels as fast as they could be supplied by the knight who carved them.

"Every man then poked other;
They said, 'This is the devil's brother,
That slays our men, and thus hem eats!'

"Their attention was then involuntarily fixed on the smoking heads before them; they traced in the swollen and distorted features the resemblance of a friend or near relation, and received from the fatal scroll which accompanied each dish the sad assurance that this resemblance was not imaginary. They sat in torpid silence, anticipating their own fate in that of their countrymen, while their ferocious entertainer, with fury in his eyes, but with courtesy on his lips, insulted them by frequent invitations to merriment. At length this first course was removed, and its place supplied by venison, cranes, and other dainties, accompanied by the richest wines. The King then apologized to them for what had passed, which he attributed to his ignorance of their taste; and assured them of his religious respect for their character as ambassadors, and of his readiness to grant them a safe conduct for their return. This boon was all that they now wished to claim; and

"King Richard spake to an old man,
'Wendes home to your Soudan!
His melancholy that ye abate;
And sayes that ye came too late.
Too slowly was your time y-guessed;
Ere ye came, the flesh was dressed,
That men shoulden serve with me,
Thus at noon, and my meynie.
Say him, it shall him nought avail,
Though he for-bar us our vitail,
Bread, wine, fish, flesh, salmon and conger;
Of us none shall die with hunger,
While we may wenden to fight,
And slay the Saracens downright,
Wash the flesh, and roast the head.
With *oo** Saracen I may well feed
Well a nine or a ten
Of my good Christian men.
King Richard shall warrant,
There is no flesh so nourissant
Unto an English man,
Partridge, plover, heron, ne swan,
Cow ne ox, sheep ne swine,
As the head of a Sarazyn.
There he is fat, and thereto tender,
And my men be lean and slender.
While any Saracen quick be,

* One.

Livand now in this Syrie,
For meat will we nothing care.
Abouten fast we shall fare,
And every day we shall eat
All so many as we may get.
To England will we nought gon,
Till they be eaten every one.'"

ELLIS'S *Specimens of Early English Metrical Romances*, vol. ii. p. 236.

The reader may be curious to know owing to what circumstances so extraordinary an invention as that which imputed cannibalism to the King of England, should have found its way into his history. Mr James, to whom we owe so much that is curious, seems to have traced the origin of this extraordinary rumour.

"With the army of the cross also was a multitude of men," the same author declares, "who made it a profession to be without money; they walked barefoot, carried no arms, and even preceded the beasts of burden on the march, living upon roots and herbs, and presenting a spectacle both disgusting and pitiable.

"A Norman, who according to all accounts was of noble birth, but who, having lost his horse, continued to follow as a foot soldier, took the strange resolution of putting himself at the head of this race of vagabonds, who willingly received him as their king. Amongst the Saracens these men became well-known under the name of *Thafurs*, (which Guibert translates *Trudentes*,) and were beheld with great horror from the general persuasion that they fed on the dead bodies of their enemies; a report which was occasionally justified, and which the king of the Thafurs took care to encourage. This respectable monarch was frequently in the habit of stopping his followers, one by one, in a narrow defile, and of causing them to be searched carefully, lest the possession of the least sum of money should render them unworthy of the name of his subjects. If even two sous were found upon any one, he was instantly expelled the society of his tribe, the king bidding him contemptuously buy arms and fight.

"This troop, so far from being cumbersome to the army, was infinitely serviceable, carrying burdens, bringing in forage, provisions, and tribute; working the machines in the sieges, and, above all, spreading consternation among the Turks, who feared death from the lances of the knights less than that further consummation they heard of under the teeth of the Thafurs."*

It is easy to conceive, that an ignorant minstrel, finding the taste and ferocity of the Thafurs commemorated in the historical accounts of the Holy wars, has ascribed their practices and propen-

* James's History of Chivalry, p. 178.

sities to the Monarch of England, whose ferocity was considered as an object of exaggeration as legitimate as his valour.

Notes to The Talisman

11.35 (Ch 2) to gab *Gaber.* This French word signified a sort of sport much used among the French chivalry, which consisted in vying with each other in making the most romantic gasconades. The verb and the meaning are retained in Scottish.

63.39 (Ch. 6) inexorable Lord of Gilsland
SIR THOMAS MULTON OF GILSLAND. He was a historical hero, faithfully attached, as is here expressed, to King Richard, and is noticed with distinction in the romance mentioned in the Introduction. At the beginning of the romance, mention is made of a tournament, in which the king returns three times with a fresh suit of armour, which acted as a disguise; and at each appearance, some knight of great prowess had a sharp encounter with him. When Richard returned the second time, the following is Mr Ellis's account of his proceedings:—"He now mounted a bay horse, assumed a suit of armour painted red, and a helmet, the crest of which was a red hound, with a long tail which reached to the earth; an emblem intended to convey his indignation against the heathen hounds who defiled the Holy Land, and his determination to attempt their destruction. Having sufficiently signalized himself in his new disguise, he rode into the ranks for the purpose of selecting a more formidable adversary; and, delivering his spear to his squire, took his mace, and assaulted Sir Thomas de Multon, a knight whose prowess was deservedly held in the highest estimation. Sir Thomas, apparently not at all disordered by a blow which would have felled a common adversary, calmly advised him to go and amuse himself elsewhere; but Richard, having aimed at him a second and more violent stroke, by which his helmet was nearly crushed, he returned it with such vigour that the king lost his stirrups, and, recovering himself with some difficulty, rode off with all speed into the forest."—ELLIS'S *Specimens*, pp. 185, 187.

67.32 (Ch. 7) El Hakim The Physician.

76.32 (Ch. 8) Azrael The Angel of Death.

80.36 (Ch. 8) the Hegira Meaning, that his attainments were those which might have been made in a hundred years.

97.15 (Ch. 10) the Assize of Jerusalem The Assisses de Jerusalem were the digest of feudal law, composed by Godfrey of

Boulogne, for government of the Latin kingdom of Palestine, when reconquered from the Saracens. "It was composed with advice of the patriarch and barons, the clergy and laity," and is, says the historian Gibbon, "a precious monument of feudatory jurisprudence, founded upon those principles of freedom which were essential to the system."

109.38 (Ch. 11) the Melec Ric Richard was thus called by the Eastern nations.

142.40 (Ch. 15) fair and false Such were the terms in which the English used to speak of their poor northern neighbours, forgetting that their own encroachments upon the independence of Scotland obliged the weaker nation to defend themselves by policy as well as force. The disgrace must be divided between Edward I. and III., who enforced their domination over a free country, and the Scots who were compelled to take compulsory oaths, without any purpose of keeping them.

209.35 (Ch. 22) burneth the tent Some preparation of opium seems to be intimated.

229.36 (Ch. 25) taught thee An universal tradition ascribed to Sir Tristrem, famous for his love of the fair Queen Ysolde, the laws concerning the practice of wood-craft, or *venerie*, as it was called, being all which related to the chase, deemed of so much consequence during the middle ages.

274.22 (Ch. 28) spouted from the veins The manner of the death of the supposed Grand Master of the Templars, was taken from the real tragedy enacted by Saladin, upon the person of Arnold or Reginald de Chatillon. This person, a soldier of fortune, had seized a castle on the verge of the desert, from whence he made plundering excursions, and insulted and abused the pilgrims who were on their journey to Mecca. It was chiefly on his account that Saladin declared war against Guy de Lusignan, the last Latin King of the Holy Land. The Christian monarch was defeated by Saladin with the loss of 30,000 men, and having been made prisoner, with Chatillon and others, was conducted before the Soldan. The victor presented to his exhausted captive a cup of sherbet, cooled in snow. Lusignan, having drank, was about to hand the cup to Chatillon, when the Soldan interfered. "Your person," he said, "my royal prisoner, is sacred, but the cup of Saladin must not be profaned by a blasphemous robber and ruffian." So saying, he slew the captive knight by a blow of his scimitar.—See GIBBON'S *History*.

277.41 (Ch. 28) canine madness

THE LEE PENNY. Since the last sheet of this volume of the present edition was printed off, a kind friend has transmitted the following curious document, by which it would appear that the alleged virtues of the Lee Penny had at one time given uneasiness to our Presbyterian brethren of Clydesdale.

(Copy)

Extract from the Assemblie Books at Glasgow, anent the Lee Penny stone.

Apud Glasgow, 21 *of October*.*

SYNOD. SESS. 2.

QUHILK day, amongest the referries of the Brethren of the Ministry of Lanark, it was proponed to the Synod that Gavin Hamilton of Raploch had pursueit an Complaint before them against Sir James Lockhart of Lee, anent the superstitious using of an Stone, set in silver, for the curing of deseased Cattle, q[lk] the said Gavin affirmed could not be lawfully usit, and that they had deferrit to give ony decisionne thairin till the advice of the Assemblie might be had concerning the same. The Assemblie having inquirit of the manner of using thereof, and particularly understood, be examination of the said Laird of Lee and otherwise, that the custom is only to cast the stone in some water, and give the deseasit Cattle thereof to drink, and that the same is done without using any words, such as Charmers and Sorcereirs use in thair unlawful practices; and considering that in nature thair are many things seen to work strange effects, whereof no human wit can give a reason, it having pleast God to give to stones and herbs a speciall vertue for healing of many infirmities in man and beast, advises the Brethren to surcease thair process, as therein they perceive no ground of Offence, and admonishes the said Laird of Lee, in the using of the said stone, to take heid that it be usit hereafter with the least scandle that possibly maybe. Extract out of the Books of the Assemblie holden at Glasgow, and subscribed at thair command.

M. ROBERT YOUNG, Clerk to the Assemblie at Glasgow.

* The year is unfortunately not given; but the Sir James Lockhart named in the extract was born in 1596, and died in 1674.

WOODSTOCK

Editorial Note

Woodstock occupies the second half of Volume 6 and the whole of Volume 7 of the 1827 *Tales and Romances*, MSS 23031 and 23032 of the Interleaved Set. Scott began to 'notify' the novel on 27 December 1830, but he did not complete the work until the end of May 1831. Cadell carried out his tasks in July and August (EEWN 19, 450–53). On 18 August Scott sent 'the long wanting introduction to Woodstock taken from Hones Every day Book' (MS 15980, f. 152r). There was further activity in the autumn. On 5 September Scott wrote to Cadell 'I send the Copy of Woodstock with the note restord 2 vols The note is in volume 1' (MS 15980, f. 165r: the '1' is imperfectly formed). During his stay in London on his way to Malta Scott sent transcriptions of the two accounts of the Woodstock events which he had had made from the originals in the British Museum (MS 15980, f. 230r). Cadell noted on 21 October that he had received from the author 'a short Introduction to Appendix to Introduction to Woodstock' (MS 21021, f. 45r). This sounds like a separate document, but if so it is not known to have survived, and it may actually be part of the corrections which Scott made in the proof of the Introduction sent to him in London on 30 September (MS 5317, f. 105r: the proof is preserved in the Interleaved Set), where the first two sentences of the final paragraph are inserted by the author. That proof as sent to Scott has some comments by the printer John Hughes, identifying areas of overlap as well as making routine typographical corrections. Cadell was working on revisions to the Introduction between 27 October and 10 January the next year (MS 21021, ff. 46r, 52r; MS 21022, f. 4v). *Woodstock* appeared on 1 August and 1 September 1832 as Volumes 39 and 40 of the Magnum.

The nineteen-page Introduction (the fluent manuscript of which is in Laidlaw's hand) is devoted almost entirely to an exploration of the sources for the strange goings-on at Woodstock (discussed in EEWN 19, 537–41). There is a characteristic sign of unease about possible accusations of book-making in the oddly-phrased sentence 'At the risk of prolonging a curious quotation, I include a page or two from Mr Hone's Every-day Book'. The most interesting feature is Scott's assertion that when composing the novel he might have missed some promising details in the account reproduced in *The British Magazine* for April 1747 (see EEWN 19, 539–41). This is very much in line with the familiar image employed in the opening paragraph, where he remembers finding himself 'still at liberty to glean another harvest out of so ample a store' already drawn on for *Peveril of the Peak* four years before. As so often he concludes, referring to the opportunities perhaps missed, 'The tree, however, must remain where it has fallen.'

As noted above, the two Appendices to the Introduction, amounting to 40 pages, reprint two accounts which Scott had encountered in the British Museum while passing through London on his way to Malta. After this expansiveness, Scott provides only a few brief footnotes (glossarial, explanatory, or indicating a source), and six endnotes, occupying (though not filling) ten pages, two of them in the first volume, the other four in the second. The first three are straightforward indications of sources, with quotations. The fourth (446–47) gives Scott an opportunity to talk about his edition of Patrick Carey's poems, carried out in ignorance of an edition of half a century earlier. The fifth (447) cites an oral source for the feather signal. And the last (447–48), one of the most attractive of Scott's briefer endnotes, is even more personal, remembering with affection Maida, the prototype of Bevis in the novel.

The Interleaved Set contains one curiosity. Between the manuscript of the Introduction and the transcription of *The Just Devil of Woodstock* there is a transcription by Laidlaw of a document running to 6 leaves headed 'Oxford Sept. 3.' giving an account of the 'sickness ⟨of⟩ & death of old Mr. Lenthal', William Lenthal (1691–62), Speaker of the House of Commons. This is haltingly endorsed by Scott 'To be inserted as refferd to ⟨as another ?tradi [or 'paper']⟩ as an illustration of Woodstock/ If Mr Cadell cannot find out which part of the Copy of Woodstock the ?comes from ?left send the whole of Woodstock to Abbotsford where the author will place it properly'. It is likely that Cadell concluded that the letter would not be relevant to any passage in the novel, a decision which the present editors would endorse.

There are four Magnum illustrations for this title. The frontispiece to Volume 39 (MAG0077 / TB348.39) was designed by William Boxall and engraved by Charles Fox. It depicts Sir Henry seated, with Alice at his feet, listening to the Evening Service of the Church of England being read by Dr Rochecliffe (EEWN 19, 135.27–37 (abridged): 'Sir Henry Lee sat . . . suited a choir of angels.'). The title-page vignette (MAG0078 / TB348.39) was designed by Edwin Landseer and engraved by William Raddon. It depicts Sir Henry's mastiff Bevis (the caption is simply 'Bevis.'). The frontispiece to Volume 40 (MAG0079 / TB348.40) was designed by James Inskipp and engraved by Augustus Fox. It depicts Sir Henry and Alice, who engages herself with needlework (EEWN 19, 205.27–30 (abridged): 'His daughter took some needle-work . . . on her parent.'). The title-page vignette (MAG0080 / TB348.40) was designed by William Collins and engraved by William Humphreys. It depicts Phoebe at the fountain, with Tomkins approaching from the Forest (EEWN 19, 325.10–17 (varied and abridged): 'As Phoebe Mayflower . . . no sense of fear.').

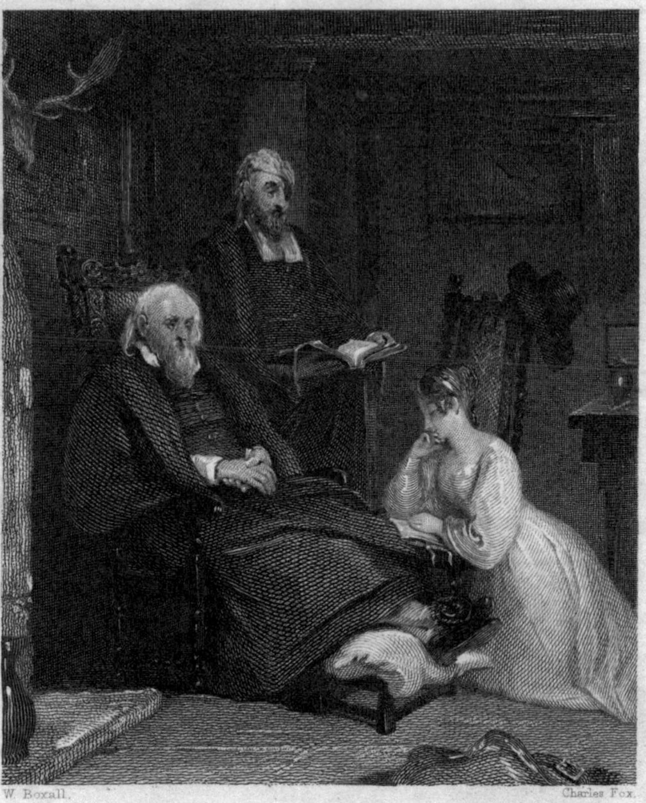

W. Boxall. Charles Fox.

WOODSTOCK.

"Sir Henry Lee sat in a wicker arm-chair by the fire, while he listened to a respectable old man, whose dilapidated dress showed still something of the clerical habit. Alice Lee kneeled at the feet of her Father, and made the responses with a voice that might have suited a choir of angels."

EDINBURGH, PUBLISHED 1832, BY ROBERT CADELL, and WHITTAKER & C? LONDON.

WAVERLEY NOVELS.

VOL. XXXIX.

WOODSTOCK.

"Bevis."

PRINTED FOR ROBERT CADELL, EDINBURGH,
AND WHITTAKER & Cº LONDON.
1832.

J. Inskipp. Augº Fox.

WOODSTOCK.

"His daughter took some needle-work, and bringing it close by the old man's side, employed her fingers on this task, bending her eyes from time to time on her parent".

EDINBURGH, PUBLISHED 1832, BY ROBERT CADELL, and WHITTAKER & Cº LONDON.

WAVERLEY NOVELS.

VOL. XL.

WOODSTOCK.

"As Phœbe Mayflower was reflecting, Fortune was malicious enough to send Tomkins to the fountain. She encouraged herself, however, and resolved to show no sense of fear."

PRINTED FOR ROBERT CADELL, EDINBURGH,
AND WHITTAKER & Cº LONDON.
1832.

Introduction to Woodstock

THE busy period of the great Civil War was one in which the character and genius of different parties were most brilliantly displayed, and, accordingly, the incidents which took place on either side were of a striking and extraordinary character, and afforded an ample foundation for fictitious composition. The author had in some measure attempted such in Peveril of the Peak; but the scene was in a remote part of the kingdom, and mingled with other national differences, which left him still at liberty to glean another harvest out of so ample a store.

In these circumstances, some wonderful adventures which happened at Woodstock in the year 1649, occurred to him as something he had long ago read of, although he was unable to tell where, and of which the hint appeared sufficient, although, doubtless, it might have been much better handled if the author had not, in the lapse of time, lost every thing like an accurate recollection of the real story.

It was not until about this period, namely, 1831, that the author, being called upon to write this Introduction, obtained a general account of what really happened upon the marvellous occasion in question, in a work termed "The Every-day Book," published by Mr Hone, and full of curious antiquarian research, the object being to give to the public a variety of original information concerning manners, illustrated by curious instances, rarely to be found elsewhere. Among other matter, Mr Hone quotes an article from the British Magazine for 1747, in the following words, and which is probably the document which the author of Woodstock had formerly perused, although he was unable to refer to the source of his information. The tract is entitled, "The Genuine History of the Good Devil of Woodstock, famous in the world, in the year 1649, and never accounted for, or at all understood to this time."

The teller of this "Genuine History" proceeds verbatim as follows:

"Some original papers having lately fallen into my hands, under the name of 'Authentic Memoirs of the Memorable Joseph Collins of Oxford, commonly known by the name of Funny Joe, and now intended for the press,' I was extremely delighted to find in them a circumstantial and unquestionable account of the most famous of all invisible agents, so well known in the year 1649, under the name of the Good Devil of Woodstock, and even adored by the people of that place, for the vexation and distress it occasioned some people they were not much pleased with. As this famous story, though related by a thousand people, and attested in all its circumstances, beyond all possibility of doubt, by people of rank, learning, and reputation, of Oxford and the adjacent towns, has never yet been generally accounted for, or at all understood, and is perfectly explained, in a manner that can admit of no doubt, in these papers, I could not refuse my readers the pleasure it gave me in reading."

There is, therefore, no doubt that, in the year 1649, a number of incidents, supposed to be supernatural, took place at the King's palace of Woodstock, which the Commissioners of Parliament were then and there endeavouring to dilapidate and destroy. The account of this by the Commissioners themselves, or under their authority, was repeatedly published, and in particular, is inserted as relation sixth of Satan's Invisible World Discovered, by George Sinclair, Professor of Philosophy in Glasgow, an approved collector of such tales.

It was the object of neither of the great political parties of that day to discredit this narrative, which gave great satisfaction both to the cavaliers and roundheads; the former conceiving that the license given to the demons, was in consequence of the impious desecration of the King's furniture and apartments, so that the citizens of Woodstock almost adored the supposed spirits, as avengers of the cause of royalty; while the friends of the Parliament, on the other hand, imputed to the malice of the fiend the obstruction of the pious work, as they judged that which they had in hand.

At the risk of prolonging a curious quotation, I include a page or two from Mr Hone's Every-day Book.

"The honourable the Commissioners arrived at Woodstock manor-house, October 13th, and took up their residence in the King's own rooms. His Majesty's bedchamber they made their kitchen, the council-hall their pantry, and the presence-chamber was the place where they sat for dispatch of business. His Majesty's dining-room they made their wood-yard, and stowed it with no other wood but that of the famous Royal Oak from the High Park, which, that nothing might be left with the name of the King about it, they had dug up by the roots, and bundled up into fagots for their firing.

"October 16th. This day they first sat for the dispatch of business. In the midst of their first debate there entered a large black dog, (as they thought,) which made a terrible howling, overturned two or three of their chairs, and doing some other damage, went under the bed, and there gnawed the cords. The door this while continued constantly shut, when, after some two or three hours, Giles Sharp, their secretary, looking under the bed, perceived that the creature was vanished, and that a plate of meat that the servants had hid there was untouched, and showing them to their honours, they were all convinced there could be no real dog concerned in the case; the said Giles also deposed on oath, that, to his certain knowledge, there was not.

"October 17th. As they were this day sitting at dinner in a lower room, they heard plainly the noise of persons walking over head, though they well knew the doors were all locked, and there could be none there. Presently after they heard also all the wood of the King's Oak brought by parcels from the dining-room, and thrown with great violence into the presence-chamber, as also the chairs, stools, tables, and other furniture, forcibly hurled about the room, their own papers of the minutes of their transactions torn, and the ink-glass broken. When all this had some time ceased, the said Giles proposed to enter first into these rooms, and, in presence of the Commissioners, of whom he received the key, he opened the door and entered the room, their honours following him. He there found the wood strewed about the room, the chairs tossed about and broken, the papers torn, and the ink-glass broken over them all as they had heard, yet no footsteps appeared of any person whatever being there, nor had the doors ever been opened to admit or let out any persons since their honours were last there. It was therefore voted, *nem. con.*, that the person who did this mischief could have entered no other way than at the keyhole of the said doors.

"In the night following this same day, the said Giles, and two other of the Commissioners' servants, as they were in bed in the same room with their honours, had their bed's feet lifted up so much higher than their heads, that they expected to have their necks broken, and then they were let fall at once with such violence as shook them up from the bed to a good distance; and this was repeated many times, their honours being amazed spectators of it. In the morning the bedsteads were found cracked and broken, and the said Giles and his fellows declared they were sore to the bones with the tossing and jolting of the beds.

"October 19th. As they were all in bed together, the candles were all blown out together with a sulphurous smell, and instantly many trenchers of wood were hurled about the room; and one of them putting his head above the clothes, had not less than six thrown at him, which wounded him very grievously. In the morning the trenchers were all found lying about the room, and were observed to be the same they had eaten on the day before, none being found remaining in the pantry.

"October 20th. This night the candles were put out as before; the curtains of the bed in which their honours lay, were drawn to and fro many times with great violence: their honours received many cruel blows, and were much bruised beside, with eight great pewter dishes, and three dozen wooden trenchers, which were thrown on the bed, and afterwards heard rolling about the room.

"Many times also this night they heard the forcible falling of many fagots by their bedside, but in the morning no fagots were found there, no dishes or trenchers were there seen either; and the aforesaid Giles attests, that by their different arranging in the pantry, they had assuredly been taken thence, and after put there again.

"October 21st. The keeper of their ordinary and his bitch lay with them: This night they had no disturbance.

"October 22d. Candles put out as before. They had the said bitch with them again, but were not by that protected; the bitch set up a very piteous cry; the clothes of their beds were all pulled off, and the bricks, without any wind, were thrown off the chimney tops into the midst.

"October 24th. The candles put out as before. They thought all the wood of the King's Oak was violently thrown down by their bedsides; they counted sixty-four fagots that fell with great violence, and some hit and shook the bed,—but in the morning none were found there, nor the door of the room opened in which the said fagots were.

"October 25th. The candles put out as before. The curtains of the bed in the drawing-room were many times forcibly drawn; the wood thrown out as before; a terrible crack like thunder was heard; and one of the servants, running to see if his master was not killed, found, at his return, three dozen trenchers laid smoothly upon his bed under the quilt.

"October 26th. The beds were shaken as before; the windows seemed all broken to pieces, and glass fell in vast quantities all about the room. In the morning they found the windows all whole, but the floor strewed with broken glass, which they gathered and laid by.

"October 29th. At midnight candles went out as before; something walked majestically through the room, and opened and shut the window; great stones were thrown violently into the room, some whereof fell on the beds, others on the floor; and at about a quarter after one, a noise was heard as of forty cannon discharged together, and again repeated at about eight minutes' distance. This alarmed and raised all the neighbourhood, who, coming into their honours' room, gathered up the great stones, fourscore in number, many of them like common pebbles and boulters, and laid them by, where they are to be seen to this day, at a corner of the adjoining field. This noise, like the discharge of cannon, was heard throughout the country for sixteen miles round. During these noises, which were heard in both rooms together, both the Commissioners and their servants gave one another over for lost, and cried out for help; and Giles Sharp, snatching up a sword, had wellnigh killed one of their honours, taking him for the spirit as he came in his shirt into the room. While they were together, the noise was continued, and part of the tiling of the house, and all the windows of an upper room, were taken away with it.

"October 30th. Something walked into the chamber, treading like a bear; it walked many times about, then threw the warming-pan violently upon the floor, and so bruised it that it was spoiled. Vast quantities of glass were now thrown about the room, and vast numbers of great stones and horses' bones were thrown in; these were all found in the morning, and the floors, beds, and walls were all much damaged by the violence they were thrown in.

"November 1st. Candles were placed in all parts of the room, and a great fire made. At midnight, the candles all yet burning, a noise like the burst of a cannon was heard in the room, and the burning billets were tossed all over the room and about the beds; and had not their honours called in Giles and his fellows, the house had assuredly been burnt. An hour after the candles went out, as usual, the crack of many cannon was heard, and many pailfuls of green stinking water were thrown on their honours in bed; great stones were also thrown in as before, the bed-curtains and bedsteads torn and broken: the windows were now all really broken, and the whole neighbourhood alarmed with the noises; nay, the very rabbit-stealers that were abroad that night in the warren, were so frightened at the dismal thundering, that they fled for fear, and left their ferrets behind them.

"One of their honours this night spoke, and in the name of God asked what it was, and why it disturbed them so? No answer was given to this; but the noise ceased for a while, when the spirit came again, and as they all agreed, brought with it seven devils worse than itself. One of the servants now lighted a large candle, and set it in the doorway between the two chambers, to see what passed; and as he* watched it, he plainly saw a hoof striking the

* Probably this part was also played by Sharp, who was the regular ghost-seer of the party.

candle and candlestick into the middle of the room, and afterwards making three scrapes over the snuff of the candle, to scrape it out. Upon this, the same person was so bold as to draw a sword; but he had scarce got it out, when he perceived another invisible hand had hold of it too, and pulled with him for it, and at last prevailing, struck him so violently on the head with the pommel, that he fell down for dead with the blow. At this instant was heard another burst like the discharge of the broadside of a ship of war, and at about a minute or two's distance each, no less than nineteen more such; these shook the house so violently, that they expected every moment it would fall upon their heads. The neighbours on this were all alarmed, and, running to the house, they all joined in prayer and psalm-singing, during which the noise still continued in the other rooms, and the discharge of cannon without, though nobody was there."

Dr Plot concludes his relation of this memorable event* with observing, that, though tricks have often been played in affairs of this kind, many of these things are not reconcilable with juggling; such as, 1st, The loud noises beyond the power of man to make, without instruments which were not there; 2d, The tearing and breaking of the beds; 3d, The throwing about the fire; 4th, The hoof treading out the candle; and, 5th, The striving for the sword, and the blow the man received from the pommel of it.

To show how great men are sometimes deceived, we may recur to a tract, entitled "*The Secret History of the Good Devil of Woodstock*", in which we find it, under the author's own hand, that he, Joseph Collins, commonly called Funny Joe, was himself this very devil;—that, under the feigned name of Giles Sharp, he hired himself as a servant to the Commissioners;— that by the help of two friends—an unknown trapdoor in the ceiling of the bedchamber, and a pound of common gunpowder—he played all these extraordinary tricks by himself;—that his fellow-servants, whom he had introduced on purpose to assist him, had lifted up their own beds; and that the candles were contrived, by a common trick of gunpowder, to be extinguished at a certain time.

The dog who began the farce was, as Joe swore, no dog at all, but truly a bitch, who had shortly before whelped in that room, and made all this disturbance in seeking for her puppies; and which, when she had served his purpose, he (Joe Sharp, or Collins,) let out, and then looked for. The story of the hoof and sword he himself bore witness to, and was never suspected as to the truth of them, though mere fictions. By the trapdoor his friends let down

* In his Natural History of Oxfordshire.

stones, fagots, glass, water, &c., which they either left there, or drew up again, as best suited his purpose; and by this way let themselves in and out, without opening the doors, or going through the keyholes; and all the noises described, he declares he made by placing quantities of white gunpowder over pieces of burning charcoal, on plates of tin, which, as they melted, exploded with a violent noise.

I am very happy in having an opportunity of setting history right about these remarkable events, and would not have the reader disbelieve my author's account of them, from his naming either white gunpowder exploding when melted, or his making the earth about the pot take fire of its own accord; since, however improbable these accounts may appear to some readers, and whatever secrets they might be in Joe's time, they are now well known in chemistry. As to the last, there needs only to mix an equal quantity of iron filings, finely powdered, and powder of pure brimstone, and make them into a paste with fair water. This paste, when it hath lain together about twenty-six hours, will of itself take fire, and burn all the sulphur away with a blue flame and a great stink. For the others, what he calls white gunpowder, is plainly the thundering powder called by our chemists *pulvis fulminans.* It is composed of three parts of saltpetre, two parts of pearl ashes or salt of tartar, and one part of flower of brimstone, mixed together and beat to a fine powder; a small quantity of this held on the point of a knife over a candle, will not go off till it melt, and then it gives a report like that of a pistol; and this he might easily dispose of in larger quantities, so as to make it explode of itself, while he, the said Joe, was with his masters.

Such is the explanation of the ghostly adventures of Woodstock, as transferred by Mr Hone from the pages of the old tract, termed the Authentic Memoirs of the memorable Joseph Collins of Oxford, whose courage and loyalty were the only wizards which conjured up those strange and surprising apparitions and works of spirits, which passed as so unquestionable in the eyes of the Parliamentary Commissioners, of Dr Plot, and other authors of credit. The *pulvis fulminans*, the secret principle he made use of, is now known to every apothecary's apprentice.

If my memory be not treacherous, the actor of these wonders made use of his skill in fireworks upon the following remarkable occasion. The Commissioners had not, in their zeal for the public service, overlooked their own private interests, and a deed was drawn up upon parchment, recording the share and nature of the advantages which they privately agreed to concede to each other; at the same time they were, it seems, loath to intrust to any one of their number the keeping of a document in which all were equally concerned.

They hid the written agreement within a flower-pot, in which a shrub concealed it from the eyes of any chance spectator. But the rumour of the apparitions having gone abroad, curiosity drew many of the neighbours to Woodstock, and some in particular, to whom the knowledge of this agreement would have afforded matter of scandal. As the Commissioners received these guests in the saloon where the flower-pot was placed, a match was suddenly set to some fireworks placed there by Sharp the secretary. The flower-pot burst to pieces with the concussion, or was prepared so as to explode of itself, and the contract of the Commissioners, bearing testimony to their private roguery, was thrown into the midst of the visitors assembled. If I have recollected this incident accurately, for it is more than forty years since I perused the tract, it is probable, that in omitting it from the novel, I may also have passed over, from want of memory, other matters which might have made an essential addition to the story. Nothing, indeed, is more certain, than that incidents which are real, preserve an infinite advantage in works of this nature over such as are fictitious. The tree, however, must remain where it has fallen.

Having occasion to be in London in October 1831, I made some researches in the British Museum, and in that rich collection, with the kind assistance of the Keepers, who manage it with so much credit to themselves and advantage to the public, I recovered two original pamphlets, which contain a full account of the phenomena at Woodstock in 1649.* The first is a satirical poem, published in that year, which plainly shows that the legend was current among the people in the very shape in which it was afterwards made public. I have not found the explanation of Joe Collins, which, as mentioned by Mr Hone, resolves the whole into confederacy. It might, however, be recovered by a stricter search than I had leisure for. In the meantime, it may be observed, that neither the name of Joe Collins, nor Sharp, occurs among the *dramatis personæ* given in these tracts, published when he might have been endangered by any thing which directed suspicion towards him, at least in 1649, and perhaps might have exposed him to danger even in 1660, from the malice of a powerful though defeated faction.

1*st August*, 1832.

* See Appendix.

APPENDIX No. I

THE WOODSTOCK SCUFFLE;

OR,

MOST DREADFUL APPARITIONS THAT WERE LATELY SEENE IN THE MANNOR-HOUSE OF WOODSTOCK, NEERE OXFORD, TO THE GREAT TERROR AND WONDERFUL AMAZEMENT OF ALL THERE THAT DID BEHOLD THEM.

[Printed in the year 1649. 4to.]

IT were a wonder if one writes,
And not of wonders and strange sights;
For ev'ry where such things affrights
Poore people,

That men are ev'n at their wits' end;
God judgments ev'ry where doth send,
And yet we don't our lives amend,
But tipple,

And sweare, and lie, and cheat, and whore,
Because the world shall drown no more,
As if no judgments were in store
But water;

But by the stories which I tell,
You'll heare of terrors come from hell,
And fires, and shapes most terrible
For matter.

It is not long since that a child
Spake from the ground in a large field,
And made the people almost wild
That heard it,

Of which there is a printed book,
Wherein each man the truth may look;
If children speak, the matter's took
For verdict.

But this is stranger than that voice,
The wonder's greater, and the noyse;
And things appeare to men, not boyes,
At *Woodstock;*

Where *Rosamond* had once a bower,
To keep her from Queen *Elinour*,
And had escap' d her poys'nous power
By good-luck,

But fate had otherwise decreed,
And *Woodstock* Mannor saw a deed,
Which is in *Hollinshed* or *Speed*
Chro-nicled;

But neither *Hollinshed* nor *Stow*,
Nor no historians such things show,
Though in them wonders we well know
Are pickled;

For nothing else is history
But pickle of antiquity,
Where things are kept in memory
From stincking,

Which otherwaies would have lain dead,
As in oblivion buried,
Which now you may call into head
With thinking.

The dreadful story, which is true,
And now committed unto view,
By better pen, had it its due,
Should see light;

But I, contented, doe indite,
Not things of wit, but things of right;
You can't expect that things that fright
Should delight.

O hearken, therefore, harke and shake!
My very pen and hand doth quake!
While I the true relation make
O' th' wonder,

Which hath long time, and still appeares
Unto the State's Commissioners,
And puts them in their beds to feares
From under.

They come, good men, imploi'd by th' State,
To sell the lands of Charles the late,
And there they lay, and long did waite
For chapmen.

You may have easy pen'worths, woods,
Lands, ven'son, householdstuf, and goods;
They little thought of dogs that wou'd
There snap-men.

But when they'd sup'd, and fully fed,
They set up remnants and to bed,
Where scarce they had laid down a head
To slumber,

But that their beds were heav'd on high;
They thought some dog under did lie,
And meant i' th' chamber (fie, fie, fie,)
To scumber.

Some thought the cunning cur did mean
To eat their mutton (which was lean)
Reserv'd for breakfast, for the men
Were thrifty;

And up one rises in his shirt,
Intending the slie cur to hurt,
And forty thrusts made at him for't,
Or fifty.

But empty came his sword again,
He found hee thrust but all in vain;
The mutton safe, hee went amain
To's fellow.

And now (assured all was well)
The bed again began to swell,
The men were frighted, and did smell
O' th' yellow.

From heaving, now the cloaths it pluckt;
The men, for feare, together stuck,
And in their sweat each other duck't.
They wished

A thousand times that it were day;
'Tis sure the divell! Let us pray.
They pray'd amain; and, as they say,
So pissed.

Approach of day did cleere the doubt,
For all devotions were run out,
They now waxt strong and something stout;
One peaked

Under the bed, but nought was there;
He view'd the chamber ev'ry where,
Nothing apear'd but what, for feare,
They leaked.

Their stomachs then return'd apace,
They found the mutton in the place,
And fell unto it with a grace.
They laughed

Each at the other's pannick feare,
And each his bed-fellow did jeere,
And having sent for ale and beere,
They quaffed.

And then abroad the summons went,
Who'll buy king's-land o' th' Parliament?
A paper-book contein'd the rent,
Which lay there;

That did contein the severall farmes,
Quit-rents, knight services, and armes;
But that they came not in by swarmes
To pay there.

Night doth invite to bed again,
The grand Commissioners were lain,
But then the thing did heave amain,
It busled,

And with great clamor fill'd their eares,
The noyse was doubled, and their feares;
Nothing was standing but their haires,
They nuzled.

Oft were the blankets pul'd, the sheete
Was closely twin'd betwixt their feete,
It seems the spirit was discreete
And civill.

Which makes the poore Commissioners
Feare they shall get but small arreares,
And that there's yet for cavaliers
One divell.

They cast about what best to doe;
Next day they would to wise men goe,
To neighb'ring towns som cours to know;
For schollars

Come not to Woodstock, as before,
And Allen's dead as a nayle-doore,
And so's old John (eclep'd the poore)
His follower;

Rake Oxford o're, there's not a man
That rayse or lay a spirit can,
Or use the circle, or the wand,
Or conjure;

Or can say (Boh!) unto a divell,
Or to a goose that is uncivill,
Nor where Keimbolton purg'd out evill,
'Tis sin sure.

There were two villages hard by,
With teachers of presbytery,
Who knew the house was hidiously
Be-pestred;

But 'lasse! their new divinity
Is not so deep, or not so high;
Their witts doe (as their meanes did) lie
Sequestred;

But Master Joffman was the wight
Which was to exorcise the spright;
Hee'll preach and pray you day and night
At pleasure.

And by that painfull gainfull trade,
He hath himselfe full wealthy made;
Great store of guilt he hath, 'tis said,
And treasure.

But no intreaty of his friends
Could get him to the house of fiends,
Hee came not over for such ends
From Dutch-land;

But worse divinity hee brought,
And hath us reformation taught,
And, with our money, he hath bought
Him much land.

Had the old parsons preached still,
The div'l should nev'r have had his wil;
But those that had or art or skill
Are outed;

And those to whom the pow'r was giv'n
Of driving spirits, are out-driv'n;
Their colledges dispos'd, and livings,
To grout-heads.

There was a justice who did boast,
Hee had as great a gift almost,
Who did desire him to accost
This evill;

But hee would not employ his gifts,
But found out many sleights and shifts;
Hee had no prayers, nor no snifts,
For th' divell.

Some other way they cast about,
These brought him in, they throw not out;
A woman, great with child, will do't;
They got one.

And she i' th' room that night must lie;
But when the thing about did flie,
And broke the windows furiously,
And hot one

Of the contractors o're the head,
Who lay securely in his bed,
The woman, shee-affrighted, fled
While they piss'd;

And now they lay the cause on her,
That e're that night the thing did stir,
Because her selfe and grandfather
Were Papists;

They must he barnes-regenerate,
(A *Hans en Kelder* of the state,
Which was in reformation gatt,)
They said, which

Doth make the divell stand in awe,
Pull in his hornes, his hoof, his claw;
But having none, they did in draw
A spay'd bitch:

But in the night there was such worke,
The spirit swaggered like a Turke;
The bitch had spi'd where it did lurke,
And howled

In such a wofull manner, that
Their very hearts went pit a pat;
The poor spay'd bitch did you know what
And fouled

The stately rooms, where kings once lay;
But the contractors shew'd the way.
But mark what now I tell you, pray,
'Tis worth it.

That book I told you of before,
Wherein were tenants written store,
A register for many more
Not forth yet;

That very book, as it did lie,
Took of a flame, no mortall eye
Seeing one jot of fire thereby,
Or taper;

For all the candles about flew,
And those that burned, burned blew,
Never kept soldiers such a doe
Or vaper.

The book thus burnt and none knew how,
The poore contractors made a vow
To worke no more; this spoil'd their plow
In that place.

Some other part o' th' house they'll find
To which the devill hath no mind,
But hee, it seems, is not inclin'd
With that grace;

But other prancks it play'd elsewhere.
An oake there was stood many a yeere,
Of goodly growth as any where,
Was hewn down,

Which into fewell-wood was cut,
And some into a wood-pile put,
But it was hurled all about
And thrown down.

In sundry formes it doth appeare;
Now like a grasping claw to teare;
Now like a dog, anon a beare,
It tumbles;

And all the windows battered are,
No man the quarter enter dare;
All men (except the glasier)
Doe grumble.

Once in the likenesse of a woman,
Of stature much above the common,
'Twas seene, but spak a word to no man,
And vanish'd.

'Tis thought the ghost of some good wife
Whose husband was depriv'd of life,
Her children cheated, land in strife
She banist.

No man can tell the cause of these
So wondrous dreadfull outrages;
Yet if upon your sinne you please
To discant,

You'le find our actions out doe hell's;
O wring your hands and cease the bells,
Repentance must, or nothing else
Appease can't.

APPENDIX No. II

THE

JUST DEVIL OF WOODSTOCK;

OR,

A TRUE NARRATIVE OF THE SEVERAL APPARITIONS, THE FRIGHTS AND PUNISHMENTS, INFLICTED UPON THE RUMPISH COMMISSIONERS SENT THITHER TO SURVEY THE MANNORS AND HOUSES BELONGING TO HIS MAJESTIE.

[London, printed in the year 1660. 4to.]

The names of the persons in the ensuing Narrative mentioned, with others.

Captain Cockaine.
Captain Hart.
Captain Crook.
Captain Carelesse.
Captain Roe.
Mr Crook, the Lawyer.
Mr Browne, the Surveyor.
Their three Servants.
Their Ordinary-keeper, and others.
The Gate-keeper, with the Wife and Servants.

Besides many more, who each night heard the noise; as Sir Gerrard

Fleetwood and his lady, with his family; Mr Hyans, with his family, and several others, who lodged in the outer courts; and during the three last nights, the inhabitants of Woodstock town, and other neighbor villages.

And there were many more, both divines and others, who came out of the country, and from Oxford, to see the glass and stones, and other stuffe, the devil had brought, wherewith to beat out the Commissioners; the marks upon some walls remain, and many, this to testifie.

THE PREFACE TO THE ENSUING NARRATIVE.

Since it hath pleased the Almighty God, out of his infinite mercy, so to make us happy, by restoring of our native King to us, and us unto our native liberty through him, that now the good may say, *magna temporum felicitas ubi sentire quæ velis, et dicere licet quæ sentias*, we cannot but esteem ourselves engaged, in the highest of degrees, to render unto him the highest thanks we can express, although, surpris'd with joy, we become as lost in the performance; when gladness and admiration strikes us silent, as we look back upon the precipiece of our late condition, and those miraculous deliverances beyond expression; freed from the slavery, and those desperate perils, we dayly lived in fear of, during the tyrannical times of that detestable usurper, Oliver Cromwell; he who had raked up such judges, as would wrest the most innocent language into high treason, when he had the cruel conscience to take away our lives, upon no other ground of justice or reason, (the stones of London streets would rise to witness it, if all their citizens were silent.) And with these judges had such councillors, as could advise him unto worse, which will less want of witness. For should the many auditors be silent, the press (as God would have it) hath given it us in print, where one of them (and his conscience-keeper, too,) speaks out, What shall we do with these men? saith he; *Æger intemperans crudelem facit medicum, et immedicabile vulnus ense recidendum.* Who these men are that should be brought to such Scicilian vespers, the former page sets forth—those which conceit *Vtopias*, and have their day-dreams of the return of, I know not what golden age, with the old line. What usage, when such a privy councillor had power, could he expect, who then had published this narrative? This much so plainly shows the devil himself dislikit their doings, (so much more bad were they than he would have them be,) severer sure then was the devil to their Commissioners at Woodstock; for he warned them, with dreadful noises, to drive them from their work. This councillor, without more ado, would have all who retain'd conceits of allegiance to their soveraign, to be absolutely cut off by the usurper's sword. A sad sentence for a loyal party, to a lawful king. But Heaven is always just; the party is repriv'd, and do acknowledge the hand of God in it, as is rightly applyed, and as justly sensible of their deliverance: in that the foundation which this councillor saith was already so well laid, is now turned up, and what he calls day-dreams are come to passe. That old line which (as with him) there seemed *aliquid divini* to the contrary, is now restored. And that rock which, as he saith, the prelates and all their adherents, nay, and their master and supporter, too, with all his posterity, have split themselves upon, is nowhere to be heard. And that posterity are safely arrived in their ports, and masters of that mighty navy, their enemies so much encreased to keep them out with. The eldest sits upon the throne, his place by birthright and descent,

Pacatumque regit Patriis virtutibus orbem;

upon which throne long may he sit, and reign in peace, that by his just government, the enemies of ours, the true Protestant Church, of that glorious martyr, our late sovereign, and of his royal posterity, may be either absolutely converted, or utterly confounded.

If any shall now ask thee why this narrative was not sooner published, as neerer to the times wherein the things were acted, he hath the reason for it in the former lines; which will the more clearly appear unto his apprehension, if he shall perpend how much cruelty is requisite to the maintenance of rebellion; and how great care is necessary in the supporters, to obviate and divert the smallest things that tend to the unblinding of the people; so that it needs will follow, that they must have accounted this amongst the great obstructions to their sales of his majestie's lands, the devil not joining with them in the security; and greater to the pulling down the royal pallaces, when their chapmen should conceit the devil would haunt them in their houses, for building with so ill got materials; as no doubt but that he hath, so numerous and confident are the relations made of the same, though scarce any so totally remarkeable as this, (if it be not that others have been more concealed,) in regard of the strange circumstances as long continuances, but especially the number of the persons together, to whom all things were so visibly both seen and done, so that surely it exceeds any other; for the devils thus manifesting themselves, it appears evidently that there are such things as devils, to persecute the wicked in this world as in the next.

Now, if to these were added the diverse reall phantasms seen at

White-Hall in Cromwell's times, which caused him to keep such nightly guards in and about his bedchamber, and yet so oft to change his lodgings; if those things done at Saint James', where the devil so joal'd the centinels against the sides of the queen's chappell doors, that some of them fell sick upon it, and others, not taking warning by it, kild one outright, whom they buried in the place, and all other such dreadful things, those that inhabited the royal houses have been affrighted with; and if to these were likewise added, a relation of all those regicides and their abettors the devil hath entred into, as he did the Gadarenes' swine, with so many more of them who hath fallen mad, and dyed in hideous forms of such distractions,—that which hath been of this within these 12 last years in England, (should all of this nature our chronicles do tell, with all the superstitious monks have writ, be put together,) would make the greater volume, and of more strange occurrents.

And now as to the penman of this narrative, know that he was a divine, and at the time of those things acted, which are here related, the minister and schoolmaster of Woodstock; a person learned and discreet, not byassed with factious humours, his name Widows, who each day put in writing what he heard from their mouthes, (and such things as they told to have befallen them the night before,) therein keeping to their own words; and, never thinking that what he had writ should happen to be made publick, gave it no better dress to set it forth. And because to do it now shall not be construed to change the story, the reader hath it here accordingly exposed.

The Just Devil of Woodstock.

The 16th day of *October*, in the year of our Lord, 1649, the commissioners for surveying and valuing his majestie's mannor house, parks, woods, deer, demesnes, and all things thereunto belonging, by name Captain Crook, Captain Hart, Captain Cockaine, Captain Carelesse, and Captain Roe, their messenger, with Mr Browne, their secretary, and two or three servants, went from Woodstock town, (where they had lain some nights before,) and took up their lodgings in his majestie's house after this manner:—The bedchamber and withdrawing-room they both lodged in and made their kitchen; the presence-chamber their room for dispatch of their business with all comers; of the council-hall their brewhouse, as of the dining-room their wood-house, where they laid in the clefts of that antient standard in the High-Park, for many ages beyond memory known by the name of the King's Oak, which they had chosen out, and caused to be dug up by the roots.

October 17th. About the middle of the night, these new guests were first awaked by a knocking at the presence-chamber door, which they also conceived did open, and something to enter, which came through the room, and also walkt about that room with a heavy step during half an hour, then crept under the bed where Captain Hart and Captain Carelesse lay, where it did seem (as it were) to bite and gnaw the mat and bed-coards, as if it would tear and rend the feather beds; which having done a while, then would heave a while, and rest; then heave them up again in the bed more high than it did before, sometime on the one side, sometime on the other, as if it had tried which captain was heaviest. Thus having heaved some half an hour, from thence it walkt out and went under the servants' bed, and did the like to them; hence it walkt into a withdrawing-room, and there did the same to all who lodged there. Thus, having welcomed them for more than two hours' space, it walkt out as it came in, and shut the outer door again, but with a clap of some mightie force. These guests were in a sweat all this while, but out of it falling into a sleep again, it became morning first before they spake their minds; then would they have it to be a dog, yet they described it more to the likeness of a great bear; so fell to the examining under the beds, where, finding only the mats scracht, but the bed-coards whole, and the quarter of beef which lay on the floor untoucht, they entertained other thoughts.

October 18th. They were all awaked as the night before, and now conceived that they heard all the great clefts of the King's Oak brought into the presence-chamber, and there thumpt down, and after roul about the room; they could hear their chairs and stools tost from one side of the room unto the other, and then (as it were) altogether josled. Thus having done an hour together, it walkt into the withdrawing-room, where lodged the two captains, the secretary, and two servants: here stopt the thing a while, as if it did take breath, but raised a hideous one, then walkt into the bed-chamber, where lay those as before, and under the bed it went, where it did heave and heave again, that now they in bed were put to catch hold upon the bed-posts, and sometimes one of the other, to prevent their being tumbled out upon the ground; then coming out as from under the bed, and taking hold upon the bed-posts, it would shake the whole bed, almost as if a cradle rocked. Thus having done here for half an hour, it went into the withdrawing-room, where first it came and stood at the bed's feet, and heaving up the bed's feet, flopt down again a while, until at last it heaved the feet so high that those in bed thought to have been set upon their heads; and having thus for two hours entertained them, went out as in the night before, but with a great noise.

October 19th. This night they awaked not until the midst of the night; they perceived the room to shake with something that walkt about the bedchamber, which having done so a while, it walkt into a withdrawing room, where it took up a brasse warming pan, and returning with it into the bedchamber, therein made so loud a noise, in these captains' own words, it was as loud and scurvie as a ring of five untuned bells rung backward; but the captains, not to seem afraid, next day made mirth of what had passed, and jested at the devil in the pan.

October 20th. These captains and their company, still lodging as before, were awakened in this night, with some things flying about the rooms, and out of one room into the other, as thrown with some great force. Captain Hart, being in a slumber, was taken by the shoulder and shaked until he did sit up in his bed, thinking that it had been one of his fellows, when suddenly he was taken on the pate with a trencher, that it made him shrink down into the bed-clothes, and all of them in both rooms kept their heads at least within their sheets, so fiercely did three dozen of trenchers fly about the rooms; yet Captain Hart ventured again to peep out to see what was the matter, and what it was that threw, but then the trenchers came so fast and neer about his ears, that he was fain quickly to couch again. In the morning they found all their trenchers, pots, and spits, upon and about their beds, and all such things as were of common use scattered about the rooms. This night there were also, in several parts of the room and outer rooms, such noises of beating at doors, and on the walls, as if that several smiths had been at work; and yet our captains shrunk not from their work, but went on in that, and lodged as they had done before.

October 21st. About midnight they heard great knocking at every door; after a while the doors flew open, and into the withdrawing-room entered something as of a mighty proportion, the figure of it they knew not how to describe. This walkt awhile about the room shaking the floor at every step, then came it up close to the bedside, where lay Captains Crook and Carelesse; and after a little pause, as it were, the bed-curtains, both at sides and feet, were drawn up and down slowly, then faster again for a quarter of an hour, then from end to end as fast as imagination can fancie the running of the rings, then shaked it the beds, as if the joints thereof had crackt; then walkt the thing into the bedchamber, and so plaied with those beds there; then took up eight peuter dishes, and bouled them about the room and over the servants in the truckle-beds; then sometimes were the dishes taken up and thrown crosse the high beds and against the walls, and so much battered; but there were more dishes wherein was meat in the same room, that were not at all removed. During this, in the presence-chamber there was stranger noise of weightie things thrown down, and, as they supposed, the clefts of the King's Oak did roul about the room, yet at the wonted hour went away, and left them to take rest such as they could.

October 22d. Hath mist of being set down; the officers, imployed in their work farther off, came not that day to Woodstock.

October 23d. Those that lodged in the withdrawing-room, in the midst of the night were awakened with the cracking of fire, as if it had been with thorns and sparks of fire burning, whereupon they supposed that the bedchamber had taken fire, and listning to it farther, they heard their fellows in bed sadly groan, which gave them to suppose they might be suffocated; wherefore they called upon their servants to make all possible haste to help them. When the two servants were come in, they found all asleep, and so brought back word, but that there were no bed-clothes upon them; wherefore they were sent back to cover them, and to stir up and mend the fire. When the servants had covered them and were come to the chimney, in the corners they found their wearing apparrel, boots, and stockings, but they had no sooner toucht the embers, when the firebrands flew about their ears so fast, that away ran they into the other room for the shelter of their cover-lids; then after them walkt something that stampt about the room as if it had been exceeding angry, and likewise threw about the trenchers, platters, and all such things in the room—after two hours went out, yet stampt again over their heads.

October 24th. They lodged all abroad.

October 25th. This afternoon was come unto them Mr Richard Crook the lawyer, brother to Captain Crook, and now deputy-steward of the mannor unto Captain Parsons and Major Butler, who had put out Mr Hyans, his majestie's officer. To entertain this new guest, the Commissioners caused a very great fire to be made, of neer the chimney-full of wood of the King's oak, and he was lodged in the withdrawing-room with his brother, and his servant in the same room. About the midst of the night a wonderful knocking was heard, and into the room something did rush, which coming to the chimney-side, dasht out the fire as with the stamp of some prodigious foot, then threw down such weighty stuffe, what ere it was, (they took it to be the residue of the clefts and roots of the King's Oak,) close by the bed-side, that the house and bed shook with it. Captain Cockaine and his fellow arose, and took their swords to go unto the Crooks. The noise ceased at their rising, so that they came to the door and called. The two brothers, though fully awaked, and heard them call, were so amazed, that they made no answer until Captain Cockaine had recovered the boldness to call very loud, and came unto the bedside; then faintly first, after some more assurance, they came to understand one another, and comforted the lawyer. Whilst this was thus, no noise was heard, which made them think the time was past of that night's troubles, so that, after some little conference, they applied themselves to take some rest. When Captain Cockaine was come to his own bed, which he had left open, he found it closely covered, which he much wondered at; but turning the clothes down, and opening it to get in, he found the lower sheet strewed over with trenchers. Their whole three dozens of trenchers were orderly disposed between his sheets, which he and his fellow endeavouring to cast out, such noise arose about the room, that they were glad to get into bed with some of the trenchers. The noise lasted a full half hour after this. This entertainment so ill did like the lawyer, and being not so well studied in the point as to resolve this the devil's law case, that he next day resolved to be gone; but having not dispatcht all that he came for, profit and perswasions prevailed with him to stay the other hearing, so that he lodged as he did the night before.

October 26th. This night each room was better furnished with fire and candle than before; yet about twelve at night came something in that dasht all out, then did walk about the room, making a noise, not to be set forth by the comparison with any other thing; sometimes came it to the bedsides and drew the curtains to and fro, then twerle them, then walk about again, and return to the bed-posts, shake them with all the bed, so that they in bed were put to hold one upon the other, then walk about the room again, and come to the servants' bed, and gnaw and scratch the wainscot head, and shake altogether in that room; at the time of this being in doing, they in the bedchamber heard such strange dropping down from the roof of the room, that they supposed 'twas like the fall of money by the sound. Captain Cockaine, not frighted with so small a noise, (and lying near the chimney,) stept out, and made shift to light a candle, by the light of which he perceived the room strewed over with broken glass, green, and some as it were pieces of broken bottles; he had not long been considering what it was, when suddenly his candle was hit out, and glass flew about the room, that he made haste to the protection of the coverlets; the noise of thundering rose more hideous then at any time before; yet, at a certain time, all vanisht into calmness. The morning after was the glass about the room, which the maid that was to make clean the rooms swept up into a corner, and many came to see it. But Mr Richard Crook would stay no longer, yet as he stopt, going through Woodstock town, he was there heard to say, that he would not lodge amongst them another night for a fee of L.500.

October 27th. The Commissioners had not yet done their work, wherefore they must stay; and being all men of the sword, they must not seem afraid to encounter with any thing, though it be the devil; therefore, with pistols charged, and drawn swords laied by their bedsides, they applied themselves to take some rest, when something in the midst of night, so opened and shut the window casements with such claps, that it awakened all that slept; some of them peeping out to look what was the matter with the windows, stones flew about the rooms as if hurled with many hands; some hit the walls, and some the beds' heads close above the pillows, the dints of which were then, and yet (it is conceived) are to be seen, thus sometime throwing stones, and sometime making thundering noise; for two hours space it ceast, and all was quiet till the morn. After their rising, and the maid come in to make the fire, they looked about the rooms; they found fourscore stones brought in that night, and going to lay them together in the corner where the glass (before mentioned) had been swept up, they found that every piece of glass had been carried away that night. Many people came next day to see the stones, and all observed that they were not of such kind of stones as are naturall in the countrey thereabout; with these were noise like claps of thunder, or report of cannon planted against the rooms, heard by all that lodged in the outer courts, to their astonishment, and at Woodstock town, taken to be thunder.

October 28th. This night, both strange and differing noise from the former first awakened Captain Hart, who lodged in the bed-chamber, who, hearing Roe and Brown to groan, called out to Cokaine and Crook to come and help them, for Hart could not now stir himself; Cockaine would faine have answered, but he could not, or look about; something, he thought, stopt both his breath and held down his eye-lids. Amazed thus, he struggles and kickt about, till he had awaked Captain Crook, who, half asleep, grew very angry at his kicks, and multiplied words, it grew to an appointment in the field; but this fully recovered Cockaine to remember that Captain Hart had called for help, wherefore to them he ran in the other room, whom he found sadly groaning, where, scraping in the chimney, he both found a candle and fire to light it; but had not gone two steps, when something blew the candle out, and threw him in the chair by the bedside, when presently cried out Captain Carelesse, with a most pittiful voice, "Come hither, O come hither, brother Cockaine, the thing's gone of me." Cockaine, scarce yet himself, helpt to set him up in his bed, and after Captain Hart, and having scarce done that to them, and also to the other two, they heard Captain Crook crying out, as if something had been killing him. Cockaine snatcht up the sword that lay by their bed, and ran into the room to save Crook, but was in much more likelyhood to kill him, for at his coming, the thing that pressed Crook went of him, at which Crook started out of his bed, whom Cockaine thought a spirit, made at him, at which Crook cried out, "Lord help, Lord save me;" Cockaine let fall his hand, and Crook, embracing Cockaine, desired his reconcilement, giving him many thanks for his deliverance. Then rose they all and came together, discoursed sometimes godly and sometimes praied, for all this while was there such stamping over the roof of the house, as if 1000 horse had there been trotting; this night all the stones brought in the night before, and laid up in the withdrawing-room, were all carried again away by that which brought them in, which at the wonted time left of, and, as it were, went out, and so away.

October 29th. Their businesse having now received so much forwardnesse as to be neer dispatcht, they encouraged one the other, and resolved to try further; therefore, they provided more lights and fires, and further, for their assistance, prevailed with their ordinary keeper to lodge amongst them, and bring his mastive bitch; and it was so this night with them, that they had no disturbance at all.

October 30th. So well they had past the night before, that this night they went to bed, confident and carelesse; untill about twelve of the clock, something knockt at the door as with a smith's great hammer, but with such force as if it had cleft the door; then ent'red something like a bear, but seem'd to swell more big, and walkt about the room, and out of one room into the other, treading so heavily, as the floare had not been strong enough to bear it. When it came into the bedchamber, it dasht against the beds' heads some kind of glass vessell, that broke in sundry pieces, and sometimes would take up those pieces, and hurle them about the room, and into the other room; and when it did not hurle the glasse at their heads, it did strike upon the tables, as if many smiths, with their greatest hammers, had been laying on as upon an anvil; sometimes it thumpt against the walls as if it would beat a hole through; then upon their heads, such stamping, as if the roof of the house were beating down upon their heads; and having done thus, during the space (as was conjectured) of two hours, it ceased and vanished, but with a more fierce shutting of the doors than at any time before.

In the morning they found the pieces of glass about the room, and observed, that it was much differing from that glasse brought in three nights before, this being of a much thicker substance, which severall persons which came in carried away some pieces of. The Commissioners were in debate of lodging there no more; but all their businesse was not done, and some of them were so conceited as to believe, and to attribute the rest they enjoyed, the night before this last, unto the mastive bitch; wherefore, they resolved to get more company, and the mastive bitch, and try another night.

October 31*st.* This night, the fires and lights prepared, the ordinary keeper and his bitch, with another man perswaded by him, they all took their beds and fell asleep. But about twelve at night, such rapping was on all sides of them, that it wakened all of them; as the doors did seem to open, the mastive bitch fell fearfully a yelling, and presently ran fiercely into the bed to them in the truckle-bed; as the thing came by the table, it struck so fierce a blow on that, as that it made the frame to crack, then took the warming-pan from off the table, and stroke it against the walls with so much force as that it was beat flat together, lid and bottom. Now were they hit as they lay covered over head and ears within the bed-clothes. Captain Carelesse was taken a sound blow on the head with the shoulder-blade bone of a dead horse, (before they had been but thrown at, when they peept up, and mist;) Browne had a shrewed blow on the leg with the backbone, and another on the head, and every one of them felt severall blows of bones and stones through the bed-clothes, for now these things were thrown as from an angry hand that meant further mischief; the stones flew in at window as shot out of a gun, nor was the bursts lesse (as from without) than of a cannon, and all the windows broken down. Now as the hurling of the things did cease, and the thing walkt up and down, Captain Cockaine and Hart cried out, In the name of the Father, Son, and Holy Ghost, what are you? What would you have? What have we done that you disturb us thus? No voice replied, (as the Captains said, yet some of their servants have said otherwise,) and the noise ceast. Hereupon Captain Hart and Cockaine rose, who lay in the bedchamber, renewed the fire and lights, and one great candle, in a candlestick, they placed in the door, that might be seen by them in both the rooms. No sooner were they got to bed, but the noise arose on all sides more loud and hideous than at any time before, insomuch as (to use the Captain's own words) it returned and brought seven devils worse than itself; and presently they saw the candle and candlestick in the passage of the door, dasht up to the roof of the room, by a kick of the hinder parts of a horse, and after with the hoof trode out the snuff, and so dasht out the fire in the chimnies. As this was done, there fell, as from the sieling, upon them in the truckle-beds, such quantities of water, as if it had been poured out of buckets, which stunk worse than any earthly stink could make; and as this was in doing, something crept under the high beds, tost them up to the roof of the house, with the Commissioners in them, until the testers of the beds were beaten down upon, and the bedsted-frames broke under them; and here some pause being made, they all, as if with one consent, started up, and ran down the stairs until they came into the Councel Hall, where two sate up a-brewing, but now were fallen asleep; those they scared much with wakening of them, having been much perplext before with the strange noise, which commonly was taken by them abroad for thunder, sometimes for rumbling wind. Here the Captains and their company got fire and candle, and every one carrying something of either, they returned into the Presence-Chamber, where some applied themselves to make the fire, whilst others fell to prayers, and having got some clothes about them, they spent the residue of the night in singing psalms and prayers; during which, no noise was in that room, but most hideously round about, as at some distance.

It should have been told before, how that when Captain Hart first rose this night, (who lay in the bedchamber next the fire,) he found their book of valuations crosse the embers smoaking, which he snacht up and cast upon the table there, which the night before was left upon the table in the presence amongst their other papers: this book was in the morning found a handful burnt, and had burnt the table where it lay; Browne the clerk said, he would not for a 100 and a 100*l.* that it had been burnt a handful further.

This night it happened that there were six cony-stealers, who were come with their nets and ferrets to the cony-burrows by Rosamond's Well; but with the noise this night from the Mannor-house, they were so terrified, that like men distracted away they ran, and left their haies all ready pitched, ready up, and the ferrets in the cony-burrows.

Now the Commissioners, more sensible of their danger, considered more seriously of their safety, and agreed to go and confer with Mr Hoffman, the minister of Wotton, (a man not of the meanest note for life or learning, by some esteemed more high,) to desire his advice, together with his company and prayers. Mr Hoffman held it too high a point to resolve on suddenly and by himself, wherefore desired time to consider upon it, which being agreed unto, he forthwith rode to Mr Jenkinson and Mr Wheat, the two next Justices of Peace, to try what warrant they could give him for it. They both (as 'tis said from themselves) encouraged him to be assisting to the Commissioners, according to his calling.

But certain it is, that when they came to fetch him to go with them, Mr Hoffman answered, that he would not lodge there one night for 500*l.*, and being asked to pray with them, he held up his hands and said, that he would not meddle upon any terms.

Mr Hoffman refusing to undertake the quarrel, the Commissioners held it not safe to lodge where they had been thus entertained any longer, but caused all things to be removed into the chambers over the gatehouse, where they staid but one night, and what rest they enjoyed there, we have but an uncertain relation of, for they went away early the next morning; but if it may be held fit to set down what hath been delivered by the report of others, they were also the same night much affrighted with dreadful apparitions, but observing that these passages spread much in discourse, to be also in particulars taken notice of, and that the nature of it made not for their cause, they agreed to the concealing of things for the future; yet this is well-known and certain, that the gate-keeper's wife was in so strange an agony in her bed, and in her bedchamber such noise, (whilst her husband was above with the Commissioners,) that two maids in the next room to her, durst not venture to assist her, but affrighted ran out to call company, and their master, and found the woman (at their coming in) gasping for breath: and the next day said, that she saw and suffered that, which for all the world she would not be hired to again.

From Woodstock the Commissioners removed unto Euelme, and some of them returned to Woodstock the Sunday se'nnight after, (the book of Valuations wanting something that was for haste left imperfect,) but lodged not in any of those rooms where they had lain before, and yet were not unvisited (as they confess themselves) by the devil, whom they called their nightly guest; Captain Crook came not untill Tuesday night, and how he sped that night the gate-keeper's wife can tell if she dareth, but what she hath whispered to her gossips, shall not be made a part of this our narrative, nor many more particulars which have fallen from the Commissioners themselves and their servants to other persons; they are all or most of them alive, and may add to it when they please, and surely have not a better way to be revenged of him who troubled them, then according to the proverb, tell truth and shame the devil.

There remains this observation to be added, that on a Wednesday morning all these officers went away; and that since then diverse persons of severall qualities, have lodged often and sometimes long in the same rooms, both in the presence, withdrawing-room, and bedchamber belonging unto his sacred Majesty; yet none have had the least disturbance, or heard the smallest noise, for which the cause was not as ordinary as apparent, except the Commissioners and their company, who came in order to the alienating and pulling down the house, which is wellnigh performed.

A SHORT SURVEY OF WOODSTOCK, NOT TAKEN BY ANY OF THE BEFORE-MENTIONED COMMISSIONERS.*

The noble seat, called Woodstock, is one of the ancient honours belonging to the crown. Severall mannors owe suite and service to the place; but the custom of the countrey giving it but the title of a mannor, we shall erre with them to be the better understood.

The mannor-house hath been a large fabrick, and accounted amongst his majestie's standing houses, because there was alwaies kept a standing furniture. This great house was built by King Henry the First, but ampleyfied with the gatehouse and outsides of the outer-court, by King Henry the Seventh, the stables by King James.

About a bow-shoot from the gate south-west, remain foundation signs of that structure, erected by King Henry the Second, for the security of Lady Rosamond, daughter of Walter Lord Clifford, which some poets have compared to the Dedalian labyrinth, but the form and circuit both of the place and ruins shew it to have been a house and of one pile, perhaps of strength, according to the fashion of those times, and probably was fitted with secret places of recess, and avenues to hide or convey away such persons as were not willing to be found if narrowly sought after. About the midst of the place ariseth a spring, called at present Rosamond's Well; it is but shallow, and shews to have been paved and walled about, likely contrived for the use of them within the house, when it should be of danger to go out.

A quarter of a mile distant from the King's house, is seated Woodstock town, new and old. This new Woodstock did arise by some buildings which Henry the Second gave leave to be erected, (as received by tradition,) at the suite of the Lady Rosamond, for the use of out-servants upon the wastes of the mannor of Bladon, where is the mother church; this is a hamlet belonging to it, though encreased to a market town by the advantage of the Court residing sometime near, which of late years they have been sensible of the want of; this town was made a corporation in the 11th year of Henry the Sixth, by charter, with power to send two burgesses to parliament or not, as they will themselves.

* This Survey of Woodstock is appended to the preceding pamphlet.

Old Woodstock is seated on the west side of the brook, named Glyme, which also runneth through the park; the town consists not of above four or five houses, but it is to be conceived that it hath been much larger, (but very anciently so,) for in some old law historians there is mention of the assize at Woodstock, for a law made in a Micelgemote (the name of parliaments before the coming of the Norman) in the days of King Ethelred.

And in like manner, that thereabout was a king's house, if not in the same place where Henry the First built the late standing pile before his; for in such days those great councils were commonly held in the King's palaces. Some of those lands have belonged to the orders of the Knights Templers, there being records which call them, *Terras quas Rex excambiavit cum Templariis.*

But now this late large mannor-house is in a manner almost turned into heaps of rubbish; some seven or eight rooms left for the accommodation of a tenant that should rent the King's meadows, (of those who had no power to let them,) with several high uncovered walls standing, the prodigious spectacles of malice unto monarchy, which ruines still bear semblance of their state, and yet aspire, in spight of envy or of weather, to shew, What kings do build, subjects may sometimes shake, but utterly can never overthrow.

That part of the park called the High-park, hath been lately subdivided by Sir Arthur Haselrig, to make pastures for his breed of colts, and other parts plowed up. Of the whole saith Roffus Warwicensis, in MS. Hen. I. p. 122, *Fecit iste Rex Parcum de Woodstock, cum Palatio infra prædictum Parcum, qui Parcus erat primus Parcus Angliæ, et continet in circuitu septem Miliaria; constructus erat Anno* 14 *hujus Regis, aut parum post.* Without the Park the King's demesne woods were, it cannot well be said now are, the timber being all sold off, and underwoods so cropt and spoiled by that beast the Lord Munson, and other greedy cattle, that they are hardly recoverable. Beyond which lieth Stonefield, and other mannors that hold of Woodstock, with other woods, that have been aliened by former kings, but with reservation of liberty for his majestie's deer, and other beasts of forrest, to harbour in at pleasure, as in due place is to be shewed.

END OF APPENDIX

Notes to Woodstock

3.35 (Preface) of that persuasion It is hardly necessary to say, unless to some readers of very literal capacity, that Doctor Rochecliffe and his manuscripts are alike apocryphal.
9.17 (Ch. 1) knife or sword This custom among the Puritans is mentioned often in old plays, and among others in the Widow of Watling Street.
9.39 (Ch. 1) sapless pottage See a curious vindication of this indecent simile here for the Common Prayer, in Note, end of Chapter.
13.33 (Ch. 1) modern events
VINDICATION OF THE BOOK OF COMMON PRAYER, AGAINST THE CONTUMELIOUS SLANDERS OF THE FANATIC PARTY TERMING IT PORRIDGE. The author of this singular and rare tract indulges in the allegorical style, till he fairly hunts down the allegory.

"But as for what you call porridge, who hatched the name I know not, neither is it worth the enquiring after, for I hold porridge good food. It is better to a sick man than meat, for a sick man will sooner eat pottage than meat. Pottage will digest with him when meat will not; pottage will nourish the blood, fill the veins, run into every part of a man, make him warmer; so will these prayers do, set our soul and body in a heat, warm our devotion, work fervency in us, lift up our soul to God. For there be herbs of God's own planting in our pottage as you call it—the Ten Commandments, dainty herbs to season any pottage in the world; there is the Lord's Prayer, and that is a most sweet pot-herb cannot be denied; then there is also David's herbs, his prayers and psalms, helps to make our pottage relish well; the psalm of the blessed Virgin, a good pot-herb. Though they be, as some term them, *cock-crowed* pottage, yet they are as sweet, as good, as dainty, and as fresh, as they were at the first. The sun hath not made them sour with its heat, neither hath the cold water taken away their vigour and strength. Compare them with the Scriptures, and see if they be not as well seasoned and crumbed. If you find any thing in them that is either too salt, too fresh, or too bitter, that herb shall be taken out and better put in, if it can be got, or none. And as in kitchen pottage there are many good herbs, so there is likewise in this church pottage, as you call it. For first, there is in kitchen pottage good water to make them; so, on the contrary, in the other pottage there is the water of life. 2. There is salt to season them; so in the other is a prayer of grace to season their hearts. 3. There is oatmeal to nourish the body, in the other is the bread of life. 4. There is thyme in them to relish them, and it is very wholesome—in the other is the wholesome exhortation not to harden our heart while it is called to-day. This relisheth well. 5. There is a small onion to give a taste—in the other is a good herb, called Lord have mercy on us. These, and many other holy herbs are contained in it, all boiling in the heart of man, will make as good pottage as the world can afford, especially if you use these herbs for digestion,—the herb repentance, the herb grace, the herb faith, the herb love, the herb hope, the herb good works, the herb piety, the herb zeal, the herb fervency, the herb ardency, the herb constancy, with many more of this nature, most excellent for digestion." *Ohe! jam satis.* In this manner the learned divine hunts his metaphor at a very cold scent, through a pamphlet of six mortal quarto pages.

29.27 (Ch. 2) a Ragged Robin The keeper's followers in the New Forest are called in popular language ragged Robins.

47.25 (Ch. 4) approaching deposition The story occurs, I think, in Froissart's Chronicles.

183.41 (Ch. 16) as David for Jonathan

Dr Michael Hudson. Michael Hudson, the *plain-dealing* chaplain of King Charles I., resembled, in his loyalty to that unfortunate monarch, the fictitious character of Doctor Rochecliffe; and the circumstances of his death were copied in the narrative of the Presbyterian's account of the slaughter of his school-fellow;—he was chosen by Charles I., along with John Ashburnham, as his guide and attendant, when he adopted the ill-advised resolution of surrendering his person to the Scots army.

He was taken prisoner by the Parliament, remained long in their custody, and was treated with great severity. He made his escape for about a week in 1647; was retaken, and again escaped in 1648, and, heading an insurrection of cavaliers, seized on a strong moated house in Northamptonshire, called Woodcroft House. He gained the place without resistance; and there are among Peck's Desiderata Curiosa several accounts of his death, among which we shall transcribe that of Bishop Kenneth, as the most correct and concise:—

"I have been on the spot," saith his Lordship, "and made all possible enquiries, and find that the relation given by Mr Wood may be a little rectified and supplied.

"Mr Hudson and his beaten party did not fly to Woodcroft, but had quietly taken possession of it, and held it for a garrison, with a good party of horse, who made a stout defence, and frequent sallies, against a party of the Parliament at Stamford, till the colonel commanding them sent a stronger detachment, under a captain, his own kinsman, who was shot from the house, upon which the colonel himself came up to renew the attack, and demand surrendry, and brought them to capitulate upon terms of safe quarter. But the colonel, in base revenge, commanded that they should not spare that rogue Hudson. Upon which Hudson fought his way up to the leads; and when he saw they were pushing in upon him, threw himself over the battlements (another account says, he caught hold of a spout or outstone), and hung by the hands as intending to fall into the moat beneath, till they cut off his wrists and let him drop, and then ran down to hunt him in the water, where they found him paddling with his stumps, and barbarously knocked him on the head."—PECK'S *Desiderata Curiosa*, Book ix.

Other accounts mention he was refused the poor charity of coming to die on land, by one Egborough, servant to Mr Spinks, the intruder into the parsonage. A man called Walker, a chandler or grocer, cut out the tongue of the unfortunate divine, and showed it as a trophy through the country. But it was remarked, with vindictive satisfaction, that Egborough was killed by the bursting of his own gun; and that Walker, obliged to abandon his trade through poverty, became a scorned mendicant.

For some time a grave was not vouchsafed to the remains of this brave and loyal divine, till one of the other party said, "Since he is dead, let him be buried."

221.33 (Ch. 19) the Old Troop

CANNIBALISM IMPUTED TO THE CAVALIERS. The terrors preceding the civil wars, which agitated the public mind, rendered the grossest and most exaggerated falsehoods current amongst the people. When Charles I. appointed Sir Thomas Lunsford to the situation of Lord Lieutenant of the Tower, the celebrated John Lillburn takes to himself the credit of exciting the public hatred against this officer and Lord Digby, as pitiless bravoes of the most bloody-minded description, from whom the people were to expect nothing but bloodshed and massacre. Of Sir Thomas Lunsford, in particular, it was reported that his favourite food was the flesh of children, and he was painted like an ogre in the act of cutting a child into steaks and broiling them. The colonel fell at the siege of Bristol in 1643, but the same calumny pursued his remains, and the credulous multitude were told,

> The post who came from Coventry,
> Riding in a red rocket,
> Did tidings tell how Lunsford fell,
> *A child's hand in his pocket.*

Many allusions to this report, as well as to the credulity of those who believed it, may be found in the satires and lampoons of the time, although, says Dr Grey, Lunsford was a man of great sobriety, industry, and courage. Butler says, that the preachers

> Made children with their tones to run for't,
> As bad as Bloodybones or Lunsford.

But this extraordinary report is chiefly insisted upon in a comedy called the *Old Troop*, written by John Lacy, the comedian. The scene is laid during the civil wars of England, and the persons of the drama are chiefly those who were in arms for the king. They are represented as plundering the country without mercy, which Lacy might draw from the life, having, in fact, begun his career as a lieutenant of cavalry, in the service of Charles I. The troopers find the peasants loath to surrender to them their provisions, on which, in order to compel them, they pretend to be in earnest in the purpose of eating the children. A scene of coarse but humorous comedy is then introduced, which Dean Swift had not, perhaps, forgotten, when he recommended the eating of the children of the poor as a mode of relieving the distresses of their parents.

"*Lieutenant.* Second me, and I'll make them bring out all they have, I warrant you. Do but talk as if we used to eat children.—Why, look you, good woman, we do believe you are poor, so we'll make a shift with our old diet—you have children in the town?

"*Woman.* Why do you ask, sir?

"*Lieutenant.* Only have two or three to supper. Flea-flint, you have the best way of cooking children.

"*Flea-flint.* I can powder them to make you taste your liquor. I am never without a dried child's tongue or ham.

"*Woman.* O! bless me!

"*Flea-flint.* Mine's but the ordinary way; but Ferret-farm is the man; he makes you the savouriest pie of a child chaldron that was ever eat.

"*Lieutenant.* A plague! all the world cannot cook a child like Mr Raggou, [a French cook or messman to the troop, and the buffoon of the piece.]

"*Raggou.* Begar me think so; for vat was me bred in the King of Mogol's kitchen? dere we kill twenty shild of a day. Take you one shild by both his two heels, and put his head between your two knees, and take your knife and slice off all buttocks,—so fashion; begar, that make a de best Scots collop in de world.

"*Lieutenant.* Ah, he makes the best pottage of a child's head and feet, however; but you must boil it with bacon—Woman, you must get bacon.

"*Woman.* O Lud—yes, sir!

"*Ferret.* And then it must be very young.

"*Lieutenant.* Yes, yes.—Good woman, it must be a fine squab child, of half a year old—a man child, dost hear?"—*The Old Troop, Act III.*

After a good deal more to this purpose, the villagers determine to carry forth their sheep, poultry, &c. to save their children. In the meantime, the Cavaliers are in some danger of being cross-bit, as they then called it; that is, caught in their own snare. A woman enters, who announces herself thus:—

"*Woman.* By your leave, your good worships, I have made bold to bring you in some provisions.

"*Ferret.* Provisions! where, where is this provision?

"*Woman.* Here, if it please you, I have brought you a couple of fine fleshy children.

"*Cornet.* Was ever such a horrid woman! what shall we do?

"*Woman.* Truly, gentlemen, they are fine squab children: shall I turn them up?—they have the bravest brawn and buttocks.

"*Lieutenant.* No, no; but, woman, art thou not troubled to part with thy children?

"*Woman.* Alas, sir, they are none of mine, they are only nurse children.

"*Lieutenant.* What a beast is this!—whose children are they?

"*Woman.* A Londoner's that owes me for a year's nursing; I hope they'll prove excellent meat; they are twins too.

"*Raggou.* Aha, but! but begar we never eat no twin shild, the law forbid that."—*Ibidem.*

In this manner the Cavaliers escape from the embarrassing consequences of their own stratagem, which, as the reader will perceive, has been made use of in the preceding chapter.

252.7 (Ch. 22) many a long year since This melancholy story may be found in the *Guardian.* An intrigue of Lord Sackville, afterwards Earl of Dorset, was the cause of the fatal duel.

275.2 (Ch. 24) men of genius This gossiping tale is to be found in the variorum Shakspeare. D'Avenant did not much mind throwing out hints in which he sacrificed his mother's character to his desire of being held a descendant from the admirable Shakspeare.

275.7 (Ch. 24) the bard's countenance D'Avenant actually wanted the nose, the foundation of many a jest of the day.

314.14 (Ch. 27) a Lindabrides A sort of court name for a female of no reputation.

344.41 (Ch. 30) a younger brother of Lord Falkland's
PATRICK CAREY. "You do not know Patrick Carey," says King

Charles in the novel; and, what is more singular, Patrick Carey has had two editors, each unknown alike to the other, except by name only. In 1771, Mr John Murray published Carey's poems, from a collection said to be in the hands of the Rev. Mr Pierrepoint Cromp. A very probable conjecture is stated, that the author was only known to private friendship. As late as 1819, the Author of Waverley, ignorant of the edition of 1771, published a second quarto from an elaborate manuscript, though in bad order, apparently the autograph of the first. Of Carey, the second editor, like the first, only knew the name and the spirit of his verses. He has since been enabled to ascertain, that the poetic cavalier was a younger brother of the celebrated Lucius Lord Carey, who fell at the battle of Newbery, and escaped the researches of Horace Walpole, to whose list of noble authors he would have been an important addition. So completely has the fame of the great Lord Falkland eclipsed that of his brothers, that this brother Patrick has been overlooked even by genealogists.

345.8 (Ch. 30) goes merrily round The original song of Carey bears Wykeham, instead of Woodstock, for the locality. The verses are full of the bacchanalian spirit of the time.

353.9 (Ch. 31) delivered the feather
SIGNAL OF DANGER BY THE TOKEN OF A FEATHER. On a particular occasion, a lady, suspecting, by the passage of a body of guards through her estate, that the arrest of her neighbour, Patrick Home of Polwarth, afterwards first Earl of Marchmont, was designed, sent him a feather by a shepherd boy, whom she dared not trust with a more explicit message. Danger sharpens the intellect, and this hint was the commencement of those romantic adventures which gave Grizzel Lady Murray the materials from which she compiled her account of her grandfather's escape, published by Mr Thomas Thomson, Deputy Register of Scotland. The anecdote of the feather does not occur there, but the author has often heard it from the late Lady Diana Scott, the lineal descendant and representative of Patrick Earl of Marchmont.

398.9 (Ch. 35) upper-leather Such a song, or something very like it, may be found in Ramsay's Tea-table Miscellany, among the wild slips of minstrelsy which are there collected.

417.8 (Ch. 37) Sir Henry Lee of Ditchley It may interest some readers to know, that Bevis, the gallant hound, one of the most handsome and active of the ancient Highland deer-hounds, had his prototype in a dog called Maida, the gift of the late Chief of Glengarry to the author. A beautiful sketch of him was made by Edwin Landseer, and afterwards engraved. I cannot suppress the avowal of some personal vanity when I mention, that a friend, going through Munich, picked up a common snuffbox, such as are sold for one franc, on which was displayed the form of this veteran favourite, simply marked as Der Lieblingshund von Walter Scott. Mr Landseer's painting is at Blair-Adam, the property of my venerable friend, the Right Honourable Lord Chief Commissioner Adam.

CHRONICLES OF THE CANONGATE

Editorial Note

Chronicles of the Canongate is unlike any other work in the Waverley Novels series in that it is not a novel but a collection of three tales in a narrative framework, beginning with an autobiographical narrative by its fictitious author-editor, Chrystal Croftangry. It appeared in two volumes in 1827, and was the first work of fiction which Scott published after the financial crash of 1826. This circumstance lies behind the presence of two unexpected names in the first edition: the 'Introduction' by this hitherto anonymous author is signed 'Walter Scott', and on the title-page the publisher appears as, not 'Archibald Constable and Co.', but 'Cadell and Co.'

Chronicles of the Canongate does not appear as one work in the Magnum. As the second volume of *Woodstock* was to appear as Volume 40, it was clear that *Chronicles* should start in Magnum Volume 41. *Chronicles* was, however, too long for one volume, and too short for two. To solve that problem the work was divided between two Magnum volumes. The contents of the first volume of *Chronicles*, containing the 'Introduction', Chrystal Croftangry's narrative, 'The Highland Widow', and 'The Two Drovers', appeared in Volume 41 of the Magnum, followed by three pieces first published in *The Keepsake for 1829*, which appeared at the end of 1828 (see *The Shorter Fiction*, EEWN 24, 143–63). The longer tale which occupies the second volume of the first edition of *Chronicles*, 'The Surgeon's Daughter', appeared in the final volume, Volume 48, after Scott's short last published novel, *Castle Dangerous*. Volume 41 was published in October 1832, the month after Scott's death, and Volume 48 concluded the series in May 1833. This arrangement had the advantage of placing all Scott's shorter works in the same volume; but by dividing *Chronicles of the*

Canongate between two volumes which were not adjacent in the Magnum it had the effect of undermining the identity of the work.

Chronicles of the Canongate had not appeared in a collected edition before an interleaved copy was called for: as a consequence Cadell had interleaved copies made of first edition volumes. What follows is puzzling as these volumes were not kept with the earlier interleaved volumes, now in the National Library of Scotland, and what has survived is scattered. It may be observed that the volumes of *Chronicles of the Canongate* which are bound uniformly with the Interleaved Set in the National Library of Scotland (MSS 23033 and 23039) are neither interleaved nor annotated. They are volumes of the octavo edition of the continuation of *Tales and Romances of the Author of Waverley*, published in 1833 (Vols 8 and 14) and are two out of nine volumes of Scott's later work bound up by Cadell to complete the series: see *Scott's Interleaved Waverley Novels*, ed. Iain Gordon Brown (Aberdeen, 1987).

The manuscript material which has been traced for the Magnum *Chronicles* is as follows:

Volume 41

1] New introductory material for *Chronicles of the Canongate* took the form of Scott's writing additional passages to appear before and after the first-edition 'Introduction'. The manuscripts of these additions are in the Huntington Library, San Marino, California, pressmarks HM 979 and HM 1982. The first mentioned, which contains the new opening, is on six leaves and is in the hand of William Laidlaw, presumably to Scott's dictation. Scott's hand is visible in the manuscript making revisions and additions, and in the last six lines of the text. MS HM 1982 contains the passage to be added at the end of the 'Introduction' and is in Scott's hand, on three leaves.

2] Scott's interleaved copy of Volume 1 of *Chronicles of the Canongate* has not been found. Another annotated volume has been identified by Professor Jane Millgate, however, in the Berg Collection of the New York Public Library. (For what is known of the previous history of this volume see Jane Millgate, *Scott's Last Edition* (Edinburgh, 1987), 58.) It is annotated not in Scott's hand but in that of his son-in-law John Gibson Lockhart. The volume is dated 1828, but the leaves are those of the first edition (1827): see EEWN 20, 325–26. It is not interleaved, and gives no evidence that it ever has been. Lockhart apparently worked on an uncut copy, and the binder who supplied the red and gilt morocco binding avoided cropping the manuscript entries by folding in the margins which contained them. This volume clearly contributed to the preparation of the

Magnum; but it is not Scott's interleaved copy, nor does it give evidence of being used as printer's copy.

Volume 48

1] The manuscripts of Scott's short Magnum 'Introduction' to 'The Surgeon's Daughter', and the source narrative by Joseph Train which follows it in Volume 48 have not been traced. There are, however, manuscripts of two other attempts at an Introduction to this work which were not used: Huntington MS HM 1982, cited above, ends on ff. 2–3 with a paragraph about 'The Surgeon's Daughter'; and William Baker and J. H. Alexander have drawn attention to a draft Introduction to the tale in Scott's hand, in the Walpole Collection at King's School, Canterbury, in a volume of 'Scott Papers, Reviews &c.', ff. 85–86 ('Scott Items in the Walpole Collection at King's School, Canterbury', *The Scott Newsletter*, 6 (Spring 1985), 6).

2] Scott's interleaved copy of Volume 2 of *Chronicles of the Canongate*, containing 'The Surgeon's Daughter', survives in the Houghton Library, Harvard, press-mark HEW 9.10.3. It is in boards, and is a rare example of an interleaved volume in the state in which Scott worked on it. It contains 189 interleaves, of which nineteen contain manuscript material in the hand of Scott and occasionally Lockhart. Some inky finger-prints may indicate that the volume was used as printer's copy.

On 23 April 1830 Scott wrote a letter to Cadell about the progress of the Magnum, adding 'I have still seven volumes of the novels besides Anne of Geierstein and Chronicles of the Canongate of which I would be the better of interleavd copy from you' (*Letters*, 11.340). Although Cadell took the interleaved copies to Abbotsford in May 1830, it is not until half way through 1831 that we have clear evidence of Scott's preparing *Chronicles of the Canongate* for the Magnum. As Scott had suffered two strokes in 1830, and a third on 17 April 1831, arrangements were being made for him to spend the coming winter in Italy. On 29 July 1831 Cadell, busy with *Woodstock*, wrote to Scott, 'The Printing & Stereotyping gets on so fast that I will in a very short time have to ask you for the Chronicles of the Canongate' (MS 3918, f. 206r). Scott showed Cadell the Introduction to *Chronicles* at Abbotsford on 9 August 1831 (MS 21043, f. 109v), and on the following day Scott wrote: 'I send you 1st vol Chronicles of the Canongate which may go to press with the General preface to which you promised to add an Appendix consisting of the account of what passd at the meeting for the theatrical fund Another Introduction specially ⟨may⟩ belonging to the tale of the

Highland widow to come in at page 146 so that the whole may proceed without interruption' (MS 15980, f. 146r). Scott's reference to the 'General Preface' here shows confusion between the item with that title written for the first volume of the Magnum series, and the newly extended 'Introduction' to *Chronicles of the Canongate*. On 12 August he wrote again to Cadell: 'I send the second Introduction to the first Volume chronicles of the Canongate . . . the Introduction comes in at the ⟨fel⟩ fly page after ⟨vol⟩ the General prolegomena' (MS 15980, f. 148r). The 'second Introduction' is the manuscript of the new material, containing information about 'The Highland Widow', which appeared in the Magnum after the first-edition 'Introduction', confusingly referred to by Scott this time as 'General prolegomena'. On the same day Cadell wrote to Scott: 'I have your parcel with the first Volume of the Chronicles for Press—there is a capital account of the theatrical dinner in Ballantynes paper which I have directed to be set up as an appendix —the proof will come to you in due course' (MS 3919, ff. 39av–39br). On 5 September Cadell recorded another meeting with Scott: 'I alluded to the arrangement of the Chronicles of the Canongate 1st Series, and that I should require a short Introduction to the Surgeons Daughter—on which he took up his pen and said he would soon give me that or any thing I wanted *in a minute*— he wrote about a page and a half & gave it to me—and said it was an Introduction to that tale . . . when I talked to him of my plan of lengthening out the first Chronicles he did not appear to follow me' (MS 21043, ff. 112v–113r). Scott either did not understand, or did not remember Cadell's plans for *Chronicles*, a failure pointing towards the need for help with the tasks to come, which would in due course be given by Lockhart. Lockhart and his family had been staying at Chiefswood on the Abbotsford estate since May 1831, making it possible that he contributed something towards *Chronicles* before Scott left Scotland on his journey to the Mediterranean on 23 September 1831.

The new materials added when *Chronicles of the Canongate* appeared in the Magnum are as follows:

Introduction: Scott added new material to the beginning and the end of the first-edition 'Introduction'. The new material is on pp. [iv]–vii and xxx–xxxiv, signed on p. xxxiv, 'W. S. / Abbotsford, *Aug.* 15, 1831.' The manuscripts of this material, cited above, were substantially rewritten before publication in the Magnum. Certainly, Scott's versions are sometimes confusing and repetitive, but one can regret such thorough rewriting, especially in the case of the concluding section, which is more coherent than Laidlaw's copy of the opening. For this reason the present volume prints Scott's additions to his first-edition 'Introduction' both as they appeared in the Magnum and in a lightly edited version of the texts of the two manuscripts in the Huntington Library. In addition, a diplomatic transcript of these manuscripts is given in the Emendation List. There is no evidence as to who rewrote the manuscripts so rigorously; but Lockhart is the most likely candidate.

Huntington MS HM 1982, which concludes the Magnum 'Introduction', gives some account of the sources of all three of the tales in *Chronicles*. As 'The Surgeon's Daughter' was destined for Volume 48 the paragraph on the third tale (see below) was omitted in Magnum 41. The fact that this omission is replaced in the Magnum by a short paragraph concluding with a personal mention of Wordsworth is evidence that Scott engaged with this part of the 'Introduction' after his initial draft. He probably added the footnote on the history of the Keith family which ends with a faulty date claiming that Mrs Murray Keith 'died not long before the date of this Introduction, (1831.)' In fact Mrs Murray Keith's dates are 1736–1818; but recalling his debt to her may have made her death seem a nearer loss. The Magnum adds eight notes to the first-edition 'Introduction', updating the material in it. Four of the notes, those making particular personal reference, add the date of writing, August 1831. Scott was surely the source for these, although there is no external evidence. The final addition to the 'Introduction', made in collaboration with Cadell, was a lengthy Appendix describing the Theatrical Fund Dinner at which Scott found himself acknowledging the authorship of the Waverley Novels, taken from the *Edinburgh Weekly Journal* of Wednesday, 28 February 1827.

Chrystal Croftangry's narrative: The Magnum adds seven footnotes and seven endnotes to this narrative. (In the first edition this narrative was untitled, as were the chapters within it. In the Magnum, however, each chapter has been given a title with Chrystal Croftangry's name in it, and the entire narrative has the running-title 'Introductory'. The New York Public Library manuscript gives the chapter headings, and instructions that they be printed in black letter, making it almost certain that they were Lockhart's work.) The Magnum retains two first-edition footnotes and expands another, which refers the reader to 'Chambers's Traditions of Edinburgh', into the Magnum endnote entitled 'Iron Rasp' (495).

The Highland Widow: the Magnum adds six footnotes (in addition to the seven first-edition footnotes) and four endnotes.

The Two Drovers: this tale had no notes in the first edition, and gains only one endnote in the Magnum.

We are left with the question: what contribution, if any, did Scott make to the new notes to the works in *Chronicles* appearing in Magnum Volume 41, after the 'Introduction' and its Appendix? We lack the interleaved volume in which Scott would have written such notes, and have only a volume annotated by Lockhart to start from. The first observation is that all the notes in these works (except the first endnote, on 'Holyrood') are indicated in Lockhart's annotated volume, and only one is suggested there which was not followed up. Short footnotes are usually complete; longer endnotes are indicated by a few words and then the direction to a printed source for a passage to quote. The writing is Lockhart's throughout. On the other hand there are a few notes which seem to imply Scott's involvement. One wonders how Lockhart could have contrived alone the pleasing reference to an Irish song: 'This is a line from a very pathetic ballad which I heard sung by one of the young ladies of Edgeworthstown in 1825. I do not know that it has ever been printed' (501). That note is in 'The Highland Widow', and there are other notes, especially in that part of the annotated volume, which raise the possibility that Lockhart sometimes worked in proximity to Scott: 'Give a note on the Masssacre of Glencoe— perhaps from *Dalrymples Memoirs*' (compare 501–03). Was Lockhart noting something Scott had said, or making a suggestion for Scott to consider? Scott is the one who knew intimately all the books cited, and Lockhart often seems to be writing down titles, gained perhaps orally, to be looked out later. This would require that the annotated volume was written before Scott left for Italy. The result, however, is quotations which readers have felt to be disproportionately long for the tales they illustrate.

The Surgeon's Daughter: For its appearance in Volume 48 of the Magnum Scott added a two page 'Introduction', signed 'W. S. / Abbotsford, *Sept.* 1831', which is probably that written for Cadell on 5 September. There also survive two earlier drafts of introductory material. One is the unused passage mentioned above in Huntington MS HM 1982, and printed on 486–90 below. The other has been described by J. H. Alexander in these words: 'This is an incoherent beginning to an introduction which was never used. It is barely legible, but appears to discuss the difficult advancement of impoverished men of medicine in Scotland. It makes use of the quotation from Johnson which stands as the first motto in the published novel. Scott is beginning to discuss his sources when he breaks off' ('Scott Items', 6). The Magnum 'Surgeon's Daughter' has nine footnotes, in addition to four first-edition footnotes. It has no endnotes and most of the footnotes are very short. All of the nine new notes are in the Houghton manuscript, seven in Scott's handwriting, and two in Lockhart's. The latter two are the note on Robert Walker in square brackets (509), and that on the same page, signed 'C.C.', which has been created, on Lockhart's instruction, out of the last paragraph of Chapter 13 in the first edition. It is noticeable that there are no notes containing long quotations from historical sources in 'The Surgeon's Daughter'. It is possible that even Scott, who certainly had intimate knowledge from boyhood of at least one Indian history, could not easily recall suitable passages for quotation, and Lockhart could not fill the gap.

There are four Magnum illustrations for this title. The frontispiece to Volume 41 (MAG0081 / TB348.41) was designed by Alexander Fraser, the elder, and engraved by James Mitchell. It depicts Hamish being handcuffed by soldiers, Elspat having fainted on the floor (EEWN 20, 110: the caption reads simply 'THE HIGHLAND WIDOW.'). The title-page vignette (MAG0082 / TB348.41) was designed by Alexander Fraser, the elder, and engraved by William Henry Watt. It depicts Hamish succumbing to the effect of the sleeping potion administered by his mother, who looks over him (EEWN 20, 97.5–8: 'I must obey you mother . . . instantly was fast asleep.'). The frontispiece to Volume 48 (MAG0095 / TB348.48) was designed by Frank Stone and engraved by Joseph Goodyear. It depicts Zilla de Monçada in her apartment, under the protection of Gordon Gray, being apprehended by her father and an armed King's Messenger, with Gray and Mr Lawford intervening (EEWN 20, 171.30–41: the legend is simply 'THE SURGEON'S DAUGHTER.'). The title-page vignette (MAG0096 / TB348.48) was designed by Frank Stone and engraved by Robert Graves. It depicts Menie Gray stepping out into the garden or parterre in the residence where she is held at Calcutta (EEWN 20, 256.18–23 (abridged): '"It may be out of it . . . into the garden.').

A. Fraser. J. Mitchell.

THE HIGHLAND WIDOW.

WAVERLEY NOVELS.

VOL. XLI.

THE HIGHLAND WIDOW.

"I must obey you mother, I feel I must, said Hamish inarticulately; "but call me when the moon rises." He sat down on the bed-reclined back, and almost instantly was fast asleep.

PRINTED FOR ROBERT CADELL, EDINBURGH,
AND WHITTAKER & C° LONDON.
1832.

Frank Stone. J. Goodyear.

THE SURGEON'S DAUGHTER.

WAVERLEY NOVELS.

VOL. XLVIII.

THE SURGEON'S DAUGHTER.

Frank Stone. Robt Graves.

"It may be out of it, then, madam", answered Miss Grey, As she spoke this she stepped through a lattice-door into the garden.

PRINTED FOR ROBERT CADELL, EDINBURGH.
AND WHITTAKER & Co LONDON.
1833.

Introduction to Chronicles of the Canongate

THE preceding volume of this Collection concluded the last of the pieces originally published under the *nominis umbra* of The Author of Waverley; and the circumstances which rendered it impossible for the writer to continue longer in the possession of his *incognito*, were communicated in 1827, in the Introduction to the first series of Chronicles of the Canongate,—consisting (besides a biographical sketch of the imaginary chronicler) of three tales, entitled "The Highland Widow," "The Two Drovers," and "The Surgeon's Daughter." In the present volume the two first named of these pieces are included, together with three detached stories, which appeared the year after in the elegant compilation called "The Keepsake." The "Surgeon's Daughter" it is thought better to defer until a succeeding volume, than to

Begin and break off in the middle.

I have, perhaps, said enough on former occasions of the misfortunes which led to the dropping of that mask under which I had, for a long series of years, enjoyed so large a portion of public favour. Through the success of those literary efforts, I had been enabled to indulge most of the tastes, which a retired person of my station might be supposed to entertain. In the pen of this nameless romancer, I seemed to possess something like the secret fountain of coined gold and pearls vouchsafed to the traveller of the Eastern Tale; and no doubt believed that I might venture, without silly imprudence, to extend my personal expenditure considerably beyond what I should have thought of, had my means been limited to the competence which I derived from inheritance, with the moderate income of a professional situation. I bought, and built, and planted, and was considered by myself, as by the rest of the world, in the safe possession of an easy fortune. My riches, however, like the other riches of this world, were liable to accidents, under which they were ultimately destined to make unto themselves wings and fly away. The year 1825, so disastrous to many branches of industry and commerce, did not spare the market of literature; and the sudden ruin that fell on so many of the booksellers, could scarcely have been expected to leave unscathed one, whose career had of necessity connected him deeply and extensively with the pecuniary transactions of that profession. In a word, almost without one note of premonition, I found myself involved in the sweeping catastrophe of the unhappy time, and called on to meet the demands of creditors upon commercial establishments with which my fortunes had long been bound up, to the extent of no less a sum than one hundred and twenty thousand pounds.

The author having, however rashly, committed his pledges thus largely to the hazards of trading companies, it behoved him, of course, to abide the consequences of his conduct, and, with whatever feelings, he surrendered on the instant every shred of property which he had been accustomed to call his own. It became vested in the hands of gentlemen, whose integrity, prudence, and intelligence, were combined with all possible liberality and kindness of disposition, and who readily afforded every assistance towards the execution of plans, in the success of which the author contemplated the possibility of his ultimate extrication, and which were of such a nature, that, had assistance of this sort been withheld, he could have had little prospect of carrying them into effect. Among other resources which occurred, was the project of that complete and corrected edition of his Novels and Romances, (whose real parentage had of necessity been disclosed at the moment of the commercial convulsions alluded to,) which has now advanced with unprecedented favour nearly to its close; but as he purposed also to continue, for the behoof of those to whom he was indebted, the exercise of his pen in the same path of literature, so long as the taste of his countrymen should seem to approve of his efforts, it appeared to him that it would have been an idle piece of affectation to attempt getting up a new *incognito*, after his original visor had been thus dashed from his brow. Hence the personal narrative prefixed to the first work of fiction which he put forth after the paternity of the "Waverley Novels" had come to be publicly ascertained: and though many of the particulars originally avowed in that Notice have been unavoidably adverted to in the prefaces and notes to some of the preceding volumes of the present collection, it is now reprinted as it stood at the time, because some interest is generally attached to a coin or medal struck on a special occasion, as expressing, perhaps, more faithfully than the same artist could have afterwards conveyed, the feelings of the moment that gave it birth. The Introduction to the first series of Chronicles of the Canongate ran, then, in these words:

[Here follows EEWN 20, 3–11.]

SUCH was the little narrative which I thought proper to put forth in October 1827: nor have I much to add to it now. About to appear for the first time in my own name in this department of letters, it occurred to me that something in the shape of a periodical publication might carry with it a certain air of novelty, and I was willing to break, if I may so express it, the abruptness of my personal forthcoming, by investing an imaginary coadjutor with at least as much distinctness of individual existence as I had ever previously thought it worth while to bestow on shadows of the same convenient tribe. Of course, it had never been in my contemplation to invite the assistance of any real person in the sustaining of my quasi-editorial character and labours. It had long been my opinion, that any thing like a literary *picnic* is likely to end in suggesting comparisons, justly termed odious, and therefore to be avoided: and, indeed, I had also had some occasion to know, that promises of assistance, in efforts of that order, are apt to be more magnificent than the subsequent performance. I therefore planned a Miscellany, to be dependent, after the old fashion, on my own resources alone, and although conscious enough that the moment which assigned to the Author of Waverley "a local habitation and a name," had seriously endangered his spell, I felt inclined to adopt the sentiment of my old hero Montrose, and to say to myself, that in literature, as in war,

> He either fears his fate too much,
> Or his deserts are small,
> Who dares not put it to the touch,
> To win or lose it all.

To the particulars explanatory of the plan of these Chronicles, which the reader is presented with in Chapter II. by the imaginary Editor, Mr Croftangry, I have now to add, that the lady, termed in his narrative, Mrs Bethune Balliol, was designed to shadow out in its leading points the interesting character of a dear friend of mine, Mrs Murray Keith,* whose death occurring shortly before had saddened a wide circle, much attached to her, as well for her genuine

* The Keiths of Craig, in Kincardineshire, descended from John Keith, fourth son of William, second Earl Marischal, who got from his father, about 1480, the lands of Craig, and part of Garvock, in that county. In Douglas's Baronage, 443 to 445, is a pedigree of that family. Colonel Robert Keith of Craig (the seventh in descent from John) by his wife, Agnes, daughter of Robert Murray of Murrayshall, of the family of Blackbarony, widow of Colonel Stirling, of the family of Keir, had one son; viz. Robert Keith of Craig, ambassador to the court of Vienna, afterwards to St Petersburgh, which latter situation he held at the accession of King George III.,—who died at Edinburgh in 1774. He married Margaret, second daughter of Sir William Cunningham of Caprington, by Janet, only child and heiress of Sir James Dick of Prestonfield; and, among other children of this marriage, were, the late well-known diplomatist, Sir Robert Murray Keith, K.B., a general in the army, and for some time ambassador at Vienna; Sir Basil Keith, Knight, captain in the navy, who died governor of Jamaica; and my excellent friend, Anne Murray Keith, who ultimately came into possession of the family estates, and died not long before the date of this Introduction, (1831.)

virtue and amiable qualities of disposition, as for the extent of information which she possessed, and the delightful manner in which she was used to communicate it. In truth, the author had, on many occasions, been indebted to her vivid memory for the *substratum* of his Scottish fictions—and she accordingly had been, from an early period, at no loss to fix the Waverley Novels on the right culprit.

In the sketch of Chrystal Croftangry's own history, the author has been accused of introducing some not polite allusions to respectable living individuals: but he may safely, he presumes, pass over such an insinuation. The first of the narratives which Mr Croftangry proceeds to lay before the public, "The Highland Widow," was derived from Mrs Murray Keith, and is given, with the exception of a few additional circumstances—the introduction of which I am rather inclined to regret—very much as the excellent old lady used to tell the story. Neither the Highland cicerone MacLeish, nor the demure waiting woman, were drawn from imagination: and on re-reading my tale, after the lapse of a few years, and comparing its effect with my remembrance of my worthy friend's oral narration, which was certainly extremely affecting, I cannot but suspect myself of having marred its simplicity by some of those interpolations, which, at the time when I penned them, no doubt passed with myself for embellishments.

The next tale, entitled "The Two Drovers," I learned from another old friend, the late George Constable, Esq. of Wallace-Craigie, near Dundee, whom I have already introduced to my reader as the original Antiquary of Monkbarns. He had been present, I think, at the trial at Carlisle, and seldom mentioned the venerable judge's charge to the jury, without shedding tears,—which had peculiar pathos, as flowing down features, carrying rather a sarcastic or almost a cynical expression.

This worthy gentleman's reputation for shrewd Scottish sense—knowledge of our national antiquities—and a racy humour, peculiar to himself, must be still remembered. For myself, I have pride in recording that for many years we were, in Wordsworth's language,

> ——a pair of friends, though I was young,
> And 'George' was seventy-two.

W. S.

ABBOTSFORD, *Aug.* 15, 1831.

APPENDIX TO INTRODUCTION

[It has been suggested to the Author, that it might be well to reprint here a detailed account of the public dinner alluded to in the foregoing Introduction, as given in the newspapers of the time; and the reader is accordingly presented with the following extract from the EDINBURGH WEEKLY JOURNAL for Wednesday, 28th February, 1827.]

THEATRICAL FUND DINNER.

Before proceeding with our account of this very interesting festival—for so it may be termed—it is our duty to present to our readers the following letter, which we have received from the President.

TO THE EDITOR OF THE EDINBURGH WEEKLY JOURNAL.

Sir,—I am extremely sorry I have not leisure to correct the copy you sent me of what I am stated to have said at the Dinner for the Theatrical Fund. I am no orator; and upon such occasions as are alluded to, I say as well as I can what the time requires.

However, I hope your reporter has been more accurate in other instances than in mine. I have corrected one passage, in which I am made to speak with great impropriety and petulance, respecting the opinions of those who do not approve of dramatic entertainments. I have restored what I said, which was meant to be respectful, as every objection founded in conscience is, in my opinion, entitled to be so treated. Other errors I left as I found them, it being of little consequence whether I spoke sense or nonsense, in what was merely intended for the purpose of the hour.

I am, sir,
Your obedient servant,
WALTER SCOTT.

Edinburgh, Monday.

The Theatrical Fund Dinner, which took place on Friday, in the Assembly Rooms, was conducted with admirable spirit. The Chairman, Sir WALTER SCOTT, among his other great qualifications, is well fitted to enliven such an entertainment. His manners are extremely easy, and his style of speaking simple and natural, yet full of vivacity and point; and he has the art, if it be art, of relaxing into a certain homeliness of manner, without losing one particle of his dignity. He thus takes off some of that solemn formality which belongs to such meetings, and, by his easy and graceful familiarity, imparts to them somewhat of the pleasing character of a private entertainment. Near Sir W. Scott sat the Earl of Fife, Lord Meadowbank, Sir John Hope of Pinkie, Bart., Admiral Adam, Baron Clerk Rattray, Gilbert Innes, Esq., James Walker, Esq., Robert Dundas, Esq., Alexander Smith, Esq., &c.

The cloth being removed, "Non Nobis Domine" was sung by Messrs Thorne, Swift, Collier, and Hartley, after which the following toasts were given from the chair:—

"The King"—all the honours.

"The Duke of Clarence and the Royal Family."

The CHAIRMAN, in proposing the next toast, which he wished to be drunk in solemn silence, said it was to the memory of a regretted prince, whom we had lately lost. Every individual would at once conjecture to whom he alluded. He had no intention to dwell on his military merits. They had been told in the senate; they had been repeated in the cottage; and whenever a soldier was the theme, his name was never far distant. But it was chiefly in connexion with the business of this meeting, which his late Royal Highness had condescended in a particular manner to patronise, that they were called on to drink his health. To that charity he had often sacrificed his time, and had given up the little leisure which he had from important business. He was always ready to attend on every occasion of this kind, and it was in that view that he proposed to drink to the memory of his late Royal Highness the Duke of York.—Drunk in solemn silence.

The CHAIRMAN then requested that gentlemen would fill a bumper as full as it would hold, while he would say only a few words. He was in the habit of hearing speeches, and he knew the feeling with which long ones were regarded. He was sure that it was perfectly unnecessary for him to enter into any vindication of the dramatic art, which they had come here to support. This, however, he considered to be the proper time and proper occasion for him to say a few words on that love of representation which was an innate feeling in human nature. It was the first amusement that the child had—it grew greater as he grew up; and, even in the decline of life, nothing amused so much as when a common tale is told with appropriate personification. The first thing a child does is to ape his schoolmaster, by flogging a chair. The assuming a character ourselves, or the seeing others assume an imaginary character, is an enjoyment natural to humanity. It was implanted in our very nature, to take pleasure from such representations, at proper times and on proper occasions. In all ages the theatrical art had kept pace with the improvement of mankind, and with the progress of letters and the fine arts. As man has advanced from the ruder stages of society, the love of dramatic representations has increased, and all works of this nature have been improved, in character and in structure. They had only to turn their eyes to the history of ancient Greece, although he did not pretend to be very deeply versed in its ancient drama. Its first tragic poet commanded a body of troops at the battle of Marathon. Sophocles and Euripides were men of rank in Athens, when Athens was in its highest renown. They shook Athens with their discourses, as their theatrical works shook the theatre itself. If they turned to France in the time of Louis the Fourteenth, that era which is the classical history of that country, they would find that it was referred to by all Frenchmen as the golden age of the drama there. And also in England, in the time of Queen Elizabeth, the drama was at its highest pitch, when the nation began to mingle deeply and wisely in the general politics of Europe, not only not receiving laws from others, but giving laws to the world, and vindicating the rights of mankind. (Cheers.) There have been various times when the dramatic art subsequently fell into disrepute. Its professors have been stigmatized; and laws have been passed against them, less dishonourable to them than to the statesmen by whom they were proposed, and to the legislators by whom they were adopted. What were the times in which these laws were passed? Was it not when virtue was seldom inculcated as a moral duty, that we were required to relinquish the most rational of all our amusements, when the clergy were enjoined celibacy, and when the laity were denied the right to read their Bibles? He thought that it must have been from a notion of penance that they erected the drama into an ideal place of profaneness, and spoke of the theatre as of the tents of sin. He did not mean to dispute, that there were many excellent persons who thought differently from him, and he disclaimed the slightest idea of charging them with bigotry or hypocrisy on that account. He gave them full credit for their tender consciences, in making these objections, although they did not appear relevant to him. But to these persons, being, as he believed them, men of worth and piety, he was sure the purpose of this meeting would furnish some apology for an error, if there be any, in the opinions of those who attend. They would approve the gift, although they might differ in other points. Such might not approve of going to the Theatre, but at least could not deny that they might give away from their superfluity, what was required for the relief of the sick, the support of the aged, and the comfort of the afflicted. These were duties enjoined by our religion itself. (Loud cheers.)

The performers are in a particular manner entitled to the support or regard, when in old age or distress, of those who had partaken of the amusements of those places which they render an ornament to society. Their art was of a peculiarly delicate and precarious nature. They had to serve a long apprenticeship. It was very long before even the first-rate geniuses could acquire the mechanical knowledge of the stage business. They must languish long in obscurity before they can avail themselves of their natural talents; and after that, they have but a short space of time, during which they are fortunate if they can provide the means of comfort in the decline of life. That comes late, and lasts but a short time; after which they are left dependent. Their limbs fail—their teeth are loosened—their voice is lost—and they are left, after giving happiness to others, in a most disconsolate state. The public were liberal and generous to those deserving their protection. It was a sad thing to be dependent on the favour, or, he might say, in plain terms, on the caprice, of the public; and this more particularly for a class of persons of whom extreme prudence is not the character. There might be instances of opportunities being neglected; but let each gentleman tax himself, and consider the opportunities *they* had neglected, and the sums of money *they* had wasted; let every gentleman look into his own bosom, and say whether these were circumstances which would soften his own feelings, were he to be plunged into distress. He put it to every generous bosom—to every better feeling —to say what consolation was it to old age to be told that you might have made provision at a time which had been neglected—(loud cheers),—and to find it objected, that if you had pleased you might have been wealthy. He had hitherto been speaking of what, in theatrical language, was called *stars*, but they were sometimes falling ones. There were another class of sufferers naturally and necessarily connected with the theatre, without whom it was impossible to go on. The sailors have a saying, every man cannot be a boatswain. If there must be a great actor to act Hamlet, there must also be people to act Laertes, the King, Rosencrantz, and Guildenstern, otherwise a drama cannot go on. If even Garrick himself were to rise from the dead, he could not act Hamlet alone. There must be generals, colonels, commanding-officers, subalterns. But what are the private soldiers to do? Many have mistaken their own talents, and have been driven in early youth to try the stage, to which they are not competent. He would know what to say to the indifferent poet and to the bad artist. He would say that it was foolish, and he would recommend to the poet to become a scribe, and the artist to paint sign-posts—(loud laughter).—But you could not send the player adrift, for if he cannot play Hamlet, he must play Guildenstern. Where there are many labourers, wages must be low, and no man in such a situation can decently support a wife and family, and save something off his income for old age. What is this man to do in latter life? Are you to cast him off like an old hinge, or a piece of useless machinery, which has done its work? To a person who had contributed to our amusement, this would be unkind, ungrateful, and unchristian. His wants are not of his own making, but arise from the natural sources of sickness and old age. It cannot be denied that there is one class of sufferers to whom no imprudence can be ascribed, except on first entering on the profession. After putting his hand to the dramatic plough, he cannot draw back; but must continue at it, and toil, till death release him from want, or charity, by its milder influence, steps in to render that want more tolerable. He had little more to say, except that he sincerely hoped that the collection to-day, from the number of respectable gentlemen present, would meet the views entertained by the patrons. He hoped it would do so. They should not be disheartened. Though they could not do a great deal, they might do something. They had this consolation, that every thing they parted with from their superfluity would do some good. They would sleep the better themselves when they have been the means of giving sleep to others. It was ungrateful and unkind, that those who had sacrificed their youth to our amusement should not receive the reward due to them, but should be reduced to hard fare in their old age. We cannot think of poor Falstaff going to bed without his cup of sack, or Macbeth fed on bones as marrowless as those of Banquo.—(Loud cheers and laughter.)—As he believed that they were all as fond of the dramatic art as he was in his younger days, he would propose that they should drink "The Theatrical Fund," with three times three.

Mr MACKAY rose, on behalf of his brethren, to return their thanks for the toast just drunk. Many of the gentlemen present, he said, were perhaps not fully acquainted with the nature and intention of the institution, and it might not be amiss to enter into some explanation on the subject. With whomsoever the idea of a Theatrical Fund might have originated, (and it had been disputed by the surviving relatives of two or three individuals,) certain it was that the first legally constituted Theatrical Fund owed its origin to one of the brightest ornaments of the profession, the late David Garrick. That eminent actor conceived that, by a weekly subscription in the Theatre, a fund might be raised among its members, from which a portion might be given to those of his less fortunate brethren, and thus an opportunity would be offered for prudence to provide what fortune had denied—a comfortable provision for the winter of life. With the welfare of his profession constantly at heart, the zeal with which he laboured to uphold its respectability, and to impress upon the minds of his brethren, not only the necessity, but the blessing of independence, the Fund became his peculiar care. He drew up a form of laws for its government, procured, at his own expense, the passing of an Act of Parliament for its confirmation, bequeathed to it a handsome legacy, and thus became the Father of the Drury-Lane Fund. So constant was his attachment to this infant establishment, that he chose to grace the close of the brightest theatrical life on record, by the last display of his transcendent talent, on the occasion of a benefit for this child of his adoption, which ever since has gone by the name of the Garrick Fund. In imitation of his noble example, Funds had been established in several provincial theatres in England; but it remained for Mrs Henry Siddons and Mr William Murray to become the founders of the first Theatrical Fund in Scotland. (Cheers.) This Fund commenced under the most favourable auspices; it was liberally supported by the management, and highly patronised by the public. Notwithstanding, it fell short in the accomplishment of its intentions. What those intentions were, he (Mr Mackay) need not recapitulate, but they failed; and he did not hesitate to confess that a want of energy on the part of the performers was the probable cause. A new set of Rules and Regulations were lately drawn up, submitted to and approved of at a general meeting of the members of the Theatre; and accordingly the Fund was re-modelled on the 1st of January last. And here he thought he did but echo the feelings of his brethren, by publicly acknowledging the obligations they were under to the management, for the aid given, and the warm interest they had all along taken in the welfare of the Fund. (Cheers.) The nature and object of the profession had been so well treated of by the President, that he would say nothing; but of the numerous offspring of science and genius that court precarious fame, the Actor boasts the slenderest claim of all; the sport of fortune, the creatures of fashion, and the victims of caprice—they are seen, heard, and admired, but to be forgot—they leave no trace, no memorial of their existence—they "come like shadows, so depart." (Cheers.) Yet humble though their pretensions be, there was no profession, trade, or calling, where such a combination of requisites, mental and bodily, were indispensable. In all others the principal may practise after he has been visited by the afflicting hand of Providence—some by the loss of limb—some of voice—and many, when the faculty of the mind is on the wane, may be assisted by dutiful children, or devoted servants. Not so the Actor—he must retain all he ever did possess, or sink dejected to a mournful home. (Applause.) Yet while they are toiling for ephemeral theatric fame, how very few ever possess the means of hoarding in their youth that which would give bread in old age! But now a brighter prospect dawned upon them, and to the success of this their infant establishment they looked with hope, as to a comfortable and peaceful home in their declining years. He concluded by tendering to the meeting, in the name of his brethren and sisters, their unfeigned thanks for their liberal support, and begged to propose the health of the Patrons of the Edinburgh Theatrical Fund. (Cheers.)

Lord MEADOWBANK said, that by desire of his Hon. Friend in the chair, and of his Noble Friend at his right hand, he begged leave to return thanks for the honour which had been conferred on the Patrons of this excellent Institution. He could answer for himself—he could answer for them all—that they were deeply impressed with the meritorious objects which it has in view, and of their anxious wish to promote its interests. For himself, he hoped he might be permitted to say, that he was rather surprised at finding his own name as one of the Patrons, associated with so many individuals of high rank and powerful influence. But it was an excuse for those who had placed him in a situation so honourable and so distinguished, that when this charity was instituted, he happened to hold a high and responsible station under the Crown, when he might have been of use in assisting and promoting its objects. His Lordship much feared that he could have little expectation, situated as he now was, of doing either; but he could confidently assert, that few things would give him greater gratification than being able to contribute to its prosperity and support; and, indeed, when one recollects the pleasure which at all periods of life he has received from the exhibitions of the stage, and the exertions of the meritorious individuals for whose aid this fund has been established, he must be divested both of gratitude and feeling who would not give his best endeavours to promote its welfare. And now, that he might in some measure repay the gratification which had been afforded himself, he would beg leave to propose a toast, the health of one of the Patrons, a great and distinguished individual, whose name must always stand by itself, and which, in an assembly such as this, or in any other assembly of Scotsmen, can never be received, (not he would say with ordinary feelings of pleasure or of delight,) but with those of rapture and enthusiasm. In doing so he felt that he stood in a somewhat new situation. Whoever had been called upon to propose the health of his Hon. Friend to whom he alluded, some time ago, would have found himself enabled, from the mystery in which certain matters were involved, to gratify himself and his auditors by allusions which found a responding chord in their own feelings, and to deal in the language, the sincere language, of panegyric, without intruding on the modesty of the great individual to whom he referred. But it was no longer possible, consistently with the respect to one's auditors, to use upon this subject terms either of mystification, or of obscure or indirect allusion. The clouds have been dispelled—the *darkness visible* has been cleared away—and the Great Unknown—the minstrel of our native land—the mighty magician who has rolled back the current of time, and conjured up before our living senses the men and the manners of days which have long passed away, stands revealed to the hearts and the eyes of his affectionate and admiring countrymen. If he himself were capable of imagining all that belonged to this mighty subject—were he even able to give utterance to all that as a friend, as a man, and as a Scotsman, he must feel regarding it, yet knowing, as he well did, that this illustrious individual was not more distinguished for his towering talents, than for those feelings which rendered such allusions ungrateful to himself, however sparingly introduced, he would, on that account, still refrain from doing that which would otherwise be no less pleasing to him than to his audience. But this his Lordship hoped he would be allowed to say, (his auditors would not pardon him were he to say less,) we owe to him, as a people, a large and heavy debt of gratitude. He it is who has opened to foreigners the grand and characteristic beauties of our country. It is to him that we owe that our gallant ancestors and the struggles of our illustrious patriots—who fought and bled in order to obtain and secure that independence and that liberty we now enjoy—have obtained a fame no longer confined to the boundaries of a remote and comparatively obscure nation, and who has called down upon their struggles for glory and freedom the admiration of foreign countries. He it is who has conferred a new reputation on our national character, and bestowed on Scotland an imperishable name, were it only by her having given birth to himself. (Loud and rapturous applause.)

Sir WALTER SCOTT certainly did not think that, in coming

here to-day, he would have the task of acknowledging, before 300 gentlemen, a secret which, considering that it was communicated to more than twenty people, had been remarkably well kept. He was now before the bar of his country, and might be understood to be on trial before Lord Meadowbank as an offender; yet he was sure that every impartial jury would bring in a verdict of Not Proven. He did not now think it necessary to enter into the reasons of his long silence. Perhaps caprice might have a considerable share in it. He had now to say, however, that the merits of these works, if they had any, and their faults, were entirely imputable to himself. (Long and loud cheering.) He was afraid to think on what he had done. "Look on't again I dare not." He had thus far unbosomed himself, and he knew that it would be reported to the public. He meant, then, seriously to state, that when he said he was the author, he was the total and undivided author. With the exception of quotations, there was not a single word that was not derived from himself, or suggested in the course of his reading. The wand was now broken, and the book buried. You will allow me further to say, with Prospero, it is your breath that has filled my sails, and to crave one single toast in the capacity of the author of these novels; and he would dedicate a bumper to the health of one who has represented some of those characters, of which he had endeavoured to give the skeleton, with a degree of liveliness which rendered him grateful. He would propose the health of his friend Bailie Nicol Jarvie, (loud applause)—and he was sure, that when the author of Waverley and Rob Roy drinks to Nicol Jarvie, it would be received with that degree of applause to which that gentleman has always been accustomed, and that they would take care that on the present occasion it should be PRODIGIOUS! (Long and vehement applause.)

Mr MACKAY, who here spoke with great humour in the character of Bailie Jarvie.—My conscience! My worthy father the deacon could not have believed that his son could hae had sic a compliment paid to him by the Great Unknown!

Sir WALTER SCOTT.—The Small Known now, Mr Bailie.

Mr MACKAY.—He had been long identified with the Bailie, and he was vain of the cognomen which he had now worn for eight years; and he questioned if any of his brethren in the Council had given such universal satisfaction. (Loud laughter and applause.) Before he sat down, he begged to propose "the Lord Provost and the City of Edinburgh."

Sir WALTER SCOTT apologized for the absence of the Lord Provost, who had gone to London on public business.

Tune—"Within a mile of Edinburgh town."

Sir Walter Scott gave, "The Duke of Wellington and the army."

Glee—"How merrily we live."

"Lord Melville and the Navy, that fought till they left nobody to fight with, like an arch sportsman who clears all and goes after the game."

Mr Pat. Robertson.—They had heard this evening a toast, which had been received with intense delight, which will be published in every newspaper, and will be hailed with joy by all Europe. He had one toast assigned him which he had great pleasure in giving. He was sure that the stage had in all ages a great effect on the morals and manners of the people. It was very desirable that the stage should be well regulated; and there was no criterion by which its regulation could be better determined than by the moral character and personal respectability of the performers. He was not one of those stern moralists who objected to the Theatre. The most fastidious moralist could not possibly apprehend any injury from the stage of Edinburgh, as it was presently managed, and so long as it was adorned by that illustrious individual, Mrs Henry Siddons, whose public exhibitions were not more remarkable for feminine grace and delicacy, than was her private character for every virtue which could be admired in domestic life. He would conclude with reciting a few words from Shakspeare, in a spirit not of contradiction to those stern moralists who disliked the Theatre, but of meekness:—"Good my lord, will you see the players well bestowed? do you hear, let them be well used, for they are the abstract and brief chronicles of the time." He then gave "Mrs Henry Siddons, and success to the Theatre-Royal of Edinburgh."

Mr Murray.—Gentlemen, I rise to return thanks for the honour you have done Mrs Siddons, in doing which I am somewhat difficulted, from the extreme delicacy which attends a brother's expatiating upon a sister's claims to honours publicly paid—(hear, hear)—yet, Gentlemen, your kindness emboldens me to say, that were I to give utterance to all a brother's feelings, I should exaggerate those claims. (Loud applause.) I therefore, Gentlemen, thank you most cordially for the honour you have done her, and shall now request permission to make an observation on the establishment of the Edinburgh Theatrical Fund. Mr Mackay has done Mrs Henry Siddons and myself the honour to ascribe the establishment to us; but no, Gentlemen, it owes its origin to a higher source—the publication of the novel of Rob Roy—the unprecedented success of the opera adapted from that popular production. (Hear,

hear.) It was that success which relieved the Edinburgh Theatre from its difficulties, and enabled Mrs Siddons to carry into effect the establishment of a fund she had long desired, but was prevented from effecting, from the unsettled state of her theatrical concerns. I therefore hope that, in future years, when the aged and infirm actor derives relief from this fund, he will, in the language of the gallant Highlander, "Cast his eye to good old Scotland, and not forget Rob Roy." (Loud applause.)

Sir WALTER SCOTT here stated, that Mrs Siddons wanted the means but not the will of beginning the Theatrical Fund. He here alluded to the great merits of Mr Murray's management, and to his merits as an actor, which were of the first order, and of which every person who attends the Theatre must be sensible; and after alluding to the embarrassments with which the Theatre had been at one period threatened, he concluded by giving the health of Mr Murray, which was drunk with three times three.

Mr MURRAY.—Gentlemen, I wish I could believe, that, in any degree, I merited the compliments with which it has pleased Sir Walter Scott to preface the proposal of my health, or the very flattering manner in which you have done me the honour to receive it. The approbation of such an assembly is most gratifying to me, and might encourage feelings of vanity, were not such feelings crushed by my conviction, that no man holding the situation I have so long held in Edinburgh, could have failed, placed in the peculiar circumstances in which I have been placed. Gentlemen, I shall not insult your good taste by eulogiums upon your judgment or kindly feeling; though to the first I owe any improvement I may have made as an actor, and certainly my success as a Manager to the second. (Applause.) When, upon the death of my dear brother the late Mr Siddons, it was proposed that I should undertake the management of the Edinburgh Theatre, I confess I drew back, doubting my capability to free it from the load of debt and difficulty with which it was surrounded. In this state of anxiety, I solicited the advice of one who had ever honoured me with his kindest regard, and whose name no member of my profession can pronounce without feelings of the deepest respect and gratitude—I allude to the late Mr John Kemble. (Great applause.) To him I applied; and with the repetition of his advice I shall cease to trespass upon your time—(Hear, hear.)—"My dear William, fear not; integrity and assiduity must prove an overmatch for all difficulty; and though I approve your not indulging a vain confidence in your own ability, and viewing with respectful apprehension the judgment of the audience you have to act before, yet be assured that judgment will ever be tempered by the feeling that you are acting for the widow and the fatherless." (Loud applause.) Gentlemen, those words have never passed from my mind; and I feel convinced that you have pardoned my many errors, from the feeling that I was striving for the widow and the fatherless. (Long and enthusiastic applause followed Mr Murray's address.)

Sir WALTER SCOTT gave the health of the Stewards.

Mr VANDENHOFF.—Mr President and Gentlemen, the honour conferred upon the Stewards, in the very flattering compliment you have just paid us, calls forth our warmest acknowledgments. In tendering you our thanks for the approbation you have been pleased to express of our humble exertions, I would beg leave to advert to the cause in which we have been engaged. Yet, surrounded as I am by the genius—the eloquence of this enlightened city, I cannot but feel the presumption which ventures to address you on so interesting a subject. Accustomed to speak in the language of others, I feel quite at a loss for terms wherein to clothe the sentiments excited by the present occasion. (Applause.) The nature of the Institution which has sought your fostering patronage, and the objects which it contemplates, have been fully explained to you. But, gentlemen, the relief which it proposes is not a gratuitous relief—but to be purchased by the individual contribution of its members towards the general good. This Fund lends no encouragement to idleness or improvidence; but it offers an opportunity to prudence, in vigour and youth, to make provision against the evening of life and its attendant infirmity. A period is fixed, at which we admit the plea of age as an exemption from professional labour. It is painful to behold the veteran on the stage (compelled by necessity) contending against physical decay, mocking the joyousness of mirth with the feebleness of age, when the energies decline, when the memory fails, and "the big manly voice, turning again towards childish treble, pipes and whistles in the sound." We would remove him from the mimic scene, where fiction constitutes the charm; we would not view old age caricaturing itself. (Applause.) But as our means may be found, in time of need, inadequate to the fulfilment of our wishes—fearful of raising expectations, which we may be unable to gratify—desirous not "to keep the word of promise to the ear, and break it to the hope"—we have presumed to court the assistance of the friends of the drama to strengthen our infant institution. Our appeal has been successful, beyond our most sanguine expectations. The distinguished patronage conferred on us by your presence on this occasion, and the substantial support which your benevolence has so liberally afforded to our institution, must impress every member of the Fund with the most grateful sentiments—sentiments which no language can express, no time obliterate. (Applause.) I will not trespass longer on your attention. I would the task of acknowledging our obligation had fallen into abler hands. (Hear, hear.) In the name of the Stewards, I most respectfully and cordially thank you for the honour you have done us, which greatly overpays our poor endeavours. (Applause.)

[This speech, though rather inadequately reported, was one of the best delivered on this occasion. That it was creditable to Mr Vandenhoff's taste and feelings, the preceding sketch will show; but how much it was so, it does *not* show.]

Mr J. CAY gave Professor Wilson and the University of Edinburgh, of which he was one of the brightest ornaments.

Lord MEADOWBANK, after a suitable eulogium, gave the Earl of Fife, which was drunk with three times three.

Earl FIFE expressed his high gratification at the honour conferred on him. He intimated his approbation of the institution, and his readiness to promote its success by every means in his power. He concluded with giving the health of the Company of Edinburgh.

Mr JONES, on rising to return thanks, being received with considerable applause, said he was truly grateful for the kind encouragement he had experienced, but the novelty of the situation in which he now was, renewed all the feelings he experienced when he first saw himself announced in the bills as a young gentleman, being his first appearance on any stage. (Laughter and applause.) Although in the presence of those whose indulgence had, in another sphere, so often shielded him from the penalties of inability, he was unable to execute the task which had so unexpectedly devolved upon him in behalf of his brethren and himself. He therefore begged the company to imagine all that grateful hearts could prompt the most eloquent to utter, and that would be a copy of their feelings. (Applause.) He begged to trespass another moment on their attention, for the purpose of expressing the thanks of the members of the Fund to the Gentlemen of the Edinburgh Professional Society of Musicians, who, finding that this meeting was appointed to take place on the same evening with their concert, had in the handsomest manner agreed to postpone it. Although it was his duty thus to preface the toast he had to propose, he was certain the meeting required no farther inducement than the recollection of the pleasure the exertions of those gentlemen had often afforded them within those walls, to join heartily in drinking "Health and prosperity to the Edinburgh Professional Society of Musicians." (Applause.)

Mr PAT. ROBERTSON proposed "the health of Mr Jeffrey,"

whose absence was owing to indisposition. The public was well aware that he was the most distinguished advocate at the bar; he was likewise distinguished for the kindness, frankness, and cordial manner in which he communicated with the junior members of the profession, to the esteem of whom his splendid talents would always entitle him.

Mr J. MACONOCHIE gave "the health of Mrs Siddons, senior—the most distinguished ornament of the stage."

Sir W. SCOTT said, that if any thing could reconcile him to old age, it was the reflection that he had seen the rising as well as the setting sun of Mrs Siddons. He remembered well their breakfasting near to the theatre—waiting the whole day—the crushing at the doors at six o'clock—and their going in and counting their fingers till seven o'clock. But the very first step—the very first word which she uttered, was sufficient to overpay him for all his labours. The house was literally electrified; and it was only from witnessing the effects of her genius, that he could guess to what a pitch theatrical excellence could be carried. Those young gentlemen who have only seen the setting sun of this distinguished performer, beautiful and serene as that was, must give us old fellows, who have seen its rise and its meridian, leave to hold our heads a little higher.

Mr DUNDAS gave "The memory of Home, the author of Douglas."

Mr MACKAY here announced that the subscription for the night amounted to L.280; and he expressed gratitude for this substantial proof of their kindness. [We are happy to state that subscriptions have since flowed in very liberally.]

Mr MACKAY here entertained the company with a pathetic song.

Sir WALTER SCOTT apologized for having so long forgotten their native land. He would now give Scotland, the Land of Cakes. He would give every river, every loch, every hill, from Tweed to Johnnie Groat's house—every lass in her cottage and countess in her castle; and may her sons stand by her, as their fathers did before them, and he who would not drink a bumper to his toast, may he never drink whisky more!

Sir WALTER SCOTT here gave Lord Meadowbank, who returned thanks.

Mr H. G. BELL said, that he should not have ventured to intrude himself upon the attention of the assembly, did he not feel confident, that the toast he begged to have the honour to propose, would make amends for the very imperfect manner in which he might express his sentiments regarding it. It had been said, that notwithstanding the mental supremacy of the present age, notwithstanding that the page of our history was studded with names destined also for the page of immortality,—that the genius of Shakspeare was extinct, and the fountain of his inspiration dried up. It might be that these observations were unfortunately correct, or it might be that we were bewildered with a name, not disappointed of the reality,—for though Shakspeare had brought a Hamlet, an Othello, and a Macbeth, an Ariel, a Juliet, and a Rosalind, upon the stage, were there not authors living who had brought as varied, as exquisitely painted, and as undying a range of characters into our hearts? The shape of the mere mould into which genius poured its golden treasures was surely a matter of little moment,—let it be called a Tragedy, a Comedy, or a Waverley Novel. But even among the dramatic authors of the present day, he was unwilling to allow that there was a great and palpable decline from the glory of preceding ages, and his toast alone would bear him out in denying the truth of the proposition. After eulogizing the names of Baillie, Byron, Coleridge, Maturin, and others, he begged to have the honour of proposing the health of James Sheridan Knowles.

Sir WALTER SCOTT.—Gentlemen, I crave a bumper all over. The last toast reminds me of a neglect of duty. Unaccustomed to a public duty of this kind, errors in conducting the ceremonial of it may be excused, and omissions pardoned. Perhaps I have made one or two omissions in the course of the evening, for which I trust you will grant me your pardon and indulgence. One thing in particular I have omitted, and I would now wish to make amends for it, by a libation of reverence and respect to the memory of SHAKSPEARE. He was a man of universal genius, and from a period soon after his own era to the present day, he has been universally idolized. When I come to his honoured name, I am like the sick man who hung up his crutches at the shrine, and was obliged to confess that he did not walk better than before. It is indeed difficult, gentlemen, to compare him to any other individual. The only one to whom I can at all compare him, is the wonderful Arabian dervise, who dived into the body of each, and in this way became familiar with the thoughts and secrets of their hearts. He was a man of obscure origin, and, as a player, limited in his acquirements, but he was born evidently with a universal genius. His eyes glanced at all the varied aspects of life, and his fancy portrayed with equal talents the king on the throne, and the clown who crackles his chestnuts at a Christmas fire. Whatever note he takes, he strikes it just and true, and awakens a corresponding chord in our own bosoms. Gentlemen, I propose "The memory of William Shakspeare."

Glee,—"Lightly tread, 'tis hallowed ground."

After the glee, Sir Walter rose, and begged to propose as a toast the health of a lady, whose living merit is not a little honourable to Scotland. The toast (said he) is also flattering to the national vanity of a Scotchman, as the lady whom I intend to propose is a native of this country. From the public her works have met with the most favourable reception. One piece of hers, in particular, was often acted here of late years, and gave pleasure of no mean kind to many brilliant and fashionable audiences. In her private character she (he begged leave to say) is as remarkable, as in a public sense she is for her genius. In short, he would in one word name—"Joanna Baillie."

This health being drunk, Mr Thorne was called on for a song, and sung, with great taste and feeling, "The Anchor's weighed."

W. MENZIES, Esq., Advocate, rose to propose the health of a gentleman for many years connected at intervals with the dramatic art in Scotland. Whether we look at the range of characters he performs, or at the capacity which he evinces in executing those which he undertakes, he is equally to be admired. In all his parts he is unrivalled. The individual to whom he alluded is (said he) well known to the gentlemen present, in the characters of Malvolio, Lord Ogleby, and the Green Man; and, in addition to his other qualities, he merits, for his perfection in these characters, the grateful sense of this meeting. He would wish, in the first place, to drink his health as an actor; but he was not less estimable in domestic life, and as a private gentleman; and when he announced him as one whom the Chairman had honoured with his friendship, he was sure that all present would cordially join him in drinking "The health of Mr Terry."

Mr WILLIAM ALLAN, banker, said, that he did not rise with the intention of making a speech. He merely wished to contribute in a few words to the mirth of the evening—an evening which certainly had not passed off without some blunders. It had been understood—at least he had learnt or supposed, from the expressions of Mr Pritchard—that it would be sufficient to put a paper, with the name of the contributor, into the box, and that the gentleman thus contributing would be called on for the money next morning. He, for his part, had committed a blunder, but it might serve as a caution to those who may be present at the dinner of next year. He had merely put in his name, written on a slip of paper, without the money. But he would recommend that, as some of the gentlemen might be in the same situation, the box should be again sent round, and he was confident that they, as well as he, would redeem their error.

Sir WALTER SCOTT said, that the meeting was somewhat in the situation of Mrs Anne Page, who had L.300 and possibilities. We have already got, said he, L.280, but I should like, I confess, to have the L.300. He would gratify himself by proposing the health of an honourable person, the Lord Chief Baron, whom England has sent to us, and connecting with it that of his "yokefellow on the bench," as Shakspeare says, Mr Baron Clerk—The Court of Exchequer.

Mr Baron CLERK regretted the absence of his learned brother. None, he was sure, could be more generous in his nature, or more ready to help a Scottish purpose.

Sir WALTER SCOTT.—There is one who ought to be remembered on this occasion. He is, indeed, well entitled to our grateful recollection—one, in short, to whom the drama in this city owes much. He succeeded, not without trouble, and perhaps at some considerable sacrifice, in establishing a theatre. The younger part of the company may not recollect the theatre to which I allude; but there are some who with me may remember by name a place called Carrubber's Close. There Allan Ramsay established his little theatre. His own pastoral was not fit for the stage, but it has its admirers in those who love the Doric language in which it is written; and it is not without merits of a very peculiar kind. But, laying aside all considerations of his literary merit, Allan was a good jovial honest fellow, who could crack a bottle with the best.—The memory of Allan Ramsay.

Mr MURRAY, on being requested, sung, "'Twas merry in the hall," and at the conclusion was greeted with repeated rounds of applause.

Mr JONES.—One omission I conceive has been made. The cause of the fund has been ably advocated, but it is still susceptible, in my opinion, of an additional charm—

> Without the smile from partial beauty won,
> Oh, what were man?—a world without a sun!

And there would not be a darker spot in poetry than would be the corner in Shakspeare Square, if, like its fellow, the Register Office, the Theatre were deserted by the ladies. They are, in fact, our most attractive stars.—"The Patronesses of the Theatre—the Ladies of the City of Edinburgh." This toast I ask leave to drink with all the honours which conviviality can confer.

Mr PATRICK ROBERTSON would be the last man willingly to introduce any topic calculated to interrupt the harmony of the evening; yet he felt himself treading upon ticklish ground when he approached the region of the Nor' Loch. He assured the company, however, that he was not about to enter on the subject of the Improvement bill. They all knew, that if the public were unanimous —if the consent of all parties were obtained—if the rights and interests of every body were therein attended to, saved, reserved, respected, and excepted—if every body agreed to it—and finally, a most essential point—if nobody opposed it—then, and in that case, and provided also, that due intimation were given—the bill in question might pass—would pass—or might, could, would, or should pass—all expenses being defrayed.—(Laughter.)—He was the advocate of neither champion, and would neither avail himself of the absence of the Right Hon. the Lord Provost, nor take advantage of the non-appearance of his friend, Mr Cockburn.—(Laughter.)—But in the midst of these civic broils, there had been elicited a ray of hope, that, at some future period, in Bereford Park, or some other place, if all parties were consulted and satisfied, and if intimation were duly made at the Kirk doors of all the parishes in Scotland, in terms of the statute in that behalf provided—the people of Edinburgh might by possibility get a new theatre.—(Cheers and laughter.)—But wherever the belligerent powers might be pleased to set down this new theatre, he was sure they all hoped to meet the Old Company in it. He should therefore propose—"Better accommodation to the Old Company in the new theatre, site unknown."—Mr Robertson's speech was most humorously given, and he sat down amidst loud cheers and laughter.

Sir Walter Scott.—Wherever the new theatre is built, I hope it will not be large. There are two errors which we commonly commit—the one arising from our pride, the other from our poverty. If there are twelve plans, it is odds but the largest, without any regard to comfort, or an eye to the probable expense, is adopted. There was the College projected on this scale, and undertaken in the same manner, and who shall see the end of it? It has been building all my life, and may probably last during the lives of my children, and my children's children. Let not the same prophetic hymn be sung, when we commence a new theatre, which was performed on the occasion of laying the foundation stone of a certain edifice, "behold the endless work begun." Play-going folks should attend somewhat to convenience. The new theatre should, in the first place, be such as may be finished in eighteen months or two years; and, in the second place, it should be one in which we can hear our old friends with comfort. It is better that a moderate-sized house should be crowded now and then, than to have a large Theatre with benches continually empty, to the discouragement of the actors, and the discomfort of the spectators.—(Applause.)—He then commented in flattering terms on the genius of Mackenzie and his private worth, and concluded by proposing "the health of Henry Mackenzie, Esq."

Immediately afterwards he said: Gentlemen,—It is now wearing late, and I shall request permission to retire. Like Partridge I may say, "*non sum qualis eram.*" At my time of day, I can agree with Lord Ogleby as to his rheumatism, and say, "There's a twinge." I hope, therefore, you will excuse me for leaving the chair.—(The worthy Baronet then retired amidst long, loud, and rapturous cheering.)

Mr PATRICK ROBERTSON was then called to the chair by common acclamation.

Gentlemen, said Mr ROBERTSON, I take the liberty of asking you to fill a bumper to the very brim. There is not one of us who will not remember, while he lives, being present at this day's festival, and the declaration made this night by the gentleman who has just left the chair. That declaration has rent the veil from the features of the Great Unknown—a name which must now merge in the name of the Great Known. It will be henceforth coupled with the name of SCOTT, which will become familiar like a household word. We have heard the confession from his own immortal lips—(cheering)—and we cannot dwell with too much, or too fervent praise, on the merits of the greatest man whom Scotland has produced.

After which, several other toasts were given, and Mr Robertson left the room about half-past eleven. A few choice spirits, however, rallied round Captain Broadhead of the 7th hussars, who was called to the chair, and the festivity was prolonged till an early hour on Saturday morning.

The band of the Theatre occupied the gallery, and that of the 7th hussars the end of the room, opposite the chair, whose performances were greatly admired. It is but justice to Mr Gibb to state, that the dinner was very handsome (though slowly served in) and the wines good. The attention of the stewards was exemplary. Mr Murray and Mr Vandenhoff, with great good taste, attended on Sir Walter Scott's right and left, and we know that he has expressed himself much gratified by their anxious politeness and sedulity.

Introduction to the Surgeon's Daughter

THE tale of The Surgeon's Daughter formed part of the second volume of Chronicles of the Canongate, published in 1827; but has been separated from the stories of The Highland Widow, &c., which it originally accompanied, and deferred to the close of this collection, for reasons which printers and publishers will understand, and which would hardly interest the general reader.

The Author has nothing to say now in reference to this little Novel, but that the principal incident on which it turns, was narrated to him one morning at breakfast by his worthy friend, Mr Train, of Castle Douglas, in Galloway, whose kind assistance he has so often had occasion to acknowledge in the course of these prefaces; and that the military friend who is alluded to as having furnished him with some information as to Eastern matters, was Colonel James Ferguson of Huntly Burn, one of the sons of the venerable historian and philosopher of that name—which name he took the liberty of concealing under its Gaelic form of *MacErries*.

W. S.

ABBOTSFORD, *Sept.* 1831.

APPENDIX TO INTRODUCTION

[*Mr Train was requested by Sir Walter Scott to give him in writing the story as nearly as possible in the shape in which he had told it; but the following narrative, which he drew up accordingly, did not reach Abbotsford until July 1832.*]

In the old Stock of Fife, there was not perhaps an individual whose exertions were followed by consequences of such a remarkable nature as those of Davie Duff, popularly called "The Thane of Fife," who, from a very humble parentage, rose to fill one of the chairs of the magistracy of his native burgh. By industry and economy in early life, he obtained the means of erecting, solely on his own account, one of those ingenious manufactories for which Fifeshire is justly celebrated. From the day on which the industrious artisan first took his seat at the Council Board, he attended so much to the interests of the little privileged community, that civic honours were conferred on him as rapidly as the Set of the Royalty* could legally admit.

To have the right of walking to church on holyday, preceded by a phalanx of halberdiers, in habiliments fashioned as in former times, seems, in the eyes of many a guild brother, to be a very enviable pitch of worldly grandeur. Few persons were ever more proud of civic honours than the Thane of Fife, but he knew well

* The Constitution of the Borough.

how to turn his political influence to the best account. The council, court, and other business of the burgh, occupied much of his time, which caused him to intrust the management of his manufactory to a near relation whose name was D*******, a young man of dissolute habits; but the Thane, seeing at last, that by continuing that extravagant person in that charge, his affairs would, in all probability, fall into a state of bankruptcy, applied to the member of Parliament for that district to obtain a situation for his relation in the civil department of the state. The knight, whom it is here unnecessary to name, knowing how effectually the Thane ruled the little burgh, applied in the proper quarter, and actually obtained an appointment for D******* in the civil service of the East India Company.

A respectable surgeon, whose residence was in a neighbouring village, had a beautiful daughter named Emma, who had long been courted by D*******. Immediately before his departure to India, as a mark of mutual affection, they exchanged miniatures, taken by an eminent artist in Fife, and each set in a locket, for the purpose of having the object of affection always in view.

The eyes of the old Thane were now turned towards Hindostan with much anxiety; but his relation had not long arrived in that distant quarter of the globe before he had the satisfaction of receiving a letter, conveying the welcome intelligence of his having taken possession of his new station in a large frontier town of the Company's dominions, and that great emoluments were attached to the situation; which was confirmed by several subsequent communications of the most gratifying description to the old Thane, who took great pleasure in spreading the news of the reformed habits and singular good fortune of his intended heir. None of all his former acquaintances heard with such joy the favourable report of the successful adventurer in the East, as did the fair and accomplished daughter of the village surgeon; but his previous character caused her to keep her own correspondence with him secret from her parents, to whom even the circumstance of her being acquainted with D******* was wholly unknown, till her father received a letter from him, in which he assured him of his attachment to Emma long before his departure from Fife; that having been so happy as to gain her affections, he would have made her his wife before leaving his native country, had he then had the means of supporting her in a suitable rank through life; and that, having it now in his power to do so, he only waited the consent of her parents to fulfil the vow he had formerly made.

The Doctor having a large family, with a very limited income to support them, and understanding that D******* had at last become a person of sober and industrious habits, he gave his consent, in which Emma's mother fully concurred.

Aware of the straitened circumstances of the Doctor, D******* remitted a sum of money to complete at Edinburgh Emma's Oriental education, and fit her out in her journey to India; she was to embark at Sheerness, on board one of the Company's ships, for a port in India, at which place, he said, he would wait her arrival, with a retinue suited to a person of his rank in society.

Emma set out from her father's house just in time to secure a passage, as proposed by her intended husband, accompanied by her only brother, who, on their arrival at Sheerness, met one C******, an old schoolfellow, captain of the ship by which Emma was to proceed to India.

It was the particular desire of the Doctor that his daughter should be committed to the care of that gentleman, from the time of her leaving the shores of Britain, till the intended marriage ceremony was duly performed on her arrival in India; a charge that was frankly undertaken by the generous sea-captain.

On the arrival of the fleet at the appointed port, D*******, with a large cavalcade of mounted Pindarees, was, as expected, in attendance, ready to salute Emma on landing, and to carry her direct into the interior of the country. C******, who had made several voyages to the shores of Hindostan, knowing something of Hindoo manners and customs, was surprised to see a private individual in the Company's service with so many attendants; and when D******* declined having the marriage ceremony performed according to the rites of the Church, till he returned to the place of his abode, C******, more and more confirmed in his suspicion that all was not right, resolved not to part with Emma, till he had fulfilled, in the most satisfactory manner, the promise he had made before leaving England, of giving her duly away in marriage. Not being able by her entreaties to alter the resolution of D*******, Emma solicited her protector C****** to accompany her to the place of her intended destination, to which he most readily agreed, taking with him as many of his crew as he deemed sufficient to ensure the safe custody of his innocent protegée, should any attempt be made to carry her away by force.

Both parties journeyed onwards till they arrived at a frontier town, where a native Rajah was waiting the arrival of the fair maid of Fife, with whom he had fallen deeply in love, from seeing her miniature likeness in the possession of D*******, to whom he had paid a large sum of money for the original, and had only intrusted him to convey her in state to the seat of his government.

No sooner was this villainous action of D******* known to C******, than he communicated the whole particulars to the commanding officer of a regiment of Scotch Highlanders that happened to be quartered in that part of India, begging at the same time, for the honour of Caledonia, and protection of injured innocence, that he would use the means in his power, of resisting any attempt that might be made by the native chief to wrest from their hands the virtuous female who had been so shamefully decoyed from her native country by the worst of mankind. Honour occupies too large a space in the heart of the Gael to resist such a call of humanity.

The Rajah, finding his claim was not to be acceded to, and resolving to enforce the same, assembled his troops, and attacked with great fury the place where the affrighted Emma was for a time secured by her countrymen, who fought in her defence with all their native valour, which at length so overpowered their assailants, that they were forced to retire in every direction, leaving behind many of their slain, among whom was found the mangled corpse of the perfidious D*******.

C****** was immediately afterwards married to Emma, and my informant assured me he saw them many years afterwards, living happily together in the county of Kent, on the fortune bequeathed by the "Thane of Fife."

J. T.

CASTLE DOUGLAS, *July*, 1832.

Introduction to the Chronicles of the Canongate, published in 1827

[Scott's original Introduction intended for the Magnum: see Editorial Note, 450–53 above]

It is remarkable, that from circumstances scarcely under my own command, my intercourse with the public had changed in a degree as sudden perhaps, and as great, as any which exists in the realms of literature—the lightness, that is, and unimportance considered.

The previous prosperity of my life had depended in some measure upon the success of a series of anonymous publications, which succeeded as much superior to their own merit as to the expectations of the public. The Author of Waverley had been able to indulge most of the tastes which a retired person might be supposed to entertain, and unquestionably, so far as worldly affairs had gone, might be esteemed fortunate in his transactions. To an easy competence derived from succession to my nearest relations, this secret source of income, like the fountain of coined gold and pearls possest by the great Persian traveller Aboulfouaris—this little supply of idle wants—enabled me without the charge of imprudence, to extend my expenditure in some lines which could not probably have been otherwise very prudent. I bought, I built, and though contented with a moderate share of the literary profits of Waverley and his successors, came to be possest of an easy fortune; and which seemed, unlike the other riches of this world, little likely to assume to itself wings and fly away. It showed however in the year 1826 that it had no more sure foundation than other sources of revenue in this transitory world. The general distress in that unlucky year of the bookselling world having taken place at once, and to an immense extent, placed the author at the mercy of those for whose transactions he had obliged himself to the extent of upwards of L.120,000; and nothing remained but the sad remedy requiring indulgence from creditors whom he could not immediately satisfy, for the purpose of turning into money valuables of every kind which he possest, and paying as speedily as was possible the debts for which he had become bound. With this purpose the author, with whatever feelings, surrendered his property like an honest man, and it became vested for the time in persons whose integrity, liberality, and general kindness, as well as prudence and knowledge, enabled them to give their assistance for carrying into execution a plan of a nature apparently gigantic, involving expenses which could not have been commanded even for a temporary purpose without their assistance.

It occurred that an edition like the present, possessing explanations upon such parts as the public had been interested in while they were in an anonymous state, might be acceptable to the readers, and if produced at a moderate expence and under favourable circumstances, would afford a considerable addition to the funds out of which payment to any extent was alone to be expected. It is needless to say, that it became necessary (all reasons for concealment being at an end) the author should avow the paternity of these tales. The following introductory preface to the Chronicles of the Canongate was written at this time, for the purpose of explaining much that it was thought necessary to elucidate concerning the present publication of what are called "The Waverley Novels."

These illustrations accordingly are given in the preface which was written upon the occasion. It is here reprinted because a laudable curiosity is reasonably attached to a coin or medal struck upon a particular occasion, which usually possesses a sharpness and precision of impress which hardly exists on those that have been current for some time in the world. I have, however, added from the newspapers of the day a more full account of what passed upon occasion of the name of the Author of Waverley being for the first time announced to the public, which (although the author, directed by the clear-headed and sagacious gentleman who undertook to act as publisher, and took on him the commercial part of the publication, had long thought of making the confession) became at last a circumstance of mere accident; for no communication existed betwixt him and his friend Lord Meadowbank, who appears, and truly, as the person who introduced the explanation. The desire of keeping together all the circumstances relating to this literary discovery will, it is hoped, apologise for the repetition of some circumstances, neither long nor of much importance, which have been already mentioned in various parts of these notes. In a word, it is the desire of the Editor that this edition should be rendered as perfect as possible, and he feels it is his duty to do all he can to accomplish his purpose, since the uncommon indulgence of the public fully authorises him to hope that the continuation of their favour will enable him, notwithstanding advancing life, and powers declining in proportion, to attain that object which he has proposed to himself, and which he may now justly consider as to a certain degree accomplished. The times, highly unfavourable certainly for literary adventure, have in this individual case proved so favourable as to authorise a hope, that the embarrassments into which the author was led by circumstances, will be extinguished by a short continuation of the same public favour which he has experienced since the commencement of the present publication under his own name, and which has already reduced these embarrassments, and provided funds to a considerable extent for the entire liquidation of what remains.

[Here the first-edition Introduction, EEWN 20, 3–11, was to follow.]

The general preface gives some account of the great change which induced the author to lay aside his incognito, or rather put it out of his power to retain it any longer. The Chronicles of the Canongate must now, like the other productions of the author, be prefaced by some introductory matter peculiar to the contents of the volumes so entitled. This cannot indeed be very long, since the works in some degree are their own commentators. Thus having resolved to make a new trial upon the public favour, the first of the kind which I had ever ventured to put forth in my own name, it struck me that something of the plan of a periodical publication might carry with it a certain degree of novelty. I did not indeed propose to request the assistance of any other person in attempting to sustain the proposed editorial labour. I have entertained an opinion that this species of giving to the public as it were a literary picknick, is almost sure to end in that sort of comparisons which are justly termed odious and are therefore to be avoided. I am also conscious perhaps from cases in which I may myself have been concerned, with what ease an author gets promises, and with how much trouble such promises are rendered good. I therefore planned a work to be dependant, as former labours, on my own resources alone, and although I had a consciousness that my spell was endangered since the Author of Waverley had "a local habitation and a name," I was determined with the Great Montrose that in literature as in war

> He either fears his fate too much,
> Or his deserts are small,
> Who dares not put it to the touch
> To win or lose it all.

Chapter 5 of the following work explains upon what plan the periodical work called the Chronicles of the Canongate was to be conducted. The lady termed in the work Mrs Bethune Baliol was an attempt to describe in its leading points the very amiable and interesting character of Mrs Murray Keith, a particular friend of the author, whose death had shortly before saddened a large circle to whom she was dear as well for her agreeable qualities, as for the extent of information which she possessed, and the delightful manner in which she was used to communicate it. She was in fact the real person who supplied the Author with some of his best stories which she afterwards recognized as they came before the public.

The first story in the Chronicles of the Cannongate after the history of the supposed Editor Chrystal Croftangry, being The Highland Widow, was derived from Mrs Keith and was told with a few additional circumstances exactly as she herself told it, and neither the Highland Cicerone MacLeish nor the demure waiting woman were ideal characters. There were instead some imaginary circumstances which I rather regret, for on reconsidering the tale with a view to the present edition, I am convinced I have injured the simplicity of the narrative, which in Mrs Keith's narration was extremely affecting.

The tale entitled The Two Drovers I learned from my old friend George Constable Esq. of Craigie Wallace, whom I have already acknowledged as the original Antiquary. I think he said he was present at the Highlanders' trial at Carlisle. He seldom mentioned the venerable judge's charge to the jury without shedding tears, which had peculiar pathos when flowing down features that had rather a sarcastic or almost a cynical expression.

The third story in the Chronicles is that of The Surgeon's Daughter, and though one would willingly believe the story too bad to be true, yet I could certainly mention some of the names under which it was currently told. Such a disclosure has, however, not made any part of my plan. If a good effect can be produced from the story itself, it will be as efficient as if the name of the criminal were attached to his action. Only I would say that my friend Colonel MacKerris, who really furnished out my tale in the oriental costume, did not stand godfather to any of the facts it contains, while he kindly consented from his eastern remembrances to furnish a costume as dazzling as that of the renowned Scheherazade herself.

Such are the prefatory documents relating to the Chronicles of the Canongate.

Notes to Chronicles of the Canongate

4.1 (Introduction) it should arrive These manuscripts are at present (August 1831) advertised for public sale, which is an addition, though a small one, to other annoyances.
4.19 (Introduction) Lord Meadowbank One of the Supreme Judges of Scotland, termed Lords of Council and Session.
5.10 (Introduction) conversation with him See, for some further particulars, the notes to Old Mortality, in the present collective edition.
5.21 (Introduction) a lady The late Mrs Goldie.
6.32 (Introduction) friends of my father James Chalmers, Esq. solicitor at law, London, who died during the publication of the present edition of these Novels. (Aug. 1831.)
8.24 (Introduction) January 1817 Lord Kinedder died in August 1822. Eheu! (Aug. 1831.)
9.11 (Introduction) their inaccessible situation I would particularly intimate the Kaim of Urie, on the eastern coast of Scotland, as having suggested an idea for the tower called Wolf's-Crag, which the public more generally identified with the ancient tower of Fast-Castle.
10.3 (Introduction) triple brass Not altogether impossible, when

it is considered that I have been at the bar since 1792. (Aug. 1831.)

15.9 (Ch. 1) the Abbey of Holyrood

HOLYROOD. The reader may be gratified with Hector Boece's narrative of the original foundation of the famous abbey of Holyrood, or the Holy Cross, as given in Bellenden's translation:

"Eftir death of Alexander the first, his brothir David come out of Ingland, and wes crownit at Scone, the yeir of God MCXXIV yeiris, and did gret justice, eftir his coronation, in all partis of his realme. He had na weris during the time of King Hary; and wes so pietuous, that he sat daylie in judgement, to caus his pure commonis to have justice; and causit the actionis of his noblis to be decidit be his othir jugis. He gart ilk juge redres the skaithis that come to the party be his wrang sentence; throw quhilk, he decorit his realm with mony nobil actis, and ejeckit the vennomus custome of riotus cheir, quhilk wes inducit afore be Inglismen, quhen thay com with Quene Margaret; for the samin wes noisum to al gud maneris, makand his pepil tender and effeminat.

"In the fourt yeir of his regne, this nobill prince come to visie the madin Castell of Edinburgh. At this time, all the boundis of Scotland were ful of woddis, lesouris, and medois; for the countre wes more gevin to store of bestiall, than ony productioun of cornis; and about this castell was ane gret forest, full of haris, hindis, toddis, and sicklike maner of beistis. Now was the Rude Day cumin, called the Exaltation of the Croce; and, becaus the samin wes ane hie solempne day, the king past to his contemplation. Eftir the messis wer done with maist solempnitie and reverence, comperit afore him mony young and insolent baronis of Scotland, richt desirus to haif sum plesur and solace, be chace of hundis in the said forest. At this time wes with the king ane man of singulare and devoit life, namit Alkwine, channon eftir the ordour of Sanct Augustine, quhilk wes lang time confessoure, afore, to King David in Ingland, the time that he wes Erle of Huntingtoun and Northumbirland. This religious man dissuadit the king, be mony reasonis, to pas to this huntis; and allegit the day wes so solempne, be reverence of the haly croce, that he suld gif him erar, for that day, to contemplation, than ony othir exersition. Nochtheles, his dissuasionis litill avalit; for the king wes finallie so provokit, be inoportune solicitatioun of his baronis, that he past, nochtwithstanding the solempnite of this day, to his hountis. At last, quhen he wes cumin throw the vail that lyis to the gret eist fra the said castell, quhare now lyis the Canongait, the staill past throw the wod with sic noyis and din of rachis and bugillis, that all the bestis were rasit fra thair dennis. Now wes the king cumin to the fute of the crag, and all his noblis severit, heir and thair, fra him, at thair game and solace; quhen suddenlie apperit to his sicht, the fairist hart that evir wes sene afore with levand creature. The noyis and din of this hart rinnand, as apperit, with awful and braid tindis, maid the kingis hors so effrayit, that na renzeis micht hald him; bot ran, perforce, ouir mire and mossis, away with the king. Nochtheles, the hart followit so fast, that he dang baith the king and his hors to the ground. Than the king kest abak his handis betwix the tindis of this hart, to haif savit him fra the strak thairof; and the haly croce slaid, incontinent, in his handis. The hart fled away with gret violence, and evanist in the same place quhare now springis the Rude Well. The pepil richt affrayitly, returnit to him out of all partis of the wod, to comfort him efter his trubill; and fell on kneis, devotly adoring the haly croce; for it was not cumin but sum hevinly providence, as weill apperis; for thair is na man can schaw of quhat mater it is of, metal or tre. Sone eftir, the king returnit to his castell; and in the nicht following, he was admonist, be ane vision in his sleip, to big ane abbay of channonis regular in the same place quhare he gat the croce. Als sone as he was awalkinnit, he schew his visione to Alkwine, his confessoure; and he na thing suspended his gud mind, bot erar inflammit him with maist fervent devotion thairto. The king, incontinent, send his traist servandis in France and Flanderis, and brocht richt crafty masonis to big this abbay; syne dedicat it in the honour of this haly croce. The croce remanit continewally in the said abbay, to the time of King David Bruce; quhilk was unhappily tane with it at Durame, quhare it is haldin yit in gret veneration."—BOECE, *book* 12, *ch.* 16.

It is by no means clear what Scottish prince first built a palace, properly so called, in the precincts of this renowned seat of sanctity. The abbey, endowed by successive sovereigns and many powerful nobles with munificent gifts of lands and tithes, came, in process of time, to be one of the most important of the ecclesiastical corporations of Scotland; and as early as the days of Robert Bruce, parliaments were held occasionally within its buildings. We have evidence that James IV. had a royal lodging adjoining to the cloister; but it is generally agreed that the first considerable edifice for the accommodation of the royal family erected here was that of James V., anno 1525, great part of which still remains, and forms the northwestern side of the existing palace. The more modern buildings which complete the quadrangle were erected by King Charles II. The nave of the old conventual church was used as the parish church of the Canongate from the period of the Reformation, until James II. claimed it for his chapel royal, and had it fitted up accordingly in a style of splendour which grievously outraged the feelings of his Presbyterian subjects. The roof of this fragment of a once magnificent church fell in in the year 1768, and it has remained ever since in a state of desolation.—For fuller particulars, see the *Provincial Antiquities of Scotland*, or the *History of Holyrood, by* MR CHARLES MACKIE.

The greater part of this ancient palace is now again occupied by his Majesty Charles the Tenth of France, and the rest of that illustrious family, which, in former ages so closely connected by marriage and alliance with the house of Stuart, seems to have been destined to run a similar career of misfortune. *Requiescant in pace!*

24.19 (Ch. 2) the Bannatyne Club This Club, of which the Author of Waverley has the honour to be President, was instituted in February 1823, for the purpose of printing and publishing works illustrative of the history, literature, and antiquities of Scotland. It continues to prosper, and has already rescued from oblivion many curious materials of Scottish History.

24.28 (Ch. 2) Somerville The ancient Norman family of the Somervilles came into this island with William the Conqueror, and established one branch in Gloucestershire, another in Scotland. After the lapse of 700 years, the remaining possessions of these two branches were united in the person of the late Lord Somerville, on the death of his English kinsman, the well-known author of "The Chase."

30.21 (Ch. 3) John Ostler See the opening scene of the first part of Shakspeare's Henry IV.

36.34 (Ch. 3) the times of the persecution

STEELE, A COVENANTER, SHOT BY CAPTAIN CREICHTON. The following extract from Swift's Life of Creichton gives the particulars of the bloody scene alluded to in the text:—

"Having drank hard one night, I (Creichton) dreamed that I had found Captain David Steele, a notorious rebel, in one of the five farmers' houses on a mountain in the shire of Clydesdale, and parish of Lismahago, within eight miles of Hamilton, a place that I was well acquainted with. This man was head of the rebels, since the affair of Airs-Moss; having succeeded to Hackston, who had been there taken, and afterward hanged, as the reader has already heard; for, as to Robert Hamilton, who was then Commander-in-chief at Bothwell Bridge, he appeared no more among them, but fled, as it was believed, to Holland.

"Steele, and his father before him, held a farm in the estate of Hamilton, within two or three miles of that town. When he betook himself to arms, the farm lay waste, and the Duke could find no other person who would venture to take it; whereupon his Grace sent several messages to Steele, to know the reason why he kept the farm waste. The Duke received no other answer, than that he would keep it waste, in spite of him and the king too; whereupon his Grace, at whose table I had always the honour to be a welcome guest, desired I would use my endeavours to destroy that rogue, and I would oblige him for ever.

* * * * * * * *

"I return to my story. When I awaked out of my dream, as I had done before in the affair of Wilson, (and I desire the same apology I made in the introduction to these Memoirs may serve for both,) I presently rose, and ordered thirty-six dragoons to be at the place appointed by break of day. When we arrived thither, I sent a party to each of the five farmers' houses. This villain Steele had murdered above forty of the king's subjects in cold blood; and, as I was informed, had often laid snares to entrap me; but it happened, that although he usually kept a gang to attend him, yet at this time he had none, when he stood in the greatest need. One of the party found him in one of the farmers' houses, just as I happened to dream. The dragoons first searched all the rooms below without success, till two of them hearing somebody stirring over their heads, went up a pair of turnpike stairs. Steele had put on his clothes, while the search was making below; the chamber where he lay was called the Chamber of Deese,* which is the name given to a room where the laird lies, when he comes to a tenant's house. Steele suddenly opening the door, fired a blunderbuss down at the two dragoons, as they were coming up the stairs; but the bullets grazing against the side of the turnpike, only wounded, and did not kill them. Then Steele violently threw himself down the stairs among them, and made towards the door to save his life, but lost it upon the spot; for the dragoons who guarded the house dispatched him with their broadswords. I was not with the party when he was killed, being at that time employed in searching at one of the other houses, but I soon found what had happened, by hearing the noise of the shot made with the blunderbuss; from whence I returned straight to Lanark, and immediately sent one of the dragoons express to General Drummond at Edinburgh."—*Swift's Works, Vol. XII.* (*Memoirs of Captain John Creichton*), pages 57–59, Edit. Edinb. 1824.

* Or chamber of state; so called from the *dais*, or canopy and elevation of floor, which distinguished the part of old halls which was occupied by those of high rank. Hence the phrase was obliquely used to signify state in general.

Woodrow gives a different account of this exploit—"In December this year, (1686,) David Steil, in the parish of Lismahagow, was surprised in the fields by Lieutenant Creichton, and after his surrender of himself on quarters, he was in a very little time most barbarously shot, and lies buried in the churchyard there."

58.6 (Ch. 6) iron rasp

IRON RASP. The ingenious Mr R. CHAMBERS's Traditions of Edinburgh give the following account of the forgotten rasp or risp.

"This house had *a pin* or *risp* at the door, instead of the more modern convenience, a knocker. The pin, rendered interesting by the figure which it makes in Scottish song, was formed of a small rod of iron, twisted or notched, which was placed perpendicularly, starting out a little from the door, bearing a small ring of the same metal, which an applicant for admittance drew rapidly up and down the *nicks*, so as to produce a grating sound. Sometimes the rod was simply stretched across the *vizzying* hole, a convenient aperture through which the porter could take cognisance of the person applying; in which case it acted also as a stanchion. These were almost all disused about sixty years ago, when knockers were generally substituted as more genteel. But knockers at that time did not long remain in repute, though they have never been altogether superseded, even by bells, in the Old Town. The comparative merit of knockers and pins was for a long time a subject of doubt, and many knockers got their heads twisted off in the course of the dispute." CHAMBERS's *Traditions of Edinburgh.*

59.13 (Ch. 6) Salisbury Crags The Rev. Mr Bowles derives the name of these crags, as of the Episcopal city in the west of England, from the same root; both, in his opinion, which he very ably defends and illustrates, having been the sites of druidical temples.

59.32 (Ch. 6) the Black Watch The well-known original designation of the gallant 42d Regiment. Being the first corps raised for the royal service in the Highlands, and allowed to retain their national garb, they were thus named from the contrast which their dark tartans furnished to the scarlet and white of the other regiments.

60.23 (Ch. 6) Each under each Shakspeare's Midsummer Night's Dream, Act IV. Sc. I.

63.22 (Ch. 6) Countess of Eglinton

COUNTESS OF EGLINTON. Susannah Kennedy, daughter of Sir Archibald Kennedy of Cullean, Bart. by Elizabeth Lesly, daughter of David Lord Newark, third wife of Alexander 9th Earl of Eglinton, and mother of the 10th and 11th Earls. She survived her husband, who died 1729, no less than fifty-seven years, and died March 1780, in her 91st year. Allan Ramsay's Gentle Shepherd, published 1726, is dedicated to her, in verse, by Hamilton of Bangour.

The following account of this distinguished lady is taken from Boswell's Life of Johnson by Mr Croker.

"Lady Margaret Dalrymple, only daughter of John Earl of Stair, married in 1700, to Hugh, third Earl of Loudoun. She died in 1777, aged *one hundred*. Of this venerable lady, and of the Countess of Eglintoune, whom Johnson visited next day, he thus speaks in his *Journey*.—'Length of life is distributed impartially to very different modes of life, in very different climates; and the mountains have no greater examples of age than the Lowlands, where I was introduced to two ladies of high quality, one of whom (Lady Loudoun) in her ninety-fourth year, presided at her table with the full exercise of all her powers; and the other, (Lady Eglintoune,) had attained her eighty-fourth year, without any diminution of her vivacity, and little reason to accuse time of depredations on her beauty.'"

* * * * * * *

"Lady Eglintoune, though she was now in her eighty-fifth year, and had lived in the retirement of the country for almost half a century, was still a very agreeable woman. She was of the noble house of Kennedy, and had all the elevation which the consciousness of such birth inspires. Her figure was majestic, her manners high-bred, her reading extensive, and her conversation elegant. She had been the admiration of the gay circles of life, and the patroness of poets. Dr Johnson was delighted with his reception here. Her principles in church and state were congenial with his. She knew all his merit, and had heard much of him from her son, Earl Alexander, who loved to cultivate the acquaintance of men of talents in every department."

* * * * * * * *

"In the course of our conversation this day, it came out that Lady Eglintoune was married the year before Dr Johnson was born; upon which she graciously said to him, that she might have been his mother, and that she now adopted him; and when we were going away, she embraced him, saying, 'My dear son, farewell!' My friend was much pleased with this day's entertainment, and owned that I had done well to force him out."

* * * * * * * *

"At Sir Alexander Dick's, from that absence of mind to which every man is at times subject, I told, in a blundering manner, Lady Eglintoune's complimentary adoption of Dr Johnson as her son; for I unfortunately stated that her ladyship adopted him as her son, in consequence of her having been married the year *after* he was born. Dr Johnson instantly corrected me. 'Sir, don't you perceive that you are defaming the Countess? For, supposing me to be her son, and that she was not married till the year after my birth, I must have been her *natural* son.' A young lady of quality who was present, very handsomely said, 'Might not the son have justified the fault?' My friend was much flattered by this compliment, which he never forgot. When in more than ordinary spirits, and talking of his journey in Scotland, he has called to me, 'Boswell, what was it that the young lady of quality said of me at Sir Alexander Dick's?' Nobody will doubt that I was happy in repeating it."

64.14 (Ch. 6) her unhappy husband The Duke of York, afterwards James II., frequently resided in Holyrood house, when his religion rendered him an object of suspicion to the English Parliament.

65.24 (Ch. 6) so was seen of it, cousin
EARL OF WINTON. The incident here alluded to is thus narrated in Nichols' Progresses of James I., Vol. III. p. 306.

"The family" (of Winton) "owed its first elevation to the union of Sir Christopher Seton with a sister of King Robert Bruce. With King James VI. they acquired great favour, who, having created his brother Earl of Dunfermline in 1599, made Robert, seventh Lord Seton, Earl of Wintoun in 1600. Before the King's accession to the English throne, his Majesty and the Queen were frequently at Seton, where the Earl kept a very hospitable table, at which all foreigners of quality were entertained on their visits to Scotland. His Lordship died in 1603, and was buried on the 5th of April, on the very day the King left Edinburgh for England. His Majesty, we are told, was pleased to rest himself at the south-west round of the orchard of Seton, on the high-way, till the funeral was over, that he might not withdraw the noble company; and he said that he had lost a good, faithful, and loyal subject."

NICHOLS' *Progresses of K. James I. Vol. III. p.* 306.

66.11 (Ch. 6) he had ever met with EXTRACT OF JOURNAL TO STELLA.—"I dined to-day (12th March, 1712,) with Lord Treasurer and two gentlemen of the Highlands of Scotland, yet very polite men." SWIFT'S *Works, Vol. III. p.* 7. *Edin.* 1824.

66.35 (Ch. 6) a Highlandman's promise
MACGREGOR of GLENSTRAE. The 2 of Octr: (1603) Allaster

MacGregor of Glenstrae tane be the laird Arkynles, bot escapit againe; bot after taken be the Earle of Argyll the 4 of Januarii, and brought to Edr: the 9 of Januar: 1604, wt: 18 mae of hes friendes MacGregors. He wes convoyit to Berwick be the gaird, conform to the Earle's promes; for he promesit to put him out of Scottis grund: Sua he keipit ane Hielandman's promes, in respect he sent the gaird to convoy him out of Scottis grund; bot yai wer not directit to pairt wt: him, bot to fetche him bak againe. The 18 of Januar, he came at evin againe to Edinburghe; and upon the 20 day, he was hangit at the crosse, and ij of his freindes and name, upone ane gallows: himself being chieff, he wes hangit his awin hight above the rest of hes freindis.—BIRRELL'S *Diary*, (*in* DALZELL'S *Fragments of Scottish History*,) p. 60–1.

71.13 (Ch. 7) incumbent at Glenorquhy This venerable and hospitable gentleman's name was MacIntyre.

71.16 (Ch. 7) towers of Kilchurn

LOCH AWE. "Loch Awe, upon the banks of which the scene of action took place, is thirty-four miles in length. The north side is bounded by wide muirs and inconsiderable hills, which occupy an extent of country from twelve to twenty miles in breadth, and the whole of this space is enclosed as by circumvallation. Upon the north it is barred by Loch Eitive, on the south by Loch Awe, and on the east by the dreadful pass of Brandir, through which an arm of the latter lake opens, at about four miles from its eastern extremity, and discharges the river Awe into the former. The pass is about three miles in length; its east side is bounded by the almost inaccessible steeps which form the base of the vast and rugged mountain of Cruachan. The crags rise in some places almost perpendicularly from the water, and for their chief extent show no space nor level at their feet, but a rough and narrow edge of stony beach. Upon the whole of these cliffs grew a thick and interwoven wood of all kinds of trees, both timber, dwarf, and coppice; no track existed through the wilderness, but a winding path, which sometimes crept along the precipitous height, and sometimes descended in a straight pass along the margin of the water. Near the extremity of the defile, a narrow level opened between the water and the crag; but a great part of this, as well as of the preceding steeps, was formerly enveloped in a thicket, which showed little facility to the feet of any but the martins and wild cats. Along the west side of the pass lies a wall of sheer and barren crags. From behind they rise in rough, uneven, and heathy declivities, out of the wide muir before mentioned, between Loch Eitive and Loch Awe; but in front they terminate abruptly in the most frightful precipices, which form the whole side of the pass, and descend at one fall into the water which fills its trough. At the north end of the barrier, and at the termination of the pass, lies that part of the cliff which is called Craiganuni; at its foot the arm of the lake gradually contracts its water to a very narrow space, and at length terminates at two rocks (called the Rocks of Brandir), which form a strait channel, something resembling the lock of a canal. From this outlet there is a continual descent towards Loch Eitive, and from hence the river Awe pours out its current in a furious stream, foaming over a bed broken with holes, and cumbered with masses of granite and whinstone.

"If ever there was a bridge near Craiganuni in ancient times, it must have been at the Rocks of Brandir. From the days of Wallace to those of General Wade, there were never passages of this kind but in places of great necessity, too narrow for a boat, and too wide for a leap; even then they were but an unsafe footway formed of the trunks of trees placed transversely from rock to rock, unstripped of their bark, and destitute of either plank or rail. For such a structure, there is no place in the neighbourhood of Craiganuni, but at the rocks above mentioned. In the lake and on the river, the water is far too wide; but at the strait, the space is not greater than might be crossed by a tall mountain pine, and the rocks on either side are formed by nature like a pier. That this point was always a place of passage, is rendered probable by its facility, and the use of recent times. It is not long since it was the common gate of the country on either side the river and the pass: the mode of crossing is yet in the memory of people living, and was performed by a little currach moored on either side the water, and a stout cable fixed across the stream from bank to bank, by which the passengers drew themselves across in the manner still practised in places of the same nature. It is no argument against the existence of a bridge in former times, that the above method only existed in ours, rather than a passage of that kind, which would seem the more improved expedient. The contradiction is sufficiently accounted for by the decay of timber in the neighbourhood. Of old, both oaks and firs of an immense size abounded within a very inconsiderable distance; but it is now many years since the destruction of the forests of Glen Eitive and Glen Urcha has deprived the country of all the trees of sufficient size to cross the strait of Brandir; and it is probable, that the currach was not introduced till the want of timber had disenabled the inhabitants of the country from maintaining a bridge. It only further remains to be noticed, that at some distance below the Rocks of Brandir, there was formerly a ford, which was used for cattle in the memory of people living; from the narrowness of the passage, the force of the stream, and the broken bed of the river, it was, however, a dangerous pass, and could only be attempted with safety at leisure and by experience."—*Notes to The Bridal of Caolchairn.*

71.43 (Ch. 7) defence and protection

BATTLE BETWIXT THE ARMIES OF THE BRUCE AND MAC-DOUGAL OF LORN. "But the King, whose dear-bought experience in war had taught him extreme caution, remained in the Braes of Balquhidder till he had acquired by his spies and outskirrers a perfect knowledge of the disposition of the army of Lorn, and the intention of its leader. He then divided his force into two columns, intrusting the command of the first, in which he placed his archers and lightest armed troops, to Sir James Douglas, whilst he himself took the leading of the other, which consisted principally of his knights and barons. On approaching the defile, Bruce dispatched Sir James Douglas by a pathway which the enemy had neglected to occupy, with directions to advance silently, and gain the heights above and in front of the hilly ground where the men of Lorn were concealed; and, having ascertained that this movement had been executed with success, he put himself at the head of his own division, and fearlessly led his men into the defile. Here, prepared as he was for what was to take place, it was difficult to prevent a temporary panic, when the yell which, to this day, invariably precedes the assault of the mountaineer, burst from the rugged bosom of Ben Cruachan; and the woods which, the moment before, had waved in silence and solitude, gave forth their birth of steel-clad warriors, and, in an instant, became instinct with the dreadful vitality of war. But although appalled and checked for a brief space by the suddenness of the assault, and the masses of rock which the enemy rolled down from the precipices, Bruce, at the head of his division, pressed up the side of the mountain. Whilst this party assaulted the men of Lorn with the utmost fury, Sir James Douglas and his party shouted suddenly upon the heights in their front, showering down their arrows upon them; and, when these missiles were exhausted, attacking them with their swords and battle-axes. The consequence of such an attack, both in front and rear, was the total discomfiture of the army of Lorn; and the circumstances to which this chief had so confidently looked forward, as rendering the destruction of Bruce almost inevitable, were now turned with fatal effect against himself. His great superiority of numbers cumbered and impeded his movements. Thrust, by the double assault, and by the peculiar nature of the ground, into such narrow room as the pass afforded, and driven to fury by finding themselves cut to pieces in detail, without power of resistance, the men of Lorn fled towards Loch Eitive, where a bridge thrown over the Awe, and supported upon two immense rocks, known by the name of the Rocks of Brandir, formed the solitary communication between the side of the river where the battle took place, and the country of Lorn. Their object was to gain the bridge, which was composed entirely of wood, and, having availed themselves of it in their retreat, to destroy it, and thus throw the impassable torrent of the Awe between them and their enemies. But their intention was instantly detected by Douglas, who, rushing down from the high grounds at the head of his archers and light-armed foresters, attacked the body of the mountaineers, which had occupied the bridge, and drove them from it with great slaughter, so that Bruce and his division, on coming up, passed it without molestation; and, this last resource being taken from them, the army of Lorn were, in a few hours, literally cut to pieces, whilst their chief, who occupied Loch Eitive with his fleet, saw, from his ships, the discomfiture of his men, and found it impossible to give them the least assistance.—TYTLER'S *Life of Bruce*.

72.2 (Ch. 7) long enough a-gone This is a line from a very pathetic ballad which I heard sung by one of the young ladies of Edgeworthstown in 1825. I do not know that it has been printed.

78.6 (Ch. 8) the Sidier Roy The Red Soldier.

89.11 (Ch. 10) Caberfae Caberfae—*Anglice*, the Stag's-head, the Celtic designation for the arms of the family of the high Chief of Seaforth.

90.27 (Ch. 10) screams and murder

MASSACRE OF GLENCOE. The following succinct account of this too celebrated event, may be sufficient for this place:—

"In the beginning of the year 1692, an action of unexampled barbarity disgraced the government of King William III. in Scotland. In the August preceding, a proclamation had been issued, offering an indemnity to such insurgents as should take the oaths to the King and Queen, on or before the last day of December; and the chiefs of such tribes, as had been in arms for James, soon after took advantage of the proclamation. But Macdonald of Glencoe was prevented by accident, rather than design, from tendering his submission within the limited time. In the end of December he went to Colonel Hill, who commanded the garrison in Fort William, to take the oaths of allegiance to the government; and the latter having furnished him with a letter to Sir Colin Campbell, Sheriff of the county of Argyll, directed him to repair immediately to Inverary, to make his submission in a legal manner before that magistrate. But the way to Inverary lay through almost impassable mountains, the season was extremely rigorous, and the whole country was covered with a deep snow. So eager, however, was Macdonald to take the oaths before the limited time should expire, that, though the road lay within half a mile of his own house, he stopped not to visit his family, and, after various obstructions, arrived at Inverary. The time had elapsed, and the sheriff hesitated to receive his submission; but Macdonald prevailed by his importunities, and even tears, in inducing that functionary to administer to him the oath of allegiance, and to certify the cause of his delay. At this time Sir John Dalrymple, afterwards Earl of Stair, being in attendance upon William as Secretary of State for Scotland, took advantage of Macdonald's neglecting to take the oath within the time prescribed, and procured from the King a warrant of military execution against that chief and his whole clan. This was done at the instigation of the Earl of Breadalbane, whose lands the Glencoe men had plundered, and whose treachery to government in negotiating with the Highland clans, Macdonald himself had exposed. The King was accordingly persuaded that Glencoe was the main obstacle to the pacification of the Highlands; and the fact of the unfortunate chief's submission having been concealed, the sanguinary orders for proceeding to military execution against his clan were in consequence obtained. The warrant was both signed and countersigned by the King's own hand, and the Secretary urged the officers who commanded in the Highlands to execute their orders with the utmost rigour. Campbell of Glenlyon, a captain in Argyll's regiment, and two subalterns, were ordered to repair to Glencoe on the first of February with a hundred and twenty men. Campbell being uncle to young Macdonald's wife, was received by the father with all manner of friendship and hospitality. The men were lodged at free quarters in the houses of his tenants, and received the kindest entertainment. Till the 13th of the month the troops lived in the utmost harmony and familiarity with the people; and on the very night of the massacre, the officers passed the evening at cards in Macdonald's house. In the night Lieutenant Lindsay, with a party of soldiers, called in a friendly manner at his door, and was instantly admitted. Macdonald, while in the act of rising to receive his guest, was shot dead through the back with two bullets. His wife had already dressed; but she was stripped naked by the soldiers, who tore the rings off her fingers with their teeth. The slaughter now became general, and neither age nor infirmity was spared. Some women, in defending their children, were killed; boys, imploring mercy, were shot dead by officers on whose knees they hung. In one place nine persons, as they sat enjoying themselves at table, were butchered by the soldiers.

In Inverriggon, Campbell's own quarters, nine men were first bound by the soldiers, and then shot at intervals, one by one. Nearly forty persons were massacred by the troops; and several who fled to the mountains perished by famine and the inclemency of the season. Those who escaped owed their lives to a tempestuous night. Lieutenant-Colonel Hamilton, who had received the charge of the execution from Dalrymple, was on his march with four hundred men, to guard all the passes from the valley of Glencoe; but he was obliged to stop by the severity of the weather, which proved the safety of the unfortunate clan. Next day he entered the valley, laid the houses in ashes, and carried away the cattle and spoil, which were divided among the officers and soldiers".—*Article* "BRITAIN;" *Encyc. Britannica—New edition.*

99.23 (Ch. 11) within the General's power

FIDELITY OF THE HIGHLANDERS. Of the strong, undeviating attachment of the Highlanders to the person, and their deference to the will or commands of their chiefs and superiors their rigid adherence to duty and principle—and their chivalrous acts of self-devotion to these in the face of danger and death, there are many instances recorded in General Stewart of Garth's interesting Sketches of the Highlanders and Highland Regiments, which might not inaptly supply parallels to the deeds of the Romans themselves, at the era when Rome was in her glory. The following instances of such are worthy of being here quoted:—

"In the year 1795, a serious disturbance broke out in Glasgow, among the Breadalbane Fencibles. Several men having been confined and threatened with corporal punishment, considerable discontent and irritation were excited among their comrades, which increased to such violence, that, when some men were confined in the guard-house, a great proportion of the regiment rushed out and forcibly released the prisoners. This violation of military discipline was not to be passed over, and accordingly measures were immediately taken to secure the ringleaders. But so many were equally concerned, that it was difficult, if not impossible, to fix the crime on any, as being more prominently guilty. And here was shown a trait of character worthy of a better cause, and which originated from a feeling alive to the disgrace of a degrading punishment. The soldiers being made sensible of the nature of their misconduct, and the consequent necessity of public example, *several men voluntarily offered themselves to stand trial*, and suffer the sentence of the law as an atonement for the whole. These men were accordingly marched to Edinburgh Castle, tried, and four condemned to be shot. Three of them were afterwards reprieved, and the fourth, Alexander Sutherland, was shot on Musselburgh Sands.

"The following demi-official account of this unfortunate misunderstanding was published at the time:—

"'During the afternoon of Monday, when a private of the light company of the Breadalbane Fencibles, who had been confined for a *military* offence, was released by that company, and some other companies who had assembled in a tumultuous manner before the guard-house, no person whatever was hurt, and no violence offered; and however unjustifiable the proceedings, it originated not from any disrespect or ill-will to their officers, but from a mistaken point of honour, in a particular set of men in the battalion, who thought themselves disgraced by the impending punishment of one of their number. The men have, in every respect, since that period conducted themselves with the greatest regularity, and strict subordination. The whole of the battalion seemed extremely sensible of the improper conduct of such as were concerned, whatever regret they might feel for the fate of the few individuals who had so readily given themselves up as prisoners, to be tried for their own and others' misconduct.'

"On the march to Edinburgh, a circumstance occurred, the more worthy of notice, as it shows a strong principle of honour and fidelity to his word and to his officer in a common Highland soldier. One of the men stated to the officer commanding the party, that he knew what his fate would be, but that he had left business of the utmost importance to a friend in Glasgow, which he wished to transact before his death; that, as to himself, he was fully prepared to meet his fate; but with regard to his friend, he could not die in peace unless the business was settled, and that, if the officer would suffer him to return to Glasgow, a few hours there would be sufficient, and he would join him before he reached Edinburgh, and march as a prisoner with the party. The soldier added, 'You have known me since I was a child; you know my country and kindred, and you may believe I shall never bring you to any blame by a breach of the promise I now make, to be with you in full time to be delivered up in the Castle.' This was a startling proposal to the officer, who was a judicious, humane man, and knew perfectly his risk and responsibility in yielding to such an extraordinary application. However, his confidence was such, that he complied with the request of the prisoner, who returned to Glasgow at night, settled his business, and left the town before daylight to redeem his pledge. He took a long circuit to avoid being seen, apprehended as a deserter, and sent back to Glasgow, as probably his account of his officer's indulgence would not have been credited. In consequence of this caution, and the lengthened march through woods and over hills by an unfrequented route, there was no appearance of him at the hour appointed. The perplexity of the officer when he reached the neighbourhood of Edinburgh may be easily imagined. He moved forward slowly indeed, but no soldier appeared; and unable to delay any longer, he marched up to the Castle, and as he was delivering over the prisoners, but before any report was given in, Macmartin, the absent soldier, rushed in among his fellow prisoners, all pale with anxiety and fatigue, and breathless with apprehension of the consequences in which his delay might have involved his benefactor.

"In whatever light the conduct of the officer (my respectable friend, Major Colin Campbell) may be considered, either by military men or others, in this memorable exemplification of the characteristic principle of his countrymen, fidelity to their word, it cannot but be wished that the soldier's magnanimous self-devotion had been taken as an atonement for his own misconduct and that of the whole, who also had made a high sacrifice, in the voluntary offer of their lives for the conduct of their brother soldiers. Are these a people to be treated as malefactors, without regard to their feelings and principles? and might not a discipline, somewhat different from the usual mode, be, with advantage, applied to them?"—Vol. II. p. 413–15. 2d Edit.

"A soldier of this regiment, (The Argyllshire Highlanders,) deserted, and emigrated to America, where he settled. Several years after his desertion, a letter was received from him, with a sum of money, for the purpose of procuring one or two men to supply his place in the regiment, as the only recompense he could make for 'breaking his oath to his God and his allegiance to his King, which preyed on his conscience in such a manner, that he had no rest night nor day.'

"This man had had good principles early instilled into his mind, and the disgrace which he had been originally taught to believe would attach to a breach of faith now operated with full effect. The soldier who deserted from the 42d Regiment at Gibraltar, in 1797, exhibited the same remorse of conscience after he had violated his allegiance. In countries where such principles prevail, and regulate the character of a people, the mass of the population may, on occasions of trial, be reckoned on as sound and trustworthy."—Vol. II. p. 218. 2d Edit.

"The late James Menzies of Culdares, having engaged in the rebellion of 1715, and been taken at Preston, in Lancashire, was carried to London, where he was tried and condemned, but afterwards reprieved. Grateful for this clemency, he remained at home in 1745, but, retaining a predilection for the old cause, he sent a handsome charger as a present to Prince Charles, when advancing through England. The servant who led and delivered the horse was taken prisoner, and carried to Carlisle, where he was tried and condemned. To extort a discovery of the person who sent the horse, threats of immediate execution in case of refusal, and offers of pardon on his giving information, were held out ineffectually to the faithful messenger. He knew, he said, what the consequence of a disclosure would be to his master, and his own life was nothing in the comparison; when brought out for execution, he was again pressed to inform on his master. He asked if they were serious in supposing him such a villain. If he did what they desired, and forgot his master and his trust, he could not return to his native country, for Glenlyon would be no home or country for him, as he would be despised and hunted out of the Glen. Accordingly he kept steady to his trust, and was executed. This trusty servant's name was John Macnaughton, from Glenlyon, in Perthshire; he deserves to be mentioned, both on account of his incorruptible fidelity, and of his testimony to the honourable principles of the people, and to their detestation of a breach of trust to a kind and honourable master, however great might be the risk, or however fatal the consequences, to the individual himself."—Vol. I. pp. 52, 53. 2d Edit.

124.8 (Ch. 12) unsophisticated state Letters from the Mountains, 3 vols.—Essays on the Superstitions of the Highlanders—The Highlanders, and other Poems, &c.

124.9 (Ch. 12) General Stewart of Garth The gallant and amiable author of the History of the Highland Regiments, in whose glorious services his own share had been great, went out Governor of St Lucie in 1828, and died in that island on the 18th of December 1829,—no man more regretted, or perhaps by a wider circle of friends and acquaintance.

146.26 (Ch. 13) what can I do more?

Robert Donn's Poems. I cannot dismiss this story without resting attention for a moment on the light which has been thrown on the character of the Highland Drover since the time of its first appearance, by the account of a drover poet, by name Robert Mackay, or, as he was commonly called, Rob Donn, *i.e.* brown Robert, and certain specimens of his talents, published in the 90th Number of the Quarterly Review. The picture which that paper gives of the habits and feelings of a class of persons with which the general reader would be apt to associate no ideas but those of wild superstition and rude manners, is in the highest degree interesting;

and I cannot resist the temptation of quoting two of the songs of this hitherto unheard of poet of humble life. They are thus introduced by the reviewer:—

"Upon one occasion, it seems, Rob's attendance upon his master's cattle business detained him a whole year from home, and at his return he found that a fair maiden, to whom his troth had been plighted of yore, had lost sight of her vows, and was on the eve of being married to a rival, (a carpenter by trade,) who had profited by the young Drover's absence. The following song was composed during a sleepless night, in the neighbourhood of Creiff, in Perthshire, and the home sickness which it expresses appears to be almost as much that of the deer-hunter as of the loving swain.

Easy is my bed, it is easy,
But it is not to sleep that I incline;
The wind whistles northwards, northwards,
And my thoughts move with it.

More pleasant were it to be with thee
In the little glen of calves,
Than to be counting of droves
In the enclosures of Creiff.
Easy is my bed, &c.

Great is my esteem of the maiden,
Towards whose dwelling the north wind blows;
She is ever cheerful, sportive, kindly,
Without folly, without vanity, without pride.
True is her heart—were I under hiding,
And fifty men in pursuit of my footsteps,
I should find protection, when they surrounded me most closely,
In the secret recess of that shieling.
Easy is my bed, &c.

Oh for the day for turning my face homeward,
That I may see the maiden of beauty:—
Joyful will it be to me to be with thee,—
Fair girl with the long heavy locks!
Choice of all places for deer-hunting
Are the brindled rock and the ridge!
How sweet at evening to be dragging the slain deer
Downwards along the piper's cairn!
Easy is my bed, &c.

Great is my esteem of the maiden
Who parted from me by the west side of the enclosed field;
Late yet again will she linger in that fold,
Long after the kine are assembled.
It is I myself who have taken no dislike to thee,
Though far away from thee am I now.
It is for the thought of thee that sleep flies from me;
Great is the profit to me of thy parting kiss!
Easy is my bed, &c.

Dear to me are the boundaries of the forest;
Far from Creiff is my heart;
My remembrance is of the hillocks of sheep,
And the heath of many knolls.
Oh for the red-streaked fissures of the rock,
Where in spring time, the fawns leap;
Oh for the crags towards which the wind is blowing—
Cheap would be my bed to be there!
Easy is my bed, &c.

"The following describes Rob's feelings on the first discovery of his damsel's infidelity. The airs of both these pieces are his own, and, the Highland ladies say, very beautiful.

Heavy to me is the shieling, and the hum that is in it,
Since the ear that was wont to listen is now no more on the watch.
Where is Isabel, the courteous, the conversable, a sister in kindness?
Where is Anne, the slender-browed, the turret-breasted, whose glossy hair pleased me when yet a boy?
Heich! what an hour was my returning!
Pain such as that sunset brought, what availeth me to tell it?

I traversed the fold, and upward among the trees—
Each place, far and near, wherein I was wont to salute my love.
When I looked down from the crag, and beheld the fair-haired stranger dallying with his bride,
I wished that I had never revisited the glen of my dreams.
Such things came into my heart as that sun was going down,
A pain of which I shall never be rid, what availeth me to tell it?

Since it hath been heard that the carpenter had persuaded thee,
My sleep is disturbed—busy is foolishness within me at midnight.
The kindness that has been between us,—I cannot shake off that memory in visions;
Thou callest me not to thy side; but love is to me for a messenger.
There is strife within me, and I toss to be at liberty;
And ever the closer it clings, and the delusion is growing to me as a tree.

Anne, yellow-haired daughter of Donald, surely thou knowest not how it is with me—
That it is old love, unrepaid, which has worn down from me my strength;
That when far from thee, beyond many mountains, the wound in my heart was throbbing,
Stirring, and searching for ever, as when I sat beside thee on the turf.
Now, then, hear me this once, if for ever I am to be without thee,
My spirit is broken—give me one kiss ere I leave this land!

Haughtily and scornfully the maid looked upon me;
Never will it be work for thy fingers to unloose the band from my curls;

Thou hast been absent a twelvemonth, and six were seeking
me diligently;
Was thy superiority so high, that there should be no end of
abiding for thee?
Ha! ha! ha!—hast thou at last become sick?
*Is it love that is to give death to thee? surely the enemy has been in
no haste.*

But how shall I hate thee, even though towards me thou hast
become cold?
When my discourse is most angry concerning thy name in thine
absence,
Of a sudden thine image, with its old dearness, comes visibly
into my mind;
And a secret voice whispers that love will yet prevail!
And I become surety for it anew, darling,
And it springs up at that hour lofty as a tower.

"Rude and bald as these things appear in a verbal translation, and rough as they might possibly appear, even were the originals intelligible, we confess we are disposed to think they would of themselves justify Dr Mackay (their Editor) in placing this herdsman-lover among the true sons of song."—*Quarterly Review, No. XC. July* 1831.

149.18 (Ch. 14) the late Mr Walker of Edinburgh [Robert Walker, the colleague and rival of Dr Hugh Blair, in St Giles's Church, Edinburgh.]

167.25 (Ch. 15) landloupers Strollers.

169.4 (Ch. 15) gled Or Kite.

169.39 (Ch. 15) clavers Tattling.

178.3 (Ch. 16) Menie Marion.

181.2 (Ch. 16) Galatian Galatian is a name of a person famous in Christmas gambols.

191.37 (Ch. 18) the Physic Garden The Botanic Garden is so termed by the vulgar of Edinburgh.

210.19 (Ch. 19) bonnie die "Pretty toy."

266.17 (Ch. 26) his present enterprise It is scarce necessary to say, that such things could only be acted in the earlier period of our Indian settlements, when the check of the Directors was imperfect, and that of the Crown did not exist. My friend Mr Fairscribe is of opinion, that there is an anachronism in the introduction of Paupiah, the Bramin Dubash of the English governor.—C. C.

THE FAIR MAID OF PERTH

Editorial Note

The Fair Maid of Perth occupies Volumes 42 and 43 of the Magnum, published on 1 November and 1 December 1832 respectively. They have an Introduction, dated 15 August 1831, and a total of not far short of a hundred notes. All 21 of the brief footnotes in the original 1828 edition are retained, and on occasion expanded, whether by an extended gloss (e.g. the slightly ostentatious addition of '*ποιητής*' to the note on 'maker' at 528) or by historical information (e.g. the note on the Brandanes at 532). The interleaved copy of this novel, preserved in the University of Texas Library in Austin, indicates that, although some of the shorter notes are Scott's own work, most of them were composed by Lockhart. Some indirect input from Scott into the Lockhart notes cannot be ruled out. (For a fuller discussion of the new annotation see EEWN 21, 407–08).

On 16 August 1831 Scott had written to Cadell: 'I inclose in this parcel the three volumes of the Chronicles of Canongate Series second with the Introduction. Anne of Geierstein comes next together with Aunt Margarets mirror' (MS 15980, f. 150r). Cadell's diary for 17 August confirms receipt: 'parcel from Sir Walter with Introduction & notes to Fair Maid of Perth' (MS 21021, f. 35v). Scott left Abbotsford for London and the Mediterranean on 23 September 1831. On 2 March 1832, with Scott still in Italy, Cadell advised the Trustees: 'it will be necessary for him [Cadell] to obtain the assistance of Mr Lockhart in the preparation of the introductions and notes for the Novels after Woodstock, very little of which had been finished by Sir Walter previously to his leaving Scotland. Stating further that Sir Walter had authorised him to apply to Mr Lockhart on all such occasions' (MS 114, p. 1). This is borne out by the comparatively few entries in Scott's hand for the interleaved copy, and by three letters from Lockhart to Cadell.

In the first, of 12 August 1832, he writes: 'As you seem to be in haste for copy I send one vol of the Maid of Perth. The Introduction must come after I hope to send it & vols 2 & 3 in a few days' (MS 21011, f. 17r). On 15 August he says: 'I have done the Notes & Introduction for the Maid of Perth but wait to see whether Morrison sends anything. Your Brownie will find some transcribing pointed out in the Introduction & in the Note at the end of Vol 3 & I had as well see the proofs of the whole novel for there are constant noddings as to the names both of Individuals & the two Clans & I cant be sure that I have corrected them all' (MS 21011, f. 19r–v). Three days later he writes further: 'I send the sheets corrected & Morrisons notes *ditto* as I as I wd wish them to appear. I have enclosed also vol II wt my notes: and the General Introduction which must be dovetailed into the old one as in the former novels in this Edition. The substance of what is said as to *Connochar* is from the Author's diary' (MS 21011, f. 21). The last sentence refers to the *Journal* entry for 5 December 1827 (390) where Scott adumbrates Conachar as, in his cowardice, a tragic not a comic figure.

The most likely interpretation of this evidence is that the Introduction referred to in Scott's letter of 16 August is the one—or some of version of it—found in MS 911, ff. 264–71 (see further below); and that at some point it was discarded, to be replaced by the published Magnum Introduction (or 'Preface') written by Lockhart in August 1832, but printed with the date of Scott's own Introduction to disguise this.

The surviving manuscript of Scott's original Introduction intended for the Magnum (evidently incomplete, since the last leaf ends with a catchword) in MS 911, ff. 264r–269r is in the hand of William Laidlaw. It differs completely from the 'Preface' published in the Magnum. In contrast to the antiquarian and source-documenting thrust of the latter it focuses on the genesis, internal and external, of *The Fair Maid*. The external genesis lies in the 'revolution' which 'took place in the public taste about the year 1828' with the arrival of the Annual as a new, and newly marketable, form. Scott's contributions, actual or promised, to some of those compelled a change of course for the second series of the Chronicles (see the *Journal*, 375, 7 November 1827, and EEWN 21, 393–94). Like the first series, this had been planned as a collection of framed short stories. Some of those were now given up for publication in annuals and 'It was therefore necessary to alter the plan of the latter part of the chronicles in size and form to adapt them more to Waverley and its successors'. The internal genesis of *The Fair Maid* is itemised in terms not of Conachar as tragic and sympathetic coward but of the twin climactic events of the clan combat and the murder of Rothsay. This supports the suggestion (EEWN 21, 396–97) that the (unhistorical) linking of those events was crucial to the novel's development. The final paragraph advances historical justification for having a Lollard priest in the novel, but in a fashion that bears on the internal workings of the narrative, as documented history in the Magnum Introduction does not: 'the awakening religious dissensions are also introduced as a key to the mysteries of the story'. This is borne out in Chapter 25, where Father Clement's heretical views require the flight of Simon and his daughter beyond the Highland line, a development necessary for the final confrontation of Conochar with Henry. (And it might be worth noting that 'A key to the mysteries' echoes the extended image in the opening paragraph to the previous chapter—the pivotal Chapter 1 of Volume 3 in the first edition—where Bonthron is recovered from the gallows). A lightly edited version of what survives of Scott's original Introduction is published in the present edition alongside its replacement, with a diplomatic (literal) transcription in the Emendation List.

The 'Preface' actually published in the Magnum picks up two topics that figured in the genesis of *The Fair Maid*: the possible exhaustion of the Highlands and Highlanders as a field for historical fiction (see EEWN 21, 391–92 and 418), and Conochar as sympathetic coward. It underlines the novel's sombre presentation of the social and political state of Scotland at the period, and discusses at some length the identity of the contending clans as a subject of antiquarian dispute, only to dismiss it drily at the end ('it is perhaps impossible to clear up thoroughly this controversy, little interesting in itself, at least to readers on this side of Inverness'). This prefigures the antiquarian documenting that makes up so much of the end of chapter notes to come. The developing story of the battle is traced from Wyntoun through the continuator of Fordoun (extended quotations from both) to the accounts (drily summarised) of Boece, Leslie, and Buchanan. In a decided shift of tone, the Preface ends with two historical anecdotes, the first of which provides a source, the second an analogue, for the devotion of Conachar's foster-brethren.

The completed annotation for the Magnum develops from the first edition in three directions. It extends the latter's glossing of individual words and phrases in the text; it expands the strictly historical notes (only three in 1828); and it swells out in antiquarian notes on the topography of Perth and on medieval customs. Many of these are by 'Mr Morrison', doubtless identical with the 'distinguished local antiquary' who supplies the note on the View from the Wicks of Baiglie for Chapter 1, or 'our local antiquary' in Chapter 6's note on The Glovers. This is David Morison or Morrison (1792–1855), from the third generation of a notable Perth family of booksellers and publishers. His grandfather Robert Morrison (1722–91), who founded the family firm, had published the 1774 edition of *The Muses Threnodie*, a major source for *The Fair Maid*. In 1819 David Morrison had become Secretary to the Literary and Antiquarian Society of Perth (founded in 1784 as the Antiquarian Society of Perth and taking 'Literary' into its title two years later). He was the author, *inter alia*, of a *Guide to the City and County of Perth*, and of catalogues of the Kinfauns library and the Kinfauns pictures which won the praises of Scott in a letter of 29 November 1828 to Lord Gray of Kinfauns (transcript in the Corson Collection in Edinburgh University Library). Scott had written to him two days earlier to acknowledge receipt of the first (and, as it turned out, only) volume of the Society's *Transactions*. The letter dwells at some length on the volume's treatment of the Gowrie conspiracy which had already been singled out for praise in the opening chapter of *The Fair Maid*, published six months earlier. Scott commends the Society's researches for having 'taken a more wide and historical view than is usual with institutions of the kind, too often dedicated to petty and puerile objects'. Something of such range is manifested in Morrison's notes for the Magnum which include a concise synopsis of the history of the High Church of St John (536), a note tinged with caustic on the Earl of Errol's Lodgings (541), and another on Morrice-Dancers (535–36).

The overall effect of those antiquarian notes is to buttress—or maybe waterlog—*The Fair Maid* as a local (in distinction from a provincial) novel. In so doing, they chime with the displacing of *St Valentine's Eve* as the primary title, with the interleaved copy notes (in Scott's hand) which flank the opening chapter, and with the historico-topographical strand in the original text from its opening chapter onwards. By contrast the near six pages of small print quoting the medieval church prayers for the ordeal by fire (taken from the Annual-style volume, *Janus*, produced by Lockhart and John Wilson in 1825), which are brought in only as an analogue to the ordeal by combat in the text, and are supplemented in turn by a cultural-historical and historical-anecdotal commentary on a case of murder tried in Edinburgh before Sir George Mackenzie in 1688, do more than smack of book-making.

The strictly historical notes can fill in detail (as that on royal mistresses for Chapter 2: 527) and may strike a thematic chord (as with that on Robert the Bruce for the same chapter, with its citation of Barbour (528), which could fortify his evoking as heroic exemplar by Catherine in her impassioned speech of Chapter 31 to Rothsay). Elsewhere they supply detailed documentation, most notably in the five-and-a-half page final note on the death of Rothsay (546–50), with its prolonged quotations from the Continuator of Fordoun, Boece, and the text of the Remission granted to Albany and Douglas by Robert III (first printed by Lord Hailes) which emphatically involves Douglas in the guilt of the Prince's murder (the MS 911 Introduction concurs in this). That can illuminate, by contrast, the complex position Scott bestows on Douglas in the novel, and the continuity of that position with *The Fair Maid*'s nuanced and incisive presentation of *realpolitik*.

There are four Magnum illustrations for this title. The frontispiece to Volume 42 (MAG0083 / TB348.42) was designed by William Allan and engraved by Charles Fox. It depicts Catharine Glover leaning over and kissing Henry Gow, asleep in a chair, with her father appearing at the door (EEWN 21, 49–50: the caption reads simply 'FAIR MAID OF PERTH.'). The title-page vignette (MAG0084 / TB348.42) was designed by David Octavius Hill and engraved by William Miller. It depicts the traveller on horseback surveying the valley of the Tay with the town of Perth in the distance (EEWN 21, 12.27–30 (with 'stretched' for 'stretching': 'He beheld stretched beneath him and its towers.') The frontispiece to Volume 43 (MAG0085 / TB348.43) was designed by Thomas Duncan and engraved by John Horsburgh. It depicts Catharine listening devoutly to instructions from Father Clement, under a rock beneath the hill of Kinnoul (EEWN 21, 145.31–34: 'At the foot of a rock a Carthusian monk.'). The title-page vignette (MAG0086 / TB348.43) was designed by David Octavius Hill and engraved by William Miller. It depicts Rothesay's barge on the Tay, as he hears the music of Louise from Henshaw's boat (EEWN 21, 323.6–8: 'A lute . . . from whence the music comes.').

W. Allan A.R.A. Chas. Fox.

FAIR MAID OF PERTH.

WAVERLEY NOVELS.

VOL. XLII.

FAIR MAID OF PERTH.

"He beheld stretched beneath him, the valley of the Tay, traversed by its ample and lordly streams; the town of Perth, with its two large meadows or Inches, its steeples, and its towers."

PRINTED FOR ROBERT CADELL, EDINBURGH.
AND WHITTAKER & C° LONDON.
1832.

T. Duncan. J. Horsburgh

FAIR MAID OF PERTH.

"At the foot of a rock which commanded the view in every direction, sat the Fair Maid of Perth, listening in an attitude of devout attention to the instructions of a Carthusian monk".

EDINBURGH, PUBLISHED 1832, BY ROBERT CADELL, and WHITTAKER & C° LONDON.

WAVERLEY NOVELS.

VOL. XLIII.

FAIR MAID OF PERTH.

'A lute' said the Duke of Rothsay, listening; 'it is, and
rarely touched. I should remember that dying fall.
Steer towards the boat from whence the music comes.'

PRINTED FOR ROBERT CADELL, EDINBURGH.
AND WHITTAKER & C° LONDON.
1832.

Preface to the Fair Maid of Perth

IN continuing the lucubrations of Chrystal Croftangry, it occurred that, although the press had of late years teemed with works of various descriptions concerning the Scottish Gael, no attempt had hitherto been made to sketch their manners, as these might be supposed to have existed at the period when the Statute-book, as well as the page of the chronicler, begins to present constant evidence of the difficulties to which the crown was exposed, while the haughty house of Douglas all but overbalanced its authority on the Southern border, and the North was at the same time torn in pieces by the yet untamed savageness of the Highland races, and the daring loftiness to which some of the remoter chieftains still carried their pretensions. The well-authenticated fact of two powerful clans having deputed each thirty champions to fight out a quarrel of old standing, in presence of King Robert III., his brother the Duke of Albany, and the whole court of Scotland, at Perth, in the year of grace 1396, seemed to mark with equal distinctness the rancour of these mountain-feuds, and the degraded condition of the general government of the country; and it was fixed upon accordingly as the point on which the main incidents of a romantic narrative might be made to hinge. The characters of Robert III., his ambitious brother, and his dissolute son, seemed to offer some opportunities of interesting contrast;—and the tragic fate of the heir of the throne, with its immediate consequences, might serve to complete the picture of cruelty and lawlessness.

Two features of the story of this barrier-battle on the Inch of Perth, the flight of one of the appointed champions, and the reckless heroism of a townsman, that voluntarily offered for a small piece of coin to supply his place in the mortal encounter, suggested the imaginary persons, on whom much of the novel is expended. The fugitive Celt might have been easily dealt with, had a ludicrous style of colouring been adopted; but it appeared to the author that there would be more of novelty, as well as of serious interest, if he could succeed in gaining for him something of that sympathy which is incompatible with the total absence of respect. Miss Baillie had drawn a coward by nature capable of acting as a hero under the strong impulse of filial affection. It seemed not impossible to conceive the case of one constitutionally weak of nerve, being supported by feelings of honour and of jealousy up to a certain point, and then suddenly giving way, under circumstances to which the bravest heart could hardly refuse compassion.

The controversy, as to who really were the clans that figured in the barbarous conflict of the Inch, has been revived since the publication of the Fair Maid of Perth, and treated in particular at great length by Mr Robert Mackay of Thurso, in his very curious "History of the House and Clan of Mackay."* Without pretending to say that he has settled any part of the question in the affirmative, this gentleman certainly seems to have quite succeeded in proving that his own worthy sept had *no* part in the transaction. The Mackays were in that age seated, as they have since continued to be, in the extreme north of the island; and their chief at the time was a personage of such importance, that his name and proper designation could not have been omitted in the early narratives of the occurrence. He on one occasion brought four thousand of his clan to the aid of the royal banner against the Lord of the Isles. This historian is of opinion that the Clan Quhele of Wyntoun were the *Camerons*, who appear to have about that period been often designated as *Macewans*, and to have gained much more recently the name of *Cameron*, i.e. *Wrynose*, from a blemish in the physiognomy of some heroic chief of the line of Lochiel. This view of the case is also adopted by Douglas in his Baronage, where he frequently mentions the bitter feuds between Clan Chattan and Clan Kay, and identifies the former sept, in reference to the events of 1396, with the Camerons. It is perhaps impossible to clear up thoroughly this controversy, little interesting in itself, at least to readers on this side of Inverness. The names, as we have them in Wyntoun, are *Clanwhewyl* and *Clachinya*, the latter probably not correctly transcribed. In the Scoti-Chronicon they are *Clanquhele* and *Clankay*. Hector Boece writes *Clanchattan* and *Clankay*, in which he is followed by Leslie; while Buchanan disdains to disfigure his page with their Gaelic designations at all, and merely describes them as two powerful races in the wild and lawless region beyond the Grampians. Out of this jumble what Sassenach can pretend *dare lucem?* The name Clanwheill appears so late as 1594, in an act of James VI. Is it not possible that it may be, after all, a mere corruption of Clan Lochiel?

The reader may not be displeased to have Wyntoun's original rhymes:

> A thousand and thre hunder yere,
> Nynty and sex to mak all clere—
> Of thre-score wyld Scottis men,

* Edinburgh, 4to, 1829.

Thretty agane thretty then,
In Felny bolnit of auld Fede,*
As thare fore-elders ware slane to dede:
Tha thre-score ware clannys twa,
Clahynnhe Qwhewyl and Clachinyha:
Of thir twa Kynnis ware tha men,
Thretty agane thretty then:
And thare thai had thair Chiftanys twa,
Scha† Ferqwharis' son wes ane of tha,
The tother Cristy Johnseone.
A selcouth thing by tha was done.
At Sanct Johnstoun besyde the Freris,
All thai enterit in Barreris
Wyth bow and ax, knyf and swerd,
To deil amang thaim thair last werd.‡
Thare thai laid on that time sa fast,
Quha had the ware§ thare at the last
I will nocht say; bot quha best had,
He was but dout bathe muth and mad.||
Fifty or má ware slane that day,
Sua few wyth lif than past away

The Prior of Lochleven makes no mention either of the evasion of one of the Gaelic champions, or of the gallantry of the Perth artisan, in offering to take a share in the conflict. Both incidents, however, were introduced, no doubt from tradition, by the continuator of Fordun, whose narrative is in these words:—

"Anno Dom. millesimo trecentesimo nonagesimo sexto, magna pars borealis Scotiæ, trans Alpes, inquietata fuit per duos pestiferos Cateranos, et eorum sequaces, viz. Scheabeg et suos consanguinarios, qui Clankay; et Cristi-Jonson, ac suos, qui Clanquhele dicebantur; qui nullo pacto vel tractatu pacificari poterant, nullâque arte regis vel gubernatoris poterant edomari, quoadusque nobilis et industriosus D. David de Lindesay de Crawford, et dominus Thomas comes Moraviæ, diligentiam et vires apposuerunt, ac inter partes sic tractaverunt, ut coram domino rege certo die convenirent apud Perth, et alterutra pars eligeret de progenie sua triginta personas adversus triginta de parte contraria, gladiis tantùm, arcubus et sagittis, absque deploidibus, vel armaturis aliis, præter bipennes; et sic congredientes finem liti ponerent, et terra pace potiretur. Utrique igitur parti summè placuit contractus, et die Lunæ proximo ante festum Sancti Michaëlis, apud North-insulam de Perth, coram Rege et Gubernatore, et innumerabili multitudine comparentes,

* *i.e.* Boiled with the cruelty of an old feud.

† *Scha* is supposed to be *Toshach, i.e.* Macintosh: the father of the chief of this sept at the time was named Ferchard. In Bower he is *Scheabeg*, *i.e.* Toschach the little.

‡ *i.e.* Fate, doom.

§ The *waur*—the worse.

|| *Muth* and *mad*, *i.e.* exhausted both in body and in mind.

conflictum acerrimum inierunt: ubi de sexaginta interfecti sunt omnes, excepto uno ex parte Clankay, et undecim exceptis ex parte altera. Hoc etiam ibi accidit, quòd omnes in præcinctu belli constituti, unus eorum locum diffugii considerans, inter omnes in amnem elabitur, et aquam de Thaya natando transgreditur; à millenis insequitur, sed nusquam apprehenditur. Stant igitur partes attonitæ, tanquam non ad conflictum progressuri, ob defectum evasi: noluit enim pars integrum habens numerum sociorum consentire, ut unus de suis demeretur; nec potuit pars altera quocumque pretio alterum ad supplendum vicem fugientis inducere. Stupent igitur omnes hærentes, de damno fugitivi conquerentes. Et cùm totum illud opus cessare putaretur, ecce in medio prorupit unus stipulosus vernaculus, staturâ modicus, sed efferus, dicens; Ecce ego! quis me conducet intrare cum operariis istis ad hunc ludum theatralem? Pro dimidia enim marca ludum experiar, ultra hoc petens, ut si vivus de palæstra evasero, victum à quocumque vestrûm recipiam dum vixero: quia, sicut dicitur, 'Majorem caritatem nemo habet, quàm ut animam suam ponat suis pro amicis.' Quali mercede donabor, qui animam meam pro inimicis reipublicæ et regni pono? Quod petiit, à rege et diversis magnatibus conceditur. Cum hoc arcus ejus extenditur, et primò sagittam in partem contrariam transmittit, et unum interficit. Confestim hinc inde sagittæ volitant, bipennes librant, gladios vibrant, alterutro certant, et veluti carnifices boves in macello, sic inconsternatè ad invicèm se trucidant. Sed nec inter tantos repertus est vel unus, qui, tanquam vecors aut timidus, sive post tergum alterius declinans, seipsum à tanta cæde prætendit excusare. Iste tamen tyro superveniens finaliter illæsus exivit; et dehinc multo tempore Boreas quievit; nec ibidem fuit, ut suprà, Cateranorum excursus."

The scene is heightened with many florid additions by Boece and Leslie, and the contending savages in Buchanan utter speeches after the most approved pattern of Livy.

The devotion of the young chief of Clan Quhele's foster-father and foster-brethren, in the novel, is a trait of clannish fidelity, of which Highland story furnishes many examples. In the battle of Inverkeithing, between the Royalists and Oliver Cromwell's troops, a foster-father and seven brave sons are known to have thus sacrificed themselves for Sir Hector Maclean of Duart—the old man, whenever one of his boys fell, thrusting forward another to fill his place at the right hand of the beloved chief, with the very words adopted in the novel—"Another for Hector!"

Nay, the feeling could outlive generations. The late much lamented General Stewart of Garth, in his account of the battle of

Killiecrankie, informs us that Lochiel was attended on the field by the son of his foster-brother. "This faithful adherent followed him like his shadow, ready to assist him with his sword, or cover him from the shot of the enemy. Suddenly the chief missed his friend from his side, and turning round to look what had become of him, saw him lying on his back with his breast pierced by an arrow. He had hardly breath, before he expired, to tell Lochiel, that seeing an enemy, a Highlander in General Mackay's army, aiming at him with a bow and arrow, he sprung behind him, and thus sheltered him from instant death. This," observes the gallant David Stewart, "is a species of duty not often practised, perhaps, by our aide-de-camps of the present day," —*Sketches of the Highlanders*, Vol. I. p. 65.

I have only to add, that the Second Series of "Chronicles of the Canongate," with the Chapter Introductory which now follows, appeared in May 1828, and had a favourable reception.

ABBOTSFORD, *Aug.* 15, 1831.

Introduction to Chronicles of the Canongate Part 2

[Scott's original Introduction intended for the Magnum: see Editorial Note, 511–12 above]

THE second part of these Chronicles was in a great measure conducted upon the same plan and by the same machinery with the first part, in which Chrystal Croftangry and Mrs Bethune Baliol were first introduced to the public. It was also intended that the stories which it was designed to publish should have been short and detached pieces of narrative, of which the author conceived he possessed a sufficient number to furnish out the second part of an entertaining miscellany. But a revolution took place in the public taste about the year 1828, when a variety of annuals were published by different editors rivalling each other in the beauty of their decorations, as well as in the literary merit of their contents. To some of these, the author of Waverley was requested to be a contributor, and it was often under circumstances which he did not think himself at liberty to refuse. In this way, a good many of the fictions, being a considerable part of the stock designed for the second part of the Chronicles of the Canongate, were given or promised to these annual collections, which were at first proper to Germany, but now became for a short time very popular with the British public; although from the expense both in art and in literature, it may be supposed that few of them turned out very profitable to the undertakers.

It was therefore necessary to alter the plan of the latter part of the Chronicles, and in size and form to adapt them more to Waverley and its successors. A part was selected of the History of Robert III., comprehending historical incidents of sufficient notoriety, but the details of which were so little known, as to allow great freedom to be taken by the narrator in the indulgence of his own fancy.

The two principal events were the combat between the Clan Chattan and the Clan Kay or Quhele, which Buchanan and our other historians state to have taken place upon the North Inch of Perth, as Pinkerton expresses it in the following passage:

> The north of Scotland being disturbed by continual feuds, between the two highland factions of Clan Kay, commanded by one Shee-beg and his relations, and Clan Quhele under a Christie Jonson, which could be appeased by no authority nor art of the king, or Fife the governor; it was at last adjusted by the Earl of Moray and Lindsay of Crawford, that the dispute should be terminated by thirty men, appointed upon either side to fight in the Royal presence at Perth. Having met on the day named before the king, governor, many nobles and a great multitude, eager to see this novelty, one of the Clan Kay felt his heart fail, and escaped by swimming across the Tay, upon which a clown who was present offered to supply his place for half a mark. A fierce battle ensued with bows, battle axes, swords, and daggers; and ended in the defeat of Clan Kay, who had only the mercenary left alive, while eleven of the opponents keeped the field. The highlanders were afterwards more quiet for a few years: but it might be said upon this occasion that a public spectacle had been appointed, to manifest to the nation that the government was without power, and the laws without force.—*Hist. of Scotland*. Vol. i, p. 51.

To this general account of a highly interesting and romantic incident, even tradition adds little more than that either the clan of M'Intosh, or that of M'Pherson, in Gaelic M'Vurich, represent the leading sept of the victorious confederacy, and it is uncertain even at this day which has the title to be preferred.

Another incident of deep importance at the time is also known at the present day, together with some circumstances of a nature uncommonly melancholy. The fate of the unfortunate David Duke of Rothesay, eldest son of Robert III., who fell a victim to the ambition of his uncle Albany and his father-in-law Douglas, seemed also a piece of real history qualified to be illustrated by fictitious narrative, since, while we know that he was actually starved to death in the dungeon tower of Falkland Castle, we are ignorant of the exact particulars attending this catastrophe.

> The royal mandate was born by Ramorgny and by another enemy of Rothsay, Sir William Lindsay, whose sister Euphemia had also been affianced to the prince, and rejected. From these circumstances it may be perceived that the scheme was laid and conducted with all the deep and dark art of consummate villainy. Albany, receiving the order with joy, resolved on its immediate enforcement, and that the bearers should be the executors. Privacy was necessary; and Rothsay was inveigled into Fife, upon pretence that he should take possession for the king of the castle of St. Andrews, till the appointment of another bishop. When the unsuspecting prince was riding with a small attendance, between Nydie and Straburn, near St. Andrews, he was seized, and held a prisoner in the castle, till the governor and his council, assembled at Culros, should determine the place of his confinement. The tower of Falkland was named; and thither Albany and Douglas, with a strong band of followers, conducted the prince, seated on a labouring horse, and covered with a russet cloke, to defend him from the falling rain. Here under the custody of John Selkirk, and John Wright, two assassins employed by Albany, the most cruel of deaths, that of famine, awaited the heir of the monarchy: and he was buried in a private manner at Lindoris, distant from the tombs of the Scottish kings, or those of his family, the conspirators not daring, by a funereal pomp, to awaken the attention and detection of the people.—*ibid.*, p. 69.

The awakening religious dissensions are also introduced as a key to the mysteries of the story, and thus not without historical authority, for in 1408 one James Resby, a follower of Wickliffe's opinions, was condemned for forty articles of heresy by a clerical court, in which Lawrence Lindores, an inquisitor, was president. He was delivered to the secular arm, and condemned to the stake at Perth, an incident which justifies the existence of the tenets held by the reforming priest introduced into the novel.

Notes to The Fair Maid of Perth

3.25 (Chrystal Croftangry's Narrative) the newest New Town of all This "newest New Town," in case Mr Croftangry's lucubrations should outlive its possession of any right to that designation, was begun, I think, in 1824, on the park and gardens attached to a quondam pretty suburban residence of the Earls of Moray—from whose different titles, and so forth, the names of the *places* and streets erected were, of course, taken. Aug. 1831.

4.5 (Chrystal Croftangry's Narrative) our present gracious Sovereign The visit of George IV. to Scotland, in August 1822, will not soon be forgotten. It satisfied many who had shared Dr Johnson's doubts on the subject, that the old feelings of loyalty, in spite of all the derision of modern wits, continued firmly rooted, and might be appealed to with confidence, even under circumstances apparently the most unfavourable. Who that had observed the state of public feeling with respect to this most amiable prince's domestic position at a period but a few months earlier, would have believed that he should ever witness such scenes of enthusiastic and rapturous devotion to his person, as filled up the whole panorama of his fifteen days at Edinburgh? Aug. 1831.

11.8 (Ch. 1) for the Tay Such is the author's opinion, founded perhaps on national pride, of the relative importance of the Scottish and the classical stream. If he should again be a blotter of paper, he hopes to be able to speak on *this* subject the surer language of personal conviction.

13.3 (Ch. 1) the matchless scene

VIEW FROM THE WICKS OF BAIGLIE. The following note is supplied by a distinguished local antiquary.

"The modern method of conducting the highways through the valleys and along the bases, instead of over the tops of the mountains, as in the days when Chrystal Croftangry travelled, has deprived the stranger of two very striking points of view on the road from Edinburgh to Perth. The first of these presented itself at the summit of one of the Ochills; and the second, which was, in fact, but a nearer view of a portion of the first, was enjoyed on attaining the western shoulder of the hill of Moredun, or Moncreiff. This view from Moncreiff (that which, it is said, made the Romans exclaim that they had found another field of Mars on the bank of another Tiber) now opens to the traveller in a less abrupt and striking manner than formerly, but it still retains many of those features which Pennant has so warmly eulogized. The view from the Ochills has been less fortunate, for the road here winds through a narrow but romantic valley amongst these eminences, and the passing stranger is ushered into Strathern, without an opportunity being offered to him of surveying the magnificent scene which in days of no ancient date every traveller from the South had spread out before him at the Wicks of Baiglie.

"But in seeking out this spot—and it will repay the toil of the ascent a thousandfold—the admirer of such scenes should not confine his researches to the Wicks of Baiglie, strictly so called, but extend them westward until he gain the old road from Kinross to the Church of Drone, being that by which Mr Croftangry must have journeyed. The point cannot be mistaken; it is the only one from which Perth itself is visible. To this station, for reasons that the critic will duly appreciate, might with great propriety be applied the language of one of the guides at Dunkeld, on reaching a bold projecting rock on Craig Vinean—"Ah, sirs, this is the *decisive point!*"

The pencil of Mr D. O. Hill was employed to give this celebrated view from the Wicks of Baiglie, as one of the illustrations of this volume.

13.23 (Ch. 1) indifferent tea Chrystal Croftangry expresses here the feelings of the author, as nearly as he could recall them, after such a lapse of years. I am, however, informed, by various letters from Perthshire, that I have made some little mistakes about names. Sure enough the general effect of the valley of the Tay, and the ancient town of Perth, rearing its grey head among the rich pastures, and beside the gleaming waters of that noblest of Scottish streams, must remain so as to justify warmer language than Mr Croftangry had at his command. Aug. 1831.

14.10 (Ch. 2) to share the Scottish throne David II., after the death of his Queen Jane, married his mistress, "ane lusty woman, Margaret Logie," and though he soon repented, and would fain have repudiated her, the Pope interesting himself in her favour, he found himself bound. As to the next generation, Boece tells us that, "After King Robert (II.) marryit the Earl of Rossis dochter, he had Elizabeth Mure (of Rowallan) in place of his wife. In the thrid year of King Robert, deceasit Euphame his Queen; and he incontinent marryit Elizabeth, lemman afore rehearsit, for the affection that he had to her bairnis."—BELLENDEN, Vol. ii, p. 452.

Robert III. himself was a son of Elizabeth Mure.

20.28 (Ch. 2) indifferently so called *Gow* is Gaelic for *Smith*.

22.17 (Ch. 2) Makar Old Scottish for *Poet*, and indeed the literal translation of the original Greek, Ποιητης.

22.28 (Ch. 2) Sir Magnus Redman He was sometime Governor of Berwick and afterwards slain at the battle of Sark in which the English were defeated.

23.34 (Ch. 2) Burn-the-wind *Burn-the-wind*, an old cant term for blacksmith, appears in Burns—

> Then *Burnewin* cam on like death,
> At every chaup, &c.

25.35 (Ch. 2) yon Highland cateran *Cateran*, or *robber*, the usual designation of the Celtic borderers on the lands of the Sassenach. The beautiful Lake of the Trosachs is supposed to have taken its name from the habits of its frequenters.

26.1 (Ch. 2) skene-occle *Skene-occle*, knife of the armpit, a species of dirk so called, used among Highlanders.

27.7 (Ch. 2) King Robert of happy memory

ROBERT BRUCE. The story of Bruce, when in sore straits, watching a spider near his bed, as it made repeated unsuccessful efforts to attach its thread, but, still persevering, at last attained the object, and drawing from this an augury which encouraged him to proceed in spite of fortune's hard usage, is familar to the reader of Barbour. It was ever after held a foul crime in any of the name of Bruce, or inheriting Gentle King Robert's blood, to injure an insect of this tribe; but indeed it is well known that compassion towards the weak formed part of his character through life; and the beautiful incident of his stopping his army when on the march in circumstances of pressing difficulty in the Ulster campaign, because a poor *lavendere* (washerwoman) was taken with the pains of childbirth, and must have been left, had he proceeded, to the mercy of the Irish Kernes, is only one of many anecdotes, that to this day keep up a peculiar tenderness, as well as pride of feeling, in the general recollection of this great man, now five hundred years mingled with the dust.

30.19 (Ch. 2) Culross girdles The girdle is the thin plate of iron used for the manufacture of the staple luxury of Scotland, the oaten cake. The town of Culross was long celebrated for its girdles.

32.5 (Ch. 3) jackmen Men wearing jacks, or armour.

34.23 (Ch. 3) Glune-amie

GLUNE-AMIE. This word has been one of the torments of the lexicographers. There is no doubt that in Perthshire, and wherever the Highlanders and the Lowlanders bordered on each other, it was a common term whereby, whether in scorn or honour, the Gaelic race used to be designated. Whether the *etymon* be, as Celtic scholars say, *Gluineamach*—i.e. *the Gartered*—(and certainly the garter has always been a marking feature in "the Garb of old Gaul") —or, as Dr Jamieson seems to insinuate, the word originally means *black cattle*, and had been contemptuously applied by the Sassenach to the herdsman, as on an intellectual level with his herd—I shall not pretend to say, more than that *adhuc sub judice lis est*.

34.32 (Ch. 3) the Shoe-gate A principal street in Perth.

38.43 (Ch. 4) the High Street

HIGH STREET. The two following notes are furnished by a gentleman well versed in the antiquities of bonny St Johnston:—

"Some confusion occasionally occurs in the historical records of Perth, from there having been two high or principal streets in that city: the North High Street, still called *the* High Street, and the South High Street, now known only as the South Street, or Shoe-gate. An instance of this occurs in the evidence of one of the witnesses on the Gowrie Conspiracie, who deponed that the Earl of Gowrie ran in from 'the High Street;' whereas the Earl's house stood in that part of the town now known as the South Street. This circumstance will explain how the Smith had to pass St Ann's Chapel and St John's Church on his way from the High Street to Curfew Row, which edifices he would not have approached if his morning walk had been taken through the more northerly of the two principal streets."

39.2 (Ch. 4) Couvrefew Street [Magnum has 'Curfew Street'.]

CURFEW STREET. "Curfew Street, or Row, must, at a period not much earlier than that of the story, have formed part of the suburbs of Perth. It was the Wynd or Row immediately surrounding the Castle Yard, and had probably been built, in part at least, soon after the Castle was rased, and its moat filled up, by Robert Bruce. There is every probability that in the days of Robert the Third, it was of greater extent than at present,—the *Castle Gable*, which now terminates it to the eastward, having then run in a line with the Skinnergate, as the ruins of some walls still bear witness. The shops, as well as the houses of the Glovers, were then, as the name implies, chiefly in the Skinnergate; but the charters in possession of the incorporation show that the members had considerable property in or adjacent to the Curfew Row, consisting not only of fields and gardens, but of dwelling-houses.

"In the wall of the corner house of the Curfew Row, adjacent to Blackfriar's Vennel, there is still to be seen a niche in the wall where the Curfew bell hung. This house formed at one time a part of a chapel dedicated to Saint Bartholomew, and in it at no very distant period the members of the Glover incorporation held their meetings."

45.36 (Ch. 5) St Macgrider A place called vulgarly Ecclesmagirdie (Ecclesia Macgirdi), not far from Perth, still preserves the memory of this old Gaelic saint from utter Lethe.

50.30 (Ch. 5) Jamie Keddie's There is a tradition that one Keddie, a tailor, found in ancient days a ring, possessing the properties of that of Gyges, in a cavern of the romantic hill of Kinnoul, near Perth.

57.10 (Ch. 6) work for the feet

THE GLOVERS. OUR local antiquary says, "The Perth artisans of this craft were of great repute, and numbered amongst them, from a very early period, men of considerable substance. There are still extant among their records many charters and grants of money and lands to various religious purposes, in particular to the upholding of the altar of St Bartholomew, one of the richest of the many shrines within the parish church of St John.

"While alluding to these evidences of the rich possessions of the old Glovers of Perth, it ought not to pass unnoticed—as Henry pinched Simon on the subject of his rival artificers in leather, the cordwainers—that the chaplain 'aikers of St Crispin,' on the Leonardhall property, were afterwards bought up by the Glovers.

"The avocations of this incorporation were not always of a peaceful nature. They still show a banner under which their forefathers fought in the troubles of the 17th century. It bears this inscription. '*The perfect honour of a craft, or beauty of a trade, is not in wealthe but in moral worth, whereby virtue gains renowne:*' and surmounted by the words, 'Grace and Peace,' the date 1604.

"The only other relic in the archives of this body which calls for notice in this place, is a leathern lash, called 'The whip of St Bartholomew,' which the craft are often admonished in the records to apply to the back of refractory apprentices. It cannot have existed in the days of our friend the Glover, otherwise its frequent application to the shoulders of Conachar, would have been matter of record in the history of that family."

66.26 (Ch. 7) the Bloody Heart The well-known cognizance of the house of Douglas.

69.27 (Ch. 7) horse and hattock *Horse and hattock*, the cry of the fairies at taking their enchanted horses, and hence a token of a mounting of any kind.

73.9 (Ch. 7) barons of Kinfauns It is generally believed that the ancient Barons of Kinfauns are now represented in the male line by a once powerful branch of the name, the Charterises of Amisfield, in Dumfries-shire. The remains of the castle, close to which is their modern residence, attest the former extent of their resources.

73.30 (Ch. 8) the East Port
EAST PORT. The following is extracted from a kind communication of the well-known antiquarian, Mr Morison of Perth:—

"The port at which the deputation for Kinfauns met, was a strongly fortified gate at the east end of the High Street, opening to the Bridge. On the north side of the street adjoining the gate, stood the chapel of the Virgin, from which the monks had access to the river by a flight of steps, still called 'Our Lady's Stairs.' Some remains of this chapel are yet extant, and one of the towers is in a style of architecture which most antiquaries consider peculiar to the age of Robert III. Immediately opposite, on the south side of the street, a staircase is still to be seen, evidently of great antiquity, which is said to have formed part of '*Gowrie's Palace*.' But as Gowrie House stood at the other end of the Watergate—as most of the houses of the nobility were situated *between* the staircase we now refer to and Gowrie House; and as, singularly enough, this stair is built upon ground, which, although in the middle of the town, is not within the burgh lands, some of the local antiquaries do not hesitate to say, that it formed part of the Royal Palace, in which the Kings of Scotland resided, until they found more secluded, and probably more comfortable, lodging in the Blackfriar's monastery. Leaving the determination of this question to those who have access to the best means for solving it, thus far is certain, that the place of rendezvous for our hero and his companions was one of some consequence in the town, where their bearing was not likely to pass unobserved. The bridge to which they passed through the gate, was a very stately edifice even in these days. Major calls it, 'Pontem Sancti Joannis ingentem apud Perth.' The date of its erection is not known, but it was extensively repaired by Robert Bruce, in whose reign it suffered by the repeated sieges to which Perth was subjected, as well as by some of those inundations of the Tay to which it was frequently exposed, and one of which eventually swept it away in 1621."

76.18 (Ch. 8) cogan na schie "Peace or war, I care not."

78.16 (Ch. 8) whose ground we ride over Every Scotchman must regret that the name of Johnstone should have disappeared from the peerage, and hope that ere long some one of the many claimants for the minor honours at least of the house of Annandale may make out a case to the satisfaction of the House of Lords. The great estates of the family are still nearly entire, and in worthy hands:—they have passed to a younger branch of the noble house of Hopetoun, one of the claimants of the elder titles.

88.33 (Ch. 9) a dignity next to that of the throne This creation, and that of the Dukedom of Albany, in favour of the King's brother, were the first instances of ducal rank in Scotland. Buchanan mentions the innovation in terms which may be considered as showing that even he partook in the general prejudice with which that title was viewed in Scotland down to a much later period. It had, indeed, been in almost every case united with heavy misfortunes—not rarely with tragic crimes.

93.30 (Ch. 9) thiggers and sorners *Thiggers* and *sorners*, sturdy beggars under various pretences.

94.21 (Ch. 9) the Galilee of the Church The *Galilee* of a Catholic Cathedral is a small side chapel to which excommunicated persons have access, though they must not enter the body of the church. Mr Surtees suggests that the name of the place thus appropriated to the consolation of miserable penitents, was derived from the text: "Ite, nunciate fratribus meis ut eant in Galileam: ibi me videbunt." Matt. xxviii. 10. See *History of Durham*, vol. i. p. lvi. Criminals claiming sanctuary, were, for obvious reasons, accustomed to place themselves in this part of the edifice.

99.16 (Ch. 10) the Brandanes The men of the Isle of Bute were called Brandanes; from what derivation is not quite certain, though the strong probability lies with Dr Leyden, who deduces the name from the Patron Saint of the islands in the Frith of Clyde—viz. St Brandin. The territory of Bute was the King's own patrimony, and its natives his personal followers. The noble family of Bute, to whom the island now belongs, are an ancient illegitimate branch of the Royal house.

100.28 (Ch. 10) the monks of Aberbrothock The complaint of the monks of Arbroath about the too great honour the Earl of Douglas had paid them in becoming their guest with a train of a thousand men, passed into a proverb, and was never forgotten when the old Scots churchmen railed at the nobility, who, in the sequel, demolished the church, out of that earnest yearning they had long felt for her goods.

102.10 (Ch. 10) The Lay of Poor Louise This lay has been set to beautiful music by a lady whose composition, to say nothing of her singing, might make any poet proud of his verses, Mrs Robert Arkwright, born Miss Kemble.

130.14 (Ch. 13) alone able to use Mr Chrystal Croftangry had not, it must be confessed, when he indited this sentence, exactly recollected the character of Rothsay, as given by the prior of Lochleven.

> A seemly person in stature,
> Cunnand into letterature.
>
> B. ix. cap. 23.

133.19 (Ch. 13) that sea-worn Hold The castle of Dunbar.

166.36 (Ch. 15) at command of my art The extent to which the science of poisoning was carried in the middle ages on the continent, is well known. The hateful practice was more and more refined, and still more generally adopted, afterwards; and we are told, among other instances of diabolical cunning, of gloves which could not be put on without inflicting a mortal disease, of letters which, on being opened, diffused a fatal vapour, &c. &c. Voltaire justly and candidly mentions it as a distinguishing characteristic of the British, that political poisonings make little, if any, figure in their history.

176.6 (Ch. 16) the Douze peers The *twelve* peers of Charlemagne, immortal in romance.

182.21 (Ch. 17) the real King The Scottish Statute Book affords abundant evidence of the extravagant and often fatal frolics practised among our ancestors under the personages elected to fill the high offices of *Quene of May*, Prince of Yule (Christmas), Abbott of Unreason, &c. &c., corresponding to the Boy Bishop of England and the French *Abbé de Liesse*, or *Abbas Letitiæ*. Shrovetide was not less distinguished by such mumming dignitaries.

183.36 (Ch. 17) the Massamore The *Massamore*, or *Massy More*, the principal dungeon of the feudal castle, is supposed to have derived its name from our intercourse with the Eastern nations at the time of the Crusades. Dr Jamieson quotes an old Latin Itinerary: "Proximus est carcer subterraneus, sive, ut *Mauri* appellant, *Mazmorra*."

189.17 (Ch. 17) Sir William Wallace The passage referred to is perhaps the most poetical one in Blind Harry's Wallace. Book v., v.180–220.

196.22 (Ch. 18) spare not, St Johnston's hunt is up!
St Johnston's Hunt is up. This celebrated Slogan or War Cry was often accompanied by a stirring strain of music, which was of much repute in its day, but which has long eluded the search of musical antiquaries. It is described by the local poet, Mr Adamson, as a great inspirer of courage.

> Courage to give, was mightily then blown
> Saint Johnston's Hunt's up, since most famous known
> By all musicians——
>
> *Muses' Threnodie, 5th Muse.*

From the description which follows, one might suppose that it had also been accompanied by a kind of war-dance.

> O! how they bend their backs and fingers tirle!
> Moving their quivering heads, their brains do whirle
> With divers moods; and as with uncouth rapture
> Transported, so do shake their bodies' structure;

Their eyes do reele, heads, arms, and shoulders move;
Feet, legs, and hands, and all their parts approve
That heavenly harmonie; while as they threw
Their browes, O mighty strain! that's brave! they shew
Great fantasie:——

Ibid. Id.

198.5 (Ch. 18) Henry Wynd

HENRY SMITH OR WYND. Mr Morrison says:—"The various designations by which Henry or Hal of the Wynd, the Gow Chrom or Bandy-legged Smith of St Johnston, was known, have left the field open to a great variety of competitors for the honour of being reckoned among his descendants. The want of early registers, and various other circumstances, prevent our venturing to pronounce any verdict on the comparative strength of these claims, but we shall state them all fairly and briefly.

"First, we have the Henry or Hendrie families, who can produce many other instances besides their own, in which a Christian name has become that of a family or tribe, from the celebrity attached to it through the great deeds of some one of their ancestors by whom it was borne. Then follow the Hals, Halls, and Halleys, among whom even some of the ancient and honourable race of the Halkets have ranged themselves. All these claims are, however, esteemed very lightly by the Wynds, who to this day pride themselves on their thewes and sinews, and consider that their ancestor being styled "Henrie Winde" by the metrical historian of the town, is of itself proof sufficient that their claim is more solid than the name would altogether imply.

"It is rather singular that, in spite of all the ill-will which Henry seems to have borne to the Celts, and the contemptuous terms in which he so often speaks of them in the text, the Gows should be found foremost among the claimants, and that the strife should lie mainly between them and their Saxon namesakes the Smiths, families whose number, opulence, and respectability, will render it an extremely difficult matter to say which of them are in the direct line, even if it should be clearer than it is, that the children of the hero were known by their father's occupation, and not by his residence.

"It only remains to notice the pretensions of the Chroms, Crooms, Crambs, or Crombies, a name which every schoolboy will associate, if not with the athletic, at least with the gymnastic exercises for which the Gow Chrom and the grammar school of Perth were equally celebrated. We need scarcely add, that while the Saxon name corresponding with the word Gow, has brought a host of competitors into the field, there has not yet started any claimant resting his pretensions on the quality expressed in the epithet *Chrom*, *i.e.* bandy-legged."

212.27 (Ch. 20) The Council-room of Perth

THE COUNCIL-ROOM. Mr Morrison says, "The places where the public assemblies of the citizens, or their magistrates, were held, were so seldom changed in former times, that there seems every reason to conclude that the meetings of the town-council of Perth were always held in or near the place where they still convene. The room itself is evidently modern, but the adjoining building, which seems to have been reared close to, if it did not actually form a part of the Chapel of the Virgin, bears many marks of antiquity. The room, in which it is not improbable the council meetings were held about the period of our story, had been relieved of part of its gloomy aspect in the reign of the third James, by the addition of one of those octagonal towers which distinguish the architecture of his favourite Cochran. The upper part of it and the spire are modern, but the lower structure is a good specimen of that artist's taste.

"The power of trying criminal cases of the most serious kind, and of inflicting the highest punishment of the law, was granted by Robert III. to the magistrates of Perth, and was frequently exercised by them, as the records of the town abundantly prove."

214.5 (Ch. 20) the entry of the morrice-dancers

MORRICE-DANCERS. Considerable diversity of opinion exists respecting the introduction of the Morrice dance into Britain. The name points it out as of Moorish origin; and so popular has this leaping kind of dancing for many centuries been in this country, that when Handel was asked to point out the peculiar taste in dancing and music of the several nations of Europe—to the French he ascribed the minuet; to the Spaniard, the saraband; to the Italian, the arietta; to the English, the hornpipe, or Morrice dance.

The local antiquary whose kindness has already been more than once acknowledged, says—

"It adds not a little interest to such an enquiry, in connexion with a story in which the fortunes of a Perth glover form so prominent a part—to find that the Glover Incorporation of Perth have preserved entire among their relics, the attire of one of the Morrice dancers, who, on some festive occasion, exhibited his paces 'to the jocose recreatment' of one of the Scottish monarchs, while on a visit to the Fair City.

"This curious vestment is made of fawn-coloured silk, in the form of a tunic, with trappings of green and red satin. There accompany it *two hundred and fifty-two* small circular bells, formed into twenty-one sets of twelve bells each, upon pieces of leather, made to fasten to various parts of the body. What is most remarkable about these bells, is the perfect intonation of each set, and the regular musical *intervals* between the tone of each. The twelve bells on each piece of leather are of various sizes, yet all combining to form one perfect intonation in concord with the leading note in the set. These concords are maintained not only in each set, but also in the intervals between the various pieces. The performer could thus produce, if not *a tune,* at least a pleasing and musical chime, according as he regulated with skill the movements of his body. This is sufficient evidence that the Morrice dance was not quite so absurd and unmeaning as might at first be supposed; but that a tasteful performer could give pleasure by it to the skilful, as well as amusement to the vulgar."

218.15 (Ch. 20) the High Church of St John's
CHURCH OF ST JOHN. "There is," says Mr Morrison, "a simplicity in the internal architecture of the building which bespeaks a very ancient origin, and makes us suspect that the changes it has undergone have in a great measure been confined to its exterior. Tradition ascribes its foundation to the Picts, and there is no doubt that in the age immediately subsequent to the termination of that monarchy it was famed throughout all Scotland. It is probable that the western part of it was built about that period, and the eastern not long afterwards, and in both divisions there is still to be seen a unity and beauty of design, which is done little justice to by the broken, irregular, and paltry manner in which the exterior has at various times been patched up. When the three churches into which it is now cut down were in one, the ceilings high and decorated, the aisles enriched by the offerings of the devotees to the various altars which were reared around it, and the arches free from the galleries which now deform all these Gothic buildings,—it must have formed a splendid theatre for such a spectacle as that of the trial by bier-right."

228.35 (Ch. 21) fighting cocks on Fastern's Even FIGHTING COCKS.—This cruel amusement was generally practised in Scotland on Shrove Tuesday so late as the last generation, and ranked with the foot-ball, the hen, and pancakes as a fitting solemnity of the festival.

231.6 (Ch. 21) the Tiger Earl Sir David Lyndsaye, first Earl of Crawford, and brother-in-law to Robert III.

236.14 (Ch. 22) Sir Simon Fraser The famous ancestor of the Lovats, slain at Halidon Hill.

236.15 (Ch. 22) Margaret Logie The beautiful mistress of David II.

244.20 (Ch. 23) to undergo the ordeal
ORDEAL BY FIRE. In a volume of miscellanies published in Edinburgh in 1825, under the name of *Janus*, there is included a very curious paper illustrative of the solemnity with which the Catholic Church in the dark ages superintended the appeal to heaven by the ordeal of *fire;* and as the ceremonial on occasions such as that in the text was probably much the same as what is there described, an extract may interest the reader.

"CHURCH-SERVICE FOR THE ORDEAL BY FIRE.

"We are all well aware that the ordeal by fire had, during many centuries, the sanction of the church, and moreover, that, considering in what hands the knowledge of those times lay, this blasphemous horror could never have existed without the connivance, and even actual co-operation, of the priesthood.

"It is only a few years ago, however, that any actual form of ritual, set apart by ecclesiastical authority for this atrocious ceremony of fraud, has been recovered. Mr Büsching, the well-known German antiquary, has the merit of having discovered a most extraordinary document of this kind in the course of examining the charter-chest of an ancient Thuringian monastery; and he has published it in a periodical work, entitled, '*Die Vorzeit*,' in 1817. We shall translate the *prayers*, as given in that work, as literally as possible. To those who suspected no deceit, there can be no doubt this service must have been as awfully impressive as any that is to be found in the formularies of any church; but words are wanting to express the abject guilt of those who, well knowing the base trickery of the whole matter, who, having themselves assisted in preparing all the appliances of legerdemain behind the scenes of the sanctuary-stage, dared to clothe their iniquity in the most solemn phraseology of religion.

"A fire was kindled within the church, not far from the great altar. The person about to undergo the ordeal was placed in front of the fire surrounded by his friends, by all who were in any way interested in the result of the trial, and by the whole clergy of the vicinity. Upon a table near the fire, the coulter over which he was to walk, the bar he was to carry, or, if he were a knight, the steel-gloves which, after they had been made red-hot, he was to put on his hands, were placed in view of all.

"Part of the usual service of the day being performed, a priest advances, and places himself in front of the fire, uttering, at the same moment, the following prayer, which is the first Mr Büsching gives:—

"'O Lord God, bless this place, that herein there may be health, and holiness, and purity, and sanctification, and victory, and humility, and meekness, fulfilment of the law, and obedience to God the Father, the Son, and the Holy Ghost. May thy blessing, O God of purity and justice, be upon this place, and upon all that be therein; for the sake of Christ, the Redeemer of the world.'

"A second priest now lifts the iron, and bears it towards the fire. A series of prayers follows; all to be repeated ere the iron is laid on the fire.

"*These are the Prayers to be said over the Fire and the Iron.*

"'1. Lord God, Almighty Father, Fountain of Light, hear us:—enlighten us, O thou that dwellest in light unapproachable. Bless this fire, O God; and as from the midst of the fire thou didst of old enlighten Moses, so from this flame enlighten and purify our hearts, that we may be worthy, through Christ our Lord, to come unto thee, and unto the life eternal.

"'2. Our Father which art in Heaven, &c.

"'3. O Lord, save thy servant. Lord God, send him help out of Zion, thy holy hill. Save him, O Lord. Hear us, O Lord. O Lord, be with us.

"'4. O God, Holy and Almighty, hear us. By the majesty of thy most holy name, and by the coming of thy dear Son, and by the gift of the comfort of thy holy Spirit, and by the justice of thine eternal seat, hear us, good Lord. Purify this metal, and sanctify it, that all falsehood and deceit of the devil may be cast out of it, and utterly removed; and that the truth of thy righteous judgment may be opened and made manifest to all the faithful that cry unto thee this day, through Jesus Christ, our Lord.'

"The iron is now placed in the fire, and sprinkled with consecrated water, both before and after it is so placed. The mass is said while the iron is heating,—the introductory scripture being,—'O Lord, thou art just, and righteous are all thy judgments.' The priest delivers the wafer to the person about to be tried, and, ere he communicates, the following prayer is said by the priest and congregation:—

"'We pray unto thee, O God, that it may please thee to absolve this thy servant, and to clear him from his sins. Purify him, O heavenly Father, from all the stains of the flesh, and enable him, by thy all-covering and atoning grace, to pass through this fire,—thy creature—triumphantly, being justified in Christ our Lord.'

"Then the Gospel:—'Then there came one unto Jesus, who fell upon his knees, and cried out, Good Master, what must I do that I may be saved? Jesus said, Why callest thou me good?' &c.

"The chief priest, from the altar, now addresses the accused, who is still kneeling near the fire:—

"'By the name of the Father, and of the Son, and of the Holy Ghost, and by the Christianity whose name thou bearest, and by the baptism in which thou wert born again, and by all the blessed relics of the saints of God that are preserved in this church, I conjure thee, Come not unto this altar, nor eat of this body of Christ, if thou beest guilty in the things that are laid to thy charge; but if thou beest innocent therein, come, brother, and come freely.'

"The accused then comes forward and communicates,—the priest saying,—'This day may the body and blood of Jesus Christ, which were given and shed for thee, be thy protection and thy succour, yea, even in the midst of the flame.'

"The priest now reads this prayer:—'O Lord, it hath pleased thee to accept our spiritual sacrifice. May the joyful partaking in this holy sacrament be comfortable and useful to all that are here present, and serviceable to the removing of the bondage and thraldom of whatsoever sins do most easily beset us. Grant also, that to this thy servant it may be of exceeding comfort, gladdening his heart, until the truth of thy righteous judgment be revealed.'

"The organ now peals, and *Kyrie Eleeison* and the Litany are sung in full chorus.

"After this comes another prayer:—

"'O God! thou that through fire hast shown forth so many signs of thy almighty power! thou that didst snatch Abraham, thy servant, out of the brands and flames of the Chaldeans, wherein many were consumed! thou that didst cause the bush to burn before the eyes of Moses, and yet not to be consumed! God, that didst send thy Holy Spirit in the likeness of tongues of fiery flame, to the end that thy faithful servants might be visited and set apart from the unbelieving generation; God, that didst safely conduct the three children through the flame of the Babylonians; God, that didst waste Sodom with fire from heaven, and preserve Lot, thy servant, as a sign and a token of thy mercy: O God, show forth yet once again thy visible power, and the majesty of thy unerring judgment: that truth may be made manifest, and falsehood avenged, make thou this fire thy minister before us; powerless be it where is the power of purity, but sorely burning, even to the flesh and the sinews, the hand that hath done evil, and that hath not feared to be lifted up in false swearing. O God! from whose eye nothing can be concealed, make thou this fire thy voice to us thy servants, that it may reveal innocence, or cover iniquity with shame. Judge of all the earth! hear us: hear us, good Lord, for the sake of Jesus Christ thy Son.'

"The priest now dashes once more the holy water over the fire, saying, 'Upon this fire be the blessing of the Father, and of the Son, and of the Holy Ghost, that it may be a sign to us of the righteous judgment of God.'

"The priest pauses; instantly the accused approaches to the fire, and lifts the iron, which he carries nine yards from the flame. The moment he lays it down he is surrounded by the priests, and borne by them into the vestry; there his hands are wrapped in linen cloths, sealed down with the signet of the church: these are removed on the third day, when he is declared innocent or guilty, according to the condition in which his hands are found. '*Si sinus rubescens in vestigio ferri reperiatur, culpabilis ducatur. Sin autem mundus reperiatur, Laus Deo referatur.*'

"Such is certainly one of the most extraordinary records of the craft, the audacity, and the weakness of mankind."

The belief that the corpse of a murdered person would bleed on the touch, or at the approach of the murderer, was universal among the northern nations. We find it seriously urged in the High Court of Justiciary at Edinburgh, so late as 1688, as an evidence of guilt. The case was that of Philip Standsfield, accused of the murder of his father, and this part of the evidence against him is thus stated in the "libel," or indictment. "And when his father's dead body was sighted and inspected by chirurgeons, and the clear and evident signs of the murder had appeared, the body was sewed up, and most carefully cleaned, and his nearest relations and friends were desired to lift his body to the coffin; and accordingly, James Row, merchand, (who was in Edinburgh in the time of the murder,) having lifted the left side of Sir James his head and shoulder, and the said Philip the right side, his father's body, though carefully cleaned, as said is, so as the least blood was not on it, did (according to God's usual method of discovering murders) blood afresh upon him, and defiled all his hands, which struck him with such a terror, that he immediately let his father's head and body fall with violence, and fled from the body, and in consternation and confusion cried, 'Lord, have mercy upon me!' and bowed himself down over a seat in the church (where the corp were inspected), wiping his father's innocent blood off his own murdering hands upon his cloaths." To this his counsel replied, that "this is but a superstitious observation, without any ground either in law or reason; and Carpzovius relates that several persons upon that ground had been unjustly challenged." It was, however, insisted on as a link in the chain of evidence, not as a merely singular circumstance, but as a miraculous interposition of Providence; and it was thus animadverted upon by

Sir George Mackenzie, the king's counsel, in his charge to the jury. "But they, fully persuaded that Sir James was murdered by his own son, sent out some chirurgeons and friends, who, having raised the body, did see it bleed miraculously upon his touching it. In which God Almighty himself was pleased to bear a share in the testimonies we produce; that Divine power, which makes the blood circulate during life, has oft times, in all nations, opened a passage to it after death upon such occasions, but most in this case."

245.32 (Ch. 23) the Skinners' Yards
SKINNERS' YARDS. "The Skinners' Yard," says Mr Morrison, "is still in the possession of that fraternity, and is applied to the purpose which its name implies. Prior to the time of the peaceable Robert, it was the court-yard of the castle. Part of the gate which opened from the town, to the drawbridge of the castle, is still to be seen, as well as some traces of the foundation of the Keep or Donjon, and of the towers which surrounded the Castle-yard. The Curfew-row, which now encloses the Skinners'-yard, at that time formed the avenue or street leading from the northern part of the town to the Dominican Monastery,"

250.4 (Ch. 23) the High Constable's lodgings
EARL OF ERROL'S LODGINGS. "The Constable's, or Earl of Errol's lodgings," says Mr Morrison, "stood near the south end of the Watergate, the quarter of the town in which most of the houses of the nobility were placed, amidst gardens which extended to the wall of the city adjoining the river. The families of the Hays had many rich possessions in the neighbourhood, and other residences in the town besides that commonly known as the Constable's Lodgings. Some of these subsequently passed, along with a considerable portion of the Carse, to the Ruthven or Gowrie family. The last of those noble residences in Perth which retained any part of its former magnificence, (and on that account styled the Palace,) was the celebrated Gowrie House, which was nearly entire in 1805, but of which not a vestige now remains. On the confiscation of the Gowrie estates, it merged into the public property of the town; and, in 1746, was presented by the magistrates to the Duke of Cumberland. His Royal Highness, on receiving this mark of the attachment or servility of the Perth rulers, asked, with sarcastic nonchalance, "If the *piece of ground* called the Carse of Gowrie went along with it?""

263.25 (Ch. 24) the slightest recollection An incident precisely similar to that in the text actually occurred, within the present century, at Oxford, in the case of a young woman who underwent the last sentence of the law for child-murder. A learned professor of that university has published an account of his conversation with the girl after her recovery.

266.28 (Ch. 25) I counsel thee These lines are still extant on the ruinous house of an Abbot, and are said to be allusive to the holy man having kept a mistress.

271.29 (Ch. 25) Primate of Scotland

> Mastere Henry of Wardlaw
> That like til Vertew was to draw,
> Chantour that time of Glasgu,
> Commendit of alkyn Vertew,
> The Pape had in affectioun,
> Baith for his fame and his resoun.
> * * * * * *
> Sua by this resoun speciale
> Of the threttinth Benet Pape,
> This Master Henry was Bischape
> Of Sanct Andrewis with honoure.
> Of Canon he was then Doctour.
>
> *Wyntoun*, B. ix. chap. 23.

276.5 (Ch. 26) Tin-Egan *Tine-egan*, or *Neidfyre*, *i.e.* forced fire. All the fires in the house being extinguished, two men produced a flame of potent virtue by the friction of wood. This charm was used, within the memory of living persons, in the Hebrides, in cases of murrain among cattle.

278.30 (Ch. 27) Mohr ar chat *i.e.* The Great Cat. The County of Caithness is supposed to have its name from Teutonic settlers of the race of the *Catti*, and heraldry has not neglected so fair an occasion for that species of painted punning in which she used to delight. *Touch not the cat but a glove*, is the motto of Mackintosh, alluding to his crest, which, as with most of the now scattered septs of the old Clan Chattan, is the Mountain Cat.

279.11 (Ch. 27) Ross and Sutherland Their territory, commonly called, after the chief of the MacKays, *Lord Reay's* country, has lately passed into the possession of the noble family of Stafford-Sutherland.

280.38 (Ch. 27) Ballough [Magnum has 'Balloch'.] *Balloch* is Gaelic for the discharge of a lake into a river.

285.42 (Ch. 27) happily situated in Scottish lakes The security no less than the beauty of the situations led to the choice of these lake islands for religious establishments. Those in the Highlands were generally of a lowly character, and in many of them the monastic orders were tolerated, and the rites of the Romish Church observed, long after the Reformation had swept both "the rooks and their nests" out of the Lowlands. The priory on Loch Tay was founded by Alexander I., and the care of it committed to a small body of monks; but the last residents in it were three nuns, who, when they did emerge into society, seemed determined to enjoy it in its most complicated and noisy state, for they came out only once a year, and that to *a market* at Kenmore. Hence that Fair is still called "Fiell na m'hau maomb," or Holy Woman's Market.

287.31 (Ch. 27) the Deasil A very ancient custom, which consists in going three times round the body of a dead or living person, imploring blessings upon him. The Deasil must be performed sun-ways, that is, by moving from right to left. If misfortune is imprecated, the party moves withershins, (German, WIDDERSINS,) that is, *against the sun*, from left to right.

287.39 (Ch. 27) permitted to enter The installation, the marriage, and the funeral of a chieftain, were the three periods of his course observed with the highest ceremony by all the clan. The latter was perhaps the most imposing of the three spectacles, from the solemnity of the occasion, and the thrilling effect produced by the coronach, sung by hundreds of voices, its melancholy notes undulating through the valleys, or reverberating among the hills. All these observances are fading away, and the occasional attempt at a gathering, for the funeral of a chief, now resembles the dying note of the coronach, faintly echoed for the last time among the rocks.

293.22 (Ch. 28) Leichtach *i.e.* Body-guard.

301.7 (Ch. 29) cailliachs Old women.

301.8 (Ch. 29) haffits *i.e.* Boxed my ears.

317.39 (Ch. 30) the mouse squeak Implying, that it was better to keep the forest than shut themselves up in fortified places.

338.42 (Ch. 32) from a granary above his prison-house Sir Alexander Ramsay of Dalhousie having irritated William Douglas, Lord of Galloway, by obtaining the Sheriffship of Teviotdale, which the haughty baron considered due to himself, was surprised in Hawick while exercising his office, and confined in Hermitage Castle until he died of famine in June, A.D. 1342. Godscroft mentions the circumstance of the grain dropping from the cornloft.—P. 75.

340.9 (Ch. 32) a bowie *i.e.* A small milk-pail.—One of the sweetest couplets in The Gentle Shepherd is—

> To bear the milk-bowie no pain was to me,
> When I at the buchting forgather'd wi' thee.

347.36 (Ch. 32) I have taken them red-hand

RED-HAND. Mr Morrison says, "the case of a person taken *red-hand* by the magistrates of Perth and immediately executed, was the main cause of the power of trying cases of life and death being taken from them and from all subordinate judicatories. A young

English officer connected with some families of rank and influence, who was stationed with a recruiting party at Perth, had become enamoured of a lady there, so young as still to be under the tuition of a dancing-master. Her admirer was in the habit of following her into the school, to the great annoyance of the teacher, who, on occasion of a ball given in his class-room in the Kirkgate, stationed himself at the door, determined to resist the entrance of the officer, on account of the scandal to which his visits had given rise. The officer came as a matter of course, and a scuffle ensued, which at last bore so threatening an aspect, that the poor dancing-master fled through the passage, or *close*, as it is called, by which there was access to the street. He was pursued by the officer with his drawn sword, and was run through the body ere he could reach the street, where the crowd usually assembled on such occasions might have protected him. The officer was instantly apprehended, and executed, it is understood, even without any form of trial; at least there is no notice of it in any of the records where it would with most probability have been entered. But the sword is still in the possession of a gentleman whose ancestors held official situations in the town at the time, and the circumstances of the murder and of the execution have been handed down with great minuteness and apparent truth of description from father to son. It was immediately afterwards that the power of the civic magistrates in matters criminal was abridged,—it is thought chiefly through the influence of the friends of this young officer."

354.34 (Ch. 33) the Gow Chrom *i.e.* A man of the hammer.

355.14 (Ch. 33) Houghmanstairs

PLOUGHMAN STARES. "This place, twice referred to in the course of our story as hateful to the Highlanders, lies near the *Stare-dam*, a collection of waters in a very desolate hollow between the hill of Birnam, and the road from Perth to Dunkeld. The *eerieness* of the place is indescribable, and is rendered yet more striking from its being within a furlong of one of the loveliest and richest scenes in Scotland—the north-west opening of Strathmore. The "dam" has been nearly drained within these few years, but the miserable patches of sickly corn which have with vast labour and cost been obtained, look still more melancholy than the solitary tarn which the barren earth seems to have drunk up. The whole aspect of the place fitted it for being the scene of the trial and punishment of one of the most notorious bands of thieves and outlaws that ever laid the Low Country under contribution. Ruthven, the sheriff, is said to have held his court on a rising ground to the north, still called the Court-hill; and there were lately, or there still may be, at the east end of the Roch-in-roy wood, some oaks on which the Highlanders were hung, and which long went by the name of the Hanged-men's-trees. The hideous appearance of the bodies hanging in chains gave the place a name which to this day grates on the ear of a Celt."—MORRISON.

359.14 (Ch. 33) the cloister garden
GARDENS OF THE DOMINICANS. "The gardens of the Dominicans surrounded the monastery on all sides, and were of great extent and beauty. Part of them immediately adjoined the North Inch, and covered all that space of ground now occupied by Atholl Place, the Crescent, and Rose Terrace, besides a considerable extent of ground to the west and south, still known by the name of the Black Friars. On a part of these grounds overlooking the North Inch, probably near the south end of the Terrace, a richly decorated summer-house stood, which is frequently mentioned in old writings as the Gilten Arbour. From the balconies of this edifice King Robert is supposed to have witnessed the conflict of the clans. What the peculiar forms, construction, or ornaments of this building were, which gained for it this title, is not even hinted at by any of the local chroniclers. It may be mentioned, however, although it is a matter of mere tradition, that the ornaments on the ceiling of the Monks' Tower (a circular watch-tower at the south-east angle of the town) were said to have been copied from those on the Gilten Arbour, by orders of the first Earl of Gowrie, at the corner of whose garden the Monks' Tower stood. This tower was taken down at the same time with Gowrie House, and many yet remember the general appearance of the paintings on the ceiling, yet it does not seem to have occurred to any one to have had them copied. They were allegorical and astronomical, representing the virtues and vices, the seasons, the zodiac, and other subjects commonplace enough; yet even the surmise that they might have been copied from others still more ancient, if it could not save them from destruction, should have entitled them to a greater share than they seem to have possessed of the notice of their contemporaries. The patience with which the antiquaries of Perth have submitted to the removal (in many cases the wanton and useless removal) of the historical monuments with which they were at one time surrounded, is truly wonderful!"—MORRISON.

377.30 (Ch. 34) I fought for my own hand Meaning, I did such a thing for my own ends, as Henry Gow fought.

379.11 (Ch. 34) the race of the Cat-a-Mountain The reader may be amused with the account of this onslaught in Boece, as translated by Bellenden.

"At this time, mekil of all the north of Scotland was hevely trublit be two clannis of Irsmen, namit Clankayis and Glenquhattanis; invading the cuntre, be thair weris, with ithand slauchter and reif. At last, it was appointit betwix the heidis-men of thir two clannis, be avise of the Erlis of Murray and Crawfurd, that xxx of the principall men of the ta clan sal cum, with othir xxx of the tothir clan, arrayit in thair best avise; and sall convene afore the king at Perth, for decision of al pleis; and fecht with scharp swerdis to the deith, but ony harnes; and that clan quhare the victory succedit, to have perpetuall empire above the tothir. Baith thir clannis, glaid of this condition, come to the North Inche, beside Perth, with jugis set in scaffaldis, to discus the verite. Ane of thir clannis wantit ane man to perfurnis furth the nowmer, and wagit ane carll, for money, to debait thair actioun, howbeit this man pertenit na thing to thaim in blud nor kindnes. Thir two clannis stude arrayit with gret hatrent aganis othir; and, be sound of trumpet, ruschit togidder; takand na respect to thair woundis, sa that thay micht distroy thair ennimes; and faucht in this maner lang, with uncertane victory: quhen ane fel, ane othir was put in his rowme. At last, the Clankayis war al slane except ane, that swam throw the watter of Tay. Of Glenquhattannis, was left xi personis on live; bot thay war sa hurt, that thay micht nocht hald thair swerdis in thair handis. This debait was fra the incarnation, MCCCXCVI yeiris."

382.29 (Ch. 35) his father's guilt and his own. The death of the Duke of Rothsay is not accompanied with the circumstances detailed by later writers in Wyntoun. The Chronicler of Lochleven says simply:—

A thousand foure hundyr yeris and twa,
All before as ye herd done,
Our lord the kingis eldest sone,
Suete and vertuous, yong and fair,
And his nerast lauchful ayr,
Honest, habil, and avenand,
Our Lord, our Prynce, in all plesand,
Cunnand into letterature,
A seymly persone in stature,
Schir Davy Duke of Rothesay,
Of Marche the sevyn and twenty day
Yauld his Saule til his Creatoure,
His corse til hallowit Sepulture.
In Lundoris his Body lies,
His Spirite intil Paradys.—B. ix. chap. 23.

The Continuator of Fordun is far more particular, and though he does not positively pronounce on the guilt of Albany, says enough to show that, when he wrote, the suspicion against him was universal; and that Sir John Ramorny was generally considered as having followed the dark and double course ascribed to him in the novel.

"Anno Domini millesimo quadringentesimo primo, obiit columna ecclesiæ robustissima, vas eloquentiæ, thesaurus scientiæ, ac defensor catholicæ fidei, dominus Walterus Treyl episcopus S. Andreæ; et etiam domina Anabella regina apud Sconam decessit, et sepulta est in Dunfermelyn. Hi enim duo, dum viverent, honorem quasi regni exaltabant; videlicet, principes et magnates in discordiam concitatos ad concordiam revocantes, alienigenas et extraneos egregiè susceptantes et convivantes, ac munificè dimissos lætificantes. Unde quasi proverbialiter tunc dictum exstitit, quòd mortuis reginâ Scotiæ, comite de Douglas, et episcopo Sancti Andreæ, abiit decus, recessit honor, et honestas obiit Scotiæ. Eodem anno quarta mortalitas exstitit in regno. Paulo ante dominus rex in consilio deputavit certos consiliarios, valentes barones et milites, juratos ad regendum et consiliandum dominum David Stewart ducem Rothsaiensem, comitem de Carrik, et principem regni, quia videbatur regi et consilio quòd immiscebat se sæpiùs effrænatis lusibus et levioribus ludicris. Propter quod et ipse consilio astrictus saniori, juravit se regimini eorum et consilio conformare. Sed mortuâ reginâ ipsius nobili matre, quæ eum in multis refrænabat, tanquam laqueus contritus fuisset, speravit se liberatum, et, spreto proborum consilio, denuo in priori levitate se totum dedit. Propter quod consilium procerum sibi assignatum quitabit se regi, et si voluisset, non tamen posse se eum ad gravitatem morum flexisse attestatur. Unde rex impotens et decrepitus scripsit fratri suo duci Albaniæ, gubernatori regni, ut arrestaretur, et ad tempus custodiæ deputaretur, donec virgâ disciplinæ castigatus, seipsum meliùs cognosceret. Non enim osculatur filium pater, sed aliquando castigat. Sed quod rex proposuit ad filii emendam, tendit ei ad noxam. Nam uterque bajulus literæ regalis ad gubernatorem de facto ostendit, se incentorem et instigatorem regi ut taliter demandaret, quod honori alterius obviaret, sicut experientiâ exitus rei patefecit. Domini enim Willelmus Lindesay de Rossy et Johannes Remorgeney milites, regis familiares et consiliarii, nuncii et portatores erant literarum regis gubernatori: quique etiam, ut dicitur, duci Rothsaiensi priùs suggesserunt, ut, post obitum episcopi Sancti Andreæ, castrum suum ad usum regis, quousque novus episcopus institueretur, reciperet et servaret: quique ipsum ducem, nihil mali præmeditatum, ad castrum Sancti Andreæ simpliciter, et cum moderata familia, equitantem, inter villam de Nidi et Stratyrum arrestaverunt, et per potentiam eundem ducem ad ipsum castrum Sancti Andreæ, sibi ad deliberandum paratum, induxerunt, et ibidem in custodia tenuerunt, quousque dux Albaniæ cum suo consilio apud Culros tento, quid de eo facerent, deliberaverunt. Qui quidem dux Albaniæ, cum domino Archibaldo II. comite de Douglas, manu validâ ipsum ad turrim de Faulkland, jumento impositum et russeto collobio chlamidatum transvexerunt: ubi in quadam honesta camerula eum servandum deputaverunt. In qua tam diu custoditus, scilicet per Johannem Selkirk et Johannem Wrycht, donec dyssenteriâ, sive, ut alii volunt, fame tabefactus, finem vitæ dedit vij. Kal. Aprilis, in vigilia Paschæ, serò, sive in die Paschæ summo mane, et sepultus est in Londoris. Præmissus verò Johannes Remorgeney tam principi, quàm domino regi, erat consiliarius, audax spiritu, et pronunciatione eloquentissimus, ac in arduis causis prolocutor regis, et causidicus disertissimus: qui, ut dicitur, ante hæc suggessit ipsi principi duci Rothsaiensi, ut patruum suum ducem Albaniæ arrestaret, et, qualicunque occasione nactâ, statim de medio tolleret: quod facere omnino princeps refutavit. Istud attendens miles, malitiæ suæ fuligine occæcatus, à cœptis desistere nequivit, hujusmodi labe attachiatus; quia, ut ait Chrysostomus, 'Coërceri omnino nequit animus pravâ semel voluntate vitiatus.' Et ideo, vice versà, pallium in alterum humerum convertens, hoc idem maleficium ducem Albaniæ de nepote suo duce Rothsaiensi facere instruxit; aliàs fine fallo, ut asseruit, dux Rothsaiensis de ipso finem facturus fuisset. Dictus insuper D. Willelmus Lindesay cum ipso Johanne Remorgeney in eandem sententiam fortè consentivit, pro eo quòd dictus dux Rothsaiensis sororem ipsius D. Willelmi Euphemiam de Lindesay affidavit, sed per sequentia aliarum matrimonia attemptata, sicut et filiam comitis Marchiæ, sic eandem repudiavit. Ipse enim, ut æstimo, est ille David, de quo vates de Breclyngton sic vaticinatus est, dicens;

Psalletur gestis David luxuria festis,
Quòd tenet uxores uxore suâ meliores,
Deficient mores regales, perdet honores.

Paulo ante captionem suam apparuit mirabilis cometes, emittens ex se radios crinitos ad Aquilonem tendentes. Ad quam visendum, cùm primò appareret, quodam vespere in castro de Edinburgh cum aliis ipse dux secedens, fertur ipsum sic de stella disseruisse, dicens; 'Ut à mathematicis audivi, huiusmodi cometes, cùm apparet, signat mortem vel mutationem alicujus principis, vel alicujus patriæ destructionem.' Et sic evenit ut prædixit. Nam, duce capto, statim in præjacentem materiam, sicut Deus voluit, redit stella. In hoc potuit iste dux Sibyllaæ prophetissæ comparari, de qua sic loquitur Claudianus:

Miror, cur aliis quæ fata pandere soles,
Ad propriam cladem cæca Sibylla taces.

The narrative of Boece attaches murder distinctly to Albany. After mentioning the death of Queen Annabella Drummond, he thus proceeds:—

"Be quhais deith, succedit gret displeseir to hir son, David, Duk of Rothesay: for, during hir life, he wes haldin in virtews and honest occupatioun: eftir hir deith, he began to rage in all maner of insolence; and fulyeit virginis, matronis, and nunnis, be his unbridillit lust. At last, King Robert, informit of his young and insolent maneris, send letteris to his brothir, the Duke of Albany, to intertene his said son, the Duk of Rothesay, and to leir him honest and civill maneris. The Duk of Albany, glaid of thir writtingis, tuk the Duk of Rothesay betwix Dunde and Sanct Androis, and brocht him to Falkland, and inclusit him in the tour thairof, but ony meit or drink. It is said, ane woman, havand commiseratioun on this Duk, leit meill fall doun throw the loftis of the toure: be quhilkis, his life wes certane dayis savit. This woman, fra it wes knawin, wes put to deith. On the same maner, ane othir woman gaif him milk of hir paup, throw ane lang reid; and wes slane with gret cruelte, fra it wes knawin. Than wes the Duke destitute of all mortall supplie; and brocht, finalie, to sa miserable and hungry appetite, that he eit, nocht allanerlie the filth of the toure quhare he wes, bot his awin fingaris: to his gret marterdome. His body wes beryit in Lundoris, and kithit miraklis many yeris eftir; quhil, at last, King James the First began to punis his slayaris; and fra that time furth, the miraclis ceissit."

The *Remission*, which Albany and Douglas afterwards received at the hands of Robert III., was first printed by Lord Hailes; and is as follows:—

"Robertus, Dei gratiâ, rex Scottorum, Universis, ad quorum notitiam præsentes literæ pervenerint, Salutem in Domino sempiternam: Cum nuper carissimi nobis, Robertus Albaniæ Dux, Comes de Fife et de Menteth, frater noster germanus, et Archibaldus Comes de Douglas, et Dominus Galwidiæ, filius noster secundum legem, ratione filiæ nostræ quam duxit in uxorem, præcarissimum filium nostrum primogenitum David, quondam Ducem Rothsaye ac Comitem de Carrick et Atholiæ, capi fecerunt, et personaliter arrestari, et in castro Sancti Andreæ primo custodiri, deindeque apud Faucland in custodia detineri, ubi ab hac luce, divinâ providentiâ, et non aliter, migrasse dignoscitur. Quibus comparentibus coram nobis, in concilio nostro generali apud Edinburgh, decimo sexto die mensis Maii, anno Domini millesimo quadringentesimo secundo, inchoato, et nonnullis diebus continuato, et super hoc interrogatis ex officio nostro regali, sive accusatis, hujusmodi captionem, arrestationem, mortem, ut superius est expressum, confitentes, causas ipsos ad hoc moventes, pro publica, ut asseruerunt, utilitate arctantes, in præsentia nostra assignârunt, quas non duximus præsentibus inserendas, et ex causâ: Habitâ deinde super hoc diligenti inquisitione, consideratis omnibus et singulis in hac parte considerandis, hujusmodi causam tangentibus, et maturâ deliberatione concilii nostri præhabitâ discussis, prænotatos Robertum fratrem nostrum germanum, Archibaldumque filium nostrum secundum jura, et eorum in hac parte participes quoscunque, viz. arrestatores, detentores, custodes, consiliarios, et omnes alios consilium, videlicet, auxilium, vel favorem eisdem præstantes, sive eorum jussum aut mandatum qualitercunque exsequentes, excusatos habemus; necnon et ipsos, et eorum quemlibet, a crimine læsæ majestatis nostræ, vel alio quocunque crimine, culpa, injuria, rancore, et offensa, quæ eis occasione præmissorum imputari possent qualitercunque, in dicto consilio nostro palam et publicè declaravimus, pronunciavimus, et diffinivimus, tenoreque præsentium declaramus, pronunciamus, et per hanc diffinitivam nostram sententiam diffinimus, innocentes, innoxios, inculpabiles, quietos, liberos, et immunes, penitus et omnimodo: Et si quam contra ipsos, sive eorum aliquem, aut aliquam vel aliquos, in hoc facto qualitercunque participes, vel eis quomodolibet adhærentes, indignationem, iram, rancorem, vel offensionem, concepimus qualitercunque, illos proprio motu, ex certa scientia, et etiam ex deliberatione concilii nostri jam dicti, annullamus, removemus, et adnullatos volumus haberi, in perpetuum. Quare omnibus et singulis subditis nostris, cujuscunque statûs aut conditionis exstiterint, districtè præcipimus et mandamus, quatenus sæpe dictis Roberto et Archibaldo, eorumque in hoc facto participibus, consentientibus, seu adhærentibus, ut præmittitur, verbo non detrahent, neque facto, nec contra eosdem murmurent qualitercunque, unde possit eorum bona fama lædi, vel aliquod præjudicium generari, sub omni pœna quæ exinde competere poterit, quomodolibet ipso jure. Datum, sub testimonio magni sigilli nostri, in monasterio Sanctæ Crucis de Edinburgh, vicesimo die mensis Maii prædicti, anno Domini millesimo quadringentesimo secundo, et regni nostri anno tertio decimo."

Lord Hailes sums up his comment on the document with words which, as Pinkerton says, leave no doubt that he considered the prince as having been murdered: viz. "The Duke of Albany and the Earl of Douglas obtained a remission in terms as ample as if they had actually murdered the heir apparent."

ANNE OF GEIERSTEIN

Editorial Note

Anne of Geierstein does not form part of the Interleaved Set. The interleaved copy, of which only Volumes 1 and 3 are known to survive, is of the first edition. Cadell had brought interleaved copies of the first editions of *Chronicles of the Canongate* and *Anne* to Abbotsford on 7 May 1830 (MS 21043, f. 40v). On 2 September Scott wrote to him a sadly confused note: 'I send you the introductions ⟨& alterations⟩ introductions of the Keepsaksale and two volumes of Anne of Geierstein Next day or the day of it you will ⟨ ? ⟩ have Anne of Geierstein Vol III' (MS 15890, f. 162r). On 6 March 1832 Cadell 'copied part of MS of Anne of Geierstein for notes for New Edition'. These must be the passages on the Troubadours and the Parliament of Love which he had suggested on 19 March 1829 should be excised from the text of the novel and saved for endnotes in the Magnum (EEWN 22, 416). The same day, 6 March, after tea, Cadell 'wrote out Notes from Anne of Geierstein' (MS 20122, f. 12v). No further record of progress has been located until 15 October 1832, after Scott's death, when Cadell received the Introduction and notes to *Anne* from Lockhart, who had apparently at least revised material produced by Scott, and may well have done more than that (MS 20122, f. 44v). On 25 October Cadell 'filled in Sir Walter Scotts corrections into Vol II of Anne of Geierstein for press' (that is, corrections either from the second volume of the interleaved copy, that is not known to have survived, or in the second half of the novel, to appear as the second Magnum volume: MS 20122, f. 46r). Two days later he received 'parcel from Lockhart with Proofs of Introduction & Notes to Anne of Geierstein' (MS 21022, f. 46r). The novel appeared as Volumes 44 and 45 of the Magnum on 1 January and 1 February 1833.

The 24-page Introduction (of which no manuscript is known to survive) is largely occupied by an account, with liberal quotation, of the latest theories on the Secret Tribunals, drawn from proofs of a forthcoming study sent by its author Francis Palgrave. This is preceded by a brief confession of historical errors resulting from the temporary unavailability of the books required: in fact, *Anne* is not noticeably more inaccurate in this respect than most of the Waverley Novels. The Introduction ends with a gratified noting of the appreciation expressed by Swiss readers.

Apart from a handful of glossarial and explanatory footnotes the volume is provided with only four endnotes, occupying 16 pages. The first consists almost entirely of a lengthy quotation from Barante's account of de Hagenbach's execution with a full translation. In Volume 45 there are the two notes extracted from the original text of the novel, as mentioned above, and a translation of Comines's account of the death of Charles the Bold.

There are four Magnum illustrations for this title. The frontispiece to Volume 44 (MAG0087 / TB348.44) was designed by William Mulready and engraved by Robert Graves. It depicts Margaret of Anjou on the ramparts of the monastery at Mont Sainte Victoire, having thrown her sable feather and red rose into the wind, with Arthur Philipson looking on (EEWN 22, 339.35–42: 'As Margaret spoke . . . back against his breast'). The title-page vignette (MAG0088 / TB348.44) was designed by Robert Trewick Bone and engraved by William Humphrys. It depicts Archibald von Hagenback in his torture-chamber surveying Francis Steinernherz preparing a two-handed sword in readiness for execution (EEWN 22, 143.12–13: 'Ha! Scharfgerichter . . . preparing for thy duty?'). The frontispiece to Volume 45 (MAG0089 / TB348.45) was designed by John West and engraved by Charles Rolls. It depicts Margaret of Anjou seated at the monastery at Mont Sainte Victoire with Arthur Philipson in attendance behind her (EEWN 22, 336.43–337.4: ' "Young man," . . . with dreadful gusts of wind.'). The title-page vignette (MAG0090 / TB348.45) was designed by John William Wright and engraved by Joshua Rolls It depicts Annette Veilchen rushing into Anne's apartment at Arnheim Castle to announce the arrival of Arthur Philipson (EEWN 22, 236.17–20: 'Annette sped up a narrow turnpike stair . . . they are come!').

W. Mulready, R.A. R. Graves.

ANNE OF GEIERSTEIN.

"As Margaret spoke, she tore from her hair the sable feather and rose, and tossed them from the battlement with a gesture of wild energy: a bickering eddy swept the feather far distant into empty space, a contrary gust of wind caught the red rose, and drove it back against his breast."

EDINBURGH, PUBLISHED 1833, BY ROBERT CADELL; and WHITTAKER & Co. LONDON.

WAVERLEY NOVELS.

VOL. XLVI.

ANNE OF GEIERSTEIN.

R. T. Bone. W. Humphrys.

"Ha! Scharfgerichter," said the knight, as he entered the folter-kammer, "thou art preparing for thy duty?"

PRINTED FOR ROBERT CADELL, EDINBURGH.
AND WHITTAKER & C° LONDON.
1833.

J. West. C. Rolls.

ANNE OF GEIERSTEIN.

"Young man," said the Queen, "the contemplation of a question so doubtful almost deprives me of reason".
As she spoke, she sunk down as one who needs rest, on a stone-seat placed on the very verge of the balcony, regardlefs of the storm, which now began to rise with dreadful gusts of wind.

EDINBURGH, PUBLISHED 1833, BY ROBERT CADELL, and WHITTAKER & Cº LONDON.

WAVERLEY NOVELS.

VOL. XLV.

ANNE OF GEIERSTEIN.

"Annette sped up a narrow turnpike stair to a closet or dressing room, where her young mistress was seated, and exclaimed with open mouth—Anne of Gei—I mean my lady Baroness, they are come, they are come!"

PRINTED FOR ROBERT CADELL, EDINBURGH.
AND WHITTAKER & C? LONDON.
1833.

Introduction to Anne of Geierstein

THIS novel was written at a time when circumstances did not place within my reach the stores of a library tolerably rich in historical works, and especially the memoirs of the middle ages, amidst which I had been accustomed to pursue the composition of my fictitious narratives. In other words, it was chiefly the work of leisure hours in Edinburgh, not of quiet mornings in the country. In consequence of trusting to a memory, strongly tenacious certainly, but not less capricious in its efforts, I have to confess on this occasion more violations of accuracy in historical details, than can perhaps be alleged against others of my novels. In truth, often as I have been complimented on the strength of my memory, I have through life been entitled to adopt old Beattie of Meikledale's answer to his parish minister when eulogizing him with respect to the same faculty. "No, doctor," said the honest border-laird, "I have no command of my memory; it only retains what happens to hit my fancy, and like enough, sir, if you were to preach to me for a couple of hours on end, I might be unable at the close of the discourse to remember one word of it." Perhaps there are few men whose memory serves them with equal fidelity as to many different classes of subjects; but I am sorry to say, that while mine has rarely failed me as to any snatch of verse or trait of character that had once interested my fancy, it has generally been a frail support, not only as to names, and dates, and other minute technicalities of history, but as to many more important things.

I hope this apology will suffice for one mistake which has been pointed out to me by the descendant of one of the persons introduced in this story, and who complains with reason that I have made a peasant deputy of the ancestor of a distinguished and noble family, none of whom ever declined from the high rank, to which, as far as my pen trenched on it, I now beg leave to restore them. The name of the person who figures as deputy of Soleure in these pages, was always, it seems, as it is now, that of a patrician house. I am reminded by the same correspondent of another slip, probably of less consequence. The Emperor of the days my novel refers to, though the representative of that Leopold who fell in the great battle of Sempach, never set up any pretensions against the liberties of the gallant Swiss, but, on the contrary, treated with uniform prudence and forbearance such of that nation as had established their independence, and with wise, as well as generous kindness, others who still continued to acknowledge fealty to the imperial crown. Errors of this sort, however trivial, ought never, in my opinion, to be pointed out to an author, without meeting with a candid and respectful acknowledgment.

With regard to a general subject of great curiosity and interest, in the eyes at least of all antiquarian students, upon which I have touched at some length in this narrative, I mean the *Vehmic* tribunals of Westphalia, a name so awful in men's ears during many centuries, and which, through the genius of Goethe, has again been revived in public fancy with a full share of its ancient terrors, I am bound to state my opinion that a wholly new and most important light has been thrown upon this matter since Anne of Geierstein first appeared, by the elaborate researches of my ingenious friend, Mr Francis Palgrave, whose proof-sheets, containing the passages I allude to, have been kindly forwarded to me, and whose complete work will be before the public ere this Introduction can pass through the press.

"In Germany," says this very learned writer, "there existed a singular jurisdiction, which claimed a *direct descent from the Pagan policy and mystic ritual of the earliest Teutons.*

"We learn from the Historians of Saxony, that the 'Frey Feld gericht,' or Free Field Court of Corbey, was, in Pagan times, under the supremacy of the Priests of the Eresburgh, the Temple which contained the Irminsule, or pillar of Irmin. After the conversion of the people, the possessions of the temple were conferred by Louis the Pious upon the Abbey which arose upon its site. The court was composed of sixteen persons, who held their offices for life. The senior member presided as the Gerefa or Graff; the junior performed the humbler duties of 'Frohner,' or summoner; the remaining fourteen acted as the Echevins, and by them all judgments were pronounced or declared. When any one of these died, a new member was elected by the Priests, from amongst the twenty-two septs or families inhabiting the Gau or district, and who included all the hereditary occupants of the soil. Afterwards, the selection was made by the Monks, but always with the assent of the Graff and of the 'Frohner.'

"The seat of judgment, the King's seat, or 'Königs-stuhl,' was always established on the greensward; and we collect from the context, that the tribunal was also raised or appointed in the common fields of the Gau, for the purpose of deciding disputes relating to the land within its precinct. Such a 'King's seat' was a plot sixteen feet in length, and sixteen feet in breadth; and when the ground was first consecrated, the Frohner dug a grave in the centre, in which each of the Free Echevins threw a handful of ashes, a coal, and a tile. If any doubt arose whether a place of judgment had been duly hallowed, the Judges sought for the tokens. If they were not found, then all the judgments which had been given became null and void. It was also of the very essence of the Court, that it should be held beneath the sky, and by the light of the sun. All the ancient Teutonic judicial assemblies were held in the open air; but some relics of solar worship may perhaps be traced in the usage and in the language of this tribunal. The forms adopted in the Free Field Court also betray a singular affinity to the doctrines of the British Bards respecting their Gorseddau, or Conventions, which were 'always held in the open air, in the eye of the light, and in face of the sun.'*

"When a criminal was to be judged, or a cause to be decided, the Graff and the Free Echevins assembled around the 'Königstuhl;' and the 'Frohner,' having proclaimed silence, opened the proceedings by reciting the following rhymes:

"Sir Graff, with permission,
I beg you to say,
According to law, and without delay,
If I, your Knave,
Who judgment crave,
With your good grace,
Upon the King's seat this seat may place.

"To this address the Graff replied:

"While the sun shines with even light
Upon Masters and Knaves, I shall declare
The law of might, according to right.
Place the King's seat true and square,
Let even measure, for justice' sake,
Be given in sight of God and man,
That the plaintiff his complaint may make,
And the defendant answer,—if he can.

"In conformity to this permission, the 'Frohner' placed the seat of judgment in the middle of the plot, and then he spake for the second time:

"Sir Graff, Master brave,
I remind you of your honour, here,
And moreover that I am your Knave;
Tell me, therefore, for law sincere,
If these mete-wands are even and sure,
Fit for the rich and fit for the poor,
Both to measure land and condition;
Tell me as you would eschew perdition.

* Owen Pugh's Elegies of Lewarch Hen, Pref., p. 46. The place of these meetings was set apart by forming a circle of stones round the *Maen Gorsedd*, or Stone of the Gorsedd.

And so speaking, he laid the mete-wand on the ground. The Graff then began to try the measure, by placing his right foot against the wand, and he was followed by the other Free Echevins in rank and order, according to seniority. The length of the mete-wand being thus proved, the Frohner spake for the third time:

"Sir Graff, I ask by permission,
If I, with your mete-wand may mete
Openly, and without displeasure,
Here the king's free judgment seat.

"And the Graff replied:

"I permit right,
And I forbid wrong,
Under the pains and penalties
That to the old known laws belong.

"Now was the time of measuring the mystic plot; it was measured by the mete-wand along and athwart, and when the dimensions were found to be true, the Graff placed himself in the seat of judgment, and gave the charge to the assembled Free Echevins, warning them to pronounce judgment, according to right and justice.

"On this day, with common consent,
And under the clear firmament,
A free field court is established here,
   In the open eye of day;
   Enter soberly, ye who may.
The seat in its place is pight,
The mete-wand is found to be right;
Declare your judgments without delay:
And let the doom be truely given,
Whilst yet the Sun shines bright in heaven.

"Judgment was given by the Free Echevins according to plurality of voices."

After observing that the author of Anne of Geierstein had, by what he calls a "very excusable poetical license," transferred something of these judicial rhymes from the Free Field Court of the Abbey of Corbey, to the Free Vehmic Tribunals of Westphalia, Mr Palgrave proceeds to correct many vulgar errors, in which the novel he remarks on no doubt had shared, with respect to the actual constitution of those last named courts. "The protocols of their proceedings," he says, "do not altogether realize the popular idea of their terrors and tyranny." It may be allowed to me to question whether the mere protocols of such tribunals are quite enough to annul all the import of tradition respecting them; but in the following details there is no doubt much that will instruct the antiquarian, as well as amuse the popular reader.

"The Court," says Mr Palgrave, "was held with known and

notorious publicity beneath the 'eye of light;' and the sentences, though speedy and severe, were founded upon a regular system of established jurisprudence, not so strange, even to England, as it may at first sight appear.

"Westphalia, according to its ancient constitution, was divided into districts called 'Freygraffschafften,' each of which usually contained one, and sometimes many, Vehmic tribunals, whose boundaries were accurately defined. The right of the 'Stuhlherr,' or Lord, was of a feudal nature, and could be transferred by the ordinary modes of alienation; and if the Lord did not choose to act in his own person, he nominated a 'Freigraff' to execute the office in his stead. The Court itself was composed of 'Freyschöppfen,' Scabini, or Echevins, nominated by the Graff, and who were divided into two classes: the ordinary, and the 'Wissenden' or 'Witan,' who were admitted under a strict and singular bond of secrecy.

"The initiation of these, the participators in all the mysteries of the tribunal, could only take place upon the 'red earth,' or within the limits of the ancient Duchy of Westphalia. Bareheaded and ungirt, the candidate is conducted before the dread tribunal. He is interrogated as to his qualifications, or rather as to the absence of any disqualification. He must be free born, a Teuton, and clear of any accusation cognizable by the tribunal of which he is to become a member.—If the answers are satisfactory, he then takes the oath, swearing by the Holy Law, that he will conceal the secrets of the Holy Vehme from wife and child—from father and mother—from sister and brother—from fire and water—from every creature upon which the sun shines, or upon which the rain falls—from every being between earth and heaven.

"Another clause relates to his active duties. He further swears, that he will 'say forth' to the tribunal all crimes or offences which fall beneath the secret ban of the Emperor, which he knows to be true, or which he has heard from trustworthy report; and that he will not forbear to do so, for love nor for loathing, for gold nor for silver nor precious stones.—This oath being imposed upon him, the new Freischopff was then intrusted with the secrets of the Vehmic tribunal. He received the password, by which he was to know his fellows, and the grip or sign by which they recognised each other in silence; and he was warned of the terrible punishment awaiting the perjured brother.—If he discloses the secrets of the Court, he is to expect that he will be suddenly seized by the ministers of vengeance. His eyes are bound, he is cast down on the soil, his tongue is torn out through the back of his neck—and he is then to be hanged seven times higher than any other criminal. And whether restrained by the fear of punishment, or by the stronger ties of mystery, no instance was ever known of any violation of the secrets of the tribunal.

"Thus connected by an invisible bond, the members of the 'Holy Vehme' became extremely numerous. In the fourteenth century, the league contained upwards of one hundred thousand members. Persons of every rank sought to be associated to this powerful community, and to participate in the immunities which the brethren possessed. Princes were eager to allow their ministers to become the members of this mysterious and holy alliance; and the cities of the Empire were equally anxious to enrol their magistrates in the Vehmic union.

"The supreme government of the Vehmic tribunals was vested in the great or general Chapter, composed of the Freegraves and all the other initiated members, high and low. Over this assembly the Emperor might preside in person, but more usually by his deputy, the Stadtholder of the ancient Duchy of Westphalia; an office, which, after the fall of Henry the Lion, Duke of Brunswick, was annexed to the Archbishopric of Cologne.

"Before the general Chapter, all the members were liable to account for their acts. And it appears that the 'Freegraves' reported the proceedings which had taken place within their jurisdictions in the course of the year. Unworthy members were expelled, or sustained a severer punishment. Statutes, or 'Reformations,' as they were called, were here enacted for the regulation of the Courts, and the amendment of any abuses; and new and unforeseen cases, for which the existing laws did not provide a remedy, received their determination in the Vehmic Parliament.

"As the Echevins were of two classes, uninitiated and initiated, so the Vehmic Courts had also a twofold character; the 'Offenbare Ding' was an Open Court or Folkmoot; but the 'Heimliche Acht' was the far-famed Secret Tribunal.

"The first was held three times in each year. According to the ancient Teutonic usage, it usually assembled on Tuesday, anciently called 'Dingstag,' or court-day, as well as 'Dienst-tag,' or serving-day, the first open or working day after the two great weekly festivals of Sun-day and Moon-day. Here all the householders of the district, whether free or bond, attended as suitors. The 'Offenbare Ding' exercised a civil jurisdiction; and in this Folkmoot appeared any complainant or appellant who sought to obtain the aid of the Vehmic tribunal, in those cases when it did not possess that summary jurisdiction from which it has obtained such fearful celebrity. Here also the suitors of the district made presentments or 'wroge,' as they are termed, of any offences committed within their knowledge, and which were to be punished by the Graff and Echevins.

"The criminal jurisdiction of the Vehmic Tribunal took the widest range. The 'Vehme' could punish mere slander and contumely. Any violation of the Ten Commandments was to be restrained by the Echevins. Secret crimes, not to be proved by the ordinary testimony of witnesses, such as magic, witchcraft, and poison, were particularly to be restrained by the Vehmic Judges; and they sometimes designated their jurisdiction as comprehending every offence against the honour of man or the precepts of religion. Such a definition, if definition it can be called, evidently allowed them to bring every action of which an individual might complain, within the scope of their tribunals. The forcible usurpation of land became an offence against the 'Vehme.' And if the property of an humble individual was occupied by the proud Burghers of the Hanse, the power of the Defendants might afford a reasonable excuse for the interference of the Vehmic power.

"The Echevins, as Conservators of the Ban of the Empire, were bound to make constant circuits within their districts, by night and by day. If they could apprehend a thief, a murderer, or the perpetrator of any other heinous crime in possession of the 'mainour,' or in the very act—or if his own mouth confessed the deed, they hung him upon the next tree. But to render this execution legal, the following requisites were necessary: fresh suit, or the apprehension and execution of the offender before daybreak or nightfall;—the visible evidence of the crime;—and lastly, that three Echevins, at least, should seize the offender, testify against him, and judge of the recent deed.

"If, without any certain accuser, and without the indication of crime, an individual was strongly and vehemently suspected; or when the nature of the offence was such as that its proof could only rest upon opinion and presumption, the offender then became subject to what the German jurists term the inquisitorial proceeding; it became the duty of the Echevin to denounce the 'Leumund,' or manifest evil fame, to the secret tribunal. If the Echevins and the Freygraff were satisfied with the presentment, either from their own knowledge, or from the information of their compeer, the offender was said to be 'verfämbt;'—his life was forfeited; and wherever he was found by the brethren of the tribunal, they executed him without the slightest delay or mercy. An offender who had escaped from the Echevins was liable to the same punishment; and such also was the doom of the party, who, after having been summoned pursuant to an appeal preferred in open court, made default in appearing. But one of the 'Wissenden' was in no respect liable to the summary process, or to the inquisitorial proceeding, unless he had revealed the secrets of the Court. He was presumed to be a true man; and if accused upon vehement suspicion, or 'Leumund,' the same presumption or evil repute, which was fatal to the uninitiated, might be entirely rebutted by the compurgatory oath of the free Echevin. If a party, accused by appeal, did not shun investigation, he appeared in the open court, and defended himself according to the ordinary rules of law. If he absconded, or if the evidence or presumptions were against him, the accusation then came before the Judges of the Secret Court, who pronounced the doom. The accusatorial process, as it was termed, was also, in many cases, brought in the first instance before the 'Heimliche Acht.' Proceeding upon the examination of witnesses, it possessed no peculiar character, and its forms were those of the ordinary courts of justice. It was only in this manner that one of the 'Wissenden' or Witan could be tried; and the privilege of being exempted from the summary process, or from the effects of the 'Leumund,' appears to have been one of the reasons which induced so many of those who did not tread the 'red earth' to seek to be included in the Vehmic bond.

"There was no mystery in the assembly of the Heimliche Acht. Under the oak, or under the lime-tree, the Judges assembled, in broad daylight, and before the eye of heaven; but the tribunal derived its name from the precautions which were taken, for the purpose of preventing any disclosure of its proceedings which might enable the offender to escape the vengeance of the Vehme. Hence, the fearful oath of secrecy which bound the Echevins. And if any stranger was found present in the Court, the unlucky intruder instantly forfeited his life as a punishment for his temerity. If the presentment or denunciation did chance to become known to the offender, the law allowed him a right of appeal. But the permission was of very little utility, it was a profitless boon, for the Vehmic Judges always laboured to conceal the judgment from the hapless criminal, who seldom was aware of his sentence until his neck was encircled by the halter.

"Charlemagne, according to the traditions of Westphalia, was the founder of the Vehmic tribunal; and it was supposed that he instituted the Court for the purpose of coercing the Saxons, ever ready to relapse into the idolatry from which they had been reclaimed, not by persuasion, but by the sword. This opinion, however, is not confirmed either by documentary evidence or by contemporary historians. And if we examine the proceedings of the

Vehmic tribunal, we shall see that, in principle, it differs in no essential character from the summary jurisdiction exercised in the townships and hundreds of Anglo-Saxon England. Amongst us, the thief or the robber was equally liable to summary punishment, if apprehended by the men of the township; and the same rules disqualified them from proceeding to summary execution. An English outlaw was exactly in the situation of him who had escaped from the hands of the Echevins, or who had failed to appear before the Vehmic Court: he was condemned unheard, nor was he confronted with his accusers. The inquisitorial proceedings, as they are termed by the German jurists, are identical with our ancient presentments. Presumptions are substituted for proofs, and general opinion holds the place of a responsible accuser. He who was untrue to all the people in the Saxon age, or liable to the malecredence of the inquest at a subsequent period, was scarcely more fortunate than he who was branded as 'Leumund' by the Vehmic law.

"In cases of open delict and of outlawry, there was substantially no difference whatever between the English and the Vehmic proceedings. But in the inquisitorial process, the delinquent was allowed, according to our older code, to run the risk of the ordeal. He was accused by or before the Hundred, or the Thanes of the Wapentake; and his own oath cleared him, if a true man; but he 'bore the iron' if unable to avail himself of the credit derived from a good and fair reputation. The same course may have been originally adopted in Westphalia; for the 'Wissend,' when accused, could exculpate himself by his compurgatory oath, being presumed to be of good fame; and it is, therefore, probable that an uninitiated offender, standing a stage lower in character and credibility, was allowed the last resort of the ordeal. But when the 'Judgment of God' was abolished by the decrees of the Church, it did not occur to the Vehmic Judges to put the offender upon his second trial by the visne, which now forms the distinguishing characteristic of the English law, and he was at once considered as condemned. The Heimliche Acht is a presentment not traversable by the offender.

"*The Vehmic Tribunals can only be considered as the original jurisdictions of the 'Old Saxons,' which survived the subjugation of their country. The singular and mystic forms of initiation, the system of enigmatical phrases, the use of the signs and symbols of recognition, may probably be ascribed to the period when the whole system was united to the worship of the Deities of Vengeance, and when the sentence was promulgated by the Doomsmen, assembled, like the Asi of old, before the altars of Thor or Woden.* Of this connexion with ancient pagan policy, so clearly to be traced in the Icelandic Courts, the English territorial jurisdictions offer some very faint vestiges; but the mystery had long been dispersed, and the whole system passed into the ordinary machinery of the law.

"As to the Vehmic Tribunals, it is acknowledged, that in a truly barbarous age and country, their proceedings, however violent, were not without utility. Their severe and secret vengeance often deterred the rapacity of the noble robber, and protected the humble suppliant; the extent, and even the abuse, of their authority was in some measure justified in an Empire divided into numerous independent jurisdictions, and not subjected to any paramount tribunal, able to administer impartial justice to the oppressed. But as the times improved, the Vehmic tribunals degenerated. The Echevins, chosen from the inferior ranks, did not possess any personal consideration. Opposed by the opulent cities of the Hanse, and objects of the suspicion and the enmity of the powerful aristocracy, the tribunals of some districts were abolished by law, and others took the form of ordinary territorial jurisdictions; the greater number fell into desuetude. Yet, as late as the middle of the eighteenth century, a few Vehmic tribunals existed in name, though, as it may be easily supposed, without possessing any remnant of their pristine power." —PALGRAVE *on the Rise and Progress of the English Commonwealth. Proofs and Illustrations.* p. 157.

I have marked *by italic letters* the most important passage of the above quotation. The view it contains seems to me to have every appearance of truth and justice—and if such should, on maturer investigation, turn out to be the fact, it will certainly confer no small honour on an English scholar to have discovered the key to a mystery, which had long exercised in vain the laborious and profound students of German antiquity.

There are probably several other points on which I ought to have embraced this opportunity of enlarging; but the necessity of preparing for an excursion to foreign countries, in quest of health and strength, that have been for some time sinking, makes me cut short my address upon the present occasion.

Although I had never been in Switzerland, and numerous mistakes must of course have occurred in my attempts to describe the local scenery of that romantic region, I must not conclude without a statement highly gratifying to myself, that the work met with a reception of more than usual cordiality among the descendants of the Alpine heroes whose manners I had ventured to treat of; and I have in particular to express my thanks to the several Swiss gentlemen who have, since the novel was published, enriched my little collection of armour with specimens of the huge weapon that sheared the lances of the Austrian chivalry at Sempach, and was employed with equal success on the bloody days of Granson and Morat. Of the ancient doublehanded *espadons* of the Switzer, I have, in this way, received, I think, not less than six, in excellent preservation, from as many different individuals, who thus testified their general approbation of these pages. They are not the less interesting, that gigantic swords, of nearly the same pattern and dimensions, were employed in their conflicts with the bold knights and men-at-arms of England, by Wallace, and the sturdy foot-soldiers who, under his guidance, laid the foundations of Scottish independence.

The reader who wishes to examine with attention the historical events of the period which the novel embraces, will find ample means of doing so, in the valuable works of Zschokké and M. de Barante—which last author's account of the Dukes of Burgundy is among the most valuable of recent accessions of European literature—and in the new Parisian edition of Froissart, which has not as yet attracted so much attention in this country as it well deserves to do.

W. S.

ABBOTSFORD, *Sept.* 17, 1831.

Notes to Anne of Geierstein

76.42 (Ch. 8) Graffslust Graff's-lust—*i. e.* Count's-delight.
78.19 (Ch. 8) Lanzknecht A private soldier of the German infantry.
93.6 (Ch. 10) the coward knights of Cornouailles The chivalry of Cornwall are generally undervalued in the Norman-French romances. The cause is difficult to discover.
125.31 (Ch. 12) double-gangers Double-walkers, a name in Germany for those aerial duplicates of humanity who represent the features and appearance of other living persons.
152.38 (Ch. 14) a man meanly born Louis XI. was probably the first king of France who flung aside all affectation of choosing his ministers from among the nobility. He often placed men of mean birth in situations of the highest trust.
175.18 (Ch. 16) noble of right There is abundant evidence that in the middle ages the office of public executioner was esteemed highly honourable all over Germany. It still is, in such parts of that country as retain the old custom of execution by stroke of sword,

very far from being held discreditable to the extent to which we carry our feelings on the subject, and which exposed the magistrates of a Scotch town, I rather think no less a one than Glasgow, to a good deal of ridicule when they advertised, some few years ago, on occasion of the death of their hangman, that "none but persons of respectable character" need apply for the vacant situation. At this day in China, in Persia, and probably in other Oriental kingdoms, the Chief Executioner is one of the great officers of state, and is as proud of the emblem of his fatal duty, as any European Lord Chamberlain of his Golden Key.

The circumstances of the strange trial and execution of the Knight of Hagenbach are detailed minutely by M. de Barante, from contemporary MS. documents; and the reader will be gratified with a specimen of that writer's narrative. A translation is also given for the benefit of many of my kind readers.

"De toutes parts, on était accouru par milliers pour assister au procès de ce cruel gouverneur, tant la haine était grande contre lui. De sa prison, il entendait retentir sur le pont et au-dessous des voûtes de la porte, le pas des chevaux, et s'enquérait à son geôlier de ceux qui arrivaient, soit pour être ses juges, soit pour être témoins de son supplice. Parfois le geôlier répondait, 'Ce sont des étrangers; je ne les connais pas.'—'Ne sont-ce pas, disait le prisonnier, des gens assez mal vêtus, de haute taille, de forte apparence, montés sur des chevaux aux courtes oreilles?' et si le geôlier répondait: 'oui,'—'Ah! ce sont les Suisses, s'écriait Hagenbach; mon Dieu ayez pitié de moi !' et il se rappelait toutes les insultes qu'il leur avait faites, toutes ses insolences envers eux; il pensait, mais trop tard, que c'était leur alliance avec la maison d'Autriche qui était cause de sa perte.

"Le 4 mai 1474, après avoir été mis à la question, it fut, à la diligence d'Hermann d'Eptingen, gouverneur pour l'archiduc, amené devant ses juges, sur la place publique de Brisach. Sa contenance était ferme et d'un homme qui ne craint pas la mort. Henri Iselin de Bâle porta la parole au nom d'Hermann d'Eptingen, agissant pour le seigneur et le pays. Il parla à peu près en ces termes:

"'Pierre de Hagenbach, chevalier, maître d'hôtel de monseigneur le duc de Bourgogne, et son gouverneur dans les pays de Ferette et Haute-Alsace, aurait dû respecter les priviléges réservés par l'acte d'engagement; mais il n'a pas moins foulé aux pieds les lois de Dieu et des hommes, que les droits jurés et garantis au pays. Il a fait mettre à mort sans jugement quatre honnêtes bourgeois de Thann; il a dépouillé la ville de Brisach de sa juridiction, et y a établi juges et consuls de son choix; il a rompu et dispersé les communautés de la bourgeoisie et des métiers; il a levé des impôts par sa seule volonté; il a, contre toutes les lois, logé chez les habitans des gens de guerre, Lombards, Français, Picards ou Flamands, et a favorisé leurs désordres et pillages. Il leur a même commandé d'égorger leurs hôtes durant la nuit, et avait fait préparer, pour y embarquer les femmes et les enfans, des bateaux qui devaient être submergés dans le Rhin. Enfin, lors même qu'il rejetterait de telles cruautés sur les ordres qu'il a reçus, comment pourrait-il s'excuser d'avoir fait violence et outrage a l'honneur de tant de filles ou femmes, et même de saintes religieuses?'

"D'autres accusations furent portées dans les interrogatories; et des témoins attestèrent les violences faites aux gens de Mulhausen et aux marchands de Bâle.

"Pour suivre toutes les formes de la justice, on avait donné un avocat à l'accusé; 'messire Pierre de Hagenbach, dit-it, ne reconnaît d'autre juge et d'autre seigneur que monseigneur le duc de Bourgogne, dont il avait commission et recevait les commandemens. Il n'avait nul droit de contrôler les ordres qu'il était chargé d'exécuter, et son devoir était d'obéir. Ne sait-on pas quelle soumission les gens de guerre doivent à leur seigneur et maître? Croit-on que le landvogt de monseigneur le Duc eût à lui remontrer et à lui résister? Et monseigneur n'a-t-il pas ensuite, par sa présence, confirmé et ratifié tout ce qui avait été fait en son nom? Si des impôts ont été demandés, c'est qu'il avait besoin d'argent. Pour les recueillir, il a bien fallu punir ceux qui se refusaient à payer. C'est ce que monseigneur le Duc, et mème l'empereur, quand its sont venus, ont reconnu nécessaire. Le logement des gens de guerre était aussi la suite des ordres du Duc. Quant à la juridiction de Brisach, le landvogt pouvait-il souffrir cette résistance?

"'Enfin, dans une affaire si grave, où il y va de la vie, convient-il de produire comme un véritable grief, le dernier dont a parlé l'accusateur? Parmi ceux qui écoutent, y en a-t-il un seul qui puisse se vanter de ne pas avoir saisi les occasions de se divertir? N'est-il pas clair que messire de Hagenbach a seulement profité de la bonne volonté de quelques femmes ou filles, ou, pour mettre les choses au pis, qu'il n'a exercé d'autre contrainte envers elles qu'au moyen de son bon argent?'

"Les juges siègérent long-temps sur leur tribunal. Douze heures entières passérent sans que l'affaire fût terminée. Le sire de Hagenbach, toujours ferme et calme, n'allégua d'autres défenses, d'autres excuses que celles qu'il avait données déjà sous la torture: les ordres et la volonté de son seigneur, qui était son seul juge, et le seul qui pût lui demander compte.

"Enfin, à sept heures du soir, à la clarté des flambeaux, les juges, après avoir déclaré qu'à eux appartenait le droit de prononcer sur les crimes imputés au landvogt, le firent rappeler, et rendirent leur sentence qui le condamna à mort. Il ne s'émut pas davantage, et demanda pour toute grâce d'avoir seulement la tête tranchée. Huit bourreaux des diverses villes se présentèrent pour exécuter l'arrêt. Celui de Colmar, qui passait pour le plus adroit, fut préfére.

"Avant de le conduire à l'échafaud, les seize chevaliers qui faisaient partie des juges requirent que messire de Hagenbach fût dégradé de sa dignité de chevalier et de tous ses honneurs. Pour lors s'avança Gaspard Hurter, héraut de l'empereur, et il dit: 'Pierre de Hagenbach, il me déplaît grandement que vous ayez si mal employé votre vie mortelle, de sorte qu'il convient que vous perdiez non-seulement la dignité et ordre de chevalerie, mais aussi la vie. Votre devoir était de rendre la justice, de protéger la veuve et l'orphelin, de respecter les femmes et les filles, d'honorer les saints prêtres, de vous opposer à toute injuste violence; et, au contraire, vous avez commis tout ce que vous deviez empêcher. Ayant ainsi forfait au noble ordre de chevalerie et aux sermens que vous aviez jurés, les chevaliers ici présens m'ont enjoint de vous en ôter les insignes. Ne les voyant pas sur vous en ce moment, je vous proclame indigne chevalier de Saint-George, au nom et à l'honneur duquel on vous avait autrefois honoré du baudrier de chevalerie.'

"Puis s'avança Hermann d'Eptingen: 'Puis-qu'on vient de te dégrader de chevalerie, je te dépouille de ton collier, chaîne d'or, anneau, poignard, éperon, gantelet.' Il les lui prit et lui en frappa le visage, et ajouta: 'Chevaliers, et vous qui désirez le devenir, j'espère que cette punition publique vous servira d'exemple, et que vous vivrez dans la crainte de Dieu, noblement et vaillamment, selon la dignité de la chevalerie et l'honneur de votre nom.' Enfin, Thomas Schutz, prevôt d'Einsisheim et maréchal de cette commission de juges, se leva, et s'adressant au bourreau, lui dit: 'Faites selon la justice.'

"Tous les juges montèrent à cheval ainsi qu' Hermann d'Eptingen. Au milieu d'eux marchait Pierre de Hagenbach entre deux prêtres. C'était pendant la nuit. Des torches éclairaient la marche; une foule immense se pressait autour de ce triste cortége. Le condamné s'entretenait avec son confesseur d'un air pieux et recueilli, mais ferme, se recommandant aussi aux prières de tous ceux qui l'entouraient. Arrivé dans une prairie devant la porte de la ville, il monta sur l'échafaud d'un pas assuré; puis, élevant la voix: 'Je n'ai pas peur de la mort, dit-il, encore que je ne l'attendisse pas de cette sorte, mais bien les armes à la main; ce que je plains, c'est tout le sang que le mien fera couler. Monseigneur ne laissera point ce jour sans vengeance pour moi. Je ne regrette ni ma vie, ni mon corps. J'étais homme; priez pour moi.' Il s'entretint encore un instant avec le confesseur, présenta la tête et reçut le coup."—M. DE BARANTE, tom. x. pp. 189–96.

TRANSLATION.

"Such was the detestation in which this cruel governor was held, that multitudes flocked in from all quarters to be present at his trial. He heard from his prison the bridge and the vaults of the gate re-echo with the tread of horses, and would ask of his jailer respecting those who were arriving, whether they might be his judges, or those desirous of witnessing his punishment. Sometimes the jailer would answer, 'these are strangers whom I know not.'—'Are not they,' said the prisoner, 'men meanly clad, tall in stature, and of bold mien, mounted on short-eared horses?' And if the jailer answered in the affirmative, 'Ah, these are the Swiss,' cried Hagenbach. 'My God, have mercy on me!' and he recalled to mind all the insults and cruelties he had heaped upon them. He considered, but too late, that their alliance with the house of Austria had been his destruction.

"On the 4th of May 1474, after being put to the torture, he was brought before his judges in the public square of Brisach, at the instance of Hermann d'Eptingen, who governed for the Archduke. His countenance was firm, as one who fears not death. Henry Iselin of Bâle first spoke in the name of Hermann d'Eptingen, who acted for the lord and the country. He proceeded in nearly these terms:—

"'Peter de Hagenbach, knight, steward of my lord the Duke of Burgundy, and his governor in the country of Ferette and Haute Alsace, was bound to observe the privileges reserved by act of compact, but he has alike trampled under foot the laws of God and man, and the rights which have been guaranteed by oath to the country. He has caused four worshipful burgesses of Thann to be put to death without trial; he has spoiled the city of Brisach, and established there judges and consuls chosen by himself; he has broken and dispersed the various communities of burghers and craftsmen; he has levied imposts of his own will; contrary to every law, he has quartered upon the inhabitants soldiers of various countries, Lombards, French, men of Picardy and Flemings, and has encouraged them in pillage and disorder; he has even commanded these men to butcher their hosts during night, and had caused boats to be prepared to embark therein women and children to be sunk in the Rhine. Finally, should he plead the orders which he had received as an excuse for these cruelties, how can he clear himself of having dishonoured so many maidens or women, even those under religious vows?'

"Other accusations were brought against him by examination, and witnesses proved outrages committed on the people of Mulhausen, and the merchants of Bâle.

"That every form of justice might be observed, an advocate was appointed to defend the accused. 'Messire Peter de Hagenbach,' said he, 'recognises no other judge or master than my lord the Duke of Burgundy, whose commission he bore and whose orders he received. He had no control over the orders he was charged to execute;—his duty was to obey. Who is ignorant of the submission due by military retainers to their lord and master? Can any one believe that the landvogt of my lord the Duke could remonstrate with or resist him? And has not my lord confirmed and ratified by his presence all acts done in his name? If imposts have been levied, it was because he had need of money; to obtain it, it was necessary to punish those who refused payment: this proceeding my lord the Duke, and the Emperor himself, when present, have considered as expedient. The quartering of soldiers was also in accordance with the orders of the Duke. With respect to the jurisdiction of Brisach, could the landvogt permit any resistance from that quarter?

"'To conclude, in so serious an affair,—one which touches the life of the prisoner,—can the last accusation be really considered a grievance? Among all those who hear me, is there one man who can say he has never committed similar imprudencies? Is it not evident that Messire de Hagenbach has only taken advantage of the good-will of some girls and women, or, at the worst, that his money was the only restraint imposed upon them?'

"The judges sat for a long time on the tribunal. Twelve hours elapsed before the termination of the trial. The Knight of Hagenbach, always calm and undaunted, brought forward no other defence or excuse than what he had before given when under the torture; viz. the orders and will of his lord, who alone was his judge, and who alone could demand an explanation.

"At length, at seven in the evening, and by the light of torches, the judges, after having declared it their province to pronounce judgment on the crimes of which the landvogt was accused, caused him to be called before them, and delivered their sentence condemning him to death. He betrayed no emotion, and only demanded as a favour, that he should be beheaded. Eight executioners of various towns presented themselves to execute the sentence; the one belonging to Colmar, who was accounted the most expert, was preferred.

"Before conducting him to the scaffold, the sixteen knights, who acted as judges, required that Messire de Hagenbach should be degraded from the dignity of knight, and from all his honours. Then advanced Gaspar Hurter, herald of the Emperor, and said: —'Peter de Hagenbach, I deeply deplore that you have so employed your mortal life, that you must lose not only the dignity and honour of knighthood, but your life also. Your duty was to render justice, to protect the widow and orphan, to respect women and maidens, to honour the holy priests, to oppose every unjust outrage: but you have yourself committed what you ought to have opposed in others. Having broken, therefore, the oaths which you have sworn, and having forfeited the noble order of knighthood, the knights here present have enjoined me to deprive you of its insignia. Not perceiving them on your person at this moment, I proclaim you unworthy Knight of St George, in whose name and honour you were formerly admitted in the order of knighthood.'

"Then Hermann d'Eptingen advanced. 'Since you are degraded from knighthood, I deprive you of your collar, gold chain, ring, poniard, spur, and gauntlet.' He then took them from him, and, striking him on the face, added:—'Knights, and you who aspire to that honour, I trust this public punishment will serve as an example to you, and that you will live in the fear of God, nobly and valiantly, in accordance with the dignity of knighthood, and the honour of your name.' At last Thomas Schulz, the provost of Einselheim, and marshal of that commission of judges, arose, and addressing himself to the executioner,—'Let justice be done.'

"All the judges, along with Hermann d'Eptingen, mounted on horseback; in the midst of them walked Peter de Hagenbach between two priests. It was night, and they marched by the light of torches; an immense crowd pressed around this sad procession. The prisoner conversed with his confessor, with pious, collected, and firm demeanour, recommending himself to the prayers of the spectators. On arriving at a meadow without the gate of the town, he mounted the scaffold with a firm step, and elevating his voice, exclaimed:—

"'I fear not death, I have always expected it; not, indeed, in this manner, but with arms in my hand. I regret alone the blood which mine will cause to be shed; my lord will not permit this day to pass unavenged. I regret neither my life or body. I was a man—pray for me!' He conversed an instant more with his confessor, presented his head, and received the blow."—M. DE BARANTE, tom. x. pp. 189–96.

196.24 (Ch. 18) Drinking Song This is one of the best and most popular of the German ditties:—

Der Rhein, der Rhein, gesegnet sei der Rhein,
Da wachsen unsre reben, &c.

222.13 (Ch. 20) the Vehmique Institution The word Wehme, pronounced Vehme, is of uncertain derivation, but was always used to intimate this inquisitorial and secret Court. The members were termed Wissenden, or Initiated, answering to the modern phrase of Illuminati. Mr Palgrave seems inclined to derive the word *Vehme* from *Ehme*, *i.e. Law*, and he is probably right.

228.33 (Ch. 20) the Red Soil The parts of Germany subjected to the operation of the Secret Tribunal, were called, from the blood which it spilt, or from some other reason, (Mr Palgrave suggests the ground tincture of the ancient banner of the district) the Red Soil. Westphalia, as the limits of that country were understood in the middle ages, which are considerably different from the present boundaries, was the principal theatre of the Vehme.

299.42 (Ch. 27) the order of the Golden Fleece The chief order of knighthood in the state of Burgundy.

318.24 (Ch. 29) corrupt the principles

THE TROUBADOURS. The smoothness of the Provençal dialect, partaking strongly of the Latin, which had been spoken for so many ages in what was called for distinction's sake the Roman Province of Gaul, and the richness and fertility of a country abounding in all that could delight the senses and soothe the imagination, naturally disposed the inhabitants to cultivate the art of poetry, and to value and foster the genius of those who distinguished themselves by attaining excellence in it. Troubadours, that is, *finders* or *inventors*, equivalent to the northern term of *makers*, arose in every class, from the lowest to the highest, and success in their art dignified men of the meanest rank, and added fresh honours to those who were born in the Patrician file of society. War and love, more especially the latter, were dictated to them by the chivalry of the times as the especial subjects of their verse. Such, too, were the themes of our northern minstrels. But whilst the latter confined themselves in general to those well-known metrical histories in which scenes of strife and combat mingled with adventures of enchantment, and fables of giants and monsters subdued by valiant champions, such as best attracted the ears of the somewhat duller and more barbarous warriors of northern France, of Britain, and of Germany—the more lively Troubadours produced poems which turned on human passion, and on love, affection, and dutiful observance, with which the faithful knight was bound to regard the object of his choice, and the honour and respect with which she was bound to recompense his faithful services.

Thus far it cannot be disputed, that the themes selected by the Troubadours were those on which poetry is most naturally exerted, and with the best chance of rising to excellence. But it usually happens, that when any one of the fine arts is cultivated exclusively, the taste of those who practise and admire its productions loses sight of nature, simplicity, and true taste, and the artist endeavours to discover, while the public learn to admire, some more complicated system, in which pedantry supersedes the dictates of natural feeling, and metaphysical ingenuity is used instead of the more obvious qualifications of simplicity and good sense. Thus, with the unanimous approbation of their hearers, the Troubadours framed for themselves a species of poetry describing and inculcating a system of metaphysical affection, as inconsistent with nature as the minstrel's tales of magicians and monsters; with this evil to society, that it was calculated deeply to injure its manners and its morals. Every Troubadour, or good Knight, who took the maxims of their poetical school for his rule, was bound to choose a lady love, the fairest and noblest to whom he had access, to whom he dedicated at once his lyre and his sword, and who, married or single, was to be the object to whom his life, words, and actions, were to be devoted. On the other hand, a lady thus honoured and distinguished, was bound, by accepting the services of such a gallant, to consider him as her lover, and on all due occasions to grace him as such with distinguished marks of personal favour. It is true, that according to the best authorities, the intercourse betwixt her lover and herself was to be entirely of a Platonic character, and the loyal swain was not to require, or the chosen lady to grant, any thing beyond the favour she might in strict modesty bestow. Even under this restriction, the system was like to make wild work with the domestic peace of families, since it permitted, or rather enjoined, such familiarity betwixt the fair dame and her poetical admirer; and very frequently human passions, placed in such a dangerous situation, proved too strong to be confined within the metaphysical bounds prescribed to them by so fantastic and perilous a system. The injured husbands on many occasions avenged themselves with severity, and even with dreadful cruelty, on the unfaithful ladies, and the musical skill and chivalrous character of the lover proved no protection to his person. But the real spirit of the system was seen in this, that in the poems of the other Troubadours, by whom such events are recorded, their pity is all bestowed on the hapless lovers, while, without the least allowance for just provocation, the injured husband is held up to execration.

319.29 (Ch. 29) Parliament of Love

HIGH AND NOBLE PARLIAMENT OF LOVE. In Provence, during the flourishing time of the Troubadours, Love was esteemed so grave and formal a part of the business of life, that a Parliament or High Court of Love was appointed for deciding such questions. This singular tribunal was, it may be supposed, conversant with more of imaginary than of real suits; but it is astonishing with what cold and pedantic ingenuity the Troubadours of whom it consisted set themselves to plead and to decide, upon reasoning which was not less singular and able than out of place, the absurd questions which their own fantastic imaginations had previously devised. There, for example, is a reported case of much celebrity, where a lady sitting in company with three persons, who were her admirers, listened to one with the most favourable smiles, while she pressed the hand of the second, and touched with her own the foot of the third. It was a case much agitated and keenly contested in the Parliament of Love, which of these rivals had received the distinguishing mark of the lady's favour. Much ingenuity was wasted on this and similar cases, of which there is a collection, in all judicial form of legal proceedings, under the title of *Arrets d'Amour*, (Adjudged cases of the Court of Love.)

400.26 (Ch. 36) he lies dead before you The following very striking passage is that in which Philip de Commines sums up the last scene of Charles the Bold, whose various fortunes he had long watched with a dark anticipation that a character so reckless, and capable of such excess, must sooner or later lead to a tragical result:

"As soon as the Count de Campo-basso arrived in the Duke of Lorrain's army, word was sent him to leave the camp immediately, for they would not entertain, nor have any communication with, such traytors. Upon which message he retir'd with his party to a Castle and Pass not far off, where he fortified himself with carts and other things as well as he could, in hopes, that if the Duke of Burgundy was routed, he might have an opportunity of coming in for a share of the plunder, as he did afterwards. Nor was this practice with the Duke of Lorrain the most execrable action that Campo-basso was guilty of; but before he left the army he conspir'd with several other officers (finding it was impracticable to attempt any thing against the Duke of Burgundy's person) to leave him just as they came to charge, for at that time he suppos'd it would put the Duke into the greatest terror and consternation, and if he fled, he was sure he could not escape alive, for he had order'd thirteen or fourteen sure men, some to run as soon as the Germans came up to charge 'em, and others to watch the Duke of Burgundy, and kill him in the rout, which was well enough contrived; I myself have seen two or three of those who were employed to kill the Duke. Having thus settled his conspiracy at home, he went over to the Duke of Lorrain upon the approach of the German army; but finding they would not entertain him, he retired to Conde.

"The German army march'd forward, and with 'em a considerable body of French horse, whom the King had given leave to be present at that action. Several parties lay in ambush not far off, that if the Duke of Burgundy was routed, they might surprise some person of quality, or take some considerable booty. By this every one may see into what a deplorable condition this poor Duke had brought himself, by his contempt of good counsel. Both armies being joyn'd, the Duke of Burgundy's forces having been twice beaten before, and by consequence weak and dispirited, and ill provided besides, were quickly broken and entirely defeated: Many sav'd themselves and got off; the rest were either taken or kill'd; and among 'em the Duke of Burgundy himself was kill'd on the spot. One Monsieur Claude of Bausmont, Captain of the Castle of Dier in Lorrain, kill'd the Duke of Burgundy. Finding his army routed, he mounted a swift horse, and endeavouring to swim a little river in order to make his escape, his horse fell with him, and overset him: The Duke cry'd out for quarter to this gentleman who was pursuing him, but he being deaf, and not hearing him, immediately kill'd and stripp'd him, not knowing who he was, and left him naked in the ditch, where his body was found the next day after the battle; which the Duke of Lorrain (to his eternal honour) buried with great pomp and magnificence in St George's Church, in the old town of Nancy, himself and all his nobility, in deep mourning, attending the corpse to the grave. The following epitaph was some time afterwards ingrav'd on his tomb:—

Carolus hoc busto Burgundæ gloria gentis
Conditur, Europæ qui fuit ante timor.

I saw a seal ring of his, since his death, at Milan, with his arms cut curiously upon a sardonix that I have seen him often wear in a ribbon at his breast, which was sold at Milan for two ducats, and had been stolen from him by a rascal that waited on him in his chamber. I have often seen the Duke dress'd and undress'd in great state and formality, and attended by very great persons; but at his death all this pomp and magnificence ceas'd, and his family was involved in the same ruin with himself, and very likely as a punishment for his having deliver'd up the Constable not long before, out of a base and avaricious principle; but God forgive him. I have known him a powerful and honourable Prince, in as great esteem, and as much courted by his neighbours, (when his affairs were in a prosperous condition,) as any Prince in Europe, and perhaps more; and I cannot conceive what should provoke God Almighty's displeasure so highly against him, unless it was his self-love and arrogance, in appropriating all the success of his enterprises, and all the renown he ever acquir'd, to his own wisdom and conduct, without attributing any thing to God. Yet to speak truth, he was master of several good qualities: No Prince ever had a greater ambition to entertain young noblemen than he, nor was more careful of their education: His presents and bounty were never profuse and extravagant, because he gave to many, and had a mind every body should taste of it. No Prince was ever more easie of access to his servants and subjects. Whilst I was in his service he was never cruel, but a little before his death he took up that humour, which was an infallible sign of the shortness of his life. He was very splendid and curious in his dress, and in every thing else, and indeed a little too much. He paid great honours to all ambassadors and foreigners, and entertain'd them nobly: His ambitious desire of fame was insatiable, and it was that which induced him to be eternally in wars, more than any other motive. He ambitiously desired to imitate the old Kings and Heroes of antiquity, whose actions still shine in History, and are so much talked of in the world, and his courage was equal to any Prince's of his time.

"But all his designs and imaginations were vain and extravagant, and turn'd afterwards to his own dishonour and confusion, for 'tis the conquerors and not the conquer'd that purchase to themselves renown. I cannot easily determine towards whom God Almighty shew'd his anger most, whether towards him who died suddenly without pain or sickness in the field of battle, or towards his subjects who never enjoy'd peace after his death, but were continually involv'd in wars, against which they were not able to maintain themselves, upon account of the civil dissentions and cruel animosities that arose among 'em; and that which was the most insupportable, was, that the very people, to whom they were now oblig'd for their defence and preservation, were the Germans, who were strangers, and not long since their profess'd enemies. In short, after the Duke's death, there was not a neighbouring state that wish'd them to prosper, nor even Germany that defended 'em. And by the management of their affairs, their understanding seem'd to be as much infatuated as their master's, for they rejected all good counsel, and pursued such methods as directly tended to their destruction; and they are still in such a condition, that though they have at present some little ease and relaxation from their sorrows, yet 'tis with great danger of a relapse, and 'tis well if it turns not in the end to their utter ruin.

"I am partly of their opinion who maintain, that God gives Princes, as he in his wisdom thinks fit, to punish or chastise the subjects; and he disposes the affection of subjects to their Princes, as he has determin'd to raise or depress 'em. Just so it has pleas'd him to deal with the House of Burgundy; for, after a long series of riches and prosperity, and six-and-twenty years' peace under three Illustrious Princes, predecessors to this Charles, (all of 'em excellent persons, and of great prudence and discretion,) it pleas'd God to send this Duke Charles, who involv'd them in bloody wars, as well winter as summer, to their great affliction and expense, in which most of their richest and stoutest men were either killed or utterly undone. Their misfortunes continu'd successively to the very hour of his death; and after such a manner, that at the last, the whole strength of their country was destroy'd, and all kill'd or taken prisoners who had any zeal or affection for the House of Burgundy, and had power to defend the state and dignity of that family; so that in a manner their losses were equal to, if not overbalanc'd their former prosperity; for as I have seen those Princes heretofore puissant, rich, and honourable, so it fared the same with their subjects; for I think, I have seen and known the greatest part of Europe; yet I never knew any province, or country, tho' perhaps of a larger extent, so abounding in money, so extravagantly fine in furniture for their horses, so sumptuous in their buildings, so profuse in their expenses, so luxurious in their feasts and entertainments, and so prodigal in all respects, as the subjects of these Princes, in my time: but it has pleased God at one blow to subvert and ruin this illustrious family. Such changes and revolutions in states and kingdoms God in his providence has wrought before we were born, and will do again when we are in our graves; for this is a certain maxim, that the prosperity or adversity of Princes are wholly at his disposal."

COMMINES, Book V. Chap. 9.

COUNT ROBERT OF PARIS

Editorial Note

No interleaved copy or relevant manuscript material for *Count Robert of Paris* are known to survive. The introductory Advertisement is in square brackets and signed by Lockhart. On 10 December 1832 Cadell 'looked over Introduction by Lockhart to Count Robert' (MS 20122, f. 52v). The notes are not in brackets, but they are very likely Lockhart's also (though Scott did send corrections to the Galignani edition from Naples): they are entirely uncreative, listing and quoting the standard sources for the novel, material mostly explored in the Historical Note and explanatory notes for EEWN 23a. The novel occupies Volume 46 and part of Volume 47 of the Magnum edition, which appeared on 1 March and 1 April 1833 respectively.

Since there is no evidence of Scott's involvement in the Advertisement or notes to *Count Robert* they have not been included in the present edition.

There are two Magnum illustrations for this title. The frontispiece to Volume 46 (MAG0091 / TB348.46) was designed by William Boxall and engraved by William Greatbatch. It depicts Robert seated on the Emperor's throne, with wolf-hound at his side (EEWN 23a, 106.32–34: 'Without a moment's hesitation . . . caress a large wolf-hound.'). The title-page vignette (MAG0092 / TB348.46) was designed by John West and engraved by Joseph Goodyear. It depicts Sebastes of Mitylene moving towards the sleeping figure of Hereward in an attempt to assassinate him (EEWN 23a, 21.25–27 (omitting 'silver' before 'corslet'): 'The assassin hovered . . . designed to protect.').

W. Boxall. W. Greatbatch.

COUNT ROBERT OF PARIS.

Without a moment's hesitation the Frank seated himself in the vacant throne of the Emperor, and extending his half armed and robust figure on the golden cushions which were destined for Alexius, he indolently began to caress a large wolf-hound.

EDINBURGH, PUBLISHED 1833, BY ROBERT CADELL, and WHITTAKER & Co. LONDON.

WAVERLEY NOVELS.

VOL. XLVI.

COUNT ROBERT OF PARIS.

The assassin hovered less than an instant over the sleeper, as if to mark the interval between the ill fitted corslet, and the body which it was designed to protect.

PRINTED FOR ROBERT CADELL, EDINBURGH,
AND WHITTAKER & C° LONDON.
1833.

CASTLE DANGEROUS

Editorial Note

No interleaved copy or relevant manuscript material for *Castle Dangerous* is known to survive. Scott was working on *Anne* in August 1831, writing on the 16th to Cadell: 'I inclose in this parcel the three volumes of the Chronicles of Canongate second with the Introduction. Anne of Geierstein comes next together with Aunt Margarets mirror' (MS 15980, f. 150r). In the Magnum the novel appeared in the second half of Volume 47 (after the conclusion of *Count Robert of Paris*) and the first part of Volume 48 (before *The Surgeon's Daughter* and a Glossary to the whole series), which appeared on 1 April and 1 May 1833 respectively, running to 466 and 492 pages respectively. The Magnum Introduction is preceded by a statement, in italics and square brackets, by Lockhart:

> The following introduction to "Castle Dangerous" was forwarded by Sir Walter Scott from Naples in February 1832, together with some corrections of the text, and notes on localities mentioned in the Novel.
>
> The materials for the Introduction must have been collected before he left Scotland, in September 1831; but in the hurry of preparing for his voyage he had not been able to arrange them so as to accompany the first edition of this Romance.
>
> A few notes, supplied by the Editor, are followed by his name in brackets.

This statement is backed up by an entry in Cadell's diary for 12 November 1832: 'wrote out letter as an Introduction to Castle Dangerous' (MS 20122, f. 48v).

The Introduction runs to only ten pages, and is entirely devoted to an indication of the written sources and topography of the novel. It is followed by an 18-page Appendix with extracts from Godscroft and Barbour in fulfilment of the pledge in the Introduction (591–92): 'As considerable liberties have been taken with the historical incidents on which this novel is founded, it is due to the reader to place before him such extracts from Godscroft and Barbour as may enable him to correct any mis-impression.' (As usual with the Magnum, readers are left to carry out their own comparison.)

As noted above, no manuscript of the Introduction is known to survive. It was corrected, and very likely more than corrected, by Lockhart: on 8 February 1833 Cadell noted that he 'wrote to Lockhart with proofs of Introduction to Castle Dangerous & Surgeons Daughter' (MS 21023, f. 9r).

Almost all of the notes are in square brackets, but some of them may well derive from information collected by Scott, and only two specifically marked as editorial have been omitted, silently, in the present edition. In particular those to 601.22–29 and 602.36–42 probably draw on material sent on 31 August 1831 by Thomas Haddow of Douglas, one of the two guides on Scott's visit there while preparing the novel. Haddow writes (MS 3919, f. 83r):

> After seeing you here some historical and other recollections occurred to me, which I imagined you might not be displeased to see. Under that impression I have committed to writing the accompanying notes, and now venture to trouble you by transmitting them.
>
> Should you think proper to peruse them, and meet with any difficulty which local opportunities might enable me to remove, it would [be] most gratifying to me to be applied to.
>
> After the parcel shall have reached you may I be permitted to expect notice of its receipt?
>
> No human being is acquainted with this communication, except my son, (a would-be Cleishbotham, unpatronized,) whose hand has been employed in transcribing.

One note derives from a letter to Scott by an unidentified informant (601–02), and one other (602–03) from a note by the minister at Douglas which may have been sent to Scott or to Lockhart.

There are two Magnum illustrations for this title. The frontispiece to Volume 47 (MAG0093 / TB348.47) was designed by Clarkson Stanfield and engraved by Samuel Sangster. It depicts Sir Aymer, guided by an old woman into the vaulted apartment of the Douglas sexton, with the page Fabian looking on from the doorway (EEWN 23b, 91–92: the caption reads simply 'CASTLE DANGEROUS.'). The title-page vignette (MAG0094 / TB348.47) was designed by Alexander Fraser, the elder, and engraved by Charles

Fox . It depicts Turnbull holding the hand of the blindfolded Lady Augusta in order to guide her (EEWN 23b, 143.24–26 (abridged): 'The trooper . . . this blinded state.').

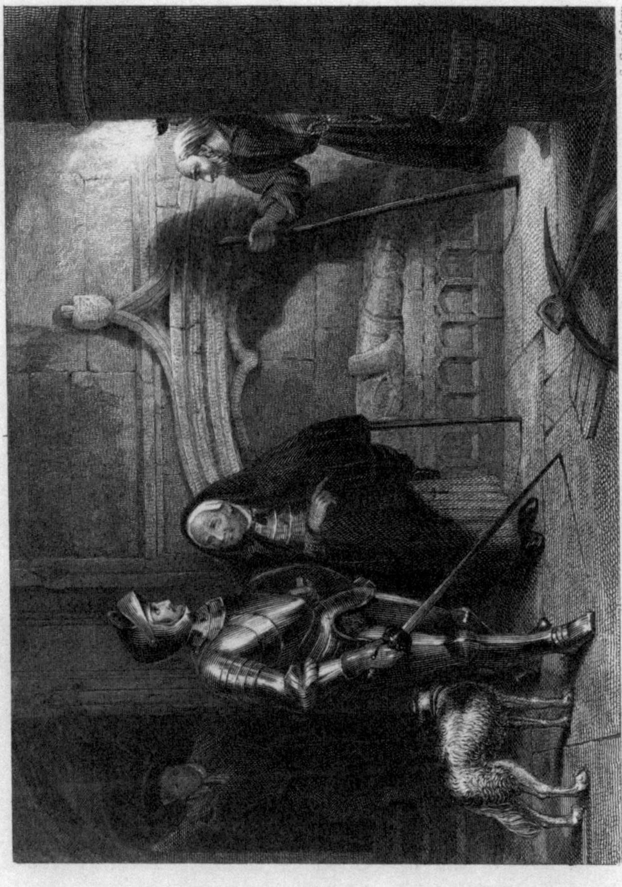

C. Stanfield, A.R.A. S. Sangster.

CASTLE DANGEROUS.

EDINBURGH, PUBLISHED 1833 BY ROBERT CADELL, & WHITTAKER & Co. LONDON.

WAVERLEY NOVELS.

VOL. XLVII.

CASTLE DANGEROUS.

A. Fraser. Chas. Fox.

"The trooper, wrapping part of a mantle round her head, lent his arm to support her in this blinded state."

PRINTED FOR ROBERT CADELL, EDINBURGH, AND WHITTAKER & Co. LONDON.

1833.

Introduction to Castle Dangerous

THE incidents on which the ensuing Novel mainly turns, are derived from the ancient Metrical Chronicle of "the Bruce," by Archdeacon Barbour, and from the "History of the Houses of Douglas and Angus," by David Hume of Godscroft; and are sustained by the immemorial tradition of the western parts of Scotland. They are so much in consonance with the spirit and manners of the troubled age to which they are referred, that I can see no reason for doubting their being founded in fact: the names, indeed, of numberless localities in the vicinity of Douglas Castle, appear to attest, beyond suspicion, many even of the smallest circumstances embraced in the story of Godscroft.

Among all the associates of Robert the Bruce, in his great enterprise of rescuing Scotland from the power of Edward, the first place is universally conceded to James, the eighth Lord Douglas, to this day venerated by his countrymen as "the Good Sir James:"

> The Gud Schyr James of Douglas,
> That in his time sa worthy was,
> That off his price and his bounté,
> In far landis renownyt was he.
>
> BARBOUR.

> The Good Sir James, the dreadful blacke Douglas,
> That in his dayes so wise and worthie was,
> Wha here, and on the infidels of Spain,
> Such honour, praise, and triumphs did obtain.
>
> GORDON.

From the time when the King of England refused to reinstate him, on his return from France, where he had received the education of chivalry, in the extensive possessions of his family,—which had been held forfeited by the exertions of his father, William the Hardy—the young knight of Douglas appears to have embraced the cause of Bruce with enthusiastic ardour, and to have adhered to the fortunes of his sovereign with unwearied fidelity and devotion. "The Douglasse," says Hollinshed, "was right joyfully received of King Robert, in whose service he faithfully continued, both in peace and war, to his life's end. Though the surname and familie of the Douglasses was in some estimation of nobilitie before those daies, yet the rising thereof to honour chanced through this James Douglasse; for, by meanes of his advancement, others of that lineage tooke occasion, by their singular manhood and noble prowess, shewed at sundrie times in defence of the realme, to grow to such height in authoritie and estimation, that their mightie puissance in mainrent,* lands, and great possessions, at length was (through suspicion conceived by the kings that succeeded) the cause in part of their ruinous decay."

In every narrative of the Scottish war of independence, a considerable space is devoted to those years of perilous adventure and suffering which were spent by the illustrious friend of Bruce, in harassing the English detachments successively occupying his paternal territory, and in repeated and successful attempts to wrest the formidable fortress of Douglas Castle itself from their possession. In the English, as well as Scotch Chronicles, and in Rymer's Fœdera, occur frequent notices of the different officers intrusted by Edward with the keeping of this renowned stronghold; especially Sir Robert de Clifford, ancestor of the heroic race of the Cliffords, Earls of Cumberland; his lieutenant, Sir Richard de Thurlewalle, (written sometimes Thruswall,) of Thirlwall Castle, on the Tippal, in Northumberland; and Sir John de Walton, the romantic story of whose love-pledge, to hold the Castle of Douglas for a year and day, or surrender all hope of obtaining his mistress's favour, with the tragic consequences, softened in the Novel, is given at length in Godscroft, and has often been pointed out as one of the affecting passages in the chronicles of chivalry.

The Author, before he had made much progress in this, probably the last of his Novels, undertook a journey to Douglasdale, for the purpose of examining the remains of the famous Castle, the Kirk of St Bride of Douglas, the patron saint of that great family, and the various localities alluded to by Godscroft, in his account of the early adventures of Good Sir James; but though he was fortunate enough to find a zealous and well-informed *cicerone* in Mr Thomas Haddow, and had every assistance from the kindness of Mr Alexander Finlay, the resident Chamberlain of his friend, Lord Douglas, the state of his health at the time was so feeble, that he found himself incapable of pursuing his researches, as in better days he would have delighted to do, and was obliged to be contented with such a cursory view of scenes, in themselves most interesting, as could be snatched in a single morning, when any bodily exertion was painful. Mr Haddow was attentive enough to forward subsequently some notes on the points which the Author had seemed desirous of investigating; but these did not reach him until, being obliged to prepare matters for a foreign excursion in quest of health and strength, he had been compelled to bring his

* Vassalage.

work, such as it is, to a conclusion.

The remains of the old Castle of Douglas are inconsiderable. They consist indeed of but one ruined tower, standing at a short distance from the modern mansion, which itself is only a fragment of the design on which the Duke of Douglas meant to reconstruct the edifice, after its last accidental destruction by fire.* His Grace had kept in view the ancient prophecy, that as often as Douglas Castle might be destroyed, it should rise again in enlarged dimensions and improved splendour, and projected a pile of building, which, if it had been completed, would have much exceeded any nobleman's residence then existing in Scotland—as, indeed, what has been finished, amounting to about one-eighth part of the plan, is sufficiently extensive for the accommodation of a large establishment, and contains some apartments the dimensions of which are magnificent. The situation is commanding; and though the Duke's successors have allowed the mansion to continue as he left it, great expense has been lavished on the environs, which now present a vast sweep of richly undulated woodland, stretching to the borders of the Cairntable mountains, repeatedly mentioned as the favourite retreat of the great ancestor of the family in the days of his hardship and persecution. There remains at the head of the adjoining *bourg*, the choir of the ancient church of St Bride, having beneath it the vault which was used till lately as the burial-place of this princely race, and only abandoned when their stone and leaden coffins had accumulated, in the course of five or six hundred years, in such a

* [The following notice of Douglas Castle, &c. is from the Description of the Sheriffdom of Lanark, by William Hamilton of Wishaw, written in the beginning of the last century, and printed by the Maitland Club of Glasgow in 1831:—

"Douglass parish, and baronie and lordship, heth very long appertained to the family of Douglass, and continued with the Earles of Douglass untill their fatall forfeiture, anno 1455; during which tyme there are many noble and important actions recorded in histories performed by them, by the lords and earls of that great family. It was thereafter given to Douglass, Earl of Anguse, and continued with them untill William, Earle of Anguse, was created Marquess of Douglass, anno 1633; and is now the principal seat of the Marquess of Douglass his family. It is a large baronie and parish, and ane laick patronage; and the Marquess is both titular and patron. He heth there, near to the church, a very considerable great house, called the Castle of Douglass; and near the church is a fyne village, called the town of Douglass, long since erected in a burgh of baronie. It heth ane handsome church, with many ancient monuments and inscriptions on the old interments of the Earles of this place.

"The water of Douglas runs quyte through the whole length of this parish, and upon either side of the water it is called Douglasdale. It toucheth Clyde towards the north, and is bounded by Lesmahagow to the west, Kyle to the southwest, Crawfurd John and Carmichaell to the south and southeast. It is a pleasant strath, plentifull in grass and corn, and coall; and the minister is well provided.

"The lands of Heysleside, belonging to Samuel Douglass, has a good house and pleasant seat, close by a wood," &c.—p. 65.]

way that it could accommodate no more. Here a silver case, containing the dust of what was once the brave heart of Good Sir James, is still pointed out; and in the dilapidated choir above appears, though in a sorely ruinous state, the once magnificent tomb of the warrior himself. After detailing the well-known circumstances of Sir James's death in Spain, 20th August, 1330, where he fell, assisting the King of Arragon in an expedition against the Moors, when on his way back to Scotland from Jerusalem, to which he had conveyed the heart of Bruce,—the old poet Barbour tells us that—

> Quhen his men lang had mad murnyn,
> Thai debowalyt him, and syne
> Gert scher him swa, that mycht be tane
> The flesch all haly fra the bane,
> And the carioune thar in haly place
> Erdyt, with rycht gret worschip, was.
>
> The banys haue thai with thaim tane;
> And syne ar to thair schippis gane;
> Syne towart Scotland held thair way,
> And thar ar cummyn in full gret hy.
> And the banys honorabilly
> In till the Kyrk off Douglas war
> Erdyt, with dule and mekill car.
> Schyr Archebald his sone gert syn
> Off alabastre, bath fair and fyne,
> Ordane a tumbe sa richly
> As it behowyt to swa worthy.

The monument is supposed to have been wantonly mutilated and defaced by a detachment of Cromwell's troops, who, as was their custom, converted the kirk of St Bride of Douglas into a stable for their horses. Enough, however, remains to identify the resting-place of the great Sir James. The effigy, of dark stone, is cross-legged, marking his character as one who had died after performing the pilgrimage to the Holy Sepulchre, and in actual conflict with the infidels of Spain; and the introduction of the HEART, adopted as an addition to the old arms of Douglas, in consequence of the knight's fulfilment of Bruce's dying injunction, appears, when taken in connexion with the posture of the figure, to set the question at rest. The monument, in its original state, must have been not inferior in any respect to the best of the same period in Westminster Abbey; and the curious reader is referred for farther particulars of it to "The Sepulchral Antiquities of Great Britain, by Edward Blore, F.S.A." London, 4to, 1826; where may also be found interesting details of some of the other tombs and effigies in the cemetery of the first house of Douglas.

As considerable liberties have been taken with the historical incidents on which this novel is founded, it is due to the reader to place before him such extracts from Godscroft and Barbour as may enable him to correct any mis-impression. The passages introduced in the Appendix, from the ancient poem of "The Bruce," will moreover gratify those who have not in their possession a copy of the text of Barbour, as given in the valuable quarto edition of my learned friend Dr Jamieson, as furnishing on the whole a favourable specimen of the style and manner of a venerable classic, who wrote when Scotland was still full of the fame and glory of her liberators from the yoke of Plantagenet, and especially of Sir James Douglas, "of whom," says Godscroft, "we will not omit here, (to shut up all,) the judgment of those times concerning him, in a rude verse indeed, yet such as beareth witness of his true magnanimity and invincible mind in either fortune:—

> Good Sir James Douglas (who wise, and wight, and worthy was,)
> Was never overglad in no winning, nor yet oversad for no tineing;
> Good fortune and evil chance he weighed both in one balance."

W. S.

APPENDIX No. I

Extracts from "The History of the Houses of Douglas and Angus. By Master DAVID HUME of Godscroft." Fol. Edit.

* * * AND here indeed the course of the King's misfortunes begins to make some halt and stay by thus much prosperous successe in his own person; but more in the person of Sir James, by the reconquests of his owne castles and countries. From hence he went into Douglasdale, where, by the means of his father's old servant, Thomas Dickson, he took in the Castle of Douglas, and not being able to keep it, he caused burn it, contenting himself with this, that his enemies had one strength fewer in that country than before. The manner of his taking of it is said to have beene thus:—Sir James taking only with him two of his servants, went to Thomas Dickson, of whom he was received with tears, after he had revealed himself to him, for the good old man knew him not at first, being in mean and homely apparell. There he kept him secretly in a quiet chamber, and brought unto him such as had been trusty servants to his father, not all at once, but apart by one and one, for fear of discoverie. Their advice was, that on Palmsunday, when the

English would come forth to the church, and his partners were conveened, that then he should give the word, and cry the Douglas slogan, and presently set upon them that should happen to be there, who being dispatched, the Castle might be taken easily. This being concluded, and they come, so soon as the English were entered into the church with palms in their hands, (according to the costume of that day,) little suspecting or fearing any such thing, Sir James, according to their appointment, cryed too soon (a Douglas, a Douglas!) which being heard in the church, (this was Saint Bride's church of Douglas,) Thomas Dickson, supposing he had beene hard at hand, drew out his sword, and ran upon them, having none to second him but another man, so that, oppressed by the number of his enemies, he was beaten downe and slaine. In the mean time, Sir James being come, the English that were in the chancel kept off the Scots, and having the advantage of the strait and narrow entrie, defended themselves manfully. But Sir James encouraging his men, not so much by words, as by deeds and good example, and having slain the boldest resisters, prevailed at last, and entring the place, slew some twenty-six of their number, and tooke the rest, about ten or twelve persons, intending by them to get the Castle upon composition, or to enter with them when the gates should be opened to let them in: but it needed not, for they of the Castle were so secure, that there was none left to keep it save the porter and the cooke, who knowing nothing of what had hapned at the church, which stood a large quarter of a mile from thence, had left the gate wide open, the porter standing without, and the cooke dressing the dinner within. They entred without resistance, and meat being ready, and the cloth laid, they shut the gates, and tooke their refection at good leasure.

Now that he had gotten the Castle into his hands, considering with himselfe (as he was a man no lesse advised than valiant) that it was hard for him to keep it, the English being as yet the stronger in that countrey, who if they should besiege him, he knewe of no reliefe, he thought better to carry away such things as be most easily transported, gold, silver, and apparell, with ammunition and armour, whereof he had greatest use and need, and to destroy the rest of the provision, together with the Castle itselfe, then to diminish the number of his followers for a garrison there where it could do no good. And so he caused carrie the meale and malt, and other cornes and graine, into the cellar, and laid all together in one heape: then he took the prisoners and slew them, to revenge the death of his trustie and valiant servant, Thomas Dickson, mingling the victuals with their bloud, and burying their carkasses in the heap of corne: after that he struck out the heads of the barrells and puncheons, and let the drink runn through all; and then he cast the carkasses of dead horses and other carrion amongst it, throwing the salt above all, so to make all together unusefull to the enemie; and this cellar is called yet the Douglas Lairder. Last of all, he set the house on fire, and burnt all the timber, and what else the fire could overcome, leaving nothing but the scorched walls behind him. And this seemes to be the first taking of the Castle of Douglas, for it is supposed that he took it twice. For this service, and others done to Lord William his father, Sir James gave unto Thomas Dickson the lands of Hisleside, which hath beene given him before the castle was taken as an encouragement to whet him on, and not after, for he was slain in the church: which was both liberally and wisely done of him, thus to hearten and draw men to his service by such a noble beginning. The Castle being burnt, Sir James retired, and parting his men into divers companies, so as they might be most secret, he caused cure such as were wounded in the fight, and he himselfe kept as close as he could, waiting ever for an occasion to enterprise something against the enemie. So soone as he was gone, the Lord Clifford being advertised of what had happened, came himselfe in person to Douglas, and caused re-edifie and repair the Castle in a very short time, unto which he also added a Tower, which is yet called Harries Tower from him, and so returned into England, leaving one Thurswall to be Captain thereof.—Pp. 26–28.

* * * * * * * * *

He (Sir James Douglas) getting him again into Douglasdale, did use this stratagem against Thurswall, Captain of the Castle, under the said Lord Clifford. He caused some of his folk drive away the cattle that fed near unto the Castle, and when the Captain of the garrison followed to rescue, gave orders to his men to leave them and to flee away. Thus he did often to make the Captain slight such frays, and to make him secure, that he might not suspect any further end to be on it; which when he had wrought sufficiently (as he thought), he laid some men in ambuscado, and sent others away to drive such beasts as they should find in the view of the Castle, as if they had been thieves and robbers, as they had done often before. The Captain hearing of it, and supposing there was no greater danger now than had been before, issued forth of the Castle, and followed after them with such haste that his men (running who should be first) were disordered and out of their ranks. The drivers also fled as fast as they could till they had drawn the

Captain a little way beyond the place of ambuscado, which when they perceived, rising quickly out of their covert, they set fiercely upon him and his company, and so slew himself and chased his men back to the Castle, some of whom were overtaken and slain, others got into the Castle and so were saved. Sir James, not being able to force the house, took what booty he could get without in the fields, and so departed. By this means, and such other exploits, he so affrighted the enemy, that it was counted a matter of such great jeopardy to keep this Castle, that it began to be called the adventurous (or hazardous) Castle of Douglas: Whereupon Sir John Walton being in suit of an English lady, she wrote to him that when he had kept the adventurous Castle of Douglas seven years, then he might think himself worthy to be a suitor to her. Upon this occasion, Walton took upon him the keeping of it, and succeeded to Thurswall; but he ran the same fortune with the rest that were before him.

For, Sir James having first dressed an ambuscado near unto the place, he made fourteen of his men take so many sacks, and fill them with grass, as though it had been corn, which they carried in the way toward Lanark, the chief market town in that county: so hoping to draw forth the Captain by that bait, and either to take him or the Castle, or both.

Neither was this expectation frustrate, for the Captain did bite, and came forth to have taken this victual (as he supposed.) But ere he could reach these carriers, Sir James, with his company, had gotten between the castle and him: and these disguised carriers, seeing the Captain following after them, did quickly cast off their upper garments, wherein they had masked themselves, and throwing off their sacks, mounted themselves on horseback, and met the Captain with a sharp encounter, he being so much the more amazed that it was unlooked for: wherefore, when he saw these carriers metamorphosed into warriors, and ready to assault him, fearing (that which was) that there was some train laid for them, he turned about to have retired into the Castle; but there also he met with his enemies; between which two companies he and his followers were slain, so that none escaped; the Captain afterwards being searched, they found (as it is reported) his mistress's letters about him. Then he went and took in the Castle, but it is uncertain (say our writers) whether by force or composition; but it seems that the Constable, and those that were within, have yielded it up without force; in regard that he used them so gently, which he would not have done if he had taken it at utterance. For he sent them all safe home to the Lord Clifford, and gave them also provision and money for their entertainment by the way. The Castle, which he had burnt only before, now he razeth, and casts down the walls thereof to the ground. By these and the like proceedings, within a short while he freed Douglasdale, Attrick Forest, and Jedward Forest, of the English garrisons and subjection.—*Ibid. page 29.*

APPENDIX No. II

[Extracts from THE BRUCE.—"Liber compositus per Magistrum Johannem Barber, Archidiaconnum Abyrdonensem, de gestis, bellis, et virtutibus, Domini Roberti Brwyss, Regis Scocie illustrissimi, et de conquestu regni Scocie per eundem, et de Domino Jacobo de Douglas."—Edited by John Jamieson, D.D., F.R.S.E., &c. &c. Edinburgh, 1820.]

Now takis James his wiage
Towart Dowglas, his heretage,
With twa yemen, for owtyn ma;
That wes a symple stuff to ta,
A land or a castell to win.
The quhethir he yarnyt to begyn
Till bring purposs till ending;
For gud help is in gud begynnyng,
For gud begynnyng, and hardy,
Gyff it be folowit wittily,
May ger oftsyss unlikly thing
Cum to full conabill ending.
Swa did it here: but he wes wyss
And saw he mycht, on nakyn wyss,
Werray his fa with evyn mycht;
Tharfor he thocht to wyrk with slycht.
And in Dowglas daile, his countré,
Upon an evynnyng entryt he.
And than a man wonnyt tharby,
That was off freyndis weill mychty,
And ryche of moble, and off cateill;
And had bene till his fadyr leyll;
And till him selff, in his yowthed,
He haid done mony a thankfull deid.
Thom Dicson wes his name perfay.
Till him he send; and gan him pray,
That he wald cum all anerly
For to spek with him priuely.
And he but daunger till him gais:
Bot fra he tauld him quhat he wais,
He gret for joy, and for pité;
And him rycht till his houss had he;

Quhar in a chambre priuely
He held him, and his cumpany,
That nane had off him persaving.
Off mete, and drynk, and othyr thing,
That mycht thaim eyss, thai had plenté.
Sa wrocht he thorow sutelté,
That all the lele men off that land,
That with his fadyr war duelland,
This gud man gert cum, ane and ane,
And mak him manrent euir ilkane;
And he him selff fyrst homage maid.
Dowglas in hart gret glaidschip haid,
That the gud men off his cuntré
Wald swagate till him bundyn be.
He speryt the conwyne off the land,
And quha the castell had in hand.
And thai him tauld all halily;
And syne amang them priuely
Thai ordanyt, that he still suld be
In hiddillis, and in priweté,
Till Palme Sonday, that wes ner hand,
The thrid day eftyr folowand.
For than the folk off that countré
Assemblyt at the kyrk wald be;
And thai, that in the castell wer,
Wald als be thar, thar palmys to ber,
As folk that had na dreid off ill;
For thai thoucht all wes at thair will.
Than suld he cum with his twa men.
Bot, for that men suld nocht him ken,
He suld ane mantill haiff auld and bar,
And a flaill, as he a thresscher war.
Undyr the mantill nocht for thi
He suld be armyt priuely.
And quhen the men off his countré,
That suld all boune befor him be,
His ensenye mycht her hym cry,
Then suld thai, full enforcely,
Rycht ymyddys the kyrk assaill
The Ingliss men with hard bataill
Swa that nane mycht eschap tham fra;
For thar throwch trowyt thai to ta
The castell, that besid wes ner.
And quhen this, that I tell you her,
Wes diuisyt, and undertane,
Ilkane till his howss hame is gane;
And held this spek in priueté,
Till the day off thar assembly.

The folk upon the Sonounday
Held to Saynct Bridis kyrk thair way;
And tha that in the castell war
Ischyt owt, bath les and mar,
And went thair palmys for to ber;
Owtane a cuk and a porter.

James off Dowglas off thair cummyng,
And quhat thai war, had witting;
And sped him till the kyrk in hy.
Bot or he come, too hastily
Ane off his criyt, "Dowglas! Dowglas!"
Thomas Dikson, that nerrest was
Till thaim that war off the castell,
That war all innouth the chancell,
Quhen he "Dowglas!" swa hey herd cry,
Drew owt his swerd; and fellely
Ruschyt amang thaim to and fra.
Bot ane or twa, for owtyn ma,
Than in hy war left lyand,
Quhill Dowglas come rycht at hand,
And then enforcyt on thaim the cry.
Bot thai the chansell sturdely
Held, and thaim defendyt wele,
Till off thair men war slayne sumdell.
Bot the Dowglace sa weill him bar,
That all the men, that with him war,
Had comfort off his wele doyng;
And he him sparyt nakyn thing,
Bot provyt swa his force in fycht,
That throw his worschip, and his mycht,
His men sa keynly helpyt than,
That thai the chansell on thaim wan.
Than dang thai on swa hardyly,
That in schort tyme men mycht se ly
The twa part dede, or then deand.
The lave war sesyt sone in hand,
Swa that off thretty levyt nane,
That thai ne war slayne ilkan, or tane.

James off Dowglas, quhen this wes done,
The presoneris has he tane alsone;
And, with thaim off his cumpany,
Towart the castell went in hy,
Or noyiss, or cry, suld ryss.
And for he wald thaim sone suppriss,
That levyt in the castell war,
That war but twa for owtyn mar,
Fyve men or sex befor send he,
That fand all opyn the entré;
And entryt, and the porter tuk
Rycht at the gate, and syne the cuk.
With that Dowglas come to the gat,
And entryt in for owtyn debate;
And fand the mete all redy grathit,
With burdys set, and clathis layit.
The gaitis then he gert sper,
And sat, and eyt all at layser.
Syne all the gudis turssyt thai
That thaim thocht thai mycht haiff away;
And namly wapnys, and armyng,
Siluer, and tresour, and clethyng.

Vyctallis, that mycht nocht tursyt be,
On this maner destroyit he.
All the victalis, owtane salt,
Als quheyt, and flour, and meill, and malt
In the wyne sellar gert he bring;
And samyn on the flur all flyng.
And the presoneris that he had tane
Rycht thar in gert he heid ilkane;
Syne off the townnys he hedis outstrak:
A foule mellé thar gane he mak.
For meile, and malt, and blud, and wyne,
Ran all to gidder in a mellyne,
That was unsemly for to se.
Tharfor the men off that countré
For swa fele thar mellyt wer,
Callit it the "Dowglas Lardner."
Syne tuk he salt, as Ic hard tell,
And ded horss, and sordid the well;
And brynt all, owtakyn stane;
And is forth, with his menye, gayne
Till his resett; for him thoucht weill,
Giff he had haldyn the castell,
It had bene assegyt raith;
And that him thoucht to mekill waith.
For he ne had hop off reskewyng.
And it is to peralous thing
In castell assegyt to be,
Quhar want is off thir thingis thre;
Victaill, or men with thair armyng,
Or than gud hop off rescuyng.
And for he dred thir thingis suld faile,
He chesyt furthwart to trawaill,
Quhar he mycht at his larges be;
And swa dryve furth his destané.

On this wise wes the castell tan,
And slayne that war tharin ilkan.
The Dowglas syne all his menye
Gert in ser placis depertyt be;
For men suld wyt quhar thai war,
That yeid depertyt her and thar.
Thaim that war woundyt gert he ly
In till hiddillis, all priuely;
And gert gud leechis till thaim bring
Quhill that thai war in till heling.
And him selff, with a few menye,
Quhile ane, quhile twa, and quhile thre,
And umquhill all him allane,
In hiddillis throw the land is gane.
Sa dred he Inglis men his mycht,
That he durst nocht wele cum in sycht.
For thai war that tyme all weldand
As maist lordis, our all the land.

Bot tythandis, that scalis sone,

Off this deid that Dowglas has done,
Come to the Cliffurd his ere, in hy,
That for his tynsaill wes sary;
And menyt his men that thai had slayne,
And syne has to purpos tane,
To big the castell up agayne.
Thar for, as man of mekill mayne,
He assemblit gret cumpany,
And till Dowglas he went in hy.
And biggyt wp the castell swyth;
And maid it rycht stalwart and styth
And put tharin victallis and men.
Ane off the Thyrwallys then
He left behind him Capitane,
And syne till Ingland went agayne.

Book IV. v. 255–462.

BOT yeit than James of Dowglas
In Dowglas Daile travailland was;
Or ellys weill ner hand tharby,
In hyddillys sumdeill priuely.
For he wald se his gouernyng,
That had the castell in keping:
And gert mak mony juperty,
To se quhethyr he wald ische blythly.
And quhen he persavyt that he
Wald blythly ische with his menye,
He maid a gadring priuely
Off thaim that war on his party;
That war sa fele, that thai durst fycht
With Thyrwall, and all the mycht
Off thaim that in the castell war.
He schupe him in the nycht to far
To Sandylandis: and thar ner by
He him enbuschyt priuely,
And send a few a trane to ma;
That sone in the mornyng gan ga,
And tuk catell, that wes the castell by,
And syne withdrew thaim hastely
Towart thaim that enbuschit war.
Than Thyrwall, for owtyn mar,
Gert arme his men, forowtyn baid;
And ischyt with all the men he haid:
And folowyt fast eftir the cry.
He wes armyt at poynt clenly,
Owtane [that] his hede wes bar.
Than, with the men that with him war,
The catell folowit he gud speid,
Rycht as a man that had na dreid,
Till that he gat off thaim a sycht.
Than prekyt thai with all thar mycht,
Folowand thaim owt off aray;
And thai sped thaim fleand, quhill thai
Fer by thair buschement war past:

And Thyrwall ay chassyt fast.
And than thai that enbuschyt war
Ischyt till him, bath les and mar,
And rayssyt sudanly the cry.
And thai that saw sa sudanly
That folk come egyrly prikand
Rycht betuix thaim and thair warand,
Thai war in to full gret effray.
And, for thai war owt off aray,
Sum off thaim fled, and sum abad.
And Dowglas, that thar with him had
A gret mengye, full egrely
Assaylyt, and scalyt thaim hastyly:
And in schort tyme ourraid thaim swa,
That weile nane eschapyt thaim fra.
Thyrwall, that wes thair capitane;
Wes thar in the bargane slane:
And off his men the mast party.
The lave fled full effraytly.

Book V. v. 7–62.

Notes to Castle Dangerous

19.14 (Ch. 2) this outpost of Hazelside [Hazelside Place, the fief granted to Thomas Dickson by William the Hardy, seventh Lord Douglas, is still pointed out about two miles to the southwest of the Castle Dangerous. Dickson was sixty years of age at the time when Lord James first appeared in Douglasdale. His heirs kept possession of the fief for centuries; and some respectable gentlemen's families in Lanarkshire still trace themselves to this ancestor.—*From Notes by Mr Haddow.*]

58.19 (Ch. 7) the most interesting objects of pursuit [The following is an extract from a letter received by Sir Walter Scott, some time after the publication of the novel:—

"When it is wished to kill any of the cattle at Chillingham, the keeper goes into the herd on horseback, in which way they are quite accessible, and singling out his victim, takes aim with a large rifle-gun, and seldom fails in bringing him down. If the poor animal makes much bellowing in his agony, and especially if the ground be stained with his blood, his companions become very furious, and are themselves, I believe, accessory to his death. After which, they fly off to a distant part of the park, and he is drawn away on a sledge. Lord Tankerville is very tenacious of these singular animals; he will on no account part with a living one, and hardly allows of a sufficient number being killed, to leave pasturage for those that remain.

"It happened on one occasion, three or four years ago, that a party visiting at the castle, among whom were some *men of war*, who had hunted buffaloes in foreign parts, obtained permission to do the keeper's work and shoot one of the wild cattle. They sallied out on horseback, and duly equipped for the enterprise, attacked their object. The poor animal received several wounds, but none of them proving fatal, he retired before his pursuers, roaring with pain and rage, till, planting himself against a wall or tree, he stood at bay, offering a front of defiance. In this position the youthful heir of the castle, Lord Ossulston, rode up to give him the fatal shot. Though warned of the danger of approaching near to the enraged animal, and especially of firing without first having turned his horse's head in a direction to be ready for flight, he discharged his piece; but ere he could turn his horse round to make his retreat, the raging beast had plunged his immense horns into its flank. The horse staggered and was near falling, but recovering by a violent effort, he extricated himself from his infuriated pursuer, making off with all the speed his wasting strength supplied, his entrails meanwhile dragging on the ground; till at length he fell, and died at the same moment. The animal was now close upon his rear, and the young Lord would unquestionably have shared the fate of his unhappy steed, had not the keeper, deeming it full time to conclude the *day's diversion*, fired at the instant. His shot brought the beast to the ground, and running in with his large knife, he put a period to its existence.

"This scene of gentlemanly pastime was viewed from a turret of the castle by Lady Tankerville and her female visitors. Such a situation for the mother of the young hero, was any thing but enviable."]

92.1 (Ch. 9) solitary situation [This is a most graphic and accurate description of the present state of the ruin. Its being occupied by the sexton as a dwelling-place, and the whole scene of the old man's interview with De Valence, may be classed with our illustrious author's most felicitous imaginings.—*Note by the Rev. Mr* S*TEWART of Douglas.*]

150.31 (Ch. 17) foregoing each advantage on either side The ominous name of Bloodmire-Sink or Syke, marks a narrow hollow to the northwest of Douglas Castle, from which it is distant about the third of a mile. Mr Haddow states, that according to local tradition, the name was given in consequence of Sir James Douglas having at this spot intercepted and slain part of the garrison of the castle while De Walton was in command.

182.2 (Ch. 20) among the feet of the combatants [The fall of this brave stripling by the hand of the English governor, and the stern heroism of the father in turning from the spot where he lay, "a model of beauty and strength," that he might not be withdrawn from the duty which Douglas had assigned him of protecting the Lady of Berkely, excites an interest for both, with which it is almost to be regretted that history interferes. It was the old man, Thomas Dickson, not his son, who fell. The *slogan*, "a Douglas, a Douglas," having been prematurely raised, Dickson, who was within the church, thinking that his young Lord with his armed band was at hand, drew his sword, and with only one man to assist him, opposed the English, who now rushed to the door. Cut across the middle by an English sword, he still continued his opposition, till he fell lifeless at the threshold. Such is the tradition, and it is supported by a memorial of some authority—a tombstone, still to be seen in the churchyard of Douglas, on which is sculptured a figure of Dickson, supporting with his left arm his protruding entrails, and raising his sword with the other in the attitude of combat.]—*Note by the Rev. Mr* S*TEWART* *of Douglas*.

THE SHORTER FICTION

Editorial Note

As explained in the editorial introduction to EEWN 24, xi, five of the eight shorter fiction pieces included in that volume did not appear in the Magnum: it is likely that Scott's failing memory did not recollect them in 1831. But the three stories which were republished in the Magnum, 'My Aunt Margaret's Mirror', 'The Tapestried Chamber', and 'Death of the Laird's Jock', do not feature in the Interleaved Set, because these three stories, first published in the *Keepsake for 1829*, did not appear in any of the earlier collections of Scott's works which were used to make up the Interleaved Set. However, the manuscripts of the introductions to the last two stories, which would normally have been bound into the Interleaved Set, survive separately (MS 911, ff. 270–71), but that of 'My Aunt Margaret's Mirror' appears to have been lost. Scott did not annotate any of these three stories.

In a retrospective entry in his journal on 20 December 1830 covering the period since 5 September Scott noted that Cadell had proposed 'assembling all my detachd works of fiction [and] Articles in annuals so that the whole, supposing I write as is proposed Six new volumes, will run the Collection to fifty when it is time to close it' (*Journal*, 613). At this stage Scott was still working on the introductions to earlier novels but, in a list apparently written by Cadell in July 1831, 'Annual tales' is listed as one of the contents of the final volume of the Magnum (MS 869, f. 180r). Scott seems to have been clear from the beginning that 'My Aunt Margaret's Mirror' was one of the proposed inclusions, and on 12 August 1831, when sending the three volumes of *The Fair Maid of Perth* with their introduction, he promised that 'Anne of Geierstein comes next together with Aunt Margaret's mirror'. He also asked Cadell for information on 'what other small pieces fall into my last volume for I am not sure that without your assistance I can remember them all' (MS 15980, f. 150r). His uncertainty about the 'other small pieces' is explained in another letter to Cadell of 18 August when he reported that 'I fear I have lost or mislaid the Keepsake or laid it by so well that I have forgot where I put it. I have vol which has the house of Aspen but not that with Aunt Margaret's mirror & other little trifles I should like to have a list of the whole which you think should be included in the Magnum' (MS 15980, f. 152r). Cadell responded the same day that 'The *Magic Mirror* I think had with it *The Tapestried Chamber* in the Keepsake of 1829 —I am not aware of any other, what may be termed "*Works of Fiction*"' (MS 3919, f. 41r). Perhaps Cadell felt that 'Death of the Laird's Jock', being an account of an allegedly historical incident, could not be classed as fiction. Scott's uncertainty about the other two stories may explain the fact that the introduction to 'My Aunt Margaret's Mirror' is relatively long (at least as printed in the Magnum) while their introductions are extremely short: very possibly he went ahead and wrote the introduction to 'My Aunt Margaret's Mirror' and only added the others once it was clear which other stories were to be included. In the event Scott's introduction to 'The Tapestried Chamber' which we give below was radically rewritten and expanded for the Magnum, probably by Lockhart, and his introduction to 'Death of the Laird's Jock' not used at all.

This edition prints for the first time Scott's original introductions to the two shorter stories but, in the absence of a manuscript, there is no alternative to printing the Magnum version of the introduction to 'My Aunt's Margaret's Mirror'. Although it is very probable that this too was rewritten by Lockhart it contains much material which was clearly Scott's own, being based on his own personal recollections. In this introduction Scott reveals that the story, whose source was originally ascribed to the narrator's fictional Aunt Margaret, of the Bothwell family of Earl's Closes, was actually derived from his real great-aunt, Margaret Swinton, his maternal grandmother's sister, a source which helps explain the many fictionalised autobiographical references in the story's original introduction. In introducing 'Death of the Laird's Jock' Scott similarly revealed his source, the Lichfield poet Anna Seward.

Introduction to My Aunt Margaret's Mirror

THE species of publication which has come to be generally known by the title of *Annual*, being a miscellany of prose and verse, equipped with numerous engravings, and put forth every year about Christmas, had flourished for a long while in Germany, before it was imitated in this country by an enterprising bookseller, a German by birth, Mr Ackermann. The rapid success of his work, as is the custom of the time, gave birth to a host of rivals, and, among others, to an Annual styled The Keepsake, the first volume of which appeared in 1828, and attracted much notice, chiefly in consequence of the very uncommon splendour of its illustrative accompaniments. The expenditure which the spirited proprietors lavished on this magnificent volume, is understood to have been not less than from ten to twelve thousand pounds sterling!

Various gentlemen of such literary reputation that any one might think it an honour to be associated with them, had been announced as contributors to this Annual, before application was made to me to assist in it; and I accordingly placed with much pleasure at the Editor's disposal a few fragments, originally designed to have been worked into the Chronicles of the Canongate, besides a MS. Drama, the long-neglected performance of my youthful days—The House of Aspen.

The Keepsake for 1828 included, however, only three of these little prose tales—of which the first in order was that entitled "My Aunt Margaret's Mirror." By way of *introduction* to this, when now included in a general collection of my lucubrations, I have only to say, that it is a mere transcript, or at least with very little embellishment, of a story that I remembered being struck with in my childhood, when told at the fireside by a lady of eminent virtues, and no inconsiderable share of talent, one of the ancient and honourable house of Swinton. She was a kind relation of my own, and met her death in a manner so shocking, being killed in a fit of insanity by a female attendant who had been attached to her person for half a lifetime, that I cannot now recall her memory, child as I was when the catastrophe occurred, without a painful re-awakening of perhaps the first images of horror that the scenes of real life stamped on my mind.

This good spinster had in her composition a strong vein of the superstitious, and was pleased, among other fancies, to read alone in her chamber by a taper fixed in a candlestick which she had had formed out of a human skull. One night this strange piece of furniture acquired suddenly the power of locomotion, and, after performing some odd circles on her chimney-piece, fairly leaped on the floor, and continued to roll about the apartment. Mrs Swinton calmly proceeded to the adjoining room for another light, and had the satisfaction to penetrate the mystery on the spot. Rats abounded in the ancient building she inhabited, and one of these had managed to ensconce itself within her favourite *memento mori.* Though thus endowed with a more than feminine share of nerve, she entertained largely that belief in supernaturals, which in those times was not considered as sitting ungracefully on the grave and aged of her condition; and the story of the Magic Mirror was one for which she vouched with particular confidence, alleging indeed that one of her own family had been an eye-witness of the incidents recorded in it.

I tell the tale as it was told to me

Stories enow of much the same cast will present themselves to the recollection of such of my readers as have ever dabbled in a species of lore to which I certainly gave more hours, at one period of my life, than I should gain any credit by confessing.

August, 1831.

Introduction to The Tapestried Chamber

This, as well as the preceding tale, is one of those stories that serve to amuse society under a certain impression of feeling and moods of mind which visit almost all in their turn. The original teller of the story was, to me at least, the celebrated Miss Seward, who, among other excellencies, possessed that delightful talent, which enables those who have it to read or recite with the greatest possible effect, and upon whom it is needless to make any remark saving that she did so.

Introduction to Death of the Laird's Jock

The last story from the Keepsake regards a circumstance of Scottish antiquities preserved on the borders of both countries. It was natural that, not unacquainted with the circumstances, I should endeavour to find some story which might be peculiarly adapted to painting.

EMENDATION LIST

The base-text for this collection of the Introductions and notes Scott wrote for the forty-eight volume edition entitled *Waverley Novels* (1829–33) is a specific set gifted by Adolphus Jack to the University of Aberdeen, except for Volume 16 (which is an 1850 reprint) and Volumes 28, 31, and 32 (which are missing). For these four volumes copies owned by the EEWN have been used. All emendations to this base-text, whether verbal, orthographic, or punctuational, are listed below, with the exception of certain general categories of emendation described in the next paragraph, and of those errors which result from accidents of printing.

The typographical presentation of headings, of letters and of quotations has been standardised. In particular, the inverted commas which are normally used for displayed verse quotations have not been reproduced, in accordance with the practice adopted by the Edinburgh Edition. Ambiguous end-of-line hyphens in the base-text have normally been interpreted in accordance with the predominant usage in the Magnum Introductions and notes, failing which following the most usual contemporaneous practice.

Each entry in the list below is keyed to the text by page and line number; the reference is followed by the new, EEWN reading, then in brackets the reason for the emendation, and after the slash the base-text reading that has been replaced. Occasionally, some explanation of the editorial thinking behind an emendation is required, and this is provided in a brief note.

The principles for emendation are described in the Introduction (25a, lxxi–lxxxiii). Most emendations are derived from the holograph materials found in the Interleaved Set of the Waverley Novels, and most involve the replacement of one reading by another; these are listed with the simple explanation '(MS)'. Where the manuscript reading adopted by the EEWN has required editorial intervention to normalise spelling or punctuation, the exact manuscript reading is given in the form: '(MS actual reading)'. Where the new reading has required editorial interpretation of the manuscript, the explanation is given in the form '(MS derived: actual reading)'. In transcriptions from manuscript, deletions are enclosed ⟨thus⟩ and insertions ↑thus↓; superscript letters are lowered without comment. Some emendations to quotations are derived from the actual source rather than the manuscript transcription; these are labelled '(source)'. Corrections of matters of fact (dates, page references, etc.) are labelled '(Editorial)'; those deriving from other printings of the Magnum are labelled '(another state)'.

IVANHOE

11.8 like (MS) / likely

11.41 this purpose (MS) / this intention

12.3 attract attention in every bosom (MS) / attract general attention

12.5 mix themselves with (MS) / mix with

12.33 scarce (MS) / scarcely

12.34 species (MS) / kind

13.25 Thus the Eastern (MS derived: Thus eastern) / The Eastern

15.21 wones (MS won ↑s↓) / wert

15.22 thou should (MS and source) / should thou
The MS modernises the source's 'thou schuld'.

15.33 producing (MS) / procuring

16.4 eat (MS) / eaten

16.18 promises to requite his hospitality at least (MS) / promises, at least, to requite his hospitality

16.20 consents (MS) / agrees

16.41 Passilodion (MS and source) / Passelodion

17.14 *taking* (MS) / taking

17.19 which he proves unable to satisfy, an (MS which he ⟨has unable⟩ proves unable to satisfy an) / which, if he proves unable to satisfy, is an

17.22 has even seen (MS) / has seen

18.7 is (MS) / are

18.26 Vol. 25a. pp. 34–36. (Editorial) / Vol. I. p. 65. (not in MS)

18.33 these (MS) / those

18.35 were all the (MS) / were the

20.21 species (MS) / sort

21.8 land of the warriors (MS Land of the warriors) / band of warriors

21.29 planks from (ISet print) / planks of the bridge from

22.16 If (MS) / Of

22.16 revenues, were (MS revenues were) / revenues, some were

22.18 they (MS) / who

22.19 If, on (MS If on) / But if, on

23.15 abbacy (source: abbacie) / Abbey (MS as Magnum)
It is the abbacy (the ownership of the abbey and all its perquisites), not simply the abbey, that Allan Stewart has obtained.

23.30 Dunure (MS and source) / Denure

24.2 leasing (source) / lie (MS as Magnum)
In Scott's instructions to Cadell regarding the transcript to be made from Bannatyne he stipulates that 'I would wish the transcript to be made in ordinary spelling except such words as are particularly Scotch which we will explain below' ([3 December 1829]: *Letters*, 11. 268).

24.7 man (MS and source) / must

24.18 off (Editorial) / of
The MS and source both have 'of' but Scott's general direction that the 'ordinary spelling' be used requires correction to 'off'.

24.27 practisian (source) / partisan (MS as Magnum)
The source has 'practisiane' (schemer, conspirator).

24.42 Dunure (MS and source) / Denure

25.17 Dunure (Editorial) / Denure (MS as Magnum)

26.10 justice (the oppressed as said is) could neither help him (MS and source) / justice could neither help the oppressed

26.13 Dunure (MS) / Denure (source: Dvnvre)

26.16 Dunure (ms derived: Dunver) / Denure (source: Dvnver)

26.31 mea (MS and source) / more
27.21 retain what they (MS) / retain the prey which they
27.32 *Armoiries* (MS) / *Armoirers*
27.35 ADDITION TO NOTE (Editorial) / ADDITION TO NOTE ATTACHED TO PAGE 99 (MS Addition to note upon Ivanhoe attachd to chapter XXVIII p. 494)
27.36 stated, it (MS stated it) / stated in Note at page 99, it
27.38 potent (MS) / patent
28.5 enquiries, and hence the (MS enquiries and hence the) / enquiries; and hence give them the
28.16 convey (MS) / carry
28.30 wilder (MS) / wild
28.30 their times (MS) / the time
28.39 romancers (MS) / romances
29.4 Fancy (MS) / fancy
29.28 with the clans of Border (MS) / with Border
29.31 murtherers (MS) / murderers
29.31 or in (MS) / and in
30.8 species (MS) / sort
30.11 to do more than take a (MS) / to take more than a
30.13 irresistibly (MS) / considerably
30.14 waste (MS) / write
30.27 curving outward (MS) / turning outward
31.12 Northmen, yet heathen, swept (MS derived: North-men yet heaten) / Northmen swept
31.12 brought back to (MS) / brought to
31.13 of more polished (MS of more polishd) / of polished
31.23 force (MS) / manner
The MS is difficult to read ('force' or 'form').
31.23 direction (MS) / curve
31.23 causeway where it suddenly changes its course, would (MS causeway where it suddenly changes its course would) / causeway, would
31.26 Coehorn (MS) / Cohorn
31.33 regularity of execution in (MS) / regularity in
31.34 scarce (MS) / scarcely
32.4 afterward (MS) / afterwards
32.29 described by Gough:— (MS described by ⟨Grose⟩ ↑Gough↓.) / described:—
32.32 situate (MS and source) / situated
32.37 is double (MS and source) / are double
33.7 been (MS and source) / extended
33.11 sides (MS and source) / side
34.6 filled (MS and source) / piled
34.17 upon (MS) / on

THE MONASTERY

42.19 to their (MS) / with their
42.20 suited the scenery of the proposed story well (MS) / suited well the scenery of the proposed story
42.27 used. (MS) / used in composition.
42.28 had yet further (MS) / possessed farther
43.5 producing (MS) / presenting
43.17 Somerville's (MS Somervilles) / Sommerville's
43.20 to naming or alluding to the irritable race (MS) / to any one who

might name or allude to the race
43.25 the beings (Editorial) / the irritable beings (MS as Magnum)
43.38 less romantic (MS) / less of romantic
43.41 even one (Editorial) / one even
The 'even' is not in the MS, and was probably inserted at a subsequent stage in the wrong position.
43.43 Vol. 25a. Pp. 275–76. (Editorial) / Vol. II. P. 179. (not in MS)
44.4 with it in (MS) / with scenes of the Monastery in
44.6 all particulars (MS) / all the particulars
44.26 farther (MS) / further
45.15 though (MS) / although
45.30 this subject (MS) / the subject
45.34 who has spent (MS) / who, having spent
45.36 and when at length emancipated from these (MS) / from which he has been at length emancipated
45.38 discovers (MS) / discerns
45.43 relieving the vacuity of such a mind (MS) / relieving vacuity of such a kind
46.4 any who (MS) / any one who
46.9 The work (MS) / This work
46.10 whatever the (MS) / whatever may be the
46.13 been cautious (MS) / been more cautious
46.28 like (MS) / likely
47.10 as subject (MS) / as being subject
47.13 sprites (MS) / spirits
47.19 du Compte de Gabalis (MS) / de Compte du Gabalis
47.22 even an afflicting (MS even an ⟨affecting⟩ afflicting) / even afflicting
47.24 unite (MS) / uniting
48.9 and even the (MS) / and the
48.19 a love of frolic (MS) / a frolic
48.33 She is scarce (MS) / The White Lady is scarcely
48.34 or inclination (MS) / or the inclination
48.37 authority (MS) / superiority
49.3 to exculpate (MS) / with the purpose of exculpating
49.8 of our own time (MS) / of the time
49.10 humours (MS) / humour
49.15 transcendental (MS) / transcendent
49.17 a "choice (MS) / "a choice
49.22 species (MS) / description
49.27 After acknowledgment (MS after acknowlegement) / After the acknowledgment
49.33 own. But (MS) / own; but
50.5 as (MS) / for
50.5 in (MS) / of
50.20 may (MS) / might
50.27 scarce (MS) / scarcely
50.33 and the (MS) / and therefore the
50.41 with great (MS) / with a great
51.1 same human (MS) / same truth of human
51.9 of almost all (MS) / of all
51.9 constitution permits (MS) / constitutions permit
51.15 of primitive human beings, find (MS of primitive human being ⟨are thus⟩ find) / of human beings in a primitive state, find
51.30 when that folly (MS) / when the peculiar kind of folly
51.31 discharge on what has no longer an existence (MS) / discharge of

ridicule on what has ceased to exist
51.34 continue on (MS) / continue to exist on
51.35 upon the whole a more (MS) / some other more
51.39 on what (MS) / or what
51.40 over that (MS) / on that
52.9 as portraits (MS) / being portraits
52.18 and as a (MS) / and because he is a
52.23 awake (MS) / awaken
52.24 mirth (MS) / laughter
52.26 failure to delineate the (MS) / failure in the delineation of the
52.27 objection (MS) / obejction
52.36 narrative had (MS story had) / narrative has
52.41 the more (MS) / this more
53.9 launched on (MS launchd on) / launched in
53.10 preserve (MS) / pursue
53.10 every one (MS) / in every case
53.11 that are (MS) / which are
53.22 Lives and Adventures (MS) / lives and adventures
53.22 who run through (MS) / who are described as running through
53.23 incur (MS) / encountering
53.23 adventures, only (MS adventures only) / adventures, which are only
53.24 happened to, or been witnessed by, the (MS happend to or been witnessd by the) / happened to be witnessed by the
53.26 links beads (MS connects beads) / links the beads
53.41 formal (MS) / penal
53.42 species (MS) / sort
53.42 be said (MS) / be especially said
54.21 burthen (MS) / burden
54.33 Like (MS) / like
54.34 men, he took (MS men he too) / men, took
54.39 See Note at 57.26–58.15 (Editorial) / See Note at the end of Chapter V. page 72 (not in MS)
55.3 Somerville (MS) / Sommerville
55.4 Somerville (MS) / Sommerville
55.6 Glenmayne (MS derived: Glemean) / Gleamer
55.35 Jedidiah (Editorial) / Jedediah (not in MS)
56.7 Jedidiah (MS) / Jedediah
56.15 domestics (MS) / domestic
56.20 in such a case (MS) / at such a time
56.25 at (MS) / of
56.39 discerned (MS discernd) / discovered
57.2 found they (MS) / found, however, they
57.4 apprehension (MS) / apprehensions
57.19 directly (MS) / distinctly
57.29 *Itinerarium* (source) / *Iter* (MS Iter)
57.39 is a small (MS and source) / was a small
58.9 ruins (MS) / river
58.30 minded their play more (MS) / liked their play better
59.10 of a loose (MS and source) / of loose
59.39 Ballads, (Editorial) / Ballads. (MS as Magnum)
60.3 species (MS) / sort
60.6 seek (MS) / search
60.17 James V. (Editorial) / James VI. (MS James VI)
61.10 for the (MS and source) / considering the
61.36 presently (MS and source) / promptly

62.19 in expense of apparel (MS in expence of apparel) / in the expense of his apparel
62.23 At this (MS) / By this
62.25 Park at (MS) / gate of
62.34 bade away (MS) / bade him have away
64.40 those (MS) / them
65.15 prudent (MS) / sage
65.15 provident and discreet (MS) / prudent and decent
65.18 accompt (MS) / account
67.8 scarce (MS) / scarcely
67.21 censures as (MS) / conceives
67.36 Scottish man (MS) / Scotsman
68.3 excepting that they had both (MS excepting that the had both) / except that they both held
68.18 same with those of (MS) / same of
69.15 result (MS) / results

THE ABBOT

78.5 upon (MS) / on
78.37 Aristarch (MS) / aristarch
79.18 predecessor (MS) / predecessors
79.21 *essais* (MS essais) / Essays
80.25 attempts on the (MS) / attempts to please the
80.27 out (MS) / forth
81.9 I did (MS) / The author did
81.13 I flinched (MS I flinchd) / The writer shrunk
81.14 did I (MS) / did he
81.15 I had (MS) / he had
81.19 I am (MS) / I was
81.32 object (MS) / origin
83.21 and were closely (MS) / and closely
84.3 gentry themselves (MS) / gentry
84.10 Border (MS border) / Borders
84.21 the last (MS) / this last
84.23 or some (MS) / or by some
84.23 on his (MS) / in his
84.24 next (MS) / on the following
85.15 story my father told me (MS) / story told me by my father
85.16 might (MS) / may
85.19 the inhabitants' accommodation (MS derived: the inhabitant's accomodation) / the accommodation of the inmates
85.21 the rest (MS) / the part that was untenanted
85.22 pitched down (MS pitchd down) / deposited
85.23 and two (MS) / to which
85.26 it fell through some trap-door, or breach in the stair, warning (MS derived: it fell through some trap-door or breach in the stair and fell to a great depth warning) / the animal fell through a trap-door, or aperture in the stair, thus warning
85.28 ancient (MS) / old
85.44 celebrate a mass (MS) / celebrate mass
86.10 circumstance (MS) / circumstances
86.25 to these indecent (MS derived: to thes indecent) / to the indecent
86.30 listened to (MS listend to) / admired
86.35 providing (MS) / provided

86.42 was now (Editorial) / were now (MS as Magnum)
88.3 holytide (MS holitide) / holyday
89.1 performer (source) / former (MS as Magnum)
89.2 Sampson's (source) / Sympson's (MS as Magnum)
89.2 Vow-breaker (MS and source: vow breaker) / Law-breakers
89.10 and braveries (MS and source) / his braveries
90.28 cumand (MS and Bannatyne) / cum
The MS reads 'cum And'. For the Bannatyne Club edition of the untraced MS source see 658, note to 90.14–91.2.
90.37 hamberis (Bannatyne) / harberis (MS as Magnum)
91.12 preassit (Bannatyne) / prensit (MS as Magnum)
91.16 fra thair said purpois, quhill (Bannatyne: fra thair said purpois quhill) / fra, quhill (MS fra [new page] quhill)
92.23 toward (MS and source) / towards
92.24 toward thee into (MS and source) / towards thee unto
92.25 "Put (Editorial) / 'Put
92.27 me."'" (Editorial) / me.'"
93.24 *Hazard yet* (MS and source) / *Hazard, yet*
93.27 FOY (MS) / FOY
93.38 be; (another state) / be (MS as Magnum)
94.7 picture (MS) / portrait
94.15 who (MS) / that
95.6 upon (MS) / on
95.42 James Drysdale (MS and source) / Jasper Dryfesdale
95.44 avowed (MS) / averred
96.6 his cloak (MS) / the cloak
96.15 which had (MS) / who had
97.2 be bereft (MS and source) / be reft
97.9 castle. But (MS Castle. But) / castle; but
97.22 favour. He (MS) / favour; since he
97.31 nearer (source) / near (MS as Magnum)
97.34 wonted (ms and source) / wanted
97.35 weed (ms and source) / hood
97.38 is,' and (another state) / is, and (MS is; and)
98.9 470 (Editorial) / 490 (MS as Magnum)
98.20 tower (another state) / door (MS Tower)
99.20 Cicerone (MS) / cicerone
99.24 at considerable (MS) / at a considerable
99.43 the said footmen (MS derived and source) / the footmen
100.9 with (source) / by (MS as Magnum)
100.9 by (MS and source) / through
100.13 in others' (MS and source) / in the others'
100.17 the vaunt guard. On the other part the Regent led the battle, and the Earl of Morton the vaunt guard. But (source: the vauntguard. On the other part the regent led the battle; and the earl of Morton the vauntguard) / the vaunt guard. But (MS the Vaunt Guard: But)
100.34 flanks (MS and source) / flank
101.38 SUUM (MS) / SUUM
102.8 successores nostri (source) / successors mei (MS as Magnum)
102.13 pro fabrica (MS and source: p fabrica) / et fabrica
102.43 concerted (MS) / connected

KENILWORTH

111.21 memory (MS Memory) / memories

111.37 patonce (Editorial) / patonee (MS and source: Patonee)
See EEWN 11, 500 (note to 117.38).
112.16 who (MS and source) / whom
112.17 him from the (MS and source) / him the
113.23 Butler (Editorial) / Butter (MS as Magnum)
This is a misprint in Ashmole: see the Explanatory Note at 663.
114.4 had (MS) / has
114.9 Rake (MS) / baker
For a full discussion of this emendation see 25a, lxxii.
114.27 Old (Editorial) / Ancient (MS as Magnum)
116.12 leave me to (MS and source) / leave to
117.24 FORSTER (Editorial) / FOSTER (not in MS)
For the spelling of this name see EEWN 11, 425.
117.25 Forster (Editorial) / Foster (MS as Magnum)
118.23 Forster (Editorial) / Foster (MS as Magnum)
119.17 Bacseg (MS and source) / Baereg
120.14 'twas (MS and source) / it was
120.22 sour-eyelidded (MS) / sour-eyelided
The source has 'sour eie-lidded'. Another state of the Magnum has the MS reading.
120.29 pp. 509–12 (Editorial) / p. 500 (MS as Magnum)
122.11 as is (MS and source) / as it is
122.20 will: by whose instructions no doubt but (MS and source) / will—by whose instructions, no doubt; but
123.7 See p. 121 above (Editorial) / See vol. xxii., p. 344 (not in MS)
123.16 festivities. [new paragraph] I am indebted . . . the possession of Mr Badnall.—See Plan, p. 110 above. (another state) / festivities.
Another state of the Magnum, which follows Scott's manuscript fairly closely, and which is adopted here, ends 'See Plan, end of volume.'
MS **reading:** festivities [new paragraph] I am indebted for a curious ground plan of the Castle of Kenilworth as it existed in Queen Elizabeths time to the voluntary kindness of Richard Baduall Esquire ⟨of⟩ of Olerbank near Liverpool. From his obliging communication I learn that the original Sketch was found among the manuscrips of the celebrated J. J. Rousseau when he left England. These were left by the philosopher to care of his friend Mr Davenport and past from his legatee into the possession of Mr. Baduall (the plan is worth Mr Cadell It may I think be engraved on a single page and come in here)
123.39 26 (Editorial) / 25 (MS as Magnum)
124.17 who has had (MS) / who had
127.14 thereof, and xvj (MS therof, and xvj) / thereof, xvj
127.17 BOARDE (MS) / BORDE
The MS spelling is preserved in another state of the Magnum.
128.3 p. 114 (Editorial) / p. x (not in MS)

THE PIRATE

136.5 about (MS) / of
136.16 touches (MS) / borders
136.16 their board (MS) / the Board
136.21 frolic (MS) / expedition
137.13 we ran over to the (MS we⟨m⟩ ran over ↑ to the ↓) / we made a run to the
The 'a' of 'ran' in the MS is very open.
137.29 attained (MS attaind) / obtained

137.35 found fate (MS) / found that fate
137.37 into (MS) / to
137.38 party, he (MS party he) / party, and he
137.40 which would be otherwise so satisfactory (MS) / which, but for these embitterments, would be otherwise so pleasing
137.43 a poem which I then was threatening the public with, and was (MS derived: a poem which I then was threatening the ⟨?subj⟩ publick and was) / a poem with which I was then threatening the public, and was It appears that 'with' was inserted in the wrong place.
138.2 much (MS) / remarkable
138.3 nameless (MS) / anonymous
138.3 making way on the public (MS making way on the publick) / making its way to popularity
138.7 islands (MS) / isles
138.8 character (MS) / events
138.9 p. 144 (Editorial) / p. 136 (not in MS)
138.15 indeed (MS) / induced
138.15 further (MS) / farther
138.29 pay was so adequate to their wants (MS) / pay, however inadequate to the expenses of a capital, was fully adequate to their wants
138.30 their departure (MS) / their approaching departure
138.34 in which (MS) / from which
138.37 upon (MS) / on
138.38 been. (MS) / been, the tone of the society in these sequestered but interesting islands.
138.41 Merrilies (MS) / Merrilees
139.1 shall (MS) / will
139.11 Norna (MS) / Norna's
140.2 Berserkar (MS) / Berserkars
140.26 this (MS) / that
140.35 two, they (MS two they) / two more, they
141.25 poor man (MS) / preacher
141.25 stranger (MS) / poor missionary
141.26 waked (MS) / watched
141.28 doors (MS) / door
141.38 dispel (MS dispell) / refute
142.19 shunned (MS shund) / shuddered
142.19 suction attending (MS) / suction supposed to attend
143.3 hath (MS and source) / has
143.29 amongst (MS) / among
143.30 *oremus* (MS) / *oramus*
143.43 like (MS) / likely
144.5 Millie. Her (MS Millie Her) / Millie; her
144.7 prayer (MS) / prayers
144.9 mariner (MS Mariner) / mariners
144.11 pretensions. Her (MS) / pretensions; her
144.14 she (MS) / the inhabitant
144.15 near (MS) / nearly
144.35 an excellent excuse (MS) / an excuse
144.37 unassisted, that, no person belonging to the vessel surviving, she (MS ?unassisted that no person belonging to the vessell surviving she) / unassisted, so that, there being no survivor, she
145.11 for (MS) / of
145.27 Crusoe been (MS) / Crusoe ever been
145.31 the islands (MS) / one island

146.6 See note to Chapter II., p. 140. Norse Fragments. (Editorial) / See Note I. To Chapter II., p. 29. Norse Fragments. (MS See Note 1st. Chapter II)
146.9 at invading (MS) / to invade
146.10 with (MS) / by
146.14 to action (MS) / into action
146.35 *Mascharарum* (MS and source) / *Maccharârum*
146.40 an hexagonal (MS and source) / an triagonal
147.2 nimble (MS) / nimbly
149.47 can (MS) / canst
149.54 *Lout* (MS Lout) / *Loot*
151.10 a (MS) / the
151.14 somewhat (MS some what) / rather
151.40 frolic (MS frolick) / work
151.42 cell. But (MS) / cell; but
152.1 have been (MS) / be
152.16 Archipelagos (Editorial) / Archipelago (MS as Magnum)
152.16 came ashore (MS) / landed
152.18 They remained in the island by force, and on bad terms with the inhabitants, till spring returned, and then effected their departure. (MS They remaind in the island by force and on bad terms with the inhabitants till spring returnd & then effected their departure.) / These strangers are remembered as having remained on the island by force, and on bad terms with the inhabitants, till spring returned, when they effected their escape.
153.19 There was a (MS) / These were, a
153.21 animals. The (MS) / animals; the
153.32 none (MS non) / no songstress
153.35 knowst (MS) / knowest
153.37 rites and the song itself as (MS) / rites as
153.38 promote.'—'Nevertheless (MS promote" "Nevertheless) / promote, and the song itself as unlawful.'—'Nevertheless
The problem seems to be that a song cannot be included within 'matters', but the revision produced repetition.
154.5 species (MS speces) / sort
154.6 powerful (MS) / tuneful
154.12 in spring (MS) / in the spring
154.17 of great name (MS) / of name
154.43 given (MS) / pledged
155.1 hand through (MS) / hand, while pronouncing it, through
155.8 Minna. (MS) / Minna in the higher ranks.
155.18 Arkwright (MS) / Ark wright
155.31 pp. 30–31 of this volume (Editorial) / vol. xvii. p. 335, of this edition (MS vol. p. of this edition)
156.8 parapets (MS) / parapet
156.8 them (MS) / it
156.17 clan-tune (MS Clan-tune) / clan-term
156.19 to that of (MS) / to the tune of
156.20 Sorceresses and fortune-tellers. (MS Sorceresses and fortune-tellers) / [no text]
157.5 storm (MS) / storms
157.7 a place (MS) / the place
157.24 unbroken (MS) / unbroke
The MS reading is found in another state of the Magnum.
157.31 promise, Note to Chapter 10, pp. 154–55 of this volume (Editorial)

/ promise, Note to Chapter II., p. 50, of this volume (MS promise here quoted ⟨as⟩ attachd to Chapter XXVI.)

157.34 species (MS) / kind

158.7 hint of joyous indulgence (MS) / kind of joyous explanation

158.11 the man (MS) / this man

158.27 eaglets (MS) / eagles

158.30 escape into (MS) / get among

158.38 sate (MS) / sat

158.40 was (MS) / is

159.17 circuit (MS) / circle

159.25 lakes (MS) / lake

THE FORTUNES OF NIGEL

167.3 Muse (MS and source) / man

167.22 after a full provision to such as might have claims on (MS) / after making a full provision for such relations as might have claims upon

167.33 sustains (MS) / supports

167.35 departments (MS) / situations

167.36 author (MS) / founder

167.38 occasion (MS) / opportunity

168.10 them (MS) / him

168.11 in place (MS) / instead

168.15 steadiness (MS) / integrity

168.20 attractive for the public; because (MS attractive for the publick because) / attractive; because

168.21 flourished, was of a character which gave (MS flourishd was of a character which gave) / flourished, gave

168.23 it admitted of much greater (MS) / it afforded greater

168.30 where the ancient (MS) / when the ancient

168.35 demanded for the effect of (MS ⟨dep⟩ demanded for the effect of) / necessary to give effect to

168.40 character (MS) / characters

168.42 as belonging (MS) / which belongs

169.12 felon-knight (MS felon knight) / fellow-knight

169.13 damsel.* And (MS damsel* And) / damsel;* but

169.15 was to (MS) / was about to

169.34 run into (MS and source) / run next into

170.11 virtues (MS and source) / virtue
Stowe has 'vertues'.

170.15 measure (MS and source) / manner

170.26 seemed to be at work (MS derived: seemd to be [end of line] work) / seemed at work

170.37 Vice (MS) / vice

170.38 with gross (MS) / in its gross

170.41 Vice (MS) / vice

171.7 sometime (MS and source) / sometimes
The MS has 'sometime⟨s⟩'.

171.9 done. ——— The (MS done ——— The) / done. The
Scott indicates an omission.

171.10 hereabouts (MS and source) / hereabout

171.20 paid to (MS) / paid by each individual to

171.31 Richard (Editorial) / Patrick (MS as Magnum)

171.34 the reign of Edward III. (Editorial) / the reign of Edward. (MS the [end of line] of Edward)

171.36 vol. i. (Editorial) / vol. ii. (MS Vol II)
171.38 talents or (MS talents ⟨?or⟩ or) / talent nor
172.5 brothers of fortune educate (MS) / men of fortune, brothers, educate
172.27 read for (MS) / read a first time for
172.35 Belfonds (MS and source) / Belfords
173.36 Williams (MS and source) / Withnam
174.22 above (MS and source) / about
174.33 indeed might (MS) / indeed it might
174.34 goods, the (MS goods the) / goods, that the
176.18 *Alicis* (source) / *Alicia* (MS missing)
176.19 *obruta* (source) / *abruta* (MS missing)
176.21 *passa* (source) / *pressa* (MS missing)
176.33 *ante* (source) / *antea* (MS missing)
176.42 wonder (MS) / admiration
177.3 [no text] (Editorial) / **Motion*—Puppet-show. (MS as Magnum) Magnum changed 'motion' at EEWN 13, 27.22 to 'pageant', necessitating the moving of the Ed1 note to the present occurrence of the word.
177.7 for (MS) / on account of
177.9 "through (MS and source) / "which, through
The MS has no quotation mark.
177.13 of this (MS) / attending the
177.23 forwards (MS) / forward
178.5 ever circular (MS and source) / even circular
Dalyell has 'euer'.
178.5 hands ever in that walk fiddling about his [a (MS hands ever in that walk fidling about his [a) / hands are in that walk ever fiddling about —— [a
178.13 *Fragments of Scotish History*, pp. 85, 87 (Editorial) / *Sketches of Scottish History*, p. 86 (MS Sketches of Scotish History p. 86)
178.19 since (MS) / ago
178.22 far inadequate (MS) / little adequate
178.27 more (MS) / most
178.31 in company (MS) / present
178.33 coat?—indeed (MS coat indeed) / coat—auld-fashioned?—indeed
178.37 heard (MS) / happened to hear
178.38 accused in ancient times of very little attention to (MS) / accused of paying very little attention in ancient times to
178.40 name as if there (MS) / name, as if conjecturing there
179.10 invokes (MS) / makes
179.20 betray something (MS) / make public some secret
179.25 from her description in (MS) / from the description of her in
179.26 were (MS) / was
179.31 scaffolds (MS and source) / scaffold
The MS has 'Scaffolds'.
179.43 it (MS) / his preserver
180.8 limitations (MS and source) / limitation
180.8 set (source) / made (MS as Magnum)
180.9 as that he asked it for was (MS and source) / as the action for which he asked it for was
The source (*Secret History*) reads 'as that he asked it for, was'.
180.18 you, Coventry, Lord Keeper? (MS and source) / you Lord Keeper, Coventry?
The MS has 'you Coventry Lord Keeper?'
180.19 sur-replied (MS and source) / replied

181.2 house (MS) / homes
181.3 to the (MS) / to be placed in the
181.6 strictly pursued respecting useful (MS) / pursued with great strictness in respect to useful
181.9 second (MS) / next
181.32 purer (MS and source) / pure
181.37 vented (MS and source) / vended
181.40 academy of honour, and (source: academy of honour—and) / academy, and (MS academy and)
181.45 Learn there (source) / Learn us (MS Learn thus)
182.2 their tongue, [new line] As (source) / the tongue? [new line] As (MS their tongue [new line] As)
Another state of the Magnum also has 'their'.
182.3 says? (source) / says. (MS says)
182.30 Elizabeth, having (MS Elizabeth having) / Elizabeth, by having
182.31 sort (MS) / sect
182.38 who (MS) / that
183.19 served the flesh up so well (MS) / served up the flesh of that unclean animal so well
183.29 repels (MS repells) / repelled
184.23 o'er night (MS) / in might (source: ore night)
185.23 aware his (MS) / aware that his
185.24 the sovereign (MS the Sovereign) / his sovereign
185.27 71 (Editorial) / 70 (MS as Magnum)
185.37 were (MS) / was
187.5 Lucy (MS and source) / Letitia
187.6 J. (MS and source) / L.
188.19 789 (Editorial) / 389 (MS as Magnum)
189.27 occasion by (MS and source) / occasionally
190.7 leglen-girth (MS) / leglin-girth
190.8 *leglen* (MS) / *leglin*
190.12 leggen-girth (MS) / leglin girth
191.10 on the walls (MS) / in the same state
191.31 rank (MS) / ranks
191.32 when (MS) / if

PEVERIL OF THE PEAK

205.6 species (MS) / sort
205.7 Falstaff was of (MS) / Falstaff of
205.18 stocked (MS stockd) / stored
205.22 the daily (MS) / their daily
207.21 1650. Of (another state) / 1650 Of (not in MS)
208.22 Chapter 20, p. 260 (Editorial) / Chapter VI., p. 129 (not in MS)
208.40 a not unfrequent compact at (MS) / a compact not unfrequent at
209.19 broad Scottish (MS) / loud Scotch
The adjective is malformed in the MS.
209.25 found their (MS) / found that their
212.46 vol. ii. (Editorial) / vol. iii. (MS missing)
213.31 438 (Editorial) / 338 (MS missing)
234.16 at contrasting (MS) / to contrast
236.27 any one know that she had seen her except her mother (MS) / any one except her mother know that she had seen her
236.34 wished (MS wishd) / waited
236.36 were (MS) / are

237.2 time (MS) / times
237.9 these (MS) / them
237.28 certain she (MS) / certain that she
238.20 Ronalds-way (MS) / Ronalds-wing
238.21 Hango Hill (MS Hango-Hill) / Hange Hall
239.25 for a goblin (MS) / for goblin
239.34 violences (MS) / violence
241.33 scarce (MS) / scarcely
242.32 Man (Editorial) / Wales (MS missing)
245.39 constant (MS) / common
246.9 material (MS) / materials
246.10 with (MS) / of
246.12 [no text] (Editorial) / *Beneath the only one of the four churches in Castle Rushin, which is or was kept a little in repair, is a prison or dungeon, for ecclesiastical offenders. "This," says Waldron, "is certainly one of the most dreadful places that imagination can form; the sea runs under it through the hollows of the rock with such a continual roar, that you would think it were every moment breaking in upon you, and over it are the vaults for burying the dead. The stairs descending to this place of terrors are not above thirty, but so steep and narrow, that they are very difficult to go down. A child of eight or nine years not being able to pass them but sideways."—WALDRON'S *Description of the Isle of Man, in his Works,* p. 105, folio.
Most of this note (keyed to 155.15 'the vault under the chapel') is present in the MS, but it is also included in the next one, on 'Sodor, or Holm-Peel'. See Editorial Note, 197.
246.31 unaccessible (MS and source) / inaccessible
247.43 indeed in the (MS and source) / indeed the
248.42 all together (MS and source) / altogether
257.22 horribly roaring, disappeared (source) / horribly disappeared (MS missing)
260.18 of Chapter 15, page 246 of this volume (Editorial) / of Chapter I., page 24 of this volume (MS of the Chapter)
260.31 a prentice (MS and source) / an apprentice
262.42 oath (MS) / oaths
262.42 species (MS) / sort
263.3 consults (MS and source) / councils
263.23 courage (MS) / energy
263.42 Unrigg (Editorial) / Unwin (not in MS)
265.7 CHALLONER (MS Challoner) / CHALLERSON
Scott's word is ambiguous: he most likely intended 'Challoner' which was understandably read as 'Challerson'.
265.42 viii (Editorial) / vii (MS VII)
266.1 SERVICE (MS Service) / SCENE
266.6 composition (MS and source) / compensation
266.8 this while (source) / that which (MS this which)
266.20 be here remarked (MS be here remarkd) / be, however, remarked
267.7 received accordingly (MS) / accordingly received
268.29 made him capable of rendering himself for a time as agreeable (another state) / rendered him as capable for a time of rendering himself agreeable (MS renderd him as capable for a time of rendering himself agreeable)
270.40 573 (Editorial) / 173 (not in MS)
272.6 187–88 (Editorial) / vol. xxvii., Note to Chapter XII. (MS vol. p.)
273.1 impudent (source) / intimate (MS as Magnum)

274.2 This insurrection . . . punished as traitors. (proofs) / [no text]
MS **reading:** Note [new line] This insurrection took place in 1660 Those engaged in it believed themselves invulnerable and invincible. They proclaimd the Millenium and disturbd London grealy The day after their mad rebelellion they were put down & subdued and their leaders not having the good fortune to be considerd as madmen were tried and punishd as traitors.
See explanatory note, 687 below.

275.28 Brantome tells us . . . expired. (MS Brantome tells us of a court lady who chose to have that tune playd which was Dying and as the ⟨as⟩ ↑at↓ the end of the burden repeated "*Oui; tout verlore et a bons anciens*," and therewith expired.) / [no text]

280.33 say seven (source) / say six (MS as Magnum)

281.23 wadding his horse at (MS and source) / wadding at

288.33 page 272 (Editorial) / page 145 (not in MS)

QUENTIN DURWARD

297.11 chivalry, however overstrained and fantastic many of its doctrines may appear to us, had in it this point of excellence, that it founded (MS derived: chivalry however overstaind—and fantastic many of its doctrines may appear to us had in it this point of excellence that it founded) / chivalry had in it this point of excellence, that however overstrained and fantastic many of its doctrines may appear to us, they were all founded

297.13 was deprived, it is (MS was deprived it is) / were deprived, it would be

297.16 Amongst (MS) / Among

297.17 Knight (MS) / knight

297.23 for corrupting (MS) / to corrupt

297.36 claim (MS) / consider
The MS word is ill formed.

299.25 forwards (MS) / forward

299.25 in defence (MS) / in the defence

299.26 sword (MS derived: sort) / exertions

299.29 and supply (MS) / and to supply

299.29 with means (MS) / with the means

299.32 or (MS) / and

299.35 defences (MS) / defence

300.8 impending (MS) / theatened

300.12 but even meritorious (MS) / but meritorious

300.13 his fiat (MS) / the monarch's fiat

300.16 evident such (MS) / evident that such

300.24 often by (MS) / often accompanied by

300.28 where (MS) / when

300.35 upon (MS) / on

300.43 See note, Disguised Herald, 321–23 below. (Editorial) / See note, Disguised Herald, at end of Chapter XVI., Vol. XXXII. (MS In Note upon Chap: ⟨l⟩IX (*The printer will adapt this referennce to the edition*)

301.9 like (MS) / likely

301.28 for forgiveness (MS) / for the forgiveness

301.29 for prolongation (MS) / for the prolongation

301.32 for some choice (MS) / for supposed

303.11 1483 (Editorial) / 1485 (MS as Magnum)

303.39 Flanders: (MS) / Flanders;

304.8 the feudal superior (MS) / a feudal superior

304.10 appear contradictory of both the (MS appear contradictory of ⟨the⟩ both the) / appear to exist as a contradiction both of the
304.17 there no one (MS) / no one there
304.19 degree (MS) / extent
304.22 whom Burgundy (MS) / whom the Duke of Burgundy
304.28 this romance (MS) / the romance
304.35 which (MS) / that
305.8 and hazards (MS) / and its hazards
305.13 neglect the attendance (MS neglect ⟨his urgen⟩ the attendanc) / neglect attendance
305.27 conveyed (MS conveyd) / convoyed
305.31 his own father (MS) / his father
305.37 dominions (MS) / possessions
305.43 versatile (MS) / variable
306.9 best of (MS) / best part of
306.10 prejudice against (MS) / not less for
306.13 rivers, are (MS rivers are) / rivers. They are
306.22 without a clasp (MS without a clasp⟨d⟩) / without clasp
306.37 upon (MS) / on
306.43 and ascertain (MS) / and thus maintain
307.29 indolence (MS) / idleness
307.36 in act (MS) / in the act
307.42 more (MS) / rather
307.43 to the Law (MS) / from the law
308.38 to consult these (MS) / to these
309.9 who were displaced, and, flying (MS who were displaced and flying) / who, displaced, and flying
309.15 where (MS) / when
310.1 Scottish men (MS) / Scotsmen
310.31 made (MS) / given
310.32 returned (MS returnd) / made
311.1 upon (MS) / on
311.6 Dammartin (MS and source) / Dammarten
311.8 d'embarras à (source) / d'ambarras a (MS d'ambara a)
311.25 her course (MS) / its course
311.26 she (MS) / he
311.27 her (MS) / his
312.12 part (MS) / feature
312.14 otherwise they (MS) / they otherwise
312.15 forms or principles (MS) / form or principle
312.28 annex (MS) / attribute
312.35 as the (MS) / as being the
312.38 adopt (MS) / follow
313.2 *sie* (MS sie) / *sic*
313.3 away! May (MS away May) / away; may
313.13 species (MS) / sort
313.33 bourd . . . bourd (MS) / boord . . . boord
313.37 Charolois (MS) / Charalois
313.37 much (MS) / great
314.23 murthered (MS murtherd) / murdered
314.27 fourteen (Editorial) / fifteen (MS 15)
At 314.3 MS has 'in 1467'. This was corrected to 'in 1468' in print, but the later numeral was left unchanged.
315.12 Arras (MS) / Arves
315.16 immense (MS) / great

315.21 Marche (MS) / Marck
316.2 Charolois (MS) / Charalois
316.7 Charolois (Editorial) / Charalois (not in MS)
316.30 d'Urfé (MS D'Urfé⟨e⟩) / de Urfé
316.34 suspicion, seeing so many of his enemies were assembled, that (MS suspicion seeing so many of his enemies were assembled that) / suspicion, that
317.14 King in (MS) / King of France in
317.22 or (MS) / nor
317.26 assisting to subdue with his arms, the (MS assisting to subdue with his arms the) / employing his troops in subduing, the
317.36 was (MS) / had
317.38 contrived (MS contrved) / constructed
318.21 affliction (MS afliction) / affection
318.38 in face of (MS) / in the face of
319.4 give the (MS) / give to the
319.10 Charles the VIIth's (Editorial) / Charles the Vth's (MS Charles Vths)
319.16 with violence (MS) / with a violence
319.40 the destined (MS) / his destined
320.6 fine (MS) / fair
320.14 foreseeing (MS) / foretelling
320.16 write or read (MS) / read or write
320.19 forwards (MS) / forward
320.31 Nancy (Editorial) / Morat (MS as Magnum)
321.15 sensible he (MS) / sensible that he
321.16 forwards (MS) / forward
323.5 tract (MS) / course
323.9 work (MS) / tract
323.16 feodary (MS feodarie) / feudatory
323.27 fifteenth (Editorial) / fourteenth (MS 14)
323.27 perfect (MS derived: persect) / general
325.6 crime (MS) / crimes
325.9 fourteen (Editorial) / four (MS as Magnum)
325.11 fourth (Editorial) / third (MS as Magnum)

SAINT RONAN'S WELL

333.28 restoring (MS) / redeeming
333.30 Spaw (MS) / Spa
333.32 accompt-books (MS accompt Books) / account-books
336.17 *Diversoria* (MS) / *Diversaria*
336.37 this species of duty (MS) / this duty
337.21 their (MS) / these
338.11 all that art can add its highest decorations to from less abundant sources. (MS all that art can adds its highest decorations to from less abundant sources) / all to which art can add its highest decorations, when drawn from less abundant sources.
338.13 separately by the Poet, are (MS separately by the Poet Are) / separately, are
338.35 for a murder (MS) / for murder
338.43 satire, once very popular (MS satire once very popular) / satire, very popular
340.43 himself (MS) / itself
341.2 he (MS) / it
341.4 he (MS it / it

341.4 his master (Editorial) / its master (MS its Master)
341.5 his life (MS) / its life

REDGAUNTLET

350.11 better (MS) / more
351.1 failing (MS) / falling
351.22 forwards (MS) / forward
351.27 singular (MS) / singularly
351.42 Scottishman (MS) / Scotchman
352.12 Lochiel, and attainted (MS derived: Lochiel ⟨was found⟩ an attainted) / Lochiel, attainted
352.39 upon private (MS) / upon his private
353.18 King (MS) / king
354.31 prescribed to him (MS) / prescribed him
355.23 like (MS) / likely
355.38 sacrificed all (MS) / sacrificed their all
356.27 be claimant (MS be clamant) / be a claimant
356.31 egotistic (MS) / egotistical
357.6 were hereafter likely (MS) / were, after that event, likely
357.10 stings (MS) / sting
357.14 alongst (MS) / along
358.2 King and the Queen (MS King & the Queen) / King and Queen
358.4 in usurpation. (MS) / in the usurpation of the family of Hanover.
358.8 but of (MS) / but those of
359.41 occupying unnecessarily the time of the court. (MS) / occupying the time of the court unnecessarily.
360.17 old (MS) / auld
360.42 swelled (MS) / swollen
361.29 catch i'faith (MS and source) / catch
362.36 afflictions befall (MS) / afflictions befell
363.21 for preservation (MS) / for the preservation
363.23 Campbell (Editorial) / Cameron (not in MS) See the Explanatory Note, 700.
363.29 like (MS) / likely
363.35 after (MS) / afterwards
364.10 sate (MS) / sat
364.31 you living (MS) / you when living
364.34 should (MS) / ought to
365.2 opinion he (MS) / opinion that he
365.29 dram. (MS) / dram of spirits.
365.38 to their performing (MS) / to performing
366.6 title of Lord (MS) / title of lord
366.8 husbands' (another state) / husband's (MS husbands)
366.8 they remain plain Mistresses distinguished only by their Lords' family name (MS they remain plain Mistresses distinguishd only by their Lords family name) / they are distinguished only by their lords' family name
366.13 carles Lords (MS) / carles lords
366.14 carlines Ladies (MS) / carlines ladies
367.40 difficulty saved (MS dificulty saved) / difficulty was saved
368.6 by the visitation of providence (MS) / of disease
368.12 Southron (MS) / Southern
370.3 EEWN **reading:** character. George III., it is said . . . soundness of policy.

MS **derived:** George the second it is said had a police of his own whose agency was so efficiency that the Sovereign was able to tell his prime Minister that the Pretender was in London. The prime Minister began immediatly to talk of measures to be taken warrants to be procurd Messengers and guards to be got in readiness "Pooh pooh' said the good naturd sovereign since I have found him ⟨abo⟩ out leave me alone to deal with him "And what said the minister "is your Majesties purpose on so important a case" "To leave himself" said George IId "and when he tires he will go back again" The truth of this story does not depend on that of the lifting of the guantlet; and while the latter could be but an idle bravado the former express George IIds goodness of heart & soundness of policy
Magnum reading: character.
A change in the size of the writing makes it clear that Scott added this paragraph to the ISet note after the main part of that note had been composed. For the Magnum several lines were added to the beginning of the ISet manuscript note and the last section was omitted. Another state preserves the original version. The present edition follows the Dryburgh Edition in adding the last section to the base-text.

370.27 in theology (MS) / on theology
370.39 device (MS) / decree

THE BETROTHED

377.33 those (MS) / the
378.35 coevals (MS) / contemporaries
379.3 *Presbyterian* (MS) / Presbyterian
379.11 Deutscher (source) / Deutschen (MS as Magnum)
379.14 Weissenhorn (source) / Wiessenhorn (MS as Magnum)
382.42 M.R.S.L. (from title-page of volume) / M.R.S.I. (MS as Magnum)
383.8 set it by (MS) / kept it
383.10 woven in with (MS) / interwoven with
383.43 Waverley, present edition, vol. 25a, 65 (note to 17.30) (Editorial) / Waverley, present edition, vol. i. p. 38, and note. (MS Waverly present edition Vol. I. P. 38–49 & note)
384.7 Algar retiring (MS and source) / Algar returning
The MS 'retiring' is imperfectly formed.
384.37 ABBOTSFORD, *1st June*, 1832. (another state) / [no text] (MS as Magnum)
386.12 recollections of the abbacies (MS) / Recollections of the Abbacies

THE TALISMAN

393.10 well nigh (MS) / almost
393.30 corrector, a situation in which I had not hitherto stood, and was not ever willing to place myself. (MS Corrector a situation in which I had not hitherto stood and was not ever willing to place myself.) / corrector.
394.5 sufficiently (MS) / successfully
394.5 acknowledged masters (MS acknowleged masters) / acknowledged to be masters
394.8 EEWN **reading:** them. At the utmost . . . scribbler like myself. [new paragraph] The period
MS **derived:** them. At the utmost European manners & those of the middle ages in which I was allowd to be in some degree at home

should accupy the larger part of ⟨the⟩ a tale on the subject of the Crusades. With regard to the other or smaller portion which was necessarily the least important I imagined that it was possible by keeping in generals to avoid any remarkable errors or anachronisms. The extreme simplicity as well as unchanging character⟨s⟩ of eastern manners ⟨of⟩ are taught us early in the enchanting terms which our early infancy learns and our manhood and age recalls to mind often without the exertion even of the faculty of volition So that in some degree every person of a lively imagination is supplied with a stock of articles to use the shopkeerers phrase upon a true oriental pattern Books of travels are numerous and for history and events the Bibliotheque Orientale was at hand to supply them [new paragraph] If an author therefore was not disposed to venture out of his depth he is in no great danger of drowning and methought this species of general acquaintance might very well serve the turn of an ignorant scribbler like myself. [new paragraph] The period
Magnum reading: them. [new paragraph] The period

394.35 opposed in the scales to (MS oppose in the scales to) / opposed to
394.39 they (MS) / each
395.30 p. 397 (Editorial) / p. xv (MS No I)
396.1 Douglas, too impatient (MS) / Douglas, impatient
396.9 antient (MS) / aged
396.25 many experiences (MS) / much experience
396.33 them, excepting (MS them excepting) / them, "excepting
396.36 condemn. (MS) / condemn."
396.38 by a mad dog (MS) / by mad dogs
397.19 *Specimens of Early English Metrical Romances* (Editorial) / *History of Chivalry* (MS Hist. of Chivalry)
397.27 ABBOTSFORD, *1st July*, 1832. (another state) / *1st July*, 1832. (MS [no text])
398.11 That (MS and source) / Tho'
402.17 on the (MS) / in their
The source has 'in the'.
403.33 pp. 185, 187 (Editorial) / pp. 193, 194 (not in MS)
404.1 for government (MS) / for the government
404.20 Ysolde, the (MS Ysolde the) / Yseult—the
404.22 being all which related to the chase, deemed (MS derived: being all which related to the laws of the chase deemd) / being those that related to the rules of the chase, which were deemed

WOODSTOCK

413.5 afforded an ample (proof correction) / afforded ample
413.23 give to the public a (MS and proof) / give a
417.27 crack (MS and source) / clack
419.19 great stink (MS and source) / bad smell
421.10 writes (source) / unites
421.18 and whore (MS and source) / and ——
The MS has '& Whore', source 'and Whore'.
423.21 day; (MS and source) / day
423.24 So pissed. (MS and source: so pissed.) / * * *
425.36 While they piss'd; (MS and source: while they piss'd;) / * * *
425.48 A spay'd bitch: (MS and source) / * * *
The MS has 'a Spay'd Bitch:', source 'a Spay'd-Bitch:'.
426.7 pat; [new line] The poor spay'd bitch did you know what [new line]

And fouled (MS and source: pat, [new line] The poore Spay'd-Bitch did you know what [new line] and fouled) / pat [new line]
*   *   *   * [new line] *   *   *
Another state of the Magnum gives the semi-colon after 'pat'.

429.5 this councillor (MS and source) / the councillor
430.2 nightly (MS and source) / mighty
434.13 his sheets (MS and source) / the sheets
434.34 frighted (MS and source) / frightened
434.37 some as (MS and source) / some of it as
443.11 piety (MS and source) / feeling
The source has 'Piety'.
443.31 week (Editorial) / year (MS as Magnum)
443.33 Northamptonshire (Editorial) / Lincolnshire (MS as Magnum)
443.33 Woodcroft (MS) / Woodford
443.40 Woodcroft (source) / Woodford (MS as Magnum)
444.28 amongst the (MS derived: amongsthe) / among the
445.5 tones (MS and source) / lives
445.30 Ferret-farm (MS and source) / Foordfarm
446.2 *Ferret* (MS (Feret) and source) / *Ford*
446.13 *Ferret* (MS and source) / *Ford*
446.24 Londoner's (MS and source: Londoners) / laundress
447.4 Pierrepoint Cromp (Editorial) / Pierspoint Crimp (MS as Magnum)
447.10 his verses (MS) / the verses
447.12 Lucius (Editorial) / Henry (MS ⟨Lucius⟩ ↑Henry↓)
447.39 the most handsome (MS) / the handsomest
448.4 Lieblingshund (MS derived: Lieblinshund) / lieblung hund

CHRONICLES OF THE CANONGATE

463.15 MacLeish (MS) / Macturk
463.16 waiting woman (MS) / washingwoman
482.7 Ogleby (Editorial) / Ogilvie (no MS; source as Magnum)
482.39 volume (Editorial) / series (no MS)

486.25 [The following is a diplomatic (literal) transcript of the manuscript of Scott's original Magnum Introduction (Huntington MSS HM 979 and 1982), which is the base text for the reading text in the present edition. The first manuscript is in Laidlaw's hand, except for the final six lines which are largely in Scott's hand. Scott has also made some additions or revisions either above the line of text or on a verso: these are indicated in bold. The second manuscript, intended to appear after the Ed1 Introduction, is in Scott's hand.]

[MS HM 979]

⟨Introduction to the Chronicles of the Canongate, published in 1827⟩ It is remarkable that from circumstances scarcely under my own command my intercourse with the Public had changed in a degree **as sudden** perhaps as remarkable as any which exists in the realms of literature, the ⟨like-⟩ lightness that is & unimportance considered. ↑N.L.↓ The previous prosperity of my life had depended in some measure upon the ⟨unmerited⟩ success **unmerited perhaps** of a series of anonimous publications which succeeded as much superior to their own merit as to the expectations of the public. The author of waverly had been able to indulge most of the tastes which a retired person might ⟨in⟩ be supposed to entertain & unquestionably so far as worldly affairs had gone might be esteemed fortunate in his transactions. To an easy ⟨fortune⟩ **competence** derived from succession to my nearest relations this secret source of income like the ⟨fountain of wealth⟩ **fountain of coind golld and pearls** possest by the great Persian traveller ⟨Abulfurres⟩ Abulfouares, this little supply of idle wants enabled me without the charge of imprudence to extend my expenditure in some lines which could not probably have been otherwise very prudent. I bought I built & **though contented with a very moderate share of the literary profits of Waverley and his successors** came to ⟨vest⟩ be possest of an easy fortune; and which seemed little **Like the other riches of this world** likely to have assumed to itself wings & fly away. It shewed however in the year seventeen hundred & twenty seven that it had no more sure foundation than other sources of revenue in this transitory world. The general distress **in that unlucky** of the Bookselling world having taken place at once & to an immense extent placed the author at the mercy of those ⟨w⟩ for whose transactions he had obliged himself to the extent of upwards of one hundred **& twenty** thousand pounds & nothing remained but the sad remedy **requiring requiring indulgence from creditors whom he could not immediatly for the purpose** of turning into money ⟨every⟩ valuable of every kind which the author possest & paying as ⟨far⟩ **speedily** as was possible the debts for which he had become bound. With this purpose the author with whatever feelings surrendered his property like an honest man & it became vested for the time in persons whose integrity liberality & general kindness as well as prudence **& knowlege** enabled them to give their assistance for carrying into execution a plan ⟨of⟩ of a nature apparently gigantic involving expenses which could not have been commanded even for a temporary purpose without their assistance. ↑N.L.↓ It occurred that an Edition like the present possessing explanations upon such parts as the public had been interested in while they were in an anonymous state might be acceptable to the readers & if produced at a moderate expence & under favourable circumstances would afford a considerable addition to the funds out of which payment to any extent was alone to be expected. It is needless to say that it became necessary (all reasons for concealment being at an end) the author should avow the paternity of these tales. The following introductory preface to the Chronicles of the Canongate was written at this time for the purpose of explaining much that it was thought necessary to elucidate concerning the present publication of what are called "The Waverly Novels"

These illustrations accordingly are given in the ⟨following⟩ preface which was written upon the occasion. It is here reprinted because a laudable curiosity is reasonably attatched to a coin or medal which is struck upon a particular occasion [caret] usually possesses a sharpness & precision of impress which hardly exists on those that have been current for some time in the world. I have however added from the newspapers of the day a more full account of what passed upon occasion of the name of the author of Waverly being for the first time anounced to the Public which although ⟨I⟩ **the author directed by the clea clear headed and sagacious Gentleman who undertook to act as publisher & took on him the commercial part of the publication** had long thought of making the confession became at last a circumstance of mere accident; for no communication existed betwixt ⟨me⟩ **him** & ⟨my⟩ **his** friend Lord meadow bank whose appears and truly as the person who introduced the explanation. The desire of keeping together all the circumstances relating to this literary discovery will ⟨not⟩ it is hoped apologise for the repetition of some circumstances neither long nor of much importance **which have been already mentiond in various parts of these notes**. In a word it is the desire of the Editor that this edition should be rendered as perfect as possible & he feels it is his duty to do all he can to accomplish his purpose since the uncommon indulgence of the public **fully** authorises him to hope that the continuation of their favour will enable him not withstand notwith standing advancing life & powers declining in proportion to attain that object which he has proposed to himself & which he may now justly consider as to a certain degree accomplished. The times highly unfavourable certainly for literary adventure have in this ⟨case⟩ individual case proved so favourable as to authorise a hope that the embarrassments into which the author was led by circumstances will be extinguished by a short continuation of the same public favour which he has experienced since the commencement of present publication under his own name

⟨Walter Scott⟩

and which has already reduced these embarassments and provided funds to a considerable extent for the entire liquidation of what remains
[Go on with printed introduction vol I Chronicles of Canongate All who

[MS HM 1982]

Introduction to Chronicles of the Canongate to come in after the Fly leaf & prefatory matter
The general preface ⟨cont⟩ already pre face gives some account of the great change which induced the other to lay aside his incognito or rather put it out of his power to retain it any longer The Chronicles of the Canongate must now like the other productions of the author be prefaced by some introductory matter peculiar to the contents of the volumes so ⟨ent⟩ entitled. These cannot indeed be very long since the works in some degree are their own commentators Thus having resolved to make a new trial upon the publick favour the first of the kind which I had ever ventured to put forth in my own name it struck me that something of the plan of a periodical publication might carry with it a certain degree of novelty. I did not indeed propose to request the assistance of any other person in attempting to sustain the proposed editorial ⟨tas⟩ labour. I have entertaind an opinion that this species of giving to the publick as it were a literary Pick Nick is almost sure to end in that species of comparaisons which are justly termd ⟨odilious⟩ odious and are therefore to be avoided. I am also conscious perhaps from cases in which I may myself have been concernd with what ⟨each⟩ ↑ease↓ an author gets promises and with how much trouble such promises ar renderd good I therefore pland a work to be dependant as former labours on my own resources alon and although I had a consciousness that my spell was endangerd since the Author of Waverley had "a local habitation and a name I was determind with the Great Montrose that in literature as in war

He either fears his fate too much
Or his deserts are small
Who dares not put it to the touch
To win or lose it all

The following work chapters 2d explains upon what plan the periodical work calld the Chronicles of the Canongate was to be conducted. The lady termd in the work Mrs Bethune Baliol ⟨wals⟩ was ⟨an⟩ an attempt to describe in its leading points the very amiable and interesting character of Mrs Murray Keith a particular friend of the author whose death had shortly before saddend a large circle to which she was dear as well for her agreeable qualities as for the extent of information which she possessd and the delightul ⟨ ? ⟩ manner in which she was used to communicate it She was in fact the real person who supplied the Author with some of his best stories which ↑ s ↓ he afterwards recognized as they came before the publi.

The first story in the ⟨tales⟩ Chronicles of the Cannongate after the history of the supposed Editor Chrystal Croftangry ↑ being the highland Widow ↓ was derived from Mrs Keith and was told with a few additional circumstances exactly as Mrs Murray Keith herself told the story and neither the highland Cicerone MacLeish nor the demure waiting woman were ideal characters. There were indeed some imaginary circumstances which I rather regret for on reconsidering the tale with a view to the present Edition I am convinced I have injured the simplicity of the narative which in Mrs Keiths narration was extremely affecting

The Tale entitled the two drovers I learnd from my old friend George Constable Esq of ⟨Craic⟩ ↑ Craigie ↓ Wallace whom I have already acknowledged as the original Antiquary I think he said he was present at the Highlanders trial at Carlisle He seldom mentiond the venerable judges charge to the Jury without shedding tears which had peculiar pathos when flowing down features which had rather a sarcastic or almost a cynical expression

The third story in the Chronicles is that of the Surgeons daughter and though one would willingly believe the story too bad to be true yet I could certainly mention some of the names under which the story was currently told Such a disclosure has however made no part any part of my plan If a good effect can be produced from the story itself it will be as efficient as if the name of the criminal were attachd to his action Only I would say that my freind colonel Mac Kerris who really furnished out my tale in the oriental costume did not stand Godfather to any of the facts it contains while he kindly consented from his eastern remembrances to furnish a costume as dazzling as that of the renownd Schehezade herself

Such are the prefatory documents relating to the Chronicles of the Canongate

---

490.36 Urie (Editorial) / Uric (no MS)
491.36 dissuasionis (source) / dissuasion is (no MS)
491.41 staill (source) / staik (no MS)
492.41 nave (Editorial) / name (no MS)
493.18 Somervilles (MS Someville) / Sommervilles
493.22 Somerville (MS) / Sommerville
496.15 (Lady Eglintoune,) had (source: (Lady Eglintoune) had) / Lady Eglintoun,) had (no MS)
498.31 grew (source) / grows (no MS)
500.9 outskirrers (source) / outskirries (no MS)
505.22 2d (Editorial) / 3d (no MS)
505.39 2d (Editorial) / 3d (no MS)
506.23 2d (Editorial) / 3d (no MS)

THE FAIR MAID OF PERTH

520.24 former (Editorial) / latter (MS missing)
See [Robert Douglas], *The Baronage of Scotland* (Edinburgh, 1798), 356.

521.45 Bowar (Editorial) / Bowar (MS missing)

523.18 [The following is a diplomatic (literal) transcript of the manuscript of Scott's Introduction for the Magnum (MS 911, ff. 264r–269r), which is the base text for the reading text in the present edition. It is in the hand of William Laidlaw, except where otherwise indicated.]

Introduction to the Chronicles of the Canongate Part II
[endorsed by Scott:] Second Series / Comes in at Chapter I of second Series

The second part of these chronicles was in a great measure conducted upon the same plan & by the same machinery with the first part in which Crystal Croftangry & Mrs Beaton Baliol were first introduced to the public. It was also intended that the stories which it was ⟨in⟩ designed to publish should have been short & detatched pieces of narrative of which the author conceived he possessed a sufficient number to furnish out the second part of an intertaining miscellany. But a revolution took place in the public taste about the year 1828 when a variety of annuals were published by different editors rivaling each other in the beauty of their decorations as well as in the literary merit of their contents. To some of these the author of Waverly was requested to be a contributor & it was often under circumstances wh. he did not think himself at liberty to refuse. In this way a good many of the fictions being a considerable part of the stock designed for the second part of the Chronicles of the Canongate was given or promised to these annual collections which were at first proper to Germany but now became for a short time very popular with the British public although from the expence both in art & in literature it may be supposed that few of them turned out very profitable to the undertakers.

It was therefore necessary to alter the plan of the latter part of the chronicles ↑ & ↓ in size & form to adopt them more to Waverly and its successors A part was selected of the History of Robert III comprehending historical incidends of sufficient notoriety but the details of which were so little known as to allow great freedom to be taken by the narrator in the indulgence of his own fancy.

The two principal events were the combat between the Clan Chattan & the Clan Kay or Qu ↑ h ↓ ele which Buchanan & our other historians state to have taken place upon the north Inch of Perth as Pinkerton expresses it in the following passage

[in the margin: '1396'] The north of Scotland being disturbed by continual feuds between the two highland factions of Clan Kay commanded by one Shee-beg & his relations & Clan Quhele ⟨quhele⟩ under a Christie Johnson which could be appeased by no authority nor art of the King, or Fyfe the Governor; it was at last adjusted by the Earl of Moray & Lindsay of Crawford that the dispute should be terminated by thirty men, appointed upon either side to fight in the Royal presence at Perth. Having met on the day named before the King, Governor ↑ many Nobles ↓ & a great multitude, eager to see this novelty, one of the Clan Kay felt his heart fail & escaped by swimming across the Tay, upon which a Clown who was present offered to supply his place for half a mark. A fierce battle ensued with bows battle axes swords & daggers; & ended in the defeat of Clan Kay who had only the mercenary left alive while eleven of the opponents keeped the field. The highlanders were afterwards more quiet for a few years: but it might be said upon this occasion that a public spectacle had been appointed to manifest to the nation that the Government was without power & the laws without force.

Hist. of Scotland Vol. I Page 51.

To this general account of a highly interesting & romantic incident even tradition adds little more than that either the clan of M'Intosh or that of M'Pherson, in Gaelic M'vurich represent the leading sept of the victorious confederacy, & it is uncertain even at this day which has the title to be prefered.

Another incident of deep importance at the time is also known at the present day together with some circumstances of a nature uncommonly melancholy: The fate of the unfortunate David Duke of Rothesay eldest son of Robert III who fell a victim to the ambition of his uncle Albany & his father in law Douglas seemed also a piece of real history qualified to be illustrated by fictitious narrative since ↑ while ↓ we know that he was actually starved to death in the dungeon tower of Falkland Castle we are ignorant of the exact particulars attending this catastrophy.

"The royal mandate was born by Ramorny & by another enemy of Rothsay Sir William Lindsay whose sister Euppemia had also been affianced to the Prince & rejected. From these circumstances it may be perceived that the ⟨ ? ⟩ ↑ scheme ↓ was laid & conducted with all the deep & dark art of consummate villainy. Albany receiving the order with joy resolved on its immediate enforcement & that the bearers should be ↑ the ↓ executors. Privacy was necessary & Rothsay was inveigled into Fife, upon pretence that he should take possession for the King of the castle of St. Andrews untill the appointment of ⟨a new⟩ ↑ another ↓ Bishop. When the unsuspecting Prince was riding with a small attendance between Nydie and Straburn near St. Andrews he was siezed & held a prisoner in the castle till the Governor & his Council assembled at Culross should determine the place of his confinement. The tower of Falkland was named, & thither Albany & Douglas with a strong band of followers, conducted the Prince, seated on a labouring horse & covered with a russset cloke to defend him from the falling rain. Here under the custody of John Selkirk & John Wright two assas ↑ s ↓ ins employed by Albany, the most cruel of deaths that of famine awaited the heir of the monarchy: and he was buried in a private manner at Lindoris, distant from the tombs of the Scottish Kings or those of his family; the conspirators not daring by a funereal pomp to awaken the attention & detection of the people

The awakening religious dissensions are also introduced as a key to the mysteries of the story & thus not without historical authority for in 1408 one James Resby a follower of Wiccliffe's opinions was condemned for forty articles of heresy by a clerical court in which Lawrence Lindores an inquisitor was president. He was ⟨condemned⟩ delivered to the secular arm & condemned to the stake at Perth, an incident which justifies the existance of the tenets held by the reforming Priest introduced into the novel. [catch-word: 'The ro-']

526.21 Such is the author's opinion . . . personal conviction. (MS derived: Such is the authors opinion founded perhaps on national pride of the

relative importance of the Roman & ⟨the⟩ classical stream If he should again be a blotter of paper the Editor hopes to be able to speak on *this* subject the surer language of personal conviction) / Such is the author's opinion, founded perhaps on feelings of national pride, of the relative claims of the classical river and the Scottish one. Should he ever again be a blotter of paper, he hopes to be able to speak on this subject the surer language of personal conviction. Aug. 1831.
Lockhart alters Scott's note.

527.33 Margaret (source) / Catharine (MS as Magnum)

527.40 ii (Editorial) / i (MS i)

528.2 He was sometime Governor of Berwick . . . defeated. (MS) / Sir Magnus Redman, sometime Governor of Berwick, fell in one of the battles on the Border which followed on the treason of the Earl of March, alluded to hereafter.
Lockhart rewrites Scott's note, perhaps because he has failed to decipher 'Sark', or perhaps in an attempt to correct an historical inaccuracy: see the explanatory note at 721 below.

528.13 *Skene-occle*, knife of the armpit, a species of dirk so called, used among Highlanders. (MS Knife of the armpit a species of dirk so calld used among highlanders) / *Skene-occle*, i.e. knife of the armpit—the Highlanders' stiletto.
Lockhart rewrites Scott's note.

530.36 *Horse and hattock* . . . any kind. (MS The cry of the fairies at taking their enchanted horses & hence ⟨take⟩ a token of a mounting of any kind.) / *Horse and hattock*, the well-known cry of the fairies at mounting for a moonlight expedition, came to be familiarly adopted on any occasion of mounting.
Lockhart rewrites Scott's note.

531.3 antiquarian (MS) / antiquary

531.4 Kinfauns met (proof) / Kinfauns must have met
The contribution by Morison is bound in to the interleaved copy in printed form. Several changes, rejected for the present edition, were made at a subsequent stage.

531.23 access to the best means (proof) / more leisure

531.24 for our hero and (proof) / for the hero of the tale and

531.27 edifice even in these days. (proof) / edifice.

532.8 *Thiggers* and *sorners*, sturdy beggars under various pretences. (MS Thiggers & sorners ↑ sturdy beggars ↓ under ⟨vindi⟩ various pretences) / *Thiggers* and *sorners*, i.e. sturdy beggars, the former, however, being, as the word implies, more civil than the latter.
Lockhart rewrites Scott's note.

534.2 all their parts (source) / all parts (not in MS)

536.33 FIGHTING COCKS.—This cruel amusement . . . the festival. (MS Fighting ⟨Cocks⟩ Cocks This cruel amusement was ⟨generally⟩ ↑ generally ↓ practised in Scotland ⟨up⟩ on Shrove tuesday so late as the last generation and rankd with the foot-ball the hen and pancakes as a fitting solem [end of line] solemnity of the festival) / [no text]
Scott's note was replaced by a version by Lockhart keyed to 168.7: '*Fastern's E'en*, the evening before the commencement of the fast,——*Anglicé—Shrove-tide*, the season of being shriven, or of confession and absolution, before beginning the penance of Lent. The cockfights, &c., still held at this period, are relics of the Catholic carnival that preceded the weeks of abstinence.'

542.3 on (MS) / in

545.39 Meaning, I did such a thing for my own ends, as Henry Gow fought

(MS Expressd "I did such a thing for my own as Henry Gow fought) / Meaning, I did such a thing for my own pleasure, not for your profit Lockhart misreads Scott in the process of tidying up the original MS note.

ANNE OF GEIERSTEIN

568.16 [The version of the Barante passage given in the Magnum is so full of errors that it has, exceptionally, been judged appropriate to emend by replacing it with the original. The only change that has been made is an abbreviation of the final paragraph, as introduced by the Magnum, presumably for dramatic effect. The substitution has resulted in a number of Editorial changes to the competent translation in the Magnum, as noted in the entries below.]
EEWN **reading:** "De toutes parts . . . pp. 189–96. (source)
Magnum reading: "De toutes parts on etait accourus par milliers pour assister au proces de ce cruel gouverneur, tant la haine etait grande contre lui. De sa prison, il entendait retentir sur le pont le pas des chevaux, et s'enquerait a son geôlier de ceux qui arrivaient: soit pour être ses juges, soit pour être témoins de son supplice. Parfois le geôlier repondait, 'Ce sont des etrangers; je ne les connais pas.' 'Ne sont—ce pas,' disait le prisonnier, 'des gens assez mal vêtus, de haute taille, de forte apparence, montés sur des chevaux aux courtes oreilles?' et si le geôlier repondait: 'Oui,'—' Ah ce sont les Suisses,' s'écriait Hagenbach. 'Mon Dieu, ayez pitie de moi !' et il se rappelait toutes les insultes qu'il leur avait faites, toutes ses insolences envers eux. Il pensait, mais trop tard, que c'était leur alliance avec la maison d'Antriche qui etait cause de sa perte. Le 4 Mai 1474, après avoir èté mis a la question, it fut, a la diligence d'Hermann d'Eptingen, gouverneur pour l'archiduc, amené devant ses juges, sur la place publique de Brisach. Sa contenance était ferme et d'un homme qui ne craint pas la mort. Henri Iselin de Bâle porta la parole au nom d'Hermann d'Eptingen, agissant pour le seigneur du pays. Il parla à peu près en ces termes: Pierre de Hagenbach, chevalier, maitre d'hôtel de Monseigneur le Duc de Bourgogne, et son gouverneur dans le pays de Sératte et Haute-Alsace, aurait dû respecter les privileges reservés par l'acte d'engagement; mais il n'a pas moins frotte aux pieds les lois de Dieu et des hommes, que les droits jurés et garantis au pays. Il a fait mettre à mort sans jugement quatre honnêtes bourgeois de Sératte; il a depouillé la ville de Brisach de sa juridiction, et y a établi juges et consuls de son choix; il a rompu et dispersé les communautés de la bourgeoisie et des mètiers; il a levè des impôts par sa seule volonté; il a, contre toutes les lois, logè chez les habitans des gens de guerre—Lombards, Français, Picards, ou Flamands; et a favorisê leur disordres et pillages. Il leur a même commande d'égorger leurs hôtes durant la nuit, et avait fait préparer, pour y'embarquer les femmes et les enfans, des batteaux qui devaient être submergés dans le Rhin. Enfin, lors même qu'il rejetterait de telles cruantes sur les ordres qu'il a reçus, comment pourrait il s'excuser d'avoir fait violence et outrage a l'honneur de tant de filles et femmes, et même de saintes religieuses?" [new paragraph] "D'autres accusations furent portèes dans les interrogatoires; et des temoins attesterent les violences faites aux gens de Mulhausen et aux Marchands de Bâle. [new paragraph] "Pour suivre toutes les formes de la justïce, on avait donnè un avocat à l'accusè. 'Messire Pierre de Hagenbach, dit-il, ne reconnaît d'autre

juge et d'autre seigneur que Monseigneur le Duc de Bourgogne, dont il avait commission, et recevait les commandemens. Il n'avait nul droit de contrôler les ordres qu'il etait chargé d'exécuter; et son devoir etait d'obéir. Ne sait-on pas quelle soumission les gens de guerre doivent a leur seigneur et maitre? Croit-on que le landvogt de Monseigneur le Duc eût à lui remontrer et à lui resister? Et monseigneur n'a'til pas ensuite, par sa présence, confirmé et ratifiè tout ce qui avait ètè fait en son nom? Si des impôts ont ètè demandés, c'est qu'il avait besoin d'argent. Pour les recueillir, il a bien fallu punir ceux qui se refusaient à payer. C'est ce que Monseigneur le Duc, et même l'empereur, quand ils sont venus, ont reconnu nécessaire. Le logement des gens de guerre ètait aussi la suite des ordres du Duc. Quant à la juridiction de Brisach; le landvogt pouvait-it souffrir cette resistance? Enfin dans une affaire si grave, où il y va de la vie, convient-il de produire comme un veritable grief, le dernier dont a parlé l'accusateur? Parmi ceux qui écoutent, y en a-t-il un seul qui puisse se vanter de ne pas avoir saisi les occasions de se divertir? N'est-il pas clair que Messire de Hagenbach a seulement profité de la bonne volontè de quelques femmes ou filles; ou, pour mettre les choses au pis, qu'il n'a exercè d'autre contrainte envers elles qu'au moyen de son bon argent?' [new paragraph] "Les juges siègérent long temps sur leur tribunal. Douze heures entières passérent sans que l'affaire fût terminée. Le Sire de Hagenbach, toujours ferme et calme, n'allégua d'autres défenses, d'autres excuses, que celles qu'il avait donné déjà sous la torture—les ordres et la volonté de son seigneur, qui etait son seul juge, et le seul qui pût lui demander compte. [new paragraph] "Enfin, à sept heures du soir, à la clarté des flambeaux, les juges, après avoir déclaré qu'à eux appartenait le droit de prononcer sur les crimes imputés au landvogt, le firent rappeler; et rendirent leur sentence qui le condamna à mort. Il ne s'èmut pas advantage; et demanda pour toute grace d'avoir seulement la tête tranchée. Huit bourreaux des diverses villes se presentérent pour exécuter l'arrêt. Celui de Colmar, qui passait pour le plus adroit, fut preferé. Avant de le conduire à l'èchafaud, les seize chevaliers qui faisaient partie des juges requirent que Messire de Hagenbach fût dégradé de sa dignité de chevalier et de tous ses honneurs. Pour lors s'avança Gaspard Hurter, héraut de l'empereur; et il dit: 'Pierre de Hagenbach, il me deplaît grandement que vous ayez si mal employé votre vi emortelle: de sorte qu'il convient que vous perddiez non-seulement la dignité et ordre de chevalerie, mais aussi la vie. Votre devoir était de rendre la justice, de proteger la veuve et l'orphelin; de respecter les femmes et les filles, d'honorer les saintes prêtres; de vous apposer a toute injuste violence; et, au contraire, vous avez commis tout ce que vous deviez empêcher. Ayant ainsi forfait au noble ordre de chevalerie, et aux sermens que vous aviez jurés, les chevaliers ici preséns m'ont enjoint de vous en ôter les insignes. Ne les voyant pas sur vous en ce moment, je vous proclame indigne chevalier de Saint George, au nom et à l'honneur duquel ou vous avait autrefois honoré de l'ordre de chevalerie.' Puis s'avança Hermann d'Eptingen: 'Puis qu'on vient de te dégrader de chevalerie, je te depouille de ton collier, chaîne d'or, anneau, poignard, eperon, gantelet.' Il les lui prit et lui en frappa le visage, et ajouta: 'Chevaliers, et vous qui desirez le devenir, j'espére que cette punition publique vous servira d'exemple, et que vous vivrez dans la crainte de Dieu, noblement et vaillamment, selon la dignité de la chevalerie et l'honneur de votre nom.' Enfin, le prevôt d'Einsilheim et marechal de cette commission de juges, se leva, et s'adressant au bourreau lui dit: 'Faites selon la justice.' [new paragraph] "Tous les juges monterent à cheval ainsi qu' Hermann d'Eptingen. Au milieu d'eux marchait Pierre de Hagenbach, entre deux prêtres. C'etait pendant la nuit. Des torches exclairaient la marche; une foule immense se pressait autour de ce triste cortège. Le condamné s'entretenait avec son confesseur d'un air pieux et recueilli, mais ferme; se recommandant aussi aux prières de tous ceux qui l'entouraient. Arrive dans une prairie devant la porte de la ville, il monta sur l'echaffand d'un pas assuré; puis elevant la voix;— [new paragraph] "'Je n'ai pas peur de la mort,' dit-il; 'encore que je ne l'attendisse pas de cette sorte, mais bien les armes a la main; que je plains c'est tout le sang que le mien fera couler. Monseigneur ne laissera point ce jour sans vengeance pour moi. Je ne regrette ni ma vie, ni mon corps. J'etais homme—priez pour moi.' Il s'entretint encore un instant avec son confesseur, presenta la tête et reçut le coup."— M. DE BARANTE, tom. x. p. 197.

571.9 the bridge and the vaults of the gate re-echo (Editorial) / the bridge re-echo
571.26 the lord and the country (Editorial) / the lord of the country
571.27 terms:— [new paragraph] "'Peter (Editorial) / terms:—'Peter
571.29 Ferette (Editorial) / Seratte
571.33 Thann (Editorial) / Seratte
572.2 maidens or women (Editorial) / women and maidens
572.23 quarter? [new paragraph] "'To conclude (Editorial) / quarter? To conclude
572.36 explanation. [new paragraph] "At length (Editorial) / explanation. At length
573.19 knighthood.' [new paragraph] "Then (Editorial) / knighthood.' Then
573.27 last Thomas Schulz, the provost (Editorial) / last the provost
574.1 pp. 189–96 (Editorial) / p. 197
574.5 sei (source) / see

CASTLE DANGEROUS

594.13 for (source) / or (no ms)
597.12 hart (source) / part (no ms)
600.16 462 (Editorial) / 460 (no ms)
601.20 7–62 (Editorial) / 10–60 (no ms)

MY AUNT MARGARET'S MIRROR

There are no emendations to this text.

THE TAPESTRIED CHAMBER

607.23 EEWN **reading:** This, as well as the preceding tale . . . that she did so. MS **reading:** The Tapestried Chamber or The Lady in the Sack [new paragraph] This as well as the proceeding tale is one of those stories which served to amuse society under a certain impression of feeling & moods of Mind which visit almost all in their turn. The original teller of the story was to me at least was the celebrated Miss Seward who among other excellencies possessed that delightfull talent which enables thosse who have it to read or recite with the greatest possible effect & upon whom it is needless to make any remark saving that she did so.

Magnum reading: This is another little story, from the Keepsake of 1828. It was told to me many years ago, by the late Miss Anna Seward, who, among other accomplishments that rendered her an amusing inmate in a country house, had that of recounting narratives of this sort with very considerable effect; much greater, indeed, than any one would be apt to guess from the style of her written performances. There are hours and moods when most people are not displeased to listen to such things; and I have heard some of the greatest and wisest of my contemporaries take their share in telling them. [new line] *August, 1831.*

THE DEATH OF THE LAIRD'S JOCK

607.32 EEWN **reading:** The last story . . . adapted to painting.
MS **reading:** The last story which ⟨it⟩ ↑ the Keepsake ↓ regards i⟨.⟩s a circumstance of Scottish antiquities preserved on the borders of both Countries. It was natural that not unacquainted with ⟨those⟩ the Circumstances I should endeavour to find some ⟨one⟩ ↑ story ↓ which might be peculiarly adapted to Poetry.
Magnum reading: The manner in which this trifle was introduced at the time to Mr F. M. Reynolds, editor of The Keepsake of 1828, leaves no occasion for a preface. [This sentence, in square brackets, is followed by the date on a new line] *August, 1831.*

END-OF-LINE HYPHENS

All end-of-line hyphens in the whole of the text of the present volume are soft unless included in the list below. The hyphens listed are hard and should be retained when quoting.

2.17	Dun-Dornadilla
4.28	death-song
29.12	Commander-in-chief
29.36	signal-word
36.38	thought-patterns
50.42	back-woodsmen
57.28	Bridge-End
62.28	presence-chamber
64.19	Border-meeting
78.12	ill-managed
85.44	hunting-mass
100.7	brother-in-law
105.12	re-entered
111.8	romance-writer
130.29	Sword-Dance
147.21	sword-dance
150.18	right-hand
155.37	pigeon-house
161.16	source-indicating
161.25	first-edition
162.8	title-page
172.35	decoy-duck
189.13	tilt-yard
196.9	horse-racing
197.17	first-edition
197.30	title-page
205.19	well-remembered
208.4	over-estimated
228.1	fair-haired
232.27	Deputy-Governour
236.7	mansion-house
237.38	Hango-hill
251.40	Kirk-Merlugh
262.5	Somerset-house
262.12	Attorney-General
269.2	moss-covered
271.18	turkey-cock
271.43	sixty-third
274.11	Rye-House
274.21	Club-House
278.19	court-martial
285.6	a-year
305.5	*in-folio*
306.28	Petit-Jean
314.32	*Schwarz-reiters*
322.37	coat-armour
334.4	watering-place
337.22	building-leases
338.35	non-appearance
355.24	free-will
356.20	non-resistance
359.23	Westminster-Hall
361.23	Chap-Book
367.26	Forty-Five
381.26	mansion-house
383.13	well-known
384.24	sixty-three
386.36	*cap-à-piè*
417.15	warming-pan
417.31	rabbit-stealers
428.34	day-dreams
430.38	brew-house
431.39	withdrawing-room
432.31	withdrawing-room
437.21	shoulder-blade
437.25	bed-clothes
453.35	running-title
462.7	quasi-editorial
463.24	Wallace-Craigie
469.14	Drury-Lane
481.40	moderate-sized
490.38	Fast-Castle
492.38	north-western
493.38	Commander-in-chief
503.18	self-devotion
509.14	herdsman-lover
523.11	aide-de-camps
537.36	steel-gloves
542.34	Stafford-Sutherland
543.40	*red-hand*
559.15	König-stuhl
562.35	serving-day
567.9	men-at-arms
578.7	self-love
592.26	re-conquests

EXPLANATORY NOTES

In these notes a comprehensive attempt is made to identify Scott's sources, and all quotations, references, historical events, and historical personages, to explain proverbs, and to translate difficult or obscure language in what he himself has written. However, the Magnum includes numerous extracts from a wide range of sources, some of them of considerable length; no attempt has been made to provide comprehensive explanatory notes on these quoted passages. When a quotation has not been recognised this is stated: any new information from readers will be welcomed. Books in the Abbotsford Library are identified by reference to the appropriate page of the *Catalogue of the Library at Abbotsford*. Biblical References are to the Authorised Version. Plays by Shakespeare are cited without authorial ascription, and references are to *William Shakespeare: The Complete Works*, edited by Peter Alexander (London and Glasgow, 1951, frequently reprinted).

The following publications are distinguished by abbreviations, or are given without the names of their authors:

Barante [A. G. P. Brugière, Baron] de Barante, *Histoire des Ducs de Bourgogne de la Maison de Valois, 1364–1477*, 3rd edn, 13 vols (Paris, 1825–26: the second part of Vol. 11 and Vols 12 and 13 are designated as 4th edn).

Barbour John Barbour, *The Bruce*, ed. A. A. M. Duncan (Edinburgh, 1997).

Biographia Scoticana [John Howie of Lochgoin], *Biographia Scoticana; or, an Historical Account of the Lives and Memorable transactions, of the Most Eminent Scots Worthies* (Leith, 1816; originally published 1775): *CLA*, 71.

Child *The English and Scottish Popular Ballads*, ed. Francis James Child, 5 vols (Boston and New York).

CLA [J. G. Cochrane], *Catalogue of the Library at Abbotsford* (Edinburgh, 1838).

Comines Philippe de Comines, *Mémoires* [indicating book and chapter], in Petitot (see below), Vols 11–13.

Don Quixote Miguel de Cervantes, *The History of the Ingenious Gentleman, Don Quixote of La Mancha*, tr. Motteux, [rev. J. G. Lockhart], 5 vols (Edinburgh, 1822): *CLA*, 85.

EEWN *The Edinburgh Edition of the Waverley Novels*, 30 vols (Edinburgh, 1993–2012).

Holinshed *Holinshed's Chronicles of England, Scotland, and Ireland*, 6 vols (London, 1807–08): *CLA*, 29.

ISet The Interleaved Set of the Waverley Novels, National Library of Scotland MSS 23001–41.

Journal *The Journal of Sir Walter Scott*, ed. W. E. K. Anderson (Oxford, 1972).

Kennet [John Hughes and White Kennet], *A Complete History of England*, 3 vols (London, 1706): *CLA*, 249.

Letters *The Letters of Sir Walter Scott*, ed. H. J. C. Grierson and others, 12 vols (London, 1932–37).

Lockhart J. G. Lockhart, *Memoirs of the Life of Sir Walter Scott, Bart.*, 7 vols (Edinburgh, 1837–38).

MAG Peter Garside and Ruth M. McAdams, *Illustrating Scott: A Database of Printed Illustrations to the Waverley Novels, 1814–1901* ⟨http://illustratingscott.lib.ed.ac.uk⟩.

Magnum Walter Scott, *Waverley Novels*, 48 vols (Edinburgh, 1829–33).

Minstrelsy Walter Scott, *Minstrelsy of the Scottish Border*, ed. T. F. Henderson, 4 vols (Edinburgh, 1902).

ODEP *The Oxford Dictionary of English Proverbs*, 3rd edn, rev. F. P. Wilson (Oxford, 1970).

ODNB *The Oxford Dictionary of National Biography*, ed. H. C. G. Matthew and Brian Harrison (Oxford, 2004); online edn, ed. Lawrence Goldman (2009).

OED *The Oxford English Dictionary*, 2nd edn, 20 vols (Oxford, 1989).

Palgrave Francis Palgrave, *The Rise and Progress of the English Commonwealth* (London, 1832).

Petitot [Claude Bernard] Petitot, *Collection complète des mémoires relatifs a l'histoire de France*, first series, 52 vols (Paris, 1819–26): *CLA*, 49.

Prose Works *The Prose Works of Sir Walter Scott, Bart.*, 28 vols (Edinburgh, 1834–36).

Ramsay *A Collection of Scots Proverbs* (1737), in *The Works of Allan Ramsay*, 6 vols (Edinburgh and London, [1945]–1974), Vol. 5, ed. Alexander M. Kinghorn and Alexander Law, 59–133.

Ray J[ohn] Ray, *A Compleat Collection of English Proverbs*, 3rd edn (London, 1737): *CLA*, 169.

Secret History *Secret History of the Court of James the First*, [ed. Walter Scott], 2 vols (Edinburgh, 1811).

Somers' Tracts *A Collection of Scarce and Valuable Tracts . . .*, 2nd edn, ed. Walter Scott, 13 vols (London, 1809–15).

TB William B. Todd and Ann Bowden, *Sir Walter Scott: A Bibliographical History 1796–1832* (New Castle, Delaware, 1998).

Waldron (1731) George Waldron, 'A Description of the Isle of Man . . .', in *The Compleat Works, in Verse and Prose, of George Waldron*, 2 parts, [ed. Theodosia Waldron] ([London], 1731), 2.[91]–191: *CLA*, 261.

Weber *Tales of the East*, ed. Henry Weber, 3 vols (Edinburgh, 1812): *CLA*, 43.

Wyntoun *De Orygynale Cronykil of Scotland, be Androw of Wyntoun*, ed. David Macpherson, 2 vols (London, 1795): *CLA*, 8. The references to Macpherson's edition are to volume and page; they are followed by book and line numbers, and chapter numbers from the edition by F. J. Amours, 6 vols (Edinburgh and London, 1903–14).

IVANHOE

10.4 L'Enfant Gâté *French* the spoilt child.

10.15–17 "Reverse the spell," . . . shown see Thomas Parnell, 'A Fairy Tale in the Ancient English Style' (1722), lines 97–99.

10.18 professor practitioner.

11.14 Men bless their stars and call it luxury see Joseph Addison, *Cato* (1713), 1.4.71.

11.27–28 wonder that they please no more see Samuel Johnson, *The Vanity of Human Wishes* (1749), line 264.

11.34–35 the Scottish Novels, as they were then exclusively termed for examples of this nomenclature see [John Hamilton Reynolds], *The Press, or Literary Chit-chat* (London, 1822), 130, and Isaac Pocock, *Nigel; or, The Crown Jewels* (London, 1823), p. iii.

11.36–42 It was his purpose . . . hereafter mentioned see EEWN 8, 409–10.

12.7–14 The idea . . . race of nobles see [John Logan], *Runnamede, A Tragedy* (London, 1783). The Saxons and Normans enter as indicated at the outset of the play, which was performed in Edinburgh in 1784. Logan (1748–88) is called 'unfortunate' because he was forced to demit his charge as an Edinburgh minister on account of personal failings and his theatrical activity.

12.27 what is called Historical Romance the first occurrence of the term recorded by *OED* is in the title of [Thomas Leland], *Longsword, Earl of Salisbury. An Historical Romance*, 2 vols (London, 1762). Its general currency is suggested by Jane Austen's use in a letter of 1 April 1816, and Scott himself employed it, at Archibald Constable's suggestion (MS 677, f. 39r: 15 August 1821), for the collected series *Historical Romances* including *Ivanhoe*, *The Monastery*, *The Abbot*, and *Kenilworth*.

12.34–36 a species of continuation . . . stranger for a full account of the spurious Fourth Series of *Tales of my Landlord* by William Fearman see EEWN 9, 360–62.

12.40–13.2 After a considerable portion . . . the Author of Waverley see EEWN 8, 409–10.

13.3–6 of opinion with Dr Wheeler . . . their favour see Maria Edgeworth, 'Manœuvring', *Tales of Fashionable Life*, 6 vols (London, 1809–1812), 3 (1809), 95. Dr Wheeler says 'sham upon sham is too much for any man'.

13.25–27 the Eastern tale-teller . . . Bagdad see 'The Robber Caliph; or, the Adventures of Haroun Alraschid with the Princess of Persia and the beautiful Zutulbe', in Weber, 1.475–96.

13.28–30 Scottish tradition . . . the Goodman of Ballengeigh the tradition is central in *The Lady of the Lake* (1810): see *Poetical Works*, 8.350–53. 'A steep path leading to the town [Stirling], and now carried round the castle, was called *Balloch-geich*. James V., who sometimes travelled through the country in disguise, when questioned who he was, always answered, "the goodman of Ballochgeich."': James Playfair, *A Geographical and Statistical Description of Scotland*, 2 vols (Edinburgh, 1819), 1.332.

13.32–35 There must have been a Norman original . . . charcoal-man *The Tale of Rauf Coilʒear* is the first item in the unpaginated *Select Remains of the Ancient Popular Poetry of Scotland*, [ed. David Laing] (Edinburgh, 1822): *CLA*, 6. In his introduction Laing conjectures that 'in common with the greater number of the ancient tales and romance in our vernacular language, [it] may possibly be traced to some *Norman* original', though no such original has been located.

13.38–14.1 The poem of John the Reeve . . . such an incident see Thomas Percy, *Reliques of Ancient English Poetry*, 4th edn, 3 vols (London, 1794), 3.179: *CLA*, 172.

13.41–42 Dr Irvine of the Advocates' Library David Irving (1778–1860) was Librarian of the Faculty of Advocates 1820–48.

14.1–2 the King and the Tanner of Tamworth 'K. Edward IV. and the Tanner of Tamworth', included in Percy, 2.83–92 (Child, 273).

14.2 the King and the Miller of Mansfield included in Percy, 3.179–89 (Child, 273, Appendix III).

14.3 others on the same topic e.g. 'King Edward III and the Shepherd' (see note to 16.30–31 below). For other examples see Child, 5.73–74.

14.3–9 the peculiar tale . . . the British Bibliographer see Sir Egerton Brydges and Joseph Haslewood, *The British Bibliographer*, 4 (1814), 81–95.

14.9–14 From thence it has been transferred . . . the Hermite 'The Kyng and the Hermyt' is included in *Ancient Metrical Tales*, ed. Charles Henry Hartshorne (London, 1829), 293–315: *CLA*, 105. Hartshorne's citation of *The British Bibliographer* as his source is on p. xxiv, and he reproduces its text exactly. In the quotations that follow (found at 300–05) Scott modernises the spelling and introduces several verbal changes: 'were' (Magnum 'wert') for 'wonys'; 'eat never' for 'ete non'; 'will lap' for 'schall lape'; and 'softly to lye' for 'softly to lyke'.

14.18–19 from his temper . . . Edward IV. Edward IV's 'preferred mode of kingship was probably the careless affability he showed to overawed visitors to his court' (*ODNB*).

14.27–29 Saint Julian . . . due homage Julian the Hospitaller, a probably mythical saint, is patron of innkeepers, boatmen, and travellers.

15.30–31 the forest laws see note to 18.33–39 below.

15.45–46 good fellow the poem has '"Thou semys a felow," seyd the frere' (305).

16.2 white bread fine white bread as opposed to the coarse brown variety usual in medieval times.

16.11–15 fustian words . . . pantnere the 'fustian words' (found in *Ancient Metrical Tales*, ed. Charles Henry Hartshorne (London, 1829), 308–09: *CLA*, 105) are gibberish. The Dryburgh Edition suggests that *fusty bandias* means 'thirsty comrades', and *strike pantnere* 'cut open the wine-skin; broach the cask'. But no support has been found for these or any other meanings. Compare 'Passelodion' and 'Berafriend' at 16.41 (the poem has 'passilodion' and 'berafrynde').

16.30–31 In Mr Hartshorne's collection . . . King Edward and the Shepherd 'A Tale of King Edward and the Shepherd': Hartshorne (see previous note), 35–80.

16.38–17.1 to wish with Falstaff . . . to be had see *1 Henry IV*, 1.2.80–81.

16.43 I warrant . . . the glass see the chorus of Richard Brinsley Sheridan's song 'Here's to the maiden of Bashful fifteen': *The School for Scandal* (1779), 3.3 (*The Dramatic Works of Richard Brinsley Sheridan*, ed. Cecil Price, 2 vols (Oxford, 1973), 1.398).

17.1–9 On such an occasion . . . escape so there are various versions and interpretations of this jingle. Scott's conjecture involves a contemporary of Edward, Prince of Wales (1330–76), a member of the Hampden family who had owned land in Buckinghamshire since before the Norman Conquest (but not Wing or Ivinghoe in that county, or Tring in Hertfordshire). The most famous Hampden was John (1595–1643), a prominent opponent of Charles I.

17.33–34 a roll of Norman warriors . . . Front-de-Bœuf 'front de buf' appears in the roll in MS Adv. 19.2.1 (The Auchinleck Manuscript), ff. 105v–107r (106r).

17.36 the freedom of the Rules the liberty granted to a Scottish advocate to plead at the English bar.

18.22–23 The motto . . . taken leave Scott had indicated his retirement in the Advertisement to *The Antiquary* (EEWN 3, [3].29–33). In the Advertisement to *Rob Roy* he apologises for failing to keep that resolution, not mentioning the intervening first series of *Tales of My Landlord*, which had been published by William Blackwood and John Murray rather than Constable and Longman (EEWN 5, 3.1–17 and 482 (note to 1.3–4)). He again retired 'from the field' at the end of the third series (EEWN 7b, 183.18–19).

18.28–30 Mr Skene of Rubislaw . . . in these novels James Skene of Rubislaw, Aberdeen (1775–1864), a long-standing friend of Scott, published *A Series of Sketches of the Existing Localities Alluded to in the Waverley Novels. Etched from Original Drawings* (Edinburgh, 1829): *CLA*, 339.

18.33–39 A most sensible grievance . . . passion for hunting the New Forest in Hampshire (only partly covered by trees) was set apart as a hunting-ground by William the Conqueror in 1079. Although restrictions on activities in royal hunting areas had been in force in the late Anglo-Saxon period, William imported a much more rigorous Continental system which made life difficult for local inhabitants.

19.3–8 Amongst the ruins . . . his chase see William Stewart Rose, 'The Red King', published as an appendix to his translation of Pierre Jean-Baptiste Legrand d'Aussy's *Partenopex de Blois* (London, 1807), [175]–217 (189): *CLA*, 185. Scott combines the first two lines of a stanza with the last four of its predecessor. The first two lines are very different in the original: 'Among the fragments of the church,/ A raven there had found a perch,—'.

19.11–20 The Charter of the Forest . . . Richard Thomson see *An Historical Essay on the Magna Charta of King John*, ed. Richard Thomson (London, 1829), 331: *CLA*, 124. Scott's paraphrase comes close to quotation. The reference is to the Forest Charter of Henry III (1217), which somewhat reduced the severity of the penalties introduced by William the Conqueror (reigned 1066–87) and further intensified by William Rufus (1087–1100). Thomson's book is ornamented with engraved borders and vignettes on every page.

19.25–27 a set of sable functionaries . . . Castle Spectre M. G. Lewis, *The Castle Spectre* (London, 1798), especially 35: *CLA*, 213.

20.1–7 John of Rampayne . . . the prisoner see *Ancient Engleish Metrical Romancës*, ed. Joseph Ritson, 3 vols (London, 1802), 1.clxxxvii–clxxxix: *CLA*, 174.

20.15–16 consult Dame Juliana Berners' book on the subject see *The Book containing the Treatises of Hawking; Hunting; Coat-Armour; Fishing; and Blasing of Arms* (The Book of St Alban's), [ed. Joseph Haselwood] (London, 1810), *passim*: *CLA*, 208.

20.16–18 The origin of this science . . . Ysolte see EEWN 8, 521 (note to 49.9). In Arthurian romance Ysolte (Isolde) was the wife of King Mark of Cornwall and lover of Tristrem (Tristan).

20.21–23 This species of masquerade . . . heraldry for this explanation of the origins of heraldic supporters see the entry on 'supporters' in the 'Glossary of the several terms used in the science of heraldry' provided by Thomas Robson, *The British Herald*, 3 vols (Sunderland, 1830), Vol. 3 (unpaginated): *CLA*, 265. It is now thought that supporters, usually animal figures, were introduced to fill up the vacant spaces between the shield and its circular setting.

20.33–36 All readers . . . Fountain's Abbey see 'Robin Hood and the Curtall Fryer' (Child, 123), in *Robin Hood: a Collection of all the Ancient Poems, Songs, and Ballads, now extant, relative to that celebrated English outlaw* . . ., [ed. Joseph Ritson], 2 vols (London, 1795), 2.[58]–65: *CLA*, 174. Ritson notes ([58]): 'In fact, he is no fryer at all, but a monk of Fountains abbey [in Yorkshire], which was of the Cistercian order'.

21.4 the joyous science minstrelsy (*Provençal* gai saber).

21.40–41 For more particulars . . . referred to see Francis Drake, *Eboracum; or, The History and Antiquities of the City of York* . . . (London, 1736), 83–84.

21.41–43 The author's mistake . . . Bossal House Robert Belt pointed out the error in a letter of 18 March 1828 (MS 3906, ff. 149–50). Scott replied from Abbotsford on 2 April: 'I am honoured with your interesting letter pointing out an anachronism in Ivanhoe for which I thank you kindly and will correct it on the first opportunity I do acknowledge I am ap[t] to treat dame History with too little ceremony, and when she will not walk my way I sometimes drag her whether she will or no, at the same time in the present and other cases in the present and other cases I have blundered from a lazy way of trusting to a good memory instead of correcting it by referring to the Chronicle. There was some apology for that in Ivanhoe for all the while [I] was busying with the two last volumes I was visited from time to time with such dreadful cramps in the stomach that no one thought I could have survived. In describing the scene in the castle (I dictated to a friend) I fainted twice, and then to it again. As I shall be in town in the course of next week I will study for an opportunity of thanking you in person, meantime I am your obliged humble Servant Walter Scott' (copy of the original in the possession of Belt's daughter: Bodleian Library, Oxford, MS Eng Lett B 16, f. 56r). Scott did indeed meet Belt in London on 2 May (*Journal*, 466–67). On 29 January 1829 he informed him that 'I have made due palinode for my error about the *locus* of the Danish battle in a new edition of Ivanhoe which will shortly appear and I hope you will find Stamford duly replaced in its honour': see Cedric C. Brown, 'Sir Walter Scott, Robert Belt, and *Ivanhoe*', *Scottish Literary Journal*, 8:2 (December 1981), 38–43 (41).

22.3–5 This horrid species of torture . . . concealed wealth Guatimozin (*c.* 1495–1522), the last Aztec emperor, was tortured by being placed on a grate over a bed of live coals.

22.8–10 after the fall of the Catholic Church . . . by law in 1560 the Scottish Parliament ended papal control of the Church in Scotland and established a new Church, Calvinist in doctrine and Presbyterian in governance. These changes were ratified by the Crown in 1572.

22.17–18 Lord James Stewart, the Prior of St Andrews James Stewart (1532–1570), created Earl of Moray in 1562, was an illegitimate son of James V King of Scots. He derived his income from his position as Commendator of the Priory of St Andrews, to which he was appointed in 1538.

22.35–23.5 Bannatyne . . . the national poor Richard Bannatyne (d. 1605) was secretary to the leading Scottish religious reformer John Knox (*c.* 1514–1572). The Earl of Cassilis was Gilbert Kennedy (*c.* 1541–1576), who succeeded as 4th Earl in 1558. A Catholic until 1566, he continued to support Mary Queen of Scots after her exile to England in 1568 rather than the young James VI who had been crowned the previous year. The Reformers hoped to create from the existing Church revenues a national endowment for the support of the ministry, education, and poor relief, but the vested interests of the commendators enjoying the revenues of the old ecclesiastical foundations proved insuperable and they retained their incomes.

23.11–27.10 The Earl of Cassilis' Tyranny . . . Amen. Amen. see Richard Bannatyne, *Journal of the Transactions in Scotland, during the Contest between the Adherents of Queen Mary, and those of her Son, 1570, 1571, 1572, 1573*, [ed. J. G. Dalyell] (Edinburgh, 1806), 55–59, 65–67 (*CLA*, 19). The transcription, in an unidentified hand, modernises most of the orthography and a few of the words of the original, and the process has been continued after the copying process. Cassilis's torturing of Allan Stewart occurred in 1570. Dunure castle is on the Ayrshire coast 10km S of Ayr: it was ruined by the end of the 17th century.

26.5–6 the celebrated George Buchanan . . . the same Abbacy Buchanan (1506–82)—poet, historian, and administrator—was granted the temporalities of Crossraguel Abbey in 1564.

27.22–25 it appears by some papers in my possession . . . confes-

sion the papers in question have not been identified. A *country keeper* was an official charged with apprehending delinquents in a particular district.

27.26–28 The author . . . metal upon metal see the anonymous review by Nassau Senior in *The Quarterly Review*, 26 (October 1821), 109–48 (135).

27.32–34 the Goddess of Armoiries . . . presides over *armoiries* is French for 'coats of arms'. In Greek mythology Pallas Athene, daughter of Zeus, was born fully armed.

27.37–40 the arms, which were assumed . . . metal upon metal Godefroy (*c.* 1060–1100) was the second son of Count Eustache of Boulogne (Boulogne-sur-mer) and may have been born in that town. He became Lord of Bouillon (in modern Belgium) in 1076 and is usually known as Godefroy de Bouillon (Godfrey of Bouillon). In 1099 he led the taking of Jerusalem from the Islamic forces, ending the First Crusade, and until his death the following year at the siege of Acre was the first head of the Kingdom of Jerusalem. His coat of arms consists of a large cross with crutch-shaped terminations (*counter-potent*), with a small version in each of the angular spaces. These are gold (*or*) and are, in defiance of the usual rule of heraldry, placed on another metal background (*argent*, silver).

27.40–28.12 The heralds . . . Second Edition see John Ferne, *The Blazon of Gentrie* (London, 1586: *CLA*, 24), 238–39, and Alexander Nisbet, *A System of Heraldry*, 2nd edn, 2 vols (Edinburgh, 1804: *CLA*, 11), 1.113, where the Latin term *arma inquirenda*, meaning 'doubtful or problematic arms', is employed.

28.13–19 The author has some idea . . . the Grand Cyrus in Pt 2, Bk 2 (separately paginated) of Madeleine de Scudéry's *Artamenes, or The Grand Cyrus*, trans. F. G., 2 vols (London, 1653–54), the King of Assyria, assuming the name Philidaspes, kidnaps the fair Mandana; when her lover Artamenes besieges Babylon the king sneaks her out of the city, dressing his retinue in white for camouflage against the snow (1.130–31). Scott conflates this escape with Philidaspes's earlier appearance to Mandana covered in blood from the battlefield, with his plume shorn and his armour hacked (1.123). The conflagration occurs in yet another episode (1.135–36). (Adapted from *Ivanhoe*, ed. Ian Duncan (Oxford, 1996), 517)

28.25–26 Stern to inflict . . . in death see 'To A. S. Cottle, from Robert Southey', in *Icelandic Poetry, or The Edda of Saemund*, trans. A. S. Cottle (Bristol, 1797), xxxiv. The Southey reads 'That laugh'd in death'; 'who smiled in death' comes from James Thomson, *Summer*, edition of 1746, line 1493, in *The Seasons*, ed. James Sambrook (Oxford, 1981).

28.37–29.6 The interchange . . . Cœur-de-Lion see *Richard Cœur de Lyon* in *Specimens of Early English Metrical Romances*, ed. George Ellis, 3 vols (London, 1805), 2.[172, misnumbered 93]–279: *CLA*, 105. The incident occurs at 193–94. The term *fancy* refers to prize-fighting. In his edition of *Ivanhoe* (Oxford, 1996) Ian Duncan notes (517–18) that in 'A Lytell Geste of Robyn Hode' Robin exchanges buffets with the King, who is disguised as an abbot, and when he recognises him kneels and swears allegiance: see *Robin Hood: a Collection of all the Ancient Poems, Songs, and Ballads, now extant, relative to that celebrated English outlaw . . .*, [ed. Joseph Ritson], 2 vols (London, 1795), 1.[1]–80, The seventh fytte (63–73): *CLA*, 174.

29.16 Patrico hedge-priest; uneducated, vagabond priest.

29.25 the fighting parson . . . Sir John Oldcastle Sir John the parson of Wrotham, who was given to carrying out robberies on Newmarket Heath, features prominently and belligerently in *The first part Of the true and honorable historie, of the life of Sir John Old-castle, the good Lord Cobham* (London, 1600).

29.27–33 There exists a monition . . . for the occasion the 'monition' has not been located.

29.34–38 In the ordinances . . . the Grand Master's mouth see EEWN 8, 562 (note to 305.36): the motto does not appear elsewhere in the Templars' Rule.
29.43–30.3 From the ballads . . . not distinctly told see EEWN 8, 534 (note to 121.20).
30.5–12 When I last saw . . . transient view of Coningsburgh see EEWN 8, 573 (note to 368.16).
30.20–21 Pennant . . . Glenelg see Thomas Pennant, *A Tour in Scotland, and Voyage to the Hebrides; MDCCLXXII*, 2 parts (London, 1790), 1.394: *CLA*, 4. At the end of his description of Glenelg (Inverness-shire), Pennant refers to 'the *Dune of Dornadilla*' 18 km SE of Tongue (Sutherland), but he does not provide an engraving of it.
31.26 some Vauban or Coehorn Sebastien Le Prestre (1633–1707), Marquis of Vauban, and Menno van Coehoorn (1641–1704) were notable military engineers, French and Dutch respectively.
32.30–34.6 The castle is large . . . filled with stones see William Camden, *Britannia: or, a Chorographical Description of . . . England, Scotland, and Ireland . . .*, trans. Richard Gough, 2nd edn, 4 vols (London, 1806), 3.267–68: *CLA*, 232. The transcription, by John Buchanan, is verbally accurate.
34.12–14 The resuscitation of Athelstane . . . fantastic character most prominent among reviewers voicing objection to this point was Francis Jeffrey in *The Edinburgh Review*, 33 (January, 1820), 1–54 (43).

THE MONASTERY

42.37 Superstitious eld a phrase also found in John Abraham Heraud, 'The Legend of St. Loy', 3.353 (stanza 18), in *The Legend of St. Loy; With Other Poems* (London, 1820), 114: see *CLA*, 162.
43.1 Boldside or Boleside, 3 km S of the centre of Galashiels.
43.7 Oberon and Queen Mab Oberon is king of the fairies in *A Midsummer Night's Dream*. Queen Mab (*Queen* meaning 'female') is 'the fairies' midwife', who delivers secret hopes in the form of dreams: see *Romeo and Juliet*, 1.4.53–94.
43.8–12 Father Chaucer . . . the place in Scott's time Chaucer was regularly termed 'the father of English poetry'. For the lines quoted see 'Sir Thopas', *The Canterbury Tales*, VII, lines 814–16.
43.17–18 Lord Somerville's . . . Pavilion John Southey Somerville (1765–1819) succeeded his uncle as 15th Baron Somerville in 1796. Scott wrote a 'Character' on his death: *Prose Works*, 4.309–21.
43.20–21 the irritable race compare Horace (65–8 BC), *Epistles*, 2.2.102: 'genus irritabile vatum' (the fretful tribe of bards).
43.33–35 mea paupera regna . . . Drumthwacket the Latin phrase means 'my poor territories'. For Sir Dugald Dalgetty's territory and use of the phrase see EEWN 7b, 234 (note to 16.15) and 245 (note to 67.13).
43.36 the water-bull a legendary amphibious animal.
44.37–41 One of these . . . on the ruin Hillslap was built by Nicol Cairncross in 1585. Colmslie dates from earlier in the century. Both towers were ruined by Scott's time, but Hillslap was restored as a residence in the 1970s. Gilbert Innes (1751–1832) of Stow, 10 km N of Galashiels, was Deputy Governor of the Royal Bank of Scotland. The Centenary edition notes (10.425): 'Mr. John Borthwick of Crookston [1787–1845], in a note to the publisher (June 14, 1843), says that Sir Walter has reversed the proprietorship of these towers—that *Colmslie* belonged to Mr. Innes of Stow, while *Hillslap* forms part of his estate of Crookston. He adds—"In proof that the

tower of Hillslap, which I have taken measures to preserve from injury, was chiefly in his head, as the tower of *Glendearg*, when writing the Monastery, I may mention that, on one of the occasions when I had the honour of being a visitor at Abbotsford, the stables then being full, I sent a pony to be put up at our tenant's at Hillslap:—'Well,' said Sir Walter, 'if you do that, you must trust for its not being *lifted* before to-morrow to the protection of Halbert Glendinning against Christie of the Clinthill.' At page 58, vol. iii. first edition [EEWN 9, 254.11], the '*winding stair*' which the monk ascended is described. The winding stone stair is still to be seen in Hillslap, but not in either of the other two towers." It is, however, probable, from the Goat's-Head crest on Colmslie, that that tower also had been of old a possession of the Borthwicks.'

44.41–43 a third, the house of Langshaw . . . shooting box Langshaw Tower, dating from the 16th century, with a 17th-century extension, was occupied until the 18th century when part of it was used as a school: it is now ruined. George Baillie (1763–1841) of Jerviswood (Lanarkshire) and Mellerstain (Berwickshire), was MP for Berwickshire 1796–1818.

45.8–9 Miss Raylands, in the Old Manor House at the opening of Charlotte Smith's novel *The Old Manor House*, 4 vols (London, 1793) the reader is introduced to the manor's occupant Miss Rayland, 'the only survivor of the three co-heiresses of Sir Hildebrand Rayland': *CLA*, 333.

45.11–14 Colmslie stands . . . the whippers of Colmslie this version of the rhyme varies from other traditional forms: see [T. C. Cairncross], 'A Lost House. Cairncross of Colmslie', *Border Magazine*, 10 (1905), 138–40 (140).

45.18 Utinam hanc . . . amicis *Latin* I wish that I may fill this [house] also with my friends. See 'Socrates ad Amicos' (Socrates to his Friends), by Gaius Julius Phaedrus (*c.* 15 BC–*c.* AD 50), line 7.

46.5–8 This erroneous identification . . . Chambers see Robert Chambers, *Illustrations of the Author of Waverley*, 2nd edn (Edinburgh, 1825), 201–08. The 'Mr O——n' proposed by Chambers as the original of Clutterbuck was Adam Ormiston (d. 1835), a small landowner of Melrose.

46.14–18 I think it is in the Spectator . . . a whole parish see *The Spectator*, 568 (16 July 1714), by Joseph Addison. [Richard Allestree], *The Whole Duty of Man* (London, 1658) was an immensely popular devotional work for almost a century after its first appearance.

46.29 Crambe bis cocta *Latin* cabbage twice boiled.

46.39–41 Machinery remained . . . Horace 'nec deus intersit, nisi dignus vindice nodus/ inciderit' (*Latin* let no god [deus ex machina] intervene, unless a difficulty come worthy of such a deliverer): Horace (65–8 BC), *Ars Poetica* (The Art of Poetry), lines 191–92.

47.4–5 Even the last . . . rest again see George Crabbe, *The Library* (1781), lines 579–80 ('lingering fiction').

47.19 Entretiens du Compte de Gabalis [Nicolas de Montfaucon de Villars], *Le Comte de Gabalis, ou entretiens sur les sciences secretes* (Paris, 1670): compare the two English versions in *CLA* 143, 152.

47.19–25 The ingenious Compte de la Motte Fouqué . . . ingratitude see Friedrich, Baron de la Motte Fouqué, 'Undine', in *Die Jahreszeiten* (Berlin, Spring 1811).

47.32 Milesian Irish. In fable, Milesius was a Spanish king whose sons were reputed to have conquered Ireland *c.* 1300 BC.

47.38–39 May Mollach . . . Hairy Arms 'It is reported That a familiar Spirit ordinarily haunted The Family of Tullochgorm, and attended for Intelligence and Drudgery. This Ghost was commonly called Meg Mulloch as having The Loof of her Hand hairy [Gaelic *molach*]': 'The Genealogy of

The Grants said to be written by Mr. James Chapman, Minister of Cromdall &c. in Anno 1729', 109 (www.clangrant.org/history/ct.htm). See for an earlier mention Coleman O. Parsons, *Witchcraft and Demonology in Scott's Fiction* (Edinburgh and London, 1964), 160. Parsons also cites (161) a spirit advising a player of a board game, found in Martin Martin, *A Description of the Western Islands of Scotland* (London, 1703), 320: compare *CLA*, 5.

48.5 Mine would if I were human see *The Tempest*, 5.1.20.

48.22–24 liable to be subjected . . . philosophy Rosicrucianism, dating from the 16th century, was (like the Gnosticism developed 14 centuries earlier) a system of secret knowledge, said to give its initiates power over elemental beings.

48.38–39 esprit follet *French* hobgoblin.

49.18 choice spirit of the age see *Julius Caesar*, 3.1.164.

49.38–39 Amadis . . . Oriana Amadis is the hero, and Oriana the heroine, of the late medieval Spanish or Portuguese romance *Amadis de Gaula*. Scott owned English and French translations: *CLA*, 106, 112, 115.

49.43 Euphues and his England for this book by John Lyly, published in 1580, see EEWN 9, 437.

50.4–5 the romances of Calprenade and Scuderi Gauthier de Costes de la Calprenède (1614–63) and Madeleine de Scudéry (1608–1701) wrote long prose romances in French.

50.6 the long reign of Louis XIV. 1643–1715.

50.8–12 Molière and Boileau . . . Les Précieuses Ridicules *Les Précieuses ridicules*, by Jean-Baptiste Poquelin (1622–73), known as Molière, appeared in 1659. The Hôtel Rambouillet, the Paris town house of Cathérine de Vivonne (1588–1665), Marchioness of Rambouillet from 1611, attracted an influential literary coterie. Molière's colleague, the poet and critic Nicholas Boileau (1636–1711), advocated good judgment in literature and attacked excess.

50.36–37 as Lear says . . . lendings see *King Lear*, 3.4.105–06.

50.40 the bard of Chios Chios, an island off the coast of Asia Minor, claimed to be the birthplace of Homer.

50.41–42 my friend Mr Cooper the American James Fenimore Cooper (1789–1851), whose series of novels known as *The Leather-stocking Tales* (1823–41) are centred on North American Indian life. Scott and Cooper met and bonded in Paris in 1826, and again in London in 1828: Edgar Johnson, *Sir Walter Scott: The Great Unknown*, 2 vols (London, 1970), 2.1002–03, 1051–52.

51.13–14 As free as nature . . . ran John Dryden, *The Conquest of Granada* (1672), Part 1, 1.208, 210.

51.30 shoots folly as it flies see Alexander Pope, *An Essay on Man* (1733–34), 1.13.

52.7–8 Don Armado . . . Holofernes characters in *Love's Labour's Lost*.

52.8 Nym and Pistol Pistol appears in *2 Henry IV*, and both characters in *Henry V* and *The Merry Wives of Windsor*.

52.12 Mercutio the quick-witted and flamboyant friend of Romeo in *Romeo and Juliet*.

52.27 incredulus odi *Latin* Horace (65–8 BC), *Ars Poetica* (The Art of Poetry), line 188: 'quodcumque ostendis mihi sic, incredulus odi' (whatever you thus show me, I discredit and abhor).

53.21 Gil Blas, Roderick Random *Gil Blas* is a picaresque novel by Alain-René Lesage, published 1715–35 and translated into English in 1749 by Tobias Smollett, whose own picaresque novel *The Adventures of Roderick Random* had appeared in 1748.

53.32 nature boon John Milton, *Paradise Lost* (1667, rev. 1674), 4.242.

53.34 Tom Jones Henry Fielding's novel *Tom Jones, a Foundling* appeared in 1749.
53.42–43 tout genre . . . ennuyeux *French* all styles are good except the boring kind. See the Preface to Voltaire (François-Marie Arouet), *L'Enfant prodigue* (1736).
54.23–24 If it isna weel bobbit . . . again see the traditional song 'The Bob o' Dumblane', a version of which was transmitted by Robert Burns to James Johnson in autumn 1795 for *The Scots Musical Museum*, but not included, probably because of its obscene overtones: see *The Poems and Songs of Robert Burns*, ed. James Kinsley, 3 vols (Oxford, 1968), 2.804, 3.1487–88.
54.29–30 the same civil and quiet person . . . David Kyle the proprietor of the George in 1830 was William Davidson whose dates are given as 1752–1857. David Kyle was Master of the Masonic lodge in Melrose in 1786.
55.4–6 Lord Somerville . . . Glenmayne and Leaderfoot for Lord Somerville see note to 43.17–18 above. For Kyle see previous note. Glenmayne and Leaderfoot are on the N bank of the Tweed: the former slightly upstream from Abbotsford, the latter 7 km downstream at the junction with Leader Water.
55.8 Thomas Thomson Thomson (1768–1852), who became Deputy Clerk Register in 1806 and Principal Clerk of Session in 1828, was an eminent legal antiquary and editor of historical documents such as charters.
55.13–16 the subject . . . Haig of Bemerside the Haigs, descended from the Norman Peter de Haga, have lived at Bemerside (4 km E of Melrose) since the 12th century. The late 13th-century Thomas Learmont, or Thomas of Erceldoune, was known as Thomas the Rhymer. He is credited with the authorship of numerous fragments of prophetic verse. For this couplet, one of 'sundry rhymes, passing for his prophetic effusions, . . . still current among the vulgar', see *Minstrelsy*, 4.117–18.
55.19–21 The same story . . . No Song, no Supper for 'The Friars of Berwick' and Allan Ramsay's 'The Monk and the Miller's Wife' see EEWN 9, 445 (note to 12.24–26). The former, anonymous, poem was ascribed by John Pinkerton to William Dunbar in his *Ancient Scotish Poems*, 2 vols (London, 1786: *CLA*, 173), 1.x–xi 'largely because he wished to show him as Chaucer's equal in narrative art' (*The Poems of William Dunbar*, ed. Priscilla Bawcutt, 2 vols (Glasgow, 1998), 1.17). The 'modern farce' is Prince Hoare's *No Song No Supper: An Opera, in two Acts* (Dublin, 1792): it was produced at the Theatre Royal, Edinburgh on 19 May 1820 and on 19 May and 24 August 1821. The first two works reach their climax with the revealing of a concealed clerical lover on the return home of the offended husband. In Hoare the wife is virtuous and her would-be seducer is a lawyer.
55.25 before the avowal was made Scott was induced to acknowledge formally his authorship at the Theatrical Fund Dinner on 23 February 1827: Lockhart, 7.17–20. *Woodstock* (1826) was the last of his novels to be published anonymously.
55.42–56.2 This note . . . genuine in the ISet Scott added the second paragraph to the original Ed1 note (EEWN 9, 29). *Tales of My Landlord, New Series, containing Pontefract Castle*, was advertised in October 1819 and published early in the following year by William Fearman. Rumour ascribed the spurious novel to the playwright and actor Thomas John Dibdin (1771–1841), but Sharon Ragaz tentatively suggests as a more plausible candidate one of Fearman's authors, J. M. H. Hales: 'The Spurious *Tales of My Landlord*', *The Library*, 10:1 (March 2009), 41–56 (51–52).
56.3–7 In consequence . . . Simon Pure letters by John Ballantyne and William Fearman were printed in *Blackwood's Edinburgh Magazine*, 6

(November 1819), 217–19. (A letter by Ballantyne had appeared towards the end of the preceding month in *The Edinburgh Evening Courant* and *The Morning Chronicle*: see the article by Sharon Ragaz referred to in the previous note, 44.) The expression 'the real Simon Pure', meaning 'the authentic article', derives from a victim of impersonation in Susannah Centlivre's comedy *A Bold Stroke for a Wife* (1718).

56.25–27 Rose Castle . . . Mary, Lady Clerk of Pennycuick Rose Castle, 13 km S of Carlisle, has been the seat of the Bishop of Carlisle since the 13th century. Rose Mary Appleby, daughter of Joseph Dacre-Appleby of Kirklington, Cumberland, born at Rose Castle in 1745, married Sir John Clerk, 5th Baronet of Penicuik, who succeeded in 1784 and died in 1798; she died in 1834. The Jacobite Donald Macdonald of Kinlochmoidart (b. *c.* 1705) was captured in Lanarkshire and executed at Carlisle on 18 October 1746.

56.31–35 It is only a year or two . . . Sheriff of Selkirkshire Gines de Passamonté is the puppeteer in *Don Quixote*, 4.119–21: Part 2 (1615), Ch. 27. Scott was appointed Sheriff-Depute of Selkirkshire in 1799. 'Depute' was dropped from the title by an Act of 1828 (9 Geo. IV. c. 29. para. 22).

57.1 But with the morning cool reflection came compare Nicholas Rowe, *The Fair Penitent* (1703), 1.1.162: 'At length the morn and cold indifference came'.

57.4 the Rhadamanth of the district in Greek mythology, Rhadamanthus is one of the judges in the infernal regions.

57.30–58.2 In another journey . . . to exhibit it see Alexander Gordon, *Itinerarium Septentrionale* (London, 1726), 165–66 (*CLA*, 11): there is an engraving of the remains of the bridge at Plate 64. The transcription, in an unidentified hand, on an inserted leaf, is verbally accurate.

58.6 Mr John Mercer Scott refers to his neighbour John Mercer in *Letters*, 5. 498–99 (27 September [1819]) and 6.305 ([December 1820]).

58.8 Mr David Kyle for David Kyle see note to 54.29–30 above.

58.11–15 I, Sir John Pringle . . . the bridge belonged the Pringles of Smailholm and Galashiels obtained a charter of Redhead and Whytbank in 1510. Scott may have been thinking of John Pringle who succeeded as laird of Smailholm and Galashiels in 1535 and died *c.* 1566. According to another account the stone bore the name of Sir Robert Pringle, a 15th-century forebear of John: see Alex. Pringle, *The Records of the Pringles or Hoppringills of the Scottish Border* (Edinburgh, 1933), 126–28.

58.17 Old Parr, or Henry Jenkins Henry Jenkins, who died in 1670, claimed to have been born *c.* 1501 and to have recollections of Fountains Abbey before the dissolution of the monasteries in 1539. Thomas Parr, who died in 1635, claimed to have been born in 1483.

58.20–31 A brood of wild-geese . . . ever since Scott slightly emends the Ed1 note, inserting 'one of' before 'the uppermost islands' and adding the final two sentences. For the proverb, concerning MacFarlane's geese, first recorded in the early 17th century, see *ODEP*, 497. Originally Scott wrote 'Why they were said to like their play better than their meat, I could never learn, but the proverb is in general use.' He deleted that and substituted the present story, a source for which has not been identified.

58.32–59.7 There are many instances . . . Gavin Wilson Scott expands the Ed1 note (EEWN 9, 145) by adding the material after 'masonic lodges'. Gavin Wilson published *A Collection of Masonic Songs, and Entertaining Anecdotes, for the use of all the Lodges* (Edinburgh, 1788: *CLA*, 171), but it does not contain such names.

59.9–17 "Yorke," says Camden . . . the girdle see William Camden, *The History or Annals of England, during the whole Life and Reign of Elizabeth* *late Queen thereof* (first published in Latin 1615–25, translated into English 1625–29), in Kennet, 2.361–676 (540): *CLA*, 249. Scott's transcription (which breaks off, lacking the last 6 words) modernises the original and has two minor verbal differences: 'York' for 'This Yorke', and 'of man' for 'of a man'. At a subsequent stage 'brought' replaced 'first brought' (the reading in the source and Scott's transcription), eliminating a repetition.

59.22–60.2 Thomas Stukely ... profligate Thomas Stukely for Stukely and the works cited in the final paragraph see EEWN 9, 471 (note to 159.31). *CLA*, 172 lists the 2nd edn (1784) and the 3rd ('new') edn (1810) of Evans.

60.9–14 in Yetholm Loch ... ruinous tower Yetholm Loch is 2 km W of Town Yetholm. The scanty remains of Lochside Tower were already on a peninsula rather than an island by the beginning of 1835: John Baird, 'Parish of Yetholm', in *The New Statistical Account of Scotland*, 15 vols (Edinburgh, 1845), 5.[159]–76 (164), dated January 1835.

60.15–18 It was of Lochwood ... this remark the ruins of the 15th-century Lochwood Tower are situated 24 km NE of Dumfries. It was occupied by the Johnstones from the late 12th to the early 18th century.

60.21–24 There is an ancient ... canting herald Scott alters and expands with the final sentence his Ed1 note. *Canting heraldry* is a form of punning arms in which the heraldic devices suggest the bearer's name or title.

60.32–33 A practice of the same kind ... Portland the Isle of Portland, Dorset, was not connected by road to the mainland until 1839. It had a number of distinctive customs, including the insistence that a betrothed woman should be pregnant before the marriage ceremony could take place.

60.35–61.14 If it were necessary ... the State Trials James Ormiston of that Ilk ('Black Ormiston') was executed in 1573. For his confession see *Ancient Criminal Trials in Scotland*, ed. Robert Pitcairn, 3 vols (Edinburgh, 1829–33), Vol. 1, Part 2, 513: *CLA*, 278. Scott modernises the original and introduces several verbal variants: 'which God is ↑ this day ↓ punishing' for 'quhilk my God this day is punishing'; 'and most high minded' for 'and heich myndit'; 'unclean of my body' for 'filthie of my body, abusing myself dyvers ways'; 'shed the innocent' for 'shed innocent'; 'he had pleased' for 'he pleasit'; 'It is' for 'For its'; 'in which' for 'quhilk'; and 'yet God' for 'ȝit my God'.

61.20–42 When all things were quiet ... accordingly was performed see *Memoirs of Robert Cary* [ed. Scott, with Robert Naunton's *Fragmenta Regalia*] (Edinburgh, 1808), 73–74. Scott's transcription is for the most part verbally faithful, but there are two noteworthy variants: 'took leave of him' for 'took our leaves of him', and 'very honest' for 'very worthy honest'. At a subsequent stage 'would promptly grant' replaces 'would presently grant', avoiding an unfortunate repetition.

62.11–12 Bonds enter'd into ... the triumph day see *Richard II*, 5.2.65–66.

62.13–15 Jonson informs us ... apparel Ben Jonson, *Every Man out of his Humour* (1616), 1.2.40–42. The quotation was apparently added at proof stage.

62.16–35 In the Memorie of the Somerville family ... spears again for the anecdote see *Memorie of The Somervilles* [ed. Scott], 2 vols (Edinburgh, 1815), 1.389–93. Scott tells much of the story in his own words, but from 'You are very brave' to the end is a paraphrase with much of the phraseology of the *Memorie*.

62.42–64.11 Fastidius ... more humanity see Ben Jonson, *Every Man out of his Humour* (1600), 4.6.66–127. The transcription, by Anne Scott, is presumably from *The Works of Ben Jonson*, ed. W. Gifford, 9 vols (London, 1816), 2.153–56 (*CLA*, 209). It has several verbal variants, most or all of them probably inadvertent (a few others were corrected at a subsequent stage): 'he came' for 'he comes'; 'his body' for 'his whole body'; 'sleeves' for 'sleeve'; 'light' for 'lights'; 'up, about' for 'up, which I wore about'; 'brim' for 'brims'; 'pounds' for 'pound'; 'to my former manner of defence' for 'to the former manner of my defence'; 'hilt' for 'hilts'; 'ruffles' for 'ruffle'; 'somewhat of a' for 'somewhat a'; and 'Ride' for 'Rid'.

64.12–13 Lord James Stewart . . . Murray for the Regent Murray see EEWN 9, 435 and 482 (note to 286.20–21).

64.26–30 That they would not care to steal . . . ere this see *The State Papers and Letters of Sir Ralph Sadler, Knight-Banneret*, ed. Arthur Clifford and Scott, 3 vols (Edinburgh, 1809), 2.116. Scott alters the opening words of the quotation to fit it to his text. He modernises and slightly adjusts the original.

64.33 biberes, caritas see EEWN 9, 484 (note to 310.5–6) and 472 (note to 171.34–35).

64.36–67.2 There is one of these charters . . . nostri vicesimo the original Latin charter, which is transcribed in a careful copperplate hand, is now in the National Records of Scotland (Melrose Charters, GD. 55/362). It may be translated thus:

CHARTER OF KING ROBERT I TO THE ABBOT AND COMMUNITY OF MELROSE.

Charter concerning a pittance of one hundred pounds.

Robert, by the grace of God King of Scots, greets all honest men throughout his whole land. Know that we, for the salvation of our own soul and of the souls of the Kings of Scotland our predecessors and successors have granted, bestowed and by this our present charter confirmed to God and to the Blessed Virgin Mary and to those men of religion the Abbot and Community of Melrose and to their successors for all time to come an annuity of one hundred pounds sterling, payment to be made each year from our rents in the Burgh of Berwick upon Tweed on the term-days of Pentecost and St Martin in winter in equal portion, or from our new customs of the aforementioned Burgh if our aforementioned rents are not able to provide the said sum of money, or from our new customs of our Burghs of Edinburgh and Haddington if our rents and customs of the town of Berwick for any reason are not sufficient for this purpose. The said sum of money of one hundred pounds is to be paid to them each year in whole and in full without any objection before all other assignations of whatever kind that have been made or are to be made by us for the daily provision for all time to come to each monk of the aforementioned monastery when eating in the Refectory one adequate supply of rice cooked with milk, of almonds, of pulse or of other foods of the same sort that have been procured in the country, and that supply of food is to be called the King's Mess for all time. And if any monk for any good reason does not wish to eat from the said Mess or is not able to take a meal nonetheless food is to be served to him from the said Mess and is to be taken to the gate for the benefit of the poor. Nor is it our pleasure that because of the existence of our aforementioned Mess the food of the said Community which is usually provided and served up to them communally by ancient rule should be in any way diminished in quality or reduced in quantity. In addition it is our pleasure and decree that the Abbot of that same monastery for the time being, with the consent of the more sage members of the Community, shall specially appoint one prudent and decent monk to receive, direct and expend the whole sum of the aforementioned money for the benefit of the community in accordance with our desire and intention, as noted above, and to render every year to the Abbot and the Superiors of the Community a faithful account of the money thus received. And it is our pleasure that in return for our aforementioned donation and in perpetual memory of us the said men of religion shall be bound yearly and for all time to come to clothe fifteen poor men at the feast of St Martin in winter and to feed them on the same day, delivering to each of them four ells of large and broad cloth or six ells of narrow cloth and to each of them one new pair of shoes according to their order. And if in any year the said men of religion shall default from these arrangements or from any of them, it is our pleasure that what has been omitted shall be paid twice over on more suitable days under the supervision of our chief forester of Selkirk for the time being, and that the said double payment shall be made before the next birthday of our Lord following the aforementioned feast of St Martin. In witness whereof we have instructed that our seal be appended to this our charter, in the presence of the venerable fathers in Christ, William, John, William and David, by the grace of God bishops of St Andrews, Glasgow, Dunkeld and Moray, Bernard, Abbot of Arbroath and Chancellor, Duncan, Malise and Hugh, Earls of Fife, Strathearn and Ross, Walter the Steward of Scotland, James, Lord Douglas and Alexander Fraser our Chamberlain, knights of Scotland. At Arbroath, on the tenth day of January in the twentieth year of our reign.

67.8–32 The late excellent . . . Caledonia, p. 579 in the second paragraph Scott provides a paraphrase of a passage from George Chalmers, *Caledonia: or, An Account, Historical and Topographic, of North Britain . . .*, 3 vols (London, 1807–24), 1.579: *CLA*, 1. The sentence quoted by Chalmers and reproduced at the beginning of the paragraph is from the unpaginated 'Preface' to David Hume of Godscroft, *The History of the Houses of Douglas and Angus* (Edinburgh, 1644; reissued in 1648 for sale in London), A2r: *CLA*, 3.

68.35–69.2 The acute pen . . . the royal family of Stewart in this paragraph , which is in the hand of John Buchanan, Scott summarises Chalmers's *Caldedonia* (see previous note), 1.572–73. Chalmers is referring to David Dalrymple (Lord Hailes), *Annals of Scotland*, 2 vols (Edinburgh, 1776–79), 1.358–62: Appendix 8 ('Of the Origin of the House of Stewart'): *CLA*, 4.

69.4–7 The contrivance . . . Das Peter Manchen a version of the story can be found in the opening pages of Ch[ristian] H[einrich] Spies[s], *Das Petermänchen. Geistergeschichte aus dem dreizehnten Jahrhunderte* (Dwarf Peter. Ghost story from the thirteenth century), 2nd edn, 2 parts (Prague and Leipzig, 1793). There the blacksmith is a tailor and the horse-shoe a ball of thread. In the 1790s Scott 'not only went through the prose plays of Goethe and Schiller, but even some of the now forgotten romances of Spiess, *then* an eminent manufacturer for the Minerva press of Germany. Among these I have heard him speak with peculiar interest of the "Petermänchen," a production of *diablerie*, which his own genius had probably invested with interest, such as no other reader could have discerned in it' ([R. P. Gillies], *Recollections of Sir Walter Scott, Bart.* (London, 1837), 72). Scott's ascription to Johann Ludwig Tieck may have arisen from Tieck's pseudonym Peter Lebrecht (used for the *Volksmärchen* of 1797, which is in the library at Abbotsford: *CLA*, 53).

69.29–30 that "law in our members . . . our minds" see Romans 7.23: 'I see another law in my members, warring against the law of my mind, and bringing me into captivity to the law of sin which is in my members'.

THE ABBOT

78.31 without my gown and band *literally* without my clerical attire. The phrase has not been located elsewhere.

78.37–79.4 Even the Aristarch Johnson . . . only a few see James Boswell, *The Life of Samuel Johnson*, ed. George Birkbeck Hill, rev. L. F. Powell, 6 vols (Oxford, 1934–50), 1.419 (1 July 1763): 'To be sure, he [Churchill] is a tree that cannot produce good fruit: he only bears crabs. But, Sir, a tree that produces a great many crabs is better than a tree which produces only a few.'

79.15–23 a passage in Grimm's Correspondence . . . the French nation the passage in question has not been located. It has not been found in Friedrich Melchior Grimm and Denis Diderot, *Mémoires historiques* . . ., 2nd edn, 7 vols (London, 1814): *CLA*, 37. In 1758 the French man of letters Voltaire (François-Marie Arouet: 1694–1778) settled at Ferney, close to the Swiss frontier.

79.29 If he fall in . . . swim *1 Henry IV*, 1.3.194.

80.17–20 in the same manner . . . from one quarter see *Don Quixote*, 3.263–64: Part 2 (1615), Ch. 14, where the celebrated weathercock is stationary for more than a week with a constant north wind.

80.26–27 Jack the Giant-killer . . . coat of darkness referring to the old nursery tale in which Jack is invisible when he puts on his magic coat.

80.29–32 In my school days . . . the other forth see *The Merchant of Venice*, 1.1.140–43.

80.33–36 his shafts . . . sevenfold shield see Homer, *The Iliad*, 8.261–72 (and, for a description of the shield 7.244–76).

80.40–81.1 a mode by which . . . a direct address to the readers Scott may have had in mind e.g. the reformed rake Belford, who expresses consistently sensible sentiments in Samuel Richardson's epistolary novel *Clarissa* (1747–48).

81.1–5 A pleasing French writer . . . personages of the tale see *Histoire du Prince Soly*, by Henri Pajon (d. 1776), in *Voyages imaginaires* . . ., 36 vols (Amsterdam, 1787–89), 25.1–222: *CLA*, 45. In Ch. 6 (147–60) 'le génie des romans' explains to Prince Soly (or Prenany) that he has authorial control over the events of the prince's life.

81.12–13 the place of deposit of the great Robert Bruce's heart on the death in 1329 of Robert I, King of Scots from 1306, his heart was embalmed and was to have been taken to Jerusalem by Sir James Douglas. When Douglas was killed in battle against the Moslems of Granada the heart was brought back to Melrose Abbey for burial. A lead casket probably containing the heart was exhumed in 1996 and re-interred in 1999.

81.20–23 the example . . . Mr Colman's drama in William Godwin's novel *Things as They Are; or, The Adventures of Caleb Williams*, 3 vols (London, 1794), the contents of a mysterious chest mentioned in the opening pages of the narrative are never disclosed to the narrator or the reader. In 1796 George Colman, the Younger adapted the work for the stage as *The Iron Chest* (1796). (In the second edition of his novel, also published in1796, Godwin substituted 'trunk' for 'chest'.) See the edition by Maurice Hindle (London, 1988), xxiii–xxiv, 9, 137–38, 171, 173, and 326.

81.39–40 like Mungo in the Padlock . . . comprehend see [Isaac Bickerstaff], *The Padlock: A Comic Opera*, new edition (London, [1789]), 18.

82.11–12 Alfred . . . Bruce Alfred the Great, King of England 871–901; Elizabeth I, Queen of England 1558–1603; Sir William Wallace (d. 1305), Scottish patriot. For the Bruce see note to 81.12–13.

82.16–17 is . . . "brought home" recoups himself.
82.24 Hotspur's task . . . roaring loud see *1 Henry IV*, 1.3.192.
83.12–15 The tracts . . . p. 258 see Thomas M'Crie, *The Life of John Knox* (Edinburgh, 1812), 266–67: *CLA*, 4. There is only one tract involved, Knox's record of the 1661 disputation on transubstantiation at Maybole in Ayrshire with the Abbot of the nearby Crossraguel Abbey, Quentin Kennedy (1520–64): see EEWN 10, 472 (note to 7.12–15).
83.19–22 Glendonwyne of Glendonwyne . . . Earls of Douglas for the Glendonwyne family see EEWN 10, 475 (note to 26.30–31). Sir Adam Glendonwyn of that Ilk was 'at all times a firm and faithful friend of King Robert Bruce [who defeated the English army at Bannockburn near Stirling in 1314], and a constant companion of James lord Douglas, called *Good Sir James*' ([Robert Douglas], *The Baronage of Scotland* (Edinburgh, 1798), 234). Douglas goes on to note that Sir Adam's second son, Sir Simon, 'died in the field by the side of the brave earl of Douglas at the memorable battle of Otterburn [Northumberland] in the year 1388'.
83.30 in dubio *Latin* in doubt.
84.4 One of the Somervilles Sir John Somervile, 2nd Baron of Cambusnethan or Camnethan, Lanarkshire, succeeded his father when he fell at Flodden in 1513, and died in 1553. For his sobriquet see *Memorie of The Somervilles*, [ed. Walter Scott], 2 vols (Edinburgh, 1815 [1816]), 1.305.
84.9–11 Saint Cuthbert . . . Tillmouth Chapel see EEWN 10, 480–81 (note to 58.28).
84.18 Sir Francis Blake Delaval Delaval (1727–71), proprietor of Seton Delaval, Northumberland, had a reputation for eccentricity.
84.30–33 An expression . . . Lancaster for the reputed dying expression of Sir Ralph Percy (1425–64) at Hedgeley Moor, Northumberland, see [John Hall], *Hall's Chronicle; containing the History of England* . . . (London, 1809), 260: *CLA*, 28. In fact Percy switched allegiance several times between the Houses of Lancaster and York.
84.42–85.10 And you shall learn . . . how does my dow? see *Minstrelsy*, 3.286 (stanzas 22–24 of 'Fause Foodrage'). The stanzas are, effectively, translated by Scott from Scots into English for the Magnum.
85.11 Earnest-money this gloss was inserted after the ISet.
85.17 1729 this correct date replaces the '1733' of the ISet manuscript note.
85.31–32 the same commodity . . . Augeas in Greek mythology one of the labours of Hercules was to cleanse the stables in which Augeas, King of Elis, housed his great herd of oxen, and which were never cleaned, by diverting a river through them.
85.34–40 A fanatic nun . . . a believer for Elizabeth Barton see EEWN 10, 485 (note to 94.38–39). In 1533 Henry VIII rejected the authority of the Pope and divorced Catherine of Aragon in order to marry Anne Boleyn. Sir Thomas More was one of those who protested, and this led to his execution in 1535.
86.5–9 We learn . . . captivated with it see *Life of Napoleon Buonaparte* (first published in 9 vols in 1827), Ch. 63: *Prose Works*, 14.219.
86.12 Saturnalia a Roman festival celebrated for 3 days in mid-December, including licence for slaves.
86.12–13 the modern Carnival the festivities held in Roman Catholic countries during the days before Ash Wednesday, pre-eminently that in Venice.
86.30–32 the gross novels . . . the clergy satirical treatments of the clergy can be found in e.g. 'The Summoner's Tale' from *The Canterbury Tales*; 'The Friars of Berwick', formerly attributed to William Dunbar (*c.* 1460–*c.* 1513);

and several of the *novelle* in *Il Decameron* by Giovanni Boccaccio (1313–75), and of those by Matteo Bandello (1485–1561).

87.6–88.48 The reader may be amused . . . Act II. Scene I. this entire passage, text and footnote, transcribed by an unidentified hand, is taken from *Provincial Antiquities of Scotland* (*Prose Works*, 7.202–03: originally published 1826). The quotation from *Sir John Oldcastle* which constitutes the footnote is 4.41–69 in the edition by Jonathan Rittenhouse (New York and London, 1984). The transcriptions are verbally faithful. Borthwick Castle is situated 20 km SE of Edinburgh.

88.6 But oh . . . forgot in *Hamlet*, 3.2.130, the catchphrase appears as 'For O, for O, the hobby-horse is forgot!' The form with 'But . . . but' is found in *Love's Labour's Lost*, 3.1.25–26.

88.7–9 There is a very comic scene . . . dance with the hobby-horse see John Fletcher, *Women Pleas'd* (performed *c.* 1620, published 1647), 4.1.

88.14–89.11 The hobby-horse . . . besides the hobby-horse? see Francis Douce, *Illustrations of Shakespeare*, 2 vols (London, 1807), 2.467–68. John Buchanan's transcription has several verbal variants, 3 of them (unusually for Buchanan) clearly errors, emended in the present text.

89.28–90.5 I came once myselfe . . . to God's word see Hugh Latimer, *Fruitfull Sermons* (London, 1635), 73v–74r: *CLA*, 71. The transcription, by Anne Scott, is generally accurate.

90.14–91.26 Vpon the xxi day . . . the same tolbouyth see *A Diurnal of Remarkable Occurrents that have passed within the country of Scotland since the death of King James the Fourth till the Year M.D.LXXV. from a manuscript of the sixteenth century, in the possession of Sir John Maxwell of Pollock, Baronet* (Edinburgh, 1833), 283–85 (ff. 103r–104r of the manuscript). The transcription here, in an unidentified hand, corresponds closely to this version published by the Bannatyne Club the year after Scott's death, but the transcriber gives 'solistatnis' for 'solistatiouns' (90.21), 'yaire' for 'thairto' (90.26), 'vyris' for 'vtheris' (90.32), 'harberis' for 'hamberis' (90.37, meaning 'hammers' and emended for the present edition), 'thar' for 'thai' (90.39), 'on their coming' for 'or their cuming' (90.43), 'then schote' for 'thaj shot' (91.5), and 'prensit' for 'preassit' (91.12, emended for the present edition); the words 'thair said purpois' are omitted after 'stay fra' (91.17, emended for the present edition), and 'servueis' appears as 'services' (91.24). The three emendations are made to avoid nonsense.

91.27–35 John Knox . . . made satisfaction see John Knox, *The Historie Of the Reformation of the Church of Scotland* ([London, 1587]; repr., [ed. David Buchanan], London, 1644), 281: *CLA*, 2. Knox defines 'four hours penie' as 'afternoons Pinte' (i.e. penny ale at 4 pm)'.

91.36–92.1 These rude rhymes . . . 2 vols [John Wedderburn et al], *Ane Compendiovs Booke, of Godly and Spiritvall Songs. Collectit out of sundrie partes of the Scripture, with sundrie of other Ballates changed out of prophaine sanges, for avoyding of sinne and harlotrie, with augmentation of sundrie gude and godly Ballates, not contained in the first Edition* (Edinburgh, 1621) is reprinted in Vol. 2 of *Scotish Poems, of the Sixteenth Century*, [ed. J. G. Dalyell], 2 vols (Edinburgh, 1801: *CLA*, 173). 'The Paip, that pagane full of pryd' can be found on pp. 191–94 of the separately paginated section occupied by Wedderburn, the lines used (and varied) by Scott being stanzas 1 and 6. In the original 1621 edition it is to be found on M2v–M3r. Scott's version is a composite one: see EEWN 10, 490 (note to 114.13–30).

92.3–6 The Saint Swithin . . . expected for St Martin (as mentioned in the novel) see EEWN 10, 490 (note to 117.8–10). The English equivalent is St Swithin, Bishop of Winchester (d. 863), whose festival is 15 July.

92.14–26 'Thus,' said the illustrious Misnar . . . vex me see Sir

Charles Morell [i.e. James Ridley], 'The Inchanters; or Misnar, the Sultan of India. Tale the Sixth'. First published in *The Tales of the Genii* . . ., 2 vols (London, 1764), 1.220–2.39, this was reprinted (as 'The Enchanters; or, Misnar the Sultan of the East') in Weber, where the passage quoted occurs at 3.473. The transcription from Weber, in the hand of Anne Scott, is verbally accurate.

92.34–35 To call him up . . . Cambuscan bold? see John Milton, *Il Penseroso* (composed 1631?, published 1645), lines 109–10. The reference is to Geoffrey Chaucer's unfinished 'Squire's Tale' in *The Canterbury Tales*.

92.39–93.16 They cross'd the moat . . . right glad they were see Samuel Taylor Coleridge, *Christabel* (composed 1797–1800, published 1816), 1.123–44. Scott first heard the poem in an oral rendition by John Stoddart, probably in 1800. Anne Scott's transcription has two verbal variants from the published version: 'this distress' for 'thy distress', and 'from weariness' for 'for weariness'.

93.18–39 Seyten, or Seyton . . . enough for me for Seyton see EEWN 10, 495 (note to 142.4). The portrait, painted in the 1570s, is now owned by the National Galleries of Scotland (NG 2274). The Latin inscription and English motto, which are cropped at the right edge of the canvas, mean 'Patient in adversity, generous in prosperity. Keep venturing on.' Most of the information in this note evidently derives from the account of George in Sir Richard Maitland, *The History of the House of Seytoun* (Glasgow, 1829), [55]–60: *CLA*, 280.

93.40 pride which aped humility see Samuel Taylor Coleridge, 'The Devil's Thoughts' (1799), line 24. The expression has become proverbial: *ODEP*, 647.

93.42–43 Je suis ni roy . . . Coucy this French couplet means 'I am neither king, nor prince; I am the Seigneur de Coucy'. The sentiment is associated with Enguerrand III (*c*. 1182–1242), who succeeded as Seigneur de Coucy in 1191 and aspired to royal state.

94.4 Seton Castle Seton Castle, 18 km E of Edinburgh, was replaced by the present castle designed by Robert Adam in 1790.

94.5–9 there exists a beautiful family-piece . . . near Melrose this group portrait, painted in 1572 by Frans Pourbus the Elder, is now owned by the National Galleries of Scotland (NG 2275). It is reproduced (ascribed to Sir Antonio More) in John Pinkerton's unpaginated *The Scotish Gallery* (London, 1799): *CLA*, 8. The Somervilles and Setons have been linked by marriage since the 16th century. The Pavilion is situated on the N side of the Tweed half-way between Melrose and Abbotsford.

94.25–26 Knox associates Lord Ruthven with Lindesay see EEWN 10, 503 (note to 186.33–34).

94.35–36 the Earl of Athole . . . Throgmorton John Stewart (d. 1579) succeeded as 4th Earl of Atholl in 1542. For Maitland and Throgmorton see EEWN 10, 475 and 507 (notes to 25.17 and 206.27).

94.43–95.5 Submitting . . . regent see John Knox, *The Historie of the Reformation of the Church of Scotland* ([London, 1587]; repr., [ed. David Buchanan], London, 1644), 499: *CLA*, 2.

95.8–11 Gan . . . betrayed for Ganelon and his bad reputation see EEWN 10, 509 (note to 229.12).

95.19–24 At fairs he play'd . . . Habbie's dead stanza 5 of *The Life and Death of the Piper of Kilbarchan, or The Epitaph of Habbie Simpson*, by Robert Sempill (d. between 1660 and 1669), published posthumously and anonymously in the last decade of the century.

95.25–29 This was the name . . . Hell's black grammar Hecate was the Greek goddess of magic and witchcraft. The phrase 'hell's black grammar' is found in Robert Burns, 'On the Late Captain Grose's Peregrinations thro' Scotland, collecting the Antiquities of that Kingdom' (1793), line 21.

95.30–35 By an ancient . . . grey man according to the legendary account given by David Hume of Godscroft, in *The History of the Houses of Douglas and Angus* (Edinburgh, 1644; reissued in 1648 for sale in London: *CLA*, 3), 3–4, the house of Douglas was founded by a Scottish king, Solvathius, *c.* 767, the first bearer of the name being a noble warrior called Sholto: 'the King being desirous to know of his Lievetenants the particulars of the fight, and inquiring for the Author of so valiant an act, the Nobleman being there in person, answer was made unto the King in the Irish tongue (which was then onely in use) *Sholto Du glasse*, that is to say, Behold yonder black, gray man'.

95.38–40 A romancer . . . a tether of Scott uses the proverb which appears in the first sentence on 3 November 1809 in a letter to George Ellis: *Letters*, 2.268. The occurrence in the letter is the only example cited in *ODEP*, 343.

95.41–96.2 an expression . . . p. 278 see George Chalmers, *The Life of Mary, Queen of Scots*, 2 vols (London, 1818), 1.278n: *CLA*, 2. For Dryfesdale see EEWN 10, 508 (note to 217.42).

96.7–11 I have on an ancient piece of iron . . . Sharpe the Latin motto means 'Faith/fidelity/trustworthiness spurns/despises gifts'. James Sharp (b. 1618) became Archbishop of St Andrews in 1661 and was murdered by a band of Covenanters in 1679. The grate, still at Abbotsford, is illustrated in Mary Monica Maxwell Scott, *Abbotsford: The Personal Relics and Antiquarian Treasures of Sir Walter Scott* (London, 1893), [vii] and described by Scott in *Reliquiæ Trotcosienses*, ed. Gerard Carruthers and Alison Lumsden (Edinburgh, 2004), 32. The actual motto on the grate is 'Fides dona superat': faith (or fidelity or trustworthiness) triumphs over gifts.

96.17 the Debateable Land see EEWN 10, 474 (note to 18.38–39).

96.18–19 A favourite . . . of James V see EEWN 10, 526 (note to 330.26).

96.20–22 The names . . . quotation see EEWN 10, 526 (note to 330.28–29).

96.23–25 Sir John Holland's poem . . . Mr David Laing for Richard Holland, called 'Sir John' by Scott, see EEWN 10, 527 (note to 335.27–30). The third publication of the Bannatyne Club, founded by Scott in 1823 to publish old Scottish documents, was Holland's *The Buke of the Howlat* (Edinburgh, 1823), edited by David Laing (1793–1878), who acted as secretary from the society's foundation to its dissolution in 1861.

96.27–97.4 In the dangerous expedition . . . September 24, 1562 for the quotations see George Chalmers, *The Life of Mary, Queen of Scots*, 2 vols (London, 1818), 1.86, 87: *CLA*, 2. The transcriptions are in Anne Scott's hand: the first has two verbal variants from Chalmers ('watches' for 'watche', and 'and a knapscap' for 'and knapscap').

97.18 the English ambassador Drury Sir William Drury (1527–79) exercised an ambassadorial role in Scotland between 1559 and 1576.

97.30–98.8 But after . . . no less affection see Robert Keith, *The History Of the Affairs of the Church and State in Scotland* (Edinburgh, 1734), 469–70: *CLA*, 11. The transcription, in Anne Scott's hand, has several verbal variants, but only one ('near' for 'nearer') is sufficiently serious to warrant emendation.

98.40–99.12 I am informed . . . Mr MacVean's system for MacVean's letter, dated 12 November 1829, see MS 869, f. 105r. For Scott's erroneous recollection of Grahame's work see EEWN 10, 530 (note to 360.43).

99.14–30 In the celebrated field of battle . . . at the great stane the battle of Killiecrankie, mentioned in the second paragraph, was fought in 1689 on level ground just N of the pass of that name. A stone is still pointed out as marking, according to popular belief, the spot where fell John Graham (1648?–89), created 1st Viscount of Dundee in 1688. Faskally House is a little S of the pass of Killiecrankie.

99.37–100.41 The Regent was out on foot . . . some dikes see *The Memoirs of Sir James Melvil of Halhill*, ed. George Scott, 3rd edn (London, 1752), 181–83: *CLA*, 8. The transcription, by Anne Scott, has several verbal variants, mostly of small significance, but a sentence important for the sense is omitted and has been restored in the present text (see the Emendation List). For the Laird of Grange see EEWN 10, 475 (note to 25.18). Alexander Home of Manderston, Berwickshire, died in 1593. 'Lord Hume' is a different Alexander Home (*c.* 1525–75), who became 5th Lord Home in 1551 and married *c.* 1558 Margaret Ker of Cessford, the sister of Sir William Ker of Cessford (d. 1600). Sir James Balfour of Pittendreich (*c.* 1525–83) was a notorious as a political turncoat.

101.18–22 We have already seen . . . quantity or quality for the Bruce's concern for this matter see 64–67 above.

101.32–102.27 A very curious letter . . . vicesimo quarto a facsimile of the Latin letter (Scottish Record Office, Melrose Charters GD. 55/364) is included in *Liber Sancte Marie de Melros*, 2 vols (Edinburgh, 1837), 329–30 (continuous pagination). For Thomas Thomson see 651 above (note to 55.8). There is one small error in the transcription made for Scott, presumably from the original manuscript, in the same careful copperplate hand as a similar document in *The Monastery* (65–67 above): 'successores mei' is now emended to 'successores nostri' (102.24). The charter may be translated thus: 'Robert by the grace of God King of Scots, to David his highly beloved son, and to his successors for all time to come: Greeting, and just as they may reign with his blessing, so may they hold to his precepts. My dearest son, worthy is the son deemed to be judged who strives hard to imitate his father's conduct in all things good and to follow his devout will; nor does he properly assume for himself the title of heir who does not adhere to the salutary behaviour of his predecessor: desirous therefore that those feelings of devout affection and true love which we have conceived towards the monastery of Melrose, where we have made arrangements for our heart to be buried with particular devotion, and towards the Monks who serve God in that place, the extreme holiness of whose life urges us to this end, continue to be expressed with true devotion by you and by our successors for all time to come, so that by your loving attitude shown to the said Monks for our sake after our death they themselves may be inspired to pray for us more fervently and more vigorously, we instruct you as strongly as we can, urgently supplicate you and enjoin you with all our heart to permit them to enjoy freely the assignations which we have conferred anew on these same Monks for the fabric of their church, and also all our other donations, increasing these if necessary rather than diminishing them, giving kindly ear to their petitions and faithfully defending and protecting them against invaders and enemies. This exhortation, supplication and precept, you, my son, and my successors for all time to come, are to take care to fulfil with outstanding zeal, if you wish to have our blessing, along with the blessing of the son of the most high King who taught sons to do their fathers' will in all things good, declaring that he had come into the world to do the will not of himself but of his father. In witness of the devotion we feel towards the aforesaid place, so loved and chosen by us, we are sending you this present letter to the aforesaid Monks for them to show to our successors hereafter. Given at Cardross on the eleventh day of May in the twenty-fourth year of our reign.'

102.28–37 If this charter . . . in the Abbey of Melrose the suggestion of forgery was raised again in 1953: see Archibald A. M. Duncan, 'The *Acta* of Robert I', *Scottish Historical Review*, 32 (1953), 1–39 (18–22). But Duncan has more recently concluded, in his edition of *The Acts of Robert I King of Scots 1306–1329*, that the document is genuine, partly on palaeographic grounds, and partly because 'the argument . . . that the king intended his heart to go to the Holy Land is irrelevant, since it is likely that he also intended it to be brought back for burial at Melrose, an intention stated in this letter' (*Regesta Regum Scottorum, 1153–1424*, 5: Edinburgh, 1988), 626.

KENILWORTH

111.2–3 A certain degree . . . Queen Mary in the immediately preceding novel *The Abbot* (1820).
111.4 her sister and her foe see Robert Burns, 'Lament of Mary Queen of Scots on the Approach of Spring' (1793), line 34, where Mary calls Elizabeth 'My sister and my fae'.
111.6–8 the candid Robertson . . . the subject see William Robertson, *The History of Scotland . . . during the reigns of Queen Mary and of King James VI. . . .*, 3rd edn, 2 vols (London, 1760), 2.245: *CLA*, 4. Robertson observes: 'Whoever undertakes to write the History of Scotland finds himself obliged, frequently, to view her [Elizabeth] in a very different, and in a less amiable light. Her authority in that kingdom, during the greater part of her reign, was little inferior to that which she possessed in her own. But this authority, acquired at first by a service of great importance to the nation, she exercised in a manner extremely pernicious to its happiness. By her industry in fomenting the rage of the two contending factions; by supplying the one with partial aid; by feeding the other with false hopes; by ballancing their power so artfully, that each of them was able to distress, and neither of them to subdue the other; she rendered Scotland long the seat of discord, confusion, and bloodshed: and her craft and intrigues, effecting what the valour of her ancestors could not accomplish, reduced that kingdom to a state of dependance on England. The maxims of policy, often little consonant to those of morality, may, perhaps, justify this conduct. But no apology can be offered for her behaviour to Queen Mary; a scene of dissimulation without necessity; and of severity beyond example. In almost all her other actions, Elizabeth is the object of our highest admiration; in this, we must allow that she not only laid aside the magnanimity which became a Queen, but the feelings, natural to a woman.'
111.31–114.3 At the west end . . . anno 1588 see Elias Ashmole, *Antiquities of Berkshire*, 3 vols (London, 1719), 1.149–54: *CLA*, 245. The passage is modernised in its presentation, in the hand of John Buchanan, but verbally it follows the original with almost entire faithfulness: Buchanan has changed 'yet without' to 'still without' (113.3), presumably to avoid the repetition of 'yet' a few words later. A few lines later a necessary 'and' was inserted before 'was afterwards' (12–13), and another before 'what a grief' (35).
111.31–35 the ruins of a manor . . . Godstow from its foundation in 685 to its dissolution in 1539 Abingdon Abbey owned Cumnor, 6 km W of Oxford. Cumnor Place was built in the 1330s as a residence for the Abbot and a sanatorium for the monks. In 1546 it, together with Godstow Nunnery, 4 km NW of Oxford, was assigned by Henry VIII to George Owen, his physician (with Oliver Bridges), and Owen's son William in turn assigned it to Anthony Forster in 1561. On Forster's death in 1572 the manor passed to Leicester, and two years later he assigned it to Henry Lord Norreys of Rycote (*c.* 1525–1601).

111.36–37 Abington arms . . . martletts see EEWN 11, 500 (note to 117.38).
112.14–15 Dr Walter Bayly . . . university Walter Bayley (1529–93) was Regius Professor of Medicine from 1561 to 1582.
112.42 about three miles distant in fact 5 miles (8 km).
113.14–15 made away killed.
113.23 Bald Butler Ashmole has 'Butter': the name of this otherwise unidentified person is given as 'Bald Buttler' in *Leicester's Commonwealth*, ed. D. C. Peck (Athens, Ohio, 1985), 81 (see Peck's note at 199).
113.28–29 Sir John Robertsett for Amy Robsart's father (Hugh in the novel) see EEWN 11, 476.
113.39 Dr Babington at the time of Amy's death Francis Babington (d. 1569?) was Rector of Lincoln College and Vice-Chancellor.
114.1–2 Cornbury Lodge Leicester's Cornbury House is near Charlbury, 20 km NW of Oxford.
114.2–3 Baker . . . Killingworth see Richard Baker, *A Chronicle of the Kings of England From the Time of the Romans Goverment unto the Raigne of our Soveraigne Lord King Charles* (London, 1643): 'The Raigne of Queen Elizabeth', 82.
114.4–5 the author of Leicester's Commonwealth see EEWN 11.473, 482. *CLA*, 258, has the 1641 edition with the erroneous attribution to the Jesuit Robert Parsons (1546–1610). Although he may well have facilitated its production, the principal author was probably Charles Arundell (1540–87), perhaps with the collaboration of other members of the conservative Roman Catholic group driven from Court by Leicester and his associates in 1582. See D. C. Peck's introduction to his edition of *Leicester's Commonwealth* (Athens, Ohio, 1985).
114.12–13 The only way . . . did it see *A Yorkshire Tragedy* (London, 1608), C3r: 'So, the surest waie to charme a womans tongue/ Is break hir neck, a pollitician did it.'
114.20–28 Mickle and Langhorne . . . liberal contributions among the contributions made by William Julius Mickle (1735–88) to *Old Ballads, Historical and Narrative, with some of modern date*, ed. Thomas Evans, 4 vols (London, 1784) is the ballad of 'Cumnor Hall' (4.130–35): *CLA*, 172. Mickle's archaic spelling is modernised in the Magnum text, in accordance with Scott's instruction in the ISet ('The printer will restore the usual spelling in these lines'): the original may be found in *Kenilworth: A Romance*, ed. J. H. Alexander (London, 1999), 393–96. John Langhorne (1735–79) is best known for *The Country Justice* (1774–77): when Scott was 15 he identified some lines from this poem on his only encounter with Robert Burns (Lockhart, 1.136–37).
114.32–117.20 Cumnor Hall John Buchanan's transcription is entirely accurate verbally. At 116.12 both Buchanan and the original 1782 and (modernised) 1810 editions of Evans have 'Then leave me to mourne' ('mourn' in 1810): the 'me', redundant metrically but helpful for the sense, was omitted at a subsequent stage.
114.39–44 The tradition . . . Sir Robert Sibbald's Copy on 29 December 1829 David Laing sent Scott a transcript of 'Informations and Manners, by Ben Jonson to W. D., 1619': MS 3911, f. 208r. This was a copy by the physician and antiquarian Sir Robert Sibbald (1641–1722) of a lost original set of notes by the poet William Drummond of Hawthornden (1585–1649) on his conversations with the poet and playwright Ben Jonson (1572–1637). Laing published the 'Informations' in *Archaeologia Scotica: or, Transactions of the Society of Antiquaries of Scotland*, 4:2 (1833), 241–70, the quoted passage being on p. 258.

117.29–118.18 In the north wall . . . for a difference see Elias Ashmole, *Antiquities of Berkshire*, 3 vols (London, 1719), 1.143–45: *CLA*, 245. The original Latin inscription, which survives in St Michael's Church, Cumnor, in black letter on brass plates (the last 6 lines on 3 small plates), has several variants from Ashmole's text, the most significant being: 'Eloquio' for 'Eloquii' (117.41, the former being grammatically superior), 'fides.' for 'fides,' (117.43, the former being preferable), 'Sic quod' for 'Si quod' (118.3), and 'Sed quae' for the repeated 'Si quod' (118.4, Ashmole's readings of these last two being erroneous). Since the Magnum reproduces Ashmole accurately no corrections have been made in the present text, but in the following translation the original inscription is respected:

> Anthony Forster, noble descendant of his race,
> Lord of Cumnor, was a man of Berkshire,
> An esquire, as was his father Richard
> Who was formerly of Evelith in Shropshire.
> Four sons issued from this line,
> From this line Anthony was the fourth.
> Wise in mind, excellent in spirit, active in body,
> His discourse was pleasant, his speech learned.
> There was honesty in his actions, charm in his conversation,
> Gravity in his demeanour, sincerity in his worship.
> Piety towards his country and a welcome openness towards the poor
> Are to be counted up and added to his other good qualities.
> So Death, which takes all things, has not taken everything away,
> But to those things which Death has taken, fame has given life.
> He knew how to pluck melodiously the sounding strings of the cithara, and to play on the Aonian lyre.
> He took pleasure in planting tender shoots in the earth, and in building beautiful houses with wondrous art.
> He was skilled at shaping many kinds of speech with well-ordered tongue, and at writing many things with well-educated hand.

Scott's ascription to Forster of multilingual ability probably involves a misreading of 'Composita varias lingua formare loquelas/ Doctus' which implies he had a command of language rather than languages.

118.33–37 The name of Lambourne . . . another man for a murderer called Lambourne see Scott's letter to Mrs Hughes of 24 August [1829]: 'There was a Lambourne executed the other day. I wonder if he is one of your Cumnor acquaintances' (*Letters*, 11.230); also his query to her husband John on 9 December of that year: 'Pray did not one Lambourne of those parts commit a very cruel murder some time since and would there be any harm in putting it into the notes of Kenilworth? If so perhaps you would give me the date. In our country I should hesitate about this, for fear of getting a dirk in my wame for tacking awa' the guid name of an honest family, but you are not I think so touchy in Berkshire' (*Letters*, 11. 273–74). John replied on 2 January 1830 (MS 3912, ff. 43r–44r): 'I have made out some particulars about the man whom I believe you ⟨par⟩ more especially alluded to. He is of a Cumnor stock of Lambourns, and perhaps one of the most notorious rascals in this part of the world; his nominal vocation, dealing in spavined, blind, or foundered hacks though by all accounts he would as soon steal them. . . . He is called Gipsy Lambourn, from his having married a gipsy: a middle aged man at present I believe, and said to be worth some money. I have found him out to be the same dealer who sold a blind horse as sound to an unsuspicious friend of mine, who could not afterwards find his chapman. Furthermore, he narrowly escaped hanging a few years ago, being detected with a stolen coach horse, whose eyelids he had burnt & otherwise altered it, as a disguise. He was saved by witnesses whom he brought out of Wales to perjure themselves. He has relations at Cumnor, not much better than himself. But I cannot make out that the Lambourn who was hanged for the murder of his wife was a man of this country, or any relation of the notable worthy above mentioned. I am not certain as to the place where the murder was committed, some say near London; some in Hampshire. The circumstances I think were that being separated from his wife, who went to service in consequence of some disagreement, he met her accidentally, attacked & cut her head nearly off.'

118.38–39 the jolly Black Bear . . . Cumnor for the change of the inn's name to The Black Bear see EEWN 11, 482 (note to 1.30). It was announced by Mary Anne Hughes in a letter of 19 February [1821], MS 3892, f. 41r: 'the landlord of the Jolly Ringers has this week put up the sign of "the black Bear, by Giles Gosling."'.

118.41 The expressions are proverbial. this sentence was added to the Ed1 note (EEWN 11, 34) in the ISet.

119.1–3 The Leicester cognizance . . . ragged staff Leicester's father was John Dudley (1504–53) created Earl of Warwick in 1547 and Duke of Northumberland in 1551. The bear and ragged staff had first been used together by Richard Neville (1428–71), Earl of Warwick from 1449.

119.4 Sir Francis Drake, Morgan Sir Francis Drake (1540–96) was an admiral exceptionally active against the Spaniards: he was knighted in 1581. Sir Henry Morgan (*c.* 1635–1688) was similarly active, and (though accused of exceeding his commission) was knighted in 1674 and appointed lieutenant-governor of Jamaica.

119.8–9 a long ballad . . . Weber see EEWN 11, 494 (note to 79.37–40).

119.10–13 This verse of an old song . . . merry-men the two lines in the note are not from Wager's play (see EEWN 11, 494: note to 80.4–7) but from 'Agaynste a Comely Coystrowne', lines 17–18, by John Skelton (*c.* 1460–1529).

119.17–24 The burial place . . . horse-shoes there see William Camden, *Britannia: or, a Chorographical Description of . . . England, Scotland, and Ireland . . .*, trans. Richard Gough, 2nd edn, 4 vols (London, 1806), 1.221. Scott's transcription has several verbal variants: most notably he omits the words after 'fourth' in Camden's 'supporting a fourth larger lying flat on them like a cromlech'.

119.31–37 Of late his offices . . . more conspicuous on 19 February [1821] Mary Anne Hughes wrote to Scott: 'Wayland Smith is in perfect preservation at the distance of not two miles from this place, & Lord Craven has enclosed it with a plantation: the village children religiously believe the old Legend of the visionary Smith & often visit the spot to hear the clink of his hammer' (MS 3892, f. 41r–v). With a letter of 15 March (ff. 75–76) she sent a sketch of the Smithy.

119.38 Orvietan see EEWN 11, 502 (note to 130.43).

120.1–6 Naunton . . . too many for them for Naunton see EEWN 11.481. On pp. 209–10 he records that on his deathbed Sussex warned his friends: 'beware of the gipsey, meaning Leicester, for he will be too hard for you all; you know not the best so well as I do.'

120.12–25 He was a tall, handsome, bold man . . . the bold face for the quotation see John Aubrey, *Letters written by Eminent Persons in the Seventeenth and Eighteenth Centuries*, 2 vols (London, 1813), Vol. 2, Pt 2, 509–12: *CLA*, 149. Sir Robert Harley (1579–1656) had his seat at Brampton Bryan, Herefordshire, 15 km W of Ludlow. Sir Thomas Overbury (1581–1613) was a prominent figure at court, made sewer to the king and knighted in 1608. Scott's modernised transcription is generally verbally accurate, apart from some revisions that may be stylistic, e.g. 'handsome, bold' for 'handsome, and bold', 'judged ⟨of⟩ ↑in↓' for 'judged on', and 'the bold face' for 'a bold face' in the couplet. The first two sentences and the last two are separated by a long passage which Scott silently omits.

120.36–121.6 Being confined in the Tower . . . the captive Paladin for the incident in the Tower see a letter endorsed 26 July [1592] from Sir Arthur Gorges to Sir Robert Cecil, printed in Arthur Cayley, Jun., *The Life of Sir Walter Ralegh, Knt*, 2nd edn, 2 vols (London, 1806), 1.128–30: *CLA*, 236.

121.18–22 When council sits . . . a God's name compare Robert Langham's *Letter* (for which see EEWN 11, 473), lines 1579–86: 'Noow syr, if the Councell sit, I am at hand, wait at an inch I warrant yoo. If any make babling, peas (say I) woot ye whear ye ar? If I take a lystenar, or a priar in at the chinks, or at the lokhole, I am by and by in the bonez of him: but noow they keep good order, they kno me well inough: If a be a freend, or such one az I like: I make him sit doun by me on a foorm, or a cheast, Let the rest wallk a Gods name.'

121.31–122.32 Dr Julio . . . p. 23 Julio is identified by D. C. Peck as Guilio Borgarucci (d. *c.* 1581): *Leicester's Commonwealth* (Athens, Ohio, 1985), 274–75. For Parsons see note to 114.4–5. For the quotation see Peck, 82–83. In the 1641 edition owned by Scott (*CLA*, 258) the extract is on pp. 23–24. John Buchanan's transcription is verbally accurate. The short passage omitted reads: 'but might have spared the yong childe in her belly, which she was enforced to make away (cruelly and unnaturally) for clearing the house against the good mans arrivall'. The omission is made in Buchanan's transcript, whether on his own initiative or by Scott's direction cannot be determined. Douglas Howard (1543–1608), eldest daughter of William Howard of Effingham, married John Sheffield, 2nd Baron Sheffield, in 1560. Dorothy Braye (1530–1605), married William Knollys (*c.* 1545–1632) shortly after the death of her first husband Edmund Brydges, 2nd Baron Chandos in 1573. Rowland Crompton was yeoman of the Earl of Essex's cellar, and Richard Lloyd was another of Essex's men. For Walter Bayley see note to 112.14–15 above.

123.1–12 The original . . . Birmingham see EEWN 11, 473.

123.17–24 I am indebted . . . Mr Badnall Scott added this paragraph to the Ed1 note. The plan was sent by Richard Badnall, of Olive Vale, near Liverpool, on 26 May 1830 (MS 3913, f. 134r–v). The philosopher Jean-Jacques Rousseau (1712–78) spent a year in England in 1766–67 at Wootton Hall, Derbyshire, the residence of Richard Davenport.

123.29–35 I was required . . . beside her see *Memoirs of his Own Life by Sir James Melville of Halhill. M.D.XLIX.–M.D.XCIII.*, [ed. Thomas Thomson] (Edinburgh, 1827), 119–20: CLA, 277. Scott's transcription has 3 small verbal variants, as well as omitting 'at Westmester' after 'solemnity'.

123.42–124.12 As then . . . into English the appearance of the lines of verse in the ISet, with two alterations, suggests that this is probably Scott's own translation, made on the spot. *ODNB* notes that the Harrington anecdote is first recorded in the late 18th century.

124.14–127.33 Furniture of Kenilworth . . . the princely pleasures of Kenilworth Hamper sent the copy of the inventory, beautifully transcribed, on 2 June 1829, as he notes in a letter of 11 November that year (MS 3911, f. 43r). For the Magnum Scott added the following paragraph at 302.33, drawing on the first section of the material quoted in the note:

'The livery cupboards were loaded with plate of the richest description, and the most varied; some articles tasteful, some perhaps grotesque, in the invention and decoration, but all gorgeously magnificent, both from the richness of the work and value of the materials. Thus the chief table was adorned by a salt, ship-fashion, made of mother-of-pearl, garnished with silver and divers warlike ensigns, and other ornaments, anchors, sails, and sixteen pieces of ordnance. It bore a figure of Fortune, placed on a globe, with a flag in her hand. Another salt was fashioned of silver, in form of a swan in full sail. That chivalry might not be omitted amid this splendour, a silver Saint George was presented, mounted and equipped in the usual fashion in which he bestrides the dragon. The figures were moulded to be in some sort useful. The horse's tail was managed to hold a case of knives, while the breast of the dragon presented a similar accommodation for oyster knives.' (Scott also incorporated the eagle chandelier in the text at the beginning of the previous chapter.)

127.35–128.15 Death of the Earl of Leicester . . . Heaven now hates for the Sibbald transcription see note to 114.39–44 above. The epitaph is included in Laing's *Archaeologia Scotica* article (see the same note), 258n.

THE PIRATE

136.2 Quoth he, there was a ship see Samuel Taylor Coleridge, 'The Rime of the Ancyent Marinere' (1798), line 10: 'There was a Ship, quoth he'.

136.9 the Northern Light-House Service the Commissioners of Northern Lighthouses was a body established by Act of Parliament in 1786 to oversee the construction and maintenance of lighthouses round the coast of Scotland and the Isle of Man.

136.19 Mr Robert Stevenson 1772–1850. His greatest achievement was designing and constructing the Bell Rock lighthouse (1807–10), which Scott and his fellow voyagers visited on this trip, and of which Scott said 'no description can give the idea of this slight, solitary, round tower, trembling amid the billows' (Lockhart, 3.137). He was grandfather of the novelist Robert Louis Stevenson.

136.21–23 Selkirkshire . . . a seaport in its circuit Scott was appointed Sheriff-Depute (or simply Sheriff, principal local law officer) of Selkirkshire in 1799, an office he retained until his death. For Corporal Trim's attribution of a coast to Bohemia see Lawrence Sterne, *Tristram Shandy* (1759–67), 8.19, following Shakespeare's stage direction to this effect in *The Winter's Tale*, 3.3.

137.3–4 the Ultima Thule of the ancients Thule was a northern island (perhaps Iceland, Norway, or—as here—the Shetlands) mentioned by Pytheas, a Greek navigator of the 4th century BC. 'Ultima Thule' (farthest Thule) is the uttermost point attainable.

137.9–10 an American cruiser on 18 June 1812 the United States of America declared war on Great Britain, and for the next two years (until December 1814) a sporadic conflict resulted in the resolution of conflicting claims to Canada. America realised that it could not successfully invade and hold Canada, and Britain that it could not successfully invade and hold America: see Philip R. N. Katcher, *The American War 1812–1814* (Reading, 1984), 19.

137.13 Morven Morvern, a peninsula in Lochaber on the W coast of Scotland, the closest part of the mainland to the Isle of Mull.

137.14–15 the Giant's Causeway . . . Staffa a distinctive volcanic basalt formation runs under the sea between the N of Ireland and Scotland, surfacing at the Giant's Causeway on the N coast of Co. Antrim and the Isle of Staffa.

137.31–32 The world of waters . . . were we see 'A wet sheet and a flowing sea', lines 15–16, in Allan Cunningham, *The Songs of Scotland, Ancient and Modern*, 4 vols (London, 1825), 4.208–09: *CLA*, 165.

137.36–37 a lady . . . friendship Harriet Katherine Townshend (1773–1814), who became Duchess of Buccleuch in 1812 on the succession of her husband Charles William Henry Scott as 4th Duke of Buccleuch. She died on 24 August 1814.

137.37–39 The subsequent loss . . . the world William Erskine (1768–1822) was appointed a judge with the title Lord Kinedder in January 1822 but died in distressing circumstances in August of the same year.

137.43 the "Lord of the Isles" the fifth and last of Scott's long poems, published in January 1815.

138.12–13 several of them . . . correspondents of my father presumably clients or legal colleagues of Walter Scott, senior (1729–99), who was a solicitor.

138.17 Udaller see EEWN 12, 605.

138.27 Fort Charlotte first constructed in the 17th century, the fort was rebuilt in 1781 and named after Queen Charlotte, consort of George III.

138.40–41 the character of Norna . . . Meg Merrilies in fact Norna attracted high praise from several of the original reviewers, and the reviewer for *Blackwood's Edinburgh Magazine* (probably J. G. Lockhart) made Scott's own point, comparing her favourably with Meg Merrilies in *Guy Mannering*: 'these two characters are not only *discriminated*, but, if we may so speak, *contrasted*. Meg Merrilies, interesting as she is, is, after all, a lesser personage than Norna' (10 (December 1821), 718). Scott is probably recalling the anonymous review by Nassau Senior in *The Quarterly Review*, 26 (January 1822), 454–74 (472): 'Norna is a more palpable copy than any of the preceding characters. . . . The first and the best . . . was Meg Merrilies: and even she touched the borders of nature; and all her successors, down to Magdalen Græme [in *The Abbot*], have gone farther and farther in transgressing them. But hitherto they have had a method in their madness—their features have been exaggerated, but they have been imposing and consistent. Norna is a perfect busy-body, and wastes her energy in restlessness and an affectation of activity as undignified and figetty as that of the Weird Sister.'

139.6–7 a Norwood prophetess a celebrated gipsy fortune-teller, Margaret Finch, who lived at the present Gipsy Hill, Norwood, Surrey: she died aged 109 in 1740.

139.17–18 The pleasure is as great . . . to cheat see Samuel Butler, *Hudibras*, Part 2 (1664), 3.1–2: *CLA*, 182, 242.

139.19–24 Indeed, as I have observed elsewhere . . . difficulty see Scott's discussion of the explanations offered at the end of their apparently supernatural fictions by Horace Walpole and Ann Radcliffe in his biographical notices of those writers (1823, 1825): *Prose Works*, 3.317–18, 369–75.

139.37 the value . . . ten shillings sterling see Arthur Edmonston, *A View of the Ancient and Present State of the Zetland Islands* . . ., 2 vols (Edinburgh, 1809), 1.135, 153: *CLA*, 19. Ten shillings is 50 pence.

139.39 unstable as water Genesis 49.4.

139.39–140.5 The sagas . . . madness see EEWN 12, 506 (note to 15.17).

140.6 bang bhang, Indian hemp.

140.8 Fair Isle island midway between Orkney and Shetland.

140.20 Mr Baikie of Tankerness James Baikie (1786–1869) succeeded his father as 8th laird of Tankerness, 13 km E of Kirkwall, in 1817.

140.25 North Ronaldshaw North Ronaldsay, the most northerly of the Orkney Isles.

140.31–34 Now the storm . . . the darken'd air Thomas Gray, 'The Fatal Sisters. An Ode' (1768), lines 1–4. The ode is an English version of a Norse poem included, with a Latin translation, in Thomas Bartholin, *Antiqvitatum Danicarum de causis contemptæ a Danis adhuc gentilibus mortis* (Copenhagen, 1689), 617–24: *CLA*, 99. The title means '[A book] of Danish antiquities: on the reasons for death being scorned by the still-heathen Danes'.

141.15 Ancient Picts the oldest known inhabitants of what is now Scotland, who lived in the E, N of the Tay estuary.

141.19 Mr S— Mr Stevenson: see note to 136.19.

141.41–142.2 the wondrous tales . . . juvenile readers Erik Pontoppidan (1698–1764), Bishop of Bergen (not Uppsala) 1747–54, published his *Det förste forsög paa Norges naturlige historie* at Copenhagen in 1752–53, including descriptions of the merman and mermaid, great sea snakes, and the kraken. Scott owned the English version, *The Natural History of Norway*, 2 parts (London, 1755: *CLA*, 265), where the creatures feature in Part 2, Ch. 8 (183–218). The first edition of William Guthrie's *A New Geographical, Historical, and Commercial Grammar* was published in London in 1770 . It went through a bewildering variety of editions up to 1827. The rumoured sea-creatures were treated with increasing scepticism as successive editions appeared, being demoted to a footnote in the 20th edition (1805 and 1806) and finally disappearing entirely in the 23rd edition, 'studiously revised and carefully corrected', in 1819.

142.8–9 What hidest thou . . . mysterious Sea? see Felicia Hemans, 'The Treasures of the Deep' (1825), lines 1–2. The second line reads 'Thou hollow-sounding and mysterious main!'.

142.34 Sir Joseph Banks Banks (1743–1820) was an eminent natural scientist and served as President of the Royal Society from 1778 until his death.

142.41–42 the Black Brunswickers in 1815 the Black Brunswickers were a volunteer regiment formed by the Duke of Brunswick in 1809: they played a prominent part in the battles of Quatre Bras and Waterloo in June 1815.

143.3–6 My music since . . . another song Thomas Tusser, *An hundreth good pointes of husbandrie* (London, 1557), dedicatory epistle, lines 25–28: see *CLA*, 177.

143.8–14 At the period supposed . . . now held in 1643 Charles I granted Orkney and Shetland to William, 7th Earl of Morton. A subsequent dispute led to their annexation to the Crown in 1669. In 1707 they were returned to the Earl of Morton by one of the last pieces of legislation by the Scottish Parliament (a Private Act of the United Kingdom Parliament confirmed this in 1742), and in 1766 they were bought from him by Sir Lawrence Dundas of Kerse (1712–81). His grandson, also Lawrence (1766–1839), succeeded his father Thomas (1741–1820) as Baron Dundas of Aske, a title conferred in 1784.

143.20 chapman's drouth proverbial phrase: *The Scottish National Dictionary*, *chapman*, 1.

143.30 Saint Ronald St Rognvald (*c.* 1103–58), who as Earl of Orkney in 1137 began building the Cathedral in Kirkwall in honour of St Magnus, canonised in 1135. Rognvald is said to have been canonised in 1192.

143.34–39 The King of Sweden . . . 1555 see Olaus Magnus, *Historia de Gentibvs Septentrionalibvs* (Rome, 1555), 116–17: *CLA*, 185. The translation is taken, with some variation and apparent reference to the 1555 original, from *A Compendious History of the Goths, Swedes, & Vandals and Other Northern Nations* (London, 1658), 45: *CLA*, 64.

144.14 Eolus god of the winds in Classical mythology. In *The Aeneid*, 1.50–59 Virgil depicts him as keeping the winds imprisoned in a cave.

144.21 Hecaté Greek goddess of the underworld, protectress of enchanters and witches.

145.12 Sanda and the Pentland Skerries or Sanday, one of the N isles of Orkney; and a set of rocky islets between Orkney and the Scottish mainland. Robert Stevenson's first work for the Commissioners of the Northern Lights was the double lighthouse on the Pentland Skerries, completed in 1794. The Sanday lighthouse on Start Point was completed in 1806.

145.27–29 Had Robinson Crusoe . . . desert island Crusoe experienced great difficulty in learning how to grind his corn during his third year on the desert island: Daniel Defoe, *The Life and Strange Surprizing Adventures of Robinson Crusoe* (1719), ed. W. R. Owens (London, 2008), 144–48.

146.5 See Hibbert's Description . . . p. 470 see Samuel Hibbert, *A Description of the Shetland Islands* (Edinburgh, 1822), 470: *CLA*, 5. Scott anglicises the speeches as reported by Hibbert: 'Death to da head that wears nae hair'; 'Here's first to . . . wir wordy land-maister, an wir lovin meat-mither, helt ta man, death to fish, and guid growth i' da grund'; 'God open the mouth of the gray fish, an haud his hand about da corn'.

146.8–9 Montrose . . . Scotland on 27 April 1650, at Carbisdale in Ross-shire, on the S side of the Kyle of Sutherland, the Covenanters defeated forces partly levied in Orkney by James Graham (1612–50), who had succeeded as 5th Earl of Montrose in 1626. For Strathnaver see EEWN 12, 538 (note to 140.30–31).

146.17 Sir John Urry Urry, or Hurry, a professional soldier, was executed at Edinburgh on 29 May 1650 after the defeat at Carbisdale (see previous note).

146.21 Wind-changing Warwick . . . no more see *3 Henry VI*, 5.1.57.

146.22 Strachan Archibald Strachan (d. 1652), an officer serving Parliament in the English Civil War, and who transferred to the Scottish Covenanting armies in 1649.

146.28–147.11 Of their Dancing in Arms . . . most wise reason see Olaus Magnus (as in note to 143.34–39) 517 (1555, in Latin) and 167–68 (1658, in English). Olaus Magnus (1490–1557) was in 1544 appointed Archbishop of Uppsala by the Pope (hence 'the Primate'), although Sweden was no longer a Catholic country.

147.16–17 Seven Champions of Christendom for the champions see [Richard Johnson], *The most famous History of the Seauen Champions of Christendome: Saint George of England, Saint Dennis of Fraunce, Saint Iames of Spaine, Saint Anthonie of Italie, Saint Andrew of Scotland, Saint Pattricke of Ireland, and Saint Dauid of Wales* . . . (London, 1596): compare *CLA*, 106.

147.18 All's Well that Ends Well nothing in *All's Well that Ends Well* can be called a dramatic interlude, but Scott may be half-recollecting the play in Act 5 of *Love's Labour's Lost* in which the comic characters present the nine worthies (although only five appear and two of those are not traditional worthies).

147.18–20 This dramatic curiosity . . . Mewbie, Zetland James Scott (d. 1860), son of John Scott of Melby (1760–1850), sent a copy of a copy (see 151.4–8) of the manuscript account of the sword-dance quoted on 11 December 1829: MS 3911, f. 137r. Neither James Scott's copy nor either of the original manuscripts has been located: his copy was transcribed by John Buchanan for the Magnum. The Hazlar (or Haslar) Hospital was the Royal Naval Hospital at Gosport, Hampshire, founded in 1746.

147.20–22 Mr Hibbert . . . the sword-dance Hibbert (see note to 146.5) has an extended description of the sword-dance at 555–60.
151.10–11 Waller's Battle of the Summer Islands see *The Works of Edmund Waller Esqr.* (London, 1729), 83–95: *CLA*, 195. 'The Battel of the Summer-Islands' is a vivid account of the hunting of two whales in Bermuda.
151.13–152.11 The Dwarfie Stone . . . direct worshippers in the Magnum this chapter endnote replaces the Ed1 footnote.
151.14–15 it has been rather undervalued . . . Mr Barry see George Barry, *The History of the Orkney Islands* (Edinburgh, 1805), 39, where the hermit's cell conjecture later in the note appears. Modern archaeology considers it to be a Neolithic chambered tomb; unusually it is not built of stones but cut from a single piece of rock.
151.40–41 cui bono *Latin* who would be the better for it? What good would it do?
152.5 Pillow cold, and sheets not warm see Richard Crashaw, 'An Epitaph vpon a Yovng Married Covple Dead and Bvyred Together' (1652), line 13: 'Pillow hard, & sheetes not warm'.
152.11 Dii Manes *Latin* protecting deities.
152.30–154.34 There lived in the same territory . . . cap. 4 Thomas Bartholin, *Antiqvitatum Danicarum de causis contemptæ a Danis adhuc gentilibus mortis* (Copenhagen, 1689), 688–93: *CLA*, 99. Bartholin (see note to 140.31–34) provides a Latin translation of his Old Norse account.
155.5 Circle of Stennis Neolithic stone circle about 6 km NE of Stromness. Scott visited the site in 1814.
155.9–11 An elder brother . . . West Indies in 1780–82 George Bridges Rodney (1718–92) commanded the British naval force which successfully defended the British West Indies against invasion by the French. Robert Scott (1767–87) joined the Royal Navy in 1778 and took part in this campaign.
155.17–18 these lines . . . Derbyshire Frances Crawford Kemble (1787–1849) married the Derbyshire millowner Robert Arkwright in 1805. The song appeared as *The Pirate's Farewell, A Ballad, By Sir Walter Scott Bart. The Music by Mrs. Robert Arkwright*, printed on paper with the watermark 1828. The four stanzas are set with only two small verbal changes.
155.19–21 The celebrated Sortes Virgilianæ . . . futurity see EEWN 12, 553 (note to 224.6–8).
155.22–27 It is worth while saying . . . the Bannatyne Club see EEWN 12, 556 (note to 245.8).
155.36–156.6 Accordingly, Torfæus assures us . . . William the Lion of Scotland see Thormodus Torffæus, *Orcades Seu Rerum Orcadensium Historiæ* (Copenhagen, 1715), 131: *CLA*, 1. William the Lion was King of Scots 1165–1214.
155.43 See the Eyrbiggia Saga see *Eyrbyggia-saga*, ed. G. J. Thorkelin (Copenhagen, 1787), 10–11: *CLA*, 64.
156.13–19 The MacRaws . . . that of Caberfae see EEWN 12, 554 (note to 260.33–34).
156.20 Sorceresses and fortune-tellers this glossarial note was omitted in the Magnum.
156.30 the bicker of Saint Magnus compare James Wallace, *An Account of the Islands of Orkney* (London, 1700), 63 (*CLA*, 15): '*Buchanan* tells a Story, which is still believ'd here and talk'd of as a truth, though now there be nothing of it. That at *Scapa* a place about a mile of *Kirkwal* to the South, there was kept a large cup, and when any new Bishop landed there, they filled it with strong Ale, and offer'd it to him to drink, and if he happened to drink it of chearfully, they promised to themselves a Noble Bishop, and many good years in his time.'

156.41 Jokul . . . common use exceptionally, this unchanged Ed1 note is here repeated for convenience.
157.3 Hercules in Roman mythology a figure of great strength given to undertaking tasks involving formidable physical prowess.
157.3 Rorie Mhor of Dunvegan see the entry for 15 September in James Boswell, *Tour to the Hebrides* (1785): 'We looked at Rorie More's horn . . . It holds rather more than a bottle and a half. Every Laird of M'Leod, it is said, must, as a proof of his manhood, drink it off full of claret, without laying it down'.
157.5–11 Luggie . . . Scalloway see John Brand, *A New Description of Orkney, Zetland, Pightland-Firth, and Caithness* (Edinburgh 1703), 110–11.
157.15 learned friend possibly Dr Arthur Edmonston of Lerwick, but the letter has not been traced.
157.19 the Heptarchy collective name for the Anglo-Saxon kingdoms of what is now England during the period AD 500–850.
158.28 the reverend gentleman . . . the island the minister on Hoy and Graemsay from 1796 to 1849 was the Rev. Gavin Hamilton (1762–1849).
158.37 Avery Henry Avery (1659–1696?), a celebrated pirate of the last decade of the 17th century, known as Captain John Avery, who brought off the biggest single act of piracy to be recorded. The source of the story has not been found.
159.2 Standing Stones of Stennis see note to 155.5.
159.33–36 The Northern Popular Antiquities . . . solemn occasions see *Prose Works*, 5.359–61. Scott's abstract originally appeared in *Illustrations of Northern Antiquities*, [ed. Henry Weber, Robert Jamieson, and Walter Scott] (Edinburgh, 1814).

THE FORTUNES OF NIGEL

167.2–3 But why . . . the Man of Ross see Alexander Pope, *Moral Essays: Epistle III. To Allen Lord Bathurst* (1733), lines 249–50, where the first line reads: 'But all our praises why should Lords engross?'.
167.5–7 Having, in the tale . . . by right the heroine of *The Heart of Mid-Lothian* (1818) is the lowly-born Jeanie Deans.
167.17 George Heriot for George Heriot (1563–1624) see EEWN 13, 526–27.
167.27–30 The Hospital . . . an institution the building, designed by the mason William Wallace in a late Gothic cum Renaissance style, is situated next to Greyfriars Kirk on the N side of the Old Town. It was begun in 1628, but the first students were not admitted until 1659. George Heriot's continues at the present as an independent co-educational day school for pupils aged 3 to 18.
168.9 a word spoken in season Isaiah 50.4; compare Proverbs 15.23.
168.25–28 Lady Mary Wortley Montague . . . lowlands in a letter of 1 April 1717, Lady Mary praises Sofia, Bulgaria, for its situation where mountains yield to plains; on 21 July 1747 she described her favourite retreat of Lóvere on Lake Iseo, N Italy, underneath the foothills of the Alps, as 'a place the most beautifully romantic I ever saw in my life'; and on 11 December 1758 she wrote: 'I have found, wherever I have travelled, that the pleasantest spots of ground have been in the vallies which are encompassed with high mountains' (*The Works of the Right Honourable Lady Mary Wortley Montagu*, [ed. James Dallaway], 6th edn, 5 vols (London, 1817), 2.150–51, 4.20, 5.66: *CLA*, 202).

169.6–7 the chivalrous language of Sir Philip Sydney's Arcadia the euphuistic (affectedly periphrastic and high-flown) language found notably in Sidney's *Arcadia* (1590), and spouted by Sir Piercie Shafton in *The Monastery* (1820).
169.7–8 the ceremonial of the tilt-yard . . . Place de Carrousel for an account of tilting in the period see G. P. V. Akrigg, *Jacobean Pageant* (London, 1962), 162–63. *Carrousel* is a French term designating formal tournaments involving various sports and entertainments, popular in the 17th century, *place* being the ground on which they were held.
169.9 Knight of the Bath member of an order of chivalry which originally—from the reign of Henry IV (1399–1413) until 1661—involved an inaugural ceremonial bath symbolising purity.
169.10–13 Lord Herbert of Cherbury . . . damsel *The Life of Edward Lord Herbert, of Cherbury. Written by himself. With a prefatory memoir*, [ed. Horace Walpole; the memoir by Scott] (Edinburgh and London, 1809), 93–95: *CLA*, 201. Edward Herbert (1582?–1648) was created Baron of Cherbury in 1629.
169.15–18 the hour was already arrived . . . experiment Francis Bacon developed his rationalistic theories most notably in *Novum Organum* (New Instrument), published in 1620.
169.22–23 Bardolph, Nym, Pistol, Peto . . . Falstaff the five characters appear in one or more of *1 Henry IV*, *2 Henry IV*, *Henry V*, and *The Merry Wives of Windsor*.
169.25–27 had, since the commencement . . . buckler see EEWN 13, 614–15 (note to 249.19). The 'Low Country wars' had begun in 1585 when Queen Elizabeth sent the Earl of Leicester to support Dutch resistance to Spanish rule.
169.27–170.16 so that a historian says . . . most places see *Somers' Tracts*, 2.262–304 (266). Scott has made several verbal changes, some of them perhaps inadvertent (e.g. 'peculiar' for 'particular'; 'countenance' for 'maintenance'; 'walk in the street' for 'walk the streets'), others probably designed to enhance the style and smooth the passage for his readers (e.g. 'unpunished and unregarded' for 'unpunished nor regarded'; 'consumed' for 'and consume'). After 'the nobility' he omits the following words: 'and not a little as was suspected from the Earl of Northampton, which persons, although of themselves they were not able to attempt any enterprise, yet faith, honesty, and other good acts, were little set by'.
170.22–25 to use the old simile . . . reservoirs see Arthur Murphy, *The Citizen* (London, 1763), 9 (Act 1, Scene 2): 'The father is a reservoir of riches, and the son is a fountain to play it all away in vanity and folly'. Scott may also have in mind George Colman (the Younger), *The Heir at Law* (Dublin, 1798), 35 (Act 3, Scene 1): 'His heart swells with pleasure as he drives through his fat native soil, which ruddy labour has cultivated; 'till he reaches this grand reservoir of opulence'.
170.41–42 the words of Burke . . . grossness see Edmund Burke, *Reflections on the Revolution in France* (1790), ed. Conor Cruise O'Brien (Harmondsworth, 1968), 170.
171.1–16 according to Sir John Harrington . . . happens see *Nugæ Antiquæ*, ed Thomas Park, 2 vols (London, 1804), 1.351–52: *CLA*, 190. The passage occurs in a letter of 1606. Scott abridges it, and he introduces several verbal variants: 'recollection' for 'remembrance'; 'an assistant and partaker' for 'an humble presenter and assistant'; 'but never did I see' for 'but I neer did see'; and 'good order and sobriety' for 'good order, discretion, and sobriety'.
171.26–29 Alsatia is elsewhere explained . . . law see EEWN 13, 181.34–182.1.

171.29–172.1 These privileges . . . 1608 see John Stow, *A Survey of the Cities of London and Westminster*, rev. John Strype and others, 6 books (London, 1720: *CLA*, 208), 3.267–69. The references are to Sir Richard Gray (not Scott's 'Sir Patrick Grey') of Codnor (Derbyshire) and to Hugh de Courtney (1303–77), who succeeded as Earl of Devon in 1340. Stow says that Sir Hugh rebuilt the friary *c.* 1350. Edward I reigned 1272–1307, and Edward III 1327–77.

171.36–44 For the gross debauchery . . . client for Sir Ralph Winwood's *Memorials* and James Howell's letters see EEWN 13, 550–51 (note to 19.34–30.6) and 540: neither of these contains much, if anything, that could be termed 'gross debauchery'. For 'the Bawdy' in the letters between King James and Buckingham, see Kennet, 2.697n: *CLA*, 249. For Isaac D'Israeli's defence of James see EEWN 13, 524.

172.1–4 Shadwell . . . Terence for the quotations from *The Squire of Alsatia* in the following paragraph and accompanying footnote see *The Dramatick Works of Thomas Shadwell*, 4 vols (London, 1720), 4.[6] and [11]: *CLA*, 217. The quotation in the text of the paragraph is verbally almost entirely accurate; that in the footnote is slightly modernised and has one stylistic change resulting in 'Flanders, who has run from his colours, and retreated' for '*Flanders*, run from his Colours, retreated'. The Earl of Dorset and Middlesex was Lionel Cranfield Sackville (1688–1765), who succeeded as 7th Earl of Dorset and 2nd Earl of Middlesex in 1706. For 'the Adelphi of Terence' see EEWN 13, 623 (note to 299.38–40).

172.29–30 according to the trick *Measure for Measure*, 5.1.502.

173.6 hoity toity, whisky frisky Mercurius Spur [Cuthbert Shaw], *The Race* (London, 1765), 25. This echoes [Isaac Bickerstaff], *Love in a Village* (London, 1763), 32 (Act 2, Scene 3, Air 18): *'hoity toity, / Wisking, firisking'*.

173.15–174.27 David Ramsay . . . Life and Times, p. 46 for Ramsay see EEWN 13, 528. The anecdote relating to him is taken from Scott's edition of Francis Osborne's *Historical Memoirs on the Reigns of Elizabeth and King James* included in *Secret History*. In an note in that edition (1.264–66) Scott first observes: 'Ben Jonson ridicules the romantic wagers which were then laid, by introducing Sir Puntarvolo, in Every Man out of his Humour [(1600), 2.3 and 3.4], giving the odds upon the performance of a journey to Constantinople, by himself, his cat, and his dog.' He then continues with the quotation from Lilly, which is taken from *The Life of William Lilly . . . Wrote by himself* (first published 1715), in *The Lives of those Eminent Antiquaries Elias Ashmole, Esquire, and Mr. William Lilly, written by themselves* (London, 1774), 47–48: *CLA*, 149. John Williams (1582–1650) was Bishop of Lincoln 1621–41, before becoming Archbishop of York. A footnote on 1.265, taken over from *Eminent Antiquaries*, observes that John Scott 'lived in Pudding-Lane, and had some time been a page (or such like) to the Lord Norris'. The quotation was transcribed for the ISet by Anne Scott: there are a number of misreadings or approximations, most significantly 'the west end' for 'the west side' (5), 'also, but one were' for 'all but one, were' (14), and 'any such like actions' for 'any in such like actions' (20); also a few modernisations of the expression.

174.36–41 It's true your carelessness . . . power, nor virtue see William Ramesay, *Vox Stellarum. Or, The Voice of the Starres: Being a short Introdvction To The Judgement of Eclipses, and the Annuall Revolutions of the World* (London, 1652 [1651]), A3v: *CLA*, 143. Scott's transcription modernises the original.

175.7 that being dead he yet speaketh see Hebrews 11.4.

175.11 Gladsmuir a hamlet 5 km W of Haddington, E Lothian.

175.17 the riot of 17th December, 1596 a tumult arising from a fictitious plot by Roman Catholics to massacre king, councillors, and Presbyterian clergy. The object of the scare was apparently to strengthen the hand of the clergy, but it backfired when James blamed them and the citizens of Edinburgh, imposing a set of punitive measures.

175.32–33 His picture . . . a lost original the portrait hangs in the Council Room at George Heriot's School (see note to 167.27–30 above). It was copied in 1698 by John Scougal (*c.* 1645–1737?) from an original, now lost, by the Flemish portraitist Paul van Somer (1576–1621).

175.34–39 His fair hair . . . enjoy it see *Historical and Descriptive Account of George Heriot's Hospital, including a memoir of the founder* (Edinburgh: J. Cunningham, 15 Bank Street; and J. & J. Johnstone, 134 High Street, 1827: *CLA*, 6), 7–8. Scott's transcription is mostly accurate. James and John Johnstone were publishers and engravers.

175.42–176.37 I may add . . . Book iii, page 228 R. Harris Barham, Rector of St Gregory by St Paul (which, he says 'before the fire of London formed one of the Towers of Old St Pauls and occupied the space of ground now filled by Queen Anne's statue'), wrote to Scott on 7 July 1830 (MS 3919, f. 210r) with the brief extract from the register quoted and mentioning, as a possible convenient source for the inscription, John Stow's *A Survey of the Cities of London and Westminster*, rev. John Strype and others, 6 books (London, 1720: *CLA*, 248), where it appears at 3.228. The Latin inscription may be translated thus:

To his most devout and most dear wife, Alison Heriot, daughter of James Primrose, His Royal Majesty's Clerk to the Privy Council of the Kingdom of Scotland, a woman most highly endowed with all good qualities of mind and body and with a devout manner of life, her most sorrowing husband George Heriot, Esquire, Jeweller to the King, the Queen and the Princes Henry and Charles, has dutifully and with many tears erected this monument, as she well deserves.

She died on the 16th day of April in the year of our salvation 1612, and in the 20th year of her life, in the very flower of her youth, and has left me, her parents and her friends to yearn most sadly for her.

Here lies Alison Primrose, overwhelmed by cruel fate,
Like a rose that has suffered from untimely handling.
Not yet twice ten circling years had she completed,
Beautiful, chaste, a joy to her father and her husband,
When she passed away in pregnancy, never, alas, a mother, and so
Came care and grief to her father, care and grief to her husband.
She has gone, yet not completely removed, but only taken to a different place:
Now she is the prime Rose of the Heavens, who was previously a rose of the earth.

The transcription of the inscription has not survived, but the Magnum text has several variants, including four gross errors which are corrected in the present text from Stow; 'sanctiori Concilio' in Stow may be a mistake, deriving from the first word of the sentence, for the usual 'Secreto Concilio'.

176.38–177.3 I am certain . . . the royal palfrey James's saying is found in a letter from Lord Thomas Howard to Sir John Harington: see EEWN 13, 561 (note to 47.2). The final recommendation forms part of the same anecdote in *Nugæ Antiquæ*: in a later Magnum note it is paraphrased from Lucy Aikin (see 679 below).

177.6–28 The English agreed . . . these curious proclamations see

Scott's edition of Osborne (referred to in the note to 28.38 above), 1.144–45. In his note to this passage (1.143–44n) Scott quotes a proclamation of the Scottish Privy Council dated 10 May 1611, which includes the words 'bot ydill rascallis, and poore miserable bodyis'. The same proclamation imposes penalties on sea captains as stated: *The Register of the Privy Council of Scotland*, 9, ed. David Masson (Edinburgh, 1889), 173–74. Scott adds: 'In another proclamation, the Council state, that one of the pretexts under which these unseemly Scottish supplicants resorted to court, was to demand payment of old debts due to them by James, which they gravely say, "is, of all kind of importunity, the maist unpleasing to his majesty."' He is referring to a proclamation of 21 November 1615 (*Register*, 10, ed. David Masson (Edinburgh, 1891), 408).

177.30 Curtsying this gloss was added after the ISet.

177.31–39 A biblical commentary . . . leave it still see EEWN 13, 566 (note to 64.19–20). The work in question is apparently Alexander Gil, *The Sacred Philosophie of the Holy Scriptvre* . . . (London, 1635), a commentary on the Apostles' Creed. It is a folio volume of 196 + 232 pages, but the quatrain does not appear in it and its source has not been traced elsewhere.

177.43–178.12 He was of a middle stature . . . with God see *Fragments of Scotish History*, [ed. J. G. Dalyell] (Edinburgh, 1798), 'Desultory Reflections on the State of Ancient Scotland' (separately paginated), 84 and 87: *CLA*, 4. The passage is also found in Weldon, in *Secret History*, 2.[1]–2 and 9. Scott modernises and anglicises the spelling; he omits two pages silently before 'He would make'; he censors Dalyell's 'his fingers euer in that valke fidling about his cod peece'; he changes 'one straine' to 'a strain'; and he alters the sense of the last sentence: 'He had need of grate assurance, rather then hopes, yat wold make daylie so bold with God'.

178.15–179.6 Sir Mungo Malagrowther . . . china shop the 'most worthy and respectable baronet' has not been identified. There is an additional reference to this endnote at 107.36 ('person's daughter').

179.11–12 Dalhousie . . . ornament see Allan Ramsay, 'To the Right Honourable, William Earl of Dalhousie' (1720), lines 1–2: *stoup* means 'pillar' in this instance.

179.14–21 Mrs Anne Turner . . . his master, King James for Anne Turner and the Overbury affair see EEWN 13, 578–79 (note to 102.14–19).

179.26 the poem called Overbury's Vision R[ichard] N[iccols], *Sir Thomas Overbury's Vision*, in *The Harleian Miscellany*, [2nd edn], ed. Thomas Park, 10 vols (London, 1808–13), 7.178–89: *CLA*, 29. The description of Mrs Turner is on p. 183.

179.26–38 There were produced . . . the Secret History of King James *The Narrative History of King James, for the First fourteen Years* is not actually included in *Secret History*. (It is to be found in *Somers' Tracts*, 2.262–304.) However the passage quoted appears in one of Scott's editorial footnotes in *Secret History* (2.225n): it is an accurate verbal reproduction of the *Somers' Tracts* text (2.332). The work which attracted the footnote is *Aulicus Coquinariæ* (The Kitchen Courtier), now known to be by William Sanderson: Scott's ascription to Peter Heylyn follows David Irving, *The Lives of the Scotish Poets*, 2 vols (Edinburgh, 1804), 2.266n (*CLA*, 18). Scott's transcription of the 'curious passage' has two verbal changes ('scaffold' for 'scaffolds', and 'shewd to such' for 'shewed by such'): the first would appear to be inadvertent and is emended in the present text (the structure is not for an execution); the second may be a deliberate change of sense and is retained. Scott normalises the unorthodox '*Coquinariæ*' of the title to '*Coquinarius*'.

179.42–180.9 In reality . . . to the King for the quotation, very loosely transcribed (or perhaps remembered) by Scott, see his edition of Anthony

Weldon's *The Court and Character of King James* in *Secret History*, 1.320–21. The original reads: 'upon which day, as Sir John Ramsey, after Earl of Holdernes, for his good service in that preservation was the principal guest, so did the king grant him any boon he would aske that day; but had such limitations set to his asking, as made his suit unprofitable unto him, as that he asked it for, was unserviceable to the king'. For John Ramsay, see EEWN 13, 525.

180.17–26 On this opposition . . . his word see Weldon in *Secret History*, 2.32–33. Scott changes Weldon's 'rendering the seale' to 'rendering up the seals', presumably to avoid an ambiguous referent with the following 'it', and adapts the quotation slightly to make it fit into his text.

180.28–31 The cruel civil wars . . . Earl of Morton see EEWN 13, 579 (note to 109.5–6).

181.16–17 Falstaff will learn . . . skirted page *The Merry Wives of Windsor*, 1.3.80–81.

181.19–182.23 The Host of the New Inn . . . hemp circle see Ben Jonson, *The New Inne* (1631), 1.3.39–88. Several of the verbal differences between Scott's transcription and the original may well be misreadings: notably, 'brushing' for 'breeding' (181.27); 'turn' for 'tune' (181.32); 'academy and' for 'academy of honour, and' (181.40, corrected in the present text as an error); and the omission of a line 'Grave Nestor and the wise Ulysses practised,' (182.1/2). But Scott's substitution of 'kiss' for 'mount' (182.8) is clearly deliberate censorship, and some other changes may possibly be intentional: 'this desperate' for 'that desperate' (181.22); 'gracefully' for 'gracefuler' (181.31); 'The language' for 'His language' (181.32); 'And common' for 'Or common' (181.38); 'And two' for 'Or two' (182.11).

182.25–36 Lord Henry Howard . . . Lord Privy Seal the Latin phrase *infesti regibus*, meaning 'troublesome or dangerous to kings' occurs towards the end of the 'Epistle Dedicatorie' of *A defensatiue* (London, 1583): *CLA*, 149. Northampton's father, also Henry (1517–47), who bore the courtesy title Earl of Surrey from 1524, introduced blank verse into English. From 1601 the younger Henry was involved in elaborate correspondence preparing the way for James's succession to the English throne in 1603, conducted principally by Robert Cecil (1563–1612), who was to be created Earl of Salisbury in 1605. Robert was the son of William Cecil (1521–98), created Baron Burghley in 1571.

182.36–38 According to De Beaumont . . . ever lived Christophe de Harlay (1569–1616), Count of Beaumont, was a French ambassador in London 1601–07. His comment has not been traced, but Lucy Aikin says that Northampton 'has been justly stigmatised as "the greatest flatterer and calumniator of the age"' (*Memoirs of The Court of King James the First*, 2nd edn, 2 vols (London, 1822), 1.440–41: *CLA*, 254) and she refers to Beaumont at 1.342. According to Weldon, in *Secret History* (1.327), Northampton was 'the grossest flatterer of the world'.

182.44–47 The 24 of November . . . shot of pistol see *The Diarey of Robert Birrel*, in *Fragments of Scottish History*, [ed. J. G. Dalyell] (Edinburgh, 1798), 2nd item (separately paginated), 130: *CLA*, 4. Scott modernises and anglicises the quotation. Sir Alexander Bruce (d. 1600), 3rd laird of Airth, succeeded his father before 8 March 1552. Sir John Wemyss (1513?–1572) succeeded his father as laird of Wemyss in 1544.

183.2–5 I knew the Hectors . . . Sir Willie see *The Scowrers* (1691), 1.1.105–08, in *The Dramatick Works of Thomas Shadwell*, 4 vols (London, 1720), 4.313: *CLA*, 217. The speaker is Tope, a *scourer* (night street roisterer). Scott's transcription has two apparent misreadings: 'these days' for 'those Days' and 'Garden' for '*Tavern*'.

183.10–20 The exertion . . . venison for Brantôme's account of the siege of Leith in 1560 see *Des Couronnels françois*, 5 (M. de Martigues) in *Œuvres complètes de Pierre de Bourdeille, Abbé séculier de Brantome*, ed. J. A. C. Buchon, 2 vols (Paris, 1842), 1.634 (compare *CLA*, 121). The Brusquet anecdote relates to Piero Strozzi, and is found in *Vies des grands capitaines estrangers et françois*, 1.69 ('Le Mareschal de Strozze'): *Œuvres complètes*, 1.169–70.

183.30–184.10 Were't not for us . . . May prattle see *The Third Part of Miscellany Poems*, ed. John Dryden (London, 1716), 338, 340, 341: compare *CLA*, 203. The prison at Wood Street ('Wood Street Compter'), W of Guildhall, dated from 1555; it finally moved to Giltspur Street, Newgate, in 1791. There is some minor reworking of the first part of the main quotation in Scott's transcription, and two stanzas are omitted in the middle of the second part.

184.15–34 Burbage . . . p. 193 Roscius (Quintus Roscius Gallus, d. 62 BC) was a celebrated Roman actor. The quotation, with some reworking, is from Richard Corbet, 'Iter Boreale' (1647), lines 339–52, in *The Poems of Richard Corbet*, 4th edn, ed. Octavius Gilchrist (London, 1807), 156–204 (193–94): *CLA*, 248 (see also EEWN 13, 592: note to 150.28–32). Scott introduces 3 significant verbal variants: 'field' for 'bed'; 'in night' for 'ore night', leading to the printed 'in might' (emended in the present text); and 'that Richard' for 'King Richard'. Gilchrist adds a note: 'From this passage we learn that Richard Burbage, the *alter Roscius* of Camden, was the original representative of Shakespeare's Richard the Third.' Camden applies the Latin tag to the actor Richard Burbage (1567?–1619) in a note of his death on 9 March 1619 ('Richardus Burbadge alter Roscius obiit'): *Gulielmi Camdeni Annales Ab Anno 1603, ad Annum 1623* (London, 1691), 42. Market Bosworth is in Leicestershire.

184.40–42 that fatal banquet . . . that age see Thomas Warton, *The History of English Poetry*, 4 vols (London, 1774–81), 4.77n: 'Robert Green was killed by a surfeit of pickled herrings and Rhenish wine. This was in 1592. At which fatal banquet Thomas Nash was present' (compare *CLA*, 103, 184). Green(e) and Nash(e) were prominent miscellaneous writers.

184.46 coquetting with these words replace the 'ogling' found in Ed1 and EEWN 13, 191.43.

184.47–185.3 Of the cant words . . . Slang Dictionary the terms *Harman-beck* ('a Beadle'), *Huff* ('a Bullying Fellow'), *drab* ('a Whore, or Slut'), and *Bil-boa* ('a Sword') are included in B. E., *A New Dictionary of the Terms Ancient and Modern of the Canting Crew* (London, [1699]; unpaginated): *CLA*, 131.

185.4–8 Only three copies . . . Captain Clutterbuck see EEWN 13, 619 (note to 267.40–44). The 'library at Kennaquhair' is Scott's own collection at Abbotsford, 'Kennaquhair' being the fictitious name for Melrose in *The Monastery*. Scott deletes in the ISet the phrase also found in Ed1 and EEWN 13 'now M. P. for a great university': Richard Heber (1774–1833) resigned his Oxford University parliamentary seat in 1825, it was thought because of a homosexual relationship.

185.13 the accursed race . . . habitation see Matthew 8.32 (Mark 5.13; Luke 8.33).

185.13–15 Ben Jonson . . . swine see EEWN 13, 555 (note to 30.23–24).

185.19–20 the coronation of George IV. Scott was present at the coronation in Westminster Abbey and the subsequent feast in Westminster Hall, on 19 July 1821.

185.28–42 The king . . . put on for this quotation, which is substantially modernised and smoothed by Scott, see Roger Coke, *A Detection of the Court and State of England During the Four Last Reigns and the Inter-Regnum*, 3rd edn (London, 1697), 71: compare *CLA*, 237.
186.1–4 the author . . . uncertain the bottle in Scott's possession was presented to him by his amanuensis George Huntly Gordon. It is illustrated in Mary Monica Maxwell Scott, *Abbotsford: The Personal Relics and Antiquarian Treasures of Sir Walter Scott* (London, 1893), Plate XXII.
186.6–15 However, in his old age . . . one or two Weldon in *Secret History*, 2.3. Scott makes three minor verbal changes to the original.
186.24–187.23 Frederigo Zucchero . . . interest of the scene the description, accurately transcribed by John Buchanan, is Item 31 in *Catalogue of Pictures, Principally of the Italian Schools, The Property of a Gentleman* (Edinburgh, 1827): the painting is said to be on panel, 2 feet by 1 foot 8 inches. Annotations by Charles Kirkpatrick Sharpe in the copy of this catalogue in the Victoria and Albert Museum (shelf mark 23.E (3)) identify the gentleman as Francis Grant, give the date of the sale as 20 March 1827, and observe that the painting was bought in for 20 guineas. (In his initial list of points to be annotated at the beginning of Vol. 21 of the ISet Scott includes 'Grants picture'.) Scott viewed the paintings on 5 February and noted in his *Journal* (275) that there was 'a very knowing catalogue by Frank Grant himself'. The work was sold again two years later at an auction of paintings from the sequestrated estate of James Stuart of Dunearn, which Scott again viewed, apparently with a view to selecting paintings for the Duke of Buccleuch (*Letters*, 11.121–22). Writing to the Duke he refers (122) to 'a picture of James VI and his court in Greenwich park a curiosity & said to be well drawn but stiffer than ten pokers all pretence to perspective laid aside and very confused. Still you might fancy it for some odd corner so I mention it.' The painting is not in the Buccleuch Collection and has not been traced elsewhere. The improbable description is probably a tongue-in-cheek performance (Scott's 'knowing' perhaps bearing the modern significance) by Grant, who was a friend of the Scott family, and who was to paint a cabinet picture of Scott in 1831; but it is conceivable that Scott himself was the author. Federico Zucchero, or Zuccaro (*c.* 1542–1609) visited England from March to August 1575, when he painted portraits of Queen Elizabeth and the Earl of Leicester. He has been credited with many other British portraits, but the attributions are very dubious, and in particular he can hardly have been responsible for British portraits of later date, such as several of James VI and I as an adult, or the 'Greenwich' scene. The letter partly paraphrased in the description is printed in Lucy Aikin, *Memoirs of The Court of King James the First*, 2nd edn, 2 vols (London, 1822), 1.326–30: *CLA*, 254. Aikin's source describes it as from 'Lord Thomas Howard to sir John Harrington'. She identifies the writer as most likely Thomas Howard, Viscount Bindon, who succeeded his brother in 1590, and died in 1611 (330n). For Harington, see EEWN 13, 561 (note to 47.2).
187.26–34 On one occasion . . . he was rowed ashore for this incident see EEWN 13, 561 (note to 47.23–24).
187.34–38 At Lochmaben . . . most admired disorder the source of this anecdote has not been located. The *vendisse*, or vendace, was a species of whitefish found only in Bassenthwaite and Derwent Water in the English Lake district and the Castle and Mill Lochs at Lochmaben, Dumfriesshire. By the beginning of the 21st century it survived only in Derwent Water. In *Macbeth*, 3.4.109–10 Lady Macbeth says to her husband, after the appearance of Banquo's ghost at the banquet: 'You have displac'd the mirth, broke the good meeting,/ With most admir'd disorder'.

188.2–3 it is now much injured . . . that sort the steam-engine in question was 'for supplying the garrison with water from the Thames': see *A new and improved History and Description of the Tower of London* (London, 1827), 5.
188.4–10 These memorials . . . the Tower of London for John Bayley's description of the inscriptions in the Beauchamp or Cobham Tower, see his *The History and Antiquities of the Tower of London*, 2nd edn (London, 1830), 131–74: *CLA*, 187. The inscriptions were discovered in 1796, when the tower was being converted for use as a mess-room for the garrison: John Brand, 'Account of Inscriptions discovered on the Walls of an Apartment in the Tower of *London*', *Archaeologia*, 13 (1800), 68–99 (with a full set of engraved plates: Brand's paper was read on 17 November 1796).
188.11 The celebrated Court Jester see EEWN 13, 530.
188.12–23 Wilson informs us . . . p. 690 Scott paraphrases and quotes Arthur Wilson, *The History of Great Britain, Being the Life and Reign of King James the First* (London, 1653), as reprinted in Volume 2 of Kennet. In the second passage referred to, Wilson notes (2.690) that 'Proclamations were sent abroad, to forbid the making or carrying of Pistols under a Foot long in the Barrel'.
188.27–40 The criminal . . . printer was pardoned for 10 years from 1572 Queen Elizabeth carried on a protracted courtship of François (1554–85), Duke of Alençon 1566–76, of Anjou from 1576, younger brother of Henri III King of France, and thus as part of her European political strategy succeeded in preventing him assisting the Dutch in their struggle against Spain. *The Discoverie of a Gaping Gvlf whereinto England is like to be swallowed by an other French mariage, if the Lord forbid not the banes, by letting her Maiestie see the sin and punishment thereof.* ([London], 1579), written by John Stubb(e)s, or Stubb(e) (*c.* 1541–1590), was printed by Hugh Singleton (d. in or before 1593). William Page, a London gentleman, was not technically the publisher, but he sent 50 copies to Sir Richard Greenfield in Cornwall for distribution to friends: see H. J. Byrom, 'Edmund Spenser's First Printer, Hugh Singleton', *Library*, 4th series, 14:2 (September 1933), 121–56 (141).
188.40–189.5 I remember . . . religion see William Camden, *The History or Annals of England, during The whole Life and Reign of Elizabeth late Queen thereof* (first published in 1630), in Kennet, 2.361–653 (487): *CLA*, 249. Scott introduces some minor re-working of the original, with 6 changes of small words.
189.11–14 The celebrated Archie Armstrong . . . amusement for the encounters between David Droman and Archie Armstrong, see Weldon, in *Secret History*, 1.400–01.
189.17–190.5 But to make this more plain . . . sported enough see John Webster, *The Displaying of Supposed Witchcraft* (London, 1677), 124: *CLA*, 153. The transcriber John Buchanan is verbally faithful to the original.
190.7–14 A leglen-girth . . . the Green see EEWN 13, 636 (note to 361.5).
190.20–191.14 Lady Lake . . . fine and imprisonment for the Lady Lake affair see EEWN 13, 639 (note to 368.30–31). For 'the historian Wilson's expression' (27) see Arthur Wilson, *The History of Great Britain, Being the Life and Reign of King James the First* (London, 1653), as reprinted in Kennet, 2.711.
191.15–22 Clarendon remarks . . . cavaliers see Edward, Earl of Clarendon, *The History of the Rebellion and Civil Wars in England*, 3 vols (Oxford, 1702–04), 2.268: *CLA*, 24. The citizens' military exercises are mocked by e.g. Thomas Middleton (1580–1627) in *Anything for a Quiet Life* (first published, posthumously, in 1662), 1.131–33: 'such a day being at the Artillery-

Garden, one of my neighbors in courtesie to salute me with his Musquet, set a fire my Fustian and Apes Breeches'.

191.28–29 His well labouring sword . . . the King see *2 Henry IV*, 1.1.126–28: 'that furious Scot,/ The bloody Douglas, whose well-labouring sword/ Had three times slain th' appearance of the King'.

PEVERIL OF THE PEAK

205.3 I might have now drawn a line presumably following the completion of the preceding novel *The Fortunes of Nigel* in May 1822.

205.9–10 Embowl'd? . . . eat me to-morrow see *1 Henry IV*, 5.4.111–13

205.13–14 those new tricks . . . getting old see Ray, 99, 142; *ODEP*, 805.

205.27–28 the Archbishop of Granada's apoplexy in *The Adventures of Gil Blas of Santillane* by René le Sage, first published in French in 1715–35, and included in Tobias Smollett's English translation in *Ballantyne's Novelist's Library*, [ed. Walter Scott], 10 vols (Edinburgh, 1821–25), 4.5–294, the picaresque hero Gil Blas's master, the Archbishop of Grenada, is 'seized with a fit of the apoplexy'. His homilies show signs of his mental deterioration: 'sometimes the good old prelate repeated the same thing over and over; sometimes rose too high, or sunk too low: it was a vague discourse, the rhetoric of an old professor'.

206.1 Thomas Scott, already mentioned in these notes in the General Preface: see EEWN 25a, 19–20.

206.13–14 some memorials . . . Desiderata Curiosa see EEWN 14, 604. See the Historical Note in EEWN 14 generally for the references that follow.

207.25–26 with whom connected, or by whom begot see Alexander Pope, 'Elegy to the Memory of an Unfortunate Lady' (1717), line 72.

207.29 the famous crown-stealer in 1671 Colonel Thomas Blood (*c.* 1618–1680) attempted to steal the crown jewels.

207.31–32 the celebrated Duke of Buckingham George Villiers (1628–87), who succeeded his murdered father shortly after his birth, was a noted wit and eminent playwright.

207.41–42 I spoke according to the trick see *Measure for Measure*, 5.1.502–03.

208.8–9 than the memory of Virgil . . . Dido see EEWN 14, 626 (note to 11.33–34).

208.12 The fine sketch of Mignon see EEWN 14, 606.

210.7–10 The following Notices . . . the Isle of Man the *Historical Notices* which follow (xvi–l), including all the footnotes, were published in London, presumably in 1823. According to John Christian, who sent the pamphlet on 16 July 1830, the author was Mark Wilks (*c.* 1760–1831), a Manx officer with the East Indian Company until his retirement in 1818. The text was sent directly to the Magnum printers, who followed it with almost complete verbal faithfulness.

210.19–31 The venerable Dr Dryasdust . . . represented them see EEWN 14, 9–11.

210.34 Hampden, or Sydney John Hampden (1595–1643) resisted Charles I's demands for 'ship-money' to finance his navy. Sir Philip Sidney (1554–86) was a much-admired soldier, courtier, and poet.

210.35 Lady Jane Grey, or Rachel Russel Lady Jane Grey, or Dudley (1537–54), executed by Queen Mary, was widely regarded as a protestant martyr. Lady Rachel Russell (1637–1723), also a convinced protestant, was particularly admired for her fortitude at the time of the execution for treason in 1683 of her second husband William Russell.

211.42–43 the companion . . . Spanish romance George Villiers (1592–1628) was created Duke of Buckingham in 1623, in which year he accompanied the future Charles I to Spain in an unsuccessful attempt to conclude a royal match with the infanta.

212.40 Published in . . . 1779 Francis Peck, *Desiderata Curiosa*, new edn, 2 vols (London, 1779): *CLA*, 240. Wilks (see note to 210.7–10 above) quotes from Peck's second volume with some freedom in the pages that follow. The page references are sometimes approximate, but they have been corrected in the present edition only when seriously misleading.

212.41 fortiter calumniari aliquid adhærebit a standard Latin tag: 'Fling lots of scandal and some is bound to stick'.

213.18–19 Sacheverill's Account . . . 1702 William Sacheverell, *An Account of the Isle of Man* (London, 1702): *CLA*, 22.

213.21–22 Hutchinson's . . . History of Cumberland William Hutchinson, *The History of the County of Cumberland*, 2 vols (Carlisle, 1794).

214.41–42 Feltham's Tour . . . being governor John Feltham, *A Tour through the Island of Mann, in 1797 and 1798* (Bath, 1798), 161 has 'John Greenhaugh governor'.

218.35 Chaloner . . . 1656 James Chaloner, *A Short Treatise of The Isle of Man* (London, 1656; appended to *The Vale-Royall of England*): see note to 264.43–265.7 below.

221.39 Rolt's History of the Isle of Man [Richard] Rolt, *The History of the Island of Man* (London, 1773).

228.1–230.10 I am enabled . . . sickens our soul writing to Scott on 14 June 1830 J. R. Oswald offered to send, *inter alia*, this 'Poetical Legend or Lament in the Manx Language composed on his [Christian's] Death and to this day a popular Ballad with the country people here' (MS 3913, f. 197r–v). The manuscript does not appear to have survived.

230.12–233.35 At the Court at Whitehall . . . Richard Browne the transcriptions of these edicts do not appear to have survived.

234.32–235.30 Major-General Blunt . . . my own defence the long quotation is from Thomas Shadwell, *The Volunteers, or The Stock-Jobbers* (1693), in *The Works of Thomas Shadwell, Esq*, 4 vols (London, 1720: *CLA*, 218), 4.437–39 (3.1). The short quotation is found at 4.419 (1.2). Scott's transcription has several verbal differences from the original, but most of these do not appear in the Magnum: evidently reference was made to the source. An exception is 'I prithee, friend' for 'Look you, *Mr. Welford*' (235.29).

235.36–37 the person by whom it was witnessed for Margaret Swinton as Scott's childhood informant see EEWN 7a, 333, and especially EEWN 24, 153–54, 187–96, where it is suggested that the alleged connection between Margaret and the Lord President's Dalrymple family may have arisen from a confusion by Scott of two Lady Primroses resulting in a false linkage.

236.7–8 the old mansion-house of Swinton this is situated 7 km N of Coldstream in Berwickshire.

237.6 writer solicitor.

237.8–20 Among them was a young Englishman . . . Caley fell dead for a full account of John Cayley's death see James Grant, *Cassell's Old and New Edinburgh*, 3 vols (London, [1884–87]), 2.243–45.

238.5 Vallis Negotii *Latin* hill of business.

238.18–32 I am obliged . . . effusion of blood Malew is a parish in the SE of the Isle of Man. The certification of the register of burials by its Vicar from 1817 to 1830, another William Christian (b. 1779), is included in the Train papers (MS 874, f. 237r: see the Editorial Note, 194–95 above), as are the details about Colquit and the execution in the third paragraph (from remarks by Henry R. Oswald, a Manx surgeon: MS 874, ff. 249v–250r, with copy also by Oswald at ff. 255r–266r). His predecessor, who was suspended, was William Christian: see William Harrison, *An Account of the Diocese of Sodor and Man* (Douglas, 1879), 127. The certification has been seriously misread: the manuscript readings are restored in the present text.

238.39 flagrantibus odiis *Latin* when the flames of hate were at their highest; in an atmosphere of intense hate.

238.42 Haddon Hall see EEWN 14, 613–14.

239.8–9 Anne, Duchess of Buccleuch and Monmouth in 1663 Anne Scott (1651–1732), Countess of Buccleuch, married James, an illegitimate son of Charles II, created Duke of Monmouth in 1662. After his execution in 1685 she became Duchess of Buccleuch in her own right.

239.15–23 The ejection . . . preference for 'Black Bartholomew' see EEWN 14, 654 (note to 136.36–39). Edmund Calamy (1600–66), his son of the same name (1634–85), and William Reynolds (1625–98) were ejected from their livings in 1662. At the same time Richard Baxter (1615–91) chose nonconformity because of his objection to the exclusive nature of the Act of Uniformity.

239.26–28 I have elsewhere noticed . . . Hugenot see 207.38–40.

239.29–31 The celebrated insurrection . . . 1661 see EEWN 14, 650 (note to 108.33–34).

239.42–241.28 It was after the King's return . . . satisfaction see *Original Memoirs, Written During the Great Civil War; being the Life of Sir Henry Slingsby, and Memoirs of Capt. Hodgson*, [ed. Walter Scott] (Edinburgh, 1806), 165–81. The division between quotation and summary is somewhat arbitrary: the note offers what is essentially a paraphrase of Hodgson, using some of his actual words. The opening sentences run in the original: 'It was after the King's return to London, one night a parcel of armed men besets my house at Coalley-hall, near Halifax, and, in an unseasonable hour in the night, demands entrance; and my servants within having some discourse with them on the outside, they gave threatening language, put their pistols in at the windows; and my wife being with child, and for fear of frightening the rest, I ordered the doors to be opened, and they came in, Joseph Lyster, Sir John Armitage's clerk, who had a warrant to apprehend me for treason, and Lawrence Johnston, and several others. After they had presented a pistol to my breast, (that Johnston did) I advised them to civil deportment, seeing I had let them in in the night; and so they shewed me their authority to apprehend me: And it was under the hands and seals of Sir John Kaye, and Sir John Armitage, knight and baronet, lieutenants . . .'. The remainder is more loosely paraphrased. For 'Prince Henry's observation' in the penultimate paragraph see *1 Henry IV*, 1.2.41–42.

242.20–31 The Contest . . . Chap. 2 Magnus Olaus (1490–1557), *A Compendious History of the Goths, Svvedes, & Vandals and Other Northern Nations* (London, 1658), 166.

242.33–243.26 In almost all the great parishes . . . nocturnal dancers Waldron (1731), 154–55. The transcription, on a paper apart, does not appear to have survived. A short paragraph has been excised from the original before 'Christmas is ushered in'.

243.34–245.28 Insula Monæ . . . my Isle of Man this document, provided by the bibliographer Thomas Frognall Dibdin (1776–1847), does not appear to have survived.

245.28–36 I am told . . . the fair-haired William Dhône the Magnum text has 'The countenance was of a light complexion, with fair and almost effeminate blue eyes, and an oval form of face'. The relevant information is included in the series of comments on *Peveril of the Peak* by Henry R. Oswald (see the Editorial Note, 195 above): MS 874, f. 251r (copy by Oswald at f. 256v). Scott uses Oswald's words for the greater part of his note. *Dhône* means 'fair' in Manx.

245.40–246.12 Whalley the Regicide . . . invaded and dispossessed for Whalley see EEWN 14, 657 (note to 148.7–12). For the painstakingly detailed comment on the tradition referred to, see Ezra Stiles, *A History of Three of the Judges of King Charles I* (Hartford, 1794), Ch. 4. James Fenimore Cooper's tale, published anonymously, is *The Borderers* (London, 1829), also known as *The Wept of Wish-ton-wish*.

246.18–250.7 Peel, or Pile-Town . . . conceiving see Waldron (1731), 2.103–09. John Buchanan has transcribed the passage accurately.

250.15–18 a dog . . . termed Mauthe see *Sir John Froissart's Chronicles*, trans. Thomas Johnes, 4 vols (Hafod, 1805), 4.657–58: *CLA*, 28. *Mauthe doog* is a rendering of the Manx *moddey dhoo*, *moddey* meaning 'dog' and *dhoo* 'black'.

250.31–259.41 'Tis this ignorance . . . accounted for see Waldron (1731), 2.125–40. The transcription has not survived, but the verbal accuracy (only one emendation is required) suggests that like that on Sodor it was probably the work of John Buchanan.

260.3 Mr Crofton Croker Thomas Crofton Croker published (anonymously) *Researches in the South of Ireland, illustrative of the scenery, architectural remains, and the manners and superstitions of the peasantry* (London, 1824), *Fairy Legends and Traditions of the South of Ireland*, 3 vols (London, 1825–28: *CLA*, 341), and *Legends of the Lakes; or, Sayings and Doings at Killarney*, 2 vols (London, 1829: *CLA*, 251).

260.4 the author of the Fairy Mythology T[homas] K[eightley], author of *The Fairy Mythology*, 2 vols (London, 1828: *CLA*, 180).

260.23–261.7 13th January . . . the Apostle James see John Lauder (Lord Fountainhall), *The Decisions of the Lords of Council and Session*, 2 vols (Edinburgh, 1759–61), 1.439–40, 440–41. Scott's transcription of the first quotation has several verbal variants, which are not present in a duplicate transcription he made originally for insertion in the Introduction: 'a stage' for 'his stage', 'by which' for 'whereby', 'an apprentice' for 'a prentice', and 'quoted' for 'cited'. These are probably deliberate. In the second quotation Scott has 'christend' for 'called', again probably intentional though resulting in a 'Christian . . . christened' jingle in the Magnum.

261.13–262.38 He was now in his trine exaltation . . . remembered for the quotations see Roger North, *Examen: or, An Enquiry into the credit and veracity of a Pretended Complete History* (London, 1740), 205–06, 225. John Buchanan's transcription is verbally accurate.

263.1–6 A narrative . . . such fires the title-page of the pamphlet (London, 1679) says that it is 'By Capt. *William Bedloe*': Scott wrote simply 'the same lately engaged', the anonymous 'person' coming in at a subsequent stage. For the line of poetry see John Dryden, *Absalom and Achitophel* (1681–82), 2.96.

263.41–42 haud aliena a Scævolæ studiis *Latin* not at all foreign to the interests of Scaevola: see Cicero, *Ad Atticum* (68–44 BC), 4.16.3. Quintus Mucius Scaelova (d. 82 BC) was an eminent orator and jurist.

263.42 Mr Christian of Unrigg for John Christian of Unrigg see 194–95 above.

264.20–34 Mr Train . . . his men in safety Thomas Stanley (b. before 1485, d. 1521) succeeded his grandfather as 2nd Earl of Derby in 1504. The verses quoted are stanzas 50–52 of a Manx poem sent to Scott by Train on 2 March 1830 with an English translation by Thomas Curphy of Douglas in the Isle of Man (the stanzas are at MS 874, ff. 204r–205r). In a further letter from Train sent on 16 July there is an account of a 'Tradition which is very popular both in Man and in Galloway', with a passage on McCulloch including a slightly varied version of the stanzas quoted and most of the other information in the *Peveril* note (ff. 232v–234Br). Scott appears to have used this second version as his starting-point, but he has introduced a number of deliberate stylistic variants and has replaced the obscure 'knee guinea-men' in the fourth line with 'vassals'. The original (in the version at ff. 233v–234r) runs:

> Then came Thomas Derby born King
> It was he that wore the Golden Crupper
> There was not one Lord in England itself
> With so many knee guinea-men as he had
> On Scotchmen he revenged himself
> He went over to Kirkcudbright
> And there made such havoc of houses
> that some of them are yet uninhabited
> Was not that bonny in a youth
> to revenge himself while he was young
> Before his beard had brown round his mouth
> And to carry his men home with him safe

264.43–265.7 The following is the deposition . . . 1653 the source of the quotation, included in Train's letter of 16 July referred to in the preceding explanatory note, has not been identified. The author referred to is presumably James Chaloner, whose brief treatise *A Short Treatise of The Isle of Man* appears at the end of William Smith and William Webb, *The Vale-Royall of England or, The County Palatine of Chester* (London, 1656). Chaloner's 'Epistle Dedicatory' is dated 1653. The quotation is not in the *Treatise*, and no other work by Chaloner has been found. The Magnum text introduces some modernisation and regularisation of the sense of Train's transcription, presumably to make things easier for the reader.

265.25–26 James MacCulloch . . . connexion James Murray McCulloch (1768–1857), of Ardwall in Wigtownshire, was the brother-in-law of Scott's brother Tom.

265.35–42 It is certain . . . Mahometan David Hume, *The History of England*, 8 vols (London, 1796–97), 8.72: *CLA*, 28. Scott's transcription is verbally accurate.

266.2–19 The crowd was prodigious . . . the mob see Roger North, *Examen: or, An Enquiry into the credit and veracity of a pretended Complete History* (London, 1740), 204–05. Scott's transcription has several verbal variants, most of them probably intentional, e.g.: 'were it a cat or a dog' for 'were it Cat or Dog'; 'so that every one' for 'so as almost every one'; 'two thumping divines' for 'two other thumping divines'; 'did contradict' for 'ever contradicted'; and 'founded' for 'derived'. He also omits several words, resulting in 'and I never met' for 'and, although I have often mentioned it, as now I do, with Precaution, yet I never met'. One clear error is corrected in the present text.

266.32–34 He was successor . . . regicide for a list of those suggested as regicidal executioner see Walter Thornbury and Edward Walford, *Old and New London*, 6 vols (London, [1879–85]), 3.350–51.

266.35–38 A Scottish gentleman . . . his toothpick the source of the anecdote has not been identified.

267.13–21 The epitaph . . . wise one for the epitaph see EEWN 14, 677–78 (note to 278.40–279.3).

267.22–25 The Duchess of Portsmouth . . . a Catholic for the Duchess of Portsmouth see EEWN 14, 678 (note to 279.22).
267.26–27 Anthony Ashley Cooper . . . the period for Shaftesbury see EEWN 14, 659 (note to 157.29–31).
267.28–29 Such was the extravagance . . . eloquence for this attribution see EEWN 14, 679 (note to 280.40–43).
267.37 Elkana Settle for Settle see EEWN 14, 682 (note to 294.16–17).
268.2–4 Even in the days of chivalry . . . not dubb'd in *Don Quixote*, 3.31: Part 1 (1605), Bk 4, Ch. 17 (or Part 1, Ch. 44), Quixote delegates the punishment of socially inferior offenders to his squire Sancho Panza.
268.7–8 a satire imputed to Dryden . . . Mulgrave John Sheffield (1647–1721), who succeeded as 3rd Earl of Mulgrave in 1658, was probably the author of *Essay on Satire*, which circulated in manuscript in 1679 and whose misattribution led to the attack on Dryden.
268.8–10 If he falls upon me . . . a cudgel see *The Letters of John Wilmot, Earl of Rochester*, ed. Jeremy Treglown (Oxford, 1980), 120 (Spring, 1676: to Henry Savile).
268.16–19 Bennet, Earl of Arlington . . . Cabal for Arlington see EEWN 14, 641 (note to 65.4–6). The word *cabal* was wittily made to refer to Clifford (Thomas Clifford of Chudleigh), Arlington, Buckingham, Ashley (Lord Shaftesbury), and Lauderdale (Charles Maitland, 3rd Earl of Lauderdale).
268.27–31 Mary . . . Charles II for Mary and her father see EEWN 14, 683 (note to 296.7–9).
268.33–269.43 Letter from the Dead to the Living . . . J. Jerningham the original letter is bound into the ISet. It is reproduced with verbal accuracy in the Magnum. George William Stafford-Jerningham (1771–1851) was 8th Baron Stafford from 1824.
270.8–9 Jernigan . . . garters see EEWN 14, 682 (note to 292.7).
270.15–39 The conversation . . . mortis see Roger North, *Examen: or, An Enquiry into the Credit and Veracity of a Pretended Complete History* (London, 1740), 572–73. Scott's transcription has a dozen verbal variants from the original, mostly very minor, but one may note in particular: 'bravery' for 'Braveur'; 'every Protestant Englishman' for 'every true *Protestant* and *Englishman*'; the insertion of '(viz that none can imagine without seeing it as I have)'; and 'instrument' for 'Engine'.
271.3 Geoffrey Hudson for Hudson see EEWN 14, 610–11.
271.21–28 Jeffrey strait was thrown . . . deliver me see 'Jeffereidos, *on the Captivity of* Jeffery', in *The Works of Sr William D'avenant Kt* (London, 1673), 224–28 (228): *CLA*, 207. Scott's version is approximate. The original runs: 'For *Jefferey* strait was throwne; whilst faint and weak,/ The cruel Foe, assaults him with his Beak,/ A Lady-Midwife now, he there by chance/ Espy'd, that came along with him from *France*:/ A heart nours'd up in War; that n're before/ This time (quoth he) could bow, now doth implore:/ Thou that delivered'st hast so many, be/ So kinde of nature, to deliver me!'
272.1–3 Jeffrey Hudson . . . Sir Hans Sloan's Museum Anthony Van Dyck's *Queen Henrietta Maria with Sir Jeffrey Hudson* (1633) is in the National Gallery of Art, Washington DC. The collection amassed by Sir Hans Sloane became the nucleus of the British Museum on his death in 1753.
272.10 Coventry's Act Coventry's Act (22 & 23 Car II c. 1) was passed in February 1670.
272.12 Then a noted actor for Mohun see EEWN 14, 702 (note to 389.35).

272.16–26 There was another sham plot . . . for a snack see North, 311. Scott modernises some of the phraseology. The words omitted are 'which allied itself to *Dangerfield*, by the Pretence of steering the *Popish-Plot* upon the Presbyterians'. The pamphlet attested by Blood as giving a true account is entitled *A Just Narrative of the Hellish New Counter-Plots of the Papists, to cast the Odium of their Horrid Treasons upon the Presbyterians . . .* (London, 1679).
272.41–273.3 I walked with him . . . at this scene see *Memoirs, illustrative of the Life and Writings of John Evelyn*, ed. William Bray, 2 vols (London, 1818), 1.412–13: *CLA*, 240. Scott alters the passage, mainly to make it intelligible out of context, but his reading of 'impudent' as 'intimate' was almost certainly inadvertent and is emended for the present text.
273.5–9 A story of this nature . . . later editions for the story see EEWN 14, 706–07 (note to 410.23–25).
273.13–28 Dined at Mr Treasurer's . . . insinuating see *Memoirs, illustrative of the Life and Writings of John Evelyn*, ed. William Bray, 2 vols (London, 1818), 1.413: *CLA*, 240. Scott's transcription is largely faithful verbally.
273.34–35 Barrington or Major Semple . . . chevalier d'industrie Sir Jonah Barrington (1756/57–1834) was in 1830 removed from his position as judge of the Irish court of Admiralty for alleged financial misappropriation. James George Semple (1759–1815) was an adventurer given to obtaining goods by false pretences. The French term *chevalier d'industrie* means 'swindler'.
274.2–7 This insurrection . . . punished as traitors this footnote was deleted, by implication, by Scott at proof stage to make room for an expansion of the text. See *Scott's Interleaved Waverley Novels*, ed. Iain Gordon Brown (Aberdeen, 1987), 24, 115.
274.8–9 Sir Thomas Armstrong for Armstrong see EEWN 14, 716 (note to 448.27–28).
274.14–19 Charles . . . Cibber's Apology see *An apology for the life of Mr. Colley Cibber . . . Written By Himself* (London, 1740), 80. According to Cibber Charles said : '*Pray, what is the Meaning, . . . that we never see a Rogue in a Play, but, Godsfish! they always clap him on a black Perriwig? when, it is well known, one of the greatest Rogues in* England *always wears a fair one?*'.
274.23–30 The place of meeting . . . unusual occasions the Magnum text reads: 'care not for expense; you will find most of them at the Club-House in Fuller's Rents.' Fuller's Rents was situated just S of Fleet Street in the Temple precincts opposite Chancery Lane, but it was destroyed in the Great Fire of 1666. The Green Ribbon Club, an anti-Court body, met in the King's Head Tavern very close by, on the E side of Chancery Lane at the junction with Fleet Street. For the quotation, variously altered by Scott, see North, 572: 'Their Seat was in a Sort of Carfour at *Chancery-Lane End*, a Centre of Business and Company most proper for such Anglers of Fools. The House was double balconied in the Front, as may be yet seen, for the Clubsters to issue forth in fresco with Hats and no Peruques; Pipes in their mouths, merry Faces, and dilated Throats, for vocal Encouragement of the Canaglia below, at Bonfires, on usual and unusual Occasions.' North explains that the institution was originally known as the King's Head Club, but 'upon Occasion of the Signal of *a Green Ribbon*, agreed to be worn in their Hats in the Days of *Street Engagements*, like the Coats of Arms of valiant Knights of old, whereby all the Warriors of the Society might be distinguished, and not mistake Friends for Enemies they were called also *The Green Ribbon Club*'.
274.39–275.27 I omit the share . . . out of order for the quotation see Roger North, *The Life Of the Honourable Sir Dudley North . . .* (London,

1744), 158: *CLA*, 243. The transcription, which is missing from the ISet, is verbally almost entirely accurate.

275.28–31 Brantome tells us . . . expired this note was omitted in the Magnum. For the death of Mademoiselle de Limeuil, maid of honour to Cathérine de Médicis, Queen Consort of France 1547–59, as recounted by Pierre de Bourdeille, seigneur de Brantôme, see 'De l'Amour des dames pour les vaillants hommes', Discourse 6, in *Œuvres du Seigneur de Brantome*, new edn, 8 vols (Paris, 1787), 4.507: *CLA*, 121: 'Quand l'heure de sa fin fut venue, elle fit venire à soy son valet . . . qui s'appelloit Julien et sçavoit très-bien joüer du violon. *Julien*, luy dit-elle, *prenez vostre violon et sonnez moy toujours jusques à ce que me voyez morte (car je m'y en vais), la défaite des Suisses, et le mieux que vous pourrez; et quand vous serez sur le mot*: Tout est perdu, *sonnez-le par quatre ou cinq fois, le plus piteusement que vous pourrez;* ce que fit l'autre, et elle-mesme luy aidoit de la voix, et quand ce vint, *tout est perdu,* elle le réïtera par deux fois; et se tournant de l'autre costé du chevet, elle dit à ses compagnes: *Tout est perdu à ce coup, et à bon escient*; et ainsi décéda' (When her last hour arrived she summoned her attendant Julien, who was an excellent violinist. 'Julien,' she said, 'take your violin and until you see I have expired (for that's where I'm heading) keep playing the defeat of the Swiss in your best manner; and when you get to 'All is lost' play it four or five times, as expressively as you can.' He did this, and she sang along as he played, repeating 'all is lost' twice. Then turning in her bed she said to her companions: 'Now indeed all is lost, and I know it for sure.' And so she died).

276.18 History of Colonel Thomas Blood in 1662 the Act of Settlement (277.2) restored confiscated lands to 'innocent Catholics', compensating the current holders with lands elsewhere, leading to Thomas Blood's planned rising in response the following year. The Solemn League and Covenant of 1643 (277.17) had involved the establishment of Presbyterian church government in England and Ireland. For the long quotation at 346–50, which like almost the whole note is in the hand of John Buchanan and is verbally accurate, see John Bayley, *The History and Antiquities of the Tower of London*, 2nd edn (London, 1830), 191–95: *CLA*, 187. The remaining material concerning Blood in this note is to be found in two publications: the pamphlet *Remarks on the Life and Death of the famed Mr Blood* (1680), reprinted in *Somers' Tracts*, 8.442–44; and Thomas Carte, *An History of the Life of James Duke of Ormonde*, 3 vols (London, 1735–36), especially 2.268–69, 420–23 (*CLA*, 27). The quotation from the former at 341–44 and from the latter at 344–46, which like the whole note are in the hand of John Buchanan, have a number of small verbal changes only one of which requires emendation.

287.30–31 There's such divinity . . . little of its will see *Hamlet*, 4.5.120–22.

QUENTIN DURWARD

297.28–30 Goethe's conception . . . Faust *Faust* is the principal work of Johann Wolfgang von Goethe. Scott refers to thc first part, published in 1808, in which Mephistopheles plays a major role. The second part was not published until 1832.

297.30–31 that which has been formed by Byron . . . Milton see Byron's *Cain* (1821) and John Milton's *Paradise Lost* (1667, rev. 1674).

297.36–37 which have induced Burns and others . . . Paradise Lost Robert Burns expressed admiration for Milton's Satan on several occasions: see Thomas Crawford, *Burns: A Study of the Poems and Songs*, 2nd edn (Edinburgh, 1965), 218. The most celebrated proponents (known to Scott) of a similar view were: John Dryden, in 'Dedication of the Æneis' (1697); Joseph Addison, in *The Spectator*, 309 (23 February 1712); Philip Dormer Stanhope, Earl of Chesterfield, in *Letters . . . to his Son*, 4 vols (London, 1774), 2.138; and William Godwin, in *An Enquiry Concerning Political Justice*, 2 vols (London, 1793), 1.261–62.

298.11–12 the principles of Machiavel in *Il Principe* (The Prince: written 1513, published 1532) Niccolò Machiavelli advocates ruthlessness in the pursuit of political objectives.

298.21–22 his creating the Virgin Mary . . . guards this commission is probably imaginary. François [Eudes] de Mézeray, *Histoire de France, depuis Faramond iusqu'à maintenant*, 3 vols (Paris, 1643–51: *CLA*, 46) records that Louis placed Boulogne 'sous l'hommage de la sainte Vierge' (2.177).

298.22–26 the cunning that admitted . . . mysteries compare Antoine Varillas, *Histoire de Louis XI.*, 2 vols (The Hague, 1689), 2.354: 'Loüis ne viola jamais le serment qu'il avoit accoûtumé de faire, qui étoit celuy de *Pâques-Dieu*' (Louis never broke the oath which he was accustomed to make, that of *God's Easter*).

298.35–36 the war termed "for the public good" see EEWN 15, 504 (1465).

299.11–13 In the fourteenth century . . . other resources Charles Mills dates the 'commencement of the decline in chivalry' from the civil strife which arose in France during the last decade of the 14th century and which spread to England during the dynastic struggle of the 15th century: 'The civil wars in England operated as fatally upon the noble order of knighthood as the civil wars in France had done in that country. In those contests, far fiercer than national hostilities, there was a ruthlessness of spirit that mocked the gentle influences of chivalry' (*The History of Chivalry or Knighthood and its times*, 2 vols (London, 1825), 2.99; compare 203–07: *CLA*, 231).

299.19–22 the good old knight's Durindarte . . . pure gold in the early 12th-century *Chanson de Roland* the sword of the champion Roland sword is called Durandal. It appears in *Don Quixote*, 4.108 (Part 2 (1615), Ch. 26) as Durindana, the weapon of Orlando (Roland). 'Durindarte' is a form found in Middle High German. The Ebro is the river in NE Spain into which flows the Jalòn, noted from Classical times for the production of high-quality steel at Bilbilis (modern Calatayud), birthplace of Martial (Marcus Valerius Martialis: *c.* AD 40–104). See his *Epigrams*, 4.55.11, 14–15: 'saevo Bilbilin optimam metallo . . . quam fluctu tenui set inquieto/ armorum Salo temperator ambit' (*Latin* Bilbilis, excellent in steel for war . . . which with its small but troublous stream, Salo, armour's temperer, encircles). Compare *Othello*, 5.2.256: 'a sword of Spain, the ice-brook's temper'.

300.1–3 those mentioned by Burke . . . grossness see Edmund Burke, *Reflections on the Revolution in France* (1790), ed. Conor Cruise O'Brien (Harmondsworth, 1968), 170.

300.6 his mistresses were of inferior rank in *Les Chroniques de Jean de Troyes* Jean de Roye (in Petitot, 14.40–41) notes that Louis brought back with him from Lyon to Orleans two mistresses, the widow and wife respectively of merchants.

300.7 Agnes Sorel Agnès Sorel (1422–50) was the high-minded and influential mistress of Charles VII.

300.8–9 his heroic father . . . England for Charles VII see EEWN 15, 524 (note to 67.11–13).

300.15 Tristram l'Hermite . . . Marshalsea for Tristram, see EEWN 15, 503. A 'Marshalsea' or 'marshalcy' was a military force under the command of a royal officer.

300.16–18 as his descendant Francis . . . dominions François I, King of France 1515–47, courted popularity by elevating the aristocracy to social equality with himself as 'the first gentleman of France'.

301.19 the Knight without Fear and Reproach Pierre du Terrail (*c.* 1473–1524), Chevalier de Bayard, a noted French captain, was known as the knight 'sans peur et sans reproche'.

301.20 the gallant Francis I François I (see note to 300.16–18) was celebrated for his military exploits.

301.28–29 wearied Heaven . . . his life see Antoine Varillas, *Histoire de Louis XI.*, 2 vols (The Hague, 1689), 2.255: 'Il engageoit à prier pour luy ceux qui passoient pour Saints . . . Mais il vouloit que l'on demandât seulement la santé de son corps à Dieu, depeur que l'on ne se rendît importun en demandant aussi celle de son esprit' (He enlisted those who were considered saints to pray for him . . . but he desired that they should only ask God for his bodily health, fearing that they would make themselves importunate by requesting also the health of his soul).

301.29–31 With a poverty of spirit . . . plundered him Comines observes (6.12: Petitot, 12.401) that Louis gave his doctor Jacques Cottier 54,000 crowns in five months, but that Cottier 'estoit si trés-rude, que l'on ne diroit point à un valet les outrageuses et rudes parolles, qu'il luy disoit' (was so rough that one would not have given a valet the outrageous and coarse language he gave him).

301.31–38 In his extreme desire of life . . . cloisters for the relics requested of Pope Sixtus IV, and sent, see Comines (6.10: Petitot, 12.391). For the hermit, see Comines (6.8: Petitot, 12.376–78): Comines calls him 'frere Robert', but he was in fact St Francis de Paulo (1416–1507: canonised 1519). Louis's foundation of 'two convents' is recorded by Nathaniel William Wraxall, *The History of France, under the Kings of the Race of Valois*, 3rd edn, 2 vols (London, 1807), 1.150: *CLA*, 204.

301.41–302.3 Making any mention . . . at once see P. Mathieu, *The History of Lewis the Eleventh*, trans. Edward Grimeston, 2 vols (London, 1614), 2.107 and Claude de Seyssel in *Supplément aux Mémoires de Messire Philippe de Comines, Seigneur d'Argenton*, [ed. Jean Godefroy] (Brussels, 1713), 295–96. The St Eutropius in question was probably the first Bishop of Saintes (Charente-Maritime), a 3rd-century martyr.

302.7–14 So great were the well-merited tortures . . . superior regions see Comines (6.12: Petitot, 12.396): 'je veux faire comparaison des maux et douleurs qu'il a fait souffrir à plusieurs, à ceux qu'il a soufferts avant mourir: pour ce que j'ay esperance qu'ils l'auront mené en paradis, et que ce aura esté partie de son purgatoire' (I wish to draw a comparison between the evils and sorrows he made many suffer and those he suffered before his death, for I hope they will have conducted him to Paradise and will have been part of his purgatory).

302.18–303.9 Pygmalion . . . ce monstre François de Salignac de la Mothe Fénelon (1651–1715), *Les Aventures de Télémaque*, Book 3, in *Œuvres Complètes*, ed. [Jean Edme Auguste] Gosselin, 10 vols (Paris, 1851–52), 6.413. The transcription does not appear to have survived, but the passage in the Magnum is verbally accurate. Pygmalion is the tyrannical King of Tyre and from the time of the work's composition was recognised as a satirical portrait of Louis XIV, King of France 1643–1715. The passage appears as follows in the translation by Tobias Smollett, *The Adventures of Telemachus, the Son of Ulysses* (originally published posthumously in 1776), ed. Leslie A. Chilton and O. M. Brack, Jr (Athens [Georgia], and London, 1997), 29–30: 'Pygmalion, tormented by an insatiable thirst after riches, becomes every day more and more miserable and hateful to his subjects. To be wealthy at Tyre is criminal:

avarice rendering him distrustful, suspicious, cruel, he persecutes the rich, and fears the poor.

It is still more criminal at Tyre to be virtuous: for to such Pygmalion thinks himself insufferable on account of his baseness and injustice; and as virtue condemns him, he hates and reviles her in return. Every thing disturbs, frets, and disquiets him; he is afraid of his own shadow, and sleeps neither night nor day: to complete his misery, the gods heap riches upon him which he dares not enjoy. What he covets in order to make him happy, is the very circumstance that prevents his being so. As he regrets whatever he gives away, and is always afraid of losing what he has, so he torments himself continually to increase his wealth. He is scarce ever seen, but is generally alone, immured in the most secret part of his palace, melancholy and dejected. Even his friends dare hardly approach him, for fear of becoming the objects of his distrust; and a terrible guard with naked swords and pikes extended continually surround his palace. There are thirty apartments that have a communication one with another, with each an iron door, and six strong bolts. In these he shuts himself up; nor is it ever known in which of them he sleeps; but it is said he never sleeps two nights successively in the same, for fear of being assassinated. He is a stranger to every sweet enjoyment; and to friendship, the sweetest of all: if any one exhorts him to indulge in pleasure, he declines the attempt; sensible that joy flies far from him, and will not take possession of his heart. His eyes that fiercely gleam with cruel fire, incessant roll about on every side: alarmed by the least noise that strikes his ear, he turns pale, and stands aghast; and black corroding care is ever painted on his wrinkled face. He speaks little, sighs often, fetching deep groans from the bottom of his heart, and unable to conceal the remorse that preys upon his vitals. The most exquisite dishes can give him no pleasure; and his children, far from being the objects of his hope, excite his fears, and thus become his most dangerous enemies: he has not been one moment during his whole life in security and free from danger, and it is only by making away with all those whom he dreaded, that he hath hitherto preserved himself. Fool! not to see that the cruelty, in which he trusts for his safety, will one day prove his ruin! Some one of his domestics, as distrustful as himself, will not fail soon to deliver the world from such a monster.'

303.34–35 the Duke of Gueldres, and William de la Marck see respectively note to 305.28–38 below and EEWN 15, 502–03.

304.7–17 The right of the feudal superior . . . his liege lord in principle land was held on feudal tenure in return for military services. If a woman who inherited was unmarried, her feudal lord had an interest in her marriage and was therefore allowed to select for her a husband who would be an appropriate vassal for rendering military service.

304.37–38 during the author's incognito the Waverley novels up to *Woodstock* (1826) were published anonymously.

304.38–39 as Lucio expresses it, spoken "according to the trick" *Measure for Measure*, 5.1.502–03.

305.1–6 This editio princeps . . . De Bure see Guillaume-François de Bure, *Bibliographie instructive*, 7 vols (Paris, 1763–68), 4.93 (Item 3714): *CLA*, 39.

305.10–21 Saint Hubert . . . Brabant Hubert (*c.* 656–727) was the eldest son of Bertrand, Duke of Aquitaine. He found favour at the court of Austrasia, the eastern French kingdom, of which the 'mayor of the palace', or virtual sovereign, was Pépin the Younger, or Pépin l'Héristal (d. 714). He became Bishop of Maastricht *c.* 705, and first Bishop of Liège in 721, when the see was moved from Maastricht. He was regarded as a saint by the 9th century. The standard soubriquet 'Apostle of the Ardennes' refers to the hill country where he spend ten years as a hermit, and where as bishop he carried out a vigorous programme of evangelisation.

305.25 the derivation *OED* explains that the term derives from the Latin *convenire* ('come together', 'assemble').

305.28–38 This was Adolphus . . . 1477 see EEWN 15, 520 (note to 48.10–28). Scott could have found some support for the striking of Arnoul, mentioned in Ed1 and repeated in this note, in Barante, 10.57: 'parfois l'on vit son fils . . . menacer son vieux père' (sometimes his son could be observed threatening his aged father). Cathérine de Bourbon (*c.* 1440–69), the daughter of Charles I (d. 1456), Duke of Bourbon and Auvergne, was in fact Adolphe's wife (they married in 1463): Adolphe's mother was Cathérine de Clèves, daughter of Philippe le Bon of Burgundy's sister Marie and Adolphe IV, Duke of Clèves. In 1471 Adolphe was imprisoned by Charles the Bold, to whom Arnoul sold the reversion of Gueldres and Zutphen the following year, and on Arnoul's death in 1473 they were incorporated into Burgundy. Adolphe remained in prison until after the Duke's death at Nancy in 1477, when the people of Ghent liberated him in the hope that he (rather than the French dauphin) would marry Marie of Burgundy (1457–82). He was however killed in that year while fighting the French. In the same year Marie married Maxmilian I of Austria (1459–1519), who laid claim to Gueldres, but Adolphe's son Charles of Egmont (1467–1538) recovered his inheritance in 1492.

305.39–306.4 This part . . . 1475 see EEWN 15, 520 (note to 49.1–2).

306.5–6 his possession . . . Saint Quentin see EEWN 15, 520 (note to 49.16–18).

306.8–11 It was a part . . . the fair sex this judgment has not been found elsewhere.

306.20–21 The weapon is now in my possession the dirk is preserved at Abbotsford.

306.28–29 Petit-Jean see EEWN 15, 503–04.

306.35–309.3 In a former volume . . . in that kingdom for the remarks on gypsies in the Magnum introduction to *Guy Mannering* referred to in the first sentence, see EEWN 25a, 109–13. Most of the material in this note is taken, or derived, from two works: John Hoyland's *A Historical Survey of the Customs, Habits, and Present State of the Gypsies* (York, 1816: *CLA*, 202) and *Dissertation on the Gipseys . . . from the German of H. M. G. Grellmann* (London 1807). Hoyland ([17]–19) gives the translation (somewhat abridged from the French) of the passage from Étienne Pasquier, *Les Recherches de la France* (Paris, 1665), 359–60 (Bk 4, Ch. 19). Scott's transcription of Hoyland introduces many verbal variants: some of these are clearly deliberate, apparently intended in part to make the passage easier for modern readers; others may be misreadings, e.g. 'wore two silver rings' for 'one or two silver rings'. The two paragraphs following the quotation in the note paraphrase more of the translation in Hoyland, 19–20.

309.6 Timur or Tamerlane for this 14th-century Tartar warrior and his conquest of Hindostan see Edward Gibbon, *The Decline and Fall of the Roman Empire* (1776–88), Ch. 65.

309.21 an individual the person in question has not been identified.

309.24 like the royal Hal . . . in his own language see *1 Henry IV*, 2.4.17–18.

309.40–41 See Note on the Gipsies . . . Chapter the reference is to the previous note, an endnote in the Magnum.

310.1–8 In 1474 . . . the said year, 1474 see [Jean de Roye], *Les Chroniques de Jean de Troyes* (Petitot, 13.455–56).

310.14–15 the Duke of Clarence, Henry V's brother Thomas

(1387–1421), the second son of Henry IV, was created Duke of Clarence in 1412.

310.30–43 The alleged origin . . . decisive Scott adds this anecdote to the Ed1 note (EEWN 15, 102). James Gregory (1753–1821) was a leading Edinburgh physician.

311.7–10 Qu'ils n'auroient pas beaucoup d'embarras . . . puisse dire *French* it is true they won't have much trouble feeding the children born of their union; but it will take place, whatever people may say about it. Nathaniel William Wraxall, *The History of France, under the Kings of the Race of Valois*, 3rd edn, 2 vols (London, 1807), 1.143.

311.12–27 A friendly, though unknown correspondent . . . Chronicle the 'unknown correspondent' has not been identified. For the incident referred to by Jean de Roye see EEWN 15, 499–500.

311.38 the "Cent Nouvelles Nouvelles" see EEWN 15, 515 (note to 26.21–23).

311.41–312.6 Galeotti . . . one of his scholars for Galeotti see EEWN 15, 536–37 (note to 152.38–42). *De egregie, sapienter, iocose dictis ac factis Regis Mathiae ad ducem Iohannem eius filium liber* (Book concerning the remarkable, wise, humorous sayings and deeds of King Matthias, for his son Duke John) was first published at Vienna in 1563. *De homine* (the title varies in different editions) was first published in Venice *c.* 1475, and was attacked for its advocacy of salvation by works rather than by faith. Sixtus IV (Francesco della Rovere, 1414–84) was Pope from 1471.

312.10 more than eleven years from April 1469 till December 1480. Duclos says 12 years: Charles Pineau-Duclos, *The History of Lewis XI., King of France*, 2 vols (London, 1746; first published as *Histoire de Louis XI*, 3 vols (Paris, 1745)), 1.292. Comines (6.7: Petitot, 12.369) wrongly calculates 14.

312.12–313.11 It was a remarkable part . . . punishment employed with the exception of the penultimate sentence of the first paragraph, and the second paragraph, which are based on local and personal knowledge, this account derives from Hoyland and Grellmann (see note to 306.35–309.3 above). *Nuts*, or *Nats*, are an itinerant class of entertainers and fortune-tellers found in S Asia.

313.12–15 A similar story . . . a contribution the source of this anecdote has not been identified.

313.17–23 Vox quoque . . . sees them see EEWN 15, 544 (note to 198.36–38). For the commentators see *P. Virgilii Maronis Opera*, ed. Jacobus Emmenessius, 3 vols (Louvain and Amsterdam, 1680: *CLA*, 226), 1.161n, citing Bk 8, Ch. 22 [34] of Pliny's *Natural History*.

313.28–32 when the Dutch . . . England the Netherlands were a French province from 1810 to 1813.

313.33–34 A sooth bourd . . . the Scot see James Kelly, *A Complete Collection of Scotish Proverbs* (London, 1721), 3; *ODEP*, 753.

313.35–38 Fought by the insurgents . . . slaughter for the battle of St Trond see EEWN 15, 547 (note to 216.19–26).

313.40–314.25 In assigning the present date . . . before Saint Lambert's cathedral the details derive from Barante, 12.247–51. Barante has the boar's head simply 'sur la manche' (on the sleeve: 12.247), and De la Marck first wounds the bishop with 'un coup dans la gorge' (a blow to the throat: 12.249).

314.32–41 He that at this day . . . enemies see Fynes Moryson, *An Itinerary*, 3 parts (London, 1617), 3.165. Scott's modernised transcription has several small verbal variants, most notably 'themselves black' for 'themselues al blacke'.

315.1–6 D'Hymbercourt . . . but in vain for Humbercourt see EEWN 15, 501. For the incident involving Mary of Burgundy see Comines (5.17: Petitot, 12.285–86).

315.8–10 Philip des Comines . . . action for Comines see EEWN 15, 500. For this opening comment see EEWN 15, 274.2–7. The Magnum version of this sentence reads: 'The person whom he particularly addressed was a lively-looking man, with an eye of great vivacity, which was corrected by an expression of reflection and gravity about the mouth and upper lip—the whole physiognomy marking a man who saw and judged rapidly . . .'.

315.12–14 Sleidan . . . noble presence for Jean Sleidan's remark see *Les Memoires de Messire Philippe de Commines . . . Auec . . . deux Epistres de Iean Sleidan, en la recommandation de l'Autheur* (Rouen, 1625), 843, 846.

315.14–38 The learned Monsieur Petitot . . . not without difficulty Petitot's note in Vol. 13 of the *Mémoires* simply refers to Ch. 4 of *Memoires de Messire Olivier de la Marche* in Petitot, 10.299–391. Comines appears at 382, his party actually led by 'Charles de Challon [Châlons], comte de Joingny, cousin germain [first cousin] de monsieur le prince d'Orange [Guillaume VII, who acceeded in 1463 and died in 1475]'. Adolphe de Clèves, Seigneur de Ravestain (1425–92), was a nephew of Philip the Good. At 10.327 the leopard is mounted on a unicorn. The expression 'fierce vanities' is from *Henry VIII*, 1.1.54. For the story of the collector of shadows, see Adelbert von Chamisso, *Peter Schlemihl's wundersame Geschichte* (The wonderful story of Peter Schemihl), ed. Friedrich Baron de la Motte Fouqué (Nuremberg, 1814). Hercules, a hero of Classical legend, was commanded by King Eurystheus to carry out a number of demanding tasks. The French *Arbre d'or* means 'golden tree'; 'arms of courtesy' are blunted weapons.

315.39 tam Marte quam Mercurio the Latin tag means 'as much Mars as Mercury [the Roman gods of war and eloquence]', i.e. equally distinguished in war and diplomacy.

315.40 troupe dorée *French* golden band; i.e. choice company or élite.

316.1–20 After the battle . . . chap. xiii see Comines (1.13: Petitot, 11.420–22), which has 'quatre ou cinq personnes' (four or five persons). For Montereau see EEWN 15, 533 (note to 125.20–23).

316.27–38 The arrival . . . 1468 see Comines (2.5: Petitot, 11.468–70). The three brothers were: Philippe, Count of Bresse (1438–97), who became Duke of Savoy in 1496; Jean Louis (1447–82), who became Bishop of Geneva in 1460; and Jacques, Count of Romont (1450–86). For de Lau and de Rivière see EEWN 15, 552–53 (note to 276.31–32). Pierre d'Urfé (d. 1508) was Seigneur of Urfé and La Bastie; the romance writer was actually Honoré d'Urfé (1528–1625). 'The Euphuist' is Sir Piercie Shafton in *The Monastery* (1820), whose high-flown language had not met with critical approval. For St Andrew and Burgundy see EEWN 15, 554 (note to 284.41–42).

316.39–41 This gesture . . . Richard III. the tradition can be traced back to Shakespeare's time in the mannerism characteristic of the actor Richard Burbage in the role of Richard III, and apparently referred to in Samuel Rowlands, *The Letting of Humours Blood In The Head Vaine, &c.* (Edinburgh, 1814: a reproduction of the edition of 1611, edited by Scott), A2r: 'Gallants, *like* Richard *the Usurper, swagger, / That had his hand continuall on his Dagger*'. It is based on historical record, and Scott's 'fierce character' suggests that he is recalling Thomas Holinshed's description of Richard's 'fierce nature' which finds expression in this obsessive movement: 'the dagger which he ware, he would (when he studied) with his hand plucke vp & downe in the sheath to the midst, neuer drawing it fullie out' (*Holinshed's Chronicles of England, Scotland, and Ireland*, 6 vols (London, 1807–08), 3.447: *CLA*, 29).

See Andrew Gurr, *The Shakespearean Stage 1574–1642*, 3rd edn (Cambridge, 1992), 114, 210.

316.42 An Earl of Douglas, so called see EEWN 15, 554–55 (note to 286.31–32).

316.43–317.2 The famous apparition . . . spectre see EEWN 15, 556 (note to 297.24–25).

317.31–33 These particulars . . .. History of France, vol. i see Comines (2.9: Petitot, 11.486–88), and Nathaniel William Wraxall, *The History of France, under the Kings of the Race of Valois*, 3rd edn, 2 vols (London, 1807), 1.111–14n: *CLA*, 204.

317.34–43 Louis kept . . . his last illness see note to 312.10 above, and EEWN 15, 541 (note to 172.39–41).

318.2–40 Prayer of Louis XI. . . . increasing the slander this note considerably expands that in Ed1 (EEWN 15, 311). For the source in Brantôme see EEWN, 556 (note to 295.38–41). Scott's translation is mostly faithful to the original. For the Duke of Guienne see EEWN 15, 560–61 (notes to 325.39–326.1 and 331.18–19). For Our Lady of Clery see EEWN 15, 557 (note to 310.14). Saint Jean d'Angély (Charente-Maritime) was a Benedictine Abbey founded in the 9th century.

318.41–319.1 Varillas . . . indicated see Antoine Varillas, *Histoire de Louis XI*, 2 vols (The Hague, 1689), 2.331.

319.6–10 he was certainly . . . Charles the VIIth's reign Mathieu notes this knighting after the siege of Fronsac (Gironde) in 1451: P. Mathieu, *The History of Lewis the Eleventh*, trans. Edward Grimeston, 2 vols (London, 1614), 2.201. For the elder Dunois see EEWN 15, 528 (note to 94.18–22). Charles VII was King of France 1422–61.

319.12–321.2 The death of Martius Galeotti . . . such indignities see EEWN 15, 559–60 (note to 321.24–26). Angelo Cato (Angelus Catho, d. 1494) acted as one of Charles the Bold's doctors before transferring his allegiance to become Louis's doctor and almoner (spiritual executive) after Charles was defeated by the Swiss at Grandson and Morat in 1476.

321.3–10 The story is told . . . author concerned see EEWN 15, 561–62 (note to 333.31–32).

321.21–39 After the death of Louis . . . united with learning for Anne of Beaujeu see EEWN 15, 527 (note to 90.6–7). For the historian's imprisonment see Comines (6.12: Petitot, 12.402). The elegy by Pierre de Ronsard (1524–85) is recorded by Petitot, who quotes the last 5 lines (11.139n): for the whole 48–line poem see the *Œuvres complètes*, ed. Jean Céard, Daniel Ménager, and Michel Simonin, 2 vols (n.p., 1994), 2.937–40.

321.41 Disguised Herald the first cross-reference to this endnote reads 'For a remarkable instance of this, see note, at the end of the Chapter.'

321.42 feciales a Roman college of priests, who sanctioned treaties when concluded, and demanded satisfaction from the enemy before a formal declaration of war.

322.7–24 Exercising that knowledge . . . the great world the incident is found in Comines (4.7: Petitot, 12.133–38).

322.27–323.24 I have heard some . . . feudatorie to England for the first quotation see John Ferne, *The Blazon of Gentrie* (London, 1586), 161–62: *CLA*, 24. Scott's transcription has a small number of minor verbal changes, most of them apparently designed to make things easier for his readers. The paragraph which follows paraphrases a passage on pp. 97–98, beginning with the assertion: 'Christ was a Gentleman, as to his flesh, by the part of his mother: (as I haue read) and might if hee had esteemed, of the vayne glorye of this worlde (whereof he often sayde, his kingdome was not) haue borne coat-armour.' The title-page of the Abbotsford copy bears the name of 'Thomas Drysdaill Islay Hereauld' and the date 1619. The passage which attracted the comment quoted is on p. 141. The comment has been written in a large formal hand ('half-text' is the Scots term) before and partly over a faded and cropped original marginal observation (now mostly illegible) in secretary hand. The offending words in the text have been scored out, probably by the earlier commentator. Scott's version of the 'half-text' comment is slightly varied. Judas Maccabaeus (d. 160 BC) was the leader of Jewish rebellions against the Syrians (see 1 and 2 Maccabees in the Apocrypha). The four doctors are: St Ambrose (*c.* 339–97), Bishop of Milan; St Augustine (354–430), Bishop of Hippo; St Jerome (Eusebius Hieronymous, *c.* 342–420), biblical scholar; and St Gregory (*c.* 540–604), Pope from 590 (Gregory I or the Great). The 'hopeful young friend' was Thomas Shortreed (1796–1826), son of Scott's old friend Robert Shortreed, Sheriff-substitute of Roxburghshire: see the Centenary Edition of the Waverley Novels, 25 vols (Edinburgh, 1871), 16.483n and James C. Corson, *Notes and Index to Sir Herbert Grierson's Edition of the Letters of Sir Walter Scott* (Oxford, 1979), 648. The Abbotsford copy of Ferne has Shortreed's name on the first flyleaf, and inside the front cover, with the date 'February 1819', possibly when the gift was made. Scott has written on the second flyleaf: 'This scarce book was the gift of a deceased young friend Thomas Shortreed'.

323.30–34 It is almost unnecessary . . . Scoonhoven Guillaume I married Johanna van Arschot van Schoonhoven (d. 1506) before 1463.

323.36–324.43 The Duke of Burgundy . . . the preceding chapter see Comines (2.10–13: Petitot, 11.489–511).

325.5–17 We have already noticed . . . Bishop of Liege's death see EEWN 15, 502–03.

325.18–22 An old rhyme . . . fought his adversary see EEWN 15, 569 (note to 398.28–29).

SAINT RONAN'S WELL

333.5 celebrare domestica facta *Latin* sing of deeds at home. Horace, *De arte poetica* (On the Art of Poetry), line 287.

333.16–17 from the authoress of Evelina to her of Marriage *Evelina*, by Fanny Burney (1752–1840), appeared in 1778, and *Marriage*, by Susan Ferrier (1782–1854), in 1818.

333.18 Edgeworth, Austin, Charlotte Smith Maria Edgeworth (1767–1849), Jane Austen (1775–1817), and Charlotte Smith (1749–1806).

333.35–36 mars the custom of his exercise compare *Hamlet*, 2.2.289: 'forgone all custom of exercises'.

334.40–41 These affectations . . . they dare see *The Rehearsal* (1672), largely by George Villiers, 2nd Duke of Buckingham. In Drawcansir's brief appearance towards the end of 4.1 'dare' is the predominating term, culminating in the couplet 'I drink, I huff, I strut, look big and stare,/ And all this I can do, because I dare'.

335.11 the license of doing what is good in his own eyes see e.g. Deuteronomy 12.8: 'Ye shall not do after all the things that we do here this day, every man whatsoever is right in his own eyes.'

335.27–28 shoot folly as it flies Alexander Pope, *An Essay on Man* (1733–34), 1.13.

335.41–336.13 the English critics . . . his ordinary style most of the English reviews found *Saint Ronan's Well* inferior and commonplace, though Meg Dods was often admired. In Scotland the *Edinburgh Magazine*, the *Scotsman*, and the *Edinburgh Literary Gazette* thought highly of some of the character sketches, but none of them was unreservedly enthusiastic.

336.16–20 In a colloquy of Erasmus . . . on the road 'Diversoria' ('Inns') was published in 1523 in the *Colloquies* of the Dutch humanist Erasmus (1466–1536): see *CLA*, 139. A translation by Craig R. Thompson can be found in *Collected Works of Erasmus* (Toronto), 39 (1997), 370–75 (371).

336.23–24 Jenny Dods . . . the Peebles road see EEWN 16, 449 (note to 6.14).

337.39–42 The foundress . . . Jerusalem see EEWN 16, 451–52 (note to 19.29). Joanna Southcott (1750–1814) was a visionary claiming prophetic powers who attracted a number of followers who believed themselves to be heirs to the new Jerusalem: she still has a small company of devotees.

337.43 King's Evil it was believed that scrofula, or the king's evil, could be cured by the touch of royalty. The practice of touching began in England and France in the 11th century and continued until the early 18th century in England and the early 19th century in France.

338.3–4 The said piper . . . mystery see EEWN 16, 453 (note to 24.34).

338.7–14 The Dark Ladye . . . entitled Love in 1798–1800 Coleridge wrote an unfinished poem entitled 'The Ballad of the Dark Ladié' which was not published until it appeared posthumously in his *Poetical Works* in 1834. It is not known how Scott became acquainted with this fragment spoken by a woman whose situation has similarities with that of Clara Mowbray. On 21 December 1799 Coleridge published a poem entitled 'Introduction to the Tale of the Dark Ladié' in *The Morning Post*; the following year that poem, which is not about the 'Dark Ladié', appeared, with stanzas omitted, in *Lyrical Ballads* (1800) under the title 'Love'. Wordsworth sent a copy of the second edition of *Lyrical Ballads* to the Whig politician Charles James Fox (1749–1806) on 14 January 1801, which Fox acknowledged on 25 May (*The Letters of William and Dorothy Wordsworth*, ed. Ernest De Selincourt, 2nd edn, *The Early Years 1787–1805*, rev. Chester L. Shaver (Oxford, 1967), 312–15, 337).

338.15–18 The late Dr Gregory . . . severe regimen see EEWN 16, 458 (notes to 60.19–21, 60.31, 60.41–61.4).

338.20 Bogle . . . Goblin the usual Scots meaning of *bogle* is 'ghost' (see EEWN 16, glossary 495), which accords with the cow-boy's having 'a sheet about him' (103.8–9). As Scott adds a note explaining bogle as 'goblin', the Magnum text alters 'sheet' to 'shirt'.

338.21–23 A kettle of fish . . . pastoral poetry 'piscatory eclogues' are poems in dialogue form featuring fishermen. Authors of such poems include Jacopo Sanazarro, who published several *Piscatoria* in 1526, and Moses Browne, whose *Piscatory Eclogues* appeared in 1729. A *fête-champêtre* is a rural entertainment.

338.39 the celebrated Cossack leader, Platoff Count Matvei Ivanovich Platov (1757–1818), a Russian general who commanded a Cossack corps in the Napoleonic wars.

338.43–339.3 This satire . . . minister of Dunbar see EEWN 16, 470–71 (note to 150.32).

339.5–6 the style of Arbuthnot John Arbuthnot (1667–1735), a distinguished physician, was a friend of Jonathan Swift and produced a number of acerbic satirical works.

339.9–26 At the same time . . . in his own house see [Simon Haliburton with Thomas Hepburn], *Memoirs of Magopico*, 2nd edn (Edinburgh, 1761), 20. Scott's transcription has a number of verbal differences from the original, notably: 'his lamb' for 'his tiend lamb', 'his house neither washed nor plastered' for 'his linen neither washed nor plaited', and 'in his power lawfully to beget' for 'in his power to beget'.

339.29–30 Kilruddery . . . Lord Meath Kilruddery House, Bray, Co. Wicklow has been the seat of the Earls of Meath since the creation of the peerage in 1627.

339.34 the scene in which Bottom rehearsed his pageant see *A Midsummer Night's Dream*, 3.1.

339.36–42 The Arnaouts . . . back to Morven Scott's transcription of part of Byron's long note to *Childe Harold's Pilgrimage*, Canto 2 (1812), line 338 has 'struck me by' for 'struck me forcibly by' and 'but a milder' for 'with a kinder': these were restored to the original reading, presumably by an intermediary, and the restoration is accepted in the present text.

340.12 the celebrated case of Murdison and Millar see *Information for James Montgomery of Stanhope, Esq; his Majesty's Advocate, for his Majesty's Interest, Pursuer; against Alexander Murdison Tenant in the Farm of Ormiston alias Wormiston, in the County of Peebles, and John Miller Shepherd to the said Alexander Murdison, both now Prisoners in the Tolbooth of Edinburgh, Pannels* ([Edinburgh], 1773). Neither this pamphlet, which is dated 1 February 1773, nor a successor dated 10 February, goes into many of the details provided by Scott. The Vale of Leithen joins Tweeddale at Innerleithen, Peeblesshire, a little to the E of Glenormiston.

341.36 Non omnis moriar *Latin* Horace, *Odes*, 3.30.6 ('I shall not altogether die').

342.3–4 The Cook . . . Family Management published with a different subtitle in 1826, *The Cook and Housewife's Manual* [by Christian Isobel Johnstone], was revised and enlarged for a 4th edition (Edinburgh, 1829) with the subtitle as given by Scott. The work was frequently republished during the rest of the 19th century.

REDGAUNTLET

351.42–352.1 a young Scottishman . . . the royal family Alexander Murray, brother of Lord Elibank, planned this assassination attempt in 1752–53, but he failed to carry it out: see David Daiches, *Charles Edward Stuart* (London, 1973), 286–88.

352.5 Sir Robert Walpole the Whig administration of Walpole (1676–1745) lasted almost without interruption from 1721 to 1742. The Jacobite plots of the early 1750s were handled by his successor Henry Pelham (1694–1754).

352.11 Doctor Archibald Cameron Scott owned a biography of Cameron (1707–53): *An Historical Account of the Life, Actions, and Conduct of Dr. Archibald Cameron, Brother to Donald Cameron of Lochiel* . . . (London, 1753: *CLA*, 91). Donald (*c.* 1700–48) was active during the 1745 Uprising. For Samuel Johnson's favourable view of Archibald's activities see James Boswell, *Life of Samuel Johnson*, ed. George Birkbeck Hill and L. F. Powell, 6 vols (Oxford, 1934–50), 1.146–47. Euan Macpherson of Cluny (1706–64), Chief of Clan Chattan (or Vuirich) escaped government troops in 1755, fleeing to France where he died the following year.

353.26 Dr King's Anecdotes of his Own Times for the passages quoted, which are verbally accurate, see William King, *Political and Literary Anecdotes of his Own Times* (London, 1818), 196–97, 204–09: *CLA*, 256. King (1685–1763) was leader of the Jacobite faction in the University of Oxford. The passages were transcribed by William Laidlaw, who acted as amanuensis for all but the opening pages of the Introduction.

353.27 Lady Primrose Anne Primrose (d. 1775) was the widow of Hugh,

3rd and last Viscount Primrose (d. 1741).

354.7–9 he had a mistress . . . Leicester House Clementine Walkinshaw (*c.* 1720–1802) became Charles's mistress in 1746 and joined him on the Continent in June or July 1752. Her elder sister Catherine was mistress of the bedchamber to the Dowager Princess of Wales at Leicester House, in London's Leicester Square, from 1767 to 1772.

355.13–14 his unhappy grandfather James II, who was forced to abdicate in 1688.

355.18–19 prohibiting the residence of Charles . . . dominions under the Peace of Aix-la-Chapelle (1748) France was required to expel Charles from its territories.

355.39–356.44 But the most odious part . . . ill rewarded see King's *Political and Literary Anecdotes* (note to 353.26 above), 201–03, quoted with verbal accuracy. A *pistole* was a gold coin, as was a *louis d'or*.

357.4 the death of his father the Old Pretender died in 1766.

357.32 a tale which had been told see Psalm 90.9: 'we spend our years as a tale that is told'.

358.1 a gentleman of fortune in Perthshire Laurence Oliphant, who succeeded his father, of the same name, as Laird of Gask in 1767 and died in 1792; see T. L. Kington Oliphant, *The Jacobite Lairds of Gask* (London, 1870), 427. (The manuscript has 'Mr. Oliphant of Gask'.) In a copy of a letter of Oliphant dated 14 July 1787 he refers to 'the Ks health' (MS 874, f. 487v).

358.28–29 fallen into the sere and yellow leaf see *Macbeth*, 5.2.23.

359.6–16 One of the nine-steps . . . without assistance Scott added the first and last of these sentences to the Ed1 note (EEWN 17, 2).

359.17–25 The Hall . . . but his own Scott inserted 'the Courts of Justice' into the Ed1 note (EEWN 17, 3).

359.27–31 Sir John Nisbett . . . jurisprudence see EEWN 17, 447 (notes to 4.9).

359.39 Sir Thomas Hope two of the sons of the leading advocate Sir Thomas Hope of Craighall (1573–1646) were appointed lords of session: Sir John Hope (*c.* 1603–54) in 1632 (taking the title Lord Craighall), and Sir Thomas Hope of Kerse (1606–43) in 1641.

360.3–4 Mathieson . . . Dr Adams Alexander Matheson, rector (headmaster) of the High School 1759–68, was succeeded by Alexander Adam (1741–1809), who died in office.

360.8–9 when Members of Parliament . . . the cover the many abuses of the franking system (see EEWN 17, 449: note to 6.32–36), which led to a seven-fold increase in franked packets in the 50 years up to 1763, were the subject of repeated complaints and investigations during the 18th century. In 1764, 1784, and 1795 a number of restrictions were introduced, but the privilege was not abolished till the introduction of the Penny Postage in 1840. For a full account see George Brumell, *A Short Account of the Franking System in the Post Office: 1652–1840* (Bournemouth, 1936), 5–13.

360.17–20 The old man's mear's dead . . . Dundee the words and tune of this song are attributed to Patrick, 'Patie', or Peter Birnie (active around the turn of the 17th century), though the words may have been by another; they were re-worked by Burns (for words, tune, and commentary see *The Poems and Songs of Robert Burns*, ed. James Kinsley, 3 vols (Oxford, 1968), no. 585 and note).

360.30–31 Rob Roy . . . Alan Mhor Cameron for Rob Roy and Cameron see EEWN 17, 454 (notes to 16.15–16 and 16.16).

361.23–24 the Chap-Book, called the History of Buckhaven see EEWN 17, 466 (note to 72.5–6).

361.25–41 The original . . . set to music see EEWN 17, 468 (note to 78.16–22). The revised version of *The Guardian, Cutter of Coleman-Street*, in which the lines do not feature, was published in 1663. The catch was set by Philip Knapton in 1825: see the Bibliography by John P. Anderson in Charles Duke Yonge, *Life of Sir Walter Scott* (London, 1888), xxxv.
362.1 Blind Rorie see EEWN 17, 470 (note to 83.27–28).
362.6–7 Blind Jack of Knaresborough between 1765 and 1792 John Metcalf (1717–1810) built some 300 km of turnpike roads, mainly in the N of England.
362.23–363.2 those less known . . . a walnut all of the people named except for Earlshall and 'Dumbarton Douglas' have entries in the appendix to John Howie, *Biographia Scoticana; or, an Historical Account of the Lives, Characters, and Memorable Transactions, of the Most Eminent Scots Worthies* (Leith, 1816; originally published 1775: *CLA*, 71): Middleton (xxiiif), Rothes (xxviiif), Lauderdale (xxxf, the final phrase of the note being on xxxi), Bonshaw (xxxiif), Dalyell (Dalziel, xxxivf), and Mackenzie (M'Kenzie, xl).
363.3–4 The reader is referred . . . History of Scotland see Robert Lindsay of Pitscottie, *The Cronicles of Scotland*, ed. John Graham Dalyell, 2 vols (Edinburgh, 1814), 1.96–100n: *CLA*, 8.
363.7–8 Sir Robert Grierson of Lagg for Sir Robert in sources known to Scott see Coleman O. Parsons, *Witchcraft and Demonology in Scott's Fiction* (Edinburgh and London, 1964), 179–84.
363.13–23 a Highland lady . . . a gentleman named Campbell four Independent Companies were established in 1725 and another two in 1729 to 'watch' the Highlands: they were amalgamated with 4 new companies in 1739 to form the 43rd (later the 42nd) Regiment of Foot, known as the Black Watch. The identity of 'Mrs C— of B—' and the commander in her story is discussed at length by Graham Tulloch and Judy King in the Historical Note to 'Phantasmagoria', Scott's earlier version of the anecdote published in *Blackwood's Edinburgh Magazine* in 1818 (EEWN 24, 182–86). They conclude that the commander's name is correctly given in 'Phantasmagoria' as Campbell, rather than Cameron (a name inserted at proof stage in the Magnum), but they are unable to determine which of the many Campbells who were officers in the various Companies is the gentleman in question, and as to 'Mrs C—— of B——' they cannot attempt 'even an educated guess'.
364.42 Peter Peebles for Peebles see 752 below (erratum for EEWN 17: note to 116.26–27).
365.42–43 Tradition . . . Lord Kames see EEWN 17, 486 (note to 135.41–42).
366.12–13 James V. . . . Justice James V founded the College of Justice, which includes the supreme Scottish civil and criminal courts, in 1532. No specific source for the anecdote has been located.
366.20 the close of the American war the 'American war' ended with Great Britain's recognition of the independence of the United States in the Treaty of Paris of 1782.
366.21 Sir James Graham of Netherby the Graham Baronetcy of Netherby, 3km N of Longtown in Cumberland, was created in 1783 for James Graham (1761–1824).
367.1–2 Old Niel Gow . . . Nathaniel Niel Gow (1727–1807) and his son Nathaniel (1763–1831) were leading folk musicians and composers. Niel is called 'Old' to distinguish him from Nathaniel's composer son Niel (1794–1823).
367.8–19 The captivity . . . quite so long Rachel Erskine (1679–1745) became Lady Grange on her marriage (probably in 1707) to James Erskine, a lord of session with the title Lord Grange. Following their

separation in 1730 she threatened to disclose his involvement in the 1715 Jacobite uprising. He had her held in captivity on North Uist and then for 8 years on the remote island of St Kilda and staged a mock funeral for her in Edinburgh. Elizabeth Canning (1734–73) 'became the centre of the most famous English criminal mystery of her century' (*ODNB*). She claimed to have been abducted on 1 January 1753 and subjected to ill treatment, but she was convicted of perjury the following year and transported to New England. Public opinion was divided as to her guilt or innocence (the novelist and magistrate Henry Fielding being her most prominent defender), and the truth has never been ascertained.

367.24 the British Linen Company a leading Scottish bank, established in 1746. Known as the British Linen Bank from 1906, it was taken over by the Bank of Scotland in 1971 and finally ceased operations in 2000.

367.27–28 the opening . . . George Street the George Street Assembly Rooms opened in 1787.

367.36–37 the real name was MacEwan, or Macmillan for a similar story with one Donald MacLaren as its progatonist see EEWN 17, 442.

367.38–39 An old gentleman of the author's name Walter Scott (1653–1729), known as 'Beardie', was Scott's great-grandfather. See 'Memoirs', *Scott on Himself*, ed. David Hewitt (Edinburgh, 1981), 2–3.

369.31–370.5 upon the coronation . . . the Pretender was in London George III was crowned on 22 September 1761. Since the 14th century the office of sovereign's champion has been held by the head of the Dymoke family. David Daiches notes of a similar tradition: 'The story that he [the Young Pretender] was present in disguise at the coronation of George III on [22] September 1761, and let fall a white kid glove from the gallery in response to the ritual challenge by Dymock, the Champion of England, in defence of the right of the newly-crowned king, is a romantic fiction, as apparently are all other stories of Charles's later visits to England or Ireland' (*Charles Edward Stuart* (London, 1973), 295).

370.19–20 The Highland regiments . . . Earl of Chatham see EEWN 17, 517 (notes to 317.34–36 and 318.26–32).

370.36 the Act 15 Geo. III. chapter 28th enacted in 1775.

THE BETROTHED

377.2–5 The Tales of the Crusaders . . . the author's own taste the friends and the occasion or occasions of their suggestion have not been identified.

377.14 a dwarf more ways than one see Laurence Sterne, *The Life and Opinions of Tristram Shandy, Gentleman* (1760–67), 4.25.

377.29–30 the celebrated year of projects (eighteen hundred and twenty-five) for the proliferation of new joint stock companies in 1824 and 1825 see *A List of Joint-Stock Companies, the proposals for which are now, or have been lately, before the public* (London, 1825). The list includes 276 companies, with others awaiting approval, gas and railroad projects being particularly prominent. Reprinted from *The Monthly Repository of Theology and General Literature* for February 1825, it is offered as 'a record of the state of the public mind, in the course of the year 1824, and the beginning of the year 1825. There has been no instance of extravagance equal to this which we now exhibit, since the infamous South-Sea Bubble in the year 1720' (p. [3]).

378.12–15 Scottish tradition . . . a hero of antiquity the story is not in the *Minstrelsy* but in Note F to *The Lay of the Last Minstrel*: *Poetical Works*, 6.236.

378.25–26 civilians experts in civil law.
378.32 bongré, malgré *French* willy-nilly.
379.1 Keep the cradle rowing the song has not been identified.
379.8 many a brave fellow, and many a bauld feat see James Hogg, 'The Fray of Elibank', line 234, published in *The Mountain Bard* (1807).
379.9–14 The tale of the Noble Moringer . . . 1533 see 'Der edle Möringer' in *Sammlung Deutscher Volkslieder*, ed. [Johann Gustav] Büsching and [Friedrich Heinrich] von der Hagen (Berlin, 1807), 102–15: *CLA*, 47. The details of the poem's origin are given at 391–93 of the collection. The quotations that follow in the Introduction are taken from Scott's own translation of the poem made in 1819 and published the following year in *The Edinburgh Annual Register, for 1816*, ccccxcv–ccccci.
381.21–24 There is also . . . romantic dramas see Johann Ludwig Tieck, *Leben und Tod der heiligen Genoveva*, in his *Romantische Dichtungen*, 2 parts (Jena, 1799–1800), 2.[1]–330: *CLA*, 53.
381.31 the lord and lady of Haighhall the owners of Haigh Hall, at Wigan in Lancashire, in 1830 were James Lindsay (1783–1869) and his wife Maria. In 1825 James became 7th Earl of Balcarres on the death of his father Alexander (b. 1752), who had married Elizabeth Bradshaigh Dalrymple, heiress of the Braidshaigh estate on the extinction of the male line. James replaced the building which had its origin in Norman times with the existing construction in 1827–40.
381.33–382.12 Sir William Bradshaghe 2d . . . An: Dom: 1315 this page, which is unique in the Magnum, reproduces a passage of prose in John Roby, *Traditions of Lancashire*, 2 vols (London, 1829: *CLA*, 197), 1.[45], in the style of a genealogical document or a monumental inscription. Roby states that his source was 'the genealogical roll of the Bradshaighs'. The passage was transcribed for Scott by John Buchanan, and has beside it a direction in the hand of William Laidlaw that it be printed 'in Anglo-Saxon type'. The drawing at the foot is taken from the monument to the Bradshaighs in Wigan Church. The mysterious 'IN. 8. E 2.' and the date 'An: Dom: 1315' are not in Roby.
381.45 congetringe that he favoured conjecturing that he resembled.
382.17–25 Mab's Cross . . . Traditions of Lancashire see John Roby, *Traditions of Lancashire*, 2 vols (London, 1829), 1.46, 83: *CLA*, 197. Roby notes (83) that Lady Mabel 'performed a weekly penance, going bare-footed from Haigh to a place outside the walls at Wigan, where a stone cross was erected, which bears to this day the name of "MAB'S CROSS."'
383.7 receipt for making an epic poem 'A Receit to make an *Epick* Poem' by Alexander Pope was published in Richard Steele's periodical *The Guardian*, No. 78, 10 June 1713. A revised version appeared subsequently as Chapter 15 of *Peri Bathous: or, Martinus Scriblerus, His Treatise of the Art of Sinking in Poetry* (1728).
383.17 Gryffyth Ap Edwin Gruffudd ap Llywelyn pursued border warfare against the English until his death in 1063.
383.18–384.34 This prince . . . put to sea see George Lyttelton, *The History of the Life of King Henry the Second*, 3rd edn, 6 vols (London, 1769), 2.338–41: *CLA*, 236. William Laidlaw's transcription is verbally almost entirely accurate.
383.18–20 Algar . . . Edward the Confessor one of Llywelyn's main allies was Ælfgar, an earl of Mercia, who had been briefly outlawed for treason against Edward the Confessor (King of England 1042–66) in 1055 and succeeded his father as Earl of Mercia and 'Earl' or 'Count' of Chester in 1057. He died *c.* 1062.
383.25 the Earl of Hereford Ralph ('the timid'), nephew of Edward

the Confessor, became Earl of Hereford *c.* 1052 and died in 1057. His soubriquet derives from the defeat described in this passage, which took place on 24 October 1055 and resulted in the sack of Hereford. On his death the Earldom of Hereford was transferred to Harold Godwineson (born *c.* 1022), who became King of England as Harold II in 1066 and was killed the same year at the Battle of Hastings.

384.22 Leofrick, Earl of Mercia Leofric, who became Earl of Mercia perhaps in the late 1020s, died in 1057 and was succeeded by his son Ælfgar.

385.1–2 the Fair of Leipsic the book fair at Leipzig was the largest in Germany between 1632 and 1945.

385.4 Walladmor a novel in three volumes (Berlin, 1824), purporting to be freely translated from the English of Walter Scott ('Frei nach dem Englischen des Walter Scott'). The author was Willibald Alexis (Georg Wilhelm Heinrich Häring).

385.20–24 in the History of the Gwydir family . . . Christmas even see John Wynne, *The History of the Gwedir Family*, [ed. Daines Barrington] (London, 1770), 118: *CLA*, 245.

385.25–33 See Madoc . . . Howell Dha see Robert Southey, *Madoc* (1805), note to Part 1, 2.96. Scott's transcription is verbally somewhat approximate. King Hwyel Dda (Hywel the Good) was the first codifier of Welsh law in the 10th century.

385.42–386.8 A very honourable testimony . . . their lives Scott transcribes (with 'valiantly' for 'willingly') from George Lyttelton, *The History of the Life of King Henry the Second*, 3rd edn, 6 vols (London, 1769), 2.372: *CLA*, 236.

386.9 contumelious epithet see EEWN, 18a, 385 (note to 47.28).

386.11–14 Old Henry Jenkins . . . by measure Henry Jenkins, who died in 1670 at the reputed age of 169, 'remembered the Abbot of Fountains-abbey very well, before the dissolution of the monasteries': Henry Wilson, *Wonderful Characters*, 3 vols (London, 1821–26), 1.412–14 (413). The source of the roast-beef measurement has not been traced.

386.16–32 The Welsh were excellent bowmen . . . an end to the war for the first paragraph see George Lyttelton, *The History of the Life of King Henry the Second*, 3rd edn, 6 vols (London, 1769), 2.373: 'those of South-Wales, and, particularly the province of Guent, or Monmouth, which was then a part of that kingdom, were accounted the best archers, not being inferior, in the use of the long bow, to the Normans themselves' (*CLA*, 236). For the second paragraph see 2.361–62 in the same work: the final sentence uses some of Lyttelton's words.

386.38 Eudorchawg see EEWN, 18a, 379 (note to 19.40).

386.41–43 Manlius . . . a gigantic Gaul when the Gauls pressed southwards towards Rome in 361 BC Titus Manlius defeated a gigantic enemy in single combat and took from him his ornamental neck-chain (*torquis*).

386.43–387.3 Aneurin . . . wreathed with the Eudorchawg see the Welsh poem *Y Gododdin*, attributed to Aneirin, which commemorates the Battle of Catraeth (probably Catterick, Yorkshire) *c.* 600, when the British Gododdin were outnumbered and defeated by the Angles. The number 300 is mentioned in stanza 10, and the gold chains in stanza 65.

387.14–22 the noble Mortimer . . . spoken of *1 Henry IV*, 1.1.38–46.

387.30–388.18 From thence we went . . . to be gone suddenly see *Memoirs of Lady Fanshawe . . . written by herself*, new edn (London, 1830), 91–93: *CLA*, 303. The transcription, in an unidentified hand, has several small verbal variants from the original, which may mostly have been made deliberately on stylistic grounds, and a small correction was introduced for the Magnum text. For the 'Bahr-Geist' see EEWN, 18a, 397 (note to 126.40).

388.24–26 It was thus . . . Nejara see *Sir John Froissart's Chronicles*, trans. Thomas Johnes, 5 vols (Hafod, 1803–10), 1.732 (Ch. 239): *CLA*, 28. Sir John Chandos (d. 1370) was one of the commanders at the battle of Nájera, Castile on 3 April 1367, between an Anglo-Gascon army, led by Edward the Black Prince, and Franco-Castilian forces.
388.27–39 Such an expression . . . the first blow the French brigand Louis Mandrin (b. 1725) was broken on the wheel on 26 May 1755 at Valence, Drôme.

THE TALISMAN

393.2 one or two friends probably James Ballantyne and Robert Cadell. For their general dissatisfaction with *The Betrothed* which led to it being laid aside for a while in favour of *The Talisman* see EEWN 18b, 283–85 and EEWN 18a, 284–87.
393.7–8 the playbill . . . . left out the first citations of this proverbial story given by *ODEP*, 345–46 are from Wordsworth and Byron (1793 and 1818 respectively). The playbill has not been located: it may be Scott's embellishment.
393.13–16 I was as thickly wrapped . . . Goshen see Exodus 10.21–23: 'And the Lord said unto Moses, Stretch out thine hand toward heaven, that there may be darkness over the land of Egypt, even darkness which may be felt./ And Moses stretched forth his hand toward heaven; and there was a thick darkness in all the land of Egypt three days: . . . but all the children of Israel had light in their dwellings'. Goshen is a region in the Nile delta.
393.18–19 its struggles for freedom against a Mohamedan tyrant Greece came under Ottoman rule in the 15th century. In 1821 there was a general uprising, which met with a ruthless response. The struggle continued until 1828 when, with the help of Britain, France, and Russia, the Turks were finally defeated. Greece's independence achieved formal international recognition at a conference held in London in 1832.
393.22 surveyed by British eyes . . . travellers the early 1820s saw the publication of several accounts of tours of Palestine, including a collection of 'views' by Cooper Willyams.
393.28 the Travellers' Club a London club, founded in 1819 for gentlemen who had travelled abroad and the provision of hospitality to distinguished foreign visitors. It moved to its present quarters in Pall Mall in 1832.
393.28–29 thrown his shoe over Edom see Psalm 60.8 (also 108.9): 'Moab is my washpot; over Edom will I cast out my shoe'.
393.32 the author of Anastasius for this and most of the other authors and works referred to in this paragraph see EEWN 18b, 370. Alain-René Lesage (1668–1747) is best known for his picaresque novel *Gil Blas* (1715–35), which Tobias Smollett translated into English in 1749 (see *CLA*, 63).
394.26 the Bibliotheque Orientale see EEWN 18b, 379.
394.43–395.1 a violation of the truth . . . Mr Mills see EEWN 18b, 319.
395.6 Prince David of Scotland for David, Earl of Huntington, see EEWN 18b, 372.
395.10–12 I had already brought upon the field . . . as a disguised knight Richard I had played a prominent part in *Ivanhoe* (1820), for most of the action disguised as the Black Knight.
395.20–22 Do you think . . . so wildly from it? see EEWN 18b, 427 (note to 252.43–253.2).

395.23 an ancient romance . . . Norman for *Richard Cœur de Lyon* see EEWN 18b, 366.
395.31–32 A principal incident . . . derived for the incident see EEWN 18b, 94 (and 82), and for the Lee Penny EEWN 18b, 369. The term 'periapt' in the sentence which follows is another word for 'amulet'.
395.40 Sir Simon Lockhart of Lee and Cartland although the Sir Simon Lockhart credited with bringing the amulet to Scotland is a 14th-century figure (EEWN 18b, 369), the progenitor of the Lanarkshire family, also called Symon Locard, was contemporary with the action of the novel.
395.43–396.3 James, the Good Lord Douglas . . . killed there Sir James Douglas (1288?–1330) fell in battle with the Moors in southern Spain.
396.14–15 a pebble . . . the Lower Empire the 'Lower Empire' is the Roman Empire from the time of Constantine in the early 4th century. The small red stone in question is actually set in a groat of Edward I, King of England 1272–1307: the talisman still survives in the possession of the Lockhart family.
396.30–36 The most remarkable part . . . condemn see 405.5–30 and explanatory note at 706 below.
397.9–18 could no longer repress . . . impetuosity *Specimens of Early English Metrical Romances*, ed. George Ellis, 3 vols (London, 1805), 2.230: *CLA*, 105.
397.21–22 the followers . . . Old Man of the Mountain the Assassins, followers of Rashid al-Din As-sinan (d. 1192), who was known as *shaykh al-jabal* ('mountain chief', mistranslated by the Crusaders as 'the old man of the mountain').
397.28 Appendix to Introduction for the quotations from *Richard Cœur de Lion* and Ellis's summary, accurately transcribed by William Laidlaw, see *Specimens of Early English Metrical Romances*, ed. George Ellis, 3 vols (London, 1805), 2.225–36: *CLA*, 105. The sentence introducing the second quotation is Scott's.
402.12–40 Mr James . . . the Thafurs see G. P. R. James, *The History of Chivalry* (London, 1830), 178–79: *CLA*, 301. Scott's transcription has several minor verbal variants, most notably 'beheld with' for 'held in' and 'a narrow' for 'any narrow'. The phrase 'the same author' refers to Guibert de Nogent (d. 1124).
403.7 The verb . . . Scottish this sentence was added to the original Ed1 note (EEWN 18b, 11). The word *gabber* is recorded by John Jamieson in *An Etymological Dictionary of the Scottish Language* (Edinburgh, 1808), with the meaning 'jabber', 'gibber', 'talk incoherently'. The *Scottish National Dictionary* notes that it is probably onomatopoeic in origin, but that it may possibly be an intensive of *gab*, from the Old French *gaber* mentioned by Scott.
403.9 Sir Thomas Multon of Gilsland for Sir Thomas see note to EEWN 18b, 395 (note to 56.29).
403.17–33 He now mounted . . . into the forest see *Specimens of Early English Metrical Romances*, ed. George Ellis, 3 vols (London, 1805), 2.187: *CLA*, 105. The account of the tournament begins on 185.
403.36–37 Meaning . . . a hundred years this note first appears in the 8vo *Tales and Romances*.
404.2–6 It was composed . . . the system Gibbon's actual words are: 'From these materials ["the public and private advice of the Latin pilgrims who were the best skilled in the statutes and customs of Europe"], with the counsel and approbation of the patriarch and barons, of the clergy and laity, Godfrey composed the ASSIZE OF JERUSALEM, a precious monument of feudal jurisprudence': Edward Gibbon, *The History of the Decline and Fall of the Roman Empire* (originally published 1776–88), ed. Oliphant Smeaton,

introd. Christopher Dawson, 6 vols (London, 1966; first published 1904), 6.89.

404.13–16 The disgrace . . . keeping them the reigns of the first three Edwards of England (1272–1307, 1307–27, and 1327–77) covered the Wars of Independence, but Edward II is excluded from this note because his defeat by Robert the Bruce at Bannockburn in 1314 resulted in a brief period of real Scottish independence from its neighbour. Scott sums up the general procedure of the Scots in a comment on the aftermath of the defeat of the young King David II at Neville's cross in 1346: 'the Scots, as usual, were no sooner compelled to momentary submission, than they began to consider the means of shaking off the yoke': *Tales of a Grandfather* [*First series*] (1828), *Prose Works*, 22.227.

404.19–23 An universal tradition . . . the middle ages see EEWN 18b, 424 (note to 229.36).

404.34–40 The victor . . . scimitar for Gibbon's actual words see EEWN 18b, 376–77 (note 10).

405.5–30 Extract . . . at Glasgow a copy of this document with a few small verbal variants from Scott's version and different spellings appeared in '*The Virtues of the* LEE STONE', *The Scots Magazine*, 49 (December 1787), 609–10. It is there headed '*Copy of an Act of the Synod and Assembly. Apud Glasgow, the 25th October*'.

WOODSTOCK

413.25–26 Among other matter . . . 1747 for the article in *The British Magazine* see EEWN 19, 539–40. Scott quotes the version in William Hone, *The Every-Day Book*, 2 vols (London, 1826–27), 2, columns 582–90. William Laidlaw's transcriptions from Hone are verbally fairly accurate. He makes a few apparently inadvertent changes: for instance he abridges 'my readers their share of the pleasure' to 'my readers the pleasure' (414.8), and at 415.10 he transcribes 'over their heads' as 'over heads', which became 'over head' at a late proof stage. At least one change seems to be intended as an enhancement: at 415.39–40 Hone's 'the candles were blown out' becomes 'the candles were all blown out together'. An authorial input to the transcription process may be suspected. Other changes may or may not have been intentional, as with the substitution of 'if his master was not killed' for 'if his masters were not killed' (416.31). Apart from an understandable misreading of Laidlaw's 'crack' as 'clack' at 417.27, corrected in the present edition, no significant changes were made in proof, though Scott inserted the footnote on 417. The quotation from Hone's commentary continues virtually uninterrupted to 419.27 ('with his masters'), with the paragraph 'If my memory be not treacherous . . . equally concerned' (419.37–420.2) as a detached extract of the same nature. Although this material is essentially a quotation it is presented as a summary and treated with more freedom than the acknowledged quotations: numerous verbal changes, mostly stylistic and clarificatory, are made in the course of Laidlaw's holograph, and to a much lesser extent by Scott in the surviving author's proof, and by Scott and/or others at further proof stages. One small bowdlerisation ('bad smell' for 'great stink', 419.19) made at a late proof stage has been reversed in the present text.

414.13–16 The account . . . George Sinclair see EEWN 19, 539 and 548 (note 24).

419.21 pulvis fulminans *Latin* an explosive mixture of potassium nitrate, potassium carbonate, and sulphur.

419.37–420.14 If my memory be not treacherous . . . the visitors

assembled the incident of the exploding flower-pot was in fact included in Mary Hughes's transcription from the account in *The Beauties of all the Magazines* sent in 1824 (see EEWN 19, 422).

421.3 The Woodstock Scuffle the tract is modernised typographically, and in general faithfully reproduced verbally; but the unknown transcriber has made an error in the first line, misreading 'writes' as 'unites' (corrected in the present text), and there are several post-transcript omissions on the grounds of decency (now restored): 'whore' (421.18); 'so pissed.' (423.24); 'while they piss'd;' (425.36); 'a Spay'd-Bitch:' (425.48); and 'The poore Spay'd-Bitch did you know what/ and fouled' (426.7–8).

422.3 in Hollinshed or Speed the story of Rosamond appears in *Holinshed's Chronicles of England, Scotland, and Ireland*, 6 vols (London, 1807–08), 2.200: *CLA*, 29; it is also in John Speed, *The Historie of Great Britaine* . . ., 2nd edn (London, 1623), 525–26: see *CLA*, 232.

422.5 Stow John Stow, *The Annales of England* (London, [1600]).

425.42 Hans en Kelder child in the womb.

427.20 The Just Devil of Woodstock the transcription is in an unknown hand. There are only a handful of mostly minor verbal variants from the original. Two Magnum variants evidently result from misreadings of the transcription and are emended in the present edition, restoring 'nightly' for 'mighty' (430.2) and 'his sheets' for 'the shoots' (431.13).

428.14 magna temporum felicitas . . . sentias *Latin* great is the happiness of times in which you may think what you like and say what you think.

428.25–26 the stones of London streets . . . silent see Luke 19.40, where Jesus, entering Jerusalem and acclaimed by a large crowd, says to a group of disapproving Pharisees: 'I tell you that, if these should hold their peace, the stones would immediately cry out'.

428.31–32 Æger intemperans . . . recidendum *Latin* an intemperate patient makes the doctor rough, and a sore which cannot be cured must be cut away with the knife.

428.33 such Scicilian vespers on Easter Monday 1282, on the stroke of the vesper bell, the Sicilians massacred their detested French rulers.

429.16 Pacatumque . . . orbem Virgil, *Eclogue* 4, line 17: 'And rules with the virtues of his father a world restored to peace'.

430.9–10 the devil hath entred into . . . swine see Matthew 8.28–34.

441.13 Terras . . . cum Templariis *Latin* lands which the King exchanged with the Templars.

441.26–29 Fecit . . . aut parum post *Latin* That king made the park of Woodstock, with the palace within the park aforesaid, which park was the first park in England, and is seven miles in circumference; it was made in the 14th year of this king's reign or a little later.

442.5–7 This custom . . . Watling Street see EEWN 19, 555 (note to 9.15–17).

442.17–443.13 But as for what you call porridge . . . digestion see Gyles Calfine, *The Book of Common Prayer Confirmed by sundry Acts of Parliament, and briefly Vindicated against the Contumelious slanders of the Fanatique Party, Tearming it Porrage* (London, 1660), 2–4. The transcription, in Scott's hand, has numerous verbal variants, notably the standardisation of 'porrage' and 'pottage' to 'pottage', and the probable misreading of 'cold winter' as 'cold water' (442.33), as well as a number of short omissions made for no obvious reason. Some of his changes are probably intended to smooth or otherwise enhance the style of the original: at 443.7 he substitutes 'many other holy herbs' for 'many wholesome herbs', presumably to avoid repeating 'wholesome' a little earlier, but introducing a change in the sense.

443.13–14 Ohe! jam satis *Latin* Oh, that's enough!

443.16–17 the New Forest in SW Hampshire.
443.18–19 The story . . . Froissart's Chronicles see EEWN 19, 571 (note to 47.20–25).
443.21 Michael Hudson Hudson (1605–48) became one of the King's chaplains in 1643.
443.26 John Ashburnham Ashburnham (1602/03–1671) was appointed groom of the bedchamber to Charles I in 1628 and was one of his closest supporters during the civil war.
443.30–31 He made his escape . . . 1647 Charles escaped from captivity for a week in November 1647.
443.37–444.13 I have been on the spot . . . on the head for this passage quoted from Bishop White Kennet see Francis Peck, *Desiderata Curiosa*, new edn, 2 vols (London, 1779), 2.379–80: *CLA*, 240. Scott's transcription has a handful of small verbal changes, the most important of which is an inadvertent substitution of 'Woodford' for Peck's 'Woodcroft', resulting in 'Woodford' being adopted on both occasions in the Magnum (they are corrected in the present text). Peck notes (379n): 'The bishop gave me leave, many years ago, to copy this account from a vol. of his own MS. collections'.
444.14–21 Other accounts . . . a scorned mendicant the material in this paragraph derives from Anthony Wood, *Athenae Oxonienses*, 2nd edn, 2 vols (London, 1721), 2, column 114: *CLA*, 232.
444.22–24 For some time . . . let him be buried see Da[vid] Lloyd, *Memoires* . . . (London, 1668), 625.
444.26–445.6 The terrors . . . or Lunsford Zachary Grey is cited in an edition by Treadway Russell Nash of Samuel Butler's *Hudibras*, 3 vols (London, 1793), 3.428: *CLA*, 242. The couplet quoted from Butler is Part 3, 2.1111–12. For Grey's original note, which lists several mentions of Lundford, see his edition of *Hudibras*, 2 vols (London, 1744), 2.311–13.
445.20–446.27 Lieutenant. Second me . . . forbid that see John Lacy, *The Old Troop: or, Monsieur Raggou* (London, 1672), 32–33, 36 (Act 3, Scene 1): *CLA*, 220. Scott's transcription is verbally extremely loose. Thus, Raggou's speech reads in the original: 'Begar me tink so; for vat was me bred in de King of *Mogul*'s kitchen for, tere ve kill twenty shild of a day? Take you one shild by both his two heels, and put his head between your two leg, den take your great a knife and slice off all de buttack, so fashion; begar, dat make a de best Scotts Collop in de varle'. Scott's version amounts to a wholesale re-writing—for what purpose is unclear. He also effects some bowdlerisation, such as 'plague' for 'pox' (445.33) and 'woman' for 'whore' (446.17), and makes things easier for his readers by substituting 'feet' for 'purtenance' (innards) at 445.42.
446.31–33 This melancholy story . . . the fatal duel see EEWN 19, 613 (note to 252.6).
446.34–35 This gossiping tale . . . the variorum Shakspeare see *The Plays of William Shakespeare*, 5th edn, rev. Isaac Reed, 21 vols (London, 1803), 1.127n: *CLA*, 210.
447.1–9 Patrick Carey has had two editors . . . the autograph of the first for the manuscript and the two editions see *CLA*, 107, 155. The editions are: [Patrick Carey], *Poems, from a Manuscript, Written in the Time of Oliver Cromwell* (London, 1771); and *Trivial Poems, and Triolets . . . By Patrick Carey*, [ed. Walter Scott] (London, 1819).
447.11–17 the poetic cavalier . . . genealogists for the Careys see EEWN 19, 627 (note to 344.39–345.8). For Walpole's work see Horace Walpole, *A Catalogue of the Royal and Noble Authors of England, Scotland, and Ireland . . . enlarged and continued to the present time by Thomas Park, F.S.A.*, 5 vols (London, 1806): *CLA*, 340. The first edition appeared in 1758.

447.22–25 On a particular occasion . . . Earl of Marchmont Patrick Hume (1641–1724) was created Earl of Marchmont in 1697. The memoirs of his daughter Grisell (1665–1746) were written by her daughter, also Grisell (1693–1759), who in 1710 married Alexander Murray, heir to the baronetcy of Stanhope. Thomas Thomson edited *Memoirs of the Lives and Characters of the Right Honourable George Baillie of Jerviswood, and of Lady Grisell Baillie. By their daughter, Lady Murray of Stanhope* (Edinburgh, 1822): *CLA*, 254. Lady Diana Hume Campbell (1735–1827) was the third daughter of Hugh, the 3rd and last Earl of Marchont (d. 1794). In 1754 she married Walter Scott, 11th Laird of Harden.

447.35–36 Such a song . . . Miscellany see EEWN 19, 633 (note to 397.40–398.9).

447.38–448.7 It may interest some readers . . . Commissioner Adam Alexander Ranaldson Macdonell of Glengarry (1771–1828) presented Maida to Scott early in 1816. The hound died in late October 1824. Sir Edwin Henry Landseer (1802–73) sketched Maida, and the other dogs at Abbotsford, during his visit in early October 1824. In 1827 he used the drawing for a painting of the aged Maida and another deerhound, *A Study at Abbotsford*. This was acquired by William Adam of Blair-Adam, Fife (1751–1839), who was Lord Chief Commissioner of Jury Court, Scotland 1815–30. It is now in the Tate Gallery, London (NO1532). An engraving appeared in *The Keepsake for 1829*, ed. Frederic Mansel Reynolds, facing 258, as the centrepiece of 'Description of the Engraving entitled A Scene at Abbotsford. By the Author of Waverley' (258–61). Landseer made a second portrait of Maida in 1832 to be engraved for the title page of the first Magnum *Woodstock* volume (Vol. 39). The German means 'The darling dog of Walter Scott'. The friend who visited Munich has not been identified, and the current location of the snuffbox is not known.

CHRONICLES OF THE CANONGATE

460.2 preceding volume Magnum Volume 40 contains the second half of *Woodstock* (1826).

460.3 nominis umbra *Latin* the shadow of a name: Lucan (AD 39–65), *Pharsalia*, 1.135.

460.12–13 The Keepsake a fashionable miscellany publication. Three stories by Scott appeared in *The Keepsake for 1829*, published in late 1828, and were included in Volume 41 of the Magnum: 'My Aunt Margaret's Mirror', 'The Tapestried Chamber', and 'Death of the Laird's Jock'.

460.15 Begin and break off in the middle not identified.

460.16–19 I have, perhaps, said enough . . . public favour most notably in the Introduction to the first edition of *Chronicles* (EEWN 20, 3–4) and the General Preface (25a, 20–21).

460.22–24 the secret fountain . . . the Eastern Tale for 'the traveller of the Eastern Tale' Scott's original manuscript version has 'the great Persian traveller Aboulfouaris' (see 487.5 below). This was probably changed because the allusion is to the fountain pouring forth diamonds and pearls in the 21st Night of *Arabian Nights Entertainment* (Weber, 1.26) rather than to anything in the story of Aboufouaris in Weber's second volume.

460.28 I bought, and built, and planted compare the phrase attributed to Julius Caesar 'veni, vidi, vici' (I came, I saw, I conquered). Scott bought the original farmhouse in 1811.

460.30–33 My riches . . . fly away see Proverbs 23.5: 'Wilt thou set thine eyes upon that which is not? for riches certainly make themselves wings; they fly away as an eagle toward heaven.'

460.33–35 The year 1825 . . . booksellers for the economic circumstances of 1825 and Scott's financial crash see the 'Introduction', EEWN 25a, xiii–xiv.
461.6 trading companies the two companies with which Scott was particularly involved were the printing firm of James Ballantyne & Co., and the publishing firm Archibald Constable & Co.
461.8–9 he surrendered . . . his own this is misleading since through an entail Scott passed Abbotsford to his son on his marriage in 1825, with the result that it was inaccessible to his creditors.
461.10 gentlemen these were the Trustees appointed to manage the estates of Scott and his printer James Ballantyne, and who supported the production of the Magnum edition as a contribution to the repayment of the outstanding debts.
461.36 The Introduction for the original publication of this Introduction see EEWN 20, 3–11 and notes on 379–83.
462.5–6 shadows of the same convenient tribe a reference to Scott's use of fictitious co-authors and editors in his earlier novels, for instance Jedidiah Cleishbotham, Peter Pattieson, Laurence Templeton, and Captain Clutterbuck.
462.9 picnic a fashionable social entertainment in which each person present contributed a share of the provisions.
462.16 a local habitation and a name *A Midsummer Night's Dream*, 5.1.18.
462.17–23 my old hero Montrose . . . lose it all see 'I'll never love thee more', lines 13–16, by James Graham (1612–50), who succeeded his father as 5th Earl of Montrose in 1626. He plays a prominent role in *A Legend of the Wars of Montrose* (1819). The poem is included in e.g. *Ancient and Modern Scottish Songs, Heroic Ballads, etc.*, [ed. David Herd], 2nd edn, 2 vols (Edinburgh, 1776), 1.236–37 (*CLA*, 171).
462.29–463.6 Mrs Murray Keith . . . the right culprit see EEWN 20, 410 (Historical Note to 'The Highland Widow').
462.31–46 The Keiths of Craig . . . (1831.) Scott's footnote adds personal knowledge to the genealogical entries of the Keiths in [Robert Douglas], *The Baronage of Scotland* (Edinburgh, 1798), 443–45. Mrs Anne Murray Keith (1736–1818) is entered on 445 simply under the name 'Anne'.
463.24–26 George Constable . . . the original Antiquary see EEWN 20, 6.24–35 and the Magnum expansion of the 'Advertisement' to *The Antiquary* in 25a, 140.
463.35–36 a pair of friends . . . seventy-two see William Wordsworth, 'The Fountain' (1800), lines 3–4: 'A pair of Friends, though I was young, / And Matthew seventy-two.'
464.3–7 [It has been . . . 1827.] the square parentheses are in the source.
464.9 Theatrical Fund Dinner see EEWN 20, 380 (note to 4.19–20). A humorous entry in Scott's *Journal* for 22 February gives 'two or three simple rules' for presiding at such an event (280–81). The account follows *The Edinburgh Weekly Journal* faithfully, but it inserts '(Loud and rapturous applause.)' at 471.41–42, and at 481.43–482.3 the original reads: 'He then rose, and commenting in flattering terms on the genius of Mackenzie, and his private worth, proposed "the health of Henry Mackenzie, Esq."'.
464.34 the Assembly Rooms an elegant public building opened in George Street in Edinburgh's New Town in 1787.
465.6 the Earl of Fife James Duff (1776–1857), who succeeded as 4th Earl of Fife in 1811, had fought with the Spanish against Napoleon.
465.7 Lord Meadowbank Alexander Maconochie (1777–1861), lawyer

and politician, was Lord Advocate in 1816–19 and became a judge in 1819 with the title Lord Meadowbank.

465.7 Sir John Hope of Pinkie, Bart. Sir John Hope (1781–1853) succeeded as 11th Baronet of Pinkie and Craighall in 1801.

465.7 Admiral Adam Sir Charles Adam (1780–1853) was promoted to rear-admiral in 1825.

465.8 Baron Clerk Rattray James Clerk Rattray of Craighall (1763–1831), Baron of Exchequer from 1809.

465.8 Gilbert Innes, Esq. (1751–1832), the immensely wealthy Deputy Governor of the Royal Bank of Scotland.

465.8 James Walker, Esq. James Walker of Dalry (1790–1856), lawyer.

465.8–9 Robert Dundas, Esq. Robert Dundas of Arniston (1799–1838), lawyer.

465.9 Alexander Smith, Esq. a lawyer resident at 7 Argyle Square, Edinburgh.

465.10 Non Nobis Domine *Latin* 'Not unto us, O Lord', the opening words of Psalm 115, which continues 'but unto thy name give glory'. The Latin version of this text has since the 16th century been used as a canon, and is here being sung as a grace after dinner.

465.11 Messrs Thorne, Swift, Collier, and Hartley a professional quartet: James Thorne, Nicholas Swift, and William Hartley appear in the Edinburgh Post-Office Directory as teachers of music.

465.14 Duke of Clarence William, Duke of Clarence (1765–1837), was the third son of George III. He succeeded his elder brother, George IV, in 1830 becoming King William IV.

465.28–29 Duke of York Frederick, Duke of York (1763–1827) was the second son of George III, and was long regarded as heir to his brother, George IV. He had a military career and died on 5 January 1827. The Royal Dukes were patrons of the Drury Lane Theatrical Fund and attended the annual dinners held in its support from 1818.

465.30–31 a bumper a drink full to the brim, especially in readiness for drinking a toast.

466.11–12 Its first tragic poet . . . Marathon Aeschylus (525–456 BC), who fought at the Battle of Marathon (490 BC) when the Greeks defeated an invading Persian army.

466.15 the time of Louis the Fourteenth Louis XIV reigned in France from 1643 to 1715.

466.18–19 the time of Queen Elizabeth Elizabeth was Queen of England from 1568 to 1603.

466.27–32 What were the times . . . to read their Bibles? this seems to suggest, oddly, that laws against the theatre were a feature of pre-Reformation culture, rather than of 17th-century British culture. A reporting error may be involved.

466.34 the tents of sin this expression is used in the Scottish Metrical Psalter version of Psalm 84.10, where the King James Bible reads 'the tents of wickedness'.

467.40 Garrick David Garrick (1717–79), celebrated actor, playwright and theatre manager, particularly associated with Drury Lane Theatre in London.

468.5 the artist to paint sign-posts—(loud laughter) the laughter is occasioned by an allusion to the fall-back profession of the would-be artist Dick Tinto in Ch. 1 of *The Bride of Lammermoor* (1819).

468.31–33 We cannot think . . . Banquo for Falstaff's love of a cup of sack see *1 Henry IV*, 2.4, especially lines 110–13. Macbeth says to the Ghost of Banquo 'Thy bones are marrowless, thy blood is cold': *Macbeth*, 3.4.94.

468.36 three times three nine cheers.
468.37 Mr Mackay Charles Mackay (1787–1857), one of the actors in the Edinburgh Theatre Royal Company.
469.1 the first legally constituted Theatrical Fund the Theatrical Fund at the Theatre Royal Drury Lane was founded by David Garrick in 1766, apparently following Thomas Gull's similar institution at the Covent Garden Theatre the previous year. To protect his foundation Garrick ensured that it was incorporated by Act of Parliament in 1775–76. It still survives.
469.17 the last display of his transcendent talent in its early years the Theatrical Fund was supported by benefit performances; in 1818 these were replaced by an annual dinner. Garrick retired from the stage in 1776, and his final performance at Drury Lane took place on 10 June when he appeared as Don Felix in *The Wonder* (1714) by Susanna Centlivre. It was a benefit performance which raised £311 12*s.* 6*d.* for the Theatrical Fund. (George Winchester Stone, Jr and George M. Kahrl, *David Garrick: A Critical Biography* (Carbondale, Illinois, 1979), xx, and *ODNB*).
469.21–22 Mrs Henry Siddons and Mr William Murray Mrs Henry Siddons (1783–1844), born Harriet Murray, married Henry Siddons (1774–1815), son of the celebrated actress Sarah Siddons (1755–1831). Harriet was the sister of William Henry Murray (1790–1852), actor and theatre manager, who had become manager of the Edinburgh Theatre Royal in 1815 on the death of his brother-in-law who had held that post. Murray remained as manager until his retirement in 1851.
469.22–23 the first Theatrical Fund in Scotland The Edinburgh Fund 'for the relief and support of decayed performers' was founded in 1819; Scott had been a patron from its foundation (James C. Dibdin, *The Annals of the Edinburgh Stage* (Edinburgh, 1888), 290–91).
469.42–43 come like shadows, so depart *Macbeth*, 4.1.111.
470.18 Lord Meadowbank see note to 465.7.
470.19 his Noble Friend see note to 465.6.
470.42 he would beg leave to propose a toast this is the toast in which Scott's authorship of the Waverley Novels was revealed to those present. Lockhart explains the context: 'Lord Meadowbank had come on short notice, and was asked abruptly on his arrival to take a toast which had been destined for a noble person who had not been able to appear. He knew that this was the first public dinner at which the object of his toast had appeared since his misfortunes, and taking him aside in the anteroom, asked him whether he would consider it indelicate to hazard a distinct reference to the parentage of the Waverley Novels, as to which there had, in point of fact, ceased to be any obscurity from the hour of Constable's failure. Sir Walter smiled, and said, "Do just as you like—only don't say much about so old a story."' (Lockhart, 7.17). Scott's own account of the circumstances is in a letter of 8 March [1827] to Lady Louisa Stuart: 'Besides the joke had lasted long enough and I was tired of it. I had not however the most distant intention of chusing the time and place where the thing actually took place for mounting the confessional. Ld Meadowbank who is a kind and clever little fellow but somewhat bustling and forward said to me in the drawing room "Do you care any thing about the mystery of the Waverly novels now"—"Not I" I replied "the secret is too generally known"—I was led to think from this that he meant to make some jocular allusion to Rob Roy [. . .] But when instead of skirmish of this kind he made a speech in which he seriously identified me with the Author of Waverley I had no opportunity of evasion and was bound either to confess or deny and it struck me while he was speaking it was as good and natural an occasion as I could find for making my avowal. And so out it came to the great astoundishment of all the hearers' (*Letters*, 10.173).

471.15 darkness visible John Milton, *Paradise Lost* (1667, rev. 1674), 1.63.

471.41–42 Loud and rapturous applause Lockhart adds 'Long before Lord Meadowbank ceased speaking, the company had got upon chairs and tables, and the storm of applause that ensued was deafening' (Lockhart, 7.19). The phrase does not appear in the *Edinburgh Weekly Journal* version of the report.

472.2–3 communicated to more than twenty people Lockhart names many of these (7.21).

472.12 Look on't again I dare not *Macbeth*, 2.2.52.

472.17–18 The wand was now broken, and the book buried see Prospero renouncing his powers in *The Tempest*, 5.1.54–57, and his lines in the Epilogue, 11–13.

472.24–25 Bailie Nicol Jarvie the actor Charles Mackay who was famous for taking the part of Bailie Nicol Jarvie in stage productions of *Rob Roy* (1817), Scott's novel in which the character appears. Of several stage adaptations of that novel the most successful was that by Isaac Pocock, a version of which was first performed in Edinburgh in 1819.

472.29 PRODIGIOUS! an allusion to Dominie Sampson in Scott's *Guy Mannering* whose exclamation this was.

473.1 Within a mile of Edinburgh town a popular song by the English dramatist and song-writer Thomas D'Urfey (1653?–1723) with a tune sometimes ascribed to Henry Purcell.

473.2–3 The Duke of Wellington and the army Arthur Wellesley (1769–1852), military leader and hero of the Peninsular War and the battle of Waterloo, was created Duke of Wellington in 1814. He was prime minister 1828–30.

473.4 How merrily we live 'How merrily we live who soldiers be', a glee for three voices by Michael East (*c.* 1580–1648).

473.5 Lord Melville and the Navy Robert Saunders Dundas (1771–1851), who succeeded as 2nd Viscount Melville in 1811, was First Lord of the Admiralty during and after the Napoleonic wars. He and Scott were friends.

473.8 Mr Pat. Robertson Peter Robertson (1794–1855), lawyer, described by Scott as 'the facetious Peter Robertson' (*Journal*, 202: 20 September 1826). Patrick, a Gaelic name, was commonly 'anglicised' as Peter in Lowland Scotland.

473.26–28 Good my lord . . . of the time *Hamlet*, 2.2.516–19.

473.43 the opera adapted from that popular production for the success of the stage version of *Rob Roy* see James C. Dibdin, *The Annals of the Edinburgh Stage* (Edinburgh, 1888), 286–90.

474.7–8 Cast his eye to good old Scotland, and not forget Rob Roy these are a variant of the last words of the play, spoken by Rob Roy, in I[saac] Pocock, *Rob Roy Macgregor* (London, 1818), 80.

474.36–37 the late Mr John Kemble John Kemble (1757–1823), a distinguished actor, brother of Sarah Siddons.

475.1–2 the widow and the fatherless two categories of the needy frequently mentioned in the Bible, for instance in James 1.27, which commends visiting 'the fatherless and widows in their affliction'.

475.8 Mr Vandenhoff John M. Vandenhoff (1790–1861) appeared at the Theatre Royal, Edinburgh, between 1822 and 1857.

475.28 the veteran on the stage Samuel Johnson, *The Vanity of Human Wishes* (1749), line 308: 'Superfluous lags the Vet'ran on the Stage'.

475.31–32 the big manly voice . . . whistles in the sound see *As You Like It*, 2.7.161–63.

475.37–38 to keep the word . . . the hope see *Macbeth*, 5.8.21–22.
476.8–11 [This speech . . . does not show.] the square parentheses are in the source.
476.12 Mr J. Cay John Cay (1790–1865), of North Charlton in Northumberland, lawyer, and Sheriff of Linlithgow from 1822.
476.12 Professor Wilson John Wilson (1785–1854), Professor of Moral Philosophy at Edinburgh University 1820–51, and a writer under the name of 'Christopher North'.
476.19 the Company of Edinburgh i.e. 'the Theatrical Company of Edinburgh', the wording in the slightly fuller account printed as *An Account of the First Edinburgh Theatrical Fund Dinner* (Edinburgh, 1827), 15.
476.20 Mr Jones an actor at the Theatre Royal, Edinburgh, between 1819 and 1825.
476.34–35 the Edinburgh Professional Society of Musicians the Musical Society of Edinburgh, formally constituted in 1728, had a body of salaried vocal and instrumental performers.
476.43 Mr Jeffrey Francis Jeffrey (1773–1850), lawyer, writer, and critic.
477.7 Mrs Siddons, senior Sarah (1755–1831), née Kemble, wife of the actor William Siddons (1744–1808), a celebrated actress admired particularly for her success in tragic parts. Mrs Siddons, junior, was her daughter-in-law. Scott had seen Sarah Siddons in one of her most famous parts, Lady Macbeth (Lockhart, 1.213).
477.22 Mr Dundas see note to 465.8–9.
477.22–23 Home, the author of Douglas John Home (1722–1808), Church of Scotland minister and playwright, famous for his play *Douglas* first staged in Edinburgh in 1756.
477.26–27 [We are happy . . . liberally.] the square parentheses are in the source.
477.30 Scotland, the Land of Cakes this name, referring to the oat and barley cakes of the Scots, is best known from Robert Burns, 'On the Late Captain Grose's Peregrinations thro' Scotland' (1789), whose opening line reads 'Hear, Land o' Cakes, and brither Scots'.
477.38 Mr H. G. Bell Henry Glassford Bell (1803–74), lawyer, poet, and historian.
478.16–17 Baillie, Byron, Coleridge, Maturin Joanna Baillie (1762–1851) Scottish playwright and poet; Lord Byron (1788–1824), poet and patron of the theatre whose plays, or 'dramatic poems', have been read rather than performed; Samuel Taylor Coleridge (1772–1834), poet and critic, author of a political play *Osorio* (1797); Charles Robert Maturin (1780–1824), novelist and playwright.
478.18 James Sheridan Knowles a native of Cork (1784–1862) who gained a reputation in Ireland and Britain as both an actor and a prolific playwright.
478.29–31 the sick man . . . better than before no specific allusion, or precise meaning, has been identified.
478.33–35 the wonderful Arabian dervise . . . their hearts Scott is perhaps recalling the mandarin Fum-Hoam, who plays a prominent part in the *Chinese Tales* in the third volume of Weber. When he first appears he asserts that he has 'appeared in all part of the world in very different forms; have consequently been of all religions, and all sects' (3.341), and at 3.392 he tells how he 'entered into the body of a young man' who became a dervish.
478.43 Lightly tread, 'tis hallowed ground a glee for three voices popular in the early 19th century.
479.6–7 One piece of hers . . . of late years Joanna Baillie's Highland

play *The Family Legend* was performed 9 times at the Edinburgh theatre in 1810 with help from Scott.

479.13 The Anchor's weighed a popular song of the early 19th century with words by Samuel James Arnold (1774–1852) and music by John Braham (1777?–1856) who was celebrated for singing it and other sea songs.

479.14 W. Menzies, Esq., Advocate William Menzies, Advocate, is named as one of Scott's co-subscribers to Henri L. Dubois' novel *Adolphe and Selanie* (Edinburgh, 1824).

479.20–21 Malvolio, Lord Ogleby, and the Green Man Malvolio is a character in *Twelfth Night*; Lord Ogleby is a character in *The Clandestine Marriage*, by George Colman the Elder and David Garrick, first performed in 1766; Dibdin recalls Daniel Terry playing 'his original part of Mr Green' in the Haymarket piece, *The Green Man*, in December 1818 (James C. Dibdin, *The Annals of the Edinburgh Stage* (Edinburgh, 1888), 284).

479.28 Mr Terry Daniel Terry (1789–1829), actor and playwright who adapted Scott's novels for the stage, starting with *Guy Mannering* in 1816.

479.29 Mr William Allan, banker William Allan of Glen, the banker who was to be Lord Provost of Edinburgh from 1829 to 1831.

480.2 Mrs Anne Page . . . possibilities see *The Merry Wives of Windsor*, 1.1.56 ('Seven hundred pounds').

480.5–6 the Lord Chief Baron, whom England has sent to us Sir Samuel Shepherd (1760–1840), lawyer, politician, and friend of Scott. He served as Lord Chief Baron of the Court of Exchequer in Scotland from 1819 to 1830. Shepherd was an Englishman; but more than that, the Scots Court of Exchequer used English legal forms.

480.6–7 yokefellow on the bench alluding to Lear's words to the Fool in *King Lear*, 3.6.37–38: 'And thou, his yoke-fellow of equity,/ Bench by his side.' Mr Baron Clerk is referred to earlier as 'Baron Clerk Rattray' (see note to 465.8).

480.12–20 There is one . . . his little theatre in 1736 Allan Ramsay (1684–1758) opened a theatre in Carrubber's Close, running northwards from the High Street in the Old Town of Edinburgh, staging plays and popular entertainments; but it was forced to close finally in 1739 by the Theatre Licensing Act of 1737 and hostility from some quarters in the city.

480.20–21 His own pastoral . . . it is written Ramsay's pastoral drama *The Gentle Shepherd* was published in 1725. The 'Doric language' (rustic or dialect speech) here means the Scots language.

480.26–27 'Twas merry in the hall this old English ballad is included in *The Lyre: A Collection of the most approved English, Irish, and Scottish songs, ancient and modern* (Edinburgh, 1824), 177–78 with the heading 'Sung by *Mr Murray*, as *Sir Mark Chase*, in *A Roland for an Oliver*'. The farce of that name, by Thomas Morton, was produced in 1819: the ballad does not appear in the printed version.

480.29 Mr Jones see note to 476.20.

480.32–33 Without the smile . . . a world without a sun! Thomas Campbell, *The Pleasures of Hope* (1799), Part 2, lines 23–24.

480.35 Shakspeare Square the square, built between 1772 and 1778, in which was Edinburgh's Theatre Royal, opened in 1769, where North Bridge meets Princes Street.

480.35 the Register Office Register House, the domed building at the north end of North Bridge in Edinburgh's New Town, designed by Robert Adam (1728–92) to house Scotland's public records, was mostly built between 1774 and 1788.

480.43 the Nor' Loch the loch to the N of the Castle and the Old Town of Edinburgh which was drained, beginning in 1759, to assist the northward spread of the city into the New Town.

481.1–2 the Improvement bill an Improvement Bill was going through Parliament in 1827, proposing several controversial building schemes for Edinburgh. Most relevant to Robertson's intervention is the Bill's prohibition of 'building south of Princes Street east of the Mound, "excepting always a Public Theatre or Playhouse"' (A. J. Youngson, *The Making of Classical Edinburgh* (Edinburgh, 1966), 181).

481.12 Mr Cockburn Henry Cockburn (1779–1854), writer and (as judge) Lord Cockburn from 1834.

481.14 Bereford Park Bearford's or Barefoots Parks, the fields to the N of the North Loch which were bought by the city in 1716 and on which the first part of the New Town was built.

481.18 a new theatre in the event the theatre which had opened in 1769 was not replaced at this date, but it was remodelled in 1828. Illustrations of the theatre before and after the alterations can be seen in *A History of Scottish Theatre*, ed. Bill Findlay (Edinburgh, 1998), 113–17, 165.

481.30 the College projected on this scale The Old College of the University of Edinburgh was embarked on to the massive plans of Robert Adam. The foundation stone was laid in 1789, but building (and funding) stopped in 1793 when Britain became involved in war against Revolutionary France. It was only after the Napoleonic Wars that construction resumed, now to revised plans by William Henry Playfair (1790–1857). The foundation stone of Playfair's plan was laid in March 1817.

481.36 behold the endless work begun not identified.

482.3 Henry Mackenzie, Esq. a Scottish writer (1745–1831) best known for his novel of sensibility, *The Man of Feeling* (1771).

482.6 non sum qualis eram *Latin* I am not what I was (Horace, *Odes*, 4.1.3). Partridge is the schoolmaster prone to humorous misfortunes in Henry Fielding, *Tom Jones* (1749); he uses the expression in 15.12 and 18.5.

482.7 Lord Ogleby see George Colman [the Elder] and David Garrick, *The Clandestine Marriage* (London, 1766), 23 (1.2).

482.26 the 7th hussars a cavalry regiment formed in Scotland in 1690.

482.31 Mr Gibb there was an Edinburgh lawyer in the 1820s called John Gibb, but this is perhaps rather an unidentified caterer.

483.7–8 Mr Train, of Castle Douglas see EEWN 20, 380 (note to 5.5).

483.19–21 [Mr Train . . . July 1832.] the square parentheses are original.

483.25–26 The Thane of Fife 'Thane' in Scottish history is a term for a person holding lands of the king, a lord; this phrase, humorously used, alludes to the title of Macduff in *Macbeth*, 4.1.71–72.

484.12 the East India Company see EEWN 20, 447–48 (Historical Note to 'The Surgeon's Daughter').

485.20 Pindarees Pindaris, a group of mounted raiders active in Central India from the late 17th to early 19th centuries.

487.4–5 the fountain of coined gold and pearls . . . Aboulfouaris see note to 460.22–24.

487.8 I bought, I built see note to 460.28.

487.11–12 unlike the other riches . . . fly away see note to 460.30–33.

488.8–10 the clear-headed and sagacious gentleman . . . the publication Robert Cadell.

489.7 picknick see note to 462.9.

489.15 a local habitation and a name *A Midsummer Night's Dream*, 5.1.18.

489.17–20 He either fears . . . lose it all see note to 462.17–23.

489.25–31 Mrs Murray Keith . . . before the public see note to 462.29–463.6.
489.43–490.1 George Constable . . . the original Antiquary see note to 463.24–26.
490.13–14 Colonel MacKerris . . . the oriental costume see EEWN 20, 491–92 (note to 288.3).
490.16 a costume . . . the renowned Scheherazade herself Scheherazade is the narrator of the *Arabian Nights' Entertainments* in Weber, but there is no emphasis on her costume there.
490.21–22 These manuscripts . . . for public sale see EEWN 20, 380 (note to 4.5).
490.34 Eheu! *Latin* Alas!
490.36 the Kaim of Urie situated on the coast 2 km N of St Cyrus, Kincardineshire. For more details see EEWN 7a, 338 (note 15).
491.6–492.27 Eftir death of Alexander the first . . . gret veneration see Hector Boece, *The History and Chronicles of Scotland*, tr. John Bellenden, 2 vols (Edinburgh, 1821), 2.297–98: *CLA*, 4. The transcription contains minor changes throughout, some of them replacing Scots with standard English spellings.
491.41 staill band of huntsmen.
493.4–6 For fuller particulars . . . Charles Mackie the books referred to are Scott's *Provincial Antiquities and Picturesque Scenery of Scotland* (London and Edinburgh, 1819–26) and Charles Mackie, *The History of the Abbey, Palace, and Chapel-Royal of Holyroodhouse* (Edinburgh, 1819).
493.7–11 The greater part . . . career of misfortune following the July Revolution of 1830 the French royal family lived at Holyrood Palace until their departure for Austria in 1832.
493.11 Requiescant in pace *Latin* may they rest in peace.
493.23–24 the well-known author of "The Chase" William Somerville (1675–1742) whose poem on hunting, *The Chace*, was published in 1735.
493.25–26 See the opening scene . . . Henry IV rather, see *1 Henry IV*, 2.1.9–10.
493.31–495.5 Having drank hard . . . the churchyard there the passage is from the 2nd edition of Scott's edition of Swift. It is transcribed with minor changes, including the incorporation in the final paragraph of the quotation from Wodrow, which is printed as a footnote in the Swift edition (its origin is Robert Wodrow, *The History of the Sufferings of the Church of Scotland*, 2 vols (Edinburgh, 1721–22), 2.589: *CLA*, 11).
495.7–26 Iron Rasp . . . Traditions of Edinburgh this note replaces the short Ed1 footnote. The quotation comes from Robert Chambers, *Traditions of Edinburgh*, 2 vols (Edinburgh, 1825), 1.236–37: *CLA*, 332. There are a few minor changes in the transcription, and a footnote on the usage of 1702 is omitted.
495.27–30 The Rev. Mr Bowles . . . druidical temples see W[illiam] L[isle] Bowles (1762–1850), *Hermes Britannicus* (London, 1828), Ch. 5 and p. 143.
495.31–36 The well-known designation . . . the other regiments see EEWN, 20, 419 (note to 77.13).
495.37–38 Shakespeare's Midsummer Night's Dream, Act IV. Sc. I *A Midsummer Night's Dream*, 4.1.120–21.
495.40–497.14 Susannah Kennedy . . . repeating it Susanna Montgomerie (1690–1780), wife of Alexander Montgomerie, 9th Earl of Eglinton, was a society hostess and literary patron. The quotations in the note come from James Boswell, *The Life of Samuel Johnson, LLD . . . A New Edition. With Numerous Additions and Notes, by John Wilson Croker*, 5 vols (London,

1831), 3.67n, 70, 71, and 96: *CLA*, 188. Scott contributed notes to the first three volumes of this edition. The last three quotations are at 5.374, 375, and 401 of the edition by George Birkbeck Hill, rev. L. F. Powell, 6 vols (Oxford, 1934–50).

497.15–18 The Duke of York . . . the English Parliament James, Duke of York and Mary Beatrice (see EEWN 20, 406: note to 64.14–15), regarded with suspicion because of their Catholicism, took refuge at Holyrood for several months between 1679 and 1682.

497.22–35 The family . . . loyal subject the quotation follows closely John Nichols, *The Progresses, Processions, and Magnificent Festivities of King James the First*, 4 vols (London, 1828), 3.306n.

497.43–498.13 The 2 of Octr: . . . hes freindis this anecdote, with some Scots forms altered, comes from Robert Birrel's Diary 1532–1605, printed in *Fragments of Scotish History*, [ed. J. G. Dalyell] (Edinburgh, 1798), 60–61: *CLA*, 4.

498.15 MacIntyre see EEWN 20, 416 (note to 71.13).

498.17–500.4 Loch Awe, upon the banks . . . by experience see John Hay Allan, *The Bridal of Caölchairn; and other poems* (London, 1822), 277–79: *CLA*, 165. The original is followed closely.

500.7–501.18 But the King . . . the least assistance see Patrick Fraser Tytler, *Lives of Scottish Worthies*, 3 vols (London, 1831–33), 1.413–15: *CLA*, 332.

501.19–21 This is a line . . . in 1825 see EEWN 20, 417 (note to 72.1–2).

501.22 The Red Soldier see EEWN 20, 419 (note to 78.6).

501.29–503.12 In the beginning . . . officers and soldiers this account of the Massacre of Glencoe comes, with omissions and alterations, from the *Encyclopaedia Britannica*. The passage is in all editions between the 2nd (1778) and the 6th (1823); in the 6th edition it is at 4.490–91.

503.25–506.22 In the year 1795 . . . the individual himself see David Stewart of Garth, *Sketches of the Character, Manners, and Present State of the Highlanders of Scotland*, 2nd edn, 2 vols (Edinburgh, 1822), 2.413–15 and 281n, 1.52–54: compare *CLA*, 19.

506.24–26 Letters from the Mountains . . . other Poems, &c. see EEWN 20, 433 (note to 124.6).

506.27–31 The gallant and amiable author . . . December 1829 see EEWN 20, 433 (note to 124.8–9).

507.4–509.13 Upon one occasion . . . true sons of song a faithful reproduction of *The Quarterly Review*, 45 (No. 90: July 1831), 371–73.

509.15–17 [Robert Walker . . . Edinburgh.] Robert Walker (1716–83), clergyman and author of *Sermons on Practical Subjects* (Edinburgh, 1765), and Hugh Blair (1718–1800), clergyman and man of letters. Of the two, who served together at St Giles' in Edinburgh, Walker was a Calvinist and Blair a 'moderate'. The square parentheses are original.

509.27–32 It is scarce necessary . . . C. C. in the Magnum the final paragraph of Ch. 13 in Ed1 is presented as a footnote, with the addition of Crystal Croftangry's initials.

THE FAIR MAID OF PERTH

519.35–37 Miss Baillie . . . filial affection an entry in Scott's *Journal* (390: 5 December 1827) makes it clear that he has in mind Edward in Joanna Baillie's tragedy *Ethwald*, which appeared in the second volume of her *A Series of Plays in Which it is Attempted to Delineate the Stronger Passions of the Mind*, 2 vols (London, 1798, 1802). The young heir to the Mercian throne shakes off a moment of cowardice in his first battle when informed that his father is hard pressed on the field.

520.3–21 The controversy . . . the line of Lochiel Mackay (*CLA*, 272) argues his case on pp. 50–52. He refers to Wyntoun, 2.373 (9.1607a: 15).

520.21–25 This view of the case . . . the Camerons see [Robert Douglas], *The Baronage of Scotland* (Edinburgh, 1798), 348, 356. But it is Clan Chattan who are identified with the Macphersons by Douglas.

520.29 In the Scoti-Chronicon . . . Clankay see 521.27–522.29 and note below.

520.30–31 Hector Boece writes . . . Leslie in Hector Boece's *Scotorvm Historiæ Prima Gentis Origine* (Paris, 1574), 335r the names are given as 'Clankay & Clankquhete'; in *The History and Chronicles of Scotland . . . translated by John Bellenden*, 2 vols (Edinburgh, 1821), 2.469 they appear as 'Clankayis and Glenquhattannis': *CLA*, 4. In John Leslie's *De Origine Moribus & rebus gestis Scotorum* (Rome, 1675; originally published 1578), 252 they are 'Clankaya, & Clanquhattana': *CLA*, 6.

520.31–34 Buchanan . . . the Grampians George Buchanan describes the rival clans as 'two families' of an 'unquiet and turbulent set of mortals': *The History of Scotland*, 5th edn, 2 vols (Edinburgh, 1762), [trans. from the Latin by William Bond], 1.438 (*CLA*, 9).

520.34 dare lucem *Latin* produce light.

520.35–36 The name Clanwheill . . . James VI. the 'clanchewill' appears in Act 37 of 1594 in *The Acts of the Parliaments of Scotland*, 4.71.

520.40–521.21 A thousand . . . past away see Wyntoun, 2.373–74 (9.17.1601–20: 15). The original has 'had þan Chiftanys twá' for 'had thair Chiftanys twa'.

521.27–522.29 Anno Dom. . . . excursus *Joannis de Fordun Scotichronicon cum Supplementis ac Continuatione Walteri Boweri*, ed. Walter Goodall, 2 vols (Edinburgh, 1759), 2.420–21: *CLA*, 12. The Latin passage may be translated as follows: 'In the year of our Lord one thousand three hundred and ninety-six, a great part of the north of Scotland, beyond the mountains, was disturbed by two pestilent caterans and their followers; namely, Scheabeg and his kin, of the Clan Kay, and Cristi Jonson, with his kin, called the Clan Quhele, who by no paction or management could be pacified, and by no art of the King or governor could be subdued, until the noble and active Lord, David of Lindesay and Crawford, and the Lord Thomas, Earl of Moray, applied to the task their diligence and powers, and so arranged matters betwixt the parties that they agreed to meet before the King on a certain day at Perth, and each to select thirty of his tribe to oppose thirty from the other side, equipped only with swords, bows and arrows, without doublets and with no other weapons apart from axes, by which encounter an end might be put to the strife, and the land enjoy peace. This contract highly pleased both parties; and on the Monday immediately before the feast of St Michael, on the North Inch of Perth, before the King, governor, and an immense multitude, they compeared and entered into a most fierce conflict, in which, out of the sixty, all were killed save one of the Clan Kay and eleven of the opposite side. It also fell out there, that, after they were all assembled in the lists, one of them, looking around for a mode of escape, slipped away from the whole body into the river Tay, and crossed it by swimming. He was pursued by thousands, but never caught. The two parties stood thereupon astonished, as unable to proceed with the engagement on account of the want of the fugitive; for the party having its numbers entire would not consent to let one be taken away; nor could the other party by any reward induce anyone to supply the place of the one who had escaped. At that, all were stunned and stood rooted to the spot, complaining of the loss of the fugitive. And that whole business seemed even likely to break short, when lo! into the midst of the space there broke a common mechanic, low in stature, but fierce in aspect, saying, "Here am I! who will induce me to enter with these workmen into this theatric game? I will try the sport for half-a-mark, asking but this beyond, that, if I come living out of these lists, I shall receive my bread from one of you for as long as I live; because, as it is said, 'greater love hath no man than that he layeth down his life for his friends.' With what reward shall I be gifted, then, who lay down my life for the enemies of the state and the realm?" What he desired was granted to him by the King and several nobles. With that the man drew his bow, and sent the first arrow into the opposite band, killing one of them. Immediately thereafter the arrows fly, they level their axes, they flash their swords, they strive with each other, and as butchers deal with oxen in the shambles, so do the parties fearlessly massacre one another. Nor was there one found among so many who, from want of will or heart, sought to shrink behind the backs of others, or to escape the terrible slaughter. The volunteer who arrived on the scene after the others finally escaped unhurt. After this event, the North was quiet for a long time; nor did the caterans make excursions thence as formerly.'

523.2–12 This faithful adherent . . . present day see David Stewart, *Sketches of the Character, Manners, and Present State of the Highlanders of Scotland*, 2 vols (Edinburgh, 1822), 1.65n: *CLA*, 19. There are two small verbal variants from the original.

523.21–524.2 The second part of these Chronicles . . . to the undertakers in January 1828 Scott was approached on successive days with requests to edit journals. The first of these requests, by the voluminous publishers Saunders and Otley, was probably for a literary journal rather than a fashionable annual: they attempted such journals in 1827 and 1829. But the second request concerned *The Keepsake*, to which Scott eventually agreed to contribute three stories originally intended for *Chronicles of the Canongate*: for a full account see EEWN 24, 143–51. Scott's suggestion that he had contributed many such items to annuals is misleading.

524.12 Pinkerton the two passages quoted are from John Pinkerton, *The History of Scotland from the Accession of the House of Stuart to that of Mary*, 2 vols (London, 1797), 1.51–52, 69: *CLA*, 4. The final paragraph of the Introduction is a paraphrase of 1.88–89.

526.3–8 This "newest New Town," . . . taken see EEWN 21, 470 (notes to 3.24 and 3.24–25).

526.10–20 The visit . . . fifteen days at Edinburgh the future Prince Regent and George IV married Caroline of Brunswick in 1795. They separated soon afterwards. However, on George's accession to the throne in 1820, Caroline returned to England to assert her role as Queen Consort. She had considerable popular support, but despite this the King barred her from attending his coronation in 1821. She died some weeks later. Samuel Johnson repeatedly referred to the unpopularity of the Hanoverian monarch: see 'Hanover, House of' in the index to James Boswell, *Life of Samuel Johnson*, ed. George Birkbeck Hill, rev. L. F. Powell, 6 vols (Oxford, 1934–50), and especially 3.155–56 (17 September 1777).

526.21–23 Such is the author's opinion . . . the classical stream popular history has it that when Agricola's soldiers first saw the River Tay and the Inches of Perth they exclaimed, 'Ecce Tiber! Ecce Campus Martius!' However there is nothing in Tacitus's *Agricola* to support the story. An early source is Henry Adamson's poem *The Muses Threnodie*, ed. James Cant (Perth, 1774: *CLA*, 17; originally published 1638), in which Scott found much useful information on Perth and its history (see EEWN 21, 466). The following passage occurs at pp. 86–87:

> And there, hard by a river-side, they found
> The fairest and most pleasant plat of ground
> That since by bank of *Tiber* they had been,
> The like for beauty seldom had they seen, . . .
> So equal fair, which when they did espy,
> Incontinent they *campus Martius* cry.

526.28 a distinguished local antiquary presumably Mr Morrison: see the Editorial Note, 512–13 above.

526.36–527.7 the hill of Moredun, or Moncrieff . . . the Wicks of Baiglie for these heights see EEWN 21, 475 (notes to 12.30–31 and 12.24).

526.40–527.1 those features which Pennant has so warmly eulogized Thomas Pennant, a Welsh naturalist and antiquary, published his *A Tour in Scotland. MDCCLXIX* at Chester in 1771. The passage referred to here occurs at 69: 'Ascended the hill of *Moncrief*; the prospect from thence is the glory of *Scotland*, and well merits the eulogia given it for the variety and richness of its views'.

527.17–18 the decisive point a path alongside the River Tay at Dunkeld leads up to Craig Vinean forest. Nearby is a viewpoint over the Tay valley—presumably the one from which the Dunkeld guide is speaking. Lower down is the Hermitage, an ornamental woodland garden created in the 1750s, later the location of Ossian's Hall which provides a view over the Falls of Braan.

527.19 Mr D. O. Hill David Octavius Hill (1802–70) was a Perth-born painter and illustrator. Through his collaboration with Robert Adamson (1821–48) he pioneered the creation of the art of photography in Scotland.

527.31–40 David II. . . . p. 452 see EEWN 21, 475 (note to 14.8–10). The quotations are rather loosely taken from Hector Boece, *The History and Chronicles of Scotland . . . translated by John Bellenden*, 2 vols (Edinburgh, 1821), 2.449, 452: *CLA*, 4.

527.43–528.1 Old Scottish . . . ποιητης the four-word Ed1 note is expanded by Lockhart.

528.2 Sir Magnus Redman see EEWN 21, 477 (note to 22.27–28). Lockhart rewrites Scott's original note, which is here restored since it is no more inaccurate than its replacement. Sir Matthew Redman was Captain of Berwick in 1381. He was active in the Battle of Otterbourne 7 years later, but no record has been found that his death *c.* 1390 was in battle. More than half a century after Sir Matthew's death a warrior of the same name died in the Battle of Sark, fought on the shores of the Solway Firth in 1449. See W[illiam] Greenwood, *The Redmans of Levens and Harewood* (Kendal, 1905), 57–69, 90–91.

528.7–8 Then Burewin . . . every chaup see EEWN 21, 477 (note to 23.34).

528.11–12 The beautiful Lake . . . frequenters the suggested derivation of the name of Loch Katrine is not accepted by modern scholars.

528.16–32 The story of Bruce . . . with the dust for 'the beautiful incident' see Barbour, 16.272–96. *Kernes* are Irish fighters, fast-moving and lightly-armed.

528.35 The town of Culross a royal burgh in Fife, on the N coast of the Firth of Forth.

529.1 the Garb of old Gaul title of, and phrase in, an 18th-century song commemorating role of Scottish soldiers in the winning of Canada from the French during the Seven Years War. It is credited to Sir Henry Erskine (1710–65), but there is an alternative tradition that the words were originally composed in Gaelic by a soldier of the 42nd Highland Regiment of Foot (the Black Watch), with several officers claiming to have translated it into English: see the *ODNB* article on Erskine. Fitted to the march composed by the soldier-musician John Reid (1722?–1807) when a lieutenant-captain in the regiment, it is said to have become a favourite song of loyal Highlanders.

529.2 Dr Jamieson Dr John Jamieson (1759–1838), antiquarian and lexicographer, is best known for his *An Etymological Dictionary of the Scottish Language*, 2 vols (Edinburgh, 1808). A *Supplement*, again in 2 volumes, followed in 1825: at 1.494–95 Jamieson records that *glunimie* is given as a fondling name to a cow, and that it appears to be the same as *glunyie-man*, applied to a rough boorish man, or a Highlander. Jamieson's work remained the standard source of information on Scots until the appearance of the *Scottish National Dictionary* in which Jamieson's information is repeated but different derivations are suggested.

529.5 adhuc sub judice lis est the tag, from Horace, *Ars Poetica*, line 78, runs in full: 'grammatici certant et adhuc sub iudice lis est' (scholars dispute, and the case is still before the court).

529.8–9 a gentleman well versed . . . St Johnston presumably Morrison.

529.15 the Gowrie Conspiracie see EEWN 21, 475 (note to 12.16).

529.28 the Castle was rased Bruce besieged and took Perth in January 1313. Barbour describes the rasing of its towers and walls (9.455–60).

529.35 incorporation a legalised society or company. The Glovers in Perth were chartered as such in 1165.

529.41 Saint Bartholomew Bartholomew figures in Matthew 10.3, Mark 3.18, Luke 6.14, and Acts 1.13 as one of the 12 apostles. Martyred in Armenia, according to tradition, by flaying and beheading, his most usual emblem is the flaying knife and he is the patron saint of, among others, all craftsmen who work in skins.

530.5–6 a ring . . . Gyges in Greek legend King Gyges found a ring which rendered the wearer invisible.

530.19 St Crispin St Crispin and his twin brother Crispinian, martyred for their faith in the 3rd century, were identified as the patron saints of cobblers, tanners, and leather-workers.

530.39–43 It is generally believed . . . their resources the Amisfield branch of the Charteris family built Amisfield Tower, some 8 km N of Dumfries, *c.* 1600. It has been in continuous occupation ever since, being extended in 1837.

531.27–28 Major calls it, 'Pontem Sancti Joannis apud Perth' see John Major, *Historia Majoris Britanniæ*, new edn (Edinburgh, 1740; first pbd 1521), 138: *CLA*, 4.

531.29–32 it was extensively repaired . . . frequently exposed see EEWN 21, 478–79 (note to 36.36) and 505 (note to 258.17–21).

531.40–42 The great estates . . . elder titles James Johnstone, 2nd Marquess of Annandale 1721–30, was succeeded by his half-brother George Vanden-Bempde. When George died in 1792 the marquessate became extinct and the earldom dormant. Between 1792 and 1879 various unresolved claims to the title were made. However in 1985 a claim to the earldom by Patrick Hope-Johnstone was recognised by the House of Lords.

532.2–5 Buchanan . . . a much later period see George Buchanan, *The History of Scotland*, 5th edn, 2 vols (Edinburgh, 1762), [trans. from the Latin by William Bond], 1.440: 'This vain title of honour was then first celebrated in Scotland, a great increase of ambition, but none at all to virtue;

neither did it afterwards thrive with any who enjoyed it' (*CLA*, 9).

532.13–16 Mr Surtees . . . p. lvi Robert Surtees (1779–1834) was historian and antiquary of his native county of Durham. The suggested derivation (or, at least, the appropriateness) of 'galilee' appears in his *The History and Antiquities of the County Palatine of Durham*, 3 vols (London, 1816–23), 1.lvi (note g): *CLA*, 261. The sentence from the Vulgate means: 'Go and tell my brethren to go to Galilee: there they will see me'.

532.19–26 The men of the Isle of Bute . . . the Royal house Lockhart adds the final sentence to the Ed1 note in the interleaved copy. The reference to John Leyden was added at a subsequent stage. St Brandin occurs more frequently as St Brendan or Brandon. A 6th-century Irish monastic saint, he is remembered for his legendary quest for the 'Isle of the Blessed' or St Brendan's Island (recounted in the 9th-century Voyage of St Brendan the Navigator). Perhaps it is the story of his voyagings which explains his status as patron saint of the islands in the Firth of Clyde. For the derivation (which is not disputed by the *Scottish National Dictionary*) see *Scottish Descriptive Poems; with some illustrations of Scottish Literary Antiquities*, ed. J. Leyden (Edinburgh, 1803), 134–35. Robert II, King of Scots 1371–90, appointed his illegitimate son Sir John Stewart as Hereditary Sheriff of Bute. His descendant in Scott's time was John Crichton-Stuart (1793–1848) who succeeded his grandfather as 2nd Marquess of Bute in 1814.

532.30 a proverb unidentified.

532.34 The Lay of Poor Louise Frances Crawford Kemble (1787–1849) married Robert Arkwright (1783–1859) in 1805. Scott's *Journal* records several instances of her singing during his visit to London in April-May 1828. In the last of those entries (14 May) he writes: 'I have received as much pleasure from that lady's musick as sound could ever give me' (475). Two printings of her setting of *Poor Louise: A Ballad by Sir W. Scott* dated [1845?] and [1877] are preserved in the British Library.

532.41–42 A seemly person . . . letterature see Wyntoun, 2.397 (9.2155–56: 21): the lines are reversed.

533.8–10 Voltaire . . . their history see a passage in the article on 'Government' in the *Dictionnaire Philosophique* (1764): 'Cette dureté de mœurs, qui a fait de leur île le théâtre de tant de sanglantes tragédies, n'a-t-elle pas contribué aussi à leur inspirer une franchise généreuse? [new paragraph] N'est-ce pas ce mélange de leurs qualités contraires qui a fait couler tant de sang royal dans les combats et sur les échafauds, et qui n'a jamais permis qu'ils employassent le poison dans leurs troubles civils, tandis qu'ailleurs, sous un gouvernement sacerdotal, le poison était une arme si commune?' (Has this disposition to harshness, which has made their island a stage for so many bloody tragedies, not also contributed to inspire in them a generous frankness? Is it not this combination of contrasting features which has caused so much royal blood to run in battles and on scaffolds, and which has never permitted the use of poisoning in their civil troubles, while elsewhere, under a priestly dispensation, poison was so commonly employed as a weapon?): *Œuvres complètes*, ed. Louis Moland, 52 vols (Paris, 1877–85), 19.295.

533.11–12 The twelve peers . . . romance in the cycle of heroic legend that accrued to the historical Charlemagne a band of twelve, the most notable being Roland and Oliver, stand at the head of his warriors.

533.13–18 The Scottish Statute Book . . . Abbas Letitiæ see *The Laws and Acts of Parliament Made by King James the First, and his Royal Successors*, ed. Sir Thomas Murray of Glendook, 2 vols (Edinburgh, 1682), 1.307 (20 June 1555): *CLA*, 11. The Act is also included in *Acts of the Parliaments of Scotland*, 2 (1814), 500 (Act 40 of 1555): *CLA*, 1. The French and Latin expressions mean 'abbot of jubilation', 'abbot of gaiety'.

533.23–25 Dr Jamieson . . . Mazmorra see the entry for 'massimore' in John Jamieson, *An Etymological Dictionary of the Scottish Language*, 2 vols (Edinburgh, 1808).

533.26–28 The passage referred to . . . 220 see EEWN 21, 499 (note to 189.15–19). The line numbers cited are those in *The Bruce; and Wallace*, [ed. John Jamieson], 2 vols (Edinburgh, 1820): *CLA*, 4.

533.35–534.5 Courage to give . . . Great fantasie Henry Adamson, *The Muses Threnodie*, ed. James Cant (Perth, 1774: *CLA*, 17; originally published 1638), 133.

534.8–535.2 Mr Morrison says . . . bandy-legged Having received this note from Morrison Lockhart deleted a much briefer note on the same subject by Scott keyed to the last sentence of the novel: 'It is generaly believed that the hero of the wynd is represented in the male line by the eminently respectable race of the smythes of Methven in Perthshire; & there is at least nothing inconsistent w[ith] this tradition in the date of their Earliest Charter'. The allusion in the final paragraph, though recognised by every schoolboy in Scott's time, has not been identified.

535.16 Cochran Thomas [Robert] Cochrane (d. 1482) was a mason or architect at the court of James III, and a favourite of the king, who may have created him Earl of Mar. His taste for ornate gothic work is evident at Auchindoun Castle, Banffshire (derelict by the early 18th century), for which he was probably responsible.

535.27–30 when Handel . . . Morrice dance the origin of this statement has not been located.

536.19–32 Tradition . . . bier-right for St John's Church see EEWN 21, 479 (note to 39.1). The building was divided into two churches in 1598, and a third church inserted *c.* 1773.

536.34–37 This cruel amusement . . . the festival in Scott's time Shrove Tuesday, the day before the beginning of the penitential season of Lent, was marked by special games of football, throwing objects at poultry, and the consumption of pancakes.

536.38 Sir David Lyndsaye see EEWN 21, 503 (note to 225.41).

536.40–41 The famous ancestor . . . Halidon Hill see EEWN 21, 504 (note to 236.13–15).

537.2–6 In a volume . . . the ordeal of fire *Janus; or, the Edinburgh Literary Almanack* was published by Oliver and Boyd in Edinburgh in November 1825, dated 1826. Its compilation was the work of Lockhart and John Wilson ('Christopher North'). 'Church-Service for the Ordeal by Fire' is the second item in this collection (44–49).

537.17–21 Mr Büsching . . .. 1817 Johann Gustav Gottlieb Büsching (1783–1829), a German archaeologist and folklorist: the Abbotsford Library contains several of his books (*CLA*, 47, 48, 63, 102). The prayers appear in 'Feierliche Gebräuche beim Beweise der Unschuld eines Beklagten durch glühende Eisen' (Solemn procedures for proving the innocence of an accused person by red-hot iron'), *Die Vorzeit, oder Geschichte, Dichtung, Kunst und Literatur des Vor- und Mittel-Alters* (Past Times, or History, Poetry, Art and Literature of the Middle Ages and the Preceding Age) (Erfurt), 1 (1817), 86–96. There is a small amount of abridgement and paraphrase of the prayers, but the narrative is heightened by additions such as the charter-chest.

540.10–12 Si sinus . . . referatur *Latin* If there is found a red weal where the mark of the iron has been, he is to be regarded as culpable. But if he is found to be free from damage, let praise be given to God.

540.21–541.8 And when his father's dead body . . . in this case see

The Tryal of Philip Standsfield, son to Sir James Standsfield, of New-Milns, for The Murther of his Father, And Other Crimes Libell'd against him, Feb. 7. 1688 (Edinburgh, 1688), 4–5, 7, 35. The Magnum version is verbally almost entirely faithful.

540.43–541.1 Sir George Mackenzie Mackenzie (1636/38–91) became Lord Advocate in 1677. His most important publication was *The Institutions of the Law of Scotland* (Edinburgh, 1684).

541.21–22 The Constable's . . . lodgings see EEWN 21, 500 (note to 194.1–2).

541.32–33 the celebrated Gowrie House . . . now remains Gowrie House, built by the family in the 16th century, was demolished in 1809 to make way for the new County Buildings.

541.38 the Carse of Gowrie a stretch of fertile, low-lying country on the N shore of the Firth of Tay between Perth and Dundee.

541.40–542.2 An incident . . . her recovery in fact the incident referred to here happened in the 17th century, not the 19th. Anne Green was a young woman hanged for infanticide in Oxford in 1650. Her body was taken in its coffin to the university to be used in an anatomy lecture. The coffin was opened in the presence of several well-known Oxford doctors including William Petty (Reader in Anatomy), Thomas Willis, Ralph Bathhurst, and Henry Clerke. After the opening she was observed to breathe: she survived and was reprieved. The 'learned professor' was Richard Watkins, 'a Scholler in Oxford', who published *Newes from the Dead* there anonymously in 1651. See J. Trevor Hughes, 'Miraculous Deliverance Of Anne Green: an Oxford case Of resuscitation in the seventeenth century', *British Medical Journal*, 285 (Issue 6357, 18–25 December 1982), 1792–93.

542.3–5 These lines . . . kept a mistress see EEWN 21, 506 (note to 266.26–28). The lines are above a door of the 16th-century Abbot House, Dunfermline.

542.7–18 Mastere Henry of Wardlaw . . . then Doctour see Wyntoun, 2.400 (9.2229–34, 2240–44: 21). The original has 'alkyn gud ẅertew' and 'fame, and þis resowne'. For Wardlaw see EEWN 21, 487 (note to 92.13).

542.32–35 Their territory . . . Stafford-Sutherland in 1829 tens of thousands of acres in the Reay country in the northern Highlands were bought by George Granville Leveson-Gower (1758–1833), who succeeded his father as 2nd Marquess of Stafford in 1803. He married Elizabeth (1765–1839), Countess of Sutherland, in 1785 and was created Duke of Sutherland in the year of his death.

542.43–44 the rooks and their nests alluding to the proverb 'Ding down the nests, and the rooks will flee away': John Kelly, *A Complete Collection of Scotish Proverbs Explained and Made Intelligible To The English Reader* (London, 1721), 88–89 (*CLA*, 169). Kelly notes: 'This Proverb was unhappily apply'd at the Reformation to the destroying of many stately Cathedrals, and Collegiate Churches'.

542.44–543.1 The priory on Loch Tay . . . body of monks Priory Island, at the E end of Loch Tay, Perthshire, was granted by Alexander I, King of Scots 1107–24, to monks from Scone Abbey in 1122.

543.11 against the sun these three words were inserted in the Ed1 note.

543.27–34 Sir Alexander Ramsay . . . P. 75 see EEWN 21, 514 (note to 338.38–39).

543.37–38 To bear the milk-bowie . . . wi' thee see 'When first my dear laddie gade to the green hill', lines 3–4, in *The Gentle Shepherd* (1725): *The Works of Allan Ramsay*, 6 vols (Edinburgh and London, [1945]–1974), Vol. 3, ed. Alexander M. Kinghorn and Alexander Law, 71.

543.40–544.25 Mr Morrison says . . . this young officer Morrison's story here is problematic. The mention of a dancing master and a recruiting party seems to suggest an 18th-century setting. Such an instant execution was certainly not normal by that period. Mr Morrison admits there is no record of such an event but suggests that the details were handed down by word of mouth. The Burgh Court of Perth would have had the authority of the Sheriff Court

546.1–23 At this time . . . yeiris Hector Boece, *The History and Chronicles of Scotland . . . translated by John Bellenden*, 2 vols (Edinburgh, 1821), 2.469: *CLA*, 4.

546.28–42 A thousand foure hundyr yeris and twa . . . intyl Paradys Wyntoun, 2.396–97 (9.2148–62: 21).

546.43–548.43 The Continuator of Fordun . . . Sibylla taces *Joannis de Fordun Scotichronicon, cum Supplementis et Continuatione Walteri Boweri*, ed. Walter Goodall, 2 vols (Edinburgh, 1759), 2.430–32: *CLA*, 12. The Latin passage may be translated as follows:

In the year of our Lord 1401 there died a most solid pillar of the church, a vessel of eloquence, a treasure-house of knowledge, and a defender of the catholic faith, the lord Walter Trail, bishop of St Andrews; Queen Annabel also died at Scone and was buried at Dunfermline. During their lifetimes these two held high the dignity of the kingdom, as it were, namely by reconciling princes and nobles who had fallen out, by welcoming and entertaining in splendid fashion strangers and foreigners and sending them away happy with lavish gifts. So at that time the saying arose, like a proverb, that with the deaths of the Queen of Scotland, the Earl of Douglas and the Bishop of St Andrews the glory of Scotland came to an end, her dignity departed and her nobility passed away. In the same year a fourth death occurred in the kingdom. A little earlier the king in council appointed certain counsellors, powerful barons and soldiers, under oath to control and advise the lord David Stewart, Duke of Rothesay, Earl of Carrick, and a prince of the realm, because the king and his council thought that he was engaging too often in unrestrained amusements and in rather trifling diversions. Because even he was held in check by wiser counsel, he swore that he would accept their guidance and advice. But on the death of his noble mother the queen, who had restrained him in many respects, it was as if his halter had been worn through: he looked forward to being free, neglected the counsel of honest men and gave himself up entirely again to his previous trifling pursuits. Because he rid himself of the advice of the noble lords that had been offered to him, he declared to the king that even if he had wanted he could not have adopted a serious way of life. So the king, weak and enfeebled, wrote to his brother the Duke of Albany, governor of the realm, to the effect that he should be arrested and kept in custody for a time, until he was chastened by the rod of discipline and came to a better understanding of himself. For a father does not only kiss his son, but sometimes chastises him. But the king's proposals for bettering his son brought about his hurt. For each of the two men who carried the king's letter to the governor actually showed that he had incited and urged the king to make such a request, which militated against the dignity of both of them, as the outcome of the event clearly showed. It was the lords William Lindsay of Rossie and John Ramorney, military men, friends and counsellors of the king, who were the messengers and bearers of the king's letter to the governor: they, it is said, previously suggested to the Duke of Rothesay that after the death of the Bishop of St Andrews he should take control of the bishop's castle and keep it for the use of the king until a new bishop was installed: as the duke, anticipating no evil, was riding in all innocence with only a small entourage to St Andrews Castle, they arrested him between the village of Nidus and Strathyre, and by force brought the duke to St Andrews

Castle, which was ready to be handed over to them, and kept him in custody there until the Duke of Albany had discussed with his council at a meeting in Culross what to do with him. The Duke of Albany, along with the lord Archibald, second Earl of Douglas, put him on a mule, disguised him with a russet tabard and transported him forcibly to the tower of Falkland, where they arranged for him to be kept prisoner in a small but decent room. He was kept in custody there for a long time, namely by John Selkirk and John Wright, until he was weakened either by dysentery or, as others will have it, by hunger, and he died late on 26 March, Easter Eve, or very early on Easter Day, and was buried at Lindores. The aforementioned John Ramorney was a counsellor both to the prince and to the lord king, bold in spirit and most eloquent in speech, and a spokesman for the king and a most skilled advocate in difficult legal cases: it is said that he previously suggested to the prince himself, the Duke of Rothesay, that he should arrest his uncle the Duke of Albany and, seizing whatever opportunity he could, should remove him from the scene: this the prince absolutely refused to do. Taking note of this, the soldier, blinded by the filthy grime of his own wickedness, gave himself up to this disgraceful behaviour and refused to abandon his schemes; because, as Chrysostom says, 'A mind that has once been corrupted by wicked desire cannot in any way be held in check.' So the tables were turned and, putting the boot on the other foot [*literally* transferring his cloak to the other shoulder], he encouraged the Duke of Albany to commit this same crime against his nephew the Duke of Rothesay: otherwise, as he asserted, the Duke of Rothesay would without doubt have made an end of Albany himself. The abovementioned lord William Lindsay happened to be of the same mind as John Ramorney, since the Duke of Rothesay was betrothed to Euphemia Lindsay, the sister of lord William, but had broken off the engagement by essaying subsequent marriages with other women, such as the daughter of the Earl of March. Indeed, I reckon he is that David about whom the prophet of Brecklington prophesied, saying

> For his merry deeds David will be sung of as licentious;
> Because he regards other men's wives as better than his own
> His royal morals will be lacking, and he will destroy his dignity.

Shortly before he was arrested there appeared a remarkable comet, sending out a long tail of rays pointing towards the north. When it first appeared, the duke and others went off by themselves to see it one evening in Edinburgh Castle, and he is said to have talked about the star, saying 'As I have heard from the mathematicians, when a comet like this appears it signals either the death or a change in the fortunes of some prince, or the destruction of some country.' And so it came to pass, just as he had predicted. For after the duke was arrested the star returned to its previous state, as God wished. In this respect the duke could be compared with the prophetess, the Sibyl, about whom Claudian said

> I wonder why you, who usually reveals to others their destiny,
> remain a silent and unseeing Sibyl in relation to your own fate.

549.4–25 Be quhais deith . . . miraclis ceissit Hector Boece, *The History and Chronicles of Scotland . . . translated by John Bellenden*, 2 vols (Edinburgh, 1821), 2.475–76: *CLA*, 4.

549.26–550.42 The Remission . . . the heir apparent see David Dalrymple of Hailes, *Annals of Scotland*, 3rd edn, 3 vols (Edinburgh, 1819), 3.57–60: *CLA*, 5. The Latin passage may be translated thus: 'Robert, by the grace of God King of Scots, to all those to whose attention these present letters may come, [sends] eternal greetings in the Lord: inasmuch as recently our dearly beloved Robert, Duke of Albany, Earl of Fife and Menteith, our brother, and Archibald, Earl of Douglas and Lord of Galloway, our son-in-law by reason of his marriage to our daughter, caused our very dearly beloved eldest son David, formerly Duke of Rothesay and Earl of Carrick and Atholl, to be taken prisoner and arrested by them in person, and to be at first imprisoned in St Andrews Castle and then kept in custody in Falkland, where he is known to have departed this life by no other means than by God's providence; these men appearing before us in our general council which began to meet in Edinburgh on the 16th day of May in the year of our Lord 1402 and continued for several days thereafter, having faced questions, or rather accusations, about this matter in accordance with our royal office, and confessing the capture, arrest and death as indicated above, alleged in our presence the reasons which impelled them to this deed, summarising them as being for the public good, as they asserted, reasons which we have thought should not be included in these presents, for good cause: a thorough enquiry having been undertaken into this matter and each and every factor that required to be considered in the case and that related to its cause having been considered and discussed after mature deliberation by our council, we have excused the aforementioned Robert our brother and Archibald our son-in-law, together with all those who shared in this with them, namely those who arrested, detained, guarded and counselled, and all others who offered them advice, help or support, or who followed their orders or instructions in any way whatsoever: moreover in our said council we have openly and publicly declared, pronounced and definitively stated, and by the tenor of these presents we now declare, pronounce and state by this definitive opinion of ours, that the two men themselves and each one of their followers are innocent, guiltless and blameless of the crime of lèse-majesté against us or of any other crime, fault, injury, malice and offence of any kind which could be imputed to them in any way whatsoever on the occasion of the aforementioned deeds, and that they are completely and absolutely free, discharged and immune. And if we have conceived against them, or against any of them, male or female, singular or plural, who have participated in any way in this act, or against those who supported them in any way whatsoever, any indignation, anger, rancour or offence, these we annul, remove and wish to be regarded as annulled in perpetuity, on our own initiative, on the basis of sure knowledge and also as a result of the deliberations of our aforementioned council. Therefore to each and every one of our subjects, of whatever state or condition, we issue a strict injunction and command that they neither slander by word or deed the frequently aforementioned Robert and Archibald and their fellow-participators, conspirators and adherents in this act, as aforementioned, nor murmur against them in any way whatsoever, to cause their good name to be harmed or any prejudice to be formed against them, subject to every penalty which is competent thereanent under any law whatsoever. Given, under the witness of our Great Seal, in the abbey of Holyrood in Edinburgh, on the 20th day of the aforementioned month of May, in the year of our Lord 1402 and the thirteenth reign of our reign.' In his *The History of Scotland from the Accession of the House of Stuart to that of Mary*, 2 vols (London, 1797: *CLA*, 4), John Pinkerton interprets the Latin pardon as implying the guilt of Albany and Douglas. He refers to its publication by Dalrymple in his *Remarks on the History of Scotland* (Edinburgh, 1773), 278–84; but he does not specifically comment on the remark quoted at the end of this Magnum note which is reprinted on 3.60 of the 1819 *Annals of Scotland*.

ANNE OF GEIERSTEIN

557.2–7 This novel . . . country see EEWN 22, 411–16.
557.13–19 old Beattie of Meikledale's answer . . . one word of it Scott tells this anecdote of Thomas Beattie (1736–1826) in his 'Memoirs': *Scott on Himself*, ed. David Hewitt (Edinburgh, 1981), 26–27.
557.26–558.2 one mistake . . . the imperial crown Scott's depiction of Emperor Friedrich III in the novel is complicated by the confusion of Friedrich and Duke Siegmund of Austria, but he does in general suggest that the Emperor was well-disposed to the Confederates (see EEWN 22, 512–13, and for Duke Leopold III 22, 514). The complaining letter, presumably from a modern Zimmermann, has not been located.
558.9–10 through the genius of Goethe . . . ancient terrors see EEWN 22, 506.
558.13–14 the elaborate researches of . . . Mr Francis Palgrave in the pages that follow Scott quotes, with almost complete faithfulness, from Palgrave, Part 2, cxliv–clvii.
558.21 the Historians of Saxony most notably Henricus Meibomius, *Irmensvla Saxonica* (Helmstedt, 1612), cited by Palgrave on p. cxliv. In the course of his account Palgrave also cites (cxl) Jacob Grimm, *Irmenstraße und Irmensäule* (Vienna, 1815) and Friedrich Heinrich von der Hagen, *Irmin, seine Säule, seine Straße und sein Wagen* (Breslau, 1817), but Grimm has nothing about Corbey, and Hagen only notes Meibomius.
558.23–26 the Eresburgh . . . its site the Irminsul, a wooden column representing the Yggdrasil, or world tree, situated on the Eresberg, now Obermarsberg, North Rhine-Westphalia, was burned by Charlemagne in 772. Charlemagne's son Louis the Pious (798–840), King of France and Holy Roman Emperor from 814, founded the Benedictine abbey of Corvey nearby in 822.
559.45–47 Owen Pugh's Elegies of Lewarch Hen . . . the Gorsedd *The Heroic Elegies and other Pieces of Llywarç Hen, Prince of the Cumbrian Britons: with a literal translation, by William Owen* (London, 1792), xlvi: *CLA*, 156. Owen (later Owen Pughe) defines *Maen Gorsedd* as 'the Stone of the Assembly'.
560.35–36 the Free Field Court . . . Westphalia see EEWN 22, 506, 541 (note to 219.21–37).
562.17–19 an office . . . Cologne Henry the Lion (1129–95) made many conquests in Germany, but in 1180 he was defeated by the Emperor and deprived by the Emperor of all his territories except Brunswick and Lüneburg (though he was no longer a duke). His Duchy of Saxony was dismantled, and the western part, Westphalia, given to the Archbishopric of Cologne. A *stadtholder* is a viceroy.
565.42–43 Asi . . . Thor or Woden the Asi, or Æsir, are actually the main tribe of Norse gods, including their chief Woden, or Odin, and Thor.
566.32–35 the necessity . . . occasion Scott left Abbotsford for his voyage to Malta and Naples on 23 September 1831, six days after the date of this Introduction.
566.41–567.7 I have in particular . . . these pages for Sempach (1386), and Grandson and Morat (1476), see EEWN 22.514–16.
567.10–11 Wallace . . . Scottish independence Sir William Wallace (d. 1305) was a leading defender of Scottish independence against Edward I, King of England.
567.13–17 Zschokké . . . Froissart 'Zschokké' is Heinrich Zschokke, author of *Des Schweizerlands Geschichte für das Schweizervolk*, 2nd (revised) edn (Aarau, 1824). For Barante see 641 above. The Chronicles of Jean Froissart (*c.* 1337–*c.* 1404) occupy Vols 10–25 of *Collection des Chroniques*

Nationales Françaises, ed. J. A. Buchon, 47 vols (Paris, 1824–26): *CLA*, 50–51.

567.26–28 The chivalry of Cornwall . . . discover in *Sir Tristrem*, Fytte 1, Stanza 91, none of the Cornish knights will defend the freedom of their country against the English, and it is left to Tristrem to do so. Scott believed *Sir Tristrem* to be an original composition by a 13th-century Scottish poet Thomas of Erceldoune, not a version of an Anglo-Norman poem; but in his edition of the romance (*Poetical Works*, 5.423) he notes an incident from a French prose version in which only one Cornish knight attempts to rescue Ysonde from Palamedes.

567.32–35 Louis XI. . . . highest trust see *Quentin Durward*, EEWN 15, 515 (note to 25.28–32).

568.9–10 as any European Lord Chamberlain . . . Key as Keeper of the Royal Palace of Westminster the Lord Chamberlain has hanging at his hip the golden key to the palace.

568.16–571.5 De toutes partes . . . reçut le coup the quotation from Barante in the Magnum is so replete with errors that it has been judged best (exceptionally) to reproduce the original, as indicated in the Emendation List.

574.3–6 This is one of the best . . . reben, &c. see EEWN 22, 539 (note to 196.20–24).

574.7–12 The word Wehme . . . probably right Scott adds the final sentence to the Ed1 note. He is probably recalling the note in Palgrave, cl, where the candidate swears 'by the Holy Law': 'Ich gelobe bey der heilingen *Ehe*. The employment of *Ehe* for law, is a pure Anglo-Saxonism—Ae, or Æþa. In a secondary sense it signifies marriage; and perhaps any lawful obligation.'

574.15–16 Mr Palgrave suggests . . . the district for this insertion into the Ed1 note see Palgrave, cxlixn. (This note is omitted in the quotation at 560–66 above.)

574.23–576.3 The Troubadours . . . execration this and the following note were originally part of the text of the novel. For Cadell's suggestion that they should become Magnum notes, see EEWN 22, 416.

576.5–24 High and Noble Parliament of Love . . . the Court of Love see previous note. The 'case of much celebrity' is among those described in [C. F. Bouche], *Essai sur l'histoire de Provence* (Marseille, 1785), 2.284.

576.30–579.36 As soon as the Count . . . at his disposal see Comines, 5:8–9 (Petitot, 12.235–41). The translation is found in *The Memoirs of Philip de Comines*, trans. [Thomas] Uvedale, 2 vols (London, 1712), 1.446–55. 'One Monsieur Claude of Bausmont . . . ante timor' is interpolated from part of a long footnote in Uvedale, whose text is reproduced in general with verbal accuracy, though there are a few short omissions. The Latin epitaph means 'Charles, the glory of the Burgundian nation, who was formerly the terror of Europe, is commemorated by this tomb.'

CASTLE DANGEROUS

588.17–20 The Gud Schyr James . . . was he see Barbour, 1.29–32.

588.22–25 The Good Sir James . . . did obtain the lines have not been found in Patrick Gordon, *The Famous History Of the Renown'd and Valiant Prince, Robert Sirnamed, The Bruce, King of Scotland, &c.* (Dort, 1615; rptd Edinburgh, 1718): *CLA*, 169.

588.34–589.5 The Douglasse . . . ruinous decay see *Holinshed's Chronicles of England, Scotland, and Ireland*, 6 vols (London, 1807–08), 5.341–42: *CLA*, 29. The original has 'was ioifullie receiued' and 'other of the same linage'.

589.12–14 in Rymer's Fœdera . . . stronghold see the index to Thomas Rymer and Robert Sanderson, *Foedera*, 3rd edn, ed. George Holmes, 10 vols (The Hague, 1739–45: *CLA*, 23), for several references to Robert de Clifford around the time of the novel's action, one to Sir John de Walton (1316), and one to Sir Richard de Thurewalle (1322).

589.18–23 the romantic story . . . chronicles of chivalry Scott himself cites the de Walton story as an 'affecting instance' in his 'Essay on Chivalry' (1818): *Prose Works*, 6.36–37.

589.31–33 Mr Thomas Haddow . . . Mr Alexander Finlay . . . Lord Douglas for Haddow's and Finlay's guidance during Scott's visit to Douglas see Lockhart, 7.295. Archibald Douglas (1773–1844) succeeded his father as 2nd Baron Douglas in 1827. See also the Editorial Note at 584 above.

590.7–9 the ancient prophecy . . . splendour the source of the prophecy has not been identified.

590.26–47 [The following notice . . . p. 65.] the quotation is a verbally faithful reproduction of William Hamilton of Wishart, *Descriptions of the Sheriffdoms of Lanark and Renfrew, compiled about M.DCCX* (Glasgow, 1831: *CLA*, 280), 64–65. The square parentheses are original.

591.10–26 Quhen his men . . . swa worthy see Barbour 20.579–86, 592–600 (faithfully reproduced).

591.40–44 the curious reader . . . house of Douglas see Edward Blore, *The Monumental Remains of Noble and Eminent Persons, comprising The Sepulchral Antiquities of Great Britain* (London, 1826), No. 5.

592.6–7 the text of Barbour . . . Jamieson John Jamieson's edition of *The Bruce; and Wallace* was published in Edinburgh (2 vols) in 1820: *CLA*, 4.

592.11–17 of whom . . . one balance see David Hume of Godscroft, *The History of the Houses of Douglas and Angus* (Edinburgh, 1644; reissued in 1648 for sale in London: *CLA*, 3), 52. Hume begins 'We will not omit', and has 'in an old rude verse', 'fortune, good or bad.', and 'for no winning'.

592.24–596.5 And here indeed . . . subjection see Hume, 26–28, 29–30. There are several verbal variants, most significantly: 'costume' for 'custome' (593.6); 'or he' for 'for he' (594.13, emended in the present text); and 'that it began' for 'which began' (595.9).

596.15–601.19 Now takis James . . . full effraytly see Barbour, 4.255–462, 5.7–62 in the first volume of John Jamieson's edition of *The Bruce; and Wallace*, 2 vols (Edinburgh, 1820). The numbering in A. A. M. Duncan's edition is 5.255–462, 6.381–436. The extracts are verbally accurate, except 'in part' for the original 'in hart' (597.12), emended in the present text. The square parentheses in the headnote are original.

601.23 William the Hardy for William the Hardie see EEWN 23b, 387. The square parentheses surrounding this note are original.

601.30–602.29 [The following is an extract . . . enviable."] these 4 paragraphs were added by an intermediary to the Ed1 note (EEWN 23b, 58). The square parentheses are original.

602.30–35 [This is a most graphic and accurate description . . . Douglas.] Alexander Stewart (1781–1862) was minister at Douglas 1820–58. The square parentheses are original.

602.43–603.18 [The fall . . . Rev. Mr Stewart of Douglas. for Alexander Stewart see previous note. The Dickson tombstone is now lost. The square parentheses are original.

THE SHORTER FICTION

606.2–5 The species of publication . . . in Germany German annuals date from the 1760s.

606.6–7 imitated . . . Mr Ackermann Rudolph Ackermann (1764–1834) published *Forget Me Not*, the first British annual, in November 1822.
606.15–16 Various gentlemen . . . associated with them *The Keepsake for 1829* (published on 1 November 1828) included pieces by Coleridge, Mary and the late Percy Shelley, Southey, and Wordsworth.
606.19–20 a few fragments . . . the Chronicles of the Canongate see EEWN24, 143–51.
606.21–22 The House of Aspen published in *The Keepsake for 1830*, 2–66.
606.29–34 a lady of eminent virtues . . . half a lifetime Margaret Swinton, sister of Scott's maternal grandmother, Jean; she died, in the manner described, in 1780 at the age of 70.
607.8 memento mori an object intended to remind the viewer of death.
607.16 I tell the tale as it was told to me a common catch phrase used in relation to a story which is hard to believe.
607.26 the celebrated Miss Seward Anna Seward (1742–1809) whose *Poetical Works* were edited by Scott in 3 volumes (Edinburgh, 1810).

ADDENDA AND CORRIGENDA

This list attends to errors in the text, and editorial matter; it corrects notes and glosses which are wrong, or for which new information has been found, and it adds notes for the identification of quotations and proverbs which were previously missed. It also changes all cross-references to Scott's fiction, plus the Magnum Introductions and notes, to the volumes of the EEWN. It does not correct editorial or typographical inconsistencies in the presentation of material (such as the spacing in note tags, and the use of 'MS' rather than 'manuscript' in discursive prose), nor mistakes which all readers can correct for themselves (such as reversed speech marks), nor printing faults such as defective letters or random dots of ink.

Readings to be replaced or added appear between bars or on separate lines without bars. There are three forms of cross-reference: references to distinct sections such as a poem or a whole Introduction have volume and page numbers; whole notes have volume and page number with 'note to 000.00' added; extracts from the texts and Introductions, and from within notes, have a volume number, plus page and line numbers in the form '000.00–00'.

The list also contains a subsidiary emendation list for *Kenilworth*. Since the publication of the EEWNedition of that novel in 1993, five missing leaves have come to light. The emendations which would have been made had these leaves been known will be found in the *Kenilworth* section (737–38).

The editors gratefully acknowledge the information received from A. MacC. Armstrong (*Ivanhoe*), Roy McHattie (*The Pirate* and *Quentin Durward*), A. G. McLaren (*Kenilworth*), Silvia Mergenthal (*Redgauntlet*), Geoffrey Plowden (*Saint Ronan's Well*), Sharon Ragaz (*Saint Ronan's Well*), Graham Robertson (*Redgauntlet*), and Mark Weinstein (*Kenilworth*).

IVANHOE: EEWN 8

112.7 for |answer—*Desdichado*| read |answer—"*Desdichado*|

331.16 for |Beaumanoir," ye| read |Beaumanoir, "ye|

403.4 for |Proofs;| read |Proofs|

422.7 for |on| read |upon|

422.8 for |(Magnum, 17.350)| read |(EEWN 25b, 34: note to 376.17)|

423.6 for |(17.192)| read |(EEWN 25b, 29: note to 292.4)|

431.23 for |(Magnum, 17.111.16–36)| read |(EEWN 25b, 27.35–28.12)|

438.19 for |(Magnum, 16.47.31)| read |(EEWN 25b, 20: note to 37.38)|

438.20 for |(17.335–39)| read |(EEWN 25b, 30–34: note to 368.36)|

438.21 for |(16.329–35)| read |(EEWN 25b, 22–27: note to 182.26)|

454 [note 7] for printed note read |EEWN 25b, 11.11–19.|

455 [note 10] for printed note read |EEWN 25b, 12.7–14.|

456 [note 47] for printed note read |EEWN 25b, 12.40–13.2.|

457 [note 66, line 19] for |(Magnum, 18.iii)| read |(EEWN 25b, 42.2–7)|

497.27 for |the band of warriors| read |the land of the warriors|

497.28 for |(Magnum, 16.262)| read |(EEWN 25b, 21.6–9)|

499.37 for |(17.170)| read |(EEWN 25b, 28–29: note to 281.17)|

502.42 for |by Favine| read |by Favine (André Favyn)|

503.52 for |*Sports*| read |*The Sports*|

504 **Title page motto**
for |taken leave'.| read |taken leave' (EEWN 25b, 18: note to 1.6).|

506 **9.33 Mr Strutt . . . Queen-Hoo-Hall**
[last line] for |(Magnum, 1.xv–xvi)| read |(EEWN 25a, 13.3–5, 23–25)|

508 **13.21 Arthur's oven**
[last line] for |*Waverley* (1.109.17–22)| read |*Waverley* (1814) (EEWN 1, 38.17)|

508 **15.10–11 In . . . the river Don**
add at end of note |The expression 'merry England' is proverbial: *ODEP*, 528.|

511 **20.14 curse of St Withold**
for |*Waverley* (1.188.15–190.8)| read |*Waverley* (1814), EEWN 1, 64–65|

511 **20.31–33 ranger of the forest . . . trade**
[line 2] for |those| read |these|
[lines 4–5] for |(Magnum, 16.17)| read |(EEWN 25b, 18.33–19.11)|

512 **21.38 Front-de Bœuf**
for |(16.xx)| read |(EEWN 25b, 17.33–34)|

512 **22.2 Malvoisin**
add at end of note |It was also the name of a Bishop of St Andrews who died in 1238.|

513 **25.15–17 two attendants . . . eastern country**
[line 2] for |(16.38)| read |(EEWN 25b, 19–20: note to 25.17)|

515 **29.40–41 every land . . . fashions**
Delete final sentence and replace with |*Laugh* is a Scots word meaning law, legal institutions, custom.|

520 **49.8 new-fangled jargon**
[line 1] for |'the| read |'The|
[last line] for |(Magnum, 16.68–69)| read |(EEWN 25b, 20.12–20)|

522 **51.20 Ivanhoe**
[last line] for |(Magnum, 16.xviii–xix)| read |(EEWN 25b, 16.37–17.12)|

522 add |**52.42–43 a love to his neighbour, or to himself** see e.g. Matthew 19.19: 'Thou shalt love thy neighbour as thyself'.|

529 add |**87.1 as pale as death** proverbial: *ODEP*, 608.|

530 for |**97.27–28 'tis**| read |**97.27–28 'tis**|

531 **106.2–3 after the fashion . . . moulinet**
[line 1] for |(1.26.5–9)| read |(1823) EEWN 15, 32.9–12|
[line 3] for |it in| read |it by|

537 **140.31 Pass on, whosoever thou art**
[lines 6–7] for |(Magnum, 16.xviii)| read |(Magnum: EEWN 25b, 16.35–36)|

538 add |**146.23 eating of the fat and drinking of the strong** see Nehemiah 8.10: 'eat the fat, and drink the sweet'.|

538 **148.29–30 sirvente . . . vulgar English**
[line 1] for |Magnum, 16.262| read |Magnum (EEWN 25b, 20.38–21.7)|
[line 5] for |*Lays*:| read |*Lays*;|

541 add |**164.7–8 as like . . . to another** compare the proverb 'As like as two peas': *ODEP*, 851.|

542 **176.9 Stamford . . . Welland**
for |(16.314)| read |(EEWN 25b, 21.15–20)|

543 add |**176.41–44 Spencer and Drayton . . . Poly-Olbion** Edmund Spenser refers to 'the fatall Welland' in *The Faerie Queene*, Book 4 (1596), 11.35.1. The line attributed to Michael Drayton has not been found, but in his *Poly-Olbion* (1612, 1622), 10.205, he calls the Cheshire Dee 'an ominous Flood'.|

543 **182.26–29 on that warm couch . . . lest the roast should burn**
for |(Magnum, 16.329–35)| read |(EEWN 25b, 23.11–25.13).|
547 **210.39 cor meum eructavit**
for |44.1| read |44.2|
551 **244.35–36 Something resembling . . . black shield**
[last line] for |(17.99)| read |(EEWN 25b, 27.29–31)|
554 **269.23 scalds**
for |ancient| read |old|, and for |(Magnum 17.148)| read |(EEWN 25b, 28.23)|
554 **269.28–29 barbarous hymn**
[line 1] for |(17.148)| read |(EEWN 25b, 28.22–31)|
[last line] for |the wild strains which animated her forefathers during the time of Paganism.| read |the wilder strains which animated her forefathers during their times of Paganism and untamed ferocity.|
556 **281.23–24 I will stand thy blow . . . mine**
for |(17.170)| read |(EEWN 25b, 29.1–5)|
558 add |**290.9 filthy lucre** 1 Timothy 3.3.|
560 add |**302.33 zealous to slaying** see Abraham Cowley, *Cutter of Coleman-Street* (1663), 5.6.|
562 **305.26 Conrade Mountfitchet**
add at end of note |But he may have adopted the name from the Essex parish of Stansted Mountfitchet in which Stansted airport is now situated.|
568 add |**336.12–13 under the shadow of the throne** see lines 5–6 of the hymn based on the opening verses of Psalm 90 by Isaac Watts (1674–1748): 'Under the shadow of thy throne/ Thy saints have dwelt secure'.|
571 add |**354.3 Sir Davit ap Morgan ap Griffith ap Hugh** compare 'an antient Briton called Madoc ap-Morgan, ap-Jenkin, ap-Jones' in Tobias Smollett, *The Expedition of Humphry Clinker* (1771), ed. Thomas J. Preston and O. M. Brack, Jr (Athens, Georgia, and London, 1988), 234: J. Melford to Sir Watkin Phillips, 3 September.|
571 add |**356.36–37 show a clean pair of heels** proverbial: Ray, 70; *ODEP*, 729.|
573 **368.16 this ancient Saxon fortress**
[line 3] for |(17.338–39)| read |(EEWN 25b, 33.2–4)|
[line 11] for |(Magnum, 17.335)| read |(EEWN 25b, 30.10–12)|
573 **368.35 various monuments**
[line 2] for |Magnum, 17.338| read |Magnum (EEWN 25b, 32.39–33.1)|
574 **372.30 oratory**
for |(17.339)| read |(EEWN 25b, 33.30–43)|
576 **385.34 basnet-cap**
[line 6] for |(1.40.2–3)| read |(EEWN 18a, 27.38–39)|

THE MONASTERY: EEWN 9

227.25 for |was-sell| read |wassell|
380.17 for |(Magnum, 18.72)| read |(EEWN 25b, 57–58: note to 63.23)|
380.18 for |(Magnum, 19.353)| read |(EEWN 25b, 67–68: note to 346.10)|
383.42 for |(Magnum, 19.394–95)| read |(EEWN 25b, 68–69: note to 346.17)|
396 [note 1] for printed note read |EEWN 25b, 42.2–7.|
443 **6.9 Kennaquhair**
for |(18.xlvii)| read |(EEWN 25b, 54.28–29)|

444 **8.24 mine honest . . . the George**
for |(18.xlvii–xlviii)| read |(EEWN 25b, 54: note to 8.25)|

444 **10.16–17 my Lord's boats**
[line 1] for |(18.lii)| read |(EEWN 25b, 55: note to 10.18)|
[lines 2–3] for |Lord Sommerville| read |Lord Somerville|

444 **11.15–16 Mr Deputy Register of Scotland**
for |(18.lv)| read |(EEWN 25b, 55: note to 11.16)|

444 **11.27–28 to exchange their own old Mumpsimus for his new Sumpsimus**
[line 7] for |unreasonably| read |unreasonably: see *ODEP*, 114|

445 **11.41 De Haga**
for |(18.lvi)| read |(EEWN 25b, 55: note to 11.42)|

447 **18.33–36 an ancient Border-knight . . . magic power**
for |(18.1xxiii)| read |(EEWN 25b, 55: note to 18.37)|

449 **25.40–42 the national adage . . . wind said no**
for the printed note read |proverbial: see James Kelly, *A Complete Collection of Scotish Proverbs* (London, 1721), 285; *ODEP*, 692.|

452 **29.41–42 to bring down . . . the bonnets of Bonny Dundee**
for |2.218.21–24| read |EEWN 5, 189.6–9|

453 add |**34.31 better fed than taught** proverbial: Ray, 189; *ODEP*, 53.|

458 **62.42–43 a bridge . . . the curious**
[line 6] for |(18.72)| read |(EEWN 25b, 57–58: note to 63.23)|

462 add |**89.25–26 all in the day's work** proverbial: *ODEP*, 9.|

462 add |**94.11–12 I am fasting from every thing but sin** see *Don Quixote*, 5.316: Part 2 (1615), Ch. 73.|

463 **98.11 Flodden**
Add at end of note |*ODEP*, 500 accepts 'there were more lost at Flodden' as proverbial, but gives only this example.|

466 add |**122.2 a fair word . . . in season** see Proverbs 15.23: 'a word spoken in due season, how good is it!'|

466 **126.14–15 made two pairs of legs . . . hands**
for |Cheviot, 245| read |*ODEP*, 607|

467 **127.25–26 the proverb of MacFarlane's geese**
for |(18.184)| read |(EEWN 25b, 58.26–31)|

470 **151.39–40 Richard Cœur de Lion . . . carbonadoed**
[lines 6–7] for |*The Talisman* (38.xvi–xx)| read |*The Talisman* (EEWN 25b, 399–402)|

471 **159.31 Rowland Yorke, Stukely**
[line 4] for |in Latin 1615, 1627; in English 1630| read |in Latin 1615–25; in English 1625–29|

480 add |**273.13 do we not pray to be liberated from temptation?** in the Lord's Prayer: Matthew 6.13 and Luke 11.4.|

481 add |**281.18 the knowledge which causeth not to err** see Proverbs 19.27: 'Cease, my son, to hear the instruction that causeth to err from the words of knowledge.'|

484 **310.5–6 the indulgentiæ—the gratias—the biberes—the weekly mess of boiled almonds**
[last line] for |(19.281–82)| read |(EEWN 25b, 65–67)|

485 **318.19 ill hearing makes ill rehearsing**
for |Cheviot, 201| read |*ODEP*, 399|

488 add |**346.9–10 men have seen it in the tree . . . the fountain** see David Hume of Godscroft, *The History of the Houses of Douglas and Angus* (Edinburgh, 1644; reissued in 1648 for sale in London: *CLA*, 3), unpaginated 'Preface': 'We do not know them [the Douglasses] in the fountain, but in the stream'.|

THE ABBOT: EEWN 10

410 [note 2] for printed note read |EEWN 25b, 78.2–35.|
416 [note 88] for |(21.238)| read |(EEWN 25b, 95–96: note to 314.29)|
473 **15.24 the Græmes of Heathergill, in Nicol-forest**
[line 3] for |(Magnum, 20.20, note)| read |(Magnum: EEWN 25b, 83: note to 15.24|
477 **34.34 his caution for a grey groat against . . . water**
for |30| read |75–76|
477 for |**34.41–42 put as ‘twere**| read |**34.41–42 put as ’twere**|
479 **50.20–21 demure . . . cream**
for |*Henry IV*| read |*1 Henry IV*|
480 **58.28 Saint Cuthbert’s cell**
[line 3] for |(Magnum, 20.121)| read |(EEWN 25b, 84.8–13)|
481 **63.19 bird in thy bosom**
for |(20.112)| read |(EEWN 25b, 84: note to 63.19)|
486 add |**101.10 the end crowns the work** proverbial: *ODEP*, 220.|
490 **117.8–10 Saint Martin of Bullions . . . rainy days**
[line 5] for |(Magnum, 20.223, note)| read |(Magnum: EEWN 25b, 92: note to 117.8)|
491 **124.3–5 spirits . . . dragged over the threshold**
for |(20.236–37)| read |(EEWN 25b, 92.30–93.16)|
497 **149.31 a maiden from Halifax**
[line 4] for |(Magnum, 20.286)| read |(Magnum: EEWN 25b, 94: note to 149.41)|
499 **163.23 Laird of Macfarlane’s geese . . . their meat**
[line 4] for |Chieftain. His Majesty| read |chieftain. His majesty|
[line 7] for |observed,—| read |observed—|, and for |liked their play better| read |minded their play more|
[line 8] for |(Magnum, 18.184, note) . . . accompanying note there.| read |(EEWN 25b, 58: note to 127.37). This Magnum note to *The Monastery* is an expansion of that in the first edition (EEWN 9, 127.38–43).|
508 **217.42 Dryfesdale**
[line 9] for |(21.238)| read |(EEWN 25b, 95–96: note to 314.29)|
510 for |**237.46**| read |**237.40**|
512 **244.40 Mother Nicneven**
for |(Magnum, 21.117)| read |(Magnum: EEWN 25b, 95: note to 246.41)|
526 **329.3 broken clan**
for |(Magnum, 21.265, note)| read |(Magnum: EEWN 25b, 96: note to 329.3)|
526 **330.28–29 the Ladies Sandilands and Olifaunt**
for |(21.268)| read |(EEWN 25b, 96: note to 330.29)|
526 **331.11 Donald nan Ord**
[line 2] for |Edward| read |Edmund|
530 **360.43 Castle of Crookstone . . . Darnley**
[line 2] for |(21.339)| read |(EEWN 25b, 99.1–4)|

KENILWORTH: EEWN 11

Since the publication of *Kenilworth* in the EEWN a further five leaves have come to light. Three of these, in the collection at Veste Coburg, Germany, are leaves 38 to 40 of Volume 1, corresponding to 1.195.16 to 1.212.13 of the first edition, or EEWN 11, 76.12–82.7. Two leaves are privately owned, namely leaves 16 and 17 of Volume 2, corresponding to 2.85.3 to 2.96.19 of the first edition, or EEWN 11, 157.86–161.36. A further leaf is recorded as being in the library of the Massachusetts Historical Society, Boston, but it has been missing for some years: this is leaf 15 of Volume 2.

The following emendations would have been included in the EEWN text had the five leaves been available at the time.

76.32 day. In (MS day ⟨i⟩ ↑I↓n) / day; in
76.34 Varney (Magnum) / his old friend and associate Foster (MS as Ed1) This is an updated version of the entry in EEWN 11.
77.9 rate—you (MS rate "you) / rate. You
77.9 distance betwixt (MS) / distance that is betwixt
77.10 farther—good (MS) / farther—Good
77.14 sunk (MS) / sank
77.26 sprung (MS) / sprang
77.28 Tressilian—it (MS) / Tressilian—It
77.35 mista'en (MS) / mistaken
78.3 the very (MS) / thy very
78.13 out—and will bear him out—in (MS out and will bear him—out in) / out in
78.18 inquiring (MS) / enquiries
78.39 right and fitting (MS) / right or fitting
79.3 discourse (MS) / discourses
79.8 occasion of (MS) / occasion for
79.10 unfortunate than (MS) / unfortunate lady than
80.2 There's (MS) / Here's
80.13 with our discretion (MS) / with discretion
80.30 achievement (MS) / achievements
80.37 at the ale (MS) / at the ale-house
81.33 into (MS) / upon
82.4 itself—she (MS) / itself. She
82.5 time—And (MS) / time—and
82.19 either have (MS) / have either
82.23 brief—is (MS breif—is) / brief—*is*
157.6 I beg you once more join (MS I beg you once more join) / I bid you once more to join
157.26 is. This (MS) / is—this
157.35 we (MS) / We
158.2 easily and fairly. (MS easily & fairly—) / easily.
158.4 peace—wait (MS) / peace. Wait
158.5 tide: it (MS) / tide; it
158.12 suspicion (MS) / suspicions
158.13 see or you (MS) / see—or than you
158.36 conceived (MS) / perceived
159.9 his secret (MS) / the secret
160.19 opportunity (MS) / opportunities
160.36 chess-queen (MS Chess-Queen) / heart The printing of 'heart' was probably an eye-slip, which occasioned the loss of a particularly fine reading.
161.10 threads (MS) / thread
161.16 similies—unless (MS) / similies, unless
161.18 insinuate (MS) / intimate
161.33 hastily together, and (MS hastily together and) / hastily, and
163.19 o' Love (MS) / a' Love
163.28 lays (MS) / toys

299 and also 301, 303, 305, 307 (running head) for |[Chap. 31]| read |[Chap. 32]|

334.16 for |whom| read |whom:|

412.25 for |25 May| read |19 May|

412.27 for |(23 and 24)| read |(22 and 23)|

432 [note 50] for |form, and the references are to Volumes 5 and 6 of the 8vo *Historical Romance* texts used by Scott.| read |form.|

464 add (after existing entry for 334.16) |334.16 with whom: (8vo) / with whom|

465 [337.22, lines 1 and 4] add |how| after |astounded Leicester|

473.22 for |page 479| read |pages 479–80|

477 [note 22] for |482| read |481|

478 [note 23] for |481| read |482 (Tilley)|

482 **2.9–10 What, ho! . . . Hostler**
for |1.1| read |2.1|

483 **4.12–15 Troth, sir . . . dead and gone**
for |3.2.1–50| read |3.2.1–51|

484 **9.40 pull their hat over their brows**
for |4.3.208| read |4.3.208–09|

484 **10.15–17 their pouch . . . dancing in it**
for |proverb| read |proverbs|. Before the full stop add |and 'The devil dances in an empty pocket' (*ODEP*, 180)|

485 **12.15 match me this catch**
for |1–3| read |14–16|

486 **15.32 a jackanape, simpering at a chesnut**
for the printed note read |a monkey smiling foolishly at a roasted chestnut which he thinks is too hot to hold.|

486 **16.22–28 town-stocks . . . pinfold . . . shelled pea-cod**
for |1.4.192| read |1.4.197|

486 add |**16.37 a trout tickled** a way of catching trout in the hand, used of those who are easily beguiled: compare *Twelfth Night*, 2.5.19–20.|

489 **34.1 cutter's law**
for |(*Woodstock*, 1826, 3.66 (Ch. 27))| read |(*Woodstock*, EEWN 19, 294.43–295.1)|

489 add |**36.33 as the haft is to the knife** apparently proverbial. Scott uses variants of the saying in *The Pirate* (EEWN 12, 297.35–36) and *Quentin Durward* (EEWN 15, 249.18–19).

490 **45.32–36 motto**
for |*Kenilworth*.| read |*Kenilworth*: see EEWN 25b, 114–17.|

491 **53.42–43 to the very outrance**
for |3.1.71| read |3.1.70–71|

491 add |**58.17 he that climbs a ladder . . . first round** proverbial: *ODEP*, 127.|

493 **73.34–39 Woodstock**
for |where he kept| read |where his grandson Henry II is said to have kept|

493 **74.36 the fiend may take all**
for |1.3.70| read |1.3.73|

494 **79.28–29 old Sir Roger Robsart**
for the printed note read |apparently a fictitious character, probably intended to be the father of Amy's father Sir John Robsart (see Historical Note, 476). In *The Battle of Floddon Field* (see next note) the fierce fighter is the father of Bryan Tunstall and not a Robsart.|

497 add |**95.13 ugly as sin** proverbial: *ODEP*, 853.|

497 **95.29–30 I would have given them the candle to hold**
for |1.4.37| read |1.4.37–38|

498 add |**106.4 the best friends must part** proverbial: *ODEP*, 290.|

499 **110.24 mareschal**
for the printed note read |the last English usage of *mareschal* in the sense of 'farrier' recorded by *OED* is dated *c.* 1720. The French *maréchal* with that meaning was becoming obsolete in French usage in Scott's time.|

500 **115.27 Edmund. I have cause to weep**
for |2.4.281| read |2.4.283|

500 **119.27–28 worse heraldry than metal upon metal**
for |See Note G . . . this point.| read |See EEWN 25b, 27.36–28.12 for a discussion of this point in a Magnum note to *Ivanhoe*.|

500 **122.27 hold the end of a feast . . . fray**
[line 2] for |4.2.74–75| read |4.2.76–77|

501 **126.5–6 Ban . . . man**
for |2.2.172–73| read |2.2.173–74|

504 **148.33 vogue la galère**
before the final full stop add |: compare *CLA*, 118|

505 **156.10 Do you bandy looks and words with me . . .?**
for |1.4.81| read |1.4.83|

506 **167.15–16 a vain and unjust pretence to the throne of England**
[line 8] add before the full stop |and Mary was their granddaughter|

506 **168.8 golden opinions from all sorts of men**
for |1.7.33| read |1.7.32–33|

508 **179.23–24 with the flight of a lapwing**
for |3.1.24| read |3.1.24–25|

508 **182.22 the Scotch wild cattle**
for |(22.342)| read |(EEWN 25b, 121: note to 182.22)|

512 **211.37 crown imperial**
for |4.1.246| read |4.1.257|

513 add |**223.14–15 she hath my head under her girdle** proverbial: Ray, 196; *ODEP*, 360–61.|

515 **245.30 as the play says, 'God be with your labour!'**
add at end of note |In his letters Scott habitually (but wrongly) attributes the phrase to Ophelia in *Hamlet*: see James C. Corson, *Notes and Index to Sir Herbert Grierson's Edition of the Letters of Sir Walter Scott* (Oxford, 1979), 185 (note to 332 (b)).

515 in **246.19 a sea of troubles** delete |see|

516 **247.33–34 But age has clawed me . . . song says**
for |sings a stanza from it in *Hamlet*, 5.1.69–72| read |sings this stanza from it in *Hamlet*, 5.1.71–74|

516 **252.13–14 treading on the kibes . . . worship**
for |5.1.133| read |5.1.137–38|

517 add |**257.31 as thou art powerful be merciful** proverbial: see *ODEP*, 778 ('As you are stout/strong be merciful'). James Kelly explains the proverb thus: '*As you are stout be merciful.* Spoken in a taunting manner to them that threaten us, whom we are not afraid of' (*A Complete Collection of Scotish Proverbs Explained and Made Intelligible to the English Reader* (London, 1721), 39: *CLA*, 169).|

517 add |**267.7–8 I knew where the shoe pinched** proverbial: Ray, 156; *ODEP*, 725.|

517 **267.9–10 I promised . . . gaberdine**
for |2.3.108–09| read |2.3.112|

517 **273.17–18 the porcelain clay of the earth**
add at end of note |For the origin of the phrase ('the porcelain clay of human kind') see John Dryden, *Don Sebastian* (1690), 1.1.240.|

518 add |**273.34 live and let others live** proverbial: Ray, 131; *ODEP*, 473.|

518 add |**274.14–15 I have . . . head under my belt** proverbial: Ray, 196; *ODEP*, 360–61.|

518 **279.6 a hole in this same Tressilian's coat**
for |3.6.80| read |3.6.78–81|

519 add |**281.35–36 turn them all round his finger** proverbial: *ODEP*, 847.|

519 **284.31 fierce vanities**
for |1.1.53| read |1.1.54|

519 **285.40 Saint Barnaby**
for the third line read |was the longest day. See Ray, 39, and Spenser, *Epithalamion* (1595), lines|

521 add |**299.42–300.1 Be Faithful, Brave, and Fortunate** compare 'Essay on Chivalry', *Prose Works*, 6.68 ('Be faithful, bold, and fortunate').|

521 **303.13 Sir Pandarus of Troy**
for |1.3.69| read |1.3.72|

521 **311.35 fair Callipolis**
for |2.4.164| read |2.4.169|

521 **312.12–15 I have heard the sea . . . a town stormed**
for |1.2.196–205| read |1.2.196–206|

522 **313.41 then, element do thy work**
for |5.2.309| read |5.2.314|

522 add |**316.14 acting as they would be done by** proverbial, deriving from Luke 6.31: Ray, 131; *ODEP*, 191.|

524 add |**349.33 victors of the world** Richard Blackmore, *Alfred* (London, 1723), 4.320 (p. 120).|

524 **360.23 they are tilting here**
for |2.3.173| read |2.3.175|

524 in |**362.35 the general massacre . . . 1012**| read |**1002**|

525 add |**376.25–26 the frozen snake . . . bosom** see Aesop's fable of the Farmer and the Snake.|

526 **389.2–3 a springe, Tony, to catch a pewit**
for |5.3.293| read |5.2.298|

529 delete |**chesnut** stale joke 15.32|

534 **jackanape**
for printed gloss read |ape 15.32; ape-like person 192.5, 360.22|

534 **linsey-wolsey**
for |see note 21.22| read |made of wool and linen material, nonsensical 21.22|

534 **long-breathed**
for printed gloss read |able to sustain violent exercise of the lungs for a long time 29.20; long-winded 381.14|

535 **muster**
for printed gloss read |pattern, assembling or coming together 151.43, 351.43|

537 **quadrille**
for printed gloss read |one of four costumed groups 351.25, 352.3|

542 delete |Donningham| and its dot

THE PIRATE: EEWN 12

416.37 for |£1.37½| read |£1.57½|
426.11 for |(1823)| read |(issued 1823; dated 1824)|
426.13 for the first |(1824)| read |(1825)|
448 [note 9] for |2.44–55| read |EEWN 14, 144.32–148.41|
449 [note 32] for printed note read |EEWN 25b, 138.39–139.24.|
486.34 for |farther| read |further|
492.7 for |in| read |upon|
495 [note 4] for printed note read |EEWN 25b, 138.15–19.|
496 [note 23] for |Magnum, 24.x–xi| read |Magnum (EEWN 25b, 138.39–139.24).
496 [note 28] for printed note read |EEWN 25b, 138.35–38.|
501 **4.10 superstition of the country**
[last line] for |Magnum, 25.50| read |Magnum (EEWN 25b, 154–55: note to 213.14)|
505 **12.3 plantie-cruive**
for |Magnum, 24.13| read |Magnum (EEWN 25b, 139: note to 12.3)|
506 **15.17 Berserkar**
[last line] for |Magnum, 24.19| read |Magnum (EEWN 25b, 139–40: note to 15.21)|
507 **17.21 daring adventures**
for |Magnum, 24.23| read |Magnum (EEWN 25b, 140: note to 17.23)|
507 **17.31–38 still preserved amongst them . . . wild poems**
[line 6] for |Magnum, 24.29–30| read |Magnum (EEWN 25b, 140–41: note to 18.3)|
507 **18.25 marine monsters**
for |(Magnum, 24.30–31)| read |(Magnum: EEWN 25b, 141–42: note to 18.28)|
507 **19.22 warlike sword-dance**
[line 6] for |(Magnum, 24.266–71)| read |(EEWN 25b, 146–51: note to 141.36)|
510 **26.30 the scarf**
for |(Magnum, 24.44)| read |(Magnum: EEWN 25b, 142.39–41)|
510 **27.1–2 new chamberlain's new Scots tacksman**
[line 7] for |Earl| read |Earls|, and for |Islands| read |islands|
[lines10–11] for |(Magnum, 24.65)| read |(EEWN 25b, 143.8–12)|
511 add |**27.28 take any port in a storm** proverbial: *ODEP*, 15.|
512 add |**31.28 like oil to the flame** proverbial: Ray, 141; *ODEP*, 587.|
514 **36.20 poor Tusser**
for |Magnum, 24.62| read |Magnum (EEWN 25b, 143: note to 36.22)|
515 add |**40.19 good people were scarce** proverbial: *ODEP*, 322.|
515 add |**40.21 self-preservation as the first law of nature** proverbial: *ODEP*, 712.|
516 add |**41.31–32 as I live by bread** compare Luke 4.4.|
516 **44.31 Portugal pieces**
for the printed note read |gold coins from Portugal.|
519 **50.6–12 cloak . . . crimson cloth**
for |(Magnum, 25.21–23)| read|(EEWN 25b, 153.2–12)|
520 add |**53.11–12 those that are made in God's image** see Genesis 1.26.|
520 **53.22 take the beetle to you**
for |Magnum, 24.94| read |EEWN 25b, 143: note to 53.22|
520 **56.28 as poor as Job**

add to note |The phrase is proverbial: Ray, 225; *ODEP*, 638.|

521 delete |**57.43 the careful skipper will sleep still enough** see Job 3.13.|

521 **58.26–27 the chapman's drouth**
for |(Magnum, 24.103)| read |(Magnum: EEWN 25b, 143: note to 58.27)|

521 **59.9 test upon it**
for |(Magnum, 24.105)| read |(EEWN 25b, 143: note to 59.9)|

521 **59.13 say an oraamus to Saint Ronald**
[lines 1–2] for |Magnum, 24.105| read |Magnum (EEWN 25b, 143: note to 59.14)|
[line 2] for |*oramus*| read |*oremus*|
[line 4] for |*Oramus* is Latin for 'we pray'| read |An *oremus* is a Latin prayer introduced by the word meaning 'let us pray'|

522 **65.19–20 selling favourable winds**
[line 4] for |(Magnum, 24.viii)| read |(EEWN 25b, 138.8–11)|
[line 5] for |Winds', in Magnum, 24.136–37| read |Winds' in the Magnum (EEWN 25b, 143–44: note to 65.20)|

522 **70.34–35 do you some capital injury**
for |Magnum, 24.137| read |Magnum (EEWN 25b, 144–45: note to 70.35)|

523 **75.17–18 mair wrecks ere winter**
for |Magnum, 24.137–38| read |Magnum (EEWN 25b, 145: note to 75.18)|

527 **88.21 the white linen raiment**
for the printed note read |see Revelation 19.8, 14, and (for 'raiment') Matthew 28.3.|

527 **90.36–37 little mills which manufacture their grain**
[line 8] for |one island| read |the islands|
[line 9] for |(Magnum, 24.198)| read |(EEWN 25b, 145: note to 105.23)|

527 **93.2 Maiden-skerrie**
for the final sentence read |See Scott's footnote at 253.39–41.|

528 **96.22 has taken a serpent into his bosom**
for the printed note read |in Aesop's fable of the Farmer and the Snake a man finds a frozen snake and puts it in his bosom to warm it; it revives and stings him.|

530 **105.23–26 the impudence to call a corn-mill . . . paltry mill-stone**
for |Magnum, 24.198| read |Magnum (EEWN 25b, 145: note to 105.23)|

530 add |**105.31 The mair cost the mair honour** proverbial: Ray, 90; *ODEP*, 145.|

535 add |**132.39–40 your burning blighting falcon eyes . . . rout about** see e.g. William Falconer (1732–69), *The Shipwreck*, ed. James Stanier Clarke (London, 1804: *CLA*, 197), 59 (Canto 2, line 178): 'With ardent eye, the Falcon marks his prey'.|

536 add |**133.11–12 as bold as a lion** proverbial: *ODEP*, 72.|

537 **139.19 Spoken like an angel**
for |I Corinthians| read |1 Corinthians|

538 **140.28–29 Montrose**
[last line] for |Magnum, 24.259| read |Magnum (EEWN 25b, 146: note to 140.31)|

538 **140.41 John Urry, or Hurry**
[line 4] for |Magnum, 24.260| read |Magnum (EEWN 25b, 146.16)|

538 **141.36 the sword-dance**
for |Magnum, 24.266–71| read |Magnum (EEWN 25b, 146–51: note to 141.36)|

538 **144.9 Mermaids**
[last line] for |at 24.31| read |(EEWN 25b, 141–42: note to 18.28)|

542 **160.43 Operam et oleum perdidi**
add to end of note |Plautus (*c.* 254–184 BC), *Pœnulus*, line 332.|

543 **165.29–30 a fool may ask . . . answer**
for the printed note read |proverbial: *ODEP*, 274.|

545 add |**178.28–32 no closing of the eyes . . . tasted of slumber**
compare Proverbs 6.10: 'Yet a little sleep, a little slumber, a little folding of the hands to sleep'.|

545 **179.9–10 Mine is no day-light tale—by that lamp it must be told**
for |Mirror', in Magnum, 41.306–07| read |Mirror': EEWN 24, 53.27–54.5|

545 **180.14–15 the Dwarfie Stone**
for |Magnum, 24.350–51| read |Magnum (EEWN 25b, 151–52: note to 180.27)|

547 **186.14–17 sport as the tortures of the dog-fish afford the fisherman . . . in blindness and agony**
for |Magnum, 24.348| read |Magnum (EEWN 25b, 152: note to 186.17)|

548 **194.32 The moral bard**
for |ed. Claire Lamont (Oxford, 1981), 330| read |EEWN 1, 353.11–12|

548 **195.42 the subject of inquiry**
for |Magnum, 25.21–23| read |Magnum (EEWN 25b, 152–54: note to 204.30)|

549 **197.29 fash his beard**
add at end of note |Compare *ODEP*, 246.|

549 **201.19–20 Spaniards . . . 1588**
for |a note at Magnum, 25.15| read |a Magnum note (EEWN 25b, 152: note to 201.20)|

551 **213.14 the promise of Odin**
for |Magnum, 25.50| read |Magnum (EEWN 25b, 155.2–5)|

552 **215.9–10 various spectres in which sailors of all nations have implicit faith**
for |Magnum, 25.43| read |Magnum note (EEWN 25b, 155: note to 215.10)|

552 **215.11 Coffin-key**
for |Magnum, 25.43| read |Magnum: EEWN 25b, 155.12–15|

553 **224.6–8 A line of Virgil . . . future events**
for |(Magnum, 25.60)| read |(Magnum, EEWN 25b, 155: note to 224.7)|

556 **245 motto**
for |Magnum, 25.98| read |Magnum (EEWN 25b, 155: note to 245.6)|

557 **253.19 Burghs and Picts-houses**
[line 2] for |Magnum at 17.335–39| read |Magnum (EEWN 25b, 30.17–31.36)|
[line 4] for |Magnum, 25.124| read |Magnum: EEWN 25b, 155–56: note to 254.9|

558 **260.33–34 Peter MacRaw's . . . Caberfae**
for |Magnum, 25.127| read |Magnum: EEWN 25b, 156: note to 260.35|

559 **267.44–45 remedy is peculiar to the isles of Thule**
for |(25.140)| read |(EEWN 25b, 156: note to 268.1|

559 **268.1 a narrative connected with Scottish antiquities**
for |ed. Claire Lamont (Oxford, 1981), 340| read |EEWN 1, 363–64 (363.13–14)|

559 add |**269.29 two flowers on the same stalk** see *A Midsummer Night's Dream*, 3.2.211, where Helena remembers Hermia and herself as resembling 'Two lovely berries moulded on one stem'.|

560 add |**277.2 for love or money** proverbial: *ODEP*, 493.|

560 **279.13 a horn full of old coins**
for |Magnum, 25.174| read |Magnum (EEWN 25b, 157: note to 279.15)|

561 for |**279.40 apicibus**| read |**279.40 in apicibus**|

561 **280.5 in nomine**
for the printed note read |short for 'in nomine Domini' (*Latin* in the name of the Lord).|

561 **280.17–19 Lindsays . . . braes of Islay**
[line 5] for |Islay,| read |Islay|

561 **283.37–38 the word Shogh**
for the printed note read |interpretable as an equivalent to Gaelic *Sealdh*, meaning 'Yes indeed'.|

563 **291.2–3 grouse, more plentiful in Orkney**
for |Magnum, 25.183| read |Magnum (EEWN 25b, 157: note to 291.4)|

565 add |**292.20–21 what is got over his back is spent—you wot how** 'What is got over the devil's back is spent under his belly': Ray, 97; *ODEP*, 329.|

565 add |**297.35–36 as the blade to the hilt** apparently proverbial. Variants of the saying are also used in *Kenilworth* (EEWN 11, 36.33) and *Quentin Durward* (EEWN 15, 249.18–19).|

566 **308.32–33 our hands were clasped within the circle of Odin**
for |note, Magnum, 25.50| read |note, EEWN 25b, 155.1–8|

567 **311.1–2 the mightiest as well as the most miserable of beings**
for |Magnum 25.225| read |Magnum (EEWN 25b, 157–58: note to 311.2)|

567 **312.1 birds of prey**
for |(Magnum, 25.226)| read |(Magnum: EEWN 25b, 158.20–22)|

567 **316.9–12 fired off his pistols . . . pleasantry**
[line 3] for |sat| read |sate|
[line 5] for |(Magnum, 25.233)| read |(EEWN 25b, 158.36–40)|

571 **332.35–38 Here are half a dozen of warrants . . . presently**
for |(Magnum, 28.189–91)| read |(Magnum: EEWN 25b, 239–41: note to 109.18)|

571 **335.26–28 mickle bicker . . . ever was brewed**
[last line] for |25.157| read|EEWN 25b, 156.42–157.4|

576 **359.22–23 this singular monument of antiquity**
for |Magnum, 25.315–16| read |Magnum (EEWN 25b, 159: note to 359.21)|

THE FORTUNES OF NIGEL: EEWN 13

x.10 for |*Francis*| read |*Frances*|
129.8 for |"So| read |So|
411.23 for |im-pressed| read |impressed|
411.24 for |ques-tionable| read |questionable|

433 The diagrammatic stemma is wrong: the second and third editions are identical to the first, but have new title pages; they do not derive from a marked-up copy of the first edition.

450.37 for |to heard| read |to have heard|

517.33 for |Huntingdon| read |Huntinglen|

521.29 for |(26.xiv–xv)| read |(EEWN 25b, 172.1–4)|

521.41 for |Explatory| read |Explanatory|

525.39 for |(26.x–xi)| read |(EEWN 25b, 170.1–25)|

527.47 for |(26.194–95)| read |(EEWN 25b, 180.11–27)|

528.3 for |(26.xi)| read |(EEWN 25b, 170.26–32)|

528.10 for |(26.130)| read |(EEWN 25b, 178–79: note to 84.41)|

531.38 for |read a first time for| read |read for|

531.39 for |(26.vi, xvi)| read |(EEWN 25b, 168.19, 172.25–28)|

541.37 for |[White Kennet,] *A Complete History of England*, 3 vols (London, 1706)| read |[John Hughes and White Kennet], *A Complete History of England*, 3 vols (London, 1706), 2.661–792|

545 **8.33 Letters . . . Oxford**
[line 5] for |(1773–1833)| read |(1774–1833)|

548 **13.18 Kennaquhair**
for |(18.xlvii)| read |(EEWN 25b, 54.28–29)|

555 **30.23–24 English pock-pudding swine**
[line 7] for |(1.219)| read |(EEWN 25a, 75: note to 103.24)|
[line 9] for |(27.176)| read |(EEWN 25b, 185: note to 297.35)|

560 **42.41 the groaning cheese**
for |(3.29)| read |(EEWN 25a, 115: note to 17.26)|

562 **48.19 Portugal piece**
for the printed note read |gold coin from Portugal.|

566 **64.19–20 a learned man . . . one quill**
for |(26.91)| read |(EEWN 25b, 177: note to 64.20)|

571 add |**73.37–38 It's ill taking the breeks . . . Highlandman** not found in traditional proverb books, but possibly an adaptation of 'It is ill getting Breeks aff a bare Arse' (Ramsay, 93; see also Ray, 296, and *ODEP*, 84, 802). However the wording 'Its ill taking a Breek off an Highlandman' is found in a manuscript 'Collection of Scots Proverbs' in the Abbotsford Library (*CLA*, 169), unfoliated, under 'I', no. 248. As Highlanders wore a plaid, or kilt, the proverb means you cannot do the impossible. Scott also uses the expression in *Waverley*, EEWN 1, 245.33–34 and in *Rob Roy*, EEWN 5, 220.21.|

578 **102.14–19 Mistress Turner . . . starch**
[line 5] for |(26.167)| read |(EEWN 25b, 179.21–23)|

587 **136.36–38 such bandying . . . thrice**
for |(26.239)| read |(EEWN 25b, 182–83: note to 136.38)|

588 **144.22–23 Maitre de Cuisine . . . pourtant**
[last line] for |(26.258)| read |(EEWN 25b, 183: note to 144.36)|

590 **145.38 cuckoo's nest . . . city of London**
for |(26.258–59)| read |(EEWN 25b, 183–84: note to 145.41)|

590 **147.8 a hog in armour**
for |*ODEP*, 147.8| read |*ODEP*, 376|

591 **148.34 Burbage . . . the Fortune**
for |(26.259)| read |(EEWN 25b, 184: note to 150.28)|

592 **150.28–32 Burbage . . . imagination**
[line 2] for |(26.259)| read |(EEWN 25b, 184: note to 150.28)|

596 **164.34 the cloven foot**
add at end of note |Showing the cloven foot is proverbial: *ODEP*, 129.|

620 **288.11–18 Scaandalum Maagnatum . . . Roman tongue**
[line 5] for |Here he| read |Here Moniplies|
621 add |**287.14 rather have her room than her company** proverbial: *ODEP*, 683.|
625 **306.27–32 Not that celebrated pistol . . . Mhic-Allastair-More**
for |(27.202)| read |(EEWN 25b, 185: note to 306.34)|
625 **307.15 the leathern bottle**
for |(27.202–03)| read |(EEWN 25b, 185–86: note to 307.17)|
628 **326.24–25 in some slight sort**
for the printed note read |**326.24–25 to confess . . . redress** proverbial: *ODEP*, 248. The expression 'in some slight sort' means 'to a little extent'.|
629 add |**334.7–8 when she is again trusted . . . the fox to keep** proverbial: *ODEP*, 285.|
634 **354.38–39 some monopoly . . . knighthood**
[line 8] for |he would charge| read |he could charge|
636 **361.5 casting a leglen-girth**
for |(27.301)| read |(EEWN 25b, 190: note to 361.5)|
637 **364.20–21 Prayer-Book . . . amazement**
for the printed note read |the opening and closing words of the Form of Solemnization of Matrimony in the Book of Common Prayer are 'Dearly beloved' and 'amazement'.|
641 add |**380.27 drank like a fish** proverbial: *ODEP*, 203.|
642 add |**384.40–41 Curse not . . . bed-chamber** see Ecclesiastes 10.20.|
642 add |**387.14–15 there are as gude fish . . . out of it** proverbial: *ODEP*, 263.|
647 add |**404.1–2 slew, and took possession** see 1 Kings 21.19.|

PEVERIL OF THE PEAK: EEWN 14

603.46 for |(28.vi)| read |(EEWN 25b, 206.11–12)|
605.43 for |(28.ix–x)| read |(EEWN 25b, 207.38–208.4)|
606.42 for |(Magnum, 28.viii–ix)| read |(EEWN 25b, 207.17–23)|
606.46 for |(28.x)| read |(EEWN 25b, 208.10–18)|
606.49 for |(xi–xiv)| read |(208.28–210.3)|
611.7 for |(30.77)| read |(EEWN 25b, 271.17–29)|
613.3 for |(28.101)| read |(EEWN 25b, 238–39: note to 63.32)|
625 **10.38–39 truths severe in fairy fiction dressed**
[line 2] for |(28.lxxxiii)| read |(EEWN 25b, 234.8–12)|
630 **21.26–27 Cuckolds and Roundheads**
for |*Woodstock*, 3 vols (Edinburgh, 1826), 1.141–42| read |*Woodstock* (1826), EEWN 19, 63.1–4|
632 **31.29 The sun is on our side of the hedge now**
for |(28.189)| read |(EEWN 25b, 239–41: note to 109.18; 240.18–19)|
633 **32.20–24 motto**
add to note |The second line alludes to the proverb 'Good wine needs no bush' (Ray, 169; *ODEP*, 326).|
637 **49.8–9 The pannel . . . gradually continued to slide back**
for |(28.92–94)| read |(EEWN 25b, 235–37: note to 49.21)|
640 **58.9–10 he passed from the judgment-seat . . . soul's sake**
for |(28.94)| read |(EEWN 25b, 238.11–13)|
642 **66.37 held as my page**
for |(28.107)| read |(EEWN 25b, 239.5–8)|

647 add |**86.17–18 many one caresses the infant . . . keeper** proverbial: Ray, 286; *ODEP*, 429.|

648 **97.33–35 Bitterer indeed . . . valiantly for the truth**
for |Acts 5.4| read |Acts 5.41|

648 **101.10 the Dobby's Walk**
for |(28.171)| read |(EEWN 25b, 239: note to 101.10)|

652 **114.29–31 one of those physiognomies . . . misfortune**
[line 2] for |(28.200–01)| read |(EEWN 25b, 245: note to 114.31)|

654 **136.36–39 the fatal edict . . . belly-gods and thieves**
[line 7] for |(28.145)| read |(EEWN 25b, 239.15–18)|

657 **150.34–37 Castle of Holm-Peel . . . place of residence**
for |(29.24–28)| read |(EEWN 25b, 246–50: note to 151.10)|

660 **159.33 gentle coz**
for |1.5.66| read |1.5.63|

662 for |**179.43 cry aloud**| read |**179.43 cry aloud and spare not**|

662 **181.28–32 motto**
for |l.65| read |1.65|

662 add |**187.13 thick, and palpable** the phrase occurs in the first paragraph of the Dedication in the Authorised Version of the Bible.|

663 **197.18–19 the Mauthe Dog**
for |in Magnum, 29.26–28| read |in a Magnum note (EEWN 25b, 248.30–249.36)|

663 **203.12–16 The Countess had seen her . . . her retinue**
[line 2] for |(29.129)| read |(EEWN 25b, 260–61: note to 203.16)|

667 add |**214.28 the lion's share** proverbial: *ODEP*, 467.|

677 **278.29–31 The Plot is non-suited . . . ranting on t'other**
[line 2] for |(29.287)| read |(EEWN 25b, 266–67: note to 278.30)|
[line 12] for |accordingly received| read |received accordingly|

677 **278.40–279.3 the epitaph . . . made upon**
[line 15] for |(29.266)| read |(EEWN 25b, 267.18–21)|

679 **280.40–43 as my good Lord said . . . the King**
for |(29.270)| read |(EEWN 25b, 267: note to 280.43)|

679 **281.32–33 Little Anthony . . . begot it himself**
for |(29.272)| read |(EEWN 25b, 267: note to 281.33)|

682 **292.7 Jerningham**
for |(29.309–10)| read |(EEWN 25b, 268–70: note to 299.41)|

682 **294.16–17 this Settle is so dull a rascal . . . take**
for |(29.295)| read |(EEWN 25b, 267: note to 294.16)|

696 **359.39 sad-eyed prophets**
for |Henry V| read |*Henry V*|

699 **375.37–38 the bien morts, who bing out to tour at you**
for |(30.106)| read |(EEWN 25b, 272: note to 375.38)|

701 **384.42 nose slit as wide as Coventry's**
for |(30.123)| read |(EEWN 25b, 272: note to 384.42)|

704 **400.35–36 no time to change my satin buskins for riding boots**
[line 5] for |(30.155)| read |(EEWN 25b, 272: note to 400.36)|

706 **410.23–25 Buckingham, falling a little behind . . . occasion**
[penultimate line] for |(30.177)| read |(EEWN 25b, 273: note to 412.24)|

711 **423.37–40 there was once a fuax . . . the aice**
[line 7] for |(30.200)| read |(EEWN 25b, 273–74: note to 424.9)|

715 add |**444.26 the bird was flown** proverbial: *ODEP*, 61.|

718 add |**455.14 the lady . . . foreign accent** the Duchess had accompanied Queen Henrietta Maria when she went into exile in 1644.|

723 **492.43–493.1 I only used . . . her faculties**
[line 2] for |(30.337)| read |(EEWN 25b, 275–76: note to 493.1)|

735 **minauderie(s)**
for |conquettish 115.26| read |coquettish manner or air, coquetry, flirtation, affectation 115.26|

738 **pursuivant**
for |royal| read |state|

743 **whenever**
for |418.39| read |101.13, 418.39|

QUENTIN DURWARD: EEWN 15

18.5 for |"temple and tower,"| read |'temple and tower,'|
297.23 for |sad thou| read |sad as thou|
404.40 for |1822 letter| read |1823 letter|
424.17 for |***Historical Romances****. . . . Historical Romances*| read |***Novels and Romances****. . . . Novels and Romances*|
425.40 for |15 January 1831| read |16 January 1831|
446.29 for |'(late proofs).| read |'(late proofs)'.|
448 for |18.5 "temple and tower,"| read |18.5 'temple and tower,'|
480 add |297.23 sad as thou (MS) / sad thou|
488 360.12 delete |(MS as Ed1)|
497.4 for |1467| read |1477|
498 for |Catherine| read |Cathérine|
500.3 for |Magnum, 31.174–75n| read |Magnum: EEWN 25b, 311: note to 112.31|
506 [note 8] for |(32.156–57)| read |(EEWN 25b, 315: note to 274.10)|
507.29 for |*History of Louis*| read |*History of Lewis*|
508.1 for |P. Mathieu,| read |[P. Mathieu,]|

509 **4.12 land and beeves**
for |3.2.300| read |3.2.306|

516 **29.3 his "fair cousin of Burgundy"**
for |Charolais' (Petitot| read |Charolais': Petitot|

519 **47.2 Glen-houlakin . . . Glen of the Midges**
[line 4] for |Edward| read |Edmund|

519 **47.27–29 I am of the Douglasses' mind . . . squeak**
[line 3] for |205–06.| read |205–06, and David Hume of Godscroft, *The History of the Houses of Douglas and Angus* (Edinburgh, 1644; reissued in 1648 for sale in London: *CLA*, 3), 259, 350.|

522 **61.9–10 I would have known thee . . . stilts**
[line 2] for |rivers. They are| read |rivers, are|
[last line] for |(Magnum, 31.72n)| read |(Magnum: EEWN 25b, 306.12–15)|

524 **70.35–36 our old Scottish proverb . . . kindred**
for |31.90| read |(EEWN 25b, 306: note to 70.36)|

525 add |**74.11–12 "heathen hounds"** see *The Ancient, Honorable, Famous, and delightfull Historie of Huon of Bourdeaux* . . ., trans. Sir John Bourchier, Lord Berners, 3rd edn (London, 1601), G5v (Ch. 32).|

537 **154.1–3 in the eastern character . . . cabalistic characters**
[line 4] for |1.125 etc.| read |1.125 etc.: *CLA*, 53.|

550 **258.22–26 To maintain . . . their share**
for |Magnum, 32.123| read |Magnum (EEWN 25b, 314.31–42)|

555 **287.31–32 silver shall be the screen . . . altar**
for |cited in Magnum, 32.252| read |followed in Magnum (EEWN 25b, 320.26–33)|

556 **297.24–25 the Wild Huntsman**
[line 5] for |(32.194)| read |(EEWN 25b, 316–17: note to 297.25)|

557 **310.15 the following extraordinary prayer**
for |(32.234–35)| read |(EEWN 25b, 318.29–36)|
559 add |**319.12 first frown of fortune** see *King Lear*, 5.3.6: 'false Fortune's frown'. The Shakespearean phrase is very common, but 'the first frown of fortune' is Scott's own, first used here.|
559 **321.24–26 this only I can tell . . . your Majesty**
[line 2] for |(32.251)| read |(EEWN 25b, 319.19–27)|
561 **333.31–32 Booted-Head**
[line 13] for |(32.271n)| read |(EEWN 25b, 321.8–10)|
568 **390.8 for two and a plack**
for |(Magnum, 32.381)| read |(Magnum: EEWN 25b, 325: note to 390.8)|
570 **400.41–401.11 as Ariosto . . . Stanza 16**
for |And how| read |'And how|
575 for |**colour** appearance| read |**colour** *noun* appearance|
575 for |**colour** disguise| read |**colour** *verb* disguise|
580 **feudatory**
for |holders| read |holder|

SAINT RONAN'S WELL: EEWN 16

394.36 for |'1728'| read |'1828'|
414 [note 67] for |28 vols| read |48 vols|
449 **6.28 Quaere aliud hospitium**
[line 2] for |*Diversaria*| read |*Diversoria*|
[last line] for |(Magnum, 33.13)| read |(Magnum: EEWN 25b, 336: note to 6.28)|
449 **7.17–18 even after the nineteenth century had commenced**
[last line] for |(33.14–15)| read |(EEWN 25b, 336–37: note to 7.21)|
450 **8.39 they maun hae a hottle**
for |(Magnum, 33.18)| read |(Magnum: EEWN 25b, 337: note to 8.39)|
451 **19.29 Luckie Buchan**
[lines 6–7] for |(Magnum, 33.38)| read |(Magnum: EEWN 25b, 337: note to 19.30)|
452 add |**21.24–25 he jumped . . . like a cock at a grossart** proverbial: Ray, 223; *ODEP*, 415.|
455 for |**33.20 Trustees' school**| read |**33.20 Trustees' School**|
461 add |**81.18 what must be shall be** a common proverbial expression in various languages.|
462 add |**87.43–88.2 my tongue . . . an unruly member** see James 3.5–8.|
462 **91.26 counsel learned in the law**
for the printed note read |Alexander Pope, *Satires of Horace Imitated* (1733), Satire 1, line 8; see also 2 *Henry IV*, 1.2.128–29.|
462 add |**92.39–40 as broken a ship's come to land** proverbial: Ray, 282; *ODEP*, 723.|
463 add |**94.43 mony ane come for wool . . . shorn** proverbial: Ray, 170; *ODEP*, 913–14.|
463 **95.40 service is nae inheritance**
add at end of note |Proverbial: Ray, 155; *ODEP*, 716.|
464 add |**98.10 drive the nail too far** compare the proverbs 'Drive the nail that will go' and 'Drive the nail to the head' (*ODEP*, 204).|
464 add |**99.30 you start at a shadow** proverbial: Ray, 174; see *ODEP*, 5.|
464 add |**100.30–31 as changeable as a weathercock** proverbial: *ODEP*, 875.|

464 add |**101.41–42 we have two strings to our bow** proverbial: Ray, 138; *ODEP*, 852.|

464 **102.40 the Raw-head and Bloody-Bones**
add to end of note |Proverbial: *ODEP*, 665. See also Samuel Butler, *Hudibras*, Part 3 (1680), 2.682.|

464 **105.11 peculiar cogniac**
for |Baronet's| read |Baronet|

464 **106.20 come up to the scratch**
add at end of note |Proverbial: *ODEP*, 706.|

465 **110.31 kettle of fish**
[line 2] for |cauldron| read |caldron|
[line 3] for |salt, to| read |salt to|
[line 5] for |(Magnum, 33.210)| read |(Magnum: EEWN 25b, 338.21–27)|

465 add |**114.38 a prettier kettle of fish** proverbial: *ODEP*, 421.|

466 **126.10 meat and mess**
for the printed note read |**126.10 meat and mess never hindered wark** proverbial: Ray, 300; *ODEP*, 521 ('Meat and mass never hindered any man').|

467 **132.5 no proof that a crime has been committed**
[line 2] for |for murder| read |for a murder|
[lines 3–4] for |(Magnum, 33.247)| read |(Magnum: EEWN 25b, 338: note to 132.5)|

469 add |**140.28–29 reckoned without her host** alluding to the proverb 'He that reckons without his host must reckon again' (*ODEP*, 667; compare Ray, 289).|

470 **150.32 Mag-Pico**
[line 3] for |Magnum, 33.287| read |EEWN 25b, 338–39: note to 150.32|

473 **165.34 When Greek . . . tug of war**
add at end of note |Proverbial: *ODEP*, 336.|

474 **165.38 Piquet**
[line 3] for |the minor| read |the major or elder|
[line 4] for |the major or elder| read |the minor|
Add at end of note |In the standard 18th-century work on the game, the rule upon which Mowbray insists and which allows him to win reads: 'If you [the Elder-hand] call a Point, and do not shew it, you reckon nothing for it; and the Younger-hand may shew, and reckon his Point.' (Edmond Hoyle, *Mr. Hoyle's Games of Whist, Quadrille, Piquet, Chess, and Backgammon*, 13th edn (London, [1763?]), 154: *CLA*, 134).|

480 **218.24 Clarissa Harlowe**
for |*Clarissa Harlowe* (1747–48)| read |*Clarissa* (1747–48)|

480 **222.14–15 the McIntoshes**
for |(Magnum, 34.79)| read |(Magnum: EEWN 25b, 340: note to 222.15)|

481 **226.14–15 There is a Heaven above us . . . each other**
add to end of note |The expression 'Heaven is above all' is proverbial: *ODEP*, 365.|

482 **240.20 What if I should personate the bridegroom**
for |text at 271.11–273.8 for a discussion| read |text at 271.11–273.8 and note to 273.13–14 for a discussion|

482 add |**242.33 the congregation of the righteous** Psalm 1.5.|

483 add |**253.37 marrying and giving in marriage** Matthew 24.38.|

485 **265.29 Law is a lick-penny**
for |4.39.15 (Ch. 39)| read |EEWN 6, 355.37–38|

485 **265.38 With your counsel learned in the law**
for the printed note read |see Alexander Pope, *Satires of Horace Imitated* (1733), Satire 1, line 8; see also *2 Henry IV*, 1.2.128–29.|

486 **281.29 hail fellow well met**
for |Apperson, 342; and *ODEP*, 277| read |Apperson, 277; and *ODEP*, 342|

486 **282.35–36 Vergeben sie . . . wenig**
[line 2] for |(Magnum, 34.188)| read |(Magnum, EEWN 25b, 340: note to 282.36)|

487 **282.37–40 Rauchen sie . . . topf**
for |(Magnum, 34.188)| read |(Magnum, EEWN 25b, 340: note to 282.40)|

487 **289.9 bing folks on the low toby**
for |(Magnum, 34.200)| read |(Magnum, EEWN 25b, 340: note to 289.9)|

488 **293.3 paullo post futurum**
for the printed note read |*Latin, literally* shortly after the future. The phrase is used to describe the future perfect tense in Greek, and as used in this context means that Mr Pot is always 'about to have received his supplies'.|

489 **310.42 mony words mickle drought**
add at end of note |Proverbial: Ray, 300; *ODEP*, 916.|

490 add |**322.25 to-morrow is a new day** proverbial: *ODEP*, 829.|

490 **324.32–33 Tippoo's prison at Bangalore**
for |In 1798, Wellesley invaded Mysore, and Tippoo was killed in 1799, defending| read |In 1799, Sir Arthur Wellesley (1769–1852), the future Duke of Wellington, invaded Mysore, and Tippoo was killed defending|

492 add |**353.1 as rich as a Jew** in *Castle Rackrent* (1800) Maria Edgeworth writes of 'the old proverb of "*as rich as a Jew*"': ed. Jane Desmarais, Tim McLoughlin, and Marilyn Butler (London, 1999), 23 (*The Novels and Selected Works of Maria Edgeworth*, ed. Marilyn Butler and Mitzi Myers, 12 vols (London, 1999–2003), 1). The phrase is recorded in the late 17th century. It is also used in *The Betrothed*, EEWN 18a, 5.14.|

493 **371.15–16 the Peninsula, where war was then at the hottest**
[line 2] for |English| read |British|

494 **adust**
for the printed gloss read |*either* in a dusty condition, affected by dust *or* tawny 154.7|

506 for |**skylark**| read |**sky-lark**|

REDGAUNTLET: EEWN 17

98.16 for |father's| read |guidsire's|
100.36 for |father| read |guidsire|
154.39 for |b[?]ood| read |blood|
420 add |98.16 guidsire's (18mo) / father's (MS fathers)|
420 add |100.36 guidsire (18mo) / father (MS as Ed1)|
443 [note 6] for printed note read |EEWN 25b, 367: note to 222.34.|
445 add before **1.5** |**title page epigraph** *As You Like It*, 2.3.69–70.|

446 **2.37–38 pin a losen, head a bicker, and hold the bannets**
for |(1.xci–xcvi)| read |(EEWN 25a, 46–49)|

447 **4.10–11 from the corner of the bench, and with covered head**
for |(Magnum, 35.9)| read |(Magnum: EEWN 25b, 359.36–38)|

448 **4.30 circle of consanguinity**
for |*Rob Roy*, 1.241–42| read |*Rob Roy* (1818), EEWN 5, 87.15–32.|

448 **5.40 quid tibi cum lyra?**
for |and to Ovid| read |and Ovid|

450 **9.5 Luckie Simpson's cow**
for |(1.114–15)| read |(EEWN 25a, 70.20–42)|

456 **20.21–22 struck them with their barbed spears**
for |*Guy Mannering*, 2.61.12–14| read |*Guy Mannering* (1815), EEWN 2, 136.16–19|

456 add |**22.18 sat like a tower** see John Milton, *Paradise Lost* (1667; rev. 1674), 1.591.|

465 in note to 69.21 for |**'twere**| read |**'twere**|

473 **89.16–17 Major Weir . . . that was burnt**
[line 5] for |wizardry| read |fornication|

474 **90.20–21 said he had given him blood instead of burgundy**
for |(10.381)| read |(EEWN 25a, 200.10–12)|

476 **96.28–29 Dumbarton Douglas . . . country and king**
for |(1589–74)| read |(1589–1660)|

476 **97.1–2 the savage Highland Amorites . . . water**
[last line] for |Magnum, 10.319| read |Magnum: EEWN 25a, 197.12|

478 **103.16 Sowport, frae the Nicol Forest**
for the printed note read |Sowport (Solport) is a parish 15 km N of Carlisle in Nicol Forest, a district once heavily wooded, stretching S from the modern Kershope Forest. See *Minstrelsy*, 2.163, 166; see also David Macpherson, *Geographical Illustrations of Scottish History* (London, 1796): *CLA*, 3.|

480 add |**113.30 Love once and love no more** compare John Milton, *Lycidas* (1638), line 131: 'smite once, and smite no more'.|

481 **116.26–27 Peter Peebles**
[line 4] for |opinion that he| read |opinion he|
[line 5] for |(Magnum, 35.241)| read |(EEWN 25b, 365.2–3)|
[lines 6–10] for |No litigant . . . single prototype.| read |According to Graham Robertson (an EEWN reader) Peter or Patrick Peebles belonged to Linlithgow. He was the son of John Peebles, cowper, and his wife Agnes Simpson. He married Margaret Robertson on 2 April 1743, and they had 11 children. In the 1780s he was trading as a baker, but became insolvent: he transferred his property to trustees on 13 November 1784, and on 8 August 1794 the trustees sold the property on behoof of creditors.|

481 **116.29 as poor as Job**
add to end of note |The phrase is proverbial: Ray, 225; *ODEP*, 638.|

484 **126.23–24 zealous . . . even to slaying**
add to end of note |The expression 'zealous even to slaying' occurs in Abraham Cowley, *Cutter of Coleman-Street* (1663), 5.6.|

485 **131.2–3 drive the swine through our bonny hanks of yarn**
for |(35.253)| read |(EEWN 25b, 365: note to 131.3)|

486 **134.22 make a spoon or spoil a horn**
for |(35.259)| read |(EEWN 25b, 365: note to 134.22)|

486 **135.41–42 an acute metaphysical judge**
[line 4] for |(35.262)| read |(EEWN 25b, 365: note to 135.41)|

487 **137.36 transporting persons**
for |(36.76)| read |(EEWN 25b, 367: note to 215.7)|

488 add |**143.30 hissing-hot** see note to 218.40.|

489 add |**150.6 bite as well as bark** compare the proverb 'Great barkers are no biters': *ODEP*, 30 (see also Ray, 76).|

495 add |**186.9–10 as thirsty as sorrow is said to be** alluding to the proverb 'Sorrow is always dry': *ODEP*, 754.|

500 **214.34–37 although, even of late years . . . temporary purpose**
for |(36.76)| read |(EEWN 25b, 367: note to 215.7)|

503 **229.23–24 one may love the Kirk . . . rigging of it**
add at end of note |See Ray, 123; *ODEP*, 490.|

504 **232.19 Turnpenny**
For |(see Magnum, 36.145)| read |(see Magnum: EEWN 25b, 368–69: note to 251.6)|

504 **232.33–35 like the man who met the devil . . . say to them**
for the printed note read |see [Daniel Defoe], *The Farther Adventures of Robinson Crusoe*, 2nd edn (London, 1719), 295 (*CLA*, 125): 'like the Man who met the Devil, if they [parties of Tartars] had nothing to say to us, we had nothing to say to them'.|

507 **248.31–32 Merry Thoughts . . . small Hours**
[line 2] for |*Miscellany*'| read |*Miscellany*|

509 **258.27 the devil a**
for the printed note read |**258.27–28 the devil a crumb . . . my bread** proverbial: Ray, 180; *ODEP*, 95. The expression 'the devil a' means 'never a'.|

510 add |**261.9–10 no scum . . . uppermost** the proverbial nature of the image is suggested by [George Huddesford], *The Scum Uppermost when the Middlesex Porridge-Pot Boils Over!!* (London, 1802).|

514 **299.36–39 five blood-specks . . . miseries**
for |(36.230–31)| read |(EEWN 25b, 369: note to 299.39)|

518 add |**324.20 hast risen from thy wrong side** proverbial: *ODEP*, 678–79.|

518 **326.11–12 The King's keys . . . patent**
for |(Magnum, 5.305; EEWN 3, 167.13n| read |(Magnum, EEWN 25a, 150: note to 167.13)|

521 add |**349.35–36 Not a Popish dog or cat . . . his Majesty** in *Peveril of the Peak*, EEWN 14, 280.40–43, Chiffinch talks of 'these times, when, as my good Lord said in the House, there should not be a Popish man-servant, nor a Popish maid-servant, not so much as dog or cat, left to bark or mew about the King!' Scott attributes this remark to Shaftesbury in the Magnum (25b, 267.28–29). David Hume attributes the *mot* to a 'noble peer' and quotes him as saying: 'I would not have . . . so much as a popish man or a popish woman to remain here; not so much as a popish dog or a popish bitch; not so much as a popish cat to pur or mew about the king' (*The History of England* [originally published 1754–62], 8 vols (London, Edinburgh, and Glasgow, 1805), 8.85: compare *CLA*, 28).

522 **355.36–357.42 note, Number D. . . . annihilate even the semblance of a royal party in Great Britain**
for |(Magnum, 35.xii–xvi)| read |(EEWN 25b, 354.6–355.6)|

535 **plack**
for |stirling| read |sterling|

THE BETROTHED: EEWN 18a

371 **6.3 Walladmor**
for |be by Friedrich August Herbig, freely| read |be freely|

378 add |**17.9 profited him nothing** see 1 Corinthians 13.3.|

389 **72.13–17 motto**
add to end of note |Its author was Sir Gilbert Elliot (1722–77), who succeeded as 3rd Baronet of Minto in 1766.|

398 for |**143.1 Timon of the woods**| read |**143.18 Timon of the woods**| and move note down 3 lines

407 **203.14 singular fortification**
[line 10] for |(1498 or 1499–*c.* 1575)| read |(d. *c.* 1575)|
[line 11] for |(d. 1546)| read |(d. 1544)|

THE TALISMAN: EEWN 18b

308.2 for |the whole of| read |the first half of|
369.37 for |Edward IV of England (1461–83)| read |Edward I of England (1272–1307)|
369.40 for |(38.viii–xi)| read |(EEWN 25b, 395.37–396.43)|
384 delete note to 13.21 His age could not exceed thirty
428 add |**267.20–21 Slay not soul and body** see Matthew 10.28: 'And fear not them which kill the body, but are not able to kill the soul: but rather fear him which is able to destroy both soul and body in hell.'
430 **277.33 the celebrated talisman**
for |000| read |369|

WOODSTOCK: EEWN 19

350.34 for |says| read |say|
426.25 for |afforded ample| read |afforded an ample|
464 [note 25] for |Magnum, 39.vi| read |EEWN 25b, 414.10–18|
465 [note 36] for printed note read |EEWN 25b, 413.2–10.|
465 [note 37] for |(39.iii–lxiv)| read |(EEWN 25b, 413–41)|
466 [note 71] for printed note read |EEWN 25b, 173.1–9.|
467 [note 115] for printed note read |EEWN 25b, 442.14–15.|
548 [note 15] for printed note read |EEWN 25b, 421–27.|
548 [note 17] for |Magnum, 39.xx| read |EEWN 25b, 420.22–38|
548 [note 22] for |Magnum, 39.xxxvii–xli| read |EEWN 25b, 428–30|
548 [note 28] for |Magnum, 39.vi| read |EEWN 25b, 414.10–18|
548 [note 34]
[line 2] for |39.v, vii–xviii| read |EEWN 25b, 413.18–419.36|
[line 3] for |on xv| read |at 418.15|
[line 4] for |on xviii| read |at 419.27|
[line 6] for |xv| read |418|
550 [note 64] for |(40.395)| read |(EEWN 25b, 447–48: note to 417.8)|
552 **3.3 the Rev. J. A. Rochecliffe, D.D.**
for |(Magnum, 39.lxixn)| read |(Magnum: EEWN 25b, 442: note to 3.35)|
555 **8.24 Bevis**
for |(40.395)| read |(EEWN 25b, 447–48: note to 417.8)|
555 **9.15–17 carried their Bibles . . . sword**
for |(39.7)| read |(EEWN 25b, 442: note to 9.17)|
556 **9.39 her ordinances, dry bran and sapless pottage**
for |(39.8, 22–23)| read |(EEWN 25b, 442–43: note to 13.33)|
564 **29.27 a Ragged Robin**
for |(39.46)| read |(EEWN 25b, 443: note to 29.27)|
581 **87.22** for |**look back**| read |**look not back**|
581 delete note |**87.23–24 look not back**|
583 **96.29 broad Portugal pieces**
for the printed note read |gold coins from Portugal.|
584 **105.11–16 Sometimes it is a pack of hounds . . . the stag is gone**
[line 6] for |(32.194)| read |(EEWN 25b, 316–17: note to 297.25)|
587 **117.14–16 tampering with him . . . seal with**
for |1227–28| read |127–28|
599 **183.21–33 Forced over the battlements . . . cut off and destroyed**

[line 2] for |(39.346–47)| read |(EEWN 25b, 443–44: note to 183.41)|
[line 5] for |43–45.| read |43–45: compare *CLA*, 240.|

605 **215.17 a hungry tyke . . . rough bane**
for the printed note read |proverbial: see *ODEP*, 196.|

606 **219.5–6 Lunsford's light-horse . . . babe-bolter**
for |(40.43–45)| read |(EEWN 25b, 444–46: note to 221.33)|

606 **219.42–220.3 Then let the health go round . . . kiss the ground**
[line 6] for |(8.343)| read |(EEWN 25a, 277: note to 323.29)|

607 **221.37–42 Miss Edgeworth . . . pocket**
for |(40.43)| read |(EEWN 25b, 444.40–43)|

613 add |**252.8 pocketing a little wrong** proverbial: *ODEP*, 636.|

620 **303.15–17 nisi dignus . . . masculine**
for |*De Arte Poetica*| read |*Ars Poetica*|

626 **335.41–42 give this feather to Mistress Alice Lee**
[line 2] for |(40.296)| read |(EEWN 25b, 447.31–34)|

631 add |**383.8–9 puffed and blew like a grampus** *ODEP*, 330, gives this as the first example of the proverbial saying.|

CHRONICLES OF THE CANONGATE: EEWN 20

118.24 indent line

354 [note 228] for |*The Waverley Novels*, 41.[iii]–vii, xxx–xxxiv| read |EEWN 25b, 460–63|

355 [note 232] for |*The Waverley Novels*, 48.[149]–50| read |EEWN 25b, 482–83|

355 [note 237]
[line 1] for |*The Waverley Novels*, 48.[151]–157| read |EEWN 25b, 483–86|
[line 3] for |*The Waverley Novels*, 9.227–36| read |EEWN 25a, 178.42–182.32|

380 **4.19–20 public meeting . . . Theatrical Fund**
[last line] for |(41.[xxxv]–lxxiii)| read |(EEWN 25b, 464–82)|

380 **5.9 that celebrated wanderer**
for |9.222–27| read |EEWN 25a, 176.16–178.33|

381 **5.23 Lockerby**
for |(Magnum, 9.227–28, 233–35)| read |(Magnum: EEWN 25a, 181.17–182.25)|

381 **5.40–41 I am unable to present to the public**
[last line] for |(11.142–47)| read |(EEWN 25a, 290–93)|

381 **6.38–39 one of the few surviving friends of my father**
for |(41.xvii)| read |(EEWN 25b, 490: note to 6.32)|

381 **7.1–2 the Baron of Bradwardine and Colonel Talbot**
[lines3–4] for |(*Waverley*, ed. Claire Lamont (Oxford, 1981), 225–26, 260–61, 312–13)| read |*Waverley* (1814), EEWN 1, 240.42–41.16, 277.3–278.22, 333.15–334.40)|

383 **9.5 Wolf's Hope**
[last line] for |(41.xxiv)| read |(EEWN 25b, 490.36–39)|

383 for |**10.20**| read |**10.12**|; for |**10.28**| read |**10.20**|; for |**11.1**| read |**10.36**|; for |**11.8**| read |**10.43**|; for |**11.9–11**| read |**11.2–3**|; and for |**11.26**| read **11.18**|

387 **17.27 the congregation of the just**
add to end of note |The phrase as given by Scott is found in the 16th

and 17th centuries, sometimes meaning the company of the redeemed in Heaven.|

387 add |**19.29 The light of life . . . was trembling in the socket** proverbial: *ODEP*, 100.|

388 **22.1 played small game than sat out**
add at end of note |See also *ODEP*, 631.|

390 add |**25.6 chambering and wantonness** Romans 13.13.|

390 add |**25.9 brute beasts** 2 Peter 2.12; Jude verse 10.|

391 add |**27.26 the eyes . . . of my understanding** see Ephesians 1.18.|

392 for |**30.29 in terrorem**| read |**30.29 in terrorem to**|

393 **33.25 some feudal Bastille**
for |(32.219n–220n)| read |(EEWN 25b, 317: note to 309.39)|

398 **48.19 Tomanthoulich**
for |000.00| read |127.2 (435 below)|

400 **53.17 Mrs Martha Bethune Baliol**
[line 4] for |(41.xxxii)| read |(EEWN 25b, 462.27–29)|

401 **55.30 ship-shape and Bristol fashion**
add at end of note |Proverbial: *ODEP*, 724.|

403 **59.30 the fortunes of Britain in 1715**
for |*Waverley*, ed. Claire Lamont (Oxford, 1981), 338| read |*Waverley* (1814), EEWN 1, 361.13–14|

411.38 for |Macturk, nor the demure washing-woman| read |MacLeish, nor the demure waiting woman|

413 [note 7] for |41.xxxiii–xxxiv| read |EEWN 25b, 463.11–19|

413 [note 10] for |Magnum, 41.xxxii| read |EEWN 25b, 462.24–463.6|

413 [note 16] for printed note read |EEWN 25b, 463.11–22.|

416 **71.13 incumbent at Glenorquhy**
for |(41.128)| read |EEWN 25b, 498: note to 71.13)|

422 add |**90.20 put your head under the belt** proverbial: Ray, 196; *ODEP*, 360–61.|

422 **90.30–31 the unhappy house of Glenlyon**
[line 5] for |*Glenlyon*,| read |*Glenlyon*|

425 add |**108.10 ever fair and false** first used in the form 'you Scots are ever fair and false' in *The Fortunes of Nigel* (EEWN 13, 381.37–38), and glossed in a Magnum note to *The Talisman* (404 above, note to 142.40). It fuses the proverbs 'There is many (a) fair thing full false' (Ray, 305; *ODEP*, 240), and 'False as a Scot' (Ray, 221; *ODEP*, 243). It was considered proverbial by the end of the 19th century: see Andrew Cheviot, *Proverbs, Proverbial Expressions, and Popular Rhymes of Scotland* (Paisley and London, 1896), 99.|

426 **111.13 the Black Tree of the Law**
for |*Quentin Durward*, 3 vols (Edinburgh, 1823), 1.54–55| read |*Quentin Durward* (1823), EEWN 15, 43.11–12|

427 add |**118.26 spread out the heavens** see Isaiah 40.22.|

431 [note 7] for printed note read |EEWN 25b, 463.23–30.|

434 **125.30 Glunamie**
for |42.74| read |EEWN 25b, 528–29: note to 34.23|

434 **126.17–18 McCombich (or, son of my friend)**
[line 3] for |*Waverley*, ed. Claire Lamont (Oxford, 1981), 74–75| read | *Waverley* (1814), EEWN 1, 80.13|

435 **127.26 walk the deasil round you**
[line 9] for |*Waverley*, ed. Claire Lamont (Oxford, 1981), 118| read |*Waverley* (1814), EEWN 1, 124.19–28|
[last line] for |(1.255)| read |(EEWN 25a, 77: note to 124.24)|

439 **136.9–10 the fords of Frew**
[last line] for |(*Rob Roy*, 3 vols (Edinburgh, 1818), 3.7.24–8.1)| read |(EEWN 5, 227.41–42)|

440 **137.5–6 A hundred curses on the swine eaters**
for |*Waverley*, ed. Claire Lamont (Oxford, 1981), 118| read |*Waverley* (1814), EEWN 1, 125.21–22|

440 **137.15 he sees his own blood!**
[lines 2–3] for |*The Fortunes of Nigel*, 3 vols (Edinburgh, 1822), 1.26| read |*The Fortunes of Nigel* (1822), EEWN 13, 28.23|

441 **139.43–140.2 the Eskdale . . . Lustruther**
[line 6] for |(3.228–30)| read |(EEWN 25a, 116.30–32)|
[line 8] for |(3.271)| read |(EEWN 25a, 120.31–37)|

449.10 for |(000)| read |(408)|

456 [note 3] for printed note read |EEWN 25b, 483.5–8.|

456 [note 5] for |Magnum, 48.151–57| read |EEWN 25b, 483–86|

466 **176.32 Menie**
for |(48.219)| read |(EEWN 25b, 509: note to 178.3)|

467 **181.2–3 Galatian, or Sir William Wallace, or Robin Hood**
[line 3] for |(48.224)| read |(EEWN 25b, 509: note to 181.2)|

476 for |**234 motto**| read |**235 motto**|

479 **247.9 black robe of his order, very much torn and patched**
for |*The Talisman*, in *Tales of the Crusaders*, 4 vols (Edinburgh, 1825), 4.71| read |*The Talisman* (1825), EEWN 18b, 159.30|

491 **288.3 friend and neighbour, Colonel MacKerris**
[penultimate line] for |(48.150)| read |(EEWN 25b, 483.10–14)|

499 **derogation**
for |loss or honour| read |loss of honour|

THE FAIR MAID OF PERTH: EEWN 21

389.23 for |Rob is| read |Rob's|

389.23 for |take| read |tak|

409.5 for |(Magnum, 42.359)| read |(EEWN 25b, 533.19)|

409.23 for |(Magnum, 42.89)| read |(EEWN 25b, 529.8–9)|

409.24 for |(Magnum, 1.176)| read |(EEWN 25b, 531.3)|

417.23 for |see Magnum, 42.59)| read |see Magnum, 42.59, emended at EEWN 25b, 527.33)|

418 [note 1] for the printed note read |*Rob Roy* (1818), EEWN 5, 215.33–34.|

420 [note 80] for |Centre| read |Center|

472 in |**6.25 'London prentice bold'**| read |**'prentice**|

472 for |**8.13 Open Sesamun**| read |**8.13 Open Sesamum**|

474 **11.16 Lady Mary Wortley Montague**
[line 6] for |The passage to which Scott refers has not been identified.| read |In a letter of 1 April 1717, Lady Mary praises Sofia, Bulgaria, for its situation where mountains yield to plains; on 24 July 1749 she described her favourite retreat of Lóvere on Lake Iseo, N Italy, underneath the foothills of the Alps, as 'a place the most beautifully romantic I ever saw in my life'; and on 11 December 1758 she wrote: 'I have found, wherever I have travelled, that the pleasantest spots of ground have been in the vallies which are encompassed with high mountains' (*The Works of the Right Honourable Lady Mary Wortley Montagu*, [ed. James Dallaway], 6th edn, 5 vols (London, 1817), 2.150–51, 4.20, 5.66 (*CLA*, 202).|

475 **12.24 the Wicks of Beglie**
[line 2] for |Magnum, 42.title-page| read |EEWN 25b, 516|

[line 3] for |see Magnum, 42.24–25| read |526–27: note to 13.3|

475 **15.2–4 To-morrow is Saint Valentine's Day . . . with the kite**
for |4–5.46| read |4.5.46|

476 **16.19–24 What have we . . . in my company**
for |(2.271.2–5)| read |(EEWN 5, 206.38–41|

477 **22.27–28 English Warden . . . Redman**
for |(Magnum, 42.43)| read |(EEWN 25b, 528.2–4)|

477 **23.36 St Leonard's Crags**
for |1.271.17–272.15| read |EEWN 6, 95.26–96.12|

477 **25.8** for |**the head**| read |**thy head**|

477 **30.19 Culross girdles**
for |see Magnum, 52.57n| read |see Magnum note, EEWN 25b, 528: note to 30.19|

479 in **38.35–37** for |**love's darts**| read |**Love's darts**|

480 **50.30 Jamie Keddie's ring**
for |(42.102)| read |(EEWN 25b, 530: note to 50.30)|

481 **59.29–30 the sins of vanity . . . easily beset**
for |151.17| read |28.36|

482 add |**64.19 put your fingers in the fire** proverbial: Ray, 190; *ODEP*, 657.|

483 **69.27 horse and hattock**
for |see Magnum, 42.140| read |see EEWN 25b, 530: note to 69.27|

483 **70.8–30 It was the custom . . . in the field**
for |2.44.22–23| read |EEWN 15, 147.18–19|

485 **79.2 their Oliver meet with a Rowland**
for |tit for tat| read |tit for tat: Ray, 208; *ODEP*, 682|

488 **93.30 thiggers and sorners**
for |see Magnum, 42.190| read |see EEWN 25b, 532: note to 93.30|

488 **94.21 the Galilee of the Church**
for |see Magnum, 42.191n| read |see Magnum, EEWN 25b, 532: note to 94.21|

490 **106.33–34 a Court of Love and Music . . . Count Aymer**
[line 7] for |qualiWcation| read |qualification|

492 **123.41 in the manner**
for the printed note read |in the act of doing something unlawful: see *OED*, mainour[2]; Numbers 5.13; *1 Henry IV*, 2.4.303.|

493 **130.14–15 writing materials . . . the churchman was alone able to use**
[line 6] for |(Magnum, 42.260)| read |(EEWN 25b, 532: note to 130.14)|

498 **170.1–8 My dog and I . . . my dog and I**
add at end of note |See also *Letters*, 8.367 and note.|

504 **236.13–15 the skull of Wallace . . . Margaret Logie**
[line 4] for |(Magnum, 43.86)| read |(EEWN 25b, 536: note to 236.15|

504 for |**239.27 Opiserque**| read |**239.27 Opiferque**|

506 add |**263.33 as black as a wolf's mouth** proverbial: *ODEP*, 167–68.|

506 **266.26–28 old makar, . . . counsel thee**
[line 5] for |in| read |on|
[last line] for |Magnum, 43.146| read |EEWN 25b, 542: note to 266.28|

507 **276.5 Tin-Egan**
for |(Magnum, 43.165)| read |(EEWN 25b, 542: note to 276.5)|

508 **278.30 Mohr ar chat**

for |(Magnum, 43.170)| read |(EEWN 25b, 542.25)|

509 **289.34 poor as Job**
add at end of note |The phrase is proverbial: Ray, 225; *ODEP*, 638.|

510 **301.8 hand has warmed my haffits**
for |Magnum, 43.215)| read |EEWN 25b, 543: note to 301.8)|

512 **317.39 better to hear the lark sing than the mouse squeak**
[lines 1–2] for |Implying that| read |Implying, that|
[line 4] for |see Magnum, 43.247).| read |EEWN 25b, 543: note to 317.39). For the saying see Andrew Cheviot, *Proverbs, Proverbial Expressions, and Popular Rhymes of Scotland* (Paisley and London, 1896), 205–06, and David Hume of Godscroft, *The History of the Houses of Douglas and Angus* (Edinburgh, 1644; reissued in 1648 for sale in London: *CLA*, 3), 259, 350.|

512 add |**319.4–5 as if he trode upon eggs** proverbial: *ODEP*, 218.|

512 **322.4 Saint Andrew with his shored cross**
for |*Flodden*| read |*Floddon*|

514 **338.38–39 How long held out . . . of Hermitage**
for |(Magnum, 43.287)| read |(EEWN 25b, 543: note to 338.42)|

518 **377.30 I fought for my own hand**
[line 5] for |here and in *Rob Roy* (2.296.19–20)| read |here, as well as in *Rob Roy* (1818), EEWN 5, 215.33–34, and *The Fortunes of Nigel* (1822), EEWN 13, 350.20–22,|

ANNE OF GEIERSTEIN: EEWN 22

321.4 for |overfriends| read |over friends|
418.12 for |one-volume| read |two-volume|
512.39 for |commomly| read |commonly|
518 [note 23] for |*A a Series*| read |*A Series*|
521.13 for |(Paris, 1819)| read |(Paris, 1819–26)|

522 **6.5–7 had invaded the Forest Cantons . . .. Russwyl**
for |000| read |514|

523 **13.1–6 Geierstein . . . lord of the castle**
[lines 8–9] for |Various places . . . Scott's invention.| read |Geierstein is the name of a mountain near Lenggries in the Bavarian Alps. It appears in E. T. A. Hoffmann, *Lebens-Ansichten des Katers Murr* (Life and Opinions of the Tom-Cat Murr), 2 parts (Berlin, 1828: first published 1819–21), 1.16 etc.

530 **93.6 the coward knights of Cornouailles**
for |(44.173)| read |(EEWN 25b, 567: note to 93.6)|

530 **94.31 with the beard . . . Spaniard says**
for |1.156| read |EEWN 14, 72.22–25|

534 **142.15 Bohemians . . . Escossais**
for |1.32| read |EEWN 15, 34.29|

541 **219.21–37 They appeared anxiously engaged . . . rightly done**
for |(44.ix)| read |(EEWN 25b, 559–60)|

544 **244.24–25 the Wild Huntsman**
[line 5] for |(32.194)| read |(EEWN 25b, 316–17)|

546 **265.17–21 Louis XI. . . . descriptions**
for |*Quentin Durward*, 3.264.23–24| read |*Quentin Durward* (1823), EEWN 15, 364.22–24|

552 **283.8 King of Sicily**
for |511| read |511–12|

552 add |**284.19 as the scum . . . uppermost** the proverbial nature of

the image is suggested by [George Huddesford], *The Scum Uppermost when the Middlesex Porridge-Pot Boils Over!!* (London, 1802).|

554 **303.3 Martin Blok**
for |2.212| see |EEWN 15, 242.20|

559 add |**337.22 walls have ears** proverbial: *ODEP*, 864.|

578 for |**ttête-du-pont**| read |**tête-du-pont**|

COUNT ROBERT OF PARIS: EEWN 23a

400.46 for |6.22| read |36.22|

424.15 for |emenda-tions| read |emendations|

424.31 delete |A number of footnotes . . . the final volumes of the EEWN.|

503.28 for |*History*| read |*The History*|

513 **40.32 Waes hael, Kaisar mirrig und machtigh**
for |cā sere| read |cāsere|

518 **77.39–41 The Prophet Balaam . . . to him**
for |23.27–28| read |22.27–28|

531 add |**180.3 Stone walls can hear** proverbial: *ODEP*, 864.|

533 **209.12–13 the troth . . . Odin**
[last line] for |Magnum, 25.50, 315.16| read |Magnum: EEWN 25b, 154–55: note to 213.14; 159: note to 359.21|

534 **215.25–27 The Saxons . . . Rome**
[line 21] for |as well God| read |as well as God|

537 add |**250.27–30 "Tancred," says Mr James, "whose valour . . . truth."** see G. P. R. James, *The History of Chivalry* (London, 1830), 88.|

537 **261.27–29 Grammaticus . . . ibit**
for |Satire| read |*Satire*|

542 add |**315.37 a sea of trouble** see *Hamlet*, 3.1.59.|

CASTLE DANGEROUS: EEWN 23b

261.1 for |(47.245)| read |(EEWN 25b, 583.16–19)|

262.10 delete |As with all of the *Tales and Romances* texts . . . supplementary volumes.|

388.33 for |(47.306)| read |(EEWN 601: note to 19.14)|

388.33 for |Douglas Haddow| read |Thomas Haddow|

405.3 for |Lockhart, the| read |Lockhart, omitted in the present edition, the|

409 **150.30 the Bloody Sykes**
[line 2] for |(48.87)| read |(EEWN 25b, 602: note to 150.31)|

409 add |**156.28–29 his Hotspur-like disposition to tire of the recitation** see *1 Henry IV*, 3.1, where Glendower wearies Hotspur with his store of Welsh omens.|

416 **207.7–8 My plough . . . the furrow**
for |therefore| read |therefore,|

THE SHORTER FICTION: EEWN 24

147.36 for |19 January| read |29 January|

195.26 for |Pringle| read |Primrose|

195.27 for |Pringle| read |Primrose|

239 add |**21.14 without form and void** Genesis 1.2.|

स्टार

अंग्रेज़ी – हिन्दी
हिन्दी – अंग्रेजी

शब्द कोश

Edited and Compiled by

JOSEPH W. RAKER
RAMA SHANKAR SHUKLA

32,000 से अधिक शब्दों का
पर्यायवाची अनुवाद

सम्पादक :

जोज़फ डब्लू. रेकर
रमाशंकर शुक्ल

भूमिका

श्री सुधाकर पांडे
(प्रधान मंत्री, नागरी प्रचारिणी सभा)

STAR

ENGLISH-HINDI
HINDI-ENGLISH
COMBINED DICTIONARY

with
a detailed glossory of official terms

STAR
ENGLISH - HINDI HINDI - ENGLISH DICTIONARY

This Edition : 2008

Price : Rs. 260/-

Star Publications (P) Ltd.
4/5, Asaf Ali Road, New Delhi-110002
E-mail : starpub@vsnl.net

Printed at Star Print-O-Bind, Delhi.

Index क्रम

नये संस्करण की भूमिका

यह अत्यंत प्रसन्नता की बात है कि अंग्रेजी, हिन्दी व हिन्दी अंग्रेजी कोश का नवीन संशोधित परिवर्धित संस्करण हिन्दी जगत के सम्मुख है। जब इसका प्रकाशन हुआ था उस समय इस कोश की उपयोगिता और गुण धर्म के कारण मैंने यह आशा व्यक्त की थी, कि हिन्दी का प्रशासनिक जगत, सामान्य शिक्षा जगत, और हिन्दी प्रेमी इस कोश का इसके गुण धर्म के कारण सम्मान करेंगे। मेरी यह धारणा यथार्थ निकली और इस कोश ने अपनी एक प्रतिष्ठा स्थापित की।

कोश रचना निरन्तर चलने वाली प्रक्रिया है। यह कार्य उसे उपयोगी और अद्यतन बनाने में सहायक होता है। इस कोश के नवीन संस्करण में भी शब्दों की संख्या बढ़ी है, अर्थों में यथाकिंचित आवश्यकतानुसार परिष्कार किया गया है और इसे और अधिक उपयोगी बनाने का यत्न किया गया है। पहले संस्करण के बाद इसमें जो संशोधन परिवर्धन किया गया है उसने इसकी उपयोगिता को और बढ़ा दिया है।

ऐसे उपयोगी ग्रन्थ के प्रकाशन और सम्पादन के लिए मैं इसके प्रकाशक और सम्पादक को बधाई देता हूं।

मई २००२
नई दिल्ली

पं. सुधाकर पाण्डेय

भूमिका

यद्यपि भारत में कोश रचना की पद्धति संसार से सबसे पुरानी है किन्तु आधुनिक कोश रचना की वैज्ञानिक पद्धति अंग्रेजों की देन है। 18वीं और 19वीं शताब्दी में एक बड़ा व्यापक अनुष्ठान हिन्दी, हिन्दुस्तानी और अंग्रेजी के कोशों के निर्माण को लेकर हुआ जिसमें ईसाई मिशनरियों, प्रशासनिक अधिकारियों ने बड़े पैमाने पर योगदान दिया और 19 वीं शताब्दी के अन्त तक इस दिशा में जो भी महत्वूर्ण कार्य हुए वे सारे एक प्रकार से उन्हीं की देन है। सन् 1808 में विलियम हंटर के हिन्दुस्तानी–इंग्लिश कोश से इस काम का शुभारम्भ हुआ और बराबर इसके संस्करण होते रहे। एम.टी. आदम, डा. गिल क्राइस्ट, जान शेक्सपीयर आदि ने इस दशा में प्रारम्भिक कार्य किये। लेकिन यह सारा का सारा कार्य रोमन लिपि में होता था।

1829 में पादरी एम.टी. आदम के कोश में सबसे पहले देवनागरी लिपि का भी प्रयोग हुआ। जान शेक्सपीयर इस दिशा में सन् 1861 तक बराबर महत्वपूर्ण कार्य करते रहे। फैलेन ने "ए न्यू हिन्दुस्तानी–इंग्लिश डिक्शनरी" का निर्माण किया जो कोश विधा की दृष्टि से इनमें सबसे अधिक महत्वपूर्ण माना गया। 19वीं शताब्दी के अन्त में भारत में इस संबंध में जागरण आरम्भ हुआ और कोश रचना की प्रक्रिया स्वतः आरम्भ हुई। अनेक विद्वानों ने हिन्दी–अंग्रेजों कोश के संबंध में समय–समय पर काम किए, साथ ही शासन की ओर से भी व्यापक पैमाने पर कार्य किया गया।

सबने अपनी–अपनी दृष्टि से कार्य किए और सबके काम की अपनी विशेषताएं हैं, किन्तु लोक और ज्ञान दोनों को संतुलित मात्रा में रखकर कोश रचना की प्रक्रिया की दृष्टि से "हिन्दी–अंग्रेजी/अंग्रेजी–हिन्दी शब्दकोश" का एक अभिनव अवदान इस दिशा में हैं, जिसकी अपनी विशेषताऐं हैं।

अंग्रेजी से हिन्दी के अनेक कोश है और हिन्दी से अंग्रेजी के भी कोश कई हैं, किन्तु संयुक्त रूप से कोई ऐसा कोश नहीं है जिसके माध्यम से एक ही कोश के द्वारा दोनों कार्य सिद्ध हो सकें। पठन–पाठन तथा सरकारी क्षेत्र में इसकी आवश्यकता अत्यन्त व्यापक रूप से अनुभव की जा रही थी जिसका

समाधान प्रस्तुत कोश के माध्यम से होता है। इसकी शब्द सम्पदा भी व्यावहारिक रूप से पर्याप्त है और जन साामान्य और सामान्यतः विद्‌वत जगत का काम इससे चल सकता है। इसके साथ ही एक अच्छी बात है कि शब्दों के अंग्रेजी अच्चारण देवनागरी लिपि में भी दिय गये हैं जिससे उच्चारण का संज्ञान सामान्य रूप से अध्ययता को हो जायेगा। इसके साथ ही शब्द चयन की प्रक्रिया में सजगता बरती गई है और यह प्रयत्न किया गया है कि वांछित शब्द सम्पदा इस कोश में आ जायें।

आज सरकार में हिन्दी के कामकाज के लिए कोशों की आवश्यकता का अनुभव बड़े व्यापक पैमाने पर किया जा रहा है और इसके निराकरण के लिए इस कोश में प्रशासनिक शब्दावली भी दे दी गई है, जिससे सामान्य व्यवहार में अत्यन्त सुविधा मिलेगी। शब्दों की अर्थ साधना में भी सजगता बरती गई है। इस तरह मेरी दृष्टि में संयुक्त रूप में प्रकाशित यह "अंग्रेजी–हिन्दी व हिन्दी अंग्रेजी कोश" इस दिशा में एक गौरवशाली, गम्भीर और लोक–हितकारी प्रयास है। मुझे विश्वास है कि सभी क्षेत्रों में इसके गुण होने के कारण सम्मान होगा और ज्ञानजगत इसे गरिमा प्रदान करेगा।

दीपावली
3.11.1994

सुधाकर पांडेय
(प्रधानमंत्री)
नागरी प्रचारिणी सभा
वाराणसी

List of abbreviations used in the Dictionary

संकेत-चिन्ह् जो इस कोष में प्रयुक्त किये गये हैं

abbr.	abbreviation.	*interj.*	interjection.
adj.	adjective.	*L.*	Latin.
adjs.	adjectives.	*mas.*	masculine.
adv.	adverb.	*med.*	medicine.
advs.	adverbs.	*mus.*	music.
alg.	algebra.	*n. ns.*	noun, nouns.
archt.	architectur.	*nout.*	nautical.
arith.	arithmetic.	*pass.*	passive.
aux.	auxiliary.	*pers.*	person.
contr.	contracted.	*phr.*	phrase.
cf.	compare.	*opp.*	opposite.
chem.	chemistry.	*pl.*	plural.
comb.	combination.	*n. sing.*	noun singular.
comp.	comparative.	*pr. part.*	present participle.
conj.	conjunction.	*p. t.*	past tense.
demons.	demonstrative.	*pres.t.*	present tense.
dim.	diminutive.	*p.p.*	past participle.
e.g.	for example.	*pref.*	prefix
esp.	especially.	*prep.*	preposition.
fut.	future.	*pron.*	pronoun.
fem.	feminine.	*Rom.*	Roman.
gram.	grammar.	*sing.*	singular.
Geog.	geography.	*suf.*	suffix.
Gr.	Greek.	*usu.*	usually.
i.e.	that is.	*v.t.*	verb intransitive.
in.	inches.	*v. t.*	verb transitive.
indef.	indefinite.	*yd. (s)*	yard (s).

अं. ग.	अंकगणित	ब. व.	बहुवचन
ए. व.	एकवचन	बी. ग.	बीज गणित
इ	इत्यादि	शि. वि.	शिल्प विद्या
औ. शा.	औषधि शास्त्र	शा. प.	शासनपद्धति
न. लि.	नपुंसक लिंग	सं.	संगीत
नौ. वि.	नौ विद्या	स्त्री. लि.	स्त्रीलिंग
पु. लि.	पुलिंग		

KEY OF TRANSLITERATION

VOWELS

Nagri character	sign	Roman	Pronunciation
अ		a	As *a* in beggar
आ	ा	A	As *a* in father
इ	ि	i	As *i* in sin
ई	ी	ee	As *ee* in meet
उ	ु	u	As *u* in pull
ऊ	ू	oo	As *oo* in pool
ऋ	ृ	ri	As *ri* in rich
ए	े	a	As *a* in gate
ऐ	ै	ai	As *a* in fat
ओ	ो	o	As *o* in hole
औ	ौ	au	As *o* in hot
अं	ं	an	As *an* in kangaroo
अँ	ँ	an	As *an* in the French—pronunciation of restaurant
अः	:	a:	Short form of ah!
ह्रस्व ए		e	As *e* in bed

CONSONANTS

Nagri character	Roman character	Pronunciation
Gutturals		
क	k	As *k* in ankle
ख	kh	
ग	g	As *g* in go
घ	gh	As *gh* in gherao
ङ	n	As *n* in hunger
Palatals		
च	c	As *ch* in church
छ	ch	

ज	j	As *j* in jar
झ	jh	
ञ	n	As *n* in punch
Cerebrals		
ट	T	As *t* in top
ठ	TH	
ड	D	As *d* in doll
ढ	DH	
ण	n	As *n* in nut
Dentals		
त	t	As *t* in French matron
थ	th	As *th* in thin
द	d	As *th* in leather
ध	dh	
न	n	As *n* in nut

There is no sign in english to represent the sounds of ड़. and ढ़ the following symbols are for them : R for ड़, Rh of ढ़ ।

Lately, certain sounds of the persian language have gained currency which are expressed by placing a dot below the corresponding letters of nagri. we shall try to imitate these sounds thus:

क़	k	As *Q* in 'quran', the sacred book of Islam
ख़	kh	As *Kh* in the name of the persian poet Umar Khaiyam
ग़	g	As *Gh* in the name of the urdu poet Ghalib
ज़	z	As *z* in zinc
फ़	f/F	As *f* in father

In Nagri every letter represents a complete sound so that it can be uttered by itself. But every consonant has a half-form also which cannot be pronounced by itself.

the half form च is ᳵ   the half form of द is द्

Whenever two consonants are conjoined the resultant conjunct, in some cases, assumes a new shape, e.g....,

क्ष ज्ञ ट्ट ट्ठ ड्ड त्त द्द द्ध द्व

द्ध झ द्य त्र ट्य ह्य क्र ध्र ट्र

त्र द्र श्र ह्व हृ ह ह्

Nagri is primarily a syllabic script. every letter of nagri represents a complete sound. Howerer, every complete sound may not be represented by a single letter, e.g..., पश्चात् (pash-čat) contains two syllabes, but four letters. To this extent, Nagri detracts from the syllabic character.

❑❑❑

उच्चारण-सम्बंधी विवरण

किसी भी भाषा का शुद्ध उच्चारण किसी अन्य भाषा के माध्यम से हो ही नहीं सकता क्योंकि प्रत्येक भाषा का अपना स्वतंत्र स्वभाव, व्यक्तित्व व चरित्र होता है तथा उसके प्रबुद्ध मूल प्रयोक्ता ही उसके शुद्ध उच्चारण की कसौटी होते हैं। प्रत्येक भाषा में कुछ ध्वनियाँ ऐसी होती हैं, जो अन्य भाषाओं में नहीं होतीं। अँग्रेज़ी में ख, घ, झ, त, ध, फ, भ, ठ, ड, ढ, ढ़, ण आदि ध्वनियाँ नहीं हैं।

उच्चारण के प्रतीकों व संकेतों का निर्धारण व चयन करते समय सरलता को प्रमुख ध्येय ही लक्ष्यों को ध्यान में रखा गया है।

संकेत व प्रतीक (Hints and symbols)

(अ) स्वर (Vowels)

प्रतीक		ध्वनि	उदाहरण		उदाहरण	
अॅ,		लघु अ	ago	अ गो	atom	ऐ टॅम
अ		सामान्य अ	under	अन् डॅर	but	बट
ऑ,	ॉ	लघु आ	out	ऑउट	about	अॅ बॉउट
आ,	ा	सामान्य आ	answer	आन् सॅः	fast	फ़ास्ट
इ,	ि	इ	It	इट	fit	फ़िट
ई,	ी	ई	eat	ईट	beat	बीट
उ,	ु	उ	foot	फुट	put	पुट
ऊ,	ू	ऊ	ooze	ऊज़	fruit	फ्रूट
ऍ,	ॅ	लघु ए	air	ऍ अॅः	pair	पॅ अॅर
ए,	े	सामान्य ए	aim	एम	fame	फ़ेम
ऐ	ॅै	लघु ऐ	ebb	ऐबॅ	self	सैल्फ़ॅ
ऐ,	ै	सामान्य ऐ	act	ऐक्ट	fact	फ़ैक्ट
ओॅ	, ोॅ	लघु ओ	omission	ओॅ मिशॅन	November	नोवैमॅ् बॅर
ओ,	ो	सामान्य ओ	oak	ओक	soak	सोक
औॅ,	ौॅ	लघु औ	on	औनॅ	pot	पौॅट
औ,	ौ	सामान्य औ	all	औल	fall	फ़ौल

संयुक्त स्वर (diphthongs)

कुछ शब्दों के उच्चारण में दो स्वरों की ध्वनियाँ मिल जाती हैं तथा ये दोनों लघु ध्वनियाँ संयुक्त रूप में एक इकाई मानी जाती हैं:

संयुक्त स्वर		उदाहरण		उदाहरण
ऑइ	eye	ऑइ	try	ट्रॉइ
ऑउ	out	ऑउट	now	नॉउ
इअ॒	ear	इअ॒:	real	रिअ॒ल
औ॑इ	oil	औ॑इल	boy	बौ॑इ
ऍअ॒	air	ऍअ॒:	mare	मे॑अ॒र
उअ॒	poor	पुअ॒:	doer	डुअ॒र

व्यंजन (Consonants)

विभिन्न शब्दों में व्यंजनों के उच्चारण सामान्य व्यंजन प्रतीकों के माध्यम से प्रस्तुत किए गए हैं। अतः इनके लिए न किसी व्याख्या की आवश्यकता है न उदाहरण की।

वर्तनी की समानता के कारण यदि दो या दो से अधिक शब्दों का उच्चारण बिल्कुल समान है तो अनावश्यक पुनरावृत्ति को बचाते हुए, क्रम में प्रथम दिए गए शब्द का ही उच्चारण अंकित किया गया है।

अंग्रेजी के उच्चारण किन्हीं कठोर नियमों से नहीं बँधे हैं। अतः विविधता व विभिन्नता इसके मुख्य लक्षण हैं। वैकल्पिक व्यवस्थाओं का बाहुल्य है। अनेक शब्द दो या अधिक प्रकार से उच्चारित होते हैं। ऐसे मामलों में अधिक प्रचलित उच्चारण को प्रथम दिया गया है तथा शेष उच्चारण/उच्चारणों के केवल परिवर्तित अंश को देकर लुप्त अंश डैश (–) से प्रदर्शित किया गया है।

इस संबंध में अक्षर r का संक्षिप्त विवेचन आवश्यक है:

1. Consonant के तुरंत पश्चात् आने वाला r अनिवार्य रूप से ध्वनित होता है, यथा try (ट्रॉइ), brown (ब्रॉउन)।

2. Vowel के तुरंत पश्चात् आने वाला r ध्वनिरहित (unsounded) रहता है, यद्यपि कुछ कोशों में इसे ध्वनित माना है। प्रस्तुत कोश में कई स्थानों पर इसे ध्वनिरहित भी दर्शाया गया हैं, यथा far (फा:), Chair (चे॑अ॒:)।

3. Vowel के पश्चात् आने वाला r कोश में दिए उच्चारण में ध्वनिरहित होते हुए भी ध्वनित हो जाता है यदि वाक्य अथवा मुहावरे में ऐसे r के आगे आने वाला शब्द Vowel से प्रारंभ होता है, यथा :

Where did he go? वे˘ अँः डिड ही गो ?

Where is he now? वे˘ अॅर इज़ ही नॉउ ?

4. कोश में ध्वनिरहित r को एक विशेष चिंह्न (:) से दर्शाया गया है।

जिस प्रकार हिंदी का सामान्य पाठक या प्रयोक्ता 'श' व 'ष' की ध्वनि के सूक्ष्म भेद से प्रायः अनभिज्ञ होता है, उसी प्रकार अंग्रेज़ी में `V' तथा `W' की ध्वनि में तात्त्विक भेद होते हुए भी सामान्य पाठक इन दोनो को एक ही ध्वनि 'व' प्रदान करता है। अतः प्रस्तुत कोश में उच्चारण के सरलीकरण के पक्ष में इन दोनों अक्षरों को समान ध्वनि का द्योतक माना गया है।

बलाघात (Stress)

अंग्रेज़ी भाषा की उच्चारण–पद्धति के अनुरूप प्रत्येक शब्द के उच्चारण को पदांशों (syllables) में विभक्त किया गया है। एकपदीय शब्दों (monosyllables) पर यह नियम लागू ही नहीं होता। ऐसे अंशों अथवा खंडों को उच्चारण में स्पष्ट रूप से दिखाया गया है। दो या दो अधिक पदांशों (syllables) वाले शब्द के उच्चारण में बलाघातित पदांशों (stressed syllables) को काले मोटे मुद्रण से स्पष्ट दिखाया गया है। कुछ शब्दों में दो पद बलाघातित है।

❑❑❑

ROMAN & HINDI NUMBER

			Sanskrit		Hindi	
			Cardinals	*Ordinals*	*Cardinals*	*Ordinals*
I	1	१	एक	प्रथम	एक	पहला
II	2	२	द्वि	द्वितीय	दो	दूसरा
III	3	३	त्रि	तृतीय	तीन	तीसरा
IV	4	४	चतुर्	चतुर्थ	चार	चौथा
V	5	५	पंच (न्)	पंचम	पांच	पांचवां
VI	6	६	षष्	षष्ठ	छः	छठा
VII	7	७	सप्त (न्)	सप्तम	सात	सातवां
VIII	8	८	अष्ट (न्)	अष्टम	आठ	आठवां
lX	9	९	नव (न्)	नवम	नौ	नवां
X	10	१०	दस (न्)	दशम	दस	दसवां

XI	11	११	ग्यारह
XII	12	१२	बारह
XIII	13	१३	तेरह
XIV	14	१४	चौदह
XV	15	१५	पन्द्रह
XVI	16	१६	सोलह
XVII	17	१७	सत्रह
XVIII	18	१८	अठारह
XIX	19	१९	उन्नीस
XX	20	२०	बीस
XXI	21	२१	इक्कीस
XXII	22	२२	बाईस
XXIII	23	२३	तेईस
XXIV	24	२४	चौबीस
XXV	25	२५	पच्चीस
XXVI	26	२६	छब्बीस
XXVII	27	२७	सत्ताईस

XXVIII	28	२८	अट्ठाईस
XXIX	29	२६	उन्तीस
XXX	30	३०	तीस
XXXI	31	३१	इकतीस
XXXII	32	३२	बत्तींस
XXXIII	33	३३	तेंतीस
XXXIV	34	३४	चौंतींस
XXXV	35	३५	पैंतीस
XXXVI	36	३६	छतीस
XXXVII	37	३७	सैंतीस
XXXVIII	38	३८	अड़तीस
XXXIX	39	३६	उन्तालीस
XL	40	४०	चालीस
XLI	41	४१	इकतालीस
XLII	42	४२	बयालीस
XLIII	43	४३	तैंतालीस
XLIV	44	४४	चौवालीस
XLV	45	४५	पैंतालीस
XLVI	46	४६	छियालीस
XLVII	47	४७	सैंतालीस
XLVIII	48	४८	अड़तालीस
IL	49	४६	उनचास
L	50	५०	पचास
LI	51	५१	इक्यावन
LII	52	५२	बावन
LIII	53	५३	तिरपन
LIV	54	५४	चौवन
LV	55	५५	पचपन
LVI	56	५६	छप्पन

LVII	57	५७	सत्तावन
LVIII	58	५८	अट्ठावन
LIX	59	५६	उनसठ
LX	60	६०	साठ
LXI	61	६१	इकसठ
LXII	62	६२	बासठ
LXIII	63	६३	तिरसठ
LXIV	64	६४	चौंसठ
LXV	65	६५	पैंसठ
LXVI	66	६६	छियासठ
LXVII	67	६७	सड़सठ
LXVIII	68	६८	अड़सठ
LXIX	69	६६	उनहत्तर
LXX	70	७०	सत्तर
LXXI	71	७१	इकहत्तर
LXXII	72	७२	बहत्तर
LXXIII	73	७३	तिहत्तर
LXXIV	74	७४	चौहत्तर
LXXV	75	७५	पचहत्तर
LXXVI	76	७६	छिहत्तर
LXXVII	77	७७	सतहत्तर
LXXVIII	78	७८	अठहत्तर
LXXIX	79	७६	उनासी
LXXX	80	८०	अस्सी
LXXXI	81	८१	इक्यासी
LXXXII	82	८२	बयासी
LXXXIII	83	८३	तिरासी
LXXXIV	84	८४	चौरासी
LXXXV	85	८५	पचासी

LXXXVI	86	८६	छियासी
LXXXVII	87	८७	सत्तासी
LXXXVIII	88	८८	अट्ठासी
XIC	89	८९	नवासी
XC	90	९०	नब्बे
XCI	91	९१	इक्यानवे
XCII	92	९२	बानवे
XCIII	93	९३	तिरानवे
XCIV	94	९४	चौरानवे
XCV	95	९५	पंचानवे
XCVI	96	९६	छियानवे
XCVII	97	९७	सत्तानवे
XCVIII	98	९८	अट्ठानवे
XCIX	99	९९	निन्यानवे

OFFICLAL TERMINOLOGY OF RANKS AND WORDS WITH EQUIVALENT TERMS USED IN HINDI

(as adopted by Government of India)

A

Abandonment परित्यजन, परित्याग

Abridgment न्यूनन

Abrogation निराकरण

Absence अनुपस्थिति, गैरहाज़िर, अभाव

Absentee अनुपस्थित, गैरहाज़िर

Academic शैक्षणिक

Academic Qualification शैक्षणिक अर्हता, शैक्षणिक योग्यता

Academy अकादमी

Accept स्वीकार करना, मानना

Acceptance स्वीकृति, प्रतिग्रहण (विधि)

Access प्रवेश, पहुँच

Account लेखा, खाता, हिसाब, गणना

Accountant लेखाकार

Accrual प्रापण, प्रोद्भवन

Accrued प्राप्त, प्रोद्भव, उपार्जित

Accusation अभियोग

Accused अभियुक्त

Achievement उपलब्धि

Acknowledgement रसीद

Acknowledge प्राप्ति स्वीकार करना, पावनी देना,

Acknowledgement पावती, अभिस्वीकृति (विधि)

Acquisition अर्जन

Act अधिनियम

Act of misconduct कदाचार

Acting (as in acting director) कार्यकारी

Actionable wrong अभियोज्य दोष

Ad hoc तदर्थ

Adaptation अनुकूलन

Additional अतिरिक्त, अपर (पदनाम में)

Address (स) पता अभिभाषण, सवाधन, मानपत्र, संबोधित करना

Addressed संबोधित

Addressed पानेवाला

Adherence अनुषक्ति

Adhoc तदर्थ

Adhoc committee तदर्थ समिति

adhoc indent तदर्थ माँगपत्र

Adjournment अवधिदान, स्थगन

Administer प्रशासन करना

Administered प्रशासित

Administering authority	प्रशासन प्राधिकारी,
Administration	प्रशासन
Administrative	प्रशासनीय, प्रशासी
Administrative ability	प्रशासन-योग्यता
Administrative approval	प्रशासनिक अनुमोदन
Administrative function	प्रशासनीय कृत्य
Administrative sanction	प्रशासनिय मंजूरी
Administrator General	महाप्रशासक
Admiralty	नौकाधिकरण, नावाधिकरण
Admissible	ग्राह्य
Admission fee	प्रवेश-शुल्क
Admission form	प्रवेश-पत्र
Adoption	दत्तक ग्रहण, दत्तक स्वीकरण
Adress of welcome	अभिनंदन-पत्र
Adult suffrage	वयस्क मताधिकार
Adulteration	अपमिश्रण
Advance	अग्रिम धन, पेशगी
Advance copy	अग्रिम प्रति
Adverse	प्रतिकूल
Adverse entry	प्रतिकूल प्रविष्टि
Advertisement	विज्ञापन
Advice	मंत्रणा, परामर्श, सलाह, सूचना, संज्ञापन
Advisory Council	मत्रंणा-परिषद्
Advise	मंत्रणा देना
Advocate	अधिवक्ता
Advocate General	महाधिवक्ता
Affect	प्रभाव डालना, प्रभावित करना
Affect prejudicially	प्रतिकूल प्रभाव डालना
Affidavit	शपथपत्र, हलफनामा
Affirmation	प्रतिज्ञान
Age limit	आयु सीमा
Age of retirement	सेवा-निवृत्ति आयु
Age of superannuation	अधिवर्षिता आयु
Agency	अभिकरण, एजेंसी
Agenda	कार्यसूची
Agent	अभिकर्त्ता, एजेंट
Agreement	सहमित, करार, अनुबंध
Air Force	विमान-बल, वायुसेना
Air navigation	विमान-परिवहन
Air traffic	विमान-यातायात
Air-ways	वायु-पथ
Airport	विमानपत्तन
Alien	अन्यदेशीय
Alienate	अन्य संक्रामण करना
Alienation	अन्य संक्रामरण, परकीयकरण
Allegation	अभिकथन, आरोप
Allegiance	निष्ठा
Allocation	बँटवारा
Allot	बाँट लगाना
Allotment	बाँट, आंबटन
Allotment order	आबंटन आदेश

Allowance भत्ता
Amendment संशोधन
Amnesty सर्वक्षमा
Amount राशि, रकम, मात्रा
Analogous सदृश, अनुरूप
Annual वार्षिक
Annual financial Statement वार्षिक वित्त-विवरण
Annuity वार्षिकी
Annulment रद्दी करण
Appeal अपील, अपील करना
Appear उपस्थित होना
Appellate tribunal अपील अधिकरण
Appended संलग्न
Applicant आवेदक
Application आवेदन, अर्जी, प्रयोज्यता, लागू होना
Appoint नियुक्त करना
Appointee नियुक्त व्यक्ति
Appointment नियुक्ति
Appropriation Bill विनियोग विधेयक
Approve अनुमोदन करना
Arbitral Tribunal मध्यस्थ न्यायाधिकरण
Arbitratior मध्यस्थ
Area क्षेत्र
Argument तर्क, बहस
Article अनुच्छेद, वस्तु नियम
Articles नियमावली
Armed Forces सशस्त्र सेना
As the case may be यथास्थिति, यथाप्रसंग
Assemble जमा होना, समवेत होना
Asembly सभा, जमाव
Assent अनुमति
Assert दृढ़ता से कहना, जोर देकर कहना
Assessment निर्धारण
Assignment समर्पण
Associate सह, सम्मिलित करना
Association संघ, सगम (विधि) संस्था
Assurance of property सम्पत्ति हस्तान्तरण पत्र
Assure आश्वस्त करना
Attached office संलग्न कार्यालय
Attention ध्यान
Attachment कुर्की, टाँच
Attendance register उपस्थिति रजिस्टर, हाज़िरी रजिस्टर
Attestation अनुप्रमाणन, तसदीक
Attorney-General महान्यायवादी
Audio-visual publicity दश्य-श्रव्य प्रचार
Audit लेखा-परीक्षा, गणना-परीक्षा
Auditor-general महालेखा-परीक्षक
Authentic प्रमाणिक
Authenticate प्रमाणित करना
Authentication प्रमाणीकरण
Authority प्राधिकारी, प्राधिकार, प्राधिकरण
Authorize प्राधिकृत करना
Autonomous स्वायत

Autonomy	स्वायत्तता, स्वायत्त शासन
Auxiliary	सहायक
Available	प्राप्य, उपलब्ध
Avoidable	परिहार्य
Award	पंचाड्ग्गा
Awareness	भान, बोध जागरूकता

B

Background	पृष्ठभूमि
Bail	प्रतिभूति, जमानत
Balance sheet	तुलन-पत्र
Ballot	मतपत्र, मतदान
Bank	बैंक अधिकोष
Banker's mortgage	बैंक बंधक
Banking	महाजनी, अधिकोषण
Bankruptcy	दिवाला
Basic education	बुनियादी शिक्षा
Basic pay	मूल वेतन
Belief	विश्वास
Beneficial	लाभप्रद
Benefit	हित, लाभ, फायदा, सुविधा
Benefit of doubt	संदेह लाभ
Betting	पण लगाना, पण क्रिया
Bicameral	दोघरा, द्विगृही
Biennial	द्विवार्षिक
Bill	विधेयक,बिल
Bill of exchange	विनिमय-पत्र
Bill of indemnity	परिहार-विधेयक, क्षतिपूर्ति-बिल
Bill of lading	वहन-पत्र
Biodata	जीवनवृत्त
Birth certificate	जन्म प्रमाण पत्र
Birth date	जन्म तिथि, जन्म तारीख
Black list	काली सूची
Black listing	काली सूची में नाम लिखना
Black market	चोर बाजार, काला बाज़ार
Blue print	ब्ल्यू प्रिन्ट
Board	मंडली, बोर्ड, परिषद्
Board of Directors	निदेशक बोर्ड, निदेशक मंडल
Body	निकाय
Body Corporate	निगम-निकाय
Body governing	शासी-निकाय
Bona Vacancia	स्वामिहीनत्व
Bonafide	वास्तविक
Booklet	पुस्तिका
Borrowing	उधार-ग्रहण
Boundary	सीमा
Boycott	बहिष्कार
Break in service	सेवा में व्यवधान
Broadcasting	प्रसारण
Budget	बजट, आय-व्ययक
Budget estimate	बजट प्राक्कलन, बजट अनुमान
Bumper	बम्पर, जोरदार, भरपूर
Bureau	ब्यूरो
Bureaucracy	अधिकारी तंत्र, नौकरशाही

Business	व्यवसाय, कारोबार
By hand	दस्ती
By post	डाक से, डाक द्वारा
Bye-election	उपनिर्वाचन
Bye-law	उपविधि

C

Cablegram	समुद्री-तार
Calculation	परिकलन
Calling	आजीविका
Camp	शिविर
Cancel	रद्द करना
Cancellation of allotment	आबंटन रद्द करना
Cancellation of indent	इडेंट रद्द करना, माँग-पत्र रद्द करना
Candidate	अभ्यार्थी, अम्मीदवार
Cantonment	कटक, छावनी
Capacity	सामर्थ्य
Capital	मूलधन, पूँजी
Capital Value	मूलधन, मूल्य
Capitation tax	प्रतिव्यक्ति कर
Carriage	परिवहन
Carry out	पालन करना
Carry over	अग्रनयन
Casting vote	निर्णायक मत
Casual	आकस्मिक, अनियत
Casual leave	आकस्मिक छुट्टी
Casualty	हताहत
Cattle pound	पशु-अवरोध, काँजी-हौज
Cause	वाद
Cause of Action	वादवूल
Cease fire	अस्त्र विराम
Celebration	समारोह
Cell	प्रकोष्ठ, कक्ष
Census	जन-गणना
Central Intelligence Bureau	केन्द्रीय-गुप्त-वार्ता-विभाग
Central registry	केन्द्रीय पंजीकरण
Central revenue	केन्द्रीय राजस्व
Centre	केन्द्र
Ceremony	समारोह
Certificate	प्रमाण-पत्र
Certificate of fitness	आरोग्य प्रमाण-पत्र, दुरुस्ती, प्रमाण-पत्री
Certificate of posting	डाक प्रमाण-पत्र, तैनाती-प्रमाण-पत्र
Certification	प्रमाणन, प्रमाणीकरण
Certiorari	उत्प्रेक्षण-लेख
Cess	उपकार
Chairman	सभापति, अध्यक्ष
Channel	माध्यम, सरणि
Character Certificate	चरित्र प्रमाण-पत्र
Character roll	चरित्र पंजी

Charge	भार, भारित करना
Charge report	कार्यभार रिपोर्ट
Charge sheet	आरोप-पत्र
Charge (n.)	दोषारोप, अभियुक्ति
Charitable	दातव्य
Charitable and religious endowments	दात्वय तथा धार्मिक धर्मस्व
Charitable institution	दातव्य संस्था
Charity	खैरात, पूर्त
Check post	जाँच-चौकी
Cheque	चेक, धनादेश
Chief	मुख्य, प्रधान
Chief Commissioner	मुख्य आयुक्त
Chief Election Commissioner	मुख्य निर्वाचन आयुक्त
Chicf judge	मुख्य न्यायाधीश
Chief justice	मुख्य न्यायाधिपति
Chief minister	मुख्य-मंत्री
Chronological order	कालक्रम
Circular	गश्ती चिट्ठी, परिपत्र
Circumstances	परिस्थितियाँ
Citizenship	नागरिकता, पौरत्व
City allowance	नगर-भत्ता
Civil	व्यावहारिक, असैनिक
Civil Court	व्यवहार न्यायालय, व्यवहारालय, दीवानी या व्यवहार अदालत
Civil wrong	व्यवहार विषयक अपकृत्य
Claim	दावा
Clarification	स्पष्टीकरण
Clause	धारा
Co-existence	सह-अस्तित्व
Code	संहिता
Code of conduct	आचरण संहिता
Code telegram	कोड तार
Coinage	टंकण
Colonization	उपनिवेशन
Column	स्तंभ
Commencement	प्रारंभ
Commerce	वाणिज्य
Commercial	वाणिज्य-सम्बन्धी
Commission	आयोग
Commission agent	कमीशन एजेंट, दलाल
Commissioner	आयुक्त
Committee	समिति
Committee, Select	प्रवर समिति
Committee, Standing	स्थायी समिति
Common good	सार्वजनिक कल्याण
Common Seal	सामान्य मुद्रा, सामान्य मुहर
Communicate	संचार करना
Communication	संचार, संसूचना, पत्रव्यवहार
Communication, means of	संचार साधन
Communique	विज्ञप्ति
Community	लोकसमाज, समुदाय
Commuted leave	परिवर्तित छुट्टी

Company	समवाय, कम्पनी
Compassion	अनुकंपा
Compassion allowance	अनुकंपा भत्ता
Compensation	प्रतिकर, क्षतिपूर्ति
Compensatory leave	प्रतिपूरक छुट्‌टी
Competent	सक्षम
Competitive examination	प्रतियोगिता परीक्षा
Complaint	फरियाद, शिकायत
Complaint book	शिकायत पुस्तिका
Comptroller and Auditor General	नियंत्रण तथा महालेखा-परीक्षक
Computation	संगणना
Concession	रियायत
Concurrence	सहमति
Concurrent	समवर्ती
Condemn	अनुपयोगी घोषित करना, दण्डनीय घोषित करना, निन्दा करना
Concurrent list	समवर्ती सूची
Condition	शर्त
Conditions of service	सेवा की शर्तें
Conference	सम्मेलन
Confession	संस्वीकृति
Confidence, want of	विश्वास का अभाव
Confirm	पुष्टि करना
Confirmation	पुष्टि
Conscience	अन्तःकरण
Consent	सम्मति
Consent, previous	पूर्व सम्मति
Consequential	आनुषंगिक
Consideration	विचार, प्रतिफल
Consolidated Fund	संचित निधि
Constituency	निर्वाचन-क्षेत्र
Constituency, territorial	प्रादेशिक निर्वाचन-क्षेत्र
Constituent-Assembly	संविधान सभा
Constitution	संघटन, गठन, संविधान
Construe	अर्थ करना
Consul	वाणिज्य-दूत
Consultation	परामर्श
Consumption	अपभोग
Contact	संपर्क
Contagious	सांसर्गिक
Contain	समाविष्ट करना
Contempt	अवमान
Contempt of Court	न्यायालय का अवमान
Contest	(स) विवाद प्रतियोगिता (क्रि.) लडना (निर्वाचन)
Context	संदर्भ, प्रसंग
Contingency allowance	आकस्मिकता भत्ता
Contingency-Fund	आकस्मिकता निधि
Contract	संविदा
Contravention	प्रतिकूलता, उल्लंघन
Contribution	अंशदान, योगदान
Control	नियंत्रण
Controlling officer	नियंत्रण अधिकारी
Controversy	विवाद, प्रतिवाद
Convention	अभिसमय, प्रथा, रूढ़ि, परंपरा

Converance	सम्पत्ति हस्तांतरण
Conveyance allowance	वाहन भत्ता
Convicted	सिद्धदोष, अभिशस्त, दोश प्रमाणित
Conviction	दोषसिद्धि, अभिशस्ति
Cooperation	सहयोग, सहकारिता
Co-operative	सहकारी, सहयोगशील
Copy	प्रतिलिपि, नकल, प्रति
Copyright	प्रतिलिपि अधिकार, कॉपीराइट, स्वत्वाधिकार
Corporation	निगम
Corporation, Sole	एकल निगम
Corporation-tax	निगम-कर
Correspondence	पत्राचार
Correspondent	संवाददाता, संपर्की
Corresponding	तद्नरूप
Corrupt	भ्रष्ट
Cost	परिव्यय, खर्च, लागत
Cottage industry	कुटीर उद्योग
Council	परिषद्
Council of ministers	मंत्रिपरिषद्
Council of States	राज्यसभा
Council, Regional	प्रादेशिक परिषद्
Council. Tribal	जनजाति-परिषद्
Countervailing duty	प्रतिशुल्क
Court	न्यायालय
Court Martial	सेनान्यायालय
Court of Ward	प्रतिपालक-अधिकरण
Court. Civil	व्यवहार-न्यायालय
Court, Criminal	दण्ड-न्यायालय
Court, District	संघ-न्यायालय
Court, Federal	उच्च-न्यायालय
Court, High	उच्च न्यायालय
Court, magistrate	दंडाधिकारी-न्यायालय
Court, Session	सत्र-न्यायालय
Court, subordinate	अधीन-न्यायालय
Court, Supreme	उच्चतम न्यायालय
Covering letter	सहपत्र
Credit	प्रत्यय, साख, पत्त, आकलन
Crime	अपराध
Criminal	अपराधी, आपराधिक,दण्ड सम्बन्धी
Criminal law	दण्ड-विधि
Cross breed	संकर
Crossed Cheque	क्रॉस चेक, रेखित चेक
Currency	चल अर्थ मुद्रा-प्रचलन
Custom	रूढ़ि,आचार
Custom duty	बहिः-शुल्क, सीमा-शुल्क
Custom, Frontier	शुल्क, सीमान्त
Cypher (Cipher)	बीज लेख, शून्य, सिफर
Cypher telegram	बीज लेख तार

D

Daily note	दैनिक नोट, दैनिक टिप्पणी
Damages	नुकसानी (विधि), हर्ज़ाना (सामान्य)
Data	आधार सामग्री आँकड़े
Dead account	निष्क्रिय लेखा
Dealing assistant	संबधित सहायक
Dealing hand	संबधित कर्मचारी
Dearness Allowance	महँगाई भत्ता
Death anniversary	पुण्यतिथि
Death-cum-retirement	मृत्यु-निवृत्ति उपदान
Debate	वाद-विवाद
Debenture	ऋण-पत्र
Debit	विकलन
Debt	ऋण
Decision	विनिश्चय
Declaration	घोषणा
Declaration form	घोषणा पत्र ·
Decree	आज्ञप्ति, कुर्की
Dedication	समर्पण
Deduction	कटौती, घटाना
Deed	विलेख
Defence	प्रतिरक्षा
Deface	विरूपित करना
De facto	वस्तुतः
Defamation	मानहानि
Degradation	पद घटाना, ग्रेड घटाना
Delay	विलंब
Deliberation	पर्यालोचन, विचार-विमर्श
Delimitation	परिसीमन
Demand	अभियाचना, माँग
Demarcation	सीमांकन
Demi-official (D.O)	अर्ध-शासकीय
Demi-official letter (D.O)	अर्ध-शासकीय पत्र
Demobilisation	सैन्य-वियोजन
Democratic	लोकतांत्रिक
Demonstration	निदर्शन, प्रदर्शन, निरूपण
Demotion	पदावनति
Department	विभाग
Departmental	विभागीय
Departmental enquiry	विभागीय जाँच
Deposit	निपेक्ष,जमा
Depositor	जमा करनेवाला, जमाकर्ता
Deprive	वंचित करना
Deputy Chairman	उपसभापति
Deputy Commissioner	उपायुक्त, मण्डलायुक्त
Deputy President	उपराष्ट्रपति
Deputy Speaker	उपाध्यक्ष
Derogation	अप्रतिष्ठा, अपमान
Descent	उदभव
Design	रूपांकण, तक्ष
Designation	पदनाम, पद
Despatch	(सं.) प्रेषण, रवानगी (कि.) प्रेषित करना, रवाना करना, भेजना

Detail	ब्यौरा, विवरण
Detrimental	अहितकारी
Devotion	निष्ठा
Diary	डायरी,दैनिकी, दैनंदिनी
Dignity	गौरव, मर्यादा, गरिमा
Diploma	डिप्लोमा
Diplomat	राजनयज्ञ
Diplomatic	राजनयिक
Diplomatic bag	राजनयिक डाक
Direct	प्रत्यक्ष, सीधा (क्रि.) निदेश देना
Direction	निर्देश
Directive	(स.) निदेश (वि.) निदेशात्मक
Disability	निर्योग्यता
Discharge	निर्वहन,पालन, उन्मोचन, सेवा-मुक्ति, कार्य-मुक्ति, छुट्टी
Disciplinary	अनुशासन-सम्बन्धी
Discipline	अनुशासन
Discovery	आविष्कार
Discretion	स्वविवेक
Discrimination	विभेद
Discussion	विचार-विमर्श, चर्चा, बहस
Dismiss	पदच्युत करना, बरखास्त करना
Dismissal	पदच्युति, बरखास्तगी
Disobedience	अवज्ञा
Disperse	विसर्जन करना
Disposal	निपटान, निर्वतन
Dispose of	निपटाना
Dispute	विवाद
Disqualification	अनर्हता
Disqualified	अयोग्य, अनर्ह
Disqualify	अनर्ह या अयोग्य ठहराना
Dissent	विमति
Dissolution	विघटन
Distribution	अवतरण, विभाजन
District	जिला
District Board	जिलापरिषद्
District Council	जिलासभा
District Fund	जिलानिधि
Ditto	यथोपरि, जैसे ऊपर
Dividend	लाभांश
Divorce	विवाह-विच्छेद, तलाक
Document	दस्तावेज़, प्रलेख
Domicile	अधिवास
Domiciled	अधिवासी
Donation	दान, संदान (विधि)
Doubtful	संदिग्ध
Down payment	तत्काल अदायगी
Drawee	अदाकर्ता
Drawing	ड्राइंग, रेखाचित्र
Due date	नियत तिथि
Dues	देय राशि
Dullness	मतिमान्ध
During good behaviour	सदाचार पर्यन्त
During the pleasure of the president	राष्ट्रपति-प्रसाद पर्यन्त
Duty	शुल्क-कर्तव्य
Duty. Costom	सीमा-शुल्क
Duty. Death	मरण-शुल्क, मृत्युकर

Duty. Estate	सम्पत्ति-शुल्क	Duty. Stamp	मुद्रांक-शुल्क
Duty. Excise	उत्पादन-शुल्क	Duty. Succession	उत्तराधिकार-शुल्क
Duty. Export	निर्यात-शुल्क	Duty, declaration	मृत्यकालिक कथन
Duty. Import	आयात-शुल्क		

E

Earned leave — अर्जित अवकाश, अर्जित छुट्टी
Earnest money — बयाना
Economic — आर्थिक
Edition — संस्करण
Education — शिक्षा
Efficiency — दक्षता, कार्यकुशलता
Efficiency bar — दक्षता रोध
Efficiency of Administration — प्रशासन कार्य-क्षमता
Efficient — दक्ष
Elect — निर्वाचित करना
Elected — निर्वाचित, चुने हुए
Election — निर्वाचन, चुनाव
Election Commissioner — निर्वाचन आयुक्त
Election, Direct — प्रत्यक्ष निर्वाचन
Election, General — साधारण निर्वाचन
Election, Indirect — परोक्ष निर्वाचन
Electoral roll — निर्वाचन नामावली
Electorate — निर्वाचक-गण, निर्वाचन-क्षेत्र
Eligibility — पात्रता, योग्यता
Eligible — लिये जाने योग्य
Embarrassment — उलझन, शर्मिन्दा
Embezzlement — गबन
Emergency — आपात स्थिति
Emergent — आपाती
Emigration — उत्प्रवास
Emoluments — उपलब्धियाँ
Employee — कर्मचारी
Employer — नियोक्ता
Employment — नौकरी, रोजगार, सेवायोजन, व्यवसाय,
Employment oriented — रोजगार उन्मुख
Employer's liability — नियोजक-दत्वय,
Enactment — अधिनियमन
Enclair telegram — शब्दबद्ध तार
Encroachment — अधिक्रमण
Encumbered Estate — भारग्रस्त सम्पदा
Endorsed — पृष्ठांकित, अकित
Endorsement — पृष्ठाकंन, सही करना, समर्थन
Endowment — धर्मस्व
English version — अंग्रेजी अनुवाद
Engagement — वचन-बन्ध
Engineering — यन्त्र-शास्त्र
Enquiry — पूछताछ, जाँच

Enroll (enrol)	भर्ती करना, (नाम) दर्ज करना
Enrolment	नाम दर्ज करना, नामांकन
Enrolment number	नामाकंन संख्या
Enterainment	मनोंरजन
Enterprise	उद्यम
Entitled	अधिकारी, हकदार
Entrust	न्यस्त करना, सौंपना
Entry	प्रविष्टि, दाखिला
Equal Protection of Laws	विधियों का समान- संरक्षण
Equality	समता
Equipment	उपकरण, साधन
Equivalent	(सं.) तुल्यांक, तुल्यमान, पर्याय (वि.) तुल्य, समकक्ष
Equilibrium	संतुल्य
Error	त्रुटि, भूल, गलती
Escheat	राजगामी धन
Escort	अनुरक्षक
Essential	अनिवार्य
Essential qualification	अनिवार्य योग्यता
Establishment	स्थापना, (स) संस्था
Estate	सपदा
Estimate	आँक, प्राक्कलन, आगणन अनुमान
Evidence	साक्ष्य,गवाही, प्रमाण
Ex-cadre post	संवर्गबाह्य पद
Exception	अपवाद
Excess profit	अतिरिक्त लाभ
Excise duty	उत्पादन शुल्क
Exclude	अपवर्जन करना
Exclusion	अपवर्जन
Exclusive Jurisdiction	अन्नय क्षेत्राधिकार
Executive	कार्य पालिका, कार्यपालक
Executive committee	कार्यकारिणी समिति
Executive council	कार्य परिषद्
Executive power	काय्रकारी शक्ति
Executive staff	कार्यपालक कर्मचारी वर्ग,
Exempt	(वि.) छूट प्राप्त (क्रि.) छूट देना
Exemption	छूट, माफी
Exercise	प्रयोग करना
Exercise of power	शाक्ति प्रयोग
Ex-officio	पदेन
Expedite	शीघ्र कार्यवाई करना, शीघ्र निपटान
Expenditure	व्यय, खर्च
Experience	अनुभव
Expert	विर्शषज्ञ
Expiry	समाप्ति
Explanation	व्याख्या, स्पष्टीकरण
Explosives	विस्फोटक
Export	निर्यात
Expost facto	कार्योत्तर
Express delivery	तुरंत वितरण, एकसप्रेस डाक
Expression	अभिव्यक्ति, वाक्यांश

Extend विस्तार करना, फैलाना
Extension of leave छुट्टी बढ़ाना
Extension of service सेवावधि बढ़ाना
External बाह्य, वैदेशिक, विदेश
External Affairs वैदेशिक कार्य
Extra duty allowance अतिरिक्त ड्यूटी भत्ता
Extra terrtorial operation राज्य क्षेत्रातीत प्रवर्तन
Extradition प्रत्यर्पण
Extraordinary leave असाधारण छुट्टी
Extraordinary असाधारण
Extraordinary gazette असाधारण राजपत्र
Eyewitness चश्मदीद गवाह, प्रत्यक्ष साक्षी

F

Face value अंकित मूल्य
Facility सुविधा
Fact तथ्य
Factory कारखाना
Fair copy स्वच्छ प्रति
Faith धर्म-भावना, श्रद्धा
Faithful विश्वासपात्र
Famine relief अकाल राहत
Fare भाड़ा, किराया
Farewell विदाई
Fault दोष, चूक
Favour अनुग्रह, कृपा, पक्षपात, पक्ष
Federal संघ
Federal Court संघ न्यायालय
Fee देय, शुल्क
Fellow अध्येता, सदस्य
Festival advance त्यौहार अग्रिम, त्यौहार पेशगी
Figures आँकड़े
File (सं.) मिसिल, फाइल, संचिका (क्रि.) फाइल करना, दाखिला करना
Finance (सं.) वित्त (क्रि.) रुपया लगाना
Finance bill वित्त विधयेक
Finance Commission वित्तायोग
Finance statement वित्तीय विवरण
Financial वित्तीय, वित्त संबंधी
Financial obligation वित्तीय भार
Financial sanction वित्तीय मंजूरी, वित्तीय संस्वीकृति
Financial year वित्तीय वर्ष, वित्त-वर्ष
Fine अर्थ-दण्डे
Fire services अग्निशमन सेवा
Fire risk आग का खतरा
First aid प्रथमोपचार, प्रथम उपचार

Fishery — मीन-क्षेत्र, मीन पण्य
Fit — योग्य, उपयुक्त
Fitness certificate — स्वस्थता प्रमाण-पत्र
Fixation — नियतन, स्थिर करना
Follow up action — अनुवर्ती कार्यवाही
Follow up negotiation — अनुवर्ती बातचीत
Foot note — पांद टिप्पणी
For the time being — तत्समय, उपस्थित समय के लिए
Forbid — निषेध करना
Forbidden — निपिद्ध
Forces — बल, सेना
Forecast — पूर्वानुमान
Foreign — विदेश
Foreign affairs — विदेशीय कार्य
Foreign collaboration — विदेशी सहयोग
Foreign exchange — विदेशी मुद्रा
Foreign trade — विदेश व्यापार
Foreword — प्राक्कथन
Forged — कूटरचित
Form — फॉर्म, प्रपत्र, रूप
Formula — सूत्र
Formulated — सूत्रित
Forwarding letter — अग्रेषण पत्र
Forwarding note — अग्रेषण टिप्पणी
Foundation — शिलान्यास, नीवं, आधार, प्रतिष्ठान
Freedom — स्वतन्त्रता, स्वातंत्र्य, आजादी
Freight — वस्तु- भाड़ा
Frequency — आवृत्ति, बारबारता
Frequent — बारंबार
Fresh receipt (F.R) — नई आवती
From (in letters) — प्रेषक
Frontiers — सीमान्त
Function — कृत्य, समारोह
Functional — कार्य संबंधी, कार्यात्मक
Function. Administrative — प्रशासकीय कृत्य
Fund — निधि
Fundamental — मूल, मौलिक, आधारिक,
Future market — वायदा बाजार

G

Gallantry award — शौर्य पुरस्कार
Gallery — दीर्घा, गैलरी, वीथि
Gambling — द्यूत, जुआ
Gazette — राजपत्र, गजट
Gazetted — राजपत्रित
Gazetted holiday — राजपत्रित अवकाश, राजपत्रित छुट्टी
Gazetted officer — राजपत्रित अधिकारी
Gazetted post — राजपत्रित पद
Gazetteer — गज़ेटियर

General — साधारण, सामान्य, आम, जनरल, प्रधान, महा

General administration — सामान्य प्रशासन

General budget — सामान्य बजट

General Conditions of contract — ठेके की सामान्य शर्तें, संविदा की सामान्य शर्तें

General Election — साधारण निर्वाचन

General provident fund — सामान्य भविष्य निधि, सामान्य निर्वाह, निधि

Generation — पीढ़ी, जनन, उत्पादन, प्रतिभा प्रतिभाशाली, प्रकृति

Genuine signature — वास्तविक हस्ताक्षर असली हस्ताक्षर

Gift — उपहार, भेंट

Gist — सार

Give effect to — कार्यान्वित करना

Golden jubilee — स्वर्ण-जयंती

Good behaviour — सद्व्यवहार

Good Character — सच्चरित्र, सच्चरित्रता

Goodwill — साख

Good wishes — शुभकामना

Govern — शासन करना

Governance — शासन

Government — सरकार

Government of business — सरकारी काम

Government of India — भारत सरकार

Government of India concern — भारत सरकार का प्रतिष्ठान

Government of State — राज्य की सरकार

Government Provident Fund — सरकारी भविष्य निधि, सरकारी निर्वाह निधि

Governor — राज्यपाल

Gradation — श्रेणीकरण, पदक्रम

Gradation list — पदक्रम सूची

Grand total — सर्वयोग

Grant — (सं.) अनुदान (क्रि.) स्वीकार करना, प्रदान करना

Grant-in-aid — सहायता अनुदान

Grantee — अनुदानग्राही, अनुदान पानेवाला

Granter — अनुदाता

Gratuity — उपदान

Grievance — शिकायत

Gross negligence — घोर प्रमाद, भारी लापरवाही

Gross total — सकल योग

Gross value — कुल मूल्य, सकल मूल्य

Guarantee — प्रत्याभूमि, अनुदान पाने वाले

Guardian — अभिभावक

Guidance — मार्गदर्शन

Guidelines — मार्गदर्शी सिद्वांत

Guiltless — निरपराध

Guilty — दोषी

H

Habeas Corpus — बन्दी-प्रत्यक्षीकरण
Half pay leave — अर्धवेतन छुट्टी
Hand bill — परचा
Handcuff — हथकड़ी
Handicrafts — हस्तशिल्प, दस्तकारी
Handloom — हाथ करघा
Hazardous — संकटमय
Head of account — लेखा शीर्ष
Headman — मुखिया
Headquarter — मुख्यालय, हेडक्वार्टर
Heir — वारिस
Herewith — इसके साथ
High Court — डच्च न्यायालय
High priority — उच्च प्राथमिकता
Highlights — मुख्य बातें, प्रमुख आकर्षण, मुख्य विशेषताएँ
Highway — राजपथ, राजमार्ग
Hindi teaching scheme — हिन्दी शिक्षण योजना
Hindrance — बाधा, अड़चन
Home district — गृह जिला
Honorarium — मानदेय
Honorary — अवैतनिक
Honour — (सं.) सम्मान, प्रतिष्ठा (क्रि.) सकारना, सम्मान करना
Hours of business — कार्य समय
Hours of employment — काम के घंटे
House — सदन
House of people — लोक-सभा
House rent — मकान किराया
House rent allowance — मकान किराया भत्ता
Human rights — मानव अधिकार

I

Identical representation — समान अभ्यावेदन
Identification mark — पहचान-चिन्ह शिनाख्त-चिन्ह
Identity — पहचान
Identity card — पहचान-पत्र
Illegal — अवैद्य
Illegal practice — अवैद्याचरण
Illustrated — सचित्र, सोदाहरण
Immediate — तत्काल, अव्यवहित, आसन्न
Immuned — उन्मुक्त
Immunity — उन्मुक्ति
Impose — दोषारोप या कर लगाना

Impeachment	महाभियोग
Implement	(सं.) औज़ार (क्रि.) परिपालन करना, कार्यावित करना
Implementation	परिपालन, कार्यान्वयन
Implementing	परिपालन
Import	आयात
Impression	छाप, मन पर प्रभाव
Impressive	प्रभावोत्पादक
Imprisonment	कारावास, कैद
Improvement	सुधार, संशोधन, समुन्नति, अभिवृद्धि
Improvement Trust	सुधार-प्रन्यास
In advance	पहले से, अग्रिम
Inauguration	उद्घाटन
Incapacity	असमर्थता
Incidental	प्रांसगिक
Incidental expenditure	प्रासंगिक व्यय
Income tax	आयकर
Incompetency	अक्षमता
Incompetent	अक्षम
Incomplete	अधूरा
Incorporation	निगमन
Incumbent of an office	पदधारी
Indebtedness	ऋणग्रस्तता
Indent	माँग-पत्र
Independent note	स्वतंत्र टिप्पणी
Index	अनुक्रमणिका, अनुक्रमणी, सूचक
Individual	व्यक्ति, व्यष्टि, वैयक्तिक, व्यक्तिगत
Industry	उद्योग
Inefficiency	अदक्षता
Ineligibility	अपात्रता
Infants	शिशु
Infectious	सांक्रमिक
Inflation	स्फीति, मुद्रा स्फीति
Influence	प्रभाव
Influence undue	अयुक्त प्रभाव
Informal	अनौपचारिक
Information	सूचना, वार्ता
Inheritence	दाय, उत्तराधिकार
Initial pay	प्रारंभिक वेतन
Initials	आद्यक्षर
Initiate	उपक्रमण करना, दीक्षा देना
Injury	क्षति
Inland waterways	अन्तर्देशीय जलपथ
Inoperative	अप्रवृत्त
Inquiry	पूछताछ, जाँच
Insolvency	दीवाला
Inspection	पर्यवेक्षण, निरीक्षण
Inspection certificate	निरीक्षण प्रमाण-पत्र
Inspection report	निरीक्षण रिपोर्ट
Institution	संस्था
Instruction	अनुदेश, हिदायत
Instrument	लिखित, संविदा, विलेख, दलील, उपकरण, साधन
Insurance	बीमा
Insured	बीमा किया हुआ, बीमाकृत
Integrity	सत्यनिष्ठा, ईमानदारी, अखंडता

Intelligence	आसूचना
Intelligible	बोधगम्य
Intensive	गहन, प्रकृष्ठ, तीव्र
Intercourse	समागम
Interdepartmental	अंर्तविभागीय
Interdepartmental reference	अंर्तविभागीय पत्राचार
Interest	ब्याज़
Interfere	हस्तक्षेप करना
Interference	हस्तक्षेप
Interim	अंतरिम
Interim order	अंतरिम आदेश
Interim relief	अंतरिम सहायता
Interim reply	अंतरिम उत्तर
International	अन्तर्राष्ट्रीय
Interpretation	निर्वाचन, व्याख्या
Interruption	बाधा, विध्न, व्यवधान, क्रमभंग
Intervene	बीच में पड़ना, अन्तःक्षेप करना, दखल देना
Interview	साक्षात्कार, भेंट
Intestacy	इच्छापत्र-हीनत्व, निर्वसीयतता
Intestate	इच्छापत्र-हीन निर्वसीयत
Intimate	सूचना देना, प्रज्ञापित करना
Intimation	प्रज्ञापन, सूचना
Introduce	पुरः स्थापना करना
Introduction	पुरः स्थापना
Invalid	अमान्य, असमर्थ
Invalidity pensions	असमर्थता निवृत्ति वेतन
Investigation	अन्वेषण, तफतीश, जाँच-पड़ताल
Invitation	निमंत्रण, आमंत्रण, माँगना
Invitation of tender	निविदा माँगना, टेंडर माँगना
In vogue	प्रचलित
Invoice	बीजक
Involved	अतंर्निहित, फँसा हुआ, संबद्ध, अतर्ग्रस्त, ग्रस्त, सहयोग
Inward register	आवक रजिस्टर, आवक पंजी
Irregularity	अनियमितता
Irrelevant	असंबद्ध, विसंगत
Issue	वाद-पद
Issue register	निर्गम-रजिस्टर

J

Job	नौकरी, कार्य
Job work	छुटपुट काम, फुटकर काम
Joining date	कार्यग्रहण तारीख
Joning report	कार्यारंभ प्रतिवेदन
Joining time	कार्यारंभ काल
Joint committee	संयुक्त समिति

Joint family — अविभक्त या संयुक्त कुटुम्ब या परिवार
Journal — दैनिकी, रोजनामचा, पत्रिका, जनरल
Jubilee — जयंती
Judge — न्यायाधीश
Judge, Additional — अपर न्यायाधीश
Judge, Extra — अतिरिक्ति न्यायाधीश
Judgement — निर्णय
Judicial — न्यायिक, अदालती
Judicial enquiry — न्यायिक जाँच, अदालती जाँच
Judicial power — न्यायिक शक्ति या अधिकार
Judicial proceeding — न्यायिक कार्यवाही, न्यायिक कार्यरीति
Judicial stamp — न्यायिक मुद्रांक
Judiciary — न्यायपालिका
Jurisdiction — क्षेत्राधिकार
Justice — न्याय, न्यायमूर्ति
Justice, Chief — मुख्य न्यायाधीश
Justification — तर्कसंगति, आचित्य
Justify — न्यायोचित ठहरना, सफाई देना,

K

Key map — मूल नक्शा
Kidnapping — अपहरण
Knowledgable — बहुज्ञ, जानकार

L

Labour — श्रम
Labour Union — श्रमिक संघ
Land mortgage bank — भूमि बंधक बैंक
Land owner — भू-स्वामी
Land Records — भू-अभिलेख
Land Revenue — भू-राजस्व
Landtenures — भू-धृति
Last pay certificate (L P C) — अंतिम वेतन प्रमाण-पत्र
Latest — नवीनतम
Law — विधि
Law and order — कानून और व्यवस्था
Law of Nations — राष्ट्रों की विधि
Lay off — कामबन्दी
Lay out — अभिन्यास, नक्शा
Leap year — लीप-वर्ष
Lease for life — आजीवन पट्टा
Leave — (सं.) छुट्टी, अवकाश, अनुमति (क्रि.) छोड़ना

Leave account छुट्टी का लेखा
Leve allowance छुट्टी भत्ता
Leave reserve छुट्टी रिज़र्व
Leave salary छुट्टी का वेतन
Leave vacancy अवकाश रिक्त, छुट्टी रिक्त
Leave with pay वैतानिक छुट्टी, सवेतन छुट्टी
Leave without pay अवैतनिक छुट्टी, बिना वेतन छुट्टी
Ledger folio खाता फोलियो, खाता पन्ना
Legal कानूनी, विधिक
Legally वैद्य रूप से, कानूनी तौर पर
Legislation विधान
Legislative Assembly विधान सभा
Legislative Council विधान परिषद्
Legislative power विधायिनी शक्ति
Legislature विधांन-मंडल
Letter head सरनामा, शीर्षनामा
Letter of acceptance स्वीकृति-पत्र
Letter of authority प्राधिकार-पत्र
Letter of Credit प्रत्ययपत्र
Levy आरोपण, उद्ग्रहंण उगाहना
Liability दायित्व
Libel अपमान लेख
Liberty स्वाधीनता

Licence अनुज्ञप्ति, लाइसेंस
Lien पुनर्ग्र हणाधिकार, धारणाधिकार
Lieutenant Governor उप राज्यपाल
Life annuty आजीवन वार्षिकी
Life insurance जीवन बीमा
Limitation परिसीमा
List सूची
List of business कार्य-सूची
List, Concurrent समवर्ती सूची
List, State राज्य-सूची
List, Union संघ सूची
Livelihood जीविका
Loan कर्ज़, ऋण
Local area स्थानीय क्षेत्र
Local authorities स्थानीय प्राधिकारी
Local board स्थानीय मण्डली
Local body स्थानीय निकाय
Local Government स्थानीय शासन
Local Self Government स्थानीय स्वशासन
Lock-up बन्दीखाना
Log book लॉग बुक
Logic तर्कशास्त्र, तर्क
Loss of resale पुर्नविक्रय में हानि
Lower age limit निम्न आयु सीमा
Lower House प्रथम सदन
Lunacy उन्माद
Lunatic उन्मत्त

M

Machinery of government — शासन-व्यवस्था
Magazine — गोदाम, बारूदघर, आयुधागार, पत्रिका
Mail train — डाक गाड़ी
Maintain — रखना, भरण-पोषण करना, अनुरक्षण करना, बनाए रखना
Maintenance — अनुरक्षण, रखना, भरण-पोषण
Maintenance allowance — भरण-पोषण भत्ता
Major — वयस्क, प्राप्तवय, मुख्य, मेजर (पद)
Major head — मुख्य शीर्ष
Majority — बहुमत, वयस्कता, बालिगपन, प्राप्तवयता, बहुसंख्यक
Management — प्रबंध
Manager — प्रबंधक, मैंनेजर, व्यवस्थापक
Mandamus — परमादेश
Manifesto — घोषणा-पत्र
Manpower — जनशक्ति
Manufacture — निर्माण
Manuscript — पांडुलिपि, हस्तलेख
Marginal note — हाशियाा टिप्पणी
Marginally noted — हाशिए पर अकित, पार्श्वीकित
Marital status — वैवाहिकी स्थिति
Maritime shipping — समुद्र-नौवहन
Mark sheet — अंक सूची
Martyr — हुतात्मा, शहीद
Mass — (सं.) जनसमूह (वि.) सामूहिक, व्यापक
Mass consumption — सामूहिक उपभोग
Maternity — प्रसूति, मार्तृत्व
Maternity home — प्रसूति गृह
Maternity leave — प्रसूति छुट्टी
Maternity relief — प्रसूति सहायता, प्रसूति साहाम्य
Maturity — परिपक्वता, प्रौढ़ता, पूर्णता
Maximum — अधिकतम, ज्यादा से ज्यादा
Maximum average pay — अधिकतम औसत वेतन
Merchandise marine — वणिक-पोता
Mediation — मध्यगता
Mediator — मध्यग
Medical aid — चिकित्सा-सहायता
Medical cerificate of fitness — स्वस्थता प्रमाण-पत्र
Medical certicate of sickness — बीमारी का प्रमाण-पत्र
Medical certificate — चिकित्सा प्रमाण -पत्र
Medical examination — स्वास्थ्य परीक्षा

Medical leave चिकित्सा छुट्टी
Medical report चिकित्सा रिपोर्ट
Medium माध्यम
Member सदस्य
Memo ज्ञापन, मेमो
Memo of demands माँग-पत्र
Memorandum ज्ञापन
Mental deificiency मनोवैकल्य
Mental weakness मनोदौर्बल्य
Merchandise marks पुण्य-चिह्न
Merit गुण
Meritorious service सराहनीय सेवा
Merits and demerits गुण-दोष, गुणावगुण
Methodology कार्यप्रणाली, प्रणाली-विज्ञान
Migrant प्रवासी
Migration प्रवास
Migration certificate प्रवास प्रमाण - पत्र
Mileage मील दूरी
Mileage allowance मील भत्ता
Mind Unsound विकृत चित्त
Mineral खनिज
Mineral resources खनिज-सम्पत्
Minimum wages कम से कम मज़दूरी, न्यूनतम वेतन
Mining settlement खनि-वसति
Ministerial लिपिवर्गीय, अनुसचिवीय
Ministerial staff लिपिकवर्गीय कर्मचारी
Minor अवयस्क, अल्पवयस्क, नाबालिग
Minor head लघु शीर्ष, गौण शीर्ष
Minority अल्पसंख्यक, अल्पसंख्य, अल्प-संख्यक वर्ग, अल्पमत, अवयस्कता
Minutes कार्यवृत्त, टिप्पणी
Migration प्रव्रजन
Misbehaviour दुर्व्यहार, कदाचार
Miscellaneous फुटकर, विविध
Mischief शरारत, उत्पात, रिष्टि (विधि)
Misconduct कदाचार
Mismanagement कुप्रबंध
Misuse (सं.) कटुपयोग, दुरुपयोग
Mode ढंग, प्रकार, रीति
Moderation अनुशोधन
Modification आशोधन, तरकीब, रूपांतर
Momentum संवेग, गतिमात्रा
Memorial स्मारक
Monetary limit आर्थिक सीमा
Money bill धन-विधेयक
Mortality मृत्यूसंख्या, मृत्युदर
Mortality rate मृत्यूदर
Mortgage बंधक, गिरवी, रेहन
Mortgager (mortgagor) बंधककर्त्ता
Mortuary मुर्दाघर
Most immediate अति तात्कालिक
Most urgent अति तुरंत, परम आवश्यक
Motion of confidence विश्वास-प्रस्ताव

Motion of no-confidence
अविश्वास-प्रस्ताव

Motivation अभिप्रेरणा

Movement register संचलन पंजिका, संचलन, संचलन पंजिका रजिस्टर

Municipal area नगर-क्षेत्र

Municipal Committee
नगर-समिति

Municipal Corporation
नगरनिगम

Municipal Tramways
नगररथ्यायान, नगर ट्राम वे

Museum संग्रहालय

Muster roll उपस्थिति नामावली

Myth मिथक

N

Name plate नामपट्ट

National (सं.) राष्ट्रीक (वि.) राष्ट्रीय

National anthem राष्ट्रगान

National calendar राष्ट्रीय कैलेंडर, राष्ट्रीय पंचांग

National economy राष्ट्रीय अर्थव्यवस्था

National flag राष्ट्रध्वज, राष्ट्रीय झंडा

National highway राष्ट्रीय राजमार्ग

National language राष्ट्रभाषा

National Savings Certificate
राष्ट्रीय बचत-पत्र, प्रमाण-पत्र

National Savings Scheme
राष्ट्रीय बचत योजना

National Song राष्ट्र-गान

Nationalism राष्ट्रवाद

Nationality राष्ट्रीयता

Native Language देशीय भाषा

Naturalization देशीयकरण

Naval नौसेना-सम्बन्धी

Navigation नौ-परिवहन

Necessary action आवश्यक कार्यवाई

Neglect of duty कर्त्तव्य की उपेक्षा

Negligence उपेक्षा, प्रमाद, गफलत

Negligible नगण्य

Negotiable instrument
परक्राम्य लिखत

Negotiation (समझौते की) बातचीत, परक्रामण

Net income शुद्ध आय

News Bulletin समाचार बुलेटिन

News paper समाचार-पत्र

News reel न्यूज़रील, समाचार-दर्शन

No-confidence motion
अविश्वास प्रस्ताव

Nomination नाम-निर्देशन, नामन, नामांकन

Nomination paper नामन-पत्र, नामज़दगी-पत्र

Nominee नामिती, नामित व्यक्ति

Non-effective अप्रभावी
Non-gazetted अराजपत्रित
Note sheet टिप्पणी-पत्र
Notice board सूचना पट्ट, नोटिस बोर्ड
Notice in writing लिखित सूचना
Notice of discharge कार्य मुक्ति सूचना, कार्य मुक्ति नोटिस
Notification अधिसूचना
Notorious कुख्यात
Null and void बातिल और शून्य

O

Oath शपथ
Oath of office पद-शपथ
Oath of secrecy गोपनीयता-शपथ
Oath taking ceremony शपथ-ग्रहण समारोह
Objection आपत्ति
Obligation आभार
Obvious स्पष्ट
Occasional यदाकदा, अनियत, प्रासंगिक
Occupation उपजीविका, धंधा
Occurrence घटना
Offence अपराध
Offender अपराधी
Offensive आक्रमणात्मक, अप्रिय
Offensive goods बदबूदार माल
Office bearer पदाधिकारी
Office copy कार्यालय प्रति, दफ्तर की प्रति
Office manual कार्यालय मैन्युअल
Office memorandum कार्यालय-ज्ञापन
Office order कार्यालय आदेश
Offiicer अधिकारी, अफसर
Official (सं.) पदधारी (वि.) शासकीय
Official business सरकारी काम
Official correspondence सरकारी पत्र-व्यवहार,
Official language राजभाषा
Official residence पदावास
Official secret सरकारी गुप्ति
Officiate स्थानापन्न होना
Officiating स्थानापन्न
Officiating allowance स्थानापन्न भत्ता
Officiating appointment स्थानापन्न नियुक्ति
Officiating pay स्थानापन्न वेतन
Okay (OK) सब ठीक, अच्छा
On probation परिवीक्षाधीन
Open fire गोली चलाना
Opening balance आदि शेष, रोकड़ जमा
Opinion राय, मत
Order in Council परिषद् आदेश
Order आदेश, क्रम
Order of precedence पूर्वता-क्रम
Order of priority अग्रता क्रम
Order of seniority वरिष्ठता-क्रम

Order Standing	स्थायी आदेश
Ordinance	अध्यादेश
Orientation	अभिविन्यास
Organization	संघटन
Oriented	उन्मुख
Out of date	पुराना, गतावधिक
Out of order	खराब, चालू नहीं, बिगड़ी दशा में अव्यवस्थित
Out of stock	स्टॉक में नहीं
Out of turn	बिन बारी
Outpost	सीमा चौकी
Output	उत्पादन, उत्पाद
Outstation	बाह्य स्थान
Outstation allowance	बाह्य स्थान भत्ता
Outward register	जावक रजिस्टर
Over age	अधिक आयु
Over payment	अधिक भुगतान
Over writing	अधिलेखन, लिखे पर लिखना
Overall charge	समग्र प्रभार
Overdue payment	खड़ा भुगतान
Over estimate	(सं.) आधि-आंकलन,
Overhauling	जीर्णो द्धार, पूरी मरम्मत, ओवरहॉल
Overtime	अतिरिक्ति समय

P

Package	पैकेज़
Panel	नामिका
Panic	आतंक
Parcel	पार्सल
Parliament	संसद
Part-time	अंशकालिक
Partnership	भागिता, सांझेदारी
Pass	पारण आदेश या परिचयपत्र
Pass book	पास-बुक
Passed	पारित, तीर्ण
Passport	पारपत्र, पहचान पत्र
Patent	पेटेंट, एकस्व
Pay order	अदायगी आदेश
Pay roll	वेतन-पत्रक
Pay scale	वेतन-मान
Pay slip	वेतन-पर्ची
Payable	देय, भुगतान
Payee	पानेवाला, आदाता
Pecuniary Jurisdiction	आर्थिक क्षेत्राधिकार
Penal rent	दंड-स्वरूप किराया
Penalty	शास्ति, दण्ड
Pending	अनिर्णीत, पड़ा हुआ, रुका हुआ,
Pension	निवृत्ति वेतन
Permission	अनुज्ञा
Percentage	प्रतिशतता, प्रतिशत दर
Performance	निष्पादन, पालन
Performance efficiency	निष्पादन दक्षता

Performance register — निष्पादन रजिस्टर
Permission — अनुज्ञा, अनुमति
Permit — (सं.) अनुज्ञा-पत्र, परमिट (कि.) अनुज्ञा देना, अनुमति देना
Perpetual succession — शास्वत उत्तराधिकार
Perquisite — परिलब्धि
Personal law — स्वीय विधि
Personal pay — वैयक्तिक वेतन
Personnel — कार्मिक
Perspective — संदर्श, परिप्रेक्ष्य
Perusal — अवलोकन, देखना
Physical education — व्यायाम शिक्षा
Physical fitness certificate — शारीरिक स्वस्थता प्रमाण-पत्र
Physically handicapped — विकलांग
Piracy — जल-दस्युता
Plead — वकालत करना
Pledge — गिरवी रखना
Pledgee — गिरवीदार
Pledger — गिरवीकर्त्ता
Point of order — व्यवस्था का प्रश्न
Police — आरक्षक
Police force — आरक्षक दल
Policy — (बीमा) पॉलिसी नीति
Policy of insurance — बीमा-पत्र
Poll — मतदान
Polling — मतदान
Pollution — प्रदूषण
Port-quarantine — पत्तन-निरोधा
Possession — कब्ज़ा
Post — पद, डाक, केन्द्र
Post graduate — स्नातकोत्तर
Postal address — डाक-पता
Postpone — मुल्तवी करना
Postponement — मुल्तवी
Preamble — प्रस्तावना
Precedent — पूर्व उदाहरण
Preceding — पूर्ववर्ती
Precis — संक्षेप
Preface — प्रस्तावना
Preference — अधिमान
Prefix — पूर्वयोजना, आरंभ में जोड़ना
Prejudice — (सं.) प्रतिकूल प्रभाव, पूर्वग्रह (कि.) प्रतिकूल प्रभाव डालना
Preliminary enquiry — प्रारंभिक जाँच
Premium — बीमा-किस्त
Prescribed — विहित, निर्धारित
Prescribed form — विहित फॉर्म, निर्धारित फॉर्म
Presentation — प्रस्तुतीकरण
Preside — पीठासीन होना, सभापतित्व करना
President — राष्ट्रपति
Presiding officer — अधिष्ठाता
Press — मुद्रणालय, प्रेस, समाचार-पत्र
Press censorship — प्रेस सेंसरी
Press communique — प्रेस-विज्ञप्ति
Press conference — पत्रकार सम्मेलन
Press copy — प्रेस-प्रति

Press gallery पत्रकार दीर्घा, पत्रकार गैलरी
Press note प्रेस -नोट
Prevail प्रचलित होना, अभिभावी होना, विद्यमान होना
Preventive detention निवारक निरोध
Previous and later references पिछले और बाद के हवाले
Previous reference पूर्व संदर्भ, पूर्व निर्देश, पिछला हवाला
Primary education प्राथमिक शिक्षा
Printer मुद्रक
Priority प्राथमिकता, अग्रता
Priority grading प्राथमिकता, की कोटियाँ
Priority indent प्राथमिकता माँग-पत्र
Prisoner काराबन्दी
Privileges विशेषाधिकार
Probation परिवीक्षा, परख, आजमाइश
Proceedings कार्यवाही
Process आदेशिका, विधि
Procesion जुलूस, शोभा-यात्रा
Proclamation उद्घोषणा
Proclamation of Emergency आपात की उद्घोषणा
Professional व्यवसायिक, वृत्तिक
Proficiency certificate प्रवीणता प्रमाण-पत्र
Prohibited प्रतिषिध, निषिध
Prohibiton प्रतिरोध-निषेध
Promotion प्रोन्नति, पदोन्नति, तरक्की, वर्धन
Promulgation प्रख्यापन
Proportional representation अनुपाती प्रतिनिधित्व
Proposal प्रस्थापना
Prorogue सत्रावसान
Prospectively भविष्यलक्षी प्रभाव से
Prospectus विवरण-पत्रिका
Protection संरक्षण
Protest विरोध, प्रतिवाद
Provide उपलब्ध कराना, प्रावधान करना
Provided बशर्ते, परंतु
Provision उपबंध, शर्त, व्यवस्था
Provisional अनंतिम, अस्थायी, अंतःकालीन
Porvisional list अनंतिम सूची
Proxy प्रतिपत्री
Public service commission लोक-सेवा आयोग
Public debt राष्ट्र-ऋण
Public demand सार्वजनिक अभियाचना
Public fund लोकनिधि
Public good लोकहित, जनहित
Public health लोक-स्वास्थ्य
Public notification सार्वजनिक अधिसूचना, लोक अधिसूचना

Public order	सार्वजनिक व्यवस्था
Public safety	लोक सुरक्षा, जन सुरक्षा
Public Service	लोक-सेवा
Publication	प्रकाशन
Punish	दंड देना, सज़ा देना
Punishable	दंडनीय
Punitive	दंडात्मक
Purchase	(सं.) क्रय, खरीद (क्रि.) खरीदना
Put up	प्रस्तुत करना
Put-up-slip	पेशपर्ची

Q

Qualification	अर्हता, योग्यता
Qualifying examination	अर्हक परीक्षा
Quarantine	निरोधा
Quasi-permanency	स्थायिक्ता
Question	प्रश्न
Question hour	प्रश्न-अवधि
Question of Law	विधि प्रश्न
Questionable	शंकास्पद, संदिग्ध
Questionnaire	प्रश्नावली, प्रश्नमाला
Quinquennial	(सं.) (वं) पंचवार्षिक
Quorum	कोरम
Quotation	भाव, दर, दर सूची, निविदा, कोटेशन
Quote	उद्धृट करना, दर बताना

R

Rank	पद, ओहदा, श्रेणी, पंक्ति
Rate list	दर-सूची
Rate of interest	ब्याज दर
Ratification	अनुसमर्थन
Reading	पठन, वाचन
Reassessment	पुनर्निर्धारण
Receipt	आय, आवती, प्राप्ति, रसीद
Receipt book	रसीद बही
Receipt register	आवती पंजिका, रसीद रजिस्टर
Receive	प्राप्त करना, लेना, अगवानी करना,
Recent	हाल ही का, नया, अभिनव
Recognised	मान्य, मान्यता प्राप्त, अभिज्ञात
Recognition	मान्यता, पहचान, अभिज्ञान
Recommend	सिफारिश करना
Recommendation	सिफारिश, संस्तुति

Reconciliation	समाधान
Recovery	वसूली
Record of rights	अधिकाराभिलेख
Recreuitment	भर्ती
Recurring	आवर्तक
Redemption charges	विमोचन-भार
Referee	निर्देशी, रेफरी
Reference	संदर्भ, निर्देश, हवाला
Reformatory	सुधारालय
Refresher Course	पुनश्चर्या
Refreshment	जलपान, उपाहार
Refuge	शरण, आश्रय
Refugee	शरणार्थी
Refundable to	लौटाई जाने योग्य
Regional Commissioner	प्रादेशिक आयुक्त
Regional Council	प्रादेशिक परिषद
Regional fund	प्रादेशिक-निधि
Registered	पंजीकृत
Registered acknowledgement	रजिस्ट्री रसीदी डाक
Registered and insured articles	रजिस्ट्री और बीमा की गई वस्तुएँ
Registration	पंजीयन, पंजीकरण, निबन्धन
Regret	(सं.) खेद (कि.) खेद प्रकट करना
Regualr cadre	नियमित संवर्ग, नियमित काडर
Regularisation	नियमितीकरण
Regulation	विनियम
Reject	अस्वीकार करना
Rejection	अस्वीकार, अस्वीकृति, नामंजूरी
Relevancy	सुसंगति
Relevant	सुसंगत
Relief	सहायता, राहत, बदल, अनुतोष
Relieve	भारमुक्त करना, नौकरी से छुट्टी देना
Relinquishment	त्याग, छोड़ना
Relinquishment of charge	कार्यभार-त्याग
Remains	प्रतिप्रेषण
Reminder	स्मरण-पत्र, अनुस्मारक
Remission	परिहार
Remote	दूरवर्ती, सुदूर, परोक्ष
Removal	निष्कासन, हटाया जाना
Remuneration	पारिश्रमिक
Repay	शोधन करना, चुकाना, लौटाना
Replacement	प्रतिस्थापन, एवजी
Replenishment	पुनःपूर्ति
Representation	प्रतिनिधित्व अभ्यावेदन
Representative	प्रतिनिधि
Reprieve	प्रविलम्बन करना
Reproduce	समुद्धृत करना
Repugnancy	विरोध
Repugnant	विरुद्ध
Reputation	प्रसिद्धि, ख्याति
Requirement	अपेक्षा, आवश्यकता

Requisit	(सं.) अपेक्षित गुण, आवश्यक गुण (वि.) आवश्यक
Requisition	अधिग्रहण
Requisition slip	माँग-पर्ची
Reservation	आरक्षण
Reserved forest	रक्षित वन
Resign	त्यागपत्र देना, इस्तीफा देना
Resignation	त्यागपत्र, इस्तीफा
Resolution	संकल्प, प्रस्ताव
Resort	(सं.) आश्रय (क्रि.) आश्रय लेना
Respite	विराम
Restriction	प्रतिबंध, रोक
Retail price	फुटकर कीमत, खुदरा कीमत
Retire	निवृत्त होना
Retirement	निवृत्ति
Retrenchment	छँटनी
Revenue	राजस्व
Revenue stamp	रसीदी टिकट
Reverse	उत्क्रम, प्रतिलोम, विपर्यास, उल्टा
Reversion	प्रत्यावर्तन
Reverted	प्रत्यावर्तित
Review	(सं.) समीक्षा, पुनर्विलोकन (क्रि.) समीक्षा करना
Revise	परिशोधित करना, दोहराना
Revision	पुनरीक्षण, दोहराना, पारिशोधन
Revoke	प्रतिसंहार करना
Reward	पारितोषिक, पुरस्कार
Risk	ज़ोखिम, ख़तरा
Roll number	पंजीक्रम, रोल नंबर
Rough copy	कच्ची नकल
Rule of the road	पथ नियम
Ruler	शासक
Rules and regulation	नियम-विनिमय
Rules of business	कार्य-संचालन नियमावली
Running commentary	चल-विवरण, चल वृत्तांत
Rustication	विनिष्कासन

S

Safe-custody	निरापद अभिरक्षा, सुरक्षित अभिरक्षा
Safeguard	सुरक्षण
Safety	संरक्षा, सुरक्षा, क्षेम
Sale	विक्रय, बिक्री
Sales tax	विक्रयकर, बिक्रीकर
Sample survey	नमूना सर्वेक्षण
Sanction previous	पूर्व स्वीकृति
Sanctioned projects	मंजूर परियोजनाएँ, संस्वीकृत परियोजनाएँ

Sanctioning authority	मंजूरीदाता प्राधिकारी
Sanctioning order	मंजरी आदेश
Sanitary	सफाई संबंधी, स्वास्थ्यकर
Satisfaction	संतोष, संतुष्टि, तुष्टि
Saving account	बचत खाता
Savings	बचत
Scale of pay	वेतनमान
Schedule of demands	माँग-अनुसूची
Schedule of supply	पूर्ति-अनुसूची
Scheduled bank	अनुसूचित बैंक
Scheduled caste	अनुसूचित जाति
Scheduled tribe	अनुसूचित जनजाति
Scholarship	छात्रवृत्ति
Scrutinizer	संवीक्षक
Scrutinity	संवीक्षा, छानबीन
Secret ballot	गुप्त-मतदान
Secret letter	गुप्त पत्र
Security	प्रतिभूति, ज़मानत, सुरक्षा
Security bond	प्रतिभूति-बंधपत्र
Security deposit	प्रतिभूति जमा, जमानत जमा
Select committee	प्रवर समिति
Self contained	स्वतः पूर्ण
Self explanatory	स्वतः स्पष्ट
Self interest	स्वार्थ, निजीलाभ, आत्महित
Self defence	आत्मरक्षा
Semi-skilled	अर्ध-कुशल
Semi-skilled labour	अर्ध-कुशल श्रमिक
Senate	सीनेट, वरिष्ठ सभा
Senior	वरिष्ठ
Seniority	वरिष्ठता
Sentence	दंडादेश
Serial list	क्रम-सूची
Service book	सेवा-पंजी, सेवा पुस्तिका
Service charges	सेवा-भार
Service postge stamp	सरकारी डाक-टिकट
Service roll	सेवा-वृत्त
Service sheet	सेवा-पत्र
Session	सत्र
Set up	(सं.) व्यवस्था, ढाँचा (क्रि) स्थापित करना
Settlement	बंदोबस्त, निपटारा
Sewage	वाहित मल
Share	(सं.) अंश, भाग (क्रि.) भागी होना, साझी होना
Share holder	शेयरधारी, शेयरहोल्डर
Shift	पारी
Short notice	अल्प सूचना
Short notice term	अल्पकालीन पाठ्यक्रम
Signature pad	हस्ताक्षर पैड
Significant	महत्वपूर्ण, सार्थक
Signify	व्यक्त करना, प्रकट करना
Simultaneous	एक साथ, एक ही समय पर,

Single transferable vote एकल संक्रमणीय मत निक्षेप
Sinking fund निक्षेप निधि
Smuggle चोरी से लाना, चोरी से ले जाना
Smuggler चोरी से लाने वाला, चोरी से ले जाने वाला
Smuggling तस्कर व्यापार, तस्करी
Social custom सामाजिक रूढ़ि
Social insurance सामाजिक बीमा
Social work समाज-कार्य
Solemn सत्यनिष्ठ, गंभीर
Solvent शोधनक्षम
Sovereign प्रभु
Spare copy अतिरिक्ति प्रति
Speaker अध्यक्ष
Speech Freedom वाक्स्वातंत्र्य
Speed breaker गतिरोधक
Sphere गोला, क्षेत्र
Spokesman प्रवक्ता
Staff कर्मचारी-वृन्त
Stamp duties मुद्रांक-शुल्क
Standing commission स्थायी आयोग
Standing order स्थायी आदेश
State Banquet राजभोज
State funds राज्यनिधि
Stationary स्थिर, अचल
Stationery लेखन-सामग्री
Status quo यथापूर्व स्थिति
Statutory कानूनी, विधिक, सांविधिक
Stay order रोकन का आदेश
Steering committee विषय निर्वाचन समिति
Stencil स्टेंसिल
Stenograhy आशुलिपि
Stigma लांछन, कलंक, धब्बा
Stimulate उत्तेजित करना
Stipend वृत्तिक, वज़ीफा
Strike हड़ताल, आघात करना
Study leave अध्ययनार्थ छुट्टी
Sub division उपप्रभाग, सबडिवीज़न, उपखंड
Subject matter वाद-विषय
Submission निवेदन, अधीनता स्वीकार करना, प्रस्तुतीकरण, पेशी
Subordinate office अधीनस्थ कार्यालय
Subrodinate officer अधीन अधिकारी
Subordinate services अधीनस्थ सेवाएँ
Subordinate staff अधीन कर्मचारी वर्ग, अधीनस्थ स्टाफ
Subscribe चंदा, या शुल्क देना, ग्राहक बनना
Substitute (सं.) एवजी, प्रतिस्थापित (क्रि.) प्रतिस्थापित करना
Substitution प्रतिस्थापन, के स्थान पर रखना
Suburb उपनगर

Subversive activities	ध्वंसात्मक कार्य
Succession	उत्तराधिकार
Successor	उत्तराधिकारी
Sue	वाद लाना
Suffer	सहना, पीड़ित करना
Sufficient	पर्याप्त
Suffix	अनुयोजन, अंत में जोड़ना
Suggestion	सुझाव, परामर्श
Suit, Civil	व्यवहारबाद
Sum	राशि, रकम, योगफल, जोड़
Summon	आहान
Superannuation	अधिवर्षिता
Superficial	ऊपरी, सतही
Superfluous	अतिरिक्त
Superintendence	अधीक्षण
Supersession	अधिक्रमण
Supervision	पर्यवेक्षण, देखरेख
Supervisory	पर्यवेक्षी
Supplement	(सं.) जोड़बंध, अनुपूरक, (कि.) जोड़ना, अनुपूरण
Supplementary	अनुपूक
Supplementary budget	अनुपूरक बजट
Supplementary cost	अनुपूरक लागत
Supplementary demand	अनुपूरक माँग
Supplementary grant	अनुपूरक अनुदान
Supplementary question	अनुपूरक प्रश्न
Supreme	सर्वोच्च
Supreme command	सर्वोच्च समादेश
Surcharge	अधिभार
Surety bond	ज़मानत बंध-पत्र
Surplus report	अधिशेष रिपोर्ट
Surprise check	आकस्मिक जाँच
Surprise visit	आकस्मित निरीक्षण
Surrender	अभ्यर्पण, समर्पित करना
Suspend	निलम्बित करना
Sympathy	सहानुभूति, सवेंदना

T

Tableau	झाँकी
Tabular	सारणीबद्ध
Tactful	व्यवहारकुशल, चातुर्यपूर्ण
Tactless	अव्यवहारिक, चातुर्यहीन
Taskforce	कार्यदल
Tax	कर
Tax, Calling	आजीविका-कर
Tax, Capitation	प्रतिव्यक्ति कर
Tax, Corporation	निगम-कर
Tax, Employment	नौकरी-कर
Tax, Entertainment	प्रमोद-कर
Tax, Export	निर्यात-कर
Tax, Income	आयकर

Tax, Profession वृत्ति-कर
Tax, Sales विक्रय-कर
Tax, Terminal सीमा-कर
Tax, Trades व्यापार-कर
Taxation कर लगाना, कराधान
Technical data तकनीकी आधार-सामग्री
Technical qualification तकनीकी योग्यता, तकनीकी अर्हता
Technical term पारिभाषिक शब्द, तकनीकी शब्द
Technical Training शिल्पी प्रशिक्षण
Telegram तार
Telegraphic address तार पता
Teller गणक
Temper मिज़ाज, स्वभाव
Temperament स्वभाव, प्रकृति, मिज़ाज
Temporary appointment अस्थायी नियुक्ति
Tenant कृषक, किसान, आसामी
Tender (सं.) टेंडर, निविदा, (क्रि.) टेंडर देना
Tender, Legal विधि-मान्य
Tension तनाव
Tenet (कार्मिक) सिद्धांत, नियम
Tenure पदावधि
Tenure of office पदावधि
Term अवधि
Term loan आवधिक कर्ज़, मियादी कर्ज़
Termination (of services) समाप्ति
Terms of delivery (माल) देने की शर्तें, परिदान की शर्तें
Terms and conditions निबंधन और शर्तें
Territorial charges प्रादेशिक भार
Territorial Jurisdiction प्रादेशिक क्षेत्राधिकार
Territorial waters जल-प्रांगण
Territory राज्य-क्षेत्र
Testament वसीयत
Testimonial शंसापत्र
Text (of a letter) कलेवर, मजमून
Thankful कृतज्ञ, आभारी
Thesis शोध प्रबंध, स्थापना
Thoroughly पूर्णतया
Thoughtful विचारशील
Threat धमकी, आशंका, खतरा
Tolls पथ-कर
Top priority परम अग्रता
Top secret परम गुप्त
Tour programme दौरा-कार्यक्रम
Trace (सं.) लेश, सुराग (क्रि.) खोजना, पता लगाना, अनुरेखण
Trade mark ट्रेडमार्क, व्यापार चिन्ह
Trade Union कार्मिक या व्यापार संघ
Traffic यातायात
Trailer अनुयान
Trainee प्रशिक्षणार्थी
Training प्रशिक्षण, टेनिंग
Training centre प्रशिक्षण केन्द
Training period प्रशिक्षण काल

Tramcar	रथ्यायान, ट्रामकार
Transaction	संचालन, सौदा, लेन-देन, संव्यवहार
Transcription	प्रतिलेखन, अनुलेखन,
Transfer	(सं.) बदली, अंतरण (क्रि.) बदली होना
Transition	संक्रमण
Transmission	प्रसारण, पारेषण (डार-तार)
Transport	परिवहन
Transportation	परिवहन, निर्वासन
Travelling allowance	यात्रा भत्ता
Treasure troves	निखात निधि
Treasury deposit receipt	खज़ाना जमा रसीद
Treaty	संधि
Trek	दुर्गम यात्रा
Tribal Area	जनजाति-क्षेत्र
Tribe	जनजाति
Tribunal	न्यायाधिकरण
Trinnial	त्रैवार्षिक
Trophy	वैजयंती, ट्रॉफी
True copy	पक्की नकल, सही प्रतिलिपि
Trust	न्यास, ट्रस्ट, विश्वास
Trustee	न्यासी
Turn down	अस्वीकार कर देना
Turnout	उत्पाद, उपस्थिति
Tution fee	शिक्षा-शुल्क
Type script	टाइप प्रति
Type subject	टाइप-विषय
Typewriter	टाइपराइटर
Typewriting	टाइपकारी, टंकण

U

Umpire	निर्णेता, अंपायर
Unauthorised	अप्राधिकृत
Unconstitutional	असाविधानिक, असंवैधिनिक
Under certiticate of posting	डाक प्रमाणित
Under consideration	विचाराधीन
Under consumption	अल्पोपभोग
Under developed	अल्पविकसित
Under estimate	अव-आकलन
Under examination	परीक्षाधीन
Underground	भूमिगत
Undesirable	अवांछनीय
Undertaking	उपक्रम, वचन
Undignified	अशोभनीय, अभद्र
Undischarged	अनुन्मुक्त
Unemployment	बेकारी, बेरोज़गारी
Unexpected	अप्रत्याशित
Unofficial	अशासनिक, अशासकीय

Union parliament	संसद
Union Territory	संघ राज्य-क्षेत्र
Unique	अनुपम, अपूर्व
Unity	एकता
Universal	सार्वभौम, सार्वजनीक
Union	संघ
Upgrade	ग्रेड बढ़ाना
Upgrading	उन्नयन
Upper age limit	ऊपरी आयु सीमा
Upset	गड़बड़ कर देना
Urban	नगरीय, शहरी
Usage	प्रयोग, चलन, प्रथा
Useful	उपयोगी
Useless	बेकार, अनुपयोगी

V

Vacancy	रिक्तता
Vacant post	रिक्त पद
Vacation	अवकाश
Vaccination	टीका
Vaccine	टीका
Vagrancy	आहिंडन, आवारागर्दी
Validation	विधिमान्यकरण
Validity	विधिमान्यता
Validity date	मान्यता तारीख
Valuable	बहुमूल्य, मूल्यवान
Valuation	मूल्यांकन, मूल्यन
Value	मूल्य
Vanity	झूठा घमंड
Variation	विभिन्नता, परिवर्तन
Variety	किस्म, प्रकार
Vegetarian	निरामिष, शाकाहारी
Verbal	मौखिक
Verification	सत्यापन
Verified copy	सत्यापित प्रति
Vest	निहित होना
Veto	वीटो, निषेधाधिकार
Vice	उप
View	दृश्य, दृष्टि
Views	दृष्टिकोण
Vigilance	सतर्कता, चौकसी
Vigorous	ज़ोरदार
Village council	ग्राम-परिषद
Violation	अतिक्रमण
Virtue	सद्गुण
Vision	दृष्टि
Visit	(सं.) आगमन (क्रि.) आना-जाना
Visitor	आगंतुक, परिदर्शक
Vital	जीवनधार
Viz	अर्थात् नामतः
Vocation	व्यवसाय
Voluntary settlement	स्वैच्छित निपटारा
Volunteer	स्वयंसेवक
Vote of no confidence	अविश्वास प्रस्ताव
Vote of thanks	धन्यवाद प्रस्ताव
Vote, Casting	निर्णायक-मत
Voter	मतदाता
Votes of credit	प्रत्ययानुदान

Votes on account लेखानुदान
Voting by ballot मतपत्र द्वारा मतदान

W

Wage मज़दूरी
Wage Differential मज़दूरी अंतर
Wage Inspector मज़दूरी निरीक्षक
Wage Living निर्वाह मज़दूरी
Wagon Controller मालडिब्बा नियंत्रक
Waiting list प्रतीक्षा-सूची
Waive प्रतीक्षा–सूची
Ward Boy वार्ड परिचर
Warehouse माल गोदाम; भांडागार
Warning चेतावनी
Warrant of precedence पूर्वता–अधिपत्र, पूर्वता–वारंट
Warrant वारंट, अधिपत्र
Warrant Officer वारंट अधिकारी
Waste-paper basket रद्दी की टोकरी
Watchman चौकीदार, प्रहरी, वाचमैन
Watch and ward पहरा व निगरानी
Watch dog निगरानी करनेवाला
Water Works जलकल विभाग
Ways and Means Committee अर्थोपाय समिति
Way-bill मार्गपत्रक
Wear and tear टूट-फूट
Weather मौसम
Wedding (of records) (अभिलेखों की छँटाई)
Weed-out छँटाई करना
Weekly arrear statement बचे हुए कामों का साप्ताहिक विवरण
Welcome address स्वागत-भाषण
Welfare Commissioner कल्याण आयुक्त
Welfare Officer कल्याण अधिकारी
Welfare state कल्याणकारी राज्य
Well versed सुप्रवीण
Wharf घाट
Wharfage घाट–भाड़ा
Whereabouts ठौर–ठिकाना, अता–पता
Whereas जबकि
Whisper (सं.) कानाफूसी (क्रि.) फुसफुसाना
White paper श्वेतपत्र
Wild life वन्य जीव
Will इच्छा-पत्र, वसीयत
Winding up समापन
Wipe out मिटा देना
Wireless बेतार
Withdrawl वापिस लेना

Withhold	रोक लेना
Without delay	अविलंब
Withstand	सहन करना
Witness	साक्षी, गवाह
Working committee	कार्य-सीमिति
Working days	कार्य–दिवस, काम के दिन
Working knowledge	कार्य साधक ज्ञान
Work Order Clerk	कार्य आदेश क्लर्क
Writ	लेख, लिखित आदेश
Write off	बट्टे खाते डालना

Y

Yardstick	मानदंड
Year	वर्ष
Year-book	शब्द कोश
Yearly	वार्षिक
Yesman	हाँ में हाँ मिलाने वाला
Yield	उपज, पैदावार
Youth	यौवन, युवक
Youth Welfare Officer	युवक कल्याण अधिकारी

Z

Zeal	जोश, उत्साह
Zenith	चरमसीमा
Zero hour	शून्य काल
Zigzag	टेढ़ा-मेढ़ा
Zonal	आंचालिक, ज़ोनल
Zonal coordination	आंचलिक समन्वय, जोनल समन्वय
Zonal Council	आंचालिक परिषद्
Zonal Office	आंचलिक कार्यालय, ज़ोनल दफ़्तर
Zoological Garden	चिड़ियाघर
Zoological survey	प्राणि सर्वेक्षण

Aa

A ए, अ, ऐ, the First letter of the english alphabet. अंग्रेजी वर्णमाला का पहिला अक्षर।

a ए, अॅ *a.* one एक ; any कोई।

aback *अॅ बैक adv.* backwards पीछे की ओर; by surprise भौचक्का।

abaction *ए-बैक्'शन् n.* (Low.) the stealing of a number of cattle at once (शा० प०) एक साथ बहुत-से पशुओं की चोरी।

abactor *(ए-बैकट्र) -n.* cattlethief पशु-चोर।

abandon *अॅ बैन् डॅन v.t.* to desert, to forsake त्याग देना।

abase *अॅ बेस v.t.* to disgrace अपमानित करना।

abasement *अॅ बेस् मॅन्ट n.* disgrace अपमान।

abash *अॅ बैश v.t.* to make ashamed लज्जित करना।

abate अॅ बेट *v.t.* to lessen कम करना; *v.i.* to become less कम होना।

abatement *अॅ बेट् मॅन्ट n.* mitigation कमी; deduction छूट।

abbey *ऐ बि n.* monastery ईसाई मठ।

abbreviate *अॅ ब्री वि एट v.t.* to shorten संक्षिप्त करना।

abbreviation *अॅ ब्री वि ए शॅन n.* shortening संक्षिप्तीकरण।

abdicate *ऐब् डि केट v.t.* to relinquish त्यागना; *v.i.* to resign power सत्ता त्यागना।

abdication *ऐब् डि के शॅन n.* act of abdication an office पद-त्याग।

abdomen *ऐब डॅ मॅन, ऐब् डो मॅन* the lower belly पेट-उदर।

abdominal *ऐब् डो मि नॅल a.* pertaining to the lower belly पेट-संबंधी।

abduct *ऐब् डक्ट v.t.* to take away by force or fraud, to entice away अपहरण करना, बहका ले जाना, निकाल ले जाना।

abduction *ऐब् डक् शॅन n.* act of abducting अपहरण।

abed *अॅ बॅड adv.* on or in bed बिस्तर पर।

aberrance *एब' -अर्-एन्स्- n.* deviation from rectitude धर्मनिष्ठा से विचलन या विचलित होना।

abet *अॅ बॅट v.t.* to encourage in a bad sense उकसाना।

abetment *अॅ बॅट मॅन्ट n.* act of abetting उकसाव।

abeyance *अॅ बे अॅन्स n.* suspension ठहराव।

abhor *अॅब् हौः v.t.* to. detest घृणा करना।

abhorrence *अॅब् हौः रॅन्स n.* detestation घृणा।

abide *अॅ बॉइड v.i.* to dwell रहना; to wait for (की) प्रतीक्षा करना ; to stay in a place टिकना; *v.t.* to endure सहन करना।

abiding *अॅ बॉइ डिड्ंग a.* permanent स्थायी; stable टिकाऊ।

ability *अॅ बि लि टि n.* skill कौशल; capability योग्यता।

abject *ऐब् जैक्ट a.* mean अधम, नीच।

ablaze *अॅ ब्लेज़ adv.* in a blaze जलता हुआ।

ablactate *एब्-लेक्' टेट् v. t.* to wean from the breast, छाती का दूध पिलाना।

ablactation *एब्-लेक्-टे'-शन् n.* the act of weaning from the mother's breast, माता का दूध पिलाने की क्रिया।

able *ए ब्ल a.* talented योग्य; clever निपुण।

ablepsy *ऐब्-लेप्'-सि n.* lowness of sight. दृष्टिशून्यता, अन्धापन।

ablush *ए-ब्लश् adv.* in a blushing state. लज्जित होते हुए, झेंपते हुए।

ablution *एब्-ल्यू'-शन् n.* washing of the body before ceremonial rites. कोई धार्मिक कार्य करने के पहले शरीर इत्यादि को शुद्ध करना।

abnegate *ऐब्'-नि-गेट् v. t.* to deny. त्याग करना।

abnegation *ऐब-नि-गे-शन् -n.* renunciation. त्याग।

abnormal *ऐब् नौः मॅल a.* not normal असामान्य।

aboard *अॅ बौःड adv.* in a ship नौका पर।

abode *अॅ बोड n.* residence घर, निवास-स्थल।

abolish *अॅ बौ ˘ लिश v.t.* to put an end to उन्मूलन करना।

abolition *ऐ बॅ लि शॅन* act of abolishing उन्मूलन।

abominable *अॅ बौं मि नॅ ब्ल a.* loathsome घृणित, घिनौना।

aboriginal *ऐ बॅ रि जि नॅल a.* primitive आदिम, मूल।

aborigines *ऐ बॅ रि जि नीज़ n. pl.* original inhabitants मूल निवासी।

abort *एब्-ऑर्ट्- v. i.*to miscarry in giving birth. गर्भपात होना।

abortion *अॅ बौः शॅन n.* mis-carriage गर्भपात।

abortive *अॅ बौः टिव a.* unsuccessful निष्फल; immature अधूरा।

abound *अॅ बॉउंड v.i.* to be plentiful प्रचुर मात्रा में होना।

about[1] *अॅ बॉउट adv.* nearly लगभग; here and there इधर-उधर।

about[2] *prep.* near to के समीप; relating to के विषय में।

above[1] *अॅ बव adv.* to or in a higher place ऊपर।

above[2] *prep.* more than से अधिक; to or in a higher place than से ऊपर।

abreast *अॅ ब्रैस्ट adv.* side by side बराबर में।

abridge *अॅ ब्रिज v.t.* to make shorter संक्षेप करना।

abridgement *अॅ ब्रिज् मॅन्ट n.* summary संक्षेप, सार।

abroad *अॅ ब्रौड़ adv.* in a foreign country विदेश में।

abrogate *एब्'-रो-गेट् v. t.* to repeal or cancel by authority, to annul. आज्ञानुसार हटाना, रद्द करना, मोडना या तोड़ना।

abrupt *अॅ ब्रप्ट a.* sudden आकस्मिक।

abruption *ऐब्-रप्'-शन् n.* a sudden breaking off. एकाएक टूटने का कार्य।

abscess *ऐब्-सेस- n.* collection of pus formed in some part of organ of the body. व्रण, शरीर के किसी भाग में मवाद भर जाना।

absonant *ऐब्'-सॉनन्ट्- adj.* absurd,

unreasonable. निरर्थक, न्याय-विरुद्ध।

abscond *ॲब् स्कौ ॅन्ड, ऐब् — v.i.* to fly from justice फ़रार होना।

absence *ऐब् सॅन्स n.* state of being absent अनुपस्थिति।

absent[1] *ऐब् सॅन्ट a.* not present अनुपस्थित।

absent[2] *ऐब् सै ॅन्ट, ॲब्– v.t.* to keep away from अनुपस्थित रखना।

absolute *ऐब् सॅ ल्यूट a.* complete पूर्ण; unlimited असीम; despotic निरंकुश।

absolutely *ऐब् सॅ ल्यूट् लि adv.* completely पूर्ण रूप से।

absolve *ऐब् ज़ौल्व, ॲब् —v.t.* to acquit, to pardon दोषमुक्त करना।

absorb *ॲब् सॉःब्, ऐब्– v.t.* to soak up सोखना; to engross लिप्त करना।

abstain *ॲब् स्टेन्, ऐब्–v.i.* to refrain बचना।

abstract[1] ऐब् स्ट्रैक्ट *a.* not concrete अमूर्त; existing in the mind only भावात्मक।

abstract[2] *n.* summary सारांश।

abstract[3] *ऐब् स्ट्रैक्ट v.t.* to separate अलग करना; to epitomise संक्षिप्त करना।

abstraction *ऐब् स्ट्रैक् शॅन n.* act of abstrating अमूर्तीकरण; absence of mind मतिहीनता।

absurd *ॲब् सॅःड a.* unreasonable असंगत; foolish विवेकहीन।

absurdity *ॲब् सॅः डि टि n.* foolishness मूर्खता; that which is absurd मूर्खता का कार्य।

abundance *ॲ बन् डॅन्स n.* plenty आधिक्य, प्रचुरता।

abundant *ॲ बन् डॅन्ट a.* plentiful प्रचुर।

abuse[1] *ॲ ब्यूज़ v.t.* to revile गाली देना; to make bad use of दुरुपयोग करना।

abuse[2] *ॲ ब्यूस n.* offencive language गाली, अपशब्द।

abusive *ॲ ब्यू सिव a.* insulting अपमानजनक।

abut *अ-बट्' v. t. & i.* (p.t. **abutted**) to join at a boundary, to meet. सीमा पर एकत्रित होना, मिलना; Abutment (-मेन्ट), Abuttal (अल्) -ns. junction, boundary. मिलन-स्थान, सीमा।

abyss *ॲ बिस n.* hell रसातल।

academic *ऐ कॅडै ॅ मिक a.* of learning and teaching विद्यामूलक; scholarly शास्त्रीय।

academy *ॲ कै डॅ मि n.* society of learned men अकादमी।

acarpous *अ-कार्'-डिअक् adj.* not producing fruit, sterile. फल न उत्पन्न करने वाला (वृक्ष), अनऊपजाऊ, बाँझ।

accede *अक्ॅ सीड v.t.* to agree (to) मान लेना।

accelerate *ऐक् सै ॅ लॅ रेट v.t.* to increase the speed of (की) गति बढ़ाना।

acceleration *ऐक् सै ॅ लॅ रे शॅन n.* act of accelerating गतिवृद्धि; increase of velocity वेग-वर्धन।

accent[1] *ऐक् सॅन्ट n.* tone of the voice स्वर; stress बलाघात।

accent[2] *ऐक् सै ॅन्ट v.t.* to express or note the accent of (का) स्वरोच्चारण करना।

accept *ॲक् सैप्ट, ऐक्– v.t.* to admit स्वीकार करना; to receive लेना।

acceptable *अॅक् सैपॅ् टॅ ब्ल a.* pleasing प्रिय; that may be accepted स्वीकार्य।

acceptance *अॅक् सैपॅ् टॅन्स n.* act of accepting स्वीकृति।

access *ऐक् सैॅ स n.* approach पहुँच; means of approach प्रवेश।

accession *ऐक् सैॅ शॅन n.* act of acceding सहमति; augmentation अभिवर्धन; coming to the throne राज्याभिषेक।

accessory *ऐक् सैॅ सॅ रि n.* an accomplice साथी; adjunct उपसाधन।

accident *ऐक् सि डॅन्ट n.* an unfortunate event दुर्घटना।

accidental *ऐक् सि डैॅन् ट्ल a.* happening by chance आकस्मिक।

accipitral *एक्-सि-पिट्रल् adj.* like a hawk, keen-sighted. (श्येन पक्षी) बाज की तरह का, तीक्ष्ण दृष्टिवाला।

acclaim[1] *अॅ क्लेम v.t.* to applaud जय जयकार करना।

acclaim[2] *अॅ क्लेम n.* applause जयकार।

acclamation *ऐक् लॅ मे शॅन n.* shout of applause जयघोष।

acclimatise *अॅ क्लॉइ मॅ टॉइज़ v.t.* to habituate to a new climate जलवायु का अभ्यस्त बनाना।

accommodate *अॅ कौॅ मॅ डेट v.t.* to adjust अनुकूल बनाना।

accommodation *अ कौॅ मॅ डे शॅन n.* lodging निवास; convenience सुविधा।

accompaniment *अॅ कम् पॅ नि मॅन्ट n.* that which accompanies सहायक वस्तुएं; the subordinate parts in music संगत, साज़।

accompany *अॅ कम् पॅ नि v.t.* to go with साथ देना; to play music to support (a singer) संगत करना।

accomplice *अॅ कम् प्लिस n.* helper in wrong doing अपराध का साथी।

accomplish *अॅ कौमॅ प्लिश,–कम्– v.t.* to finish successfully पूर्ण करना।

accomplished *अॅ कौमॅ प्लिश्ड,–कम् a.* skilled पारंगत।

accomplishment *अॅ कौमॅ् प्लिश् मॅन्ट, –कम्– n.* achievement उपलब्धि; skillfulness दक्षता, निपुणता; embellishment अलंकरण।

accord[1] *अॅ कॉःड v.t.* to make to agree सहमत करना; to concede स्वीकार करना; *v.i.* to agree सहमत होना।

accord[2] *n.* agreement सहमति harmony तालमेल, सामंजस्य।

accordingly *अॅ कॉः डिङ्ग् लि adv.* consequently तद्नुसार।

account[1] *अॅ कॉउन्ट n.* narration वर्णन; importance महत्व; a reckoning गणना; register of facts relating to money खाता; reason कारण।

account[2] *v.t.* to reckon गणना करना; to consider विचार करना; to value महत्त्व देना।

accountable *अॅ कॉउन् टॅ ब्ल a* responsible, answerable उत्तरदायी।

accountancy *अॅ कॉउन् टॅन् सि n.* the office or work of an accountant मुनीमी।

accountant *अॅ कॉउन् टॅन्ट n.* person who keeps financial accounts मुनीम।

accredit *अॅ क्रैॅ डिट v.t.* to trust विश्वास करना; to accept as true

सच मानना; to authorise अधिकृत करना।

accrementition *अक्'-क्रे-मेन्- टिश्'-अन् -n* gradual increase क्रमिक वृद्धि।

accrete *अक्-क्रीट्' v. t.* to grow together. साथ उगना; *adj.* growing together साथ उगने वाला।

accrue *ॲ क्रू v.i.* to increase वृद्धि होना; to come as a product उपार्जित होना।

accumulate *ॲ क्यू म्यु लेट v.t.* to heap up ढेर लगाना; to amass संग्रह करना; *v.i.* to increase greatly बढ़ना।

accumulation *ॲ क्यू म्यु ले शॅन n.* heaping ढेर, संचय; collection संग्रह।

accuracy *ऐ क्यु रॅ सि n.* exactness शुद्धता।

accurate *ऐ क्यू रिट a.* free from error शुद्ध; exact ठीक।

accursed *ॲ कॅः सिड a.* doomed शापित; unfortunate अभागा।

accusation *ऐ क्यू ज़े शॅन n.* impeachment अभियोग; that of which one is accused आरोप।

accuse *ॲ क्यूज़ v.t.* to blame दोषारोपण करना; to bring charge against अपराधी ठहराना।

accused *ॲ क्यूज्ड n.* one charged with a crime अपराधी व्यक्ति।

accustom *ॲ कस् टॅम v.t.* to habituate आदी बनाना।

accustomed *ॲ कस् टॅम्ड a.* habituated आदी।

ace एस *n.* playing card with one spot इकाई, पासे या ताश का एक्का।

acentric *ऐ-से न्'-ट्रिक् -adj.* not centred. केन्द्र में स्थित न रहने वाला।

acephalous *ए-सेफ्'-अ-लॉस् adj.* headless, without a chief. बिना सिर का, बिना चौधरी या सरदार का।

acephalus *अ-सेफ्' -अ-लस् -n.* a verse defective at the beginning. ऐसी कविता जो आरम्भ में दोषपूर्ण हो।

acetify *अ-सेट्'-इ-फाइ v. t.* (*p.t.* **acetified**) to turn in to vinegar. सिरका बनाना, खट्टा करना।

ache[1] एक *n* pain पीड़ा।

ache[2] *v.i.* to suffer from pain पीड़ा होना।

achieve *ॲ चीव v.t.* to attain, to gain हासिल करना; to win जीतना।

achievement *ॲ चीव् मॅन्ट n.* attainment प्राप्ति, उपलब्धि; success सिद्धि, सफलता।

achromatic *ऐक्-रो-मेट्'-इक —adj.* free from colour. बिना रंग का।

acid[1] *ऐ सिड a* sour अम्ल, खट्टा, तीखा।

acid[2] *n* sour substance अम्ल, तेजाब।

acidity *ॲ सि डि टि n.* quality of being sour खट्टापन, अम्लता।

acknowledge *ॲक् नौ˘ लिज v.* to admit to be true स्वीकारना; to report receipt of पावती भेजना; to express thanks for धन्यवाद देना।

acknowledgement *ॲक् नौ˘ लिज् मॅन्ट n.* recognition स्वीकृति; receipt रसीद।

acne *ऐक्'-नि n.* a disease which is marked by pimples. मुँहासा, डोंड़सा।

acorn *ए कौःन n.* fruit of oak बलूत का फल।

acoustic *अ कूस् टिक a.* pertaining to sense of hearing श्रवणेंद्रिय-संबंधी।

acoustics *अ कूस् टिक्स n. sing.* science of sound ध्वनिशास्त्र।

acquaint *अ क्वेन्ट v.t.* to make familiar to परिचय कराना; to inform सूचना देना।

acquaintance *अ क्वेन् टॅन्स n.* familiarity परिचय; person with whom one is acquainted परिचित व्यक्ति।

acquest *अ-क्वेस्ट् ' n.* self-acquired property. अपनी कमाई हुई सम्पत्ति।

acquiesce *ऐ क्वि ऐसॅ v.i.* to agree सम्मत या राज़ी होना।

acquiescence *ऐँ क्वि ऐ ॅ सॅन्स n.* giving a quiet assent मौन स्वीकृति, रज़ामंदी।

acquire *अ क्वॉइअ: v.t.* to attain प्राप्त करना, अधिकार में करना।

acquirement *अ क्वॉइअ: मॅन्ट n.* act of acquiring उपार्जन; attainment प्राप्ति; the thing acquired अर्जित वस्तु।

acquisition *ऐ क्वि ज़ि शॅन n.* act of acquiring अभिग्रहण; gain प्राप्ति; thing acquired अर्जित पदार्थ।

acquit *अ क्विट v.t.* to declare not guilty (of a crime) निर्दोष घोषित करना; to set free *मुक्त करना;* to conduct (कर्त्तव्य) पूरा करना।

acquittal *अ क्वि ट्ल n.* setting free from a charge दोषमुक्ति या रिहाई।

acre *ए कॅ: n.* a measure of land एकड़, 4840 वर्गगज़।

acreage *ऐ कॅ रिज n.* area of land measured in acres एकड़ों में नाप।

acrimony ऐ क्रि मॅ नि *n.* bitterness of temper, manner or language रूखापन, उग्रता।

acrobat *ऐ क्रॅ बैट n.* performer of clever gymnastic exercises नट, कलाबाज़।

across[1] *अ क्रौ ॅस adv.* from one side to the other आर-पार, आगे को।

across[2] *prep.* from side to side of के आर-पार।

act[1] *ऐक्ट n.* deed कार्य; state of reality वास्तविकता; part of a play नाटक का अंक; law विधि।

act[2] *v.i.* to do something करना, व्यवहार करना; to take part in a play अभिनय करना; *v.t.* to do करना; to perform (का) अभिनय करना।

acting *ऐक् टिङ्ग n.* action कार्य; mode of performing a part in a play अभिनय।

action *ऐक् शॅन n.* a deed कार्य; operation अभियान; suit मुक़दमा।

activate *ऐक् टि वेट v.t.* to make active सक्रिय बनाना; to increase the energy of (की) शक्ति बढ़ाना।

active *ऐक् टिव a.* busy सक्रिय, व्यस्त; quick चपल।

activity *ऐक् टि वि टि n.* agility स्फूर्ति, चपलता; state of being active सक्रियता; (*pl.*) doings कार्यकलाप।

actor *ऐक् टॅ: n.* one who acts कार्यकर्त्ता; a stage-player अभिनेता।

actress *ऐक् ट्रिस n.* a female stage-player अभिनेत्री।

actual *ऐक् ट्यु अॅल, –चु–a.* real वास्तविक; existing in fact यथार्थ।

actually *ऐक् ट्यु अॅ लि, –चु–adv.* as a matter of fact वस्तुतः।

acumen *अ क्यू मै ॅन n.* sharpness कुशाग्रता।

acute *ॲ क्यूट a.* sharp पैना, तीव्र; penetrating अंतर्भेदी।

adage *ऐ डिज n.* a proverb कहावत; a maxim सूक्ति।

adamant[1] *ऐ डॅ मॅन्ट a.* unyielding हठी।

adamant[2] *n.* a very hard substance कठोर पदार्थ।

adapt *ॲ डैप्ट v.t.* to adjust (में) सामंजस्य स्थापित करना; to suit अनुकूल बनाना।

adaptation *ॲ डैप् टे शॅन n.* act of adapting अनुकूलन।

adays *अ-डेज्' adv.* now-a-days, at present. आजकल, इन दिनों।

add *ऐड v.t.* to join to जोड़ना; to annex संलग्न करना; to say further आगे कहना।

addict[1] *ॲ डिक्ट v.t.* to apply habitually (का) आदी होना।

addict[2] *ऐ डिक्ट n.* a slave to a habit व्यसनी।

addiction *ॲ डिक् शॅन n.* state of being addicted व्यसनलिप्तता; devotion आसक्ति।

addition *ॲ डि शॅन n.* act of adding जोड़ने की क्रिया; the thing added जोड़ी गई वस्तु; increase वृद्धि।

additional *ॲ डि शॅ नॅल a.* added अतिरिक्ति।

addle *ऐडल् adj.* rotten, barren सड़ा (गन्दा); बाँझः *v.t.* to make rotten, to confuse सड़ाना, घबड़ाना।

address[1] *ॲ ड्रैसॅ v.t.* to speak directly to संबोधित करना, निवेदन करना; to write a name and destination on (पर) पता लिखना।

address[2] *ऐड् रैसॅ n.* speech व्याख्यान, बोलने का ढंग; place to which letters may be directed पता, *(pl.)* courtship प्रेमाचार।

addressee *ऐड् रै ˘ सी n.* one addressed पत्र पाने वाला।

adduce *ॲ ड्यूस v.t.* to bring forward प्रस्तुत करना; to cite उद्धृत करना।

adept[1] *ऐ डैप्ट n.* one fully skilled निपुण व्यक्ति।

adept[2] *ॲ डैप्ट a.* well skilled निपुण, पारंगत।

adequacy *ऐ डि क्वॅ सि n.* quality of being adequate पर्याप्तता, प्रचुरता।

adequate *ऐ डि क्वॅट, –क्विट– a.* sufficient पर्याप्त, competent सक्षम।

adhere *ॲड् हिॲ: v.i.* to stick चिपकना; to remain firm दृढ़ रहना।

adherence *ॲड् हिॲ रॅन्स n.* state of adhering चिपकना; attachment लगाव; fidelity निष्ठा।

adhesion *ॲड ही ज़ॅन n.* act or state of sticking चिपकाव।

adhesive[1] *ॲड् ही सिव n.* a substance used for sticking things together चिपकाने वाला पदार्थ, गोंद।

adhesive[2] *a.* sticky चिपकनेवाला, चिपकानेवाला, चिपचिपा, लसलसा।

adhibit *ऐड्-हिबिट् v. t.* to put on, to use, to administer, to apply, to attach. रखना, धरना, प्रयोग करना, जोड़ना।

ad hoc *ऐड् हौकॅ* for this special purpose तदर्थ।

adieu[1] *ॲ ड्यू n.* a farewell विदाई।

adieu[2] *interj.* farewell अलविदा।

adiure *ऐ-जूर्' v. t.* to charge under oath or penalty, to request earnestly शपथपूर्वक आज्ञा देना अथवा कहना, आग्रहपूर्वक प्रार्थना करना।

adjacent *अॅ जे सॅन्ट a.* lying near समीपवर्ती।

adjective *ऐ जिक् टिव n.* a word added to a noun to qualify it विशेषण।

adjoin *अॅ जौ˘ इन v.t.* to join to (से) जोड़ना; *v.i.* to be next अगला होना।

adjourn *अॅ जॅः न v.t.* to postpone स्थगित करना; *v.i.* to be postponed स्थगित होना।

adjournment *अॅ जॅः न् मॅन्ट n.* postponement स्थगन।

adjudge *अॅ जज v.t.* to determine judicially निर्णय करना।

adjunct *ऐ जङ्क्ट n.* a thing or person joined to another अनुबद्ध वस्तु या व्यक्ति।

adjuration *ऐ-जू-रे'शन् n.* solemn oath शपथ।

adjust *अॅ जस्ट v.t.* to regulate नियमित करना; to adapt अनुकूलित करना।

adjustment *अॅ जस्ट्मॅन्ट n.* act of adjusting अनुकूलन; arrangement व्यवस्था।

administer *अॅड् मि निस् टॅः v.t.* to manage प्रबंध करना; to govern शासन करना; to distribute वितरित करना।

administration *अॅड् मि निस् ट्रे शॅन n.* the act of administering प्रबंधन; the government प्रशासन।

administrative *अॅड् मि निस् ट्रॅ टिव a.* concerned with administration प्रशासन-संबंधी।

administrator *अॅड् मि निस् ट्रे टॅः n.* one who manages or directs प्रशासक।

admirable *ऐड् मॅ रॅ ब्ल a.* worthy or being admired प्रशंसनीय।

admiral *ऐड् मॅ रॅल n.* the chief commander of a navy नौसेनाध्यक्ष।

admiration *ऐड् मि रे शॅन n.* the act of admiring प्रशंसा।

admire *अॅड् मॉइअॅः v.t.* to express or to have a high opinion of प्रशंसा करना, गुण गाना।

admissible *अॅड् मि सि ब्ल a.* that may be admitted or allowed ग्राह्य, स्वीकार्य।

admission *अॅड् मि शॅन n.* admittance प्रवेश; anything admitted or conceded स्वीकारोक्ति।

admit *अॅड् मिट v.t. & i.* to allow to enter प्रवेश की अनुमति देना; to grant स्वीकार करना।

admittance *अॅड् मि टॅन्स n.* entrance प्रवेश; permission to enter प्रवेशाज्ञा।

admonish *अॅड् मौ˘ निश v.t.* to warn चेताना; to reprove mildly ताड़ना देना।

admonition *ऐड् मॅ नि शॅन n.* warning, caution चेतावनी; gentle reproof ताड़न।

adnascent *ऐड्-नेस्'-एन्ट् adj.* growing to or upon. बढ़ता हुआ।

ado *अॅ डू n.* trouble परेशानी; stir हलचल।

adobe *ए-डो'-बि-n.* sub-dried brick धूप में सुखाई हुई ईंट।

adolescence *ऐ डो˘ लै˘ सॅन्स n.* the state or time of being adolescent किशोरावस्था।

adolescent *ऐ डो˘ लै˘ सॅन्ट a. & n.* (one) passing from childhood to maturity किशोर।

adopt *अ डौप्ट v.t.* to take and treat as a child गोद लेना; to apply अपनाना।

adoption *अ डौप् शॅन n.* act of adopting अंगीकरण; taking as a child दत्तक-ग्रहण।

adorable *अ डौ रॅ ब्ल a.* worthy to be adored आराध्य।

adoration *ऐ डॅ रे शॅन n.* worship आराधना; veneration श्रद्धा।

adore *अ डों:, अ डौं: v.t.* to worship पूजा करना, to love intensely अधिक प्रेम करना।

adorn *अ डौ:न v.t.* to deck सजाना, श्रृंगार करना; to beautify सुंदर बनाना।

adscititious *ऐड्-सि-टिश्'-अस् adj* assumed, added, additional स्वीकृत, माना हुआ, जोड़ा हुआ, परिशिष्ट।

adscript *ऐड-स्क्रिप्ट् adj. & n.* written after, a serf. बाद में लिखा हुआ, दास।

adulation *ऐ ड्यु ले शॅन n.* servile flattery चापलूसी।

adult[1] *अ डल्ट a.* grown to maturity वयस्क।

adult[2] *n.* grown-up person वयस्क व्यक्ति।

adulterate *अ डल् टॅ रेट v.t.* to debase by mixing with something inferior or spurious (में) मिलावट करना।

adulteration *अ डल् टॅ रे शन n.* act of adulterating मिलावट।

adultery *अ डल् टॅ रि n.* violation of the marriage bed परस्त्रीगमन, व्यभिचार।

advance[1] *ॲड् वान्स v.t.* to put forward आगे बढ़ाना; to promote पद में उन्नति करना; to pay before due time पेशगी देना; *v.i.* to go forward आगे बढ़ना; to make progress प्रगति करना।

advance[2] *n.* payment beforehand पेशगी; loan उधार; going forward प्रगति।

advancement *ॲड् वान्स् मॅन्ट n.* progress प्रगति।

advantage[1] *ॲड् वान् टिज n.* gain or benefit लाभ; favourable state अनुकूल परिस्थिति।

advantage[2] *v.t.* to benefit or to profit लाभ पहुंचाना।

advantageous *ऐड् वॅन् टे जॅस a.* useful उपयोगी, लाभदायक।

advent *ऐड् वैन्ट n.* arrival आगमन।

adventure *ॲड् वैन् चॅः n.* enterprise साहस; a bold undertaking साहसिक कार्य।

adventurous *ॲड् वैन् चॅ रॅस a.* darting साहसी; full of hazard जोखिम से भरा।

adverb *ऐड् वॅःब n.* क्रिया-विशेषण।

adverbial *ॲड् वॅः बि ॲल a.* pertaining to adverb क्रिया-विशेषण-संबंधी।

adversary *ऐड् वॅः सॅ रि n.* an opponent वैरी, शत्रु, दुश्मन।

adverse *ऐड् वॅःस a.* hostile विपरीत, विरूद्ध; harmful हानिकर।

adversity *ॲड् वॅः सि टि n.* misfortune दुर्भाग्य; calamity विपत्ति।

advert *अड्-वर्ट v. t.* to draw the attention to, to refer to ध्यान दिलाना, उद्देश्य करना।

advertise *ऐड् वॅः टॉइज़ v.t.* to publish a notice of विज्ञापन करना; to announce घोषित करना।

advertisement *अॅड़ वॅः टिस् मॅन्ट n.* act of advertising विज्ञापन; a public notice सूचना।

advice *अॅड़ वॉइस n.* councel परामर्श, उपदेश; information सूचना।

advisable *अॅड़ वॉइ जॅ ब्ल a.* worthy to be recommended अनुमोदनीय; proper उचित।

advisability *ऐड़-वाइ-जे-बि-लिटि n.* expediency. शीघ्र होने की योग्यता।

advise *अॅड़ वॉइज़ v.t.* to counsel परामर्श देना; to inform सूचना देना।

advocacy *ऐड़ वॅ कॅ सि n.* the function of an advocate वकालत; defence पक्षपोषण।

advocate[1] *ऐड़ वॅ किट –केट n.* one who pleads वकील; supporter समर्थक।

advocate[2] *ऐड़ वॅ केट v.t.* to plead in favour of वकालत करना; to support पक्षपोषित करना।

aerial[1] *ऍ अॅ रि अॅल a.* belonging to the air हवाई; unreal अवास्तविक।

aerial[2] *n.* an antenna एंटिना।

aeriform *एअर्-इ-फॉर्म adj.* of the form of air, gaseous, unreal वायु के समान, गैस के सदृश, अवास्तविक।

aerify *एअर्'-इ-फाइ- v. t.* to fill with air वायु से पूर्ण करना या भरना।

aerodrome *ऍ अॅ रॅ ड्रोम n.* the landing place of aircraft हवाई अड्डा।

aeronautics *ऍ अॅ रॅ नौ टिक्स n.pl.* the science or art of aerial navigation विमान चालन-विज्ञान।

aeroplane *ऍ अॅ रॅ प्लेन n.* aircraft हवाई जहाज़।

aesthetic *ईस् थै˘ टिक a.* pertaining to aesthetics सौंदर्यशास्त्र-संबंधी।

aesthetics *ईस् थै˘ टिक्स n.pl.* the principles of taste and art सौंदर्यशास्त्र।

aestival *ई-स्टि-वल् adj.* pertaining to summer. ग्रीष्म ऋतु सम्बन्धी।

afar *अॅ फ़ाः adv.* from a far distance दूर से; at a far distance दूरी पर।

affable *ऐ फॅ ब्ल a.* courteous सुशील, मिलनसार।

affair *अॅ फे˘अॅ : n.* business मामला।

affect *अॅ फ़ैॅक्ट v.t.* to act upon प्रभावित करना; to pretend स्वांग भरना।

affectation *अॅ फ़ैक् टे शॅन n.* pretence स्वांग, दिखावा।

affection *अॅ फ़ै˘क् शॅन n.* attachment अनुराग; love प्यार।

affectionate *अॅ फ़ै˘क्शॅ नॅट –निट a.* full of affection प्रीतिमय; loving प्यारा।

affidavit *ऐ फि डे विट n.* a written declaration on oath शपथपत्र, हलफ़नामा।

affiliation *अॅ फ़ि लि ए शॅन n.* association संपर्क, संबंध; act of affiliating संबंधन।

affinity *अॅ फ़ि नि टि n.* relation संबंध; similarity समानता; attraction आकर्षण।

affirm *अॅ फ़ः म v.t.* to assert दृढ़ता के साथ कहना; to ratify विधिपूर्वक पुष्ट करना; to declare दावे से कहना।

affirmation *ऐ फ़ः मे शॅन n* a solemn declaration पुष्टीकरण।

affirmative *अॅ फ़ः मॅ टिव a.* positive सकारात्मक।

affix *अॅ फ़िक्स v.t.* to attach जोड़ना; to fix चिपकाना।

afflict *अॅ फ़्लिक्ट v.t.* to cause pain सताना।

affliction *अॅ फ़्लिक् शॅन n.* distress यातना, संताप।

affluence *ऐ फ़्लु अॅन्स n.* prosperity संपन्नता।

affluent *ऐ फ्लु अॅन्ट a.* prosperous धनवान्।

afford *अॅ फ़ौःड v.t.* to give देना; to supply जुटाना।

afforest *अॅ फ़ौ ॅ रिस्ट v.t.* to cover with forest वन लगाना।

affray *अॅ फ़्रे n.* public noisy quarrel हंगामा।

affront[1] *अॅ फ़्रॅन्ट v.t.* to insult अपमानित करना।

affront[2] *n.* disrespect अपमान।

afield *अफ़ील्ड्'-adv.* in or on the field खेत में अथवा खेत पर।

aflame *अॅ फ़्लेम adv.* in a flaming state जलता हुआ; on fire आग पर।

afloat *अॅ फ़्लोट adv.* in a floating state बहता हुआ।

afoot *अॅ फुट adv.* in active progress सक्रिय स्थिति में।

afore *अ-फोर् prep. & adv.* before, in front of, previously आगे, सामने, प्राचीन काल में।

afraid *अॅ फ़्रेड a.* frightened भयभीत।

afresh *अॅ फ़्रै ॅश adv.* anew नए सिरे से।

after[1] *आफ़् टॅः prep.* later than के बाद में।

after[2] *adv.* later in time उसके बाद, जब।

after[3] *conj.* later than the time when उसके बाद जब।

after[4] *a.* subsequent आगामी।

afterwards *आफ़् टॅः वॅःड्ज़ adv.* later बाद में।

again *अॅ गेन adv.* once more फिर, पुनः; moreover इसके अतिरिक्त।

against *अॅ गॅन्स्ट अॅ गेन्स्ट prep.* in front of के सामने; in contrast to से विषमता में; in a position of hostility to के विरोध में।

agamist *ऐग्'-आ-मिस्ट् n.* one who is against marriage. विवाह-विरोधी।

agape *अॅ गेप adv.,* a having the mouth open मुंह खोले हुए।

agaze *अगेज़्' adv.* gazing टकटकी लगाकर देखता हुआ।

age *एज n.* lifetime आयु; epoch युग; oldness बुढ़ापा।

aged *ऐ जिड a.* very old वृद्ध; एज्ड of the age of की अवस्था का।

agency *ए जॅन् सि n.* office of an agent अभिकरण, आढत; branch शाखा; means साधन, माध्यम्।

agenda *अॅ जै ॅन् डॅ n. pl.* list of items to be discussed कार्यसूची।

agent *ए जॅन्ट n.* representative प्रतिनिधि; spy जासूस।

aggravate *ऐ ग्रॅ वेट v.t.* to irritate उत्तेजित करना; to worsen बिगाड़ना।

aggravation *ऐ ग्रॅ वे शॅन n.* irritation उत्तेजना; increase वृद्धि।

aggregate *ऐ ग्रि गेट v.t.* to accumulate संचित करना; to collect संग्रह करना; to combine संयुक्त करना; *v.i.* to assemble एकत्र होना; to be added संयुक्त होना।

aggression *अॅ ग्रै ॅ शॅन n.* attacking आक्रमण; intrusion अतिक्रमण।

aggressive *अॅ ग्रै ॅ सिव a.* offensive आक्रामक; having angry temperament क्रोधी।

aggressor *अॅ ग्रै ॅ सॅः n.* one who

attacks आक्रामक।

aggrieve *अॅ ग्रीव v.t.* to afflict with pain सताना, पीड़ित करना।

aghast *अॅ गास्ट a.* surprised आश्चर्यचकित, भयाक्रांत।

agile *ऐ जॉइल a.* active चपल, फुरतीला।

agility *अॅ जि लि टि n.* activeness चपलता; nimbleness स्फूर्ति।

agitate *ऐ जि टेट v.t.* to excite उत्तेजित करना; to disturb घबरा देना; to stir up हिलाना।

agitation *ऐ जि टे शॅन n.* excitement उत्तेजना; stirring आलोड़न; protest आंदोलन।

agist *अ-जिस्ट्' v. t.* to take others' cattle to feed for a sum कुछ धन लेकर चराने के लिए दूसरे के पशु ले जाना।

aglow *अॅ ग्लो adv.* in a glowing state चमकता हुआ।

agnus *ऐग्'-नस् n.* a lamb. भेड़ या बकरी का बच्चा; मेमना।

ago *अॅ गो adv.* in the past बहुत समय पहले।

agog *अ-गॉग्' adj. & adv.* on the move, expectant, in eager excitement. गतिमान, आशायुक्त, आतुर।

agonist *अग्'-ऑ-निस्ट् n.* a combatant, a champion. योद्धा, लड़ाका।

agonize *ऐ गॅ नॉइज़ v.t.* to cause to suffer pain कष्ट देना।

agony *ऐ गॅ नि n.* anguish of mind यंत्रणा।

agronomy *ऐग्'-रॉन्'-अऐ'-मि n.* rural economy. ग्रामीण व्यवस्था।

agoraphobia *ऐ-गॅरा-फ़ो'-बि-आ n.* fear of crowds. भीड़ से डर लगना।

agrarian *अॅ ग्रॅ अॅ रि अॅन a.* relating to agriculture कृषि-संबंधी; relating to land भूमि-संबंधी।

agree *अॅ ग्री v.i.* to concur सहमत होना; to suit अनुकूल होना; to say yes राज़ी होना; *v.t.* to accept as correct सही मान लेना।

agreeable *अॅ ग्री अॅ ब्‌ल a.* ready to agree सहमत; consentaneous स्वीकार्य; suitable उपयुक्त।

agreement *अॅ ग्री मॅन्ट n.* contract समझौता, अनुबंध; concord सहमति।

agricultural *ऐग् रि कल् चॅ रॅल a.* pertaining to agriculture कृषि-संबंधी

agriculture *ऐग् रि कल् चॅः n.* land cultivation कृषि।

agriculturist *ऐग्रिकल्चॅरिस्ट n.* farmer किसान।

ague *ए'-ग्यू- n.* a. kind of malarial fever accompanied with shivering जूड़ी, बुखार।

ahead *अॅ हैˇड adv.* further on आगे की ओर; in advance प्रगति की ओर।

aheap *अ-हीप् adv.* in a heap, trembling with fear ढेर में, डर से कांपता हुआ।

aid[1] एड *n.* help सहायता; helper सहायक; ingredient उपादान।

aid[2] *v.t* to help सहायता देना।

aigrette *एग्'-रिट् n.* white heron, tuft of feathers or hair सफेद सारस पक्षी, बाल या परों का गुच्छा।

ail *एल v.t.* to trouble सताना; to make sick बीमार करना; *v.i.* to be ill बीमार होना।

ailment *एल् मॅन्ट n.* illness बीमारी।

aim[1] *एम n.* purpose प्रयोजन; intention अभिप्राय; target लक्ष्य।

aim² *v.i.* to take aim लक्ष्य साधना।

air *ऍअ:* *n.* fluid we breathe हवा; atmosphere वायुमण्डल।

aircraft *ऍ अ: क्राफ्ट* *n.* aeroplane विमान।

airy *ऍ अ रि* *a.* full of air हवादार; unsubstantial हवाई; of air वायु-संबंधी।

ajar *अ जा:* *adv.* partly open अधखुला।

akin *अ किन* *a.* related by blood सगा; of like nature समान प्रकृति वाला।

alacrious *अलैक्रि-अस्* *adj.* cheerful, happy, प्रसन्न, खुश।

alacrity *अ लैक् रि टि* *n.* briskness फुरती; readiness तत्परता।

alamort *आल'-मॉर्ट* *adj.* semi-dead, dejected अधमरा, उत्साहहीन, उदास।

alarm¹ *अ ला:म* *n.* notice of danger खतरे की सूचना; warning चेतावनी; fear भय।

alarm² *v.t.* to give notice of danger खतरे की सूचना देना।

alas *अ लैस* *interj.* cry of grief हा! हाय ! आह !

albeit *ऑल् बी इट* *conj.* even if, although यद्यपि, हालांकि।

albion *ऐल्-बि-अन्* *n.* ancient name for england. इंग्लैंड का प्राचीन नाम।

album *ऐल् बॅम* *n.* a blank book for the insertion of photographs etc. चित्राधार।

albumen *ऐल्-ब्यू-मिन्* *n.* a thick substance, the white of eggs गाढ़ा पदार्थ, अंडे की सफेदी।

alchemy *ऐल् कॅ मि, –कि–* *n.* the science of transmutation of other metals into gold कीमियागीरी।

alcohol *ऐल् कॅ होलॅ* *n.* pure spirit मद्यसार।

ale *एल* *n.* a beverage यवसुरा, बीयर।

alegar *अल्'-इ-गर्* *n.* a sour or ale or its vinegar. खट्टी शराब या इसका सिरका।

alert *अ लॅ:ट* *a.* watchful सतर्क; nimble फुरतीला; brisk तेज़।

alertness *अ लॅ:ट निस* *n.* watchfulness सतर्कता; nimbleness फुरतीलापन।

algebra *ऐल् जि ब्रॅ* *n.* method of calculating by symbols बीजगणित।

alias¹ *ए लि ऐस, –ॲस–* *n.* an assumed name उपनाम।

alias² *adv.* otherwise अन्यथा।

alibi *ऐ लि बॉइ* *n.* the fact of being elsewhere अन्यत्र उपस्थिति।

alien *ए ल्यॅन* *a.* foreign विदेशीय; strange अजनबी।

alienate *ए ल्यॅ नेट* *v.t.* to transfer हस्तांतरित करना; to turn away पृथक् करना; to estrange पराया करना।

aliferous *ए-लिफ्'-अर्-अस्* *adj.* having wings. परवाला, परदार।

alight *अ लॉइट* *v.i.* to land नीचे आना।

align *अ लॉइन्* *v.t.* to arrange in a line पंक्तिबद्ध करना; to regulate by a line श्रेणीबद्ध करना।

alignment *अ लॉइन् मॅन्ट* *n.* laying out by a line पंक्तियोजना; setting in a line सीध-निर्धारण।

alike¹ *अ लॉइक* *a.* similar समान।

alike² *अ लॉइक* *adv.* in a similar manner समान रूप से

aliment *एल्'-इ-मेन्ट्* *n.* a nourishment, food, support

पोषण, पुष्टिकर पदार्थ, आहार, आश्रय।

alimony *ऐल्'-इ-मन्'-इ n.* an allowance given to a woman when separated from her husband परित्यक्त पत्नी के भरण-पोषण का भत्ता।

alin *अ-लिन्' adj.* related by blood, of a similar character सगोत्र (सजातीय, सगा), समान प्रकृति का।

aliquot *ऐल्'-इ-क्वॉट् n. & adj.* an internal factor of a number which divides another without a remainder. पूरा भाग देने वाली संख्या, किसी पूर्ण विभाजक संख्या का।

alive *ॲ लॉइव a.* living जीवित; lively जागरूक; active क्रियाशील; in existence अस्तित्वमय।

alkali *ऐल्'-क-लाइ n.* खट्टापन हटाने का पदार्थ जैसे सोडा, पोटास।

all[1] *औल a.* comprising every individual one समस्त; any कोई; every प्रत्येक।

all[2] *n.* everybody, everything सबकुछ, सर्वस्व; the whole संपूर्णता।

all[3] *adv.* whole पूर्णतया।

all[4] *pron.* the whole number सब।

allay *ॲ ले v.t.* to calm शांत करना; to reduce कम करना।

allegation *ऐ लि गे शॅन n.* the act of alleging आरोपण; citation अभिकथन।

allege *ॲ लैॅज v.t.* to subject to allegation आरोपित करना; to give as a reason कारणस्वरूप प्रस्तुत करना।

allegiance *ॲ ली जॅन्स n.* loyalty निष्ठा।

allegorical *ऐ लॅ गौॅरि कॅल a.* relating to allegory अन्योक्ति-'संबंधी।

allegory *ऐ लि गौॅरि, ऐ लैॅगॅ रि n.* symbolical narration अन्योक्ति, दृष्टांत।

allergy *ऐ लॅ: जि n.* hyper-sensitivity प्रत्यूर्जता; antipathy चिढ़।

alleviate *ॲ ली वि एट v.t.* to lessen, to relieve, to mitigate, to comfort. हल्का कर देना, छुटकारा देना, कम करना।

alleviation *ॲ ली वि ए शॅन n.* mitigation उपशमन; lessening कमी।

alley *ऐ लि n.* a narrow lane गली; a walk in a garden वीथिका; a passage पगडंडी।

alliance *ॲ लॉइ ॲन्स n.* friendship मैत्री; treaty संधि।

alligator *ऐ लि गे टॅ; n.* a large reptile घड़ियाल की जाति का जलजंतु।

alliterate *एल्-लिट'-अर्-एट' v. t.* to use words begining with the same letter. एक ही अक्षर से आरम्भ होने वाले शब्दों का प्रयोग करना।

alliteration *ॲ लि टॅ रे शॅन n.* the recurrence of the same initial sound अनुप्रास।

allocate *ऐ लॅ केट v.t.* to set apart for a particular purpose निर्धारित करना।

allocation *ऐ लॅ के शॅन n.* act of allocating विनियोजन; allotment आवंटन।

allot *ॲ लौॅट v.t.* to distribute बांटना; to assign नियत करना।

allotment *ॲ लौॅट मॅन्ट n.* act of alloting बँटाई; share हिस्सा।

allow *ॲ लॉउ v.t.* to permit अनुमति देना; to assign नियत करना; to grant or give देना।

allowance *ॲ लॉउ ॲन्स n.* permission अनुमति, अनुज्ञा; amount given भत्ता; rebate छूट।

alloy *ऐ लों ̆इ, अॅ लौ ̆इ n.* a mixture of metals मिश्रित धातु; baser element खोट।

allude *अॅ ल्यूड v.i.* to mention indirectly इंगित करना।

alluminate *अल्यू'-मिन्-एट्' v. t.* to adorn with ornaments. to illuminate. आभूषणों से सुसज्जित करना, सजाना।

allure *अॅ ल्यूअॅः v.t.* to attract आकर्षित करना।

allurement *अॅ ल्यूअॅः मॅन्ट n.* act of alluring प्रलोभन; fascination आकर्षण।

allusion *अॅ ल्यू ज़ॅन n.* indirect reference इशारा, संकेत।

allusive *अॅ ल्यू सिव a.* hinting, refering indirectly सांकेतिक।

ally[1] *अॅ लॉइ v.t.* to join संबद्ध करना, जोड़ना।

ally[2] *अॅ लॉइ, ऐ लॉइ n.* friend मित्र; anything near to another in classification समवर्गी।

almanac *औल्मॅ नैक n.* a register of the days, weeks and months of the year with astronomical events, anniversaries etc. पंचांग।

almighty *औल् मॉइ टि a.* omnipotent सर्वशक्तिमान।

almond *आ मॅन्ड n.* a kind of dry fruit and its tree बादाम और उसका वृक्ष।

almost *आल् मोस्ट adv.* very nearly करीब-करीब।

alms *आम्ज़ n.* relief given out of pity to the poor भिक्षा।

aloft *अॅ लौफ़्ट adv.* on high ऊंचे पर; in the air आकाश में।

alone *अॅ लोन a.* single अकेला; unaccompanied एकांकी; only एकमात्र।

along[1] *अॅ लौ ̆ ङंग adv.* lengthwise लंबाई में onward आगे; together साथ में।

along[2] *prep.* by the side of की बग़ल में; lengthwise by के समानांतर।

aloof *अॅ लूफ adv.* at a distance दूर; apart अलग।

aloud *अॅ लॉउड adv.* loudly ऊँची आवाज़ में।

alp *ऐल्प् n.* a high mountain, a mountain peak, ऊँचा पहाड़, पर्वत की चोटी।

alpha *ऐल्'-फ़ा n.* the first letter of the greek alphabet {A, a}, the first, ग्रीक वर्णमाला का पहिला अक्षर, आदि, आरम्भ।

alphabet *ऐल् फॅ बै ̆ट n.* letters used in writing a language वर्णमाला।

alphabetical *ऐल् फॅ बै ̆टि कॅल a.* in order of an alphabet वर्णक्रमानुसारी।

alphonsion *ऐल्-फ़ॉन'-सिन् n.* an in strument for extracting bullets. शरीर में से बंदूक की गोली निकालने का यन्त्र।

alpinist *ऐल्'-पिन्-इस्ट् n.* a climber on high mountains. ऊँचे पहाड़ पर चढ़ने वाला।

already *औल् रै ̆ डि adv.* by this time अब तक; by that time तब तक; before a given time पहले ही।

also *औल् सो adv.* in addition साथ ही; too और, भी।

altar *ऑल् टः n.* place for offerings बलिवेदी।

alter *औल् टॅ:* *v.t.* to change परिवर्तित करना; *v.i.* to be changed परिवर्तित होना।

alteration *औल् टॅ रे शॅन* *n.* change परिवर्तन; modification संशोधन।

altercation *औल् टॅ: के शॅन* *n.* quarrel झगड़ा।

alternate[1] *औल् टॅ: निट* *a.* happening by turns क्रम से होने वाला।

alternate[2] *औल् टॅ: नेट* *v.t.* to change back and forth आगे-पीछे करना।

alternative[1] *औल्टॅ: नॅ टिव* *n.* choice विकल्प।

alternative[2] *a.* affording a choice between two things वैकल्पिक।

although *औल् दो* *conj.* even though यद्यपि।

altimeter *ऑल्-टि-मि-टर्* *n.* an instrument for measuring heights. ऊँचाई नापने का एक प्रकार का यन्त्र।

altitude *ऐल् टि ट्यूड* *n.* height above sea-level ऊँचाई।

altivalent *ऑल्'-टिव्'-ए-लेन्ट्* *adj.* flying high. ऊँचा उड़ने वाला।

alto *ऐल्-टो* *n.* highest male voice. पुरुष का गायन में सबसे ऊँचा अलाप।

altogether *औल् टॅ गै दॅ:* *adv.* entirely पूर्णरूप से; in all कुल मिलाकर।

aluminium *ऐ ल्यु मि नि ॲम* *n.* a light white metal अल्युमीनियम।

alumna *अलम्'-ना* *n.* a woman graduate. उपाधि प्राप्त विदुषी।

always *औल् वॅज़, –वेज़–* *adv.* at all times सर्वदा।

alveary *ऐल्'-वि-अ-रि* *n.* the hive of bees. मधुमक्खी का छत्ता।

alvine *ऐल्'-वाइ-न्* *adj.* pertaining to the belly. पेट या तोंद सम्बन्धी।

am *ऐम* first person sing. present tense of 'be' हूं।

amalgam *ॲ मैल् गॅम* *n.* alloy of mercury पारद-मिश्रण; a combination or mixture मिश्रण।

amalgamate *ॲ मैल् गॅ मेट* *v.t.* to mix मिश्रित करना, मिलाना; *v.i.* to be mixed मिल जाना।

amalgamation *ॲ मैल् गॅ मे शॅन* *n.* mixing मिश्रण।

amass *ॲ मैस* *v.t.* to collect एकत्र करना।

amateur *ऐ मॅ टॅ: ट्यूॲ:* *n.* non-professional person अव्यवसायी, शौक़ीन व्यक्ति; an inexperienced person अनुभवहीन व्यक्ति।

amatory *ऐम्'-अ-टर्-इ* *adj.* expression of love. प्रेम उत्पन्न करने वाला, प्रेम का भाव दिखलाने वाला।

amauriosis *ऐम्-ओ-रो'-सिस्* *n.* partial or total loss of sight थोड़ी या पूर्ण दृष्टि-हीनता।

amaze *ॲ मेज़* *v.t.* to fill with great surprise विस्मित करना।

amazement *ॲ मेज़ मॅन्ट* *n.* surprise विस्मय।

ambassador *ऐम् बै सॅ डॅ:* *n.* envoy of a country in another country राजदूत।

amberite *ऐम्'-बर्-आइट्* *n.* a smokeless explosive बिना धुएें का बारूद।

ambient *ऐम्'-बि-ऍन्ट्* *adj.* surrounding, encompassing, circumfused. चारों ओर रहने वाला, व्यापक।

ambiguity *ऐम् बि ग्यु इ टि* *n.* state of being ambiguous संदिग्धता।

ambiguous *ऐम् बि ग्यु अॅस a.* indistinct अस्पष्ट; having more than one meaning अनेकार्थी।

ambition *ऐम् बि शॅन n.* strong desire महत्वाकांक्षा; an object of such a desire महत्वाकांक्षा का विषय।

ambitious *ऐम् बि शॅस a.* full of ambition महत्वाकांक्षी।

ambry *ऐम्-ब्रि' n.* a wall cupboard, a pantry. दीवाल की अलमारी, भण्डार।

ambulance *ऐम् ब्यु लॅन्स n.* van for the sick रोगी-वाहन।

ambulant *ऐम्-ब्यू-लेन्ट् adj.* moving here and there. इधर-उधर घूमने वाला।

ambulate *ऐम्'-ब्यू-लेट्' v.t.* to move about. इधर-उधर घूमना।

ambush *ऐम् बुश n.* lying in wait to make a surprise attack घात।

ameliorate *अॅ मी लि अॅ रेट v.t.* to make better सुधारना; *v.i.* to become better सुधरना।

amelioration *अॅ मी लि अॅ रे शॅन n.* improvement सुधार।

amen *आ मै˘न, ए —interj.* so be it ऐसा ही हो, तथास्तु।

amenable *अॅ मी नॅ ब्ल a.* responsive प्रतिसंवेदी।

amend *अॅ मे˘न्ड v.t.* to correct संशोधन करना; to improve परिशोध करना; *v.i.* to become better सुधरना।

amendment *अॅ मैन्ड मॅन्ट n.* correction दोष-शोधन; reformation सुधार।

amends *अॅ मेन्डज़ n.pl.* compensation क्षतिपूर्ति।

amenorrhoea *अ-मेन्'-ओर्-री-आ n.* suppression of menstruation स्त्रियों का मासिक धर्म बन्द होना।

amiability *ए मि अॅ बि लि टि n.* sweetness of temper सुशीलता; friendliness मैत्रीभाव।

amiable *ए मि अॅ ब्ल a.* good tempered सौम्य; lovable प्रेमपात्र।

amicable *ऐम्'-इ-के-ब्ल् adj.* friendly, done in a friendly way. मित्रवत्, मित्रभाव का।

amid *अॅ मिड prep.* in or into the middle of मध्य में; during के दौरान।

amiss *अॅ मिस adv.* improperly अनुचित रूप में; wrongly अशुद्ध रूप में।

amity *ऐ मि टि n.* friendship मित्रता।

ammunition *ऐ म्यु नि शॅन n.* military projectiles अस्त्र-शस्त्र।

amnesia *एम्-नी'-सिया n.* loss of memory. स्मृति-शक्ति का लेप, स्मृति-हीनता।

amnesty *ऐम् नैसॅ टि n.* general pardon सर्वक्षमा।

among, amongst *अॅ मङ्ग, अॅ मङ्ग्स्ट prep.* surrounded by से घिरा; in the middle of के बीच में।

amoral *ऐ मौ˘ रॅल a.* not moral नैतिकता-निरपेक्ष।

amount[1] *अॅ मॉउन्ट n.* sum of money राशि; quantity मात्रा; total योग।

amount[2] *v.i.* to result (in) परिणाम होना।

amount[3] *ए-माउन्ट्' v. t.* to result in, to be equivalent to परिणाम होना, बराबर होना।

amorous *ऐ मॅ रॅस a.* inclined to love प्रेमातुर; relating to love प्रेम-विषयक।

amour *अ मुअः, ऐ n.* love प्रेम।

ampere *ऐम् पे˘ अः n.* unit of electric current विद्युत् धारा की इकाई।

amphibious *एम्-फ़िब'-इ-अस् adj.* able to live in air and water द्विधा गति वाला, स्थल तथा जल में रहने योग्य।

amphitheatre *ऐम् फि थि अ टः n.* रंगभूमि, अंखाड़ा।

ample *ऐम् पल a.* quite enough प्रचुर, पर्याप्त; spacious विस्तीर्ण।

amplification *ऐम् प्लि फि के शॅन n.* act of amplifying विस्तारण; enlargement प्रवर्धन।

amplifier *ऐम् प्लि फॉइ अः n.* appliance for amplifying sound ध्वनिविस्तारक।

amplify *ऐम् प्लि फॉइ v.t.* to enlarge बढाना; *v.i.* to speak copiously विस्तार से व्याख्या करना।

amuck *अ मक adv.* with a mad desire पगलाकर।

amulet *ऐ म्यु लै˘ट n.* a charm against evils or witchcraft ताबीज।

amuse *अ म्यूज़ v.t.* to entertain (का) मनोरंजन करना।

amusement *अ म्यूज़् मॅन्ट n.* entertainment मनोरंजन।

an *ऐन, अॅन art*, one, any एक, कोई।

anabaptism *एन्-ए-बेप्'-टिज्म् n* rebaptism. दुबारा नामकरण।

anachronism *एन्'-एक्रॉ-नि-ज्म् n.* error in regard to time. कालगणना का भ्रम।

anaclisis *एन्-आक्'-लाइ-सिस् n.* bed sore. चारपाई पर निरन्तर पड़े रहने से उत्पन्न फोडा।

anadem *एन्'-आ-डेम् n.* a garland. माला।

anaemia *अ नी मि अ n.* lack of blood रक्ताल्पता।

anaesthesia *ऐ निस् थी ज़्य n.* insensibility संज्ञाहीनता, बेहोशी।

anaesthetic *ऐ निस् थै˘ टिक n. a.* (a substance) producing insensibility निश्चेतक।

anal *ए-नल् adj.* pertanining to or near anus, under the tail गुदा सम्बन्धी या गुदा के समीप का, पूँछ के नीचे का।

analogous *अ नै लौ˘गॅस a.* similar सदृश, अनुरूप।

analogy *अ नै लॅ जि n.* likeness सादृश्य, अनुरूपता।

analyse *ऐ न लॉइज़ v.t.* to subject to analysis विश्लेषण करना; to split up into parts (वाक्य) विच्छेद करना।

analysis *अ नै लि सिस n.* act of analysing विश्लेषण; (*gram.*) splitting up into parts वाक्य-विग्रह।

analyst ऐ नॅ लिस्ट *n.* one who analyses विश्लेषणकर्ता।

analytic,—al *ऐ नॅ लि टिक्,–टि कॅल a.* pertaining to analysis विश्लेषणात्मक।

anamnesis *एन्-आम्'-नी-सिस् n.* recollection of previous existence पूर्व जन्म का स्मरण।

anamorphous *एन्'-आ-मॉर्फ्-अस् adj.* abnormally developed. विकृत अंग वाला।

anarchism *ऐ नॅः किज्म n.* political theory favouring anarchy अराजकतावाद।

anarchist *ऐ नॅः किस्ट n.* person supporting anarchism अराजकतावादी।

anarchy *ऐ नॅ: कि n.* lawlessness अराजकता; disorder अव्यवस्था।

anatomy *ॲ नै टॅ मि n.* science of structure of bodies शरीर-रचना-विज्ञान।

ancestor *ऐन् सिस् टॅ: n.* forefather पूर्वज।

ancestral *ऐन् सै ॅस ट्रॅल a.* relating to ancestors पैतृक।

ancestry *ऐन् सिस् ट्रि n.* lineage वंशावली; descent कुल-परंपरा।

anchor *ऐङ् कॅ: n.* device for holding a ship at rest लंगर।

anchorage *ऐङ् कॅ रिज n.* duty on anchoring लंगरशुल्क; place where a ship anchors लंगर-गाह।

ancient *एन् शॅन्ट a.* old प्राचीन; antique पुरानी चलन का।

ancon *ऐनकान n.* elbow. कोहनी।

and *ऐन्ड, ॲन्ड ॲन् conj.* a connecting particle और, तथा।

androphagi *ऐन्-ड्रॉफ्'-एजि n. pl.* cannibals. नरभक्षक लोग।

anecdote *ऐ निक् डोट n.* short account of an interesting incident रूचिकर घटना, चुटकुला।

anemometer *एन्-इ--मॉम्-इट्-अर n.* an instrument for measuring the force of wind. वायु की शक्ति नापने का यंत्र।

anew *ॲ न्यू adv.* afresh नए सिरे से; again फिर।

anfractuous *ऐन्-फ्रेक्-ट्यु-अस् adj.* intricate, circuitous. पेचीला, चक्करदार।

angel *एन् जॅल n.* a divine messenger देवदूत।

anger *ऐङ् गॅ: n.* resentment क्रोध, रोष।

angina *ऐन्-जाइ'-ना n.* quinsy गला सूखने का रोग, गण्डमाला।

angle[1] *ऐङ्.'-गल् n. & v. t.* a fishhok, to fish with a hook. मछली पकड़ने की बंसी, बंसी से मछली फँसाना।

angle[2] *ऐङ्: ग्ल n.* inclination of two lines meeting in a point कोण; corner कोना।

angry *ऐङ् ग्रि a.* wrathful क्रोधित।

anguish *ऐङ् ग्विश n.* agony पीड़ा; grief कष्ट; extreme pain परिताप।

angular *ऐङ् ग्यु लॅ: a.* having corners कोणयुक्त; relating to angles कोण-संबंधी।

anigh *अ-नाइ'- adv. pref.* near to, at hand समीप, पास में।

animal *ऐ नि मॅल n.* quadruped चौपाया, जानवर; living being जीव, प्राणी।

animate[1] *ऐ नि मेट v.t.* to enliven जीवन युक्त करना; to present through animation चल कारटून के रूप में प्रस्तुत करना।

animate[2] *ऐ नि मिट,– मेट a.* living जीवित।

animation *ऐ नि मे शॅन n.* enlivement सजीवता; invigoration प्रोत्साहन।

animosity *ऐ नि मौ ॅ सि टि n.* active enmity वैर, शत्रुता।

animus *ऐन्'-इ-मस् n.* hostile spirit or intention. द्वेष, विरोधपूर्ण भावना या इच्छा।

aniseed *ऐन्'-इ-सीड़ n.* the seeds of anise plant. सौंफ का बीज।

ankle *ऐङ् क्ल n.* joint connecting the leg with the foot टख़ना।

anklet *ऐङ्: क् लिट n.* an ornament for the ankle नुपूर।

annalist *ऐ नॅ लिस्ट n.* historian, a writer of annals. इतिहासकार, इतिहास-लेखक।

annals *ऐ नॅल्ज़ n.pl.* yearwise story of events वार्षिक वृत्तांत।

annectant *अ-नेक्ट्'-अन्ट् adj.* connecting. जोड़ने वाला, संयोजक।

annex *ॲ नैक्स v.t.* to connect संबद्ध करना; to attach शामिल करना; to take possession of अधिकार करना।

annexation *ऐ नैक् से शॅन n.* appendix परिशिष्ट; appending संयोजन।

annihilate *ॲ नॉइ हि लेट v.t.* to destroy नष्ट करना; to abolish उन्मूलन करना।

annihilation *ॲ नॉइ हि ले शॅन n.* destruction ध्वंस।

anniversary *ऍ: नि वॅ: सॅ रि n.* yearly celebration of an event जयंती।

announce *ॲ नॉउंस v.t.* to declare घोषणा करना।

announcement *ॲ नॉउंस् मॅन्ट n.* declaration घोषणा।

annoy *ॲ नौ ँइ v.t.* to vex चिढ़ाना; to irritate उद्विग्न करना।

annoyance *ॲ नौँइ ॲन्स n.* vexation खीज, चिढ़; irritation उत्तेजना।

annual *ऐ न्यू ॲल a.* yearly वार्षिक।

annuitant *ऐ'-न्यू'-टेन्ट् n.* one who receives an annuity वार्षिक वेतन या वृत्ति पाने वाला मनुष्य।

annuity *ॲ न्यू इ टि n.* yearly grant वार्षिक अनुदान।

annul *ॲ नल v.t.* to repeal रद्द करना।

annulet *ऐ'-न्यु-लेट् n.* a small ring छोटी, अँगूठी या मुँदरी।

anoint *ॲ नौ ँइन्ट v.t.* to apply oil or ointment to (पर) तेल या मरहम लगाना।

anomalous *ॲ नौँ मॅ लॅस a.* irregular अनियमित।

anomaly *ॲ नौँ मॅ लि n.* irregularity अनियमितता; deviation from rule नियम-विरोध।

anon *अ-नॉन'-adv.* quickly, soon presently, then again शीघ्र अभी।

anonymity[1] *ऐ'-नॉन-इम्-इट्-इ n.* the condition of being anonymous. अज्ञात होने की अवस्था।

anonymity[2] *n.* namelessness अनामता।

anonymous *ॲ नौँनि मॅस a.* nameless अनाम; not bearing (author's) name (लेखक के) नाम-रहित।

another *ॲ न दॅ: a.* any other अन्य; different भिन्न।

answer[1] *आन् सॅ: n.* reply उत्तर; solution समाधान।

answer[2] *v.t.* to reply to उत्तर देना; to respond to प्रतिक्रिया के रूप में करना; *v.i.* to reply उत्तर देना; to be accountable उत्तरदायी होना।

answerable *आन् सॅ रॅ ब्ल a.* that may be answered उत्तर दिया जाने-योग्य; responsible उत्तरदायी।

ant *ऐन्ट n.* a pismire चींटी।

antacid *एन्ट्-एस'-इड् adj. & n.* removing acidity. खट्टापन हटाने वाला, अम्लत्व-नाशक पदार्थ।

antagonism *ऐन टै गॅ निज़्म n.* hostility बैर, शत्रुता; opposition सक्रिय विरोध।

antagonist *ऐन् टै गॅ निस्ट n.* opponent विपक्षी।

antagonize *ऐन् टै गॅ नॉइज़ v.t.* to

rouse opposition वैरी बनाना; to counteract प्रतिकार करना।

antarctic *ऐन् टा: क् टिक a.* relating to the south pole दक्षिणध्रुवीय।

antecede *ऐन्'-टि-सीड्'-v.t.* to go before or happen before time. समय से पूर्व घटित होना।

antecedent[1] *ऐन् टि सी डॅन्ट n.* that which goes before पूर्वगामी; (*gram.*) the noun to which a relative refers पूर्वपद।

antecedent[2] *a.* prior पूर्ववर्ती।

antedate *ऐन्'-टि-डेट् n.* a date before the exact time. स्थिर काल से पूर्व का समय।

antelope *ऐन'-टि-लोप' n.* a genus of deer like ruminant. एक प्रकार का हिरन या मृग।

antenatal *ऐन्'-टि-ने'-टल् adj.* previous to birth. उत्पत्ति के पूर्व का।

antennae *ऐन् टै ˘ नॅ n. (pl.)* an aerial एंटिना; the feeler of an insect स्पर्शशृंगिका।

antenuptial *ऐन्'-टि-नप्'-शल् adj.* before nuptials, occurring before marriage. विवाह से पूर्व होने वाला।

anthem *ऐन्'-थेम् n.* a hymn or song, sacred song sung in praise of god. ईश्वर-स्तुति, स्तुतिरूप गायन, भजन।

anthology *ऐन् थौ˘ लॅ जि n.* collection of literary pieces चयनिका।

anthropoid *ऐन्'-थ्रॉ-पॉयड् adj.* resembling man in form only. केवल आकार में मनुष्य के सदृश।

anti *ऐन्-टि pref.* in the sense of against, in place of "उपसर्ग जिसका अर्थ विपरीत स्थान में होता है।

anti-aircraft *ऐन् टि ऍ ऑ: क्राफ्ट a.* used against enemy aircraft विमान-भेदी।

antic *ऐन् टिक n.* odd or ridiculous action, queer behaviour अजीब कार्य अथवा व्यवहार।

anticardium *एन्'-टि-कार्-डि-अम् n.* the pit of the stomach. नाभि, ठोढ़ी।

anticipate *ऐन् टि सि पेट v.t.* to forestall पूर्वानुमान करना; to expect पहले से आशा करना; to foretaste पूर्वानुभव करना।

anticipation *ऐन् टि सि पे शॅन n.* expectation प्रत्याशा; forestate पूर्वानुमान।

antidote *ऐन् टि डोट n.* medicine that counteracts posion विषमारक औषधि।

antinomy *ऐन्'-टि-नॉ-मि n.* a conflict of authority अधिकार-विरोध।

antipathy *ऐन् टि पॅ थि n.* dislike घृणा; opposition विरोध, शत्रुता।

antiphony *ऐन्'-टि-फ़ॉनि n.* echo, response प्रतिध्वनि, प्रतिगान।

antipodes *ऐन'-टि-पॅडी-जू n. pl.* those who live on opposite sides of the globe. भूमण्डल के विपरीत सिरों पर रहने वाले, प्रतिलोम।

antiquarian[1] *ऐन् टि क्वे˘ अॅ रि अॅन a.* pertaining to antiquaries पुरातत्व-विषयक।

antiquarian[2] *n.* one versed in antiquities पुरातत्ववेत्ता।

antiquary *ऐन ।टि क्वॅ रि n.* one versed in antiquities पुरातत्ववेत्ता।

antiquated *ऐन टि क्वे टिड a.* ancient प्राचीन; old-fashioned अप्रचलित।

antique *ऐन् टीक a.* ancient पुरातन; old-fashioned दकियानूसी, अप्रचलित।

antiquity *ऐन् टी क्वि टि n.* ancientness पुरातनता; *(pl.)* relics पुरावशेष; ancient times प्राचीनकाल।

antiseptic[1] *ऐन् टि सैपॅ टिक n.* a substance that resists putrefaction रोगाणुरोधक औषधि।

antiseptic[2] *a.* counteracting putrefaction रोगाणुरोधक।

antithesis *ऐन् टि थि सिस n.* contrast विपर्यय; opposition विरोध।

antitheist *एन्'-टि-थी'-इस्ट् n.* one who does not believe in god's existence. नास्तिक, अनीश्वरवादी;

antler *ऐन्ट् लॅः n.* a branch of a stag's horn बारहसिंह की शाखादार सींग।

antonym *ऐन् टॅ निम n.* a word of opposite meaning विलोम।

anus *ए नॅस n.* the lower opening of the bowels मलद्वार, गुदा।

anvil *ऐन् विल n.* blacksmith's iron-block निहाई (लोहार की)।

anxiety *ऐङ् ज़ॉइ ॲ टि a.* state of being anxious परेशानी; concern चिंतां।

anxious *ऐङ्क् शॅस a.* causing concern चिंताजनक; concerned चिंतित; eager उत्सुक, उतावला।

any[1] *ऐ नि a.* some कोई।

any[2] *adv.* in any degree किसी सीमा तक।

anyhow *ऐ नि हॉउ adv.* in some way or the other किसी न किसी तरीके से।

apace *ॲ पेस adv.* quickly शीघ्रता से।

apart *ॲ पाःट adv.* separately अलग से; aside एक ओर।

apartment *ॲ पाःट् मॅन्ट n.* a room कक्ष।

apathy *ऐ पॅ थि n.* want of feeling भावहीनता; indifference उदासीनता।

ape[1] *एप n.* a tailless monkey कपि, पुच्छहीन बंदर; imitator अनुकरण करनेवाला।

ape[2] *v.t.* to imitate अनुकरण करना।

aperture *ऐ पॅः ट्युॲः n.* a hole छिद्र।

apex *ए पैक्स n.* summit शिखर।

aphorism *ऐफ्'-ऑ-रिज़्म् n.* adage, maxim, definition कहावत (सूत्र), वचन।

apiary *ऐ पि ॲ रि n.* place for apiculture मधुमक्खीपालन-स्थान।

apiculture *ए पि कल् चॅः n.* bee-keeping मधुमक्खी–पालन।

apish *ए पिश a.* ape-like वानर-सदृश।

apnoea *एप्'-नीआ n.* stoppage of breathing. साँस की रुकावट, श्वासावरोध।

apologize *ॲ पौ लॅ जॉइज v.i.* to express regret खेद प्रकट करना।

apologue *ऐप्'-ॲ'-लॉग् n.* fable, parable or a moral story, a tale. उपदेशपूर्ण कहानी, उपाख्यान।

apology *ॲ पौ लॅ जि n.* regretful acknowledgement of offence स्वदोष-स्वीकार।

apostle *ॲ पौ ॅ स्ल n.* preacher of religion धर्मप्रचारक।

apostrophe *ॲ पौसॅ ट्रॅ फि n.* a mark(') indicating contraction of a word वर्णलोप या संबंधकारक का चिह्न।

apotheosis *अप्'-ऑथि-ऑसिस्* *n.* making god-like देवता तुल्य निर्माण।

apparatus *ऐ पॅ रे टॅस* *n.* set of instruments उपकरण।

apparel[1] *अॅ पै रॅल* *n.* clothing वस्त्र।

apparel[2] *v.t.* to dress वस्त्र पहनना।

apparent *अॅ पै रॅन्ट, पे ॅ अॅ* *a.* that may be seen प्रत्यक्ष।

appeal[1] *अॅ पील* *n.* the removal of a case to a higher court अपील।

appeal[2] *v.t.* to make an earnest request प्रार्थना करना; to refer to superior court अपील करना.; *v.i.* to suplicate विनती करना; to be interesting आकर्षित अथवा प्रभावित करने का गुण रखना।

appear *अॅ पिअॅ:* *v.i.* to become visible दृष्टिगोचर होना; to seem प्रतीत होना।

appearance *अॅ पिअॅ रॅन्स* *n.* appearing प्रकटन; outward look बाह्याकृति; presence उपस्थिति; rise उदय।

appease *अॅ पीज़* *v.t.* to pacify शांत करना; to comfort सांत्वना देना।

appellant *अॅ पै ॅ लॅन्ट* *n.* one who appeals अपीलकर्त्ता।

append *अॅ पैन्ड* *v.t.* to add संलग्न करना; to annex नत्थी करना।

appendage *अॅ पैन् डिज* *n.* appendix परिशिष्ट, संलग्नक।

appendicitis *अॅ पैन् डि सॉइ टिस* *n.* a disease of intestine उपांत्रशूल।

appendix[1] *अप्'-पेन्ड्-इक्स्* *n.* *(pl.* **appendices** इ-सीज्) anything added in the end परिशिष्ट, शेष संग्रह।

appendix[2] *अॅ पैन् डिक्स* *n.* supplement परिशिष्ट।

appetence *ऐप्'-पिट्-एन्स्* *n.* desire, longing अभिलाषा, इच्छा।

appetent *(ऐप-पीटेंट)-* *adj.* desiring अति उत्सुक।

appetite[1] *ऐ पि टॉइट* *n.* a strong desire for food भोजनेच्छा।

appetite[2] *n.* hunger भूख; desire इच्छा।

appetizer *ऐ पि टॉइ ज़ॅ:* *n.* something causing appetite क्षुधावर्धक वस्तु।

applaud *अॅ प्लौड* *v.t.* to extoll हर्षध्वनि-द्वारा अनुमोदन करना; to commend प्रशंसा करना।

applause *अॅ प्लौज़* *n.* praise loudly expressed हर्षध्वनि; acclamation प्रशंसा।

apple *ऐ पल* *n.* an edible fruit सेब; the pupil of the eye पुतली।

appliance *अॅ प्लॉइ अॅन्स* *n.* instrument उपकरण; thing applied उपाय, युक्ति; act of applying प्रयोग।

applicable *ऐप् लि कॅ बल* *a.* fit to be applied प्रयोग में लाया जाने-योग्य।

applicant *ऐप् लि कॅन्ट* *n.* one who applies प्रार्थी।

application *ऐप् लि के शॅन* *n.* request प्रार्थना; petition अर्ज़ी; using अनुप्रयोग।

apply *अॅ प्लॉइ* *v.t.* to enforce लागू करना; to use प्रयोग में लाना; *v.i.* to make a request आवेदन करना; to be relevant लागू होना।

appoint *अॅ पौ ॅइन्ट* *v.t.* to employ नियुक्त करना; to nominate मनोनीत करना; to fix निश्चित करना।

appointment *अॅ पौ ॅइन्ट मॅन्ट* *n.* act

of appointing नियुक्ति; engagement मिलने का समय; office held नौकरी।

apportion अॅ पौः शॅन *v.t.* to divide बांटना।

apposite अप्'-पॉ-जिट् *adj* proper, well put, suitable, appropriate योग्य, सगंत (यथार्थ)।

apposite² ऐ पॅ ज़िट *a.* suitable संगत।

appositely अप-पॉ जिट (लि) *adv.* suitably उचित रीति से।

approbate एप्'-प्रो'-बेट् *v.t.* to approve, to sanction. अनुमोदन करना, स्वीकार करना।

appraise अॅ प्रेज़ *v.t.* to estimate मूल्यांकन करना; to fix the price of (का) मूल्य निर्धारित करना।

appreciable अॅ प्री शि अॅ ब्ल *a.* noticeable उल्लेखनीय, ध्यातव्य।

appreciate अॅ प्री शि एट *v.t.* to estimate justly मूल्यांकन करना; to esteem highly सम्मान करना; to raise in value मूल्य बढ़ाना; *v.i.* to increase in value महंगा हो जाना।

appreciation अॅ प्री शि ए शॅन *n.* estimation मूल्यांकन, परख; recognition प्रशंसा; raise in value मूल्यवृद्धि।

apprehend ऐ प्रि हैन्ड *v.t.* to arrest बंदी बनाना; to understand सीखना; to fear डरना।

apprehension ऐ प्रि हैन् शॅन *n.* arrest गिरफ्तारी; fear आशंका; understanding समझ।

apprehensive ऐ प्रि हैन् सिव *a.* fearful आशंकित।

apprentice अॅ प्रैन् टिस *n.* learner of a trade प्रशिक्षु।

apprise अॅ प्राइज *v.t.* to notify सूचित करना।

approach¹ अॅ प्रोच *v.t.* to come near to (के) पास पहुंचना; to approximate से मिलता-जुलता होना; *v.i.* to come near पहुंचना।

approach² *n.* act of approaching आगमन; way, path मार्ग; method विधि।

approbation ऐ प्रॅ बे शॅन *n.* approval अनुमोदन।

appropriate¹ अॅ प्रो प्रि एट *v.t.* to take and use as one's own हड़प लेना; to authorise for some specific use प्रयोजन विशेष के लिए अधिकृत करना।

appropriate² अॅ प्रो प्रि इट *a.* suitable उपयुक्त।

appropriation अॅ प्रो प्रि ए शॅन *n.* act of appropriating स्वायत्तीकरण।

approval अॅ प्रू वॅल *n.* approbation अनुमोदन; sanction स्वीकृति।

approve अॅ प्रूव *v.t.* to give approval of अनुमोदन करना; to agree सहमति देना।

approximate अॅ प्रौकॅ सि मिट *a.* very near अत्यंत समीप; almost correct प्रायः शुद्ध।

appricot ए प्रि कौॅट *n.* a fruit like peach ख़ूबानी।

appurtenance अप्-पर-टिन्'-एन्स् *n.* belonging, an accessory सम्पत्ति का स्वामित्व, लगाव।

apron ए प्रॅन *n.* garment worn over the front part of the body पेटबंद।

apt ऐप्ट *a.* suitable संगत, उपयुक्त; quick-witted योग्य; prone उद्यत।

aptitude ऐप् टि ट्यूड *n.* tendency

रूझान; fitness औचित्य।

aquarium *अ'-क्वेर्'-इ-अम् n.* pond in which living aquatic plants or animals are kept जल के पौधों या जन्तुओं के पालने का जलाशय।

aquarius *अ'-क्वेर्-इ-अस् n.* the 11th sign of zodiac कुम्भ राशि।

aqueduct *ऐ-'क्वि-डक्ट् n.* an artificial channel कृत्रिम जलमार्ग, नहर।

arable *ऐ र् ब्ल a. & n.* (land) fit for ploughing जुताई-योग्य (भूमि)।

arbiter *आ: बि टॅ: n.* arbitrator मध्यस्थ।

arbitrary *आ: बि ट्रॅ रि a.* based on discretion मनमाना; despotic निरंकुश; capricious स्वेच्छाचारी।

arbitrate *आ: बि ट्रे ट v.t.* to decide as an arbitrator मध्यस्थता करना।

arbitration *आ: बि ट्रे शॅन n.* decision by an arbiter पंचफ़ैसला।

arbitrator *आ: बि ट्रे टॅ: n.* arbiter मध्यस्थ।

arc *आ: क n.* part of a circle चाप।

arcade *आर्'-केड्' n.* row of arches supported on columns. खम्भों पर बनी हुई मेहराबें।

arch[1] *आ:च n.* vault तोरण, मेहराब।

arch[2] *v.t.* to form into an arch मेहराबदार बनाना।

arch[3] *a.* chief प्रधान; crafty चालाक।

archaic *आ: के इक a.* obsolete अप्रचलित।

archangel *आ: केन् जॅल n.* angel of highest rank प्रधान देवदूत।

archbishop *आ: च् बि शॅप n.* chief bishop प्रमुख पादरी।

archer *आ: चॅ: n* a bowman धनुर्धर।

architect *आ: कि टैक्ट n.* one who plans building वास्तुकार।

architecture *आ: कि टेक् चॅ: n.* art or science of buildings वास्तुकला; style of building निर्माण-शैली।

archives *आ: कॉइव्ज n.pl.* place for keeping records अभिलेखागार।

Arctic आ: क् टिक *a.* of the north polar regions उत्तरीध्रुव-संबंधी

ardent *आ: डॅन्ट a.* eager उत्साही; fervid उत्कट; burning ज्वलंत।

ardour *आ: डॅ: n.* eagerness उत्साह; enthusiasm जोश।

arduous *आ: ड्यू अॅस a.* hard-working परिश्रमी; difficult कठिन, श्रमसाध्य।

area *ऍ अॅ रि अॅ n.* surface measure क्षेत्रफल; region भूभाग; field of study अध्ययन-क्षेत्र।

areca *आर्'-इ-का n.* betel-nut palm सुपारी का वृक्ष।

arefaction *एरि'-फ़ेक्'-शन् n.* act of drying सुखाने का कार्य।

arena *अॅ री नॅ n.* open space for combatants अखाड़ा।

argil *आर्'-जिल् n.* potter's clay, alumina. कुम्हार की मिट्टी, एल्यूमिना।

argue *आ: ग्यू v.t.* to show reasons for प्रमाणित करना; *v.i.* to present reason तर्क प्रस्तुत करना।

argument *आ: ग्यू मॅन्ट n.* plea तर्क, युक्ति; debate वादविवाद।

argute *आर्'-ग्यूट' adj.* sharp, shrill तीखा, कर्कश (शब्द)।

arid *एर्-इड् adj.* parched with heat गरमी से झुलसा हुआ।

aries *एर्-ईज् n.* the Ram. मेष राशि।

aright[1] *ए-राइट् adv.* rightly, without mistake, to the right side उचित रीति से, ठीक, दाहिनी ओर।

aright² *अ॑ रॉइट adv.* rightly ठीक प्रकार से।

arise *अ॑ रॉइज़ v.i.* to rise उदित होना; to ascend ऊपर उठना; to get up जागना; to appear प्रकट होना।

aristocracy *ऐ रिस् टौ॑ क्रॅ सि n.* ruling body of nobles कुलीनतंत्र; nobility अभिजात वर्ग।

aristocrat *ऐ रिस् टॅ क्रैट, अ॑ रिस् n.* person of noble birth कुलीन व्यक्ति।

aristophanic *एर्'-इस्-टॉ फेनइक adj.* witty, shrewd. हँसमुख, चतुर।

arithmetic *अ॑ रिथ् मै॑टिक n.* science of numbers अंकगणित।

arithmetical *अ॑ रिथ् मै॑ टि कॅल a.* pertaining to arithmetic अंकगणित-संबंधी।

ark *आर्क् n.* a chest, a box, a large boat तिजोरी, बक्स, बड़ी नाक।

arm¹ *आःम n.* limb from the shoulder to the hand भुजा; sleeve आस्तीन; *(pl.)* weapons हथियार।

arm² *v.t.* to equip with weapons हथियारों से सुसज्जित करना; *v.i.* to prepare for war युद्ध के लिए तैयारी करना।

armada *आः मा डॅ, आः मै डॅ n.* a fleet of armed ships युद्धपोतों का बेड़ा।

armament *आः मॅ मॅन्ट n. (pl.)* weaponry युद्ध-सामग्री।

armature *आः मॅ ट्युअॅः n.* a moving part of an electromagnetic device विद्युत्-चुंबकीय यंत्र का घूमता हुआ भाग।

armistice *आः मिस् टिस n.* truce युद्धविराम।

armlet *आर्म्'-लेट् a.* an ornament worn round the ram, a small inlet of sea. जोशन (बाजूबन्द), समुद्र की शाखा।

armour *आः मॅः n.* a defensive covering कवच।

armoury *आः मॅ रि n.* a repository of arms शास्त्रागार।

army *आः मि n.* military forces सेना; a large number दलबल।

around¹ *अ॑ रॉउन्ड prep.* on all sides of के चारों ओर।

around² *adv.* on every side सब ओर; in all directions चारों ओर; nearby आसपास।

arouse *अ॑ रॉउज़ v.t.* to awaken जगाना; to stir into action क्रियाशील बनाना, चेताना।

arraign *अर्'-रेन् v. t.* to accuse, to find fault with, to impeach. अपराधी ठहराना, दोष लगाना, कलंक लगाना।

arrange *अ॑ रेन्ज् v.t.* to set in a rank क्रम में रखना; to put in order व्यवस्थित करना; *v.i.* to make plans in advance व्यवस्था करना।

arrangement *अ॑ रेन्ज् मॅन्ट n.* setting in a rank क्रमस्थापन; order व्यवस्था; *(pl.)* plans योजनाएं।

arrant *आर्'-रेन्ट n.* notorious, downright कुख्यात, अत्यन्त (निपट),

array¹ *अ॑ रे v.t.* to dress वस्त्रों से अलंकृत करना; to equip सेना को शस्त्र सज्जित करना।

array² *n.* order क्रम; order of a battle व्यूह-रचना; attire वस्त्र।

arrears *अ॑ ,रिअॅःज़ n.pl.* unpaid amount बकाया।

arrest¹ *अ॑ रैस्ट v.t.* to seize हिरासत में लेना; to stop रोकना।

arrest² *n.* seizure by warrant गिरफ़्तारी।

arrival *अॅ राॅइ वॅल n.* act of arriving आगमन; thing that arrives आगत वस्तु।

arrive *अॅ राॅइव v.i.* to reach पहुंचना; to attain a position of success सफलता पाना।

arrogance *ऐ रॅ गॅन्स n.* undue assumption of importance घमंड, गर्व।

arrogant *ऐ रॅ गॅन्ट a.* overbearing अक्खड़, हेकड़।

arrow *ऐ रो n.* a straight, pointed missile made to be shot from a bow तीर, बाण।

arrowroot *ऐ रो रूट n.* starchy food made from the powdered root of a plant अरारोट।

arsenal *आः सॅ नॅल n.* armoury आयुधागार।

arsenic *आः सॅ निक n.* a poisonous powder संखिया।

arson *आः सॅन n.* criminal act of setting fire आगज़नी।

art *आःट n.* creation of beauty कला; skill कुशलता; cunning चालाकी; artistic product कलाकृति।

artery *आः टॅ रि n.* tube or vessel that conveys blood from the heart रक्तवाहिनी, धमनी।

artful *आःट् फुल a.* crafty चालाक; skillful निपुण।

arthritis *आर्-थ्राइ'-टिस् n.* gout, inflammation of joints जोड़ों की सूजन।

artichoke *आर्'-टि-चोक् n.* a kind of edible plant. चुकन्दर, हाथी चक।

article *आः टि क्ल n.* a clause in an agreement अनुच्छेद; a piece of writing लेख, रचना; an item वस्तु, नग; a part of speech used before nouns उपपद।

articulate *आः टि क्यु लिट a.* jointed जोड़दार; clear स्पष्ट; able to express one's thoughts with ease अभिव्यक्तिक्षम।

artifice *आर्-टि-फाइस् n.* crafty contrivance, skill, device, fraud धूर्तता, चालाकी, साधन, छल।

artificial *आः टि फि शॅल a.* not natural कृत्रिम; imitated नकली।

artillery *आः टि लॅ रि n.* big guns तोपें; gunnery तोपखाना।

artisan *आः टि ज़ैन n.* a handicraftsman शिल्पी, दस्तकार।

artist *आः टिस्ट n.* one practising a fine art चित्रकार, कलाकार।

artistic *आः टिस् टिक a.* concerned with art कलात्मक।

artless *आःट् लिस a.* simple सीधा, सरल; guileless छल-कपट-रहित; natural स्वाभाविक।

as¹ *ऐज़, ॲज adv.* to such an extent इस सीमा तक; for example उदाहरणस्वरुप।

as² *conj.* although यद्यपि; since क्योंकि; to which degree जितना; like समान; in the manner in which जिस प्रकार।

as³ *pron.* who, which, that जो, जिसने, जिसको।

asafoetida *ऐस्-आ-फोटिडा n.* a kind of resinous gum. हींग।

asbestos *ऐस्'-बेस्'-टस् n.* an incombustible fibrous mineral न जलने वाली एक तन्तुमय धातु, अदह।

ascend *अॅ सैन्ड v.t.* to go up (पर) चढ़ना; *v.i.* to go up ऊपर जाना।

ascent *अॅ सैन्ट n.* an up-slope चढाव; a going up चढ़ाई।

ascertain *ऐ सॅः टेन v.t.* to find out for certain निश्चित करना।

ascetic[1] *अॅ सै ॅ टिक n.* person leading self-denying life तपस्वी।

ascetic[2] *a.* leading a life of severe self-discipline तपस्यापूर्ण।

ascribe *अॅस् क्रॉइब v.t.* to attribute मढ़ना, लगाना, आरोपित करना।

ash *ऐश n.* the dust or remains of anything burnt राख; *(pl.)* remains of human body after cremation भस्मि, अवशेष।

ashamed *अॅ शेम्ड a.* affected with shame शर्मिंदा, लज्जित।

ashore *अॅ शौः, अॅ शो ॅः adv.* on the shore किनारे पर।

aside[1] *अॅ सॉइड adv.* on or to one side, apart एक ओर, अलग।

aside[2] *n.* words spoken in an undertone स्वगतकथन।

asinine *ऐस्'-इन्-आइन् adj.* pertanining to asses, foolish गदहे से सम्बन्धित, मूर्ख।

ask *आस्क v.t.* to put a question पूछना; to request निवेदन करना; to demand मांगना; to inquire पूछताछ करना।

asleep *अॅ स्लीप adv. & a.* in a sleeping state सोता हुआ; dead मृत; numb सुन्न।

aspect *ऐस् पैक्ट n.* appearance आकृति; position, phase अवस्थिति; view दृष्टिकोण; direction of facing पहलू।

asperse *एस्-पर्स v. t.* to defame, to culminate. निन्दा करना, कलंक लगाना।

aspirant *अॅस् पॉइ रॅन्ट n.* one who aspires उच्चाकांक्षी व्यक्ति।

aspiration *ऐस् पि रे शॅन n.* eager; desire अभिलाषा, लालसा।

aspire *अॅस् पॉइअॅः v.t.* to be filled with ambition महत्वाकांक्षा करना।

ass *ऐस n.* a small animal of the horse genus गदहा; a dull, stupid fellow मूर्ख व्यक्ति।

assail *अ-सेल्'v. t.* to make a violent attack आक्रमण करना, चढ़ाई करना।

assassin *अॅ सै सिन n.* murderer हत्यारा।

assassinate *अॅ सै सि नेट v.t.* to murder हत्या करना।

assassination *अॅ सै सि ने शॅन n,* murder हत्या, वध।

assault[1] *अॅ सौल्ट n.* a sudden attack धावा, चढाई; rape बलात्कार।

assault[2] *v.t.* to make an attack upon आक्रमण करना।

assemble *अॅ सैम् ब्ल v.t.* to collect एकत्र करना; to put together the parts of (के) पुरज़े जोड़ना; *v.i.* to meet together एकत्र हो जाना।

assembly *अॅ सैम्ब् लि n.* the act of assembling जमाव; a company assembled समाज, मंडली; a body of persons सम्मेलन।

assent[1] *अॅ सैन्ट v.i.* to express agreement सहमत होना।

assent[2] *n.* an agreement सहमति; consent अनुमति।

assert *अॅ सॅःट v.t.* to make a claim to (one's right) (अधिकारों का) दावा करना; to declare firmly निश्चयपूर्वक कहना।

assess *अ॑ सैसॅ v.t.* to determine (tax etc.) (कर आदि) निर्धारित करना; to estimate अनुमान लगाना; to evaluate आंकना।

assessment *अ॑ सैसॅ मॅन्ट n.* act of assessing कर-निर्धारण; evaluation मूल्यांकन।

asset *ऐ सै॑ ट n. (pl.)* property संपत्ति; useful quality or skill उपयोगी गुण अथवा कौशल।

assibilate *एस्-सिब्'-इ-लेट्' v. t.* to utter a hissing sound, to make sibilant सीत्कार (सुसकार) सहित बोलना।

assign *अ॑ सॉइन v.t.* to allot आवंटन करना; to designate, to appoint नियुक्त करना; to specify निर्धारित करना।

assignee *अ॑ सॉइ नी n.* one to whom any right or property is assigned संपत्ति-भागी।

assimilate *एस्-सिम्'-इ-लेट्'- v. t.* to make like to, to compare with, to absorb into the system. सदृश करना, तुलना करना, पचाना (परिपाक करना); *v. i.* to be absorbed एकीभूत होना, पचना।

assimilation *एस-सिम-इले'-शन् n,* समीकरण, परिपाक, परिणाम।

assist *अ॑ सिस्ट v.t.* to help सहायता करना; *v.i.* to render help हाथ बंटाना।

assistance *अ॑ सिस् टॅन्स n.* help, aid सहायता।

assistant *अ॑ सिस् टॅन्ट n.* one who assists, helper सहायक।

associate[1] *अ॑ सो॑ शि एट v.t.* to join जोड़ना; to unite सयुंक्त करना, मिलाना; to make a partner साथी बनाना; *v.t.* to be joined मिलना, जुड़ना।

associate[2] *अ॑ सो शि इट a.* connected जुड़ा हुआ; accompanying सहकारी।

associate[3] *n.* a partner or colleague सहकर्मी; a companion साथी।

association *अ॑ सो सि ए शॅन n.* society संगति; union संघ; intimacy घनिष्टता।

assoil *एस्'-सॉयल्' v. t.* to free from guilt or sin, to forgive पाप से मुक्त करना, क्षमा करना।

assort *अस्'-सॉर्ट्' v. t. & i.* to arrange into groups, to agree यथाक्रम करना, वर्गीकरण करना, छाँटना, एकमत होना।

assuage *अ॑ सवेज v.t.* to soften मृदु करना।

assume *अ॑ स्यूम v.t.* to take for granted मान लेना; to seize (अधिकार) छीन लेना; to suppose कल्पना करना।

assumption *अ॑ सम्प् शॅन n.* taking for granted पूर्वधारणा; that which is taken for granted मान्यता; arrogance घमंड; supposition कल्पना; act of taking upon oneself धारण।

assurance *अ॑ शुअ॑ रॅन्स n.* confidence विश्वास; sureness निश्चय; insurance बीमा; security प्रतिभूति; impudence धृष्टता।

assure *अ॑ शुअ॑: v.t.* to make sure सुनिश्चित करना; to insure बीमा करना; to reasure विश्वास दिलाना।

astatic *ए-स्टेट्'-इक् adj.* not keeping on fixed position अस्थिर।

asterisk *ऐस् टॅ रिस्क* *n.* star-like sign तारक चिह्न।

asterism *ऐस्-टर-इज्म्* *n.* a cluster of three stars. तीन तारों का चिन्ह।

asteroid *ऐस्'-टीर्-'ऑ एड* *adj.& n.* of the form of a star, a star fish, a small star तारे के आकार का, तारा मीन, एक छोटा तारा।

asthma *ऐस् मॉ* *n.* a disease making breathing difficult दमा।

astir *अ-स्टर्'* *adv.* in motion, in excitement गतिशील, उत्तेजना में।

astonish *ॲस् टौ˘ निश* *v.t.* to surprise greatly, to amaze विस्मित करना।

astonishment *ॲस् टौ˘ निश् मंट* *n.* amazement विस्मय।

astound *एस्'-टाउन्ड्'* *v.t.* to surprise, to cause fear, to amaze चकित करना, भयभीत करना, घबड़ा देना।

astray *ॲस् ट्रे* *adv., a.* out of the right way पथभ्रष्ट।

astrologer *ॲस् ट्रौ लॅ जॅ:* *n.* one versed is astrology ज्योतिषी।

astrology *ॲस् ट्रौ˘ लॅ जि* *n.* science of foretelling events by stars ज्योतिष।

astronaut *ऐस्. ट्रौ˘नौ˘ट* *n.* one engaged in space travel अंतरिक्ष-यात्री।

astronomer *ॲस् ट्रौ˘ नॅ मॅ:* *n.* one versed in astronomy खगोलशास्त्री।

astronomy *ॲस् ट्रौ˘ नॅ मि* *n.* science of the heavenly bodies खगोलशास्त्र।

asunder *ॲ सन् डॅ:* *adv.* apart अलग-अलग; into parts टुकड़ों में।

asylum *ॲ सॉइ लॅम* *n.* place of shelter शरण-स्थल।

at *ऐट* *prep.* on पर; over ऊपर; in में; towards की ओर; near के पास।

atheism *ऐ थि इज़्म* *n.* disbelief in the existence of God or gods नास्तिकता।

atheist *ए थि इस्ट* *n.* person who does not believe in the existence of God or gods नास्तिक।

athirst *अ-थर्स्ट'* *adj.* thirsty, wanting drink, eager प्यासा, उत्सुक।

athlete *ऐथ् लीट* *n.* sportsman व्यायामी, कसरती, क्रीड़ा-प्रतियागी।

athletic *ऐथ् लै˘ टिक* *a.* strong बलवान; of athletes कसरती।

athletics *ऐथ् लै˘ टिक्स* *n. pl.* athletic sports क्रीड़ा, खेलकूद।

athwart *आ-थ्वर्ट्* *prep.* across, transversely, from side to side, in opppsition to पार, आर-पार, एक ओर से दूसरी ओर, विपरीत अवस्था में।

atlas *ऐट् लॅस* *n.* a book of maps मानचित्रावली।

atmosphere *ऐट् मॅस् फ़िॲ:* *n.* the gaseous envelope that surrounds the earth वायुमंडल; environment पर्यावरण।

atoll *एट्'-ऑल्* *n.* ring-shaped corel reef. मूँगे का वृत्ताकार पहाड़।

atom *ऐ टॅम* *n.* smallest particle of an element अणु, परमाणु; anything very small सूक्ष्म वस्तु।

atomic *ॲ टौ˘ मिक* *a.* pertaining to atoms अणु-संबंधी।

atone *ॲ टोन* *v.i.* to make amends (for wrong) प्रायश्चित करना।

atonement *ॲ टोन् मॅन्ट* *n.* act of atoning प्रायश्चित।

atrocious अ ट्रो शॅस *a.* very cruel नृशंस; appalling भयंकर।

atrocity अ ट्रौ सि टि *n.* cruelty क्रूरता, नृशंसता।

attach अॅ टैच *v.t.* to seize by legal authority कुर्क करना; to connect, to join मिलाना; to fix जोड़ना; to assign प्रदान करना।

attache अॅ टै शे *n.* a technical expert on a diplomatic staff दूतावास का अधिकारी।

attachment अॅ टैच् मॅन्ट *n.* state of being attached लगाव; something attached संलग्न वस्तु।

attack[1] अॅ टैक *n.* an assault हमला; a fit दौरा; hostile criticism कड़ी आलोचना।

attack[2] *v.t.* to assault आक्रमण करना; to criticise आलोचना करना।

attain अॅ टेन *v.t.* to reach or accomplish पहुंचना।

attainment अॅ टेन् मॅन्ट *n.* act of attaining प्राप्ति उपलब्धि; *(pl.)* skill क्षमता, कौशल।

attaint अट्'-टेन्ट् *v. t.* to stain, to insult कलुषित करना, अपमानित करना।

attempt[1] अॅ टॅम्प्ट *v.t.* to try प्रयत्न करना।

attempt[2] *n.* effort प्रयास; attack आक्रमण।

attend अॅ टॅन्ड *v.t.* to be present at (में) उपस्थित होना; to accompany (के) साथ होना; to give heed to (पर) ध्यान देना; to take care of (की) देखभाल करना; *v.i.* to take care देखभाल करना; to be present उपस्थित होना।

attendance अॅ टैन् डॅन्स *n.* the act of being present उपस्थिति; the number of people present उपस्थित लोग।

attendant अॅ टैन् डॅन्ट *n.* one who attends another परिचारक, सेवक।

attention अॅ टैन् शन् *n.* attending to something or someone ध्यान; drill position of standing straight and still सावधान।

attentive अॅ टैॅन् टिव *a.* paying attention सतर्क।

attest अॅ टैॅस्ट *v.t.* to certify प्रमाणित करना; to give evidence of साक्ष्य देना।

attire[1] अॅ टाइअॅ: *n.* dress परिधान।

attire[2] *v.t.* to dress वस्त्र पहनाना।

attitude ऐ टि ट्यूड *n.* outlook दृष्टिकोण; posture of the body मुद्रा।

attorney अॅ टॅ: नि *n.* a person with legal authority to act for another प्रतिनिधि; lawyer वकील।

attract अॅ ट्रैक्ट *v.t.* to draw to oneself आकर्षित करना; to charm लालायित करना।

attraction अॅ ट्रैक् शॅन *n.* charm आकर्षण; something that attracts आकर्षक वस्तु।

attractive अॅ ट्रैक् टिव *a.* having the power to attract आकर्षक।

attribute[1] अॅ ट्रि ब्यूट *v.t.* to ascribe आरोपित करना।

attribute[2] ऐ ट्रि ब्यूट *n.* an inherent quality आंतरिक गुण।

auction[1] औक् शॅन *n.* public sale नीलाम।

auction[2] *v.t.* to sell by auction नीलाम करना।

audible *औ डि ब्ल a.* loud enough to be heard श्रव्य।

audience *औ डि अॅन्स n.* a body of listeners श्रोतागण; a ceremonial interview औपचारिक साक्षात्कार।

audit[1] *औ डिट n.* formal verification of an account-book अंकेक्षण।

audit[2] *v.t.* to make an audit of (का) अंकेक्षण करना।

auditive *ऑड्-इट्'-इव् adj.* pertaining to hearing श्रवण-सम्बन्धी।

auditor *औ डि टॅः n.* one who audits accounts अंकेक्षक।

auditorium *औ डि टौ रि अॅम n.* the space allotted to the hearers श्रोताकक्ष।

auger *ऑ गॅः n.* a tool for boring holes बरमा।

aught *औट n.* anything कोई वस्तु।

augment *औग् मॅन्ट v.t.* to increase बढ़ाना; *v.i.* to grow larger बढ़ना।

augmentation *औग् मैनॅ टे शॅन n.* increase संवर्धन, वृद्धि।

August *औ गस्ट n.* eighth month of the year अगस्त।

august *औ गस्ट n.* venerable भव्य।

aunt *आन्ट n.* father's or mother's sister बुआ, मौसी, चाची।

auriform *ऑ'-रि-फार्म् adj.* earshaped कान की आकृति का।

aurilave *ऑ'-रि-लेव् n.* instrument for cleaning the ears कानखोदनी।

aurora *ऑ'-रोरा-n.* dawn, colour of sky at sunrise तड़का, अरूणोदय।

auspicate *ऑ'-स्पि-केट् v.t.* to initiate, to inaugurate, to foreshow दीक्षा देना, अभिमन्त्रित करना, भविष्य बतलाना।

auspice *ऑ'-स्पिस् n. (usu. in pl.)* observations for the sake of omen, protection, patronage *(pl.)* under the patronage of शकुन-विचार, रक्षा, संरक्षण, शरण में।

auspicious *औस् पि शॅस a.* favourable शुभसूचक।

austere *औस् टिअॅः a.* very plain सरल, सादा।

authentic *औ थैनॅ टिक a.* genuine प्रामाणिक; true असली।

author *औ थॅः n.* the writer of a book or article etc. लेखक।

authoritative *औ थौ ˘ रि टॅ टिव a.* official आधिकारिक; reliable विश्वसनीय।

authority *औ थौ ˘ रि टि n.* legal power or right शक्ति या अधिकार; an expert विशेषज्ञ; permission आज्ञा; a person or body holding power अधिकारी सत्ता।

authorize *औ थॅ रॉइज़ v.t.* to empower प्राधिकृत करना।

autobiography *औ टॉ˘ बॉइ ऑ˘ ग्रॅ फि n.* a person's life written by himself आत्मकथा।

autocracy *औ टौ ˘ क्रॅ सि n.* an absolute government by one man, despotism एकतंत्र, राजशाही।

autocrat *औ टॅ क्रैट n.* an absolute sovereign निरंकुश शासक।

autocratic *औ टॅ क्रे टिक a.* despotic एकतंत्रीय, निरंकुश।

autograph *औ टॅ ग्राफ n.* a person's own handwriting or signature स्वाक्षर या हस्ताक्षर।

automatic *औ टॅ मै टिक a.* self operating (machine) स्वचालित (यंत्र);

done without thinking अविवेचित।

automobile *औ टॅ मो बील n.* motor car मोटरकार।

autonomous *औ टौ ँ नॅ मॅस a.* functioning independently स्वायत्त।

autumn *औ टॅम n.* season between winter and summer पतझड़।

auxiliary[1] *औग् ज़ि लि ॲ रि a.* helping सहायक।

auxiliary[2] *n.* helping verb सहायक क्रिया; *(pl.)* troops serving with another nation सहायक सेना।

avale *अवे'-ल् v.t.* to come down नीचे उतरना; *v. t.* to lower नीचे उतारना।

avail *ॲ वेल v.t.* to benefit लाभ पहुंचाना; *v.i.* to be of use उपयोगी होना।

available *ॲ वे लॅ बृल a* within reach पहुंच के अंदर; obtainable प्राप्य।

avarice *ऐ वॅ रिस n.* eager desire for wealth लालसा, लालच।

avenge *ॲ वै ॅन्ज v.t.* to take vengeance for प्रतिशोध लेना।

avenue *अ-वेन्-यू n.* a walk bordered by trees, way of approaching, wide street वृक्षों से आच्छादित मार्ग, द्वार, मार्ग, चौड़ी सड़क।

average[1] *ऐ वॅ रिज n.* medium औसत।

average[2] *a.* midway between extremes औसत दर्जे का।

average[3] *v.t.* to find the average of माध्य निकालना; to amount to as an average (का) औसत होना।

averse *ॲ वॅ:स a.* opposed विपरीत; unwilling अनिच्छुक।

aversion *ॲ वॅ: शॅन n.* hatred घिन, घृणा; antipathy द्वेष।

avert *ॲ वॅ:ट v.t.* to prevent रोकना; to turn away (one's eyes etc.) (आंखें) बचा लेना।

aviary *ए'-वि-अ-रि n.* a place for keeping birds चिड़ियाखाना, पक्षीशाला।

aviation *ए वि ए शॅन n.* art and science of flying विमानचालन।

aviator *ऐ वि ए टॅ: n.* pilot of an aeroplane विमानचालक।

avid *एव्'-इड़ adj.* greedy eager लालची, उत्सुक।

avidity *एव इडइ-टि adv.* earnest desire उत्कट इच्छा।

avidly *एव इडलि adv.* eagerly उत्सुकता से।

avoid *ॲ वौ ॅइड v.t.* to keep away from से बचना; to shun टालना।

avoidance *ॲ वौ ॅइ डॅन्स n.* act of avoiding बचाव।

avow *ॲ वॉउ v.t.* to confess स्वीकार करना; to declare घोषणा करना।

avulsion *ए-वल्-शन् n.* dividing or tearing away पृथक्करण, अलगाव।

await *ॲ वेट v.t.* to wait for (की) प्रतीक्षा करना; to expect आशा करना।

awake[1] *ॲ वेक v.t.* to rouse from sleep जगाना; *v.i.* to become aware सचेत होना।

awake[2] *a* roused from sleep, aware सचेत।

award[1] *ॲ वौ:ड v.t.* to grant प्रदान करना; to make a judicial decision निर्णय करना।

award[2] *n.* prize पुरस्कार; judicial decision न्यायिक निर्णय।

aware *ॲ वेॲ: a.* conscious, attentive जानकर, अवगत।

away *अॅ वे adv.* from here यहां से; far, apart दूर, अलग।

awe *औ n.* reverent wonder विस्मय; respect, combined with fear and reverence भयमिश्रित श्रद्धा।

awful *औ फुल a.* terrifying डरावना; impressive प्रभावशाली; very great अति महान।

awhile *अॅ व्हॉइल adv.* for a short time कुछ देर के लिए।

awkward *औक् वॅःड a.* clumsy भद्दा; delicate नाजुक; uncomfortable कष्टकर।

axe *ऐक्स n.* a tool for chopping wood कुल्हाड़ी।

axis *ऐक् सिस n.* the line on which something revolves अक्षरेखा।

axle *ऐक् सल n.* a rod on which a wheel turns धुरी।

Bb

B *बी-ब्* the second letter of the English alphabet, (Mus.) the seventh note, (Alg.) the second known quantity. अंग्रेजी वर्णमाला का दूसरा अक्षर, (स०) सातवाँ सुर, (बीजगणित में) दूसरा ज्ञात परिमाण।

babble[1] *बै ब्ल n.* foolish talk बकवास; confused sounds बड़बड़ाहट।

babble[2] *v.i.* to talk foolishly बकवास करना; to murmur बड़बड़ाना।

babe *बेब n.* baby बच्चा।

babel *बे -बल् n.* a high structure, a scene of confusion, tumult, meaningless noise ऊँची इमारत, उपद्रव, कोलाहल, बलवा, विप्लव, निरर्थक शब्द।

baboon *बा-बून् n.* a kind of large monkey. एक प्रकार का बड़ा बन्दर, लंगूर।

baby *बे बि n.* very young child शिशु।

bachelor *बै चॅ लॅः n.* unmarried man अविवाहित व्यक्ति।

back[1] *बैक n.* the rear part of the human body कमर; the hinder part पिछला भाग।

back[2] *adv.* backwards पिछली तरफ़।

backbite *बेक् बॉइट v.t.* to speak evil of secretly चुग़ली खाना।

backbone *बेक् बोन n.* spine रीढ़; main support आधार।

background *बैक् ग्रॉउन्ड n.* parts situated in the rear पृष्ठभूमि; a person's origin, education etc. पृष्ठिका।

backhand *बैक्-हैन्ड् n.* writing which is leaning to left बाई ओर झुका हुआ लेख।

backslide *बैक्-स्लाइड् v.i.* to fall into sin पतित होना।

backward *बेक् वॅःड a.* retarded in development पिछड़ा हुआ।

backward(s) *बैक् वॅःड्ज़ adv.* towards the rear पीछे की ओर; towards the past भूतकाल की ओर।

bacon *बे कॅन n.* meat of pig शूकर-मांस।

bacteria *बेक् टिअॅ रिअॅ n.pl.* microscopic organisms जीवाणु।

bad *बैड a.* not good बुरा; unwel

अस्वस्थ; serious गंभीर; harmful हानिकारक; immoral अनैतिक।

badge *बैज* *n.* a distinguishing emblem बिल्ला।

badger *बै जॅः* *n.* small grey animal बिज्जू।

badly *बैड़-लि* *adv.* cruelly defectively क्रूरता से, बुरे प्रकार से।

badminton *बेड़ मिन् ॲन* *n.* a court game played over a net बैडमिंटन।

baffle *बै फ़्ल* *v. t.* to make useless विफल कर देना; to defeat परास्त करना।

bag[1] *बैग* *n.* a flexible container थैला।

bag[2] *v. i.* to put into a bag थैले में रखना; to capture पकड़ना।

baggage *बै गिज* *n.* luggage यात्री-सामान।

bagpipe *बैग्-पाइप्* *n.* a kind of wind-instrument मसक बाजा।

bail[1] *बेल* *n.* security given for release ज़मानत; the person who gives such security ज़मानत देने वाला।

bail[2] *v. t.* to liberate from custody of security ज़मानत पर रिहा करना।

bailable *बे लॅ ब्ल* *a.* that may be bailed जिसकी ज़मानत हो सके।

bailiff *बे लिफ़्* *n.* landlord's agent कारिंदा।

bait[1] *बेट* *n.* temptation प्रलोभन।

bait[2] *v.t.* to furnish with a bait लुभाना; to harass तंग करना; to annoy क्रोध दिलाना।

bake *बेक* *v.t.* to cook in an oven सेंकना, गर्मी से पकाया जाना।

baker *बे कॅः* *n.* one whose occupation is to bake bread नानबाई।

bakery *बे कॅ रि* *n.* place for baking बेकरी।

balance[1] *बै लॅन्स* *n.* a pair of scales तराजू; equilibrium संतुलन; the sum due on an account देय राशि।

balance[2] *v.t.* to bring to an equilibrium संतुलित करना।

balcony *बैल् कॅ नि* *n.* platform projecting from a window छज्जा।

bald *बौल्ड* *a.* without hair on the head गंजा; bare नंगा; unadorned अनलंकृत।

bale[1] *बेल* *n.* a bundle or package of goods गांठ।

bale[2] *v.t.* to make into bales की गांठ बनाना।

baleful *बेल् फुल* *a.* calamitous संकटपूर्ण; deadly घातक; harmful हानिकारक।

baleen *बे-लीन्* *n.* whalebone ह्वेल मछली की हड्डी।

ball *बौल* *n.* a round body गेंद; a bullet गोली; an entertainment of dancing एक प्रकार का नृत्य।

ballad *बै लॅड* *n.* a short narrative poem गाथा-गीत।

ballet *बै ले* *n.* a theatrical exhibition of dancing and pantomimic action बैले नृत्य।

balloon *बॅ लून* *n.* a large bag filled with gas गुब्बारा।

ballot[1] *बै लॅट* *n.* a little ticket or paper used in voting मतपत्र; voting by this means गुप्त मतदान।

ballot[2] *v.i.* to vote by ballot गुप्त मतदान करना।

balm *बाम* *n.* a fragrant and healing ointment मरहम, बाम।

balsam *बाल्-सम्* *n.* a kind of aromatic healing substance, a flower of the rainy season. पीड़ा हरने वाली सुगंधित औषधि, गुलमेंहदी।

bam *बैम्* *n.* falsehood, a hoax झूठ, कपट; *v.t.* to cheat ठगना, धोखा देना।

bamboo *बैम् बू* *n.* a tropical plant of the reed kind बांस।

ban[1] *बैन* *n.* an order prohibiting something प्रतिबंध।

ban[2] (*—nn—*) *v.t.* to prohibit प्रतिबंधित करना।

banal *बै नॅल, बे नॅल* *a.* hackneyed घिसा-पिटा; vulgar निम्नस्तरीय।

banana *बॅ ना नॅ* *n.* a gigantic plant and its fruit केला।

band *बैन्ड* *n.* a strip of cloth etc. पट्टी, फ़ीता; a group of evil men गिरोह; a musical group संगीत-मंडली।

bandage[1] *बैन् डिज* *n.* a cloth for a wound पट्टी।

bandage[2] *v.t.* to bind with a bandage (पर) पट्टी बांधना।

bandit *बैन् डिट* *n.* robber डाकू, लुटेरा।

bang[1] *बैङ्ग* *v.t.* to slam धम से बंद करना।

bang[2] *n.* heavy knock ज़ोरदार दस्तक।

bangle *बैङ् ग्ल* *n.* ornament worn round the arm चूड़ी।

banish *बै निश* *v.t.* to send into exile निर्वासित करना।

banishment *बै निश् मॅन्ट* *n.* act of banishing निष्कासन; exile निर्वासन।

banjo *बैन् जो* *n.* a stringed musical instrument एक प्रकार का बाजा।

bank[1] *बैङ्क* *n.* ground rising from the side of a river कूल, किनारा; place where money is deposited बैंक, अधिकोष; a mound टीला।

bank[2] *v.t.* to deposit (money) in a bank बैंक में (धन) जमा करना; *v.i.* to keep money in a bank बैंक में पैसा रखना; (with '*on*', '*upon*') to base one's hopes आशा करना, भरोसा रखना।

banker *बैङ् कॅः* *n.* one who deals in money रुपये का लेन-देन करने वाला; one who works in a bank बैंक-कर्मी।

bankrupt *बैङ् क्रप्ट* *n.* & *a.* insolvent दिवालिया।

bankruptcy *बैङ् क्रप्ट् सि* *n.* state of being a bankrupt दिवालियापन।

banner *बैनॅः* *n.* flag ध्वज; large cloth carrying a slogan बैनर।

banquet[1] *बैङ् क्विट* *n.* a formal feast भोज, दावत।

banquet[2] *v.t.* to treat with a feast दावत देना; to feast दावत लेना।

bantam *बैन्-टम्* *n.* a dwarf fowl, a shortman नाटा मुरगा, नाटा पुरुष।

banter[1] *बैन् टॅः* *v.t.* to make fun मज़ाक़ उड़ाना।

banter[2] *n.* fun मज़ाक।

bantling *बान्ट्'-लिङ्ग्* *n.* a young child, a brat बच्चा, छोकरा।

banyan *बैन् यॅन* *n.* an Indian tree of the fig genus बरगद।

baptism *बैप् टिज़्म* *n.* a ceremonial immersion in water दीक्षा-स्नान, बपतिस्मा।

baptize *बैप् टॉइज़* *v.t.* to administer baptism दीक्षा-स्नान कराना।

bar[1] *बाः* *n.* a long piece of metal

छड; obstruction बाधा, रुकावट; legal profession वकालत।

bar² (*-rr-*) *v.t.* to prevent रोकना; to keep out अलग करना।

barb *बा:ब* *n.* the point which stands backward in an arrow or fish-hook बाण या बंसी का कांटा।

barbarian¹ *बा: बे ॅ अ रि अॅन* *a.* uncivilized असभ्य, जंगली।

barbarian² *n.* a person in a savage state जंगली व्यक्ति; an uncultured person असभ्य व्यक्ति।

barbarism *बा: बॅ रिज़्म* *n.* state of being uncivilised असभ्यता।

barbarity *बा: बै रि टि* *n.* cruelty क्रूरता, बर्बरता।

barbarous *बा: बॅ रॅस* *a.* in the state of barbarism असभ्य; cruel क्रूर।

barbed *बा:ब्ड* *a.* provided with barbs कांटेदार।

barber *बा: बॅ:* *n.* a man's hair-dresser हज्जाम।

bard *बा:ड* *n.* a. Celtic minstrel भाट, चारण; a poet कवि।

bare¹ *बे ॅ अ:* *a.* uncovered नंगा; empty खाली।

bare² *v.t.* to make naked नंगा करना।

barely *बे ॅ अ: लि* *adv.* poorly अभाव में; merely केवल; hardly मुश्किल से।

bargain¹ *बा: गेन* *n.* agreement, contract संविदा; a gainful transaction सौदा।

bargain² *v.t.* to make a bargain सौदा करना।

barge *बा:ज* *n.* boat नाव।

bark¹ *बा:क* *n.* the outer ring of a tree छाल; the cry of a dog कुत्ते की भौंक।

bark² *v.t.* to make the sound of a dog भौंकना।

barley *बा: लि* *n.* a species of grain जौ।

barn *बा:न* *n.* a building for grain खत्ती, कोठार।

barnacles *बार्न्-ए-क्ल्स्* *n.* pl. iron placed on the nose of horses for shoeing नाल बाँधते समय घोड़े का नथुना पकड़ने की सँड़सी।

barometer *बॅ रौ ॅ मि टॅ:* *n.* an instrument for measuring the pressure of atmosphere वायुदाबमापी।

barouche *बा-रूश्'* *n.* a kind of double-seated four-wheeled carriage एक प्रकार की चौपहिया गाड़ी।

barrack *बै रॅक* *n.* a building for soldiers सेनावास।

barrage *बै राज़,* *n.* dam बांध; heavy gun-fire भारी गोलाबारी।

barrator *बैर्'-रे-ट्र* **(-er)** *ns.* a troublesome litigant झगड़ालू, अदलतिया।

barrel *बै रॅल* *n.* a round wooden cask पीपा; the tube of a gun बंदूक की नाल।

barren *बै रॅन* *n* sterile बांझ; unproductive अनुपजाऊ।

barricade *बै रि केड* *n.* a barrier बाधा, रुकावट।

barrier *बै रि अ:* *n.* fence घेरा; obstruction अवरोध।

barrister *बै रिस् टॅ:* *n.* a counsellor at law बैरिस्टर, वकील।

barter¹ *बा: टॅ:* *v.t.* to exchange in commerce (की) अदला-बदली करना; *v.i.* to exchange one thing for another वस्तु-विनिमय करना।

barter² *n.* exchange विनिमय।

barton *बार्टन्* *n.* a farmyard, out house खलिहान, बाहरी मकान।

basal *बेसल्* *adj.* pertaining to base, fundamental आधार सम्बन्धी, मौलिक।

base[1] *बेस* *n.* starting point प्रस्थान-बिंदु; foundation आधार, नींव।

base[2] *a.* worthless खोटा, नीच; low in value घटिया।

base[3] *v.t.* to place on a basis आधारित करना।

baseless *बेस् लिस* *a.* without base निराधार; groundless निर्मूल।

basement *बेस् मॅन्ट* *n.* the ground floor of a building तहख़ाना।

bashful *बैश् फुल* *a.* modest, shy संकोची।

basial *बे'-सिअल्* *n.* pertaining to kissing चुम्बन सम्बन्धी।

basic *बे सिक* *a.* fundamental मौलिक, बुनियादी।

basil *बेस्'-इल्* *n.* a kind of aromatic medicinal herb, tanned sheep-skin. तुलसी, कमायी हुई भेड़ की खाल।

basin *बे सन* *n.* a shallow dish चिलमची; a depression in the earth's surface तलहटी; country drained by a river घाटी।

basis *बे सिस* *n.* the underlying principle आधारभूत सिद्धांत; the basic supporting factor मूलाधार।

bask *बास्क* *v.i.* to lie in warmth or in the sun धूप सेंकना; to enjoy ease and prosperity आनंद लेना।

basket *बास् किट* *n.* a domestic vessel made of twigs डलिया, टोकरी।

baslard *बीस्'-लर्ड्* *n.* a small dagger worn on by gentlemen, a girdle पेटी में लगाने की छोटी कटार, पेटी, कमरबन्द।

bass *बास्* *n.* inner bark of lime tree, the lowest part in music नींबू के पेड़ की भीतरी छाल, गायन में सबसे नीचा सुर।

bastard[1] *बैस् टॅःड* *n.* an illegitimate child अवैध संतान।

bastard[2] *a.* illegitimate अवैध।

bat[1] *बैट* *n.* a flying mammal चमगादड़।

bat[2] *n.* a club for striking a ball बल्ला; a batsman बल्लेबाज़।

bat[3] (*-tt-*) *v. i.* to wield a bat बल्लेबाज़ी करना *v.t.* to strike with a bat बल्ले से मारना या फेंकना।

batch *बैच* *n.* a group or number of persons जत्था, टोली; a set of similar objects घान।

bath *बाथ* *n.* immersion in water स्नान।

bathe *बेद* *v. t.* to immerse in water नहलाना; *v. i.* to take a bath स्नान करना।

baton *बै टॅन* *n.* a short heavy stick सोंटा, छड़ी।

batsman *बैट्स'-मैन्* *n.* one who wields the bat in cricket बैट पकड़कर क्रिकेट खेलने वाला, बल्लेबाज।

battalion *बॅ टै ल्यॅन* *n.* a body of soldiers बटालियन, वाहिनी।

battery *बै टॅ रि* *n.* an apparatus for originating an electric current बैटरी; unit of artillery तोपख़ाना; attack आक्रमण।

battle[1] *बै ट्ल* *n.* encounter of two armies युद्ध।

battle[2] *v. i.* to contend in fight युद्ध लड़ना।

bawd *बॉड्* *n.* a procurer or

procuress स्त्रियों को बहकाकर कुकर्म कराने वाली स्त्री।

bawl *बॉल्* *n.i.* to speak noisily, to shout चिल्लाकर बोलना, चिंग्घाड़ मारना, चिल्लाना; *n.* a loudcry चिंग्घाड़।

bawn *बॉन्* *n.* cattle-fold पशुपाला।

bay *बे* *n.* an arm of the sea खाड़ी।

bayard *बे'-आ-ई* *n.* a brave or chivalrous person वीर मनुष्य।

bayonet *बे ॲ निट* *n.*, a dagger-like weapon fixed to a rifle संगीन।

be[1] *बी* *v.t.* होना।

be[2] *बी* *pref.* added to nouns & adjs. to form verbs. संज्ञा इत्यादि शब्दों में क्रिया बनाने के लिये जोड़ा हुआ उपसर्ग यथा-be-set, bescorch, Bedim, Be-friend. इत्यादि।

beach *बीच* *n.* the shore of the sea समुद्र-तट।

beacon *बी कॅन* *n.* light to direct seamen प्रकाश-स्तंभ; a signal of danger संकेतक।

bead *बीड* *n.* a little ball strung on a thread मनका।

beadle *बी'-ड्ल्* *n.* the servant of a company, church officer किसी कम्पनी या व्यवसाय संघ का नौकर, गिरजे का पदाधिकारी।

beak *बीक* *n.* a bird's bill चोंच।

beaker *बी कॅ:* *n.* a glass vessel used by chemists बीकर।

beam[1] *बीम* *n.* a long squared piece of timber or concrete शहतीर, बीम; a ray of light किरण; cross bar of a balance तराजू की डंडी।

beam[2] *v. i.* to send out light चमकना; to smile happily मुस्कराना।

bean *बीन* *n.* vegatable सेम, बोड़ा।

bear[1] *बे˘ ॲ:* *n.* a large carnivorous quadruped भालू।

bear[2] *v.t.* to carry ले जाना; to support संभालना; to produce पैदा करना; to endure सहन करना; to behave व्यवहार करना।

beard *बिॲ:ड* *n.* the hair on the chin दाढ़ी।

bearing *बे˘ ॲ रिङ्ग* *n.* demeanour व्यवहार, आचरण।

beast *बीस्ट* *n.* any four-footed animal पशु; a brutal man क्रूर व्यक्ति।

beastly *बीस्ट् लि* *a.* brutal नृशंस, क्रूरतापूर्ण।

beat[1] *बीट* *v. t.* to hit, to strike पीटना; to stir फेंटना; to thrash कूटना; to defeat पराजित करना; *v. t.* to throb धड़कना।

beat[2] *n.* a stroke चोट; throb धड़कन; ,round गश्त।

beautiful *ब्यू टि फुल* *a.* lovely सुंदर।

beautify *ब्यू टि फ़ाइ* *v. t.* to make beautiful सजाना।

beauty *ब्यू टि* *n.* loveliness, grace सौंदर्य।

beaver *बी वॅ:* *n.* a fur-coated animal ऊदबिलाव; its fur लोमचर्म।

because *बि कौज़* *conj.* for the reason that क्योंकि।

beck *बेक्* *n.* a brook, a mountain stream. पहाड़ी नाला या नदी।

beckon[1] *बेक्'-अन्'* *v.t.* & *i.* to summon, to call attention by gestures or nodding पुकारना, संकेत करना।

beckon[2] *बै˘ कॅन* *v. t.* to call by a signal or gesture इशारे से बुलाना; *v.i.* to make a gesture इशारा करना।

become *बि कम* *v. i.* to come to be हो जाना; *v. t.* to suit शोभा देना।

becoming *बि क मिङ्ग* *a.* fit उपयुक्त; graceful सुहावना।

bed *बै˘ड* *n.* something to sleep or rest on शय्या, चारपाई; bottom of a river नदीतल; a garden plot क्यारी।

bedevil *बि डै˘ बिल* *v. t.* to confuse भरमाना; to torment सताना।

bedding *बेड़-डिड़्ग* *n.* materials used for making a bed. शयन सामग्री।

bedight *बि-डाइट्′* *v.t.* to adorn. सजाना।

bed-time *बेड़-टाइम्* *n.* time for going to sleep निद्रा का समय।

bee *बी* *n.* the insect that makes honey शहद की मक्खी।

beech *बीच्* *n.* a kind of common forest tree एक प्रकार का जगंली वृक्ष।

beef *बीफ़* *n.* the flesh of an ox, bull or cow गोमांस।

beehive *बी-हाइव्′* *n.* artificial dwelling for bees मधुमक्खी का कृत्रिम घर।

beer *बिअ:* *n.* an alcoholic drink made from malt बियर, यवसुरा।

beet *बीट* *n.* an edible plant चुकंदर।

beetle *बी ट्ल* *n.* an insect with four wings भृंग, झींगुर।

befall *बि फ़ौल* *v. t.* to happen to (पर) बीतना; *v. i.* to happen घटित होना।

before[1] *बि फ़ो:* *prep.* in front of के सामने; in the presence of के समक्ष; earlier than से पहले।

before[2] *adv.* in time preceding पूर्व में; in the past भूत में; onward आगे की ओर; in front सामने।

before[3] *conj.* previous to the time when इससे पहले कि; rather than इसके बजाय कि।

beforehand *बि फ़ो: हैन्ड* *adv.* in advance पहले ही।

befriend *बि फ्रैंन्ड* *v. t.* to act as a friend to मित्र बनाना।

beg *बैग* (*-gg-*) *v. t.* to ask in charity भीख में मांगना; to ask earnestly निवेदन करना; to take for granted मान लेना; *v. i.* to ask or live upon alms भीख मांगना।

beget *बि गै˘ट* *v. t.* to produce जन्म देना।

beggar *बै˘ गॅ:* *n.* one who begs भिखारी।

begin *बि गिन* (*-nn-*) *v. t.* to start प्रारंभ करना; *v. i.* to be started प्रारंभ होना।

beginning *बि गि निङग* *n.* the start प्रारंभ।

begird *बि-गर्ड्* *v.t.* to encircle, to surround लपेटना, घेरना।

beguile *बि गॉइल* *v. t.* to practise guile on ठगना; to charm मोहित करना; to pass (time etc.) pleasantly आनंद के साथ (समय आदि) बिताना।

behalf *बि हाफ़* *n.* interest, favour, benefit हित, लाभ।

behave *बि हेव* *v. i.* to act आचरण करना।

behaviour *बि हे व्यॅ:* *n.* conduct, way of behaving आचरण।

behead *बि है˘ड* *v. t.* to cut off the head of (का) सिर काटना।

behind[1] *बि हॉइन्ड* *adv.* in the rear

पीछे की ओर; backwards पिछड़ी स्थिति में।

behind² *prep.* in the rear of के पीछे; remaining after से बाद में; inferior to से पिछड़ा हुआ।

behold *बि होल्ड v. t.* to look at with attention ध्यान से देखना।

being *बि इङ्ग n.* existence अस्तित्व; a creature प्राणी, जीवधारी।

belabour *बि ले बॅ: v. t.* to beat soundly पीटना।

belated *बि-लेट्'- इड़adj.* coming too late बहुत देर से आने वाला।

belch¹ *बैल्च v. t.* to send (smoke, flames etc.) out उगलना; *v. i.* to send out gas from the stomach noisily through the mouth डकार लेना।

belch² *n.* act or sound of belching डकार।

belief *बि लीफ़ n.* conviction धारणा; faith, trust विश्वास; a religious tenet धार्मिक आस्था।

believe *बि लीव v. t.* to give belief to विश्वास करना; to have confidence in (पर) भरोसा रखना।

bell *बेलॅ n.* a hollow, metal, cup-shaped instrument that rings when struck घंटी, घंटा।

belle *बेलॅ n.* a lady of great beauty सुंदरी।

bellicose *बे ॅलि कोस a.* warlike युद्धप्रिय, लड़ाकू।

belligerency *बि लि जॅ रॅन् सि n.* being warlike युद्धप्रियता।

belligerent¹ *बि लि जॅ रॅन्ट a.* waging war युद्धरत।

belligerent² *n.* a nation or state waging war युद्धरत राज्य।

bellow *बॅ ॅ लो v. i.* to roar like a bull चिंघाड़ना, गरजना।

bellows *बै ॅ लोज़ n. pl.* an instrument for creating stream of air धौंकनी।

belly *बै ॅ लि n.* abdomen, stomach पेट, उदर।

belong *बि लौ ॅङ्ग v. i.* to be, the property (of) (का) होना, (की) संपति होना; to be connected संबद्ध होना; to be a member or inhabitant सदस्य अथवा निवासी होना।

belongings *बि लौ ॅङ् गिङ्ग्ज़ n. pl.* personal possessions व्यक्तिगत माल-असबाब।

beloved¹ बि ल विड *a.* greatly loved परमप्रिय।

beloved² *n.* darling प्रियतम, प्रेयसि।

below¹ *बि लो adv.* beneath नीचे।

below² *prep.* lower than से नीचे।

belt *बैल्ट n.* a girdle पेटी; a band पट्टा; a strip of land इलाक़ा, क्षेत्र।

belvedere *बेल्'-वि-डिअर् n.* a raised turret or pavilion to view scenery दृश्य देखने का ऊँचा चबूतरा या मंच।

bemask *बि-मास्क्' v. t.* to conceal, to mask छिपाना, बुरके से ढाँपना।

bemire *बि-मायर्' v. t.* to stain with mud कीचड़ पोतना, कीचड़ से गन्दा करना।

bemuse *बि-म्यूज' v. t.* to stupefy, to confuse बुद्धिहीन करना, व्यग्र करना।

bench *वैन्च n.* a long seat बेंच, तिपाई; body of judges न्यायपीठ; a court of law अदालत।

bend¹ बैन्ड *n.* curve मोड़, झुकाव।

bend² *v. t.* to curve मोड़ना; to turn घुमाना; *v.i.* to become curved

मुड़ना; to stoop झुकना; to yield हार मानना; to turn घूमना।

beneath[1] *बि नीथ adv.* in a lower place नीचे।

beneath[2] *prep.* below, under के नीचे।

benefaction *बेन्-इ-फेक'-शन् n.* gift for a good cause, charitable donation धर्मदान, उपकार, दान-दक्षिणा।

benefice *बेन्-इ-फाइस् n.* a church living पादरी की वृत्ति।

beneficial *बै ॅनि फ़ि शॅल a.* conferring benefit लाभकारी।

benefit[1] *बै ॅ नि फ़िट n.* allowance भत्ता; a favour कृपा; advantage लाभ।

benefit[2] *v. t.* to do a service to लाभ पहुँचाना; *v.i.* to gain advantage लाभान्वित होना।

benevolence *बि नै ॅ वॅ लॅन्स n.* kindness कृपा, दया।

benevolent *बि नै ॅ वॅ लॅन्ट a.* kind कृपालु, दयालु।

benight *बि'-नाइट्' v. t.* to cover with darkness अंधेरा करना।

benign *बि'-नाइन्' adj* gentle, fortunate, kind कृपालु, सुखप्रद, दयालु।

benignly *(बि-नाइन-लि) adv.* kindly दयालुता से।

benison *बेन्'-इ-सन् n.* a blessing. benediction वरदान, आशीर्वाद।

bent *बैन्ट n.* natural inclination रूझान।

bequeath *बि क्वीद v. t.* to leave by will वसीयत में देना।

bereave *बि रीव v. t.* to deprive of बंचित करना।

bereavement *बि रीव् मॅन्ट n.* being bereaved वियोग; loss by death मृत्यु के कारण क्षति।

berth *बॅ:थ n.* sleeping place in a ship or train शायिका।

beside *बि सॉइड prep.* by the side of के पास में; compared with की तुलना में।

besides[1] *बि सॉइड्ज़ prep.* in addition to के अतिरिक्त।

besides[2] *adv.* moreover साथ ही, इसके अतिरिक्त।

beslaver *बिस्'-लेवर् v. t.* to flatter very much बड़ी चापलूसी करना, चाटुकारी करना।

besiege *बि-सीज्' v. t.* to assail, to lay siege to आक्रमण करना, घेर लेना।

bestow *बि स्टो v. t.* to give प्रदान करना।

bestrew *बेस-ट्रयू' v. t.* to scatter about छितराना, फैलाना, छींटना।

bet[1] *बै ॅट (-tt-) v.i.* to wager शर्त लगाना।

bet[2] *n.* a pledge made in betting शर्त।

betel *बी ट्ल n.* leaf used for chewing पान।

betray *बि ट्रे v.t.* to deal treacherously with विश्वासघात करना; to reveal प्रकट करना।

betrayal *बि ट्रे ॲल n.* betraying or being betrayed विश्वासघात।

betroth *बि ट्रोद v. t.* to promise to marry वाग्दान करना।

betrothal *बि ट्रो दॅल n.* mutual contract of marriage वाग्दान।

better[1] *बै ॅ टॅः a.* superior बेहतर; improved in health पहले से स्वस्थ।

better[2] *adv.* in a more excellent

manner और अच्छे ढंग से; more अपेक्षाकृत अधिक।

better[3] *v. t.* to improve सुधारना।

betterment *बैं टः मॅन्ट n.* improvement सुधार, उन्नति।

between *बि ट्वीन prep.* in the middle of के मध्य।

beverage *बैं वॅ रिज n.* liquor मदिरा।

bewail *बि वेल v. t.* to mourn for पर शोक मनाना।

beware *बि वें अः v.i.* to take care (of) सचेत या चौकस रहना।

bewilder *बि विल् डः v. t.* to puzzle, to confuse उलझन में डालना, भ्रमित करना।

bewitch *बि विच v.t.* to enchant (पर) जादू करना; to fascinate मोहित करना।

beyond[1] *बि यॉन्ड prep.* on the further side of के उस ओर; out of the reach of की पहुंच से बाहर; above से ऊपर।

beyond[2] *adv.* at a distance दूरी पर, परे।

bi *बाइ pref.* in the sense of, "twice, doubly, twofold" दोहरा, दुबारा, दुगना।

biangular *बाइ-एङ्ग्'-यु-लर् adj.* having two angles दो कोण का।

bias[1] *बॉइ ॲस n.* prejudice पक्षपात।

bias[2] *v. t.* to prejudice, to influence unfairly पक्षपातपूर्ण बनाना।

biaxial *बाइ'-एक्स्-इ-अल् adj.* with two axes दो धुरा (या अक्ष) वाला।

bibber *बिब्'-बर् n.* one given to drinking पियक्कड़

bible *बाइ'-ब्ल् n.* the sacred book of the Christian Church ईसाइयों की धर्म-पुस्तक।

bibliography *बिब् लि आ ग्रॅ फि n.* a list of books ग्रंथ-सूची।

bibliographer *बिब्-लिऑ-ग्रेफर् n.* a compiler of a history of literary books साहित्यिक ग्रन्थों का इतिहास-लेखक।

bicentenary *बाइ-सेन्'-टे-न्-अ-रि adj.* occurring after two hundred years दो सौ वर्ष पर होने वाला।

biceps *बॉइ सैप्स n.* the muscle in front of the upper arm द्विशिर पेशी।

bicker *बिक्'-अर् v. t.* to quarrel, to run quickly कलह करना (विवाद करना)।

bicycle *बॉइ सि क्ल n.* a two-wheeled vehicle propelled by the rider बाइसिकिल।

bid[1] *बिड v.t.* to say as greeting अभिवादन करना; to order आदेश देना; to offer (a price) (बोली) लगाना।

bid[2] *n.* offer of price *बोली;* effort प्रयत्न।

bidder *बिड्'-अर् n.* one who bids दाँव या बाजी लगाने वाला।

bide *बाइड v. t. (p. t.* Bided) to dwell, to remain, to await, to endure रहना, ठहरना, प्रतीक्षा करना, सहना।

biennial *बाइ-एनिअल् adj.* recurring or happening every two years दो साल में होने वाला।

bier *बिॲः n.* a frame for carrying the dead to the grave अरथी।

big *बिग a.* great महान; large बड़ा; important महत्त्वपूर्ण।

bigamy *बि गॅ मि n.* practice of having two wives or husbands at the same time द्विविवाह-प्रथा।

bight *बाइट् n.* a loop; a curve or recess, a small bay, झूलन, घुमाव,

छोटी खाड़ी।

bigot *बि गॅट n.* a person in pervious to argument कट्टर या धर्मांध व्यक्ति।

bigotry *बि गॅ ट्रि n.* state or quality of being a bigot कट्टरता, धर्मांधता।

bile *बॉइल n.* fluid secreted by the liver पित्त; anger, ill temper चिड़चिड़ापन।

bilingual *बॉइ लिङ् ग्वॅल a.* capable of using two languages द्विभाषी।

bill *बिल n.* bird's beak चोंच; draught of a proposed new law विधेयक; poster इश्तहार; statement of money बिल, प्राप्यक।

billion *बिल् यॅन n.* (France, U.S.A.) one thousand million एक अरब; (Brit.) one million, millions दस खरब।

billow[1] *बि लो n.* wave लहर।

billow[2] *v.i.* to roll in large waves लहराना।

biliteral *बाइ-लिट्,'-अर्'-अल adj.* consisiting of two letters दो अक्षरों का।

bilk *बिल्क् v. t.* to cheat, to elude धोखा देना, छलना।

bimenasl *बाइ-मेन्-सल adj.* occurring once in two months दो महीने में एक बार होने वाला।

bimonthly *बाइ-मन्थ्'-लि adj.* once in two months, also twice a month दो महीने में एक बार, महीने में दो बार।

binary *बाइ-न-रि adj.* double, involving pairs दोहरा (द्विगुण) जोड़ा।

bind *बॉइन्ड v.t.* to tie बांधना; to fasten (a book) (किताब पर) जिल्द बांधना।

binding *बॉइन् डिङ्ग a.* compelling अनिवार्य।

binocular *बॉइ नौ ॅक्यु लॅःज़ n.pl.* small telescope for both eyes दूरबीन।

biographer *बॉइ औॅ ग्रॅ फ़ॅः n.* writer of a biography जीवनी-लेखक।

biography *बॉइ औ ॅ ग्रॅ फ़ि n.* an account of one's life and character जीवनी।

biologist *बॉइ औॅ लॅ जिस्ट n.* a scientist who studies biology जीव विज्ञानी।

biology *बॉइ औॅ लॅ जि n.* science of life जीव विज्ञान।

bioscope *बायो-स्कोप् n.* a cinematograph. चलते-फिरते कार्य का चित्र लेना और इसी को परदे पर चलते-फिरते दिखलाना।

biped *बॉइ पैॅड n.* an animal with two feet द्विपाद।

birch *बर्च् n.* a kind of smooth-barked tree, a bundle of its twings used for flogging भोजपत्र, बालकों को मारने का कोड़ा।

bird *बॅःड n.* a feathered creature पक्षी।

birdlime *बर्ड्'-लाइम n.* a viscous stuff which is used in catching birds चिड़िया पकड़ने का लासा।

birth *बॅःथ n.* being born जन्म।

biscuit *बिस्किट n.* hard bread made into cake बिस्कुट।

bisect *बॉइ सैक्ट v. t.* to cut into two द्विविभाजित करना।

bisexual *बाइ-सेक्स्-युअल् adj.* having both sexes in one स्त्री तथा पुरुष जाति के अंगों का एक ही व्यक्ति में होना, द्विलिंगीय।

bishop *बि शॅप n.* clergyman बिशप,

धर्माध्यक्ष।

bison *बाई'-सन् (जन्)* *n.* a large wild animal like ox जंगली साँड।

bisque *बिस्क्* *n.* unglazed white porcelain, a rich meat or fish soup बिना पालिश की हुई चीनी मिट्टी मांस या मछली का स्वादिष्ट झोल या रसा या जायकेदार शोरबा।

bit *बिट* *n.* a very small piece टुकड़ा; the mouthpiece of a bridle लगाम की मुखरी।

bitch *बिच्* *n.* female of a dog, fox or wolf कुतिया, सियारिन, मादा भेड़िया।

bite[1] *बॉइट* *v. t.* to cut or sever with the teeth काटना; to sting डसना; to eat into खा जाना।

bite[2] *n.* wound made by biting घाव, काट; a mouthful मुंहभर अंश; a sting दंश।

bitter *बि टॅः* *a.* sharp to the taste कडुवा; full of ill-will द्वेषपूर्ण; distressing पीड़ादायक; severe तेज़।

bi-weekly *बाइ-वीक्'-लि* *adj.* twice in every week सप्ताह में दो बार, अर्ध-साप्ताहिक।

bizarre *बिजार्* *adj.* odd, fantastic झक्की, पागल।

blab *ब्लाब्* *v. t. & i.* (*p. t.* Blabbed) to talk foolishly, to reveal secrets बड़बड़ करना, भेद खोल देना।

black *ब्लैक* *a.* destitute of light प्रकाश-रहित; dark-complexioned सांवला; wicked दुष्टतापूर्ण।

blacken *ब्लै कॅन* *v. t.* to make black काला करना।

blackmail[1] *ब्लैक् मेल* *n.* extortion by intimidation भयादोहन।

blackmail[2] *v.t.* to subject to blackmail भयादोहन करना।

blacksmith *ब्लैक् स्मिथ* *n.* a craftsman who works in iron लोहार।

bladder *ब्लै डॅः* *n.* bag like part of the body in which urine collects मूत्राशय।

blade *ब्लेड* *n.* cutting part of a sword, knife etc. फलक; flat part of an oar पतवार का चपटा भाग; leaf पत्ती।

blain *ब्लेन्* *n.* an in flamed boil, a blister व्रण, फफोला, छाला, फोड़ा।

blame[1] *ब्लेम* *v. t.* to censure निंदा करना, दोष लगाना; to hold responsible उत्तरदायी ठहराना।

blame[2] *n.* censure निंदा; fault दोष।

blanch *ब्लांश्* *v. t. & i* to grow pale with fear भय से पीला पड़ जाना।

bland *ब्लान्ड्* *adj.* gentle, polite, mild नम्र, विनीत, मृदु।

blank[1] *ब्लैङ्क* *a.* unmarked, unwritten कोरा; empty खाली, रिक्त।

blank[2] *n.* empty space रिक्त स्थान।

blanket *ब्लैङ् किट* *n.* a warm covering for a bed कंबल।

blare *ब्लेअर्* *v. t.* to utter loudly चिल्लाकर बोलना।

blast[1] *ब्लास्ट* *n.* violent explosion of gunpowder विस्फोट; loud noise धमाका।

blast[2] *v.i.* to destroy नष्ट करना; to blow up उड़ा देना।

blaze[1] *ब्लेज़* *n.* flame ज्वाला; a bright glow चमक।

blaze[2] *v.i.* to burn brightly दहकना; to shine like a flame चमकना।

bleach *ब्लीच्* *v. t.* to whiten धोना, सफेद करना।

blear *ब्लिअर्* *v. t.* to make dull, to

make dim sighted मन्द करना, चौंधा देना।

bleat[1] *ब्लीट n.* the cry of a sheep, goat etc. मिमियाहट।

bleat[2] *v. i.* to utter a bleat मिमियाना।

bleb *ब्लेब् n.* small blister or bubble on skin फफोला।

bleed *ब्लीड v. i.* to emit blood खून बहना; to feel pain दर्द अनुभव करना।

blemish *ब्लै ˘ मिश n.* mark of imperfection धब्बा; fault दोष।

blend[1] *ब्लैन्ड v. t.* to mix together मिलाना; *v.i.* to be mixed मिलना।

blend[2] *n.* a mixture मिश्रण।

bless *ब्लैसॅ v. t.* to wish happiness to आशीर्वाद देना; to consecrate अभिमंत्रित करना; to endow with प्रदान करना; to glorify गौरवान्वित करना।

blether (-Blather) *ब्लेद् (ब्लाद्)-अर् v. i.* to talk nonsense बड़बड़ (बकवाद) करना।

blight *ब्लाइट् n.* a disease of plants, mildewrust वनस्पति रोग, पाला, गेरूई।

blind *ब्लॉइन्ड a.* destitute of sight अंधा; wanting discernment विवेकशून्य; thoughtless विचारहीन।

blindage *ब्लाइन्ड्'- एज् n.* screen for troops फौज के लिये आच्छादन।

blindfold *ब्लॉइन्ड् फोल्ड v. t.* to cover the eyes of (की) आंखों पर पट्टी बांधना।

blindness *ब्लाइन्ड्'- नेस् n.* state of being blind, ignorance, a shade अन्धता, अज्ञान, पर्दा।

blink *ब्लिड़क v. t. & i.* to wink पलक मारना (आंखें छिपाना), तुच्छ समझना; *n*- glance, glimmer, wink झलक, टिमटिमाहट, निर्मीलन।

bliss *ब्लिस n.* perfect happiness परमानंद।

blister *ब्लिस् टॅः n.* a thin bladder on the skin फफोला।

blizzard *ब्लिजाड़् n.* a blinding snowstorm चौंधानेवाली बर्फ की आँधी।

bloc *ब्लौकॅ n.* a group of nations or parties गुट।

block[1] *ब्लौकॅ n.* heavy piece of wood or stone कुंदा, शिलाखंड; a lump of solid matter खंड, पिंडक; a group of houses भवन-समूह; obstruction बाधा, रुकावट।

block[2] *v.t.* to obstruct अवरुद्ध करना।

blockade *ब्लौ ˘ केड n.* a close siege by troops or ships घेराबंदी।

blockhead *ब्लौक् है ˘ड n.* a stupid fellow मूर्ख व्यक्ति।

blood *ब्लड n.* red liquid flowing through the body रक्त, ख़ून; relationship संबंध, नाता; descent वंश।

bloodshed *ब्लड़ शै ˘ड n.* the shedding of blood रक्तपात।

bloody *ब्ल डि a.* stained with blood रक्तरंजित; cruel निर्दय।

bloom[1] *ब्लूम n.* the flowering state फलने-फूलने का समय; a time of beauty यौवन; flower पुष्प।

bloom[2] *v.i.* blossom बहार आना; to flourish फलना-फूलना।

blossom[1] *ब्लौ ˘ सॅम n.* flower of a plant बौर, मंजरी; state of flowering पुष्पणकाल।

blossom[2] *v.i.*, to bloom खिलना; to flourish फलना-फूलना

blot[1] *ब्लौ ˘ट n.* a spot or stain दाग, धब्बा।

blot[2] *(-tt-) v. t.* to stain (पर) धब्बा लगाना; to soak up ink etc. from (से) स्याही आदि सुखाना।

blouse *ब्लॉउज़ n.* outer garment from neck to waist ब्लाउज़।

blow[1] *ब्लो v.i.* (of the wind) to move (हवा का) बहना; to produce a current of air (from the mouth) फूंक मारना *v. t.* to drive by means of a current of air उड़ाना; to cause to sound बजाना।

blow[2] *n.* a stroke of the fist घूंसा; a shock झटका।

blue[1] *ब्लू n.* colour of cloudless sky नीलवर्ण।

blue[2] *a.* of a blue colour नीले रंग का; sky-coloured आकाश-नील।

bluff[1] *ब्लफ v. t.* to deceive or mislead by a pretence धोखा देना।

bluff[2] *n.* pretence दिखावा, धोखा।

blunder[1] *ब्लन् डः n.* serious mistake भारी भूल।

blunder[2] *v.i.* to make a serious mistake भारी भूल करना।

blunt *ब्लन्ट a.* dull on the edge or point कुंद, भोथरा; outspoken मुंहफट स्पष्टवादी।

blur *ब्लर् n.* a stain, a spot, a blemish धब्बा, कलंक।

blurt *ब्लर्ट् v. t.* to utter abruptly or unadvisedly. बिना समझे बोल उठना।

blush[1] *ब्लश n.* reddening of the face due to shame झेंप।

blush[2] *v.i.* to go red in the face झेंपना।

boar *बौः n.* male of swine सूअर।

board[1] *बौःड n.* a piece of timber, broad and thin तख्ता; food भोजन; a council समिति।

board[2] *v. t.* to enter (a ship, train etc.) (में) सवार होना; to furnish with meals भोजन देना; *v.i.* to take one's meals भोजन लेना।

boast[1] *बोस्ट v.i.* to brag डींग मारना।

boast[2] *n.* bragging शेख़ी, डींग।

boat[1] *बोट n.* a small ship नाव।

boat[2] *v.i.* to sail a boat नाव खेना।

bodice *बौˇ डिस n.* a woman's garment above waist चोली।

bodily[1] *बौˇ डि लि a.* relating to the body शारीरिक।

bodily[2] *adv.* corporeally सशरीर।

body *बौˇ डि n.* a human being or an animal काया, देह; group of people समिति; a corpse शव।

bodyguard *बौˇ डि गाःड n.* a guard to protect somebody अंगरक्षक।

bog[1] *बौˇग n.* morass दलदल।

bog[2] *(-gg-) v.i.* to be stuck फंस जाना।

bogle *बो'-ग्ल् n.* phantom, bugbear, agoblin प्रेत, पिशाच।

bogus *बौ गॅस a.* sham, not genuine खोटा, जाली।

boil[1] *बौˇइल n.* a sore swelling or tumour फोड़ा।

boil[2] *v.i.* to bubble from the action of heat उबलना; to be cooked by boiling पकना *v. t.* to prepare by boiling उबालकर बनाना।

boiler *बौˇइ लॅः n.* a vessel in which a thing is boiled देग।

bold *बोल्ड a.* daring निडर; courageous साहसी; impudent धृष्ट।

boldness *बौल्ड़ निस n.* fearlessness निर्भीकता; impudence धृष्टता।

bolt[1] *बोल्ट n*. a bar of a door सिटकनी; a headed metal pin, काबला; discharge of lightening गाज, वज्रपात।

bolt[2] *v. t*. to fasten सिटकनी लगाना।

bomb[1] *बौमॅ n*. an iron shell filled with explosive material बम।

bomb[2] *v. t*. to attack with a bomb (पर) बम गिराना।

bombard *बैमॅ् बाःड v. t*. to attack with bombs (पर) बमबारी करना।

bombardment *बौमॅ् बाःड् मॅन्ट n*. act of bombarding बमबारी।

bomber *बौ˘ मॅः n*. an aircraft used to carry bombs बमवर्षक।

bonafide[1] *बो नॅ फॉइ डि adv*. in good faith सद्भावपूर्वक।

bonafide[2] *a* genuine सद्भावपूर्ण; सदाशयी।

bond *बौन्ड n*. a solemn agreement अनुबंध; that which binds बंधन; link, union संबंध, मेलभाव।

bondage *बौन्ॅ डिज n*. slavery दासता।

bone *बोन n*. hard substance forming animal's skeleton हड्डी।

bonfire *बौन्ॅ फॉइअॅः n*. large fire in the open air expressive of joy उत्सवाग्नि।

bonnet *बौ˘ निट n*. hat with strings टोप; cover of motor vehicle engine ढक्कन, बोनिट।

bonten *बॉन्'-टेन् n*. a narrow woollen fabric. ऊनी कपड़े की पट्टी।

bonus *बो नॅस n*. premium, extra payment बोनस, अधिलाभ।

book[1] *बुक n*. printed or written literary work पुस्तक।

book[2] *v. t*. to reserve (room, ticket etc.) सुरक्षित करा लेना; to charge with legal offence आरोपित करना।

book-keeper *बुक्'-कीप्'-अर् n*. a keeper of accounts मुनीम, हिसाब करने वाला।

book-mark *बुक्'-मार्क् n*. a card for marking a page in a book पुस्तक में पृष्ठ संकेत के रखने का कार्ड।

book-seller *बुक-सेल्'-अर् n*. one who sells books पुस्तक बेचने वाला।

book-worm *बुक्'-वर्म् n*. an indiscriminate reader of books किताबों का कीड़ा (सदा पुस्तक पढ़ने वाला)।

bookish *बु किश n*. fond of study पढ़क्कू, अव्यावहारिक।

booklet *बुक् लिट n*. a little book पुस्तिका।

boon *बून n*. favour, gift or grant वरदान।

boor *बु-अर् n*. peasant, a rude fellow किसान (देहाती), गँवार; **Boorish** *(-इश्) adj*. rude in manners, illiterate.

boost[1] *बूस्ट n*. encouragement प्रोत्साहन; help सहारा; upward push बढ़ावा।

boost[2] *v. t*. to push up बढ़ावा देना; to encourage प्रोत्साहित करना; to increase बढ़ाना।

boot *बूट n*. covering for the foot जूता; luggage compartment in a car सामान-धानी।

booth *बूथ n*. a temporary shed मंडप, कोष्ठ।

booty *बू टि n*. spoil, plunder लूट, लूट का माल।

booze *बूज् v. i*. to drink deeply

अधिक मदिरा पीना।

border[1] *बौः डॅः* *n.* boundary सीमांत; margin किनारी।

border[2] *v.t.* to provide with border किनारी लगाना; to adjoin (से) लगा हुआ होना।

bore[1] *बौः* *v. t.* to make a hole in छेदना, बेधना; to weary उबा देना।

bore[2] *n.* the hole made by boring छेद; a tiresome person उबानेवाला व्यक्ति।

born *बॉर्न्* (p. p. of Bear) brought forth जन्मा हुआ, पैदा हुआ; **Born rich** (rich-from birth) जन्म का धनी।

borne *बार्न* *adj.* carried, supported, defrayed लाया हुआ, आश्रय दिया हुआ, व्यय किया हुआ।

borrow *बौ ˘ रो* *v. t.* to receive as a loan उधार लेना।

bosom *बु ज़ॅम* *n.* breast छाती; seat of the affections हृदय।

boss *बौसॅ* *n.* master मालिक।

botany *बौ ˘ टॅ नि* *n.* the science which treats of plants वनस्पति विज्ञान।

botch *बॉच्* *v. t.* & *n.* to repair badly, a clumsy patch, an eruptive swelling on skin पैबन्द लगाना, पैबन्द, फोड़ा।

both[1] *बोथ* *a.* each of two दोनों।

both[2] *pron.* one and the other दोनों लोग।

both[3] *conj.* alike, equally समान रूप से।

bother *बौ ˘ दॅः* *v. t.* to annoy तंग करना; *v.i.* to trouble oneself परेशान होना।

botheration *बौ ˘ दॅ रे शॅन* *n.* act of bothering, state of being bothered झंझट, परेशानी ।

bottle *बौ ˘ ट्ल* *n.* a narrow-mouthed vessel of glass etc. बोतल।

bottler *बॉट्'-लर्* *n.* one who bottles liquors बोतनों में शराब भरने वाला।

bottom *बौ ˘ टॅम* *n.* the lowest part तह; the ground under water तल; the foundation आधार; the lower side निचला भाग; the origin उद्गम; the lowest part of a ship etc. पैंदा।

bough *बॉउ* *n.* branch of a tree टहनी, शाखा।

boulder *बोल्'-डर्* *n.* a large water-wom rounded stone पानी से घिसा हुआ चिकना बड़ा गोल पत्थर।

bouncer *बाउन्'-सर्* *n.* a boaster, a bully, a liar शेखीबाज या घमंडी, झूठा।

bound *बॉउन्ड* *n. pl.* limits सीमा।

boundary *बॉउन् डॅ रि* *n.* border सीमारेखा।

bountiful *बॉउन् टि फुल* *a.* abundant प्रचुर, भरपूर; generous उदारतापूर्ण।

bounty *बॉउन् टि* *n.* gift दान, उपहार; generosity उदारता; gratuity इनाम।

bouquet *बु के, बु के* *n.* a bunch of flowers गुलदस्ता।

bout *बॉउट्* *n.* a turn at work, fit of illness, trial of strength काम की पारी, बीमारी का दौरा, शक्ति-परीक्षा।

bow[1] *बॉउ* *v. t.* to bend झुकाना; *v.i.* to bend झुकना; to yield हार मानना।

bow[2] *n.* act of bowing नमन।

bow[3] *n.* an instrument to shoot

arrows धनुष।

bowel *बॉउ ॲल* *n. (pl.)* the intestines आंतें; the interior part अंदरूनी भाग।

bower *बॉ उ ॲ:* *n.* shady retreat कुंज।

bowl[1] *बोल* *n.* a round hollow dish कटोरा; wooden ball लकड़ी की गेंद।

bowl[2] *v.i.* to send a ball to the batsman गेंदबाजी करना; *v. t.* (with 'out') to dismiss (a batsman) by hitting the wicket आउट करना।

box *बौक्स* *n.* a case of wood, metal etc. संदूक, बकस; a container for holding things डिब्बा; a small enclosure in a court कटघरा।

boxing *बौक् सिङ्ग* *n.* act or art of fighting with the fists मुक्केबाज़ी।

boy *बौ ॅइ* *n.* a male child लड़का, बालक।

boycott[1] *बौ ॅइ कौ ॅट (-tt-)* *v. t.* to refuse to deal with or participate in बहिष्कार करना।

boycott[2] *n.* refusal of dealings or participation बहिष्कार।

boyhood *बॉय्'-हुड्* *n.* boyish age, state of being a boy लड़कपन।

brace *ब्रेस्* *n.* a couple, a thing that tightens, *(pl.)* trouser suspenders, a pair, boring instrument used by carpenters युगल (जोड़ा), बन्धन, (ब०व) पतलून लटकाने का पट्टा, जोड़ा, बढ़ई का बरमा।

bracelet *ब्रेस-लेट्* *n.* an ornament for the wrist. पहुँची, कंगल, बाजू।

brag[1] *ब्रैग (-gg-)* *v. i.* to boast डींग मारना।

brag[2] *n.* boast डींग।

braille *ब्रेल्* *n.* printing in relief (letters for the blind) अन्धों के लिये उभरे अक्षरों में छपी पुस्तक।

brain *ब्रेन* *n.* the nervous matter within the skull दिमाग़।

brake[1] *ब्रेक* *n.* a contrivance for retarding the motion of wheels ब्रेक।

brake[2] *v. t. v.i.* ब्रेक लगाना।

branch *ब्रान्च* *n.* the shoot of a tree or plant डाली; section, subdivision शाखा, उपखंड।

brand *ब्रान्ड्* *n.* mark made by hot iron, trade mark, a sword तपे लोहे का चिन्ह, व्यापारिक चिन्ह, तलवार।

brandy *ब्रैन् डि* *n.* a strong spirit; distilled from wine ब्रांडी।

brangle *ब्राङ्गल* *v. t.* to quarrel कलह करना, झगड़ना।

brass *ब्रास* *n.* a yellow alloy of copper and zinc पीतल।

brave *ब्रेव* *a.* daring साहसी; bold निडर; valiant बहादुर।

bravery *ब्रे वॅ रि* *n.* courage बहादुरी, साहस।

brawl *ब्राल्* *v. i. & n.* to engage in a noisy quarrel, murmur कलह करना, विवाद।

bray[1] *ब्रे* *n.* cry of an ass गधे की रेंक।

bray[2] *v. i.* (of an ass) to cry रेंकना।

breach *ब्रीच* *n.* state of being broken विच्छेद; infringement उल्लंघन।

bread *ब्रै ॅड* *n.* food made of flour or meal baked रोटी; livelihood जीविका।

breaden *ब्रॉड्'-एन्* *v. t. & i.* to make or grow broad चौड़ा करना या होना।

breadth *ब्रै ॅड्थ* *n.* width, distance from side to side चौड़ाई।

break[1] *ब्रेक v. t.* to separate into pieces तोड़ना; to shatter चूर-चूर करना; to destroy नष्ट करना; to fail to observe पालन न करना; to violate भंग करना, उल्लंघन करना; *v.i.* to be broken टूट जाना।

break[2] *n.* act of breaking भंजन; gap अंतराल; a broken part दरार।

breakage *ब्रे किज n.* act of breaking तोड़ने की क्रिया; damage caused by breaking टूटने से हुई क्षति; state of being broken टूट-फूट।

breakdown *ब्रेक् डॉउन n.* accidental stoppage अचानक का अवरोध।

breakfast *ब्रेक् फ़ॅस्ट n.* the first meal in the day नाश्ता।

breakneck *ब्रेक्´-नेक् n.* asteep place, a great fall करारा, गिराव, adj. hazardous आपत्तिजनक।

breast *ब्रेस्ट n.* the fore part of a body छाती, सीना; either of the milk glands of a woman स्तन, कुच।

breath *ब्रेथॅ n.* air used in the act of breathing श्वास; respiration श्वसन।

breathe *ब्रीद v. i.* to draw into and eject air from the lungs सांस लेना।

breeches *ब्रि चिज़ n. pl.* a garment similar to trousers बरजिस, जांघिया।

breed[1] *ब्रीड v.t.* to bring up पालन-पोषण करना; to educate सिखाना; *v.i.* to produce offspring प्रजनन करना।

breed[2] *n.* race, generation जाति, नस्ल।

breeze *ब्रीज़ n.* gentle wind समीर, बयार।

breviary *ब्री-वी-य-रि n.* a book containing prayers स्तोत्र-संग्रह।

brevity *ब्रै ˘ वि टि n.* shortness संक्षिप्तता।

brew *ब्रू v. t.* to make (beer, ale etc.) (शराब) खींचना, बनाना; to contrive (a plot etc.) (योजना) बनाना; *v. i.* to make beer शराब बनाना; to be in preparation निर्माणाधीन होना।

brewery *ब्रु अॅ रि n.* a place where brewing is carried on यवसुरा निर्माणशाला।

bribe[1] *ब्रॉइब n.* a gift to corrupt the conduct घूस, रिश्वत।

bribe[2] *v. t.* to offer or give a gift to रिश्वत देना।

brick *ब्रिक n.* a lump of clay used in building ईंट।

bride *ब्रॉइड n.* a woman about to be, or newly married दुलहन, नववधू।

bridegroom *ब्रॉइड् ग्रुम n.* a man about to be, or newly married दुल्हा, वर।

bridge *ब्रिज n.* a structure across a river etc. to furnish a passage पुल।

bridle *ब्रॉइ ड्ल n.* the harness on the head of a horse including the straps etc. लगाम।

brief *ब्रीफ़ a.* short संक्षिप्त।

brigade *ब्रि गेड n.* subdivision of an army वाहिनी।

brigadier *ब्रि गॅ डिअॅः n.* the officer who commands a brigade ब्रिगेडियर।

bright *ब्रॉइट a.* clear स्पष्ट; shining

चमकदार; cheerful मुदित; clever तीव्रबुद्धि।

brighten *ब्रॉइ टॅन v. t.* to make bright चमकाना *v. i.* to become bright चमकना।

brilliance *ब्रि ल्यॅन्स n.* state of being brilliant चमक, दीप्ति।

brilliant *ब्रि ल्यॅन्ट a.* shining चमकदार; of great talents प्रतिभाशाली।

brim *ब्रिम् n.* the upper edge of anything कंठ, मुख, किनारा।

brine *ब्राइन् n.* salt water, the sea, tears खारा पानी, समुद्र, आँसू।

bring *ब्रिङ्ग v. t.* to lead or cause to come लाना।

brinjal *ब्रिन्'-जॉल् n.* fruit of egg-plant, egg-apple बैंगन, भंटा।

brink *ब्रिङ्क n.* edge of a steep place कगार।

brisk *ब्रिस्क् adj.* active, lively, full of spirit तीव्र, चपल।

bristle *ब्रिस्'-स्ल् n.* the stiff hair of swine सुअर के कड़े बाल; *v. t.* to cause hair to stand रोमांचित होना, पुलकित होना, रोवाँ खड़ा होना।

british *ब्रिट्'-इश् adj.* pertaining to England, of British empire आंग्लदेशीय, अंग्रेज़।

brittle *ब्रि ट्ल a.* apt to break टूटने-योग्य।

broad *ब्रौड a.* wide चौड़ा; general सामान्य।

broadcast[1] *ब्रौड कास्ट n.* act of broadcasting प्रसारण।

broadcast[2] *v. t.* to scatter (seed) बखेरना; to make widely known प्रचारित करना; to send out by radio or television प्रसारित करना।

brocade *ब्रो-केड् n.* fabric with raised pattem in gold-thread or silk किमखाब, ज़रीदार या बूटेदार कपड़ा।

broccoli *ब्रॉक्-ऑ-लि n.* cabbage with edible flower, फूलगोभी।

brochure[1] *ब्रो शुअँ: n.* a pamphlet विवरणिका।

brochure[2] *ब्रा-शूर n.* a stitched booklet सिली हुई छोटी पुस्तक।

broker *ब्रो कँ: n.* an agent who buys and sells for others दलाल।

brood *ब्रडू n.* batch of birds or animals, offspring पशु या पक्षियों के बच्चे।

brook *ब्रुक n.* a small stream नाला, छोटी नदी।

broom *ब्रूम n.* a brush for sweeping झाडू।

bronze *ब्रॉञ्ज् n. & adj.* brown alloy of copper and tin काँसा, कस्कुट का, काँसे का।

broth *ब्रौथॅ n.* thick soup शोरबा।

brothel *ब्रॉथू'-थ्ल् n.* house of ill-fame (prostitution) वेश्यालय, रंडी का घर।

brother *ब्र दँ: n.* son of the same parents भाई।

brotherhood *ब्र दँ: हुड n.* state or quality of being brother भ्रातृत्व।

brow *ब्रॉउ n.* ridge over eyes भौंह।

brown[1] *ब्रॉउन a.* reddish yellow भूरा।

brown[2] *n.* reddish yellow colour भूरा रंग।

browse *ब्राउज् n.* new leaves of trees. नई पत्तियाँ, पंखड़ी।

bruise *ब्रूज् n.* injury by blow. आघात, चोट।

bruit *ब्रूट्* *n.* report, rumor सूचना (जन-प्रवाद), झूठी खबर या झूठा समाचार।

brush *ब्रश* *n.* an instrument to clean by rubbing or sweeping सफ़ाई का ब्रश; painter's large pencil रंग भरने का ब्रश; the tail of a fox लोमड़ी की पूंछ।

brustle *ब्रस्-स्ल्* *v. t.* to rustle, to crackle खड़खड़ाना।

brutal *ब्रू टॅल* *a.* cruel क्रूर, निर्दय।

brute *ब्रूट* *n.* an animal पशु।

bubble *ब ब्ल* *n.* a ball of liquid filled with air बुलबुला।

bucket *ब किट* *n.* a vessel in which water is drawn or carried बाल्टी।

buckle *ब क्ल* *n.* a metal clasp for fastening belt, strap etc. बकसुआ।

bud *बड* *n.* the first shoot of a leaf कली।

budge *बज्* *v. i. & n.* to make the slightest movement, to give way, lambskin fur सरकना, घिसकना, हिलना, मेमने का बाल।

budget *बज्-इट्* *n.* contents of a bag or bundle, a stock, annual estimate of acconts कोष (संग्रह), पूँजी, आय-व्यय का वार्षिक अनुमान।

buff *बफ्* *n.* leather of buffalo or oxhide, a blow भैंस या बैल का चमड़ा, घूँसा।

buffalo *ब फॅ लो* *n.* a species of ox भैंस, भैंसा।

buffoon *ब फून* *n.* jester मसखरा।

bug *बग* *n.* a small blood-sucking insect खटमल।

bugle *ब्यू-ग्ल्* *n.* a small trumpet of brass बिगुल, सिंगी, तुरही।

build[1] *बिल्ड* *v. t.* to construct निर्माण करना।

build[2] *n.* general shape or structure गठन, रचना।

building *बिल् डिङ्ग* *n.* a house or other structure भवन, निर्माण।

bulb *बल्ब* *n.* a round root कंद; glass container of electric lamp filament बल्ब।

bulk *बल्क* *n.* magnitude विस्तार; size आकार।

bulky *बल् कि* *a.* of great bulk भारी, बड़ा।

bull *बुल* *n.* the male cattle सांड।

bulldog *बुल् डौ ॅग* *n.* a species of dog एक प्रकार का कुत्ता।

bull's eye *बुल्ज्'-आइ* *n.* the centre of a target. निशाना लगाने का गोल बिन्दु।

bullet *बु लिट* *n.* a small round missile shot from firearm गोली।

bulletin *बु लि टिन* *n.* an official report विज्ञप्ति।

bullock *बु लक* *n.* a young bull बैल।

bully[1] *बु लि* *n.* an overbearing quarrelsome fellow धौंसिया।

bully[2] *v. t.* to insult and overbear धौंसियाना, भयभीत करना।

bulwark *बल्'-वर्क्* *n.* rampart, fortification, breakwater, a principle. दुर्ग का प्राचीन, कोट, दुर्गीकरण, बाँध, सिद्धान्त।

bumper *बम्प्'-अर* *n.* a cup filled up to the brim, anything unusual or abundant. मुँह तक भरा हुआ प्याला, कोई असामान्य पदार्थ।

bumpy *बम्प्'-इ* *adj.* abounding in bumps. उछलने वाला, कूदने वाला।

bunch *बन्च* *n.* a cluster of things गुच्छा; group of people जनसमूह।

bundle *बन् ड्ल* *n.* a package पुलिंदा।

bungalow *बङ् गॅ लो* *n.* a house with only ground floor बंगला।

bungle¹ *बङ् ग्ल* *v. t.* to mismanage बिगाड़ना *v. i.* to act clumsily भद्दे ढंग से काम करना।

bungle² *n.* bungling घपला।

bunk *बङ्क्* *n.* a sleeping berth सोने के लिये पटरी; *v. t.* to clear off हटा देना।

bunker *बङ् कॅ:* *n.* underground shelter तहख़ाना, सेनावास।

buoy *बॉय्'* *n.* an anchored floating seamark for showing navigable course जहाज़ का मार्ग दिखलाने का लंगर पर बँधा हुआ पीपा।

buoyancy *बॉय्'-आन्-सि* *n.* the floating power of liquids तरल पदार्थ की प्लवनशीलता, उतराव, हल्कापन।

burden¹ *ब: ड्न* *n.* load बोझा।

burden² *v. t.* to load लादना।

burdensome *ब: ड्न् सॅम* *a.* heavy भारी; oppressive कष्टकारी।

bureau *ब्यू-रो'* *n.* (*pl.* **Bureaux** —रोज़) a writing desk, office, department दराज वाल मेज़, लेखन-स्थान, दफ्तर, मुहकमा।

Bureacuracy *ब्यू-रो'-क्र-सि* *n.* government through officials अनियन्त्रित शासन, कर्मचारियों द्वारा चलाया जाने वाला राज्य, नौकरशाही।

bureaucrat *ब्यू-रो'-क्रेट्* *n.* an advocate of bureaucracy, an official कर्मचारी शासन-पद्धति का अनुयायी।

burglar *बॅ: ग्लॅ:* *n.* one who robs a house by night चोर।

burglary *ब: ग्लॅ रि* *n.* the act of a burglar चोरी।

burial *बै ˘ रि अॅल* *n.* act of burying दफ़न।

burk *बर्क्* *v. t.* to avoid, to suppress, to hush up टालना, (जनश्रुति) दबाना, चुपके से तय कर देना।

burn¹ *ब:न* *v. t.* to consume with fire जलाना; to inflame उत्तेजित करना, *v. i.* to be on fire जलना; to be inflamed with desire उत्तेजित होना।

burn² *n.* a hurt caused by fire जलने की चोट।

burrow *बर्'-रो* *n.* a hole in the earth made by rabbits, for shelter बिल, माँद।

burst¹ *ब:स्ट* *v. i.* to fly or break open फट पड़ना; to enter with violence तीव्रता से प्रवेश करना; *v.t.* to break by force फोड़ना; to open suddenly तीव्रता से खोलना।

burst² *n.* a violent disruption प्रस्फोट, विस्फोट।

bury *बै ˘ रि* *v. t.* to put into the grave दफनाना; to hide in the earth ज़मीन में गाड़ना या छिपाना।

bus *बस* *n.* a large motor vehicle for passengers बस।

bush *बुश* *n.* shrub झाड़ी; woodland जंगल।

business *बिज् निस* *n.* occupation पेशा; concern सरोकार; trade व्यवसाय।

businessman *बिज़् निस् मॅन* *n.* a man engaged in trade or commerce व्यापारी।

bustle *बस्-सल्* *v. t.* to stir oneself, to hurry कार्य में लगना, जल्दी से काम करना

busy *बि ज़ि* *a.* occupied व्यस्त; actively engaged कार्यरत।

but[1] *बट* *prep.* except के अतिरिक्त।

but[2] *conj.* yet, still किंतु, फिर भी।

butcher[1] बु *चें:* *n.* one who kills animals for market क़साई।

butcher[2] *v. t.* to kill (animals) for food हत्या करना।

butter[1] *ब टें:* *n.* an oily substance obtained from cream by churning मक्खन।

butter[2] *v. t.* to spread butter on (पर) मक्खन लगाना।

butterfly *ब टें: फ्लॉइ* *n.* an insect with large colourful wings तितली।

buttermilk *ब टें:* मिल्क *n.* the milk that remains after the butter is separated मट्ठा।

buttock *ब टॅक* *n.* back of hip चूतड़।

button[1] *ब टॅन* *n.* fastener sewn on clothes बटन।

button[2] *v. t.* to fasten with buttons बटन लगाना।

buy *बॉइ* *v. t.* to purchase ख़रीदना।

buyer *बॉइ अॅ:* *n.* purchaser क्रेता।

buzz[1] *बज़* *v. i.* to make a low humming sound गुंजन करना।

buzz[2] *n.* a humming sound भिनभिनाहट।

by[1] *बॉइ* *prep.* near के समीप; during के दौरान; through से होकर; not later than तक।

by[2] *adv.* near पास में; past पास से होकर।

bye-bye *बॉइ बॉइ* *interj.* goodbye नमस्कार।

by-election *बॉइ इ लैक् शॅन* *n.* parliamentary election during the term of the parliament उपचुनाव।

bylaw, bye-law *बॉइ लौ* *n.* an accessory law उपनियम।

bypass *बॉइ* पास *n.* a road that avoids a town उपमार्ग।

by-product *बॉइ प्रौ˘ डक्ट* *n.* a secondary product उपोत्पादन।

byre *बॉइ अॅ:* *n.* a cow-house गोशाला।

byword *बॉइ वॅ:ड* *n.* a proverb लोकोक्ति; an object of scorn घृणा का पात्र।

Cc

C *सी* the third letter of the english alphabet, the first note in the natural major scale. अंग्रेजी वर्णमाला का तीसरा अक्षर, (सं०) पहिला सुर; it is sounded as '*k*' before *a, o, u, l* and *r*, but before *e, i* and *y*, it is sounded as '*s*', when combined with *h*, it is sound as *k* or '*ch*'. इसका उच्चारण a, o, u, l तथा r के पूर्व रहने पर '*क्*' *e, i*, और *y* के पूर्व रहने पर '*स्*' होता है, *ch* का उच्चारण '*च्*' तथा '*क्*' होता है।

cab *कैब* *n.* a covered one-horse carriage घोड़ागाड़ी।

cabaret *कैब्'-आ-रे* *n.* a tavern सराय।

cabbage *कै बिज* *n.* a culinary vegetable बन्दगोभी, करमकल्ला।

cabin *कै बिन* *n.* a hut कुटीर; an apartment in a ship जहाज़ की कोठरी।

cabinet *कै बि निट,–नै ˘ट* *n.* outer case of television, radio etc. पेटिका; the ministers of state मंत्रि-मंडल; a piece of furniture with drawers or shelves अलमारी।

cable[1] *के ब्ल* *n.* a strong rope रस्सा; wire conveying electric power, telegraph signals etc. डोरी; submarine telegraphic message समुद्रीतार।

cable[2] *v. t.* to send by ocean telegraph सतुद्रीतार से भेजना।

cache *काश* *n.* a hiding place for concealing treasure, provisions or ammunition. रत्न, भोजन-सामग्री तथा गोली-बारूद छिपाने का स्थान।

cachet *काशे* *n.* a stamp, a capsule containing medicine. मोहर, औषध भरने की छोटी पतली शीशी।

cackle *केक्-क्ल्* *v. i.* to make sound like a duck or hen, to talk idly, to boast कूकना, अव्यक्त शब्द करना, डींग हाँकना।

cactus *कैक् टॅस* *n.* a spiny shrub नागफनी।

cad *कैड्* *n.* a person of mean nature and manners नीच प्रवृत्ति तथा अशिष्ट आचरण का मनुष्य।

cadet *कॅ डै˘ट* *n.* a young man in a military school सैनिक छात्र।

cadge *काज्'* *v. i.* to go about peddling or begging भीख माँगते फिरना।

cadmium *कैड्'-मि-अम्* *n.* a metal like tin टीन के समान एक धातु।

cafe *कै फ़े* *n.* coffee-house काफ़ीघर।

cage *केज* *n.* an enclosure of wire for birds and beasts पिंजड़ा।

cain *कैन्* *n.* a murderer, rent paid in kind हत्यारा, वस्तु द्वारा चुकाया गया किराया।

cake *केक* *n.* baked, sweetened, breadlike food केक; a compact mass टिकिया।

calamity *कॅ लै मि टि* *n.* great misfortune विपत्ति।

calcium *कैल्'-सि-अम्* *n.* the base of metallic lime चूने का तत्त्व या सार।

calculate *कैल् क्यु लेट* *v. t.* to compute गणना करना; to estimate अनुमान लगाना।

calculator *कैल्-क्यू-लेटर्* *n.* one who or that which calculates जोड़ने वाला, गणना करने का यन्त्र।

calculation *कैल् क्यु ले शॅन* *n.* estimate अनुमान; process or result of calculating गणन।

calendar *कै लिन् डॅः* *n.* a table of months and days in the year पंचांग।

calf *काफ़* *n.* young of a cow or some other animal बछड़ा; fleshy back part of leg below the knee पिंडली।

call[1] *कौल* *v. t.* to ask or command to come पुकारना।

call[2] *n.* vocal utterance पुकार; a short visit भेंट।

caller *कॉल्'-अर्* *n.* one who pays a visit भेंट करने वाला मनुष्य।

calligraphy *कैल्-लिग्-रे-फि* *n.* the art of beautiful handwriting सुन्दर लिखावट की कला।

calling *कौ लिङ्ग* *n.* vocation पेशा।

callow *कैल्'-लो adj.* not covered with feathers, inexperienced पंखहीन (बिना पर का), अनुभवशून्य (कोरा), नातर्जुबेकार।

callous *कै लॅस a.* hardened कठोर।

calm[1] *काम n.* still, quiet शांत।

calm[2] *n.* tranquility शांति।

calm[3] *v. t.* make calm शांत करना।

calmative *का-मे-टिव् adj.* possessing soothing or sedative effect शान्ति लाने वाली (औषध)।

calorie *कैल्'-ऑर्-इ n.* unit of heat तापमान की (इकाई), माप।

calumniate *कैल्'-अम्-नि-एट् v. t.* to slander निन्दा करना, झूठा अभियोग लगाना।

camel *कै मॅल n.* a large, desert animal with humped back ऊँट।

camera कै मॅ रॅ *n.* an apparatus for taking photographs कैमरा।

camlet *केम'-लिट् n.* light cloth of wool or silk used for making cloaks लबादा बनाने का ऊनी या रेशमी हल्का वस्त्र।

camp[1] *कैम्प n.* an encampment शिविर, पड़ाव।

camp[2] *v. i.* to encamp पड़ाव डालना।

campaign *कैम् पेन n.* a series of efforts आंदोलन; a series of military operations अभियान।

camphor *कैम् फ़ः n.* a strong smelling white substance कपूर।

can[1] *कैन n.* a metal container डिब्बा।

can[2] *(-nn-) v. t.* to put in a can डिब्बे में बंद करना।

can[3] *v. aux.* to be able समर्थ होना; to be possible संभव होना।

canal *कॅ नैल n.* an artificial water course नहर; duct in the body नली।

canard *का-नार्ड् n.* a fabricated story (झूठी) कल्पित कथा।

cancel *कैन् सॅल v. t.* to cross out काट देना; to annual रद्द करना; to call off वापस लेना; to neutralise व्यर्थ कर देना।

cancellation *कैन्-सैल्-ले-शन् n.* act of abolishing काटने का कार्य, रदद्।

cancer *कैन् सॅः n.* malignant growth in the body कैंसर।

candid *कैन् डिड a.* ingenuous मासूम; frank स्पष्टवादी, निष्कपट।

candidate *कैन् डि डेट n.* one who seeks office or post प्रत्याशी; one who takes an examination परीक्षार्थी।

candle *कैन् ड्ल n.* a stick of wax with wick मोमबत्ती।

candour *कैन् डॅः n.* frankness स्पष्टवादिता; sincerity निष्कपटता।

candy[1] *कैन् डि n.* crystallized sugar मिसरी।

candy[2] *v. t.* to conserve with sugar पागना।

cane[1] *केन n.* a reed बेंत।

cane[2] *v. t.* to beat with a cane बेंत से मारना।

canister *कै निस् टॅः n.* a small box with a lid कनस्तर।

cannon *कै नॅन n.* a large gun तोप।

cannonade *कैन्-नन्-एड्' n. v. & t.* continous gun-fire, to bombard निरन्तर गोलों की वर्षा, निरन्तर गोला चलाना।

canon *कान्-अॅन् n.* a law or rule, a kind of type, church decree विधि (नियम, व्यवस्था), एक प्रकार का टाइप, गिरजाघर की डिगरी।

canopy *कै नॅ पि n.* covering over throne, bed etc. चंदोवा, छतरी।

canteen *कैन् टीन n.* a place where provisions etc. are sold जलपान-गृह।

canter *कान्ट्'-अर् n.* an easy gallop, a beggar कदम चाल, भिखमंगा।

canton *कैन्-टॅन् n.* a small division of a country, a distinct state किसी देश का छोटा विभाग, प्रदेश, भाग।

cantonment *कैन् टून् मॅन्ट n.* part of a town occupied by troops छावनी।

canvas *कैन् वॅस n.* cloth for painting on चित्रफलक, कैनवास।

canvass *कैन् वॅस v. t.* to solicit votes वोट मांगना।

cap[1] *कैप n.* covering for the head टोपी; lid ढक्कन।

cap[2] *(-pp-) v. t.* to put a cap on टोपी पहनाना।

capability *कै पॅ बि लि टि n.* quality of being capable सामर्थ्य।

capable *के पॅ ब्ल a.* having sufficient skill or power योग्य; competent सक्षम।

capacious *कॅ पे शॅस a.* roomy विशाल, लंबा-चौड़ा।

capacity *क पै सि टि n.* power of holding क्षमता; ability योग्यता।

cape *केप n.* point of land running into sea अंतरीप।

capital[1] *कै पि टॅल n.* chief town राजधानी; money, funds पूंजी; a large-sized letter बड़ा अक्षर।

capital[2] *a.* punishable by death मृत्युदंड-योग्य; chief मुख्य; excellent उत्तम, उत्कृष्ट।

capitalist *कै पि टॅ लिस्ट n.* owner of capital पूंजीपति।

capitulate *कै-पिट्-यू-लेट् v. t.* to surrender on terms किसी शर्त पर शत्रु के अधीन हो जाना।

caprice *कॅ प्रीस n.* whim, freak मौज, सनक।

capricious *कॅ प्रि शॅस a.* full of caprice सनकी, मनमौजी।

capricorn *केप्-रि-कार्न n.* the tenth sign of the zodiac मकर राशि।

capsicum *केप्'-साइज्'n.* a kind of tropical plant बड़ी लाल मिर्च।

capsize *कैप् सॉइज़ v. i.* to be overturned उलट जाना।

capsular *कैप'-स्यूल्-अर् adj.* pertaining to capsule.बीजकोष-सम्बन्धी।

captain *कैप् टिन n.* leader, commander कप्तान।

captaincy *कैप् टिन् सि n.* the rank, post or commission of a captain कप्तान का पद, कप्तानी।

caption *कैप् शॅन n.* heading or short title शीर्षक।

captivate *कैप् टि वेट v. t.* to charm, to fascinate मुग्ध करना, आकर्षित करना।

captive[1] *कैप् टिव n.* one taken prisoner in war बंदी।

captive[2] *a.* kept in bondage बंदी बना हुआ।

captivity *कैप् टि वि टि n.* state of being a captive बंदी दशा।

capture[1] *कैप् चॅ: v. t.* to make prisoner बंदी बनाना।

capture[2] *n.* act of taking prisoner बंदीकरण।

car *का: n.* motorcar मोटरगाड़ी; coach

गाड़ी का डिब्बा, कोच।

carat *कै रॅट n.* a measure of the purity of gold करात, कैरट।

caravan *कै रॅ वैन, n.* a company of travellers कारवाँ, काफ़िला।

carbide *कार्'-बाइड् n.* a compound of carbon with other elements दूसरे तत्वों के साथ कार्बन का यौगिक।

carbon *काः बॅन n.* pure charcoal कारबन।

card *काःड n.* a thick stiff paper पत्रक; a playing card ताश का पत्ता।

cardamom *कार्डा-मम् n.* an aromatic pungent spice एला, इलायची।

cardboard *काःड् बौःड n.* thin, stiff board made of paper pulp गत्ता।

cardiac (al) *कार्'-डि-एक् (-अल)adjs.* pertaining to the heart. हृदय सम्बन्धी।

cardinal[1] *काः डि नॅल a.* chief प्रधान।

cardinal[2] *n.* a dignitary in the Roman Catholic church next to the pope कार्डिनल।

care[1] *कै ॅअः n.* attention सावधानी; worry चिंता; charge देखरेख।

care[2] *v. i.* to be concerned चिंतित होना; to look after देखरेख करना।

career *कॅ रिॲः n.* progress through life प्रगति; profession व्यवसाय; rapid motion तीव्र गति।

careful *कै ॅ ॲः फुल a.* solicitous चिंतित; cautious सावधान, सचेत।

careless *के ॅ ॲः लिस a.* heedless लापरवाह; incautious असावधान।

caress *कॅ रै ॅस v. t.* to fondle पुचकारना।

cargo *काः गो n.* the goods in a ship पोतभार।

caricature *कै रि कॅ ट्युॲः n.* a portrait or description so exaggerated as to excite ridicule व्यंग्य-चित्र।

carious *केरि-अस् adj.* rotten, ulcerated सड़ा हुआ, गलित।

carl *कार्ल् n.* a mean fellow, a rustic, a husbandman, a clown नीच पुरुष, गँवार मनुष्य, किसान, खेतिहर, विदूषक, भांड।

carnage *कार्-नेज् n.* great slaughter of men संहार, हत्याकाण्ड।

carnival *कार्नि-वल् n.* a riotous festival, revelry आनन्द उत्सव।

carol *कारोल् n.* joyous song आनन्द का गीत, स्त्रोत।

carpal *कार्-पल् adj.* pertaining to wrist कलाई का।

carpenter *काः पिन् टॅः n.* one who works in timber बढ़ई।

carpentry *काः पिन् ट्रि n.* the trade, art or work of a carpenter बढ़ईगीरी।

carpet *काः पिट n.* a woven fabric for covering floors क़ालीन, दरी।

carriage *कै रिज n.* act of carrying ढुलाई; vehicle गाड़ी; cost of carrying भाड़ा।

carrier *कै रि ॲः n.* one who carries for hire वाहक; an attachment fixed to a bicycle साइकिल का कैरियर।

carrot *कै रॅट n.* a yellowish or reddish esculent root of a tapering form गाजर।

carry *कै रि v. t.* to bear ले जाना; to transport पहुंचाना; to support संभालना; to have with one साथ रखना।

cart *का:ट* *n.* a carriage of burden with two wheels छकड़ा।

cartage *का: टिज* *n.* act of carrying in a cart ढुलाई का काम; price paid for carting भाड़ा।

carton *कार्टन्* *n.* a cardboard (pasteboard) box for holding goods सामान रखने का दफ्ती का बक्स।

cartoon *का: टून* *n.* a humorous or satirical drawing व्यंग्य-चित्र, हास्य चित्र; a sequence of drawings telling a story कार्टून-कथा।

cartridge *का: ट्रिज* *n.* a case containing charge of a gun कारतूस।

carve *का:व* *v. t.* to engrave उत्कीर्ण करना; to cut काटना; to sculpture मूर्ति का रूप देना।

cascade *कैस् केड* *n.* waterfall जलप्रताप।

case *केस* *n.* suit मुक़दमा; matter मामला; problem समस्या; box संदूक; state of affairs स्थिति; *(gram.)* relation of words in a sentence कारक।

cash[1] *कैश* *n.* ready money नक़द धन।

cash[2] *v. t.* to turn into money नगदी में बदलना।

cashier *कै शिअ:* *n.* one who has charge of money कोषाध्यक्ष, खज़ांची।

casing *केस्'-इङ्ग्* *n.* a covering ढ़प्पन, ढकना।

cask *कास्क्'* *n.* a wooden vessel for holding liquors पीपा, कठवत।

casket *कास्क्'-इट्* *n.* a small box used for keeping jewels, letter or cremated ashes जवाहरात, पत्र या शव की राख रखने का बक्सा।

cassette *कै सै ॅट* *n.* a plastic container of film कैसिट।

cast[1] *कास्ट* *v. t.* to throw फेंकना; to scatter छितराना; to mould ढालना।

cast [2] *n.* a throw निक्षेपण; a mould ढांचा; set of actors अभिनेतावृंद; squint भेंगापन।

caste *कास्ट* *n.* social rank जाति।

castigate *कैस् टि गेट* *v. t.* to chastise फटकारना; to punish दंड देना।

casting *कास्ट्'-इङ्ग्* *n.* a moulding धातु को गलाकर ढलाई।

cast-iron *कास्ट्'-आयरन्* *n.* iron melted and cast in moulds कान्ती लोहा, ढला हुआ लोहा।

castle *का स्ल* *n.* a fortified building दुर्ग; (chess) a piece (शतरंज) हाथी।

castor oil *कास् टॅ: औ ॅइल* *n.* a medicinal oil obtained from tropical plant रेंडी का तेल।

castral *कास्-ट्रल्* *adj.* pertaining or belonging to a camp खेमे का।

casual *कै ज़्यु अॅल्* *a.* happening by chance आकस्मिक।

casualty *कै ज़्यु अॅल् टि* *n.* accident दुर्घटना; the victim of an accident दुर्घटना का शिकार।

cat *कैट* *n.* a domestic animal of the feline tribe बिल्ली।

catalogue *कै टॅ लौगॅ* *n.* a list सूचीपत्र।

cataract *कै टॅ रैक्ट* *n.* waterfall जलप्रताप; an eye-disease मोतियाबिंद।

catch[1] *कैच* *v. t.* to take hold of पकड़ना; to be in time for (bus etc.) (बस आदि) पकड़ना; to hear

सुनना; to find out पाना; to contract (cold etc.) (कोई रोग) ग्रहण करना।

catch[2] *n.* act of catching पकड़ने की क्रिया; what is caught शिकार; trick, deception चाल, धोखा; device for holding the door shut अर्गला।

categorical *कै टि गौ ˘ रि कॅल a.* pertaining to a category श्रेणीगत; unqualified and unconditional सुनिश्चित, निरपेक्ष।

category *कै टि गॅ रि n.* class, division श्रेणी, पद।

cater *के-टर् v. i.* to provide food or amusement भोजन या मनोरंजन का प्रबंध करना।

caterpillar *कैट्'-अर्-पिल्-लर् n.* the larva of a moth or insect, a rapacious person कीड़ा, झिनगा, लोभी आदमी।

cathedral *कॅ थी ड्रॅल n.* the principal church प्रधान गिरजाघर।

catholic *कै थॅ लिक a.* liberal उदार।

cattle *कै ट्ल n. pl.* animals like cows, bulls मवेशी।

cauliflower *कौ ˘ लि फ़्लॉउ ॲ: n.* a variety of cabbage फूलगोभी।

causal *कॉ'-जल् adj.* expressing cause हेतुक, कारण बतलाने वाला।

causality *कॉज़्'-एल्-इट्-ई n.* the agency of a cause, relation of cause and effect कारणत्व, कारण और परिणाम का परस्पर सम्बन्ध।

cause[1] *कौज़* reason कारण; purpose उद्देश्य।

cause[2] *v.t.* to bring about उत्पन्न करना, का कारण बनना।

causeway *काज़्'-वे n.* a raised road over water or through a marsh बाँध, पुल।

caustic *कौस् टिक a.* burning or corrosive दाहक; biting तीखा।

caution[1] *कौ शॅन n.* warning चेतावनी; care सतर्कता।

caution[2] *v. t.* to warn चेतावनी देना।

cautious *कौ शॅस a.* having caution सतर्क।

cavalry *कै वॅल् रि n.* mounted troops वख्तरबंद सेना।

cave *केव n.* den गुफा।

cavern *कै वॅ:न n.* a large cave गुफ़ा।

cavil *काव्'-इल् v. t.* to raise captious objection झूठी निन्दा करना, दोष निकालना।

cavity *के वि टि n.* a hollow place रंध्र, गुहा।

caw[1] *कौ n.* cry of crow काँव-काँव।

caw[2] *v. i.* to cry like a crow काँव-काँव करना।

cease *सीस v. i.* to stop बंद होना; *v. t.* to put a stop to बंद करना।

ceaseless *सीस् लिस a.* without end, incessant निरंतर, निर्विराम।

cedar *सी'-डार् n.* a kind of tree देवदार का वृक्ष।

ceiling *सी लिङ्ग n.* the upper inside surface of a room भीतरी छत।

celebrate *सै ˘ लि ब्रेट v. t. & i.* to honour by solemn rites उत्सव या त्योहार मनाना।

celebrated *सै ˘ लि ब्रे टिड a.* famous प्रसिद्ध।

celebration *सै ˘ लि ब्रे शॅन n.* the act of celebration उत्सव, समारोह; ceremonious performance अनुष्ठान।

celebrity *से-लेब्-रिट्-ई n.* fame,

reknown कीर्ति, प्रसिद्धि, प्रशंसा, यश।

celestial *सि-लेस्ट्-इअल् adj.* heavenly, divine, beautiful दिव्य, स्वर्गीय, सुन्दर।

celibacy[1] *सेल्-इब्'-एस्-ई n.* unmarried life अविवाहित जीवन, कुँआरापन, ब्रह्मचर्य।

celibacy[2] *सै ॅ लि बॅ सि n.* unmarried state ब्रह्मचर्य, अविवाहित जीवन।

cell *सै ॅल n.* a small room कोठरी; cavity कोटर; a group of people गुट; minute basic unit of living matter कोशिका; device converting chemical energy into electric energy बैटरी।

cellar *सै ॅ लॅः n.* an underground apartment used for storage तहख़ाना।

cellular *सेल्'-ल्यू-लर् adj.* having small cavities छोटे छिद्रवाला, जालीदार।

cement[1] *सि मैंन्ट n.* fine mortar सीमेंट।

cement[2] *v. t.* to join firmly together जोड़ना।

cemetery *सै ॅ मि टॅ रि n.* a burial place क़ब्रिस्तान।

cense *सेन्स् v. t.* to perfume with burming incense धूप देना।

censer *सेन्स्'-सर् n.* a licensing officer, a harsh critic दोष, निरीक्षक, गुण-दोष विवेचक।

censor[1] *सैनॅ् सॅः n.* one who examines manuscripts etc. before they are published निरीक्षक, नियंत्रक।

censor[2] *v. t.* to examine निरीक्षण करना।

censorious *सेन्-सोर्-'इ-अस् adj.* fault-finding दोष निकालने वाला।

censorship *सेन्-सर्'-शिप् n.* the office of a censor लाइसेन्स देने वाले का पद।

censure[1] *सैनॅ् शॅः n.* reproof निंदा।

censure[2] *v. t.* to blame निंदा करना।

census *सैॅन् सॅस n.* an official count of population जनगणना।

cent *सेन्ट् n.* a hundred, a coin which is the hundredth part of a dollar सौ, एक सिक्का।

centenarian *सैनॅ् टि नैॅ अॅ रि अॅन n.* a person who is a hundred years completed of age शतायु व्यक्ति।

centenary *सैनॅ् टि नॅ रि n.* period of a hundred years सौ वर्ष का समय; commemoration of an event a hundred years earlier शताब्दी महोत्सव।

centennial *सेन्ट्-ए-नि-यल् adj. n.* hundredth anniversary सौवीं वर्षगाँठ।

center *सेन्-टर् n.* a waist-belt कमरबन्द, कमर की पेटी।

centigrade *सैनॅ् टि ग्रेड a.* divided into a hundred degrees सौ अंशों में विभाजित।

centipede *सेन्ट्-इ-पीड् n.* a many footed crawling insect गोजर, कनखजूरा।

central *सैनॅ् ट्रॅल a.* placed in the centre केंद्रीय; chief मुख्य।

centre *सैनॅ् टॅः* middle point केंद्र।

centrifugal *सेन्-ट्रिफ्'-यू-गल् adj.* tending to fly off form centre केन्द्र से हट जाने वाली (प्रवृत्ति)।

centuple *सेन्'-ट्यू-पल् n. & adj.* hundredfold सौगुना।

century *सैनॅ चु रि* *n.* hundred सौ, शतक; a hundred years शताब्दी।

ceramics *से-रेम्-इक्स् n.* the art of pottery, objects made of clay कुम्हारी विद्या, मिट्टी के पात्र।

cerated *सेर्'-एट्-एड् adj.* covered with wax मोम से ढँका हुआ।

cereal[1] *सिॲ रि ॲल n.* grain used as food अन्न।

cereal[2] *a.* pertaining to corn अन्नमय।

cerebral *सेर्-रि-ब्रल् adj.* pertaining to cerebrum प्रधान मस्तिष्क सम्बन्धी।

ceremonial *सै ˘ रि मो नि ॲल a.* relating to ceremony समारोहपूर्ण।

ceremonious *सै ˘ रि मो नि ॲस a.* formal औपचारिक।

ceremony *सै ˘ रि मॅ नि n.* religious rites धर्मक्रिया; solemnity समारोह; formalism शिष्टाचार।

certain *सॅः टॅन a.* fixed निश्चित; inevitable अवश्यंभावी; unquestionable निर्विवाद; reliable विश्वसनीय।

certainly *सॅः टॅन् लि adv.* without doubt निःसंदेह।

certainty *सॅः टॅन् टि n.* fixed or real state निश्चितता; truth सत्य; fact तथ्य; inevitability अवश्यंभाविता।

certificate *सॅः टि फ़ि किट n.* a written testimony प्रमाण पत्र।

certify *सॅः टि फॉइ v. t.* to testify प्रमाणित करना।

cerumen *सि-रु'-मेन् n.* wax secreted by the ear कान का खूँट।

cession *सेशन् n.* giving up, yielding, परित्याग, समर्पण।

cesspool *सैसॅ पूल n.* a pit into which drains empty हौदी।

chain *चेन n.* a series of links ज़ंजीर; a line of things connected श्रृंखला; that which binds बेड़ी, बंधन।

chair *चे ˘ ॲः n.* a seat कुर्सी; an official seat पद।

chairman *चेअर्'-मेन् n.* one who controls a committee सभापति।

chaice *चे-इस् n.* goblet, a cup of bowl प्याला, पात्र।

chaise *चेज़ n.* a pleasure-carriage आनन्द की सवारी, गाड़ी।

chalk *चौक n.* white calcareous earth of carbonate of lime चाक।

challenge[1] *चै लिन्ज n.* summons to fight चुनौती; objection आपत्ति।

challenge[2] *v. t.* to summon to fight चुनौती देना।

chamber *चैम् बॅः n.* an apartment कक्ष; an office कार्यालय; a hall of justice of legislation सदन।

chamberlain *चेम्'-बर्-लेन् n.* a high officer in a king's court राजमहल का एक प्रधान कर्मचारी।

champion[1] *चैम् पि ॲन n.* supporter समर्थक; winner सर्वजेता।

champion[2] *v. t.* to support समर्थन करना।

chance *चान्स n.* that which happens unawares संयोग; luck, fortune भाग्य; opportunity अवसर।

chancellor *चान् सि लॅः n.* highest authority of a university कुलाधिपति।

chancery *चान्सरी n.* the highest court of justice प्रधान न्यायालय, दीवानी की बड़ी अदालत।

change[1] *चेन्ज v. t.* to make different बदल देना; to exchange विनिमय

करना; *v. i.* to become different बदल जाना।

change² *n.* alteration परिवर्तन।

channel *चैन'- नल् n.* a bed of running water स्त्रोत, नाला, समुद्रस्त्रोत, तरल पदार्थ का मार्ग, दिशा, द्वार।

chant *चान्ट्' n.* song गीत, स्तोत्र, भजन।

chaos *के औसॅ n.* utter confusion अव्यवस्था।

chaotic *कै औ ˘ टिक* a pertaining to chaos अव्यवस्था-संबंधी।

chapel *चै पॅल n.* place of worship पूजास्थल।

chapter *चैप् टॅ: n.* a division of a book अध्याय।

character *कै रिक् टॅ: n.* distinctive qualities of a person or thing चरित्र, लक्षण; a person in fiction or drama पात्र।

charge¹ *चा:ज v. t.* to load आवेशित करना; to put a price on (के) दाम मांगना; to lay a responsibility on (पर) दायित्व डालना; to command आदेश देना; to accuse दोष देना।

charge² *n.* an assault धावा; order आदेश; price मूल्य; accusation दोषारोपण; accumulation of electricity आवेश।

chariot *चे रि ॲट n.* a stately carriage with two or four wheels रथ।

charitable *चै रि टॅ बल् a.* characterised by charity दानशील; for charity दानार्थ; kindly दयावान।

charity *चै रि टि n.* kindness दयाभाव; almsgiving भिक्षादान; benefaction परोपकार; charitable institution दानी संस्था।

charm¹ *चा: म n.* attractiveness आकर्षण; magic spell जादू-टोना।

charm² *v. t.* to attract लुभाना; to delight आनंद देना।

chart *चा:ट n.* map मानचित्र, नक़्शा; graph, table चार्ट, लेखा।

charter *चा: टॅ: n.* declaration घोषणापत्र; privilege प्राधिकार; deed of hire अवक्रय-पत्र।

chase¹ *चेस v. t.* to pursue पीछा करना।

chase² *n.* pursuit पीछा।

chaste *चेस्ट a.* pure शुद्ध, पवित्र; undefiled अभ्रष्ट; simple सादा।

chastity *चैस् टि टि n.* quality of being chaste शुचिता, शुद्धता।

chat¹ *चैट n.* familiar talk बातचीत, गपशप।

chat² *(-tt-) v. i.* to talk familiarly बातचीत करना, गपशप करना।

chatter *चै टॅ: v. t.* to talk idly बकवास करना; to chirp rapidly चहचहाना; (of teeth) to rattle or knock together कटकटाना।

chauffeur *शौ फ़ॅ: n.* a private cardriver कार-चालक।

cheap *चीप a.* low in price सस्ता; inferior घटिया।

cheapen *ची पॅन v. t.* to reduce price of सस्ता करना; to degrade (का) स्तर गिराना; *v. i.* to be reduced in price or worth सस्ता या घटिया होना।

cheat¹ *चीट v. t.* to defraud ठगना।

cheat² *n.* one who deceives छलिया, ठग।

check¹ *चै कॅ v. t.* to verify जांचना; to restrain नियंत्रित करना।

check² *n.* a stop रोक, अवरोध; control नियंत्रण।

checkmate चैक् मेट *n.* winning situation in chess शहमात; complete defeat करारी हार।

cheek *चीक n.* side of face below the eye कपोल, गाल।

cheep *चीप् v. i.* to chirp or pipe like a young bird चिड़िया के बच्चे की तरह चीं-चीं करना या सीटी बजाना।

cheer[1] *चिअॅ: n.* shout of applause जयजयकार; gladness प्रसन्नता; encouragement प्रोत्साहन।

cheer[2] *v. t.* to comfort धैर्य बंधाना; to gladden आनंदित करना; to encourage by shouts (की) जयजयकार करना।

cheerful *चिअॅ: फुल a.* gay प्रसन्न।

cheerless *चिअॅ: लिस a.* gloomy उदास; dejected निराश।

cheese *चीज़ n.* coagulated milk pressed into a firm mass and used as food पनीर।

chemical[1] *कै ॅ मि कॅल a.* pertaining to chemistry रसायन-संबंधी।

chemical[2] *n.* substance obtained by a chemical process रासायनिक पदार्थ।

chemise *शि मीज़ n.* a girl's undergarment शमीज़।

chemist *कै ॅ मिस्ट n.* pharmacist भेषजज्ञ; dealer in medicinal drugs औषध-विक्रेता।

chemistry *कै ॅ मिस् ट्रि n.* science of elements and compounds रसायन-शास्त्र।

cheque *चैकॅ n.* an order for money चेक।

cherish *चै ॅ रिश v. t.* to treat with tenderness दुलारना; to foster पोसना।

cheroot *शै ॅ रूट n.* small cigar सिगार।

chess *चैसॅ n.* a game played by two on a board divided into sixty four squares शतरंज का खेल।

chest *चैस्ॅट n.* the part of the body containing the heart and lungs वक्षस्थल; a big strong box तिजोरी।

chestnut *चैस्ॅट् नॅट n.* large, reddish brown nut or its tree पांगर।

chew *चू v. t.* to crush with teeth चबाना।

chevalier *शेव्-अ-लिअर् n.* a knight, a gallant. महावीर, अश्वारोही।

chicken *चि किन n.* a young hen चूजा।

chide *चॉइड v. t.* to scold, to rebuke झिड़की देना।

chief[1] *चीफ़ n.* leader मुखिया।

chief[2] *a.* principal मुख्य।

chieftain *चीफ़् टॅन n.* chief of a clan or tribe मुखिया।

child *चॉइल्ड (pl.* children) *n.* infant बच्चा; offspring संतान।

childhood *चॉइल्ड् हुड n.* state of being a child शैशव; time when one is a child शैशवकाल।

childish *चॉइल् डिश a.* of or like a child बचकाना; silly मूर्खतापूर्ण।

chill *चिल n.* unpleasant coldness ठिठुरन।

chilli *चि लि n.* dry red pepper लाल मिर्च।

chilly *चि लि a.* cold ठंडा।

chiliad *किल्-इ-आड् n.* a thousand years. एक हजार वर्ष का काल।

chimney *चिम् नि n.* a passage for smoke चिमनी।

chimpanzee *चिम् पैन् ज़ी n.* an anthropoid ape वनमानुष।

chin *चिन n.* part of the face under the mouth ठोड़ी।

china *चॉइ नॅ n.* fine earthenware चीनी मिट्टी के बरतन।

chirp[1] *च:प v.i.* to make a short shrill sound चींचीं करना।

chirp[2] *n.* short shrill sound चींचीं।

chisel[1] *चि ज़ॅल n.* a steel tool छेनी।

chisel[2] *(-ll-) v. t.* to cut with a chisel छेनी से काटना।

chit *चिट n.* informal note पर्ची।

chivalrous *शि वॅल् रॅस् a.* full of valour शौर्यवान; courteous शिष्ट; generous उदार।

chivalry *शिवॅल् रि n.* bravery शौर्य; courtesy शिष्टता; system of knighthood क्षात्र-परंपरा।

chlorine *क्लार्'-इन् n.* a suffocating gas. साँस घुटाने वाली एक गैस।

chloroform *क्लोरो-फॉर्म् n.* a liquid for producing insensibility बेहोश करने की एक प्रसिद्ध तरल औषधि।

choice *चौ ॅइस n.* selection पसंद; option विकल्प।

choir *क्वॉइॲ: n.* a group of singers गायक-मंडली।

choke *चोक v. t.* to block up अवरुद्ध करना; to stop breathing of गला घोंटना; *v. i.* to suffer choking गला घुटना।

cholera *कौ ॅ लॅ रॅ n.* a disease accompanied by diarrhoea and vomiting हैज़ा।

chocolate *चॉकलेट् n.* a kind of sweatmeat containing sugar, coco and flour चीनी, कोको और मैदा की एक प्रकार की मिठाई।

choose *चूज़ v. t.* to take by preference चुनना, छांटना।

chop *चौपॅ (-pp-) v. t.* to cut into small pieces काटना।

chord *कौ:ड n.* string of a musical instrument तार, तंत्री, emotional response भावनात्मक प्रतिक्रिया।

choroid *को-रॉइड़ n.* the membrane which lines the eye-ball आँख की पुतली की भीतर की झिल्ली।

chorus *कौ रॅस n.* a company of singers गायक-दल; a refrain टेक; a song is sung by a band of singers वृंदगान।

Christ *क्राइस्ट n.* Jesus of Nazarath मसीहा।

Christendom *क्रि स्न् डॅम n.* the Christian world ईसाई जगत्।

Christian[1] *क्रिस् ट्यॅन n.* follower of Christ ईसाई।

Christian[2] *a.* following Christ ईसाई मतानुयायी; relating to Christ or His religion ईसाई धर्म-संबंधी।

Christianity *क्रिस् टि ऐ नि टि n.* the religion of Christ ईसाई धर्म।

Christmas *क्रिस् मॅस n* festival of the birth of Christ ईसा-जन्मोत्सव।

chrome *क्रोम् n.* a yellow pigment and colour पीला रंग।

chronic *क्रौ ॅ निक a.* continuing a long time जीर्ण, पुराना।

chronicle *क्रौ ॅ नि क्ल n.* an historical account of events in order of time इतिहास।

chronology *क्रॅ नौ ॅ लॅ जि n.* arrangement of events according to their dates घटनाक्रम, कालक्रम।

chronograph *क्रान-ओ-ग्राफ् n.* an

instrument to record time with great accuracy सूक्ष्म रीति से समय नापने का एक प्रकार यन्त्र।

chuckle *चक्'-क्ल् v. i.* to laugh in a suppressed manner, to cackle; to show signs of glee मुँह बन्द करके हँसना, प्रसन्नता के चिन्ह दिखलाना।

chum *चम् n.* a familiar friend, a chamber fellow, a kind of fish लँगोटिया यार, पुराना मित्र, एक प्रकार की मछली।

church *चःच n.* building for Christian public worship गिरजाघर।

churchyard *चःच् याःड n.* a burial ground attached to a church क़ब्रिस्तान।

churl *चर्ल् n.* an ill-bred fellow, a rustic देहाती, गँवार मनुष्य।

churn¹ *चॅःन v. t. & i.* to stir (something) vigorously बिलोना, मथना।

churn² *n.* large milk can दूध का मटका; vessel for making butter दूध मथने का पात्र।

cigar *सि गाः n.* a tobacco roll for smoking सिगार।

cigarette *सि गॅ रै ॅट n.* finely cut tobacco rolled in paper for smoking सिगरेट।

cinema *सि नि मॅ n.* building used for showing of films सिनेमाघर; art of making movies चलचित्र।

cinnabar *सिन्'-नाबार् n.* vermilion सिंगारिफ, सिन्दूर।

cinnamon *सिन्-नामन् n.* the aromatic inner bark of a tree. दालचीनी, दालचीनी का वृक्ष।

cipher, cypher *सॉइ फॅः n.* the figure 0 शून्य का अंक; secret writing बीज लेख; a person of no importance नगण्य व्यक्ति।

circle *सॅः क्ल n.* a perfectly round flat figure वृत्; something like a circle घेरा; cycle परिक्रमा।

circuit *सॅः किट n.* circumference परिधि; area क्षेत्र, going round परिक्रमा; path of an electric current परिपथ।

circumfluence *सर्-कम'-फ्लु-एन्स् n.* flowing round on all sides जल का चौफेर बहाव।

circumspect *सर्'-कम्-स्पेक्ट् adj.* cautious, wary सावधान, जाग्रत, चौकन्ना।

circular¹ *सॅः क्यु लॅः a.* round गोल।

circular² *n.* a paper addressed to a number of persons परिपत्र।

circulate *सॅः क्यु लेट v. i.* to move round प्रसारित होना, *v. t.* to send round प्रसारित करना।

circulation *सॅः क्यु ले शॅन n.* act of circulating प्रसारण; flow of blood रक्त-संचार; extent of sale of a newspaper समाचार-पत्र का प्रसार।

circumference *सॅः कम् फॅ रॅन्स n.* the bounding line of a circle परिधि।

circumstance *सॅः कॅम्स् टॅन्स n.* a particular fact or event घटना; *(pl.)* conditions connected with an event or person परिस्थितियां।

circus *सॅः कॅस n.* arena for sports and games अखाड़ा; a travelling show of trained animals, clowns, acrobats, etc.सर्कस।

cist *सिस्ट् n.* a stone chest, a grave of prehistoric times पत्थर का सन्दूक, प्राचीन काल की समाधि, कब्र।

citadel *सि टॅ डॅल* *n.* a fortress in or near a city नगर-दुर्ग, गढ़ी।
cite *सॉइट* *v. t.* to summon to appear in a court अदालत में तलब करना; to quote उद्धृत करना।
citizen *सि टि ज़ॅन* *n.* an inhabitant of a city नगर-निवासी; an inhabitant of a state नागरिक।
citizenship *सि टि ज़ॅन् शिप* *n.* the rank of a citizen नागरिकता।
citric *सि-ट्रिक्* *adj.* pertaining to citron or lemon नींबू की खटाई का।
city *सि टि* *n.* a large town शहर, नगर।
civic *सि विक* *a.* relating to civil affairs नागरिक; of a city नगर का।
civics *सि विक्स* *n.* study of civic life and affairs नागरिकशास्त्र।
civil *सि विल* *a.* relating to people मानव-समाज-संबंधी; not military असैनिक; cultured सभ्य।
civilian *सि वि लि ॲन* *n.* non-military person असैनिक व्यक्ति।
civilization *सि वि लॉइ ज़ेशॅन* *n.* state of being civilized सभ्यता, शिष्टता।
civilize *सि वि लॉइज़* *v. t.* to bring out of barbarity; सभ्य बनाना।
clack *क्लाक्* *n.* & *v. i.* a clattering noise, to make a sudden sharp noise कर्कश शब्द, खड़खड़ाहट, एकाएक खड़खड़ाहट का शब्द करना।
claim¹ *क्लेम* *n.* act of claiming दावा; assertion दृढ़ कथन।
claim² *v. t.* to demand as a right दावा करना; to assert दृढ़तापूर्वक कहना।
claimant *क्ले मॅन्ट* *n.* the person making a claim दावेदार।
clamber *क्लेम्-बर* *v. i.* to climb with difficulty कठिनता से चढ़ना।
clamour¹ *क्लै मॅः* *n.* loud noise कोलाहल।
clamour² *v. i.* to engage in noisy shouting कोलाहल करना।
clamp *क्लैम्प्* *n.* a clasp or hand used to hold things together पाहू, कोनिया, शिकंजा,
clan *क्लैन* *n.* a tribe आदिम जाति, कबीला।
clandestine *क्लेन्-डेस्'-टाइन्* *adj.* hidden, secret छिपा हुआ, गूढ़ गुप्त।
clap¹ *क्लैप (-pp-)* *v. i.*, to strike the hands together ताली बजाना; *v.t.* to strike gently थपथपाना।
clap² *n.* loud explosive noise कड़क; sound of the palms of the hands struck together करतल ध्वनि।
clarify *क्लै रि फॉइ* *v. t.* to make clear स्पष्ट करना; *v. i.* to become clear स्पष्ट होना।
clarification *n.* स्पष्टीकरण।
clarion *क्लैरिॲन* *n.* a kind of trumpet तुरही।
clarity *क्ले-रिट्'ई* *n.* purity, clearness सफाई, स्वच्छता, शुद्धता।
clash¹ *क्लैश* *n.* encounter मुठभेड़; collision टक्कर; conflict संघर्ष।
clash² *v. t.* to strike against someone टकराना; *v.i.* to disagree violently असहमत होना; to coincide एक ही समय होना।
clasp *क्लास्प्* *n.* a contrivance for fastening, embrace, reach अँकुरा (बलकस), आलिगंन, पहुँच।
class *क्लास* *n.* rank of persons or

things श्रेणी; group of students taught together कक्षा।

classic[1] *क्लै सिक a.* of the first rank उत्कृष्ट: of the highest quality सर्वोत्तम।

classic[2] *n.* a literary work or writer of recognised excellence उत्कृष्ट कृति अथवा लेखक।

classical *क्लै सि कॅल a.* pertaining to best art and literature शास्त्रीय; of the highest quality अति उत्कृष्ट; pertaining to the ancient times प्राचीनकाल-संबंधी।

classification *क्लै सि फ़ि के शॅन n.* act of classifying वर्गीकरण।

classify *क्लै सि फ़ॉइ v. t.* to categorise वर्गीकृत करना।

clause *क्लौज़ n.* component part of a sentence वाक्यांश; a single proviso in law धारा, अनुच्छेद।

claw *क्लौ n.* foot with pointed nails पंजा।

clay *क्ले n.* earth मिट्टी।

clean[1] *क्लीन* a. neat साफ़-सुथरा; clear-cut स्वच्छ; pure पवित्र।

clean[2] *v. t.* to purify साफ़ करना।

cleanliness *क्लीन् लि निस n.* purity; स्वच्छता।

cleanse *क्लैन्ज़ v. t.* to make clean परिमार्जन करना।

clear[1] *क्लिअॅ: a.* neat साफ़-सुथरा; pure शुद्ध; distinct स्पष्ट।

clear[2] *v. t.* to make clear साफ़ करना; to remove हटाना; to pass over लांघना *v. i.* to become clear स्वच्छ होना।

clearance *क्लिअॅ रॅन्स n.* making clear निकासी।

clearly *क्लिअॅ: लि adv.* obviously स्पष्ट रूप से।

cleft *क्लफट् n.* a fissure, a crack, a split फाँक, फटन, दरार।

clergy *क्लॅ: जि n.* body of ministers of Gospel याजकगण।

clerical *क्लै˘ रि कॅल a.* pertaining to clergy याजकीय; pertaining to a clerk लिपिक-विषयक।

clerk *क्ल:क n.* an office worker क्लर्क, लिपिक।

clever *क्लै˘ वॅ: a.* skilful चतुर, होशियार।

clew *क्लू n.* a ball of thread or yarn, the corner of a sail डोरे की रील या गोली, पाल का कोना।

click *क्लिक् n.* a catch in machinery, a sharp short sound खटका, चटखनी, खटके का शब्द।

client *क्लॉइ अॅन्ट n.* the employer of a lawyer मुवक्किल; a customer ग्राहक।

cliff *क्लिफ n.* a steep rock खाड़ी चट्टान।

climate *क्लॉइ मिट n.* weather conditions जलवायु।

climax *क्लॉइ मैक्स n.* apex शिखर; culmination चरम, उत्कर्ष।

climb[1] *क्लॉइम n.* act of climbing चढ़ाई।

climb[2] *v.i.* to mount चढ़ाई पर जाना; to progress प्रगति करना; *v. t.* to ascend (पर) चढ़ना।

cling *क्लिङ्ग v. i.* to stick, to adhere चिपटना; to be firmly attached लगाव मानना।

clinic *क्लि निक n.* place for medical treatment चिकित्सालय।

clink *क्लिङ्क् n.* a sharp ringing sound, a prison झनझन शब्द,

कारागृह।

cloak *क्लोक* *n.* a loose upper garment चोग़ा।

clock *क्लौकॅ* *n.* time measuring instrument घड़ी।

clod *क्लॉड्* *n.* a lump of earth, a lout मिट्टी का ढोंका, मूर्ख।

cloister *क्लॉयस्ट्-अर्* *n.* a convent, a monastery, a covered walk, a nunnery, मठ, विहार (आश्रम), वृक्षों से ढका हुआ मार्ग, संन्यासिनियों का आश्रम।

close[1] *क्लोज़* *n.* end अंत, समाप्ति।

close[2] *a.* near समीप; intimate घनिष्ट; careful सावधानीपूर्ण।

close[3] *v. t.* to shut बंद करना; to end समाप्त करना।

closet *क्लौ ˘ ज़िट* *n.* small room कोठरी।

closure *क्लो ज़ॅः* *n.* act of closing समापन।

clot[1] *क्लौ ˘ट* *n.* semi-solid lump थक्का।

clot[2] *(-tt-)* *v. t.* to form into clots थक्का बनाना; *v. i.* coagulate थक्का बनना।

cloth *क्लौथॅ* *n.* a woven material or fabric कपड़ा।

clothe *क्लोद* *v. t.* to put clothes on कपड़े पहनाना।

clothes *क्लोद्ज़* *n. pl.* garments परिधान।

clothing *क्लो दिङ्ग* *n.* garments collectively परिधान।

cloud *क्लॉउड* *n.* condensed visible water vapour बादल।

cloudy *क्लॉउ डि* *a.* overcast with clouds मेघाच्छादित; not clear धुंधला।

clove *क्लोव्* *n.* a kind of pungent, aromatic spice लवंग।

clown *क्लॉउन* *n.* jester or buffoon विदूषक, मसख़रा।

club *क्लब* *n.* an association of persons सभा, गोष्ठी; a cudgel गदा; one of the suits at cards चिड़ी।

clue *क्लू* *n.* hint सूत्र, संकेत।

clumsy *क्लम् ज़ि* *a.* unskilled अनाड़ी; ill-made भौंडा; shapeless बेडौल।

cluster[1] *क्लस् टॅः* *n.* bunch गुच्छा।

cluster[2] *v. i.* to gather in a cluster समूहबद्ध होना।

clutch *क्लच* *n.* tight grasp पकड़, चंगुल; a mechanical device in automobiles क्लच।

clutter *क्लट्'-अरॅ* *v. t.* to run with confused noise चिल्लाकर दौड़ना।

co *कॉ* *n.* an *abbr.* for Company. 'कम्पनी' शब्द का संक्षिप्त रूप।

coach *कोच* *n.* a large four wheeled carriage बग्घी; railway carriage रेलगाड़ी का डिब्बा; tutor, instructor प्रशिक्षक।

coachman *कोच् मॅन* *n.* driver of a coach गाड़ीवान।

coal *कोल* *n.* a black mineral used as fuel कोयला।

coalition *को अॅ लि शॅन* *n.* union, alliance सम्मिलन, मेल।

coarse *कौःस* *a.* inferior घटिया; rough खुरदुरा; unrefined अशिष्ट।

coast *कोस्ट* *n.* sea-shore समुद्र-तट।

coat *कोट* *n.* man's upper garment कोट; layer तह, परत।

coating *कोटिङ्ग* a layer of paint, cloth for coats रंग की तह, कोट बनाने का कपड़ा।

coax *कोक्स v. t.* to persuade बहलाना; to wheedle मनाना।

cobalt *को-बॉल्ट् n.* a metal like nickel गिलट के समान एक सफेद धातु।

cobbler *कौबॅ लॅः n.* shoe-mender मोची।

cobra *को ब्रॅ n.* a venomous snake with a hood फनदार विषैला साँप।

cobweb *कौबॅ वैबॅ n.* spider's web मकड़ी का जाला।

cocaine *को-केन्' n.* a drug producing local insensibility कोकीन।

cock *कौकॅ n.* male of a domestic fowl मुर्गा; tapped spout टोंटी; lever in a gun बंदूक का घोड़ा।

cocker *कॉक्-अर् v. t.* to pamper, to cuddle लाड़ करना, दुलार करना।

cockle *कॉक्-क्ल् v. i.* to bulge, to pucker or wrinkle फूलना, झुर्री पड़ना।

cock-pit *कौकॅ पिट n.* pilot's seat or compartment in an aircraft वायुयान में चालक-कक्ष।

cockroach *कौकॅ रोच n.* the black beetle तिलचट्टा।

coconut *को को नॅट n.* large edible nut नारियल।

code *कोड n.* systematic collection of laws संहिता; a secret language संकेत–लिपि।

co-education *को ऐ˘ ड्यु के शॅन n.* education of boys and girls together सहशिक्षा।

coefficient *को-एफ'-इश्-इअन्ट् n* a joint factor, a number or quantity that multiplies another number गुणक, गुणा करने वाली संख्या।

co-exist *को ऐगॅ ज़िस्ट v. i.* to exist at the same time सहवर्ती होना।

co-existence *को ऐगॅ ज़िस् टॅन्स n.* existence at the same time सहअस्तित्व।

coffee *कौ ˘ फ़ि n.* seeds of coffee tree कॉफ़ी के बीज़; drink made from them इनसे बना पेय।

coffin *कौ ˘ फ़िन n.* box for corpse शव-पेटिका, ताबूत।

cog *कॉग् n.* the catch or tooth of a wheel by which it drives another wheel पहिये का दाँता।

cogent *को'-जेन्ट् adj.* forcible, convincing, powerful प्रबल, निश्चित, विश्वस्त, बलवान।

cognate *कॉग्-नेट् adj.* skin in origin, related of allied to सगोत्री, सम्बन्धी।

cognizance *कौगॅ नि ज़ॅन्स n.* (law) knowledge जानकारी।

cohabit *को-हैब्-इट् v. t.* to dwell together as husband and wife. पति-पत्नी के समान सहवास करना।

coherent *को हिअॅ रॅन्ट a.* showing logical consistency सुसंगत; sticking together संस्क्त।

cohesive *को-हे'-सिव् adj.* producing union एकता लाने वाला, संयुक्त होने वाला।

coif *कॉइफ् n.* a cap or covering for the head टोपी, टोप।

coin *कौ˘इन n.* metal money सिक्का, मुद्रा।

coinage *कौ ˘इ निज n.* currency सिक्का, मुद्रा; act of coining money सिक्का-ढलाई।

coincide *कॉइन्-साइड्' v. i.* to occupy the same position, to agree

समान या अनुरूप होना, ठीक-ठीक बैठना, सहमत होना।

coir *कॉइर्* *n.* coconut fibre which is used for making ropes, matting नारियल की जटा जो रस्सी, चटाई आदि बनाने के लिये काम में लाई जाती है।

coke *कोक्* *v. t.* to convert coal in to solid substance पत्थर के कोयले को ठोस बनाना।

cold[1] *कोल्ड* *a.* chilly शीतल, ठंडा; indifferent उदासीन।

cold[2] *n.* absence of heat ठंडक, शीत; catarrh सर्दी, जुकाम।

collaborate *कॅ लै बॅ रेट* *v. i.* to work conjointly सहयोग करना।

collaboration *कॅ लै बॅ रे शॅन* *n.* cooperation सहयोग।

collapse *कॅ लैप्स* *v. i.* to fall to pieces एकाएक गिरना; to lose heart हिम्मत हारना।

collar *कौ˘ लॅः* *n.* neckband कॉलर।

colleague *कौ˘ लीग* *n.* co-worker सहकर्मी।

collect *कॅ लैक्ट* *v. t.* to gather संग्रह करना, इकट्ठा करना; *v. i.* to come together इकट्ठा होना।

collection *कॅ लैक् शॅन* *n.* act of collection संचयन, संकलन; the thing collected संचित वस्तु।

collective *कॅ लैक् टिव* *a.* of a group सामूहिक।

collector *कॅ लैक् टॅः* *n.* one who collects संग्राहक, वसूल करनेवाला।

college *कौ˘ लिज* *n.* institution for higher education महाविद्यालय।

collide *कॅ लॉइड* *v. i.* to strike against one-another टकराना, भिड़ना।

collision *कॅ लि ज़ॅन* *n.* act of colliding भिड़त; conflict संघर्ष।

collusion *कॉल्यूजन* *n.* a secret compact for a fraudulent purpose, deceit जाल, कपट, दलबन्दी।

colon[1] *को लॅन* *n.* a punctuation mark (;) अपूर्ण विराम।

colon[2] large intestine बड़ी अंतड़ी।

colonel *कॅः नॅल* *n.* an army officer कर्नल।

colonial *कॅ लो नि ॲल* *a.* pertaining to colonies औपनिवेशिक।

colony *कौ˘ लॅ नि* *n.* body of people who settle in a new country उपनिवेश; country so settled बस्ती।

colour[1] *क लॅः* *n.*, hue, tint रंग; paint रोग़न।

colour[2] *v. t.* to paint रंगना; to disguise (का) रूप बदल देना; to distort तोड़-मरोड़ देना।

colter *कोल्टर्* *n.* the cutting iron of a plough हल का फार।

column *कौ˘ लॅम* *n.* a tall, erect pillar स्तंभ; upright division of a printed page कॉलम।

coma *को मॅ* *n.* unnatural deep sleep लंबी मूर्च्छा, अचेतन अवस्था।

comb *कोम* *n.* an instrument for arranging hair कंघा; the crest of a cock कलग़ी; mass of honey cells मधुमक्खियों का छत्ता।

combat[1] *कौमॅ् बॅट* *n.* fight संग्राम, युद्ध।

combat[2] *(-tt-)* *v. t.* to oppose विरोध करना।

combatant[1] *कौमॅ् बॅ टॅन्ट* *n.* a fighter योद्धा।

combatant[2] *a.* fighting युद्धशील।

combination *कौम्ँ बि ने शॅन n.* union सम्मिलन; association संगठन।

combine *कॅम् बॉइन v. t.* to unite मिलाना; to join together जोड़ना; *v. i.* to come together मिल जाना।

come *कम v. i.* to arrive पहुंचना; to move towards a person or place आना।

comedian *कॅ मी डि अॅन n.* a comic actor हास्य-अभिनेता।

comedy *कौ˘ मि डि n.* a stage play with happy ending सुखांतकी।

comet *कौ˘ मिट n.* a heavenly body with a tail of light धूमकेतू, पुच्छलतारा।

comfit *कम्'-फिट् n.* a sweetmeat, sugarplum, confection. मिठाई, लायचीदाना, मेवों की मिठाई।

comfort[1] *कम् फ़:ट n.* relief आराम; consolation सांत्वना।

comfort[2] *v. t.* to console सांत्वना देना।

comfortable *कम् फॅ: टॅ बल a.* free from hardship शांतिप्रद, सुखद; full of comfort आरामदायक।

comic[1] *कौ˘ मिक a.* amusing आनंदप्रद; pertaining to comedy सुखांतकी–संबंधी।

comic[2] *n.* magazine full of strip cartoons हास्यरस की पत्रिका।

comical *कौ˘मि कॅल a.* funny मज़ाकिया, हास्यपूर्ण

comma *कौ˘ मॅ n.* punctuation mark (,) अल्पविराम-चिह्न।

command[1] *कॅ मान्ड n.* order आदेश, आज्ञा; control नियंत्रण।

command[2] *v. t.* to order आदेश देना; to control वश में रखना।

commandant *कौ˘ मॅन् डैन्ट n.* commanding officer of a military organization सेनानायक।

commander *कॅ मान् डॅ: n.* person who commands नायक; rank below captain in the navy सेनानायक।

commemorate *कॅ मै˘ मॅ रेट v. t.* to serve as a memorial of (का) कीर्तिमान होना; to honour the memory of (का) पुण्यस्मरण करना।

commemoration *कॅ मै˘ मॅ रे शॅन n.* act of commemorating स्मरणोत्सव।

commence *कॅ मैन्स v. t.* to begin प्रांरभ करना; *v. i.* make a beginning प्रारंभ होना।

commencement *कॅ मैन्स् मॅन्ट n.* beginning प्रारंभ।

commend *कॅ मैन्ड v. t.* to speak good of (की) प्रशंसा करना; to entrust सौंपना।

commendable *कॅ मैन् डॅ ब्ल a.* praiseworthy प्रशंसनीय।

commendation *कॅ मैन् डे शॅन n.* admiration प्रशस्ति, प्रशंसा।

comment[1] *कौ˘ मैन्ट v. i.* to make remarks टिप्पणी करना; *v. t.* to say by way of remarks टिप्पणी के रूप में कहना।

comment[2] *n.* explanatory remarks टीका–टिप्पणी।

commentary *कौ˘ मैन् टॅ रि n.* a series of comments टीका-टिप्पणी; an explanatory essay व्याख्यात्मक निबंध।

commentator *कौ˘ मैन् टे टॅ: n.* an annotator भाष्यकार, टीकाकार; person who relays commentary विवरणकार।

commerce *कौ ˘ मॅःस n.* trade वाणिज्य।

commercial *कॅ मॅः शॅल a.* pertaining to commerce वाणिज्यक; with a profit motive लाभ के उद्देश्यवाला।

commiserate *कम्-मिज्'-एरेट् v. t.* to feel or show pity for दया करना, करुणा दिखाना।

commission *कॅ मि शॅन n.* a body entrusted with some special duty आयोग; act of performing कृत्य; payment by percentage for doing something दलाली; delegated authority कार्याधिकार।

commissioner *कॅ मि शॅ नॅः n.* supreme authority of a commissionery आयुक्त, मंडलायुक्त।

commissure *कॉम्-मि'-श्योर् n.* a place where two bodies unite दो पदार्थो का मिलन-स्थल।

commit *कॅ मिट v. t.* to entrust सौंपना; to do (an offence or mistake) (अपराध आदि) करना; to pledge प्रतिज्ञा करना।

committee *कॅ मि टि n.* a select body made for some special business समिति।

commodity *कॅ मौँ˘ डि टि n.* anything useful माल, वस्तु।

common *कौ ˘ मॅन a.* belonging to all or several सामान्य, साधारण; public सार्वजनिक; ordinary मामूली।

commoner *कौ˘ मॅ नॅः n.* one of the common people सामान्य व्यक्ति।

commonplace *कौ˘ मॅन् प्लेस a.* ordinary सामान्य।

commonwealth *कौ ˘ मॅन् वैल्थ n.* republic गणतंत्र; (cap.) federation of self governing states राष्ट्रमंडल।

commotion *कॅ मो शॅन n.* agitation उत्तेजना; noisy confusion शोरगुल।

commove *कॅमाव v. t.* to excite, to agitate उत्तेजित करना।

communal *कौ ˘ म्यु नॅल a.* sectarian सांप्रदायिक।

commune *कॉम्-म्यून v. t.* to hold intimate intercourse with सम्भाषण करना, बातचीत करना।

communicate *कॅ म्यु नि केट v. t.* to impart देना, पहुंचाना; to reveal प्रकट करना, सूचित करना।

communication *कॅ म्यु नि के शॅन n.* act of communicating संप्रेषण; information सूचना; means of exchanging message संचार-व्यवस्था।

communique *कॉम्-म्यूनीक् n.* an official statement which is given to the press सरकारी विज्ञप्ति।

communism *कौ˘ म्यु निज़्म n.* vesting of property in the community साम्यवाद।

community *कॅ म्यु नि ़टि n.* society समाज; social group संप्रदाय; similarity सामान्यता।

commute *कम्यूट् v. t.* to interchange or exchange अदल-बदल करना।

compact[1] *कॅम् पैक्ट a.* closely packed together सघन, ठोस; neatly fitted सुगठित।

compact[2] *कौमॅ पैक्ट n.* agreement संविदा, समझौता।

companion *कॅम् पै न्यॅन n.* comrade साथी; associate सहचर।

company *कम् पॅ नि n.* association संगठन; party टोली; group of persons assembled समवाय।

comparative *कॅम पै रॅ टिव a.* estimated by comparison तुलनात्मक।

compare *कॅम् पे ॅ अ॑: v. t.* to liken समान बताना; *v. i.* to be like or equal समान होना।

comparison *कॅम् पै रि सॅन n.* act of comparing तुलना; comparative estimate मिलान।

compartment *कॅम् पा:ट् मॅन्ट n.* section कक्ष, विभाग; partition of a railway carriage रेलगाड़ी का डिब्बा।

compass *कॅम् पॅस n.* instrument for showing north दिक् सूचक, कुतुबनुमा; , *(pl.)* instrument for drawing circles परकार।

compassion *कॅम पै शॅन n.* sympathy सहानुभूति।

compel *कॅम् पैलॅ (-ll-) v. t.* to overpower विवश करना; to force (पर) दबाव डालना।

compensate *कौमॅ् पैनॅ् सेट v.t.* to make up for (की) क्षतिपूर्ति करना।

compensation *कौमॅ् पैनॅ् से शॅन n.* recompense क्षतिपूर्ति।

compete *कॅम् पीट v. i.* to be in rivalry प्रतिस्पर्धा करना।

competence *कौ मॅ् पि टॅन्स n.* capability सामर्थ्य, क्षमता।

competent *कौमॅ् पि टॅन्ट a.* capable सक्षम, समर्थ।

competition *कौमॅ् पि टि शॅन n.* act of competing प्रतियोगिता; rivalry प्रतिस्पर्धा।

competitive *कॅम् पै ॅ टि टिव a.* of the nature of competition प्रतियोगी।

compile *कम्पाइल् v. t.* to collect materials from various authors, to amass संकलित करना, संग्रह करना।

complacent *कम्-प्ले-सेन्ट् adj.* self-satisfied सन्तुष्ट।

complain *कॅम् प्लेन v. i.* to express feelings of discontent शिकायत करना।

complaint *कॅम् प्लेन्ट n.* act of complaining फ़रियाद; an ailment कष्ट, रोग; grievance उलाहना।

complaisance *कॉम्पलेजैन्स् n.* politeness, civility शिष्टाचार, भलमन्सी।

complaisant *कॉम्-प्ले-जान्ट् adj.* desirous or pleasing, obliging अनुरोधी, आज्ञानुकूल।

complement *कौमॅ् प्लि मॅन्ट n.* that which completes पूरक।

complementary *कौमॅ् प्लि मैनॅ् टॅ रि a.* acting as a complement अनुपूरक।

complete[1] *कॅम् प्लीट a.* entire पूर्ण; finished समाप्त।

complete[2] *v. t.* to finish पूरा करना; to make perfect पूर्णता प्रदान करना।

completion *कॅम् प्ली शॅन* the act of being finished समापन; accomplishment पूर्ति।

complex[1] *कौमॅ् प्लैक्स a.* complicated जटिल; composite मिश्रित।

complex[2] *n.* obsession मनोग्रंथि; group of related buildings भवन-समूह।

complexion *कॅम् प्लैकॅ् शॅन n.* colour

of the face वर्ण।

compliance *कम्-प्लाई-एन्स्* *n.* consent, submission स्वीकृति, आज्ञानुकूलता, आज्ञाकारिता।

compliant *कम्-प्लाइ-एन्ट्* *adj.* yielding obliging सरल प्रकृति का, आज्ञाकारी, संकोची।

complicate *कौमॅ् प्लि केट* *v. t.* to make complex उलझाना।

complication *कौमॅ् प्लि के शॅन* *n.* entangled condition उलझन।

compliment[1] *कौमॅ् प्लि मॅन्ट* *n.* praise प्रशंसा; *(pl.)* greetings अभिवादन।

compliment[2] *कौमॅ् प्लि मैंन्ट* *v. t.* to praise प्रशंसा करना।

comply *कॅम् प्लॉइ* *v. i.* to act in accordance पालन करना।

component *कम्पॉनेन्ट्* *adj.* forming part of a whole साधक, अंगभूत।

compose *कॅम् पोज़* *v. t.* to constitute निर्मित करना; to write लिखना; to settle तय करना; to calm (oneself) शांत होना।

composition *कौमॅ् पॅ ज़ि शॅन* *n.* act of composing संयोजन; literary or musical work रचना; act of setting types मुद्रायोजन, अक्षर-योजन।

compositor *कॅम् पौ ॅ ज़ि टॅः* person who sets types for printing अक्षर-योजक।

compost *कौमॅ् पौस्ॅट* *n.* compound manure मिश्रित खाद।

composure *कम्पोजर्* *n.* calmness, tranquility शान्ति।

compound[1] *कौमॅ् पॉउन्ड* *n.* enclosed area अहाता।

compound[2] *a.* made up of two or more combined parts यौगिक।

compound[3] *n.* something made up of two or more combined parts यौगिक; *(gram.)* word composed of two or more smaller words समास।

compound[4] *कॅम् पॉउन्ड* *v. i.* to mix together मिलाना; to settle तय करना।

compounder *कम्पाउण्डर्* *n.* one who compounds or mixes things पदार्थों को मिलाने वाला, औषधि बनाने वाला।

comprehend *कौमॅ् प्रि हैन्ॅड* *v. t.* to understand समझना; to include सम्मिलित करना।

comprehension *कौमॅ् प्रि हैन्ॅ शॅन* *n.* faculty of understanding बोध, समझ, धारणा।

comprehensive *कौमॅ् प्रि हैन्ॅ सिव* *a.* extensive व्यापक।

compress *कॅम् प्रैसॅ* *v. t.* to press दबाना; to condense संक्षिप्त करना।

compromise[1] *कौमॅ् प्रॅ मॉइज़* *n.* settlement समझौता।

compromise[2] *v. t.* to settle by mutual agreement निपटारा करना।

compulsion *कॅम् पल् शॅन* *n.* act of compelling बाध्यकरण; state of being compelled बाध्यता।

compulsory *कॅम् पल् सॅ रि* *a.* constraining बाध्यकर; obligatory अनिवार्य।

compunction *कम्पङ्क्शन्* *n* the pricking of conscience, regret मनोव्यथ, पश्चाताप।

computation *कम्प्यूटेशन्* *n.* estimate, reckoning गणना, गिनती।

compute *कम्-पयूट्* *v.t.* to reckon to number, to calculate गणना करना, गिनना, लेखा करना।

comrade *कौमॅ रिड* *n.* companion साथी; an associate सहयोगी।

conation *को-ने-शन्* *n.* the effort of will-power इच्छा शक्ति का प्रयत्न।

concave *कॉन्-केव्* *adj.* curved, hollow, vaulted or arched नतोदर, खोखला।

conceal *कॅन् सील* *v. t.* to hide छिपाना।

concede *कन्सीड्* *v.t.* to allow, to admit स्वीकार करना, अंगीकार करना।

conceit *कॅन् सीट* *n.* self flattering opinion आत्मश्लाघा।

conceive *कॅन् सीव* *v. t.* to form in the womb गर्भ प्रदान करना; to take into mind विचार करना; *v. i.* to become pregnant गर्भवती होना।

concentrate *कौनॅ सैनॅ ट्रेट* *v. t.* to condense गाढ़ा करना; to bring together इकट्ठा करना; to focus केंद्रित करना।

concentration *कौनॅ सैनॅ ट्रे शॅन* *n.* act of concentrating एकाग्रता; state of being concentrated संकेंद्रण।

concept *कौनॅ सैप्ट* *n.* an object conceived by the mind संकल्पना।

conception *कॅन् सैपॅ शॅन* *n.* act of conceiving अवधारण; inception of pregnancy गर्भधारण।

concern[1] *कॅन् सःन* *v. t.* to have a relation to (से) संबंधित होना; to make anxious चिंतित करना।

concern[2] *n.* care, anxiety चिंता; affair मामला; a business व्यवसाय।

concert[1] *कौनॅ सॅःट* *n.* a programme of music संगीत-गोष्ठी।

concert[2] *कॅन् सॅःट* *v. t.* to arrange (में) सामंजस्य स्थापित करना।

concession *कॅन् सै˘ शॅन* *n.* act of conceding छूट, रियायत; thing conceded रियायत में दी गई वस्तु; special privilege विशेष सुविधा।

conch *कौ˘ङ्क, कौन्च* *n.* sea-shell शंख।

conciliate *कन्सिलिएट* *v.t.* to pacify, to win over, to reconcile शान्त करना, सान्त्वना देना, मनाना।

concise *कॅन् सॉइस* *a.* brief संक्षिप्त, सारगर्भित।

conclude *कॅन् क्लूड* *v. t.* to deduce निष्कर्ष निकालना; to end समापन करना; *v. i.* to come to an end समाप्त होना।

conclusion *कॅन् क्लू ज़ॅन* *n.* decision निर्णय; end उपसंहार।

conclusive *कॅ क्लू सिव* *a.* decisive निर्णायक।

concoct *कॅन् कौकॅ्ट* *v. t.* to make up (a dish) पकाना; to plan (की) योजना बनाना; to fabricate गढ़ना।

concoction *कॅन् कौकॅ शॅन* *n.* fabrication मनगढ़ंत कहानी।

concord *कौ˘ङ् कौःड* *n.* agreement समझौता; harmony सामंजस्य।

concrescence *कन्-क्रे-सन्स्* *n.* growing together एक साथ उगना या बढ़ना, सहवृद्धि।

concrete[1] *कौनॅ क्रीट, कौङ्* –*n.* mixture of cement, sand etc. used in building कंकरीट।

concrete[2] *a.* actual यथार्थपूर्ण; not abstract मूर्त; solid ठोस।

concrete[3] *कॅङ् क्रीट v. t.* to cover with concrete कंकरीट से भरना; to solidify ठोस रूप देना।

concubinage *कॅन्-क्यु-बिन्-एज् n.* the state of being a concubine वेश्यापन।

concubine *कौन्ँ क्यु बॉइन n.* woman kept as wife उपपत्नी।

conculcate *कॉन्-कल्-केट् v.t.* to trample under feet पैरों से कुचलना।

condemn *कॅन् डैमॅ v. t.* to blame निंदा करना; to declare unfit for use निकम्मा ठहराना।

condemnation *कॅन् डैमॅ ने शॅन n.* act of condemning निंदा; state of being condemned तिरस्कार।

condense *कॅन् डैन्स v. t.* to concentrate गाढ़ा करना; to abridge संक्षिप्त करना; *v. t.* to become dense गाढ़ा होना।

condite *कॉन-डाइट् v.t.* to preserve, to pickle अचार, मुरब्बा इत्यादि बनाना।

condition *कॅन् डि शॅन n.* situation परिस्थिति; a modifying circumstance शर्त; state अवस्था।

conditional *कॅन् डि शॅ नॅल a.* depending on conditions प्रतिबंधात्मक; not absolute सशर्त।

condole *कॅन् डोल v. i.* to grieve with another शोक प्रकट करना।

condolence *कॅन डो लॅन्स n.* act of condoling शोक।

condonation *कॉन-डोनेशन् n.* act of forgiving, forgiveness अपराध क्षमा करने का कार्य, क्षमा-प्रदान।

conduct[1] *कौन्ँ डक्ट n.* behaviour आचार-व्यवहार; management संचालन।

conduct[2] *कॅन् डक्ट v. t.* to lead नेतृत्व करना; to guide मार्ग दिखाना; to behave आचरण करना।

conductor *कॅन् डक् टॅः n.* a leader नेता; a director निर्देशक; a body that transmits heat, electricity etc. सुचालक; a person incharge of a bus कंडक्टर।

cone *कोन् n.* a solid circular figure tapering to a point शंकु, नोकदार आकृति।

confectioner *कॅन् फ़ैक् शॅ नॅः n.* one who makes and sells sweetmeats हलवाई।

confectionery *कॅन् फ़ैक् शॅ नॅ रि n.* sweetmeats in general मिष्ठान; place where sweetmeats are prepared हलवाईखाना, मिष्ठान गृह।

confer *कॅन् फॅः v. i.* to consult together वार्तालाप करना *v. t.* to give or bestow प्रदान करना।

conference *कौन्ँ फ़ॅ रॅन्स n.* assembly सभा, सम्मेलन; meeting for consultation परामर्श।

confess *कॅन् फ़ैॅस v. t.* to admit स्वीकार करना; to own as a crime, debt etc. मानना; *v. i.* to declare one's sins पापों को कह देना।

confession *कॅन् फ़ैॅ शॅन n.* admission of a fault पाप-स्वीकारोक्ति; act of confessing पाप-स्वीकरण।

confidant *कौन्ँ फ़ि डैन्ट n.* a confidential विश्वासपात्र मित्र।

confide *कॅन् फ़ॉइड v. i.* to trust विश्वास करना; *v. t.* tell in confidence गुप्त रूप से बताना।

confidence *कौन्ँ फ़ि डॅन्स n.* faith, trust विश्वास; self-reliance आत्मविश्वास; boldness साहस।

confident *कौन्ँ फ़ि डॅन्ट a.* having confidence आश्वस्त।

confidential *कौन्ँ फ़ि डैन्ँ शॅल a.* trustworthy विश्वस्त; secret गुप्त।

confine *कॅन् फ़ॉइन v. t.* to imprison क़ैद करना; to restrain प्रतिबंधित करना; to limit सीमित करना।

confinement *कॅन् फ़ॉइन् मॅन्ट n.* imprisonment कारावास; being in bed for child birth प्रसूति।

confirm *कॅन् फ़:म v. t.* to strengthen दृढ़ बनाना; to prove to be true पुष्टि करना; to administer confirmation स्थायी करना; to make sure विश्वस्त होना।

confirmation *कौन्ँ फ़: मे शॅन n.* act of confirming पुष्टीकरण; proving right प्रमाणीकरण; corroboration समर्थन।

confiscate *कौन्ँ फ़िस् केट v. t.* to size by authority ज़ब्त करना।

confiscation *कौन्ँ फ़िस् के शॅन n.* forfeiture ज़ब्ती।

conflict[1] *कौन्ँ फ़्लिक्ट n.* struggle संघर्ष; clashing of views टकराव।

conflict[2] *कॅन् फ़्लिक्ट v. i.* to clash संघर्ष करना।

confluence *कौन्ँ फ़्लु ॲन्स n.* place where two rivers unite संगम।

confluent *कॉन्-फ्लू-अन्ट् adj.* flowing together एक साथ बहता हुआ।

conformity[1] *कॉन-फॉर्म्-इट्-इ n.* likeness, congruity, compliance अनुरूपता, समानता, आज्ञा पालन।

conformity[2] *कॅन् फ़ौ:–मि टि n.* likeness समनुरूपता; compliance अनुपालन।

confraternity *कॉन्-फर-टर्-निटी n.* brotherhood बन्धुत्व, भाईचारा।

confrontation *कौन्ँ फ़्रॅन् टे शॅन n.* opposition विरोध, आमना-सामना।

confuse *कॅन फ़्यूज़ v. t.* to put into disorder अव्यवस्थित करना; to disconcert भ्रम में डालना।

confusion *कॅन् फ़्यू ज़ॅन n.* confoundment भ्रम; disorder अव्यवस्था।

confute *कन्फ्यूट् v.t.* to prove to be false, to disprove झूठा सिद्ध करना, असिद्ध करना।

conge *कॉन्-जे n.* farewell. विदाई

congenial *कॅन् जी नि ॲल a.* agreeable अनुकूल।

conglutinate *कॅन्-ग्लू-टिन्-एट् v.t.* to stick together with glue सरेस से चिपकाना या बैठाना।

congratulate *कॅन् ग्रै ट्यु लेट v. t.* to felicitate बधाई देना।

congratulation *कॅन् ग्रै ट्यु ले शॅन n.* act of congratulating बधाई।

congress *कौ ँङ् ग्रैसॅ n.* assembly सभा, सम्मेलन।

conjecture[1] *कॅन् जैँक् चॅः n.* guess अटकल, अनुमान।

conjecture[2] *v. t.* decide by guess अनुमान से निर्णय करना; *v. i.* to make a guess अटकल लगाना।

conjugal *कौन्ँ जु गॅल a.* pertaining to marriage वैवाहिक।

conjugate *कॉन्-जू-गेट् v.t. & i.* to inflect verbs, to marry, to unite sexually क्रियापद के रूप चलाना, विवाह करना, सम्भोग करना।

conjunct *कॉन्-जङक्ट् adj.* joined together, associated संयुक्त मिला हुआ।

conjunctiva *कॉन्-जङ्क्-टाइवा n.* the membrane which connects the inner eyeball with eyelid आंख के भीतरी भाग की झिल्ली।

conjuncture *कन्-जङ्क्ट-चर् n.* a combination of events, occasion, a crisis संयोग, घटना, अवसर।

conjure[1] *कंज्यूर v.t.* to appeal solemnly निष्ठापूर्वक अनुरोध करना।

conjure[2] *कंज्यूर v.i.* to act by magical influence जादू करना, मन्त्र वश करना।

connect *कॅ नैक्ट v. t.* to join जोड़ना; to unite संबद्ध करना; *v. i.* to associate मिलना।

connection *कॅ नैक् शॅन n.* act of connecting संयोजन; relationship संबंध, link कड़ी।

connivance *कनाइवान्स् n.* act of winking at a fault, collusion उपेक्षा, आनाकानी।

conquer *कौ ˘ङ् कॅः v. t.* to gain victory over जीतना *v. i.* to be victorious विजयी होना।

conquest *कौ ˘ङ्क्वैस्ट n.* victory विजय।

conscience *कौ ˘न्शॅन्स n.* sense of right and wrong पुण्य-अपुण्य-विवेक।

conscious *कौन्ॅ शॅस a.* sensible सचेतन, wakeful जाग्रत।

consecrate *कॉन्सि-क्रेट् v.t.* to set apart as sacred, to hallow, to sanctify धार्मिक कार्य के लिए उत्सर्ग कर देना पवित्र करना (संस्कार करना), प्रतिष्ठा करना।

consecutive *कन्सिक्यूटिव् adj.* following in order निरन्तर (लगातार), क्रमागत।

consecutively *(टिव्-लि) adv.* in a consecutive manner यथाक्रम, क्रम से।

consensus *कन्सेन्सस् n.* agreement, unanimity अनुकूलता, एकमत।

consent[1] *कॅन् सैन्ट n.* permission अनुज्ञा; agreement सहमति।

consent[2] *v. i.* to agree सहमत होना।

consent[3] *कन्सेन्ट् v.t.* to agree, to yield, to comply सहमत होना, मान लेना, स्वीकार करना।

consequence *कौन्ॅ सि क्वॅन्स n.* result परिणाम; significance महत्व।

consequent *कौन्ॅ सि क्वॅन्ट a.* following as a consequence अनुगामी, अनुवर्ती।

conservative[1] *कॅन् सॅः वॅ टिव a.* opposed to great or sudden change रूढ़िवादी।

conservative[2] *n.* a conservative person रूढ़िवादी व्यक्ति।

conserve *कॅन् सॅःव v. t.* to save from damage सुरक्षित रखना; to preserve संरक्षित करना।

consider *कॅन् सि डॅः v. t.* to think over विचार करना; to regard मानना; to contemplate सोचना; to make allowance for (का) ध्यान रखना।

considerable *कॅन सि डॅ रॅ बल a.* important महत्वपूर्ण; adequate यथेष्ट।

considerate *कॅन् सि डॅ रिट a.* having consideration for others दूसरे का ध्यान रखने वाला।

consideration *कॅन् सि डॅ रे शॅन n.* careful thought विचार, मनन; something kept in mind लिहाज़, ध्यान; compensation क्षतिपूर्ति; importance महत्व।

considering *कन्सिडरिंग् prep.* in view of विचार करते हुए, समझते हुए।

consign[1] *कन्साइन् v.t.* to hand over,

to deliver, to transmit सौंपना, देना (अर्पण करना), भेजना।

consign[2] *कॅन् सॉइन v. t.* to send भेजना; to entrust सुपुर्द करना।

consignment *कॅन् सॉइन् मॅन्ट n.* consigning प्रेषण; goods consigned प्रेषित माल !

consist *कॅन् सिस्ट v. i.* to be composed (of) (का) बना होना, (में) निहित होना।

consistence,-cy *कॅन् सिस् टॅन्स, –टॅन् सि n.* degree of density घनापन; harmony सामंजस्य।

consistent *कॅन् सिस् टॅन्ट a.* compatible युक्तिसंगत; not contradictory अविरोधी।

consolation *कौनॅ् सॅ ले शॅन n.* solace सांत्वना।

console *कॅन् सोल v. t.* to give comfort सांत्वना देना।

consolidate *कॅन् सौ˘ लि डेट v. t.* to make solid संघटित करना; to unite into one समेकन करना।

consolidation *कॅन् सौ˘ लि डे शॅन n.* act of consolidating चकबंदी; state of being consolidated घनी भवन।

consonance *कॉन्सॅनन्स् n.* agreement, harmony, concord अविरोध, अनुरूपता, एकलय, मेल।

consonant *कौनॅ् सॅ नॅन्ट n.* letter always sounded with a vowel व्यंजन।

consort *कॉनसॅर्ट् n.* husband or wife, companion पति या पत्नी, संगी, साथी।

conspectus *कन्स्पेक्ट्-अस् n.* general view, synopsis सामान्य दृश्य, सारांश, रूपरेखा।

conspicuous *कॅन् स्पि क्यु अॅस a.* remarkable सुस्पष्ट; eminent विशिष्ट।

conspiracy *कॅन् स्पि रॅ सि n.* a plot षड्यंत्र।

conspirator *कॅन् स्पि रॅ टॅः n.* a plotter षड्यंत्रकर्त्ता।

conspire *कॅन् स्पॉइअॅः v. i.* to make secret plans षड्यंत्र रचना; to work together मिल जाना।

constable *कन् स्टॅ ब्ल n.* a policeman सिपाही।

constant *कौनॅ् स्टॅन्ट a.* uninterrupted निर्बाध, सतत्; invariable स्थिर।

constellation *कॉन्स्टलेशन n.* a number of fixed stars grouped together नक्षत्रों का समूह, नक्षत्रमण्डल।

constipation *कौनॅ् स्टि पे शॅन n.* costiveness क़ब्ज़, मलावरोध।

constituency *कॅन् स्टि ट्यु अॅन् सि n.* body of electors मतदाता-क्षेत्र।

constituent[1] *कॅन् स्टि ट्यु अॅन्ट n.* a component part घटक; elector मतदाता, निर्वाचक व्यक्ति।

constituent[2] helping to form a whole अंशभूत, संघटक; having the power to make a constitution संविधान-निर्माणकारी।

constitute *कौनॅ् स्टि ट्यूट v. t.* to form निर्मित करना; to appoint नियुक्त करना।

constitution *कौनॅ् स्टि ट्यू शॅन n.* a system of fundamental laws विधान; general physical structure of a person शारीरिक गठन।

constrict *कॉन्स्ट्रिक्ट् v.t.* to compress, to contract दबाना, सिकोड़ना।

construct *कॅन् स्ट्रक्ट v. t.* to build निर्माण करना; to form रचना करना।

construction *कॅन् स्ट्रक् शॅन n.* act of constructing निर्माण; structure बनावट; something constructed निर्मित वस्तु।

consult *कॅन् सल्ट v. t.* to take advice from (से) परामर्श लेना।

consultation *कौनॅ् सल् टे शॅन n.* act of consulting परामर्श।

consume *कॅन् स्यूम v. t.* to use up उपयोग में लाकर समाप्त कर देना; to destroy नष्ट करना।

consumption[1] *कॅन् सम्प् शॅन n.* act of consuming उपयोग।

consumption[2] Tuberculosis *n.* तपेदिक, क्षयरोग।

contact[1] *कौनॅ् टैक्ट n.* touch स्पर्श; coming together संपर्क; close union or juncture of bodies संयोग।

contact[2] *कॅन् टैक्ट, कौनॅ् टैक्ट v. t.* to get into touch with (से) संपर्क स्थापित करना।

contagious *कॅन् टै जॅस a.* caught or communicated by contact संसर्गज, संक्रामक।

contain *कॅन् टेन v. t.* to hold अंतर्विष्ट करना; to restrain नियंत्रित करना; to include समाविष्ट करना।

contaminate *कन्टामिनेट् v.t.* to pollute, to corrupt दूषित करना (भ्रष्ट करना), अपवित्र या कलंकित करना।

contemplate *कौनॅ् टैमॅ् प्लेट v. t.* to consider विचार करना; to meditate on (पर) मनन या चिंतन करना; to intend इरादा रखना।

contemplation *कौनॅ् टैमॅ् प्ले शॅन n.* deep thought मनन, चिंतन; thoughtful view अवलोकन।

contemporary *कॅन् टैमॅ् पॅ रॅ रि a.* belonging to the same time समकालीन; of the present time समसामयिक।

contempt *कॅन् टैम्प्ट n.* disrespect अपमान; disobedience to rules अवज्ञा; scorn घृणा।

contemptuous *कॅन् टैम्पॅ ट्यु अॅस a.* full of contempt तिरस्कारपूर्ण।

contend *कॅन् टैॅन्ड v. i.* to oppose विरोध करना; to strive संघर्ष करना; to argue बहस करना; *v. t.* to assert earnestly दृढ़तापूर्वक कहना।

content[1] *कॅन् टैन्ट a.* satisfied संतुष्ट; pleased आनंदित।

content[2] *v. t.* to satisfy संतुष्टि प्रदान करना।

content[3] *n.* satisfaction संतुष्टि।

content[4] *कौनॅ् टैन्ट n. (pl.)* that which is contained अंतर्वस्तु; index of topics in a book विषय-सूची।

contention *कॅन् टैनॅ् शॅन n.* dispute विवाद कलह; argument तर्क।

contentment *कॅन् टैन्ट् मॅन्ट n.* state of being contented संतोष।

contest[1] *कॅन् टैस्ॅट v. t.* to strive for प्राप्त करने का दावा करना; *v. i.* to strive संघर्ष करना; to participate in competition प्रतियोगिता में भाग लेना।

contest[2] *कौनॅ् टैस्ॅट n.* competition प्रतियोगिता; struggle संघर्ष।

context *कौनॅ् टैक्स्ट n.* the part which precedes or follows a passage quoted प्रसंग।

continent *कौनॅ् टि नॅन्ट n.* one of the main land masses महाद्वीप।

continental *कौनॅ् टि नैनॅ् ट्ल a.* pertaining to a continent महाद्वीपीय।

contingency *कन्-टिन्-जेन्-सि n.* a fortuitous event आकस्मिक घटना।

continual *कन्टिन्युअल् adj.* without interruption, incessant सतत, निरन्तर।

continuation *कॅन् टि न्यु ए शॅन n.* succession, prolongation जारी रखने या रहने की स्थिति; extension विस्तार; resumption पुनरारंभ।

continue *कॅन् टि न्यु v. i.* to remain in a state or place रहना; to go on जारी रहना; *v. t.* to carry on जारी रखना; to resume पुन; प्रारंभ करना; to prolong बनाए रखना।

continuity *कौनॅ् टि न्यु इ टि n.* state of being continuous निरंतरता।

continuous *कॅन् टि न्यु अॅस a.* going on without break अविरत, निरंतरत।

contour *कौनॅ् टुअॅ: n.* outline रूपरेखा।

contra *कॉन्-ट्रा pref.* in the sense of against विमुख, विपरीत अर्थ का उपसर्ग।

contraception *कॉन्ट्रेसेप्शन् n.* prevention of conception. गर्भधारण न करना, गर्भ अवरोध।

contract[1] *कौनॅ् ट्रैक्ट n.* agreement संविदा।

contract[2] *कॅन ट्रैक्ट v. t.* to make shorter सिकोड़ना; to make a contract for (का) ठेका लेना; to become liable for (का) ज़िम्मा लेना; to catch, to acquire ग्रहण करना; *v. i.* to become shorter सिकुड़ना।

contrapose *कॉन्ट्रपोज v.t.* to place over against a thing विपरीत स्थिति या अवस्था में रखना।

contractor *कॅन् ट्रैक् टॅ: n.* person that enters into contracts ठेकेदार।

contradict *कौनॅ् ट्रॅ डिक्ट v. t.* to oppose विरोध करना; to assert the contrary of खंडन करना।

contradiction *कौनॅ् ट्रॅ डिक् शॅन n.* a contrary assertion प्रतिवाद; inconsistency with itself अंतर्विरोध।

contrary *कौनॅ् ट्रॅ रि a.* opposite विरोधी; unfavourable प्रतिकूल।

contrast[1] *कॅन् ट्रास्ट, –ट्रैस्ट v. t.* to set in opposition विषमता दिखाना; *v. i.* to stand in contrast विषम होना।

contrast[2] *कौनॅ् ट्रास्टं, –ट्रैस्ट n.* opposition विरोध, विषमता।

contribute *कॅन् ट्रि ब्यूट v. t.* to give in common with others देना; *v.i.* to give a part अंशदान करना।

contribution *कौनॅ् ट्रि ब्यू शॅन n.* act of contributing योगदान; that which is contributed चंदा, अंशदान।

control[1] *कॅन् ट्रोल n.* restraint संयम, नियंत्रण; superintendence संचालन।

control[2] *(-ll-) v. t.* to restrain (पर) नियंत्रण करना; to regulate संचालित करना।

controller *कन्ट्रोलर् n.* one who has authority to control, one who checks expenditure अध्यक्ष, हिसाब-किताब जांचने वाला।

controversy *कौनॅ् ट्रॅ वॅ: सि, कॅन् ट्रौॅ वॅ: सि n.* dispute, debate विवाद।

contuse *कन्ट्यूज़् v.t.* to injure with out breaking skin, to beat and bruise कुचलना, भीतरी घाव करना।

conundrum *कनण्ड्रम् n.* a riddle, a puzzle प्रहेलिका, पहेली।

convene *कन्ँ वीन v. t.* to cause to assemble आयोजित करना, बुलाना।

convener *कॅन् वी नॅः n.* one who calls an assembly together संयोजक।

convenience *कॅन् वी नि अॅन्स n.* ease सुविधा; comfort आराम।

convenient *कॅन् वी नि अॅन्ट a.* suitable उपयुक्त; providing convenience सुविधाजनक; comfortable आरामदायक।

convent *कौन्ँ वैन्टॅ n.* a body of monks or nuns धर्मसंघ; a monastery मठ।

convention *कॅन् वैन्ँ शॅन n.* recognised social custom प्रथा; assembly सभा, सम्मेलन।

conversant[1] *कौन्ँ वॅः सॅन्ट, कॅन् वॅः–a.* proficient प्रवीण, दक्ष।

conversant[2] *कनवर्सेन्ट् adj.* well-acquainted versed, proficient परिचित, निपुण (कुशल)।

conversation *कौन्ँ वॅः सेशॅन n.* talk वार्तालाप, संवाद।

converse *कन्वर्स् v.t.* to talk, to hold intercourse with सम्भाषण करना, बोलना, वार्तालाप करना।

conversion *कॅन् वॅः शॅन n.* act of converting रूपांतरण; change of religion धर्म-परिवर्तन।

convert[1] *कॅन् वॅःट v. t.* to change रूपांतरित करना; to change the religion of (का) मत-परिवर्तन करना।

convert[2] *कौन्ँ वॅःट n.* person who has changed his religion धर्मपरिवर्तित व्यक्ति।

convey *कॅन् वे v. t.* to communicate सूचित करना; to deliver सौंपना; to carry पहुंचाना।

conveyance *कॅन् वे अन्स n.* vehicle सवारी, वाहन; act of conveying संप्रेषण।

convict[1] *कॅन विक्ट v. t.* to declare guilty अपराधी घोषित करना।

convict[2] *कौन्ँ विक्ट n.* a convicted person सिद्धदोष, अपराधी।

conviction *कॅन् विक् शॅन n.* finding someone guilty दोषसिद्धि; a settled belief धारणा, आस्था।

convince *कॅन् विन्स v. t.* to persuade by argument or proof विश्वास दिलाना।

convivial *कन्विविअल् adj.* befitting a feast jovial उत्सव-सम्बंधी, प्रफुल्ल।

convocation *कॉन्-वो-के-शन् n.* a calling together an assembly of cleargy or members of a university समागम, सभा (समाज), पादरियों का संघ, विश्वविद्यालय के सदस्यों की सभा, दीक्षान्त समारोह।

convoke *कन्वोक् v.t.* to call together, to assemble पुकारना, बुलाना, इकट्ठा करना।

convolve *कन्वाल्व् v.t.* to roll or wind together लपेटना।

coo[1] *कू n.* cry of doves कूजन।

coo[2] *v. i.* to make a cry of doves कूजना।

cook[1] *कुक v. t.* to prepare (food) by heating (भोजनादि) पकाना।

cook[2] *n.* person who cooks food रसोइया।

cooker *कु कॅः n.* apparatus for cooking कुकर।

cool[1] *कूल a.* moderately cold शीतल; unexcited उत्तेजनाहीन; uninterested उदासीन।

cool[2] *v. i.* to lose heat ठंडा होना; *v.t.* to make cool ठंडा करना।

cooler *कू लॅः n.* vessel for cooling शीतलक, कूलर।

coolie *कू लि n.* unskilled workman or porter मज़दूर, कुली।

co-operate *को औ ॅ पॅ रेट v. i.* to work together मिलकर काम करना।

co-operation *को औ ॅ पॅ रे शॅन n.* working together सहकारिता।

co-operative *को औ ॅ पॅ रॅ टिव a.* pertaining to co-operation सहकारी, सहयोगी।

co-ordinate[1] *को औॅः डि नेट a.* equal in degree, status etc. समकक्ष।

co-ordinate[2] *कौ औॅः डि नेट v. t.* to arrange in due order समायोजन करना।

co-ordination *को औॅः डि ने शॅन n.* act of co-ordinating समायोजन, सामंजस्य।

coot *कूट् n.* a water fowl, a stupid fellow जल पक्षी, मूर्ख व्यक्ति।

co-partner *को पाःट् नॅः n.* joint partner सहभागी।

cope *कोप v. i.* to deal successfully डटकर मुकाबला करना।

coper *कोप्-अर् n.* a horse-dealer घोड़ों का सौदागर, घोड़ों का व्यापारी।

copper *कौ ॅ पॅः n.* reddish-brown metal तांबा।

coppice *कॉप्-पिस् n.* small trees grown for periodical cutting a thicket जंगल, झाड़ी (टट्टी)।

coprology *कॉप्-रॉ-लॉ-जि n.* moral impurity in art and literature कला-कौशल या साहित्य की अश्लीलता।

copulate *कॉप्-यू-लेट v.i.* to unite sexually मैथुन करना।

copy[1] *कौ ॅ पि n.* reproduction of a thing प्रतिलिपि; imitation अनुकृति।

copy[2] *v. t.* to reproduce (की) नक़ल करना; to imitate अनुकरण करना।

coral *कौ ॅ रॅल n.* a hard red substance मूंगा।

cord *कौःड n.* string, a thin rope डोरी।

cordial *कौः डि अॅल a.* hearty हार्दिक।

corbel *कॉर्-बेल् n.* a projection of stone, timber or iron in a building, a niche घोड़िया, ताखा।

cordate *कॉर्डेट् adj.* heart-shaped हृदय (पान) के आकार का।

core *कोर् n.* a homy capsule, the central part of anything, the heart अर्न्तभाग, भीतरी हिस्सा (गुद्दा), हृदय।

coriander *कॉर्-रि-एन्-डर् n.* an annual plant whose fruits are aromatic and carminative धनियां।

corinth *कॉ-रिन्थ n.* a small fruit, currant, a fine city of Greece, a prostitute house किसमिस, मुनक्का, यूनान का सुन्दर नगर, वेश्यालय।

cork *कॉर्क् n.* bark of cork-oak, a bottle-stopper काग, बोतल का डट्टा।

cormorant *कॉरमॉरेण्ट् n.* a voracious sea-bird, a rapacious man एक प्रकार की बड़ी समुद्री चिड़िया, पेटू मनुष्य, भुक्खड़ आदमी।

corn *कौःन* *n*. seed बीज; grain अनाज; painful horny growth on foot or toe घट्टा।

cornea *कॉर्निआ* *n*. the interior transparent membrane of the eye-ball कनीनिका, आंखों की पुतली।

corner *कौः नंः* *n*. angle enclosed by two walls, sides etc. कोण, कोना; region भूभाग।

cornet *कॉर्निट्* *n*. a brass wind musical instrument like trumpet, an ice-cream cone, a lady's head dress, a troop of cavalary, a cavalry officer तुरही के प्रकार का एक बाजा, मलाई की कुल्फी, औरतों की कुल्फी-नुमा टोपी, घुड़सवार पलटन, पलटन का अफसर।

cornicle *कॉर्-नि-क्ल्* *n*. a little horn छोटा सींग।

coronation *कौ˘ रॅ ने शॅन* *n*. crowning ceremony of a king राज्याभिषेक।

coronet *कॉर्-अ-निट्* *n*. a small crown, a garland छोटा, मुकुट, माला।

corporal *कौः पॅ रॅल* *a*. bodily दैहिक, शारीरिक।

corporate *कॉर्-पॅ-रेट्* *adj*. forming a body united मिला हुआ, संयुक्त।

corporation *कौ : पॅ रे शॅन* *n*. body governing a town निगम; a large trading concern व्यापार संघ।

corps *कौः* *n*. body of troops सैन्य निकाय।

corpse *कौःप्स* *n*. dead body शव।

correct[1] *कॅ रैक्ट* *a*. without a mistake दोष-रहित; right सही, शुद्ध।

correct[2] *v. t.* to make correct संशोधन करना।

correction *कॅ रैक् शॅन* *n*. act of correcting संशोधन, सुधार; something put in place of what is wrong शुद्धि।

correlate *कौ˘ रि लेट* *v. t.* to bring into reciprocal relation सहसंबंधी बनाना।

correlation *कौ˘ रि ले शॅन* *n*. mutual relationship पारस्परिक संबंध।

correspond *कौ˘ रिस् पौन्ड* *v. i.* to write and receive letters पत्र-व्यवहार करना; to be in agreement मेल खाना; to be similar समान होना।

correspondence *कौ˘रिस् पौनॅ डॅन्स* *n*. state of corresponding सामंजस्य; intercourse by letters पत्र-व्यवहार; similarity समानता।

correspondent *कौ˘ रिस् पौनॅ टॅन्ट* *n*. a writer of letters पत्र-व्यवहारी; news-paper-reporter संवाददाता।

corridor *कौ˘ रि डौः* *n*. a passage in the building, train, etc. गलियारा।

corroborate *कॉरॉबॅरेट्* *v.t.* to confirm by evidence, to strengthen प्रमाणित करना, पुष्ट करना।

corrosive *कॉरोजिव* *adj*. tending to corrode (तीव्र नाशक) खाने वाला।

corrupt[1] *कॅ रप्ट* *v. t.* to make rotten दूषित करना; to cause moral decay in भ्रष्ट करना।

corrupt[2] *a*. rotten दूषित; lacking moral values भ्रष्ट; dishonest बेईमान।

corruption *कॅ रप् शॅन* *n*. act or process of corrupting दूषण; state of being corrupt भ्रष्टता; moral debasement नैतिक पतन।

cosier *कोजिअर्* *n.* cobbler मोची।

cosmetic[1] *कौज़् मैˇ टिक* *a.* designed to increase beauty सौंदर्यवर्धक।

cosmetic[2] *n.* preparation designed to increase beauty अंगराग।

cosmic *कॉज़्-मिक्* *adj.* of the universe, rising or settig with the sun. जगत्-संबंधी, सूर्य के साथ उदय या अस्त होने वाली।

cost[1] *कौˇस्ट* *v. t.* to have as price के मूल्य का होना; to entail loss or sacrifice of (की) हानि सहना या बलिदान करना।

cost[2] *n.* price मूल्य, लागत।

costal *कॉस्ट्-अल्* *adj.* pertaining to ribs or side of body पसली संबंधी।

cote *कोट्* *n.* a shed, a shelter for animals झोंपड़ी, पशुओं के लिये घेरा, बाड़ा।

costly *कौस्ट्लि* *a.* of a high price महंगा; valuable मूल्यवान।

costume *कौस्ॅ ट्यूम* *n.* an established mode of dress पोशाक, पहनावा।

cosy *कौ ज़ि* *a.* comfortable आरामदायक।

cot *कौˇट* *n.* small bed खटिया, चारपाई।

cottage *कौˇ टिज* *n.* small country house झोंपड़ी, कुटिया।

cotton *कौˇ टॅन* *n.* soft substance like wool कपास, रूई; thread or cloth made of this सूती धागा या कपड़ा।

couch *कॉउच* *n.* a sofa सोफ़ा।

cough[1] *कौफ़ॅ* *n.* act of coughing खांसी।

cough[2] *v. i.* to expel air from lungs suddenly with a harsh noise खांसना।

council *कॉउन् सिल* *n.* an assembly for consultation परिषद्, समिति।

councillor *कॉउन् सि लॅः* *n.* a member of a council पार्षद, सभासद।

counsel[1] *काउन् सॅल* *n.* advice परामर्श, मंत्रणा; advocate अधिवक्ता।

counsel[2] *v. t.* to advise परामर्श देना।

counsellor *कॉउन् सॅ लॅः* *n.* one who counsels सलाहकार, परामर्शदाता।

count[1] *कॉउन्ट* *n.* act of counting गणना; the number counted संख्या।

count[2] *v. t.* to reckon, to calculate गिनना; to include सम्मिलित करना; to consider to be मानना; *v. i.* to name the numerals in order गिनती गिनना; to have merit or value महत्वपूर्ण होना।

countenance *कॉउन् टि नॅन्स* *n.* the human face मुखाकृति; favour, support समर्थन।

counter[1] *कॉउन् टॅः* *n.* a table on which money is counted पटल, काउंटर।

counter[2] *v. t.* to act in opposition to (का) विरोध करना।

counteract *काउन्ट्-अर्-एक्ट्* *v.t.* to hinder, to defeat, to neutralize रोकना, हराना, निष्फल करना।

countercharge *काउन्ट्-अर्-चार्ज़्* *n.* a charge brought against an accuser अभियोक्ता (फरियादी) के विरुद्ध अभियोग या नालिश।

counterfeit *कॉउन् टॅः फ़िट* *a.* sham, not genuine खोटा, कृत्रिम; made in imitation नक़ली।

counterfeiter *काउन्ट्-अर्-फीटर्* *n.* a forger, a cheat जालसाज, नक़ली सिक्का बनाने वाला, ठग।

countermand *काउन्ट्-अर्-मान्ड्* *v.t.* to revoke, to cancel a previous order प्रतिकूल आदेश देना, पहिली आज्ञा को काट देना।

counterpart *कॉउन् टॅः पॉःट* *n.* a person or thing identical to another प्रतिवस्तु।

countersign *कॉउन् टॅः सॉइन* *v. t.* to sign (a document) already signed प्रतिहस्ताक्षरित करना।

countess *काउनट्-ऐस्* *n.* the wife of a count or Earl इंग्लैंड के काउन्ट या अर्ल (उपाधिधारियों) की स्त्री, बेगम।

countless *कॉउन्ट् लिस* *a.* innumerable अनगिनत।

country *कन् ट्रि* *n.* a state or kingdom देश; a large tract of land भूभाग; rural parts देहात, गांव।

county *कॉउन् टि* *n.* a division of a country प्रदेश, ज़िला; a shire प्रबंध-मंडल।

coup *कू* *n.* a blow, a successful stroke चोट, सच्चा आघात।

couple[1] *क पल* *n.* a pair जोड़ा; husband and wife पति-पत्नी।

couple[2] *v. t.* to join together जोड़ना; to unite संयोजित करना; *v. i.* to associate मिल जाना।

couplet *कप् लिट* *n.* two lines of rhymed verse दोहा।

coupon *कू पॅन* *n.* ticket etc. entitling the holder to receive something कूपन, पर्णिका।

courage *क रिज* *n.* bravery बहादुरी, पराक्रम, साहस।

courageous *कॅ रे जॅस* *a.* bold, fearless निडर।

courier *कु रि अॅः* *n.* a messenger संदेशवाहक।

course *कौःस* *n.* syllabus पाठ्यक्रम; channel of water जलमार्ग; path रास्ता; line of action कार्यप्रणाली; series शृंखला।

court[1] *कौःट* *n.* hall of justice न्यायालय; a royal palace राजदरबार; playground for certain games खेल का मैदान; wooing प्रणय-निवेदन।

court[2] *v. t.* to woo प्रणय-निवेदन करना; to seek, to invite निवेदन करना, आमंत्रित करना।

courteous *कॅ ट्यॅस* *a.* polite विनम्र, शिष्ट।

courtesan *कौः टि ज़ैन* *n.* a prostitute वेश्या, गणिका।

courtesy *कॅः टॅ सि* *n.* quality of being courteous सौजन्य; polite behaviour शिष्टाचार।

courtier *कौः ट्यॅः* *n.* member of a sovereign's court दरबारी।

courtship *कौःट् शिप* *n.* wooing प्रणय-निवेदन, प्रेमालाप।

courtyard *कौःट् याःड* *n.* an enclosure round or near a house आंगन, चौक।

cousin *क ज़न* *n.* the son or daughter of an uncle or aunt चचेरा, ममेरा, फुफेरा या मौसेरा भाई या बहिन।

covenant *कव्नेण्ट्* *n.* a compact, a bargain, a mutual agreement or contract पारस्परिक स्वीकृति, पण, सौदा, सट्टा, ठीका।

cover[1] *क वॅः* *v. t.* to place or spread over ढंकना; to include सम्मिलित करना; to be sufficient for के लिए पर्याप्त होना; to travel over (की) यात्रा करना; to hide छिपा लेना।

cover[2] *n.* something that covers आवरण, आच्छादन; concealment

छिपाव; lid ढक्कन; shelter आड़; protection बचाव।

coverlet *क वॅः लिट* *n.* bed-cover पलंगपोश।

covet *क. वि-ट्* *v.t.* to desire eagerly लोभ करना, लालच करना।

cow[1] *कॉउ* *n.* the female of a bull गाय।

cow[2] *v. t.* to frighten डराना।

coward *कॉउ ॲःड* *n.* a timid person कायर।

cowardice *कॉउ ॲः डिस* *n.* want of courage कायरता।

cower *काउ्-अर्* *v.i.* to stand in a bent position, to crouch from fear दबकना, भय से सिकुड़ना।

coy *कौ˘इ* *a.* modest विनीत।

cozy *को-जि* comfortable सुखकर।

crab *क्रैब* *n.* a crustaceous fish with strong claws केकड़ा।

crack[1] *क्रैक* *n.* a split दरार; a sudden sound कड़क; flaw दोष, कमी।

crack[2] *v. i.* to make a sudden sharp sound कड़कना; to split टूटना, दरार पड़ना; to break with a sound टूटना; *v. t.* to break with a sharp noise तोड़ना।

cracker *क्रै कॅः* *n.* firework पटाखा।

crackle *क्राक्-क्ल्* *v.t.* to make a cracking sound कड़ाके का शब्द करना।

cradle *क्रै ड्ल* *n.* an infant's bed पालना।

craft *क्राफ़्ट* *n.* skilled trade हस्त-कौशल; art कारीगरी; trickery चालाकी।

craftsman *क्राफ़्ट्स् मॅन* *n.* one skilled in a craft शिल्पी।

crafty *क्राफ़् टि* *a.* cunning कुटिल, चालाक।

cram *क्रैम (-mm-)* *v. t.* to stuff ठूंसना; to memorise रटना; *v. i.* to feed to excess ठूंस-ठूंस कर खाना।

crambo *क्राम्-बो* *n.* a game of rhyming तुकबंदी का खेल।

crane *क्रेन* *n.* a large wading bird with long legs सारस; a machine for lifting heavy weights क्रेन, भारोत्तोलन यंत्र।

crankle *क्राङ्क्-क्ल्* *v.t.* to twist, to turn ऐंठना, घुमाना।

crash[1] *क्रैश* *v. i.* to fall to pieces with a loud noise धमाके के साथ ध्वस्त होना; to collide टकराना; to fall with a crash धमाके के साथ गिरना; to make a loud noise धमाका करना; *v. t.* to cause to fall and break गिराकर ध्वस्त करना।

crash[2] *n.* sudden loud noise धमाका; collision टक्कर; loud, violent fall धमाके के साथ पतन।

crass *क्रास्* *adj.* thick, gross, stupid घना, मूर्ख, अनाड़ी।

crate *क्रेट्* *n.* a large framework, a case or basket for carrying glass, fruit ढाँचा, झाँप, टोकरी।

crave *क्रेव* *v.t.* to beg earnestly, to long for याचना करना, मांगना।

craw *क्रॉ* *n.* the crop or throat or stomach of insects or birds पक्षियों या कीड़ों का सिर या गला या पेट।

crawl[1] *क्रौल* *v. t.* to creep रेंगना; to advance slowly घिसटना।

crawl[2] *n.* crawling movement रेंग; slow pace मंदगति।

craze *क्रेज़* *n.* insanity, mania उन्माद, पागलपन।

crazy *क्रे ज़ि* *a.* insane सनकी, झक्की;

madly eager अत्यंत उत्साहपूर्ण।

creak[1] *क्रीक v. i.* to make a sharp grating sound चरमराना।

creak[2] *n.* sharp grating sound चरमराहट।

cream *क्रीम n.* the fatty part of milk मलाई; the best part of anything सार; a cosmetics for the face क्रीम।

crease *क्रीस n.* line made by folding तह का निशान; wrinkle सिकुड़न।

create *क्रि एट v. t.* to bring into existence सर्जन करना।

creation *क्रि ए शॅन n.* the act of creating सर्जन; the universe सृष्टि; created things रचना।

creative *क्रि-एट्-इव् adj.* having power to create, that creates उत्पन्न करने की शक्ति वाला, उत्पादक।

creator *क्रि ए टॅ: n.* maker निर्माता; (cap.) the Supreme Being विधाता।

creature *क्री चॅ: n.* an animate being प्राणी।

credible *क्रै ˘ डॅ ब्ल a.* worthy of belief प्रामाणिक, विश्वसनीय।

credit *क्रै˘ डिट n.* good name प्रसिद्धि, साख; faith, belief विश्वास; money due जमा धन।

creditable *क्रै˘ डि टॅ ब्ल a.* bringing honour श्रेयस्कर।

creditor *क्रै˘ डि टॅ: n.* one to whom a debt is due ऋणदाता।

credulity *क्रेड्-यू-लिटि adj.* too ready to believe, unsuspecting सहज में विश्वास करने योग्य, सन्देह शून्य।

creed[1] *क्रीड् n.* a religious belief, a set opinion on any subject धर्म, स्वीकृत मत।

creed[2] *क्रीड n.* any system of belief मत, पंथ।

creek *क्रीक् n.* a small inlet on the sea-coast a small harbour खाड़ी, बन्दरगाह।

creep *क्रीप v. i.* to move as a reptile रेंगना; to crawl पेट के बल खिसकना।

creeper *क्री पॅ: n.* a creeping plant लता।

cremate *क्रि मेट v. t.* to dispose of (a human body) by the burning दाहसंस्कार करना।

cremation *क्रिमेशन n.* act of cremating दाहसंस्कार।

crest *क्रैस्ट n.* a tuft on the head of certain birds कलगी।

crevet *क्रेव्-ऍट् n.* a melting pot used by goldsmiths सोना-चांदी गलाने की सुनार की घरिया।

crew *क्रू n.* ship's, boat's or aircraft's company चालकदल; a gang कर्मीदल।

crib *क्रिब् n.* a receptacle for fodder, a but, a small bed for children, situation चरनी, झोपड़ी, पालना, स्थिति।

cricket *क्रि किट n.* a small jumping insect झींगुर; a game played with bat and ball क्रिकेट।

crime *क्राइम n.* act or offence punishable by law अपराध।

crimp *क्रिम्प् n.* an agent who entraps men for soldiers सिपाहियों की भरती करने वाला।

crimple *क्रिम्-पल् v.t.* to contract or chrink, to curl सिकोड़ना, मोड़ना।

criminal[1] *क्रि मि नॅल n.* person committing a crime अपराधी व्यक्ति।
criminal[2] *a.* guilty of crime अपराधी; of crime आपराधिक।
crimson *क्रिम् ज़ॅन* a deep red गहरा लाल।
cringe *क्रिन्ज v. i.* to flatter with mean servility चापलूसी करना।
cripple *क्रि प्ल n.* a lame person विकलांग व्यक्ति।
crisis *क्रॉइ सिस n.* difficult and dangerous time संकटकाल।
crisp *क्रिस्प a.* brisk फुरतीला; brittle ख़स्ता।
criterion *क्रॉइ टिऑरि ॲन n.* standard of judgement मापदंड।
critic *क्रि टिक n.* one skilled in judging literary or artistic work समालोचक; a reviewer समीक्षक; fault-finder छिद्रान्वेषी।
critical *क्रि टि कॅल a.* relating to criticism समालोचनात्मक; faultfinding दोषदर्शी; relating to crisis संकटपूर्ण।
criticism *क्रि टि सिज़्म n.* the art of criticising आलोचना; censure छिद्रान्वेषण।
criticize *क्रि टि सॉइज़ v. t.* to judge critically (की) समालोचना करना; to find fault with (की) निंदा करना।
croak *क्रोक् n.* a deep hoarse sound of a frog or crow कौवे के कांव-कांव या मेंडक के टरटों का शब्द।
crockery *क्रौ ॅ कॅ रि n.* vessels formed of clay मिट्टी के बरतन।
crocodile *क्रौ ॅ कॅ डॉइल n.* a large aquatic reptile घड़ियाल।
croesus *क्रो-सस् n.* a wealthy or rich person धनी, अमीर आदमी।
crook *क्रुक a* hook, bend, curve, a shepherd's hooked staff. झुकाव, घुमाव, कमान, गडरिया की लग्गी।
crop *क्रॉप n.* agricultural production फ़सल, उपज।
cross[1] *क्रौसॅ v. t.* to move or go across पार करना; to intersect काटना; to oppose विरोध करना; to cancel by marking with a cross काट-कूट देना।
cross[2] *n.* mark made by drawing one line across another गुणा अथवा जमा का चिन्ह; symbol of Christianity सलीब; hybrid संकर।
cross[3] *a.* angry अप्रसन्न; peevish चिड़चिड़ा; transverse तिरछा।
crossing *क्रौ ॅ सिङ्ग n.* act of going across पार जाने की क्रिया; place where two roads, railways, etc. cross चौराहा।
crotchet *क्रॉचेट् n.* a musical note, half of a minim, a whimsical fancy संगीत विद्या का चिन्ह, झक।
crouch *क्रॉउच v. i.* to bend low, to lie close to the ground झुकना, ज़मीन से सट जाना।
crow[1] *क्रो n.* a black bird कौआ; cry of a cock मुर्ग़े की बांग।
crow[2] *v. i.* to cry as a cock बांग देना; to boast डींग मारना।
crowd *क्रॉउड n.* unorganized collection of people or things भीड़, जनसमूह।
crown[1] *क्रॉउन n.* an ornament for the head in the form of a wreath राजमुकुट; head शीर्ष; perfection पूर्णता।

crown² *v. t.* to make (someone) wear a crown मुकुट पहनाना; to adorn गौरवान्वित करना।

crucial *क्रू-शल्* *adj.* searching, critical छानबीन करने वाला, प्रामाणिक।

crude *क्रूड* *a.* unrefined अशोधित; wanting in culture अशिष्ट।

cruel *क्रु ॲल* *a.* savage, brutal नृशंस।

cruelty *क्रु ॲल टि* *n.* quality of being cruel नृशंसता; mercilessness दयाहीनता।

cruise *क्रूज्* *v.i.* to sail to and for making no particular port. समुद्र में इधर-उधर यात्रा करना।

cruiser *क्रू जॅः* *n.* speedy warship युद्धपोत।

crumb *क्रम* *n.* the soft part of bread रोटी का गूदेदार भाग; a fragment टुकड़ा।

crumble *क्रम् बल* *v. t.* to break into small pieces टुकड़े-टुकड़े करना; *v. i.* to become small pieces टुकड़े-टुकड़े होना।

crump *क्रम्प्* *adj.* crooked ऐंठा टेढ़ा।

crusade *क्रू सेड* *n.* war on religious ground धर्मयुद्ध।

crush *क्रश* *v. t.* to press with force दबाना; to squeeze भींचना; to force out by squeezing निचोड़ना; to pound पीसना; to subdue परास्त करना।

crust *क्रस्ट* *n.* the hard outer coat of anything छाल; the hard surface of a loaf पपड़ी, छिलका।

crutch *क्रच* *n.* support आधार; support for a lame person बैसाखी।

cry¹ *क्रॉइ* *n.* scream क्रंदन; loud utterance चिल्लाहट; clamour कोलाहल; call of animal पशु की बोली।

cry² *v. i.* to utter a shrill loud sound चिल्लाना; to weep रोना।

cryptography *क्रिप्टोग्राफ़ि* *n.* the art of writing in secret characters गुप्त (सांकेतिक) लिखन की विद्या।

crystal *क्रिस् टॅल* *n.* pure transparent quartz मणिभ, स्फटिक; a superior kind of glass बढ़िया कांच।

cub *कब* *n.* the young of certain animals पुशुशावक।

cube *क्यूब* *n.* a regular solid body with six equal square sides घनक्षेत्र।

cubic, –al *क्यू बिक, क्यू बि कॅल* *a.* having the shape of a cube घनीय।

cubiform *क्यूब-इ-फार्म* *adj.* of the form of cube घनाकार।

cuckold *कक्-ओल्ड्* *n.* the husband of an unfaithful wife व्यभिचारिणी स्त्री का पति।

cuckoo *कु कू* *n.* a singing bird of black colour कोयल।

cucumber *क्यू कम् बॅः* *n.* a plant of the gourd family and its fruit खीरा, ककड़ी।

cudgel *क जॅल* *n.* a short and thick stick गदा।

cue *क्यू* *n.* hint संकेत; the last words of an actor's speech अभिनेता के संवाद के अंतिम शब्द।

cuff¹ *कफ़* *n.* a stroke with the open hand तमाचा; wrist band कफ़, कलाई-बंद।

cuff² *v. t.* strike with the open hand तमाचा मारना।

cuisine *क्वी-जीन्* *n.* style of cooking, cookery पकाने की विधि।
cullet *कल्-लिट्* *n.* refuse glass for remelting दुबारा गलाने के लिये कांच के टुकड़े।
culminate *कल्-मिन्-ऍट्* *v.i.* to reach the highest point उच्चतम स्थान पर पहुंचना, परम कोटि को प्राप्त करना।
culpable *कल् पॅ ब्ल* *a.* blame-worthy सदोष, आपराधिक।
culprit *कल् प्रिट* *n.* offender, guilty person अपराधी।
cult *कल्ट* *n.* sect पंथ; संप्रदाय; a system of religious belief धर्म-संप्रदाय।
cultivate *कल् टि वेट* *v. t.* to till (ground) जोतना; to develop विकसित करना।
cultrate *कल्-ट्रेट्* *adj.* shaped like the edge of a knife छुरी की धार के समान बना हुआ।
cultural *कल् चॅ रॅल* *a.* pertaining to culture सांस्कृतिक।
culture *कल् चॅः* *n.* pattern of social behaviour संस्कृति; cultivating खेती; artificial rearing पालन; growth of bacteria जीवाणुओं की वृद्धि।
culvert *कल-वर्ट्* *n.* an arched channel carrying water under or over a road सड़क के नीचे से या ऊपर से पानी के जाने की मेहराबदार नाली या पुलिया।
cunning[1] *क निङ्ग* *a* artful, crafty चालाक, मक्कार।
cunning[2] *n.* artifice, craftiness चालाकी, चतुरता।
cup *कप* *n.* a drinking vessel प्याला।
cupboard *क बॅः ड* *n.* an enclosed set of shelves in the kitchen अलमारी।
Cupid *क्यू पिड* *n.* the Roman love-god कामदेव।
cupidity *क्यू पि डि टि* *n.* covetousness अर्थलिप्सा।
curable *क्युअॅ रॅ ब्ल* *a.* that may be cured आरोग्य-साध्य।
curative *क्युअॅ रॅ टिव* *a.* tending to cure रोगनिवारक।
curb[1] *कॅःब* *n.* check, control निग्रह, नियंत्रण।
curb[2] *v. t.* to control नियंत्रण करना।
curcuma *कुर्क्यूमा* *n.* turmeric हल्दी।
curd *कॅःड* *n.* coagulated milk दही।
cure[1] *क्युअॅः* *n.* medical treatment इलाज; remedy दवाई, औषध।
cure[2] *v. t.* to heal उपचार करना।
curfew *कॅः फ्यू* *n.* order for people to remain indoors निषेधाज्ञा।
curiosity *क्युअॅ रि ऑ सि टि* *n.* state of being curious जिज्ञासा; inquisitiveness कुतूहल।
curious *क्युअॅ रि अॅस* *a.* having eagerness to know जिज्ञासु; strange अद्‌भुत।
curl *कर्ल्* *n.* a spiral lock of hair, act of curling घुंघराला बाल, ऐंठन।
currant *कर्-ऍन्ट्* *n.* dried fruit of grape सूखा अंगूर, दाख, मुनक्का, किशमिश।
currency *क रॅन् सि* *n.* money in circulation in a country मुद्रा; state of being in use चलन।
current[1] *क रॅन्ट* *n.* flow of electricity विद्युत्धारा; stream of water धारा; flow प्रवाह।
current[2] *a.* of the present time वर्तमान, सामयिक; in general use प्रचलित।

curriculum *कॅ रि क्यु लॅम* *n.* prescribed course of study पाठ्यक्रम।

curse[1] *कॅःस* *n.* invocation of evil अभिशाप; misfortune दुर्भाग्य।

curse[2] *v. t.* to wish for a curse (for someone) अभिशाप देना।

cursory *कॅः सॅ रि* *a.* superficial सतही, सरसरी।

curt *कॅःट* *a.* brief संक्षिप्त; rude अशिष्टतापूर्ण।

curtail *कॅः टेल* *v. t.* to shorten संक्षिप्त करना; to reduce घटाना।

curtain *कॅः ट्न* *n.* piece of cloth hung at a window etc. आवरण, परदा; a screen in a theatre यवनिका।

curve[1] *कॅः व* *n.* bending without angles वक्र, घुमाव।

curve[2] *v. t.* to bend into a curve मोड़ना; *v. i.* to be bent into a curve मुड़ना।

cushion[1] *कु शॅन* *n.* a kind of pillow मसनद।

cushion[2] *v. t.* to provide cushion गद्दों से सजाना।

custard *कस् टॅःड* *n.* a composition of mild and eggs, sweetened and baked or boiled दूध की लपसी।

custodian *कस् टो ड्यॅन* *n.* guardian संरक्षक; care-taker निधिपाल।

custody *कस् टॅ डि* *n.* detention हिरासत; guarding निगरानी।

custom *कस् टॅम* *n.* established usage रीति, प्रथा; toll tax सीमा-शुल्क।

customary *कस् टॅ मॅ रि* *a.* habitual, usual प्रथागत।

customer *कस् टॅ मॅः* *n.* person who purchases things ख़रीददार, ग्राहक।

cut[1] *कट (-tt-)* *v. t.* to hew and fell काटकर गिरा देना; to reap (फ़सल) काटना; to trim or pare कुतरना, छांटना; to abridge कम करना; to injure घाव करना; to intersect द्विभाजित करना।

cut[2] *n.* act of cutting कटाव, कटाई; a blow प्रहार; wound caused by a sharp edge घाव, चोट; reduction कमी।

cutis *क्यूट्-इस्* *n.* true skin भीतरी त्वचा।

cuvette *कूव्-ऍट्* *n.* a trench sunk along the middle of a dry ditch सूखी खाई के बीच में खोदा हुआ गड्ढ़ा।

cycle *सॉइक्ल* *n.* a bicycle साइकिल; circle चक्र; recurrence आवर्तन।

cyclic *सॉइ क्लिक* *a.* recurring in cycles चक्रीय।

cyclist *सॉइ क्लिस्ट* *n.* the rider of a cycle साइकिल-सवार।

cyclone *सॉइ क्लोन* *n.* a circular storm चक्रवात।

cyclostyle[1] *सॉइ क्लॅ स्टॉइल* *n.* apparatus for printing copies from a stensil चक्रलेखित्र।

cyclostyle[2] *v. t.* to produce (copies) from stensil चक्रलिपित करना।

cylinder *सि लिन् डॅः* *n.* a roller-shaped object of uniform diameter बेलन।

cynic *सि निक* *n.* person who sees no good in anything निंदक, मानवद्वेषी।

cypher see cipher.

cypress *सॉइ प्रॅस* *n.* an evergreen tree with very dark foliage सरू।

Dd

D *डी* the fourth letter of the English alphabet *(mus.)* the second note of natural major scale. अंग्रेजी वर्णमाला का चौथा अक्षर, (सं.) द्वितीय स्वर, रे (ऋषभ); **D Block** *n.* डी अक्षर की आकृति का टुकड़ा d-contraction for the words 'had' and 'would' 'हाड्' तथा 'वुड्' शब्द का छोटा रूप।

dabble *डै ब्ल v. i.* to splash about in liquid with hands or feet इधर-उधर पानी उलीचना; to do something as a hobby शौक़िया कुछ काम करना।

dacoit *डॅ कौ ॅ इट n.* robber डाकू।

dacoity *डॅ कौ ॅ इ टि n.* robbery डकैती।

dad, daddy *डैड, डै डि n.* a child's word for father पिता।

daffodil *डै फ़ॅ डिल n.* yellow narcissus पीला नरगिस।

daft *डाफ़्ट् adj.* foolish, insane, crazy मूर्ख, पागल, झक्की।

dagger *डै गॅः n.* a short sharp-pointed sword खंजर।

daily[1] *डे लि a.* happening or being everyday दैनिक।

daily[2] *adv.* everyday प्रतिदिन।

daily[3] *n.* a newspaper published everyday दैनिक समाचार-पत्र।

dainty[1] *डेन् टि a.* nice सुरुचिपूर्ण; delicate नाजुक; elegant रमणीय।

dainty[2] *n.* something nice लालित्यपूर्ण वस्तु; a delicacy स्वादिष्ट खाद्य।

dairy *डे ॅ अॅ रि n.* a shop where milk, butter etc. are sold दुग्धशाला।

dais *डे इस, डेस n.* raised platform मंच।

daisy *डे ज़ि n.* a small white flower with a yellow centre एक श्वेत पुष्प।

dale *डेल n.* a place between hills घाटी।

dam *डैम n.* a bank to confine or raise water बांध।

damage[1] *डै मिज n.* harm हानि; money claimed as compensation हरजाना।

damage[2] *v. t.* to cause damage क्षति पहुंचाना।

dame *डेम् n.* a lady-keeper of a boarding house, the wife of a knight or a baronet स्त्री (महिला), गृहिणी, नवाबिन।

damn *डैम v. t.* to condemn to hell शाप देना।

damnation *डाम्-ने-शन् n.* eternal punishment in hell नरक-दण्ड, नरक-यातना।

damp[1] *डैम्प a.* moist आर्द्र।

damp[2] *n.* moist air नम हवा; fog कोहरा।

damp[3] *v. t.* to moisten गीला करना; to dispirit निरुत्साह करना।

damsel *डाम्-ज़ल् n.* a young unmarried woman; a girl कुमारी कन्या, युवती, कुमारी, बालिका, लड़की।

dance[1] *डान्स* rhythmical movement of body and feet नृत्य।

dance[2] *v. t.* to cause to dance नचाना; *v. i.* to move with measured steps नाचना।

dandelion *डाण्डिलायन्* *n.* a common yellow flowered plant पीले फूल का एक प्रकार का पौधा।

dandle *डान्-इल्* *v.t.* to fondle or toss a child on knee or arms, to pet, to play with बच्चे को घुटनों पर या गोद में झुलाना, लाड करना।

dandruff *डैन् ड्रॅफ़* *n.* dead skin in small scales among the hair रूसी।

dandy *डैन् डि* *n.* a fop छैला।

danger *डेन् जॅः* *n.* risk संकट, जोखिम; something likely to cause harm भय का कारण।

dangerous *डेन् जॅ रॅस* *a.* full of danger खतरनाक, भयंकर।

dangle *डैङ् ग्ल* *v. t.* to swing झुलाना।

dank *डाङ्क्* *adj.* damp, oozy, moist पानी रसता हुआ, तर, गीला।

dap *डाप्* *v.i.* (p.t. dapped.) to dip lightly, to bounce जल में थोड़ा-सा डुबाना, कूदना।

dare *डे˘ अॅः* *v. i.* to be bold enough हिम्मत रखना; *v. t.* to offer a challenge चुनौती देना।

daring[1] *डे˘ अॅ रिङ्ग* *n.* boldness निर्भीकता।

daring[2] *a.* bold निर्भीक, हिम्मत वाला।

dark[1] *डाःक* *a.* blackish सांवला; clouded अंधकारमय।

dark[2] *n.* absence of light अंधकार; ignorance अज्ञानता।

darkle *डार्-कल्* *v.i.* to lie concealed छिपे रहना।

darling[1] *डाः लिङ्ग* *n.* one dearly beloved प्रियतम।

darling[2] *a.* dearly beloved प्यारा, चहेता।

dart *डार्ट्* *n.* a light javelin a pointed missile, a rapid motion, the sting of a poisonous insect बर्छी, शंकु, तीव्र गति, जहरीले कीड़े का डंक।

dash[1] *डैश* *v. i.* to rush forward झपटना; *v. t.* to smash तोड़ देना; to throw फेंक देना, पटक देना; to destroy नष्ट करना; to discourage हतोत्साह करना।

dash[2] *n.* a sudden rush झपट्टा; vigour उत्साह; smartness फुरती; a stroke of the pen पड़ी रेखा (–); short race छोटी दौड़; striking टक्कर।

date[1] *डेट* *n.* statement of time दिनांक; age काल; period समय; a datepalm or its fruit खजूर।

date[2] *v. t.* to mark with date तिथ्यंकित करना।

daub[1] *डौब* *n.* a smear पुताई।

daub[2] *v. t.* to smear पोतना।

daughter *डौ टॅः* *n.* one's female child आत्मजा, पुत्री।

daunt *डौन्ट* *v. t.* to frighten भयभीत करना।

dauntless *डौन्ट् लिस* *a.* fearless निर्भीक।

dawdle *डा ड्ल्* *v.i.* to idle विलम्ब करना।

dawn[1] *डौन* *n.* a day-break प्रभात, उषा।

dawn[2] *v. i.* to become day सुबह होना; to appear प्रकट होना।

day *डे* *n.* the time of light दिन; date तिथि; time from sunrise to sunset दिन का समय; period काल।

daze[1] *डेज़* *n.* bewilderment स्तब्धता।
daze[2] *v. t.* to bewilder स्तब्ध करना।
dazzle[1] *डै ज़ल* *n.* dazzling light चकाचौंध।
dazzle[2] *v. t.* to daze or overpower with strong light चकाचौंध करना।
deacon *डी-क्न* *n.* an order of clergy below bishop and priest छोटा पादरी।
dead *डै ॅड* *a.* lifeless मृत, निर्जीव; motionless गतिहीन; inactive निष्चेष्ट; no longer functioning बंद पड़ा हुआ।
deadlock *डै ॅड़ लौकॅ* *n;.* complete failure to reach agreement गतिरोध।
deadly *डै ॅड़ लि* *a.* fatal घातक; implacable कठोर; fearful भयंकर।
deaf *डैफ़ॅ* *a.* incapable of hearing बधिर, बहरा।
deal[1] *डील* *n.* quantity मात्रा; bargain सौदा; business transaction व्यापारिक लेन-देन।
deal[2] *v. i.* to transact business व्यापार करना; to act कार्य करना।
dealer *डी लॅः* *n.* distributer बांटनेवाला; trader व्यापारी।
dealing *डी लिङ्ग* *n. (pl.)* transaction व्यापार-संबंध; behaviour व्यवहार।
dean *n.* the head of a cathedral, the head of a faculty in a college गिरजाघर या कालेज का अध्यक्ष।
dear *डिअॅः* *a.* beloved प्रिय, प्यारा; costly महंगा; precious मूल्यवान।
dearth *डॅःथ* *n.* scarcity दुर्लभता।
death *डै ॅथ* *n.* decease देहांत; murder वध; end अंत।
debar *डि बाः (-rr-)* *v. t.* to prevent (पर) रोक लगाना; to prohibit वर्जित करना।
debase *डि बेस* *v. t.* to lower in quality or value (का) अवमूल्यन करना; to degrade पतित करना।
debate[1] *डि बेट* *n.* discussion विचार-विमर्श; controversy विवाद।
debate[2] *v. t.* to dicuss (पर) बहस करना; to argue तर्क-वितर्क करना।
debauch[1] *डि बौच* *v. t.* to corrupt भ्रष्ट करना; to pervert व्यभिचारी बनाना।
debauch[2] *n.* lewdness लंपटता, व्यभिचारिता।
debauchee *डि बौ ची* *n.* a dissipated person विषयी।
debauchery *डि बौ चॅ रि* *n.* lewdness व्यभिचारिता।
debility *डि बि लि टि* *n.* physical weakness कृशता, क्षीणता।
debit[1] *डै ॅ बिट* *n.* the left hand side of an account नामखाता; entry in account of sum owed ऋणांकन।
debit[2] *v. t.* to enter as due (का) ऋणांकन करना।
debris *डे ब्रि* *n.* rubbish कूड़ा-करकट; wreckage मलबा।
debt *डै ॅट* *n.* what is owed ऋण, उधार; obligation आभार।
debtor *डै ॅ टॅः* *n.* one indebted क़र्जदार।
decade *डै ॅ केड* *n.* period of ten years दशाब्दी।
decadent *डै ॅ कॅ डॅन्ट, डि के डॅन्ट* *a.* declining पतनोन्मुख।
decamp *डि कैम्प* *v. i.* to make off secretly चुप-चुप भाग जाना।

decay[1] *डि के* putrefaction क्षय; decomposition सड़न।

decay[2] *v. i.* to waste नष्ट होना; to decline ह्रास होना।

decease[1] *डि सीस n.* departure from this life मृत्यु।

decease[2] *v. i.* to die मर जाना।

deceit *डि सीट n.* fraud धोखा; a lie झूठ।

deceive *डि सीव v. t.* to mislead धोखा देना; to delude बहकाना, ठगना।

December *डि सैम् बॅः n.* last month of the year वर्ष का अंतिम माह, दिसंबर।

decency *डी सॅन् सि n.* state or quality of being decent शालीनता; decorum औचित्य।

decennary *डि-सेन्-रि n.* a period of ten years दस वर्ष का काल।

decent *डी सॅन्ट a.* proper उचित, शोभनीय; respectable सम्माननीय।

deception *डि सैपॅ शॅन n.* act of deceiving ठगी; artifice practised चालाकी; fraud धोखा।

decide *डि सॉइड v. t.* to settle (का) निबटारा करना; to determine निर्णय पर पहुंचना।

decillion *डि-सिलियन n.* the tenth power of a million दस लाख को इसी से दस बार गुणा करके बनी हुई संख्या।

decimal *डै˘ सि मॅल a.* tenth दसवां, दशम; reckoned by ten दशमलव।

decimate *डेस्-सि-मेट् v.t.* to destroy a tenth part दशम भाग नष्ट करना।

decision *डि सि ज़ॅन n.* judgement निर्णय; determination निश्चय।

decisive *डि सॉइ सिव a.* conclusive निर्णयात्मक; showing firmness दृढ़तापूर्ण।

deck[1] *डैकॅ n.* the platform or floor of a ship जहाज़ का फ़र्श।

deck[2] *v. t.* to adorn सजाना।

declaration *डैकॅ लॅ रे शॅन n.* act of declaring घोषणा।

declare *डि क्ले˘ अॅः v. t.* to announce formally घोषित करना; to tell explicitly स्पष्ट बता देना; to testify प्रमाणित करना; to reveal प्रकट करना।

decline[1] *डि क्लॉइन n.* decay ह्रास; deterioration घटाव।

decline[2] *v. t.* to refuse इंकार करना; *v. i.* to slope down झुकना, नीचा होना; to grow weaker कमज़ोर होना; to go down ढलना; to decay क्षीण होना।

declivous *डि-क्लिव्-अस् adj.* bent down-wards नीचे को झुका हुआ।

decompose *डी कॅम् पोज़ v. t.* to separate into original elements (का) अपघटन करना; *v. i.* to decay सड़ना।

decomposition *डि कौमॅ पॅ ज़ि शॅन n.* decay सड़न।

decontrol *डी-कण्ट्रोल् v.t.* to release from government control सरकारी नियन्त्रण हटाना।

decorate *डै˘ कॅ रेट v. t.* to ornament अलंकृत करना; to honour with a badge or medal पदक से सम्मानित करना।

decoration *डै˘ कॅ रे शॅन n.* act of decorating अलंकरण; that which adorns अलंकार; a badge or medal पदक।

decorum डि कौ रॅम *n.* propriety of speech or behaviour शिष्टाचार।

decrease[1] डी क्रीस *v. t.* to make less कम करना; *v. t.* to grow less कम होना।

decrease[2] डी क्रीस *n.* gradual diminution ह्रास।

decree[1] डि क्री *n.* an edict राजाज्ञा, आज्ञप्ति; a judicial decision न्यायिक निर्णय।

decree[2] *v. i.* to issue an order आज्ञप्ति देना; *v. t.* to determine judicially निर्णय करना।

decrement डे-क्रिमेन्ट् *n.* decrease, waste कमी, नाश।

dedicate डैˇ डि केट *v. t.* to devote wholly समर्पण करना; to inscribe (a book etc.) to a person or cause (पुस्तक आदि) समर्पित करना।

dedication डैˇ डि के शॅन *n.* act of devoting to some person समर्पण।

deduct डि-डक्ट् *v.t.* to take away, to subtract हटाना (कम करना) घटाना।

deed डीड *n.* action कृत्य; a written agreement प्रसंविदा; document दस्तावेज़; feat करतब।

deem डीम् *v.i.* to believe, to consider, to determine, to judge विश्वास करना, विचारना, इरादा, निर्णय करना।

deep डीप *a.* being far below the surface गहरा; not obvious गहन, रहस्यपूर्ण; grave in sound भारी; mysterious रहस्यमय।

deer डिअ: *n.* a quadruped with horns हरिण।

defamation डैˇ फ़ॅ मे शॅन *n.* act of defaming मान-हानि।

defame डि फ़ेम *v. t.* to slander बदनाम करना।

default डि-फॉल्ट् *n.* defect, neglect of duty, failure to act or appear दोष, अपराध, अनुपस्थिति।

defeat[1] डि फ़ीट *n.* loss of battle पराजय।

defeat[2] *v. t.* to win a victory over परास्त करना।

defect डि फ़ैक्ट, डी फ़ैक्ट *n.* want अभाव; a blemish दोष।

defence डि फ़ैन्स *n.* a guarding against danger रक्षा; protection बचाव; fortification मोर्चाबंदी; a defendant's plea सफ़ाई।

defend डि फ़ैन्ड *v. t.* to guard रक्षा करना; to support पक्ष लेना।

defendant डि फ़ैन् डॅन्ट *n.* a defender प्रतिवादी।

defensive डि फ़ैन् सिव serving for defence सुरक्षात्मक।

deference डैˇ फ़ॅ रॅन्स *n.* respect, regard सम्मान।

defiance डि फ़ाइ अॅन्स *n.* act of defying अवज्ञा; a challenge चुनौती।

deficit डैˇ फ़ि सिट *n.* deficiency of revenue घाटा।

deficient डिफ़िशन्ट् *adj.* incomplete, wanting, defective अपूर्ण, न्यून, हीन।

defile डि-फ़ाइल् *n.* a narrow way, a gorge संकुचित मार्ग, दर्रा।

define डि फ़ाइन *v. t.* to explain exactly परिभाषा देना।

definite डैˇ फ़ि निट *a.* having fixed limits सीमांकित; precise निश्चित; clear सुस्पष्ट।

definition डैˇ फ़ि नि शॅन *n.* the act

of defining निश्चयन; a brief description of a thing by its properties परिभाषा।

deflation *डि-फ्ले-शन्* *n.* reducing the value of paper money (करेन्सी) नोट का मूल्य कम करना।

deflect *डि-फ्लेक्ट्* *v.t. & i.* to turn aside, to bend down, to deviate from the right path हटाना, झुकाना (मोड़ना) बुरे मार्ग पर जाना।

deft *डेफ़्ट्* *adj.* skilful, clever, dexterous कुशल, चतुर, निपुण।

degrade *डि ग्रेड* *v. t.* to reduce to a lower rank (का) दरजा घटाना; to debase भ्रष्ट करना।

degree *डि ग्री* *n.* a title awarded by a university उपाधि; measure मात्रा; rank कोटि, श्रेणी।

dehort *डिहॉर्ट्* *v.i.* to dissuade, to exhort बहकाना।

deist *डी-इस्ट्* *n.* one who professes deism ईश्वरवादी, आस्तिक।

deity *डी-इ-टि* *n.* divinity, a god or goddess ईश्वर, देवता या देवी।

deject *डि जैक्ट* *v. t.* to dishearten हतोत्साह करना।

dejection *डि जैक् शॅन* *n.* depression निराशा।

delay *डि-ले* *v.t. & i.* (p.t. delayed) to postpone, to hinder, to linger, to put off time विलम्ब करना, समय बिताना, देर करना।

delibate *डेल्-इ-बेट्* *v.t.* to taste, to sip स्वाद लेना, चूसना।

deligate[1] *डै ˘ लि गिट* *n.* a representative प्रतिनिधि।

delegate[2] *डै ˘ लि गेट* *v. t.* to send as deputy प्रतिनिधि के रूप में भेजना; to entrust (duties, rights etc.) (कर्त्तव्य, अधिकार आदि) सौंपना।

delegation *डै ˘ लि गे शॅन* *n.* deputation प्रतिनिधान; a body of delegates प्रतिनिधिमंडल।

delete *डि लीट* *v. t.* to eliminate काट देना।

deliberate[1] *डि लि बॅ रेट* *v. i.* to weigh well in one's mind विचारना; to discuss विचार-विमर्श करना।

deliberate[2] *डि लि बॅ रिट* *a.* done on purpose जानबूझ कर किया हुआ।

deliberation *डि लि बॅ रे शॅन* *n.* careful consideration and discussion विचार-विमर्श।

delicate *डै ˘ लि किट* *a.* soft, tender मुलायम; fine उत्तम, बढ़िया; needing great care नाजुक; critical संकटपूर्ण।

delicious *डि लि शॅस* *a.* highly pleasing to the taste स्वादिष्ट।

delight[1] *डि लॉइट* *n.* that which yields great pleasure आनंद का साधन; a high degree of pleasure आनंद।

delight[2] *v. t.* to affect with great pleasure आनंद देना; *v.i.* to take great pleasure आनंद लेना।

deliver *डि लि वॅः* *v. t.* to hand over सौंपना; to give birth जन्म देना; to utter or present (speech etc.) बोलना; to release मुक्त करना।

delivery *डि लि वॅः रि* *n.* distribution वितरण; child-birth प्रसव; handing over सुपुर्दगी; style of speaking भाषण-शैली।

delta *डैल् टॅ* *n.* a space between diverging mouths of a river नदी मुख-भूमि।

delude *डि-ल्यूड़* *n.t.* to impose upon, to deceive मोहित करना, ठगना (छलना)।

delusion *डि-ल्यू-जन्* *n.* a false impression or opinion, deception fallacy मोह, भ्रम, इन्द्रजाल, माया।

demand[1] *डि मान्ड* *n.* requirement आवश्यकता; claim दावा; desire इच्छा; act of demanding अभ्यर्थना।

demand[2] *v. t.* to ask authoritatively मांग करना; to require चाहना।

demarcation *डी-मार्क्-ऍ-शन्* *n.* the marking of boundaries, division, a fixed limit सीमा रेखा का निर्धारण, विभाग, निश्चित सीमा।

dement *डि मेन्ट्* *v.t.* to drive mad उनमत्त करना, पागल करना।

demerit *डी मै ˘ रिट* *n.* fault दोष; undesirable quality अवगुण।

democracy *डि मौ ˘ क्रॅ सि* *n.* a government by the people प्रजातंत्र, लोकतंत्र।

democratic *डै ˘ मॅ क्रै टिक* *a.* connected with democracy प्रजातंत्रात्मक।

demolish *डि मौ ˘ लिश* *v. t.* to destroy ध्वस्त करना; to put an end to समाप्त करना।

demon *डी मॅन* *n.* ghost प्रेत; devil राक्षस; evil-minded person नरपिशाच।

demonetize *डीमॉनिटाइज्* *v.t.* to deprive of standard value as money धातु के सिक्कों का मूल्य घटना।

demonstrate *डै ˘ मॅन् स्ट्रेट* *v. t.* to exhibit प्रदर्शन करना; to give proof of (का) प्रमाण देना।

demonstration *डै ˘ मॅन् स्ट्रे शॅन* *n.* act or process of demonstrating प्रदर्शन।

demoralize *डि मौ ˘ रॅ लॉइज़* *v. t.* to corrupt the moral of नैतिक पतन करना; to deprave उत्साह भंग करना।

demur[1] *डि मॅः* *n.* objection आपत्ति।

demur[2] *(-rr-)* *v. t.* to object आपत्ति करना।

demurrage *डि-मर्-रेज्* *n.* an allowance made for undue detention of goods माल का समय से अधिक रुकावट का हरजाना।

den *डैनॅ* *n.* a cave गुहा; a lair मांद; a haunt अड्डा।

dengue *डेङ्ग्-गू* *n.* a severe tropical fever accompanied by acute pain in the joints. लंगड़ा ज्वर।

denial *डि नॉइ अॅल* *n.* denying नकार; refusing a request अस्वीकृति; statement that something is not true खंडन।

denote *डि नोट* *v. i.* to indicate घोषित करना; to imply (का) अर्थ रखना।

denounce *डि नॉउन्स* *v. t.* to accuse publicly दोषारोपण करना; to stigmatize निंदा करना।

dense *डैन्स* *a.* thick, compact घना, सघन।

density *डैन्ॅ सि टि* *n.* closeness, compactness सघनता; mass per unit of volume घनत्व।

dentist *डैन्ॅ टिस्ट* *n.* a dental surgeon दंत-चिकित्सक।

denude *डि-नयूड़* *v.t.* to make nude or naked नंगा करना।

denunciation *डि-नन्-सि-ऍ-शनं* *n.* act of denouncing a public menace, a threat अनिष्ट प्रकाशन, सार्वजनिक भर्त्सना।

deny *डि नॉइ v. t.* to refuse to admit अस्वीकार करना; to contradict खंडन करना।

depart *डि पाःट v. i.* to leave प्रयाण करना; to start प्रस्थान करना; to die परलोक सिधारना।

department *डि पाःट् मॅन्ट n.* a separate part भाग; a distinct branch विभाग।

departure *डि पाः चॅः n.* act of leaving a place प्रस्थान, प्रयाण; going away विचलन; death देहत्याग।

depauperate *डि-पॉ-पर-ऍट् v.t.* to impoverish दरिद्र करना या बनाना।

depend *डि पैन्ड v. i.* to rest or rely solely निर्भर होना; to trust भरोसा करना।

dependant *डि पैनॅ् डॅन्ट n.* one who depends on another आश्रित; follower अनुचर।

dependence *डि पैनॅ् डॅन्स n.* state of being dependent पराधीनता।

dependent *डि पैनॅ् डॅन्ट a.* depending निर्भर।

depict *डि पिक्ट v. t.* to paint carefully चित्रांकित करना; to describe in words वर्णन करना।

deplorable *डि प्लौ रॅ बल a.* lamentable शोचनीय; grievous खेदजनक।

deploy *डि-प्लॉय् v.t.* to open out or extend in a line, to spread out पंक्ति में रखना, फैलाना।

deponent *डि-पो-नेन्ट् n.* one who gives testimony in a court, a witness अदालत में साक्षी देने वाला व्यक्ति, गवाह।

deport *डि-पोर्ट् v.t.* to behave, to transport or banish व्यवहार करना (चेष्टा करना), देश बाहर निकालना।

depose *डि पोज़ v. t.* to dethrone पदच्युत करना; to divest of office अपदस्थ करना; *v. i.* to bear witness गवाही देना।

deposit[1] *डि पौँ ज़िट n.* thing deposited जमा; anything given as security प्रतिभूति।

deposit[2] *v. t.* to give as deposit निक्षेप करना।

depot *डैँ पो n.* a store-house संग्रहागार।

depreciate *डि-प्री-शि-एट् v.t. & i* to diminish value of, to fall in value, to regret. मूल्य घटना, दाम कम होना, पछताना।

depredate *डे-प्रि-डेट् v.t.* to plunder, to prey upon, to devour लूटना, शिकार करना, खा जाना।

depress *डि प्रैसॅ v. t.* to cast a gloom over उदास करना; to press down अवनत करना।

depression *डि प्रैँ शॅन n.* state of being depressed उदासी; dejection विषाद; a hollow गर्त।

deprive *डि प्रॉइव v. t.* to dispossess, to take from (से) वंचित करना।

depth *डैॅथ n.* distance downwards गहराई; deep place गहरा स्थान; abstruseness विदग्धता; intensity विचार-गांभीर्य।

deputation *डैँ प्यु टे शॅन n.* a body of persons sent on a mission शिष्टमंडल।

depute *डि प्यूट v. t.* to appoint as a substitute प्रतिनिधि के रूप में नियुक्त करना; to send with a special commission किसी विशेष कार्य के लिए भेजना।

deputy *डै ॅ प्यु टि* *n.* a person appointed to act for another प्रतिनिधि।

derail *डि रेल* *v. t.* to cause to leave the rails पटरी से उतारना; *v.i.* to go off the rails पटरी से उतर जाना।

derive *डि रॉइव* *v. t.* to draw or receive प्राप्त करना; to trace the etymology of (का) मूल खोजना।

descend *डि सैन्ड* *v. i.* to come or go down नीचे आना या जाना; to slope down ढालू होना; to spring (from) वंशज होना।

descendant *डि सैन् डॅन्ट* *n.* offspring from an ancestor वंशज।

descent *डि सैन्ट* *n.* coming down उतार; ancestry वंश; sudden attack आक्रमण; handing down हस्तांतरण।

describe *डिस् क्रॉइब* *v. t.* to trace out चित्रण करना; to give an account of वर्णन करना।

description *डिस् क्रिप् शॅन* *n.* act of describing निरूपण; account विवरण।

descriptive *डि स्क्रिप् टिव* *a.* serving to describe वर्णनात्मक।

desert[1] *डि ज़ॅःट* *v. t.* to leave, to forsake त्यागना; *v. i.* to quit हट जाना।

desert[2] *डै ॅ ज़ॅःट* *n.* vast sandy plane रेगिस्तान; uninhabited tract निर्जन स्थान।

deserve *डि ज़ॅःव* *v. t.* to be worthy of (का) अधिकारी होना।

design[1] *डि ज़ॉइन* *v. t.* to make a plan of (की) योजना बनाना; to intend इरादा रखना; to plot षड्यंत्र रचना; to sketch खाका बनाना।

design[2] *n.* an outline sketch रूपरेखा, खाका; working plan योजना; a pattern नमूना; purpose, intention उद्देश्य, इरादा।

desirable *डि ज़ॉइअॅ रॅ ब्ल* *a.* worthy of desire वांछनीय; pleasing, attractive आकर्षक।

desire[1] *डि ज़ॉइअॅः* *n.* eagerness to obtain or enjoy अभिलाषा; longing इच्छा; lust वासना।

desire[2] *v.t.* to wish for the possession or enjoyment of (की) कामना करना; to ask मांगना।

desirous *डि ज़ॉइअॅ रॅस* *a.* full of desire इच्छुक।

desk *डै ॅस्क* *n.* an inclining table to write or read upon डैस्क, मेज़।

despair[1] *डिस् पे ॅ अॅः* *n.* a hopeless state निराशा।

despair[2] *v. i.* to give up all hope निराश होना।

desperate *डैसॅ पॅ रिट* *a.* reckless, ready to do anything दुःसाहसी; beyond hope निराशाजनक।

despicable *डैसॅ पि कॅ ब्ल* *a.* contemptible घृणित, तिरस्कार-योग्य।

despise *डिस् पॉइज़* *v. t.* to hold in contempt घृणा करना।

despot *डैसॅ पौ ॅट* *n.* an absolute ruler निरंकुश शासक।

destination *डैसॅ टि ने शॅन* *n.* goal गंतव्य; purpose उद्देश्य।

destiny *डैसॅ टि नि* *n.* predetermined fate नियति, भवितव्यता।

destroy *डिस् ट्रौ ॅइ* *v. t.* to pull down नष्ट करना, ध्वसत करना; to kill मारना।

destruction *डिस् ट्रक् शॅन n.* ruin विनाश; death मृत्यु।

detach *डि टैच v. t.* to separate अलग करना।

detachment *डि टैच् मॅन्ट n.* act of detaching अलग करने की क्रिया; aloofness अलगाव; absence of attachment अनासक्ति।

detail[1] *डी टेल n.* particular ब्यौरा; small or unimportant part गौण बात।

detail[2] *डि टैल v. t.* to relate in full विस्तृत विवरण देना।

detain *डि टेन v. t.* to withhold, to prevent from leaving रोके रखना।

detect *डि टैक्ट v. t.* to discover, to find out खोजना, पता लगाना।

detective[1] *डि टैक् टिव a.* employed in detecting जासूसी।

detective[2] *n.* a police officer whose duty is to detect criminals जासूस।

determination *डि टॅः मि ने शॅन n.* firmness of purpose दृढ़ संकल्प; act of determining निश्चयन।

determine *डि टॅः मिन v. t.* to decide निश्चय करना; to establish निर्धारित करना; to settle तय करना।

dethrone *डि थ्रोन v. t.* to depose, to remove from throne गद्दी से उतारना।

develop *डि वैॅ लॅप v. t.* to cause to grow विकसित करना; to elaborate विस्तृत करना; to treat (film) with chemicals to bring out image (चित्र) उभारना; *v. i.* to grow विकसित होना।

development *डि वैॅ लॅप् मॅन्ट n.* act or process of developing विकास; expansion विस्तार; growth वृद्धि।

deviate *डी वि एट v. i.* to stray, to turn away भटकना, विचलित होना।

deviation *डी वि ए शॅन n.* turning aside विचलन।

device *डि वॉइस n.* contrivance जुगत, तरकीब, जुगाड़; scheme योजना।

devil *डैॅ विल n.* an evil spirit शैतान; a very wicked person नर-पिशाच।

devise *डि वॉइज़ v. t.* to think out सोच लेना; to contrive (की) जुगत निकालना।

devoid *डि वौॅइड a.* destitute, empty (of) रहित, विहीन।

devote *डि वोट v. t.* to set apart by vow अर्पित करना; to apply closely to लगाना।

devotee *डैॅ वोॅ टी n.* one wholly devoted समर्पित व्यक्ति; a zealous worshipper भक्त।

devotion *डि वो शॅन n.* act of devoting or state of being devoted समर्पण; (*pl.*) prayers प्रार्थनाएं; devoutness भक्तिभाव।

devour *डि वॉउअॅ; v. t.* to swallow up निगल जाना; to read eagerly धुन के साथ पढ़ना।

dew *ड्यू n.* moisture from atmosphere condensed into drops on the surface, grass etc. ओस।

diabetes *डॉइअॅ बी टीज़ n.* disease characterized by sugar in blood मधुमेह।

diagnose *डॉइ अॅग् नोज़ v. t.* to ascertain from symptoms the true nature of (disease) (का) निदान करना।

diagnosis *डॉइ ॲग् नो सिस n.* process of diagnosing निदान।

diagram *डॉइ ॲ ग्रैम n.* drawing to explain something आरेख, रेखालेख।

dial *डॉइ ॲल n.* face of a clock etc. डायल, अंकपट्ट।

dialect *डॉइ ॲ लैक्ट n.* spoken language peculiar to a region उपभाषा, बोली।

dialogue *डॉइ ॲ लौगॅ n.* conversation संवाद; discussion विचार-विमर्श।

diameter *डॉइ ऐ मि टॅः n.* straight line drawn from side to side through the centre of a circle व्यास।

diamond *डॉइ ॲ मॅन्ड n.* a very hard precious stone हीरा।

diarrhoea *डॉइ ॲ रि ॲ n.* excessive frequency of bowel movements अतिसार, दस्त।

diary *डॉइ ॲ रि n.* a register of daily events दैनंदिनी, डायरी।

dice[1] *डॉइस n. pl.* small cubes marked with spots (1 to 6) on the sides पासे।

dice[2] *v. i.* to play with dice पासे का खेल खेलना।

dictate *डिक् टेट v. t.* to deliver as an order आदेश देना; to say or read for another, to transcribe लिखवाना।

dictation *डिक् टे शॅन n* dictating श्रुतलेख; order or direction आदेश।

dictator *डिक् टे टॅः n.* one invested with absolute authority तानाशाह, अधिनायक।

diction *डिक् शॅन n.* choice of words शब्द-चयन।

dictionary *डिक् शॅ नॅ रि n.* a book containing the words arranged alphabetically with their meanings शब्दकोश।

dictum *डिक् टॅम n.* an authoritative saying आदेश-वाक्य; maxim सिद्धांत-वाक्य।

didactic *डॉइ डैक् टिक a.* designed to teach उपदेशात्मक।

die[1] *डॉइ v. i.* to come to the end of life मरना; to come to an end नष्ट होना।

die[2] *n.* small cube with numbered faces पासा।

diet *डॉइ ॲट n.* food भोजन; food prescribed medically पथ्य।

differ *डि फ़ॅः v. i.* to vary पृथक् होना; to disagree असहमत होना; to be unlike असमान होना।

difference *डि फ़ॅ रॅन्स n.* discrimination भेदभाव; unlikeness असमानता; dissimilarity भिन्नता; disagreement मतभेद।

different *डि फ़ॅ रॅन्ट a.* separate भिन्न; dissimilar असमान।

difficult *डि फ़ि कॅल्ट a.* not easy दुर्बोध, जटिल hard to please कठिनाई से प्रसन्न होने वाला।

difficulty *डि फ़ि कॅल् टि n.* hardness to be done कठिनाई; obstacle बाधा।

dig[1] *डिग n.* excavation खुदाई।

dig[2] *(-gg-) v.t.* to break up (ground) with a spade खोदना।

digest[1] *डॉइ जैस्ट; डि v. t.* prepare (food) in the stomach for assimilation पचाना; to think over carefully and take into the mind आत्मसात करना।

digest² *डॉइ जैस्ट n.* a collection (of laws) संकलन, संग्रह; systematic summary सार, संकलन।

digestion *डि जै˘ श्‌न n.* act of digesting पाचन; process or power of digesting food पाचन-क्रिया।

digit *डि जिट n.* a finger उंगली; anyone of the figures (0 to 9) अंक।

dignify *डिग् नि फ़ॉइ v.t.* to invest with dignity शोभायुक्त करना, गौरवान्वित करना।

dignity *डिग् नि टि n.* honourable place गौरवपूर्ण स्थान।

dilemma *डि लै˘ मॅ, डॉइ– n.* a situation of difficult or doubtful choice दुविधा।

diligence *डि लि जॅन्स n.* steady application परिश्रम, उद्यम।

diligent *डि लि जॅन्ट a.* steady in application, industrious परिश्रमी।

dilute¹ *डॉइ ल्यूट v. t.* to make thinner पतला करना; *v.i.* to become thinner पतला होना।

dilute² *a.* weakened by diluting पतला।

dim¹ *डिम a.* not bright धुंधला; not seen clearly अस्पष्ट।

dim² *(-mm-) v. t.* to make dim धुंधला करना; *v.i.* to become dim धुंधला होना।

dimension *डि मैन्‌ श्‌न, डॉइ– n.* extention in a single direction आयाम; *(pl.)* measure of a thing, its size, capacity etc. लंबाई-चौड़ाई।

diminish *डि मि निश v. t.* to make less कम करना; *v.i.* to grow less कम होना।

din *डिन n.* loud continued noise कोलाहल।

dine *डॉइन v. t.* to host dinner खाना खिलाना; *v.i.* to have dinner भोजन करना।

dinner *डि नॅः n.* banquet प्रीतिभोज; main meal of the day भोजन।

dip¹ *डिप n.* act of dipping ग़ोता; hollow गड्ढा।

dip² *(-pp-) v. t.* to put (something) into liquid डुबकी देना; *v.i.* to plunge ग़ोता लगाना।

diploma *डि प्लो मॅ n.* educational certificate प्रमाण-पत्र।

diplomacy *डि प्लो मॅ सि n.* the art or practice of conducting international negotiations कूटनीति; skill in dealing with people व्यवहार-कुशलता।

diplomat *डिप् लॅ मैट n.* one engaged in official diplomacy राजनयिक; person clever at dealing with people कूटनीतिज्ञ।

diplomatic *डिप् लॅ मै टिक a.* pertaining to diplomacy कूट-नीतिक।

dire *डॉइअॅः a.* terrible, dreadful भयानक, भीषण।

direct¹ *डि रैक्ट, डॉइ–, डॅ– a.* straight सीधा; not ambiguous सुस्पष्ट; immediate तात्कालिक।

direct² *v. t.* to point or aim at (की ओर) संकेत या लक्ष्य करना; to show the right course to मार्ग दिखाना; to conduct संचालन करना; to order आदेश देना।

direction *डि रैक् श्‌न, डॉइ– n.* act of directing संचालन; guidance मार्गदर्शन; command निर्देश; control नियंत्रण।

director *डि रैक् टः, डॉइ–* *n.* one who directs निर्देशक।

directory *डि रैक् टॅ रि* *n.* reference book with the list of persons with various details निर्देशिका।

dirt *डॅःट* *n.* mud कीचड़; dust धूल; any filthy substance गंदगी।

dirty *डॅः टि* *a.* unclean मलिन; filthy गंदा।

disability *डिस् अॅ बि लि टि* *n.* lack of ability अक्षमता; state of being disabled विकलांगता।

disable *डिस् ए ब्ल* *v. t.* to make unable अक्षम बनाना; to cripple विकलांग बनाना।

disabled *डिस् ए ब्ल्ड* *a.* crippled विकलांग।

disadvantage *डिस् अॅड् वान् टिज* *n.* unfavourable circumstance प्रतिकूल अवस्था; hindrance बाधा।

disagree *डिस् अॅ ग्री* *v. i.* to have different opinions असहमत होना; to prove unsuitable अनुपयुक्त सिद्ध होना।

disagreeable *डिस् अॅ ग्रि अॅ ब्ल* *a.* unpleasant अरुचिकर, अप्रिय; unsuitable प्रतिकूल।

disagreement *डिस् अॅ ग्री मॅन्ट* *n.* absence of agreement असहमति; difference of opinion मतभेद।

disappear *डिस् अॅ पिअॅः* *v. i.* to vanish from sight अदृश्य होना।

disappearance *डिस् अॅ पिअॅ रॅन्स* *n.* disappearing लोप, तिरोभाव।

disappoint *डिस् अॅ पौ ॅइन्ट* *v. t.* to frustrate हताश करना to defeat the fulfilment of निष्फल करना।

disapproval *डिस् अॅ प्रू वॅल* *n.* disapproving निरनुमोदन, अस्वीकार।

disapprove *डिस् अॅ प्रूव* *v. t.* to reject अस्वीकृत करना; to censure (की) निंदा करना।

disarm *डिस् आःम* *v. t.* to deprive of arms निःशस्त्र करना।

disarmament *डिस् आः मॅ मॅन्ट* *n.* act or state of being disarmed निःशस्त्रीकरण।

disaster *डि ज़ास् ट्रॅः* *n.* calamity आपदा; sudden misfortune दुर्भाग्य।

disastrous *डि ज़ास् ट्रॅस* *a.* calamitous संकटपूर्ण; ruinous विनाशपूर्ण।

disc *डिस्क* *n.* thin, flat, circular object like a coin चकती।

discard *डिस् कॉःड* *v. t.* to throw away निकाल फेंकना; to reject रद्द करना।

discharge[1] *डिस् चाःज* *v. t.* to unload भारमुक्त करना; to relieve of a charge सेवा मुक्त करना; to fire (a gun) (गोली) चलाना; to perform अदा या पूरा करना।

discharge[2] *n.* release मुक्ति; unloading अवतारण; dismissal बरखास्तगी; emission रिसाव, बहाव; performance पालन, संपादन; payment अदायगी।

disciple *डि सॉइ प्ल* *n.* follower अनुयायी।

discipline *डि सि प्लिन* *n.* slef-control आत्मसंयम; training शिक्षण; orderly conduct अनुशासन; a subject or field of study अध्ययन का विषय या क्षेत्र।

disclose *डिस् क्लोज़* *v. t.* to reveal प्रकट करना।

discomfort *डिस् कर्मफॅःट* *n.* uneasi-

ness असुविधा, बेचैनी।
disconnect *डिस् कॅ नैक्ट v. t.* to detach वियोजित करना।
discontent *डिस् कॅन् टैन्ट n.* dissatisfaction असंतोष।
discontinue *डिस् कॅन् टि न्यू v. t.* to give up त्याग देना; to put an end to समाप्त कर देना; *v. i.* to come to an end समाप्त हो जाना, रुक जाना।
discord *डिस् कौःड n.* strife अनबन, कलह; disagreement विसंगति; dissonance बेसुरापन।
discount *डिस् कॉउन्ट n.* reduction छूट।
discourage *डिस् कॅ रिज v. t.* to dissuade हतोत्साह करना।
discourse *डिस् कौःस् n.* a speech or lecture प्रवचन।
discourteous *डिस् कॅः टि अॅस a.* impolite अविनीत; rude अभद्र।
discover *डिस् कवॅः v. t.* to find out पता लगाना, खोजना।
discovery *डिस् क वॅ रि n.* act of discovering अन्वेषण; thing discovered खोजी गई वस्तु।
discretion *डिस् क्रै ॅ शॅन n.* prudence समझदारी; freedom to act as one thinks fit स्वविवेक।
discriminate *डिस् क्रि मि नेट v. t.* to distinguish between (में) भेद करना; to single out for special favour पक्षपात करना; *v.i.* to be discerning पहचान करना।
discrimination *डिस् क्रि मि ने शॅन n.* ability to discriminate विभेदन-क्षमता; partiality पक्षपात।
discuss *डिस् कस v. t.* to hold conversation about (पर) विचार-विनिमय करना।
disdain[1] *डिस् डेन n.* scorn घृणा।
disdain[2] *v. t.* to scorn घृणा करना।
disease *डि ज़ीज़ n.* sickness बीमारी।
disguise[1] *डिस् गॉइज़ n.* disguised state छद्मवेश।
disguise[2] *v. t.* to change the appearance of (का) वेश बदलना; to hide the truth of छिपाना।
dish *डिश n.* plate, bowl etc. used for serving food तश्तरी; contents of dish तश्तरी-भर।
dishearten *डिस् हाः ट्न v. t.* to cause to lose courage or confidence हतोत्साह करना।
dishonest *डिस् औॅ निस्ट a.* not honest बेईमान।
dishonesty *डिस् औॅ निस् टि n.* being dishonest बेईमानी।
dishonour[1] *डिस् औॅ नॅः v. t.* to treat disgracefully अनादर करना; to refuse to pay (a cheque) (चेक को) अस्वीकृत करना।
dishonour[2] *n.* want of honour अनादर; person or thing that brings disgrace अनादर का कारण।
dislike[1] *डिस् लॉइक v. t.* not to like नापसंद करना।
dislike[2] *n.* feeling of not liking अरुचि, नफ़रत।
disloyal *डिस् लौॅइ अॅल a.* unfaithful विश्वासघाती।
dismiss *डिस् मिस v. t.* to reject (law suit) without further hearing खारिज़ करना; to send away बर्खास्त करना।
dismissal *डिस् मि सॅल n.* dismissing or being dismissed बरख़ास्तगी।
disobey *डिस् अॅ बे v. t.* to refuse or fail to obey अवज्ञा करना।

disorder *डिस् औः डॅः n.* confusion अव्यवस्था; slight illness विकार; rioting उपद्रव।

disparity *डिस् पै रि टि n.* inequality असमानता; great difference अंतर।

dispensary *डिस् पैन् सॅ रि n.* a place where medicines are dispensed औषधालय, दवाखाना।

disperse *डिस् पॅःस v. t.* to scatter बिखेरना; to diffuse छितराना।

displace *डिस् प्लेस v. t.* to remove from its place विस्थापित करना; to remove from office पदच्युत करना।

display[1] *डिस प्ले v. t.* to exhibit प्रदर्शित करना।

display[2] *n.* exhibition प्रदर्शन।

displease *डिस प्लीज़ v. t.* to annoy, to offend नाराज़ करना।

displeasure *डिस् प्लै ˘ ज़ॅः n.* annoyance, anger नाराज़गी, क्रोध।

disposal *डिस् पो ज़ॅल n.* act or power of disposing व्यवस्था; selling विक्रय; control नियंत्रण; getting rid of निपटारा।

dispose *डिस् पोज़ v. t.* to arrange व्यवस्थित करना; to settle मामला निपटाना; to incline प्रवृत्त करना।

disprove *डिस् प्रूव v. t.* to prove false असत्य सिद्ध करना।

dispute[1] *डिस् प्यूट n.* controversy विवाद; quarrel झगड़ा।

dispute[2] *v. i.* to discuss विचार–विमर्श करना; *v.t.* to call in question संदेह करना; to argue तर्क-वितर्क करना।

disqualification *डिस क्वौ ˘ लि फ़ि के शॅन n.* disqualifying or being disqualified अयोग्यता; that which disqualifies अयोग्यता का आधार।

disqualify *डिस् क्वौ ˘ लि फ़ॉइ v. t.* to make ineligible अयोग्य ठहराना या बनाना।

disquiet *डिस् क्वॉइ ॲट n.* uneasiness बेचैनी; anxiety चिंता।

disregard[1] *डिस् रि गाःड n.* neglect उपेक्षा; insult अपमान।

disregard[2] *v. t.* to pay no attention to उपेक्षा करना।

disrepute *डिस् रि प्यूट n.* bad name, disgrace अपयश, बदनामी।

disrespect *डिस् रिस् पैक्ट n.* want of respect अनादर।

disrupt *डिस रप्ट v. t.* to break up भंग करना।

dissatisfaction *डिस् सै टिस् फ़ैक् शॅन n.* state of being dissatisfied असंतोष।

dissatisfy *डिस् सै टिस् फ़ॉइ v. t.* to fail to satisfy असंतुष्ट करना, नाराज़ करना।

dissect *डि सैक्ट v. t.* to cut apart काटना, विच्छेदन करना; to examine or criticise in detail अवलोकन अथवा आलोचना करना।

dissection *डि सैक् शॅन n.* act of cutting up anatomically विच्छेदन; act of separating into parts for the purpose of critical examination विश्लेषण।

dissimilar *डि सि मि लॅः a.* not similar असमान।

dissolve *डि ज़ौल्व v.t.* to melt पिघलाना; to put an end to समाप्त करना; *v. i.* to be melted पिघलना; to disappear लुप्त होना।

dissuade *डि स्वेड v. t.* to exhort

against, to persuade not to न करने के लिए समझाना।

distance *डिस् टॅन्स n.* extent of interval between two things दूरी, फ़ासला; aloofness अलगाव।

distant *डिस् टॅन्ट a.* not close दूर का; lying at a distance दूरस्थ।

distil *डिस् टिल (-ll-) v. t.* to vaporise and recondense (a liquid) आसवन करना; to purify शुद्ध करना; *v.i.* to tickle down, to fall in drops टपकना।

distillery *डिस् टि लॅ रि n.* the building where distilling is carried on आसवनी।

distinct *डिस् टिङ्क्ट a.* separated by some mark पृथक्, अलग; definite निश्चित; clear स्पष्ट।

distinction *डिस् टिङ्क् शॅन n.* difference अंतर; special honour विशेष सम्मान; unusual quality विशिष्टता।

distinguish *डिस् टिङग्विश v. i.* to recognize difference अंतर लाना या समझना; *v.t.* to recognise पहचानना; to honour सम्मानित करना।

distort *डिस् टौःट v. t.* to twist तोड़-मरोड़ देना; to put out of shape विकृत करना।

distress[1] *डिस् ट्रैसॅ n.* anguish of body or mind कष्ट, परेशानी; affliction मुसीबत।

distress[2] *v. t.* to afflict with pain or anguish परेशान करना।

distribute *डिस् ट्रि ब्यूट v. t.* to deal out बांटना, वितरित करना; to spread फैलाना।

distribution *डिस् ट्रिब्यू शॅन n.* act of distributing वितरण; spreading over a large area फैलाव, विस्तार; division विभाजन।

district *डिस् ट्रिक्ट n.* an administrative unit जनपद, ज़िला।

distrust[1] *डिस् ट्रस्ट n.* lack of trust अविश्वास।

distrust[2] *v. t.* to have no trust in (में) विश्वास न रखना।

disturb *डिस् टःब v. t.* to throw into disorder अस्तव्यस्त करना; to agitate उत्तेजित करना; to interrupt बाधा डालना।

ditch डिच *n.* a long narrow channel dug into the earth खाई।

ditto *डि टो n.* the same (as stated before) यथोपरि; ditto mark („) तथैव चिह्न (”)।

dive[1] *डॉइव v. i.* to plunge under surface of water ग़ोता लगाना; to go under water पानी के नीचे जाना; to go to a lower level नीचे स्तर पर आ जाना।

dive[2] *n.* act of diving गोता; a descent under water पानी के नीचे पैठ; a plunge down through the air हवा में नीचे की ओर झपट्टा।

diverse *डॉइ वॅःस,* ***डॉइ*** *वॅःस a.* various, different विविध।

divert *डॉइ वॅःट v. t.* to turn aside मोड़ना, ध्यान हटाना; to amuse मनोरंजन करना।

divide *डि वॉइड v. t.* to separate into parts विभक्त करना; to cause to disagree मतभेद पैदा करना; to distribute बांटना; *v. i.* to be separated विभक्त होना।

divine *डि वॉइन a.* heavenly, like a god दैवी, दिव्य; excellent उत्कृष्ट।

divinity *डि वि नि टि n.* the state of being divine दिव्यता; the study of theology धर्मशास्त्र; a god or deity देवता।

division *डि वि ज़ॅन n.* act of dividing विभाजन; separation अलगाव; partition बंटवारा; disagreement मतभेद; part of an army (सेना में) डिवीज़न।

divorce[1] *डिवौःस* legal dissolution of marriage तलाक़; separation अलगाव।

divorce[2] *v. t.* to put away by divorce तलाक़ देना।

divulge *डॉइ वॅल्ज v. t.* to disclose प्रकट करना।

do *डू, डु v. t.* to perform करना; to finish पूरा करना; to work out हल करना; to suit (के लिए) उपयुक्त होना; to have as a job पेशे के रूप में करना।

docile *डो सॉइल a.* submissive विनम्र; easily managed वश्य।

dock *डौकॅ n. (pl.)* dockyard गोदी; place in court where a prisoner stands कटघरा।

doctor *डौकॅ् टॅः n.* a qualified practitioner of medicine चिकित्सक; person who holds doctorate विद्यावारिधि।

doctorate *डौकॅ् टॅ रिट n.* the degree of a doctor डॉक्टर की उपाधि।

doctrine *डौकॅ् ट्रिन n.* set of principles सिद्धांत, मत।

document *डौ˘ क्यु मॅन्ट n.* written proof or evidence दस्तावेज़।

dodge[1] *डौ˘ ज n.* dodging चकमा।

dodge[2] *v. t.* to evade by cunning चकमा देना।

doe *डो n.* the female of deer, rabbit etc. मृग, ख़रगोश आदि की मादा।

dog[1] *डौगॅ n.* a domesticated animal of the wolf family कुत्ता।

dog[2] *(-gg-) v. t.* to keep close behind पीछा करना।

dogma *डौगॅ् मॅ n.* a doctrine or belief धर्ममत।

dogmatic *डौगॅ् मै टिक a.* relating to dogma धर्ममत-संबंधी।

doll *डौ˘ल n.* a child's toy गुड़िया।

dollar *डौ˘ लॅः n.* the unit of money in U.S.A. and some other countries डॉलर।

domain *डॅ मेन n.* territory under one government शासन-क्षेत्र; field of knowledge ज्ञानक्षेत्र।

dome *डोम n.* hemispherical roof गुंबद।

domestic[1] *डॅ मैसॅ् टिक, डो˘– a.* of the household घरेलू; not foreign देशीय; tamed (animals) पालतू।

domestic[2] *n.* a household servant घरेलू नौकर।

domicile *डौ˘ मि सॉइल, – सिल n.* family residence आवास।

dominant *डौ˘ मि नॅन्ट a.* governing प्रमुख; ascendant ऊर्ध्वगामी।

dominate *डौ˘ मि नेट v. t.* to rule शासन करना; to predominate over (से) श्रेष्ठ होना।

domination *डौ˘ मि ने शॅन n.* rule शासन; superiority श्रेष्ठता।

dominion *डॅ मि नि अॅन n.* sovereign authority प्रभुत्व; a governed territory उपनिवेश।

donate *डो˘ नेट v. t.* to make a donation of दानस्वरूप देना।

donation डोॅ ने शॅन *n.* (act of) giving दान।

donkey डौॅङ् कि *n.* ass गधा।

donor डोनॅः *n.* one who donates दाता, दानी।

doom[1] डूम *n.* fate भाग्य; ruin विनाश; judicial sentence सज़ा।

doom[2] *v. t.* to condemn to punishment दंड देना; to destine to destrucrtion (के) भाग्य में विनाश बदा होना।

door डौः, डौॅः *n.* the entrance of a house or room दरवाज़ा; means of approach प्रवेश-मार्ग।

dose डोज़ *n.* the quantity of medicine given at one time खुराक।

dot[1] डौॅट *n.* a small round spot बिंदु।

dot[2] *(-tt-) v. t.* to mark with a dot or dots बिंदु लगाना; to sprinkle छितराना।

double[1] ड बल *a.* twofold दोगुना; forming a pair युग्मित; deceitful धोखेबाज़।

double[2] *v. t.* to make two-fold दोहरा करना; to increase by adding an equal amount to दोगुना करना।

double[3] *n.* twice as much दोगुनी मात्रा; a duplicate प्रतिरूप।

doubt[1] डॉउट *v. i.* to waver in opinion of judgment संदेह करना; to suspect शंका करना; *v.t.* to deem uncertain अनिश्चित मानना; to distrust विश्वास न करना।

doubt[2] *n.* a wavering in opinion ऊहापोह; uncertainty अनिश्चितता; suspicion शंका, संदेह।

dough डो *n.* pasty mass of flour गुँथा हुआ आटा।

dove डव *n.* a pigeon पड़की, फ़ाखता।

down[1] डॉउन *adv.* to, in or towards a lower position नीचे की ओर; immediately तुरंत।

down[2] *prep.* from a higher part to a lower part of के नीचे की ओर; at a lower part of के निचले भाग में; along के किनारे।

down[3] *v. t.* to hit and make fall मारकर गिरा देना।

downfall डॉउन् फौल *n.* a fall from power पतन; cause of ruin बर्बादी का कारण।

downpour डॉउन् पौः *n.* heavy rainfall भारी वर्षा।

downright[1] डॉउन् रॉइट *adv.* completely पूरी तरह से।

downright[2] *a.* straight forward स्पष्टवादी।

downward डॉउन् वॅःड *a.* moving, going, to what is low अधोगामी।

downward, downwards डॉउन् वॅःड्ज़ *adv.* towards what is lower नीचे की ओर।

dowry डॉउ रि *n.* property which a woman brings to her husband in marriage दहेज।

doze[1] डोज़ *n.* a nap ऊँघ, झपकी।

doze[2] *v. i.* to sleep lightly ऊँघना।

dozen ड ज़न *n.* a set of twelve दर्जन।

draft[1] ड्राफ्ट *v. t.* to draw the preliminary version or plan of (का) प्रारूप तैयार करना।

draft[2] *n.* a written order for payment of money बैंक ड्राफ्ट; a preliminary version मसविदा।

draftsman ड्राफ़्ट्स् मॅन *a.* one who

drafts documents or makes plans दस्तावेज़-लेखक, नक़्शानवीस।

drag[1] *ड्रैग* *n.* obstruction to progress बाधा।

drag[2] *(-gg-) v. t.* to pull along with effort घसीटना।

dragon *ड्रै गॅन* *n.* a mythical winged reptile सपक्ष नाग; a fierce person खूंखार व्यक्ति।

drain[1] *ड्रेन* *n.* a channel for removing liquid अपवाहिका; sewer गंदी नाली।

drain[2] *v. t.* to draw off gradually धीरे-धीरे निकालना; *v.i.* to flow off बह जाना।

drainage *ड्रे निज* *n.* draining जलनिकास; system of drains जल-प्रणाली।

dram *ड्रैम* *n.* a small drink of liquor (मदिरा का) छोटा घूंट; a unit of measure (1/16 or 1/8 of an ounce) ड्राम (1/16 या 1/8) औंस।

drama *ड्रा मॅ* *n.* stage-play नाटक; series of events घटनाचक्र।

dramatic *ड्रॅ मै टिक* *a.* pertaining to drama नाटक-संबंधी; exciting उत्तेजक; sudden आकस्मिक।

dramatist *ड्रै मॅ टिस्ट* *n.* a writer of plays नाटककार।

draper *ड्रे पॅ:* *n.* dealer in cloth and cloth goods वस्त्र विक्रेता।

drastic *ड्रैस् टिक* *a.* forceful, severe कठोर, प्रबल।

draught[1] *ड्राफ़्ट* *n.* current of air through apertures झिरियों में से आने वाली हवा; act of drawing खिंचाव; dose of medicine दवा की खुराक; act of drinking पान, पीने की क्रिया; quantity drunk at once घूंट; plan or layout मसौदा; quantity of fish caught in a net एक बार में जाल में फंसी मछली।

draught[2] *v.t.* see draft.

draw[1] *ड्रौ* *v.t.* to pull along खींचना, घसीटना; to inhale (सांस) लेना; to sketch अंकित करना; to attract आकर्षित करना; to take from (well, etc.) निकालना; to receive (from bank) (बैंक से) निकालना।

draw[2] *n.* act of drawing कर्षण; unfinished game अनिर्णीत खेल।

drawback *ड्रौ बैक* *n.* shortcoming कमी, त्रुटि; disadvantage असुविधा।

drawer *ड्रौ:, ड्रौ ॅ अॅ:* *n.* a box-like container which slides in and out of furniture दराज; one who draws pictures चित्रकार; one who draws money धन निकालने वाला; *(pl.)* an undergarment जांघिया।

drawing *ड्रौ इङ्ग* *n.* art of drawing by lines चित्रांकन; a picture in lines चित्रकारी।

drawing-room *ड्रौ इङ्ग् रूम* *n.* a sitting room बैठक।

dread[1] *ड्रैॅड* *n.* object of fear विभीषिका; great fear भय, आशंका।

dread[2] *v.t.* to fear greatly (से) भयभीत होना।

dread[3] *a.* exciting fear आतंकमय।

dream[1] *ड्रीम* *n.* vision during sleep स्वप्न; reverie दिवास्वप्न।

dream[2] *v. i.* to fancy things during sleep स्वप्न देखना; *v.t.* to see or imagine in a dream स्वप्न में देखना।

drench *ड्रैॅन्च* *v. t.* to make thoroughly wet सराबोर कर देना।

dress[1] *ड्रैसॅ* *n.* clothing, garment पोशाक, परिधान।

dress[2] *v. t.* to clothe (वस्त्र) पहनाना; to apply dressing to (पर) पट्टी बांधना; to prepare (food) for table (भोजन) तैयार करना; *v.i.* to put on clothes वस्त्र पहनना।

dressing *ड्रै ˘ सिङ्ग* *n.* dress or clothes वस्त्र, परिधान; bandage मरहमपट्टी।

drill[1] *ड्रिल* *n.* pointed instrument for making holes बरमा, बेधनी; physical training क़वायद, ड्रिल।

drill[2] *v. t.* to bore (में) छेद करना।

drink[1] *ड्रिङ्क* *n.* liquid for drinking पेयपदार्थ; liquor शराब।

drink[2] *v. t.* to take in (liquid) पीना; *v.i.* to take alcohol शराबी होना।

drip[1] *ड्रिप* *n.* action or sound of falling in drops टपकन, चुअन।

drip[2] *(-pp-)* *v. i.* to fall in drops टपकना; *v. t.* to cause to fall in drops टपकाना।

drive[1] *ड्रॉइव* *v. t.* to cause to move हांकना; to operate and steer (car etc.) (कार आदि) चलाना; to force (a nail etc.) ठोंकना; to convey in vehicle वाहन-द्वारा ले जाना; to urge, to impel बाध्य करना; *v.i.* to keep car etc. going कार चलाना; to go by car etc. कार आदि द्वारा जाना।

drive[2] *n.* act of driving संचालन; journey in a vehicle; सवारी से यात्रा; campaign आंदोलन।

driver *ड्रॉइ वँः* *n.* one who drives चालक।

drizzle[1] *ड्रि ज़्ल* *n.* rain in fine drops फुहार।

drizzle[2] *v. i.* to rain in small drops फुहार पड़ना।

drop[1] *ड्रौपॅ* *n.* tiny ball of liquid बूंद; fall पतन।

drop[2] *(-pp-)* *v. i.* to fall in drops टपकना; to fall गिरना; *v. t.* to cause to fall in drops टपकाना; to allow to fall गिराना।

drought *ड्रॉउट* *n.* continuous failure of rain अनावृष्टि, सूखा।

drown *ड्रॉउन* *v.i.* to die by suffocation in water डूबकर मरना; *v.t.* to kill by suffocation in water डुबाकर मारना; to submerge डुबा देना।

drug *ड्रग* *n.* medical substance औषधि; narcotic नशीली वस्तु।

druggist *ड्र गिस्ट* *n.* person who sells drugs औषध-विक्रेता।

drum[1] *ड्रम* *n.* musical instrument sounded by beating ढोल, नगाड़ा, tympanum of the ear कान का परदा; cylindrical barrel पीपा।

drum[2] *(-mm-)* *v.i.* to play a drum ढोल बजाना।

drunkard *ड्रङ्कॅःड* *n.* drunken person शराबी।

dry[1] *ड्रॉइ* *a.* not wet सूखा; not interesting नीरस; indifferent उदासीन; having prohibition शराबबंदी वाला।

dry[2] *v. i.* to become dry सूखना; *v.t.* to remove the moisture from सुखाना।

dual *ड्यूअॅल* *a.* two- fold दोहरा; of two द्वैत।

duck[1] *डक* *n.* common water-bird बतख़।

duck² *v.i.* to dip under water डुबकी लगाना; to escape by hiding छिपकर भाग निकलना।

due¹ *ड्यू a.* payable देय; that ought to be paid प्राप्य; proper उचित।

due² *n.* that which is owed उधार, ऋण; anything due दातव्यधन; right अधिकार; (*pl.*) fees शुल्क।

due³ *adv.* exactly बिल्कुल; directly सीधा।

duel¹ *ड्यु ॲल, ड्यू– n.* two-sided contest द्वंद्वयुद्ध।

duel² *डयु ॲल (-ll-) v. i.* to fight a duel द्वंद्वयुद्ध करना।

duke *ड्यूक n.* sovereign of a small state शासक, राजा।

dull¹ *डल a.* sluggish मंद; dim निष्प्रभ; cheerless उदास; blunt कुंठित; not brisk निष्क्रिय।

dull² *v. t.* to make dull मंद बनाना; to make dim धुंधला करना; *v.i.* to become dull मंद होना।

duly *ड्यू लि adv.* in a proper way विधिवत्।

dumb *डम a.* unable to speak गूंगा।

dunce *डन्स n.* stupid person मूर्ख आदमी।

dung *डङ्ग n.* animal excreta गोबर।

duplicate¹ *ड्यू प्लि किट a.* exactly like मिलता-जुलता।

duplicate² *n.* exact copy प्रतिलिपि।

duplicate³ *ड्यू प्लि केट v. t.* to make an exact copy of (की) प्रतिलिपि बनाना।

duplicity *ड्यु प्लि सि टि n.* double dealing दुरंगापन, कपट।

durable *डयूअॅ रॅ बल a.* long lasting स्थायी, टिकाऊ।

duration *ड्युअॅ रे शॅन n.* time a thing continues कालावधि।

during *डयूअॅ रिङ्ग prep.* in the course of पर्यंत।

dusk *डस्क n.* twilight गोधूलि।

dust¹ *डस्ट n.* finely powdered dirt धूल।

dust² *v.t.* to remove dust form (से) धूल झाड़ना।

duster *डस् टॅः n.* a cloth for removing dust झाड़न।

dutiful *ड्यू टि फुल a.* attentive to duty कर्त्तव्यनिष्ठ।

duty *ड्यू टि n.* moral or legal obligation कर्त्तव्य; tax on import or export शुल्क, कर।

dwarf *ड्वौःफ़ n.* very undersized person बौना।

dwell *ड्वैॅल v. i.* to live in a place रहना, बसना।

dwelling *ड्वैॅ लिङ्ग n.* habitation, house घर, निवास-स्थान।

dwindle *डिविन् ड्ल v. t.* to diminish gradually, to decline क्षीण होना।

dye¹ *डॉइ v. t.* to give a new and permanent colour to रंगना।

dye² *n.* a colouring substance रंग।

dynamic *डॉइ नै मिक a.* concerned with force गत्यात्मक; very energetic स्फूर्त।

dynamics *डॉइ नै मिक्स n. pl.* the science which investigates the action of force गतिविज्ञान।

dynamite *डॉइ नॅ मॉइट n.* powerful explosive बारूद।

dynamo *डॉइ नॅ मो n.* machine that generates electricity विद्युत् शक्ति-यंत्र।

dynasty *डि नॅस् टि, डॉइ–* *n.* succession of rulers belonging to one family राजवंश।

dysentery *डि सॅन् ट्रि* *n.* disease characterized by diarrhoea with blood and mucus पेचिश।

Ee

E *ई* the fifith letter of the English alphabet, the third note of the natural diatonic scale. अंग्रेजी वर्णमाला का पाँचवाँ अक्षर, गायन में तृतीय स्वर।

each[1] *ईच* *a.* every one separately considered प्रत्येक।

each[2] *pron.* each thing, person, group etc. प्रत्येक।

eager *ई गॅ:* *a.* excited by desire व्यग्र; keen इच्छुक।

eagle *ई ग्ल* *n.* a large bird of prey गरुड़।

ear *इअॅ:* *n.* organ of hearing कान; a spike, as of corn बाली।

early[1] *अॅ: लि* *adv.* before the usual time सामान्य समय से पूर्व; in the first part of the day सवेरे के समय।

early[2] *a.* appearing before expected आशा से पूर्व होनेवाला; belonging to the first part of the day सवेरे-सवेरे होनेवाला; referring to the near future निकट भविष्य से संबद्ध।

earn *अॅ:न* *v. t.* to gain by labour अर्जित करना; to deserve (के) योग्य होना।

earnest *अॅ: निस्ट* *a.* ardent, zealous जोशीला; serious गंभीर।

earth *अॅ:थ* *n.* the globe we inhabit पृथ्वी; the world सृष्टि; dry land स्थल; the soil मिट्टी।

earthen *अॅ: थॅन* *a.* made of earth मृण्मय।

earthly *अॅ:थ् लि* *a.* worldly सांसारिक।

earthquake *अॅ:थ् क्वेक* *n.* a shaking of the earth भूकंप।

ease[1] *ईज़* *n.* freedom from difficulty चैन; rest आराम; facility सुगमता।

ease[2] *v. t.* to give ease to सुविधा देना; to free from pain (का) दुःख दूर करना; to free from trouble (का) कष्ट निवारण करना।

east[1] *ईस्ट* *n.* the part of the sky where the sun rises पूर्व दिशा।

east[2] *adv.* in or toward the east पूर्व की ओर।

east[3] *a.* of the east पूर्वीय।

easter *ईस् टॅ:,* *n.* Christian festival held on Sunday after Good Friday ईस्टर, पुनरुत्थान पर्व।

eastern *ईस् टॅ:न* *a.* belonging to the east पूर्व-संबंधी; oriental प्राच्य।

easy *ई ज़ि* *a.* not difficult सरल; carefree निश्चित; comfortable आरामदेह।

eat *ईट* *v. t.* to chew and swallow (food) खाना; to destroy नष्ट करना; *v.i.* to take food भोजन करना।

eatable[1] *ईटॅ ब्ल* *n.* (*pl.*) anything used as food खाद्य पदार्थ।

eatable[2] *a.* fit to be eaten खाने-योग्य।

ebb[1] *ऐ ॅब* *n.* flowing back of tide भाटा, उतार; decline अवनति।

ebb[2] *v. i.* to flow back उतर जाना; to decay क्षीण हो जाना, कमज़ोर पड़ना।

ebony *ऐॅबॅ नि* *n.* black wood आबनूस।

echo[1] *ऐ ॅ को* *n.* repetition of a sound by reflection प्रतिध्वनि ।

echo[2] *v. t.* to repeat, as echo प्रतिध्वनित करना; to imitate closely (की) अनुकृति करना; *v.i.* to resound गूंजना; to be repeated दोहराया जाना।

eclipse *इ क्लिप्स* *n.* obscuring of light from one heavenly body by another ग्रहण।

economic *ई कॅ नौ ॅ मिक, ऐ ॅ–* *a.* pertaining to economy आर्थिक।

economical *ई कॅ नौ ॅ मि कॅल* *a.* frugal मितव्ययी।

economics *ई कॅ नौ ॅ मिक्स, ऐ ॅ–* *n.* (*sing.*) science dealing with wealth अर्थशास्त्र।

economy *ई कौ ॅ नॅ मि* *n.* structure of economic life अर्थव्यवस्था; thrifty use of resourses मितव्ययिता।

edge *ऐॅज* *n.* cutting side of a blade धार; border किनारा।

edible *ऐ ॅ डि ब्ल* *a.* fit to be eaten भोज्य।

edifice *ऐ ॅ डि फ़िस* *n.* large building भवन।

edit *ऐॅ डिट* *v. t.* to prepare (book, film, etc.) for publication संपादन करना।

edition *इ डि शॅन* *n.* form in which something is published संपादन का स्वरूप; number of copies of a new publication संस्करण।

editor *ऐ ॅ डि टॅः* *n.* one who edits a book, film, etc. संपादक।

editorial[1] *ऐ ॅ डि टौ रि ॲल* *a.* pertaining to or written by an editor संपादकीय।

editorial[2] *n.* an article written by an editor संपादकीय लेख।

educate *ऐ ॅ ड्यु केट* *v. t.* to teach, train or develop by schooling शिक्षा देना।

education *ऐ ॅ ड्यु के शॅन* *n.* act of educating शिक्षण; instruction and discipline शिक्षा।

efface *इ फ़ेस* *v. t.* to rub or wipe out रगड़कर मिटा देना।

effect[1] *इ फ़ैक्ट* *n.* impression प्रभाव; result परिणाम; (*pl.*) property संपत्ति।

effect[2] *v. t.* to produce उत्पन्न करना; to execute अमल में लाना।

effective *इ फ़ैक् टिव* *a.* producing the effect desired or intended प्रभावशाली।

effeminate *इ फ़ै ॅ मि निट* *a.* womanish, unmanly स्त्रैण, पौरुषहीन, कायर।

efficacy *ऐ ॅ फ़ि कॅ सि* *n.* power to produce effect प्रभावोत्पादकता।

efficiency *इ फ़ि शॅन् सि* *n.* competence निपुणता, क्षमता।

efficient *इ फ़ि शॅन्ट* *a.* capable योग्य, निपुण; producing a result फलोत्पादक।

effigy *ऐ ॅफ़ि जि* *n.* the image or likeness of a person पुतला।

effort *ऐ ॅ फ़ॅःट* *n.* endeavour, exertion प्रयास।

egg *ऐॅग* *n.* an oval body laid by a female bird or fish अंडा; ovum डिंब।

ego *ई गो, ऐ˘ गो n.* the self अहंकार, दंभ।

egotism *ऐ˘गों˘ टिज़्म n.* an exaggerated love of self, self-exaltation अहंभाव।

eight *एट n.* the number next above seven आठ (8)।

eighteen *ए टीन a.* the number next above seventeen अठारह (18)।

eighty *ए टि n.* the number equal to ten times eight अस्सी (80)।

either[1] *ऑइ दॅः, ई– a., pron.* one or the other दो में से कोई; one of two दो में से एक; each प्रत्येक।

either[2] *adv.* (used after a negative phrase) moreover इसके साथ-साथ।

eject *इ जैक्ट v. t.* to throw out बाहर फेंकना।

elaborate[1] *इ लै बॅ रेट v. t.* to state in details विस्तार से कहना।

elaborate[2] *इ लै बॅ रिट a.* detailed विस्तृत; complicated जटिल।

elapse *इ लैप्स v. t.* to slip or glide away गुज़रना।

elastic *इ लैस् टिक a.* flexible लचीला।

elbow *ऐ˘ल् बो n.* joint where the arm bends कोहनी; angle, bend मोड़।

elder[1] *ऐ˘ल् डॅः a.* of earlier birth ज्येष्ठ, अग्रज।

elder[2] *n.* person of greater age आयु में बड़ा व्यक्ति; an old person वृद्ध व्यक्ति।

elderly *ऐ˘ल् डॅः लि a.* somewhat old सयाना, वयोवृद्ध।

elect *इ लैक्ट v. t.* to choose by vote निर्वाचित करना; to select चयन करना।

election *इ लैक् शॅन n.* act of choosing by vote चुनाव, निर्वाचन।

electorate *इ लैक् टॅ रिट n.* a body of electors निर्वाचक मंडल।

electric *इ लैक् ट्रिक a.* containing, conveying or produced by eletricity विद्युतीय।

electricity *इ लैक् ट्रि सि टि n.* the electric power विद्युत्।

electrify *इ लै˘क् ट्रि फ़ॉइ v. t.* to communicate elecricity to (का) विद्युतीकरण करना।

elegance *ऐ˘ लि गॅन्स n.* quality of being elegant प्रांजलता; refinement शिष्टता।

elegant *ऐ˘ लि गॅन्ट* a graceful रमणीय; refined परिष्कृत।

elegy *ऐ˘ लि जि n.* a poem or a song expressive of sorrow and lamentation शोकगीत।

element *ऐ˘ लि मॅन्ट n.* basic thing मूलवस्तु; ingredient मूलतत्त्व।

elementary *ऐ˘लि मैन्ॅ टॅ रि a.* simple, ordinary सामान्य।

elephant *ऐ˘ लि फ़ॅन्ट n.* a huge quadruped having a long trunk and tusks हाथी।

elevate *ऐ˘ लि वेट v. t.* to raise उन्नत करना; to refine or dignify शुद्ध अथवा गरिमामय बनाना।

elevation *ऐ˘ लि वे शॅन n.* act of raising उन्नयन; a rise in rank उन्नति; a height ऊंचाई।

eleven *इ लै˘ व्न n.* number next above ten ग्यारह (11)।

elf *ऐल्फ़ n.* a fairy परी; a mischievous little creature बौना प्राणी।

eligible *ऐ˘ लि जि ब्ल a.* fit to be

chosen ग्राह्य, वरणीय; suitable उपयुक्त।

eliminate *इ लि मि नेट v. t.* to set aside, to throw off हटाना।

elimination *इ लि मि ने शॅन n.* leaving out निष्कासन, हटाव।

elope *इ लोप v. i.* to run away with a lover सहपलायन करना।

eloquence *ऐ˘ लॅ क्वॅन्स n.* power of making a moving speech वाक्पटुता।

eloquent *ऐ˘ लॅ क्वॅन्ट a.* having eloquence वाक्पटु; fluent in speech भाषणपटु।

else[1] *ऐ˘ल्स a.* other अन्य; additional अतिरिक्त।

else[2] *adv.* otherwise अन्यथा।

elucidate *इ ल्यू सि डेट v. t.* to make clear स्पष्ट करना।

elude *इ ल्यूड v. t.* to avoid से बचना; to baffle (की) समझ में न आना।

elusion *इ ल्यू ज़ॅन n.* act of eluding छल, कपट; evasion टालमटोल।

elusive *इ ल्यू सिव a.* practising elusion मायावी; evasive टालमटोल वाला।

emancipation *इ मैन् सि पे शॅन n.* liberation मुक्ति।

embalm *इम् बाम v. t.* to preserve (a dead body) by aromatics शवलेप करना।

embankment *इम् बैङ्क् मॅन्ट n.* act of embanking तटबंधन; artificial mound तटबंध।

embark *इम् बा:क, ऐमॅ् v. t.* to put on board a ship पोतारोहण करना; *v. i.* (with 'on') to engage in (में) लगना।

embarrass *इम् बै रॅस v. t.* to involve in difficulties मुश्किल में डालना; to hamper बाधा डालना।

embassy *ऐमॅ् बॅ सि n.* the mission, charge or residence of an ambassador दूतावास।

embitter *इम् बि टॅ:, ऐमॅ्– v. t.* to make bitter कड़वा बनाना।

emblem *ऐमॅ् ब्लॅम n.* symbol प्रतीक।

embodiment *इम् बौ˘ डि मॅन्ट, ऐमॅ्– n.* representation in bodily form मूर्तरूप।

embody *इम् बौ˘ डि, ऐमॅ्– v. t.* to give bodily form मूर्तरूप देना; to give a definite form निश्चित रूप देना।

embolden *इम् बोल् डॅन, ऐमॅ्- v. t.* to encourage प्रोत्साहित करना।

embrace[1] *इम् ब्रेस, ऐमॅ्– v. t.* to take within the arms आलिंगन करना; to include सम्मिलित करना।

embrace[2] *n.* act of embracing आलिंगन।

embroidery *इम् ब्रौ˘इ डॅ रि, ऐमॅ्– n.* ornamental needle-work क़सीदाकारी।

embryo *ऐमॅ् ब्रि ओ n.* unborn offspring भ्रूण।

emerald *ऐ˘ मॅ रॅल्ड n.* green precious stone पन्ना।

emerge *इ मॅ:ज v. i.* to become manifest प्रकट होना।

emergency *इ मॅ: जॅन् सि n.* an unexpected situation demanding urgent action आपातकाल।

eminance *ऐ˘ मि नॅन्स n.* state of being eminent श्रेष्ठता; superiority उच्चता।

eminent *ऐ˘ मि नॅन्ट a.* distinguished, outstanding प्रतिष्ठित।

emissary *ऐँ मि सॅ रि* *n.* one sent on private business दूत।

emit *इ मिट (-tt-)* *v. t.* to send out बाहर भेजना।

emolument *इ मौॅ ल्यु मॅन्ट* *n.* profit arising from office or employment परिलाभ; salary वेतन।

emotion *इ मो शॅन* *n.* strong feeling भावावेश।

emotional *इ मो श नॅल* *a.* given to emotion भावुक; appealing to the emotions भावोत्तेजक; emotion-charged भावपूर्ण।

emperor *ऐम्ॅ पॅ रॅ:* *n.* ruler of an empire सम्राट्।

emphasis *ऐम्ॅ फ़ॅ सिस* *n.* stress बलाघात; importance महत्व; vigour of speech ओजपूर्ण कथन।

emphasize *ऐम्ॅ फ़ॅ सॉइज़* *v. t.* to place emphasis on महत्व देना।

emphatic *इम् फ़ै टिक, ऐम्ॅ–* *a.* impressive प्रभावी; strong मज़बूत।

empire *ऐम्ॅ पॉइअॅ:* *n.* dominion of an emperor साम्राज्य।

employ *इम् प्लौॅइ, ऐम्ॅ–* *v. t.* to keep at work नियोजित करना; to make use of काम में लाना।

employee *ऐम्ॅ प्लौॅइ ई* *n.* one who works for an employer कर्मचारी।

employer *ऐम्ॅ प्लौॅइ अॅ:* *n.* one who employs नियोजक।

employment *ऐम्ॅ प्लौॅइ मॅन्ट* *n.* act of employing नियोजन; appointment नियुक्ति।

empower *इम् पॉउ अॅ:, ऐम्ॅ–* *v. t.* to authorise अधिकार देना; to enable समर्थ बनाना।

empress *ऐम्ॅ प्रिस* *n.* the consort of an emperor महारानी, साम्राज्ञी।

empty[1] *ऐम्प् टि* *a.* containing nothing खाली।

empty[2] *v. t.* to make empty खाली करना; *v. i.* to become empty खाली होना।

emulate *ऐ ॅ म्यु लेट* *v. t.* to strive to equal or excel (की) बराबरी की चेष्टा करना; to imitate अनुकरण करना।

enable *इ ने बृल* *v. t.* to make able योग्य बनाना; to empower शक्ति देना; to authorise अधिकार देना।

enact *इ नैक्ट* *v. t.* to make into law कानून का रूप देना; to act the part of (का) अभिनय करना।

enamel *इ नै मॅल* *n.* preservative coating on metal तामचीनी; hard coating on teeth दंतवल्क।

enamour *इ नै मॅ:* *v. t.* to inspire with love प्रेमासक्त करना; to charm अनुरक्त करना।

encase *इन् केस, ऐन्ॅ–* *v. t.* to enclose in a case डिब्बे में बंद करना।

enchant *इन् चान्ट, ऐन्ॅ–* *v. t.* to fill with delight प्रसन्न करना; to put a spell on (पर) जादू करना।

encircle *इन् सॅ: कृल, ऐन्ॅ–* *v. t.* to surround घेरना।

enclose *इन् क्लोज़* *v. t.* to shut in on all sides चारों ओर से घेरना; to envelope लिफ़ाफ़े में बंद करना।

enclosure *इन् क्लो ज़ॅ: ऐन्ॅ–* *n.* that which is enclosed (in a letter) संलग्नक; space fenced off अहाता, घेरा।

encompass *इन् कम् पॅस, ऐन्ॅ–* *v. t.* to surround घेरना; to go round (की) प्रदक्षिणा करना।

encounter[1] इन् *कॉउन् टॅः, ऐन्ँ–* *n.* clash between hostile factions भिड़ंत।

encounter[2] *v. t.* to meet unexpectedly अनायास भेंट होना; to meet in conflict से भिंड़त होना।

encourage इन् *क रिज* *v. t.* to give courage प्रोत्साहित करना।

encroach इन् *क्रोच, ऐन्ँ–* *v. i.* to advance beyond the proper limits अतिक्रमण करना।

encumber इन् *कम् बॅः, ऐन्ँ–* *v. t.* to load, to burden भाराक्रान्त करना।

encyclopaedia *ऐन्ँ सॉइ क्लोँ पी ड्यॅ* *n.* a collection of articles on one or more branches of knowledge विश्वकोश।

end[1] ऐन्ड *v. t.* to put an end to समाप्त करना; *v.i.* to come to an end समाप्त होना।

end[2] *n.* limit सीमा; extremity किनारा; conclusion समाप्ति; death मृत्यु; result परिणाम; purpose उद्देश्य।

endanger इन् *डे न् जॅः, ऐ न्–* *v. t.* to bring into danger विपत्ति में डालना।

endear इन् *डिअॅः ऐन्ँ–* *v.t.* to make dear प्यारा बनाना।

endearment इन् *डिअॅः मॅन्ट, ऐन्ँ–* *n.* tender affection प्रीति; *(pl.)* affectionate embrace प्रेमालिंगन।

endeavour[1] इन् *डै वॅः, ऐन्ँ–* *n.* earnest effort प्रयास, प्रयत्न।

endeavour[2] *v.i.* to try earnestly प्रयत्न करना।

endorse इन् *डौःस, ऐन्ँ–* *v. t.* to confirm समर्थन करना; to write one's name on the back of पृष्ठांकित करना, पृष्ठांकन करना।

endow इन् *डॉउ, ऐन्ँ–* *v. t.* to give (money property etc.) to provide regular income वृत्तिदान करना; to furnish (with) प्रदान करना।

endurable इन् *ड्युअॅ रॅ ब्ल* *a.* that can be endured सहनीय।

endurance इन् *ड्युअॅ रॅन्स* *n.* ability to last स्थायित्व; ability to stand hardship सहनशीलता।

endure इन् *ड्युअॅः, ऐन्ँ–* *v.t.* to tolerate सहन करना; *v.i.* to last टिकना, चालू रहना।

enemy *ऐ नि मि* *n.* one who is unfriendly शत्रु; an opponent विरोधी; hostile force शत्रु सेना।

energetic *ऐ नॅः जै टिक* *a.* vigorous शक्तिशाली; full of energy ऊर्जायुक्त।

energy *ऐ नॅः जि* *n.* power (electrical, atomic etc.) ऊर्जा; vigour शक्ति; force बल।

enfeeble इन् *फी ब्ल, ऐन्ँ–* *v. t.* to weaken दुर्बल करना।

enforce इन् *फौःस, ऐन्ँ–* *v. t.* to compel बाध्य करना; to strengthen बल प्रदान करना।

enfranchise इन् *फ्रैन् चॉइज़, ऐन्ँ–* *v.t.* to admit to the right of voting मताधिकार देना; to set free मुक्त करना।

engage इन् *गेज, ऐन्ँ–* *v. t.* to employ काम पर लगाना; to hire किराये पर करना; to betroth सगाई या वाग्दान करना; to attract आकर्षित करना; to occupy घेरना; to begin fighting with से लड़ना; *v.i.* to promise वचन देना; to busy oneself (with) (में) व्यस्त रखना।

engagement *इन् गेज् मॅन्ट, ऐनॅ्–* *n.* agreement to marry वाग्दान; social or business commitment कार्यक्रम; promise वादा, देनदारी; battle, conflict मुठभेड़।

engine *ऐनॅ् जिन* *n.* a machine worked by heat or other energy यंत्र, इंजन।

engineer *ऐनॅ् जि निअॅ:* *n.* person skilled in a branch of engineering अभियंता।

English[1] *इङ्ग् लिश* *a.* relating to England आंग्ल, बरतानवी।

English[2] *n.* the people of England अंग्रेज़ लोग; language of England अंग्रेजी भाषा।

engrave *इन् ग्रेव, ऐनॅ्–* *v. t.* to carve उत्कीर्ण करना।

engross *इन् ग्रौ ॅस, ऐनॅ्–* *v.t.* to occupy completely बुरी तरह व्यस्त रखना।

engulf *इन् गल्फ़, ऐनॅ्–* *v.t.* ιo swallow निगलना; to submerge निमग्न करना।

enigma *इ निग् मॅ* *n.* riddle पहेली; mystery रहस्य।

enjoy *इन् जौ ॅइ, ऐनॅ्–* *v. t.* to take pleasure in (का) रस लेना; to have use or benefit of (का) प्रयोग या लाभ भोगना।

enjoyment *इन् जौ ॅइ मॅन्ट, ऐनॅ्–* *n.* pleasure आनंद; satisfaction संतुष्टि; possession and use उपभोग।

enlarge *इन् ला:ज, ऐनॅ्–* *v. t.* to make larger (का) विस्तार करना; to amplify बढ़ाना।

enlighten *इन् लॉइ टॅन, ऐनॅ्–* *v. t.* to elevate by knowledge प्रबुद्ध करना; to cause to understand सूचित करना।

enlist *इन् लिस्ट, ऐनॅ्–* *v. t.* to enrol (का) नाम लिखना; to obtain प्राप्त करना।

enliven *इन् लॉइ वॅन, ऐनॅ्–* *v. t.* to make lively सजीव करना; to put life into (में) जान डालना।

enmity *ऐनॅ् मि टि* *n.* hostility शत्रुता; ill-will विद्वेष।

ennoble *इ नो बॅल, ऐॅ–* *v. t.* to make noble उदात्त बनाना; to make a member of the nobility अभिजात वर्ग का सदस्य बनाना।

enormous *इ नौ: मॅस* *a.* huge विशाल।

enough[1] *इ नफ़* *a.* adequate यथेष्ट; sufficient पर्याप्त।

enough[2] *adv.* sufficiently पर्याप्त मात्रा में।

enquire *इन् क्वॉइअॅ:* see inquire.

enquiry *इन् क्वॉइअॅ रि* see inquiry.

enrage *इन् रेज़, ऐनॅ्–* *v. t.* to make angry क्रुद्ध करना।

enrapture *इन् रैप् चॅ:, ऐनॅ्–* *v. t.* to transport with pleasure or delight प्रफुल्ल करना।

enrich *इन् रिच, ऐनॅ्–* *v. t.* to make rich संपन्न बनाना; to add to बढ़ाना।

enrol *इन् रोल (-ll-)* *v. t.* to enlist भरती करना।

enshrine *इन् श्रॉइन, ऐनॅ्–* *v. t.* to enclose in a shrine प्रतिष्ठापित करना; to preserve with great care संजोना।

enslave *इन् स्लेव, ऐनॅ्–* *v.t.* to reduce to slavery दास बनाना।

ensue *इन् स्यू, ऐनॅ्–* *v.i.* to follow, to come after पीछे घटित होना।

ensure *इन् श्युअॅ:, ऐनॅ्–* *v. t.* to make safe सुरक्षित रखना; to make sure सुनिश्चित करना।

entangle *इन् टैङ् गल, ऐनॅ्–* *v. t.* to ensnare फंदे में फंसाना; to perplex उलझाना।

enter *ऐनॅ् टॅ:* *v. t.* to go (come) into प्रवेश करना; to penetrate प्रविष्ट करना; to join का सदस्य बनना; to write, to register लिखना।

enterprise *ऐनॅ् टॅ: प्रॉइज़* *n.* undertaking उद्यम; business उपक्रम; bold or dangerous undertaking जोखिम का काम।

entertain *ऐनॅ् टॅ: टेन* *v. t.* to amuse (का) मनोरंजन करना; to keep in mind ध्यान में रखना; to consider पर विचार करना।

entertainment *ऐनॅ् टॅ: टेन् मॅन्ट* *n.* recreation मनोरंजन।

enthrone *इन् थ्रोन, ऐनॅ्–* *v. t.* to place on a throne सिंहासनारूढ़ करना।

enthusiasm *इन् थ्यू ज़ि ऐज़्म, ऐनॅ्–* *n.* keen interest, eagerness उत्साह, उमंग।

enthusiastic *इन् थ्यू ज़ि ऐस् टिक, ऐनॅ्–* *a.* full of enthusiasm उत्साही।

entice *इन् टॉइस, ऐनॅ्–* *v. t.* to tempt लुभाना।

entire *इन् टॉइअॅ:, ऐनॅ्–* *a.* whole, complete संपूर्ण।

entirely *इन् टॉइअॅ: लि, ऐनॅ्–* *adv.* completely संपूर्णतः।

entitle *इन् टॉइ ट्ल, ऐनॅ्–* *v. t.* to give claim to दावेदार बनाना; to qualify समर्थ बनाना; to give title to उपाधि देना।

entity *ऐनॅ् टि टि* *n.* being सत्ता, अस्तित्व; reality वास्तविकता।

entomology *ऐनॅ् टॅ मौ ˘ लॅ जि* *n.* science of insects कीटविज्ञान।

entrails *ऐनॅ् ट्रेल्ज़* *n. pl.* intestines अंतड़ियां।

entrance *ऐनॅ् ट्रॅन्स* *n.* act of entering प्रवेश; door, gate प्रवेश-द्वार।

entrap *इन् ट्रैप, ऐनॅ्– (-pp-)* *v. t.* to trick बहकाना; to catch as if in a trap फंसाना।

entreat *इन् ट्रीट, ऐनॅ्–* *v. t.* to beg earnestly अनुनय करना।

entreaty *इन् ट्री टि, ऐनॅ्–* *n.* earnest request विनती।

entrust *इन् ट्रस्ट* *v. t.* to put into care of (की) देख-रेख में रखना; to trust (someone) with सौंपना।

entry *ऐनॅ् ट्रि* *n.* act of entering प्रवेश; entrance प्रवेश-द्वारः; an item recorded प्रविष्टि।

enumerate *इ न्यू मॅ रेट* *v. t.* to count गिनना; to mention one by one एक-एक करके बताना।

envelop *इन् वै ˘ लॅप, ऐनॅ्–* *v. t.* to cover आवृत्त करना, ढकना; to surround entirely पूरी तरह घेरना।

envelope *ऐनॅ् वि लोप, औनॅ्–* *n.* cover for letter लिफ़ाफ़ा।

enviable *ऐनॅ् वि अॅ ब्ल* *a.*, causing envy ईर्ष्या-योग्य।

envious *ऐनॅ् वि अॅस* *a.* full of envy ईर्ष्यालु।

environment *इन् वॉइअॅ रॅन् मॅन्ट* *n.* physical surroundings पर्यावरण; conditions of life परिवेश।

envy[1] *ऐनॅ् वि* *v.* jealousy ईर्ष्याः a desired object चाह की वस्तु।

envy[2] *v. t.* to feel jealous of (से) ईर्ष्या रखना।

epic *ऐ˘ पिक n.* poetic account of the deeds of a legendary hero महाकाव्य।

epidemic *ऐ˘ पि डै˘ मिक n.* wide-spread occurrence of disease महामारी।

epigram *ऐ˘ पि ग्रैम n.* short witty saying विदग्धोक्ति।

epilepsy *ऐ˘ पि लैपॅ् सि n.* a disease of nervous system अपस्मार, मिरगी।

epilogue *ऐ˘ पि लौगॅ n.* conclusion उपसंहार।

episode *ऐ˘ पि सोड n.* interesting incident घटना।

epitaph *ऐ˘ पि टाफ़ n.* inscription on a tombstone समाधिलेख।

epoch *ई पौकॅ n.* period of history marked by notable events युग।

equal[1] *ई क्वॅल a.* the same in size, quantity, degree, etc. समान; identical समरूप।

equal[2] *(-ll-) v. t.* to be equal to के समान होना।

equal[3] *n.* person or thing equal to another समकक्ष व्यक्ति या वस्तु।

equality *ई क्वौ˘ लि टि n.* state of being equal समानता; uniformity समरूपता।

equalize *ई क्वॅ लॉइज़ v. t.* to make equal बराबर करना।

equate *इ क्वेट v. t.* treat as equal समान मानना; to make equal समान बनाना।

equation *इ क्वे शॅन n.* balancing संतुलन; mathematical expression समीकरण।

equator *इ क्वे टॅ: n.* an imaginary line round the earth विषुवत् रेखा।

equilateral *ई क्वि लै टॅ रॅल a.* having all sides equal समबाहु।

equip *इ क्विप (-pp-) v. t.* to fit out सज्जित या लैस करना।

equipment *इ क्विप् मॅन्ट n.* necessary apparatus उपस्कर, साज़-सामान।

equitable *ऐ˘ क्वि टॅ ब्ल a.* fair, just न्यायोचित।

equivalent *इ क्वि वॅ लॅन्ट a.* equal in value, amount, etc. सम, तुल्य; of the same meaning समानार्थी।

equivocal *इ क्वि वॅ कॅल a.* of double meaning द्वयर्थक; of doubtful meaning भ्रमात्मक।

era *इॅ अॅ रॅ n.* epoch काल, युग।

eradicate *इ रै टि केट v. t.* to wipe out उन्मूलन करना।

erase *इ रेज़ v. t.* to scrape out (रगड़कर) मिटाना।

erect[1] *इ रैक्ॅट v. t.* to build निर्माण करना; to found स्थापित करना; to fix in an upright position सीधा खड़ा करना।

erect[2] *a.* upright सीधा खड़ा हुआ।

erection *इ रैक् शॅन n.* act of erecting उत्थापन; a building, a structure निर्माण।

erode *इ रोड v. t.* to wear away क्षय करना to eat into खा जाना, काट देना।

erosion *इ रो ज़ॅन n.* act of eroding क्षरण, कटाव।

erotic *इ रौ˘ टिक a.* amorous शृंगारिक।

err *ऐ˘: v. i.* to make a mistake भूल करना।

errand *ऐ˘ रॅन्ड n.* verbal message संदेश; purpose of a journey यात्रा का उद्देश्य।

erroneous *इ रो नि ॲस a.* wrong, अशुद्ध, गलत; mistaken भ्रमपूर्ण।

error *ऐ˘ रॅः n.* mistake भूल।

erupt *इ रप्ट v. i.* to break out suddenly प्रस्फुटित होना।

eruption *इ रप् शॅन n.* outbreak प्रस्फुटन, विस्फोट; rash on the skin फोड़े-फुंसी।

escape[1] *इस् केप n.* outlet निकास; flight पलायन।

escape[2] *v.i.* to get free मुक्त होना; to get off safely सुरक्षित निकल जाना; to go unpunished अदंडित बच जाना; *v.t.* to elude (से) बचना; to be forgotten by (से) भुला दिया जाना।

escort[1] *ऐसॅ् कौःट n.* guard अनुरक्षी।

escort[2] *इस् कौःट v. t.* to accompany as an escort (की) रक्षार्थ साथ जाना।

especial *इस् पै˘ शॅल ऐसॅ्– a.* particular विशिष्ट।

essay[1] *ऐ˘ से n.* piece of prose written on a given topic निबंध।

essay[2] *v. t.* to try to do (का) प्रयत्न करना; to make experiment of परखना।

essayist *ऐ˘ से इस्ट n.* a writer of essays निबंधकार।

essence *ऐ˘ सॅन्स n.* distinctive element of a thing सार, तत्व, concentrated extract of a substance आसव।

essential *इ सैनॅ् शॅल, ऐ˘– a.* necessary आवश्यक; fundamental मूलभूत; मौलिक।

establish *इस् टैब् लिश, ऐसॅ्– v. t.* to set up (की) स्थापना करना; to prove प्रमाणित करना; to settle स्थिर करना।

establishment *इस् टैब् लिश मॅन्ट, ऐसॅ्– n.* act of establishing स्थापना; business settlement अधिष्ठान।

estate *इस् टेट, ऐसॅ् n.* landed property भूसंपत्ति।

esteem[1] *इस् टीम, ऐसॅ्– n.* regard आदर, मान; recognition मान्यता।

esteem[2] *v. t.* to respect आदर करना; to consider मान्यता देना।

estimate[1] *ऐसॅ् टि मिट,–मेट n.* valuing in mind अनुमान; rough calculation आकलन।

estimate[2] *ऐसॅ् टि मेट v. t.* to evaluate मूल्यांकन करना।

estimation *ऐसॅ् टि मे शॅन n.* opinion, judgement मत; reckoning आकलन; regard सम्मान।

etcetera *ऐ˘ट सै˘ट्रॅ* (usually written etc.) and other things तथा अन्य वस्तुएं; and so on इत्यादि।

eternal *इ टॅः नॅल* perpetual, everlasting शाश्वत, सनातन।

eternity *इ टॅः नि टि n.* time without end अनंत काल।

ether *ई थॅः n.* a colourless liquid made from alcohol *ईथर,* outer space व्योम।

ethical *ऐ˘ थि कॅल a.* relating to morals नैतिक।

ethics *ऐ˘ थिक्स n. (pl.)* treatise on morals नीतिग्रंथ।

etiquette *ऐ˘ टि कैट n.* customary rules of behaviour शिष्टाचार।

etymology *ऐ˘ टि मौ˘ लॅ जि n.* study or science of origin of words व्युत्पत्तिशास्त्र।

eunuch *यू नॅक n.* castrated man नपुसंक, हिजड़ा।

evacuate *इवै क्यु एट v. t.* to vacate खाली करना; to remove हटा देना।

evacuation *इ वै क्यु ए शॅन n.* being or getting vacated शून्यीभवन, शून्यीकरण; withdrawal परित्याग; removal निकास।

evade *इ वेड v. t.* to avoid टालना; to escape from (से) बचना।

evaluate *इ वै ल्यु एट v. t.* to find out the value of (का) मूल्यांकन करना।

evaporate *इ वै पॅ रेट v. i.* to turn to vapour भाप बनाना; to vanish लुप्त हो जाना; *v. t.* to convert into vapour भाप बनाना; to extract moisture from सुखाना।

evasion *इ वे ज़ॅन n.* act of evading अपवंचन; excuse बहाना; equivocation अस्पष्ट कथन।

even[1] *ई वॅन a.* uniform सम, एकरूप; level समतल; equal समगुण।

even[2] *v. t.* to make even or smooth सम करना।

even[3] *adv.* still और भी; equally समान रूप से।

evening *ईव् निङ्ग n.* close of the day संध्या।

event *ई वैन्ट n.* important happening घटना।

eventually *ई वैनॅ ट्यु अॅ लि adv.* ultimately, in the end अंततः।

ever *ई˘ वॅः adv.* always, at all times सर्वदा; at any time किसी भी समय।

evergreen[1] *ऐ˘ वॅः ग्रीन a.* always fresh सदाबहार।

evergreen[2] *n.* tree or shrub having foliage throughout the year सदाबहार पेड़, पौधा आदि।

everlasting *ऐ˘ वॅः लास् टिङ्ग a.* eternal चिरस्थायी।

every *ऐवॅ रि a.* each प्रत्येक।

evict *इ विक्ट v. t.* to expel by legal process बेदख़ल करना।

eviction *इ विक् शॅन n.* expulsion बेदख़ली।

evidence *ऐ˘ वि डॅन्स n.* testimony साक्ष्य, गवाही; proof प्रमाण।

evident *ऐ˘ वि डॅन्ट a.* obvious सुस्पष्ट।

evil[1] *ई वल n.* that which is not good अशुभ।

evil[2] *a.* wicked दुष्ट; bad निंद्य।

evoke *इ वोक v. t.* to call up, to summon पुकारना, आह्वान करना।

evolution *ई वॅ ल्यू शॅन n.* gradual development विकास।

evolve *इ वौ˘ल्व v.t.* to develop विकसित करना; *v.i.* to be developed विकसित होना; to undergo slow changes धीरे-धीरे परिवर्तित होना।

ewe *यू n.* a female sheep भेड़।

exact *इग् ज़ैक्ट a.* precise यथार्थ; absolutely correct ठीक।

exaggerate *इग् ज़ै जॅ रेट, ऐगॅ– v. t.* to magnify unduly अतिरंजना करना।

exaggeration *इग् ज़ै जॅ रे शॅन n.* statement in excess of the truth अतिशयोक्ति।

exalt *इग् ज़ौल्ट v. t.* to raise in rank पदोन्नत करना; to extol सराहना करना।

examination *इग् ज़ै मि ने शॅन, ऐगॅ– n.* test of knowledge परीक्षा; close inspection जांच-पड़ताल।

examine *इग् ज़ैं मिन, ऐग्– v. t.* to test परीक्षा करना; to inspect (की) जांच करना।

examinee *इग् ज़ै मि नी n.* one under examination परीक्षार्थी।

examiner *इग् ज़ै मि नें: n.* one who examines परीक्षक।

example *इग् ज़ाम् प्ल, ऐग्– n.* instance उदाहरण; specimen नमूना।

excavate *ऐक्स् कॅ वेट v. t.* to hollow खोखला करना; to dig out खोदना।

excavation *ऐक्स् कॅ वे शॅन n.* excavating or being excavated उत्खनन।

exceed *इक् सीड, ऐक्– v.t.* to go beyond (से) अधिक होना।

excel *इक् सैॅल, ऐक्– v.i.* to be leading अग्रगण्य होना; *v.t.* to be superior to (से) श्रेष्ठ होना।

excellence *ऐक् सॅ लॅन्स n.* superiority उत्कृष्टता।

excellency *ऐक् सॅ लॅन् सि n.* title of honour मान्यवर।

excellent *ऐक् सॅ लॅन्ट a.* of great virtue or worth उत्कृष्ट।

except[1] *इक् सैप्ट, ऐक्– v. t.* to leave out छोड़ देना।

except[2] *prep.* leaving out के अतिरिक्त।

exception *इक् सैप् शॅन, ऐक्– n.* exclusion अपवाद; objection आपत्ति।

excess[1] *इक् सैसॅ n.* superabundance अति, बाहुल्य; surplus अधिशेष; intemperance असंयम।

excess[2] *a.* additional अतिरिक्त, फ़ालतू।

exchange[1] *इक्स् चेन्ज, ऐक्सॅ– n.* giving and taking of one thing for another विनिमय; (cap.) stock exchange विनिमय-केंद्र; central telephone exchange दूरभाष केंद्र।

exchange[2] *v. t.* to change for another विनिमय करना।

excise *ऐक् सॉइज इक्– n.* tax on certain home commodities उत्पादन-शुल्क, आबकारी।

excite *इक् साइट, ऐक्– v. t.* to rouse उत्तेजित करना; to call into activity जाग्रत करना।

exclaim *इक्स् क्लेम, ऐक्स्– v.i.* to speak suddenly चिल्लाना; *v.t.* to say suddenly चिल्लाकर कहना।

exclamation *ऐक्स् क्लॅ मे शॅन n.* uttered expression of surprise विस्मयोद्‌गार।

exclude *इक्स् क्लूड, ऐक्स्– v. t.* to leave out निकालना।

exclusive *इक्स् क्लू सिव, ऐक्स्– a.* admitting no others अनन्य singular, sole एकमात्र; reserved to a few विशिष्ट।

excommunicate *ऐक्स् कॅ म्यू नि केट v. t.* to expel from the community समाज से बहिष्कृत करना।

excursion *इक्स् कॅ: शॅन् ऐक्स्– n.* outgoing पर्यटन; pleasure trip आमोद-विहार।

excuse[1] *इक्स् क्यूस v.t.* to pardon क्षमा करना; to free from blame दोषमुक्त करना।

excuse[2] *n.* ground for being excused बहाना।

execute *ऐक् सि क्यूट v. t.* to carry out पालन करना; to put to death judicially फांसी देना; to give effect to कार्यान्वित करना।

execution *ऐक् सि क्यू शॅन n.* putting into effect क्रियान्वयन; putting to death judicially फांसी का दंड।

executioner *ऐक् सि क्यू शॅ नॅः n.* one employed to execute criminals जल्लाद, फांसी देने वाला।

exempt[1] *इग् ज़ैम्प्ट, ऐगॅ्– v. t.* to free मुक्त करना; to grant immunity माफ़ करना।

exempt[2] a not liable शुल्क से मुक्त।

exercise[1] *ऐक् सॅः सॉइज़ n.* putting in practice प्रयोग; exertion of the body for health कसरत; military drill क़वायद; a school task for practice अभ्यास।

exercise[2] *v. t.* to put into practice प्रयोग करना; to improve by practice अभ्यास द्वारा विकसित करना; *v.i.* to take exercise व्यायाम करना।

exhaust *इग् ज़ौस्ट, ऐगॅ्– v. t.* to tire out थका देना; to use up समाप्त कर देना; to draw off बाहर निकालना; to discuss thoroughly विस्तृत व्याख्या करना।

exhibit[1] *इग् ज़ि बिट, ऐगॅ्– n.* something exhibited प्रदर्शनीय वस्तु।

exhibit[2] *v. t.* to show दिखाना, प्रदर्शित करना।

exhibition *ऐक् सि बि शॅन n.* public show प्रदर्शनी; display प्रदर्शन।

exile[1] *ऐक् सॉइल, ऐगॅ् ज़ॉइल n.* expulsion from one's country देश-निष्कासन।

exile[2] *v. t.* to expel from one's country देश से निकालना।

exist *इग् ज़िस्ट, ऐगॅ्– v.i.* to be in existence अस्तित्व रखना; to live जीवित होना।

existence *इग् ज़िस् टॅन्स, ऐगॅ्– n.* state of being अस्तित्व; life जीवन।

exit *ऐक् सिट, ऐगॅ् ज़िट n.* departure प्रस्थान; passage out बहिर्गमन-द्वार।

expand *इक्स् पैन्ड, ऐक्स्– v.t.* to spread out फैलाना; to enlarge फुलाना; *v.i.* to increase बढ़ना; to spread फैलना।

expansion *इक्स् पैन् शॅन, ऐकॅस्– n.* spread फैलाव; extension विस्तार, प्रसार; increase वृद्धि।

ex-parte[1] *ऐकॅस् पाः टि a.* one sided एकपक्षीय।

ex-parte[2] *adv.* in the interest of one side only एक के पक्ष में।

expect *इक्स् पैक्ट, ऐकॅस्– v. t.* to hope for आशा करना; to await प्रतीक्षा करना।

expectation *ऐकॅस् पै क् टे शॅन n.* expecting उम्मीद; future prospects अपेक्षा, आशा।

expedient *इक्स् पी ड्यॅन्ट, ऐकॅस्– a.* suitable उपयुक्त; advantageous लाभकारी।

expedite *ऐकॅस् पि डॉइट v. t.* to hasten जल्दी करना।

expedition *ऐकॅस् पि डि शॅन n.* exploration खोजयात्रा; organised march or journey अभियान; promptness शीघ्रता।

expel *इक्स् पैलॅ, ऐक्सॅ– (-ll-) v. t.* to discharge in disgrace निकाल देना; to banish निष्कासित करना।

expend *इक्स् पैन्ड, ऐकॅस्– v. t.* to spend खर्च करना; to consume उपभोग करना।

expenditure *इक्स् पॅनॅ डि चॅः, ऐकॅस्– n.* money spent लागत; expense खर्च।

expense *इक्स् पॅन्स, ऐक्स्–* *n.* expenditure खर्च; cost लागत।

expensive *इक्स् पैन् सिव, ऐक्स्–* *a.* costly महंगा।

experience[1] *इक्स् पिअॅ रि अॅन्स, ऐक्स्–* *n.* the gaining of knowledge and skill on the basis of practical life and observation अनुभव; observation निरीक्षण, अवलोकन; the event घटना।

experience[2] *v. t.* to undergo, to have an experience of झेलना, भोगना।

experiment *इक्स् पै ˘ रि मॅन्ट, ऐक्स्–* *n.* something done to test a theory परीक्षण।

expert[1] *ऐक्स् पॅ:ट* *a.* having familiar knowledge विशेषज्ञ।

expert[2] *n.* one skilful in something कुशल व्यक्ति।

expire *इक्स् पॉइअॅ:, ऐक्स्–* *v.i.* to lapse (अवधि) समाप्त होना; to die मरना।

expiry *इॅक्स् पॉइअॅ रि, ऐक्सॅ्–* *n.* end or termination (of a period of time) अवसान।

explain *इक्स् प्लेन, ऐक्स्–* *v. t.* to account for (का) कारण बताना; to make plain स्पष्ट करना; to illustrate the meaning of (का) अर्थ बताना।

explanation *ऐक्स् प्लॅ ने शॅन* *n.* exposition व्याख्या; meaning अर्थ।

explicit *इक्स् प्लि सिट, ऐक्स्–* *a.* clearly stated सुस्पष्ट, definite सुनिश्चित।

explode *इक्स् प्लोड, ऐक्स्–* *v. t.* to cause to blow up (का) विस्फोट करना; *v.i.* to burst with a loud report फटना।

exploit[1] *ऐक्स् प्लौ ˘इट* *n.* a heroic act पराक्रम।

exploit[2] *इक्स् प्लौ ˘इट, ऐक्स्–* *v. t.* to make gain out of (से) लाभ उठाना; to turn to use उपयोग करना; to make gain at the expense of (का) शोषण करना।

exploration *ऐक्स् प्लॅ रे शॅन* *n.* travel for the sake of discovery अन्वेषण; act of searching thoroughly जांच-पड़ताल।

explore *इक्स् प्लौ:, ऐक्स्–* *v.t.* to search खोजना; to examine thoroughly छानबीन करना।

explosion *इक्स् प्लो ज़ॅन, ऐक्स्–* *n.* blast विस्फोट; loud report धमाका; sudden increase अचानक वृद्धि।

explosive[1] *इक्स् प्लो सिव, ऐक्स्–* *n.* explosive material विस्फोटक पदार्थ।

explosive[2] *a.* causing explosion विस्फोटक।

exponent *ऐक्स् पो नॅन्ट, इक्स्–* *n.* expounder प्रतिपादक।

export[1] *ऐक्स् पौ:ट* *n.* act of exporting निर्यात; goods that are exported निर्यात की जाने वाली वस्तुएं।

export[2] *ऐक्स् पौ: ट* *v. t.* to send out of a country निर्यात करना।

expose *इक्स् पोज़, ऐक्स्–* *v. t.* to uncover उघाड़ना; to display प्रदर्शित करना; to disclose प्रकट करना।

express[1] *इक्स् प्रैसॅ, ऐक्स्–* *v. t.* to put into words कहना, वर्णन करना; to make known अभिव्यक्त करना।

express[2] *a.* definitely stated स्पष्ट रूप से कथित; speedy तीव्रगामी।

express[3] *n.* express train द्रुतगामी रेलगाड़ी।

expression *इक्स् प्रै˘ शॅन, ऐकॅस्–* *n.* act, power or mode of representing अभिव्यंजना; features मुखाकृति।

expressive *इक्स् प्रै˘ सिव, ऐकॅस्–* *a.* vividly representing अभिव्यंजनापूर्ण; full of expression भावाभिव्यक्तिपूर्ण।

expulsion *इक्स् पल् शॅन, ऐकॅस्–* *n.* banishment निष्कासन।

extend *इक्स् टैन्ड, ऐक्स्–* *v. t.* to stretch out विस्तृत करना; to exert to the full तानना; to widen चौड़ा करना।

extent *इक्स् टैन्ट, ऐक्स्–* *n.* size आकार; scope क्षेत्र; degree सीमा।

external *ऐकॅस् टः नॅल* *a.* exterior बाह्य; foreign विदेशी।

extinct *इक्स् टिङ्क्ट, ऐकॅस्–* *a.* extinguished बुझा हुआ; no longer existing विलुप्त।

extinguish *इक्स् टिङ् ग्विश, ऐक्सॅ–* *v.t.* to put out बुझाना; to destroy नष्ट करना।

extol *इक्स् टौ˘ल, ऐकॅस्–* *v. t.* to praise highly प्रशंसा करना।

extra[1] *ऐकॅस् ट्रॅ* *a.* additional अतिरिक्त; more than usual फ़ालतू।

extra[2] *adv.* additionally, more than usually असामान्य रूप से।

extract[1] *ऐकॅस् ट्रैक्ट* *n.* distilled substance निचोड़; essence सार।

extract[2] *इक्स् ट्रैक्ट, ऐक्स्–* *v. t.* to draw out by distillation अर्क़ निकालना; to extort ऐंठना।

extraordinary *इक्स् ट्रौः डि नॅ रि* *a.* unusual असाधारण; exceptional अपूर्व।

extravagance *इक्स् ट्रै वि गॅन्स, ऐकॅस्–* *n.* immoderation उच्छृंखलता; lavish expenditure फ़िजूलख़र्ची।

extravagant *इक्स् ट्रै वि गॅन्ट, ऐकॅस्–* *a.* wasteful अपव्ययी; immoderate असंयमी; excessive अत्यधिक।

extreme[1] *इक्स् ट्रीम्, ऐकॅस्–* *a.* farthest दूरतम; excessive अति अधिक; far from moderate उग्र क्रांतिकारी।

extreme[2] *n.* utmost degree अधिकतम मात्रा; one of opposite ends सिरा, किनारा।

extremist *इक्स् ट्री मिस्ट, ऐकॅस्–* *n.* holder of extreme opinion अतिवादी।

exult *इग् ज़ल्ट, ऐगॅ–* *v. i.* to rejoice exceedingly उल्लसित होना।

eye *ऑइ* *n.* organ of sight आंख।

eyeball *ऑइ बौल* *n.* globe of the eye नेत्र-गोलक।

eyelash *ऑइ लैश* *n.* hair fringing the eyelid बरौनी।

eyelet *ऑइ लिट* *n.* a small hole for a rope etc. to pass through सूराख़।

eyewash *ऑइ वौश* *n.* lotion for the eyes नेत्रधावन; pretence बहाना।

Ff

F ऍफ़ the sixth letter of the English and Latin alphabet, the fourth note of the natural diatonic scale. अंग्रेजी या रोम की वर्णमाला का छठा अक्षर, गायन में चौथा सुर।

fable फ़े ब्ल *n.* a tale with a moral नीति कथा; legend पौराणिक कथा; an untrue statement झूठी बात।

fabric फ़ै ब्रिक *n.* cloth कपड़ा; framework, structure भवन।

fabricate फ़ैब् रि केट *v.t.* to forge जालसाज़ी के रूप में करना; to construct निर्माण करना; to invent गढ़ना।

fabrication फ़ैब् रि के शॅन *n.* fabricating गढ़ाई, संरचना; forgery जालसाज़ी; invention छल रचना, गढ़त; something fabricated गढ़ी गई वस्तु।

fabulous फ़ै ब्यू लॅस *a.* unbelievable अविश्वसनीय; amazing आश्चर्यजनक।

facade फ़ॅ साड *n.* false appearance मुखौटा; front face of building मकान का अग्रभाग।

face[1] फ़ेस *n.* front of head चेहरा; front part of anything अग्रभाग।

face[2] *v.t.* to be opposite to (के) आमने-सामने होना; to meet boldly सामना करना।

facet फ़ैसिट *n.* aspect पहलू।

facial फ़े शॅल *a.* pertaining to face मुख-संबंधी।

facile फ़ै सॉइल *a.* easy सुगम।

facilitate फ़ॅ सि लि टेट *v.t.* to make easier आसान कर देना।

facility फ़ॅ सि लि टि *n.* convenience सुविधा।

fac-simile फ़ैक् सि मि लि *n.* exact copy प्रतिकृति।

fact फ़ैक्ट *n.* truth सत्य; reality यथार्थ।

faction फ़ैक्शॅन *n.* strife within a party दलबंदी।

factious फ़ैक् शॅस *a.* quarrelsome झगड़ालू।

factor फ़ैक् टॅः *n.* an agent अभिकर्त्ता; cause कारण; any of the numbers which, when multiplied, form a product गुणक।

factory फ़ैक् टॅ रि *n.* building where things are manufactured कारख़ाना।

faculty फ़ै कॅल् टि *n.* department of learning संकाय; mental and physical ability क्षमता।

fad फ़ैड *n.* craze सनक।

fade फ़ेड *v.i.* to grow pale or dim धीमा पड़ना; to lose colour रंग का उड़ना।

faggot फ़ै गॅट *n.* bundle of sticks for fuel ईधन की लकड़ियों का गट्ठर।

fail फ़ेल *v.i.* to be unsuccessful असफल होना; to stop functioning काम बंद कर देना।

failure फ़ेल् यॅः *n.* lack of success असफलता।

faint[1] फ़ेन्ट *a.* dim धुंधला; weak कमज़ोर।

faint[2] *v.i.* to swoon मूर्च्छित होना।

fair[1] *फ़ेऑ़:* *a.* beautiful सुंदर; clear साफ़; impartial निष्पक्ष; white-complexioned गौरवर्ण।

fair[2] *n.* periodical market पैंठ, मेला; exhibition प्रदर्शनी।

fairly *फ़े˘ ऑ़: लि* *adv.* justly निष्पक्ष रूप से; reasonably न्यायसंगत ढंग से; in a satisfactory degree पर्याप्त मात्रा में।

fairy *फ़े˘ अॅ रि* *n.* small mythical being परी।

faith *फ़ेथ* *n.* confidence, trust विश्वास; belief निष्ठा; religion धर्म।

faithful *फ़ेथ् फ़ुल* *a.* loyal वफ़ादार; accurate यथार्थ।

falcon *फ़ौल् कॅन* *n.* a bird of prey of the hawk family बाज़, श्येन।

fall[1] *फ़ौल* *v.i.* to drop, to come down freely गिरना; to become lower कम होना; to decrease घटना; to hang down लटकना; to perish नष्ट होना; to collapse ढहना; to happen घटित होना; to lose power पतन होना।

fall[2] *n.* falling पतन; coming down, decrease पतन; collapse विनाश; defeat पराजय; moral debasement नैतिक पतन।

fallacy *फ़ै लॅ सि* *n.* a mistaken idea or argument भ्रांति, तर्काभास।

fallow *फ़ैलो* *n.* (of land) ploughed but not planted परती।

false *फ़ौल्स* *a.* wrong ग़लत; deceptive भ्रामक; not real अवास्तविक; faithless निष्ठाहीन; sham नक़ली।

falter *फ़ौल् टॅ:* *v.i.* to walk or move unsteadily लड़खड़ाना; to speak in a shaky voice हकलाना।

fame *फ़ेम* *n.* reputation यश, कीर्ति।

familiar *फ़ॅ मि लि ऑ़:* *a.* well-known जाना-पहचाना; knowing something or someone well जानकार।

family *फ़ै मि लि* *n.* parents and children taken together परिवार; a group of related things श्रेणी, वर्ग।

famine *फ़ै मिन* *n.* serious shortage of food अकाल, दुर्भिक्ष।

famous *फ़े मॅस* *a.* very well-known प्रसिद्ध, विख्यात।

fan *फ़ैन* *n.* device of giving air पंखा।

fanatic[1] *फ़ॅ नै टिक* *a.* unreasonably zealous in religion मतांध।

fanatic[2] *n.* a person filled with unreasonable enthusiasm धर्मांध व्यक्ति।

fancy[1] *फ़ैन् सि* *n.* imagination कल्पना; whim सनक।

fancy[2] *v.t.* to imagine कल्पना करना; to like पसंद करना।

fantastic *फ़ॅन् टैस् टिक* *a.* wildly wonderful विलक्षण।

far[1] *फ़ॉ:* *adv.* at or to a great distance दूर; very much कहीं अधिक।

far[2] *a.* distant दूरस्थ।

far[3] *n.* distance दूरी।

farce *फ़ा:स* *n.* comedy of extravagant humour प्रहसन; absurd and pointless proceedings, mockery मज़ाक़, तमाशा।

fare *फ़ेˇऑ़:* *n.* price for passage भाड़ा, किराया; food खाना; passenger सवारी।

farewell[1] *फ़े˘ऑ़: वैलॅ* *n.* well-wishing at parting विदा।

farewell[2] *interj.* good-bye अलविदा।

farm *फ़ा:म* *n.* agricultural land

कृषि-भूमि।

farmer *फ़ाःमॅः n.* cultivator किसान।

fascinate *फ़ै सि नेट v.t.* to charm मोहित करना; to render motionless वशीभूत करना।

fascination *फ़ै सि ने शॅन n.* act of fascinating आकर्षण, सम्मोहन।

fashion *फ़ै शॅन n.* style of dress भूषाचार, फ़ैशन; mode, manner तरीक़ा, रीति।

fashionable *फ़ै शॅ नॅ बल a.* fond of fashion फ़ैशनपरस्त, शौक़ीन मिजाज़।

fast[1] *फ़ास्ट a.* rapid तीव्र; ahead of time तेज़, आगे; loyal पक्का, सच्चा; unfading (colour) पक्का (रंग)।

fast[2] *adv.* rapidly तेज़ी से।

fast[3] *n.* going without food उपवास।

fast[4] *v.i.* to go without food उपवास करना।

fasten *फ़ा सॅन v.t.* to tie बांधना; to fix firmly जकड़ना।

fat[1] *फ़ैट a.* fleshy मांसल; oily स्निग्ध; thick मोटा।

fat[2] *n.* oily substance चिकनाई; substance found in animal bodies वसा, चर्बी।

fatal *फ़े टॅल a.* causing destruction or death घातक।

fate *फ़ेट n.* destiny भाग्य; final issue अंतिम परिणाम।

father *फ़ा दॅः n.* a male parent पिता।

fathom[1] *फ़ै दॅम v.t.* to measure depth थाह लेना; to comprehend भलीभांति समझ लेना।

fathom[2] *n.* a measure of depth (6 feet) फ़ैदम, गहराई का माप (6 फुट)।

fatigue[1] *फ़ॅ टीग n.* weariness थकान।

fatigue[2] *v.t.* to cause fatigue थकाना।

fault *फ़ौल्ट n.* error भूल; mistake ग़लती; blemish अवगुण।

faulty *फ़ौल् टि a.* having a fault or faults दोषपूर्ण।

fauna *फ़ौनॅ n.* animal world प्राणि-जगत्, जीव-जंतु।

favour[1] *फ़े वॅः n.* partiality पक्षपात; help सहायता; support अनुमोदन।

favour[2] *v.t.* to give support to समर्थन करना; to give unfair help or advantage पक्षपात करना।

favourable *फ़े वॅ रॅ बल a.* conducive अनुकूल।

favourite[1] *फ़े वॅ रिट a.* esteemed प्रीतिभाजन।

favourite[2] *n.* a darling प्रेमपात्र; a minion चहेता।

fear[1] *फ़िअॅः n.* dread भय; anxiety चिंता; apprehension आशंका।

fear[2] *v.i.* to have fear, to be afraid डरना; *v.t.* to regard with fear (से) डरना; to have an uneasy feeling of आशंकित होना।

fearful *फ़िअॅः फुल a.* causing fear भयानक, भयावह; frightened भयभीत।

feasible *फ़ी ज़ॅ बल a.* possible संभव; practicable शक्य।

feast[1] *फ़ीस्ट n.* festivity उत्सव; banquet प्रीतिभोज।

feast[2] *v.i.* to hold a feast दावत का आयोजन करना; *v.t.* to entertain sumptuously दावत देना।

feat *फ़ीट n.* a deed of great courage or skill साहसिक कार्य।

feather *फ़ै˘ दॅः n.* one of the light coverings that grow from a bird's skin पंख।

feature *फ़ी चॅः n.* characteristic लक्षण; prominent trait वैशिष्ट्य;

face मुखाकृति।

February *फ़ै ब् रू अॅ रि n.* second month of the year फ़रवरी।

federal *फ़ै ड रॅल a.* pertaining to union of states संघीय।

federation *फ़ै डॅ रे शॅन n.* union of states संघ, राज्य संघ।

fee *फ़ी n.* the money paid for help or advice received शुल्क।

feeble *फ़ी ब्ल a.* weak कमज़ोर।

feed[1] *फ़ीड v.t.* to give food to भोजन देना; to foster पालन-पोषण करना।

feed[2] *n.* plentiful meal भोजन; fodder चारा।

feel *फ़ील v.t.* to touch स्पर्श करना; to examine by touching छूकर परखना; to consider मानना; to be sensitive to महसूस करना; *v.i.* to take ill बुरा मान जाना; to come to know जानकारी होना।

feeling *फ़ी लिङ्ग n.* the sense of touch स्पर्श; ability to feel स्पर्श क्षमता; physical sensation शारीरिक अनुभूति; emotion भावना; sympathy सहानुभूति, opinion मत, धारणा।

feign *फ़ेन v.t.* to make a show or pretence of बहाना करना।

felicitate *फ़ि लि सि टेट v.t.* to congratulate बधाई देना।

felicity *फ़ि लि सि टि n.* good fortune सौभाग्य।

fell *फ़ैलॅ v.t.* to cause to fall गिराना; to cut down (a tree) (पेड़) काट डालना।

fellow *फ़ै लौ n.* companion साथी; member सदस्य; partner सहभागी; research student शोधछात्र।

female[1] *फ़ी मेल a.* pertaining to woman kind स्त्री-जाति-विषयक।

female[2] *n.* a female animal मादा।

feminine *फ़ै मि निन a.* pertaining to women नारी-सुलभ; (*gram.*) of the gender to which female names belong स्त्रीलिंग।

fence[1] *फ़ैन्स n.* enclosure चहारदीवारी; barrier for enclosing घेरा, बाड़ा।

fence[2] *v.t.* to enclose घेरना; to defend रक्षा करना।

fend *फ़ैन्डॅ v.t.* to ward off बाहर रोक देना; to defend रक्षा करना।

ferment[1] *फ़ः मैन्टॅ n.* agitation हंगामा; substance that excites fermentation ख़मीर।

ferment[2] *v.t.* to excite उत्तेजित करना; to excite fermentation in (में) ख़मीर उठाना।

fermentation *फ़ः मैनॅ टे शॅन n.* fermenting or being fermented किण्वन; unrest, excitement उपद्रव, उत्तेजना।

ferocious *फ़ॅ रो शॅस a.* savage, fierce क्रूर, ख़ूंखार।

ferry[1] *फ़ै रि n.* boat नाव।

ferry[2] *v.t.* to carry or convey over water नाव से पार उतारना।

fertile *फ़ः टॉइल a.* fruitful फलदायक; able to produce abundantly उपजाऊ।

fertility *फ़ः टि लि टि n.* quality of being fertile उर्वरता।

fertilize *फ़ः टि लॉइज़ v.t.* to make fertile उर्वर बनाना।

fertilizer *फ़ः टि लॉइ जः n.* manure खाद, उर्वरक।

fervent *फ़ः वैन्ट a.* zealous उत्साही; burning उत्तप्त।

fervour *फ़: वॅ:* *n.* warmth of feeling, zeal जोश।

festival *फ़ैस् टि वॅल, –टॅ–* *n.* joyful cele-bration आनंदोत्सव; a day or period of public rejoicing त्यौहार, पर्व।

festive *फ़ैसॅ् टिव* *a.* joyous, mirthful उल्लासमय।

festivity *फ़ैस् टि वि टि* *n.* social mirth आनंदमंगल; joyfulness हर्षोल्लास।

festoon *फ़ैसॅ् टून* *n.* a string of flowers, foliage etc. suspended in a curve or curves बंदनवार।

fetch *फ़ैचॅ* *v.t.* to bring लाना; to obtain as price मूल्य के रूप में प्राप्त करना।

fetter[1] *फ़ै ॅ टॅः* *n.* chain ज़ंजीर; *(pl.)* chain for the feet बेड़ी।

fetter[2] *v.t.* to put fetters on बेड़ी डालना; to restrain बंधन लगाना।

feud *फ़्यूड* *n.* hostility वैमनस्य, वैर; a fief सामंत।

feudal *फ़्यू डॅल* *a.* pertaining to feuds सामंती।

fever *फ़ी वॅ:* *n.* disease marked by great bodily heat ज्वर; agitation अशांति।

few *फ़्यू* *a.* not many थोड़े से।

fiasco *फ़ि ऐस् को* *n.* an ignominious failure पूर्ण असफलता।

fibre *फ़ॉइ बॅ:* *n.* a thread रेशम, तंतु: nature प्रकृति; texture बनावट।

fickle *फ़ि कल* *a.* changeable चंचल, अस्थिर।

fiction *फ़िक् शॅन* *n.* literature in the form of novels, tales etc. कथा-साहित्य; falsehood झूठ, मनगढ़ंत बात।

fictitious *फ़िक् टि शॅस* *a.* imaginary काल्पनिक; counterfeit मनगढ़ंत।

fiddle[1] *फ़ि ड्ल* *n.* violin सारंगी, बेला।

fiddle[2] *v.i.* to play on a violin सारंगी बजाना; to waste time समय बरबाद करना।

fidelity *फ़ि डै ॅ लि टी, फ़ॉइ–* *n.* faithfulness निष्ठा।

fie *फ़ॉइ* *interj.* an exclamation denoting disapprobation धिक्कार।

field *फ़ील्ड* *n.* a piece of land suitable for tillage कृषि-भूमि; playground खेल का मैदान; battle ground युद्ध का मैदान; area of knowledge or interest कार्य-क्षेत्र।

fiend *फ़ीन्ड* *n.* devil प्रेत; cruel person क्रूर व्यक्ति।

fierce *फ़िअ:स* *a.* ferocious उग्र, प्रचंड; savage हिंस्र; violent प्रबल।

fiery *फ़ॉइ अ रि* *a.* consisting of fire आग्नेय; like fire अग्निवत्; impetuous जोशीला; fierce प्रचंड।

fifteen *फ़िफ़् टीन* *n.* ten plus five पंद्रह (15)।

fifty *फ़िफ़् टि* *n.* the number next above 49 पचास (50)।

fig *फ़िग* *n.* kind of fruit अंजीर।

fight[1] *फ़ॉइट* *n.* struggle लड़ाई, झगड़ा; fighting spirit लड़ने की चाह।

fight[2] *v.t.* to engage in conflict with किसी के विरुद्ध लड़ना; to contend against विरोध करना; *v.i.* to strive प्रयत्न करना।

figment *फ़िग् मॅन्ट* *n.* fabrication काल्पनिक वस्तु।

figurative *फ़िग् यू रॅ टिव* *a.* metaphorical लाक्षणिक; full of figures of speech आलंकारिक।

figure[1] *फ़ि गॅ:* *n.* a numerical symbol अंक; shape, form आकार, रूप;

human shape मानव-आकृति; a diagram रेखाचित्र; ornament of speech अलंकार।

figure[2] *v.t.* to picture in the mind कल्पना करना; to appear in में प्रदर्शित होना।

file[1] *फ़ॉइल n.* record संचिका; collection of data आंकड़ों का संग्रह।

file[2] *v.t.* to put in a file फ़ाइल में रखना; to refer to a court मुक़दमा चलाना।

file[3] *n.* a roughened tool for smoothing or shaping रेती।

file[4] *v.t.* to apply file to रेती लगाना।

file[5] *n.* row of people मनुष्यों की पंक्ति।

file[6] *v.i.* to march one behind the other पंक्ति में चलना।

fill *फ़िल v.t.* to make full पूरा भरना; to furnish (an office) with an occupant (पद) ग्रहण करना; *v. i.* to become full भर जाना।

film[1] *फ़िल्म n.* motion picture चलचित्र; membrane झिल्ली।

film[2] *v.t.* to make a motion picture of चलचित्र का रूप देना।

filter[1] *फ़िल् टॅः n.* a device through which air, water etc. can pass in order to remove solid particles निस्यंदक, छन्ना।

filter[2] *v.t.* to cause to pass through a filter छानना; *v.i.* to pass through a filter छनना।

filth *फ़िल्थ n.* foul matter कचरा, गंदगी; obscenity अश्लीलता।

filthy *फ़िल् थि a.* unclean अस्वच्छ; foul गंदा, मैला।

fin *फ़िन n.* propelling organ of fish मीनपक्ष।

final *फ़ॉइ नॅल a.* last अंतिम; definite सुनिश्चित; conclusive समापक।

finance[1] *फ़ॉइ नैन्स, फ़ि– n.* revenue वित्त, अर्थ; money affairs अर्थ-व्यवस्था।

finance[2] *v.t.* to manage financially (की) अर्थ-व्यवस्था करना।

financial *फ़ॉइ नैन् शॅल a.* pertaining to finance वित्तीय, आर्थिक।

financier *फ़ॉइ नैन् सि अॅः, फ़ि– n.* one who administers public revenue वित्त-प्रबंधक।

find *फ़ॉइन्ड v.t.* to come across प्राप्त करना; to discover खोजना; to experience अनुभव करना।

fine[1] *फ़ॉइन n.* a sum of money to be paid as a penalty जुर्माना।

fine[2] *v.t.* to impose a fine on जुर्माना करना।

fine[3] *a.* of very good quality उत्तम, उत्कृष्ट; delicate, thin पतला, महीन; enjoyable आनंददायक; pleasant सुहावना; healthy स्वस्थ।

finger[1] *फ़िङ्गॅः n.* one of the five parts at the end of the hand उंगली।

finger[2] *v.t.* to touch with fingers उंगलियों से छूना।

finish[1] *फ़ि निश v.t.* to end समाप्त करना; to complete पूरा करना; to refine परिष्कृत करना; *v.i.* to come to an end समाप्त होना; to be completed पूरा होना।

finish[2] *n.* the last part अंत; perfection पूर्णता; polish परिष्कार।

finite *फ़ॉइ नॉइट a.* having an end or limit सीमित; (*gram.*) a form of verb एक प्रकार की क्रिया।

fir *फ़ॅः n.* kind of timber देवदारू।

fire[1] *फ़ाइअॅः n.* state of burning अग्नि; conflagration अग्निकांड; ardour जोश; shooting of fire arms गोलाबारी।

fire[2] *v.t.* to discharge (गोली) छोड़ना; to cause to burn जलाना; to bake सेंकना; पकाना।

firm[1] *फ़ॅ:म* *a.* stable स्थायी; strong मज़बूत; steady दृढ़; hard कठोर; fixed निश्चित।

firm[2] *n.* a commercial house व्यवसाय–संघ।

first[1] *फ़ॅ:स्ट* *a.* chief प्रमुख; foremost सबसे आगेवाला।

first[2] *n.* first place प्रथम स्थान; first class प्रथम श्रेणी।

first[3] *adv.* in the first place प्रथमतः।

fiscal *फ़िस् कॅल* *a.* pertaining to the public treasury राजकोषीय; financial वित्तीय।

fish[1] *फ़िश* *n.* a well-known aquatic vertebrate मछली; the flesh of this animal used as food मछली का मांस।

fish[2] *v.i.* to catch fish मछली पकड़ना; to search for तलाश करना।

fisherman *फ़ि शॅ: मॅन* *n.* one whose occupation is to catch fish मछुआरा।

fissure *फ़ि शॅ:* *n.* a cleft, a cleavage दरार।

fist *फ़िस्ट* *n.* closed and clenched hand घूंसा।

fistula *फ़िस् ट्यु लॅ* *n.* a deep, narrow, sinuous ulcer नासूर, नाड़ी–व्रण।

fit[1] *फ़िट (-tt-) v.t.* to be suited to के लिए उपयुक्त होना; to be properly adjusted to में ठीक से बैठ जाना; to arrange or adjust बैठाना; *v.i.* to be correctly adjusted ठीक से बैठना; to be of the right size उचित आकार का होना।

fit[2] *a.* well-suited उपयुक्त; proper उचित; ready तैयार; in good condition अच्छी हालत में।

fit[3] *n.* a sudden attack of illness दौरा; a passing state, mood लहर, तरंग, सनक।

fitful *फ़िट् फुल* *a.* irregular अस्थिर।

fitter *फ़ि टॅ:* *n.* one who assembles the parts of a machine मिस्तरी।

five *फ़ॉइव* *n.* the number next after four पांच (5)।

fix[1] *फ़िक्स* *v.t.* to set जमा देना; to assign, to appoint निर्धारित करना, तय करना; *v.i.* to become firm or solidified पक्का या कड़ा हो जाना।

fix[2] *n.* a difficult situation परेशानी।

flabby *फ़्लै बि* *a.* weak दुर्बल; soft शिथिल।

flag *फ़्लैग* *n.* bunting, piece of cloth with a design used as an emblem ध्वज, झंडा।

flagrant *फ़्ले ग्रॅन्ट* *a.* enormous अति, घोर; outrageous दारुण।

flame[1] *फ़्लेम* *n.* blaze of fire ज्वाला; beam of lilght तेज़ लपट; rage क्रोध।

flame[2] *v.i.* to kindle प्रदीप्त होना; to take fire दहकना; to be angry क्रुद्ध होना।

flannel *फ़्लै न्ल* *n.* kind of woollen cloth फ़लालेन।

flare[1] *फ़्ले˘ ॲ:* *v.i.* to spread फैलना; to widen out चौड़ा होना; to blaze up भभक उठना।

flare[2] *n.* sudden blaze भड़क, भभक।

flash[1] *फ़्लैश* *n.* momentary gleam of light कौंध, दमक; sudden burst of feelings भाव-स्फुरण।

flash² *v.t.* to cause to flash चमकाना; to send by sudden means तत्क्षण प्रसारित करना; *v.i.* to sparkle brilliantly कौंधना।

flask *फ़्लास्क* *n.* narrow-necked bottle सुराही।

flat¹ *फ़्लैट* *a.* smooth and level चौपट, चौरस; spread out फैला हुआ; dull नीरस; uniform एक समान; downright साफ़-साफ़, कोरा।

flat² *n.* suite of rooms on one floor of a building भवन-खंड, कमरों का सैट; flat part of anything चपटा भाग।

flatter *फ़्लै टॅ* *v.t.* to overpraise चापलूसी करना; to coax फुसलाना।

flattery *फ़्लै टॅ रि* *n.* insincere praise चापलूसी।

flavour *फ़्लै वॅः* *n.* sweet smell सुवास, सुगंध; taste आस्वाद।

flaw *फ़्लौ* *n.* defect दोष।

flea *फ़्ली* *n.* a small blood-sucking insect पिस्सू।

flee *फ़्ली* *v.i.* to run away रफूचक्कर होना।

fleece¹ *फ़्लीस* *n.* sheep's wool ऊन।

fleece² *v.t.* to shear (की) ऊन कतरना; to plunder लूटना।

fleet *फ़्लीट* *n.* a number of warships under one commander जहाज़ी बेड़ा; a number of vehicles working under one command जत्था, बेड़ा।

flesh *फ़्लैशॅ* *n.* soft part between skin and bone मांस; soft substance of fruit गूदा; the body शरीर; sensual appetite दुर्वासना।

flexible *फ़्लै ॅक् सॅ ब्ल* *a.* pliant लचीला; adaptable अनुकूलनीय।

flicker¹ *फ़्लि कॅः* *n.* an unsteady light टिमटिमाहट, झिलमिलाहट।

flicker² *v.t.* to burn unsteadily टिमटिमाना।

flight *फ़्लॉइट* *n.* passing through the air उड़ान; fleeing पलायन; ladder सीढ़ी।

flimsy *फ़्लिम् ज़ि* *a.* thin पतला, झीना; weak क्षीण।

fling *फ़्लिङ्ग* *v.t.* to throw violently फेंकना।

flippancy *फ़्लि पॅन् सि* *n.* undue levity छिछोरापन।

flirt¹ *फ़्लॅःट* *n.* person who flirts चोचलेबाज़ व्यक्ति।

flirt² *v.i.* to make a show of love दिखावटी प्रेम करना।

float *फ़्लोट* *v.i.* to be borne on water उतरना, तैरना; to flow बहना; to hang around मंडराना; *v.t.* to cause to be conveyed on water प्रवाहित करना।

flock¹ *फ़्लौकॅ* *n.* company of animals or birds झुंड; group समूह।

flock² *v.i.* to gather or go in crowds एकत्र होना।

flog *फ़्लौगॅ* *(-gg-)* *v.t.* to beat or strike पीटना, प्रहार करना; to lash कोड़े लगाना।

flood¹ *फ़्लड* *n.* a great flow of water जलप्लावन; a deluge बाढ़; abundance प्रचुरता।

flood² *v.t.* to overflow जलमग्न करना; to deluge बाढ़ग्रस्त करना।

floor¹ *फ़्लौः* *n.* surface तल; bottom of the room फ़र्श; storey in a building मंज़िल, तल्ला।

floor² *v.t.* to furnish with a floor (में) फ़र्श बनाना।

flora *फ़्लौ रॅ* *n.* vegetation in a region वनस्पति।

florist *फ़्लौ ˘ रिस्ट* *n.* seller of flowers फूल-विक्रेता; producer of flowers पुष्पोत्पादक।

flour *फ़्लॉउअॅ:* *n.* finely ground meal आटा।

flourish *फ़्ल रिश* *v.i.* to thrive फलना-फूलना।

flow[1] *फ़्लो* *n.* stream प्रवाह; rise of tide ज्वार।

flow[2] *v.i.* to run (as water) प्रवाहित होना; to move in a stream घूमना।

flower *फ़्लॉउ अॅ:* *n.* a blossom पुष्प; choicest part सर्वोत्तम भाग।

flowery *फ़्लॉउ अॅ रि* *a.* full of flowers पुष्पमय; embellished with figurative language अलंकृत।

fluent *फ़्लु अॅन्ट* *a.* flowing प्रवाह-युक्त।

fluid[1] *फ़्लु इड, फ़्लू–* *a.* capable of flowing तरल; changeable परिवर्तनीय।

fluid[2] *n.* substance capable of flowing द्रव्य।

flush[1] *फ़्लश* *v.i.* to blush लज्जा से लाल हो जाना; to flow suddenly or violently तेज़ी से या अचानक बहना; to be excited उत्तेजित होना; *v. t.* to cleanse by rush of water पानी के बहाव द्वारा साफ करना; to excite उत्तेजित करना।

flush[2] *n.* sudden flow of blood to the face लज्जा भाव-जनित चेहरे की लाली; excitement उत्तेजना; flow of water प्रवाह; elation आनंदातिरेक।

flute[1] *फ़्लूट* *n.* a small wind-instrument with holes and keys बांसुरी।

flute[2] *v.i.* to play on a flute बांसुरी बजाना।

flutter[1] *फ़्ल टॅ:* *n.* flapping movement फड़फड़ाहट।

flutter[2] *v.t.* to flap rapidly फड़फड़ाना, फड़फड़ करना।

fly[1] *फ़्लॉइ* *n.* a two-winged insect मक्खी।

fly[2] *v.i.* to move through the air on wings उड़ना; to travel by an aircraft वायुयान-द्वारा यात्रा करना; to pilot an aircraft वायुयान उड़ाना; to move swiftly तेज़ी से गुज़रना।

foam[1] *फ़ोम* *n.* froth फेन, झाग।

foam[2] *v.t.* to froth झाग पैदा करना।

focal *फ़ो कॅल* *a.* belonging to a focus नाभीय।

focus[1] *फ़ोकॅस* *n.* point at which rays of light, heat, etc. meet किरण-केंद्र; centre of interest अभिरुचि-केंद्र, केंद्र-बिंदु।

focus[2] *(-s-or-ss-)* *v.t.* to bring to focus फ़ोकस करना; to concentrate संकेंद्रित करना।

fodder *फ़ौ ˘ डॅ:* *n.* food for cattle चारा।

foe *फ़ो* *n.* enemy शत्रु।

fog *फ़ौगॅ* *n.* thich mist कोहरा।

foil *फौ ˘ इल* *v.t.* to frustrate निष्फल करना; to baffle हरा देना।

fold[1] *फ़ोल्ड* *n.* the doubling or doubled part of any flexible substance तह, परत; enclosure for sheep भेड़शाला, बाड़ा।

fold[2] *v.t.* to double मोड़ना; to embrace बांहों में भरना; *v.i.* to become folded मुड़ना।

foliage *फ़ो लि इज* *n.* leaves collectively पर्णसमूह।

folk *फ़ोक* *n.* people in general.

follow *फौ ˘ लो* *v.t.* to attend on

अनुगमन करना; to conform to अनुसरण करना; to understand समझना; to engage in पेशे के रूप में करना; to result from (का) परिणाम होना; to pursue पीछा करना; to come after के बाद आना।

follower *फ़ौ॑ लो ऑ:* *n.* disciple शिष्य; attendant अनुचर; imitator अनुकर्ता।

folly *फ़ौ॑ लि* *n.* foolishness मूर्खता।

foment *फ़ौ॑ मैन्ट* *v.t.* to apply warm lotions to सेंकना; to stir up भड़काना।

fond *फ़ौन्ड* *a.* having a liking शौकीन; doting चाहनेवाला; foolish मूर्खतापूर्ण।

fondle *फ़ौ॑ न् ड्ल* *v.t.* to caress दुलारना, पुचकारना।

food *फ़ूड* *n.* what one feeds on भोजन।

fool *फ़ूल* *n.* stupid person मूर्ख व्यक्ति; jester मसखरा।

foolish *फ़ुलिश* *a.* stupid मूर्ख; marked with folly मूर्खतापूर्ण।

foolscap *फ़ूल्ज़ कैप* *n.* printing paper measuring 17" × 131/2" 17"×131/2" नाप का कागज।

foot *फ़ुट* *n.* part of the body used for standing पांव, पैर; base आधार; lower end निचला सिरा; measure of 12 inches फ़ुट।

for[1] *फ़ौ:* *prep.* with the prupose of के हेतु; in exchange for के बदले में; in support of के पक्ष में; because of के कारण; meant for के लिए; in respect of के उपलक्ष्य में; for the length or duration of की दूरी अथवा अवधि के लिए; in spite of के बावजूद; in search of की तलाश में, towards की ओर।

for[2] *conj.* because क्योंकि।

forbid *फ़ॅ: बिड* *v.t.* to prohibit निषिद्ध करना।

force[1] *फ़ौ:स* *n.* strength शक्ति; compulsion अनिवार्यता, body of troops सैन्य-बल; violence बल प्रयोग।

force[2] *v.t.* to compel बाध्य करना; to break open तोड़ना।

forceful *फ़ौ:स् फ़ुल* *a.* full of force सशक्त, बलशाली।

forcible *फ़ौ:स् सॅ ब्ल* *a.* done by force बलात संपादित।

forearm[1] *फ़ौर: आ:म* *n.* arm between elbow and the wrist प्रबाहु।

forearm[2] *v.t.* to arm beforehand पहले से शस्त्रसज्जित करना।

forecast[1] *फ़ौ: कास्ट* *n.* prediction पूर्वानुमान।

forecast[2] *फ़ौ: कास्ट* *v.t.* to foresee पूर्वानुमान करना; to predict भविष्यवाणी करना।

forefather *फ़ौ: फ़ादॅ* *n.* ancestor पूर्वज।

forefinger *फ़ौ: फ़िङ्गॅ:* *n.* finger next to thumb तर्जनी।

forehead *फ़ॉ: हेड* *n.* forepart of the head माथा, मस्तक।

foreign *फ़ौ॑ रिन* *a.* belonging to another country विदेशीय; alien पराया; inappropriate असंगत; irrelevant अप्रासंगिक।

foreigner *फ़ौ रिनॅ:* *n.* one who belongs to another country विदेशी व्यक्ति।

foreknowledge *फ़ौ: नौ॑ लिज* *n.* knowledge beforehand अग्रज्ञान, पूर्वज्ञान।

foreleg *फ़ौ: लैगॅ* *n.* a quadruped's

front leg अगली टांग।

forelock *फ़ौ: लौकॅ n.* lock of hair on the forehead माथे पर की अलक।

foreman *फ़ौ: मॅन n.* workman in charge of other workers अग्रणी, अगुआ।

foremost *फ़ौ: मोस्ट a.* first in rank or dignity सर्वोत्तम, सर्वोपरि।

forenoon *फ़ौ: नून n.* morning पूर्वाह।

forerunner *फ़ो: र नॅ: n.* precursor अग्रदूत।

foresee *फ़ौ:सी v.t.* to see or know beforehand पहले से ही देख या जान लेना।

foresight *फ़ौ: सॉइट n.* act or power of foreseeing दूरदर्शिता; prudence अग्रदृष्टि।

forest *फ़ौ: रिस्ट n.* wood, jungle जंगल, वन।

forestall *फ़ौ: स्टौल v.t.* to guard against in advance रोकथाम करना; to anticipate पूर्व से ही देख या जान लेना।

forester *फ़ौ रिस् टॅ: n.* one who watches a forest वनरक्षक।

forestry *फ़ौ रिस् ट्रि n.* science of caring for forests वानिकी, वनविज्ञान।

foretell *फ़ौ: टैलॅ v.t.* to predict भविष्यवाणी करना।

forethought *फ़ौ: थौॅट n.* a thinking beforehand पूर्व विचार; foresight दूरदृष्टि।

forever *फ़ॅ रै ॅ वॅ: adv.* for always सदैव के लिए।

forewarn *फ़ौ: वौ:न v.t.* to warn beforehand पूर्व चेतावनी देना; to give previous notice to पूर्व सूचना देना।

foreword *फ़ौ: वॅ:ड n.* preface भूमिका।

forfeit[1] *फ़ौ: फ़िट v.t.* to lose by penalty ज़ब्त हो जाना।

forfeit[2] *n.* penalty, fine जुरमाना; thing forfeited अपवर्तित वस्तु।

forfeiture *फ़ौ: फ़ि चॅ: n.* act of forfeiting अपवर्तन, ज़ब्ती।

forge[1] *फ़ौ:ज n.* place where metal is worked मिस्तरी-खाना; smithy लोहार की दुकान; furnace भट्ठी।

forge[2] *v.t.* to shape (metal) by heating (धातु को) तपाकर गढ़ना; to make बनाना; to make a fraudulent copy of (की) जाली नक़ल करना।

forgery *फ़ौ: जॅ रि n.* forging of a document etc. जालसाज़ी; forged document जालसाज़ी वाला दस्तावेज़।

forget *फ़ॅ: गै ॅट v.t.* to lose the remembrance of भूल जाना; to neglect की उपेक्षा करना।

forgetful *फ़ॅ: गै ॅट् फुल a.* apt to forget भुलक्कड़; neglectful लापरवाह।

forgive *फ़ॅ: गिव v.t.* to pardon क्षमा करना।

forgo *फ़ौ: गो v.t.* to renounce त्याग देना; to do without के बिना काम चलाना।

forlorn *फ़ॅ: लौ:न a.* deserted परित्यक्त; miserable दु:खी, अभागा।

form[1] *फ़ौ:म n.* shape आकार; type, kind प्रकार; structure ढांचा; style शैली; condition दशा; formality औपचारिकता, शिष्टाचार; printed paper with spaces to be filled in प्रपत्र; class कक्षा।

form² *v.t.* to shape बनाना; to develop विकसित करना; to organise गठित करना; *v.i.* to take shape निर्मित होना, बनना।

formal *फ़ौ: मॅल a.* ceremonious औपचारिक; apparent दिखाऊ, ऊपरी; related to form आकारिक।

format *फ़ौ: मैट n.* get-up of a book ग्रंथ का आकार।

formation *फ़ौ: मे शॅन n.* forming निर्माण; thing formed निर्मित वस्तु; structure रचना, बनावट।

former¹ *फ़ौ: मॅ: a.* earlier in time पूर्वकालिक; first named पहला।

former² *pron.* first named thing or person पूर्वोक्त वस्तु या व्यक्ति।

formerly *फ़ौ: मॅ: लि adv.* in time past गतकाल में।

formidable *फ़ौ: मि डॅ बल a.* exciting fear or apprehension भयावह; difficult कठिन।

formula *फ़ौ: म्यु लॅ n.* rule नियम, सूत्र; recipe नुसखा।

formulate *फ़ौ: म्यु लेट v.t.* to express in a formula सूत्रबद्ध करना; to put into a precise and comprehensive statement निश्चित व शुद्ध रूप में प्रस्तुत करना।

forsake *फ़ॅ: सेक v.t.* to abandon त्याग देना।

forswear *फ़ौ: स्वे ॅ अॅ: v.t.* to renounce upon oath त्यागना; to deny on oath क़सम खाकर इनकार करना।

fort *फ़ौ:ट n.* a fortified place क़िला।

forte *फ़ौ: टि n.* something in which a person excels विशिष्टता।

forth *फ़ौ:थ adv.* forward आगे; out बाहर।

forthcoming *फ़ौ:थ् क मिङ्ग a.* coming forth आगामी; ready for use, available उपलब्ध।

forthwith *फ़ौ:थ् विद adv.* without delay तुरंत।

fortify *फ़ौ: टि फ़ॉइ v.t.* to strengthen मज़बूत करना।

fortitude *फ़ौ: टि ट्यूड n.* patient courage धैर्य।

fort-night *फ़ौ:ट् नॉइट n.* two weeks पखवारा।

fortress *फ़ौ: ट्रिस n.* a fort क़िला।

fortunate *फ़ौ: चॅ निट a.* having good fortune भाग्यशाली; coming by good luck भाग्य-जनित।

fortune *फ़ौ: चॅन n.* luck, chance भाग्य, दैवयोग; wealth धन, संपत्ति।

forty *फ़ौ:टि n.* four tens चालीस (40)।

forum *फ़ौ: रॅम n.* a place for open discussion मंच।

forward¹ *फ़ौ: वॅ:ड a.* lying in front अग्रिम; advanced अग्रवर्ती; impudent ढीठ।

forward² *adv.* onward आगे की ओर; towards the future भविष्य में; to the front आगे।

forward³ *v.t.* to send forward अग्रसारित करना; to send भेजना।

fossil *फ़ौ ॅ सिल n.* remains of a prehistoric animal or plant जीवाश्म।

foster *फ़ौ ॅस् टॅ: v.t.* to encourage प्रोत्साहन देना; to bring up पोषण करना।

foul *फ़ॉउल a.* unfair नियमविरूद्ध; dishonest बेईमान; evil smelling बदबूदार; abusive गाली-भरा।

found *फ़ॉउन्ड v.t.* to establish स्थापित करना; to start building

(की) बुनियाद रखना।

foundation *फ़ॉउन् डै शॅन n.* basis आधार; solid ground or base on which a building rests बुनियाद, नींव; act of founding संस्थापन।

founder *फ़ॉउन् डॅः n.* one who lays a foundation stone संस्थापक।

foundry *फ़ॉउन् ड्रि n.* art of casting ढलाई की कला; the place of casting ढलाई-घर।

fountain *फ़ाउन् टिन n.* spring of water झरना; artificial jet of water फ़व्वारा।

four *फ़ौः n.* the number next after three (4) चार।

fourteen *फ़ौः टीन n.* the number next after thirteen (14) चौदह।

fowl *फ़ॉउल n.* domestic cock or hen पालतू मुर्गा या मुर्गी।

fowler *फ़ॉउ लॅः n.* one who kills or traps birds चिड़ीमार।

fox *फ़ौक्स n.* a small animal of the dog family लोमड़ी।

fraction *फ़ैक् शॅन n.* small part of a whole अंश; (maths) any part of a unit भिन्न।

fracture[1] *फ़ैक्चॅः n.* breaking of a bone अस्थिभंग।

fracture[2] *v.t.* to cause to break तोड़ना।

fragile *फ़्रै जॉइल a.* easily broken or damaged भंगुर।

fragment *फ़्रैग् मॅन्ट n.* piece broken off खंडित अंश; an incomplete part अंश।

fragrance *फ़्रेग् रॅन्स n.* sweet smell सुवास, खुशबू।

fragrant *फ़्रैग् रॅन्ट a.* sweet- smelling सुगंधित।

frail *फ़्रेल a.* weak, delicate कमज़ोर, सुकुमार।

frame[1] *फ़्रैम v.t.* to make बनाना; to surround with a frame (पर) चौखट लगाना।

frame[2] *n.* main structure of a building ढांचा; human or animal shape पंजर; surrounding part चौखटा; part of spectacles फ्रेम।

frachise *फ़्रैन् चॉइज़ n.* right to vote मताधिकार।

frank *फ़्रैङ्क a.* outspoken निष्कपट, स्पष्टवादी।

frantic *फ़्रैन् टिक a.* wildly excited उत्तेजित।

fraternal *फ्र˘ टॅः नॅल a.* brotherly भ्रात्रीय।

fraternity *फ़्रॅ टॅः नि टि n.* brotherly feeling भ्रातृत्व; a body of men associated by a common interest भ्रातृसंघ।

fratricide *फ़्रै ट्रि सॉइट n.* the act of killing one's brother or sister भाई/बहिन की हत्या; one who does so भ्रातृहंता।

fraud *फ़्रोड n.* deceit धोखा; trickery चालबाज़ी।

fraudulent *फ़्रौ ड्यु लॅन्ट a.* using fraud कपटी, कपटपूर्ण।

fraught *फ़्रौट a.* full (of) भरा हुआ।

fray *फ़्रे n.* a fight लड़ाई, मुकाबला।

free[1] *फ़्री a.* independent आत्मनिर्भर; not controlled by others स्वाधीन; not occupied खाली, अव्यस्त; not subject to cost or tax मुफ्त, निःशुल्क; unhindered निर्बाध; exempt मुक्त; not literal स्वतंत्र।

free[2] *v.t.* to set at liberty मुक्त करना।

freedom *फ़्री डॅम n.* state of being free स्वतंत्रता।

freeze *फ़्रीज v.i.* to be congealed by cold जम जाना; to be hardened into ice बर्फ बनना; *v.t.* to chill ठिठुराना; to change into ice बर्फ में बदलना; to fix स्थिर करना।

freight *फ़्रेट n.* charge for the transportation of goods भाड़ा।

French[1] *फ़्रैन्च a.* pertaining to France. फ़्रॉन्स-संबंधी।

French[2] *n.* the language of France फ़्रॉन्स की भाषा।

frenzy *फ़्रैन् ज़ि n.* violent agitation of the mind उन्माद।

frequency *फ़्री क्वॅन् सि n.* frequent occurrence बारंबारता।

frequent *फ़्री क्वॅन्ट n.* that takes place repeatedly बार-बार होने वाला।

fresh *फ़ ॅश a.* unused अप्रयुक्त; new नया, ताज़ा; full of health, not tired अश्रांत; additional अतिरिक्त; inexperienced अनुभवहीन।

fret[1] *फ़्रैटॅ n.* irritation चिड़चिड़ापन।

fret[2] *(-tt-) v.t.* to cause to worry चिंतित करना; *v.i.* to worry चिंतित होना।

friction *फ़्रिक् शॅन n.* rubbing रगड़; disagreement मनमुटाव।

Friday *फ़्रॉइ डे, –डि n.* sixth day of the week शुक्रवार।

fridge *फ़्रिज n.* refrigerator प्रशीतियंत्र।

friend *फ़्रैन्ड n.* intimate associate मित्र; an ally सहायक।

fright *फ़्रॉइट n.* terror, sudden fear भीति, भय।

frighten *फ़्रॉइ ट्न v.t.* to make afraid भयभीत करना।

frigid *फ़्रि जिड a.* cold ठंडा; without feeling or spirit भावशून्य, उदासीन।

frill *फ़्रिल n.* an ornamental edging झालर।

fringe[1] *फ़्रिन्ज n.* an ornamental border of hanging threads झब्बेदार किनारा।

fringe[2] *v.t.* to furnish with frill झब्बा लगाना।

frivolous *फ़्रि वॅ लॅस a.* trifling तुच्छ; not serious छिछोरा।

frock *फ़्रौकॅ n.* a monk's robe चोग़ा, लबादा; a dress worn by a woman or a baby फ़्रॉक।

frog *फ़्रौगॅ n.* an amphibious animal मेढक।

frolic[1] *फ़्रौ ॅ लिक n.* gaiety प्रसन्नता; merry making उछलकूद।

frolic[2] *(-ck-) v.i.* to jump playfully उछलकूद करना।

from *फ़्रौम, फ़्रॅम prep.* expressing point of departure, source, distance, cause, change of state etc. से।

front[1] *फ़्रन्ट n.* fore part अग्रभाग; position directly ahead अगवाड़ा, आगा; battle line or area मोरचा।

front[2] *a.* at the front of सामने का, सामने वाला।

front[3] *v.t.* to face के सामने होना।

frontier *फ़्रन् टिअ: n.* border of a country सीमांत।

frost *फ़्रौस्ट n.* snow तुषार, हिम; cold शीत; frozen dew जमी ओस।

frown[1] *फ़्राउॅन n.* stern look तेवर।

frown[2] *v.i.* to winkle eyebrows भौहें चढ़ाना।

frugal *फ्रू गॅल a.* economical मितव्ययी; cheap सस्ता।

fruit *फ्रूट n.* seed and its envelope फल; advantage लाभ।

fruitful *फ्रूट् फुल a.* very productive फलोत्पादक; profitable लाभकारी।

frustrate *फ्रस् ट्रेट v.t.* to balk कुंठित करना; to make vain विफल करना।

frustration *फ्रस् ट्रे शॅन n.* despondency हताशा।

fry[1] *फ्रॉइ v.t.* to cook with fat घी आदि में छोंकना; *v.i.* to be cooked in fat छुंकना।

fry[2] *n.* young fish पोना।

fuel *फ्यू ॲल n.* material for burning ईंधन; something that feeds passion उद्दीपक वस्तु।

fugitive[1] *फ्यू जि टिव a.* fleeting भगोड़ा; transitory क्षणभंगुर।

fugitive[2] *n.* absconder भगोड़ा।

fulfil *फुल् फ़िल v.t.* to complete पूर्ण करना; to comply with कार्यरूप में परिणत करना।

fulfilment *फुल् फिल मॅन्ट n.* completion पूर्ति; accomplishment निर्वाह।

full[1] *फुल a.* filled up भरपूर, पूरा; entire समग्र, अशेष; abundant भरपूर।

full[2] *adv.* fully पूर्णतया; very अत्यंत।

fullness *फुल् निस n.* completion परिपूर्णता; abundance प्रचुरता।

fully *फु लि adv.* entirely पूर्ण रूप से।

fumble *फ़म् ब्ल v.i.* to grope about awakwardly टटोलना; to attempt or handle something bunglingly गड़बड़ कर देना।

fun *फ़न n.* merriment आमोद-प्रमोद।

function[1] *फ़ङ् क् शॅन n.* performance उत्सव; duty, work कर्त्तव्य, कार्य।

function[2] *v.i.* to operate, to work काम करना।

functionary *फ़ङ् क् शॅ नॅ रि n.* an official अधिकारी।

fund *फ़न्ड n.* treasure ख़ज़ाना, निधि; stock, supply भंडार, आपूर्ति।

fundamental *फ़न् डॅ मैन्ॅ टॅल a.* basic आधारभूत; essential तात्विक।

funeral *फ्यू नॅ रॅल n.* disposal of the dead अंत्येष्टि; the procession taking a dead body to a cemetery शव-यात्रा।

fungus *फ़ङ् गॅस n.* toadstool कवक, फफूंद।

funny *फ़ नि n.* full of fun मज़ाकिया।

fur *फ़ॅ: n.* soft fine hair of certain animals पशुलोम।

furious *फ्युॲ रि ॲस a.* wild, savage उग्र; enraged क्रोधोन्मत्त।

furl *फ़ॅ: ल v.t.* to roll up लपेटना; to wind up समेटना।

furlong *फ़ॅ: लौ ङ्ग n.* an eighth of a mile फर्लांग।

furnace *फ़ॅ: निस n.* enclosed structure for producing great heat अग्निकुंड, भट्ठी।

furnish *फ़ॅ: निश v.t.* to equip सुसज्जित करना; to supply उपलब्ध कराना।

furniture *फ़ॅ: नि चॅ: n.* decorative household equipment साज-सज्जा, फ़र्नीचर।

furrow *फ़ रो n.* trench made by a plough हलरेखा, कूंड़।

further[1] *फ़ॅ: दॅ: adv.* more और अधिक; in addition इसके अतिरिक्त; to a greater distance और आगे की ओर।

further² *a.* additional अतिरिक्त, और अधिक; more distant और आगे स्थित।

further³ *v.t.* to help forward आगे बढ़ाना।

fury *फ्युअॅ रि* *n.* violent passion उन्माद।

fuse¹ *फ्यूज़* *v.t.* to melt पिघला देना; to blend मिला देना; *v.i.* to be melted पिघल जाना।

fuse² *n.* wire inserted in an electric circuit as a safety device फ़्यूज़ तार।

fusion *फ़्यू ज़ॅन* *n.* blending, melting विलयन, संलयन।

fuss¹ *फ़स* *n.* flurry गड़बड़ी।

fuss² *v.i.* to make fuss गड़बड़ी करना।

futile *फ्यू टॉइल* *a.* worthless निरर्थक; serving no useful end व्यर्थ।

futility *फ्यू टि लि टि* *n.* quality of being futile निरर्थकता।

future¹ *फ्यू चॅः* *a.* that is to be भावी; (*gram.*) pertaining to the time to come भविष्यत्कालिक।

future² *n.* the time to come भविष्य।

Gg

G जी the seventh letter of the English alphabet, the fifth note of the diatonic scale. अंग्रेजी वर्णमाला का सातवाँ अक्षर, गायन में पाँचवाँ स्वर; It has a hard sound before a, o, u, l and r and is sounded soft before e, i, y इसका उच्चारण a, o, u, l तथा r के पूर्व रहने पर 'ग' तथा e, i, y के पूर्व रहने पर 'ज' होता है; it is silent in some words, कुछ शब्दों में इसका उच्चारण नहीं होता, यथा, "gnat-नॉट्" "gnaw-नॉ" इत्यादि में।

gabble *गै ब्ल* *v.i.* to talk fast or without meaning ऊलजलूल बातें करना।

gadfly *गैड् फ्लॉइ* *n.* a fly which stings cattle डांस।

gag¹ *गैग* *(-gg-)* *v.t.* to stop up (somebody's mouth) with cloth etc. (किसी के मुंह) में कपड़ा ठूंसना; to deprive of free speech अभिव्यक्ति की स्वतंत्रता से वंचित करना।

gag² *n.* cloth etc. used to stop up somebody's mouth कपड़ा आदि जो किसी के मुंह में ठूंसा जाय।

gaiety *गे अॅ टि* *n.* cheerfulness, liveliness प्रफुल्लता, आमोद-प्रमोद, मौज-मस्ती।

gain¹ *गेन* *v.t.* to obtain प्राप्त करना; to get as advantage लाभ के रूप में प्राप्त करना; to earn कमाना; to reach पहुंचना।

gain² *n.* profit लाभ; increase वृद्धि।

gainsay *गेन् से* *v.t.* to deny प्रतिवाद करना।

gait *गेट* *n.* manner of walking चाल।

galaxy *गै लॅक् सि* *n.* milky way आकाश गंगा; an assemblage of splendid persons विशिष्ट व्यक्तियों की मंडली।

gale *गेल n.* a strong wind तेज़ हवा, अंधड़।

gallant[1] *गै लॅन्ट a.* handsome सुंदर; brave बहादुर; attentive to ladies रमणीरंजक।

gallant[2] *n.* lover प्रेमी; fashionable young man छबीला नौजवान।

gallantry *गै लॅन् ट्रि n.* bravery बहादुरी; courtesy शिष्टता; attentiveness to ladies नारी भक्ति।

gallery *गै लॅ रि n.* a covered passage दीर्घा; room for the exhibition of works of art चित्रशाला।

gallon *गै लॅन n.* a liquid measure of four quarts or eight points गैलन।

gallop[1] *गै लॅप n.* fastest pace of horse चौकड़ी।

gallop[2] *v.t.* to cause to move fast सरपट दौड़ाना; *v.i.* to move very fast सरपट दौड़ना।

gallows *गै लौज़ n. sing.* wooden frame for hanging criminals फांसी का तख़्ता; hanging फांसी।

galore *गॅ लौः adv.* in abundance प्रचुर मात्रा में।

galvanize *गैल् वॅ नॉइज़ v.t.* to coat with zinc जस्ता या क़लई चढ़ाना; to stimulate प्रेरित करना।

gamble[1] *गैम् बॅल v.i.* to play for high stakes जुआ खेलना; to take a chance दांव लगाना।

gamble[2] *n.* game of chance for money जुआ, द्यूतक्रीड़ा।

gambler *गैम् ब्लॅः n.* one who gambles जुआरी।

game[1] *गेम n.* sport of any kind खेल, क्रीड़ा; trick चाल, छल; animals or birds hunted शिकार।

game[2] *v.i.* to gamble जुआ खेलना।

gander *गैन् डॅः n.* a male goose हंस।

gang *गैङ्ग n.* band of criminals गिरोह।

gangster *गैङ्ग् स्टॅ n.* member of a criminal gang लुटेरों के गिरोह का सदस्य।

gap *गैप n.* opening दरार; breach in continuity क्रमभंग; interval अंतराल।

gape *गेप v.i.* to open the mouth wide मुंह फाड़ना; to yawn जम्हाई लेना; to stare with open mouth देखते रह जाना।

garage *गैराःज़, –रिज n.* building in which motor-vehicles are housed यानशाला, गैरेज।

garb[1] *गाःब n.* dress परिधान।

garb[2] *v.t.* to clothe परिधान पहनाना।

garbage *गाः बिज n.* refuse कूड़ा-कचरा।

garden *गाः ड्न n.* park, ground on which flowers are cultivated उद्यान, बाग़।

gardener *गाःड् नॅः n.* one engaged in gardening माली।

gargle *गाः ग्ल v.i.* to wash the throat ग़रारे करना; *v.t.* to wash (the throat) ग़रारे-द्वारा (गला) साफ़ करना।

garland[1] *गाः लॅन्ड n.* wreath of flowers माला, हार।

garland[2] *v.t.* to deck with garland माला पहनाना।

garlic *गाः लिक n.* strongly flavoured onion-like bulb लहसुन।

garment *गा: मॅन्ट* *n.* an article of clothing वस्त्र, परिधान।

garter *गा: टॅ:* *n.* band used to support a stocking मोज़ाबंध।

gas *गैस* *n.* any air-like substance गैस; gasoline पैट्रोल।

gasket *गैस् किट* *n.* a piece of metal or rubber used for sealing गैसकेट अवरोधक डोरी।

gasp[1] *गास्प* *n.* a sudden, sharp intake of breath हाँफा।

gasp[2] *v.i.* to struggle for breath हांफना।

gassy *गै ॅसि* *a.* full of gas गैस-युक्त।

gastric *गै ॅस् ट्रिक* *a.* belonging to the stomach जठर-संबंधी।

gate *गेट* *n.* entrance द्वार; passage into a building, city or enclosure फाटक।

gather *गै दॅ:* *v.t.* to collect एकत्र करना; to pick तोड़ना; to conclude निष्कर्ष निकालना; *v.i.* to assemble इकट्ठा होना।

gaudy *गौ डि* *a.* showy दिखाऊ; gay भड़कीला।

gauge *गेज* *n.* a measuring instrument पैमाना; a device for measuring rain वर्षामापी यंत्र।

gauntlet *गौन्ट् लिट* *n.* iron glove of armour हस्तत्राण।

gay *गे* *a.* gaudy भड़कीला; merry प्रफुल्लित; lively ज़िंदादिल।

gaze[1] *गेज़* *v.t.* to look fixedly एकटक देखना।

gaze[2] *n.* fixed look टकटकी।

gazette *गॅ ज़ैॅट* *n.* official newspaper containing list of government appointments etc. गज़ट, राजपत्र।

gear *गिअॅ:* *n.* cogged wheel गरारी; equipment उपस्कर।

geld *गैल्ड* *v.t.* to castrate बधिया करना।

gem *जै मॅ* *n.* any precious stone रत्न।

gender *जैन् डॅ:* *n.* grammatical classification of sexes लिंग।

general *जै ॅ नॅ रॅ ल* *a.* ordinary साधारण; belonging to all सार्वजनिक।

generally *जै ॅ नॅ रॅ लि* *adv.* in a general or collective manner सामान्यतः।

generate *जै ॅ नॅ रेट* *v.t.* to produce पैदा करना।

generation *जै ॅ नॅ रे शॅन* *n.* descendants, race पीढ़ी; production उत्पादन।

generator *जै ॅ नॅ रे टॅ:* *n.* producer उत्पादक, जनित्र।

generosity *जै ॅ नॅ रौ ॅ सि टि* *n.* nobleness उदारता।

generous *जै ॅ नॅ रॅस* *a.* liberal उदार; ample प्रचुर।

genius *जी नि अॅस, जी न्यॅस* *n.* special inborn faculty of any individual प्रतिभा; person endowed with natural talent प्रतिभाशाली व्यक्ति।

gentle *जैन् ट्ल* *a.* noble कुलीन; refined भद्र; mild, moderate मंद।

gentleman *जैन् ट्ल् मॅन* *n.* a man of good social position भद्रपुरुष।

gentry *जैन् ट्रि* *n.* class of gentle people कुलीनलोग।

genuine *जै ॅ न्यु इन* *a.* original असली; natural अकृत्रिम; real यथार्थ।

geographer जि औ ॅ ग्रॅ फॅः *n.* person having knowledge of geography भूगोलवेत्ता।

geographical जि अॅ ग्रै फ़ि कॅल *a.* pertaining to geography भौगोलिक।

geography जि औ ॅ ग्रॅ फ़ि *n.* science of sufrace of the earth and its inhabitants भूगोल।

geological जि अॅ लौ ॅ जि कॅल *a.* pertaining to geology भूविज्ञानीय।

geologist जि औ ॅ लॅ जिस्ट *n.* person having the knowledge of geology भूविज्ञान-वेत्ता।

geology जि औ ॅ लॅ जि *n.* science relating to the history and development of the earth's crust भूविज्ञान।

geometrical जि अॅ मै ॅ ट्रि कॅल *a.* relating to geometry रेखागणितीय।

geometry जि औ ॅ मॅ ट्रि *n.* study of lines, angles and figures रेखागणित।

germ जॅ :म *n.* origin स्रोत; microbe जीवाणु; bacillus रोगाणु।

germicide जॅः मि सॉइड *n.* substance that kills germs जीवाणुनाशी।

germinate जॅः मि नेट *v.i.* to sprout अंकुरित होना; to begin to grow as seeds बढ़ना।

germination जॅः मि ने शॅन *n.* act of germinating अंकुरण।

gerund जै ॅ रॅन्ड *n.* a kind of verbal noun क्रियावाचक संज्ञा।

gesture जैसॅ् चॅः *n.* a posture or motion of the body or limbs चेष्टा, संकेत।

get गै ॅट *v.t.* to obtain प्राप्त करना; to earn कमाना; to catch ग्रहण करना; to receive प्राप्त करना; *v.i.* to become होना।

ghastly गाःस्ट् लि *a.* hideous घिनावना; frightful भयानक।

ghost गोस्ट *n.* the soul of man प्रेतात्मा; disembodied spirit भूत।

giant जॉइ अॅन्ट *n.* demon दैत्य; man of extraordinary stature भीमकाय व्यक्ति।

gibbon गि बॅन *n.* a type of ape लंगूर।

gibe[1] जॉइब *v.i.* to scoff ताना मारना; to mock हंसी उड़ाना।

gibe[2] *n.* a scoff उपहास; taunt ताना।

giddy गि डि *a.* dizzy चक्कंर से आक्रांत; causing giddiness चकरानेवाला; flighty अत्यधिक, चपल।

gift गिफ्ट *n.* present उपहार; talent प्रतिभा।

gifted गिफ़् टिड *a.* talented प्रतिभाशाली।

gigantic जॉइ गैन् टिक *a.* of immense size भीमकाय।

giggle गि गल *v.i.* to laugh in a silly manner फूहड़ढंग से हंसना।

gild गिल्ड *v.t.* to cover with gold (पर) सोना चढ़ाना; to adorn with lustre चमकाना।

gilt गिल्ट *a.* gold-coloured सुनहरा।

ginger जिन्जॅः *n.* the root of a tropical plant अदरक।

gipsy जिप् सि *n.* see gypsy.

giraffe जि राफ़, –रैफ़ *n.* a ruminant animal with spotted coat and very long neck and legs जिराफ़।

gird *गॅ:ड v.t.* to put belt round पेटी से बांधना; to encircle घेर लेना।

girder *गॅ: डॅ: n.* beam of wood or steel शहतीर, गर्डर।

girdle[1] *गॅ: ड्ल n.* waist belt मेखला, करधनी।

girdle[2] *v.t.* to bind with girdle पेटी से बांधना।

girl *गॅ:ल n.* a female child कन्या, लड़की; maid servant सेविका।

girlish *गॅ: लिश a.* like a girl बालिकावत्।

gist *जिस्ट n.* summary सारांश, सार।

give *गिव v.t.* to bestow प्रदान करना; to offer सौंपना; to present प्रस्तुत करना; to pay चुकाना; to donate दान करना; to communicate भेजना।

glacier *ग्लै सिअॅ: n.* a mobile mass of ice or snow हिमनद।

glad *ग्लैड a.* pleased प्रसन्न; cheerful प्रसन्नचित; giving pleasure आनंदकारी।

gladden *ग्लै ड्न v.t.* to make glad प्रसन्न करना।

glamour *ग्लै मॅ: n.* charm आकर्षण; fascination मोहकता।

glance[1] *ग्लान्स n.* momentary look झांकी, दृष्टिपात।

glance[2] *v.i.* to looke briefly दृष्टिपात करना; to allude संकेत करना; to fly off, to pass quickly तेज़ी से गुज़र जाना।

gland *ग्लैन्ड n.* secreting structure in plant or animal ग्रंथि, गांठ।

glare[1] *ग्लेॅअॅ: n.* dazzling light दीप्ति, चमक; overpowering lustre चौंध।

glare[2] *v.i.* to give a very bright light चमकना, दमकना; to stare fiercely आंखे तरेरना।

glass *ग्लास n.* a hard brittle substance कांच; drinking glass गिलास; mirror दर्पण; (*pl.*) spectacles चश्मा।

glaucoma *ग्लौ कों मॅ n.* an eye-disease सबलबाय।

glaze[1] *ग्लेज़ v.t.* to furnish with glass शीशा लगाना; to cover with a glass-like substance चमकीला पदार्थ चढ़ाना।

glaze[2] *n.* a glass like substance शीशे-जैसा पदार्थ।

glazier *ग्ले ज्यॅ: n.* one who glazes windows कांच का काम करने वाला।

glee *ग्ली n.* feeling of joy or delight उल्लास।

glide *ग्लॉइड v.t.* to move along smoothly and slowly सरकना, फिसलना; (of an aircraft) to fly without use of engine विसर्पण करना।

glider *ग्लॉइ डॅ: n.* motorless aircraft विसर्पक।

glimpse *ग्लिम्प्स n.* a fleeting view झलक।

glitter[1] *ग्लि टॅ: v.i.* to shine with bright light चमचमाना।

glitter[2] *n.* lustre चमक।

global *ग्लो बॅल a.* relating to the whole world सार्वभौम, विश्वव्यापी; globe-shaped ग्लोब के आकार का।

globe *ग्लोब n.* the earth पृथ्वी; something spherical or rounded गोलक; sphere with map of earth ग्लोब।

gloom *ग्लूम n.* feeling of sadness उदासी, विषाद; darkness अंधकार।

gloomy *ग्लू मि a.* dark अंधकारपूर्ण;

dejected उदास, खिन्न।

glorification *ग्लौ रि फ़ि के शॅन n.* exaltation to honour and dignity प्रशस्ति।

glorify *ग्लौ रि फ़ॉइ v.t.* to make glorious महिमामंडित करना; to exalt गुणगान करना।

glorious *ग्लौ रि ॲस a.* exalted कीर्तिकर; splendid तेजस्वी; magnificent शोभायुक्त।

glory *ग्लौ रि n.* dignity महिमा; honour गौरव, यश।

gloss *ग्लौसॅ n.* surface shine ऊपरी चमक; shiny surface चमकदार सतह; deceptive appearance झूठा दिखावा।

glossary *ग्लौ ˘ सॅ रि n.* a list of words with their meanings शब्दावली।

glossy *ग्लौ˘ सि a.* smooth and shining चमकदार।

glove *ग्लव n.* covering for the hand दस्ताना।

glow[1] *ग्लो v.i.* to shine चमकना।

glow[2] *n.* shining heat दीप्ति; brightness उज्ज्वलता।

glucose *ग्लू कोस n.* sugar found in fruit etc. फल-शर्करा, ग्लूकोज़।

glue *ग्लू n.* a sticky substance सरेस।

glut[1] *ग्लट (-tt-) v.t.* to feed to satiety छकाना, तृप्त करना।

glut[2] *n.* surfeit आधिक्य।

glutton *ग्ल ट्न n.* one who eats too much पेटू, खाऊ।

gluttony *ग्ल टॅ नि n.* excessive eating पेटूपन।

glycerine *ग्लि सॅ रीन, –रिन n.* a sweet liquid used in chemistry and industry ग्लिसरीन।

go *गो v.i.* to proceed जाना; to depart विदा लेना; to function चलना, काम करना; to elapse गुज़र जाना; to reach पहुंचना; to start प्रस्थान करना; to become होना।

goad[1] *गोड n.* sharp pointed stick अंकुश।

goad[2] *v.t.* to drive with a goad अंकुश से हांकना; to urge forward प्रेरित करना।

goal *गोल n.* aim, end लक्ष्य, उद्देश्य।

goat *गोट n.* a horned quadruped बकरी।

gobble *गौ ˘ ब्ल n.* to swallow in lumps भकोसना।

goblet *गोबॅ लिट n.* large drinking cup without a handle चषक, पानपात्र।

god *गौ ˘ड n. (cap.)* The Creater परमात्मा; superhuman being देवता।

goddess *गौ ˘डिस n.* a female god देवी।

godhead *गो ˘ड़ है ˘ड n.* state of being a god देवत्व।

godly *गौ ˘ड़ लि a.* pious धार्मिक।

godown *गो डॉउन n.* warehouse गोदाम।

godsend *गौ ˘ड़ सैन्ड n.* a windfall वरदान।

goggles *गौ˘ ग्लज़ n. pl.* protective spectacles धूप का चश्मा।

gold *गोल्ड n.* a costly yellow metal स्वर्ण, सोना।

golden *गोल् डॅन a.* of gold, of the colour of gold सुनहरा, स्वर्णिम।

goldsmith *गोल्ड् स्मिथ n.* worker in gold स्वर्णकार।

golf *गौ ॅल्फ़* *n.* a game गॉल्फ़।

gong *गो ॅङ्ग* *n.* a metal disc which sounds when struck घंटा, घड़ियाल।

good[1] *गुड* *a.* comendable प्रशंसनीय; proper उचित; excellent उत्तम, श्रेष्ठ; well-behaved सदाचारी; adequate पर्याप्त; virtuous गुणवान।

good[2] *n.* benefit लाभ, हित; *(pl.)* wares सामान; property संपत्ति।

good-bye *गुड् बॉइ* *interj.* farewell अलविदा।

goodness *गुड् निस* *n.* excellence उत्तमता; benevolence उदारता।

goodwill *गुड् विल* *n.* well-wishing सद्भावना; credit साख; reputation ख्याति।

goose *गूस* *n.* female swan हंसिनी; silly person मूर्ख व्यक्ति।

gooseberry *गुज़् बै ॅरि* *n.* a prickly bush एक झाड़ी।

gorgeous *गौः जॅस* *a.* splendid भव्य।

gorilla *गॅ रि लॅ* *n.* great African ape वनमानुष।

gospel *गौसॅ् पॅल* *n.* set of noble doctrines सिद्धांतावलि; teaching of Christ ईसा का उपदेश।

gossip *गौ ॅ सिप* *n.* idle talk गपशप; rumour अफ़वाह; a person who talks idly गप्पी।

gourd *गुअॅःड* *n.* a large fleshy vegetable लौकी।

gout *गॉउट* *n.* disease of swelling of the joints गठिया, वातरोग।

govern *ग वॅःन* *v.t.* to rule शासित करना; to direct निर्देशित करना; to control नियंत्रित करना।

governance *ग वॅः नॅन्स* *n.* act or manner of governing शासन, शासन-विधि।

governess *ग वॅः निस* *n.* a woman employed to teach the children of rich family and to live with them अध्यापिका।

government *ग वॅःन् मॅन्ट* *n.* ruling or managing body शासन, सरकार; system of governing शासन–पद्धति।

governor *ग वॅः नॅः* *n.* head of state राज्यपाल; controller नियंत्रक।

gown *गॉउन* *n.* loose flowing outer garment चोग़ा, लबादा।

grab *ग्रैब (-bb-)* *v.t.* to seize or grasp suddenly छीनना।

grace[1] *ग्रे ॅस* *n.* beauty सौंदर्य; charm आकर्षण; favour, mercy कृपा; delay, postponement विलंब, स्थगन; a short prayer before a meal भोजन से पहले की प्रार्थना।

grace[2] *v.t.* to add grace to (की) शोभा बढ़ाना।

gracious *ग्रें शॅस* *a.* charming रमणीय; kind दयालु।

gradation *ग्रे डे शॅन* *n.* degree श्रेणी; state of being arranged in ranks श्रेणी-व्यवस्था।

grade[1] *ग्रेड* *n.* degree श्रेणी; rank पदक्रम; class कक्षा।

grade[2] *v.t.* to arrange according to grade वर्गीकरण करना।

gradual *ग्रै ड्यु अॅल* *a.* advancing by degrees क्रमिक।

graduate[1] *ग्रै ड्यु एट* *v.i.* to receive a university degree स्नातक होना।

graduate[2] *n.* one who has obtained a university degree स्नातक।

graft[1] *ग्रॉःफ़्ट* *n.* inserting of small piece of plant into another

कलम; planting रोपण।

graft² *v.t.* to insert a graft in (पर) क़लम लगाना।

grain *ग्रेन* *n.* seed of food plant अनाज; a tiny bit दाना।

grammar *ग्रै मॅ:* *n.* science of language व्याकरण।

grammarian *ग्रॅ मे˘ ॲ रि ॲन* *n.* one who is versed in grammar व्याकरणवेत्ता।

gramme *ग्रैम* *n.* a unit of mass in the metric system, gram ग्राम।

gramophone *ग्रै मॅ फ़ोन* *n.* machine for reproducing music etc. recorded on flat discs ग्रामोफ़ोन (वाद्य)।

grannary *ग्रै नॅ रि* *n.* store house for grain अन्नभंडार, कोठार।

grand *ग्रैन्ड* *a.* magnificent भव्य; great महान्।

grandeur *ग्रैन् जॅ:* *n.* splendour उत्कर्ष; dignity शान, वैभव।

grant¹ *ग्रॉन्ट* *v.t.* to bestow प्रदान करना; to admit स्वीकार करना; to consent अनुमति देना।

grant² *n.* something bestowed अनुदान।

grape *ग्रेप* *n.* fruit of vine अंगूर।

graph *ग्रैफ़* *n.* a diagram रेखाचित्र।

graphic *ग्रै फ़िक* *a.* of graph आलेखी; pictorial चित्रात्मक; vivid स्पष्ट।

grapple¹ *ग्रै पल* *n.* a seizing पकड़; small anchor with several claws of arms कांटा।

grapple² *v.i.* to come to grips (with) भिड़ना; to cope (with) से निपटना।

grasp¹ *ग्रास्प* *v.t.* to seize and hold कसकर पकड़ लेना; to accept eagerly उत्सुकता से ग्रहण करना; to comprehend समझ लेना।

grasp² *n.* grip पकड़; comprehension समझ, बोध।

grass *ग्रॉस* *n.* common herbage घास।

grate¹ *ग्रेट* *n.* frame-work of bars जाली; frame-work for holding fire आतशदान।

grate² *v.t.* to rub hard घिसना; to grind (दांत) पीसना; to irritate चिढ़ाना।

grateful *ग्रेट् फुल* *a.* thankful आभारी, कृतज्ञ; pleasing सुखद।

gratification *ग्रे टि फ़ि के शॅन* *n.* feeling of satisfaction संतोष; gift पारितोषिक।

gratis *ग्रे टिस* *adv.* without payment निःशुल्क।

gratitude *ग्रै टि ट्यूड* *n.* thankfulness कृतज्ञता।

gratuity *ग्रॅ ट्यु इ टि* *n.* something given in return for service उपदान; a tip मुक्त भेंट; donation दान।

grave¹ *ग्रेव* *n.* a hole dug to bury the dead क़ब्र।

grave² *a.* serious गंभीर; dignified, solemn महत्त्वपूर्ण।

gravitate *ग्रै वि टेट* *v.i.* to be attracted आकर्षित होना।

gravitation *ग्रै वि टे शॅन* *n.* force of attraction between bodies गुरुत्वाकर्षण।

gravity *ग्रै वि टि* *n.* gravitational attraction गुरुत्वाकर्षण; seriousness गंभीरता।

graze¹ *ग्रेज़* *v.i.* to eat grass चरना; *v.t.* to eat or feed on (growing grass) चराना; to rub lightly हलका-सा रगड़ना।

graze² *n.* scratch खरोंच।

grease¹ *ग्रीस n.* oily matter ग्रीज़।

grease² *v.t.* to lubricate चिकना करना; to bribe घूस देना।

greasy *ग्री सि, –ज़ि a.* oily चिकना; fatty चर्बीदार।

great *ग्रेट a.* big, large विशाल; pre-eminent महान्; lofty उदात्त।

greed *ग्रीड n.* eager desire लोलुपता।

greedy *ग्री डि a.* eagerly desirous लालची।

Greek¹ *ग्रीक n.* language of Greece युनानी भाषा; native of Greece युनान-निवासी।

Greek² *a.* of Greece or Greek यूनान या यूनानी से संबंधित।

green¹ *ग्रीन a.* of the colour of leaves हरित, हरा-भरा; immature अनाड़ी; unripe अपक्व; fresh ताज़ा।

green² *n.* green colour हरा रंग; (*pl.*) green vegetables हरी सब्ज़ियां; area of grass घास का मैदान।

greenery *ग्री नॅ रि n.* vegetation वनस्पति की हरियाली।

greet *ग्रीट v.t.* to salute अभिवादन करना; to welcome स्वागत करना; to send good wishes शुभकामनाएं भेजना।

grenade *ग्रि नेड n.* small bomb thrown by the hand हथगोला।

grey *ग्रे a.* brown भूरा; dim धुंधला; aged वृद्ध।

greyhound *ग्रे हॉउन्ड n.* swift, slender dog used for racing and hunting एक प्रकार का कुत्ता।

grief *ग्रीफ़ n.* sorrow शोक; affliction व्यथा; distress विपत्ति।

grievance *ग्री वॅन्स n.* cause for complaint शिकायत।

grieve *ग्रीव v.t.* to make sorrowful दुःख देना; *v.i.* to feel grief शोक मानना।

grievous *ग्री वॅस a.* painful कष्टदायक; severe गहरा।

grind *ग्रॉइन्ड v.i.* to be crushed or rubbed together पिसना; *v.t.* to reduce to powder by crushing पीसना; to oppress सताना।

grinder *ग्रॉइन् डॅः n.* apparatus for grinding पीसने का उपकरण।

grip¹ *ग्रिप (-pp-) v.t.* to hold fast पकड़ना।

grip² *n.* firm hold जकड़न; understanding समझ; handle मूठ।

groan¹ *ग्रोन v.i.* to utter deep rumbling sound in distress कराहना।

groan² *n.* deep moan कराह।

grocer *ग्रोसॅः n.* dealer in staple foods, general household supplies पंसारी।

grocery *ग्रो सॅ रि n.* articles sold by grocer किराना, पंसारी का सामान; trade of a grocer पंसारी का व्यवसाय।

groom¹ *ग्रूम n.* one incharge of horses साइस; bridegroom दूल्हा।

groom² *v.t.* to feed and look after (घोड़ों को) चारा देना व देखभाल करना; to train प्रशिक्षित करना।

groove¹ *ग्रूव n.* furrow नाली।

groove² *v.t.* to cut grooves in नालीदार बनाना।

grope *ग्रोप v.t.* to seek by groping टटोलकर तलाशना; *v.i.* to feel about टटोलना।

gross¹ *ग्रोस n.* twelve dozen बारह

दर्जन (144)।

gross² *a.* bulky मोटा; solid ठोस; heavy भारी; not refined, vulgar अशिष्टतापूर्ण।

grotesque *ग्रौ ˘ टैस्क a.* deformed भोंडा, विकृत; absurd बेतुका।

ground *ग्राउंड n.* earth, land पृथ्वी, भूमि; surface धरातल; basis आधार; reason कारण; bottom of sea समुद्रतल।

group¹ *ग्रुप n.* number of persons or things together समूह; section of a party समुदाय, टोली।

group² *v.t.* to place in groups वर्गीकृत करना।

grow *ग्रो v.t.* to cause to grow उगाना; to produce पैदा करना; to develop विकसित करना; *v.i.* to develop विकसित होना; to increase बढ़ना; to be produced उत्पन्न होना।

grower *ग्रौ अॅ: n.* cultivator कृषक, उत्पादक।

growl¹ *ग्रॉउल v.i.* to make guttural sound of anger गुर्राना।

growl² *n.* angry guttural sound गुर्राहट।

growth *ग्रोथ n.* growing वर्धन; development विकास; increase वृद्धि; production उपज, उत्पादन।

grudge¹ *ग्रज v.t.* to be unwilling to give देने को तैयार न होना।

grudge² *n.* secret enmity वैमनस्य, द्रोह।

grumble *ग्रम् ब्ल v.i.* to murmur बड़बड़ाना; to express discontent असंतोष प्रकट करना।

grunt¹ *ग्रन्ट n.* pig's cry सुअर की आवाज़; gruff noise घुरघुर।

grunt² *v.i.* to make a gruff sound घुरघुरना।

guarantee¹ *गै रॅन् टी n.* assurance आश्वासन।

guarantee² *v.t.* to give guarantee of का आश्वासन देना; to agree to be responsible for का दायित्व लेना।

guard¹ *गॉ:ड v.i.* to be careful सतर्क रहना; to watch पहरा देना; *v.t.* to protect बचाना।

guard² *n.* watchman पहरेदार; protection बचाव; caution सतर्कता; watchfulness रखवाली; sentry संतरी; weariness चौकसी; official in charge of train रेलगाड़ी का गार्ड।

guardian *गॉ: ड्यॅन n.* one who guards or takes care अभिभावक।

guava *ग्वा वॅ n.* kind of fruit अमरूद।

guerilla *गॅ रि लॅ n.* one engages in irregular warfare छापामार सैनिक।

guess¹ *गैस n.* random surmise अनुमान, अटकल।

guess² *v.i.* to make a conjecture अनुमान लगाना; *v.t.* to conjecture अनुमान से कहना।

guest *गैस्ट n.* visitor received and entertained अतिथि।

guidance *गॉइ डॅन्स n.* leadership नेतृत्व; direction निर्देशन।

guide¹ *गॉइड v.t.* to direct पथप्रदर्शन करना; to lead नेतृत्व करना।

guide² *n.* one who or that which guides पथ प्रदर्शक; leader नेता; guide-book प्रदर्शिका।

guild *गिल्ड n.* corporation संघ, निकाय।

guile *गॉइल n.* deceit छल-कपट।

guilt *गिल्ट n.* offence अपराध; sin पाप।

guilty *गिल् टि a.* having done wrong अपराधी; showing guilt दोषमय।

guise *गॉइज़ n.* external appearence बाह्य वेश; manner शैली, ढंग; dress वेश।

guitar *गि टाः n.* a musical instrument सितार, गिटार।

gulf *गल्फ़ n.* indentation in coast खाड़ी; abyss खाई; a wide gap चौड़ा फासला।

gull[1] *गल n.* sea-bird जलमुर्गी।

gull[2] *n.* a dupe मूर्ख।

gull[3] *v.t.* to dupe, to cheat ठगना।

gulp *गल्प n.* quantity swallowed at a time कौर, ग्रास; mouthful घूंट।

gum *गम n.* firm fleshy tissue surrounding the bases if teeth मसूढ़ा; sticky substance गोंद।

gun *गन n.* firearm बंदूक।

gust *गस्ट n.* sudden blast of wind झोंका; violent burst of passion भावावेग।

gutter *गॅ टॅः n.* channel नाली, मोरी।

guttural *ग टॅ रॅल a.* pertaining to the throat कंठ-संबंधी।

gymnasium *जिम् ने ज़्यॅम n.* place or building for gymnastics व्यायामशाला।

gymnast *जिम् नैस्ट n.* one skilled in gymnastics व्यायामी।

gymnastic *जिम् नैस् टिक a.* pertaining to atheletic exercises व्यायाम-संबंधी।

gymnastics *जिम् नैस् टिक्स n. pl.* atheletic exercises व्यायाम विद्या।

Hh

H एच (ऍइच्) the eighth letter of the English alphabet, a symbol for hydrogen in Chemistry. अंग्रेजी वर्णमाला का आठवाँ अक्षर, रसायन शास्त्र में 'हाइड्रोजन' नामक तत्व के लिए संकेत।

habeas corpus *हे बि ॲस कोः पॅस n.* a writ issued to produce a prisoner in court बंदी प्रत्यक्षीकरण।

habit *हैबिट n.* custom आदत; dress पोशाक।

habitable *है बि टॅ बल a.* fit to live in निवास्य, रहने-योग्य।

habitat *है बि टैट n.* natural dwelling (of plants, animals) प्राकृतिक वास।

habitation *है बि टै शॅन n.* dwelling घर; act of living निवास।

habituate *हॅ बि ट्यु एट v. t.* to accustom आदी बनाना।

hack *हैक v.t.* to cut roughly बेरहमी से काटना।

hag *हैग n.* an ugly old woman डायन।

haggard *है गॅःड a.* exhausted थका-मांदा; wild-looking जंगली।

haggle *है ग्ल v.i.* to argue about price सौदेबाज़ी करना।

hail[1] *हेल n.* frozen rain ओला; intense shower बौछार।

hail[2] *v.i.* to falls as hail ओला गिरना।

hail³ *v.t.* to greet अभिवादन करना; to call out to पुकारना; *v. i.* to come (from) आना।

hair *हे ॲः* filament issuing from the skin of an animal or human body बाल, केश।

hale *हेल a.* robust, healthy भला-चंगा।

half¹ *हाफ़ n.* one of two equal parts आधा भाग।

half² *a.* forming half आधा।

hall *हौल n.* large room बड़ा कमरा।

hallmark *हौल् माःक n.* mark of excellence विशिष्टता-चिन्ह।

hallow *है लो v.t.* to make holy पवित्र करना।

halt¹ *हौल्ट v. t.* to bring to a halt रोकना; *v.i.* to stop marching रुकना।

halt² *n.* short stop रुकाव, ठहराव; stopping place पड़ाव।

halve *हाव v.t.* to divide into two equal parts आधा-आधा बांटना।

hamlet *हैम् लिट n.* small village खेड़ा, गांवड़ी।

hammer¹ *है मॅः n.* a tool with a heavy head हथौड़ा; the part of a gun that explodes the charge बंदूक का घोड़ा।

hammer² *v.t.* to beat with, or as with, a hammer पीटना।

hand¹ *हैन्ड n.* part of the arm below the wrist हाथ; worker कार्यकर्त्ता; style of writing लिखने का ढंग; signature हस्ताक्षर; help सहायता; pointer on the dial घड़ी आदि की सूई; applause प्रशंसा।

hand² *v.t.* to pass by hand देना, पहुंचाना।

handbill *हैन्ड् बिल n.* a loose printed sheet etc. to be circulated विज्ञप्ति, इश्तहार।

handbook *हैन्ड् बुक n.* manual, guide-book पुस्तिका, गुटका।

handcuff¹ *हैन्ड् कॅफ़ n.* a pair of metal rings हथकड़ी।

handcuff² *v.t.* to put handcuffs on हथकड़ी-लगाना।

handful *हैन्ड् फुल n.* as much as the hand will grasp or hold मुट्ठीभर; small quantity or number अल्पमात्रा या संख्या।

handicap¹ *हैन् डि कैप (-pp-) v.t.* to place at a disadvantage बाधा डालना।

handicap² *n.* disadvantage बाधा; physical disability अपंगता।

handicraft *हैन् डि क्राफ़्ट n.* work performed by the hand हस्तशिल्प।

handiwork *हैन् डि वॅःक n.* product of manual labour दस्तकारी।

handkerchief *हैङ् कॅः चिफ़ n.* a small piece of cloth रूमाल।

handle¹ *हैन् ड्ल n.* that part of an object which is held in the hand हत्था।

handle² *v.t.* to control नियंत्रण करना; to feel, use or hold with the hand छूना, छेड़-छाड़ करना।

handsome *हैन् सॅम a.* good-looking सुंदर; generous उदार।

handy *हैन् डि a.* convenient for use सुविधाजनक; skilled in using the hands सिद्धहस्त।

hang *हैङ्ग v.t.* to suspend लटकाना; to put to death by suspending by the neck फांसी देना।

hanker *हैङ् कॅः* *v.i.* to crave लालायित होना।

haphazard *हैप् है जॅःड* *a.* without order or planning अव्यवस्थित।

happen *है पॅन* *v.t.* to come by chance संयोगवश होना; to occur घटित होना।

happening *है पॅ निङ्ग* *n.* occurrence घटना।

happiness *है पि निस* *n.* state of being happy सुख; enjoyment of pleasure आनंद; good luck सौभाग्य।

happy *है पि* *a.* feeling pleasure प्रसन्न; feeling contentment संतुष्ट; lucky भाग्यशाली।

harass *हे रॅस* *v.t.* to vex तंग करना; to fatigue with importunity थका देना।

harassment *है रॅस् मॅन्ट* *n.* act of harassing उत्पीड़न, परेशानी।

harbour[1] *हाः बॅः* *n.* shelter आश्रम; a haven for ships बंदरगाह।

harbour[2] *v.t.* to shelter शरण देना; to maintain बनाए रखना।

hard *हाःड* *a.* not soft कड़ा; solid ठोस; firm दृढ़; difficult to understand कठिन; difficult to do दुष्कर।

harden *हाः ड्न* *v.t.* to make hard कड़ा बनाना; to make unfeeling कठोर बनाना; *v.i.* to become hard कड़ा होना।

hardihood *हाः डि हुड* *n.* quality of being hardy साहसिकता।

hardly *हाः ड् लि* *adv.* scarcely मुश्किल से ही।

hardship *हाःड् शिप* *n.* suffering मुसीबत; discomfort कष्ट।

hardy *हाः डि* *adj.* bold साहसी; tough, strong बलशाली।

hare *हैॲः* *n.* a swift rodent खरगोश।

harm[1] *हाःम* *n.* injury चोट; damage क्षति; evil बुराई।

harm[2] *v.t.* to hurt चोट पहुंचाना; to damage क्षति पहुंचाना।

harmonious *हाः मो नि ॲस* *a.* having harmony सामंजस्यपूर्ण; sweet sounding श्रुतिमधुर।

harmonium *हाः मो नि ॲम* *n.* a musical wind-instrument हारमोनियम।

harmony *हाः मॅ नि* *n.* concordance सामंजस्य; agreement in relation समरसता; pleasing combination of musical notes संगत, सुरीलापन; peace शांति।

harness[1] *हाः निस* *n.* equipment साज-सज्जा; apparatus उपकरण।

harness[2] *v.t.* to equip with armour साज़बद्ध करना; to utilise power or energy का उपयोग करना।

harp *हाःप* *n.* a musical instrument वीणा।

harsh *हाःश* *a.* rough रूखा, कठोर; jarring कर्कश; cruel निर्दयतापूर्ण।

harvest *हाः विस्ट* *n.* crops gathered in उपज; product of any act परिणाम।

haverster *हाः विस् टॅः* *n.* reaper फ़सल काटने-वाला; reaping machine फ़सल काटने की मशीन।

haste *हेस्ट* *n.* quickness of movement, hurry शीघ्रता।

hasten *है स्न* *v.i.* to hurry शीघ्रता करना; *v.t.* to cause (something) to happen sooner जल्दी कराना।

hasty *हैस् टि* *a.* characterised by haste शीघ्रतापूर्ण; quick-tempered हड़बड़िया।

hat *हैट* *n.* covering for the head टोप।

hatchet *है चिट* *n.* small axe कुल्हाड़ी।

hate[1] *हेट* *n.* intense dislike घृणा।

hate[2] *v.t.* to dislike intensely घृणा करना।

haughty *हौ टि* *a.* proud दंभी, अभिमानी; arrogant उद्धत।

haunt[1] *हौन्ट* *v.t.* to frequent (में, पर) प्रायः जाना; to vex परेशान करना।

haunt[2] *n.* place frequently visited अड्डा।

have *हैव* *v.t.* to own, to possess (का) स्वामी होना; to be affected with (से) ग्रसित होना; to be obliged (to do) (के लिए) बाध्य होना; to contain रखना; to get प्राप्त करना।

haven *हे व्न* *n.* harbour बंदरगाह।

havoc *है वॅक* *n.* destruction विध्वंस।

hawk *हौक* *n.* a bird of falcon family बाज़।

hawker *हौ कॅ:* pedlar फेरीवाला।

hawthorn *हौ थौःन* *n.* a thorny tree वन-संजली।

hay *हे* *n.* dried grass सूखी घास।

hazard[1] *है जॅः ड* *n.* chance संयोग; risk जोखिम।

hazard[2] *v.t.* to risk संकट में डालना; to venture (का) ख़तरा मोल लेना।

haze *हेज़* *n.* vapour or mist कुहरा।

hazy *हे ज़ि* *a.* misty धुंधला; uncertain अनिश्चित; full of confusion उलझन-भरा।

he *ही* *pron.* a male person or animal already named वह, उसने।

head[1] *है˘ड* *n.* the topmost part of the body सिर; mind मस्तिष्क; chief, leader मुखिया, नेता; top चोटी; that part of a weapon which is used for striking नोक; front अग्रभाग; climax चरम बिंदु; topic विषय।

head[2] *v.t.* to be the chief of का नेतृत्व करना; *v.i.* to move forward आगे बढ़ना।

headache *है डेक* *n.* pain in the head सिरदर्द।

heading *है˘ डिङ्ग* *n.* title शीर्षक।

headlong *है ड् लौ˘ ङ्ग* *adv.* with the head foremost सिर के बल।

headstrong *हैड् स्ट्रौ˘ ङ्ग* *a.* self-willed स्वेच्छाचारी।

heal *हील* *v.i.* to grow well ठीक होना; *v.t.* to make well स्वस्थ बनाना।

health *हैल्थ* *n.* sound bodily and mental condition स्वास्थ्य; freedom from disease आरोग्य।

healthy *है ल्थ् थि* *a.* in good health स्वस्थ; wholesome स्वास्थ्यवर्धक।

heap[1] *हीप* *n.* mass of things ढेर; collection संग्रह।

heap[2] *v.t.* to amass संचय करना; to pile up ढेर लगाना।

hear *हिअॅ:* *v.t.* to perceive by the ear सुनाई पड़ना; to listen ध्यान देना, कान लगाना; to be told बताया जाना; to try (a case) (मुक़दमे की) सुनवाई करना।

hearsay *हिअॅ: से* *n.* rumour अफ़वाह।

heart *हाःट* *n.* organ which makes blood circulation हृदय; bosom उर; courage साहस; central part केंद्र; essence सार।

hearth *हा:थ n.* part of room where fire is made चूल्हा; home घर।

heartily *हा: टि लि adv.* sincerely हृदय से।

heat[1] *ही ट n.* warmth ऊष्मा, गर्मी; sensation of warmth हरारत; anger क्रोध; passion जोश।

heat[2] *v.t.* to make hot गर्म करना; to agitate उत्तेजित करना; *v.i.* to become hot गर्म होना।

heave *हीव v.i.* to lift उठाना; to throw फेंकना; to utter (a sigh) (आह) भरना।

heaven *है˘ व्‌न n. (pl.)* sky आकाश; dwelling place of gods देवलोक।

heavenly *है˘ व्‌न् लि a.* divine दिव्य; celestial स्वर्गीय।

hedge[1] *है˘ ज n.* close row of bushes झाड़ी की बाड़।

hedge[2] *v.t.* to surround with hedge बाड़ लगाना; to obstruct रोकना।

heed[1] *हीड v.t.* to keep in mind ध्यान में रखना।

heed[2] *n.* care देखभाल; attention सावधानी।

heel *हील n.* back part of human foot एड़ी; part of shoe supporting this जूते का पिछला भाग।

hefty *है˘ फ़् टि a.* heavy भारी; muscular हृष्ट-पुष्ट।

height *हॉइट n.* state of highness ऊंचाई; top चोटी; extremity पराकाष्ठा; quality of being high उच्चता।

heighten *हॉइ ट्‌न v.t.* to make higher ऊंचा करना।

heinous *ही नॅ स a.* odious घृणित, जघन्य; atrocious नृशंस।

heir *ऍ अॅ: n.* successor उत्तराधिकारी।

hell *है˘ल a.* the abode of the damned नरक; misery दुर्दशा।

helm *है˘ल्म n.* steering apparatus पतवार।

helmet *है˘ल्‌मिट n.* covering of armour for the head शिरस्त्राण।

help[1] *हैल्प v.t.* to assist सहायता करना।

help[2] *n.* assistance सहायता; one who assists सहायक।

helpful *है˘ल्प् फुल a.* giving help सहायक; useful लाभदायक।

helpless *है˘ ल्प् लिस a.* wanting assistance असहाय।

helpmate *है˘ल्प्‌मेट n.* assistant सहायक; wife सहधर्मिणी।

hemisphere *है˘ मि स्फ़ि अॅ: n.* half of the globe or map गोलार्ध।

hemp *हैम्प n.* an intoxicating drug भांग; jute जूट, सनई।

hen *हैनॅ n.* female domestic fowl मुर्गी।

hence *है˘न्स adv.* from here यहां से; from now अब से; for this reason इसी कारण से, अतः।

henceforth *है˘न्स् फ़ौ:थ adv.* from now onwards अब से आगे; in future भविष्य में।

henceforward *है˘न्स् फ़ौ: वॅ:ड adv.* from now onwards अब से आगे।

henchman *हैन्च् मॅन n.* trusty follower विश्वसनीय अनुचर।

henpecked *है˘न् पैक्ड a.* governed by his wife जोरू का गुलाम।

her[1] *हॅ: pron.* objective and possessive case of 'she' उस (स्त्री) को; उस (स्त्री); का।

her² *a.* belonging to her उसका।
herald¹ *है ॅ रॅल्ड n.* forerunner अग्रदूत; proclaimer उद्घोषक।
herald² *v.t.* to announce घोषित करना; to proclaim approach of (के) आगमन की सूचना देना।
herb *हॅःब n.* plant or shrub used in medicine जड़ी-बूटी।
herculean *हॅः क्यु लि ॲन a.* requiring extraordinary strength अत्यंत कठिन।
herd *हॅःड n.* company of animals feeding or travelling together पशु-समूह।
herdsman *हॅःड्ज़ मॅन n.* keeper of a herd चरवाहा।
here *हिअॅः* in this place यहां, इधर; in this present life इस लोक में।
hereabouts *हिअॅ रॅ बॉउट्स adv.* near this place आसपास।
hereafter *हिअॅर आफ़् टॅः adv.* after this time इसके बाद।
hereditary *हि रै ॅ डि टॅ रि n.* discending or coming by inheritance वंशानुगत।
heredity *हि रै ॅ डि टि n.* hereditary transmission of qualities आनुवंशिकता।
heritable *है ॅ रि टॅ ब्ल a.* that may be inherited वंशागत।
heritage *है ॅ रि टिज n.* that which is inherited विरासत।
hermit *हॅः मिट n.* saint संन्यासी; one who lives in solitude वानप्रस्थ, एकांतवासी।
hermitage *हॅः मि टिज n.* hermit's cell कुटी।
hernia *हॅः न्यॅ, n.* a rupture in the weak spot in the stomach wall हर्निया, अंत्रवृद्धि।
hero *हिअॅ रो n.* distinguished brave person योद्धा; illustrious person नायक।
heroic *हि रो ॅ इक a.* befitting a hero वीरोचित; pertaining to hero नायक-संबंधी।
heroine *है ॅ रो ॅ इन n.* principal female figure नायिका, वीरांगना।
heroism *है ॅ रो ॅ इज़्म n.* bravery वीरता; boldness साहस।
herring *है ॅ रिङ्ग n.* a common, edible, sea-water fish हिलसा।
hesitant *है ॅ ज़ि टॅन्ट a.* inclined to hesitate संशयशील।
hesitate *है ॅ ज़ि टेट v.i.* to hold back or delay in making a dicision संकोच करना; to vacillate दुविधा में पड़ना।
hesitation *है ॅ ज़ि टे शॅन n.* wavering संकोच, हिचकिचाहट; vacillation असमंजस।
hew *ह्यू v.t.* to cut with an axe कुल्हाड़ी से काटना।
heyday *है डे n.* time of greatest prosperity and power सर्वोत्तम समय।
hibernation *हॉइ बॅः ने शॅन n.* passing winter in deep sleep शीतनिद्रा।
hiccup *हि कप n.* spasm of the breathing organs with an abrupt cough-like sound हिचकी।
hide¹ *हॉइड n.* skin of an animal पशुचर्म, चमड़ा।
hide² *v.t.* to conceal छिपाना।
hideous *हि डि ॲस a.* horrible भयंकर, भीषण; extremely ugly घिनौना।

hierarchy *हॉ इ अॅ राः कि n.* system of persons arranged in graded order पदक्रम, अनुक्रम।

high *हॉइ a.* tall, lofty ऊँचा।

highly *हॉइ लि adv.* to a high degree अत्यधिक मात्रा में।

Highness *हॉइ निस n.* (cap.) title of honour महाराज; the state of being High उच्चता।

highway *हाई वे n.* a public road राजपथ।

hilarious *हि ले˘ अॅ रि अॅस a.* gay, extravagantly merry उल्लसित।

hilarity *हि लै रि टि n.* gaiety प्रफुल्लता।

hill *हिल n.* small mountain पहाड़ी; mound टीला।

hillock *हि लॅक n.* small hill टीला।

him *हिम pron.* objective of 'he' उसे, उसको।

hinder *हिन् डॅः v.t.* to prevent, to keep back बाधा पहुंचाना, अड़चन डालना।

hindrance *हिन् ड्रॅन्स n.* act of hindering अवरोध।

hint[1] *हिन्ट n.* distant or indirect indication संकेत।

hint[2] *v.i.* to indicate indirectly इशारा करना।

hip *हिप n.* either side of body below waist and above thigh नितंब, कूल्हा।

hire[1] *हॉइअॅः n.* wages for service पारिश्रमिक; price paid for the use of anything भाड़ा।

hire[2] *v.t.* to give on hire किराए पर देना।

hireling *हॉइअॅः लिङ्ग n.* one who serves for wages भाड़े से रोज़ी कमानेवाला।

his *हिज़ pron.* belonging to him उसका।

hiss[1] *हिस n.* sibilant sound सिसकारी, फुफकार।

hiss[2] *v.i.* to make a sibilant sound फुफकारना।

historian *हिस् टौ रि अॅन n.* writer of history इतिहासकार।

historic *हिस् टौ˘ रिक a.* famous in history इतिहास-प्रसिद्ध।

historical *हिस् टौ˘ रि कॅल a.* relating to history ऐतिहासिक।

history *हिस् टॅ रि n.* knowledge of past events इतिहास; account of an event वृत्तांत; life-story इतिवृत्त।

hit[1] *हिट (-tt-) v.t.* to strike प्रहार करना; to come against with force टकराना; to wound the feelings of मर्माहत करना; to find पा लेना; to score (रन) बनाना।

hit[2] *n.* blow प्रहार; success सफलता; a taunting remark ताना, व्यंग्य।

hitch *हिच n.* an impediment अड़चन; a knot गांठ; a jerky movement झटकोला।

hither *हि दॅः adv.* to this place इस स्थान पर।

hitherto *हि दॅः टू adv.* to this time अब तक।

hive *हॉइव n.* a colony of bees मधुमक्खी का छत्ता।

hoarse *हौःस a.* discordant, harsh कर्कश, बेसुरा।

hoax[1] *हौक्स n.* deceptive trick चकमा।

hoax[2] *v.t.* to trick by a practical joke चकमा देना।

hobby *हौ˘ बि n.* favourite pursuit

followed as an amusement शौक़, अभिरुचि।

hobby-horse *हौ˘ बि हौःस* *n.* a wooden horse as a toy कठघोड़ा।

hockey *हौ˘ कि* *n.* game played with a stick and ball हॉकी का खेल।

hoist *हौ˘ इस्ट* *v.t.* to lift upward by means of a tackle फहराना; to heave up ऊपर उठाना।

hold[1] *हौल्ड* *n.* grasp पकड़; influence प्रभाव।

hold[2] *v.t.* to grasp पकड़ना; to have capacity for (की) क्षमता रखना; to carry on चालू रखना; to detain रोकना; to celebrate मनाना; to believe विश्वास करना; to occupy धारण करना।

hole[1] *होल* *n.* cavity छेद; hollow place ख़ाली स्थान; pit कुंड।

hole[2] *v.t.* to put into a hole छेद में डालना; to make a hole in खोदना।

holiday *हौ˘ लि डे* *n.* day of exemption from labour अवकाश का दिन; a festival त्योहार।

hollow[1] *हौ˘ लो* *a.* having an empty space खोखला; empty ख़ाली; unreal निरर्थक।

hollow[2] *n.* hole छेद; cavity गड्ढा।

hollow[3] *v.t.* to make hollow खोखला करना।

holocaust *हौ˘ लॅ कौस्ट* *n.* complete destruction सर्वनाश।

holy *हो लि* *a.* sacred पावन, पवित्र; pure शुद्ध; saintly पुण्यात्मा।

homage *हौ˘ मिज* *n.* tribute श्रद्धांजलि; reverence श्रद्धा।

home *होम* *n.* residence निवास; house मकान; native place जन्म स्थान।

homicide *हौ˘ मि सॉइड* *n.* manslaughter मानव-हत्या; killer हत्यारा।

homoeopath *हो मि ओ˘ पैथ* *n.* one who practices homeopathy समचिकित्सक।

homeopathy *हो मि औ˘ पॅ थि* *n.* a treatment of disease using drugs that in a healthy man would cause the disease मितव्ययी चिकित्सा।

homogeneous *हौ˘ मो जी नॅस* *a.* of the same kind or nature सजातीय।

honest *औ˘ निस्ट* *a.* upright, just ईमानदार; truthful सत्यवादी।

honesty *औ˘ निस् टि* *n.* uprightness ईमानदारी; truthfulness सत्यवादिता।

honey *ह नि* *n.* sweet thick fluid produced by bees शहद।

honeycomb *ह नि कोम* *n.* mass of waxy cells formed by bees मधुकोश।

honeymoon *ह नि मून* *n.* a holiday taken immediately after marriage प्रमोदकाल, सुहागरात।

honorarium *औ˘ नॅ रे˘ अॅ रि अॅम* *n.* voluntary fees paid to a professional man for his services मानदेय।

honorary *औ˘ नॅ रॅ रि* *a.* without salary अवैतनिक; conferring honour सम्मानार्थ।

honour[1] *औ˘ नॅः* *n.* respect आदर।

honour[2] *v. t.* to confer an honour on सम्मानित करना; to accept and pay when due भुगतान करना।

honourable *औ˘ नॅ रॅ ब्ल* *a.* worthy of honour माननीय।

hood हुड *n.* covering for the head शिरोवेष्टन, टोप।

hoodwink हुड़ विङ्क *v.t.* to deceive आंख में धूल झोंकना।

hoof हूफ़ *n.* part of an animal's foot खुर।

hook हुक *n.* an object of bent form अंकुश; curved cutting tool हंसिया।

hooligan हू लि गॅन *n.* a violent noisy person आवारा, गुंडा।

hoot[1] हूट *n.* owl's cry उल्लू की बोली; cry of disapproval or derision घृणासूचक शोर।

hoot[2] *v.i.* to make a hoot घृणा-सूचक शोर करना; *v.t.* to make hoots at शोर करके भगाना।

hop[1] हौ ॅप *(-pp-) v. i.* to leap on one leg फुदकना; to move in jumps कुलॉच मारते हुए चलना।

hop[2] *n.* the action of hopping कूद, उछाल; a short jump कुलॉच।

hope[1] होप *v.t.* to expect and desire (की) आशा रखना; *v.i.* to entertain hope आशावान होना।

hope[2] *n.* feeling of expectation and desire आशा; basis of hoping आशा का आधार।

hopeful होप् फुल *a.* having hope आशावान्; giving hope आशापूर्ण।

hopeless होप् लिस *a.* without hope निराश; worthless निकम्मा।

horde हौःड *n.* multitude भीड़, झुंड।

horizon हॅ रॉइ ज़न् *n.* circle in which earth and sky seem to meet क्षितिज; limit of knowledge etc. ज्ञान आदि की सीमा।

horn हौःन *n.* outgrowth on the head सींग; funnel-shaped mouth piece शृंगी, तुरही।

hornet हौः निट *n.* kind of wasp भिड़, बर्रे।

horrible हौ ॅ रि ब्ल *a.* terrible भीषण; dreadful भयंकर।

horrify हौ ॅ रि फ़ॉइ *v.t.* to strike with horror भयभीत करना।

horror हौ ॅ रॅः *n.* fear भय; intense repugnance घृणा, आतंक।

horse हौःस *n.* hoofed animal used for riding and draught घोड़ा।

horticulture हौ : टि कल् चॅः *n.* art of gardening बाग़बानी।

hose होज़ *n.* covering for the legs or feet जुर्राब; flexible water pipe रबर का पाइप।

hosiery हो ज़ॅ रि *n.* knitted goods होज़री।

hospitable हौ ॅस् पि टॅ ब्ल *a.* welcoming and generous towards guests अतिथि-सत्कार करने वाला।

hospital हौ ॅस् पि ट्ल *n.* institution for treatment चिकित्सालय।

hospitality हौ ॅस् पि टै लि टि *n.* welcome or entertainment of guests आतिथ्य, अतिथि-सत्कार।

host होस्ट *n.* one who entertains a stranger or guest मेज़बान।

hostage हौ ॅस् टिज *n.* person held as a pledge until certain demands are met बंधक।

hostel हौ ॅस् टॅल *n.* residence for students छात्रावास।

hostile हौ ॅस् टॉइल *a.* opposed विरोधी; unfriendly शत्रुतापूर्ण।

hostility हौ ॅस् टि लि टि *n.* opposition विरोध; enmity शत्रुता।

hot हौ ॅट *a.* very warm गर्म, तप्त; violent उग्र, प्रचंड; excited उत्तेजित;

angry क्रुद्ध।

hotchpotch *हौचॅ् पौचॅ* *n.* jumble घालमेल।

hotel *हो टै˘ल, ओ–* *n.* commercial establishment providing lodging and meals होटल, विश्रामालय।

hound *हाउॅन्ड* *n.* dog used in hunting शिकारी कुत्ता।

hour *ऑउअॅ:* *n.* 60 minutes or 24th part of a day घंटा।

house[1] *हॉउस* *n.* dwelling place मकान; family परिवार।

house[2] *v.t.* to provide house for घर दिलाना; to shelter आश्रय देना।

how *हॉउ* *adv.* in what way कैसे; in what condition किस रूप में।

however[1] *हॉउ ऐ˘ वॅ:* *adv.* in whatever way चाहे जैसे।

however[2] *conj.* nevertheless, all the same तथापि, फिर भी।

howl[1] *हॉउल* *v.t.* to utter with outcry चिल्लाकर कहना; *v.i.* to cry चीख़ना।

howl[2] *n.* a yell चीख़।

hub *हब* *n.* nave of a wheel नाभि।

hubbub *ह बब* *n.* uproar कोलाहल; confused noise of many voices हुल्लड़।

huge *ह्यूज* *a.* enormous वृहत्, विशाल।

hum[1] *हम (-mm-)* *v. i.* to make a sound like bees गुंजन करना; *v.t.* to sing with closed lips गुनगुनाना।

hum[2] *n.* humming गुंजन।

human *ह्यू मॅन* *a.* of man मानवीय।

humane *ह्यू मेन, ह्यु–* *a.* benevolent, kind दयालु।

humanitarian *ह्यू मै नि टे˘ अॅ रिअॅन* *a.* benevolent लोकोपकारी।

humanity *ह्यू मै नि टि, ह्यु–* *n.* human beings in general मानव जाति; human nature मानवता, मानव-स्वभाव; kindness दयाभाव।

humanize *ह्यू मॅ नाइॅज़* *v.t.* to make human मानवीय बनाना; to make humane दयावान बनाना; *v.i.* to become human मानवीय बनना; to become humane दयावान बनना।

humble *हम् ब्ल* *a.* modest विनम्र।

humdrum *हम् ड्रम* *a.* dull नीरस; commonplace घिसा-पिटा।

humid *ह्यू मिड* *a.* damp, moist नम, गीला।

humidity *ह्यू मि डि टि* *n.* moisture नमी, आर्द्रता।

humiliate *ह्यू मि लि एट, ह्यु–* *v.t.* to mortify (का) मान-मर्दन करना।

humiliation *ह्यू मि लि ए शॅन, ह्यु–* *n.* degradation मान-मर्दन।

humility *ह्यू मि लि टि* *n.* modesty विनम्रता।

humorist *ह यू मॅ रिस्ट* *n.* humorous talker or writer विनोदी, हास्यकार।

humorous *ह्यू मॅ रॅस* *a.* having a sense of humour विनोदपूर्ण, हास्यपूर्ण।

humour *ह्यू मॅ:* *n.* amusement परिहास।

hunch *हन्च* *n.* hump कूबड़।

hundred *हन् ड्रॅड* *n.* ten times ten (100) सौ।

hunger *हङ् गॅ:* *n.* need for food भूख; strong desire लालसा।

hungry *हङ् ग्रि* *a.* having desire for food भूखा; greedy लालची।

hunt[1] *हन्ट* *v.t.* to seek out to kill or capture (का) शिकार करना; to try to find ढूढंना; *v.i.* to go for hunt शिकार के लिए जाना।

hunt[2] *n.* the act of hunting आखेट; search तलाश।

hunter *हन् टॅः* *n.* one who hunts शिकारी।

huntsman *हन्ट्स् मॅन* *n.* hunter आखेटक; man incharge of the hounds during a hunt शिकारी कुत्तों की देखरेख करने वाला।

hurdle[1] *हः ड्ल* *n.* obstacle बाधा।

hurdle[2] *v.t.* to enclose with durdles (में) बाधा खड़ी करना।

hurl *हॅःल* *v.t.* to fling with violence उछालना।

hurrah *हु राः* *interj.* exclamation of joy or applause आनंद या प्रशंसासूचक उद्घोष।

hurricane *ह रि कॅन, –केन* *n.* cyclonic storm झंझावात।

hurry[1] *हरि* *v.t.* to hasten तेज़ी से करना; *v.i.* to move or act with impatient haste उतावली दिखाना।

hurry[2] *n.* undue haste अतिशीघ्रता; agitation व्यग्रता।

hurt[1] *हॅःट* *v.t.* to cause pain to चोट पहुंचाना; to damage क्षति पहुंचाना।

hurt[2] *n.* injury चोट, आघात; damage क्षति।

husband *हज़् बॅन्ड* man to whom a woman is married पति।

husbandry *हज़् बॅन् ड्रि* *n.* business of a farmer काश्तकारी; careful management सुव्यवस्था।

hush[1] *हश* *n.* silence निस्तब्धता।

hush[2] *v.i.* to become silent शांत होना; *v.t.* to make silent शांत करना।

husk *हस्क* *n.* dry thin covering of certain fruits भूसी, छिलका।

husky *हस् कि* *a.* full of husks छिलकेदार; dry शुष्क।

hut *हट* *n.* small temporary dwelling कुटीर।

hyaena, hyena *हॉइ ई नॅ* *n.* a wild animal related to dog लकड़बग्घा।

hybrid[1] *हॉइ ब्रिड* *a.* crossbred संकर जाति का।

hybrid[2] *n.* mongrel संकर, दोग़ला।

hydrogen *हॉइ ड्रि जॅन* *n.* a gas which produces water when combined with oxygen उदजन।

hygiene *हॉइ जीन* *n.* science or art of preserving health स्वास्थ्य-विज्ञान।

hygienic *हॉइ जी निक* *a.* pertaining to health स्वास्थ्यकर, स्वास्थ्य-संबंधी।

hymn *हिम* *n.* song of praise स्तुति; song or worship ईश-भजन।

hyperbole *हॉइ पॅः बॅ लि* *n.* exaggeration अतिशयोक्ति।

hypnotism *हिप् नॅ टिज़्म* *n.* a sleep-like condition caused by artificial means सम्मोहन।

hypnotize *हिप् नॅ टॉइज़* *v.t.* to affect with hypnotism सम्मोहित करना।

hypocrisy *हि पौ ँ क्रॅ सि* *n.* concealment of true character or belief मिथ्याचार, आडंबर।

hypocrite *हि पॅ क्रिट* *n.* one who practises hypocrisy पाखंडी।

hypocritical *हि पॅ क्रि टि कॅल* *a.* pertaining to hypocrisy पाखंडी।

hypothesis *हॉ इ पौ ँ थि सिस* *n.*

supposition कल्पना; proposition परिकल्पना।

hypothetical *हॉइ पॅ थै˘ टि कॅल a.* conjectural काल्पनिक।

hysteria *हिस् टिॲ रिॲ n.* mental disorder with emotional outbursts हिस्टीरिया, वातोन्माद।

hysterical *हिस् टै˘ रि कॅल a.* suffering from hysteria हिस्टीरिया से प्रभावित; caused by hysteria हिस्टीरिया-जनित।

Ii

I आइ the ninth letter of the English alphabet, it is sounded as short or long 'i' or like the sound of the letter itself. In Roman numberals I represents 'one' in Chemistry I represents iodine. अंग्रेजी वर्णमाला का नवाँ अक्षर, इसका उच्चारण 'इ' 'ई' तथा 'आइ' होता है; रोम की संख्या-माला में यह 'एक' का सूचक होता है; रसायनशास्त्र में यह 'आयडिन' के लिये प्रयुक्त होता है।

I *ऑइ pron. (pl. we)* first person singular in the subjective case मैं, मैंने।

ice *ऑइस n.* frozen water बर्फ़।

iceberg *ऑइस् बॅःग n.* floating mass of ice हिमशैल।

icicle *ऑइ सि क्ल n.* pointed piece of ice formed by the freezing of dripping water हिमलंब।

icy *ऑइ सि a.* very cold बरफ़ीला।

idea *ऑइ डि ॲ n.* opinion, belief विचार, मत; plan योजना; conception अवधारणा।

ideal[1] *ऑइ डि ॲल a.* existing in idea or fancy आदर्श; existing only in idea काल्पनिक।

ideal[2] *n.* conception of something that is perfect आदर्श।

idealism *ऑइ डिॲ लिज़्म n.* tendency to seek perfection in every thing आदर्शवाद।

idealist *ऑइ डिॲ लिस्ट n.* one who holds the doctrine of idealism आदर्शवादी।

idealistic *ऑइ डिॲ लिस् टिक a.* pertaining to idealism आदर्शात्मक।

idealize *ऑइ डिॲ लॉइज़ v.t.* to make ideal आदर्श बनाना; to embody in an ideal form आदर्शरूप देना।

identical *ऑइ डैन् टि कॅल a.* the same वही; exactly alilke बिल्कुल समान।

indentification *ऑइ डैन् टि फ़ि के शॅन n.* act of identifying अभिनिर्धारण; establishing identity पहचान।

identify *ऑइ डैन् टि फ़ॉइ v.t.* to make to be the same (से) तादात्म्य स्थापित करना; to establish the identity of पहचानना।

identity *ऑइ डैन् टि टि n.* sameness समरूपता; proof of who the person or thing really is पहचान।

ideocy *इ डि ॲ सि n.* state of being an idiot मूर्खता।

idiom *इ डि ॲम n.* language of a

people or country बोली, भाषा; a group of words whose meaning must be taken together मुहावरा।

idiomatic *इ डि अॅ मै टिक a.* using idioms मुहावरेदार।

idiot *इ डि अॅट n.* a foolish person मूर्ख व्यक्ति।

idiotic *इ डि औ ˘ टिक a.* full of foolishness मूर्खतापूर्ण।

idle *ऑइ ड्ल a.* not working निष्क्रिय, बेकार; lazy आलसी; useless व्यर्थ का।

idleness *ऑइ ड्ल् निस n.* inaction निष्क्रियता; sloth आलस्य; uselessness व्यर्थता।

idler *ऑइ ड्लॅ: n.* one who idles निष्क्रिय व्यक्ति; lazy person आलसी व्यक्ति।

idol *ऑइ डॅल n.* image of a deity देव-प्रतिमा; object of devotion भक्तिभाजन।

idolater *ऑइ डौ ˘ लॅ टॅ: n.* a worshipper of idols मूर्तिपूजक।

if *इफ़ conj.* on condition that यदि; whether याकि।

ignoble *इग् नो ब्ल a.* shameful, dishonourable शर्मनाक।

ignorance *इग् नॅ रॅन्स n.* want of knowledge अज्ञान।

ignorant *इग् नॅ रॅन्ट a.* wanting knowledge or information अनजान।

ignore *इग् नौ: v.t.* to take no notice of (की) उपेक्षा करना।

ill[1] *इल a.* sick बीमार; bad बुरा।

ill[2] *adv.* badly ग़लत ढंग से; imperfectly अपूर्णरूप से; unfavourably बुराई करते हुए।

ill[3] *n.* evil बुराई; misfortune दुर्भाग्य, मुसीबत।

illegal *इ ली गॅल a.* not legal अवैध; contrary to law कानून-विरोधी।

illegibility *इ लै ˘ जि बि लि टि n.* being illegible अपठनीयता।

illegible *इ लै ˘ जि ब्ल a.* that connot be read अपठनीय।

illegitimate *इ लै जी टि मिट a.* not legitimate अवैध; not authorized by law ग़ैरक़ानूनी।

illicit *इ लि सिट a.* not permitted निषिद्ध; unlawful, lawless अवैध।

illiteracy *इ ली टॅ रॅ सि n.* inability to read and write निरक्षरता।

illiterate *इ लि टॅ रिट a.* not able to read and write निरक्षर।

illness *इल् निस n.* state of being ill रूग्णता; ailment रोग।

illogical *इ लौ ˘ जि कॅल a.* not logical तर्कविरुद्ध।

illuminate *इ लू मि नेट v.t.* to light up जगमगा देना; to decorate अलंकृत करना; to make clear स्पष्ट करना।

illumination *इ लू मि ने शॅन n.* act of illuminating प्रदीपन; the light provided प्रकाश; clarification व्याख्या, स्पष्टीकरण; (*pl.*) display of coloured lights for decoration प्रकाश-द्वारा सजावट।

illusion *इ लू ज़ॅन n.* false conception भ्रम; misleading appearance मरीचिका।

illustrate *इ लॅस् ट्रेट v.t.* to explain by example उदाहरण देकर स्पष्ट करना; to furnish (books etc.) with pictures सचित्र बनाना।

illustration *इ लॅस् ट्रे शॅन n.* act of illustrating चित्रण; an example उदाहरण; design to illustrate the text of a book चित्र।

image *इ मिज n.* representation of a person or thing made in wood or stone मूर्ति; a close likeness प्रतिरूप; a reflection बिंब, प्रतिबिंब।

imagery *इ मि जॅ रि n.* use of images or figures of speech बिंब-विधान।

imaginary *इ मै जि नॅ रि a.* existing only in imagination काल्पनिक; unreal अवास्तविक।

imagination *इ मै जि ने शॅन n.* power of imagining कल्पनाशक्ति; what is imagined कल्पित वस्तु।

imaginative *इ मै जि नॅ टिव a.* having or using imagination कल्पनाशील, कल्पनात्मक।

imagine *इ मै जिन v.t.* to form a picture of in the mind कल्पना करना।

imitate *इ मि टेट v.t.* to follow as a model or example अनुकरण करना; to copy नक़ल करना; to mimic नकल उतारना।

imitation *इ मि टे शॅन n.* copy नक़ल; act of imitating अनुकरण; counterfeit नक़ली रूप।

imitator *इ मि टि टॅः n.* one who imitates अनुकरण करनेवाला।

immaterial *इ मॅ टिअॅ रि अॅल a.* unimportant महत्वहीन; not having physical substance अभौतिक,अमूर्त।

immature *इ मॅ ट्युअॅः a.* not mature अपरिपक्व; not fully developed अविकसित।

immaturity *इ मॅ ट्युअॅ रि टि n.* state or quality of being immature अपरिपक्वता।

immeasurable *इ मै˘ ज़ॅ रॅ बल a.* boundless अमित, असीमित।

immediate *इ मी डि अॅट a.* without delay तात्कालिक; relating to the present time वर्तमान संबंधी; nearest निकटस्थ।

immemorial *इ मि मौ रि अॅल a.* going back beyond the reach of memory अति प्राचीन।

immense *इ मैन्॑स a.* very large विशाल।

immensity *इ मैनॅ सि टि n.* vastness विशालता।

immerse *इ मॅः स v.t.* to put under the surface of liquid डुबाना; to involve, to engross तल्लीन करना।

immersion *इ मॅः शॅन n.* immersing or being immersed निमज्जन।

immigrant *इ मि ग्रॅन्ट n.* one who immigrates into a country आप्रवासी।

immigrate *इ मि ग्रेट v.i.* to come into a country for permanent residence आप्रवासन करना।

immigration *इ मि ग्रे शॅन n.* act of removing into a country for settlement आप्रवासन।

imminent *इ मि नॅन्ट a.* likely to come or happen soon निकटस्थ।

immodest *इ मौ˘ डिस्ट a.* not modest अविनीत, निर्लज्ज; indecent अशिष्ट।

immodesty *इ मौ˘ डिस् टि n.* want of modesty निर्लज्जता।

immoral *इ मौ ˘ रॅल* *a.* not moral अनैतिक; depraved भ्रष्ट, चरित्रहीन।

immorality *इ मौ˘ रै लि टि* *n.* quality of being immoral अनैतिकता; immoral conduct अनैतिक आचरण।

immortal *इ मौः टॅल* *a.* not mortal अमर; imperishable अमिट; never forgotten अविस्मरणीय।

immortality *इ मौः टै लि टि* *n.* condition or quality of being immortal अमरता।

immortalize *इ मौः टॅ लॉइज़* *v.t.* to render immortal अमर बनाना।

immovable *इ मू वॅ ब्ल* *a.* motionless अचल; fixed (property) अडिग, स्थिर (संपत्ति)

immune *इ म्यून* *a.* safe, secure प्रतिरक्षित।

immunity *इ म्यू नि टि* *n.* protection बचाव, प्रतिरक्षा।

immunize *इ म्यू नॉइज़* *v.t.* to make immune प्रतिरक्षित करना।

impact *इम् पैक्ट* *n.* effect प्रभाव; the shock of a moving body that strikes against another संघात।

impart *इम् पाःट* *v.t.* to give देना; to communicate बताना।

impartial *इम् पाः शॅल* *a.* not partial निष्पक्ष।

impartiality *इम् पाः शि ऐ लि टि* *n.* state or quality of being impartial निष्पक्षता।

impassable *इम् पा सॅ ब्ल* *a.* that cannot be passed अलंघ्य।

impasse *इम् पास, ऐम्–* *n.* deadlock गतिरोध।

impatience *इम् पे शॅन्स* *n.* condition or quality of being impatient अधीरता, व्यग्रता।

impatient *इम् पे शॅन्ट* *a.* eager, restless अधीर, व्यग्र।

impeach *इम् पीच* *v.t.* to charge with a crime अभियोग लगाना; to call in question संदेह करना।

impeachment *इम् पीच् मॅन्ट* *n.* impeaching अभियोग।

impede *इम् पीड* *v.t.* to obstruct, to hinder (में) बाधा डालना।

impediment *इम् पै˘ डि मॅन्ट* *n.* obstruction बाधा; a defect of speech हकलाहट।

impenetrable *इम् पै˘ नि ट्रॅ ब्ल* *a.* that cannot be penetrated अभेद्य।

imperative *इम् पै˘ रॅ टिव* *a.* urgent अत्यावश्यक, अनिवार्य; obligatory आदेशात्मक।

imperfect *इम् पॅः फ़िक्ट* *a.* not perfect अपूर्ण, अधूरा।

imperfection *इम् पॅः फैकॅ् शॅ* *n.* want of perfection अपूर्णता।

imperial *इम् पिअॅ रि अॅल* *a.* royal शाही; concerned with an empire साम्राज्यिक, साम्राज्य-संबंधी।

imperialism *इम् पिअॅ रि अॅ लिज़्म* *n.* policy of extending a country's empire and influence साम्राज्यवाद।

imperil *इम् पै˘ रिल* *(-ll-)* *v.t.* to put in danger संकट में डालना।

imperishable *इम् पै˘ रि शॅ ब्ल* *a.* that cannot perish अक्षय।

impersonal *इम् पॅः सॅ नॅल* *a.* not personal अवैयक्तिक; having no existence as a person व्यक्तित्वहीन।

impersonate *इम् पॅः सॅ नेट* *v.t.* to

pretend to be (another person) (का) छद्म रूप धारण करना; to act the part of (का) अभिनय करना।

impersonation *इम् पॅः सॅ ने शॅन n.* act of impersonating पररूप धारण।

impertinence *इम् पॅः टि नॅन्स n.* rudeness गुस्ताख़ी।

impertinent *इम् पॅः टि नॅन्ट a.* rude गुस्ताख, ढीठ।

impetuosity *इम् पै˘ ट्यु औ˘ सि टि n.* quality of being empetuous प्रचंड, जल्दबाज़।

impetuous *इम् पै˘ ट्यु ॲस a.* acting without consideration अविवेकी; rash जल्दबाज़; moving or acting energetically प्रचंड, तीव्र।

implement[1] *इम् प्लि मॅन्ट n.* tool उपकरण; instrument औज़ार।

implement[2] *इम् प्लि मॅन्ट v.t.* to carry out कार्यान्वित करना।

implicate *इम् प्लि केट v.t.* to involve फंसाना।

implication *इम् प्लि के शॅन n.* being involved in a crime उलझाव; something suggested निहितार्थ।

implicit *इम् प्लि सिट a.* implied अंतर्निहित; unquestioning निर्विवाद।

implore *इम् प्लौः v.t.* to beg प्रार्थना करना, याचना करना।

imply *इम् प्लॉइ v.t.* to involve (में) अंतर्निहित होना।

impolite *इम् पॅ लॉइट a.* discourteous, rude अशिष्ट अभद्र।

import[1] *इम् पौःट v.t.* to bring (goods) into the country (माल) आयात करना।

import[2] *इम् पौःट n. (pl.)* goods imported आयात; importance महत्व।

importance *इम् पौः टॅन्स n.* being important महत्व।

important *इम् पौः टॅन्ट a.* of great consequence महत्वपूर्ण।

impose *इम् पोज़ v.t.* to lay (penalties, tax etc.) लगाना; to enforce लागू करना।

imposing *इम् पो ज़िङ्ग a.* impressive प्रभावशाली।

imposition *इम् पॅ ज़ि शॅन n.* act of imposing आरोपण; that which is imposed लागू की गई वस्तु; deception धोखा।

impossibility *इम् पौ˘ सॅ बि लि टि n.* state of being impossible असंभवता।

impossible *इम् पौ˘ सि ब्ल a.* that cannot be done असंभव।

impostor *इम् पौसॅ टॅः n.* person pretending to be what he is not पाखंड़ी।

imposture *इम् पौसॅ चॅः n.* fraud committed by an impostor पाखंड।

impotence *इम् पॅ टॅन्स n.* state of being impotent नपुसंकता।

impotent *इम् पॅ टॅन्ट a.* unable to copulate नपुंसक; powerless दुर्बल।

impoverish *इम् पौ˘ वॅ रिश v.t.* to make poor निर्धन कर देना।

impracticability *इम् प्रैक् टि कॅ बि लि टि n.* state of being impracticable अव्यावहारिकता।

impracticable *इम् प्रैक् टि कॅ ब्ल a.* that cannot be put into effect अव्यवहार्य।

impress *इम् प्रैस् v.t.* to influence

deeply प्रभावित करना; to make a mark on (पर) चिन्ह लगाना।

impression *इम् प्रै ˘ शॅन n.* effect on mind प्रभाव; vague notion विचार, मत; mark made by pressing छाप, चिन्ह; separate printing of a book संस्करण।

impressive *इम् प्रै ˘ सिव a.* effective प्रभावशाली।

imprint[1] *इम्-प्रिन्ट v.t.* to mark by print or pressure छापना।

imprint[2] *इम् प्रिन्ट n.* lasting effect प्रभाव; mark छाप।

imprison *इम् प्रि ज़न v.t.* to put in prison बंदी बनाना।

improper *इम् प्रौ ˘ पॅ: a.* not suitable अनुचित; indecent अभद्र; incorrect असंगत, ग़लत।

impropriety *इम् प्रो ˘ प्रॉइ अॅ टि n.* unsuitability अनौचित्य; incorrectness ग़लती।

improve *इम् प्रूव् v.t.* to make better सुधारना; *v.t.* to become better सुधरना।

improvement *इम् प्रूव् मॅन्ट n.* state of being improved सुधार।

imprudence *इम् प्रू डॅन्स n.* state or quality of being imprudent अविवेक, नासमझी।

imprudent *इम् प्रू डॅन्ट a.* unwise अविवेकी।

impulse *इम् पल्स n.* sudden inclination of act अंतःप्रेरणा; impelling force आवेग।

impulsive *इम् पल् सिव a.* acting on impulse आवेगशील।

impunity *इम् प्यू नि टि n.* exemption from punishment दंड-मुक्ति।

impure *इम् पयुअॅ:, –प्यौ: a.* adulterated, polluted मिलावटी, प्रदूषित; defiled अशुद्ध।

impurity *इम् प्यूअॅ रि टि n.* adulteration मिलावट; unholiness अपवित्रता।

impute *इम् प्यूट v.t.* to ascribe (पर) लांछन लगाना।

in *इन prep.* a preposition that expresses inclusion within limits of space, time, circumstance, sphere etc. में, के भीतर।

inability *इन् अॅ बि लि टि n.* incapability अक्षमता; being unable असमर्थता।

inaccurate *इन् ऐ क्यु रिट a.* not accurate अशुद्ध, ग़लत।

inaction *इन् ऐक् शॅन n.* idleness आलस्य; lack of action अकर्मण्यता।

inactive *इन् ऐक् टिव a.* inert निष्क्रिय; idle आलसी।

inadmissible *इन् अॅड् मि सि बल a.* not acceptable अस्वीकार्य; not allowable अमान्य।

inanimate *इन् ऐ नि मिट a.* lifeless निर्जीव; senseless अचेतन; dull सुस्त।

inapplicable *इन् ऐप् लि कॅ बल a.* not applicable अप्रयोज्य।

inattentive *इन् अॅ टैन् टिव a.* careless, neglectful असावधान।

inaudible *इन् औ डि बल a.* not able to be heard अश्राव्य।

inaugural *इन् औ ग्यु रॅल a.* pertaining to inauguration उद्घाटन-संबंधी।

inauguration *इन् औ ग्यु रे शॅन n.* beginning, opening उद्घाटन।

inauspicious *इन् औस् पि शॅस a.* ill-omened अशुभ, अमांगलिक।

inborn *अन् बोःन a.* implanted by nature सहज; born in जन्मजात।

incalculable *इन कैल् क्यु लॅ ब्‌ल a.* too great to be calculated गणनातीत; that cannot be reckoned beforehand जिसका पहले से अनुमान न हो सके।

incapable *इन् के पॅ ब्‌ल a.* incompetent अक्षम, असमर्थ; not capable अशक्त।

incapacity *इन् कॅ पै सि टि n.* powerlessness शक्तिहीनता; inability असमर्थता।

incarnate[1] *इन् का: निट a.* invested with body देहयुक्त, अवतारी; personified मूर्तिमान।

incarnate[2] *इन् का: नेट v.t.* to give human form to साकार रूप में रखना।

incarnation *इन् का: ने शॅन n.* incarnate form अवतार; the taking of human shape अवतरण।

incense[1] *इन् सैन्स v.t.* to make angry चिढ़ाना, क्रुद्ध करना।

incense[2] *इन् सैन्स n.* substance that gives off pleasant fumes when burnt सुगंध, हवन सामग्री।

incentive *इन् सैन् टिव n.* encouragement प्रोत्साहन; stimulus उद्‌दीपन।

inception *इन् सैप् शॅन n.* beginning आरंभ।

inch *इन्च n.* one-twelfth of a foot. इंच।

incident *इन् सि डॅन्ट n.* event घटना।

incidental *इन् सि डैन् टॅल a.* occasional आकस्मिक।

incite *इन सॉइट v.t.* to instigate उत्तेजित करना।

inclination *इन् क्लि ने शॅन n.* bent झुकाव; natural aptness अभिरुचि; desire इच्छा।

incline *इन् क्लॉइन v.i.* to lean झुकना; to be disposed रुझान होना; *v.t.* to bend मोड़ना; to cause to lean झुकाना।

include *इन् क्लूड v.t.* to add to, to take in सम्मिलित करना।

inclusion *इन् क्लू ज़ॅन n.* act of including अंतर्वेशन, समावेश।

inclusive *इन् क्लू सिव a.* including, enclosing सम्मिलित।

incoherent *इन् को ˘ हिअॅ रॅन्ट a.* inconsistent असंगत; irrelevant असंबद्ध।

income *इन कॅम् n.* profit लाभ; revenue आय।

incomparable *इन् कौम् पॅ रॅ ब्‌ल a.* matchless अनुपम; unique अनोखा।

incompetent *इन् कौम् पि टॅन्ट a.* wanting adequate power अक्षम; unqualified अयोग्य।

incomplete *इन् कॅम् प्लीट a .* not complete, imperfect अधूरा।

inconsiderate *इन् कॅन् सि डॅ रिट a.* thoughtless अविवेकी; lacking in regard for the feelings of others दूसरों का ध्यान न रखने वाला।

inconvenient *इन कॅन् वी न्यॅन्ट a.* causing uneasiness असुविधाजनक।

incorporate[1] *इन् कौः पॅ रेट v.t.* to include सम्मिलित करना; to form into a corporation निगमित करना।

incorporate[2] *इन् कौः पॅ रिट a.* included सम्मिलित; corporated निगमित।

incorporation इन कौः पॅ रे शॅन *n.* act of incorporating संयोजन।

incorrect इन कॅ रैक्ट *a.* not correct, faulty अशुद्ध, ग़लत।

incorrigible इन् कौ ˘ रि जॅ ब्ल *a.* beyond correction असंशोधनीय।

incorruptible इन् कॅ रप् टॅ ब्ल *a.* not capable of fault अदूषणीय; honest ईमानदार।

increase[1] इन् क्रीस *v.t.* to make greater in size, number etc. बढ़ाना; *v.i.* to grow in size etc. बढ़ना।

increase[2] *n.* growth विस्तार, वृद्धि।

incredible इन् क्रै ˘ डॅ ब्ल *a.* that cannot be believed, difficult to believe in अविश्वसनीय।

increment इन् क्रि मॅन्ट *n.* increase वृद्धि; increase in salary वेतन-वृद्धि।

incriminate इन् क्रि मि नेट *v.t.* to charge with a crime (पर) अभियोग लगाना; to blame (पर) दोष लगाना।

incubate इन् क्यु बेट *v.i.* to sit on eggs for hatching अंडे सेना; *v.t.* to hatch (eggs) by sitting on them (अंडे) सेना।

inculcate इन् कल् केट *v.t.* to impress on the mind मन में बैठाना।

incumbent[1] इन् कम् बॅन्ट *n.* one who holds an office पदग्राही।

incumbent[2] *a.* lying on आश्रित।

incur इन कॅः *v.t.* to become liable to (का) दायित्व लेना; to bring upon oneself to suffer झेलना।

incurable इन क्युअॅ रॅ ब्ल *a.* not admitting of cure अचिकित्स्य, असाध्य।

indebted इन डै ˘ टिड *a.* owing money ऋणी; grateful आभारी।

indecency इन् डी सॅन् सि *n.* impudence अशिष्टता; unbecomingness अनौचित्य।

indecent इन् डी सॅन्ट *a.* immodest अभद्र; unbecoming अनुचित; obscene अश्लील।

indecision इन् डि सि ज़ॅन *n.* want of decision असमंजस।

indeed इन् डीड *adv.* in fact वास्तव में; undoubtedly निस्संदेह।

indefensible इन् डि फ़ैन् सॅ ब्ल *a.* that cannot be excused or justified असमर्थनीय; that cannot be defended अरक्षणीय।

indefinite इन् डै ˘ फ़ि निट *a.* uncertain, undetermined अनिश्चित।

indemnity इन् डै ˘ म् नि टि *n.* security from damage or loss क्षति या हानि से सुरक्षा।

independence इन् डि पैन् डॅन्स *n.* freedom स्वतंत्रता; self- reliance स्वावलंबन।

independent इन् डि पैन् डॅन्ट *a.* free स्वतंत्र; self-governing स्वावलंबी।

indescribable इन् डि स्क्रॉइ बॅ ब्ल *a.* that cannot be described अवर्णनीय।

index इन् डैक्स *n. (pl. indices)* pointer सूचक, संकेत; list सूची; the forefinger तर्जनी।

Indian इन् डि अॅन, इन् ड्यॅन *a.* residing in India भारतीय।

indicate इन् डि केट *v.t.* to point out संकेत करना; to make known सूचित करना।

indication इन् डि के शॅन *n.* act of

indicating संकेत करना; hint संकेत।

indicative *इन् डि कॅ टिव a.* pointing out परिचायक।

indicator *इन् डि के टॅः n.* that which or one who indicates सूचक।

indict *इन् डॉइट v.t.* to charge with crime अभियोग लगाना।

indictment *इन् डॉइट् मॅन्ट n.* formal charge अभियोग।

indifference *इन् डि फ़ॅ रॅन्स n.* unconcern उदासीनता।

indifferent *इन् डि फ़ॅ रॅन्ट a.* unconcerned उदासीन; neutral निष्पक्ष।

indigenous *इन् डि जे˘ नॅस a.* native born or produced देशज।

indigestible *इन् डि जैसॅ् टॅ ब्ल a.* not digestible अपचनीय।

indigestion *इन् डि जैसॅ् चॅन n.* want of digestion अपच, अजीर्ण।

indignant *इन डिग् नॅन्ट a.* feeling or showing justifiable anger क्रुद्ध।

indignation *इन् डिग् ने शॅन n.* anger क्रोध, क्षोभ।

indigo *इन् डि गो n.* violet blue dye नील।

indirect *इन् डि रैक्ट a.* not direct अप्रत्यक्ष; not straight to the point, round about घुमावदार; (gram.) reported (speech) प्रतिवेदित।

indiscipline *इन डि सि प्लिन n.* want of discipline अनुशासनहीनता।

indiscreet *इन् डिस् क्रीट a.* lacking in caution, not carefully considered असावधानीपूर्ण, नासमझी का।

indiscretion *इन् डिस् क्रै˘ शॅन n.* inattention अनवधान; want of descretion अविवेक।

indiscriminate *इन् डिस् क्रि मि निट a.* disorderly विश्रृंखल; lacking discrimination अंधाधुंध।

indispensable *इन् डिस् पैनॅ् सॅ ब्ल a.* absolutely necessary अपरिहार्य।

indisposed *इन् डिस् पोज़्ड a.* unwell अस्वस्थ; not inclined अनच्छुिक।

indisputable *इन् डिस् प्यू टॅ ब्ल a.* beyond dispute निर्विवाद।

indistinct *इन् डिस् टिङ्क्ट a.* not distinct अस्पष्ट।

individual *इन् डि वि ड्यु ॲल a.* personal व्यक्तिगत।

individualism *इन् डि वि ड्यु ॲ लिज़्म n.* principle of asserting one's independence व्यक्तिवाद।

individuality *इन् डि वि ड्यु ऐ लि टि n.* separate and distinct existence वैयक्तिकता।

indivisible *इन् डि वि ज़ॅ ब्ल a.* that cannot be divided अविभाज्य।

indolent *इन् डॅ लॅन्ट a.* lazy, inactive आलसी, निष्क्रिय।

indomitable *इन् डौ˘ मि टॅ ब्ल a.* not to be overcome दुर्दमनीय, अदम्य।

indoor *इन् डौः a.* practised or used within a building भीतरी, आभ्यंतरिक।

indoors *इन् डौःज़ adv.* in or into a building भवन के अंदर।

induce *इन् ड्यूस v.t.* to motivate प्रेरित करना; to instigate भड़काना।

inducement *इन् डॅयूस् मॅन्ट n.* incentive अभिप्रेरण; persuation प्रलोभन।

induct *इन् डक्ट v.t.* to install प्रतिष्ठापित करना।

induction *इन् डक् शॅन n.* installation अधिष्ठापन।

indulge *इन् डल्ज v.t.* to please प्रसन्न करना; to gratify तृप्त करना; *v.i.* to yield to a desire लिप्त रहना या होना।

indulgence *इन् डल् जॅन्स n.* favour अनुग्रह, कृपा; giving way to one's desires अतिभोग, लिप्तता।

indulgent *इन् डल् जॅन्ट a.* characterised by indulgence लिप्त; doing favour कृपालु।

industrial *इन् डस् ट्रि ॲल a.* relating to industry औद्योगिक।

industrious *इन् डस् ट्रि ॲस a.* hardworking मेहनती।

industry *इन् डस् ट्रि n.* any branch of trade or manufacture उद्योग; assiduity अध्यवसाय।

ineffective *इन् इ फैक् टिव a.* not effective अप्रभावी; useless निष्फल।

inert *इ नॅ:ट a.* inactive निष्क्रिय; having no power of motion गतिहीन, स्थिर।

inertia *इ नॅ: श्यॅ n.* motionlessness निश्चेष्टता।

inevitable *इन् ऐ॓ वि टॅ ब्ल a.* unavoidable अपरिहार्य।

inexact *इन् इग् ज़ैक्ट a.* not exact अशुद्ध।

inexorable *इन् ऐक् सॅ रॅ ब्ल a.* hardhearted निष्ठुर; unbending अनमनीय।

inexpensive *इन् इक्स् पै॓न् सिव a.* economical मितव्ययी; cheap सस्ता।

inexperience *इन् इक्स् पिॲ रि ॲन्स n.* want of experience अनुभवहीनता।

inexplicable *इन् ऐक्स् प्लि कॅ ब्ल a.* that cannot be explained अव्याख्येय, अपरिभाष्य।

infallible *इन् फै लॅ ब्ल a.* not liable to fail अचूक; not able to make a mistake त्रुटिरहित।

infamous *इन् फ़ॅ मॅस a.* notorious बदनाम।

infamy *इन् फ़ॅ मि n.* being infamous अपकीर्ति; public dishonour बदनामी।

infancy *इन् फ़ॅन् सि n.* early childhood बचपन; early stage प्रारंभिक अवस्था।

infant *इन् फ़ॅन्ट n.* baby बच्चा, शिशु।

infanticide *इन् फ़ैन् टि सॉइड n.* the murder of a child शिशुबध।

infantile *इन् फ़ॅन् टॉइल a.* pertaining to infant शिशु-संबंधी; having characteristics of infancy बालोचित।

infantry *इन् फ़ॅन् ट्रि n.* soldiers fighting on foot पैदल सेना।

infatuate *इन् फ़ै ट्यु एट v.t.* to turn to folly मूढ़ बनाना; to inspire with shallow love मोहित करना।

infatuation *इन् फ़ै ट्यु ए शॅन n.* enchantment सम्मोह।

infect *इन् फ़ैक्ट v.t.* to corrupt भ्रष्ट करना; to taint संदूषित करना; to fill with disease germs रोगाणु युक्त करना।

infection *इन् फ़ैक् शॅन n.* act of infecting संक्रमण; disease resulting from infection छूत की बीमारी।

infectious *इन् फ़ैक् शॅस a.* infecting with disease संक्रामक; quickly influencing others शीघ्र प्रभावी।

infer *इन् फ़ॅः (-rr-) v.t.* to conclude निष्कर्ष निकालना; to estimate अनुमान करना।

inference *इन् फ़ॅ रॅन्स n.* that which is inferred or deduced अनुमान; conclusion निष्कर्ष।

inferior *इन् फ़िअॅ रि अॅः a.* of poor quality घटिया; lower in rank अवर।

inferiority *इन् फ़िअ रि औँ रि टि n.* poorness in quality घटियापन; degradation अपकर्ष।

infernal *इन् फ़ॅः नॅल a.* belonging to lower regions नारकीय।

infinite *इन् फ़ि निट a.* endless अनंत, असीम।

infinity *इन् फ़ि नि टि n.* (*maths.*) countless or indefinite number (गणित) अनंत संख्या।

infirm *इन् फ़ॅःम a.* physically weak कमज़ोर, अशक्त; irresolute अस्थिर।

infirmity *इन् फ़ॅः मि टि n.* despondency अवसन्नता; unstability अदृढ़ता; weakness दुर्बलता।

inflame *इन् फ़्लेम v.t.* to excite उत्तेजित करना; to cause to flame प्रज्वलित करना; *v.i.* to become excited उत्तेजित होना; to burst into flame जलना।

inflammable *इन् फ्लै मॅ बल a.* combustible ज्वलनशील; excitable उत्तेजनशील।

inflammation *इन फ़्लॅ मे शॅन n.* state of being inflamed प्रज्वलन; kindling of passions उत्तेजन; swelling with heat and pain प्रदाह, सूजन।

inflammatory *इन् फ़्लै मॅ टॅ रि a.* tending to inflame प्रज्वलनकारी; pertaining to swelling सूजन-संबंधी।

inflation *इन् फ़्ले शॅन n.* undue increase in the quantity of money मुद्रास्फीति, मुद्राप्रसार।

inflexible *इन् फ्लैक् सॅ ब्ल a.* unbending अनमनीय; rigid कड़ा।

inflict *इन् फ़्लिक्ट v.t.* to impose forcibly थोपना; to cause suffering to पीड़ा पहुंचाना।

influence[1] *इन् फ्लु अॅन्स n.* ability or power to affect others प्रभाव।

influence[2] *v.t.* to affect प्रभाव डालना।

influential *इन फ़्लु ऐन् शॅल a.* having much influence प्रभावशाली।

influenza *इन फ़्लु ऐन् ज़ॅ n.* epidemic virus disease श्लेष्मा ज्वर।

influx *इन् फ्लक्स n.* flowing in अंतःप्रवाह।

inform *इन् फ़ौःम v.t.* to give information to सूचना देना; to tell बताना।

informal *इन् फ़ौः मॅल a.* unceremonious अनौपचारिक।

information *इन् फ़ॅः मे शॅन n.* news ख़बर, समाचार; act of informing सूचना।

informative *इन फ़ॅः मॅ टिव a.* affording information सूचनापूर्ण; instructive शिक्षाप्रद।

informer *इन फौ: मॅ:* *n.* one who informs against another मुख़बिर।

infringe *इन फ्रिन्ज v.t.* to violate उल्लंघन करना।

infringement *इन् फ्रिन्ज् मॅन्ट n.* violation अतिक्रमण, उल्लंघन।

infuriate *इन् फ्युअॅ रि एट v.t.* to enrage क्रुद्ध करना।

infuse *इन फ़्यूज़ v.t.* to inspire अनुप्राणित करना; to moisten तर करना, भिगोना।

infusion *इन् फ़्यू ज़ॅन n.* act of infusing निषेचन; liquid extract निषेचक।

ingrained *इन् ग्रेन्ड a.* inherent अंतर्निहित; deep-rooted गहरा।

ingratitude *इन् ग्रै टि ट्यूड n.* unthankfulness कृतघ्नता।

ingredient *इन् ग्री ड्यॅन्ट n.* component अवयव, घटक।

inhabit *इन् है बिट v.t.* to dwell in (में) वास करना।

inhabitable *इन् है बि टॅ बुल a.* that can be lived in आवास-योग्य।

inhabitant *इन् है बि टॅन्ट n.* resident निवासी।

inhale *इन् हेल v.i.* to breathe in सांस लेना *v.t.* to draw into the lungs सांस-द्वारा खींचना।

inherent *इन् हिअॅ रॅन्ट a.* in-born जन्मजात।

inherit *इन् है˘ रिट v.t.* to get as heir उत्तराधिकार में पाना; to derive from ancestors पूर्वजों से प्राप्त करना।

inheritance *इन् है˘ रि टॅन्स n.* that which is or may be inherited उत्तराधिकार, विरासत।

inhibit *इन् हि बिट v.t.* to prevent रोकना।

inhibition *इन् हि बि शॅन n.* act of restraining अवरोध।

inhospitable *इन हौसॅ् पि टॅ बुल a.* not hospitable असत्कारशील।

inhuman *इन् ह्यू मॅन a.* brutal अमानवीय।

inimical *इ नि मि कॅल a.* unfriendly विरोधी; harmful हानिकर।

inimitable *इ नि मि टॅ बुल a.* unmatched अद्वितीय; not worth imitating अननुकरणीय।

initial[1] *इ नि शॅल a.* of or related to the beginning प्रारंभिक।

initial[2] *n. (usu. pl.)* first letters of a person's name आद्याक्षर।

initial[3] *(-ll-) v.t.* to put one's initials on आद्याक्षरित करना।

initiate *इ नि शि एट v.t.* to start, to begin सूत्रपात करना, आरंभ करना।

initiative *इ नि शि अॅ टिव n.* first step, lead पहल; ability to act independently स्वतंत्र रूप से कार्य करने की योग्यता।

inject *इन् जैक्ट v.t.* to force in अंतःक्षिप्त करना, इंजेक्शन देना।

injection *इन् जैक् शॅन n.* act of injecting अंतःक्षेप, इंजेक्शन।

injudicious *इन् जू डि शॅस, –जू– a.* not judicious अविवेकी।

injunction *इन् जङ्क् शॅन n.* judicial order आदेश।

injure *इन् जॅ: v.t.* to damage क्षति करना; to inflict bodily hurt on घायल करना।

injurious *इन् जुअॅ रि अॅस a.* hurtful, wrongful हानिकर, अनिष्टकर।

injury *इन् जॅ रि n.* hurt क्षति, चोट।

injustice *इन् जस् टिस n.* act of unfairness अन्यायपूर्ण कृत्य; want of justice अन्याय।

ink *इङ्क n.* coloured liquid used for writing and printing स्याही।

inkling *इङ्क लिङ्ग n.* dim notion, slight hint आभास, संकेत।

inland[1] *इन् लॅन्ड, –लैन्ड a.* confined to a country अंतर्देशीय; within a country आंतरिक।

inland[2] *इन् लैन्ड adv.* in the interior of a country अंदर-अंदर।

in-laws *इन् लौज़ n. (pl.)* relatives by marriage ससुरालवाले।

inmate *इन् मेट n.* one of a number of persons living together संवासी।

inmost *इन् मोस्ट a.* secret गुप्त; most inward अंतरतम।

inn *इन n.* public house सराय।

innate *इ नेट a.* inborn जन्मजात; inherent अंतर्भूत।

inner *इ नॅः a.* internal अंदरूनी।

innermost *इ नॅः मोस्ट a.* inmost अंतरतम।

innings *इ निङ्गज़ n. (sing.)* (cricket) duration of batting पारी; period of power प्रभुत्व की अवधि।

innocence *इ नॅ सॅन्स n.* freedom from legal guilt निरपराधता; blamelessness निर्दोषिता।

innocent *इ नॅ सॅन्ट a.* ignorant of evil निर्दोष; knowing nothing of evil or wrong भोला-भाला।

innovate *इ नो˘ वेट v.t.* to renew नया बनाना; to improve सुधारना।

innovation *इ नो˘ वे शॅन n.* act of innovating नवोन्मेष।

innovator *इ नो˘ वे टॅः n.* one who brings new changes प्रवर्तक।

innumerable *इ न्यू मॅ रॅ ब्ल a.* countless असंख्य।

inoculate *इ नौ˘ क्यु लेट v.t.* to vaccinate टीका लगाना।

inoculation *इ नौ˘ क्यु ले शॅन n.* vaccination टीकाकरण।

inoperative *इन् औ˘ पॅ रॅ टिव a.* not working निष्क्रिय; having no effect अप्रभावी।

inopportune *इन् औ˘ पॅः ट्यून a.* unseasonable असामयिक।

input *इन् पुट n.* amount of power put in लगाई गई शक्ति का परिमाण; data fed into a computer कंप्यूटर में भरी गई सामग्री।

inquest *इङ् क्वैस्ट n.* judicial inquiry क़ानूनी जांच।

inquire *इन् क्वॉइअॅः v.t.* to investigate जांच करना; *v.i.* to make an examination अनुसंधान करना।

inquiry *इन् क्वाइअॅ रि n.* investigation जांच; act of enquiring पूछताछ।

inquisition *इन् क्वि ज़ि शॅन n.* judicial inquiry न्यायिक जांच; searching examination परीक्षण।

inquisitive *इन् क्वि ज़ि टिव a.* eager to know जिज्ञासु।

insane *इन् सेन a.* crazy उन्मादी; of unsound mind भ्रांतचित।

insanity *इन् सै नि टि n.* mental disorder उन्माद, विक्षिप्तता।

insatiable *इन् से श्यॅ ब्ल a.* that cannot be satisfied अतोषणीय।

inscribe *इन् स्क्रॉइब v.t.* to engrave उत्कीर्ण करना; to mark चिह्नित करना।

inscription *इन् स्क्रिप् शॅन n.* act of inscribing उत्कीर्णन; record inscribed on stone etc. अभिलेख, शिलालेख।

insect *इन् सैक्ट n.* small invertebrate creature कीट, कृमि।

insecticide *इन् सै ॅक् टि सॉइड n.* insect-killing substance कीटनाशी औषधि।

insecure *इन् सि कयुअॅः a.* unsafe अरक्षित।

insecurity *इन् सि क्युअॅ रि टि n.* want of safety असुरक्षा।

insensibility *इन् सैनॅ सि बि लि टि n.* lack of feeling असंवेदन; unconsciousness संज्ञाहीनता।

insensible *इन् सैनॅ सि ब्ल a.* unconscious बेसुध; without sensation संवेदन-शून्य।

inseparable *इन् सै ॅ पॅ रॅ ब्ल a.* that cannot be separated अवियोज्य।

insert *इन् सॅःट v.t.* to put in सन्निविष्ट करना।

insertion *इन् सॅः शॅन n.* act of putting in सन्निवेश।

inside[1] *इन् सॉइड n.* the inner side भीतरी भाग।

inside[2] *prep.* within के अंदर; into अंदर की ओर।

inside[3] *a.* of, in, on the inside अंदरूनी; secret गुप्त।

inside[4] *adv.* indoors, within अंदर।

insight *इन् सॉइट n.* imaginative penetration सूक्ष्मदृष्टि।

insignificance *इन् सिग् नि फ़ि कॅन्स n.* unimportance महत्वहीनता; meaninglessness निरर्थकता।

insignificant *इन् सिग् नि फ़ि कॅन्ट a.* unimportant महत्वहीन; meaningless निरर्थक।

insincere *इन् सिन् सिअॅः a.* not sincere निष्ठाहीन।

insincerity *इन् सिन् सै ॅ रि टि n.* faithlessness निष्ठाहीनता।

insinuate *इन् सि न्यु एट v.t.* to hint इशारा करना; to suggest indirectly परोक्ष रूप से अथवा चालाकी से सुझाना।

insinuation *इन् सि न्यु ए शॅन n.* sarcasm कटाक्ष; coaxing उकसावा; indirect hint परोक्ष संकेत।

insipid *इन् सि पिड a.* tasteless स्वादहीन; uninteresting अरुचिकर।

insipidity *इन् सि पि डि टि n.* tastelessness स्वादहीनता; spiritlessness उत्साहहीनता।

insist *इन् सिस्ट v.t.* to persist in pressing आग्रह करना; to emphasise ज़ोर देना।

insistence *इन सिस् टॅन्स n.* persistence अनुरोध, आग्रह; emphasis बल।

insistent *इन सिस् टॅन्ट a.* persistent आग्रहपूर्ण।

insolence *इन् सॅ लॅन्स n.* impudence गुस्ताख़ी, अविनय।

insolent *इन् सॅ लॅन्ट a.* impudent गुस्ताख, अविनीत।

insoluble *इन् सौ ॅ ल्यु ब्ल n.* that cannot be solved असाध्य, असमाधेय; that cannot be dissolved अघुलनशील।

insolvency *इन् सौलॅ वॅन् सि n.* bankruptcy दिवालियापन।

insolvent *इन् सौलॅ वॅन्ट a.* not able to pay one's debt दिवालिया।

inspect *इन् स्पै ॅक्ट v.t.* to examine परीक्षण करना।

inspection *इन् स्पैक् शॅन n.* close examination निरीक्षण, परीक्षण।

inspector *इन् स्पैक् टॅ: n.* one who inspects निरीक्षक।

inspiration *इन् स्पि रे शॅन n.* stimulation प्रेरणा; source of inspiring प्रेरणा-स्रोत।

inspire *इन् स्पॉइअॅ: v.t.* to induce प्रेरित करना।

instability *इन् स्टॅ बि लि टि n.* want of stability अस्थिरता।

install *इन् स्टौल v.t.* to put in a position or rank नियुक्त करना; to place in an office ceremoniously पदारूढ़ करना।

installation *इन् स्टौ ले शॅन् –स्टॅ– n.* act of installing अधिष्ठापन।

instalment *इन् स्टौल् मॅन्ट n.* one of a series of partial payments किस्त।

instance *इन् स्टॅन्स n.* example दृष्टांत।

instant[1] *इन् स्टॅन्ट n.* moment निमिष, क्षण।

instant[2] *a.* urgent आवश्यक; immediate तात्कालिक।

instantaneous *इन् स्टॅन् टे न्यॅस a.* immediate तात्कालिक।

instantly *इन् स्टॅन्ट् लि adv.* at once तुरंत।

instigate *इन् स्टि गेट v.t.* to provoke उकसाना, भड़काना।

instigation *इन् स्टि गे शॅन n.* instigating, being instigated भड़कावा, उकसाहट।

instil *इन् स्टिल (-ll-) v.t.* to drop in टपकाना; to infuse into the mind चित्त में बैठाना।

instinct *इन् स्टिङ्क्ट n.* impulse प्रवृत्ति; intuition अंतःप्रेरणा।

instinctive *इन् स्टिङ्क् टिव a.* based on instinct प्रवृत्तिमूलक।

institute *इन् स्टि ट्यूट n.* organisation संस्था।

institution *इन स्टि ट्यू शॅन n.* act of establishing प्रतिष्ठापन; organisation संस्था।

instruct *इन स्ट्रक्ट v.t.* to direct हिदायत करना; to teach शिक्षा देना।

instruction *इन स्ट्रक् शॅन n.* direction अनुदेश, हिदायत; act of teaching शिक्षण।

instructor *इन् स्ट्रक् टॅ: n.* teacher शिक्षक; one who instructs अनुदेशक।

instrument *इन् स्टु मॅन्ट n.* tool औज़ार; apparatus उपकरण; document दस्तावेज़।

instrumental *इन् स्टु म ॅन् टॅल a.* serving as a means सहायक; relating to musical instrument वाद्य-विषयक।

instrumentalist *इन् स्टु मैन् टॅ लिस्ट n.* player of a musical instrument वादक।

insubordinate *इन् सॅ बौ: डि निट a.* disobedient अवज्ञाकारी।

insubordination *इन् सॅ बौ: डि ने शॅन n.* disobedience अवज्ञा।

insufficient *इन् सॅ फ़ि शॅन्ट a.* inadequate अपर्याप्त।

insular *इन् स्यु लॅ: a.* of an island द्वीपीय; narrow-minded संकीर्णमना।

insularity *इन स्यु लै रि टी n.* state of being insular द्वीपीयता; narrow-mindedness मानसिक संकीर्णता।

insulate *इन् स्यु लेट v.t.* to separate, to isolate पृथक् करना; to cover in order to prevent the passage of heat or electricity विद्युत्-ऊष्मारोधी बनाना।

insulation *इन् स्यु ले शॅन n.* act of separating पृथक्करण; resisting flow of heat or electricity तापावरोधन, विद्युत्रोधन।

insulator *इन् स्यु ले टॅ: n.* separator पृथक्कारी; non conductor विसंवाहक।

insult[1] *इन् सल्ट n.* dishonour अपमान, तिरस्कार।

insult[2] *इन् सल्ट v.t.* to dishonour अनादर करना।

insupportable *इन् सॅ पौः टॅ ब्ल a.* unbearable असहनीय।

insurance *इन् शुअॅ रॅन्स, –शौ– n.* act or system of insuring बीमा।

insure *इन् शुअॅ:, –शौः v.t.* to make sure सुनिश्चित करना; to secure बीमा करना।

insurgent[1] *इन सॅ: जॅन्ट a.* rebellious विद्रोही।

insurgent[2] *n.* a rebel विद्रोही व्यक्ति।

insurmountable *इन् सॅः मॉउन् टॅ ब्ल a.* impassable दुस्तर, अलंघ्य।

insurrection *इन् सॅ रैकॅ शॅन n.* rebellion विद्रोह।

intact *इन् टैक्ट a.* undamaged अक्षुण्ण।

intangible *इन् टैन् जि ब्ल a.* that cannot be grasped or touched अमूर्त।

integral *इन् टि ग्रॅल a.* necessary for completeness संपूर्णता के लिए अनिवार्य, अविभाज्य।

integrity *इन् टैगॅ रि टि n.* unimpaired state समग्रता; wholeness संपूर्णता; honesty ईमानदारी।

intellect *इन् टि लैक्ट n.* intelligence प्रज्ञा, बुद्धि।

intellectual[1] *इन् टि लैकॅ ट्यु अॅल a.* of or relating to intellect बौद्धिक।

intellectual[2] *n.* intellectual person बुद्धिजीवी।

intelligence *इन् टै ˘ लि जॅन्स n.* intellectual skill प्रज्ञा; news, information सूचना।

intelligent *इन् टै˘ लि जॅन्ट a.* having intellect बुद्धिमान्।

intelligentsia *इन् टै˘ लि जैन्ट् सि अॅ n.* intellectuals as a class बुद्धिजीवी-वर्ग।

intelligible *इन् टै ˘ लि जॅ ब्ल a.* easy to understand सुबोध।

intend *इन् टैन्ड v.t.* to fix the mind upon इरादा करना; to purpose प्रयोजन रखना।

intense *इन् टैन्स a.* high in degree अत्यधिक; ardent जोशीला; violent प्रचंड।

intensify *इन् टैनॅ सि फ़ॉइ v.t.* to make intense घनीभूत करना; to become more intense घनीभूत होना।

intensity *इन टैनॅ सि टि n.* ardour उत्कटता; acuteness तीव्रता; quality of being intense आधिक्य।

intensive *इन् टैनॅ सिव a.* dense सघन; sharp प्रखर।

intent[1] *इन् टैन्ट n.* purpose अभिप्राय।

intent[2] *a.* concentrating दत्तचित्त; eager उत्सुक।

intention *इन् टैनॅ् शॅन n.* purpose आशय; aim लक्ष्य।

intentional *इन् टैनॅ् शॅ नॅल a.* done on purpose सोद्देश्य, जानबूझकर किया गया।

intercept *इन् टॅः सैप्ट v.t.* to stop and seize inpassage मार्ग में रोकना; to obstruct (में) बाधा डालना।

interception *इन् टॅः सैपॅ् शॅन n.* act of intercepting अवरोधन।

interchange[1] *इन् टॅः चेन्ज n.* to give and take mutually परस्पर विनिमय करना; to exchange विनिमय करना।

interchange[2] *इन् टॅः चेन्ज v.* mutual exchange परस्पर विनिमय।

intercourse *इन् टॅः कौःस n.* copulation, coitus संभोग; meeting समागम।

interdependence *इन् टॅः डिपैनॅ् डॅन्स n.* mutual dependence परस्पर निर्भरता।

interdependent *इन् टॅः डि पैनॅ् डॅन्ट a.* mutually dependent परस्पर निर्भर।

interest *इन् ट्रिस्ट, – टॅ रॅस्ट n.* right अधिकार; benefit हित; concern सरोकार; disposition towards a thing दिलचस्पी; sum paid for the use of money ब्याज।

interested *इन् ट्रिस् टिड, इन् टॅ रॅस् टिड a.* taking interest रुचि लेने वाला; not impartial पक्षपातपूर्ण; having an interest हितबद्ध।

interesting *इन् ट्रिस् टिङ्ग, इन् टॅ रॅस् टिङ्ग a.* arousing interest रुचिकर।

interfere *इन् टॅः फ़िअॅः v.i.* to intervene हस्तक्षेप करना; to come in the way विघ्न डालना।

interference *इन् टॅः फ़िअॅ रॅन्स n.* act of interfering हस्तक्षेप।

interim *इन् टॅ रिम n.* provisional अंतरिम।

interior[1] *इन् टिअॅ रिअॅः a.* situated within आंतरिक।

interior[2] *n.* the inside आंतरिक भाग; inland areas भीतरी प्रदेश।

interjection *इन् टॅः जैकॅ् शॅन n.* an exclamatory word or phrase विस्मयादिबोधक।

interlock *इन् टॅः लौकॅ v.t.* to clasp in each other गूंथना; *v.i.* to be locked together गुंथ जाना।

interlude *इन् टॅः ल्यूड n.* interval अंतराल; short piece introduced between the acts of a drama विष्कंभक।

intermediary *इन् टॅः मी ड्यॅ रि n.* mediator मध्यस्थ।

intermediate *इन् टॅः मी ड्यॅट a.* happening between two others मध्यवर्ती।

interminable *इन् टॅः मि नॅ ब्ल a.* endless अनंत; very long बहुत लंबा।

intermingle *इन् टॅः मिङ् ग्ल v.t.* to mix together परस्पर मिश्रित करना; *v.i.* to be mixed together परस्पर मिश्रित होना।

intern *इन् टॅःन v.t.* to confine within fixed bounds नज़रबंद कर देना।

internal *इन् टॅः नॅल a.* inner भीतरी, आंतरिक; of the home affairs of a country देशीय।

international *इन् टॅः नै शॅ नॅल a.* transcending national limits अंतर्राष्ट्रीय।

interplay *इन् टॅ: प्ले n.* mutual action अन्योन्य क्रिया।

interpret *इन् टॅ: प्रिट v.t.* to elucidate व्याख्या करना; to explain the meaning of (का) विवेचन करना।

interpreter *इन् टॅ: प्रि टॅ: n.* person who gives an immediate translation of words spoken in another language दुभाषिया।

interrogate *इन् टैॅ रॅ गेट v.t.* to put question to प्रश्न करना।

interrogation *इन् टैॅ रॅ गे शॅन n.* act of interrogating पूछताछ; question mark प्रश्नवाचक चिन्ह।

interrogative[1] *इन् टॅ रौॅ गॅ टिव a.* indicating a question प्रश्नात्मक; (*gram.*) expressed as a question प्रश्नवाचक।

interrogative[2] *n.* word used in asking question प्रश्नवाचक शब्द।

interrupt *इन् टॅ रप्ट v.t.* to break continuity of (का) क्रमभंग करना; to obstruct बाधा डालना।

interruption *इन् टॅ रप् शॅन n.* hindrance बाधा, अवरोध; break in continuity क्रमभंग।

intersect *इन् टॅ: सैक्ट v.t.* to divide by cutting or crossing काटना; *v.i.* to cut or cross each other एक-दूसरे को काटना।

intersection *इन् टॅ: सैक् शॅन* :. intersecting प्रतिच्छेदन; crossroads चौराहा।

interval *इन् टॅ: वॅल n.* intermission मध्यांतर।

intervene *इन् टॅ: वीन v.i.* to interfere हस्तक्षेप करना।

intervention *इन् टॅ: वैन् शॅन n.* interference हस्तक्षेप; interposition व्यवधान।

interview[1] *इन् टॅ: व्यू n.* meeting of persons face to face साक्षात्कार।

interview[2] *v.t.* to have an interview with (से) साक्षात्कार करना।

intestinal *इन् टैस् टि नॅल a.* pertaining to the intestines आंत्र-संबंधी।

intestine *इन् टैस् टिन n. (usu. pl.)* lower part of alimentary canal आंत, आंत्र।

intimacy *इन् टि मॅ सि n.* close familiarity घनिष्ठता।

intimate[1] *इन् टि मिट a.* close घनिष्ठ; innermost आभ्यंतर; closely acquainted परिचित।

intimate[2] *इन् टि मेट v.t.* to make known बताना; to show clearly स्पष्ट प्रदर्शित करना।

intimation *इन् टि मे शॅन n.* announcement सूचना, घोषणा; hint संकेत।

intimidate *इन् टि मि डेट v.t.* to frighten भयभीत करना।

intimidation *इन् टि मि डे शॅन n.* act of intimidating संत्रास।

into *इन् टु prep.* के अंदर, में।

intolerable *इन् टौ ॅ लॅ रॅ बल a.* that cannot be endured असह्य।

intolerance *इन् टौ ॅ लॅ रॅन्स n.* quality or state of being intolerant असहिष्णुता।

intolerant *इन् टौ ॅ लॅ रॅन्ट a.* not tolerant असहिष्णु।

intoxicant *इन् टौक् सि कॅन्ट n. & a.* intoxicating (agent) मादक (द्रव्य)।

intoxicate *इन् टौक् सि केट v.t.* to make drunk मदोन्मत्त करना; to elate excessively अत्यधिक उल्लासित करना।

intoxication *इन् टौक् सि के शॅन n.* drunkenness मादकता।

intransitive *इन् ट्रैन् सि टिव,– ट्रान्– a. (verb)* not taking an object अकर्मक।

interpid *इन् ट्रै ˘ पिड a.* without fear निडर; brave बहादुर।

intrepidity *इन् ट्रि पि डि टि n.* fearlessness निर्भीकता।

intricate *इन् ट्रि किट a.* complicated जटिल; puzzling पेचीदा।

intrigue[1] *इन् ट्रीग v.t.* to conspire षड्यंत्र करना।

intrigue[2] *n.* secret plotting षड्यंत्र; secret love-affair गुप्त प्रेम-संबंध।

intrinsic *इन् ट्रिन् सिक a.* inherent, essential अंतर्भूत, तात्त्विक।

introduce *इन् ट्रॅ ड्यूस v.t.* to bring in (का) सूत्रपात करना; to preface (की) भूमिका लिखना; to make known परिचय कराना।

introduction *इन् ट्रॅ डक् शॅन n.* act of introducing परिचय; preface भूमिका; thing introduced उपक्रम।

introductory *इन् ट्रॅ डक् टॅ रि a.* serving to introduce परिचयात्मक।

introspect *इन् ट्रो ˘ स्पैक्ट v.i.* to look into आत्मनिरीक्षण करना।

introspection *इन् ट्रो ˘ स्पै ˘ क् शॅन n.* act of observing the process of one's own mind अंतर्दर्शन।

intrude *इन् ट्रूड v.t.* to force in घुसेड़ना; *v.i.* to enter without invitation अनुचित रूप से घुस पड़ना।

intrusion *इन् ट्रू ज़ॅन n.* encroachment अतिक्रमण।

intuition *इन् ट्यू इ शॅन, –ट्यू– n.* instinctive understanding अंतर्बोध।

intuitive *इन् ट्यू इ टिव a.* perceived by intuition अंतःप्रज्ञात्मक।

invade *इन् वेड v.t.* to attack (पर) आक्रमण करना; to encroach upon (में) घुसपैठ करना।

invalid[1] *इन् वै लिड a.* void, null अमान्य; not valid अप्रामाणिक।

invalid[2] *इन् वै लिड, –लीड a.* disabled अपंग।

invalid[3] *n.* an invalid person अपंग व्यक्ति।

invalidate *इन् वै लि डेट v.t.* to make of no effect अमान्य करना; to render invalid अप्रामाणिक ठहराना।

invaluable *इन् वै ल्यु अॅ बल a.* priceless अमूल्य।

invasion *इन् वे ज़ॅन n.* attack, assault हमला, चढ़ाई।

invective *इन् वैक् टिव n.* abusive language गाली-गलौज।

invent *इन् वैन्ट v.t.* to create (something) new आविष्कार करना; to make up गढ़ना।

invention *इन् वैन् शॅन n.* that which is invented आविष्कार; act of inventing आविष्करण।

inventive *इन् वैन् टिव a.* able to invent आविष्कारशील।

inventor *इन् वैन् टॅः n.* one who invents आविष्कारक।

invert *इन् वॅःट v.t.* to turn upside down पलटना, औंधा करना; to change the order of (का) क्रम भंग करना।

invest *इन् वैस्ट v.t.* to put (money) in (धन) लगाना; to decorate सजाना।

investigate *इन् वैस् टि गेट v.t.* to search अनुसंधान करना; to inquire into (की) जांच-पड़ताल करना।

investigation *इन् वैस् टि गे शॅन n.* research अनुसंधान; act of examination जांच-पड़ताल।

investment *इन् वै ˘ स्ट् मॅन्ट n.* act of investing पूंजी-निवेश; money invested लगाया गया धन।

invigilate *इन् वि जि लैट v.t.* to supervise निरीक्षण करना।

invigilation *इन् वि जि ले शॅन n.* act of invigilating निरीक्षण।

invigilator *इन् वि जि ले टॅः n.* one who invigilates निरीक्षक।

invincible *इन् विन् सि ब्ल a.* unconquerable अपराजेय।

inviolable *इन् वॉइ अॅ लॅ ब्ल a.* that cannot be violated अनुल्लंघनीय।

invisible *इन् वि ज़ॅ ब्ल a.* not capable of being seen अंतर्धान; that cannot be seen अदृश्य।

invitation *इन् वि टे शॅन v.* act of inviting आमंत्रण; written solicitation निमंत्रण-पत्र।

invite *इन् वॉइट v.t.* to ask politely to come आमंत्रित करना।

invocation *इन् वों˘ के शॅन n.* prayer वंदना; invoking आह्वान।

invoice *इन् वौ˘ इस n.* bill बीजक।

invoke *इन् वोक v.t.* to call on (का) आह्वान करना; to ask earnestly for के लिए विनती करना।

involve *इन् वौ˘ल्व v.t.* to entangle फंसाना; to be necessary for (के लिए) आवश्यक होना।

inward *इन् वॅःड a.* situated within आंतरिक।

inwards *इन् वॅःड्ज adv.* towards the inside अंदर की ओर, अंदर को; into the mind or soul अंतरात्मा में।

irate *ऑइ रेट a.* angry, enraged क्रुद्ध, नाराज़।

ire *ऑइअॅः n.* anger, rage क्रोध, नाराज़गी।

Irish[1] *ऑइअॅरिश a.* of Ireland आयरलैंड का।

Irish[2] *n.* the Irish language आयरलैंड की भाषा; the people of Ireland आयरलैंड के निवासी।

irksome *अॅःक् सॅम a.* tedious बोझिल, उबा देनेवाला।

iron[1] *ऑइ अॅन n.* a common metal लोहा; appliance used for smoothing clothes इस्तरी।

iron[2] *v.t.* to smooth with iron (पर) इस्तरी करना।

ironical *ऑइ रौ ˘ नि कॅल a.* containing irony व्यंग्यात्मक; saying something meaning the opposite वक्रोक्तिपूर्ण।

irony *ऑइअॅ रॅ नि n.* sarcastic use of words व्यंग्य।

irradiate *इ रे डि एट v.i.* to shine प्रदीप्त होना; *v.t.* to light up प्रकाशित करना।

irrational *इ रै शॅ नॅल a.* not rational तर्कशून्य।

irreconcilable *इ रै ˘ कॅन् सॉइ लॅ ब्ल a.* inconsistent असंगत; unfit for agreement समझौते के अयोग्य।

irrecoverable *इ रि क वॅः रॅ ब्ल a.* that cannot be recovered or remedied अपूरणीय।

irrefutable *इ रै˘ फ़्यु टॅ ब्ल a.* that

cannot be refuted अकाट्य।

irregular *इ रै ॅ ग्यु लॅः* *a.* not regular अनियमित; disorderly क्रमविरूद्ध।

irregularity *इ रै ॅ ग्यु लै रि टि* *n.* the quality of being irregular अनियमितता।

irrelevant *इ रै ॅ लि वॅन्ट* *a.* not to the point असंबद्ध; not relevant विसंगत।

irrespective *इ रि स्पै ॅक् टिव* *a.* not having regard (of) निरपेक्ष।

irresponsible *इ रिस् पौ ॅन् सॅ ब्ल* *a.* without a sense of responsibility अनुत्तरदायी, लापरवाह।

irrigate *इ रि गेट* *v.t.* to water by means of canals etc. सींचना।

irrigation *इ रि गे शॅन्* *n.* act of irrigating सिंचाई।

irritable *इ रि टॅ ब्ल* *a.* easily annoyed चिड़चिड़ा।

irritant[1] *इ रि टॅन्ट* *a.* irritating उत्तेजक, प्रकोपक।

irritant[2] *n.* irritant substance उत्तेजक पदार्थ; something that irritates the mind उत्तेजक बातें।

irritate *इ रि टेट* *v.t.* to provoke चिढ़ाना; to stimulate उकसाना।

irritation *इ रि टे शॅन* *n.* act of irritating उत्तेजना; annoyance चिड़चिड़ाहट; burning sensation जलन।

irruption *इ रप् शॅन* *n.* sudden increase अचानक वृद्धि; breaking in सेंध।

island *ऑइ लॅन्ड* *n.* mass of land surrounded by water टापू।

isle *ऑइल* *n.* island टापू।

isobar *ऑइ सो ॅ बाः* *n.* line on map connecting places of equal barometric pressure समदाब रेखा।

isolate *ऑइ सॉ लेट,–सॅ–* *v.t.* to separate from others पृथक् करना।

isolation *ऑइ सॅ ले शॅन* *n.* separation अलगाव; segregation पार्थक्य।

issue[1] *इ स्यू, इ श्यू, इ शू* *v.i.* to go out निकलना; to result परिणाम होना; *v.t.* to give or send out निकालना; to publish प्रकाशित करना; to distribute वितरित करना।

issue[2] *n.* a going out निकास, निर्गमन; publication प्रकाशन; discharge स्राव; offspring संतान; topic of discussion विचारणीय-विषय; question, dispute विवाद; outcome, result परिणाम।

it इट *pron.* वह, यह।

Italian[1] *इ टैल्यॅन* *a.* of Italy इटली का, इटली से संबद्ध।

Italian[2] *n.* language of Italy इटली की भाषा; native of Italy इटली-निवासी।

italic *इ टै लिक* *a.* sloping (letters, type) तिरछा (लेखन, मुद्रण)।

italics *इ टै लिक्स* *n. pl.* letters in slanting type तिरछा मुद्रण।

itch[1] इच *n.* irritating sensation खुजली; constant teasing desire बेचैनी।

itch[2] *v.i.* to have an itch खुजली होना।

item *ऑइ टॅम* *n.* subject विषय; entry in account मद।

ivory *ऑइ वॅ रि* *n.* hard substance of tusks of elephant हाथी-दांत।

ivy *ऑइ वि* *n.* climbing, clinging, evergreen plant आइवी, सदाबहार लता।

Jj

J जे the tenth letter of the English alphabet, developed from I, not found in English books before the middle of the seventeenth century. अक्षर 'I' से विकसित अंगेजी वर्णमाला का दसवाँ अक्षर, सत्रहवीं शताब्दी के मध्य तक इस अक्षर के स्थान में अंग्रेजी पुस्तकों में प्रायः I अक्षर का ही प्रयोग होता था; **J-pen** (a broad-pointed nib) चौड़ी नोक की निब (जीभी) जिस पर अक्षर 'J' छपा होता है।

jab *जैब (-bb-) v.t.* to stab भोंक देना।

jabber *जै बॅ: v.t.* to utter indistinctly बड़बड़ करना।

jack[1] *जैक n.* labourer मज़दूर; servant सेवक; machine for raising heavy weights उत्तोलक।

jack[2] *v.t.* to lift with a jack जैक-द्वारा उठाना।

jackal *जै कौल n.* wild dog-like animal सियार।

jacket *जै किट n.* wrapper of a book पुस्तकावरण; short coat जाकेट।

jade *जेड n.* worn-out horse मरियल घोड़ा; a green precious stone हरितमणि।

jail *जेल n.* prison कारागृह, बंदीगृह।

jailer *जै लॅ: n.* officer incharge of a jail कारापाल।

jam[1] *जैम n.* fruit preserved मुरब्बा; block or stoppage due to crowding अवरोध।

jam[2] *(-mm-) v.t.* to press into a small space ठूंसना; to cause to stick together अटकाना, चिपकाना; to apply fiercely ज़ोर से लगाना; to squeeze भींचना, कुचलना; to block up by crowding भीड़ से रोकना; *v.i.* to become stuck अटक जाना; to become unworkable ठप हो जाना।

jar *जा: n.* vessel of glass etc. जार, मर्तबान; conflict संघर्ष; shock झटका; harsh sound कर्कश ध्वनि।

jargon *जा: गॅन n.* chatter अनर्गल वार्तालाप; language used by a particular group वर्ग-बोली।

jasmine, jessamine *जैस् मिन्, जै ˘सॅ मिन n.* fragrant white flower चमेली।

jaundice[1] *जौन् डिस n.* a disease marked by yellowness of eyes and skin पीलिया; bitterness कटुता; prejudice पक्षपात।

jaundice[2] *v.t.* to affect with jaundice पीलिया ग्रस्त करना।

javelin *जैव् लिन n.* spear thrown in sports भाला, बरछा।

jaw *जौ n.* bony part holding the teeth जबड़ा।

jay *जे n.* a noisy bird of brilliant plumage नीलकंठ।

jealous *जै˘ लॅस a.* envious ईर्ष्यालु; distrustful, suspicious संशयशील, शंकालु; taking watchful care सतर्क, चौकन्ना।

jealousy *जै˘ लॅ सि n.* envy ईर्ष्या।

jean *जीन n.* strong cotton cloth मज़बूत सूती कपड़ा, जीन; *(pl.)* trousers of strong cotton cloth, usu., blue नीले कपड़े का पाज़ामा।

jeer *जिअॅः v.i.* to laugh mockingly मज़ाक उड़ाना।

jelly *जै ˘ लि n.* food made of fruit-syrup अवलेह, जेली।

jeopardize *जै ˘ पॅः डॉइज़ v.t.* to put in danger खतरे में डालना।

jeopardy *जै ˘ पॅः डि n.* danger ख़तरा।

jerk *जॅःक n.* jolt झटका।

jerkin *जॅः किन n.* a sleeveles jacket मिरज़ई।

jerky *जॅः कि a.* moving or coming by jerks झटकेदार।

jersey *जॅः ज़ि n.* close fitting woollen upper garment जर्सी।

jest[1] *जैस्ट n.* joke हंसी; taunt ताना।

jest[2] *v.i.* to make a jest व्यंग्य करना।

jet *जै ˘ट n.* stream of liquid gas etc. धारा, धार; small hole छेद, सुराख; spout टोटी; aircraft propelled by a jet engine जैट विमान; a black mineral संगमूसा, कृष्णाष्म।

Jew *जू n.* one of Hebrew race यहूदी।

jewel[1] *जू अॅल n.* a precious stone रत्न, मणि।

jewel[2] *(-ll-) v.t.* to aborn with jewels रत्नमंडित करना।

jeweller *जू अॅ लॅः n.* one who deals in or makes jewels जौहरी।

jewellery *जू अॅ लॅ रि n.* jewels in general रत्न, रत्नाभूषण।

jingle[1] *जिङ् ग्ल n.* a clinking sound झनकार; short rhyme used in advertising विज्ञापन-गीत।

jingle[2] *v.i.* to produce clinking sound झनझनाना।

job *जौबॅ n.* work काम; specific duty कर्त्तव्य; regular paid position नौकरी।

jobber *जौ ˘ बॅः n.* one who buys and sells as a broker दलाल, आढ़तिया; person who jobs ठेके पर काम करनेवाला व्यक्ति।

jobbery *जौ ˘ बॅ रि n.* public business done dishonestly भ्रष्टाचार।

jocular *जौ ˘ क्यु लॅः a.* humorous विनोदप्रिय; given to jokes हंसी-मज़ाक़ करनेवाला।

jog *जौगॅ (-gg-) v.t.* to shake धकेलना, हिलाना; to stimulate चेताना; *v.i.* to move by jogs इधर-उधर या ऊपर-नीचे हिलना; to trudge धीरे-धीरे दौड़ना।

join *जौ ˘ इन v.t.* to connect जोड़ना; to unite संबद्ध करना; to come into association with साथ देना; *v.i.* to be connected जुड़ना; to unite संबद्ध होना।

joiner *जौ ˘इ नॅः n.* maker of finished woodwork बढ़ई, मिस्तरी; one who joins योजक, जोड़नेवाला।

joint *जौ ˘ इन्ट n.* joining जोड़; place where two things meet संधिस्थल।

jointly *जौ ˘इन्ट् लि adv.* together मिलजुलकर।

joke[1] *जोक n.* jest परिहास।

joke[2] *v.i.* to make jokes हंसी-मज़ाक़ करना।

joker *जो कॅः n.* one who jokes विदूषक, जोकर; extra card in a pack ताश का अतिरिक्त पत्ता।

jollity *जौ ˘ लि टि n.* merrymaking आमोद-प्रमोद, राग-रंग।

jolly *जौ ˘ लि a.* merry प्रफुल्ल, प्रसन्न; expressing mirth विनोदशील।

jolt[1] *जौ ˘ल्ट n.* sudden jerk झटका; आघात।

jolt² *v.t.* to shake with a sudden jerk हिचकोले देना।

jostle¹ *जौॅ स्‌ल n.* hustle and bustle धक्कमधक्का।

jostle² *v.t.* to push (as in a crowd) धक्का देना।

jot¹ *जौॅ ट n.* a tiny particle कण।

jot² *(-tt-) v.t.* to make a quick written note संक्षेप में लिख देना।

journal *जॅ: नॅल n.* daily news-paper दैनिक समाचार-पत्र; diary दैनंदिनी; magazine पत्रिका।

journalism *जॅ: नॅ लिज़्म n.* profession or writing for public jounals पत्रकारिता।

journalist *जॅ: नॅ लिस्ट n.* one who writes for public journals पत्रकार।

journey¹ *जॅ: नि n.* travel यात्रा; excursion सैर।

journey² *v.i.* to travel यात्रा करना।

jovial *जो व्यॅल a.* full of jollity उल्लासपूर्ण; joyous प्रसन्नचित।

joviality *जो वि ऐ लि टि n.* liveliness जिंदादिली; humorousness विनोदप्रियता।

joy *जौॅइ n.* gladness हर्ष, आनंद।

joyful, joyous *जौॅइ फुल जौॅइ ॲस n.* full of joy हर्षित, आनंदित।

jubilant *जू बि लॅन्ट a.* shouting for joy उल्लसित।

jubilation *जू बि ले शॅन n.* rejoicing आनंदोत्सव।

jubilee *जू बि ली n.* an occasion of rejoicing आनंदोत्सव का अवसर; a special anniversary of an event esp. the 50th पचासवीं वर्षगांठ।

judge¹ *जज n.* an officer appointed to try cases in a law court न्यायाधीश; one who decides in a dispute, contest etc. निर्णायक; an arbiter पंच।

judge² *v.i.* to act as a judge निर्णय करना; *v.t.* to form an opinion about आंकना; to decide तय करना।

judgement *जज् मॅन्ट n.* verdict निर्णय; opinion धारणा; discrimination विवेक।

judicature *जू डि कॅ चॅ: n.* court न्यायालय; system of courts न्याय-व्यवस्था; jurisdiction न्यायाधिकार।

judicial *जु डि शॅल, जू– a.* of or by a court of law न्याय-संबंधी, न्यायिक।

judiciary *जु डि शि ॲ रि, जू– n.* system of courts and judges न्यायतंत्र।

judicious *जु डि शॅस, जू– a.* possessing sound judgement विवेकशील।

jug *जग n.* vessel with a handle जग।

juggle *जॅ़ ग्‌ल v.t.* to conjure जादूगरी करना।

juggler *जॅ़ग् लॅ: n.* one who practises jugglery बाज़ीगर।

juice *जूस n.* sap of vegetables or fruits सूप, रस।

juicy *जूसि a.* containing much juice रसदार।

jumble¹ *जम् ब्‌ल n.* confused mixture घालमेल; confusion अस्तव्यस्तता।

jumble² *v.t.* to mix confusedly गड्मड्ड करना।

jump¹ *जम्प n.* leap छलांग; sudden rise अकस्मात वृद्धि।

jump² *v.i.* to spring upwards कूदना;

v.t., to pass over with a jump लांघना।

junction *जङ्क् शॅन n.* joining संधि, संयोजन; place or point of union संधि-स्थल।

juncture *ज़ङ्क् चॅः n.* joining, union संधि-स्थल; a point of time समय, अवसर।

jungle *जङ् ग्ल n.* land with dense growth of trees जंगल, वन।

junior[1] *जू न्यॅः a.* lower in standing or rank अवर, कनिष्ठ।

junior[2] *n.* a junior person अवर व्यक्ति।

junk *जङ्क n.* rubbish कूड़ा-करकट, कचरा।

jupiter *जू पि टॅः n.* name of a planet बृहस्पति ग्रह।

jurisdiction *जुअॅ रिस् डिक् शॅन n.* legal authority न्याय-सीमा; limits within which legal authority may be exercised अधिकार-क्षेत्र।

jurisprudence *जुअॅ रिस् प्रू डॅन्स n.* science of knowledge of law न्यायशास्त्र।

jurist *जुअॅ रिस्ट n.* an expert in law क़ानूनविद, विधिवेत्ता।

juror *जु अॅ रॅः n.* member of a jury जूरी का सदस्य।

jury *जुअॅ रि n.* a body of persons sworn to render a verdict on a law case न्यायपीठ।

juryman *जुअॅ रि मॅन n.* member of a jury जूरी का सदस्य।

just[1] *जस्ट a.* fair उचित; in accordance with facts युक्तिसंगत; according to justice न्यायोचित।

just[2] *adv.* exactly वस्तुतः, merely केवल; quite recently अभी-अभी।

justice *जस् टिस n.* judicial decision अदालती निर्णय; judge न्यायाधीश।

justifiable *जस् टि फ़ॉइ अॅ ब्ल a.* that may be justified न्याय; reasonable तर्कसंगत।

justification *जस् टि फ़ि के शॅन n.* rationality औचित्य; reasonableness तर्कसंगतता।

justify *जस् टि फ़ॉइ v.t.* to make just न्यायसंगत बनाना; to prove to be just उचित प्रमाणित करना।

justly *जस्ट् लि adv.* honestly, fairly न्यायतः, उचित रूप में।

jute *जूट n.* a fibre जूट, पटसन।

juvenile *जू वि नॉइल a.* pertaining to youth किशोर-संबंधी; having youth यौवनमय; suited to youth युवकोचित।

Kk

K के the eleventh letter of the English alphabet (it is not pronounced before N), the symbol of potassim in chemistry. अंग्रेजी वर्णमाला का ग्याहवाँ अक्षर, इस अक्षर का उच्चारण 'एन' अक्षर के पूर्व रहने पर नहीं होता है, रसायन शास्त्र में 'पोटाशिअम' के लिए सांकेतिक चिन्ह।

keen *कीन a.* eager इच्छुक; sharp

तेज़; enthusiastic उत्साही।

keenness *कीन् निस n.* eagerness उत्सुकता, उत्कंठा; sharpness तीव्रता; zeal उत्साह।

keep *कीप v.t.* to retain possession of पास रखना; to store सुरक्षित रखना; to maintain बनाए रखना; to fulfil पूरा करना, निभाना; to tend देख-रेख करना।

keeper *की पॅ: n.* one who or that which keeps रक्षक; attendant देखभाल करनेवाला।

keepsake *कीप् सेक n.* something kept in memory of the giver स्मृतिचिन्ह।

kennel *कै˘ नॅल n.* hut to shelter a dog कुत्ताघर।

kerchief *कॅ: चिफ़ n.* head-cloth औढ़नी; handkerchief रूमाल।

kernel *कॅ : न्ल n.* seed within a hard shell गुठली; soft inner part of nut गिरी; the core सार।

kerosene *कै˘ रॅ सीन n.* a thin oil used as fuel मिट्टी का तेल।

ketchup *कै˘ चॅप n.* sauce of vinegar, potatoes etc. चटनी।

kettle *कै ट्ल n.* a metal container पतीली, केतली।

key[1] *की n. (pl.keys)* instrument for locking and unlocking चाबी; a book of answers कुंजी; solution समाधान।

key[2] *v.t.* to lock with a key चाबी से बंद करना; to put a key into (lock) (ताले में) चाबी लगाना।

kick[1] *किक n.* a hit with the foot ठोकर।

kick[2] *v.t.* to hit with the foot ठोकर से मारना।

kid *किड n.* young goat मेमना; child बच्चा।

kidnap *किड् नैप (-pp-) v.t.* to steal (a human being) for ransom (मानव का) अपहरण करना।

kidney *किड् नि n.* the organ which secretes urine गुर्दा।

kill[1] *किल v.t.* to put to death मारना, बध करना; to destroy नष्ट करना; to waste व्यर्थ खोना।

kill[2] *n.* act of killing हत्या, वध; animals killed in hunt शिकार।

kiln *किल्न, किल n.* large oven for baking or drying भट्टा।

kin *किन n.* family, relatives परिजन, सगे-संबंधी।

kind[1] *कॉइन्ड n.* sort क़िस्म, प्रकार।

kind[2] *a.* benevolent कृपालु; gentle सज्जनतापूर्ण।

kindergarten *;किन् डॅ: गा: ट्न n.* infant school बाल-विहार।

kindle *किन् ड्ल v.t.* to set fire to सुलगाना; to light चमकाना; to inflame भड़काना।

kindly *कॉइन्ड् लि adv.* in a friendly, considerate way कृपया।

king *किङ्ग n.* monarch सम्राट्, राजा; (chess) the main piece बादशाह।

kingdom *किङ्ग्-डॅम n.* monarchial state साम्राज्य, राज्य।

kinship *किन् शिप n.* blood relationship सगोत्रता; similarity समानता।

kiss[1] *किस् n.* a touch with the lips चुंबन।

kiss[2] *v.t.* to touch with the lips चूमना।

kit *किट n.* small wooden tub कठौता, लकड़ी का टब; material, tools etc. in a container साज़-सामान।

kitchen *कि चिन n.* place where food is cooked रसोईघर।

kite *कॉइट n.* light frame covered with paper for flying in the air पतंग; a bird of the hawk family चील।

kith *किथ n.* relatives रिश्तेदार।

kitten *कि ट्न n.* a young cat बिल्ली का बच्चा।

knave *नेव n.* a rogue दुष्ट, धूर्त; jack at cards (ताश) गुलाम।

knavery *ने वॅ रि n.* villainy, roguery धूर्तता, दुष्टता।

knee *नी n.* joint below thigh घुटना।

kneel *नील v.i.* to rest and fall on knees घुटने टेकना।

knife *नॉइफ़ n.* instrument for cutting चाकू।

knight[1] *नॉइट n.* warrior योद्धा।

knight[2] *v.t.* to confer kinghthood on नाइट की उपाधि देना।

knit *निट (-tt-) v.t.* to weave बुनना।

knock *नौकॅ v.t.* to strike, to hit मारना, प्रहार करना; to rap खटखटाना।

knot[1] *नौ ॅट n.* tightened loop गांठ।

knot[2] *(-tt-) v.t.* to tie बांधना।

know *नो v.t.* to be informed about जानना; to be aware of से सचेत होना; to have under-standing of (की) जानकारी होना।

knowledge *नौ ॅ लिज n.* understanding जानकारी; learning ज्ञान; information सूचना; acquaintance परिचय।

Ll

L ऍल the twelfth letter of the English alphabet, a symbol for 50 in Roman numerals. अंग्रेजी वर्णमाला का बारहवाँ अक्षर, रोमन संख्या में ५० के लिए संकेत।

label[1] *ले बल n.* a card marked and attached to an object लेबिल, नामपत्र।

label[2] *(-ll-) v.t.* to attach a label to लेबिल लगाना।

labial *ले ब्यॅल a.* of the lips ओष्ठसंबधी।

laboratory *लै बॅ रॅ टॅ रि, लॅ बौ ॅ —n.* a building or room where scientific tests are carried out प्रयोगशाला।

laborious *लॅ बौ रि ॲस a.* hard-working परिश्रमी; tedious कठिन, श्रमसाध्य।

labour[1] *ले बॅ: n.* hard work परिश्रम; working class श्रमिक वर्ग; pain of child birth प्रसव-पीड़ा।

labour[2] *v.i.* to work hard कठिन परिश्रम करना।

laboured *ले बॅ:ड a.* showing signs of great effort यत्नसिद्ध: forced, not natural अस्वाभाविक।

labourer *ले बॅ रॅ: n.* working man श्रमिक।

labyrinth *लै बि रिन्थ n.* an intricate network of winding passages भूलभुलैया; complicated situation उलझन।

lac, lakh *लैक* *n.* the number one hundred thousand एक लाख, सौ हज़ार।

lace[1] *लेस* *n.* a cord used for fastening shoe etc. फ़ीता, तस्मा; delicate ornamental work made of threads जाली।

lace[2] *v.t.* to fasten with laces फ़ीतों से बांधना।

lacerate *लै-सॅ-रेट* *v.t.* to tear चीरना, फाड़ना; to rend, to wound चीर-फाड़ करना; to afflict यंत्रणा देना।

lachrymose *लैक्-रि-मोस* *a.* full of tears अश्रुपूर्ण, साश्रु; shedding tears, given to weeping रुदनकारी।

lack[1] *लैक* *n.* need, want कमी, अभाव।

lack[2] *v.t.* to have less than enough of (का) अभाव होना।

lackey *लै कि* *n.* a manservant or footman नौकर, टहलुआ।

lacklustre *लैक्-लॅस्-ट्रॅः* *a.* wanting lustre निस्तेज, निष्प्रभ।

laconic *लॅ कौ ॅ निक* *a.* (speech) terse अल्पाक्षरिक, संक्षिप्त।

lactate *लैक्-टेट* *v.i.* to secrete milk दुग्ध स्रावित करना।

lactometer *लै क्-टौ-मि-टॅरः* *n.* apparatus for measuring the density of milk दुग्धमापी।

lactose *लैक्-टोस* *n.* milk sugar दुग्धशर्करा।

lacuna *लॅ क्यू नॅ* *n.* (*pl. -nas, -nae- नी*) missing part कमी; gap अंतराल।

lacy *ले-सि* *a.* like lace, having lace लेसदार, झालरदार।

lad *लैड* *n.* boy लड़का।

ladder *लै डॅः* *n.* a narrow frame with steps or rungs for climbing up or down सीढ़ी।

lade *लेड* (*p.p. / laden*) *v.t.* to burden, to load लादना।

ladle[1] *लै ड्ल* *n.* spoon with long handle and big bowl करछुल।

ladle[2] *v.t.* to serve with a ladle करछुल से देना।

lady *ले डि* *n.* polite name for a woman महिला।

lag *लैग* *v.i.* to walk or move too slowly धीरे-धीरे चलना; to hang back or linger पीछे रह जाना।

laggard *लै-गॅःड* *n.* one who lags behind फिसड्डी व्यक्ति; weak person शक्तिहीन व्यक्ति।

lagoon *लॅ-गून* *n.* shallow lake near the sea समुद्र के पास की झील।

lair *ले ॅ अँः* *n.* den मांद।

lake *लेक* *n.* a large stretch of water surrounded by land झील।

lama *ला मॅ* *n.* a Buddhist priest of Tibet लामा।

lamb *लैम* *n.* a young sheep मेमना।

lambaste *लैम्-बेस्ट* *v.t.* to beat मारना, पीटना; to thrash कूटना; to reprimand डांटना-फटकारना।

lame[1] *लेम* *a.* limping, crippled in leg लंगड़ा; unconvincing असंतोषजनक, कच्चा।

lame[2] *v.t.* to make lame पंगु बनाना।

lament[1] *लॅ मैन्ट* *v.i.* to feel or show great sorrow शोक प्रकट करना; *v.t.* to mourn for विलाप करना।

lament[2] *n.* expression of grief विलाप, शोक।

lamentable *लै मॅन् टॅ ब्ल* *a.* distressing शोचनीय; regrettable खेद-योग्य।

lamentation *लै मॅन् टे शॅन* *n.* act

of lamenting विलाप।

lambkin *लैम्-किन n.* a little lamb छोटा मेमना।

laminate *लै-मि-नेट v.t.* to make into a thin plate पतली परत का रूप देना; to make by putting layers together परत मिलाकर बनाना।

lamp *लैम्प n.* a glass-covered light दीपक, लैंप।

lampoon¹ *लैम् पून n.* a harsh satire कटाक्षपूर्ण रचना।

lampoon² *v.t.* to satirise (पर) व्यंग्य करना।

lance¹ *लान्स n.* a spear, a sharp-pointed weapon with a long handle बल्लम।

lance² *v.t.* to pierce चुभाना।

lancer *लान् सॅः n.* soldier armed with a lance बल्लमधारी योद्धा।

lancet *लान्-सिट a.* a surgical instrument छुरिका, नश्तर, शल्य-यंत्र।

land¹ *लैन्ड n.* solid part of the earth भूमि; country देश; region क्षेत्र।

land² *v.i.* to set on shore from a ship पोत से उतरना; *v.t.* to bring (an aeroplane) to surface from the air (जहाज़ को) उतारना।

landing *लैन् डिङ्ग n.* the flat space at the top of a flight of stairs चौकी; coming ashore from a ship अवतरण।

landscape *लैन्ड् स्केप n.* natural inland scenery परिदृश्य; a picture of landscape प्राकृतिक दृश्य-चित्र।

lane *लेन n.* a narrow road गली; area of road for one stream of traffic एक ही प्रकार के यातायात-हेतु निर्दिष्ट पथ।

language *लैङ् ग्विज n.* human speech भाषा।

languish *लैङ् ग्विश v.i.* to bocome dispirited मुरझाना, क्षीण होना।

lank *लैङ्क a.* flaccid कृश, क्षीण; tall and thin लंबा और पतला; straight and flat (बाल) सीधा और चपटा।

lantern *लैन् टॅःन n.* a container with glass sides for holding a light लालटेन।

lap *लैप n.* front part from the waist to the knees of a sitting person गोदी।

lapse¹ *लैप्स v.i.* to fall to bad ways पतित हो जाना; to end from disuse कालातीत हो जाना।

lapse² *n.* a slight mistake त्रुटि, भूल।

lard *लाःड n.* rendered fat of the hog सुअर की चरबी।

large *लाःज a.* big बड़ा; generous उदार।

largesse *लाः-जॅस n.* generous giving उदार दान; gift so given दिया गया दान।

lark *लाःक n.* a small bird that sings clearly and seetly and flies very high भरत, भरुहि।

lascivious *लॅ सि वि ॲस a.* lustful कामुक।

lash¹ *लैश a.* to strike with a lash कोड़ा मारना।

lash² *n.* a whip-stroke कोड़े का आघात; a whip चाबुक, कोड़ा।

lass *लैस n.* girl लड़की, किशोरी।

last¹ *लास्ट a.* coming at the end अंतिम; most recent गत, पिछला।

last² *adv.* after all others सबके अंत में; on the last occasion पिछली बार।

last[3] *v.i.* to remain in good condition टिकना, बना रहना।

last[4] *n.* that which comes at the end अंतिम वस्तु।

lastly *लास्ट् लि adv.* finally अंतिम तौर से।

lasting *लास् टिङ्ग a.* durable टिकाऊ।

latch *लैच n.* a fastening for a door or gate कुंडी, डंडाला।

late[1] *लेट a.* coming after the appointed time विलंबित; delayed पिछेता; recent पिछला, हाल का; deceased स्वर्गीय; that was recently but now is not भूत-पूर्व।

late[2] *adv.* after proper time विलंब से; recently हाल ही में।

lately *लेट् लि* recently हाल ही में।

latent *ले टॅन्ट a.* hidden गुप्त, अंतर्निहित।

lath *लाथ n.* slip, thin slip of wood छेपट, लकड़ी का पतला लंबा टुकड़ा।

lathe[1] *लेद n.* machine for turning and shaping articles of wood, metal etc. खराद।

lathe[2] *लेद n.* a machine for shaping wood or metal ख़राद मशीन।

lather *ला दॅः, लै दॅः n.* froth made by soap and water झाग।

latitude *लै टि ट्यूड n.* the distance north or south of the equator, measured in degrees अक्षांश; freedom from narrow restrictions छूट।

latrine *लॅ ट्रीन n.* lavatory शौचालय।

latter *लै टॅः a.* the second of two पिछला; later बाद वाला।

lattice *लै टिस n.* a network of bars crossed diagonally जाल, जालक।

laud[1] *लौड v.t.* to praise प्रशंसा करना।

laud[2] *n.* praise प्रशंसा।

laudable *लौ डॅ ब्ल a.* worthy of praise प्रशंसनीय।

laugh[1] *लाफ n.* act or sound expressing delight हंसी।

laugh[2] *v.i.* to express delight हंसना।

laughable *ला फ़ॅ ब्ल a.* ridiculous हास्यास्पद; comical, amusing हास्यकर, मनोरंजक।

laughter *लाफ़् टॅः n.* act or sound of laughing हंसी, हास्य।

launch[1] *लौन्च v.t.* to set (a newly built vessel) afloat (नया पोत) समुद्र में उतारना; to send off a (rocket) (प्रक्षेपास्त्र) छोड़ना।

launch[2] *n.* act of launching जलावतरण; a power-driven boat नाव।

launder *लौन् डॅः v.t.* to wash and iron (clothes) (कपड़े) धोना और प्रेस करना।

laundress *लौन् ड्रिस n.* woman who washes the dresses धोबिन।

laundry *लौन् ड्रि n.* a place where clothes are washed धुलाईघर।

laurel *लौ रॅल n.* a shrub with glossy evergreen leaves जयपत्र।

laureate[1] *लौ-रि-इट a.* crowned with a laurel wreath लोरल भूषित।

laureate[2] *n.* a perosn who is honoured for some achievement विशिष्ट सम्मान-प्राप्त व्यक्ति।

lava *लावॅ n.* rock-matter that flows in a molten state from volcanoes लावा।

lavatory *लै वॅ टॅ रि n.* a room where

one can wash one's hands and face प्रच्छालन-कक्ष; flush toilet शौचालय।

lavender *लै-विन्-डर:* *n.* plant with fragrant pale lilac flowers एक प्रकार का सुगंधित पौधा जिसके फूल पीले रंग के होते हैं।

lavish[1] *लै विश* *a.* abundant प्रचुर; extravagant अपव्ययी।

lavish[2] *v.t.* to spend abundantly दिल खोलकर ख़र्च करना।

law *लौ* *n.* any regulation which people must obey क़ानून।

lawful *लौ फुल* *a.* legal वैध; rightful उचित; agreeable to law न्यायसम्मत।

lawless *लौ लिस* *a.* illegal अवैध; contrary to law न्याय-विरुद्ध।

lawn *लौन* *n.* a piece of ground covered with grass घास का मैदान।

lawyer *लौ यँ:* *n.* someone who is expert in matters connected with the law विधिवक्ता, वकील।

lax *लैक्स* *a.* not strict ढीला; negligent बेपरवाह।

laxative[1] *लैक् सॅ टिव* *n.* a mild purgative रेचक औषधि।

laxative[2] *a.* causing easy bowel movement रेचक।

laxity *लैक् सि टि* *n.* state or quality of being lax रेचन; losseness ढिलाई, शिथिलता।

lay[1] *ले* *v.t.* to put (something) down रखना।

lay[2] *a.* not expert अविशेषज्ञ; relating to persons who are not priests अयाजकीय।

lay[3] *n.* a short narrative poem गीत।

layer *ले अँ:* *n.* single thickness of some substance spread over another परत, तह।

layman *ले मॅन* *n.* a person who is not expert साधारण व्यक्ति।

laze *लेज़* *v.i.* to be idle सुस्त रहना, आलस्य करना।

laziness *ले ज़ि निस* *n.* state or quality of being lazy आलस्य।

lazy *ले ज़ि* *n.* indolent आलसी, सुस्त।

lea *ली* *n.* open country, meadow, pasture खुला मैदान, चरागाह।

leach *लीच* *v.t.* to drain away by percolation घोलकर बहाना; to percolate through something निथारना।

lead[1] *लै ॅड* *n.* a metal सीसा; thin stick of graphite (पेंसिल का) सुरमा।

lead[2] *लीड* *v.t.* to guide मार्गदर्शन करना; to be the head or leader of (की) अगुवाई करना।

lead[3] *n.* guidance मार्गदर्शन।

leaden *लै ॅ ड्न* *a.* heavy बोझिल; made of lead सीसे का।

leader *लीडॅ:* *n.* person that leads अगुआ; guiding head नेता।

leadership *ली-डर:-शिप* *n.* state or quality of being a leader नेतृत्व, नायकत्व।

leaf *लीफ़* *n.* (*pl. leaves* लीव्ज़) broad green part on the stem of a plant पत्ती; a sheet of paper पन्ना; a thin sheet of metal वर्क़।

leaflet *लीफ़ लिट* *n.* a small pamphlet पत्रक, पुस्तिका।

leafy *लीफ़ि* *a.* full of leaves पत्तियों से भरा हुआ।

league *लीग* *n.* association of nations, groups, individuals संघ।

leak[1] *लीक* *n.* creak दरार; leacking रिसाव।

leak[2] *v.i.* to escape out through opening रिसना; *v.t.* to give out (information) (रहस्य) प्रकट कर देना।

leakage *ली किज* *n.* a leaking रिसन।

lean[1] *लीन* *n.* thin पतला, दुबला।

lean[2] *v.i.* to bend झुकना; to rest in a sloping position तिरछा होना; *v.t.* to cause to rest against झुकाना।

leap[1] *लीप* *v.i.* to jump कूदना; to pass over or jump लांघना।

leap[2] *n.* act of leaping कूद, उछाल।

learn *लॅःन* *v.i.* to get knowledge सीखना; *v.t.* to come to know जानना; to memorize रटना।

learned *लॅः निड* *a.* having much knowledge विद्वान scholarly पंडित।

learner *लॅः नॅः* *n.* a pupil शिष्य; a beginner नौसिखिया।

learning *लॅः निङ्ग* *n.* education शिक्षा; erudition विद्वत्ता।

lease[1] *लीस* *n.* contract for a specified time and fixed payment पट्टा।

lease[2] *v.t.* to give or get by a lease पट्टे पर देना या पाना।

least[1] *लीस्ट* *a.* smallest possible अल्पतम।

least[2] *adv.* to the smallest extent कम-से-कम मात्रा में।

leather *लै˘ दॅः* *n.* animal skin prepared for use चमड़ा।

leave[1] *लीव* *n.* absence from duty अवकाश; period of such absence अवकाश-अवधि; departure विदा।

leave[2] *v.t.* to go away from छोड़ना; to abandon त्यागना; to let remain रहने देना; *v.i.* to depart विदा होना, प्रस्थान करना।

lecture[1] *लै ˘क् चॅः* *n.* discourse व्याख्यान; reproof फटकार।

lecture[2] *v.i.* to deliver lecture भाषण देना; *v.t.* to scold फटकारना।

lecturer *लैकॅ् चॅ रॅः* *n.* a college or university teacher प्रवक्ता, व्याख्याता।

ledger *लै˘ जॅः* *n.* book containing accounts खाता-बही।

lee *ली* *n.* shelter आश्रयण शरण; quarter towards which the wind blows ओट, वायुप्रतिकूल-पार्श्व, अनुवात।

leech *लीच* *n.* a blood-sucking worm जोंक।

leek *लीक* *n.* vegetable of the onion genus प्याज़ जैसी सब्ज़ी।

left[1] *लैफ़्ट* *a.* denoting the part opposed to the right of the body बायां।

left[2] *n.* the side opposite to the right वाम, वामपक्ष।

leftist *n.* person following leftism, progressive person वामपंथी व्यक्ति, प्रगतिवादी व्यक्ति।

leg *लैगॅ* *n.* a limb of the body टांग; support of a table, chair etc. पाया; a stage of a journey मंज़िल।

legacy *लै˘ गॅ सि* *n.* bequest वसीयत।

legal *ली गॅल* *a.* permitted by law क़ानूनी, वैध।

legality *ली गै लि टि* *n.* condition; or character of being legal वैधता।

legalize *ली गॅ लॉइज़* *v.t.* to make legal क़ानूनी बनाना।

legend *लैˇ जॅन्ड n.* a story handed down from the past किंवदंती।

legendary *लैˇ जॅन् डॅ रि a.* famous प्रसिद्ध; known only in legends पौराणिक।

leghorn *लैˇ-गहौरःन n.* small breed of domestic fowl एक प्रकार की पालतू मुर्ग़ी; hat made of fine straw चटाई का बना टोप।

legible *लैˇ जॅ ब्‌ल, –जि– a.* readable सुपाठ्य।

legibly *लैˇ जि ब्लि adv.* so as to be read सुपाठ्य रूप में।

legion *ली जॅन n.* division of an army सैन्य-टुकड़ी; a vast number भीड़, विशाल संख्या।

legionary *ली-जॅ-नॅ-रि n.* member of a legion सेना का सदस्य।

legislate *लैˇ जिस् लेट v.i.* to make or enact a law or laws क़ानून बनाना।

legislation *लैˇ जिस् ले शॅन n.* act of making a law or laws विधि-निर्माण; laws or statutes enacted विधान।

legislative *लैˇ जिस् लॅ टिव a.* capable of or pertaining to the enacting of laws विधायी।

legislator *लैˇ जिस् ले टॅः n.* one who makes laws क़ानून-निर्माता।

legislature *लैˇ जिस् ले चॅः n.* law-making body विधानमंडल।

legitimacy *लि जि टि मॅ सि n.* state or quality of being legitimate, legality वैधता।

legitimate *लि जि टि मिट a.* accordant with law न्यायसंगत; following by logical or natural sequence तर्कसंगत; born of legally married parents वैध।

leisure[1] *लैˇ ज़ॅः n.* freedom from occupation अवकाश; vacant time ख़ाली समय।

leisure[2] *a.* vacant ख़ाली; फुरसत का।

leisurely[1] *लैˇ ज़ॅः लि a.* unhurried मंथर।

leisurely[2] *adv.* without haste or hurry धीरे-धीरे।

lemon *लैˇ मॅन n.* an acid fruit of the orange kind नींबू।

lemonade *लैˇ मॅ नेड n.* a drink made from lemon juice, sugar and water शिंकजी।

lend *लैन्ड v.t.* to furnish on condition of the thing being returned उधार देना।

length *लैˇङ्‌ग्थ n.* state or quality of being long लंबाई, विस्तार; duration of time अवधि।

lengthen *लैˇङ्‌ग् थॅन v.t.* to make longer लंबा करना; *v.i.* to become longer लंबा होना।

lengthy *लैˇ ङ्‌ग् थि a.* somewhat long विस्तृत, बहुत लंबा।

lenience, leniency *लीन् यॅन्स, –यॅन् सि n.* quality of being lenient उदारता।

lenient *लीन् यॅन्ट a.* acting without rigour, mild उदार, कोमल।

lens *लैन्ज़, n.* glass लैंस।

lentil *लैन् टिल n.* a kind of bean plant मसूर का पौधा; seed of this plant मसूर।

Leo *ली-ओ n.* the 5th sign of the Zodiac सिंह राशि।

leonine *ली अॅ नॉइन, लि– a.* of a lion सिंह-विषयक; like a lion सिंह जैसा।

leopard *लैॅ पॅःड* *n.* a large carnivorous animal of the cat genus, with a spotted skin तेंदुआ।
leper *लै ॅ पॅः* *n.* one affected with leprosy कोढ़ी, कुष्ठरोगी।
leprosy *लैपॅ् रॅ सि* *n.* a foul contagious disease कोढ़, कुष्ठ।
leprous *लैपॅ् रॅस* *a.* affected with leprosy कुष्ठ-पीड़ित।
less[1] *लैसॅ* *a.* smaller in quantity अपेक्षाकृत कम।
less[2] *n.* smaller quantity, part of amount अपेक्षाकृत कम मात्रा या भाग।
less[3] *adv.* to a smaller extent अपेक्षाकृत कम सीमा तक; not so much इतना नहीं।
less[4] *prep.* with the deduction of, minus को निकालकर।
lessee *लै ॅ सी* *n.* the person to whom a lease is given पट्टेदार।
lessen *लैॅ सन्* *v.t.* to make less कम करना, घटाना; *v.i.* to become less कम होना, घटना।
lesser *लै ॅ सॅः* *a.* not so great as the other लघुतर।
lesson *लैॅ सन्* *n.* portion which a pupil learns at one time पाठ; example उदाहरण।
lest *लैस्ॅट* *conj.* for fear that इस डर से कि; in order that not ताकि नहीं।
let *लैॅट* *v.t.* to allow अनुमति देना; to lease पट्टे पर देना।
lethal *ली थॅल* *a.* fatal प्राणघातक।
lethargic *लै ॅ थाः जिक* *a.* drowsy निश्चेष्ट; dull सुस्त; wanting in energy शक्तिहीन।
lethargy *लै ॅ थॅः जि* *n.* morbid drowsiness तंद्रा; dullness सुस्ती।
letter *लै ॅ टॅः* *n.* a mark used as the representative of sound वर्ण; a written message पत्र; (*pl.*) literature and learning साहित्य व विद्या।
level[1] *लै ॅ वल्* *n.* plane सतह; standard स्तर; rank in a scale of values दरजा।
level[2] *a.* perfectly flat and even समतल; equal in importance or rank समस्तर।
level[3] *(-ll-) v.t.* to make level समतल करना; to demolish गिरा देना; to equalize एकबराबर करना।
lever[1] *ली वॅः* *n.* a bar used for raising weights etc. उत्तोलक।
lever[2] *v.t.* to move (something) with a lever उत्तोलक से हटाना।
leverage *ली वॅ रिज* *n.* action or power of a lever उत्तोलन, उत्तोलक की शक्ति।
levity *लैॅ वि टि* *n.* lack of seriousness छिछोरापन।
levy[1] *लैॅ वि* *v.t.* to raise वसूल करना; to collect एकत्र करना।
levy[2] *n.* act of levying करारोपण; collection, realisation उगाही; amount levied आरोपित राशि; enrolment of troops भरती।
lewd *लूड, ल्यूड* *a.* indecent अशिष्ट, भद्दा; lustful कामुक।
lexicography *लैक्ॅ सि कौगॅ् रॅ फि* *n.* dictionary-writing कोश-रचना।
lexicon *लैक्ॅ सि कॅन* *n.* a dictionary शब्दकोश।
liability *लॉइ ॲ बि लि टि* *n.* state of being liable ज़िम्मेदारी, दायित्व; (*pl.*) debts देयधन।
liable *लॉइ ॲ बल्* *a.* answerable उत्तरदायी, ज़िम्मेदार; subject (to) संभाव्य।

liaison *लि ए ज़ॅन, ली–* *n.* an illicit intimacy between a man and a woman जार संबंध; connection संबंध।

liar *लॉइ अ:* *n.* one who utters falsehood झूठा, असत्यवादी।

libel[1] *लॉइ बॅल* *n.* a defamatory writing निंदालेख; written accusation अभियोग-पत्र; defamation परिवाद।

libel[2] *(-ll-)* *v.t.* to defame falsely झूठ के सहारे बदनाम करना।

liberal *लि वॅ रॅल* *a.* generous उदार; bountiful दानशील; broad-minded उदारचेता।

liberalism *लि बॅ रॅ लिज़्म* *n.* the principles and views of liberals उदारवाद।

liberality *लि बॅ रै लि टि* *n.* generosity उदारता।

liberate *लि बॅ रेट* *v.t.* to free मुक्त करना, स्वाधीन करना।

liberation *लि बॅ रे शॅन* *n.* act of liberating विमुक्तिकरण; being liberated मुक्ति-प्राप्ति।

liberator *लि बॅ रे टॅ:* *n.* one who liberates मुक्तिदाता।

libertine *लि बॅ: टॉइन, –टीन,–टिन* *n.* morally dissolute person नैतिक रूप से पतित व्यक्ति।

liberty *लि बॅ: टि* *n.* state or condition of one who is free स्वतंत्रता।

librarian *लॉइ ब्रे˘ अॅ रि अॅन* *n.* the keeper of a library or collection of books पुस्तकालयाध्यक्ष।

library *लॉइ ब्रॅ रि* *n.* a collection of books पुस्तक-संचय; building for a collection of books पुस्तकालय।

licence *लॉइ सॅन्स* *n.* authority or liberty given to do something अनुज्ञा-पत्र; wrong use of freedom स्वच्छंदता।

license *लॉइ सॅन्स* *v.t.* to give a licence to अनुज्ञा देना।

licensee *लॉइ सॅन् सी* *n.* one to whom a licence is granted अनुज्ञापत्रधारी।

licentious *लॉइ सैन् शॅस* *a.* sexually immoral व्यभिचारी; dissolute पतित।

lick[1] *लिक* *v.t.* to pass the tongue over the surface of जीभ से चाटना; to touch lightly हल्का स्पर्श करना।

lick[2] *n.* act of licking चाटने की क्रिया।

lid *लिड* *n.* a movable cover of a vessel or box ढक्कन; eyelid पलक।

lie[1] *लॉइ* *v.i.* to be or put oneself flat in a resting position लेटना; to be resting flat पड़ा रहना; to remain रहना; to exist अस्तित्व रखना; to consist (in) निहित होना।

lie[2] *v.i.* to make an untrue statement झूठ बोलना।

lie[3] *n.* untruth असत्य; false statement असत्य भाषण।

lien *लिअॅन* *n.* legal claim वैध अधिकार।

lieu *ल्यू* *n.* place स्थान।

lieutenant *लैफ़ टै˘ नॅन्ट* *n.* a junior officer in the army or navy लैफ़्टिनेन्ट।

life *लॉइफ़* *n.* time from birth to death जीवनकाल, animate existence जीवन, प्राण; spirit आत्मा; way of living जीवन-शैली; vigour जोश, उत्साह; a biography जीवनी।

lifeless *लॉइफ़् लिस* *a.* deprived of life जीवन-रहित; dead मृत।

lifelong *लॉइफ़् लौ ॅङ्ग* *a.* lasting through life आजीवन।

lift¹ *लिफ़्ट* *n.* lifter उत्तोलक, उत्थापक; raising उत्थान; ride in car etc. सवारी।

lift² *v.t.* to raise to a higher position उन्नत बनाना; to raise उठाना; to steal चुराना to remove हटाना।

light¹ *लॉइट* *n.* that by which objects are rendered visible प्रकाश; brightness चमक; enlightenment ज्ञानोदय; flame लपट; way of viewing दृष्टिकोण।

light² *a.* bright चमकीला, ज्योतिर्मय; not heavy हलका; easy सरल; easy to digest सुपाच्य; easy to endure सहनीय; gentle मंद।

light³ *v.t.* to set burning जलाना; to give light to प्रकाशित करना; *v.i.* to take fire जलना; to brighten चमकना, प्रकाशित होना।

lighten *लॉइ ट्न* *v.i.* to become brighter चमकदार होना; to become light हलका होना; *v.t.* to illuminate प्रकाशित करना; to make lighter हलका करना।

lighter *लॉइ टॅः* *n.* device for lighting cigarettes etc. लाइटर।

lightly *लॉइट् लि* *adv.* in a light way हलके से, धीरे से; slightly मामूली सी मात्रा में; with little consideration बिना सोचे-विचारे।

lightening *लॉइट् निङ्ग* *n.* the sudden and vivid flash that precedes thunder, produced by a discharge of atmospheric electricity आकाशीय विद्युत्।

lignite *लिग्- नॉइट* *n.* brown coal भूरा कोयला।

like¹ *लॉइक* *a.* similar अनुरूप।

like² *n.* liking पसंद; something similar समान प्रकार।

like³ *v.t.* to be pleased with पसंद करना; to wish चाहना; to choose चयन करना।

like⁴ *prep.* similar to के समान।

likelihood *लॉइक् लि हुड* *n.* probability संभव्यता।

likely *लॉइक् लि* *a.* probable संभाव्य; suitable उपयुक्त।

liken *लॉइ क्न* *v.t.* to compare तुलना करना।

likeness *लॉइक् निस* *n.* similarity अनुरूपता।

likewise *लॉइक् वॉइज़* *adv.* in like manner उसी तरह।

liking *लॉइ किङ्ग* *n.* inclination पसंद, रुचि; fondness शौक़।

lilac *लॉइ- लॅक* *n.* European tree of olive family नीलक; light purple colour हलका बैंगनी रंग।

lily *लि लि* *n.* a bulbous flowering plant कुमुदिनी।

limb *लिम* *n.* organ अवयव; branch शाखा।

limber¹ *लिम्- बॅरः* *v.t.* to make flexible लचीला बनाना; *v.i.* to be flexible लचीला होना।

limber² *n.* shaft of vehicle गाड़ी का जुआ; detachable fore-part of a guncarriage तोपगाड़ी का अगला भाग।

lime¹ *लॉइम* *n.* any viscous substance चूना; a sticky substance लासा।

lime² *v.t.* to treat with lime चूना लगाना।

lime³ *n.* a tree of the lemon family चकोतरा।

limelight *लॉइम् लॉइट n.* an intense white light used for lighting the stage तीव्र प्रकाश; great publicity लोकप्रसिद्धि।

limit¹ *लि मिट n.* boundary सीमा, परिसीमा, restriction प्रतिबंध।

limit² *v.t.* to bound सीमित करना; to restrain रोक लगाना।

limitation *लि मि टे शॅन n.* act of limiting परिसीमन; restriction बाधा, रुकावट।

limited *लि मि टिड a.* narrow संकुचित; restricted नियंत्रित।

limitless *लि मिट् लिस a.* boundless, having no limits असीम।

line¹ *लॉइन n.* thread-like marking रेखा; route मार्ग, पथ; row of soldiers etc. पंक्ति; method पद्धति; series श्रेणी, क्रम; field of activity पेशा, कार्य-क्षेत्र; railway track रेल-मार्ग; advice सलाह।

line² *v.t.* to mark out with lines (रेखा) खींचना; to sketch, रेखांकन करना; to put in line पंक्तिबद्ध करना; *v.i.* to take a place in a line पंक्ति में खड़ा होना।

line³ *v.t.* to provide with an inside covering अस्तर लगाना।

lineage *लि नि इज n.* descendents in a line from a common progenitor वंशावली।

linen *लि नॅन n.* cloth made of flax क्षोमवस्त्र।

linger *लिङ् गॅः v.i.* to delay विलंब करना; to remain long ठहरना; *v.t.* to spend wearily जैसे-तैसे बिताना।

lingo *लिङ्गो n. (pl. -es)* language not understood विदेशी भाषा; despised language तिरस्कृत भाषा।

lingua franca *लिङ् ग्वॅ फ्रैङ् कॅ n.* language used for communication between people of different mother tongues सामान्य भाषा, लोकभाषा।

lingual *लिङ् ग्वॅल a.* pertaining to the tongue or language जिह्वा अथवा भाषा-संबंधी।

linguist *लिङ् ग्विस्ट n.* person skilled in languages भाषाविद्।

linguistic *लिङ् ग्विस् टिक a.* relating to language भाषा-संबंधी, भाषा-वैज्ञानिक।

linguistics *लिङ् ग्विस् टिक्स n.* the science of language भाषा-विज्ञान।

lining *लॉइ निङ्ग n.* the covering of the inner surface of anything अस्तर।

link¹ *लिङ्क n.* anything connected शृंखला, संपर्क; ring of a chain ज़ंजीर की कड़ी।

link² *v.t.* to join, to connect जोड़ना।

linseed *लिन् सीड n.* seed of flax plant अलसी।

lintel *लिन् ट्ल n.* top piece of door or window सरदल।

lion *लॉइ ॲन n.* a carnivorous animal of the cat family शेर।

lioness *लॉइ ॲ निस n.* female lion शेरनी, सिंहनी।

lip *लिप n.* one of the two fleshy parts covering the front teeth अधर, ओठ।

liquefy *लिक् वि फ़ॉइ v.t.* to make liquid द्रव बनाना; *v.i.* to become liquid द्रव बनना।

liquid¹ *लिक् विड a.* fluid तरल; not

solid जो ठोस न हो; clear स्पष्ट।

liquid[2] *n.* fluid द्रव पदार्थ।

liquidate *लिक् वि डेट v.t.* to pay or settle (a debt) (ऋण) चुकाना; to arrange affairs of and dissolve (a company) परिसमाप्त करना; to wipe out, to kill मिटा देना, नष्ट करना।

liquidation *लिक् वि डे शॅन n.* act of liquidating परिशोधन; dissolution विघटन; bankruptcy दिवालियापन।

liquor *लिकॅः n.* spirituous fluid आसव, मदिरा; beverage पेय पदार्थ।

lisp[1] *लिस्प v.t.* to speak with faulty pronunciation of 's' and 'z' तुतलाना।

lisp[2] *n.* a lisping manner of speech तुतलाहट।

list[1] *लिस्ट n.* a roll or catalogue सूचीपत्र।

list[2] *v.t.* to enlist सूचीबद्ध करना।

listen *लि स्न v.i.* to hearken सुनना; to follow advice ध्यान देना।

listener *लिस् नॅः n.* one who listens श्रोता।

listless *लिस्ट् लिस a.* having no wish इच्छा-रहित; indifferent उदासीन।

lists *लिस्ट्स n. pl.* field for combat अखाड़ा।

literacy *लि टॅ रॅ सि n.* condition of being literate साक्षरता।

literal *लि टॅ रॅल a.* according to the letter शब्दशः; connected with letters आक्षरिक; taking words in their usual sense शाब्दिक।

literary *लि टॅ रॅ रि a.* pertaining to literature साहित्यिक।

literate *लि टॅ रिट a.* able to read and write साक्षर।

literature *लि टॅ रि चॅः n.* collective writings of a country or period साहित्य, साहित्यिक रचना।

litigant *लि टि गॅन्ट n.* person engaged in a law-suit विवादी, मुक़दमेबाज़।

litigate *लि टि गेट v.t.* to contest in law (पर) मुक़दमेबाज़ी करना; *v.i.* to carry on a lawsuit बाद करना।

litigation *लि टि गे शॅन n.* a lawsuit वाद, मुक़दमा; going to law मुक़दमेबाज़ी।

litre *ली टॅः n.* metric unit of capacity लीटर (माप)।

litter[1] *लि टॅः n.* rubbish left scattered about बिखरा हुआ कूड़ा-करकट; young of an animal produced at one birth पशु के एक ब्यांत के बच्चे; portable couch पालकी; straw etc. as bedding for animals तृणशैय्या।

litter[2] *v.t.* to strew with litter कूड़े-करकट से गंदा करना; to bring forth (young) जन्म देना।

litterateur *ली-टे-रा-टरः n.* literary person साहित्यिक व्यक्ति।

little[1] *लि ट्ल a.* small in size or extent लघु, छोटा; small in extent or quantity अनधिक; petty नगण्य; mean तुच्छ।

little[2] *adv.* slightly थोड़ा-सा।

little[3] *n.* a small quantity अल्प मात्रा।

littoral *लि-टॅ-रॅल a.* belonging to the seashore or to lands near the coast समुद्रतटीय, तटवर्ती।

liturgical *लि-टॅरः-जि-कॅल* *a.* pertaining to form of worship पूजापद्धति-संबंधी।

live[1] *लिव* *v.i.* to exist अस्तित्व रखना; to be alive जीवित रहना; to dwell निवास करना; to have life प्राणधारी होना; *v.t.* to lead बिताना।

live[2] *लॉइव* *a.* having life जीवंत; alive जीवित; energetic ओजस्वी; carrying electric current विद्युन्मय; flaming सुलगता हुआ; (of broadcast) transmitted during the actual performance सीधा (प्रसारण)।

livelihood *लॉइव् लि हुड* *n.* means of living आजीविका।

lively *लॉइव् लि* *a.* active सक्रिय; vigorous ओजस्वी; vivid स्पष्ट।

liver *लि वॅः* *n.* the organ which secretes the bile यकृत, जिगर।

livery *लि वॅ रि* *n.* uniform provided for servants नौकरों की वरदी।

living[1] *लि विङ्ग्* *a.* having life जीवंत; existing वर्तमान; alive सप्राण।

living[2] *n.* means of subsistence जीविका।

lizard *लि ज़ॅःड* *n.* a four-footed tailed reptile छिपकली।

load[1] *लोड* *n.* burden बोझ, भार; amount carried at a time बोझ, खेप; grievous weight शोक-भार।

load[2] *v.t.* to put a load on लादना; to charge (gun) (बंदूक में) गोली भरना; to put a length of film into (a camera) (कैमरे में) रील भरना।

loadstar *लोड्-स्टारः* *n.* pole-star ध्रुवतारा।

loadstone *लोड्-स्टोन* *n.* a magnet चुंबक पत्थर।

loaf[1] *लोफ़* *n.* a mass of bread formed by the baker पावरोटी।

loaf[2] *v.i.* to lounge आवारागर्दी करना; to pass time idly आलस्य में समय बिताना।

loafer *लो फॅः* *n.* a lounger आवारा आदमी।

loan[1] *लोन* *n.* lending उधार; sum of money lent ऋण राशि।

loan[2] *v.t.* to lend उधार देना।

loath *लोथ* *a.* not inclined, reluctant अनिच्छुक।

loathe *लोद* *v.t.* to feel disgust at (से) घृणा रखना।

loathsome *लोद् सॅम* *a.* exciting disgust घिनौना, वीभत्स; disgusting घृणास्पद।

lobby *लौ ˘ बि* *n.* an appartment giving admission to others उपांतिका; an entrance-hall प्रवेश-कक्ष; waiting room प्रतीक्षा-कक्ष।

lobe *लोब* *n.* broadrounded segmental division पिंडक, पिंडिका; soft lower part of the ear कान का कोमल भाग।

lobster *लौ˘ब्-स्टॅरः* *n.* large strong clawed edible crustacean महाचिंगट, समुद्री झींगा।

local *लो कॅल* *a.* pertaining to a particular place स्थानीय, देशीय।

locale *लो˘ काल* *n.* the scene of a particular event घटना-स्थल।

locality *लो˘ कै लि टि* *n.* area, district, place स्थान।

localize *लो कॅ लॉइज़* *v.t.* to make local स्थानीय बनाना।

locate *लो˘ केट* *v.t.* to attribute to a place स्थान से जोड़ना; to find the place of के स्थान का पता

लगाना; to establish in a place स्थापित करना।

location *लो ˘ के शॅन n.* situation स्थिति; place स्थान; act of locating स्थान-निर्धारण।

lock[1] *लौकॅ n.* a tuft or ringlet of hair लट।

lock[2] *v.t.* to fasten (door, chest etc.) (का) ताला लगाना; to close fast बंद करना; *v.i.* to become locked बंद हो जाना।

lock[3] *n.* a device for fastening door, lid etc. ताला; the mechanism which fires a gun बंदूक का घोड़ा; a condition which makes movement impossible अवरोध।

locker *लौ ˘ कॅः n.* small cupboard that may be locked तालेदार अलमारी।

locket *लौ ˘ किट n.* a little case worn as an ornament सोने या चांदी का कुंडा, लॉकेट।

locomotive *लो कॅ मो टिव n.* a steam engine वाष्प इंजिन; automatic machine or engine स्वचालित यंत्र या इंजिन।

locus *लो-कॅस (pl.-ci) n.* place, location स्थान, अवस्थिति; the line or surface constituted by all positions of a point or line बिंदुपथ, रेखापथ।

locust *लो कॅस्ट n.* a destructive winged insect टिड्डी।

locution *लो ˘-क्यू-शॅन n.* mode of speaking वाक्शैली, भाषण-शैली; phrase मुहावरा।

lodge[1] *लौ ˘ज n.* abode आवास; tent खेमा, तंबू।

lodge[2] *v.t.* to furnish with a dwelling ठहराना; to place रखना; to infix बैठा देना; *v.t.* to live रहना।

lodging *लौ ˘ जिङ्ग n.* temporary habitation अस्थायी आवास।

loft *लौफ्ट n.* upper room अटारी, मचान; gallery in a hall or church दीर्घा।

lofty *लौफ़् टि a.* high in position उन्नत; haughty अभिमानी।

log *लौगॅ n.* bulky piece of wood लट्ठा, कुंदा; detailed record of voyages of ship, aircraft etc. यात्रा-दैनिकी।

logarithim *लौं- गॅ- रिथ्म n.* the power of a fixed number घात, प्रमापक, लघुगणक।

loggerhead *लौ ˘- गरः- है ˘ड n.* blockhead, dunce मूढ़, स्थूलबुद्धि; apparatus or iron लौह-यंत्र।

logic *लौ ˘ जिक n.* science and art of reasoning तर्कशास्त्र।

logical *लौ ˘ जि कॅल a.* of or according to logic तर्कसम्मत; proved by logic तर्कसिद्ध।

logician *लौ ˘ जि शॅन n.* person skilled in logic तर्कशास्त्री।

loin *लौ ˘इन n.* lower part of the back कटि, नितंब।

loiter *लौ ˘इ टॅः v.i.* to dawdle आवारागर्दी करना।

loll *लौ ˘ल v.i.* to dangle (the tongue) (जीभ) लपलपाना; to lie lazily about सुस्ती में पड़े रहना; to hang out लटकना; *v.t.* to let hang out लटकाना।

lollipop *लौ ˘ लि पौपॅ n.* a large sweet on a stick for sucking चूसने की मिठाई।

lone *लोन a.* solitary अकेला, एकाकी।

loneliness *लोन् लि निस n.* state of being lonely निर्जनता, एकाकीपन।

lonely *लोन् लि a.* unaccompanied एकाकी; uninhabited निर्जन।

lonesome *लोन् सॅम a.* solitary निर्जन; feeling lonely एकाकी।

long[1] *लौ ॅङ्ग a.* not short लंबा; extended दीर्घ।

long[2] *adv.* for a long time लंबे समय तक; at a distant time बहुत दिन पूर्व अथवा पश्चात्।

long[3] *v.i.* to yearn लालायित होना।

longevity *लौन् जे ॅ वि टि n.* great length of life दीर्घायुता।

longing *लौ ॅङ् गिङ्ग n.* yearning तीव्र इच्छा।

longitude *लौन्ॅ जि ट्यूड n.* distance measured in degrees east or west of the standard meridian देशांतर।

look[1] *लुक v.i.* to seem प्रतीत होना; to give attention अभिमुख होना।

look[2] *a.* appearance रूप, आकृति; view दृष्टिपात।

loom[1] *लूम n.* machine for weaving करघा।

loom[2] *v.i.* to appear indistinctly धुंधला दिखाई देना; to seem ominously close पास ही मंडराना।

loop *लूप n.* coil कुंडली; snare फंदा; branch of a railway line रेलवे-शाखा।

loop-hole *लूप् होल n.* a narrow vertical opening in a wall for defence रंध्र; means of escape बचाव का रास्ता।

loose[1] *लूॅ:स a.* unbound बंधनमुक्त; slack शिथिल; unrestrained अव्यवस्थित; vague अस्पष्ट; dissolute लंपट।

loose[2] *v.t.* to set free मुक्त करना; to make loose ढीला करना; to relax शिथिल करना।

loosen *लू स्न v.t.* to set free रिहा करना; to make loose ढीला करना; *v.i.* to become loose ढीला होना; to open खुलना।

loot[1] *लूट n.* plunder लूटमार।

loot[2] *v.i.* to plunder लूटपाट करना; *v.t.* to plunder लूटना।

lop[1] *लौपॅ (-pp-) v.t.* to cut off the top or ends of छांटना; to cut away छिन्न-भिन्न कर डालना।

lop[2] *n.* act of lopping काट-छांट।

lord *लौ:ड n.* master स्वामी; (cap.) God प्रभु।

lordly *लौ:ड् लि a.* like or becoming of a lord राजोचित; haughtly घमंडी।

lordship *लौ:ड् शिप n.* state of being a lord आधिपत्य, स्वामित्व।

lore *लौॅ:, लौ: n.* learning विद्या।

lorry *लौ ॅ रि n.* a wagon without sides or with low sides ठेला।

lose *लूज़ v.t.* to miss खो देना; to fail to keep गंवा देना; to waste व्यर्थ व्यय करना; to be defeated in (में) हार जाना; *v.i.* to suffer loss हानि उठाना; to fail असफल होना।

loss *लौ ॅस n.* losing हानि; diminution ह्रास; defeat पराजय।

lot[1] *लौ ॅट n.* destiny भाग्य; item at auction बोली के लिए वस्तु; an area of land भूभाग; share भाग।

lot[2] *n.* large quantity or number बड़ी मात्रा या संख्या; collection ढेर।

lotion *लो शॅन n.* medicinal or cosmetic liquid लोशन।

lottery *लौ ॅ टॅ रि n.* a competition at which prizes are awarded by drawing lots लॉटरी।

lotus *लो टॅस n.* water lily कमल।

loud *लॉउड a.* noisy कोलाहलपूर्ण; making a great sound उच्चस्वर युक्त।

lounge[1] *लॉउन्ज़ v.i.* to loll मटरगश्ती करना; to idle मौज करना।

lounge[2] *n.* state or act of lounging पर्यटन-प्रवृत्ति; entrance or sitting room बरामदा।

louse *लॉउस n.* a parasitic insect living in the hair and skin जूं।

lovable *लॅ व बल a.* worthy of love प्रीतिकर, प्रेम-योग्य।

love[1] *लव n.* fondness प्रणय; affection वात्सल्य।

love[2] *v.t.* to be fond of प्रेम करना; *v.i.* to be in love प्यार होना।

lovely *लॅव् लि a.* loving प्रिय, प्रियकर; beautiful सुंदर, मनोरम।

lover *लॅ वः n.* one who loves प्रेमी।

loving *ल विङ्ग a.* affectionate अनुरागशील।

low[1] *लो a.* not of high rank निम्न; contemptible घृणित; not loud मंद (स्वर); below the surface निचला; depressed उदास; cheap सस्ता।

low[2] *adv.* in a low position निम्न स्थिति में।

low[3] *v.i.* to make the noise of cow रंभाना।

low[4] *n.* sound made by cows रंभाहट।

lower *लो अः v.t.* to make low झुकाना; to lessen कम करना; to dilute अपकृष्ट करना; to degrade गिराना; to weaken कमज़ोर करना; *v.i.* to become lower or less कम होना, नीचा होना।

lowliness *लो लि निस n.* humility दीनता; simplicity सादगी; modesty विनम्रता।

lowly *लो लि a.* modest विनयशील; humble दीन; simple सरल, सादा।

loyal *लौ ॅइ अॅल a.* faithful निष्ठावान।

loyalist *लौ ॅइ अॅ लिस्ट n.* one who supports the government in times or revolt राजभक्त।

loyalty *लौ ॅइ अॅल् टि n.* faithfulness निष्ठा; loyal conduct निष्ठापूर्ण आचरण।

lubricant *लू ब्रि कॅन्ट n.* lubricating substance चिकनाई।

lubricate *लू ब्रि केट v.t.* to apply a lubricant to चिकनाना।

lubrication *लू ब्रि के शॅन n.* act of lubricating स्नेहन।

lucent *लू सन्ट a.* bright, shining चमकदार।

lucerne *लू सॅःन n.* clover-like plant used for feeding animals रिजका।

lucid *लू सिड,ल्यू– a.* shining चमकदार; easily understood सुबोधगम्य।

lucidity *लू सि डि टि, ल्यू– n.* brightness चमक; clearness स्पष्टता; quality of being lucid सुबोधगम्यता।

luck *लक n.* fortune भाग्य; chance संयोग।

luckily *ल कि लि adv.* fortunately सौभाग्य से।

luckless *लक् लिस a.* unfortunate अभागा, दुर्भाग्यपूर्ण।

lucky *ल कि a.* fortunate भाग्यशाली; auspicious मंगलप्रद।

lucrative *लू क्रॅ टिव a.* profitable लाभप्रद; bringing in money अर्थकर।

lucre *लू कॅः n.* money, wealth धन, दौलत।

luggage *ल गिज n.* traveller's belongings असबाब, सामान।

lukewarm *लूक् वौःम, ल्यूक्– a.* tepid गुनगुना; indifferent उदासीन।

lull[1] *लल v.t.* to make (one) sleep by patting थपकियां देकर सुलाना; to quiet शांत करना; *v.i.* to become calm शांत होना।

lull[2] *n.* interval of calm शांति-काल।

lullaby *ल लॅ बॉइ n.* song to lull children to sleep लोरी।

luminary *लू मि नॅ रि, ल्यू– n.* a body that gives off light ज्योति-नक्षत्र; a person distinguished for his learning महान विद्वान्।

luminous *लू मि नॅस ल्यू– a.* giving light प्रकाशमान; easily understood सुबोधगम्य।

lump[1] *लम्प n.* mass पिंड; heap ढेर; swelling सूजन।

lump[2] *v.t.* to throw into a confused mass ढेर लगाना; *v.i.* to gather in lump एकत्र होना।

lunacy *लू नॅ सि, ल्यू– n.* insanity पागलपन; mad behaviour पागलपन का व्यवहार।

lunar *लू नॅः, ल्यू– a.* of the moon चंद्रमा-संबंधी, चाँद्र।

lunatic[1] *लू नॅ टिक n.* a mad man पागल व्यक्ति।

lunatic[2] *a.* mad पागल।

lunch[1] *(-eon) लन्च, लन् शॅन n.* midday meal मध्याह्न-भोजन।

lunch[2] *v.i.* to take lunch भोजन करना; *v.t.* to provide lunch for भोजन देना।

lung *लङ्ग* respirating organ in animals फेफड़ा।

lunge[1] *लन्ज n.* a sudden movement forward झपट्टा; a sword-thrust तलवार का वार।

lunge[2] *v.i.* to thrust with a sword तलवार घोंपना; to move forward suddenly झपट्टा मारना।

lurch[1] *लॅःच n.* a sudden roll to one side अचानक एक ओर को लड़खड़ाना।

lurch[2] *v.i.* to move in an awkward manner लड़खड़ाना।

lure[1] *ल्यूअॅः n.* enticement प्रलोभन; bait चारा, चुग्गा।

lure[2] *v.t.* to entice प्रलोभित करना; to attract आकर्षित करना।

lurk *लःक v.i.* to be concealed दुबकना; to lie in wait घात में होना।

luscious *ल शॅस a.* most pleasing in taste सुस्वाद।

lush *लश a.* juicy रसीला; luxuriant प्रचुर।

lust *लस्ट n.* sexual desire काम-वासना; strong desire लालसा।

lustful *लस्ट् फुल a.* full of lust कामुक।

lustre *लस् टॅः n.* glow चमक, द्युति; beauty सौंदर्य।

lustrous *लस् ट्रॅस a.* bright, shining चमकदार।

lusty *लस् टि a.* healthy and strong हृष्ट-पुष्ट।

lute *लूट, ल्यूट n.* a stringed musical instrument वीणा।

luxuriance *लग् जुअॅ रि अॅन्स, लक् सुअॅ– n.* abundance प्रचुरता।

luxuriant *लग़् जुॲ रि ॲन्ट, लक् सुॲ–* *a.* abundant प्रचुर; richly ornamented (style) अत्यलंकृत (शैली)।

luxurious *लग़् जुॲ रि ॲ स, लक् सुॲ–* *a.* furnished with luxuries विलासमय; fond of luxuries विलासप्रिय।

luxury *लक् शॅ रि* *n.* enjoyment of the best and costliest विलासिता; (*pl.*) things giving such enjoyment विलास-साधन।

lynch *लिन्च* *v.t.* to put to death without trial बिना मुक़दमे के मार डालना।

lyre *लॉइॲ:* *n.* an instrument like the harp वीणा।

lyric[1] *लि रिक* *a.* intended for singing गेय।

lyric[2] *n.* short poem for singing गीतिकाव्य।

lyrical *लि रि कॅल* *a.* of lyric poetry गेय काव्य से संबंधित; having the qualities of a lyric गेय।

lyricist *लि रि सिस्ट* *n.* writer of lyrics प्रगीतकार, गीतिकाव्यकार।

Mm

M ऍम the thirteenth letter of the English alphabet, in Roman notation used for 1000. अंग्रेजी भाषा का तेरहवाँ अक्षर, रोमन अंकमाला में १००० के लिए प्रयुक्त अंक।

macabre *मॅ काबॅ:* *a* horrible भयानक।

mace *मेस* *n.* a club with a spiked head कीलदार गदा; a staff of office सोंटा।

macerate *मै-सॅ-रेट* *v.t.* to soften by steeping भिगोकर मुलायम करना; *v.i.* to undergo maceration भीगकर मुलायम होना।

machine *मॅ शीन* *n.* an apparatus consisting of inter-related parts कल, यंत्र।

machinery *मॅ शी नॅ रि* *n.* machines in general यंत्र-प्रणाली; moving parts of a machine किसी यंत्र के चलने वाले भाग।

mad *मैड* *a.* insane पागल; very enthusiastic अति उत्साहपूर्ण; excited उत्तेजित; angry क्रुद्ध।

madam *मॅ डॅम* *n.* courteous form of address to a lady महोदया।

madden *मै डॅन* *v.t.* to make mad पागल करना।

madrigal *मैड़-रि-गॅल* *n.* a lyrical peom गीत, कजरी ; a pastrol song ग्राम्यगीत।

maestro *मा ऐ ॅस् ट्रो* *n.* out-standing musician संगीतज्ञ; master of any art कलाविद।

magazine *मै गॅ ज़ीन* *n.* periodical publication पत्रिका; a place for storing explosives बारूदख़ाना, शस्त्रागार; appliance for supplying cartridges automatically to gun मैगज़ीन।

maggot *मै-गॅट* *n.* a legless grub कीट, कृमि; a fad सनक।

magic[1] *मै जिक* *n.* enchantment इंद्रजाल, जादू।

magic[2] *a.* done by magic ऐंद्रजालिक; possessing magic जादूभरा।

magical *मै जि कॅल a.* pertaining to magic जादू-संबंधी।

magician *मॅ जि शॅन n.* one versed in magic जादूगर।

magisterial *मै जिस् टिॲ रि ॲल a.* pertaining to a magistrate दंडाधिकारी-संबंधी।

magistracy *मै जिस् ट्रॅ सि n.* body of magistrates दंडाधिकारीगण; office of a magistrate दंडाधिकरण।

magistrate *मै जिस् ट्रिट, –ट्रेट n.* one who has power of putting the law in force दंडाधिकारी।

magnanimity *मैग् नॅ नि मि टि n.* quality of being magnanimous उदारहृदयता।

magnanimous *मैग् नै नि मॅस a.* generous उदार हृदय, विशाल-हृदय।

magnate *मैग् नेट n.* a noble महापुरुष।

magnet *मैग् निट n.* lode-stone चुंबक; person or thing that attracts आकर्षक व्यक्ति या वस्तु।

magnetic *मैग् नै˘ टिक a.* pertaining to magnet चुंबकीय; able to attract आकर्षक।

magnetism *मैग् नि टिज़्म n.* cause of the attractive power of the magnet चुंबकत्व; personal charm and attraction व्यक्तिगत सौंदर्य व आकर्षण।

magnificent *मैग् नि फि सॅन्ट a.* pompous भव्य, शानदार।

magnify *मैग् नि फ़ॉइ v.t.* to enlarge विस्तीर्ण करना; to exaggerate बढ़ा-चढ़ाकर कहना; to give praise to प्रशंसा करना।

magnitude *मैग् नि ट्यूड n.* importance महत्व; size आकार; greatness विशालता, महानता।

magpie *मैगॅ पॉइ n.* a black and white bird related to the crow मुटरी; person who chatters much बातूनी व्यक्ति।

mahogany *मॅ हौ˘ गॅ नि n.* a tree yielding reddish brown wood तून।

mahout *मॅ हॉउट n.* a man who drives an elephant महावत।

maid *मेड n.* virgin कुमारी; female servant सेविका।

maiden[1] *मे ड्न n.* girl कन्या; a young unmarried woman अविवाहित युवती।

maiden[2] *a.* unmarried अविवाहित; first प्रथम; (cricket) (an over) scoring no runs (ओवर) जिसमें कोई रन न बना हो।

mail[1] *मेल n.* post डाक; train carrying mail डाक-गाड़ी।

mail[2] *v.t.* to post डाक में डालना; to send by post डाक-द्वारा भेजना।

mail[3] *n.* armour made of rings or plates of metal कवच।

main[1] *मेन a* chief प्रधान।

main[2] *n.* principal pipe-line carrying water, electricity etc. मुख्य पाइप लाइन अथवा विद्युत् परिपथ; chief part मुख्य भाग; strength, power शक्ति।

mainly *मेन् लि adv.* chiefly मुख्य रूप से; for the most part अधिकांशतः।

mainstay *मेन् स्टे n.* chief support मुख्य सहारा।

maintain *मेन् टेन, मै˘न्–, मॅन्– v.t.* to keep in existence बनाए रखना;

to keep up, to continue जारी रखना; to preserve सुरक्षित रखना; to assert, to affirm दृढ़तापूर्वक कहना; to support पालन करना।

maintenance *मेन् टि नॅन्स n.* supporting निर्वाह; keeping in working order अनुरक्षण; means of support भरण-पोषण का साधन।

maize *मेज़ n.* staple cereal मक्का।

majestic *मॅ जै ॅस् टिक a.* stately राजसी; sublime तेजस्वी।

majesty *मै जिस् टि n.* grandeur भव्यता; royal state प्रभुसत्ता।

major[1] *मे जॅः a.* main, chief मुख्य; significant महत्त्वपूर्ण; serious गंभीर; greater बड़ा।

major[2] *n.* army officer next above captain मेजर; one who has come of age वयस्क।

majority *मॅ जौ ॅ रि टि n.* the great number बहुमत; coming of age वयस्कता; excess of votes on one side मतों की बढ़त।

make[1] *मेक v.t.* to construct निर्माण करना; to produce उत्पादन करना; to prepare तैयार करना; to persuade प्रेरित करना।

make[2] *n.* brand मार्का; structure बनावट; type प्रकार।

Maker *मे कॅः n.* one who makes निर्माता; (cap.) The Creator स्रष्टा, विधाता।

maladjustment *मैल् अॅ जस्ट् मॅन्ट n.* improper adjustment कु-समायोजन।

maladministration *मैल् अॅड् मि नि स्ट्रे शॅन n.* bad administration दुर्व्यवस्था, कुशासन।

malady *मै लॅ डि n.* illness बीमारी।

malaria *मॅ ले अॅ रि अॅ n.* a fever passed on by mosquitoes मलेरिया।

maladroit *मै-लॅ-ड्रौ ॅइट a.* unskillful, clumsy फूहड़, अनाड़ी।

malafide[1] *मे-लॅ-फ़ॉइ-डि a.* illintentioned, having bad designs दुर्भावपूर्ण; treacherous कपटपूर्ण, जाली।

malafide[2] *adv.* in bad faith, treacherously दुर्भावपूर्वक, बेईमानी से।

malaise *मै-लेज़ n.* uneasiness बेचैनी, व्याकुलता; feeling of sickness or discomfort रुग्णता, अनमनापन।

malcontent[1] *मैल् कॅन् टैन्ट a.* dissatisfied असंतुष्ट।

malcontent[2] *n.* a person who is discontented असंतुष्ट व्यक्ति।

male[1] *मेल a.* masculine पुलिंग; pertaining to male sex पुरुषजातीय।

male[2] *n.* male person or animal पुरुष अथवा नर पशु।

malediction *मै-लि-डिक्-शॅन n.* evil speaking, curse शाप, अभिशाप।

malefactor *मै-लि-फ़ैक्-टरः n.* evil doer, criminal दुष्कर्मी, अपराधी।

maleficent *मॅ-लै ॅ-फ़ि-सॅन्ट a.* hurtful अनिष्टकारी, अपकारी।

malice *मै लिस n.* ill-will द्वेष-भावना।

malicious *मॅ लि शॅस a.* bearing ill-will विद्वेषपूर्ण; moved by ill-intention विद्वेषी।

malign[1] *मॅ लॉइन v.t.* to speak evil of निंदा करना; to defame बदनाम करना; to tell lies about के विषय में झूठ बोलना।

malign[2] *a.* evil in influence

अनिष्टकर; harmful हानिकर।

malignancy *मॅ लिग् नॅन सि* *n.* malice विद्वेष; ill-will दुर्भावना।

malignant *मॅ लिग् नॅन्ट* *a.* disposed to do harm अहितकर; ill-intentioned दुर्भावनापूर्ण।

malignity *मॅ लिग् नि टि* *n.* a deep rooted ill-will गहन द्वेषभाव; malignant character विषालुता।

malleable *मै लि अॅ ब्ल* *a.* capable of being hammered into shape जिसे पीट-पीट कर कोई आकार दिया जा सके; easily trained शिक्षणीय।

malmsey *माम्-ज़ि* *n.* strong and sweet wine मधुर मदिरा।

malnutrition *मैल् न्यू ट्रि शॅन्, –न्यु–* *n.* imperfect or faulty nutrition कुपोषण।

malpractice *मैल् प्रैक् टिस* *n.* misconduct दुराचार; corruption भ्रष्टाचार; neglect of duty कर्त्तव्य-विमुखता।

malt *मौːॅल्ट, मौल्ट* *n.* barley grain prepared for brewing ह्विस्की बनाना, माल्ट।

mal-treatment *मैल् ट्रीट् मॅन्ट* *n.* ill-treatment दुर्व्यवहार।

mamma *मॅ मा* *n.* mother माता।

mammal *मै मॅल* *n.* class of animals that suckle their young स्तनपायी।

mammary *मै-मॅ-रि* *a.* relating to the breasts स्तन-संबंधी।

Mammon *मै मॅन* *n.* wealth संपत्ति; (cap.) god of greed कुबेर।

mammoth[1] *मै मॅथ* *n.* large sized elephant विशालकाय हाथी।

mammoth[2] *a.* collosal विशालकाय।

man[1] *मैन* *n.* human being नर मनुष्य; person व्यक्ति; human race मानव-जाति; adult male पुरुष; piece use in chess (चैस) पैदल।

man[2] *(-nn)* *v.t.* to supply with men for service or defence सेवा अथवा रक्षा-हेतु मनुष्य प्रदान करना।

manage *मै निज* *v.t.* to administer प्रबंध करना; to control नियंत्रित करना; to conduct संचालित करना; *v.i.* to conduct affairs काम चलाना।

manageable *मै नि जॅ ब्ल* *a.* governable नियंत्रण-योग्य; that can be managed जिसकी व्यवस्था की जा सके।

management *मै निज् मॅन्ट* *n.* body of managers प्रबंध समिति; act or art of managing प्रबंधन।

manager *मै नि जॅː* *n.* one who manages प्रबंधक।

managerial *मै नॅ जिअॅ रिअॅल* *a.* of managers प्रबंधकों से संबंधित।

mandate *मैन् डेट* *n.* command अधिदेश; order आदेश; authority given to representatives by voters जनादेश।

mandatory *मैन् डॅ टॅ रि* *a.* containing a mandate अधिदेश-प्राप्त; compulsory अनिवार्य।

mane *मीन* *n.* long hair on the back of the neck (of horse etc.) अयाल।

manes *मे नीज़, मा–* *n. pl.* spirits of the dead पितृ, पितर।

manful *मैन् फुल* *a.* brave, energetic पराक्रमी।

manganese *मैङ् गॅ नीज़, मैङ् गॅ नीज़* *n.* a metallic element मैंगनीज़।

manger *मेन् जॅː* *n.* trough for food

of horses and cattle नांद।

mangle *मैङ् ग्ल v.t.* to cut up badly, to hack क्षत-विक्षत करना; to spoil विकृत करना।

mango *मैन् गो n. (pl. oes)* a pear-shaped fruit आम; the tree bearing this fruit आम का पेड़।

manhandle *मैन् हैन् ड्ल v.t.* to treat roughly (से) मार-पीट करना; to move by physical strength शारीरिक शक्ति से हटाना।

manhole *मैन्-होल n.* a hole large enough to admit a man प्रवेश-छिद्र।

manhood *मैन् हुड n.* manly quality पुरुषत्व; human nature मनुष्यत्व।

mania *मे न्यॅ n,* violent madness उन्माद; craze सनक; extreme enthusiasm धुन, अति उत्साह।

maniac *मे नि ऐक n.* a mad man पागल व्यक्ति।

manicure *मै-नि-क्युअरः n.* professional treatment for hands and nails नख-प्रसाधन।

manifest[1] *मै नि फ़ैस्ॅट a.* perceptible व्यक्त, स्पष्ट।

manifest[2] *v.t.* to make clear प्रकट करना; to show clearly स्पष्ट दिखा देना।

manifestation *मै नि फ़ैस् टे शॅन n.* clarification स्पष्टीकरण; demonstration प्रदर्शन।

manifesto *मै नि फ़ैस् टो n.* public written declaration of intentions, opinion and motives of a party or body घोषणापत्र।

manifold *मै नि फ़ोल्ड a.* various in kind बहुविध, विविध।

manipulate *मॅ नि प्यु लेट v.t.* to falsify झुठलाना; to handle with skill सावधानी से चलाना; to manage (की) व्यवस्था करना।

manipulation *मॅ नि प्यु ले शॅन n.* act of manipulating छल-साधन।

mankind *मैन् कॉइन्ड n.* human race मानव-जाति; (मैन् कॉइन्ड) the male sex पुरुष-जाति।

manlike *मैन्-लॉइक a.* like a man मनुष्यवत्; masculine, manly पुरुषोचित।

manliness *मैन् लि निस n,* manhood पुरुषत्व; bravery पौरुष।

manly *मैन् लि a.* having a man's qualities पुरुषोचित।

manna *मैन् n.* food of Israelites in the wilderness दिव्यान्न।

mannequin *मे-नि-किन n.* dummy figure पुतला, पंजर; woman employed to wear and display clothes कपड़े पहनकर प्रदर्शित करने वाली नौकरानी।

manner *मै नॅः n.* good behaviour शिष्टाचार; method रीति, ढंग; (*pl.*) habits and customs रीति-रिवाज; (*pl*) social behaviour सामाजिक आचरण; style शैली।

mannerism *मै नॅ रिज़्म n.* artificiality कृत्रिमता; peculiarity of style or manner शैली-वैशिष्ट्य।

mannerly *मै नॅः लि a.* well-behaved शिष्ट।

manoeuvre[1] *मॅ नू वॅः n.* startagem चालाकी; piece of dexterous management विदग्धता planned movement (of armed forces) युक्तिचालन; (*pl.*) training exercises प्रशिक्षण-अभ्यास।

manoeuvre[2] *v.i.* to perform a manoeuvre चालाकी का व्यवहार करना; *v.t.* to cause to perform a manoeuvre चालाकी कराना; to make by manoeuvre चालाकी से बनाना; to manage with skill होशियारी से साधना।

manor *मै नॅः n.* land belonging to a lord जागीर, ज़मींदारी।

manorial *मॅ-नौ˘-रि-अॅल a.* pertaining to a manor जागीर-संबंधी।

mansion *मैन् शॅन n.* a large house विशाल भवन।

mantel *मैन् ट्ल n.* ornamental structure over and in front of fire place कार्नस, अंगीठी।

mantle[1] *मैन् ट्ल n.* a loose cloak लबादा; covering आवरण; a hood for a gas jet गैस लालटेन की बत्ती।

mantle[2] *v.t.* to cover ढक लेना; to conceal छिपाना।

manual[1] *मैन् यु अॅल a.* of the hand हाथका, दस्ती; physical शारीरिक।

manual[2] *n.* hand book or handy compendium of large subject नियमावली, गुटका।

manufacture[1] *मैन् यु फ़ैक् चॅः v.t.* to produce, to make निर्माण करना; to invent गढ़ना।

manufacture[2] *n.* act or process of manufacturing औद्योगिक निर्माण; anything manufactured निर्मित वस्तु।

manufacturer *मैन् यु फ़ैक् चॅ रॅः n.* one who manufactures things उत्पादक, निर्माता।

manumission *मै-न्यू-मि-शॅन n.* release from slavery दास्यमुक्ति, छुटकारा।

manumit *मै-न्यू-मिट (-tt-) v.t.* to release from slavery दासता से मुक्त करना; to set free मुक्त करना।

manure[1] *मॅ न्युयअॅः n.* fertilizer खाद।

manure[2] *v.t.* to enrich with fertilizing substance खाद देना।

manuscript *मैन् यु स्क्रिप्ट n.* book etc. written by hand पांडुलिपि।

many *मै˘ नि a.* numerous अनेक।

map[1] *मैप n.* representation of the surface of the earth or of any part of it मानचित्र।

map[2] *(-pp-) v.t.* to make a map of (का) मानचित्र बनाना।

mar *माः (rr-) v.t.* to damage क्षति पहुंचाना।

marathon *मै रॅ थॅन n.* long distance race लंबी दौड़; test of endurance धैर्य की परीक्षा।

maraud *मै-रौड v.i.* to rove in quest or plunder लूटमार करते फिरना।

marauder *मॅ-रौ-डरः n.* one who raids or plunders लुटेरा, उपद्रवी।

marble *माः ब्ल n.* granular crystalline limestone संगमरमर; *(pl)* works of art in marble संगमरमर की कलाकृतियां; small ball of glass, clay etc. used in children's game गोली।

march[1] *माःच n* border सीमांत; border district सीमांत प्रांत; departure प्रस्थान, कूच; (MARCH) the third month of the year मार्च का महीना।

march[2] *v.i.* to walk in rhythmical military manner क़दम से क़दम मिलाकर चलना; *v.t.* to force to go जाने के लिए बाध्य करना।

mare *मे˘ अॅः n.* female horse घोड़ी।

margarine *मा:-जॅ-रीन, -गॅ-* *n.* butterlike substance made from vegetable oils and fats कृत्रिम मक्खन।

margin *मा: जिन* *n.* space round the page of a book हाशिया; edge किनारा; border सीमांत; difference between selling and buying prices क्रय-विक्रय मूल्य का अंतर।

marginal *मा: जि नॅल* *a.* pertaining to margin सीमावर्ती; barely sufficient मामूली-सा।

marigold *मै रि गोल्ड* *n.* plant with yellow flowers गेंदा।

marine *मॅ रीन* *a.* pertaining to navy जलसेना-संबंधी; concerned with the sea समुद्रीय।

mariner *मै रि नॅ:* *n.* sailor पोतवाहक।

marionette *मै-रि-अॅ-नैॅट* *n.* puppet moved by strings कठपुतली।

marital *मै रि ट्ल, मॅ रॉइ ट्ल* *a.* pertaining to marriage वैवाहिक, दांपत्य-संबंधी; relating to husband पति-विषयक।

maritime *मै रि टॉइम* *a.* pertaining to the sea समुद्री; bordering on the sea तटीय।

mark[1] *मा:क* *n.* target लक्ष्य, निशाना; stamp मुहर; spot धब्बा; sign चिन्ह; fame प्रसिद्धि।

mark[2] *v.t.* to make a mark on अंकित करना; to indicate लक्षित करना।

marker *मा:-कर:* *n.* person or tool that marks चिन्हक; one who marks the score in games अंकगणक।

market[1] *मा: किट* *n.* place for buying and selling बाज़ार।

market[2] *v.t.* to buy and sell in a market क्रय-विक्रय करना।

marketable *मा: कि टॅ ब्ल* *a.* fit for the market विक्रेय।

marksman *मा: क्स् मॅन* *n.* one who shoots well निशानेबाज़।

marl *मारल* *n.* limy clay used as manure चिकनी मिट्टी।

marmalade *मार:-मॅ-लेड* *n.* jam फलपाग, मुरब्बा।

maroon[1] *मॅ रून* *n.* brownish red colour भूरा लाल रंग।

maroon[2] *a.* brownish red भूरे लाल रंग का।

maroon[3] *v.t.* to leave (someone) on deserted island or coast (किसी को) निर्जन द्वीप अथवा समुद्रतट पर छोड़ना; to isolate अलग-थलग कर देना।

marriage *मै रिज* *n.* wedding विवाह, शादी।

marriageable *मै रि जॅ ब्ल* *a.* fit for marriage विवाह-योग्य।

marry *मै रि* *v.t.* to wed (से) शादी करना, विवाह करना; *v.i.* to be wedded विवाह करना।

Mars *मा:स* *n.* the god of war युद्ध का देवता; a planet मंगल ग्रह।

marsh *मा:श* *n.* swamp दलदल।

marshal[1] *मा: शॅल* *n* chief military officer सेनापति।

marshal[2] *(-ll-)* *v.t.* to arrange in order क्रमबद्ध करना; to conduct (somebody) with ceremony (किसी को) विधिपूर्वक ले चलना।

marshy *मा: शि* *a.* swampy दलदली।

marsupial *मार:-स्यू-पि-अॅल* *n.* an order of mammals having a pouch for carrying their young शिशुधानी जीव।

mart *मा:ट n.* market बाज़ार; centre of commerce वाणिज्य-केंद्र।

marten *मर:-टॅन n.* an animal close akin to the weasels नेवले जैसा एक जंतु।

martial *मा: शॅल a.* brave, warlike रणप्रिय बहादुर; of or belonging to war सामरिक, जंगी।

martinet *मार:-टि-नै ॅट n.* strict disciplinarian कठोर अनुशासक।

martyr *मा: टॅ: n.* one suffering death for his faith शहीद; one who suffers in one cause कष्ट-भोगी।

martyrdom *मा: ट डॅम n.* self-sacrifice आत्मबलिदान।

marvel[1] *मा: व्ल n.* a wonder कौतुक; a wonderful example अद्‌भुत उदाहरण।

marvel[2] *(-ll-) v.i.* to wonder विस्मित हो जाना।

marvellous *मा: वि लॅस a.* wonderful आश्चर्यजनक, अद्‌भुत।

mascot *मैस्-कॅट n.* supposed bringer of good luck शुभंकर; a talisman ताबीज़।

masculine *मैस् क्यु लिन, मास्– a.* relating to males पुरुषोचित; denoting male gender (व्या.) पुंलिंग।

mash[1] *मैश n.* grain, bran etc. cooked for animals दलिया; any substance softened and crushed मसला हुआ पदार्थ।

mash[2] *v.t.* to crush मसलना।

mask[1] *मास्क n.* face-cover मुखौटा; disguise छद्‌मवेश।

mask[2] *v.t.* to disguise छद्‌मवेश धारण करना; to cover (face) with a mask (चेहरा) मुखौटे से ढंकना।

mason *मै स्न n.* brick and stone layer राजगीर।

masonry *मै स्न् रि n.* stone-work, brick-work चिनाई; art of mason राजगीरी।

masquerade *मास्-कॅ-रेड n.* assembly of persons wearing masks at a ball नकाबयुक्त सहनृत्य; disguise छद्‌मवेशधारण; pretence, false show दिखावा, धोखा।

mass[1] *मैस n.* lump of matter पदार्थ पिंड; quantity मात्रा।

mass[2] *v.i.* to gather जमा करना, जमा होना।

massacre[1] *मै सॅ कॅ: n.* indiscriminate slaughter जनसंहार।

massacre[2] *v.t.* to slaughter indicriminately जनसंहार करना।

massage[1] *मै साज़ n.* rubbing of the body मालिश।

massage[2] *v.t.* to apply massage to (की) मालिश करना।

masseur *मै सॅ: n.* one who gives massage अंगमर्दक।

massive *मै सिव a.* large; heavy and solid विशाल, भारी व ठोस; impressive प्रभावशाली।

massy *मै सि a.* solid ठोस; heavy भारी।

mast *मास्ट n.* sail-pole मस्तूल।

master[1] *मास् टॅ: n.* teacher शिक्षक; owner स्वामी; husband पति; expert विशेषज्ञ; employer नियोक्ता; captain of ship कप्तान।

master[2] *v.t.* to overcome वशीभूत करना; to become expert in (की) विशेष योग्यता प्राप्त करना।

masterly *मास् टॅ: लि a.* like a master स्वामिज़नोचित; most excellent अद्वितीय।

masterpiece *मास् टॅः पीस n.* outstanding creation or work सर्वोत्कृष्ट कृति।

mastery *मास् अॅ रि n.* autharity प्रभुत्व; masterly skill and knowledge दक्षता।

masticate *मैस्-टि-केट v.t.* to chew चबाना।

masturbate *मैस्-टरः-बेट v.i.* to stimulate one's own genital organ हस्तमैथुन करना।

mat *मैट n.* a floor covering चटाई; a piece of material used to wipe shoes पायंदाज़।

matador *मै-टॅ-डौः n .* man who kills the bull in bullfights वृषहंता।

match[1] *मैच n.* pairing जोड़; contest प्रतियोगिता; an equal सदृश व्यक्ति; union by marriage विवाह-संबंध।

match[2] *v.i.* to be alike समान होना; to encounter मुक़ाबला करना; *v.t.* to be equal to (के) समान होना; to treat as equal समान मानना।

match[3] *n.* a short stick tipped with material that ignites when rubbed दियासलाई।

matchless *मैच् लिस a.* unique, having no equal अद्वितीय, बेजोड़।

mate[1] *मेट n.* companion साथी, मित्र; husband or wife जीवनसंगी; an officer on a ship सहायक पोताधिकारी; one of a pair of mated animals पशुओं के जोड़े में से एक।

mate[2] *v.t.* to come together for the purpose of having sexual intercourse जोड़ा खाना; *v.t.* to cause to unite for the purpose जोड़ा खिलाना।

mate[3] *n.* checkmate शहमात।

mate[4] *v.t.* to checkmate शहमात देना।

material[1] *मॅ टिअॅ रि अॅल a.* physical भौतिक; corporal दैहिक; essential तात्त्विक।

material[2] *n.* substance from which something can be made पदार्थ; facts, happenings तथ्य, घटना।

materialism *मॅ टिअॅ रि अॅ लिज़्म n.* theory that only material things exist भौतिकवाद; love of material things सांसारिकता, मायाजाल।

materialize *मॅ टिअॅ रि अॅ लॉइज़ v.t.* to cause to assume bodily form मूर्तरूप देना; to execute कार्यान्वित करना; *v.i.* to take a material form कार्यान्वित होना।

maternal *मॅ टॅः नॅल a.* of a mother मातृक; motherly मातृवत्।

maternity *मॅ टॅः नि टि n.* state or relation of mother मातृत्व।

mathematical *मै थि मै टि कॅल a.* pertaining to or done by mathematics गणितशास्त्रीय।

mathematician *मै थि मॅ टि शॅन n.* one versed in mathematics गणितशास्त्री।

mathematics *मै थि मै टिक्स n (pl. or sing)* science of magnitude and numbers गणित।

matinee *मै टि ने n.* public entertainment held in the afternoon अपराह्नकालीन लोकमनोरंजन।

matriarch *मेट्-रि-आःर्क n.* woman who dominates her family कुलमाता।

matricidal *मॅ-ट्रि-सॉइ-डॅल a.* pertaining to muder of one's own mother मातृघातक।

matricide *मे ट्रि सॉइड n.* murder of mother मातृवध; murderer of mother मातृहंता।

matriculate *मॅ ट्रि क्यु लेट v.t.* to be enrolled in a college or university महाविद्यालय अथवा विश्वविद्यालय में भरती होना।

matriculation *मॅ ट्रि क्यु ले शॅन n.* entrance examination प्रवेशिका–परीक्षा।

matrimonial *मै ट्रि मोन् यॅल a.* pertaining to marriage वैवाहिक।

matrimony *मै ट्रि मॅ नि n.* wedlock, marriage परिणय, विवाह।

matrix *मे-ट्रिक्स (pl. -es, -rices) n.* womb गर्भाशय; mould, that in which anything is embedded सांचा।

matron *मै ट्रॅन n.* married woman विवाहिता; one in-charge of nursing and domestic arrangements कार्याधीक्षिका।

matter[1] *मै टॅः n.* material पदार्थ; goods सामान; subject विषय; importance महत्व; affair मामला।

matter[2] *v.i.* to be of importance महत्वपूर्ण होना।

mattock *मै टॅक n.* a digging tool like a pickaxe गैंती, फावड़ा।

mattress *मै ट्रिस n.* bed made of stuffed bag गद्दा।

mature[1] *मॅ ट् यु अॅः a.* fully developed परिपक्व; grown up प्रौढ़; due for payment देय।

mature[2] *v.i.* to develop विकसित होना; to come to ripeness परिपक्व होना; *v.t.* to bring to full development विकसित करना।

maturity *मॅ ट्युअॅ रि टि n.* state of being mature परिपक्वता।

maudlin *मौड़-लिन a.* silly मूर्खतापूर्ण; sickly sentimental भावुकतापूर्ण।

maul[1] *मौल n.* heavy wooden hammer मूसल।

maul[2] *v.t.* to handle roughly (से) बुरा व्यवहार करना; to beat or injure पीटना, चोट पहुंचाना।

maulstick *मौल्-स्टिक n.* stick used by painters as a rest for the hand (चित्रकारी के समय) हाथ टेकने की छड़ी।

maunder *मौन्-डरः v.t.* to wander idly भटकते हुए घूमना-फिरना; to grumble, to mutter लापरवाही से बड़बड़ाना।

mausoleum *मौ सॅ लि अॅम n.* a magnificent tomb मक़बरा, समाधि।

mawkish *मौ किश a.* insipid रूखा; sentimental भावुक।

maxilla *मैक्-सि-लॅ (pl. -lae) n.* upper jaw bone जंभिका, ऊपर का जबड़ा।

maxim *मैक् सिम n.* proverb उक्ति, कहावत; rule of conduct नियम; general truth सूक्ति।

maximize *मैक् सि मॉइज़ v.t.* to raise to the highest degree उच्चतम सीमा तक बढ़ाना।

maximum[1] *मैक् सि मॅम a.* greatest अधिकतम, उच्चतम।

maximum[2] *n.* greatest quantity, degree etc. अधिकतम मात्रा, सीमा आदि।

May *मे n.* fifth month of the year मई मास।

may *मे* *v. aux.* expresses possibility, permission, opportunity, wish, request etc. संभावना, अनुमति, अवसर, इच्छा, प्रार्थना आदि की अभिव्यक्ति करता है।

mayor *मे˘ अॅः* *n.* the head of a corporation नगरप्रमुख।

maze *मेज़* *n.* an area of intricate pathways टेढ़े-मेढ़े मार्गोंवाला प्रदेश; labyrinth भूलभुलैया।

me *मी, मि* *pron.* first personal objective pronoun मुझको, मुझे।

mead *मीड* *n.* honey and water fermented and flavoured शहद की मदिरा (मद्यासव)।

meadow *मै˘ डो* *n.* pasture land चारागाह।

meagre *मी गॅः* *a.* scanty, thin थोड़ा, अल्प; insufficient अपर्याप्त।

meal *मील* *n.* ground grain आटा; food भोजन; occasion for eating भोजन का समय।

mealy *मी लि* *a.* meal-covered आटे से ढका; soft कोमल।

mean[1] *मीन* *a.* average माध्य, औसत; intermediate मझला; low in rank or birth नीच।

mean[2] *n.* an average मध्यमान; middle position मध्यस्थिति; *(pl.)* medium माध्यम, साधन।

mean[3] *v.t.* to intend अभिप्राय रखना; to purpose उद्देश्य रखना।

meander *मि ऐन् डॅः* *v.i.* to wind about चक्कर लगाना।

meaning *मी निङ्ग* *n.* sense intended अभिप्राय।

meaningful *मी-निङ्ग्-फुल* *a.* significant, purposeful अर्थपूर्ण, सार्थक।

meaningless *मी-निङ्ग्-लिस* *a.* senseless, without significance निरर्थक, निष्प्रयोजन।

meanness *मीन्-निस* *n.* lowleness नीचता, कमीनापन; baseness अधमता।

means *मीन्ज़* *n. (pl.)* resources साधन; money धन; medium माध्यम।

meanwhile *मीन् वॉइल –ह्वॉइल* *adv.* in the intervening time इसी बीच में।

measles *मी ज़ल्ज़* *n. sing.* a contagious disease in man खसरा।

measurable *मै˘ ज़ॅ रॅ ब्‌ल* *a.* that may be measured परिमेय।

measure[1] *मै˘ ज़ॅः* *n.* size नाप; unit इकाई; extent सीमा; plan योजना।

measure[2] *v.t.* to find length or quantity of नापना; *v.i.* to take measurements नाप लेना; to be of a specified measure नाप में कुछ होना।

measureless *मै˘ ज़ॅः लिस* *a.* boundless असीमित।

measurement *मै˘ ज़ॅः मॅन्ट* *n.* dimension नाप; act of measuring नपाई।

meat *मीट* *n.* the flesh of animals used as food मांस।

mechanic[1] *मि कै निक* *n.* skilled workman मिस्त्री।

mechanic[2] *a.* mechanicalयांत्रिक।

mechanical *मि कै नि कॅल* *a.* pertaining to machines यांत्रिक; machine like यंत्रवत्।

mechanics *मि कै निक्स* *n.* science of machinery यांत्रिकी।

mechanism *मै˘ कॅ निज़्म* *n.* way in which something works क्रियाविधि; system तंत्र।

medal *मैॅ ड्ल n.* piece of metal in the form of coin given as reward पदक।

medallist *मैॅ डॅ लिस्ट n.* one who has gained a medal पदक-प्राप्त व्यक्ति।

maddle *मैॅ ड्ल v.i.* to interfere unnecessarily बाधा डालना।

media *मी डि अॅ n. pl.* see medium

mediaeval, medieval *मैॅ डि ई वॅल a.* of Middle Ages मध्ययुग का।

median *मी-डि-अॅन a.* situated in the middle मध्यस्थ; passing through the middle मध्यगामी।

mediate *मी डि एट v.i.* to act as intermediary मध्यस्थता करना; *v.t.* to settle through mediation मध्यस्थता द्वारा निपटाना।

mediation *मी डि ए शन n.* act of mediating मध्यस्थता।

mediator *मी डि ए टॅः n.* one who mediates मध्यस्थ।

medical *मैॅ डि कॅल a.* relating to the art of physician आयुर्वैज्ञानिक।

medicament *मैॅ डि कॅ मॅन्ट, मैॅ डि– n.* औषध तत्व।

medicinal *मैॅ डि सि न्ल a.* having medical properties औषधीय, औषधगुणयुक्त।

medicine *मैॅड् सिन n.* substance used for treatment of disease औषधि; study of the science of healing चिकित्साशास्त्र।

medico *मैॅ डि को n.* medical practitioner चिकित्सक; student of medical science चिकित्सा विज्ञान का विद्यार्थी।

mediocre *मी डि ओ कॅः, मी डि ओ कॅः a.* ordinary सामान्य; average औसत दर्जे का।

mediocrity *मी डि औॅ क्रि टि n.* middling degree सामान्य अवस्था।

meditate *मैॅ डि टेट v.t.* to consider deeply (पर) विचार करना; *v.i.* to be occupied in contemplation मनन करना।

mediation *मै डि टे शॅन n.* deep thought ध्यान मनन।

meditative *मैॅ डि टॅ टिव, –टे– a.* given to meditation मननशील।

medium[1] *मी ड्यॅम n (pl.) media मी डि अॅ,- ms)* a middle state मध्यस्थिति; something intermediate in nature or degree मध्यवर्ती वस्तु; an intervening substance माध्यम; an agency, means साधन; means of communicating news संचार-साधन।

medium[2] *a.* about halfway between extremes मंझला, मझोला।

meek *मीक a.* mild, submissive विनम्र, सौम्य।

meet[1] *मीट n.* meeting बैठक।

meet[2] *v.t.* to come face to face with (से) मिलना; to satisfy पूरा करना; *v.i.* to come together भेंट होना।

meeting *मी टिङ्ग n.* an assembly, a gathering सभा; coming together मुलाक़ात, भेंट।

megalith *मैॅ-गॅ-लिथ n.* huge stone महा पाषाण।

megalithic *मैॅ-गॅ-लि-थिक a.* of huge stone महापाषाणीय; belonging to Stone Age पाषाणयुगीन।

megaphone *मैॅ गॅ फ़ोन n.* device for increasing volume of sound ध्वनिप्रवर्धी।

melancholia *मैॅ लॅन् को ल्यॅ n.*

morbid melancholy विषाद-रोग।

melancholic *मै ॅ लॅन् कौ ॅ लिक a.* disordered by melancholy विषादग्रस्त।

melancholy[1] *मै ॅ लॅन् कौ ॅ लि n.* dejection खिन्नता, अवसाद।

melancholy[2] *a.* sad खिन्न, दुखी; low-spirited निराश; causing sadness दुःखद।

melee *मै ॅ-ले n.* confused conflict हंगामा; turmoil, stampede भगदड़।

meliorate *मी-लि-ऑ-रेट v.t.* to make better सुधारना, संवारना; *v.i.* to grow better सुधरना, अच्छा बनना।

mellow *मै ॅ लो a.* soft मृदु; well matured परिपक्व, समझदार।

melodious *मि लो ड्यॅस a.* sweet-sounding सुरीला।

melodrama *मै ॅ लो ड्रा मॅ n.* an exciting and sensational play उत्तेजक व सनसनीखेज़ नाटक; over dramatic behaviour अतिनाटकीय व्यवहार।

melodramatic *मै ॅ लो ॅ ड्रॅ मै टिक a.* pertaining to melodrama अतिनाटकीय; sensational सनसनीखेज़; emotional भावुकतापूर्ण।

melody *मै ॅ लॅ डि n.* tune लय, राग; sweetness मधुरता।

melon *मै ॅ लॅन n.* juicy guard तरबूज़।

melt *मै ॅल्ट v.i.* to become liquid from solid पिघलना, गलना; *v.t.* to cause to melt गलाना, पिघलाना।

member *मैमॅ् बॅः n.* any of the individuals making up a body or society सदस्य; limb अंग, अवयव।

membership *मैमॅ् बॅः शिप n.* state of being a member सदस्यता; number of members सदस्य-संख्या।

membrane *मै ॅम्-ब्रेन n.* thin flexible solid sheet or film त्वक, झिल्ली।

memento *मि मैनॅ् टो n.* something kept or given as a reminder स्मृतिचिह्न।

memo *मै ॅ मो n.* short for 'memorandum'.

memoir *मै ॅम् वाः n.* short life history संक्षिप्त जीवनवृत्त; record of events इतिहास; *(pl.)* a person's written account of his own life आत्मचरित।

memorable *मै ॅ मॅ रॅ ब्ल a.* deserving to be remembered स्मरणीय; remarkable विलक्षण।

memorandum *मै ॅ मॅ रैन् डॅम n. (pl. da, -dums)* something to be remembered; स्मरण-पत्र; representation ज्ञापन-पत्र।

memorial[1] *मॅ मौ रि ॲल n.* monument स्मारक।

memorial[2] *a.* pertaining to memory स्मरण-विषयक।

memory *मै ॅ मॅ रि n.* remembrance स्मृति; faculty of remembering; स्मरण-शक्ति; commemoration यादगार।

menace[1] *मै ॅ नॅस n,* threat धमकी; apprehension भीति; curse अभिशाप।

menace[2] *v.t.* to threaten धमकी देना।

mend *मैन्ड v.t.* to repair मरम्मत करना; to correct ठीक करना; to improve सुधारना।

mendacious *मै ॅन्-डे-शॅस a.* lying, untruthful मिथ्यावादी।

menial[1] *मी न्यॅल, मी नि ॲल a.* degrading तुच्छ; suitable for domestic servants दासोचित।

menial[2] *n.* domestic servant सेवक।

meningitis *मै ॅ-निन्-जॉइ-टिस n.* inflammation of the membranes of the brain गर्दन-तोड़ बुखार, मस्तिष्कावरणशोथ।

menopause *मै ॅ-नॅ-पौज़ n.* ending of menstruation रजोनिवृत्ति।

menses *मैनॅ् सि:ज़ n. pl.* monthly discharge from the uterus ऋतुस्राव।

menstrual *मैनॅ् स्ट्रू ॲल a.* of the menses ऋतुस्राव विषयक।

menstruation *मैन् स्ट्रू ए शॅन n.* periodic discharge from the uterus ऋतुस्राव।

mental *मैनॅ् ट्‌ल a.* pertaining to mind मानसिक; done in the mind मनोगत।

mentality *मैनॅ् टै लि टि n.* way of thinking मनोवृत्ति; mental power बौद्धिक शक्ति।

mention[1] *मैनॅ् शॅन n.* reference उल्लेख।

mention[2] *v.t.* to make mention of चर्चा करना।

mentor *मैनॅ् टॅ: n.* counsellor सलाहकार।

menu *मै ॅ न्यू n.* list of dishes भोज्य-सूची।

mercantile *मॅ: कॅन् टॉइल a.* pertaining to merchants वाणिज्य–संबंधी; commercial व्यापारिक।

mercenary *मॅ: सॅ नॅ रि a.* working only for money धनार्थी; influenced by greed लालची।

mercerise *मॅ: सॅ रॉइज़ v.t.* to give lustre (to cotton fabrics) by treating with chemicals (सूती कपड़ों को) रसायनों-द्वारा चमकीला बनाना।

merchandise *मॅ: चॅन् डॉइज़ n.* goods bought and sold माल, सौदा।

merchant *मॅ: चॅन्ट n.* trader व्यापारी।

merciful *मॅ: सि फुल a.* kind, full of mercy दयालु, कृपालु।

merciless *मॅ: सि लिस* pitiless, cruel क्रूर, निष्ठुर।

mercurial *मॅ:क्युअॅ-रि-ॲल a.* containing mercury पारदमय; alert, clever चुस्त, चालाक; unsteady चंचल, अस्थिर।

mercury *मॅ: क्यु रि n.* silvery metallic element पारद; (cap.) the planet nearest the sun बुद्ध।

mercy *मॅ: सि n.* clemency दया; compassion अनुकंपा।

mere *मिअॅ: a.* only केवल; not more than मात्र।

merge *मॅ:ज v.t.* to absorb मिला लेना; *v.i.* to be absorbed मिल जाना।

merger *मॅ: जॅ: n.* absorption विलयन; joining together एकीकरण।

meridian *मॅ-रि-डि-ॲन a.* of or at midday दोपहरी का; at culmination or highest point उत्तम सर्वोच्च।

merit[1] *मैॅ रिट n.* good quality सद्‌गुण; worth योग्यता; desert अर्हता।

merit[2] *v.t.* to deserve के योग्य होना।

meritorious *मै ॅ रि टौ रि ॲस a.* qualified गुणी; worthy योग्य; praiseworthy प्रशंसनीय।

mermaid *मॅ: मेड n.* a woman with a fish's tail in place of legs जलपरी।

merman *मॅः मेन n.* man with a fish's tail in place of legs जलपुरुष।

merriment *मैˇ रि मॅन्ट n.* joy आनंद आमोद-प्रमोद।

merry *मैˇ रि a* joyous, cheerful सानंद, प्रसन्न।

mesh[1] *मैˇश n.* net, network जाली; one of the open spaces in a net जाल या जाली का छिद्र।

mesh[2] *v.t.* to catch in a mesh जाल में पकड़ना या फंसाना।

mesmerism *मैˇज़् मॅ रिज़्म n.* hypnotism सम्मोहन।

mesmerize *मैˇज़् मॅ रॉइज़ v.t.* to hypnotize सम्मोहित करना; to hold spell-bound मंत्रमुग्ध करना।

mess[1] *मैˇस n.* hotel भोजनालय; confusion गड़बड़झाला; trouble परेशानी; dirt गंदगी।

mess[2] *v.i.* to eat meals भोजन करना; *v.t.* to spoil बिगाड़ देना; to put into disorder अस्त-व्यस्त करना।

message *मैˇ सिज n.* errand समाचार, सूचना; teaching संदेश।

messenger *मैˇसिन् जॅः n.* message-bearer संदेशवाहक।

messiah *मि सॉइ अॅ n.* Christ ईसा मसीह; Saviour मोक्षदाता, रक्षक।

Messrs *मैˇ-सॅःज n.* (abbrev. of messieurs) used as the pl. of Mr. सर्वश्री।

metabolism *मैˇ टॅ बॅ लिज़्म n.* chemical process of living body शरीर की रासायनिक प्रक्रिया।

metal *मैˇ ट्ल n.* opaque elementary substance धातु; broken stone for making roads रोड़ी, गिट्टी।

metallic *मि टै लिक a.* consisting to metal धातुमय; like metal धातुवत्।

metallurgy *मैˇ टै लॅः जि n.* science applied to metals (रसा.) धातुकर्म विज्ञान।

metamorphosis *मैˇ टॅ मौः फ़ॅ सिस n.* transformation रूपांतरण।

metaphor *मैˇ टॅ फ़ॅः n.* a figure of speech based on comparison रूपक।

metaphysical *मैˇ टॅ फ़ि ज़ि कॅल a.* pertaining to metaphysics तात्विक; abtruse गूढ़, सूक्ष्म।

metaphysics *मैˇटॅ फ़ि ज़िक्स n. sing.* branch of philosophy concerned with nature of existence, truth and knowledge तत्वमीमांसा।

mete मीट *v.t.* to apportion बांटना; to measure नापना।

meteor *मी ट्यॅः n.* shooting star उल्का।

meteoric *मी-टि-औˇ-रिक a.* of the atmosphere मौसम-संबंधी; swift तीव्र; brilliant चमकीला।

meteorologist *मी-टि-अॅ-रौˇ-लॅ-जिस्ट n.* one who studies weather and climate ऋतुविज्ञानी।

meteorology *मी ट्यॅ रौˇ लॅ जि n.* study of weather and climate मौसम विज्ञान।

meter *मी टॅः n.* apparatus for measuring मापक।

method *मैˇ थॅड n.* mode ढंग, विधि; manner कार्यविधि; procedure पद्धति।

methodical *मि थौˇ डि कॅल a.* systematic सुव्यवस्थित।

metre *मी टॅ:* *n.* unit of length in the metric system मीटर; verse rhythm छंद।
metric *मै ॅट् रिक* *a.* pertaining to metre मीटर-संबंधी।
metrical *मैटॅ् रि कॅल* *a.* of metre छंद संबंधी; composed in verse छंदोबद्ध; connected with measurement मापीय।
metropolis *मिट्रो ॅ पॅ लिस* *n.* capital of a country राजधानी।
metropolitan[1] *मै ॅ ट्रो पौ लि टॅन* *a.* of a metropolis राजधानी का अथवा उससे संबंधित।
metropolitan[2] *n.* person living in a metropolis राजधानी-निवासी।
mettle *मै ॅ-ट्ल* *n.* spirit, courage उत्साह, दिलेरी; temperament स्वभाव की विशेषता।
mettlesome *मै ॅ-ट्ल्-सॅम* *a.* high spirited तेजस्वी, साहसी।
mew[1] *म्यू* *v.i.* to cry as a cat म्याऊँ-म्याऊँ करना।
mew[2] *n.* cat's cry म्याऊँ।
mezzanine *मै ॅ- ज़ॅ- नीन* *n.* room below the stage (प्रेक्षागृह में) रंगभूमि का तहख़ाना।
mica *मॉइ कॅ* *n.* a glittering scaly metal अभ्रक।
microfilm *मॉइ-क्रॅ-फ़िल्म* *n.* photographic film for preserving a microscopic record of a document सूक्ष्म, फ़िल्म, अणुचित्र।
micrology *माइ-क्रौ ॅ-लॅ-जि* *n.* study of microscopic objects सूक्ष्म-पदार्थ-विज्ञान, सूक्ष्मविज्ञान।
micrometer *मॉइ-क्रौ ॅ-मि-टर:* *n.* instrument for measuring minute distances or angles सूक्ष्ममापी।
microphone *मॉ इ क्रॅ फ़ोन* *n.* sound amplifier ध्वनिविस्तारक।
microscope *मॉइ क्रॅ स्कोप* *n.* instrument for magnifying minute objects सूक्ष्मदर्शी यंत्र।
microscopic *मॉइ क्रॅस् कौ ॅ पिक* *a.* very minute अति सूक्ष्म।
microwave *मॉइ-क्रॅ-वेव* *n.* a very short wavelength सूक्ष्म तरंग।
mid *मिड* *a.* middle मध्यवर्ती।
midday *मिड् डे* *n.* noon मध्याह्न।
middle[1] *मि ड्ल* *a.* intermediate मध्यवर्ती।
middle[2] *n.* middle position मध्यस्थिति; waist कमर।
middleman *मि ड्ल् मैन* *n.* intermediary बिचौलिया।
middling *मिड्-लिङ्ग* *a.* mediocre मध्यम श्रेणी का; moderate साधारण।
midget *मि-जिट* *n.* a small person वामन पुरुष; something very small लघु वस्तु।
midland *मिड्-लैन्ड* *n.* interior of the country; central part मध्यदेश।
midnight *मिड् नॉइट* *n.* 12 o' clock at night अर्द्धरात्रि।
mid-off *मिड्-औ ॅफ़* *n.* fielder near the bowler on the 'off' side (क्रिकेट) बल्लेबाज़ के आधे दाएं खड़ा खिलाड़ी।
mid-on *मिड्-औ ॅन* *n.* fielder near the bowler on the 'on' side (क्रिकेट) बल्लेबाज़ के आधे बाएं खड़ा खिलाड़ी।
midriff *मिड्-रिफ़* *n.* the part of a woman's garment that fits over the diaphragm मध्यपट।
midst *मिड्स्ट* *n.* middle मध्य।

midsummer *मिड़ स मॅः* *n.* middle of summer मध्यग्रीष्म ऋतु।

midwife *मिड़ वॉइफ़* *n.* woman who assists in child birth दाई, धात्री।

might *मॉइट* *n.* strength, power पराक्रम, शक्ति।

mighty *मॉइ टि* powerful शक्तिशाली; brave, बहादुर; very great अति महान।

migraine *मी ग्रेन* *n.* severe headache on one side आधासीसी।

migrant *मॉइ-ग्रॅन्ट* *n.* one who migrates प्रवासी।

migrate *मॉइ ग्रेट* *v.i.* to change one's abode to another country प्रव्रजन करना।

migration *मॉ इ ग्रे शॅन* *n.* state or act of migrating प्रव्रजन।

mike *मॉइक* *n.* see microphone.

milch *मिल्च* *a.* milk-giving दुधारू।

mild *मॉइल्ड* *a.* gentle शांत; soft हल्का; calm शांत।

mildew *मिल्-ड़्यू* *n.* disease of plants caused by the growth of minute fungi चेंपा, काई, फफूंदी।

mile *मॉइल* *n.* measure of distance (1760 yards) मील।

mileage *मॉइ लीज* *n.* allowance per mile प्रतिमील भत्ता; miles travelled यात्रा की हुई मीलें; distance in miles मीलों में दूरी।

milestone *मॉइल्-स्टोन* *n.* a stone showing distnace in miles मील का पत्थर; an important stage or event महत्वपूर्ण स्थिति, घटना आदि।

milieu *मी-ल्यू* *n.* environment वातावरण; surrounding परिवेश।

militant[1] *मि लि टॅन्ट* *a.* bellingerant युद्धप्रिय; using violence हिंसाकारी।

militant[2] *n.* a person disposed to fight युद्धकर्त्ता।

military[1] *मि लि टॅ रि* *a.* pertaining to soldiers सैन्य; warlike सामरिक।

military[2] *n.* army सेना।

militate *मि लि टेट* *v.i.* to fight युद्ध करना।

militia *मि लि शॅ* *n.* military force of citizens for home service नागरिक सेना।

milk[1] *मिल्क* *n.* white fluid with which mammals feed their young दूध।

milk[2] *v.t.* to draw milk from दुहना; *v.i.* to yield milk दूध देना, दुधारू होना।

milky *मिल् कि* *a.* like milk दूधिया।

mill[1] *मिल* *n.* machine for grinding चक्की।

mill[2] *v.t.* to pass through a mill पीसना।

millennium *मि लै ˘ नि अॅम* *n.* a period of a thousand years सहस्राब्दि; period of peace and happiness स्वर्ण युग।

miller *मि लॅः* *n.* owner of a mill चक्कीवाला, आटा पीसनेवाला।

millet *मि-लिट* *n.* a well-known food grain बाजरा।

milliner[1] *मि-लि-नरः* *n.* one who makes or sells women's headgear, trimmings etc. नारी-वस्त्र-निर्माता।

milliner[2] *मि लि नॅः* *n.* one who makes head-dresses, hats etc. for females स्त्रियों के शिरोवस्त्रों का निर्माता।

millinery *मि नि नॅ रि* *n.* occupation of a milliner महिला वस्त्र-निर्माण।

million *मिल् यॅन n.* a thousand thousand दस लाख (1,000,000)।

millionaire *मिल् यॅ ने ॅ अँ: n.* very rich person धनपति।

millipede *मि-लि-पीड n.* a worm with many legs बहुपादधारी कीट।

mime¹ *मॉइम n.* play without dialogue संवादरहित नाटक; farcical play of real life प्रहसन; a buffoon विदूषक, ठिठोलिया।

mime² *v.i.* to act as a mime स्वांग भरना।

mimesis *मि-मै ॅ-सिस n.* imitation or representation in art अनुकरण, निकटतम सादृश्य।

mimic¹ *मि मिक a.* imitative अनुकरणात्मक।

mimic² *n.* one who imitates नक़लची, नक़्क़ाल।

mimic³ *v.t. (-cked, -cking)* to imitate (की) नकल उतारना।

mimicry *मि मिक् रि n.* imitation (often for sport or ridicule) नक़ल।

minaret *मि नॅ रै ॅट n.* tall, slender tower of a mosque मीनार।

mince *मिन्स v.t.* to cut or chop (meat) into very small pieces (मांस) काटना; to soften or moderate (words) बात को हल्का या कम करके बताना।

mind¹ *मॉइन्ड n.* memory स्मृति; remembrance स्मरण; thought, idea विचार; opinion मत; intention इरादा; purpose उद्देश्य; intellect बुद्धि; understanding समझ; attention ध्यान।

mind² *v.t.* to take offence at (का) बुरा मानना; to care for (की) चिंता करना; to attend to (पर) ध्यान देना; to be cautious about के बारे में सतर्क रहना, to be concerned about के विषय में चिंतित रहना; *v.i.* to be careful सावधान या सतर्क रहना।

mindful *मॉइन्ड् फुल a.* careful सावधान।

mindless *मॉइन्ड्-लिस a.* stupid मूर्ख, मंदबुद्धि; unmindful लापरवाह।

mine¹ *मॉइन pron.* belonging to me मेरा।

mine² *n.* deep hole from which minerals are dug out खान; hidden deposit of explosive बारूदी सुरंग।

miner *मॉइ नॅ: n.* one who works in a mine खनिक।

mineral¹ *मि नॅ रॅल n.* matter got by mining खनिज।

mineral² *a.* of minerals खनिज-संबंधी।

mineralogist *मि नॅ रॅ लॅ जिस्ट n.* one who is versed in the science of minerals खनिज-विज्ञानी।

mineralogy *मि नॅ रॅ लॅ जि n.* science of the properties of mineral substances खनिज शास्त्र।

mingle *मिङ् ग्ल v.t.* to mix मिलाना; *v.i.* to be mixed मिल जाना।

miniature¹ *मि न्यॅ चॅ:, मि नि अँ चॅ: n.* small picture, book or model सूक्ष्म चित्र, पुस्तक या मूर्ति।

miniature² *a.* minute लघु, छोटा।

minim *मि-निम n.* (music) the shortest note अर्द्धस्वर; short downstroke in handwriting अक्षरों की नीचे निकली नोक, बिंदुक; least part अल्पतम भाग।

minimal *मि नि मॅल* *a.* least अल्पतम।

minimize *मि नि मॉइज़* *v.t.* to reduce to the minimum घटाना, कम करना।

minimum[1] *मि नि मॅम* *n. (pl. -ms, minima)* smallest amount न्यूनतम मात्रा।

minimum[2] *a.* least possible अल्पतम।

minion *मिन् यॅन* *n.* favourite कृपापात्र; servile follower खुशामदी टट्टू।

minister[1] *मि निस् टॅः* *n.* departmental administrator in a state मंत्री।

minister[2] *v.i.* to give care or aid ध्यान या सहायता देना; to give service सेवा करना।

ministrant *मि-निस्-ट्रॅन्ट* *a.* administering सेवारत; attendant सेवक।

ministry *मि निस् ट्रि* *n.* a body of ministers मंत्रिमंडल; act of ministering मंत्रित्व।

mink *मिङ्क* *n.* small animal of the weasel kind ऊदबिलाव जाति का एक जंतु।

minor[1] *मॉइ नॅः* *a.* lesser छोटा, लघु; not risky or serious हल्का; under age नाबालिग़, अवयस्क।

minor[2] *n.* person under the age of 18 अवयस्क व्यक्ति।

minority *मॉइ नौ˘ रि टि* *n.* minor's state अवयस्कता; lesser number अल्प संख्या; a class or section numbering less than the one in majority अल्पसंख्यक।

minster *मिन्-स्टॅः* *n.* an abbey church आश्रम-गिरजा।

mint[1] *मिन्ट* *n.* an aromatic plant पुदीना।

mint[2] *n.* place where money is coined टकसाल।

mint[3] *v.t.* to coin (money) (सिक्के) ढालना।

minus[1] *मॉइ नॅस* *prep.* without के बिना।

minus[2] *a.* indicating subtraction ऋणात्मक; negative नकारात्मक।

minus[3] *n.* the sign of subtraction ऋण का चिह्न (–)।

minuscule *मि-नॅस्-क्यूल* *a.* small cursive script अंग्रेज़ी वर्णमाला के छोटे अक्षर।

minute[1] *मॉइ न्यूट* *a.* very small बहुत छोटा।

minute[2] *मि निट* *n.* 60th part of an hour मिनट; *(pl.)* record of proceedings of a meeting विवरण।

minutely *मॉइ न्यूट् लि* *adv.* closely, carefully सूक्ष्मता से, ध्यानपूर्वक; attending to small details बारीकी से।

minx *मिङ्क्स* *n.* a pert young girl कुलच्छनी; jade जिद्दी एवं हठी लड़की।

miracle *मि रॅ क्ल* *n.* marvel चमत्कार; supernatural event अलौकिक घटना।

miraculous *मि रै क्यु लॅस* *a.* marvellous चमत्कारिक; surprising आश्चर्यजनक।

mirage *मि राज़* *n.* deceptive sight of water in a desert मृगमरीचिका; illusion भ्रम।

mire[1] *मॉइअॅः* *n.* swampy ground दलदल; mud कीचड़।

mire[2] *v.t.* to cause to stick in mire दलदल में फंसाना; to soil with mud सानना, कीचड़ लगाना; *v.i.* to sink in mire कीचड़ या दलदल में पड़ना।

mirror[1] *मि रॅः n.* looking glass दर्पण।
mirror[2] *v.t.* to reflect प्रतिबिंबित करना।
mirth *मॅःथ n.* joy, merriment आनंद, आमोद-प्रमोद।
mirthful *मॅःथ् फुल a.* full of mirth आनंदपूर्ण।
misadventure *मिस् अॅड् वैन्ँ चॅः n.* mishap दुर्घटना; ill-luck दुर्भाग्य।
misalliance *मिस्-अॅ-लॉइ-अॅन्स n.* unsuitable alliance बेमेल संबंध; marriage with one of lower rank बेमल विवाह।
misanthrope *मिस् अॅन् थ्रोप n.* hater of mankind मानवद्वेषी।
misapplication *मिस्-ऐप-लि-के-शॅन n.* misuse अनुचित प्रयोग, दुरुपयोग।
misapprehend *मिस्-ऐ-प्रि-हैन्ड v.t.* to take or understand in a wrong sense (का) मिथ्याबोध करना, उलटा या ग़लत समझना।
misapprehension *मिस्-अॅ-प्रि-हैॅन्-शॅन n.* misunderstanding मिथ्या-बोध, भ्रम।
misappropriate *मिस् अॅ प्रो प्रि एट v.t.* to take and use wrongfully दुरुपयोग करना; to embezzle ग़बन करना।
misappropriation *मिस् अॅ प्रो प्रि ए शॅन n.* act of misappropriating दुरुपयोग; embezzlement ग़बन।
misbehave *मिस् बि हेव v.i.* to behave ill बुरा व्यवहार करना।
misbehaviour *मिस् बि हेव् यॅः n.* bad behaviour, misconduct बुरा व्यवहार।
misbelief *मिस्-बि-लीफ़ n.* belief in false doctrine भ्रांत धारणा।
miscalculate *मिस् कैल् क्यु लेट v.t.* to reckon (amounts etc.) wrongly ग़लत गणना करना।
miscalculation *मिस् कैल् क्यु ले शॅन n.* erroneous calculation अशुद्ध गणना।
miscall *मिस-कौल v.t.* to call by a wrong name ग़लत या अशुद्व नाम से पुकारना।
miscarriage *मिस् कै रिज n.* abortion गर्भपात; failure असफलता, विफलता।
miscarry *मिस् कै रि v.i.* (of plan, etc.) to fail (योजना आदि का) विफल होना; (of letters etc.) not to reach the right destination अपवाहित होना; to bring forth young prematurely गर्भपात होना।
miscellaneous *मि सि लेन् यॅस a.* mixed मिश्रित; diverse कई तरह का, विविध।
miscellany *मि सै लॅ नि, मि सि– n.* mixture of various kinds, medley विविधतापूर्ण संग्रह।
mischance *मिस् चान्स n.* bad luck दुर्भाग्य।
mischief *मिस् चिफ़ n.* misconduct दुर्व्यवहार, शरारत; harm हानि; hurt चोट।
mischievous *मिस् चि वॅस a.* full of pranks शरारतपूर्ण; having harmful effect हानिप्रद।
misconceive *मिस्-कॅन्-सीव v.t.* to conceive wrongly मिथ्या अर्थ लगाना; to mistake ग़लत समझना।
misconception *मिस् कॅन् सैप् शॅन n.* wrong idea ग़लत धारणा।
misconduct *मिस् कौन्ँ डॅक्ट n.* misbehaviour दुराचरण।
misconstrue *मिस्-कॅन्-स्ट्रू v.t.* to

interpret wrongly (का) अर्थ ठीक न लगाना, ग़लत समझना।

miscreant *मिस् क्रि ॲन्ट n.* a scoundrel, a rascal धूर्त, बदमाश।

misdeed *मिस् डीड n.* evil deed दुष्कर्म।

misdemeanour *मिस-डि-मी-नरः n.* misdeed, bad conduct दुष्कर्म, दुराचरण; petty crime सामान्य अपराध।

misdirect *मिस् डि रैक्ट v.t.* to give the wrong information गुमराह करना।

misdirection *मिस् डि रैक् शॅन n.* wrong direction बहकावा, अपनिदेशन।

miser *मॉइ जॅः n.* money-hoarder कंजूस।

miserable *मि ज़ॅ रॅ ब्ल a.* very unhappy अति दुःखपूर्ण; causing misery दुःखदायी; worthless निकम्मा; squalid घिनौना।

miserly *मॉइ-ज़ॅः-लि a.* niggardly कृपणतापूर्ण।

misery *मि ज़ॅ रि n.* distress मुसीबत; great unhappiness तकलीफ़, विपत्ति; poverty कंगाली।

misfire *मिस् फ़ॉइॲः v.i.* to (of a gun) to fail to go off (बंदूक) न दग़ना; (of a motor engine) to fail to ignite (इंजन) चालू न होना।

misfit *मिस् फ़िट n.* an improper thing or person अनुपयुक्त वस्तु या आदमी।

misfortune *मिस् फ़ौ ँः चॅन n.* ill-luck दुर्भाग्य।

misgive *मिस्-गिव (-gave, -given) v.t.* to suggest apprehensions, to fill with forebodings अविश्वास करना; *v.i.* to have apprehensive forebodings अशुभ की आशंका करना।

misgiving *मिस् गि विङ्ग n.* doubt संदेह।

misguide *मिस् गॉइड v.t.* to mislead गुमराह करना।

mishap *मिस् हैप n.* minor accident दुर्घटना।

misjudge *मिस् जज v.t.* to judge wrongly ग़लत निर्णय करना।

mislead *मिस लीड v.t.* to lead into error बहकाना; to lead astray भटका देना; to give false information to ग़लत सूचना देना।

mismanagement *मिस् मै निज् मॅन्ट n.* bad management कुप्रबंध।

mismatch *मिस्-मैच v.t.* to match unsuitably अनुपयुक्त ढंग से जोड़े में रखना।

misnomer *मिस् नो मॅः n.* wrong name मिथ्या नाम।

misplace *मिस् प्लेस v.t.* to put in a wrong place ग़लत जगह रखना।

misprint[1] *मिस् प्रिन्ट n.* mistake in printing छापे की भूल।

misprint[2] *v.t.* to print wrongly ग़लत छापना।

misrepresent *मिस् रैप् रि ज़ैन्ट v.t.* to give a false account of (का) अयथार्थ विवरण देना।

misrule *मिस् रुल n.* bad government कुशासन।

miss[1] *मिस n.* unmarried girl कुमारी।

miss[2] *v.t.* to fail to hit चूकना; to lose खोना; to omit छोड़ना।

missile *मि सॉइल n.* a weapon that is thrown or shot प्रक्षेपास्त्र।

mission *मि शॅन n.* special work विशेष कार्य; party of persons sent for special work विशेष कार्यदल; political message राजनीतिक संदेश।

missionary *मि शॅ नॅ रि n.* religious instructor धर्म प्रचारक।

missis, missus *मि-सिस्, -सिज़ n.* mistress of the house स्वामिनी, मालकिन; wife पत्नी।

missive *मि-सिव n.* written message लिखित संदेश।

mist *मिस्ट n.* water vapour in fine drops कुहासा, कुहरा।

mistake[1] *मिस् टेक n.* an error भूल।

mistake[2] *v.t.* to understand or do wrongly ग़लत समझना या करना।

mister *मिस् टॅः n.* title of courtesy to man श्री, श्रीमान, महोदय।

mistletoe *मि-स्ल्-टो n.* an evergreen shrubby plant आकाश बेल, अमर बेल।

mistreat *मिस्-ट्रीट v.t.* to treat ill (से) दुर्व्यवहार करना।

mistress *मिस् ट्रिस n.* female head of a house गृहस्वामिनी; lady teacher शिक्षिका; beloved प्रेयसि; woman living with a man as a wife उपपत्नी, रखैल।

mistrust[1] *मिस् ट्रस्ट n.* disbelief अविश्वास।

mistrust[2] *v.t.* to disbelieve अविश्वास करना।

misty *मिस् टि a.* full of mist कुहासे वाला।

misunderstand *मिस् ऑन् डॅः स्टैन्ड v.t.* to understand wrongly ग़लत समझना।

misunderstanding *मिस् ऑन् डॅः स्टैन् डिङ्ग n.* mistaken idea ग़लतफ़हमी।

misuse[1] *मिस् यूस n.* improper use or treatment दुरुपयोग।

misuse[2] *मिस् यूज़ v.t.* to use badly (का) दुरुपयोग करना।

mite[1] *मॉइट n.* dot, iota कण; small amount अल्प धन, अल्प मात्रा; a small thing छोटी वस्तु; small child शिशु।

mite[2] *n.* a tick, cattle-louse किलनी, चिचड़ी।

mithridate *मिथ्-रि-डेट n.* an antidote to poison विषमार औषधि, ज़हर मोहरा।

mitigate *मि टि गेट v.t.* to lessen कम करना।

mitigation *मि टि गे शॅन n.* act of mitigating अल्पीकरण।

mitre **मॉइ-टॅः** *n.* bishop's headdress पादरी का शिरोवस्त्र, किरीट।

mitten *मि-ट्न n.* glove without a separate cover for each finger बिना उंगलियों का दस्ताना; glove for the hand and wrist हाथ व कलाई का दस्ताना; a bosing glove मुक्केबाज़ी का दस्ताना।

mix *मिक्स v.i. & v.t.* to mingle मिलना, मिलाना।

mixture *मिक्स् चॅः n.* mixed product मिश्रित वस्तु; act of mixing मिश्रण।

moan[1] *मोन v.i.* to lament विलाप करना।

moan[2] *n.* a lament विलाप; low sound of pain कराह।

moat[1] *मोट n.* a deep trench खंदक, परिखा, खाई।

moat[2] *v.t.* to surround with a moat के चारों ओर खाई खोदना।

mob[1] मौ˘ब *n.* disorderly crowd भीड़; the common people जनसाधारण।

mob[2] *(-bb-) v.t.* to crowd round के चारों ओर भीड़ लगाना।

mobile मो बॉइल, –बिल *a.* movable चल, गतिशील; often changing परिवर्तनशील।

mobility मो ˘ बि लि टि *n.* being mobile गतिशीलता।

mobilize मो बि लॉइज़ *v.t.* to collect (troops) for active service युद्ध के लिए (सेना) एकत्रित करना; to organise संगठित करना; *v.i.* to become organised संगठित होना।

mock[1] मौकॅ *v.i.* to scoff (at) हंसी उड़ाना; *v.t.* to ridicule उपहास करना।

mock[2] *a.* sham, imitation दिखावटी, कृत्रिम।

mockery मौ˘ कॅ रि *n.* ridicule मज़ाक़; travesty स्वांग, दिखावा।

modality मो-डै-लि-टि *n.* method रीति; terms, style वृत्तित्व; quality of being limited by a condition निश्चयमात्रा।

mode मोड *n.* method विधि; prevailing fashion चालू रिवाज।

model[1] मौ ˘ ड्ल *n.* pattern नमूना; ideal आदर्श।

model[2] *(-ll-) v.t.* to mould गढ़ना, ढालना; to make a model of का नमूना बनाना।

moderate[1] मौ ˘ डॅ रिट *a.* temperate मध्यम; limited सीमित; mild नरम।

moderate[2] मौ ˘ डॅ रेट *v.t.* to pacify शांत करना; to lessen कम करना।

moderation मौ˘ डॅ रे शॅन *n.* quality of being moderate संयम, संतुलन; freedom from excess अतिहीनता।

modern मौ ˘ डॅःन *a.* new नया; of the present times आधुनिक।

modernity मौ ˘ डॅः नि टि *n.* being modern आधुनिकता।

modernize मौ ˘ डॅः नॉइज़ *v.t.* to adapt to modern ideas, style or language आधुनिकीकरण करना।

modest मौ˘ डिस्ट *a.* mild नरम; bashful शर्मीला; moderate मामूली, मर्यादित।

modesty मौ˘ डिस् टि *n.* politeness नरमी; shyness संकोच।

modicum मौ-डि-कॅम *n.* small quantity अल्प परिमाण।

modification मौ ˘ डि फ़ि के शॅन *n.* change परिवर्तन।

modify मौ ˘ डि फ़ॉइ *v.t.* to change बदलना; to make less severe (की) कठोरता कम करना; *(gram.)* to qualify the sense of के अर्थ को संयत करना।

modulate मौ ˘ ड्यु लेट *v.t.* to adjust ठीक करना; to regulate व्यवस्थित करना।

moil मौ˘इल *v.i.* to toil, to drudge कठोर परिश्रम करना।

moist मौ˘ इस्ट *a.* damp नम, गीला।

moisten मौ ˘इ स्न *v.t.* to make moist नम करना; *v.i.* to become moist नम होना।

moisture मौ˘ इस् चॅः *n.* dampness नमी, गीलापन।

molar[1] मो लॅः *n.* a grinding tooth दाढ़।

molar[2] *a.* relating to the grinding teeth दाढ़-विषयक।

molasses मॅ लै सिज़ *n.* treacle शीरा।

mole *मोल* *n.* a small burrowing animal छछूंदर; small, dark spot on the skin तिल।

molecular *मौ ˘-लै ˘-क्यु-लरः* *a.* pertaining to smallest particle, atomic आणविक, अणुक।

molecule *मौ ˘-लि-क्यूल* *n.* smallest particle of any substance अणु।

molest *मौ˘ लस्ट, मॅ–* *v.t.* to vex तंग, करना; छेड़खानी करना।

molestation *मौ˘ ल˘स् टे शॅन* *n.* act of molesting छेड़खानी।

molten *मोल्-टॅन* *a.* melted पिघला हुआ।

moment *मो मॅन्ट* *n.* instant क्षण।

momentary *मो मॅन् टॅ रि* *a.* lasting for a moment क्षणिक।

momentous *मौ˘ मै˘न्टस, मॅ–* *a.* weighty महत्वपूर्ण; important आवश्यक।

momentum *मौ˘ मैन् टॅम, मॅ–* *n.* force of a moving body or machine गति-मात्रा।

monarch *मौ˘ नॅःक* *n.* supreme ruler राजा।

monarchy *मौ ˘ नॅः कि* *n.* government in which the supreme power is lodged in a single person एकतंत्र।

monastery *मौ˘ नॅस् टॅ रि* *n.* monk-house मठ।

monasticism *n.* corporate monastic life वानप्रस्थ, संन्यासभाव; system of living in monastery मठवाद।

Monday *मन् डे,–डि* *n.* second day of the week सोमवार।

monetary *म नि टॅ रि* *a.* relating to money आर्थिक।

money *म नि* *n.* currency मुद्रा; wealth संपत्ति।

monger *मङ्-गरः* *n.* dealer, trader वणिक, व्यापारी।

mongoose *मौन्ॅ गूस* *n.* a small animal noted for killing snakes नेवला।

mongrel *मङ्-ग्रल* *a.* mixed in reed संकरजातीय, दोग़ला, मिलाजुला।

monitor *मौ˘ नि टॅः* *n.* senior pupil in a school appointed to instruct and look after juniors छात्रनायक; a screen in a television studio टेलिविज़न का पर्दा।

monitory *मौ˘-नि-टॅ-रि* *a.* giving admonition or warning उपदेशात्मक, शिक्षाप्रद।

monk *मङ्क* *n.* male inhabitant of a monastery मठवासी।

monkey *मङ् कि* *n.* long tailed quadrumanous animal बंदर।

monochromatic *मौ˘-नॅ-क्रॅ-मै-टिक* *a.* of one colour or wavelength only एकवर्णी, एक रंग में रंगनेवाला; completely colour-blind वर्णांध।

monocle *मौ-नॅ-क्ल* *n.* a single eye-glass एक आंख का चश्मा।

monocular *मौ ˘-नौ ˘-क्यु-लरः* *a.* one eyed काना, एकाक्षी, एकनेत्री।

monody *मौ˘-नॅ-डि* *n.* mournful ode or poem शोकगीत; song for one voice एकस्वरगीत।

monogamy *मौ ˘ नौ ˘ गॅ मि, मॅ–* *n.* the marrying of only one at a time एकविवाह-प्रथा।

monogram *मौ ˘ नॅ ग्रैम* *n.* a design of letters interwoven नाम-चिह्न।

monograph *मौ ˘ नॅ ग्राफ़* *n.* scholarly writing on a single subject प्रबंध।

monogynous *मौँ-नौँ-जि-नॅस a.* having one wife एकपत्नीक; mating with one female एक स्त्री केसरी।

monolatry *मौ ॅ-नौ ॅ-लॅ-ट्रि n.* worship of one god एकदेव पूजा।

monolith *मौ ॅ नौ ॅ लिथ, n.* single large block of stone एकाश्म।

monologue *मौँ नॅ लौँ ग n.* a speech by one person एकालाप।

monopolist *मॅ नौ ॅ पॅ लिस्ट n.* person who has a monopoly एकाधिकारी।

monopolize *मॅ नौ ॅ पॅ लॉइज़ v.t.* to hold the monopoly of पर एकाधिकार करना।

monopoly *मॅ नौॅ पॅ लि n.* sole trading power or privilege एकाधिकार।

monosyllable *मौ ॅ नॅ सि लॅ बल n.* word of a single syllable एकाक्षर।

monosyllabic *मौ ॅ नॅ सि लै बिक a.* having only one syllable एकाक्षरीय।

monotheism *मौँ नौँ थी इज़्म n.* belief in only one God एकेश्वरवाद।

monotheist *मौ ॅ नो ॅ थी इस्ट n.* a believer in only one God एकेश्वरवादी।

monotonous *मॅ नौ ॅ टॅ नॅस a.* dull नीरस; lacking in variety एकरस; wearisome उबा देनेवाला।

monotony *मॅ नौ ॅ टॅ नि n.* dullness नीरसता; absence of variety एकरसता।

monsoon *मौन्ँ सून n.* seasonal wind मौसमी हवा; season marked by heavy rains बरसात का मौसम।

monster *मौन्ँ स्टॅः n.* giant राक्षस, दैत्य; very cruel person अत्यंत क्रूर व्यक्ति; huge person, animal or thing विशालकाय व्यक्ति, पशु आदि।

monstrous[1] *मौ ॅन्-स्ट्रॅस a.* devilish राक्षसी, नृशंस; horrible विकटरूप, डरावना, भयंकर; enormous विशाल, वृहत; huge, bulky भारी; out of the common course of nature असंगत।

monostrous[2] *मौन्ँ स्ट्रॅस n.* huge विशालकाय; horrible डरावना।

month *मन्थ n.* any of the twelve divisons of a year माह, महीना।

monthly[1] *मन्थ्लि a.* done or happening once a month or every month मासिक।

monthly[2] *adv.* once a month प्रतिमाह।

monthly[3] *n.* a magazine published every month मासिक पत्रिका।

monument *मौ ॅ न्यु मॅन्ट n.* statue, memorial स्मारक।

monumental *मौ ॅ न्यु मै ॅन् ट्ल a.* serving as a monument स्मारकीय; of lasting value स्थायी महत्व का; very great अति महान।

moo *मू v.i.* to low रंभाना।

mood *मूड n.* mental state or feeling मनोदशा, मनःस्थिति।

moody *मू डि a.* bad tempered बदमिज़ाज; gloomy उदास; changeable in mood चंचल मनोदशा वाला।

moon *मून n.* earth's satellite चंद्रमा।

moor[1] *मुअॅः, मौः n.* tract of open, uncultivated land बंजर प्रदेश।

moor[2] *v.t.* to secure (ship) with chains or ropes (जलयानको) बांधना।

moorings *मू रिङ्ग्ज़ n. pl.* chains, ropes etc. by which a ship is moored लंगर; something providing stability टिकने या रुकने का साधन।

moot *मूट n.* discussion वादविवाद, बहस।

mop[1] *मॉ᷃प n.* broom झाड़ू।

mop[2] *(-pp-) v.t.* to wipe or clean झाड़पोंछ करना।

mope *मोप v.i.* to yield to low spirits, to be sad or listless उदास होना, विषण्ण होना।

moral[1] *मॉ᷃ रॅल a.* relating to morality नैतिक; virtuous सदाचारपूर्ण।

moral[2] *n.* practical lesson सीख, शिक्षा; *(pl.)* moral principles नैतिक नियम।

morale *मॉ᷃ राल, मॅ– n.* temper or state of mind as expressed in action हौसला, मनोबल।

moralist *मॉ᷃ रॅ लिस्ट n.* one who teaches morals नैतिक शिक्षक; one who inculcates or practises moral duties नैतिकतावादी।

morality *मॅ रै लि टि n.* moral principles and conduct सदाचार; moral quality नैतिकता; a kind of drama teaching moral lesson नीति-नाटक।

moralize *मॉ᷃ रॅ लॉइज़ v.t.* to give a moral interpretation of नैतिक व्याख्या करना; *v.i.* to deal with moral aspects नीतिगत बात करना।

morbid *मौः बिड a.* diseased बीमार, रुग्ण; gruesome घिनावना या घिनापन।

morbidity *मौ᷃ः बिडिटि n.* diseased state रुग्णता; state of being gruesome घिनावनापन।

more[1] *मौः, मौ᷃ः a.* greater in number or quantity अधिक।

more[2] *adv.* to a greater extent अधिक मात्रा में।

moreover *मौः रो वॅः adv.* besides इसके अतिरिक्त।

morganatic *मौरः- गॅ- नै- टिक a.* of marriage between persons of unequal rank अनुमोल (विवाह)।

morgue *मौरःग n.* place where dead bodies are laid out for identification, mortuary शवगृह, मुर्दाघर।

moribund *मौ᷃-रि-बन्ड a.* about to die, in a dying state मृतप्राय, मरणासन्न।

morning *मौः निङ्ग n.* the first part of the day सुबह।

moron *मौ᷃-रौ᷃न n.* feeble-minded person मंदबुद्धि व्यक्ति।

morose *मॅ-रोस a.* gloomy म्लान, उदास; sour-tempered कर्कश, चिड़चिड़ा; severe कठोर।

morphia *मौः फ़्यॅ n.* narcotic extract of opium अफ़ीम का सत्त्व।

morrow *मौ᷃ रो n.* next day आगामी दिन।

morsel *मौः सॅल n.* tiny piece टुकड़ा; mouthful ग्रास।

mortal[1] *मौः ट्ल a.* subject to death नाशवान, नश्वर; deadly घातक।

mortal[2] *n.* human being मानव-प्राणी।

mortality *मौः टै लि टि n.* state of being mortal नश्वरता; number of deaths मृतकों की संख्या; death-rate मृत्यु-दर।

mortar *v.t.* to bombard with a

mortar (पर) गोलाबारी करना; to join or plaster with mortar चूने से जोड़ना, चूना लगाना।

mortgage[1] *मौः गिज n.* pledge of property as security for debt बंधक, गिरवी।

mortgage[2] *v.t.* to pledge as security बंधक रखना।

mortagagee *मौः गॅ जी n.* receiver of pledge गिरवीदार।

mortgator *मौः गॅ जौः n.* one who pledges गिरवी रखने वाला।

mortify *मौः टि फ़ॉइ v.t.* to humiliate अपमानित करना; to subdue by self denial आत्म-त्याग-द्वारा दमन करना; *v.i.* to be affected with gangrene (मांस का) सड़ जाना।

mortuary *मौरः-ट्यु-ॲ-रि n.* morgue शवशाला, मुर्दाघर; payment to the parish priest मृत्यु-कर।

mosaic *मोॅ ज़े इक n.* pattern made by coloured bits of stone पच्चीकारी; this process of decoration पच्चीकारी की विधि।

mosque *मौॅस्क n.* muslim temple मसजिद।

mosquito *मॅस् की टो, मौॅस्– n. (pl.-toes)* stinging gnat मच्छर।

moss *मौॅस् n.* soggy ground or soil दलदल, कीचड़; small plant with no woody material काई, शैवाल।

most[1] *मोस्ट a.* greatest सबसे अधिक।

most[2] *adv.* in the greatest degree सर्वाधिक मात्रा में।

most[3] *n.* greatest number, amount of degree सर्वाधिक संख्या या मात्रा।

mote *मोट n.* particles of dust रजकण, धूलिकण; seed or other particle in wool or cotton (कपड़ों या ऊन में) दाना, गांठ; speck, stain or blemish चित्ती, धब्बा।

motel *मो-टैॅल n.* hotel with accommodation and servicing facilities for cars कार आदि रखने की व्यवस्था वाला होटल।

moth *मौॅथ n.* a nocturnal insect like butterfly शलभ, पतंगा।

mother[1] *मदॅः n.* female parent माता।

mother[2] *v.t.* to act as mother to (की) मां होना।

motherhood *म दॅः हुड n.* state of being a mother मातृत्व।

motherlike *म-दरः-लॉइक a.* like a mother, befitting a mother मातृवत्, मातृसुलभ।

motherly *म दॅः लि a.* like mother मां-जैसा।

motif *मोॅ टीफ़ n.* theme मूल भाव।

motion[1] *मो शॅन n.* a proposal formally made in an assembly प्रस्ताव; gesture चेष्टा; moving from place to place गति।

motion[2] *v.i.* to make a gesture इशारा करना; *v.t.* to direct (somebody) by gesture संकेत-द्वारा बताना।

motionless *मो शॅन् लिस a.* still स्थिर।

motivate *मो टि वेट* to provide with an incentive प्रेरित करना।

motivation *मो टि वे शॅन n.* act of motivating प्रेरणा।

motive *मो टिव n.* intention इरादा; that which causes somebody to act प्रेरणा, उद्देश्य।

motley *मौॅट् लि a.* multi-coloured बहुरंगी; of various sorts पंचमेल।

motor[1] *मो टॅः* *n.* that which imparts motion गति देनेवाला; machine to supply motive power मोटर; motorcar कार।

motor[2] *v.i.* to travel by car मोटरगाड़ी से यात्रा करना; *v.t.* to equip with motor मोटर लगाना; to carry by motor car कार से ले जाना।

motorist *मो टॅ रिस्ट* *n.* person who drives a car मोटर-चालक; person who travel in a car कार-यात्री।

mottle *मौ ˘-ट्ल* *n.* yarn of two colours दुरंगा सूत; blotched appearance, condition or surface धब्बेदार स्थिति।

motto *मौ ˘ टो* *n. (pl. -es)* a word, phrase or sentence expressing ideals of a group आदर्श-वाक्य।

mould[1] *मोल्ड* *n.* a hollow object in which metal etc. is cast सांचा; pattern for shaping नमूना; character चरित्र; shape, form आकार।

mould[2] *v.t.* to shape आकार देना।

mould[3] *n.* fungoid growth caused by dampness फफूंदी।

mould[4] *n.* loose or surface earth ढीली मिट्टी, बारीक मिट्टी।

mouldy *मोल् डि* *a.* covered with mould फफूंदीदार; stale बासी; old fashioned पुराना, घिसा-पिटा।

moult *मोल्ट* *v.i.* to cast feathers पंख या अन्य आवरण गिराना; *v.t.* to shed गिराना, हटाना (पंख आदि)।

mound *मॉउन्ड* *n.* small hill टीला; heap of earth ढेर।

mount[1] *मॉउन्ट* *n.* hill पहाड़ी।

mount[2] *v.t.* to climb चढ़ना; to get on to (a horse etc.) पर सवार होना; to supply with a horse घोड़ा देना; to put and fix in position (पर) चौखटा चढ़ाना; *v.i.* to increase बढ़ना।

mount[3] *n.* that on which a thing is supported or fitted धारक, आधार; a horse घोड़ा।

mountain *मॉउन् टिन* *n.* high hill पहाड़।

mountaineer *माउन् टि निअँः* *n.* mountain-climber पहाड़ पर चढ़ने वाला, पर्वतारोही।

mountainous *मॉउन् टि नॅस* *a.* of a mountain पहाड़ी, पर्वतीय।

mourn *मौःन* *v.i.* to lament, to bewail विलाप करना; *v.t.* to feel sorrow for (पर) विलाप करना।

mourner *मौः नॅः* *n.* one who mourns विलाप करनेवाला।

mournful *मौःन् फुल* *n.* sad, sorrowful दुःखी, शोकाकुल।

mourning *मौः निङ्ग* *n.* lamentation मातम, विलाप।

mouse *मॉउस* *n. (pl. mice)* small rodent चूहा।

moustache *मस् टाश* *n.* hair on upper lip मूंछ।

mouth[1] *मॉउथ* *n.* facial opening मुंह।

mouth[2] *v.t.* to speak (words) with too much movement of the jaws (शब्दों को) जबड़ों को बहुत घुमाकर बोलना; to utter pompously कृत्रिमता के साथ बोलना; to take (food) into the mouth (भोजन) मुंह में रखना; to touch with the mouth मुंह से छूना।

mouthful *मॉउथ् फुल* *n.* morsel कौर, निवाला।

movable *मू वॅ बल* *a.* capable of being moved सर्पी; (property) that can be shifted चल (संपत्ति)।

movables *मू वॅ ब्ल्ज़ n. pl.* goods, commodities, furniture चल संपत्ति।

move[1] *मूव n.* change of place and position स्थान-परिवर्तन; something done to achieve purpose कार्यवाही; (chess) player's turn चाल, बारी।

move[2] *v.t.* to change position of हटाना, खिसकाना; to stir emotions of द्रवित करना; to incite भड़काना; to propose for consideration प्रस्तावित करना; *v.i.* to change place or posture हटना; to shake हिलना; to take action कार्यवाही करना।

movement *मूव् मॅन्ट n.* act of moving गति; agitation to bring about some desired result आंदोलन।

mover *मू वॅः n.* a person who puts a proposal प्रस्तावक।

movies *मू विज़ n.pl.* cinema pictures चलचित्र।

mow *मो v.t.* to cut down (grass) (घास) काटना।

much[1] *मच a* great in quantity अधिक।

much[2]*adv.* greatly, to a great extent अधिक मात्रा में।

mucilage *म्यू-सि-लिज n.* glue found in plants लासा; any sticky substance चिपचिपा पदार्थ; gum गोंद।

muck *मक n.* dung गोबर; manure खाद; anything worthless कबाड़; rubbish कूड़ाकरकट; mess गंदगी।

mucous *म्यू कॅस a.* like mucus कफ़ जैसा; covered with mucus श्लेष्मा-युक्त।

mucus *म्यू कॅस n.* sticky substance produced by the mucous membrane श्लेष्मा।

mud *मड n.* mire कीचड़।

muddle[1] *म ड्ल n.* confusion, disorder अव्यवस्था, गड़बड़ी।

muddle[2]*v.t.* to confuse भ्रम में डालना; to bewilder घबरा देना; to mismanage अव्यवस्थित करना।

muffle *म फ़्ल v.t.* to wrap, to cover लपेटना, ढकना।

muffler *मफ़् लॅः n.* scarf worn round the neck गुलूबंद।

mug *मग n.* cup or jug जलपात्र।

muggy *म-गि a.* close and damp उमसदार; foggy धुंधभरा।

mulatto *म्यू-लै-टो n.* offspring of a negro and person of European stock (हब्शी और गौरे का) वर्णसंकर।

mulberry *मल् बॅ रि n.* a juicy fruit शहतूत।

mule *म्यूल n.* offspring of an ass and a mare खच्चर।

mulish *म्यू-लिश a.* like a mule खच्चर जैसा; obstinate जिद्दी, हठीला।

mull[1] *मल n.* muddle घालमेल।

mull[2] *v.t.* to bungle गड़बड़ करना।

mullah *(मु-ला, म-ला) n.* Muslim learned in theology मुल्ला, मौलवी।

mullion *मल्-यॅन n.* upright division between the lights of windows वातायन-दंड।

multifarious *मॅल् टि फ़े ॅअॅ रि ॲस a.* many and varied विभिन्न प्रकार के।

multiform *मल्-टि-फ़ौःम n.* having many forms, polymorphic

बहुरूपी, नानारूपी।

multilateral *मल्-टि-लै-टॅ-रॅल a.* with several parties or participants बहुदेशीय, अनेकराष्ट्रीय; many-sided अनेकभुजीय, बहुपार्श्विक।

multiparous *मल्-टि-पॅ-रॅस a.* producing more than one at a birth बहुप्रसवा, बहुप्रसवीय।

multiple[1] *मल् टि पल a.* having many parts बहुखंडीय।

multiple[2] *n.* quantity which contains another an exact number of times गुणज, अपवर्त्य।

multiped *मल्-टि-पैँड n.* many footed animal बहुपाद पशु।

multiplex *मल्-टि-प्लैक्स a.* multiple, having many parts or forms अनेक तत्वीय, बहुविध, बहुरूप; cinema hall with many screens कई परदों वाला छविग्रह।

multiplicand *मल्-टि-प्लि-कॅन्ड, मल्-टि-प्लि-कैन्ड n.* quantity to be multiplied by another गुण्य राशि।

multiplication *मल् टि प्लि के शन n.* process of multiplying गुणन।

multiplicity *मल् टि प्लि सि टि n.* state of being great in number बहुलता।

multiply *मल् टि प्लॉइ v.t.* to increase many times गुणा करना।

multitude *मल् टि ट्यूड n.* crowd भीड़; the common people जनसाधारण; state of being many बहुलता, आधिक्य।

mum[1] *मम a.* silent चुप।

mum[2] *n.* silence चुप्पी।

mumble *मम् ब्ल v.i.* to speak indistinctly बुदबुदाना।

mummer *म-मॅ: n.* actor in a dumb show मूक अभिनेता।

mummy[1] *म मि n.* embalmed dead body ममी, परिरक्षित शव।

mummy[2] *n.* mother माँ, मम्मी।

mumps *मम्प्स n. sing.* disease with painful swellings in the neck कनपेड़ा, गलसुआ।

munch *मन्च v.t.* to chew चबाना; *v.i.* to chew with marked action of the jaws जुगाली करना।

mundane *मन् डेन a.* worldly सांसारिक।

municipal *म्यू नि सि पॅल, म्यु– a.* belonging to the local self-government of a town नगरपालिका-संबंधी।

municipality *म्यू नि सि पै लि टि, म्यु– n.* local self-government of a town नगरपालिका।

munificent *म्यू-नि-फ़ि-सॅन्ट a.* bountiful दानशील, दाता।

muniment *म्यू-नि-मॅन्ट n.* a record making good a claim अधिकार-पत्र; *(pl.)* furnishings, equipment etc. सामान, सामग्री, उपकरण।

munitions *म्यू नि शॅन्स n. pl.* military stores युद्ध-सामग्री।

mural[1] *म्युअॅ रॅल a.* having to do with a wall भित्तीय।

mural[2] *n.* a painting done on a wall भित्तिचित्र।

murder[1] *मॅ: डॅ: n.* unlawful manslaughter हत्या।

murder[2] *v.t.* to kill मारना, हत्या करना; to spoil बिगाड देना।

murderer *मॅ: डॅ रॅ: n.* killer हत्यारा, खूनी।

murderous *मॅ: डॅ रॅस a.* capable of murder प्राणघातक।

murmur[1] मँ: मँ: *n.* low utterance, grumble गुनगुनाहट, बड़बड़ाहट।

murmur[2] *v.t.* to utter in low tone गुनगुनाना, *v.i.* to grumble बड़बड़ाना।

muscle म स्‌ल *n.* the tissue that forms the muscles of the body मांसपेशी।

muscovite मस्‌-कॅ-वॉइट *n.* common white mica श्वेत अभ्रक।

muscular मस्‌ क्यु लँ: *a.* strong शक्तिशाली; of or relating to the muscles मांसपेशीय।

muse[1] म्यूज़ *v.i.* to ponder ध्यान लगाना, मनन करना।

muse[2] *n.* the goddess of poetry सरस्वती।

museum म्यू ज़ि ॲम, म्यु– *n.* repository of wonderful things अजायबघर।

mush मश *n.* meal boiled in water दलिया; anything pulpy गूदा, गूदेदार वस्तु; sentimentality भावुकता।

mushroom मश्‌ रूम *n.* edible fungus कुकुरमुत्ता।

music म्यू ज़िक *n.* art of harmonious sounds संगीत।

musical म्यू ज़ि कॅल *a.* belonging to music सांगीतिक।

musician म्यू ज़ि शॅन्‌, म्यु– *n.* one skilled in music संगीतकार।

musk मस्क *n.* strong perfume कस्तूरी।

musket मस्‌ किट *n.* hand-gun बंदूक़।

musketeer मस्‌ कि टिॲ: *n.* soldier who uses a musket बंदूक़धारी सिपाही।

muslin मस्‌ लिन *n.* thin, fine, cotton-cloth मलमल।

must[1] मस्ट *aux.v.* to be obliged आवश्यक होना, अनिवार्य होना; to be certain निश्चित होना।

must[2] *n.* something one must do अनिवार्यता।

must[3] *n.* newly pressed grape juice द्राक्षारस।

mustache मॅस्‌-टाश *n.* moustache मूँछ।

mustang मस्‌-टैङ्‌ग *n.* wild horse मसतुरंग, जंगली घोड़ा।

mustard मस्‌ टॅ:ड *n.* an oil plant सरसों।

muster[1] मस्‌ टॅ: *v.t.* to collect (as troops) एकत्र करना; *v.i.* to assemble एकत्र होना।

muster[2] *n.* assembling of troops सैनिक-सभा।

musty मस्‌ टि *a.* mouldy फफूंददार; stale बासी।

mutation म्यू टे शन *n.* change परिवर्तन।

mutative म्यु-टॅ-टिव *a.* changing, mutable परिवर्तनशील, परिवर्तनीय।

mute[1] म्यूट *a.* dumb गूंगा; silent शांत, चुप।

mute[2] *n.* one who cannot speak गूंगा व्यक्ति।

mutilate म्यू टि लेट *v.t.* to injure or disfigure by cutting a piece from अंगभंग करना, विकृत करना।

mutilation म्यू टि ले शॅन, म्यु– *n.* removal of some essential part अंगच्छेद।

mutinous म्यू टि नॅस *a.* rebellious विद्रोही, बाग़ी।

mutiny[1] म्यू टि नि *n.* revolt against constituted authority ग़दर, बग़ावत।

mutiny[2] *v. i.* to rise against lawful authority बग़ावत करना।

mutter *म टॅः v.i.* to utter words with compressed lips बड़बड़ाना; *v.t.* to utter with a low murmuring voice बड़बड़ाकर कहना।

mutton *म ट्न n.* flesh of sheep भेड़ का मांस।

mutual *म्यू ट्यु ॲल a.* reciprocal पारस्परिक, आपसी।

muzzle[1] *म ज़्ल n.* mouth and nose of an animal थूथन; cover for mouth and nose मोहरा, छींका; open end of gun नालमुख।

muzzle[2] *v.t.* to put muzzle on (पर) छींका लगाना; to prevent from expressing opinion प्रतिबंधित करना।

my *मॉइ a.* belonging to me मेरा, मेरी।

myalgia *मॉइ-ऐल्-जि-ॲ n.* pain in muscle पेशी-पीड़ा, पुट्ठो में दर्द।

myopia *मॉइ ओ पि ॲ n.* shortsightedness अल्पदृष्टि।

myopic *मॉइ औ ˘ पिक a.* short sighted निकटदृष्टिक।

myosis *मॉइ-ओ-सिस n.* abnormal contraction of the pupil of the eye तारासंकोच।

myriad[1] *मि रि ॲड n.* very great number विशाल संख्या।

myriad[2] *a.* innumerable असंख्य।

myrrh *मॅः n.* an aromatic gum गंधरस।

myrtle *मॅः-ट्ल n.* an evergreen shrub with beautiful and fragrant leaves विलायती मेंहदी, हिना।

myself *मॉइ- सैल्फ़, मि- pron.* used for 'I' or 'me' (for emphasis) मैं स्वयं, स्वयं मैं।

mysterious *मिस् टिअ रि ॲस a.* containing mystery रहस्यमय।

mystery *मिस् टॅ रि n.* something above human intelligence रहस्य; anything inexplicable रहस्यपूर्ण वस्तु।

mystic[1] *मिस् टिक a.* of hidden meaning or spiritual power रहस्यवादी।

mystic[2] *n.* one who seeks union with God and realization of truth रहस्यवादी।

mysticism *मिस् टि सिज़्म n.* belief that knowledge of God is obtainable through prayer and contemplation रहस्यवाद।

mystify *मिस् टि फ़ॉइ v.t.* to perplex intentionally भ्रमित करना।

myth *मिथ n.* a tale with supernatural characters or events पौराणिक कथा; invented story कल्पित कथा; imaginary person or object काल्पनिक व्यक्ति या वस्तु।

mythical *मि थि कॅल a.* relating to myth पुराणकथा-संबंधी; existing only in myth पौराणिक; fictitious कल्पित।

mythological *मि थॅ लौ ˘ जि कॅल a.* relating to or proceeding from mythology पौराणिक; unreal अयथार्थ।

mythology *मि थौ ˘ लॅ जि n.* science or doctrine of myths पुराण विद्या; myths collectively पुराण-संग्रह।

Nn

N ऍन् the fourteenth letter of the English alphabet, (in Chemistry) symbol for nitrogen, an indefinite number in mathematics, (in printing) a measurement equal to half em. अंग्रेजी भाषा का चौदहवाँ अक्षर, (रसायनशास्त्र में) नाइट्रोजन द्रव्य के लिए संकेत, गणित में अज्ञात संख्या, (छापे में) एक परिणाम जो 'एम्' का आधा होता है।

nab *नैब (-bb-) v.t.* to arrest बंदी बनाना; to seize छीनना।

nabob *ने-बौबॅ n.* wealthy person धनाढ्य व्यक्ति।

nadir *ने डिअॅ: n.* point opposite zenith अधोबिंदु, पादबिंदु; lowest point निम्नतम बिंदु।

nag[1] *नैग n.* a small horse टट्टू।

nag[2] *(-gg-) v.t.* to scold constantly बुरी-भला कहना; to cause pain to कष्ट देना।

nail[1] *नेल n.* the horny substance at the end of the human fingers नाखून; a sharp metal peg कील।

nail[2] *v.t.* to fasten or stud with nails कीलों से जड़ना।

naive *ना ईव, नॉइ– a.* artless भोला-भाला; ingenious निष्कपट।

naivete, naivety *ना ईव् टे, नॉइ n.* artlessness भोला-भालापन।

naked *ने किड a.* bare अनावृत; nude नंगा; evident स्पष्ट।

name[1] *नेम n.* that by which a person or thing is designated नाम; reputation ख्याति; famous person ख्याति प्राप्त व्यक्ति।

name[2] *v.t.* to give name to नाम रखना; to call by name नाम से पुकारना; to mention का उल्लेख करना; to appoint नियुक्त करना; to entitle शीर्षक देना; to nominate मनोनीत करना; to specify निश्चित करना।

namely *नेम् लि adv.* that is to say अर्थात्; for example उदाहरण के तौर पर।

namesake *नेम सेक n.* person or thing with the same name as another नामराशि।

nap[1] *नैप (-pp-) v.i.* to have a short sleep झपकी लेना।

nap[2] *n.* a short sleep झपकी।

nap[3] *n.* a card game ताश का एक खेल।

nape *नेप n.* back of the neck ग्रीवासंधि, घाटिका।

napkin *नैप् किन n.* handkerchief रूमाल।

narcissism *नार-सि-सिज़्म n.* abnormal love and admiration for oneself आत्ममोह, आत्मरति।

narcissus *ना:रसि-सॅस (pl. -es, -ssi) n.* daffodil genus of the Amaryllis family नरगिस, इंदिरापुष्प।

narcosis *नार-को-सिस n.* drowsiness उनींदापन; unconsciousness संज्ञाहीनता।

narcotic *ना: कौॅ टिक n.* a substance which relieves pain and produces sleep नशीली औषधि।

narrate *नै रेट, नॅ–* *v.t.* to tell or relate बताना, सुनाना।

narration *नै रे शॅन, नॅ–* *n.* the telling of a story कथन।

narrative[1] *नै रॅ टिव* *n.* story कथा; account वर्णन।

narrative[2] *a.* in the form of a story कथात्मक।

narrator *नै रे टॅ:, नॅ–* *n.* one who narrates वाचक, वर्णनकर्त्ता।

narrow[1] *नै रो* *a.* not wide or broad संकीर्ण, परिमित; small लघु, छोटा; not liberal अनुदार।

narrow[2] *v.t.* to make narrow संकरा करना; *v.i.* to become narrow संकरा होना।

nasal[1] *ने ज़ॅल* *a.* of the nose, for the nose नाक का, नाकार्थ।

nasal[2] *n.* nasal sound नासिक्य।

nascent *नै सन्ट* *a.* coming into being उदीयमान।

nasty *नास् टि* *a.* dirty गंदा; filthy गर्हित, घिनौना; obscene अश्लील; dangerous ख़तरनाक।

natal *ने-टॅल* *a.* of or connected with birth प्रसव-संबंधी; native जन्मकालीन, जन्मजात।

natant *ने-टॅन्ट* *a.* floating, swimming प्रवहमान, प्लवमान।

nation *ने शॅन* *n.* body of people inhabiting the same country राष्ट्र।

national *नै शॅ नॅल* *a.* pertaining to a nation राष्ट्रीय।

nationalism *नै शॅ नॅ लिज़्म* *n.* strong devotion to one's own nation राष्ट्रप्रेम, राष्ट्रीयता।

nationalist *नै शॅ नॅ लिस्ट* *n.* one who is attached to one's country राष्ट्रवादी।

nationality *नै शॅ नै लि टि* *n.* quality of being national राष्ट्रीयता; national quality or feeling राष्ट्रीय गुण या भावना।

nationalization *नै शॅ नॅ लॉइ ज़ै शॅन* *n.* act of nationalizing राष्ट्रीयकरण।

nationalize *नै शॅ नॅ लॉइज़* *v.t.* to make national राष्ट्रीय बनाना; to bring under national control (का) राष्ट्रीयकरण करना।

native[1] *ने टिव* *a.* inborn जन्मजात; born in a particular place स्थान-विशेष पर जन्मा; found in pure state शुद्ध रूप में प्राप्त; pertaining to the place of one's birth जन्मस्थानीय।

native[2] *n.* one born in a place मूल निवासी।

nativity *नॅ टि वि टि* *n.* birth जन्म।

natural *नै च् रॅल* *a.* pertaining to nature प्राकृतिक; provided by nature प्रकृतिप्रदत्त; not artificial अकृत्रिम; inborn जन्मजात, स्वाभाविक; normal सामान्य; illegitimate अवैध।

naturalist *नै च् रॅ लिस्ट* *n.* one versed in natural science or natural history प्रकृतिविज्ञानी।

naturalize *नै च् रॅ लॉइज़* *v.t.* to admit to citizenship नागरिकता प्रदान करना; to accustom to new climate नई जलवायु का अभ्यस्त बनाना।

naturally *नै च् रॅ लि* *adv.* in a natural manner सहजतः; according to nature स्वभावतः।

nature *ने चॅ:* *n.* inborn quality

जन्मजात गुण; disposition प्रवृत्ति; kind, sort प्रकार; the universe with all its phenomena प्रकृति-जगत्; life force जीवनशक्ति; natural scenery प्राकृतिक दृश्य; temperament स्वभाव।

naughty *नौ टि a. (-tier, -tiest)* mischievous उद्दंड; hurtful अनिष्टकारी।

nausea *नौ स्यॅ n.* feeling or inclination to vomit मतली, वमनेच्छा।

nautic(al) *नौ-टि-कॅल a.* of or pertaining to ships, to sailors or to navigation नाविकीय, नौचालन-संबंधी, नौका-विषयक।

naval *ने वॅल a.* pertaining to ships जहाज़ी, नौचालन-संबंधी; pertaining to navy नौसेना-संबंधी।

nave *नेव n.* hub, central part of a wheel through which the axle passes चक्रनाभि।

navigable *नै वि गॅ ब्ल a.* that may be navigated नौगम्य।

navigate *नै वि गेट v.i.* to sail नौचालन करना; *v.t.* to direct the course of (का) संचालन करना।

navigation *नै वि गे शॅन n.* act of navigating नौचालन; art of conducting ships नौचालन-विद्या; sea-voyage नौ-यात्रा।

navigator *नै वि गे टॅः n.* one who directs the course of a ship दिक्चालन-निर्देशक; one who navigates or sails नाविक।

navy *नै वि n.* all the ships of war belonging to a nation जहाज़ी बेड़ा, नौसेना।

nay *ने adv.* no नहीं; not only so but ऐसा ही नहीं अपितु; yet more और भी; in point of fact वास्तव में।

neap *नीप a.* (of tides) of smallest range लघु, नीचा।

near[1] *निअॅः a.* not distant in place, time or degree समीपी; intimate घनिष्ट।

near[2] *prep.* close to के पास।

near[3] *adv.* at or to a short distance पास ही, थोड़ी दूरी पर।

near[4] *v.i.* to approach, to come near पास आना।

nearly *निअॅः लि adv.* closely घनिष्ट रूप से; almost लगभग।

neat *नीट a.* pure शुद्ध; clean निर्मल; without water added अमिश्र।

nebula *नैॅ-ब्यु-लॅ (pl. -lae) n.* group of very distant stars आकाशगंगा, नीहारिका; little cloudiness मामूली मेघच्छन्नता; slight opacity of the cornea आंख की फूली।

necessary[1] *नै सि सॅ रि n.* anything indispensable requisite आवश्यक वस्तु।

necessary[2] *a.* such as must be अवश्यंभावी; essential आवश्यक; indispensable अनिवार्य।

necessitate *निसैॅ सि टैट v.t.* to make necessary आवश्यक बनाना।

necessity *नि सैॅ सि टि n.* condition of being necessary आवश्यकता; something that is necessary आवश्यक वस्तु; poverty निर्धनता।

neck *नैक् n.* part of an animal's body between the head and the trunk गर्दन, ग्रीवा।

necklace *नैक् लिस n.* string of beads, precious stones etc. worn round the neck कंठहार।

necklet *नैॅक्-लिट्* *n.* ornament for neck कंठाभूषण।

necromancer *नैॅक्-रौॅ-मैन्-सरः* *n.* sorcerer ओझा, पैशचिक, ऐंद्रजालिक।

necropolis *नैॅक्-रौॅ-पॅ-लिस* *n.* graveyard, cemetery समाधिस्थल, कब्रिस्तान।

nectar *नैकॅ टॅः* *n.* the fabled drink of the gods अमृत।

need[1] *नीड* *n.* poverty निर्धनता; misfortune दुर्भाग्य; necessity आवश्यकता।

need[2] *v.t.* to want आकांक्षा करना; to require (की) आवश्यकता होना।

needful *नीड़ फुल* *a.* necessary, requisite आवश्यक।

needle *नी ड़ल* *n.* an instrument for inter-weaving thread सुई, सुआ।

needless *नीड़-लिस* *a.* not needed, unnecessary निष्प्रयोजन, अनावश्यक।

needs *नीड़ज़* *adv.* of necessity अनिवार्यतः।

needy *नी डि* *a.* being in need ज़रूरतमंद; poor निर्धन।

nefandous *नि-फ़ैन्-डॅस* *a.* abominable घृणास्पद, दुष्टतापूर्ण।

nefarious *नि फ़ेॅ अॅ रि अॅस* *a.* wicked in the extreme दुष्टतापूर्ण।

negation *नि गे शॅन* *n.* a denial इंकार; contradiction विरोध।

negative[1] *नै ॅ गॅ टिव* *a.* implying denial or negation निषेधात्मक; not positive नकारात्मक।

negative[2] *n.* a proposition by which something is denied नकारात्मक कथन।

negative[3] *v.t.* to reject अस्वीकार करना; to prove to be untrue ग़लत सिद्ध करना; to neutralize निष्प्रभावी कर देना।

neglect[1] *निग् लैक्ट* *v.t.* to treat with no regard उपेक्षा करना; to overlook पर ध्यान न देना; to leave undone अनकिया छोड़ देना।

neglect[2] *n.* want of care or attention उपेक्षा, अवहेलना।

negligence *नेगॅ लि जॅन्स* *n.* quality of being negligent लापरवाही; neglect उपेक्षा।

negligent *नैगॅ लि जॅन्ट* *a.* lacking in care लापरवाह।

negligible *नैगॅ लि जॅ ब्ल* *a.* too small तुच्छ; unimportant महत्त्वहीन।

negotiable *नि गो शि अॅ ब्ल* *a.* that may be negotiated संधि-वार्ता योग्य।

negotiate *नि गो शि एट* *v.t.* to arrange by conference; बात-चीत द्वारा व्यवस्था करना; to bargain or discuss सौदा या वार्ता करना।

nagotiation *नि गो शि ए शॅन* *n.* discussion विचार-विमर्श, वार्ता।

negotiator *नि गो शि ए टॅः* *n.* one who negotiates वार्ताकार।

Negress *नी ग्रिस* *n. (pl.-es)* a Negro woman or girl हबशिन।

Negro *नी ग्रो* *n. (pl.-es)* member of the black African race हबशी।

neigh[1] *ने* *v.i.* to utter the cry of a horse हिनहिनाना।

neigh[2] *n.* cry of a horse हिनहिनाहट।

neighbour *ने बॅः* *n.* one who lives or dwells near another पड़ोसी।

neighbourhood *ने बॅः हुड* *n.* condition of being neighbours पड़ोस।

neighbourly *ने बॅः लि a.* friendly मित्र-जैसा; helpful सहायक; befitting a good neighbour अच्छे पड़ोसी-जैसा।

neither *नॉइ दॅः, नी– a., conj. & pron.* not either कोई भी नहीं (दो में से)।

Nemesis *नै ॅ-मि-सिस n.* deserved fate नियति Greek goddess of retribution प्रतिरोध देवी।

neolithic *नी-ओ ॅ-लि-थिक a.* of the later or more advanced Stone Age नवपाषाणकालिक, उत्तर पाषाणकालीन।

neon *नी-औ ॅन n.* a colourless inert gas (at atomic no. 10) found in atmosphere (रसा.) एक अक्रिय गैस, (गैसीय तत्व परमाणु क्रमांक १०)।

nephew *नैफ़्यूः नैव्यू n.* son of a brother or sister भतीजा या भांजा।

nepotism *नै ॅ पॅ टिज़्म n.* undue patronage of relations भाई-भतीजावाद।

Neptune *नैपॅ ट्यून n.* god of the sea वरूण; name of a planet एक ग्रह का नाम।

nerve *नॅःव n.* one of the fibrous threads in bodies, whose function is to convey sensation and originate motion स्नायु; *pl.* condition of being easily worried or irritated घबराहट, चिड़चिड़ाहट; boldness साहस।

nerveless *नॅःव् लिस a.* wanting strength of will शक्तिहीन, संकल्पहीन।

nervous *नॅः वॅस a.* pertaining to nerves स्नायविक; easily agitated अधीर; timid डरपोक।

nescience *नै ॅश्-यॅन्स, नै ॅ-शॅन्स n.* want of knowledge अज्ञान, अविद्या, नासमझी।

nest[1] *नै ॅस्ट n.* structure prepared for egg-laying by birds निलय, घोंसला, नीड़; shelter, resort आश्रयस्थल; den अड्डा; accumulation, tangled mass समुदाय, झुंड।

nest[2] *v.t.* to put into a nest घोंसले में रखना; *v.i.* to go into a nest घोंसले में जाना।

nether *नै-दरः a.* lower निम्नस्थ, निचला।

nestle *नै ॅ स्ल v.i.* to settle oneself comfortably चैन से बैठना।

nestling *नैस्ट् लिङ्ग n.* a bird too young to leave the nest घोंसलावासी बच्चा।

net[1] *नै ॅट n.* a fabric or wire जाली; a fabric of string and cord जाल; trap जाल।

net[2] *(-tt-) v.t.* to take in a net जाल में फंसाना; to cover with a net जाल या जाली से ढंकना।

net[3] *a.* remaining after all deductions शुद्ध; final अंतिम।

net[4] *(-tt-) v.t.* to gain as a net profit शुद्ध लाभ के रूप में कमाना।

nettle[1] *नै ॅ-ट्ल n.* common weed with stinging hair बिच्छू-बूटी।

nettle[2] *v.t.* to sting डंक मारना; to sting with annoyance क्रोध दिलाना, खिझाना।

network *नै ॅट्-वर्क n.* system of lines तंत्र; any structure in the form of a net जाली, जाल।

neurologist *न्युअॅ रौ ॅ लॅ जिस्ट n.* one expert in neurology तंत्रिका-विज्ञानी।

neurology *न्युअॅ रौ ॅ लॅ जि n.* science and study of nerves तंत्रिका-विज्ञान।

neurosis *न्युअॅ-रो-सिस् n.* functional derangement through disordered nervous system (चि.) तंत्रिका-रोग, स्नायुरोग; mental disturbance विक्षेप, उन्माद।

neuter¹ *न्यू टॅः a.* neither masculine nor feminine नपुंसक (लिंग)।

neuter² *n.* a neuter word नपुंसक लिंग का शब्द; neuter gender नपुंसक लिंग।

neutral *न्यू ट्रॅल a.* indifferent उदासीन; helping neither side in war or quarrel तटस्थ।

neutralize *न्यू ट्रॅ लॉइज़ v.t.* to render neutral or inoperative तटस्थ बनाना।

neutron *न्यूट्-रौ ॅन n.* uncharged particle of about the same mass as proton न्यूट्रान, क्लीवाणु।

never *नै ॅ वॅः adv.* at no time कभी नहीं; not at all बिल्कुल नहीं।

nevertheless *नै ॅ वॅः दॅ लैसॅ conj.* however, in spite of that तिस पर भी, तथापि।

new *न्यू a.* recent in origin नया; fresh ताज़ा; modern आधुनिक; novel नये ढंग का; inexperienced अनुभवरहित; not familiar अनजान।

news *न्यूज़ n. (sing.)* recent or new information ख़बर, समाचार।

next¹ *नै ॅ क्स्ट a.* nearest in place, time, rank or degree दूसरा, अगला।

next² *adv.* after this इसके उपरांत।

nib *निब n.* pen-point निब।

nibble¹ *नि ब्ल v.t.* to take little bites of कुतरकर खाना।

nibble² *n.* act of nibbling कुतरने की क्रिया।

nice *नॉइस a.* agreeabe बढ़िया; satisfactory संतोषजनक; friendly मैत्रीपूर्ण; kind दयालु; fine उत्तम; careful सावाधानीपूर्ण; subtle सूक्ष्म, बारीकी का।

nicety *नॉइ-सि-टि n.* fineness सूक्ष्मता; refinenment परिष्कारण, संशोधन; exactness of treatment ठीक व्यवहार; delicacy सुकुमारता; delicate management सुव्यवस्था।

niche *निच n.* a recess in a wall ताक़, आला; a suitable place or job in life उचित स्थान का कार्य।

nick *निक n.* the precise point निशान, चिह्न; cut कटान; notch दाँता; precise time ऐन मौका।

nickel *नि क्ल n.* a valuable metal of a white colour गिलट, निकल।

nickname¹ *निक् नेम n.* a name given in contempt or jest उपनाम।

nickname² *v.t.* to give a nickname to उपनाम देना।

nicotine *नि कॅ टीन n.* poisonous substance in tobacco निकोटीन।

niece *नीस n.* daughter of one's brother or sister भतीजी, भांजी।

niggard *नि गॅःड n.* a mean, stingy person कमीना, कंजूस व्यक्ति।

niggardly *नि गॅःडॅ लि a.* miserly कंजूस।

nigger *नि-गॅः n.* negro हब्शी; black larva काला डिंभक

nigh¹ *नॉइ adv.* nearly लगभग।

nigh² *prep.* near to के पास।

night *नॉइट n.* time of darkness

between sunset and sunrise रात्रि, रात।

nightingale *नॉइ टिङ् गेल n.* small migratory bird that sings at night बुलबुल।

nightly *नाइट् लि a. & adv.* (done) by night or every night रात का, रात के समय।

nightmare *नॉइट् मे ॅ अ: n.* frightening dream दु:स्वप्न।

nighty, nightie *नॉइ-टि n.* nightgown सोते समय पहनने का वस्त्र।

nihilism *नॉइ-इ-लिज़्म, -हि- n.* belief in nothing शून्यवाद, नाशवाद; denial of all reality of all objective growth of truth अनस्तित्ववाद, नास्तिकवाद; nothingness शून्यता; extreme scepticism अतिशय संशयवाद।

nil *निल n.* nothing कुछ नहीं।

nimble *निम् ब्ल a.* quick moving चपल, फुरतीला; sharp (mind) तीव्र (बुद्धि)।

nimbus *निम्-ब्ल (pl.-es, -bi) n.* a rain-cloud जलमेघ, वर्षामेघ; a halo आभाचक्र।

nine *नॉइन n., a.* (the number) next after eight नौ (9)।

nineteen *नॉइन् टीन n.,* a. (the number) next after 18 उन्नीस (19)।

nineteenth *नॉइन्-टीन्थ a.* next after eighteenth उन्नीसवां।

ninetieth *नॉइन्-टि-इथ a.* last of ninety नब्बेवां; equal to one of ninety equal parts नब्बेवां (अंश)।

ninth *नॉइन्थ a.* next after the eighth नवां।

ninety *नॉइन् टि n., a.* (the number) next after 89 नब्बे (90)।

nip *निप (-pp.-) v.t.* to press hard दबाना, कुचलना; to stop the growth of (का) विकास रोकना।

nipple *नि प्ल n.* point of a breast, teat स्तनाग्र।

nitrogen *नॉइ ट्रि जॅन, –ट्रॅ– n.* one of the gases making up the air नत्रजन।

no[1] *नो a.* not any कोई नहीं, कुछ नहीं, not at all बिल्कुल नहीं।

no[2] *adv.* not नहीं।

no[3] *n.* refusal, denial मना, इंकार।

nobility *नो ॅ बि लि टि n.* state or quality of being noble भलमनसाहत; the nobles as a class कुलीन वर्ग।

noble[1] *नो ब्ल a.* free from meanness उत्तम; belonging to aristocracy अभिजात्य वर्ग का।

noble[2] *n.* a person of noble birth कुलीन व्यक्ति।

nobleman *नो-ब्ल्-मॅन n.* one who is noble or of high rank कुलीनपुरुष, महानुभाव।

nobody *नो बॅ डि pron.* no person कोई नहीं; a person of no importance महत्वहीन व्यक्ति।

nocturnal *नौक् टॅ: नॅल a.* of, in, by night रात का, रात में; active by night रात में क्रियाशील।

nod *नौ ॅड (-dd-) v.i.* to make a slight bow (सहमति में) सिर हिलाना; to move up and down ऊपर-नीचे हिलना; *v.t.* to indicate by a nod गर्दन के संकेत से बताना।

node *नोड n.* knot ग्रंथि, गांठ; swelling सूजन; knob घुंडी।

noise *नौ ॅइज़ n.* sound of anykind शोर।

noisy *नौ ॅइ ज़ि a. (-sier, -siest)* full of noise कोलाहलपूर्ण; making much noise कोलाहलकारी।

nomad *नौ ॅ मॅड, नो मैड n.* one who leads a wandering or pastoral life यायावर, ख़ानाबदोश।

nomadic *नौ ॅ मै डिक a.* of nomads भ्रमणशील।

nomenclature *नौ ॅ मैन् क्लॅ चॅः, नो मैन् क्ले चॅः n.* system of names नामावली, नामपद्धति।

nominal *नौ ॅ मि न्ल a.* existing only in name जिसका अस्तित्व केवल नाम का हो; inconsiderable अविचारणीय, बहुत थोड़ा।

nominate *नौ ॅ मि नेट v.t.* to designate or propose for an office नामांकित करना।

nomination *नौ ॅ मि ने शॅन n.* state of being nominated नामांकन; act of nominating नामांकन की क्रिया।

nominee *नौ ॅ मि नी n.* person nominated नामांकित व्यक्ति।

non-alignment *नौ ॅन्-अॅ-लॉइन्-मॅन्ट n.* policy of not taking sides in international politics तटस्थता, गुटनिरपेक्षता।

nonchalance *नौनॅ् शॅ लॅन्स n.* indifference उदासीनता।

nonchalant *नौनॅ् शॅ लॅन्ट a.* indifferent उदासीन।

none[1] *नन pron.* not any, not one कोई नहीं, एक भी नहीं।

none[2] *adv.* in no way किसी रूप में नहीं; in no degree लेशमात्र नहीं।

nonentity *नौ ॅ नैनॅ् टि टि n.* nonexistent thing अस्तित्वहीन वस्तु; person of no importance तुच्छ व्यक्ति।

nonetheless *नन् दॅ लैसॅ adv.* nevertheless फिर भी; however तो भी।

nonpareil[1] *नौनॅ् पॅ रै ॅल a.* unequalled, matchless अद्वितीय।

nonpareil[2] *n.* person or thing unrivalled अद्वितीय व्यक्ति या वस्तु।

nonplus *नौनॅ् प्लस, v.t.* to confound, to bewilder completely हक्का-बक्का कर देना, कर्त्तव्यविमूढ़ करना।

nonsense *नौनॅ् सॅन्स n.* words without meaning बकवास; things of no importance महत्वहीन बात।

nonsensical *नौनॅ् सैनॅ् सि कॅल a.* destitute of sense अर्थहीन; absurd बेहूदा।

nook *नुक n.* out of the way place अलग का स्थान।

noon *नून n.* midday दोपहर।

noose[1] *नूस n.* a running loop फंदा।

noose[2] *v.t.* to catch in a noose फंदे में फंसाना; to make a noose of का फंदा बनाना।

nor *नौः conj* and not और न।

norm[1] *नौःम n.* standard मानक; model नमूना।

norm[2] *n.* rule नियम; required standard मानक, प्रतिमान।

normal *नौः मॅल a.* regular नियमित; usual सामान्य।

normalcy *नौः मॅल् सि n.* state of being normal सामान्यता, सामान्य स्थिति।

normalize *नौः मॅ लॉइज़ v.t.* to make normal सामान्य बना देना।

north[1] *नौःथ n.* a region opposite to the south उत्तर।

north[2] *a.* in, or or from, the north उत्तरी।

north[3] *adv.* to or towards the

north उत्तर की ओर।

northerly[1] नौः दँः लि *a.* coming from the north उत्तरी।

northerly[2] *adv.* towards the north उत्तर की ओर।

northern नौः दँःन *a.* of the north उत्तरी।

nose[1] नोज़ *n.* the organ of smell नाक, नासिका; sense of smell सूंघने की शक्ति।

nose[2] *v.t.* to discover by smell सूंघ कर पता लगाना।

nosegay नोज़्-गे *n.* a bunch of flowers गुलदस्ता।

nosey, nosy नो-ज़ि *a.* inquisitine जिज्ञासु, कुतूहली।

nostalgia नौसॅ टैल् जिॲ *n.* homesickness घर की याद; wistful longing for something of the past बीते दिनों की याद।

nostril नोॅस् ट्रिल *n.* one of the two apertures of the nose नथुना।

nostrum नौॅस्-ट्रॅम *n.* secret, quack or patent mdicine (चि.) गुप्त औषधि, रामबाण।

not नौ ॅट *adv.* a word that expresses negation ना, नहीं।

notability नो-टॅ-बि-लि-टि *n.* fame, repute प्रसिद्धि, प्रख्याति; any notable thing स्मरणीय वस्तु; peculiarity विशिष्टता।

notable नो टॅ ब्‌ल *a.* worthy of note ध्यातव्य; remarkable उल्लेखनीय, प्रशंसनीय।

notary नो-टॅ-रि *n.* officer authorised to certify deeds, documents and contract set विपत्र-प्रमाणक, लेख्य-प्रमाणक।

notation नो-टे-शॅन *n.* representation of numbers or quantities अंकन, संकेतन; system of signs or symbols संकेत-पद्धति, अंकन-पद्धति।

notch नौ ॅच *n.* nick दांता, दंतुरण; indentation खांच, खांचा; narrow pass संकीर्ण पथ, तंग रास्ता।

note[1] नोट *n.* a mark, sign, or token चिह्न; brief record of facts टिप्पणी; a communication in writing पत्र; bank note कागज़ी मुद्रा; *(pl.)* short annotation व्याख्या; fame प्रसिद्धि; notice सूचना।

note[2] *v.t.* to notice ध्यान देना; to record अंकित कर लेना।

noteworthy नोट् वँः दि *a.* worthy of observation or notice उल्लेखनीय, ध्यातव्य।

nothing[1] न थिङ्ग *n.* not anything कुछ नहीं।

nothing[2] *adv.* not at all बिल्कुल नहीं।

notice[1] नो टिस *a.* information सूचना; intimation, warning चेतावनी; heed or attention ध्यान।

notice[2] *v.t.* to give attention to ध्यान देना; to observe देख लेना।

notification नो टि फि के शॅन *n.* act of notifying सूचना; announcement विज्ञप्ति, घोषणा।

notify नो टि फ़ॉइ *v.t.* to make known ज्ञापित करना; to inform सूचना देना।

notion नो शॅन *n.* idea, opinion mental conception धारणा, विचार।

notional नो-शॅ-नॅल *a.* theoretical सैद्धांतिक; imaginary काल्पनिक, कल्पनापूर्ण; having a full menaing of its own बोधात्मक; of the nature of notion मनोगत, वैचारिक।

notoriety नो˘ टॅ रॉइ ॲ टि *n.* state of being notorious कुख्याति।
notorious नो˘ टौ˘ रि ॲस *a.* widely known (esp. in a bad sense) कुख्यात।
notwithstanding[1] नौ˘ ट् विद् स्टैन् डिङ्ग *prep.* in spite of के बावजूद।
notwithstanding[2] *adv.* nevertheless, all the same फिर भी।
notwithstanding[3] *conj.* although यद्यपि।
nought नौ˘ट *n.* not anything कुछ नहीं; cipher शून्य (0)।
noun नॉउन *n.* a person, thing or idea संज्ञा।
nourish न रिश *v.t.* to feed खिलाना-पिलाना; to supply with nutriment पोषण करना; to encourage बढ़ाना, प्रोत्साहित करना।
nourishment न रिश् मॅन्ट *n.* act of nourishing पोषण; nutrition पोषण आहार।
novel[1] नौ˘ वॅल *a.* new नया; strange अद्‌भुत।
novel[2] *n.* a fictitious prose narrative उपन्यास।
novelette नौ˘ वॅ लैˇट *n.* short novel लघु उपन्यास।
novelist नौ˘ वॅ लिस्ट *n.* writer of novels उपन्यासकार।
novelty नौ˘ वॅल् टि *n.* quality of being novel नवीनता; something new कोई नयी वस्तु।
november नो˘ वैˇम् बॅः *n.* eleventh month of the year नवंबर।
novice नौ˘ विस *n.* one who is new in any business नौसिखुआ।
now[1] नॉउ *adv.* at the present time अब, इस समय; immediately तुरंत।
now[2] *conj.* since क्योंकि।
nowhere नो वेˇ ॲः, हेˇ ॲः *adv.* not in any place कहीं नहीं।
noxious नौˇक्-शॅस *a.* hurtful अनिष्टकारक, अहितकर।
nozzle नौ˘ ज़ल *n.* pointed spout टोंटी।
nuance न्यू-ॲन्स *n.* delicate degree or shade of difference सूक्ष्म भेद या अंतर।
nubile न्यू-बॉइल,-बिल *a.* marriageable (woman) विवाह-योग्य (स्त्री); sexually attractive मोहक।
nuclear न्यू क्लि ॲः *a.* relating to nucleus परमाण्वीय; constituting a nucleus नाभिकीय।
nucleus नयू क्लि ॲस *n.* centre केंद्र; core of the atom अणु का केंद्र।
nude[1] न्यूड *a.* naked नग्न, निर्वस्त्र।
nude[2] *n.* a naked figure नग्न मानव-चित्र।
nudity न्यू डि टि *n.* state of being nude नग्नता।
nudge *v.t.* to poke or push gently टबोकना।
nugget न-गिट *n.* lump of gold स्वर्णपिंड।
nuisance न्यू स्न्स *n.* that which annoys or is offensive परेशानी का कारण।
null नल *a.* of no force or validity रद्द, अमान्य।
nullification न लि फ़ि के शॅन *n.* act of nullifying निष्प्रभावीकरण।
nullify न लि फ़ॉइ *v.t.* to make null and void निष्प्रभावी करना, रद्द करना।
numb नम *a.* having diminished power of sensation or motion, अवसन्न सुन्न; stupefied स्तब्ध,

संज्ञाशून्य; without feeling भावनारहित।

number[1] नम् बॅ: *n.* symbol saying how many संख्या; one issue of a periodical or newspaper पत्रिका का अंक; *(gram.)* classification as to singular or plural (व्या.) वचन।

number[2] *v.t.* to give a number to पर अंक डालना; to include as part of a total में जोड़ना।

numberless नम्-बरः-लैस *a.* innumerable, countless अगणित, असंख्य, संख्यातीत।

numeral नयू-मॅ-रॅल *a.* pertaining to, consisting of, or expressing, number संख्यात्मक, संख्यावाचक।

numerator न्यू मॅ रे टॅः *n.* number above the line in a vulgar fraction अंश।

numerical न्यू मै ॅ रि कॅल, न्यु– *a.* belonging to numbers संख्यात्मक।

numerous न्यू मॅ रॅस *a.* great in number, many अनेक, बहुत।

nun नन *n.* a female monk ईसाई भिक्षुणी।

nunnery न नॅ रि *n.* a convent of nuns भिक्षुणियों का मठ।

nuptial नप् शॅल *a.* of marriage वैवाहिक।

nuptials नप् शॅल्ज़ *n. pl.* marriage विवाह।

nurse[1] नॅःस *n.* woman attendant in a hospital परिचारिका।

nurse[2] *v.t.* to act as a nurse to (की) परिचारिका का कार्य करना; to look after carefully ढंग से देखभाल करना।

nursery नॅः सॅ रि *n.* place in which children are nursed and taken care of शिशु-सदन; place where trees, plants etc. are propagated free seed पौधशाला।

nurture[1] नॅः चॅः *n.* education शिक्षा; training प्रशिक्षण; nourishment भोजन, पोषण।

nurture[2] *v.t.* to bring up पालन-पोषण करना; to educate शिक्षित करना।

nut नट *n.* fruit containing a seed or kernel within a covering गिरीदार मेवा; hollow metal collar into which a screw fits ढिबरी।

nutrition न्यु ट्रि शॅन, न्यू– *n.* receiving foods भोजन-ग्रहण; act of nourishing पोषण।

nutritious न्यु ट्रि शॅस, न्यू– *a.* serving to nourish पोषक (भोजन); promoting growth वृद्धिकारक।

nutritive न्यू ट्रि टिव *a.* pertaining to nutrition पोषण-संबंधी।

nuzzle न-ज़ल *n.t.* to sniff सूंघना; to burrow with the nose नाक से खोदना; to touch with the nose नाक से छूना; to rub with the nose नाक से रगड़ना।

nylon नॉइ-लॅन, -लौ ॅन *n.* a strong elastic synthetic material used in hosiery and textile नाइलॉन।

nymph निम्फ़ *n.* goddess of the mountains, forests, meadows, or waters परी।

Oo

O ओ the fifteenth letter of the English alphabet, symbol for oxygen Chemistry. अंग्रेजी वर्णमाला का पन्द्रहवाँ अक्षर, रसायन शास्त्र प्राणवायु (ऑक्सीजन या उद्‌जन) के लिये सांकेतिक अक्षर।

oak *ओक* *n.* a valuable tree of many species शाहबलूत।

oar *औः, औ ः* *n.* a long piece of timber used to propel a boat चप्पू।

oarsman *औः ज़् मॅन* *n.* one who rows at the oar नाविक, मल्लाह।

oasis *ओ ए सिस* *n.* *(pl.-ses ओ ए सीज़)* fertile spot where there is water in a desert नख़लिस्तान।

oat *ओट* *n.* a cereal plant valuable for its grain जई।

oath *ओथ* *n.* solemn declaration शपथ।

obduracy *औब् ड्यु रॅ सि* *n.* state or quality of being obdurate हठ, ज़िद।

obdurate *औब् ड्यु रिट* *a.* stubborn हठी, ज़िद्दी।

obedience *ॲ बी ड्यॅन्स* *n.* quality of obeying आज्ञाकारिता।

obedient *ॲ बी डॅयन्ट* *a.* submissive to authority आज्ञाकारी।

obeisance *ओ˘ बे सॅन्स* *n.* a bow or courtesy to show respect श्रद्धापूर्ण नमन।

obesity *ओ˘ बी सि टि* *n.* opulence, fatness मोटापा।

obey *ॲ बे, ओ˘ बे* *v.t.* to comply with की आज्ञा मानना; *v.i.* to submit to authority आज्ञाकारी होना।

obituary *ॲ बि ट्यु ॲ रि* *a.* printed notice or account of somebody's death निधन-सूचना।

object[1] *औब् जिक्ट* *n.* end लक्ष्य; person or thing to which feeling or action is directed पात्र, विषय, purpose उद्देश्य; material thing वस्तु; *(gram.)* objective case (व्या.) कर्मकारक।

object[2] *ॲब् जैक्ट* *v.t.* to state in opposition विरोधस्वरूप कहना; *v.i.* to make a protest विरोध करना।

objection *ॲब् जै˘क् शॅन* *n.* act of objecting आपत्ति।

objectionable *ॲब् जै˘क् शॅ नॅ ब्ल* *a.* justly liable to objections आपत्तिजनक।

objective[1] *ॲब् जै˘क् टिव, औब्-* *n.* goal लक्ष्य; purpose उद्देश्य; the objective case कर्मकारक।

objective[2] *a.* having existence outside the mind वस्तुगत; real वास्तविक; uninfluenced by personal feelings or opinions तटस्थ, निष्पक्ष; *(gram.)* of the object (व्या.) कर्मवाची।

oblation *ओ˘ ब् ले शॅन* *n.* offering made to God or a god नैवेद्य, चढ़ावा, बलि।

obligation *औ˘ ब् लि गे शॅन* *n.* that which morally obliges बंधन, आभार; duty कर्त्तव्य; responsibility उत्तरदायित्व।

obligatory *ॲब् लि गॅ टॅ रि* *a.* imposing an obligation बाध्यकर, अनिवार्य।

oblige *अॅ ब्लॉइज v.t.* to compel विवश करना; to help or gratify with a small service उपकृत करना।

oblique *अॅब् लीक, ओ ॅब्- a.* slanting तिरछा।

obliterate *अॅब् लि टॅ रेट, औबॅ् लि- v.t.* to destroy entirely पूर्णतः विनष्ट करना।

obliteration *अॅब् लि टॅ रे शॅन n.* act of obliterating विनाश, विलोपन।

oblivion *अॅ ब्लि वि अॅन n.* state of being forgotten विस्मरण।

oblivious *अॅ ब्लि वि अॅस a.* having no memory (of) स्मृतिहीन।

oblong[1] *औबॅ् लौ ॅ ङ्ग a.* of rectangular shape आयताकार।

oblong[2] *n.* a rectangle more long than broad आयत।

obnoxious *औबॅ् नौकॅ् शॅस, अॅब्- a.* extremely unpleasant अप्रिय।

obscene *औबॅ् सीन a.* normally repugnant अश्लील।

obscenity *औबॅ् सै ॅ नि टि n.* state or qulaity of being obscene अश्लीलता।

obscure[1] *अॅब् स्क्युअॅः, औबॅ्- a.* not easily understood गूढ; hidden गुप्त; faint धुंधला।

obscure[2] *v.t.* to conceal छिपाना।

obscurity *अॅब् स्कुअॅ रि टि, औबॅ्- n.* state or quality of being obscure गूढ़ता; something that is obscure गूढ़ विचार, भाव आदि।

observance *अॅब् ज़ॅः वॅन्स n.* the keeping of a law, custom, festival etc. अनुपालन; a custom or ceremony रिवाज़, रीति, प्रथा।

observant *अॅब् ज़ॅः वॅन्ट a.* carefully attentive सावधान, सतर्क; mindful of laws, customs etc. अनुपालक।

observation *औबॅ् ज़ॅः वे शॅन n.* watching and noting निरीक्षण; ability to notice अवलोकन-क्षमता; *(usu.pl.)* comment, remark टिप्पणी।

observatory *अॅब् ज़ॅः वॅ टॅ रि n.* a place for astronomical observations वैधशाला।

observe *अॅब् ज़ॅःव v.t.* to take notice of अवलोकन करना; to celebrate मनाना; to keep, to follow पालन करना; to comment टिप्पणी-स्वरूप कहना।

obsess *अॅब् सैसॅ v.t.* to occupy the mind continually अभिभूत करना, परेशान करना।

obsession *अॅब् सै ॅ शॅन n.* state of being obsessed परेशानी; something that obsesses परेशानी का कारण।

obsolete *औ ॅब् सॅ लीट a.* out of date पुराना; no longer in use अप्रचलित।

obstacle *औबॅ् स्टॅ कल n.* hindrance, inpediment बाधा, रुकावट।

obstinacy *औबॅ् स्टि नॅ सि n.* state or quality of being obstinate हठ, ज़िद।

obstinate *औबॅ् स्टि निट a.* stubborn हठी, ज़िद्दी।

obstruct *अॅब् स्ट्रक्ट v.t.* to block up अवरूद्ध करना।

obstruction *अॅब् स्ट्रक् शॅन n.* act of obstructing अवरोध obstacle बाधा।

obstructive *अॅब् स्ट्रक् टिव a.* hindering बाधक।

obtain *अॅब् टेन v.t.* to acquire प्राप्त करना; *v.i.* to be customary प्रचलित होना।

obtainable *अॅब् टे नॅ ब्ल a.* available प्राप्य।

obtuse *अॅब् टयूस a.* dull मंदबुद्धि; (an angle) of more than 90 degrees अधिक (कोण); blunt, not pointed भोथरा; stupid मूर्ख, भौंदू।

obvious *औबॅ वि अॅस a.* evident स्पष्ट; manifest प्रकट।

occasion[1] *अॅ के ज़ॅन n.* opportunity अवसर; cause, reason कारण; need आवश्यकता।

occasion[2] *v.t.* to be the cause of का कारण बनना।

occasional *अॅ के ज़ॅ न्ल a.* happening only now and then यदा-कदा होनेवाला; produced for some special event अवसर विशेष के लिए।

occasionally *अॅ के ज़ॅ नॅ लि adv.* not regularly यदा-कदा।

occident *औकॅ सि डॅन्ट n.* the west पश्चिम।

occidental *औकॅ सि डैनॅ ट्ल a.* western पाश्चात्य।

occult *औ ॅ कल्ट a.* hidden गुप्त, छिपा हुआ; supernatural अलौकिक।

occupancy *औ ॅ क्यु पॅन् सि n.* fact of occupying दख़ल; residing निवास।

occupant *औ ॅ क्यु पॅन्ट n.* an occupier दख़लकार।

occupation *औ ॅ क्यु पे शॅन n.* act of taking possession क़ब्ज़ा, अधिकार; employment रोज़गार; vocation व्यवसाय।

occupier *औ ॅ क्यु पॉइ अॅ: n.* tenant दख़लदार।

occupy *औ ॅ क्यु पॉइ v.t.* to take possession of अधिकार में करना; to inhabit में रहना; to take up (time) (समय) लेना।

occur *अॅ कॅ: (-rr-) v.i.* to happen घटित होना; to come into the mind ध्यान में आना।

occurrence *अॅ क रॅन्स n.* happening, event घटना।

ocean *ओ शॅन n.* the large area of sea महासागर।

oceanic *ओ शि ऐ निक a.* of the ocean समुद्री, महासागरीय।

octagon *औकॅ टॅ गॅन n.* a plane figure having eight angles and sides अष्टकोण।

octangular *औकॅ टैङ् ग्यू लॅ: a.* having eight angles अष्टकोणीय।

octave *औकॅ टिव n.* a stanza of eight lines अष्टपदी।

October *औकॅ टो बॅ: n.* tenth month of the year अक्टूबर।

octogenarian[1] *औकॅ टो ॅ जि नॅ ॅ अॅ रि अॅन a.* of an age from 80 to 89 अस्सी से नवासी वर्षीय।

octogenarian[2] *a.* person of an age from 80 to 89 अस्सी से नवासी वर्षीय व्यक्ति।

octroi *औकॅ ट्रॉव n.* local tax चुंगी।

ocular *औकॅ यु लॅ: a.* of eye or sight आंखों या दृष्टि से संबंधित।

oculist *औकॅ यु लिस्ट n.* specialist in eye diseases नेत्ररोग-विशेषज्ञ।

odd *औ ॅड a.* not even विषम (संख्या); strange अद्भुत; unpaired अयुग्म; extra अतिरिक्त।

oddity *औ ॅ डि टि n.* singularity अनोखापन; odd person or thing अनोखा व्यक्ति या वस्तु।

odds *औ ˘ ड्ज़ n. pl.* inequalities असमानताएं; difference in favour of one फ़र्क; chances संभावनाएं।

ode *ओड n.* a lyric poem in the form of address संबोध गीत।

odious *ओ डि अॅस a.* hateful, repulsive घृणास्पद।

odium *ओ ड्यॅम n.* widespread dislike घृणाभाव।

odorous *ओ डॅ रॅस a.* fragrant सुगंधित।

odour *ओ डॅः n.* smell गंध।

offence *औ ˘ फ़ैन्स, अॅ- n.* illegal act अपराध; transgression of law क़ानून का उल्लंघन; displeasure अप्रसन्नता; attacking आक्रमण; insult अपमान।

offend *अॅ फ़ैन्ड v.t.* to displease नाराज़ करना; to insult अपमानित करना; *v.i.* to do wrong, to commit an offence अपराध करना।

offender *अॅ फ़ैनॅ डॅः n.* one who offends अपराधी।

offensive[1] *अॅ फ़ैनॅ सिव a.* causing offence अपमानजनक; causing displeasure or annoyance अप्रसन्नताजनक; aggressive आक्रामक।

offensive[2] *n.* act of attacking वार, आक्रमण; a sustained effort अनवरत प्रयत्न।

offer[1] *औ ˘ फ़ः v.t.* to present (for acceptance of rejection) प्रस्तुत करना; to tender देना; to propose प्रस्तावित करना; *v.i.* to occur घटित होना, प्रस्तुत होना।

offer[2] *n.* act of offering प्रस्ताव; something offered भेंट, बलि।

offering *औ ˘ फ़ॅ रिड़्ग n.* gift उपहार; oblation भेंट, चढ़ावा।

office *औ ˘ फ़िस n.* place where official or professional work is done कार्यालय; a government department सरकारी विभाग; position पद; duty कर्त्तव्य, कार्य।

officer *औ ˘ फ़ि सॅः n.* person invested with an office अधिकारी।

official[1] *अॅ फ़ि शॅल a.* authoritative आधिकारिक; pertaining to office पदीय।

official[2] *n.* one holding office पदाधिकारी।

officially *अॅ फ़ि शॅ लि adv.* in an official manner or capacity अधिकृत रूप से।

officiate *अॅ फ़ि शि एट v.i.* to perform official duties किसी पद पर काम करना।

officious *अॅ फ़ि शॅस a.* too eager to serve सेवा के लिए उतावला।

offing *औ ˘ फ़िड़्ग n.* the distant part of the sea visible from the shore दृश्य क्षितिज।

offset[1] *औफ़ॅ सै˘ट, औफ़् - v.t. (-tt-)* to compensate क्षतिपूर्ति करना; to counterbalance संतुलित करना।

offset[2] *n.* a method of printing ऑफ़सैट छपाई।

offshoot *औ ˘फ़् शूट n.* shoot of a plant प्रशाखा।

offspring *औ˘फ़् स्प्रिड़्ग n.* child or children संतति।

oft *औ˘फ़्ट adv.* often प्रायः।

often *औ˘ फ़्न, औ- adv.* frequently प्रायः।

ogle[1] *ओ गॅल v.t. & v.i.* to look amorously (at) प्रेम-भरी दृष्टि से देखना, घूरना, ताकना।

ogle[2] *n.* amorous stare प्रेम-भरी चितवन।

oil[1] औ ॅइल *n.* easily burning liquid तेल।

oil[2] *v.t.* to apply oil to तेल लगाना।

oily औ ॅइलि *a. (lier, -liest)* like oil तेल जैसा; greasy चिकना; too smooth and fawning चापलूसीपूर्ण।

ointment औ ॅइन्ट् मॅन्ट *n.* a grease applied to the skin मरहम।

old ओल्ड *a.* aged बूढ़ा; not new or fresh पुराना; antiquated प्राचीन।

oligarchy औ ॅ लि गॉः कि *n.* government in which the supreme power is in a few hands अल्पतंत्र।

olive औ ॅ लिव *n.* an evergreen tree जैतून।

olympiad औ ॅ लिम् पि ऐड *n.* period of four years between olympic games ओलिंपिक खेलों के बीच की चार वर्ष की अवधि।

omega ओ मि गॅ *n.* a letter of the Greek alphabet ग्रीक वर्णमाला का अंतिम अक्षर; end अंत।

omelet (te) औमॅ् लिट *n.* dish of eggs beaten and fried with seasoning आमलेट।

omen ओ मै ॅन *n.* a sign of a future event (good or bad) शकुन।

ominous ओॅ मि नॅस *a.* suggesting future trouble, inauspicious अमंगलकारी।

omission ओॅ मि शॅन *n.* act of omitting अनाचरण; something omitted चूक, त्रुटि।

omit ओॅ मिट *(-tt-) v.t.* to pass over or neglect पर ध्यान न देना; to fail to include छोड़ देना।

omnipotence औ ॅम् नि पॅ टॅन्स *n.* almighty or unlimited power सर्वशक्तिमत्ता।

omnipotent औमॅ् नि पॅ टॅन्ट *a.* all-powerful सर्वशक्तिमान।

omnipresence आमॅ् नि प्र ॅ ज़ॅन्स *n.* presence in every place at the same time सर्वव्यापकता।

omnipresent औमॅ् नि प्रै ॅ ज़ॅन्ट *a.* present in all places at the same time सर्वव्यापी।

omniscience औमॅ् नि ॅसि अॅन्स *n.* universal knowledge सर्वज्ञता।

omniscient औमॅ् नि सि अॅन्ट *a.* having universal knowledge सर्वज्ञ।

on[1] औनॅ *prep.* above and touching: at पर; near के पास; towards की ओर; concerning के विषय में; during के दौरान।

on[2] *adv.* forward आगे की ओर; continuously अनवरत रूप से; in action चालू हालत में।

once वन्स *adv.* for one time एक बार; formerly पहले; ever कभी।

one[1] वन *a.* single एक; the same वही, समान; united एक जुट।

one[2] *pron.* a person कोई व्यक्ति; a thing कोई वस्तु।

oneness वन् निस *n.* unity एकता; uniformity एकरूपता।

onerous औ ॅ नॅ रॅस *a.* burdensome भारी।

onion अन् यॅन *n.* an edible bulb of pungent flavour प्याज़।

on-looker औनॅ् लु कॅः *n.* spectator दर्शक।

only[1] ओन् लि *a.* single अकेला; alone मात्र।

only[2] *adv.* for one purpose alone मात्र।

only[3] *conj.* but then, however किंतु, तथापि।

onomatopoeia *औ˘ नॅ मै टॉ पि अॅ n.* formation of a word by using sounds that suggest the object to be named ध्वनि अनुकरणात्मक शब्द।

onrush *औनॅ् रश n.* strong onward rush or flow प्रवाह।

onset *औनॅ् सै˘ट n.* assault हमला, चढ़ाई।

onslaught *औनॅ् स्लौट n.* fierce attack भीषण आक्रमण।

onus *ओ नॅस n.* burden भार; responsibility उत्तरदायित्व।

onward[1] *औनॅ् वॅःड a.* advanced अग्रवर्ती; forward, progressive प्रगतिशील।

onward[2], **onwards** *औनॅ् वॅःड़्ज़ adv.* forward आगे की ओर।

ooze[1] *ऊज़ n.* soft liquid mud कीचड़, पंक।

ooze[2] *v.i.* to pass out slowly रिसना; *v.t.* to emit रिसाना, बाहर फेंकना।

opacity *ओ˘ पै सि टि n.* quality of being opaque अपारदर्शिता।

opal *ओ पॅल n.* a precious stone displaying variegated colours ओपल, दूधिया पत्थर।

opaque *ओ˘ पेक a.* not transparent अपारदर्शी।

open[1] *ओ पॅन a.* not covered खुला; not closed खुला।

open[2] *v.t.* to cause to be open खोलना; to unfold खोलना; to start चालू करना; to establish स्थापित करना; to spread out फैलाना; *v.i.* to become open खुलना; to be started चालू होना।

opening *ओ पे निङ्ग n.* opportunity अवसर; beginning आरंभ; first performance प्रारंभिक प्रदर्शन; open space खुली जगह।

openly *ओ पॅन् लि adv.* in an open manner खुले रूप में।

opera *औ˘ पॅ रॅ n.* a dramatic composition set to music and sung and acted on the stage संगीत-नाटक।

operate *औ˘ पॅ रेट v.t.* to cause to function चलाना, चालू करना; to manage (का) संचालन करना; *v.i.* to function काम करना, चलना; to carry out a surgical operation शल्यक्रिया करना; to carry out military movements सैनिक कार्यवाही करना।

operation *औ˘ पॅ रे शॅन n.* act of surgery शल्यक्रिया; strategic military movement सैनिक अभियान; act or method of operating संचालन।

operative *औ˘ पॅ रॅ टिव a.* in operation चालू; effective लागू; of surgical operations शल्यक्रियात्मक।

operator *औ˘ पॅ रे टॅः n.* one who operates प्रचालक।

opine *ओ˘ पॉइन v.t.* to have the opinion that मानना, सोचना।

opinion *ॲ पिन् यॅन n.* belief विश्वास; view, judgement मत, धारणा; estimation अनुमान।

opium *ओ प्यॅम n.* a narcotic drug अफ़ीम।

opponent *ॲ पो नॅन्ट n.* one who opposes विरोधी व्यक्ति, प्रतिद्वंद्वी।

opportune *औ˘ पॅः ट्यून a.* timely अवसरोचित; suitable उचित।

opportunism *औ˘ पॅः ट्यु निज़्म n.*

policy of doing what is expedient अवसरवादिता।

opportunity *औ ॅ पॅ: ट्यू नि टि n.* favourable time or chance सुअवसर।

oppose *अॅ पोज़ v.t.* to offer resistance to विरोध करना।

opposite *औ ॅ पॅ ज़िट a.* contrary विरोधी; facing सामने वाला; adverse प्रतिकूल।

opposition *औ ॅ पॅ ज़ि शॅन n.* act of opposing विरोध; resistance प्रतिरोध; party opposing that in power विरोधी दल; contrast प्रतिकूलता।

oppress *अॅ प्रॅ ॅस v.t.* to harass तंग करना; to govern with tyranny क्रूरतापूर्वक शासन करना; to weigh down दबाना, दमन करना।

oppression *अॅ प्रै ॅ शॅन n.* act of oppressing दमन।

oppressive *अॅ प्रै ॅ सिव a.* hard to endure दमनकारी, असहनीय; unjustly severe अत्याचारी।

oppressor *अॅ प्रै ॅ सॅ: n.* one who oppresses दमनकर्त्ता; cruel ruler क्रूर शासक।

opt *ऑप्ट v.i.* to make a choice चयन करना, विकल्प छांटना।

optic *औपॅ टिक a.* pertaining to sight दृष्टि-संबंधी; relating to the science of optics प्रकाशकीय।

optician *औपॅ टि शॅन n.* person skilled in optics चश्मे का निर्माता।

optimism *औ ॅप् टि मिज़्म n.* hopeful view of things आशावाद।

optimist *औपॅ टि मिस्ट n.* one who believes in optimism आशावादी।

optimistic *औपॅ टि मिस् टिक a.* relating to or characterized by optimism आशान्वित, आशावादी।

optimum[1] *औपॅ टि मॅम n.* the most favourable condition अनुकूलतम परिस्थिति।

optimum[2] *a.* most favourable अनुकूलतम, सर्वोत्तम।

option *औपॅ शॅन n.* choice विकल्प; right to choose चयनाधिकार; thing that is or may be chosen चयन की गई या की जानेवाली वस्तु।

optional *औ ॅप् शॅ नॅल a.* depending on choice वैकल्पिक; not compulsory ऐच्छिक।

opulence *औ ॅप् यु लॅन्स n.* wealth धन-संपत्ति; abundance प्रचुरता, बाहुल्य।

opulent *औपॅ यु लॅन्ट a.* wealthy धनाढ्य, समृद्ध; luxuriant प्रचुर, भरपूर।

oracle *औ ॅ रॅ कॅल n.* prophetic wisdom देववाणी; person regarded as a source of wisdom आप्तपुरूष; shrine देवस्थल, तीर्थ-मंदिर।

oracular *अॅ रै क्ज़ लॅ: a.* of or like an oracle देववाणीय, देववाणीसदृश; with a hidden meaning रहस्यपूर्ण, गूढ़ार्थक।

oral *औ रॅल a.* spoken rather than written मौखिक; of or administered through the mouth मुखीय या मुख से दी जाने वाली (औषधि)।

orally *औ रॅ लि adv.* in an oral manner मौखिक रूप से; through the mouth मुखद्वार से।

orange[1] *औ ॅ रिन्ज n.* a citrus fruit संतरा; the tree bearing this fruit संतरे का पेड़; reddish yellow colour नारंगी रंग।

orange² *a.* reddish yellow नारंगी।

oration *औ रे शॅन n.* formal speech भाषण, व्याख्यान।

orator *औ ॅ रॅ टः n.* skilled or eloquent speaker कुशल वक्ता।

oratorical *औ ॅ रॅ टौ ॅ रि कॅल a.* of orator or oration भाषण-संबंधी, व्याख्यानीय।

oratory *औ ॅ रॅ टॅ रि n.* the art of public speaking भाषणकला।

orb *औःब n.* globe पृथ्वी-मंडल; sphere गोला।

orbit *औः बिट n.* the path of a planet or comet परिक्रमापथ, कक्षा।

orchard *औः चॅःड n.* peice of ground with fruit-trees फलोद्यान।

orchestra *औँः किस् ट्रॅ n.* body of musicians वादकवृंद।

orchestral *औँः कैस् ट्रॅल a.* of, for, by an orchestra वाद्यवृंदीय।

ordeal *औः डील n.* severe test, trial by fire and water अग्नि-परीक्षा।

order¹ *औः डॅः n.* command आदेश; request to supply goods आदेश, आदेश-पत्र; way in which things are placed in relation to one another अनुक्रम; obedience to the laws प्रशासनिक व्यवस्था; rank or class in society श्रेणी।

order² *v.t.* to command आदेश देना; to arrange व्यवस्थित करना; to direct निर्देशित करना।

orderly¹ *औः डॅः लि a.* in accordance with good order सुव्यवस्थित; regular नियमित।

orderly² *n.* an officer's messenger in the army अर्दली।

ordinance *औः डि नॅन्स n.* order given by authority अध्यादेश।

ordinarily *औः डि नॅ रि लि adv.* in an ordinary manner साधारणतः।

ordinary *औः डि नॅ रि a.* average, common सामान्य।

ordnance *औःड् नॅन्स n.* artillery तोपखाना; ammunition गोला-बारूद; military department in charge of ammunition आयुध-विभाग।

ore *औः n.* a metal bearing mineral कच्ची धातु।

organ *औः गॅन n.* instrument or means माध्यम; a musical instrument with sounding pipes वाद्यराज; part of an animal अवयव, अंग।

organic *औः गै निक a.* pertaining to or acting as an organ आंगिक; pertaining to the animal and vegetable world जैव; having a systematic arragnement of parts संगठित।

organism *औः गॅ निज़्म n.* organic structure शरीर-रचना; a body exhibiting organic life जीव।

organization *औः गॅ नॉइ ज़े शॅन n.* act or process of organizing संघटन, व्यवस्थापन।

organize *औः गॅ नॉइज़ v.t.* to establish and systematize संघटित करना; to put into working order सुव्यवस्थित करना; to make preparations for (की) तैयारी करना।

orient¹ *औ रि ॲन्ट n.* East पूर्व।

orient² *v.t.* to orientate (भवन आदि) का मुंह पूर्व की ओर करके बनाना।

oriental¹ *औ रि ऐनॅ् ट्ल a.* eastern प्राच्य, पूर्वी।

oriental² *n.* a native of some eastern country पूर्ववासी।

orientate *औ रि ऐन्॑ टेट* *v.t.* to orient (भवन आदि) पूर्व की ओर मुंह करके बनाना।

origin *औ˘ रि जिन* *n.* source स्त्रोत, मूल; beginning उद्‌गम।

original[1] *अॅ रि जॅ न्‌ल* *a.* pertaining to origin मूल, मौलिक; first, earliest प्रारंभिक।

original[2] *n.* origin, source मूल रूप।

originality *अॅ रि जि नै लि टि* *n.* quality or state of being original मौलिकता।

originate *अॅ रि जि नेट* *v.t.* to give origin toउद्‌भूत करना; to produce निर्मित करना; *v.i.* to have origin उद्‌भूत होना।

originator *अॅ रि जि ने टॅ:* *n.* one who or that which originates प्रवर्तक, जन्मदाता।

ornament[1] *औ: नॅ मॅन्ट* *n.* that which adarns or embellishes आभूषण, अलंकरण।

ornament[2] *औ: नॅ मैन्ट* *v.t.* to decorate अलंकृत करना।

ornamental *औ : नॅ मेन्॑ ट्‌ल* *a.* pertaining to ornament शोभाकारी, आलंकारिक।

ornamentation *औ: नॅ मैन्॑ टे शॅन* *n.* ornaments or decorations सजावट; beautification अलंकरण।

orphan[1] *औ: फ़॑न* *n.* child bereaved of father or mother, or of both अनाथ बालक।

orphan[2] *v.t.* to cause to be an orphan अनाथ बनाना।

orphanage *औ: फ़॑ निज* *n.* home for orphans अनाथालय।

orthodox *औ: थॅ डौक्॑स* *a.* conventional परंपरागत; holding accepted views रूढ़िवादी।

orthodoxy *औ: थॅ डौक्॑ सि* *n.* quality or state of being orthodox रूढ़िवादिता।

oscillate *औ˘ सि लेट* *v.i.* to swing दोलन करना; *v.t.* to cause to swing दोलन कराना।

oscillation *औ˘ सि ले शॅन* *n.* act of oscillating दोलन।

ossify *औ˘ सि फ़ॉइ* *v.t.* to make hard like bone अस्थिवत् बनाना; to change into bone अस्थि का रूप देना; to make rigid कठोर बनाना; *v.i.* become hard like bone अस्थिवत् बनना; to be changed into bone अस्थि का रूप लेना; to become rigid कठोर बनना।

ostracize *औसॅ ट्रॅ सॉइज़* *v.t.* to banish by ostracism, to expel निर्वासित करना।

ostrich *औसॅ ट्रिच* *n.* a large running bird of Africa शुतुरमुर्ग़।

other[1] *अ दॅ:* *a.* not the same दूसरा; remaining शेष; different भिन्न; more अन्य, और।

other[2] *pron.* other person or thing अन्य व्यक्ति या वस्तु।

otherwise[1] *अ दॅ: वॉइज़* *adv.* in another way भिन्न प्रकार से; in other conditions अन्य दशाओं में; in other respects अन्य मामलों में।

otherwise[2] *conj.* if not, or else अन्यथा, नहीं तो।

otter *औ˘ टॅ:* *n.* a fish-eating aquatic mammal ऊदबिलाव।

ottoman *औ˘ टॅ मॅन* *n.* a cushioned seat without back or arms, used as a box दिवान।

ounce *ऑउन्स* *n.* twelfth part of a

pound troy औंस।

our *ऑउअः pron.* of or belonging to us हमारा, हमारे, हमारी।

oust *ऑउस्ट v.t.* to drive out of office or power निकाल देना, हरा देना।

out *ऑउट adv.* away from home घर से दूर; in the open air खुले में; away from बाहर; no longer in office अपदस्थ; on strike हड़ताल पर; no longer alight बुझी स्थिति में।

out-balance *ऑउट् बै लॅन्स v.t.* to outweigh से भारी या महत्वूपर्ण होना।

outbid *ऑउट् बिड v.t.* to offer a higher price than (से) बढ़कर बोली बोल देना।

outbreak *ऑउट् ब्रेक n.* sudden beginning (of war or disease) आरंभ, प्रकोप।

outburst *ऑउट बॅःस्ट n.* bursting out (of anger, cheers etc.) प्रस्फोटन।

outcast[1] *ऑउट् कास्ट n.* one driven out from society जातिच्युत व्यक्ति।

outcast[2] *a.* driven out from home or society बहिष्कृत।

outcome *ऑउट् कम n.* result or effect of an event परिणाम, नतीजा।

outcry *ऑउट् क्रॉइ a.* loud shout चीख़, चिल्लाहट; protest विरोध।

outdated *ऑउट् डे टिड a.* made out of date पुराना।

outdo *ऑउट् डू v.t.* to do more or better than से अच्छा होना, पछाड़ना।

outdoor *ऑउट् डौः a.* existing or being done out of doors बाह्य, बाहरी।

outer *ऑउ टॅः a.* concerning the outside बाह्य।

outfit[1] *ऑउट् फ़िट n.* set of garments worn together कपड़ों का जोड़ा।

outfit[2] *(-tt-) v.t.* to equip सज्जित करना।

outgrow *ऑउट् ग्रो v.t.* to grow too large for से अधिक बढ़ जाना।

outhouse *ऑउट् हॉउस n.* an out building उपभवन।

outing *ऑउ टिङ्ग n.* short pleasure trip सैर-सपाटा।

outlandish *ऑउट् लैन् डिश a.* seeming odd and out of place अजीब, विदेशी।

outlaw[1] *ऑउट् लौ n.* fugitive from law अपराधी।

outlaw[2] *v.t.* to ban (पर) प्रतिबंध लगाना; to make illegal अवैध घोषित करना।

outline[1] *ऑउट् लॉइन n.* rough sketch रूपरेखा; general plan सामान्य योजना।

outline[2] *v.t.* to sketch चित्रित करना; to summarize संक्षेप में प्रस्तुत करना।

outlive *ऑउट् लिव v.i.* to live longer than से अधिक समय तक जीवित रहना।

outlook *ऑउट् लुक n.* attitude दृष्टिकोण; future prospect भावी संभावना।

outmoded *ऑउट् मो डिड a.* out of fashion अप्रचलित, पुराना।

outnumber *ऑउट् नम् बॅः v.t.* to be greater in number than (से) संख्या में अधिक होना।

outpatient *ऑउट् पे शॅन्ट n.* person visiting a hospital for treatment बहिरोंगी।

outpost *ऑउट् पोस्ट n.* observation

post at a distance दूरवर्ती चौकी।

output *ऑउट् पुट n.* quantity of goods produced or work done उत्पादन।

outrage[1] *ऑउट् रेज,-रिज n.* injurious violence नृशंसता।

outrage[2] *v.t.* to offend grossly का घोर अपमान करना; to injure चोट पहुंचाना; to violate भंग करना; to ravish का शील भंग करना।

outright[1] *ऑउट् रॉइट adv.* entirely पूर्णतया; openly स्पष्ट रूप से।

outright[2] *a.* thorough पूरा, समग्र; open, plain स्पष्ट।

outrun *ऑउट् रन v.t.* to run faster than से तेज़ दौड़ना; to go beyond से आगे निकल जाना।

outset *ऑउट् सै ॅट n.* start प्रांरभ।

outshine *ऑउट् शॉइन v.t.* to surpass (को) मात कर देना; to shine more brightly than (से) बढ़कर चमकना।

outside[1] *ऑउट् सॉइड a.* external बाह्य।

outside[2] *n.* the external surface बाहरी सतह।

outside[3] *adv.* on or to the outside बाहर की ओर।

outside[4] *prep.* at or on the outside of के बाहर; beyond the limits of की सीमा से परे।

outsider *ऑउट् सॉइ डः n.* person outside from a specific group बाहरी व्यक्ति।

outsize *ऑउट् सॉइज़ a.* larger than usual अधिमाप, सामान्य से बड़ा।

outskirts *ऑउट् स्कॅःट्स n.pl.* outlying parts of a town बाह्याचंल, नगरोपांत।

outspoken *ऑउट् स्पो कॅन a.* frank in saying what one thinks स्पष्टवादी।

outstanding *आउट् स्टैन् डिङ्ग a.* eminent विशिष्ट; unresolved अनिर्णीत; still to be paid बक़ाया।

outward[1] *ऑउट् वॅःड a.* situated outside बाह्य; apparent ऊपरी।

outward[2]**, outwards** *adv.* towards the outside बाहर की ओर।

outwardly *ऑउट् वॅःड् लि adv.* in appearance देखने में।

outweigh *ऑउट् वे v.t.* to exceed in weight or inportance से अधिक भारी या महत्वपूर्ण होना।

outwit *ऑउट् विट (-tt-) v.t.* to get the better of by cunning से अधिक चालबाज़ होना।

oval[1] *ओ वॅल a.* egg-shaped अंडाकार।

oval[2] *n.* something egg-shape अंडाकार वस्तु।

ovary *ओ वॅ रि n.* female egg-producing organ अंडाशय।

ovation *ओ ॅ वे शॅन n.* expression of popular acclaim जय जयकार।

oven *अ वॅन n.* small furnace चूल्हा।

over[1] *ओ वॅः prep.* above के ऊपर; on, upon पर; more than से अधिक; across के आर-पार।

over[2] *adv.* above ऊपर की ओर; in excess अधिक; too much हद से ज़्यादा।

over[3] *n.* (cricket) delivery of six balls from one end ओवर।

overact *ओ वॅः रैक्ट v.t.* to act (something) in an exaggerated way अत्याभिनय करना।

overall[1] *ओ वॅ रौल n.* loose fitting garment लबादा।

overall[2] *a.* including everything, total कुल।

overawe ओ वॅ: रो *v.t.* to fill with fear and subdue आतंकित करना।

overboard ओ वॅ: बोःड़ *adv.* over the side of a ship into the water (जहाज़) पर से।

overburden ओ वॅ: बॅ: ड्न *v.t.* to load with excessive weight भाराक्रांत करना, अधिक बोझ डालना।

overcast ओ वॅ: कास्ट *a.* covered over by clouds मेघाच्छन्न।

overcharge[1] ओ वॅ: चाःज *v.t. & i.* to charge higher price (from) (से) अधिक मूल्य वसूलना।

overcharge[2] *n.* excessive charge अधिमूल्य।

overcoat ओ वॅ: कोट *n.* heavy coat ओवरकोट।

overcome ओ वॅ: कम *v.t.* to overwhelm अभिभूत कर देना; to be victorious over पर विजयी होना।

overdo ओ वॅ: डू *v.t.* to do too much (की) अति करना; to cook too much बहुत अधिक पका देना।

overdose[1] ओ वॅ: डोस *n.* excessive dose of medicine (ओषधि की) अतिमात्रा।

overdose[2] *v.t.* to give too large a dose औषधि की अति मात्रा देना।

overdraft ओ वॅ: ड्राफ़्ट *n.* amount of money drawn in excess of deposit जमा से अधिक निकाली राशि।

overdraw ओ वॅ: ड्रौ *v.t.* to exaggerate अतिरंजित करना; to draw a sum in excess of (one's credit balance in a bank) (खाते में जमा) से अधिक धन निकालना।

overdue ओ वॅ: ड्यू *a.* beyond the time fixed विलंबित।

overhaul[1] ओ वॅ: हौल *v.t.* to repair मरम्मत करना; to examine and set in order निरीक्षण करके ठीक करना; to overtake से आगे निकलना।

overhaul[2] *n.* thorough repairing पूरी मरम्मत।

overhear ओ वॅ: हिअॅ: *v.t.* to hear secretly चुपके से सुनना; to hear by chance संयोग से सुनना।

overjoyed ओ वॅ: जौॅइड *a.* greatly delighted अति प्रसन्न।

overlap[1] ओ वॅ: लैप (*-pp-*) *v.t.* to go over and beyond the edge of कुछ अंश तक ढक लेना।

overlap[2] *n.* the ogverlapping part ढकने वाला भाग।

overleaf ओ वॅ: लीफ़ *adv.* on the other side of the leaf पन्ने की दूसरी ओर।

overload[1] ओ वॅ: *v.t.* to put too great a load on अधिक भार से लादना।

overload[2] *n.* too great a load क्षमता से अधिक भार।

overlook ओ वॅ: लुक *v.t.* to ignore (की) अनदेखी करना; to have a view of from above ऊपर से देखना।

overnight[1] ओ वॅ: नॉइट *adv.* during the night रात के समय; throughout the night रात-भर।

overnight[2] *a.* lasting a night, done at night रात्रि भर का।

overpower ओ वॅ: पॉउ अॅ: *v.t.* to overcome by superior force पराजित करना।

overrate औ वॅ: रेट *v.t.* to have too high an opinion of को अनावश्यक महत्व देना।

overrule ओ वॅ: रुल *v.t.* to disallow रद्द करना।

overrun *ओ वँ: रन v.t.&i.* to spread over and occupy रौंद डालना; to go beyond in time से अधिक समय तक चलना।

oversee *ओ वँ: सी v.t.* to supervise पर्यवेक्षण करना।

overseer *ओ वँ: सिअँ: n.* one who supervises पर्यवेक्षक।

overshadow *ओ वँ: शै डो v.t.* to throw a shadow over पर छाया डालना; to cause to seem less important का महत्व कम करना।

oversight *ओ वँ: सॉइट n.* failure to notice something दृष्टिभ्रम, चूक।

overt *ओ वँ:ट, ओˇ वँ:ट a.* manifest प्रकट।

overtake *ओ वँ: टेक v.t.* to catch up and pass in the same direction (से) आगे निकल जाना।

overthrow[1] *ओ वँ: थ्रो v.t.* to cause the fall of (का) तख़्ता उलट देना।

overthrow[2] *n.* defeat पराजय; ruin विनाश।

overtime[1] *ओ वँ: टॉइम adv.* after the usual hours सामान्य समय के पश्चात्।

overtime[2] *n.* time spent at work after the usual hours अधिसमय।

overture *ओ वँ: ट्युअँ: n.* piece of orchestral music वाद्यसंगीत; proposal initiating negotiations संधि-प्रस्ताव।

overwhelm *ओ वँ: हैˇल्म v.t.* to overpower अभिभूत करना; to overcome by force पराजित करना।

overwork[1] *ओ वँ: वँ:क v.i.* to work too hard and too long अतिश्रम करना; *v.t.* to cause to work too hard अतिश्रम कराना।

overwork[2] *ओ वँ: वँ:क n.* working to much or too long अतिश्रम।

owe *ओ v.t.&i.* to be under obligation to pay क़र्ज़दार होना; to have duty to render कर्त्तव्य से बंधा होना।

owl *ऑउल n.* a nocturnal bird उल्लू।

own[1] *ओन a.* belonging or relating to oneself अपना, निजी।

own[2] *v.t.* to possess का स्वामी होना; to admit स्वीकार करना।

owner *ओ नँ: n.* person who owns something स्वामी।

ownership *ओ नँ: शिप n.* the state of being an owner स्वामित्व।

ox *औक्स n. (pl. oxen)* castrated bullock बैल।

oxygen *औक् सि जॅन n.* gas necessary for life ऑक्सीजन।

oyster *औˇ इस् टँ: n.* kind of shellfish शुक्ति।

Pp

P पी the sixteenth letter of the English alphabet, chemical symbol for phosphorus. अंग्रेजी वर्णमाला का सोलहवाँ अक्षर फ़ास्फ़ोरस् (स्फुर्) नामक तत्व के लिए रासायनिक संकेत।

pace[1] *पेस n.* step पग; walk, gait चाल; rate of movement गति।

pace[2] *v.i.* to step, to walk चलना; *v.t.* to cross by walking चलकर तय

करना।

pacific *पॅ सि फ़िक a.* calm, tranquil शांत, स्थिर; pacifying शांतिप्रद।

pacify *पै सि फ़ॉइ v.t.* to allay शांत करना; to give peace to शांति लाना।

pack[1] *पैक n.* bundle, bale गठरी, बोझ; set of playing cards ताश की गड्डी; band of animals शिकारी कुत्तों, भेड़ियों इत्यादि का समुदाय।

pack[2] *v.t.* to stuff माल से भरना; to make into a bundle गठरी बांधना; *v.i.* to make up bundles गठरी बनाना।

package *पै किज n.* bundle,packet छोटी गठरी; charge for packing गठरी बनाने का भाड़ा।

packet *पै किट n.* small parcel or pack, bundle छोटा पार्सल या पुलिंदा।

packing *पै किङ्ग n.* material used in making a packet बांधने की सामग्री; act of one who packs बांधने का कार्य।

pact *पैक्ट n.* agreement बंधेज; इक़रारनामा; contract ठेका, संधि।

pad[1] *पैड n.* cushion गद्दी; soft saddle काठी; block of blotting paper सोख़्ता या कागज़ की गड्डी; sole of animals पशुओं के पैर के नीचे का कोमल भाग।

pad[2] *(-dd-) v.t.* to make soft with pad गद्देदार बनाना।

padding *पै डिङ्ग n.* material used for stuffing गद्दी।

paddle[1] *पै ड्ल v.i.* to move feet in water पानी में पैर मारना; to row नाव चलाना।

paddle[2] *n.* a short oar छोटा डांड़ा।

paddy *पै डि n.* rice in the husk धान।

page[1] *पेज n.* boy servant छोकरा, लड़का; one side of a leaf of a book पुस्तक के पत्र का एक ओर का भाग।

page[2] *v.t.* to number the pages of (पुस्तक आदि के) पन्ने में अंक डालना।

pageant *पै जॅन्ट n.* pomp आडंबर, लीला; show तमाशा।

pageantry *पॅ जॅन् ट्रि n.* pompous spectacle आडंबर, तड़क-भड़क; show (collectively) तमाशा।

pagoda *पॅ गो डॅ n.* pyramidal temple पगोड़ा, मेरु-मंदिर।

pail *पेल n.* bucket बाल्टी।

pain[1] *पेन n.* anguish दुःख; suffering पीड़ा; distress क्लेश; *(pl.)* trouble, exertion, throes of child birth कष्ट, परेशानी, प्रसव-वेदना।

pain[2] *v.t.* to cause pain to पीड़ा देना दुःख देना।

painful *पेन्फुल a.* distressing, full of pain दुःखदायी।

painstaking *पेन्स् टे किङ्ग a.* diligent, laborious परिश्रमी, उद्यमी।

paint[1] *पेन्ट n.* pigment, colouring matter रंग।

paint[2] *v.t.* to colour रंगना; to portray चित्र बनाना; to describe वर्णन करना।

painter *पेन् टॅः n.* picture-maker, portrayer चित्रकार।

painting *पेन् टिङ्ग n.* picture in paint रंगा हुआ चित्र; art of representing objects by colours चित्रकला।

pair[1] *पे अः n.* set of two जोड़ा; man and his wife दंपती।

pair[2] *v.t.* to join in pairs जोड़ा लगाना

या मिलाना; *v.i.* to be grouped in two's जोड़ों का रूप लेना।

pal *पैल n.* friend मित्र।

palace *पै लिस n.* king's residence राजभवन, महल।

palanquin *पै लॅन् कीन n.* men-borne covered conveyance शिविका, पालकी।

palatable *पै लॅ टॅ ब्ल a.* tasteful, savoury स्वादिष्ट।

palatal *पै लॅ ट्ल a.* pertaining to the palate तालु-संबंधी।

palate *पै लिट n.* roof of the mouth तालु; taste स्वाद।

palatial *पॅ ले शॅल a.* like a palace भवन-जैसा; magnificent भव्य।

pale[1] *पेल n.* enclosure बाड़ा।

pale[2] *a.* wan पीला; dim, not bright धुंधला।

pale[3] *v.i.* to turn pale पीला होना।

palette *पै लिट n.* artist's flat board to mix colours on चित्रकार की रंग मिलाने की पटिया।

palm[1] *पाम n.* inner surface of hand हथेली।

palm[2] *v.t.* to conceal in the palm of hand हथेली में छिपाना।

palm[3] *n.* a tropical tree ताड़ का पेड़; symbol of victory विजय-चिह्न।

palmist *पा मिस्ट n.* one who deals in palmistry हस्तरेखा-सामुद्रिक विद्या में निपुण।

palmistry *पा मिस् ट्रि n.* art of telling fortune by the hand हस्त रेखा-सामुद्रिक विद्या।

palpable *पैल् पॅ ब्ल a.* plain, obvious स्पष्टगोचर, स्पष्ट, प्रत्यक्ष।

palpitate *पैल् पि टेट v.i.* to pulsate, to throb धड़कना, कांपना।

palpitation *पैल् पि टे शॅन n.* pulsation, beating of heart धड़कन।

palsy *पौल् ज़ि n.* paralysis पक्षाघात।

paltry *पौल् ट्रि a.* trivial, worthless तुच्छ; mean नीच।

pamper *पैम् पॅ: v.t.* to gratify the wishes of संतुष्ट करना; to indulge too much बहुत अधिक लाड करना।

pamphlet *पैम्फ़् लिट n.* thin, unbound book पैम्फ़्लेट, पर्चा; a short treatise छोटी पत्रिका।

pamphleteer *पैम्फ़् लि टिअ: n.* writer of pamphlets पर्चा लिखने वाला, पत्रिकाकार।

panacea *पै नॅ सि अॅ n.* cure for all ills रामबाण।

pandemonium *पैन् डि मो न्यॅम n.* abode of evil spirits पिशाच-निवास; disordely place अव्यवस्थित स्थान; din and uproar बड़ा उपद्रव।

pane *पेन n.* piece of glass in a window कांच की पट्टी।

panegyric *पै नि जि रिक n.* eulogy स्तुति; laudation प्रशंसा।

panel[1] *पै न्ल n.* raised or sunk portion in a door द्वारफलक, दिलहा; a piece of wood on which a picture is painted तैलचित्र बनाने की तख़्ती group of persons forming a team मंडल।

panel[2] *(-tt-) v.t.* to form with panels दिलहा या चौखटा लगाना।

pang *पैङ्ग n.* sharp pain व्यथा, संताप, वेदना।

panic *पै निक n.* terror त्रास, आतंक; sudden fear अकस्मात् भय।

panorama *पै नॅ रॉ मॅ; रै मॅ n.* extensive wiew निरंतर दृष्टिगत दृश्य; a picture of objects in all directions चित्रमाला; wide view इर्द-गिर्द का दृश्य।

pant[1] पैन्ट *v.i.* to gasp हांफना; to yearn तीव्र इच्छा करना।

pant[2] *n.* gasp धड़कन।

pantaloons *पै ॅन् टॅ लूनज़ n. pl.* tightly fitting trousers पतलून।

pantheism *पैन् थी इज़्म n.* the doctrine that the universe is God. विश्वदेवतावाद, सर्वेश्वरवाद।

pantheist *पैन् थी इस्ट n.* one who believes in pantheism सर्वेश्वरवादी।

panther *पैन् थॅः n.* a variety of leopard चीता, तेंदुआ।

pantomime *पैन् टॅ मॉइम n.* dumb-show मूकाभिनय; a theatrical show स्वांग।

pantry *पैन् ट्रि n. (pl. pantries)* room for storing food or untensils भंडारघर।

papacy *पे पॅ सि n.* office of the Pope पोप (रोम के सबसे बड़े पादरी) का पद; authority or jurisdiction of the Pope पादरी का अधिकार अथवा कार्यक्षेत्र।

papal *पे पल a.* relating to the Pope पोप-संबंधी।

paper *पे पॅः n.* thin flat sheet used for writing कागज़; newspaper समाचारपत्र; article, essay लेख; documents चिट्ठी-पत्री; set of examination questions प्रश्नपत्र।

par *पाः n.* equality of value सममूल्य; state of equality समता, बराबरी।

parable *पै रॅ ब्ल n.* story with a moral lesson नीतिकथा।

parachute *पै रॅ शूट n.* umbrella-like apparatus used to retard the descent of a falling body पैराशूट, हवाई छतरी।

parachutist *पै रॅ शू टिस्ट n.* one who uses a parachute हवाई छतरी से उतरने वाला सैनिक।

parade[1] *पॅ रेड n.* military display परेड, क़वायद; show, ostentation आडंबर; military exercise सैन्य-व्यायाम; public walk टहलने का मार्ग।

parade[2] *v.t.* to display प्रदर्शित करना; *v.i.* to go about in military procession परेड करना।

paradise *पै रॅ डॉइस* heaven स्वर्ग; a place of bliss परम आनंद का सुंदर स्थान।

paradox *पै रॅ डौक्स n.* a seeming contradiction असत्याभास, परस्पर विरूद्ध मत।

paradoxical *पै रॅ डौ ॅक् सि क्ल a.* of the nature of a paradox असत्याभास रूप का।

paraffin *पै रॅ फ़िन n.* wax like hydrocarbon mixture used in candles मोमबत्ती बनाने का एक प्रकार का पदार्थ, मृद्धसा।

paragon *पै रॅ गॅन n.* a perfect example of excellence, a model आदर्श या अत्युत्तम पदार्थ।

paragraph *पै रॅ ग्राफ़ n.* section of chapter or book अनुच्छेद, प्रकरण।

parallel[1] *पै रॅ लै ॅल a.* continuously at equal distances समानांतर; equal in all essential parts सदृश।

parallel[2] *v.t.* to represent as similar समानांतर करना; to compare तुल्य करना।

parallelism *पै रॅ लै ॅ लिज़्म n.* resemblance, comparison समानता।

parallelogram *पै रॅ लैॅ लॅ ग्रैम n.* a quadrilateral with opposite sides parallel समानांतर चतुर्भुज।

paralyse *पै रॅ लॉइज़ v.t.* to affect with paralysis लकवा मारना; to make ineffectal शक्तिहीन करना।

paralysis *पै रॅ लि सिस n.* a disease with damaged nervous system पक्षाघात, लकवा रोग।

paralytic *पै रॅ लि टिक a.* affected with paralysis लकवा मारा हुआ।

paramount *पै रॅ मॉउन्ट n.* superior to all others सर्वश्रेष्ठ, सर्वोत्तम।

paramour *पै रॅ मुअ: n.* an illicit lover अवैध प्रेमी; mistress प्रेमिका।

paraphernalia *पै रॅ फ़: ने ल्यॅ n. pl.* odds and ends सामग्री; equipment साज़-सामान।

paraphrase[1] *पै रॅ फ्रेज़ n.* meaning of a passage in other words टीका; free translation अन्वय।

paraphrase[2] *v.t.* to put into other words संक्षिप्त व्याख्या करना।

parasite *पै रॅ सॉइट n.* animal or plant living on another परोपजीवी जंतु या पौधा।

parcel[1] *पा: स्ल n.* a packet पार्सल; a portion खंड; a bundle पोटली, गठरी।

parcel[2] *(-ll-) v.t.* to divide into portions खंड करना, बांटना।

parch *पा:च v.t.* to roast भूनना; to scorch झुलसाना।

pardon[1] *पा: ड्न v.t.* to forgive, to excuse क्षमा करना।

pardon[2] *n.* forgiveness क्षमा।

pardonable *पा: डॅ नॅ ब्ल a.* excusable क्षमा के योग्य।

parent *पे रॅ अॅ रॅन्ट n.* father or mother माता या पिता; origin उद्गम।

parentage *पे अॅ रॅन् टिज n.* lineage जाति, कुल; parenthood वल्दियत।

parental *पॅ रैनॅ ट्ल a.* pertaining to parents पैतृक; affectionate प्रिय।

parenthesis *पॅ रै˘ न् थि सिस n. (pl.-ses)* sentence inserted into another निक्षेपवाक्य, अप्रधान वचन; brackets कोष्ठक ( ) का चिह्न।

parish *पै रिश n.* district under one clergyman पादरी का प्रदेश।

parity *पै रि टि n.* analogy समानता; equality बराबरी।

park[1] *पा:क n.* large enclosed piece of ground पार्क; ground in a town for recreation क्रीडावन, सर्वसामान्य के घूमने का बग़ीचा।

park[2] *v.t.* to inclose in a park पार्क बनाना; to leave (vehicle) for a short time (मोटर आदि) मोटर चौक में खड़ा करना।

parlance *पा: लॅन्स n.* way of speaking संभाषण की शैली; conversation वार्ता।

parley[1] *पा: लि n.* mutual discourse बातचीत; conference संभाषण-सभा।

parley[2] *v.i* to hold discussion सभा करना।

parliament *पा: लॅ मॅन्ट n.* legislative assembly संसद।

parliamentarian *पा: लॅ मैनॅ टे˘ अॅ रि अॅन n.* one skilled in parliamentary matters संसदवेत्ता; member of parliament संसद-सदस्य।

parliamentary *पाः लि मैँ न् टॅ रि a.* pertaining to parliament संसदीय।

parlour *पाः लॅः n.* sitting room बैठक।

parody[1] *पै रॅ डि n.* burlesque imitation हास्यानुकृति।

parody[2] *v.t.* to imitate in parody (की) पैरोडी लिखना।

parole[1] *पॅ रोल n.* conditional release of a prisoner पैरोल, सावधि मुक्ति, कारावकाश।

parole[2] *v.t.* to place on parole कारा से मुक्त करना।

parricide *पै रि सॉइड n.* murderer of a parent माता-पिता की हत्या करने वाला; murder of a parent मातृ-पितृहत्या।

parrot *पै रॅट n.* bird with short hooked beak तोता।

parry[1] *पै रि v.t.* to turn aside रोकना; to evade छेकना।

parry[2] *n.* act of parrying छेकान।

parson *पाः स्न n.* clergyman पादरी।

part[1] *पाः ट n.* share अंश; portion भाग; section खंड; role of an actor नाटक के पात्र का नियोग।

part[2] *v.t.* to divide बांटना; to separate अलग करना; *v.i.* to depart विदा होना।

partake *पाः टेक v.i. (p.t.-took, p.p.-taken)* to share भाग लेना, साक्षी होना।

partial *पाः शॅल a.* forming only a part आंशिक; incomplete अपूर्ण; biased पक्षपाती।

partiality *पाः शि ऐ लि टि n.* bias पक्षपात; fondness स्नेह।

participate *पाः टि सि पेट v.i.* to take part हिस्सा लेना; to share साक्षी होना।

participant *पाः टि सि पॅन्ट n.* partaker भाग लेने वाला।

participation *पाः टि सि पे शॅन n.* act of participating हिस्सेदारी, शिरकत।

particle *पाः टि क्ल a.* atom कण; very small quantity लेश।

particular[1] *पॅः टि क्यु लॅः a.* distinct पृथक्; special विशिष्ट; private व्यक्तिगत; careful सावधान; exact निश्चित।

particular[2] *n. (pl.)* detailed account विस्तृत वर्णन।

partisan[1] *पाः टि ज़ैन n.* a partyman पक्षधर।

partisan[2] *a.* prejudiced पक्षपातपूर्ण।

partition[1] *पाः टि शॅन n.* division into parts बंटवारा; section हिस्सा; dividing wall अलगानेवाली दीवार।

partition[2] *v.t.* to divide into sections बंटवारा करना, बांटना।

partner *पाःट् नॅः n.* companion साथी; associate in business सहकारी, साझीदार; husband or wife जीवन-साथी।

partnership *पाःट् नॅः शिप n.* state of being a partner साझेदारी, साझा; joint business सम्मिलित धंधा।

party *पाः टि n. (pl. parties)* a body of individuals दल; company समुदाय, समाज; one of two litigants मुक़दमा करनेवाला; side पक्ष।

pass[1] *पास v.i.* to go by चले जाना; to die मर जाना; to get success परीक्षा में उत्तीर्ण होना; to cease समाप्त हो जाना; to elapse बीत जाना; to happen घटित होना; to be enacted पारित होना; to be current फैलना; *v.t.* to cross पार करना; to undergo with success उत्तीर्ण करना; to circulate घुमाना; to spend बिताना; to hand over देना; to enact पारित करना।

pass[2] *n.* a narrow way दर्रा; permission पास, पार-पत्र; success (in examination) सफलता (परीक्षा में) condition दशा, हालत; thrust वार।

passage *पै सिज n.* act of going past गमन; voyage यात्रा; way through मार्ग; part of a book or speech अवतरण; enactment पारण।

passenger *पै सिन् जॅः n.* one who travels by public conveyance यात्री मुसाफ़िर।

passion *पै शॅन n.* strong emotion चित का आवेग; ardour भावावेग; love प्रेम।

passionate *पै शॅ निट a.* vehement तीव्र, तीक्ष्ण; irascible क्रोधी; lustful कामुक; moved by passion आवेशपूर्ण।

passive *पै सिव a.* inactive निष्क्रिय; unresisting निश्चेष्ट।

passport *पास् पौःट n.* license to travel abroad पार-पत्र।

past[1] *पास्ट a.* gone by बीता हुआ; belonging to an earlier period पहले का।

past[2] *n.* beyond times भूतपूर्व काल।

past[3] *prep.* beyond के आगे; out of reach of की पहुंच के बाहर; after के बाद।

paste[1] *पेस्ट n.* mixture of flour and water used as an adhesive आटे की लेई, साना हुआ आटा; soft composition लुगदी।

paste[2] *v.t.* to stick with paste लेई से चिपकाना।

pastel *पैस् टैॅल, पॅस् टैॅल n.* coloured chalk रंगीन खड़िया।

pastime *पास् टॉइम n.* game क्रीड़ा, खेल; recreation मन-बहलाव।

pastoral *पास् टॅ रॅल a.* relating to a bishop or shepherd पादरी या गड़रिये से संबंधित; relating to country life ग्रामीण जीवन-संबंधी।

pasture[1] *पास् चॅः n.* grass for food of cattle चारा घास; grazing ground चरागाह।

pasture[2] *v.t.* to feed on grazing चराना; *v.i.* to graze चरना।

pat[1] *पैट (-tt-) v.t.* to tap थपथपाना, ठोकना।

pat[2] *n.* light quick blow, tap थपकी।

pat[3] *adv.* exactly निश्चित रूप से; at a proper time उचित समय पर।

patch[1] *पैच v.t.* to repair, to mend मरम्मत करना।

patch[2] *n.* piece of cloth sewed on garment चिप्पड़, पैबंद।

patent[1] *पे टॅन्ट a.* evident स्पष्ट; manifest प्रत्यक्ष।

patent[2] *n.* writing granting exclusive right to invention पेटेन्ट, एकस्व।

patent[3] *v.t.* to secure a patent for. (आविष्कार की) रजिस्ट्री कराना।

paternal *पॅ टॅः न्ल a.* fatherly, hereditary पैतृक।

path *पाथ n.* way मार्ग; footway पगडंडी।

pathetic *पॅ थैॅ टिक a.* heart-touching हृदयस्पर्शी; full of pathos कारुणिक।

pathos *पे थौ˘स n.* power of exciting pity करुणा।

patience *पे शॅन्स n.* endurance सहनशीलता; forbearance धैर्य।

patient[1] *पे शॅन्ट a.* having endurance सहनशील; full of patience धैर्ययुक्त; not hasty जल्दी न करनेवाला।

patient[2] *n.* a person under medical treatment रोगी।

patricide *पैट् रि सॉइड n.* murder of father पितृहत्या; murderer of father पितृहंता।

patrimony *पैट् रि मॅ नि n.* property inherited from ancestors पैतृक धन, विरासत।

patriot *पै ट्रि ॲट, पे- n.* person who loves his country देशभक्त।

patriotic *पै ट्रि औ˘ टिक a.* inspired by the love of one's country देशभक्तिपूर्ण।

partiotism *पै ट्रि ॲ टिज़्म, पे- n.* love of one's country देशभक्ति।

patrol[1] *पॅ ट्रोल (-ll-) v.i.* to go the rounds as a patrol पहरा देना, रक्षा करना; *v.t.* to pass round as a guard (का) पहरा देना।

patrol[2] *n.* marching round by a guard रक्षा के निमित्त चक्कर लगाने की क्रिया; patrolling person or persons पहरेदार।

patron *पे ट्रॅन n.* supporter पोषक; protector संरक्षक।

patronage *पैट्रॅ निज n.* support सहायता; act of patronising संरक्षत्व।

patronize *पैट् रॅ नॉइज़ v.t.* to act as a patron towards आश्रय देना, सहायता देना।

pattern *पै टॅ:न n.* a model सांचा; design नमूना।

paucity *पौ सि टि n.* scarcity कमी; smallness of quantity न्यूनता।

pauper *पौ पॅ: n.* a poor person दरिद्र।

pause[1] *पौज़ n.* short interval or stop विराम, ठहराव।

pause[2] *v.i.* to cease for a time विश्राम करना, ठहरना।

pave *पेव v.t.* to form (surface) with stone or brick (पर) पत्थर या ईंट बैठाना, मार्ग बनाना।

pavement *पेव् मॅन्ट n.* paved floor पत्थर या ईंट का फ़र्श; footpath सड़क की पटरी।

pavilion *पॅ वि ल्यॅन n.* tent तंबू, ख़ेमा; ornamental building for concerts. etc. मंडप।

paw[1] *पौ n.* animal's foot with claws पंजा, चंगुल।

paw[2] *v.t.* to scratch with the paw or paws. पंजे से खुरचना।

pay[1] *पे v.t. (p.t. paid)* to discharge (debt) ऋण चुकाना; to reward बदला देना; to give salary वेतन देना।

pay[2] *n.* salary वेतन।

payable *पे ॲ बॅल a.* justly due देय; that may or ought to be paid शोधनीय।

payee *पे ई n.* person to whom money is paid or is due रुपया पानेवाला।

payment *पे मॅन्ट n.* act of paying भुगतान; discharge of debt चुकौता; amount paid अदा की गई राशि।

pea *पी n.* plant with seeds in pods मटर।

peace *पीस n.* state of quiet शांति; freedom from war अविरोध; harmony मैत्री।

peaceable *पी सॅ ब्ल a.* disposed to peace शांतिप्रिय; calm, unworried अव्याकुल।

peaceful *पीस् फुल a.* free from war, noise, disturbance शांत।

peach *पीच n.* आड़ू।

peacock *पी कौ ॅक n.* a large bird with rich plumage मोर।

peahen *पी हैनॅ n.* female of the peacock मयूरी।

peak *पीक n.* pointed top शिखर; hill's sharp top पहाड़ की चोटी।

pear *पेअॅः n.* a well-known fruit नाशपाती।

pearl *पॅःल n.* a whitish gem मोती।

peasant *पे ॅ ज़ॅन्ट n.* countrymen working on land किसान, खेतिहर।

peasantry *पे ॅ ज़ॅन् ट्रि n.* peasants as a class किसान-वर्ग।

pebble *पै ॅ ब्ल n.* small roundish stone पत्थर की गोली, कंकड़।

peck[1] *पैकॅ n.* measure of two gallons दो गैलन की तौल।

peck[2] *v.i.* to strike (at) with the beak चोंच मारना।

peculiar *पि क्यू ल्यॅः a.* unusual असाधारण; strange, odd विलक्षण।

peculiarity *पि क्यु लि ऐ रि टि n.* distinguishing feature विशेषता; oddity विलक्षणता।

pecuniary *पि क्यु न्यॅ रि a.* relating to money धन-संबंधी, आर्थिक।

pedagogue *पै ॅ डॅ गौगॅ n.* teacher of children बाल-शिक्षक; school master बाल-अध्यापक।

pedagogy *पै ॅ डॅ गौ ॅ गि, -जि n.* science of teaching शिक्षणशास्त्र।

pedal[1] *पै ॅ ड्ल n.* lever to be pressed by the foot पैडल, किसी यंत्र का पैर से चलाने का भाग।

pedal[2] *(-ll-) v.t.* to move with the pedal पैडल से चलाना; *v.i.* to use a pedal पैडल का प्रयोग करना।

pedant *पै ॅ डॅन्ट n.* one who makes a display of his learning विद्याडंबरी।

pedantic *पि डै ॅन् टिक n.* making a vain display of learning पांडित्य दिखलाने वाला।

pedantry *पै ॅ डॅन् ट्रि n.* vain display of learning विद्याडंबर।

pedestal *पै ॅडिस् ट्ल n.* base of a column पाद-पीठ, चौकी; pillar भवन का स्तंभपाद।

pedestrian *पि डै ॅस् ट्रि ॲन n.* one who walks on foot पादचारी या पैदल चलनेवाला यात्री।

pedigree *पै ॅ डि ग्रि n.* lineage, line of ancestors वंशावली।

peel[1] *पील v.t.* to strip off (skin, bark) (से) छिलका या छाल उतारना।

peel[2] *n.* skin of fruit or vegetables छिलका, छाल।

peep[1] *पीप v.i.* to look through a crevice चोरी से देखना, झांकना।

peep[2] *n.* a look through a small opening झांकी।

peer *पिअॅः n.* a nobleman शिष्टजन।

peerless *पि ॅअॅः लिस a.* matchless अनुपम।

peg[1] *पैगॅ n.* nail, pin कील, खूंटी।

peg[2] *(-gg-) v.t.* to fasten with pegs खूंटियों से बांधना, खूंटे से बांधना, स्थिर करना।

pelf *पै ˘ल्फ़* *n.* money, riches धन-दौलत।

pell-mell *पैल्ँ मै ˘ल* *adv.* in utter confusion व्याकुलता से।

pen[1] *पै ˘न* *n.* a writing instrument लेखनी।

pen[2] *(-nn-)* *v.t.* to write लिखना।

penal *पी न्ल* *a.* relating to punishment दंडविषयक।

penalize *पी नॅ लॉइज़* *v.t.* to impose penalty on दंड देना।

penalty *पै˘ नॅल् टि* *n.* self-imposed suffering तपस्या; repentance प्रायश्चित्त; punishment दंड।

pencil[1] *पैन्ँ सॅल* *n.* an instrument of black lead for writing पेंसिल।

pencil[2] *(-ll-)* *v.t.* to write with a pencil पेंसिल से लिखना अथवा चित्र बनाना।

pending[1] *पैन्ँ डिङ्ग* *prep.* during के दौरान।

pending[2] *a.* undecided अनिर्णीत; awaiting settlement विचाराधीन।

pendulum *पैन्ँ ड्यु लॅम* *n.* suspended body swinging to and fro पेंडुलम, दोलक।

penetrate *पै˘ नि ट्रे˘ट* *v.t.* to pierce चुभाना; to understand (का) अर्थ समझना; *v.i.* to spread व्याप्त होना।

penetration *पै˘ नि ट्रे˘ शॅन* *n.* act of penetrating प्रवेशन; act of piercing बेधन।

penis *पै˘ निस* *n.* male organ of copulation शिश्न, लिंग।

penniless *पै˘ नि लिस* *a.* poor निर्धन; having no money दरिद्र।

penny *पै˘ नि* *n.* a coin worth one twelfth of a shilling अंग्रेज़ी सिक्का जो प्रायः एक आने के बराबर होता है।

pension[1] *पैन्ँ शॅन* *n.* allowance paid to retired people पेंशन, पूर्व सेवावृत्ति।

pension[2] *v.t.* to grant pension पेंशन देना।

pensioner *पैन्ँ शॅ नॅः* *n.* a person who is receiving pension पेंशन पाने वाला व्यक्ति।

pensive *पैन्ँ सिव* *a.* sadly thoughtful चिंताग्रस्त।

pentagon *पैन्ँ टॅ गॅन* *n.* figure having five angles पंचकोण, पंचभुज।

peon *पी ॲन* *n.* office messenger चपरासी।

people[1] *पी प्ल* *n.* persons in general जन; persons who are forming a state जनता; *(pl.)* race, tribe जाति।

people[2] *v.t.* to fill with people, to populate बसाना, मनुष्यों से पूर्ण करना।

pepper[1] *पै˘ पॅः* *n.* a plant and its pungent seed गोल मिर्च।

pepper[2] *v.t.* to put pepper on मिर्च मिलाना।

per *पॅः* *prep.* by से, द्वारा; for प्रति।

perambulator *पॅ रै˘म् ब्यु ले टॅः* *n.* baby carriage बच्चागाड़ी।

perceive *पॅः सीव* *v.t.* to know through senses जानना; to understand समझना; to observe देखना।

perceptible *पॅः सैपॅ टि ब्ल* perceivable देखने या समझने योग्य।

per cent *पॅः सैन्ट* *adv.* in each hundred प्रति सैकड़ा।

percentage *पॅः सॅन्ँ टिज* *n.* rate per hundred फ़ीसदी, फ़ी सैकड़ा।

perception *पॅ: सैपॅ शॅन n.* discernment बोध; knowledge through the senses अनुभव।

perceptive *पॅ: सैपॅ टिव a.* having perception प्रत्यक्ष ज्ञानशील।

perch[1] *पॅ:च n.* a fresh water fish मीठे जल की मछली; bird's resting place चिड़ियों के बैठने का अड्डा; measure of 5½ yards 5½ गज़ की नाप।

perch[2] *v.i.* to sit on a perch अड्डे पर बैठना; *v.t.* to place on a perch ऊंचे पर रखना।

perennial[1] *पॅ रैनॅ यॅल a.* lasting through the whole year वर्ष-भर रहने वाली; perpetual, everlasting चिरस्थायी।

perennial[2] *n.* a plant lasting more than two years बारहमासी पौधा।

perfect[1] *पॅ: फ़िक्ट a.* complete संपूर्ण; faultless निर्दोष; unspoilt उत्तम; whole अखंड।

perfect[2] *पॅ: फ़िक्ट, पॅ: फ़ैक्ट v.t.* to accomplish पूर्ण करना; to make faultless निर्दोष बनाना।

perfection *पॅ: फ़ैकॅ शॅन n.* the state of being perfect परिपूर्णता, निर्दोषता उत्तमता।

perfidy *पॅ: फ़ि डि n.* treachery, violation of trust विश्वासघात।

perforate *पॅ: फ़ॅ रेट v.t.* to make holes in छेद करना।

perforce *पॅ: फ़ौ:स adv.* by force बलपूर्वक, हठ से।

perform *पॅ: फ़ौ:म v.t.* to do करना; to accomplish पूर्ण करना; to act नाटक करना; *v.i.* to play on a musical instrument बाजा बजाना।

performance *पॅ: फ़ौ: मॅन्स n.* act of perfoming पूर्ति; acting अभिनय; deed कार्य; achievement उपलब्धि।

performer *पॅ: फ़ौ˘ मॅ: n.* one who accomplishes कार्य करने वाला; one who performs as an actor or musician नाटक करनेवाला।

perfume[1] *पॅ: फ़्यूम n.* fragrance सुंगध; scent इत्र।

perfume[2] *पॅ: फ़्यूम v.t.* to put perfume on सुगंधित करना।

perhaps *पॅ: हैप्स adv.* possibly कदाचित्, संयोगवश।

peril[1] *पै˘ रिल n.* hazard विपत्ति; risk आशंका; danger ख़तरा।

peril[2] *(-ll-) v.t.* to expose to danger विपत्ति में डालना।

perilous *पै˘ रि लॅस a.* dangerous, risky संकटमय।

period *पिअॅ रि अॅड n.* a portion of time समय, कालावधि; era युग; full stop पूर्ण विराम; sentence वाक्य।

periodical[1] *पिअॅ रि औ˘ डि कॅल n.* magazine published at regular intervals पत्रिका, नियतकालिक पत्रिका, सावधिक पत्र।

periodical[2] *a.* recurring at regular intervals नियतकालिक।

periphery *पॅ रि फ़ॅ रि n.* boundary बाहरी सीमा; circumference परिधि।

perish *पै˘ रिश v.i.* to die मरना; to decay सड़ना; to be destroyed नाश होना।

perishable *पै˘ रि शॅ ब्‌ल a.* liable to perish नाश होने-योग्य।

perjure *पॅ: ज़ॅ: v.i.* to make a false statement झूठी गवाही देना; to forswear प्रतिज्ञा भंग करना।

perjury *पॅ: जॅ रि n.* false swearing

झूठी गवाही या शपथ।

permanence, -cy *पॅ: मॅ नॅन्स,- नान्सि n.* state or quality of being permanent स्थिरता, नित्यता।

permanent *पॅ: मॅ नॅन्ट a.* fixed स्थिर; stable स्थायी; abiding नित्य; lasting टिकाऊ।

permissible *पॅ: मि सि ब्ल a.* allowable आज्ञा पाने-योग्य।

permission *पॅ: मि शॅन n.* act of permitting आज्ञा; authorisation अनुमति।

permit[1] *पॅ: मिट (-tt-) v.t.* to allow आज्ञा देना।

permit[2] *पॅ: मिट n.* written permission or license परमिट, प्रानुमति-पत्र।

permutation *पॅ: म्यु टे शॅन n.* interchange परिवर्तन, उलट-पुलट।

pernicious *पॅ: नि शॅस a.* injurious अपकारक; deadly, destructive नाशक।

perpendicular[1] *पॅ: पैन्ँ डि क्यु लँ: a.* at right angles लंबरूप; vertical खड़े बल का।

perpendicular[2] *n.* perpendicular line समकोणिक रेखा।

perpetual *पॅ: पैˇ ट्यु अॅल a.* lasting forever नित्य; permanent सतत्; continuous लगातार।

perpetuate *पॅ: पैˇ ट्यु एट v.t.* to make perpetual जारी रखना।

perplex *पॅ: प्लैक्स v.t.* to bewilder व्याकुल करना, घबराना; to puzzle चक्कर में डालना।

perplexity *पॅ: प्लैक् सि टि n.* bewilderment व्यग्रता; intricacy झंझट।

persecute *पॅ: सि क्यूट v.t.* to oppress पीड़ा देना, कष्ट देना; to harass सताना; to treat cruely चोट पहुंचाना।

persecution *पॅ: सि क्यू शॅन n.* oppression, harassment उत्पीड़न।

perseverance *पॅ: सॅ विअॅ रॅन्स n.* continued diligence अध्यवसाय; steadfastness दृढ़ता।

persevere *पॅ: सि विअॅ: v.i.* to proceed diligently अध्यवसाय में लगा रहना; to make constant effort निरंतर प्रयत्न करना।

persist *पॅ: सिस्ट v.i.* to continue steadily दृढ़ रहना।

persistence *पॅ: सिस् टॅन्स n.* perseverance अध्यवसाय; steadiness दृढ़ता।

persistent *पॅ: सिस् टॅन्ट a.* steady दृढ़; persevering आग्रही।

person *पॅ: सॅन n.* individual human being मनुष्य, व्यक्ति; human body मानव-शरीर।

personage *पॅ: सॅ निज n.* notable person श्रेष्ठ पुरुष, संभ्रांत जन।

personal *पॅ: सॅ न्ल a.* individual व्यक्तिगत; private निजी।

personality *पॅ: सॅ नैˇ लि टि n.* distinctive character व्यक्तित्व; a well-known person संभ्रांत व्यक्ति।

personification *पॅ: सौˇ नि फ़ि के शॅन n.* act of personifying मानवीकरण; embodiment मूर्तीकरण।

personify *पॅ: सौˇ नि फ़ॉइ v.t.* to represent as a person मानवीकरण करना; to be a model of (का) मूर्तरूप होना।

personnel *पॅ: सॅ नॅल् n.* staff employed in a service कार्यकर्त्ता वर्ग, कर्मचारी-दल।

perspective *पॅ: स्पैक् टिव n.* apparent relation between two aspects परिप्रेक्ष्य; view, prospect दृश्य।

perspiration *पॅ: स्पॅ री शॅन n.* sweat पसीना।

perspire *पॅ: स्पॉइअॅ: v.i.* to sweat पसीना निकलना।

persuade *पॅ: स्वेड v.t.* to influence by argument फुसलाना; to prevail on मनाना; to induce उकसाना।

persuasion *पॅ: स्वे शॅन n.* act of persuading प्रतीतीकरण; inducement प्रोत्साहन।

pertain *पॅ: टेन v.i.* to belong उपांग होना; to have reference (to) संदर्भ रखना; to concern संबद्ध होना।

pertinent *पॅ: टि नॅन्ट a.* proper योग्य, ठीक; relevant उचित।

perturb *पॅ: टॅ:ब v.t.* to disquiet, to disturb व्याकुल करना; to agitate घबराना।

perusal *पि रू ज़ॅल n.* reading carefully अध्ययन, वाचन, पठन।

peruse *पॅ रूज़ v.t.* to read carefully चित्त लगाकर पढ़ना।

pervade *पॅ: वेड v.t.* to permeate (में) व्याप्त होना।

perverse *पॅ: वॅ:स a.* perverted विकृत; stubborn दुराग्रही; wicked दुष्ट; intractable उद्दंड।

perversion *पॅ: वॅ: शॅन n.* being perverted विकृति; moral corruption आचारभ्रष्टता।

perversity *पॅ: वॅ: सि टि n.* being perverse दुःशीलता; stubbornness दुराग्रह।

pervert *पॅ: वॅ:ट v.t.* to lead astray, to mislead सन्मार्ग से हटाना; to debase, to corrupt दुषित करना।

pessimism *पै ॅ सि मिज़्म n.* tendency to see the worst side of things निराशावाद।

pessimist *पै ॅ सि मिस्ट n.* one who, believes in pessimism निराशावादी।

pessimistic *पै ॅ सि मिस् टिक a.* pertaining to pessimism निराश, निराशावादी।

pest *पैस्ॅट n.* plague महामारी; harmful thing नाशकारक वस्तु।

pesticide *पै ॅस्टिसैड n.* a chemical use for killing pest कीटनाशक (दवा)।

pestilence *पैसॅ् टि लॅन्स n.* plague प्लेग; epidemic महामारी।

pet[1] *पै ॅट n.* animal kept with affection प्यारा, पालतू जानवर।

pet[2] *(-tt-) v.t.* to treat with affection प्यार करना, पोसना।

petal *पै ॅ ट्ल n.* leaf-like part of a flower फूल की पंखुरी, दलपत्र।

petition[1] *पि टि शॅन n.* entreaty, request याचिका, अर्ज़ी, प्रार्थना।

petition[2] *v.t.* to present petition to (को) प्रार्थना-पत्र भेजना।

petitioner *पि टि शॅ नॅ: n.* one who petitions निवेदक, अभ्यर्थी।

petrol *पै ॅट्रो ल n.* refined petroleum पेट्रोल।

petroleum *पि ट्रो ल्यॅम n.* mineral oil खनिज तैल।

petticoat *पै ॅ टि कोट n.* woman's undergarment पेटीकोट।

petty *पै ॅ टि a.* small छोटा; on a small scale अल्प; unimportant तुच्छ, क्षुद्र; mean नीचतापूर्ण।

petulance *पै ॅ ट्यु लॅन्स n.* peevishness दुःशीलता।

petulant *पै˘ ट्यु लॅन्ट a.* peevish कर्कश; irritable चिड़चिड़ा।

phantom *फ़ैन् टॅम n.* apparition प्रेत की छाया; spectre, ghost प्रेत।

pharmacy *फ़ाः मॅ सि n.* preparation and dispensing of drugs औषधि बनाने की विद्या; dispensary औषधालय, दवाख़ाना।

phase *फ़ेज़ n.* stage अवस्था; state स्थिति; aspect पहलू।

phenomenal *फ़ि नौ˘ मि न्ल a.* relating to phenomena प्रकृतिविषयक; remarkable अद्‌भुत।

phenomenon *फ़ि नौ˘ मि नौनॅ n. (pl. phenomena)* anything remarkable अद्‌भुत पदार्थ; scene दृश्य।

phial *फ़ॉइ ॲल n.* small bottle शीशी, छोटी बोतल।

philanthropic *फ़ि लॅन् थ्रौ˘ पिक a.* loving mankind सर्वजन-उपकारी, लोकानुरागी; benevolent उदार।

philanthropist *फ़ि लैन् थ्रॅ पिस्ट n.* one devoted to philanthropy मनुष्य मात्र से प्रेम करनेवाला व्यक्ति, जन-हितैषी, समाजसेवी।

philanthropy *फ़ि लैन् थ्रॅ पि n.* love of mankind विश्वप्रेम, लोकोपकार।

philological *फ़ि लॅ लौ˘ जि कॅल a.* of philology भाषाशास्त्रीय।

philologist *फ़ि लौ˘ लॅ जिस्ट n.* one who expert in philology भाषाविद्।

philology *फ़ि लौ˘ लॅ जि n.* linguistic science भाषाविज्ञान।

philosopher *फ़ि लौ˘ सॅ फ़ॅः n.* a person versed in philosophy तत्वज्ञानी, दार्शनिक।

philosophical *फ़ि लॅ सौ˘ फ़ि कॅल a.* given to philosophy दार्शनिक; pertaining to philosophy तत्वविज्ञान-संबंधी।

philosophy *फ़ि लौ˘ सॅ फ़ि n.* search for knowledge दर्शनशास्त्र; study of realities and general principles तत्व विज्ञान।

phone *फ़ोन n.* telephone फ़ोन, 'टेलीफ़ोन' शब्द का छोटा रूप।

phonetic *फ़ॅ नै˘ टिक a.* relating to vocal sounds ध्वनि-संबंधी।

phonetics *फ़ॅ नै˘ टिक्स n. sing.* science of vocal sounds ध्वनि-विज्ञान, स्वर-शास्त्र।

phosphate *फ़ौ˘स् फ़ेट n.* any salt of phosphoric acid फॉस फ़ौरस तत्व से बना हुआ लवण, भास्वीय लवण।

phosphorus *फ़ौस् फ़ॅ रॅस n.* inflammable element appearing luminous in the dark फ़ास् फ़ोरस, एक जलनेवाला तत्व जो अंधेरे में चमकता है, भास्वर।

photo *फ़ो टो n. (pl. -s)* photograph फ़ोटो।

photograph[1] *फ़ो टॅ ग्राफ़,-ग्रैफ़ v.t.* to take photo of फ़ोटो उतारना।

photograph[2] *n.* picture obtained by photography फ़ोटोचित्र।

photographer *फ़ॅ टौ˘ ग्रॅ फ़ॅः n.* one who takes photographs फ़ोटो उतारने वाला।

photographic *फ़ो टॅ ग्रै फ़िक a.* relating to photography फ़ोटो-संबंधी।

photography *फ़ॅ टौ˘ ग्रॅ फ़ि n.* art of taking photographs फ़ोटो खींचने की कला।

phrase[1] *फ़्रेज़ n.* group of words मुहावरा; expression उक्ति; mode of expression वाक्यशैली।

phrase[2] *v.t.* to express in words शब्दों में व्यक्त करना।

phraseology *फ़े ज़ि औ˘ लॅ जि n.* choice of words शब्दचयन; manner of expression कथनशैली।

physic[1] *फ़ि ज़िक n.* science of medicine औषधि-शास्त्र; medicine औषधि।

physic[2] *(-ck-) v.t.* to remedy इलाज करना, देवा देना।

physical *फ़ि ज़ि कॅल a.* material पदार्थ विज्ञान-संबंधी; bodily शारीरिक; earthly पार्थिव।

physician *फ़ि ज़ि शॅन n.* medical practitioner डॉक्टर, वैद्य चिकित्सक।

physicist *फ़ि ज़ि सिस्ट n.* one skilled in physics भौतिकशास्त्री।

physics *फ़ि ज़िक्स n. sing.* science dealing with matter and energy भौतिक विज्ञान, पदार्थ-विज्ञान।

physiognomy *फ़ि ज़ि औ˘ नॅ मि n.* science of reading the face आकृति देखकर चरित्र बतलाने की विद्या; face मुख की आकृति।

physique *फ़ि ज़ीक n.* bodily structure शरीर-रचना, डीलडौल।

pianist *पिॲ निस्ट n.* performer on piano पियानोवादक।

piano *प्यै नो, प्या- n. (pl. -s)* a musical instrument पियानो।

pick[1] *पिक v.t.* to pluck तोड़ना; to gather इकट्ठा करना; to select carefully चुनना; to peck at चोंच मारना।

pick[2] *n.* a pick-axe फावड़ा; selection चुनाव; the best thing सबसे उत्तम पदार्थ।

picket[1] *पि किट n.* pointed stake नोकदार छड़; small group of men on police duty सैन्य दल।

picket[2] *v.t.* to station (men) as pickets पहरे पर तैनात करना।

pickle[1] *पि क्‌ल n.* things preserved in brine, vinegar etc. अचार, मुरब्बा; vinegar सिरका।

pickle[2] *v.t.* to preserve in pickle अचार या मुरब्बा बनाना।

picnic[1] *पिक् निक n.* pleasure excursion पिकनिक, वनभोजन, घर के बाहर का आमोद।

picnic[2] *(-ck-) v.i.* to take part in picnic पिकनिक में भाग लेना।

pictorical *पिक् टौ रि ॲल a.* forming pictures, graphic सचित्र, चित्रमय।

picture[1] *पिक् चॅः n.* painting चित्र; mental image दृश्य; beautiful object अति सुंदर पदार्थ; cinema चलचित्र।

picture[2] *v.t.* to represent in a picture (का) चित्र खींचना, स्पष्ट वर्णन करना; to describe graphically चित्रात्मक वर्णन करना।

picturesque *पिक् चॅ रैस्क् a.* graphic (का) चित्र के समान सुंदर; vivid स्पष्ट।

piece[1] *पीस n.* portion भाग; part खंड; coin मुद्रा; gun बंदूक; small composition छोटी रचना; a single object एक अकेली वस्तु।

piece[2] *v.t.* to mend by patching (पर) चिप्पड़ लगाना; to put together, to join जोड़ना।

pierce *पिॲःस v.t.* to perforate छेदना; to make a way through घुसाना; *v.i.* to enter प्रवेश करना।

piety *पॉइ ॲ टि n.* devotion to God

ईश्वरभक्ति; religiosity धर्म-परायणता; devotion भक्ति।

pig *पिग n.* a swine सुअर; a young swine सुअर का बच्चा; mass of unforged metal बिना ढाली गई धातु।

pigeon *पि जिन n.* a bird of the dove family कबूतर।

pigmy *पिग् मि n.* pygmy बौना।

pile[1] *पॉइल n.* beam लट्ठा; heap ढेर; pyre चिता।

pile[2] *v.t.* to heap (up) ढेर लगाना; to amass इकट्ठा करना।

piles *पॉइल्ज़ n.* a rectum disease, haemorrhoids बवासीर।

pilfer *पिल् फ़: v.t.* to steal in small quantities थोड़ा-थोड़ा करके चुराना।

pilgrim *पिल् ग्रिम n.* a traveller to a sacred place तीर्थयात्री।

pilgrimage *पिल् ग्रि मिज n.* journey to holy place तीर्थयात्रा।

pill *पिल n.* small ball of medicine गुटिका, गोली।

pillar *पि लॅ: n.* column स्तंभ, खंभा, आधार।

pillow[1] *पिलो n.* cushion for the head तकिया।

pillow[2] *v.t.* to lay on a pillow, to use as a pillow तकिया लगाना।

pilot[1] *पॉइ लॅट n.* one who flies an aircraft पाइलट, विमान-चालक।

pilot[2] *v.t.* to guide मार्ग दिखलाना; to act as pilot to (का) चालक होना।

pimple *पिम् प्ल n.* small pus-filled spot on the skin मुंहासा।

pin[1] *पिन n.* short, thin, sharp pointed stiff wire with a round head आलपीन; peg खूंटी।

pin[2] *(-nn-) v.t.* to fasten with a pin आलपीन से नत्थी करना।

pinch[1] *पिन्च v.t.* to nip, to squeeze between thumb and finger चिकोटी काटना; to steal बलपूर्वक धन लेना; to afflict दुःख देना।

pinch[2] *v.* painful squeeze चिकोटी; nip कोंचन, चुभन; amount that can be taken between thumb and finger चुटकी-भर।

pine[1] *पॉइन n.* an evergreen tree चीड़ का वृक्ष, देवदार।

pine[2] *v.i.* to languish विलाप करना; to yearn लालायित होना।

pine-apple *पॉइन् ऐ प्ल n.* a juicy fruit अनन्नास tree bearing this fruit उसका पेड़।

pink[1] *पिङ्क n.* a garden flower एक सुगंधित फूल; light rose colour प्याज़ी रंग।

pink[2] *a.* of light rose colour हल्के गुलाबी रंग का।

pinkish *पिङ् किश a.* rather pink हल्का गुलाबी।

pinnacle *पि नॅ क्ल n.* pointed turret on roof अटारी, कलश; highest point चरम सीमा; mountain peak पर्वतशिखा।

pioneer[1] *पॉइ अॅ निअॅ: n.* path maker मार्ग-निर्माता explorer प्रथम अन्वेषक; leader अगुआ, नेता।

pioneer[2] *v.t.* to lead, to guide मार्ग दिखलाना, मार्ग बतलाना।

pious *पॉइ अॅस a.* holy पवित्र; godly धार्मिक; devout भक्तिमान।

pipe[1] *पॉइप n.* a flute, wind instrument बांसुरी; tube नली; note of a bird पक्षी का गायन; smoking pipe पाइप; windpipe श्वासनली।

pipe[2] *v.i.* to play on a pipe बांसुरी या सीटी बजाना।

piquant *पी कॅन्ट* *a.* sharp तीखा; lively सरस; interesting रुचिकर; pungent चटपटा; stimulating उत्तेजक।

piracy *पॉइअॅ रॅ सि* *n.* sea-robbery समुद्री डकैती।

pirate[1] *पॉइअॅ रिट* *n.* sea-robber समुद्री डाकू।

pirate[2] *v.t.* to rob on the high seas समुद्री जहाज़ पर डाका डालना।

pistol *पिस् ट्ल* *n.* small firearm पिस्तौल।

piston *पिस् टॅन* *n.* a sort of plunger पिस्टन, पिचकारी का डंडा।

pit[1] *पिट* *n.* deep hole in ground गड्ढ़ा; depression शरीर पर छोटे गर्त; covered hole as a trap for wild animals पशुओं को फंसाने का गड्ढा।

pit[2] *(-tt-) v.t.* to mark with small dents or scars छोटे गड्ढे बनाना।

pitch[1] *पिच* *n.* black sticky substance made from coaltar तारकोल; elevation ऊंचाई; elevation of note in music स्वरमान; slope ढाल; throw फेंक; (cricket) ground between the wickets विकटों के बीच का भूभाग।

pitch[2] *v.t.* to throw फेंकना; to set up भूमि पर गाड़ना, स्थिर करना।

pitcher *पि चॅः* *n.* large earthen jug घड़ा, मटका।

piteous *पि टि अॅस* *a.* arousing pity दीन, दयनीय।

pitfall *पिट फ़ौल* *n.* covered pit for catching animals फंसाने का जाल; hidden danger गुप्त संकट।

pitiable *पि टि अॅ ब्ल* *a.* deserving pity दया का पात्र, दीन।

pitiful *पि टि फुल* *a.* full of pity compassionate दयापूर्ण, करुणामय।

pitiless *पि टि लिस* *a.* hard-hearted, merciless निर्दय, कठोर।

pitman *पिट् मॅन* *n.* a miner खान में काम करनेवाला श्रमिक।

pittance *पि टॅन्स* *n.* small allowance क्षुद्र वेतन; inadequate wages अल्प पारिश्रमिक।

pity[1] *पि टि* *n.* sympathy दया; compassion करुणा।

pity[2] *v.t.* to feel pity for (पर) दया करना, तरस खाना।

pivot[1] *पि वॅट* *n.* pin on which some thing turns चूल या कील जिस पर कोई यंत्र घूमता है; main basis प्रधान आधार।

pivot[2] *v.t.* to furnish with pivot चूल लगाना; to turn on a pivot चूल पर घुमाना।

playcard *प्लै काःड* *n.* poster विज्ञापन-पत्र।

place[1] *प्लेस* *n.* spot स्थल; portion of land भूमि; stage स्थिति; rank श्रेणी; calling उद्यम, room स्थान; office पद; residence निवास।

place[2] *v.t.* to appoint नियुक्त करना; to invest लगाना; to put रखना।

placid *प्लै सिड* *a.* quiet शांत; mild नम्र; gentle सौम्य।

plague[1] *प्लेग* *a.* pestilence प्लेग, महामारी; serious trouble उत्पात; calamity विपत्ति।

plague[2] *v.t.* to cause trouble पीड़ा देना, कष्ट देना।

plain[1] *प्लेन* *a.* smooth चौरस; level

सपाट; ordinary सामान्य; obvious प्रत्यक्ष; simple सीधा।

plain[2] *n.* a piece of level land मैदान।

plaintiff *प्लेन् टिफ़ n.* person who brings an action at law अभियोगी, वादी, मुद्दई।

plan[1] *प्लैन n.* scheme योजना; diagram मानचित्र; sketch ढांचा।

plan[2] *(-nn-) v.t.* to make plan of योजना बनाना।

plane[1] *प्लेन n.* smooth surface चौरस भूमि; stage जीवन-स्थिति; carpenter's tool for smoothing wood बढ़ई का रंदा।

plane[2] *v.t.* to make smooth with a plane चौरस करना।

plane[3] *a.* perfectly level चौरस।

plane[4] *n.* wing of an aeroplane वायुयान का पंख; aeroplane वायुयान।

planet *प्ले निट n.* heavenly body revolving round the sun नक्षत्र, ग्रह।

planetary *प्लै नि टॅ रि a.* relating to a planet ग्रह-संबंधी।

plank[1] *प्लैङ्क n.* long flat piece of sawn timber लकड़ी का तख़्ता।

plank[2] *v.t.* to cover with planks तख़्ते लगाना।

plant[1] *प्लान्ट n.* a young or small tree पौधा; establishment equipped with machinery कारख़ाना।

plant[2] *v.t.* to put (plants) in the ground to grow जमाना; to put firmly स्थिर करना।

plantain *प्लैन् टिन n.* banana tree केले का वृक्ष।

plantation *प्लैन् टे शॅन n.* act of planting रोपाई, वृक्षारोपण; planting खेत; grove उद्यान; colony नव उपनिवेश, बस्ती।

plaster[1] *प्लास् टॅ: n.* mixture of lime, water etc. for coating walls भीत पर लगाने का पलस्तर; piece of cloth spread with medicinal substance औषधि का लेप।

plaster[2] *v.t.* to cover (a wall) with plaster पलस्तर लगाना; to put a plaster on लेप लगाना।

plate[1] *प्लेट n.* a shallow dish प्लेट; a thin sheet of metal पत्तर, चद्दर।

plate[2] *v.t.* to cover with thin coating of some metal मुलम्मा करना।

plateau *प्लै टो n. (pl.-s)* tableland पठार।

platform *प्लैट् फ़ौ:म n.* raised level floor मंच; a structure for speakers at public meetings चबूतरा, मचान।

platonic *प्लॅ टौ॓ निक a.* pertaining to Plato तत्वज्ञानी, प्लेटो-संबंधी।

platoon *प्लॅ टून n.* body of soldiers पलटन, पैदल सेना।

play[1] *प्ले n.* movement गति; activity क्रियाशीलता; amusement हंसी, विनोद; sport खेल, क्रीड़ा; dramatic piece नाटक; dramatic performance अभिनय; gambling जुआ।

play[2] *v.i.* to sport खेलना; to perform a play नाटक करना; to gamble जुआ खेलना; to frolic कूद-फांद मचाना; to perform on an instrument of music बाजा बजाना; *v.t.* to execute संपन्न करना; to employ oneself in the game of (कोई खेल) खेलना।

player *प्ले अॅ: n.* one who plays a

game खिलाड़ी actor अभिनेता; person who plays a musical instrument वादक।

plea *प्ली n.* defendant's statement तर्क; reason, cause हेतु, कारण; excuse बहाना; request प्रार्थना।

plead *प्लीड v.i.* to argue in support of a claim वकालत करना, पक्ष-समर्थन करना; to make earnest appeal निवेदन करना; plead *v.t.* to bring forward as a plea तर्क के रूप में प्रस्तुत करना।

pleader *प्ली डः n.* advocate अधिवक्ता, वकील।

pleasant *प्लै ॅ ज़ॅन्ट a.* giving pleasure मनोहर, सुहावना।

pleasantry *प्लै ॅ ज़ॅन् ट्रि n.* gaiety आनंद; humour हंसी।

please *प्लीज़ v.t.* to be agreeable to प्रसन्न करना; to delight आनंदित करना; to gratify संतुष्ट करना; to seem good to रुचिकर या अच्छा लगना।

pleasure *प्लै ̈ ज़ंः n.* enjoyment आनंद; delight सुख; choice रुचि; will अभिलाषा।

plebiscite *प्लैॅबि सिट, -सॉइट n.* vote by all citizens जनमत-संग्रह।

pledge[1] *प्लैजॅ n.* promise प्रतिज्ञा; hostage, pawn बंधक।

pledge[2] *v.t.* to pawn बंधक रखना; to promise वचन देना; to vow प्रतिज्ञा करना।

plenty *प्लैनॅ् टि n.* abundance बहुतायत; sufficiency प्रचुरता।

plight *प्लॉइट n.* distressing state दुर्दशा।

plod *प्लौ ॅड (-dd-) v.i.* to walk wearity थके क़दमों से चलना; to work slowly धीरे-धीरे काम करना।

plot[1] *प्लौ ॅट n.* piece of ground भूमि; secret plan गुप्त योजना; conspiracy कूट-प्रबंध; outline उपन्यास या नाटक का कथानक।

plot[2] *(-tt-) v.t.* to make a diagram or plan of रूपरेखा या ख़ाका बनाना; *v.i.* to make secret plans कपट प्रबंध करना।

plough[1] *प्लॉउ n.* an instrument for turning up soil हल; *v.t.* break up (land) with a plough हल से (भूमि) जोतना।

plough[2] *v.i.* to use a plough हल से जुताई करना।

ploughman *प्लॉउ मॅन n.* man who guides a plough हलवाहा।

pluck[1] *प्लक v.t.* to pick off तोड़ना; to snatch छीनना; to gather इकट्ठा करना; to twitch ऐंठना।

pluck[2] *n.* courage साहस; short sharp pull झटका।

plug[1] *प्लग n.* stopper डाट; tobacco pressed hard गुल्ली; an electricity device प्लग।

plug[2] *(-gg-) v.t.* to stop with a plug डाट लगाकर बंद करना।

plum *प्लम n.* a stone fruit आलूबुखारा, आलूचा, बेर; tree bearing it आलूबुखारे का पेड़।

plumber *प्लम् बॅः n.* workman who fits pipes for water पानी का नल बैठानेवाला, नलकार।

plunder[1] *प्लन् डॅः v.t.* to take by force, to rob लूटना।

plunder[2] *n.* booty लूट का माल; act of plundering लूटमार।

plunge[1] *प्लन्ज v.t.* to immerse डुबाना; to dive ग़ोता लगाना।

plunge[2] *n.* act of plunging, immersion डुबकी।

plural प्लुॅ रॅ˘ल *a.* more than one, denoting plurality अनेक, बहुवचन।

plurality प्लु अॅ रै लि टि *n.* state of being plural अनेकता; majority अधिकता।

plus[1] प्लस *a.* to be added अधिक।

plus[2] *n.* the sign + जोड़ने का चिह्न (+)।

ply[1] प्लॉइ *v.t.* to wield काम में लाना; to work at पर काम करना; to supply आपूर्ति करना; to urge अनुरोध करना; to keep busy व्यस्त रखना; *v.i.* to run चालू रहना।

ply[2] *n.* layer परत; strand लड़।

pneumonia न्यू मो न्यॅ *n.* inflammation of lungs न्यूमोनिया, फेफड़ों की सूजन।

pocket[1] पौ˘ किट *n.* small bag inserted in garment पाकिट जेब; pouch खलीता; cavity कोटरिका।

pocket[2] *v.t.* to put into one's pocket जेब में रखना; to appropriate अपने काम में लाना।

pod पौ˘ड *n.* long seed vessel फली।

poem पो इम *n.* composition in verse पद्यकाव्य; piece of poetry कविता।

poesy पो इ ज़ि *n.* poetic composoition काव्य-रचना; poetic art काव्य-कला।

poet पो इट *n.* writer of poems कवि।

poetaster पो˘ इ टैस् टॅः *n.* petty poet क्षुद्र कवि; rhymer तुक्कड़।

poetess पो इ टिस *n. fem.* female poet कवयित्री।

poetic पो ऐ˘ टिक *a.* pertaining to poetry कविता-संबंधी।

poetics पो ऐ˘ टिक्स *n.* theory of poetry काव्यशास्त्र।

poetry पो˘ इ ट्रि *n.* poem कविता; poetic composition काव्य-रचना; versified composition पद्य, काव्य।

poignacy पौ˘इ ग्नॅन् सि *n.* sharpness तीखापन; keenness तीक्ष्णता; quality of being poignant मार्मिकता।

poignant पौ˘इ ग्नॅन्ट *a.* sharp तीखा; moving मर्मवेधी pungent उत्कट।

point[1] पौ˘ इन्ट *n.* dot बिंदु; sharp end यंत्र की नोक; cape अंतरीप; occasion अवसर; punctuation mark विरामचिह्न unit of scoring अंक; argument तर्क; meaning अर्थ; hint संकेत; moment क्षण, purpose उद्देश्य; stage स्थिति।

point[2] *v.t.* to make pointed नोकदार बनाना; to aim निशाना लगाना; to indicate संकेत करना; to show दिखाना; to fill with mortar सीमेंट से भरना।

poise[1] पौ˘इज़ *v.t.* to balance in weight तौलना; to hold in equilibrium संतुलित रखना; *v.i.* to be balanced संतुलित होना।

poise[2] *n.* equilibrium संतुलन, indecision असमंजस।

poison[1] पौ˘इ ज़्न *n.* substance causing death विष, गरल; something harmful हानिकारक वस्तु।

poison[2] *v.t.* to give poison to ज़हर देना; to kill with poison मारना, नष्ट करना; to currupt दूषित करना।

poisonous पौ˘इ ज़ॅ नस *a.* venomous विषैला, ज़हरीला।

poke[1] पोक *v.t.* to push ढकेलना; to

jab कोचना; to stir up कुरेदना।

poke² *n.* nudge धक्का।

polar *पो लॅः n.* pertaining to the pole or poles ध्रुवीय; close to the poles ध्रुव के समीप का।

pole *पोल n.* long piece of wood लंबा डंडा; a measure of 5½ yards 5½ गज़ की नाप; either of the two ends of a magnet ध्रुव चुंबक के दोनों छोर।

police *पॅ लीस n.* body of civil officers for enforcing order पुलिस, आरक्षी।

policeman *पॅ लीस् मॅन n.* a member of police force पुलिस का सिपाही।

policy *पौˇ लि सि n.* line of conduct नीति dexterity युक्ति; statecraft राज्य-शासन-पद्धति; contract of insurance बीमा-पत्र।

polish¹ *पौˇ लिश v.t.* to make glossy चमकाना; to refine स्वच्छ करना; *v.i.* to become glossy चमकना।

polish² *n.* substance for polishing पॉलिश; shine चमक; elegance शोभा; refinement शिष्टता।

polite *पॅ लॉइट a.* refined शिष्ट; polished in manners विनीत।

pliteness *पॅ लॉइट् निस n.* refinement शिष्टता; courtesy विनय।

politic *पौˇ लि टिक a.* showing policy नीति-चतुर; sagacious बुद्धिमान।

political *पॅ लि टि कॅल a.* pertaining to the state राजनीतिक।

politician *पौˇ लि टि शॅन n.* one versed or engaged in politics राजनीतिज्ञ।

politics *पौˇ लि टिक्स n. pl. (used as sing.)* science of government राजनीतिशास्त्र।

polity *पौˇ लि टि n.* system of government राज्यशासनपद्धति, राजतंत्र।

poll¹ *पोल n.* head मस्तक; list of voters निर्वाचकों की नामावली; voting मतदान।

poll² *v.t.* to shear बाल काटना; to receive (votes) वोट पाना; *v.i.* to vote वोट देना।

pollen *पौˇ लिन n.* fertilizing dust of flowers पराग।

pollute *पॅ ल्यूट v.t.* to corrupt, to desecrate दूषित करना, भ्रष्ट करना।

pollution *पॅ ल्यू शॅन n.* act of polluting प्रदूषण; defilement अपवित्रीकरण।

polo *पो लो n.* game played on horseback पोलो, चौगान।

polygamous *पौˇ लि गॅ मॅस a.* practising polygamy एक से अधिक पत्नीवाला।

polygamy *पौˇ लि गॅ मि n.* custom of marrying several persons बहुविवाह।

polyglot¹ *पौˇ लि ग्लौट n.* person knowing several languages बहुभाषी, बहुभाषाविद्।

polyglot² *a.* knowing several languages बहुभाषाविद्।

polytechnic¹ *पौˇ लि टैक् निक a.* dealing with various arts and crafts पॉलीटेकनीक, विविधकला-विषयक।

polytechnic² *पौˇ लि टैक् निक n.* college dealing with various arts and crafts विविधकला विद्यालय।

polytheism *पौ ॅ लि थि इज़्म n.* belief in many gods बहुदेववाद।

polytheist *पौ ॅ लि थि इस्ट n.* person believing in many gods बहुदेवपूजक।

polytheistic *पौ ॅ लि थि इस् टिक a.* pertaining to polytheism बहुदेववादी।

pomp *पौम्प n.* splendid display आडंबर, विभव, ठाटबाट।

pomposity *पौम् पौ ॅ सि टि n.* being pompous आडंबर।

pompous *पौम् पॅस a.* displaying pomp आडंबरी, विभवयुक्त।

pond *पौन्ड n.* pool छोटा तालाब।

ponder *पौन् डॅ: v.t.* to weigh in the mind मन में तौलना to consider विचार करना।

pony *पो नि n.* small horse टट्टू छोटा घोड़ा।

poor *पुअॅ: a.* wretched दीन; paltry तुच्छ; indigent दरिद्र; mean अधम; luckless अभागा; humble विनीत; infertile अनुपजाऊ; needy ज़रूरतमंद; weak निर्बल।

pop¹ *पौप (-pp-) v.i.* to make a small smart sound फट की आवाज होना, धमाका होना; to enter suddenly अचानक आ धमकना; to issue forth at once बाहर निकलना; *v.t.* to put suddenly पटक देना; to offer with a quick sudden motion फुरती से प्रस्तुत करना।

pop² *n.* small smart sound फट, फटाक।

pope *पोप n.* head of Roman Catholic Church पोप, रोम का बड़ा पादरी।

poplar *पौप् लॅ: n.* name of a tree चिनार।

poplin *पौप् लिन n.* shiny cotton cloth पॉपलीन कपड़ा।

populace *पौ ॅ प्यु लॅस n.* the common people साधारण लोग, जन-समूह।

popular *पौ ॅ प्यु लॅ: a.* pertaining to the masses लौकिक; liked by the people सर्वप्रिय; prevalent प्रचलित।

popularity *पौॅ प्यु लै रि टि n.* quality of being popular लोकप्रियता; social fame प्रसिद्धि।

popularize *पौ ॅ प्यु लॅ रॉइज़ v.t.* to make popular लोकप्रिय या प्रसिद्ध बनाना।

populate *पौॅ प्यु लेट v.t.* to fill with inhabitants जनपूर्ण करना, बसाना।

population *पौॅ प्यु लेॅ शॅन n.* people living in a place or country जनसंख्या, आबादी।

populous *पौ ॅ प्यु लॅस a.* thickly populated जनपूर्ण, घना आबाद।

porcelain *पौ:स् लिन, -लेन् n.* fine earthenware चीनी के बर्तन।

porch *पौ:च n.* portico ड्योढी, ओसारा।

pore *पौ: n.* tiny opening in the skin रोमकूप।

pork *पौ:क n.* pig's flesh as food सुअर का मांस।

porridge *पौॅ रिज n.* food of oatmeal boiled in water लपसी, हलुआ।

port *पौ:ट n.* harbour बंदरगाह।

portable *पौ: टॅ ब्ल a.* that may be easily carried ले जाने-योग्य, वहनीय।

portage *पौ: टिज n.* act of carrying ढुलाई; transport charges ले जाने का भाड़ा।

portal *पौः ट्ल n.* imposing doorway सदर दरवाज़ा।

portend *पौः टैन्ड v.t.* to be an omen of शकुन, बतलाना; to foretell पहिले से सूचना देना।

porter *पौः टॅः n.* doorkeeper द्वारपाल, दरबान; a carrier कुली।

portfolio *पौःट् फ़ो˘ ल्यो n. (pl. -s)* flat portable case for loose papers खुले पत्र, मानचित्र आदि रखने का बस्ता; office of a minister मंत्री का विभाग।

portico *पौःटि को n. (pl. es)* a covered walk at the entrance of a building, porch द्वार-मंडप, बरसाती।

portion[1] *पा ःशॅन, n.* part, share अंश, भाग; dowry दहेज; fate भाग्य।

portion[2] *v.t.* to divide into shares बांटना।

portrait *पौः ट्रिट n.* picture of a person छविचित्र, व्यक्तिचित्र।

portraiture *पौः ट्रि चॅः n.* art of portraying चित्रण, आलेखन, चित्रकारी; portrait चित्र।

portray *पौः ट्रे˘ v.t.* to make a picture of (का) चित्र बनाना; to describe vividly वर्णन करना।

portrayal *पौ ः ट्रे ॲल n.* act of portraying चित्रलेखन; description वर्णन।

pose[1] *पोज़ v.i.* to assume attitude मुद्रा बनाना, विशेष स्थिति में बैठना; to affect or pretend बनना, दिखावा करना; *v.t.* to puzzle स्तंभित करना, चक्कर में डालना।

pose[2] *n.* position मुद्रा, स्थिति; artistic posture छवि।

position[1] *पॅ ज़ि शॅन n.* place स्थान; situation स्थिति; status पदवी; attitude अंगस्थिति।

position[2] *v.t.* to place in position रखना।

positive *पौ˘ ज़ि टिव a.* definite निश्चित, sure, certain पक्का, greater than zero धनराशि का; affirmative सकारात्मक; constructive रचनात्मक।

possess *पॅ ज़ैसॅ v.t.* to own अधिकार में रखना; to have and hold धारण करना; to be full of (से) युक्त होना; to have possession of अधिकार में लेना; to influence अधिकार में लेना; प्रभावित करना।

possession *पॅ ज़ै˘ शॅन n.* ownership अधिकार; something possessed अधीन पदार्थ; occupancy आधिपत्य।

possibility *पौ˘ सि बि लि टि n.* state or quality of being possible संभावना।

possible *पौ˘ सि ब्ल a.* practicable, probable होने-योग्य, संभाव्य।

post[1] *पोस्ट n.* upright piece of wood, metal etc. खंभा, थूनी।

post[2] *v.t.* to stick on some post खंभे पर लगाना; to fix up in some public place (पर) सार्वजनिक विज्ञापन लगाना।

post[3] *n.* office पद; power, authority अधिकार; postal department डाक विभाग; place where soldier is stationed चौकी।

post[4] *v.t.* to station (soldiers) in a particular spot नियुक्त करना; to place (letter) in the post office (चिट्ठी) छोड़ना; *v.i.* to hasten on वेग से यात्रा करना।

post[5] *adv.* in haste शीघ्रता से।

postage *पोस् टिज n.* charge for the carrying of letters डाक-महसूल।

postal *पोस् ट्ल a.* relating to the carrying of mails डाक-संबंधी।

post-date *पोस्ट् डेट v.t.* to put (on a letter, cheque etc.) a date later than the actual one उत्तरदिनांकित करना।

poster *पोस् टॅः n.* large advertising bill पोस्टर, विज्ञापन; one who posts bills विज्ञापन चिपकानेवाला।

posterity *पौॅस् टैॅ रि टि n.* descendants संतति, वंश; future generations भावी पीढ़ी।

posthumous *पौॅस् थ्यु मॅस a.* coming or happening after death मरणोत्तर।

postman *पौस्ट् मॅन n.* letter-carrier डाकिया, पत्रवाहक।

postmaster *पोस्ट् मास् टॅः n.* official-in-charge of a post-office पत्रपाल, डाकपति।

post-mortem[1] *पोस्ट् मौः टॅम a.* taking place after death मृत्यु के पश्चात्।

post-mortem[2] *n.* medical examination made after death शव-परीक्षा।

post-office *पौस्ट् औॅ फ़िस n.* office in-charge of postal service डाकघर।

postpone *पौस्ट् पोन v.t.* to put off to a later time स्थगित करना, टालना।

postponement *पोस्ट पोन् मॅन्ट n.* act of postponing स्थगन, विलंबन।

postscript *पोस् स्क्रिप्ट n.* addition to letter, book etc. अनुलेख, पत्र, समाप्त करने पर लिखा हुआ, अंश, पुनश्च।

posture *पौसॅ चॅः n.* way of holding the body मुद्रा; attitude of the body आसन; position of the body अंग-विन्यास; condition, state दशा।

pot[1] *पौ ॅट n.* a metallic or earthenware vessel पात्र, भांड, गमला।

pot[2] *(-tt-) v.t.* to put in a pot पात्र में रखना।

potash *पौ ॅ टैश n.* alkali used in soap etc. पोटाश, सज्जी, खार।

potassium *पॅ टै श्यॅम n.* white metallic element पोटैशियम, पोटाश का आधारभूत तत्व, दहातु।

potato *पॅ टे टो n. (pl. -es)* plant with tubers आलू का पौधा; one of the tubers आलू।

potency *पो टॅन सि n.* power, might शक्ति; efficacy प्रभावशीलता।

potent *पो टॅन्ट a.* powerful, mighty प्रबल, बलवान।

potential[1] *पों ॅ टैन्ॅ शॅल a.* possible शक्य; latent प्रच्छन्न।

potential[2] *n.* possibility संभावना।

pontentiality *पो ॅ टैन्ॅ शि ऐ लि टि n.* possibility संभावना; latent capacity शक्यता।

potter *पौ ॅ टॅः n.* maker of earthenware vessels कुम्हार।

pottery *पौ ॅ टॅ रि n.* earthenware मिट्टी के पात्र; business of the potter कुम्हार का व्यापार।

pouch *पॉउच n.* small bag थैली।

poultry *पोल् ट्रि n.* domestic fowls घरेलू मुर्गी, बत्तख इत्यादि।

pounce[1] *पॉउन्स v.i.* to make a downward swoop झपटना, आक्रमण करना।

pounce[2] *n.* sudden attack झपट्टा।

pound[1] *पॉउन्ड n.* unit of weight

पौंड, आध सेर तौल; monetary unit एक मुद्रा-विशेष।

pound[2] *v.t.* to beat to pieces कूटना; to crush to powder पीसना।

pour *पौः v.i.* to flow or issue forth बहना, निकलना; to rain havily ज़ोरदार वर्षा होना; *v.t.* to let flow out बहाना; to emit उगलना।

poverty *पौˇ वँः टि n.* state of being poor दरिद्रता; want कमी; scarcity अभाव।

powder[1] *पॉउ डँः n.* solid matter in dry fine particles पाउडर; dust बुकनी; gunpowder बारूद।

powder[2] *v.t.* to reduce to dust बुकनी करना; to sprinkle with powder छिड़कना।

power *पॉउ अँः n.* strength शक्ति; energy ऊर्जा; force बल; authority अधिकार; influence प्रभाव; state राज्य; government शासन।

powerful *पॉउ अँः फुल a.* having power, strong शक्तिशाली; forceful बलशाली; influential प्रभावशाली।

practicability *प्रैक् टि क् बि लि टि n.* quality or state of being practicable करणीयता, साध्यता।

practicable *प्रैक् टि कँ ब्ल a.* that may be done or effected करने योग्य; feasible संभव।

practical *प्रैक् टि क्ल a.* given to action व्यावहारिक; relating to practice अभ्यास-संबंधी, प्रायोगिक; useful उपयोगी; virtual वास्तविक।

practice *प्रैक् टिस n.* habit अभ्यास; exercise of any profession व्यवसाय; actual performance क्रिया, कार्य; custom प्रथा।

practise *प्रैक् टिस v.t.* to do repeatedly अभ्यास करना; to put into practice कार्यान्वित करना।

practitioner *प्रैक् टि शँ नँः n.* professional man व्यवसायी।

pragmatic *प्रैग मै टिक a.* concerned with practical consequence व्यवहारमूलक।

pragmatism *प्रैग् मँ टिज़्म n.* pedantry पांडित्य का अभिमान; matter of factness व्यवहारवाद।

praise[1] *प्रेज़ n.* commendation प्रशंसा, स्तुति।

praise[2] *v.t.* to commend, to admire प्रशंसा करना, स्तुति करना।

praiseworthy *प्रेज़् वँः दि a.* deserving praise सराहने-योग्य।

prank *प्रैङ्क n.* playful trick क्रीड़ा, खेल।

prattle[1] *प्रै ट्ल v.i.* to talk like a child बचकानी बातें करना।

prattle[2] *n.* childish talk बचकानी बात।

pray *प्रे v.i.* to offer prayers to God प्रार्थना करना; to entreat विनती करना।

prayer *प्रेˇ अँः n.* act of praying to God प्रार्थना; worship स्तुति, भजन।

preach *प्रीच v.i.* to deliver sermon धर्म का उपदेश करना; to give moral advice to नैतिक शिक्षा देना।

preacher *प्री चँः n.* one who preaches धर्मोपदेशक।

preamble *प्री ऐम् ब्ल n.* introduction भूमिका।

precaution *प्रि कौ शॅन n.* care taken in advance चौकसी, सावधानी।

precautionary *प्रि कौ शॅ नॅ रि a.* for the sake of precaution सतर्कता के तौर पर किया गया।

precede *प्रि सीड* to go before आगे होना, पूर्वकालीन होना।

precedence *प्रि सी डॅन्स, प्रै˘ सि डॅन्स n.* act of preceding पूर्व आगमन; priority प्राथमिकता; superiority श्रेष्ठता।

precedent *प्रै˘ सि डॅन्ट n.* some previous case taken as a rule दृष्टांत, पूर्वोदाहरण, नज़ीर।

precept *प्री सैप्ट n.* rule नियम; maxim नीतिवचन; direction निर्देश; moral instruction उपदेश।

preceptor *प्रि सैपॅ टॅः n.* moral teacher उपदेशक, गुरू।

precious *प्रै˘ शॅस a.* of great value मूल्यवान; costly महंगा; dear प्रिय।

precis *प्रे˘ सी n.* summary संक्षेप; abstract सार।

precise *प्रि सॉइस n.* definite निश्चित; exact यथार्थ।

precision *प्रि सि ज़ॅन n.* exactness यथार्थता; accuracy शुद्धता।

precursor *प्रि कॅः सॅः, प्री- n.* forerunner अग्रदूत, पूर्वगामी।

predecessor *प्री डि सै˘ सॅः n.* previous occupant of a position पूर्वाधिकारी; a thing that has been replaced by another of its kind पूर्ववर्ती वस्तु।

predestination *प्री डैसॅ टि ने शॅन n.* the doctrine that God has ordained everything पूर्वनियति; destiny भाग्य।

predetermine *प्री डि टॅः मिन v.t.* to decide in advance पहले से निर्णय कर लेना।

predicament *प्रि डि कॅ मॅन्ट n.* difficult or awkward situation कठिन परिस्थिति।

predicate *प्रै˘ डि किट n. (gram.)* what is said about the subject in the sentence (व्या.) विधेय।

predict *प्रि डिक्ट v.t.* to foretell भविष्यवाणी करना।

prediction *प्रि डिक् शॅन n.* prophecy भविष्यवाणी।

predominance *प्रि डौ˘ मि नॅन्स n.* superiority प्रबलता, प्रभुता।

predominant *प्रि डौ˘ मि नॅन्ट a.* chief प्रमुख; prevailing प्रबल।

predominate *प्रि डौ˘ मि नेट v.i.* to be the main or controlling element प्रमुख होना, प्रबल होना।

pre-eminence *प्री ऐ˘ मि नॅन्स n.* superiority श्रेष्ठता, उत्कृष्टता।

pre-eminent *प्री ऐ˘ मि नॅन्ट a.* outstanding श्रेष्ठ, उत्कृष्ट।

preface[1] *प्रै˘ फ़िस n.* introduction प्रस्तावना।

preface[2] *v.t.* to provide with a preface (की) भूमिका लिखना।

prefect *प्री फ़ैक्ट n.* student who helps a teacher in maintaining discipline अनुशासनपालक छात्र।

prefer *प्रि फ़ः v.t.* to like better अपेक्षाकृत अधिक पंसद करना।

preference *प्रै˘ फ़ॅ रॅन्स n.* act of preferring पसंद; that which is preferred पसंद की वस्तु; liking something more than another तरजीह।

preferential *प्रै˘ फ़ॅ रैनॅ शॅल a.* giving preference, relating to preference तरजीही।

prefix[1] *प्री फ़िक्स n.* syllable placed before another to form a new compound word उपसर्ग।

prefix[2] *प्री फ़िक्स v.t.* to add a prefix to उपसर्ग लगाना।

pregnancy *प्रैग् नॅन् सि n.* state of being pregnant गर्भावस्था; the period of remaining pregnant गर्भावस्था की अवधि।

pregnant *प्रैग् नॅन्ट a.* containing unborn young within the body गर्भवती।

prehistoric *प्री हिस् टौ˘ रिक a.* of the period before recorded history प्रागैतिहासिक।

prejudice *प्रै जु डिस n.* preconceived opinion पूर्वधारणा; bias पक्षपात; injury, harm हानि, क्षति, चोट।

prelate *प्रै˘ लॅट, -लिट n.* bishop or other churchman of equal or higher rank धर्माधिकारी।

preliminary[1] *प्रि लि मि नॅ रि a.* introductory प्राथमिक।

preliminary[2] *n (pl. -ries) (usu pl.)* preliminary action, measures etc. प्रारंभिक कार्यवाही।

prelude[1] *प्रै˘ ल्यूड n.* introductory piece of poetry मंगलाचरण; something preparatory प्रस्तावना।

prelude[2] *v.t.* to introduce परिचित कराना; to preface प्रस्तावना लिखना।

premarital *प्री मै रि टॅल a.* occurring before marriage विवाह से पूर्व का।

premature *प्रै˘ मॅ ट्युअ: a.* happening or done before the proper time कालपूर्व।

premeditate *प्रि मै˘ डि टेट, प्री- v.t.* to consider or plan in advance पूर्वयोजन करना।

premeditation *प्रि मै˘ डि टे शॅन, प्री- n.* consideration or planning in advance पूर्वचिंतन।

premier[1] *प्रै˘ म्यॅ:, प्री- a.* first in position or importance सर्वप्रथम, प्रमुख।

premier[2] *n.* prime minister प्रधानमंत्री।

premiere *प्रै˘ मि ऍअ: n.* first performance of a play, film, etc. प्रथम प्रदर्शन।

premium *प्री म्यॅम n.* instalment paid for an insurance policy बीमा शुल्क।

premonition *प्री मॅ नि शॅन n.* foreboding पूर्वबोध।

preoccupation *प्री औ˘ क्यु पे शॅन, प्रि- n.* mental concentration or absorption मानसिक व्यस्तता।

preoccupy *प्री औ˘ क्यु पॉइ, प्रि- v.t.* to engross attention of तल्लीन करना।

preparation *प्रै˘ पॅ रे शॅन n.* act of preparing तैयारी; something prepared तैयार की गई वस्तु।

preparatory *प्रि पै रॅ टॅ रि a.* introductory प्रारंभिक; serving as a preparation उपक्रमात्मक।

prepare *प्रि पे`अ: v.t.* to make ready तैयार करना; to make बनाना; *v.i.* to get ready तैयार होना।

preponderance *प्रि पौन् डॅ रॅन्स n.* quality of being greater in number, strength, influence, etc. प्रधानता, प्राबल्य, प्रमुखता।

preponderate *प्रि पौन् डॅ रेट v.i.* to be of greater power, influence or importance प्रबल, प्रमुख, प्रधान होना।

preposition *प्रै˘ पॅ ज़ि शॅन n.* word used with a noun or pronoun to show its relation with another word पूर्वसर्ग।

prerequisite[1] *प्री रैकॅ वि ज़िट a.* required as a prior condition पूर्वापेक्षित।

prerequisite[2] *n.* something required as prior condition पूर्वापेक्षा।

prerogative *प्रि रौ˘ गॅ टिव n.* exclusive right परमाधिकार, विशेषाधिकार।

prescience *प्रै˘ शि ॲन्स n.* foreknowledge पूर्वबोध।

prescribe *प्रि स्कॉइब v.t.* to lay down as a rule निर्धारित करना; to advise (a medicine) for treatment नुसख़े में लिखना।

prescription *प्रि स्क्रिप् शॅन n.* act of prescribing निर्धारण; thing prescribed निर्धारित वस्तु; doctor's written direction नुसख़ा; medicine prescribed निर्धारित औषधि।

presence *प्रै˘ ज़ॅन्स n.* state of being present उपस्थिति।

present[1] *प्रै˘ जॅन्ट a.* now existing विद्यमान; being in the place in question उपस्थित।

present[2] *n.* present time वर्तमान समय।

present[3] *प्रि ज़ैन्ट v.t.* to offer for show or approval प्रस्तुत करना; to make a gift of उपहारस्वरूप देना।

presentation *प्रै˘ ज़ॅन् टे शॅन n.* act of offering a present उपहार प्रदान करना; the gift which is presented भेंट, उपहार; act of presenting प्रस्तुतीकरण।

presently *प्रै˘ ज़न्ट् लि adv.* soon शीघ्र।

preservation *प्रै˘ ज़ॅः वे शॅन n.* act of preserving परिरक्षण।

preservative[1] *प्रि ज़ॅः वॅ टिव n.* something which preserves परिरक्षक।

preservative[2] *a.* tending to preserve, having the quality of preserving परिरक्षी।

preserve[1] *प्रि ज़ॅःव v.t.* to keep safe सुरक्षित रखना; to make a preserve (fruits) (फलों का) मुरब्बा बनाना; to maintain बनाए रखना।

preserve[2] *n.* something that is preserved परिरक्षित वस्तु।

preside *प्रि ज़ॉइड v.i.* to be chairman or president of a meeting सभापति होना।

president *प्रै˘ ज़ि डॅन्ट n.* head of a republic राष्ट्रपति; one who presides सभापति; chief officer of an organisation अध्यक्ष।

presidential *प्रै˘ ज़ि डैन् शॅल a.* of or concerned with the president अध्यक्षीय।

press[1] *प्रैसॅ v.t.* to push against दबाना; to force (पर) दबाव डालना; to squeeze out निचोड़ना; to make smooth by ironing इस्त्री करना; to compel बाध्य करना; to insist ज़ोर देना; to emphasize बल देना; *v.i.* to throng भीड़ लगाना; to hasten जल्दी करना।

press[2] *n.* a printing machine छपाई की मशीन; printing house छापाख़ाना; newspapers collectively समाचार-पत्र; reporters, journalists संवाददाता, पत्रकार; crowd भीड़; stress बल; cupboard अलमारी।

pressure *प्रै˘ शॅः n.* act of pressing दबाव; moral force नैतिक दबाव; distress or difficulty कष्ट, परेशानी; compulsion बाध्यता।

pressurize *प्रै˘ शॅ रॉइज़ v.t.* to put pressure on (पर) दबाव डालना।

prestige *प्रैसॅ टीज़ n.* esteem प्रतिष्ठा।

prestigious *प्रैसॅ टि जॅस a.* relating to prestige प्रतिष्ठा-संबंधी।

presume *प्रि ज़्यूम v.t.* to take for granted मानना; to suppose to be true सत्य समझना; to venture (का) साहस करना।

presumption *प्रि ज़म्प् शॅन n.* something presumed कल्पना; something which seems likely अनुमान, संभावना; arrogance घमंड, अकड़।

presuppose *प्री सॅ पोज़ v.t.* to imply (का) अभिप्राय होना; to take for granted मान लेना; to require के लिए आवश्यक होना।

presupposition *प्री सॅ पो ज़ि शॅन n.* presupposing पूर्वधारणा।

pretence *प्रि टैन्स n.* act of pretending बहाना; simulation दिखावा, ढोंग; pretext बहाना।

prtend *प्रि टैन्ड v.t.* to feign का बहाना करना; to simulate का ढोंग करना।

pretension *प्रि टैनॅ शॅन n.* claim true or false दावा; pretext बहाना।

pretentious *प्रि टैनॅ शॅस a.* full of pretension मिथ्याभिमानी, मिथ्या दावेदार।

pretext *प्री टैक्स्ट n.* an ostensible reason or motive बहाना।

prettiness *प्रि टि निस n.* attractiveness सुंदरता, रम्यता।

pretty[1] *प्रि टि a. (-tier, -tiest)* pleasing सुंदर; attractive आकर्षक।

pretty[2] *adv.* fairly, quite बहुत कुछ, काफ़ी हद तक।

prevail *प्रि वेल v.i.* to gain the victory or superiority विजय अथवा श्रेष्ठता प्राप्त करना; to be in force लागू होना; to succeed सफल होना; to predominate प्रबल होना, हावी होना।

prevalance *प्रै˘ वॅ लॅन्स n.* being prevalent प्रचलन, व्यापकता।

prevalent *प्रै˘ वॅ लॅन्ट a.* prevailing व्याप्त, फैला हुआ; predominant प्रबल।

prevent *प्रि वैन्ट v.t.* to stop or intercept रोकना; to impede में बाधा डालना।

prevention *प्रि वैनॅ शॅन n.* the act of preventing निवारण, रोकथाम।

preventive *प्रि वैनॅ टिव् a.* tending to prevent निवारक।

previous *प्री व्यॅस a.* preceding पूर्ववर्ती, पहला।

prey[1] *प्रे n.* a bird or animal hunted by another शिकार; victim पीड़ित, बलि।

prey[2] *v.i. (with 'on' or 'upon')* to seize and devour prey शिकार करना; to make attacks for plunder धावा बोलना; to exert a harmful pressure on mind मस्तिष्क के लिए हानिप्रद होना।

price[1] *प्रॉइस n.* cost मूल्य; worth महत्व।

price[2] *v.t.* to fix the price of (का) मूल्य निर्धारित करना; to mark the price of मूल्यांकित करना।

prick[1] *प्रिक n.* slender pointed thing that can pierce कांटा; sharp point नोक; being pricked चुभन; puncture by a prick छेद; sting डंक; remorse पीड़ा।

prick[2] *v.t.* to pierce with a prick चुभाना; to spur प्रेरित करना; to fill with remorse पीड़ा पहुंचाना।

pride[1] *प्राइॅड n.* state or quality of being proud अभिमान; inordinate self-esteem दंभ, घमंड, अहंकार; cause of pride अभिमान का आधार।

pride[2] *v.t.* to indulge (oneself) in pride अभिमान करना।

priest *प्रीस्ट n.* clergyman पुरोहित।

priestess *प्रीस् टिस n.* a female clergy पुजारिन।

priesthood *प्रीस्ट् हुड n.* office of a priest पौरोहित्य; the whole body of priests पुरोहित-वर्ग।

prima facie *प्रॉइ मॅ फ़े शि adv.* at first view or appearance प्रथम द्रष्टया।

primarily *प्रॉइ मॅ रि लि adv.* in the first place प्रथमतः; originally मूलतः।

primary *प्रॉइ मॅ रि a.* first प्रथम; chief प्रधान; original मूल; elementary प्राथमिक।

prime[1] *प्रॉइम a.* foremost मुख्य; first प्रथम; original मूल; fundamental आधारभूत; first in rank or importance etc. सर्वश्रेष्ठ।

prime[2] *n.* the best part उत्कर्ष; youth यौवन; full health पूर्ण स्वास्थ्य।

primer *प्रॉइ मॅः n.* an elementary education book प्रवेशिका।

primeval *प्रॉइ मी वॅल a.* of the earliest age or time आदि युगीन।

primitive *प्रि मि टिव a.* of the earliest time आदिम, पुरातन; crude अपरिष्कृत; uncivilized असभ्य।

prince *प्रिन्स n.* son of a king राजकुमार।

princely *प्रिन्स् लि a.* splendid शानदार; generous उदार; stately राजसी।

princess *प्रिन् सैसॅ n.* daughter of a king or emperor राजकुमारी।

principal[1] *प्रिन् सि पॅल n.* head प्रधान व्यक्ति; head of an educational institution प्रधानाचार्य; sum of money lent मूलधन।

principal[2] *a.* first प्रथम; chief प्रधान; most important अत्यधिक महत्वपूर्ण।

principle *प्रिन् सॅ प्ल n.* fundamental law सिद्धांत; uprightness ईमानदारी; element विशिष्ट तत्व; rule of conduct आचार, नियम।

print[1] *प्रिन्ट v.t.* to reproduce in ink छापना; to cause to be reproduced in ink छपवाना; to make a positive picture from (a negative) (नैगेटिव) से फ़ोटो तैयार करना; to stamp (fabric) with coloured design (कपड़े) की छपाई करना।

print[2] *n.* mark made by pressure छाप, निशान; printed calico छींट; printed matter मुद्रित सामग्री।

printer *प्रिन् टॅः n.* one who prints मुद्रक।

prior[1] *प्राइ अॅः a.* earlier पूर्ववर्ती।

prior[2] *n.* chief of a religious house मठाध्यक्ष।

prioress *प्रॉइ अॅ रिस n.* female prior

मठाध्यक्षा।

priority *प्रॉइ औ ˘ रि टि n.* being prior प्रथमता; precedence पूर्वता।

prison *प्रि ज़्न n.* place of confinement बंदीगृह, कारागार; confinement कैद।

prisoner *प्रि ज़् नें: n.* one shut up in a prison बंदी।

privacy *प्रॉइ वॅ सि n.* state of being private एकांत।

private *प्रॉइ विट a.* confidential गुप्त; personal व्यक्तिगत; not open to the public असार्वजनिक; not having official character ग़ैर सरकारी।

privation *प्रॉइ वे शॅन n.* lack of the necessaries of life अभाव, असुविधा; hardship कठिनाई; act of depriving वंचन।

privilege *प्रि वि लिज n.* personal favour सुविधा; separate and personal advantage विशेषाधिकार।

prize[1] *प्रॉइज़ n.* reward पुरस्कार, पारितोषिक।

prize[2] *v.t.* to value highly कद्र करना।

probability *प्रौ ˘ बॅ बि लि टि n.* likelihood संभावना।

probable *प्रौ ˘ बॅ ब्ल a.* likely संभावित।

probably *प्रौ ˘ बॅब् लि adv.* possible संभवतया।

probation *प्रौ ˘ बे शॅन, प्रॅ- n.* period of trial परिवीक्षा काल; proof प्रमाण; trial परिवीक्षा।

probationer *प्रौ ˘ बे शॅ नें:, प्रॅ- n.* one on probation परिवीक्षार्थी।

probe[1] *प्रोब v.t.* to investigate thoroughly जांच-पड़ताल करना।

probe[2] *n.* thorough investigation जांच-पड़ताल।

problem *प्रौबॅ् लॅम n.* question proposed for solution प्रश्न; matter difficult to deal with समस्या।

problematic *प्रौबॅ् लॅ मै टिक a.* of the nature of a problem समस्यात्मक।

procedure *प्रॅ सी जॅ: n.* an established method of doing things कार्यपद्धति।

proceed *प्रो सीड, प्रॅ- v.i.* to go forward अग्रसर होना; to continue in an activity कार्य जारी रखना।

proceeding *प्रॅ सी डिङ्ग, प्रो- n.* course of action कार्यवाही; *(pl.)* official record कार्यवाही की अधिकृत रपट; *(pl.)* legal action क़ानूनी कार्यवाही।

proceeds *प्रो सीड्ज़ n. pl.* price or profit मूल्य अथवा मुनाफ़ा।

process *प्रो सैसॅ n.* series of action or changes प्रक्रिया; growth, progress प्रगति, विकास; method of operation कार्यविधि; action of law क़ानूनी कार्यवाही।

procession *प्रॅ सै ˘ शॅन n.* train of persons in formal order जुलूस।

proclaim *प्रॅ क्लेम v.t.* to announce publicly घोषणा करना।

proclamation *प्रौक् लॅ मे शॅन n.* an official public announcement घोषणा।

proclivity *प्रॅ क्लि वि टि n.* tendency, inclination प्रवृत्ति, झुकाव।

procrastinate *प्रो ˘ कैस् टि नेट v.i.* to delay action टालमटोल करना।

procrastination *प्रो ˘ क्रैस् टि ने शॅन*

n. procrastinating टालमटोल।

proctor *प्रौक् टः* *n.* an official of the college who maintains discipline अनुशासन-अधिकारी।

procure *प्रॅ क्युअंः* *v.t.* to obtain प्राप्त करना।

procurement *प्रॅ क्युअंः मॅन्ट* *n.* act of obtaining प्राप्ति।

prodigal *प्रौ डि गॅल* *a.* extravagant, wasteful अपव्ययी।

prodigality *प्रौ ˘ डि गै लि टि* *n.* extravagance अपव्ययिता; generosity उदारता।

produce[1] *प्र ˘ ड्यूस* *v.t.* to manufacture उत्पादन करना; to supply पूर्ति करना; to exhibit प्रदर्शित करना; to give birth to पैदा करना।

produce[2] *प्रौ˘ ड्यूस* *n.* what is produced उत्पादन; agricultural products कृषि-उत्पादन।

product *प्रौ ˘ डॅक्ट* *n.* that what is produced उत्पाद; result परिणाम; number resulting from multiplication गुणनफल।

production *प्रॅ डक् शॅन* *n.* product उत्पाद; act or process of producing उत्पादन।

productive *प्रॅ डॅक् टिव* *a.* having the power of producing उत्पादक।

productivity *प्रौ डक् टि वि टि* *n.* being productive उत्पादकता।

profane[1] *प्रॅ फ़ेन* *a.* vulgar अश्लील; not sacred अपवित्र।

profane[2] *v.t.* to pollute, to desecrate अपवित्र करना।

profess *प्रॅ फ़ैसॅ* *v.t.* to confess publicly खुले-आम स्वीकार करना; to assert दावे के साथ कहना; to pretend ढोंग करना; to declare belief in आस्था दिखलाना; to declare openly खुलेआम दावा करना।

profession *प्रॅ फ़ै ˘ शॅन* *n.* occupation पेशा, व्यवसाय; avowal घोषणा।

professional *प्रॅ फ़ै ˘ शॅ नॅल* *a.* pertaining to a profession व्यवसाय-संबंधी।

professor *प्रॅ फ़ै ˘ सॅः* *n.* teacher of the highest rank in a university प्राध्यापक।

proficiency *प्रॅ फ़ि शॅन् सि* *n.* skill प्रवीणता, निपुणता।

proficient *प्रॅ फ़ि शॅन्ट* *a.* skilled, expert प्रवीण, निपुण।

profile[1] *प्रो फ़ील, -फ़ॉइल* *n.* character sketch रेखाचित्र; side view पार्श्वचित्र।

profile[2] *v.t.* to draw in profile (का) रेखाचित्र बनाना।

profit[1] *प्रौ˘ फ़िट* *n.* advantage, benefit लाभ; financial gain मुनाफ़ा।

profit[2] *v.t.* to benefit लाभ पहुंचाना; financial gain लाभ प्राप्त करना।

profitable *प्रौ˘फ़ि टॅ बॅल* *a.* yielding profit लाभकारी।

profiteer[1] *प्रौ˘ फ़ि टिअॅः* *n.* one who makes excessive profits in times of scarcity मुनाफ़ाखोर।

profiteer[2] *v.i.* to make excessive profits मुनाफ़ाखोरी करना।

profligacy *प्रौफ़् लि गॅ सि* *n.* immorality अनैतिकता, दुश्चरित्रता; wastefulness अपव्ययिता, उड़ाऊपन।

profligate *प्रौफ़् लि गिट* *a.* shamlessly immoral अनैतिक, दुश्चरित्र; reckless लापरवाह; wasteful उड़ाऊ, अपव्ययी।

profound *प्र फ़ॉउन्ड a.* deep अथाह; deep in skill or knowledge गहन; abstruse गूढ़, दुर्बोध।

profundity *प्रॅ फ़न् डि टि n.* depth गहराई; being profound गांभीर्य।

profuse *प्रॅ फ़्यूज़ a.* lavish प्रचुर।

profusion *प्रॅ फ्यू ज़ॅन n.* abundance प्रचुरता।

progeny *प्रौ ˘ जि नि n.* offspring संतान; descendants वंशज; children बच्चे।

programme[1] *प्रो ग्रैम n.* plan of proceedings योजना; broadcast on radio or television कार्यक्रम।

programme[2] *v.t.* to make a programme of (का) कार्यक्रम बनाना।

progress[1] *प्रो ग्रैॅस n.* development विकास, प्रगति।

progress[2] *प्र ˘ ग्रै ˘ स प्रो ˘- v.i.* to improve सुधार होना; to move forward प्रगति करना।

progressive *प्रॅ ग्रै ˘ सिव, प्रो ˘- a.* advocating progress प्रगतिशील; progressing by degrees उन्नतिशील।

prohibit *प्रॅ हि बिट, प्रो˘- v.t.* to forbid रोकना, मना करना।

prohibition *प्रो˘ हि बि शॅन n.* act of prohibitng निषेध; the banning of alcoholic drinks मद्यनिषेध।

prohibitive *प्रो˘ हि बि टिव, प्र˘- a.* implying prohibition निषेधक; (of prices) very high अति ऊंचे (मूल्य)।

prohibitory *प्रो˘ हि बि टॅ रि, प्रॅ- a.* designed to prohibit something निषेधात्मक।

project[1] *प्रौ˘ ज़ेक्ट n.* scheme योजना; plan परियोजना।

project[2] *प्रौ˘ ज़ेक्ट v.t.* to plan योजना बनाना; to throw फेंकना; to cause (a shadow, picture, etc.) to fall (on a surface) डालना; *v.i.* to stick out, to jut out बाहर निकला होना।

projectile[1] *प्रॅ˘जैक् टॉइल, प्रौ जिक्- n.* heavy missile प्रक्षेपणास्त्र।

projectile[2] *a.* that can be sent forward or thrown प्रक्षेप्य।

projection *प्रॅ जै˘क् शॅन, प्रो˘- n.* act of projecting प्रक्षेपण; something that juts out बाहर निकला भाग।

projector *प्रो ˘ जैक् टॅ:, प्रॅ- n.* that which casts something forward प्रक्षेपित्र।

proliferate *प्रॅ लि फ़ॅ रेट, प्रो˘- v.i.* to grow rapidly प्रचुर मात्रा में उत्पन्न होना; *v.t.* to reproduce rapidly प्रचुर मात्रा में उत्पन्न करना।

proliferation *प्रॅ लि फ़ॅ रे शॅन, प्रो˘- n.* rapid growth तीव्र बृद्धि।

prolific *प्रॅ लि फ़िक, प्रो˘- a.* fruitful फलदायक; producing much बहुत उपज देनेवाला।

prologue *प्रो लौगॅ n.* preface, introduction भूमिका; introductory part of a poem मंगलाचरण।

prolong *प्र˘ लौङ्ग, प्रौ˘ v.t.* to make longer लंबा करना।

prolongation *प्रो ˘ लौङ गे शॅन n.* making longer दीर्घीकरण।

prominence *प्रौ मि नॅन्स n.* state of being prominent विशिष्टता।

prominent *प्रौ˘ मि नॅन्ट a.* eminent विशिष्ट; important महत्वपूर्ण; standing out बाहर निकला हुआ।

promise[1] *प्रौ ˘ मिस n.* pledge, undertaking वादा, प्रतिज्ञा; hope or likelihood of success प्रत्याशा।

promise² *v.t.* to give one's word वचन देना; to give cause for expecting आशान्वित करना।

promising *प्रौ ˘ मि सिङ्ग a.* giving promise or grounds for good hopes आशाजनक, होनहार।

promissory *प्रौ ˘ मि सॅ रि a.* containing a promise or binding declaration वचनात्मक, प्रतिज्ञात्मक।

promote *प्रॅ मोट v.t.* to help forward बढ़ावा देना; to encourage प्रोत्साहित करना; move up to higher rank पदोन्नत करना।

promotion *प्रॅ मो शॅन n.* act of promoting पदोन्नयन; encouragement प्रोत्साहन; advancement विकास।

prompt¹ *प्रौम्प्ट a.* ready तत्पर; done without delay त्वरित।

prompt² *v.t.* to urge प्रेरित करना; to remind (an actor) of forgotten words अनुबोधन करना।

prompter *प्रौम्प् टॅः n.* one who prompts, actors अनुबोधक।

prone *प्रोन a.* lying face downwards अधोमुख; inclined इच्छुक, प्रवृत्त।

pronoun *प्रो नॉउन n.* word used instead of a noun सर्वनाम।

pronounce *प्रॅ नॉउन्स v.t.* to declare or affirm घोषणा करना; to utter उच्चारण करना; to give one's opinion अपना मत व्यक्त करना।

pronunciation *प्रॅ नॅन् सि ए शॅन n.* act or mode of pronouncing something उच्चारण, उच्चारण-शैली।

proof¹ *प्रूफ़ n.* evidence प्रमाण; trial परीक्षण; *(print.)* an impression in printing for correction प्रूफ़।

proof² *a.* impenetrable अभेद्य; able to resist प्रतिरोध करने-योग्य।

prop¹ *प्रौप n.* pole or beam used as a support टेक, थूनी।

prop² *(-pp-) v.t.* to support सहारा देना।

propaganda *प्रौ ˘ पॅ गैन् डॅ n.* spreading of information or ideas to advance a cause प्रचार।

propagandist *प्रौ ˘ पॅ गैन् डिस्ट n.* one who actively spreads propaganda प्रचारक।

propagate *प्रौ ˘ पॅ गेट v.t.* to spread widely प्रसारित करना; to multiply by generation or reproduction उपजाना, बढ़ाना; to diffuse फैलाना।

propagation *प्रौ ˘ पॅ गे शॅन n.* act of propagating प्रसारण; diffusion फैलाव।

propel *प्रॅ पैˇल, प्रोˇ- (-ll) v.t.* to drive forward ठेलना।

proper *प्रौ ˘ पॅः a.* correct, suitable उपयुक्त; appropriate उचित; decent समुचित; *(gram.)* denoting individual person or place (व्या.) व्यक्तिवाचक।

property *प्रौ ˘ पॅः टि n.* possession संपत्ति; attribute गुणधर्म; special quality विशेषता।

prophecy *प्रौ ˘ फ़ि सि n.* prediction भविष्यकथन।

prophesy *प्रौ फ़ि सॉइ v.t.* to predict पहले से बता देना; *v.i.* to make a prophecy भविष्यकथन करना।

prophet *प्रौ ˘ फ़िट n.* (*fem. prophetess*) a devinely inspired religious leader पैगंबर; a person who predicts the future

भविष्यद्रष्टा।

prophetic *प्रॅ फ़ै ॅ टिक a.* pertaining to a prophet पैग़ंबरी; unfolding future events भविष्यसूचक।

proportion[1] *प्रॅ पौ: शॅन n.* comparative relation अनुपात; comparison तुलना; symmetry सममिति; just or equal share अंश।

proportion[2] *v.t.* to adjust in due proportion समानुपातन करना।

proportional *प्रॅ पौ : शॅ न्‌ल a.* proportionate समानुपातिक।

proportionate *प्रॅ पौ : शॅ निट a.* having a due proportion समानुपाती, सापेक्ष।

proposal *प्रॅ पो ज़ॅल n.* that which is proposed प्रस्ताव; offer of marriage विवाह-प्रस्ताव; suggestion सुझाव।

propose *प्र ॅ पोज़ v.t.* to offer for consideration प्रस्तावित करना; to nominate मनोनीत करना; *v.i.* to make a proposal प्रस्ताव करना; to offer onself in marriage विवाह-प्रस्ताव; सुझाव।

proposition *प्रौ ॅ पॅ ज़ि शॅन n.* proposal प्रस्ताव; a statement कथन; a theorem साध्य।

propound *प्रॅ पॉउन्ड v.t.* to put forward for consideration or solution प्रस्तावित करना।

proprietary *प्रॅ प्रॉइ अॅ टॅ रि a.* belonging to a proprietor मालिकाना।

proprietor *प्रॅ प्रॉइ अॅ टॅ: n.* an owner स्वामी।

propriety *प्रॅ प्रॉइ अॅ टि n.* state of being proper उपयुक्तता; justness औचित्य; proper behaviour मर्यादा।

prorogue *प्रॅ रोग, प्रो ॅ v.t.* to suspend (a legislative session) (सत्र का) अवसान करना।

prosaic *प्रो ॅ ज़े इक a.* uninteresting नीरस; commonplace सामान्य।

prose *प्रोज़ n.* speech or language not in verse गद्य।

prosecute *प्रौ ॅ सि क्यूट v.t.* to pursue at law (पर) मुक़दमा चलाना।

prosecution *प्रौ ॅ सि क्यूशन n.* act of prosecuting अभियोजन।

prosecutor *प्रो ॅ सि क्यू टॅ: n.* one who prosecutes अभियोक्ता।

prosody *प्रौ ॅ सॅ डि n.* the rules of metre or versification छंदशास्त्र।

prospect *प्रौसॅ् पैक्ट n.* outlook दृष्टिकोण; reasonable hope आशा; expectation अपेक्षा; a distant view परिदृश्य।

prospective *प्रॅस् पैक् टिव a.* hoped for प्रत्याशित; future भावी।

prospsectus *प्रॅस् पैक् टॅस n. (pl. es)* a printed statement of some enterprise proposed विवरण-पुस्तिका।

prosper *प्रौसॅ् पॅ: v.i.* to increase in wealth समृद्ध होना; to succed सफल होना।

prosperity *प्रौसॅ् पै ॅ रि टि n.* flourishing state समृद्धि; success सफलता; good fortune सौभाग्य।

prosperous *प्रौसॅ् पॅ रॅस a.* flourishing समृद्ध; successful सफल; fortunate भाग्यशाली।

prostitute[1] *प्रौसॅ् टि ट्यूट n.* a woman who offers sexual intercourse in return for payment वेश्या।

prostitute[2] *v.t.* to put to wrong

use (को) भ्रष्ट करना, दुरूपयोग करना।

prostitution *प्रौसॅ टि ट्यू शॅन n.* practice of prostituting oneself वेश्यावृत्ति; misuse दुरूपयोग।

prostrate[1] *प्रौ ॅस् ट्रेट,-ट्रिट a.* lying flat दंडवत् पड़ा हुआ; overcome पराजित; overthrown गिराया हुआ।

prostrate[2] *प्रौसॅ ट्रेट v.t.* to throw flat on ground गिरा देना; to render helpless असहाय कर देना।

prostration *प्रौसॅ ट्रे शॅन n.* act of lying flat दंडवत् अवस्था; complete exhaustion पूर्ण श्रांति।

protagonist *प्रो ॅ टै गॅ निस्ट n.* supporter पक्षपोषक; chief character नायक; principal actor मुख्य अभिनेता।

protect *प्रॅ टैक्ट v.t.* to shield from danger ख़तरे से रक्षा करना।

protection *प्रॅ टैक् शॅन n.* defence रक्षा; shelter शरण, आश्रय; act of protecting बचाव; that which protects रक्षक।

protective *प्रॅ टैक् टिव a.* giving protection संरक्षी; serving as protection रक्षात्मक।

protector *प्रॅ टैक् टः n.* one who protects रक्षक।

protein *प्रो टीन n.* an organic substance found in some foods प्रोटीन।

protest[1] *प्रो टैस्ट n.* formal declaration of dissent प्रतिवाद, विरोध।

protest[2] *प्रॅ टैस्ट v.i.* to make a formal declaration of opposition प्रतिवाद करना; to raise an objection आपत्ति करना; *v.t.* to assert दृढ़तापूर्वक कहना।

protestation *प्रो ॅ टेसॅ टे शॅन n.* a solemn declaration गंभीर घोषणा; an act of protest विरोध।

prototype *प्रो टॅ टॉइप n.* an original type or model आदिरूप।

proud *प्राउंड a.* feeling proper pride स्वाभिमानी; boastful घमंडी, दंभी; arrogant अक्खड़; self respecting आत्मसम्मानपूर्ण; stately शानदार।

prove *प्रूव v.t.* to try by experiment प्रमाणित करना; to establish the truth or reality of सिद्ध करना; *v.i.* to be found by experience or trial प्रमाणित होना।

proverb *प्रौ ॅ वॅःब n.* a popular saying लोकोक्ति; maxim कहावत।

proverbial *प्रॅ वॅः ब्यॅल a.* widely known सर्वविदित; of the nature of a proverb लोकोक्तीय।

provide *प्रॅ वॉइड v.i.* to make preparation तैयारी करना; *v.t.* to supply मुहैया करना; to equip सुसज्जित करना; to stipulate शर्त लगाना; to give प्रदान करना।

providence *प्रौ ॅ वि डॅन्स n.* foresight दूरदृष्टि; (cap.) the care which God exercises over His creatures ईश-कृपा; (cap.) God ईश्वर।

provident *प्रौ ॅ वि डॅन्ट a.* thrifty मितव्ययी; showing foresight दूरदर्शी।

providential *प्रौ ॅ वि डैनॅ शॅल a.* accomplished by divine providence दैवकृत; lucky शुभ।

province *प्रौ ॅ विन्स n.* state प्रांत; sphere of action कार्यक्षेत्र।

provincial *प्रॅ विन् शॅल a.* of a province प्रांतीय; narrow-minded

संकीर्णतापूर्ण।

provincialism *प्रॅ विन् शॅ लिज़्म n.* the quality of being provincial प्रांतीयता; narrow-mindedness संकीर्णता।

provision *प्रॅ वि ज़न n.* act of providing व्यवस्थापन; stores provided भंडार; clause in any statute धारा।

provisional *प्रॅ वि ज़ॅ न्ल a.* temporary अस्थायी।

proviso *प्रॅ वॉइ ज़ो n. (pl. -s)* condition शर्त।

provocation *प्रौ˘ वॅ के शॅन n.* act of provoking उत्तेजन; cause of resentment चिढ़ने का कारण।

provocative *प्रॅ वौ˘ कॅ टिव a.* exciting उत्तेजक।

provoke *प्रॅ वोक v.t.* to irritate चिढ़ाना; to stimulate प्रदीप्त करना; to incite भड़काना।

prowess *प्रॉउ इस n.* bravery वीरता; gallantry शौर्य; boldness and dexterity in war निर्भीकता।

proximate *प्रौक् सि मॅट a.* nearest समीपी; in closest relationship निकट संबंधी।

proximity *प्रौक् सि मि टि n.* state of being proximate निकटता।

proxy *प्रौक् सि n.* authorised agent or substitute अधिकृत कार्यकर्ता अथवा स्थानापन्न व्यक्ति।

prude *प्रूड n.* a person of extreme propriety अति औचित्यवादी व्यक्ति।

prudence *प्रू डॅन्स n.* quality of being prudent विवेक, सावधानी।

prudent *प्रू डॅन्ट a.* sensible and wise विवेकी; सावधान।

prudential *प्रू डैनॅ शॅल, प्र- a.* marked by prudence विवेकपूर्ण।

prune *प्रून v.t.* to cut away parts of (tree, etc.) छंटाई करना; to take out unnecessary part from अनावश्यक अंश निकाल देना।

pry *प्रॉइ v.i.* to peep narrowly ताक-झांक करना।

psalm *साम n.* sacred song धार्मिक भजन।

pseudonym *स्यू डो निम,-डॅ- n.* false or feigned name छद्‌नाम।

psyche *सॉइ कि n.* human soul आत्मा; human mind मानव-मस्तिष्क; mentality मानसिकता।

psychiatrist *सॉइ कॉइ ॲ ट्रिस्ट n.* expert in psychiatry मनश्चिकित्सक।

psychiatry *सॉइ कॉइ ॲ ट्रि n.* treatment of mental illness मनश्चिकित्सा।

psychic *सॉइ किक a.* belonging to the soul आध्यात्मिक; psychological मनोवैज्ञानिक।

psychological *सॉइ कॅ लै˘ जि कॅल a.* pertaining to psychology or science of mind मनोवैज्ञानिक।

psychologist *सॉइ कौ˘ लॅ जिस्ट n.* one who is conversant with psychology मनोविज्ञानी।

psychology *सॉइ कौ˘ लॅ जि n.* that branch of knowledge which deals with the mind मनोविज्ञान।

psychopath *सॉइ को˘ पैथ n.* patient of mental disorder मनोरोगी।

psychosis *सॉइ को सिस n.* severe mental disorder मनोविकृति।

psychotherapy *सॉइ को˘ थै˘ रॅ पि*

n. treatment of disease by psychological methods मनश्चिकित्सा।

puberty *प्यू बॅ: टि n.* sexual maturity तारूण्य।

public[1] *पब् लिक a.* pertaining to a whole community सार्वजनिक; for the use of benefit of all सर्वोपयोगी।

public[2] *n.* people as a whole जनता।

publication *पब् लि के शॅन n.* act of publishing प्रकाशन; announcement घोषणा; something published प्रकाशित सामग्री (पुस्तक आदि)।

publicity *पब् लि सि टि n.* business of advertising प्रचार।

publicize *पब् लि सॉइज़ v.t.* to give publicity to प्रचारित करना।

publish *पब् लिश v.t.* to cause to be printed and offered for sale प्रकाशित करना; to make public सार्वजनिक बनाना।

publisher *पब् लि शॅ: n.* one who publishes (especially books) प्रकाशक।

pudding *पु डिङ्ग n.* a sweet dish पुडिंग।

puddle[1] *पड़ल n.* small, dirty pool डबरा, पोखर।

puddle[2] *v.t.* to make muddy गंदला करना।

puerile *प्यु अॅ रॉइल a.* trivial तुच्छ; suitable only for a child बचकाना।

puff[1] *पफ़ n.* sudden emission of breath फूंक; a whiff कश; short blast of wind झोंका; pad गदिया; swelling सूजन।

puff[2] *v.i.* to breathe hard after exertion तेज़ी से सांस लेना; to take puffs in smoking कश मारना; *v.t.* to drive with a blast फूँकना; to inflate फुलाना; to inflate with pride घमंड से भरना; to praise extravagantly अति प्रशंसा करना।

pull[1] *पुल v.t.* to draw or move towards oneself खींचना; to remove by drawing out उखाड़ना; to pluck खींचना।

pull[2] *n.* act of pulling खिंचाई; effort परिश्रम; influence प्रभाव, दबाव।

pulley *पु लि n.* grooved wheel घिरनी।

pullover *पुल् ओ वॅ: n.* sweater, jersey स्वेटर, ज़रसी।

pulp[1] *पल्प n.* soft juicy part of a fruit गूदा; soft mass of rags or wood लुग़दी।

pulp[2] *v.t.* to crush into pulp लुग़दी बनाना।

pulpit *पुल् पिट a.* raised platform in temple प्रवचन-मंच।

pulpy *पल् पि a.* full of pulp गूदेदार।

pulsate *पल् सेट, पल् सेट v.i.* to beat or throb धड़कना।

pulsation *पल् से शॅन n.* single beat or throb धड़कन; throb फड़कन।

pulse[1] *पल्स n.* regular beat of arteries नब्ज़, नाड़ी-स्पंदन।

pulse[2] *v.i.* to beat or throb स्पंदित होना।

pulse[3] *n* edible seeds of pod-bearing plants दाल।

pump[1] *पम्प n.* machine for raising water or extracting air पंप।

pump[2] *v.t.* to raise, put in, take out with pump पंप से उठाना, रखना, निकालना; *v.i.* to work a pump पंप चलाना।

pumpkin *पम्प् किन n.* a variety of gourd कद्दू।

pun[1] *पन n.* play on words यमक, श्लेष।

pun[2] *(-nn-) v.i.* to make a pun यमक या श्लेष का प्रयोग करना।

punch[1] *पन्च n.* an instrument for driving holes in metal etc. पंच, छेदक; blow or thrust मुक्का।

punch[2] *v.t.* to perforate with a punch पंच से छेद करना; to hit with the fist मुक्का मारना।

punctual *पङ्क् ट्यु अॅल a.* made or done at the exact time समयानुकूल; observant of appointed time समय का पाबंद।

punctuality *पङ्क् ट्यु ऐ लि टि n.* quality of being punctual समय की पाबंदी।

punctuate *पङ्क् ट्यु एट v.t.* to insert punctuation marks in में विराम-चिह्न लगाना; to interrupt में रुकावट पैदा करना।

punctuation *पङ्क् ट्यु ए शॅन n.* practice of punctuating विराम-चिह्न-विधान।

puncture[1] *पङ्क् चॅः n.* act of pricking छेदन; small hole thus made छिद्र।

puncture[2] *v.t.* to pierce with a small point नोक से छेद करना।

pungency *पन् जॅन् सि n.* sharpness तीव्रता; bitterness तीखापन।

pungent *पन् जॅन्ट a.* biting तीक्ष्ण; sharp तीव्र।

punish *प निश v.t.* to inflict penalty on दंड देना; to cause to suffer कष्ट पहुंचाना।

punishment *प निश् मॅन्ट n.* penalty दंड।

punitive *प्यू नि टिव a.* inflicting punishment दंडात्मक।

puny *प्यू नि a.* small and weak छोटा व दुर्बल।

pupil *प्यू प्ल n.* disciple शिष्य; aperture in the iris through which the rays of light pass पुतली।

puppet *प पिट n.* a small figure in human form mechanically worked पुतली; person who is a mere tool अधीन व्यक्ति।

puppy *प पि n.* young dog पिल्ला।

purblind *पॅः ब्लॉइंड* dim-sighted चुंधा।

purchase[1] *पॅः चॅस n.* thing bought ख़रीदी गई वस्तु; buying क्रय, ख़रीद।

purchase[2] *v.t.* to buy ख़रीदना।

pure *प्युअॅः a* unmixed अमिश्रित; clear स्पष्ट; clean साफ़; chaste पवित्र; genuine असली।

purgation *पॅः गे शॅन n.* purification शुद्धि; purging of the bowels विरेचन।

purgative[1] *पॅः गॅ टिव n.* substance having the power to purge विरेचक पदार्थ।

purgative[2] *a.* having the power to purge शोधक, विरेचक।

purgatory *पॅः गॅ टॅ रि n.* place of temporary suffering for the purification of soul शुद्धि का स्थान।

purge *पॅःज v.t.* to make pure or clean पवित्र करना; to evacuate the bowels of रेचन करना।

purification *प्युअॅ रि फ़ि के शॅन n.*

act of purifying शुद्धिकरण।

purify *प्युअॅ रि फ़ॉइ v.t.* to make pure or clear पवित्र करना; to free from admixture शुद्ध करना; to free from guilt or sin पापरहित करना।

purist *प्युअॅ रिस्ट n.* one excessively nice in the use of words etc. शुद्धिवादी।

puritan *प्युअॅ रि टॅन n.* person strict in morals नियमनिष्ठ व्यक्ति।

puritanical *प्युअॅ रि टै नि कॅल a.* very strict in morals नैतिकतावादी।

purity *प्युअॅ रि टि n.* state or quality of being pure शुद्धता, शुचिता।

purple *पॅ: प्ल a., n.* (colour) produced by mixing red and blue बैंगनी (रंग)।

purport[1] *पॅ: पॅ:ट n.* general intention or meaning सामान्य आशय अथवा अर्थ।

purport[2] *v.t.* to signify, to imply आशय या अभिप्राय रखना; to claim to be दावा करना।

purpose[1] *पॅ: पॅस n.* end, aim उद्देश्य; intention आशय, प्रयोजन; determination निश्चय।

purpose[2] *v.t.* to have as one's purpose उद्देश्य रखना।

purposely *पॅ: पॅस् लि adv.* intentionally जानबूझकर, सोद्देश्य।

purr[1] *पॅ: n.* pleased noise which a cat makes म्याऊँ; vibrating sound (as that of a car engine) घुरघुर।

purr[2] *v.i.* (of a cat) to make a pleased noise म्याऊँ करना; (of a car-engine) to make a vibrating sound घुरघुर करना।

purse[1] *पॅ:स n.* small money bag बटुआ; money धन।

purse[2] *v.t.* to put in a purse बटुए में रखना।

pursuance *पॅ: स्यु अॅन्स, -स्यू- n.* carrying out पालन।

pursue *पॅ: स्यू v.t.* to chase पीछा करना; to continue जारी रखना; to have as an aim or purpose (का) लक्ष्य रखना।

pursuit *पॅ: स्यूट n.* chase पीछा; attempt to obtain लक्ष्य; occupation धंधा।

purview *पॅ: व्यू n.* scope क्षेत्र; limit सीमा; sphere परिधि।

pus *पस n.* yellowish matter produced by supuration पीव, मवाद।

push[1] *पुश v.t.* to press agaist with force धकेलना; to enforce (पर) ज़ोर देना; to urge प्रोत्साहित करना; to extend बढ़ाना; to press दबाना।

push[2] *n.* act of pushing धक्का; determination निश्चय; vigorous effort or enterprise घोर प्रयत्न।

put *पुट (-tt-) v.t.* to place in any position or situation रखना; to apply लगाना; to propose प्रस्तावित करना; to express अभिव्यक्त करना।

puzzle[1] *प ज़्ल n.* problem समस्या, पहेली; state of bewilderment उलझन।

puzzle[2] *v.t.* to perplex उलझन में डालना।

pygmy (pigmy) *पिग् मि n.* dwarf बौना।

pyorrhoea *पॉइ अॅ रि अॅ n.* a disease of the gums पायरिया।

pyramid *पि रॅ मिड n.* solid structure built in ancient Egypt पिरामिड।

pyre पॉइ अ: *n.* large pile of wood for burning a dead body चिता।

python पॉइ थौनॅ,-थॅन *n.* a large snake that crushes its prey अजगर।

Qq

Q क्यू the seventeenth letter of the English alphabet, this letter was absent in the Anglo-Saxon alphabet, it is alsways followed by 'u' in English words, Roman numeral for 500. अंग्रेजी वर्णमाला का सत्रहवाँ अक्षर, अंग्रेजी की प्राचीन लिपि में इसका प्रयोग न था, kw से इस अक्षर का उच्चारण प्रकट होता था, अंग्रेजी के शब्दों में Q के बाद सर्वदा 'u' आता है, रोमन संख्या में ५०० के लिये संकेत।

quack[1] क्वैक *v.i.* to make the cry of a duck बतख़ की तरह टर्राना।

quack[2] *n.* cry of a duck बतख़ का शब्द; pretending physician ठगविद्या करनेवाला, नीमहकीम।

quackery क्वै कॅ रि *n.* pretension to medical skill नीमहकीमी।

quadrangle क्वौ ॅड़ रैङ् ग्ल *n.* open four-sided court चौकोर आंगन; a figure with four angles चतुर्भुज।

quadrangular क्वौ ॅ ड्रैङ् ग्यु लॅ: *a.* four-sided चतुष्कोणीय।

quadrilateral क्वौ ॅड़ रि लै ॅ टॅ रॅल *a. & n.* four-sided (figure) चार भुजा की (आकृति)।

quadruped क्वौ ॅड़ रू पै ॅड *n.* four-footed animal चौपाया, चतुष्पद।

quadruple[1] क्वौ ॅड़ रू प्ल *a.* four-fold चौगुना।

quadruple[2] *v.t.* to make four-fold चौगुना करना।

quail क्वेल *n.* a small bird like partridge बटेर।

quaint क्वेन्ट *a.* strange, unusual, old-fashioned विचित्र, विलक्षण, पुराने ढंग का।

quake[1] क्वेक *v.i.* to shake, to tremble कांपना, थर्राना।

quake[2] *n.* quaking कंपकंपी, थर्राहट।

qualification क्वौ ॅ लि फ़ि के शॅन *n.* ability योग्यता; restriction मर्यादा, विशिष्टता।

qualify क्वौ ॅ लि फ़ॉइ *v.i.* to become fit to do a particular thing योग्य बनना; to pass a test or examination परीक्षा या प्रतियोगिता में उत्तीर्ण होना; *v.t.* to moderate, to limit सीमित करना; to make fit योग्य बनाना।

qualitative क्वौ ॅ लि टॅ टि व *a.* relating to quality जाति, स्वभाव या गुण-संबंधी।

quality क्वौ ॅ लि टि *n.* nature or worth of anything गुण, जाति; rank पद; nature स्वभाव, लक्षण।

quandary क्वौनॅ् डॅ रि *n.* perplexity दुविधा, व्याकुलता, घबराहट।

quantitative क्वौनॅ् टि टॅ टिव *a.* relating to quantity परिणाम संबंधी।

quantity क्वौनॅ् टि टि *n.* amount

परिमाण, विस्तार, मात्रा, अंश।

quantum *क्वौन्ँ टॅम n.* desired amount आवश्यक परिमाण या मात्रा।

quarrel[1] *क्वौ˘ रॅल n.* angry dispute कलह, झगड़ा; disagreement विवाद।

quarrel[2] *(-ll-) v.i.* to argue or disagree angrily with somebody झगड़ना।

quarrelsome *क्वौ˘ रॅल् सॅम a.* fond of quarrels झगड़ालू, लड़ाका।

quarry[1] *क्वौ˘ रि n.* place where stone, slate etc. is got out of ground खदान, खान।

quarry[2] *v.i.* to work in a quarry खान से पत्थर निकालना।

quarter[1] *क्वौ˘ टः n.* fourth of any thing चतुर्थ भाग; post स्थान; direction दिशा; lodgings ठहरने का स्थान।

quarter[2] *v.t.* to divide into four equal parts चार भाग करना; to lodge ठहराना।

quarterly[1] *क्वौ : टः लि a.* coming each quarter तीसरे महीने, होनेवाला, त्रैमासिक।

quarterly[2] *n.* three-monthly magazine त्रैमासिक पत्रिका।

queen *क्वीन n.* wife of a king राजपत्नी; woman who rules a country महारानी, रानी; a piece in chess (शतरंज में) वज़ीर; card with the picture of queen (ताश में) बेग़म।

queer *क्विअॅः a.* strange, very unusual अनूठा, विलक्षण।

quell *क्वैलॅ v.t.* to overcome वश में करना; to suppress दबाना; to allay शांत करना।

quench *क्वैन्च v.t.* to damp down or put out (fire) (आग या प्यास) बुझाना, दबाना, to put an end to (something) शांत करना, चुप कर देना।

query[1] *क्विअॅ रि n. (pl. queries)* question प्रश्न, पूछताछ।

query[2] *v.t.* to ask questions प्रश्न करना।

quest[1] *क्वै˘स्ट n.* search अन्वेषण, खोज, अनुसंधान।

quest[2] *v.t.* to search खोज करना।

question[1] *क्वैस् चॅन n.* enquiry प्रश्न, जांच; point of debate विवाद या विचार का विषय।

question[2] *v.t.* to ask for information प्रश्न पूछना, जांचना; to interrogate पूछताछ करना; to doubt संदेह करना।

questionable *क्वैस् चॅ नॅ ब्ल a.* doubtful संदेहयुक्त, अनिश्चित।

questionnaire *क्वैस् चॅ ने˘ अॅः n.* a list of questions प्रश्नमाला।

queue *क्यू n.* line of people waiting their turn पंक्ति, क़तार।

quibble[1] *क्वि ब्ल n.* evasive answer वाक्छल, वक्रोक्ति, शब्द-श्लेष।

quibble[2] *v.i.* to indulge in quibble वाक्छल करना, टेढ़ा बोलना, शब्द-श्लेष का प्रयोग करना।

quick[1] *क्विक a.* swift, hasty फुरतीला, प्रस्तुत, तीव्र।

quick[2] *n.* sensitive flesh शरीर का जीवित (मर्म) भाग।

quicksand *क्विक् सैन्ड n.* loose, wet sand नदी या समुद्र का-धसकनेवाला बालू का किनारा।

quicksilver *क्विक सिल् वॅः n.* mercury पारद, पारा।

quiet[1] *क्वॉइ ॲट a.* calm, silent निश्चल, शांत, सौम्य, चुपचाप।

quiet[2] *n.* calmness शांति, स्थिरता।

quiet[3] *v.t.* to make calm स्थिर करना; *v.i.* to be calm शांत होना।

quilt *क्विल्ट n.* padded coverlet रज़ाई, तोषक, गद्दा, तोषक की खोली।

quinine *क्वि नीन n.* bitter drug for malaria कुनैन।

quintessence *क्विन् टै ॅ सॅन्स n.* purest form शुद्धतम रूप, essential feature मुख्य लक्षण, embodiment मूर्तरूप।

quit *क्विट (-tt-) v.t.* to leave छोड़ना, त्यागना।

quite *क्वॉइट adv.* wholly सर्वथा, पूरी तरह से, बिलकुल।

quiver[1] *क्वि वॅः n.* arrow case तरकस।

quiver[2] *v.i.* to tremble कांपना, थर्राना।

quixotic *क्विक् सौ ॅ टिक a.* idealistic आदर्शपूर्ण; chivalrous वीरतापूर्ण।

quiz[1] *क्विज़ n.* general knowledge test सामान्य ज्ञान-परीक्षा।

quiz[2] *v.t.* to question, to interrogate प्रश्न पूछना।

quorum *क्वौ ॅ रॅम n.* minimum number for a meeting कोरम, किसी सभा के कार्य के लिए सभासदों की निर्दिष्ट संख्या।

quota *क्वो ॅ टॅ n.* assigned share कोटा, अंश, स्थिर भाग।

quotation *क्वो ॅ टे शॅन n.* citation उद्धरण; market rate प्रचलित मूल्य।

quote *क्वो ॅट v.t.* to cite किसी के शब्द का उद्धरण करना; to state (price) मूल्य बतलाना।

quotient *क्वो शॅन्ट n.* number obtained by dividing one number by another भागफल।

Rr

R आर् the eighteenth letter of the English alphabet, Roman numeral for 80. अंग्रेजी वर्णमाला का अठारहवाँ अक्षर, अस्सी संख्या के लिए संकेत; **The three R's** (*reading, writing and arithmetic*) पढ़ना, लिखना तथा अंकगणित–ये तीन "आर्स्" कहलाते हैं।

rabbit *रै बिट n.* burrowing rodent allied to the hare ख़रगोश।

rabies *रे बीज़ n.* viral disease transmitted by dogs जलातंक।

race[1] *रेस n.* descendant वंश; class वर्ग; sect जाति; running दौड़; contest प्रतिस्पर्धा।

race[2] *v.i.* to run swiftly तेज़ दौड़ना।

racial *रे शॅल a.* pertaining to race or lineage कुल या वंश-संबंधी।

racialism *रे शॅ लिज़्म n.* characteristics of a race किसी जाति की विशिष्टता।

rack[1] *रैक v.t.* to distort मरोड़ना; to torture सताना।

rack[2] *n.* an instrument of torture शिकंजा।

racket *रै किट n.* a confused din शोरगुल; the bat used in tennis टेनिस का बल्ला; dishonest way of getting money तिकड़म, चालाकी।

radiance रे *डि अॅन्स,-ड्यॅन्स n.* lustre कांति; brilliancy चमक।

radiant रे *डि अॅन्ट, -ड्यॅन्ट a.* issuing rays किरणें फैलानेवाला; beaming चमकीला।

radiate रे *डि एट v.t.* to emit rays of (light) विकीर्ण करना; to spread out प्रसारित करना; *v.i.* to sparkle जगमगाना।

radiation रे *डि ए शॅन n.* beamy brightness रश्मि-प्रकाश; spreading out प्रसारण; emission of rays विकिरण।

radical रै *डि कॅल a.* essential तत्वरूप; original असली; fundamental मौलिक; drastic उग्र।

radio[1] रे *डि ओ n.* wireless telegraphy or telephony बिना तार का यंत्र, रेडियो।

radio[2] *v.t.* to transmit by wireless telegraphy बिना तार के (समाचार) भेजना।

radish रै *डिश n.* salad plant with a white or red edible root मूली।

radium रे *ड्यॅम,* रे *डि अॅम n.* an intensely radioactive element रेडियम धातु।

radius रे *डि अॅस,* रे *ड्यॅस n. (pl. radii* रे डि ऑइ) a straight line from the centre of a circle to the circumference अर्द्धव्यास, त्रिज्या।

rag[1] रैग *n.* rough separate fragment चिथड़ा; torn piece of woven material वस्त्रखंड; roofing stone or tile खपरैल।

rag[2] *(-gg-) v.t.* to tease कष्ट देना; to play rough jokes upon भद्दी हंसी करना।

rage[1] रेज *n.* violent anger क्रोध; violence उत्पात; enthusiasm उत्साह।

rage[2] *v.i.* to be furious with anger क्रोध करना।

raid[1] रेड *n.* hostile incursion आक्रमण, धावा; sudden visit by authorities छापा।

raid[2] *v.t.* to make a raid on पर छापा मारना या धावा बोलना *v.i.* to carry out a raid छापा मारना।

rail[1] रेल *n.* horizontal bar of wood or metal छड़; railing घेरा; a railway रेलमार्ग।

rail[2] *v.t.* to inclose with rails छड़ों से घेरना *v.i.* to use abusive language गाली देना।

raling रे *लिङ्ग n.* a fence घेरा, कठघरा।

raillery रे *लॅ रि n.* good humoured teasing दिल्लगी, परिहास, मज़ाक़।

railway रेल् *वे n.* road having iron rails laid in parallel lines on which carriages run रेलपथ।

rain[1] रेन *v.i.* to fall in drops from the clouds वर्षा होना, बरसना; *v.t.* to send down बरसाना।

rain[2] *n.* cloud-water वर्षा।

rainy रे *नि a.* having much rain वर्षावाला।

raise रेज़ *v.t.* to lift उठाना; to construct निर्माण करना; to elevate ऊपर उठाना; to increase बढ़ाना; to bring forward प्रस्तुत करना; to collect एकत्र करना।

raisin रे *ज़्न n.* dried grape किशमिश।

rally[1] रै *लि v.t.* to re-unite समेटना, फिर से जोड़ना; to attack with raillery दिल्लगी करना; *v.i.* to recover strength or vigour शक्ति जुटाना; to come together एकत्र होना।

rally² *n.* coming together संगठन; recovery of strength शक्ति-संचय; inprovement during illness स्वास्थ्य-लाभ; (tennis etc.) long exchange of continuous strokes लंबी भिड़ंत; gathering or assembly जमघट।

ram¹ *रैम* *n.* uncastrated male sheep मेढ़ा, भेड़ा।

ram² *(-mm-) v.t.* to strike against with force टक्कर मारना; to stuff भर देना।

ramble¹ *रैम् बल* *v.t.* to roam carelessly about घूमना।

ramble² *n.* irregular excursion पर्यटन, भ्रमण।

rampage¹ *रैम् पेज* *v.i.* to dash about violently क्रोध में इधर-उधर दौड़ना।

rampage² *n.* angry or violent behaviour क्रोधपूर्ण व हिंसात्मक आचरण।

rampant *रैम् पॅन्ट* *a.* unrestrained अनियंत्रित; violent तीक्ष्ण; aggressive आक्रामक।

rampart *रैम् पाःट,-पॅःट* *n.* parapet or bulwark क़िले की दीवार; defence सुरक्षा।

rancour *रैङ्कॅः* *n.* deep-seated enmity गहरी शत्रुता; malignity विद्वेष।

random *रैन् डॅम* *a.* done without definite object एकाएक किया हुआ।

range¹ *रेन्ज* *v.t.* to place in order क्रम से रखना; *v.i.* to move, to wander घूमना; to vary within limits सीमाओं के बीच होना।

range² *n.* scope कार्यक्षेत्र; extent सीमा; series of mountains पर्वत-श्रेणी; reach पहुंच; limit सीमा; variety विभिन्नता; distance covered by a shot गोली की मार; place where shooting is carried on चांदमारी।

ranger *रेन् जॅः* *n.* official connected with a forest or park वनपाल।

rank¹ *रैङ्क* *n.* row, line पंक्ति; official grade पद; a social class वर्ग; high position in society प्रतिष्ठा।

rank² *v.t.* to classify वर्गीकृत करना; to put in a class किसी श्रेणी में रखना; *v.i.* to have a place स्थान रखना।

rank³ *a.* (of plants) growing too luxuriantly अत्यधिक बढ़नेवाला; foul smelling बदबूदार; coarse अशिष्ट, गंवारू; extreme नितांत।

ransack *रैन् सैक* *v.t.* to search thoroughly छान मारना, खोजना; to plunder लूटना।

ransom¹ *रैन् सॅम* *n.* release from captivity by payment रिहाई; price paid for redemption or pardon निष्कृतिधन।

ransom² *v.t.* to pay ransom for धन देकर छुड़ाना; to set free in exchange for ransom धन लेकर छोड़ना।

rape¹ *रेप* *n.* sexual assault on बलात्कार; violation उल्लंघन।

rape² *v.t.* to make sexual assualt on (से) बलात्कार करना।

rapid *रै पिड* *a.* quick, swift तीव्र।

rapidity *रे पि डि टि* *n.* quickness तीव्रता।

rapier *रे पिअॅः* *n.* a light sword हल्की तलवार।

rapport रै पौः *n.* harmony मेल, घनिष्ठता।

rapt रैप्ट *a.* wholly absorbed तन्मय।

rapture रैप् चँः *n.* extreme joy or pleasure हर्षातिरेक।

rare रे˘ अँः *a.* not frequent यदाकदा होनेवाला; uncommon असाधारण; very valuable मूल्यवान; thin विरल।

rascal रास् कॅल *n.* a scoundrel धूर्त व्यक्ति।

rash रैश *a.* hasty जल्दबाज़; over-bold दुस्साहसी।

rat रैट *n.* a small rodent चूहा।

rate[1] रेट *v.t.* to appraise मूल्यांकन करना; to consider मानना; to fix the value of का मूल्य निर्धारित करना।

rate[2] *n.* proportion अनुपात; price मूल्य; degree of speed गति की मात्रा; reckoning दर।

rather रा दँः *adv.* more readily अधिक तत्परता से; somewhat कुछ-कुछ।

ratify रै टि फ़ॉइ *v.t.* to confirm पुष्टि करना।

ratio रे शिओ *n. (pl. ratios)* relation or proportion अनुपात।

ration रै शॅन *n.* daily allowance of provisions रसद, राशन।

rational रै शॅ नॅल *a.* endowed with reason बुद्धिसंपन्न; reasonable तर्कसंगत; sensible विवेकशील, समझदार।

rationale रै शिअॅ ना लि *n.* logical basis तर्कसम्मत आधार।

rationality रै शॅ नै लि टि *n.* the quality of being rational तर्कसंगतता; the power of reasoning तर्कशक्ति।

rationalize रै शॅ नॅ लॉइज़ *v.t.* to justify by plausible resoning तार्किक आधार पर उचित बताना।

rattle[1] रै ट्ल *v.i.* to clatter खड़खड़ाना; *v.t.* to say or repeat (something quickly) जल्दी-जल्दी कहना या दुहराना।

rattle[2] *n.*short sharp′ sound खड़खड़।

ravage[1] रे विज *n.* devastation विध्वंस।

ravage[2] *v.t.* to cause violent destruction to तहस-नहस करना।

rave रेव *v.i.* to be delirious बड़बड़ाना।

raven रे व्न *n.* a black bird like crow काला कौआ।

ravine रॅ वीन *n.* a deep narrow valley कंदरा।

raw रौ *a.* not manufactured अनिर्मित; uncooked अपक्व; inexperienced अनुभवरहित; untrained अप्रशिक्षित; crude फूहड; cold and damp ठंडा और नम।

ray रे *n.* line of light किरण।

raze रेज़ *v.t.* to scratch out खुरचना, मिटाना; to lay level with the ground भूमिसात करना।

razor रे ज़ः *n.* knife for shaving off hair उस्तरा।

reach रीच *v.t.* to extend फैलाना, बढ़ाना; to gain प्राप्त करना; to attain to पर पहुंचना।

react रि ऐक्ट, री- *v.i.* to act upon the doer प्रतिकार करना, प्रतिक्रिया करना।

reaction रि ऐक् शॅन, री- *n.* reciprocal action प्रतिक्रिया; counteraction विरूद्ध क्रिया।

reactinary *रि ऐक् शॅ नॅ रि, री-* *a.* implying reaction प्रतिकार करने वाला।

read *रीड* *v.t.* *(pt. & p.p. read रैॅड)* to look at and understand (written matter) पढ़ना; to learn by reading शिक्षा प्राप्त करना; to utter बोलना; to interpret व्याख्या करना; to study अध्ययन करना; *v.i.* to be able to understand what is written पढ़ने की क्षमता रखना।

reader *री डॅः* *n.* one who reads पाठक; teacher in university रीडर; textbook for reading in class पाठमाला।

readily *रैॅ डि लि* *adv.* promptly शीघ्रता से; cheerfully सुख से।

readiness *रैॅ डि निस* *n.* quickness तत्परता; willingness इच्छा।

ready *रैॅ डि* *a.* prepared तैयार; willingly disposed उद्यत; present at hand उपस्थित।

real *रिअॅल* *a.* actual वास्तविक; genuine असली।

realism *रिअॅ लिज़्म* *n.* regarding things as they are यथार्थ।

realist *रिअॅ लिस्ट* *n.* person who believes in realism यथार्थवादी।

realistic *रिअॅ लिस् टिक* *a.* pertaining to realism यथार्थवादी।

reality *रि ऐ लि टि, री-* *n.* state or quality of being real वास्तविकता; actuality सच्चाई।

realization *रि अॅ लॉइ ज़े शॅन* *n.* full awareness अनुभूति, अहसास; obtaining प्राप्ति; collection वसूली।

realize *रि अॅ लॉइज़* *v.t. & i.* to make real वास्तविक बनाना; to convert into money रुपये में बदलना; to acquire प्राप्त करना; to be fully conscious of अनुभव करना; to collect वसूल करना।

really *रिअॅ लि* *adv.* actually वास्तव में; in truth वस्तुतः।

realm *रैॅल्म* *a.* kingdom राज्य; region क्षेत्र।

ream *रीम* 480 sheets of paper रिम (कागज़ का)।

reap *रीप* *v.t.* to cut with a scythe काटना; to gather (harvest) (फ़सल) एकत्र करना; to receive as fruit of previous activity कर्म के फल के रूप में पाना।

reaper *री पॅः* *n.* a person who reaps लुनेरा; a reaping machine फ़सल कट।

rear[1] *रिअॅः* *n.* back part पिछला भाग; last part of army, fleet etc. सेना, बेड़े आदि का सबसे अंतिम भाग।

rear[2] *v.t.* to bring up पालन-पोषण करना; to raise, to lift up उठाना; *v.i.* to rise on hind legs पिछली टांगों पर खड़ा होना।

reason[1] *री ज़्न* *n.* justification औचित्य; cause कारण; sanity विवेक; rational ground तर्क।

reason[2] *v.i.* to make use of one's reason बुद्धि से काम लेना; to argue तर्क करना; *v.t.* to say by way of argument तर्कस्वरूप कहना; to persuade by argument समझाना।

reasonable *री ज़ॅ नॅ ब्ल* *a.* logical तर्कसंगत; able to reason तर्कशील; moderate यथोचित।

reassure *री अॅ शुअॅः* *v.t.* to assure anew पुनः विश्वास दिलाना।

rabate *री बेट* *n.* deduction छूट।

rebel[1] *रि बैलॅ (-ll-) v.i.* to revolt विद्रोह करना।

rebel[2] *रै बल n.* one who rebels विद्रोही।

rebellion *रि बैलॅ यॅन n.* act of rebelling, revolt बग़ावत।

rebellious *रि बैलॅ यॅस a.* pertaining to rebellion विद्रोहमूलक; mutinous बाग़ी।

rebirth *री बॅःथ n.* being born again पुनर्जन्म; revival पुनरूत्थान।

rebound[1] *रि बॉउन्ड v.i.* to spring or bound back प्रतिक्षिप्त होना; to come back upon oneself स्वयं पर प्रतिघात करना।

rebound[2] *री बॉउन्ड n.* act of rebounding प्रतिक्षेप, उच्छलन।

rebuff[1] *रि बफ़ n.* snubbing झिड़की; defeat पराजय।

rebuff[2] *v.t.* to check रोकना; to snub झिड़कना।

rebuke[1] *रि ब्यूक v.t.* to reprove sharply फटकारना, डांटना।

rebuke[2] *n.* reproof फटकार।

recall[1] *रि कौल v.t.* to call or bring back, to summon back वापस बुलाना; to recollect स्मरण करना।

recall[2] *n.* a call to return वापस बुलाना; ability to remember स्मरण-क्षमता।

recede *रि सीड v.i.* to go back or away पीछे या दूर जाना; to become distant दूरी पर होना।

receipt *रि सीट n.* act of receiving प्राप्ति; a written acknowledgement of something received पावती।

receive *रि सीव v.t.* to accept स्वीकार करना; to take लेना; to get प्राप्त करना; to greet स्वागत करना।

receiver *रि सी वॅः n.* one who accepts stolen goods चोर-हटिया; earpiece of telephone चोग़ा; official taking public money गृहीता, रिसीवर; person who takes something पानेवाला।

recent *री सन्ट a.* new नया, ताज़ा; that has lately happened हाल का।

recently *री सन्ट् लि adv.* lately, not long ago हाल ही में।

reception *रि सैपॅ शॅन n.* welcome स्वागत; formal social gathering स्वागत-समारोह; signals recieved अभिग्रहण।

receptive *रि सैपॅ टिव a.* such as to receive readly शीघ्र-ग्रहणकारी।

recess *रि सैसॅ n.* period of retirement अवकाश; vacation अनध्याय; niche ताक़, आला; hollow कोटरिका; hidden place गुप्त स्थान।

recession *रि सैॅ शॅन n.* withdrawal वापसी; period of reduced economic activity व्यापारिक मंदी।

recipe *रै ॅ सि पि n.* medical prescription नुसखा; direction for preparing a dish पाक-विधि; expedient उपाय।

recipient *रि सि पि ॲन्ट n.* one who receives प्रापक।

reciprocal *रि सि प्रॅ कॅल a.* mutual पारस्परिक।

reciprocate *रि सि प्रॅ केट v.t.* to exchange आदान-प्रदान करना; to give and take mutually अदल-बदल करना।

recital *रि सॉइ ट्ल n.* narration विवरण, वृत्तांत; a programme of music संगीत का कार्यक्रम; act of reciting गायन-प्रस्तुति।

recitation रै˘ सि टे शॅन *n.* recital from memory पाठ।

recite रि सॉइट *v.t.* to repeat aloud सुनाना।

reckless रैकॅ् लिस *a.* heedless, careless लापरवाह; rash जल्दबाज़।

reckon रै˘ कॅन *v.t.* to count गिनती करना; to consider मानना; to include सम्मिलित करना; to estimate अनुमान लगाना; to calculate गणना करना।

reclaim रि क्लेम *v.t. & i.* to claim back वापिस मांगना; to make fit for cultivation कृषि-योग्य बनाना; to recover पुनः प्राप्त करना; to reform सुधारना।

reclamation रै˘ क्लॅ मे शॅन *n.* reform सुधार; making fit for cultivation भूमि-सुधार।

recluse रि क्लूस *n.* person who lives alone एकांतवासी।

recognition रै˘ कॅग् नि शॅन *n.* acknowledgement मान्यता; formal identification पहचान।

recognize रै˘ कॅग् नॉइज़ *v.t.* to know again पहचान लेना; to acknowledge formally मान्यता देना; to indicate appreciation of मानना।

recoil[1] रि कौ˘इल *v.i.* to move or start back पीछे हटाना; to rebound वापस निकल जाना।

recoil[2] a starting or falling back वापसी, प्रतिक्षेप।

recollect रै˘ कॅ लैक्ट *v.t.* to remember स्मरण करना।

recollection रै˘ कॅ लैक् शॅन *n.* remembrance स्मरण।

recommend रै कॅ मैन्ड *v.t.* to praise प्रशंसा करना; to speak well of, to make acceptable संस्तुति करना; to advise सलाह देना।

recommendation रै˘ कॅ मैन् डे शॅन *n.* favourable representation संस्तुति।

recompense[1] रै˘ कॅम् पैन्स *v.t.* to compensate क्षतिपूर्ति करना; to make amends for प्रतिफल देना।

recompense[2] *n.* reward पुरस्कार compensation क्षतिपूर्ति।

reconcile रै˘ कॅन् सॉइल *v.t.* to make friendly again से मेलमिलाप कराना; to harmonize में सामंजस्य करना; to accept स्वीकार करना।

reconciliation रै˘ कॅन् सि लि ए शॅन *n.* renewal of friendship मित्रता का नवीनीकरण।

record[1] रि कौःड *v.t.* to preserve in writing अंकित करना; to register पंजीकृत करना।

record[2] रै कौःड *n.* an unbeaten performance कीर्तिमान; official report अभिलेख; facts known ज्ञात तथ्य; a disc for a gramophone ग्रामोफ़ोन रिकार्ड।

recorder रि कौःडॅ *n.* one who records लेखक, कार्यालय का रिकार्ड रखनेवाला।

recount रि कॉउन्ट *v.t.* to tell in detail ब्योरा देना।

recoup रि कूप *v.t.* to compensate क्षतिपूर्ति करना।

recourse रि कौःस *n.* resort to a possible help आश्रय।

recover रि क वॅः *v.t.* to get back वापिस पाना; *v.i.* to grow well स्वस्थ होना।

recovery *रि क वॅ रि n.* act of recovering वसूली; regaining health स्वास्थ्य-लाभ।

recreation *रैॅ क्रि ए शॅन n.* entertainment मनोरंजन; source of recreation मनोरंजन का साधन।

recruit[1] *रि क्रूट n.* newly enlisted soldier रंगरूट; a new member नया सदस्य।

recruit[2] *v.t.* to enlist in the army भर्ती करना; to engage नियुक्त करना।

rectangle *रैक् टैङ् ग्ल n.* a quadrilateral with right angles आयत।

rectangular *रैक् टैङ् ग्यु लॅः a.* shaped like a rectangle आयताकार।

rectification *रैक् टि फ़ि के शॅन n.* act of rectifying समाधान, शुद्धि।

rectify *रैक् टि फ़ॉइ v.i.* to correct सही करना; to purify शुद्ध करना।

rectum *रैॅक् टॅम n.* the lowest part of the large intestine opening at the anus गुदा, मलद्वार।

recur *रि कॅः (-rr-) v.i.* to happen again पुनरावृत्ति होना।

recurrence *रि क रॅन्स n.* return पुनरागमन; repetition पुनरावृत्ति।

recurrent *रि क रॅन्ट a.* recurring from time to time आवर्तक।

red[1] *रैॅड a.* of a colour resembling that of arterial blood लाल रंग का।

red[2] *n.* colour resembling that of arterial blood लाल रंग।

redden *रै ड्न v.t.* to make red; *v.i.* to become red लाल होना।

reddish *रै डिश a.* somewhat red ललछौहां।

redeem *रि डीम v.t.* to rescue मुक्त करना; to ransom धन देकर छुड़ाना; to free from sin पाप से मुक्त करना; to make up for की कमी पूरी करना।

redemption *रि डैम्प् शॅन n.* deliverance from sin, atonement प्रायश्चित-द्वारा पाप-मुक्ति; release छुटकारा।

redouble *रि ड ब्ल, री- v.t.* to increase बढ़ाना; to intensify घनीभूत करना; *v.t.* to be increased बढ़ना, अधिक होना।

redress[1] *रि ड्रैसॅ v.t.* to remedy उपाय करना; to readjust दुबारा दुरूस्त करना; to rectify शुद्ध करना; to compensate क्षतिपूर्ति करना।

redress[2] *n.* act of redressing सुधार, शुद्धि; compensation क्षतिपूर्ति।

reduce *रि ड्यूस v.t.* to decrease कम करना; to change बदलना; to slim पतला करना।

reduction *रि डक् शॅन n.* act of reducing न्यूनन; diminution कमी; subjugation पराभव।

redundance *रि डन् डॅन्स n.* being redundant फालतूपन।

redundant *रि डन् डॅन्ट a.* superfluous फ़ालतू; not needed अनावश्यक।

reel[1] *रील n.* a bobbin for thread चर्खी; (cinema) length of film रील; a staggering motion लड़खड़ाहट।

reel[2] *v.i.* to stagger लड़खड़ाना।

refer *रि फ़ॅः v.t.* to send भेजना; to assign सौंपना; to submit प्रस्तुत करना; to ascribe से संबद्ध करना; *v.i.* to allude हवाला देना; to make mention ज़िक्र करना।

referee *रै ˘ फ़ रीं n.* an umpire निर्णयकर्त्ता।

reference *रै ˘ फ़ रॅन्स n.* act of referring निर्देशन; mention ज़िक्र, चर्चा; connection संदर्भ, प्रसंग; testimonial प्रमाण-पत्र; citation उद्धरण।

referendum *रै ˘ फ़ रैन् डॅम n.* the referring of a question to the people for final approval जनमत-संग्रह।

refine *रि फ़ॉइन v.t.* to purify शुद्ध करना; to free from defects सुधारना।

refinement *रि फ़ॉइन् मॅन्ट n.* act of refining शुद्धता; fineness of taste or feeling शिष्टता।

refinery *रि फ़ॉइ नॅ रि n.* place and apparatus for refining sugar, metals, etc. परिशोधनशाला।

reflect *रि फ़्लैक्ट v.t.* to throw back (heat, light etc.) परावर्तित करना; to send back an image of प्रतिबिंबित करना; to express प्रकट करना; *v.i.* to meditate चिंतन करना।

reflection *रि फ़्लैक् शॅन n.* act of reflecting परावर्तन; censure निंदा; consideration विचार; meditation ध्यान।

reflective *रि फ़्लैक् टिव a.* throwing back परावर्तक; contemplative चिंतनशील।

reflector *रि फ़्लैक् टॅ: n.* one who reflects प्रतिक्षेपक।

reflex[1] *री फ्लैक्स n.* an involuntary action अनैच्छिक क्रिया।

reflex[2] *a.* involuntary अनैच्छिक; reflected परावर्तित।

reflexive *रि फ़्लैक् सिव a*, reflective कर्त्ता-संबंधी।

reform[1] *रि फ़ौःम v.t.* to make better सुधारना; to correct दोष हटाना।

reform[2] improvement सुधार; removal of defects दोषनिवृति।

reformation *रै ˘ फ़ः मे शॅन n.* act of reforming सुधार।

reformatory[1] *रै ˘फ़ः मॅ टॅ रि n.* an institution for reclaiming young criminals सुधार-गृह।

reformatory[2] *a.* tending to produce reform सुधारात्मक।

reformer *रि फ़ौः मॅः n.* one who reforms सुधारक।

refrain[1] *रि फ़्रेन v.i.* to abstain (from) (से) अलग रहना।

refrain[2] *n.* burden of a song or poem टेक, स्थायी।

refresh *रि फ़्रैशॅ v.t.* to revive नया करना; to freshen ताज़ा करना।

refreshment *रि फ़्रैशॅ मॅन्ट n.* act of refreshing ताज़गी; light food, drink etc. जलपान।

refrigerate *रि फ़्रिजॅ रेट v.t.* to cool शीतल करना।

refrigeration *रि फ़्रिजॅ रे शॅन n.* freezing, cooling प्रशीतन।

refrigerator *रि फ़्रि जॅ रे टॅः n.* an apparatus for cooling or for making ice शीतक यंत्र, प्रशीतित्र।

refuge *रै ˘ फ़्यूज n.* shelter शरण; place of shelter शरणस्थल।

refugee *रै ˘ फ़्यू जी n.* one who seeks refuge शरणार्थी।

refulgence *रि फ़ल् जॅन्स n.* brightness चमक, दीप्ति।

refulgent *रि फ़ल् जॅन्ट a.* shining, bright देदीप्यमान।

refund[1] *रि फ़न्ड* *v.t.* to pay back लौटाना।

refund[2] *री फ़न्ड* *n.* repayment धन की वापसी।

refusal *रि फ़्यू ज़ॅल* *n.* denial of something offered अस्वीकृति; rejection प्रतिषेध।

refuse[1] *रि फ़्यूज़* *v.t.* to make refusal of अस्वीकार करना; to deny मना करना; to reject प्रतिषेध करना।

refuse[2] *रै ॅ फ़्यूस* *n.* rubbish, useless matter अवशिष्ट, मल।

refutation *रै ॅ फ़्यु टे शॅन, -फ़्यू-* *n.* disproof खंडन।

refute *रै ॅ फ़्यूट* *v.t.* to disprove खंडन करना; to rebut by argument तर्क से असत्य ठहराना।

regal *री गॅल* *a.* royal राजकीय, शाही।

regard[1] *रि गाःड* *v.t.* to notice carefully ध्यान से देखना; to respect आदर करना; to take into account विचार करना; to consider मानना; to relate to से संबद्ध होना।

regard[2] *n.* look दृष्टि; attention ध्यान; respect सम्मान; point, matter मामला।

regenerate *री जै ॅ नॅ रेट* *v.t.* to generate anew फिर से उत्पन्न करना; to bring into a better state सुधारना; to reform morally (में) नैतिक सुधार लाना; *v.i.* to grow again पुनः विकसित होना।

regeneration *रि जै ॅ नॅ रे शॅन* *n.* act of regenerating सुधार, उत्थान; reproduction पुनर्जन्म।

regicide *रै ॅ जि सॉइड* *n.* murder of a king राजहत्या; murderer of a king राजहंता।

regime *रे ज़ीम* *n.* administration प्रशासन; system व्यवस्था।

regiment *रै ॅ जि मॅन्ट* *n.* unit of army commanded by a colonel सैन्यदल।

regiment[2] *रै ॅ जि मैन्टॅ* *v.t.* to organize, संगठित करना, to discipline नियंत्रित करना।

region *री जॅन* *n.* area, territory भूभाग; part of the body शरीरांग; tract of land मंडल; sphere क्षेत्र।

regional *री जॅ नॅल* *a.* pertaining to a region क्षेत्रीय, मंडलीय।

register[1] *रै ॅ जिस् टॅः* *n.* list सूची; record book पंजिका; written record लेखा; range of voice स्वर-विस्तार।

register[2] *v.t.* to enter in register पंजीकृत करना; to record दर्ज करना; to show दर्शाना; to set down in writing लिपिबद्ध करना।

registrar *रै ॅ जिस् ट्राः* *n.* officer charged with keeping registers पंजीयक, कुलसचिव।

registration *रै ॅ जिस् ट्रे शॅन* *n.* act of registering पंजीकरण; getting registered पंजीयन।

registry *रै ॅ जिस् ट्रि* *n.* registration पंजीयन, पंजीकरण; place where registers are kept लेखागार।

regret[1] *रि ग्रै ॅट (-tt-)* *v.i.* to be sorry for दुःखी होना।

regret[2] *n.* sorrow, feeling of sadness खेद।

regular *रै ॅ ग्यु लॅः* *a.* formal औपचारिक; usual सामान्य; systematic यथारीति; orderly यथाक्रम; recurring uniformly नियमित; fixed नियत।

regularity *रै ॅ ग्यु लै रि टि n.* state or character of being regular नियमितता।

regulate *रै ॅ ग्यु लेट v.t.* to adjust by rule नियमित करना; to direct निर्देश करना; to put in order क्रम में रखना।

regulation *रै ॅ ग्यु ले शॅन n.* act of regulating व्यवस्थापन; rule नियम।

regulator *रै ॅ ग्यु ले टॅः n.* one who or that which regulates प्रबंधकर्त्ता, नियंत्रक।

rehabilitate *री ॲ बि ले टेट v.t.* to restore to a former capacity or position पूर्व अवस्था में लाना।

rehabilitation *री ॲ बि लि टे शॅन n.* act of restoring forfeited rights or privileges पुनर्निवेशन।

rehearsal *रि हॅः सॅल n.* preparatory performance of a play पूर्व-प्रयोग, नाटक का प्रारंभिक अभिनय।

rehearse *रि हॅःस v.t.* to repeat दुहराना; to practise अभ्यास करना; to say over again पुनः कहना।

reign[1] *रेन v.i.* to govern राज्य करना; to be supreme सर्वोपरि होना।

reign[2] *n.* period of a king's rule राज्यकाल।

reimburse *री इम् बॅःस v.t.* to repay लौटाना।

rein[1] *रेन n.* narrow strap to guide a horse लगाम; means of restraint नियंत्रण।

rein[2] *v.t.* to restrain रोकना; to control नियंत्रित करना।

reinforce *री इन् फौःस v.t.* to strenghten by new assistance सुदृढ़ बनाना।

reinforcement *री इन् फौःस् मॅन्ट n.* act of reinforcing सुदृढ़ीकरण।

reinstate *री इन् स्टेट v.t.* to restore to a former position बहाल करना; to replace पुनः स्थापित करना।

reinstatement *री इन् स्टेट् मॅन्ट n.* restoration to former position बहाली; re-establishment पुनः स्थापन का कार्य।

reiterate *री इ टॅ रेट v.t.* to repeat again and again बार-बार दुहराना।

reiteration *री इ टॅ रे शॅन n.* repetition पुनरावृत्ति।

reject *रि जैक्ट v.t.* to discard अस्वीकार करना; to forsake त्यागना।

rejection *रि जै ॅक् शॅन n.* refusal to accept or grant अस्वीकार।

rejoice *रि जौ ॅइस v.i.* to be glad प्रसन्न होना; to gladden आनंदित होना; *v.t.* to make joyful आनंदित करना।

rejoin *रि जौ ॅइन v.t.* to join again फिर से जोड़ना; to answer to a reply प्रत्युत्तर देना।

rejoinder *रि जो इन् डॅः n.* an answer to reply प्रत्युत्तर।

rejuvenate *रि जू वि नेट v.t.* to restore to youth पुनः युवा बनाना; *v.i.* to become young again पुनः तरुण बनना।

rejuvenation *रि जू वि ने शॅन n.* act of rejuvenating नई जवानी।

relapse[1] *रि लैप्स v.i.* to return to a former state पहली दशा में आना।

relapse[2] *n.* falling back, either in health or morals पतन, पलटा।

relate *रि लेट v.t.* to tell, to recount बताना, विवरण देना; to bring into relation with से संबद्ध करना; to refer to से संबद्ध होना।

relation *रि ले शॅन n.* act of relating संबंध; act of describing वर्णन; reference संदर्भ; connection संबंध, रिश्ता।

relative[1] रै˘ *लॅ टिव a.* having relation or reference सापेक्ष; (*gram.*) showing relation संबंधसूचक।

relative[2] *n.* one allied by blood संबंधी, रिश्तेदार।

relax *रि लैक्स v.t.* to loosen or weaken शिथिल करना; *v.i.* to become loosened or slack शिथिल होना।

relaxation *री लैक् से शॅन n.* act of relaxing शिथिलीकरण; state of being relaxed शिथिलता।

relay[1] *रि ले n.* fresh team or group नई टोली; a broadcast from one station transmitted by another प्रसारण।

relay[2] *v.t.* to transmit (a broadcast) from another station प्रसारित करना।

release[1] *रि लीस v.t.* to liberate मुक्त करना; to allow to be published, seen or known प्रकाशित या प्रदर्शित करना।

release[2] *n.* liberation मुक्ति; releasing प्रकाशन, प्रदर्शन।

relent *रि लैन्ट v.i.* to soften in temper नरम पड़ना।

relentless *रि लैन्ट् लिस a.* pitiless, unmerciful दयाहीन।

relevance रै˘ *लि वॅन्स n.* state or quality of being relevant प्रासंगिकता।

relevant रै˘ *लि वॅन्ट a.* to the purpose प्रासंगिक।

reliable *रि लॉइ अॅ बल a.* trustworthy विश्वसनीय।

reliance *रि लॉइ अॅन्स n.* trust विश्वास; confidence भरोसा।

relic रै˘ *लिक n.* remaining fragment निशानी; memento स्मारक-चिह्न; *(pl.)* remains अवशेष।

relief *रि लीफ़ n.* lessening or ending of pain आराम, चैन; help सहायता; release from duty भार मुक्ति; one who relieves another एवज़, भारग्राही; prominence प्रमुखता; reinforcements कुमुक।

relieve *रि लीव v.t.* to remove or lessen हटाना या कम करना; to release from duty कर्त्तव्यमुक्त करना; to assist सहायता करना।

religion *रि लि जॅन n.* any system of faith and worship धर्म।

religious *रि लि जॅस a.* pertaining to religion धार्मिक; devout धर्मात्मा।

relinquish *रि लिङ् क्विश v.t.* to renounce, to leave छोड़ना, त्याग देना।

relish[1] रै˘ *लिश v.t.* to enjoy the taste of स्वाद लेना; to like पसंद करना।

relish[2] *n.* taste, flavour स्वाद, सुवास; liking पसंद।

reluctance *रि लक् टॅन्स n.* unwillingness अनिच्छा।

reluctant *रि लक् टॅन्ट a.* unwilling अनिच्छुक।

rely *रि लॉइ v.i.* to depend (upon) निर्भर होना; to trust विश्वास करना।

remain *रि मेन v.i.* to continue in a place or condition रहना; to last टिकना; to exist बच जाना।

remainder *रि मैन् डॅः n.* that which

remains बचा हुआ अंश; residue शेष।

remains *रि मैन्ज़ n. (pl.)* what remains over अवशेष; ruins खंडहर; dead body मृत शरीर।

remand[1] *रि मान्ड v.t.* to send back to jail पुनः जेल भेजना।

remand[2] *n.* being remanded जेल-वापसी।

remark[1] *रि मा:क n.* notice निरीक्षण; comment टिप्पणी।

remark[2] *v.t.* to observe, to notice ध्यान से देखना या सुनना; to utter by way of comment टिप्पणीस्वरूप कहना।

remarkable *रि मा: कॅ ब्ल a.* worthy of remark विलक्षण; extraordinary असाधारण।

remedial *रि मी ड़्यॅल a.* intended to cure उपचारी।

remedy *रै ˘ मि डि n.* that which cures a disease चिकित्सा; means of redress उपाय।

remedy[2] *v.t.* to cure चिकित्सा करना; to repair ठीक करना।

remember *रि मैमॅ बॅ: v.t.* to have in the memory स्मरण रखना; to have (something) in remembrance याद करना; to convey greetings नमस्ते कहना।

remembrance *रि मैमॅ ब्रॅन्स n.* memory स्मृति; memorial स्मारक; token चिह्न।

remind *रि मॉइन्ड v.t.* to put in mind याद दिलाना; to cause to remember याद कराना।

reminder *रि मॉइन् डॅ: n.* something that helps somebody to remember something स्मरणपत्र।

reminiscence *रै ˘ मि नि सॅन्स n.* recollection स्मरण।

reminiscent *रै ˘ मि नि सॅन्ट a.* reminding (of) स्मृति रखने या जगानेवाला।

remission *रि मि शॅन n.* abatement कमी, घटाव; pardon क्षमा; remitting or debt ऋण-भुगतान।

remit *रि मिट (-tt-) v.t.* to relax शिथिल करना; to send (money etc.) by post डाक-द्वारा (पैसा आदि) भेजना; to forgive क्षमा करना।

remittance *रि मि टॅन्स n.* act of remitting प्रेषण; the sum or thing remitted भेजा हुआ धन।

remorse *रि मौ:स n.* reproach of conscience पश्चाताप, ग्लानि।

remote *रि मोट a.* distant in place of conscience दूरस्थ, दूरवर्ती; widely separated असंबद्ध; slight अल्प।

removable *रि मू वॅ ब्ल a.* that may be removed हटाने-योग्य।

removal *रि मू वॅल n.* act of removing हटाने का कार्य; dismissal पदच्युति; elimination निराकरण।

remove *रि मूव v.t.* to displace हटाना; to dismiss पदच्युत करना।

remunerate *रि म्यू नॅ रेट v.t.* to reward for service मज़दूरी देना।

remuneration *रि म्यू नॅ रे शॅन n.* reward पुरस्कार, पारितोषिक; compensation प्रतिफल।

remunerative *रि म्यू नॅ रॅ टिव a.* profitable लाभकारी।

renaissance *रॅ ने सॅन्स n.* rebirth, revival पुनर्जन्म, पुनरुत्थान।

render *रैन् डॅ: v.t.* to give in return लौटाना; to deliver up सौंपना;

to present प्रस्तुत करना; to cause to become बनाना; to translate अनुवाद करना।

rendezvous *रॉन् डि वू n.* place of meeting मिलन-स्थल; appointment पूर्वनिश्चित भेंट।

renew *रि न्यू v.t.* to make new again नया करना; to replace पूर्व अवस्था में लाना; to grow or begin again पुनः प्रारंभ करना; to make valid again नवीकरण करना।

renewal *रि न्यू अॅल n.* renewing नवीकरण; being renewed नवीभवन।

renounce *रि नॉउन्स v.t.* to give up छोड़ना; to disown अपनाने से इनकार करना।

renovate *रैॅ नोॅ वेट,-नॅ- v.t.* to renew नया करना; to restore to freshness अच्छी अवस्था में लाना।

renovation *रैॅ नोॅ वे शॅन n.* renovating नवीकरण।

renown *रि नॉउन n.* reputation, fame यश, कीर्ति।

renowned *रि नॉउन्ड a.* eminent, famous प्रसिद्ध।

rent[1] *रैन्ट n.* money payable yearly for the use of land etc. मालगुजारी; payment for hire किराया।

rent[2] *v.t.* to occupy or use for rent किराये पर लेना; to allow to be used for rent किराये पर देना।

renunciation *रि नन् सि ए शॅन n.* self-denial आत्मत्याग; act of renouncing त्याग।

repair[1] *रि पेॅ अॅः v.t.* to refit मरम्मत करना; to put right again ठीक करना।

repair[2] *n.* repairing मरम्मत।

raparable *रैॅ पॅ रॅ बॅल a.* that can be made good क्षतिपूर्ति-योग्य।

repartee[1] *रैॅ पाः टी n.* smart, ready and witty reply व्यंग्य-उक्ति, क्षिप्र उत्तर।

repatriate[1] *री पैट् रि एट v.t.* to restore to one's own country स्वदेश भेजना।

repatriate[2] *n.* repatriated person प्रत्यावर्तित व्यक्ति।

repatriation *री पैट् रि ए शॅन n.* act of returning to one's own country देश-प्रत्यावर्तन।

repay *रि पे v.t.* to pay back or again वापस करना, चुका देना; to pay in return प्रतिदानस्वरूप देना।

repayment *रि पे मॅन्ट n.* act of repaying money वापसी; the sum repaid वापस की हुई राशि।

repeal[1] *रिपील v.t.* to revoke निरस्त करना।

repeal[2] *n.* act of repealing निरसन।

repeat *रि पीट v.t.* to do or utter again फिर से करना या कहना, दुहराना; *v.i.* to recur आवृत्ति करना।

repel *रि पैलॅ (-ll-) v.t.* to drive back पीछे को हटाना; to cause a feeling of dislike in (में) घृणा उत्पन्न करना।

repellent[1] *रिपैॅ लॅन्ट a.* tending to repel विकर्षक; disgusting घृणास्पद।

repellent[2] *n.* something that repels विकर्षक वस्तु।

repent *रि पैन्ट v.i.* to feel regret for something done or left undone पश्चात्ताप करना।

repentance *रि पैन्ॅ टॅन्स n.* contrition पश्चात्ताप।

repentant *रि पैन्ॅ टॅन्ट a.* repenting पछतावा करनेवाला।

repercussion *री पॅ: क शॅन n.* reverberation प्रतिध्वनि; act of driving behind प्रतिघात; effect प्रभाव।

repetition *रै ˘ पि टि शॅन n.* that which is repeated आवृत्ति; act of doing or uttering a second time पुनरुक्ति, दुहराव।

replace *रि प्लेस v.t.* to put again in the former place पुनः स्थापित करना; to take the place of (का) स्थान लेना।

replacement *रि प्लेस् मॅन्ट n.* replacing प्रतिस्थापन; substitution प्रतिस्थापन।

replenish *रि प्लै ˘ निश v.t.* to fill again फिर से भरना।

replete *रि प्लीट a.* filled परिपूर्ण, भरपूर।

replica *रैपॅ लि कॅ n.* facsimile प्रतिकृति।

reply[1] *रि प्लॉइ v.i.* to answer उत्तर देना *v.t.* to say by way of answer उत्तर में कहना।

reply[2] *n.* response, answer उत्तर।

report[1] *रि पौःट v.t.* to give an account of का विवरण देना; to relate कहना, बयान करना; to complain about शिकायत करना; *v.i.* to act as a reporter संवाददाता का कार्य करना; to present oneself उपस्थित या प्रस्तुत होना।

report[2] *n.* an account विवरण; statement बयान; rumour अफ़वाह; repute नाम; sound of an explosion धमाका।

reporter *रि पौः टॅः n.* one who reports to the newspaper संवाददाता।

repose[1] *रि पोज़ n.* peace शांति; composure आराम; sleep नींद।

repose[2] *v.i.* to rest आराम करना; *v.t.* to lay at rest आराम से लिटा देना; to place रखना; to lean झुकाना, टेकना।

repository *रि पौ ˘ ज़ि टॅ रि n.* warehouse भंडार-गृह।

represent *रैपॅ रि ज़ैन्ट v.t.* to describe वर्णन करना; to show प्रदर्शित करना; to denote द्योतित करना; to be substitute for (का) प्रतिनिधित्व करना; to symbolize (का) प्रतीक होना।

representation *रैपॅ रि ज़ैनॅ टे शॅन n.* act of representing प्रतिनिधित्व; likeness प्रतिरूप; a polite protest विरोध-पत्र।

representative[1] *रैपॅ रि ज़ैनॅ टॅ टिव n.* one who or that which represents प्रतिनिधि।

representative[2] *a.* showing प्रदर्शक, द्योतक; acting for others प्रतिनिधिक।

repress *रि प्रैस v.t.* to suppress शमन करना; to restrain रोकना।

repression *रि प्रै ˘ शॅन n.* check नियंत्रण; restraint दबाव।

reprimand[1] *रैपॅ रि मान्ड n.* severe reproof for a fault घुड़की, लताड़।

reprimand[2] *v.t.* to administer a sharp rebuke to निंदा करना, झिड़कना।

reprint[1] *री प्रिन्ट v.t.* to print again पुनः मुद्रित करना।

reprint[2] *री प्रिन्ट n.* a second or new edition पुनर्मुद्रण।

reproach[1] *रि प्रोच v.t.* to charge severly with a fault धिक्कारना।

reproach[2] *n.* censure धिक्कार; disgrace तिरस्कार।

reproduce *री प्रॅ ड्यूस v.t.* to produce copy of की प्रतिलिपि प्रस्तुत करना; to bring forth as offspring संतान के रूप में जन्म देना; to grow again पुनः विकसित करना; to create again पुनः बनाना।

reproduction *री प्रॅ डक् शॅन n.* process of reproducing पुनरुत्पादन; copy प्रतिकृति; bringing forth offspring प्रजनन।

reproductive *री प्रॅ डक् टिव a.* reproducing पुनरुत्पादक।

reproof *रि प्रूफ़ n.* blame निंदा; rebuke फटकार।

reptile *रैपॅ टॉइल n.* an animal that moves on its belly, or by means of small short legs रेंगनेवाला जंतु।

republic *रि पब् लिक n.* state in which the supreme power is vested in elected representatives प्रजातंत्र राज्य।

republican[1] *रि पब् लि कॅन a.* pertaining to or consisting of a republic लोकतंत्र-संबंधी।

republican[2] *n.* one who favours republican government लोकतंत्रवादी।

repudiate *रि प्यू डि एट v.t.* to reject अस्वीकार करना; to disown परित्याग करना।

repudiation *रि प्यू डि ए शॅन n.* rejection अस्वीकृति, तिरस्कार; disowning परित्याग।

repugnance *रि पग् नॅन्स n.* aversion घृणा।

repugnant *रि पग् नॅन्ट a.* distasteful अरुचिकर, घृणास्पद।

repulse[1] *रि पल्स v.t.* to repel खदेड़ना; to resist successfully प्रतिशोध करना।

repulse[2] *n.* driving back खदेड़ने की क्रिया; rebuff पराजय।

repulsion *रि पल् शॅन n.* feeling of aversion घृणा, अरुचि; act of repulsing हटाने की क्रिया, पराजय।

repulsive *रि पल् सिव a.* repellent प्रतिकारक, पीछे हटानेवाला; forbidding निषेधक।

reputation *रैॅ प्यु टे शॅन n.* repute प्रसिद्धि, ख्याति; good name नेकनामी; fame यश।

repute[1] *रि प्यूट v.t.* to estimate गणना करना; to consider मानना।

repute[2] *n.* reputation यश, कीर्ति।

request[1] *रि क्वैस्ट v.t.* to petition, to demand for प्रार्थना करना।

request[2] *n.* asking प्रार्थना; demand मांग, आकांक्षा; thing asked for मांगी गई वस्तु।

requiem *रैॅक् वि ऐमॅ n.* a service for the dead मृतकों की शांति के लिए प्रार्थना।

require *रि क्वॉइअॅः v.t.* to need की आवश्यकता रखना; to demand मांगना।

requirement *रि क्वॉइअॅः मॅन्ट n.* demand मांग, आवश्यकता; something necessary आवश्यक वस्तु।

requisite[1] *रैकॅ वि ज़िट a.* necessary आवश्यक।

requiste[2] *n.* thing needed for some purpose आवश्यक वस्तु।

rquisition[1] *रैकॅ वि ज़ि शॅन n.* demand मांग।

requisition[2] *v.t.* to make a demand upon or for मांगना, प्रार्थना

करना।

requite *रि क्वॉइट v.t.* to repay, to give in return लौटाना, बदले में देना।

rescue[1] रैस्॒ *क्यू v.t.* to deliver from confinement, danger or evil मुक्त करना।

rescue[2] *n.* deliverance निस्तार; liberation मुक्ति।

research[1] *रि सॅःच v.i.* to carry out investigation अनुसंधान करना।

research[2] *n.* critical investigation अनुसंधान, अन्वेषण।

resemblance *रि ज़ैम्॒ ब्लॅन्स n.* likeness सादृश्य होना।

resemble *रि ज़ैम्॒ ब्लॅ v.t.* to be like के सदृश होना।

resent *रि ज़ैन्ट v.t.* to feel indignation for बुरा मानना; to be angry at (पर) क्रोध करना।

resentment *रि ज़ै ॅट् मॅन्ट n.* deep sense of insult अपमान; indignation नाराज़गी, अप्रसन्नता।

reservation *रै ॅ ज़ॅः वे शॅन n.* concealment छिपाव, दुराव; doubt संदेह; act of reserving आरक्षण।

reserve *रि ज़ःव v.t.* to keep in store बचा रखना; to set apart अलग करना।

rservoir *रै ॅ ज़ॅः व्वाः n.* a place where anything is kept in store संग्रह, कोश; an artificial lake to supply a town with water जलाशय।

reside *रि ज़ॉइड v.i.* to have one's abode, to dwell निवास करना।

residence *रै ॅ ज़ि डॅन्स n.* abode निवासस्थान।

resident[1] *रै ॅ ज़ि डॅन्ट a.* residing निवासी।

resident[2] *n.* one who resides रहने वाला।

residual *रि ज़ि ड्यु ॲल a.* left after a part is taken शेष (भाग)।

residue *रै ॅ ज़ि ड्यू n.* remainder अवशेष।

resign *रि ज़ॉइन v.t.* to give up छोड़ना; to surrender सौंपना; to renounce त्यागना; *v.t.* to give up office त्यागपत्र देना।

resignation *रै ॅ ज़िग् ने शॅन n.* act of resigning परित्याग; state of being resigned समर्पण।

resist *रि ज़िस्ट v.t.* to withstand रोकना; to struggle against संघर्ष करना; to oppose विरोध करना।

resistance *रि ज़िस् टॅन्स n.* opposition विरोध; hindrance बाधा।

resistant *रि ज़िज़् टॅन्ट a.* making resistance बाधक।

resolute *रै ॅ ज़ॅ ल्यूट a.* determined कृतसंकल्प; steadfast दृढ़।

resolution *रै ॅ ज़ॅ ल्यू शुन n.* determination निश्चय, संकल्प; solution समाधान; formal expression of opinion प्रस्ताव।

resolve *रि ज़ॉल्व v.t.* to analyse विश्लेषण करना; to determine निश्चय करना; to divide into parts विभक्त करना; to solve का समाधान करना।

resonance *रै ॅ ज़ॅ नॅन्स n.* state or quality of being resonant प्रतिध्वनि; prolongation of sound by vibrations गूंज।

resonant *रै ॅज़ॅ नॅन्ट a.* resounding गुंजायमान।

resort[1] *रि ज़ौःट v.i.* to have recourse सहारा लेना; to go frequently प्रायः जाना।

resort² *n.* recourse आश्रय; act of resorting गमन; haunt गमन-स्थान।

resound *रि जॉउन्ड v.i.* to echo गूंजना।

resource *रि सौःस n.* any source of aid or support साधन, संबल; means of support उपाय, सहारा।

resourceful *रि सौःस् फुल a.* quick at finding resources उपाय-कुशल; having resources साधन-संपन्न।

respect¹ *रिस् पैक्ट v.t.* to regard आदर करना; to have consideration for का ध्यान रखना।

respect² *n.* regard आदर; estimation सम्मान, मान्यता; reference संदर्भ; *(pl.)* regards अभिवादन।

respectful *रिस् पैक्ट् फुल a.* showing respect श्रद्धालु।

respective *रिस् पैक् टिव a.* relating severally each to each अपने-अपने, निजी।

respiration *रैस्पि रे शॅन n.* breathing श्वसन।

respire *रिस् पॉइअॅः v.i.* to breathe सांस लेना।

resplendent *रिस् प्लैन् डॅन्ट a.* very bright देदीप्यमान।

respond *रिस् पौन्ड v.i.* to answer उत्तर देना; to react प्रतिक्रिया दिखाना; to act in answer to some action प्रत्युत्तर-स्वरूप कुछ करना।

respondent *रिस् पौन् डॅन्ट n.* one who responds, defendant प्रतिवादी।

response *रिस् पौन्स n.* answer, reply उत्तर; reaction प्रतिक्रिया।

responsibility *रिस् पौन् सि बि लि टि n.* state of being responsible उत्तरदायित्व।

responsible *रिस् पौन् सॅ ब्ल a.* answerable उत्तरदायी।

rest¹ *रैस्ट v.i.* to be still स्थिर होना; to lie in sleep सोना; to die मरना; to be satisfied संतुष्ट होना; to take rest आराम करना; *v.t.* to give rest to आराम देना; to place on support सहारा देना।

rest² *n.* repose विश्राम; remainder अवशेष; ease शांति; faith विश्वास; *(with pl. verb)* others अन्य।

restaurant *रैस्ॅ टॅ रॅन्ट n.* establishment for the sale of refreshment भोजनालय।

restive *रैस्ॅ टिव a.* stubborn अड़ियल; restless बेचैन; impatient अधीर।

restoration *रैस्ॅ टॅ रे शॅन n.* bringing back वापसी; recovery पूर्वावस्था की प्राप्ति; repairing मरम्मत।

restore *रिस् टौः v.t.* to repair मरम्मत करना; to cure स्वस्थ करना; to renew नवीकरण करना; to give back लौटाना।

restrain *रिस् ट्रेन v.t.* to hold back नियंत्रित करना; to restrict प्रतिरोध करना, सीमित करना।

restrict *रिस् ट्रिक्ट v.t.* to limit सीमाबद्ध करना; to curb दबाना।

restriction *रिस् ट्रिक् शॅन n.* limitation सीमा, बंधन; restraint संयम।

restrictive *रिस् ट्रिक् टिव a.* tending to restrict प्रतिबंधक।

result¹ *रि ज़ल्ट v.i.* to rise as a consequence परिणाम होना।

result² *n.* consequence परिणाम; effect प्रभाव।

resume[1] *रि ज़्यूम v.t.* to take up again पुनः प्राप्त करना; to begin again दुबारा आरंभ करना; *v.i.* to continue after interruption पुनः चालू होना।

resume[2] *रि ज्यू मे,- ज़्यु- n.* summary सार, संक्षेप।

resumption *रि ज़म्प् शॅन n.* act of resuming पुनर्ग्रहण; fresh start पुनरारंभ।

resurgence *रि सॅः जॅन्स n.* rising again पुररुत्थान।

resurgent *रि सॅः जॅन्ट a.* reviving पुनरुत्थानशील।

retail[1] *री टेल v.t. & i.* to sell in small quantities फुटकर बिक्री करना या होना।

retail[2] *री टेल n.* the sale of commodities in small quantities फुटकर बिक्री।

retail[3] *adv.* by retail खुदरा द्वारा।

retail[4] *a.* connected with or engaged in retail खुदरा।

retailer *री टे लॅः n.* one who retails फुटकर विक्रेता।

retain *रि टेन v.t.* to hold back रोक रखना; to engage services of नौकर रखना।

retaliate *रि टै लि एट v.i.* to revenge प्रतिकार करना; to return injury for injury बदले में चोट करना।

retaliation *रि टे लि ए शॅन n.* return of like for like प्रतिकार।

retard *रि टाःड v.t.* to render slower धीमा करना; to keep back रोकना; to impede development of (का) विकास अवरूद्ध करना।

retardation *रि टॉः डे शॅन n.* diminution in speed गतिरोध; obstruction बाधा।

retention *रि टैन् शॅन n.* maintenance अवधारणा; memory स्मृति; power of retaining धारणा-शक्ति।

retentive *रि टैन् टिव a.* having power to retain धारणा-शक्ति वाला।

reticence *रै˘ टि सॅन्स n.* being reticent अल्पभाषिता।

reticent *रै˘ टि सॅन्ट a.* reserved in speech अल्पभाषी।

retina *रै˘ टि नॅ n.* one of the coats of the eye, where visual impressions are received आंख के पिछले भाग का चित्रपट।

retinue *रै˘ टि न्यू n.* train of attendants नौकर-चाकर, सेवकवृंद।

retire *रि टॉइ अॅः v.i.* to withdraw from business or active life व्यापार या सक्रिय जीवन को त्यागना; *v.t.* to remove from service सेवामुक्त करना।

retirement *रि टॉइअॅः मॅन्ट n.* act of retiring कार्यमुक्ति; retired life अवकाशप्राप्त जीवन।

retort[1] *रि टौःट v.t.* to repay in kind जैसे को तैसा लौटाना; to answer back quickly मुंहतोड़ जवाब देना।

retort[2] *n.* retorting answer मुंह तोड़ जवाब।

retouch *री टच v.t.* to improve by new touches परिष्कृत करना, सुधारना।

retrace *रि ट्रेस v.t.* to go over again पर वापस जाना।

retread[1] *री ट्रै˘ड v.t.* to put a new tread on (a worn tyre) (पुराने टायर पर) नई रबर चढ़ाना।

retread[2] *n.* renovated tyre रबर चढ़ा टायर।

retreat *रि ट्रीट v.i.* to draw back पीछे हटना।

retrench *रि ट्रैन्च v.t.* to cut down (expenditure) (व्यय) घटाना; *v.i.* to economize अल्पव्यय करना।

retrenchment *रि ट्रैन्च् मॅन्ट n.* economy व्यय में कमी।

retrieve *रि ट्रीव v.t.* to recover पुनः प्राप्त करना; to repair सुधारना; to rescue बचाना।

retrospect *रै ॅ ट्रो ॅ स्पैक्ट n.* backward view पश्चात् दृष्टि; review of past time सिंहावलोकन; survey of past events बीती बांतों की जांच।

retrospection *रि ट्रौ ॅस् पैक् शॅन n.* looking back सिंहावलोकन, पश्चदर्शन।

retrospective *रि ट्रौ ॅस् पैक् टिव a.* looking back पश्चदर्शी; applying to the past पूर्वप्रभावी।

return[1] *रि टॅःन v.i.* to go or come back लौटना; *v.t.* to give or send back लौटाना; to elect चुनना; to reply उत्तर देना।

return[2] *n.* returning वापसी; profit लाभ; official report विवरणी; recurrence आवृत्ति।

revel[1] *रैॅ व्ल (-ll-) v.i.* to feast with noise jollity मद्यपान का उत्सव मनाना; to delight आनंद लेना।

revel[2] *n.* merriment आमोद-प्रमोद।

revelation *रै ॅ वि ले शॅन n.* revealing प्रकटन।

reveller *रै ॅ वॅ लॅः n.* one who revels मौज उड़ाने वाला।

revelry *रै ॅ वॅल् रि n.* noise festivity, jollity रंगरलियां।

revenge[1] *रि वैन्ज v.t.* to avenge बदला लेना।

revenge[2] *n.* retaliation for wrong done प्रतिकार।

revengeful *रि वैॅन्ज् फुल a.* vindictive प्रतिशोधी।

revenue *रै ॅ वि न्यू n.* income आय; the annual income of a state राज्य की वार्षिक आय।

revere *रि विअॅः v.t.* to have deep respect for सम्मान करना; to regard as sacred पुनीत मानना।

reverence *रै ॅ वॅ रॅन्स n.* act of respect सत्कार; veneration आदर।

reverend *रै ॅ वॅ रॅन्ड a.* worthy of reverence माननीय।

reverent *रै ॅ वॅ रॅन्ट a.* showing reverence श्रद्धालु।

reverential *रै ॅ वॅ रे ॅ न् शॅल a.* marked by reverence श्रद्धापूर्ण।

reverie *रै ॅ वि रि n.* day-dream दिवास्वप्न।

reversal *रि वॅः सॅल n.* act of reversing उल्टाव, विपर्यय।

reverse[1] *रि वॅःस a.* opposite विपरीत; inverted उल्टा।

reverse[2] *n.* the contrary विपर्यय, उल्टा; the back surface पीछे का भाग; misfortune दुर्भाग्य; defeat पराजय।

reverse[3] *v.t.* to turn the other way अधोमुख करना; to invert उलटना; to annual रद्द करना; to do the opposite of के विपरीत करना; *v.i.* to go in the opposite direction विपरीत दिशा में जाना।

reversible *रि वॅः सि ब्ल a.* that can be reversed उलटने अथवा

पलटने योग्य।

revert *रि वॅःट v.i.* to return to the original person लौट आना; to return to former state पूर्वस्थिति में लौटना।

review¹ *रि व्यू v.t.* to reconsider पुनर्विचार करना; to inspect निरीक्षण करना; to write reviews of (की) समीक्षा करना।

review² *n.* re-examination पुनर्परीक्षण; revision पुनर्निरीक्षण; a critical account समीक्षा।

revise *रि वॉइज़ v.t.* to look over again दुबारा विचार करना; to re-examine दुबारा जांचना; to reconsider and amend faults of पुनः संशोधन करना।

revision *रि वि ज़ॅन n.* act of revising संशोधन; what is revised संशोधित वस्तु।

revival *रि वॉइ वॅल n.* act or reviving पुररुत्थान; restoration to life or vigour पुनरुज्जीवन; restoration to use पुनः प्रचलन।

revive *रि वॉइव v.i.* to return to life पुनर्जीवित होना; to come back into use पुनः प्रचलित होना; to recover new vigour उत्प्राणित होना; *v.t.* to bring again to life पुनर्जीवित करना।

revocable *रैॅ वौ कॅ ब्ल a.* capable of being revoked खंडन करने-योग्य।

revocation *रैॅ वॅ के शॅन n.* repeal निरसन।

revoke *रि वोक v.t.* to repeal रद्द करना; to withdraw हटाना, वापस लेना।

revolt¹ *रि वोल्ट v.i.* to cast off allegiance राजद्रोह करना; to rise against a ruler राजशासन के विरुद्ध उठना; to rise to rebellion बलवा करना।

revolt² *n.* rebellion बलवा, राजद्रोह।

revolution *रैॅ वॅ ल्यू शॅन n.* act of revolving चक्कर; rotation परिभ्रमण; overthrow of existing political institutions क्रांति।

revolutionary¹ *रैॅ वॅ ल्यू शॅ नॅ रि a.* pertaining to or tending to produce a revolution क्रांतिकारी।

revolutionary² *n.* an instigator of a revolution क्रांतिकारी।

revolve *रि वौल्व v.i.* to turn round चक्कर खाना, घूमना; *v.t.* to rotate घुमाना।

revolver *रि वौल् वॅः n.* pistol with revolving mechanism रिवाल्वर।

reward¹ *रि वौःड n.* return for services or for merit पारितोषिक, पुरस्कार; sum of money offered for some service इनाम।

reward² *v.t.* to give a reward to इनाम देना।

rhetoric *रैॅ टॅ रिक n.* art of effective speech वाक्पटुता।

rhetorical *रि टौॅ रि कॅल a.* high flown, showy शब्दाडंबरपूर्ण।

rheumatic *रू मै टिक a.* relating to rheumatism गठिया-संबंधी; caused by rheumatism गठिया-ग्रस्त।

rheumatism *रू मॅ टिज़्म n.* a painful disease with swollen joints गठिया।

rhinoceros *रॉइ नौ सॅ रॅस n. (pl. -es)* a large thick-skinned animal with one or two horns on the nose गैंडा।

rhyme[1] *रॉइम n.* sameness of sound of the endings of two or more words तुक।

rhyme[2] *v.i.* to make verses पद्य लिखना।

rhymester *रॉइम् स्टॅः n.* one who makes rhymes पद्यकार, तुक्कड़।

rhythm *रि दम b.* measured flow of words ताल, लय।

rhythmic, -al *रिद् मिक, - मि कॅल a.* pertaining to rhythm तालबद्ध।

rib *रिब n.* one of the curved bones in chest पसली; hinged rod of umbrella frame छाते की तीली।

ribbon *रि बॅन n.* narrow woven band of silk or stain साटन या रेशम का पतला फ़ीता।

rice *रॉइस n.* a cereal plant धान, मूंजी; its seeds as food चावल।

rich *रिच a.* wealthy धनी; valuable बहुमूल्य; costly क़ीमती; ample प्रचुर।

riches *रि चिज़ n. pl.* wealth धन।

richness *रिच् निस a.* quality or state of being rich धनाढ्यता; abundance प्रचुरता।

rick *रिक n.* stack of hay etc. गरी, पोरौटी।

rickets *रि किट्स n.* a disease of childhood causing softening of the bone सूखा रोग।

rickety *रि कि टि a.* suffering from rickets सूखा रोगी।

rickshaw *रिक् शौ n.* a light two-wheeled carriage drawn by man रिक्शा।

rid *रिड v.t.* to make free मुक्त करना।

riddle[1] *रिड्ल n.* puzzle पहेली।

riddle[2] *v.i.* to use riddles पहेली कहना।

ride[1] *रॉइड (p.t.* rode *रोड; p.p.* ridden *रि ड्न) v.t.* sit on and control पर सवारी करना; to be carried on पर ले जाया जाना; *v.i.* to go on horseback or in vehicle घोड़ा या गाड़ी से जाना।

ride[2] *n.* journey on horseback or in a vehicle घोड़ा या गाड़ी से यात्रा; a riding track पथ मार्ग।

rider *रॉइ डॅः n.* one who rides सवार; supplementry clause अनुवृद्धि।

ridge *रिज n.* mountain range पर्वतपृष्ठ; rough top of anything चोटी; any narrow elevation संकरा ऊंचा भाग।

ridicule[1] *रि डि क्यूल v.t.* to make fun of उपहास करना; to mock ठिठोली करना।

ridicule[2] *n.* mockery उपहास।

ridiculous *रि डि क्यु लॅस a.* deserving to be ridiculed हास्यास्पद; absurd बेहूदा।

rifle[1] *रॉइ फ़्ल v.t.* to search and rob खोजकर लूटना; to make spiral grooves in में झिरी काटना।

rifle[2] *n.* a gun with grooved barrel राइफ़ल।

rift *रिफ़्ट n.* cleft, fissure दरार, फटन।

right[1] *रॉइट a.* just न्याय; true सच्चा; correct सही; of the right hand दाहिनी ओर का।

right[2] *adv* rightly उचित रीति से; correctly सही प्रकार से; to the right side दाहिनी ओर को।

right[3] *n.* justice न्याय; authority अधिकार; truth सत्यता; right hand side दायाँ भाग।

right[4] *v.t.* to do justice to न्याय करना; to put in a proper position उचित स्थान में रखना।

righteous *रॉइ चॅस* *a.* just न्यायपरायण; holy पवित्र; honest ईमानदार।

rigid *रि जिड* *a.* not flexible कड़ा; harsh कठोर; strict दृढ़; severe कर्कश।

rigorous *रि गॅ रॅस* *a.* severe कर्कश; strict दृढ़।

rigour *रि गॅः* *n.* hardship कठिनता; strictness दृढ़ता; harshness कठोरता।

rim *रिम* *n.* edge, border किनारा; outer ring of a wheel नेमि।

ring[1] *रिङ्ग* *n.* circle of metal अंगूठी; circular course चक्रपथ; enclosure for circus performance घेरा, रिंग; ringing sound घंटी।

ring[2] *(rang रैङ्ग; rung रङ्ग)* *v.t.* to cause (bell) to sound (घंटी) बजाना; to telephone टेलिफ़ोन करना; *v.i.* to give a resonant sound बजना; to resound गूंजना।

ringlet *रिङ्ग् लिट* *n.* curly lock of hair अलक, बालों का लच्छा।

ringworm *रिङ्ग् वॅःम* *n.* a skin disease दाद।

rinse *रिन्स* *v.t.* to wash out धो डालना; to remove soapy water from खंगालना।

riot[1] *रॉइ अॅट* *n.* violent public disturbance दंगा; disorder अव्यवस्था, उपद्रव।

riot[2] *v.t.* to take part in a riot बलवा करना।

rip *रिप* *(-pp-)* *v.t.* to cut or tear apart फाड़ना; *v.i.* to become torn फटना।

ripe *रॉइप* *a.* mature पक्व, पका हुआ; fully developed पूर्ण विकसित।

ripen *रॉइ पॅन* *v.i.* to become ripe पकना; *v.t.* to make ripe पकाना।

ripple[1] *रिप ल* *n.* small wave on the surface of water लहर।

ripple[2] *v.t.* to move slightly in waves लहराना।

rise[1] *रॉइज़* *(p.t. rose रोज़ p.p. risen रि ज़न)* to get up उठना; to stand erect सीधा खड़ा होना; to ascend चढ़ना; to appear above the horizon उगना, निकलना; to come to life जीवित होना; to revolt बलवा करना।

rise[2] *n.* upslope, ascent चढ़ाव; upward progress उन्नति; rising उठान; increase वृद्धि; coming up उदय; origin उद्‌गम, विकास।

risk[1] *रिस्क* *v.t.* to take the chance of जोखिम उठाना; to put in danger ख़तरे में डालना।

risk[2] *n.* possibility of loss or injury जोखिम; possibility of danger ख़तरा।

risky *रिस् कि* *a.* hazardous संकटमय, ख़तरनाक।

rite *रॉइट* *n.* religious ceremony धार्मिक उत्सक, अनुष्ठान।

ritual[1] *रि ट्यु अॅल, -चु-* *n.* prescribed order of rites धार्मिक संस्कार।

ritual[2] *a.* concerning rites धार्मिक रीति-संबंधी।

rival[1] *रॉइ वॅल* *n.* competitor प्रतिस्पर्धी, प्रतिद्वंद्वी।

rival[2] *(-ll-)* *v.t.* to be a rival of का प्रतिद्वंद्वी होना।

rivalry *रॉइ वॅल् रि* *n.* keen competition होड़ प्रतिस्पर्धा।

river *रि वॅः* *n.* large natural flow of water नदी।

rivet[1] *रि विट* *n.* a metal pin कीलक, रिपट।

rivet[2] *v.t.* to fasten with rivets कीलक से जोड़ना; to concentrate केंद्रित करना।

rivulet *रि व्यु लिट* *n.* small stream नाला।

road *रोड* *n.* open paved way सड़क।

roam *रोम* *v.i.* to wander about aimlessly घूमना-फिरना।

roar[1] *रौः* *n.* loud deep sound as of a lion गर्जन।

roar[2] *v.i.* to make loud deep sound as of a lion गर्जन करना।

roast[1] *रोस्ट* *v.t.* to cook by exposing directly to heat भूनना; *v.i.* to be cooked in this way भुनना।

roast[2] *a.* that has been roasted भुना हुआ।

roast[3] *n.* joint of roasted meat भुना हुआ मांस; operation of roasting भुनने की क्रिया।

rob *रौ ॅब (-bb-)* *v.t.* to deprive by force लूटना।

robber *रौॅबॅः* *n.* one who robs लुटेरा, डाकू।

robbery *रौॅ बॅ रि* *n.* act of robbing लूटपाट, डकैती।

robe[1] *रोब* *n.* loose outer garment लबादा।

robe[2] *v.t.* to dress कपड़े पहनाना; *v.i.* to put on robes कपड़े पहनना।

robot *रो बौ ॅट* *n.* a man-like mechanical being यंत्र-मानव।

robust *रो बस्ट* *a.* strong and healthy हृष्ट-पुष्ट।

rock[1] *रौकॅ* *v.t.* to sway strongly झुलाना, हिलाना; *v.i.* to be swayed हिलना, झोंके खाना।

rock[2] *n.* large mass of stone चट्टान।

rocket *रौ ॅ किट* *n.* missile प्रक्षेपास्त्र; projectile राकेट।

rod *रौ ॅड* *n.* bar of wood or metal छड़।

rodent *रो डॅन्ट* *n.* a gnawing animal कृतंक।

roe *रो* *n.* a small deer छोटा हिरन।

rogue *रोग* *n.* a knave, a scoundrel दुष्ट।

roguery *रो गॅ रि* *n.* conduct of a rogue दुष्टता।

roguish *रो गिश* *a.* of the nature of a rogue दुष्टतापूर्ण

role *रोल* *n.* part that an actor plays भूमिका; part played in any job कार्य, योगदान।

roll[1] *रोल* *n.* rolling motion लुढ़काव; piece of paper etc. rolled up काग़ज़ आदि, बेलनाकार लिपटा हुआ; anything rolled round टिकिया; list सूची; official list of people उपस्थिति-पंजिका।

roll[2] *v.i.* to move in the same direction घूमना, लुढ़कना; to go round चक्कर खाना; to revolve on its axis धुरे पर घूमना; *v.t.* to wind round लपेटना; to smooth out with roller पर बेलन फेरना।

roll-call *रौल् कौल* *n.* calling of names हाज़िरी, उपस्थिति।

roller *रो लॅः* *n.* a cylinder-shaped object for smoothing or flattening बेलन, रोलर।

romance *रो ॅ मैन्स, रॅ-* *n.* a love affair प्रेम-लीला; tale of chivalry शौर्य-गाथा; idealized tale

अयथार्थपूर्ण कथा।

romantic *रोॅ मैन् टिक, रॅ-* *a.* characterised by romance रोमानी; dealing with love प्रेम-प्रसंगयुक्त; unpractical, remote from reality अव्यावहारिक।

romp[1] *रौम्प* *v.i.* to play boisterously प्रगल्भता से खेलना।

romp[2] *n.* a noisy game उछल-कूद, हुड़दंगी खेल-कूद।

rood *रूड* *n.* cross of Christ ईसामसीह के सूली पर चढ़ने का चित्र; quarter of an acre चौथाई एकड़।

roof[1] *रूफ़* *n.* upper covering of a building supported by its walls छत, पाटन; top of anything ऊपर का भाग।

roof[2] *v.t.* to cover with a roof छत से पाटना।

rook[1] *रूक* *n.* a bird of crow family कौआ; cheat धोखेबाज़, ठग।

rook[2] *v.t.* to swindle ठगना।

room *रूम* *n.* apartment in a house कमरा; space स्थान; opportunity अवसर।

roomy *रूमि* *a.* spacious विस्तीर्ण, विशाल।

roost[1] *रूस्ट* *n.* pole on which a bird rests at night अड्डा, बसेरा।

roost[2] *v.i.* to perch बसेरा लेना, बैठना।

root[1] *रूट* *n.* underground part of a plant जड़; origin आधार, कारण; basis from which a word is derived धातु।

root[2] *v.i.* to become established जड़ जमना; *v.t.* to cause to take root की जड़ जमाना।

rope[1] *रोप* *n.* strong thick cord रस्सी।

rope[2] *v.t.* to bind with a rope रस्सी से बांधना।

rosary *रो ज़ॅ रि* *n.* a string of beads for counting prayers सुमिरनी, माला; rose garden गुलाब-उद्यान।

rose *रोज़* *n.* a prickly bush bearing beautiful fragrant flower गुलाब का पौधा; its flower गुलाब; pink colour गुलाबी रंग।

roseate *रो ज़ि अट, -इट* *a.* rose-coloured गुलाबी।

rostrum *रौसॅ ट्रॅम* *n.* public platform मंच।

rosy *रो ज़ि* *a.* rose-coloured गुलाबी; hopeful उज्ज्वल।

rot[1] *रौॅट* *n.* decay दुर्गंध, सड़न।

rot[2] *(-tt-)* *v.i.* to undergo decay सड़ना; to perish gradually नाश होना।

rotary *रो टॅ रि* *a.* acting by rotation, revolving घूमनेवाला।

rotate *रोॅ टैट* *v.i.* to revolve चक्कर खाना; to move round on axis धुरी पर घूमना; *v.t.* to cause to move round घुमाना।

rotation *रोॅ टे शॅन* *n.* act of rotating चक्कर; regular succession नियमित आवर्तन।

rote *रोट* *n.* repetition दुहराव mechanical performance यंत्रवत् क्रिया।

rouble *रू बॅल* *n.* Russian silver coin रूस का सिक्का, रूबल।

rough *रफ़* *a.* of uneven or irregular surface ऊबड़खाबड़; harsh रूखा, कठोर; ill-mannered अशिष्ट; unfinished अपरिष्कृत; approximate लगभग।

round[1] *रॉउन्ड* *a.* cylindrical बेलनाकार; full, complete पूर्ण; roughly correct लगभग सही।

round[2] *adv.* circularly चक्रवत्; on all sides चारों ओर।

round[3] *n.* round object गोल वस्तु; circumference परिधि; series क्रम; stage स्थिति।

round[4] *v.t.* to make circular गोल करना; to move round के चारों ओर चक्कर लगाना; *v.i.* to become round गोल होना।

rouse *रॉउज़* *v.i.* to wake from sleep जगाना; to provoke temper of उत्तेजित करना।

rout[1] *रॉउट* *v.t.* to put to disorderly flight भगदड़ करना।

rout[2] *n.* assembly of revellers हुड़दंगी भीड़; utter defeat घोर पराजय; disorderly retreat भगदड़।

route *रूट* *n.* passage taken for a journey मार्ग।

routine[1] *रू टीन* *n.* regular course of action नियमित कार्यक्रम।

routine[2] *a.* regular, ordinary नैत्य, सामान्य।

rove *रोव* *v.i.* to wander aimlessly भटकना, घूमना।

rover *रो वॅ:* *n.* wanderer घुमंतू।

row[1] *रो* *n.* a line of things or persons पंक्ति।

row[2] *v.t.* to move (a boat) by using oars (नाव) खेना; to carry in a boat नाव से ले जाना; *v.i.* to be an oarsman खेवनहार होना।

row[3] *n.* journey or outing in a boat नाव-द्वारा यात्रा अथवा भ्रमण; distance rowed खेयी हुई दूरी।

row[4] *रॉउ* *n.* uproar हुल्लड़; quarrel झगड़ा; disturbance उपद्रव।

rowdy *रॉउ डि* *a.* turbulent, noisy उपद्रवी, कोलाहलपूर्ण।

royal *रौइॅ अॅल* *a.* kingly राजसी।

royalist *रौ ॅइ अॅ लिस्ट* *n.* supporter of a king or queen राजभक्त।

royalty *रौ ॅइ अॅल् टि* *n.* royal persons राजघराने के सदस्य; royal dignity or power राजसी गौरव अथवा सत्ता; sum paid to the owner of copyright रायॅल्टी।

rub[1] *रब* *(-bb-)* *v.t.* to move (one thing) on the surface (of another) घिसना, रगड़ना; to clean or polish साफ़ या चमकदार करना; to massage मालिश करना; to chafe रगड़ना; to remove by friction मिटाना; *v.i.* to come into contact with friction रगड़ खाना; to be worn by friction मिट जाना।

rub[2] *n.* rubbing रगड़; impediment बाधा; difficulty कठिनाई।

rubber *र बॅ:* *n.* an elastic substance रबड़; person who rubs घिसने या रगड़ने वाला व्यक्ति।

rubbish *र बिश* *n.* worthless material कूड़ा-करकट; nonsense बकवास।

rubble *र ब्ल* *n.* fragments of stone etc. मलबा।

ruby *रू बि* *n.* a precious stone माणिक; deep red colour गहरा लाल रंग।

rude *रूड* *a.* impolite असभ्य; coarse भद्दा; vulgar गंवारूँ; uneducated अशिक्षित।

rudiment *रू डि मॅन्ट* *n. (pl.)* basic principles मूल तत्त्व; an elementary fact प्रारंभिक तथ्य।

rudimentary रू *डि मैन्ँ टॅ रि a.* basic प्रारंभिक मूल।

rue रू *v.t.* to grieve for पर दुःखी होना; to repent of (पर) पश्चाताप करना।

rueful रू *फुल a.* feeling regret दुःखी, उदास।

ruffian रफ़् *यॅन n.* violent lawless person गुंडा।

ruffle र *फ़ल v.t.* to annoy चिढ़ाना।

rug *रग n.* floor-mat ग़लीचा; a coverlet आच्छादन।

rugged र *गिड a.* rough खुरदरा, ऊबड़-खाबड़; not refined अशिष्ट; wrinkled (face) झुर्रीदार।

ruin[1] रू *इन n.* destruction विनाश; downfall पतन; *(pl.)* remains of a building or city खंडहर।

ruin[2] *v.t.* to destroy नष्ट करना; to spoil बिगाड़ना।

rule[1] *रूल n.* principle सिद्धांत; set of regulations नियम; government शासन; measuring stick पैमाना।

rule[2] *v.t.* to govern शासन करना; to give a decision निर्णय देना।

ruler रू *लॅ: n.* one who rules शासक, राजा; stick for measuring or ruling lines पैमाना।

ruling रू *लिङ्ग n.* decision made by an authority व्यवस्था, आदेश, निर्णय।

rum[1] *रम n.* a spirit शराब।

rum[2] *a.* strange विलक्षण; queer भद्दा।

rumble[1] *रम् ब्ल v.i.* to make a sound like thunder गड़गड़ाहट का शब्द करना।

rumble[2] *n.* rumbling sound गड़गड़ाहट।

ruminant[1] रू *मि नॅन्ट a.* (animal) that chews the cud जुगाली करने वाला।

ruminant[2] *n.* cud-chewing animal जुगाली वाला पशु।

ruminate रू *मि नेट v.i.* to chew the cud जुगाली करना; mediate चिंतन करना।

rumination रू *मि ने शॅन n.* chewing the cud जुगाली; meditation चिंतन, मनन।

rummage[1] र *मिज v.i.* to turn things over for search ढूंढ मचाना; *v.t.* to search thoroughly (का) चप्पा-चप्पा छान मारना।

rummage[2] *n.* search छान-बीन।

rummy र *मि n.* a card game ताश का रमी खेल।

rumour[1] *रूमॅ: n.* unverified statement अफ़वाह।

rumour[2] *v.t.* to circulate by way of rumour अफ़वाह फैलाना।

run[1] *रन (p.t. ran रैन; p.p. run) v.i.* to move quickly on foot दौड़ना; to rush शीघ्रता करना; to escape बच भागना; to move from one place to another चलना; to function काम करना; to spread फैलना; to flow बहना; to revolve घूमना; to continue चालू रहना; *v.t.* to cross by running दौड़कर पार करना; to expose oneself (to risk) (खतरा) मोल लेना; to cause to run दौड़ाना; to manage चलाना।

run[2] *n.* act of running दौड़; rush झपट्टा; tendency प्रवृत्ति; period अवधि; sequence क्रम; score of one at cricket क्रिकेट का एक 'रन'।

rung *रङ्ग* *n.* crossbar of a ladder सीढ़ी का डंडा।

runner *र नँः* *n.* one who runs धावक; messenger संदेशवाहक, हरकारा।

rupee *रू पी* *n.* coin of India रुपया।

rupture[1] *रप् चँः* *n.* breach of relation संबंध-विच्छेद; fracture टूटन।

rupture[2] *v.t.* to break तोड़ना; to burst फोड़ना; *v.i.* to break टूटना; to burst फूटना।

rural *रु अॅ रॅल* *a.* pertaining to the countryside देहाती, ग्रामीण।

ruse *रूज़* *n.* a trick चाल, धोखा।

rush[1] *रश* *n.* period of great activity व्यस्तता का समय; sudden attack झपट्टा।

rush[2] *v.t.* to carry along rapidly तेज़ी से ले जाना; to attack suddenly अचानक हमला करना; to cause to move violently तेज़ी से दौड़ाना; *v.i.* to move violently झपटना।

rush[3] *n.* a plant that grows in marshes जलबेंत।

rust[1] *रस्ट* *n.* reddish-brown coating on iron ज़ंग, मोरचा; a disease of plants रतुआ।

rust[2] *v.i.* to become rusty मोरचा खा जाना; *v.t.* to affect with rust ज़ंग लगाना।

rustic[1] *रस् टिक* *a.* unsophisticated ग्राम्य, गंवारू।

rustic[2] *n.* a country man गँवार।

rusticate *रस् टि केट* *v.t.* to expel (a student) from college as punishment (छात्र को) दंडस्वरूप निष्कासित करना।

rustication *रस् टि के शॅन* *n.* act of rusticating निष्कासन।

rusticity *रस् टि सि टि* *n.* being rustic गँवारूपन।

rusty *रस् टि* *a.* covered with rust ज़ंग खाया हुआ।

rut *रट* *n.* deep groove made by passage of wheels लीक; settled habit पक्की आदत।

ruthless *रूथ् लिस* *a.* pitiless, cruel निर्दय।

rye *रॉइ* *n.* a grain used for fodder and bread राई; plant bearing it राई का पौधा।

Ss

S *ऍस्* the nineteenth letter of the English alphabet, any object shaped like S. Roman numeral for 70 or 70,000. अंग्रेजी वर्णमाला का उन्नीसवाँ अक्षर, इस अक्षर के आकार का कोई पदार्थ, रोमन संख्या में ७० अथवा ७०,००० के लिए संकेत; Collar of S (a collar composed of links in the form of S.) जंजीर या पट्टा जिसमें S अक्षर के आकार की कड़ियाँ गुथी होती हैं।

sabbath *सै बॅथ* *n.* day of rest and worship विश्राम और पूजा का दिन।

sabotage[1] *सै बॅ टाज़* *n.* willful destruction तोड़फोड़।

sebotage[2] *v.t.* to perform an act of sabotage against से तोड़-फोड़ करना।

sabre[1] *से बॅ:* *n.* sword with curved blade कृपाण, तलवार।

sabre[2] *v.t.* to strike a sabre कृपाण से घायल करना।

saccharin *सै कॅ रिन* *n.* an artificial sweetener सैकरिन।

saccharine *सै कॅ रॉइन* *a.* resembling sugar शर्करा-जैसा; very sweet अति मधुर।

sack[1] *सैक* *n.* large bag of hemp बोरी, बोरा; dismissal बरख़ास्तगी; plunder लूट।

sack[2] *v.t.* to rob लूटना; to dismiss from a job बरख़ास्त करना।

sacrament *सैक् रॅ मॅन्ट* *n.* religious ceremony धार्मिक उत्सव, धार्मिक संस्कार।

sacred *से क्रिड* *a.* holy पवित्र; divine अलौकिक; religious धार्मिक; adorable पूजनीय।

sacrifice[1] *सैक् रि फ़ाईस* *n.* offering अर्पण; abandonment त्याग; surrender समर्पण।

sacrifice[2] *v.t.* to offer to a god on an alter बलिदान करना, भेंट चढ़ाना; *v.i.* to make a sacrifice त्याग करना।

sacrificial *सैक् रि फ़ि शॅल* *a.* pertaining to sacrifice बलिदान-संबंधी।

sacrilege *सैक् रि लिज* *n.* profanation of sacred things अपवित्रीकरण।

sacrilegious *सैक् रि लि जॅस* *a.* profane देवत्व का अपहारी।

sacrosanct *सैक् रो ˘ सैङ्क्ट* *a.* sacred पवित्र; worthy of protection रक्षणीय।

sad *सैड* *a.* unhappy दुःखी; sorrowful उदास।

sadden *सै ड्न* *v.t.* to make sorrowful दुःखी करना।

saddle[1] *सै ड्ल* *n.* rider's seat to be placed on a horse's back काठी।

saddle[2] *v.t.* to put a saddle on (घोड़े) की पीठ पर ज़ीन कसना।

sadism *से डिज़्म, सा-, सै-* *n.* delight in cruelty परपीड़न-रति।

sadist *से डिस्ट* *n.* person guilty of sadism पर पीड़न कामुक।

safe[1] *सेफ़* *a.* free from danger निरापद; involving on risk सुरक्षित।

safe[2] *n.* chest for keeping valuables तिजोरी।

safeguard[1] *सैफ़् गा:ड* *n.* defence, protection बचाव, रक्षा।

safeguard[2] *v.t.* to protect रक्षा करना।

safety *सेफ़् टि* *n.* security, freedom from danger सुरक्षा।

saffron[1] *सैफ़् रॅन* *n.* purple flowered crocus केसर, जाफ़रान; orange colour केसरिया रंग।

saffron[2] *a.* of the colour of saffron केसरिया।

sagacious *सॅ गे शॅस* *a.* gifted with acute समझदार, बुद्धिमान।

sagacity *सॅ गै सि टि* *n.* quickness of discernment चतुराई; farsightedness दूरदर्शिता।

sage[1] *सेज* *n.* venerable man ऋषि, संत; a wise man मनीषी।

sage[2] *a.* wise बुद्धिमान।

sail[1] *सेल* *n.* canvas spread to catch wind and propel a boat पाल; act of sailing खेवन; journey upon the water जल-यात्रा।

sail[2] *v.i.* to travel by water जलयात्रा करना; to move smoothly शांत रूप से चलना; *v.t.* to voyage across नाव से पार करना।

sailor *से लॅः* *n.* seaman नाविक, मल्लाह।

saint *सेन्ट* *n.* a holy person संत।

saintly *सेन्ट् लि* *a.* befitting a saint पुण्यात्मा।

sake *सेक* *n.* cause कारण; purpose उद्देश्य।

salable *से लॅ ब्ल* *a.* fit for sale विक्रेय।

salad *से लॅड* *n.* dish of uncooked vegetables सलाद।

salary *से लॅ रि* *n.* pay वेतन।

sale *सेल* *n.* act of selling बिक्री।

salesman *सेल्स् मॅन्* *n.* one who sells विक्रेता।

salient *सेल् यॅन्ट* *a.* chief, prominent मुख्य।

saline *से लॉइन* *a.* salty नमकीन, खारा।

salinity *सॅ लि नि टि* *n.* quality of being saline खारापन।

saliva *सॅ लॉइ वॅ* *n.* spittle लार।

sally[1] *सै लि* *n.* leap छलांग; sudden rush झपट्टा; excursion विहार।

sally[2] *v.i.* to make a sally झपट्टा मारना।

saloon *सॅ लून* *n.* large public room बैठक; a large reception room स्वागत-कक्ष।

salt[1] *सौल्ट, सौ ॅल्ट* *n.* chloride of sodium नमक; pungency तीखापन; wit बुद्धि।

salt[2] *v.t.* to sprinkle with salt नमक छिड़कना।

salty *सौल् टि* *a.* tasting of salt नमकीन।

salutary *सै ल्यु टॅ रि* *a.* wholesome, having a good result लाभकारी, स्वास्थ्यप्रद।

salutation *सैल् यू टै शॅन* *n.* greeting अभिवादन।

salute[1] *सॅ ल्यूट* *v.t.* to make salutation to नमस्कार करना; to honour आदर करना।

salute[2] *n.* a gesture of respect अभिवादन, नमन, firing of guns as a mark of honour सलामी।

salvage[1] *सैल् विज* *n.* rescue of property from loss at sea, or from fire नाशरक्षण; property so saved रक्षित संपत्ति।

salvage[2] *v.t.* to protect from loss क्षति से बचाना।

salvation *सैल् वे शॅन* *n.* deliverance from sin पापों से मुक्ति, उद्धार।

same *सेम* *a.* uniform अभिन्न, वही, तुल्य; unchanged अपरिवर्तित; identical वही; aforesaid पूर्वोक्त।

sample[1] *साम् प्ल* *n.* speciman नमूना।

sample[2] *v.t.* to take or give sample of की बानगी लेना या देना; to try, to test जांच करना; to select छांटना, चुनना।

sanatorium *सै नॅ टौ रि ॲम* *n.* health-resort आरोग्यआश्रम।

sanctification *सैङ्क् टि फ़ि के शॅन* *n.* act of sanctifying पवित्रीकरण।

sanctify *सैङ्क् टि फ़ॉई* *v.t.* to purify from sin पाप से मुक्त करना।

sanction[1] *सैङ्क् शॅन* *n.* approval अनुमोदन; penalty for breaking law प्रतिबंध।

sanction[2] *v.t.* to authorise आज्ञा देना, अधिकृत करना।

sanctity *सैङ्क् टि टि n.* holiness पवित्रता; purity पवित्रता।

sanctuary *सैङ्क् ट्यु अॅ रि n. (pl.-ries)* holy place मंदिर; place of refuge शरणस्थल; a reservation where animals may not be hunted पशुविहार।

sand *सैन्ड n.* minute fragments of stone बालू, रेत।

sandal *सैन् ड्ल n.* shoe consisting of sole attached by straps चप्पल, खड़ाऊं।

sandalwood *सैन् ड्ल् वुड n.* a kind of fragrant wood चंदन।

sandwich[1] *सैन् विज n.* thin slices of bread सैंडविच।

sandwich[2] *v.t.* to place (something) between two objects दो पदार्थों के बीच में (कुछ) रखना।

sandy *सैन् डि a.* like sand बालू जैसा; consisting of sand रेतीला।

sane *सेन a.* of sound mind स्वस्थ चित्त का।

sanguine *सैङ् ग्विन a.* of the colour of blood रक्त वर्ण का; hopeful आशायुक्त; confident विश्वासयुक्त।

sanitary *सै नि टॅ रि a.* hygienic आरोग्यकर; pertaining to health स्वास्थ्य-संबंधी।

sanity *सै नि टि n.* state of being sane स्थिरबुद्धिता; health of mind मानसिक स्वास्थ्य।

sap[1] *सैप n.* the juice that circulates in plants रस; vigour, energy शक्ति।

sap[2] *(-pp-) v.t.* to weaken निर्बल बनाना; to drain away the life and strength of शक्तिहीन करना।

sapling *सैप् लिङ्ग n.* young tree छोटा पौधा।

sapphire *सै फ़ॉइअ: n.* a blue precious stone नीलम; deep blue गहरा नीला रंग।

sarcasm *सा: कैज़्म n.* ironical remark व्यंग्य कथन; taunt ताना।

sarcastic *सा: कैस् टिक a.* ironical व्यंग्यपूर्ण, कटु; taunting ताने-भरा।

sardonic *सॉ: डौ˘ निक a.* scornful निंदापूर्ण।

satan *सै टॅन n.* the Devil शैतान।

satchel *सै चॅल n.* a small bag थैला, झोला।

satellite *सै टॅ लॉइट n.* planet revolving round another उपग्रह; hanger on पिछलग्गू।

satiable *सै श्यॅ ब्ल a.* that can be satisfied तृप्त।

satiate *सै शि एट v.t.* to gratify to the full तृप्त कर देना।

satiety *सॅ टॉइ अॅ टि n.* being satiated तृप्ति अघाव।

satire *सै टॉइअ: n.* irony, sarcasm उपहास, व्यंग्य; work using satire व्यंग्यपूर्ण कृति।

satirical *सॅ टि रि कॅल a.* containing satire व्यंग्यपूर्ण; characterized by satire व्यंग्यात्मक; fond of satire व्यंग्यप्रिय।

satirist *सै टॅ रिस्ट n.* one who writes a satire व्यंग्य-लेखक।

satirize *सै टि रॉइज़ v.t.* to ridicule in a satirical manner व्यंग्य करना।

satisfaction *सै टिस् फ़ैक् शॅन n.* gratification of desire संतोष, तृप्ति।

satisfactory *सै टिस् फ़ैक् टॅ रि a.* satisfying संतोषजनक।

satisfy *सै टिस् फ़ॉइ v.t.* to gratify fully संतुष्ट करना; to convince क़ायल करना; to fulfil पूरा करना।

saturate *सै चॅ रेट v.t.* to impregnate thoroughly with परिपूर्ण करना; to wet thoroughly तरबतर कर देना।

saturation *सै चॅ रे शॅन n.* act of saturating संतुष्टि, संतृप्ति।

Saturday *सै टॅः डे,-डि n.* last day of the week शनिवार।

sauce *सौस n.* chutney चटनी; impudence धृष्टता।

saucer *सौ सॅः n.* shallow vessel for placing a cup of tea on तश्तरी।

saunter *सौन्टॅः v.t.* to stroll बेकार घूमना; to walk in a leisurely manner टहलना।

savage[1] *सै विज a.* wild जंगली; uncivilized अशिष्ट; cruel निर्दय।

savage[2] *n.* member of a savage tribe हबशी।

savagery *सै वि जॅ रि n.* cruelty क्रूरता; barbarity वहशीपन।

save[1] *सेव v.t.* to make or keep safe सुरक्षित रखना; to keep or store for future बचत करना; to hoard (money) (धन) संचित करना; to defend रक्षा करना।

save[2] *prep.* except के सिवाय, के अलावा।

saviour *से व्यॅः n.* one who saves from destruction रक्षक, उद्धारक।

savour[1] *से व्यॅः n.* taste स्वाद; flavour रस; smell गंध।

savour[2] *v.t.* to have a particular smell or taste सुगंधित अथवा स्वादिष्ट होना; to suggest the presence (of) का आभास देना; *v.t.* to give flavour to स्वादिष्ट बनाना; to have flavour of की गंध रखना।

saw[1] *सौ n.* a cutting tool आरा।

saw[2] *v.t.* to cut with a saw आरे से काटना।

say[1] *से v.t.* to speak, to utter बोलना, कहना; to assume कल्पना करना।

say[2] *n.* speech व्याख्यान, कथन; share in decision निर्णय में भागीदारी।

scabbard *स्कै बॅःड n.* sheath for a sword or a dagger म्यान।

scabies *स्कै बीज़ n.* a skin disease causing itching खुज़ली।

scaffold *स्कै फ़ॅल्ड n.* temporary platform for building workmen पाड़; gallows फांसी का तख़्ता।

scale[1] *स्केल n.* hard flake on a fish, reptile, etc. शल्क; thin layer पपड़ी; a graduated measure मापक; ratio of size between a thing and a model or map of it पैमाना; dish of a balance पलड़ा; extent सीमा; *(pl.)* an instrument for measuring weight तराजू।

scale[2] *v.t.* to weigh in scales तराजू में तोलना; to have weight of का वज़न रखना; to climb पर चढ़ना; to remove scales from से शल्क हटाना; *v.i.* to come off in scales पपड़ी के रूप में उतरना।

scalp *स्कैल्प n.* skull खोपड़ी; skin and hair of head सिर की त्वचा और बाल।

scamper[1] *स्कैम् पॅः v.i.* to run about इधर-उधर दौड़ना।

scamper[2] *n.* short, quick run छोटी, तेज़ दौड़।

scan *स्कैन (-nn-) v.t.* to examine minutely सूक्ष्म परीक्षण करना; to scrutinize जांचना।

scandal *स्कैन् ड्ल n.* defamation बदनामी, मानहानि; back-biting चुगुली; malicious talk अपवाद।

scandalize *स्कैन् डॅ लॉइज़ v.t.* to defame बदनाम करना; to shock आघात पहुंचाना।

scant *स्कैन्ट a.* not sufficient अपर्याप्त, स्वल्प।

scanty *स्कैन् टि a.* small in size or amount कम, न्यून।

scapegoat *स्केप् गोट n.* person blamed for other's faults बलि का बकरा।

scar[1] *स्का: n.* mark of a sore or wound घाव का निशान।

scar[2] *(-rr-) v.t.* to mark with scar धब्बा लगाना।

scarce *स्कैॅ अ:स a.* not plentiful अल्प; rare विरल; uncommon दुर्लभ।

scarcely *स्कॅ अ:स् लि adv.* not quite, almost not मुश्किल से ही।

scarcity *स्कॅ अ: सि टि n.* state of being scarce विरलता, न्यूनता, अल्पता, दुर्लभता।

scare[1] *स्कॅअ: n.* sudden alarm अकारण भय।

scare[2] *v.t.* to terrify डराना; to drive away by frightening डराकर भगाना।

scarf *स्का:फ़ n.* a strip of fabric worn over the shoulders, round the neck or over the hair गुलूबंद, दुपट्टा।

scatter *स्कै टॅ: v.t.* to throw here and there फैलाना, छितराना; *v.i.* to go in different directions बिखरना, फैलना।

scavenger *स्कै विन् जॅ: n.* person employed to keep the streets clean by removing refuse सफ़ाई कर्मचारी, मेहतर।

scene *सीन n.* place of action घटना-स्थल; subdivision of a play नाटक का दृश्य; view दृश्य; episode घटना; display of strong emotion तमाशा, प्रदर्शन; a stage set for a performance of a play मंचसज्जा।

scenery *सी नॅ रि n.* landscape representation of a scene दृश्यभूमि; the blackcloth etc. used on the stage of a theatre मंच-सज्जा।

scenic *सी निक a.* of the stage नेपथ्य-संबंधी; picturesque सुंदर, चित्रात्मक।

scent[1] *सैन्ट n.* agreeable odour सुगंध; perfume इत्र; trail खोज; clue सुराग़।

scent[2] *v.t.* to smell सूंघना; to fill with fragrance सुगंधित करना; to discover by smelling गंध-द्वारा पता लगाना; to suspect संदेह करना।

sceptic *स्कैपॅ् टिक n.* atheist नास्तिक; one who maintains doubt or disbelief संदेहवादी।

sceptical *स्कैपॅ् टि क्ल a.* incredulous संशयात्मक।

scepticism *स्कैपॅ् टि सिज़्म n.* a disbelieving state of mind संदेहवाद, संशयात्मकता।

sceptre *सैपॅ् टॅ: n.* ornamental staff as symbol of royal power राजदंड।

schedule[1] *शैॅ ड् यूल n.* programme कार्यक्रम; time-table सारणी; table of details or appended table अनुसूची।

schedule² *v.t.* to make a list of अनुसूची बनाना।

scheme¹ *स्कीम n.* system पद्धति; plan योजना; contrivance उपाय।

scheme² *v.i.* to form a plan योजना बनाना; *v.t.* to contrive उपाय करना।

schism *सिज़्म n.* faction फूट; group resulting from faction विच्छिन्न संप्रदाय।

scholar *स्कौ ॅ लॅः n.* learned person विद्वान्; pupil शिष्य।

scholarly *स्कौ ॅ लॅः लि a.* learned विद्वान्, विद्वत्तापूर्ण।

scholarship *स्कौ ॅ लॅः शिप n.* erudition पांडित्य; allowance given to a student छात्रवृत्ति।

scholastic *स्कॅ लैस् टिक a.* pertaining to a scholar विद्वान्-संबंधी; educational शिक्षा-विषयक; academic शास्त्रीय।

school *स्कूल n.* educational institution विद्यालय, पाठशाला; branch of study शिक्षा की शाखा; group of artists, thinkers etc. with common beliefs संप्रदाय।

science *सॉइ ॲन्स n.* systematic knowledge विज्ञान।

scientific *सॉइ ॲन् टि फ़िक a.* pertaining to science वैज्ञानिक।

scientist *सॉइ ॲन् टिस्ट n.* one who is versed in science वैज्ञानिक।

scintillate *सिन् टि लेट v.i.* to sparkle चमकना।

scintillation *सिन् टि ले शॅन n.* lustre, glitter चमक।

scissors *सि ज़ॅःज़ n. pl.* a cutting instrument कैंची।

scoff¹ *स्कौफ़् n.* taunt ताना।

scoff² *v.i.* to jeer (at) उपहास करना।

scold *स्कोल्ड v.t.* to find fault with दोष निकालना; to rebuke, to reprimand फटकारना।

scooter *स्कू टॅः n.* light, motorcycle स्कूटर।

scope *स्कोप n.* sphere of action or observation क्षेत्र; opportunity for action गुंजाइश।

scorch *स्कौच v.t.* to burn or discolour (surface) with heat झुलसाना।

score¹ *स्कोः, स्कौंः n.* set of twenty एक कोड़ी (बीस); reckoning गणना; number of points made by a player in certain games खेल के अंक; reason कारण; scratch खरौंच।

score² *v.t.* to gain (points) in a game खेल में (अंक या रन) बनाना; to cross out काटना; to mark चिह्नित करना; *v.i.* to keep tally of points अंकों या रनों का हिसाब रखना।

scorer *स्कौ ॅ रॅः n.* person who keeps a record of points, goals, runs, etc, scored in a game गणक; player who scores goals, runs etc. गोल या रन बनाने वाला खिलाड़ी।

scorn¹ *स्कौःन n.* extreme contempt तिरस्कार; derision घृणा।

scorn² *v.t.* to hold in contempt तिरस्कार करना, घृणा करना।

scorpion *स्कौः प्यॅन n.* a small animal with a poisonous sting in its long tail बिच्छू।

Scot *स्कौ ॅट n.* native of Scotland स्कॉटलैंड का निवासी।

Scotch¹ *स्कौचॅ a.* of Scotland स्कॉटलैंड-संबंधी।

Scotch² *n.* people of Scotland

स्कॉटलैंड निवासी; a kind of whisky एक प्रकार की शराब।

scot-free *स्कौ ॅट् फ़्री a.* unharmed सुरक्षित, निरापद।

scoundrel *स्कॉउन् ड्रॅल n.* rogue, rascal दुष्ट।

scourge¹ *स्कॅ:ज n.* whip कोड़ा; severe affliction महान् कष्ट; calamity विपत्ति।

scourge² *v.t.* to flog कोड़े मारना; to punish severely कड़ा दंड देना।

scout¹ *स्कॉउट n.* boy scout बालचर; spy गुप्तचर।

scout² *v.i.* to act as a scout बालचर के रूप में काम करना; to act as spy गुप्तचर्या करना।

scowl¹ *स्कॉउल v.i.* to frown त्योरी चढ़ाना।

scowl² *n.* a bad-tempered look भ्रूभंग, त्योरी चढ़ी दृष्टि।

scramble¹ *स्क्रैम् ब्ल v.i.* to climb ऊपर चढ़ना; to struggle for something संघर्ष करना; *v.t.* to mix up मिला देना; to cook (eggs) beaten up with milk दूध के साथ फेंटकर (अंडे) पकाना।

scramble² *n.* scrambling संघर्ष; rough climb ऊबड़-खाबड़ चढ़ाई; disorderly proceeding अव्यवस्थित कार्यवाही।

scrap *स्क्रैप n.* rejected metal pieces रद्दी, धातु; smallest piece छोटा टुकड़ा।

scratch¹ *स्क्रैच n.* mark of injury खरोंच।

scratch² *v.t.* to mark (surface) with something sharp खुरचना, खरोंचना; to draw along घसीटना; to rub घिसना; to cancel रद्द करना; to withdraw वापस लेना; *v.i.* to use the nail or claws नाखूनों या पंजों का प्रयोग करना।

scrawl¹ *स्क्रौल v.t.* to write or draw hastily तेज़ी से लिखना या घसीटना।

scrawl² *n.* poor writing घसीट।

scream¹ *स्क्रीम v.i.* to make a sudden cry चीख़ना; *v.t.* to utter in a scream चीख़ कर कहना।

scream² *n.* shrill cry चीख़।

screen¹ *स्क्रीन n.* surface on which films are shown चित्रपट; device to shelter from light etc. परदा।

screen² *v.t.* to shelter, to hide बचाना, छिपाना; to show (film) चित्रपट पर दिखाना; to scrutinize परखना, जांचना।

screw¹ *स्क्रू n.* a metal peg पेच।

screw² *v.t.* to fasten (with a screw) पेच से कसना।

scribble¹ *स्क्रि ब्ल v.t.* to write or draw carelessly घसीट में लिखना या खींचना; *v.i.* to make meaningless marks उलटी-सीधी लकीरें खींचना।

scribble² *n.* careless writing घसीट।

script *स्क्रिप्ट n.* handwriting लिखावट; manuscript पांडुलिपि।

scripture *स्क्रिप् चॅः n.* sacred writings of a religion धर्मग्रंथ।

scroll *स्क्रोल n.* roll of paper used for writing कागज़ का खर्रा; ornamental design कटावदार डिज़ाइन।

scrutinize *स्क्रू टि नॉइज़ v.t.* to make thorough examination of सावधानी से जांच करना।

scrutiny *स्क्रू टि नि n.* thorough examination सूक्ष्म जांच; critical investigation समीक्षा; official examination of votes मतपत्रों की जांच।

scuffle[1] *स्क फ़्ल n.* confused brief fight हाथापाई।

scuffle[2] *vi.* to take part in a confused fight हाथापाई करना।

sculptor *स्कल्प् टः n.* one who carves on wood or stone पत्थर या लकड़ी पर नक़्क़ाशी करनेवाला, मूर्तिकार।

sculptural *स्कल्प् चॅ रॅल a.* pertaining to sculpture प्रतिमा-निर्माण-संबंधी।

sculpture *स्कल्प् चॅः n.* art of carving in relief on stone, wood or clay मूर्तिकला।

scythe[1] *सॉइद n.* a manual reaping implement दांती, दरांती।

scythe[2] *v.t.* to cut with scythe दरांती से काटना।

sea *सी n.* the ocean सागर; large quantity विशाल मात्रा; vast expanse दीर्घ विस्तार।

seal[1] *सील n.* impression attached to a document, significant mark मुहर।

seal[2] *n.* an aquatic flesh-eating mammal मांसाहारी समुद्री स्तनधारी जंतु।

seal[3] *v.t.* to stamp with seal मुहर लगाना; to close up tightly अच्छी तरह बंद करना; to decide तय करना।

seam[1] *सीम n.* the line of sewing where pieces of cloth are joined सीवन; line of junction of two planks संधिरेखा; thin layer परत।

seam[2] *v.t.* to join by a seam सिलाई से जोड़ना।

seamy *सी मि a.* marked with seams सीवनदार; sordid घिनौना।

search[1] *सॅःच n.* act of searching खोज; inquiry जांच।

search[2] *v.t.* to seek out खोजना; to probe जांच करना।

season[1] *सी ज़्न n.* period of the year marked by different climatic conditions ऋतु; time when something is plentiful किसी वस्तु की प्रचुरता का समय; proper time उचित समय।

season[2] *v.t.* to render mature and fit for use परिपक्व बनाना; to add flavouring to स्वादिष्ट बनाना; to make experienced अभ्यस्त बनाना।

seasonable *सी ज़ॅ नॅ ब्ल a.* opportune उचित समय पर होने वाला।

seasonal *सी ज़ॅ नॅल a.* happening only at a particular season मौसमी।

seat[1] *सीट n.* thing to sit on बैठने का आसन, गद्दी; location स्थिति, स्थान; legislative constituency निर्वाचन-क्षेत्र; buttocks चुतड़; bose आधार।

seat[2] *v.t.* to cause to sit बैठाना; to fix firmly जमाना; to provide seats बैठने का स्थान देना।

secede *सि सीड v.i.* to withdraw formally from a larger body पृथक् हो जाना।

secession *सि सै˘ शॅन n.* act of seceding अपगमन, अलगाव।

secessionist *सि सै˘ शॅ निस्ट n.* one favouring secession अलगाववादी।

seclude *सि क्लूड v.t.* to separate from society समूह से अलग करना;

to keep aloof अलग रखना।

secluded *सि क्लू डिड a.* separated from society एकांत अकेला, निर्जन।

seclusion *सि क्लू ज़ॅन n.* privacy एकांतता।

second[1] *सै˘ कॅन्ड a.* next after first दूसरा।

second[2] *n.* one who follows another अनुयायी; sixtieth part of a minute मिनट का साठवां भाग; inferior goods घटिया माल।

second[3] *v.t.* to support अनुमोदित करना।

secondary *सै˘ कॅन् डॅ रि a.* next in importance गौण; supplementary अनुपूरक।

seconder *सै˘ कॅन् डॅः n.* one who supports a resolution प्रस्ताव का अनुमोदक।

secrecy *सी क्रॅ सि n.* privacy एकांतता; concealment गुप्तता।

secret[1] *सी क्रिट a.* concealed छिपा हुआ; remote, quiet शांत।

secret[2] *n.* something kept from view or knowledge गुप्त भेद; the real source मुख्य स्रोत या कारण; something mysterious रहस्यपूर्ण वस्तु।

secretariat (e) *सैकॅ रॅ टे˘ ॲ रि ॲट n.* secretarys' department सचिवालय।

secretary *सैकॅ रि ट्रि n.* an administrative or executive officer of an organization सचिव, मंत्री।

secrete *सि क्रीट v.t.* to conceal छिपाना; to produce by secretion स्त्रावित करना।

secretion *सि क्री शॅन n.* process of secreting स्त्रवण; matter secreted स्त्राव।

secretive *सिक् रि टिव a.* habitually keeping things secret गोपनशील।

sect *सैक्ट n.* religious party or faction पंथ, संप्रदाय, मत।

sectarian *सैक् टे˘ ॲ रि ॲन a.* pertaining to a particular sect किसी विशेष मत या पंथ-संबंधी।

section *सैक् शॅन n.* division अनुभाग, भाग; subdivision of a book अनुच्छेद; part of a whole खंड, अंश।

sector *सैक् टॅः n.* field of business activity व्यावसायिक क्षेत्र; military area of operation सैन्य कार्यवाही का क्षेत्र।

secure[1] *सि क्युॲः a.* safe सुरक्षित; firmly fixed सुदृढ़।

secure[2] *v.t.* to free from anxiety सुरक्षित करना; to obtain प्राप्त करना; to make strong दृढ़ करना।

security *सि क्युॲ रि टि n.* safety सुरक्षा; undertaking to obtain release of a prisoner ज़मानत; thing pledged as guarantee प्रतिभूति।

sedan *सि डैन n.* a covered chair carried by two men पालकी।

sedate[1] *सि डेट a.* serious गंभीर; calm शांत।

sedate[2] *v.t.* to soothe by drugs दवा से आराम पहुंचाना।

sedative[1] *सै˘ डॅ टिव a.* having a soothing effect शामक।

sedative[2] *n.* sedative drug शामक औषध।

sedentary *सै˘ डॅन् टॅ रि a.* sitting आसीन, बैठा हुआ; accustomed to sitting बैठे रहने का आदी।

sediment *सै˘ डि मॅन्ट n.* matter

which settles at the bottom of a liquid तलछट।

sedition *सि डि शॅन n.* conduct or speech tending to breach of public piece विद्रोह, विप्लव।

seditious *सि डि शॅस a.* inclined to sedition विप्लवकारी।

seduce *सि ड्यूस n.* to lead astray बहकाना; to tempt लुभाना; to attract आकर्षित करना।

seduction *सि डक् शॅन n.* act of seducing सतीत्व-हरण; tempting to an evil action दुष्प्रेरणा।

seductive *सि डक् टिव a.* alluring लुभावना।

see *सी v.t.* to perceive देखना; to be cognizant of पर ध्यान देना; to find out मालूम करना, ढूंढना; to make sure आश्वस्त करना; to visit भेंट करना; to consult परामर्श करना; to reflect विचार करना; to accompany के साथ जाना; *v.i.* to have the power of sight दृष्टि रखना।

seed[1] सीड *n.* plant's element of life बीज; prime cause मूल कारण; semen वीर्य।

seed[2] *v.t.* to sow with seed बोना; *v.i.* to produce seed बीज उगाना।

seek *सीक v.t. (p.t. & p.p. sought)* to ask for मांगना; to try प्रयास करना; *v.i.* to search खोज करना।

seem *सीम v.i.* to appear जान पड़ना; to look दिखाई पड़ना।

seemly *सीम् ली a.* proper, befitting उपयुक्त, उचित।

seep *सीप v.i.* to tickle through slowly रिसना।

seer *सिअॅः n.* prophet सिद्धपुरुष, दृष्टा।

seethe *सीद v.i.* to boil उबलना; to be agitated उत्तेजित होना।

segment[1] *सै ॅग् मॅन्ट n.* part cut off from something भाग, खंड।

segment[2] *v.t.* to divide into segments विभाजित करना; *v.i.* to be divided into segments विभक्त होना।

segregate *सैगॅ रि गेट v.t.* to isolate पृथक् करना।

segregation *सैगॅ रि गे शॅन n.* separation अलगाव, वियोग।

seismic *सॉइज़् मिक a.* pertaining to earthquakes भूकंप-संबंधी।

seize *सीज़ v.t.* to take possession of by force छीनना; to grasp पकड़ना।

seizure *सीज़ॅः n.* act of seizing पकड़; possession by force ज़ब्ती।

seldom *सैलॅ डॅम adv.* not often यदा-कदा, कभी-कभार।

select[1] *सि लैक्ॅट v.t.* to choose as the best चुनना।

select[2] *a.* choice चुनिंदा; excellent उत्कृष्ट।

selection *सि लैकॅ शॅन n.* act of selecting चयन।

selective *सि ल क् टिव a.* capable of selection चयन-योग्य।

self *सैल्फ़ n. (pl. selves)* person's own individuality व्यक्तित्व; one's own interest स्वार्थ; sameness एकता।

selfish *सै ॅल् फ़िश a.* devoted to personal profit स्वार्थी।

selfless *सै ॅल्फ़ लिस a.* unselfish स्वार्थरहित।

sell *सै ॅल v.t. (p.t. & p.p. sold)* to dispose of in exchange for money बेचना; to deal in (की) दुकान

करना; *v.i.* to be sold बिकना।

seller *सैॅ लॅः n.* one who sells विक्रेता; something that is sold बिकने वाली वस्तु।

semblance *सैम्ँ ब्लॅन्स n.* likeness सादृश्य; false appearance दिखावा।

semen *सी मैनॅ n.* male generative fluid of animals वीर्य, शुक्र।

semester *सि मैॅस् टॅः n.* a half year term अर्द्धवार्षिक सत्र।

seminal *सी मि न्ल a.* of semen वीर्य-संबधी।

seminar *सैॅ मि नाः n.* meeting for discussion गोष्ठी।

senate *सैॅ निट n.* legislative body प्रबंधकारिणी समिति; governing body of a university विश्वविद्यालय की प्रशासनिक समिति।

senator *सैॅ नॅ टॅः n.* member of a senate समिति-सदस्य।

senatorial[1] *सैॅ नॅ टौ रि ॲल a.* of a senate or senator प्रशासनिक समितीय अथवा समिति-सदस्यीय।

senatorial[2] *a.* pertaining to senate प्रशासनिक समिति-संबंधी।

send *सेन्ड v.t.* to cause to go भेजना; to dispatch प्रेषित करना।

senile *सी नॉइल a.* pertaining to old age वृद्धावस्था-संबंधी।

senility *सि नि लि टि n.* weakness in old age बुढ़ापे की दुर्बलता।

senior[1] *सी न्यॅः a.* superior in age वयोवृद्ध; of a higher rank बड़े पद का।

senior[2] *n.* superior उच्च व्यक्ति; elder person वयोवृद्ध व्यक्ति।

seniority *सी नि औॅ रि टि n.* condition of being senior वरीयता।

sensation *सैन्ँ से शॅन n.* feeling अनुभूति; excitement उत्तेजना, सनसनी; strong impression संवेदना।

sensational *सैन्ँ से शॅ नॅल a.* pertaining to the sense of perception संवेदनात्मक; producing excited interest सनसनीख़ेज़।

sense[1] *सैन्ॅस n.* faculty of perception इंद्रिय; mental alertness चेतना; consciousness होश; meaning अर्थ; judgment विवेक, समझ।

sense[2] *v.t.* to perceive, to understand अनुभव करना, समझना।

senseless *सैॅन्स् लिस a.* foolish मूर्ख, मूर्खतापूर्ण; unconscious बेहोश।

sensibility *सैॅन् सि बि लि टि n.* sensitiveness संवेदनशीलता।

sensible *सैन्ँ सि ब्ल a.* reasonable, wise समझदार; aware जागरूक, अवगत; perceptible by the senses इंद्रिय-ग्राह्य।

sensitive *सैन्ँ सि टिव a.* quick to receive impressions संवेदनशील; easily offended तुनुकमिज़ाज; emotional भावुक; easily affected नाजुक; responsive to slight changes सूक्ष्मग्राही।

sensual *सैन्ँ स्यु ॲल a.* lustful कामुक, कामुकतापूर्ण।

sensualist *सैन्ँ स्यु ॲ लिस्ट n.* a lustful person भोगवादी, कामी।

sensuality *सैन्ँ स्यु ऐ लि टि n.* indulgence of sensual pleasures कामुकता।

sensuous *सैन्ँ स्यु ॲस a.* appealing to the senses इंद्रिय-संबंधी।

sentence[1] *सैन्ँ टॅन्स n.* group of words giving complete meaning वाक्य; penalty imposed by the court दंड।

sentence² *v.t.* to pass sentence on दंड देना।

sentience *सैन् शॅन्स n.* quality of being sentient संवेदन, चेतना।

sentient *सैन् शॅन्ट a.* capable of feeling संवेदनशील।

sentiment *सैन् टि मॅन्ट n.* tendency to be moved by feeling भावुकता; emotion भाव; opinion मत, विचार।

sentimental *सैन् टि मैन् ट्ल a.* having a tendency to be moved by feeling भावुक; full of emotion भावुकतापूर्ण।

sentinel *सैन् टि न्ल n.* sentry संतरी, पहरेदार।

sentry *सैन् ट्रि n.* soldier on watch संतरी।

separable *सै ॅ पॅ रॅ ब्ल a.* capable of being separated वियोज्य, पृथक्करणीय।

separate¹ *सै ॅ पॅ रेट v.t.* to divide अलग करना; to put apart हटाना; *v.i.* to withdraw अलग होना, हटना।

separate² *सै ॅ पॅ रिट a.* divided विभक्त; existing apart अलग।

separation *सै ॅ पॅ रे शॅन n.* disconnection पृथक्करण; being disconnected पृथक्भवन; division विभाजन।

sepsis *सैप् सिस n.* pus forming bacteria पूर्ति, पूतिता।

September *सॅप् टै ॅम् बॅः n.* ninth month of the year सितंबर।

septic *सैप् टिक a.* caused by sepsis पूतिक, विषाक्त।

sepulchre *सै ॅ पॅल् कॅः n.* tomb समाधि, मक़बरा।

sepulture *सै ॅ पॅल् चॅः n.* burial दफ़न।

sequel *सी क्वॅल n.* consequence परिणाम; continuation, remaining part शेष।

sequence *सी क्वॅन्स n.* succession अनुक्रम; successive order क्रम।

sequester *सि क्वैस् टॅः v.t.* to seclude अलग करना।

serene *सि रीन a.* calm, tranquil शांत; unclouded मेघरहित।

serenity *सि रै ॅ नि टि n.* quality of being serene शांति।

serf *सॅःफ n.* a land-worker, कृषि-मज़दूर, land slave कृषि दास।

serge *सॅःज n.* a strong woollen cloth सर्ज, एक प्रकार का कपड़ा।

sergeant *साः जॅन्ट n.* non-commissioned army-officer सारजेंट।

serial¹ *सिॲ रि ॲल a.* belonging to a series क्रमिक, आनुक्रमिक; published in instalments धारावाहिक।

serial² *n.* periodical publication or presentation धारावाहिक।

series *सिॲ रीज़ n. (sing. & pl.)* sequence क्रम अनुक्रम; (maths.) a set of numbers forming a progression माला, श्रेणी, शृंखला।

serious *सिॲ रि ॲस a.* sincere गंभीर; of importance महत्वूपर्ण; causing concern चिंताजनक; thoughtful विचारशील।

sermon *सॅः मॅन n.* moral or religious discourse नीतिवचन, धर्मोपदेश।

sermonize *सॅ : मॅ नॉइज़ v.i.* to talk like a preacher धर्मोपदेशक होना; *v.t.* to preach धार्मिक शिक्षा देना।

serpent *सॅः पॅन्ट n.* snake सर्प; a treacherous person धूर्त; धोखेबाज़ व्यक्ति।

serpentine *सॅः पॅन् टॉइन n.* winding like a serpent सर्पिल; sly धूर्त, चालाक।

servant *सॅः वॅन्ट n.* one who serves सेवक; employee कर्मचारी।

serve[1] *सॅःव v.t.* to work for (की) नौकरी करना; to perform duties for (की) सेवा करना; to place (food, etc.) on the table (भोजन आदि) परोसना; to be satisfactory for के लिए उपयुक्त होना; to undergo भुगतना; to deliver (a summons, etc.) (समन) तामील करना; to meet the needs of (की) आवश्यकता पूरी करना; *v.i.* to put the ball into play सर्विस करना।

serve[2] *n.* act of serving ball सर्विस।

service[1] *सॅः विस n.* being a servant नौकरी; act of service सेवा; *(pl.)* armed forces सेना; help सहायता; system, organization व्यवस्था; attendance ख़िदमत, टहल; use प्रयोग; maintenance of vehicle रख-रखाव; a set of dishes, cups, etc. बरतन; (tennis) serving सर्विस; legal notification तामील; serving of food खाना परोसने की क्रिया।

service[2] *v.t.* to overhaul पूरी तरह से जांच करके सुधारना।

serviceable *सॅः वि सॅ ब्ल a.* in working order चालू हालत में; durable टिकाऊ।

servile *सॅः वॉइल a.* slavish दासतापूर्ण; cringing लल्लो-चप्पो करनेवाला, खुशामदी।

servility *सॅः वि लि टि n.* servile behaviour or attitude दासता, जी-हुजूरी।

session *सैˇ शॅन n.* meeting of court न्यायालय की बैठक; meeting of Parliament संसद-सत्र; academic term शिक्षण-सत्र।

set[1] *(-tt-) v.t.* to put रखना; to fix बैठाना, जमाना; to apply लगाना; to make ready तैयार करना; to establish स्थापित करना; to allot नियत करना; to arrange (a table) व्यवस्थित करना; to start चालू करना; to settle निश्चित करना; *v.i.* to sink डूबना, छिपना; to become firm कड़ा होना, जमना।

set[2] *a.* fixed स्थिर; prescribed निर्धारित; conventional रूढ़िगत; formal औपचारिक।

set[3] *n.* a group of people with common qualities एक-जैसे लोगों का समूह, गुट; a group of things श्रेणी; receiver for radio or television सैट।

settle *सैˇ ट्ल v.i.* to come to rest बैठना; to subside नीचे जाना, बैठना; to take up residence बसना; *v.t.* to arrange व्यवस्थित करना; to decide तय करना; to pay अदा करना।

settlement *सैˇ ट्ल् मॅन्ट n.* act of settling निपटारा; agreement समझौता; payment भुगतान; decision निर्णय; determination निर्धारण; colony उपनिवेश; subsidence धंसन।

settler *सैˇट् लॅः n.* colonist उपनिवेशी।

seven[1] *सैˇ व्न n.* the number next to six सात की संख्या (7)।

seven[2] *a.* one more than six सात।

seventeen *सैˇ व्न् टीन n., a.* (the number) next after sixteen सत्रह (17)।

seventeenth *सै˘ वॅनॅ टीन्थ a.* next after the 16th सत्रहवां।
seventh *सै˘ वृन्थ a.* next after the 6th सातवां।
seventieth *सै˘ वन् टीथ a.* next after the 69th सत्तरवां।
seventy *सै˘ वृन् टि n., a.* (the number) next after 69 सत्तर (70)।
sever *सै˘ वॅः v.t.* to cut off काट देना; to break off तोड़ देना; *v.i.* to come apart टूटना, अलग होना।
several *सै˘ वॅ रॅल a.* a few, some कई; separate अलग; individual व्यक्तिगत; various विभिन्न; different भिन्न।
severance *सै˘ वॅ रॅन्स n.* severing पृथक्ता; disconnection विच्छेद।
severe *सि विअॅः a.* strict कड़ा; hard to do कठिन; rigorous कठोर; harsh सख़्त, कठोर।
severity *सि वै˘ रि टि n.* quality of being severe कठोरता, कठिनता।
sew *सा v.t. (p.t. sewed सोड; p.p.* sewn सोन) to fasten with stitches टांकना, सिलना; to make (garment) by stitching (कपड़ा) सिलना; *v.i.* to work with needle सिलाई करना।
sewage *स्यू इज n.* refuse conveyed in sewer गंदा पानी, मलजल।
sewer *स्यु अॅः n.* underground drain for refuse मलप्रणाल, नाला।
sewerage *स्यु अॅ रिज n.* system of drains मलव्यवस्था।
sex *सैक्स n.* state of being male or female लिंग; sexual activity यौन-क्रिया।
sexual *सैक् स्यु अॅल a.* pertaining to sex लैंगिक।
sexuality *सैक् स्यु ऐ लि टि n.* the quality of being sexual लैंगिकता; sexual desire काम-वासना।
sexy *सै˘क् सि n.* inclined to sexual indulgence कामुक; much concerned with sexuality कामोत्तेजक।
shabby *शै बि a.* worn and torn फटा-पुराना, जीर्ण-शीर्ण; poorly dressed फटेहाल; disgraceful घृणित, घिनौना।
shackle[1] *शै कल n.* metal ring for prisoner's wrist or ankle बेड़ी।
shackle[2] *v.t.* to fasten with shackles बेड़ी डालना।
shade[1] *शेड n.* slight darkness छाया; the darker part of a picture चित्र का काला भाग; a slight amount थोड़ी मात्रा; covering for a lamp दीपक का ढकना; ghost भूत, प्रेत।
shade[2] *v.t.* to shield from light ओट में करना; to mark(a picture) with different degrees of shade छायित करना।
shadow[1] *शै डो n.* dark projection of something छाया, परछाईं; slight trace आभास; indistinct image अस्पष्ट बिंब; gloom विषाद; inseparable companion अविभाज्य साथी।
shadow[2] *v.t.* to cast shadow over आच्छादित करना; to follow closely के पीछे लगा रहना।
shadowy *शै डो इ a.* having shadow or shade छायादार; like a shadow छायावत्।
shaft *शाफ़्ट n.* handle of a tool or weapon दस्ता, मूठ; a ray of light किरण; pole कड़ी; arrow तीर।
shake[1] *शेक v.i. (p.t. shook शुक, p.p.*

shaken शेकन) to move to and fro or up and down हिलना; to shudder कांपना; *v.t.* to cause to move हिलाना; to dismay भयभीत करना।

shake² *n.* act of shaking झटका; tremor कंपन।

shaky *शे कि* *a.* unsteady अस्थिर, कंपायमान; unreliable अविश्वसनीय।

shallow *शैलो* *a.* not deep उथला; superficial सतही।

sham¹ *शैम (-mm-) v.i.* to pretend बहाना करना।

sham² *n.* pretence दिखावा, बहाना।

sham³ *a.* pretended दिखावटी।

shame¹ *शेम* *n.* feeling of guilt शरम, हया; public disgrace कलंक।

shame² *v.t.* to cause to feel shame लज्जित करना।

shameful *शेम् फुल* *a.* disgraceful लज्जाजनक।

shameless *शेम् लिस* *a.* with no sense of shame निर्लज्ज।

shampoo¹ *शैम् पू* *n.* a lotion for washing hair केशमार्जक; act of washing hair with shampoo केशामार्जन।

shampoo² *v.t.* to wash with shampoo शैंपू से धोना।

shanty *शैन् टि* *a.* roughly built hut झोपड़ी, कुटी।

shape¹ *शेप* *n.* outward form आकार; a pattern नमूना; condition दशा।

shape² *v.t.* to form आकार देना, बनाना; *v.i.* to develop विकसित होना।

shapely *शेप् लि* *a.* of pleasing shape सुघड़, सुंदर।

share¹ *शे ॅ अ:* *n.* portion हिस्सा, भाग; contribution योगदान; unit of ownership in a public company शेयर।

share² *v.t.* to distribute बांटना; to have in common में सहभागी होना।

share³ *n.* blade of a plough फाल।

shark *शा:क* *n.* a large, ferocious fish हांगर, सोर; a swindler ठग, धूर्त।

sharp¹ *शा:प* *a.* able to cut पैना; keen तेज़; pointed नुकीला; abrupt, sudden तीव्र; pungent चरपरा; clever चतुर; crafty चालाक; shrill तीखा; brisk फुरतीला; steep खड़ा।

sharp² *adv.* promptly ठीक समय से।

sharpen *शा: पॅन* *v.t.* to make sharp तेज़ करना; to become sharp तेज़ होना।

sharpener *शा: पॅ नॅ:* *n.* something that sharpens धार तेज़ करने का साधन।

sharper *शा: पॅ:* *n.* a swindler ठग, बेईमान।

shatter *शै टॅ:* *v.t.* to break in pieces चूर-चूर कर देना; to destroy नष्ट करना; *v.i.* to be damaged नष्ट होना।

shave¹ *शेव* *v.t.* to cut close मूंडना, हजामत बनाना; to pare away काटना; *v.i.* to remove hair with a razor हजामत करना।

shave² *n.* act of shaving or being shaved हजामत।

shawl *शौल* *n.* piece of fabric to cover woman's shoulders or to wrap a body शॉल।

she *शी* *pron.* third person singular feminine pronoun वह (स्त्री)।

sheaf *शीफ़* *n. (pl. sheaves शीव्ज़)* a bundle of corn पूला, पूली।

shear *शिअ:* *v.t.* to cut the wool off (a sheep) (भेड) मूंड़ना।

shears *शिअ:ज़* *n. pl.* large pair of scissors कैंचा।

shed[1] *शैड* *(-dd-) v.t.* to let fall गिरा देना; to cause to flow बहाना।

shed[2] *n.* roofed shelter सायबान, छप्पर।

sheep *शीप* *n. (pl. sheep)* a grass-eating animal भेड़।

sheepish *शी पिश* *a.* shy संकोची; timid दब्बू; stupid भौंदू।

sheer *शिअ:* *a.* complete, thorough निरा, कोरा; absolute परिपूर्ण; very thin महीन।

sheet[1] *शीट* *n.* a large piece of cloth or any thin material चादर; wide expanse विस्तार।

sheet[2] *v.t.* to cover with a sheet (पर) चादर डालना।

shelf *शैल्फ़* *n. (pl. shelves शैल्वॅज)* a horizontal board fixed to a wall टांड, ताक।

shell[1] *शै˘ल* *n.* hard outer case खोल; husk छिलका; explosive projectile गोला।

shell[2] *v.t.* to take shell from छीलना; to take out of shell छीलकर निकालना; to fire at with shells (पर) गोले बरसाना।

shelter[1] *शैल्ॅ टॅ:* *n.* protection बचाव, पनाह; refuge शरणस्थल।

shelter[2] *v.t.* to give protection to पनाह देना; *v.i.* to take shelter पनाह लेना।

shelve *शैल्व* *v.t.* to put on shelf ताक़ पर रखना; to postpone dealing with टालना; to cease to employ नौकरी से हटा देना।

shepherd *शै ˘ पॅ:ड* *n.* man who tends sheep गड़ेरिया।

shield[1] *शील्ड* *n.* a piece of armour carried on arm ढाल; protective plate कवच; any protective device रक्षा का साधन।

shield[2] *v.t.* to protect, to save बचाना, रक्षा करना।

shift[1] *शिफ़्ट* *v.t.* to cause to move हटाना; to transfer स्थानांतरित करना; *v.i.* to move हटना; to be transferred स्थानांतरित होना।

shift[2] *n.* change परिवर्तन; a group of workmen who start work as another group finishes पाली; time of the working of this group पाली की अवधि; dodge चकमा।

shifty *शिफ़् टि* *a.* deceitful धोखेबाज़; evasive बहानेबाज़।

shilling *शि लिङ्ग* *n.* a former British coin शिलिंग।

shilly-shally[1] *शि लि-शै लि* *v.i.* to waver हिचकिचाना।

shilly-shally[2] *n.* wavering, indecision हिचकिचाहट, अनिर्णय।

shin *शिन* *n.* front of lower leg टांग के नीचे का अगला भाग।

shine[1] *शॉइन* *v.i. (p.t. & p.p. shone शॉनॅ)* to give out light चमकना।

shine[2] *n.* brightness चमक।

shiny *शॉइ नि* *a.* bright, glossy चमकदार।

ship[1] *शिप* *n.* a large sea-going vessel जहाज़।

ship[2] *(-pp-) v.t.* to put on, or send by ship जहाज़ पर लादना या भेजना; *v.i.* to embark जहाज़ पर चढ़ना; to take service in ship जहाज़ पर

नौकरी करना।

shipment *शिप् मॅन्ट n.* act of shipping जहाज़ पर लदान; quantity of goods shipped नौभार।

shire *शॉइअॅ: n.* country प्रांत।

shirk *शॅ:क v.t.* to avoid (से) जी चुराना।

shirker *शॅ: कॅ: n.* one who avoids work कामचोर।

shirt *शॅ:ट n.* garment for upper part of body कमीज़।

shiver *शि वॅ: v.i.* to tremble कांपना।

shoal[1] *शोल n.* a large number of fish swimming together मछलियों का झुंड।

shoal[2] *n.* a shallow place in the sea समुद्र में उथला स्थान।

shock[1] *शौकॅ n.* violent impact झटका; emotional disturbance सदमा; collision टक्कर; effect of electric current on nerves बिजली का झटका; nervous weakness दहशत।

shock[2] *v.t.* to horrify भयभीत करना; to disgust (में) घृणा-भाव उत्पन्न करना; to cause shock to (में) दहशत उत्पन्न करना।

shoe[1] *शू n.* an outer covering for the foot जूता; metal rim put on horse's hoof नाल; metal tip शाम।

shoe[2] *v.t.* to provide with shoes जूते पहनाना, नाल लगाना।

shoot[1] *शूट v.t.* to kill with a missile गोली से मारना; to send (missile) (गोली) छोड़ना या दागना; *v.i.* to sprout अंकुरना; to photograph फ़ोटो लेना।

shoot[2] *n.* a young branch टहनी; shooting competition अस्त्र प्रतियोगिता; hunting expedition शिकार।

shop[1] *शौपॅ n.* place where goods are sold दुकान।

shop[2] *(-pp-) v.i.* to visit shops to buy ख़रीददारी करना।

shore *शौ: n.* coast समुद्रतट।

short[1] *शौ:ट a.* not long छोटा; not tall नाटा; not enough अपर्याप्त कम; brief अल्पकालीन।

short[2] *adv.* abruptly अचानक; not far enough पास ही।

shortage *शौ: टिज n.* lack अभाव, कमी।

shortcoming *शौ:ट् कॅ मिङ्ग n.* failure, defect दोष, अवगुण।

shorten *शौ:ट्न v.t.* to make short छोटा या कम करना; to become short कम या छोटा होना।

shortly *शौ:ट् लि adv.* soon शीघ्र ही।

shorts *शौ:ट्स n. pl.* short trousers निकर, हाफ़पैन्ट।

shot *शौ ॅट n.* act of shooting मार; sound made by a fire-arm बंदूक की आवाज़; range पहुंच; marksman निशानेबाज; photograph फ़ोटो।

shoulder[1] *शोल् डॅ: n.* part of the body next to head कंधा।

shoulder[2] *v.t.* to undertake (का) दायित्व लेना; to take on one's shoulders कंधों पर लेना।

shout[1] *शॉउट n.* loud cry चीख़, चिल्लाहट।

shout[2] *v.i.* to cry in a loud voice चिल्लाना, चीख़ना; *v.t.* to say loudly चिल्लाकर कहना।

shove[1] *शव v.t.* to push धकेलना।

shove[2] *n.* a strong push ठेला, धक्का।

shovel[1] *श वृल n.* a spade-like instrument बेलचा।

shovel[2] *(-ll-) v.t.* to move with a shovel बेलचे से हटाना।

show[1] शो *v.t. (p.t. showed, p.p.shown)* to expose to view दिखाना; to display प्रदर्शित करना; to explain समझाना; to prove सिद्ध करना।

show[2] *n.* display प्रदर्शन; exhibition प्रदर्शनी; spectacle दृश्य; entertainment तमाशा; ostentation तड़क-भड़क; pretence दिखावा, बहाना।

shower[1] *शॉउ अॅः n.* short fall of rain बौछार; outpouring झड़ी; a. kind of bath फुहारा-स्नान।

shower[2] *v.t.* to bestow liberally बरसाना; *v.i.* to take bath in shower फुहारा-स्नान करना।

shrew *श्रू n.* an animal like a mouse छछूंदर; a bad tempered woman कर्कशा, लड़ाकी स्त्री।

shrewd *श्रूड a.* intelligent बुद्धिमान, समझदार; crafty चालाक।

shriek[1] *श्रीक n.* a shrill cry चीख़।

shriek[2] *v.i.* to scream चीख़ना; *v.t.* to utter in a scream चीख़कर कहना।

shrill *श्रिल a.* sharp in tone तेज़, तीक्ष्ण (आवाज़)।

shrine *श्रॉइन n.* holy place, place of worship पवित्र स्थान, मंदिर।

shrink *श्रिङ्क v.i. (p.t. shrank, p.p.shrunk)* to become smaller सिकुड़ना; to draw back पीछे हटना; *v.t.* to make smaller सिकोड़ना।

shrinkage *श्रिङ् किज n.* process of shrinking सिकुड़न।

shroud[1] *श्रॉउड n.* cloth in which a dead body is wrapped कफ़न; a covering आवरण, परदा।

shroud[2] *v.t.* to cover, to hide ढकना, छिपाना।

shrub *श्रब n.* a bushy plant झाड़ी।

shrug[1] *श्रग (-gg-) v.t.* to raise (shoulders) as sign of indifference (कंधे) उचकाना; *v.i.* to raise shoulders कंधे उचकाना।

shrug[2] *n.* shrugging कंधे उचकाने की क्रिया।

shudder[1] *श डॅः v.i.* to tremble with horror कांप उठना।

shudder[2] *n.* shuddering कंपकंपी।

shuffle[1] *श फ़्ल v.i.* to move feet without lifting them पैर घसीटना; to act evasively टाल-मटोल करना; *v.t.* to mix (cards) (पत्ते) फेंटना; to mingle मिलाना; to evade टालना।

shuffle[2] *n.* shuffling घसीटन; change फेर-बदल; mixing मिश्रण।

shun *शन (-nn-) v.t.* to avoid (से) बचना; to keep away from (से) दूर रहना।

shunt *शन्ट v.t.* to push aside अलग धकेलना; to divert दूसरी ओर मोड़ना; to move (train) to another line (गाड़ी को) दूसरी पटरी पर हटाना।

shut *शट (-tt-) v.t.* to close बंद करना; *v.i.* to be closed बंद होना।

shutter *श टॅः n.* movable window screen झिलमिली; device controlling entry of light to the lens of a camera कैमरा-कपाट।

shuttle[1] *श ट्ल n.* a device used to pass thread of weft through the warp ढरकी, भरनी; holder of the lower thread in a sewing machine शटल; train running to and fro over short distance शटल गाड़ी।

shuttle² *v.t., v.i.* to move backwards and forwards like a shuttle आगे-पीछे, इधर-उधर चलना-फिरना या चलाना-फिराना।

shuttlecock *श ट्ल् कौकॅ n.* article used as a ball in badminton चिड़िया।

shy¹ *शॉइ n. (shyer, shyest)* bashful संकोची, लज्जालु; (of animals) easily scared बिदकने या भड़कने वाले (पशु); reluctant अनिच्छुक।

shy² *v.i.* to start back in fear बिदकना, भड़कना।

sick *सिक a.* inclined to vomit मिचलीग्रस्त; not well or healthy अस्वस्थ; wearied थका हुआ, तंग आया हुआ।

sickle *सि क्ल n.* reaping hook हंसिया, दरांती।

sickly *सिक् लि a.* unhealthy अस्वस्थ, रुग्ण।

sickness *सिक् निस n.* illness बीमारी; vomiting मचली।

side¹ *सॉइड n.* surface सतह; part of body right or left पार्श्व; region क्षेत्र; aspect पहलू; party पक्ष; faction गुट; दल; extremity सिरा; direction दिशा।

side² *v.i.* to take up cause (of) पक्ष लेना।

siege *सीज n.* besieging घेराबंदी।

siesta *सि ऐसॅ टॅ n.* short sleep after midday meal दोपहर की झपकी।

sieve¹ *सीव n.* device for sifting छलनी।

sieve² *v.t.* to sift, to strain छानना।

sift *सिफ़्ट v.t.* to pass through a sieve छानना; to examine closely बारीकी से जांच करना।

sigh¹ *सॉइ n.* long audible breath आह।

sigh² *v.i.* to heave a sigh आह भरना; *v.t.* to utter with a sigh आह भरकर कहना।

sight¹ *सॉइट n.* faculty of seeing दृष्टि; seeing दर्शन; thing seen दृश्य; *(pl.)* places of interest दर्शनीय स्थान; range of vision दृष्टि-क्षेत्र।

sight² *v.t.* to catch sight of देखना, दिखाई पड़ना।

sightly *सॉइट् लि a.* pleasant to look at रमणीय, सुंदर।

sign¹ *सॉइन n.* gesture संकेत; mark चिह्न, निशान; symbol प्रतीक।

sign² *v.t.* to put signature on (पर) हस्ताक्षर करना; *v.i.* to make gesture संकेत करना।

signal¹ *सिग् नॅल n.* token, sign संकेत।

signal² *a.* remarkable उल्लेखनीय।

signal³ *(-ll-) v.t.* to make signals to (को) संकेत करना; *v.i.* to send information by signals संकेत का प्रयोग करना।

signatory *सिग् नॅ टॅ रि n.* one who signs a document हस्ताक्षरकर्त्ता।

signature *सिग् नॅ चॅः n.* person's name written by himself हस्ताक्षर।

significance *सिग् नि फ़ि कॅन्स n.* importance महत्व।

significant *सिग् नि फ़ि कॅन्ट a.* meaningful अर्थपूर्ण; important महत्वपूर्ण।

signification *सिग् नि फ़ि के शॅन n.* meaning अर्थ, तात्पर्य।

signify *सिग् नि फ़ॉइ v.t. (p.t. signified)* to mean अर्थ रखना; to indicate द्योतित करना; to imply तात्पर्य रखना।

silence[1] *सॉइ लॅन्स n.* absence of noise शांति; lack of speech मौन।

silence[2] *v.t.* to make silent चुप करना; to repress दबाना, दमन करना।

silencer *सॉइ लॅन् सॅ: n.* device to reduce noise of engine exhaust etc. साइलैंसर।

silent *सॉइ लॅन्ट a.* making no sound शांत; not pronounced अनुच्चरित।

silhouette *सि ल्यु ऐ ॅट n.* outline of an object seen against light पार्श्व छायाचित्र।

silk *सिल्क n.* fibre made by silkworms रेशम।

silken *सिल् कॅन a.* made of silk रेशमी; like silk रेशम-जैसा; soft कोमल।

silky *सिल् कि a.* like silk रेशम-जैसा; soft कोमल; smooth चिकना।

silly *सि लि a.* foolish, stupid मूर्ख; indicating folly मूर्खतापूर्ण।

silt[1] *सिल्ट n.* fine sediment deposited by water रेग, गाद।

silt[2] *v.t.* to fill with silt रेगयुक्त करना; to be choked with silt रेग से अवरूद्ध हो जाना।

silver *सिल् वॅ: n.* white precious metal चांदी; silverware चांदी का सामान; silver-coins चांदी के सिक्के।

silver[2] *a.* made of silver चांदी से बना; of the colour of silver श्वेत, चांदी जैसा; bright चमकदार।

silver[3] *v.t.* to coat with silver (पर) चांदी चढ़ाना।

similar *सि मि लॅ: a.* of the same kind सदृश, तुल्य।

similarity *सि मि लै रि टि n.* likeness समानता; resemblance समरूपता।

simile *सि मि लि n.* a figure of speech involving comparison between two things उपमा।

similitude *सि मि लि ट्यूड n.* likeness समानता; comparison तुलना।

simmer *सि मॅ: v.i.* to boil gently खदकना; to be in a state of suppressed anger अंदर-अंदर उबलना, नाराज़ होना।

simple *सिम् पल a.* plain सादा; not complicated सरल; mere निरा, खालिस; guileless सीधा-सादा; stupid मूर्ख; ordinary सामान्य।

simpleton *सिम् पल् टॅन n.* foolish person बुद्धू, भोंदू।

simplicity *सिम् प्लि सि टि n.* simpleness सादगी; artlessness निष्कपटता।

simplification *सिम् प्लि फ़ि के शॅन n.* act of simplifying सरलीकरण।

simplify *सिम् प्लि फ़ॉइ v.t.* to make simple सरल बनाना।

simultaneous *सि मल् टे न्यॅस a.* happening at the same time समकालिक।

sin[1] *सिन n.* violation of moral or divine law पाप-कर्म।

sin[2] *(-nn-) v.i.* to commit sin पाप

करना।

since[1] *सिन्स prep.* after से, के बाद।

since[2] *conj.* from the time when के बाद से; because क्योंकि।

since[3] *adv.* from then till now तब से अब तक; ago पहले।

sincere *सिन् सिअॅ: a.* honest ईमानदार; genuine सच्चा; unaffected अकृत्रिम; straight-forward निष्कपट।

sincerity *सिन् सैˇ रि टि n.* honesty सच्चाई ईमानदारी; quality of being sincere निष्कपटता।

sinful *सिन् फुल a.* wicked पापी; tending to sin पापमय।

sing *सिङ्ग v.i.* to utter musical sounds गाना; *v.t.* to utter musically गाकर सुनाना।

singe[1] *सिन्ज v.t.* to burn surface of झुलसाना।

singe[2] *n.* a slight burn झुलसन।

singer *सिङ् गॅ: n.* one who sings गायक।

single[1] *सिङ् ग्ल a.* only one केवल एक; unmarried अविवाहित; for one person only एक व्यक्ति-हेतु; for a journey in one direction एक ओर की यात्रा-हेतु।

single[2] *n.* a single ticket एकतरफ़ा टिकट; a single run at cricket एक रन; *(pl.)* match between two players only इकहरा मैच।

single[3] *v.t.* (with 'out') to pick चुनना, छांटना।

singular *सिङ् ग्यु लॅ: a.* remarkable अद्वितीय, उल्लेखनीय; unusual असाधारण; (gram.) denoting one person or thing एकवचन।

singularity *सिङ् ग्यु लै रि टि n.* strangeness अनोखापन।

singularly *सिङ् ग्यु लॅ: लि adv.* peculiarly, strangely अनोखे ढंग से।

sinister *सि निस् टॅ: a.* ominous अशुभ, अनिष्टकारी; threatening भयावह; unlucky दुर्भाग्यपूर्ण।

sink[1] *सिङ्क v.i.* (sank, sunk) to be submerged डूबना; to go down below the horizon अस्त होना, छिपना; to decline in value मूल्य में कमी आना; *v.t.* to cause to sink डुबोना; to make by digging खोदकर बनाना (कुआं, आदि)।

sink[2] *n.* a basin in kitchen चहबच्चा।

sinner *सि नॅ: n.* one who sins पापी।

sinuous *सि न्यु अॅस a.* winding टेढ़ा-मेढ़ा, घुमावदार।

sip[1] *सिप (-pp-) v.t.* to drink bit by bit चुस्की लगाकर पीना।

sip[2] *n.* act of sipping चुस्की।

sir *सॅ: n.* a respectful form of address to a man श्रीमान, महोदय।

siren *सॉइअॅ रिन, - रॅन n.* loud hooter used as a warning or as a time-signal भोंपू; mythical nymph who lured sailors to destruction जलपरी; an alluring woman मोहिनी।

sister *सिस् टॅ: n.* daughter of same parents बहन; a senior nurse उपचारिका, नर्स; nun मठवासिनी।

sisterhood *सिस् टॅ: हुड n.* relation of sister बहनापा; society of women महिला संघ।

sisterly *सिस् टॅ: लि a.* like a sister भगिनीवत्।

sit *सिट (-tt-) v.i.* to be seated बैठना; to incubate अंडे सेना; to be in session अधिवेशन होना; to take examination परीक्षा देना; to fit ठीक बैठना; *v.t.* to cause to sit बैठाना।

site *सॉइट n.* location स्थान; space for a building निर्माण-स्थल।

situation *सि ट्यू ए शॅन n.* a site, a position स्थान, स्थल; state of affairs परिस्थिति; employment, post नौकरी, पद।

six *सिक्स n., a.* (the number) next after five छः (6)।

sixteen *सिक्स् टीन n., a.* six more than ten सोलह (16)।

sixteenth *सिक्स् टीन्थ a.* the last of sixteen सोलहवां।

sixth *सिक्स्थ a.* the last of six छठा, छठवां।

sixtieth *सिक्स् टि ॲथ a.* the last of sixty साठवां।

sixty *सिक्स् टि n., a.* ten times six साठ (60)।

sizable *सॉइ ज़ॅ ब्ल a.* of considerable size विशाल, बड़ा।

size[1] *सॉइज़ n.* degree of largeness आकार; dimension लंबाई-चौड़ाई, विस्तार।

size[2] *v.t.* to arrange according to size आकार-क्रम में रखना।

sizzle[1] *सि ज़्ल v.i.* to make a hissing sound छुन-छुन की ध्वनि करना।

sizzle[2] *n.* hissing sound छुन-छुन की ध्वनि।

skate *स्केट n.* steel blade attached to boot for gliding over ice स्केट।

skate[2] *v.t.* to glide on skates स्केटों पर फिसलना।

skein *स्केन n.* length of yarn coiled into a bundle लच्छी, अंटी।

skeleton *स्कै ँ लि ट्न n.* bony framework of an animal body कंकाल, अस्थिपंजर; any framework or outline ढांचा, रूपरेखा।

sketch[1] *स्कै ँच n.* rough drawing कच्चा खाका; brief account संक्षिप्त वर्णन; a short humorous play हास्य नाटिका।

sketch[2] *v.t.* to make a sketch of (का) नक़्शा बनाना; to give a brief account of (का) संक्षिप्त वर्णन करना; *v.i.* to practise the art of making sketches नक़्शे बनाना।

sketchy *स्कै ँ चि a.* omitting detail संक्षिप्त; incomplete अधूरा।

skid[1] *स्किड (-dd-) v.i.* to slide or slip फिसलना।

skid[2] *n.* act of skidding फिसलने की क्रिया; a piece of wood fixed to a wheel to act as a brake उड़ीक, आंट।

skilful *स्किल् फुल a.* expert निपुण, कुशल; showing skill कौशलपूर्ण।

skill *स्किल n.* dexterity, expertness निपुणता, कौशल।

skin[1] *स्किन n.* the natural outer covering of an animal body त्वचा, खाल; the outer layer of a fruit फल का छिलका; thin film of the top of a liquid milk पपड़ी, मलाई।

skin[2] *(-nn-) v.t.* to remove skin of (की) खाल या छिलका उतारना।

skip[1] *स्किप (-pp-) v.i.* to leap slightly फुदकना, कुदकना; to practise rope jumping रस्सी कूदना; *v.t.* to pass over or omit छोड़ जाना।

skip[2] *n.* act of skipping उछाल, कूद।

skipper *स्कि पॅः n.* captain of a ship or team कप्तान।

skirmish[1] स्कॅ: *मिश n.* small battle झड़प।

skirmish[2] *v.t.* to take part in a skirmish झड़प में भाग लेना।

skirt[1] *स्कॅ:ट n.* woman's garment hanging from waist घाघरा; lower part of woman's dress पल्ला; outlying part, border किनारा, बाहरी भाग।

skirt[2] *v.t.* to move along the edge of (के) किनारे-किनारे चलना।

skit *स्किट n.* a slight amusing play प्रहसन।

skull *स्कल n.* the body covering of brain खोपड़ी, कपाल।

sky[1] *स्कॉइ n.* the upper atmosphere of the earth आकाश।

sky[2] *v.t.* to hit (a criket ball) high (गेंद) ऊंची उछालना।

slab *स्लैब n.* a thick broad piece पटिया।

slack *स्लैक a.* loose ढीला; sluggish सुस्त; careless असावधान, लापरवाह; not busy निष्क्रिय।

slacken *स्लै कॅन v.t.* to make slack ढीला करना; to make idle सुस्त करना; *v.i.* to become slack ढीला होना; to become idle सुस्त होना।

slacks *स्लैक्स n. (pl.)* loose trousers ढीला-ढाला पाजामा।

slake *स्लेक v.t.* to satisfy, to quench (thirst) (प्यास) बुझाना।

slam[1] *स्लैम (-mm-) v.t.* to shut noisily ज़ोर से बंद करना; to put down violently पटकना।

slam[2] *n.* noisy shutting धम।

slander[1] *स्लान् डॅ: n.* false statement meant to damage a person's reputation झूठी निंदा।

slander[2] *v.t.* to utter slander about (की) झूठी निंदा करना।

slanderous *स्लान् डॅ रॅस a.* tending to slander निंदात्मक।

slang *स्लैङ्ग n.* colloquial language बोलचाल की भाषा, अपरिष्कृत भाषा।

slant[1] *स्लान्ट v.t.* to tilt तिरछा करना, झुकाना; *v.i.* to move obliquely मुड़ना, घूमना।

slant[2] *n.* a tilt झुकाव, तिरछापन; slope ढाल।

slap[1] *स्लैप n.* a blow with an open hand चांटा, तमाचा।

slap[2] *(-pp-) v.t.* to strike with an open hand तमाचा मारना।

slash[1] *स्लैश v.t.* to make a long cut चीर देना; to strike at पीटना; to reduce in length छोटा करना; to criticise severely कड़ी आलोचना करना।

slash[2] *n.* act of slashing अल्पीकरण; long cut चीरा।

slate *स्लेट n.* stone which splits in flat sheets परतदार पत्थर; piece of this stone स्लेट, पटिया।

slattern *स्लै टॅ:न n.* a slut फूहड़ स्त्री।

slatternly *स्लै टॅ:न् लि a.* slovenly, untidy फूहड, बेशऊर।

slaughter[1] *स्लौ टॅ: n.* killing of animals पशुवध; massacre नरसंहार।

slaughter[2] *v.t.* to kill वध करना।

slave[1] *स्लेव n.* a person without freedom or personal rights दास; one dominated by another or some crazy idea किसी व्यक्ति या सनक आदि का गुलाम।

slave[2] *v.i.* to work like a slave दासता में काम करना।

slavery *स्ले वॅ रि n.* condition of a slave दासता; practice of owning slaves दास-प्रथा।

slavish *स्ले विश a.* servile दासतापूर्ण।

slay *स्ले v.t.* to kill वध करना।

sleek *स्लीक a.* glossy चिकना; shiny चमकदार।

sleep[1] *स्लीप v.i.* to slumber सोना।

sleep[2] *n.* slumber नींद।

sleeper *स्ली पॅ: n.* one who sleeps सोने वाला; a berth in a sleeping car शयनिका; a heavy beam स्लीपर, सिलीपट।

sleepy *स्ली पि a.* drowsy उनींदा; inactive निष्क्रिय; apt to make one sleep निद्राकारी।

sleeve *स्लीव n.* part of a garment that covers the arm (वस्त्र की) आस्तीन; cover आवरण।

sleight *स्लॉइट n.* dexterity कौशल; trickery चाल, करतब।

slender *स्लैनॅ् डॅ: n.* slim, narrow पतला; कमज़ोर; slight अल्प थोड़ा।

slice[1] *स्लॉइस n.* thin, flat piece cut off फांक, कतला; share अंश, भाग।

slice[2] *v.t.* to cut into slices फांकों या कतलों के रूप में काटना।

slick *स्लिक a.* sleek चिकना; sly चालाक, शरारती; smooth-tongued मिठबोला।

slide[1] *स्लॉइड v.i.* to slip smoothly सरकाना; to glide फिसलना; *v.t.* to cause to glide फिसलाना; to pass imperceptibly चुपके से खिसकाना।

slide[2] *n.* act of sliding सरकन, फिसलन; smooth surface चिकनी सतह; piece of glass to be viewed under microscope स्लाइड।

slight[1] *स्लॉइट a.* slim, frail पतला, कमज़ोर; small थोड़ा, अल्प।

slight[2] *n.* insult अपमान।

slight[3] *v.t.* to disregard अपमानित करना।

slim[1] *स्लिम a.* slender, thin पतला, छरहरा।

slim[2] *(-mm-) v.i.* to become slim पतला होना, वज़न कम करना।

slime *स्लॉइम n.* greasy, thick liquid mud कीचड़।

slimy *स्लॉइ मि a.* consisting of mud पंकयुक्त; like mud पंकवत्; covered with slime पंकिल।

sling *स्लिङ्ग n.* a leather loop used for throwing stones गोफन, गुलेला; bandage for supporting wounded limb गलपट्टी।

slip[1] *स्लिप (-pp-) v.i.* to slide फिसलना; to move away quietly खिसक जाना; to make a small error साधारण ग़लती करना।

slip[2] *n.* act of slipping सर्पण, सरक; a slight error साधारण ग़लती; pillow-cover खोल; a narrow strip of paper परची।

slipper *स्लि पॅ: n.* a light shoe for indoor use घरेलू प्रयोग की चप्पल।

slippery *स्लि पॅ रि a.* apt to cause slipping फिसलन वाला; hard to hold पकड़ में न आने वाला।

slipshod *स्लिप शौ ॅड a.* slovenly फूहड़िया; careless असावधानीपूर्ण।

slit[1] *स्लिट n.* a long, narrow opening दरार।

slit[2] *(-tt-) v.t.* to make a slit in (में) दरार करना।

slogan *स्लो गॅन n.* distinctive phrase (in advertising or electioneering) नारा।

slope[1] *स्लोप n.* a slant, an inclination up or down ढाल।

slope[2] *v.i.* to have a slope ढालू होना; *v.t.* to cause to slope ढालू बनाना।

sloth *स्लोथ n.* laziness, indolence आलस्य, काहिली; idleness निष्क्रियता।

slothful *स्लोथ् फुल n.* lazy आलसी; inactive निष्क्रिय, निठल्ला।

slough[1] *स्लॉउच n.* swamp, marsh दलदल।

slough[2] *स्लफ़ n.* cast-off skin of snake केंचुली।

slough[3] *v.t.* to shed (skin) (केंचुली) गिराना; *v.i.* to fall off गिरना, अलग हटना।

slovenly *स्ल् वॅन् लि a.* untidy मैला-कुचैला; careless लापरवाह।

slow[1] *स्लो a*, taking a long time धीमा; moving not less than normal speed मंद गतिवाला; dull-witted मंदबुद्धि।

slow[2] *v.i.* to get slow धीमा होना; *v.t.* to make slow धीमा करना।

slowly *स्लो लि adv.* at a slow speed धीमी गति से।

slowness *स्लो निस n.* quality of being slow धीमापन।

sluggard *स्ल गॅःड n.* a slow lazy person सुस्त आलसी व्यक्ति।

sluggish *स्ल गिश a.* lazy सुस्त, आलसी; slow मंदगति; inactive निष्क्रिय।

sluice *स्लुः स n.* a gate or door to control flow of water जलद्वार; flow of water through a sluice-gate जलद्वार से जल-प्रवाह।

slum *स्लम n.* part of a town with dirty, poor unhygienic condition गंदी बस्ती।

slumber[1] *स्लम् बॅः v.i.* to sleep सोना।

slumber[2] *n.* sleep नींद।

slump[1] *स्लम्प n.* sudden decline (of prices) मंदी; sudden fall अकस्मात् पतन।

slump[2] *v.i.* to collapse गिर पड़ना।

slur *स्लॅः n.* a stain कलंक, धब्बा; stigma बदनामी।

slush *स्लश n.* mud कीचड़।

slushy *स्ल शि a.* muddy कीचड़दार।

slut *स्लट n.* a dirty woman of bad reputation गंदी बदनाम स्त्री।

sly *स्लॉइ a.* (slyer, slyest) deceitful धोखेबाज़; playful, mischievous शरारती।

smack[1] *स्मैक n.* taste, flavour स्वाद; heroin अफ़ीम।

smack[2] *v.i.* to taste स्वाद देना; to give suggestion आभास देना।

smack[3] *n.* a small fishing vessel मत्स्य नौका।

smack[4] *n.* a slap चांटा; sound of a blow चटाक-पटाक।

smack[5] *v.t.* to slap चांटा मारना; *v.i.* to make a sound like a blow चपत की ध्वनि उत्पन्न करना।

small[1] *स्मौल a.* little छोटा; unimportant तुच्छ, महत्वहीन।

small[2] *n.* slender part of the back intestine कमर का पतला भाग।

smallness *स्मौल् निस* quality of being small छोटापन।

smallpox *स्मौल् पौक्स n.* a contagious disease चेचक।

smart[1] *स्माःट a.* brisk, active फुरतीला; clever, witty चतुर, हाज़िर-जवाब; well-dressed बना-ठना; severe कड़ा, कठोर।

smart² *v.i.* to feel pain टीस लगना।

smart³ *n.* sharp pain टीस।

smash¹ *स्मैश* *v.t.* to break violently झटके से तोड़ना; to strike hard कड़ी चोट करना; to destroy नष्ट करना; *v.i.* to break टूटना; to dash (against) टकराना।

smash² *n.* heavy blow भारी प्रहार; collision टक्कर।

smear¹ *स्मिअ:* *v.t.* to cover or mark with something oily सानना, पोतना; defame बदनाम करना।

smear² *n.* an oily mark दाग़, धब्बा; defamation बदनामी।

smell¹ *समैॅल* *n.* faculty of perceiving odour घ्राणशक्ति; odour गंध।

smell² *v.t.* to perceive by nose सूंघना; to suspect शंका करना; *v.i.* to give out odour महकना, गंध देना; to use the nose गंध का अनुभव करना।

smelt *स्मैल्ट* *v.t.* to melt (ore) पिघलाना, गलाना; to separate (metal) from ore (धातु) अलग करना।

smile¹ *स्मॉइल* *n.* expression of pleasure on the face मुस्कान।

smile² *v.i.* to wear a smile मुस्काना; to be favourable प्रसन्न होना; *v.t.* to show by smile मुस्कान-द्वारा प्रदर्शित करना।

smith *स्मिथ* *n.* worker in iron, gold, etc. धातु-कर्मी।

smock *स्मौकॅ* *n.* loose outer garment लबादा, लंबा कुर्ता।

smog *स्मौगॅ* *n.* fog mixed with smoke धूम-कोहरा।

smoke¹ *समोक* *n.* cloudy mass of carbon rising from anything burning धुआं; act of smoking tobacco धूम्रपान।

smoke² *v.i.* to give off smoke धुआं छोड़ना; to inhale the fumes of tobacco धूम्रपान करना; *v.t.* to use for smoking (बीड़ी, हुक्का आदि) पीना।

smoky *स्मो कि* *a.* giving out much smoke धुंधुआता; like smoke धुआं-जैसा; filled with smoke धुआंयुक्त।

smooth¹ *स्मूद* *a.* not rough चिकना; even of surface हमवार; free from obstacles निर्विघ्न; calm शांत।

smooth² *v.t.* to make smooth चिकना करना; to quieten शांत करना।

smother *स्म दॅ:* *v.t.* to suffocate दम घोंटना; to suppress दबाना; to cover thickly ढकना।

smoulder *स्मोल् डॅ:* *v.i.* to burn slowly without flame सुलगना; (of feelings) to exist in suppressed state घुटन होना।

smug *स्मग* *a.* self-satisfied आत्म-संतुष्ट, दंभी।

smuggle *स्म् ग्ल* *v.t.* to import or export without paying customs duties तस्करी करना; to take secretly चोरी से लेना।

smuggler *स्मग् लॅ:* *n.* one who smuggles तस्कर।

snack *स्नैक* *n.* light hasty meal हल्का भोजन।

snag *स्नैग* *n.* difficulty कठिनाई; obstacle रोड़ा, बाधा।

snail *स्नेल* *n.* a slow-moving small animal with a shell घोंघा।

snake[1] *स्नेक n.* serpent सर्प।

snake[2] *v.i.* to move like a serpent रेंगना।

snap[1] *स्नैप (-pp-) v.t.* to break तोड़ना; to take a quick photograph of (का) एकाएक फ़ोटो लेना; to bite काटना; to take eagerly झपट लेना; *v.i.* to break टूटना; to make a sharp sound कड़कना; to speak sharply कड़क कर बोलना।

snap[2] *n.* act of snapping तड़क; snapshot आशुचित्र; sound of breaking कड़क; a bite काट, कर्तन; spell (of cold) (ठंड का) दौर।

snap[3] *a.* sudden आकस्मिक; without planning अनियोजित।

snare[1] *स्ने ॅअ: n.* trap with a slip-knot जाल, फंदा temptation ललचाव।

snare[2] *v.t.* to catch in a snare फंसाना।

snarl[1] *स्ना:ल n.* a growl गुर्राहट; *a.* tangle उलझन; confusion गड़बड़झाला।

snarl[2] *v.i.* to growl गुर्राना।

snatch[1] *स्नैच v.t.* to seize quickly छीनना; to take ग्रहण करना।

snatch[2] *n.* grab बलपूर्वक ग्रहण; fragment टुकड़ा; short spell दौर।

sneak[1] *स्नीक v.i.* to slink आंख बचाकर आना-जाना; to act in a mean, underhand manner चालाकी का व्यवहार करना।

sneak[2] *n.* a pettly thief उचक्का; an informer मुख़बिर।

sneer[1] *स्निअॅ: v.i* to express contempt अवहेलना दिखाना।

sneer[2] *n.* expression of contempt तिरस्कार, अवहेलना।

sneeze[1] *स्नीज़ v.i.* to make a sneeze छींकना।

sneeze[2] *n.* sudden outburst of air through the nose and mouth छींक।

sniff[1] *स्निफ़ v.i.* to inhale with a sharp hiss सूं-सूं करना; (with 'at') to express disapproval अस्वीकृति अभिव्यक्त करना; *v.t.* to smell सूंघना।

sniff[2] *n.* act or sound of sniffing सुड़क।

snob *स्नौबॅ n.* person whose basis of respect and contempt is social and financial status वर्गदंभी।

snobbery *स्नौ ॅ बॅ रि n.* quality of being snobbish वर्गदंभ।

snobbish *स्नौ ॅ बिश* of or like a snob दंभपूर्ण।

snore[1] *स्नौ:, स्नौॅं: v.i.* to breathe noisily when asleep खर्राटे लेना।

snore[2] *n.* noisy breath in sleep ख़र्राटा।

snort[1] *स्नौ:ट v.i.* to make contemptuous noise by driving breath through nostrils फुंकारना, फुफकारना।

snort[2] *n.* act or sound of snorting फुफकार।

snout *स्नॉउट n.* animal's projecting nose थूथन, थूथनी।

snow[1] *स्नो n.* frozen vapour बरफ़, तुषार।

snow[2] *v.i.* to fall as snow बरफ़ गिरना।

snowy *स्नो इ a.* covered with snow बरफ़ीला as white as snow बरफ़ जैसा सफ़ेद।

snub[1] *स्नब (-bb-) v.t.* to treat with

contempt or neglect झिड़कना, अनदेखी करना, कोई महत्व न देना।

snub[2] *n.* snubbing words or behaviour झिड़की, अपमान।

snuff *स्नफ़ n.* powdered tobacco for inhaling through the nose सुंघनी।

snug *स्नग n.* warm, comfortable गर्म, आरामदायक; neat and tide साफ़-सुथरा।

so[1] *सो adv.* to such an extent इतना; in such a manner ऐसे, इस प्रकार; very अत्यंत।

so[2] *conj.* therefore अतः।

soak[1] *सोक v.t.* to drench भिगोना; to absorb सोखना; to steep डुबोना; *v.i.* to lie in liquid भीगना।

soak[2] *n.* soaking शुष्कन।

soap[1] *सोप n.* a detergent compound साबुन।

soap[2] *v.t.* to apply soap on साबुन लगाना।

soapy *सो पि a.* like soap साबुन जैसा; containing soap साबुनयुक्त।

soar *सौः, सौंः v.i.* to fly high ऊंची उड़ान भरना, ऊंचा उड़ना; to increase बढ़ना।

sob[1] *सौबॅ (-bb-) v.i.* to weep with short catches of breath सुबकना।

sob[2] *n.* act or sound of sobbing सुबकी।

sober *सो बॅ a.* not drunk अमत्त; temperate संयमी; serious गंभीर; not showy सादा।

sobriety *सो ब्राइॅ अॅ टि n.* state of being sober गांभीर्य, सादगी, संयम।

sociability *सो शॅ बि लि टि n.* quality of being sociable मिलनसारी।

sociable *सो शॅ ब्ल a.* friendly, ready to mix with other people मिलनसार।

social *सो शॅल n.* relating to society सामाजिक; gregarious संघचारी; sociable मिलनसार।

socialism *सो शॅ लिज्म n.* system of state ownership of the wealth of a country समाजवाद।

socialist[1] *सो शॅ लिस्ट n.* an advocate of socialism समाजवादी।

socialist[2] *a.* concerned with socialism समाजवादी।

society *सॅ सॉइ अ टि n.* social community समाज; a group formed for a specific purpose संस्था; companionship संग-साथ।

sociology *सो सि औॅ लॅ जि n.* study of growth and behaviour of human societies समाजशास्त्र।

sock *सौकॅ n.* a short stocking मौज़ा; removable inner sole of a shoe पैतावां, भीतरी तल्ला।

socket *सौॅ किट n.* a hollow into which something fits गर्तिका, साकेट।

sod *सौॅड n.* a lump of earth with grass तृणभूमि।

sodomite *सौॅ डॅ मॉइट n.* one who practises sodomy लौंडेबाज़।

sodomy *सौॅ डॅ मि n.* sexual intercourse between males लौंडेबाजी।

sofa *सौ फ़ॅ n.* a long padded seat with raised back and arms सोफ़ा।

soft *सौफ़्ट n.* not hard कोमल, मुलायम; mild विनम्र; subdued धीमा, मंद; quiet शांत; lenient नरम, ढीला; over sentimental अति भावुक; (water) containing few mineral salts मृदु; non-alcoholic अमादक; compassionate दयालु।

soften *सौ ˘ फ़्न v.t.* to make soft कोमल बनाना; to make mild विनम्र करना; to mollify शांत करना; to lighten हल्का करना; to mitigate कम करना; to make less loud धीमा या मंद करना; *v.i.* to become soft मुलायम होना; to become lenient नरम होना।

soil[1] *सौ˘इल n.* earth, ground मिट्‌टी; country देश।

soil[2] *v.t.* to make dirty गंदा करना; *v.i.* to become dirty गंदा होना।

sojourn[1] *सौ ˘ जॅःन, स जॅःन v.i.* to stay for a time ठहरना, कुछ समय के लिए रुकना।

sojourn[2] *n.* short stay ठहराव, प्रवास।

solace[1] *सौ ˘ लॅस v.t.* to console सांत्वना देना।

solace[2] *n.* consolation सांत्वना।

solar *सौ लॅः a.* of the sun सौर, सूर्य का।

solder[1] *सौल् डॅः n.* easily melted alloy used to join metals रांगा, टांका।

solder[2] *v.t.* to join by means of solder झालना, टांके से जोड़ना।

soldier[1] *सोल् जॅः n.* one serving in army सैनिक।

soldier[2] *v.i.* to serve in army सैनिक के रूप में काम करना।

sole[1] *सोल n.* underside of foot पैर का तलवा; under part of boot तल्ला।

sole[2] *v.t.* to fit with sole (में) तल्ला लगाना।

sole[3] *a.* single, only एकमात्र, अकेला।

solemn *सौ ˘ लॅम a.* earnest, grave गंभीर; formal औपचारिक; impressive प्रभावशाली।

solemnity *सॅ लैमॅ् नि टि n.* quality of being solemn गंभीरता।

solemnize *सौ ˘ लॅम् नॉइज़ v.t.* to celebrate समारोह मनाना; to make solemn गंभीर बनाना।

solicit *सॅ लि सिट v.t.* to request earnestly विनती करना।

solicitation *सॅ लि सि टे शॅन n.* soliciting विनती, प्रार्थना।

solicitor *सॅ लि सि टॅः n.* a lawyer confined to lower courts only न्यायाभिकर्त्ता।

solicitious *सॅ लि टि टॅस a.* anxious चिंतित; eager उत्कंठित।

solicitude *सॅ लि सि ट्यूड n.* anxiety चिंता; eagerness उत्कंठा।

solid[1] *सौ ˘ लिड a.* not hollow ठोस; compact सुगठित; firm दृढ़ कड़ा; cubic घनाकार; unmixed खालिस, शुद्ध; reliable विश्वसनीय; massive भारी।

solid[2] *n.* a body of three dimensions पिंड; solid substance ठोस पदार्थ।

solidarity *सौ˘ लि डै रि टि n.* unity in support of common interests एकता, एकजुटता।

soliloquy *सॅ लि लॅ क्वि n.* thoughts spoken by a person when alone स्वगत।

solitary *सौ ˘ लि टॅ रि a.* alone, single अकेला; remote दूरस्थ।

solitude *सौ ˘ लि ट्यूड n.* state of being alone अकेलापन; loneliness एकाकीपन; seclusion एकांत; lonely place एकांत स्थान।

solo[1] *सो लो n. (pl. -s-)* music for one performer एकल संगीत-रचना।
solo[2] *a.* performed by one person एकल।
solo[3] *adv.* by oneself अकेले।
soloist *सो लो ॅ इस्ट n.* person who gives a solo एकल गायक या वादक।
solubility *सौ ॅ ल्यु बि लि टि n.* quality of being soluble घुलनशीलता, समाधेयता।
soluble *सौ ॅ ल्यु बल a.* capable of being dissolved in liquid घुलनशील; that can be solved or explained समाधेय।
solution *सॅ ल्यू शॅन n.* answer to a problem समाधान; dissolving विलयन; liquid with something dissolved in it घोल।
solve *सै ॅल्व v.t.* to work out हल करना; to find answer to समाधान करना।
solvency *सौल्ॅ वॅन् सि n.* ability to pay all one's debts ऋण-शोध-क्षमता।
solvent[1] *सौल्ॅ वॅन्ट a.* able to pay all one's debts ऋणशोधक्षम; able to dissolve विलायक।
solvent[2] *n.* liquid with power of dissolving विलायक द्रव।
sombre *सोम्ॅ बॅः a.* dark-coloured कालिमामय; gloomy निराशाजनक, विषादपूर्ण।
some[1] *सॅम a.* one or other कोई; unspecified in number or quantity कुछ।
some[2] *pron.* an indefinite number or quantity कुछ।
somebody[1] *सम् बॅ डि pron.* some person कोई (व्यक्ति)।
somebody[2] *n.* a person of importance विशिष्ट व्यक्ति।
somehow *सम् हॉउ adv.* in some way or the other जैसे-तैसे।
someone *सम् वॅन pron.* somebody कोई (व्यक्ति)।
somersault[1] *स मॅः सौल्ट n.* tumbling head over heels कलाबाज़ी।
somersault[2] *v.i.* to turn a somersault कलाबाज़ी खाना।
something[1] *सम् थिङ्ग pron.* an unexpected thing or event कुछ।
something[2] *adv.* somewhat कुछ-कुछ, कुछ सीमा तक।
sometime *सम् टॉइम adv.* at some time कभी-कभी, किसी समय।
sometimes *सम् टॉइम्ज़ adv.* occasionally कभी-कभी।
somewhat *सम् हौ ॅट adv.* slightly, to some degree कुछ-कुछ।
somewhere *सम् ह्वेॲः adv.* in some place कहीं, किसी जगह।
somnambulism *सौम्ॅ नैम् ब्यु लिज़्म n.* sleep-walking निद्राभ्रमण।
somnambulist *सौम्ॅ नैम् ब्यु लिस्ट n.* sleep-walker निद्राचारी।
somnolence *सौम्ॅ नॅ लॅन्स n.* drowsiness निद्रालुता।
somnolent *सौम्ॅ नॅ लॅन्ट n.* drowsy उनींदा; causing sleep निद्राजनक।
son *सॅन n.* male child पुत्र।
song *सौ ॅङ्ग n.* act of singing गायन; a musical composition गाना।
songster *सौ ॅङ्ग् स्टॅः n.* a singer गायक।
sonic *सौ ॅ निक a.* relating to sound ध्वनि-संबंधी।
sonnet *सौ ॅ निट n.* a fourteen-line

poem चतुर्दश-पदी।

sonority *सॅ नौ ˘ रि टि n.* quality of being sonorous निनादिता; being melodious सुरीलापन।

soon *सून adv.* in a short time जल्दी, शीघ्र; early सवेरे; quickly शीघ्रता से, जल्दी से।

soot[1] *सूट n.* a black substance deposited by smoke काजल, कालिख।

soot[2] *v.t.* to cover with soot काजल लगाना।

soothe *सूद v.t.* to make calm शांत करना; to make (pain etc.) less sharp (पीड़ा) कम करना।

sophism *सौ ˘ फ़िज़्म n.* false reasoning intended to deceive, specious argument कुतर्क, भ्रामक तर्क, हेत्वाभास।

sophist *सौ ˘ फिस्ट n.* falacious reasoner कुतर्की, भ्रामक तार्किक।

sophisticate *सॅ फ़िस् टि केट v.t.* to make artificial कृत्रिम बनाना; to spoil बिगाड़ना, भ्रष्ट करना।

sophisticated *सॅ फ़िस् टि के टिड a.* complicated जटिल; artificial कृत्रिम; experienced in worldly ways दुनियादारी में निपुण।

sophistication *सॅ फ़िस् टि के शॅन n.* artificiality कृत्रिमता; worldly wisdom दुनियादारी।

sorcerer *सौः सॅ रॅः n.* magician जादूगर।

sorcery *सौ : सॅ रि n.* witchcraft, magic जादू।

sordid *सौ ˘ डिड a.* mean, squalid नीच, घिनौना; ignoble base पतित, निम्नकोटि का।

sore[1] *सौः, सौंः a.* painful पीड़ादायक; sad, grieved दुःखी; resentful नाराज़।

sore[2] *n.* ulcer, boil फोड़ा।

sorrow[1] *सौ ˘ रो n.* grief दुःख, पीड़ा।

sorrow[2] *v.i.* to grieve दुःखी होना।

sorry *सौ ˘ रि a.* feeling grief दुःखी; feeling regret खेदपूर्ण।

sort[1] *सौःट n.* kind, class प्रकार।

sort[2] *v.t.* to arrange in groups श्रेणी के अनुसार रखना।

soul *सोल n.* the spirit आत्मा; example, model नमूना, आदर्श।

sound[1] *सॉउन्ड a.* in good condition अच्छा-खासा, सही-सलामत; healthy स्वस्थ; correct सही; undamaged अक्षत।

sound[2] *v.i.* to make sound ध्वनि करना; to seem प्रतीत होना; *v. t.* to cause to sound बजाना; to convey (some impression) (आभास) देना; to pronounce, to utter उच्चारण करना, बोलना; to find depth of (की) गहराई नापना; to ascertain views of (के) विचार जानना।

sound[3] *n.* what is heard ध्वनि।

soup *सूप n.* liquid food made by boiling meat, vegetables etc. शोरबा।

sour[1] *सॉउअँः a.* acid खट्टा; ill-tempered चिड़चिड़ा; disagreeable अप्रिय; bitter कटु।

sour[2] *v.t.* to make sour खट्टा करना; *v.i.* to become sour खट्टा होना।

source *सौःस n.* origin उद्गम, स्रोत; the starting point of a river निकास; primary cause मूल कारण; means साधन।

south[1] *सॉउथ n.* the direction opposite to north दक्षिण।

south[2] *n.* lying in the south दक्षिण में स्थित; (wind) blowing from south दक्षिणी।

south[3] *adv.* towards the south दक्षिण की ओर।

southerly *स दः लि a.* (of winds) blowing from the south दक्षिणी।

southern *स दॅःन a.* pertaining to the south दक्षिणी।

souvenir *सू वॅ निअॅः n.* a keepsake, memento यादगार, स्मारिका, स्मृति-चिह्न।

sovereign[1] *सौवॅ् रिन n.* king, queen राजा, रानी; a gold coin worth 20 shillings (20 शिलिंग के बराबर) एक स्वर्ण मुद्रा।

sovereign[2] *a.* supreme सर्वश्रेष्ठ; excellent उत्तम; highest सार्वभौम।

sovereignty *सौवॅ् रिन् टि n.* supreme power प्रभुसत्ता; dominion राज्य; independent state स्वतंत्र राज्य।

sow[1] *सो v.t.* (sowed सोड; sown सोन) to place (seed) in the ground बोना; *v.i.* to do sowing बुआई करना।

sow[2] *सॉउ n.* a female pig सुअरी।

space[1] *स्पेस n.* distance दूरी; area, room जगह; period अवधि, समय; expanse विस्तार; region beyond earth's atmosphere अंतरिक्ष।

space[2] *v.t.* to palce at intervals फ़ासले में रखना।

spacious *स्पे शॅस a.* wide, extensive विस्तृत।

spade[1] *स्पेड n.* a tool for digging फावड़ा, कुदाल।

spade[2] *v.t.* to big with a spade फावड़े से खोदना।

span[1] *स्पैन n.* the distance between the tips of the thumb and the little finger when stretched बालिश्त, बित्ता; the distance between the arches of a bridge पुल के मेहराबों के बीच की दूरी; the full width of anything चौड़ाई; extent सीमा।

span[2] *(-nn-) v.t.* to stretch over के ऊपर फैला होना; to measure with hand बालिश्त से नापना।

Spaniard *स्पैन् यॅःड n.* a native of Spain स्पेन का निवासी।

spaniel *स्पैन यॅल n.* a breed of dog with long silky hair and large ears कुत्ते की एक नस्ल।

Spanish[1] *स्पै निश a.* of Spain, pertaining to Spain स्पेन का, स्पेन देश से संबंधित।

Spanish[2] *n.* the language of Spain स्पेन की भाषा; *(pl.)* the people of Spain स्पेन के लोग।

spanner *स्पै नॅः n.* a tool or gripping nut etc. रिंच, पाना।

spare[1] *स्पे ॅअॅः v.t.* to leave unhurt बख़्श देना; to show mercy (पर) दया करना; to abstain from using प्रयोग में न लाना; to do without के बिना काम चलाना; to give away दे देना।

spare[2] *a.* additional अतिरिक्त, फालतू; in reserve सुरक्षित; thin, lean पतला-दुबला; scanty अल्प, अपर्याप्त।

spare[3] *n.* spare part फ़ालतू पुरज़ा।

spark[1] *स्पाःक n.* a small glowing particle चिनगारी; a small flash caused by an electric discharge स्फुलिंग, बिजली के तारों की

चिनगारी; vigour उत्साह; a trace लेश।

spark² *v.i.* to give out sparks चमकना, चिनगारी निकलना।

spark³ *n.* gay and elegant fellow बांका, छैला।

sparkle¹ *स्पाः क्ल v.i.* to give out flashes of light चमकना, चिनगारी देना।

sparkle² *n.* act of sparkling चमक; a small spark छोटी चिनगारी; glitter चमक।

sparrow *स्पै रो n.* a small brownish bird गौरैया।

sparse *स्पाःस a.* scanty अपर्याप्त, कम; thinly scattered छितराया हुआ।

spasm *स्पैज़्म n.* sudden convulsive (muscular) contraction ऐंठनयुक्त जकड़न; sudden burst of activity क्रिया-कलाप का दौरा।

spasmodic *स्पैज़् मौॅ डिक a.* occurring in spasms रुक-रुक कर झटके से होनेवाला।

spate *स्पेट n.* flood बाढ़; *n.* sudden rush आधिक्य, प्रचुरता।

spatial *स्पे शॅल a.* pertaining to space, of space स्थान-विषयक।

spawn¹ *स्पौन n.* eggs of fish or frog जलजीवों के अंडे।

spawn² *v.i.* (of fish or frog) to cast eggs अंडे देना।

speak *स्पीक (spoke, spoken) v.i.* to utter words बोलना; to talk बातचीत करना; to address an audience भाषण देना; to be able to use a language कोई भाषा बोलने की योग्यता रखना; to express अभिव्यक्त करना।

speaker *स्पी कॅः n.* one who speaks वक्ता; an orator भाषण देनेवाला।

spear¹ *स्पिअॅः n.* a long pointed weapon भाला।

spear² *v.t.* to pierce or wound with a spear भाले से बींधना या घायल करना।

spearhead¹ *स्पिअॅः है ॅड n.* the pointed head of a spear भाले की नोक; leader, main force नेता, मुख्य शक्ति।

spearhead² *v.t.* to act as a spearhead for नेतृत्व करना।

special *स्पै ॅ शॅल a.* beyond the usual असाधारण; particular विशिष्ट; distinct स्पष्ट; limited सीमित।

specialist *स्पै ॅ शॅ लिस्ट n.* an expert in some field विशेषज्ञ।

speciality *स्पै ॅ शि ऐ लि टि n.* special quality विशेषता; subject on which one has special knowledge विशेष योग्यतावाला विषय।

specialization *स्पै ॅ शॅ लॉइ ज़े शॅन n.* act of specializing विशिष्टीकरण; state of being specialized विशेषज्ञता।

specialize *स्पै ॅ शॅ लॉइज़ v.i.* to become a specialist विशेषज्ञ बनना; *v.t.* to make special विशिष्ट बनाना।

species *स्पी शीज़ n.* a group having some common characteristics जाति, वर्ग; sort क़िस्म, भेद।

specific *स्पि सि फ़िक a.* definite निश्चित; particular विशिष्ट।

specification *स्पै ॅ सि फ़ि के शॅन n.* act of specifying विशिष्ट निर्देशन; detailed description of something विशेष उल्लेख।

specify *स्पै ˘ सि फ़ॉइ v.t.* to state definitely or in detail निश्चित रूप से अथवा विस्तार से कहना।

specimen *स्पै ˘ सि मिन, -मॅन n.* a sample नमूना; a item in a collection बानगी।

speck *स्पैकॅ n.* a tiny spot or particle धब्बा, दाग़।

spectacle *स्पैक् टॅ क्ल n.* a sight दृश्य; a public dispaly प्रदर्शन, प्रदर्शनी; *(pl.)* eye-glasses चश्मा, ऐनक।

spectacular *स्पैक् टै क्यु लॅः a.* impressive भव्य, प्रभावशाली; showy दिखाऊ, भड़कीला; magnificent शानदार।

spectator *स्पैक् टे टॅः n.* on-looker दर्शक।

spectre *स्पैक् टॅः n.* ghost भूत; image of something unpleasant काली छाया।

speculate *स्पै ˘ क्यु लेट v.i.* to conjecture अटकल लगाना; to engage in risky commercial transactions सट्टेबाजी करना, सट्टा लगाना।

speculation *स्पै ˘ क्यु ले शॅन n.* act of speculating अटकलबाज़ी; meditation चिंतन, मनन; risky commercial transaction सट्टेबाज़ी।

speech *स्पीच n.* faculty of speaking वाणी; language भाषा; conversation वार्तालाप; discourse भाषण; way of speaking बोली।

speed[1] *स्पीड n.* swiftness तेज़ी, शीघ्रता; rate of progress गति, चाल।

speed[2] *v.i.* to move quickly तेज़ी से चलना, जल्दी करना; *v.t.* to increase the speed of (की) गति बढ़ाना।

speedily *स्पी डि लि adv.* with speed, quickly तेज़ी से।

speedy *स्पी डि a.* quick, rapid, nimble तीव्र; चपल, फुर्तिला; prompt तात्कालिक।

spell[1] *स्पैलॅ n.* magic formula मंत्र; enchantment जादू; fascination सम्मोहन।

spell[2] *v.t.* to name or write the letters of (a word) in their proper order हिज्जे करना; to indicate संकेत करना।

spell[3] *n.* period of time अवधि, समय; period of activity or duty पारी।

spend *स्पैन्ड v.t.* to pay out व्यय करना; to pass (time) (समय) बिताना; to use up completely ख़त्म करना।

spendthrift *स्पैन्ड् थ्रिफ़्ट n.* wasteful person अपव्ययी व्यक्ति।

sperm *स्पॅःम n.* the seminal fluid of a male animal, semen शुक्राणु, वीर्य।

sphere *स्फ़िअॅः n.* a globe, a ball गोला; range क्षेत्र; status स्तर।

spherical *स्फ़ै ˘ रि क्ल a.* shaped like a sphere गोलाकार।

spice[1] *स्पॉइस n.* aromatic pungent vegetable substance मसाला; anything that adds flavour or interest etc. चटपटी सामग्री।

spice[2] *v.t.* to season with spices मसालों से छोंकना; to flavour स्वादिष्ट बनाना।

spicy *स्पॉइ सि a.* flavoured with spices मसालेदार; interesting रुचिकर।

spider *स्पॉइ डॅः n.* a small eight-legged creature which spins web मकड़ी।

spike[1] *स्पॉइक n.* a sharp point नोक; a rob with a sharp point नोकदार छड़; a large nail कील; an ear of corn अनाज की बाल।

spike[2] *v.t.* to pierce with a spike कील से बींधना; to put spikes on (पर) की लगाना।

spill[1] *स्पिल v.i.* to flow over, to fall out छलकना; *v.t.* to cause or allow to flow over छलकाना; to upset, to cause to fall गिरा देना; to shed (blood) (खून) बहाना।

spill[2] *n.* fall गिराव, पतन; amount spilt छलकन; a thin strip of wood, twisted paper etc. for lighting fire, candle etc. बत्ती, शलाका।

spin[1] *स्पिन (-nn-) v.i.* to revolve rapidly घूमना; to twist thread सूत कातना; to produce a web जाला बुनना; *v.t.* to make (yarn) from fibres (सूत) कातना; to produce (a web) (जाला) बनाना; to cause to revolve घुमाना; to narrate सुनाना।

spin[2] *n.* spinning motion चक्रण, घुमाव; turning movement of a diving aircraft वायुयान का घुमावदार उतार।

spinach *स्पि निज n.* a leafy vegetable पालक।

spinal *स्पॉइ न्ल a.* of the spine मेरुदंडीय।

spindle *स्पिन् ड्ल n.* the rob by which thread is twisted in spinning तकला।

spine *स्पॉइन n.* the backbone मेरुदंड, रीढ़; a spiky growth on a plant or on the body of an animal कांटा; a ridge कंटक; back of a book पीठ, पुश्त।

spinner *स्पि नँः n.* a person who spins कातनेवाला; the machine that spins कताई-मशीन।

spinster *स्पिन् स्टॅः n.* unmarried woman अविवाहिता स्त्री।

spiral[1] *स्पॉइ रॅल n.* continuous curve सर्पिल आकार; circular motion सर्पिल गति; coil कुंडली।

spiral[2] *a.* formed like or running in a spiral घुमावदार, पेचदार; coiling around a fixed line in constantly changing series of planes कुंडलित।

spirit *स्पि रिट n.* the soul आत्मा; a ghost प्रेत; courage साहस; disposition स्वभाव; alcoholic drink मद्यसार; meaning अर्थ, भाव।

spirited *स्पि रि टिड a.* vigorous उत्साही; lively सजीव, उत्प्राणित।

spiritual *स्पि रि ट्यु अॅल, -चु- a.* pertaining to the spirit आत्मिक; relating to the higher soul आध्यात्मिक।

spiritualism *स्पि रि ट्यु अॅ लिज़्म, चु- n.* doctrine of the existence of spirit distinct from matter अध्यात्मवाद।

spiritualist *स्पि रि ट्यु अॅ लिस्ट, -चु- n.* one who believes in spiritualism अध्यात्मवादी।

spirituality *स्पि रि ट्यु ऐ लि टि, -चु- n.* quality of being spiritual आध्यात्मिकता।

spit[1] *स्पिट (-tt-) v.i.* to eject saliva थूकना; *v.t.* to eject from the mouth थूककर निकालना।

spit[2] *n.* act of spitting थूकने की क्रिया; spittle, saliva थूक।

spite *स्पॉइट n.* malice द्वेष।

spittle *स्पि ट्ल n* saliva थूक।

spittoon *स्पि टून n.* vessel to spit into पीकदान।

splash[1] *स्प्लैश v.i.* (of a liquid) to fall about in drops छिड़का जाना; to throw water etc. about पानी आदि इधर-उधर उलीचना या फेंकना; *v.t.* to cause to fall about in drops छिड़कना, उलीचना; to scatter बखेरना; to display prominently प्रदर्शित करना; दिखावा करना।

splash[2] *n.* act of splashing छिड़काव; sound of splashing छप-छप; liquid thrown about छींटा, छपाका; a noticeable patch धब्बा; extravagant display दिखावा।

spleen *स्प्लीन n.* an organ in the abdomen तिल्ली; morose temper उदासी, अनमनापन।

splendid *स्प्लैँन् डिड a.* magnificent शानदार, भव्य; excellent उत्तम, उत्कृष्ट।

splendour *स्प्लैनँ डः n.* magnificence भव्यता, वैभव; brightness चमक, दीप्ति।

splinter[1] *स्प्लिन् टः n.* a thin fragment किरच, छिपटी।

splinter[2] *v.t.* to break into splinters किरचों या छिपटियों में तोड़ना; *v.i.* to come off as splinters किरचों या छिपटियों में टूटना।

split[1] *स्प्लिट (-tt-) v.i.* to come apart lengthwise चिरना, फटना; to become disunited विभाजित होना; *v.t.* to break lengthwise चीरना, फाड़ना; to divide into shares हिस्सों में बांटना; to make disunited विभाजित करना।

split[2] *n.* act of splitting चीरने या फाड़ने का कार्य; a crack दरार, झिरी; division विभाजन।

spoil[1] *स्पौ ँइल v.t.* to damage, to ruin नष्ट कर देना; to plunder लूटना; to harm the character of बिगाड़ देना; *v.i.* to be damaged बिगड़ जाना।

spoil[2] *n.* booty लूट, लूट का माल; profit लाभ।

spoke *स्पोक n.* the radial bar of a wheel अर, आरा।

spokesman *स्पोक्स् मॅन n.* one who deputed to speak for others प्रवक्ता।

sponge[1] *स्पन्ज n.* a synthetic substance absorbing liquids स्पंज।

sponge[2] *v.t.* to wipe with sponge स्पंज से पोंछना या सोखना।

sponsor[1] *स्पौनॅ् सॅः n.* an advertiser who pays for a radio or television programme प्रायोजक; one promoting something उन्नायक।

sponsor[2] *v.t.* to act as a sponsor for प्रयोजित करना।

spontaneity *स्पौनॅ् टॅ नी इ टि n.* quality of being spontaneous स्वाभाविकता, स्वतः प्रवृत्ति।

spontaneous *स्पौनॅ् टे न्यॅस a.* voluntary स्वैच्छिक; natural स्वाभाविक स्वतः स्फूर्त।

spoon[1] *स्पून n.* a utensil with a shallow bowl at the end of a handle चम्मच।

spoon[2] *v.t.* to lift with a spoon चम्मच से उठाना।

spoonful *स्पून् फुल n.* the quantity contained by a spoon चम्मच-भर मात्रा।

sporadic *स्पॅ रै डिक, स्पौ ॅ-* *a.* scattered, occurring here and there छुट-पुट।

sport[1] *स्पौःट* *n.* fun, amusement मनोरंजन; athletic games खेल-कूद; mockery मज़ाक़; enjoyment आनंद।

sport[2] *v.i.* to play about, to amuse oneself खिलवाड़ करना, मन बहलाना।

sportive *स्पौः टिव* *a.* playful क्रीड़ाशील, विनोदी।

sportsman *स्पौःट्स् मॅन* *n.* one who engages in sports खिलाड़ी।

spot[1] *स्पौ ॅट* *n.* a tiny mark or stain निशान, धब्बा; blemish दोष; pimple मुंहासा place स्थान।

spot[2] *(-tt-)* *v.t.* to mark with spots धब्बे डालना; to detect खोजना, पता लगाना; to observe देखना।

spotless *स्पौ ॅट् लिस* *a.* unblemished दोषरहित; pure शुद्ध, साफ़-सुथरा।

spousal *स्पॉउ ज़ॅल* *n.* marriage विवाह।

spouse *स्पॉउज़* *n.* husband or wife पति अथवा पत्नी।

spout[1] *स्पॉउट* *n.* a narrow tube on a vessel through which liquid is poured out टोंटी; a pipe that takes water down from a roof पनाला; strong jet of water धारा।

spout[2] *v.i.* to gush, to pour out तेज़ी से बाहर निकलना।

sprain[1] *स्प्रेन* *n.* injury caused by wrenching मोच।

sprain[2] *v.t.* to injure by twisting violently मुड़काना, मोच करना।

spray[1] *स्प्रे* *n.* fine drops of liquid फुहार; a device for producing fine drops of liquid फुहारा।

spray[2] *n.* a branch, a twig टहनी; floral ornament फूलों का आभूषण।

spray[3] *v.t.* to sprinkle with shower of fine drops छिड़कना।

spread[1] *स्प्रै ॅड* *v.i.* to stretch फैलना; to become known प्रचारित होना; *v.t.* to apply a thin layer of लगाना; to open out बिछाना; to scatter बिखेरना।

spread[2] *n.* extent विस्तार; increase वृद्धि; a cloth covering for a bed or table पलंगपोश, मेज़पोश।

spree *स्प्री* *n.* a frolic, a romp मौज-मस्ती, उछल-कूद

sprig *स्प्रिग* *n.* a small twig टहनी; offshoot शाखा।

sprightly *स्प्रॉइट् लि* *a.* lively, brisk उत्साहपूर्ण, फुरतीला।

spring[1] *स्प्रिड़्ग* *v.i.* to leap उछलना; to come into being अस्तित्व में आना; to appear प्रकट होना; to grow उगना; *v.t.* to develop विकसित करना।

spring[2] *n.* a leap उछाल; a source of water सोता, जल-स्रोत; elasticity लचक; piece of metal with much resistance कमानी; the first season of the year बसंत ऋतु।

sprinkle *स्प्रिंङ् कॅल* *v. t.* to scatter in small drops छिड़कना।

sprint[1] *स्प्रिन्ट* *v.i.* to run a short distance at full speed खूब तेज़ी से दौड़ना।

sprint[2] *n.* a short fast run थोड़ी तेज़ी से दौड़।

sprout[1] *स्प्रॉउट* *v.i.* to put forth shoots अंकुरित होना; to spring up, to begin to grow उगना।

sprout[2] *n.* a new shoot अंकुर।

spur[1] *स्पॅ:* *n.* a pricking instrument attached to a horseman's heel महमेज़; the spike on a cock's leg कंट, खांग; stimulus प्रेरणा; a projecting part of a mountain range पर्वत-स्कंध।

spur[2] *(-rr-) v.t.* to prick with spurs एड़ लगाना।

spurious *स्प्यूॲ रि ॲस* *a.* not genuine नक़ली।

spurn *स्पॅ:न* *v.t.* to reject with scorn ठुकरा देना, अस्वीकार करना।

spurt[1] *स्पॅ:ट* *v.i.* to gush out फूट निकलना; to make a sudden effort झपट्टे से काम करना।

spurt[2] *n.* a gush, a jet तेज़ धार; a short sudden effort झपट्टा।

sputnik *स्पुट् निक* *n.* an artificial satellite कृत्रिम उपग्रह।

sputum *स्प्यू टॅम* *n.* saliva, spittle लार, थूक।

spy[1] *स्पॉइ* *n.* one who watches and reports secretly जासूस, गुप्तचर।

spy[2] *v.i.* to act as a spy जासूसी करना; *v.t.* to catch sight of देखना।

squad *स्क्वौ ˘ड* *n.* a small party दस्ता, टुकड़ी।

squadron *स्क्वौ ˘ड् रॅन* *n.* a division of cavalry regiment, fleet or aircraft स्क्वाड्रॅन, दस्ता।

squalid *स्क्वौ ˘लिड* *a.* dirty, uncared-for गंदा, घिनावना।

squalor *स्क्वौ ˘लॅ:* *n.* squalid state गंदगी, घिनावनापन।

squander *स्क्वौन् ˘डॅ:* *v.t.* to spend or use wastefully उड़ा देना, अपव्यय करना, गंवाना।

square[1] *स्क्वे ˘ॲ:* *n.* an equilateral rectangle वर्ग; anything is such a shape चौकोर टुकड़ा; open space मैदान, चौक; product of a number multiplied by itself वर्गफल; instrument for drawing right angle गुनिया।

square[2] *a.* of the shape of a square वर्गाकार; honest ईमानदार; even, quits बराबर; level समतल।

square[3] *v.t.* to make square वर्गाकार बनाना; to find square of (का) वर्ग निकालना; to tally मिलान करना; to pay चुकता करना; to bribe घूस देना।

squash[1] *स्क्वौशॅ* *v.t.* to crush into a pulp भुरता बना देना; to press or squeeze दबाना, भींचना; to repress (का) दमन करना।

squash[2] *n.* juice of crushed fruit फल-रस-पेय; crowd भीड़।

squat *स्क्वौट* *v.i.* to sit on heels उकडूं बैठना; to sit बैठना; to sit with the legs crossed पालथी मारना।

squeak[1] *स्क्वीक* *v.i.* to make short shrill sound चूं-चूं करना।

squeak[2] *n.* a short shrill sound चूं-चूं की ध्वनि।

squeeze *स्क्वीज़* *v.t.* to press दबाना, भींचना to press moisture from निचोड़ना; to pack tightly ठूंसकर भरना; to obtain by extortion तंग करना, विवश करना।

squint[1] *स्क्विन्ट* *v.i.* to have eyes looking different ways भेंगा होना; to glance side ways कनखी मारना।

squint[2] *n.* squinting position of eye-balls भेंगापन; sideways glance कनखी।

squire *स्क्वॉइअ:* *n.* the chief landowner जमींदार; a young gentleman attending on a knight अनुचर; one who escorts a lady अनुरक्षक।

squirrel *स्क्वि रॅल* *n.* a small rodent with a bushy tail गिलहरी।

stab[1] *स्टैब (-bb-) v.t.* to wound with a sharp pointed weapon छुरे से घायल करना; to push (a knife etc.) into somebody (छुरा) घोपना।

stab[2] *n.* act of stabbing धार-दार हथियार से प्रहार।

stability *स्टॅ बि लि टि* *n.* quality of being stable स्थायित्व।

stabilization *स्टे बि लॉइ ज़े शॅन* *n.* making stable स्थिरीकरण; being stable स्थिरीभवन।

stabilize *स्टे बि लॉइज़, स्टै-* *v.t.* to make stable स्थिर बनाना।

stable[1] *स्टे ब्ल* *a.* firm, steady स्थिर, दृढ़।

stable[2] *n.* building for horses अस्तबल।

stable[3] *v.t.* to put into a stable अस्तबल में रखना।

stadium *स्टे ड़्यॅम* *n.* a sports ground स्टेडियम, क्रीड़ा-स्थल।

staff[1] *स्टाफ़* *n.* a stick, a pole सोंटा, लाठी, डंडा; personnel कर्मचारीगण।

staff[2] *v.t.* to provide with personnel कर्मचारी प्रदान करना।

stag *स्टैग* *n.* a male deer हिरण।

stage[1] *स्टेज* *n.* a platform मंच; platform of theatre रंगमंच; dramatic art or profession नाट्यकला अथवा व्यवसाय; a step in development अवस्था, स्थिति, चरण; stopping place of a journey पड़ाव; distance between stopping places मंज़िल।

stage[2] *v.t.* to put (a play) on the stage (का) मंचन करना; to arrange in a dramatic manner नाटकीय ढंग से आयोजित करना।

stagger[1] *स्टै गॅ:* *v.i.* to walk unsteadily लड़खड़ाकर चलना; *v.t.* to astound, to startle चौंका देना; to shock धक्का पहुंचाना; to cause to walk or move unsteadily लड़खड़ा देना।

stagger[2] *n.* a reeling movement लड़खड़ाहट।

stagnant *स्टैग् नॅन्ट* *a.* not moving स्थिर; foul, impure गंदा; sluggish मंद, गतिहीन।

stagnate *स्टैग् नेट* *v.i.* to be stagnant स्थिर या गतिहीन होना; to cease to develop विकसित न होना।

stagnation *स्टैग् ने शॅन* *n.* state or quality of being stagnant गतिहीनता, विकासहीनता।

staid *स्टेड* *a.* sober, sedate गंभीर, शांतमना।

stain[1] *स्टेन* *n.* spot, mark धब्बा, निशान; staining material अभिरंजक।

stain[2] *v.t.* to mark, to spot (पर) धब्बे लगाना; to apply staining material to अभिरंजक लगाना; to bring disgrace upon कलंकित करना।

stainless *स्टेन् लिस* *a.* free from stain बेदाग़; so made that it will not stain जंगरोधी।

stair *स्टे ॲ:* *n.* one of a series of steps पैड़ी; *(pl.)* set of steps ज़ीना, सोपान।

stake[1] *स्टेक* *n.* sharpened stick or

post खूंटा; execution by burning अग्निदंड; money risked in gamling बाज़ी की रक़म।

stake[2] *v.t.* to risk (का) जोखिम लेना; to support with stakes खूंटों का सहारा देना; to wager (की) बाज़ी लगाना।

stale[1] स्टेल *a.* not fresh बासी; hackneyed घिसापिटा, पुराना; dull अरुचिकर; tired थका हुआ।

stale[2] *v.t.* to make stale बासी करना; *v.i.* to become stale बासी होना।

stalemate स्टेल् मेट *n.* (chess) position from which no further move is possible ज़िच; deadlock गतिरोध।

stalk[1] स्टौक *n.* a plant's stem डंठल।

stalk[2] *v.i.* to walk in a stiff and stately manner शान से अकड़कर चलना; to follow stealthily चोरी-चोरी पीछा करना।

stalk[3] *n.* stiff manner of walking गर्वीली चाल; act of stalking game लुक-छिप कर शिकार।

stall[1] स्टौल *n.* a compartment for one animal in a cattle-shed थान; erection for display and sale of goods छोटी दुकान; a seat in a cathedral आसन; front seat in a theatre अग्रिम आसन; a finger sheath अंगुली-त्राण।

stall[2] *v.t.* to put in a stall थान पर रखना; to delay टालना; to hinder रोकना; *v.i.* (of a motor engine) to stop unintentionally अचानक रुक जाना; (of an aircraft) to lose flying speed (वायुयान की) उड़ने की गति समाप्त होना।

stallion स्टैल् यॅन *n.* uncastrated horse बिना बधिया किया घोड़ा।

stalwart[1] स्टौल् वॅःट *a.* strong, sturdy मज़बूत, हृष्ट-पुष्ट; staunch loyal निष्ठावान।

stalwart[2] *n.* a stalwart person पक्का समर्थक।

stamina स्टै मि नॅ *n.* power of endurance दम-ख़म, शक्ति।

stammer[1] स्टै मॅः *v.i.* to speak haltingly हकलाना।

stammer[2] *n.* halting speech हकलाहट।

stamp[1] स्टैम्प *n.* stamping with the foot पैर की थाप; imprinted mark छाप; appliance for marking मोहर, मुद्रा; a printed piece of paper stuck on letters etc. डाक टिकट; characteristic mark लक्षण।

stamp[2] *v.i.* to put down foot with force पैर पटकाना; *v.t.* to impress mark on मुद्रांकित करना; to affix postage stamp on (पर) टिकट लगाना; to fix in memory स्मृति में बिठाना।

stampede[1] स्टैम् पीड *n.* sudden rush of panic-stricken animals or people भगदड़।

stampede[2] *v.i.* to run in panic भगदड़ मचना; *v.t.* to cause stampede (में) भगदड़ मचाना।

stand[1] स्टैन्ड *v.i.* to remain upright खड़ा होना या रहना; to rise to one's feet उठ खड़ा होना; to remain मौजूद होना; to be situated स्थित होना; to cease to move स्थिर रहना; to offer oneself as a candidate चुनाव में खड़ा होना; to be symbol (of) प्रतीक होना; *v.t.* to set in upright position खड़ा करना; to endure सहन करना।

stand² *n.* stopping of motion ठहराव; position taken up मोरचा; a piece of furniture used as support धानी; a stall on which goods are displayed दुकान; place for vehicles to stand अड्डा।

standard¹ *स्टैन् डॅःड* *n.* a model by which other things are judged मानक; level स्तर; a banner, flag झंडा; a measure माप; class कक्षा।

standard² *a.* usual सामान्य; of recognized authority प्रामाणिक।

standardization *स्टैन् डॅः डॉइ ज़े शॅन* *n.* act of standardizing मानकीकरण।

standardize *स्टैन् डॅः डॉइज़* *v.t.* to regulate by a standard (का) मानकीकरण करना।

standing *स्टैन् डिङ्ग* *n.* rank or position दरजा या स्थान; reputation ख्याति; duration अवधि।

standpoint *स्टैन्ड् पौँ इन्ट* *n.* point of view दृष्टिकोण।

standstill *स्टैन्ड् स्टिल* *n.* stoppage विराम।

stanza *स्टैन् ज़ॅ* *n.* a group of lines of verse forming a unit बंद, छंद।

staple¹ *स्टे पल* *n.* main product मुख्य उपज; fibre रेशा; raw material कच्चा माल; a bent piece of wire for fastening sheets of paper स्टेपल।

staple² *a.* chief, basic मुख्य, प्रधान।

star¹ *स्टाः* *n.* a twinkling heavenly body तारा; asterisk तारक; an outstanding actor or actress प्रसिद्ध अभिनेता अथवा अभिनेत्री; luck भाग्य; a star shaped badge सितारा।

star² *(-rr-) v.t.* to mark with a star or stars तारांकित करना; *v.i.* to be a famous actor or actress प्रसिद्ध अभिनेता अथवा अभिनेत्री होना।

starch¹ *स्टाःच* *n.* a white food substance found esp. in grain and potatoes श्वेत सार; a powdered form of this substance used for stiffening linen कलफ़।

starch² *v.t.* to stiffen with starch (पर) कलफ़ लगाना।

stare¹ *स्टे ॅअः* *v.i.* to look fixedly घूरना; to be obvious or visible स्पष्ट दिखाई देना।

stare² *n.* a fixed gaze टकटकी।

stark¹ *स्टॉःक* *n.* bleak फीका, निरानंद; absolute निरा, कोरा।

stark² *adv.* completely सरासर, पूर्ण रूप से।

starry *स्टा रि* *a.* full of stars तारामय; consisting of stars तारों से जड़ा; bright चमकदार।

start¹ *स्टाःट* *v.t.* to begin प्रारंभ करना; to set going चालू करना; *v.i.* to begin प्रारंभ होना; to make sudden movement चालू होना; to be set up स्थापित होना।

start² *n.* beginning प्रारंभ; abrupt movement प्रस्थान; act of setting शुभारंभ, स्थापना; advantage conceded रिआयत; a sudden movement due to surprise चौंक।

startle *स्टाः ट्ल* *v.t.* to alarm, to give a fright to चौंकाना।

starvation *स्टाः वे शॅन* *n.* suffering or death caused by lack of food भूखमरी।

starve *स्टाःव* *v.i.* to suffer or die

from hunger भूखों मरना; *v.t.* to cause to suffer or die from hunger भूखों मारना।

state[1] स्टेट *n.* condition अवस्था, दशा; place, situation स्थिति; politically organized people राज्य; government सरकार; rank पद; pomp शान, ठाठ-बाट।

state[2] *v.t.* to express in words कहना।

stateliness *स्टेट् लि निस n.* splendour, pomp शान।

stately *स्टेट् लि a.* splendid imposing शानदार, भव्य।

statement *स्टेट् मॅन्ट n.* act of stating कथन; expression in words अभिव्यक्ति; account विवरण।

statesman *स्टेट्स् मॅन n.* an eminent politician राजनेता।

static *स्टै टिक n.* motionless स्थिर, गतिहीन।

statics *स्टै टिक्स n. sing.* science dealing with bodies at rest स्थैतिकी, स्थिति-विज्ञान।

station[1] *स्टे शॅन n.* a stopping place for railway trains स्टेशन; rank or social position स्थिति, पद।

station[2] *v.t.* to put in position रखना, तैनात करना।

stationary *स्टे शॅ नॅ रि a.* not moving स्थिर, अचल।

stationer *स्टे शॅ नॅः n.* one who sells stationery लेखन-सामग्री-विक्रेता।

stationery *स्टे शॅ नॅ रि n.* writing materials लेखन-सामग्री।

statistical *स्टॅ टिस् टि कॅल a.* pertaining to statistics सांख्यिकीय।

statistician *स्टै टिस् टि शॅन n.* one expert in statistics सांख्यिकीविद्।

statistics *स्टॅ टिस् टिक्स n.* facts shown in numbers आंकड़े; science that studies such facts सांख्यिकी।

statue *स्टै ट्यू n.* a figure cast in stone or metal मूर्ति, प्रतिमा।

stature *स्ट चॅः n.* bodily height क़द, ऊंचाई; greatness महानता, उच्चता।

status *स्टे टॅस n.* position, rank पद, स्थान; prestige प्रतिष्ठा।

statute *स्टै ट्यूट n.* written law संविधि, क़ानून।

statutory *स्टै ट्यु टॅ रि a.* defined or authorized by statute वैधानिक, क़ानूनी।

staunch *स्टौन्च a.* reliable, trustworthy विश्वसनीय, निष्ठावान।

stay[1] *स्टै v.i.* to remain रहना; to sojourn ठहरना, टिकना; to pause रुकना थमना; to wait प्रतीक्षा करना; to endure चलना, बना रहना; *v.t.* to stop रोकना; to hinder बाधित या अवरुद्ध करना; to postpone स्थगित करना।

stay[2] *n.* sojourning ठहराव; check रोक; restraint बंधन; postponement स्थगन; support टेक, सहारा।

steadfast *स्टैॅड् फ़ास्ट a.* firm resolute दृढ़, अटल।

steadiness *स्टैॅ डि निस n.* quality of being steady दृढ़ता तत्परता।

steady[1] *स्टैॅ डि a.* firm दृढ़ regular नियमित; temperate धीर, संतुलित।

steady[2] *v.t.* to make firm दृढ़ बनाना; *v.i.* to become steady दृढ़ बनना।

steal *स्टील v.i.* to commit theft चोरी करना; to move silently चोरी-चोरी आना या जाना; *v.t.* to take unlawfully चुराना।

stealthily *स्टील् थि लि adv.* secretly चोरी-छुपे।

steam[1] स्टीम *n.* vapour of boiling shift water भाप; the power of steam वाष्प-शक्ति।

steam[2] *v.i.* to give off steam भाप छोड़ना; to rise in vapour भाप निकलना; to move by steam power वाष्प-निकलना; वाष्प-शक्ति से चलना; *v.t.* to cook or treat with steam भाप से पकाना या भाप देना।

steamer *स्टी मॅः n.* a steamship स्टीमर; vessel in which food is cooked by being steamed भापतापी पात्र।

steed *स्टीड n.* a horse घोड़ा।

steel *स्टील n.* a hard alloy of iron and carbon इस्पात; a weapon of steel, esp. a sword लोहे का शस्त्र, विशेषतया तलवार।

steep[1] *स्टीप a.* sloping sharply तीव्र ढलान वाला।

steep[2] *v.t.* to soak, to saturate भिगोना, तर करना।

steeple *स्टी प्ल n.* church tower with spire मीनार।

steer *स्टिअॅः v.t.* to guide or direct the course of (का) मार्गदर्शन करना; *v.i.* to respond to guidance दिशा निर्देशन को मानना।

stellar *स्टै˘ लॅः a.* relating to stars तारकीय, नक्षत्रीय।

stem[1] *स्टैमॅ n.* stalk डंठल; trunk तना; a long slender part पतली डंडी; the front part of a ship जलयान का अग्र भाग; the unchanging part of a word धातु, मूल शब्द।

stem[2] *(-mm-) v.i.* to arise पैदा होना, उठना।

stench *स्टैन्च n.* unpleasant smell दुर्गंध, बदबू।

stencil[1] *स्टैन् सिल n.* a thin sheet with letters or patterns cut in it स्टैंसिल; the pattern made from it इससे बनी छाप।

stencil[2] *(-ll-) v.i.* to make a pattern by means of a stencil स्टेंसिल से नमूना या चित्र बनाना।

stenographer *स्टै˘ नौ˘ ग्रॅ फॅ n.* a writer of shorthand आशुलिपिक।

stenography *स्टै˘ नौ˘ ग्रॅ फ़ि n.* shorthand writing आशुलिपि।

step[1] *स्टैपॅ n.* act of stepping क़दम; sound made by stepping पदचाप; mark made by foot पंदचिह्न manner of walking चाल; distance covered by stepping once डग, पग; a rung, a stair सीढ़ी का डंडा, पैड़ी; measure उपाय।

step[2] *(-pp-) v.i.* to move and set down foot चलना; *v.t*, to measure in paces डगों से नापना।

steppe *स्टैपॅ n.* a large treeless plain घास का मैदान।

stereotype[1] *स्टै˘ रि अॅ टॉइप n.* a metal plate for printing cast from set up type मुद्रण-फलक; a fixed pattern घिसा-पिटा, स्थिर नमूना।

stereotype[2] *v.t.* to make stereotype of (को) घिसा-पिटा रूप देना।

stereotyped *स्टै˘ रि अॅ टाइप्ड a.* conventional परंपरागत, रूढ़िबद्ध।

sterile *स्टै˘ रॉइल a.* (woman) not able to produce offspring बांझ; (land) not able to produce any crop बंजर, ऊसर; free from germs जीवाणुरहित।

sterility *स्टै ˘ रि लि टि n.* inability to produce offspring बांझपन; inability to produce any crop बंजरपना; being without germs जीवाणुहीनता।

sterilization *स्टै ˘ रि लॉइ ज़े शॅन n.* rendering a woman unable to produce offspring बंध्यीकरण; freeing from germs जीवाणुनाशन।

sterilize *स्टै ˘ रि लॉइज़ v.t.* to render (a woman) unable to produce offspring बांझ बनाना; to make free from germs जीवाणुरहित बनाना।

sterling[1] *स्टॅ: लिङ्ग a.* genuine, true खरा, असली; of solid worth पक्का; dependable विश्वसनीय।

sterling[2] *n.* genuine British money खरी ब्रिटिश मुद्रा।

stern[1] *स्टॅ:न a.* severe, strict कठोर, कड़ा।

stern[2] *n.* rear part of a ship जलयान का पिछला भाग।

stethoscope *स्टै ˘ थॅस् कोप n.* an instrument for listening to heart-beats and breath-sounds etc. स्टैथौस्कोप, परिश्रावक।

stew[1] *स्ट्यू n.* a dish of meat and vegetables cooked slowly धीमी आंच में पकाया भोजन; state of excitement उत्तेजना।

stew[2] *v.t.* to cook slowly in a closed vessel बंद बरतन में धीरे-धीरे पकाना; *v.i.* to be cooked gently धीरे-धीरे पकना।

steward *स्ट्यु अॅ:ड n.* one who manages another's property प्रबंधक; one who organizes the catering in a club etc. खाद्य-प्रबंधक; one who helps to run functions समारोह-संचालक; one who waits on passengers in a ship or aircraft खिदमतगार।

stick[1] *स्टिक n.* a long thin piece of wood लाठी, लकड़ी, डंडा; a wand छड़ी।

stick[2] *v.t.* to stab, to pierce चुभोना, घोंपना; to fasten with gum चिपकाना; to push into or through आर-पार निकालना; *v.i.* to adhere चिपकना; to come to stop अटक जाना, रुक जाना; to be fastened लगना, अटकना।

sticker *स्टि कॅ: n.* an adhesive label चिप्पी, स्टिकर।

stickler *स्टिक् लॅ: n.* a person who insists on something आग्रही।

sticky *स्टि कि n.* adhesive चिपचिपा; difficult जटिल।

stiff *स्टिफ़ n.* not easily bent अनम्य; rigid कठोर; difficult कठिन, जटिल; not easily moved कड़ा; thick, viscous गाढ़ा; excessive अत्यधिक।

stiffen *स्टि फ़ॅन v.t.* to make stiff कड़ा या कठोर बनाना; *v.i.* to become stiff कड़ा या कठोर बनना।

stifle *स्टि फ़्ल v.t.* to suffocate (का) दम घोटना; to suppress दबाना; *v.i.* to feel suffocated दम घुटना।

stigma *स्टिग् मॅ n.* a mark of shame कलंक, लांछन।

still[1] *स्टिल a.* motionless स्थिर, अचल; noiseless चुप, शांत।

still[2] *adv.* to this time अब तक; yet तथापि; motionlessly स्थिर अवस्था में, noiselessly शांत रूप में।

still[3] *v.t.* to silence, to make quiet शांत करना।

still⁴ *n.* a single picture from a cinema film अचल चित्र; deep silence नीरवता, सन्नाटा; an apparatus for distilling भभका।

stillness *स्टिल् निस n.* the state or quality of being still शांति, स्थिरता।

stilt *स्टिल्ट n.* a pole with footrest for walking, raised from ground पैरबांसा।

stimulant *स्टि म्यु लॅन्ट n.* drug etc. acting as a stimulus प्रेरक पदार्थ।

stimulate *स्टि म्यु लेट v.t.* to rouse up, to stir up उभारना, उद्दीप्त करना, प्रेरित करना।

stimulus *स्टि म्यु लॅस n.* that which stimulates प्रेरणा, प्रोत्साहन।

sting¹ *सिटङ्ग v.t.* to wound with a sting डंक मारना; to inflict sharp pain तीव्र पीड़ा पहुंचाना; *v.i.* to feel sharp pain तीव्र पीड़ा होना।

sting² *n.* pointed tail of insects like wasps etc. डंक; a. cause of mental pain मानसिक वेदना का कारण।

stingy *स्टिन् जि a.* niggardly, miserly कंजूस, मक्खीचूस।

stink¹ *स्टिङ्क v.i.* to give out offensive smell बदबूदार होना।

stink² *n.* stench, unpleasant smell बदबू, दुर्गंध।

stipend *स्टॉइ पैन्ड n.* a salary esp., of a clergyman वृत्ति, वज़ीफ़ा।

stipulate *स्टि प्यु लेट v.t.* to put forward as a necessary condition शर्त लगाना।

stipulation *स्टि प्यु ले शॅन n.* provision व्यवस्था; condition शर्त।

stir *स्टॅ: (-rr-) v.i.* to move हिलना; to be roused उमड़ना; *v.t.* to cause to move हिलाना; to rouse भड़काना।

stirrup *स्टि रॅप n.* a support hung from a saddle for the rider's feet रकाब।

stitch¹ *स्टिच n.* movement of a needle in sewing सीवन; the amount of thread left by such a movement टांका; sharp pain हूक, पार्श्वशूल।

stitch² *v.t.* to sew सिलना; *v.i.* to do needlework सिलाई करना।

stock¹ *स्टौकॅ n.* material stored माल, सामान; reserve भंडार; farm animals पशुधन; reputation प्रतिष्ठा; ancestry वंश; capital of a company मूलधन, पूंजी; tree trunk तना; money lent to the government सरकारी ऋण।

stock² *v.t.* to keep, to store (का) भंडारण करना; to supply with livestock पशुधन की आपूर्ति करना; to keep (goods) in readiness for sale बिक्री के लिए रखना।

stock³ *a.* kept in store for sale बिक्री के लिए उपलब्ध; hackneyed घिसा-पिटा।

stocking *स्टौ˘ किङ्ग n.* a close fitting covering for leg and foot मौज़ा।

stoic *स्टो˘ इक n.* one who endures pain without complaining वैरागी, तापस, साधु।

stoke *स्टोक v.t.* to feed with fuel (में) ईधन झोंकना; *v.i.* to act as stoker ईंधन का काम करना।

stoker *स्टो कॅ: n.* one who feeds the fire with fuel ईंधन झोंकने वाला।

stomach[1] स्ट मॅक *n.* abdomen पेट; appetite भूख; desire इच्छा।
stomach[2] *v.t.* to endure, to put up with बरदाश्त करना।
stone[1] स्टोन *n.* a piece of rock पत्थर; gem रत्न, नगीना; hard seed of fruit गुठली; hard deposit formed in kidneys पथरी, अश्मरी; a unit of weight, 14 pounds 14 पाउंड का बट्टा।
stone[2] *v.t.* to throw stones at (पर) पत्थर फेंकना; to take the stones out of (fruit) (फल से) गुठली निकालना।
stony स्टो नि *a.* full of stones, covered with stones पथरीला; hard कठोर; cold भावशून्य।
stool स्टूल *n.* a backless chair स्टूल, चौकी; excrement विष्टा।
stoop[1] स्टूप *v.i.* to lean forward or down झुकना; to lower oneself morally नैतिक रूप से गिरना; *v.t.* to bend forwards and downwards झुकाना।
stoop[2] *n.* stooping position of the body झुकाव।
stop[1] स्टॉप *(-pp-) v.t.* to bring to halt रोकना; to prevent न करने देना; to interrupt (में) रूकावट पैदा करना; to suspend रोक देना; to fill up (an opening) (छेद आदि) भर देना; to bring to an end बंद करना, समाप्त करना; *v.i.* to come to a halt रुकना; to stay ठहरना।
stop[2] *n.* stopping विराम; punctuation mark विरामचिह्न; a. fixed point at which buses etc. stop बस-स्टॉप; (music) a divice for regulating pitch खूंटी।
stoppage स्टौ ˘ पिज *n.* ceasing to work रूकावट; state of being stopped अवरोध।
storage स्टौ रिज *n.* a place for storing गोदाम, भंडार; act of storing भंडारण, संचयन।
store[1] स्टौ:, स्टौं: *n.* a stock of things भंडार; abundance प्रचुरता; shop दुकान; place for keeping goods गोदाम।
store[2] *v.t.* to lay up बचा रखना; to put in a godown or warehouse गोदाम में रखना।
storey स्टौ रि *n.* horizontal division of a building मंज़िल, खंड।
stork स्टौ:क *n.* a large wading bird सारस।
storm[1] स्टौ:म *n.* violent weather with wind, rain, hail etc. झंझावत, तूफान; an assault on a fortress धावा; violent outbreak उपद्रव, हुल्लड़।
storm[2] *v.i.* to shout angrily (at) गुस्से से चीख़ना; *v.t.* to capture अधिकार में करना; to force an entry into (में) ज़बरदस्ती घुस जाना।
stormy स्टौ: मि *a.* like storm, characterised by storm तूफ़ानी; violent प्रचंड।
story स्टौ रि *n.* a narrative कहानी।
stout स्टॉउट *a.* strong, though मज़बूत, कड़ा; brave, resolute बहादुर, संकल्पशील; fat स्थूलकाय।
stove स्टोव *n.* an apparatus for cooking, heating etc. स्टोव, अंगीठी।
stow स्टो *v.t.* to pack, put away carefully बांधकर रख देना।
straggle स्ट्रै ग्ल *v.i.* to spread in

an irregular manner तितर-बितर हो जाना, बिखर जाना; to drop behind while on the march पिछड़ जाना; to stray away from the main group भटक जाना।

straggler *स्ट्रे ग्लॅ:* *n.* one who straggles भटकैया।

straight[1] *स्ट्रेट* *a.* without bend सीधा, ऋजु; honest ईमानदार; neat, tidy साफ़-सुथरा; outspoken स्पष्टवादी।

straight[2] *adv.* in a straight line सीधे; without delay तुरंत।

straighten *स्ट्रे टॅन* *v.t.* to make straight सीधा करना।

straightforward *स्ट्रेट फ़ौ: वॅ:ड* *a.* honest ईमानदार; without evasion स्पष्ट सीधा-सादा; easy to understand सरल।

straightway *स्ट्रेट् वे* *adv.* immediately तुरंत।

strain[1] *स्ट्रेन* *v.t.* to stretch tightly कसकर तानना; to weaken by over-exertion अधिक श्रम से थकाना; to filter छानना; *v.i.* to make great effort ज़ोरदार प्रयत्न करना।

strain[2] *n.* great effort ज़ोरदार प्रयास; stretching force तनाव, खिंचाव, fatigue थकान; great demand मांग; injury from being sprained over-work मोच; घोर परिश्रम।

strait *स्ट्रेट* *n.* a channel of water connection two seas जलडमरूमध्य।

straiten *स्ट्रे टॅन* *v.t.* to make narrow संकीर्ण बनाना; to press with poverty ग़रीबी से दबाना।

strand[1] *स्ट्रैन्ड* *v.i.* to run a ground भूग्रस्त होना; to be left in difficulties परेशानी में छूटना; *v.t.* to cause to run a ground भूग्रस्त करना; to leave in difficulties परेशानी में छोड़ना।

strand[2] *n.* one single string or wire of rope लड़; shore समुद्र-तट।

strange *स्ट्रेन्ज* *a.* odd अनोखा, अटपटा; uncommon असामान्य; wonderful अद्‌भुत, आश्चर्यजनक; foreign विदेशी; singular अद्वितीय।

stranger *स्ट्रेन् जॅ:* *n.* an unknown person अजनबी; foreigner विदेशी; one unaccustomed अनुभवहीन अथवा नौसिखिया व्यक्ति।

strangle *स्ट्रैङ् गल* *v.t.* to kill by throttling गला घोंटकर मारना; to suppress दबाना।

strangulation *स्ट्रैङ् ग्यु ले शॅन* *n.* strangling श्वास-अवरोधन।

strap[1] *स्ट्रैप* *n.* a strip of leather or other material पट्टा।

strap[2] *(-pp-)* *v.t.* to hit with a strap पट्टे से मारना; to fasten with a strap पट्टे से बांधना।

strategem *स्ट्रै टि जॅम* *n.* a plan, a trick चाल, छल।

strategic *स्ट्रॅ टी जिक* *a.* pertaining to strategy युद्धनीति-विषयक; of value for strategy युद्धनीति की दृष्टि से महत्वपूर्ण।

strategist *स्ट्रै टि जिस्ट* *n.* one skilled in strategy युद्धनीतिज्ञ।

strategy *स्ट्रै टि जि* *n.* art of war युद्ध-कौशल; overall plan समूची योजना।

stratum *स्ट्रै टॅम, स्ट्रा टॅम* *n. (pl.-ta)* layer of rock स्तर।

straw *स्ट्रौ n.* stalks of grain भूसा; a single stalk तिनका।

strawberry *स्ट्रौ बॅ रि n.* a creeping plant with red fruit झरबेरी; its fruit झरबेर।

stray[1] *स्ट्रे v.i.* to wander घूमना; to digress भटकना; to get lost खो जाना।

stray[2] *a.* strayed भटका हुआ; occasional बिरला, कोई-कोई।

stray[3] *n.* a lost child or animal भटका हुआ बच्चा या पशु; an isolated example इक्का-टुक्का मामला।

stream[1] *स्ट्रीम n.* a river, a brook नदी, नाला; steady flow प्रवाह तांता।

stream[2] *v.i.* to flow बहना; to float on air लहराना।

streamer *स्ट्री मॅः n.* a long, narrow flag पताका।

streamlet *स्ट्रीम् लिट n.* a small stream, brook नदिया, नाला।

street *स्ट्रीट n.* a road in town or village गली, सड़क।

strength *स्ट्रै ङ्ग्थ n.* quality of being strong शक्ति, बल; toughness मज़बूती, कड़ापन; vehemence प्रचंडता; full number of people लोगों की पूरी संख्या।

strengthen *स्ट्रैङ् थॅन v.t.* to make stronger मज़बूत बनाना; *v.i.* to become stronger शक्तिशाली बनना।

strenuous *स्ट्रै न्यु अॅस a.* energetic ज़ोरदार; using great effort अध्यवसायी।

stress[1] *स्ट्रैसॅ n.* emphasis बल; tension तनाव; strain घोर श्रम; fatigue थकान; pressure दबाव; effort प्रयत्न accent बलाघात।

stress[2] *v.t.* to emphasize (पर) बल देना; to put accent on (पर) बलाघात करना।

stretch[1] *स्ट्रैचॅ v.t.* to extend फैलाना; to exert to utmost (पर) पूरा ज़ोर लगाना; to tighten कसना; to reach out आगे बढ़ाना; *v.i.* to extend फैलना; to have elasticity नम्य होना।

stretch[2] *n.* act of stretching तनाव, खिंचाव; expance विस्तार; spell दौर, वार।

stretcher *स्ट्रै चॅः n.* an appliance on which a disabled person is carried मरीज़ को ले जाने का चौखटा, स्ट्रेचर।

strew *स्ट्रुः v.t.* to scatter बिखेरना।

strict *स्ट्रिक्ट a.* severe कठोर, सख़्त; without exception अपवादरहित; accurate, precise विशुद्ध।

stricture *स्ट्रिक् चॅः n.* severe criticism कटु आलोचना; constriction निकोचन।

stride[1] *स्ट्रॉइड v.i.* to walk with long steps लंबे डग मारना।

stride[2] *n.* a long step लंबा डग।

strident *स्ट्रॉइ डॅन्ट a.* harsh in tone कर्कश; loud कर्णभेदी।

strife[1] *स्ट्रॉइफ n.* conflict संघर्ष, झगड़ा।

strike[1] *स्ट्रॉइक v.t.* to deal a blow to मारना; to attack आक्रमण करना; to produce (fire) by friction घर्षण-द्वारा (अग्नि) उत्पन्न करना; to hit against टकराना; to enter the mind of (के) मन में आना; to arrive at (पर) पहुंचना; to affect प्रभावित करना; to discover खोज निकालना; to cancel, to cross out काट देना; to indicate (the hour) by strokes बजाना; *v.i.* to deal a blow घूंसा मारना; to make an attack आक्रमण करना; to sound बजना; to cease work हड़ताल करना।

strike² *n.* act of stopping work हड़ताल; discovery of oil etc. by drilling तेल की खोज; a sudden attack by aircraft हवाई हमला।

striker *स्ट्राँइ कँ:* *n.* one who is on strike हड़तालकर्त्ता।

string¹ *स्ट्रिङ्ग* *n.* a thin cord रस्सी, डोरी; length of wire in violins, guitars etc. तंत्री, तार; series शृंखला, तांता।

string² *v.t.* to supply with strings तार या तंत्री से सज्जित करना; to put on a string धागे में गूंथना; to hang on a string डोरी पर लटकाना।

stringency *स्ट्रिन् जॅन् सि* *n.* severity सख़्ती, कड़ाई।

stringent *स्ट्रिन् जॅन्ट* *a.* strict, rigid कठोर, सख्त।

strip¹ *स्ट्रिप* *n.* a long narrow piece पट्टी।

strip² *(-pp-)* *v.t.* to lay bare नंगा करना; to remove outer covering of उघाड़ना; to deprive वंचित करना; *v.i.* to undress कपड़े उतारना, नंगा होना।

stripe¹ *स्ट्रॉइप* *n.* a narrow mark, band धारी; mark on a uniform to show rank फ़ीता।

stripe² *v.t.* to mark with stripes (पर) धारी बनाना।

strive *स्ट्रॉइव* *v.i.* to try hard, to struggle भरसक प्रयत्न करना, संघर्ष करना।

stroke¹ *स्ट्रोक* *n.* blow प्रहार; sudden action, occurrence घटना; mark of pen घसीट; mark of brush स्पर्श; chime of clock टनटन; single movement of the hand or hands हाथ का घुमाव।

stroke² *v.t.* to pass hand lightly over (पर) हाथ फेरना।

stroke³ *n.* a stroking movement हाथ फेरने की क्रिया।

stroll¹ *स्ट्रोल* *v.i.* to walk in a leisurely manner टहलना, चहलक़दमी करना।

stroll² *n.* a leisurely walk चहलक़दमी।

strong *स्ट्रौ ँङ्ग* *a.* powerful शक्तिशाली; robust हृष्ट-पुष्ट; firm दृढ़; difficult to break पक्का, मज़बूत; intense गहन; emphatic ज़ोरदार; not diluted गाढ़ा; ardent प्रगाढ़।

stronghold *स्ट्रौँङ्ग् होल्ड* *n.* a fort क़िला, गढ; a centre of some beliefs or activities केंद्र।

structural *स्ट्रक् चॅ रॅल* *a.* pertaining to structure संरचनात्मक।

structure *स्ट्रक् चँ:* *n.* manner of construction संरचना, बनावट; something constructed निर्माण।

struggle¹ *स्ट्र ग्ल* *v.i.* to contend resolutely संघर्ष करना; to make great effort भरसक प्रयत्न करना।

struggle² *n.* violent effort संघर्ष।

strumpet *स्ट्रम् पिट* *n.* a prostitute वेश्या।

strut¹ *स्ट्रट* *(-tt-)* *v.i.* to walk in a conceited manner इठलाना, अकड़कर चलना।

strut² *n.* conceited walk गर्वीली चाल; a rigid support टेक।

stub *स्टब* *n.* a tree stump ठूंठ; a short piece of pencil पेंसिल का टुकड़ा; a short remaining part of a cigarette सिगरेट का बचा हुआ भाग।

stubble *स्ट ब्ल* *n.* stumps of cut grain after reaping खूंटी, ठूंठी; short growth of beard दाढ़ी के छोटे बाल।

stubborn *स्ट बॅःन* *a.* obstinate हठीला, जिद्दी।

stud[1] *स्टड* *n.* a nail with a large head गुलमेख; a double-headed button दुहरा बटन।

stud[2] *(-dd-)* *v.t.* to set with studs जड़ना।

student *स्ट्यू डॅन्ट* *n.* one who studies at a college etc. विद्यार्थी, छात्र; a studious person अध्येता।

studio *स्ट्यू डि ओ* *n.* the work, room of an artist, photographer etc. शिल्पशाला; building where film, television or radio shows are made or broadcast प्रसारण-कक्ष, प्रसार-भवन।

studious *स्ट्यू ड्यॅस* *a.* devoted to study अध्ययनशील।

study[1] *स्ट डि* *v.i.* to be engaged in learning अध्ययन करना; *v.t.* to examine carefully (का) गूढ़ निरीक्षण करना; to make study of (का) अध्ययन करना; to show concern for के विषय में चिंतित होना।

study[2] *n.* devotion to gaining knowledge अध्ययन; subject studied अध्ययन का विषय; a room for studying in अध्ययनकक्ष; scrutiny जांच।

stuff[1] *स्टफ़* *n.* material पदार्थ; raw material कच्चा माल; any substance कोई पदार्थ।

stuff[2] *v.t.* to fill tightly ठूंसकर भरना; to fill (animal's skin) with material (पशु-चर्म में) कुछ भरना; to fill with seasoned mixture (में) मसाला भरना।

stuffy *स्ट फ़ि* *a.* lacking fresh air घुटन-भरा; dull उबाऊ; conventional परंपरागत।

stumble[1] *स्टम् ब्ल* *v.i.* to trip and nearly fall ठोकर खाना; to falter लड़खड़ाना।

stumble[2] *n.* act of stumbling ठोकर।

stump[1] *स्टम्प* *n.* ramnant of a tree ठूंठ; what is left after cutting or breakage अंश, टुकड़ा; (cricket) one of the three upright sticks that form the wicket डंडा, स्टंप।

stump[2] *v.t.* to puzzle चकरा देना; to strike the vicket of (को) आउट करना; *v.i.* to walk clumsily पैर पटककर चलना।

stun *स्टन* *(-nn-)* *v.t.* to knock senseless चोट मारकर अचेत करना; to amaze आश्चर्यचकित करना।

stunt[1] *स्टन्ट* *v.t.* to check growth of (का) विकास रोकना।

stunt[2] *n.* a feat of dexterity of daring करतब; a sensational idea for gaining publicity प्रचार-साधन।

stupefy *स्ट्यू पि फ़ॉइ* *v.t.* to make stupid मूर्ख बनाना।

stupendous *स्ट्यू पैन् डॅस* *a.* amazing आश्चर्यजनक; huge विशाल।

stupid *स्ट्यू पिड* *a.* foolish, silly मूर्ख, बुद्धू; slow-witted मंदबुद्धि।

stupidity *स्ट्यू पि डि टि* *n.* foolishness मूर्खता।

sturdy *स्टॅः डि* *a.* strong, rigorous तगड़ा, हृष्ट-पुष्ट; strongly built मज़बूत।

sty, stye *स्टॉइ* *n.* inflammation on the edge of eye-lid अंजनहारी।

style *स्टॉइल* *n.* manner of writing, speaking etc. शैली; sort प्रकार; fashion in dress फ़ैशन; manner ढंग, तरीक़ा; design बनावट।

subdue *सॅब् ड्यू* *v.t.* to bring under control वश में करना; to make quieter, softer, gentler धीमा करना।

subject[1] *सब् जिक्ट* *n.* theme, topic विषयवस्तु; a branch of knowledge as a course of study विषय; *(gram.)* person or thing about which something is said कर्त्ता; one under power of another अधीन व्यक्ति; *(pl.)* citizens प्रजा।

subject[2] *a.* owing allegiance पराधीन; subordinate अधीन; dependent निर्भर; आधारित; liable (to) संभाव्य।

subject[3] *सब् जैक्ट* *v.t.* to cause to undergo के लिए बाध्य करना; to subdue अधीन करना।

subjection *सब् जैक् शॅन* *n.* subjecting or being subjected आधिपत्य।

subjective *सब् जिक् टिव* *a.* based on personal feelings आत्मपरक, व्यक्तिनिष्ठ; *(gram.)* of the subject कर्तृपदीय।

subjudice *सब् जू डि सि* under judicial consideration विधि-विचाराधीन।

subjugate *सब् जु गेट* *v.t.* to subdue अधीन करना; to overecome पराभूत करना।

subjugation *सब् जु गे शॅन* *n.* act of subjugating आधिपत्य।

sublet *सब् लै ॅट* *(-tt-)* *v.t.* to let (property) which is already rented शिकमी देना, उप पट्टे पर देना।

sublimate *सब् लि मेट* *v.t.* to direct (low instincts and energies) into more desirable channels (का) उदात्तीकरण करना; to refine परिशुद्ध करना।

sublime[1] *सॅब् लॉइम* *a.* elevated उदात्त; eminent उत्कृष्ट; majestic भव्य।

sublime[2] *n.* that which fills one with reverence उदात्तता।

sublimity *सब् लि मि टि* *n.* sublime quality उदात्तता, भव्यता।

submarine[1] *सब् मॅ रीन* *n.* a vessel designed to stay under water पनडुब्बी।

submarine[2] *a.* existing under the surface of the sea अंतःसागरी।

submerge *सॅब् मॅःज* *v.i.* to go under water डूबना, ग़ोता लगाना; *v.t.* to place under water डुबोना।

submission *सॅब् मि शॅन* *n.* yielding समर्पण obedience ; आज्ञापालन; humility विनम्रता।

submissive *सॅब् मि सिव* *a.* willing to obey आज्ञाकारी; meek विनीत विनम्र।

submit *सॅब् मिट* *v.t.* to put forward प्रस्तुत करना; to put (oneself) under the control of another (की) अधीनता स्वीकार करना; to suggest सुझाव देना; *v.i.* to surrender झुकना, हार मानना।

subordinate[1] स ˘ बौः डि निट *a.* of lower rank मातहत; less important गौण, कम महत्व का; *(gram.)* dependent अधीन, आश्रित।

subordinate[2] *n.* one who is lower in rank अधीनस्थ कर्मचारी।

subordinate[3] सॅ बौः डि नेट *v.t.* to treat as subordinate गौण समझना, कम महत्व देना।

subordination सॅ बौः डि ने शॅन *n.* act of subordinating अधीनीकरण; state of being subordinate अधीनता।

subscribe सॅब् स्क्रॉइब *v.t.* to pay (a sum of money) to a cause चंदे के रूप में देना; to write (one's name) at the foot of a document दस्तावेज़ के नीचे (अपना नाम) लिखना।

subscription सॅब् स्क्रिप्शॅन *n.* act of subcribing अंशदान; the money raised by subcribing चंदा, चंदे की राशि।

subsequent सॅब् सि क्वॅन्ट *a.* later, following उत्तरवर्ती, आगामी।

subservience सॅब् सॅः व्यॅन्स *n.* quality of being subservient उपयोगिता; servile submissiveness चापलूसी, दासतापूर्ण विनीतता।

subservient सॅब् सॅः व्यॅन्ट *a.* giving too much respect (to,), servile श्रद्धापूर्ण; useful सहायक।

subside सॅब् सॉइड *v.i.* to sink down धंसना, धसकना; to settle नीचे बैठ जाना; to lessen, to abate कम होना; to come to an end समाप्त होना।

subsidiary सॅब सि ड़यॅ रि *a.* supplementary पूरक; secondary गौण; auxiliary सहायक।

subsidize सब् सि डॉइज़ *v.t.* to give a subsidy to आर्थिक सहायता देना।

subsidy सब् सि डि *n.* money granted as help आर्थिक सहायता।

subsist सब् सिस्ट, सॅब्- *v.i.* to exist, to sustain life बना रहना, जीवित रहना।

subsistence सब् सिस् टॅन्स *n.* the means by which one supports life जीवन-यापन का साधन; livelihood जीविका।

substance सब् स्टॅन्स *n.* matter पदार्थ; essence सार; wealth धन-संपत्ति; a particular kind of matter तत्व; meaning, gist अर्थ, भावार्थ।

substantial सॅब् स्टैन् शॅल *a.* of ample amount पर्याप्त; of a material nature भौतिक; firm, solid दृढ़ ठोस basic, essential तात्त्विक; of real worth वास्तविक; financially sound संपन्न, धनी।

substantially सब् स्टैन् शॅ लि *adv.* considerable पर्याप्त मात्रा में; essentially तत्वतः।

substantiate सॅब् स्टैन् शि एट *v.t.* to establish by proof प्रमाणित करना।

substantiation सॅब् स्टैन् शि ए शॅन *n.* act of substantiating प्रमाणीकरण।

substitute[1] सब् स्टि ट्यूट *n.* person or thing acting for another स्थानापन्न।

substitute[2] *v.t.* to put as a substitute for (की) एवज़ में रखना; *v.t.* to serve as substitute (for) एवज़ के रूप में काम करना।

substitution सॅब् स्टि ट्यू शॅन *n.*

act of substituting प्रतिस्थापन।

subterranean *सॅब् टॅ रे न्यॅन a.* underground भूमिगत।

subtle *स ट्ल n.* elusively thin or tenuous सूक्ष्म; fine or delicate in meaning बारीक; mysterious रहस्यपूर्ण; mentally acute कुशाग्र-बुद्धि; crafty चालाक; complicated जटिल।

subtlety *स ट्ल् टि n.* tenuousness सूक्ष्मता; fineness बारीकी; complicacy जटिलता; mental acuteness विलक्षणता; craftiness चालाकी।

subtract *सॅब् ट्रैक्ट v.t.* to take away from, to deduct घटाना।

subtraction *सॅब् ट्रैक् शॅन n.* act of subtracting घटाव।

suburb *सब् अॅ:ब n.* outlying area of a city उपनगरीय क्षेत्र।

suburban *सॅ बॅ: बॅन a.* belonging to the suburbs उपनगरीय; narrow minded संकीर्णतापूर्ण।

subversion *सब् वॅ: शॅन n.* act of subverting or being subverted समाप्ति, विनाश।

subversive *सब् वॅ: सिव a.* tending to subvert विनाशक, उपद्रवकारी।

subvert *सॅब् वॅ:ट v.t.* to overthrow उलट देना, पलट देना; to corrupt विकृत करना।

succeed *सॅक् सीड v.i.* to get success सफल होना; to take over a position, rank etc. उत्तराधिकारी होना; *v.t.* to come after के पश्चात् घटित होना।

success *सॅक् सैसॅ n.* a favourable result सफलता; attainment of wealth संपन्नता; a successful person or thing सफल व्यक्ति अथवा वस्तु।

successful *सॅक् सैसॅ फुल a* having success सफल; having attained wealth etc. संपन्न।

succession *सॅक् सै˘ शॅन n.* coming of one thing after another अनुक्रमण; a series सिलसिला, तांता a succeeding पदारोहण, राज्यारोहण; line of those entitled to succeed one another वंशक्रम।

successive *सॅक् सै˘ सिव a.* following one after another क्रमिक, आनुक्रमिक।

successor *सॅक् सै˘ सॅ: n.* person who succeeds another in position or rank उत्तराधिकारी।

succour[1] *स कॅ: n.* help in distress परेशानी में सहायता।

succour[2] *v.t.* to help in distress परेशानी में सहायता करना।

succumb *सॅ कम v.i.* to yield हार मानना; to die मर जाना।

such[1] *सच a.* of the kind indicated ऐसा, इस प्रकार का; like, similar समान प्रकार की; so very इतना।

such[2] *pron.* such persons or things ऐसे व्यक्ति अथवा वस्तुएं।

suck[1] *सक v.t.* to draw into the mouth चूसना; to hold and dislove in mouth पपोलना; to draw in सोखना।

suck[2] *n.* sucking चूषण; breast-feeding स्तनपान।

suckle *स क्ल v.t.* to feed from the breast स्तनपान कराना।

sudden *स ड्न n.* abrupt आकस्मिक; hurried शीघ्रतापूर्ण।

suddenly *स ड्न् लि adv.* abruptly, unexpectedly अचानक, अकस्मात्।

sue *स्यू, सू v.t.* to prosecute (पर) मुक़दमा चलाना; to seek justice from (से) न्याय की प्रार्थना करना; *v.i.* to make an entreaty विनती करना।

suffer *स फ़ॅः v.t.* to undergo भुगतना, झेलना; to tolerate सहना; *v.i.* to be damaged हानि होना; to be unwell अस्वस्थ होना।

suffice *सॅ फ़ॉइस v.i.* to be sufficient पर्याप्त होना।

sufficiency *सॅ फ़ि शॅन् सि n.* sufficient quantity पर्याप्त मात्रा; quality of being sufficient प्रचुरता।

sufficient *सॅ फ़ि शॅन्ट a.* enough, adequate पर्याप्त।

suffix[1] *स फ़िक्स n.* a letter or letters added at the end of a word प्रत्यय।

suffix[2] *v.t.* to add, to annex to the end जोड़ना, प्रत्यय लगाना।

suffocate *स फ़ॅ केट v.t.* to kill by deprivation of oxygen दम घोटकर मारना; to cause difficulty in breathing दम घोटना; *v.i.* to be killed by suffocation दम घुटकर मरना; to have difficulty in breathing दम घुटना।

suffocation *स फ़ॅ के शॅन n.* state of being suffocated घुटन।

suffrage *सफ़् रिज n.* right to vote मताधिकार।

sugar[1] *शु गॅः n.* a sweet vegetable-substance चीनी, शकर।

sugar[2] *v.t.* to sweeten or mix with sugar (में) चीनी डालना, मीठा करना।

suggest *सॅ जैस्ट v.t.* to propose प्रस्तावित करना; to bring into the mind जताना, लक्षित करना; to hint संकेत करना।

suggestion *सॅ जैस् चॅन n.* proposal प्रस्ताव; hint संकेत; idea or plan suggested सुझाव; hypnosis सम्मोहन।

suggestive *सॅ जैस् टिव a.* productive of ideas विचारोत्तेजक; evocative उद्दीपक; tending to suggest something improper अश्लीलतापूर्ण।

suicidal *स्यु इ सॉइ ड्ल a.* of suicide आत्महत्या-संबंधी; harmful to one's own interests आत्मघाती।

suicide *स्यु इ सॉइड n.* self murder आत्महत्या; action destructive to one's interests आत्मघात।

suit[1] *स्यूट n.* a set of clothing सूट; action at law मुक़दमा; a formal request प्रार्थना, विनती; a pack at cards ताश का रंग; asking a woman's hand in marriage विवाह-प्रस्ताव।

suit[2] *v.t.* to make appropriate to उपयुक्त बनाना; to match (से) मेल खाना; to be fitting अनुकूल होना; to satisfy संतुष्ट करना।

suitability *स्यू टॅ बि लि टि n.* quality of being suitable उपयुक्तता।

suitable *स्यू टॅ ब्ल a.* fitting, proper उपयुक्त; becoming उचित, शोभनीय; convenient सुविधाजनक।

suite *स्वीट n.* a set of matching furniture मेल खाता हुआ फर्नीचर; a set of rooms कमरों का सैट; a number of attendants नौकर-चाकर; a musical composition in several parts वाद्य संगीत-रचना।

suitor *स्यू टॅः n.* one who sues वादी; wooer प्रेमी; petitioner प्रार्थी,

आवेदक; one asking for marriage विवाह-प्रस्तावक।

sullen *स लॅन a.* unwilling to talk or be sociable रूठा हुआ; morose उदास, दुःखी dismal निरानंद; dull नीरस।

sulphur *सल् फ़ॅः n.* light yellow nonmetallic element गंधक।

sulphuric *सल् फ़्युअॅ रिक a.* containing sulphur गंधक-युक्त।

sultry *सल् ट्रि a.* hot and humid उमसदार।

sum[1] *सम n.* amount of money धनराशि; total योग, जोड़; a summary सारांश; an arithmetical problem गणित का प्रश्न।

sum[2] *(-mm-) v.t.* to add up जोड़ना, योग निकालना; to summarize (का) संक्षिप्त विवरण देना।

summarily *स मॅ रि लि adv.* speedily शीघ्रतापूर्वक; abruptly तुरंत।

summarize *स मॅ रॉइज़ v.t.* to make summary of संक्षिप्त करना; to present briefly संक्षेप में प्रस्तुत करना।

summary[1] *स मॅ रि n.* a brief account संक्षेप, संक्षिप्त विवरण।

summary[2] *a.* brief संक्षिप्त; done quickly शीघ्रतापूर्ण; without attention to small matters सरसरे ढंग से किया हुआ।

summer *स मॅः n.* the warmest season ग्रीष्म ऋतु।

summit *स मिट n.* top, peak चोटी।

summon *स मॅन v.t.* to demand attendance of बुला भेजना; to call on पुकारना; to bid (witness) appear in court गवाही के लिए सम्मन देना; to gather up बटोरना।

summons *स मॅन्ज़ n.* an order to appear in court सम्मन, अदालत का बुलावा।

sumptuous *सम्प् ट्यु अॅस a.* lavish महंगा, ख़र्चीला; magnificent वैभवशाली, शानदार।

sun[1] *सन् n.* the luminous body round which the planets move सूर्य; light and warmth from the sun धूप; any fixed star नक्षत्र।

sun[2] *(-nn-) v.t.* to expose to sun's rays धूप में रखना।

Sunday *सन् डि,-डे n.* the first day of the week रविवार।

sunder *सन् डॅः v.t.* to separate अलग करना।

sundary *सन् ड्रि a.* various विभिन्न।

sunny *स नि a.* like the sun सूर्यवत्; warm गर्म; bright उजला; cheerful प्रसन्नचित।

sup *सप (-pp-) v.i.* to take supper रात्रि का भोजन करना; *v.t.* to take by sips सुकड़ना।

superabundance *सूॅ प र बन् डॅन्स n.* very great quantity आधिक्य, प्रचुरता।

superabundant *सूॅ प र बन् डॅन्ट a.* very abundant प्रचुरतापूर्ण, भरपूर।

superb *स्यू पॅःब a.* excellent, splendid उत्तम, शानदार।

superficial *स्यू पॅः फि शॅल a.* of the surface ऊपरी, पृष्ठकीय; not thorough अगंभीर, छिछला।

superficiality *स्यू पॅः फि शि ऐ लि टि n.* the quality of being superficial छिछलापन, पल्लव ग्राहिता।

superfine *स्यू पॅः फ़ॉइन a.* very fine अति उत्तम, over-refined अति परिष्कृत।

superfluity *स्यू पॅः फ़्यु इ टि n.* excess आधिक्य; unnecessary amount फ़ालतू मात्रा।

superfluous *स्यू पॅः फ़्लु ॲस a.* unnecessary फ़ालतू; excessive अति अधिक।

susperhuman *स्यू पॅः ह्यू मॅन a.* beyond ordinary human size or capacity अतिमानवीय; supernatural अलौकिक।

superintend *स्यू पॅः इन् टैन्ड v.t.* to have charge of (का) अधीक्षण करना; to supervise (की) देखभाल करना; to direct (का) संचालन करना।

superintendence *स्यू पॅः इन् टैनॅ डॅन्स n.* superintending देख-रेख, संचालन।

superintendent *स्यू पॅः इन् टैनॅ डॅन्ट n.* a senior police officer अधीक्षक; a manager, controller प्रबंधक, नियंत्रक।

superior *स्यु पिॲ रि ॲः a.* higher in rank, quality or position उच्च, वरिष्ठ; greater in quality or quantity श्रेष्ठतर, बेहतर।

superiority *स्यु पिॲ रि औ˘ रि टि n.* quality of being superior श्रेष्ठता, उच्चता।

superlative[1] *स्यु पॅ लॅ टिव a.* of the highest quality सर्वश्रेष्ठ; *(gram.)* denoting the quality of being the best of the highest श्रेष्ठतासूचक।

superlative[2] *n. (gram.)* the superlative form उत्तमावस्था।

superman *स्यू पॅः मैन n.* a man of abnormal mental and physical ability अतिमानव।

supernatural *स्यु पॅः नै च् रॅल a.* beyond physical laws अलौकिक।

supersede *स्यु पॅः सीड v.t.* to take the palce of (का) स्थान लेना; to set aside, to discard हटा देना, निकाल फेंकना।

supersonic *स्यू पॅः सौ˘ निक a.* moving faster than sound पराध्वनिक।

superstition *स्यू पॅः टि शॅन n.* an unreasoning belief in magic, charms etc. अंधविश्वास।

superstitious *स्यू पॅः स्टि शॅस a.* based on or involving superstition अंधविश्वासी।

supertax *स्यू पॅः टैक्ट n.* additional tax अधिकर।

supervise *स्यू पॅः वॉइज़ v.t.* to direct निर्देशित करना; to superintend अधीक्षण करना, संचालन करना।

supervision *स्यू पॅः वि ज़ॅन n.* act of supervising देख-रेख, निरीक्षण।

supervisor *स्यू पॅः वॉइ जॅः n.* one who supervises पर्यवेक्षक, निरीक्षक।

supper *सपॅः n.* the last meal of the day रात्रि का भोजन।

supple *स पॅल a.* pliable सुनम्य; flexible लचीला, ढीला।

supplement[1] *स्प् लि मॅन्ट n.* something added to fill up deficiency परिशिष्ट; extra and separate addition to a periodical परिशिष्ट।

supplement[2] *सप् लि मैन्ट v.t.* to add to जोड़ देना; to supply deficiency of पूरा करना।

supplementary *सप् लि मैनॅ टॅ रि a.* additional पूरक।

supplier *स प्लॉइ ॲः n.* person or firm supplying goods प्रदायक, संभरक।

supply[1] सॅ प्लॉइ *v.t.* to furnish आपूर्ति करना; to make available उपलब्ध कराना; to provide प्रदान करना।

supply[2] *n.* stock, store भंडार; supplying आपूर्ति।

support[1] सॅ पौःट *v.t.* to hold up संभालना; to sustain पालना, भरण-पोषण करना; to help, to encourage सहारा या प्रोत्साहन देना; to advocate समर्थन करना।

support[2] *n.* favour पक्ष, सहारा; person or thing that supports सहारे का साधन।

suppose सॅ पोज़ *v.t.* to assume मान लेना, कल्पना करना; to imagine, to think समझना, सोचना; to accept as likely (की) संभावना समझना।

supposition स पॅ ज़ि शॅन *n.* assumption कल्पना; conjecture अनुमान।

suppress सॅ प्रैसॅ *v.t.* to crush कुचलना; to put down (का) दमन करना; to conceal छिपाना।

suppression सॅ प्रैसॅ शॅन *n.* suppressing or being suppressed दमन, concealment गोपन।

supremacy सॅ प्रैॅ मॅ सि *n.* position of being supreme उच्चता, सर्वश्रेष्ठता।

supreme स्यु प्रीम *a.* highest in authority or rank सर्वोच्च; the greatest possible अधिकतम।

surcharge[1] सॅः चाःज *n.* an additional charge अधिशुल्क; additional load अधिभार।

surcharge[2] *v.t.* to overload अधिभार लगाना; to make an additional charge अधिशुल्क लगाना।

sure शुअॅः, शौः, शौः *a.* certain निश्चित; trustworthy विश्वसनीय; without doubt असंदिग्ध।

surely शुअॅः लि, शौः -, शौः *adv.* certainly निश्चित रूप से; undoubtedly निःसंदेह।

surety शुअॅ टि, शौःटि *n.* security ज़मानत; one who makes himself responsible for another's obligations ज़मानतदार।

surf सॅःफ *n.* waves breaking on the shore समुद्र की तटीय लहरें।

surface[1] सॅः फिस exterior बाह्य भाग; the top of a liquid सतह, तल; outward appearance ऊपरी दिखावा।

surface[2] *v.i.* to come to the surface ऊपर आना, उजागर होना; *v.t.* to cause to come to the surface ऊपर लाना; to put a surface on (पर) सतह पर परत चढ़ाना।

surfeit सॅः फ़िट *n.* excess अतिरेक, आधिक्य; disgust caused by excess परितृप्ति ऊब।

surge[1] सॅःज *n.* a large wave महोर्मि, हिलोरा; a rush of emotion आवेश; sudden increase रेला।

surge[2] *v.i.* to move in large waves हिलोर मारना; to swell उमड़ना।

surgeon सॅः जॅन *n.* a doctor who performs operations शल्य चिकित्सक, शल्यकार।

surgery सॅः जॅ रि *n.* medical treatment by operation शल्य-चिकित्सा; science of treating diseases by operation शल्य-विज्ञान; a room for surgical operation शल्य-कक्ष।

surmise[1] सॅः मॉइज़ *n.* guess, conjecture अनुमान।

surmise² *v.t. & v.i.* to guess, to conjecture अनुमान करना; अंदाज़ा लगाना।

surmount *सॅ: मॉउन्ट v.t.* to overcome, to get over (पर) विजय पाना।

surname *सॅ: नेम n.* family name कुलनाम।

surpass *सॅ: पास v.t.* to go beyond (से) बढ़चढ़कर होना; to excel (से) श्रेष्ठ होना; to exceed (से) अधिक होना।

surplus *सॅ: प्लॅस n.* what remains over in excess अधिशेष, आवश्यकता से अधिक वस्तु।

surprise¹ *सॅ: प्रॉइज़ n.* something unexpected अप्रत्याशित घटना या तथ्य; what takes unawares आश्चर्यजनक बात; astonishment आश्चर्य, अचरज।

surprise² *v.t.* to cause surprise to आश्चर्यचकित करना; to astonish अचरज में डालना; to come upon unexpectedly अचानक आ पहुंचना।

surrender¹ *सॅ रैॅन् डॅ: v.t.* to yield, to give into (से) हार मानना, समर्पण करना; to give up possession of छोड़ देना, त्याग देना; *v.i.* to cease resistance घुटने टेकना।

surrender² *n.* act of surrendering आत्मसमर्पण, हार।

surround *सॅ रॉउन्ड v.t.* to encompass घेरना।

surroundings *सॅ रॉउन् डिङ्ज n. pl.* environment पास-पड़ोस, प्रतिवेश।

surtax *सॅ: टैक्स n.* additional tax अधिकर।

surveillance *सॅ: वे लॅन्स n.* close watch, supervision निगरानी।

survey¹ *सॅ: वे n.* a general view सर्वेक्षण; a map or record नक़्शा, आलेख।

survey² *सॅ: वे v.t.* to look at as a whole सर्वेक्षण करना; to measure in order to make a map नक्शा बनाने-हेतु भूमापन करना; to examine the condition of (का) निरीक्षण करना।

survival *सॅ: वॉइ वॅल n.* continuation of existence उत्तरजीविता, उत्तरजीवन; an old-fashioned person पुराने तौर-तरीकों वाला व्यक्ति।

survive *सॅ: वॉइव v.i.* to continue to live बना रहना, जीवित बचना; *v.t.* to outlive के बाद तक जीवित रहना; to come alive through से बच जाना।

suspect¹ *सॅस् पैक्ट v.t.* to doubt the innocence of (पर) संदेह करना; to mistrust (पर) अविश्वास करना; to feel, to believe समझना, महसूस करना।

suspect² *सस् पैक्ट a.* of suspected character संदिग्ध।

suspect³ *n.* suspected person संदिग्ध व्यक्ति।

suspend *सॅस् पैन्ड v.t.* to hang up लटकाना; to cause to cease for a time बंद करना, रोक देना; to debar from an office निलंबित करना; to keep inoperative बंद रखना, स्थगित रखना।

suspense *सॅस् पैॅन्स n.* state of uncertainty अनिश्चय की स्थिति; anxiety, worry चिंता, दुविधा।

suspension *सॅस् पैनॅ शॅन n.* state of being suspended प्रलंबन; something suspended लटकी

वस्तु; debarring from an office निलंबन; ceasure for a time आस्थगन।

suspicion *सॅस् पि शॅन n.* suspecting संदेह, शक; slight trace पुट, रमक।

suspicious *सॅस् पि शॅस a.* full of suspicion शक्की, शंकालु; arousing suspicion संदेहजनक।

sustain *सॅस् टेन v.t.* to keep, to hold up संभालना, थामना; to keep going बनाए रखना; to keep alive जीवित रखना; to undergo भुगतना, झेलना।

sustenance *सस् टि नॅन्स n.* that which sustains, food भोजन, जीवनाधार।

swagger[1] *सवै गॅः v.i.* to boast डींग मारना; to strut इठलाना।

swagger[2] *n.* strutting gait इठलाती चाल; boastful manner डींग, अकड़।

swallow[1] *स्वौ लो v.t.* to pass (food or drink) down the throat निगलना; to engulf सटक लेना; to endure सहन करना; to accept credulously आंख मूंदकर विश्वास करना।

swallow[2] *n.* act of swallowing निगरण, निगलने की क्रिया; amount swallowed निगली हुई मात्रा।

swallow[3] *n.* a migratory bird अबाबील।

swamp[1] *स्वौम्प n.* boggy land दलदल।

swamp[2] *v.t.* to entangle in swamp दलदल में फंसाना; to overwhelm अभिभूत करना; to flood आप्लावित करना।

swan *स्वौन n.* a large white-necked water-bird हंस।

swarm[1] *स्वौःम n.* a large cluster of insects दल, झुंडः a vast crowd भीड़, जमघट।

swarm[2] *v.i.* to form a swarm झुंड में होना; to gather in large numbers भीड़ लगाना।

swarthy *स्वौःदि a.* dark-complexioned सांवला।

sway[1] *स्वे v.i.* to swing unsteadily डोलना, हिलना-डुलना; to incline to one side एक ओर झुकना; to fluctuate घटना-बढ़ना; *v.t.* to cause to sway हिलाना; to influence प्रभावित करना।

sway[2] *n.* swaying movement दोलन; rule, dominion शासन, influence प्रभाव।

swear *स्वे ॲः v.t.* to promise on oath शपथपूर्वक वचन देना; to cause to take an oath क़सम खिलाना; *v.i.* to take an oath सौगंध खाना।

sweat[1] *स्वैॅट n.* perspiration पसीना।

sweat[2] *v.i.* to perspire पसीना आना; to toil कड़ा परिश्रम करना।

sweater *स्वैॅटः n.* a knitted jersey स्वेटर।

sweep[1] *स्वीप v.i.* to effect cleaning with broom झाडू लगाना; to pass swiftly तेज़ी से निकल जाना; to extend फैलना; *v.t.* to clean with a broom झाडू से साफ़ करना; to carry away उड़ा ले जाना।

sweep[2] *n.* act of sweeping झाडूः बुहारी, साफ़-सफ़ाई; sweeping motion घुमाव; wide curve मोड़; range प्रभाव-क्षेत्र, मार; a chimney-sweeper चिमनी साफ़ करनेवाला; a long oar लंबा डांड।

sweeper *स्वी पॅः n.* a person who sweeps झाड़ू लगानेवाला; a thing that sweeps अपमार्जक।

sweet[1] *स्वीट a.* tasting like sugar मीठा; agreeable रुचिकर, सुहावना; charming आकर्षक; fresh ताज़ा; fragrant सुगंधित; tuneful मधुर; beloved प्यारा।

sweet[2] *n.* a small piece of sweet food मिष्टान; sweet course भोजनोपरांत मिष्टान्न का दौर।

sweeten *स्वी ट्न v.t.* to make sweet मीठा करना।

sweetmeat *स्वीट् मीट n.* sweetened delicacy मिष्ठान्न।

sweetness *स्वीट् निस n.* the quality of being sweet मिठास।

swell[1] *स्वै ̆ल v.i.* to increase in volume बढ़ना; to expand सूजना, फूलना; to bulge out उभरना; to be puffed up प्रफुल्लित होना; *v.t.* to cause to grow in volume बढ़ाना; to puff up प्रफुल्लित करना।

swell[2] *n.*a act of swelling फुलाव, बढ़ाव; bulging उभार; an increase in amount वृद्धि; a long and unbroken wave महातरंग।

swift *स्विफ़्ट a.* rapid, quick तीव्र; prompt तत्पर।

swim[1] *स्विम (-mm-) v.i.* to move and support oneself in water तैरना; to float उतराना; to glide smoothly विसर्पण करना; to feel dizzy चकराना।

swim[2] *n.* act of swimming तैराकी।

swimmer *स्वि मॅः n.* one who swims तैराक।

swindle[1] *स्विन् ड्ल v.t.* to cheat ठगना।

swindle[2] *n.* fraud, act of swindling ठगी, झांसा।

swindler *स्विन्ड् लॅः n.* one who swindles झांसिया, ठग।

swine *स्वॉइन n.* a pig सूअर; a contemptible person घृणित व्यक्ति।

swing[1] *स्विङ्ग v.i.* to move to and fro झूलना, डोलना; to turn घूम जाना; to hang लटकना; to move to and fro in a swing झूले पर झूलना; *v.t.* to cause to move to and fro झुलाना, डोलाना; to cause to turn घुमाना; to brandish घुमाना।

swing[2] *n.* act of swinging दोलन; seat hung to swing on झूला, हिंडोला; fluctuation अस्थिरता, उतार-चढ़ाव; rhythm लय।

swiss[1] *स्विस n.* a native of switzerland स्विटजरलैंड का निवासी।

swiss[2] *a.* of switzerland, pertaining to Switzerland स्विटज़रलैंड का या उससे संबंधित।

switch[1] *स्विच n.* a device for turning electric current on and off स्विच, बटन; a sudden change भारी परिवर्तन; a flexible twig टहनी; a tress of false hair कृत्रिम बालों का लट।

switch[2] *v.t.* to shift or change बदलना; to affect (current) with switch स्विच-द्वारा (विद्युत्) चालू करना; to change abruptly अचानक परिवर्तित करना; *v.i.* to shift बदलना।

swoon[1] *स्वून n.* a faint मूर्च्छा, बेहोशी।

swoon[2] *v.i.* to faint मूर्च्छित होना।

swoop[1] *स्वूप v.i.* to dive as a hawk झपट्टा मारना।

swoop² *n.* act of swooping झपट्टा।

sword *सौःड n.* a weapon with a long blade and hilt तलवार।

sycamore *सि कॅ मौः n.* a kind of fig tree गूलर।

sycophancy *सि कॅ फ़ॅन् सि n.* the quality of being a sycophant चाटुकारिता, चापलूसी।

sycophant *सि कॅ फ़ॅन्ट n.* one using flattery to gain favour चापलूस।

syllabic *सि लै बिक n.* in, of, or in syllables उच्चारण की इकाई से संबंधित।

syllable *सि लै ब्ल n.* a separate unit of sound in speech उच्चारण-इकाई।

syllabus *सि लॅ बॅस n.* the outline of a course of study पाठ्यक्रम।

sylph *सिल्फ़ n.* a spirit of the air परी; a slender graceful woman सुंदर तरुणी।

sylvan *सिल् वॅन a.* of forests or trees वृक्षीय, वनीय।

symbol *सिम् बॅल n.* sign चिह्न; a thing representing something प्रतीक।

symbolic *सिम् बौ˘ लिक a.* using or used as a symbol प्रतीकात्मक।

symbolism *सिम् बॅ लिज़्म n.* use of symbols in art and literature प्रतीकवाद।

symbolize *सिम् बॅ लॉइज v.t.* to be a symbol of (का) प्रतीक होना; to use a symbol or sympbols for प्रतीक-द्वारा प्रस्तुत करना।

symmetrical *सि मै˘ ट्रि कॅल a.* having symmetry सममित।

symmetry *सि मि ट्रि n.* proportion between parts सममिति; balance संतुलन।

sympathetic *सिम् पॅ थै˘ टिक a.* showing sympathy, having sympathy सहानुभूतिपूर्ण।

sympathize *सिम् पॅ थॉइज़ v.i.* to feel or express sympathy सहानुभूति रखना।

sympathy *सिम् पॅ थि n.* feeling for another in pain etc. सहानुभूति; compassion दया।

symphony *सिम् फ़ॅ नि n.* a composition for full orchestra वाद्यवृंद रचना; harmony of sounds सुरीलापन।

symposium *सिम् पो ज़्यॅम (pl. -ms, -sia) n.* conference, meeting विचार-गोष्ठी; a book of contributions by several authors on one topic निबंध-संग्रह।

symptom *सिम्प् टॅम n.* a change in physical or mental condition indicating illness or healthiness लक्षण; sign, token चिह्न, आसार।

symptomatic *सिम्प् टॅ मै टिक a.* serving as a symptom (of) लक्षणसूचक।

synonym *सि नॅ निम n.* a word with the same meaning as another पर्याय।

synonymous *सि नौ˘ नि मॅस a.* (word) having the same meaning as another पर्यायवाची, समानार्थी।

synopsis *सि नौ˘प् सिस n.* summary संक्षेप; outline रूपरेखा।

syntax *सिन् टैक्स n. (gram.)* arrangement of words in a sentence वाक्य-रचना।

synthesis *सिन् थै ˘ सिस (pl.-theses) n.* putting together, combination संश्लेषण।

synthetic[1] *सिन् थैˇ टिक a.* produced by synthesis संश्लेषणात्मक; artificial कृत्रिम।

synthetic[2] *n.* a product of synthesis कृत्रिम उत्पादन।

syringe[1] *सि रिन्ज n.* a device for taking up fluids from or injecting them into the body पिचकारी।

syringe[2] *v.t.* to clean or treat with a syringe पिचकारी से धोना या फहारना।

syrup *सि रॅप n.* a solution of sugar and water or sugar and fruit juice चाश्नी, शरबत।

system *सिस् टॅम n.* a complex, whole organization तंत्र; method तरीक़ा; classification वर्गीकरण; plan योजना; order क्रम-व्यवस्था।

systematic *सिस् टॅ मै टिक a.* methodical पद्धतिबद्ध; based on a system व्यवस्थित।

systematize *सिस् टि मॅ टॉइज़ v.t.* to reduce to system सुव्यवस्थित करना; to arrange methodically क्रमबद्ध करना।

Tt

T टी the twentieth letter of the English alphabet, anything shaped like the letter T. अंग्रेजी वर्णमाला का बीसवाँ अक्षर, इस अक्षर के आकार का कोई पदार्थ; **To cross the T's** (to be very precise.) निश्चित या स्पष्ट होना।

table[1] *टे बल n.* a piece of furniture मेज़; food भोजन; an arrangement of facts or figures in columns तालिका।

table[2] *v.t.* to lay on the table for discussion प्रस्तुत करना।

tablet *टैब् लिट n.* a pill टिकिया, गोली; a small pad of writing paper पटिया, तख़्ती; slab पट्टी, फलक।

taboo[1] *टॅ बू n.* prohibition निषेध; thing prohibited वर्जित वस्तु।

taboo[2] *a.* forbidden निषिद्ध।

taboo[3] *v.t.* to place under taboo निषिद्ध करना।

tabular *टै ब्यु लॅः a.* arranged in tables तालिकाबद्ध।

tabulate *टै ब्यु लेट v.t.* to arrange in tables तालिकाबद्ध करना।

tabulation *टै ब्यु ले शॅन n.* act of tabulating सारणीयन।

tabulator *टै ब्यु लॅ टॅः n.* person or machine that tabulates सारणीयक।

tacit *टै सिट a.* silent, implied मौन, अनकहा।

taciturn *टै सि टॅःन a.* saying very little अल्पभाषी।

tackle[1] *टै कल n.* equipment साज़-सामान; set of ropes, pulleys etc. रस्से, घिरनी आदि; (football) act of stopping an opponent विरोधी पर क़ाबू।

tackle² *v.t.* to grapple (से) भिड़ना; to take in hand हाथ में लेना; to challenge चुनौती देना।

tact *टैक्ट n.* skill in dealing with people or situations व्यवहार-कौशल, सूझ-बूझ।

tactful *टैक्ट् फुल a.* showing tact व्यवहार कुशल।

tactician *टैक् टि शॅन n.* an expert on tactics रणनीतिज्ञ; one who can manage a situation skilfully कार्य-सम्पादन में निपुण व्यक्ति।

tactics *टैक् टिक्स n. (with sing v.)* art of handling troops, ships in battle रणनीति; adroit management of a situation युक्ति, नीति-कौशल।

tactile *टैक् टॉइल a.* relating to the sense of touch स्पर्श-योग्य।

tag¹ *टैग n.* metal tip to a shoe-lace फ़ीते की घुंडी; a label tied to something लेबुल; much quoted saying घिसा-पिटा कथन।

tag *(-gg-) v.t.* to append संलग्न करना; to trail behind (के) पीछे-पीछे चलना।

tail *टेल n.* flexible prolongation of animal's spine पूंछ; portion at the back of something पिछला भाग; lowest part निचला भाग; *(pl.)* reverse side of a coin सिक्के का पृष्ठ भाग।

tailor¹ *टे लॅः n.* maker of garments दरज़ी।

tailor² *v.t.* to make (garments) (कपड़े) सिलना।

taint¹ *टेन्ट n.* defect, flaw दोष; infection छूत।

taint² *v.t.* to infect दूषित करना; सड़ाना; *v.i.* to be infected दूषित होना, सड़ना।

take टेक *v.t.* to grasp पकड़ना, लेना; to get प्राप्त करना; to carry ले जाना; to eat or drink ग्रहण करना।

tale *टेल n.* story कहानी; report विवरण; malicious rumour अफ़वाह।

talent *टै लॅन्ट n.* natural ability प्रतिभा, ancient weight or money प्राचीन तौल या मुद्रा।

talisman *टै लिज़् मॅन n.* amulet तावीज़।

talk¹ *टौक v.i.* to speak बोलना; *v.t.* to express in speech कहना; to discuss (पर) विचार विमर्श करना।

talk² *n.* speech, lecture भाषण; conversation वार्तालाप; rumour अफ़वाह।

talkative *टौ कॅ टिव a.* fond of talking बातूनी।

tall *टौल a.* above average in height लंबा, ऊंचा।

tallow *टै लो n.* animal fat चरबी।

tally¹ *टै लि n.* account लेखा, हिसाब; a duplicate प्रतिरूप।

tally² *v.t.* to correspond अनुरूप होना; to keep record लेखा रखना।

tamarind *टै मॅ रिन्ड n.* a tropical tree इमली का वृक्ष; its fruit इमली।

tame¹ *टेम a.* subdued शांत, सौम्य; lacking in energy निस्तेज; domesticated पालतू uninteresting नीरस; submissive दब्बू।

tame² *v.t.* to make tame पालतू बनाना, पालना; to subdue वश में करना।

tamper *टैम् पॅः v.i.* to meddle, to interfere हस्तक्षेप करना, छेड़-छाड़

करना।

tan[1] *टैन (-nn-) v.i.* to go brown भूरा होना; *v.t.* to cause to go brown भूरा करना; to convert (animal hide) to leather (खाल को) चमड़े का रूप देना।

tan[2]*a.,n.* (of) brown colour of skin भूरे रंग की त्वचा (वाला)।

tangent *टैन् जॅन्ट n.* line that just touches a curve स्पर्शज्या।

tangible *टैन् जॅ ब्‌ल a.* that can be touched स्पर्शनीय; definite निश्चित concrete ठोस।

tangle[1] *टैङ् ग्‌ल n.* confused mass उलझन; muddle गुत्थी, जटिल स्थिति।

tangle[2] *v.t.* to twist together उलझाना।

tank *टैङ्क n.* a large container टंकी; a big reservoir तालाब; an armoured fighting vehicle टैंक।

tanker *टैङ् कॅः n.* ship or lorry for carrying liquids तेल-पोत, टंकी-ट्रक।

tanner *टै नॅः n.* one who tans hides चर्म-शोधक।

tannery *टै नॅ रि n.* palce where leather is made चर्म-शोधनशाला।

tantalize *टैन् टॅ लॉइज़ v.t.* to tease by keeping something just out of reach तरसाना, ललचाना।

tantamount *ट्रैन टॅ मॉउन्ट a.* equal, equivalent in value or significance समान, तुल्य।

tap[1] *टैप n.* valve with handle to regulate flow of fluid टोंटी; slight blow थपकी।

tap[2]*(-pp-) v.t.* to draw liquid from (से) द्रव निकालना; to put tap in टोंटी लगाना; to strike gently थपकी देना।

tape[1] *टेप n.* a narrow long strip फ़ीता, पट्टी, टेप।

tape[2] *v.t.* to record on magnetic tape टेप करना, अभिलेखन करना।

taper[1] *टे पॅः v.i.* to become gradually thin towards one end एक सिरे की ओर पतला होता जाना।

taper[2]*n.* a very thin candle पतली मोमबत्ती; a narrowing पतलापन।

tapestry *टै पिस् ट्रि n.* cloth into which design in woven दीवार दरी, चित्र कंबल।

tar[1] *टाः n.* thick black liquid distilled from coal डामर, तार-कोल।

tar[2]*(-rr-) v.t.* to coat with tar (पर) तार-कोल पोतना।

target *टाः गिट n.* mark to be shot at निशाना; thing aimed at लक्ष्य, उद्देश्य; object of criticism आलोचना का विषय; butt उपहास का पात्र।

tariff *टै रिफ़ n.* tax levied on imports सीमा-शुल्क।

tarnish *टॉः निश v.t.* to make discoloured बदरंग करना; to discredit बट्टा लगाना; *v.i.* to become discoloured बदरंग होना।

task[1] *टास्क n.* a piece of work set or undertaken कार्य।

task[2] *v.t.* to assign task to कार्य सौंपना।

taste[1] *टेस्ट n.* flavour स्वाद; sense of tasting ज़ायका; preference पसंद; judgement समझ, निर्णयशक्ति।

taste[2]*v.t.* to find the taste of चखना; *v.i.* to have specific flavour विशिष्ट स्वाद रखना।

tasteful *टेस्ट् फुल a.* showing good taste रुचिकर।

tasty *टेस् टि a.* pleasant to taste स्वादिष्ट।

tatter[1] *टै टॅः n.* ragged piece चिथड़ा।

tatter[2] *v.t.* to make ragged चिथड़े करना; *v.i.* to become ragged चिथड़ा होना।

tattoo[1] *टॅ टू n.* beat of drum and bugle call ढोल व बिगुल का नाद; military spectacle सेना का प्रदर्शन; mark of tattooing लीला गोदे का चिह्न।

tattoo[2] *v.i.* to mark skin with pricks and colours लीला गोदना।

taunt[1] *टौन्ट v.t.* to reproach contemptuously ताना मारना।

taunt[2] *n.* an insulting reproach ताना, कटाक्ष।

tavern *टै वॅःन n.* an inn, a public house सराय, मधुशाला।

tax[1] *टैक्स n.* compulsory payment imposed by government कर।

tax[2] *v.t.* to impose tax on (पर) कर लगाना।

taxable *टैक् सॅ ब्ल a.* liable to tax कर-योग्य।

taxation *टैक् से शॅन n.* levying of taxes करारोपण।

taxi[1] *टैक् सि n.* motor car that may be hired with driver टैक्सी।

taxi[2] *v.i.* to go in a taxi टैक्सी में जाना।

tea *टी n.* dried leaves of a shrub चाय की पत्ती; a drink made from them चाय (पेय)।

teach *टीच v.t.* to instruct शिक्षा देना; to educate पढ़ाना।

teacher *टी चॅः n.* one who teaches शिक्षक।

teak *टीक n.* a tree and its timber सागौन का पेड़ व लकड़ी।

team *टीम n.* a set of players टीम; a set of people working together टोली; two or more animals working together जोड़ी।

tear[1] *टे ॅ अॅः v.t.* to pull apart, to rend फाड़ना, चीरना; *v.i.* to become split फट जाना।

tear[2] *n.* a hole, a cut, a split खोंच, चीरा।

tear[3] *टिअॅः n.* drop of fluid coming from the eye आंसू।

tearful *टिअॅः फुल a.* inclined to weep रोंआसा; with tears अश्रुपूर्ण।

tease *टीज़ v.t.* to irritate, to annoy चिढ़ाना, परेशान करना; to pull apart fibres of (का) रोआँ उठाना।

teat *टीट n.* nipple स्तनाग्र।

technical *टैक् नि कॅल n.* involving technique तकनीकी।

technicality *टैक् नि कै लि टि n.* a technical quality or state प्राविधिकता।

technician *टैकॅ नि शॅन n.* one skilled in a particular technique तकनीक जाननेवाला।

technique *टैकॅ नीक n.* method of performance प्रविधि; skill required by a performer कौशल, निपुणता।

technological *टैकॅ नॅ लौ ॅ जि कॅल a.* relating to technology प्रौद्योगिकीय।

technologist *टैकॅ नौ ॅ लॅ जिस्ट n.* one skilled in technology प्रौद्योगिकीविद्।

technology *टैकॅ नौ ॅ लॅ जि n.* science applied to practical needs

प्रौद्योगिकी।

tedious *टी ड्यॅस a.* causing fatigue or boredom उबाने या थकानेवाला, नीरस।

tedium *टी ड्यॅम n.* monotony नीरसता, ऊब।

teem *टीम v.i.* to abound प्रचुरता में होना; to swarm उमड़ना, बड़ी संख्या में आना।

teenager *टीन् ए जॅः n.* one in his (her) teens किशोर, किशोरी।

teens *टीन्ज़ n. pl.* years of life from 13 to 19 किशोरावस्था।

teethe *टीद v.i.* (of baby) to grow first teeth दूध के दांत निकलना।

teetotal *टी टो ट्ल a.* pledged to abstain from alcohol मद्यत्यागी।

teetotaller *टी टो टॅ लॅः n.* one who abstains from alcoholic drinks मद्यत्यागी।

telecast *टै˘ लि कास्ट n.* a television programme दूरदर्शन-कार्यक्रम।

telecast[2] *v.t.* to broadcast by television दूरदर्शन से प्रसारित करना।

telecommunications *टै˘ लि कॅ म्यू नि के शॅन्ज़ n.* communications by cable, telegraph, telephone, etc. दूरसंचार।

telegram *टै˘ लि ग्रैम n.* message sent by telegraph तार-संदेश।

telegraph[1] *टै˘ लि ग्राफ़, -ग्रैफ़ n.* apparatus for sending messages speedily तार-यंत्र।

telegraph[2] *v.t.* to communicate by telegraph तार-द्वारा भेजना।

telegraphic *टै˘ लि ग्रै फ़िक* sent by telegraph तार-द्वारा प्रेषित; suitable for telegraph तार-योग्य।

telegraphist *टि लै˘ ग्रै फ़िस्ट n.* one who works telegraph तार-यांत्रिक।

telegraphy *टि लै˘ ग्रॅ फ़ि, टै˘- n.* science of telegraph तारसंचार।

telepathic *टै˘ लि पै थिक a.* relating to telepathy दूर-संवेदी।

telepathist *टि लै˘ पॅ थिस्ट, टै˘- n.* one who studies or practises telepathy दूरसंवेदनविद्।

telepathy *टि लै˘ पॅ थि n.* action of one mind on another at a distance दूरसंवेदन।

telephone[1] *टै˘ लि फ़ोन n.* apparatus for communicating sound to hearer at a distance दूरभाष।

telephone[2] *v.t.* to communicate by telephone दूरभाष से कहना; *v.i.* to speak by telephone दूरभाष का प्रयोग करना।

telescope *टै˘ लि स्कोप n.* optical instrument for magnifying distant objects दूरबीन।

telescopic *टै˘ लि स्कौ˘ पिक a.* pertaining to telescope दूरबीनी; acting as a telescope दूरबीन जैसा।

televise *टै˘ लि वॉइज़ v.t.* to transmit by television दूरदर्शन से प्रसारित करना।

television *टै˘ लि वि ज़ॅन n.* system of producing on screen images of distant objects, events etc. दूरदर्शन।

tell *टैलॅ v.t.* to let know बताना; to inform सूचित करना; to order आदेश देना; to count गिनना।

teller *टै˘ लॅः n.* narrator कथक; bank cashier खजांची।

temper[1] *टै मॅ पॅः n.* frame of mind

मानसिकता; anger क्रोध; degree of hardness of steel इस्पात की कठोरता।

temper[2] *v.t.* to moderate कम करना, मंद करना; to harden कठोर बनाना; to bring to proper condition उचित दशा में लाना।

temperament *टैमॅ पॅ रॅ मॅन्ट n.* natural disposition स्वभाव, प्रकृति।

temperamental *टैमॅ पॅ रॅ मैन् टॅल a.* caused by temperament स्वाभाविक।

temperance *टैमॅ पॅ रॅन्स n.* moderation संयमन; abstinence, esp. from alcohol मद्यत्याग।

temperate *टैमॅ पॅ रिट a.* showing moderation संयमी; neither too hot nor too cold शीतोष्ण।

temperature *टैमॅ पॅ रि चॅः n.* degree of heat or cold तापमान।

tempest *टैमॅ पिस्ट n.* violent storm तूफ़ान।

tempestuous *टैमॅ पैसॅ ट्यु अॅस a.* stormy तूफ़ानी।

temple[1] *टैमॅ पल n.* building for worship मंदिर, देवालय।

temple[2] *n.* flat side on either side of forehead कनपटी।

temporal *टैमॅ पॅ रॅल a.* concerned with time कालिक; earthly, worldly सांसारिक।

temporary *टैमॅ पॅ र रि a.* not permanent अस्थायी, अल्पकालिक।

tempt *टैम्प्ट v.t.* to attract, to allure लुभाना; to induce प्रेरित करना, उकसाना।

temptation *टैम्प् टे शॅन n.* act of tempting प्रलोभन; thing that tempts प्रलोभन-विषय।

tempter *टैम्प् टॅः n.* one who tempts लुभानेवाला।

ten *टैन् n., a.* (number) next after nine दस (10)।

tenable *टै ॅ नॅ बल a.* that can be defended समर्थनीय, प्रतिपाद्य।

tenacious *टि ने शॅस, टै ॅ- a.* holding firmly मज़बूत पकड़ वाला; (of memory) retentive तीव्र (स्मृति)।

tenacity *टि नै सि टि n.* quality of being tenacious तीव्रता।

tenancy *टै नॅन् सि n.* use of house, building or land in return for rent किरायेदारी, काश्तकारी।

tenant *टै ॅ नॅन्ट n.* one who holds house, land etc. on rent or lease किरायेदार, काश्तकार।

tend *टैन्ड v.i.* to be inclined प्रवृत्त होना।

tendency *टैन् डॅन् सि n.* inclination, bent झुकाव, प्रवत्ति।

tender[1] *टैन् डॅः n.* an offer to do work according to a contract निविदा।

tender[2] *v.t.* to make an offer प्रस्तुत करना।

tender[3] *n.* one who tends सेवक, टहलुआ।

tender[4] *a.* not tough or hard मुलायम; easily injured सुकुमार, कोमल; loving स्नेहशील; gentle सौम्य।

tenet *टै ॅ निट्, टी नै ॅट n.* doctrine, belief सिद्धांत, मत।

tennis *टै ॅ निस n.* game played with ball and racket टैनिस।

tense[1] *टैन्स n.* modification of verb to show time of action काल।

tense[2] *a.* stretched tight कसा हुआ, तना हुआ; emotionally strained तनावग्रस्त।

tension *टैन् शॅन n.* state of being stretched कसाव, तनाव; mental strain मानसिक उद्विग्नता।

tent *टैन्ट n.* movable shelter of canvas तंबू, डेरा।

tentative *टैन् टॅ टिव a.* done as a trial, experimental आज़माइशी।

tenure *टै ˘ न्यूअॅ: n.* holding of an office or property धारण; length of time of holding an office कार्यकाल।

term[1] *टॅ:म n.* word, expression शब्द; limited period of time अवधि; period during which courts sit, schools are open etc. सत्र; *pl.* relationship संबंध; *pl.* conditions शर्तें।

term[2] *टॅ:म v.t.* to name, to describe पुकारना, वर्णन करना।

terminable *टॅ: मि नॅ बल a.* that can be terminated समाप्य।

terminal[1] *टॅ: मि नल a.* forming an end अंतिम; occurring each term सात्रिक, अवधिक।

terminal[2] *n.* end of a wire used to make an electrical connection सिरा; end of a railway line, bus line etc. अंतिम स्टेशन।

terminate *टॅ: मि नेट v.t.* to bring to an end समाप्त करना; *v.i.* to come to an end समाप्त होना।

termination *टॅ: मि ने शॅन n.* ending समाप्ति।

terminological *टॅ: मि नॅ लौ ˘ जि कॅल a.* of terminology पारिभाषिक शब्दावली से संबंधित।

terminology *टॅ: मि नौ ˘ लॅ जि n.* terms used in a particular science पारिभाषिक शब्दावली।

terminus *टॅ: मि नॅस n. (pl. termini)* the last station of a railway, bus or air journey अंतिम स्टेशन।

terrace *टै ˘ रॅस n.* raised level place चबूतरा; level cut out of a hill पहाड़ी से काटकर बनाया गया चौरस भाग; a row of similar houses joined together भवन-पंक्ति।

terrible *टै ˘ रि बल a.* causing great fear भयानक; serious गंभीर; excessive घोर, भारी।

terrier *टै ˘ रि अॅ: n.* a breed of dog कुत्ते की एक नस्ल।

terrific *टॅ रि फ़िक a.* terrible भयावह; very great अति अधिक।

terrify *टै ˘ रि फ़ॉइ v.t.* to frighten, to fill with fear भयभीत करना, आतंकित करना।

territorial *टै ˘ रि टौ रि अॅल a.* of territory क्षेत्रीय, प्रादेशिक।

territory *टै ˘ रि टॅ रि n.* region क्षेत्र; area of knowledge ज्ञान-क्षेत्र।

terror *टै ˘ रॅ: n.* great fear आतंक; cause of fear भय का कारण।

terrarism *टै ˘ रॅ रिज़्म n.* use of terror to achieve an end आतंकवाद।

terrorist *टै ˘ रॅ रिस्ट n.* person who uses violence for an end आतंकवादी।

terrorize *टै ˘ रॅ रॉइज़ v.t.* to force or oppress by terror or violence आतंकित करना।

terse *टॅ:स a.* concise, expressed in a few words संक्षिप्त।

test[1] *टै ˘ स्ट v.t.* to put to the proof जांचना, परखना।

test² *n.* trial परीक्षण, जांच; examination परीक्षा; criterion कसौटी।

testament *टैसॅ टॅ मॅन्ट n.* a will वसीयत; one of the two main parts of the Bible बाइबिल के दो भागों में से एक।

testicle *टैसॅ टि कल n.* either of two male reproductive glands अंडग्रंथि।

testify *टैसॅ टि फ़ॉइ v.i.* to give evidence प्रमाण देना; *v.t.* to serve as proof of प्रमाणित करना।

testimonial *टैसॅ टि मो न्यॅल n.* certificate of character, ability etc. प्रमाणपत्र।

testimony *टैसॅ टि मॅ नि n.* a statement of proof साक्ष्य, गवाही; affirmation कथन, घोषणा।

tete-a-tete *टे टा टेट n.* private conversation व्यक्तिगत वार्तालाप।

tether¹ टै ˘ दॅ: *n.* a rope or chain for fastening a grazing animal रस्सी, पगहा।

tether² *v.t.* to tie up with a tether पगहे से बांधना।

text *टैकॅस्ट n.* the main part of a book मूल पाठ; a short quotation from the Bible बाइबिल से उद्धृत पाठ।

textile¹ *टैकॅस् टॉइल a.* concerned with weaving वस्त्र-उद्योग-संबंधी।

textile² *n.*, woven cloth of fabric वस्त्र, कपड़ा।

textual *टैकॅस् ट्यु ॲल n.* of a text मूल पाठ-विषयक।

texture *टैकॅस् चॅ: n.* way in which a cloth is woven बुनावट; structure गठन; tissue तंतु।

thank¹ *थैङ्क v.t.* to say thanks to धन्यवाद देना; to express gratitude to के प्रति आभार व्यक्त करना।

thank² *n. (used as pl.)* words of gratitude आभार-प्रदर्शन।

thankful *थैङ्क् फुल a.* grateful कृतज्ञ, आभारी।

thankless *थैङ्क् लिस a.* unrewarding, unprofitable व्यर्थ, अलाभकारी; ungrateful कृतघ्न।

that¹ दैट *a.* वह।

that² *dem. pron.* वह, उसने।

that³ *rel. pron.* जो, जिसने, जिसे।

that⁴ *adv.* ताकि।

that⁵ *conj.* कि।

thatch¹ *थैच n.* roofing made of straw ,छप्पर।

thatch² *v.t.* to roof (a house) with straw, reeds etc. (पर) छप्पर डालना।

thaw¹ थौ *v.i.* to melt पिघलना; (of person) to become warmer or more genial पसीजना, प्रभावित होना; *v.t.* to cause to melt पिघलाना; to make more genial दयाद्रवित करना।

thaw² *n.* melting द्रवण, पिघलन, गलन।

theatre *थि ॲ टॅ: n.* place where plays etc. are performed नाट्यशाला; dramatic works नाट्यकृतियां; large room with tiered seats व्याख्यान-कक्ष; surgical operating room शल्य-कक्ष।

theatrical *थि ऐट् रि कॅल a.* of, for the theatre नाट्यशाला-विषयक, नाट्यशाला-हेतु; exaggerated अतिरंजित; showy दिखावटी, कृत्रिम।

theft *थैफ़्ट n.* stealing चोरी।

their *दें ॲ: a.* of them उनका।

theirs *देॲ:ज pron.* belonging to

them उनका।

theism *थी इज़्म, थि-* *n.* belief in the existence of one God आस्तिकता।

theist *थी इस्ट, थि-* *n.* a believer in God आस्तिक।

them *दैमॅ* *pron.* to those (persons or things) उनको, उन्हें।

thematic *थि मै टिक* *a.* relating to theme विषयगत।

theme *थीम* *n.* subject विषय।

then[1] *दैनॅ* *adv.* at that time उस समय; next तत्पश्चात्; in that case ऐसी स्थिति में; also, moreover साथ ही।

then[2] *a.* existing, in office at that time तत्कालीन।

thence *दैन्स* *adv.* from there वहां से; for that reason अतः, उस कारण से।

theocracy *थि औ˘ क्रॅ सि* *n.* government by a deity or priesthood धर्मतंत्र, पुरोहिततंत्र।

theologian *थि अॅ लो ज्यॅन* *n.* advanced student of theology धर्मविज्ञानी, धर्मतत्त्वज्ञ।

theological *थि अॅ लौ˘ जि कॅल* *a.* concerned with theology धर्मविज्ञान-विषयक।

theology *थि औ˘ लॅ जि* *n.* study of God and religion धर्मविज्ञान, ईश्वरमीमांसा।

theorem *थि अॅ रॅम* *n.* proposition which can be demonstrated by argument प्रमेय।

theoretical *थि अॅ रॅ टि कॅल* *a.* concerned with theory only सैद्धांतिक; speculative विचारात्मक।

theorist *थि अॅ रिस्ट* *n.* person who forms theories सिद्धांतशास्त्री।

theorize *थि अॅ रॉइज़* *v.i.* to form theories, to speculate सिद्धांत स्थापित करना।

theory *थि अॅ रि* *n.* system of rules and principles सैद्धांतिक ज्ञान; rules and reasoning सिद्धांत।

therapy *थै˘ रॅ पि* *n.* medical treatment उपचार, चिकित्सा।

there *दे˘अॅः* *adv.* at that place वहां।

thereabouts *दे˘ अॅ रॅ बॉउट्स* *adv.* near that place, number, quantity etc. वहीं कहीं, लगभग उतना।

thereafter *दे˘ अॅ राफ़् टॅः* *adv.* after that तदनंतर।

thereby *दे˘ अॅः बॉइ* *adv.* by that means उसके द्वारा।

therefore *दे˘ अॅः फ़ौः* *adv.* for that reason अतः।

thermal *थॅः मॅल* *a.* pertaining to heat ऊष्मीय।

thermometer *थॅः मौ˘ मि टॅः* *n.* an instrument for measuring temperature तापमापी।

thermos (flask) *थॅः मौसॅ (फ़्लास्क)* *n.* vacuum flask थर्मस।

thesis *थी सिस* *n. (pl. theses)* written work submitted for degree or diploma शोध-ग्रंथ।

thick[1] *थिक* *a.* not thin मोटा; dense घना; viscous गाढ़ा; throaty (voice) भर्राई हुई (आवाज़)।

thick[2] *n.* most crowded part सर्वाधिक भीड़वाला भाग।

thick[3] *adv.* abundantly प्रचुर मात्रा में; rapidly and in large numbers अंधाधुंध, लगातार।

thicken *थि कॅन* *v.i.* to grow thick मोटा होना; *v.t.* to make thick मोटा

बनाना।

thicket *थि किट n.* thick growth of small trees झुरमुट।

thief *थीफ़ n.* one who steals चोर।

thigh *थॉइ n.* upper part of leg जंघा, रान।

thimble *थिम् ब्ल n.* cap protecting end of finger when sewing अंगुश्ताना।

thin[1] *थिन a.* of little thickness पतला; lacking density: छितराया हुआ; not fat दुबला।

thin[2] *(-nn-) v.t.* to make thin पतला करना; *v.i.* to become thin पतला होना।

thing *थिङ्ग n.* a material वस्तु; *(pl.)* belongings सामान; a fact तथ्य; topic विषय; matter मामला।

think *थिङ्क v.t.* to consider मानना; to believe विश्वास करना; *v.i.* to reflect विचारना; to imagine कल्पना करना; to hold opinion मत रखना।

thinker *थिङ् कॅ: n.* a person who thinks विचारक।

third[1] *थॅ:ड a.* the last of three तीसरा।

third[2] *n.* one of three equal parts तिहाई भाग।

thirdly *थॅ:ड् लि adv.* in the third place तीसरे स्थान पर।

thirst[1] *थॅस्ट n.* desire to drink प्यास; craving, yearning तीव्र इच्छा।

thirst[2] *v.i.* to have thirst प्यासा होना; to be eager इच्छुक होना।

thirsty *थॅ:स् टि a.* wanting some thing to drink प्यासा; eager, desirous इच्छुक।

thirteen[1] *थॅ: टीन n.* the number above twelve तेरह की संख्या (13)।

thirteen[2] *a.* one more than twelve तेरह।

thirteenth[1] *थॅ: टीन्थ a.* the last of thirteen तेरहवां।

thirtieth[1] *थॅ: टि इथ a.* the last of thirty तीसवां।

thirtieth[2] *n.* one of thirty equal parts तीसवां भाग।

thirty[1] *थॅ: टि n.* the number three times ten तीस की संख्या (30)।

thirty[2] *a.* three times ten तीस।

thistle *थि स्ल n.* a prickly wild plant ऊंटकटारा।

thither *दि दॅ: adv.* in that direction उस ओर; to that place वहां को।

thorn *थौ:न n.* a prickle कांटा।

thorny *थौ:नि a.* full of thorns कंटकमय; troublesome कष्टप्रद।

thorough *थ रॅ a.* complete पूर्ण।

thoroughfare *थ रॅ फ़ेॅअ: n.* a road that the public has the right to use आम रास्ता।

though[1] *दो conj.* in spite of the fact that यद्यपि।

though[2] *adv.* nevertheless, however तथापि।

thought *थौट n.* process of thinking मनन; consideration सोच-विचार; an idea विचार; intention इरादा, मंतव्य।

thoughtful *थौट् फुल a.* considerate लिहाज़ करनेवाला; engaged in meditation मननशील।

thousand[1] *थॉउ ज़ॅन्ड n.* the number ten times a hundred हज़ार की संख्या (1000)।

thousand[2] *a.* ten times a hundred हज़ार।

thrall *थ्रौल n.* slave दास।

thralldom *थ्रौल् डॅम n.* bondage, slavery दासता।

thrash *थ्रैस v.t.* to beat soundly पीटना, छेतना; to defeat soundly बुरी तरह हरा देना।

thread[1] *थ्रॅड n.* fine cord धागा; yarn सूत; a spiral ridge on a screw पेंच की चूड़ी; theme, meaning कथावस्तु, अर्थ।

thread[2] *v.t.* to put thread in to (में) धागा डालना; to put (beads, pearls, etc.) on a thread (मनके, मोती आदि) धागे में पिरोना।

threadbare *थ्रै ॅड़् बे ॅअ: a.* worn thin जीर्ण, फटा-पुराना; hackneyed, much used घिसा-पिटा।

threat *थ्रै ॅट n.* declaration of intention to harm or injure धमकी; a warning of danger ख़तरे की चेतावनी; a source of danger ख़तरे का कारण।

threaten *थ्रै ॅट्न v.t.* to use threats to or towards धमकी देना; to utter a threat of (की) धमकी देना; *v.i.* to be a source of danger ख़तरा होना।

three[1] *थ्री n.* the number next above two तीन की संख्या (3)।

three[2] *a.* one more than two तीन।

thresh *थ्रैशॅ v.t.* to beat the grain out कूट-छेत कर दाना निकालना; *v.i.* to beat wheat etc. take out grain कूटने-पीटने का काम करना।

thresher *थ्रै ॅ शॅ: n.* threshing machine मड़ाई की मशीन।

threshold *थ्रै ॅ शोल्ड n.* stone or plank under a door way दहलीज़; entrance प्रवेश-द्वार; star+ प्रारंभ।

thrice *थ्रॉइस adv.* three times तीन बार।

thrift *थ्रिफ़्ट n.* economy, frugality मितव्ययिता।

thrifty *थ्रिफ़् टि a.* economical, frugal मितव्ययी।

thrill[1] *थ्रिल n.* a sudden feeling of excitement पुलक, सिहरन।

thrill[2] *v.t.* to cause to feel a thrill पुलकित करना; *v.i.* to feel a thrill पुलकित होना।

thrive *थ्राइव v.i.* to grow well, to flourish फलना-फूलना, समृद्ध होना।

throat *थ्रोट n.* front part of the neck गला, कंठ; gullet हलक़।

throaty *थ्रो टि a.* (of voice) hoarse, guttural भर्राई हुई, बैठी हुई (आवाज़)।

throb[1] *थ्रौबॅ (-bb-) v.i.* to quiver strongly, to pulsate धड़कना, स्पंदित होना।

throb[2] *n.* pulsation, vibration स्पंदन, कंपन।

throe *थ्रो n. (usu pl.)* sharp pain, esp. of child-birth तीव्र पीड़ा, विशेषतया प्रसव-पीड़ा।

throne[1] *थ्रोन n.* the seat of a king or queen राजगद्दी, सिंहासन।

throne[2] *v.t.* to place on throne, to declare king राजगद्दी पर बिठाना, अभिषेक करना।

throng[1] *थ्रौ ॅङ्ग n.* crowd भीड़।

throng[2] *v.t.* to fill with crowd ठसाठस भर देना, भीड़ से भरना; *v.i.* to crowd इकट्ठा होना, भीड़ लगाना।

throttle[1] *थ्रौ ॅ ट्ल n.* device to control flow of fuel to an engine उपरोधक।

throttle[2] *v.t.* to strangle गला घोंटना; to suppress दबाना; to control नियंत्रित करना।

through[1] *थ्रू prep.* from end to end of के आर-पार; from one side to the other of से होकर; from beginning to end of के प्रारंभ से अंत तक; by means of के द्वारा as a result of के परिणाम स्वरूप।

through[2] *adv.* from beginning to end आद्योपांत; to the end अंत तक।

through[3] *a.* going nonstop बिना रुके जानेवाला।

throughout[1] *थ्रू ऑउट adv.* in every part सर्वत्र all through सदैव, आद्योपांत।

throughout[2] *prep.* in every part of के प्रत्येक भाग में।

throw[1] *थ्रो v.t.* to fling फेंकना; to cause to fall गिरा देना।

throw[2] *n.* act of throwing फेंक; distance to which something is thrown फेंक की दूरी; a chance (of dice) चाल।

thrust[1] *थ्रस्ट v.t.* to push violently धक्का देना; to stab घोंपना।

thrust[2] *n.* a violent push ज़ोरदार धक्का; lunge, stab प्रहार, घोंप; propulsive force or power उछाल; stress बल; cutting remark कटु कथन।

thud[1] *थड n.* dull, heavy sound धम, धड़ाम का स्वर।

thud[2] *(-dd-) v.i.* to make a dull sound धम की आवाज़ करना।

thug *थग n.* a brutal violent person गुंडा।

thumb[1] *थम n.* short thick finger of the human hand अंगूठा।

thumb[2] *v.t.* to dirty with the thumb अंगूठे से गंदा करना; to signal for lift in a vehicle (अंगूठे से) संकेत करना।

thump[1] *थम्प n.* dull, heavy blow मुक्का, प्रहार, sound of a heavy blow धम का स्वर।

thump[2] *v.t.* to strike with a heavy blow मुक्का मारना; *v.i.* to fall heavily धम से गिरना।

thunder[1] *थन् डॅः n.* loud noise accompanying lightening गरज़, गड़गड़ाहट।

thunder[2] *v.i.* to rumble with thunder गरजना; to make noise like thunder बादल की तरह गड़गड़ाना; *v.t.* to utter loudly कड़क कर कहना।

thunderous *थन् डॅ रॅस a.* giving out thunder गर्जनशील।

Thursday *थॅःज़् डे,-डि n.* fifth day of the week गुरूवार।

thus *दस adv.* in this way इस प्रकार; therefore अतः।

thwart *थ्वौःट v.t.* to prevent रोकना।

tiara *टि आ रॅ n.* a jewelled head ornament, coronet मुकुट।

tick[1] *टिक n.* a light sound as made by a watch टिक-टिक की ध्वनि; a tiny creature that sucks the blood of animals चिचड़ी; a small mark (✓) सही का चिह्न (✓)।

tick[2] *v.i.* to make a light sound like that of a watch टिक-टिक करना; *v.t.* to mark with a tick (पर) सही का चिह्न लगाना।

ticket *टि किट n.* card or paper entitling holder to admission, travel etc. टिकट; label लेबुल।

tickle *टि कल v.t.* to touch, poke (part of body) to produce laughter गुदगुदाना; to amuse (का)

मन बहलाना, हंसाना।

ticklish *टिक् लिश a.* sensitive to tickling गुदगुदी अनुभव करनेवाला; tricky, difficult जटिल।

tidal *टॉइ डॅल a.* of a tide or tides ज्वारीय।

tide *टॉइड n.* the regular rise and fall of the sea ज्वार।

tidings *टॉइ डिङ्ग्ज़ n. pl.* news समाचार।

tidiness *टॉइ डि निस n.* neatness स्वच्छता; orderliness सुव्यवस्था।

tidy[1] *टॉइ डि a.* neat साफ़-सुथरा; orderly सुव्यवस्थित।

tidy[2] *v.t.* to put in order सुव्यवस्थित करना।

tie[1] *टॉइ v.t.* to fasten बांधना; to restict सीमित करना; *v.i.* to score the same number of points in a game खेल में बराबर-बराबर अंक प्राप्त करना।

tie[2] *n.* a neck-tie टाई, कंठबंध; a knot गांठ; something used for fastening बंधनी; equal score in a game अंकों की समानता; connecting link कड़ी।

tier *टिअॅ: n.* a row of seats placed one behind and above another पीछे की ओर क्रमशः उठती हुई कुर्सियों की पंक्ति।

tiger *टॉइ गॅ: n.* a large carnivorous feline animal बाघ।

tight *टॉइट a.* firmly stretched कसा हुआ, तना हुआ; firmly fastened मज़बूत बंधा हुआ; fitting too closely तंग।

tighten *टॉइ ट्न v.t.* to make tight कसना, तानना; *v.i.* to become tight तनना, तंग होना।

tigress *टॉइ ग्रिस n.* a female tiger बाघिन।

tile[1] *टॉइल n.* a piece of baked clay used for covering roofs, floors, walls etc. खपरा, खपरैल।

tile[2] *v.t.* to cover with tiles खपरों से पाटना।

till[1] *टिल prep.* upto the time of के समय तक।

till[2] *n. conj.* to the time that जब तक कि।

till[3] *v.t.* to cultivate, to plough जोतना, जुताई करना।

tilt[1] *टिल्ट v.i.* to come into a sloping position झुकना, तिरछा होना; *v.t.* to incline, to cause to slope झुकाना।

tilt[2] *n.* sloping position झुकाव।

timber *टिम् बॅ: n.* wood used in building इमारती लकड़ी।

time[1] *टॉइम n.* duration including past, present and future समय; a period अवधि; era, age युग; moment क्षण; occasion मौक़ा; opportunity अवसर; leisure अवकाश।

time[2] *v.t.* to measure the duration of का समय नापना; to choose the proper moment for के लिए उचित समय का चयन करना।

timely *टॉइम् लि a.* opportune समयोचित।

timid *टि मिड a.* easily frightened भीरु, डरपोक।

timidity *टि मि डि टि n.* quality of being timid भीरुता।

timorous *टि मॅ रॅस a.* timid भीरु।

tin[1] *टिन n.* a malleable metal टिन, टीन; a can, a canister टिन का

डिब्बा, कनस्तर।

tin[2] *(-nn-) v.t.* to pack in tins डिब्बों में रखना।

tincture[1] *टिङ्क् चें:* *n.* a slight suggestion of taste or colour झलक; a substance dissolved in alcohol घोल।

tincture[2] *v.t.* to colour, to tint (पर) हल्का रंग चढ़ाना (का) पुट देना।

tinge[1] *टिन्ज* *n.* slight trace, flavour आभा, झलक।

tinge[2] *v.t.* to colour, flavour slightly की पुट देना।

tinker *टिङ्कं:* *n.* mender of kettles and pans ठठेरा, कसेरा।

tinsel *टिन् सॅल* *n.* glittering metallic substance for decoration पन्नी; anything sham and showy भड़कीली वस्तु।

tint[1] *टिन्ट* *n.* colour रंग, वर्ण; shade of colour, tinge आभा; झलक।

tint[2] *v.t.* to colour, to tinge रंगना।

tiny *टॉइ नि* *a.* very small बहुत छोटा।

tip[1] *टिप* *n.* thin, pointed end of something नोक, पतला सिरा।

tip[2] *(-pp-) v.t.* to put a point on नोकदार बनाना; to cover a tip with something सिरे पर शाम चढ़ाना।

tip[3] *n.* gratuity for personal service बख़्शिश; hint संकेत, सुझाव, युक्ति।

tip[4] *(-pp-) v.t.* to give a tip to बख़्शिश देना।

tip[5] *n.* place where rubbish is dumped घूरा।

tip[6] *(-pp-) v.t.* to tilt उलट देना; to touch lightly हल्का-सा छूना; *v.i.* to topple over उलट जाना।

tipsy *टिप् सि* *a.* slightly drunk हल्के नशे में।

tirade *टॉइ रेड* *n.* a long outburst of scolding फटकार-भरा भाषण।

tire *टॉइॲ:* *v.t.* to make weary थका देना; *v.i.* to become weary थक जाना; (with, 'of') to lose interest or linking for something ऊबना।

tiresome *टॉइॲ: सॅम* *a.* wearysome थकाऊ।

tissue *टि स्यू-श्यू* *n.* a finely woven fabric महीन कपड़ा; substance of animal body, plant, etc. ऊतक; fine, soft, paper used as handkerchief पतला, मुलायम काग़ज़।

titanic *टॉइ टै निक* *a.* immense विशाल, भीमकाय।

tithe *टाइद* *n.* tenth part of a farmer's produce paid as tax for the upkeep of the clergy दशमांश कर।

title *टॉइ ट्ल* *n.* name of a book पुस्तक का नाम; heading शीर्षक; appellation उपाधि legal right अधिकार।

titular *टि ट्यू लॅं:* *a.* held by virtue of a title औपाधिक; pertaining to title उपाधि-संबंधी nominal नामधारी, नाम का।

toad *टोड* *n.* animal like large frog भेक, टोड।

toast[1] *टोस्ट* *n.* a slice of bread browned by heat डबल रोटी का सिका हुआ टुकड़ा; act of toasting शुभकामना।

toast[2] *v.t.* to drink to the health or success of (के) स्वास्थ्य या सफलता के लिए पीना; to make brown by heating सेंकना; *v.i.* to become brown by heat सिकना।

tobacco *टॅ बै को* *n.* a plant and its leaves used for smoking, chewing or snuff तंबाकू।

today[1] *टॅ डे* *adv.* on this day आज; nowadays आजकल।

today[2] *n.* this day यह दिन।

toe[1] *टो* *n.* a digit of foot पैर की उंगली; the front of an animal's foot खुर, सुम; front of a shoe or sock जूते या मौज़े का पंजा।

toe[2] *v.t.* to touch with the toe पैर से छूना।

toffee *टौ ˘ फ़ि* *n.* a sticky sweet made of sugar and butter टॉफी।

toga *टोगॅ* *n.* loose outer garment चोग़ा।

together *टॅ गै ˘ दॅः* *adv.* in company साथ-साथ; in one place एक जगह; at the same time एक ही समय; continuously लगातार।

toil[1] *टौ ˘इल* *n.* hard work कठिन परिश्रम।

toil[2] *v.i.* to work hard कठिन परिश्रम करना।

toilet *टौ˘इ लिट* *n.* a lavatory शौचघर; process of washing, dressing प्रसाधन; articles used for this प्रसाधन-सामग्री।

toils *टौ ˘इल्ज़* *n. pl.* snares, nets जाल, चंगुल।

token *टो कॅन* *n.* a symbol प्रतीक; a metal tag used as a coin or ticket सांकेतिक मुद्रा, सिक्का।

tolerable *टौ˘ लॅ रॅ बल* *a.* bearable सहनीय; fairly good संतोषजनक, कामचलाऊ।

tolerance *टौ˘ लॅ रॅन्स* *n.* ability to endure opinions or behaviour different from one's own सहनशीलता, सहिष्णुता।

tolerant *टौ˘ लॅ रॅन्ट* *a.* having tolerance सहिष्णु, सहनशील।

tolerate *टौ˘ लॅ रेट* *v.t.* to endure सहन करना; to allow, to permit होने देना, अनुमति देना।

toleration *टौ˘ लॅ रे शॅन* *n.* practice of allowing religious freedom धार्मिक सहिष्णुता।

toll[1] *टोल* *n.* tax paid for the use of a road or a bridge पथकर; loss damage हानि, क्षति।

toll[2] *n.* sound of bell घंटा-नाद।

toll[3] *v.t.* to ring (a bell) at regular intervals घंटा बजाना; *v.i.* to ring with regular strokes बजना।

tomato *टॅ मा टो* *n.* *(pl.-es)* a red, juicy fruit टमाटर।

tomb *टूम* *n.* grave क़ब्र।

tomboy *टौमॅ् बौ ˘इ* *n.* a girl who likes rough, boyish games मरदानी लड़की।

tomcat *टौमॅ् कैट* *n.* a male cat बिलाव, विडाल।

tome *टोम* *n.* a large, heavy book विशाल ग्रंथ।

tomorrow[1] *टॅ मौ ˘ रो* *n.* the day after today आने वाला कल।

tomorrow[2] *adv.* on the day after today कल को।

ton *टन* *n.* a measure of weight टन।

tone *टोन* *n.* quality of voice स्वर, ध्वनि; quality of musical sound तान, सुर; intonation लहज़ा, स्वर-शैली; healthy condition स्वस्थ स्थिति।

tone[2] *v.t.* to give a particular tone of sound तानबद्ध करना; *v.i.* to be in harmony मेल खाना।

tongs *टौँ ङ्‌ग्ज n. pl.* large pincers चिमटा, संडसी।

tongue *टङ्‌ग n.* the muscular organ inside mouth जीभ; language भाषा।

tonic[1] *टौ ˘ निक a.* concerned with tone तान-विषयक; invigorating शक्तिवर्धक।

tonic[2] *n.* medicine that increases general health स्वास्थ्यवर्धक औषधि; keynote मूलस्वर।

to-night[1] *टॅ नॉइट n.* this night आज की रात।

tonight[2] *adv.* on this night आज रात को।

tonne *टन n.* a metric ton मीटरी टन।

tonsil *टौन्‌ सिल n.* gland in throat गुलतुंडिका, टॉन्सिल।

tonsure *टौन्‌ शॅः n.* the shaving of the top of the head of a person मुंडन।

too टू *adv.* excessively बहुत अधिक; also भी।

tool *टूल n.* an instrument or appliance औज़ार; means to an end साधन; a servile helper कठपुतली, गुलाम।

tooth *टूथ n.* bone-like projection in gums दांत; cog, prong दांता।

toothache *टूथ्‌ एक n.* pain in a tooth दांत-दर्द।

toothsome *टूथ्‌ सॅम a.* pleasant to eat स्वादिष्ट ।

top[1] *टौपॅ n.* summit चोटी; highest rank सर्वोच्च पद; lid ढक्कन; the upper surface ऊपरी तल।

top[2] *(-pp-) v.t.* to provide a top for (पर) चोटी लगाना; to reach the top of की चोटी पर पहुंचना; to surpass (से) श्रेष्ठ होना; to cut the tops off (के) सिरे काटना।

top[3] *n.* a child's spinning toy लट्टू।

topaz *टो पैज़ n.* a transparent yellow mineral पुखराज।

topic *टौ ˘ पिक n.* subject for discussion विषय।

topical *टौ ˘ पि कॅल a.* of present interest सामयिक।

topographer *टॅ पौ ˘ ग्रॅ फ़ॅ- n.* an expert in topography स्थलाकृति-विशेषज्ञ।

topographical *टौ˘ पॅ ग्रै फ़ि कॅल a.* pertaining to topography स्थलाकृतिक।

topography *टॅ पौ ˘ ग्रॅ फ़ि n.* surface features of a place स्थलाकृति; description of these features स्थलाकृति का वर्णन।

topple *टौ˘ पल v.i.* to fall over उलट जाना, गिर जाना; *v.t.* to cause to fall over उलट देना, गिरा देना।

topsy turvy[1] *टौपॅ सि टॅः वि a.* upside down औंधा, उलटा-पुलटा; confused, disordered अस्तव्यस्त।

topsy turvy[2] *adv.* upside down उलट-पुलट स्थिति में।

torch *टौःच n.* burning brand मशाल; a small portable electric lamp टॉर्च।

torment[1] *टौः मैन्ट n.* intense suffering यातना।

torment[2] *टौः मैन्ट v.t.* to torture यातना देना।

tornado *टौः ने डो n. (pl. -es)* a violent storm तूफ़ान।

torpedo[1] *टौः पी डो n. (pl.-es)* an under-water missile पनडुब्बी।

torpedo² *v.t.* to strike or sink with torpedo पनडुब्बी से आक्रमण करना या डुबोना।

torrent *टौ ˘ रॅन्ट* *n.* a rushing stream प्रचंड धारा।

torrential *टौ ˘ रैन् शॅल* *a.* resembling a stream प्रचंड धारा जैसा।

torrid *टौ ˘ रिड* *a.* very hot अति उष्ण।

tortoise *टौ: टॅस* *n.* a slow-moving reptile with four legs and a hard shell कछुआ।

tortuous *टौ : ट्यु अॅस, - चु-* *a.* winding टेढ़ा-मेढ़ा।

torture¹ *टौ: चॅः* *n.* severe pain यातना, संताप।

torture² *v.t.* to subject to torture यातना देना, सताना।

toss¹ *टौसॅ* *v.t.* to throw up उछालना; to jerk झटका देना; *v.i.* to throw a coin into the air to decide something सिक्का उछालना।

toss² *n.* tossing movement उछाल।

total¹ *टो ट्ल* *a.* complete, whole, entire संपूर्ण, समूचा।

total² *n.* whole amount पूर्ण मात्रा।

total³ *(-ll-)* *v.t.* to find the total जोड़ना; *v.i.* to amount to कुल जोड़ होना।

totality *टो ˘ टै लि टि* *n.* entirety संपूर्णता।

touch¹ *टच* *v.t.* to come into contact with के संपर्क में आना; to put hand on स्पर्श करना, छूना; to reach तक पहुंचना; to affect emotions of का हृदय छूना; to deal with का ज़िक करना; to interfere with के साथ छेड़-छाड़ करना।

touch² *n.* act of touching स्पर्श; contact संपर्क; slight stroke हल्की थपकी।

touchy *ट चि* *a.* easily offended, sensitive नाराज़, उत्तेजित, संवेदनशील।

tough *टफ़* *a.* strong मज़बूत, दृढ़; stiff कड़ा, कठोर; difficult कठिन।

toughen *ट फ़ॅन* *v.t.* to make tough कड़ा बनाना; *v.i.* to become tough कड़ा होना।

tour¹ *टुअॅः* *n.* travelling round, excursion भ्रमण, यात्रा।

tour² *v.i.* to go on excursion भ्रमण करना; *v.t.* to make tour of का भ्रमण करना।

tourism *टुअॅ रिज़्म* *n.* business of organising tours पर्यटन।

tourist *टुअॅ रिज़्ट* *n.* a person travelling for pleasure पर्यटक।

tournament *टु अॅः नॅ मॅन्ट, टौः -* *n.* a contest decided by a series of matches खेलकूद-प्रतियोगिता।

towards *टॅ वॉःड्ज* *prep.*, in the direction of की ओर; in relation to के संबंध में; near के लगभग; for the purpose of के हेतु।

towel¹ *टॉउ अॅल* *n.* cloth for drying something तौलिया, गमछा।

towel² *(-ll-)* *v.t.* to dry or rub with a towel तौलिये से पोंछना।

tower¹ *टॉउ अॅः* *n.* a tall narrow building मीनार; fortress क़िला।

tower² *v.i.* to rise to a great height ऊंचा उठना।

town *टॉउन* *n.* centre of population larger than a village क़सबा।

township *टॉउन् शिप* *a.* small town क़सबा।

toy¹ *टौ ˘इ* *n.* a child's plaything खिलौना।

toy[2] *v.i.* to trifle खिलवाड़ करना।

trace[1] *ट्रेस n.* track left by something खोज, निशान; indication संकेत; minute quantity अल्प मात्रा।

trace[2] *v.t.* to draw out खींचना; to copy by means of tracing paper अनुरेखित करना; to find, to discover ज्ञात करना; to find the track of (का) सुराग़ पा लेना; to describe वर्णन करना (के) विकास की रूपरेखा प्रस्तुत करना।

traceable *ट्रे सॅ ब्ल a.* capable of being traced खोजने-योग्य।

track[1] *ट्रैक n.* a path made by use मार्ग; direction दिशा; a set of railway lines रेलपथ; a path laid out for races दौड़-पट्टी, दौड़-मार्ग; trail खोज।

track[2] *v.t.* to follow trail of खोज पर चलना; to find by following trail खोज निकालना, ढूंढ लेना।

tract[1] *ट्रैक्ट n.* a wide expance विस्तृत भूभाग।

tract[2] *n.* pamphlet, treatise पुस्तिका।

traction *ट्रैक् शॅन n.* action of drawing, pulling कर्षण, खिंचाव।

tractor *ट्रैक् टः n.* a motor vehicle for pulling ट्रैक्टर।

trade[1] *ट्रैड n.* commerce व्यापार; buying and selling क्रय-विक्रय; any profitable pursuit लाभकारी धंधा।

trade[2] *v.i.* to engage in trade व्यापार करना; to buy and sell क्रय-विक्रय करना; *v.t.* to exchange की अदला-बदली करना।

trader *ट्रेड़ः n.* a merchant व्यापारी।

tradesman *ट्रेड़्जिमॅन n.* shopkeeper दुकानदार; a skilled worker कुशल कारीगर।

tradition *ट्रॅ डि शॅन n.* the handing down from generation to generation of ideas, beliefs, customs, etc. परंपरा।

traditional *ट्रॅ डि शॅ नॅल a.* pertaining to tradition परंपरागत, पारंपरिक।

traffic[1] *ट्रै फिक n.* the movement of vehicles on roads and streets यातायात; illicit trade अवैध व्यापार।

traffic[2] *(-ck-) v.i.* to trade in illicit goods अवैध वस्तुओं का व्यापार करना।

tragedian *ट्रॅ जी ड्यॅन n.* writer of tragedy त्रासदीकार; actor in tragedy त्रासदी-अभिनेता।

tragedy *ट्रै जि डि n.* a play concerned with suffering and having a sad ending दुःखांत नाटक; a sad or calamitous event दुःखद घटना।

tragic *ट्रै जिक a.* of tragedy दुःखांत; calamitous अनर्थकारी, विपत्तिपूर्ण।

trail[1] *ट्रेल n.* track मार्ग; trace खोज, चिह्न thing that trails पुछल्ला; a rough path पगडंडी।

trail[2] *v.t.* to drag behind one घसीटना; to hunt by following tracks खोज के आधार पर पीछा करना; *v.i* to be drawn behind घसीटना; to move wearily धीरे-धीरे से चलना।

trailer *ट्रे लॅः n.* a vehicle pulled by another यान के पीछे लगा यान; extracts from a film shown to advertise it in advance फिल्म की झलकियां।

train[1] *ट्रेन* *n.* line of railway coaches joined to locomotive रेलगाड़ी; a series, succession क्रम, तांता; attendants following an important person परिकर।

train[2] *v.t.* to give teaching and practice प्रशिक्षण देना; to cause (plants) to grow in a particular way पोधों को विशेष ढंग से बढ़ाना; to aim (gun, etc.) बंदूक से निशाना लगाना।

trainee *ट्रे नी* *n.* one who is being trained प्रशिक्षणार्थी।

training *ट्रे निङ्ग* *n.* practical education प्रशिक्षण।

trait *ट्रेट* *n.* a distinguishing feature विशेषता, लक्षण।

traitor *ट्रे टः* *n.* one guilty of treason विश्वासघाती, देशद्रोही।

tram *ट्रैम* *n.* vehicle running on rails laid on roadway ट्रामगाड़ी।

trample *ट्रैम् पल* *v.t.* to tread heavily on कुचलना, रौंदना।

trance *ट्रान्स* *n.* unconsciousness बेहोशी; ecstasy आत्मविस्मृति।

tranquil *ट्रैङ् क्विल* *a.* calm, quiet शांत।

tranquility *ट्रैङ् क्वि लि टि* *n.* tranquil state शांति।

tranquillize *ट्रैङ् क्वि लाइज़* *v.t.* to make calm शांत करना।

transact *ट्रैन् ज़ैक्ट, ट्रान्-* *v.t.* to carry through संपादित करना।

transaction *ट्रैन् ज़ैक् शॅन, ट्रान्-* *n.* the act of transacting संपादन; business transacted संपादित कार्य।

transcend *ट्रेन् सैन्ड ट्रान्-* *v.t.* to go beyond the range of (human experience, understanding, etc.) मानव के अनुभव, समझ आदि से बढकर होना।

transcendent *ट्रेन् सैन् डॅन्ट, ट्रान्-* *a.* surpassing, excelling (human experience, etc.) अनुभवातीत।

transcribe *ट्रैन् स्क्रॉइब ट्रान्-* *v.t.* to copy in writing की लिखित प्रतिलिपि तैयार करना।

transcription *ट्रैन् स्क्रिप् शॅन, ट्रान्-* *n.* transcribing प्रतिलिपि-लेखन; something trancribed प्रतिलिपि।

transfer[1] *ट्रैन्स् फ़ः, ट्रान्स्-* *n.* movement from one situation to another स्थानातंरण।

transfer[2] *(-rr-)* *v.t.* to move or send from one situation to another स्थानांतरित करना।

transferable *ट्रैन्स् फ़ॅ रॅ ब्ल, ट्रान्स्-* *a.* that can be transferred स्थानांतरणीय।

transfiguration *ट्रैन्स् फ़ि ग्यु रे शॅन, ट्रान्स-* *n.* transfiguring रूपांतरण।

transfigure *ट्रैन्स् फ़ि गॅः, ट्रान्स्-* *v.t.* to alter the appearance of रूपांतरित करना।

transform *ट्रैन्स् फ़ोःम, ट्रान्स्-* to change in appearance or nature (का) रूप बदल देना।

transformation *ट्रैन्स् फ़ॅ मे शॅन, ट्रान्स्-* *n.* being transformed रूपांतरण।

transgress *ट्रेन्स् ग्रैसॅ, ट्रान्स्-* *v.t.* to go beyond अतिक्रमण करना; to break (law, agreement, etc.) भंग करना; *v.i.* to sin पाप करना।

transgression *टैन्स् ग्रै˘ शॅन, ट्रान्स्-* *n.* transgressing अतिक्रमण, उल्लंघन; sin पाप।

transit *ट्रैन् जिट, ट्रान्-* *n.* the passing of something from one place to another परिवहन; conveying or being conveyed प्रेषण।

transition *ट्रैन् जि शॅन्, ट्रान्-* *n.* change from one state to another परिवर्तन।

transitive *ट्रैन् जि टिव, ट्रान्-* *n.* (of a verb) having an object सकर्मक क्रिया।

transitory *ट्रैन् जि टॅ रि, ट्रान्-* *n.* not lasting long अस्थायी।

translate *ट्रैन्स् लेट, ट्रान्स* *v.t.* to turn from one language into another अनुवाद करना।

translation *ट्रैन्स् ले, ट्रान्स्-* *n.* act of translating अनुवाद; something translated अनूदित अंश।

transmigration *ट्रैन्ज़् मॉइ ग्रे शॅन, ट्रान्ज़्-* *n.* passage (of soul) into another body देहांतरण, पुनर्जन्म।

transmission *ट्रैन्ज् मि शॅन, ट्रान्ज़्-* *n.* transference संचारण, प्रेषण।

transmit *ट्रैन्ज़् मिट, ट्रान्ज़्-* *(-tt-)* *v.t.* to pass on प्रेषित करना; to communicate पहुंचाना।

transmitter *ट्रैन्ज़् मि टॅः, ट्रान्ज़्-* *n.* somebody or something that transmits प्रेषक।

transparent *ट्रैन्स् पे ॅ अॅ रॅन्ट, ट्रान्स्-* *a.* that can be seen through पारदर्शी; obvious स्पष्ट।

transplant *ट्रैन्स् प्लान्ट, ट्रान्स्-* *v.t.* to move and plant in another place प्रतिरोपित करना।

transport[1] *ट्रैन्स् पौःट, ट्रान्स्-* *v.t.* to carry from one place to another ले जाना; to enrapture आनंदविभोर करना।

transport[2] *n.* conveying or being conveyed परिवहन; means of carrying परिवहन-साधन।

transportation *ट्रैन्स् पौ : टे शॅन* *n.* transporting परिवहन।

trap[1] *ट्रैप* *n.* device for catching animals ढका हुआ गड्ढा; U shaped section of a brain pipe पाइप का U के आकार का मोड़।

trap[2] *(-pp-)* *v.t.* to take in a trap जाल में फंसाना; to capture by trick धोखा देकर पकड़ना।

trash *ट्रैश* *n.* worthless material कूड़ा-करकट।

travel[1] *ट्रै व्ल* *(-ll-)* *v.i.* to make a journey यात्रा करना; to move, to go चलना।

travel[2] *n.* travelling यात्रा।

traveller *ट्रै वॅ लॅः* *n.* person on a journey यात्री।

tray *ट्रे* *n.* a flat receptacle of wood, metal, etc. used for carrying small articles ट्रे।

treacherous *ट्रै चॅ रॅस* *a.* disloyal विश्वासघाती; unreliable अविश्वसनीय; deceitful धोखेबाज़।

treachery *ट्रै चॅ रि* *n.* betrayal विश्वासघात; deceit धोखा।

tread[1] *ट्रै ॅड* *v.t.* to set foot on (पर) पैर रखना या चलना; to trample कुचलना, रौंदना; to oppress दमन करना।

tread[2] *n.* act or manner of stepping पदचाप; treading गमन, चलने की क्रिया; upper surface of step पैड़ी का ऊपरी तल; part of rubber tyre in contact with ground टायर का बाहरी भाग।

treason *ट्री ज़न* *n.* disloyalty

निष्ठाहीनता; betrayal of trust विश्वासघात।

treasure[1] *ट्रै ˘ ज़्ः n.* stored wealth भंडार, ख़ज़ाना; riches धन-दौलत।

treasure[2] *v.t.* to store up संचित करना; to prize बहुमूल्य समझना; to cherish संजोना।

treasurer *ट्रै ˘ ज़् रः n.* official in charge of funds कोषाध्यक्ष।

treasury *ट्रै˘ ज़ॅ रि n.* place for treasure खज़ाना; government department in charge of finance राजकोष।

treat[1] *ट्रीट v.t.* to deal with बरताव करना; पेश आना; to regard समझना, मानना; to give medical care to इलाज करना; (with 'of') to discourse on विवेचन करना; to entertain at one's expense की आवभगत करना।

treat[2] *n.* a special pleasure मनोरंजन, आनंद; feast दावत।

treatise *ट्री टिज़ n.* a long essay dealing with a particular subject प्रबंध, विस्तृत निबंध।

treatment *ट्रीट् मॅन्ट n.* act or manner of treating व्यवहार; manner of handling संपादन; a doctor's dealing with an illness इलाज।

treaty *ट्री टि n.* a signed contract between states संधि, समझौता।

tree *ट्री n.* a large plant पेड़; a diagram showing the descent of a family वंशवृक्ष।

trek[1] *ट्रैकॅ (-kk-) v.i.* to make a long, difficult journey on foot पैदल लंबी व कठोर यात्रा करना, पैदल चलना।

trek[2] *n.* a long, difficult journey on foot लंबी, कठोर पैदल यात्रा।

tremble *ट्रैमॅ् ब्ल v.i.* to shiver कांपना; to shake हिलना; to feel anxiety चिंतित होना।

tremendous *ट्रि मैन्ॅ डॅस a.* vast, immense विशाल; amazing आश्चर्यजनक।

tremor *ट्रै ˘ मः n.* shaking कंपन; minor earthquake भूंकप का हलका झटका।

trench[1] *ट्रैन्ॅच n.* a long, narrow ditch खाई, खंदक़।

trench[2] *v.t.* to surround with a trench के चारों ओर खाई खोदना; to cut grooves in (में) खांचा बनाना।

trend *ट्रैन्डॅ n.* direction, tendency रूख़, प्रवृत्ति।

trespass[1] *ट्रैसॅ पॅस v.i.* to intrude on property of another अनाधिकार प्रवेश करना; to encroach अतिक्रमण करना।

trespass[2] *n.* act of trespassing अतिक्रमण।

trial *ट्रॉइ अॅल n.* act of testing जांच, परीक्षण; severe affliction मुसीबत, संकट; court-hearing मुक़दमा।

triangle *ट्रॉइ ऐङ् ग्ल n.* a figure with three angles त्रिभुज।

triangular *ट्राइ ऐङ् ग्यु लॅः a.* in the shape of a triangle त्रिभुजाकार।

tribal *ट्रॉइ ब्ल a.* of a tribe or tribes जनजातीय।

tribe *ट्रॉइब n.* a primitive race जनजाति; a large family descended from one ancestor वंश।

tribulation *ट्रि ब्यु ले शॅन n.* misery, trouble, affliction मुसीबत, संकट।

tribunal *ट्रॉइ ब्यू न्ल, ट्रि- n.* a court

of justice न्यायालय; body appointed to inquire into and decide a specific matter न्यायाधिकरण।

tributary[1] *ट्रि ब्यु टॅ रि n.* stream flowing into another सहायक नदी।

tributary[2] *a.* auxiliary सहायक; contributory सहयोगी, सहकारी; paying tribute करदायी।

trick[1] *ट्रिक n.* deception धोखा; feat of skill चाल, चालाकी; illusion भ्रम; knack तरीक़ा।

trick[2] *v.t.* to cheat, to deceive धोखा देना।

trickery *ट्रि कॅ रि n.* deception धोखा।

trickle *ट्रि कल v.i.* to flow gently or in small drops टपकना; *v.t.* to cause to flow in small drops टपकाना।

trickster *ट्रिक् स्टॅः n.* a cheat, one who practises trickery कपटी, धोखेबाज़।

tricky *ट्रि कि a.* crafty चालाक; difficult, involved जटिल।

tricolour[1] *ट्रि कॅ लॅः a.* three coloured तिरंगा।

tricolour[2] *n.* tricolour flag तिरंगा झंडा।

tricycle *ट्रॉइ सि कल n.* three-wheeled cycle तिपहिया साइकिल।

trifle[1] *ट्रॉइ फ़ल n.* something insignificant नगण्य वस्तु; small amount अल्पमात्रा।

trifle[2] *v.i.* to toy खिलवाड़ करना; not to treat seriously मज़ाक में लेना।

trigger *ट्रि गॅः n.* catch or lever of a gun लिबलिबी, घोड़ा।

trim[1] *ट्रिम a.* neat, tidy साफ़-सुथरा।

trim[2] *n.* decoration सज्जा; state of being trim साफ़-सुथरापन।

trim[3] *(-mm-) v.t.* to prune छांटना; to decorate सजाना; to adjust संवारना; to put in good order सुव्यवस्थित करना।

trinity *ट्रि नि टि n.* a group of three त्रिक, त्रयी; state of being three त्रित्व।

trio *ट्री ओ n.* a set of three त्रिक, त्रयी।

trip[1] *ट्रिप (-pp-) v.t.* to cause to stumble गिरा देना; to cause to mistake ग़लती कराना; *v.i.* to skip फुदकना; to dance नाचना; to stumble ठोकर खाना; to mistake चूक जाना।

trip[2] *n.* a short journey for pleasure सैर stumble लड़खड़ाहट; nimble step फुदकन; error भूल-चूक।

tripartite *ट्राइ पाः टॉइट a.* having three parts त्रिपक्षीय, त्रिभागीय।

triple[1] *ट्रि पल a.* threefold तिगुना।

triple[2] *v.t., v.i.* to treble तिगुना करना या होना।

triplicate[1] *ट्रिप् लि किट a.* threefold तिगुना।

triplicate[2] *n.* one of a set of three copies तीन प्रतियों में से एक।

triplicate[3] *v.t.* to make threefold तिगुना करना।

triplication *ट्रिप् लि के शॅन n.* making threefold त्रिगुणन।

tripod *ट्रॉइ पौ ॅड n.* stool, stand, etc. with three legs तिपाई।

triumph[1] *ट्रॉइ अॅम्फ़ n.* victory, success विजय, सफलता; joy in a victory विजयोल्लास।

triumph[2] *v.i.* to achieve victory or success विजय या सफलता प्राप्त करना; to exult खुशी मनाना।

triumphal *ट्रॉइ अम् फ़ॅल* *a.* of victory विजय-संबंधी; for victory विजय-हेतु।

triumphant *ट्रॉइ अम् फॅन्ट* *a.* having triumphant विजयी; showing joy in victory विजयोल्लसित।

trivial *ट्रि वि ॲल* *a.* trifling नगण्य; slight हल्का।

troop[1] *ट्रुप* *n.* a group of persons or animals दल, टोली; a unit of cavalry रिसाला; *(pl.)* soldiers सैनिक।

troop[2] *v.i.* to move in a troop टोली में चलना।

trooper *ट्र पॅः* *n.* a horse-soldier घुड़सवार सैनिक।

trophy *ट्रो फि* *n.* prize, award पुरस्कार, पारितोषिक; memorial of victory विजय-स्मारक।

tropic *ट्रौ ॅ पिक* *n.* one of the two imaginary circles between the equator and the poles कर्क अथवा मकर रेखा।

tropical *ट्रौ ॅ पि कॅल* *a.* pertaining to the tropics उष्ण कटिबंधीय; very hot अति उष्ण।

trot[1] *ट्रौ ॅट* *(-tt-)* *v.i.* (of a horse) to move at medium pace दुलकी चलना; *v.t.* to cause a horse to move thus दुलकी चलाना।

trot[2] *n.* the pace between a walk and a canter दुलकी।

trouble[1] *ट्र बल* *n.* disturbance व्यवधान; worry चिंता; a difficulty कठिनाई।

trouble[2] *v.t.* to cause worry to चिंतित करना; to annoy परेशान करना; *v.i.* to take pains कष्ट उठाना।

troublesome *ट्र बल् सॅम* *a.* causing trouble कष्टप्रद, चिंताजनक, असुविधाजनक।

troupe *ट्रूप* *n.* a company of performers मंडली।

trousers *ट्रॉउ ज़ॅःस* *n. pl.* two legged outer garment covering the body from waist to ankles पतलून, पायजामा।

trowel *ट्रॉउ ॲल* *n.* flat-bladed tool for spreading mortar करनी।

truce *ट्रूस* *n.* temporary cessation of fighting युद्धविराम।

truck *ट्रक* *n.* a wheeled vehicle for moving goods ट्रक।

true *ट्रू* *a.* in accordance with facts तथ्यात्मक; faithful निष्ठावान; exact, correct सही, शुद्ध; genuine खरा, असली।

trump[1] *ट्रम्प* *n.* card of suit temporarily ranking above others तुरुप।

trump[2] *v.t.* to play a trump card on (पर) तुरुप मारना।

trumpet[1] *ट्रम् पिट* *n.* a brass wind instrument तुरही।

trumpet[2] *v.i.* to blow a trumpet तुरही बजाना; to make a noise like a trumpet तुरही जैसा शोर करना; *v.t.* to advertise loudly ज़ोर-ज़ोर से प्रचार करना।

trunk *ट्रङ्क* *n.* main stem of a tree पेड़ का तना; a person's body excluding head and limbs धड़; box for clothes बक्स, संदूक; the snout of an elephant हाथी की सूंड।

trust[1] *ट्रस्ट* *n.* confidence विश्वास; firm belief आस्था; reliance भरोसा; responsibility दायित्व; combination of producers for mutual benefit न्यास; property held for another धरोहर।

trust[2] *v.t.* to rely on (पर) भरोसा करना; to believe in का विश्वास करना; to expect, to hope आशा करना; to entrust सौंपना।

trustee *ट्रस् टि* *n.* a person who holds property in trust for another न्यासी।

trustful *ट्रस्ट् फुल* *a.* inclined to trust विश्वासी।

trustworthy *ट्रस्ट् वँः दि* *a.* reliable भरोसे का; dependable निर्भर करने योग्य; honest ईमानदार।

trusty *ट्रस् टि* *n.* faithful निष्ठावान; reliable विश्वसनीय।

truth *ट्रूथ* *n.* state of being true सच्चाई; something that is true वास्तविकता।

truthful *ट्रूथ् फुल* *a.* accustomed to speak the truth सत्यवादी; accurate, exact सही, सच।

try[1] *ट्रॉइ* *v.i.* to attempt, to endeavour प्रयत्न करना; *v.t.* to test जांचना, परखना; to strain दबाव डालना; to put on trial in a law court मुक़दमा चलाना।

try[2] *n.* effort प्रयत्न।

trying *ट्राइ इङ्ग* *a.* upsetting चिंताजनक; annoying परेशान करनेवाला; difficult दुष्कर।

tryst *ट्रिस्ट* *n.* appointment to meet पूर्व निश्चित भेंट; place appointed मिलन-स्थल।

tub *टब* *n.* open, wooden vessel like bottom half of barrel टब, नांद; small, round container गोल बरतन; bath स्नान।

tube *ट्यूब* *n.* a long, hollow cylinder नली; flexible cylinder with cap to hold paste etc. ट्यूब; underground railway भूमिगत रेल-प्रणाली।

tuberculosis *टयु बँः क्यु लो सिस* *n.* a wasting disease of the lungs क्षेय रोग, तपेदिक़।

tubular *ट्यू ब्लु लॅः* *a.* like a tube नलिकाकार।

tug *टग (-gg-)* *v.t.* to pull hard ज़ोर से खींचना; to drag घसीटना।

tuition *ट्यु इ शॅन* *n.* private teaching अनुशिक्षण।

tumble[1] *टम् ब्ल* *v.i.* to fall गिर जाना; to roll about लुढ़कना, करवटें बदलना; *v.t.* to cause to fall गिरा देना; to throw carelessly फेंक देना।

tumble[2] *n.* a fall गिराव, पतन; state of disorder अव्यवस्था।

tumbler *टम्ब् लॅः* *n.* a flat bottomed drinking glass गिलास; acrobat कलाबाज़।

tumour *ट्यू मॅः* *n.* an abnormal growth in or on the body अर्बुद।

tumult *ट्यू मल्ट* *n.* violent uproar तीव्र कोलाहल, शोर।

tumultuous *ट्यु मल् ट्यु अस* *a.* noisy कोलाहलपूर्ण।

tune[1] *ट्यून* *n.* melody धुन; correctness of pitch स्वरसंगति; harmony सामंजस्य, ताल-मेल।

tune[2] *v.t.* to put in tune समस्वरित करना; to adjust the mechanism of की ट्यूनिंग करना।

tunnel[1] *ट न्‌ल n.* underground passage सुरंग।

tunnel[2] *(-ll-) v.i.* to make a tunnel सुरंग बनाना; *v.t.* to make a tunnel through के आर-पार सुरंग बनाना।

turban *टॅ: बॅन n.* man's head dress पगड़ी, साफ़ा।

turbine *टॅ: बॉइन, -बिन n.* an engine driven by a stream of water, steam or gas टरबाइन।

turbulence *टॅ: ब्यु लॅन्स n.* disorder गड़बड़ी अशांति; violence उग्रता, उपद्रव।

turbulent *टॅ: ब्यु लॅन्ट a.* disturbed अशांत; disorderly अस्त-व्यस्त; violent उग्र।

turf *टॅ:फ n.* top layer of soil matted with grass तृणभूमि।

turkey *टॅ: कि n.* a large bird reared for food पीरू।

turmeric *टॅ: मॅ रिक n.* हल्दी।

turmoil *टॅ: मौ ˘ इल n.* confusion घबराहट; commotion खलबली; agitation हलचल।

turn[1] *टॅ:न v.i.* to revolve घूमना; to change direction मुड़ना; to change बदल जाना; *v.t.* to cause to go round घुमाना; to alter direction of मोड़ना; to convert परिवर्तित करना; to shape on lathe गढ़ना, खरादना।

turn[2] *n.* act of turning घुमाव; revolution चक्कर; a change in direction मोड़; a bend मोड़; a change of state परिवर्तन; period, spell पारी।

turner *टॅ: नॅ: n.* person who works with a lathe खरादी।

turnip *टॅ: निप n.* a plant with an edible root शलजम।

turpentine *टॅ: पॅन् टॉइन n.* an oil used in painting तारपीन।

turtle *टॅ: ट्‌ल n.* sea tortoise समुद्री कच्छप।

tusk *टस्क n.* long side tooth sticking out from the closed mouth गजदंत, खांग।

tussle[1] *ट स्‌ल n.* a struggle संघर्ष।

tussle[2] *v.i.* to struggle संघर्ष करना।

tutor *ट् यू टॅ: n.* private teacher निजी शिक्षक।

tutorial[1] *ट्यु टौ रि ॲल a.* pertaining to a tutor शिक्षकीय।

tutorial[2] *n.* a period of instruction by a tutor निजी शिक्षक के शिक्षण का समय।

twelfth[1] *टवैल्फ़्त a.* the last of twelve बारहवां।

twelfth[2] *n.* one of twelve equal parts बारहवां भाग।

twelve[1] *ट्वैल्व n.* the number next above eleven बारह की संख्या (12)।

twelve[2] *n.* one more that eleven बारह।

twentieth[1] *ट्वैन्ँ टि इथ a.* last of twenty बीसवां।

twentieth[2] *n.* one of twenty equal parts बीसवां भाग।

twenty[1] *टवैन्ँ टि a.* twice ten बीस (20)।

twenty[2] *n.* the number twice ten बीस की संख्या।

twice *टवॉइस adv.* two times दो बार।

twig *ट्विग n.* a small branch टहनी।

twilight *ट्वॉइ लॉइट n.* faint light before sunrise or after sun-set धुंधला प्रकाश।

twin[1] *ट्विन n.* one of two born together जुड़वां जोड़े में से एक।

twin[2] *a.* being a twin जुड़वां।

twinkle[1] *ट्विङ् क्ल v.i.* to shine with a wavering light झिलमिलाना; to sparkle चमकना।

twinkle[2] *n.* act of twinkling झिलमिलाहट, चमक।

twist[1] *ट्विस्ट v.t.* to wind together गूथना; to bend out of shape ऐंठ या मरोड़ देना; to wrench मुड़काना; to distort विकृत करना; to wind ऐंठना; *v.i.* to curve मुड़ना, घूमना।

twist[2] *n.* act of twisting ऐंठन; a wrench मरोड़; distortion विरूपण।

twitter[1] *ट्वि टॅः n.* chirping चहक, चहचहाहट।

twitter[2] *v.i.* to chirp चहकना।

two[1] *टूँ n.* the number next above one दो की संख्या (2)।

two[2] *a.* next above one दो।

twofold *टू फ़ोल्ड a.* double दोगुना।

type[1] *टॉइप n.* class श्रेणी; sort प्रकार pattern नमूना; block bearing a letter used for printing टाइप।

type[2] *v.t.* to print with type-writer टंकित करना।

typhoid *टॉइ फ़ौॅइड n.* acute fever affecting intestines आंत्रज्वर, मियादी बुख़ार।

typhoon *टॉइ फून n.* violent storm प्रचंड तूफ़ान।

typhus *टॉइ फ़ॅस n.* fever with dark spots on body तंद्रिक ज्वर।

typical *टि पि क्ल a.* true to type प्रारूपिक characteristic विशिष्ट।

typify *टि पि फ़ॉइ v.t.* to serve as type/model of (का) प्रारूप होना।

typist *टॉइ पिस्ट n.* one who operates type-writer टंकक।

tyranny *टि रॅ नि n.* harsh and unjust rule तानाशाही, निरंकुशता; oppression अत्याचार, नृशंसता।

tyrant *टॉइ रॅन्ट n.* a cruel, harsh ruler तानाशाह, निरंकुश शासक।

tyre *टॉइअॅः n.* rubber ring over rim of road vehicle टायर।

Uu

U यू The fifth vowei and the twenty-fisrt letter of the English alphabet. अंग्रेजी भाषा का पाँचवाँ स्वर तथा इक्कीसवाँ अक्षर, इसका उच्चारण 'अ', 'उ', 'यु' तथा 'यू' होता है

udder *अ डॅः n.* milk-secreting organ of a cow etc. अयन।

uglify *अग् लि फ़ॉइ v.t.* to make ugly कुरूप बनाना, बिगाड़ना।

ugliness *अग् लि निस n.* quality of being ugly कुरूपता।

ugly *अग्लि a.* unpleasant to look at कुरूप, भद्दा, dangerous ख़तरनाक।

ulcer *अल् सॅः n.* an infected spot on the body फोड़ा, व्रण।

ulcerous *अल् सॅ रॅस a.* of ulcer व्रणीय, having an ulcer व्रणयुक्त।

ulterior *अल् टिअॅः रि अॅः a.* concealed, hidden गुप्त; situated beyond बाह्य, remote दूरस्थ, undisclosed परोक्ष।

ultimate *अल् टि मिट a.* last अंतिम, most significant सर्वोच्च महत्व का।

ultimately *अल् टि मिट्लि adv.* finally अंततः।

ultimatum *अल् टि मे टॅम n.* final terms offered अंतिमेत्थम, अंतिम शर्त।

umbrella *अम् ब्रै ˘ लॅ n.* a covered light framework used to give protection against rain, sun, etc. छाता।

umpire[1] *अम् पॉइअॅः n.* referee निर्णायक।

umpire[2] *v.t., v.i.* to act as umpire (in) (में) निर्णायक होना।

unable *अन् ए ब्ल a.* not able असमर्थ।

unanimity *यू नॅ नि मि टि n.* state of being unanimous मतैक्य, सर्वसम्मति।

unanimous *यू नैनि मॅस a.* in complete agreement सर्वसम्मत।

unaware *अन् अॅ वें अॅः a.* not knowing, ignorant अनभिज्ञ, अनजान।

unawares *अन् अॅ वे ˘ अॅःज़ adv.* unknowingly अनजाने में; unexpectedly अकस्मात्।

unburden *अन् बॅः ड्न v.t.* to relieve of a load का बोझ उतारना।

uncanny *अन् कै नि a.* weird, mysterious अलौकिक रहस्यमय।

uncertain *अन् सॅः ट्न a.* changing constantly अपरिवर्तनशील; doubtful अनिश्चित, संदिग्ध; irresolute ढुलमुल।

uncle *अङ् क्ल n.* brother of father ताऊ, चाचा, brother of mother मामा।

uncouth *अन् कूथ a.* rough, clumsy भद्दा, boorish गंवार, vulgar असभ्य।

under[1] *अन् डॅः prep.* below के नीचे, less than से कम, subordinate to के मातहत, included in में शामिल, in the time of के समय में, known by की जानकारी में।

under[2] *adv.* in lower place or condition नीचे, नीचे की ओर।

under[3] *a.* lower नीचे वाला।

undercurrent *अन् डॅः क रॅन्ट n.* current running under the surface अंतर्धारा।

underdog *अन्डॅः डौगॅ n.* one who is ill-used दलित व्यक्ति।

undergo *अन् डॅः गो, v.t.* to experience, to pass through भुगतना, सहना, से गुज़रना।

undergraduate *अन् डॅः ग्रै ड्यु इट n.* a student who has not yet taken a degree पूर्वस्नातक।

underhand *अन् डॅः हैन्ड a.* sly, secret चालाकीपूर्ण, गुप्त।

underline *अन् डॅः लॉइन v.t.* to put line under रेखांकित करना, to emphasize पर बल देना।

undermine *अन् डॅः मॉइन v.t.* to make a tunnel under के नीचे सुरंग बनाना, to weaken gradually दुर्बल या क्षीण करना।

underneath[1] *अन् डॅ नीथ adv.* below नीचे।

underneath[2] *prep.* under के नीचे।

understand *अन् डॅः स्टैन्ड v.t.* to grasp the meaning of (का) अर्थ समझना, to take for granted मानना।

undertake *अन् डॅः टेक v.t.* to make oneself responsible for (का) दायित्व लेना; to enter upon चालू करना, to promise वचन देना।

undertone *अन् डॅः टोन n.* low tone मंद स्वर, underlying quality आंतरिक गुण।

underwear *अन् डॅः वेंॲ n.* underclothing अधोवस्त्र, अंतरीय।

underworld *अन् डॅः वॅःल्ड n.* criminals and their associates अपराधी वर्ग, निम्नवर्ग; abode of the dead अधोलोक।

undo *अन् डॅ v.t.* to ruin नष्ट करना, to unfasten, to open खोलना।

undue *अन् ड्यू a.* improper अनुचित, excessive बहुत अधिक।

undulate *अन् ड्यू लेट v.i.* to move up and down like waves लहराना, लहरदार होना।

undulation *अन्ड्ययू ले शॅन n.* act of undulating तरंगण, लहराने की क्रिया।

unearth *अन्ॲःथ v.t.* to dig up खोदकर निकालना; to discover खोजना।

uneasy *अन् ई ज़ि a.* restless बेचैन, अशांत; anxious चिंतित।

unfair *अन् फ़ॅॲः a*, unjust अनुचित, अन्यायपूर्ण।

unfold *अन् फ़ोल्ड v.t.* to open, to spread out खोलना, फैलाना; to reveal प्रकट करना।

unfortunate *अन् फ़ौः चॅ निट a.* unlucky दुर्भाग्यपूर्ण, regrettable खेदजनक।

ungainly *अन् गेन् लि a.* awkward, clumsy भद्दा।

unhappy *अन् है पि a.* sorrowful दुःखद, दुःखपूर्ण; not suitable अनुपयुक्त।

unification *यु नि फ़ि के शॅन n.* act of unifying एकीकरण; state of being unified एकीभवन।

union *यू न्यॅन n.* joining into one संयोजन, state of being joined एकता, federation संघ।

unionist *यू न्यॅ निस्ट n.* supporter of union संघवादी।

unique *यू नीक a.* having no equal अद्वितीय।

unison *यूनि ज़्न n.* the same pitch स्वरैक्य, harmony सामंजस्य।

unit *यू निट n.* single thing or person इकाई, standard quantity मात्रक; group of people or things with one purpose श्रेणी।

unite *यूनॉइट v.t.* to join into one एक करना मिलाना; to connect जोड़ना; to associate से मिलना, *v.i.* to become one एक होना, to combine जुड़ जाना, मिलना।

unity *युनिटि n.* state of being one एकता; harmony सामंजस्य, uniformity एकरूपता।

universal *यूनिवॅः सॅल a.* relating to all things or all people विश्वव्यापी।

universality *यूनिवॅः सैॅलिटि n.* quality of being universal विश्वव्योपकता।

universe *यूनि वॅःस n.* the whole of creation, sun, stars and everything that exists विश्व, ब्रह्मांड।

university *यू नि वॅः सि टि n.* an educational institution for higher studies विश्वविद्यालय।

unjust *अन् जस्ट a.* unfair अन्यायी, अन्यायपूर्ण।

unless *अन् लैसॅ conj.* if not यदि नहीं।

unlike[1] *अन् लॉइक a.* not similar

असमान।

unlike² *prep.* different from से भिन्न।

unlikely *अन् लॉइक् लि a.* improbable असंभाव्य।

unmanned *अन् मैन्ड a.* not provided with a crew कर्मीदल रहित।

unmannerly *अन् मै नँः लि a.* rude, ill-bred अशिष्ट, असभ्य।

unprincipled *अन् प्रिन् सि प्ल्ड a.* dishonest बेईमान; without any principles सिद्धांतहीन।

unreliable *अन् रि लॉइ अँ ब्ल a.* that cannot be relied upon अविश्वसनीय।

unrest *अन् रैस्ट n.* disturbed condition अशांति; restlessness बेचैनी।

unruly *अन् रु लि a.* badly behaved, disorderly उपद्रवी, उच्छृखंल; uncontrolled अनियंत्रित।

unsettle *अन् सॅ : टल v.t.* to upset, to distress अशांत करना; to disturb अस्तव्यस्त करना।

unsheathe *अन् शीद v.t.* to take out of the sheath म्यान से निकालना।

until¹ *अन् टिल prep.* upto the time of तक।

until² *conj.* to the time that जब तक कि।

untoward *अन् टो ॅ अँःड a.* inconvenient असुविधाजनक; unfortunate दुर्भाग्यपूर्ण।

unwell *ॲन् वैलॅ a.* not well अस्वस्थ।

unwittingly *अन् वि टिङ्ग् लि adv.* unknowingly अनजाने में।

up¹ *अप adv.* to a higher position ऊपर की ओर; completely पूर्ण रूप से finished समाप्त।

up² *prep.* to a higher level of के ऊपर, along के साथ-साथ।

upbraid *अप् ब्रेड v.t* to reproach फटकारना।

upheaval *अप् ही वॅल n.* a violent disturbance उथल-पुथल।

uphold *अप् होल्ड v.t* to support संभालना, to maintain कायम रखना।

upkeep *अप् कीप n* act, process or cost of keeping something in good repair अनुरक्षण, मरम्मत।

uplift¹ *अप् लिफ़्ट v.t.* to lift up ऊपर उठाना; to improve सुधारना।

uplift² *n.* lifting up उत्थान; improvement सुधार, विकास।

upon *ॲपॉ ॅन prep.* on पर, के ऊपर।

upper *अप् पॅः a.* higher, situated above ऊपरी, ऊपर वाला।

upright *अप् रॉइट a.* erect खड़ा, सीधा; honest सच्चा, ईमानदार।

uprising *अप् रॉइ ज़िङ्ग, - n.* a revolt उपद्रव।

uproar *अप् रौः n.* tumult कोलाहल; disturbance गुलगपाड़ा।

uproarious *अप् रौ रि ॲस a.* very noisy कोलाहलपूर्ण।

uproot *अप् रूट v.t.* to pull out by the roots उखाड़ना।

upset *अप् सै ॅट (-tt-) v.t.* to turn upside down उलटना, to distress परेशान या चिंतित करना।

upshot *अप् शौ ॅट n.* outcome, result परिणाम।

upstart *अप् स्टाःट n.* one who has gained power or wealth quickly कल का नवाब।

up-to-date *अप् टॅ डेट a.* of the present time सामयिक; of the newest sort आधुनिकतम, नवीनतम।

upward *अप् वॅ:ड* *a.* moving up उर्ध्वगामी।

upwards *अप् वॅ:ड्ज़* *adv.* towards a higher place ऊपर की ओर।

urban *अॅ: बॅन* *a.* concerned with a town नगरीय।

urbane *अॅ:बेन* *a.* civilized, refined सुसभ्य, शिष्ट।

urbanity *अॅ: बै नि टि* *n.* refinement सौम्यता; politeness सुसभ्यता, विनम्रता।

urchin *अॅ: चिन* *n.* a mischievous young boy नटखट लड़का।

urge[1] *अॅ:ज* *v.t* to exhort earnestly समझाना, to entreat विनती करना; to drive on प्रेरित करना।

urge[2] *n.* strong desire तीव्र इच्छा अथवा हाजत।

urgency *अॅ: जॅन् सि* *n.* quality or state of being urgent अत्यावश्यकता।

urgent *अॅ: जॅन्ट* *a.* pressing अत्यंत महत्वपूर्ण, needing attention at once अति आवश्यक।

urinal *यू अॅ रि न्ल* *n.* place for urination मूत्रालय, a vessel into which urine may be passed मूत्रपात्र।

urinary *यु अॅ रि नॅ रि* *a.* of urine मूत्रीय।

urinate *युअॅ रि नेट* *v.i.* to discharge urine लघुशंका करना।

urination *युअॅ रि नेशॅन* *n.* act of urinating मूत्र-त्याग।

urine *युअॅ रिन* *n.* the waste fluid that is passed out of the body मूत्र।

urn *अॅ:न* *n.* a metal vessel for serving tea and other liquids कलश;, a vessel for the ashes of the dead भस्म-कलश, अस्थि-कलश।

usage *यू ज़िज* *n.* act of using प्रयोग; custom प्रथा, method of using प्रयोग का ढंग।

use[1] *यूस* *n.* value उपयोगिता, ability to use प्रयोग करने की क्षमता, right to use प्रयोगाधिकार, profit लाभ।

use[2] *v.t.* to employ काम में लाना, to consume प्रयोग-द्वारा समाप्त करना, to treat (से) व्यवहार करना।

useful *यूसॅ फुल* *a.* of use उपयोगी; helpful सहायक, serviceable प्रयोज्य।

usher[1] *अ शॅ:* *n.* one showing people to seats प्रवेशक।

usher[2] *v.t.* to act as an usher to अंदर ले जाना; to introduce (का) सूत्रपात करना, to announce घोषित करना।

usual *यू जु अॅल* *a.* normal, ordinary सामान्य।

usually *यू जु अॅ लि* *adv.* as a rule नियमत; generally सामान्यतः।

usurer *यू ज़ॅ रॅ:* *n.* person whose business is usury सूदख़ोर।

usurp *यू ज़ॅ:प* *v.t.* to seize wrongfully हड़पना, हथियाना।

usurpation *यू जॅ: पेशॅन* *n.* act of usurping अनाधिकार ग्रहण।

usury *यूजॅ रि, -ज़ॅ:-* *n.* lending of money at excessive interest सूदख़ोरी, excessive interest ब्याज की ऊंची दर।

utensil *यू टैनॅ् स्ल, -सिल* *n.* vessel बरतन, implement in domestic use घरेलू उपकरण।

uterus *यू टॅ रॅस* *n. (pl. uteri)* womb गर्भाशय।

utilitarian *यू टि लि टै ॅ अॅ रि अॅन a.* useful rather than beautiful उपयोगी।

utility *यू टि लि टि n.* usefulness उपयोगिता, benefit लाभ, something useful उपयोगी वस्तु।

utilization *यू टि लॉइ ज़े शॅन n.* act of utilising उपयोग, प्रयोग।

utilize *यू टि लॉइज़ v.t.* to make use of प्रयोग करना।

utmost[1] *अट् मोस्ट a.* farthest दूरतम, greatest अधिकतम।

utmost[2] *n.* greatest possible amount अधिकतम मात्रा।

utopia *यू टो प्यॅ n .* an imaginary state where everything is perfect आदर्श राज्य।

utopian *यू टो पि अॅन a.* ideally perfect आदर्श, impracticable अव्यावहारिक।

utter[1] *अ टॅः v.t.* to make (sound) with the mouth मुंह से (ध्वनि) उत्पन्न करना; to say कहना, to put (false money etc.) into circulation (जाली मुद्रा) चलाना।

utter[2] *a.* complete, absolute पूर्ण, निरा।

utterance *अ टॅ रॅन्स n.* way of speaking बोली, something said कथन; expression अभिव्यक्ति।

utterly *अ टॅः लि adv.* completely पूर्णतया।

Vv

V वी the twenty-second letter of the English alphabet, used as a Roman numeral representing 5 or fifth, representing an object or mark having the shape of the letter (V), short from for "verb". अंग्रेजी वर्णमाला का बाईसवाँ अक्षर, रोमन संख्या में ५ अंक या पाँचवें के लिए प्रयुक्त, अक्षर (V) के आकार की वस्तु या चिन्ह को दिखलानेवाला, 'verb' का छोटा सा रूप।

vacancy *वे कॅन् सि n.* emptiness ख़ालीपन; unfilled post रिक्त पद।

vacant *वे कॅन्ट a.* unoccupied ख़ाली, रिक्त; showing lack of understanding समझ-रहित।

vacate *वॅ केट v.t.* to leave empty ख़ाली करना; to give up (a job, a house etc.) (पद, मकान आदि) त्यागना।

vacation *वॅ के शॅन n.* a holiday अवकाश; act of vacating परित्याग।

vaccinate *वैक् सि नेट v.t.* to inject with a vaccine टीका लगाना।

vaccination *वैक् सि ने शॅन n.* inocculation with a vaccine टीकाकरण।

vaccinator *वैक् सि ने टॅः n.* one who inocculates with a vaccine टीका लगाने वाला।

vaccine *वैक् सीन n.* substance used for inocculation टीका-द्रव्य।

vacillate *वै सि लेट v.i.* to waver डावांडोल होना; to hesitate हिचकिचाना।

vacuum *वै क्यु अॅम n. (pl. vacuums, vacua)* space completely empty of substance or gas शून्य, निर्वात।

vagabond[1] *वै गॅ बौन्ड n.* person with no fixed home आवारा, घुमक्कड़ व्यक्ति।

vagabond[2] *a.* roving घुमंतू

vagary *वे गॅ रि n.* whim, eccentricity सनक, मौज।

vagina *वॅ जॉइ नॅ* passage from womb to exterior योनि।

vague *वेग a.* not clear अस्पष्ट।

vagueness *वेग् निस n.* quality of being vague अस्पष्टता।

vain *वेन a.* useless व्यर्थ; foolish मूर्ख, मूर्खतापूर्ण; conceited दंभी, अहंकारी।

vainglorious *वेन् ग्लौ रि ॲस a.* boastful दंभी।

vainglory *वेन् ग्लौ रि n.* boastfulness दंभ, अहंकार।

vainly *वेन् लि adv.* fruitlessly व्यर्थ।

vale *वेल n.* valley घाटी।

valiant *वैल् यॅन्ट a.* brave दिलेर, वीरतापूर्ण।

valid *वै लिड a.* sound उचित; accpetable according to law वैध।

validate *वै लि डेट v.t.* to make valid मान्य बनाना।

validity *वॅ लि डि टि n.* soundness ठोसपना; legal force वैधता; reasonableness तर्कसंगतता।

valley *वै लि n.* river, basin घाटी।

valour *वै लॅ: an* bravery शौर्य, वीरता, साहस।

valuable *वै ल्यु ॲ ब्ल a.* of great value उपयोगी, मूल्यवान।

valuation *वै ल्यु ए शॅन n.* estimating the worth of something मूल्यांकन; estimated worth अनुमानित मूल्य।

value[1] *वै ल्यू n.* worth महत्व; utility उपयोगिता; price मूल्य; (pl.) principles सिद्धांत।

value[2] *v.t.* to estimate value of (का) मूल्य आंकना; to hold in respect सम्मान करना।

valve *वाल्व n.* वाल्व।

van *वैन n.* a covered vehicle for goods बंद गाड़ी; a railway carriage बंद माल डिब्बा।

vanish *वै निश v.i.* to disappear लुप्त हो जाना।

vanity *वै नि टि n.* excessive pride, conceit मिथ्याभिमान; worthlessness सारहीनता।

vanquish *वैङ् क्विश v.t.* to overcome पराजित करना।

vaporize *वे पॅ रॉइज़ v.t.* to convert into vapour वाष्प में बदल देना; *v.i.* to be converted into vapour वाष्प में बदल जाना।

vaporous *वे पॅ रॅस a.* like vapour वाष्प जैसा; containing vapour वाष्पमय।

vapour *वे पॅ: n.* gaseous form of a substance वाष्प।

variable *वे ॲ रि ॲ ब्ल a.* changeable परिवर्तनीय, परिवर्तनशील।

variance *वे ॲ रि ॲन्स n.* disagreement अनबन; difference of opinion मतभेद।

variation *वे ॲ रि ए शॅन n.* alteration परिवर्तन; extent of change विभिन्नता।

varied *वे ॲ रिड a.* diverse विभिन्न; modified परिवर्तित।

variety *वॅ रॉइ ॲ टि n.* diversity विविधता; sort, kind प्रकार।

various *वे ॅ ऑ रि ॲस a.* of several kinds विविध; different विभिन्न।

varnish[1] *वाः निश n.* a liquid applied to wood to make it glossy रोग़न।

varnish[2] *v.t.* to cover with varnish रोग़न करना।

vary *वे ॅ ऑ रि v.t.* to make different बदल देना; *v.i.* to become different बदल जाना।

vasectomy *वै सैक् टौ ॅ मि n.* opertion performed on men to cause sterility नसबंदी।

vaseline *वै सि लीन n.* a jelly-like petrolium-pruduct वैसलीन।

vast *वास्ट a.* immense विशाल।

vault[1] *वौल्ट n.* an arched ceiling मेहराबी छत; cellar तहख़ाना।

vault[2] *n.* a leap aided by hands हाथों की सहायता से कूद।

vault[3] *v.i.* to make a vault कूदना।

vegetable[1] *वै ॅ जि टॅ ब्ल n.* edible plant साग, शाक; part of plant used as food सब्जी, तरकारी।

vegetable[2] *a.* having to do with plants शाकसंबंधी; made from plants वनस्पति से निर्मित।

vegetarian[1] *वै ॅ जि टे ॅ ऑ रि ॲन n.* one who does not eat meat शाकाहारी।

vegetarian[2] *a.* of vegetables निरामिष।

vegetation *वै ॅ जि टे शॅन n.* plants collectively पेड़-पौधे, वनस्पति।

vehemence *वी ऑ मॅन्स n.* quality of being vehement तीव्रता; vigour उत्साह, जोश।

vehement *वी ऑ मॅन्ट a.* vigorous ओजपूर्ण; impetuous प्रचंड, उग्र; forceful प्रबल।

vehicle *वी इ क्ल n.* means of conveying वाहन, सवारी; means of expression अभिव्यक्ति का माध्यम।

vehicular *वि हि क्यु लॅः a.* related to vehicles यानीय; consisting of vehicles यानयुक्त।

veil[1] *वेल n.* light material to cover face or head ओढ़नी, दुपट्टा; mask, cover परदा, नक़ाब।

veil[2] *v.t.* to cover with a veil ढकना, छिपाना, (पर) परदा डालना।

vein *वेन n.* tube in body taking blood to heart शिरा; a rib in a leaf शिरा; a seam of mineral in rock धारी, पट्टी; mood मनोदशा।

velocity *वि लौ ॅ सि टि n.* speed गति, वेग।

velvet *वैल् विट n.* soft silky fabric with a thick short pile मख़मल।

velvety *वैल् वि टि a.* of or like velvet मख़मली; soft मुलायम।

venal *वी नॅल a.* guilty of taking or willing to take, bribes घूसख़ोर; corrupt भ्रष्ट।

venality *वी नै लि टि n.* quality of being venal घूसख़ोरी, भ्रष्टता।

vender, vendor *वैन् डॅः n.* one who sells विक्रेता।

venerable *वै ॅ नॅ रॅ ब्ल a.* worthy of reverence आदरणीय, श्रद्धेय।

venerate *वै ॅ नॅ रेट v.t.* to regard with great respect आदर करना, श्रद्धाभाव रखना।

veneration *वै ॅ नॅ रे शॅन n.* deep respect श्रद्धा, समादर।

vengeance *वैन् जॅन्स n.* revenge प्रतिशोध।

venial *वी नि अॅल a.* excusable क्षम्य; not serious, minor लघु, गौण, छोटी- मोटी (त्रुटि)।

venom *वै˘ नॅम n.* poison विष; spite, malice विद्वेष, बैर।

venomous *वै˘ नॅ मॅस a.* poisonous विषैला; spiteful द्वेषपूर्ण।

vent *वैन्ट n.* a narrow hole छेद, सूराख; outlet (for feelings) निकास।

ventilate *वैनॅ् टि लेट v.t.* to supply with fresh air हवादार बनाना; to bring into discussion प्रकाश में लाना, अभिव्यक्त करना।

ventilation *वैनॅ् टि ले शॅन n.* ventilating or being ventilated वातापूर्ति हवादारी।

ventilator *वैनॅ् टि ले टॅः n.* a device for ventilating वातायनी, हवाकश।

venture[1] *वैनॅ् चॅः n.* risky undertaking जोखिम।

venture[2] *v.t.* to risk जोखिम में डालना; *v.i.* to dare साहस करना।

venturesome *वैनॅ् चॅः सॅम a.* ready to take risks साहसिक; risky जोखिम-भरा।

venturous *वैनॅ् चॅ रॅस a.* adventurous साहसी।

venue *वै˘ न्यू n.* meeting-place सभा-स्थल; location स्थान।

veracity *वॅ रै सि टि n.* truthfulness सच्चाई, वास्तविकता।

verendah *वॅ रैन् डॅ n.* open partly enclosed porch on outside of house दालान, बरामदा।

verb *वॅःब n. (gram.)* part of speech expressing action or being *(व्या.)* क्रिया।

verbal *वॅः बॅल a.* concerning words शाब्दिक; spoken (rather than written मौखिक; relating to a verb क्रिया-संबंधी।

verbally *वॅः बॅ लि adv.* orally मौखिक रूप में।

verbatim[1] *वॅः बे टिम a.* literal शाब्दिक।

verbatim[2] *adv.* word for word शब्दशः।

verbose *वॅः बोस a.* wordy, having more words than needed शब्दबहुल, शब्दाडंबरपूर्ण।

verbosity *वॅः बौ˘ सि टि n.* quality of being verbose शब्दाडंबर, शब्दबहुलता।

verdant *वॅः डॅन्ट a.* green and fresh हरा-भरा।

verdict *वॅः डिक्ट n.* decision of a jury अभिनिर्णय; opinion मत।

verge *वॅःज n.* edge किनारा; grass-border घासदान किनारा; brink सीमा, छोर।

verification *वै˘ रि फ़ि के शॅन n.* act of verifying सत्यापन; search for proof प्रमाणन।

verify *वै˘ रि फ़ॉइ v.t.* to check the truth of सत्यापित करना; to test the accuracy of जांच करना।

verisimilitude *वै˘ रि सि मि लि ट्यूड n.* lifelikeness सत्याभास।

veritable *वै˘ रि टॅ ब्लि a.* real, genuine वास्तविक सच्चा।

vermillion[1] *वॅः मिल् यॅन n.* bright red colour गहरा लाल रंग।

vermillion[2] *a.* bright red गहरा लाल।

vernacular[1] *वॅः नै क्यु लॅः n.* language of a country or district सामान्य भाषा, जनसाधारण की भाषा।

vernacular[2] *a.* native देशी; of vernacular भाषागत।

vernal *वॅः नॅल a.* of spring वासंतिक, वसंतकालीन।

versatile *वॅः सॅ टॉइल a.* clever at many different things बहुमुखी।

versatility *वॅ सॅ टि लि टि n.* quality of being versatile बहुमुखी प्रतिभा-संपन्नता।

verse *वॅःस n.* stanza छंद; poetry काव्य; line of poetry पद्यपंक्ति।

versed *वॅःस्ट a.* skilled, expert निष्णात, प्रवीण।

versification *वॅः सि फ़ि के शॅन n.* art of versifying पद्यरचना; metre छंद।

versify *वॅः सि फ़ॉइ v.t.* to turn into verse पद्यबद्ध करना; *v.i.* to write verse पद्यरचना करना।

version *वॅः शॅन n.* account from one person's point of view कथन, बयान; translation अनुवाद।

versus *वॅः सॅस prep.* against बनाम, विरूद्ध।

vertical *वॅः टि क्ल a.* upright खड़ा, ऊपर सीधा।

verve *वॅःव n.* enthusiasm उत्साह; vigour ओज।

very *वै ॅ रि a.* identical वही; truly such यही; extreme बिल्कुल।

vessel *वै ॅ स्ल n.* a container for holding a liquid बरतन; a ship जहाज़ जलयान; duct वाहिका।

vest[1] *वैस्ट n.* undergarment for the trunk फतूही।

vest[2] *v.t.* to furnish (से) संपन्न करना; to endow प्रदान करना; to clothe (को) कपड़े पहनाना।

vestige *वैस् टिज n.* a small trace अवशेष, निशानी।

vestment *वैस्ट् मॅन्ट n.* robe worn by clergy परिधान, चोग़ा।

veteran[1] *वै ॅ टॅ रॅन n.* a person with long experience अनुभवी व्यक्ति।

veteran[2] *a.* old hand experienced अनुभवी, पुराना।

veterinary *वै ॅ टॅ रि नॅ रि a.* of, concerning, the health of animals पशुचिकित्सा-संबंधी।

veto[1] *वी टो n. (pl.-es)* power to reject or disallow something निषेधाधिकार।

veto[2] *v.t.* to enforce veto against निषिद्ध करना, (की) मनाही करना।

vex *वैक्स v.t.* to annoy तंग करना; to distress परेशान करना।

vexation *वैक् से शॅन n.* annoyance परेशानी; source of annoyance परेशानी का कारण।

via *वॉइअॅ prep.* by way of के मार्ग से, से होकर।

viable *वॉइ अॅ ब्ल a.* workable व्यवहार्य; capable of surviving and growing जीवन-क्षम।

vial *वॉइ अॅल n.* small bottle शीशी।

vibrate *वॉइ ब्रेट v.i.* to move to and fro rapidly कंपायमान होना; (of sunds) to quiver आवाज़ का कांपना; *v.t.* to cause to move to and fro rapidly कंपायमान करना; to cause to quiver कंपाना।

vibration *वॉइ ब्रे शॅन n.* act of vibrating कंपन।

vicar *वि काः n.* clergyman in charge of a parish पुरोहित।

vicarious *वि के ॅअॅ रि अॅस a.* performed, suffered, etc. in place of another प्रतिनिधि मूलक; taking the place of another स्थानापन्न; felt by imagining oneself in another's place परानुभूतिमूलक।

vice *वाइस* *n.* an immoral habit व्यसन; immoral conduct अनैतिक आचरण; sexual immorality चरित्रहीनता; a fault दोष, बुराई।

viceroy *वॉइस् रौ ॅइ* *n.* (fem. vicereine) ruler on behalf of a sovereign वाइसराय।

vice-versa *वॉइ सि वॅ: सॅ* *adv.* the other way round विलोमतः।

vicinity *वि सि नि टि* *n.* closeness समीपता; neighbourhood पड़ोस।

vicious *वि शॅस* *a.* wicked दुष्ट, धूर्त; spiteful द्वेषपूर्ण; ferocious ख़तरनाक।

vicissitude *वि सि सि ट्यूड* *n.* change of fortune भाग्य का फेर; ups and downs उतार-चढ़ाव।

victim *विक् टिम* *n.* one harmed or killed शिकार; animal or person slain as a sacrifice बलिभाजन।

victimize *विक् टि मॉइज़* *v.t.* to make a victim of को शिकार बनाना, हानि पहुंचाना; to punish unfairly अकारण दंडित करना।

victor *विक् टॅ:* *n.* conqueror, winner विजेता।

victorious *विक् टौ रि ॲस* *a.* triumphant विजयी।

victory *विक् टॅ: रि* *n.* success in a contest or battle विजय।

victuals *वि ट्ल्ज़* *n. pl.* food, provisions खाद्य, खाद्य-सामग्री।

vie *वॉइ* *v.i.* to compete होड़ लगाना, मुक़ाबला करना।

view[1] *व्यू* *n.* act of seeing अवलोकन; scene, prospect दृश्य; picture चित्र, तस्वीर; opinion मत, धारणा।

view[2] *v.t.* to look at देखना; to survey पर्यवलोकन करना; to consider विचार करना; मानना।

vigil *वि जिल* *n.* wakefulness through the night रतजगा; watchfulness रखवाली।

vigilance *वि जि लॅन्स* *n.* watchfulness निगरानी, रखवाली।

vigilant *वि जि लॅन्ट* *a.* watchful सतर्क, चौकस।

vigorous *वि गॅ रॅस* *a.* strong शक्तिशाली; energetic ओजस्वी।

vile *वॉइल* *a.* shameful, disgusting घिनावना, नीचतापूर्ण; despicable घृणित, घृणा-योग्य।

vilify *वि लि फ़ॉइ* *v.t.* to speak ill of की निंदा करना; to slander बदनाम करना।

villa *वि लॅ* *n.* large, luxurious, country house देहाती बंगला; a detached suburban house उपनगरीय भवन।

village *वि लिज* *n.* a small group of houses in country area गांव, देहात।

villager *वि लि जॅ:* *n.* village-dweller देहाती, ग्रामीण।

villain *वि लॅन* *n.* a wicked person खल, दुष्ट; chief wrong-doer (in drama or novel) खलनायक।

vindicate *विन् डि केट* *v.t.* to clear of blame दोषमुक्त करना; to justify उचित बताना; to establish the truth of सच सिद्ध करना।

vindication *विन् डि के शॅन* *n.* act of vindicating दोष-मुक्ति।

vine *वॉइन n.* climbing plant bearing grapes अंगूर की बेल।
vinegar *वि नि गँः n.* acid liquor सिरका।
vintage *विन् टिज n.* the grape harvest द्राक्षा-संचयन; wine अंगूरी शराब।
violate *वॉइ अॅ लेट v.t.* to break (law, agreement, etc.) भंग करना; उल्लंघन करना; to commit rape on (से) बलात्कार करना; to profane अपवित्रत करना।
violation *वॉइ अॅ ले शॅन n.* act of violating उल्लंघन; rape बलात्कार; desecration अपवित्रीकरण।
violence *वॅइ अॅ लॅन्स n.* state of being violent हिंसा; intensity तीव्रता, उग्रता; use of force बल-प्रयोग।
violent *वॉइ अॅ लॅन्ट a.* marked by violence हिंसात्मक; involving physical attack आक्रामक; intense तीव्र, उग्र।
violet *वॉइ अॅ लिट n.* a small plant with bluish-purple or white flowers बनफ़ंशा; purple blue colour बैंगनी रंग।
violin *वॉइ अॅ लिन n.* a four stringed musical instrument वायलिन।
violinist *वॉइ अॅ लि निस्ट n.* a violin-player वायलिन-वादक।
virgin[1] *वॅः जिन n.* a girl who has not had sexual intercourse कुंआरी, अक्षत यौवना।
virgin[2] *n.* without experience of sexual intercourse अक्षत; pure पवित्र; untilled (land) बिना जोती हुई भूमि।
virginity *वॅः जि नि टि n.* state of being virgin कौमार्य; chastity शुचिता, पवित्रता।
virile *वि रॉइल a.* (man) capable of copulation संभोग-शक्तियुक्त; strong, forceful शक्तिशाली।
virility *वि रि लि टि n.* sexual power संभोग-क्षमता; masculine strength पौरुष।
virtual *वॅः ट्यु अॅल a.* so in effect, though not in appearance or name वास्तविक।
virtue *वॅः चू, -ट्यू- n.* moral goodness नैतिकता; a specific good quality सद्‌गुण; merit योग्यता।
virtuous *वॅः ट्यु अॅस, -चु- a.* morally good नेक, सद्‌गुणी; chaste पावन, शुद्ध।
virulence *वि रु लॅन्स, -र्यु- n.* quality of being virulent विषाक्तता; harmfulness हानिप्रदता; malice द्वेषभाव।
virulent *वि रू लॅन्ट, -र्यु- a.* poisonous विषाक्त; malicious द्वेषपूर्ण।
virus *वॉइ रॅस n.* poisonous element causing infectious diseases विषाक्त तत्व।
visage *वि ज़िज n.* the human face चेहरा।
visibility *वि ज़ि बि लि टि n.* degree of clarity of atmosphere दृश्यता; distance at which something can be seen दृष्टिसीमा।
visible *वि ज़ि ब्ल a.* that can be seen दृश्यमान, दृष्टिगोचर।
vision *वि ज़ॅन n.* sight दृष्टि; imagination कल्पना; dream स्वप्न; insight अंतर्दृष्टि।
visionary[1] *वि ज़ॅ नॅ रि a.* belonging to a vision काल्पनिक, अवास्तविक; impractical अव्यावहारिक; dreamy

स्वप्निल; idealistic आदर्शवादी।

visionary[2] *n.* a dreamer स्वप्न-दृष्टा; impractical person अव्यावहारिक व्यक्ति।

visit[1] *वि ज़िट n.* act of visiting भेंट; stay ठहराव; official call दौरा।

visit[2] *v.t.* to go to see से मिलने जाना; to stay as a guest with के यहां ठहरना; *v.i.* to make a visit दौरा करना।

visitor *वि ज़ि टः n.* a guest मेहमान; a tourist पर्यटक; one who comes for a visit भेंटकर्ता।

vista *विस् टॅ n.* view दृश्य।

visual *वि ज़्यु ॲल a.* concerned with seeing दृष्टि-विषयक; visible दृश्य।

visualize *वि ज़्यु ॲ लॉइज़ v.t.* to form mental image of की सजीव कल्पना करना।

vital *वॉइ ट्ल a.* necessary for life प्राणाधार; of great importance अति आवश्यक animated सजीव।

vitality *वॉइ टै लि टि n.* liveliness, energy जीवन-शक्ति।

vitalize *वॉइ टॅ लॉइज़ v.t.* to give life to जीवन प्रदान करना; to lend vigour to शक्ति देना।

vitamin *वॉइ टॅ मिन, वि- n.* विटामिन।

vitiate *वि शि एट v.t.* to spoil बिगाड़ना; to corrupt भ्रष्ट करना।

vivacious *वि वे शॅस a.* gay आनंदपूर्ण; sprightly फुरतीला।

vivacity *वि वै सि टि n.* quality of being vivacious ज़िंदादिली; gaiety आनंदमयता।

viva-voce[1] *वॉइ वॅ वो सि adv.* by word of mouth मौखिक रूप में।

viva-voce[2] *a.* oral मौखिक।

viva-voce[3] *n.* oral examination मौखिक परीक्षा।

vivid *वि विड a.* bright चमकदार; lively सजीव; clear स्पष्ट।

vixen *विक् सॅन n.* a female fox लोमड़ी; a spiteful woman कर्कशा।

vocabulary *वॅ कै ब्यु लॅ रि, वो ॅ- n.* list of words शब्द-सूची; stock of words शब्द-भडांर।

vocal *वो कॅल a.* of voice वाणी-विषयक; spoken कथित; expressive of feelings by speaking मुखर, मुखरित।

vocalist *वो कॅ लिस्ट n.* a singer गायक।

vocation *वो ॅ के शॅन n.* profession, trade व्यवसाय; special aptitude विशेष रूझान।

vogue *वोग n.* fashion प्रचलन।

voice[1] *वौ ॅइस n.* sound that comes from the mouth आवाज़; quality of sound स्वर; expression अभिव्यक्ति; opinion मत, विचार।

voice[2] *v.t.* to express अभिव्यक्त करना।

void[1] *वौ ॅइड a.* empty रिक्त, खाली; not legally bound रद्द।

void[2] *v.t.* to make invalid रद्द करना; to empty out ख़ाली करना।

void[3] *n.* empty space शून्य, रिक्ति।

volcanic *वौलॅ् कै निक a.* of or like a volcano ज्वालामुखीय।

volcano *वौलॅ् के नो n. (pl.-es)* a mountain discharging lava, gases, ashes etc. ज्वालामुखी।

volition *वो ॅ लि शॅन n.* power of willling संकल्प-शक्ति; act of willing संकल्प।

volley[1] *वौ ॅ लि n.* simultaneous discharge of a number of missiles बौछार; rush of oaths, questions, etc. झड़ी; act of volleying उड़ती गेंद पर मार।

volley[2] *v.t* to discharge दाग़ना; (tennis) to return (ball) before it hits ground टप्पा लगने से पहले गेंद को लौटाना; *v.i.* to be dischrged दाग़ना, बौछार होना।

volt *वोल्ट n.* unit of electric potential वोल्ट।

voltage *वोल टिज n.* electric force measured in volts वोल्टता।

volume *वौ˘ ल्यूम n.* a large amount ढेर, राशि; loudness ध्वनि की तीव्रता; space occupied आयतन; bulk, mass मात्रा; book पुस्तक; part of book bound in one cover जिल्द।

voluminous *वॅ ल्यू मि नॅस a.* extensive विशाल, भारी।

voluntarily *वौ˘ लॅन् टॅ रि लि adv.* in a voluntary manner स्वेच्छा से।

voluntary *वौ˘ लॅन् टॅ रि a.* done by free will स्वैच्छिक।

volunteer[1] *वौ˘ लॅन् टिअ: n.* one who offers to do something of his own free will स्वयंसेवक।

volunteer[2] *v.t.* to give of offer voluntarily स्वेच्छा से देना; *v.i.* to offer oneself of one's own free will स्वयं को प्रस्तुत करना।

voluptuary *वॅ लप् ट्यु अॅ रि n.* one given to luxury and sexual pleasures विषयासक्त, भोगी।

voluptuous *वॅ लप् ट्यू अॅस a.* full of sexual pleasure भोगपूर्ण; giving sexual plelasure विलासप्रद; seeking sexual pleasure विलासप्रिय; sexually attractie कामोत्तेजक; showing sexual desire कामुक।

vomit[1] *वौ˘ मिट v.t.* to eject through the mouth मुंह से उलट देना; *v.i.* to eject contents of stomach through the mouth उलटी करना।

vomit[2] *n.* act of vomiting वमन-क्रिया; matter vomited उलटी, वमन।

voracious *वॅ रे शॅस a.* greedy लालची; very hungry अति भूखा; desiring much तीव्र इच्छावाला।

votary *वो टॅ रि n.* (fem. votaress) a person devoted to some pursuit, service or cause भक्त, अनुयायी।

vote[1] *वोट n.* formal expression of choice मतदान; right to express this choice मताधिकार; ballot मतपत्र; decision reached by voting चुनाव का निर्णय।

vote[2] *v.i.* to express choice by ballot मत देना; *v.t.* to grant by vote स्वीकृत करना।

voter *वो टॅ: n.* person who votes मतदाता; one who has the right to vote मताधिकारी।

vouch *वॉउच v.i.* (with 'for') to guarantee आश्वासन देना; to make oneself responsible दायित्व लेना।

voucher *वॉउ चॅ: n.* a documentary record of an expense paid व्यय की रसीद।

vouchsafe *वॉउच् सेफ़ v.t.* to condescend, to grant or do (something) देने या करने की कृपा करना।

vow[1] *वॉउ n.* pledge or solemn promise व्रत, प्रतिज्ञा।

vow[2] *v.t.* to promise solemnly, to take a vow for का व्रत लेना।

vowel *वॉउ अॅल,-इल n.* a speech sound made without contact of tongue, teeth or lips स्वर।

voyage[1] *वौ˘इ इ जॅः n.* one who undertakes a voyage समुद्र-यात्रा।

voyage[2] *v.i.* to make a voyage समुद्र-यात्रा करना।

voyager *वौ˘इ इजॅः n.* one who undertakes a voyage समुद्र-यात्री।

vulgar *वल् गॅः a.* coarse, ill-mannered भद्दा, अशिष्ट; obscene अश्लील; common सामान्य।

vulgarity *वल् गै रि टि n.* coarseness गंवारपन, अभद्रता; obscenity अश्लीलता।

vulnerable *वल् नॅ रॅ ब्ल a.* liable to be hurt or wounded छेद्य; open to attack जिस पर वार किया जा सके।

vulture *वल् चॅः n.* a large bird that feeds on carrion गिद्ध।

Ww

W डब्ल्यू the twenty third letter of the English alphabet, with the sound of a consonant when beginning a syllable and of a vowel if it does not begin a syllable. अंग्रेजी वर्णमाला का तेइसवाँ अक्षर, इसका उच्चारण किसी सिलेब्ल या मात्रा के आदि में व्यञ्जन, अन्यथा स्वर होता है।

wade *वेड v.i.* to walkthrough water or something that hinders progress पानी आदि में होकर गुज़रना; to walk with difficulty कठिनाई से चलना।

waddle *वौ˘-ड्ल v.i.* to walk with a rolling gait डगमगाकर चलना; to toddle इठलाती चाल चलना।

waft[1] *वौफ़्ट, वौफ़्ट, वाफ़्ट v.t.* to carry lightly and smoothly through air or over water हवा या पानी-द्वारा फैलाना।

waft[2] *n.* breath or puff of air महक, गमक।

wag[1] *वैग (-gg-) v.i.* to move rapidly from side to side हिलना; *v.t.* to cause to move rapidly from side to side हिलाना।

wag[2] *n.* wagging movement दोलन, हिलने की क्रिया।

wage[1] *वेज v.t.* to engage in में लगना; to carry on चालू रखना।

wage[2] *n.(usu. pl.)* payment for work done मज़दूरी।

wager[1] *वे जॅः n.* a bet शर्त।

wager[2] *v.i.* to bet शर्त लगाना, बाज़ी लगाना।

wagon *वै गॅन n.* a four-wheeled vehicle for heavy loads चौपाहिया गाड़ी; railway freight-truck मालडिब्बा।

wail[1] *वेल v.i.* to mourn, to cry out in grief or pain बिलखना, रोना, विलाप करना।

wail[2] *n.* mournful cry विलाप।

wain *वेन n.* wagon बैलगाड़ी, मालगाड़ी का डिब्बा।

waist *वेस्ट n.* part of the body between hips and ribs कमर।

waistband *वेस्ट्-बैन्ड n.* band on a

garment fitting round the waist कमरबंद।

waistcoat *वेस्ट्-कोट* *n.* a short sleeveless garment worn under the coat वास्कट।

wait[1] *वेट* *v.i.* to stay in one place प्रतीक्षा करना; to delay acting थोड़ी देर रुकना; to act as attendant सेवा-टहल करना; *v.t.* to postpone टालना।

wait[2] *n.* act of waiting प्रतीक्षा; period of waiting प्रतीक्षाकाल।

waiter *वे टॅः* *n.* attendant on guests at a hotel बैरा।

waitress *वेट्-रिस* *n.* a female waiter परिचारिका, सेविका।

waive *वेव* *v.t.* to forgo छोड़ देना; not to insist on पर ज़ोर न देना; to put aside हटा देना।

wake[1] *वेक* *v.t.* to rouse from sleep जगाना; to rouse from inactivity सचेत करना; *v.i.* to stop sleeping जगना; to rise into action सचेत होना, क्रियाशील होना।

wake[2] *n.* vigil जागरण; all night watch beside corpse शव की पूरी रात की रखवाली।

wake[3] *n.* track left behind in water by a moving ship अनुजल।

wakeful *वेक् फुल* *a.* sleepless निद्रा-रहित; on the watch सजग, चौकन्ना।

walk[1] *वौक* *v.i.* to move on foot at ordinary pace चलना; *v.t.* to cause to move on foot चलाना; to go over on foot चलकर पार करना।

walk[2] *n.* act of walking सैर, भ्रमण; gait चाल; journey on foot पदयात्रा; path मार्ग; profession पेशा, व्यवसाय।

wall[1] *वौल* *n.* solid upright erection of brick, stone, etc. दीवार; barrier रोक।

wall[2] *v.t.* to surround with a wall दीवार से घेरना; to block up with a wall दीवार से रोकना।

wallet *वौ ˘ लिट* *n.* a small folding case that fits the pocket or handbag थैली।

wallop *वौ-लॅप* *v.t.* to strike with force (पर) आघात करना; to beat soundly बुरी तरह पीटना।

wallow *वौ ˘ लो* *v.i.* to roll around (in mud) लोट-पोट करना; to revel मस्ती लूटना, गुलछर्रे उड़ाना।

walnut *वौल् नट* *n.* an edible nut with a hard shell अखरोट; the tree bearing this अखरोट का पेड़; its wood अखरोट की लकड़ी।

walrus *वौल्-रॅस* *n.* an aquatic webfooted carnivorous animal, sea horse समुद्री घोड़ा।

wan *वौनॅ* *a.* pale, looking ill पीला, विवर्ण।

wand *वौन्ड* *n.* a thin rod छड़ी।

wander *वौन्ॅ डॅः* *v.i.* to roam, to ramble घूमना; to go astray भटकना; to deviate विषय से हट जाना।

wane[1] *वेन* *v.i.* (of the moon) to decrease in size घटना, छोटा होना; to decline ह्रास होना।

wane[2] *n.* decline, decrease ह्रास, अवनति।

want[1] *वौन्ट* *v.t.* to need की आवश्यकता होना; to desire की इच्छा रखना; to lack का अभाव होना।

want[2] *n.* need आवश्यकता; deficiency अभाव; desire इच्छा।

wanton *वौन्ँ टॅन a.* dissolute लंपट; without motive उद्देश्यहीन; unrestrained संयमहीन।

war[1] *वौ: n.* fighting between nations युद्ध; state of hostility शत्रुता; conflict संघर्ष।

war[2] *(-rr-) v.i.* to make war लड़ना, युद्ध करना।

warble[1] *वौ: ब्ल v.i.* to sing with a trilling sound कूजना।

warble[2] *n.* trilling sound कूजन।

warbler *वौ: ब्लॅ: n.* bird that warbles गायक पक्षी।

ward[1] *वौ:ड n.* one who is under the care of a guardian आश्रित; a divison (of city, hospital etc.) वार्ड; guardianship संरक्षकत्व।

ward[2] *v.t.* to protect रक्षा करना।

warden *वौ: ड्न n.* a person in charge of a hostel, college etc. वार्डन, रक्षक।

warder *वौ: डॅ: n.* jailer जेलर, कारापाल।

wardrobe *वौ:ड् रोब n.* piece of furniture for hanging clothes in कपड़ों की अलमारी; a person's supply of clothes वस्त्र, कपड़े।

wardship *वौ:ड्-शिप n.* protection, custody अभिरक्षा।

ware *वे ॅ अँ: n. (pl.)* goods, articles सामान, वस्तुएं।

warehouse *v.t.* to deposit in a warehouse गोदाम में रखना; to store up जमा करना।

warfare *वौ: फे ॅअँ: n.* making war संग्राम condition of being at war युद्ध की स्थिति।

warlike *वौ: लॉइक a.* fond of war युद्धप्रिय; ready for war युद्ध के लिए तत्पर; valiant बहादुर।

warm[1] *वौ:म a.* moderately hot गुनगुना; (of clothing) serving to maintain heat गरम कपड़े; affectionate स्नेहपूर्ण; enthusiastic उत्साहपूर्ण; hearty हार्दिक; sympathetic सहानुभूतिपूर्ण।

warm[2] *v.t.* to make warm गरम करना; *v.i.* to become warm गरम होना।

warmth *वौ:म्थ n.* mild heat गरमी, गरमाहट; cordiality हार्दिकता; emotion भावुकता।

warn *वौ:न v.t.* to put on guard सचेत करना; to admonish चेतावनी देना; to give advance information to पूर्वसूचना देना।

warning *वौ: निङ्ग n.* notice of danger etc. पूर्वसूचना; admonition चेतावनी।

warrant[1] *वौ ॅ रन्ट n.* authority अधिकार; document giving authority आज्ञापत्र।

warrant[2] *v.t.* to guarantee (का) ज़िम्मा लेना; to authorize अधिकार देना।

warrantee *वौ ॅ रॅन् टी n.* person given a warranty व्यक्ति जिसे आश्वस्त किया गया हो।

warrantor *वौ : रॅन् टॅ: n.* person giving warranty आश्वासनदाता।

warranty *वौ ॅ रॅन् टि n.* authority अधिकार; assurance आश्वासन।

warren *वौ-रिन, -रॅन n.* an area of land where rabbits have their burrows खरगोशों का बाड़ा; a confused mass of streets गलियों की भूल-भुलैया।

warrior *वौ˘ रि ॲ:* *n.* fighter योद्धा।

wart *वौ:ट* *n.* small hard growth on skin मस्सा।

wary *वे˘ॲ रि* *a.* watchful, cautious सतर्क, चौकस।

wash[1] *वौशॅ* *v.t.* clean with water धोना; *v.i.* to be washable पानी में धुलने-योग्य होना।

wash[2] *n.* act of washing धुलाई; clothes washed at one time धुलाई के कपड़े; bath स्नान; thin coating पतला लेप।

washable *वौ˘ शॅ ब्ल* *a.* that can be washed without damage धुलाई-योग्य।

washer *वौ˘ शॅ:* *n.* washing machine धुलाई की मशीन; a flat ring of metal, rubber, etc. that fits under a nut वाशर।

wasp *वौ˘ स्प* *n.* a winged stinging insect भिड़, ततैया।

waspish *वौ˘स्-पिश* *a.* spiteful, virulent तुनकमिज़ाज, चिड़चिड़ा।

wassail *वौ˘-स्ल,-सेल* *n.* drinking about मद्यपानोत्सव; festive occasion, revelry रंगरेलियां, उत्सव; drinking or festive song मद्यपानगीत, उत्सवगान।

wastage *वैस् टिज* *n.* amount wasted छीजन; loss हानि।

waste[1] *वेस्ट* *a.* worthless, useless निरर्थक, व्यर्थ; barren (land) बंजर भूमि।

waste[2] *n.* act of wasting बरबादी; what is wasted नष्ट पदार्थ; desert ऊसर।

waste[3] *v.t.* to use extravagantly नष्ट करना, व्यर्थ उड़ाना; to fail to take advantage of का लाभ न उठाना; to lay desolate उजाड़ देना; *v.i.* to dwindle क्षीण होना, घटना; to pine away घुलना, दुर्बल होना, सूख जाना।

wasteful *वेस्ट् फुल* *a.* extravagant अपव्ययी; causing waste विनाशकारी।

watch[1] *वौचॅ* *v.t.* to observe closely निरीक्षण करना, अवलोकन करना; to guard रखवाली करना; *v.i.* to be on watch पहरे पर होना; to keep awake जागते रहना।

watch[2] *n.* close observation अवलोकन; wakefulness चौकसी; guard चौकीदार; spell of duty पहरा; portable time-piece for the wrist घड़ी।

watchful *वौचॅ फुल* *a.* wide awake सतर्क, चौकस।

watchword *वौचॅ वॅ:ड* *n.* a slogan or rallying cry नारा, संकेतशब्द।

water[1] *वौ टॅ:* *n.* liquid found in rivers, lakes, seas etc. पानी; body of water जलाशय; tear आंसू; urine मूत्र।

water[2] *v.t.* to put water on or into (पर या में) पानी डालना; to irrigate सींचन; to give water (to an animal) पशु को पानी पिलाना; to add water to में पानी मिलाना *v.i.* to salivate मुंह में पानी भर आना (of eyes) to fill with tears आंखों में आंसू आ जाना।

waterfall *वौ टॅ: फ़ौल* *n.* perpendicular descent of water of river जल-प्रपात।

water-melon *वौ टॅ: मै˘ लॅन* *n.* a large fruit with juicy flesh तरबूज़।

waterproof[1] *वौ टॅः प्रूफ़ a.* not letting water through जलसह।

waterproof[2] *n.* waterproof garment जलसह वस्त्र।

waterproof[3] *v.t.* to make waterproof जलसह बनाना।

watertight *वौ ˘ टॅः टॉइट a.* made in such a way that water cannot penetrate जलरोधी; flawless दोषहीन, त्रुटिरहित।

watery *वौ ˘ टॅ रि a.* like water जलवत्; of water जलीय; (of eyes) running with water अश्रुमय।

watt *वौ ˘ट n.* unit of electic power वाट।

wave[1] *वेव n.* a ridge on the surface of water लहर; a waving movement संकेत, इशारा; vibration तरंग।

wave[2] *v.t.* to move to and fro हिलाना; to signal by waving हाथ हिलाकर संकेत करना; *v.i.* to be in curves घुंघराले होना।

waver *वे वॅः v.i.* to hesitate हिचकिचाना; to be unsteady अस्थिर होना।

wax[1] *वैक्स n.* soft material made by bees मोम; substance used for sealing लाख।

wax[2] *v.t.* to put wax on मोम लगाना; *v.i.* to increase बढ़ना।

way *वे n.* path मार्ग; manner ढंग, तरीका; means साधन; direction दिशा; progress प्रगति; condition दशा।

wayfarer *वे फ़े ˘अॅ रॅः n.* traveller on foot राही, पथिक।

waylay *वे ले v.t.* to ambush की घात में बैठना; to wait for and stop की तलाश में होना व रोकना।

wayward *वे वॅःड a.* wilful हठी, जिद्दी; capricious तरंगी, मौजी।

weak *वीक a.* not strong कमज़ोर, निर्बल; lacking in ability अयोग्य, अक्षम; irresolute ढुलमुल।

weaken *वी कॅन v.t. & i.* to make or become weak कमज़ोर बनाना या बनना।

weakling *वीक् लिङ्ग n.* a feeble creature कमज़ोर प्राणी।

weakness *वीक् निस n.* state of being weak कमज़ोरी; fault or defect of character चारित्रिक दोष; fondness, special liking शोक़, चस्का।

weal *वील n.* well-being कल्याण, हित, सुख-शांति।

wealth *वैल्थ n.* riches धन-दौलत; abundance प्रचुरता, बाहुल्य।

wealthy *वैल् थि a.* having wealth धनी, धनाढ्य।

wean *वीन v.t.* to accustom (a baby or a young animal) to food other than its mother's milk मां का दूध छुड़ाना; to cause (somebody) to turn away (from bad habit) किसी से बुरी आदत छुड़ाना।

weapon *वै ˘ पॅन n.* an implement to fight with हथियार।

wear *वे ˘ अः v.t.* to have on the body पहनना; to show प्रदर्शित करना; *v.i.* to last चलना।

weary[1] *विअॅ रि a.* tired थका-मांदा; tiring थकान।

weary[2] *v.t. & i.* make or become weary थकाना या थकना।

weary[3] *a.* exhausted श्रांत, क्लांत; causing weariness थकाऊ, उबाऊ;

tasteless अरुचिकर, नीरस।

weary⁴ *v.t.* to make weary श्रांत करना, थकाना; to reduce the patience of उबा देना।

weather¹ *n.* day-to-day climatic condition of a place वैँ दः मौसम।

weather² *v.t.* to expose to open air खुली हवा में रखना; to endure झेलना, सहना।

weave *वीव* *v.t.* to interlace (threads) to make fabric बुनना; *v.i.* to work at a loom बुनाई का काम करना।

weaver *वी वँः* *n.* a person who weaves at a loom बुनकर, जुलाहा।

web *वैबॅ* *n.* woven fabric कपड़ा; net spun by spider मकड़ी का जाला; membrane between toes of ducks, bats, etc. पदजाल।

webby *वै ॅ-बि* *a.* having a web झिल्लीदार; like a web झिल्ली के समान।

wed *वै ॅड (-dd-)* *v.t.* to marry (से) विवाह करना; to unite जोड़ना, मिलाना; *v.i.* to get married शादी करना।

wedding *वै ॅ डिङ्ग* *n.* marriage ceremony विवाहोत्सव, विवाह।

wedge¹ *वैजॅ* *n.* a v-shaped piece of wood or metal फन्नी, पच्चर।

wedge² *v.t.* to fasten with a wedge में पच्चर लगाना।

wedlock *वै ॅड़ लौकॅ* *n.* marriage विवाह।

Wednesday *वैन्ज़् डे, -डि* *n.* fourth day of the week बुधवार।

weed¹ *वीड* *n.* a wild plant अपतृण; a thin sickly person or animal पतला-दुबला व्यक्ति या पशु।

weed² *v.t.* to clear of weeds निराना; (with `out') to remove (something undesirable) अनावश्यक वस्तु को निकाल फेंकना।

week *वीक* *n.* period of seven days सप्ताह।

weekly¹ *वीक् लि* *a.* happening once a week साप्ताहिक।

weekly² *adv.* once a week प्रत्येक सप्ताह।

weekly³ *n.* a periodical published once a week साप्ताहिक पत्रिका।

weep *वीप* *v.i.* (wept) to shed tears रोना; to grieve दुःखी होना, विलाप करना।

weevil *वी विल* *n.* small beetle harmful to grain etc. घुन।

weigh *वे* *v.t.* to find weight of तोलना; to consider सोचना, विचारना; *v.i.* to have weight वज़नदार होना।

weight *वेट* *n.* heaviness वज़न; piece of metal of known weight बाट; something heavy बोझा; importance महत्व।

weightage *वे-टिज* *n.* price paid for the weighing of goods तोलन-व्यय; importance बढ़त।

weighty *वे टि* *a.* of great weight भारी; important महत्वपूर्ण।

weir *विअॅः* *n.* a dam across a river (नदी का) सेतु, बांध; fence of stakes set in stream for catching fish (मछली पकड़ने की) बाड़।

weird *विअॅःड* *a.* uncanny अलौकिक; strange अनोखा।

welcome¹ *वैलॅ कॅम* *a.* received gladly सुखद; freely permitted अनुमत।

welcome² *n.* freindly greeting

अभिनंदन; reception स्वागत।

welcome[3] *v.t.* to greet with pleasure स्वागत करना।

weld[1] *वैल्ड v.t.* to unite (metal) by fusion वैल्ड करना; to unite closely जोड़ना, मिलाना; *v.i.* to be capable of being welded जुड़ने योग्य होना।

weld[2] *n.* welded joint जोड़।

welfare *वैल् फ़ै ॅअ: n.* well-being कल्याण।

well[1] *वैलॅ a.* in good health स्वस्थ; suitable उपयुक्त।

well[2] *adv.* in a satisfactory manner भली-भांति; skilfully निपुणता से; intimately घनिष्टतापूर्वक; suitably औचित्यपूर्वक; fully पूर्ण रूप से; to a considerable degree पर्याप्त रूप में।

well[3] *n.* a hole sunk into the earth for water कुआं; source स्त्रोत।

well[4] *v.i.* to flow, to spring बहना, उमड़ना।

wellignton *वैॅलिङ्ग्-टॅन n.* a kind of long boot worn by men लंबा मर्दाना जूता।

well-known *वैॅल्-नोन a.* fully known सुपरिचित; celebrated सुप्रसिद्ध; notorious कुख्यात।

well-read *वैॅल्-रैॅड a.* of wide reading, learned विद्वान।

well-timed *वैॅल्-टॉइम्ड a.* oppourtune, keeping accurate time समयानुकूल।

well-to-do *वैॅल्-टु-डु a.* prosperous, well-off संपन्न, धनी, खाता-पीता।

welt *वैॅल्ट n.* band or strip of leather चमड़े का फ़ीता; lash चाबुक; a strip of leather sewed round the upper of a boot (जूते की) पट्टी, गोट।

welter *वैॅल्-टर: n.* state of turmoil विक्षोभ; agitation, surging mass आंदोलन, हंगामा; confusion असमंजस।

wen *वैॅन n.* a sebaceous cyst अर्बुद, गिल्टी।

wench *वैॅन्श n.* a damsel, girl छोकरी, लड़की; maid-servant नौकरानी।

west[1] *वैस्ॅट n.* the direction of the setting sun पश्चिम; part of country etc. lying to this side पश्चिमी भाग; occident पाश्चात्य जगत।

west[2] *a.* of the west पश्चिमी; coming from the west पछुवां।

west[3] *adv.* towards the west पश्चिम की ओर।

westerly[1] *वैसॅ् टः लि a.* situated towards the west पश्चिमी; coming from the west पछुवां।

westerly[2] *adv.* towards the west पश्चिम की ओर।

western *वैसॅ् टःन a.* of, in the west पश्चिमी; characteristic of the west पाश्चात्य।

wet[1] *वैॅट a.* having water or other liquid on a surface गीला; soaked in liquid तर; rainy बरसाती।

wet[2] *(-tt-) v.t.* to make wet गीला क.।

wetness *वैॅट् निस n.* quality of being wet गीलापन।

whack *हैक v.t.* to strike hard (with staff) (लाठी से) प्रहार; *v.i.* to strike चोट करना।

whale *हेल, n.* a large fish-shaped sea-animal वेल, हेल।

wharfage *हौः -फ़िज n.* dues paid for using a wharf घाट-शुल्क, घाट-भाड़ा।

what[1] *हौ ॅट, वौ ॅट a.* which कौनसा, कौनसे; how much कितना ? how great, how much कितना अधिक; as much as जितना।

what[2] *pron.* which thing जो वस्तु; that which जो; which thing क्या, कौन वस्तु।

what[3] *interj.* exclamation of surprise, anger etc. क्या ! उफ़ !, अरे!

whatever *हौ ॅट् ऐ ॅ वॅः, वौ ॅट्- pron.* anthing which जो कुछ भी; no matter what कुछ भी।

wheat *हीट, वीट n.* (plant producing) grain from which flour is made गेहूं का पौधा।

wheedle *वी ड़्ल v.t.* to coax, to flatter फुसलाना, चापलूसी करना।

wheel[1] *हील, वील a.* circular frame or disc पहिया; act of turning चक्र, घुमाव।

wheel[2] *v.t.* to cause to turn घुमाना; to cause to move लुढ़काना; to cause to change course मोड़ना; *v.i.* to turn घूमना; to go on a wheel लुढ़कना; to change course मुड़ना।

whelm *है ॅल्म v.t.* to plunge deep, to submerge डुबो देना; to overpower अभिभूत करना।

whelp *है ॅल्प n.* (contemptuously) young man छोकरा; young of a lion सिंहशावक; young of a dog, puppy पिल्ला।

when[1] *हैनॅं, वेनॅं adv.* at which time कब; at the time that जब।

when[2] *conj.* at the which time that जिस समय; although यद्यपि; since क्योंकि।

whence *हैन्॑स, वैन्॑स adv.* from where जहां से, कहां से।

whenever *हैनॅ् ऐ ॅ वॅः, वैनॅ्- adv. conj.* at whatever time जब कभी।

where[1] *ह्वे ॅ ॲः, वे ॅ ॲः adv.* at what place कहां; at or to the place in which जहां।

where[2] *conj.* in or at what place जहां।

whereabout, whereabouts *हे ॅअरः-ॲ-बॉउट, -बॉउट्स adv.* about where, near what? कहां

whereas *हे ॅॲ ५-ऐज़ conj.* when in fact, but on the contrary जबकि।

whereat *हे ॅॲः-ऐट conj.* at or upon which जिस पर, जहां।

wherein *हे ॅॲ :-इन् adv.* in which place or respect किस बात में, किस दृष्टि से।

whereupon *हे ॅअरः-ॲ-पौ ॅन conj.* upon which जिसपर; at or after which जिसके बाद।

wherever *हे ॅॲः-ऐ ॅ-वरः adv.* at whatever place जहां कहीं।

whet *है ॅट, वै ॅट (-tt-) v.t.* to sharpen तेज़ करना; to stimulate उकसाना, उत्तेजित करना, प्रोत्साहित करना।

whether *है ॅ दॅः, वै ॅ- conj.* if यदि; even if भले ही।

which[1] *ह्चिव विच, pron.* कौनसा; जो।

which[2] *a.* कौनसा।

whichever, whichsoever *ह्चि्-ऐ ॅ-वरः, ह्चि्-सो-ऐ ॅ-वरः pron.* everyone which, any one, no matter which जो कोई, चाहे जो।

whiff *ह्विफ़ n.* slight inhalation सांस, फूंक, sudden puff of air (हवा का)

झोंका; puff of smell गंध, गमक।

while[1] *हॉइल, वॉइल n.* period of time समय।

while[2] *conj.* during the time that जिस समय, for as long as जब जब तक; whereas जबकि; although यद्यपि।

while[3] *v.t.* (with 'away') to spend (time) idly समय गंवाना, मस्ती में काटना।

whim *हिवम विम n.* sudden passing fancy सनक, झक, मौज।

whimper *हिम्-परः v.i.* to express grief with a whining voice रिरियाना; *v.t.* to utter; low whining tone रिरियाकर कहना।

whimsical *हिम् ज़ि कॅल, विम्- a.* quaint अनोखा; full of whims झक्की, सनकी।

whine[1] *हॉइन, वॉइन v.i.* to make a thin complaining cry क्याऊँ-क्याऊँ करना, रोना-चिल्लाना; *v.t.* to utter with a whine रोते हुए कहना।

whine[2] *n.* long drawn complaining cry चिल्लाहट।

whip[1] *हिप, विप (-pp-) v.t.* to thrash छेतना; to beat फेंटना; to strike with a whip कोड़े मारना।

whip[2] *n.* lash attached to a handle कोड़ा।

whipcord *हिप्-कौ :ड n.* cord for makng whips चाबुक की डोरी।

whir *हँः n.* sound from rapid whirling motion भिनभिनाहट।

whirl[1] *हँःल, वॅःल n.i.* to turn around rapidly घूमना; to move rapidly in a circular course चक्कर खाना; *v.t.* to cause to turn around घुमाना; to cause to move in a circular course चक्कर खिलाना।

whirl[2] *n.* whirling movement घुमाव, चक्कर; giddiness चकराहट, घबराहट।

whirligig *हँः लि गिग, वॅः- n.* spinning top लट्टू; merry-go-round चक्रदोला।

whirlpool *हँःल् पूल, वॅःल्- n.* eddy भंवर।

whirlwind *हँःल् विन्ड, वॅःल्- n.* violent current of air with a spiral motion चक्रवात, बगूला।

whisk[1] *विस्क v.t.* to brush lightly झाड़ना; to remove quickly तेज़ी से उठा ले जाना; to beat to a froth फेंटना।

whisk[2] *n.* light brush कूंचा; egg-beating implement फेंटनी।

whisker *विस् कॅः n.* the stiff hair at the side of an animal's mouth पशु की मूंछ; *(pl.)* hair allowed to grow on the sides of a man's face गलमुच्छे।

whisky *हिस् कि, विस्- n.* an alcoholic drink distilled from malted grain ह्विस्की।

whisper[1] *हिस् पॅः, विस् v.t.* to speak or say (something) softly फुसफुसा कर कहना; *v.i.* to make a murmuring sound मरमराना; to rustle सरसराना।

whisper[2] *n.* a sound made softly फुसफुस; a low rustling sound सरसराहट।

whistle[1] *हि स्ल, वि- v.i.* to produce a shrill sound सीटी बजाना; *v.t.* to summon by whistle सीटी-द्वारा बुलाना; to signal by whistling सीटी से संकेत करना।

whistle[2] *n.* a shrill sound सीटी की आवाज़; instrument to make such sound सीटी।

white[1] *ह्वॉइट, वॉइट a.* of the colour of snow सफ़ेद; pale पीला; having a light coloured skin गोरा।

white[2] *n.* colour of snow सफ़ेद रंग; clothing of thin colour सफ़ेद पोशाक; clear fluid round the yolk of an egg अंडे की सफ़ेदी; white man गोरा।

whiten *ह्वाइ ट्नॅ, वाइ- v.t.* to make सफ़ेद करना; *v.i.* to become white सफ़ेद होना।

whitewash[1] *ह्वॉइट् वौशॅ, वॉइट्- n.* substance for whitening walls etc. सफ़ेदी, क़लई।

whitewash[2] *v.t.* to coat with whitewash सफ़ेदी करना; to cover up छिपाना।

whither *ह्वि दॅः, वि- adv.* where कहां।

whitish *वॉइ टिश, ह्वॉइ- a.* almost white सफ़ेद-सा।

whittle *ह्वि-ट्ल v.t.* to cut or pare with a knife चाकू से काटना या छीलना; to reduce the amount bit by bit थोड़ा-थोड़ा करके कम करना *v.i.* to cut or pare a piece of wood लकड़ी काटना या छीलना।

whiz (z) *ह्विज़ v.i.* to make a hissing sound सनसनाना।

who हू *interr. pron.* कौन, किसने; rel. pron. जो, जिसने।

whoever हू ऐ˘ *वॅः pron.* anyone who जो कोई, जो भी।

whole[1] *होल a.* complete, entire संपूर्ण; not broken साबुत, समूचा।

whole[2] *n.* complete thing or system संपूर्ण वस्तु अथवा व्यवस्था।

whole-hearted *होल्-हॉ:-टिड a.* hearty, generous, sincere हार्दिक, एकनिष्ठ।

wholesale[1] *होल् सेल n.* selling of goods in large quantities थोक बिक्री।

wholesale[2] *a.* relating to bulk-selling थोक-संबंधी, थोक का; extensive व्यापक, विशाल।

wholesale[3] *adv.* in large quantities थोक में, बहुत अधिक।

wholesaler *होल् से लॅः n.* one who trades on wholesale basis थोक व्यापारी।

wholesome *होल् सॅम a.* producing good effect हितकारी; favourable to health स्वास्थ्यकर।

wholly *हो लि adv.* entirely पूर्णतया।

whom *हूम pron.* किसे, किसको; जिसे, जिसको।

whore *हौः, हौंः n.* a prostitute वेश्या।

whose *हूज़ pron.* किसका, जिसका।

why *हवॉइ, वॉइ adv.* for what reason क्यों; for which reason, because of which जिस लिए, जिस कारण से।

wick *विक n.* stip of thread feeding flame of lamp or candle with oil दीपक की बत्ती।

wicked *वि किड a.* evil, sinful दुष्ट, पापी; very bad धूर्त, बदमाश; mischievous नटखट, शरारती।

wicker *वि कॅः n.* flexible twigs that can be woven into baskets etc. खपची, लचीली टहनी।

wicket *वि किट n.* small gate छोटा फाटक; (cricket) set of three stumps and bails विकिट।

wide[1] *वॉइड a.* broad चौड़ा; spacious

विस्तृत; liberal उदार।

wide² *adv.* to the full extent पूर्णरूप से; far from the intended target लक्ष्य से दूर; to a great distance दूर तक।

widen *वॉइ ड्न v.t.* to make wide or wider चौड़ा करना; *v.i.* to become wide or wider चौड़ा होना।

widespread *वॉइड् स्प्रैँ ड a.* extending over a wide area व्यापक, दूर तक फैला हुआ।

widow¹ *वि डो n.* a woman whose husband is dead विधवा।

widow² *v.t.* to make a widow of विधवा बनाना।

widower *वि डो ॲ: n.* man whose wife is dead विधुर।

width *विड्थ n.* breadth चौड़ाई।

wield *वील्ड v.t.* to hold and use प्रयोग में लाना; to brandish घुमाना, चलाना; to manage संभालना, नियंत्रित करना।

wife *वॉइफ़ n. (pl. wives)* a man's partner in marriage पत्नी।

wig *विग n.* artificial hair for the head बालों की टोपी, विग।

wight *वॉइट n.* a human being प्राणी।

wigwam *विग्-वैम n.* a hut कुटिया।

wild *वॉइल्ड a.* not tamed जंगली; uncivilized असभ्य; excited उत्तेजित।

wilderness *विल् डॅ: निस n.* desert, waste place बीहड़; state of desolation उजाड़।

wile *वॉइल n.* trick चाल, छल-कपट।

will¹ *विल n.* mental faculty of making decision संकल्पशक्ति; purpose उद्देश्य; volition संकल्प-व्यापार; determination संकल्प; wish इच्छा; legal document for disposal of property after death वसीयत-नामा।

will² *v.t.* to have a wish इच्छा रखना; *v.t.* to wish चाहना।

willing *वि लिङ्ग a.* ready तत्पर; given or done freely स्वैच्छिक।

willingness *वि लिङ्ग् निस n.* readiness तत्परता।

willow *वि लो n.* a tree with long thin, flexible branches भिंसा; its wood इसकी लकड़ी।

wily *वॉइ-लि a.* full of craft and cunning धूर्त, चालाक।

wimble *विम्-ब्ल n.* an instrument for boring holes बरमा, बरमी।

wimple *विम्-प्ल n.* a head dress worn by nuns शिरोवस्त्र।

win¹ *विन (-nn-) v.t.* to get by labour or effort प्राप्त करना; to reach पहुंचना; to allure लुभाना, ललचाना; to be successful in में सफल होना; *v.i.* to be victorious विजयी होना; to be successful सफल होना।

win² *n.* victory विजय।

wince *विन्स v.i.* to shrink सिकुड़ जाना; to hesitate झिझकना; to be startled चौंक जाना।

winch *विन्च n.* reel पेचक; roller चर्ख़ी; crank of wheel, axil पहिये की धुरी।

wind¹ *विन्ड n.* air in motion समीर; breath सांस; gas formed in the stomach अफारा।

wind² *v.t.* to cause to be breathless का सांस फुलाना; to get the scent of की गंध पा लेना।

wind³ *वॉइन्ड v.t.* to twist लपेटना; to make into a ball or coil का गोला

या लच्छी बनाना; to move in a spiral manner घुमाना; to tighten the spring of (a watch) घड़ी में चाबी या कूक देना।

windbag *विन्ड्-बैग* *n.* person who talks a lot but says nothing important बातूनी, गप्पी व्यक्ति।

winder *वॉइन्-डर:* *n.* one who winds मोड़नेवाला; instrument for winding चाबी भरने का यंत्र; clock or watch key घड़ी की चाबी।

windlass *विन्ड्-लॅस* *v.t.* a hand winch for pulling and lifting बेलन-चरखा।

windmill *विन्ड्-मिल* *n.* a mill driven by the wind पवनचक्की।

window *विन् डो* *n.* an opening in a wall to admit light, air etc. खिड़की।

windy *विन् डि* *a.* with much wind तूफ़ानी।

wine *वॉइन* *n.* fermented juice of grape etc. अंगूरी शराब।

wing *विङ्ग* *n.* either of the two organs of a bird by which it flies पंख; the surface supporting an aircraft in the air वायुयान का पंख।

wink[1] *विङ्क* *v.i.* to move the eyelid पलक झपकना; to give a hint, to convey amused understanding आंख से इशारा करना; to blink टिमटिमाना; to connive अनदेखी करना; *v.t.* to make (the eyes) wink (आंखो को) जल्दी-जल्दी झपकाना।

wink[2] *n.* act of winking झपक; a hint given by means of the eye आंख का इशारा; an instant पलभर।

winner *वि नॅं:* *n.* one who wins विजेता।

winnow *वि नो* *v.t.* to separate (grain) from chaf by means of a stream of air ओसाना, बरसाना।

winsome *विन् सॅम* *a.* charming आकर्षक।

winter[1] *विन् टॅं:* *n.* the coldest season शीत ऋतु।

winter[2] *v.i.* to pass the winter जाड़ा बिताना।

wintry *विन् ट्रि* *a.* cold, chilly शीतल, ठंडा; of winter शीतकालीन; lacking warmth भावशून्य।

wipe[1] *वॉइप* *v.t.* to rub so as to clean पोंछना।

wipe[2] *n.* act of wiping पोंछन।

wire[1] *वॉइअॅ:* *n.* metal drawn into thin strand तार; telegram तार।

wire[2] *v.t.* to fasten with wire तार से बांधना; to provide with wire तार लगाना; to send by telegraph तार द्वारा भेजना।

wireless[1] *वॉइअॅ लिस* *a.* without the use of wires बेतार का।

wireless[2] *n.* radio, radio set रेडियो।

wiring *वॉइअॅ रिङ्ग* *n.* system of wires for electric current बिजली के तार।

wisdom *विज़् डॅम* *n.* quality of being wise समझदारी, बुद्धिमानी।

wisdom-tooth *विज़्-डॅम-टूथ* *n.* a back tooth अक्ल दाढ़।

wise *वॉइज़* *a.* sensible, having intelligence and knowledge समझदार, बुद्धिमान।

wish[1] *विश* *n.* desire इच्छा; thing desired इच्छित वस्तु।

wish[2] *v.t.* to desire चाहना; *v.i.* to

have a desire इच्छुक होना।

wishful *विश् फुल a.* desirous आकांक्षी, इच्छुक।

wisp *विस्प n.* small bundle of straw or hay घास का गट्ठर; small broom पतली झाड़ू; tuft or shred गुच्छा; thin strand or fibre तंतु।

wistful *विस्ट् फुल a.* longing, yearning उत्कंठित; sadly pensive उदासीपूर्ण।

wit *विट n.* alertness of mind बुद्धि की प्रखरता; clever and humorous expression of ideas वाग्विदग्धता; person gifted with quickness of mind हाज़िर-जवाब व्यक्ति।

witch *विच n.* a woman having evil supernatural powers जादूगरनी; a hag डाइन; an alluring girl or woman मोहिनी।

witchcraft *विच् क्राफ़्ट n.* sorcery, use of magic जादू-टोना।

witchery *वि चॅ रि n.* witchcraft जादू-टोना; fascination, charm आकर्षण।

with *विद prep.* in the company of के साथ; as a means of के द्वारा; in the care of की देखरेख में; against विरूद्ध।

withal *वि-दौल adv.* besides के अतिरिक्त; with all or the rest सब के साथ।

withdraw *विद् ड्रौ v.t.* to draw back खींच लेना, पीछे हटाना; to take back वापस लेना to take out निकालना; *v.i.* to move back पीछे हटना, वापस जाना।

withdrawal *विद् ड्रौ ॲल n.* taking out निकासी; moving back वापसी; taking back वापसी।

withe *विद, विथ n.* a flexible twig लचीली टहनी।

wither *वि दॅः v.i.* to fade मुरझाना; *v.t.* to cause to fade मुरझा देना।

withhold *विद् होल्ड v.t.* to keep back रोक रखना; to refrain from giving देने से इनकार करना।

within[1] *विद् इन prep.* inside of, not beyond के अंदर, से अधिक नहीं।

within[2] *adv.* indoors घर में; inside अंदर।

within[3] *n.* inner side, inner part भीतरी भाग।

without[1] *विद् ऑउट prep.* not with, lacking से रहित, के बिना।

without[2] *adv.* outside बाहर की ओर।

without[3] *n.* outer side or part बाह्य भाग।

withstand *विद् स्टैन्ड v.t.* to resist, to oppose का विरोध करना to hold out against का सामना करना।

witless *विट्-लिस a.* destitute of wit बुद्धिहीन; silly मूर्ख; thoughtless विचारहीन; indiscreet विवेकहीन।

witness[1] *विट् निस n.* one who sees something प्रत्यक्ष-दर्शक; testimony गवाही; one who gives testimony गवाह; one attesting signature प्रमाण कर्त्ता।

witness[2] *v.i.* to give testimony गवाही देना; *v.t.* to see देखना; to attest प्रमाणित करना।

witticism *वि टि सिज़्म n.* witty remark चुटीला कथन।

witty *वि टि a.* clever and amusing (person) वाग्विदग्ध, हाज़िरजवाब; characterized by wit चुटीला, मज़ेदार।

wizard *वि ज़ॅःड n.* a magician

जादूगर।

wobble *वौ ˘ ब्ल v.i* to rock हिलना, लड़खड़ाना; to be uncertain अस्थिर होना; *v.t.* to cause to rock हिलाना, लड़खड़ा देना।

woe *वो n.* grief, sorrow शोक, विषाद।

woebegone *वो-बि-गौ ˘न a.* dismal, sad, उदास; beset with woe विषादमय।

woeful *वो फुल n.* sorrowful शोकपूर्ण; miserable दुःखी।

wolf *वुल्फ़ n.* a wild predatory dog-like animal भेड़िया।

woman *वु मॅन n.* adult human female नारी, स्त्री; the female sex स्त्री-जाति।

womanhood *वु मॅन् हुड n.* state of being woman नारीत्व।

womanish *वु मॅ निश n.* effeminate ज़नाना, स्त्रैण।

womanize, ise *वु-मॅ-नॉइज़ v.t.* to make effeminate स्त्रैण बनाना; *v.i.* to consort with women, esp. prostites व्यभिचार करना, वेश्यागमन करना।

womb *वूम n.* female organ of conception गर्भाशय।

wonder[1] *वन् डॅः n* astonishment आश्चर्य; a marvel अजूबा; a miracle चमत्कार।

wonder[2] *v.i.* to marvel आश्चर्य करना; *v.t.* to be doubtful about के विषय में अनिश्चित होना।

wonderful *वन् डॅः फुल a.* causing wonder आश्चर्यजनक; remarkable very fine अत्युत्तम।

wondrous *वॅन्-ड्रॅस a.* wonderful आश्चर्यजनक, अद्भुत; excellent अत्युत्कृष्ट।

wont[1] *वौन्ट a.* accustomed आदी।

wont[2] *n.* custom habit रिवाज, आदत।

wonted *वौ ˘न्-टिड़ a.* accustomed अभ्यस्त; usual सामान्य।

woo *वू v.t.* to court, to seek the love of (से) प्रणय-निवेदन करना; to coax फुसलाना।

wood *वुड n.* timber लकड़ी; fire-wood ईंधन; *(pl.)* a tract of land with growing trees जंगल।

wooden *वु डॅन a.* made of wood लकड़ी का।

woodland *वुड़-लॅन्ड n.* land covered with wood वनस्थली, वन।

woof *वूफ़ n.* the threads that cross the warp in weaving बाना।

wool *वुल n.* soft hair of sheep, goat etc. ऊन; yarn made from this ऊनी धागा।

woollen[1] *बु लॅन a.* made of wool ऊनी।

woollen[2] *n* fabric made of wool ऊनी कपड़ा; *(pl.)* clothes made of wool ऊनी वस्त्र।

word[1] *वॅःड n.* a meaningful unit of speech शब्द; message संदेश; brief remark टिप्पणी, कथन; a promise वचन, वादा; information सूचना; command आदेश।

word[2] *v.t.* to express in words शब्दों में व्यक्त करना।

wordy *वॅः डि a.* verbose शब्दाडंबरपूर्ण।

work[1] *वॅःक n.* labour श्रम; employment व्यदसाय; activity कार्य; task नियत कार्य; thing done कृत्य; production of art कृति; *(pl.)* factory कारख़ाना।

work² *v.t.* to cause to operate चालू करना, चलाना; to make, to shape बनाना, ढालना; *v.i.* to labour श्रम करना; to operate चलना; to engage in some activity काम करना; to be occupied in business धंधे में लगना।

workable *वॅ: कॅ ब्‌ल a.* that can be made to work व्यवहार्य।

workaday *वॅ: कॅ डे a.* plain, ordinary सादा, सामान्य।

worker *वॅ: कॅ: n.* a wage-earner मज़दूर।

workman *वॅ:क् मॅन n.* manual worker मज़दूर।

workmanship *वॅ:क् मॅन् शिप n.* skill of a workman शिल्प, कारीगरी।

workshop *वॅ:क् शौपॅ n.* place where things are made कारख़ाना।

world *वॅ:ल्ड n.* the universe विश्व; the planet earth भूलोक; mankind मानव-जाति; human society मानव-समाज, जगत्, दुनिया; society समाज; an area of interest रुचि-क्षेत्र।

worldling *वॅ:ल्ड्-लिङ्ग n.* one devoted exclusively to worldly pleasures सांसारिक आनंद में लिप्त व्यक्ति।

worldly *वॅ:ल्ड् लि a.* earthly पार्थिव; mundane सांसारिक; materialistic भौतिक।

worm *वॅ:म n.* small limbless creeping creature कीड़ा, कृमि; a weak spineless person कमीना आदमी; the spiral part of a screw पेंच की चूड़ी।

wormwood *वॅ:म् वुड n.* a bitter herb नागदौन; bitterness कटुता।

worn *वौ:न a.* that has been worn, showing effects of wear घिसा हुआ, फटा हुआ; exhausted वृद्ध, थका-मांदा; hackneyed घिसा-पिटा।

worry¹ *व रि n.* anxiety चिंता; a cause of anxiety चिंता का कारण।

worry² *v.i.* to be concerned चिंतित होना; *v.t.* to trouble परेशान करना।

worsen *वॅ: सॅन v.t.* to make worse बिगाड़ना; *v.i.* to become worse बिगड़ना।

worship¹ *वॅ: शिप n.* act of worshipping पूजा, उपासना; admiration प्रशंसा; a title of respect श्रीमन्।

worship² *(-pp-) v.t.* to adore पूजा करना; to love and admire के प्रति प्रेम व प्रशंसा का भाव रखना।

worshipper *वॅ: शि पॅ: n.* adorer, devotee पुजारी, उपासक।

worst¹ *वॅ:स्ट n.* the highest degree of badness, most evil state or effect सबसे बुरी बात।

worst² *a.* bad or evil in the highest degree सब से बुरा।

worst³ *v.t.* to defeat पराजित करना।

worsted *वु: स्टिड n.* woollen yarn ऊनी धागा; cloth made from this yarn ऊनी कपड़ा।

worth¹ *वॅ:थ n.* value, merit गुण; virtue गुणवत्ता; usefulness उपयोगिता; excellence उत्कृष्टता।

worth² *a.* having a certain value निश्चित मूल्य का; deserving of के लायक; possessing का स्वामी।

worthless *वॅ:थ् लिस a.* of no use व्यर्थ, निरर्थक।

worthy *वॅ: दि a.* deserving (of) के योग्य; deserving respect सम्मान्य।

would-be *वुड्-बी a.* wishing to be

इच्छुक; intended to be होने वाला।

wound[1] वुन्ड *n.* injury, hurt from cut, stab etc. घाव, ज़ख्म; a hurt to feelings ठेस।

wound[2] *v.t.* to hurt, to injure घायल करना; to pain ठेस पहुंचाना।

wrack रैक *n.* sea weed cast ashore (किनारे पर पड़ा हुआ) समुद्री शैवाल।

wraith रेथ *n.* apparition of a person about to die or newly dead प्रेत, प्रेतात्मा।

wrangle[1] रैङ् ग्ल *v.i.* to quarrel noisily लड़ना झगड़ना; to dispute बहस करना।

wrangle[2] *n.* noisy quarrel लड़ाई-झगड़ा dispute बहस, वाद-विवाद।

wrap[1] रैप *(-pp-)* *v.t.* to cover by putting something round लपेटना; to conceal छिपाना।

wrap[2] *n.* a loose garment आवरण; a shawl शाल, चादर।

wrapper रैँ पः *n.* a loose cover for a book आवरण; a strip of paper wrapped round a periodical of sending by post कागज़ की लपेटन।

wrath रौथ, रौथॅ *n.* anger क्रोध।

wreath रीथ *n.* a circle of interwoven flowers माला।

wreathe रीद *v.t.* to form into a wreath गूथना; to surround घेरना; to wind round लपेटना।

wreck[1] रैकॅ *n.* distruction of ship पोतभंग; wrecked ship पोतावशेष; ruin भग्नावशेष, विनाश।

wreck[2] *v.t.* to cause to wreck of भग्न करना, नष्ट करना।

wreckage रैॅ किज *n.* the remains of something wrecked पोतावशेष, भग्नावशेष।

wrecker रैॅ-कॅः *n.* person who causes a wreck ध्वंसकर्त्ता; one who criminally ruins anything तोड़-फोड़ करनेवाला।

wren रैनॅ *n.* a small song bird पिटपिटी, फुदकी।

wrench[1] रैन्च *n.* a violent twist मरोड़; sprain मोच; spanner रिन्च; grief of parting बिछुड़ने की पीड़ा।

wrench[2] *v.t.* to twist violently मरोड़ना, ऐंठना; to distort तोड़-मरोड़ देना; to sprain मोच देना।

wrest रैस्ट *v.t.* to take by force छीनना; to twist मरोड़ना।

wrestle रैॅ स्ल *v.i.* to struggle with an opponent so as to throw him to the ground कुश्ती लड़ना; to strive संघर्ष करना।

wrestler रैसॅ लॅः *n.* one who wrestles कुश्ती लड़ने वाला, पहलवान।

wretch रैचॅ *n.* a poor, miserable person अभागा व्यक्ति।

wretched रैॅ चिड *a.* miserable, unhappy दुःखी, अभागा।

wrick रिक *n.* sprain (हलकी) मोच, मरोड़।

wriggle[1] रि ग्ल *v.i.* to move with twisting action रेंगना; to squim कुलबुलाना।

wriggle[2] *n.* twisting movement रेंगने की क्रिया; squim कुलबुलाहट।

wring रिङ्ग *v.t.* to twist ऐंठना; to squeeze out निचोड़ना; to extort ऐंठ लेना।

wrinkle[1] रिङ् क्ल *n.* crease in the skin झुर्री; fold सिलवट; pucker शिकन।

wrinkle[2] *v.t.* to cause wrinkles in

में सिलवट डालना, झुर्री पैदा करना; *v.i.* to become wrinkled झुर्री या शिकन पड़ना।

wrist *रिस्ट n.* joint by which the hand is united to the arm कलाई, मणिबंध।

writ *रिट n.* a written command from law court हुक्मनामा।

write *रॉइट v.t.* to set down in words लिखना to compose की रचना करना; to communicate in writing लिखकर भेजना; *v.i.* to form words on paper लिखना; to be an author लेखन-कार्य करना; to send a letter पत्र भेजना।

writer *रॉइ टॅ: n.* one who writes लिखनेवाला; an author लेखक।

writhe *रॉइद v.i.* to twist the body in pain छटपटाना, तड़पना।

wrong[1] *रौँ ग a.* incorrect ग़लत, अशुद्ध; not suitable अनुपयुक्त; unjust अन्यायपूर्ण; illegal अवैध; not moral अनैतिक; sinful पापपूर्ण।

wrong[2] *adv.* in the wrong way ग़लत ढंग से।

wrong[3] *v.t.* to do wrong to से अन्याय करना।

wrongful *रौ ङ्ग् फुल a.* unjust अन्यायपूर्ण; unlawful अवैध।

wry *रॉइ a.* twisted, contorted टेढ़ा, तोड़ा-मरोड़ा; sardonic व्यंग्यपूर्ण।

Xx

X एक्स the twenty-fourth letter of the English alphabet pronounced like 'z' at the beginning of a word and ks. elsewhere; as a Roman numeral it stands for 10, the first unkonwn quantity (x) in algebra. अंग्रेजी वर्णमाला का चौबीसवाँ अक्षर, शब्द के आदि में इस अक्षर का उच्चारण "ज्" तथा अन्य स्थान में "क्स्" होता है, रोमन संख्या में यह १० के लिए प्रयुक्त होता है, बीजगणित में (x) पहिली अज्ञात संख्या के लिये यह प्रयुक्त होता है।

xerox[1] *ज़ी रौक्स n.* a photocopy छायाप्रति।

xerox[2] *v.t.* to photocpoy (की) छायाप्रति बनाना।

Xmas *क्रिस् मॅस n.* Christmas बड़ा दिन।

x-ray[1] *ऐंक्स रे n.* एक्स किरण।

x-ray[2] *a.* pertaining to x-ray एक्स-किरणीय।

x-ray[3] *v.t.* to photograph by x-rays एक्सकिरण फ़ोटो लेना।

xylophagous *ज़ाइ लौँ फ़ॅ गॅस a.* wood-eating काष्ठ-भक्षी।

xylophilous *ज़ाइ लॉ फ़ि लॅस a.* fond of eating wood काश्ठ-प्रेमी।

xylophone *ज़ॉइ लॅ फ़ोन n.* a musical instrument of wooden bars which sound when struck काष्ठ-तरंग।

Yy

Y वाई the twenty-fifth letter of the English alphabet, a Roman numeral for 150, the letter is a vowel after a consonant and a consonant after a vowel. अंग्रेजी वर्णमाला का पचीसवाँ अक्षर, रोमन् संख्या में १५० के लिये प्रयुक्त होता है, व्यन्जन के बाद इसका उच्चारण स्वर का तथा स्वर के बाद इसका उच्चारण व्यन्जन का होता है।

yacht[1] *यॉट n.* a light sailing boat हलकी नौका।

yacht[2] *v.i.* to travel in a yacht नौका-विहार करना।

yak *यैक n.* long-haired ox of Central Asia सुरागाय, चमर।

yap[1] *यैप (-pp-) v.i.* (of small dogs, etc.) to utter sharp short barks भौं-भौं करना; to talk idly बकसाव करना।

yap[2] *n.* a shrill bark भौं-भौं।

yard *या:ड n.* a unit of length (36 inches) गज़; enclosed area अहाता।

yarn *या:न n.* spun thread सूत, तागा; a tale कहानी, क़िस्सा।

yawn[1] *यौन v.i.* to open the mouth wide in sleepiness जम्हाई लेना; to be wide open चौड़ा होना।

yawn[2] *n.* act of yawning जम्हाई।

Year *यिअॅ:, यॅ: n.* twelve months वर्ष।

yearly[1] *यिअॅ: लि, यॅ:- a.* taking place every year वार्षिक।

yearly[2] *adv.* every year, once a year प्रतिवर्ष।

yearn *यॅ:न v.i.* to feel longing लालायित होना।

yearning *यॅ: निङ्ग n.* longing, desire लालसा, इच्छा।

yeast *यीस्ट n.* substance used as fermenting agent ख़मीर।

yell[1] *यैलॅ v.i.* to cry out in loud shrill tone चिल्लाना; *v.t.* to say in loud shrill tone चिल्लाकर कहना।

yell[2] *n.* a loud shrill cry चिल्लाहट, पुकार।

yellow[1] *यैं लो a.* of the colour of lemons पीला।

yellow[2] *n.* the colour of lemons पीला रंग।

yellow[3] *v.t.* to cause to become yellow पीला करना; *v.i.* to become yellow पीला होना।

yellowish *यैं लो इश a.* rather yellow पीला-सा, कुछ-कुछ पीला।

Yen *यैंन n.* Japanese monetary unit यैन, जापानी मुद्रा।

yeoman *यो मॅन n.* a small farmer छोटा ज़मींदार।

yes *यैसॅ adv.* of agreement or consent हाँ, सचमुच।

yesterday[1] *यैसॅ टॅ: डे, -डि n.* the day just pasted बीता हुआ दिन।

yesterday[2] *adv.* on the day just pasted कल; recently हाल में।

yet[1] *यैंट adv.* upto the present time अब तक; in addition इसके अतिरिक्त; still अभी तक।

yet[2] *conj.* nevertheless तथापि।

yield[1] *यील्ड v.t.* to produce पैदा करना; to provide प्रदान करना; to give up, to surrender समर्पित करना, त्याग देना; *v.i.* to submit आत्मसमर्पण करना; to surrender हार मानना।

yield[2] *n.* amount produced उपज, पैदावार; profit लाभ; result परिणाम।

yoke[1] *योक n.* a wooden bar put across the necks of oxen pulling a cart etc. कड़ी, जुआ; bond or tie बंधन, संबंध; a mark of servitude दासता; a pair of oxen बैलों की जोड़ी; part of a garment that fits the shoulders वस्त्र का कंधोंवाला भाग।

yoke[2] *v.t.* to put a yoke on (पर) जुआ रखना, जीतना; to join together जोड़ना, युग्मित करना।

yolk *योक n.* the yellow part of an egg अंडे की ज़रदी।

younder[1] *यौन् डॅः a.* that can be seen over there वहाँ का, वह वाला।

younder[2] *adv.* over there, in that direction वहाँ, उस ओर।

young[1] *यङ्ग a.* not old छोटा; immature अपरिपक्व, अनाड़ी; at an early stage of growth नवोदित।

young[2] *n.* offspring संतान, बच्चे।

youngster *यङ्ग्स्टॅः n.* a young person not yet mature enough छोकरा, लौंडा।

youth *यूथ n.* state or time of being young यौवन, तरुणाई; young man जवान युवक; young people नौजवान लोग।

youthful *यूथ् फुल a.* young युवा, तरुण।

Zz

Z जेड् the twenty-six and the last letter of the English alphabet, it has the sound of s, z, or sh अंग्रेजी वर्णमाला का छब्बीसवाँ तथा अन्तिम अक्षर, इसका उच्चारण स, ज्, तथा श होता है।

Zany *ज़े नि a.* funny in an unusual way बेहूदा, हास्यपूर्ण

zeal *ज़ील n.* great enthusiasm जोश, उत्साह।

zealot *ज़ैं लॅट n.* enthusiast उन्मादी; fanatic supporter कट्टर समर्थक।

zealous *ज़ैं लॅस a.* full of zeal, ardent जोशपूर्ण, उत्साही।

zebra *ज़ी ब्रॅ n.* striped African animal like a horse ज़ेबरा।

zenith *ज़ैं निथ n.* point of the sky exactly overhead शिरोबिंदु; the highest point चरम बिंदु, पराकाष्ठा।

zephyr *ज़ैं फ़ॅः n.* west wind पछुवाँ हवा; gentle breeze मंद समीर।

zero *ज़िअॅ रो n.* the figure 0, शून्य; nothing कुछ नहीं; freezing point हिमांक।

zest *ज़ैस्ट n.* enjoyment मज़ा, आनंद; enthusiasm उत्साह, जोश।

zigzag[1] *ज़िग् ज़ैग n.* line or course with sharp turns in alternate directions टेढ़ी-मेढ़ी रेखा।

zigzag[2] *a.* formed in a zigzag टेढ़ा-मेढ़ा।

zigzag[3] *(gg) v.i.* to go in a zigzag टेढ़ा-मेढ़ा जाना।

zinc *ज़िङ्क* *n.* a bluish-white metal जस्ता।

zip[1] *ज़िप* *n.* a whizzing sound सनसनाहट; a kind of fastener ज़िप।

zip[2] *(pp) v.t.* to open or close by means of a zip ज़िप से बंद करना या खोलना।

zodiac *ज़ो डि ऐक n* राशिचक्र।

zonal *ज़ो नॅल* *a.* of or pertaining to a zone मंडलीय।

zone *ज़ोन* *n.* one of the five climatic belts into which the earth is divided कटिबंध; any belt-like area क्षेत्र, मंडल।

zoo जू *n.* place where live animals are kept for exhibition चिड़ियाघर, जंतुशाला।

zoological *ज़ॉ अॅ लॉ जि कॅल, जु* *a.* of zoology प्राणि-विज्ञान विषयक।

zoologist *ज़ॉ ऑ लॅ जिस्ट, जु-* *n.* an expert in zoology प्राणि-विज्ञानी।

zoology *ज़ॉ ऑ लॅ जि, जु-* *n.* scientific study of animals प्राणि-विज्ञान।

zoom[1] *ज़ूम* *n.* sudden upward flight of an aircraft वायुयान की तेज़ ऊर्ध्व उड़ान; the humming sound made by such a flight ऐसी उड़ान की गूँज।

zoom[2] *v.i.* (of an aircraft) to rise steeply (वायुयान का) तेज़ी से ऊपर उठना; to move with a fast roaring noise शोर करते हुए तेज़ी से गुज़रना; to soar ऊँचा उठना।

हिन्दी-अंग्रेजी

HINDI-ENGLISH

HINDI ALPHABETS

and their romanised transliterations

अ	आ	इ	ई	उ	ऊ	ऋ
a	ã	i	i	u	ü	r
ए	ऐ	ओ	औ	अं	अः	
e	ai	o	au	am	ah	
क	ख	ग	घ	ङ		
ka	kha	ga	gha			
च	छ	ज	झ	ञ		
c	ch	ja	jha			
ट	ठ	ड	ढ	ण		
ta	tha	da	dha			
त	थ	द	ध	न		
ta	tha	da	dha	na		
प	फ	ब	भ	म		
pa	fa/pha	ba	bha	ma		
य	र	ल	व	श		
ya	ra	la	va	s		
ष		स	ह			
s/s/sh		sa	ha			

संयुक्त व्यञ्जन

क्ष	त्र	ज्ञ
ksha	tra	Jna

Abbreviations used :

अ.	अंग्रेजी English	प्र.	प्रत्यय
अ.	अरबी Arabic	वि.	विशेषण Adjective
फ./फा.	फारसी Persian	क्रि.	क्रिया Verb
स्त्री.	स्त्रीलिंग Feminine	स. क्रि.	सकर्मक क्रिया
पु.	पुंल्लिग Masculine	अ. क्रि.	अकर्मक क्रिया
बहु.	बहुवचन Plural		

अ

अ *(a)* the first letter and vowel of Devnagri alphabet.

अंक *(ank)* पु. digit; mark; issue; number; act (drama); embrace; lap.

अंकगणित *(ankganit)* पु. arithmetic.

अंकन *(ankan)* पु. numbering; notation; brand; tagging; imprinting; making; description; writing; drawing.

अंकित *(ankit)* वि. marked; labelled; tagged; written; numbered; drawn; painted.

अंकुर *(ankur)* पु. villus (pl. villi); shoot; off-shoot; sign.

अंकुरण *(ankuran)* पु. germination; sprouting.

अंकुरित *(ankurit)* वि. sprouted; germinated; budded.

अंकुश *(ankus)* पु. elephant goad; hook; uncus; prod; restraint; control.

अंकेक्षक *(ankeksak)* पु. auditor.

अंकेक्षण *(ankeksan)* पु. audit.

अंग *(ang)* पु. organ; limb; body; division; department; part; branch; area; side; aspect.

अँगड़ाई *(angrāi)* स्त्री. stretching of limbs; twisting of body.

अँगना, आँगन *(angana)* पु. courtyard.

अँगरखा *(angarkha)* पु. loose upper male garment.

अंगराग *(amgarāg)* पु. cosmetics.

अंगार, अँगारा *(angāra)* पु. ember; cinder.

अंगीकार *(angikāra)* पु. acceptance (as one's own).

अँगीठी *(amgithi)* स्त्री. brazier; ingle; fire place; grate.

अंगुल *(angul)* पु. (स्त्री. उँगली) digit; a finger's breadth.

अंगुलत्राण *(angultrān)* पु. thimble.

अंगुली, अँगुली *(amguli)* स्त्री. finger: digit.

अंगुश्ताना *(angustāna)* पु. (फा.) thimble.

अँगूठा *(amguthā)* पु. thumb.

अँगूठी *(amguthi)* स्त्री. finger-ring.

अंगूर *(angur)* पु. grape.

अँगोछा *(amgochā)* पु. towel.

अंचल *(ancal)* पु. circle; zone; region.

अंजन *(anjan)* पु. collyrium; eyesalve.

अंजर-पंजर *(anjar-panjar)* पु. physical frame; skeleton; joints of the body; parts of a machine.

अंजलि *(anjali)* स्त्री. hollow of the palm.

अंजाम *(anjām)* पु. (फ़ा.) result; consequence; end; completion.

अंजीर *(anjir)* पु. (फ़ा.) fig.

अंट-शंट *(ant-śant)* वि. absurd; incoherent irrelevant; inconsistent; random.

अंड-बंड *(and band)* वि. miscellaneous; meaningless; nonsense; incoherent; irrelevant.

अंडा (andā) पु. egg.

अंडाकार *(andākār)* वि. oval; oviform.

अंतःकरण *(antahkaran)* पु. conscience.

अंतः पुर *(antahpur)* पु. harem.

अंतः प्रेरणा *(antahprerna)* स्त्री. urge; inspiration.

अंत *(ant)* पु. end; fall; destruction; edge; result; death.

अँतड़ी *(amtri)* स्त्री. intestine.

अंततः *(antatah)* क्रि. वि. at long last; finally; ultimately; eventually.

अंततोगत्वा *(antatogatvā)* क्रि. वि. at long last; finally: ultimately; eventually.

अंतरंग *(antarang)* वि. internal; inner; intimate; private.

अंतर *(antar)* पु. difference; distance.

अंतरात्मा *(antarātma)* स्त्री. conscience. soul.

अंतराल *(antarāl)* पु. interval; space.

अंतरिक्ष *(antariks)* पु. space; sky.

अंतरिक्ष यात्री *(antariksh-yātri)* पु. astronaut.

अंतरिक्ष यान *(antariksh-yān)* पु. spaceship.

अंतरिक्ष विज्ञान *(antariksh-vijnan)* पु. meteorology.

अंतरिम *(antarim)* वि. interim.

अंतरीकरण *(antikaran)* पु. stagger (archit).

अंतरीप *(antarip)* पु. cape.

अंतर्गत *(antargat)* वि. included.

अंतर्जात *(antarjāt)* वि. innate.

अंतर्जातीय *(antarjātiya)* वि. intercaste.

अंतर्दृष्टि *(antar-dristi)* स्त्री. insight.

अंतर्देशीय *(antardeśiya)* वि. interstate; inland; (inland letter).

अंतर्द्वंद्व *(antardvand)* पु. inner conflict.

अंतर्धान *(antardhān)* पु. disappearance.

अंतर्ध्वंस *(antardhavas)* पु. sabotage.

अंतर्निहित *(antarnihit)* वि. implicit; inherent.

अंतर्मुखी *(antarmukhi)* वि. introvert.

अंतर्यामी *(antaryāmi)* वि. pervading the innerself.

अंतर्राष्ट्रीय *(antarrāśtriya)* वि. international; global.

अंतर्वस्त्र *(antarvastra)* पु. underwear; undergarment.

अंतर्विरोध *(antarvirodh)* पु. self- contradiction.

अंतर्निहित *(antarnihit)* वि. latent; concealed; rendered invisible.

अंतस्तल *(antastal)* पु. heart of hearts; mind.

अंतिम *(antim)* वि. final; last; ultimate; terminal.

अंतेवासी *(antevasi)* पु. resident pupil.

अंदर *(andar)* क्रि. पु. (फ़ा.) within; in; inside.

अंदरूनी *(andaruni)* वि. (फ़ा.) internal; inward.

अंदाज़ *(andāz)* पु. फ़ा. estimate; guess; style; mode: gesture.

अंदाज़न *(andāzan)* क्रि. पु. (फ़ा.) roughly; approximately.

अंदाजा *(andāzā)* पु. (फ़ा.) estimate; guess: conjecture; surmise.

अंधकार *(andhākar)* पु. darkness.

अंधड़ *(andhar)* पु. violent duststorm.

अंधता *(andhata)* स्त्री. blindness.

अंधविश्वास *(andhvisvās)* पु. superstition; orthodoxy.

अंधा *(andhā)* पु. a blind person.

अंधाधुंध *(andhādhund)* क्रि. वि. indiscriminately; racklessly; excessively.

अंधानुकरण *(andhānukarn)* पु. blind imitation.

अंधापन *(andhāpan)* पु. blindness.

अँधियारा *(amdhiyārā)* see. अंधकार

अंधेर *(amdher)* पु. complete lawlessness.

अँधेरा *(amdherā)* पु. darkness.

अंबर *(ambar)* पु. sky; cloud; garment.

अंबार *(ambār)* पु. (फ़ा.) heap; bulk.

अंबुधि अंबुनिधि *(ambudhi; ambunidhi)* पु. ocean.

अंश *(ams)* पु. share; part; portion; degree (of an angle); division; fragment; fraction; ingredient; contribution; passage.

अंशकालिक *(amśakalik)* वि. part-time.

अंशतः *(amstah)* क्रि. वि. partly.

अंशदान *(amśadān)* पु. contribution.

अंशदायी *(amśadāi)* वि. contributory

अकड़ *(akar)* स्त्री. rigidity; stiffness; intractibility; strut; conceit; haughtiness.

अकड़बाज़ *(akarbāz)* वि. haughty; arrogant.

अकथनीय *(a-kathaniya)* वि. indescribable; ineffable; unutterable.

अकर्मक *(a-karmak)* वि. intransitive.

अकर्मण्य *(a-karmanya)* वि. indolent; idle.

अकर्मण्यता *(a-karmanyatā)* स्त्री. indolence; inertness; idleness; inactivity.

अकल्पनीय *(a-kalpaniya)* वि. unimaginable; inconceivable.

अकल्पित *(akalpit)* वि. unimagined.

अकसर *(aksar)* क्रि. वि. (अ.) often; usually.

अकस्मात् *(akasmāt)* क्रि. वि. accidentally; suddenly.

अकाट्य *(akātya)* वि. indisputable; irrefutable.

अकादमी *(akādmi)* स्त्री. academy.

अकारण *(akāran)* वि. without any pretext; groundless; causeless; unprovoked.

अकाल[1] *(akāl)* पु. famine.

अकाल[2] *(akāl)* वि. untimely.

अकिंचन[1] *(akincan)* पु. poorman; pauper.

अकिंचन[2] *(akincan)* वि. poor; destitute.

अकुलाना *(akulāna)* अ. क्रि. to feel restless or uneasy.

अकुलाहट *(akulāhat)* स्त्री. uneasiness; restlessness.

अकुशल *(akushal)* वि. unskilled.

अकुशलता *(akushaltā)* स्त्री. inefficiency; incompetence.

अकृतज्ञ *(akritjna)* वि. ungrateful; thankless.

अकृत्रिम *(akritrim)* वि. natural; genuine; unsophisticated; unaffected.

अकेला *(akelā)* वि. alone; lonely; lonesome; solitary; sole.

अकेले *(akele)* क्रि. वि. alone; without a companion.

अक्खड़ *(akkhar)* वि. contumacious; rude and rough; headstrong; fearless.

अक्खड़पन *(akkharpan)* पु. contumacy; haughtiness; fearlessness; rudeness; incivility.

अक़्ल *(akal)* स्त्री. (अ.) wisdom; intellect; intelligence;

अक़्लमंद *(akalmand)* वि. (अ.) sagacious; intelligent; wise.

अक़्लमंदी *(akalmandi)* स्त्री. (अ.) sagacity; intelligence.

अक्षम्य *(akshamya)* वि. inexcusable; unforgivable; unpardonable.

अक्षय *(akshay)* वि. everlasting; endless; inexhaustible; eternal.

अक्षर[1] *(akshar)* पु. syllable; character; sort (print); letter.

अक्षर[2] *(akshar)* वि. undecaying; imperishable.

अक्षरशः *(aksharśah)* क्रि. वि. in toto; literaly; verbatim.

अक्षांश *(akshāmś)* पु. latitude.

अक्षुण्ण *(akshun)* वि. unbroken; unimpaired; intact; whole ; undiminished.

अखंड *(akhand)* वि. undivided; unbroken; whole; complete; indivisible; non-stop; irrevocable.

अख़बार *(akhbār)* पु. (अ.) newspaper.

अखबारनवीस *(akhbārnavis)* पु. (अ.) journalist.

अख़बारनवीसी *(akhbārnavisi)* स्त्री. (अ) journalism.

अखरना *(akharnā)* अ. क्रि. to be unpleasant; to be disagreeble; to make one feel sore; to be troublesome; to be oppressive.

अखरोट *(akhrot)* पु. walnut.

अखाड़ा *(akhārā)* पु. arena; place for exercise; congregation or abode of sadhus.

अखिल *(akhil)* वि. entire; whole; complete.

अगम *(agam)* वि. unattainable; inacessible; incomprehensible.

अगम्य *(agamya)* वि. impassable; beyond reach; inapproachable; incomprehensible.

अगर *(agar)* क्रि. वि. (फ़ा.) if.

अगरबत्ती *(agarbatti)* स्त्री. incense-stick.

अगला *(agalā)* वि. following; next; forthcoming; approaching; coming.

अगवानी *(agavāni)* स्त्री. welcome; reception.

अगाध *(agādh)* वि. profound; unfathomable; immense.

अगुआ *(aguā)* पु. leader; pioneer; forerunner.

अगोचर *(agocar)* वि. imperceptible.

अग्नि *(agni)* स्त्री. fire.

अग्निकांड *(agnikānd)* पु. arson; conflagration.

अग्निदाह *(agnidāh)* पु. cremation.

अग्र *(agra)* वि. pre-eminent; topmost; chief; fornt; first; best.

अग्रगण्य *(agraganya)* वि. leading; prominent.

अग्रगामी *(agragāmi)* वि. pioneering; foregoing; preceding.

अग्रजा *(agrajā)* स्त्री. elder sister.

अग्रणी *(agrani)* वि. foremost: leading: outstanding: prominent.

अग्रदूत *(agradüt)* पु. herald: pioneer: forerunner; harbinger.

अग्रलेख *(agralekh)* पु. editorial (journ).

अग्रसर *(agrasar)* वि. going ahead; leading.

अग्रसारण *(agrasāran)* पु. forwarding.

अग्रसारित *(agrasārit)* वि. forwarded.

अग्राह्य *(agrāhāya)* वि. unacceptable; inadmissible; ineligible; incomprehensible.

अग्रिम *(agrim)* वि. advance; first; foremost; superior.

अग्रेषण *(agreśan)* पु. forwarding.

अघ *(agha)* पु. sin; misdeed.

अघाना *(aghāna)* अ. क्रि. to be satisfied.

अचंभा *(acambhā)* पु. astonishment; wonder; surprise.

अचंभित *(acambhit)* वि. astonished; amazed; wonder-struck.

अचरज *(acaraj)* पु. astonishment; surprise.

अचल *(a-cal)* वि. constant; firm; stable; immobile; stationary.

अचलता *(a-calata)* स्त्री. firmness; immovability.

अचानक *(acanak)* क्रि. वि. suddenly.

अचार *(acār)* पु. pickles.

अचिंत *(a-cint)* वि. thoughtless; carefree.

अचिंत्य *(a-cintya)* वि. inconceivable; unknowable; beyond imagination; beyond hope; sudden.

अचिर[1] *(a-cir)* वि. prompt; recent; new; momentary.

अचूक *(a-cuk)* वि. effective; unfailing.

अचेत *(a-cet)* वि. unconscious.

अचेतन[1] *(a-cetan)* पु. lifeless object.

अचेतन[2] *(a-cetan)* वि. inanimate.

अच्छा[1] *(acchā)* वि. good; nice; fine; excellent; pleasant; pleasing; genuine; pure; righteous; agreeable; proper; suitable; befitting; satisfactory; favourable.

अच्छा[2] *(acchā)* क्रि. वि. well; nicely; excellently.

अच्छाई *(acchāi)* स्त्री. goodness; virtue; merit; excellence; advantage.

अच्छापन *(acchāpan)* पु. see अच्छाई।

अच्युत *(a-cyut)* वि. infallible; unerring; immutable.

अछूत[1] *(a-chüt)* वि. untouchable.

अछूत[2] *(a-chüt)* पु. man of low caste.

अछूता *(a-chütā)* वि. unpolluted; untouched; fresh; unused; unharnessed; unexplored.

अजगर *(ajagar)* पु. python; a huge snake.

अजनबी[1] *(ajnabi)* वि. (फ़ा.) exotic: unknown; unfamiliar: alien.

अजनबी[2] *(ajnabi)* पु. (फ़ा.) stranger.

अजब *(ajab)* वि. (अ.) wonderful; strange; peculiar; marvellous.

अजर *(a-jar)* वि. ever young; undecaying; free from old age.

अजा *(azā)* स्त्री. she-goat; goddess Durga.

अजायबघर *(ajāyb-ghar)* पु. museum.

अजिर *(ajir)* पु. courtyard; arena; wind; body; matter of senses.

अज़ीज़ *(aziz)* पु. (फा.) dear.

अजीब *(ajib)* वि. peculiar; marvellous; strange; wonderful.

अजीर्ण *(a-jïrn)* पु. constipation; indigestion; dyspepsia.

अजूबा *(ajübā)* पु. (अ.) wonder.

अजेय *(ajey)* वि. invincible; unconquerable.

अज्ञात *(a-jnāt)* वि. unknown; incognito.

अज्ञान *(a-jnān)* पु. ignorance.

अज्ञानता *(a-jnānata)* स्त्री. ignorance.

अज्ञानी *(a-jnāni)* वि. unwise: ignorant.

अज्ञेय *(a-jney)* वि. unknowable; unfit to be know.

अटकना *(ataknā)* अ. क्रि. to get stuck up; to be held up; to quarrel.

अटकल *(atkal)* स्त्री. conjecture; guess; speculation.

अटकाना *(atkānā)* स. क्रि. to detain; to hinder; to prevent; to delay; to connect; to link; to obstruct.

अटखेली *(atakheli)* see अठखेली

अटपटा *(atpatā)* वि. incongruous; absurd; unpleasant; unsavoury.

अटल *(a-tal)* वि. resolute; steadfast; firm; unwavering; immovable; irrevocable; unalterable.

अटूट *(a-tut)* वि. unbreakable; unbroken; continuous; firm.

अट्टहास, -हास्य *(attahās)* पु. horse

laugh; guffaw.

अठखेली *(athkheli)* स्त्री. frolic; merriment.

अड़ंगा *(arangā)* पु. impediment; obstacle.

अड़चन *(arcan)* स्त्री. hitch; hindrancne; obstacle; difficulty.

अड़ना *(arnā)* अ. क्रि. to be obstinate; to stick; to insist; to halt; to be restive.

अड़ाना *(arānā)* स. क्रि. to cause to obstruct; to press forward.

अडिग *(a-dig)* वि. steady; unflinching.

अड़ियल *(ariyal)* वि. stubborn: inflexible; mulish.

अड़ोस-पड़ोस *(arōs-parōs)* पु. neighbourhood.

अड्डा *(adda)* पु. meeting place; stand (for vehicles); base.

अणु *(anu)* पु. atom; molecule.

अणुबम *(anu-bam)* पु. atom bomb.

अतः, अतएव *(atah; at-ev)* अ. therefore; hence.

अतल *(a-tal)* वि. bottomless; fathomless; unffathomable.

अता-पता *(atā-patā)* पु. clue; whereabout; trace.

अति *(ati)* वि. excessive; too much; very much; extreme; absolute.

अतिकर *(ati-kar)* पु. surtax.

अतिक्रम *(ati-kram)* अतिक्रमण पु. transgression; violation; infringement.

अतिचार *(ati-cār)* पु. trespass; profanation; outrage; violation.

अतिचारी *(ati-cāri)* वि. outrageous; intrusive; profane.

अतिथि *(atithi)* पु. guest.

अतिथिपरायण *(atithi-parāyan)* वि. hospitable.

अतिथि-सत्कार *(atithi-satkār)* पु. hospitality.

अतिमानव *(ati-mānav)* पु. superman.

अतिमानवीय *(ati-mānaviya)* वि. superhuman.

अतिरंजना *(ati-ranjana)* स्त्री. exaggeration.

अतिरंजित *(ati-ranjit)* वि. exaggerated.

अतिरिक्त *(ati-rikt)* वि. additional; accessory; extra; superfluous; surplus; auxiliary.

अतिरेक *(ati-rek)* पु. superfluity; excess; exuberance; plenty; abundance; surplus; redundancy.

अतिवादी *(ati-vādi)* पु. extremist.

अतिशय *(ati-śay)* पु. excessive.

अतिशयता *(ati-śayatā)* स्त्री. surplusage; excessiveness.

अतिशयोक्ति *(ati-sayokti)* स्त्री. hyperbole.

अतिसार *(ati-sār)* पु. dysentry; diarrhoea.

अतींद्रिय *(atindriya)* वि. imperceptible; supersensible; supersensuous; extrasensory; transcendental.

अतीत *(atit)* वि. past.

अतीव *(ativ)* पु. excessive.

अतुल *(a-tul)* अतुलनीय, अतुलित, अतुल्य वि. unequalled; unparalleled; matchless; immeasurable; immense; unique.

अतृप्त *(a-trpt)* वि. unsatiated; unsatisfied.

अत्यंत *(aty-ant)* वि. much; immese.

अत्यधिक *(aty-adhik)* वि. very much; too much.

अत्यल्प *(aty-alp)* वि. very little; meagre.

अत्याचार *(aty-ā-cār)* पु. tyranny; atrocity; excess; outrage; oppression.

अत्याचारी *(aty-a-cari)* वि. atrocious; tyrannous; outrageous; oppressive.

अत्यावश्यक *(aty-āvasyak)* वि. urgent.

अत्युक्ति *(aty-ukti)* स्त्री. hyperbole.

अथक *(a-thak)* वि. untiring; unceasing; ceaseless; indefatigible.

अथवा *(athavā)* वि. either; or.

अथाह *(a-thāh)* वि. very deep; unfathomable; bottomless.

अदक्ष *(adaksh)* वि. inefficient; incompetent.

अदद *(adad)* पु. (अ.) piece; number; article; item.

अदना *(adnā)* वि. (अ.) low; inferior; insignificant; worthless; trifling; trivial.

अदब *(adab)* पु. (अ.) respect; regard; civility; etiquette; politeness; courtesy; literature.

अदम्य *(a-damya)* वि. irresistible; irrepressible.

अदरक *(adrak)* पु. ginger.

अदल-बदल *(adal-badal)* स्त्री. barter; interchange.

अदा *(adā)* स्त्री. (अ.) blandishment; coquetry; posture; graceful manner.

अदाकार *(adakār)* पु. actor; performer.

अदायगी *(adāygi)* स्त्री. payment; performance.

अदालत *(adālat)* स्त्री. court of low.

अदालती *(adālati)* वि. judicial; legal.

अदावत *(adāvat)* स्त्री. (अ.) animosity; enmity; hostility; rivalry.

अदूरदर्शिता *(adürdarsitā)* स्त्री. shortshightedness.

अदूरदर्शी *(adürdarsi)* वि. wanting in foresight; unwise; ignorant.

अदृश्य *(a-drisya)* वि. invisible.

अदृष्ट *(a-drist)* पु. fate; fortune; calamity; unforseen trouble.

अदृष्ट *(a-drișt)* वि. unforeseen; unseen.

अद्धा *(addhā)* पु. half of a bottle; half of any measure; counterfoil.

अद्‌भुत *(adbhut)* वि. marvellous; fantastic; wonderful.

अद्यतन *(adyatan)* वि. modern; latest

अद्वितीय *(a-dvitiya)* वि. unique; matchless.

अधःपतन, *(adhāh-patan)* अधःपात पु. degeneration; degradation; downfall; deterioration.

अधकचरा *(adhākacrā)* वि. half-ripe; immature; incomplete; half-baked; unassimilated.

अधखिला *(adh-khila)* वि. half-bloomed.

अधखुला *(adh-khulā)* वि. half-uncovered; half-open

अधम[1] *(adham)* वि. vile; mean; base.

अधम[2] *(adham)* पु. miscreant; villain.

अधमरा *(adh-marā)* वि. half-dead.

अधर *(a-dhar)* पु. lip; empty space.

अधर्म *(a-dharm)* पु. sinful; unrighteousness; immorality; irreligion; injustice.

अधर्मी *(a-dharmi)* वि. irreligious; sinful.

अधार्मिक *(a-dharmik)* वि. irreligious; profane; unrighteous; sacrilegeous.

अधिक *(adhik)* वि. much; extra; additional; surplus; abundant.

अधिकतम *(adhikatam)* विं. maximum; utmost.

अधिकतर *(adhikatar)* क्रि. वि. mostly.

अधिकता *(adhikatā)* स्त्री. excess; sufficiency; profusion.

अधिकरण *(adhi-karan)* पु. tribunal locative case (grammar); organ; agency; organization.

अधिकांश *(adhikāns)* वि. most; more than half.

अधिकाधिक *(adhikādhik)* वि. utmost; maximum; more and more.

अधिकार *(adhi-kār)* पु. right; mastery; claim; power; authority; command; jurisdiction; entitlement.

अधिकारी *(adhi-kāri)* पु. officer: owner; proprietor: authority.

अधिकृत *(adhi-krit)* वि. authorised; occupied; accredited; official.

अधिकोष *(adhikos)* पु. bank.

अधिक्रम, अधिक्रमण *(adhikram)* पु. supersession; encroachment.

अधिक्षेत्र *(adhiksetra)* पु. jurisdiction.

अधिगत *(adhi-gat)* वि. attained; acquired; gained; obtained; achieved.

अधिग्रहण *(adhi-grahan)* पु. acquisition.

अधिदेश *(adhi-des)* पु. mandata.

अधिनायक *(adhināyak)* पु. dictator; leader.

अधिनायकत्व *(adhi-nāyakatva)* पु. dictatroship.

अधिनायकवाद *(adhi-nāyakvad)* पु. dictatorism.

अधिनायकीय *(adhi-nāyakiya)* वि. dictatorial.

अधिनियम *(adhi-ni-yam)* पु. act of legislature.

अधिनिर्णय *(adhi-nirnay)* पु. award.

अधिपत्र *(adhi-patra)* पु. warrant

अधिप्रभार *(adhi-prabhār)* पु. surcharge.

अधिभार *(adhi-bhar)* पु. surcharge: incumbrance: overweight.

अधिमानव *(adhi-mānav)* पु. superman.

अधिमास *(adhi-mās)* पु. leap month.

अधियाचन *(adhi-yācan)* पु. requisition.

अधियुक्त *(adhi-yuktā)* वि. employed.

अधियोद्धा *(adhi-yodhā)* अधियोजक पु. employer.

अधियोजन *(adhi-yojan)* पु. employment.

अधिराज्य *(adhi-rājya)* पु. suzerian state.

अधिलाभ *(adhi-lābh)* पु. super profit; bonus.

अधिवक्ता *(adhi-vaktā)* पु. advocate.

अधिवर्ष *(adhi-varśa)* पु. leap year

अधिवेशन *(adhi-veśan)* पु. session.

अधिशासी *(adhi-śasi)* पु. executive.

अधिशुल्क *(adhi-śulk)* पु. premium.

अधिशोषण *(adhi-śośan)* पु. absorption.

अधिष्ठाता *(adhi-sthātā)* पु. president; chief; presidingdeity; dean.

अधिष्ठान *(adhi-sthān)* पु. abode; establishment, installation.

अधिष्ठापन *(adhi-sthāpan)* पु. installation.

अधिसंख्यक *(adhi-san-khyak)* वि. supernumerary.

अधिसूचना *(adhi-sucanā)* स्त्री. notification.

अधीक्षक *(adhiksak)* पु. superintendent.

अधीक्षण *(adhikśan)* पु. superintendence.

अधीन *(adhin)* वि. subordinate.

अधीनता *(adhinatā)* पु. subjection;

subordinating: dependence.

अधीनस्थ *(adhinasth)* वि. subordinate; dependent.

अधीर *(a-dhir)* वि. fidgety; restive; nervous; impatient; anxious.

अधीरता *(a-dhiratā)* स्त्री. impatience; perplexity; anxiety; petulance; nervousness.

अधूरा *(adhūrā)* वि. incomplete; imperfect.

अधूरापन *(adhūrāpan)* पु. incompleteness; imperfection.

अधेड़ *(adher)* वि. middle-aged.

अधोगति *(adhogati)* स्त्री. downfall; degradation; decline; decay; degeneration.

अधोगामी *(adhogāmi)* वि. descending; going downwards.

अधोमुख, *(adhomukh)* वि. facing downwards; dejected; depressed; drooped; prone.

अध्यक्ष *(adhy-aks)* पु. chairman; president

अध्यात्म *(adhy-ātm)* पु. spiritual contemplation.

अध्यादेश *(adhy-ā-des)* पु. ordinance.

अध्यापक *(adhy-āpak)* पु. teacher.

अध्यापन *(adhy-āpan)* पु. teaching.

अध्यापिका *(adhy-āpika)* स्त्री. lady-teacher.

अध्याय *(adhy-āy)* पु. chapter.

अध्येता *(adhy-eta)* पु. student; scholar.

अनंत *(an-ant)* वि. infinite; unending; eternal; unlimited; infinity; eternity.

अनंतर *(an-antar)* क्रि. वि. afterwards; later on.

अनगढ़ *(an-garh)* वि. crude; grotesque.

अनगिनत *(an-ginat)* वि. countless; innumerable; untold.

अनचाहा *(an-cāhā)* वि. undesired; unwanted.

अनजान *(an-jān)* वि. unacquainted; unknown; ignorant.

अनदेखा *(an-dekhā)* वि. unseen.

अनधिकार *(an-adhi-kār)* वि. unauthorised.

अनधिकृत *(anadhikrit)* वि. unauthorised; unoccupied.

अनन्नास *(anannās)* पु. pine-apple.

अनन्य *(an-anya)* वि. exclusive; matchless; unique.

अनन्यता *(an-anyatā)* स्त्री. uniqueness; exclusiveness.

अनपच *(an-pac)* अपच पु. indigestion.

अनपचा *(an-pacā)* वि. undigested; unassimilated.

अनपढ़ *(an-parh)* वि. illiterate; uneducated.

अनपेक्षित *(an-pêksit)* वि. not expected; not required; unwanted.

अनबन *(anban)* स्त्री. estrangement; rift; discord.

अनबूझ *(an-būjh)* अबूझ वि. unintelligible.

अनभिज्ञ *(an-abhi-jna)* वि. unacquainted; ignorant; unaware.

अनभिज्ञता *(an-abhi-jnatā)* स्त्री. ignorance; unawareness; unacquaintedness.

अनभ्यस्त *(anbhyast)* वि. unaccustomed.

अनमना *(an-manā)* वि. absent minded; unattentive; indifferent; indisposed.

अनमेल *(an-mel)* वि. incommensurate; discordant; inharmonious; heterogeneous; ill-matched.

अनमोल *(an-mol)* वि. invaluable; priceless.

अनम्य *(anamya)* वि. stiff; unbending; rigid; inflexible.

अनम्र *(anamra)* वि. impertinent; impudent; disrespectful; immodest.

अनर्गल *(an-argal)* वि. unrestrained; incoherent; absurd; meaningless.

अनर्थ *(an-arth)* पु. calamity; absurdity; absolutely; contrary meaning.

अनल *(anal)* पु. fire.

अनवरत *(an-ava-rat)* वि. continuous; incessant.

अनशन *(an-asan)* पु. fast; hunger strike.

अनश्वर *(a-nasvar)* वि. everlasting; immortal.

अनसुना *(an-sunā)* वि. unheard.

अनहोनी *(an-honi)* वि. improbable; impossible; miraculous.

अनागत *(an-ā-gat)* वि. yet to come; future: not attained: unknown.

अनाचार *(an-ā-cār)* पु. licentiousness; misconduct; malpractice; immorality; corruption.

अनाज *(anāj)* पु. corn; grain; cereal.

अनाड़ी *(anāri)* वि. unskilful

अनाथ *(a-nāth)* पु. orphan.

अनाथ *(a-nath)* वि. helpless; orphaned.

अनाथालय *(anāthālaya)* अनाथाश्रम पु. orphanage.

अनादर *(an-ā-dar)* पु. disrespect; disregard; insult.

अनादि *(an-ādi)* वि. eternal; everlasting.

अनाप-शनाप *(anāp-śanāp)* वि. absurd; slipslop; irrelevant.

अनाम *(a-nām)* अनामक वि. anonymous; nameless.

अनामिका *(a-nāmika)* स्त्री. ring finger.

अनायास *(an-ā-yās)* क्रि. वि. suddenly; spontaneously; involuntarily.

अनार *(anār)* पु. pomegranate.

अनावरण *(an-ā-varan)* पु. exposure; unveiling.

अनावर्तक, अनावर्ती *(an-ā-vrti)* वि. nonrecurring.

अनावश्यक *(a-nāvaśyak)* वि. unnecessary; unimportant; useless; redundant.

अनावृत *(an-ā-vrit)* वि. non-recurring; unrepeated; uncovered; unveiled.

अनावृष्टि *(anāvriśti)* स्त्री. drought; want of rain.

अनासक्त *(anāsakt)* वि. unattached, detached.

अनासक्ति *(anāsakti)* स्त्री. detachment.

अनास्था *(anāstha)* स्त्री. lack of devotedness.

अनिंद्य *(a-nindya)* अनिंदनीय वि. flawless; irreproachable; unimpeachable.

अनिच्छा *(an-ichā)* स्त्री. unwillingnes; reluctance.

अनित्य *(a-nitya)* वि. ephemeral; transient.

अनिद्रा *(a-nidrā)* वि. insomnia; sleeplessness.

अनियंत्रित *(aniyantrit)* वि. unrestrained; uncontrolled.

अनियत *(aniyat)* वि. indeterminate; indefinite.

अनियमित *(a-ni-yamit)* वि. irregular.

अनिर्णीत *(a-nir-nit)* वि. pending: inconclusive: undecided.

अनिर्दिष्ट *(anirdiśta)* वि. unspecified; unprescribed.

अनिर्वचनीय *(a-nirvacaniya)* वि. indescribable; inexpressible; ineffable.

अनिवार्य *(a-ni-vārya)* वि. compulsory; unavoidable; inevitable; obligatory; mandatory.

अनिवार्यता *(a-ni-vāryatā)* स्त्री. inevitability.

अनिश्चय *(a-niś-cay)* पु. uncertainty; indecision; incertitude.

अनिश्चित *(a-niś-cit)* वि. undecided; uncertain; unsettled; indefinite.

अनिश्ट *(an-ist)* पु. calamity.

अनीति *(a-niti)* स्त्री. impropriety; immorality; high-handedness.

अनुकंपा *(anu-kampā)* स्त्री. kindness; mercy.

अनुकरण *(anu-karan)* पु. imitation; emulation; mimicry; copy.

अनुकरणशील *(anukaransil)* वि. imitative.

अनुकरणीय *(anu-karaniya)* वि. imitable.

अनुकूलता *(anu-külata)* स्त्री. favourableness; agreeability; suitability; befittingness; conformity; congeniality.

अनुकृति *(anu-kriti)* स्त्री. emulation; imitation; copy.

अनुक्रम *(anu-kram)* पु. sequence; succession.

अनुगामी *(anu-gāmi)* पु. follower.

अनुगूँज *(anu-gumj)* स्त्री. re-echo

अनुग्रह *(anu-grah)* पु. favour; grace; benignity; obligation; kindness.

अनुचर *(anu-car)* अनुचारी पु. follower; attendant.

अनुचित *(anu-cit)* वि. unbecoming; improper; unjustified; undue.

अनुज *(anuj)* पु. younger brother.

अनुजा *(anujā)* स्त्री. younger sister.

अनुज्ञा *(anu-jnā)* स्त्री. licence; permission.

अनुज्ञापत्र *(anujnāpatra)* पु. licence; permit.

अनुत्तरदायित्व *(anuttardayitva)* पु. irresponsibility.

अनुत्तरित *(anuttarit)* वि. unreplied; unresponded; unanswered.

अनुत्तीर्ण *(anuttirna)* वि. unsuccessful.

अनुदान *(anu-dān)* पु. grant.

अनुदार *(anu-dār)* वि. illiberal; conservative.

अनुदारता *(anudārta)* स्त्री. conservatism.

अनुनय *(anu-nay)* पु. persuation; entreaty; mollification.

अनुनाद *(anu-nād)* पु. resonance; echo.

अनुनासिक *(anu-nāsik)* वि. nasal.

अनुपजाऊ *(anupjāu)* वि. unproductive; barren.

अनुपम *(an-upam)* वि. unparalleled; matchless; incomparable; unique.

अनुपमता *(anupamatā)* स्त्री. matchlessness; uniqueness.

अनुपयुक्त *(anupayukt)* वि. unsuitable; unfit; improper.

अनुपयुक्तता *(anupayuktā)* स्त्री. unsuitability; unfitness; impropriety.

अनुपयोग *(anupayog)* पु. without use.

अनुपयोगी *(anupayogi)* वि. unavailing; useless; unserviceable.

अनुपस्थित *(anupasthit)* वि. absent.

अनुपस्थिति *(anupasthiti)* स्त्री. absence.

अनुपात *(anu-pāt)* *पु.* proportion; ratio.

अनुपालन *(anupālan)* *पु.* compliance; adherence; obedience.

अनुपूरक *(anu-purak)* *वि.* supplementary.

अनुप्राणित *(anu-prānit)* *वि.* inspired; animated; enlivened.

अनुप्रास *(anu-prās)* *पु.* alliteration.

अनुबंध *(anu-bandh)* *पु.* annexure; contract; addendum.

अनुभव *(anu-bhav)* *पु.* experience.

अनुभवहीन *(anubhav-hina)* *वि.* lack of experience.

अनुभवहीनता *(anubhav-hinta)* *स्त्री.* lack of experience.

अनुभवी *(anu-bhavi)* *वि.* experienced.

अनुभूत *(anu-bhut)* *वि.* tried; proven; experimented.

अनुभूति *(anu-bhuti)* *स्त्री.* perception; feeling; realisation; sensibility.

अनुमति *(anu-mati)* *स्त्री.* permission.

अनुमान *(anu-mān)* *पु.* estimate; surmise; guess; supposition; presumption.

अनुमानित *(anu-mānit)* *वि.* approximate; estimated.

अनुमोदक *(anu-modak)* *पु.* seconder.

अनुयायी *(anu-yāyi)* *पु.* follower; adherent; disciple.

अनुरक्त *(anu-rakt)* *वि.* infatuated: enamoured.

अनुरक्ति *(anu-rakti)* *स्त्री.* infatuation.

अनुराग *(anu-rāg)* *पु.* affection; attachment.

अनुरागी *(anu-rāgi)* *वि.* affectionate; devoted.

अनुरूप *(anu-rüp)* *वि.* conformable; resemblant; analogous; similar.

अनुरोध *(anu-rodh)* *पु.* entreaty; solicitation; earnest; request.

अनुर्वर *(anur-var)* *वि.* unproductive; inferitle; sterile; barren.

अनुवाद *(anu-vād)* *पु.* translation.

अनुवादित *(anu-vādit)* अनूदित *वि.* translated.

अनुशंसा *(anuśamsa)* *स्त्री.* recommendation.

अनुशासक *(anu-śāsak)* *पु.* disciplinarian.

अनुशासन *(anu-śāsan)* *पु.* disciplined.

अनुशासनहीनता *(anu-śāsan-hinatā)* *स्त्री.* indiscipline.

अनुशासित *(anu-śāsit)* *वि.* disciplined.

अनुष्ठान *(anu-sthān)* *पु.* ceremony; ritual; rite; religious performance.

अनुसंधान *(anu-san-dhān)* *पु.* research; investigation.

अनुसंधानकर्ता *(anusandhān-kartā)* *पु.* researcher; investigator.

अनुसरण *(anu-saran)* *पु.* pursuance.

अनुसूचित *(anu-sucit)* *वि.* scheduled.

अनुसूची *(anu-suci)* *स्त्री.* schedule.

अनुस्वार *(anu-svār)* *पु.* nasal sound.

अनूठा *(anuthā)* *वि.* unique; unprecedented; wonderful; extraordinary; uncommon.

अनूदित *(anüdit)* see अनुवादित

अनूप *(anüp)* *वि.* unique; unequalled.

अनेक *(an-ek)* *वि.* numerous; many.

अनेकता *(anekatā)* *स्त्री.* *पु.* अनेकत्व diversity; plurality.

अनैतिक *(a-naitik)* *वि.* depraved; immoral.

अनैतिकता *(a-naitikata)* वी. depravity; immorality.

अनोखा *(anokhā)* वि. peculiar; queer; unique; novel; marvellous.

अनोखापन *(anokhāpan)* पु. peculiarity; queerness; novelty; uniqueness.

अनौचित्य *(anaucitya)* पु. indecency; impropriety.

अनौपचारिक *(a-naupcārik)* वि. unofficial; informal; unceremonious.

अन्न *(ann)* पु. corn; grain.

अन्नदाता *(anna-datā)* पु. bread-giver.

अन्य *(anya)* वि. other; different; another.

अन्यत्र *(anyatra)* क्रि. वि. elsewhere.

अन्यथा *(anyathā)* क्रि. वि. otherwise.

अन्यमनस्क *(anya-manask)* वि. out of sorts; absent-minded.

अन्यमनस्कता *(anya-manaskatā)* स्त्री. absent-mindedness.

अन्याय *(a-ny-āy)* पु. injustice.

अन्यायपूर्ण *(anyāypuran)* अन्यायमूलक वि. unjust.

अन्यायी *(a-ny-āyi)* unjust; unfair.

अन्योक्ति *(anyökti)* स्त्री. allegory.

अन्वय *(anv-ay)* पु. concordance; acord; agreement; natural order or sequence of words in a sentence; logical connection of cause and effect or proposition and conclusion; lineage; prose order; paraphrase.

अन्वीक्षण *(anv-iksan)* पु. microscopic examination; investigation.

अन्वेषक *(anv-eṣak)* अन्वेषी पु. explorer; enquirer; researcher.

अन्वेषण *(anv-eṣan)* पु. exploration; research; investigation.

अन्वेषित *(anv-esit)* वि. enquired; explored; investigated.

अपंग *(apang)* वि. crippled; disabled.

अपकर्ष *(apa-karś)* पु. deterioration; downfall; degeneration.

अपकार *(apa-kār)* पु. disservice.

अपकीर्ति *(apa-kirti)* स्त्री. disrepute; disgrace; infamy; ignominy.

अपक्व *(a-pakva)* वि. raw; inripe; immature.

अपच *(a-pac)* पु. dyspepsia; indigestion.

अपटु *(a-patu)* वि. unskilled; inexpert; incompetent; inefficient.

अपठित *(a-pathit)* वि. unread; unseen.

अपढ़ *(a-parh)* वि. uneducated; unlettered.

अपथ्य *(a-pathya)* वि. unwholesome.

अपदस्थ *(a-padasth)* वि. deposed; dismissed.

अपनत्व *(apnatva)* see अपनापन।

अपना *(apnā)* वि. one's own; personal; private.

अपनाना *(apnānā)* स. क्रि. to treat as one's own; to adopt; to own.

अपनापन *(apnāpan)* अपनत्व पु. feeling of ownness; affinity; cordiality.

अपमान *(apa-mān)* पु. insult; disrespect; disgrace; affront; derogation.

अपमानकारी *(apamānkāri)* अपमानजनक वि. libellous; insulting; humiliating; derogatory.

अपमानित *(apa-mnit)* वि. disgraced; insulted; disrespected; humiliated.

अपमिश्रण *(apmisran)* पु. adulteration.

अपमिश्रित *(apmisrit)* पु. adulterated.

अपयश *(apa-yaś)* पु. disrepute; infamy; disgrace.

अपराजित *(a-parā-jit)* वि. undefeated; unvanquished.

अपराजेय *(a-parā-jey)* वि. invincible.

अपराध *(apa-rādh)* पु. guilt; crime; of fence.

अपराधपूर्ण *(aprādh-purna)* वि. criminal; offensive; guilty.

अपराध-विज्ञान *(aprādh-vijnan)* पु. criminology.

अपराधी *(apa-rādhi)* पु. culprit; offender; criminal.

अपराहं *(aparâhna)* पु. afternoon.

अपरिग्रह *(aparigrah)* पु. non-possession; possessionlessress renunciation.

अपरिचित *(a-pari-cit)* वि. unacquainted.

अपरिपक्व *(aparipakva)* वि. immature; unripe.

अपरिमित *(apari-mit)* वि. limitless; enormous.

अपरिवर्तनीय *(aparivartaniya)* वि. inconvertible; unchangeable.

अपरिवर्तित *(aparivartit)* वि. unchanged; unmodified; unaltered.

अपरिष्कृत *(apariskrit)* वि. unrefined; crude; unsophisticated; coarse.

अपरिहार्य *(apari-hārya)* वि. indispensable; inevitable; unavoidable.

अपरोक्ष *(aproksh)* वि. direct; overt.

अपर्याप्त *(a-paryāpta)* वि. inadequate; insufficient.

अपर्याप्तता *(aparyāptatā)* स्त्री. inadequacy; insufficiency.

अपलक *(a-palak)* वि. unwinking; sleepless.

अपवाद *(apa-vād)* पु. exception.

अपवाह *(apa-vāh)* पु. drainage.

अपविचार *(apavicār)* पु. bad idea.

अपवित्र *(a-pavitra)* वि. unholy; impious; desecrated; profane.

अपवित्रता *(a-pavitrata)* स्त्री. unholiness; impiety; desecratedness.

अपवृद्धि *(apa-vriddhi)* स्त्री. unnatural growth; aggravation.

अपव्यय *(apa-vyay)* पु. extravagance.

अपव्ययी *(apa-vyayi)* वि. extravagant; prodigal.

अपशकुन *(apa-śakun)* पु. ill-omen.

अपशब्द *(apa-śabd)* पु. abusive language.

अपस्मार *(apa-smār)* पु. epilepsy.

अपहरण *(apa-haran)* पु. kidnapping; abduction.

अपहर्ता *(apa-hartā)* पु. kidnapper; abductor.

अपहृत *(apa-hrit)* वि. abducted; kidnapped.

अपाच्य (*apācya*) वि. indigestible.

अपाठ्य *(apthya)* वि. illegible.

अपात्र *(a-pātr)* वि. undeserving; inworthy; ineligible.

अपार *(a-pār)* वि. boundless; immense.

अपार्दर्शक *(a-pārdarśak)* वि. opaque.

अपारदर्शिता *(apārdarśitā)* स्त्री. opacity.

अपारदर्शी *(apārdarsi)* see. अपारदर्शक

अपार्थिव *(a-pārthiva)* वि. spiritual; celestial; unearthy.

अपाहिज *(apāhij)* वि. crippled; disabled.

अपितु *(api-tu)* क्रि. वि. but.

अपुष्ट *(a-puśt)* वि. unconfirmed; unauthenticated.

अपूर्ण *(a-purn)* वि. incomplete; imperfect; inconclusive.

अपूर्णता *(a-purnatā)* स्त्री. incompleteness; imperfection.

अपूर्व *(a-purv)* वि. unprecedented.

अपेक्षा *(apêksa)* स्त्री. expectation.

अपेक्षाकृत *(apekshākrit)* क्रि. वि. comparatively.; relatively.

अपेक्षित *(apêksit)* वि. expected; required; requisite.

अप्रकाशित *(apra-kāśit)* वि. unpublished; unlighted; undisclosed.

अप्रकाश्य *(apra-kāśya)* वि. unfit for publication or disclosure.

अप्रचलन *(apra-calan)* पु. non-currency; obsolescence.

अप्रचलित *(apra-calit)* वि. out-dated; obsolete; out-moded.

अप्रतिम *(apratim)* वि. matchless; unequalled.

अप्रत्यक्ष *(apraty-aks)* वि. indirect; conert.

अप्रत्याशित *(apraty-āśit)* वि. unexpected.

अप्रधान *(apra-dhān)* वि. secondary; subsidiary; minor.

अप्रयुक्त *(aprayukta)* वि. unused; unconsumed.

अप्रसन्न *(a-pra-sann)* वि. displeased; unhappy.

अप्रसन्नता *(a-pra-sannatā)* स्त्री. displeasure; unhappiness.

अप्राप्त *(a-prâpt)* वि. unachieved; unobtained.

अप्राप्य *(a-prâpya)* वि. unobtainable; unattainable; not available.

अप्रामाणिक *(a-pramānik)* वि. unauthentic; unauthoritative.

अप्रासंगिक *(a-prāsangik)* वि. out of context; irrelevant.

अप्रिय *(a-priya)* वि. unpleasant; disagreeable; undesirable.

अप्सरा *(apsarā)* स्त्री. fairy; nymph.

अफरा *(aphrā)* पु. indigestion; accumulation of wind in stomach.

अफ़वाह *(afvāh)* पु. rumour.

अफ़सर *(afsar)* पु. officer.

अफ़साना *(afsāna)* पु. tale; story.

अफ़सोस *(afsos)* पु. sorrow; grief.

अफ़ीम *(afim)* स्त्री. opium.

अफ़ीमची *(afimci)* पु. opium addict.

अब *(ab)* क्रि. वि. now

अबद्ध *(a-baddh)* वि. free; not in bondage.

अबरक *(abrak)* पु. mica.

अबला *(a-balā)* स्त्री. women.

अबूझ *(a-bujh)* वि. insolvable; unintelligible.

अबोध *(a-bodh)* वि. ignorant; innocent.

अभद्र *(a-bhadra)* वि. indecorous; indecent; undignified.

अभय *(a-bhay)* वि. fearless; undaunted.

अभागा *(a-bhāgā)* वि. unlucky; unfortunate.

अभाव *(a-bhāv)* पु. dearth; want; deficiency; scarcity; absence.

अभावग्रस्त *(abhāvgrast)* वि. scarcity; stricken; scarcity.

अभिकथन *(abhi-kathan)* पु. allegation: assertion.

अभिकर्ता *(abhi-kartā)* पु. agent.

अभिचार *(abhi-cār)* पु. exorcism; black magic; sorcery: incantation

अभिजात *(abhi-jāt)* पु. aristocrat; noble.

अभिजात्य *(abhi-jātya)* वि. aristocratic; victorious.

अभिज्ञ *(abhi-jna)* वि. well-versed.

अभिज्ञता *(abhi-jnatā)* स्त्री. familiarity; conversance; awareness.

अभिज्ञात *(abhi-jnāt)* वि. recognised.

अभिज्ञान *(abhijnan)* पु. recognition; recollection; identification.

अभिज्ञापन *(abhijnāpan)* पु. announcement.

अभिनंदन *(abhi-nandan)* पु. reception; greeting; ceremonious welcome; ovation; commemoration.

अभिनंदित *(abhi-nandit)* वि. honoured; greeted.

अभिनय *(abhi-nay)* पु. stage performance; acting.

अभिनव *(abhi-nav)* वि. novel; quite new.

अभिनिर्णय *(abhinirnay)* पु. verdict.

अभिनीत *(abhi-nit)* वि. enacted; staged.

अभिनेता *(abhi-netā)* पु. actor.

अभिनेत्री *(abhi-netri)* स्त्री. actress.

अभिनेय *(abhi-neya)* वि. stageable.

अभिनेयता *(abhi-nayatā)* स्त्री. stageability.

अभिन्न *(a-bhinn)* वि. intimate; close; identical; integral.

अभिन्नता *(a-bhinnatā)* स्त्री. sameness; oneness; identify.

अभिपुष्टि *(abhi-pusti)* स्त्री. confirmation; affirmance.

अभिप्राय *(abhi-prây)* पु. intention; motive; motif; implication; purport.

अभिभावक *(abhi-bhāvak)* पु. guardian.

अभिभाषण *(abhi-bhāśan)* पु. address.

अभिभूत *(abhi-bhut)* वि. overpowered; overwhelmed.

अभिमान *(abhi-mān)* पु. vanity; pride.

अभिमानी *(abhi-māni)* वि. arrogant; proud.

अभियंता *(abhi-yanta)* पु. engineer.

अभियान *(abhi-yān)* पु. drive; campaign; expedition.

अभियुक्त *(abhi-yukt)* पु., वि. accused.

अभियोक्ता *(abhi-yoktā)* पु. accuser.

अभियोग *(abhi-yog)* पु. accusation; charge; impeachment.

अभियोगी *(abhi-yogi)* पु. accuser.

अभियोजक *(abhi-yojak)* पु. prosecutor.

अभियोजन *(abhi-yojan)* पु. prosecution.

अभिराम *(abhi-ram)* वि. lovely; beautiful; delightful; charming.

अभिरुचि *(abhi-ruci)* स्त्री. taste; liking; interest.

अभिलाषित *(abhi-lāśit)* वि. desired; cherished.

अभिलाषा *(abhi-lāśa)* स्त्री. wish; desire.

अभिलाषी *(abhi-lāśi)* वि. desirous; wishing

अभिलेख *(abhi-lekh)* पु. record.

अभिलेखागार *(abhi-lekhāgār)* पु. archives.

अभिवादन *(abhi-vādan)* पु. salutation; felicitation.

अभिव्यंजक *(abhi-vyanjak)* वि. expressive.

अभिव्यंजना *(abhi-vyanjanā)* स्त्री. menifestation; expression.

अभिव्यंजित *(abhi-vyanjit)* वि. expressed.

अभिव्यक्त *(abhi-vy-akt)* वि. expressed; manifested.

अभिव्यक्ति *(abhi-vy-akti)* स्त्री. menifestation; expression.

अभिशाप *(abhi-śāp)* पु. calumny; curse; anathema.

अभिषेक *(abhi-sek)* पु. consecration; coronation.

अभिसार *(abhi-sar)* पु. rendezvous.

अभिसारिका *(abhi-sārika)* स्त्री. a woman who meets her lover clandestinely.

अभी *(abhi)* क्रि. वि. just now; yet; still; beginning.

अभीप्सा *(abhipsā)* स्त्री. aspiration.

अभीप्सित *(abhipsit)* वि. aspried; desired.

अभीष्ट *(abhîst)* वि. cherished; desired.

अभूतपूर्व *(abhut-purva)* वि. unprecedented.

अभेद्य *(a-bhedya)* वि. impenetrable; impregnable.

अभ्यंतर *(abhy-antar)* वि. interior; inner; internal.

अभ्यर्थन *(abhy-arthan)* पु. solicitation; prayer; welcome; reception.

अभ्यर्थी *(abhy-arthi)* पु. candidate.

अभ्यस्त *(abhy-ast)* वि. habituated; accustomed.

अभ्यागत *(abhy-ā-gat)* पु. guest; visitor.

अभ्यास *(abhy-ās)* पु. practice; drill.

अभ्युदय *(abhy-uday)* पु. prosperity advent; rise.

अभ्र *(abhra)* पु. sky; cloud.

अभ्रक *(abhrak)* पु. mica.

अमंगल *(a-mangal)* पु. evil; inauspiciousness; disaster.

अमंगलकारी *(amangal-kāri)* वि. inauspicious; disaster.

अमर *(a-mar)* पु. immortal; eternal

अमरूद *(amrud)* पु. guava.

अमर्यादित *(a-maryādit)* वि. improper; intemperate; undignified; unlimited.

अमल *(a-mal)* पु. execution; action; application; enforcement; practice.

अमला *(amlā)* फ. staff retinue; para phernalia.

अमली *(amali)* वि. practical.

अमानत *(amānat)* स्त्री. deposit; something given in trust.

अमानतदार *(amānat-dār)* पु. trustee.

अमानवीय *(amānāviya)* वि. cruel; inhuman.

अमानुषिक *(a-mānusik)* वि. beastly; inhuman.

अमान्य *(a-mānya)* वि. invalid; unacceptable.

अमावस, अमावस्या *(amāvas; amāvasya)* स्त्री. the last day of the dark fortnight.

अमिट *(a-mit)* वि. indelible.

अमित *(a-mit)* वि. enormous; immense; boundless; limitless.

अमीन *(amin)* पु. a junior officer appointed for land survey and revenue collection; bailiff.

अमीर *(amir)* वि. wealthy; noble

अमीरी *(amiri)* स्त्री. richness; wealthness: nobility.

अमुक *(amuk)* वि. so and so; such and such.

अमूर्त *(a-mürt)* वि. abstract; intangible; incorporeal.

अमूल्य *(a-mulya)* वि. valuable; precious; invaluable.

अमृत *(a-mrit)* पु. nectar.

अमोघ *(a-mogh)* वि. sure; unfailing; infallible.

अम्मा *(amma)* स्त्री. mother.

अम्ल *(amla)* पु. acid.

अम्लता *(amlata)* स्त्री. sourness; acidity.

अम्लान *(a-mlān)* वि. unfaded; bright; clear; fresh.

अयश *(a-yas)* पु. infamy; disgrace.

अयोग्य *(a-yogya)* वि. unqualified; ineligible; unworthy; unfit; incompetent; unable.

अयोग्यता *(a-yogyatā)* स्त्री. disqualification; unworthiness; unfitness; inability; incompetence.

अरक़, अर्क़ *(araq)* पु. distilled extract; essence.

अरण्य *(aranya)* पु. forest; jungle.

अरमान *(armān)* पु. aspiration.

अरसिक *(a-rasik)* वि. inaesthetic.

अराजक *(a-rājak)* वि. anarchical; chaotic.

अराजकता *(a-rājakatā)* स्त्री. anarchy; chaos; lawlessness.

अराजकतावाद *(arājaktāvad)* पु. anarchism.

अराजपत्रित *(arāj-patrit)* वि. nongazetted.

अरारूट, अरारोट *(arārut; arārota)* पु. arrow-root.

अरि *(ari)* पु. enemy; foe.

अरिष्ट *(a-rist)* पु. misfortune; disaster.

अरुचि *(a-ruci)* स्त्री. disinterestedness; dislike; aversion.

अरुचिकर *(aruci-kar)* वि. uninteresting; disagreeable; tasteless.

अरुणिमा *(arunimā)* स्त्री. reddish glow.

अरुणोदय *(arunodaya)* पु. dawn; daybreak.

अर्क़ *(arq)* see अरक़

अर्गल *(argal)* अर्गला स्त्री. drawbar.

अर्चन *(arcan)* पु. worship; adoration.

अर्चना *(arcanā)* स्त्री. see अर्चन.

अर्ज़ *(arz)* स्त्री. (अ.) request; supplication; width.

अर्जन *(arjan)* पु. earning; acquisition.

अर्जित *(arjit)* वि. acquired; earned.

अर्ज़ी *(arzi)* स्त्री. (अ.) application; petition.

अर्थ *(arth)* पु. meaning; wealth; money.

अर्थदंड *(arth-dand)* पु. fine; penalty.

अर्थव्यवस्था *(arth-vyavastha)* स्त्री. economy.

अर्थशास्त्र *(arth-sāstra)* पु. economics.

अर्थशास्त्री *(arth-śastri)* पु. economist.

अर्थहीन *(arth-hin)* वि. meaningless.

अर्थी *(arthi)* स्त्री. bier.

अर्दली *(ardali)* पु. orderly; attendant.

अर्ध *(ardh)* वि. half.

अर्धविराम *(ardh-viram)* पु. semi-colon.

अर्धचंद्र *(ardh-candra)* पु. half-moon; crescent.

अर्धवृत्त *(ardh-vrit)* पु. semi-circle.

अर्धसप्ताहिक *(ardh-saptahik)* वि. biweekly.

अर्धांगिनी *(ardh-āngini)* स्त्री. wife.

अर्पण *(arpan)* पु. surrender; offer.

अर्पित *(arpit)* वि. surrendered: offered.

अर्ह *(arha)* वि. competent: qualified.

अर्हता *(arhata)* स्त्री. qualification; competence.

अलंकरण *(alan-karan)* पु. decoration; ornamentation; adornment.

अलंकार *(alan-kār)* पु. ornament; embellishment; figure of speech; rhetoric.

अलंकृत *(alan-krit)* वि. decorated; ornamented.

अलख[1] *(a-lakh)* वि. imperceptible; invisible.

अलख[2] *(a-lakh)* पु. God

अलग *(a-lag)* वि. different; aloof.

अलगाव *(algāv)* पु. segregation; separation; isolation.

अलबेला *(albelā)* वि. frivolous; foppish.

अलभ्य *(a-labhya)* वि. rare; unattainable.

अलमारी *(almāri)* स्त्री. almirah; cupboard.

अलविदा *(alvidā)* स्त्री. (अ.) good bye.

अलस *(alas)* वि. idle; sluggish; lazy.

अलसता *(alsatā)* स्त्री. lethargy.

अलसाना *(alsānā)* अ. क्रि. to feel lazy; to be slack or sluggish.

अलसी *(alsi)* स्त्री. linseed.

अलाप, आलाप *(alāp)* पु. augmentation; tuning the voice for singing.

अलाभकर *(alābh-kar)* वि. unprofitable; uneconomical; unremunerative.

अली *(ali)* स्त्री. female friend.

अलिखित *(alikhit)* वि. unrecorded; unscripted; unwritten.

अलौकिक *(a-laukik)* वि. unworldly; supernatural.

अलौकिकता *(alaukikta)* स्त्री. supernaturalness; unworldliness.

अलप *(alpa)* वि. small; little; minute.

अल्पकालिक *(alpa-kālik)* वि. temporary; short-lived; ephemeral.

अल्पतम *(alpatam)* वि. minimal; minimum.

अल्पता *(alpata)* स्त्री. minuteness; smallness; insignificance.

अल्पबुद्धि *(alpabudhi)* वि. silly; idiotic.

अल्पभाषी *(alp-bhāshi)* वि. reserved; taciturn.

अल्पमत *(alp-mat)* पु. minority.

अल्पायु *(alpāyu)* स्त्री. young age.

अल्पाहार *(alpāhār)* पु. abstemiousness; abstinence; meagre diet.

अल्पाहारी *(alpāhāri)* वि. abstemious; abstinent.

अल्लाह *(allāh)* पु. (अ.) God.

अल्हड़ *(alhar)* वि. childishly carefree.

अल्हड़पन *(alharpan)* पु. carefree disposition.

अवकाश *(ava-kāś)* पु. leave; vacation; holiday; leisure.

अवगत *(ava-gat)* वि. informed; apprised.

अवगाहन *(ava-gāhan)* पु. bathing; immersion; profound study.

अवगुंठन *(ava-gunthan)* वि. veil; concealment.

अवगुण *(ava-gun)* पु. demerit; defect; vice; fault.

अवचेतन *(ava-cetan)* वि. subconscious.

अवज्ञा *(avajna)* स्त्री. disobedience.

अवतरण *(ava-taran)* पु. descent; landing; passage; incarnation.

अवतरित *(ava-tarit)* वि. descended; incarnated.

अवतार *(ava-tār)* पु. incarnation.

अवतीर्ण *(ava-tirn)* वि. incarnated; descended.

अवधारणा *(ava-dhāranā)* स्त्री. conception.

अवधि *(ava-dhi)* स्त्री. period; duration; term; tenure.

अवनत *(ava-nat)* वि. bent; depressed.

अवनति *(avanati)* स्त्री. degradation; decadence; downfall; degeneration.

अवनि, अवनी *(avani)* स्त्री. earth.

अवमान *(avamān)* पु. humiliation; disrespect; contempt.

अवमूल्यन *(ava-mulyan)* पु. devaluation.

अवयव *(ava-yav)* पु. portion; part;

limb; component; ingredient; constituent; organ.

अवयस्क *(avyasak)* वि. minor.

अवयस्कता *(avyasaktā)* स्त्री. minority.

अवर *(avar)* वि. junior; inferior.

अवरुद्ध *(ava-ruddh)* वि. hindered; obstructed; impeded; closed; frozen; stalled; muffled; blocked.

अवरोध *(ava-rodh)* पु. hindrance; obstruction; impediment; restraint; obstacle.

अवरोधक *(ava-rodhak)* वि. arresting; censorious.

अवरोह *(ava-roh)* पु. descension.

अवरोही *(avarohi)* वि. falling; descending; regressive.

अवर्णनीय *(avarnaniya)* वि. ineffable; indescribable.

अवलंब *(ava-lamb)* अवलंबन पु. support; dependence.

अवलि, अवली *(avali)* स्त्री. row; line.

अवलेह *(ava-leh)* पु. jelly; confection.

अवलोकन *(ava-lokan)* पु. observation; scanning; examination.

अवशिष्ट *(ava-śiṣt)* वि. remaining; residuary; residual.

अवशेष *(ava-ses)* पु. residue; remainder; remains; remnant; vestige.

अवशोषक *(avśoshak)* वि. absorption.

अवशोषण *(avśoshan)* पु. absorption.

अवश्यंभावी *(avaśyambhavi)* वि. inevitable.

अवश्य *(a-vaśya)* अवश्यमेव क्रि. वि. certainly; necessarily; definitely; surely.

अवसर *(ava-sar)* पु. chance; opportunity; occasion.

अवसाद *(avsād)* पु. gloom; languor; lassitude; dejection; melancholy; depression.

अवसान *(avasān)* पु. end; termination; terminal; death.

अवस्था *(ava-sthā)* स्त्री. state; condition.

अवस्थिति *(ava-sthiti)* स्त्री. location.

अवहेलना *(ava-helanā)* अवहेला स्त्री. neglect; desiregard; contempt.

अवांछनीय *(avānchniya)* वि. unwanted; unwelcome; undesired.

अवाक् *(avāk)* वि. stunned; wonderstruck; speechless; tongue-tied.

अवास्तविक *(avāstavik)* वि. unreal; fake.

अविकल *(avikal)* वि. unabridged; intact; indentical.

अविकसित *(avikasit)* वि. undeveloped.

अविचल *(avi-cal)* वि. motionless; steady; firm; resolute.

अविचारित *(avi-chārit)* वि. not well thought out; off hand; hasty.

अविचारी *(avi- cāri)* वि. injudicious; thoughtless.

अविजित *(avi-jit)* वि. unconquered; unvanquished.

अविद्यमान *(avidyamān)* वि. non-existent.

अविद्या *(a-vidyā)* स्त्री. ignorance; nescience.

अविनय *(avi-nay)* स्त्री. impolite; immodest; impertinent.

अविनयी *(avi-nayi)* वि. impolite; immodest; impertinent.

अविनाशी *(avi-naśi)* वि. immortal; indestructible; imperishable.

अविनीत *(avi-nit)* वि. impolite; impertinent.

अविभक्त *(avi-bhakt)* **अविभाजित** वि. undivided.

अविरल *(avi-ral)* वि. continuous; uninterrupted; incessant.

अविराम *(aviram)* वि. non-stop; incessant; continuous.

अविलंब *(avi-lamb)* क्रि. वि. without delay; at once; forwith.

अविवाहित *(avi-vāhit)* वि. unmarried; celibate.

अविवेक *(avi-vek)* पु. indiscretion; imprudence; indiscrimination.

अविश्वसनीय *(avi-śvasniya)* वि. unreliable; untrustworthy; unbelievable; incredible.

अविश्वास *(avi-svas)* पु. distrust; disbelief; lack of confidence.

अविस्मरणीय *(a-vismarniya)* वि. unforgettable.

अवैतनिक *(avaitnik)* वि. honorary.

अवैध *(a-vaidh)* वि. illegal; unlawful; illegitimate; illicit.

अवैधानिक *(a-vaidhanik)* वि. unconstitutional.

अव्यक्त *(a-vyakt)* वि. imperceptible; indistinct; obscure; not apparent or manifest; latent.

अव्यवस्था *(a-vyavastha)* स्त्री. disorder; lawlessness; disarray; confusion; chaos.

अव्यवस्थित *(a-vyavsthit)* वि. disorderly; unsystematic; chaotic.

अव्यावसायिक *(avyavsayik)* वि. non-professional.

अव्यावहारिक *(a-vyavaharik)* वि. not feasible; impractical; impracticable.

अशक्त *(a-sakt)* वि. feeble; weak; invalid.

अशक्तता *(aśaktata)* स्त्री. disability; infirmity; invalidity.

अशर्फ़ी *(asrafi)* स्त्री. (फ़ा.) a gold coin.

अशांत *(a-śant)* वि. agitated; restless; unquiet; disturbed.

अशांति *(a-santi)* स्त्री. unrest; agitation; disturbance; turbulence.

अशासकीय *(asaskiya)* वि. non-official.

अशिक्षा *(a-siksa)* स्त्री. illiteracy; absence of education.

अशिक्षित *(a-śiksit)* वि. illiterate; uneducated.

अशिष्ट *(a-śist)* वि. ill-mannered; rudeimpolite; immodest; vulgar.

अशिष्टता *(a-śistatā)* स्त्री. impoliteness; rudeness; ill-manners; valgarity.

अशुद्ध *(a-śuddh)* वि. impure; incorrect.

अशुद्धि *(a-śuddhi)* पु. mistake; error; inaccuracy.

अशुभ *(a-śubh)* वि. inauspicious; evilomened.

अशोभनीय *(a-śobhaniya)* वि. undignified; unseemly; unbecoming.

अश्क *(aśk)* पु. (फ़ा.) tears.

अश्मरी *(aśmari)* स्त्री. calculas.

अश्रु *(aśru)* पु. tear.

अश्लील *(a-ślil)* वि. obscene; vulgar.

अश्लीलता *(a-ślilatā)* स्त्री. obscenity; vulgarity.

अश्व *(aśva)* पु. horse.

अश्वशाला *(aśvaśālā)* स्त्री. stable.

अश्वारोहण *(asvārohan)* पु. horseman; cavalier.

अष्टपाद *(aśtapād)* वि. octopus.

अष्टबाहु *(aśt-bāhu)* पु. octopus.

अष्टभुज *(aśt-bhuj)* पु. octagon.

असंगठित *(asangathit)* वि. unorganised.

असंगत *(a-sangat)* वि. inconsistent; irrelevant; incoherent; anomalous; incompatible; discordant; incongruous.

असंगति *(a-sangati)* स्त्री. incoherence; irrelevance; anomaly; inconsistency; incongruity; incompatibility.

असंतुलन *(asantulan)* पु. disequilibrium; imbalance.

असंतुलित *(asantulit)* वि. erratic; unbalanced.

असंतुष्ट *(a-san-tust)* वि. discontented; dissatisfied; aggrieved.

असंतोष *(a-san-toś)* पु. discontentment; dissatisfaction; unrest.

असंदिग्ध *(a-san-digdh)* वि. definite; certain; doubtless; indubitable.

असंबद्ध *(a-sam-baddh)* वि. incoherent; irrelevant; disconnected.

असंभव *(a-sam-bhav)* वि. impossible.

असंयत *(a-sam-yat)* वि. immoderate; intemperate: unrestrained.

असंयमित *(a-sam-yamit)* वि. unrestrained.

असत्य *(a-satya)* वि. false; unture.

असत्यता *(a-satyatā)* स्त्री. falsehood; untruth.

असफल *(a-safal)* वि. unsuccessful.

असफलता *(a-safaltā)* स्त्री. failure.

असबाब *(asbāb)* पु. (अ.) luggage; baggage; goods and chattles; belongings.

असभ्य *(a-sabhya)* वि. uncivilized; savage discourteous; ill-bred

असभ्यता *(a-sabhyatā)* स्त्री. uncivility; savageness: indecency; vulgarity.

असमंजस *(a-sam-anjas)* पु. dilemma; fix.

असम *(a-sam)* वि. uneven; unequal; unmatching; dissimilar.

असमता *(a-samatā)* स्त्री. inequality: disparity: unevenness.

असमय *(a-samay)* क्रि. वि. untimely; out of season; inopportunely.

असमर्थ *(a-sam-arth)* वि. incompetent; incapable; unable; disabled.

असमर्थता *(a-sam-arthatā)* स्त्री. incompetence; incapability; inability.

असमान *(a-samān)* वि. uneven; unequal; dissimilar.

असमानता *(a-samāntā)* स्त्री. disparity; inequality; dissimilarity.

असम्मत *(a-sam-mat)* वि. dissenting.

असम्मति *(a-sam-mati)* स्त्री. disagreement; discordance.

असर *(asar)* पु. (अ.) effect; influence; impression.

असल *(asl)* वि. (अ.) original; pure; real; genuine.

असलियत *(asliyat)* स्त्री. (अ.) reality; bonafides; fact.

असली *(asli)* वि. real; true; pure; genuine.

असह *(asah)* वि. unbearable; intolerable.

असहनशील *(a-sahansil)* वि. intolerant.

असहनीय *(a-sahniya)* वि. intolerable; unbearable; unendurable.

असहमत *(a-sahmat)* वि. disagreeing; dissenting.

असहमति *(a-sahmati)* स्त्री. disagreement.

असहयोग *(a-sahyog)* पु. non-cooperation.

असहिष्णु *(a-sahisnu)* वि. intolerant; unenduring.

असह्य *(a-sahya)* वि. intolerable; unbearable.

असांसद *(asāmsad)* वि. unparliamentary.

असाधारण *(a-sādhāran)* वि. unusual; extra-ordinary; exceptional: uncommon.

असाधारणता *(a-sadharantā)* स्त्री. unusualness: uncommonness.

असाध्य *(a-sadhya)* वि. incurable; impracticable; incorrigible.

असाध्यता *(asādhyatā)* स्त्री. incorrigibility; incurability.

असामाजिक *(a-sāmājik)* वि. unsocial; unsocialble; anti-social.

असामान्य *(a-sāmānya)* वि. uncommon; exceptional; extra-ordinary.

असार *(a-sār)* वि. unsubstantial; worthless; immaterial.

असावधान *(a-sāvadhan)* वि. careless; negligent.

असावधानी *(a-sāvadhani)* स्त्री. negligence; carelessness.

असि *(asi)* स्त्री. sword.

असीम *(a-sim)* वि. boundless; unlimited; infinite.

असीमित *(a-simit)* वि. boundless; unlimited; infinite.

असुंदर *(a-sundar)* वि. ugly; charmless.

असुर *(asur)* पु. demon; devil.

असुरक्षा *(a-suraksha)* स्त्री. insecurity.

असुरक्षित *(a-surakshit)* वि. insecure; unsafe.

असुविधा *(a-suvidhā)* स्त्री. inconvenience.

अस्त *(ast)* वि. set; sunk.

अस्तबल *(astabal)* पु. (अ.) stable.

अस्तर *(astar)* पु. lining of a garment; inner coating or colour or varnish.

अस्तव्यस्त *(asta-vyast)* वि. scattered; confused; helter-skelter.

अस्तव्यस्तता *(astavyastatā)* स्त्री. disorderliness; confusion.

अस्ताचल *(astācal)* पु. the western mountain behind which the sun is supposed to set.

अस्तित्व *(astitva)* पु. existence; entity; being.

अस्त्र *(astra)* पु. weapon; missile.

अस्त्र-शस्त्र *(astra-śastra)* पु. arms and weapons; weaponary; armament.

अस्त्रशाला *(astr-śālā)* स्त्री. arsenal; armoury.

अस्त्रगार *(astrāgār)* पु. see अस्त्रशाला.

अस्थायी *(a-sthāyi)* वि. temporary.

अस्थि *(asthi)* स्त्री. bone.

अस्थि-पंजर *(asthi-panjar)* पु. skeleton of bones.

अस्थिर *(a-sthir)* वि. instable; unsteady; fickle; wavering; variable.

अस्थिरता *(a-sthiratā)* स्त्री. instability; inconsistancy; fickleness.

अस्पताल *(aspatāl)* पु. hospital.

अस्पताल गाड़ी *(aspatāl-gāri)* स्त्री. ambulance.

अस्पष्ट *(a-spaśt)* वि. obscure; vague; ambiguous; indistinct; blurred; confusing.

अस्पष्टता *(a-spastatā)* स्त्री. ambiguity; vagueness; indistinctness.

अस्पृश्य *(a-spriśya)* वि. untouchable.

अस्पृश्यता *(a-sprśyatā)* स्त्री. untouchability.

अस्मिता *(asmitā)* स्त्री. pride; vanity.

अस्वस्थ *(asvasth)* वि. unhealthy; indisposed.

अस्वस्थता *(asvasthatā)* स्त्री. illness; indisposition.

अस्वाभाविक *(asvasbhāvik)* वि. unnatural.

अस्वाभाविकता *(asvabhāviktā)* स्त्री.

unnaturalness.

अस्वीकृत *(a-svikrit)* वि. refused; rejected.

अस्वीकृति *(a-svikriti)* स्त्री. non-acceptance; rejection.

अहंकार *(ahamkār)* पु. egotism.

अहंकारी *(ahamkari)* वि. egoistical; vain.

अहमियत *(ahmiyat)* स्त्री. importance; significance.

अहलकार *(ahlkār)* पु. (अ.) clerk; functionary.

अहस्तांतरणीय *(a-hastātantarniya)* वि. non-transferable.

अहस्तांतरित *(a-hastāntrit)* वि. not transferred.

अहाता *(ahāta)* पु. (अ.) enclosure; compound; precinets; premises.

अहिंसा *(a-himsā)* स्त्री. non-violence.

अहिंसात्मक *(ahimsatmak)* वि. non-violent.

अहित *(a-hit)* पु. damage; harm; injury.

अहितकर *(ahitkar)* वि. harmful; injurious.

अहेर *(aher)* पु. hunting.

अहेरी *(aheri)* पु. hunter; stalker.

आ

आ *(ā)* the second letter and second vowel of Devnagri alphabet.

आँकड़े *(āmkre)* पु. data; statistics; figures.

आँकना *(āmkanā)* स. क्रि. to assess; to estimate; to evaluate; to appraise.

आँख *(āmkh)* स्त्री. eye.

आँगन *(āmgan)* पु. courtyard.

आँच *(āmc)* स्त्री. fire; harm.

आँचल *(āmcal)* पु. the extreme part of sari; region; border.

आंचलिक *(āmcalik)* वि. regional; zonal.

आँत *(āmt)* स्त्री. intestine.

आँतरिक *(āntarik)* वि. internal; domestic.

आंदोलन *(āndolan)* पु. movement; agitation; campaign; drive.

आँधी *(āmdhi)* स्त्री. dust storm; windstorm.

आँवला *(āmvla)* पु. emblic myrobalan.

आंशिक *(āmsik)* वि. partial; fractional; fragmentary.

आँसू *(āmsu)* पु. tear.

आइंदा *(āinda)* क्रि. वि (फ़ा.) in future.

आईना *(āinā)* पु. (फ़ा.) mirror; looking glass.

आकर *(ā-kar)* पु. treasure.

आकर्षक *(ā-karsak)* वि. attractive; charming.

आकर्षण *(ā-karsan)* पु. attraction; charm.

आकर्षित *(ā-karsit)* वि. attracted; charmed.

आकलन *(ā-kalan)* पु. estimate; calculation.

आकस्मिक *(ākasmik)* वि. sudden; abrupt; accidental.

आकस्मिकता *(ākasmikatā)* स्त्री. contingency; suddenness.

आकांक्षा *(ā-kanksā)* स्त्री. aspiration.

आकांक्षी *(ā-kanksi)* वि. aspirant.

आकार *(ā-kār)* पु. size; form; shape.

आकाश *(ā-kās)* पु. sky; space.

आकाशगंगा *(ākās-gangā)* स्त्री. milky way.

आकाशवाणी *(ākāsvāni)* स्त्री. oracle; radio voice from sky.

आकुल *(ākul)* वि. uneasy; restless; distressed.

आकुलता *(ākulatā)* स्त्री. worry; uneasiness; restlessness.

आकृति *(ā-kriti)* स्त्री. figure; shape; form.

आक्रमण *(ā-kraman)* पु. attack; invasion; aggression; assault.

आक्रमणकारी *(ākrmankāri)* वि. aggressor; invador.

आक्रामक[1] *(ā-krāmak)* पु. invader; aggressor.

आक्रामक[2] *(ā-krāmak)* वि. aggressive.

आक्रामकता *(ākrāmaktā)* स्त्री. aggressiveness.

आक्रोश *(ā-kroś)* पु. wrath; anger; resentment.

आक्षेप *(ā-ksep)* पु. accusation; allegation; charge.

आख़िरकार *(ākhirkār)* क्रि. वि. after all; in the end; at last; ultimately.

आख़िरी *(ākhiri)* वि. (अ.) ultimate; last; final.

आखेट *(ā-khet)* पु. hunting.

आख्या *(ā-khyā)* स्त्री. remark; report.

आगंतुक *(āgantuk)* पु. visitor.

आग *(āg)* स्त्री. fire; passion; lust.

आगज़नी *(āgzani)* स्त्री. arson.

आगमन *(ā-gaman)* स्त्री. arrival.

आगा *(āga)* पु. frontage; front; face.

आगामी *(ā-gāmi)* वि. forthcoming; ensuing; next; future; subsequent.

आगार *(ā-gār)* पु. depository; treasury; store house.

आगाह *(āgāh)* वि. (फ़ा.) apprised; warned; cautioned.

आगे *(āge)* क्रि. वि. forward; onward; ahead; in front; in future.

आग्नेयास्त्र *(āgneyastra)* पु. fire-arms; fire-emitting missile.

आग्रह *(ā-grah)* पु. insistence; pertinance.

आघात *(ā-ghāt)* पु. accent (ling.); shock; blow; stroke; hit; impact.

आचमन *(ā-caman)* पु. sipping water from the palm of the hand.

आचरण *(ā-caran)* पु. conduct; behaviour; practice.

आचार *(ā-cār)* पु. moral conduct; behaviour.

आचार-विचार *(ācār-vicār)* पु. manners and morals.

आचारसंहिता *(ācār-samhitā)* स्त्री. moral code.

आचार्य *(ā-cārya)* पु. professor; teacher; preceptor.

आच्छादन *(ā-chādan)* पु. covering roof.

आच्छादित *(ā-cchādit)* वि. covered.

आज *(aj)* क्रि. वि. today; at present.

आजकल *(ājkal)* क्रि. वि. now-a-days.

आजन्म *(ā-janm)* क्रि. वि. since birth; as long as one is alive.

आज़माइश *(āzmāis)* स्त्री. (फ़ा.) test; trial.

आज़ाद *(āzād)* वि. (फ़ा.) independent; free.

आज़ादी *(āzādi)* स्त्री. (फ़ा.) freedom; independence.

आजीवन *(ā-jivan)* वि. lifelong.

आजीविका *(ā-jivikā)* स्त्री. livelihood.

आज्ञा *(ā-jnā)* स्त्री. order; command.

आज्ञाकारिता *(ājnākāritā)* स्त्री. obedience.

आज्ञाकारी *(ājnākāri)* वि. obedient.

आज्ञापालक *(agnā-pālak)* वि. obedient.

आटा *(ātā)* पु. flour.

आडंबर *(ādambar)* पु. imposture; affection.

आड़ *(ar)* स्त्री. screen; cover; coverage; barricade.

आड़ा *(ārā)* वि. transverse; horizontal; oblique.

आड़ू *(arū)* पु. peach.

आढ़तिया *(ārhatiyā)* पु. commission agent; broker

आतंक *(ā-tank)* पु. terror; panic.

आतंकवाद *(ātank-vad)* पु. terrorism

आतंकित *(ā-tankit)* वि. terrorised; panicstricken; panicky.

आततायी *(ā-tatāyi)* पु. tyrant; oppressor.

आतिशबाज़ी *(ātisbāzi)* स्त्री. (फा.) fire works; display of fire works.

आतिथेय *(ātitheya)* पु. host.

आतिथ्य *(ātithya)* पु. hospitality.

आतुर *(ā-tur)* वि. eager; impatient; rash; hasty; restless.

आतुरता *(ā-turata)* स्त्री. impatience; eagerness; rashness; hastiness; restlessness.

आत्म *(ātm)* वि. pertaining to the soul; own; personal.

आत्मकथा *(ātm-kathā)* स्त्री. autobiography.

आत्मकेंद्रित *(ātm-kendrit)* वि. autocentric; egocentric.

आत्मगौरव *(ātm-gaurav)* पु. self-dignity.

आत्मघात *(ātm-ghāt)* पु. suicide.

आत्मचरित *(ātm-carit)* autobiography.

आत्मनिरीक्षण *(ātm-nirikshan)* पु. introspection; self-analysis.

आत्मनिर्भर *(ātm nirbhar)* वि. self-reliant; self-sufficient.

आत्म-प्रशंसा *(ātm-prasamsā)* स्त्री. self-praise.

आत्मबल *(ātm-bal)* पु. will power.

आत्मरक्षा *(ātm-rakshā)* स्त्री. self-defence.

आत्मविश्वास *(ātm-visvās)* पु. self-confidence.

आत्मशुद्धि *(ātm-śuddhi)* स्त्री. self-purification.

आत्मसंयम *(ātm-samyam)* पु. self-restraint.

आत्मसमर्पण *(ātm-samarpan)* पु. resignation; capitulation; surrender.

आत्महत्या *(ātm-hatyā)* स्त्री. suicide.

आत्मा *(ātmā)* स्त्री. soul; spirit.

आत्माभिमान *(ātmā-bhimān)* पु. self-respect.

आत्मानुभूति *(ātmānubhuti)* स्त्री. self-realisation.

आत्मिक *(ātmik)* वि. spiritual.

आत्मीय *(ātmiya)* पु. relatives; kith and kin.

आत्मीयता *(ātmiyatā)* स्त्री. intimacy; close affinity; cordiality.

आत्मोत्कर्ष *(ātmotkarśa)* पु. eudaemonia; self-elevation.

आत्मोन्नति *(ātmonnati)* स्त्री. self-elevation.

आदत *(ādat)* स्त्री. (अ.) habit; custom.

आदम *(ādam)* पु. (अ.) adam; man.

आदमखोर *(ādamkhor)* पु. (अ.) man-eater; cannibal.

आदमी *(ādmi)* पु. (अ.) man; person; adult; husband.

आदमीयत *(ādmiyat)* स्त्री. humanity.

आदर *(ā-dar)* पु. regard; esteem;

honour; respect; reverence.

आदरणीय *(ā-daraniy)* वि. respectable; honourable.

आदर-सत्कार *(ādar-satkār)* पु. hospitality.

आदर्श *(ā-darś)* पु. ideal; model.

आदर्शवाद *(ādarś-vād)* पु. idealism.

आदान *(ā-dān)* पु. receiving; taking; accepting; borrowing.

आदाब *(ādāb)* पु. (फ़ा.) salutation; compliment.

आदि *(ādi)* पु. beginning; origin; source.

आदिक *(ādik)* वि. initial.

आदिम *(ādim)* वि. primitive; aboriginal.

आदिवासी[1] *(ādivāsi)* पु. aborigine.

आदिवासी[2] *(ādivāsi)* वि. aboriginal.

आदी *(ādi)* वि. (अ.) habituated; accustomed.

आदेश *(ā-deś)* पु. command; behest; order.

आद्यक्षर *(ādyakshar)* पु. initials.

आद्योपांत *(ādyopānt)* क्रि. वि. from beginning to end.

आधा *(ādhā)* वि. half.

आधार *(ā-dhār)* पु. base; basis; ground; foundation.

आधारभूत *(ā-dhār-bhūt)* वि. fundamental; basic.

आधार-स्तम्भ *(ādhār-stambh)* पु. main support.

आधारित *(ā-dhārit)* वि. based; founded.

आधिकारिक *(ādhikārik)* वि. authoritative; official.

आधिक्य *(ādhikya)* पु. excess; surplus; abundance; plenty.

आधिपत्य *(ādhipatya)* पु. supremacy dominion; sovereignty

आधुनिक *(ādhunik)* वि. modern.

आधुनिकता *(ādhunikatā)* वि. modernity.

आधुनिकीकरण *(ādhunikikaran)* पु. modernisation.

आध्यात्मिक *(ādhyātmik)* वि. spiritual.

आनंद *(ā-nand)* पु. bliss; happiness; pleasure; joy; delight.

आनंदमय *(ānand-maya)* वि. blissful; delightful.

आनंदित *(ā-nandit)* वि. happy; delighted.

आन *(ān)* स्त्री. prestige; honour; dignity.

आनन *(ānan)* पु. face; mouth.

आनन-फानन *(ānan-fānan)* क्रि. वि. instantaneously; at once.

आना *(ānā)* अ. कि. to come; to reach; to arrive.

आना-कानी *(ānākāni)* स्त्री. evasion; hesitation.

आनुपातिक *(ānupātik)* वि. proportionate.

आनुवंशिक *(ānuvamśik)* वि. hereditary.

आनुवंशिकता *(ānuvanśikta)* स्त्री. heredity.

आप *(āp)* सर्व. you; one's self.

आपत्काल *(āpatkāl)* पु. emergency.

आपत्ति *(a-patti)* स्त्री. objection.

आपत्तिजनक *(āpattijanak)* वि. objectionable.

आपदा *(ā-padā)* स्त्री. calamity; peril; suffering; distress; adversity.

आपसदारी *(āpasdāri)* स्त्री. mutuality; brotherhood; fraternity.

आपसी *(āpasi)* वि. reciprocal; mutual.

आपा *(āpā)* पु. ego; vanity; arrogance; consciousness; one's own entity; self.

आपात *(ā-pat)* पु. catastrophe; emergency.

आपातिक *(āpātik)* वि. emergent; contingent.

आपूर्ति *(ā-pürti)* स्त्री. supply.

आपेक्षिक *(āpekśik)* वि. relative.

आप्लावन *(ā-plāvan)* पु. inundation; immersion.

आप्लावित *(ā-plāvit)* वि. inundated; immersed.

आफ़त *(āfat)* स्त्री. (अ.) trouble; distress; calamity; misfortune.

आफ़ताब *(āftāb)* पु. (फ़ा.) the sun.

आब *(āb)* स्त्री. brilliance; water.

आबकारी *(ābkāri)* स्त्री. (फ़ा.) excise; distillery.

आबद्ध *(ā-baddh)* वि. bound; enclosed.

आबनूस *(ābnüs)* पु. ebony.

आबपाशी *(āb-pāsi)* स्त्री. (फ़ा.) irrigation.

आबरू *(ābrü)* स्त्री. (फ़ा.) chastity; honour; dignity.

आबहवा *(āb-hawā)* स्त्री. (फ़ा.) climate.

आबाद *(ābād)* वि. (फ़ा.) populated; inhabited; flourishing; prosperous.

आबादी *(ābādi)* स्त्री. population; habitation; colony.

आभा *(ā-bhā)* स्त्री. splendour; lustre; tint; tinge.

आभार *(ā-bhār)* पु. obligation; gratitude; thankfulness.

आभारी *(ā-bhāri)* वि. grateful; obliged; thankful.

आभास *(ā-bhās)* पु. glimpse; inkling; semblance.

आभूषण *(ā-bhüsan)* पु. ornament; jewellery; decoration; embellishment.

आभूषित *(ā-bhüsit)* वि. ornamented; decorated; embellished.

आमंत्रण *(āmantran)* पु. invitation.

आमंत्रित *(ā-mantrit)* वि. invited.

आम[1] *(ām)* पु. mango.

आम[2] *(ām)* वि. (अ.) commom; general; public.

आमद *(āmad)* स्त्री. (फ़ा.) aproach; arrival; income.

आमदनी *(āmadani)* स्त्री. (फ़ा.) income

आमना-सामना *(āmnā-sāmnā)* पु. confrontation; encounter; coming face to face.

आमरण *(āmaran)* क्रि. वि. till death.

आमादा *(āmāda)* वि. (फ़ा.) bent upon; intent; adamant; determined.

आमाशय *(āmāsaya)* पु. stomach.

आमिष *(āmiś)* पु. meat.

आमुख *(ā-mukh)* पु. preamble; preface.

आमूल[1] *(ā-mül)* वि. fundamental; radical.

आमूल[2] *(ā-mül)* क्रि. वि. completely.

आमोद *(ā-mod)* पु. joy; pleasure; delight; amusement; merriment.

आय *(āye)* स्त्री. income; earning; receipt; proceeds; revenue.

आयकर *(āyekar)* पु. income tax.

आयत *(āyāt)* पु. rectangle.

आयतन *(ā-yatan)* पु. volume; bulk; capacity.

आयताकार *(āyatākār)* वि. rectangular.

आय-व्ययक (āye-vyayak) पु. budget.

आया *(āyā)* स्त्री. nurse.

आयात *(ā-yāt)* पु. import.

आयातित *(ā-yātit)* वि. imported.

आयाम *(ā-yām)* पु. amplitude; width; extension; expansion.

आयु *(āyu)* स्त्री. age.

आयुक्त *(ā-yukt)* पु. commissioner.

आयुध *(ā-yudh)* पु. armament; arms; weapon.

आयुधशाला (*āyudhsālā*) **आयुधागार** (*ayudhagar*) पु. arsenal; armoury.

आयुर्विज्ञान *(ayurvijnan)* पु. medical science.

आयुर्वेद (*āyurved*) पु. the Indian medical system; medical science.

आयोग *(ā-yog)* पु. commission.

आयोजक (*ā-yojak*) पु. sponsor; convener; organiser.

आयोजन (*ā-yojan*) पु. sponsoring; convening; planning; organising; arrangenment.

आयोजित *(ā-yojit)* वि. arranged; convened; sponsored; organised.

आरंभ *(ā-rambh)* पु. beginning; start; outset; commencement; inception; origin.

आरंभिक *(ā-rambhik)* वि. preliminary; initial; elementary.

आरक्षक *(ā-raksak)* पु. reservation; protection.

आरक्षित *(ā-raksit)* वि. reserved.

आरती *(ārati)* स्त्री. ceremonial adoration with kindled lamps.

आरसी *(ārsi)* स्त्री. mirror; looking glass.

आरा *(ārā)* पु. saw.

आराधाक *(ā-rādhak)* पु. worshipper; adorer; devotee.

आराधना *(ā-rādhaṇā)* पु. worship; adoration.

आराम *(ārām)* पु. (फ़ा.) rest; relief; comfort; ease.

आरामतलब *(ārāmtalab)* वि. (फ़ा.) indolent; easy going; slothful.

आरामदेह *(ārāmdeh)* वि. comfortable.

आरी *(āri)* स्त्री. small saw; table-saw.

आरूढ़ *(ā-rürh)* वि. ascended; mounted.

आरेख *(ārekh)* पु. diagram.

आरेखन (*ārekhan*) पु. drawing.

आरोग्य *(ārogya)* पु. health; freedom from disease.

आरोग्यशाला (*ārogyaśālā*) स्त्री. nursing home; sanitorium.

आरोप *(ā-rop)* पु. allegation; charge; projection; imposition; superimposition.

आरोपण (*ā-ropan*) पु. superimposition; imposition; transplantation.

आरोहण *(ā-rohan)* पु. ascent; embarkation; progression.

आरोही (*ā-rohi*) पु. rider.

आर्थिक *(ārthik)* वि. economic; pecuniary; financial.

आर्द्र *(ārdra)* वि. damp; wet; moist; humid.

आर्द्रता *(ardrata)* स्त्री. dampness; humidity; wetness.

आलंकारिक *(ālankarik)* वि. ornamental; decorative; figurative; rhetorical.

आलंबन *(a-lamban)* पु. dependence; support; foundation; base.

आलय *(ālay)* पु. house; abode; dwelling place; assylum.

आलस, आलस्य *(ālas; ālasya)* पु. laziness; sloth; lethargy.

आलसी *(ālsi)* वि. lazy; lethargic.

आला *(ālā)* पु. niche; recess.

आलाप *(ā-lāp)* पु. preliminary modulation of vioce for singing conversation; dialogue.

आलिंगन *(ā-lingan)* पु. embrace; clasp; hug.

आलीशान (*āliśan*) वि. (अ.) grand; magnificent; stately; superb;

imposing.

आलू *(ālu)* पु. potato.

आलूचा *(ālūcā)* पु. plum.

आलू बुख़ारा *(ālūbukhārā)* पु. dried plum.

आलेख *(ā-lekh)* पु. sketch; graph; treatise; plan; dictation; script; document; record.

आलेखन *(ālekhan)* पु. graphic representation; writing; painting; sketching; dictation.

आलोक *(ā-lok)* पु. light; lustre; enlightenment.

आलोकित *(ālokit)* वि. lit; lighted; illuminated.

आलोचक *(ālocak)* पु. critic; reviewer.

आलोचना *(ā-locanā)* स्त्री. criticism; observation; review.

आलोचनात्मक *(ālocanātmak)* वि. critical.

आलोड़न *(ā-loran)* पु. act of shaking; stirring; churning.

आलोड़ित *(ā-lorit)* वि. stirred; shaken; agitated.

आवंटन *(ā-vantan)* पु. allotment.

आवक *(āvak)* पु. arrival; incoming goods.

आवभगत *(āvbhagat)* स्त्री. hospitality; reception; welcome.

आवरण *(ā-varan)* पु. cover; wrapper; sheath; mask; coat; screen.

आवर्तक *(ā-vartak)* वि. recurring.

आवर्तन *(ā-vartan)* पु. recurrence; rotation; revolution; repetition.

आवर्ती *(ā-varti)* वि. recurring; recurrent; recursive.

आवश्यक *(āvaśyak)* वि. necessary; important; essential; obligatory; inevitable.

आवश्यकता *(āvasyakatā)* स्त्री. want; need; inevitability; necessity; requirement.

आवागमन *(āvāgaman)* पु. transmigration; coming and going; transport.

आवाज़ *(āvāz)* स्त्री. (फ़ा.) voice; sound; report; call.

आवारगी *(āvārgi)* **आवारागर्दी** *(āvārāgardi)* स्त्री. (फ़ा.) profligacy; loafing; vagrancy.

आवारा *(āvārā)* पु. (फ़ा.) vagabond; vagrant; loafer.

आवास *(ā-vās)* पु. dwelling place; residence; abode.

आवासी *(ā-vāśi)* वि. residential.

आवाह्न *(ā-vāhan)* पु. call; summoning; invocation.

आविर्भाव *(āvir-bhāv)* पु. emergency; advent; apearance; manifestation.

आविर्भूत *(āvir-bhut)* वि. emerged; manifested; risen.

आविष्करण *(āvis-karan)* आविष्कार पु. invention.

आविष्कर्त्ता *(āvis-kartā)* आविष्कार पु. inventor.

आविष्कृत *(āvis-krit)* वि. invented.

आवृत्ति *(ā-vritti)* स्त्री. frequency: repetition; recurrence; reversion: reprint.

आवेग *(ā-veg)* पु. impetus; impluse; passion; emotion.

आवेदक *(ā-vedak)* पु. applicant; petitioner.

आवदेन *(ā-vedan)* पु. application.

आवेश *(ā-ves)* पु. intense emotion; frenzy; passion; agitation.

आशंका *(ā-sanka)* स्त्री. apprehension; fear; doubt.

आशंकित *(ā-śankit)* वि. apprehensive.

आशय *(ā-śay)* पु. meaning; purport; intention; intent.

आशा *(āsā)* स्त्री. hope; aspiration.

आशाजनक *(āsājanak)* वि. hopeful.

आशातीत *(āśātit)* वि. beyond hope or expectation; unexpected.

आशावान *(āśāvān)* वि. optimistic; hopeful.

आशाहीन *(āśāhin)* वि. disappointed; disgusted; hopeless.

आशिक़ *(āśiq)* पु. (अ.) lover.

आशिक़ी *(āśiqi)* स्त्री. (अ) love-making; amorousness.

आशीर्वचन *(ā-sirvaccm)* **आशीर्वाद** पु. blessing words of benediction.

आशु *(āsu)* वि. quick; prompt; speedy; extempre.

आशुलिपि *(āśulipi)* स्त्री. shorthand; stenography.

आश्चर्य *(āscarya)* पु. surprise; astonishment; wonder.

आश्चर्यचकित *(āscaryacakit)* वि. surprised; wonder-struck; astonished.

आश्चर्यजनक *(āścaryajank)* वि. wonderful; surprising.

आश्रम *(ā-śram)* पु. hermitage; convent.

आश्रय *(ā-śray)* पु. shelter; patronage.

आश्रित *(ā-śṛit)* पु. refugee; dependant; protege.

आश्वस्त *(ā-śvast)* वि. assured; convinced.

आश्वासन *(ā-śvāsan)* पु. assurance; guarantee.

आसक्त *(ā-sakt)* वि. attached; addicted; fascinated; charmed; infatuated.

आसक्ति *(ā-sakti)* स्त्री. attachment; fascination; infatuation.

आसन *(āsan)* पु. posture; seat.

आसन्न *(ā-sann)* वि. impending; imminent; proximate; adjacent.

आसपास *(ās-pās)* क्रि. वि. near about; in the vicinity; all round; on all sides.

आसमान *(āsmān)* पु. sky; firmament.

आसमानी *(āsmāni)* वि. azure; sky-blue.

आसरा *(āsrā)* पु. shelter; reliance; support.

आसान *(āsān)* वि. (फ़ा.) easy; convenient; simple; facile.

आसानी *(āsāni)* स्त्री. convenience; facility; ease.

आसार *(āsār)* पु. (अ.) sign; symptom; breath of a wall.

आसीन *(āsin)* वि. seated.

आसुरी *(āsuri)* वि. devilish; diabolic; demonic.

आस्तिक *(āstik)* वि. theistic; devout.

आस्तीन *(āstin)* स्त्री. (फा.) sleeve.

आस्था *(ā-sthā)* स्त्री. belief; faith.

आस्वादन *(ā-svādan)* पु. relishing; tasting

आह *(āh)* स्त्री. sigh.

आहट *(āhat)* स्त्री. light sound.

आहत *(ā-hat)* वि. injured; wounded; hurt; offended; punch marked.

आहार *(ā-hār)* पु. food; meal; diet.

आहार-विज्ञान *(āhār-vijnān)* पु. dietetics.

आहिस्ता *(āhistā)* क्रि. वि. (फ़ा.) gently; slowly.

आहुति *(ā-huti)* स्त्री. oblation offered to God.

आहूत *(āhūt)* वि. invited; summoned; called.

आह्वान *(ā-hvān)* पु. invocation; summon.

इ

इ (*i*) the third letter and vowel of Devnagri alphabet.

इंगित *(ingit)* पु. indication; hint; sign; gesture; beckoning.

इंतक़ाम, इंतिकाम (*intaqām; intiqām*) पु. (अ.) revenge.

इंतज़ाम, इंतिज़ाम (*intazām; intizām*) पु. (अ.) arrangement.

इंद्रजाल (*indrājāl*) पु. white magic; jugglery; conjuration.

इंद्रधनुष (*indra-dhanuśa*) पु. rainbow.

इंद्रलोक (*indralok*) पु. heaven.

इंद्रिय (*indriya*) स्त्री. sense.

इंद्रियगोचर (*indriyagocar*) वि. perceptible; capable of being ascertained through senses.

इंसान (*insān*) पु. (अ.) man; human being.

इंसानियत (*insāniyat*) स्त्री. (अ.) humanity; gentlemanliness.

इंसानी (*insāni*) वि. (अ.) human.

इंसाफ़ (*imsāf*) पु. (अ.) fair deal; justice.

इकट्ठा (*ikatthā*) वि. collected; gathered; united.

इकतरफ़ा (*iktarfā*) वि. ex-parte; unilateral; one sided.

इकतारा (*iktārā*) पु. one-stringed musical instrument.

इक़रार (*iqrār*) पु. (अ.) agreement; promise; bond.

इक़रारनामा (*iqrār-nāmā*) पु. (अ.) deed of agreement; written agreement.

इकलौता (*iklautā*) वि. only; single.

इकाई (*ikāi*) स्त्री. unit.

इच्छा (*iccha*) स्त्री. desire; wish; will.

इच्छाचारी (*icchācāri*) वि. libertine; self willed.

इच्छापत्र (*icchāpatra*) पु. will; testament.

इच्छाशक्ति (*icchā-sakti*) स्त्री. will power.

इच्छित (*icchit*) वि. willed; desired; aspired; wished for.

इच्छुक (*icchuk*) वि. desirous; willing; wishing.

इजलास *(ijlās)* पु. (अ.) court; session.

इज़हार *(izhār)* पु. (अ.) manifestation; expression; demonstration.

इजाज़त *(ijāzat)* स्त्री. (अ.) permission.

इजाफ़ा *(izāfā)* पु. (अ.) addition; augmentation; increase; enhancement.

इज़्ज़त *(izzat)* स्त्री. (अ.) prestige; honour; respect; dignity.

इज़्ज़तदार *(izzatdār)* वि. (अ.) reputed; esteemed; respectable.

इठलाना *(ithlānā)* अ. क्रि. to strut; to act affectedly; to assume swaggering airs.

इतना[1] *(itnā)* वि. this much; so much; as this.

इतना[2] *(itnā)* क्रि. वि. too much; so much.

इतमीनान *(itminān)* पु. (अ.) assurance; conviction; trust; confidence; relief.

इति *(iti)* स्त्री. end; conclusion; termination.

इतिहास *(iti-hās)* पु. history.

इतिहासकार *(itihāskār)* पु. historian.

इत्तफ़ाक़ *(ittafāq)* पु. (अ.) coincidence;

chance; unity.

इत्तला, इत्तिला *(ittilā)* स्त्री. (अ.) intimation; information; notice.

इत्यादि *(ity-ādi)* अ. etcetera; so on and so forth.

इत्र *(itr)* पु. (अ.) perfume; scent; essence.

इत्रदान *(itr-dān)* पु. cassolette; scentcase.

इधर *(idhar)* क्रि. वि. this side; this way; here; these days; at present.

इन *(in)* वि. these.

इनक़लाब *(inqalāb)* पु. (अ.) revolution.

इनक़लाबी *(inqalābi)* वि., पु. revolutionary.

इनकार *(inkār)* पु. (अ.) refusal; denial.

इनाम *(inām)* पु. (अ.) prize.; reward.

इनायत *(onāyat)* स्त्री. (अ.) obligation; favour; grace; bestowal.

इबादत *(ibādat)* स्त्री. (अ.) worship; adoration.

इबारत *(ibārat)* स्त्री. (अ.) text, writing style; mode of writing.

इमदाद *(imdād)* स्त्री. (अ.) aid; help.

इमला *(imlā)* पु. dictation.

इमली *(imli)* स्त्री. tamarind.

इमाम (*imām*) पु. (अ.) Muslim high priest.

इमारत *(imārat)* स्त्री. (अ.) building.

इमारती *(imārati)* वि. (अ.) pertaining to building.

इम्तहान, इम्तिहान (*imtahān*) पु. (अ.) examination; test; trial.

इरादा *(irādā)* पु. (अ.) idea; intention.

इलज़ाम *(ilzām)* पु. (अ.) allegation; accusation; charge.

इलाका *(ilāqā)* पु. (अ.) circle; territory; sphere; district; zone; region; locality; area.

इलाज *(ilāj)* पु. (अ.) treatment; remedy; cure.

इलायची *(ilāyci)* स्त्री. (अ.) cardamon.

इल्तिजा *(iltijā)* स्त्री. (अ.) request; entreaty.

इल्म *(ilm)* पु. (अ.) knowledge; learning; skill.

इशारा *(isārā)* पु. (अ.) signal; sign; hint; indication; gesture.

इश्क *(iśq)* पु. (अ.) love; amour.

इश्तहार, इश्तिहार *(istahār)* पु. (अ.) poster; hand-bill; advertisement.

इष्ट *(ist)* वि. adored; favourite; favoured.

इस *(is)* सर्व. this; it .

इसरार *(isrār)* पु. (अ.) insistence; entreaty.

इसलाम *(islam)* पु. (अ.) Muslim religion.

इस्तग़ासा, इस्तिगासा (*istagāsā*) पु. (अ.) prosecution; criminal proceedings.

इस्तरी, इस्तिरी *(istri)* स्त्री. press; smoothing iron.

इस्तीफ़ा *(istifa)* पु. (अ.) resignation.

इस्तेमाल *(istemāl)* पु. (अ.) use; application; consumption

इस्पात *(ispāt)* पु. (अ.) steel.

ई

ई *(i)* the fourth letter and the fourth vowel of the Devnagri alphabet.

ईंट *(imt)* स्त्री. brick.

ईंधन *(indhan)* पु. fuel; firewood; tinder.

ईख *(ikh)* स्त्री. sugarcane.

ईजाद *(ijād)* स्त्री. (अ.) invention.

ईमान *(imān)* पु. (अ.) faith; belief; honesty; integrity; fairplay.

ईमानदार *(imāndār)* वि. (अ.) honest; faithful; upright; just; sincere.

ईमानदारी *(imāndāri)* स्त्री. honesty; integrity; faithfulness; sincerity.

ईर्ष्या *(irśyā)* स्त्री. jealousy; envy.

ईर्ष्यालु *(irśyālu)* वि. jealous; envious.

ईश्वर *(iśvar)* पु. God.

ईश्वरनिष्ठ *(iśvarnistha)* वि. theistical.

ईश्वरवाद *(iśvar-vād)* पु. theism.

ईश्वरीय *(iśvariya)* वि. Godly; divine.

ईसवी *(isvi)* वि. pertaining to Christ.

ईसा *(isā)* पु. Jesus Christ.

ईसाई *(isāi)* पु. Christian.

उ

उ *(u)* the fifth letter and vowel of the Devnagri alphabet.

उँगली *(umgli)* स्त्री. finger.

उँडेलना *(umdelnā)* स. क्रि. to pour.

उऋण *(urin)* वि. free from debt; debt free.

उकताना *(uktana)* अ. क्रि. to be fed up; to be tired (of); to get bored.

उकसाना *(uksānā)* स. क्रि. to incite; to instigate; to provoke; to raise.

उकसाहट *(uksahat)* स्त्री. instigation; excitement; provocation.

उक्त *(ukt)* वि. stated above; mentioned above; aforesaid; spoken; said.

उक्ति *(ukti)* वि. saying; statement; expression; utterance; remark; dictum.

उखड़ना *(ukharnā)* अ. क्रि. to be uprootd; to be dislodged; to be dislocated.

उखाड़ना *(ukhārnā)* स. क्रि. to uproot; to eradicate; to dig out; to dislodge.

उगना *(ugnā)* अ. क्रि. to grow; to germinate; to rise (of sun).

उगाना *(ugānā)* स. क्रि. to grow; to cause to germinate; to raise;to produce.

उगाहना *(ugāhnā)* स. क्रि. to collect; to realise; to raise.

उगाही *(ugāhi)* स्त्री. collection; realization; levy; recovery.

उग्र *(ugra)* वि. fierce; violent; aggressive.

उग्रता *(ugratā)* स्त्री. aggressiveness.

उग्रवाद *(ugravād)* पु. extremism; radicalism.

उग्रवादी *(ugravādi)* पु. extremist; radicalist.

उघड़ना *(agharnā)* अ. क्रि. to be uncovered; to be exposed; to be disclosed.

उघाड़ना *(ughārnā)* स. क्रि. to uncover; to expose; to disclose.

उचकना *(ucaknā)* अ. क्रि. to stand on tip-toe.

उचकाना *(uckānā)* स. क्रि. to raise up; to lift up.

उचक्का *(ucakkā)* पु. sneak-thief; pilferer; swindler; shop-lifter.

उचक्कापन *(ucakkāpan)* पु. swindling.

उचटना *(ucatnā)* अ. क्रि. to be weary; to feel dejected; to be interrupted; to come off.

उचित *(ucit)* वि. proper; right; appropriate; suitable; fair; reasonable; advisable.

उच्च *(ucc)* वि. tall; high; superior; lofty; elevated; noble.

उच्चतम *(uccatam)* वि. highest; best; supreme.

उच्चता *(uccatā)* स्त्री. elevation; loftiness; superiority.

उच्चारण *(uc-cāran)* पु. pronunciation.

उच्छृंखल *(uc-chrankhal)* वि. unrestrained; licentious; wanton; impertinent; disorderly; undisciplined.

उच्छ्वास *(uc-chvās)* पु. exhalation; expiration; sigh.

उछलना *(uchalnā)* अ. क्रि. to jump; to leap; to spring; to rebound.

उछाल *(uchāl)* स्त्री. leap; jump; rebound; throw; toss.

उछालना *(uchālna)* स. क्रि. to toss.

उजड़ना *(ujarnā)* अ. क्रि. to be ruined or destroyed; to be deserted; to lie waste.

उजड्ड *(ujadd)* वि. ill-mannered; boorish; rude; rough; uncivilised; clumsy.

उजड्डता *(ujaddata)* स्त्री. see. उजड्डपन

उजड्ड-पन *(ujaddāpan)* पु. rudeness; boorishness; incivility; roughness.

उजरत *(ujrat)* स्त्री. (अ.) remuneration.

उजला *(ujlā)* वि. bright; clean; white.

उजाड़ *(ujār)* वि. desolate; deserted; devastated; barren.

उजाड़ना *(ujārnā)* स. क्रि. to destroy; to ruin; to render desolate; to devastate; to spoil; to root up.

उजाला *(ujālā)* पु. light; brightness; splendour.

उज्ज्वल *(uj-jval)* वि. splendid; bright; radiant; clear; luminous; beautiful; white.

उज्ज्वलता *(uj-jvalatā)* स्त्री. splendour; brightness; shine; lustre.

उठना *(uthnā)* अ. वि. to rise; to get up; to be rented out; to expire; to pass away; to stand up; to be ready; to grow; to develop.

उठाईगिरी *(uthāigiri)* स्त्री. pilferage.

उठाऊ *(uthāü)* वि. portable.

उठान *(uthān)* पु. ascent; elevation; rise; height; blossoming youth.

उठाना *(uthānā)* स. क्रि. to lift up; to raise; to wake up; to bear; to remove; to erect; to pick up; to take up.

उड़द *(urad)* see. उरद

उड़नखटोला *(urankhatolā)* पु. legendary flying cot.

उड़नतस्तरी *(urantaśtari)* स्त्री. flying saucer.

उड़नदस्ता *(urandastā)* पु. flying squad.

उड़ना *(urnā)* अ. क्रि. to fly ; to get dim; to fade; to vanish; to explode.

उड़ान *(urān)* स्त्री. flight.

उड़ाना *(urānā)* स. क्रि. to squander; to fly; to let fly; to steal; to kidnap.

उतना *(utnā)* वि. क्रि. वि. that much; to that extent.

उतरन *(utran)* स्त्री. old; worn out clothes; cast off clothes.

उतरना *(utarnā)* अ. क्रि. to get down; to alight; to go down; to fall or diminish; to be dislocated.

उतार *(utār)* पु. descent; fall; depreciation.

उतार-चढ़ाव *(utār-carhāv)* पु. fluctuations; rise and fall; ups and downs; variation.

उतारना *(utārna)* स. क्रि. to unload; to bring down; to dislocate; to cause to disembark; to copy; to take across.

उतावला *(utāvlā)* वि. impatient; excessively eager; head strong.

उतावलापन *(utāvlāpan)* पु. impatience; rashness; hastiness; haste.

उत्कंठा *(ut-kanthā)* स्त्री. curiosity; eagerness; longing; craving..

उत्कट *(ut-kat)* वि. intense; excessive; gigantic; richly endowed.

उत्कर्ष *(ut-karś)* पु. crescendo; apotheosis; ascendence; exaltation; excellence; prosperity; eminence.

उत्कीर्ण *(ut-kirn)* वि. engraved; carved.

उत्कृष्ट *(ut-krist)* वि. excellent; outstanding; paramount; superior; highest.

उत्कृष्टता *(ut-kriśtatā)* स्त्री. eminence; superiority; excellence.

उत्कोच *(utkoc)* पु. bribe; graft.

उत्खनन *(ut-khanan)* पु. excavation.

उत्तम *(uttam)* वि. best; excellent.

उत्तमता *(uttamatā)* स्त्री. excellence; fineness.

उत्तर *(uttar)* पु. north; reply; answer defence.

उत्तरदायित्व *(uttardāyitva)* पु. accountability; responsibility; obligation.

उत्तरदायी *(uttar-dāyi)* वि. responsible; accountable; answerable.

उत्तराधिकार *(uttarādhikār)* पु. inheritance; succession.

उत्ताप *(uttāp)* पु. excessive hot; distress; affliction; ferment.

उत्ताल *(ut-tāl)* वि. violent; high.

उत्तीर्ण *(ut-tirn)* वि. passed; successful; crossed.

उत्तुंग *(ut-tung)* वि. lofty; high.

उत्तेजक *(ut-tejak)* वि. provocative; stimulating; inciting.

उत्तेजना *(ut-tejnā)* स्त्री. provocation; excitement; agitation; stimulation.

उत्तेजनाप्रद *(uttejnāprad)* वि. provocative; stimulating; exciting.

उत्तेजित *(ut-tejit)* वि. excited; provoked.

उत्तोलक *(ut-tolak)* पु. lift; lever; crane.

उत्थान *(ut-thān)* पु. rise; uplift.

उत्पत्ति *(ut-patti)* स्त्री. production; creation; origin; birth.

उत्पन्न *(ut-pann)* वि. produced; born; originated.

उत्पात *(ut-pat)* पु. mischief; nuisance riot; violence.

उत्पाती *(ut-pāti)* वि. mischievous; naughty.

उत्पाद *(ut-pād)* पु. produce; yield; product; output.

उत्पादक *(ut-pādak)* पु. producer; originator.

उत्पादकता *(ut-pādakatā)* स्त्री. productivity; fertility.

उत्पादन *(ut-pādan)* पु. production; output; produce; yield; generation.

उत्पीड़क *(u-pirak)* पु. oppressor; persecutor.

उत्पीड़न *(ut-piran)* पु. oppression; persecution; harassment.

उत्पीड़ित *(ut-pirit)* वि. oppressed; persecuted; harassed.

उत्प्रेरित *(utprerit)* वि. catalysed; activated; indued.

उत्फुल्ल *(ut-phull)* वि. blossomed; delighted; buoyant.

उत्फुल्लता *(utphullata)* स्त्री. delightfulness; blossoming; buoyancy.

उत्सर्ग *(ut-sarg)* पु. abandonment; sacrifice.

उत्सव *(ut-sav)* पु. festival; celebration; festivity.

उत्साह *(ut-sāh)* पु. enthusiasm; zeal.

उत्साहवर्धक *(utsāhvardhak)* वि. encouraging; inspiring.

उत्साहवर्धन *(utsāhvardhan)* पु. encouragement; inspiration.

उत्साही *(ut-sāhi)* पु. enthusiast.

उत्सुक *(ut-suk)* वि. eager; curious; keen; anxious.

उत्सुकता *(ut-sukatā)* स्त्री. curiosity; eagerness; anxiousness.

उथल-पुथल *(uthal-puthal)* स्त्री. turmoil; upheaval.

उथला *(uthlā)* वि. shallow.

उदधि *(uda-dhi)* पु. ocean; sea.

उदय *(ud-ay)* पु. rise; emergence.

उदर *(udār)* पु. stomach; abdomen.

उदात्त *(ud-ātt)* वि. sublime; lofty; noble.

उदार *(ud-ār)* वि. liberal; generous; magnificent; tolerant.

उदारता *(ud-āratā)* स्त्री. generosity; magnanimity; liberality; leniency.

उदास *(ud-ās)* वि. sad; gloomy; dejected.

उदासी *(ud-āsi)* स्त्री. sadness; dejection; gloom; melancholy; sullenness.

उदासीन *(ud-āsin)* वि. indifferent; disinterested; apathetic.

उदासीनता *(ud-āsinatā)* स्त्री. indifference; disinterestedness; apathy.

उदाहरण *(ud-ā-haran)* पु. illustration; example; instance; precedent.

उदित *(udit)* वि. ascended; risen; emerged.

उदीयमान *(udiyamān)* वि. promising; rising; ascending.

उद्गम *(ud-gam)* पु. source; fountainhead; origin; rising; coming up.

उद्गार *(ud-gār)* पु. expression of inner feelings; effusion.

उद्घाटन *(ud-ghātan)* पु. inauguration; uncovering; revelation.

उद्घोष *(ud-ghośa)* पु. proclamation.

उद्दंड *(ud-dand)* वि. insolent; impertinent; rude; rebellious.

उद्दीपक *(ud-dipak)* पु. stimulant; stimulus.

उद्दीपन *(ud-dipan)* पु. stimulation;

stimulus; provocation.

उद्देश *(uddes)* पु. subject of discussion; purpose; example; clarification; determination.

उद्देश्य *(ud-desya)* पु. end; purpose; aim; subject; object; motive.

उद्धारण *(ud-dhāraṅ)* पु. quotation; excerpt; citation; extract.

उद्धार *(ud-dhār)* पु. salvation; deliverance; rescue; riddance; redemption; restoration; unplift.

उद्धृत *(ud-dhrit)* वि. quoted; cited.

उद्बोध *(ud-bodh)* पु. enlightenment.

उद्बोधन *(ud-bodhan)* पु. awakening; consciousness; evocation.

उद्भव *(ud-bhav)* पु. origin; birth; descent.

उद्भूत *(udbhut)* वि. born; produced; emerged.

उद्यत *(ud-yat)* वि. ready; prepared.

उद्यम *(ud-yam)* पु. enterprise; venture; business; pursuit; diligence.

उद्यमी *(ud-yami)* वि. enterprising; diligent; industrious.

उद्यान *(ud-yān)* पु. park; garden; orchard.

उद्योग *(ud-yog)* पु. industry; labour; effort; endeavour.

उद्योगपति *(ud-yogpati)* पु. industrialist.

उद्विग्न *(ud-vign)* वि. agitated; perturbed; unquiet; troubled.

उद्वेग *(ud-veg)* पु. uneasiness; restlessness perturbation; agitation.

उद्वेलन *(udvelan)* पु. perturbation; agitation; surgency; turmoil.

उधाड़ना *(udhārna)* अ. क्रि. to be unsewn; to be ripped; to be untwisted; to be unrolled; to be unravelled.

उधार[1] *(udhār)* क्रि. वि. on that side; that way; there.

उधार[2] *(udhār)* पु. credit; loan; debt.

उधेड़ना *(udherna)* स. क्रि. to unsew; to open up; to excoriate; to unroll.

उन्नत *(un-nat)* वि. elevated; developed; high; lofty; improved; advanced.

उन्नति *(un-nati)* स्त्री. progress; rise; promotion; improvement; advancement; elevation; uplift; betterment.

उन्नयन *(un-nayan)* पु. progress; development; upliftment.

उन्मत्त *(un-matt)* वि. intoxicated; drunk; delirious.

उन्माद *(un-mād)* पु. mania; lunacy; intoxication; insanity; hysteria.

उन्मादी *(un-mādi)* वि. insance; frenzied; hysterical; intoxicated.

उन्मुक्त *(un-mukt)* वि. unrestrained; liberated; free; open.

उन्मूलन *(un-mulan)* पु. uprooting; eradication; abolition; extermination.

उपकरण *(upa-karan)* पु. equipment; apparatus; appliance; paraphernalia.

उपकार *(upa-kār)* पु. good; benefaction.

उपकारी *(upa-kari)* वि. beneficial; favourable; obliging; helping; benevolent.

उपकुलपति *(upkulpati)* पु. vice-chancellor.

उपकृत *(upkrit)* वि. grateful; obliged.

उपग्रह *(upa-grah)* पु. satellite.

उपचार *(upa-cār)* पु. treatment; remedy.

उपज *(upaj)* स्त्री. output; yield; produce; product; harvest.

उपजाऊ *(upjāü)* वि. fertile; productive.

उपजाऊपन *(upajāüpan)* पु. fertility; productivity.

उपदेश *(upa-deś)* पु. precept; sermon; preaching; teaching.

उपद्रव *(upa-drav)* पु. riot; disturbance; mischief.

उपद्रवी *(upa-dravi)* वि. riotious; rowdy; mischievous; naughty; unruly.

उपनगर *(upa-nagar)* पु. suburb.

उपनगरीय *(upa-nagariya)* वि. suburban.

उपनाम *(upa-nām)* पु. pen-name; nick-name.

उपनियम *(up-niyam)* पु. bye-law.

उपनिवेश *(upa-niveś)* पु. colony.

उपन्यास *(upa-nyās)* पु. novel.

उपन्यासकार *upa-nyāskār)* पु. novelist.

उपपति *(upapati)* पु. paramour; lover.

उपपत्नी *(upa-patni)* स्त्री. mistress; keep; concubine.

उपभुक्त *(upbhukta)* वि. used; consumed.

उपभोक्ता *(upa-bhoktā)* पु. consumer; user.

उपभोग *(upabhog)* पु. consumption; use.

उपमंत्री *(up-mantri)* पु. deputy- minister.

उपमहाद्वीप *(upa-mahādvip)* पु. subcontinent.

उपमा *(upa-mā)* स्त्री. simile; comparison; analogy.

उपयुक्त *(upa-yukt)* वि. appropriate; proper; suitable.

उपयुक्तता *(upa-yuktatā)* स्त्री. appropriateness; suitability.

उपयोग *(upa-yog)* पु. use; utilisation; utility; exploitation; consumption.

उपयोगिता *(upa-yogitā)* स्त्री. utility; usefulness.

उपयोगी *(upa-yogi)* वि. useful; helpful; serviceable.

उपरांत *(uparānt)* क्रि. वि. after; afterwards.

उपराज्यपाल *(up-rājyapāl)* पु. deputy governor.

उपराष्ट्रपति *(uparāśtrapati)* पु. vice-president.

उपरिलिखित *(upari-likhit)* वि. above mentioned.

उपर्युक्त *(uparyukt)* वि. above-mentioned; aforesaid.

उपलक्ष्य *(upa-laks)* पु. object; occasion.

उपलब्ध *(upa-labd)* वि. available.

उपलब्धि *(upa-labdhi)* स्त्री. achievement; accomplishment; realization; attainment; finding.

उपला *(uplā)* पु. dung-cake.

उपवन *(upa-van)* पु. garden; park; park land.

उपवाक्य *(up-vakya)* पु. fast.

उपविभाग *(up-vibhag)* पु. sub-division; subordinate department.

उपशाखा *(up-śākhā)* स्त्री. sub-branch; subsidiary branch.

उपसंपादक *(up-sampādak)* पु. sub-editor.

उपसंहार *(up-samhār)* पु. epilogue; conclusion; finale.

उपसभापति *(up-sabhāpati)* पु. vice president; vice-chairman.

उपसमिति *(up-samiti)* स्त्री. sub-committee.

उपसर्ग *(upa-sarg)* पु. prefix.

उपस्थित *(upa-sthit)* वि. present.

उपस्थिति *(upa-sthiti)* स्त्री. presence; attendance; roll-call.

उपहार *(upa-hār)* पु. present; gift.

उपहास *(upa-hās)* पु. mockery; derision; ridicule.

उपहासास्पद *(upa-hāsāspad)* वि. ridiculous; ludicrous; laughable.

उपादान *(upādān)* पु. ingredient; matter; factor.

उपादेय *(upādeya)* वि. useful; beneficial.

उपाधि *(upādhi)* स्त्री. degree; epithet; title.

उपाय *(upay)* पु. means; measure; way; device; remedy; cure.

उपार्जन *(upārjan)* पु. earning; acquisition.

उपालंभ *(upālambh)* पु. reproach; complaint.

उपासक *(upāsak)* पु. worshipper; adorer.

उपासना *(upāsanā)* स्त्री. worship; devotion; service.

उपास्य *(upāsya)* वि. adorable; worth worshipping.

उपेक्षा *(upeksā)* स्त्री. neglect; negligence; disregard.

उपेक्षित *(upeksit)* वि. neglected; ignored; discarded; disregarded.

उफनना *(uphananā)* अ. क्रि. to boil over; to express distress.

उफान *(uphān)* पु. boiling up; turmoil.

उबकाई *(ubkāi)* स्त्री. nausea; feeling of vomiting.

उबटन *(ubtan)* पु. a cosmetic paste annointed over the body.

उबरना *(ubarnā)* अ. क्रि. to get riddance; to be liberated; to be free.

उबलना *(ubalnā)* अ. क्रि. to boil; to simmer.

उबारना *(ubārnā)* स. क्रि. to emancipate; to liberate; to salvage.

उबाल *(ubāl)* पु. simmering; boiling; seething.

उबालना *(ubālnā)* स. क्रि. to boil.

उबासी *(ubāsi)* स्त्री. yawn.

उभय *(ubhay)* वि. both; the two.

उभयचर *(ubhayacar)* पु. amphibious.

उभरना *(ubharnā)* अ. क्रि. to emerge; to bulge out; to protrude.

उभार *(ubhār)* पु. bulging; bulge; projection; protrusion.

उभारना *(ubhārnā)* स. क्रि. to raise up; to provoke.

उमंग *(umang)* स्त्री. zeal; aspiration.

उमड़ना *(umarnā)* अ. क्रि. to swell; to burst; to flood; to overflow.

उमस *(umas)* स्त्री. sultriness; sultry weather.

उम्मीद *(ummid)* स्त्री. (फ़ा.) expectation; hope

उम्मीदवार *(ummidvār)* पु. candidate.

उम्र *(umra)* स्त्री. (अ.) age; lifetime.

उरद *(urad)* पु. a kind of pulse; black gram.

उर्वर *(urvar)* उर्वर वि. productive; fertile.

उर्वरक *(urvarak)* पु. fertiliser.

उर्वरता *(urvaratā)* स्त्री. productivity; fertility.

उलझन *(uljhan)* स्त्री. complication; fix; perplexity; entanglement.

उलझाना *(uljhānā)* स. क्रि. to complicate; to entangle; to involve.

उलझाव *(uljhāv)* पु. involvement; entanglement; complication.

उलटना *(ulatnā)* स. क्रि. to overturn; to capsize; to reverse; to subvert; to turn over.

उलट-फेर *(ulat-pher)* पु. upsetting; shuffling; changes.

उलटा *(ultā)* वि. reverse; topsy-turvy; opposite; contrary; inverted.

उलटी *(ulti)* स्त्री. vomit; vomiting.

उलाहना *(ulāhnā)* पु. complain; reproach.

उल्का *(ulkā)* स्त्री. falling star; meteor; shooting star.

उल्लंघन *(ul-langhan)* पु. violation; transgression.

उल्लसित *(ul-lasit)* वि. joyous; jubilant; radiant.

उल्लास *(ul-lās)* पु. jubiliation; joy; delight; meriment.

उल्लू *(ullü)* पु. owl; idiot.

उल्लेख *(ul-lekh)* पु. mention; reference.

उल्लेखनीय *(ul-lekhaniya)* उल्लेख वि. remarkable; worthy; of being mentioned.

उस *(us)* सर्व., वि. he or she; that; it.

उसाँस *(usams)* स्त्री. sigh.

उसूल *(usül)* पु. (अ.) principle.

उस्तरा *(ustrā)* पु. (फ़ा.) razor.

ऊ

ऊ *(ü)* the sixth letter and vowel of the Devnagri alphabet.

ऊँघ *(ümgh)* स्त्री. drowsiness.

ऊँघना *(ümghna)* अ. क्रि. to doze; to be sleepy.

ऊँच-नीच *(ümc-nic)* स्त्री. pros and cons; ups and downs; good and evil; high and low.

ऊँचा *(ümca)* वि. elevated; loft; high; loud; tall; great; eminent.

ऊँचाई *(ümcai)* स्त्री. height; altitude; elevation; loftiness.

ऊँट *(ümt)* पु. camel.

ऊटपटांग *(ütpatāmg)* वि. absurd; incoherent; ridiculous; slipslop; senseless; meaningless.

ऊत *(üt)* वि. idiot; stupid; issueless.

ऊतक *(ütak)* पु. tissue.

ऊधम *(üdham)* पु. clamour; row; uproar; hurly-burly; mischief.

ऊधमी *(üdhami)* वि. mischievous; naughty; rowdy.

ऊन *(ün)* स्त्री. wool.

ऊपर *(üpar)* अ. on; upon; above; upward; over; on the top.

ऊपरी *(üpari)* वि. upper; superficial; showy; insincere; extra.

ऊब *(üb)* स्त्री. boredom; monotony; disgust.

ऊबड़-खाबड़ *(übar-khābar)* वि. uneven; rough and rugged.

ऊबना *(übnā)* अ. क्रि. to feel bored; to feel irked.

ऊर्जा *(ürjā)* स्त्री. energy; vigour and vitality; power.

ऊर्मि *(ürmi)* स्त्री. wave; ripple; flow.

ऊलजलूल *(ül-jalül)* वि. slipslop; absurd; irrelevant; ridiculous; foolish.

ऊष्मा *(üsmā)* स्त्री. warmth; heat.

ऊसर *(üsar)* वि. barren or fallow land.

ऊहापोह *(ühāpoh)* पु. consideration of the pros and cons.

ऋ

ऋ (*r*) the seventh letter and vowel of the Devnagri alphabet.

ऋजु (*rju*) वि. straight; simple.

ऋण (*rn*) पु. debt.

ऋणग्रस्त (*rn-grast*) वि. indebted.

ऋणपत्र (*rn-patr*) पु. bond; pronote.

ऋतु (*rtu*) स्त्री. season; menstruation.

ऋषि (*rsi*) पु. sage; seer; hermit.

ए

ए (*e*) the eighth letter and vowel of the Devnagri alphabet.

एक (*ek*) वि. one; single; lone.

एकक (*ekak*) पु. unit; singlet.

एकछत्र (*ekchatr*) वि. having absolute authority; autocratic.

एकजान (*ekjān*) वि. complete union; completely identified.

एकतरफ़ा (*ek-tarfā*) वि. ex-parte; onesided; unilateral.

एकता (*ekatā*) स्त्री. unity; oneness; solidarity; integrity.

एकतारा (*ekatārā*) पु. one-stringed musical instrument.

एकत्र (*ekatr*) क्रि. वि. together; collected in one place.

एकत्रित (*ekatrit*) वि. accumulated; gathered; collected; assembled.

एकत्व (*ekatva*) पु. unity; oneness.

एकदम (*ekdam*) क्रि. वि. immediately; instantly; suddenly; in one breath.

एकमंज़िला (*ek-manjilā*) वि. having only one storey; single storeyed.

एकमत (*ek-mat*) वि. unanimous.

एकरस (*ekras*) वि. monotonous; constant; similar.

एकरसता (*ekrastā*) स्त्री. uniform; identical.

एकरूप (*ekrup*) वि. uniform; identical.

एकरूपता (*ekrüptā*) स्त्री. uniformity; identity.

एकल (*ekal*) वि. lone; solitary; singular.; single.

एकलिंगता (*ek-lingtā*) स्त्री. unisexualism.

एकलिंगी (*ek-lingi*) वि. unisexual.

एकवचन (*ek-vachan*) वि. singular.

एकसमान (*ek-samān*) वि. uniform; constant.

एकसमानता (*ek-samāntā*) स्त्री. uniformity; constancy.

एकसूत्रता (*ek-sütratā*) स्त्री. co-ordination; integration.

एकस्वरता (*ek-svartā*) स्त्री. unison; monotony.

एकांकी (*ekānke*) पु. one-act play.

एकांगी (*ekāngi*) वि. one-sided; biased; partial.

एकांत[1] (*ekānt*) पु. seclusion; isolation; solitude; privacy.

एकांत[2] *(ekānt)* वि. lonely; exclusive.
एकांतता *(ekāntatā)* स्त्री. seclusion; secludedness; privacy; solitude.
एकांश *(ekāns)* पु. unit; item.
एका *(ekā)* पु. unity, solidarity; oneness.
एकाएक *(ekā-ek)* क्रि. वि. suddenly; unexpectedly; unawared; all of a sudden.
एकाकी *(ekāki)* वि. lonely; solitary; single.
एकाकीपन *(ekākipan)* पु. feeling of loneliness.
एकाग्र *(ekāgr)* वि. concentrated.
एकाग्रता *(ekagratā)* स्त्री. concentration.
एकाधिक *(ekādhik)* वि. more than one; very few.
एकाधिकार *(ekādhikār)* पु. monopoly.
एकाधिपत्य *(ekādhiptya)* पु. autocracy; monopoly.
एकार्थक *(ekārthak)* वि. synonymous.
एकीकरण *(ekikaran)* पु. unification.
एकीकृत *(ekikrit)* वि. unified; integrated.
एकीभूत *(ekibhüt)* वि. unified; collected; together; consolidated.
एड़ *(er)* स्त्री. spur.
एड़ी *(eri)* स्त्री. heel.
एतबार *(etbār)* पु. (अ.) confidence; trust; faith.
एतराज़ *(etrāz)* पु. (अ.) objection; protest; opposition.
एलान *(elān)* पु. (अ.) announcement; declaration.
एवं *(evam)* अ. and; also.
एवज़ *(evaz)* पु. (अ.) substitution; substitute.
एहसान *(ehsān)* पु. (अ.) obligation.
एहसास *(ehsās)* पु. (अ.) feeling; consciousness; realisation.

ऐ

ऐ *(ai)* the ninth letter and vowel of the Devnagri alphabet.
ऐंचातानी *(aincātāni)* स्त्री. tugging and pulling; manipulation and manoeuvring struggle inspired by selfish motive.
ऐंठ *(aimth)* स्त्री. twist; ply; convolution; conceit; vanity; stiffness; perk; obstinacy.
ऐंठन *(aimthan)* स्त्री. twist; contortion; torsion; convolution.
ऐंठना *(aimthana)* स. क्रि. to contort; to twist; to extort; to fleece; to cramp; to be conceited.
ऐंठू *(aimthü)* वि. arrogant; perky; obstinate; conceited.
ऐच्छिक *(aicchik)* वि. voluntary; optional.
ऐतिहासिक *(aitihāsik)* वि. historic; historical.
ऐतिहासिकता *(aitihāsiktā)* स्त्री. historicity.
ऐनक *(ainak)* पु. (अ.) spectacles; eyeglasses.
ऐब *(aib)* पु. (अ.) defect; vice; flaw; fault.
ऐयाश *(aiyās)* वि. (अ.) voluptuous; debauch.
ऐयाशी *(aiyāsi)* स्त्री. debauchery; lewdness; sensuality
ऐरा-ग़ैरा *(airā-gairā)* वि. alien; rabble; inferior; having no sta-

tus; insignificant.

ऐश *(aiś)* पु. (अ.) sensuous pleasure; merriment; luxury.

ऐश्वर्य *(aiśvarya)* पु. glory and grandeur; prosperity; opulence.

ऐसा *(aisā)* क्रि. वि., वि. such; of this type; so.

ऐहिक *(aihik)* वि. mundane; secular; temporal.

ओ

ओ *(o)* the ninth letter and vowel of the Devnagri alphabet.

ओंठ *(omth)* पु. lip.

ओकाई *(okāi)* स्त्री. nausea; feeling of vomiting.

ओखली *(okhli)* स्त्री. mortar.

ओछा *(ochā)* वि. mean; petty; trifling; short; small; shallow.

ओछापन *(ochāpan)* पु. meanness; pettiness.

ओज *(oj)* पु. lustre; splendour; prowess; vigour.

ओजस्विता *(ojasvitā)* स्त्री. virility.

ओजस्वी *(ojasvi)* वि. virile; rigorous.

ओझल *(ojhal)* वि. out of sight; evanescent.

ओझा *(ojhā)* पु. exorcist.

ओट *(ot)* स्त्री. cover; shelter; screen.

ओठ *(oth)* पु. lip.

ओढ़ना[1] *(orhnnā)* स. क्रि. to cover oneself with; to own up.

ओढ़ना[2] *(orhnnā)* पु. covering; covering sheet.

ओढ़नी *(orhni)* स्त्री. woman's mantle.

ओर *(or)* स्त्री. side; direction.

ओला *(olā)* पु. hailstone; hail.

ओस *(os)* स्त्री. dew.

ओहदा *(ohdā)* पु. (अ.) post; designation; rank.

औ

औ *(au)* the tenth letter and vowel of the Devnagri alphabet.

औंधा *(aumdhā)* क्रि. वि. upside down; with the face downward.

औक़ात *(auqāt)* स्त्री. (अ.) capability; status.

औचित्य *(aucitya)* पु. appropriateness; proprietry; validity; justification.

औज़ार *(auzār)* पु. (अ.) instrument; tool.

औटाना *(autānā)* स. क्रि. to boil.

औद्योगीकरण *(audyogikaran)* वि. industrialisation.

औपचारिक *(aupacārik)* वि. formal; ceremonial.

औपचारिकता *(aup-cāriktā)* स्त्री. formality; ceremony; ceremonialism.

और *(aur)* वि. different; other; else.

औरत *(aurat)* स्त्री. (अ.) woman; wife; maid servant.

औलाद *(aulad)* स्त्री. (अ.) offspring; descendants; children.

औषध, औषधि *(auśadh)* स्त्री. medicine; drug.

औषधशाला *(ausadh-śālā)* स्त्री. pharmacy.

औषधालय *(ausdhālayā)* पु. dispensary.

औसत *(ausat)* वि. (अ.) average.

औसान *(ausān)* पु. (फ़ा.) presence of mind; wits.

क

क *(ka)* the first consonants in Devnagri alphabet.

कंकड़ *(kankar)* पु. small piece of stone; pebble.

कंकण *(kankan)* पु. bangle; a bracelet.

कंकरीट *(kankrit)* पु. mixture of gravel; lime; cement and sand; concrete.

कंकाल *(kankāl)* पु. skeleton.

कंगन *(kangan)* पु. bracelet.

कंगाल *(kangāl)* पु. poor; miserable.

कंगाली *(kangāli)* स्त्री. misery; poverty.

कँगूरा *(kamgürā)* पु. tower; parapet wall; ornament on crowns.

कंघा *(kanghā)* पु. comb.

कंचन *(kancan)* पु. wealth; gold.

कंचुक *(kancuk)* पु. brassieres; skin of a snake.

कंजूस *(kanjüs)* अ. parsimonious; miserly.

कँटीला *(kamtilā)* अ. prickly; thorny.

कंठ *(kanth)* पु. neck; the throat.

कंठस्थ *(kanthasth)* अ. learnt by heart.

कंठाग्र *(kanthāgra)* अ. learnt by heart.

कंद *(kand)* पु. esculent tuber root; sugar candy.

कंदरा *(kandarā)* स्त्री. cave.

कंधा *(kandhā)* पु. shoulder.

कंपन *(kampan)* पु. shiver; a thrill.

कंपायमान *(kampāyamān)* अ. oscillating; quivering.

कंबल *(kambal)* पु. rug; blanket.

ककड़ी *(kakri)* स्त्री. cucumber.

कक्ष *(kaks)* पु. chamber; room.

कक्षा *(kaksā)* स्त्री. class room; orbit.

कचरा *(kacrā)* पु. sweepings; rubbish

कचहरी *(kacahri)* स्त्री. court of justice; assembly.

कचूमर *(kacümar)* पु. anything well-crushed.

कचोट *(kacot)* स्त्री. lingering agony.

कच्चा *(kaccā)* अ. unripe; immature.

कछुआ *(kachua)* पु. tortoise; turtle.

कटकटाना *(katkatānā)* वि. to grind teeth.

कटना *(katnā)* वि. to be cut; to pass away time; to be ashamed; to complete; to die in battle.

कटाई *(katāi)* स्त्री. act of cutting; harvesting.

कटाक्ष *(katāks)* पु. ogling; a side-look; taunt.

कटार *(katār)* स्त्री. large knife; dagger.

कटु *(katu)* अ. sharp; unpleasant; bitter.

कटोरदान *(katordān)* पु. brass lid for keeping articles of food.

कटोरा *(katorā)* पु. big bowl; cup.

कटौती *(katauti)* स्त्री. deduction; reduction.

कट्टर *(kattar)* अ. strict; fanatic.

कठिन *(kathin)* अ. hard; difficult.

कठोर *(kathor)* अ. rough; hard; unkind.

कड़वा *(karvā)* अ. unpleasant; bitter.

कड़ा *(karā)* अ. पु. stiff; hard; stony; a ring of metal.

कड़ाही *(karāhi)* पु. big boiling pan.

कढ़ाई *(karhai)* स्त्री. the art of embroidery.

कण *(kan)* पु. jot; particle; a small fragment of rice or wheat.

क़तई *(qatai)* क्रि. अ. altogether; wholly; completely.

कतरना *(katarnā)* वि. to cut; to clip; to chip.

कतरा *(katrā)* पु. drop; fragment.

कतराना *(katrānā)* वि. to cause, to be cut out; to avoid and encounter.

कताई *(katāi)* स्त्री. spinning.

कतार *(qatār)* स्त्री. row; line.

कत्ल *(qatl)* पु. slaughter; murder.

कथन *(kathan)* पु. mention; statement; saying.

कथनी *(kathani)* स्त्री. speech; narration.

कथा *(kathā)* स्त्री. tale; fable; religious discourse.

कथानक *(kathānak)* पु. small story; the plot.

कथोपकथन *(kathopakathan)* पु. conversation; dialogue.

कथ्य *(kathya)* पु. subject matter.

कद *(kad)* पु. height; size.

कदम *(qadam)* पु. footstep; step; pace.

कदाचित *(kadācit)* अ. may be possible; by chance.

कदापि *(kadāpi)* अ. seldom.

कद्दावर *(kaddāvar)* क्रि. tall staturee; giant like.

कद्दू *(kaddu)* पु. pumpkin.

कद्र *(qadr)* स्त्री merit; appreciation; respect.

कनखी *(kankhi)* स्त्री. glance of the eye; ogle; leer.

कनस्तर *(kanastar)* पु. canister.

कनात *(qanāt)* स्त्री. screen of canvas; walls of a tent.

कनी *(kani)* स्त्री. small particle; uncooked grain of rice.

कन्नी *(kanni)* स्त्री. edge; border; ends of kite; tool of a mason.

कन्या *(kanyā)* स्त्री. girl; virgin; daughter.

कपट *(kapat)* पु. guile; fraud; hypocrisy.

कपड़ा *(kaprā)* पु. cloth; fabric.

कपाट *(kapāt)* पु. screen door; leaf.

कपाल *(kapāl)* पु. the head; skull; begging bowl.

कपास *(kapās)* स्त्री. cotton.

कपूत *(kapüt)* पु. son of bad character; undutiful son.

कपूर *(kapür)* पु. camphor.

कप्तान *(kaptān)* पु. captain.

कफ़ *(kaf)* पु. a cuff.

कफ़न *(kafan)* पु. coffin; pall; shroud.

कब *(kab)* अ. at what time; when.

कबड्डी *(kabaddi)* पु. Indian outdoor game.

कबाड़ *(kabār)* पु. worthless articles; rubbish.

कबाड़ी *(kabāri)* पु. one who sells old and broken articles.

कबीला *(qabilā)* पु. tribe.

कबूतर *(kabutar)* पु. pigeon.

कबूल *(qabul)* पु. agreement; consent; confession.

कब्ज़ *(qabz)* पु. constipation.

कब्जा *(qabzā)* पु. grip; possession.

कब्र *(qabr)* स्त्री. grave.

कब्रिस्तान *(qabaristān)* पु. cemetery; graveyard.

कभी *(kabhi)* पु. seldom; sometimes.

कमजोर *(kamzor)* वि. feeble; weak.

कमबख्त *(kambakht)* वि. unlucky; illfated; cursed.

कमनीय *(kamaniya)* वि. desirable; beautiful.

कमर *(kamar)* स्त्री. waist.

कमल *(kamal)* पु. lotus flower.

कमाई *(kamāi)* स्त्री. earnings; wages.

कमाऊ *(kamāu)* वि. laborious; earning member.

कमान *(kamān)* पु. bow; arch; command.

कमाना *(kamānā)* स. क्रि. to earn; to process.

कमानी *(kamāni)* स्त्री. spring of steel.

कमाल *(kamāl)* पु. perfection; excellence.

कमी *(kami)* स्त्री. decline; deficiency; shortage.

कमीज़ *(qamiz)* स्त्री. shirt.

कमीन *(kamiṅ)* अ. क्रि. low-born; mean.

कमीना *(kaminā)* अ. क्रि. mean; wicked.

कयामत *(qayāmat)* स्त्री. day of resurrection; last day of judgement.

कर *(kar)* पु. tusk of an elephant; hand; tax.

करतब *(kartab)* पु. work; performance; skill; jugglery.

करतार *(kartār)* पु. master; husband; the Creator.

करतूत *(kartüt)* स्त्री. misdeed; evil doing.

करना *(karnā)* स. क्रि. to act; to perform.

करनी *(karni)* स्त्री. action; deed.

करवट *(karvat)* स्त्री. sleeping on the side; turning from one side to the other side.

करामात *(karāmāt)* स्त्री. wonderful feat; miracle.

करार *(qarār)* पु. contract; agreement.

करारा *(karārā)* अ. क्रि. hard; rigid; crisp; befitting (reply).

कराहना *(karāhnā)* स. क्रि. to cry in pain; to moan.

करिश्मा *(karismā)* पु. magic; miracle.

करीना *(qarinā)* पु. manner; mode; orderliness.

करीब *(qarib)* क्रि. close by; near.

करुण *(karun)* अ. क्रि. merciful; touching.

करुणा *(karunā)* स्त्री. mercy; pity; tenderness of feeling.

करोड़ *(karor)* अ. क्रि. ten million.

कर्कश *(karkas)* अ. क्रि. husky; cruel.

क़र्ज़ *(qarz)* पु. debt; loan.

कर्ण *(karn)* पु. ear; hypotenuse; helm of a ship.

कर्तव्य *(kartavya)* पु. duty.

कर्ता *(kartā)* पु. the Creator.

कर्म *(karma)* पु. act; work; occupation; fate; grammatical object.

कर्मठ *(karmath)* अ. क्रि. active; energetic.

कर्मण्य *(karmanya)* अ. क्रि. hard working; laborious.

कलंक *(kalank)* पु. aspersion; blame.

कलंकित *(kalankit)* अ. क्रि. blemished; defamed.

कल *(kal)* अ. क्रि. melodious; yesterday; tomorrow; comfort; machine or its part.

कलई *(qalai)* स्त्री. tin; white wash; external grandeur.

कलपना *(kalpana)* स. क्रि. to grieve; to lament.

कलफ़ *(kalaf)* पु. starch; pimple or spot on the face.

कलम *(kalam)* स्त्री. pen.

कलसा *(kalsā)* पु. waterpot; jar.

कलह *(kalah)* पु. scramble; quarrel.

कला *(kalā)* स्त्री. division; moon's phase.

कलाई *(kalāi)* पु. fore-arm; wirst.

कली *(kali)* स्त्री. bud; gusset.

कलुष *(kalus)* पु. impurity; sin; dirty; sinful.

कलूटा *(kalütā)* अ. क्रि. of black complexion; sun-burnt.

कलेजा *(kaleja)* पु. heart; liver.

कल्पना *(kalpanā)* स्त्री. supposition; imagination.

कल्पनातीत *(kalpanātit)* अ. क्रि. beyond imagination; unimaginable.

कल्याण *(kalyān)* पु. welfare; good fortune.

कल्लोल *(kallol)* पु. frolic; play.

कवच *(kavac)* पु. armour; helmet.

कवयित्री *(kavayitri)* स्त्री. poetess.

कवायद *(qavāyad)* पु. military exercise; drill.

कवि *(kavi)* पु. poet.

कविता *(kavitā)* स्त्री. poem; peotry.

कवित्व *(kavitva)* पु. poetic genius.

कश *(kas)* पु. lash; whip; pulling; flogging.

कशमकश *(kaśamakas)* स्त्री. tension.

कशीदा *(kasidā)* पु. embroidery.

कष्ट *(kast)* पु. distress; pain; trouble.

कसक *(kasak)* स्त्री. griping pain; strain.

कसकना *(kasakanā)* स. क्रि. to cause a pain (or strain).

कसना *(kasanā)* स. क्रि. to tighten; to fix firmly.

कसबा *(qasbā)* पु. town.

कसम *(qasam)* स्त्री. oath.

कसर *(kasr)* स्त्री. deficiency; draw back.

कसरत *(kasrat)* स्त्री. physical exercise.

कसाई *(kasāi)* पु. butcher.

कसाव *(kasāv)* पु. astringency; tightness.

कसूर *(qasür)* पु. error; fault.

कसैला *(kasailā)* अ. क्रि. pungent; astringent.

कसौटी *(kasauti)* स्त्री. touch stone trial.

कहकहा *(qahqahā)* पु. a boisterous laugh.

कहना *(kahnā)* स. क्रि. to say; to utter.

कहा *(kahā)* पु. order; precept; saying.

कहानी *(kahāni)* स्त्री. tale; story.

कहावत *(kahāvat)* स्त्री. saying; proverb.

कॉंच *(kāmc)* पु. glass.

कॉंटा *(kāmtā)* पु. thorn; fishing hook.

कॉंटेदार *(kāntedār)* अ. क्रि. prickly; thorny.

कांड *(kāmd)* पु. sectional division; chapter; incident.

कांत *(kānt)* पु. lover; husband; pleasing; lovely.

कांति *(kānti)* स्त्री. beauty; loveliness; lustre.

कॉंपना *(kāmpnā)* स. क्रि. to shiver; to shudder.

कॉंसा *(kāmsā)* पु. bronze.

काइयाँ *(kāiyan)* अ. क्रि. shrewd; cunning.

काई *(kāi)* स्त्री. lichen; moss.

काक *(kāk)* पु. crow; cunning fellow.

काग़ज़ *(kāgaz)* पु. paper; written document.

काग़ज़ी *(kāgazi)* अ. क्रि. made of paper; paper-dealer.

काजल *(kājal)* पु. lampblack for use on eyes; soot.

काजू *(kājü)* पु. cashew-nut.

काट *(kāt)* पु. act of cutting; cut; bite; wound.

काटना *(kātnā)* स. क्रि. to cut; to bite; to reap; to trim.

काठ *(kāth)* पु. timber; wood.

काठी *(kāthi)* स्त्री. structure; frame; saddle.

काढ़ना *(kārhnā)* स. क्रि. to embroider.

कातना *(kātnā)* स. क्रि. to spin.

कार्तिक *(kārtik)* पु. the eighth month of Hindu calender.

कातिल *(qātil)* पु. murderer.

कान *(kān)* पु. ear.

काना *(kānā)* अ. क्रि. one eyed; partly rotten (fruit).

कानून *(qānün)* पु. law.

कापी *(kāpi)* स्त्री. exercise book.

काफिर *(kāfir)* पु. disbeliever in Mohammedanism, cruel, pitiless.

काफिला *(kāfila)* पु. caravan.

काफ़ी *(kāfi)* अ. क्रि. sufficient; enough; coffee.

काबू *(qābü)* पु. possession; control.

काबिल *(qābil)* अ. क्रि. qualified; able.

काम *(kām)* पु. task; employment; job; desire.

कामकाजी *(kāmkāji)* अ. क्रि. busy; active; laborious.

कामगार *(kāmgār)* पु. labourer; worker.

कामचलाऊ *(kāmcalāu)* अ. क्रि. adhoc.

कामचोर *(kāmcor)* अ. क्रि. inactive; lazy; shirker.

कामधंधा *(kām-dhandhā)* पु. occupation; work; daily work.

कामना *(kāmanā)* स्त्री. wish; desire.

कामयाब *(kāmyāb)* अ. क्रि. successful.

कामिनी *(kāmini)* स्त्री. beautiful lady; lustful woman.

कामी *(kāmi)* अ. क्रि. loving; lustful.

कामुक *(kāmuk)* अ. क्रि. sensual; amorous.

कायदा *(qāydā)* पु. regulation; practice.

कायम *(qāyam)* अ. क्रि. settled; established.

कायर *(kāyar)* अ. क्रि. timid; coward.

कायल *(qāyl)* अ. क्रि. convinced by argument.

काया *(kāyā)* स्त्री. the body; person.

कारखाना *(kārkhānā)* पु. mill; factory; workshop.

कारगर *(kārgar)* अ. क्रि. effective.

कार *(kār)* पु. cause; purpose; reason.

कारतूस *(kārtus)* पु. cartridge.

कारनामा *(kārnāmā)* पु. deed; doing.

कारबार *(kārbār)* पु. business; profession; occupation.

कारवाँ *(kārvām)* पु. caravan.

कारागृह *(kārāgreh)* पु. jail; prison.

कारावास *(kārāvās)* पु. imprisonment; captivity.

कारिंदा *(kārindā)* पु. one who works for some one; an agent.

कारिस्तानी *(kāristāni)* स्त्री. trickery; cunningness.

कारीगर *(kārigar)* पु. mechanic; craftsman; artisan.

कारोबार *(kārobār)* पु. occupation; business.

कार्य *(kārya)* पु. work; vocation; job.

कार्यकर्ता *(kārya-kartā)* पु. employee; worker.

कार्यकुशल *(kāryakusal)* अ. क्रि. efficient.

कार्यक्रम *(kārya-kram)* पु. programme.

कार्यवाहक *(kārya-vāhak)* अ. क्रि. officiating; acting.

कार्यवाही *(kāryavāhi)* स्त्री. proceedings.

कार्यसूची *(kārya-suci)* स्त्री. agenda.

कार्यान्वित *(kāryānvit)* अ. क्रि. executed.

कार्यालय *(kāryālay)* पु. office.

कालकोठरी *(kāl-kothari)* स्त्री. solitary cell.

काला *(kālā)* अ. क्रि. dark; black.

कालिख *(kālikh)* स्त्री. lampblack; stain; soot; blackness.

कालिमा *(kālimā)* स्त्री. blemish; blackness.

क़ालीन *(qālin)* पु. carpet.

काल्पनिक *(kālpanik)* अ. क्रि. unreal; imaginary.

काव्य *(kāvya)* पु. poetry.

काश *(kās)* पु. Had God willed thus! May it happen!

काश्त *(kāśt)* स्त्री. tenancy; cultivation.

काहिल *(kāhil)* अ. क्रि. indolent; lazy.

किंचित *(kincit)* अ. क्रि. somewhat; perhaps.

किंतु *(kin-tu)* पु. but.

किंवदंती *(kimvadanti)* स्त्री. false report; rumour.

किचकिच *(kic-kic)* स्त्री. useless prattling; quarrel.

कितना *(kitnā)* अ. क्रि. how much.

कितने *(kitne)* अ. क्रि. how many.

किधर *(kidhar)* अ. क्रि. where.

किनारा *(kinārā)* पु. side; edge; bank.

किफ़ायत *(kifāyat)* स्त्री. thrift; economy.

किरण *(kiran)* स्त्री. ray of light; beam.

किरायेदार *(kirāyedār)* पु. hirer; tenant.

किराना *(kirānā)* पु. grocery.

किराया *(kirāyā)* पु. hire; rent; fare.

किलकना *(kilaknā)* स. क्रि. to shout in joy.

किलकारी *(kilkāri)* स्त्री. sound of joy.

किला *(qilā)* पु. castle; fort; tower.

किवाड़ *(kivār)* स्त्री. a door-leaf.

किशमिश *(kiśmiś)* स्त्री. small stoneless raisins; currants.

किशोर *(kiśor)* अ. क्रि. youthful; adolescent.

किश्ती *(kiśti)* स्त्री. boat.

किसान *(kisān)* पु. peasant; farmer; cultivator.

किस्त *(qist)* स्त्री. portion of debt; instalment.

किस्म *(qism)* स्त्री. kind; sort; type.

किस्सा *(qissā)* पु. tale; story.

किचड़ *(kicar)* पु. clay; mud.

कीटाणु *(kitānu)* पु. germ.

कीड़ा *(kirā)* पु. worm; insect.

कीमत *(qimat)* स्त्री. cost; price; worth.

कीर्ति *(kirti)* स्त्री. fame; reputation.

कील *(kil)* स्त्री. pin; peg; nail.

कुँआरा *(kun-ārā)* अ. क्रि. unmarried; bachelor.

कुंकुम *(kunkum)* स्त्री. saffron.

कुँजड़ा *(kumjrā)* पु. vegetable vendor.

कुंजी *(kumji)* स्त्री. key.

कुंठा *(kunthā)* स्त्री. frustration.

कुंडल *(kundal)* पु. large ring worn on the ears.

कुंद *(kund)* पु. lotus flower.

कुआँ *(kuam)* पु. well.

कुकरे *(kukre)* पु. trachoma.

कुकर्म *(ku-karm)* पु. sin; misdeed.

कुख्यात *(ku-khyāt)* अ. क्रि. defamed; of bad repute.

कुचलना *(kucalnā)* स. क्रि. to tread; to crush.

कुछ *(kuch)* पु. क्रि. some; a little; anything.

कुटनी *(kutni)* स्त्री. procuress; a bawd.

कुटिल *(kutil)* अ. क्रि. cruel; crooked.

कुटी *(kuti)* स्त्री. hut; cottage.

कुटीर *(kutir)* पु. cottage.

कुटुंब *(kutumb)* पु. family.

कुढ़ना *(kurhnā)* स. क्रि. to grudge; to be angry.

कुतरना *(kutarnā)* स. क्रि. to nibble; to gnaw.

कुतूहल *(kutūhal)* पु. eagerness; curiosity.

कुत्ता *(kuttā)* पु. dog.

कुत्सित *(kutsit)* अ. क्रि. shabby; contemptible.

कुदरत *(qudrat)* स्त्री. the nature; power; God.

कुनबा *(kunbā)* पु. household; family.

कुपित *(kupit)* अ. क्रि. angry; offended; irate.

कुबड़ा *(kubrā)* अ. क्रि. household; family.

कुमक *(kumak)* स्त्री. reinforcement; aid; assistance.

कुमार *(kumār)* पु. boy; son; unmarried.

कुमुद *(kumud)* पु. lily; red lotus.

कुम्हलाना *(kumhlānā)* स. क्रि. to wither; to shrivel; to fade.

कुम्हार *(kumhār)* पु. potter.

कुरबानी *(qurbāni)* स्त्री. sacrifice.

कुरेदना *(kurednā)* स. क्रि. to scratch; to scrape.

कुर्सी *(kursi)* स्त्री. chair.

कुल *(kul)* अ. क्रि. all; entire; complete; lineage; dynasty.

कुलटा *(kulatā)* स्त्री. unchaste woman.

कुलबुलाना *(kulbulānā)* स. क्रि. to rumble; to creep; to be restless.

कुली *(quli)* पु. labourer; coolie.

कुलीन *(kulin)* अ. क्रि. well born; of noble descent; of gentle blood.

कुल्ला *(kullā)* पु. rinsing and washing of mouth; gargle.

कुल्हाड़ा *(kulhārā)* पु. exe; hatchet.

कुशल *(kuśal)* अ. क्रि. expert; skilful; safety; prosperity.

कुशाग्र *(kuśāgr)* अ. क्रि. sharp; penetrating.

कुशासन *(kuśāsan)* पु. maladministration.

कुश्ती *(kuśti)* स्त्री. duel; wrestling.

कुष्ठ *(kusth)* पु. leprosy.

कुसुम *(kusum)* पु. flower.

कुसूर *(qusūr)* पु. ommission; fault.

कुहकना *(kuhakanā)* स. क्रि. to twiter; to coo.

कुहरा *(kuhrā)* पु. fog; mist.

कुहराम *(kuhrām)* पु. uproar; lamentation.

कुहासा *(kuhāsā)* पु. fog; mist.

कूकना *(kūknā)* स. क्रि. to sob; cry of a pea cock.

कूच *(küc)* पु. departure; march.

कूचा *(kücā)* पु. a narrow path lane.

कूट *(küt)* अ. क्रि. false; counterfeit.

कूटना *(kütnā)* स. क्रि. to pound; to crush to beat.

कूड़ा *(kürā)* पु. sweepings; rubbish

कूढ़ *(kürh)* अ. क्रि. dull-headed; stupid.

कूदना *(küdnā)* स. क्रि. to leap; to jump.

कूबड़ *(kübar)* पु. hunch; hump.

कूल्हा *(külhā)* पु. bones of the hip; hip.

कृतकृत्य *(krit-kritya)* अ. क्रि. successful; happy.

कृतघ्न *(kritaghna)* अ. क्रि. thankfull; grateful.

कृतज्ञ *(kritajya)* अ. क्रि. indebted; grateful.

कृतार्थ *(kritarth)* अ. क्रि. satisfied; gratified; obliged.

कृति *(kriti)* स्त्री. a work.

कृती *(kriti)* अ. क्रि. creative; creator.

कृत्य *(kritya)* पु. duty; perforr ance; work.

कृत्रिम *(kritrim)* अ. क्रि. bogus; artificial; fictitious.

कृदंत *(kridant)* पु. participle.

कृपण *(kripan)* अ. क्रि. stingy; miser.

कृपया *(kripayā)* पु. favourable; kindly; please.

कृपा *(kripā)* स्त्री. grace; kindness; pity.

कृपालु *(kripālu)* अ. क्रि. compassionate; kind.

कृश *(kriś)* अ. क्रि. thin; lean.

कृषक *(kriśak)* पु. peasant; farmer.

कृषि *(kriśi)* स्त्री. agriculture; farming.

कृष्ण *(kriśna)* अ. क्रि. dark; black; lord Krishna.

केंचुआ *(kemcuā)* पु. earthworm.

केंचुली *(kemculi)* स्त्री. slough of a snake.

केंद्र *(kendra)* पु. centre.

केंद्रक *(kendrak)* पु. a nucleus.

केंद्रित *(kendrit)* अ. क्रि. concentrated; centralised.

केंद्रीकरण *(kendrikaran)* पु. centralisation.

केंद्रीय *(kendriya)* अ. क्रि. central.

केतली *(ketli)* पु. kettle.

केला *(kelā)* पु. banana.

केलि *(keli)* स्त्री. frolic; pastime; sport.

केवट *(kevat)* पु. boat man.

केवड़ा *(kevrā)* पु. the fragrance flowers of screnpine.

केवल *(keval)* अ. क्रि. alone; only; mere.

केसर *(kesar)* स्त्री. the tendrils of a flower; saffron.

केसरी *(kesari)* पु. lion.

कैंची *(qaimci)* स्त्री. scissors; shears.

कैंसर *(kensar)* पु. cancer.

कै *(qai)* स्त्री. vomiting; nausea.

कैद *(qaid)* स्त्री. imprisonment.

कैफियत *(kaifiyat)* स्त्री. statement; description; remarks.

कैसा *(kaisā)* अ. क्रि. of what sort; how.

कोंपल *(kompal)* स्त्री. new sprout; tender leaf.

कोई *(koi)* क्रि. anybody; a few; someone .

कोख *(kokh)* स्त्री. womb.

कोट *(kot)* पु. fort; citadel; a coat.

कोटा *(kotā)* पु. quota.

कोटि *(koti)* स्त्री. rank; category; ten million.

कोठरी *(kothri)* स्त्री. small room; cabin.

कोठा *(kothā)* पु. big room; ware house.

कोठी *(kothi)* पु. mansion; bunglow.

कोड़ा *(korā)* पु. lash; whip.

कोढ़ *(korh)* पु. leprosy.

कोण *(kon)* पु. corner; angle.

कोतवाली *(kotvāli)* स्त्री. main police station.

कोताही *(kotāhi)* स्त्री. want; deficiency.

कोप *(kop)* पु. anger; wrath.

कोफ्त *(koft)* स्त्री. tedium.

कोमल *(komal)* अ. क्रि. tender; mild; soft.

कोयल *(koyl)* स्त्री. cuckoo.

कोयला *(koylā)* पु. coal.

कौल *(qaul)* पु. agreement; contract; promise.

कौशल *(kauśal)* पु. art; welfare; skill.

क्या *(kyā)* वि. what.

क्यों *(kyom)* पु. why.

क्रम *(kram)* पु. system; chain; series.

क्रमशः *(kramshah)* क्रि. by degrees; respectively.

क्रमांक *(kramānk)* पु. roll nunber.

क्रमिक *(kramik)* अ. क्रि. serial; successive.

क्रांति *(krānti)* स्त्री. revolution.

क्रिया *(kriyā)* स्त्री. activity; action; work; verb.

क्रियात्मक *(kriyātmak)* पु. i.e., active; functional.

क्रियान्वित *(kriyānvit)* स्त्री. implementation.

क्रियाविधि *(kriyāvidhi)* स्त्री. procedure.

क्रियाशील *(kriyāsil)* अ. क्रि. active.

क्रिस्तान *(kristān)* पु. Christian.

क्रीड़ा *(krirā)* स्त्री. amusement; sport.

क्रुद्ध *(kruddh)* अ. क्रि. infuriated; angry; wrathful.

क्रूर *(krūr)* अ. क्रि. unkind; ruthless; cruel.

क्रोध *(krodh)* पु. fret; anger.

क्रोधित *(krodhit)* अ. क्रि. resentful; angry.

क्रोधी *(krodhi)* अ. क्रि. wrathful; hightempered.

क्लांति *(klanti)* स्त्री. fatigue; weariness.

क्लिष्ट *(kliśt)* अ. क्रि. difficult.

क्लेश *(kleś)* पु. trouble; suffering; pain.

क्षण *(ksan)* पु. an instant; moment.

क्षणिक *(ksanik)* अ. क्रि. momentary.

क्षत *(ksat)* अ. क्रि. hurt; wounded.

क्षति *(ksati)* स्त्री. harm; injury; wastage.

क्षतिपूर्ति *(ksatipūrti)* स्त्री. reimbursement; compensation.

क्षमता *(ksamatā)* स्त्री. fitness; ability; competence.

क्षमा *(ksama)* स्त्री. forgiveness; mercy.

क्षम्य *(ksamya)* अ. क्रि. forgivable.

क्षय *(ksay)* पु. decrease; loss; erosion.

क्षार *(kśār)* पु. alkali; alkaline; salty.

क्षितिज *(ksitig)* पु. horizon.

क्षीण *(ksin)* अ. क्रि. weak; feeble.

क्षुद्र *(ksudra)* अ. क्रि. contemptible; small.

क्षुब्ध *(ksubdh)* अ. क्रि. impatient; angry.

क्षेत्र *(ksetr)* पु. ground; field.

क्षेत्रफल *(ksetra-phal)* पु. area.

क्षेम *(ksem)* स्त्री. protection; welfare.

क्षोभ *(ksobh)* पु. excitement; agitation distress.

ख

ख *(kha)* the second consonant in Devnagri alphabets.

खँखारना *(khamkhārnā)* स. क्रि. to hawk; to make effort before spitting.

खंजर *(khanjar)* पु. poniard; dagger.

खंड *(khand)* पु. part; section.

खंडन *(khandan)* पु. denial; repudiation.

खँडहर *(khandhar)* पु. debris; the ruins.

खंडित *(khandit)* अ. क्रि. destroyed; broken.

खंदक *(khandaq)* पु. a moat round a fort; a deep ditch.

खंभा *(khambhā)* पु. post; pillar.

खचाखच *(khacā-khac)* अ. क्रि. वि. overcrowded.

खच्चर *(khaccar)* पु. mule.

खज़ाँची *(khazānci)* पु. treasurer.

खज़ाना *(khazānā)* पु. treasury; treasure.

खटकना *(khataknā)* स. क्रि. to throb; to feel disgusted.

खटका *(khatkā)* पु. fear; doubt; knocking.

खटखटाना *(khatkhatānā)* स. क्रि. to knock; to tap.

खटपट *(khatta-pat)* स्त्री. strife; wrangling; quarrel.

खटमल *(khatt-mal)* पु. a bed bug.

खटाई *(khatāi)* स्त्री. sourness; tartness.

खटाखट *(khatā-khat)* स्त्री. sound of beating; constant cliking; quickly.

खटास *(khatās)* स्त्री. tartness; sourness.

खट्टा *(khattā)* अ. क्रि. tart; sour.

खड़ा *(kharā)* अ. क्रि. erect; standing; upright.

खड्ड *(khadd)* पु. deep pit.

खत *(khat)* पु. letter; handwriting.

खतरनाक *(khatarnāk)* अ. क्रि. risky; dangerous.

खतरा *(khatrā)* पु. risk; danger.

खता *(khatā)* स्त्री. error; mistake.

खत्म *(khatm)* अ. क्रि. end; complete; finished.

खदेड़ना *(khadernā)* स. क्रि. to drive away.

खद्दर *(khaddar)* पु. hand-spun cloth.

खनकना *(khanaknā)* स. क्रि. to clink; to jingle.

खनिक *(khanik)* पु. miner.

खनिज *(khanij)* अ. क्रि. mineral substance.

खपत *(khapat)* स्त्री. consumption; sale.

खपना *(khapnā)* स. क्रि. to be used; to be consumed.

खफा *(khafa)* अ. क्रि. angry; enraged; displeased.

खबर *(khabar)* स्त्री. information; news.

खबरदार *(khabardār)* अ. क्रि. careful; cautious.

खब्त *(khabt)* पु. madness; mania.

खामियाज़ा *(khamiyāzā)* पु. compensation; loss.

खरगोश *(khargos)* पु. hare; rabbit.

खरबूज़ा *(kharbüzā)* पु. melon.

खरा *(kharā)* अ. क्रि. pure; sincere; candid.

खराब *(kharāb)* अ. क्रि. spoiled; bad; wicked; defected.

खरीद *(kharid)* स्त्री. purchase; buying.

खरीदना *(kharidnā)* स. क्रि. to purchase; to buy.

खरीदार *(kharidār)* पु. purchaser.

खरीफ *(kharif)* स्त्री. crop which is reaped in autumn.

खरोंचना *(kharomcnā)* स. क्रि. to scrape; to scratch.

खर्च *(kharc)* पु. expenditure; expense.

खर्चीला *(kharcila)* अ. क्रि. extravagant; lavish; costly; expensive.

खर्रा *(kharrā)* पु. genuine; pure.

खर्राटा *(kharrātā)* पु. snoring.

खलबली *(khalbali)* स्त्री. alarm; agitation; commotion.

खलल *(khalal)* पु. confusion; interruption.

खलिहान *(khalihān)* पु. grainary; barn.

खसखस *(khas-khas)* पु. mawseed; poppy seed.

ख़सम *(khasam)* पु. husband; master.

खसरा *(khasrā)* पु. measles.

खसोटना *(khasotnā)* स. क्रि. to pull out; to scratch.

खस्ता *(khastā)* अ. क्रि. very brittle; crisp.

खाँड *(khānd)* स्त्री. unrefined sugar.

खाँसना *(khāmsanā)* स. क्रि. to cough.

खाँसी *(khāmsi)* स्त्री. cough.

खाई *(khāi)* स्त्री. dike; ditch; trench.

खाक *(khāk)* स्त्री. dirt; ashes; anything trivial.

खाका *(khākā)* पु. map; diagram; sketch.

खाकी *(khāki)* अ. क्रि. dusky; brown.

खाट *(khāt)* स्त्री. bedstead; cot.

खाड़ी *(khāri)* स्त्री. bay; gulf.

खाता *(khātā)* पु. ledger; account.

खातिर *(khātir)* स्त्री. hospitality; for.

खातिरी *(khātiri)* स्त्री. hospitality.

खाद *(khād)* स्त्री. manure; fertilizer.

खाद्य *(khādya)* पु. food; edible.

खान *(khān)* स्त्री. mine.

खानदान *(khāndān)* पु. family.

खाना *(khānā)* स. क्रि. to eat; eatable.

ख़ाना *(khānā)* पु. house; compartment; shelf.

खानाबदोश *(khānā-bados)* पु. rover; an idle scamp.

खामी *(khāmi)* स्त्री. defect.

खामोश *(khāmoś)* अ. क्रि. taciturn; silent.

खारा *(khārā)* अ. क्रि. salty brackish.

खारिज *(khārij)* अ. क्रि. expelled; dismissed; discharged.

खारिश *(khāriś)* स्त्री. itch; scab.

खाल *(khāl)* स्त्री. skin. hide.

खालिस *(khālis)* अ. क्रि. unmixed; pure.

खाली *(khāli)* अ. क्रि. void; empty; vacant.

खास *(khās)* अ. क्रि. peculiar; special; proper.

खासा *(khāsā)* अ. क्रि. good; noble.

खासियत *(khāsiyat)* स्त्री. quality; characteristics.

खिंचाव *(khimcāv)* पु. tightness; attraction.

खिचड़ी *(khicri)* स्त्री. a dish prepared from rice and pulse boiled together; a mixture; hotch-potch.

खिड़की *(khirki)* स्त्री. window.

खिताब *(khitāb)* पु. title.

खिदमत *(khidmat)* स्त्री. duty; service.

खिन्न *(khinn)* अ. क्रि. wearied; sad;

glum; gloomy.

खिलखिलाना *(khilkhilānā)* स. क्रि. to laugh loudly.

खिलना *(khilnā)* स. क्रि. to blow; to blossom.

खिलवाड़ *(khilvār)* स्त्री. pastime; frolic.

खिलाड़ी *(khilāri)* पु. player; sportsman.

खिलाफ *(khilaf)* अ. क्रि. contrary; opposite; against.

खिलौना *(khilaunā)* पु. toy.

खिल्ली *(khilli)* स्त्री. jest; joke.

खिसकना *(khisaknā)* स. क्रि. to slip away; to move slowly.

खिसियाना *(khisiyānā)* स. क्रि. to grin; to giggle.

खींचना *(khimcnā)* स. क्रि. to wrest; to pull; to haul.

खीज/खीझ *(khijh)* स्त्री. anger; vexation.

खीरा *(khirā)* पु. cucumber.

खुजली *(khujli)* स्त्री. itch; eczema.

खुजाना *(khujānā)* स. क्रि. to scratch.

खुद *(khud)* क्रि. self; of one's own accord.

खुदगरज़ *(khudgarz)* अ. क्रि. selfseeking; selfish.

खुदरा *(khudrā)* अ. क्रि. small coins retail.

खुदा *(khudā)* पु. God; the almighty.

खुदाई *(khudāi)* स्त्री. providence; digging.

खुफिया *(khufiyā)* अ. क्रि.secret; a spy.

खुरचना *(khurcanā)* स. क्रि.to scrape to scratch.

खुरदरा *(khurdarā)* अ. क्रि. coarse; rough.

खुराक *(khurāk)* स्त्री. diet; dose.

खुर्दबीन *(khurd-bin)* स्त्री. microscope.

खुलना *(khulnā)* स. क्रि. to be unravelled; to be opened; to be untied.

खुलासा *(khulāsā)* पु. brief; summary; gist; brief.

खुल्लम-खुल्ला *(khullam-khullā)* अ. क्रि. without reservation; publicly.

खुश *(khuś)* अ. क्रि. pleased; merry; happy.

खुशकिस्मत *(khuś-kiśmat)* अ. क्रि. for tunate.

खुशखबरी *(khuś-khabri)* स्त्री. glad findings; happy news .

खुशनसीब *(khuś-naśib)* अ. क्रि. fortunate.

खुशबू *(khuśbü)* स्त्री. odour; fragrance.

खुशमिज़ाज *(khuś-mijāz)* अ. क्रि. cheerful; good-tempered.

खुशहाल *(khuś-hāl)* अ. क्रि. prosperous; in good circumstances.

खुशामद *(khuśāmad)* स्त्री. false praise; flattery.

खुशी *(khuśi)* स्त्री. delight; cheerfulness; happiness.

खुश्क *(khuśk)* अ. क्रि. withered; dry.

खुश्की *(khuśki)* स्त्री. brought; dryness.

खूँख्वार *(khümkhvār)* अ. क्रि. ferocious; cruel.

खूँटी *(khümti)* स्त्री. stubble.

खून *(khün)* पु. murder; blood.

खूनी *(khüni)* पु. murderer; assassin.

खूबसूरत *(khübsürat)* अ. क्रि. handsome; beautiful.

खूबी *(khübi)* स्त्री. goodness; speciality; merit.

खेत *(khet)* पु. field; farm.

खेतिहर *(khetihar)* पु. peasant; farmer.

खेती *(kheti)* स्त्री. agriculture; farming.

खेद *(khed)* पु. sorrow; gloominess; regret.

खेमा *(khemā)* पु. tent; pavilion.

खेल *(khel)* पु. fun; game; sport.

खेलना *(khelnā)* स. क्रि. to sport; to play; to stage.

खैर *(khair)* स्त्री. welfare; happiness; all right; well.

खैरात *(khairāt)* स्त्री. alms; charity.

खैरियत *(khairiyat)* स्त्री. safety; welfare.

खोखला *(khokhlā)* अ. क्रि. empty; hollow.

खोज *(khoj)* स्त्री. search; investigation; discovery.

खोजना *(khojnā)* अ. क्रि. to seek; to search; to investigate; to discover.

खोटा *(khotā)* अ. क्रि. faulty; defective.

खोदना *(khodnā)* स. क्रि. to scratch; to big.

खोना *(khonā)* स. क्रि. to lose; to squander.

खोपड़ी *(khopri)* स्त्री. the pate; skull.

खोलना *(kholnā)* अ. क्रि. to unfold; to open; to unbind.

खौफ *(khauf)* पु. dread; fear.

खौलना *(khaulnā)* स. क्रि. to bubble; to boil.

ख्याति *(khyāti)* स्त्री. renown; fame; repute.

ख्याल *(khyāl)* पु. attention; thought; idea; opinion.

ख्वाब *(khvab)* पु. dream.

ख्वाहमख्वाह *(khvām-khah)* पु. without any purpose; uselessly.

ख्वाहिश *(khvāhis)* स्त्री. desire; wish.

ग

ग *(ga)* the third consonant in Devnagri alphabets.

गंज *(ganj)* स्त्री. pile; bladness.

गंजा *(ganjā)* अ. क्रि. scald-headed; bald.

गठबंधन *(gatha-bandhan)* पु. a custom in marriage ceremony in which the skirts of bridegroom's and bride's mantles are tied together.

गंदगी *(gandagi)* स्त्री. impurity; dirtiness.

गंदा *(gandā)* अ. क्रि. filthy; dirty; nasty.

गंदला *(gandalā)* अ. क्रि. dirty; muddy.

गंध *(gandh)* स्त्री. odour; smell; scent.

गंभीर *(gambhir)* अ. क्रि. sober; grave; reserved.

गँवाना *(gamvānā)* स. क्रि. to waste; to lose.

गँवार *(gamvār)* अ. क्रि. vulgar; ill-bred.

गँवारू *(gamvārü)* अ. क्रि. rude; rusic.

गऊ *(gaü)* पु. cow; gentle.

गज *(gaj)* पु. elphant; yard; yardstick.

गज़ब *(gazab)* स्त्री. calamity.

गटकना *(gatknā)* स. क्रि. to eat; to swallow.; to gulp.

गट्ठर *(gatthar)* पु. big bundle; package.

गठन *(gathan)* स्त्री. construction.

गठरी *(gathri)* स्त्री. parcel; bundle.

गठिया *(gathiyā)* स्त्री. sack; pains in the joints; rheumatism.

गठीला *(gathilā)* अ. क्रि. full of knots; robust.

गड़गड़ाना *(gargarānā)* स. क्रि. to rumble; to gurgle.

गड़पना *(garapanā)* स. क्रि. to glut; to swallow.

गड़बड़ *(garbar)* स्त्री. confusion; hinddle.

गड्डी *(gaddi)* स्त्री. pack; bundle.

गड्ढा *(gaddhā)* पु. ditch; hollow.

गढ़ *(garh)* पु. castle; stronghold.

गढ़ना *(garhnā)* स. क्रि. to form; to mould.

गण *(gan)* पु. multitude; union.

गणतंत्र *(ganatantra)* पु. Republic.

गणना *(gananā)* स्त्री. calculation; counting.

गणराज्य *(ganarājya)* पु. a government by the people.

गणिका *(ganikā)* स्त्री. dancing girl; prostitute.

गणित *(ganit)* पु. mathematics.

गति *(gati)* स्त्री. movement; speed; condition.

गतिमान *(gatimān)* अ. क्रि. on the move; moving.

गदर *(gadr)* पु. rebellion.

गदगद *(gadgad)* ·अ. क्रि. overwhelmed; very happy; greatly delighted.

गद्दा *(gaddā)* पु. bed cushion.

गद्दार *(gaddār)* पु. अ. क्रि. traitor.

गद्दी *(gaddi)* स्त्री. stuffed pad; cushion.

गद्य *(gadya)* पु. prose.

गधा *(gadhā)* पु. donkey; stupid fellow.

गन्ना *(gannā)* पु. sugarcane.

गप *(gap)* स्त्री. a gossip; chat.

गपोड़ *(gapor)* पु. a gossiper.

गफ *(gaf)* अ. क्रि. thick; dense; compact.

ग़फ़लत *(gaflat)* स्त्री. mistake; carelessness.

गबन *(gaban)* पु. misappropriation of money; embezzlement.

गम *(gam)* पु. woe; sorrow.

गमला *(gamlā)* पु. flower-pot.

गमी *(gami)* स्त्री. the period of observing mourning; death.

गरज *(garaj)* स्त्री. thunder; roar.

गरज़ *(garz)* स्त्री. concern; need.

गरजना *(garajnā)* स. क्रि. to bluster; to roar.

गरदन *(gardan)* स्त्री. neck.

गरम *(garam)* अ. क्रि. burning; warm; hot; woollen (cloth).

गरमागरम *(garmā-garam)* अ. क्रि. heated; hot; fresh.

गरमागरमी *(garma-garmi)* स्त्री. exchange of hot words.

गरमाना *(garmānā)* स. क्रि. to heat up; to be in excitement.

गरमी *(garmi)* स्त्री. heat; anger; summer.

गरिमा *(garimā)* स्त्री. grace; dignity.

गरिष्ठ *(gariśth)* अ. क्रि. indigestible; heavy.

गरीब *(garib)* अ. क्रि. humble; poor.

गरुर *(garür)* पु. pride; vanity.

गर्त *(gart)* पु. pit; crack in a wall.

गर्द *(gard)* स्त्री. dust; dirt.

गर्दन *(gardan)* स्त्री. neck.

गर्दिश *(gardis)* स्त्री. bad days; difficult time.

गर्भ (garbha) पु. pregnancy; the womb.

गर्भाधान *(garbā-dhān)* पु. conception; impregnation.

गर्भाशय *(garbhāśay)* पु. uterus; womb.

गर्भिणी *(garbhini)* अ. क्रि. pregnant.

गर्व *(garv)* पु. conceit; pride; vanity.

गर्हित *(garhit)* अ. क्रि. wicked; detestable.

ग़लत *(galat)* अ. क्रि. incorrect; wrong; untrue.

ग़लतफहमी *(galat-fahmi)* स्त्री. misunderstanding.

ग़लती *(galti)* स्त्री. error; mistake.

गलना *(galnā)* स. क्रि. to be dissolved; to decay.

गला *(galā)* पु. throat; neck.

गली *(gali)* स्त्री. lane; street.

गलीचा *(galicā)* पु. carpet.

गल्प *(galp)* स्त्री. small tale.

गल्ला *(gallā)* पु. cash-box; daily income of a shop kept in a chest.

गँवाना *(ganvānā)* स. क्रि. to waste; to suffer.

गवाह *(gavāh)* पु. deponent; witness.

गवाही *(gavāhi)* स्त्री. testimony; evidence .

गवैया *(gavaiyā)* पु. singer.

गश्त *(gast)* स्त्री. beat; patrol.

गहन *(gahan)* अ. क्रि. deep; profound.

गहना *(gahnā)* पु. ornament; jewellery; to handle.

गहरा *(gahrā)* अ. क्रि. profound; deep.

गहराई *(gahrāi)* स्त्री. depth; profoundity.

गहराना *(gahrānā)* स. क्रि. to be deep; to excavate.

गाँठ *(gamth)* स्त्री. knob; knot; tie.

गांभीर्य *(gāmbhirya)* पु. gravity; depth; importance.

गाँव *(gamv)* पु. village.

गाज *(gāj)* स्त्री. roar; thunderbolt; lighting.

गाजर *(gājar)* स्त्री. carrot.

गाड़ना *(gārnā)* स. क्रि. to lay; to bury; to pitch.

गाड़ी *(gāri)* स्त्री. car; cart; carriage.

गाढ़ा *(gārhā)* अ. क्रि. dense; thick; close; hand woven cloth.

गाना *(gānā)* स. क्रि. to chant; to sing; song.

गाफिल *(gāfil)* अ. क्रि. careless; stupid; negligent.

गाय *(gay)* स्त्री. cow; meek and humble.

गायक *(gāyak)* पु. singer.

गायन *(gāyan)* पु. chant; singing.

गायब *(gāyab)* पु. lost; vanished.

गाल *(gāl)* पु. cheek.

गाली *(gāli)* स्त्री. rebuke; abuse.

गावदी *(gāvdi)* अ. क्रि. dull headed; stupid.

गाहक *(gāhak)* पु. client; purchaser; customer.

गिचपिच *(gic-pic)* अ. क्रि. not clearly written; illegible.

गिड़गिड़ाना *(girgirānā)* स. क्रि. to implore; to whine.

गिद्ध *(giddh)* पु. vulture.

गिनती *(ginti)* स्त्री. calculation; reckoning.

गिनना *(ginanā)* स. क्रि. to count; regard to estimate.

गिरगिट *(girgit)* पु. chameleon; opportunist.

गिरजाघर *(girjāghar)* पु. church.

गिरना *(girnā)* स. क्रि. to come down; to fall; to drop.

गिरफ्तार *(giraftar)* अ. क्रि. seized; arrested.

गिरवी *(girvi)* अ. क्रि. pledged; mortgaged.

गिरावट *(girāvat)* स्त्री. lapse; spill.

गिरोह *(giroh)* पु. gang.

गिला *(gilā)* पु. accusation; complaint.

गिलाफ *(gilāf)* पु. pillow-cover.

गीत (git) पु. song.

गीदड़ *(gidar)* पु. jackal; coward.

गीला *(gilā)* अ. क्रि. wet.

गुंजन *(gunjan)* पु. humming sound.

गुंजाइश *(gunjāiś)* स्त्री. capacity; accommodation.

गुंजार *(gunjār)* पु. buzzing.

गुंडा *(gundā)* पु. rogue; wicked.

गुंबद *(gumbad)* पु. vault; dome.

गुच्छा *(gucchā)* पु. bunch; tuft.

गुज़र *(guzar)* स्त्री. passing of time.

गुज़रना *(guzarnā)* स. क्रि. to cross over; to pass away.

गुज़ारना *(guzārnā)* स. क्रि. pass time.

गुज़ारा *(guzārā)* पु. livlihood; subsistence.

गुट *(gut)* पु. group; faction.

गुड़ *(gur)* पु. raw sugar; jaggery.

गुड़िया *(guriyā)* स्त्री. doll.

गुड्डी *(guddi)* स्त्री. kite doll.

गुण *(gun)* पु. quality; attainment.

गुणन *(gunan)* पु. calcualtion; mulitiplication.

गुणा *(gunā)* पु. multiplication.

गुत्थमगुत्था *(guttham-guthā)* पु. entanglement; scuffle.

गुत्थी *(gutthi)* स्त्री. entanglement; knot.

गुदगुदा *(gudgudā)* अ. क्रि. fleshy; soft.

गुदगुदाना *(gudgudānā)* स. क्रि. to titillate; to tickle.

गुनगुना *(gungunā)* अ. क्रि. slightly warm.

गुनगुनाना *(gungunānā)* स. क्रि. to buzz; to hum.

गुनहगार *(gunahgār)* अ. क्रि. guilty; sinful; criminal.

गुना *(gunā)* multiple quantity.

गुनाह *(gunāh)* पु. gilt; sin; fault.

गुप्त *(gupt)* अ. क्रि. hidden; concealed; confidential.

गुप्तचर *(guptacar)* पु. a spy detective.

गुफा *(gupphā)* स्त्री. cave.

गुबार *(gubār)* पु. dust; vexation.

गुब्बारा *(gubbārā)* पु. balloon.

गुम *(gum)* अ. क्रि. hidden; missing; lost.

गुमान *(gumān)* पु. imagination; doubt; pride.

गुमाश्ता *(gumāśtā)* पु. manager; agent.

गुर *(gur)* पु. simplified method; formula.

गुरदा *(gurdā)* पु. kidney.

गुरु *(guru)* पु. teacher; spiritual guide.

गुरुता *(gurutā)* स्त्री. weight; heaviness; greatness; gravity.

गुरुत्वाकर्षण *(grurtvā-karśan)* पु. gravitation.

गुरुघंटाल *(gurughantāl)* अ. क्रि. very crafty; great knave.

गुर्गा *(gurgā)* पु. servant; spy; low fellow.

गुर्राना *(gurrānā)* स. क्रि. to snarl; to roar; to growl.

गुलछर्रे *(gulchharre)* पु. revelry; merry-making.

गुलाब *(gulāb)* पु. rose.

गुलाबी *(gulābi)* अ. क्रि. pink; rosy; light red colour.

गुलाम *(gulām)* पु. slave.

गुसलखाना *(gusal-khānā)* पु. a bathroom.

गुस्ताख *(gustākh)* अ. क्रि. rude; arrogant.

गुस्सा *(gussā)* पु. rage; anger.

गुस्सैल *(gussail)* अ. क्रि. choleric; furious.

गूँगा *(gümgā)* अ. क्रि. dumb.

गूँज *(gümj)* स्त्री. buzzing; echo.

गूँजना *(gümjanā)* स. क्रि. to buzz; to resound; to echo.

गूंधना *(gümdhnā)* स. क्रि. to knead.

गूढ़ *(gurh)* अ. क्रि. obscure; secret.

गूदड़ *(güdar)* पु. bundle of old tattered clothes; rags.

गूदा *(gudā)* पु. pulp; essential portion of a thing.

गृह *(grh)* पु. house; residence.

गृहस्थ *(grhasth)* पु. householder.

गृहस्थी *(grhasthi)* स्त्री. household; family.

गृहिणी *(grhiṇi)* स्त्री. wife.

गेरुआ *(geruā)* अ. क्रि. red brown.

गेहुआँ *(gehuām)* अ. क्रि. of the colour of wheat.

गेहूँ *(gehum)* पु. wheat.

गैर *(gair)* अ. क्रि. alien; other.

ग़ैरत *(gairat)* स्त्री. modesty; emulation.

गोंद *(gomd)* पु. gum; wood-gum.

गो *(go)* स्त्री. a cow.

गो *(go)* पु. though.

गोचर *(gochar)* अ. क्रि. visible.

गोता *(gotā)* पु. immersion; dive.

गोद *(god)* स्त्री. lap.

गोदना *(godnā)* स. क्रि. to puncture.

गोदाम *(godām)* पु. storehouse; warehouse.

गोदी *(godi)* स्त्री. the lap; dock.

गोपी *(gopi)* स्त्री. cowherd's wife.

गोबर *(gobar)* पु. cow-dung.

गोया *(goya)* पु. as if.

गोरा *(gorā)* अ. क्रि. fair-skinned; white.

गोलंदाज *(golandaz)* पु. marksman; gunner.

गोल *(gol)* अ. क्रि. globular; round.

गोला *(golā)* पु. ball; connon ball.

गोलार्ध *(golārdh)* पु. hemisphere.

गोली *(goli)* पु. pill; bullet; tablet.

गोशाला *(gośālā)* स्त्री. cow-shed; enclosure cattle.

गोश्त *(gost)* पु. flesh.

गोष्ठी *(gośthi)* स्त्री. assembly; discourse.

गौ *(gau)* अ. क्रि. a cow.

गौण *(gaun)* अ. क्रि. secondary; inferior.

ग़ौर *(gaur)* अ. क्रि. white; fair.

ग़ौर *(gaur)* पु. considration; pondering.

गौरव *(gaurav)* पु. heaviness; pride; glory.

ग्रंथ *(granth)* पु. book; volume.

ग्रीष्म *(grisma)* पु. the summer.

ग्लानि *(glāni)* स्त्री. lassitude; repentance.

ग्वाला *(gvālā)* पु. cowkeeper; milkman.

घ

घ *(gha)* the forth consonant in Devnagri alphabets.

घंटा *(ghantā)* पु. gong; bell; hour.

घंटी *(ghanti)* स्त्री. small bell.

घटक *(ghatak)* पु. intermediary; messenger.

घटना *(ghatanā)* स्त्री. happening; incident; to decrease; to decline.

घटा *(ghatā)* स्त्री. gathering of clouds.

घटिया *(ghatiyā)* अ. क्रि. low in price; cheap; of bad quality.

घड़ा *(gharā)* पु. an earthen pot; jug.

घड़ी *(ghari)* स्त्री. time; space of 24 hours; watch.

घन *(ghan)* पु. cloud; sledgehammer; cubid.

घना *(ghanā)* अ. क्रि. thick; close.

घनिष्ठ *(ghanisth)* अ. क्रि. most intimate; close.

घपला *(ghaplā)* पु. bungling.

घबराना *(ghabrānā)* स. क्रि. to be confused; to be nervous.

घमंड *(ghamand)* पु. pride; conceit.

घमासान *(ghamāsān)* अ. क्रि. fierce.

घर *(ghar)* पु. house; home.

घराना *(gharānā)* पु. family.

घरेलू *(gharelü)* अ. क्रि. domestic; private.

घसीटना *(ghasitnā)* स. क्रि. to trail; to drag.

घहरना *(ghahranā)* स. क्रि. to thunder.

घाघ *(ghāgh)* अ. क्रि. shrewd; cunning.

घाटा *(ghātā)* पु. deficit; loss.

घात *(ghāt)* स्त्री. killing; ambush; opportunity.

घातक *(ghātak)* अ. क्रि. fatal; savage; murderer.

घायल *(ghāyal)* अ. क्रि. hurt; wounded.

घाव *(ghāv)* पु. injury; wound.

घास *(ghās)* स्त्री. grass.

घासलेट *(ghāslet)* पु. vegetable oil; inferior stuff.

घिनौना *(ghinaunā)* अ. क्रि. hateful; odious.

घिसना *(ghisnā)* स. क्रि. to be worn out; to rub.

घूँघराले *(ghümghrāle)* अ. क्रि. curly.

घुग्घू *(ghugghü)* पु. owl; fool.

घुटना *(ghutnā)* स. क्रि. to be suffocated; knee.

घुट्टी *(ghutti)* स्त्री. a medicine which is given to infants to clear out the bowels.

घुड़ *(ghur)* पु. horse.

घुड़की *(ghurki)* स्त्री. reprimand; threat; rebuking.

घुन *(ghun)* पु. wood-worn.

घुन्ना *(ghunnā)* अ. क्रि. one who conceals his emotions; malicious.

घुप्प-अंधेरा *(ghupp-andherā)* अ. क्रि. pitch dark.

घुमक्कड़ *(ghumakkar)* अ. क्रि. rover; wanderer.

घुमड़ना *(ghumarnā)* स. क्रि. gathering of clouds in the sky.

घुमाव *(ghumāv)* पु. curvature; a turning; twist.

घुलना *(ghulnā)* स. क्रि. to be lean and thin; to be dissloved in a liquid; to be melted.

घुसना *(ghusnā)* स. क्रि. to pierce; to enter; to thurst into.

घुसपैठ *(ghus-paith)* स्त्री. access; entrance; infiltration.

घुसाना *(ghusānā)* स. क्रि. to pile; to poke; to penetrate.

घुसेड़ना *(ghusernā)* स. क्रि. to pierce; to thrust in; to stuff in.

घूँसा *(ghümsā)* पु. blow with the fist; boxing.

घूँघट *(ghümghat)* पु. veil which conceals womah's face.

घूँघर *(ghümghar)* पु. curl of hair; curly.

घूँट *(ghümt)* पु. a sip; draught.

घूमना *(ghümnā)* स. क्रि. to wander;

to roam; to stroll.

घूरना *(ghürnā)* स. क्रि. to ogle; to stare; to frown.

घूरा *(ghürā)* पु. rubbish; sweepings.

घूस *(ghüs)* स्त्री. emolument; bribe.

घृणा *(ghrna)* स्त्री. hatred; dislike.

घृणित *(ghrnit)* अ. क्रि. despicable; one who is hated.

घृत *(ghrt)* पु. clarified butter; ghee.

घेरना *(ghernā)* स. क्रि. to encircle; to ecompass; to enclose.

घेरनी *(gherni)* स्त्री. handle of a spinning wheel.

घेरा *(gherā)* पु. circumference; enclosure; fence.

घेवर *(ghevar)* पु. a kind of sweetmeat.

घोंघा *(ghomghā)* पु. conch; slug; snail; foolish; worthless.

घोंसला *(ghomslā)* पु. a nest.

घोटना *(ghotnā)* स. क्रि. to rub for smoothening; to cream up; to earn to memory.

घोटाला *(ghotālā)* पु. scandal; bungling; confusion.

घोड़ा *(ghorā)* पु. horse; hammer of a gun.

घोड़ी *(ghori)* स्त्री. a mare; a song sung at the time of marriage.

घोर *(ghor)* अ. क्रि. horrible; terrible; awful.

घोल *(ghol)* पु. solution.

घोलना *(gholnā)* स. क्रि. to mix; to dissolve.

घोषणा *(ghośanā)* स्त्री. announcement; a declaration.

च

च *(ca)* the first consonants in Devnagri alphabets.

चंगा *(canga)* अ. क्रि. healthy; sound; healed.

चंगुल *(cangul)* पु. grasp; claw.

चंचरीक *(cancarik)* पु. buzzing bee.

चंचल *(cancal)* अ. क्रि. restless; unsteady; flickering.

चंचलता *(cancalatā)* स्त्री. unsteadiness; inconsistancy.

चंट *(cant)* अ. क्रि. willy; cunning; cheat.

चंड *(cand)* अ. क्रि. violent; fierce; powerful.

चंडाल *(candāl)* पु. low born; outcaste; cruel.

चंडालिका *(candālikā)* स्त्री. an epithet of Hindu Goddes Druga.

चंदन *(candan)* पु. sandalwood.

चंदराना *(candrānā)* स. क्रि. to deceive; to beguile.

चँदला *(camdlā)* अ. क्रि. bald-headed.

चंदा *(canda)* पु. moon; contribution; subscription.

चंद्र *(candra)* पु. the moon.

चंद्रमा *(candramā)* पु. the moon .

चंद्रिका *(candrikā)* स्त्री. moonlight; moonbeams.

चंपत *(campat)* अ. क्रि. disappearing; vanishing.

चंपा *(campā)* पु. the tree Michelia champacca which bears fragrant yellow flowers.

चंपू *(campü)* पु. a literary work which is composed in prose and verse.

चँवर *(camvar)* पु. whisk; flapper made of the tail of a yak.

चक *(cak)* पु. plot of land.

चकई *(cakai)* स्त्री. whirling toy like pulley; female of a ruddy goose.

चकती *(cakti)* स्त्री. patch of leather; a round plate of metal.

चकता *(caktā)* पु. blotch on the skin.

चकनाचूर *(caknācur)* अ. क्रि. broken into fragments; much weary.

चकबंदी *(cakbandi)* स्त्री. marking the boundaries of land.

चकमक *(caqmaq)* पु. a kind of hard stone; flint.

चकमा *(cakmā)* पु. deception; trick.

चकराना *(cakrānā)* स. क्रि. to revolve; to feel dizzy; to be confused.

चकल्लस *(cakallas)* स्त्री. turnoil; fust.

चकाचौंध *(cakācaumdh)* स्त्री. dazzling effects of light on the eyes.

चकित *(cakit)* अ. क्रि. suprised; astonished; amazed.

चक्कर *(cakkar)* पु. multitude; circle; whirl; wheel; vertigo.

चक्की *(cakki)* स्त्री. mill; grinding mill.

चक्र *(cakr)* पु. wheel; circular object.

चक्राकार *(cakrākār)* अ. क्रि. circular.

चक्षु *(caksu)* पु. eye.

चखना *(cakhnā)* स. क्रि. to taste.

चखाना *(cakhānā)* स. क्रि. to cause to taste.

चचा *(cacā)* पु. paternal nucle.

चची *(caci)* स्त्री. paternal aunt.

चचेरा *(cacerā)* अ. क्रि. descended from the paternal uncle; cousin brother.

चचोड़ना *(cacornā)* स. क्रि. to sip by pressing under the teeth.

चट *(cat)* अ. क्रि. quickly; instantly.

चटक *(catak)* स्त्री. splendour; brilliance; sharp; bright.

चटकना *(catkanā)* स. क्रि. to snap; to make a sound of breaking up.

चटकनी *(catkani)* स्त्री. click; bolt of a door.

चटक-मटक *(catak-matak)* स्त्री. gaudiness; wantonness; ornamentation.

चटकीला *(catkilā)* अ. क्रि. of rich colour; shining; brilliant; glittering.

चटचट *(catcat)* स्त्री. a cracking sound.

चटखनी *(catkhani)* स्त्री. tower bolt; a bolt.

चटनी *(catni)* स्त्री. sauce.

चटपटा (catpatā) अ. क्रि. delicious; saucy.

चटाई *(catāi)* स्त्री. act of licking; mat.

चटाक *(catāk)* स्त्री. a crackling sound.

चटुल *(catul)* अ. क्रि. agile; fickle; clever.

चटोरा *(catorā)* अ. क्रि. fond of spicy food greedy.

चट्टान *(cattān)* स्त्री. cliff; rock.

चट्टा-बट्टा *(cattā-battā)* पु. toy for children.

चढ़ना *(carhnā)* स. क्रि. to ascend; to rise; to go up; to attack.

चढ़ाई *(carhai)* स्त्री. invasion; ascent; assult; attack.

चढ़ावा *(carhāvā)* पु. offering to a god; religious gift.

चणक *(canak)* पु. gram.

चतुरंग *(caturang)* पु. chess; an army consisting of pedestrians;

chariots; horses and elephants.

चतुरंगिणी *(caturangini)* अ. क्रि. having four divisions of an ancient Indian army.

चतुर *(catur)* अ. क्रि. dexterous; ingenious; expert; clever.

चतुर्दिक *(caturdik)* पु. four quarters; on all sides.

चतुर्भुज *(caturbhuj)* अ. क्रि. quadrilateral; four sided figure.

चतुर्भुजी *(caturbhuji)* स्त्री. the four armed female; Vaishnava cult.

चतुर्मास *(catur-mās)* पु. four months of the rainy season.

चतुर्मुख *(catur-mukh)* अ. क्रि. four faced; God Brahma.

चतुर्विधि *(catur-vidhi)* अ. क्रि. of four types; four-fold.

चतुराई *(caturāi)* स्त्री. ingenuity; cleverness.

चना *(canā)* पु. gram.

चपटा *(captā)* अ. क्रि. flat.

चपड़ा *(caprā)* पु. shellac; kind of red insect.

चपत *(capat)* पु. slap; push; loss.

चपरनाती *(capar-nāti)* पु. foolish; stupid.

चपरासी *(caprāsi)* पु. peon.

चपल *(capal)* अ. क्रि. variable; unsteady; clever.

चपलता *(capalatā)* स्त्री. variability; nimbleness; unsteadiness.

चपला *(capalā)* स्त्री. goddess Lakshmi; lighting.

चपाती *(capāti)* स्त्री. a thin cake or bread (of the Indian style).

चपेट *(capet)* स्त्री. blow; slap; sudden misfortune.

चप्पल *(cappal)* अ. क्रि. a sandal; a slipper.

चप्पा *(cappā)* पु. fourth part; small portion.

चप्पू *(cappü)* पु. oar; paddle.

चबाना *(cabānā)* स. क्रि. to masticate; to chew; to munch.

चबारा *(cabārā)* पु. room in the upper most storey of a house.

चबूतरा *(cabütrā)* पु. stand; platform; stage; dais.

चमक *(camak)* पु. brilliancy; shining flash.

चमकना *(camaknā)* स. क्रि. to flash; to sparkle; to giltter.

चमकनी *(camakni)* स्त्री. irritable woman.

चमकाना *(camakānā)* स. क्रि. to furnish; to varnish; to sparkle.

चमकीला *(camkilā)* अ. क्रि. glittering; glossy; clear; splendid.

चमगादड़ *(camgādar)* पु. bat; vampire.

चमचम *(cam-cam)* स्त्री. kind of Bengali sweetmeat; glittering; bright.

चमचमाना *(camcamānā)* स. क्रि. to glitter; to shine; to brighten.

चमचमाहट *(camcamāhat)* पु. brightness; glow; glitter.

चमचा *(camcā)* पु. large spoon; flatterer.

चमड़ा *(camrā)* पु. skin; leather.

चमत्कार *(camatkār)* पु. wonder; marvel; surprise.

चमन *(caman)* पु. bed of a garden; small garden.

चमर *(camar)* पु. tail of a yak used as a flapper to whisk off flies.

चमाचम *(camācam)* क्रि. brightly; shining.

चमार *(camār)* पु. shoemaker; skinner; cobbler.

चमेली *(cameli)* स्त्री. the jasmine plant; fragrant flower.

चम्मच *(cammac)* पु. spoon.

चयन *(cayan)* पु. work of collecting or picking; selection.

चयनिका *(cayanikā)* स्त्री. collection.

चर *(car)* पु. secret messenger; spy; sound made when tearing cloth.

चरई *(carai)* स्त्री. manger.

चरक *(carak)* पु. spy; a secret messenger; a traveller; white leprosy on Indian system of medicine.

चरकटा *(carkatā)* पु. chaff-cutter; non entity.

चरका *(carkā)* पु. a slight wound; loss; trick; fraud.

चरख़ *(carkh)* पु. revolving wheel; lathe.

चरख़ा *(carkhā)* पु. revolving wheel; spinning wheel.

चरखी *(carkhi)* स्त्री. winch; reel.

चरचराना *(carcarānā)* स. क्रि. to crackle; to sputter.

चरण *(caran)* पु. foot; the line of poetry; root.

चरणामृत *(carnāmrit)* पु. ambrosia of the feet.

चरपरा *(carparā)* अ. क्रि. hot; pungent; acrid.

चरबी *(carbi)* स्त्री. grease; fat; tallow.

चरम *(caram)* अ. क्रि. final; last; ultimate.

चरमराना *(carmarānā)* स. क्रि. to produce a creaking sound.

चरवाई *(carvāi)* स्त्री. job wages paid for grazing cattle.

चरवाना *(carvānā)* स. क्रि. to cause to graze.

चरवाहा *(carvāhā)* पु. shepherd; herdsman.

चरस *(caras)* पु. large bucket of leather used in irrigation; intoxicating drug prepared from the flowers of hemp.

चरसी *(carsi)* पु. one who smokes.

चरागाह *(carāgāh)* पु. pasturage; meadow.

चराचर *(carācar)* अ. क्रि. sentient and lifeless; movable and immovable.

चराना *(carānā)* स. क्रि. to graze; to make a fool of .

चरित *(carit)* पु. conduct; character; biography.

चरितार्थ *(caritārth)* अ. क्रि. gratified; successful.

चरित्र *(caritr)* पु. conduct; custom; character.

चरित्रांकन *(caritrānkan)* पु. characterisation.

चर्चा *(carcā)* स्त्री. discussion; mention.

चर्चरी *(carcari)* स्त्री. song sung in the spring season; clapping of hands.

चर्पटी *(carpati)* स्त्री. a kind of thin cake.

चर्म *(carm)* पु. skin; leather.

चलन *(calan)* पु. motion; use; method; custom.

चलना *(calnā)* स. क्रि. to go; to walk; to proceed.

चलनी *(calni)* स्त्री. a sieve.

चलाऊ *(calāū)* अ. क्रि. lasting; durable.

चलायमान *(calāyamān)* अ. क्रि. movable; wavering; unsteady.

चश्मा *(caśmā)* पु. spectacles; eyeglasses; fountain; spring.

चसका *(caskā)* पु. ardent desire; relish; habit.

चस्पाँ *(caspām)* अ. क्रि. stuck; fixed; affixed.

चहकना *(cahaknā)* स. क्रि. to warble; to be talkative; to chirp.

चहचहाना *(cahcahānā)* स. क्रि. to warble; to chirp.

चहलकदमी *(cahalqadmi)* स्त्री. walking of a person at a slow pace.

चहलपहल *(cahal-pahal)* स्त्री. mirth; merriment; hustle-bustle.

चहारदीवारी *(cahār-divāri)* स्त्री. four surrounding walls of a house.

चहेता *(cahetā)* पु. dear; beloved.

चहेती *(caheti)* स्त्री. beloved.

चाँटा *(camtā)* पु. slap; blow.

चांडाल *(candāl)* पु. sinful person.

चाँद *(cāmd)* पु. moon.

चाँदनी *(camdni)* स्त्री. moonlight; bedsheet.

चाँदी *(cāmdi)* स्त्री. silver.

चाँप *(cāmp)* स्त्री. pressure thrust; lock of a gun.

चांसलर *(cānsalar)* पु. the highest officer of a University; Chancellor.

चाक *(cāk)* पु. wheel; potter's wheel; circular mark.

चाकर *(cākar)* पु. servant; menial; waiter.

चाकरनी *(cākrani)* स्त्री. house maid; female servant.

चाकरी *(cākri)* स्त्री. service; attendance.

चाकू *(cāqü)* पु. knife.

चाचा *(cācā)* पु. paternal uncle.

चाट *(cāt)* स्त्री. spicy preparation of fruits; vegetables etc.

चाटना *(cātnā)* स. क्रि. to lap; to lick.

चाटु *(cātu)* पु. favourable conversation.

चाणक्य *(canakya)* पु. famous stateman of ancient India.

चातक *(cātak)* पु. kind of cuckoo which is supposed to drink drops of rain.

चातुरी *(cāturi)* स्त्री. clerverness; art.

चातुर्य *(cāturya)* पु. skill; cleverness.

चादर *(cādar)* स्त्री. sheet; plate; bedsheet.

चान्द्रायण *(cāndrāyan)* पु. Hindu fast which is observed for one month.

चाप *(cāp)* पु. bow; semi-circle; pressure sound of stepping.

चापना *(cāpnā)* स. क्रि. to press.

चापलूस *(cāplüs)* अ. क्रि. servile; flattering; obsequious.

चापलूसी *(cāplüsi)* स्त्री. adulation; flattery.

चापी *(cāpi)* पु. archer; the god Shiva.

चाबना *(cābnā)* स. क्रि. to masticate; to chew.

चाबी *(cābi)* स्त्री. key.

चाबुक *(cābuk)* पु. whip; lash.

चाम *(cām)* पु. skin; hide; leather.

चामुंडा *(cāmundā)* स्त्री. apithet of Hindu Goddess Durga.

चाय *(cāy)* स्त्री. tea.

चारखाना *(cārkhānā)* पु. chequered cloth.

चारण *(cāran)* पु. bard; panogyrist; wandering minstrel.

चारदीवारी *(cār-divāri)* स्त्री. enclosure.

चारपाई *(cārpāi)* स्त्री. bedstead; cot; bed.

चारपाया *(cārpāyā)* पु. quadruped.

चारा *(cārā)* पु. food for cattle; fodder; pasture.

चारु *(cāru)* अ. क्रि. attrractive; elegant; beautiful.

चारुता *(cārutā)* स्त्री. beauty.

चारों ओर *(cārun-or)* क्रि. about; around; on all sides.

चाल *(cāl)* स्त्री. walk; movement; step.

चालक *(cālāk)* अ. क्रि. driver.

चालाक *(cālāk)* अ. क्रि. sharp; clever; cunning.

चालान *(cālān)* पु. invoice; a challan.

चालू *(cālü)* अ. क्रि. tenable; current; prevalent; cunning.

चाव *(cāv)* पु. ardent desire; eagerness.

चावल *(cāval)* पु. rice.

चाशनी *(cāśni)* स्त्री. syrup; taste.

चाह *(cāh)* पु. desire; will; love; liking.

चाहत *(cāhat)* स्त्री. longing; fondness; affection.

चाहना *(cāhnā)* स. क्रि. to desire; to love; to need; to want.

चाहे *(cāhe)* पु. either or.

चिउँटा *(ciumtā)* पु. black ant of bigger species.

चिउँटी *(ciumti)* स्त्री. ant.

चिंघाड़ *(cinghār)* स्त्री. shrillery.

चिंघाड़ना *(cinghārnā)* स. क्रि. to scream; to trumpet like an elephant .

चिंतक *(cintak)* अ. क्रि. musing; thinker.

चिंतन *(cintan)* पु. study; thinking; reflection.

चिंता *(cintā)* स्त्री. anxiety; worry; care.

चिंत्य *(cintya)* अ. क्रि. reflective; thinkable.

चिकन *(cikan)* स्त्री. embroidered fine muslin.

चिकना *(ciknā)* अ. क्रि. smooth; glossy; clean; slippery.

चिकनाई *(ciknāi)* स्त्री. gloss; smoothness; oiliness.

चिकनापन *(ciknāpan)* पु. greasiness; smoothness.

चिकित्सक *(cikitsak)* पु. doctor; physician.

चिकित्सा *(cikitsā)* स्त्री. treatment; medication.

चिकित्सालय *(cikitsālay)* पु. dispensary; hospital.

चिकोटी *(cikoti)* स्त्री. pinch; twitch.

चिट्ठा *(cittha)* पु. detailed report; account book.

चिट्ठी *(citthi)* स्त्री. letter.

चिड़चिड़ा *(circirā)* अ. क्रि. peevish; irritable.

चिड़िया *(ciriyā)* स्त्री. bird; sparrow.

चिढ़ *(cirh)* स्त्री. vexation; irritation; hatred.

चिढ़ना *(cirhnā)* स. क्रि. to be irritated.

चिढ़ाना *(cirhānā)* स. क्रि. to tease; to huff.

चित *(cit)* अ. क्रि. supine; attention; mind.

चितकबरा *(citkabrā)* अ. क्रि. spotted.

चितवन *(citvan)* स्त्री. glance; look.

चिता *(citā)* स्त्री. funeral pyre.

चितेरा *(citerā)* पु. painter.

चित्त *(citt)* पु. mind; supine.

चित्ती *(citti)* स्त्री. scar; spot.

चित्र *(citr)* पु. painting; picture.

चित्रण *(citran)* पु. drawing; portrayal.

चिथड़ा *(cithrā)* पु. rag; shred.

चिथाड़ना *(cithārnā)* स. क्रि. to tear to pieces.

चिनगारी *(cingāri)* स्त्री. spark; ember.

चिनाई *(cināi)* स्त्री. bilge and cantline; brick-laying.

चिपकना *(cipaknā)* स. क्रि. to stick; to cling.

चिपचिपा *(cipcipā)* अ. क्रि. waxy; limy; gummy.

चिपचिपाना *(cipcipānā)* स. क्रि. to feel sticky.

चिपटना *(cipatnā)* स. क्रि. to stick; to adhere to.

चिपटा *(ciptā)* अ. क्रि. stuck; flat.

चिबुक *(cibuk)* पु. chin.

चिमटना *(cimatnā)* स. क्रि. to embrace; to cling; to hold fast.

चिमटा *(cimtā)* पु. tongs; pincers.

चिमनी *(cimni)* स्त्री. chimney; funnel.

चिरंजीव *(cirañjiv)* अ. क्रि. blessed with longevity; son.

चिरंतन *(cirantan)* अ. क्रि. ever lasting perpetual.

चिर *(cir)* अ. क्रि. lasting for a long time; ever.

चिरना *(cirnā)* स. क्रि. to be sawed.

चिराग़ *(cirāg)* पु. light; lamp.

चिरौंजी *(ciraunji)* स्त्री. name of a tree; edible nut.

चिलगोज़ा *(cilgozā)* पु. fruit of the pine tree.

चिलचिलाना *(cilcilānā)* स. क्रि. to shine scorchingly.

चिलम *(cilam)* स्त्री. part of hubble-bubble which contains the fire.

चिलमची *(cilamaci)* स्त्री. metal basin to wash hands.

चिल्ल-पों *(cillpom)* स्त्री. scream; cry; noise.

चिल्लाना *(cillānā)* स. क्रि. to cry out; to shout.

चिल्लाहट *(cillāhat)* स्त्री. clamour; scream.

चिह्न *(cihn)* पु. sign; mark.

चिह्नित *(cihnit)* अ. क्रि. marked. stained; spotted.

चीं *(cim)* स्त्री. chirp.

चींटी *(cimti)* स्त्री. ant.

चीख *(cikh)* स्त्री. scream; shreek.

चीख़ना *(cikhnā)* अ. क्रि. to shreek; to scream.

चीज़ *(ciz)* स्त्री. commodity; thing.

चीता *(citā)* पु. panther; leopard.

चीत्कार *(citkār)* स्त्री. shouting; uproar.

चीथड़ा *(cithrā)* पु. rag.

चीनी *(cini)* स्त्री. chinese (language); sugar; a chinese.

चीर *(cir)* पु. cloth; bark of tree; rag.

चीरना *(cirnā)* स. क्रि. to rip; to cleave; to tear.

चीरा *(cirā)* पु. surgical operation.

चील *(cil)* स्त्री. kite; eagle.

चुंगल *(cungal)* पु. claw; talon; handful.

चुंगी *(cungi)* स्त्री. cess; octroi.

चुंधियाना *(cumdhiyānā)* स. क्रि. to see dimly; to be dazzled.

चुंबक *(cumbak)* पु. loadstone; magnet.

चुंबन *(cumban)* पु. kissing; kiss.

चुंबित *(cumbit)* अ. क्रि. kissed; loved.

चुकंदर *(cuqandar)* पु. beet root; beet; sugar beet.

चुकाना *(cukānā)* स. क्रि. to settle; to pay off.

चुगना *(cugnā)* स. क्रि. to pick up food with beak.

चुग़ल-ख़ोर *(cugalkhor)* पु. tell tale; back biter.

चुगली *(cugli)* स्त्री. whispering; backbiting.

चुगाई *(cugāi)* स्त्री. act of picking.

चुगाना *(cugānā)* स. क्रि. to cause to pick.

चुटकी *(cutki)* स्त्री. pinch.

चुटकुला *(cutkulā)* पु. joke.

चुड़ैल *(curail)* स्त्री. hag; witch.

चुनना *(cunanā)* स. क्रि. to extract; to pick; to gather.

चुनरी *(cunri)* स्त्री. a piece of coloured cloth worn by women.

चुनाँचे *(cunāmce)* फा. thus; therefore.

चुनाव *(cunāv)* पु. pick; choice; election; selection.

चुनिंदा *(cunindā)* अ. क्रि. selected.

चुनौती *(cunauti)* स्त्री. a challenge.

चुप *(cup)* अ. क्रि. quiet; silent.

चुपचाप *(cup-cāp)* क्रि. quietly; silently.

चुपड़ना *(cuparnā)* स. क्रि. to besmear; to flatter.

चुप्पा *(cuppā)* अ. क्रि. secretive.

चुप्पी *(cuppi)* स्त्री. silence.

चुभना *(cubhnā)* स. क्रि. to be pierced; to feel pain.

चुमकारना *(cumkārnā)* स. क्रि. to coax; to fondle; to produce a kissing sound.

चुराना *(curānā)* स. क्रि. to steal; to pinch.

चुलबुला *(culbulā)* अ. क्रि. restless; gay; fidgeting; fickleness.

चुल्ली *(culli)* स्त्री. fire place; chimney of stove.

चुल्लू *(cullü)* पु. hollowed palm; handful of liquid.

चुस्की *(cuski)* स्त्री. suck; sip.

चुसना *(cusnā)* स. क्रि. to be sucked.

चुसनी *(cusni)* स्त्री. a child's coral; feeding bottle.

चुसाना *(cusānā)* स. क्रि. to cause to be sucked.

चुस्त *(cust)* अ. क्रि. tight; narrow; active; smart.

चुस्ती *(custi)* स्त्री. agility; smartness.

चुहटना *(cuhatnā)* स. क्रि. to crush with feet; to trample.

चुहल *(cuhal)* स्त्री. merriment; jollity.

चुहिया *(cuhiyā)* स्त्री. small mice.

चूँ *(cüm)* पु. shirping of a small bird.

चूँकि *(cümki)* फा. for this; because.

चूकना *(cüknā)* स. क्रि. to slip; to err; to miss.

चूज़ा *(cüza)* पु. chicken.

चूड़ा *(cüra)* स्त्री. top; creast; bracelet.

चूड़ी *(cüri)* स्त्री. ring; bangle.

चून *(cün)* पु. wheat-meal; flour.

चूना *(cünā)* स. क्रि. to drap; to leak; mortar; lime.

चूमना *(cümnā)* स. क्रि. to kiss.

चूरन *(cüran)* पु. digestive powder.

चूरमा *(cürmā)* पु. sweetmeat made of crushed bread.

चूरा *(cürā)* पु. sawdust; broken part.

चुर्ण *(cürn)* पु. digestive powder; powder.

चूल्हा *(cülhā)* पु. stove; fire place.

चूसना *(cüsnā)* स. क्रि. to sip; to suck; to drink.

चूहा *(cühā)* पु. mouse; rat.

चूहेदानी *(cühedāni)* स्त्री. rat trap.

चेचक *(cecak)* स्त्री. small-pox.

चेट *(cet)* पु. a servant.

चेटी *(ceti)* स्त्री. female servant.

चेतना *(cetanā)* स्त्री. feeling; consciousness; to understand; to think.

चेताना *(cetānā)* स. क्रि. to acquaint; to awaken; to tease.

चेतावनी *(cetāvni)* स्त्री. warning; alarm.

चेरी *(ceri)* स्त्री. female slave.

चेला *(celā)* पु. disciple; pupil.

चेष्टा *(cesṫā)* स्त्री. bodily action; spirit; effort.

चेहरा *(cehrā)* पु. face; countenance; front part of a thing.

चैत *(cait)* पु. first month of the Hindu calender.

चैतन्य *(caitanya)* अ. क्रि. perceiving; sensitive; conscious; intelligence

चैन *(cain)* पु. rest; tranquillity; relief.

चोंगा *(comgā)* पु. funnel; telephone's receiver.

चोंच *(comc)* स्त्री. neb; bill; beak.

चोखा *(cokhā)* अ. क्रि. pure; clear; keen; fine.

चोगा *(cogā)* पु. long coat; gown.

चोचला *(coclā)* स्त्री. coquettishness; playfulness.

चोट *(cot)* स्त्री. hurt; stroke; blow; attack.

चोटी *(coti)* स्त्री. braided hair of a woman; crown; braid.

चोर *(cor)* पु. burglar; thief.

चोरी *(cori)* स्त्री. burglary; theft.

चोली *(coli)* स्त्री. blouse; bodice; brassieres.

चौंकना *(caumknā)* स. क्रि. to start up in sleep; to be alarmed.

चौंकाना *(caumkānā)* स. क्रि. to alarm to startle.

चौंगा *(caungā)* पु. wheedling; bait.

चौंधियाना *(caumdhiyānā)* स. क्रि. to flash; to daze.

चौ *(cau)* an allomorph of four.

चौक *(cauk)* पु. square plot of ground; courtyard; centre of four road.

चौकी *(cauki)* स्त्री. stool; bench for sitting; police station.

चौकीदार *(cauki-dār)* पु. sentry; guard; watchman.

चौकीदारी *(cauki-dāri)* स्त्री. the business of watchman.

चौगान *(caugān)* पु. game of polo.

चौड़ा *(caurā)* अ. क्रि. wide; broad.

चौथा *(cauthā)* अ. क्रि. the forth; fourth lunar day; forth day of somebody's death.

चौथाई *(cauthāi)* अ. क्रि. fourth part.

चौथापन *(cauthā-pan)* पु. fourth stage of life; old age.

चौदस *(caudas)* स्त्री. fourteenth day of a lunar month according to Hindu calendar.

चौधरी *(caudhari)* पु. headman of a village; foreman.

चौपड़ *(caupar)* पु. a game which is played with three long dices.

चौपाई *(caupāi)* स्त्री. metre or verse consisting of four lines.

चौबाइन *(caubāin)* स्त्री. the wife of a chaube.

चौबारा *(caubārā)* पु. open room built on the roof of a house.

चौबे *(caube)* पु. a subcaste among Brahmans.

चौमंज़िला *(cau-manzilā)* अ. क्रि. built of four storeys.

चौसर *(causar)* पु. game played with long dices.

चौहान *(cauhān)* पु. caste among Rajputs.

च्यवन *(cyavan)* पु. dripping; oozing; the name of a sage.

च्यवनप्राश *(cyavn-parās)* पु. an Ayurvedic medicine.

च्युत *(cyut)* अ. क्रि. dropped; fallen; degraded.

च्युति *(cyuti)* स्त्री. falling; perishing.

छ

छ *(cha)* member of the second pentad of consonants in Devnagri alphabet.

छँटना *(chamtnā)* स. क्रि. to be separated on being cut; to be removed; to be lean and thin.

छँटा हुआ *(chamtā huā)* अ. क्रि. selected; cunning.

छँटाई *(chamtāi)* स्त्री. retrenchment the work or wages for cleaning.

छँटनी *(chamtani)* स्त्री. retrenchment .

छंद *(chand)* पु. metre; stanza.

छंदोबद्ध *(chando-badh)* अ. क्रि. in the form of a verse.

छकड़ा *(chakrā)* पु. wooden car; cart.

छकना *(chaknā)* स. क्रि. to be satisfied; to be intoxicated.

छकाना *(chakānā)* स. क्रि. to satiate; to intoxicate; to cheat.

छक्का *(chakkā)* पु. a group of six; the sixth at cards; a six in cricket.

छगन *(chagan)* पु. baby; darling.

छछूँदर *(chachümdar)* स्त्री. mole; muskrat.

छछूंदरी *(chachumdari)* स्त्री. a vole.

छज्जा *(chajjā)* पु. terrace; balcony.

छटंकी *(chatamki)* स्त्री. a weight of one small portion.

छटकना *(chataknā)* स. क्रि. to slip off; to keep aloof.

छटपटाना *(chatpatānā)* स. क्रि. to toss; to struggle; to be restless.

छटपटी *(chatpati)* स्त्री. restlessness; struggling.

छटाँक *(chatāmk)* स्त्री. one sixteenth of approximately a kilogram.

छटा *(chatā)* स्त्री. brilliance; glory; sixth.

छटाव *(chatāv)* पु. separation.

छठ *(chath)* स्त्री. the sixth day of fortnight in a lunar month.

छठी *(chathi)* स्त्री. ceremony performed on the sixth day after child birth.

छड़ी *(chari)* स्त्री. rod; cane; stick.

छत *(chat)* स्त्री. roof; ceiling.

छतरी *(chatri)* स्त्री. umbrella.

छत्ता *(chattā)* पु. a covered footpath; carridor; bee hive.

छत्र *(chatr)* पु. umbrella; parasol.

छत्रक *(chatrak)* पु. temple; pavilion.

छत्रधारी *(chatradhāri)* अ. क्रि. carrying an umbrella; prince.

छद्म *(chadma)* पु. pretext; trick; fraud.

छद्मी *(chadmi)* अ क्रि. crafty; impersonating.

छनकना *(chanakanā)* स. क्रि. to emit a hissing sound.

छनना *(channā)* पु. filter.

छनाई *(chanāi)* स्त्री. percolation.

छपाई *(chapāi)* स्त्री. stamping; printing.

छपाका *(chapākā)* पु. the sound produced by striking against water.

छपाना *(chapānā)* स. क्रि. to cause to be printed.

छप्पर *(chappar)* पु. booth; thatched roof.

छबड़ा *(chabrā)* पु. a shallow basket.

छबि *(chabi)* स्त्री. aspect; beauty.

छबीला *(chabilā)* अ. क्रि. handsome; graceful.

छरहरा *(charahrā)* अ. क्रि. light; swift; slim and smart.

छर्रा *(charrā)* पु. small shot.

छल *(chal)* पु. deception.

छलकना *(chalaknā)* स. क्रि. to spill out; to overflow.

छलनी *(chalni)* स्त्री. strainer; sieve.

छलाँग *(chalāng)* स्त्री. spring; vault; jumping.

छलावा *(chalāvā)* पु. shadow of a ghost; magic.

छलिया *(chaliyā)* अ. क्रि. पु. artful; crafty; cunning.

छल्ला *(challā)* पु. ring worn on the fingers; bangle .

छवि *(chavi)* स्त्री. features; beauty; brilliance.

छाँटना *(chāmtnā)* स. क्रि. to sort out; to select; to cut.

छांदोग्य *(chāndogya)* पु. an Upanishad of (Hindi classic) Samaveda.

छाँव *(chāmv)* स्त्री. shadow; shade.

छाँह *(chāmh)* स्त्री. reflection; shadow; shade.

छाछ *(chāch)* स्त्री. butter-milk.

छाज *(chāj)* पु. winnowing basket; thatch.

छाजन *(chājan)* पु. covering; cloth.

छाता *(chātā)* पु. umbrella.

छाती *(chāti)* स्त्री. chest; breast; bosom.

छात्र *(chātr)* पु. pupil; scholar; student.

छात्रावास *(chātrāvās)* पु. boarding house; hostel.

छान *(chān)* स्त्री. frame work for thatching with straw.

छानना *(chānnā)* स. क्रि. to strain; to filter; to investigate.

छान-बीन *(chān-bin)* search; investigation; critical research.

छाना *(chānā)* स. क्रि. to thatch; to cover; to spread; to dominate.

छाप *(chāp)* स्त्री. stamp; print; impression; brand.

छापना *(chāpnā)* स. क्रि. to stamp; to imprint; to impress .

छापा *(chāpā)* पु. impression; stamp; seal.

छापाखाना *(chāpākhānā)* पु. printing press.

छाया *(chāyā)* स्त्री. shade; shadow.

छार *(chār)* पु. ashes; dirt.

छाल *(chāl)* स्त्री. rind; bark; skin.

छाला *(chālā)* पु. blister; pimple.

छालिया *(chaliya)* स्त्री. betel nut.

छावनी *(chavni)* स्त्री. thatch; encampment; cantonment.

छावा *(chāvā)* पु. boy; son.

छिः *(chi)* स्त्री. a word used to express contempt.

छिंकाना *(chimkānā)* स. क्रि. to cause someone to sneeze.

छिछला *(chichlā)* अ. क्रि. thin; shallow.

छिछली *(chichli)* स्त्री. play of ducks and drakes.

छिछोरा *(chichorā)* स. क्रि. trivial; petty.

छिटकना *(chitaknā)* स. क्रि. to be scattered; to be dispersed.

छिटकाना *(chitkānā)* स. क्रि. to spread all round; to scatter.

छिटकी *(chitki)* स्त्री. speck.

छिड़कना *(chiraknā)* स. क्रि. to spill; to sprinkle; to patter.

छिड़काव *(chirkāv)* पु. act of sprinkling .

छिड़ना *(chirnā)* स. क्रि. to begin; to commence.

छितरना *(chitarnā)* स. क्रि. to be scattered.

छिद्र *(chidra)* पु. hole; gap; slot; defect .

छिनना *(chinnā)* स. क्रि. to be snatched away; to be taken by force.

छिनाल *(chināl)* अ. क्रि. स्त्री. adulterous; sluttish.

छिन्न *(chinn)* अ. क्रि. cut; divided.

छिपकली *(chipkali)* स्त्री. lizard.

छिपना *(chipnā)* स. क्रि. to be concealed; to be hidden.

छिपाना *(chipānā)* स. क्रि. to cover; to hide; to conceal.

छिपाव *(chipāv)* पु. hiding; secrecy.

छिलका *(chilkā)* पु. rind; crust; peel.

छिलना *(chilnā)* स. क्रि. to be rubbed away; to be excoriated.

छींक *(chimk)* स्त्री. a sneeze .

छींकना *(chimknā)* स. क्रि. to sneeze.

छींट *(chimt)* स्त्री. drops of water.

छींटना *(chimtnā)* स. क्रि. to scatter; to diffuse.

छींटा *(chimtā)* पु. slap; casual glance; spot made by a drop water.

छीका *(chikā)* पु. net of strings for hanging..

छीछड़ा *(chichrā)* अ. क्रि. tough flesh of an animal.

छीछालेदर *(chichāledar)* स्त्री. embarrassment.

छीज *(chij)* स्त्री. diminution; waste.

छीनना *(chinnā)* स. क्रि. to take possession; to extort; to snatch.

छीना-झपटी *(chinā-jhapati)* स्त्री. extortion; forcible seizing.

छीबर *(chibar)* स्त्री. thick calico.

छीलना *(chilnā)* स. क्रि. to peel; to pare; to scrap.

छुआछूत *(chüāchüt)* स्त्री. untouchability.

छुईमुई *(chui-mui)* स्त्री. sensitive; mimosa plant.

छुगनू *(chuganü)* पु. smallbells attached to an ornament.

छुटकारा *(chutkārā)* पु. escape; exemption; riddance.

छुटपन *(chutpan)* पु. infancy; childhood.

छुट्टा *(chuttā)* अ. क्रि. free; alone; not bound.

छुट्टी *(chutti)* स्त्री. leave; vacation; holiday.

छुड़वाना *(chrvānā)* स. क्रि. to cause someone freed; to leave.

छुड़ाव *(churāv)* पु. discharge.

छुपना *(chupnā)* स. क्रि. to hide oneself.

छुरा *(churā)* पु. razor; dagger.

छुरी *(churi)* स्त्री. knife; small dagger.

छुहारा *(chuhārā)* पु. dry date palm.

छू *(chü)* पु. the act of blowing or uttering; an incantation; to disappear from sight; to fly away; to vanish.

छूट *(chüt)* स्त्री. remission; discount; rebate.

छूटना *(chütnā)* अ. क्रि. to lag; to be dismissed; to get rid of.

छूत *(chüt)* स्त्री. touch; infection; contagion.

छूना *(chünā)* स. क्रि. to touch; to feel;.

छेक *(chek)* पु. hole; division.

छेड़खानी *(cherkhāni)* स्त्री. act of provoking; teasing.

छेड़छाड़ *(cherchār)* स्त्री. teasing; provocation.

छेड़ना *(chernā)* स. क्रि. to irritate; to excite; to tease.

छेद *(ched)* पु. aperture; breach; hole.

छेदक *(chedak)* अ. क्रि. boring or cutting; divisor.

छेदना *(chednā)* स. क्रि.to perforate; to drill; to bore.

छैला *(chailā)* पु. fap; spark; dandy.

छोकरा *(chokrā)* पु. boy; lad.

छोकरी *(chokri)* स्त्री. girl.

छोटा *(chotā)* अ. क्रि. little; narrow; junior.

छोटी इलायची *(choti-ilāici)* स्त्री. cardamom.

छोड़ना *(choranā)* स. क्रि. to relinquish; to remit; to let go; to leave.

छोर *(chor)* पु. border; end; the edge

छोरा *(chorā)* पु. boy; lad.

छोला *(cholā)* पु. gram.

छौंकना *(chumknā)* पु. to fry.

छौना *(chaunā)* पु. young one.

ज

ज *(ja)* the third of the second pentad of the consonants in Devnagri alphabet.

जंग *(jang)* स्त्री. battle; fight.

जंग *(zang)* पु. rust.

जंगम *(jangam)* अ. क्रि. movable; moving; living.

जंगल *(jangal)* पु. forest; woods; wilderness.

जंगली *(jangli)* अ. क्रि. wild; savage; uncivilised.

जंगी *(jangi)* अ. क्रि. military; warlike; martial.

जंघा *(janghā)* स्त्री. thigh.

जंजाल *(janjāl)* पु. perplexity; embarrassment; entanglement.

ज़ंजीर *(zañjir)* स्त्री. shackle; chain.

जंतु *(jantu)* पु. animal; creature.

जंभाई *(jambhāi)* स्त्री. yawning.

जकड़ना *(jakarnā)* स. क्रि. to tighten; to grasp.

ज़ख़ीरा *(zakhirā)* पु. a treasure; collection; store-house.

ज़ख्म *(zakhm)* पु. injury; wound.

ज़ख्मी *(zakhmi)* अ. क्रि. injured; wounded; hurt.

जग *(jag)* पु. the universe; world.

जगत *(jagat)* पु. the universe; world.

जगदंबा *(jagdambā)* स्त्री. Hindu goddess Durga.

जगदीश *(jagadiśa)* पु. Hindu Lord of the Universe.

जगना *(jagnā)* स. क्रि. to be awakened; to be careful.

जगमगाना *(jagmagānā)* स. क्रि. to glitter; to shine; to twinkle.

जगह *(jagah)* स्त्री. place; locality; space.

जगाना *(jagānā)* स. क्रि. to raise; to awake.

जघन्य *(jaghanya)* अ. क्रि. abominable; detested; low.

जच्चा *(jaccā)* स्त्री. woman in maternity.

जज़्ब *(jazb)* अ. क्रि. assimilated; absorbed.

जज़्बा *(jazbā)* पु. feeling; emotion.

जटिल *(jatil)* अ. क्रि. very difficult; intricate.

जठर *(jathar)* पु. womb; stomach.

जड़ *(jar)* स्त्री. root; senseless; material.

जड़ता *(jaratā)* स्त्री. immovableness; stiffness.

जड़ना *(jarnā)* स. क्रि. to fit; to join; to set with jewels.

जड़ाऊ *(jarau)* अ. क्रि. studded or set with jewels.

जड़ाना *(jarānā)* स. क्रि. to cause to be set.

जड़ी *(jari)* स्त्री. a medicinal plant.

जताना *(jatānā)* स. क्रि. to make known; to remind.

जत्था *(jatthā)* पु. gang; a band.

जन *(jan)* पु. mankind; a person; people.

जनक *(janak)* पु. father; originator; the father of Sita.

जनजाति *(janajāti)* पु. a tribe.

जनता *(janatā)* पु. public; masses.

जननी *(janani)* स्त्री. mother.

जनाना *(zanānā)* अ. क्रि. female; female ward.

जनाब *(janāb)* अ. क्रि. पु. your honour; your highness; mister.

जनार्दन *(janārdan)* पु. an epithet of Hindu Lord Vishnu.

जनेऊ *(janeü)* पु. sacred thread of Hindu religion.

जनोक्ति *(janokti)* स्त्री. proverb.

जन्म *(janm)* पु. birth; production; origin.

जन्मोत्सव *(janamotsav)* पु. birthday celebration.

जप *(jap)* पु. prayer.

जपना *(japnā)* स. क्रि. to repeat silently name of any deity; to mutter prayers.

जपमाला *(japmālā)* स्त्री. a rosary for counting prayers.

जब *(jab)* क्रि. when; at whatever time.

जबड़ा *(jabrā)* पु. jaw.

जबरदस्त *(zabardast)* अ. क्रि. strong; powerful; violent.

जबरन *(jabran)* क्रि. forcible; with force.

ज़बह *(zabah)* पु. slaughter.

ज़बहा *(zabahā)* पु. spirit; courage.

ज़बान *(zabān)* स्त्री. tongue; language.

ज़बानी *(zabāni)* अ. क्रि. by word of mouth; vocal.

जवाब *(javāb)* पु. answer.

जवाबदेह *(javābdeh)* अ. क्रि. accountable; liable; subject to.

ज़बून *(zabün)* अ. क्रि. bad; wicked.

ज़ब्त *(zabt)* अ. क्रि. confiscated; forfeited.

ज़ब्ती *(zabti)* स्त्री. forfeiture; forfeit.

जब्र *(jabra)* पु. oppression; force.

जमघट *(jamghat)* पु. throng; crowd; assembly.

जमदग्नि *(jamdagni)* पु. the name of a sage.

जमना *(jamnā)* स. क्रि. to be coagulated; to be frozen; to be fixed.

जमवट *(jamavat)* स्त्री. the wooden foundation of a well.

जमहाई *(jamahāi)* स्त्री. gaping; yawning.

जमा *(jamā)* अ. क्रि. accumulated; collected; stored.

जमाई *(jamāi)* पु. son-in-law.

जमात *(jamāt)* पु. assembly; class.

जमादार *(jamādār)* पु. head of soldiers; person on guard.

ज़मानत *(zamānat)* स्त्री. bond; surety; bail.

ज़मानती *(zamānati)* पु. surety; guarantor.

ज़माना *(zamānā)* पु. time; world; age; period.

जमाव *(jamāv)* पु. crowd; accumulation.

ज़मींकन्द *(zamimkand)* पु. the yam.

ज़मींदार *(zamindār)* पु. cultivator; land-lord.

ज़मीन *(zamin)* स्त्री. land; the earth; soil; ground.

ज़मीनी *(zamini)* अ. क्रि. earthly; pertaining to the earth.

जम्बुक *(jambuk)* पु. jackal.

जम्बूद्वीप *(jambüdvip)* पु. one of the seven divisions of the world as described in the Hindu Puranas.

जम्बूरा *(jambürā)* पु. swivel; small pliers.

जम्हाई *(jamhāi)* स्त्री. yawning.

जयंत *(jayant)* अ. क्रि. victorious; triumphant.

जयंती *(jayanti)* स्त्री. jubilee; goddess Durga.

जय *(jay)* स्त्री. victory; conquest.

जयकार *(jayakār)* स्त्री. cheers; rejoicings.

जयघोषणा *(jaya-ghośanā)* स्त्री. declaration of victory.

जयद्रथ *(jayadrath)* पु. brother-in-law of king Duryodhana.

जयध्वज *(jayadhvaj)* पु. name of an ancient king of Avanti; flag of victory.

जयपत्र *(jayapatra)* पु. bond of victory.

जयमंगल *(jaya-mangal)* पु. the elephant on which a king mounts.

जयश्री *(jayśri)* स्त्री. goddess of victory.

जयस्तंभ *(jaya-stambha)* पु. the monument erected to commemorate a victory.

जया *(jayā)* स्त्री. epithet of gooddess Durga; green grass.

ज़र *(zar)* पु. riches; wealth.

जरा *(jarā)* पु. senility; old age.

ज़रा *(zarā)* अ. क्रि. little; less.

जराग्रस्त *(jarā-grast)* अ. क्रि. aged; old.

जराभीरु *(jarā-bhiru)* पु. cupid.

जरासंध *(jarāsandh)* पु. name of an ancient king of an Indian state.

ज़रिया *(zariyā)* पु. connection; means; agency.

ज़री *(zari)* स्त्री. cloth woven with gold thread.

ज़रूर *(zarür)* क्रि. of course; certainly; necessarily.

ज़रूरत *(zarürat)* स्त्री. need; want; necessity.

ज़रूरी *(zarüri)* अ. क्रि. necessary; needful; important.

ज़र्क-बर्क *(zarq-barq)* अ. क्रि. shining; brilliant.

जर्जर *(jarjar)* अ. क्रि. old; decrepit;

worn out.

जर्जरित *(jarjarit)* अ. क्रि. tattered; crushed.

ज़र्दी *(zardi)* स्त्री. yellowness; paleness.

ज़र्रा *(zarrā)* पु. particle; an atom.

जर्राह *(jarrāh)* पु. surgeon; anatomist.

जर्राही करना *(jarrāhi karnā)* स. क्रि. to operate.

जलंधर *(jalandhar)* पु. the name of a demon; dropsy.

जल *(jal)* पु. water; aqua.

ज़लज़ला *(zalzalā)* पु. earthquake.

जलन *(jalan)* स्त्री. inflammation; burning sensation; jealousy.

जलना *(jalnā)* स. क्रि. to flame; to burn.

जलनिधि *(jal-nidhi)* पु. sea; ocean.

जलपक्षी *(jal-paksi)* पु. aquatic bird.

जलपात्र *(jal-pātra)* पु. urn; flagon.

जलपान *(jal-pān)* पु. breakfast; light refreshment.

जलप्रणाली *(jal-pranāli)* स्त्री. device of water.

जलप्रपात *(jal-prapāt)* पु. waterfall.

जलप्रवाह *(jal-pravah)* पु. torrent; act of throwing something into water.

जलप्रलय *(jal-pralay)* पु. destruction by water.

जलप्लावन *(jal-plāvan)* पु. flood.

जलबेंत *(jal-bent)* पु. water-cane.

जलभँवर *(jal-bhanvar)* पु. water bee.

जलमय *(jal-maya)* अ. क्रि. watery.

जलमानुष *(jal-mānus)* पु. merman.

जलयन्त्र *(jal-yantra)* पु. an appliance to raise water; water wheel.

जलवायु *(jal-vāyu)* स्त्री. climate.

जलशास्त्र *(jal-śāstra)* पु. hydromechanics.

जलसा *(jalsā)* पु. meeting; function; social gathering.

जलसेना *(jal-senā)* स्त्री. navy.

जलस्तंभ *(jal-stambh)* पु. lighthouse water-sprout.

जलाना *(jalānā)* स. क्रि. to light; to kindle; to burn; to scold.

ज़लालत *(zalālat)* स्त्री. meanness.

जला-भुना *(jalā-bhunā)* अ. क्रि. hot-tempered.

जलार्द्र *(jalā-rādr)* अ. क्रि. moist; wet.

जलाल *(jalāl)* पु. splendour; glory; power.

जलावतन *(jalā-vatan)* पु. exile; exiled.

जलाशय *(jalāśaya)* पु. tank; lake.

ज़लील *(zalil)* अ. क्रि. wretched; base; mean.

जलूस *(jalüs)* पु. procession.

जलेबी *(jalebi)* स्त्री. a kind of sweetmeat.

जल्दी *(jaldi)* स्त्री. quickness; hurry.

जल्प *(jalp)* पु. babbling.

जल्पना *(jalpanā)* स. क्रि. to brag; to boast.

जल्लाद *(jallād)* पु. executioner; cruel person.

जवनिका *(javanikā)* स्त्री. theatrical screen.

जवाँमर्द *(javām-mard)* स्त्री. gallantry; brave; hero.

जवान *(javān)* अ. क्रि. young; youthful; brave; soldier or sepoy.

जवानी *(javāni)* स्त्री. youth.

जवाब *(javāb)* answer; reply; retaliation.

जवाबी *(javābi)* अ. क्रि. requiring a reply; pertaining to answer.

जवाहर *(javāhar)* पु. jewel; gem.

जश्न *(jaśna)* पु. merriment; festivity; festival.

जस्ता *(jastā)* पु. zinc.

जहन्नुम *(jahannum)* पु. hell.

ज़हमत *(zahmat)* स्त्री. afflication; trouble; injury.

ज़हर *(zahar)* पु. venom; poison.

ज़हरमोहरा *(zahar-mohrā)* पु. the bezoar; a kind of green stone supposed to be and antidote to poison.

ज़हरीला *(zahrilā)* अ. क्रि. poisonous; venomous.

जहाँ *(jahām)* क्रि. wherever.

जहाँगीरी *(jahāngiri)* स्त्री. kind of bracelet.

जहाँपनाह *(jahām-panāh)* पु. the protector of the world; His Imperial Majesty.

जहाज़ *(jahāz)* पु. ship; vessel; sail.

जहाज़ी *(jahāzi)* अ. क्रि. marine; nautical; sailor.

जहान *(jahān)* पु. the world.

जहानी *(jahāni)* अ. क्रि. worldly; terrestrial.

जहालत *(jahālat)* स्त्री. ignorance; barbarity; stupidity.

जहीं *(jahim)* क्रि. wherever; at whatsoever place.

ज़हीन *(zahin)* अ. क्रि. intelligent; sagacious; wise.

जहेज़ *(jahez)* पु. dowry; gift in marriage.

जाह्नु *(jāhnu)* पु. name of a sage who adopted the river Ganges as his daughter.

जाँघ *(jāmgh)* स्त्री. thigh.

जाँघिया *(jānghiyā)* पु. lower underwear; short drawers.

जाँच *(jāmc)* पु. trial; investigation.

जाँचना *(jāmcnā)* स. क्रि. to ascertain; to examine; to try; to investigate.

जागना *(jāgnā)* स. क्रि. to get up from bed; to awake; to be careful.

जागता हुआ *(jāgtā-huā)* क्रि. vigilant unwinking.

जागरण *(jāgaran)* पु. watch; vigil; wakefulness.

जागरित *(jāgarit)* अ. क्रि. wide-awake; watchful; alert.

जागरूक *(jāgarük)* अ. क्रि. wakeful; vigilant.

जागीर *(jāgir)* स्त्री. rent-free grant given as a reward property.

जागृति *(jāgrti)* स्त्री. wakefulness; and awakening.

जाज्वल्यमान *(jājvalyamān)* अ. क्रि. shining; lustrous.

जाट *(jāt)* पु. a tribe in India.

जाड़ा *(jārā)* पु. winter; cold.

जाड्य *(jādya)* पु. lack of sensation.

जातक *(jātak)* पु. child; newborn baby.

जात-पात *(jāt-pāt)* स्त्री. caste and community.

जाता *(jātā)* स्त्री. girl; daughter.

जाति *(jāti)* स्त्री. race; sex; caste; community.

ज़ाती *(jāti)* अ. क्रि. personal; individual.

जातीय *(jātiya)* अ. क्रि. pertaining to tribe or caste.

जातीयता *(jātiyatā)* स्त्री. communal feeling.

जादू *(jādü)* पु. juggling; magic; spell; charm.

जादूगर *(jādügar)* पु. juggler; magician; conjurer.

जादूगरनी *(jādügarni)* स्त्री. witch.

जादूगरी *(jādügari)* स्त्री. magic; sorcery; a charm.

जान *(jān)* स्त्री. understanding; life; spirit.

जानकार *(jānkār)* अ. क्रि. conversant; knowing; experienced.

जानकी *(jānaki)* स्त्री. daughter; Sita.

जानदार *(jāndār)* अ. क्रि. animate; having life.

जानना *(jānanā)* स. क्रि. to know; to understand.

जान-पहचान *(jān-pehcān)* स्त्री. acquaintance.

जानवर *(jānvar)* पु. animal; beast.

जाना *(jānā)* स. क्रि. to go; to depart.

जानु *(jānu)* पु. the knee.

जानी *(jāni)* अ. क्रि. dear; beloved.

जाप *(jāp)* पु. rosary for prayers.

जापक *(jāpak)* पु. one who repeats the names of a deity.

जाफ़रान *(zāfrān)* पु. saffron.

जाबालि *(jā-bāli)* पु. the preceptor of Hindu king Dasharatha.

ज़ाब्ता *(zābtā)* पु. regulation; rule.

जाम *(jām)* अ. क्रि. jammed; jam; a peg.

जामन *(jāman)* पु. rennet used in coagulating milk.

जामा *(jāmā)* पु. garment; raiment; robe.

जामाता *(jāmātā)* पु. son-in-law.

जामुन *(jāmun)* पु. black plum; jambo.

जाम्बवती *(jāmb-vati)* स्त्री. one of the wives of Lord Krishna.

जाम्बवंत *(jāmb-vant)* पु. minister of ancient Hindu King Sugreeva.

ज़ायका *(zāyqā)* पु. relish; taste.

जायदाद *(jāydād)* स्त्री. property.

ज़ाया *(jāyā)* अ. क्रि. waste; ruined.

जार *(jār)* पु. a lover; and adulterer.

जारण *(jāran)* पु. burning; reducing to ashes.

जारी *(jāri)* अ. क्रि. proceeding; running.

जाल *(jāl)* पु. mesh; net; network; plot.

जाला *(jālā)* पु. net; cobweb.

ज़ालिम *(zālim)* अ. क्रि. tyrannical; cruel; oppressive.

जाली *(jāli)* स्त्री. net; frandulant; unanthentic.

जासूस *(jāsüs)* पु. emissary; spy.

ज़ाहिर *(zāhir)* अ. क्रि. obvious; clear; plain; manifest.

जाहिल *(jāhil)* अ. क्रि. foolish; ignorant; illiterate; rude.

ज़िंदगी *(zindagi)* स्त्री. फा. life; span of life.

ज़िंदा *(zindā)* वि. फा. alive; living.

जिंस *(jims)* स्त्री. अ. commodity; cereals.

जिगर *(jigar)* पु. फा. liver; spirit; courage.

जिज्ञासा *(jijñāsā)* स्त्री. curiosity; inquisitiveness.

जिज्ञासु *(jijñāsu)* वि. inquisitive; curious.

जिठानी *(jithāni)* स्त्री. wife of husband's elder brother.

जितना *(jitnā)* वि. as much.

जितने *(jitne)* वि. as many.

ज़िदी *(ziddi)* स्त्री. अ. obstinacy; stubbornness.

जिधर *(jidhar)* क्रि. वि. in whichever direction; wherever.

जिन, जिन्न *(jin; jinn)* पु. अ. ghost; one of the spirits of lower type.

ज़िम्मेदार *(zimmedār)* वि. अ. responsible; answerable.

ज़िम्मेदारी *(zimmedāri)* स्त्री. अ. responsibility.

ज़िम्मेवार *(zimmevār)* वि. अ. responsible.

जिरह *(jirah)* स्त्री. अ. cross-examination; cross-question.

ज़िरहबक्तर *(zirahbaktar)* पु. अ. armour.

ज़िला *(zilā)* पु. अ. district.

ज़िलाधीश *(zilādhis)* पु. district magistrate of collector.

जिलाना *(jilānā)* स. क्रि. to restore to life; to give life to; to revive.

जिल्द *(jild)* स्त्री. अ. binding of book cover; a volume; skin; hide.

जिल्दबंदी *(jildbandi)* स्त्री. अ. bookbinding.

जिल्दसाज़ *(jild-sāz)* पु. अ. bookbinder.

जिल्दसाज़ी *(jild-sāzi)* स्त्री. अ. bookbinding.

जिस *(jis)* सर्व. an oblique form of; which who.

जिसका *(jiskā)* सर्व. whose.

जिसको *(jisko)* सर्व. whom.

जिस जगह *(jis-jagah)* क्रि. वि. where.

जिसमें *(jis-men)* क्रि. वि. wherein.

जी *(ji)* पु. mind; heart.

जीजा *(jijā)* पु. brother-in-law (sister's husband).

जीजी *(jiji)* स्त्री. elder sister.

जीत *(jit)* स्त्री. victory; success; triumph; conquest; advantage.

जीतना *(jitnā)* स. क्रि. to win; to conquer.

जीना *(jinā)* अ. क्रि. to live; to be alive.

ज़ीना *(zinā)* पु. फा. staircase.

जीभ *(jibh)* स्त्री. tongue.

जीमना *(jimnā)* स. क्रि. to eat; to take (food).

जीर्णता *(jirnatā)* स्त्री. senescence; senility.

जीर्णशीर्ण *(jirn-śirn)* वि. tattered; worn out; ruined.

जीव *(jiv)* पु. life; soul; creature; living being; organism.

जीवन *(jivan)* पु. life.

जीवनचरित *(jivan-carit)* पु. biography.

जीवनदायक *(jivandāyak)* वि. life-giving.

जीवनी *(jivani)* स्त्री. biography.

जीवनीकार *(jivani-kār)* पु. biographer.

जीवरसायन *(jiv-rasāyan)* पु. biochemistry.

जीवविज्ञान *(jiv-vijnān)* पु. biology.

जीवाणु *(javānu)* पु. bacteria.

जीवाणुनाशक *(jivānu-nāsak)* वि. bectericidal.

जीवाणु विज्ञान *(jivānu-vijnān)* पु. bacteriology.

जीवात्मा *(jivātmā)* पु. individual soul enshrined in the human body.

जीविका *(jivikā)* स्त्री. livelihood; subsistence.

जीवित *(jivit)* वि. living; alive.

जुकाम *(zukām)* पु. cold; catarrh.

जुग-जुग *(jug-jug)* क्रि. वि. for ages; for ever.

जुगत *(jugat)* स्त्री. means; device; measure; contrivance; skill.

जुगल *(jugal)* पु. pair; couple.

जुगलबंदी *(jugal-bandi)* स्त्री. duet

जुगाड़ *(jugār)* पु. improvisation; manipulation; procurement.

जुगाली *(jugāli)* स्त्री. rumination.

जुगुप्सा *(jugupsā)* स्त्री. dislike; aversion; disgust; abhorrence.

जुझारू *(jujhārü)* वि. combatant; berserk.

जुटना *(jutnā)* अ. क्रि. to unite; to flock; to be engaged in work; to assemble.

जुटाना *(jutānā)* स. क्रि. to collect; to unite closely together; to combine.

जुड़ना *(jurnā)* अ. क्रि. to be attached or added; to collect (as gathering).

जुड़वाँ *(jurvām)* वि. twin.

जुतना *(jutnā)* अ. क्रि. to be yoked; to be tilled; to be engaged in a drudgery.

जुताई *(jutāi)* स्त्री. ploughing; tillage.

जुदा *(judā)* वि. फा. separate; distinct.

जुदाई *(judāi)* स्त्री. separation; parting.

जुर्म *(jurm)* पु. अ. crime; offence.

जुर्माना *(jurmānā)* पु. अ. fine; penalty.

जुर्रत *(jurrat)* स्त्री. अ. courage; audacity; effrontery.

जुर्राब *(jurrāb)* स्त्री. socks; stockings.

जुलाब *(julāb)* पु. purgative.

जुलाहा *(julāhā)* पु. weaver.

जुलूस *(julüs)* पु. अ. procession.

जुल्म *(zulm)* पु. अ. injustice; oppression; tyranny.

जूँ *(jüm)* स्त्री. bouse.

जूझना *(jüjhnā)* अ. क्रि. to fight; to combat; to struggle.

जूठन *(jüthan)* स्त्री. leavings (of food; drink etc.).

जूठा *(jüthā)* वि. defiled by eating or drinking.

जूड़ी *(jüri)* स्त्री. ague; malarial fever.

जूता *(jütā)* पु. a pair of shoes; shoes; slippers; sandals.

जूही *(jühi)* स्त्री. jasmine.

जेठ *(jeth)* पु. husband's elder brother; third month of the Indian calendar.

जेठानी *(jethāni)* स्त्री. wife of husband's elder brother.

जेब *(jeb)* पु. अ. pocket.

जेबकतरा *(jeb-qatrā)* पु. pick-pocket.

जेल *(jel)* पु. prison; gaol; jail.

जैसा *(jaisā)* क्रि. वि. as; like; such as.

जैसे *(jaise)* क्रि. वि. as; as if; according as; for example; for instance.

जोंक *(jomk)* स्त्री. leech.

जो *(jo)* सर्व. who; which; what; that.

जोखिम *(jokhim)* पु. risk; danger.

जोगी *(jogi)* पु. ascetic; mendicant.

जोड़ *(jor)* पु. addition; total; sum; joint; patch; match; seam.

जोड़ना *(jornā)* स. क्रि. to join; to unite; to bind; to connect; to attach; to add; to collect; to amass; to assemble; to hoard.

जोड़ा *(jorā)* पु. pair; couple; suit.

जोड़ी *(jori)* स्त्री. pair; couple.

जोत *(jot)* स्त्री. tillage; land-holding; right to till a land; yoke strap.

जोतना *(jotnā)* स. क्रि. to plough; to till; to yoke; to harness; to work.

जोताई *(jotāi)* स्त्री. act or wages of tilling etc.

ज़ोर *(zor)* पु. फा. strength; prowess; force; stress; strain; emphasis.

ज़ोरदार *(zordār)* वि. फा. powerful; strong; influential.

जोरू *(jorü)* स्त्री. wife.

जोश *(jos)* पु. फा. zeal; fervour; vigour enthusiasm.

जोशीला *(josīlā)* वि. zealous; spirited; vigorous; enthusiastic.

जौ *(jau)* पु. barley.

जौहर *(jauhar)* पु. valour; skill; valiance.

जौहरी *(jauhri)* पु. jeweller.

ज्ञात *(jñāt)* वि. known.

ज्ञातव्य *(jñātavya)* वि. knowable; worth knowing.

ज्ञाता *(jñātā)* पु. one who knows; scholar; learned person.

ज्ञान *(jñāna)* पु. knowledge; learning.

ज्ञानी *(jñāni)* वि. wise; learned; scholarly.

ज्ञानेंद्रिय *(jñānendriya)* पु. sense organ.

ज्ञापन *(jñāpan)* पु. memorandum; act or state of giving information or instruction.

ज्ञापित *(jñāpit)* वि. made known; in formed; notified.

ज्ञेय *(jñeya)* वि. perceptible; knowable.

ज्या *(jyā)* स्त्री. bow-string; (in geom.) the chord of an arc; sine.

ज़्यादती *(zyādati)* स्त्री. excess; high-handedness; injustice.

ज़्यादा *(zyādā)* वि. more; many; much; abundant; excessive; extra.

ज्यामिति *(jyāmiti)* स्त्री. geometry.

ज्येष्ठ[1] *(jyeśth)* वि. eldest; senior most.

ज्येष्ठ[2] *(jyeśth)* पु. third lunar month.

ज्येष्ठता *(jyeśthatā)* स्त्री. state of being eldest; seniority.

ज्येष्ठा *(jyeśthā)* स्त्री. elder sister; dearest wife; Ganges; middle finger; lizard

ज्यों *(jyom)* क्रि. वि. as; as if.

ज्योति *(jyoti)* स्त्री. light; flame; lustre; vision; luminosity.

ज्योतिष *(jyotis)* पु. astrology.

ज्योतिषी *(jyotiśi)* पु. astrologer.

ज्योत्स्ना *(jyotsnā)* स्त्री. moonlight.

ज्वर *(jvar)* पु. fever.

ज्वलंत *(jvalant)* वि. brilliant; shining; apparent; evident.

ज्वार *(jvār)* स्त्री. millet; tide.

ज्वार-भाटा *(jvār-bhātā)* पु. flood tide and ebb-tide.

ज्वालामुखी *(jvālā-mukhi)* पु. volcano.

झ

झ *(jha)* the fourth letter of Devnagri alphabets.

झंकार *(jhaṁkār)* पु. tinkling; jingling; clinking sound.

झंकारना *(jhaṁkārnā)* अ. क्रि. to produce tinkling; jingling sound.

झंकृत *(jhaṁkrt)* वि. tinkled; jingled.

झंझट *(jhanjhat)* पु. botheration; annoying situation; mess; trouble; imbroglio.

झंझावात *(jhanjhāvāt)* पु. storm.

झंडा *(jhaṇḍā)* पु. flag; banner; standard.

झंडी *(jhaṇḍi)* स्त्री. bunting.

झक *(jhak)* स्त्री. whim; craze; eccentricity.

झकझक *(jhak-jhak)* स्त्री. higgling; dispute; long-drawn discussion.

झकझोरना *(jhakjhornā)* स. क्रि. to shake violently.

झकोरना *(jhakornā)* स. क्रि. to shake; to put in motion; to derive or beat (as wind or rain); to gush through.

झक्की[1] *(jhakki)* पु. crazy; eccentric; whimsical.

झक्की[2] *(jhakki)* पु. crazy person; whimsical person; crack.

झक्कीपन *(jhakkipan)* पु. craziness;

whimsicality; essentricity.

झगड़ना *(jhagarṇā)* अ. क्रि. to quarel; to dispute; to argue; to altercate; to scramble.

झगड़ा *(jhagrā)* पु. quarrel; dispute; altercation; strife.

झगड़ालू *(jhagrālü)* वि. quarrelsome; contankerous; disputatious.

झटका *(jhatkā)* पु. jerk; jolt.

झटपट *(jhatpat)* क्रि. वि. speedily; quickly; promptly.

झड़ना *(jharnā)* अ. क्रि. to drop; to fall; to fall off.

झड़प *(jharap)* स्त्री. skirmish; brawl; contention; altercation; wordy duel.

झड़पना *(jharapnā)* अ. क्रि. to fight; to contend.

झड़बेरी *(jharberi)* स्त्री. wild plum; bush.

झड़ी *(jharī)* स्त्री. continuous or incessant downpour; uninterrupted occurrence.

झनक *(jhanak)* स्त्री. tinkling clinking / jingling sound.

झनझनाना *(jhanjhanānā)* अ. क्रि. to clang; jingle; tinkle; clink; to be benumbed or cramped.

झनझनाहट *(jhanjhanāhat)* स्त्री. jingling; tinkling; numbness.

झपकाना *(jhapkānā)* स. क्रि. to wink; to blink.

झपकी *(jhapki)* स्त्री. nap or doze; blink.

झपटना *(jhapatnā)* अ. क्रि. to dash; to run; to make a sudden swoop; to pounce; to snatch or snap (at); to grab.

झपट्टा *(jhapaṭṭā)* पु. swoop; pounce.

झबरा *(jhabrā)* वि. having long hair; hairy; shaggy.

झमेला *(jhamelā)* पु. botheration; mess; entanglement; imbroglio; complicated affair.

झरझर *(jharjhar)* स्त्री. sound produced by the flow of water; murmur.

झरना *(jharnā)* पु. fall; spring; streamlet.

झरोखा *(jharokhā)* पु. small window; aperture; latticed screen.

झलक *(jhalak)* स्त्री. glimpse; glance; semblance; tinge.

झलकना *(jhalaknā)* अ. क्रि. to be reflected; to appear faintly; to carry a semblance.

झलाई *(jhalāi)* स्त्री. soldering; welding; charges for soldering.

झल्लाना *(jhallānā)* अ. क्रि. to be annoyed; to be enraged; to shout peevishly; to be irritated; to fret and fume.

झल्लाहट *(jhallāhat)* स्त्री. fretting and fuming; tantrums.

झाँकना *(jhāṁknā)* अ. क्रि. to peep; to peer.

झाँकी *(jhāṁki)* स्त्री. tableau; pageant; scene; glance; glimpse; public display of decorated idols of Hindu gods.

झाँझ *(jhāṁjh)* स्त्री. cymbal; sistrum.

झाँसा *(jhāṁsā)* पु. deception; hoax; trickery; dodge; hoodwink.

झाड़[1] *(jhār)* पु. bush; shrub.

झाड़[2] *(jhar)* स्त्री. dusting; reprimand; rebuke; exorcism.

झाड़न *(jhāran)* स्त्री. duster; sweepings; rubbish.

झाड़ना *(jhārnā)* स. क्रि. to dust; to clean; to sweep; to extort; to reprimand; to scold; to exercise; to shake off; to knock off; to show off.

झाड़-फ़ानूस *(jhār-fānus)* पु. chandelier.

झाड़ू *(jhārü)* स्त्री. broom.

झाबा *(jhābā)* पु. a big basket; pannier.

झालर *(jhālar)* स्त्री. flounce; frill; festoon.

झिकझिक *(jhik-jhik)* स्त्री. useless wrangling; discussion.

झिझक *(jhijhak)* स्त्री. hitch; hesitation; shyness.

झिझकना *(jhijhaknā)* अ. क्रि. to hesitate; to feel shy.

झिड़कना *(jhiraknā)* स. क्रि. to rebuke; to reprimand; to scold; to snub.

झिड़की *(jhirkī)* स्त्री. rebuke; reproof; snub.

झिरी *(jhirī)* स्त्री. aperture; small hole; cleft; fissure; slit; recess; chink.

झिलमिलाना *(jhilmilānā)* अ. क्रि. to flicker; to shimmer; to twinkle.

झिलमिलाहट *(jhilmilāhat)* स्त्री. twinkle; shimmer; flicker.

झिल्ली *(jhillī)* स्त्री. thin skin; pellicle; membrane; film.

झींगुर *(jhiṁgur)* पु. cricket.

झीना *(jhīnā)* वि. thin; sparsely woven.

झुँझलाना *(jhuṁjhalānā)* अ. क्रि. to be irritated or annoyed; to be peevish or fretful.

झुँझलाहट *(jhuṁjhalāhat)* स्त्री. irritation; annoyance; peevishness; fretfulness.

झुंड *(jhuṇḍ)* पु. flock; herd; crowd; group; horde.

झुकना *(jhuknā)* स. क्रि. to bend. to hang down; to droop; to be bent down; to stoop; to lean; to incline; to bow; to submit; to yield.

झुकाना *(jhukānā)* स. क्रि. to bend; to cause to drop; to tilt; to cause to stoop; to force to accept defeat; to force to yield; to cause to lean.

झुकाव *(jhukāv)* पु. stoop; bowing down; bent; inclination; twist; tilt; trend.

झुठलाना *(jhuthlānā)* स. क्रि. to be lie; to falsify.

झुमका *(jhumkā)* पु. pendant of an ear-ring; a kind of ear-ring.

झुरमुट *(jhurmut)* पु. clump of trees etc.; cluster of shrubs; shadowy grove; shrubbery.

झुर्री *(jhurrī)* स्त्री. wrinkle.

झुलसना *(jhulasnā)* अ. क्रि. to be scorched; to be charred.

झुलसाना *(jhulsānā)* स. क्रि. to scorch; to singe; to sear.

झुलाना *(jhulānā)* स. क्रि. to swing; to rock.

झूठ *(jhūth)* पु. lie; falsehood; misrepresentation; untruth.

झूठा *(jhuthā)* वि. telling lies; untrue; false; fictitious; faithless.

झूमना *(jhūmnā)* अ. क्रि. to sway to and fro; to nod the head in a gay mood or intoxication.

झूमर *(jhūmar)* पु. ornament worn on head and ear; a kind of folk dance; rocking toy; ring of people; boats etc.

झूलना *(jhūlnā)* अ. क्रि. to swing; to dangle; to oscillate.

झेंप *(jheṁp)* स्त्री. blush; shyness; bashfulness.

झेंपना *(jheṁpnā)* अ. क्रि. to feel abashed; to blush; to feel embarrassed.

झोंकना *(jhoṁkanā)* स. क्रि. to throw; to thrust or pour (something) into furnace; to spend blindly.

झोंका *(jhoṁkā)* पु. gust; breeze; current (of wind); wave; undulation.

झोंपड़ी *(jhoṁpri)* स्त्री. hut; cottage.

झोला *(jholā)* पु. wallet; bag; kit; knapsack.

ट

ट *(ṭa)* the first letter of the third pentad of the Devnagri Alphabet.

टंकक *(ṭankak)* पु. typist.

टंकण *(ṭankan)* पु. typewriting; typing; soldering; mintage; coinage.

टंकणयंत्र *(ṭankan-yantra)* पु. typewriter

टंकशाला *(ṭanksālā)* पु. mint.

टँकाई *(ṭankāi)* स्त्री. work or state of stitching or soldering; charges for stitching; pecking.

टंकित *(ṭankit)* वि. typed.

टंकित्र *(ṭankitra)* पु. typewriter.

टंकी *(ṭanki)* स्त्री. cistern; reservoir; tank.

टँगना *(ṭamgnā)* अ. क्रि. to hang; to be hung; to be suspended; to be in a state of uncertainty or indecision.

टंटा *(ṭanṭā)* पु. quarrel; wrangling; altercation; meaningless complication; botheration; trouble; disturbance.

टकटकी *(ṭakṭaki)* स्त्री. gaze; stare; fixed look.

टकराना *(ṭakrānā)* अ. क्रि. to collide; to be knocked; to clash; to quarrel; to encounter; स. क्रि. to bring into collision; to dash against; to knock (against).

टकसाल *(ṭaksāl)* स्त्री. mint; mint house.

टकसाली *(ṭaksālī)* वि. of or pertaining to a mint.

टका *(ṭakā)* पु. an old Indian copper coin equal to two pice or paises.

टक्कर *(ṭakkar)* स्त्री. collision; clash; quarrel; encounter.

टखना *(ṭakhanā)* पु. ankle.

टटोलना *(ṭatolnā)* स. क्रि. to grope; to feel; to sound (somebody).

टट्टी *(ṭaṭṭi)* स्त्री. latrine; stool; faeces; screen (made of bamboo parings; straw or reeds etc.)

टट्टू *(ṭaṭṭū)* स्त्री. undersized horse; pony.

टन *(ṭan)* पु. tinkling sound; peal; chime; ton (measure of weight).

टनटन *(ṭantan)* स्त्री. tinkling sound; sound of bells; chime.

टपकन *(ṭapkan)* स्त्री. dripping.

टपकना *(ṭapaknā)* अ. क्रि. to fall as drops; to trickle; to drip; to leak.

टपका *(ṭapkā)* पु. mango fallen from the tree when ripe; drop; continuous dropping; dripping; leakage.

टपरा *(ṭaprā)* पु. hut; cottage; thatch.

टप्पर *(ṭappar)* पु. thatch; shed; canopy; awning.

टप्पा *(ṭappā)* पु. bound; range (of a ball; bullet etc.); spring; leap; jump; a form of light classical Hindustani music employing very quick movements.

टमटम *(ṭamṭam)* स्त्री. (अ.) a tumtum; an open horse-carriage.

टरकाना *(ṭarkānā)* स. क्रि. to put off; to evade; to dispose of summarily; to parry.

टर्रटर्र *(ṭarr-ṭarr)* स्त्री. croak; deep

hoarse sound.

टर्राना *(ṭarrānā)* अ. क्रि. to croak; to grumble haughtily.

टलना *(ṭalnā)* अ. क्रि. to move; to stir; to be displaced; to slip away; to make off; to get out of the way; to be postponed; to be disobeyed.

टसुआ *(ṭasuā)* पु. tear.

टहल *(ṭahal)* स्त्री. drudgery; menial sevice; attendance.

टहलना *(ṭahalnā)* अ. क्रि. to stroll; to walk.

टहलुआ *(ṭahluā)* टहलुवा, टहलू पु. drudge; menial worker; lackey.

टाँकना *(ṭāṁknā)* पु. to stitch; to cobble; to solder; to roughen (the surface of a stone mill); to jot down; to record; to write down.

टाँका *(ṭaṁkā)* पु. stitch; solder; patch.

टाँग *(ṭāṁg)* स्त्री. leg.

टाँगना *(ṭāṁgnā)* स. क्रि. to hang; to suspend.

टाट *(ṭāṭ)* पु. sackcloth; gunny.

टाप *(ṭāp)* स्त्री. hoof (of a horse); tramp (of a horse); a bamboo frame for catching fish; hood (of tonga etc.)

टापना *(ṭāpnā)* अ. क्रि. to paw; to trample; to be left helpless; to be impatient; restless; or agitated; to repent.

टापू *(ṭāpū)* पु. island; isle.

टालना *(ṭālnā)* स. क्रि. to post-pone; to put off; to evade by subterfuge; to prevaricate; to avert; to avoid; to ignore; to fail to observe.

टिकट *(ṭikaṭ)* स्त्री. ticket; postage stamp.

टिकट-घर *(ṭikaṭ-ghar)* पु. booking office.

टिकट-बाबू *(ṭikaṭ-bābu)* पु. booking clerk.

टिकना *(ṭiknā)* अ. क्रि. to stick fast; to remain firm; to stay; to stop; to halt; to last; to continue.

टिकाऊ *(ṭikāu)* वि. lasting; durable.

टिकाऊपन *(ṭikāūpan)* पु. durability.

टिकाना *(ṭikānā)* स. क्रि. to cause to stand; to station; to encamp; to put (one) up; to lodge.

टिकिया *(ṭikya)* स्त्री. pill; tablet; small cake.

टिड्डी *(ṭiddī)* स्त्री. locust.

टिपाई *(ṭipāi)* स्त्री. copying; jotting down.

टिप्पण *(ṭippan)* पु. note; annotation; gloss; commentary.

टिप्पणी *(ṭippanī)* स्त्री. annotation; note; remark; comment.

टिप्पस *(ṭippas)* पु. manipulation; device to fulfil one's ends.

टिमटिमाना *(ṭimṭimānā)* अ. क्रि. to glimmer; to twinkle.

टीका[1] *(ṭikā)* पु. mark put on the forehead; inoculation; vaccination; ceremony before marriage; an ornament worn on the forehead.

टीका[2] *(ṭikā)* स्त्री. commentary; annotation.

टीकाकार *(ṭikākār)* पु. commentutor. annotator.

टीन *(ṭina)* स्त्री. a malleable white metal; tinplate; tin.

टीम-टाम *(ṭīm-ṭām)* स्त्री. ostentation; frippery; finishing touches; dressing.

टीस *(ṭīs)* स्त्री. shooting pain; mental agony; anguish.

टुंडी *(ṭuṇḍī)* स्त्री. navel.

टुकड़ा *(ṭukṛā)* पु. piece; fragment part; portion; division; a bit of bread.

टुकड़ी *(ṭukṛī)* स्त्री. troop; a corps (of an army). group; party; band.

टुच्चा *(ṭuccā)* वि. tow; mean; ignoble; worthless; petty; insignificant.

टुटन *(ṭūṭan)* स्त्री. twisting pain.

टूटना *(ṭūṭnā)* अ. क्रि. to be broken; fractured; cracked; damaged etc; to break; to be severed or sundered; to be dissolvd (as partnership); closed abolished etc.; to have twisting pain; to be changed (as money).

टूट-फूट *(ṭüt-phūt)* स्त्री. break-age; damage; wear and tear; damages.

टूटा-फूटा *(ṭūṭā-phuṭā)* वि. broken to pieces; damaged; demolished; worn out.

टेक *(ṭek)* स्त्री. prop; stay; support; resolve; determination; burden of a song; refrain.

टेकना *(ṭekanā)* स. क्रि. to support; to prop; to set down; to rest; to place.

टेढ़ा *(ṭerhā)* वि. bent; curved; crooked; difficult; intricate; oblique; slanting; skew.

टेढ़ापन *(ṭerḥāpan)* पु. crookedness; intricacy.

टेर *(ṭer)* स्त्री. loud call; cry for help; high pitch (music).

टेरना *(ṭernā)* स. क्रि. to call aloud; to summon; to sing loudly; to produce a sound; to call for help.

टेसू *(ṭesū)* पु. the tree butea frondosa and its flower.

टोंटी *(ṭoṁṭī)* स्त्री. spout; tap; nozzle.

टोकना *(ṭoknā)* स. क्रि. to object; to question; to interrogate; to in tervene; interrupt; to challenge; to accost.

टोकरा *(ṭokrā)* पु. a large basket; coop.

टोकरी *(ṭokrī)* स्त्री. basket.

टोटका *(ṭotkā)* पु. totem; witchcraft; sorcery.

टोटा *(ṭotā)* पु. loss; damage; want; deficiency; scarcity; butt end (of a cigarette etc.)

टोना *(ṭonā)* पु. totem; witchcraft; sorcery; spell.

टोपा *(ṭopā)* पु. large-size headwear (worn during winter).

टोपी *(ṭopī)* स्त्री. cap; cover.

टोली *(ṭolī)* स्त्री. band; batch; troupe; herd; group.

टोह *(ṭoh)* स्त्री. search; reconnaissance; whereabouts; sounding; hunt-out.

टोहना *(ṭohnā)* स्त्री. क्रि. to grope; to search; to trace; to feel for; to touch; to reconnoitre.

ठ

ठ *(ṭha)* the second letter of the third pentad of the Devnagri alphabets.

ठंड *(ṭhaṇḍ)* स्त्री. cold; chill.

ठंडा *(ṭhaṇḍā)* वि. cold; cool; soothed; extinguished; passionless; unresponsive.

ठंडाई *(ṭhaṇḍai)* वि. cooling drink.

ठक-ठक *(ṭhak-ṭhak)* स्त्री. repeated knock or tapping sound.

ठकुराई *(ṭhakurāī)* ठाकुरी स्त्री. rank or status of thakur; the region or land which is under a thakur; lordliness; supremacy; haughtiness.

ठग *(ṭhag)* पु. cheat; swindler.

ठगई *(ṭhagai)* स्त्री. cheating; dupery.

ठगना *(ṭhagnā)* स. क्रि. to cheat; to swindle.

ठगी *(ṭhagī)* स्त्री. cheating; trickery; swindling.

ठटरी *(ṭhatri)* स्त्री. skeleton; bier.

ठट्ठा *(ṭhaṭṭhā)* पु. banter; fun; joke; jest.

ठठेरा *(ṭhaṭherā)* पु. tinker; brazier.

ठठोली, ठिठोली *(ṭhaṭholī)* स्त्री. jesting; fun.

ठनना *(ṭhananā)* अ. क्रि. to be determined or resolved; to come to hostilities.

ठप *(ṭhapp)* क्रि. वि. at a stand still; reduced to a state of inactivity.

ठप्पा *(ṭhappā)* पु. die; stamp; impression; broad silver lace; mould.

ठमक *(ṭhamak)* स्त्री. halt; gait with thumping steps.

ठर्रा *(ṭharrā)* पु. mountry liquor.

ठलुआ *(ṭhaluā)* वि. out of employment; idle.

ठसक *(ṭhasak)* स्त्री. swagger; coquetry; dignity; vanity; affectation; uppishness.

ठसका *(ṭhasakā)* पु. kind of dry cough; push; shock.

ठसाठस *(ṭhasā-thas)* वि. packed; filled to capacity.

ठहरना *(ṭhaharnā)* अ. क्रि. to stop; to stay; to wait; to stabilise.

ठहराना *(ṭhaharānā)* स. क्रि. to cause to stand or stay; to top; to cause to lodge.

ठाँये *(ṭhāṁy)* स्त्री. sound of a gun shot.

ठाँव *(ṭhāṁv)* पु. place; station; residence.

ठाकुर *(ṭhākur)* पु. deity; god; lord; master; chief; leader; landlord; highly honoured person.

ठाट, ठाठ *(ṭhāṭ)* पु. pomp; splendour; maginficence; joy; luxury; style; fashion.

ठाट-बाट *(ṭhāt-bāt)* पु. pomp and show.

ठाठदार *(ṭhāth-dār)* वि. pompous; gorgeous; magnificent; glorious.

ठानना *(ṭhānanā)* स. क्रि. to resolve; to determine.

ठिकाना *(ṭhikānā)* पु. abode; place.

ठिठकना *(ṭhithaknā)* अ. क्रि. to stop short; to stand amazed.

ठीक[1] *(ṭhik)* क्रि. properly; correctly; truly; rightly; well; suitably; usefully.

ठीक[2] *(ṭhik)* वि. right; true; correct; accurate; fit; good (health); proper; suitable; useful.

ठीक-ठाक *(ṭhik-thāk)* वि. fit; proper; accurate.

ठीकरा *(ṭhīkrā)* पु. broken piece of earthen ware.

ठुकराना *(ṭhukrānā)* स. क्रि. to kick away; to put aside contemptuously; to reject; to turn down.

ठुड्डी *(ṭhuḍḍi)* स्त्री. chin; parched grain that does not expand or swell.

ठुमकना *(ṭhumaknā)* अ. क्रि. to strut; to walk with dancing gait; to take steps in such a manner in dancing that the bells may give systematic jingling sound.

ठुमका *(ṭhumkā)* पु. delicate or slow jerk of the feet.

ठूँठ *(ṭhūṁṭh)* पु. stump (of a tree); an amputated hand or arm.

ठूँसना *(ṭhūṁsnā)* स. क्रि. to stuff; to thrust in; to eat greedily.

ठेंगा *(ṭheṁgā)* पु. thumb (used only to show contempt).

ठेका *(ṭhekā)* पु. contract.

ठेकेदार *(ṭheke-dār)* पु. contractor.

ठेकेदारी *(ṭheke-dāri)* स्त्री. contractorship.

ठेलना *(ṭhelnā)* स. क्रि. to push and move.

ठेला *(ṭhelā)* पु. bullock cart; wheel barrow; trolley; violent push.

ठेस *(ṭhes)* स्त्री. knock; emotional shock; blow.

ठोंकना *(ṭhomknā)* स्त्री. to beat; to hammer; to drive (a nail); to pat.

ठोकर *(ṭhokar)* स्त्री. stumbling; knock.

ठोस *(ṭhos)* वि. solid; sound.

ठौर *(ṭhaur)* पु. place; opportunity.

ड

ड *(ḍa)* the third letter of the pentad of Devnagri alphabets.

डंक *(ḍaṅk)* पु. sting; nib (of a pen).

डंका *(ḍaṅkā)* पु. kettle drum.

डंगर[1] *(ḍaṅgar)* पु. quadruped; cattle.

डंगर[2] *(ḍaṅgar)* वि. lean and thin; stupid; foolish.

डंठल *(ḍaṇṭhal)* पु. stem; stalk.

डंड *(ḍaṇḍ)* पु. rod; an athletic exercise.

डंडा *(ḍaṇḍā)* पु. stick; staff; club; bar.

डंडी *(ḍaṇḍi)* स्त्री. pole or shaft (of a vehicle); lever; handle; beam of a scale; stem; stalk; branch.

डकराना *(ḍakrānā)* अ. क्रि. to bellow (as an ox); to weep loudly

डकार *(ḍakār)* पु. belch; burp.

डकारना *(ḍakāranā)* अ. क्रि. to belch; to swallow down; to embezzle.

डकैत *(ḍakait)* पु. decoit; robber.

डकैती *(ḍakaiti)* स्त्री. decoity; robbery; piracy.

डग *(ḍag)* पु. pace; step in walking.

डगमग *(ḍagmag)* वि. tottering; trembling; staggering; unsteady; wavering.

डगमगाना *(ḍagmagānā)* अ. क्रि. to falter; to stagger; to waver; to lurch.

डगर *(ḍagar)* स्त्री. path; track.

डटना *(ḍaṭnā)* अ. क्रि. to stand firmly.

डढ़ियल *(ḍarhiyal)* वि. having a long beard.

डपट *(ḍapaṭ)* स्त्री. reprimand.

डपटना *(ḍapaṭnā)* स. क्रि. to rebuke; to reprimand.

डफली *(ḍaphli)* स्त्री. tabor; tambourine.

डबडबाना *(ḍabḍabānā)* अ. क्रि. to be tearful; to be filled with tears.

डब्बा *(ḍabbā)* पु. a tiny box.

डर *(ḍar)* पु. terror; fear; fright; scare; doubt; apprehension.

डरना *(ḍarnā)* अ. क्रि. to be afraid; to fear; to apprehend.

डराना *(ḍarānā)* स. क्रि. to frighten; to terrify; to scare; to threaten.

डरावना *(ḍarāvnā)* वि. terrible; horrible; frightful; dreadful.

डलिया *(ḍaliyā)* स्त्री. small open basket.

डली *(ḍali)* स्त्री. lump; piece.

डसना *(ḍasnā)* स. क्रि. to bite; to sting.

डाँट *(ḍāmṭ)* स्त्री. reprimand; scolding.

डायन *(ḍāin)* स्त्री. witch; quarrelsome ugly woman; hag; sorceress.

डाक *(ḍāk)* स्त्री. mail; post.

डाकखाना *(ḍāk-khānā)* पु. post of fice.

डाकपाल *(ḍākpāl)* पु. postmaster.

डाका *(ḍākā)* पु. robbery; dacoity.

डाकिया *(ḍākiyā)* पु. postman.

डाक्टर *(ḍākṭar)* पु. (अं.) doctor; a medical practitioner; doctorate in any subject.

डांटना *(ḍāṭnā)* स. क्रि. to stuff; to stop up; to scold; to reprimand.

डाढ़ *(ḍāṛh)* स्त्री. molar.

डाढ़ी *(ḍāṛhī)* स्त्री. beard.

डायरी *(ḍāyrī)* स्त्री. diary.

डाल *(ḍāl)* स्त्री. branch.

डालना *(ḍālnā)* स. क्रि. to put in; to pour; to thrust upon; to put on.

डाली *(ḍāli)* स्त्री. small branch; twig; small basket; basket in which presents are kept.

डाह *(ḍāh)* स्त्री. envy; jealousy; malic.

डिगाना *(ḍigānā)* स. क्रि. to cause to stumble; to shake (from faith etc.); to remove; to shift; to cause to budge.

डिबिया *(ḍibiyā)* स्त्री. small box or casket; case.

डिब्बा *(ḍibbā)* पु. box; chest; railway compartment.

डींग *(ḍiṁg)* स्त्री. bragging; boasting.

डीलडौल *(ḍil-ḍaul)* पु. stature; size. shape; physique; body.

डुगडुगी *(ḍugḍugī)* स्त्री. small kettle-drum.

डुबकी *(ḍubkī)* स्त्री. dip; dive; act of diving; plunge.

डुबाना *(ḍubānā)* to plunge; to drown; to dip; to ruin.

डुलाना *(ḍulānā)* स. क्रि. to cause to move; to shake; to swing; to make unsteady or shaky; to take out for a walk etc.

डूबना *(ḍubnā)* अ. क्रि. to sink; to be drowned; to set (as sun); to be destroyed; to be ruined; to be absorbed; be engrossed; be lost (in business or study or thought etc.); to sink; to faint.

डेरा *(ḍerā)* पु. camp; temporary abode; encampment.

डैना *(ḍainā)* पु. wing (of bird).

डोंगी *(ḍoṁgi)* स्त्री. a small boat; dug-out.

डोर *(ḍor)* स्त्री. string; thread; the kite-flying thread; support;

डोरा *(ḍorā)* पु. cord; string for sewing or stitching.

डोरी *(ḍori)* स्त्री. string; cord.

डोल *(ḍol)* पु. bucket; round shallow pail.

डोलना *(ḍolnā)* अ. क्रि. to swing; to oscillate; to walk about; to move about; to waver; to swerve.

डौल *(ḍaul)* पु. shape; form; build; appearance; method; device; type.

ड्योढ़ी *(ḍyoṛhī)* स्त्री. main gate of a house; vestibule; threshold.

ढ

ढ *(ḍha)* the fourth letter of the third pentad of the Devnagri alphabets.

ढंग *(ḍhaṅg)* पु. manner; procedure; mode; method; sign; demeanour.

ढँढोरची *(ḍhaṁḍhorcī)* पु. drummer.

ढँढोरा *(ḍhaṁḍhorā)* पु. proclamation by beat of drum.

ढकना[1] *(ḍhaknā)* पु. cover; lid.

ढकना[2] *(ḍhaknā)* to cover.

ढकेलना *(ḍhakelnā)* स. क्रि. to push; to thrust forward; to shove.

ढकोसला *(ḍhakoslā)* पु. hypocrisy; sham; humbug; imposture.

ढर्रा *(ḍharrā)* पु. method; mode. style; attitude; behaviour.

ढलकना *(ḍhalaknā)* अ. क्रि. to flow down; to roll; to trickle down.

ढलकाना *(ḍhalkānā)* स. क्रि. to shed; to pour; to cause to roll down; to spill (milk etc.).

ढलना *(ḍhalnā)* अ. क्रि. to be moulded or cast.

ढलाई *(ḍhalāī)* स्त्री. casting; moulding; the cost of casting; mintage; brassage.

ढलान *(ḍhalān)* पु. slope; descent.

ढहना *(ḍhahnā)* अ. क्रि. to fall or tumble down; to be destroyed or razed; to be reduced to ruins; to crash down; to collapse.

ढाँचा *(ḍhāṁcā)* पु. frame-work; setup; frame; plan; skeleton; carcass.

ढाढ़स *(ḍhāṛhas)* पु. solace; consolation.

ढाना *(ḍhānā)* स. क्रि. to knock down. to pull down; to raze (a building etc.) to demolish; to topple down.

ढाबा *(ḍhābā)* पु. thatched roofing of hut; kind of hotel.

ढाल *(ḍhāl)* स्त्री. slope; style; fashion; mode; shield.

ढालना[1] *(ḍhālnā)* स. क्रि. to pour out; to drink.

ढालना[2] *(ḍhālnā)* स. क्रि. to mould or cast.

ढाली *(ḍhālī)* पु. soldier wearing armour.

ढालू *(ḍhālū)* वि. sloping; declivous.

ढिंढोरची *(ḍhindhorčhi)* पु. one who proclaims by beat of drum.

ढिंढोरा *(ḍhiṁdhorā)* पु. public proclamation by beat of drum.

ढिठाई *(ḍhiṭhāī)* स्त्री. impudence; obduracy; audacity; temerity.

ढिलाई *(ḍhilāi)* स. क्रि. the state of sluggishness; relaxation; looseness; sloth; indolence; idleness; leniency.

ढीठ *(ḍhiṭh)* वि. obstinate; stubborn; impudent; impertinent; bold; daring; fearless; shameless.

ढीठता *(ḍhiṭhātā)* स्त्री. (पु. ढीठपन) impertinence; obduracy.

ढील *(ḍhīl)* स्त्री. laxity; slackness; leniency; undue delay; looseness.

ढीला *(ḍhīlā)* वि. loose; slack; not strict; lenient.

ढीलापन *(ḍhilāpan)* पु. act or state of looseness; sluggishness.

ढुलकना *(ḍhulaknā)* अ. क्रि. to roll

down; to spill; to be inclined.

ढुलना *(ḍhulnā)* अ. क्रि. to be carried (load etc.).

ढुलमुल *(ḍuhlmul)* वि. shaking; tottering; wavering; unsteady.

ढेर *(ḍher)* पु. heap; pile; accumulation; bulk.

ढेला *(ḍhelā)* पु. clod; lump of earth; piece of brick; stone etc.

ढोंग *(ḍhoṁg)* पु. hypocrisy; imposture; dissimulation.

ढोंगी[1] *(ḍhoṁgī)* पु. hypocrite; impostor.

ढोंगी[2] *(ḍhoṁgī)* वि. hypocritical; fradulent.

ढोना *(ḍhonā)* स. क्रि. to carry; to bear on shoulder or head.

ढोर *(ḍhor)* पु. cattle.

ढोल *(ḍhol)* पु. drum.

ढोलक *(ḍholak)* स्त्री. small drum; kettle drum.

ढोलकिया[1] *(ḍholkiyā)* पु. one who plays on a small drum; drummer.

ढोलकी *(ḍholkī)* स्त्री. small drum.

त

त *(ta)* the first letter of the fourth pentad of Devnagri alphabets.

तंग *(taṇg)* वि. (फ़ा.) strait; narrow; tight; distracted; troubled; vexed; fed up; distressed; poor; badly off.

तंगदस्त *(taṇgdast)* वि. (फ़ा.) short of money.

तंगदस्ती *(taṇgdastī)* स्त्री. (फ़ा.) shortage of money.

तंगहाल *(taṇghāl)* वि. (फ़ा.) distressed; destitute.

तंगी *(taṇgī)* स्त्री. straitness; narrowness; tightness; closeness; distress; difficulty; scarcity; poverty.

तंतु *(tantu)* पु. thread; cord; rope; string; fibre; cobweb; filament; tissue.

तंतुवाद्य *(tantu-vādya)* पु. stringed musical instrument.

तंत्र *(tantra)* पु. model; type; system; frame work; charm; spell; sorcery.

तंत्रिका *(tantrikā)* स्त्री. kind of creeper; nerve; fibre; wire; string of a musical instrument.

तंत्रिका विज्ञान *(tantrika-vijnan)* पु. neurology.

तंत्री *(tantrī)* पु. one who plays on a stringed instrument; practitioner of enchantments.

तंदुरूस्त *(tandurüst)* वि. sound in body; healthy; vigorous.

तंदुरूस्ती *(tandurüsti)* स्त्री. health; bodily vigour.

तंद्रा *(tandrā)* स्त्री. lassitude; weariness; exhaustion; drowsiness; sleepiness; sluggishness

तंद्रालु *(tandrālu)* वि. sleepy; drowsy; lethargic.

तंद्रिल *(tandril)* वि. drowsy; sleepy.

तंबाकू *(tambākü)* पु. tobacco.

तंबूरा *(tambürā)* पु. a four-stringed musical instrument.

तक़दीर *(taqdīr)* स्त्री. (अ.) luck; fortune; fate; destiny; lot.

तकना *(taknā)* स. क्रि. to stare; to look.

तकनीक *(taknik)* स्त्री. technique.

तकनीकी *(takniki)* वि. technical.

तक़रार *(takrār)* स्त्री. (अ.) contention; dispute; controversy; altercation; quarrel; wrangling.

तक़रीर *(taqrir)* स्त्री. (अ.) speech; lecture.

तकली *(takli)* स्त्री. small spindle.

तकलीफ़ *(taklīf)* स्त्री. (अ.) pain; agony; difficulty; trouble; distress; inconvenience; suffering; ailment.

तकल्लुफ़ *(takalluf)* पु. (अ.) formality.

तकिया *(takiyā)* पु. (फ़ा.) pillow; cushion; abode of a faqir.

तकुआ *(takuā)* पु. spindle.

तख़्त *(takht)* पु. (फ़ा.) throne; seat made of planks.

तख़्ता *(takhtā)* पु. (फ़ा.) plank; board.

तख़्ती *(takhtī)* स्त्री. small wooden plate; school boy's small board for writing.

तगड़ा *(tagrā)* वि. robust; stout; strong; powerful.

तचना *(tacnā)* अ. क्रि. to be scorched; to be exposed to severe heat; to be grieved.

तट *(taṭ)* पु. bank (of a river); coast; shore; beach.

तटबंध *(taṭbandh)* पु. embankment; dike.

तटवर्ती *(taṭvartī)* पु. coastal; pertaining to a coast or bank; littoral.

तटस्थ *(tattastha)* वि. neutral; non-aligned.

तटस्थता *(tattasthatā)* स्त्री. non-alignment; neutrality.

तटीय *(taṭīya)* वि. pertaining to a bank; neutrality.

तड़क *(taṛak)* स्त्री. cracking; snapping; crack-mark.

तड़क-भड़क *(taṛak-bharak)* स्त्री. pomp and show; pageantry; glitter; pompousness; ostentation; tawdriness.

तड़का *(taṛkā)* पु. early morning; dawn; browning spices in heated oil or ghee.

तड़प *(taṛap)* स्त्री. tossing or rolling about in agony; restlessness; restivity; anxious eagerness or ardent desire; yearning; longing; smart.

तड़पना *(taṛapnā)* अ. क्रि. to toss or roll about in agony; to be restless; to writhe in pain; to be anxiously eager (for); to be eagerly desirous; to long (for).

तड़पाना *(taṛpānā)* स. क्रि. to render restless; to torment; to cause writhing pain.

तड़ाग *(taṛāg)* पु. pond; tank.

तड़ातड़ *(taṛātaṛ)* क्रि. वि. with successive reports; with promptitude; instantaneously.

तड़ित् *(tarit)* स्त्री. lightening.

तड़ी *(taṛi)* स्त्री. braggadocio; slap; blow; fraud; deceit; bluff; ascendancy; overbearing conduct; show of superiority.

ततैया *(tataiyā)* स्त्री. wesp; chilli.

तत्काल *(tatkāl)* क्रि. वि. at once; immediately; instantaneously.

तत्कालीन *(tatkālin)* वि. the then; contemporary.

तत्त्व *(tattva)* पु. element; essence; substance; reality; truth.

तत्त्वज्ञान *(tattva-jnān)* पु. knowledge of the truth of reality; philosophy.

तत्त्वत: *(tattvaṭah)* क्रि. वि. essentially; materially.

तत्पर *(tatpar)* वि. ready; prepared; exclusively engaged (in).

तत्परता *(tatpartā)* स्त्री. readiness; preparedness; devotion; concentration; alacrity; promptness.

तत्पश्चात् *(tatpascāt)* क्रि. वि. there after; hence-forth.

तथा *(tathā)* क्रि. वि. so; and; also; as well as; so; thus; in that manner.

तथाकथित *(tathā-kathit)* वि. so called.

तथ्य *(tathyā)* पु. truth; reality; fact; data; substance.

तदनंतर *(tadanantar)* क्रि. वि. immediately after that; there upon; then; thereafter.

तदनुकूल *(tadanukül)* क्रि. वि. conforming to that; consistent with that; accordingly.

तदनुसार *(tadanusār)* क्रि. वि. accordingly.

तदबीर *(tadbīr)* स्त्री. (अ.) device; contrivance; way; means; plan.

तन *(tan)* पु. (अ.) body.

तनख़्वाह *(tankhāh)* स्त्री. (फ़ा.) pay; salary.

तनना *(tannā)* अ. क्रि. to be pulled tight; to be stretched; to stand erect in an affected manner; to be tense; to run into temper.

तनया *(tanayā)* स्त्री. daughter.

तनाव *(tanāv)* पु. tension; tautness; hostility; rivalry; state or quality of being stretched; tenseness.

तनुज *(tanuj)* पु. son.

तन्मय *(tanmay)* वि. completely engrossed or absorbed (in).

तन्मयता *(tanmayatā)* स्त्री. state of being fully engrossd or absorbed (in); trance; concentration.

तप *(tap)* पु. religious austerity; bodily mortification; penance asceticism; tenacity; perseverance.

तपन *(tapan)* स्त्री. warming; heating; burning; mental distress; grieving; pining; heat; warmth; burning sensation.

तपना *(tapnā)* अ. क्रि. to be heated; to burn with pain or grief; to be angry; to be irritated; to pass through experience; to be seasoned; to practise self; mortification.

तपस *(tapas)* पु. sun; ascetic; hermit.

तपस्या *(tapasyā)* स्त्री. penance; austerity; self-mortification.

तपस्विनी *(tapasvinī)* स्त्री. female devotee; female ascetic.

तपस्वी *(tapasvī)* पु. ascetic; hermit.

तपाना *(tapānā)* स. क्रि. to heat; to warm; to tease; to irritate; to inflict suffering (on one's body).

तपेदिक *(tapediq)* स्त्री. (फ़ा.) tuberculosis.

तप्त *(tapt)* वि. heated; burnt; redhot; flushed with rage; distressed; pained; afflicted.

तफ़रीह *(tafrīh)* स्त्री. (अ.) amusement; merriment; recreation.

तफ़सील *(tafsīl)* स्त्री. (अ.) details; particulars.

तबदील *(tabdīl)* वि. (अ.) changed; altered; exchanged.

तबदीली *(tabdīlī)* स्त्री. (अ.) change alteration; exchange.

तबला *(tablā)* पु. (अ.) small tambourine; a percussion instrument.

तबादला *(tabādlā)* पु. (अ.) transfer; exchange; barter.

तबाह *(tabāh)* वि. (फ़ा.) ruined; destroyed; undone.

तबीयत *(tabīyat)* स्त्री. (अ.) state of mental or physical health; nature; disposition; temperament.

तम *(tam)* पु. darkness; gloom.

तमक *(tamak)* स्त्री. rage; passion.

तमतमाना *(tamtamānā)* अ. क्रि. to redden with anger or heat; to become or grow red (in the face); to glow; to sparkle.

तमन्ना *(tamannā)* स्त्री. (अ.) wish; desire; longing; aspiration.

तमाचा *(tamācā)* पु. (फ़ा.) slap; thump.

तमाम *(tamām)* वि. (अ.) all; whole; entire; finished; ended.

तमाशा *(tamāśā)* पु. (अ.) entertainment; show; sight; spectacle; anything strange or curious; fun; jest; joke (fig.)

तमीज़ *(tamīz)* स्त्री. (अ.) etiquette; decorum; discrimination; sense or ability to do a particular work; discernment; discretion.

तय *(tay)* वि. decided; settled; fixed.

तरंग *(taraṇg)* स्त्री. wave; billow; ripple; emotion; ecstasy; fancy; whim; caprice; melody.

तरंगित *(taraṇgit)* वि. wavy; tossing with waves; rippling; overflowing tremulous; waving; high spirited; ecstatic.

तर *(tar)* वि. (फ़ा.) moist; damp; wet; soaked; fresh.

तरकश *(tarkaś)* पु. (फ़ा.) quiver.

तरकारी *(tarkárī)* स्त्री. vegetable.

तरकीब *(tarkīb)* स्त्री. (अ.) means; device; contrivance; mode; method.

तरक़्क़ी *(taraqqī)* स्त्री. (अ.) progress; improvement; advancement; elevation; promotion; increase; increment.

तरजीह *(tarjīh)* स्त्री. (अ.) preference; precedence; priority.

तरतीब *(tartīb)* स्त्री. (अ.) order; arrangement; system.

तरना *(tarnā)* अ. क्रि. to be ferried; to pass; to attain salvation.

तरफ़ *(taraf)* स्त्री. (अ.) side; direction; party; group.

तरफ़दारी *(tarafdārī)* स्त्री. (फ़ा.) partiality; partisanship, bias.

तरबूज़ *(tarbüz)* पु. (फ़ा.) watermelon.

तरमीम *(tarmim)* स्त्री. (अ.) amendment; modification.

तरल *(taral)* वि. liquid; fluid.

तरलता *(tarlatā)* तरलाई स्त्री. fluidity; liquidity; tremulousness; unsteadiness; fickleness.

तरस *(taras)* पु. pity; compassion; mercy.

तरसना *(tarasnā)* अ. क्रि. to pine; to long or desire eagerly.

तरह *(tarah)* स्त्री. sort; kind; manner; mode.

तराई *(tarāī)* स्त्री. land lying at the foot of a watershed or on the banks of a river; foothill; act of wetting or soaking (a plastered wall or roof etc.).

तराज़ू *(tarāzü)* स्त्री. (फ़ा.) scales; balance.

तराना *(tarānā)* पु. (फ़ा.) song; mode of singing.

तरावट *(tarāvat)* स्त्री. moisture; freshness; coolness.

तराशना *(tarāśnā)* स. क्रि. to trim; to pare; to chisel; to cut; to carve;

to shape; to fashion.

तरी *(tari)* स्त्री. (फ़ा.) moisture; dampness; humidity; wetness.

तरीक़ा *(tariqā)* पु. (अ.) means; device; method; mode; manner.

तरु *(tarü)* पु. tree.

तरुण *(taruṇ)* वि. young; youthful; juvenile; newly-born or produced (tree etc.).

तरुणी *(truni)* स्त्री. young or youth ful women.

तरेड़ *(tarer)* स्त्री. crack; crevice.

तरेरना *(tarernā)* स. क्रि. to look in oblique manner.

तरोताज़ा *(tarotāzā)* वि. (फ़ा.) fresh; refreshed; revived.

तर्क *(trk)* पु. argument; contention; plea; science of reasoning; logic; discussion; disputation

तर्कशास्त्र *(tarkśāstrā)* पु. logic; science of reasoning.

तर्कसंगत *(tark-sangat)* वि. logical; justifiable; approapriate.

तर्कहीन *(trk-hina)* वि. illogical.

तर्ज़ *(tarz)* स्त्री. (अ.) manner; mode; style; form; shape; fashion; tune.

तर्पण *(tarpan)* पु. state of being pleased or satisfied; gratification; presenting libations to the gods; or to the names of deceased an cestors.

तल *(tal)* पु. bottom; base; surface.

तलछट *(talchat)* स्त्री. sediment; dregs; silt.

तलवा *(talvā)* पु. sole of shoe.

तलवार *(talvār)* स्त्री. sword; sabre.

तलहटी *(talhaṭi)* स्त्री. sub-mountian region.

तला *(talā)* पु. bottom; lowest part; base; sole of a shoe.

तलाक़ *(talāq)* पु. (अ.) divorce.

तलाक़नामा *(talāqnāmā)* पु. divorce deed.

तलाश *(talāś)* स्त्री. (तु.) search; quest.

तलाशना *(talāśnā)* स. क्रि. to search; to investigate.

तलाशी *(talāśi)* पु. तु. search.

तली *(tali)* स्त्री. bottom.

तलैया *(talaiyā)* स्त्री. small tank or pond.

तल्लीन *(tallin)* वि. absorbed; engrossed; immersed.

तल्लीनता *(tallinatā)* स्त्री. concentration; deep devotion; deep involvement; absorption.

तवा *(tavā)* पु. iron plate for baking bread; frying pan; gramophone record.

तवायफ़ *(tavāyaf)* स्त्री. (अ.) prostitute; harlot.

तशरीफ़ *(taśrif)* वि. (अ.) honour; prestige; elderliness.

तश्तरी *(taśtari)* स्त्री. (फ़ा.) plate; saucer.

तसल्ली *(tasalli)* स्त्री. (अ.) consolation; comfort; solace; contentment; satisfaction.

तसवीर *(tasvir)* स्त्री. (अ.) picture; painting; photograph.

तस्करी *(taskari)* स्त्री. smuggling; theft; robbery.

तह *(tah)* स्त्री. (फ़ा.) layer; stratum; fold; plait; bottom.

तहक़ीक़ात *(tahqiqāt)* स्त्री. (अ.) inquiry; investigation.

तहख़ाना *(tahkhānā)* पु. (फ़ा.) cellar; cell.

तहज़ीब *(tahzib)* स्त्री. (अ.) etiquette; civilization; culture.

तहलका *(tahalkā)* पु. (अ.) commotion; excitement; stir.

तहस-नहस *(tahs-nahas)* वि. destroyed; ruined; devastated.

तहसील *(tahsīl)* स्त्री. (अ.) subdivision of a district; office or court of a tahsildar.

ताँता *(tāmtā)* पु. series; influx; succession.

ताई *(tāi)* स्त्री. wife of father's elder brother; aunt.

ताईद *(tāīd)* स्त्री. confirmation; support.

ताऊ *(tāū)* father's elder brother; uncle.

ताक[1] *(tāk)* पु. look; glance; gaze; watch; look-out.

ताक़[2] *(tāq)* पु. (अ.) niche; shelf.

ताक़त *(tāqat)* स्त्री. (अ.) capability; ability; power; strength; might; force.

ताक़तवर *(tāqatvar)* वि. (अ.) forceful; strong; mighty; vigorous.

ताकना *(tāknā)* स. क्रि. to look at; to stare at; to watch for.

ताज *(tāj)* पु. (अ.) crown; diadem; tiara; cret; tuft; plume.

ताज़गी *(tāzgī)* स्त्री. (फ़ा.) freshness; newness.

ताजपोशी *(tājposhī)* स्त्री. coronation; crowning.

ताज़ा *(tāzā)* वि. (फ़ा.) fresh; new; raw; green; recent.

ताज्जुब *(tājjub)* पु. (अ.) wonder; astonishment; amazement; surprise.

ताड़ *(tār)* पु. palm-tree of fan palm.

ताड़ना[1] *(tāṛnā)* स. क्रि. to conjecture; to guess; to understand; to perceive; to discover; to find out; to chide; to reprimand.

ताड़ना[2] *(tāṛnā)* स्त्री. reprimand; admonition; rebuke.

ताड़ी *(tārī)* स्त्री. fermented juice of palm-tree; taddy.

तात्कालिक *(tātkālīk)* वि. instantaneous; immediate; simultaneous; contemporary.

तात्पर्य *(tātparyā)* पु. objet; intent; import; sum and substance.

तात्त्विक *(tāttvik)* पु. elemental; fundamental; essential; substantial.

तानना *(tānanā)* स. क्रि. to tighten; to pitch (as tent); to string up.

ताना *(tānā)* पु. warp; taunt; sarcastic remark.

ताना-बाना *(tānā-bānā)* पु. warp and woof.

तानाशाह *(tānāsāh)* पु. (फ़ा.) dictator; tyrant.

तानाशाही *(tānāsāhi)* स्त्री. (फ़ा.) dictatorship; dictatorial rule; arbitrariness.

ताप *(tāp)* पु. warmth; temperature; fever; affliction; pain; agony; heat.

तापना *(tāpnā)* अ. क्रि. to warm oneself (at or over a fire); to bask (in the sun or before fire).

तापमान *(tāpmān)* पु. temperature.

तापस *(tāpas)* पु. ascetic.

तापसी *(tāpasī)* वि. pertainging to asceticism.

ताबड़-तोड़ *(tābaṛ-toṛ)* क्रि. वि. in quick succession; immediately.

ताबूत *(tābüt)* पु. (अ.) bier; coffin.; cist.

ताबेदार *(tābedār)* वि. (अ.) dependent; obedient; subservient; servile.

ताबेदारी *(tābedāri)* स्त्री. (फ़ा.) subservience; servility.

तामसिक *(tāmasik)* वि. dark; pertaining to ignorance.

तामीर *(tāmīr)* पु. (अ.) construction; building.

तामील *(tāmil)* स्त्री. (अ.) execution; service.

ताम्र *(tāmr)* पु. copper.

तार *(tār)* पु. wire; chord; telegraphic message; telegram; uninterrupted series.

तारक *(tārak)* पु. liberator; deliverer; saviour; protector; star; planet.

तारघर *(tārghar)* पु. telegraph office.

तारतम्य *(tāratmya)* पु. sequence; compatibility of values; harmony.

तारना *(tārnā)* स. क्रि. to enable (one) to cross; to free; to rid; to deliver.

तारपीन *(tārpīn)* पु. turpentine.

तारांकित *(tārānkit)* वि. marked with an asterisk; starred.

तारा *(tārā)* पु. star; luck; pupil of the eye; pearl.

तारिका *(tārikā)* स्त्री. film star; actress; star.

तारीख़ *(tārīkh)* स्त्री. (अ.) date; history; chronicle.

तारीफ़ *(tārīf)* स्त्री. (अ.) praise; commendation; speciality or significant quality; introduction (of a person).

तारुण्य *(tāruṇya)* पु. youth; youthfulness.

तार्किक[1] *(tārkik)* पु. dialectician; logician.

तार्किक[2] *(tārkik)* वि. logical; rational; logistic.

ताल *(tāl)* पु. pond; tank.

ताल-मेल *(tāl-mail)* पु. harmony; coordination; adjustment.

ताला *(tālā)* पु. lock.

तालाबंदी *(tālābandi)* स्त्री. lock-out;

तालाब *(tālāb)* पु. pond; pool; tank.

ताली *(tālī)* स्त्री. key; clapping (of hands); applause.

तालीम *(tālīm)* स्त्री. (अ.) education; instruction.

तालू *(tālū)* पु. palate;.

ताव *(tāv)* पु. hat; anger; sheet of paper.

तावीज़ *(tāvīz)* पु. (अ.) amulet.

ताश *(tāś)* पु. playing cards; game of cards.

तासीर *(tāsīr)* स्त्री. (अ.) impression; effect.

तिकड़म *(tikṛam)* पु. manipulation; manoeuvre; device; expedient.

तिकड़ी *(tikṛī)* स्त्री. three of cards; trio; group of three.

तिकोना *(tikonā)* वि. three-cornered; triangular.

तिक्त *(tikt)* वि. bitter; pungent; acrid.

तिगुना *(tigunā)* वि. three fold; three times; triple.

तिजारत *(tijārat)* पु. (अ.) trade; commerce; business.

तिजारती *(tijārati)* वि. commercial; pertaining to trade; mercantile.

तिजोरी *(tijorī)* स्त्री. (अ.) iron safe; chest.

तितर-बितर *(titar-bitar)* वि. scattered; dispersed.

तितली *(titlī)* स्त्री. butterfly.

तिथि *(tithi)* स्त्री. date.

तिनका *(tinkā)* स्त्री. grass; straw.

तिपाई *(tipāi)* स्त्री. tripod.

तिबारा *(tibārā)* क्रि. वि. for the third time.

तिमाही *(timāhi)* वि. quarterly.

तिमिर *(timir)* पु. darkness; gloom.

तिरंगा *(tiraṇgā)* वि. tri-coloured.

तिरछा *(tirchā)* वि. slanting; oblique; awry; askew.

तिरछापन *(tirchāpan)* पु. slant; skewness; obliquity; obliqueness.

तिरना *(tirnā)* अ. क्रि. to float.

तिरपाल *(tirpāl)* terpaulin.

तिरस्कार *(tiras-kār)* पु. contempt; opprobrium; disregard.

तिरस्कार्य *(tiaraskārya)* वि. contemptible.

तिरस्कृत *(tiras-kṛt)* वि. disregarded; insulted; condemned.

तिराहा *(tirāhā)* पु. junction of three roads of paths.

तिरोहित *(tirôhit)* वि. vanished; disappeard; removed or withdrawn from sight; covered; concealed; hidden.

तिल *(til)* पु. the sesamum plant; mole; pupil of the eye.

तिलक *(tilak)* पु. mark on the forehead; ornament worn of forehead.

तिलचटा *(tilcaṭṭā)* पु. cockroach.

तिलमिलाना *(tilmilānā)* अ. क्रि. to writhe in agony; to be dazzled; to fret and fume.

तिलमिलाहट *(tilmilāhat)* स्त्री. restlessness; tossing about; rage.

तिलांजलि *(tilānjalī)* स्त्री. a handful of water mixed with sesamum seeds offered to the deceased ancestors; abandonment; giving up once and for all.

तिलिस्म *(tilism)* वि. (अ.) talisman; mystry; a structure based on a spell.

तिलिस्मी *(tilismī)* वि. (अ.) magical; mystical; talismanic.

तिल्ली *(tillī)* स्त्री. spleen; spleenitis; kernel of sesamum.

तिहरा *(tihrā)* वि. triple; triplicate; threefold.

तिहाई *(tihāī)* वि. third part; one third.

तीक्ष्ण *(tīkśṇ)* वि. sharp; pungent; violent; vehement; quick; keen; intelligent; penetrating.

तीक्ष्णता *(tīksnātā)* स्त्री. sharpness; pungency.

तीखा *(tīkhā)* वि. biting; sharp.

तीखापन *(tīkhāpan)* स्त्री. bitterness; sharpness.

तीतर *(tītar)* पु. patridge.

तीमारदार *(tīmārdār)* पु. (फ़ा.) attendant; a person attending on a patient.

तीमारदारी *(tīmārdārī)* स्त्री. (फ़ा.) attendance or nursing (of a patient).

तीरंदाज़ *(tīrandāz)* पु. (फ़ा.) bowman; archer.

तीरंदाज़ी *(tīrandāzi)* स्त्री. (फ़ा.) archery; bowmanship.

तीर[1] *(tir)* पु. shore; bank.

तीर[2] *(tir)* पु. (फ़ा.) arrow; shaft.

तीर्थ *(tirth)* पु. place of pilgrimage.

तीर्थयात्रा *(tīrthyatrā)* स्त्री. pilgrimage.

तीर्थयात्री *(tīrth-yātrī)* पु. pilgrim.

तीर्थाटन *(tīrthātan)* पु. pilgrimage.

तीली *(tīlī)* स्त्री. (फ़ा.) matchstick; skewer; wooden or iron bar or wire (as of a bird-cage; etc.); spoke.

तीव्र *(tīvrā)* वि. much; exceeding; excessive; sharp; keen; acute; intense; fast.

तीव्रता *(tīvrātā)* स्त्री. violence; sharpness; fastness; acuteness; intensity.

तीसरा *(tīsrā)* वि. third.

तुक *(tuk)* स्त्री. rhyme; harmony; coordination; propriety; suitability.

तुकबंदी *(tukbandi)* स्त्री. rhyming; versification; crude-poetry.

तुकांत *(tukānt)* वि. having terminal alliteration; rhymed.

तुच्छ *(tucch)* वि. petty; worthless; insignificant; contemptible; smal; little; trivial.

तुच्छता *(tucchatā)* स्त्री. pettiness; worthlessness; despicableness; insignificance; meanness; triviality.

तुड़ाना *(turānā)* स. क्रि. to cause to break; to break; rend; tear; to change (a coin or currency note in to smaller ones).

तुतलाना *(tutlānā)* अ. क्रि. to lisp.

तुतलाहट *(tutlāhat)* स्त्री. lisping.

तुनकना *(tunaknā)* अ. क्रि. to be petulant or pettish; to get into temper.

तुनक-मिज़ाज *(tunak-mizāj)* वि. fretful; peevish; touchy; irritable; petulant.

तुम *(tum)* सर्व. you.

तुम्हारा *(tumhārā)* सर्व. your; yours.

तुम्हीं *(tumhī)* सर्व. you alone; you only.

तुम्हें *(tumhen)* सर्व. to you; unto you.

तुरंग *(turang)* पु. horse.

तुरंगशाला *(turangshālā)* स्त्री. stable.

तुरंगी *(turangī)* पु. horse rider.

तुरंत *(turant)* क्रि. वि. at once; quickly; forthwith; instantly.

तुलना[1] *(tulnā)* स्त्री. comparison.

तुलना[2] *(tulnā)* अ. क्रि. to be weighed.

तुलनात्मक *(tulnātmak)* वि. comparative.

तुलवाई *(tulvāi)* स्त्री. act of weighing; the price paid for weighment.

तुलवाना *(tulvānā)* स. क्रि. to have (a thing) weighed.

तुला *(tulā)* स्त्री. balance or scale; pair of scales; libra; the seventh sign of the zodiac.

तुल्य *(tulya)* वि. equal (to); equivalent; resembling; similar; analogous (to).

तुषार *(tusār)* वि. frost.

तुष्ट *(tust)* वि. satisfied; contented; pleased; glad.

तुष्टता *(tustatā)* वि. satisfacton; appeasement; gratification.

तुष्टि *(tusti)* स्त्री. satisfaction; gratification; contentment; pleasure; delight.

तुष्टीकरण *(tustīkaran)* पु. placation; appeasement.

तू *(tū)* सर्व. thou.

तू-तड़ाक *(tū-tarāk)* स्त्री. uncivil and rude language.

तू-तू, मैं-मैं *(tū-tū; main-main)* स्त्री. altercation; squabble.

तूती *(tūtī)* स्त्री. a kind of musical instrument resembling a flute or clarionet.

तूफ़ान *(tūfān)* पु. (अ). storm; tempest; hurricane.

तूफ़ानी *(tūfānī)* वि. (अ.) stormy; tempestuous; (fig.) riotous; boisterous; violent.

तूल *(tūl)* पु. cotton cloth of red colour; dark red colour; length; prolixity; heap.

तूलिका *(tūlikā)* स्त्री. painter's brush.

तृण *(tṛn)* पु. grass; blade of grass; straw.

तृप्त *(tṛpt)* वि. satiated; satisfied.

तृप्ति *(tṛpti)* स्त्री. satisfaction; satiety.

तृषा *(tṛśā)* स्त्री. thirst.

तृष्णा *(tṛśṇā)* स्त्री. thirst; strong desire; eagerness; longing; greed; craving.

तेंदुआ *(tenduā)* पु. leopard.

तेग़ *(teg)* स्त्री. (फ़ा.) sword; scimitar.

तेज़[1] *(tej)* पु. splendour; glory; refulgence.

तेज़[2] *(tej)* वि. (फ़ा.) sharp; acute; fast; violent; fiery; pungent; acrid; swift; quick; smart; intelligent; quick-witted; effective; efficacious (as medicine); dear; costly.

तेजपात *(tejpāt)* पु. leaf of the laurus cassia.

तेजवंत *(tejvanta)* वि. virile; glorious; strong; mighty; shining; brilliant.

तेजवान् *(tajvān)* वि. luminous; refulgent; brilliant; impressive; glorious.

तेजस्वी *(tejasvī)* वि. brilliant; splendid; bright.

तेज़ाब *(tezāb)* पु. (फ़ा.) acid.

तेज़ाबी *(tezābī)* वि. (फ़ा.) acidic.

तेज़ी *(tezī)* स्त्री. (फ़ा.) sharpness; haste; quickness; pungency; dearness; intensity.

तेरा *(terā)* सर्व. thy; thine; yours.

तेल *(tel)* पु. oil.

तेवर *(tevar)* पु. oilman.

तेवर *(tevar)* पु. angry look; frown; eyebrow.

तैनात *(taināt)* वि. (अ.) appointed; posted; engaged.

तैनाती *(tainātī)* स्त्री. appointment; posting; deployment; engagement.

तैयार *(taiyār)* वि. (अ.) willing; prepared; ready; finished; completed.

तैयारी *(taiyārī)* स्त्री. (अ.) preparation; preparedness; readiness; arrangement.

तैरना *(tairnā)* अ. क्रि. to swim; to float.

तैराक *(tairāk)* पु. swimmer.

तैराकी *(tairākī)* स्त्री. swimming.

तैल *(tail)* पु. oil.

तैश *(taiś)* पु. (अ.) rage; wrath.

तैसा *(taisā)* वि. of that manner; of like manner; similar.

तोंद *(tomd)* स्त्री. protuberant belly; potbelly; paunch; tummy.

तोंदल *(tomdal)* वि. pot-bellied.

तोड़ *(tor)* पु. breaking; breach; fracture; rupture; antidote; countermeasure.

तोड़ना *(torṇā)* स. क्रि. to break; to tear; to rend; to pluck (fruit etc.); to fracture; to violate (a vow or law etc.); to disband; to sever; to sunder (a tie; or friendhsip etc.).

तोड़-फोड़ *(toṛ-foṛ)* स्त्री. breaking and smashing; sabotage.

तोतला *(tatlā)* वि. lispring; lisper.

तोता *(totā)* पु. parrot; matchlock (of a gun).

तोप *(top)* स्त्री. (तु.) cannon.

तोपख़ाना *(topkhānā)* पु. (तु.) artillery

तोपची *(topci)* पु. (तु.) gunner.

तोबा *(tobā)* स्त्री. (अ.) vow to sin no more; vow to desist from doing something again.

तोरण *(toran)* पु. arch; gateway; decorations of a gateway; festoon.

तोलना *(tolnā)* स. क्रि. to weigh.

तोहफ़ा *(tohfā)* पु. (अ.) gratuitous gift; present.

तौर *(taur)* पु. (अ.) manner; mode;

conduct; demeanour.

तौर-तरीक़ा *(tour-tarikā)* पु. way of acting; manner; deportment.

तौल *(taul)* स्त्री. weight or quantity measured by the balance; standard weight or measure of weight.

तौलना *(taulnā)* स. क्रि. to weight; to balance; to judge; to estimate.

तौलाई *(taulāi)* स्त्री. weighment; price paid for having (a thing) weighed.

त्यक्त *(tyakt)* वि. left; abandoned; forsaken; deserted.

त्याग *(tyāg)* पु. abandonment; deserting; parting; renunciation; sacrifice; abdication; resignation.

त्यागना *(tyāgnā)* स. क्रि. to abandon; to give up; to rellinquish; to renounce.

त्यागी *(tyāgī)* पु. renouncer; recluse.

त्याज्य *(tyājya)* वि. abandonable; worth abandoning.

त्यों *(tyoṁ)* क्रि. वि. thus; so; then; at the same time.

त्योरी *(tyorī)* स्त्री. eye-brow; frwn; angry look.

त्योहार *(tyohār)* पु. festival; festivity.

त्रसित, त्रस्त *(trast)* वि. harrowed; oppressed; tormented.

त्राण *(trān)* पु. protection; defence; salvation; deliverance; shelter; help; protection for the body; guard; armour.

त्राणकर्ता *(trān-kartā)* पु. protector; saviour.

त्राता *(trātā)* पु. protector; defender; saviour.

त्रास *(trās)* स्त्री. alarm; fear; dread; terror; scare; affliction; pain; torment; torture.

त्रासदी *(trāsadi)* स्त्री. tragedy.

त्राहि *(trāhi)* अ. save ! deliver ! mercy !

त्राहिमाम *(trāhimān)* अ. protect me; save me.

त्रिकोण *(trikon)* पु. triangular object; trinagle.

त्रिज्या *(trijyā)* स्त्री. radius.

त्रिदोष *(tridosh)* पु. disorder of the three humours of the body.

त्रिभुज *(tribhuj)* पु. triangle.

त्रिभुवन *(tribhuvan)* पु. three worlds (heaven; earth and the lower region).

त्रिमूर्ति *(trimūrti)* स्त्री. trinity; the Hindu triad (Brahma; Vishnu and Shiva).

त्रिया *(triyā)* स्त्री. woman.

त्रिलोक *(trilok)* पु. three worlds (heaven; earth and the lower region).

त्रुटि *(truti)* स्त्री. error; mistake; flaw; defect.

त्रुटिपूर्ण *(trutīpūran)* वि. erroneous; defective.

त्रेता *(tretā)* पु. the second yug or silver age of the Hindus (comprising 1;296;000 years).

त्रैलोक्य *(trailokya)* वि. pertaining to the three-worlds.

त्वक् *(tvak)* पु. the skin; bark.

त्वचा *(tvacā)* स्त्री. skin; hide; bark; rind.

त्वरित *(tvarit)* वि. quick; swift; speedy; accelerted.

थ

थ *(tha)* the second letter of the fourth pentad of the Devnagri alphabets.

थकना *(thaknā)* अ. क्रि. to be tired; to be wearied; to be fatigued; to be fed up; to be exhausted.

थकान *(thakān)* स्त्री. weariness; fatigue; exhaustion; lassitude.

थकाना *(thakānā)* स. क्रि. to weary; to tire; to fatigue; to exhaust; to enervate.

थकावट *(thakāvat)* स्त्री. fatigue; weariness; exhaustion.

थक्का *(thakkā)* पु. anything congealed or conglomerated; clot; lump.

थन *(than)* पु. uddar; teat.

थपकना *(thapaknā)* स. क्रि. to pat; to strike or pat gently with the palm.

थपकी *(thapki)* स्त्री. pat; tap.

थपथपाना *(thapthapānā)* अ. क्रि. to pat with the palm.

थपेड़ा *(thaperā)* पु. blow; stroke; buffet.

थप्पड़ *(thappar)* पु. slap.

थमना *(thamnā)* अ. क्रि. to stop.

थमाना *(thamānā)* स. क्रि. to entrust; to recline.

थरथराना *(thartharānā)* अ. क्रि. to vibrate; to tremble; to shudder.

थरथराहट *(thartharāhat)* स्त्री. vibration; quivering; trembling.

थर्राना *(tharrānā)* अ. क्रि. to tremble; to shudder; to vibrate; to quiver.

थल *(thal)* पु. dry ground; land.

थलचर *(thalchar)* पु. terrestrial animal.

थाती *(thāti)* स्त्री. anything given in charge; trust; accumulated wealth; riches.

थान *(thān)* पु. full length of cloth; place; stall; abode; residence.

थाना *(thānā)* पु. police station.

थानेदार *(thanedār)* पु. officer in charge of police station; police sub-inspector.

थानेदारी *(thānedarī)* स्त्री. the office or functions of a police-inspector.

थामना *(thāmnā)* स. क्रि. to hold; to grasp; to clutch; to seize; to catch; to prop; to support.

थाल *(thāl)* पु. large round flat plate or dish of metal.

थाली *(thālī)* स्त्री. small Indian metal plate.

थाह *(thah)* स्त्री. depth; bottom.

थिगली *(thigli)* स्त्री. patch stitched on clothes to cover holes.

थिरकना *(thiraknā)* (अ.) क्रि. to dance nimbly; to move or dance with expressive action and gesture.

थू *(thü)* (अ.) fie!; pooh!; damn!.

थूक *(thük)* पु. spit; saliva; sputum.

थूकना *(thüknā)* (अ.) क्रि. to spit; to expel from mouth.

थूथनी *(thüthnī)* स्त्री. snout of an animal; muzzle.

थैला *(thailā)* पु. largle bag; sack.

थैली *(thaili)* स्त्री. small bag; sack; purse or money bag.

थोक *(thok)* वि. wholesale.

थोक विक्रेता *(thokvikretā)* पु. wholesaler.

थोड़ा *(thorā)* वि. little; scanty; small.

थोथा *(thothā)* वि. unsubstantial; immaterial; hollow; empty; worthless; meaningless; senseless.

थोपना *(thopnā)* स. क्रि. to plaster; to impose.

द

द *(da)* the third letter of the fourth pentad of the Devnagri alphabets.

दंग *(daṅg)* वि. (फ़ा.) wonderstruck; astonished; amazed.

दंगल *(daṅgal)* पु. (फ़ा.) a wrestling tournament.

दंगा *(daṅgā)* पु. disturbance; riot; row.

दंगेबाज़ *(daṅge-bāz)* वि. riotous; rowdy.

दंड *(daṇḍ)* पु. stick; staff; rod; sceptre; wand; fine; penalty; punishment.

दंडनीय *(daṇḍniyā)* वि. punishable; culpable.

दंड-विधान *(daṇḍ-vidhān)* पु. penal code.

दंड-विधि *(daṇḍ-vidhi)* स्त्री. criminal law.

दंडात्मक *(daṇḍātmak)* वि. punitive; penal.

दंडित *(daṇḍit)* वि. punished; fined.

दंत *(dant)* पु. tooth.

दंतकथा *(dant-kathā)* स्त्री. legend; anecdote; fable.

दंत-चिकित्सक *(dant-çikitsak)* पु. dentist; dental surgeon.

दंत-चिकित्सा *(dant-çikitsā)* स्त्री. dentistry.

दंपती *(dampati)* पु. couple; husband and wife.

दंभ *(dambh)* पु. conceit; vainglory; vanity.

दंभी *(dambhi)* वि. conceited; vainglorious.

दक़ियानूस[1] *(daqiyānüs)* वि. (अ.) old-fashioned; conservative; obscurant.

दक़ियानूस[2] *(daqiyānüs)* पु. (अ.) obscurantist; conservative.

दक़ियानूसी *(daqiyānüsi)* वि. (अ.) obscurantist; conservative.

दक्खिन *(dakkhin)* पु. south; right.

दक्ष *(daks)* वि. expert; dexterous; adroit; skilful.

दक्षता *(dakṣatā)* स्त्री. competence; efficiency; dexterity.

दक्षिण *(dakṣin)* पु. south; right.

दक्षिणा *(dakṣiṅā)* स्त्री. fee or present to the officiating priest.

दख़ल *(da<u>kh</u>al)* पु. (अ.) access; posession; occupation; intervention.

दग़ा *(dagā)* पु. (फ़ा.) deceit; deception; treachery; perfidy; cheating.

दग़ाबाज़ *(dagābāz)* वि. (फ़ा.) deceitful; treacherous; fraudulent.

दग़ाबाज़ी *(dagābāzi)* स्त्री. treachery; deceitfulness; fraud.

दग्ध *(dagdh)* वि. burnt; scorched; tormented; pained distressed.

दढ़ियल *(darhiyal)* वि. bearded.

दत्तक *(dattak)* पु. adopted son.

दत्तचित्त *(datt-cit)* वि. fully attentive; concentrated.

ददौरा *(dadaurā)* पु. dump.

दधि *(dadhi)* पु. curd.

दधिसुत *(dadhisut)* पु. lotus; moon; pearl; poison.

दनदनाना *(dandanānā)* अ. क्रि. to go as fast as a shot; to shoot forth.

दनादन *(danādan)* क्रि. वि. non stop; incessantly.

दफ़न *(dafan)* पु. (अ.) burial.

दफ़नाना *(dafnānā)* स. क्रि. (अ.) to bury.

दफा *(dafā)* स्त्री. time; turn; section; in a code of law.

दफ़्तर *(daftar)* पु. (फ़ा.) office.

दफ़्तरी *(daftarī)* पु. (फ़ा.) bookbinder; one who keeps office and office papers in order.

दफ़्ती *(daftī)* स्त्री. (अ.) board; cardboard; mill-board.

दबंग *(dabang)* वि. fearless; bold; domineering.

दबना *(dabnā)* (अ.) क्रि. to be pressed down; to be buried; to bend (under pressure of weight); bo be subdued; to yield; to be pacified; to be concealed; to be hushed up.

दबाना *(dabānā)* स. क्रि. to press down; to stroke (the limb); to suppress; to repress; to subdue; to dominate; to hush up; to restrain; to curb; to check.

दबाव *(dabāv)* पु. suppression; in fluence; restraint; compulsion; pressure; duress.

दबोचना *(dabocanā)* स. क्रि. to seize suddenly; to grasp.

दब्बू *(dabbū)* वि. tame; of meek or submissive nature.

दब्बूपन *(dabbūpan)* पु. submissiveness; tameness.

दम *(dam)* पु. breath; moment; life; stamina; endurance; puff.

दमक *(damak)* स्त्री. glow; brilliance; flash; glimmer.

दमकना *(damaknā)* (अ.) क्रि. to shine; to glimmer; to glitter.

दमकल *(damkal)* पु. fire engine; fire extinguisher.

दमदार *(damdār)* वि. strong; forceful.

दमन *(daman)* पु. suppression; repression; subjugation; self-restraint.

दमनकारी *(damankārī)* वि. oppressive; suppressive; repressive.

दमनात्मक *(damanātmak)* वि. coercive; oppressive; suppressive.

दमा *(damā)* पु. (फ़ा.) asthma.

दया *(dayā)* स्त्री. mercy; pity; compassion.

दयामय *(dayāmay)* वि. merciful; kind; compassionate.

दयालु *(dayālu)* वि. merciful; compassionate; kind-hearted; generous.

दयालुता *(dayālutā)* स्त्री. kindness; mercy; compassion.

दयावान् *(dayāvān)* दयाशील वि. compassionate; merciful; kind; generous.

दरख्वास्त *(dar-khāst)* स्त्री. (फ़ा.) request; application; petition.

दरगाह *(dar-gāh)* स्त्री. (फ़ा.) shrine.

दरजा *(darjā)* पु. (अ.) rank; standard; class.

दरबान *(darbān)* पु. (फ़ा.) doorkeeper; gate-keeper; porter.

दरबार *(dar-bār)* पु. (फ़ा.) royal court; hall of audience.

दरबारी *(dar-bāri)* पु. (फ़ा.) courtier.

दरवाज़ा *(darvāzā)* पु. (फ़ा.) door; gate.

दराज़ *(darāz)* स्त्री. (फ़ा.) drawes.

दरार *(darār)* स्त्री. crevice; crack; breach; rift; fissure; cleavage.

दरिंदा *(darindā)* पु. (फ़ा.) flesh eating animal; carnivore.

दरिद्र *(daridra)* वि. poor; wretched.

दरिद्रता *(daridratā)* स्त्री. penury; poverty; misery; destitution.

दरिद्री *(daridrī)* वि. poor; wretched.

दरिया *(dariyā)* स्त्री. (फ़ा.) river.

दरियादिल *(dariyādil)* वि. (फ़ा.) liberal; large-heated; magnanimous.

दरियादिली *(driyādilī)* स्त्री. large-heartedness; magnanimity; liberality.

दरी *(darī)* स्त्री. cotton carpet.

दर्जन *(darjan)* पु. dozen.

दर्जा *(darjā)* पु. (अ.) degree; class; category; grade; status.

दर्जिन *(darjin)* स्त्री. (फ़ा.) female tailor; wife of a tailor.

दर्ज़ी *(darzī)* पु. (फ़ा.) tailor.

दर्द *(dard)* पु. (फ़ा.) pain; ache; affliction.

दर्दनाक *(dardnāk)* वि. (फ़ा.) painful; piteous; tragic.

दर्प *(darp)* पु. pride; arrogance; vanity; haughtiness.

दर्पण *(darpaṇ)* पु. mirror; looking glass.

दर्रा *(darrā)* पु. (फ़ा.) mountain pass.

दर्शक *(darśak)* पु. spectator; visitor.

दर्शन *(darśan)* पु. visit; sight; view; appearance; meeting; philosophical system.

दर्शनशास्त्र *(darśan-sāstra)* पु. philosophy.

दर्शनीय *(darśanīya)* वि. worth seeing.

दल *(dal)* पु. petal; leaf; team; party; faction; batch; swarm; herd; group.

दलदल *(daldal)* पु. marsh; swamp; bog.

दलना *(dalnā)* स. क्रि. to grind coarsely; to mill; to cursh.

दलबंदी *(dalbandī)* स्त्री. party formation; groupism; party-politics; factionalism.

दलबदलू *(dalbadlū)* पु. defectionist; defector.

दलाल *(dalāl)* पु. (अ.) broker; commission-agent.

दलाली *(dalālī)* स्त्री. (फ़ा.) business of broker; commission of a broker; brokerage.

दलित *(dalit)* वि. crushed; downtrodden; oppressed.

दलील *(dalīl)* स्त्री. (अ.) plea; argument.

दवा *(davā)* स्त्री. (अ.) medicine; drug.

दवाख़ाना *(davākhānā)* पु. (अ.) dispensary; hospital.

दवात *(davāt)* स्त्री. ink-pot.

दशक *(daśak)* पु. a group of ten; decade.

दशमलव *(daśamlav)* पु. decimal.

दशा *(daśā)* स्त्री. state; condition.

दशाब्द *(daśābda)* पु. decade.

दशाब्दी *(daśābdi)* स्त्री. see दशाब्द.

दस्त *(dast)* पु. (फ़ा.) loose stools; hand.

दस्तक *(dastak)* स्त्री. knock or rap.

दस्तकार *(dastakār)* पु. (फ़ा.) handicraftman; artisan.

दस्तकारी *(dastakāri)* स्त्री. (फ़ा.) handicraft; craftsmanship.

दस्तख़त *(dastakhat)* पु. (फ़ा.) signature.

दस्ता *(dastā)* पु. (फ़ा.) handle; helve; haft; quire of paper; a squad (of troops etc).

दस्ताना *(dastānā)* पु. (फ़ा.) handglove.

दस्तावर *(dastāvar)* वि. (फ़ा.) purgative; laxative.

दस्ती *(dastī)* वि. (फ़ा.) carried or delivered by hand.

दस्तूर *(dastūr)* पु. (फ़ा.) custom; fashion; system; routine.

दस्यु *(dasyu)* पु. thief; robber; bandit; pirate.

दस्युता *(dasyutā)* स्त्री. robbery; dacoity; banditry.

दहकना *(dahaknā)* (अ.) to burn with red hot flame; to blaze.

दहकाना *(dahkānā)* स. क्रि. to cause to blaze.

दहन *(dahan)* पु. burning; combustion; inflammation.

दहनशील *(dahanśila)* वि. combustible; inflammable.

दहना *(dahnā)* स. क्रि. to burn; to persecute; to torture; अ. क्रि. to be burnt.

दहलना *(dahalnā)* (अ.) क्रि. to tremble with fear; to be alarmed or terrified.

दहला *(dahlā)* पु. (फ़ा.) playing card with ten pips.

दहलाना *(dahlānā)* स. क्रि. to overawe; to terrify.

दहलीज़ *(dahlīz)* स्त्री. (फ़ा.) doorstill; threshold.

दहशत *(dahśat)* स्त्री. (फ़ा.) fear; fright; terror; dismay; alarm.

दहाड़ *(dahār)* स्त्री. roar; loud cry.

दहाड़ना *(dahārnā)* (अ.) क्रि. to roar; to cry or shout aloud.

दही *(dahī)* पु. curds.

दहेज़ *(dahez)* पु. dowry.

दाँत *(dāṁt)* पु. tooth.

दाँता *(dāṁtā)* पु. notch; cog or tooth (of a wheel or saw etc.)

दाँती *(dāṁti)* स्त्री. sickle; scythe.

दांपत्य[1] *(dāmpatya)* पु. matrimonial relationship.

दाँपत्य[2] *(dāmpatya)* वि. conjugal; marital.

दाँव *(dāṁv)* पु. opportunity; chance; time; turn; trick (wrestling); trick; stratigem.

दाँव-पेच *(dāṁv-penč)* पु. manoeuvres; tactics.

दाई *(dāī)* स्त्री. nurse; midwife.

दाख़िल *(dākhil)* वि. (फ़ा.) admitted; entered; inserted.

दाख़िल-ख़ारिज *(dākhil-khārij)* पु. mutation; change of name of owner.

दाख़िला *(dākhilā)* पु. (फ़ा.) entry; admission.

दाग़ *(dāg)* पु. (फ़ा.) spot; stain; stigma; blemish.

दाग *(dag)* पु. cremation; lighting the pyre.

दाग़दार *(dāgdār)* वि. specked; scared; carked; branded; stained.

दाग़ना *(dāgnā)* स. क्रि. to brand; to canterize; to fire (a gun etc.).

दाग़ी *(dāgī)* वि. (फ़ा.) marked; spotted; stained; branded; disgraced.

दाड़िम *(dāṛim)* पु. pomegranate.

दाढ़ *(dāṛh)* स्त्री. molar.

दाढ़ी *(dāṛhī)* स्त्री. beard.

दाता *(dātā)* पु. giver; donor.

दादा *(dādā)* पु. paternal grandfather; elder brother; leader of a gang; gangster; hoodlum.

दादागीरी *(dādāgiri)* स्त्री. gangsterism; hooliganism; heroship.

दान *(dān)* पु. act of giving; donation; charity.

दानव *(dānav)* पु. giant; demon.

दाना *(dānā)* पु. (फ़ा.) corn; seed.

दानी[1] *(dānī)* पु. donor; benefactor.

दानी[2] *(dānī)* वि. munificent; generous; charitable.

दानेदार *(dāne-dār)* वि. (फ़ा.) granular; granulated.

दाब़ *(dāb)* पु. pressure; suppression; dominance.

दाबना *(dābnā)* स. क्रि. to press; to keep under control; to bury.

दाम *(dām)* पु. price; value; money.

दामाद *(dāmād)* पु. son-in-law.

दामिनी *(dāminī)* स्त्री. lightning.

दायरा *(dāyrā)* पु. (अ.) circle; ring; range; jurisdiction; scope.

दायाँ *(dāyāṁ)* वि. right.

दायित्व *(dāyitva)* पु. responsibility; onus.

दारिद्रय *(dāridrya)* पु. poverty; indigence.

दारुण *(dārun)* वि. severe; frightful; horrible; terrible; dire.

दारू *(dārū)* स्त्री. (फ़ा.) alcohol; liquor.

दार्शनिक[1] *(dārśanik)* पु. philosopher.

दार्शनिक[2] *(dārśanik)* वि. philosophical pertaining to philosophy.

दार्शनिकता *(dārśaniktā)* स्त्री. philosophical attitude.

दाल *(dāl)* स्त्री. pulse.

दालान *(dālān)* पु. verandah.

दाँव *(dāv)* पु. attempt; wrestling bout; opportune time; remedy; trick; winning move.

दाँव-पेच *(dāv-pech)* पु. trickery.

दावत *(dāvat)* स्त्री. (अ.) feast; banquet; invitation.

दावतनामा *(dāvatnāmā)* पु. written invitation.

दावा *(dāvā)* पु. (अ.) lawsuit claim contention; assertion.

दास *(dās)* पु. slave; servant; vassal.

दासता *(dāsatā)* स्त्री. slavery; vassal age.

दास-प्रथा *(dās-prathā)* स्त्री. slavery.

दासी *(dāsī)* स्त्री. female or maid servant; chambermaid.

दाह *(dāh)* पु. burning; sensation of burning; heat; cremation.

दाहक *(dāhak)* वि. burning; causing heat; inflammatory.

दाह-कर्म *(dāh-karm)* पु. cremation.

दाह-क्रिया *(dāh-kriyā)* स्त्री. cremation.

दाहना *(dāhnā)* स. क्रि. to burn; to torture; to torment.

दाह-संस्कार *(dāh-saṁskār)* पु. funeral rites.

दाहिना *(dāhinā)* वि. situated at the right hand.

दाहिने *(dāhine)* क्रि. वि. to the right.

दिक़्क़त *(diqqat)* स्त्री. (अ.) difficulty; trouble.

दिखना *(dikhnā)* (अ.) क्रि. to be seen; to appear; to be visible.

दिखलाना *(dikhlānā)* स. क्रि. to show; to demonstrate; to exhibit; to display.

दिखाना *(dikhānā)* स. क्रि. to show; to display; to exhibit; to demonstrate.

दिखावट *(dikhāvaṭ)* स्त्री. mere show; ostentation.

दिखावटी *(dikhāvaṭī)* वि. showy; pretentious; artificial.

दिखावा *(dikhāvā)* पु. show; ostentation; pretension; imposture.

दिग्दर्शन *(digdarśan)* पु. a general outline or survey of the subject; direction; guidance.

दिग्विजय *(digvijay)* स्त्री. universal conquest.

दिग्सूचक *(digsučak)* स्त्री. compass.

दिठौना *(diṭhaunā)* पु. a patch or a black mark put on the forehead of a child to guard against the influence of a malignant eye.

दिन *(din)* पु. day; day time.

दिनकर *(dinkar)* पु. the sun.

दिनचर्या *(din-čaryā)* स्त्री. daily routine.

दिनांक *(dinānk)* पु. date.

दिनांकित *(dainānkit)* वि. dated.

दिमाग़ *(dimāg)* पु. (अ.) brain; mind; intellect.

दिमाग़ी *(dimāgi)* वि. (अ.) mental; related to the mind.

दिया *(diyā)* पु. earthen lamp.

दियासलाई *(diyāsalāi)* स्त्री. match-stick.

दिल *(dil)* पु. (फ़ा.) heart; courage.

दिलकश *(dilkas)* वि. (फ़ा.) attractive.

दिलखुश *(dil-khus)* वि. (फ़ा.) pleasant.

दिलचस्प *(dilčaspa)* वि. (फ़ा.) interesting.

दिलचस्पी *(disčaspi)* वि. (फ़ा.) interest.

दिलजोई *(diljoi)* स्त्री. (फ़ा.) consolation; xolace.

दिलदार *(dildār)* वि. (फ़ा.) of a good heart and loving nature; amorous; large-hearted.

दिलपसंद *(dilpasand)* वि. (फ़ा.) favourite.

दिलफेंक *(dilphenk)* वि. (फ़ा.) of romantic disposition; flirtacious.

दिलरुबा *(dilrubā)* वि. (फ़ा.) charming; bewitching; enchanting.

दिलासा *(dilāsā)* पु. consolation; solace;

दिली *(dilī)* वि. hearty; cordial.

दिलेर *(diler)* स्त्री. (फ़ा.) courageous; daring; brave.

दिलेरी *(dilerī)* स्त्री. (फ़ा.) courageousness; bravery.

दिल्लगी *(dillagī)* स्त्री. jest; joke; fun.

दिल्लगीबाज़ *(dillagībāz)* वि. jocular; jocose.

दिवंगत *(divaṁgat)* वि. deceased; late.

दिवस *(divas)* पु. day.

दिवाकर *(divākar)* पु. the sun.

दिवाला *(divālā)* पु. bankruptcy; insolvency.

दिवालिया *(divāliyā)* पु. bankrupt; insolvent.

दिवास्वप्न *(divāsvpna)* पु. day dreaming; reverie.

दिव्य *(divya)* वि. celestial; supernatural; divine; brilliant; charming; beautiful.

दिशा *(diśā)* स्त्री. direction; side; trend.

दिसावर *(disāvar)* पु. foreign country; foreign mart.

दिसावरी *(disāvarī)* वि. imported; belonging to another country.

दिहाड़ी *(dihāṛī)* स्त्री. work-day; daily working hours of a labourer; daily wages of a labourer.

दीक्षांत *(dikshānt)* पु. conclusion of a phase of education.

दीक्षांत-समारोह *(dikshānt-samāroh)*

पु. convocation.

दीक्षा *(dīkṣā)* स्त्री. initiation.

दीक्षार्थी *(dīkṣārthi)* पु. catechumen; postulant.

दीक्षित *(dīkṣit)* वि. initiated.

दीखना *(dikhanā)* (अ.) क्रि. to be visible; to appear; to be in sight.

दीदी *(dīdī)* स्त्री. elder sister.

दीन *(dīn)* वि. poor; miserable; humble.

दीनता *(dinatā)* स्त्री. misery; poverty; humility; meekness.

दीप *(dīp)* पु. lamp; lantern; light.

दीपक *(dīpak)* पु. lamp; lantern.

दीपावलि, दीपावली *(dipāvali)* स्त्री. Hindu festival of lights; row of lights.

दीपिका *(dīpikā)* स्त्री. small lamp; moonlight.

दीप्त *(dīpt)* वि. blazing; flaming; shining; bright; brilliant; acute; gorgeous; illuminated.

दीप्ति *(dīpti)* स्त्री. brightness; splendour; brilliance; lustre; luminosity; glow.

दीमक *(dīmak)* स्त्री. white ant; termite.

दीया *(dīyā)* पु. lamp.

दीयासलाई *(dīyāsalaī)* स्त्री. match stick.

दीर्घ *(dīrgh)* वि. long; big; large.

दीर्घकाय *(dīrghkāya)* वि. gigantic; tall and bulky.

दीर्घता *(dīrghatā)* स्त्री. length; largeness; bigness.

दीर्घसूत्री *(dīrghsutri)* वि. slow; dilatory; procrastinating.

दीर्घा *(dīrghā)* स्त्री. corridor; gallery.

दीर्घायु *(dīrghāyu)* वि. long-living.

दीर्घायुता *(dīrghāyutā)* स्त्री. longevity.

दीवट *(divat)* स्त्री. lamp-stand.

दीवान *(dīvān)* पु. (फ़ा.) royal court; court minister; collected works of a poet.

दीवाना *(dīvānā)* वि. (फ़ा.) mad; insane; nympholeptic; crazy.

दीवानापन *(divānāpan)* पु. nympholepsy; craziness; insanity.

दीवानी *(divānī)* वि. (फ़ा.) pertaining to a civil court as opposed to the criminal one; mad (female).

दीवार *(dīvār)* स्त्री. (फ़ा.) wall.

दीवाली *(diwāli)* see दीपावली

दुःख *(dukh)* पु. trouble; pain; grief; distress; suffering.

दुःखद *(dukhad)* वि. painful; grievous; troublesome; unfortunate; sorrowful.

दुःखी *(dukhī)* वि. sad; aggrieved; troubled; afflicted.

दुःसाध्य *(dussādhya)* वि. difficult to be performed or accomplished; difficult to be managed or dealt with; arduous.

दुःसाहस *(dussāhas)* पु. audacity; temerity.

दुःस्वप्न *(dusvapna)* पु. nightmare.

दुआ *(duā)* स्त्री. (अ.) prayer; blessing; benediction.

दुकान *(dukān)* स्त्री. (फ़ा.) shop.

दुकानदार *(duukāndār)* पु. (फ़ा) shopkeeper.

दुकानदारी *(dukāndārī)* स्त्री. (फ़ा.) shopkeeping.

दुखड़ा *(dukhṛā)* पु. tale of woes; sorrowful story.

दुखना *(dukhnā)* (अ.) क्रि. to pain to ache.

दुखाना *(dukhānā)* स. क्रि. to trouble;

to cause pain; to torment; to hurt.

दुखित *(dukhit)* वि. distressed; griefstricken.

दुखिया *(Dukhiya)* वि. aflicted; in pain or distress.

दुग्ध *(dugdh)* पु. milk; milky juice of plants; sap.

दुग्धशाला *(dugdhsālā)* स्त्री. dairy.

दुतकार *(dutkār)* स्त्री. reproof; reprimand; upbraiding.

दुतकारना *(dutkārnā)* स. क्रि. to reprimand; to rebuke slightingly.

दुतरफ़ा *(dutarfā)* वि. bilateral; two sided.

दुधमुँहा[1] *(dudhmumhā)* वि. suckling.

दुधमुँहा[2] *(dudhmumhā)* पु. suckling baby; infant.

दुधार, दुधारू *(dudhār; dudhārū)* वि. milch; giving milk.

दुनिया *(duniyā)* स्त्री. (अ.) world.

दुनियादार *(duniyādār)* वि. (अ.) absorbed in worldly affairs; worldly; worldly wise.

दुनियादारी *(duniyādāri)* स्त्री. (अ.) worldly wisdom; worldliness.

दुपट्टा *(dupaṭṭā)* पु. a kind of mantle or piece of linen in which there are two layers; a cloth loosely worn over the shoulder.

दुपहर *(dupahar)* पु. noon; mid-day.

दुबकना *(dubaknā)* (अ.) क्रि. to cower; to crouch; to be concealed; to lurk.

दुबला *(dublā)* वि. slim; lean; thin.

दुभाषिया *(dubhāsiyā)* पु. interpreter; one who knows two languaes.

दुम *(dum)* स्त्री. (फ़ा.) tail; hindmost part.

दुमदार *(dumdār)* वि. (फ़ा.) having a tail; pointed at the back.

दुरभिसंधि *(durabhi-sanādhi)* स्त्री. conspiracy; secret plot.

दुराग्रह *(durāgreh)* पु. contumacy; importunity; obduracy; pertinacity; undue insistence; fanaticism.

दुराग्रही *(durāgrehi)* वि. obdurate; pertinacious; mulish; importunate; unduly insistent.

दुराचार *(durācār)* पु. misconduct; moral-turpitude; depravity.

दुराचारी *(duracari)* वि. wicked; immoral; licentious.

दुराव *(durāv)* पु. concealment.

दुराशा *(durāsā)* स्त्री. hoping against hope; false hope.

दुरुपयोग *(durupyog)* पु. misuse; abuse.

दुरूस्त *(durust)* वि. (फ़ा.) proper; sound; mended; repaired; fit; correct.

दुरूह *(dur-ūh)* वि. abstruse; recondite; unintelligible.

दुरूहता *(dur-ūhtā)* स्त्री. abstruseness; unintelligibility.

दुर्गंध *(durgandh)* स्त्री. bad smell; stench; stink; obnoxious smell; bad odour.

दुर्ग *(dur-g)* पु. fort; castle ; citadel.

दुर्गति *(dur-gati)* स्त्री. distress; misery; poverty.

दुर्गम *(dur-gam)* वि. difficult to be traversed or travelled over; impassable; hard to be understood.

दुर्गुण *(dur-gun)* पु. defect; fault; flaw; vice.

दुर्घटना *(dur-ghatnā)* स्त्री. accident; mishap.

दुर्जन *(dur-jan)* पु. bad man; villain; scoundrel.

दुर्जनता *(dur-jantā)* स्त्री. wickedness;

villainy; rascality.

दुर्जेय *(dur-jeya)* वि. invincible; difficult to be conquered or won.

दुर्दम *(dur-dam)* वि. indomitable; irrepressible; unyielding; difficult to subdue.

दुर्दम्य *(dur-damya)* वि. impregnable; invincible; recalcitrant.

दुर्दशा *(durdaśā)* स्त्री. sad plight; misery; adversity.

दुर्दांत *(dur-dānt)* वि. invincible; impregnable.

दुर्बल *(durbal)* वि. of little strength; weak; feeble; thin; slender; emaciated; lean.

दुर्बलता *(durbaltā)* स्त्री. weakness; feableness; thinness; debility.

दुर्बुद्धि *(durbudhi)* वि. evil minded; wicked; silly; foolish; stupid.

दुर्बोध *(dur-bodh)* वि. unintelligible; abstruse; obscure.

दुर्भावना *(durbhāvanā)* स्त्री. evil thought; bad inclination.

दुर्भिक्ष *(durbhiksh)* पु. famine.

दुर्लंघ्य *(durlanghya)* वि. impassable; difficult to cross; insurmountable.

दुर्लभ *(durlabh)* वि. difficult to be obtained or found; scarce; rare.

दुर्लभता *(durlabhtā)* स्त्री. scarcity; unavailability; rarity.

दुर्वचन *(dur-vačan)* पु. bad or harsh language; abuse.

दुर्विनीत *(dur-vinita)* वि. ill-mannered; impudent.

दुर्वृत्त *(dur-vritt)* वि. depraved; wicked; evil-minded.

दुर्व्यवस्था *(dur-vyavsthā)* स्त्री. mismanagement.

दुर्व्यवहार *(dur-vyavahār)* स्त्री. illtreatment; misconduct; misbehaviour.

दुर्व्यसन *(dur-vyasan)* पु. bad propensity; vice; addiction.

दुलत्ती *(dulatti)* स्त्री. kick with the two hind legs (as by an ass or a horse).

दुलराना *(dularānā)* स. क्रि. to fondle; to caress.

दुलहन, दुलहिन *(dulhan)* स्त्री. bride.

दुलहा *(dulhā)* पु. bridegroom.

दुलहिन *(dulhin)* see दुलहन

दुलार *(dulār)* पु. fondling affection.

दुलारना *(dulārnā)* स. क्रि. to fondle; to show affection to; to love; to pet; to caress.

दुलारा *(dulārā)* वि. beloved; darling.

दुविधा *(duvidhā)* स्त्री. dilemma; fix.

दुशाला *(duśāla)* पु. shawl; double shawl.

दुश्चरित्र[1] *(duś-čaritra)* पु. misdoing; ill conduct; depravity; profligacy.

दुश्चरित्र[2] *(duś-čaritra)* वि. degenerate; profligate.

दुश्चिंता *(duś-cinta)* स्त्री. anxiety.

दुश्मन *(duśman)* पु. (फ़ा.) enemy; foe.

दुष्कर *(duśkar)* वि. difficlt to be performed or accomplished; hard to be done.

दुष्कर्म *(duśkarm)* पु. evil act; misdeed; sin; vice.

दुष्ट[1] *(duṣṭ)* वि. wicked; bad; vile; knavish; malevolent.

दुष्ट[2] *(duṣṭ)* पु. scoundrel; rascal; scamp.

दुष्टता *(duṣtatā)* स्त्री. badness; wickedness; viciousness; knavery; malevolence; mischievousness.

दुष्टात्मा *(duśtātmā)* वि. of bad nature; evil-minded; wicked; malicious.

दुस्सह *(dussah)* वि. unbearable; intolerable.

दुस्साध्य *(dussādhya)* वि. hardened; difficult to treat.

दुस्साहस *(dussāhas)* पु. recklessness.

दुहत्था *(duhatha)* वि. provided with two handles.

दुहना *(duhnā)* स. क्रि. to milk; to squeeze; to exploit.

दुहरा *(duhrā)* वि. two-fold; double folded.

दुहराना *(duhrānā)* स. क्रि. to repeat; to revise.

दुहाई *(duhāī)* स्त्री. cry for help or mercy of justice; complaint; appeal; invocation.

दूत *(dūt)* पु. courier; messenger; emissary; ambassador; envoy.

दूतावास *(dūtāvās)* पु. embassy; consulate.

दूध *(dūdh)* पु. milk; milky juice of certain plants.

दूधिया[1] *(dūdhiyā)* वि. milk white; milky; containing or abounding in milk; juicy.

दूधिया[2] *(dūdhiyā)* पु. milk-vendor; white ash colour.

दून *(dūn)* स्त्री. valley.

दूना *(dūnā)* वि. double; twice as much.

दूभर *(dūbhar)* वि. onerous; burdensome; difficult to be borne; difficult; arduous.

दूरंदेश *(dūrandeś)* वि. (फ़ा.) far-sighted

दूरंदेशी *(dūrandeśī)* स्त्री. (फ़ा.) far-sightedness.

दूर *(dūr)* क्रि. वि. away; beyond; far off.

दूरगामी *(dūrgāmī)* वि. far-reaching.

दूरदर्शक *(dūrdarśak)* पु. telescope.

दूरदर्शन *(dūrdarśan)* television.

दूरदर्शिता *(dūrdarśitā)* स्त्री. farsightedness; farsight; sagacity; prudence.

दूरदृष्टि *(dūr-dṛsti)* स्त्री. farsightedness.

दूरबीन *(dūrbina)* स्त्री. telescope; field-glass.

दूरभाष *(dūrbhaś)* पु. telephone.

दूरमुद्रक *(dūrmudrak)* पु. teleprinter.

दूरमुद्रण *(dūrmudran)* पु. teleprinting.

दूरलेख *(dūrlekh)* पु. telegram.

दूरलेखी *(dūrlekhi)* वि. telegraphic.

दूरवर्ती *(dūr-verti)* वि. far removed; remote; distant.

दूरवीक्षक *(dūrvikshak)* पु. telescope.

दूरसंचार *(dūr-sančar)* पु. tele-communication.

दूरी *(dūrī)* स्त्री. distance; remoteness.

दूल्हा *(dūlhā)* पु. bridegroom.

दूषण *(dūṣan)* पु. fault; blemish; defect; contamination; pollution; stigma; defilement; prostitution.

दूषित *(dūṣit)* वि. blemished; defiled; spoiled; contaminated; polluted; stigmatic; defective; corrupted; vitiated; sulllied.

दूसरा *(dūsrā)* वि. second; next; another; different.

दूहना *(dūhnā)* स. क्रि. to milk.

दृढ़ *(dirḥ)* वि. fixed; firm; tough; strong; irrevocable; confirmed; firmly fastened; shut fast; tense; fortis.

दृढ़ता *(diṛatā)* स्त्री. firmness; strength; resoluteness; toughness.

दृश्य[1] *(dṛśyā)* वि. visible; spectacular; visual.

दृश्य[2] *(dṛśyā)* पु. scene; spectacle; scenery; sight.

दृश्यता *(dṛśyāta)* स्त्री. visulality; visibility.

दृष्टांत *(drāstānt)* पु. example; instance; illustration; (in rhet.) a figure of speech in which an assertion or statement is illustrated by example.

दृष्टा *(drāstā)* पु. seer.

दृष्टि *(dṛsṭi)* स्त्री. eye-sight; vision.

दृष्टिकोण *(dṛsṭikon)* पु. point of view.

दृष्टिगत *(dṛsṭigat)* वि. seen; perceived; viewed.

दृष्टिगोचर *(drsṭi-gočar)* वि. visible; perceptible.

दृष्टिपात *(dṛsṭi-pāt)* पु. look; glance; act of seeing.

दृष्टिहीन *(dṛsṭi-hin)* वि. nerve blind.

देखना *(dekhnā)* स. क्रि. to see; to look; to observe; to perceive; to search; to feel (as pulse); to supervise; to manage; to weigh well; to consider.

देखभाल, देखरेख *(dekh-bhāl)* स्त्री. care; supervision; observation.

देदीप्यमान *(dedīpyamān)* वि. shining intensely; resplendent; brilliant.

देन *(den)* स्त्री. act of giving; gift; contribution.

देनदार *(dendār)* पु. debtor.

देनदारी *(dendāri)* स्त्री. liability; indebtedness.

देना *(denā)* स. क्रि. to give; to grant; to lay (eggs); to pay (a debt etc.); to confer; to bestow; to entrust; to assign.

देय[1] *(dey)* पु. worth-giving; to be paid; payable; due.

देय[2] *(dey)* पु. dues.

देयता *(deyatā)* स्त्री. indebtedness; liability.

देर *(der)* स्त्री. delay; period of time; a long while.

देरी *(derī)* स्त्री. delay.

देव *(dev)* पु. deity; god; a respectable person; a huge fellow of thing.

देवता *(devatā)* पु. deity; a god; divinity; image of a deity; idol.

देवत्व *(devatvā)* पु. godhood; godliness; divinity.

देवदार *(devdār)* पु. devdar; cedar.

देवदासी *(devdāsī)* स्त्री. temple dancer; dancing girl dedicated to a deity.

देवदूत *(devdūt)* पु. angel.

देवर *(devar)* पु. husband's younger brother.

देवरानी *(devrānī)* स्त्री. wife of husband's younger brother.

देवलोक *(devlok)* पु. abode of gods.

देववाणी *(dev-vāni)* स्त्री. oracle; Sanskrit; language of gods.

देवसभा *(davsabhā)* स्त्री. pantheon.

देवस्थान *(devsthān)* पु. abode of gods; temple.

देवांगना *(davāṁganā)* स्त्री. god's spouse; a celestial damsel; goddess.

देवालय *(davālay)* पु. temple; pagoda;

देवी *(devī)* स्त्री. a female deity; a respectful title applied to a lady.

देश *(deś)* पु. place; region; country; part; portion; province; protion of a body or region.

देशत्याग *(deś-tyāg)* पु. expatriation.

देशद्रोह *(deś-droh)* पु. treason.

देशद्रोही *(deś-drohi)* पु. traitor; fifth columnist.

देश-निकाला *(deś-nikālā)* पु. expatriation; exile; banishment.

देशप्रेम *(deś-prem)* पु. patriotism.

देशप्रेमी[1] *(deś-premi)* पु. patriot.

देशप्रेमी[2] *(deś-premi)* वि. patriotic.

देशभक्त *(deś-bhakt)* पु. patriot.

देशभक्ति *(deś-bhakti)* स्त्री. patriotism.

देशवासी *(deś-vāsi)* पु. compatriot.

देशांतर *(deśāntar)* पु. another country; longitude.

देशांतरण *(deśāntran)* पु. migration; transmigration.

देशांतरित *(deśāntarit)* वि. transmigrated.

देशाटन *(deśātan)* पु. roaming or wandering through a country; touring in a country or countries.

देशी *(deśī)* वि. belonging to a province; local; indigenous.

देशीय *(deśīya)* वि. domestic; native.

देसावर *(desāvar)* पु. foreign country; place from which goods are sent for.

देसावरी *(desāvarī)* वि. of or belonging to a foreign country; imported.

देह *(deh)* स्त्री. body.

देहांत *(dehānt)* पु. death.

देहात *(dehāt)* पु. village.

देहाती[1] *(dehātī)* वि. rural; pertaining to a village; rustic; uncivilized.

देहाती[2] *(dehātī)* पु. villager.

देहावसान *(dehāvasān)* पु. death demise.

दैत्य *(daityā)* पु. demon. evil spirit.

दैनिक *(dainik)* वि. daily; diurnal.

दैनिकी *(dainikī)* स्त्री. daily diary.

दैन्य *(dainyā)* पु. poverty; indigent; humbleness; meekness; depression; miserable state.

दैव *(daiv)* पु. fate; destiny; luck; fortune.

दैवयोग *(daivyog)* पु. accident; chance.

दैशिक *(daiśik)* वि. relating to the country; indigenous.

दैहिक *(daihik)* वि. physical; corporeal.

दोआब *(doāb)* पु. tract of country between two rivers.

दोग़ला *(doglā)* वि. cross-bred; hybrid.

दोज़ख़ *(dozakh)* पु. (फ़ा.) hell.

दो तरफ़ा *(do-tarfa)* see दुतरफ़ा

दोनों *(donoṁ)* सर्व. वि. both.

दोमट *(domat)* स्त्री. loam.

दोयम *(doyam)* वि. (फ़ा.) second rate; second (in order of merit).

दोलक *(dolak)* पु. pendulum; oscillator.

दोष *(doś)* पु. defect; fault; demerit; crime ; sin; guilt; blame; blemish; weak-point; error.

दोषपूर्ण *(dośpūrna)* वि. defective; faulty.

दोषमुक्त *(doś-mukta)* वि. guiltless; acquitted.

दोषमुक्ति *(dośmukti)* स्त्री. acquittal.

दोषारोपण *(dośāropan)* पु. accusation; charge.

दोषी[1] *(doṣī)* वि. faulty; defective; wicked; guilty.

दोषी[2] *(doṣī)* पु. sinner; guilty person; one who is at fault.

दोस्त *(dost)* पु. (फ़ा.) friend.

दोस्ताना[1] *(dostānā)* पु. (फ़ा.) friendship; friendliness.

दोस्ताना[2] *(dostānā)* पु. (फ़ा.) friendly; worthy of a friend.

दोस्ती *(dosti)* स्त्री. (फ़ा.) friendship; amity.

दोहरा *(dohrā)* वि. bouble; having two folds; dual.

दोहा *(dohā)* पु. couplet.

दौड़ *(dauṛ)* स्त्री. race.

दौड़ना *(dauṛanā)* (अ.) क्रि. to run; to run about.

दौड़ाना *(dauṛānā)* स. क्रि. to cause to run; to run (brush etc.)

दौर *(daur)* पु. going round; moving in a circle; round (of wine etc.)

दौरा *(daurā)* पु. going round; a revolution; a turn; tour; fit; attack of a disease.

दौरान *(daurān)* पु. (अ.) duration; period.

दौलत *(daulat)* स्त्री. wealth; riches; opulence; good fortune; prosperity; happiness.

दौलतख़ाना *(daulatkhānā)* पु. (अ.) residence.

दौलतमंद *(daulatmand)* वि. (अ.) wealthy; opulent; rich; prosperous.

दौहित्र *(douhitrā)* पु. daughter's son; grandson.

द्युति *(dyuti)* स्त्री. light; brightness; splendour; radiance; lustre.

द्युत *(dyūt)* पु. gambling.

द्युतक्रीड़ा *(dyūt-krirā)* स्त्री. gambling.

द्योतक *(dyotak)* वि. bringing into light; making clear; significant; indicative; exponent.

द्योतन *(dyotan)* पु. indication; signification.

द्रव *(drav)* पु. fluid; liquid; liquid substance.

द्रवण *(dravaṇ)* पु. melting.

द्रवणांक *(dravanānk)* पु. melting point.

द्रवता *(dravatā)* स्त्री. liquidity; fluidity.

द्रवित *(dravit)* वि. melted; liquified; moved (by emotion).

द्रव्य *(dravya)* पु. thing; material; matter; elementary substance; any possession; wealth; goods; property; money.

द्रष्टव्य *(draśtavya)* वि. visible; perceptible; pleasing to sight; lovely; beautiful.

द्रष्टा *(draśtā)* पु. spectator; witness; viewer.

द्राक्षा *(drākṣā)* स्त्री. grape; vine.

द्रुत *(drut)* वि. quick; swift; speedy; dissolved; melted.

द्रुतगामी *(drutgāmi)* वि. fast moving; quick; light-footed.

द्रोह *(droh)* पु. malice; hostility.

द्रोही *(drohi)* वि. hostile; disloyal; treacherous; perfidious.

द्वंद्व *(dvandva)* पु. pair; couple; duel; pair of conflicting ideas; thoughts and tendencies; struggle; strife.

द्वंद्व युद्ध *(dvandva-yudh)* पु. duel fighting.

द्वंद्वात्मक *(dvandvātmak)* वि. conflicting.

द्वार *(dvār)* पु. door; gate entrance; an aperture of the human body; opening.

द्वारपाल *(dvārpāl)* पु. porter; gatekeeper.

द्वारा *(dvārā)* क्रि. वि. through; through the medium or agency (of).

द्विगुणित *(dvigunit)* वि. doubled.

द्विज *(dvija)* पु. Brahman religious man.

द्वित्व *(dvitva)* पु. duplication; repetition; duplication of a consonant in a word.

द्विपक्षी, द्विपक्षीय *(dvi-pakshi)* *वि.* bilateral; dipartite.

द्विरूक्ति *(dvi-rukti)* *स्त्री.* repetition; reiteration.

द्विवार्षिक *(dvi-varśik)* *वि.* biennial.

द्विविध *(dvi-vidh)* *वि.* of two kinds of types.

द्विविधा *(dvi-vidhā)* *स्त्री.* dilemma; suspense; uncertainty; quandary.

द्वीप *(dvip)* *पु.* island; isle.

द्वेष *(dveś)* *पु.* malice; spite; malignity hostility; hatred; malevolence.

द्वेषपूर्ण *(dveś-pūran)* *वि.* malicious.

द्वेषी *(dveśī)* *वि.* malicious; hostile; inimical.

द्वैत *(dvait)* *पु.* duality; duplicity; discrimination; pair; couple; dualism.

ध

ध *(dha)* the fourth letter of the fourth pentad of the Devnagri alphabets.

धंधा *(dhandhā)* *पु.* occupation; vocation; business; trade; work in general.

धँसना *(dhaṁsnā)* *(अ.)* *क्रि* to sink; to pierce; to stick; to enter; to run (into); to penetrate.

धँसाना *(dhaṁsānā)* *स. क्रि.* to cause to sink; to pierce; to stick; to thrust.

धक *(dhak)* *स्त्री.* palpitation.

धकापेल[1] *(dhakāpel)* *स्त्री.* shoving and pushing; jostling.

धकापेल[2] *(dhakāpel)* *क्रि. वि.* vigorously; vehemently.

धकियाना *(dhakiyānā)* *स. क्रि.* to push about; to thrust ahead.

धकेलना *(dhakelnā)* *स. क्रि.* to shove; to push; to jostle.

धक्कमधक्का *(dhakkamdhakkā)* *पु.* shoving and pushing; jostling.

धक्का *(dhakkā)* *पु.* push; shock; jog; jolt; loss; damage; setback.

धज्जी *(dhajjī)* *स्त्री.* strip; shred; rag; tatter.

धड़ *(dhar)* *पु.* trunk (of the body); body; stem; trunk (of the tree).

धड़कन *(dharkan)* *स्त्री.* palpitation; throb; pulsation.

धड़कना *(dharkanā)* *(अ.)* *क्रि.* to throb; to palpitate.

धड़काना *(dharkānā)* *स. क्रि.* to frighten; to alarm; to terrify; to cause to beat or palpitate.

धड़धड़ाना *(dhardharānā)* *(अ.)* *क्रि.* to make a rattling or banging sound; to knock at the door violently.

धड़ल्ले से *(dharalle-se)* *क्रि. वि.* fearlessly; without hesitation or hitch.

धड़ा *(dharā)* *पु.* counter-balance; counter balancing weight; tare; weight of five seers; faction; block; bloc.

धड़ाधड़ *(dharādhar)* *क्रि. वि.* one after another; in quick succession; incessantly; with the quick succession of rattling sounds; quickly with loud report; with a crash.

धड़ाबंदी *(dharābandi)* स्त्री. counterpoise; counterbalancing; factionalism.

धड़ाम *(dharām)* स्त्री. crash; thud.

धतूरा *(dhatürā)* पु. stramonium.

धधकना *(dhadhakanā)* (अ.) क्रि. to burn fiercely; to flare up.

धधकाना *(dhadhakānā)* स. क्रि. to cause to blaze of flare up.

धन *(dhan)* पु. property; wealth; money; capital; plus.

धनराशि *(dhanrāsi)* स्त्री. amount; sum.

धनवान *(dhan-vān)* वि. rich; wealthy.

धनाढ्य *(dhanadhya)* वि. opulent; rich; wealthy.

धनादेश *(dhanādes)* पु. money-order; draft (issued by bank).

धनिक *(dhanik)* वि. rich; wealthy.

धनिकतंत्र *(dhaniktantra)* पु. plutocracy.

धनिया *(dhaniyā)* पु. coriander seed.

धनी *(dhani)* वि. rich; opulent; wealthy.

धनु *(dhanu)* पु. bow; ninth sign of the zodiac.

धनुर्धर *(dhanurdhar)* पु. archer; bowman.

धनुष *(dhanus)* पु. bow; arch.

धन्य[1] *(dhanya)* (अ.) 'well done'; 'bravo'; fortunate ! what happiness!.

धन्य[2] *(dhanya)* वि. blessed; fortunate; lucky; happy; praiseworthy.

धन्यवाद *(dhanyavād)* पु. expression of gratitude; thanks.

धब्बा *(dhabbā)* पु. stain; blot; stigma; slur; blemish.

धम *(dham)* स्त्री. thud.

धमकाना *(dhamkānā)* (अ.) क्रि. to threaten; to menace; to intimidate.

धमकी *(dhamki)* स्त्री. threat; menace.

धमन-भट्टी *(dhaman-bhattī)* स्त्री. blast furnace.

धमाका *(dhamāka)* पु. explosion; crack; crash; blast.

धमाचौकड़ी *(dhamācaukri)* स्त्री. noise; tumult; bustle; turmoil; gambol; frolic.

धरती *(dharti)* स्त्री. the earth; ground; land; soil.

धरना[1] *(dharnā)* स. क्रि. to place; to put; to keep; to catch; to seize; to apprehend; to hold; to pledge.

धरना[2] *(dharnā)* पु. sitting doggedly to enforce compliance of a demand.

धरपकड़ *(dhar-pakar)* स्त्री. mass arrests.

धरा *(dharā)* स्त्री. the earth.

धरातल *(dharātal)* पु. surface of the earth; surface.

धराशायी *(dharāsāyi)* वि. fallen on the ground; razed to the ground; fallen flat.

धरित्री *(dharitrī)* स्त्री. the earth.

धरोहर *(dharōhar)* स्त्री. deposit; trust (money or article); inheritance; inherited property etc.

धर्म *(dharm)* पु. essential or inherent quality; attribute; duty; prescribed course of conduct; religion.

धर्मग्रंथ *(dharm-granth)* पु. sacred book or scripture.

धर्मच्युत *(dharm-cyut)* वि. deviated from religion or duty.

धर्मज्ञ *(dharmajna)* वि. well-versed in theology.

धर्म-तंत्र *(dharm-tantra)* पु. theocracy.

धर्मनिंदा *(dharm-nindā)* स्त्री. blasphemy.

धर्मनिरपेक्ष *(dharm-nirpeksha)* वि. secular.

धर्मनिरपेक्षता *(dharm-nirpekśtā)* स्त्री. secularism.

धर्मनिष्ठ *(dharm-niśth)* वि. religious minded; devout.

धर्मनिष्ठा *(dharm-nisthā)* स्त्री. piety; devotedness; religious faith.

धर्मपत्नी *(dharm-patni)* स्त्री. lawful wife.

धर्मपरायण *(dharm-parāyan)* वि. religious; religious-minded; devout.

धर्मपरायणता *(dharm-parāyanatā)* स्त्री. religiousity.

धर्मभीरू *(dharm-bhirü)* वि. god-fearing; scrupulous.

धर्मयुद्ध *(dharm-yuddha)* पु. religious war; crusade.

धर्मशाला *(dharmsālā)* स्त्री. inn; hostelry.

धर्मशास्त्र *(dharm-śāstra)* पु. theology.

धर्मांध *(dharmāndh)* वि. fanatic.

धर्मांधता *(dharmāndhatā)* स्त्री. fanaticism; bigotry.

धर्माडंबर *(dharmādambar)* पु. religiosity.

धर्मात्मा[1] *(dharmātmā)* वि. religious; pious; righteous; saintly.

धर्मात्मा[2] *(dharmātmā)* पु. good or noble person; virtuous man; saint.

धर्मार्थ *(dharmārtha)* वि. charitable.

धर्मिणी *(dharminī)* स्त्री. wife.

धर्मोपदेश *(dharmopadeśa)* पु. sermon; religious discourse; catechesis.

धर्मोपदेशक *(dharmopadeshak)* पु. religious preacher; ecclesiast.

धवल *(dhaval)* वि. white; clean; unsullied; bright.

धवलता *(dhavaltā)* स्त्री. whiteness; brightness; clearness; fairness.

धसक *(dhasak)* स्त्री. depression; sagging; sinking; pungent smell emitted by dry leaf; chillies etc.

धसकन *(dhaskan)* स्त्री. depression; sagging; sinking.

धसकना *(dhaskanā)* अ. क्रि. to be depressed; to sag; to feel jealous.

धसका *(dhaskā)* पु. a disease of lungs (in animals); dry cough; bronchitis.

धसना *(dhasanā)* अ. क्रि. to be ruined or destroyed; to sink; to penetrate.

धाँधली *(dhāṁdhli)* स्त्री. chaotic condition; disorder; trick; cheating; arbitrary conduct; arbitrariness.

धाक *(dhāk)* स्त्री. sway; control; awe.

धाकड़ *(dhākar)* वि. daring; dashing; bold; dauntless; influential; commanding.

धागा *(dhāgā)* पु. thread.

धातु *(dhātu)* स्त्री. metal; constituent element or essentail ingredient of the body; verbal root.

धातु-विज्ञान *(dhātu-vijnān)* पु. metallurgy.

धान *(dhān)* पु. rice in the husk; paddy; rice-plant.

धानी *(dhānī)* वि. light green.

धान्य *(dhānya)* पु. cereal.

धान्यागार *(dhānyāgār)* पु. granary; barn.

धाम *(dhām)* पु. a dwelling place; abode; residence; seat of a deity; place of pilgrimage; sacred place.

धार *(dhār)* स्त्री. flow; stream; current; sharp edge.

धारक *(dhārak)* पु. holder; bearer; debter

धारण *(dhāran)* पु. holding; bearing; wielding; wearing; keeping; maintenance; retention.

धारणा *(dhāranā)* स्त्री. idea; view; concept; notion; impression; power of retention; receptive power of mind.

धारदार *(dhārdār)* वि. sharp.

धारा *(dhārā)* स्त्री. stream; current; line of descending fluid; flow; continuous line or series.

धाराप्रवाह *(dhārāpravāh)* वि. fluent; non-stop; incessant.

धारी *(dhāri)* स्त्री. stripe; line.

धारीदार *(dhāridār)* वि. lined; streaked; striped.

धार्मिक *(dhārmik)* वि. religious; pious; pertaining to religion; scriptural; theological.

धावा *(dhāvā)* पु. sortie; attack; assault; raid; charge.

धिक्कार *(dhikkār)* पु. reproach; censure; curse; condemnation.

धिक्कारना *(dhikkārnā)* स. क्रि. to reproach; to censure; to curse; to damn.

धींगामुश्ती *(dhiṁga-mus'ti)* स्त्री. dealing; high handedness.

धीमा *(dhīmā)* वि. slow; faint; dim; dull; tardy; slow; lazy; inactive; gentle; mild; soft.

धीमे *(dhīme)* क्रि. वि. slowly; mildly; in a low tone.

धीर[1] *(dhīr)* वि. patient; firm; grave; sober; strongminded; steady; resolute.

धीर[2] *(dhīr)* पु. consolation; solace; patience.

धीरज *(dhiraj)* पु. patience; fortitude; steadiness; consolation; composure.

धीरता *(dhiratā)* स्त्री. patience; fortitude; composure.

धीरे *(dhīre)* क्रि. वि. slowly; mildly.

धीरे-धीरे *(dhīre-dhīre)* क्रि. वि. slowly; mildly.

धुंध *(dhundh)* स्त्री. haze; dimness; mist; fog; dust cloud; dimsightedness; purblindness.

धुँधलका *(dhuṁdhalkā)* पु. twilight; darkishness.

धुँधला *(dhumdhalā)* वि. hazy; misty; foggy; darkish; smoky; blurred; vague; dull; dim.

धुँधुलाना *(dhuṁdhlānā)* (अ.) क्रि. to 'be hazy; misty or foggy; to become dull or dim; to be blurred.

धुँधलापन *(dhuṁdhlāpan)* पु. haziness; dimness.

धुआँ *(dhuāṁ)* पु. smoke.

धुआँधार *(dhuaṁdhār)* वि. torrential; violent; fluent; eloquent; incessant and excessive.

धुकर-पुकर *(dhukar-pukar)* स्त्री. suspense; palpitation.

धुत *(dhut)* वि. steeped; stupefied; besotted; intoxicated.

धुन *(dhun)* स्त्री. assiduity; application perseverance; ardent desire; ardour; mania; fad; craze.

धुनना *(dhunnā)* स. क्रि. to card or comb; to beat thoroughly.

धुनाई *(dhunāi)* स्त्री. carding; combing; wages of carding; beating;

thrashing.

धुरंधर *(dhurandhar)* वि. pre-eminent; learned; leading; foremost; chief.

धुरा *(dhurā)* प. axle.

धुलना *(dhulnā)* (अ.) क्रि. to be washed or cleansed; to become free of blemishes.

धुलवाना *(dhulvānā)* स. क्रि. to get washed; to have cleansed.

धुलवाई *(dhulvāī)* स्त्री. work of getting something washed; charges paid for washing.

धुलाई *(dhulāī)* स्त्री. washing; a wash; washing charges.

धुलाना *(dhulānā)* स. क्रि. to cause to be washed or cleaned; to get (a thing) washed.

धुनी *(dhūnī)* स्त्री. fire lit by a Hindu ascetic; burning of incense; fumigation.

धूप[1] *(dhüp)* स्त्री. sunlight; sunshine; heat of the sun.

धूप[2] *(dhüp)* स्त्री. incense; a fragrant substance.

धूप-घड़ी *(dhüp-ghari)* स्त्री. sundial.

धूपदान *(dhüpdān)* पु. incense pot; incensory.

धूपदानी *(dhüpdāni)* स्त्री. small censer; incensory.

धूम *(dhüm)* स्त्री. bustle; tumult; celebrity; display; pomp; fanfare; fame; eclat; boom.

धूमकेतु *(dhüm-ketu)* पु. leg comet.

धूमधाम *(dhüm-dhām)* स्त्री. pomp and show; eclat; fanfare.

धूमिल *(dhümil)* वि. dim; blurred; vague; smoky; smoke-coloured.

धूम्र *(dhümra)* पु. smoke.

धूम्रपान *(dhuṁrapan)* पु. smoking.

धूर्त[1] *(dhürt)* पु. cheat; knave; rascal; rogue.

धूर्त[2] *(dhürt)* वि. deceitful; roguish.

धूर्तता *(dhürtatā)* स्त्री. knavery; fraudulence; cunningness; cheating; rascality; roguery.

धूल *(dhül)* स्त्री. dust.

धूसर *(dhüsar)* वि. dust-coloured; grey; dusty.

धृष्ट *(dhrst)* वि. impudent; shameless; insolent; arrogant.

धृष्टता *(dhusṛatā)* स्त्री. impudence; insolence; arrogance; audacity.

धैर्य *(dhairya)* पु. patience; fortitude; steadiness; firmness.

धैर्यवान *(dhairyvān)* वि. patient.

धोखा *(dhokhā)* पु. fraud; cheating; deception; delusion; blunder; mistake; false appearance.

धोखा-धड़ी *(dhokhā-dhari)* स्त्री. fraud; deception; sharp practice.

धोखेबाज़ *(dhokhe-bāz)* वि. deceitful.

धोखेबाज़ी *(dhokhe-bāzi)* स्त्री. deceit; fraud; imposture; cheating.

धोती *(dhoti)* स्त्री. loose garment for legs cotton saree.

धोना *(dhonā)* स. क्रि. to wash; to cleanse; to launder; to remove.

धोबिन *(dhobin)* स्त्री. washerwoman; launderess; washerman's wife.

धोबी *(dhobī)* पु. washerman; launderer.

धौंकनी *(dhauṁkanī)* स्त्री. bellows; blower; blow-pipe.

धौंस *(dhauṁs)* स्त्री. threat; bluster; awesome demeanour; brow-beating; over-whelming influence; awe; sway.

धौल-धप्पड़ *(dhaul-dhapper)* पु. slapping and boxing; exchange of blows.

ध्यान *(dhyān)* पु. attention; advertency; heed; thinking;

reflection. consideration; care; meditation; contemplation; concentration of mind.

ध्रुव *(dhruv)* वि. firm; resolute.

ध्रुवतारा *(dhruv-tārā)* पु. pole star.

ध्रुवीकरण *(dhruvkaran)* पु. polarisation.

ध्रुवीय *(dhruvīya)* वि. polar.

ध्वंस *(dhvams)* पु. destruction; demolition; ruin; devastation; sabotage.

ध्वंसक *(dhvaṁsak)* पु. destroyer; devastator.

ध्वंसन *(dhvaṁsan)* पु. destruction; devastation.

ध्वंसात्मक *(dhvaṁsātmak)* वि. destructive.

ध्वंसावशेष *(dhvansāvśeśa)* पु. wreckage; rubble; ruins; remains; debris.

ध्वज *(dhvaj)* पु. flag; banner.

ध्वजा *(dhvajā)* स्त्री. flag; banner.

ध्वजारोहण *(dhvajārohan)* पु. hoisting of a flag.

ध्वनि *(dhvani)* स्त्री. sound; echo; voice; implied meaning; suggested sense.

ध्वनित *(dhvanīt)* वि. sounded; implied; suggested; hinted.

ध्वनिरोधी *(dhvanirodhi)* वि. sound-proof.

ध्वनि-विज्ञान *(dhvani-vijnān)* पु. phonetics; phonology; acoustics.

ध्वन्यात्मक *(dhvanayātmak)* वि. phonetic.

ध्वन्यार्थ *(dhvanyārtha)* पु. suggested meaning; implied sense.

ध्वस्त *(dhvast)* वि. fallen; ruined; dilapidated; destroyed; devastated.

न

न *(na)* the fifth letter of the fourth pentad of the Devnagri alphabets.

नंग-धड़ग *(nang-dharang)* वि. stark naked; nude.

नंगा *(naṅgā)* वि. naked; nude; bare; uncovered; without ornament.

नंगापन *(naṅgāpan)* पु. shamelessness; nakedness.

नंदलाल *(nand-lāl)* पु. Lord Krishna.

नंदिनी *(nandinī)* स्त्री. daughter; goddess Durga; the Ganges.

नंदी *(nandī)* वि. speaker of a prelude or benediction in drama; name of the door-keeper of Shiva; his chief attendant; or of the bull which he rides.

नंदोई *(nandoī)* पु. the husband of husband's sister.

नंबरी *(numbarī)* वि. notorious; bearing a number; numbered.

नककटा, नकटा *(nakkatā)* वि. noseclipt; noseless; flatnosed; snubnosed; shameless.

नकचढ़ा *(nakcaṛhā)* वि. fastidious; peevish; illtempered.

नक़द *(naqad)* पु. cash money.

नक़दी *(naqdī)* स्त्री. cash money; ready money; hard cash.

नक़ब *(naqab)* स्त्री. (अ.) house-breaking; burglary.

नक़ल *(naql)* स्त्री. (अ.) imitation; copy; duplicate transcript; mimicry.

नक़लची *(naqalcī)* पु. (अ.) one who copies by unfair means; imitator; mimic.

नक़ली *(naqlī)* वि. (अ.) imitated; imitation; fabricated; spurious; artificial; counterfeit; false; fake; dummy.

नक़ाब *(naqāb)* स्त्री. mask; veil; visor; vizard.

नकारना *(nakārnā)* स. क्रि. to negate; to deny; to refuse; to rejected to dishonour (a cheque).

नकारात्मक *(nakārātmak)* वि. negative; implying refusal or denial.

नकेल *(nakel)* स्त्री. nose-string; nose halter.

नक़्क़ारख़ाना *(naqqārkhānā)* पु. (फ़ा.) kettle-drum chamber.

नक़्क़ारची *(naqqārcī)* पु. (फ़ा.) kettle-drummer.

नक़्क़ाल *(naqqāl)* पु. (अ.) cheat; imitator; mimic; mimicker.

नक़्क़ाशी *(naqqāśī)* स्त्री. (अ.) carving; engraving.

नक़्शा *(naqśā)* पु. (अ.) map; mode; pattern; structure; design; plan; sketch; draft; chart.

नक़्शानवीस *(naqśā-navis)* पु. draftsman.

नक़्शानवीसी *(naqśā-navisi)* स्त्री. draftmanship.

नक्षत्र *(nakśatra)* पु. star.

नक्षत्र-विद्या *(nakśatra-vidyā)* स्त्री. astronomy.

नख *(nakh)* पु. nail; a pear-like fruit.

नख़रा *(nakhrā)* पु. (फ़ा.) coquetry; feminine airs and graces; unwillingness.

नख़रेबाज़ *(nakhrebāz)* वि. (फ़ा.) coquettish.

नख़लिस्तान *(nakhalistān)* वि. (फ़ा.) oasis.

नग *(nag)* पु. precious stone; gem; jewel; mountain; piece; article.

नगर *(nagar)* पु. city; town.

नगर-निगम *(nagar-nigam)* पु. municipal corporation.

नगर-निगमाध्यक्ष *(nagar-nigamādhyaksh)* पु. mayor.

नगर-निवासी *(nagar-nivāsi)* पु. citizen.

नगरपालिका *(nagar-pālikā)* स्त्री. municipality.

नगर-प्रमुख *(nagar-pramukh)* पु. mayor.

नगरवासी *(nagar-vāsi)* पु. inhabitant of a city; citizen.

नगरीकरण *(nagarikaran)* पु. urbanisation.

नगरीय *(nagarīya)* वि. urban; of or pertaining to the city.

नगाड़ा *(nagārā)* पु. kettle drum.

नगीना *(nagīnā)* पु. precious stone; gem; jewel.

नग्न *(nagna)* वि. naked; nude; bare; uncovered.

नग्नता *(nagnatā)* स्त्री. nakedness; nudeness; shamelessness.

नचाना *(nacānā)* स. क्रि. to cause to dance; to make (one) dance; to spin (a top; etc.)

नज़दीक *(nazdik)* क्रि.वि. near; in the vicinity.

नज़र *(nazar)* स्त्री. (अ.) sight; eyesight; vision; look; glance.

नज़रबंद¹ *(nazarband)* वि. (अ.) under detention.

नज़रबंद² *(nazarband)* पु. (अ.) internee; detenu.

नज़रबंदी *(nazarbandi)* स्त्री. (अ.) detention; internment.

नज़राना *(nazrānā)* पु. gift; present.
नज़रिया *(nazariyā)* पु. view point.
नज़ला *(nazlā)* पु. (अ.) catarrah; cold.
नज़ाकत *(nazākat)* स्त्री. (फ़ा.) tenderness; delicacy; elegance; grace.
नजात *(nazāt)* स्त्री. (फ़ा.) liberation; riddance; deliverance; salvation.
नज़ारा *(nazārā)* पु. (अ.) scene; sight; view; spectacle.
नज़्म *(nazm)* स्त्री. (अ.) poem; verse.
नट *(nat)* पु. actor; acrobat.
नटखट *(naṭkhaṭ)* वि. naughty; mischievous.
नटी *(nati)* स्त्री. actress; wife of the stage-manager.
नत *(nat)* वि. bent; curved; tilted; bowed.
नति *(nati)* स्त्री. bend; curvature; inclination; bias; modesty; humbleness.
नतीजा *(natījā)* पु. (फ़ा.) result; consequence; effect; conclusion.
नत्थी *(nathī)* वि. tagged; attached.
नथ *(nath)* स्त्री. nose-ring.
नथना[1] *(nathna)* (अ.) क्रि. to be tagged; to be pierced.
नथना[2] *(nathnā)* पु. nostril.
नथनी *(nathnī)* स्त्री. small nose-ring.
नद *(nad)* पु. a big river.
नदी *(nadī)* स्त्री. river.
ननद *(nanad)* स्त्री. husband's sister.
ननदोई *(nandoi)* पु. husband of the husband's sister.
ननसाल *(nanasāl)* स्त्री. mother's paternal home.
ननिहाल *(nanihāl)* स्त्री. the house or family of maternal grandfather.
नन्हा *(nanhā)* वि. small; tiny; little; young.
नपना *(napnā)* पु. measuring device.
नपुंसक[1] *(napuṁsak)* पु. hermaphrodite (neither man nor woman); eunuch; impotent person.
नपुंसक[2] *(napuṁsak)* वि. impotent; cowardly; neuter (gender).
नपुंसकता *(napuṁsaktā)* स्त्री. impotency; cowardliness; unmanliness; being a eunuch.
नफ़रत *(nafrat)* स्त्री. (अ.) contempt; disgust; hatred.
नफ़ा *(nafā)* पु. (अ.) profit; gain.
नफ़ासत *(nafāsat)* स्त्री. (अ.) delicacy; refinement; sophistication.
नफ़ीरी *(nafīrī)* स्त्री. (फ़ा.) clarinet.
नफ़ीस *(nafīs)* वि. (अ.) nice; fine; excellent; exquisite; dainty.
नब्ज़ *(nabz)* स्त्री. (अ.) pulse.
नभ *(nabh)* पु. sky; firmament.
नभचर[1] *(nabhčar)* वि. sky-faring.
नभचर[2] *(nabhčar)* पु. one who moves in the sky; bird.
नम *(nam)* वि. moist; damp; wet.
नमक *(namak)* पु. (फ़ा.) salt.
नमकहराम *(namak-haram)* वि. ungrateful; disloyal.
नमकहरामी *(namak-harāmi)* स्त्री. (फ़ा.) imgratitude; ungratefulness.
नमकहलाल *(namak-halāl)* वि. (फ़ा.) grateful; faithful; loyal.
नमकहलाली *(namak-halāli)* स्त्री. (फ़ा.) gratitude; gratefulness; loyalty.
नमकीन *(namkīn)* वि. salty; saltish; salted; saline; brackish.
नमन *(naman)* पु. bending; flexure; deference; salutation; obeisance.
नमनीय *(namaniya)* वि. flexible; worthy of respect; respectable;

adorable; elastic.

नमस्कार *(namaskār)* पु. salutation; obeisance.

नमस्ते *(namaste)* स्त्री. a term of greeting or salutation.

नमाज़ *(namāz)* स्त्री. (फ़ा.) formal prayer (offered by muslims).

नमाज़ी *(namāzi)* पु. (फ़ा.) one meticulously regular in prayer; a devout Muslim.

नमित *(namit)* वि. bowed; bent down; caused to stoop.

नमी *(nami)* स्त्री. moisture; dampness; humidity.

नमीदार *(namidār)* वि. humid; moist.

नमूना *(namünā)* पु. (फ़ा.) specimen; sample; pattern; model; design; example; ideal.

नम्य *(namya)* वि. flexible; elastic.

नम्यता *(namyata)* स्त्री. plasticity; elasticity; flexibility.

नम्र *(namr)* वि. modest; humble; meek.

नम्रता *(namratā)* स्त्री. modesty; humility; meekness; politeness.

नम्रतापूर्ण *(namratāpürna)* वि. humble; modest.

नम्रतापूर्वक *(namratāpürvak)* क्रि. वि. humbly; meekly; submissively.

नय *(nay)* पु. policy; diplomacy; humility; farsightedness; leadership.

नयन *(nayan)* पु. eye.

नयनाभिराम *(nayanābhirām)* वि. lovely to behold; charming; beautiful; attractive.

नया *(nayā)* वि. new; novel; recent; fresh; unused; inexperienced; modern; unacquainted.

नयापन *(nayāpan)* पु. newness; novelty.

नर *(nar)* पु. man; male.

नरक *(narak)* पु. hell; infernal region; inferno; dirty and obnoxious place.

नरकुल *(narkul)* पु. reed.

नरगिस *(nargis)* स्त्री. (फ़ा.) narcissus plant and its flower.

नरम *(narm)* वि. soft; gentle; delicate; kind; merciful; moderate.

नरमी *(narmi)* स्त्री. softness; gentleness; kindness; moderateness.

नरहत्या *(nar-hatyā)* स्त्री. homicide; genocide.

नरेश *(naresa)* पु. king; prince.

नरोत्तम *(narottam)* पु. superhuman.

नर्क *(narak)* पु. hell; infernal region.

नर्तक *(nartak)* पु. male dancer.

नर्तकी *(nartaki)* स्त्री. female dancer.

नर्तन *(nartan)* पु. dance.

नर्म, नरम *(naram)* वि. (फ़ा.) soft; flexible; delicate; tender; mild; gentle; polite.

नर्मी, नरमी *(narmi)* स्त्री. softness; tenderness; mildness; politeness.

नल *(nal)* पु. pipe; tube; water-pipe; hydrant.

नलकी *(nalki)* स्त्री. narrow pipe; tube; tubule.

नलकूप *(nalküpa)* पु. tube-well.

नलकी *(nalaki)* स्त्री. tube; tubule. conduit; quiver.

नलिनी *(nalini)* स्त्री. lotus; lily.

नली *(nali)* स्त्री. tube; pipe; barrel (of gun); spout.

नवजात *(navjāt)* वि. newly born; nascent.

नवनीत *(navnit)* पु. butter.

नवम *(navam)* वि. ninth.

नवयुवक *(nava-yuvak)* पु. young man.

नवयुवती *(nava-yuvati)* स्त्री. young woman.

नवयौवन *(vava-yauvan)* पु. prime of youth.

नवयौवना *(nava-yauvanā)* स्त्री. girl just grown up to puberty; young woman.

नवागत *(navāgat)* वि. recently arrived; newcomer; guest.

नवाना *(navānā)* स. क्रि. to bend; to bow; to cause to submit.

नवाब *(navāb)* पु. (अ.) Muslim nobleman or ruler; baron; title of some Muslim rulers; aristocrat.

नवाबी[1] *(navābi)* वि. (अ.) relating to a Nawab; aristocratic.

नवाबी[2] *(navābi)* स्त्री. luxurious and lavish living; arbitrary conduct in the manner of a nawab.

नवासा *(navāsā)* पु. daughter's son.

नवीकरण *(navīkaran)* पु. renewal; renovation; rejuvenation.

नवीन *(navin)* वि. new; novel; original.

नवीनतम *(navīntam)* वि. latest; most modern.

नवीनता *(navīnatā)* स्त्री. newness; novelty; freshness; modernity; modernism.

नवीनीकरण *(navīnīkaran)* पु. renewal; rejuvenation.

नवोदा *(navodā)* स्त्री. a newly married woman; a bride.

नवोदित *(navodit)* वि. nascent; rising; young.

नशा *(naśā)* पु. intoxication; drunkenness; intoxicating substance; habit of drinking or taking intoxicants.

नशाख़ोर *(naśākhor)* वि. inebriate; given to addiction.

नशाखोरी *(naśākhorī)* स्त्री. addiction to intoxicants; inebriation.

नशाबंदी *(naśābandi)* स्त्री. prohibition.

नशीला *(naśīlā)* वि. inebriant; intoxicating; intoxicated.

नशेबाज़ *(naśebāz)* पु. inebriate; habitual drunkard.

नशेबाज़ी *(naśebāzi)* स्त्री. drug addiction alcoholism.

नश्तर *(naśtar)* पु. (फ़ा.) lancet; fleam; surgical knife.

नश्वर *(naśvar)* वि. perishable; destructible; transient; short-lived; mortal.

नश्वरता *(naśvaratā)* स्त्री. perishableness; transitoriness; evanescence.

नष्ट *(naśṭ)* वि. destroyed; ruined; annihilated; dead; perished; wasted.

नस *(nas)* स्त्री. vein; sinew; tendent; nerve; fibre.

नसबंदी *(nasbandi)* स्त्री. vasectomy.

नसल *(nasal)* स्त्री. breed; lineage; race.

नसीब *(nasīb)* पु. (अ.) luck; fate; destiny.

नसीहत *(nasīhat)* स्त्री. (अ.) teaching; precept; preaching; admonition; advice.

नसूड़िया *(nasuria)* वि. ominous; sinister; inauspicious.

नस्ल *(nasal)* पु. (अ.) breed; pedigree; geneology; offspring; progeny.

नहर *(nahar)* स्त्री. canal; channel; waterway.

नहला *(nahlā)* पु. playing card with nine pips; the nine in playing cards.

नहलाना *(nahlānā)* स. क्रि. to bathe;

to give bath.

नहान *(nahān)* पु. bath; a festival day for taking bath.

नहाना *(nahānā)* (अ.) क्रि. to bathe; to take a bath; to be smeared (with); to be soaked or drenched (in).

नहीं *(nahīṁ)* क्रि. वि. no; not; nay.

नाँद *(nāmd)* स्त्री. manger; trough.

ना *(nā)* क्रि. वि. (फ़ा.) no; not; nay.

नाइन *(nāin)* स्त्री. barber's wife; a woman of barber caste.

नाई *(nāi)* क्रि. वि. like; as.

नाई *(nāi)* पु. barber.

नाउम्मेद *(nā-ummed)* वि. (फ़ा.) hopeless; despaired; despondent; desperate; dejected; disappointed.

नाक *(nāk)* स्त्री. nose; mucus.

नाक-नक़्श *(nāk-naqśa)* पु. features; facial cut.

नाका *(nākā)* पु. extremity (of a road etc.); entrance to a road; or pass etc.; check-post.

नाकाबंदी *(nākābandi)* स्त्री. stop page of entry; shutting up a road etc.; blockade.

नाकाम *(nākām)* वि. (फ़ा.) unsuccessful; fruitless; ineffective; infructuous.

नाकामयाब *(nākāmayāb)* वि. (फ़ा.) unsuccessful.

नाकामयाबी *(nākāmayābi)* स्त्री. (फ़ा.) failure.

नाकामी *(nākāmi)* स्त्री. (फ़ा.) failure; worthlessness.

नाकारा *(nākārā)* वि. (फ़ा.) useless; worthless; unserviceable; good for nothing.

नाखुदा *(nākhuda)* पु. (फ़ा.) captain of a ship.

नाखुश *(nākhus)* वि. (फ़ा.) displeased; annoyed; unhappy.

नाखून *(nākhün)* पु. (फ़ा.) nail.

नाग *(nāg)* पु. hooded snake; cobra; serpent or snake in general; elephant.

नागफनी *(nāgphani)* स्त्री. the prickly pear; cactus.

नागर *(nāgar)* वि. relating to a city; urban; civil; civilian; clever; sharp.

नागवार *(nāgavār)* वि. (फ़ा.) unpleasant; intolerable.

नागरिक[1] *(nāgarik)* वि. living in a city or town; pertaining to city or town; civil; civililan.

नागरिक[2] *(nāgarik)* पु. citizen; civilian.

नागरिकता *(nāgarikatā)* स्त्री. citizenship; urbanity.

नागरिकशास्त्र *(nāgariksāstra)* पु. civics.

नागरिक सेना *(nāgarik senā)* स्त्री. militia.

नागरीकरण *(nāgarikaran)* पु. urbanisation; transcription into Devnagri.

नागा *(nāgā)* स्त्री. absence from work.

नाच *(nāc)* पु. dance.

नाचना *(nācnā)* (अ.) क्रि. to dance; to caper or frisk about; to run about; to move about; to act upon the instigation or dictates of an other.

नाचीज़ *(nāchiza)* वि. (फ़ा.) trifling; worthless.

नाज़ *(nāz)* पु. (फ़ा.) coquetry; airs; pride; conceit.

नाजायज़ *(nājāyaz)* वि. improper; undue; unjust; unlawful; illegitimate; illegal.

नाजुक *(nāzuk)* वि. (फ़ा.) delicate; tender; thin; slender; slim; fragile; frail; subtle; critical.

नाटक *(nātak)* पु. play; drama; acting; show; pretence.

नाटककार *(nāṭak-kār)* पु. playwright; dramatist.

नाटकीय *(nātakiya)* वि. dramatic; histrionic.

नाटकीयता *(nātakiyatā)* स्त्री. theatricalism; theatricality; dramatism.

नाटा *(nātā)* वि. dwarfish; short-statured.

नाट्यकला *(nāṭyākalā)* स्त्री. dramatic art; dramaturgy; histrionicism.

नाट्यकार *(nātyakār)* पु. playwrighter; dramatist.

नाट्यमंदिर *(nāṭyamandir)* पु. the atre.

नाट्यशाला *(nātyashālā)* पु. theatre

नाट्यशास्त्र *(nāṭya-sastra)* पु. dramatic science; dramaturgy; dramatics.

नाड़ा *(nārā)* पु. umbilical cord; tape inserted in the upper part of the trousers for binding it round the waist; trouser's string.

नाड़ी *(nāri)* स्त्री. artery; vein; pulsebeat.

नाता *(nātā)* पु. connection; relation; kinship.

नातिन *(nātin)* स्त्री. grand daughter.

नाती *(nāti)* पु. grandson.

नातेदार *(nātedār)* पु. relative; kinsman.

नातेदारी *(nātedāri)* स्त्री. relationship; kinship.

नाथ *(nāth)* पु. lord; master; husband; nose-string (of an ox etc.).

नाथना *(nāthnā)* स. क्रि. to bore the nose (of an animal); to put a string or rope in the nose hole (of an animal).

नाद *(nād)* पु. sound.

नादान *(nādān)* वि. (फ़ा.) innocent; foolish; unwise; unskilful; inefficient; ignorant.

नादानी *(nādāni)* वि. (फ़ा.) ignorance; innocence; stupidity; foolishness; unskilfulness.

नादिरशाही[1] *(nādirśāhi)* स्त्री. (अ.) tyranny; highhandedness; oppression like that of Nadir Shah.

नादिरशाही[2] *(nādirshāhi)* वि. (अ.) tyrannous; oppressive; cruel (like Nadir Shah).

नाना *(nānā)* पु. maternal grandfather; several.

नानी *(nāni)* स्त्री. maternal grandmother.

नाप *(nāp)* स्त्री. measure; measurement.

नापना *(nāpnā)* स. क्रि. to measure.

नापसंद *(nāpasand)* वि. not liked; not to one's liking; repulsive; disagreeable; displeasing; unacceptable; disapproved.

नापाक *(nāpāk)* वि. (फ़ा.) not sacred; unholy; impure; unclean; dirty; filthy; polluted; defiled; lewd; licentious; unchaste.

नाबालिग़ *(nābāligh)* वि. (फ़ा.) minor.

नाबालिग़ी *(nābālighi)* स्त्री. (फ़ा.) minority (in age).

नाभि *(nābhi)* स्त्री. the navel; the navel of a wheel; umbilicus; hub; centre; central point; focus.

नाभिक *(nabhik)* पु. nucleus.

नाभिकीय *(nābhikiya)* वि. nuclear.

नाभिकेंद्र *(nābhikendra)* वि. (फ़ा.) focal point; focus.

नामंजूर *(nā-manzur)* वि. (फ़ा.) not accepted or granted; not sanctioned; rejected; disapproved.

नाम *(nām)* पु. name; title; nomenclature; appellation; designation; reputation; fame; renown.

नामकरण *(nāmkaran)* पु. naming; giving a name; nomenclature; the ceremony of naming a child after birth.

नामज़द *(nām-zad)* वि. (फ़ा.) nominated.

नामज़दगी *(nām-jadgi)* स्त्री. (फ़ा.) nomination.

नामपट्ट *(nām-pat)* पु. sign board; name-plate.

नामर्द *(nā-mard)* वि. (फ़ा.) impotent emasculate; cowardly.

नामांकन *(nāmankan)* पु. nomination; inscription of name; enrolment.

नामांकित *(nāmānkit)* वि. nominated; enrolled.

नामाकूल *(nāmākul)* वि. (फा.) impertinent; improper; inappropriate; unreasonable; irrational.

नामावली *(nāmāvali)* स्त्री. list of names.

नामी *(nāmi)* वि. of good repute.

नामी-गिरामी *(nāmī-gārāmī)* वि. famous; renowned; reputed; eminent.

नामुनासिब *(nā-munāsib)* वि. (फ़ा.) improper; unsuitable; unbecoming. indecent.

नामुमकिन *(nāmumkin)* वि. (फ़ा.) impossible

नामोनिशान *(nāmo-nishān)* पु. trace; mark.

नायक *(nāyak)* पु. leader; guide; chief; master; head; lord; military official of a low rank; hero.

नायन *(nāyan)* स्त्री. barber's wife; woman; of the barber caste.

नायब *(nāyab)* पु. (अ) assistant. deputy; delegate.

नायबी *(nāybī)* स्त्री. assistantship. deputyship.

नायाब *(nāyab)* वि. (फ़ा.) rare; not easily available.

नायिका *(nāyīka)* स्त्री. heroine (of a literary composition); beloved or wife (in the poems of erotic sentiment).

नारंगी *(nārangī)* स्त्री. orange.

नारा *(nārā)* पु. slogan

नाराज़ *(nārāz)* वि. (फ़ा.) displeased; offended; annoyed.

नाराज़ी *(nārāzī)* स्त्री. (फ़ा.) displeasure; annoyance.

नारियल *(nāriyal)* पु. coconut.

नारी *(nāri)* स्त्री. woman; female.

नारीत्व *(naritva)* पु. womanhood.

नारेबाज़ *(nārebāz)* पु. sloganeer; slogan-monger.

नारेबाज़ी *(nārebāzī)* स्त्री. sloganeering

नाल[1] *(nāl)* स्त्री. hollow tubular stalk (as of lotus); tube; pipe; barrel; navel-string.

नाल[2] *(nāl)* पु. gambling den; amount paid to the person who arranges for gambling.

नाल[3] *(nāl)* पु. (अ.) orse-shoe.

नाला *(nālā)* पु. big drain; gutter; rivulet.

नालायक़ *(nālāyak)* वि. (फ़ा.) unworthy; unfit; incompetent; mischievous; stupid.

नालायक़ी *(nālāyakī)* स्त्री. (फ़ा.) unworthiness; worthlessness; unfitness; incompetence; stupidity.

नालिश *(nāliś)* law-suit; complaint.

नाली *(nāli)* स्त्री. drain; drain-pipe; sewer; thin pipe; conduit.

नाव *(nāv)* स्त्री. boat; ferry.

नाविक *(nāvik)* पु. sailor; seaman; boatman.

नाश *(nāś)* पु. annihilation; destruction; ruin; devastation; waste; wastefulness.

नाशक[1] *(nāśak)* वि. destructive; devastating; fatal; wasteful.

नाशक[2] *(nāśak)* पु. remover; dispeller; antidote; killer.

नाशवान *(nāśvān)* वि. perishable; mortal.

नाश्ता *(nāstā)* पु. (फ़ा.) breakfast; light repast; refreshment.

नासमझ *(nāsamajh)* वि. (फ़ा.) innocent; ignorant; unwise.

नासमझी *(nāsamjhī)* स्त्री. (फ़ा.) innocence; ignorance; folly; stupidity.

नासा *(nāsā)* स्त्री. nose; nostril.

नासिका *(nāsikā)* स्त्री. nose; trunk of an elephant.

नास्तिक *(nāstik)* पु. atheist.

नास्तिकता *(nāstikatā)* स्त्री. atheism; infidelity.

निंदक *(nindak)* पु. censurer; slanderer.

निंदनीय *(nindanīya)* वि. blameworthy; blameable; reprehensible; censurable.

निंदा *(nindā)* स्त्री. blame; censure; slander; reproof; condemnation; backbiting.

निंदित *(nindit)* वि. blamed; censured; reproved; slandered; calumniated.

निंदिया *(nindiya)* स्त्री. sleep.

निंद्य *(nīndya)* वि. censurable; contemptible.

निंबू *(nimbü)* निंबूक पु. lemon.

निःशंक[1] *(niḥ-śaṇk)* वि. free from doubt or suspicion; fearless; bold; daring.

निःशंक[2] *(niḥ-śaṇk)* क्रि. वि. without misgiving or apprehension; fearlessly; unhesitatingly.

निःशब्द *(niḥ-śabd)* वि. silent; speechless; calm; quiet.

निःशुल्क *(niḥ-sulk)* वि. duty-free; free of fee.

निःसंकोच *(niḥ-sankoc)* क्रि. वि. unhesitatingly; without reserve or shyness.

निःसंदेह *(niḥ-sandeh)* क्रि. वि. indubitably; certainly; without doubt.

निःस्पृह *(niḥ-sprh)* वि. free from desire; out of coveting; selfless; having no selfish motives.

निःस्वार्थ *(niḥ- svārth)* वि. unselfish; selfless; without any selfishness.

निःस्वार्थता *(niḥ-svārthatā)* स्त्री. selflessness; unselfishness.

निकट *(ni-kaṭ)* वि. near; close; proximate.

निकटतम *(nikat-ṭam)* वि. nearest.

निकटता *(ni-kaṭatā)* स्त्री. proximity; nearness; closeness; closeness intimacy.

निकटवर्ती *(ni-kaṭvarti)* वि. near; proximate; close; living near; neighbouring; adjacent.

निकम्मा *(nikammā)* वि. unemployed; idle; useless; worthless; good for nothing; unworthy; incapable; worthless.

निकलना *(nikalnā)* (अ.) क्रि. to come out; to appear; to rise; to get out; to escape; to be solved; to be worked out; to emanate; to be extracted; to emerge; to issue or be isued; to slink away; to be published; to be brought out; to passs away; to elapse; to turn out.

निकलवाना *(nikalvānā)* स. क्रि. to cause to take out; issue; expel etc.

निकाय *(ni-kāy)* पु. guild; association; group; class; flock; heap; collection; assemblage.

निकालना *(nikālnā)* स. क्रि. to take out; to separate; to remove; to oust; to expel; to eradicate; to eliminate; to deduct; to exclude; to discharge; to dismiss; to withdraw; to take away; to retract; to draw; to solve; to publish; to extract.

निकास *(nikās)* पु. origin; extraction; gate; exit; outlet; vent; source.

निकासी *(nikāsi)* स्त्री. clearance; departure; out-put; produce; turnout.

निकाह *(nikāh)* पु. (अ.) marriage; matrimony.

निकृष्ट *(ni-krśt)* वि. low; base; vile; inferior; inferiormost.

निकृष्टता *(ni-krstatā)* स्त्री.lowness; baselessness; vileness; contemptibleness.

निकेत *(ni-ket)* निकेतन पु. house; habitation; mansion; abode; residence.

निखट्टू[1] *(nikhaṭṭu)* वि. idle; unearning; unemployed; indolent; lazy.

निखट्टू[2] *(nikhaṭṭu)* पु. idle fellow; idler; one who earns nothing; unemployed person.

निखट्टूपन *(nikhaṭṭupan)* पु. idleness; indolence; laziness.

निखरना *(nikharnā)* (अ.) क्रि. to be cleaned; to be cleansed; to be come clear or elegant.

निखार *(nikhār)* पु. brightness; lustre; elegance.

निखारना *(nikhārnā)* स. क्रि. to cleanse; to clean; to bleach; to brighten; to make clean.

निगम *(ni-gam)* पु. corporation.

निगरानी *(nigrānī)* स्त्री. (फ़ा.) watch; guard; supervision; wardship; surveillance.

निगलना *(nigalnā)* स. क्रि. to swallow; to gulp; to devour.

निगह *(nigāh)* स्त्री. (फ़ा.) glance; sight; kind glance; favourable attention; watch; guard; observation; attention.

निगाह *(nigāh)* see निगह

निगोड़ा *(nigoṛā)* वि. idle; indolent; worthless; wretched; unfortunate

निग्रह *(ni-grah)* पु. control; restraint self-control; self-repression.

निग्रही *(ni-grahī)* पु. one who restrains.

निचला *(niclā)* पु. lower.

निचाई *(nicāi)* स्त्री. lowness; declivety; slope.

निचान *(nicān)* पु. lowness; low land; declivity; slope.

निचुड़ना *(nicuṛnā)* (अ.) क्रि. to be squeezed or pressed; to be extracted; to flow out gently; to trickle; to ooze; to drop.

निचोड़ *(nicoṛ)* पु. esence; substance; gist; that which is squeezed or pressed out; extract.

निचोड़ना *(nicoṛnā)* स. क्रि. to squeeze; to press; to wring; to extract; to squeeze out; to press out; to wring out; to exploit.

निछावर *(nichāvar)* वि. sacrifice; giving up; propitiatory offering made to ward off an evil eye; thing or money offered as above.

निज *(nij)* वि. own; one's own.

निज़ाम *(nizām)* पु. (अ.) administration; management; order.

निजी *(nijī)* वि. one's own; personal individual; relating to particular persons' private; unofficial.

निठल्ला¹ *(niṭhallā)* वि. idle; indolent; lazy; out of work or employment; unemployed.

निठल्ला² *(nithallā)* पु. idler.

निठल्लापन *(niṭhallāpan)* पु. laziness; idleness; unemployment.

निठुर *(niṭhur)* वि. cruel; hard; obdurate; ruthless; hard-hearted.

निठुरता *(nithurtā)* स्त्री. hardheartedness; cruelty; ruthlessness; obduracy; relentlessness.

निडर *(niḍar)* वि. fearless; dauntless; bold; daring; intrepid.

निडरता *(niḍartā)* स्त्री. fearlessness; dauntlessness.

निढाल *(niḍhāl)* वि. languid; wearied; spiritless.

नितंब *(nitamb)* पु. buttock; hip.

नित *(nit)* क्रि. everyday; daily.

नितांत¹ *(ni-tānt)* वि. extraordinary; excessive; absolute; complete.

नितांत² *(ni-tānt)* क्रि. वि. absolutely; excessively; quite.

नित्य¹ *(nitya)* वि. everlasting; eternal; regular.

नित्य² *(nitya)* क्रि. वि. everyday; daily; constantly; always.

नित्यता *(nityatā)* स्त्री. eternity; perpetuity.

नित्यप्रति *(nityaprati)* क्रि. वि. everyday; daily.

निथरना *(nitharnā)* (अ.) क्रि. to be dacanted; to be made clear or clean; (by letting the feculent matter subside).

निथार *(nithār)* पु. decantation; feculent matter subsiding beneath the water etc.

निथारना *(nithārnā)* स. क्रि. to decant; to make clear or clean; to purify (water or liquid by letting the feculent matter subside).

निदर्शक¹ *(ni-darśak)* पु. demonstrator; illlustrator.

निदर्शक² *(ni-darśak)* वि. pointing out; proclaiming; indicative; showing.

निदर्शन *(ni-darśan)* पु. demonstration; exemplification; instance; example; figure; illustration.

निदान¹ *(ni-dān)* क्रि. वि. in the end; at last; eventually; finally; consequently.

निदान² *(ni-dān)* पु. primary cause; the first or essential cause; (in medicine) diagnosis.

निदान गृह *(nidān-grih)* पु. clinic.

निदान-शास्त्र *(nidān-sāstra)* स्त्री. diagnostics .

निदेश *(ni-deś)* पु. direction; directive; instruction.

निदेशक¹ *(ni-deśak)* पु. director.

निदेशक² *(ni-deśak)* वि. directive.

निदेशालय *(ni-deśālay)* पु. office of the director; directorate.

निदेशिका *(ni-desikā)* स्त्री. directory.

निद्रा *(nidrā)* स्त्री. sleep; slumber.

निद्राचार *(nidrācār)* पु. somnambulism.

निद्रारोग *(nidrārog)* पु. narcolepsy.

निद्रालु *(nidrālu)* पु. sleepy; drowsy; slumberous; somnolent.

निद्रित *(nidrit)* वि. sleeping; asleep.

निधड़क *(nidharak)* क्रि. वि. fearlessly; boldly; dauntlessly.

निधन *(ni-dhan)* पु. death; demise.

निधि *(nidhi)* स्त्री. treasure; fund.

निनाद *(ninād)* पु. loud sound; noise; reverberation; resonance.

निनादित *(ni-nādit)* वि. echoing; resonant; producing sound.

निपट *(nipaṭ)* क्रि. वि. sheer; mere; quite; completely; absolutely; very much; extremely; exceedingly.

निपटना *(nipaṭnā)* see निबटना

निपटान *(niptān)* पु. disposal; settlement.

निपटाना *(niptānā)* see निबटाना

निपटारा *(nipṭārā)* see निबटारा

निपात *(ni-pāt)* पु. destruction; fall; degradation; death; throw.

निपुण *(ni-puṇ)* वि. clever; adroit; expert; skilful; dexterous.

निपुणता *(ni-puṇatā)* स्त्री. cleverness; adroitness; skilfulness; dexterity; expertness.

निपोरना *(niporṇā)* स. क्रि. to grin.

निबंध *(ni-bhandh)* पु. treatise; essay.

निबंधकार *(ni-bandhkār)* पु. eassayist.

निबंधन *(ni-bandhan)* पु. act of fastening; binding together; linkage; connection; composition; writing.

निबंधलेखक *(nibandh-lekhak)* see निबंधकार

निब *(nib)* स्त्री. nib

निबटना *(nibaṭnā)* (अ.) क्रि. to be completed; to be finished; to be disposed of; to be relieved; to be settled or decided.

निबटाना *(nibṭānā)* स. क्रि. to complete; to finish; to dispose of; to decide; to settle; to repay (debt etc.).

निबटारा *(nibṭārā)* निबटाव, निबटेरा पु. disposal; relief; settlement; termination.

निबद्ध *(ni-baddh)* वि. bound; tied; joined or fastened together; intertwined; set or inlaid; composed; written.

निबाह *(nibāh)* पु. subsistence; maintenance; livelihood; carrying on; pulling on; acommodation; adjustment.

निबाहना *(nibāhnā)* स. क्रि. to subsist; to sustain; to maintain; to support; to carry on; to pull on; to fulful; to accomplish to keep (one's) promise etc.; to accommodate; to adjust.

निबौली *(nibauli)* स्त्री. the fruit of the margosa (neem) tree.

निभना *(nibhnā)* to be fulfilled; to be accomplished; to be performed; to be effected; to maintain mutual relations; to subsist; to sustain; to be accommodated.

निभाना *(nibhānā)* स. क्रि. to fulfil; to accomplish; to perform; to continue mutual relations (with); to accommodate; to maintain; to sustain; to carry on; to pull on; to manage.

निभाव *(nibhāv)* पु. adjustment; accommodation.

निमंत्रण *(ni-mantṛan)* पु. invitaiton.

निमंत्रित *(ni-mantrit)* वि. invited.

निमग्न *(ni-magn)* वि. absorbed; engrossed; submerged.

निमज्जन *(nimajjan)* पु. dip; plunge; immersion; submersion.

निमज्जित *(nimajjit)* वि. submerged, immersed; sunken; bathed.

निमित्त *(nimitt)* पु. cause; reason; purpose; aim; pretext; factor; instrument.

निम्न *(nimn)* वि. low; depressed; lower; below; normal; mean; following; given; below.

निम्नलिखित *(nimn-likhit)* वि. following; mentioned below; undermentioned.

नियंता *(ni-yantā)* पु. controller; sustainer; ruler; governor.

नियंत्रक *(ni-yantrak)* पु. controller.

नियंत्रण *(ni-yantran)* पु. check; restraint; restriction; control.

नियंत्रित *(ni-yantrit)* वि. controlled; restrained; checked; restricted; regulated; tamed; brought under control.

नियत *(ni-yat)* वि. prescried; fixed; decided; settled; allotted; scheduled.

नियति *(ni-yati)* स्त्री. destiny; fate; luck; fortune.

नियतिवाद *(ni-yativād)* पु. determinism; fatalism.

नियम *(ni-yam)* पु. rule; law; regulation.

नियमतः *(ni-yamatah)* क्रि. वि. in accordance with a rule.

नियमन *(niyaman)* पु. regulation; control; restriction; limitation; regularisation.

नियमबद्ध *(niyam-baddh)* वि. bound by rule or rules; regulated; regular.

नियमावली *(niyamāvali)* स्त्री. rules and regulations.

नियमित *(ni-yamit)* वि. bound by rules; regulated; regular; conforming to rules; regularise.

नियमितता *(ni-yamitatā)* स्त्री. regularity.

नियमितीकरण *(ni-yamitikaran)* पु. decasualisation; regularisation.

नियमोल्लंघन *(niyamollanghan)* पु. breach of law.

नियामक[1] *(ni-yāmak)* पु. regulator; controller; ruler; manager; director.

नियामक[2] *(ni-yāmak)* वि. regulative; directive.

नियामत *(niyāmat)* पु. rare gift; divine blessing.

नियुक्त *(ni-yukt)* वि. appointed; employed; posted; fixed; settled.

नियुक्ति *(ni-yukti)* स्त्री. appointment; employment; engagement; posting.

नियोक्ता[1] *(ni-yoktā)* वि. appointing.

नियोक्ता[2] *(ni-yoktā)* पु. employer; appointer; appointing authority.

नियोजक *(ni-yojak)* पु. employer.

नियोजन *(ni-yojan)* पु. employment; planning.

नियोजित *(ni-yojit)* वि. employed; planned.

निरंकुश *(nir-ankuś)* वि. uncontrolled unfettered; unrestrained; unruly; self-willed; autocratice; despotic.

निरंकुशता *(nir-ankuśata)* स्त्री. arbitrariness; selfwilledness; unruliness; despotism; absolutism.

निरंतर[1] *(nir-antar)* वि. continuous; perpetual; uninterrupted; incessant.

निरंतर[2] *(nir-antar)* क्रि. वि. always;

ever; constantly; continually incessantly; continuously.

निरक्षर *(nir-aksar)* वि. illiterate; uneducated.

निरक्षरता *(nir-akśaratā)* स्त्री. illiteracy.

निरखना *(nirakhnā)* स. क्रि. to look at; to see; to observe; to view; to inspect; to scan; to examine closely.

निरपराध *(nir-apa-rādh)* निरपराधी वि. guiltless; innocent; faultless.

निरपवाद *(nir-apa-vād)* वि. unexceptional; blameless.

निरपेक्ष *(nir-pêkṣ)* वि. absolute; independent; neutral indifferent; unconcerned; careless; negligent; without expectation; disinterested.

निरभिमान *(nirabhimān)* वि. free from conceit; devoid of pride; humble.

निरर्थक *(nir-arthak)* वि. meaning less; nonsensical; useless; vain; unprofitable; non-significant; vain.

निरस्त *(nir-ast)* वि. cancelled; repealed.

निरस्त्र *(nir-astra)* वि. weaponless; unarmed; disarmed.

निरस्त्रीकरण *(nir-astrīkaran)* पु. disarmament.

निरस्त्रीकृत *(nir-astrīkrt)* वि. disarmed.

निरा *(nirā)* वि. pure; unalloyed; entire; complete.

निराई *(nirāī)* स्त्री. weeding; wages paid for weeding.

निराकरण *(nirākaran)* पु. refutation; repudiation; contradiction; removal; cancellation; abrogation.

निराकार[1] *(nir-ā-kār)* पु. formless; God; the universal spirit; Almighty; Brahma.

निराकार[2] *(nir-ā-kār)* वि. formless; shapeless; incorporeal.

निरादर *(nir-ā-dar)* पु. dishonour; disrespect; humiliation.

निराधार *(nir-ā-dhār)* वि. false; hollow; baseless; groundless; unfounded; without support or prop.

निराना *(nirānā)* स. क्रि. weed out.

निरापद *(nir-ā-pad)* वि. secure; safe; protected; without calamity; trouble free.

निरामिष *(nir-āmis)* वि. without meat; fleshless; vegetarian.

निरालंब *(nir-ā-lamb)* वि. helpless; having no shelter or support; destitute; baseless.

निराला *(nirālā)* विं. strange; unique; uncommon; extraordinary; peculiar; curious; odd.

निरावरण *(nir-ā-varan)* वि. without covering; uncovered; unveiled; exposed.

निराश *(nir-āś)* वि. hopeless; disappointed; desperate; frustrated.

निराशा *(nir-āsā)* स्त्री. hopelessness; despair; frustration; disappointment.

निराशाजनक *(nir-āsājanak)* वि. disappointing; hopeless; depressing.

निराशावाद *(nir-āśāvād)* पु. pessimism

निराशावादी[1] *(nir-āśāvādi)* पु. pessimist.

निराशावादी[2] *(nir-āśāvādi)* वि. pessimistic.

निराश्रित *(nir-ā-śrit)* वि. destitute.

निराश्रितता *(nir-ā-śritatā)* वि. destitution.

निराहार *(nir-ā-hār)* वि. fasting; abstaining from food; foodless.

निरीक्षक *(nir-īksak)* पु. inspector; invigilator; observer.

निरीक्षण *(nir-īksan)* पु. inspection; invigilation; observation.

निरीश्वर *(nirīshvar)* पु. Godless; atheistic.

निरीश्वरवाद *(nirīshvarvād)* पु. atheistic doctrine; atheism.

निरीह *(nir-īh)* वि. desireless; indiferent; simple; innocent; harmless.

निरूत्तर *(nir-uttar)* वि. unable to answer back; answerless; without a reply; silenced.

निरूत्साह[1] *(nir-ut-sāh)* वि. lacking spirit or courage; spiritless.

निरूत्साह[2] *(nir-ut-sah)* वि. lack of enthusiasm; spiritlessness.

निरूत्साहित *(nir-ut-sahit)* वि. discouraged; disheartened.

निरूद्देश्य *(nir-ud-desya)* वि. aimless.

निरूद्ध *(ni-ruddh)* वि. obstructed; hindered; checked; restrained; blocked.

निरूपक[1] *(nirupak)* पु. one who represents; explains etc.

निरूपक[2] *(nirupak)* वि. explanatory; determining; demonstrative; characterising; representative.

निरूपण *(ni-rupan)* पु. critical appreciation; evaluation; representation; explanation; characterisation; portrayal.

निरूपित *(ni-rupit)* वि. represented; explained; evaluated; investigated; determined; demonstrated.

निरोग *(nirog)* see नीरोग।

निरोध *(no-rodh)* पु. restraint; check; control; prevention; hindrance; obstruction; detention; constraint; condom.

निरोधक *(ni-rodhak)* वि. restraining; controlling; detaining; preventive; obstructing; hindering.

निर्गत *(nir-gat)* पु. gone out; gone forth; issued; come forth; come out; appeared; gone away; departed.

निर्गम *(nir-gam)* पु. going forth or out; going away; door; outlet; exit; clearance; issue.

निर्गुण *(nir-guṇ)* पु. devoid of all properties; without attributes.

निर्गुणी *(nir-gunī)* वि. devoid of good qualities or virtues.

निर्जन *(nir-jan)* वि. solitary; lonely (place); unpeopled; uninhabited; unfrequented; deserted; desolate.

निर्जनता *(nir-jantā)* स्त्री. loneliness; desolation; state of being deserted or uninhabited; solitude.

निर्जल *(nir-jal)* वि. without water; waterless; dry.

निर्जलन *(nir-jalan)* पु. dehydration.

निर्जीव *(nir-jiv)* वि. inanimate; lifeless; dead; spiritless.

निर्झर *(nir-jhar)* पु. waterfall; cataract; cascade.

निर्णय *(nir-nay)* पु. verdict; judgement; decision; sentence; determination; settlement; conclusion.

निर्णयात्मक *(nirnayātmak)* वि. decisive; conclusive.

निर्णायक[1] *(nir-nāyak)* पु. judge referee; umpire.

निर्णायक[2] *(nir-nāyak)* वि. decisive;

conclusive; crucial.

निर्णीत *(nir-nīt)* वि. decided; judged; concluded.

निर्दय *(nir-day)* वि. ruthless; merciless; cruel; heartless.

निर्दयता *(nir-dayatā)* स्त्री. ruthlessness; mercilessness; pitilessness.

निर्दयी *(nir-dayī)* वि. pitiless; merciless; cruel.

निर्दलीय *(nir-daliya)* वि. non-party; independent; non-partisan.

निर्दिष्ट *(nir-dist)* वि. assigned; determined; specified.

निर्देश *(nir-deś)* पु. direction instruction.

निर्देशक[1] *(nir-deśak)* पु. directive; guiding; indicative; suggestive.

निर्देशक[2] *(nir-deśak)* पु. director; guide.

निर्देशन *(nir-deśan)* पु. indication; directon; guidance; reference.

निर्देशिका *(nir-deśīkā)* स्त्री. directory; manual.

निर्दोष *(nir-doś)* वि. faultless.

defectless; flawless; guiltless; innocent; sinless; blameless.

निर्दोषता *(nir-dosatā)* स्त्री. flawlessness faultlessness; blamelessness; innocence.

निर्दोषिता *(nir-dositā)* स्त्री. innocence.

निर्द्वंद्व[1] *(nir-dvandva)* वि. uncontested; undisputed; indifferent; to independent.

निर्द्वंद्व[2] *(nir-dvandva)* क्रि. वि. freely; without any obstruction or obstacle.

निर्धन *(nir-dhan)* वि. poor; indigent.

निर्धनता *(nir-dhanatā)* स्त्री. poverty; indigence.

निर्धारक[1] *(nir-dhārak)* पु. determinant; determiner; assessor.

निर्धारक[2] *(nir-dhārak)* वि. determinative; determinant.

निर्धारण *(nir-dhāran)* पु. determination; decision; fixation; assessment.

निर्धारित *(nir-dhārit)* वि. determined; ascertained; fixed; settled; assessed; laid down; prescribed.

निर्धारिती *(nir-dhāritī)* पु. assessee.

निर्निमेष[1] *(nir-ni-meś)* वि. with fixed look; unwinking.

निर्निमेष[2] *(nir-ni-meś)* क्रि. वि. without blinking; without a wink.

निर्बल *(nir-bal)* वि. weak; feeble; frail; powerless.

निर्बलता *(nir-balatā)* स्त्री. weakness; feebleness; powerlessness.

निर्बाध *(nir-bādh)* वि. unobstructed; unhindered.

निर्बाधित *(nir-bādhitā)* वि. unrestricted.

निर्बुद्धि *(nir-buddhi)* वि. stupid; foolish.

निर्भय *(nir-bhay)* वि. fearless; intrepid; dauntless; free from all dangers.

निर्भयता *(nir-bhayatā)* स्त्री. dauntlessness; intrepidity; fearlesness.

निर्भर *(nir-bhar)* वि. dependent.

निर्भरता *(nir-bharatā)* स्त्री. dependence; reliance.

निर्भीक *(nir-bhīk)* वि. fearless; dauntless.

निर्भीकता *(nir-bhīktā)* स्त्री. fearlessness; dauntlessness.

निर्मम *(nir-mam)* वि. cruel; heartless; ruthless; devoid of affection or attachment.

निर्ममता *(nir-mamtā)* स्त्री. cruelty; heartlessness; ruthlessness.

निर्मल *(nir-mal)* वि. pure; clear;

clean; stainless; unsullied; without a blemish; chaste; without illwill; innocent; guileless.

निर्मलता *(nir-maltā)* स्री. clearness; spotlessness; stainlessness; blemishlessness; chastity; purity; innocence.

निर्मलीकरण *(nir-malikaran)* पु. purificartion.

निर्माण *(nir-mān)* पु. erection; construction; creation; formation; composition; manufacture.

निर्माणाधीन *(nir-mānādhin)* वि. under construction.

निर्माणात्मक *(nir-mānaātmak)* वि. formative; constructive.

निर्माता *(nir-mātā)* पु. constructor; builder; creator; producer; manufacturer.

निर्मित *(nir-mit)* पु. constructed; built; formed; prepared; made; manufactured.

निर्मूल *(nir-mūl)* वि. eradicated; completely uprooted; destroyed or ruined; baseless; unfounded; rootless.

निर्मूलन *(nir-mülan)* पु. eradication; uprootment; extirpation; extermination (pol.).

निर्मोह *(nir-moh)* निर्मोही वि. free from attachment; without affection.

निर्यात *(nir-yāt)* पु. export.

निर्यातक *(nir-yātak)* पु. exporter.

निर्लज्ज *(nir-lajj)* वि. shameless; brazenfaced; immodest; impudent.

निर्लज्जता *(nir-lajjatā)* स्री. shamelessness; immodesty.

निर्लिप्त *(nir-lipt)* वि. unconnected; unconcerned; not involved; indifferent; detached.

निर्लिप्ता *(nir-liptā)* स्री. non-attachment; detachment.

निर्लेप *(nir-lep)* वि. faultless; unblemished; pure; stainless; unsmeared; unanointed.

निर्वसन *(nir-varsan)* वि. unclothed; naked; nude.

निर्वस्त्र *(nir-vastra)* वि. nude.

निर्वस्त्रता *(nir-vastratā)* स्री. nudity.

निर्वाचक *(nir-vāčak)* पु. elector.

निर्वाचन *(nir-vāčan)* पु. election.

निर्वाचित *(nir-vācit)* वि. elected.

निर्वाण *(nir-vān)* पु. emancipation; salvation.

निर्वात *(nir-vāt)* पु. vacuum.

निर्वासन *(nir-vāsan)* वि. expulsion; banishment; exile; expatriation; deportation.

निर्वासित *(nir-vāsit)* वि. expelled; exiled; expatriated; banished; deported.

निर्वाह *(nir-vāh)* पु. maintenance; subsistence; performance; discharge; adjustment; accommodation.

निर्विकार *(nir-vi-kār)* वि. unchanged; unchangeable; immutable; passionless; dispassionate; stolid.

निर्विघ्न[1] *(nir-vi-ghna)* वि. uninterrupted; unobstructed; free from impedements.

निर्विघ्न[2] *(nir-vi-ghan)* क्रि. वि. without any untoward incident.

निर्विरोध[1] *(nir-virodh)* वि. unopposed; uncontested; unanimous.

निर्विरोध[2] *(nir-virodh)* क्रि. वि. without any oppossition unanimously.

निर्विवाद[1] *(nir-vi-vād)* वि. undisputed; not contradicted; universally acknowledged; uncontrovertible.

निर्विवाद[2] *(nir-vi-vād)* क्रि. वि. without any dispute or controversy; undisputedly.

निर्वैयक्तिक *(nir-vaiyaktik)* वि. impersonal.

निर्वैयक्तिकता *(nir-vaiyaktikata)* स्त्री. impersonal approach; non-individuality; objectivity; non-subjectivity.

निलंबन *(ni-lamban)* पु. suspension.

निलंबित *(ni-lambit)* वि. suspended.

निवारक *(ni-vārak)* वि. preventive; removing; setting aside; interdictory; prohibitive; precautionary.

निवारण *(ni-vāran)* पु. eradication; prevention; preclusion; release; liberation; prohibition; removal.

निवाला *(nivālā)* पु. (फ़ा.) mouthful; morsel.

निवास *(ni-vās)* पु. living; dwelling residing; residence; abode habitation; resting place; house.

निवासी *(ni-vāsi)* पु. resident; inhabitant.

निविड़ *(ni-viṛ)* वि. thick; dense; deep; impervious.

निविड़ता *(ni-virtā)* स्त्री. thickness; density; imperviousness.

निविदा *(ni-vida)* पु. tender.

निर्वृत्ति *(nir-vṛtti)* स्त्री. freedom from work; disencumbrance; completion; resignation; discontinuance of worldly acts; retirement; renunciation.

निवेदक *(ni-vedak)* पु. applecant; supplicant.

निवेदन *(ni-vedan)* पु. request; submission; application; supplication; petition.

निवेदित *(ni-vedit)* वि. requested; submitted; delivered; presented.

निशा *(nisā)* स्त्री. night.

निशाकर *(niśākar)* पु. moon.

निशाचर *(niśāchar)* पु. demon; goblin; fiend; devil; evil spirit.

निशान *(niśān)* पु. (फ़ा.) sign; mark; trace; clue; ensign; flag; banner; standard; emblem; stain; blemish; scar; impression.

निशाना *(niśānā)* पु. (फ़ा.) butt; target; mark; aim.

निशानी *(niśāni)* स्त्री. (फ़ा.) token of remembrance; memento; keepsake; memorial; sign; token; trace; clue; impression.

निशानेबाज़ *(niśānebāz)* पु. marksman; expert shot.

निशानेबाज़ी *(niśānebāzi)* स्त्री. marks manship.

निशि *(niśi)* स्त्री. night.

निश्चय *(niś-cay)* पु. determination; resolution; resolve; decision; certainty; positiveness; positive conclusion; certitude.

निश्चयात्मक *(niś-cayātmak)* वि. definite; certain; positive; decisive.

निश्चल *(niś-cal)* वि. immovable; steady; fixed; still; invariable; unchangeable.

निश्चलता *(niś-caltā)* स्त्री. immovability; steadiness; invariableness; changelessness; quiescence (psych.) .

निश्चायक[1] *(niś-cāyak)* पु. one who ascertain or determines.

निश्चायक[2] *(niś-chāyak)* वि. decisive; conclusive; definite.

निश्चिंत *(niś-cinṭ)* वि. carefree; free from worry.

निश्चिंतता *(niś-cintatā)* स्त्री. quietude; freedom from worry.

निश्चित *(niścit)* वि. certain; definite; determined; determinate.

निश्चेष्ट *(niśceśt)* वि. incapable of motion; motionless; still; effortless.

निश्चेष्टता *(niś-ceśtatā)* स्त्री. unconsciousness; inertia.

निश्छल *(nis-chal)* वि. guileless; straightforward.

निश्छलता *(niś-chaltā)* स्त्री. guilelessness; straight-forwardness; sincerity.

निश्शंक *(niś-shank)* वि. fearless; dauntless.

निश्शेष *(nis-śes)* पु. balance; residue.

निषंग *(ni-śang)* पु. quiver; sword; infatuation.

निषिद्ध *(ni-śiddh)* वि. forbidden; prohibited; banned.

निषेध *(ni-śedh)* पु. prohibition; inhibition; ban; taboo.

निषेधाज्ञा *(ni-śedhājnā)* स्त्री. prohibitory order.

निषेधात्मक *(ni-śedhātamak)* वि.Prohibitory; prohibitive.

निषेधादेश *(ni-śedhādes)* पु. interdiction.

निष्कंटक[1] *(niś-kantak)* वि. troublefree; unobstructed; smooth; secure; free from danger or nuisance.

निष्कंटक[2] *(niś-kantak)* क्रि. वि. unobstructedly; smoothly; securely; without fear or enmity; opposition or obstacle.

निष्कपट *(niś-kapat)* वि. guiltless; sincere; straightforward; honest.

निष्कपटता *(niś-kapatatā)* स्त्री. guiltlessness; sincerity; honesty; straightforwardness.

निष्कर्ष *(niś-kars)* पु. conclusion; inference; essence; chief or main point; gist; epitome.

निष्काम *(niś-kām)* वि. free from wish or desire; disinterested; unattached.

निष्कासन *(niś-kāsan)* पु. expulsion; ejectment; eviction; removal; ostracism.

निष्कासित *(niś-kāsit)* वि. expelled; truned out; ejected; ostracised.

निष्क्रिय *(niś-kriy)* वि. inactive inert; passive; idle; effortless; indolent.

निष्क्रियता *(niś-kriyatā)* स्त्री. inaction; inactivity; inertia; passivity; idleness; indolence.

निष्चेष्ट *(niś-cesta)* see निष्क्रिय।

निष्ठा *(ni-śthā)* स्त्री. firm adherence; faith; devotion; allegiance; loyalty; fidelity.

निष्ठापूर्वक *(ni-śthāpurvak)* क्रि. वि. conscientiously; faithfully.

निष्ठावान् *(ni-śthāvān)* वि. loyal; faithful; having allegiance; devoted.

निष्ठुर *(ni-śthur)* वि. merciless; ruthless; hard-hearted; pitiless; cruel; brutal; harsh.

निष्ठुरता *(ni-śthuratā)* स्त्री. ruthlessness; mercilessness; brutality; cruelty; harshness.

निष्णात *(ni-śnāt)* वि. well versed; conversant; expert.

निष्पंद *(niś-paṇd)* वि. unflickering; motionless; still steady; fixed.

निष्पक्ष *(niś-paks)* वि. unbiased; impartial; neutral; non-aligned.

निष्पक्षता *(niś-paksatā)* स्त्री. unbiasedness; partiality; newtrality.

निष्पत्ति *(nis-patti)* स्त्री. ripeness; maturity; perfection; consummation; full development; execution; implementation; completion; accomplishment; attainment; achievement.

निष्पादक *(nis-pādak)* पु. executor; maker; performer.

निष्पादन *(nis-pādan)* पु. execution; implementation; performance; performative function.

निष्पादित *(niś-pādit)* वि. executed; implemented; performed; accomplished.

निष्पाप *(niś-pāp)* वि. sinless; guiltless; free from vice.

निष्प्रभावी *(niś-prā-bhāvī)* पु. neutral.

निष्प्रभावीकरण *(niś-prā-bhāvīkaran)* पु. neutralisation.

निष्प्रयोजन *(niś-prā-yojan)* वि. aimless; vain; fruitless; useless.

निष्प्राण *(niś-prān)* वि. lifeless; inanimate; dead; spiritless; without vigour; dull; insentient.

निष्फल *(niś-phal)* वि. fruitless; unsuccessful; futile; vain; infructuous.

निस्तब्ध *(ni-śtabdh)* स्त्री. motionless; stunned; quiet; silent.

निस्तब्धता *(ni-sṭabdhatā)* स्त्री. noiselesness; quietness; motionlessness.

निस्तार *(nis-tār)* पु. riddance; liberation; release; rescue; escape; acquittal; salvation; relief; going across.

निस्तारक *(niś-tārak)* पु. one who carries across or one who brings someone across; rescurer; releaser; saviour.

निस्तारण *(niś-tāran)* पु. deliverance; lilberation; salvage; passing or converying across; disposal; accomplishment.

निस्तेज *(niś-tej)* वि. lustreless; spitless.

निस्पंद *(ni-śpand)* वि. without vibration; unwavering; steady.

निस्पृह *(nispṛh)* वि. above all desires.

निस्पृहता *(nispṛhatā)* क्रि. वि. desirelessness; unambitiousness.

निस्संकोच *(nissankoč)* क्रि. वि. unhesitatingly.

निस्संतान *(nis-san-tān)* वि. childless; issueless.

निस्संदेह *(nis-sandeh)* क्रि. वि. doubtlessly; undoubtedly; surely; certainly.

निस्सहाय *(nis-sahāy)* वि. helpless.

निस्सार *(nis-sār)* वि. unsubstantial; meaningless; worthless vain.

निःस्वार्थ[1] *(nisvārtha)* वि. selfless; unselfish.

निःस्वार्थ[2] *(nisvārtha)* क्रि. वि. without any self interest; selflessly.

निःस्वार्थता *(nisvārthatā)* स्त्री. selflessness.

निहत्था *(nihatthā)* वि. without arms; unarmed.

निहायत *(nihāyat)* क्रि. वि. (अ.) very much; exteremely; excessively.

निहारना *(nihārnā)* स. क्रि. to look at; to see.

निहाल *(nihāl)* वि. pleased; delighted; fully satisfied; gratified.

निहित *(ni-hit)* वि. latent; inherent; implicit; tacit; vested.

निहोरना *(nihoranā)* स. क्रि. to solicit; to beseech.

निहोरा *(nihorā)* पु. entreaty; solicitation.

नींद *(niṁd)* स्त्री. sleep.

नींव *(nimv)* स्त्री. foundation; base.

नीच *(nic)* वि. mean; base; vile; inferiour; low; lowly.

नीचता *(nicatā)* स्त्री. wileness; baseness; meanness; lowliness.

नीचा *(nicā)* वि. low; low lying; inferior.

नीचे *(nice)* क्रि०. वि. beneath; down; below; in the lower part or portion.

नीति *(niti)* स्त्री. policy; craftiness; diplomacy; tactics.

नीतिज्ञ *(nitijna)* पु. moralist; statesman; politician; diplomat.

नीतिपरक *(nitiparak)* वि. didactic.

नीतिवादी[1] *(nitivādi)* पु. moralist; follower of moralism.

नीतिवादी[2] *(nitivādi)* वि. pertaining to moralism.

नीतिशास्त्र *(nitisāstra)* पु. moral science; ethics.

नीतिशास्त्रीय *(nitisastria)* वि. ethical.

नीबू *(nibu)* पु. lemon.

नीम[1] *(nim)* पु. margosa tree; neem tree.

नीम[2] *(nim)* वि. (फ़ा.) half; semi; pseudo.

नीम-हकीम *(nim-hakim)* पु. quack; mountbank.

नीयत *(niyat)* स्त्री. (अ.) motive; intention.

नीर *(nir)* पु. water.

नीरज *(niraj)* पु. lotus.

नीरजा *(nirajā)* वि. dust-free.

नीरद *(nirad)* पु. cloud.

नीरव *(ni-rav)* वि. noiseless; soundless; silent; quiet; calm.

नीरवता *(ni-ravatā)* स्त्री silence; calmness; noiselessness; soundlessness.

नीरस *(ni-ras)* वि. tasteless; flavourless; insipid; sapless; without juice; wanting in charms; charmless; uninteresting; prosaic; withered or dried up; dry; (fig.) lacking aesthetic sense.

नीरसता *(ni-rasatā)* स्त्री. tastelessness; insipidness; saplessness; charmlessness; lack of aesthetic sense; prosaicism; monotony.

नीरोग *(ni-rog)* वि. free from sickness or disease; healthy.

नील *(nil)* पु. indigo.

नीलकंठ *(nilkanth)* पु. epithet of Siva; peacock.

नीलगाय *(nilgāi)* स्त्री. blue bull.

नीलम *(nilam)* नीलमणि स्त्री. saphire.

नीला *(nilā)* वि. blue; azure.

नीलापन *(nilāpan)* पु. blueness.

नीलाम *(nilām)* पु. auction; public sale.

नीलामी *(nilāmi)* वि. auction.

नीलिमा *(nilimā)* स्त्री blueness; blueishness.

नीवी *(nivi)* स्त्री. knot of the garment worn round a woman's waist; waist-cord.

नीहार *(ni-hār)* पु. fog; mist; frost.

नीहारिका *(ni-hārikā)* स्त्री. nebula.

नुक़ताचीनी (*nuqtācini*) स्त्री. (अ.) fault finding; criticism.

नुक़सान *(nuqsān)* पु. (अ.) loss; harm; damage.

नुकसानदेह (*nuqsāndeh*) वि. harmful; disadvantageous.

नुकीला *(nukilā)* वि. pointed; sharp.

नुकीलापन *(nikilāpan)* पु. pointedness; sharpness.

नुक्कड़ *(nukkar)* पु. corner.

नुक्स *(nuqs)* पु. (अ.) fault; flaw; defect; deficiency.

नुनखरा *(nunkharā)* वि. saltish; saline; brachish.

नुनखरापन *(nunkharāpan)* पु. saltishness; salineness; brakishness.

नुमाइंदगी *(numāindagi)* स्त्री. (फ़ा.) representation; delegacy.

नुमाइंदा *(numāindā)* पु. (फ़ा.) representative; delegate.

नुमाइश *(numāis)* स्त्री. (फ़ा.) exhibition.

नुमाइशी *(numāisi)* स्त्री. (फ़ा.) showy; ostensible; ostentatious; relating or pertaining to an exhibition; meant for show; display or exhibition.

नुमायाँ *(numāyān)* वि. (फ़ा.) manifest; glaring; apparent; obvious.

नुसख़ा *(nuskhā)* पु. (अ.) recipe; prescription.

नूतन *(nūtan)* वि. new; modern.

नूतनता *(nūtanatā)* स्त्री. newness; novelty.

नूपुर *(nūpur)* पु. ornament for the feet; anklet.

नूर *(nür)* पु. (अ.) light; splendour; brilliance; lustre; resplendence.

नृत्य *(nṛtya)* पु. dance.

नृत्यकला *(nṛtyakalā)* स्त्री. art of dancing.

नृत्यरचना *(nṛtyarachnā)* स्त्री. choreography.

नृत्यरूपक *(nṛtya-rüpak)* पु. ballet.

नृत्यशाला *(nṛtya-shālā)* स्त्री. dancing hall.

नृप *(nṛp)* पु. king; monarch.

नृशंस *(nṛsaṁs)* वि. cruel; tyrannous; atrocious.

नृशंसता *(nṛśamsatā)* स्त्री. cruelty; tyranny; atrocity; brutality.

नेक *(nek)* वि. (फ़ा.) good; noble; gentle; virtuous.

नेकनामी *(naknāmī)* स्त्री. (फ़ा.) good name; reputation.

नेकनीयत *(nekniyat)* स्त्री. (फ़ा.) well-intentioned; well-meaning; honest; sincere.

नेकनीयती *(nekniyatī)* स्त्री. (फ़ा.) goodness of intention; good faith; bonafides; honesty; sincerity.

नेकी *(nekī)* स्त्री. (फ़ा.) goodness; bonafides; beneficence; benevolence; charity.

नेग *(neg)* पु. customary presents given on festive occasion.

नेता *(netā)* पु. (स्त्री. नेत्री) leader; pioneer.

नेतागीरी *(netāgīrī)* स्त्री. leadership.

नेतृत्व *(netṛtva)* पु. leadership; guidance.

नेत्र *(netra)* पु. eye.

नेत्रगोलक *(netrgolak)* स्त्री. eye ball.

नेत्रदान *(netrdān)* पु. donation of eyes.

नेपथ्य *(nepathya)* पु. green room of a theatre; back stage; decoration; equipment; dress; costume.

नेवला *(nevlā)* पु. mongoose.

नेस्तनाबूद *(nestnābūd)* वि. (फ़ा.) completely destroyed; devastated.

नैतिक *(naitik)* वि. moral; ethical.

नैतिकता *(naitikatā)* स्त्री morality.

नैन *(nain)* पु. eye.

नैपुण्य *(naipunya)* पु. dexterity; adroitness.

नैया *(naiyā)* स्त्री. boat.

नैराश्य *(nairāśya)* पु. hopelessness; despair; frustration; dejection.

नैवेद्य *(naivedya)* पु. offering of eatables presented to a deity; oblation.

नैसर्गिक *(naisargik)* वि. natural; inborn; innate; spontaneous.

नैहर *(naihar)* पु. married woman's parental home.

नोक *(nok)* स्त्री. (फ़ा.) point; tip; end.

नोक-झोंक *(nok-jhoṅk)* स्त्री. (फ़ा.) sarcastic exchanges or comments altercation.

नोकदार *(nokdār)* वि. (फ़ा.) pointed; sharp.

नौकर *(naukar)* पु. (फ़ा.) domestic attendant; servant; employee.

नौकरशाह *(naukarsāh)* पु. bureaucrat.

नौकरशाही *(naukarsāhī)* स्त्री. bureaucracy.

नौकरानी *(naukarānī)* स्त्री. maidservant.

नौकरी *(naukarī)* स्त्री. service; employment; job.

नौका *(naukā)* पु. boat; ferry.

नौका-विहार *(naukā-vihār)* पु. boating.

नौचालक *(nau-cālak)* पु. navigator.

नौचालन *(nau-cālan)* पु. navigation.

नौजवान *(naujavān)* पु. youngman; youth.

नौजवानी *(naujavāni)* स्त्री. young age; youth.

नौटंकी *(nautanki)* स्त्री. kind of folk drama.

नौनिहाल *(naunihāl)* पु. growing or rising generation; youth; young people; child; baby.

नौबत *(naubat)* स्त्री. (फ़ा.) ominous turn; situation; occasion; state of affairs; large kettle drum.

नौ-विज्ञान *(nau-vijnān)* पु. nautical science.

नौशा *(nausā)* पु. (फ़ा.) bridegroom.

नौसादार *(nausādar)* पु. sal-ammoniac; ammonium chloride.

नौसिखिया[1] *(nausikhiyā)* पु. beginner; novice; fresher.

नौसिखिया[2] *(nausikhiyā)* वि. inexperienced.

नौसेना *(nausenā)* स्त्री. navy.

नौ-सेनापति *(nau-senāpati)* पु. chief of naval staff; admiral.

नौ-सैनिक[1] *(nau-sainik)* पु. naval soldier.

नौ-सैनिक[2] *(nau-sainik)* वि. naval.

न्याय *(ny-āy)* पु. justice; equity.

न्यायकर्ता *(ny-āykartā)* पु. judge.

न्यायतंत्र *(ny-āytantra)* पु. judiciary.

न्यायपरता *(ny-āyparatā)* स्त्री. justness; fairness; equitability.

न्यायपरायण *(ny-āy-parāyan)* स्त्री. just; fair; equitable.

न्यायपराणता *(ny-āy-parāyanatā)* स्त्री. justness; righteousness; equitability.

न्यायपालिका *(ny-āy-pālikā)* स्त्री. judiciary.

न्यायपीठ *(ny-āy-pitha)* पु. bench.

न्यायप्रिय *(ny-āy-priya)* वि. justice-loving.

न्यायमूर्ति *(ny-āy-murti)* पु. justice; a judge of supreme court.

न्याययवादी *(ny-āy-vādī)* पु. attorney.

न्यायशास्त्र *(ny-āy-sāstra)* पु. jurisprudence.

न्याय संगत *(ny-āy-sangat)* वि. just; justified; lawful.

न्यायाधीश *(ny-āyādhis)* पु. judge; justice.

न्यायालय *(ny-āyālaya)* पु. court of law.

न्यायिक *(ny-āyik)* वि. judicial.

न्यायोचित *(nyāyocit)* वि. just; equitable; fair; right.

न्यारा *(nyārā)* वि. separate; different; distinct; extraordinary; uncommon.

न्यून *(ny-ün)* वि. less; lower; inferior; deficient; wanting; small.

न्यूनतम *(ny-ünatam)* वि. minimum; minimal.

न्यूनता *(ny-ünatā)* स्त्री. shortage; paucity; scarcity; want; deficiency.

न्यूनीकरण *(ny-ünikaran)* पु. abatement.

न्योछावर *(nyochāvar)* see निछावर

न्योतना *(nyoutanā)* स. क्रि. to invite.

न्योता *(nyotā)* पु. invitation.

प

प *(pa)* the first letter of the fifth pentad of the Devnagri alphabets.

पंक *(paṅk)* पु. mud; mire; slime.

पंकज *(paṅkaj)* पु. lotus.

पंकिल *(paṅkil)* वि. muddy; slimy.

पंक्ति *(paṅkti)* स्त्री. queue; line; row; rank.

पंख *(paṅkh)* पु. wing; feather; arm of a fan.

पँखड़ी *(paṁkhri)* स्त्री. petal.

पंखा *(paṅkhā)* पु. fan.

पंगत *(paṅgat)* पंगति स्त्री. row of people siting at a meal; community meal.

पंगु *(paṅgu)* वि. lame; crippled.

पंगुता *(paṅgutā)* स्त्री. lameness.

पंच *(pañc)* पु. assemble of (originally) five men; member of the panchayat; body of arbitrators; juror; arbitrator.

पंचकोण *(pañckona)* पु. pentagon.

पंचनामा *(pañcnāmā)* पु. arbitration bond.

पंचनिर्णय *(pañcnirnay)* पु. judgement of an arbitrator.

पंचफैसला *(pañcfaisalā)* पु. arbitration.

पंचमी *(pañcamī)* स्त्री. fifth day of fortnight of a lunar month.

पंचमेल *(pañc-mel)* वि. having five different ingredients.

पंचशील *(pañc-sila)* पु. the five chief principles of conduct of Buddhism; the five basic principles or international conduct designed to achieve and consolidate worldpeace.

पंचांग *(pañcāng)* पु. almanac; Hindu calendar.

पंचायत *(pañcāyat)* स्त्री. village assemble; arbitration.

पंचायती *(pañcāyati)* वि. pertaining to community; common; public.

पंछी *(pañchī)* पु. bird.

पंजर *(pañjar)* पु. skeleton; frame; cage.

पंजा *(pañjā)* पु. a collection of five things; the five fingers of toes; claw; paw; the fore-part of foot wear.

पंजिका *(pañjikā)* स्त्री. small register.

पंजीकरण *(pañjīkaran)* पु. registration.

पंजीकृत *(pañjīkṛt)* वि. registered.

पंजीयक *(pañjiyak)* पु. registrar.

पंडाल *(pañdāl)* पु. huge pavilion; marquee.

पंडित *(pañdit)* पु. learned person; a title of respect of Hindus who are learned in the Brahmanical theology; a leaned man.

पंडिताई *(pañditai)* स्त्री. scholarship; the function or profession of a pandit.

पंडिताऊ *(pañditāu)* वि. pedantic; befittnig a 'pandit'; doctrinaire.

पंडितानी *(pañditāni)* स्त्री. wife of a Brahmin or learned man.

पंथ *(pañth)* पु. path; road; sect; cult.

पकड़ *(pakaṛ)* स्त्री. the act of holding or gripping; grip or hold; grasp; catch; seizure.

पकड़-धकड़ *(pakaṛ-dhakaṛ)* स्त्री. apprehension; seizure; round of arrests.

पकड़ना *(pakaṛnā)* स. क्रि. to catch; to hold; to grasp; to overtake; to capture; to apprehend.

पकना *(paknā)* (अ.) क्रि. to ripen; to be cooked; to turn grey or white (hair); to suppurate; to mature.

पकवान *(pakvān)* पु. preservable dressed food; fried delicacy.

पकवाना *(pakvānā)* स. क्रि. to cause to cook or dress.

पकाना *(pakānā)* स. क्रि. to cook; to boil; to ripen; to season.

पकौड़ा *(pakaurā)* स्त्री. a kind of fried snack.

पकौड़ी *(pakauṛi)* स्त्री. a kind of dish made of peasemeal; pastry filled with pease-meal.

पक्का *(pakkā)* वि. ripe; permanent; lasting; expert; strong; fixed; firm; fast.

पक्व *(pakva)* वि. cooked; roasted; ripel mature.

पक्कवता *(pakvatā)* स्त्री. repeness.

पक्ष *(paks)* पु. side; wing; fortnight; aspect; party; favour.

पक्षकार *(pakśkār)* पु. party

पक्षधर *(pakśdhar)* पु. supporter.

पक्षपात *(pakśpāt)* पु. partiality; favouritism.

पक्षपाती *(pakśpāti)* वि. partial; partisan.

पक्षाघात *(paksāghāt)* पु. paralysis.

पक्षी *(pakśi)* पु. bird.

पक्षी विज्ञान *(pakśi-vyjnān)* पु. ornithology.

पख़ *(pakh)* स्त्री. impediment; obstacle; hindrance.

पखवाड़ा *(pakhvārā)* पु. fortnight.

पखारना *(pakhārnā)* स. क्रि. to wash; to cleanse.

पखेरू *(pakhrü)* पु. bird.

पग *(pag)* पु. pace; step.

पगडंडी *(pagdaṇdi)* स्त्री. footpath; track.

पगड़ी *(pagṛi)* स्त्री. turban; gratification money for letting out a house.

पगना *(pagnā)* (अ.) क्रि. to be soaked in some syrup.

पगला *(paglā)* वि. mad; insane.

पगाना *(pagānā)* स. क्रि. to soak in syrup.

पगार *(pagār)* पु. wages; salary; wet earth or clay for building purposes; boundary; enclosure.

पचना *(pacnā)* अ. क्रि. to be digested.

पचाना *(pacānā)* स. क्रि. to digest; to do away with dishonestly or wrongfully; to embezzle; to assimilate.

पच्चीकारी *(paccīkārī)* स्त्री. mosaic-work; inlay work.

पछड़ना *(pacharnā)* (अ.) क्रि. to be beaten down or defeated; to be knocked down; to be floored; to be overshadowed; to be overtaken; to be left behind; to be surpassed.

पछताना *(pachtāna)* (अ.) क्रि. to repent.

पछतावा *(pachtāvā)* पु. repentance; remorse.

पछाड़ *(pachār)* स्त्री. falling back in a swoon.

पछाड़ना *(pachārnā)* स. क्रि. to throw down; to knock down; to defeat.

पट *(paṭ)* पु. garment; raiment; cloth; screen; a door panel; shutter.

पटकना *(paṭaknā)* स. क्रि. to throw down; to topple; to knock down; to abate; go down or subside (as swelling or tumour).

पटबीजना *(paṭbījnā)* पु. glow-worm.

पटरा *(paṭrā)* पु. plank.

पटरानी *(paṭrāni)* स्त्री. queen consort; chief queen.

पटरी *(paṭrī)* स्त्री. small wooden plank; bank of a canal; rail; railtrack.

पटल *(paṭal)* पु. roof; thatch; table; wooden plank; layer; (tech.) desk in parliament or legislative assembly; screen; counter; board.

पटवारी *(paṭvārī)* पु. a government functionary at the village level; who keeps land records.

पटसन *(paṭsan)* पु. jute; hemp.

पटाका *(paṭākā)* पु. cracker; slap.

पटाक्षेप *(paṭākshep)* पु. fall of curtain.

पटाख़ा *(paṭākhā)* पु. cracker.

पटाना *(paṭānā)* स. क्रि. to get settled; to settle; to persuade; to bring round.

पटाव *(paṭāv)* पु. roofing covering; covered place.

पटिया *(paṭiyā)* स्त्री. wooden or stone slan; slip of board tablet; slate.

पटु *(paṭu)* वि. skilled; dexterous; ingenius.

पटुता *(paṭutā)* वि. skilfulness; cleverness; ingenuity.

पट्ट *(paṭṭ)* पु. plate; board; plank.

पट्टा *(paṭṭa)* पु. title deed; lease; dog-collar; belt.

पट्टाकर्ता *(paṭṭākartā)* पु. leasor.

पट्टाधारी *(paṭṭādhāri)* पु. lease-holder.

पट्टिका *(paṭṭika)* स्त्री. flipper; rule; panel; fillet; pallet.

पट्टी *(paṭṭī)* स्त्री. wooden plate (for beginners to write on); misquidance; strap; strip.

पट्ठा *(paṭṭhā)* पु. wrestler; lace; broad brocade; sinew; robust youth.

पठन *(paṭhan)* पु. reading; studying; recitation.

पठन-पाठन *(paṭhan-pāṭhan)* पु. reading and teaching.

पठनशील *(paṭhan-sila)* वि. studious.

पठनीय *(paṭhaniya)* वि. readable; worth reading.

पठाना *(paṭhānā)* स. क्रि. to send (someone).

पठार *(paṭhār)* पु. plateau; table-land.

पठित *(paṭhit)* वि. studied; read.

पड़ताल *(parṭāl)* स्त्री. investigation;

remeasurement; checking.

पड़ती *(parti)* स्त्री. fallow land.

पड़ना *(parnā)* अ. क्रि. to drop; to participate; to halt; encamp; camp; to lie down; to fall.

पड़ाव *(parāv)* पु. halting place; camp; encampment.

पड़ोस *(paros)* पु. neighbourhood; vicinity.

पड़ोसी, पड़ौसी *(parosi)* वि. neighbour.

पड़ोसिन *(parosin)* स्त्री. female neighbour.

पढ़ना *(parhnā)* स. क्रि. to read; to make out; to decipher; to study.

पढ़वाना *(parhvānā)* स. क्रि. to cause (one) to be taught; to cause to be read.

पढ़ाई *(parhai)* स्त्री. study; tuition fee; education; learning.

पढ़ाना *(parhānā)* स. क्रि. to teach; to instruct; to coach; to cause to read.

पतंग *(patang)* पु. sun; bird; paper kite; moth; insect.

पतंगबाज़ *(patangbāz)* पु. kite-flier.

पतंगबाज़ी *(patangbāzi)* स्त्री. kiteflying.

पतंगा *(patangā)* पु. moth; insect; spark (of fire).

पत *(pat)* स्त्री. prestige; honour; dignity.

पतझड़, पतझर *(patjhar)* पु. autumn.

पतन *(patan)* पु. downfall; fall; degradation; decline; degeneration.

पतनशील *(patan-sila)* वि. tending to fall; decadent.

पतनाला *(patnālā)* see पनाला।

पतनोन्मुख *(patanonmukh)* वि. tending to fall; falling.

पतला *(patlā)* वि. thin; fine; flimsy; liquid; diluted.

पतलापन *(patlāpan)* पु. thinness; leanness; tenuousness; wateriness.

पतलून *(patlün)* स्त्री. pantaloon; trousers.

पतवार *(patvār)* स्त्री. rudder; helm

पता *(patā)* पु. whereabouts; address; information; knowledge.

पताका *(patākā)* स्त्री. flag; banner.

पति *(pati)* पु. husband.

पतित *(patit)* वि. fallen; degraded; wicked; sinful.

पतिधर्म *(patidharm)* पु. devotion to husband.

पतिभक्ति *(pati-bhakti)* स्त्री. fidelity to husband.

पतियाना *(pati-ānā)* स. क्रि. to trust; to rely; to believe.

पतिव्रता *(pati-vratā)* स्त्री. faithul wife; virtuous wife.

पतीली *(patili)* स्त्री. cooking vessel; kettle.

पतोहू *(patohü)* स्त्री. son's wife; daughter-in-law.

पत्तन *(pattan)* पु. port; town; city.

पत्तल *(pattal)* स्त्री. leaf-plate; food served on a leaf-plate.

पत्ता *(pattā)* पु. leaf; playing card.

पत्ती *(patti)* स्त्री. small leaf; leaf or thick plate (of metal); share.

पत्तीदार[1] *(pattidār)* वि. leafy.

पत्तीदार[2] *(pattidār)* पु. share-holder; partner.

पत्थर *(patthar)* पु. stone.

पत्नी *(patni)* स्त्री. wife.

पत्नीव्रत *(patnivrat)* पु. vow to be loyal to one's wife; fidelity to one's wife.

पत्र *(patr)* पु. leaf; letter.

पत्रक *(patrak)* पु. card; leaflet; chit.

पत्रकार *(patrakār)* पु. journalist.

पत्रकारिता *(patrakāritā)* स्त्री. journalism.

पत्र-पत्रिका *(patra-patrikā)* स्त्री. periodicals; magazines.

पत्रपेटी *(patra-petī)* स्त्री. letter-box.

पत्र-मित्र *(patra-mitra)* पु. penfriend; pen pall.

पत्रवाहक *(patr-vāhak)* पु. bearer of letter; postman.

पत्रा *(patrā)* पु. almanac.

पत्राचार *(patrācār)* पु. correspondence.

पत्रावली *(patrā-vali)* स्त्री. scroll; scroll-work; collection of letters.

पत्रिका *(patrikā)* स्त्री. magazine; periodical; journal.

पत्री *(patrī)* स्त्री. note; letter; document.

पथ *(path)* पु. path; way; road; route.

पथकर *(pathkar)* पु. toll; toll tax; road toll.

पथप्रदर्शक *(path-pradarsak)* पु. guide.

पथप्रदर्शन *(path-pradarsan)* पु. guidance.

पथभ्रष्ट *(path-bhrastha)* वि. fallen; stray; misguided.

पथराना *(pathrānā)* (अ.) क्रि. to become hard like stone; to be petrified; to harden into stone.

पथराव *(pathrāv)* पु. stoning; pelting stones.

पथरी *(pathrī)* स्त्री. stone; bladder-stone.

पथरीला *(pathrila)* वि. stone; rocky.

पथिक, पथी *(pathik)* पु. traveller; wayfarer.

पथ्य[1] *(pathya)* वि. light (meal; diet); proper; suitable; wholesome.

पथ्य[2] *(pathya)* पु. wholesome food; diet conducive to health.

पद *(pad)* पु. foot; footstep; step; pace; stride; place; line of stanza; verse; designation; status; rank; post.

पदक *(padak)* पु. medal.

पदचिह्न *(pad-cinh)* पु. foot-print; foot-mark.

पदच्युत *(pad-c̄yut)* वि. dismissed; discharged from office; degraded.

पदच्युति *(pad-cyuti)* स्त्री. dismissal; degradation.

पदत्याग *(pad-tyāg)* पु. abandonment of office; abdication; resignation.

पदत्राण *(pad-trān)* पु. shoe; footwear.

पददलित *(pad-dalit)* वि. trodden under foot; down-trodden.

पदवी *(padvī)* स्त्री. title; appelation.

पदाघात *(padāghāt)* पु. blow with the feet; kick; accent.

पदाधिकारी *(padādhikārī)* पु. officer; office-bearer; official.

पदार्थ *(padārṭh)* पु. thing; object; material; matter.

पदार्पण *(padārpan)* पु. arrival; stepping-in.

पदावनत *(padāvanat)* वि. demoted; degraded.

पदावनति *(padāvanati)* स्त्री. reversion; demotion; downgrading.

पदावली *(padāvali)* स्त्री. series of verses or words; phraseology; collection of devotional songs.

पदासीन *(padāsīna)* वि. occupying an office.

पदेन *(paden)* क्रि. वि. ex-officio; by

virtue of an office.

पदोन्नत *(padonnat)* वि. promoted.

पदोन्नति *(padonnati)* स्त्री. promotion; rise in rank or status.

पद्धति *(paddhati)* स्त्री. method; system.

पद्म *(padma)* पु. lotus.

पद्य *(padya)* पु. verse; poetry.

पद्यकार *(padyakār)* पु. versifier.

पधारना *(padhārnā)* (अ.) क्रि. to arrive; to go; to set out.

पनघट *(panghat)* पु. place for drawing water; village well.

पनडुब्बी *(pandubbī)* स्त्री. sub-marine.

पनबिजली *(panbijlī)* स्त्री. hydroelectricity.

पनस *(panas)* पु. jacktree and its fruits; thorn; a kind of snake.

पनही *(panhī)* स्त्री. footwear.

पनाला *(panālā)* पु. gutter; drain.

पनाह *(panāh)* पु. (फो.) refuge; shelter.

पनीर *(panīr)* पु. (फो.) cheese.

पन्ना *(pannā)* पु. emerald; leaf of a book; sheet; folio; beverage prepared from baked mango; tamarind and cumin seed etc.

पन्नी *(pannī)* स्त्री. plated multi-coloured paper; metalic paper; kind of coloured paper.

पपड़ी *(papṛī)* स्त्री. crust; scab; scale; dry incrustation formed on a healing wound.

पपीता *(papītā)* पु. papaya.

पय *(pay)* पु. drinkable; water.

पयस *(payas)* पु. milk.

पयाम *(payām)* पु. (फ़ा.) message.

पयोद *(payod)* पु. cloud.

पयोधर *(payodhar)* पु. cloud; breast.

परंतु *(paran-tu)* अ. but; however.

परंपरा *(param-parā)* स्त्री. tradition; convention.

परंपरागत *(param-parāgat)* वि. traditional; orthodox; customary.

परंपरावाद *(param-parāvad)* पु. conservatism; traditionalism; orthodoxy.

परंपरावादी *(param-parāvadī)* पु. traditionalist; conformist.

पर[1] *(par)* अ. but; yet; still.

पर[2] *(par)* वि. other; not one's own; posterior; different.

पर[3] *(par)* पु. on; upon; above.

पर[4] *(par)* पु. (फ़ा.) feather; wing.

परकटा *(parkātā)* वि. with feathers cut off; wing-clipped.

परकार *(parkār)* स्त्री. divider.

परकीया *(parkīyā)* स्त्री. adulteress; (in traditional Indian poetics one of the three types of heroines.)

परकोटा *(parkotā)* पु. precinct; boundary; rampart.

परख *(parakh)* पु. test; examination; trial; distinguishing faculty; probation.

परखचा *(parakhachā)* पु. fragment; shred.

परखना *(parakhnā)* स. क्रि. to test; to examine.

परखवाना *(parakhavānā)* स. क्रि. to cause to be tested or examined.

परखी *(parkhī)* स्त्री. gadget for testing corn packed in sacks.

परगना *(parganā)* पु. (फ़ा.) subdivision.

परगनाधीश *(parganādhish)* पु. subdivisional officer.

परचा *(parcā)* पु. (फ़ा.) piece of paper; chit; question paper.

परची *(parcī)* स्त्री. slip; chit.

परचून *(parcūn)* पु. provisions; grocery.

परचूनिया *(parcūniyā)* पु. grocer; retailer of provisions.

परछाईं *(parchāīm)* स्त्री. shadow; reflection.

परजीवी *(parjīvī)* वि. parasitic.

परतंत्र *(par-tantra)* वि. dependent.

परतंत्रता *(par-tantratā)* स्त्री. dependence; subjection.

परती *(partī)* स्त्री. fallow land.

परदा *(pardā)* पु. (फ़ा.) curtain; screen; secret; mystery; veil.

परदादा *(pardādā)* पु. paternal great-grandfather.

परदादी *(pardādī)* स्त्री. paternal great-grandmother.

परदेश, परदेस *(pardeś)* पु. foreign country; another country.

परदेशी, परदेसी *(pardesī)* पु. foreigner; stranger; alien.

परनाना *(parnānā)* पु. maternal great grandfather.

परनानी *(parnānī)* स्त्री. (maternal) great grandmother.

परनाला *(parnālā)* पु. drain pipe; gutter.

परनिंदा *(parnindā)* स्त्री. censure.

परपीड़क *(par-pirak)* पु. oppressor.

परपोता *(parpotā)* पु. great grandson.

परम *(param)* वि. highest; best; most; chief; principal; extreme (limit); ultimate; absolute.

परमगति *(paramgati)* स्त्री. salvation; emancipation.

परमधाम *(param-dhām)* पु. heaven.

परमपद *(param-pad)* पु. highest state or position; liberation; salvation.

परमाणु *(paramanū)* पु. atom.

परमात्मा *(paramātmā)* पु. God.

परमानंद *(paramānad)* पु. beatitude; ultimate pleasure; supreme bliss; God.

परमार्थ *(paramārth)* पु. highest good; the best end; salvation; ultimate reality.

परमावश्यक *(paramāvśyak)* वि. most essential; most urgent.

परमेश्वर *(parmeśvar)* पु. God.

परला *(parlā)* वि. of the other side or end; next in order.

परलोक *(parlok)* पु. the other world.

परलोकगमन *(parlok-gaman)* पु. demise.

परवरिश *(parvaris)* स्त्री. (फ़ा.) bringing up; fostering; nurture.

परवर्ती *(par-varti)* वि. later; subsequent.

परवश *(parvasa)* वि. under another's control dependent; subservient.

परवशता *(paarvaśatā)* स्त्री. dependence on another; subjection; subservience.

परवाना *(parvānā)* पु. (फ़ा.) warrant; order; moth.

परसना *(parasnā)* स. क्रि (फ़ा.) to serve (food); to touch; to feel by touch.

परसों *(parsoṁ)* (अ.) day before yesterday; day after tomorrow.

परस्त्रीगमन *(par-strigaman)* पु. adultery.

परस्त्रीगामी *(par-strigāmī)* वि. adulterer.

परस्पर *(paras-par)* क्रि. वि. mutually; reciprocally.

परस्परता *(paras-partā)* स्त्री. mutuality; reciprocity.

परहित *(parhit)* पु. denevolence; benefaction; beneficence.

परहितवाद *(parhitvād)* पु. altruism.

परहितवादी *(parhitvādi)* पु. altruist.

परहेज़ *(parhez)* पु. (फ़ा.) abstinence; avoidance; control of the passions; regimen.

पराकाष्ठा *(parā-kāsthā)* स्त्री. climax; culminating point; extremity; extreme.

पराक्रम *(parākram)* पु. bravery; valiance. gallantry; heroism.

पराक्रमी *(parâkramī)* वि. brave; valiant; heroic; gallant.

पराग *(parāg)* पु. pollen.

पराजय *(parā-jay)* स्त्री. defeat.

पराजित *(parā-jit)* वि. defeated; vanquished.

पराधीन *(parā-dhin)* वि. dependent on another.

पराधीनता *(parā-dhintā)* स्त्री. dependence on another; subjection; subjugation.

पराभाव *(parā-bhāv)* पु. defeat; overthrow; debacle.

पराभूत *(parā-bhūt)* वि. defeated; overthrown.

परामनोविज्ञान *(para-manovignān)* पु. parapsychology

परामर्श *(parā-marś)* पु. advice; counsel; consultation.

परामर्शदाता *(parā-marśdātā)* पु. adviser; counsel; consultant.

परायण *(parāyan)* स्त्री. absorbed; devoted.

परायणता *(parāyantā)* स्त्री. absorption; devotion.

पराया *(parāyā)* वि. belonging to another; not one's own; alien; foreign.

परावर्तक[1] *(parā-vartak)* पु. reflector.

परावर्तक[2] *(parā-vartak)* वि. reflecting; causing reflection.

पराश्रय *(parā-śray)* पु. dependence on others; subjection.

पराश्रित *(parāśṛit)* स्त्री. dependent; subjection or subjugation.

पराश्रितता *(parāsṛitatā)* स्त्री. dependence.

परास्त *(parāst)* वि. defeated; vanquished; overthrown.

परिंदा *(parinḍā)* पु. (फ़ा.) bird.

परिकल्पना *(pari-kalpanā)* स्त्री. speculation; hypothesis.

परिकल्पित *(pari-kalpit)* वि. presumed; envisaged.

परिक्रमा *(pari-kramā)* स्त्री. going round a person or an idol as an indication of reverence; circumambulation.

परिखा *(pari-khā)* स्त्री. foss; moat.

परिगणना *(pari-gananā)* स्त्री. calculation; schedule.

परिगणित *(pari- ganit)* वि. calulated; scheduled; enumerated.

परिग्रह *(pari-grah)* पु. taking; acceptance; receipt; possession; property; wife.

परिग्रहण *(pari-grahan)* पु. accession.

परिचय *(pari-cāy)* पु. acquaintance; introduction; familiarity.

परिचय-पत्र *(pari-cay-patra)* पु. letter of introduction.

परिचर्चा *(pari-cārcā)* स्त्री. discussion; symposium.

परिचर्या *(pari-caryā)* स्त्री. attendance; nursing.

परिचायक *(pari-cāyak)* पु. one who introduces.

परिचारक *(pari-cārak)* पु. male attendant.

परिचारिका *(pari-cārikā)* स्त्री. female attendant; nurse; hostess; chamber maid.

परिचारित *(pari-cārit)* वि. circulated.

परिचालन *(pri-cālan)* पु. steering; operation; circulation.

परिचित *(pari-čit)* *वि.* acquainted; familiar.

परिच्छेद *(pari-cched)* *पु.* section or chapter of a book.

परिजन *(pari-jan)* *पु.* family; household members; attendants; followers; retinue.

परिणत *(pari-ṇat)* *वि.* changed; transformed; metamorphosed.

परिणति *(pari-ṇati)* *स्त्री.* change; transformation; culmination; metamorphosis; result.

परिणय *(pari-ṇay)* *पु.* marriage wedding; wedlock.

परिणय-सूत्र *(pari-ṇay-sutra)* *पु.* bond of marriage.

परिणाम *(pari-ṇām)* *पु.* result; consequence.

परितप्त *(pari-tapta)* *वि.* hot; heated; afflicted; anguished.

परितप्ति *(pari-tapti)* *स्त्री.* heating; excessive heat; excessive suffering.

परिताप *(pari-tāp)* *पु.* scorching heat; pain; agony; repentance; penitence.

परितुलन *(pari-tulan)* *पु.* collation.

परितोष *(pari-tos)* *पु.* complete satisfaction; delight; gratification.

परित्यक्त *(pari-tyakt)* *वि.* quitted; deserted.

परत्यिक्ता *(pari-tyaktā)* *स्त्री.* abandoned woman.

परित्याग *(pari-tyāg)* *पु.* desertion; abandonment; renunciation.

परिधान *(pari-dhān)* *पु.* dress; clothes; garment; costume; robes.

परिधि *(pri-dhi)* *स्त्री.* circumference; periphery; boundary; ambit; perimeter.

परिपक्व *(pari-pakva)* *वि.* ripe; developed; matured.

परिपक्कवता *(pari-pakkvatā)* *स्त्री.* ripeness; maturity; full development.

परिपक्वासथा *(pari-pakāvāsthā)* *स्त्री.* maturity.

परिपत्र *(pari-patr)* *पु.* circular; circular letter.

परिपाटी *(pari-pātī)* *स्त्री.* convention; custom; tradition; succession; arrangement; usage.

परिपालक *(pari-pālak)* *पु.* implementer; executer; preserver.

परिपालन *(pari-pālan)* *पु.* execution; implementation; maintenance.

परिपालनीय *(pari-pālaniya)* *वि.* worth executing or implementing.

परिपालयिता *(pari-palīyitā)* *पु.* executant.

परिपालित *(pari-pālit)* *वि.* executed; maintained; implemented.

परिपूरक *(pari-pūrak)* *वि.* supplementary.

परिपूरित *(pari-pūrit)* *वि.* supplemented; fully accomplished; filled; infused or informed.

परिपूर्ण *(pari-pūrn)* *वि.* perfect; complete; full; replete; brimful; infused; imbued.

परिपूर्णता *(pari-pūrnatā)* *स्त्री.* repletion; brimfulness; perfection; completeness.

परिप्रेषक *(pari-presāk)* *पु.* despatcher; sender.

परिप्रेषण *(pari-presān)* *पु.* despatch; sending.

परिभाषा *(pari-bhāsā)* *स्त्री.* definition.

परिभाषित *(pari-bhāsit)* *वि.* defined.

परिभाष्य *(pari-bhāsya)* *वि.* definable.

परिमाण *(pari-māṇ)* पु. measure; weight; quantity; circumference; volume; amount.

परिमाप *(pari-māp)* पु. measurement; dimension; scale; perimeter.

परिमापी *(pari-māpī)* पु. perimeter.

परिमार्जन *(pari-mārjan)* पु. improvement; cleansing; purging; refinement; moderation.

परिमार्जित *(pari-marjit)* वि. improved; cleaned; purged; refined; moderated.

परिमित *(pari-mit)* वि. limited; measured; moderate.

परिमिति *(pari-miti)* स्त्री. limit; perimeter.

परिमेय *(pari-meya)* वि. measurable; limited.

परिरक्षक *(pari-rakshak)* पु. preserver; shielder; custodian; defender.

परिरक्षण *(pari-rakshan)* पु. guarding in every respect; shielding; preservation; custody.

परिवर्तन *(pari-vartan)* पु. exchange; change; alteration; conversion.

परिवर्तनशील *(pari-vartanśil)* वि. changeable.

परिवर्तनशीलता *(pari-vartanśiltā)* स्त्री. variability; changeability.

परिवर्तनीय *(pari-vartanīya)* वि. changeable; variable; alterable; interchangeable; convertible.

परिवर्तित *(pari-vartit)* वि. exchanged; changed; altered; converted.

परिवर्धित *(pari-vardhit)* वि. enlarged; developed; grown.

परिवहन *(pari-vahan)* पु. transport; transportation.

परिवहनीय *(pari-vahanīya)* वि. transportable.

परिवाद *(pari-vād)* पु. complaint; censure; scandal; calumny.

परिवादी *(pari-vādī)* पु. complainant; scandal-monger; calumniator.

परिवार *(pari-vār)* पु. family; class; house-hold; kins.

परिवेश *(pari-veś)* पु. environment; surrounding.

परिवेष्टन *(pari-veṣṭan)* पु. encirclement; wrapping; enclosure.

परिवेष्टित *(pari-vestit)* वि. enclosed; wrapped; surrounded.

परिव्यय *(pari-vyay)* पु. cost; expenditure; disbursement.

परिव्राजक *(pari-vrājak)* पु. wandering religious mendicant; ascetic.

परिशीलन *(pari-silan)* पु. critical study; perusal.

परिश्रम *(pari-śram)* पु. labour; hard work; exertion; diligence.

परिश्रमी *(pari-śramī)* वि. industrious; hard-working; diligent; laborious.

परिष्करण *(pari-skaran)* पु. finishing; retouching; refinement.

परिष्कार *(pari-śkār)* पु. refinement; embellishment; decoration.

परिष्कृत *(pari-śkṛt)* वि. purified; adorned; decorated; improved; refined; sophisticated.

परिष्कृति *(pari-śkṛti)* स्त्री. refinement; purification.

परिसर *(pari-sar)* पु. environs; premises; enclave.

परिसीमन *(pari-siman)* पु. delimitation.

परिसीमा *(pari-śimā)* स्त्री. extreme limit; precincts; boundary line.

परिसीमित *(pari-sīmit)* वि. limited; demarked.

परिस्थिति *(pari-sthiti)* स्त्री. circumstances; situation.

परिस्थितिगत *(pari-sthitigat)* वि. circumstantial.

परिहार *(pari-hār)* पु. rectification; abstention; avoidance; evasion; atonement; expiation; remission.

परिहार्य *(pari-hārya)* वि. avoidable.

परिहास *(pari-hās)* पु. joke; fun; ridicule.

परी *(parī)* स्त्री. (फ़ा.) fairy; elf; beautiful woman; nymph.

परीक्षक *(parīkṣak)* पु. examiner; investigator; tester.

परीक्षण *(parīkṣan)* पु. examination; test; trial.

परीक्षा *(parīkṣā)* स्त्री. trial; ordeal; test; examination.

परीक्षार्थी *(parīkṣārthi)* पु. examinee.

परीक्षित *(parīkṣit)* वि. audited; examined; tested; tried.

परुष *(paruṣ)* वि. hard; rough; coarse; rigid.

परुषता *(paruṣatā)* स्त्री. hardness; rigidity.

परे *(pare)* क्रि. वि. at a distance; beyond; away.

परेशान *(pareśān)* वि. (फ़ा.) worried; troubled; harassed.

परेशानी *(pareśānī)* स्त्री. (फ़ा.) worry; harassment; trouble.

परेषक *(pareśak)* पु. consignor; consigner.

परेषण *(pareśan)* पु. consignment.

परेषणी *(pareśanī)* पु. consignee.

परोक्ष *(parokṣ)* वि. imperceptible; indirect.

परोपकार *(paropkār)* पु. benevolence; philanthropy.

परोपकारी[1] *(paropkarī)* वि. benevolent; munificent.

परोपकारी[2] *(paropkarī)* पु. philanthropist; benevolent person.

परोपजीवी *(paropjīvī)* पु. parasite.

परोसना *(parosnā)* स. क्रि. to serve (food); to dish up.

परोसा *(parosā)* पु. dish of one man's meal.

पर्चा *(parcā)* पु. slip of paper; chit; paper; question paper.

पर्ची *(parcī)* स्त्री. slip of paper.

पर्ण *(parṇ)* पु. folio; leaf.

पर्णशाला *(parṇsālā)* स्त्री. hut made of leaves; bower.

पर्दा *(pardā)* see परदा

पर्यटक *(pary-aṭak)* पु. tourist.

पर्यटन *(pary-aṭan)* पु. tourism.

पर्यवेक्षक *(pary-avêkṣak)* पु. supervisor.

पर्यवेक्षण *(pary-avêkṣan)* पु. supervision.

पर्याप्त *(pary-āpt)* वि. enough; sufficient; ample; plentiful; adequate

पर्याप्तता *(pary-āptatā)* स्त्री. sufficiency; adequacy.

पर्याय *(pary-āy)* पु. synonym.

पर्यायवाचक *(pary-āyvācak)* पर्यायवाची वि. synonymous.

पर्यावरण *(pary-ā-varan)* पु. environment.

पर्व *(parv)* पु. festival; knot; section; node.

पर्वत *(parvat)* पु. mountain.

पर्वतारोहण *(parvtārohan)* पु. mountaineering.

पर्वतारोही *(parvtārohi)* पु. mountaineer.

पर्वतीय *(parvtīya)* वि. mountainous; hilly; belonging to mountains.

पलंग *(palaṅg)* पु. bedstead; bed.

पलंग-पोश *(palang-posh)* पु. bed-sheet.

पल *(pal)* पु. measure of time equal to twenty-four seconds; moment; instant.

पलक *(palak)* स्त्री. eye-lash; eyelid.

पलटन *(paltan)* स्त्री. platoon; large number.

पलटना *(palaṭnā)* स. क्रि. to alter; to over-turn; to turn; barter; to return; to change; to alter; to turn over.

पलटा *(palṭā)* पु. iron pan or ladle with a long handle; relapse; return.

पलड़ा *(palṛā)* पु. pan of balance.

पलथी *(palthī)* स्त्री. cross-legged sitting posture; squatting.

पलना[1] *(palnā)* अ. क्रि. to be brought up; to be nourished; to be reared.

पलना[2] *(palnā)* पु. cradle.

पलस्तर *(palastar)* पु. (अ.) plaster.

पलायन *(palāyan)* पु. fleeing; escape; abscondence.

पलायनवाद *(palāyanvād)* पु. escapism.

पलायनवादी[1] *(palāyanvādī)* वि. pertaining to escapism.

पलायनवादी[2] *(palāyanvādī)* पु. escapist or follower of escapism.

पलाश *(palāś)* पु. kind of tree or its leaves; its purple coloured flowers.

पलीत *(palīt)* वि. wicked; roguish; shabby.

पलीता *(palītā)* पु. wick; igniter; guncotton.

पल्लव *(pallav)* पु. new tender leaf; sprout; shoot.

पल्लवग्राही[1] *(pallav-grāhi)* वि. superficial (in knowledge) smattering.

पल्लवग्राही[2] *(pallav-grāhi)* पु. person with superficial knowledge; amateur; smatterer.

पल्ला *(pallā)* पु. end of garment; end of a saree etc.; piece of cloth; pan of a balance; door panel.

पल्लू *(pallū)* पु. end of a (female garment; broad border.

पल्लेदार *(palledār)* पु. porter; carrier of heavy burden.

पल्लेदारी *(palledārī)* स्त्री. calling of a porter; wages paid for porterage.

पवन *(pavan)* पु. air; breeze; wind.

पवन-चक्की *(pavan-cākki)* स्त्री. windmill.

पवित्र *(pavitr)* वि. sacred; sacrosanct; holy; pure; sinless; free from sensual properties.

पवित्रता *(pavitrātā)* स्त्री. purity; cleanness; sanctity.

पशु *(paśu)* पु. animal; cattle; beast.

पशु-चिकित्सक *(paśu-cīkitsak)* पु. veterinary doctor.

पशु-चिकित्सा *(paśu-cīkitsa)* स्त्री. veterinary science or therapy.

पशुता *(paśutā)* स्त्री. animality; bestiality; beastliness.

पशुधन *(paśu-dhan)* पु. livestock.

पशु-पालन *(paśu-pālan)* पु. cattle-breeding; animal husbandry.

पश्चात् *(paścāt)* क्रि. वि. after; afterwards; behind.

पश्चाताप *(paścātap)* पु. regret; repentance.

पश्चिम *(paścim)* पु. west; occident.

पश्चिमी *(paścimī)* वि. pertaining to west; western; occidental.

पश्चिमोत्तर *(paścmotār)* वि. north-western.

पसंद *(pasand)* स्त्री. (फ़ा.) liking; choice; preference.

पसरना *(pasarnā)* अ. क्रि. to be spread out; to stretch out; to stretch oneself.

पसली *(pasli̅)* स्त्री. rib.

पसाना *(pasānā)* स. क्रि. to remove the scum of (boiling rice); to pour off (the water in which some edible has been boiled).

पसारना *(pasārnā)* स. क्रि. to expand; to spread; to stretch out.

पसीजना *(pasi̅jnā)* अ. क्रि. to perspire; to ooze; to be compassionate.

पसीना *(pasi̅nā)* पु. perspiration; sweat.

पसोपेश *(paso-peś)* पु. hitch; indecision; perplexity; quandary.

पस्त *(past)* वि. (फ़ा.) defeated; weary; completely fatigued and exhausted.

पहचान *(pahcān)* स्त्री. recognition; identity; identification mark.

पहचानना *(pahcānanā)* स. क्रि. to recognise.

पहनना *(pahannā)* स. क्रि. to put on; to wear.

पहनाना *(pahanānā)* स. क्रि. to clothe.

पहनावा *(pahnāvā)* पु. dress; garment; costume.

पहर *(pahr)* पु. measure of time equal to three hours.

पहरा *(pahrā)* पु. guard; watch.

पहरेदार *(pahredar)* पु. watchman; sentry; guard.

पहरेदारी *(pahredari)* स्त्री. watchmanship.

पहल[1] *(pahl)* स्त्री. beginning; commencement; initiative.

पहल[2] *(pahl)* पु. facet.

पहलवान *(pahlvān)* पु. (फ़ा.) wrestler.

पहलवानी *(pahlvāni̅)* स्त्री. (फ़ा.) wrestling.

पहला *(pahlā)* वि. first; primary; former.

पहलू *(pahlū)* पु. (फ़ा.) side; flank; aspect; facet.

पहले *(pahale)* क्रि. वि. in the beginning; before; previously; in olden times.

पहले-पहल *(pahale-pahl)* क्रि. वि. first of all; for the first time.

पहाड़ *(pahāṛ)* पु. mountain.

पहाड़ा *(pahāṛā)* पु. multiplication table.

पहाड़ी[1] *(pahāṛi̅)* वि. pertaining to the hill; hilly; living on or near a mountain; mountainous.

पहाड़ी[2] *(pahāṛi̅)* स्त्री. hillock.

पहिया *(pahiyā)* पु. wheel.

पहुँच *(pahuṁc)* पु. reach; access; arrival; approach.

पहुँचना *(pahuṁcanā)* अ. क्रि. to reach; to arrive.

पहुँचा *(pahuṁcā)* पु. wrist.

पहुँचाना *(pahuṁcāṇā)* स. क्रि. to carry; to convey.

पहुँची *(pahuṁci̅)* स्त्री. wrist ornament.

पहेली *(paheli̅)* स्त्री. puzzle; quiz; riddle.

पांडित्य *(pāṇḍitya)* पु. scholarship; learning.

पांडित्यपूर्ण *(pāṇḍitya-purn)* वि. aureate; scholarly.

पांडुलिपि *(pāṇḍu-lipi)* स्त्री. manuscript.

पाँव *(pāṁv)* पु. foot.

पाई *(pāi̅)* स्त्री. small vertical line used in writing or printing in Devnagri characters; full stop; old copper coin.

पाक[1] *(pāk)* वि. (फ़ा.) holy; sacred; pure; clean.

पाक[2] *(pāk)* पु. cooking; maturation; Pakistan.

पाक-कला *(pāk-kala)* स्त्री. art of cooking; culinary art.

पाकशास्त्र *(pāk-sāstra)* पु. cookery.

पाकेटमार *(pāket-mār)* पु. pickpocket.

पाक्षिक *(pākṣik)* वि. biweekly; fortnightly.

पाखंड *(pākhand)* पु. hypocrisy; simulation; imposture.

पाखंडी[1] *(pākhaṇdī)* पु. hypocrite; dissembler; impostor.

पाखंडी[2] *(pākhaṇdī)* वि. dissembling; hypocritical.

पख़ाना *(pākhānā)* पु. latrine; faeces; human excrement; stool.

पागना *(pāgnā)* स. क्रि. to dip in or coat with syrup.

पागल *(pāgal)* वि. mad; insane; lunatic.

पागलपन *(pāgalpan)* पु. foolishness; madness; lunacy; insanity.

पागलख़ाना *(pāgalkhānā)* पु. lunatic asylum.

पाचक *(pācak)* वि. digestive; causing digestion.

पाचन *(pāchan)* पु. digestion.

पाजामा *(pājāmā)* पु. pyjamas; Indian trousers.

पाजी[1] *(pājī)* वि. mean; wicked; vile; crooked.

पाजी[2] *(pājī)* पु. scoundrel; rascal.

पाटना *(pātnā)* स. क्रि. to cover; to roof; to stock; to heap.

पाठ *(pāṭh)* पु. reading; religious text; lesson; text; recitation; version.

पाठक *(pāṭhak)* पु. reader; pupil; subcaste among Brahmans; reciter; teacher.

पाठदोष *(pāṭh-dōs)* पु. textual error.

पाठन *(pāṭhan)* पु. teaching.

पाठशाला *(pāṭhśāla)* स्त्री. school.

पाठ्य *(pāṭhya)* वि. readable; worth reading; legible.

पाठयक्रम *(pāṭhyakram)* पु. syllabus; course of study; curriculum.

पाणि *(pāṇi)* पु. hand.

पाणिग्रहण *(pāṇigrahan)* पु. marriage; wedding.

पाणिग्रहीत *(pāṇi-grahit)* वि. married.

पात *(pāt)* पु. fall; shedding; collapse; destruction; mode; leaf.

पातक *(pātak)* पु. sin.

पातकी[1] *(pātakī)* वि. sinner; evildoer.

पातकी[2] *(pātakī)* वि. sinful.

पातगोभी *(pāt-gobhi)* स्त्री. cabbage.

पाताल *(pātāl)* पु. underworld; hell; the lower region.

पाती *(pātī)* स्त्री. leaf; dried leaf; letter.

पात्र *(pātr)* पु. utensil; container; character (in a play etc.).

पात्रता *(pātratā)* स्त्री. eligibility.

पाथेय *(pātheya)* पु. provisions for a journey.

पाद *(pād)* पु. foot or leg; quarter; fourth part; a verse of line; fart.

पाद-टिप्पणी *(pād-tippāni)* स्त्री. foot note.

पादप *(pādap)* पु. tree.

पाद-प्रहार *(pād-prahār)* पु. kick.

पादरी *(pādrī)* पु. Christian missionary; clergy; priest; vicar.

पादाघात *(pāda-ghāt)* वि. kick.

पादुका *(pādukā)* स्त्री. wooden shoe (sandal); shoe.

पान[1] *(pān)* पु. drinking; drinking

spirituous liquors; drink; beverage.

पान² *(pān)* पु. betel-leaf.

पानगोष्ठी *(pāngosthi)* स्त्री. cocktail.

पाना¹ *(pānā)* स. क्रि. to get; to acquire; to obtain; to receive; to attain; to achieve.

पाना² *(pānā)* पु. spanner.

पानी *(pānī)* स्त्री. water; acqua.

पानीदार *(pānīdār)* वि. lustrous; respectable; honourable.

पाप *(pāp)* पु. sin; vice; evil.

पापकर्म *(pāpkarm)* पु. sin; sinful deed.

पापड़ *(pāpaṛ)* पु. thin crisp cake made of ground pulses.

पापाचार *(pāpācār)* पु. sinful conduct.

पापाचारी *(pāpācārī)* पु. sinner.

पापात्मा *(pāpātma)* वि. sinful; unholy.

पापी¹ *(pāpī)* पु. sinner.

पापी² *(pāpī)* वि. sinful; immoral.

पाबंद *(pāband)* वि. (फ़ा.) tied; fettered; habituated; to; accustomed.

पाबंदी *(pābandī)* स्त्री. (फ़ा.) restriction; control; ban; binding; obligation.

पामर¹ *(pāmar)* वि. low; wicked; crooked; mean; sinful.

पामर² *(pāmar)* पु. rascal; knave; scoundrel.

पायँ *(pāyaṁ)* पु. foot.

पायँचा *(pāyaṁcā)* पु. one of the two legs of pyjama or pants.

पायजामा *(pāijāma)* see पाजामा।

पायदान *(pāydān)* पु. foot-board; door-mat.

पायदार *(pāydār)* वि. (फ़ा.) durable; lasting.

पायदारी *(pāydarī)* स्त्री. (फ़ा.) durability.

पायल *(pāyal)* स्त्री. anklet; ankle ornament.

पाया *(pāyā)* पु. (फ़ा.) leg of a piece of furniture; pillar post; prop; support.

पारंगत *(pāramgat)* वि. expert; wellversed; well conversant.

पारंपरिक *(pāramparik)* वि. traditional; conventional.

पार *(pār)* पु. (opposite) bank; shore etc.; across.

पारखी *(pārakhī)* पु. connoisseur.

पारगमन *(pārgaman)* पु. going across; transit.

पारगामी *(pārgāmī)* वि. pervasive; pervading; going across.

पारद *(pārad)* पु. mercury.

पारदर्शक *(pārdarsak)* वि. transparent.

पारदर्शकता, पारदर्शिता *(pārdarśita)* स्त्री. transparency.

पारदर्शी *(pārdarśī)* वि. transparent.

पारपत्र *(pārpatra)* पु. passport.

पारमार्थिक *(pāramārthik)* वि. relating to a high and spiritual object; spiritual; charitable; transcendental; ultra-mundane.

पारलौकिक *(pārlaukik)* वि. relating to the next world; transcendental; ultra-mundane.

पारस *(pāras)* पु. philosopher's stone; touchstone; an object of unusual merits.

पारसाल *(pārsāl)* पु. last year.

पारस्परिक *(pārasparik)* वि. mutual; reciprocal.

पारस्परिकता *(pārasparikatā)* स्त्री. reciprocity; mutuality.

पारा *(pārā)* पु. mercury.

पारायण *(pārâyan)* पु. perusal of a

religious book; thorough reading.

पारावार *(pārâvar)* पु. sea; ocean; bank; limit.

पारित *(pārit)* वि. passed.

पारितोषिक *(pāritoṣik)* पु. reward (in terms of money); prize.

पारिभाषिक *(pāribhāṣik)* स्त्री. pertaining to definition; technical.

पारिभाषिकी *(pāribhāṣikī)* स्त्री. terminology.

पारिवारिक *(pārivārik)* वि. pertaining to a family; domestic.

पारिवारिकता *(pārivārikata)* स्त्री. family feeling; domesticity.

पारिश्रमिक *(pāriśramik)* पु. remuneration.

पारिस्थितिक *(pāristhitik)* वि. ecological; circumstantial.

पारिस्थितिकी *(pāristhitikī)* स्त्री. ecology.

पारी *(pārī)* स्त्री. turn; shift; innings.

पार्थक्य *(pārthakya)* पु. separation; difference; separateness; isolation.

पार्थक्यवाद *(pārthakyavād)* पु. separatism.

पार्थक्यवादी *(pārthakyavādī)* पु. separatist.

पार्थिव *(pārthiv)* पु. relating to earth; springing or derived from the earth; earthen; earthly.

पार्श्व *(pārśva)* पु. armpit; side; part of the body below the armpit; wing; flank; back.

पार्श्वगायक *(pārśva-gāyak)* पु. play back singer.

पार्श्वसंगीत *(pārśva-sāngit)* पु. background music.

पार्षद *(pārṣad)* पु. member of an assembly; retinue (of a god); concillor.

पालक *(pālak)* पु. protector; foster parent.

पालकी *(pālki)* स्त्री. palanquin.

पालतू *(pāltū)* वि. domesticated; tame; pet.

पालथी *(pālthī)* स्त्री. cross-legged sitting posture; squatting posture.

पालन *(pālan)* पु. upbringing; compliance; observance; protection.

पालन-पोषण *(pālan-poshān)* पु. upbringing nurture; fostering.

पालना[1] *(pālnā)* स. क्रि. to bring up; to rear; to observe; to comply; to tame; to domesticate; to keep (vow).

पालना[2] *(pālnā)* पु. cradle; crib.

पाला *(pālā)* पु. frest; opportunity (in dealing with); line of demarcation (in kabaddi etc.).

पावक *(pāvak)* पु. fire; the Sun; god of fire; god Varuna.

पावती *(pāvatī)* स्त्री. receipt.

पावन *(pāvan)* वि. holy; sacred; immaculate; pure.

पावनता *(pāvantā)* वि. holiness; sanctity; immaculation; purification; purity.

पावस *(pāvas)* स्त्री. rainy season.

पाश *(pāś)* स्त्री. tie; bond; chain; fetter; trap or net; noose; snare; lock.

पाशविक *(pāśavik)* वि. brutal; beastlike; beastly.

पाशविकता *(pāśviktā)* स्त्री. brutality; bararianism; barbarousness.

पाश्चात्य *(pāścātya)* वि. belonging to west; western; occidental; hinder; posterior; later.

पाषाण *(pāṣān)* पु. stone.

पासंग *(pāsaṅg)* पु. (फ़ा.) counterweight; make-weight.

पास *(pās)* क्रि. वि. near; nearby; at hand.

पासा *(pāsā)* पु. dice.

पाहुना *(pāhunā)* पु. guest; son-in-law.

पिंगल *(piṅgal)* पु. prosody.

पिंगलशास्त्र *(piṅgal-sāstra)* पु. science of prosody.

पिंजर *(piñjar)* पु. skeleton; physical frame.

पिंजरा *(piñjrā)* पु. cage.

पिंड *(piṇḍ)* पु. clod; lump; ball of rice of flour offered to the spirits of deceased ancestors.

पिंडली *(piṇḍlī)* स्त्री. calf of the leg.

पिंडी *(piṇḍī)* स्त्री. small lump; small round mass of anything; round skein of thread; crook.

पिक *(pik)* पु. cuckoo.

पिघलना *(pighalnā)* अ. क्रि. to melt; to be liquefied; to show pity; to be moved by emotion; to thaw.

पिघलाना *(pighalānā)* स. क्रि. to melt; to soften; to cause to move.

पिचकना *(picaknā)* अ. क्रि. to shrivel; to be squeezed; to subside; to deflate; to sag.

पिचकाना *(picakānā)* स. क्रि. to cause to sink or go down; to reduce the swelling of; to cause to deflate or shrink.

पिचकारी *(picakārī)* स्त्री. syringe; spray gun.

पिछड़ना *(picharṇā)* अ. क्रि. to lag behind.

पिछड़ा *(picharā)* वि. backward.

पिछड़ापन *(pacharāpan)* पु. backwardness.

पिछलगा *(pachalagā)* पु. follower; dependent; lackey.

पिछवाड़ा *(pichvārā)* पु. backyard; rear; hind part.

पिटना *(piṭnā)* अ. क्रि. to be defeat; to be beaten.

पिटाई *(pitāī)* स्त्री. act of beating; wages for beating or thrashing; good beating; defeat.

पिटारा *(pitārā)* पु. large basket; big chest or box.

पिता *(pitā)* पु. father; originator.

पितामह *(pitāmah)* पु. paternal grandfather.

पितामही *(pitāmahī)* स्त्री. paternal grand-mother.

पितृघात *(pitṛghāt)* पु. patricide.

पितृघाती *(pitṛghātī)* पु. patricide.

पितृत्व *(pitṛtva)* पु. fatherhood; paternity.

पित्ता *(pittā)* पु. gall bladder.

पित्ताशय *(pittāśaya)* पु. gall-bladder.

पित्ती *(pittī)* स्त्री. urticaria; skin rash.

पिद्दी *(piddī)* स्त्री. brown-backed Indian robin; insignificant creature.

पिनक *(pinak)* स्त्री. opium-induced; drowsiness; intoxicated state.

पिपासा *(pipāsā)* स्त्री. thirst; desire; greed; yearning; craving.

पिपासित, पिपासु *(pipāsu)* वि. thirsty; possessed of a yearning or craving.

पिपीलिका *(pipīlikā)* स्त्री. ant.

पियक्कड़ *(piyakkar)* पु. drunkard.

पिया *(piyā)* पु. husband.

पिरोना *(pironā)* स. क्रि. to thread; to string.

पिलपिला *(pilpilā)* वि. flabby flaccid; soft; pulpy.

पिलाना *(pilānā)* स. क्रि. to cause to drink; to put through; to fill through.

पिल्ला *(pillā)* पु. pup; puppy.

पिशाच *(piśāc)* पु. devil; hell-hound; demon; malevolent spirit.

पिष्टपेषण *(pisṭ-pesān)* पु. useless labour; repetition.

पिसना *(pisnā)* अ. क्रि. to be ground (powdered); crushing.

पिसवाना *(pisvānā)* स. क्रि. to cause to be ground or powdered.

पिसाई *(pisāī)* स्त्री. grinding; grinding charges.

पिस्ता *(pistā)* पु. pistachio nut.

पिस्तौल *(pistaul)* स्त्री. pistol.

पिस्सू *(pissū)* पु. flea.

पीक *(pīk)* स्त्री. spittle of chewed betel-leaf.

पीकदान *(pīkdān)* पु. cuspidor; spittoon.

पीछा *(pīchā)* पु. rear; back part; pursuit; chase.

पीछे *(pīche)* क्रि. वि. behind; on the backside; after; afterwards.

पीटना *(pītnā)* स. क्रि. to beat; to thrash; to defeat; to knock; to dash; to bang.

पीठ[1] *(pīth)* पु. seat made of wood; steel; etc.; seat; stand; base; bench.

पीठ[2] *(pīṭh)* स्त्री. back; upper portion; back part.

पीड़न *(pīṛan)* पु. oppression; torment.

पीड़ा *(pīṛā)* स्त्री. pain; ache; agony; tribulation.

पीड़ित *(pīṛit)* वि. pained; oppressed; afflicted; distressed.

पीढ़ा *(pīṛhā)* पु. low stool; pedestal.

पीढ़ी *(pīṛhi)* स्त्री. generation; small wooden seat.

पीत[1] *(pīt)* स्त्री. yellow; pale.

पीत[2] *(pīt)* स्त्री. yellow colour; topaz; sulphur.

पीतता *(pītatā)* स्त्री. yellowness; pallor.

पीतल *(pītal)* पु. brass.

पीताश्म *(pītaśm)* पु. topaz.

पीना *(pīnā)* स. क्रि. to sip; to drink; to tolerate; endure.

पीप *(pīp)* स्त्री. pus.

पीपल *(pīpal)* स्त्री. an Indian creeper and its fruit used in medicine.

पीपा *(pīpā)* पु. can; canister; tin; cask; barrel; drum; pontoon.

पीर[1] *(pīr)* स्त्री. (फ़ा.) spiritual guide; Muslims' saint.

पीर[2] *(pīr)* स्त्री. pain; affliction.

पीलवान *(pīlvān)* पु. elephant driver.

पीला *(pīlā)* वि. yellow; pale; pallid.

पीलापन *(pīlāpan)* पु. yellowness.

पीलिया *(pīliyā)* पु. jaundice.

पीसना *(pīsnā)* स. क्रि. to powder; to grind; to gnaw (teeth) .

पीहर *(pīhar)* पु. married woman's parental house.

पुंज *(puñj)* पु. heap; accumulation; collection; bulk.

पुंस्त्व *(puṃsatva)* पु. masculinity; manhood; virility.

पुआ *(puā)* पु. a kind of sweet flourcake.

पुआल *(puāl)* पु. paddy-straw.

पुकार *(pukār)* स्त्री. call; cry; petition; roll-call.

पुकारना *(pukārnā)* स. क्रि. to call; to cry out; to call for help; to proclaim.

पुखराज़ *(pukhrāj)* पु. topaz.

पुख़्ता *(pukhtā)* वि. (फ़ा.) strong; solid; firm; lasting; mature; expert.

पुचकारना *(pucakārnā)* स. क्रि. to fondle; to caress.

पुच्छल *(pucchal)* वि. tailed; having a tail.

पुच्छलतारा *(pucchal-tārā)* पु. comet; meteor.

पुजारी *(pujārī)* पु. worshipper; adorer; priest.

पुट *(puṭ)* पु. plating; slight mixture; seasoning; light touch.

पुट्ठा *(puṭṭhā)* पु. hip; rump; back portion of binding of a book.

पुड़िया *(puṛiyā)* स्त्री. small paper packet.

पुण्य *(puṇya)* पु. virtuous action; good deed; fruit or reward of virtue; virtue; religious merit.

पुण्यात्मा[1] *(puṇyātmā)* वि. puresouled; righteous; virtuous.

पुण्यात्मा[2] *(puṇyātmā)* पु. righteous person.

पुतला *(piutlā)* पु. effigy.

पुतली *(piutlī)* स्त्री. pupil of the eye. puppet; doll.

पुताई *(putāī)* स्त्री. white-wash; white-washing.

पुत्र *(putr)* पु. son.

पुत्रवती *(putrvati)* स्त्री. a woman blessed with a son.

पुत्रवधू *(putrvadhu)* स्त्री. daughter-in-law.

पुत्री *(putrī)* स्त्री. daughter.

पुदीना *(pudīnā)* पु. mint.

पुनः *(punaḥ)* क्रि. वि. again; oncemore.

पुनः स्थापन *(punaḥ-sthāpna)* पु. reinstatement; resettlement; restoration; re-establishment.

पुनरागम, पुनरागमन *(punara-gaman)* पु. coming again; return; reoccurrence.

पुनरावर्तन *(punarā-vartan)* पु. recapituation; relapse; recrudescence; repetition.

पुनरावर्ती *(punarā-varti)* वि. repetitive; returning; recurrent.

पुनरावलोकन *(punarā-vlokan)* पु.revision; reperusal; retrospection.

पुनरावृत्ति *(punarā-vriti)* स्त्री. repetition; return; recapitulation; circumlocution.

पुनरीक्षक *(punaraikshak)* पु. reviewer.

पुनरीक्षण *(punarikshan)* पु. review; revision.

पुनरुक्त *(punarukt)* वि. repeated; retold; reiterated.

पुनरुक्ति *(punarokti)* स्त्री. repetition; tautology.

पुनरुज्जीवन *(punarujjivan)* पु. resurrection; resuscitation; revival; regeneration.

पुनरुत्थान *(punar-uthan)* पु. renaissance; revival; resurgence; resurrection.

पुनरुत्पादन *(punar-utpadan)* पु. reproduction.

पुनरुद्धार *(punar-udhar)* पु. restoration; renovation; revival.

पुनर्गठन *(punar-gathan)* पु. reorganisation.

पुनर्जनन *(punar-jānan)* पु. regeneration; reproduction.

पुनर्जन्म *(punar-janma)* पु. rebirth; reincarnation.

पुनर्जागरण *(punar-jāgaran)* पु. renaissance; reawakening.

पुनर्गिमन *(punar-giman)* पु. re-issue; re-emergence.

पुनर्निमाण *(punar-nirmān)* पु. reconstruction.

पुनर्निर्वाचन *(punar-nirvācān)* पु. reelection.

पुनर्परीक्षण *(punar-parikshan)* पु. re-examination; retrial.

पुनर्मिलन *(punar-milan)* पु. re-union.

पुनर्मुद्रण *(punar-mudran)* पु. re-impression; re-print.

पुनर्वास *(punar-vās)* पु. re-habilitation.

पुनर्विचार *(punar-vicār)* पु. re-consideration; revision.

पुनर्वितरण *(punar-vitaran)* पु. redistribution.

पुनर्व्यवस्था *(punar-vyasthā)* स्त्री. reorganisation.

पुनर्स्थापना *(punar-sthāpan)* पु. replacement; re-installation.

पुनि *(puni)* क्रि. वि. again.

पुनीत *(punīt)* वि. pure; holy; sacred; pious.

पुर *(pur)* पु. town; city.

पुरखा *(purkhā)* पु. ancestor; forefather.

पुरजन *(purjan)* पु. inhabitants of a town.

पुरज़ा *(purzā)* पु. (फ़ा.) scarp (of paper); piece; bit; chit; component; part of machine; prescription.

पुरस्कार *(puraskār)* पु. prize; award; reward.

पुरस्कृत *(puraskrit)* वि. rewarded.

पुराण *(purān)* पु. Hindu mythology.

पुरातन *(purā-tan)* वि. ancient; archaic; antique.

पुराना *(purānā)* वि. old; ancient; worn out; experienced; out-of date; old-fashioned.

पुरालेख *(purā-lekh)* पु. epigraph.

पुरालेख विद्या *(purā-lekh-vidyā)* स्त्री. epigraphy.

पुरालेखागार *(purā-lekhāgār)* पु. archives.

पुरालेखी *(purā-lekhī)* वि. archival.

पुरी *(puri)* स्त्री. city; town.

पुरुष *(puruṣ)* पु. man; person (in grammar).

पुरुषत्व *(puruśatva)* पु. manhood; manliness; valour; masculinity.

पुरुषार्थ *(puruśarth)* पु. (human) effort or exertion.

पुरुषार्थी *(puruśarthī)* वि. industrious; painstaking; laborious.

पुरोहित *(purohit)* पु. Hindu-priest; pastor.

पुल *(pul)* पु. bridge.

पुलकन *(pulakan)* पु. titillation.

पुलकना *(pulaknā)* अ. क्रि. to experience a thrill of joy; to be delighted.

पुलकित *(pulākit)* वि. having the hair of the body erect; thrilled with joy.

पुलाव *(pulāv)* पु. spiced rice preparation.

पुलिंदा *(pulindā)* पु. bundle; sheaf; packet.

पुल्लिंग *(pulliṇg)* पु. masculine gender.

पुश्त *(puśt)* स्त्री. (फ़ा.) generation; back; back portion.

पुश्ता *(puśtā)* पु. (फ़ा.) embankment; buttress.

पुश्तैनी *(puśtainī)* वि. ancestral; hereditary.

पुष्ट *(pusṭ)* वि. nourished; strong; robust; sturdy; confirmed; well-built.

पुष्टिता *(pusṭatā)* स्त्री. confirmation; strength.

पुष्टि *(pùsṭi)* स्त्री. confirmation; affirmation.

पुष्टिकारक *(puṣṭikārāk)* वि. nutritious.

पुष्टीकरण *(puṣṭīkaraṇ)* पु. confirmation.
पुष्प *(puṣp)* पु. flower.
पुष्पराग *(pusprāg)* पु. topaz.
पुष्पांजलि *(puspānjali)* स्त्री. floral tribute.
पुष्पित *(puspit)* वि. bearing flowers flowered; luxuriant.
पुस्तक *(puṣtak)* स्त्री. book.
पुस्तकाध्यक्ष *(puṣtaka-dhyaksh)* पु. librarian
पुस्तकालय *(puṣtakālay)* पु. library.
पुस्तिका *(pustikā)* स्त्री. booklet; handbook.
पुस्तकीय *(pustakīya)* वि. pertaining to a book; found in the books; bookish.
पुहुप *(puhup)* पु. flower.
पूँछ *(pūṁch)* स्त्री. tail; back portion.
पूँजी *(pūṁji)* स्त्री. capital; assets; wealth.
पूँजीकरण *(pūṁjikaraṇ)* पु. capitalization.
पूँजीपति *(pūnjipati)* पु. capitalist.
पूँजीवाद *(pūnjivād)* पु. capitalism.
पूँजीवादी[1] *(pūnjivādī)* वि. capitalistic.
पूँजीवादी[2] *(pūnjivādī)* पु. one who believes in capitalism; follower of capitalism.
पूआ *(pūā)* पु. sweet fried small cake.
पूछ *(pūch)* स्त्री. inquiry; value; importance; respect.
पूछगछ, पूछताछ *(pūchtāch)* स्त्री. investigation; enquiry.
पूछना *(pūchnā)* स. क्रि. to enquire; to question; to interrogate; to respect.
पूजक *(pūjak)* पु. worshipper; votary; adorer; devotee.
पूजन *(pūjan)* पु. worship.
पूजना *(pūjanā)* वि. to worship; to adore.
पूजनीय *(pūjanīya)* वि. venerable; honourable; adorable.
पूजा *(pūjā)* स्त्री. worship; veneration; adoration; honour.
पूज्य *(pūjya)* वि. venerable; adorable, deserving honour.
पूत *(pūt)* पु. son.
पूरक[1] *(pūrak)* पु. supplement.
पूरक[2] *(pūrak)* वि. supplementary; complementary.
पूरब *(pūrab)* पु. seat.
पूरबी *(pūrabī)* वि. eastern.
पूरा *(pūrā)* वि. full; whole; all; entire; complete; fulfilled; thorough.
पूरित *(pūrit)* वि. filled; completed.
पूर्ण *(pūrṇ)* वि. full; filled; complete; all; entire; perfect.
पूर्णता *(pūrṇatā)* स्त्री. fullness; absoluteness; perfection.
पूर्णमासी *(pūrṇmasī)* see. पूर्णिमा
पूर्णविराम *(pūraṇ-virām)* पु. full stop.
पूर्णिमा *(pūrṇimā)* स्त्री. day of full moon.
पूर्ति *(pūrti)* स्त्री. fulfilment; filling up; supply.
पूर्व[1] *(pūrv)* वि. first; previous; former; foregoing.
पूर्व[2] *(pūrv)* पु. east.
पूर्व[3] *(pūrv)* क्रि. वि. before; beforehand.
पूर्वज *(pūrvaj)* पु. ancestor; forefather; predecessor.
पूर्वदिनांकन *(pūrv-dināṁkan)* पु. antedating.
पूर्वदिनांकित *(pūrv-dināṁkit)* वि. antedated.
पूर्वनिर्धारण *(pūrv-nirdhāran)* पु. pre-

determination.

पूर्वनिर्धारित *(pūrv-nirdhārit)* वि. predetermined.

पूर्ववत् *(pūrv-vat)* क्रि. वि. as before.

पूववर्ती[1] *(pūrv-varti)* वि. existing before; preceding; foregoing.

पूर्ववर्ती[2] *(pūrv-varti)* पु. antecedent; predecessor.

पूर्वानुमान *(pūrvānumān)* पु. forecast; prognosis; anticipation.

पूर्वापेक्षा *(pūrvāpeksā)* स्त्री. pre-requisite.

पूर्वाभास *(pūrvāsbhās)* स्त्री. prolepsis; aura; anticipation; fore-shadowing; presage; premonition; foreboding.

पूर्वाभिनय *(pūrvābhinaya)* पु. rehearsal.

पूर्वाभ्यास *(pūrv-bhyās)* स्त्री. rehearsal.

पूर्वार्द्ध, पूर्वार्ध *(pūrv-ārdh)* पु. first half.

पूर्वाह्न *(pūrvāhān)* पु. forenoon.

पूला *(pūlā)* पु. small bundle of grass or straw; sheaf.

पूस *(pūs)* पु. tenth month of Indian calendar.

पृथक् *(pṛthak)* वि. separate; different.

पृथक्करण *(prthakkarān)* पु. separation; severance; isolation; segregation.

पृथक्ता *(pṛthakatā)* पु. state or quality of being different; separateness; aloofness.

पृथक्तावाद *(pṛthaktāvad)* पु. isolationism; separatism.

पृथ्वी *(pṛthvī)* स्त्री. world; earth.

पृथ्वीलोक *(pṛthvīlok)* पु. the mortal world.

पृष्ठ *(pṛṣṭh)* पु. back; hinder part; upper side; outer surface; page.

पृष्ठभूमि *(pṛṣth-bhūmi)* स्त्री. background.

पृष्ठांकन *(pṛsthānkan)* पु. endorsement.

पृष्ठांकित *(pṛṣṭhānkit)* वि. endorsed.

पेंदा *(peṁdā)* पु. base; bottom.

पेंदी *(peṁdī)* स्त्री. bottom; anus; root or carrot or radish.

पेच *(pec)* पु. (फ़ा.) screw; trick (in wrestling); turn; winding; complication; intricacy; part of a machine.

पेचकस *(peckas)* पु. (फ़ा.) screw driver.

पेचिश *(peciś)* स्त्री. (फ़ा.) dysentery.

पेचीदगी *(pecīdagī)* स्त्री. complication; intricacy; complexity.

पेचीदा *(pecīdā)* वि. (फ़ा.) complicated; intricate.

पेट *(peṭ)* पु. belly; stomach; abdomen.

पेटी *(peṭī)* स्त्री. small box or chest; belt; girdle.

पेटू[1] *(peṭū)* वि. gluttonous.

पेटू[2] *(peṭū)* पु. glutton; gourmand.

पेटूपन *(peṭūpan)* पु. gluttony.

पेठा *(peṭhā)* पु. white gourd; kind of sweetmeat prepared of (white) gourd.

पेड़ *(peṛ)* पु. tree.

पेड़ू *(peṛū)* पु. part of the body lying between the navel and the pubic region.

पेय *(pey)* वि. drinkable; potable.

पेरना *(pernā)* स. क्रि. to crush; to torment; to exploit.

पेलना *(pelnā)* स. क्रि. to thrust in; to penetrate; to impel.

पेश *(peś)* वि. presented; forwarded.

पेशकश *(peśkaś)* स्त्री. (फ़ा.) proposal; request.

पेशकार *(peśakar)* पु. (फ़ा.) court clerk.

पेशगी *(peśagī)* स्त्री. (फ़ा.) advance; earnest money.

पेशबंदी *(peśabandī)* स्त्री. (फ़ा.) forestalling; anticipation; arrangement.

पेशा *(peśā)* पु. (फ़ा.) occupation; trade; profession; vocation; calling.

पेशानी *(peśānī)* स्त्री. (फ़ा.) forehead.

पेशाब *(peśāb)* पु. (फ़ा.) urine.

पेशाबख़ाना, पेशाबघर *(peśab-ghar)* पु. (फ़ा.) urinal.

पेशी[1] *(peśī)* स्त्री. (फ़ा.) hearing of law suit.

पेशी[2] *(peśī)* स्त्री. muscle.

पेशेवर *(peśevar)* वि. (फ़ा.) professional.

पेषक *(peśāk)* पु. grinder.

पेषण *(peśan)* पु. pulverisation; grinding; milling.

पैंठ *(paiṁṭh)* स्त्री. periodical market; marketing day.

पैकर *(paikar)* पु. (फ़ा.) retailer.

पैग़ंबर *(paigambar)* पु. (फ़ा.) prophet.

पैग़ाम *(paigām)* पु. (फ़ा.) message.

पैठ *(paiṭh)* स्त्री. access; reach; insight.

पैठना *(paiṭhanā)* अ. क्रि. to have access; to enter.

पैतरा *(paitrā)* पु. wrestling trick; stratagem; tactics; manoeuvre.

पैतरेबाज *(paitrebāz)* पु. person who knows the way of wrestling or using the arms; strategist; dodger.

पैतृक *(paitṛk)* वि. paternal; ancestral; hereditary; parental.

पैदल[1] *(paidal)* पु. footman; infantryman; pedestrain; chessman; pawn.

पैदल[2] *(paidal)* वि. pedestrian.

पैदल[3] *(paidal)* क्रि. वि. on foot.

पैदा *(paidā)* वि (फ़ा.) born; created; produced; grown; earned.

पैदाइश *(paidāiś)* स्त्री (फ़ा.) birth; production.

पैदाइशी *(paidāiśī)* वि. inborn; natural.

पैदावार *(paidāvār)* स्त्री. yield; production.

पैना *(painā)* वि. sharp; pointed; keen.

पैमाइश *(paimāiś)* स्त्री. (फ़ा.) measurement; survey (of land).

पैमाना *(paimānā)* पु. (फ़ा.) scale; measure; peg (for drinking liquor).

पैर *(pair)* पु. foot; foot-mark; footprint; threshing floor; barn.

पैरवी *(pairavī)* स्त्री. (फ़ा.) pursuit; advocacy.

पैबंद *(paiband)* पु. patch.

पैशाचिक *(paiśacik)* वि. fiendish; demonic.

पैसा *(paisā)* पु. paisa; money; wealth.

पोंगा[1] *(poṁgā)* वि. stupid; foolish.

पोंगा[2] *(poṁgā)* पु. simpleton.

पोंगापंथी[1] *(poṁgā-panthī)* स्त्री. idiocy; stupidity.

पोंगापंथी[2] *(poṁgā-panthī)* वि. foolish; stupid.

पोंछना[1] *(poṁchanā)* स. क्रि. to wipe; to cleanse; to rub out; to efface.

पोंछना[2] *(poṁchanā)* पु. duster; wiper.

पोत *(pot)* पु. ship; boat.

पोतना *(potanā)* स. क्रि. to whitewash; to smear; to coat.

पोतभार *(potbhār)* पु. cargo.

पोतवाह *(potvāh)* वि. sailor.

पोता *(potā)* पु. grandson; rent; revenue; testicle; daubing cloth or brush.

पोती *(poti)* स्त्री. grand-daughter.

पोथा *(pothā)* पु. voluminous book.

पोथी *(pothī)* स्त्री. book; booklet.

पोदीना *(podīnā) see* पुदीना

पोपला *(poplā)* वि. empty; toothless; shrivelled.

पोल *(pol)* स्त्री. emptiness; hollowness; illusion.

पोला *(polā)* वि. empty; soft; flabby; hollow.

पोशाक *(pośāk)* स्त्री. (फ़ा.) dress; uniform apparel; attire; costume.

पोशीदगी *(pośīdagī)* स्त्री. secrecy; privacy.

पोशीदा *(pośīdā)* वि. (फ़ा.) secret; hidden concealed.

पोषक[1] *(poṣak)* पु. one who feeds or nourishes.

पोषक[2] *(poṣak)* वि. nourishing; nutritive.

पोषण *(poṣan)* पु. bringing up; rearing; fostering; support; protection; nutrition; nourishment.

पोषित *(poṣit)* वि. supported; reared; brought up; nourished.

पोस्त *(post)* पु. (फ़ा.) poppy plant; poppy seed; skin; hide.

पौ *(pau)* स्त्री. early dawn.

पौआ *(pauā)* पु. quarter of a seer; quarter measure; bottle of liquor; support; backing.

पौत्र *(pautr)* पु. grand-son.

पौत्री *(pautri)* स्त्री. grand-daughter.

पौद *(paud)* स्त्री. seedling; sapling; young plant; generation.

पौदघर *(paudghar)* स्त्री. nursery.

पौधा *(paudhā)* पु. young plant; sapling.

पौर *(paur)* पु. citizen; municipal councillor; outer verandah in a house.

पौराणिक *(paurāṇik)* वि. mythological.

पौरुष *(pauruṣ)* पु. heroism; valour; manliness; masculinity; virility.

पौष्टिक *(pauṣṭik)* वि. nutritive; nutritious; restorative; alimentary.

पौष्टिकता *(paustikatā)* स्त्री. nutritiveness; nourishment.

प्याऊ *(pyāū)* स्त्री. water-booth; free water-kiosk.

प्याज़ *(pyāz)* पु. (फ़ा.) onion.

प्यादा *(pyādā)* पु. (फ़ा.) foot-soldier; footman; pedestrian; pawn (in chess).

प्यार *(pyār)* पु. love; affection; amour.

प्यारी *(pyārī)* वि. dear; beloved; lovely; pleasing.

प्याला *(pyālā)* पु. (फ़ा.) cup.

प्याली *(pyālī)* स्त्री. small cup.

प्यास *(pyās)* स्त्री. thirst; longing; craving; greed.

प्यासा *(pyāsā)* वि. thirsty.

प्रकंप *(pra-kamp)* पु. vibration; quivering; trembling.

प्रकंपित *(pra-kampit)* वि. vibrated; quivered; trembled; shivered.

प्रकट *(pra-kat)* वि. manifest; apparent; revealed; obvious; evident; ostensible.

प्रकरण *(pra-karan)* पु. context; chapter; episode; topic; case.

प्रकल्पना *(pra-kalpanā)* स्त्री. presumption; supposition; hypothesis.

प्रकांड *(pra-kānd)* वि. outstanding; eminent; profound.

प्रकार *(pra-kār)* वि. description; manner; way; method; kind; type.

प्रकारांतर *(pra-kārāntar)* पु. different method or manner.

प्रकाश *(pra-kāś)* पु. light.

प्रकाशक *(pra-kāśak)* पु. illuminator; publisher.

प्रकाशन *(pra-kāśan)* पु. publication.

प्रकाश-स्तंभ *(pra-kāś-stamb)* पु. lighthouse.

प्रकाशित *(pra-kāśit)* वि. lighted; illumined; revealed; published.

प्रकीर्ण *(pra-kirṇ)* वि. spread out; scattered; dispersed; miscellaneous.

प्रकृति *(pra-kṛti)* स्त्री. temperament; disposition; nature.

प्रकृतिस्थ *(pra-kṛtisth)* वि. composed; normal; calm and cool; natural.

प्रकोप *(pra-kop)* पु. wrath; rage; fury; epidemic; attack.

प्रकोष्ठ *(pra-kostha)* पु. fore-arm; part above the wrist; courtyard; room near the gate of a palace; lobby; chamber.

प्रक्रिया *(par-kriyā)* स्त्री. process; procedure.

प्रक्षालन *(pra-kṣālan)* पु. washing up.

प्रक्षालि्त *(pra-kṣālit)* वि. washed; cleansed; bleached.

प्रक्षेप *(pra-kṣep)* पु. throwing; casting; interpolation; projection.

प्रक्षेपक *(pra-kṣepak)* पु. projector.

प्रक्षेपण *(pra-kṣepaṇ)* पु. throw; hurling; projection.

प्रखर *(pra-khar)* वि. sharp; acute; fierce.

प्रखरता *(pra-kharatā)* स्त्री. sharpness; acuteness.

प्रख्यात *(pra-khyāt)* वि. famous; reputed; eminent; renowned.

प्रगति *(pra-gati)* स्त्री. progress; advancement; development.

प्रगतिवाद *(pra-gati-vād)* पु. progressivism.

प्रगतिवादी *(pra-gati-vādi)* पु. progressivist.

प्रगतिशील *(pra-gatiśila)* वि. progressive.

प्रगाढ़ *(pra-gāṛh)* वि. dense; thick; profound; deep.

प्रगाढ़ता *(pra-gāṛhatā)* स्त्री. profundity; denseness.

प्रगति *(pra-gati)* पु. lyrical song; lyric.

प्रगीतिकार *(pria-gitikar)* पु. lyrist; lyricist.

प्रचंड *(pra-caṇḍ)* वि. excessively violent; furious.

प्रचंडता *(pra-caṇdatā)* स्त्री. violence; furiousness; fierceness; passionateness; virulence.

प्रचलन *(pra-calan)* पु. custom; usage; currency.

प्रचलित *(pra-calit)* वि. in usage; current; in force.

प्रचार *(par-cār)* पु. prevalence; currency; propaganda; publicity.

प्रचारक *(pra-cārak)* पु. propagator; propagandist.

प्रचुर *(pracur)* वि. abundant; plentiful; copious; ample.

प्रचुरता *(pracuratā)* स्त्री. abundance; plenty; ampleness; copiousness.

प्रच्छन्न *(pra-chann)* वि. covered; hidden; disguised; covert; latent.

प्रच्छन्नता *(pra-chanata)* स्त्री. covertness; concealment; latency; stealthiness; secrecy.

प्रजनन *(pra-janan)* पु. reproduction; bringing forth; breeding.

प्रजा *(pra-jā)* स्त्री. subjects; public.

प्रजातंत्र *(pra-jātaṇtr)* पु. democracy.

प्रजातांत्रिक *(pra-jāntāntrik)* वि. democratic.

प्रजाति *(pra-jātī)* स्त्री. race.

प्रजातीय *(pra-jātya)* वि. racial.

प्रज्ञ *(pra-jña)* वि. wise; intelligent; learned.

प्रज्ञता *(pra-jñatā)* स्त्री. wisdom; intelligence; learning.

प्रज्ञा *(pra-jñā)* स्त्री. intelligence; discrimination; understanding.

प्रज्ञावान् *(pra-jñāvān)* वि. highly intelligent; intellectual.

प्रज्वलन *(pra-jvalan)* पु. ignition; setting on fire; burning; blazing.

प्रज्वलित *(pra-jvalit)* वि. burning; flaming; ignited; burnt; blazed; bright; shining.

प्रण *(praṇ)* पु. determination; pledge; vow; resolution.

प्रणय *(pra-ṇay)* पु. love; affection; amour.

प्रणाम *(pra-ṇām)* पु. salutation.

प्रणाली *(pra-ṇālī)* स्त्री. system; method; mode; channel.

प्रणेता *(pra-ṇetā)* पु. author; composer; writer; promulgator; precursor.

प्रताप *(pra-tāp)* पु. courage; heroism; glory; dignity; benedictory influence.

प्रति[1] *(prati)* स्त्री. copy; print.

प्रति[2] *(prati)* क्रि. वि. for; towards.

प्रतिकार *(prati-kār)* पु. compensation; revenge; retaliation; retribution; treatment; counteraction.

प्रतिकूल *(prati-kūl)* वि. unfavourable; adverse; repugnant; prejudicial.

प्रतिकृति *(prati-kṛti)* स्त्री. prototype replica; image; reproduction.

प्रतिक्रिया *(prati-kriyā)* स्त्री. reaction; repercussion.

प्रतिक्रियात्मक *(prati-kriyātāmak)* वि. reactionary.

प्रतिक्रियावादी[1] *(prati-kriyāvādī)* वि. reactionary.

प्रतिक्रियावादी[2] *(prati-kriyāvādī)* पु. reactionist.

प्रतिगामी *(prati-gāmī)* वि. regressive; retrogressive.

प्रतिच्छाया *(prati-chāyā)* स्त्री. reflection; shadow; facsimile; image; picture.

प्रतिज्ञा *(prati-jñā)* स्त्री. pledge; vow.

प्रतिज्ञा-पत्र *(pratignā-patra)* पु. written pledge; covenant; bond; promissory note.

प्रतिदान *(prati-dān)* पु. barter; exchange; giving back; return; redemption.

प्रतिदिन *(prati-din)* क्रि. वि. daily; everyday.

प्रतिद्वंद्वी[1] *(prati-dvandvī)* पु. antagonist; rival; contestant.

प्रतिद्वंद्वी[2] *(prati-dvandvī)* वि. opponent; rival; antagonistic.

प्रतिध्वनि *(prati-dhvani)* स्त्री. echo; reverberation.

प्रतिनिधि *(prati-ni-dhi)* पु. proxy; representative; delegate; agent.

प्रतिपक्ष *(prati-pakṣ)* पु. contesting or opposite party; opinion expressed by the opposite party; antithesis.

प्रतिपक्षी *(prati-pakṣī)* पु. opponent; adversary; adverse party.

प्रतिपादन *(prati-pādan)* पु. exposition; commencement; presentation; treatment.

प्रतिफल *(prati-phal)* पु. result; return; reward; yield.

प्रतिबंध *(prati-bandh)* पु. ban; restriction; check; condition; prohibition.

प्रतिबद्ध *(prati-baddh)* वि. committed; restricted.

प्रतिबद्धता *(prati-baddhatā)* स्त्री. commitment.

प्रतिबिंब *(prati-bimb)* पु. reflection; image.

प्रतिबिंबित *(prati-bimbit)* वि. reflected.

प्रतिभा *(prati-bhā)* स्त्री. genius; talent.

प्रतिभावान् *(prati-bhāvān)* वि. brilliant; talented.

प्रतिभाशाली *(prati-bhā-sāli)* वि. brilliant; gifted.

प्रतिभू *(prati-bhū)* पु. surety; bail.

प्रतिभूति *(prati-bhūti)* स्त्री. security; bail; security deposit; surety.

प्रतिमा *(prati-mā)* स्त्री. idol; statue; icon; image.

प्रतिमान *(prati-mān)* पु. model; exemplar; norm; pattern.

प्रतिमूर्ति *(prati-mūrti)* स्त्री. image; icon; idol; prototype; replica; embodiment.

प्रतियोगिता *(prati-yogitā)* स्त्री. competition; contest.

प्रतियोगी[1] *(prati-yogī)* पु. competitor; rival; opponent.

प्रतियोगी[2] *(prati-yogī)* वि. competitive.

प्रतिरक्षण *(prati-rakṣan)* पु. see प्रतिरक्षा

प्रतिरक्षा *(prati-rakṣā)* स्त्री. defence; immunity.

प्रतिरूप *(prati-rūp)* पु. specimen; duplicate form; prototype; image; representative; pattern; model; counterpart.

प्रतिरोध *(prati-rodh)* पु. ban; hindrance; obstruction; counteraction; resistance; opposition.

प्रतिरोधक[1] *(prati-rodhak)* पु. resistor; obstructor.

प्रतिरोधक[2] *(prati-rodhak)* पु. resistant; contestant; antagonistic; causing obstruction.

प्रतिरोधन *(prati-rodhan)* पु. resistance.

प्रतिरोधी *(prati-rodhī)* वि. resistive; obstructive; resistant; antagonistic; counteractive; hostile.

प्रतिलिपि *(prati-lipi)* स्त्री. copy; facsimile; duplicate; transcript; reproduction.

प्रतिलेख *(prati-lekh)* पु. transcript.

प्रतिवर्ष *(prati-varśa)* क्रि. per annum.

प्रतिवाद *(prati-vād)* पु. counterstatement; refutation; protest; controversy.

प्रतिवादी *(prati-vadi)* पु. defendant; respondent.

प्रतिशत *(prati-śat)* क्रि. per cent.

प्रतिशोध *(prati-śodh)* पु. revenge; vengeance; retribution.

प्रतिशोधी *(prati-śodhi)* पु. avenger.

प्रतिष्ठा *(prati-ṣṭhā)* स्त्री. fame; glory; renown; installation; establishment; dignity, status, prestige.

प्रतिष्ठान *(prati-ṣṭhān)* पु. fixing; placing, site; situation; institute; establishment; foundation.

प्रतिष्ठापन *(prati-ṣṭhāpan)* वि. fixing; placing; installation consecration.

प्रतिष्ठित *(prati-ṣṭhit)* वि. honourable;

established; installed.

प्रतिस्पर्धा *(prati-spardhā)* पु. rivalry; competition.

प्रतिहिंसक[1] *(prati-hiṃsak)* पु. one who retaliates; retaliator.

प्रतिहिंसक[2] *(prati-hiṃsak)* वि. revengefull; retaliatory.

प्रतिहिंसा *(prati-hiṃsā)* वि. counter-violence; reprisal.

प्रतीक *(pratīk)* पु. symbol; signifier emblem.

प्रतीकवाद *(pratīkvād)* पु. symbolism.

प्रतीकवादी *(pratīkvādī)* पु. symbolist.

प्रतीकात्मक *(pratīkātmak)* वि. allegorical; symbolic.

प्रतीक्षा *(pratîkṣā)* स्त्री. wait; waiting; expectation.

प्रतीक्षालय *(pratîkṣālya)* पु. waiting room.

प्रतीक्षित *(pratîkṣit)* वि. awaited.

प्रतीत *(pratît)* स्त्री. apparent; experienced.

प्रतीति *(pratîti)* स्त्री. knowledge; ascertainment; clear or distinct perception or apprehension; conviction; assurance; confidence; appearance.

प्रत्यंग *(praty-aṅg)* पु. minor parts of the body.

प्रत्यंचा *(praty-añcā)* स्त्री. bow-string.

प्रत्यक्ष *(praty-akṣ)* वि. visible; perceptible; obvious; apparent; direct.

प्रत्यय *(praty-ay)* पु. idea; belief; credit; credence; confidence; faith; testimony; suffix.

प्रत्याख्यान *(pratyākhyan)* पु. rebuttal; confutation; repudiation; denunciation.

प्रत्यादेश *(praty-ā-deś)* पु. refutation; warning; command; order; refusal.

प्रत्याशा *(praty-āśā)* स्त्री. hope; expectation anticipation.

प्रत्याशित *(praty-āśit)* वि. anticipated.

प्रत्याशी *(praty-āśī)* पु. candidate.

प्रत्युत *(praty-ut)* क्रि. वि. but; even then; on the other hand; on the contrary.

प्रत्युत्तर *(praty-uttar)* पु. rejoinder; reply; retort.

प्रत्युत्पन्न *(party-up-pann)* वि. readywitted; prompt; reborn.

प्रत्युत्पन्नमति *(praty-ut-pannmatī)* वि. ready minded; sharp; readywitted; ingenious.

प्रत्येक *(praty-ek)* वि. each; every.

प्रथम *(pratham)* वि. first; foremost; chief; principal.

प्रथमतः *(prathamatāh)* क्रि. वि. firstly; first of all; in the first place.

प्रथमा *(prathamā)* स्त्री. (gram.) nominative case.

प्रथा *(prathā)* स्त्री. custom; convention; usage; practice; system.

प्रदत्त *(pradatt)* वि. given away; bestowed; gifted; paid; paid up.

प्रदर *(pra-dar)* पु. leucorrhoea.

प्रदर्शक *(pra-darśak)* पु. demonstrator; exhibitor; showman.

प्रदर्शन *(pra-darśan)* पु. display; exhibition; demonstration; performance; show.

प्रदर्शनकारी *(pra-darśankari)* पु. showman; exhibitor demonstrator.

प्रदर्शनी *(pra-darśānī)* स्त्री. exhibition; exposition.

प्रदर्शित *(pra-darśit)* वि. exhibited; displayed; demonstrated; shown.

प्रदान *(pra-dān)* पु. gift; grant; bestowal.

प्रदाह *(pra-dāh)* पु. ignition; burning; inflammation; combustion.

प्रदीप *(pra-dīp)* पु. lamp; light; lantern.

प्रदीपन *(pra-dīpan)* पु. illumination; glow; lustre.

प्रदीप्त *(pra-dipt)* वि. lighted; illuminated; rediant; shining; roused.

प्रदूषक *(pra-dūsak)* पु. pollutant.

प्रदूषण *(pra-dūṣaṇ)* पु. pollution.

प्रदेश *(pra-deś)* पु. region; territory; province.

प्रधान[1] *(pra-dhān)* पु. chief; head; leader; president.

प्रधान[2] *(pra-dhān)* वि. prominent; leading; chief.

प्रधानता *(pra-dhānatā)* स्त्री. prominence; importance.

प्रधानाचार्य *(pra-dhānācārya)* पु. principal.

प्रधानाध्यापक *(pradhānādhyāpak)* पु. headmaster.

प्रपंच *(pra-pañc)* पु. illusory creation; delusion; mundane affairs; worldly affairs; artifice manipulation.

प्रपत्र *(pra-patra)* पु. form; proforma.

प्रपात *(pra-pāt)* पु. waterfall; cataract.

प्रपितामह *(pra-pitāmah)* पु. paternal great grandfather.

प्रपौत्र *(pra-pautr)* पु. great grandson.

प्रपौत्री *(pra-pautrī)* स्त्री. great granddaughter.

प्रफुल्ल *(pra-phull)* वि. delighted; joyful; elated; blossomed; bloomed.

प्रबंध *(pra-bandh)* पु. arrangement; management; literary composition; dissertation; thesis; treatise.

प्रबंधक, प्रबंधकर्त्ता *(pra-bandhak)* पु. organiser; manager; executive.

प्रबंधकाव्य *(pra-bandh-kavya)* पु. epic.

प्रबंधकीय *(pra-bandhkiya)* वि. managerial.

प्रबल *(pra-bal)* वि. very strong; mighty; cogent; powerful; vigorous; forceful; staunch; potent.

प्रबलता *(pra-balatā)* स्त्री. strength; forcefulness; prominence.

प्रबुद्ध *(pra-buddh)* वि. awakened; conscious; learned; enlightened; illuminated.

प्रबोध *(pra-bodh)* पु. awakening; consciousness; real knowledge.

प्रबोधन *(pra-bodhan)* पु. enlightenment; awakening; exhortation.

प्रभा *(pra-bhā)* स्त्री. light; radiance; lustre; glory; aura.

प्रभात *(pra-bhāt)* पु. day-break; dawn.

प्रभाती *(pra-bhātī)* स्त्री. morning song.

प्रभारी *(pra-bhāri)* पु. in-charge.

प्रभाव *(pra-bhāv)* पु. influence; effect; impact; impression.

प्रभावकारी *(pra-bhāv-kāri)* वि. effective; influential.

प्रभावपूर्ण *(pra-bhāv-puran)* वि. influential; effective.

प्रभावशाली *(pra-bhāv-sālī)* वि. effective; influential; impressive.

प्रभावहीन *(pra-bhāvhin)* वि. unimpressive; devoid of influence.

प्रभावित *(pra-bhāvit)* वि. influenced.

प्रभावी *(pra-bhāvī)* वि. effective;

dominant.

प्रभु *(pra-bhu)* पु. God; ruler; king; lord; master; sovereign.

प्रभुता *(pra-bhutā)* स्त्री. lordship; supremacy; sovereignty; greatness; importance; glory.

प्रभुत्व *(pra-bhutva)* पु. dominance; domination; sway; power; authority.

प्रभुत *(pra-bhūt)* वि. abundant; ample; plentiful.

प्रमत्त *(pra-matt)* वि. drunk; intoxicated; inattentive; gone crazy with power and pelf; tipsy.

प्रमाण *(pra-māṇ)* पु. measure; proof; testimony; authority.

प्रमाणन *(pra-māṇan)* पु. certification.

प्रमाण-पत्र *(pra-māṇ-patra)* पु. certificate; testimonial.

प्रमाणित *(pra-māṇit)* वि. proved; authenticated; certified.

प्रमाणीकरण *(pra-māṇikaran)* पु. attestation certification; authentication.

प्रमाणीकृत *(pra-māṇīkrt)* वि. attested; certified; authenticated.

प्रमाद *(pra-mād)* पु. negligence; carelessness; inadvertence; intoxication; insanity.

प्रमादी *(pra-mādī)* वि. negligent; careless; vain ; perfunctory.

प्रमुख *(pra-mukh)* वि. chief; cardinal.

प्रमुखता *(pra-mukhatā)* स्त्री. superiority; predominance; prominence; salience.

प्रमुद, प्रमुदित *(pra-mudit)* वि. delighted; happy; full of joy.

प्रमेय *(pra-mey)* पु. theorem.

प्रमेह *(pra-meh)* पु. diabetes.

प्रमोद *(pra-mod)* पु. merriment; joy; entertainment.

प्रमोदी *(pra-modī)* वि. jolly; delightful.

प्रयत्न *(prayatna)* पु. effort; attempt; endeavour; trial.

प्रयाण *(pra-yāṇ)* पु. setting out; departure; march (of army); death.

प्रयास *(pra-yās)* पु. effort; endeavour; attempt.

प्रयुक्त *(pra-yukt)* वि. used; employed; applied; consumed.

प्रयोक्ता *(pra-yoktā)* पु. user; consumer; experimenter.

प्रयोग *(pra-yog)* पु. use; employment; application; experiment.

प्रयोगशाला *(pra-yog-sāla)* स्त्री. laboratory.

प्रयोगात्मक *(pra-yogātmak)* वि. experimental; practical.

प्रयोजक *(pra-yojak)* पु. experimentalist; employer; one who unites; motivator; moneylender.

प्रयोजन *(pra-yojan)* पु. intention; motive; purpose; signification; use.

प्ररूप *(pra-rūp)* पु. type.

प्रलयंकार *(pra-layaṇkar)* वि. catastrophic; devastating; calamitous; disastrous.

प्रलय *(pra-lay)* स्त्री. universal dissolution or destruction; devastation; annihilation; deluge; devastating flood.

प्रलाप *(pra-lāp)* पु. delirium; incoherent talk (due to sorrow or grief); prattle.

प्रलापी *(pra-lāpī)* वि. prattling talking incoherently; delirious.

प्रलोभन *(pra-lobhan)* पु. temptation;

allurement; inducement.

प्रवंचक *(pra-vañcak)* पु. cheat.

प्रवंचना *(pra-vañcanā)* स्त्री. deceit; fraud; trickery.

प्रवक्ता *(pra-vaktā)* पु. spokesman; lecturer.

प्रवचन *(pra-vacan)* पु. (religious) discourse; sermon.

प्रवर *(pra-var)* वि. best; excellent; senior; superior.

प्रवर्तक *(pra-vartak)* पु. pioneer; innovator; one who inspires; promoter; propagator.

प्रवर्तन *(pra-vartan)* पु. pioneering; prompting; inciting; propagation; promotion; induction.

प्रवर्धन *(pra-vardhan)* amplification; magnification; development; progress; increase.

प्रवाद *(pra-vād)* पु. rumour; slander' calumny; expression; challenge.

प्रवादी *(pra-vādī)* पु. rumour monger; slanderer; calumniator.

प्रवास *(pra-vās)* पु. dwelling abroad; migration.

प्रवासी *(pra-vāsī)* पु. emigrant.

प्रवाही *(pra-vahi)* वि. fluent; flowing.

प्रविधि *(pra-vi-dhi)* स्त्री. technique.

प्रविष्टि *(pra-viṣti)* स्त्री. entrance; entry (in the register etc.); posting; particulars to be entered (in the register etc.).

प्रवीण *(pra-viṇ)* वि. proficient; skilled.

प्रवृत्त *(pra-vṛtt)* वि. engaged (in) ; occupied (with).

प्रवृत्ति *(pra-vṛtti)* स्त्री. trend; tendency.

प्रवेश *(pra-veś)* पु. entrance; entry; admission; access; approach.

प्रवेश-पत्र *(pra-veś-patra)* पु. pass; admission card; entry permit; visa.

प्रवेशिका *(pra-veśikā)* स्त्री. preliminary test; A.B.C. book; first reader.

प्रशंसक *(pra-śaṃsak)* पु. admirer; eulogist; fan.

प्रशंसनीय *(pra-śaṃsanīya)* वि. praiseworthy; laudable.; admirable commendable.

प्रशंसा *(pra-sāṃsā)* स्त्री. praise; admiration; commendation.

प्रशंसात्मक *(pra-śaṃsātmak)* वि. laudatory; appreciative.

प्रशंसित *(pra-śaṃsit)* वि. praised; admired; commended.

प्रशंस्य *(pra-śaṃsya)* see. प्रशंसनीय

प्रशस्त *(pra-śast)* वि. praised; commended; excellent; best; vast; spacious; broad; expansive.

प्रशस्ति *(pra-śāsti)* स्त्री. praise; admiration; panegyric; introduction; preface.

प्रशांत *(pra-śānt)* वि. tranquillized; composed; calm; quiet.

प्रशासक *(pra-śāsak)* पु. administrator.

प्रशासन *(pra-śāsan)* पु. administration.

प्रशासनिक *(pra-śāsanik)* वि. administrative.

प्रशिक्षक *(pra-śikṣask)* पु. instructor; trainer.

प्रशिक्षण *(pra-śiksan)* पु. training.

प्रशिक्षित *(pra-śikṣit)* वि. trained.

प्रशिक्षु *(pra-śikṣu)* पु. intern; trainee.

प्रश्न *(praśn)* पु. question; interrogation; query.

प्रश्नपत्र *(praśnpatra)* पु. question paper.

प्रश्नवाचक *(praśna-vācāk)* वि. interrogative.

प्रश्नावली *(praśnāvali)* स्त्री. list of questions.

प्रश्नोत्तर *(praśnottar)* पु. question and answer; catechism.

प्रश्रय *(pra-śray)* पु. support; patronage; backing; shelter.

प्रसंग *(pra-saṅg)* पु. context; reference; sexual intercourse; coition.

प्रसंगाधीन *(pra-saṅgadhin)* वि. under reference.

प्रसंविदा *(praśamvida)* स्त्री. covenant.

प्रसन्न *(pra-sann)* वि. pleased; happy; delighted; glad; cheerful; pure; clear.

प्रसन्नता *(prasannatā)* स्त्री. cheerfulness; clearness; purity; happiness; pleasure.

प्रसव *(pra-sav)* पु. delivery; birth.

प्रसव-पीड़ा *(pra-sav-pirā)* स्त्री. labour pain.

प्रसाद *(pra-sād)* पु. offering to an idol; meant for distribution; clearness; purity; boon; blessing; food left by a spiritual teacher; lucidity of literary style; pleasure; grace.

प्रसाधन *(pra-sādhan)* पु. make-up; toilet; dressing equipment; adornment; decoration.

प्रसार *(pra-sār)* पु. spread; stretch extension; expansion; propagation.

प्रसारक *(pra-sārak)* वि. expansive; extensive.

प्रसारण *(pra-sāraṇ)* पु. broadcast; expansion; propagation.

प्रसारित *(pra-sārit)* वि. broadcast; expanded; extended; propagated.

प्रसिद्ध *(pra-siddh)* वि. famous; well-known; reputed; renowned.

प्रसिद्धि *(pra-siddhi)* स्त्री. fame; renown; repute.

प्रसूत *(pra-sūt)* वि. born; brought forth; delivered.

प्रसूति *(pra-sūti)* स्त्री. delivery; childbirth; maternity; woman who delivers child.

प्रस्तर *(pra-star)* पु. stone; rock.

प्रस्ताव *(pra-stav)* पु. resolution; proposal; offer; motion; suggestion.

प्रस्तावक *(pra-stāvak)* पु. proposer; mover.

प्रस्तावना *(pra-stāvanā)* स्त्री. prologue; introduction; preface; preamble.

प्रस्तावित *(pra-stāvit)* वि. proposed.

प्रस्तुत *(pra-stut)* वि. presented; submitted; relevant; ready; produced; under study or discussion; offered.

प्रस्तुति *(pra-stuti)* स्त्री. presentation; submission; production.

प्रस्तुतीकरण *(pra-stutikaran)* पु. presentation.

प्रस्थान *(pra-sthān)* पु. departure; march.

प्रस्फुटन *(pra-sphuṭan)* पु. opening up; blooming; manifestation.

प्रहर *(pra-har)* पु. eighth part of a day; three hours.

प्रहरी *(pra-harī)* पु. watchman; bellman; sentinel; one who announces the hours by striking a bell.

प्रहसन *(pra-hasan)* पु. farce; farcical play.

प्रहार *(pra-hār)* पु. stroke; blow; assault.

प्रहेलिका *(pra-helikā)* स्त्री. riddle; puzzle; conundrum; enigma.

प्रह्लाद *(pra-hlād)* पु. bliss; delight;

sound; snake; an ancient country; son of Hirnyakashyapa in Hindu mythology.

प्रांजल *(prâñjal)* वि. lucid; clear; upright; honest; plain.

प्रांजलता *(prâñjalatā)* स्त्री. lucidity; clarity.

प्रांत *(prânt)* पु. province; territory; edge; border.

प्रांतीय *(prântīya)* वि. pertaining to a province; provincial.

प्रांतीयता *(prântiyatā)* स्त्री. provincialism; regionalism.

प्राकृत[1] *(prākṛt)* स्त्री. an ancient language of India.

प्राकृत[2] *(prākṛt)* वि. pertaining to nature; natural; original; uncivilized; uneducated; ordinary.

प्राकृतिक *(prākṛtik)* वि. natural; derived from nature; pertaining to human nature.

प्राक्कथन *(prākkathan)* पु. foreword.

प्रागैतिहासिक *(prāgaitihāsik)* वि. prehistoric.

प्राग्ज्ञान *(prāgnān)* पु. foreknowledge.

प्राचार्य *(prâcārya)* पु. principal.

प्राची *(prācī)* स्त्री. the east; the eastern quarter; the orient.

प्राचीन *(prācīn)* वि. ancient; old; outdated; antique.

प्राचीनता *(prācīnatā)* स्त्री. antiguity; oldness; ancientness.

प्राचीर *(prācīr)* पु. surrounding wall of city; fort etc. parapet; bulwark rampart.

प्राचुर्य *(prācūrya)* पु. abundance; plenty; exuberance.

प्राण *(prâñ)* पु. life; winds of the body; vital air; vital breath; vitality; soul; spirit.

प्राणघातक *(prâñ-ghātak)* वि. fatal; murderous.

प्राणदंड *(prâñ-dand)* पु. capital punishment.

प्राणदान *(prâñ-dān)* पु. restoration of life; gift of life; sacrifice of one's life.

प्राणप्यारा *(prân-pyāra)* वि. beloved.

प्राणांत *(prâñant)* पु. death; end of life.

प्राणांतक *(prâñāntak)* वि. fatal; mortal; causing death.

प्राणायाम *(prâñāyām)* पु. exercising control over the process of breathing.

प्राणी *(prânī)* पु. living creature; animal.

प्राणीविज्ञान *(prānī-vignān)* पु. zoology.

प्रातः[1] *(prātah)* पु morning.

प्रातः[2] *(prātah)* क्रि. वि. early in the morning; at dawn.

प्रातःकाल *(prāt-kal)* पु. morning; daybreak.

प्राथमिक *(prāthamik)* वि. first; elementary; primary; occurring in the first place.

प्राथमिकता *(prāthamikatā)* वि. precedence; priority.

प्रादुर्भाव *(prādur-bhāv)* पु. coming into existence; origin; birth; manifestation; appearance; becoming visible.

प्रादेशिक *(prādeśik)* वि. regional; territorial; provincial.

प्रादेशिकता *(prādeśikatā)* स्त्री. regionalism; territoriality.

प्राध्यापक *(prâdhy-āpak)* पु. lecturer.

प्रापक *(prâpak)* पु. payee.

प्राप्त *(prâpt)* वि. got; obtained; acquired; procured.

प्राप्तकर्त्ता *(prâptkartā)* receiver; recipient.

प्राप्तांक *(prâptānk)* पु. marks scored; marks obtained.

प्राप्ति *(prâpti)* स्त्री. gain; advantage; profit; income; receipt; act of receiving proceeds; acquisition; procuration; attainment; yield.

प्राप्तिकर्त्ता *(prâptikartā)* पु. recipient.

प्राप्य *(prâpya)* वि. attainable; procurable; acquirable; available.

प्राप्यता *(prâpyatā)* स्त्री. availability.

प्रामाणिक *(prāmāṇik)* वि. authoritative; authentic.

प्रामाणिकता *(prāmāṇikatā)* स्त्री. authenticity; genuineness.

प्रायः *(prâyaḥ)* क्रि. almost; more or less; generally; usually; often.

प्रायद्वीप *(prāyadvip)* पु. peninsula.

प्रायशः *(prâyaśah)* क्रि. वि. very often; usually; mostly; generally.

प्रायश्चित्त *(prâyaś-citt)* पु. expiation; atonements; penitence.

प्रायोगिक *(prâyogik)* स्त्री. pertaining to experiment; practical; experimental; applied.

प्रारंभ *(prârambh)* पु. commencement; beginning; starting point; inception; initiation.

प्रारंभिक *(prârambhik)* वि. initial; starting; preliminary; elementary; original; introductory.

प्रारब्ध *(prârabdh)* पु. destiny; fate; lot.

प्रारूप *(prârūp)* पु. draft; outline; proforma.

प्रार्थना *(prârthanā)* स्त्री. request; solicitation; prayer; petition; application.

प्रार्थना-पत्र *(prârthanā-patra)* पु. application.

प्रार्थनीय *(prârthanīya)* वि. worth making a request; worth soliciting.

प्रार्थित *(prârthit)* पु. requested; applied for; solicited.

प्रार्थी *(prârthī)* पु. one who prays or requests; applicant; petitioner; supplicator.

प्रालेख *(prâlekh)* पु. draft.

प्रावधान *(prāvdhān)* पु. provision.

प्राविधिक *(prāvidhik)* वि. technical.

प्राश्निक[1] *(prāshnik)* वि. pertaining to a question.

प्राश्निक[2] *(prāshnik)* interrogator; paper-setter.

प्रासंगिक *(prāsaṅgik)* वि. relevant; occasional; incidental; contingent.

प्रासंगिकता *(prāsaṅgikatā)* स्त्री. contingency; relevance.

प्रासाद *(prāsād)* पु. palace; palatial building.

प्रिय[1] *(priya)* वि. dear; darling; beloved; lovable; lovely; pleasing; pleasant; favourite.

प्रिय[2] *(priya)* वि. lover; husband.

प्रियतम[1] *(priyatam)* पु. husband.

प्रियतम[2] *(priyatam)* वि. dearest.

प्रियतमा *(priyatamā)* स्त्री. wife; beloved.

प्रियभाषी *(priya-bhasi)* वि. sweet-tongued; mealy-mouthed.

प्रिया *(priyā)* स्त्री. wife; beloved; darling.

प्रीतम *(pritam)* पु. lover; beloved.

प्रीति *(prīti)* स्त्री. love; affection.

प्रीतिभोज *(prīti-bhoj)* पु. banquet; feast.

प्रेक्षक *(prêkṣak)* पु. spectator; observer.

प्रेक्षागार *(prêkṣāgār)* पु. theatre; auditorium.

प्रेत *(prêt)* पु. ghost; goblin.

प्रेतात्मा *(prêtātmā)* पु. spirit; ghost; apparitional soul.

प्रेम *(prem)* पु. love; affection; attachment.

प्रेमपात्र *(prem-pātra)* वि. beloved; dear.

प्रेमालाप *(premālāp)* पु. love-talk; cordial talk.

प्रेमिका *(premikā)* पु. woman who loves someone; beloved (female).

प्रेमी *(premi)* पु. lover.

प्रेरक *(prêrak)* वि. inspiring; motivating.

प्रेरणा *(prêraṇā)* स्त्री. inducement; inspiration; incentive; drive.

प्रेरित *(prêrit)* वि. induced; inspired; motivated; prompted.

प्रेषक *(prêṣak)* पु. despatcher; consignor; sender; remitter.

प्रेषण *(prêṣan)* पु. despatch; consignment; transmission.

प्रेषित *(prêṣit)* वि. despatched; consigned; transmitted

प्रेषिती *(prêṣitī)* पु. addressee; consignee.

प्रोत्साहन *(prôtsāhan)* पु. encouragement; boosting up; incentive.

प्रोत्साहित *(prôtsāhit)* वि. encouraged; given incentive.

प्रोन्नत *(prônnat)* वि. raised; elevated; projected; advanced.

प्रौढ़ *(praûṛh)* वि. full grown; adult; mature.

प्रौढ़ता *(praûṛhatā)* स्त्री. maturity; adulthood.

प्रौढ़ा *(praurhā)* स्त्री. grown-up woman.

प्रौद्योगिकी *(praudyogikī)* स्त्री. technology.

प्लव *(plav)* पु. floating; swimming; thrust; small boat.

प्लावन *(plāvan)* पु. submersion; plunge; inundation; flood; deluge.

प्लावित *(plāvit)* वि. inundated; flooded; submerged.

प्लीहा *(plīhā)* पु. spleen; disease of the spleen.

फ

फ *(pha)* the second letter of the fifth pentad of the Devnagri alphabets.

फंदा *(phandā)* पु. noose; snare; loop; trick; ruse; subterfuge.

फँसना *(phaṁsnā)* अ. क्रि. to be noosed; to be ensnared; to be embroiled; to be involved; to be entangled.

फँसाना *(phaṁsānā)* स. क्रि. to ensnare, to entrap, to bait; to embroil; to get stuck up or blocked (as money etc.); to implicate; to entangle; to decoy.

फ़कीर *(faqīr)* पु. (अ.) beggar; mendicant.

फ़कीरी *(faqīrī)* स्त्री. (अ.) beggary; mendicity.

फक्कड़ *(phakkar)* वि. indigent and carefree; reckless and extravagant.

फक्कड़पन *(phakkarpan)* पु. carefreeness, carefree manner, indigence.

फ़ख़ *(fakhr)* पु. (फ़ा.) pride.

फ़ज़ीहत *(fazīhat)* स्त्री. (अ.) disgrace; insult; ignominy; infamy; heinous and hated quarrel or wrangle; embarrassment; discomfiture.

फटकना *(phatakanā)* स. क्रि. to winnow; to dust; to shake or knock off (as dust from clothes).

फटकार *(phaṭkār)* स्त्री. scolding; reprimand; rebuke; chiding.

फटकारना *(phaṭkārnā)* स. क्रि. to scold; chide; reprimand; to give (cloth) jerk; to beat (clothes) on a stone (in washing).

फटना *(phaṭnā)* अ. क्रि. to be torn; to be split; be rent; be cracked; be broken; to turn or become sour; to explode; to burst.

फटाफट *(phaṭāphaṭ)* क्रि. वि. quickly.

फटीचर *(phaṭīcar)* वि. shabby; shabbily dressed; despicable; abominable.

फटेहाल *(phaṭe-hāl)* वि. in a ragged or shabby condition; in a miserable plight.

फटेहाली *(phaṭe-hālī)* स्त्री. raggedness.

फड़क, फड़कन *(pharak)* स्त्री. thrill; throb; palpitation; pulsation.

फड़कना *(pharakanā)* अ. क्रि. to flutter; to twitch convulsively (as the eyelids etc.); to be thrilled; to be greatly delighted; to palpitate; to throb; to pulsate.

फड़फड़ाना *(pharpharānā)* स. क्रि. to flutter; to put in a flutter; to flutter.

फड़फड़ाहट *(pharpharāhaṭ)* स्त्री. flutter.

फ़तह *(fatah)* स्त्री. (अ.) victory; triumph; conquest.

फ़न *(fan)* पु. (अ.) art; craft; skill.

फ़नकार *(fankar)* पु. (अ.) artist.

फफूँद, फफूँदी *(phaphūṁdī)* स्त्री. fungus; mould.

फफ़ोला *(phapholā)* पु. blister; vesicle; eruption; scald.

फबती *(phabtī)* स्त्री. pleasantry; fun; jest; sarcastic remark; banter; dig.

फबना *(phabanā)* अ. क्रि. to become; befit; to be suitable; apt; appropriate; to look elegant; graceful; beautiful.

फ़रज़ंद *(farzand)* पु. (फ़ा.) son.

फ़रमाइश *(farmāiś)* स्त्री. (फ़ा.) thing desired or ordered; will; request; order.

फ़रमाइशी *(farmāiśī)* वि. made to order; requested; on specific request.

फ़रमान *(farmān)* पु. (फ़ा.) order; command; royal letter; charter; edict.

फ़रमाना *(farmānā)* स. क्रि. to order; command; to affirm; to declare.

फरसा *(pharsā)* पु. hatchet; axe; halberd.

फ़रार *(farār)* वि. (अ.) at large; absconding; fugitive.

फ़रियाद *(fariyād)* स्त्री. (फ़ा.) cry for help or redress; petition; complaint.

फ़रियादी *(farivadī)* पु. (फ़ा.) complainant; plaintiff; seeker of redress or justice.

फ़रेब *(fareb)* पु. (फ़ा.) fraud; treachery; duplicity; wiliness; double dealing; deception.

फ़रेबी *(farebī)* वि. (फ़ा.) fraudulent; deceptive.

फ़र्क़ *(fraq)* पु. (अ.) distinction; difference.

फ़र्ज़ *(farz)* पु. (अ.) obligation; onus; duty.

फ़र्ज़ी *(farzī)* वि. (अ.) hypothetical; supposititious; fictitious; imaginary; supposed.

फर्राटा *(pharrāṭā)* पु. fluency; promptitude fastness; haste.

फ़र्श *(farś)* पु. (अ.) floor; carper; pavement.

फल *(phal)* पु. fruit; gain; profit; advantage; result; effect; consequence; reward; requital; recompense; ironhead (of a spear; arrow etc.); blade of knife etc; plough-share; product or quotient.

फलक *(phalak)* पु. board; slab or tablet; sheet of paper; blade; sky

फलतः *(phalat)* क्रि. वि. as a result; consequently.

फलदायक *(phaldāyak)* वि. fruitful; fructuous; profitable; advantageous; productive efficacious; effective.

फलदार *(phaldār)* वि. fruit-bearing; fruitful; (weapon) having a sharp head or blade.

फलना *(phalnā)* अ. क्रि. to bear fruit; to be fulfilled; to thrive; to prosper; to break out into blisters; pimples etc.

फलप्रद *(phalprad)* वि. fruitful; bearing-fruit; efficacious.

फलस्वरूप *(phal-svarupa)* क्रि. वि. consequently; as a result.

फलाँग *(phalāṁg)* स्त्री. leap; jump; spring; long stride.

फलाँगना *(phalāṁgnā)* अ. क्रि. to spring; leap; jump.

फलाहार *(phalāhar)* पु. fruitarian diet.

फलित ज्योतिष *(phalit-jyotisa)* पु. astrology.

फली *(phalī)* स्त्री. pod of a leguminous plant.

फ़व्वारा *(favvārā)* पु. (अ.) fountain.

फ़सल *(fasal)* स्त्री. (अ.) harvest; crop; season; time.

फ़साद *(fasād)* पु. (अ.) riot; disturbance; quarrel; brawl.

फ़सादी *(fasādī)* वि. (अ.) riotous; quarrelsome; rowdy.

फ़साना *(fasānā)* पु. (फा.) story; long narrative.

फहरना *(phaharnā)* अ. क्रि. to fly (as a flag); to wave; flutter.

फहराना *(phahrānā)* स. क्रि. to cause to flutter; to wave; to hoist.

फाँक *(phāṁk)* स्त्री. piece; slice; fillet; fragment; paring.

फाँकना *(phāṁkanā)* स. क्रि. to put (something powdery) into the mouth.

फाँदना *(phāṁdanā)* (अ.) क्रि. to leap; to spring; to jump; to skip.

फाँस *(phāṁs)* स्त्री. noose; snare; splinter; knot; trap.

फाँसना *(phāṁsanā)* स. क्रि. to ensnare; to entrap; to embroil; entangle; involve; implicate.

फाँसी *(phāṁsī)* स्त्री. death by hanging; execution.

फ़ाक़ा *(fāqā)* पु. (अ.) starvation; going without food.

फागुन *(phāgun)* पु. the twelfth month of the Hindu calendar.

फाटक *(phāṭak)* पु. main gate; entrance.

फाड़ना *(phāṛanā)* स. क्रि. to tear off; to rend; to split; to open (mouth); to pull apart.

फानूस *(fānūs)* पु. (फ़ा.) chandilier.

फ़ायदा *(fāydā)* पु. (अ.) advantage; benefit; profit; gain; good result; utility; improvement.

फ़ायदेमंद *(fāyde-mand)* वि. (फ़ा.) profitable; beneficial; advantageous; efficacious.

फालतू *(fāltū)* वि. surplus; spare; extra; superfluous; useless; worthless.

फालिज *(fālij)* पु. (अ.) paralysis.

फावड़ा *(phāvṛā)* पु. mattock; spade.

फ़ासला *(fāslā)* पु. (अ.) gap; distance.

फाहा *(phāhā)* पु. flock of cotton; lint.

फ़िक़रा *(fiqrā)* पु. (अ). sentence.

फ़िक्र *(fiqr)* स्त्री. (अ.) care; concern; worry; anxiety.

फ़िक्रमन्द *(fiqrmand)* वि. (अ.) worried; anxious.

फिटकरी *(phiṭkarī)* स्त्री. alum.

फ़िदा *(fidā)* वि. (अ.) enamoured; infatuated; charmed; attracted; devoted (to).

फिरंगी *(firaṅgī)* पु. European; Englishman.

फिर *(phir)* क्रि. वि. again; afterwards; thereafter; in future.

फ़िरक़ा *(firqā)* पु. (अ.) sect; community.

फ़िरक़ापरस्त *(firqā-prasat)* वि. (अ.) sectarian.

फिरक़ापरस्ती *(firqā-parasatī)* स्त्री. (अ.) sectarianism.

फिरना *(phirnā)* (अ.) क्रि. to go round; to promenade; to ramble; to turn back; to return; to revolve; to go back (on); to turn (from).

फिर भी *(phir-bhi)* क्रि. वि. even then; inspite of that.

फिर से *(phir-se)* क्रि. वि. afresh; anew.

फ़िराक़ *(firāq)* पु. separation.

फिरौती *(phirautī)* स्त्री. act of returning; ransom; money presented in reciprocation.

फ़िलहाल *(filhāl)* क्रि. वि. (अ.) at present; for the present; for the time being.

फिस *(phis)* वि. useless; fizzled out; turned useless.

फिसड्डी *(phisaddī)* वि. backward; sluggish; trailing behind; worthless.

फिसलन *(phisalan)* स्त्री. slipperiness.

फिसलना *(phisalna)* अ. क्रि. to slip; to slide; to skid.

फीका *(phīkā)* वि. tasteless; vapid; insipid; pale; dim; faint.

फीकापन *(phīkāpan)* पु. tastelessness; dimness; insipidity.

फ़ीता *(fītā)* पु. (पुर्त.) lace; ribbon; tape (for measurement); strap.

फ़ील *(fil)* पु. (फ़ा.) elephant; bishop (chess) .

फूँकना *(phuṁknā)* अ. क्रि. to burn.

फुँकनी *(phuṁknī)* स्त्री. blow pipe (of goldsmith etc.).

फुंकवाना *(phuṁkavānā)* स. क्रि. to cause to burn.

फुंकार *(phuṁkār)* स्त्री. hissing.

फुँदना *(phuṁdnā)* पु. tassel; rosette.

फुंसी *(phuṁsī)* स्त्री. pimple; small boil; whelk.

फुजूल *(fūzūl)* वि. (अ.) unnecessary; futile; useless.

फुजूलख़र्च *(fūzu-kharč)* वि. (अ.) extravagant; prodigal; spendthrift.

फुजूलख़र्ची *(fūzu-kharcī)* स्त्री. (अ.) extravagance; prodigality.

फुटकर *(phuṭkar)* वि. miscellaneous.

फुदकना *(phudaknā)* अ. क्रि. to jump; to skip; to hop; to skip or dance about.

फुनगी *(phunagī)* स्त्री. sprout; shoot; extremity; tip; summit; cockade.

फुप्फुस *(phup-phus)* पु. lung.

फुफकार *(phuphkār)* स्त्री. hissing (of snake).

फुफकारना *(phuphkārnā)* अ. क्रि. to hiss; to make a hissing sound.

फुरती *(phurtī)* स्त्री. smartness; quickness; promptness; agility.

फुरतीला *(phurtīlā)* वि. agile; active; smart.

फुरतीलापन *(phurtīlāpan)* पु. agility; activeness; smartness; promptness.

फुरसत *(fursat)* स्त्री. (अ.) leisure; respite; spare time.

फुर्ती *(phurtī)* see फुरती

फुर्सत *(fursat)* see फुरसत

फुलझड़ी *(phulijharī)* स्त्री. a kind of fire-work; (fig) stray remark made on purpose; a provoking remark uttered in a lighter vein.

फुलवारी *(phulvārī)* स्त्री. small flower-garden.

फुलाना *(phulānā)* स. क्रि. to cause to swell; puff out; to inflate.

फुसफुस *(phusphus)* स्त्री. whisper.

फुसफुसाना *(phusphusānā)* अ. क्रि. to whisper; to speak in a low tone.

फुसफुसाहट *(phusphusāhaṭ)* स्त्री. whisper; whispering sound.

फुसलाना *(phusalānā)* स. क्रि. to coax; to cajole; to inveigh; to intice; to wheedle; to seduce; to allure.

फुहार *(phuhār)* स्त्री. drizzle.

फुहारा *(phuhārā)* पु. spring; gush; fountain; shower.

फूँक *(phūṁk)* स्त्री. breath of air; blow; puff; whiff.

फूँकना *(phūkanā)* स. क्रि. to puff; to blow; to blow or breathe (a charm or incantation); to blow up (fire etc); to set on fire; inflame; to squander away; to waste.

फूँकनी *(phūṁkni)* स्त्री. blow-pipe.

फूट *(phūt)* स्त्री. crack; split; rift; chasm; discord; dissension; large cucumber that splits up on ripening.

फूटना *(phūṭanā)* अ. क्रि. to break; crack; split; to erupt; to explode; to sprout; to shoot; to come out; to appear.

फूफा *(phūphā)* पु. husband of father's sister; uncle.

फूफी *(phūphī)* स्त्री. paternal aunt; father's sister.

फूल *(phūl)* पु. flower; blossom; ashes left after cremation.

फूलगोभी *(phū-gobhī)* स्त्री. cauliflower.

फूलदान *(phū-dān)* पु. flower vase.

फूलदार *(phū-dār)* वि. flowery; embroidered.

फूलना *(phūlnā)* अ. क्रि. to blossom; to flower; to bloom; to swell out; to be puffed.

फूहड़[1] *(phūhār)* वि. unmannerly; slovenly; coarse-grained.

फूहड़[2] *(phuhar)* स्त्री. illiterate; slut; slattern.

फूहड़पन *(phūharpan)* पु. slovenliness; untidiness.

फेंकना *(phemkanā)* स. क्रि. to throw; fling; cast; hurl; to drop; to mislay; to throw carelessly; to spend uselessly.

फेंटना *(pheṁṭanā)* स. क्रि. to beat up; to batter; to shuffle; to whisk.

फेन *(phen)* पु. froth; foam; lather.

फेनिल *(phenil)* वि. frothful; foamy; full of lather.

फेफड़ा *(phepharā)* पु. lung.

फेर *(pher)* पु. turn; twist; curvature; dilemma; to recant; perplexity; ruse; trick; subterfuge; circuitous route; detour.

फेरना *(phernā)* स. क्रि. to turn; to turn round; to turn away; to reject; to send back; to turn over; to reverse; invert; to pass (brush etc.) over.

फेरबदल *(pher-badal)* स्त्री. alteration; modification.

फेरा *(pherā)* पु. circuit; round; circumambulation; matrimonial rite according to which the bride and the bridegroom move round the sacred fire; trip.

फेरी *(pherī)* स्त्री. going round; circumambulation; hawking; pedling.

फेरीवाला *(pherīwala)* पु. hawker; pedler; itinerant merchant.

फ़ेहरिस्त *(fehrist)* स्त्री. (अ.) list inventory.

फैलना *(phailnā)* अ. क्रि. to be spread; to be diffused; to be scattered; to expand; to extend; to stretch; to become public.

फैलाना *(phailānā)* स. क्रि. to spread; to stretch; to expand; to lengthen; to draw out; to diffuse; to publicise.

फैलाव *(phailāv)* पु. stretch; expansion; publicity.

फ़ैसला *(faislā)* पु. (अ.) judgement; decision; adjudication; settlement; conclusion.

फ़ोकट *(phokaṭ)* वि. free; free of charge; gratis; without any substance.

फ़ोड़ना *(phoṛanā)* स. क्रि. to break to pieces; to explode; to split; to induce (a person) to defect.

फ़ोड़ा *(phorā)* पु. boil. tumour; abscess; ulcer.

फ़ौज *(fauj)* स्त्री. (अ.) army; crowd.

फ़ौजदार *(faujdār)* पु. army chief; police inspector.

फ़ौजदारी *(faujdārī)* स्त्री. (अ.) criminal fighting; assault; criminal breach of peace; penal offence.

फ़ौजी[1] *(faujī)* वि. (अ.) of or belonging to the army; martial

फ़ौजी[2] *(faujī)* पु. (अ.) soldier.

फ़ौरन *(fauran)* क्रि. वि. quickly; immediately; at once.

फ़ौलाद *(faulād)* पु. (अ.) steel.

फ़ौलादी *(faulādī)* वि. (अ.) made of steel; strong; stout; sturdy.

फ़ौवारा *(fauvārā)* see फव्वारा।

ब

ब *(ba)* the third letter of the fifth pentad of the Devnagri alphabets.

बंकिम *(baṅkim)* वि. oblique; curved; coquettish; showy.

बँगला[1] *(baṁglā)* पु. small bungalow.

बँगला[2] *(baṁglā)* स्त्री. Bengali language.

बंजर *(bañjar)* पु. waste land; unproductive land.

बँटना *(baṁṭanā)* अ. क्रि. to be divided or shared; to be distributed; to be partitioned.

बँटवाना *(baṁṭvānā)* स. क्रि. to cause to be shared; to be distributed or to be divided.

बँटवारा *(baṁtvārā)* पु. distribution; division; partition of property etc.

बंटाढ़ार *(banṭāḍhār)* पु. complete destruction; devastation; ruination; undoing.

बंद[1] *(band)* वि. bound; tied up; fastened; imprisoned; closed; shut; prevented; hindered; stopped; discontinued; banned.

बंद[2] *(band)* वि. closure; bund; bank; knot; string; strap; body joint.

बंदगोभी *(band-gobhi)* स्त्री. cabbage.

बंदनवार *(bandanvār)* पु. festoon of leaves of mango tree etc.

बंदर *(bandar)* पु. monkey; ape.

बंदरगाह *(bandargāh)* पु. (फ़ा.) sea port; harbour.

बंदरघुड़की *(bandar-ghurki)* स्त्री. falsethreat; inpotent threat.

बंदा *(bandā)* पु. (फ़ा.) slave or servant; devotee.

बंदिश *(bandiś)* स्त्री. (फ़ा.) tying; binding; restriction; composition; construction (in poetry).

बंदी *(bandī)* पु. prisoner; captive.

बंदीकरण *(bandīkaran)* पु. capture; incarceration.

बंदीगृह *(bandī-grih)* पु. jail; prison house.

बंदूक़ *(bandūq)* स्त्री. (फ़ा.) gun; musket.

बंदूक़ची *(bandūqacī)* पु. musketeer; gunner; gunman.

बंदोबस्त *(bandobast)* पु. (फ़ा.) arrangement; administration; survey and settlement of land.

बंध *(bandh)* पु. string; cord; knot; construction; composition; dam; tie; frame; ligature.

बंधक *(bandhak)* पु. binder; pawn; pledge; mortage; surety; hostage.

बंधन *(bandhan)* पु. fastening; binding; tying; obstacle; hindrance; ckeck; restraint; bondage.

बँधना *(bandhanā)* अ. क्रि. to be bound; fastened etc; to be restricted or regulated.

बंधु *(bandhu)* पु. friend; welस. wishser; kinsman; relation; kindred; brother.

बँधुआ *(bandhuā)* वि. captive; bonded.

बंधुजन *(bandhu-jan)* पु. kinsfolk; kinsmen.

बंधुता *(bandhutā)* स्त्री. fraternity; fraternalism; kinship; affinity.

बंधुत्व *(bandhutvā)* पु. brotherhood; fraternity.

बंध्यकरण *(bandhyakaran)* पु. sterilization; gelding; castration.

बंध्यता *(bandhyatā)* स्त्री. sterility; infertility; barrenness.

बंध्या *(bandhyā)* स्त्री. sterile woman.

बंबा *(bambā)* पु. hand-pump; waterpipe.

बंसी *(baṃsi)* स्त्री. flute; pipe; fishing hook.

बक *(bak)* पु. heron or crane; hypocrite; simulator.

बक-झक *(bak-jhak)* स्त्री. silly talk; nonsense; babble; jabbering.

बकतर *(baktar)* पु. (फ़ा.) armour.

बकतरबंद *(baktarband)* वि. (फ़ा.) armoured.

बकना *(baknā)* (अ.) क्रि. to babble; to indulge in silly talk.

बकबक *(bakbak)* see बकझक।

बकरा *(bakrā)* पु. he-goat.

बकलस *(bakalas)* पु. buckle; fibula.

बकवाद *(bakvād)* स्त्री. nonsensical or foolish talk; twaddle; tattle; gabble.

बकसुआ *(baksuā)* पु. buckle; fibula.

बक़ाया[1] *(baqāyā)* वि. (अ.) remaining; outstanding.

बक़ाया[2] *(baqāyā)* पु. arrears; remainder; balance.

बकोटना *(bakoṭanā)* स. क्रि. to lacerate or tear with the nails; scratch.

बक्की *(bakkī)* वि. talkative; chatty; voluble; loquacious.

बखानना *(bakhānanā)* स. क्रि. to explain; to expound ; to describe; to eulogize; to sing the praises of.

बख़िया *(bakhiyā)* स्त्री. (फ़ा.) fine sewing with double stitching; back-stitching.

बखुद *(bakhud)* क्रि. वि. (फ़ा.) by oneself.

बखूबी *(bakhūbi)* क्रि. वि. (फ़ा.) well; properly; duly; thoroughly; completely.

बखेड़ा *(bakheṛā)* पु. entanglement; complication; quarrel; dispute.

बख़्तर *(bakhtar)* see बकतर।

बख़्शना *(bakhśanā)* स. क्रि. to give; to grant; to bestow; to forgive; to pardon; to excuse; to spare.

बख़्शीश *(bakhśiś)* स्त्री. (फ़ा.) donation; reward; gratuity; pardon; forgiveness; tip.

बग़ल *(bagal)* स्त्री. (फ़ा.) armpit; flank; side.

बगला *(bagalā)* पु. heron.

बगावत *(bagāvat)* स्त्री. (अ.) revolt; rebellion.

बगिया *(bagiyā)* स्त्री. small garden.

बग़ीचा *(bagīcā)* पु. garden.

बगुला *(bagulā)* पु. heron.

बगूला *(bagūlā)* पु. (फ़ा.) whirlwind.

बग़ैर *(ba-gair)* क्रि. वि. (फ़ा.) without.

बग्घी *(bagghī)* स्त्री. four-wheeled carriage; victoria.

बघारना *(baghāranā)* स. क्रि. to season (vegetable; pulses; etc.) with onion and spices in heated oil or ghee.

बचकाना *(backānā)* वि. childish; immature; puerile.

बचकानापन *(backānāpan)* पु. childishness; puerility.

बचत *(bacat)* स्त्री. residue; remainder; surplus; balance; savings; profit; gain.

बचना *(bacanā)* अ. क्रि. to be saved; to be left; to remain; to escape; to avoid.

बचपन *(bacapan)* पु. infancy; childhood.

बचपना *(bacapanā)* पु. childhood; childishness or childlike action; puerility.

बचाना *(bacānā)* स. क्रि. to preserve; to protect; to shield; to save; to spare; to retain unused or unspent.

बचाव *(bacāv)* पु. protection; rescue; defence; safeguard; shielding; avoidance; escape.

बच्चा *(baccā)* पु. young one of a creature; child; infant.

बच्चागाड़ी *(baccā-gāṛī)* स्त्री. perambulator.

बच्ची *(baccī)* स्त्री. little girl; female child.

बच्चेदानी *(bacce-dāni)* स्त्री. uterus.

बछिया *(bachiyā)* स्त्री. heifer.

बछेड़ा *(bacheṛā)* पु. colt.

बछेड़ी *(bacheṛī)* स्त्री. heifer; female colt.

बजना *(bajnā)* अ. क्रि. to produce sound; to ring; to be struck; to sound.

बजरा *(bajrā)* पु. millet; doubledeck boat.

बजरी *(bajrī)* स्त्री. gravel.

बजवाना *(bajvānā)* स. क्रि. to cause to ring or play.

बजा *(bajā)* वि. (फ़ा.) proper; suitable; fit; becoming; right; just; true.

बज़ाज़ *(bazāz)* पु. (अ.) clothmerchant; draper; clothier.

बजाना *(bajānā)* स. क्रि. to play (on a musical instrument); to perform or execute; to beat (a drum; gong); to strike.

बजाय *(ba-jāy)* क्रि. वि. (फ़ा.) in place of; in lieu of; instead of.

बटन *(baṭan)* स. क्रि. switch; button.

बटना *(baṭana)* पु. to twine into rope.

बटमार *(baṭmār)* पु. highwayman; robber; brigand.

बटमारी *(baṭmārī)* स्त्री. waylaying; robbery; brigandage.

बटवाना *(batvānā)* स. क्रि. to cause to divide or distribute; to cause to make into a rope.

बटाना *(baṭānā)* स. क्रि. to get shared or divided; to get made into a rope.

बटिया *(baṭiyā)* स्त्री. footpath; small; smooth piece of stone; small pestle.

बटी *(baṭi)* स्त्री. globule; pill; tablet.

बटुआ *(baṭuā)* पु. a small bag with divisions; purse.

बटेर *(baṭer)* स्त्री. quail.

बटोरन *(baṭoran)* स्त्री. sweepings.

बटोरना *(baṭoranā)* स. क्रि. to gather up; to assemble; to accumulate; to collect; to glean; to pick.

बटोही *(baṭohī)* पु. way-farer; traveller.

बट्टा *(baṭṭā)* पु. discount; loss.

बड़बड़ *(baṛbaṛ)* स्त्री. grumbling; murmuring; muttering; useless talk.

बड़प्पन *(baṛappan)* पु. greatness; dignity; magnanimity.

बड़बड़ाना *(baṛbaṛānā)* अ. क्रि. to grumble; to murmur; to talk to one-self in anger.

बड़बड़िया *(baṛbaṛiyā)* वि. given to muttering.

बड़भागी *(baṛbhāgi)* वि. lucky; fortunate.

बड़वाग्नि *(baṛavâgni)* स्त्री. बड़वानल *(baravânal)* पु. the submarine fire; sea-fire.

बड़हल *(baṛhal)* स्त्री. jack-fruit.

बड़ा[1] *(baṛā)* वि. large; big; huge; grand; eminent; exalted; elder; superior.

बड़ा[2] *(baṛā)* क्रि. वि. very excessively; exceedingly; highly.

बड़ा[3] *(baṛā)* पु. saltish perparation of urd-pulse; elderly person; influential person.

बड़ाई *(baṛāī)* स्त्री. largeness; greatness; bigness; vastness; bulkiness; praise; laudation.

बड़ी *(baṛī)* स्त्री. dried up tiny round cakes of ground pulse; potatoes etc. large.

बड़ी माता *(baṛī-mātā)* स्त्री. small pox.

बढ़ई *(baṛhaī)* पु. carpenter.

बढ़ईगीरी *(baṛhaī-girī)* स्त्री. carpentry.

बढ़त *(baṛhat)* स्त्री. progression; lead; advantage; excess.

बढ़ती *(baṛhatī)* स्त्री. advancement; progress; promotion; enhancement; increase in riches of family; surplus.

बढ़ना *(baṛhanā)* अ. क्रि. to increase; to be enlarged; to be enhanced; to be extended; to be prolonged; to advance; to make headway; to grow.

बढ़ाना *(baṛhānā)* स. क्रि. to promote; to advance; to increase; to enhance; to enlarge; extend; stretch; to raise; to close (shop etc.); to put off (lamp etc.); to extend.

बढ़ाव *(baṛhāv)* पु. increase; augmentation; advancement; extension; enlargement; expansion; growth; development.

बढ़ावा *(baṛhāvā)* पु. inducemen incitement; encouragement, incentive; stimulus; motivation; abetment.

बढ़िया *(baṛhiyā)* वि. superior; excellent; of good quality.

बढ़ोतरी *(baṛhotrī)* स्त्री. increase; increment; advancement; promotion.

बतख़ *(batakh)* स्त्री. duck.

बतलाना *(batlānā)* बताना स. क्रि. to explain; to point out; to direct; to indicate; to state; to tell.

बतियाना *(batiyānā)* अ. क्रि. to talk; to speak; to converse.

बत्ती *(battī)* स्त्री. wick; candle; lamp; lantern; light.

बद *(bad)* वि. (फ़ा.) bad; wicked; vile; depraved.

बदअमनी *(bad-amani)* स्त्री. (फ़ा.) disturbance; disquiet;unrest.

बदइंतज़ाम *(bad-intazām)* वि. (फ़ा.) incompetent in management; maladministered.

बदइंतज़ामी *(bad-intazāmī)* स्त्री. (फ़ा.) bad management; misgovernment; maladmini-stration.

बदक़िस्मत *(bad-qismat)* वि. (फ़ा.) unfortunate; ill-fated.

बदक़िस्मती *(bad-qismatī)* स्त्री. (फ़ा.) misfortune; bad luck.

बदचलन *(bad-cālan)* वि. (फ़ा.) depraved; immoral.

बदतमीज़ *(bad-tamiz)* वि. (फ़ा.) unmannerly; uncivilised; rude; impudent.

बदतमीज़ी *(bad-tamizī)* स्त्री. (फ़ा.) unmannerliness; uncivilisedness; rudeness; impudence.

बदतर *(badtar)* वि. (फ़ा.) worse.

बदतहज़ीब *(bad-tahzib)* see बदतमीज़ ।

बददिमाग़ *(bad-dimāg)* वि. (फा.) haughty; arrogant; conceited; ilस.tempered; bad tempered.

यददिमाग़ी *(bad-dimāgī)* स्त्री. (फ़ा.) arrogance; conceitedness.

बददुआ *(bad-duā)* स्त्री. (फ़ा.) curse; malediction.

बदन *(badan)* पु. (फा.) body.

बदनसीब *(bad-nasib)* वि. (फ़ा.) unfortunate; ill-fated.

बदनसीबी *(bad-nasibi)* स्त्री. (फ़ा.) misfortune; ill-luck.

बदनाम *(badnām)* वि. (फ़ा.) defamed; infamous.

बदनामी *(badnāmī)* स्त्री. (फ़ा.) disrepute; infamy; notoriety; slander.

बदनीयत *(bad-niyat)* वि. (फ़ा.) ill-intentioned; having bad designs.

बदनुमा *(badnūmā)* वि. (फ़ा.) awkward; ugly.

बदबू *(badabū)* स्त्री. (फ़ा.) foul smell; stink; bad odour.

बदबूदार *(badabūdār)* वि. (फ़ा.) foul-smelling; stinking.

बदमज़ा *(bad-mazā)* वि. (फ़ा.) unpleansat; disagreeable; distasteful; unsavoury.

बदमाश[1] *(bad-māś)* वि. (फ़ा.) of a bad profession or way of life; immoral; wicked.

बदमाश[2] *(bad-māś)* पु. (फ़ा.) villain; rascal; miscreant.

बदमाशी *(bad-māsī)* स्त्री. (फ़ा.) bad way of living; loose conduct; villainy; rascality; wickedness.

बदमिज़ाज *(bad-mizāj)* वि. (फ़ा.) ill-tempered; tetchy; short-tempered; petulant.

बदमिज़ाजी *(bad-mizājī)* स्त्री. (फ़ा.) ill-temper; short-temper; petulance; tantrum.

बदरंग *(bad-rang)* वि. (फ़ा.) discoloured; faded; tarnished; forced out of countenance; grown pallid; (card-game) of a colour different from that of the card moved.

बदल *(bdal)* पु. change; exchange; alteration; modification.

बदलना *(badalnā)* अ. क्रि. to be substituted; to be transferred; to be transformed; to assume another form; to change; to alter; to exchange; to barter; to replace; to substitute.

बदलवाना *(badalvānā)* स. क्रि. to cause to be exchanged; to get changed; to get replaced.

बदला *(badlā)* पु. change; substitution; exchange; revenge; vengeance; retalisation; recompense; return.

बदलाव *(badlāv)* पु. change.

बदशक्ल *(bad-śakal)* वि. (फ़ा.) ugly; grotesque; deformed.

बदशगुन *(bad-śagun)* वि. (फ़ा.) inauspicious; ominous.

बदसलीक़ा *(bad-saliqā)* वि. (फ़ा.) unmannerly; slovenly.

बदसलूकी *(bad-salūqī)* स्त्री. (फ़ा.) ill-treatment; maltreatment.

बदसूरत *(bad-surat)* वि. (फ़ा.) ugly; grotesque.

बदसूरती *(bad-suratī)* वि. (फ़ा.) ugliness; grotesqueness.

बदस्तूर *(badastur)* क्रि. वि. (फ़ा.) as usual; as ever before; in the customary way.

बदहज़मी *(bad-hazmi)* स्त्री. (फ़ा.) indigestion.

बदहवास *(bad-havās)* वि. (फ़ा.) stupefied; bewildered; stunned.

बदहवासी *(bad-havāsi)* स्त्री. (फ़ा.) stupefaction; bewilderment.

बदहाल *(badahāl)* वि. (फ़ा.) miserable; destitute.

बदी *(badī)* स्त्री. (फ़ा.) badness; evil; wickedness.

बदौलत *(badaulat)* क्रि. वि. (फ़ा.) by means (of); through; owing (to); due (to); by virtue (of).

बद्ध *(baddh)* वि. bound; tied; enclosed; restrained; checked; withheld; killing.

बधाई *(badhāī)* स्त्री. song of congratulations; congratulations; greeting; felicitation.

बधावा *(badhāvā)* पु. congratulation; presents sent ceremoniously as a mark of felicitation.

बधिक *(badhik)* पु. killer; slaughterer; executioner; hunter.

बधिया *(badhiyā)* पु. castrated animal.

बधिर *(badhir)* पु. deaf man.

बधिरता *(badhiātā)* स्त्री. deafness;

बधू *(badhu)* see वधू

बनजारन *(banjaran)* स्त्री. nomadic woman.

बनजारा *(banjārā)* पु. nomad; nomadic grocer.

बनना *(bannā)* अ. क्रि. to be composed; to be made; to be prepared; to be produced; fabricated; created; to be built; to become; to feign; to assume airs; to be befooled.

बनमानुस *(ban-mānus)* पु. chimpanzee.

बनवाना *(banavānā)* स. क्रि. to cause to be made; to cause someone to make (anything).

बनाना *(banānā)* स. क्रि. to make; to build; to prepare; to make ready; to form.

बनाम (*ba-nām*) क्रि. वि. (फ़ा.) in the name (of); to the address (of); versus.

बनावट *(banāvat)* स्त्री. structure; construction; formation; workmanship; artifice; show; display; get-up; artificiality; texture; fabric.

बनावटी *(banāvaṭi)* वि. fictitious; unreal; showy; artificial; counterfeit; sham; spurious.

बनाव-सिंगार *(banāv-simhār)* पु. make-up.

बनिता *(banita)* स्त्री. wife; woman.

बनिया *(baniyā)* पु. merchant; trader; shopkeeper.

बबूल *(babūl)* पु. acacio tree.

बम[1] *(bam)* पु. shaft; large kettle-drum.

बम[2] *(bam)* पु. bomb.

बमबारी *(bambāri)* बमवर्षा स्त्री. bombing; bombardment.

बयान *(bayān)* पु. (अ.) description; declaration; exposition; statement; account.

बयाना *(bayānā)* पु. earnest-money; advance.

बयाबान *(bayābān)* पु. (फ़ा.) forest; desert land.

बरकत *(barkat)* स्त्री. (फ़ा.) affluence; increase; abundance; grace; good luck; gain.

बरख़ास्त *(bar-khāst)* वि. (फ़ा.) dismissed; discharged; dissolved.

बरख़ास्तगी *(bar-khāstagī)* स्त्री. (फ़ा.) dismissal; termination.

बरखुरदार[1] *(bar-khurdār)* वि. (फ़ा.) prosperous; flourishing; fortunate.

बरखुरदार[2] *(bar-khurdār)* पु. (फ़ा.) son; issue.

बरछा *(barchā)* पु. spear; lance.

बरछी *(barchī)* स्त्री. small spear; dagger; javelin.

बरतन *(bartan)* पु. vessel; domestic utensil.

बरतना *(baratnā)* स. क्रि. to have personal relation or dealings with; to deal with; to use; employ; apply; make use of.

बरताव *(bartāv)* पु. behaviour; treatment; dealing.

बरदाश्त *(bar-dāśt)* स्त्री. (फ़ा.) endurance; patience; forbearance.

बरबस *(barbas)* क्रि. वि. forcibly; willynilly; without any reason; in vain; unexpectedly; all of a sudden.

बरबाद *(bar-bād)* वि. (फ़ा.) ruined; destroyed; wasted.

बरबादी *(bar-bādī)* स्त्री. (फ़ा.) destruction; ruination; waste.

बरमा *(barmā)* पु. drill; auger; a kind of gimlet or borer worked with string.

बरस *(baras)* पु. year.

बरसगाँठ *(baras-gānth)* स्त्री. birth anniversary.

बरसना *(barasnā)* अ. क्रि. to rain; to fall; to give vent to anger.

बरसात *(barsāt)* स्त्री. rainy seasson.

बरसाती[1] *(barsātī)* वि. belonging to the rainy season; rainy.

बरसाती[2] *(barsātī)* स्त्री. rain coat; a room on the roof of a house to sleep during the rains; portico.

बरसाना *(barsānā)* स. क्रि. to cause to rain; to shower.

बरसी *(barsī)* स्त्री. death-anniversary.

बरात *(barāt)* स्त्री. marriage procession; marriage party.

बराती *(barātī)* पु. one who joins a marriage procession; member of a marriage party.

बराबर[1] *(bar-ābar)* वि. (फ़ा.) even; equal; parallel; etc.; matching.

बराबर[2] *(bar-ā-bar)* क्रि. वि. (फ़ा.) constantly; continuously; ever.

बराबर-बराबर *(bar-ā-bar-bar-ābar)* क्रि. वि. (फ़ा.) equally; on the basis of parity; in close proximity.

बराबरी *(barābarī)* स्त्री. equality; parity; rivalry; competition.

बरामद *(bar-āmad)* वि. (फ़ा.) recovered; seized.

बरामदगी *(bar-āmadgī)* स्त्री. (फ़ा.) recovery.

बरामदा *(barāmadā)* पु. (फ़ा.) verandah

बरी *(barī)* वि. (अ.) acquitted; absolved; discharged.

बरौनी *(baraunī)* स्त्री. eye-lashes.

बर्तन *(bartan)* see बरतन।

बर्ताव *(bartāv)* see बरताव।

बर्फ़ *(barf)* स्त्री. (फ़ा.) snow; ice.

बर्फ़ीला *(barfilā)* वि. icy; snowy.

बर्बर *(barbar)* वि. barbarian; savage; uncultured.

बर्बरता *(barbartā)* स्त्री. barbarism; savagery.

बर्बरतापूर्ण *(barbartāpurna)* वि. barbarous.

बर्राना *(barrānā)* अ. क्रि. to gobble; to talk in sleep or fever.

बल[1] *(bal)* पु. kink; twist; contortion.

बल[2] *(bal)* पु. strength; might; power; force; army; potency; vigour; vitality; emphasis; stress; accent.

बलग़म *(balgam)* पु. (अ.) phlegm.

बलबूता *(balbutā)* पु. capacity; strength.

बलवंत *(balvant)* वि. powerful; strong; vigorous; potent.

बलवती *(balvatī)* वि. strong.

बलवर्धक *(balvardhak)* वि. invigorating; nutritious; energising.

बलवा *(balvā)* पु. (अ.) riot; rebellion.

बलवान् *(balvān)* बलशाली वि. strong; powerful.

बला *(balā)* स्त्री. (अ.) calamity; affliction vile or hateful thing; misfortune; evil spirit.

बलात् *(balāt)* क्रि. वि. forcibly; all of a sudden; suddenly.

बलात्कार *(balātkār)* पु. forcible or oppressive act; outrage; rape; criminal assault.

बलात्कारी *(balātkārī)* पु. raper; rapist.

बलि *(bali)* स्त्री. sacrificial beast (in a ritual); sacrifice for a cause.

बलिदान *(balidān)* पु. sacrifice of a beast to please a deity; sacrifice of one's life.

बलिदानी[1] *(balidanī)* वि. sacrificing.

बलिदानी[2] *(balidanī)* पु. sacrificer.

बलिष्ठ *(baliśt)* वि. strongest; most powerful; very strong.

बलिहारी *(balihāri)* स्त्री. exclamation in affectionate praise and wonder; feeling of offering or submitting oneself.

बली *(balī)* वि. strong; powerful; mighty.

बलूत *(balūt)* पु. (अ.) oak.

बलैया *(balaiyā)* स्त्री. blessings.

बल्कि *(balki)* क्रि. वि. (फ़ा.) on the contrary; rather; but; etc.

बल्लम *(ballam)* पु. spear; lance.

बल्ला *(ballā)* पु. bat (in cricket); racket; pole.

बल्ली *(ballī)* स्त्री. pole; beam; pole or bamboo with which a boat is propelled.

बल्लेबाज़ *(ballebāz)* पु. batsman.

बल्लेबाज़ी *(ballebāzī)* स्त्री. batting; batsmanship.

बवंडर *(bavaṇdar)* पु. whirlwind; hurricane; typhoon; uproar.

बवाल *(bavāl)* पु. anything painful or distressing; mess.

बवासीर *(bavāsīr)* स्त्री. (अ.) piles.

बसना *(basnā)* अ. क्रि. to dwell; to inhabit; to be populated.

बसाना *(basānā)* स. क्रि. to cause to dwell; to rehabilitate; to people; to colonize.

बसीला *(basīlā)* वि. odorous; foul in smell.

बसूली *(basūlī)* स्त्री. a mason's tool for cutting bricks or stone.

बसेरा *(baserā)* पु. night's lodging; nest; bird's resting place during night; abode; dwelling; nocturnal stay.

बस्ता *(bastā)* पु. bag; school bag; portfolio; bundle.

बस्ती *(bastī)* स्त्री. inhabited place; settlement; satellite town; colony.

बहकना *(bahaknā)* अ. क्रि. to be misled; to go astray; to be excited or intoxicated.

बहकाना *(bahkānā)* स. क्रि. to mislead; to deceive; delude; to instigate.

बहकावा *(bahkāvā)* पु. misleading; delusion; inveiglement; trick; ruse.

बहन *(bahn)* see बहिन।

बहना *(bahnā)* स. क्रि. to flow; to blow; to ooze.

बहनोई *(bahnoī)* पु. sister's husband; brother-in-law.

बहरा *(bahrā)* वि. deaf.

बहरापन *(bahrāpan)* पु. deafness.

बहलना *(bahalnā)* अ. क्रि. to be amused or entertained.

बहलाना *(bahlānā)* स. क्रि. to amuse; to entertain.

बहलाव *(bahlāv)* पु. diversion; amusement; recreation; entertainment.

बहलावा *(bahlāvā)* पु. allurement; enticement; false hope.

बहस *(bahs)* स्त्री. (अ.) discussion; argument; debate; contention; pleading.

बहादुर *(bahādur)* वि. (फ़ा.) brave; valiant; bold.

बहादुरी *(bahādurī)* स्त्री. bravery; valour; boldness.

बहाना[1] *(bahānā)* स. क्रि. to cause to flow; to squander; to sell cheap.

बहाना[2] *(bahānā)* पु. (फ़ा.) excuse; pretext.

बहानेबाज़ *(bahāne-bāz)* पु. (फ़ा.) pretender.

बहानेबाज़ी *(bahāne-bāzī)* स्त्री. (फ़ा.) pretention; making an excuse.

बहार *(bahār)* स्त्री. (फ़ा.) spring or blooming season; delight; merriment; jubilance; elegance; beauty; glory; etc.

बहाली *(ba-hālī)* स्त्री. (फ़ा.) reinstatement; restoration.

बहाव *(bahāv)* पु. flow; drift; course of a river; flush; flux.

बहिन *(bahin)* स्त्री. sister.

बहिरंग *(bahirang)* वि. outer; external; outward; unessential; extraneous.

बहिर्गमन *(bahir-gaman)* पु. exit; going out.

बहिश्त *(bahiśt)* पु. heaven.

बहिष्कार *(bahiṣkār)* पु. exclusion; expulsion; removal; boycott.

बहिष्कृत *(bahiṣkrit)* वि. excluded or expelled; removed; boycotted.

बही *(bahī)* स्त्री. book of accounts; ledger.

बही-खाता *(bahī-khāta)* पु. ledger; account book; record-book; book keeping.

बहुअर्थक *(bahu-arthak)* वि. polysemantic; polysemous.

बहुआयामी *(bahu-ayāmi)* वि. variegated; having many plans or levels.

बहुज्ञ *(bahugva)* वि. versatile; scholarly; learned.

बहुज्ञता *(bahugvatā)* स्त्री. state of being welस.versed in many things; versatility; polymathy.

बहुत[1] *(bahut)* वि. much; abundant; plentiful; immense; many.

बहुत[2] *(bahut)* क्रि. वि. very; extremely.

बहुतायत *(bahutāyat)* स्त्री. muchness; abundance; plenty.

बहुतेरा *(bahuterā)* वि. very much; enough; in many ways.

बहुतेरे *(bahutere)* वि. many; numerous.

बहुधंधी *(bahu-dhandhi)* वि. engaged in many jobs; busy in multifarious activities.

बहुधा *(bahudhā)* क्रि. वि. often; frequently; usually; in many ways.

बहुपतित्व *(bahu-patitva)* पु. polyandry.

बहुपत्नीक *(bahu-patnik)* पु. polygamist.

बहुपत्नीप्रथा *(bahu-patīnprathā)* स्त्री. polygamy.

बहुभाषी[1] *(bahu-bhāshi)* पु. polyglot; multilinguist.

बहुभाषी[2] *(bahu-bhāshi)* वि. multilingual; talkative; loquacious.

बहुभुज *(bahu-bhuj)* पु. polygon.

बहुमत *(bahu-mat)* पु. many different opinions; majority opinion; majority.

बहुमुखी *(bahu-mukhi)* वि. versatile.

बहुमूल्य *(bahu-mulya)* वि. costly; precious; invaluable.

बहुरंगी *(bahu-rangi)* वि. multicoloured; many-hued.

बहुरूपिया[1] *(bahu-rupiyā)* पु. person who assumes various characters and disguises; mimic; imposter.

बहुरूपिया[2] *(bahu-rupiyā)* वि. multimorphic.

बहुल *(bahul)* वि. abundant; plentiful.

बहुलता *(bahulata)* स्त्री. immensity; multiplicity; abundance;

plenty.

बहुवचन *(bahu-vacan)* पु. the plural number.

बहुविद्याविज्ञान *(bahu-vidyavignān)* पु. polymathy.

बहुविध *(bahu-vidh)* वि. multifarious; variegated.

बहुविधता *(bahu-vidhatā)* स्त्री. multifariousness; variety.

बहुविवाह *(bahu-vivāh)* पु. polygamy; polyandry.

बहुशः *(bahuśah)* क्रि. वि. repeatedly; again and again; many a time; frequently.

बहुश्रुत *(bahuśrut)* वि. polymathic; well-informed.

बहू *(bahū)* स्त्री. son's wife; daughter-law; bride; wife.

बहेलिया *(baheliyā)* पु. fowler; hunter.

बाँकपन, बाँकपना *(bāṁkpan)* पु. curvedness; wantonness; crookedness; dandyism; foppishness.

बाँका *(bāṁka)* वि. bent; curved; wanton; dandyish; foppish; showy; chivalrous; gallant.

बाँकुरा *(bāṁkurā)* वि. brave; heroic; clever; crooked; sharp.

बाँग *(bāṁg)* स्त्री. (फ़ा.) sound; voice; crowing of a cock at dawn; call for prayer by the mullah from a mosque.

बांचना *(bāṁcnā)* स. क्रि. to read out; decipher.

बाँझ[१] *(bāṁjh)* वि. barren(woman); unfertile; sterile.

बाँझपन *(bāṁjhpan)* पु. barrenness; unproductiveness; sterility.

बाँट *(bāṁt)* स्त्री. act of dividing or distributing; part; portion; share; dealing out (cards).

बाँटना *(bāṁṭnā)* स. क्रि. to divide; to apportion; to distribute; to deal out.

बाँदी *(bāṁdī)* स्त्री. maid-servant; bondmaid; female serf.

बाँध *(bāṁdh)* पु. embankment; dam; barrage; dike.

बाँधना *(bāṁdhnā)* स. क्रि. to bind; to fasten; to tie; to wrap around; to pack; to fold; to imprison.

बांधव *(bāndhav)* पु. fraternal relations; kith and kin; brethren.

बाँबी *(bāṁbī)* बाँमी स्त्री. snake's hole; ant hill.

बाँस *(bāṁs)* पु. bamboo; pole; spinal chord.

बाँसुरी *(bāṁsurī)* स्त्री. pipe; flute.

बाँह *(bāṁh)* स्त्री. arm; sleeve.

बाअदब *(bā-adab)* वि. (फ़ा.) respectful.

बाएँ *(bāyen)* क्रि. वि. to the left; on the left hand side.

बाक़ायदा *(bāqāyadā)* वि. (फ़ा.) systematic; regular.

बाक़ी *(bāqī)* वि. (अ.) remaining; left over.

बाग *(bāg)* स्त्री. reins; bridle.

बाग़ *(bāg)* पु. (फ़ा.) garden; park.

बागड़ोर *(bāg-dor)* स्त्री. reins.

बाग़बान *(bāg-bān)* पु. (फ़ा.) gardener; horticulturist.

बाग़बानी *(bāg-bānī)* स्त्री. (फ़ा.) gardening; horticulture.

बाग़ी *(bāgī)* वि. (अ.) rebellious; revolting.

बगीचा *(bāgīcā)* पु. (फ़ा.) small garden; park.

बाघ (*bāgh*) पु. lion; tiger.

बाज़ *(baz)* पु. (फ़ा.) hawk; falcon.

बाजरा *(bājrā)* पु. species of millet; plant of millet.

बाजा *(bājā)* पु. musical instrument.

बाज़ार *(bāzār)* पु. (फ़ा.) market; market-place; bazar.

बाज़ारू *(bāzārū)* वि. pertaining to the market; low; vulgar.

बाजी *(bāzī)* स्त्री. elder sister.

बाज़ी *(bazi)* स्त्री. (फ़ा.) stake; bet; wager; play; performance; turn.

बाज़ीगर *(bāzigār)* पु. (फ़ा.) juggler; magician; conjurer.

बाज़ीगरी *(bāzigāri)* स्त्री. jugglery; conjuring; conjury.

बाट[1] *(bāt)* स्त्री. way; path; course; twine; coil; twist.

बाट[2] *(bāt)* पु. measure of weight.

बाड़ा *(bāṛā)* पु. enclosed space; enclosure; fold.

बाढ़ *(bāṛh)* स्त्री. growth; inundation; flood; abundance; plenty; profit; gain.

बाण *(bāṇ)* पु. arrow.

बात *(bāt)* स्त्री. speech; conversation; talk; discourse; thing; matter; fact; point; counsel; discussion; negotiation; utterance; statement; commitment; word; happening; excuse.

बातचीत *(bātcīt)* स्त्री. talks; conversation; discourse; negotiations; dialogue.

बातूनी *(bātūnī)* वि. talkative loquacious; garrulous.

बादल *(bādal)* पु. cloud.

बादशाह *(bādśah)* पु. (फ़ा.) king; monarch; sovereign; king in the playing cards or chess.

बादशाहत *(bādśāhat)* स्त्री. kingship; reign.

बादाम *(bādām)* पु. (फ़ा.) almond.

बादामी *(bādāmī)* वि. almond coloured; brown; almond shaped; made of or containing almonds.

बाधक *(bādhak)* वि. obstructive; hindering; impeding; resistant.

बाधा *(bādhā)* स्त्री. obstruction; hindrance impediment; bar; handicap; interference; interruption; trouble; disturbance; obsession (of an evil spirit; etc.)

बाधित *(bādhit)* वि. restricted; handicapped; barred; impeded; obstructed; obsessed.

बाध्य *(bādhya)* वि. restricted; checked; obliged; compelled.

बाध्यता *(bādhyatā)* स्त्री. duress; coercion;; obligation.

बानक *(bānak)* पु. guise; appearance; form; shape.

बानगी *(bānagī)* स्त्री. specimen; sample; fore-taste.

बानर *(bānar)* पु. monkey.

बाप *(bāp)* पु. father.

बाबा *(bābā)* पु. (फ़ा.) father; grandfather; old man; sage; ascetic.

बाबू *(bābū)* पु. educated man; gentleman; clerk.

बायाँ *(bāyaṁ)* वि. left.

बायें *(bāyeṁ)* क्रि. वि. to the left; in the opposite camp.

बारंबार *(bārambār)* क्रि. वि. again and again; repeatedly; time and again; frequently.

बारंबारता *(bārambārtā)* स्त्री. frequency.

बार[1] *(bar)* स्त्री. time; delay; turn.

बार[2] *(bar)* पु. association of lawyers; profession of lawyers; liquor shop; dancing hall.

बार-बार *(bār-bār)* क्रि. वि. again and again; time and again.

बारहबाट *(bārah-bāt)* वि. scattered all round; cast to winds; at sixes and sevens; thrown into confusion.

बारहसिंगा *(bārā-siṁhā)* पु. stag.

बारात *(bārāt)* see बरात।

बाराती *(bārātī)* see बराती।

बारिश *(bāriś)* स्त्री. (फ़ा.) rain; shower; rainy season.

बारी *(bārī)* स्त्री. turn; day of the cyclic fever.

बारी-बारी *(bārī-bārī)* से क्रि. वि. turn by turn.

बारीक *(bārīk)* वि. (फ़ा.) thin; fine; slender; subtle.

बारीकी *(bārīkī)* स्त्री. (फ़ा.) fineness; minuteness; subtlety.

बारूद *(bārūd)* स्त्री. (फ़ा.) gun powder

बारूदख़ाना *(bārūdkhanā)* पु. (फ़ा.) magazine; arsenal; armoury.

बाल *(bāl)* पु. hair.

बालक *(bālak)* पु. child; boy; ignorant person.

बालकपन *(bālakpan)* पु. boyhood.

बालटी *(bālṭi)* स्त्री. bucket.

बालपन *(bālpan)* पु. childhood.

बालम *(bālam)* पु. husband; beloved; sweetheart;.

बाला *(bālā)* स्त्री. adolescent girl; young woman.

बालानशीन *(bālā-naśin)* वि. (फ़ा.) honourable; distinguished; the best; the finest.

बालिका *(bālikā)* स्त्री. female child; young girl.

बालिग़ *(bālig)* वि. (अ.) adult.

बालिश्त *(bāliśt)* पु. (अ.) span measured by the extended thumb and little finger.

बाली *(bālī)* स्त्री. ear-ring; ear or spike of corn.

बालुका *(bālukā)* स्त्री. sand.

बालू *(bālū)* स्त्री. sand; silica.

बाल्टी *(bālṭī)* see बालटी।

बाल्यकाल *(bālyakāl)* पु. childhood.

बाल्यावस्था *(bālyavastha)* स्त्री. age of childhood.

बावड़ी *(bāvṛī)* स्त्री. deep pucca well with steps.

बावरची *(bāvarcī)* पु. (फ़ा.) cook; butler.

बावरचीख़ाना *(bāvarcīkhānā)* पु. (फ़ा.) cook-house; kitchen.

बावला *(bāvalā)* वि. mad; insane; deranged; crazy.

बावलापन *(bavlāpan)* पु. madness; craziness; insanity.

बावली *(bāvalī)* स्त्री. small tank witn steps all round.

बावेला *(bāvelā)* पु. furore; ballyo; uproar; tumult.

बाशिंदा *(bāśindā)* पु. (फ़ा.) dweller; resident; inhabitant; denizen.

वाष्पीकरण *(baśpikaran)* पु. evaporation; vaporization.

बास[1] *(bās)* पु. dwelling; residing; lodge; dress.

बास[2] *(bās)* स्त्री. foul smell; obnoxious odour.

बासा[1] *(bāsā)* वि. stale; kept overnight.

बासा[2] *(bāsā)* पु. habitat; dwelling place.

बासी *(bāsī)* see बासा।

बाहर *(bāhar)* क्रि. वि. outside; without; beyond; away.

बाहरी *(bāhrī)* वि. external; outward; outer; foreign.

बाहु *(bāhu)* स्त्री. arm.

बाहुपाश *(bāhu-pās)* पु. embrace; arm girdle.

बाहुबल *(bāhu-bal)* पु. strength of arm; muscular strength.

बाहुल्य *(bāhulya)* पु. abundance;

plenty; exuberance.

बाह्य *(bāhya)* वि. outer; external; outward; foreign; strange.

बाह्यतः *(bahyatāh)* क्रि. वि. externally.

बिंदी *(bindī)* स्त्री. dot; cypher; small vermilion mark on forehead.

बिंदु *(bindu)* पु. drop of water; detached particle; (geom.) point; zero; cipher; bull's eye (in shooting.)

बिंब *(bimb)* पु. reflection; shadow; image; disc.

बिकना *(bikanā)* अ. क्रि. to be sold; to sell; to be blind follower; to be enslaved.

बिकवाना *(bikavānā)* स. क्रि. to get sold; to cause to sell.

बिकाऊ *(bikāū)* वि. saleable; for sale.

बिक्री *(bikrī)* स्त्री. sale; circulation; act of selling; marketing; disposal.

बिखरना *(bikharnā)* अ. क्रि. to be strewn or dispersed; to be scattered or diffused (light); to spill.

बिखराना *(bikharānā)* see बिखेरना।

बिखराव *(bikhrāv)* पु. scattering; diffusion; disunity; disintegration.

बिखेरना *(bikhernā)* स. क्रि. to scatter; to strew; to diffuse; to spill.

बिगड़ना *(bigarṇā)* अ. क्रि. to be disfigured or deformed; to be spoilt; to be disordered; to be damaged; to become vicious; wicked or unruly; to be enraged.

बिगड़ैल *(bigṛail)* वि. short-tempered; peevish.

बिगाड़ *(bigāṛ)* पु. disfigurement; defacement; disorder; defect; damage; harm; injury; rift; discord.

बिगाड़ना *(bigāṛanā)* स. क्रि. to ruin; spoil; mar; to vitiate; to damage; to put out of order.

बिगुल *(bigul)* पु. (अ.) bugle.

बिचरना *(bicarnā)* अ. क्रि. to go in a leisurely manner; to walk about; to roam; to loiter; to ramble.

बिचला *(bicalā)* वि. middle; intervening; of middle class; moderate.

बिचौलिया *(bicauliyā)* पु. middleman; intermeddler; intermediary; go-between; broker.

बिच्छू *(bicchū)* पु. scorpion; a kind of grass.

बिछवाना *(bichvānā)* स. क्रि. to cause to be spread; to have (a carpet etc.) spread.

बिछाना *(bichānā)* स. क्रि. to spread; to spread out; to extend; to lay.

बिछुड़ना *(bichuṛanā)* अ. क्रि. to separate; to part company.

बिछोह *(bichoh)* पु. painful separation; parting.

बिछौना *(bichaunā)* पु. bed; bedding.

बिजली *(bijlī)* स्त्री. lightening; thunderbolt; electricity.

बिजलीघर *(bijlīghar)* पु. powerhouse; powerstation.

बिजूका, बिजूखा *(bijūkā)* पु. scarecrow.

बिटिया *(biṭiyā)* स्त्री. little daughter; girl.

बिठलाना, बिठाना *(biṭhlānā)* स. क्रि. to cause to sit; to seat; to fix; to take (a woman) as kept.

बिड़ाल *(biṛāl)* पु. he-cat.

बितंडा *(bitaṁdā)* पु. mess.

बिताना *(bitānā)* स. क्रि. to pass or spend.

बिदकना *(bidakanā)* अ. क्रि. to be scared; to shirk (from); to shy;

to be alarmed; to be startled; to be provoked.

बिदकाना *(bidakānā)* स. क्रि. to scare; to startle; to cause to recede or draw back.

बिदा *(bidā)* स्त्री. farewell; permission to depart; departure.

बिदाई *(bidāī)* स्त्री. farewell; farewell function; departure; present made by a host to a visitor; ceremonial farewell.

बिनती *(binatī)* स्त्री. request; importunity; submission.

बिनना *(binanā)* स. क्रि. to pick out (bad ones); to knit; to weave.

बिनवाना *(binavānā)* स. क्रि. to cause to be knitted or woven.

बिना[1] *(binā)* स्त्री. (अ.) cause; plea.

बिना[2] *(binā)* क्रि. वि. without.

बिनाई *(bināī)* स्त्री. knitting; weaving; picking; charges for weaving or knitting; charges for picking.

बिफरना *(bipharnā)* वि. to be visibly annoyed; to be provoked; to be startled.

बिरला *(birlā)* वि. rare.

बिरवा *(birvā)* पु. sapling;seedling.

बिरही *(birahī)* पु. lover in pangs of separation.

बिराजना *(birājanā)* अ. क्रि. to be seated gracefully; to look fine.

बिरादराना *(birādārānā)* वि. (फ़ा.) brotherly; fraternal.

बिरादरी *(birādārī)* स्त्री. (फ़ा.) community; brotherhood; fraternity.

बिल *(bil)* पु. hole; bill; bill of exchange.

बिलखना *(bilakhanā)* अ. क्रि. to weep bitterly; to lament; to wail.

बिलगाना *(bilgānā)* स. क्रि. to separate; to detach; to be separated.

बिलगाव *(bilagāv)* पु. separation parting; detachment; disintegration.

बिलना *(bilanā)* अ. क्रि. to be rolled into flat cakes.

बिलबिलाना *(bilbilānā)* अ. क्रि. to writhe; to wriggle; to be restless with pain; to toss about in torment.

बिलाव *(bilāv)* पु. tom-cat.

बिल्कुल *(bilkul)* क्रि. वि. entirely; wholly; solely; absolutely; quite.

बिल्ला *(billā)* पु. male cat; badge; insignia.

बिल्ली *(billī)* स्त्री. female cat; latch.

बिवाई *(bivāī)* स्त्री. kibe or chap on the heel; chilblain.

बिसरना *(bisarnā)* अ. क्रि. to be forgotten.

बिसराना *(bisaranā)* स. क्रि. to forget.

बिसात *(bisāt)* स्त्री. (अ.) capacity or power; sheet etc. that is spread out; chess-cloth; diceboard; etc.

बिसातख़ाना *(bisāt-khānā)* पु. (अ.) departmental store; small wares store; general store; haberdashery.

बिसाती *(bisātī)* पु. (अ.) vendor of small wares; general merchant.

बिसूरना *(bisurnā)* अ. क्रि. to cry slowly; to sob; to wail.

बिस्तर *(bistar)* पु. (फ़ा.) bed; bedding.

बिस्तरबंद *(bistarband)* पु. (फ़ा.) holdall.

बिस्मिल्लाह *(bismillāh)* स्त्री. (अ.) beginning.

बिहँसना *(bihaṁsanā)* अ. क्रि. to smile; to laugh.

बींधना *(bimdhanā)* स. क्रि. to perforate; to bore through; to pierce.

बीच *(bic)* पु. middle; midst; centre.

बीच-बचाव *(bic-bacāv)* पु. interposition; intervention; mediation.

बीचोबीच *(bico-bic)* क्रि. वि. exactly in the middle.

बीज *(bij)* पु. seed; cause; source; origin.

बीजक *(bijak)* पु. list; invoice; inventory; bill.

बीजगणित *(bij-ganit)* पु. algebra.

बीजमंत्र *(bij-mantra)* पु. keynote.

बीजारोपण *(bijāropan)* पु. sowing; initiation.

बीतना *(bitanā)* अ. क्रि. to pass; to elapse; to expire; to befall; to fappen; to occur.

बीनना *(binanā)* स. क्रि. to pick to gather; to pluck; to pickout; to select; to glean.

बीनाई *(bināi)* स्त्री. vision; eye-sight.

बीभत्स *(bibhats)* वि. abhorrent; loathsome; horrid; sinful; rotten.

बीमा *(bimā)* पु. (फ़ा.) insurance.

बीमार[1] *(bimār)* वि. (फ़ा.) sick; ill; ailing; unwell; indisposed.

बीमार[2] *(bimār)* पु. (फ़ा.) patient.

बीमारी *(bimari)* स्त्री. (फ़ा.) illness; ailment; sickness; disease.

बीवी *(bivi)* स्त्री. (फ़ा.) wife; lady.

बीहड़ *(bihar)* वि. uncultivated; uneven(land); rugged; rough; arduous; difficult to do; cut off; detached; dense; thick.

बुज़दिल *(buzdil)* वि. (फ़ा.) cowardly; timid.

बुज़दिली *(buzdili)* स्त्री. (फ़ा.) cowardice; timidity.

बुजुर्ग[1] *(buzurg)* पु. (फ़ा.) respectable man; elderly man; ancestor.

बुजुर्ग[2] *(buzurg)* वि. (फ़ा.) aged; elderly; venerable.

बुजुर्गी *(buzurgi)* स्त्री. (फ़ा.) elderliness; agedness; respectability.

बुझना *(bujhanā)* अ. क्रि. to be put out; to be extinguished; to be cooled; to be pacified; to be quenched.

बुझाना *(bujhānā)* स. क्रि. to put out; to extinguish; to quench; to cool by putting into water; to pacify; to gratify.

बुड्ढा[1] *(buḍḍhā)* वि. old; aged.

बुड्ढा[2] *(buḍḍhā)* पु. old man.

बुढ़ापा *(buṛhāpā)* पु. old age; senility.

बुढ़िया *(buṛhiyā)* स्त्री. old woman.

बुत *(but)* पु. (फ़ा.) idol; image; statue.

बुदबुदाना *(budbudānā)* अ. क्रि. to effervesce; to buddle; to gabble; mutter.

बुदबुदाहट *(budbudahat)* स्त्री. effervescence; muttering; gabbering.

बुद्धि *(buddhi)* स्त्री. perception; comprehension; intelligence; wisdom; mind; intellect; sense.

बुद्धिगम्य *(budhi-gamya)* वि. intelligible; understandable; perceptible.

बुद्धिजीवी *(budhi-jivi)* पु. mental worker.

बुद्धिमत्ता *(budhi-mattā)* स्त्री. wisdom; sagacity; intelligence.

बुद्धिमान *(budhi-mān)* वि. intelligent; brilliant; wise; prudent; sensible; sagacious.

बुद्धिमानी *(budhi-māni)* स्त्री. intelligence; widom; sagacity; prudence.

बुद्धू *(buddū)* वि. dull; stupid; foolish; blockheaded.

बुद्धपना *(buddhūpanā)* पु. foolishness; stupidity; dullardness.

बुध *(budh)* पु. wednesday; mercury (planet).

बुनना *(bunanā)* स. क्रि. to weave; to knit; to intertwine.

बुनवाना *(bunavānā)* स. क्रि. to cause to be woven; to get (a thing) woven.

बुनवाई *(bunavāī)* स्त्री. act of weaving; wages for weaving.

बुनाई *(bunāī)* स्त्री. weaving; knitting; design of weaving or knitting; weaving charges.

बुनावट *(bunāvat)* स्त्री. design or texture.

बुनियाद *(buniyād)* स्त्री. (फ़ा.) basis; ground; foundation.

बुनियादी *(buniyādī)* वि. (फ़ा.) pertaining to foundation; basic; fundamental.

बुरा *(burā)* वि. bad; evil; evilminded; immoral; villainous; ugly; ill-looking; disagreeably unpleasant; odious; hateful; faulty; defective; vicious.

बुराई *(burāī)* स्त्री. evil deeds; badness; wickendness; accusation; evil; vice; flaw; fault; defect.

बुरादा *(burādā)* पु. (फ़ा.) filings; saw-dust.

बुर्ज *(burj)* पु. (अ.) bastion; turret; tower.

बुलंद *(buland)* वि. (फ़ा.) very high; lofty; elevated; exalted.

बुलंदी *(bulandī)* स्त्री. (फ़ा.) loftiness; height.

बुलबुल *(bulbul)* स्त्री. (अ.) nightingale.

बुलबुला *(bulbulā)* पु. bubble.

बुलवाना *(bulvānā)* स. क्रि. to cause to talk; to cause to be sent for; to send for; to convene; to summon.

बुलाना *(bulānā)* स. क्रि. to call; to send for; to convene; to summon; to invite.

बुलावा *(bulāvā)* पु. call; invitation; summons.

बुवाई *(buvāī)* स्त्री. sowing; wages paid for sowing; method of sowing.

बुहारना *(buhārnā)* स. क्रि. to sweep.

बुहारी *(buhārī)* स्त्री. broom; mop.

बूँद *(būṁd)* स्त्री. drop.

बूँदा-बाँदी *(būṁdā-bāndi)* स्त्री. intermittent rain; drizzle.

बू *(bū)* स्त्री. (फ़ा.) foul smell; stink.

बूचड़ख़ाना *(būcār-khānā)* पु. slaughter-house.

बूझ *(būjh)* स्त्री. perception; understanding; intelligence; comprehension; riddle; faculty of guessing the future correctly.

बुझना *(būjhanā)* स. क्रि. to understand; perceive; make out; comprehend; to reach the depth of; to guess correctly; to pose(a riddle) for solution.

बूटेदार *(būte-dar)* वि. embroidered.

बूढ़ा *(būṛhā)* वि. old; aged; senile.

बूढ़ी *(būṛhī)* स्त्री. old woman.

बूता *(būtā)* पु. strength; power; ability; capacity; capability.

बृहत् *(bṛhat)* वि. large; big; bulky; strong.

बेंच *(beṁc)* स्त्री. (अ.) bench in general; seats of judges in courts; seats allotted to a party for its members in Parliament; etc.

बेअक़्ल *(be-aqla)* वि. (फ़ा.) stupid; senseless; foolish.

बेअदब *(be-adab)* वि. (फ़ा.) ilस.behaved; unmannerly; disrespectful; rude; impolite; impudent.

बेअदबी *(be-adabī)* स्त्री. (फ़ा.) incivility; rudeness; disrespect; impudence; impoliteness.

बेआबरू *(be-ābru)* वि. (फ़ा.) dishonoured; disgraced; humiliated; insulted.

बेइंतिहा *(be-intahā)* वि. (फ़ा.) endless; without end.

बेइंसाफ़ी *(be-insāfī)* स्त्री. (फ़ा.) injustice; wrong; inequality.

बेइज़्ज़त *(be-izzat)* वि. (फ़ा.) without honour or dignity; disgraced; humiliated; insulted.

बेइज़्ज़ती *(be-izzatī)* स्त्री. (फ़ा.) dishonour; disgrace; ignominy.

बेईमान *(be-imān)* वि. (फ़ा.) corrupt; dishonest; unscrupulous.

बेईमानी *(be-imānī)* स्त्री. (फ़ा.) dishonesty; breach of trust; unfair dealing.

बेक़द्री *(be-qadri)* स्त्री. (फ़ा.) disgrace; dishonour; disrespect.

बेक़रार *(be-qarār)* वि. (फ़ा.) restless; uneasy; disturbed in mind; impatient.

बेक़रारी *(be-qarari)* स्त्री. (फ़ा.) restlessness; uneasiness; impatience.

बेकल *(be-kal)* वि. (फ़ा.) perturbed; restless; uneasy.

बेकली *(be-kali)* स्त्री. (फ़ा.) restlessness; perturbed state of mind; uneasiness; disquiet.

बेकस *(bekas)* वि. (फ़ा.) helpless; hapless; destitute.

बेकसी *(bekasi)* स्त्री. (फ़ा.) helplessness; destitution.

बेक़सूर *(be-qasur)* वि. (फ़ा.) innocent; faultless; guiltless.

बेक़ाबू *(be-qābu)* वि. (फ़ा.) out of control; beyond control.

बेक़ायदा *(be-qāyada)* वि. (फ़ा.) unarranged; irregular; without order.

बेकार[1] *(bekār)* वि. (फ़ा.) idle; unemployed; unserviceable; good for nothing; useless.

बेकार[2] *(bekār)* क्रि. वि. (फ़ा.) to no purpose; for no rhyme or reason.

बेकारी *(bekārī)* स्त्री. (फ़ा.) the state of being unemployed; unemployment.

बेखटक *(be-khatak)* बेखटके क्रि. वि. without apprehension or doubt; fearlessly; unhesitatingly.

बेख़बर *(be-khabar)* वि. (फ़ा.) uninformed; unaware; oblivious.

बेख़बरी *(be-khabari)* स्त्री. (फ़ा.) oblivion; obliviousness; unawareness; ignorance.

बेखुदी *(be-khudi)* स्त्री. (फ़ा.) senselessness.

बेग़म *(begam)* स्त्री. (तु.) lady; title of king's wife or chieftain's wife; etc.; playing card with queen's picture.

बेग़रज़ *(begaraz)* वि. (फ़ा.) selfless; having no selfish motive or interest.

बेगाना *(begānā)* वि. (फ़ा.) not related; alien; unknown.

बेगार *(bagār)* स्त्री. (फ़ा.) forced labour without payment.

बेगुनाह *(begunāh)* वि. (फ़ा.) guiltless: innocent.

बेगुनाही *(begunāhi)* स्त्री. (फ़ा.) guiltlessness; innocence.

बेग़ैरत *(beghairat)* वि. (फ़ा.) shameless; having no self-respect.

बेघर *(be-ghar)* वि. homeless; without hearth and home.

बेचना *(becanā)* स. क्रि. to sell.

बेचारा *(be-cāra)* वि. (फ़ा.) without remedy or resources; helpless; destitute.

बेचैन *(be-cāin)* वि. uneasy; restless or disturbed.

बेचैनी *(be-cāinī)* स्त्री. (फ़ा.) uneasiness; restlessness; disquietude.

बेजा *(bejā)* वि. (फ़ा.) improper; unfair.

बेजोड़ *(bejor)* वि. unparalleled; unmatched; matchless; unprecedented; incongruous; inharmonious; dicordant.

बेटा *(beṭā)* पु. son.

बेटी *(beṭī)* स्त्री. daughter.

बेड़ा *(beṛā)* पु. fleet of boats or ships; flotilla; raft of timbers; plants etc.

बेड़ी *(beṛī)* स्त्री. fetters; shackles; boat; small fleet; bondage.

बेडौल *(be-daul)* वि. disproportionate; shapeless; ilस.fashioned; ugly; clumsy; unsymmetrical.

बेढंगा *(be-dhanga)* वि. ilस.mannered; ilस.behaved; ilस.arranged; unsystematic; ugly; unshapely.

बेढ़ब *(be-dhab)* वि. ugly; unshapely; unmannerly; rude; unmanageable; crooked; unsystematic.

बेतरतीब *(be-tartib)* वि. (फ़ा.) disorderly; ill-arranged; unsystematic.

बेतरतीबी *(be-tartibi)* स्त्री. (फ़ा.) disorderliness; absence of system; method or order.

बेतहाशा *(be-tahāśā)* क्रि. वि. (फ़ा.) at top speed; very swiftly; wildly; recklessly; indiscreetly; rashly.

बेताब *(be-tāb)* वि. (फ़ा.) restless; uneasy; impatient; restive.

बेताबी *(be-tābi)* स्त्री. (फ़ा.) restlessness; uneasiness; impatience.

बेतुका *(be-tukā)* वि. absurd; nonsensical; incoherent; irrelevant.

बेतुकापन *(be-tukāpan)* पु. absurdity; irrelevance; ridiculousness; incongruity.

बेदख़ल *(be-dakhal)* वि. (फ़ा.) dispossessed; evicted; ousted; forced out.

बेदख़ली *(be-dakhalī)* स्त्री. (फ़ा.) dispossession; ejectment; eviction.

बेदर्दी *(be-dardi)* स्त्री. (फ़ा.) cruelty; inhumanity; mercilessness.

बेदाग़ *(be-dāg)* वि. (फ़ा.) blotless; spotless; clean; stainless; without blemish; innocent; guiltless.

बेदिल *(be-dil)* वि. (फ़ा.) dejected; heartless.

बेधड़क *(be-dharak)* क्रि. वि. fearlessly; dauntlessly; recklessly; rashly.

बेधना *(bedhanā)* स. क्रि. to pierce; to perforate; to bore; to wound; to stab.

बेपनाह *(bepanāh)* वि. (फ़ा.) shelterless; homeless; very much; excessive.

बेपरदगी, बेपर्दगी *(be-pardagi)* स्त्री. (फ़ा.) nakedness; encroachment on privacy; exposure; insult.

बेपरदा *(bepardā)* वि. (फ़ा.) unveiled; barefaced; having no privacy; exposed.

बेफ़िक्र *(be-fikra)* वि. (फ़ा.) carefree.

बेफ़िक्री *(be-fikri)* स्त्री. (फ़ा.) freeness from care or anxiety; carefreeness.

बेबस *(bebas)* वि. (फ़ा.) powerless; helpless.

बेबसी *(bebasi)* स्त्री. (फ़ा.) helplessness; powerlessness.

बेबाक़ *(bebāq)* वि. (फ़ा.) forthright; intrepid; dauntless; cleared off.

बेमतलब *(be-matlab)* क्रि. वि. (फ़ा.) purposelessly; irrelevantly.

बेमिसाल *(be-misāl)* वि. (फ़ा.) unparalleled; unprecedented; unique.

बेमेल *(be-mel)* वि. without unison; unharmonious; incongruous; incoherent.

बेर[1] *(ber)* पु. jujube tree and its fruit; plum.

बेर[2] *(ber)* स्त्री. time; turn.

बेरहम *(beraham)* वि. (फ़ा.) pitiless; merciless; curel.

बेरहमी *(berahami)* स्त्री. (फ़ा.) hard-heartedness; cruelty; mercilessness.

बेरी *(berī)* स्त्री. jujube tree; plum tree.

बेरुख़ी *(berukhi)* स्त्री. (फ़ा.) indifference; neglect.

बेरोक *(berok)* वि. unobstructed unhindered; unhampered.

बेरोज़गार *(berozgār)* वि. (फ़ा.) unemployed.

बेरोज़गारी *(berozgāri)* स्त्री. (फ़ा.) unemployment.

बेल *(bel)* स्त्री. wood apple and its fruit; creeper; climber; vine; lace.

बेलग़ाम *(be-lagām)* वि. (फ़ा.) unbridled; licentious; intemperate loose-tongued.

बेलचा *(belcā)* पु. (फ़ा.) shovel.

बेलन *(belan)* पु. cylinder of wood; rolling-pin; roller.

बेलना *(belnā)* स. क्रि. to roll.

बेलाग *(belāg)* वि. without stain or blemish; faultless; without any favour regard; irreproachable; frank; forthright; straight forward.

बेवकूफ़ *(bevaquf)* वि. (फ़ा.) foolish; stupid.

बेवकूफ़ी *(bevaqufi)* स्त्री. (फ़ा.) stupidity; foolishness; want of understanding; ignorance.

बेवक़्त *(be-vaqta)* वि. (फ़ा.) untimely; inopportune.

बेवफ़ा *(be-vafā)* वि. (फ़ा.) faithless; perfidious; treacherous; disloyal.

बेवफ़ाई *(be-vafāi)* स्त्री. (फ़ा.) disloyalty; faithlessness; infidelity.

बेवा *(bevā)* स्त्री. (फ़ा.) widow.

बेशक *(beśak)* क्रि. वि. (फ़ा.) undoubtedly; doubtlessly; indeed; certainly; of course.

बेशर्म *(beśarm)* वि. (फ़ा.) shameless; impudent; immodest.

बेशर्मी *(beśarmi)* स्त्री. (फ़ा.) shamelessness; immodesty; impudence.

बेशुमार *(beśumār)* वि. (फ़ा.) countless; numberless; innumerable.

बेसब्र *(besabra)* वि. (फ़ा.) impatient; restive; fidgety.

बेसब्री *(besabri)* स्त्री. (फ़ा.) impatience; restivity; fidgetiness.

बेसहारा *(besahāra)* वि. (फ़ा.) helpless; without support.

बेसुध *(besudh)* वि. in a swoon; senseless; fainted; unaware; bewildered; absent-minded.

बेहद *(behad)* वि. (फ़ा.) boundless; endless; too much; excessive.

बेहया *(behayā)* वि. (फ़ा.) shameless; immodest.

बेहयाई *(behayāi)* स्त्री. (फ़ा.) shamelessness; impudence.

बेहाल *(behāl)* वि. (फ़ा.) in a sad plight; in a bad shape or state; afflicted; distressed.

बेहिसाब *(behisāb)* वि. (फ़ा.) countless; beyond calculation; incalculable.

बेहूदगी *(behūdagī)* स्त्री. (फ़ा.) impudence; smuttiness; valgarity.

बेहूदा *(behūdā)* वि. (फ़ा.) impudent; nonsensical; smutty; vulgar.

बेहूदापन *(behūdāpan)* पु. smuttiness; obscenity.

बेहोश *(behoś)* वि. (फ़ा.) unconscious; senseless.

बेहोशी *(behośī)* स्त्री. (फ़ा.) unconsciousness; senselessness.

बैंगन *(baiṁgan)* पु. brinjal.

बैंगनी *(baiṁgnī)* वि. of the colour of brinjal; purple; violet.

बैठक *(baiṭhak)* स्त्री. sitting room; drawing room; sitting; meeting; a kind of exercise.

बैठना *(baiṭhanā)* अ. क्रि. to sit; to be seated; to settle; to cling; to sink down; to settle down; to be adjusted; to appear (in some examination) to cave in; to crash down; to sink; to fit in.

बैठाना *(baiṭhānā)* स. क्रि. to set; to cause to settle down; to cause to sit down; to cause to be seated; to place; to establish.

बैनाम *(bai-nām)* पु. (अ.) saledeed.

बैर *(bair)* पु. enmity; hostility; animosity; ill-will.

बैरागी *(bairāgī)* पु. recluse.

बैल *(bail)* पु. bullock; ox; blockhead; fool.

बैलगाड़ी *(bailgari)* स्त्री. bullock-cart.

बैसाख *(baisākh)* पु. the second month according to the Hindu calendar.

बैसाखी *(baisākhjī)* स्त्री. a festival falling on the first day of Baisakh; crutch.

बोआई *(boāī)* स्त्री. sowing; wages paid for sowing.

बोआना *(boānā)* स. क्रि. to cause to sow.

बोझ, बोझा *(bojhā)* पु. load; burden.

बोझिल *(bojhil)* वि. heavy; massive; burdensome.

बोटी *(boṭī)* स्त्री. small bit; slice or morsel of flesh or meat; chop of flesh.

बोतल *(botal)* स्त्री. bottle.

बोदा *(boda)* वि. weak; feeble; lowspirited; dulस.headed; stupid.

बोध *(bodh)* पु. knowledge; understanding; sense; perception; enlightenment.

बोधक[1] *(bodhak)* वि. causing to know; informing; signifying.

बोधक[2] *(bodhak)* वि. indicator; one who cause to know or teach.

बोधगम्य *(bodh-gamya)* वि. comprehensible; understandable.

बोधगम्यता *(bodh-gamyatā)* स्त्री. intelligibility; intelligible; comprehensibility.

बोना *(bonā)* स. क्रि. to sow; to plant; dwarf.

बोरा *(borā)* पु. gunny bag; sack.

बोरिया *(boriyā)* स्त्री small sack or gunny bag.

बोरी *(borī)* स्त्री. small gunny bag.

बोल *(bol)* पु. utterance; phrase; sentence; speech; talk etc. opening words of song; taunt.

बोल-चाल *(boस.cāl)* स्त्री. talk; conversation; parlance; mode of speech.

बोलती *(bolatī)* स्त्री. power of speech; act of speaking.

बोलना *(bolanā)* अ. क्रि. to speak; to talk.

बोलबाला *(bol-bālā)* पु. influence; vogue; domination; sway.

बोली *(bolī)* स्त्री. speech (in general); dialect; bid (at an auction); jeer; taunt.

बौखलाना *(boukhalānā)* अ. क्रि. to talk nonsense out of passion or anger; to lose temper; to lose one's self-control in anger.

बौखलाहट *(boukhalāhat)* स्त्री. frenzy; fury; menutal agitation; wild folly.

बौछार *(bauchār)* स्त्री. heavy shower of rain; volley.

बौद्ध[1] *(bauddh)* वि. pertaining to Buddhism.

बौद्ध[2] *(bauddh)* पु. Buddhist; follower of Lord Buddha and his religion.

बौद्धिक *(bauddhik)* वि. intellectual; mental.

बौद्धिकता *(bauddhikata)* स्त्री. intellectualism.

बौना[1] *(baunā)* वि. dwarfish.

बौना[2] *(baunā)* पु. dwarf.

बौर *(baur)* पु. blossom of the mango tree.

बौराना *(baurānā)* अ. क्रि. to become crazy; to go off one's head; to blossom.

ब्याज *(byāj)* स्त्री. interest (on money).

ब्याजख़ोर *(byāj-khor)* पु. usurer.

ब्याजखोरी *(byāj-khorī)* स्त्री. usury.

ब्याह *(byah)* पु. marriage; wedding.

ब्याहना *(byahana)* पु. to marry; to wed; to give or to take in marriage.

ब्योरा *(byorā)* पु. detailed account; details; particulars; description.

ब्योरेवार *(byore-vār)* क्रि. वि. in detail.

ब्रह्मचर्य *(brahmcārya)* पु. celibacy.

ब्रह्मचारी *(brahmcārī)* पु. celibate.

ब्रह्मांड *(brahmānd)* पु. universe; cosmos; the uppermost point of the skull.

भ

भ *(bha)* the fourth letter of the fifth pentad of the Devnagri alphabets.

भंग[1] *(bhaṅg)* see भंजन।

भंग[2] *(bhaṅg)* वि. dismissed; discharge; dissolved.

भंग[3] *(bhaṅg)* स्त्री. hemp plant.

भंगिमा *(bhaṅgimā)* स्त्री. gesture; pose; posture; curvature; obliquity.

भंगी *(bhaṅgi)* पु. sweeper; scavenger.

भंगुर *(bhangur)* वि. fragile; brittle; transitory; transient.

भंगुरता *(bhaṅguratā)* स्त्री. brittleness; fragility; transience; perishability.

भंजक *(bhañjak)* पु. one who breaks; breaker.

भंजन *(bhañjan)* पु. separation; demolition; destruction; iconoclasm; fracture; breach.

भंडा *(bhaṇḍā)* पु. utensil; secret.

भंडाफोड़ *(bhaṇḍāphor)* पु. exposure; disclosure.

भंडार *(bhaṇḍār)* पु. treasury; depository; repository; storeroom; storage.

भंडारण *(bhaṇḍāran)* पु. storage.

भंडारा *(bhaṇḍārā)* पु. feast.

भंडारी *(bhaṇḍārī)* पु. store-keeper; cook; stockist.

भंड़ैती *(bhanṁṛaitī)* स्त्री. buffoonery; clownage.

भँवर *(bhaṁvar)* पु. whirlpool; vortex; eddy.

भँवरा *(bhaṁvrā)* पु. black-bee; bumble-bee.

भकोसना *(bhakosnā)* स. क्रि. to devour; to swallow hastily.

भक्त[1] *(bhakt)* वि. attached or devoted; loyal; faithful.

भक्त[2] *(bhakt)* पु. devotee; worshipper; follower.

भक्ति *(bhakti)* स्त्री. devotion; loyalty; service; worship; homage; attachment; affection; reverence.

भक्तिपरायण *(bhakti-parāyan)* वि. devoted; given to devotion.

भक्तिपूर्ण *(bhakti-purna)* वि. devotional.

भक्षक *(bhakṣak)* पु. voracious eater; devourer; glutton; eater; consumer.

भक्षण *(bhakṣan)* पु. eating; feeding; devouring.

भक्षी *(bhakṣī)* पु. eater.

भक्ष्य[1] *(bhakṣya)* वि. edible; eatable.

भक्ष्य[2] *(bhakṣya)* पु. edible; food.

भगंदर *(bhagandar)* पु. fistula in the anus.

भगदड़ *(bhagdaṛ)* स्त्री. stampede; panic.

भगवान् *(bhagavān)* स्त्री. The Supreme Being; God.

भगाना *(bhagānā)* स. क्रि. to cause to flee or escape; to cause to run away; to chase out; to elope; to kidnap; to abduct; to drive off; to remove; to dispel.

भगिनी *(bhaginī)* स्त्री. sister.

भगोड़ा *(bhagoṛā)* पु. absconder; fugitive; run-away; deserter.

भग्न *(bhagn)* वि. broken; shattered.

भग्नावशेष *(bhagnāvśes)* पु. remains; ruins; debris; relics.

भग्नाशा *(bhagnaśa)* स्त्री. despair; frustration; disppointment; dejection.

भजन *(bhajan)* पु. worship; adoration; hymn; devotional song.

भजना *(bhajanā)* स. क्रि. to worship; to repeat (God's name) with devotion.

भटकना *(bhaṭaknā)* अ. क्रि. to go astry; to lose the path; to wander about aimlessly; to be confused or perplexed; to be bewildered.

भटकाना *(bhaṭkānā)* स. क्रि. to cause to stray; to mislead; to bewilder.

भटकाव *(bhaṭkāv)* पु. aberration.

भट्ट *(bhaṭṭ)* पु. bard; scholarly Brahman.

भट्टा *(bhaṭṭā)* पु. brick kiln.

भट्ठी *(bhaṭṭhī)* स्त्री. furnace; small kiln; oven; distillery.

भड़क *(bharak)* स्त्री. ostentation; glitter.

भड़कदार *(bharakdār)* वि. ostentatious; gaudy.

भड़कना *(bharaknā)* अ. क्रि. to be blown into flame; blaze up; to get excited or enraged; to flare up; to be startled; to be scared or alarmed.

भड़काना *(bharkānā)* स. क्रि. to blow up into a flame; to kindle; to inflame; to provoke or incite; to intensify; to aggravate; to startle; scare; frighten.

भड़कीला *(bhaṛkīlā)* वि. glittering; showy; gaudy; ostentatious.

भड़कीलापन *(bhaṛkīlāpan)* पु. ostentation; tawdriness; gaudiness; flamboyance.

भड़ास *(bhaṛās)* स्त्री. accumulated grudge; stored-up spite; pent up feelings.

भडुआ *(bhaṛuā)* पु. attendant on a dancing girl; one who lives on the earnings of a prostitute; pimp; procurer; good for nothing fellow.

भतीजा *(bhatījā)* पु. nephew.

भतीजी *(bhatījī)* स्त्री. brother's daughter; niece.

भत्ता *(bhattā)* पु. allowance.

भद्दा *(bhaddā)* वि. clumsy; awkward; unseemly; slovenly; shoddy; improper; inapt; unsuitable.

भद्दापन *(bhaddāpan)* पु. awkwardness; clumsiness; vulgarity; untowardness.

भद्र *(bhadra)* वि. gentle; noble; polite; courteous; benevolent; virtuous; urbane.

भद्रता *(bhadratā)* स्त्री. courtesy; affability; gentleness; goodness; nobility; urbanity.

भनक *(bhanak)* स्त्री. low or distant sound; hum; inkling; clue.

भनभनाना *(bhanbhanānā)* अ. क्रि. to buzz; to hum.

भनभनाहट *(bhanbhanāhaṭ)* स्त्री. hum; buzz.

भन्नाना *(bhannānā)* अ. क्रि. to be infuriated; to flare up.

भबका *(bhabakā)* पु. retort; alembic; blast of furnace; sudden emission of stench.

भबकी *(bhabakī)* स्त्री. hollow threat.

भभक *(bhabhak)* स्त्री. flare (of a lamp; lantern; fire); sudden burst into flame; foul smell; stench; sudden emission of stench.

भभकना *(bhabhaknā)* अ. क्रि. to flare up; to burst suddenly into flame; to blaze; to be provoked; to burst into a fit of fury.

भभका *(bhabhkā)* see भबका।

भभूत *(bhabhūt)* स्त्री. sacred ashes.

भयंकर *(bhayaṅkar)* वि. fearful; frightful; terrible; horrible; dangerous.

भयंकरता *(bhayaṅkartā)* स्त्री. dreadfulness; fearfulness; terribleness.

भय *(bhay)* पु. fear; fright; dread; horror.

भयकर *(bhayakar)* वि. terrifying; threatening; frightening; intimidating.

भयभीत *(bhayabhīt)* वि. afraid; frightened; scared.

भयाकुल *(bhayākūl)* वि. fear-stricken; terrified; scared; horrified.

भयाक्रांत *(bhayākrant)* वि. horror stricken; terrified.

भयातुर *(bhayātyur)* see भयाकुल।

भयानक *(bhayānak)* वि. dreadful; fearful; frightening; horrible; terrible.

भयानकता *(bhayānaktā)* स्त्री. dreadfulness; terribleness.

भयावह *(bhayāvah)* पु. terrible.

भरण *(bharaṇ)* पु. nourishing; alimentation; feeding.

भरण-पोषण *(bharaṇ-pośan)* पु. maintenance; subsistence; alimentation.

भरती *(bhartī)* स्री. filling; insertion; stuffing etc.; admission; enrolment; enlistment; recruitment.

भरना *(bharnā)* स. क्रि. to pour; to fill up; to close; to choke; to make good to compensate; to fill up (vacancy etc.); to accumulate; heap up; stack; to fill; to excite; to instigate; to suffer; bear; endure; to be filled up; to be healed up (as a wound); to be replete (with); to abound in; to be choked.

भरपाई *(bhar-pai)* स्री. quittance; payment in full; receipt in full.

भरपूर[1] *(bhar-pur)* वि. full; brimful; overflowing.

भरपूर[2] *(bhar-pur)* क्रि. fully; completely thoroughly; well; very well; abundantly; excessively.

भरपेट *(bhar-pet)* वि. to the fullest satisfaction; in the fullest measure; to full capacity.

भरम *(bhram)* पु. illusion; secret.

भरमाना *(bharmānā)* स. क्रि. to confuse; to bewilder; to cause to wander; to cause to stray; to allure; to tempt; to mislead; to misdirect.

भरमार *(bharmār)* स्री. abundance; plentifulness; glut.

भरवाना *(bharvānā)* स. क्रि. to cause to fill.

भरसक *(bharsak)* वि. utmost; best possible.

भराई *(bharāī)* स्री. act of filling; stuffing; packing; charges paid therefor; nogging.

भरापूरा *(bharāpurā)* वि. wealthy; prosperous flourishing; thriving; abounding; having a large family fleshy.

भराव *(bharāv)* पु. filling; wadding padding; packing material.

भरोसा *(bharosā)* पु. support; help; hope; assurance; trust; faith; confidence.

भर्तार *(bhartār)* पु. husband.

भर्त्सना *(bhartsanā)* स्री. reproach; condemnation; censure; upbraiding.

भर्राना *(bharrānā)* अ. क्रि. to go hoarse or husky; whizz; to be choked.

भलमनसाहत *(bhalmansāhat)* स्री. gentlemanliness; civility; urbanity; decorum; noble behaviour.

भला[1] *(bhalā)* वि. good; virtuous; righteous; guiltless.

भला[2] *(bhalā)* पु. well-being; good; welfare.

भलाई *(bhalāī)* स्री. good; goodness; virtue; merit; benevolence. kindness; welfare; prosperity.

भला-चंगा *(bhalā-chāṇgā)* वि. healthy; hale and hearty; sound; satisfactory.

भला-बुरा *(bhalā-burā)* पु. pros and cons; good points and bad points; one's own interest; admonition; reproach; good and evil.

भलामानस *(bhalāmānas)* पु. gentleman.

भवदीय *(bhavadiya)* क्रि. वि. yours.

भवन *(bhavan)* पु. building; house; residence.

भवनिष्ठ *(bhavniśth)* क्रि. वि. yours faithfully.

भवितव्यता *(bhavitavyatā)* स्त्री. the inevitable fate; destiny.

भविष्य *(bhaviśya)* पु. the future.

भविष्यत् *(bhaviśyat)* पु. future.

भविष्यवक्ता *(bhaviśya-vaktā)* पु. prophet; fortuneteller; soothsayer.

भविष्यवादी *(bhaviśya-vadī)* पु. futurist; prophet.

भव्य *(bhavya)* वि. grand; gorgeous; splendid; grandiose; magnificent.

भव्यता *(bhavyatā)* स्त्री. splendour; grandiosity; magnificence.

भस्म *(bhasm)* स्त्री. ashes; cinders; medicinal powder obtained by burning metals.

भस्मसात् *(bhasmsāt)* वि. reduced to ashes; burnt to ashes.

भस्मावशेष *(bhasmāअśesh)* पु. residue in the form of ashes.

भस्मी *(bhasmī)* स्त्री. dust of lime; coal; etc.

भस्मीभूत *(bhasmībhūt)* वि. burnt to ashes.

भाँग *(bhāṁg)* स्त्री. intoxicating hemp.

भांड *(bhāṁḍ)* पु. vessel; earthenware.

भाँड *(bhāṁṛ)* पु. jester; buffoon; clown; one who cannot keep a secret; blab.

भांडार *(bhāṇḍār)* पु. stock; stockroom; godown.

भाँति *(bhāṁti)* स्त्री. manner; mode; variety; kind; sort; class; type; design.

भाँपना *(bhāṁpnā)* स. क्रि. to guess; to make out; to look through the reality of ; to divine.

भाँवर *(bhāṁvar)* स्त्री. circumambulation of sacrificial fire by the bride and bridegroom at the time of marriage.

भाई *(bhāī)* पु. brother; relative; kinsman; member of the same caste or fraternity; a form of address to equals and the dear ones.

भाईचारा *(bhāīchāra)* पु. brotherhood; fraternity; fraternisation; fraternal understanding.

भाग *(bhāg)* पु. part; portion; fraction; distribution; partition; side; division; lot; fate; luck; share.

भागना *(bhāganā)* अ. क्रि. to run; to flee; to abscond; to escape; to go away; be gone; to make off; to elope(with).

भाग-दौड़ *(bhāg-daur)* स्त्री. running about; strenuous efforts; haste.

भागफल *(bhāg-fal)* पु. quotient.

भागी *(bhāgī)* पु. sharer; partner; accomplice.

भागीदार *(bhāgī-dār)* पु. co-partner; co-sharer.

भागीदारी *(bhāgīdārī)* स्त्री. partnership.

भाग्य *(bhāgya)* पु. fortune; luck; destiny.

भाग्यवश *(bhāgyavaś)* क्रि. वि. luckily; fortunately.

भाग्यवाद *(bhāgyavād)* पु. fatalism.

भाग्यवादी[1] *(bhāgyavādī)* वि. pertaining to fate; fatalistic.

भाग्यवादी[2] *(bhāgyavādī)* पु. fatalist.

भाग्यवान् *(bhāgyavān)* वि. fortunate; lucky.

भाग्यहीन *(bhāgyahin)* वि. unlucky; unfortunate; wretched.

भाजन *(bhājan)* पु. utensil; vessel;

container; one who deserves.

भाज्य *(bhājya)* वि. divisible.

भाटा *(bhāṭā)* पु. ebb-tide; low tide.

भाड़ *(bhāṛa)* पु. parcher's oven.

भाड़ा *(bhāṛā)* पु. rent; hire; fare; freight.

भात *(bhāt)* पु. boiled rice; marriage ceremony where bridegroom's father dines with bride's father.

भादों *(bhādoṁ)* पु. sixth month of the Hindu calendar.

भान *(bhān)* पु. consciousness; awareness; inkling.

भानजा *(bhānjā)* पु. nephew (sister's son).

भानजी *(bhānjī)* स्त्री sister's daughter; niece.

भाना *(bhānā)* स. क्रि. to be agreeable to; to look good or befitting; to like.

भानु *(bhānu)* पु. the sun.

भाप *(bhāp)* स्त्री. steam; vapour.

भाभी *(bhābhī)* स्त्री. sister-in-law (elder brother's wife).

भामिनी *(bhāminī)* स्त्री. pretty woman.

भार *(bhār)* पु. load; burden; charge; trust; responsibility; onus; weight; encumbrance; mass.

भारत *(bhārat)* भारतवर्ष पु. India.

भारतवासी *(bhāratvāsī)* पु. Indian; native of India.

भारतविद् *(bhārat-vid)* पु. Indologist.

भारत-विद्या *(bhārat-vidyā)* स्त्री. Indology.

भारती *(bhāratī)* स्त्री. speech; goddess Saraswati; Mother India.

भारतीय *(bhāratīyā)* वि. born in India; Indian.

भारी *(bhārī)* वि. heavy; weighty; massive; unwieldy; great; grand; difficult; hard; large; big; bulky.

भारीपन *(bhārīpan)* पु. heaviness; weightiness; massiveness.

भार्या *(bhāryā)* स्त्री. wife; spouse.

भाल *(bhāl)* पु. forehead; lance; spear.

भाला *(bhālā)* पु. large spear; lance; javelin.

भालू *(bhālū)* पु. bear.

भाव[1] *(bhāv)* पु. disposition; temperament; emotion; sentiment; purpose; signification; meaning; gist; gesture; gesticulation.

भाव[2] *(bhāv)* पु. rate; quotation.

भावना *(bhāvanā)* स्त्री. meditation; contemplation; speculation; fancy; feeling; emotion; sentiment.

भावनात्मक *(bhāvanātmak)* वि. full of sentiment; speculative.

भावपक्ष *(bhāvpaksh)* पु. theme; thought; subject matter.

भावप्रवण *(bhāअ.pravan)* वि. sentimental; emotional.

भावप्रवणता *(bhāअ.pravanatā)* स्त्री. sentimentality; emotional disposition.

भाववाचक *(bhāअ.vācāk)* वि. abstract (gram).

भावविभोर *(bhāअ.vibhor)* वि. overwhelmed with emotion; steeped in emotion.

भावात्मक *(bhāvātmak)* वि. emotional; sentimental.

भावात्मकता *(bhāvātmakatā)* स्त्री. affectivity; emotionality.

भावानुवाद *(bhāvānuvād)* पु. paraphrase; free translation.

भावार्थ *(bhavārāth)* पु. broad explanation; exposition; inherent meaning; obvious purport; sense; substance; gist.

भावी *(bhāvī)* वि. what must take place or is destined to happen; predestined; inevitable; prospective.

भावुक *(bhāvuk)* वि. emotional; sentimental; impulsive.

भावुकता *(bhāvukatā)* स्त्री. sentimentality; impulsiveness; emotionality.

भावोत्कर्ष *(bhāvotkarśh)* पु. emotional excellence or elevation; emotional upsurge.

भावोन्मत्त *(bhāvanmatt)* वि. overwhelmed with emotion; emotioncrazy.

भाषण *(bhāṣāṇ)* पु. speech; lecture; address; conversation.

भाषा *(bhāṣā)* स्त्री. language; speech.

भाषाई *(bhāṣāī)* वि. linguistic.

भाषागत *(bhāṣāgat)* वि. linguistic.

भाषा-विज्ञान *(bhāṣā-viygān)* पु. philology; linguistics.

भाषा-विज्ञानी *(bhāṣā-viyanī)* पु. linguist; philologist.

भाषाविद् *(bhāṣā-vid)* पु. linguist; philologist.

भिंडी *(bhiṇḍī)* स्त्री. lady's finger.

भिक्षा *(bhikṣā)* स्त्री. begging; alms; charity.

भिक्षाटन *(bhikṣātan)* पु. mendicancy.

भिक्षावृत्ति *(bhikṣāvrtī)* स्त्री. beggary; mendicancy.

भिक्षु *(bhikṣu)* भिक्षुक पु. beggar; mendicant; religious mendicant; esp. Buddhist; friar.

भिखमंगा *(bhikhmaṁgā)* पु. beggar; pauper.

भिखारिणी, भिखारिन *(bhikhārin)* स्त्री. female; beggar; beggar woman.

भिखारी *(bhikhārī)* पु. beggar; mendicant.

भिगोना *(bhigānā)* पु. to wet; to drench.

भिजवाना *(bhijvānā)* स. क्रि. to cause to send; to cause to be sent; to cause to wet.

भिड़ंत *(bhirant)* स्त्री. clash; skirmish collision; confrontation; encounter; grappling.

भिड़ *(bhir)* स्त्री. wasp.

भिड़ना *(bhiraṇā)* अ. क्रि. to come into collision; to collide; to clash; to contend; to fight; to be locked in a wordy duel; to grapple.

भित्ति *(bhitti)* स्त्री. wall; reef.

भिनकना *(bhinaknā)* अ. क्रि. to buzz; to be covered with flies; to be extremely shabby.

भिनभिनाना *(bhinbhinānā)* अ. क्रि. to buzz; to hum.

भिनभिनाहट *(bhinbhināhaṭ)* स्त्री. buzzing sound.

भिन्न[1] *(bhinn)* पु. different; fraction.

भिन्न[2] *(bhinn)* वि. separate; separated; broken; split; divided; other; different; diverse.

भिन्नता *(bhinntā)* स्त्री. dissimilarity; distinction; difference.

भिश्ती *(bhiśtī)* पु. water-carrier.

भींचना *(bhīṁcnā)* स. क्रि. to squeeze; to press hard; to grasp tightly; to embrace tightly; to tighten; to hold close together.

भीख *(bhīkh)* स्त्री. begging; mendicity; charity; alms.

भीगना *(bhīgnā)* अ. क्रि. to be wet or drenched; to be soaked.

भीड़ *(bhīṛ)* स्त्री. multitude; crowd; throng; concourse; rabble; mob; excess; calamity; crisis; congestion.

भीतर *(bhitār)* क्रि. वि. in; inside; within.

भीतरी *(bhītarī)* वि. internal; inner; inward; hidden; secret; unexpressed.

भीति *(bhīti)* स्त्री. fear; apprehension; dread; terror; fright.

भीमकाय *(bhīmkaya)* वि. gigantic.

भीरु *(bhīru)* वि. timid; cowardly.

भीरुता *(bhīrutā)* स्त्री. timidity; cowardice.

भीषण *(bhīṣaṇ)* वि. fearful; frightening; awful; terrible; gruesome; tremendous.

भीषणता *(bhīṣaṇatā)* स्त्री. gruesomeness; awfulness.

भुक्खड़ *(bhūkkar)* वि. gluttonous; voracious; famished (with hunger); starved; hungry.

भुक्त *(bhukt)* वि. experienced; consumed.

भुखमरा *(bhukmarā)* वि. starved; hungry; famished.

भुखमरी *(bhukmarī)* स्त्री. starvation; hunger; famine.

भुगतना *(bhugatnā)* स. क्रि. to suffer; to undergo; to bear; to endure; to pay the penalty of; to suffer consequences of.

भुगतान *(bhugtān)* पु. payment; delivery; settlement; disposal; acquittance.

भुजंग *(bhujang)* पु. snake; serpent.

भुजबल *(bhujbal)* पु. physical strength; strength of the arms; prowess.

भुजा *(bhujā)* स्त्री. arm; hand; side of a geometrical figure.

भुनगा *(bhunagā)* पु. gnat; maggot; insect; insignificant creature or person.

भुनना *(bhunanā)* अ. क्रि. to be parched; to be roasted; to be changed into small coins; to be slaughtered with guns etc.

भुनभुनाना *(bhunbhunānā)* अ. क्रि. to mumble; to gabble; to grumble; to express indignation indistinctly.

भुनवाना *(bhunavānā)* स. क्रि. to get parched; to get changed into currency of smaller denomination.

भुनाना *(bhunānā)* स. क्रि. to get something parched; to change (into smaller denomination currency).

भुरभुरा *(bhurbhurā)* वि. crisp; friable.

भुलक्कड़ *(bhulakkar)* वि. forgetful; temperamentally prone to forgetting.

भुलाना *(bhulānā)* स. क्रि. to forget; to mislead; to bewilder; to delude.

भुस *(bhus)* पु. straw; chaff.

भू *(bhū)* स्त्री. earth; world; land; ground; soil.

भूकंप *(bhūkamp)* पु. earthquake.

भूखंड *(bhūkhand)* पु. territory; plot; tract of land.

भूख *(bhūkh)* स्त्री. appetite; hunger.

भूखा *(bhūkhā)* वि. hungry; famished; starving; desirous; craving; poor; destitute.

भूगर्भ *(bhū-garbha)* पु. interior of the earth.

भूगर्भशास्त्र *(bhū-garbhśastra)* पु. geology.

भूगर्भशास्त्री *(bhū-garbhśastrī)* पु. geologist.

भूगर्भशास्त्रीय *(bhū-garbhśastryīa)* वि. geological.

भूगोल *(bhūgol)* पु. geography.

भूचाल *(bhūcāl)* see भूकंप।

भूत[1] *(bhūt)* वि. past; gone by; been; become; produced; former; old.

भूत[2] *(bhūt)* पु. ghost; evil spirit; a creature; matter; element; past; past tense.

भूतकाल *(bhūtkāl)* पु. (gram.) past tense; the past.

भूतपूर्व *(bhūt-purva)* पु. ex; former; past; previous.

भूतल *(bhū-tal)* पु. surface of the earth; the ground.

भूदान *(bhūdān)* पु. gift of land.

भूदानी *(bhūdānī)* पु. donor of land.

भूधर *(bhū-dhar)* पु. mountain; hill.

भूनना *(bhūnanā)* स. क्रि. to roast; to broil; to parch; to scorch; to fry; to annihilate (with gun etc.); to blast; to reduce to ashes.

भूभाग *(bhū-bhag)* पु. region; place; spot; territory.

भूमंडल *(bhū-maṇḍal)* पु. terrestrial globe; the earth.

भूमध्यरेखा *(bhū-madhuarekhā)* स्त्री. equator.

भूमि *(bhūmi)* स्त्री. earth; world; ground; soil; land; place; site; region; country.

भूमिका *(bhūmikā)* स्त्री. preface; introduction; (drama) role of an actor.

भूमिगत *(bhūmigat)* वि. underground; subterranean; secret; fallen on the earth.

भूरा[1] *(bhūrā)* वि. brown; grey.

भूरा[2] *(bhūrā)* पु. brown colour.

भूरापन *(bhūrā-pan)* पु. brownness.

भूल *(bhūl)* स्त्री. forgetfulness; oversight; neglect; illusion bewilderment; slip; mistake; error; omission; failure; fault.

भूल-चूक *(bhūl-chūk)* स्त्री. errors and omissions; act of commission or omission.

भूलना *(bhūlnā)* अ. क्रि. to be forgotten; to err; to go astray; to forget; to omit; to miss.

भूलोक *(bhūlok)* पु. earth; the habitation of mortals.

भूषण *(bhūṣaṇ)* पु. ornament; jewellery; decoration; embellishment.

भूसा *(bhūsā)* पु. chaff; husk.

भूसी *(bhūsī)* स्त्री. husk; bran.

भृकुटि, भृकुटी *(bhṛkuṭī)* स्त्री. eyebrow; frown.

भृत्य *(bhṛtya)* पु. slave; servant; attendant.

भेंगा *(bheṁgā)* वि. squint-eyed.

भेंगापन *(bheṁgāpan)* पु. squint; cross eye.

भेंट *(bheṁt)* स्त्री. meeting; interview; visit; gift; present; offering.

भेंटवार्ता *(bheṁt-vārtā)* स्त्री. interview.

भेजना *(bhejnā)* स. क्रि. to send; to cause to go; to transmit; to remit; to despatch; to consign.

भेजा *(bheja)* पु. brain.

भेड़ *(bheṛ)* स्त्री. sheep; simpleton; timid person.

भेड़-चाल *(bheṛ-cāl)* स्त्री. mobmentality.

भेड़ा *(bheṛā)* पु. ram; male sheep.

भेड़िया *(bheṛiyā)* पु. wolf.

भेद *(bhed)* पु. difference; distinction; kind; sort; species; variety; secrecy; secret; mystery; hidden meaning; implication; dissension; disunion; division; schism; split.

भेदभाव *(bhed-bhāv)* पु. partition-ship; partiality; discrimination; differentiation.

भेदिया *(bhediyā)* पु. one who knows the secret; spy; secret agent.

भेरी *(bherī)* स्त्री. siren; drum.

भेष *(bheś)* पु. appearance; exterior appearance; guise; get-up.

भेंगा *(bhaingā)* वि. squint-eyed; cross-eyed.

भैंस *(bhaiṁs)* स्त्री. she-buffalo.

भैंसा *(bhaiṁsā)* पु. he-buffalo.

भैया *(bhaiyā)* पु. brother; mode of address for equals and youngsters.

भोंकना *(bhoṁknā)* अ. क्रि. to stab; to stick; to thrust; to drive in; to pierce; to prick; to bark.

भोंडा *(bhoṇḍā)* वि. ilस.shaped; uncouth; grotesque; coarsegrained; indecent; crude; ugly; unsymmetrical.

भोंडापन *(bhoṇḍāpan)* पु. grotesqueness; ugliness; indecency; crudeness; crudity.

भोंदू *(bhoṁdū)* वि. silly; boobyish; simple; stupid.

भोंपू *(bhoṁpū)* पु. kind of musical insturment; siren; a horn.

भोग *(bhog)* पु. perception (of joy or sorrow); enjoyment; suffering; sexual enjoyment; carnal pleasure; use; application; utility; result of good or evil (deeds).

भोगना *(bhoganā)* स. क्रि. to experience (pleasure or pain); to enjoy; to suffer; to undergo; to derive sexual pleasure; to copulate.

भोगी *(bhogī)* वि. enjoying; using; given to carnal pleasure; voluptuous; pleasure-seeking; sex indulgent.

भोग्य *(bhogya)* वि. enjoyable; that is to be endured or experienced.

भोज *(bhoj)* वि. banquet; feast.

भोजन *(bhojan)* पु. food; victuals; meal; diet.

भोजनालय *(bhojanalyā)* पु. mess; dining hall; restaurant.

भोजपत्र *(bhoj-patra)* पु. birch tree; the leaf and the bark of a tree.

भोज्य *(bhojya)* वि. suitable or fit to be eaten; eatable; edible.

भोथरा *(bhothrā)* वि. obtuse; blunt.

भोर *(bhor)* पु. break of day; dawn; early morning.

भोला *(bholā)* वि. natural; simple; artless; guileless; harmless; innocent; simple minded; silly; stupid; gullible.

भोलापन *(bholāpan)* पु. simpleness; simple-heartedness; innocence.

भोला-भाला *(bholā-bhālā)* वि. innocent; ingenuous; honest and simple.

भौं *(bhauṁ)* स्त्री. eyebrow.

भौंकना *(bhauṁknā)* अ. क्रि. to bark; to talk nonsensically or foolishly.

भौंरा *(bhauṁrā)* पु. a large black bee; a top.

भौंह *(bhauṁh)* स्त्री. eyebrow.

भौचक *(bhaucak)* वि. stunned; aghast; nonplussed; dumbfounded.

भौचक्का *(bhaucakkā)* see भौचक।

भौतिक *(bhautik)* वि. appertaining to the corporal elements; elemental; made of matter; mundane; worldly; physical; material.

भौतिकवाद *(bhautikvād)* पु. materialism.

भौतिकवादी *(bhautikvādī)* वि. materialistic.

भौतिकी *(bhautikī)* स्त्री. physics.

भ्रम *(bhram)* पु. illusion; misconception; doubt; suspicion; apprehension; confusion misunderstanding.

भ्रमजनक *(bhramjanak)* वि. illusory.

भ्रमण *(bhraman)* पु. roaming about; ramble; excursion; travel; going round.

भ्रमणकारी *(bharmaṇkārī)* वि. itinerant; traveller.

भ्रमणशील *(bharmaṇśil)* वि. roving; rambling; itinerant.

भ्रमर *(bhramar)* पु. large black bee; the bumble bee.

भ्रमरी *(bhramari)* स्त्री. female black bee.

भ्रमात्मक *(bhramātmak)* वि. illusory; illusive.

भ्रमित *(bhramit)* वि. illusioned; confused; mistaken; strayed; misled.

भ्रष्ट *(bhraṣt)* वि. depraved; vicious; dissolute; fallen; degraded; debased; corrupt; spoilt; decayed; ruined; broken.

भ्रष्टता *(bhraṣtata)* स्त्री. corruptness; corruption; depravity; state of being spoilt; wantonness.

भ्रष्टाचार *(bhraṣtacār)* पु. corruption; depravity; bribery; wantonness.

भ्रष्टाचारी *(bhraṣtacārī)* वि. corrupt; wanton; depraved.

भ्रांत *(bhrānt)* वि. perplexed; confused; gone astray; fallen into error.

भ्रांति *(bhrānti)* स्त्री. delusion; wrong notion; false idea or impression; uncertainty; suspense; confusion.

भ्राता *(bhrātā)* पु. brother.

भ्रातृत्व *(bhrātav)* पु. fraternity; brotherhood.

भ्रातृभाव *(bhrātṛbhāv)* पु. fraternal feeling; affection.

भ्रातृ-हत्या *(bhrātṛ-haytyā)* स्त्री. fratricide.

भ्रामक *(bhramak)* वि. misleading; deceptive; false; fallacious; causing doubt or suspicion; confusing.

भ्रू *(bhru)* पु. eyebrow; pleasing movement of the eyebrows.

म

म *(ma)* ; the fifth and final letter of the fifth pentad of the Devnagri alphabets.

मँगता *(maṁgtā)* पु. beggar; mendicant.

मंगल[1] *(maṅgal)* वि. auspicious; propitious; conferring happiness.

मंगलकलश *(mangal-kalaś)* पु. benediction; good wishes.

मंगलकारक, मंगलकारी *(mangal-karak)* वि. auspicious; propitious; benedictory; beneficial.

मंगलकार्य *(mangal-kārya)* पु. festive occasion; auspicious ceremony.

मंगलगान *(mangal-gān)* पु. auspicious song.

मंगलध्वनि *(mangal-dhvani)* स्त्री. tumultuous sound of auspicious songs etc.; music at the time of marriage or other auspicious occasions.

मंगलप्रद *(mangal-prad)* वि. benedictory.

मंगलवार *(mangal-vār)* पु. Tuesday.

मंगलसूचक *(manga स.sūcak)* वि. mangal-sucak auguring good luck; auspicious.

मंगलाचरण *(mangalā-caran)* वि. invocation.

मँगवाना *(maṁgvānā)* स. क्रि. to cause to be sent for; to send for; to cause to be fetched.

मँगाना *(mamgana)* स. क्रि. to cause to bring; to order; to send for.

मंगेतर[1] *(maṁgetar)* स्त्री. fiance or fiancee.

मंगेतर[2] *(maṁgetar)* वि. betrothed.

मंच *(mañc)* पु. dias; stage; platform; raised platform; scaffold; forum; rostrum.

मंचन *(mañcan)* पु. staging.

मंचीय *(mañciya)* वि. pertaining to the stage; theatrical.

मँजना *(maṁjanā)* अ. क्रि. to be rubbed; wiped; cleaned or polished; to be practised; to be exprienced; to be seasoned; to get proficient.

मंजरी *(mañjarī)* स्त्री. shoot; sprout spring; cluster of flowers or blossoms.

मंज़िल *(manzil)* स्त्री. inn; destination; storey; (fig.) stage.

मंज़िल *(maṁzil)* पु. a kind of cymbal.

मंजु *(mañju)* वि. beautiful; lovely; charming; pretty.

मंजुल *(mañjul)* वि. beautiful; charming; lovely.

मंजुलता *(mañjulatā)* स्त्री. prettiness; beauty.

मंजूरी *(mamzūrī)* स्त्री. approval; grant; sanction; acceptance.

मँझधार *(manjh-dār)* स्त्री. midstream; mid-current.

मँझला *(maṁjhlā)* वि. middle.

मँझोला *(maṁjholā)* वि. of medium size; middling.

मंडन *(maṇḍan)* पु. ornamentation; adornment; embellihment; corroboration; confirmation.

मंडप *(maṇḍap)* पु. open hall; temporary hall erected on ceremonial occasions; arbour; bower; tent; pavilion; canopy; building consecrated to a deity; temple.

मँडराना *(maṁḍarānā)* अ. क्रि. to fly round; to hover; to hang around; to gather thick(as clouds).

मंडल *(maṇḍal)* पु. circle; ring; coil; wheel; disc; halo; disk of the sun or moon; region; country; territory; zone; division; company; assembly; association; orbit (of a planet etc.); multitude; collection.

मंडली *(maṇḍalī)* स्त्री. team; party; association; floc; company (of singers); gang; circle; band; troupe; coterie.

मंडित *(maṇḍit)* वि. adorned; ornamented; decorated; corroborated; supported; veneered.

मंडूक *(maṇḍūk)* पु. frog.

मंत्र *(mantra)* पु. incantation; charm; spell; means; contrivance; a passage of the Vedas; a Vedic hymn; esoteric formula.

मंत्रगान *(mantragān)* पु. chant.

मंत्रणा *(mantraṇā)* स्त्री. consultation; deliberation; advice; counsel; conspiracy.

मंत्रमुग्ध *(mantra-mugdh)* वि. charmed; spell-bound.

मंत्रालय *(mantrālay)* पु. ministry.

मंत्रित्व *(mantritva)* पु. ministership.

मंत्रिमंडल *(mantri-mandal)* पु. cabinet of ministers.

मंत्री *(mantrī)* पु. minister; adviser; counsellor; secretary.

मंथन *(manthan)* पु. churning; agitating; stirring or shaking about; deep pondering over something; contemplation.

मंथर *(manthar)* वि. slow; tardy; lazy; sluggish.

मंद *(mand)* वि. slow; tardy; dim; faint; low soft; inactive; sluggish; dull; slack; weak.

मंदता *(mandatā)* स्त्री. dullness; dimness; slowness.

मंदबुद्धि *(mand-budhi)* वि. dull-witted; silly; foolish; stupid; dullard; laggard; retarded.

मंदा *(mandā)* वि. cheap; slow; tardy.

मंदिर *(mandir)* पु. temple; palace; mansion.

मंदी *(mandī)* स्त्री. slowness; tardiness; fall in prices; depression in price; slump in market.

मंशा *(maṃśā)* स्त्री. (अ.) motive; purpose; intention; purport; tenor; implication.

मंसूबा *(maṃsūbā)* पु. contrivance; plan; design; intention; will; desire; project; scheme.

मकई *(makaī)* स्त्री. maize.

मकड़ा *(makṛā)* पु. male spider.

मकड़ी *(makṛī)* स्त्री. female spider.

मकतब *(maktab)* पु. (अ.) school.

मकर *(makar)* पु. crocodile; name of the tenth sign of zodiac; the sign Capricorn.

मकररेखा *(makar-rekhā)* स्त्री. tropic of Capricorn.

मक़सद *(maqsad)* पु. (अ.) intention; motive; object; aim; desire; wish; intended sense; meaning; purport.

मक़सूद *(maqsūd)* वि. (अ.) desired; aimed; intended.

मकान *(makān)* पु. (अ.) house; home; abode; residence; dwelling.

मक्का *(makkā)* स्त्री. maize.

मक्कार *(makkār)* वि. (अ.) deceitful. cunning; crafty.

मक्खन *(makkhan)* पु. butter.

मक्खी *(makkhī)* स्त्री. fly; honey bee; the sight (of a gun).

मक्खीचूस *(makkhī-chūs)* वि. miserly; niggardly.

मख़मल *(makhmal)* स्त्री. (फ़.) velvet.

मख़मली *(makhmalī)* वि. (फ़) of velvet; velvety; soft; delicate.

मखाना *(makhānā)* पु. a kind of dry fruit (prepared by parching lotus seeds).

मखौल *(makhaul)* पु. mockery; joke; jest.

मगन *(magan)* वि. delighted; glad; happy; immersed; absorbed; deeply engaged; deeply in love; rapt; enamoured.

मगर[1] *(magar)* पु. crocodile.

मगर[2] *(magar)* क्रि. वि. (फ.) but; however; yet.

मगरमच्छ *(magarmach)* पु. crocodile.

मग़रूर *(magrūr)* वि. (अ.) proud; vain; arrogant.

मग्न *(magnā)* वि. drowned; sunk;

busy; absorbed; immersed; delighted; glad; happy.

मचना *(macna)* अ. क्रि. to be caused; to be occasioned; to happen.

मचलना *(macalnā)* अ. क्रि. to be wayward; to be refractory; to insist; to pester; to be cross; to sulk.

मचली *(macalī)* स्त्री. nausea; a tendency towards vomiting.

मचान *(macān)* पु. raised platform (for shooting wild animals).

मचाना *(macānā)* स. क्रि. to cause; to make; to raise up; stir up.

मच्छर *(macchar)* पु. mosquito.

मच्छरदानी *(maccharā-dānī)* स्त्री. mosquito net.

मछली *(machlī)* स्त्री. fish; ear-ring made in the form of a fish; muscle or tendon.

मज़दूर *(mazdūr)* पु. (फ़.) hired lobourer; worker; workman; wage-earner.

मज़दूरी *(mazdūrī)* स्त्री. (फ.) bodily labour; work; wages; remuneration.

मज़बूत *(mazbūt)* वि. (अ.) firm; fixed; fast; durable; lasting; strong; sturdy.

मज़बूर *(majbūr)* वि. (अ.) compelled; helpless.

मज़बूरी *(majbūrī)* स्त्री. compulsion; helplessness.

मजमा *(majmā)* पु. (अ.) crowd; gathering; assembly.

मज़मून *(mazmūn)* पु. (अ.) subject; topic.

मजलिस *(majlis)* स्त्री. (अ.) assembly; congregation; meeting; convention; congress; council; conference.

मज़हब *(mazhab)* पु. (अ.) belief; creed; religion; faith.

मज़हबी *(mazhabī)* वि. of or relating to a religion or sect; religious.

मज़ा *(mazā)* पु. (अ.) joy; delight; pleasure; taste; flavour; relish.

मज़ाक़ *(mazāq)* पु. (अ.) joke; jest; fun.

मज़ाक़िया *(mazāqiyā)* वि. (अ.) humorous; jolly; jocular.

मज़ार *(mazār)* पु. (अ.) tomb; grave.

मज़ेदार *(mazedār)* वि. (अ.) delicious; savoury; tasty; enjoyable packed with fun and frolic; humoursome.

मझधार *(majh-dhār)* पु. mid-stream; mid-current.

मझला *(majhalā)* वि. middle; medium.

मटकना *(maṭakanā)* अ. क्रि. to strut; to swagger.

मटका *(maṭakā)* पु. large earthen jara; big pitcher.

मटकाना *(maṭakānā)* स. क्रि. to make coquettish gestures with.

मटमैला *(maṭmailā)* वि. dusty; dust coloured; soiled.

मटर *(matar)* स्त्री. pea.

मटरगश्ती *(maṭargaśtī)* स्त्री. stroll; promenade; rambling; roving; vagrancy; vagabondage.

मटियामेट *(maṭiyā-met)* वि. completely destroyed; ruined; razed; devastated.

मट्ठा *(maṭṭhā)* पु. butter-milk.

मठ *(maṭh)* पु. monastery; abbey; temple; pagoda; priory; cloister.

मठाधीश *(maṭhā-dhiś)* पु. head of a monastery; abbot,

मढ़ना *(maṛhnā)* स. क्रि. to gild; to framel; to mount; to impose; to impute.

मढ़वाना *(maṛhvānā)* स. क्रि. to cause to be mouted or framed; to cause to be gilded.

मढ़ी *(maṛhī)* स्त्री. hutment; small monastery or temple.

मणि *(maṇi)* स्त्री. precious stone; gem; jewel; anything best of its kind.

मणिश्र *(maṇiśra)* पु. crystal.

मत *(mat)* पु. vote; opinion; judgement; belief; thought; idea; doctrine; tenet; sect; faith; creed.

मतदाता *(matdātā)* पु. voter.

मतदान *(matdān)* पु. polling; voting.

मतपत्र *(mat-patra)* पु. ballot; ballot paper.

मतभेद *(mat-bhed)* पु. difference of opinion; dissension; disagreement.

मतलब *(matlab)* पु. (अ.) aim; purpose; motive; meaning; self-interest; concern.

मतलबी *(matlabī)* पु. (अ.) selfish; self-seeking self-concerned.

मतली *(matlī)* स्त्री. nausea.

मतवाला *(matvala)* वि. intoxicated; drunk; wild; wayward; tipsy; passionate.

मतवालापन *(matvālāpan)* पु. intoxicatedness; drunkenness; waywardness; tipsiness.

मताधिकार *(matādhikār)* पु. franchise; suffrage.

मति *(matī)* स्त्री. intellect; understanding; sense; opinion; view.

मतिभ्रम *(mati-bhram)* पु. delusion; confusion of mind; hallucination.

मतिमंद *(mati-mand)* वि. dull; imbecile; backward; retarded.

मतैक्य *(mataikya)* पु. unanimity.

मत्था *(mathā)* पु. forehead.

मत्स्य *(matsya)* पु. fish.

मत्स्यपालन *(matsya-pālan)* पु. fish-culture; fish-farming.

मथना *(mathnā)* स. क्रि. to churn; to stir round; to ponder; to consider.

मथनी *(mathnī)* स्त्री. churner.

मद[1] *(mad)* पु. intoxication; drunkenness; delight; rapture; passion; pride; arrogance; juice that oozes from and elephant's temples.

मद[2] *(mad)* स्त्री. column; head; account-head.

मदद *(madad)* स्त्री. (अ.) assistance; help; aid; rescue; reinforcement.

मददगार *(madad-gār)* पु. (अ.) assistant; helper; supporter.

मदरसा *(madrasā)* पु. (अ.) school; institution of higher education during Muslim period.

मदहोश *(madahoś)* वि. (फ़ा.) dead drunk; intoxicated; out of senses; confounded; stupefied; unconscious senseless.

मदहोशी *(madahośī)* स्त्री. (फ.) drunkenness; senselessness; intoxicatedness.

मदारी *(madārī)* पु. conjurer; juggler; trickster.

मदिरा *(madirā)* स्त्री. spirituous liquor; wine.

मदिरालय *(madirālaya)* पु. bar; public drinking house.

मदोन्मत्त *(madonmat)* वि. intoxicated with spirituous liquor; drunk; intoxicated with passion; pride or wealth.

मद्धिम *(maddhim)* वि. middle; moderate; medium; ordinary; common; dull; faint; faded (as colour etc.).

मद्य *(madya)* पु. liquor; wine; alchohol.

मद्य-निषेद्य *(madya-niśedh)* पु. prohibition.

मद्यपान *(madya-pān)* पु. drinking; intoxication.

मधु *(madhu)* पु. honey; spirituous liquor; any sweet intoxicating drink; juice or nectar of flowers.

मधुकर *(madhukar)* पु. large black bee.

मधुप *(madhūp)* पु. large black bee; honey-bee.

मधुमास *(madhumās)* पु. spring.

मधुमेह *(madhu-meh)* पु. diabetes.

मधुर *(madhur)* वि. sweet; pleasant; pleasing; melodious; mellifluous; charming; attractive.

मधुरता *(madhuratā)* स्त्री. sweet-ness; pleasantness; mellifluence; melodiousness.

मधुरभाषी *(madhurbhāsī)* वि honey-tongued; sweet-spoken.

मधुशाला *(madhuśālā)* स्त्री. bar; public drinking house; tavern.

मध्य *(madhya)* पु. middle; centre; medium tempo; middle octave; interlude.

मध्यकालीन *(madhya-kālīn)* वि. medieval.

मध्यम *(madhyam)* वि. medium; intermediate; slow; dim; fair; passable; mediocre; so-so.

मध्यमा *(madhyamā)* स्त्री. middle finger.

मध्यमार्ग *(madhy-mārg)* पु. via media; middle course; golden mean.

मध्ययुगीन *(madhya-yugīn)* see मध्यकालीन।

मध्यवर्ती *(madhya-varti)* वि. lying in the middle; central; intermediary.

मध्यस्थ *(madhyasth)* पु. middle man; mediator; arbitrator.

मध्यस्थता *(madhyasthatā)* स्त्री. mediatorship; arbitration.

मध्यांतर *(madhyāntar)* पु. recess; interval.

मध्याह्न *(madhyāhan)* पु. mid-day; noon.

मन *(man)* पु. mind (considered as the seat of perception and passion); inclination; psyche; heart; soul; spirit; disposition; mood; temper; desire; longing; weight equal to forty seers.

मनका *(mankā)* पु. bead; rosary.

मनगढ़ंत *(man-garhant)* वि. fabricated; concocted.

मनचला *(man-calā)* वि. fickle-minded; fidgety; frivolous.

मनचाहा *(man-cāhā)* वि. desired or wished; favourite; done of one's own accord; to one's own wish.

मनन *(manan)* पु. deliberation; reflection; meditation.

मननशील *(manansīl)* वि. thoughtful; meditative; contemplative.

मनपसंद *(manpasand)* वि. favourite; to one's liking; after one's own heart.

मनभावन *(man-bhāvan)* वि. charming; attractive; pleasing; favourite; beloved.

मनमाना *(man-mānā)* वि. pleasing one's own mind; arbitrary; licentious; self-willed.

मनमानापन *(man-mānāpan)* पु. arbitrariness.

मनमानी *(man-māni)* स्त्री. arbitrariness; arbitrary conduct; self-will; wilfulness.

मनमुटाव *(man-mutāv)* पु. estrangement; antagonism; rift; rupture; bad blood; ilस.feeling.

मनमौजी *(man-mauji)* वि. whimsical; self-willed; capricious.

मनमौजीपन *(man-māujipan)* पु. capriciousness; whimsicality.

मनवांछित *(man-vānchit)* वि. desired.

मनसूबा *(mansūbā)* पु. (अ.) plan; design; intention; project; scheme.

मनस्ताप *(manastāp)* पु. mental pain; anguish; remorse; affliction; mental agony.

मनस्वी *(mansavī)* पु. intelligent; high-souled; high-minded; thoughtful; contemplative; single-minded.

मनहूस *(manhūs)* वि. (अ.) illomened; inauspicious; ilस.fated; gloomy.

मनाना *(manana)* स. क्रि. to persuade; to prevail upon; to propitiate; to assuage; to appease; to invoke; to call upon (god); to celebrate; to perform.

मनाही *(manāhi)* स्त्री. prohibition; ban; forbiddance.

मनीषी *(maniśi)* वि. wise; learned; intelligent; clever; prudent; thoughtful.

मनुज *(manuj)* पु. human being; man.

मनुजता *(manujatā)* स्त्री. humanity.

मनुष्य *(manuśyā)* पु. man.

मनुष्यता *(manuśyatā)* स्त्री. manhood; humanity; aggregate of human qualities.

मनुहार *(manuhār)* स्त्री. appeasement; pacification; flattery; adulation; persuation.

मनोकामना *(mano-kāmanā)* स्त्री. heart's desire; wish.

मनोज *(manoj)* पु. Cupid; the god of love.

मनोज्ञ *(manogna)* वि. pleasing; lovely; beautiful; charming.

मनोनियोग *(mano-niyog)* पु. application of mind; attention.

मनोनीत *(manonita)* वि. taken by the mind; nominated.

मनोबल *(manobal)* पु. moral strength; morale.

मनोयोग *(manoyog)* वि. close attention; concentration; single-mindedness.

मनोरंजक *(mano-ranjak)* वि. interesting; amusing; recreative; entertaining.

मनोरंजन *(mano-ranjan)* पु. amusement; recreation; entertainment.

मनोरथ *(manorath)* पु. wish; desire; longing.

मनोरम *(mano-ram)* वि. attractive; pleasing; charming; lovely; beautiful.

मनोरमता *(mano-ramatā)* स्त्री. loveliness; comeliness.

मनोवांछित *(mano-vānchit)* वि. desired; wished; longed for.

मनोविकार *(mano-vikār)* पु. emotion; feeling; passion; psychic disorder; mental disorder.

मनोविकारी *(mano-vikārī)* वि. psychiatric.

मनोविज्ञान *(mano-vignān)* पु. psychology.

मनोवैज्ञानिक *(mano-vaignānik)* पु. psychological.

मनोव्यथा *(mano-vyathā)* स्त्री. mental agony; anguish; affliction.

मनोहर *(manohar)* वि. captivating; fascinating; alluring; beautiful; lovely; charming.

मनौती *(manauti)* स्त्री. appeasement; offering promised to a deity for fulfilment of some desire.

मन्मथ *(manmath)* पु. Cupid; lovegod.

ममता *(mamatā)* स्त्री. affection; attachment.

मयंक *(mayaṅk)* पु. moon.

मयस्सर *(mayassar)* वि. (अ.) attainable; available.

मयूर *(mayūr)* पु. peacock.

मयूरी *(mayūrī)* स्त्री. pea-hen.

मरज़ी *(marzī)* स्त्री. (अ.) desire; wish; inclination; pleasure; assent; consent.

मरण *(maraṇ)* पु. death; demise; expiration; mortality.

मरणासन्न *(maraṇāsan)* वि. on the verge of death; moribund.

मरणोत्तर *(maraottar)* वि. posthumous.

मरतबान *(martabān)* पु. jar.

मरना *(marnā)* अ. क्रि. to die; to expire; to fade; to wither; to labour or toil hard; to suffer hardship; to be dead or out (as in a game); to be absorbed.

मरमर *(marmar)* पु. marble.

मरमरा *(marmarā)* वि. brittle.

मरमरी *(marmarī)* वि. of marble; made of marble; like marble.

मरम्मत *(marammat)* स्त्री. (अ.) repair; mending; (fig.) punishment given with the object of mending someone.

मरहम *(marham)* पु. (अ.) ointment; balm.

मरहमपट्टी *(marhampaṭī)* स्त्री. dressing; bandage.

मरियल *(mariyal)* वि. sickly; feeble; rickety.

मरीचिका *(marīcikā)* स्त्री. mirage; illusion.

मरीज़ *(marīz)* पु. (अ.) sick person; patient.

मरु *(maru)* पु. desert.

मरुस्थल *(marusthal)* पु. desert land.

मरोड़ *(maror)* स्त्री. turn; bend; twist; convolution; contortion; wrench.

मरोड़ना *(maroṛnā)* स. क्रि. to turn; to bend; to twist; to contort; to wring.

मरोड़ा *(maroṛā)* पु. convolution; dysentery.

मर्कट *(markaṭ)* पु. monkey.

मर्ज़ *(marz)* पु. (अ.) ailment; disease.

मर्ज़ी *(marzi)* स्त्री. (अ.) wish; desire.

मर्त्यलोक *(martyalok)* पु. world; habitation of mortals; earth.

मर्द *(mard)* पु. (फ.) man; male; brave and strong man; husband.

मर्दानगी *(mardānagī)* स्त्री. (फ.) manliness; bravery; courage; prowess.

मर्दाना *(mardānā)* वि. (अ.) male; man-like; maculine brave; valorous; manful.

मर्दुमशुमारी *(mardum-śumāri)* स्त्री. (फ.) census.

मर्म *(marm)* पु. implied meaning; quintessence; secret; mystery; core or vital part of the body; weak; vulnerable or mortal point; secret recess (of the heart; etc.).

मर्मज्ञ *(marmagna)* वि. knowing mysteries; familiar with the most secret or recondite portions of subject; deeply versed.

मर्मभेदी *(marmbhedī)* वि. moving;

touching; poignant; excessively painful; heart-rending.

मर्मातक *(marmātak)* वि. poignant; heartrending; mortal.

मर्यादा *(maryādā)* स्त्री. limit boundary; ambit; propriety of conduct; decorum; decency; established usage; social code; custom; rank; station; dignity.

मर्यादित *(maryādit)* वि. limited; limited by propriety; dignified.

मल *(mal)* पु. rubbish; dirt; filth; any excretion of the body; excrement; faeces.

मलद्वार *(maldvar)* पु. anus.

मलना *(malnā)* स. क्रि. to rub; to massage; to anoint; to smear.

मलबा *(malbā)* पु. rubbish; refuse; debris.

मलमल *(malmal)* स्त्री. muslin.

मलवाना *(malvānā)* स. क्रि. to have or get (a thing) rubbed; to cause to be massaged.

मलाई *(malāī)* स्त्री. kneading; rubbing; the wages paid for kneading or rubbing; cream of milk.

मलाल *(malāl)* पु. (अ.) grief; anguish; remorse; compunction.

मलाशय *(malāśaya)* पु. rectum.

मलिन *(malin)* वि. dirty; filthy; tarnished; stained; obscured; dull or dim (light etc.); sad; downcast; melancholy; sombre.

मलिनता *(malinatā)* स्त्री. dirtiness; filthiness; impurity; squalor; sadness; sombreness.

मलीन *(malīn)* वि. dirty; shabby; melancholy.

मलेरिया *(maleriyā)* पु. malaria.

मल्ल *(mall)* पु. professional wrestler or boxer.

मल्लाह *(mallāh)* पु. (अ.) sailor; mariner; boatman.

मवेशी *(maveśī)* पु. cattle.

मशक़्क़त *(maśaqqat)* स्त्री. (अ.) toil; hard labour.

मशगूल *(maśgūl)* वि. (अ.) busy; occupied; absorbed.

मशवरा *(maśvarā)* पु. (अ.) consultation; advice; counsel.

मशहूर *(maśahūr)* वि. (अ.) famous; welस.known; celebrated; reputed; notorious.

मशाल *(maśāl)* स्त्री. (अ.) torch.

मशालची *(maśalcī)* पु. (अ.) torchbearer.

मसका *(maskā)* पु. butter; flattery; adulation.

मसख़रा¹ *(maskharā)* वि. (अ.) funny; humoursome.

मसख़रा² *(maskharā)* पु. (अ.) jester; joker; buffoon; clown.

मसख़रापन *(maskharāpan)* पु. buffoonery; jesting; funniness; clownage.

मस्जिद *(masjid)* स्त्री. (अ.) mosque.

मसनद *(masnad)* पु. (अ.) bolster; big pillow.

मसनूई *(masnui)* वि. (अ.) artificial; contrived.

मसरूफ़ *(masrūf)* वि. (अ.) busy; occupied.

मसलना *(masalnā)* स. क्रि. to rub to pieces; to press hard; to bruise; to crush.

मसला *(maslā)* पु. (अ.) issue; question; problem.

मसहरी *(masahrī)* स्त्री. mosquitonet.

मसान *(masān)* पु. cremation ground; crematory.

मसाना *(masānā)* पु. (अ.) urinary bladder.

मसाला *(masālā)* पु. spicery; spices; condiments; material; ingredients; etc.

मसि *(masi)* स्त्री. ink.

मसीह *(masīh)* पु. (अ.) Jesus Christ.

मसीहा *(masīhā)* पु. (फ.) Messiah; one endowed with powers to revive the dead.

मसूड़ा, मसूढ़ा *(masūṛā)* पु. gum (of the teeth).

मसोसना *(masosanā)* (अ.) क्रि. to suppress (an emotion etc.).

मसौदा *(masaudā)* पु. (अ.) draft.

मस्त *(mast)* वि. intoxicated; drunk; carefree; overjoyed; delighted.

मस्तक *(mastak)* पु. head; forehead.

मस्तिष्क *(mastiṣk)* पु. cerebrum; brain.

मस्ती *(mastī)* स्त्री. joy; sexual excitement; intoxication; youthful vigour.

मस्तूल *(mastūl)* पु. (पुर्त.) mast.

मस्सा *(massā)* पु. wart.

महँगा *(mahaṁgā)* वि. dear; expensive; costly.

महँगाई *(mahaṁgāī)* स्त्री. dearness; expeniveness; costliness.

महंत *(mahant)* पु. head of a monastery; abbot; monk.

महक *(mahak)* स्त्री. fragrance; odour; aroma.

महकदार *(mahakdār)* वि. fragrant; odoriferous; aromatic.

महकना *(mahaknā)* अ. क्रि. to give out sweet smell or fragrance.

महकमा *(mahakmā)* पु. (अ.) department.

महकाना *(mahkānā)* स. क्रि. to exhale (scent); to perfume; to scent.

महज़ *(mahz)* वि. (अ.) mere; only; sheer.

महतारी *(mahtārī)* स्त्री. mother.

महत् *(mahat)* वि. great; big; large; huge; high; eminent; distinguished; intense; gross; thick; dense.

महत्तम *(mahattam)* वि. greatest; biggest; maximum; maximal.

महत्ता *(mahattā)* स्त्री. greatness; magnitude; importance; significance.

महत्त्व *(mahattva)* पु. importance; significance; greatness; magnitude.

महत्वपूर्ण *(mahattvapuran)* वि. important; significant; material.

महत्वाकांक्षा *(mahatvā-kānkshā)* स्त्री. ambition; aspiration.

महत्त्वाकांक्षी *(mahatvā-kānkshī)* वि. ambitious; aspiring.

महफ़िल *(mahfil)* स्त्री. (अ.) assembly; congregation; private gathering; recreational assembly.

महबूब *(mahbūb)* पु. (अ.) lover.

महबूबा *(mahbūbā)* स्त्री. (अ.) beloved.

महराब *(mahrāb)* स्त्री. (अ.) arch.

महल *(mahal)* पु. (अ.) palace; palatial mansion.

महल्ला *(mahallā)* पु. (अ.) ward (in a town or city); locality.

महसूल *(mahsūl)* पु. (अ.) tax; duty; custom; portage; revenue; commission; freight.

महा *(mahā)* वि. ample; excessive; great; illustrious; mighty.

महाकाय *(mahākāvya)* वि. large; mammoth; gigantic; bulky.

महाकाव्य *(maha-kāvya)* पु. epic.

महाजन *(mahājan)* पु. merchant; tradesman; money-lender; a great or eminent man; a very distinguished person.

महात्मा *(mahātmā)* पु. saintly person; saint; enlightened soul.

महान *(mahān)* महान् वि. great; eminent.

महानगर *(mahānagar)* पु. metropolis.

महानता *(mahānatā)* स्त्री. greatness; eminence; nobility.

महापौर *(mahāpaur)* पु. mayor.

महामना *(mahāmanā)* वि. high-minded noble-minded; magnanimous.

महामात्य *(mahāmātya)* पु. prime minister; premier.

महामारी *(mahāmārī)* स्त्री. an epidemic.

महारत *(mahārat)* स्त्री. (अ.) practice; expertise.

महारथी *(mahārathī)* पु. great warrior; leading luminary in any field of knowledge or activity.

महाराज *(mahārāj)* पु. great king; supreme sovereign; respectful address; cook.

महाराजा *(maharajā)* पु. king of kings; potentate.

महालेखापाल *(mahalekhāpāl)* पु. accountant general.

महावट *(mahāvat)* स्त्री. winter rains.

महावत *(mahāvat)* पु. mahout; elephant-driver.

महावर *(mahāvar)* पु. red colour used by ladies to beautify their feet.

महाविद्यालय *(mahāvidyālaya)* पु. college.

महाशय *(mahāsay)* पु. gentleman.

महासंघ *(mahāśangh)* पु. federation; confederation.

महासचिव *(mahā-sāciv)* secretary general.

महासागर *(mahā-sagar)* पु. ocean.

महि *(mahi)* स्त्री. earth.

महिमा *(mahimā)* स्त्री. greatness; glory; dignity; exaltation.

मही *(mahī)* स्त्री. earth; ground; soil.

महीन *(mahīn)* वि. fine; thin; soft.

महीना *(mahīnā)* पु. month; menses.

महोत्सव *(mahotsava)* पु. great festival; great rejoicing; big celebration.

महोदय *(mahôday)* पु. an honorific term; sir; gentleman.

महोदया *(mahôdayā)* स्त्री. madam.

माँ *(māṁ)* स्त्री. mother.

माँग *(māṁg)* स्त्री. request; requirement; want; demand; parting of the hair (on the head).

माँगना *(māṁganā)* स. क्रि. to ask for; to request for; to demand; to claim.

माँग-पत्र *(māṁg-patra)* पु. memorandum of demands; order form; indent.

मांगलिक *(māṅgalik)* वि. bendictory; auspicious; propitious.

माँझना *(māṁjhanā)* स. क्रि. to cleanse; to scrub; to polish; to practise; to exercise.

माँद *(māṁd)* स्त्री. den.

माँदा *(māṁdā)* वि. (फ.) fatigued; tired; ailing; indisposed.

मांस *(māṁs)* पु. flesh; meat.

मांसपेशी *(māṁs-peśi)* स्त्री. muscle.

मांसाहारी *(maṁsāhāri)* वि. nonvegetarian; carnivorous.

माकूल *(māqūl)* वि. (अ.) proper; appropriate; fair; reasonable; fit; suitable.

माखन *(mākhan)* पु. butter.

माचिस *(mācis)* स्त्री. match-box.

मातम *(mātam)* पु.(अ.) grief; mourning; lamentation.

मातम-पुरसी *(matam-pursi)* स्त्री. condolence.

मातहत *(mātahat)* वि. subordinate; subservient.

मातहती *(mātahati)* स्त्री. subordination; subservience.

माता *(mātā)* स्त्री. mother; respectful term of address to an elderly woman; smalस.pox.

मातुल *(mātul)* पु. maternal uncle; mother's brother.

मातृ *(mātṛ)* स्त्री. mother.

मातृत्व *(mātṛtva)* पु. maternity; motherhood.

मातृ-भाषा *(mātṛ-bhāsā)* स्त्री. mother-tongue.

मातृ-भूमि *(mātṛ-bhumi)* स्त्री. mother land; home land.

मात्र *(mātr)* क्रि. वि. only; merely; sheerly.

मात्रा *(mātrā)* स्त्री. measure; quantity; dose (of medicine); the length of time required to pronounce a syllable; duration; voweस.mark in Devnagri script.

मात्रिक *(mātrik)* वि. or pertaining to a voweस.mark; based on the number of Matras; durative.

माथा *(māthā)* पु. forehead.

माथा-पच्ची *(māthā-pāci)* स्त्री. taxing of brains; mental over-exertion.

मादक *(mādak)* वि. intoxicating; stupefying.

मादकता *(mādaktā)* स्त्री. intoxication; drunkenness.

मादा *(mādā)* स्त्री. (फ.) female.

माधुर्य *(mādhurya)* पु. sweetness; pleasantness.

माध्यम *(mādhyam)* वि. means; medium; vehicle.

मानक *(mānak)* पु. standard;norm.

मानकीकरण *(mānakikaran)* पु. standardization.

मानचित्र *(māncitra)* पु. map; chart.

मानदंड *(māndand)* पु. standard; criterion.

मानद *(mānad)* वि. honorary.

मानदेय *(manadeya)* पु. honorarium.

मानता *(mānatā)* स्त्री. importance; recognition; reckoning (as great; powerful etc.).

मानना *(mānana)* स. क्रि. to admit; to accept; to confess; to acknowledge; to respect; revere; esteem; to assume; to suppose; to take for granted; to obey; to agree; to condescend; to acquiesce.

माननीय *(mānaniya)* वि. honourable, venerable; respectable.

मानव *(mānav)* पु. human being.

मानवजाति *(mānaअ.jāti)* स्त्री. human species; mankind.

मानवजाति विज्ञान *(mānav-jāti-vigynān)* पु. ethnology.

मानवजाति विज्ञानी *(mānav-jāti-vigyani)* पु. ethnologist.

मानवजातीय ***(mānavjātiya)*** **वि.** eth-nic.

मानवता ***(mànavatā)*** **स्त्री.** humanity; **mankind; human quality.**

मानवतावाद *(mānavatāvād)* पु. humanism.

मानवपूजा *(mānav-pujā)* स्त्री. anthropolatry.

मानवप्रेम *(mānav-prem)* पु. philanthropy.

मानवविज्ञान *(mānav-vignān)* पु. anthropology.

मानवविज्ञानी *(mānav-vignāni)* पु.

anthropologist.

मानविकी *(mānavikī)* स्त्री. humanities.

मानवीकरण *(mānavikaran)* पु. humanization; personification.

मानवीय *(mānavīya)* वि. pertaining to mankind; humanitarian; human.

मानवोचित *(mānavočit)* वि. befitting a human being.

मानस *(mānas)* पु. mind; heart; soul; psyche; man; human being.

मानसिक *(mānasik)* वि. of or pertaining to the mind; mental; psychic.

मानहानि *(mānhāni)* स्त्री. insult; defamation; contempt.

मानी *(mānī)* वि. haughty; proud; self-respecting; entitled to respect; highly honoured.

मानुष *(mānuś)* पु. man.

मानुषिक *(mānusik)* वि. of or pertaining to mankind.

मानुषी[1] *(mānusī)* स्त्री. woman.

मानुषी[2] *(mānusī)* वि. of or pertaining to mankind.

मानो *(māno)* क्रि. वि. supposing; as though; as if; as it were.

मान्य *(mānya)* वि. valid; tenable; acceptable; honourable; venerable; respectable.

मान्यता *(mānyatā)* स्त्री. recognition; acceptability; validity.

माप *(māp)* पु. measure; measurement; size; dimension.

मापक *(māpak)* पु. measurer; surveyor; meter.

मापतौल *(māptaul)* पु. measurement; a system of measures and weights; complete assessment of weight; measure etc.

मापदंड *(māp-dand)* पु. yardstick; standard; touchstone; criterion.

मापना *(māpana)* स. क्रि. to measure; to survey; to scale.

माफ़ *(māf)* वि. (अ.) excused; condoned; forgiven; pardoned.

माफ़िक़ *(māfiq)* वि. (अ.) suitable; agreeable; favourable; befitting.

माफ़ी *(māfi)* स्त्री. (अ.) forgiveness; pardon; exemption; condonation.

मामला *(māmalā)* पु. matter; occurrence; happening; business; affair; case; cause or suit (in law).

मामा *(māmā)* पु. maternal uncle.

मामी *(māmī)* स्त्री. maternal aunt.

मामूली *(māmūlī)* वि. (अ.) ordinary; common-place; customary; usual; a little; negligible; marginal.

मायका *(māyakā)* पु. paternal house of a married woman.

माया *(māyā)* स्त्री. divine and formless power of the Supreme Being; extraordinary or supernatural power; magical or wonderful power; enchantment; illusion of magic; delusion; prosperity; opulence; riches.

मायावी[1] *(māyāvī)* पु. magician ; juggler.

मायावी[2] *(māyāvī)* वि. deceptive; deceitful.

मायूस *(māyūs)* वि. (अ.) frustrated; disappointed; dejected.

मायूसी *(māyūsī)* स्त्री. (अ.) disappointment; despair.

मारना *(mārnā)* स. क्रि. to kill; slay; slaughter; to beat; to strike; to hit; to counteract; to turn ineffective (poison etc.); to overcome conquer; defeat; to destroy; ruin; to win in a game of cards or chess; to master; to subdue; tame; mortify (affections; appetites or lusts).

मारपीट *(mārpit)* स्त्री. scuffle; exchange of blows; mutual fighting.

मार्ग *(mārg)* पु. way; road; path; route; course; means; contrivance; transit; passage.

मार्गदर्शक *(mārg-darśak)* पु. guide; conductor; pilot.

मार्गदर्शन *(mārg-darśan)* पु. guidance; pilotage.

मार्मिक *(mārmik)* वि. vital; affecting the vital parts; poignant; touching; moving.

माल *(māl)* पु. (अ.) goods; stock; merchandise; dainty; delicious dish; household goods or effects; riches; money; property; wealth; rent or revenue (from land).

मालकिन *(mālkin)* स्त्री. lady owner; land lady; mistress.

मालगाड़ी *(mālgāṛī)* स्त्री. (अ.) goods train.

मालगुज़ारी *(mālguzārī)* (अ.) land revenue.

मालगोदाम *(mālgodām)* पु. warehouse; store-house; godown.

मालटा *(mālaṭā)* पु. a kind of citrus fruits.

मालदार *(māldār)* वि. (अ.) wealthy; rich; moneyed.

मालभाड़ा *(mālbhāṛā)* पु. freight; freight charges.

माला *(mālā)* स्त्री. row; line; series; wreath; garland; collection; group; string (of beads etc.).

मालिक *(mālik)* पु. (अ.) proprietor; owner; master; the Supreme Being; husband.

मालिन *(mālin)* स्त्री. wife of gardener; female gardener or flower-seller.

मालिन्य *(mālinya)* पु. sullenness; rancour; estrangement; uncleanliness; dirtiness; pollution; impurity.

मालिश *(māliś)* स्त्री. (अ.) shampooing; massage.

माली[1] *(mālī)* पु. gardener; florist; flower-seller.

माली[2] *(māli)* वि. financial; fiscal; economic.

मावा *(māvā)* पु. milk inspissated by boiling.

मास *(mās)* पु. month; meat.

मासिक *(māsik)* वि. monthly; happening every month.

मासिकधर्म *(māsik-dharm)* पु. monthly course; menstruation.

मासूम *(māsūm)* वि. (अ.) innocent; guiltless; simple; pitiable; deserving mercy.

मासूमियत *(masumiyat)* स्त्री. (अ.) innocence; harmlessness; guiltlessness.

माह *(māh)* पु. (फ.) month.

माहवारी *(māhvarī)* स्त्री. (फ़ा.) monthly course; menstruation.

माहिर *(māhir)* वि. (अ.) skilful; proficient; expert.

माहौल *(māhaul)* पु. atmosphere; environment; milieu.

मिक़दार *(miqdār)* स्त्री. (अ.) quantity; measure.

मिचना *(micnā)* अ. क्रि. to be shut or closed.

मिचलाना *(miclānā)* अ. क्रि. to feel like vomiting; to feel nausea.

मिचली *(miclī)* स्त्री. nausea; qualm.

मिचौनी, मिचौली *(micaunī)* स्त्री. the game of hide and seek.

मिज़ाज *(mizāj)* पु. (अ.) nature; temperament; diposition; health; pride; haughtiness.

मिटना *(miṭanā)* अ. क्रि. to be effaced or erased; to be destroyed; to be annihilated; to be undone; to be extinct.

मिटाना *(miṭānā)* स. क्रि. to efface; to erase; to rub or to blot out; to destroy; to ruin.

मिट्टी *(miṭṭī)* स्त्री. earth; clay; dust.

मिट्टी का तेल *(mitti-ka-tel)* पु. kerosene.

मिठाई *(miṭhāī)* स्त्री. sweetmeat; sweets.

मिठास *(miṭhās)* स्त्री. sweetness.

मितभाषी *(mitbhasi)* वि. temperate in speech; teciturn.

मितव्ययिता *(mit-vyatitā)* स्त्री. economy; thriftiness.

मितव्ययी *(mit-vyayi)* वि. economical; thrifty; frugal.

मित्र *(mitr)* पु. friend; ally; comrade.

मित्रता *(mitratā)* स्त्री. friendship; intimacy.

मिथ्या[1] *(mithyā)* वि. false; untrue; feigned; spurious; sham; illusory; fake.

मिथ्या[2] *(mithyā)* पु. untruth; falsehood; illusion.

मिथ्याचार *(mithyācār)* पु. imposture.

मिन्नत *(minnat)* स्त्री. (अ.) entreaty; request; humble and earnest supplication.

मिमियाना *(mimiyānā)* अ. क्रि. to bleat; to speak submissively; to speak cringingly.

मियाद *(miyād)* see मीआद।

मियादी *(miyādī)* see मीआदी।

मियान *(miyān)* स्त्री. (फ़ा.) scabbard; sheath.

मिरगी *(mirgī)* स्त्री. epilepsy.

मिर्च *(mirc)* स्त्री. chillies; pepper.

मिलता-जुलता *(miltā-jultā)* वि. resembling partially; almost identical or similar.

मिलन *(milan)* पु. union; contact; meeting.

मिलनसार *(milansār)* वि. sociable; friendly; affable.

मिलना *(milnā)* अ. क्रि. to be mixed; to be mingled; to be blended; to join; to unite; to come together; to come into contact; to meet; to be discovered; to be revealed; to be found; to be obtained; to come to hand; be acquired; to defect; to harmonize; to correspond.

मिलवाना *(milvānā)* स. क्रि. to cause to be joined; to cause to be united; to cause to be reconciled.

मिलाई *(milāī)* स्त्री. act of mixing; act of causing a meeting; visit (esp. paid to a prisoner of a patient).

मिलान *(milān)* पु. reconciliation (of accounts); comparison; tallying of accounts; collation; matching.

मिलाना *(milānā)* स. क्रि. to mix; mingle; to blend; to connect; to join; to unite; to introduce (one person to another); to reconcile; to reconcile (accounts); to compare; to cause (someone) to defect to one's side; to tune.

मिलाप *(milāp)* पु. rapproachement; reconciliation; union; unity; social converse.

मिलावट *(milāvat)* स्त्री. adulteration.

मिलावटी *(milāvatī)* वि. adulterated; spurious.

मिलीभगत *(milībhagat)* स्त्री. collusion; league; sinister alliance.

मिश्र *(miśra)* वि. mixed; blended; combined; having an alloy.

मिश्रण *(miśraṇ)* पु. combination; mixture; blend; adulteration.

मिश्रित *(miśrit)* वि. mixed; mingled; blended.

मिश्री *(miśrī)* वि. candy.

मिष्टभाषी *(miṣṭ-bhasī)* वि. softspoken; honey-tongued.

मिष्टान्न *(miṣṭānn)* पु. confectionary; sweetmeat.

मिसाल *(misāl)* स्त्री. (अ.) example; precedent.

मिस्तरी *(mistrī)* स्त्री. artisan; craftsman; mechanic.

मीआद *(mīyvād)* स्त्री. (अ.) limit of time; period; term; usance.

मीआदी *(mīyādī)* वि. lasting for a certain period.

मीचना *(mīcnā)* स. क्रि. to shut or close (the eyes).

मीज़ान *(mīzān)* स्त्री. (अ.) total; balance; pair of scales.

मीठा[1] *(mīṭhā)* पु. sweet; pleasant; agreeable; slow; slight; mild.

मीठा[2] *(mīṭhā)* पु. sweets.

मीत *(mīt)* पु. friend.

मीन *(mīn)* स्त्री. fish; twelfth sign of the zodiac; pisces.

मीन-मेख *(mīn-mekh)* पु. uncharitable criticism; fault-finding.

मीनार *(mīnār)* स्त्री. (अ.) tower; minaret; steeple.

मीमांसक *(mīmāṃsak)* पु. exponent; commentator.

मीमांसा *(mīmāṃsā)* स्त्री. reflection; consideration; investigation of truth; name of one of the six systems of Hindu philosophy in which vedic rituals are stipulated; interpretative exposition; scholarly commentary.

मुंडन *(muṇḍan)* पु. shaving of the head; tonsure.

मुँडना *(muṁḍnā)* अ. क्रि. to be shaved; (fig.) to be fleeced; to be swindled.

मुँडाई *(muṁḍāī)* स्त्री. shaving charges; act of shaving.

मुँडाना *(mumḍānā)* स. क्रि. to get shaved; to have tonsured.

मुँड़ासा *(mimṛāsā)* पु. a kind of turban.

मुँडेर *(muṁḍer)* स्त्री. parapet.

मुँदना *(muṁdanā)* अ. क्रि. to be shut or closed; to be covered or hidden.

मुंशी *(mumśī)* पु. (अ.) scribe; clerk; teacher of Persian of Urdu.

मुंसिफ़ *(mumṣif)* पु. (अ.) an officer of judiciary; officer of the civil court below the rank of a subjudge.

मुँह *(muṁh)* पु. mouth; face; countenance; aperture; orifice; opening.

मुँहज़ोर *(muṁh-zor)* वि. insolent; impertinent; impudent.

मुँहज़ोरी *(muṁh-zorī)* स्त्री. insolence; impudence; high spiritedness; hard-mouthedness.

मुंहतोड़ *(muṁh-tor)* वि. apt; befiting; crushing; incontrovertible; retaliatory.

मुँहफट *(mumh-fat)* वि. loose tongued; outspoken.

मुँहासा *(mumhāsā)* पु. pimple.

मुअत्तल *(muattal)* वि. (अ.) suspended; held in abeyance.

मुअत्तली *(muattalī)* पु. (अ.) suspension.

मुआयना *(muāyanā)* पु. (अ.) inspection; visit.

मुआवज़ा *(muāvazā)* पु. (अ.) compensation; recompense; remuneration; indemnity.

मुक़दमा *(muqadmā)* पु. (अ.) law-suit; suit; cause.

मुक़दमेबाज़ *(muqadmebāz)* पु. (अ.) litigant.

मुक़द्दर *(muqaddar)* पु. (अ.) fate; destiny; luck.

मुकम्मल *(mukammal)* वि. (अ.) complete; entire; whole; accomplished.

मुकरना *(mukaranā)* अ. क्रि. to deny; to go back upon one's word.

मुक़र्रर *(muqarrar)* वि. (अ.) settled; fixed; established; appointed; posted.

मुक़ाबला *(muqābalā)* पु. (अ.) encounter; confrontation; comparison; competition; collation; equality.

मुक़ाम *(muqām)* पु. (अ.) halt; stay; place; site; residence.

मुकुट *(mukuṭ)* पु. diadem; crown.

मुक्का *(mukkā)* पु. punch; thump; blow of fist.

मुक्केबाज़ *(mukke-bāz)* पु. boxer; pugilist.

मुक्केबाज़ी *(mukke-bāzī)* स्त्री. fisticuffs; pugilism; boxing.

मुक्त *(mukt)* वि. set free; liberated; released; absolved; thrown; cast; discharged; hurled; unfettered; exonerated.

मुक्ता *(muktā)* स्त्री. pearl.

मुक्ति *(mukti)* स्त्री. release; liberation; deliverance; salvation; absolution of the soul from metempsychosis; emancipation.

मुख *(mukh)* स्त्री. mouth; face; front; fore-part; facade; opening; aperture.

मुख़तार *(mukhtār)* पु. (अ.) legal agent.

मुखपत्र *(mukhpatra)* पु. manifesto; organ.

मुखपृष्ठ *(mukhpristh)* पु. title page; front page.

मुखबंध *(mukh-bandh)* पु. preface.

मुख़बिर *(mukhbir)* पु. (अ.) spy; reporter; informer.

मुखर *(mukhar)* वि. talkative; garrulous; loquacious; vociferous; noisy; making a continuous sound; cheeky; explicit; outspoken.

मुखरता *(mukhartā)* स्त्री. vociferousness; talkativeness; outspokenness; explicitness.

मुख़ालफ़त *(mukhālafat)* स्त्री. (फ़ा.) opposition; antagonism.

मुखावरण *(mukhāvaran)* पु. mask; cover-design.

मुखिया *(mukhiyā)* पु. chief; leader.

मुखौटा *(mukhauṭā)* पु. mask.

मुख़्तसर *(mukhtasar)* वि. (अ.) brief.

मुख्य *(mukhya)* वि. chief; principal; main; major; important; prominent; cardinal.

मुख्यतः *(mukhyatāh)* क्रि. वि. primarily; mainly; chiefly; predominantly; pre-eminantly.

मुख्यता *(mukhyātā)* स्त्री. pre-eminence; distinction; prominence.

मुख्यमंत्री *(mukhya-mantri)* पु. chief minister.

मुख्यालय *(mukhyālaya)* पु. headquarters.

मुग्ध *(mugdh)* वि. fascinated; perplexed; infatuated.

मुग्धता *(mugdhatā)* स्त्री. fascination; infatuation.

मुजरिम *(mujarim)* पु. (अ.) criminal; offender.

मुटापा *(muṭāpā)* पु. fatness; plumpness; obesity.

मुट्ठी *(muṭṭhī)* स्त्री. fist; grasp (of the hand); handful; a measure equal to the breadth of fist.

मुठभेड़ *(muṭh-bher)* स्त्री. collision; clash; skirmish; meeting; encounter; confrontation.

मुठिया *(muthiyā)* स्त्री. handle or hilt; the round plump stick with which a cotton carder strikes the string of his bow.

मुड़ना *(muṛnā)* अ. क्रि. to be turned; to be twisted; to bend; to turn; to turn back.

मुदर्रिस *(mudarris)* पु. (अ.) school teacher.

मुदित *(mudit)* वि. pleased; delighted; happy.

मुद्दई *(muddaī)* पु. (अ.) plaintiff.

मुद्दत *(muddat)* स्त्री. (अ.) period; length of time; duration; usance.

मुद्दा *(muddā)* पु. (अ.) object; purport; intention; issue; theme.

मुद्रक *(mudrak)* पु. printer.

मुद्रण *(mudraṇ)* पु. printing; marking; sealing; stamping.

मुद्रणालय *(mudraṇālaya)* पु. printing press.

मुद्रांकन *(mudrānkan)* पु. stamping; sealing.

मुद्रा *(mudrā)* स्त्री. seal; signet; stamp; ring embedded with name or personal mark; currency; money; coins; mien; countenance; pose; posture.

मुद्रित *(mudrit)* वि. sealed; stamped; printed; marked; closed.

मुनादी *(munādī)* स्त्री. (अ.) proclamation.

मुनाफ़ा *(munāfā)* पु. (अ.) gain; profit.

मुनाफ़ाख़ोर *(munāfākhor)* पु. (अ.) profiteer.

मुनाफ़ाख़ोरी *(munāfākhorī)* स्त्री. profiteering.

मुनासिब *(munāsib)* वि. (अ.) proper; suitable; reasonable.

मुनि *(muni)* पु. ascetic; hermit.

मुनीम *(munīm)* पु. clerk of a merchant; accountant.

मुफ़लिस *(muflis)* वि. (अ.) poor; indigent.

मुफ़लिसी *(muflisī)* स्त्री. (अ.) poverty; pauperdom.

मुफ़्त *(muft)* वि. (फ.) free of charge; gratis.

मुबारक *(mubārak)* वि. (अ.) auspicious; blessed; fortunate.

मुबारकबाद *(mubārakbād)* स्त्री. (अ.) congratulations; felicitations.

मुमकिन *(mumkin)* वि. (अ.) possible; feasible.

मुरग़ा *(murgā)* पु. cock.

मुरग़ी *(murgī)* स्त्री. hen.

मुरझाना *(murjhānā)* अ. क्रि. to wither; fade; droop; to become dejected or dispirited.

मुरदा[1] *(murdā)* पु. (फ.) corpse; dead body.

मुरदा[2] *(murda)* वि. (फ.) dead; lifeless.

मुरब्बा *(murabbā)* पु. (अ.) jam; square; conserve.

मुराद *(murād)* स्त्री. (अ.) wish; longing; desire; inclination; object; purport; tenor.

मुरौवत *(murauvat)* स्त्री. (अ.) gentility; obligingness; benevolence; politeness; affability.

मुर्ग़ *(murg)* मुर्ग़ा *(murgā)* see मुरग़ा।

मुर्गी *(murgī)* स्त्री. see मुरग़ी।

मुलम्मा *(mulammā)* पु. (अ.) gilding; gilt; plating; veneer; coating; external show; ostentation.

मुलाक़ात *(mulāqāt)* स्त्री. (अ.) meeting; visit; interview; acquaintance.

मुलाज़मत *(mulāzamat)* स्त्री. (अ.) employment; service.

मुलाज़िम *(mulāzīm)* पु. (अ.) employee; servant; attendant.

मुलायम *(mulāyam)* वि. (अ.) soft; tender; delicate.

मुलायमियत *(mulāyamiyat)* स्त्री. (अ.) softness; tenderness; gentleness; generosity.

मुल्क *(mulk)* पु. (अ.) country; territory; region.

मुशायरा *(muśayarā)* पु. (अ.) poetic symposium.

मुश्किल[1] *(muśkil)* वि. (अ.) difficult; hard; tough.

मुश्किल[2] *(muśkil)* स्त्री. (अ.) difficulty; hardship.

मुष्टि *(muṣṭi)* स्त्री. fist; fist-blow.

मुसकराना *(muskarānā)* अ. क्रि. to smile.

मुसकान *(muskān)* स्त्री. smile.

मुसकाना *(muskānā)* see मुसकराना

मुसलमान *(musalmān)* पु. (अ.) Mohammedan; Muslim.

मुसाफ़िर *(musāfir)* पु. (अ.) traveller; wayfarer. passenger.

मुसीबत *(musībat)* स्त्री. (अ.) trouble; difficulty; calamity; misfortune; disaster.

मुस्टंडा[1] *(musṭaṇḍā)* वि. strong- bodied; stout.

मुस्टंडा[2] *(musṭaṇḍā)* पु. rough and robust fellow.

मुस्तक़िल *(mustaqil)* वि. (अ.) stable; permanent; confirmed.

मुस्तैद *(mustaid)* वि. (अ.) ready; prepared; alert; active; agile; vigilant.

मुस्तैदी *(mustaidī)* स्त्री. (अ.) readiness; alertness; promptitude; vigilance.

मुहताज *(muhtāj)* वि. (अ.) dependent; needy; indigent; destitute; poor.

मुहब्बत *(muhabbat)* स्त्री. (अ.) love; affection; fondness.

मुहर *(muhar)* स्त्री. seal; stamp; gold coin.

मुहरा *(muharā)* पु. front part; prey; victim; a pawn or piece of chess.

मुहर्रिर *(muharrir)* पु. (अ.) clerk; scribe.

मुहलत *(muhlat)* स्त्री. (अ.) grace period; leave of absence from work.

मुहल्ला *(muhallā)* पु. locality; ward; street.

मुहाना *(muhānā)* पु. mouth of a river; estuary.

मुहावरा *(muhāvrā)* पु. (अ.) idiom; phrase; practice; habit.

मुहावरेदार *(muhāvaredār)* वि. idiomatic.

मुहिम *(muhim)* स्त्री. (अ.) expedition; campaign; arduous job.

मुहूर्त *(muhūrt)* पु. auspicious moment; auspicious beginning.

मूँग *(mūṁg)* स्त्री. a kind of lentil; green pluse.

मूँगफली *(mūṁgfali)* स्त्री. pea-nut.

मूँगा *(mūṁgā)* पु. coral.

मूँछ *(mūṁch)* स्त्री. moustache; whiskers.

मूँज *(mūṁj)* स्त्री. a kind of long fibre (of which ropes are made).

मूँड़ *(ṁūṁr)* पु. head.

मूँड़ना *(mūṁdanā)* स. क्रि. to shave; to tonsure; to cozen; to cheat; to fleece.

मूँदना *(mūṅdnā)* स. क्रि. to close; to shut; to cover; to hide.

मूक *(mūk)* वि. dumb; mute; speechless; dummy.

मूक अभिनय *(mūk-abhinaya)* पु. pantomime; mummery.

मूक अभिनेता *(mūk-abhinetā)* पु. mime.

मूठ *(mūth)* स्त्री. hilt; handle; act of sorcery; grip; knob.

मूढ़ *(mūṛh)* वि. foolish; silly; stupid; stupefied; infatuated.

मूढ़ता *(mūṛhatā)* स्त्री. stupidity; simplicity; folly.

मूतना *(mūtnā)* अ. क्रि. to discharge urine; to make water; to piss.

मूत्र *(mūtra)* पु. urine; piss.

मूत्राशय *(mūtrāśya)* पु. urinary bladder; vesica.

मूर्ख *(mūrkh)* वि. stupid; foolish; idiotic.

मूर्खता *(mūrkhatā)* स्त्री. stupidity; folly; idiocy; silliness.

मूर्च्छा *(mūrcchā)* स्त्री. swoon; fainting; unconsciousness; fit; trance.

मूर्च्छित *(mūrchit)* वि. fainted; swooned; out of senses.

मूर्ति *(mūrti)* स्त्री. image; figure; form; idol; statue; icon.

मूर्तिकला *(mūrti-kalā)* स्त्री. sculpture.

मूर्तिकार *(mūrti-kār)* पु. sculptor.

मूर्तिपूजा *(mūrti-pujā)* स्त्री. image-worship; idolatry; iconolatry.

मूर्तिभंजक *(mūrti-bhanjik)* पु. iconoclast.

मूर्तिशास्त्र *(mūrti-śastra)* पु. iconology.

मूल[1] *(mūl)* वि. original.

मूल[2] *(mūl)* पु. root; ground work; beginning; origin; source; cause; original text; principal (sum).

मूलतः *(mūltāh)* क्रि. वि. basically; fundamentally; primarity.

मूली *(mūlī)* स्त्री. radish.

मूल्य *(mūlya)* स्त्री. cost; price; worth; value.

मूल्य-निर्धारण *(mūlya-nirdhāran)* पु. evaluation; assessment.

मूल्यवान *(mūlyavān)* मूल्यवान् वि. costly; valuable; precious.

मूल्यांकन *(mūlyānkan)* पु. assessment; evaluation; appraisal.

मूल्यांकित *(mūlyānkit)* वि. valued; denominated.

मूषक *(mūṣak)* पु. rat; mouse.

मूसल *(mūsal)* स्त्री. pestle; pounder.

मूसलाधार *(mūslādhār)* वि. heavy or torrential (rain).

मूसली *(mūslī)* स्त्री. small pestle.

मृग *(mṛg)* पु. deer; antelope.

मृगछौना *(mṛgchannā)* पु. fawn.

मृगतृष्णा *(mṛg-trśna)* स्त्री. mirage; unaccomplishable desire.

मृगया *(mṛgayā)* स्त्री. hunting.

मृगी *(mṛigi)* स्त्री. female deer; a hind.

मृत *(mṛt)* वि. dead; deceased; defunct; extinct.

मृतक[1] *(mṛtak)* पु. dead body; corpse.

मृतक[2] *(mṛtak)* वि. deceased.

मृत्यु *(mṛtyu)* स्त्री. death; demise.

मृत्युलोक *(mṛtyulok)* पु. the mortal world.

मृदु *(mṛdu)* पु. soft; delicate; tender; benign.

मृदुता *(mṛduatā)* स्त्री. softness; tenderness.

मृदुल *(mṛdul)* वि. soft; tender; delicate; gentle; mild.

मृदुलता *(mṛdulatā)* स्त्री. softness; sweetness; mildness; gentleness.

मेंड *(meṁṛ)* स्त्री. hedge (raised to separate fields); border; balk.

मेंह *(meṁh)* पु. rain.

मेंहदी *(meṁhdī)* स्त्री. myrtle; henna.

मेखला *(mekhalā)* स्त्री. belt; girdle; waist-band.

मेघ *(megh)* पु. cloud.

मेज़ *(mez)* पु. table.

मेज़बान *(mezbān)* पु. (फ.) host.

मेढक *(meḍhak)* पु. frog.

मेढ़ा *(meṛhā)* पु. ram; tud.

मेथी *(methī)* स्त्री. the plant finugreek and its seed.

मेदा *(medā)* पु. (अ.) stomach.

मेधा *(medhā)* स्त्री. mental vigour or power; intellect; understanding.

मेधावी *(medhāvī)* वि. possessed of extraordinary mental power; intelligent; brilliant.

मेम *(mem)* स्त्री. lady; madame; queen (in playing cards).

मेमना *(memnā)* पु. lamb; kid.

मेरा *(merā)* सर्व. my; mine.

मेल *(mel)* पु. reconciliation; agreement; concord; intimacy; amity; friendship; rapprochement; mixture combination; match; kind; quality; mail (train); mode; scale.

मेल-जोल *(mel-jol)* पु. reconciliation; compromise; friendship.

मेला *(melā)* पु. crowd; multitude; throng; large concourse of people; fair.

मेवा *(mevā)* पु. (फ.) dry fruit.

मेहतर *(mehtar)* पु. (फ़.) sweeper; scavenger.

मेहतरानी *(mchtrānī)* स्त्री. wife of a sweeper; sweeper woman.

मेहनत *(mehnat)* स्त्री. (अ.) labour; toil; hard work; industry; exercise.

मेहनतकश *(mehnatkas)* वि. (अ.) hard working painstaking.

मेहनती *(mehnatī)* वि. laborious; diligent; hard-working.

मेहमान *(mehmān)* पु. (फ.) guest.

मेहरबान *(mehrbān)* वि. (फ़) kind; compassionate.

मेहरबानी *(meharbānī)* स्त्री. (फ.) kindness; compassion; favour.

मैं *(maiṁ)* सर्व. I; me.

मैत्री *(maitrī)* स्त्री. friendship; intimacy; cordiality.

मैदान *(maidān)* पु. (फ.) extensive plain; plains; field; playground; battle- field.

मैना *(mainā)* स्त्री. myna.

मैया *(maiyā)* स्त्री. mother.

मैल *(mail)* पु. dirt; filth; scum; rancour; sullenness; grudge; grouse.

मैला *(mailā)* वि. dirty; filthy; foul; unclean.

मैलापन *(mailāpan)* पु. dirtiness; filthiness.

मोक्ष *(mokṣ)* पु. emancipation; deliverance; freedom; salvation; release from worldly existence; final beatitude.

मोचक *(mocak)* वि. redemptive.

मोचन *(mocan)* पु. release; liberation; deliverance redemption.

मोची *(mocī)* पु. shoemaker; cobbler.

मोज़ा *(mozā)* पु. (फ़) stockings; socks.

मोटा *(moṭā)* वि. fat; plump; corpulent; thick; coarse; rough.

मोटाई *(moṭāī)* स्त्री. fatness; plumpness; corpulence; thickness.

मोटापन, मोटापा *(moṭāpan)* मोटापा पु. fatness; plumpness; thickness; obesity.

मोठ *(moṭh)* स्त्री. lentil.

मोड़ *(moṛ)* पु. turn; bend; twist; turning point; (fig.) a new direction; orientation; fold.

मोड़ना *(moṛnā)* स. क्रि. to turn; to turn back; to bend; to twist; to fold.

मोती *(moti)* पु. pearl.

मोतीझरा *(motījharā)* पु. typhoid.

मोम *(mom)* पु. wax.

मोमजामा *(momjāmā)* पु. oil cloth.

मोमबत्ती *(mombatti)* स्त्री. candle stick.

मोर *(mor)* पु. peacock.

मोरचा *(morcā)* पु. rust; battle-front.

मोरचाबंदी *(morcābandi)* स्त्री. stratagem; battle-array; deployment of army.

मोरनी *(mornī)* स्त्री. pea-hen.

मोह *(moh)* पु. attachment; love; affection; infatuation; delusion of mind.

मोहक *(mohak)* वि. infatuating; charming; fascinating; seductive.

मोहभंग *(mohbhang)* पु. disillusionment; disenchantment.

मोहरा *(mohrā)* पु. chessman; opening the mouth of a container; van; vanguard; forepart of an army.

मोहित *(mohit)* वि. fascinated; charmed; enamoured; infatuated; deluded.

मोहिनी[1] *(mohinī)* वि. fascinating; charming.

मोहिनी[2] *(mohinī)* स्त्री. illusion; charm; spell.

मौका *(mauqā)* पु. (अ.) chance; occasion; opportunity; place of occurrence; situation; site.

मौखिक *(maukhik)* वि. oral; viva voce (test) verbal

मौखिकी *(maukhikī)* वि. oral; verbal.

मौज *(mauj)* स्त्री. (अ.) whim; caprice; fancy; delight; ecstasy; wave; surge.

मौज़ा *(mauzā)* पु. (अ.) village; socks.

मौज़ूँ *(mauzūṁ)* वि. (अ.) reasonable; befitting; suitable.

मौजूद *(maujaūd)* वि. (फ.) present; existing.

मौजूदगी *(maujūdagī)* स्त्री. (फ़.) existence; presence.

मौजूदा *(maujūdā)* वि. (अ.) existing; current; present.

मौत *(maut)* स्त्री. (फ.) death; demise.

मौन[1] *(maun)* वि. mumsilent; speechless.

मौन[2] *(maun)* पु. silence; taciturnity.

मौरूसी *(maurūsī)* वि. (अ.) hereditary; patrimonial.

मौलिक *(maulik)* वि. radical; primordial; fundamental.

मौलिकता *(maulikatā)* स्त्री. originality.

मौसम *(mausam)* पु. (अ.) season; weather; opportune time.

मौसमविज्ञान *(mausam-vygan)* पु. meteorology.

मौसमी *(mausamī)* वि. (अ.) seasonal; of the season.

म्याऊँ *(myāṁv)* स्री. mew.

म्यान *(myān)* स्री. (फ़.) sheath; scabbard.

म्लान *(mlān)* वि. languid; weary; gloomy.

म्लेच्छ[1] *(mlecch)* वि. lowly; unclean dirty; shabby.

य

य *(ya)* the first of the four semivowels of the Devnagri alphabets.

यंत्र *(yantra)* पु. instrument; mechanical contrivance; machine; amulet; talisman; mystical diagram.

यंत्रचालित *(yantra-cālit)* वि. mechanized; machine-operated.

यंत्रणा *(yantrāṇā)* स्री. pain; anguish; affliction; torture.

यंत्रमानव *(yantra-manāv)* पु. robot.

यंत्रवत् *(yantra-vat)* क्रि. वि. like a machine; mechanically.

यंत्रविद् *(yamtra-vid)* पु. engineer.

यंत्रित *(yantrit)* वि. mechanised.

यकायक *(yakāyak)* क्रि. वि. all at once; suddenly; immediately.

यक़ीन *(yaqīn)* पु. (अ.) confidence; faith; trust; certainty; assurance; belief.

यक़ीनन *(yaqīnan)* क्रि. वि. (अ.) certainly; surely.

यकृत *(yakrit)* पु. liver.

यक्ष्मा *(yakṣmā)* पु. tuberculosis; consumption.

यज्ञ *(yajña)* पु. religious ceremony in which oblations were offered; sacrifice.

यज्ञोपवीत *(yajño-pavit)* पु. sacrificial hall; house or place for keeping the sacrificial fire.

यज्ञशाला *(yajñā-śālā)* स्री. sacred thread; a Hindu ceremony in which a child is introduced to wearing the sacred thread.

यती *(yatī)* पु. ascetic; monk.

यतीम *(yatīm)* पु. (अ.) orphan.

यतीमख़ाना *(yatīm-khānā)* पु. (अ.) orphanage.

यत्न *(yatn)* पु. effort; endevour; means; device; care.

यत्नपूर्वक *(yatn-purvak)* क्रि. वि. with care; with effort or attempt.

यत्र-तत्र *(yatr-tatr)* अ. here and there; there and every where.

यथा *(yathā)* अ. as; according to; thus; for example; for instance.

यथायोग्य *(yathā-yojua)* क्रि. वि. according as one deserves.

यथार्थ *(yathārth)* वि. accurate; realistic.

यथार्थतः *(yathārthtah)* क्रि. वि. truly; rightly; exactly; realistically.

यथार्थता *(yathârthatā)* स्री. reality; correctness; accuracy; exactness; exactitude.

यथार्थवाद *(yathārthvād)* पु. realism.

यथार्थवादी *(yatharthvādī)* वि. realistic.

यथेष्ट *(yathêṣṭ)* वि. according to wish or desire; sufficient; enough; adequate; requisite.

यथोचित *(yathochit)* वि. befitting; due; proper; appropriate; reasonable; rightful.

यदा-कदा *(yadā-kadā)* क्रि. वि. now and then; occasionally; sometimes.

यदि *(yadi)* क्रि. वि. if; in case; provided that.

यद्यपि *(vadyapi)* क्रि. वि. even if; although; though.

यम *(yam)* पु. the god of death; selfrestraint; self-control; twin.

यमदूत *(yamdūt)* पु. messenger of death.

यमपुरी *(yampuri)* स्त्री. infernal world.

यमलोक *(yamlok)* पु. see यमपुरी।

यव *(yav)* पु. barley; corn.

यवन *(yavan)* पु. Mohammadan.

यश *(yaś)* पु. glory; splendour; praise; reputation.

यशस्वी *(yaśasvi)* वि. reputed; renowned; glorious celebrated.

यशोगान *(yasogyan)* पु. encomium; eulogy.

यष्टि *(yaṣṭi)* स्त्री. stick; staff; branch; twig; arm; creeper; sugarcane.

यह[1] *(yah)* सर्व. he; she; this; it.

यह[2] *(yah)* वि. this.

यहाँ *(yahāṁ)* सर्व. here; at this place.

यही *(yahī)* सर्व. certainly this.

यहूदिन *(yahūdin)* स्त्री. Jewess.

यहूदी *(yahūdī)* पु. Jew.

यांत्रिक[1] *(yāntrik)* वि. mechanical; working like a machine.

यांत्रिक[2] *(yāntrik)* पु. mechanist.

यांत्रिकता *(yāntrikatā)* स्त्री. mechanism.

यांत्रिकी *(yāntrikī)* स्त्री. mechanics.

यांत्रिकीकरण *(yāntrikīkaran)* पु. mechanization.

या *(yā)* क्रि. वि. or; either.

याचक *(yācak)* क.पु. beggar; mendicant.

याचकता *(yācakatā)* स्त्री. begging; mendicancy.

याचिका *(yācikā)* स्त्री. petition; request.

याजक *(yājak)* पु. sacrificer; sacrificing priest.

यातना *(yātanā)* स्त्री. torment; torture.

यातायात *(yātâyāt)* पु. traffic; transport.

यात्रा *(yātrā)* स्त्री. journey; travel; wayfaring; trip; tour; pilgrimage; march.

यात्री *(yātrī)* पु. traveller; wayfarer; passenger; pilgrim.

याद *(yād)* स्त्री. (फा.) remembrance; recollection; memory; commemoration.

यादगार *(yādgār)* स्त्री. (फ़ा.) monument; memorial; memento.

याददाश्त *(yād-dāśt)* स्त्री. (फ़ा.) memory.

यानी *(yānī)* क्रि. वि. (अ.) that is to say; viz.; i.e.

यापन *(yāpan)* पु. spending or passing (time).

याम *(yām)* पु. period of three hours; time; restraint; progress; conveyance; road.

यामिनी *(yāminī)* स्त्री. night.

यायावर[1] *(yāyavār)* वि. frequently travelling; vagrant; nomadic; itinerant.

यायावर[2] *(yāyavār)* पु. nomad; wanderer.

यार *(yār)* पु. (फ़ा.) friend; companion; paramour; lover; supporter.

यारी *(yārī)* स्त्री. friendship; romantic intimacy; illicit love.

युक्त *(yukt)* वि. joined; united; connected; attached; combined; included; fitted with; befitting; suitable; proper.

युक्ति *(yukti)* स्त्री. means; contrivance; device; argument; plea; union; junction; combination; artifice; tactics; manoeuvre; skill.

युक्तिसंगत *(yuktiśangat)* वि. reasonable; rational.

युग *(yug)* पु. period; era; epoch; age of the world according to Puranas; pair; couple.

युगल *(yugal)* पु. pair; couple; duet.

युगांतर *(yugāntar)* पु. succeeding epoch; advent of a new epoch.

युत *(yut)* वि. mixed.

युद्ध *(yuddh)* पु. war; battle; combat.

युद्धक्षेत्र *(yuddh-chātra)* पु. battlefield; war zone.

युद्धविराम *(yuddh-virām)* पु. ceasefire; armistice; truce.

युयुत्सु *(yuyutsu)* स्त्री. belligerence; bellicosity; pugnacity.

युवक *(yuvak)* पु. youth; youngman.

युवती *(yuvatī)* स्त्री. young woman; damsel.

युवराज *(yuvrāj)* पु. heir-apparent; crown-prince.

युवराश्री *(yuvrāśri)* स्त्री. princess.

युवा *(yuvā)* वि. young.

युवावस्था *(yuvā-vasthā)* स्त्री. young age; youth.

यों *(yoṁ)* अ. thus; in this way.

योग *(yog)* पु. compound; yoga system of philosophy; concentration of mental faculties; device; remedy; (arith.) addition; (astro.) conjunction.

योगक्षेम *(yog-ksem)* पु. wel स.being

योगदान *(yogdān)* पु. contribution; participation.

योगफल *(yogfal)* पु. sum; total.

योगासन *(yogāsan)* पु. posture of performing yoga practices.

योगी *(yogī)* पु. follower of the yoga sysem of philosophy; Shiva.

योग्य *(yogya)* पु. qualified; able; proper; fit; suitable; deserving; capable; eligible; meritorious; worthy.

योग्यता *(yogyatā)* स्त्री. suitability; propriety; fitness; ability; capability; quality; qualification; eligibility; competence; worthiness; merit.

योग्यतापूर्वक *(yogyatāpurvak)* क्रि. वि. ably; efficiently.

योजक *(yojak)* पु. connecter; copula.

योजन *(yojan)* पु. joining; uniting; fixing; measure of distance.

योजना *(yojanā)* स्त्री. scheme; plan; project.

योजनाबद्ध *(yojanāvadh)* वि. planned; programmed.

योजित *(yojit)* वि. planned; employed; used; joined; connected; united; arranged.

योद्धा *(yoddhā)* पु. fighter; warrior; soldier; combatant.

योनि *(yoni)* स्त्री. place of birth or origin; female organ of generation; vagina; one class out of 84 lakh classes of creatures according to Puranas; sex.

यौगिक[1] *(yougik)* वि. relating to the religious practice of yoga philosophy.

यौगिक² *(yougik)* पु. compound.

यौन *(yaun)* वि. sexual.

यौन-विज्ञान *(yaun-vyhgan)* पु. sexology.

यौनाचार *(yaunācār)* पु. sex indulgence.

यौवन *(yauvan)* पु. youth; puberty.

र

र *(ra)* the second of the semivowels of the Devnagri alphabets.

रंक *(raṅk)* पु. beggar; pauper; poor person.

रंग *(raṅg)* पु. glamour; beauty; amusement; mode; manner; whim; mood; influence; colour; hue; dye; complexion; trump in playing cards; suit; kind; category; gaiety.

रंग-ढंग *(raṅg-dhaṅg)* पु. manners; demeanour; conduct.

रंगत *(raṅgat)* स्त्री. colour; complexion; tint; condition.

रंगदार *(raṅgdār)* वि. coloured.

रंगना *(raṁgnā)* स. क्रि. to colour; to dye; to paint; to write excessively; to infatuate; to influence.

रंग-बिरंगा *(raṅg-bīraṅgā)* वि. of various colours; multicoloured; colourful; of diverse kinds; variegated.

रंगभूमि *(raṅg-bhumi)* स्त्री. place of amusement; stage; theatre.

रंगमंच *(raṅg-mañch)* पु. stage for acting.

रंगमहल *(raṅg-mahal)* पु. private apartment; the apartment meant for amorous sport.

रंगरूट *(raṅgrūt)* पु. recruit.

रंगरूप *(raṅgrūp)* पु. physical appearance; looks; complexion and figure.

रँगरेली *(raṅg-relī)* स्त्री. rejoicing; merriment; pleasure; revelry.

रँगवाई *(raṁgvāī)* स्त्री. act of getting (clothes) dyed; charges paid for dyeing.

रँगवाना *(raṁgvānā)* स. क्रि. to cause to be dyed; to get dyed.

रंगशाला *(raṁgsālā)* स्त्री. theatre; place of making mirth or enjoyment.

रंगसाज़ *(raṁgsáj)* पु. (फ़ा.) painter; colourman.

रंगसाज़ी *(raṁgsázī)* स्त्री. (फ़ा.) mixing or making colours; painting.

रँगाई *(raṁgāī)* स्त्री. act of colouring or dyeing; charges paid for colouring etc.

रँगाना *(raṁgānā)* स. क्रि. to cause to be coloured or dyed; to get dyed.

रंगारंग *(raṁgāraṅg)* वि. of various colours; of different sorts; variegated; colourful.

रंगीन *(raṅgīn)* वि. (फ़ा.) coloured; painted; colourful; gay; lively; jovial.

रंगीनी *(raṅgīnī)* स्त्री. being coloured; being of various colours; elegant or colourful make-up; colourfulness; sportiveness; gaiety; mirthfulness.

रँगीला *(raṁgīlā)* वि. gay; merry; jovial; gaudy; showy; colourful.

रंज *(rañj)* पु. (फ़ा.) sorrow; grief; affliction; sadness; gloominess.

रंजन *(rañjan)* पु. act of colouring; dyeing or painting; entertainment; amusement.

रंजिश *(rañjiś)* स्त्री. (फ़ा.) animosity; ill-feeling; malice; estrangement.

रंजीदा *(rañjīdā)* वि. (फ़ा.) grieved; sorrowful; sad; gloomy.

रँडापा *(raṇḍāpā)* पु. widowhood.

रंडी *(randi)* स्त्री. harlot; prostitute.

रँडुआ *(raṁḍuā)* पु. widower.

रँदना *(raṁdanā)* स. क्रि. to plane.

रंदा *(randā)* पु. carpenter's plane.

रंध्र *(randhra)* पु. hole; aperture; stomata; orifice; pore.

रँभाना *(raṁbhānā)* अ. क्रि. to low.

रई *(raī)* स्त्री. churning staff; churner.

रईस *(raīs)* पु. (अ.) rich or wealthy man; nobleman.

रईसी *(raīsī)* स्त्री. state of being wealthy.

रक़म *(raqam)* स्त्री. (अ.) amount; capital; sum.

रकाब *(rakāb)* स्त्री. stirrup.

रकाबी *(rakābī)* स्त्री. dish; plate; platter.

रक़ीब *(raqīb)* पु. (अ.) rival.

रक्त *(rakt)* पु. blood; red colour.

रक्तचाप *(raktchāp)* पु. blood- pressure.

रक्तपात *(raktpāt)* पु. bloodshed.

रक्षक *(rakṣak)* पु. protector; preserver; guardian; keeper; guard; escort.

रक्षण *(rakṣaṇ)* पु. act of guarding; protection; preservation.

रक्षा *(rakṣā)* स्त्री. defence; protection.

रक्षात्मक *(rakṣātmāk)* वि. protective; defensive.

रक्षित *(rakṣit)* वि. protected; preserved; secured.

रक्षी *(rakṣī)* पु. guard; protector; watch; sentinel.

रखना *(rakhanā)* स. क्रि. to put; to place; to lay; to take into possession; to keep; to employ; to appoint; to keep as wife or husband.

रखवाना *(rakhvānā)* स. क्रि. to cause to be kept; to have (a thing) placed in charge or custody; to cause to employ or appoint; to cause to maintain.

रखवाला *(rakhvālā)* पु. guard; keeper; custodian; caretaker; watchman.

रखवाली *(rakhvālī)* स्त्री. protection; safe guarding; custody; watch; guard; care; watchmanship.

रखाना *(rakhānā)* स. क्रि. to cause to keep; to guard; to watch; to take care of; to maintain.

रखेल, रखेली *(rakhail)* स्त्री. concubine; keep (girl).

रग *(rag)* स्त्री. artery; vein; nerve.

रगड़ *(ragar)* स्त्री. rubbing; abrasion; friction; rub; bruise.

रगड़ना *(ragaṛnā)* स. क्रि. to rub; to bruise.

रगड़ा *(ragṛā)* पु. mark of friction or rubbing; rubbing; a rub; quarrel or animosity which lasts for some time; bruise; toil.

रचना *(racnā)* स्त्री. formation; structure; fabrication; literary production; composition creation; fabric; construction.

रचनाकार *(racnākār)* पु. composer;

author; creator maker.

रचनात्मक *(racnātamak)* वि. constructive; formative.

रचयिता *(racayitā)* पु. author; composer; creator; maker.

रचित *(racit)* वि. made; formed; created; composed; constructed; stained.

रज *(raj)* स्त्री. dust; pollen of flowers; second of the three constituent qualities of all substances; menstruation.

रजकण *(rajkan)* पु. dust particles.

रजत[1] *(rajat)* पु. silver.

रजत[2] *(rajat)* वि. silvery; made of silver.

रजतपट *(rajatpat)* पु. silver-screen; cinema; screen.

रजनी *(rajanī)* स्त्री. night.

रजनीपति *(rajanīpatī)* पु. moon.

रजवाहा *(rajvāhā)* पु. distributory; small canal.

रजस्वला *(rajsalavā)* स्त्री. woman during the menses.

रज़ा *(razā)* स्त्री. (अ.) wish; will; desire; permission; consent.

रज़ाई *(rajāī)* स्त्री. quilt.

रज़ामंद *(razāmand)* वि. (अ.) willing; agreeable.

रज़ामंदी *(razāmandī)* स्त्री. (अ.) willingness; consent.

रजोधर्म *(razo-dhram)* पु. menstruation.

रज्जु *(rajju)* पु. rope; cord; string.

रटंत *(raṭant)* स्त्री. cramming; learning by heart or repetition.

रट *(raṭ)* स्त्री. constant repetition; reiteration.

रटना *(raṭnā)* स. क्रि. to cram; to repeat; to learn by heart.

रण *(raṇ)* पु. battle; war.

रणकौशल *(raṇkauśal)* पु. war strategy; tactics of war.

रणक्षेत्र *(raṇkśhetra)* पु. battle-field.

रणपोत *(raṇpot)* पु. battleship.

रणभूमि *(raṇbhumi)* स्त्री. battleground; field of battle.

रणभेरी *(raṇbherī)* स्त्री. battle bugle; war trumpets.

रणस्थल *(raṇasthal)* पु. battle-field.

रत *(rat)* वि. engaged; absorbed; busy.

रतजगा *(ratjagā)* पु. vigil.

रति *(rati)* स्त्री. sexual union; coition; copulation; (in lit.) sentiment of love; name of the goddess of love personified as wife of Cupid.

रतौंधी *(rataumdhī)* स्त्री. night-blindness; nyctalopia.

रत्न *(ratn)* पु. jewel; gem; precious stone; most outstanding personality.

रत्नाकर *(ratnākar)* पु. sea; ocean.

रथ *(rath)* पु. chariot.

रथवान *(rathvān)* पु. charioteer.

रद्द *(radd)* वि. (अ.) rejected; cancelled; annulled.

रद्दा *(raddā)* पु. stratum (of a wall); layer (of bricks).

रद्दी[1] *(raddī)* वि. (अ.) waste; worthless; inferior.

रद्दी[2] *(raddi)* स्त्री. (अ.) waste material or product; waste-paper.

रद्दोबदल *(raddobadal)* स्त्री. (अ.) change; alteration; modification; reshuffling.

रपटन *(rapaṭan)* स्त्री. slipperiness.

रपटना[1] *(rapaṭnā)* अ. क्रि. to slip; to slide; to act or move rapidly.

रपटना[2] *(rapaṭnā)* वि. slippery.

रपटाना *(rapṭānā)* स. क्रि. to cause to

move rapidly.

रफ़ू *(rafū)* पु. (अ.) darning.

रफ़ूगर *(rafū-gar)* पु. (अ.) darner.

रफ़ू-चक्कर *(rafū-chakkar)* पु. mischieveous disappearance.

रफ़्तार *(raftār)* स्त्री. (फ़ा.) pace; speed; velocity.

रबड़ *(rabar)* स्त्री. rubber tree and the product made from its juice.

रबड़ी *(rabṛī)* स्त्री. thickened milk.

रबी *(rabī)* स्त्री. (अ.) the spring harvest.

रमण *(ramaṇ)* पु. pleasing or delightful act; sexual union; cohabitation; walk; stroll; saunter.

रमणा, रमणी *(ramaṇī)* स्त्री. charming woman; beautiful young woman; damsel.

रमणीक *(ramaṇīk)* वि. beautiful; lovely; pleasant; charming; winsome; attractive.

रमणीकता *(ramaṇīkyatā)* स्त्री. beauty; charm; prettiness; attractiveness.

रमणीय *(ramaṇiya)* स्त्री. charming; beautiful; lovely.

रमणीयता *(ramaṇīkyatā)* स्त्री. beauty; charm; loveliness; prettiness.

रमना *(ramanā)* अ. क्रि. to be absorbed; to be devoted; to roam; to wander about.

रव *(rav)* पु. noise; tumult; uproar; sound; echo; hum; buzz.

रवन्ना *(ravannā)* पु. passage permit; waybill.

रवानगी *(ravānagī)* स्त्री. departure; setting out.

रवाना *(ravānā)* वि. (फ़ा.) set out; departing.

रवानी *(ravānī)* स्त्री. fluency; flow.

रवि *(ravi)* पु. the Sun.

रविवार *(ravivār)* पु. Sunday.

रवैया *(ravaiya)* पु. behaviour; conduct; manner. fashion.

रश्मि *(raśmi)* स्त्री. ray of light; beam.

रस *(ras)* पु. sap; juice; soup; broth; relish (one of the six senses); (in lit.) pleasure; delight; happiness.

रसज्ञ *(rasajna)* पु. one who knows Rasa or true essence; one who understands and appreciates poetry; connoisseur.

रसज्ञता *(rasajnatā)* स्त्री. connoisseurship; capability to relish or appreciate; aesthetic sense.

रसद *(rasad)* स्त्री. (फ़ा.) supplies of food which travellers or soldiers carry with them; food stuff; ration; provisions.

रसना *(rasnā)* स्त्री. tongue; rein; rope; cord.

रसरंग *(rasraṅg)* पु. enjoyment derived from love; sport of love; sexual union.

रसहीन *(ras-hīn)* वि. sapless; insipid; unsavoury; dry; dull.

रसातल *(rasātal)* पु. lowest of the seven regions under the earth; nether world; lower world or hell in general.

रसायन *(rasāyan)* पु. chemistry; alchemy.

रसायनज्ञ *(rasāyanajna)* पु. chemist.

रसायन विज्ञान *(rasāyan-vignan)* पु. chemistry.

रसायनवेत्ता *(rasāyan-vetā)* पु. chemist.

रसायनशाला *(rasāyan-śālā)* स्त्री. chemical laboratory.

रसायनशास्त्र *(rasāyan-śastra)* पु. chemistry.

रसायनशास्त्री *(rasāyan-śastrī)* पु. chemist; scholar of chemistry.

रसास्वादन *(rasā-svādan)* पु. relishing; enjoyment of any poetic sentiment in literature.

रसिकता *(rasikatā)* स्त्री. sense of taste; quality of being aesthetic.

रसिया *(rasiyā)* पु. epicure; man of amorous disposition; type of folk song.

रसीद *(rasīd)* स्त्री. (फ़ा.) receipt.

रसोइया *(rasoiyā)* पु. cook.

रसोई *(rasoī)* स्त्री. cooked or dressed food; kitchen.

रसौली *(rasaulī)* स्त्री. tumour.

रस्म *(rasm)* स्त्री. (अ.) custom; practice; ceremony; ritual; formality.

रस्मी *(rasmī)* स्त्री. customary; formal; ceremonial.

रस्साकशी *(rassakasi)* स्त्री. tug-of war; tussle.

रस्सी *(rassī)* स्त्री. rope; cord.

रहज़न *(rahzaṇ)* पु. (फ़ा.) highway man.

रहन *(rahn)* पु. (फ़ा.) mortgage; pledge; pawn; way of living.

रहन-सहन *(rahn-shan)* पु. mode of living.

रहना *(rahanā)* अ. क्रि. to dwell; to live; to reside; to exist; to stay; to remain.

रहम *(raham)* पु. (अ.) mercy; kindness; pity; compassion.

रहमत *(rahmat)* स्त्री. (अ.) mercy; kindness; compassion.

रहस्य *(rahasya)* पु. secret; mystery in spiritualism.

रहस्यपूर्ण *(rahasya-purn)* वि. mysterious; secretive.

रहस्यवाद *(rahasya-vad)* पु. mysticism.

रहस्यवादी[1] *(rahasyavādī)* वि. mystical.

रहस्यवादी[2] *(rahasyavādī)* पु. mystic.

रहित *(rahit)* वि. devoid; without; void(of); separated (from); free (from).

राँगा *(rāṁgā)* पु. pewter.

राँड *(raṁḍ)* स्त्री. widow.

राई *(rāī)* स्त्री. mustard-like oil seed; small particle.

राक्षस *(rākṣas)* पु. demon; devil; monster.

राक्षसी[1] *(rākṣasī)* वि. demon-like; devilish; monstrous.

राक्षसी[2] *(rākṣasī)* स्त्री. female demon.

राख *(rākh)* स्त्री. ashes.

राग *(rāg)* पु. love; affection; attachment; colour (particularly red); melodic mode or structure with a fixed sequence of notes; melody; passion; emotion.

राग-द्वेष *(rāg-dveṣ)* पु. love and hatred.

राज *(rāj)* पु. kingdom; state; rule; government; mason.

राज़ *(rāz)* पु. (फ़ा.) secret.

राजकीय *(rājakiya)* वि. royal; kingly. official; governmental.

राजकुमार *(rājkumār)* पु. king's son; prince.

राजकुमारी *(rājkumārī)* स्त्री. king's daughter; princess.

राजकुल *(rājkul)* पु. king's family; royal race or dynasty.

राजगद्दी *(rājgaddi)* स्त्री. king's throne; royal throne.

राजगीर *(rājgīr)* पु. mason.

राजगीरी *(rājgīrī)* स्त्री. masonary.

राजतंत्र *(rājtantra)* पु. monarchy.

राजतंत्रीय *(rājtantrīya)* पु. monarchial.

राजतिलक *(rājtilak)* पु. coronation.

राजदूत *(rājdūt)* पु. king's envoy; ambassador.

राजदूतावास *(rājdūtāvās)* पु. embassy; diplomatic mission.

राजद्रोही[1] *(rāj-drohī)* पु. traitor; rebel; seditionist.

राजद्रोही[2] *(rāj-drohī)* वि. seditious.

राजधानी *(rājdhanī)* स्त्री. capital city.

राजनय *(rājnay)* पु. diplomacy.

राजनयिक *(rājnayik)* पु. diplomat.

राजनीति *(rājnītī)* स्त्री. statesman ship; politics.

राजनीतिक *(rājnītik)* वि. political.

राजनीतिज्ञ *(rājnitijna)* पु. politician.

राजनीतिशास्त्र *(rājnitiśastra)* पु. political science.

राजनेता *(rājnetā)* पु. statesman.

राजपत्र *(rājpatra)* पु. gazzette.

राजपत्रित *(rājpatrit)* वि. gazzetted.

राजपथ *(rājpath)* पु. national highway.

राज-पाट *(rāj-pāt)* पु. royal throne and kingdom.

राजभक्त *(rājbhakt)* पु. loyalist; one loyal to the ruler.

राजभक्ति *(rājbhaktī)* स्त्री. loyalty towards the king or the state.

राजभवन *(rājbhavan)* पु. place of king; royal mansion or residence.

राजमहल *(rājmahal)* पु. royal residence; palace.

राजमार्ग *(rājmārg)* see राजपथ।

राजमुकुट *(rājmukut)* पु. diadem; crown.

राजयक्ष्मा *(rājyaksmā)* पु. tuberculosis.

राजवंश *(rājvan's)* पु. royal race or family; dynasty.

राजशाही *(rājsāhī)* वि. royal.

राजस्व *(rāzasva)* पु. revenue of a king or state.

राजा *(rājā)* पु. king; sovereign; monarch; ruler.

राज़ी *(rāzī)* वि. (अ.) willing; agreeable; pleased; contented.

राज़ीनामा *(rāzīnāmā)* पु. (अ.) agreement; written consent; rapprochement.

राज्य *(rājyā)* पु. kingdom; royalty; sovereignty; reign; country; kingdom; dominion; realm; unit of a federation of states; state; polity.

राज्यतंत्र *(rājyatantra)* पु. monarchy; system of administration; or government.

राज्य-परिषद् *(rājya-priśad)* स्त्री. council of States; Upper House.

राज्यपाल *(rājya-pāl)* पु. Governor of a State.

राज्यमंडल *(rājya-mandal)* पु. confederation; confederacy.

राज्यसभा *(rājya-sabhā)* स्त्री. Council of states; state assembly.

राज्याभिषेक *(rājyābhiśek)* पु. coronation.

रात *(rāt)* स्त्री. night.

रार *(rār)* स्त्री. quarrel; fray; dispute.

रात्रि *(rātri)* स्त्री. night.

रात्रिचर[1] *(rātri-cār)* वि. nocturnal.

रात्रिचर[2] *(rātri-cār)* पु. demon; nocturnal-being.

रात्रि भोजन *(rātri-bhojan)* पु. dinner.

रान *(rān)* स्त्री (फ़ा.) thigh.

रानी *(rānī)* स्त्री. king's wife; queen.

रामबाण *(rāmbān)* पु. unfailing remedy; sure cure; panacea.

रामराज्य *(rām-rajya)* पु. golden rule; welfare-state; reign of Lord Rama.

राय *(rāy)* स्त्री. counsel; advice; opinion.

राल *(rāl)* स्त्री. resin; saliva; spittle.

राशि *(rāśi)* स्त्री. heap; mass; pile; accumulation; fraction; sign of the zodiac; amount; quantity.

राष्ट्र *(rāsṭra)* पु. nation; country people.

राष्ट्रगान *(rāsṭra-gān)* पु. national anthem.

राष्ट्रपति *(rāsṭra-patī)* पु. president of a country.

राष्ट्रभाषा *(rāsṭra-bhāsā)* स्त्री. national language.

राष्ट्रमंडल *(rāsṭra-mandal)* पु. Commonwealth of nations.

राष्ट्रवाद *(rāsṭravād)* पु. nationalism.

राष्ट्रवादी[1] *(rāsṭravādi)* वि. nationalistic.

राष्ट्रवादी[2] *(rāsṭravādi)* पु. nationalist.

राष्ट्रसंघ *(rāsṭra-sangh)* पु. League of Nations.

राष्ट्रीय *(rāṣṭrīya)* वि. national.

राष्ट्रीयकरण *(rāsṭrīyakaran)* पु. nationalisation.

राष्ट्रीयकृत *(rāsṭriyakṛt)* वि. nationalised.

राष्ट्रीयता *(rāsṭrīyatā)* स्त्री. nationalism.

रास्ता *(rāstā)* पु. (फ़ा.) road; way; path; passage; course; route; approach.

राह *(rāh)* स्त्री. (फ़ा.) see रास्ता।

राहगीर *(rāhgīr)* पु. (फ़ा.) traveller; wayfarer; pedestrian.

राहज़न *(rāhzan)* पु. (फ़ा.) highwayman.

राहज़नी *(rāhjanī)* स्त्री. (फ़ा.) highway robbery.

राहत *(rāhat)* स्त्री. (अ.) rest; ease; relief; freedom; from toil or trouble etc.

राही *(rāhī)* see राहगीर।

रिआया *(riāyā)* स्त्री. (अ.) subjects; people.

रिक्त *(rikt)* वि. empty; vacant.

रिक्तता *(riktatā)* वि. emptiness; vacancy.

रिक्ति *(rikitī)* स्त्री. vacancy.

रिझाना *(rijhānā)* स. क्रि. to please; to captivate; to charm.

रिपु *(ripu)* पु. enemy; foe; opponent.

रिपुता *(riputā)* स्त्री. enmity; hostility.

रिमझिम *(rim-jhim)* स्त्री. drizzling.

रियासत *(riyāsat)* स्त्री. (अ.) state of being wealthy; nobleness; estate; regality; princely state.

रियासती *(riyāsatī)* वि. of or belonging to a state or estate.

रिश्ता *(riśtā)* पु. (फ़ा.) relation; relationship; affinity.

रिश्तेदार *(riśtedār)* पु. (फ़ा.) relative; relation; kinsman.

रिश्तेदारी *(riśtedārī)* स्त्री. (फ़ा.) relationship; kinship.

रिश्वत *(riśvat)* स्त्री. (अ.) bribe.

रिश्वतख़ोर *(riśvatkhor)* पु. (अ.) one who takes bribe.

रिहा *(rihā)* वि. (फ़ा.) released; liberated; set free.

रिहाइश *(rihāiś)* स्त्री. residence; lodging.

रिहायशी *(rihāysī)* वि. residential.

रिहाई *(rihāī)* स्त्री. liberation; freedom; release; acquittal.

रीछ *(rīch)* पु. bear.

रीझना *(rījhnā)* अ. क्रि. to be inclined; to be infatuated; to be charmed.

रीठा *(rīṭhā)* पु. soap-wart; soap-nut.

रीढ़ *(rīṛh)* वि. back-bone; spine.

रीढ़दार *(rīṛh-dār)* वि. spiny; vertebral.

रीत *(rīt)* वि. custom; practice; convention; vogue; mode.

रीता *(rītā)* वि. empty; void.

रीतापन *(rītāpan)* पु. emptiness; vacancy; voidness.

रीति *(rīti)* स्त्री. custom; fashion; practice; convention; style.

रीति-रिवाज *(rīti-rivaj)* पु. customs and practices.

रूंड *(rūnḍ)* पु. headless body; tree devoid of branches; leaves; etc.; torso.

रूआँ *(ruāṁ)* पु. soft thin hair of the body.

रुआँसा *(ruāṁsā)* वि. on the verge of weeping.

रूआब *(ruāb)* पु. commanding or awe-inspiring presence; dignity; awe; great influence.

रूई *(ruī)* स्त्री. cotton.

रूकना *(ruknā)* अ. क्रि. to stop; to halt; to rest; to be hindered; to stay; to pause.

रुकवाना *(rukvānā)* स. क्रि. to cause to be stopped.

रुकावट *(rukāvaṭ)* स्त्री. obstruction; check; hindrance; bar; barricade; blockade; resistance; interruption.

रुख़[1] *(rukh)* पु. (फ़ा.) face; countenance; facet; aspect; direction; trend; facade; attitude.

रुख़[2] *(rukh)* क्रि. वि. (फ़ा.) in the direction; towards.

रुख़सत *(rukhsat)* स्त्री. (अ.) permission; departure; leave.

रुखाई *(rukhai)* स्त्री. roughness; dryness; rudeness; indifference.

रुग्ण *(rugṇ)* वि. diseased; sick; unwell; indisposed; morbid.

रुग्णता *(rugṇatā)* स्त्री. sickness; indisposition; illness; diseased condition.

रुचि *(ruci)* स्त्री. liking; taste; interest; relish; fancy.

रुचिकर *(rucikar)* वि. causing pleasure; interesting; tasteful; relishing.

रुचिर *(rucir)* वि. agreeable; lovely; pleasant; winsome.

रुचिरता *(ruciratā)* स्त्री. agreeableness; pleasantness.

रुझान *(rujhān)* पु. inclination; aptitude; trend.

रुतबा *(rutbā)* पु. (अ.) rank position; status.

रुदन *(rudan)* पु. weeping; wailing; lamentation.

रुद्ध *(ruddh)* वि. obstructed; hindered; choked; closed.

रुधिर *(rudhir)* पु. blood.

रुधिर-विज्ञान *(rudhir-vygan)* पु. haematology.

रुधिर-स्त्राव *(rudhir-śtrāv)* पु. haemorrhage.

रुनझुन *(runjhun)* स्त्री. tinkling sound.

रुपया *(rupayā)* पु. rupee; money.

रुलाई *(rulāī)* स्त्री. act of weeping; readiness to weep; verge of weeping or crying.

रुलाना *(rulānā)* स. क्रि. to cause to weep; to make (one) cry or weep.

रुष्ट *(ruṣṭ)* वि. enraged; wrathful;

displeased; offended.

रुष्टता *(ruṣṭatā)* स्त्री. state of being angry or offended; displeasure; annoyance.

रुँधना *(rūṁdhnā)* स. क्रि. to obstruct or restrain; to block; to surround.

रूखा *(rūkhā)* वि. rough; coarse; dry; harsh; blunt; curt; unsympathetic.

रूखापन *(rūkhāpan)* पु. dryness; curtness; bluntness; roughness; inconsiderateness; coldness.

रूठना *(rūṭhanā)* अ. क्रि. to be irritated; to be vexed; to be offended or displeased.

रूढ़ि *(rūṛhi)* स्त्री. tradition; convention; usage.

रूढ़िगत *(rūṛhigat)* वि. stereotyped; conventional.

रूढ़िग्रस्त *(rūṛhigrast)* वि. conventionalistic; convention bound; conservative.

रूढ़िवाद *(rūrhivād)* पु. conservatism; traditionalism; conventionalism.

रूढ़िवादी *(rūṛhivādī)* वि. conservative; conventionalistic.

रूप *(rūp)* पु. appearance; form; shape; way; method; beauty; grace; image; mould; type; version.

रूपक *(rūpak)* पु. image; likeness; silver ornament; play; drama; allegory; metaphor.

रूबरू *(rūbarū)* क्रि. वि. (फ़ा.) face to face.

रूपरेखा *(rūprekhā)* स्त्री. sketch; outline; synopsis; blue-print.

रूपवंत *(rūpvant)* वि. having a beautiful form or figure; handsome.

रूपवती *(rūpvatī)* वि. beautiful or well formed (woman).

रूपवान् *(rūpvān)* see रूपवंत।

रूप-विज्ञान *(rūp-vignān)* पु. morphology.

रूप-सज्जा *(rūp-sajjā)* स्त्री. makeup.

रूपसी *(rūpsī)* स्त्री. very beautiful woman.

रूपांतर *(rūpāntar)* पु. change of appearance or form; adaptation.

रूपांतरण *(rūpantraṇ)* पु. transformation; commutation; modification; metamorphosis.

रूपांतरित *(rūpāntarit)* वि. commuted; transformed.

रूपोश *(rūpoś)* वि. (फ़ा.) veiled; absconding.

रूमाल *(rūmāl)* पु. (फ़ा.) handkerchief.

रूसना *(rūsnā)* अ. क्रि. to get displeased; to be angry; to sulk.

रूह *(rūh)* स्त्री. (अ.) soul; spirit; vital principle; spirit or essence.

रेंकना *(reṁkanā)* अ. क्रि. to bray.

रेंगना *(reṁganā)* अ. क्रि. to creep; to crawl.

रेखा *(rekhā)* स्त्री. line; mark; newly grown whiskers in early youth.

रेखांकन *(rekhānkaṇ)* पु. drawing of lines; line work.

रेखांकित *(rekhānkit)* वि. underlined.

रेखागणित *(rekhā-ganit)* पु. geometry.

रेखाचित्र *(rekha-chitr)* पु. sketch; line drawing; figure; plan-design; outline map.

रेगमाल *(regmāl)* पु. (फ़ा.) sand paper.

रेगिस्तान *(regiśtan)* पु. sandy region or tract; desert.

रेगिस्तानी *(regiśtani)* वि. sandy; of or

pertaining to a desert.

रेचक *(recāk)* वि. purgative; cathartic.

रेचन *(recān)* पु. purgation; purging of bowels.

रेज़गारी *(rezgārī)* स्त्री. small coin; change (of money).

रेणु *(reṇu)* **रेणुका** *(reṇukā)* स्त्री. dust; sand; a grain of dust or sand; an atom; a small particle.

रेत *(ret)* स्त्री. earth; sand.

रेतना *(retnā)* स. क्रि. to rub or smoothen with a file; to file or sharpen; to rasp.

रेता *(retā)*see रेत।

रेती *(retī)* स्त्री. file; rasp.

रेतीला *(retīlā)* वि. sandy.

रेल-पेल *(rel-pel)* स्त्री. crowd; throng; rush; abundance; profusion; exuberance; jostle; melee; stampede.

रेवड़ *(revaṛ)* पु. flock (of goats or sheep).

रेशम *(reśam)* पु. (फ़ा.) silk.

रेशमी *(reśami)* वि. silken; made or woven of silk.

रेशा *(reśā)* पु. (फ़ा.) fibre; grain; staple.

रेशेदार *(reśedār)* वि. (फ़ा.) fibrous.

रेह *(reh)* स्त्री. fossil alkali (used for washing and making soap); impure nitrate of soda; saline soil.

रेहन *(rehn)* पु. (फ़ा.) pledging pawning; mortgage.

रैन *(rāin)* स्त्री. night

रोंगट *(roṁgatā)* पु. hair (of the body).

रोएँदार *(royen-dār)* वि. hairy; woolly.

रोक *(rok)* स्त्री. ban; check; restraint; prevention; obstacle; stay; barrier; prohibition; embargo.

रोकड़ *(rokaṛ)* स्त्री. cash; ready money.

रोकड़िया *(rokaṛiyā)* पु. cash keeper; cashier; treasurer.

रोकना *(roknā)* स. क्रि. to hinder; to impede; to retard; to prevent; to intercept; to obstruct; to resist; to protect; to detain; to hold.

रोग *(rog)* पु. ailment; sickness; disease.

रोगग्रस्त *(rog-grast)* वि. sick; diseased; ill.

रोगनाशक *(rog-nāśak)* वि. curative; preventive; prophylactic.

रोग-विज्ञान *(rog-vignān)* पु. pathology.

रोगाणु *(rogānū)* पु. germs which cause diseases.

रोगिणी *(rogiṇī)* स्त्री. diseased female.

रोगी *(rogī)* पु. patient.

रोगी-गाड़ी *(rogī-garī)* स्त्री. ambulance.

रोचक *(rocak)* वि. interesting; engaging; entertaining; pleasant.

रोचकता *(rocakatā)* स्त्री. appealableness; agreeableness; pleasantness.

रोज़ *(roz)* पु. (फ़ा.) day.

रोज़गार *(rozgār)* पु. (फ़ा.) profession; vocation; occupation; employment.

रोज़नामचा *(roznāmcā)* पु. (फ़ा.) daybook; diary; daily account book.

रोज़मर्रा *(rozmarā)* क्रि. वि. (फ़ा.) daily; every day.

रोज़ाना *(rozānā)* क्रि. वि. (फ़ा.) every day; daily.

रोज़ी *(rozī)* स्त्री. (फ़ा.) means of subsistence; livelihood.

रोज़ी-रोटी *(rozī-roṭī)* स्त्री. livelihood.

रोड़ा *(roṛā)* पु. a fragment of stone or brick etc.; obstruction; hindrance.

रोड़ी *(roṛī)* स्त्री. gravel rubble; hardcore.

रोदन *(rodan)* पु. weeping; wailing; lamentation.

रोधक *(rodhak)* वि. obstructive; prohibitive.

रोधन *(rodhan)* पु. obstruction; impediment; obstacle; hindrance.

रोना *(ronā)* अ. क्रि. to weep; wail; lament.

रोपण *(ropan)* पु. act of setting up or erecting; act of raising; planting or sowing.

रोपना *(ropanā)* स. क्रि. to set up; to erect; to raise; to plant; to sow; to transplant.

रोब *(rob)* पु. (अ.) awe; terror; awful influence of one's greatness or power; sway; dignity; impressiveness.

रोबदार *(robdār)* वि. (अ.) aweinspiring; influential.

रोबीला *(robīlā)* see रोबदार।

रोम *(rom)* पु. thin and fine hair of the body; pore.

रोमकूप *(romkūp)* पु. pore of the skin.

रोमांच *(romānc)* पु. thrill (of rapture; horror; surprise; horripilation.

रोमांचक *(romāncak)* वि. thrilling.

रोमांचित *(romāncīt)* वि. thrilled; horripilated.

रोली *(rolī)* स्त्री. mixture of turmeric and lime which is used in marking tilak on forehead.

रोशन *(rośan)* वि. (फ़ा.) bright; shining; lighted.

रोशनदान *(rośandān)* पु. (फ़ा.) hole for admitting light; skylight; ventilator.

रोशनाई *(rośanāī)* स्त्री. ink.

रोशनी *(rośanī)* स्त्री. light; illumination.

रोष *(roṣ)* पु. anger; wrath; rage.

रौंदना *(raumdanā)* स. क्रि. to trample; to tread down; to crush.

रौनक़ *(raunaq)* स्त्री. (फ़ा.) brightness; lustre; splendour; hustle and bustle; crowd or throng.

ल

ल *(la)* the third of the semi-vowel series of the Devnagri alphabets.

लँगड़ा *(lamgṛā)* पु. cripple; lame man; a species of mango.

लँगड़ाना *(lamgṛānā)* अ. क्रि. to limp.

लँगड़ापन *(lamgṛāpan)* पु. lameness.

लंगर *(langar)* पु. (फ़ा.) anchor; public kitchen alms-house; privy cover worn by the wrestlers.

लंगूर *(langūr)* पु. long tailed black faced monkey; baboon.

लँगोट, लँगोटा *(lamgoṭ)* पु. a strip of cloth worn to protect the private parts; loin cloth.

लँगोटी *(lamgoṭī)* स्त्री. small loin cloth.

लंघन *(langhan)* पु. violation; transgression; fast.

लंघनीय *(langhanīya)* वि. that can

be traversed or passed over; passable.

लंपट *(lampaṭ)* वि. lascivious; disolute; libertine; lewd; profligate.

लंपटता *(lampaṭatā)* स्त्री. dissoluteness; lewdness; lasciviousness; profligacy; debauchery.

लंबा *(lambā)* वि. long; lengthy; tall; great; large; spiacious.

लंबाई *(lambāī)* स्त्री. length; tallness; height.

लंबित *(lambit)* वि. prolonged; lengthened; penduline; pending .

लंबी *(lambī)* see. लंबा।

लंबोदर[1] *(lambodar)* वि. pot-bellied; long-bellied; paunchy; gluttonous.

लंबोदर[2] *(lambodar)* पु. epithet of god Ganesh; glutton.

लकड़दादा *(lakaṛ-dādā)* पु. great great grand-father.

लकड़बग्घा *(lakar-bagghā)* पु. hyena.

लकड़हारा *(lakaṛ-hārā)* पु. woodman; woodcutter.

लकड़ी *(lakaṛī)* स्त्री. wood; timber; firewood; fuel; crutches.

लक़वा *(laqvā)* पु. (अ.) paralysis.

लकीर *(lakīr)* स्त्री. line; streak.

लकुटी *(lakuṭī)* स्त्री. small stick or cane.

लक्षण *(laksan)* पु. distinctive mark; sign; symptom; token; any mark or feature of the body (indicating good or bad luck); feature; character; attribute.

लक्षित *(lakṣit)* वि. denoted; indicated; implied; seen; observed; beheld; discerned; discovered; known (from signs); indicated; implied; marked; distinguished.

लक्ष्मी *(lakṣmī)* स्त्री. fortune; prosperity; wealth; grace; splendour; lustre; woman symbolising fortune and prosperity; Lakshmi; goddess of wealth.

लक्ष्य *(lakṣya)* स्त्री. target; aim; object; goal; implication or implied meaning.

लक्ष्यपूर्ति *(laksyapūrtī)* स्त्री. fulfilment of the aim.

लक्ष्यवेध *(laksyaved)* पु. hitting the target.

लक्ष्यसिद्धि *(laksyasīdhī)* स्त्री. attainment of one's aim or goal.

लखना *(lakhanā)* स. क्रि. to see; behold; perceive; to understand; to mark out; to keep an eye on.

लखपति *(lakhpatī)* पु. millionaire; wealthy person.

लगन *(lagan)* स्त्री. devotion; perseverance; application; auspicious hour.

लगना *(lagnā)* अ. क्रि. to be close; be contiguous; to be fastened; to be stitched;\to be attached; to be joined; to hang about; to haunt; to be invested; to be spent; to gall; pinch; rub; to affect; to have the intended or natural effect; to take root; to become rooted; to be burnt or scorched (as food in cooking); to be related; to seem; to appear.

लगभग *(lagbhag)* क्रि. वि. almost; about; nearly.

लगातार *(lagātār)* क्रि. वि. constantly; continuously; regularly.

लगान *(lagān)* पु. land revenue; rent.

लगाना *(lagānā)* स. क्रि. to put together (figures); to sum up; to add; to put in order; to arrange; to plant; to set; to put (to work); to apply; to use; to employ; to engage; to construe; to infuse or imbue.

लगाम *(lagām)* स्त्री. (फ़ा.) reins; bridle.

लगाव *(lagāv)* पु. bond; link; contact; relation; attachment; affection; inclination; propensity.

लग्न[1] *(lagn)* वि. adhered or clung to; stuck; held fast.

लग्न[2] *(lagn)* वि. the rising of the sun or of the planets; an auspicious or lucky moment; wedding ceremony.

लघु *(laghu)* वि. little; small; diminutive; sober; trifling; trivial.

लघुतम *(laghutam)* वि. minimum; lowest; smallest.

लघुता *(laghutā)* स्त्री. smallness; littleness; insignificance; absence of dignity; humiliation.

लघुशंका *(laghuśankā)* स्त्री. urination.

लचक *(lacak)* स्त्री. flexibility; elasticity; resilience.

लचकदार *(lacakdār)* वि. elastic; flexible.

लचकना *(lacaknā)* अ. क्रि. to bend; to be bent; to receive a sprain or strain.

लचकाना *(lacakānā)* स. क्रि. to cause to bend; to bend.

लचकीला *(lacakīlā)* वि. flexible; elastic; resilient.

लचर *(lacar)* वि. untenable; weak; ineffective.

लचीला *(lacīlā)* वि. flexible; elastic.

लचीलापन *(lacīlāpan)* पु. flexibility; elasticity.

लच्छेदार *(lachedār)* वि. having fine shreds; amusing; fascinating.

लजाना *(lajānā)* अ. क्रि. to feel shy; to blush.

लजालू *(lajālū)* वि. bashful.

लज़ीज *(lazīz)* वि. (अ.) tasty; delicious.

लजीला *(lajīlā)* वि. shy; bashful; modest.

लजीलापन *(lajīlāpan)* पु. bashfulness.

लज़्ज़त *(lazzat)* स्त्री. (अ.) taste; flavour; relish.

लज्जा *(lajjā)* स्त्री. shame; modesty; shyness.

लज्जालु *(lajjālu)* वि. baskful; modest; shy.

लज्जाशील *(lajjaśil)* वि. of modest disposition;modest; bashful.

लज्जित *(lajjit)* वि. ashamed; abashed.

लट *(laṭ)* स्त्री. curl; ringlet; lock of hair; matted or tangled hair.

लटकना *(laṭaknā)* अ. क्रि. to hang in air; to be in a suspense; to keep in a state of indecision; to be delayed; to sling; to lop.

लटका *(laṭkā)* पु. formula; tip; device; affected movement or mannerism.

लटकाना *(laṭkānā)* स. क्रि. to hang; to suspend; to tilt; to keep (one) waiting; to delay.

लटा *(laṭā)* वि. wicked; mean; weak; emaciated; improverished.

लट्टू *(laṭṭū)* पु. spinning top.

लट्ठ *(laṭṭh)* पु. staff; cudgel.

लट्ठबाज़ *(laṭṭhbāz)* वि. skilled in wielding a cudgel; quarrelsome.

लट्ठा *(laṭṭhā)* पु. beam; log; rafter; coarse kind of long cloth; a kind of white cloth; measuring rod or pole measuring 5{1}/4 of hand space.

लठिया *(laṭhiyā)* स्त्री. small stick.

लड़ *(laṛ)* स्त्री. string (of pearls; etc.); strand (of a rope or cord); row; line; series.

लड़कपन *(laṛakpan)* पु. boyhood; childhood; childishness.

लड़का *(laṛka)* पु. boy; son.

लड़की *(laṛki)* स्त्री. girl; maid; daughter.

लड़खड़ाना *(laṛkharānā)* अ. क्रि. to stagger; to stumble; to stutter; to falter (in speech).

लड़खड़ाहट *(larkharāhat)* स्त्री. staggering; stumbling.

लड़ना *(laṛnā)* अ. क्रि. to fight; to quarrel; to collide (with); to wreste; to make war; to give battle; to debate; to argue; to contend; to struggle.

लड़ाई *(laṛāī)* स्त्री. fighting; battle; war; wrestling; duel; quarrel; brawl; wordy duel; dispute; discord; histility; struggle.

लड़ाई-झगड़ा *(laṛāī-jhagrā)* पु. broil; altercation; quarrel; enmity; hostility.

लड़ाका *(laṛākā)* वि. pugnacious; quarrelsome; contentious; bellicose.

लड़ाकू *(laṛākū)* वि. used in battle; (arms' ships etc.); warlike; quarrelsome; bellicose.

लड़ाना *(laṛānā)* स. क्रि. to cause to fight; to make (two persons or animals) fight; to instigate; to collide; to cause to wrestle.

लड़ी *(laṛī)* स्त्री. string (of pearls; or flowers; etc.) chain; strand (of rope or cord).

लड्डू *(laḍḍū)* पु. ball-shaped sweetmeat.

लत *(lat)* स्त्री. addiction.

लता *(latā)* स्त्री. vine; creeper; branch.

लताड़ *(latār)* स्त्री. scolding; reprimand; rebuke.

लताड़ना *(latāṛnā)* स्त्री. to scold or to reprimand.

लतीफ़ा *(latīfā)* पु. (अ.) witty anecdote; witticism; pleasantry; jest; joke.

लत्ता *(lattā)* पु. scrap of cloth; rag; tatter; cloth.

लथपथ *(lath-path)* वि. soaked; saturated; drenched; clogged; besmeared.

लथेड़ना *(latheṛnā)* स. क्रि. to draggle; to smear.

लदना *(ladanā)* अ. क्रि. to be loaded; to be laden; to be borne; to be carried; to be finished; to be over.

लदवाना *(ladvānā)* स. क्रि. to cause to be loaded to cause to load.

लदान *(ladān)* पु. act of loading.

लद्धड़ *(laddhar)* वि. lethargic; slothful.

लपकना *(lapaknā)* अ. क्रि. to rush forth; to go out with gusto; to catch; take a catch (a ball; etc.).

लपट *(lapaṭ)* स्त्री. flame; blaze; blast of fragrance; smell; fragrance; blister.

लपलपाना *(laplapānā)* अ. क्रि. to be resilient or flexible (as a cane); to resile; to brandish (as sword); to bring out again and again (tongue).

लपलपाहट *(laplapāhaṭ)* स्त्री. resilience; flexibility.

लपसी *(lapsī)* स्त्री. glutinous kind of food; sticky substance.

लपेट *(lapeṭ)* स्त्री. folding; twisting;

covering; fold; coil; plait; girth; circumference; compass.

लपेटना *(lapeṭānā)* स. क्रि. to wind or to twine; to roll up; to fold or wrap; (fig.) to involve; to implicate.

लफ़ंगा[1] *(lafaṅgā)* पु. (फ़ा.) loafer; vagabond.

लफ़ंगा[2] *(lafaṅgā)* वि. (फ़ा.) roguish; vagabondish.

लफ़्ज *(lafz)* पु. (अ.) word.

लफ्फ़ाज़ *(laffāz)* वि. (अ.) verbose; talkative.

लफ़्फ़ाज़ी *(laffāzi)* स्त्री. (फ़ा.) verbosity; talkativeness; use of high sounding phraseology.

लब *(lab)* पु. (फ़ा.) lip.

लबरेज़ *(labrez)* वि. (फ़ा.) full to the brim.

लबादा *(labādā)* पु. (फ़ा.) cloak; gown; robe; apron.

लबालब *(labālab)* क्रि. वि. upto the brim.

लब्धि *(labdhi)* स्त्री. acquirement; attainment; achievement; (arith.) quotient.

लभ्य *(labhāya)* वि. attainable; obtainable; within reach.

लमहा *(lamhā)* पु. (अ.) moment.

लय[1] *(lay)* पु. merger; immersion; fusion; dissolution; extinction; destruction.

लय[2] *(lay)* स्त्री. tempo; rhythm; tune.

लरज़ना *(larzanā)* अ. क्रि. to shake; to quiver; to tremble; to be frightened.

ललक *(lalak)* स्त्री. craving; yearning; longing.

ललकना *(lalaknā)* अ. क्रि. to long or crave; to yearn.

ललकार *(lalkār)* स्त्री. challenge; boost to fight.

ललकारना *(lalkārnā)* स. क्रि. to hold out a challenge; to throw the gaunlet to; to halloo.

ललचना *(lalacanā)* अ. क्रि. to be tempted or allured.

ललचाना *(lalcānā)* स. क्रि. to tempt; to allure; अ. क्रि. see ललचाना।

ललना *(lalanā)* स्त्री. woman; beautiful lady.

लला *(lalā)* पु. dear child (boy).

ललाट *(lalāṭ)* पु. forehead.

ललाम *(lalāṁ)* वि. beautiful; lovely; charming; handsome.

ललित *(lalit)* वि. lovely; beautiful; elegant; graceful.

ललितकला *(lalitkalā)* स्त्री. fine art.

लल्लो-चप्पो *(lallo-cāppo)* स्त्री. wheedling; adulation; flattery; coaxing; huggery.

लवण *(lavan)* पु. salt.

लवणता *(lavaṇatā)* स्त्री. salinity; beauty.

लवलीन *(lavalīn)* वि. absorbed; engrossed.

लश्कर *(laśkar)* पु. (फ़ा.) host; multitude; army.

लसदार *(lasdār)* वि. sticky; adhesive; glutinous.

लसलसा *(laslasā)* वि. adhesive; glutinous; sticky.

लसलसाना *(laslasānā)* अ. क्रि. to be viscous; to be sticky.

लसीला *(laslīā)* वि. adhesive; viscous.

लसीलापन *(laslīāpan)* पु. adhesiveness; stickiness.

लस्सी *(lassī)* स्त्री. cold drink made of churned curd mixed with water and sugar.

लहँगा *(lahaṁgā)* पु. loose skirt or petticoat.

लहक *(lahak)* स्त्री. flame; blaze; glare; glitter; flash.

लहकना *(lahaknā)* अ. क्रि. to bend or wave; to rise up into a flame; to blaze up.

लहकाना *(lahkānā)* स. क्रि. to cause to warble or quiver; to incite; to instigate; to blow up (a fir).

लहज़ा *(lahzā)* पु. (अ.) tone; accent; intonation; delivery.

लहर *(lahar)* स्त्री. wave; ripple; surge; caprice; fancy; ecstasy; transport; rapture.

लहरदार *(lahardār)* वि. wavy; undulatory; sinuous.

लहरा *(lahrā)* पु. wave; recreation; merry-making; tune; spell of rain.

लहराना *(lahrānā)* अ. क्रि. to shimmer; to fluctuate; to undulate; to be in ecstasy.

लहरियादार *(lahirādār)* वि. corrugated; wavy; meandering; having a wavy pattern.

लहलहाना *(lahlahnānā)* अ. क्रि. to be verdant; to flourish or bloom; to wave; to undulate.

लहसुन *(lahsun)* पु. garlic.

लहू *(lahū)* पु. blood.

लहू-लुहान *(lahū-lūhān)* वि. smeared in blood; soaked in blood.

लाँघना *(lāṁghanā)* स. क्रि. to jump or spring over; to cross; to go beyond; to pass over; to transgress; to violate.

लांछन *(lāñchan)* पु. blame; slur; stigma; blemish; slander.

लाक्षणिक *(lākṣaṇik)* वि. expressing indirectly or figuratively; metaphorical; allegorical; symbolical; acquainted with marks or signs.

लाक्षणिकता *(lākṣaṇikatā)* स्त्री. metonymy.

लाक्षा *(lākṣā)* स्त्री. a kind of red dye; lac; shellac.

लाख *(lakh)* वि. a hundred thousand; lac.

लाग *(lāg)* स्त्री. attachment; affection; competition; enmity; hostility; rancour; support.

लाग-डाट *(lāg-dāt)* स्त्री. rancour; rivalry; competition.

लागत *(lāgat)* स्त्री. cost.

लागू *(lāgū)* वि. applied; enforced; applicable.

लाचार *(lācār)* वि. (अ.) helpless; destitute; hopeless; compelled; obliged; constrained.

लाचारी *(lācārī)* स्त्री. (अ.) helplessness; inability.

लाज *(lāj)* स्त्री. shame; sense of decency; shyness; bashfulness; modesty; honour.

लाजवंती *(lājvantī)* स्त्री. modest; coy; blushing woman; the plant touch-me-not.

लाजवाब *(lāj-javāb)* वि. (अ.) peerless; unique; speechless; silent.

लाज़िम *(lāzim)* लाज़िमी वि. inevitable; obligatory; compulsory.

लाठी *(lāṭhi)* स्त्री. staff; stick; cudgel.

लाड़ *(lāṛ)* पु. affection; caress endearament; fondling.

लाड़ला *(lāṛalā)* वि. darling; dear; beloved.

लात *(lāt)* स्त्री. leg; kick.

लादना *(lādanā)* स. क्रि. to load; to burden; to saddle (one) with (responsibility).

लानत *(lānat)* स्त्री. (अ.) curse; condemnation; reproach; rebuke; censure.

लानत-मलामत *(lānat-malāmat)* स्त्री. (अ.) reproof; reproach; curse.

लाना *(lānā)* स. क्रि. to bring; to fetch; to bring forward; to present; to produce.

लापता *(lāpatā)* वि. (अ.) missing; absconding.

लापरवाह *(lāparvāh)* वि. (अ.) careless; carefree; negligent; inattentive; heedless.

लापरवाही *(lāparvāhī)* स्त्री. (अ.) carelessness; negligence; heedlessness.

लाभ *(lābh)* पु. advantage; benefit; gain; profit.

लाभकर *(lābhkar)* वि. profitable; beneficial; advantageous.

लाभांश *(lābhāṇs)* पु. dividend; bonus.

लाम *(lām)* पु. army; war-front.

लामबंदी *(lāmbandī)* स्त्री. mobilization (of army).

लामिसाल *(lamisāl)* वि. (अ.) matchless; peerless; unique.

लायक़ *(lāyaq)* वि. (अ.) worthy; able; capable; competent.

लार *(lār)* स्त्री. saliva; spittle; string; series; row; train.

लाल[1] *(lal)* पु. son; darling; pet;ruby.

लाल[2] *(lal)* वि. red; ruddy.

लालच *(lālac)* पु. temptation; greed.

लालची *(lālaci)* वि. greedy; avaricious.

लालन-पालन *(lālan-pālan)* पु. rearing; upbringing.

लाल फ़ीताशाही *(la स.fitāsāhi)* स्त्री. red tapism.

लाल बुझक्कड़ *(lā स.bhujākkar)* वि. ignorant fool who thinks himself wise enough to answer every question.

लालसा *(lālasā)* स्त्री. longing; ardent desire; yearning.

लालायित *(lālāyit)* वि. eager; tempted; enamoured.

लालित्य *(lālitya)* पु. gracefulness; grace; beauty; charm; delicacy.

लालिमा *(lālimā)* पु. redness; reddishness.

लाली *(lālī)* स्त्री. redness; ruddishness; a darling daughter; rouge; lipstick.

लावण्य *(lāvaṇya)* पु. beauty; loveliness; charm.

लावारिस *(lāvāris)* वि. (अ.) heirless; having or leaving no heir; to which there is no heir; (property); unclaimed.

लाश *(lāś)* स्त्री. dead body; corpse carcass.

लासानी *(lā-sānī)* वि. (अ.) matchless; uncomparable; peerless.

लिंग *(liṅg)* पु. mark; spot; sign; token; genital organ; phallus deity representing Shiva; gender; sign of gender or sex.

लिए *(liye)* क्रि. वि. for; for the sake (of); on account (of).

लिखत *(likhat)* स्त्री. writing.

लिखत-पढ़त *(likhat-parhat)* स्त्री. documentation; document, written deed.

लिखना *(likhanā)* स. क्रि. to write; to register; to note down; to copy; to compose (a work etc.).

लिखवाना *(likhavānā)* स. क्रि. to cause to be written or recorded.

लिखाई *(likhāī)* स्त्री. act of writing; wages or remuneration for writing or copying; art or business of writing.

लिखाना *(likhānā)* स. क्रि. to cause to write; to dictate.

लिखा-पढ़ा *(likhā-parhā)* वि. educated; literate.

लिखा-पढ़ी *(likhā-parhī)* स्त्री. correspondence; written agreement.

लिखावट *(likhāvaṭ)* स्त्री. manner of writing; handwriting.

लिखित *(likhit)* वि. written; recorded.

लिटाना *(liṭānā)* स. क्रि. to cause to lie down; to lay (one) down.

लिथड़ना *(litharṇā)* अ. क्रि. to be besmeared.

लिपटना *(lipaṭanā)* अ. क्रि. to cling (to); to adhere (to); to twine or coil (round); to embrace; to concentrate on a work.

लिपटाना *(lipaṭānā)* स. क्रि. to fold to wrap (round) to twine or wind (round etc.); to embrace.

लिपना *(lipanā)* अ. क्रि. to be washed over; to be white-washed; to be smeared; to be plastered or coated.

लिपवाना *(lipavānā)* स. क्रि. to cause to plaster; to cause to smear.

लिपाई *(lipāī)* स्त्री. act or plastering; wages paid for plastering.

लिपि *(lipi)* स्त्री. writing; script.

लिपिक *(lipik)* लिपिकार पु. scribe; clerk.

लिपिबद्ध *(lipibadh)* वि. written; recorded.

लिप्त *(lipt)* वि. attached; involved; engrossed.

लिप्यंतरण *(lipyantran)* पु. transcription; transliteration.

लिप्सा *(lipsā)* स्त्री. ardent desire for getting or regaining; lure; greed.

लिफ़ाफ़ा *(lifāfā)* पु. (अ.) cover of a letter; envelope; wrapper; outward case; outward show.

लिबास *(libās)* पु. (अ.) apparel; clothes; dress; attire.

लियाक़त *(liyāqat)* स्त्री. (अ.) skill; ability; merit; propriety; fitness.

लिसलिसा *(lislisā)* वि. viscous.

लिहाज़ *(lihāz)* पु. (फ़ा.) respect; deference; regard; consideration; shame; hesitation.

लिहाज़ा *(lihāzā)* क्रि. वि. (अ.) therefore; thus; consequently.

लिहाफ *(lihāf)* पु. (अ.) quilt.

लीक *(lik)* स्त्री. mark (of a cart wheel); wheeस.track; rut; track; trace; established practice; custom; rule.

लीख *(līkh)* स्त्री. tiny louse.

लीचड़ *(licaṛ)* वि. sluggish; slothful; clumsy; stingy.

लीन *(līn)* वि. completely absorbed; completely merged; devoted; engrossed; vanished; disappeard.

लीपना *(līpanā)* स. क्रि. to plaster; to coat; to smear.

लीपा-पोती *(līpā-potī)* स्त्री. plastering and white washing; patching up

लीला *(līlā)* स्त्री. play; sport; stage representation (of the deeds of divine incarnations); mysterious acts or happenings.

लुंगी *(luṅgi)* स्त्री. cloth-sheet worn round legs.

लुंज *(luṁj)* वि. crippled (parson).

लुंजपुंज *(luṁj-puṁj)* वि. flaccid and feeble; without muscles; mangled and mutilated.

लुका-छिपी *(lūkā-cipī)* स्त्री. hide and seek; clandestine existence.

लुकाना *(lukānā)* स. क्रि. to hide; to conceal.

लुगदी *(lugdī)* स्त्री. pulp.

लुगाई *(lūgāī)* स्त्री. woman; wife.

लुच्चा *(luccā)* वि. base; depraved; lewd.

लुटना *(luṭanā)* अ. क्रि. to be plundered; to be robbed; to be deprived.

लुटाना *(luṭānā)* स. क्रि. to squander; to give away liberally; to sell at a very cheep rate.

लुटिया *(luṭiyā)* स्त्री. small round utensil.

लुटेरा *(luṭerā)* पु. plunderer; robber; bandit; free booter.

लुढ़कना *(lurhaknā)* अ. क्रि. to roll down; to topple over; to tumble down.

लुत्फ़ *(lutf)* पु. (अ.) fun; pleasure; enjoyment; elegance; grace; beauty.

लुप्त *(lupt)* वि. dropped; elided; obsolete; out of use; extinct.

लुब्ध *(lubdh)* वि. charmed; attracted; covetous; greedy; avaricious.

लुभाना *(lubhānā)* अ. क्रि. to be allured;tempted; to tantalize; to allure to tempt.

लुभावना *(lubhāvanā)* वि. charming; attractive; alluring.

लुहार *(luhār)* पु. blacksmith.

लू *(lū)* स्त्री. hot wind of summer; sun-stroke.

लूट *(lūt)* स्त्री. plunder; robbery; booty; spoil.

लूटना *(lūṭanā)* स. क्रि. to plunder; to rob; to charge exorbitantly; to extort.

लूला *(lūlā)* वि. handless; crippled; handicapped.

लेई *(leī)* स्त्री. adhesive paste prepared from fine flour.

लेकिन *(lekin)* क्रि. वि. but; however; yet.

लेख *(lekh)* पु. handwriting; written document; article.

लेखक *(lekhak)* पु. writer; author.

लेखन *(lekhan)* पु. writing; painting; sketching.

लेखनी *(lekhanī)* pen.

लेखा *(lekhā)* पु. account; calculation; return.

लेखाकार *(lekhākār)* पु. accountant.

लेखा-जोखा *(lekhā-jokhā)* पु. calculation of accounts.

लेखा-परीक्षक *(lekhā-pariksak)* पु. auditor.

लेखा-परीक्षण *(lekhā-pariksan)* पु. auditing.

लेखा-परीक्षा *(lekhā-pariksā)* स्त्री. audit.

लेखा-बही *(lekhā-bahī)* स्त्री. account book; cash-book.

लेखिका *(lekhikā)* स्त्री. authoress.

लेटना *(leṭanā)* अ. क्रि. to repose; rest; to lie down; to lie prostrate.

लेन-देन *(len-den)* पु. money-transaction; money-lending.

लेना *(lenā)* स. क्रि. to hold; grasp; lay hold of; to get; obtain; to buy; purchase; to seize; capture; take possession of; to borrow.

लेना-देना *(lenā-denā)* पु. transaction; dealing; concern.

लेप *(lep)* पु. smearaing; plastering; coating; plaster in general; ointment; liniment.

लेपना *(lepanā)* स. क्रि. to coat; to anoint.

लैंगिक *(laingik)* वि. sexual; phallic.

लोई *(loi)* स्त्री. a kind of woollen blanket; small ball of doughed flour to be spread into bread.

लोक *(lok)* पु. the world; the earth; people or subjects.

लोककथा *(lok-kathā)* लोकगाथा स्त्री. popular legend; folk-tale.

लोकगीत *(lokgīt)* पु. folk song.

लोकतंत्र *(loktantra)* पु. democracy.

लोकतांत्रिक *(loktāntrik)* वि. democratic.

लोकनाट्य *(loknātya)* पु. folk-drama.

लोकनिधि *(loknidhī)* स्त्री. public fund.

लोकनीति *(lokniti)* स्त्री. folk-ethics; public policy.

लोकनृत्य *(lok-nrtya)* पु. folk-dance.

लोकप्रिय *(lokpriya)* वि. popular.

लोकप्रियता *(lokpriyatā)* स्त्री. popularity.

लोकमत *(lokmat)* पु. public opinion.

लोकसंपर्क *(lok-sampark)* पु. public relations.

लोकसभा *(loksabhā)* स्त्री. House of the people; House of Commons.

लोकसाहित्य *(lok-sāhitya)* पु. folkliterature.

लोकसेवक *(lok-sevak)* पु. public servant.

लोकसेवा-आयोग *(lok-sevā-āyog)* पु. Public Service Commission.

लोकहित *(lok-hit)* पु. public welfare; public interest.

लोकाचार *(lokācār)* पु. common practice; popular or general custom.

लोकातीत *(lokātīt)* वि. extra-mundane; transcendent (al).

लोकोक्ति *(lokākit)* स्त्री. proverb; popular saying.

लोकोत्तर *(lokottar)* वि. supernatural; transcendental; extra-worldly.

लोकोपकार *(lokopakār)* पु. public welfare; philanthropy.

लोकोपकारी[1] *(lokopakārī)* वि. pertaining to public good; philanthropic; humanitarian.

लोकोपकारी[2] *(lokopakārī)* पु. philanthropist.

लोकोपयोगी *(lokopayogī)* वि. useful for people in general.

लोच *(loc)* स्त्री. flexibility; elasticity.

लोचदार *(locdār)* वि. elastic; flexible.

लोचन *(locan)* पु. eye.

लोटना *(loṭnā)* अ. क्रि. to welter; to roll.

लोट-पोट *(lot-pot)* स्त्री. rolling or tossing about.

लोटा *(loṭā)* पु. a small round metal utensil.

लोढ़ा *(loṛhā)* पु. stone pestle; pounder.

लोप *(lop)* पु. omission; dropping; extinction; elision.

लोपन *(lopan)* पु. concealment; extinction.

लोभ *(lobh)* पु. eagerness; desire; longing; temptation; covetousness; greediness; avarice.

लोभी *(lobhī)* वि. covetous; greedy; avaricious.

लोम *(lom)* पु. hair on the body of men or animal; fur.

लोमहर्षक *(lomharsak)* वि. horripilating; thrilling.

लोमड़ी *(lomrī)* स्त्री. fox.

लोरी *(lorī)* स्त्री. lullaby.

लोलुप *(lolup)* वि. covetous; greedy; very desirous; very eager.

लोलुपता *(lolupatā)* स्त्री. covetousness; greed; eager desire or longing.

लोहा *(lohā)* पु. iron.

लोहार *(lohār)* पु. blacksmith.

लोहित *(lohit)* वि. red; red-coloured;

scarlet.

लोहिया *(lohiyā)* पु. iron-seller.

लाहू *(lohū)* पु. blood.

लौंग *(lauṁg)* स्त्री. clove; nose-stud.

लौ *(lau)* स्त्री. flame; glow; devotion; ardent desire; longing; craving.

लौकिक *(laukik)* वि. wordly; mundane; customary.

लौट *(lauṭ)* स्त्री. return.

लौटना *(lauṭanā)* अ. क्रि. to return; to turn back; to go back on one's word; turn; to change.

लौटाना *(lauṭānā)* स. क्रि. to return; to send back.

लौह[1] *(lauh)* पु. iron; weapon; arm.

लौह[2] *(lauh)* वि. made of iron or copper; red.

व

व *(va)* the fourth of the semivowel series of the Devnagri alphabets.

वंग *(vang)* पु. name of Indian State Bengal

वंचक *(vañcak)* पु. cheat; deceiver; sharper; jackal; domesticated mongoose.

वंचना[1] *(vañcanā)* स्त्री. cheating; deception; deceit; fraud.

वंचना[2] *(vañcanā)* स. क्रि. to deceive; to cheat.

वंचित *(vañcit)* वि. deprived; devoid; deceived; cheated.

वंदन *(vandan)* पु. reverence; worship; praise; salutation; invocation.

वंदना *(vandanā)* स्त्री. adoration; salutation; invocation.

वंदनीय, वंद्य *(vandanīya)* वि. worthy of worship; adorable; worthy of reverence.

वंध्य *(vandhya)* वि. unproductive; sterile; fruitless; faulty; defective.

वंध्यकरण *(vandhyakaran)* पु. sterilization.

वंध्यता *(vandhyatā)* स्त्री. sterility.

वंध्या *(vandhyā)* स्त्री. sterile woman or cow.

वंश *(vaṃś)* पु. species; lineage; dynasty; family.

वंशगत *(vaṃśgat)* वि. ancestral; lineal.

वंशज *(vaṃśaj)* पु. progeny; descendant.

वंश-परंपरा *(vaṃś-paramparā)* स्त्री. lineage; family tradition.

वंशवृत्त *(vaṃśvrit)* पु. genealogy.

वंशानुक्रम *(vaṃsā-nukram)* पु. genealogy; family succession; pedigree.

वंशानुगत *(vaṃśanugat)* see वंशगत।

वंशावली *(vaṃśavali)* स्त्री. pedigree.

वंशी *(vaṃśī)* स्त्री. flute; pipe.

वकालत *(vakālat)* स्त्री. (अ.) legal practice; pleadership; advocacy.

वकालत-नामा *(vakālat-nāmā)* पु. power of attorney.

वकील *(vakīl)* पु. (अ.) attorney; pleader; lawyer; counsellor.

वक़्त *(vaqt)* पु. (अ.) time; opportunity.

वक्तव्य *(vaktavya)* पु. speech; statement; condemnation.

वक्ता *(vaktā)* पु. spokesman; speaker; lecturer; learned person.

वक्तृत्व *(vaktṛatva)* पु. ability to speak well; eloquence; elocution.

वक्र *(vakr)* वि. curved; curled; bent; crooked; cunning; cruel.

वक्रगति *(vakrgatī)* वि. reserve.

वक्रोक्ति *(vakrokti)* स्त्री. pun; equivocation; insinuation.

वक्ष *(vakṣa)* पु. breast; bosom; chest.

वक्षस्थल *(vakṣ-sthal)* पु. breast chest.

वग़ैरह *(vagairah)* क्रि. वि. etcetera.

वचन *(vacan)* पु. speech; utterance; promise; (gram). number.

वचनबद्ध *(vacan-badh)* वि. committed.

वचनबद्धता *(vacan-badhatā)* स्त्री. commitment.

वचनभंग *(vacanbhang)* पु. breach of promise.

वज़न *(vazan)* पु. (अ.) load; weight; importance; value.

वज़नदार *(vazandār)* वि. (अ.) heavy; weighty; important.

वज़नी *(vazanī)* वि. heavy; important.

वज़ह *(vajah)* स्त्री. reason; cause; source.

वज़ीफ़ा *(vazīfā)* पु. (अ.) scholarship; stipend.

वज़ीर *(vazīr)* पु. (अ.) minister; secretary; ambassador; a chessman.

वज्र *(vajra)* पु. Lord Indra's weapon; lightening; thunderbolt; any fatal weapon.

वज्रपात *(vajrapāt)* पु. the fall of a thunderbolt; a stroke of lightening.

वज्राघात *(vajrāghāt)* पु. calamity; stroke of lightening or thunderbolt.

वट *(vaṭ)* पु. banyan tree.

वणिक् *(vaṇik)* पु. merchant; trader.

वतन *(vatan)* पु. (अ.) native country; native place.

वत्स *(vats)* पु. child; offspring.

वत्सल *(vatsal)* पु. affectionate.

वत्सलता *(vatsalatā)* स्त्री. fondness; affection.

वदन *(vadan)* पु. mouth; face; countenance.

वध *(vadh)* पु. murder; slaughter.

वधशाला *(vadhsālā)* स्त्री. slaughter home.

वधु *(vadhū)* स्त्री. bride; wife.

वन *(van)* पु. forest;woods; garden.

वनमानुष *(van-mānush)* पु. chimpanzee.

वनराज *(van-rāj)* पु. lion; king of forest.

वनरोपण *(van-ropan)* पु. afforestation.

वनवर्धन *(van-vardhan)* पु. selviculture.

वनवास *(van-vas)* पु. exile; banishment.

वनवासी *(van-vāsī)* पु. one who lives in a forest; an exile.

वनविज्ञान *(van-vijnān)* पु. forestry.

वनस्थली *(vanasthalī)* स्त्री. woodland.

वनस्पति *(vanaspati)* स्त्री. vegetation.

वनस्पति-विज्ञान *(vanaspati-vijnān)* पु. botany.

वनिता *(vanitā)* स्त्री. woman.

वन्य *(vanya)* वि. growing or produced in woods; wild; uncultured; savage.

वफ़ा *(vafā)* पु. (अ.) dutifulness; faithfulness; loyality; fulfilment of a promise.

वफ़ादार *(vafādār)* वि. (अ.) faithful; honest; true; loyal.

वफ़ादारी *(vafādārī)* स्त्री. (अ.) faithfulness; fidelity; loyalty; sincerity; dutifulness.

वबाल *(vabāl)* पु. (अ.) difficulty; burden; curse.

वमन *(vaman)* पु. vomiting; vomit.

वय *(vay)* पु. age; youth; bird; vitality; health.

वयस्क[1] *(vayask)* वि. relating to age; mature; major; adult (in law).

वयस्क[2] *(vayask)* पु. adult; major.

वयस्कता *(vayaskatā)* स्त्री. adulthood.

वयोवृद्ध *(vayo-vridh)* वि. old; elderly; venerable.

वर *(var)* पु. selection; choice; bridegroom; husband; boon; blessing; gift; present.

वरक़ *(varaq)* पु. (अ.) sheet of paper; leaf of a book; foil of gold or silver; petal.

वरज़िश *(varziś)* स्त्री. (फ़ा.) exercise; physical labour.

वरण *(varaṇ)* पु. choice; selection; choice of a partner for marriage; request; protection; riddance.

वरदान *(vardān)* पु. favour; blessing; boon.

वरदी *(vardī)* स्त्री. (अ.) uniform.

वरन् *(varan)* अ. but; on the other hand.

वरना *(varnā)* क्रि. वि. otherwise; else.

वरम *(varam)* पु. (अ.) swelling.

वराह *(varāh)* पु. boar; hog; pig.

वरिष्ठ *(variṣṭh)* वि. great and respectable; senior; high etc.

वरिष्ठतता *(variṣṭhtatā)* स्त्री. seniority.

वरीयता *(varīyatā)* seniority.

वरुण *(varuṇ)* पु. Vedic god of water; the planet Neptune.

वर्ग *(varg)* पु. class; community; species; party; faction; group; square.

वर्गहीन *(varghin)* प. classless.

वर्गीकरण *(vargīkaraṇ)* पु. classification; grouping.

वर्गीकृत *(vargikṛt)* वि. classified.

वर्जन *(varjan)* पु. prohibition; restriction; avoidance.

वर्जनीय *(varjanīya)* वि. worth deserting or forsaking; restricted; worth prohibiting; improper; undesirable.

वर्जित *(varjit)* वि. forbidden; left; remaining; devoide; excluded unacceptable; prohibited.

वर्ण *(varṇ)* पु. colour; dye; caste.

वर्णक्रम *(varṇkarm)* पु. alphabetical arrangement; spectrum.

वर्णन *(varṇan)* description; account; colouring; writing; praise; mention.

वर्णनात्मक *(varṇātmak)* वि. descriptive.

वर्णनीय *(varṇanīya)* वि. fit to be described.

वर्णमाला *(varṇmālā)* स्त्री. alphabet.

वर्णव्यवस्था *(varṇvyavasthā)* स्त्री. caste system.

वर्णसंकर *(varṇsaṁkar)* वि. from parents of different castes.

वर्णाश्रम *(varanāśram)* पु. Hindu system of communities.

वर्तनी *(vartanī)* स्त्री. spelling (of a word).

वर्तमान *(vartamān)* वि. existing; current; in force; present.

वर्तिका *(vartikā)* स्त्री. wick (of a

lamp); stick; pointed brush.

वर्तुल *(vartul)* वि. round; circular; orbiculate.

वर्दी *(vardi)* uniform.

वर्द्धन, वर्धन *(vardhan)* पु. act of increasing or growing; increase; growth.

वर्म *(varm)* पु. (अ.) inflammation; swelling.

वर्ष *(varṣ)* पु. year.

वर्षगाँठ *(varṣ-gānth)* स्त्री. birth anniversary; birthday.

वर्षण *(varṣaṇ)* पु. falling of rain.

वर्षा *(varṣā)* स्त्री. rains; monsoon.

वल्कल *(valkal)* पु. bark of a tree; garment made of bark.

वल्द *(vald)* पु. (अ.) son (of).

वल्दियत *(valdiyat)* स्त्री. (अ.) fathers name; parentage.

वल्मीक *(valmik)* पु. ant-hill.

वल्लभ[1] *(vallabh)* पु. beloved; dear; chief.

वल्लभ[2] *(vallabh)* पु. beloved person; husband.

वल्लरि, वल्लरी *(vallari)* स्त्री. creeper; sprout.

वश *(vaś)* पु. power; capacity; control.

वशीकरण *(vaśīkaran)* पु. overcoming by charms; spell etc.; means of subjugating or fascinating.

वशीभूत *(vaśībhūt)* subjudigated; undercontrol; fascinated; enchanted.

वसंत *(vasant)* पु. spring season.

वसन *(vasan)* पु. cloth; clothes; dress; garment; apparel; attire; dwelling; residing.

वसा *(vasā)* स्त्री. fat; marrow; pith.

वसीअत, वसीयत *(vasīyat)* स्त्री. (अ.) will; testament; bequest; legacy.

वसीयतनामा *(vasīyat-nāmā)* पु. (अ.) will.

वसुंधरा *(vasundharā)* स्त्री. the earth.

वसूल *(vasūl)* वि. (अ.) received; collected (funds; etc.).

वसूली *(vasūlī)* स्त्री. receipt; realisation; recovery; collection.

वस्तु *(vastu)* स्त्री. thing; material; object; article.

वस्तुतः *(vastutaha)* क्रि. वि. actually; in reality.

वस्तुनिष्ठ *(vastunisth)* वि. objective.

वस्तुस्थिति *(vastu-sthiti)* स्त्री. reality.

वस्त्र *(vastra)* पु. cloth; clothes.

वह *(vah)* सर्व. that; he; she.

वहन *(vahan)* पु. carrying; bearing; conveying.

वहम *(vaham)* पु. (अ.) false doubt or notion; superstition.

वहशत *(vahśat)* स्त्री. savagery; embarrassment; excitement.

वहशी *(vahsī)* वि. barbarous; savage; rustic.

वहशीपन *(vahśīpan)* पु. savagery; barbarousness; madness.

वहाँ *(vahāṁ)* क्रि. वि. there.

वहीं *(vahīṁ)* क्रि. वि. at that very place; there itself.

वही *(vahi)* सर्व. that very one; the same; he himself; the same.

वह्नि *(vahni)* पु. fire.

वांछनीय *(vāñchanīya)* वि. desirable; worthy of desire.

वांछनीयता *(vāñchanīyatā)* स्त्री. desirability.

वांछित *(vāñchit)* वि. wished; desired.

वाक़ई *(vāqaī)* क्रि. वि. (अ.) really; actually.

वाक़िफ़ *(vāqif)* वि. (अ.) conversant; familiar.

वाक़फ़ीयत *(vāqafiyat)* स्त्री. (अ.) acquaintance; knowledge; familiarity.

वाक् *(vāk)* स्त्री. speech; expression; saying.

वाक्पटु *(vāk-patu)* वि. eloquent; skilled in speech.

वाक्पटुता *(vāk-patutā)* स्त्री. eloquence.

वाक्य *(vākya)* पु. sentence.

वाग्जाल *(vāg-jāl)* पु. equivocation; multiloquence; grandiloquence.

वाग्दान *(vāg-dan)* पु. betrothal; engagement.

वाङ्मय *(vāṅmay)* पु. literature; treatise.

वाचक *(vacak)* पु. reader; speaker; messenger; important word; noun; name.

वाचन *(vācan)* पु. perusal; statement; narration.

वाचनालय *(vācanālya)* पु. reading room.

वाचाल *(vācāl)* वि. talkative; garrulous.

वाचालता *(vācālatā)* स्त्री. talkativeness; loquaciousness; garrulity.

वाजिब *(vājib)* वि. (अ.) reasonable; proper.

वाटिका *(vāṭikā)* स्त्री. small garden.

वाणिज्य *(vānijya)* पु. commerce; trade.

वाणिज्यदूत *(vānijya-dut)* पु. commercial counsel.

वाणी *(vāṇī)* स्त्री. voice; words; speech; tongue; the goddess of speech; Saraswati.

वात *(vāt)* पु. air; air as one of the three humours of body; gout.

वातानुकूलन *(vātānukulān)* पु. air-conditioning.

वातानुकूलित *(vātānukulit)* वि. air-conditioned.

वातायन *(vātāyan)* पु. ventilator; window.

वातावरण *(vātāvaran)* पु. atmosphere; environment.

वात्सल्य *(vātsalya)* पु. affection or tenderness towards offspring.

वाद *(vād)* पु. discussion; controversy; suit; case; dispute; theory.

वादक *(vādak)* पु. musician; speaker; debator on religious scriptures etc.; a special style of beating drum.

वादन *(vādan)* पु. playing upon a musical instrument.

वाद-विवाद *(vād-vivād)* पु. dispute; controversy; discussion.

वादा *(vādā)* पु. (अ.) promise; pledge for repayment of debt.

वादी *(vādī)* पु. plaintiff; appellant; complainant; (music) keynote; expounder of a theory.

वाद्य *(vādya)* पु. musical instrument.

वाद्यवृंद *(vādya-vrṇd)* पु. orchestra.

वाद्यसंगीत *(vādya-saṁgita)* पु. instrumental music.

वानर *(vānar)* पु. monkey; ape.

वापस *(vāpas)* वि. (फ़ा.) returned.

वापसी *(vāpsī)* स्त्री. return; retreat.

वाम *(vām)* वि. left; opposite; adverse; wicked. vile; bad.

वामन *(vāman)* वि. dwarfish; bent; mean; low.

वामपंथ *(vām-panth)* पु. leftism.

वामपंथी *(vām-panthī)* पु. leftist; follower of leftism.

वामा *(vāmā)* स्त्री. woman; goddess Durga; Lakshmi; Saraswati; Gauri; mother of Tirthankar Parshvanath.

वायदा *(vāydā)* पु. (अ.) promise.

वायस *(vāyas)* पु. crow.

वायु *(vāyu)* स्त्री. air; breath.

वायुमंडल *(vāyumandal)* पु. atmosphere.

वायुमिति *(vāyumiti)* स्त्री. aerometrics.

वायुयान *(vāyuyān)* पु. aeroplane.

वायुलेखी *(vāyu-lekhi)* पु. aerograph.

वायुविज्ञान *(vāyu-vygnan)* पु. aerology.

वायुसेना *(vāyusenā)* स्त्री. air-force.

वायुमार्ग *(vāyumarg)* पु. air-route.

वार *(vār)* पु. day (of the week); assault; attack; blow; lid; door.

वारदात *(vārdāt)* स्त्री. (अ.) incident; occurrence.

वारना *(vārnā)* स. क्रि. to wave (anything) round or over one as a means of averting evil etc.; to sacrifice.

वारांगणा वारांगना *(vārānganā)* स्त्री. prostitute; harlot.

वारा-न्यारा *(vāra-nyārā)* पु. huge gains; heavy profits; settlement; reconciliation; termination.

वारि *(vāri)* पु. water; rain; circle.

वारिज *(vārij)* पु. lotus; fish; conch.

वारिद *(vārid)* पु. cloud.

वारिस *(vāris)* पु. (अ.) heir; successor.

वारुणी *(vāruṇī)* स्त्री. wine.

वार्त्ता, वार्ता *(vārtā)* स्त्री. conversation; talk; speech; rumour.

वार्त्ताकार, वार्ताकार *(vārtākār)* पु. speaker; talker.

वार्त्तालाप *(vārtālāp)* पु. conversation; parley; talk.

वार्षिक *(vārṣik)* वि. annual; yearly.

वालिद *(vālid)* पु. (अ.) father.

वालिदा *(vālidā)* स्त्री. (अ.) mother.

वालदैन *(vāldain)* पु. (अ.) parents.

वावैला *(vāvailā)* पु. (अ.) wailing.

वाष्प *(vāṣp)* पु. steam; vapour; tear.

वास *(vās)* पु. dwelling; living; residence; home; house; smell; flavour.

वासना *(vāsanā)* स्त्री. desire; longing; craving; lust.

वासर *(vāsar)* पु. day.

वासी *(vāsī)* वि. resident; inhabitant.

वास्तव *(vāstav)* पु. substance; reality; fact; truth.

वास्तविक *(vāstavik)* वि. actual; real; true; factual; substantial.

वास्तविकता *(vāstavikatā)* स्त्री. reality.

वास्ता *(vāstā)* पु. (अ.) relationship; connection; friendship.

वास्तु *(vāstu)* पु. building; site; foundation of a house.

वास्तुकला *(vāstukalā)* स्त्री. architecture.

वास्तुविद् *(vāstuvid)* पु. architect.

वास्ते *(vāste)* क्रि. (अ.) for the sake (of); on account (of); by reason (of); on or in behalf of.

वाह *(vāh)* क्रि. वि. (फ़ा.) well done ! fine ! excellent !

वाहक *(vāhak)* पु. porter; carrier; charioteer; rider; bearer; conductor.

वाहन *(vāhan)* पु. conveyance; carriage vehicle.

वाहवाही *(vāhvāhi)* स्त्री. (फ़ा.) cheers; applause.

वाहिनी *(vāhinī)* स्त्री. army; a division of army.

वाहियात *(vāhiyāt)* वि. (फ़ा.) useless;

nonsensical; worthless; vulgar.

विंदु *(vindu)* पु. see बिंदु।

विकट *(vi-kaṭ)* वि. difficult; ticklish; formidable; horrible; dreadful; huge; ugly.

विकराल *(vi-karāl)* वि. dreadful; horrible; frightful; formidable.

विकर्षण *(vi-karśan)* पु. pulling under; dragging; dislike; hatred; disinclination; repulsion; aversion.

विकल *(vi-kal)* वि. restless; uneasy; maimed; scared; discouraged; incomplete; belittled.

विकलता *(vi-kalatā)* स्त्री. scare; uneasiness; discouragement.

विकलांग *(vi-kalāṅg)* वि. multimated; maimed; disabled.

विकल्प *(vi-kalp)* पु. option; alternative; uncertainty; ambiguity.

विकसित *(vi-kasit)* वि. developed; budded; blown; bloomed.

विकार *(vi-kār)* पु. perversion; defilement; disorder; deterioration; disease.

विकास *(vi-kas)* पु. budding; blooming; development; evolution; growth.

विकासवाद *(vikāsvād)* पु. evolutionism.

विकासशील *(vikāsīl)* वि. developing.

विकीर्ण *(vi-kīrn)* वि. scattered; dishevelled; full; famous.

विकृत *(vi-kṛt)* वि. defiled; corrupted; deformed; disfigured; transformed; unnatural; incomplete; agitated.

विकृति *(vi-kṛti)* स्त्री. changed form; disfigurement; modification; transformation; deformation; corruption; abnormal or sudden event disease; excitement; lust; animosity; abortion.

विक्रम *(vi-kram)* स्त्री. valour; power; bravery; movement; manner; way; path; stability.

विक्रमी *(vi-kramī)* वि. valiant; heroic; related to Vikram.

विक्रांत *(vi-krānt)* वि. valiant; mighty; pre-eminent; heroic; radiant; effulgent.

विक्रेता *(vi-kretā)* पु. salesman; seller; vendor; dealer.

विक्षत *(vikshat)* वि. wounded; hurt; injured.

विक्षिप्त *(vi-kṣipt)* वि. mad lunatic; crazy; bewildered; perplexed; thrown; scattered.

विक्षिप्तता *(vi-kṣiptatā)* स्त्री. lunacy; bewilderment; restlessness.

विक्षुब्ध *(viksubdha)* स्त्री. agitated; disturbed; restless; indignant.

विक्षेपण *(vi-kṣepaṇ)* पु. dissemination; throwing; despatch; shaking; pulling bowstring; hindrance.

विक्षोभ, विक्षोभण *(vikšobn)* पु. agitation; perturbation; disorder; disturbance; mental restlessness.

विख्यात *(vi-khyāt)* वि. famous; renowned; designated; recognised.

विगत *(vi-gat)* वि. past; last; destitute or deprived; dead.

विगलित *(vi-galit)* वि. dissolved; melted (heart); disappeared; oozy; oozing.

विग्रह *(vi-grah)* पु. analysis; quarrel; discord; war; battle; shape; form; body; statue; idol; enlargement; extension; division.

विग्रही *(vi-grahī)* वि. warlike; bellicose; idolatrous.

विघटन *(vi-ghaṭan)* पु. breaking up; destruction; ruin; disintegration.

विघटनकारी *(vi-ghaṭankārī)* वि. destructive; disruptive.

विघ्न *(vi-ghna)* पु. obstacle; impediment; disturbance; hindrance; obstruction; disruption.

विघ्नकारी *(vi-ghnakārī)* वि. causing obstacle or interruption; impeding; hindering; disturbing.

विचरण *(vi-caraṇ)* पु. wandering; walk; saunter; ramble; tour.

विचरना *(vi-carnā)* अ. क्रि. to wander; to walk; to saunter.

विचलित *(vi-calit)* वि. moved or deviated (from promise; principle or place); unsteady; fickle; troubled; disturbed; restless.

विचार *(vi-cār)* पु. reflection; deliberation; pondering; view; thought; idea; consideration.

विचारिक *(vi-cārak)* पु. thinker; philosopher.

विचारगोष्ठी *(vi-cār-gośthi)* स्त्री. seminar.

विचारणीय *(vi-cāraṇīya)* वि. needing consideration or deliberation; doubtful; under consideration; verifiable.

विचारधारा *(vi-cār-dhārā)* स्त्री. ideology.

विचारना *(vi-cārnā)* स. क्रि. to think; deliberate.

विचारपूर्ण *(vi-cār-puran)* स्त्री. thoughtful; reflective.

विचारपूर्वक *(vi-car-purvak)* क्रि. वि. thoughtfully.

विचार मग्न *(vicār-magan)* वि. engrossed in thought; pensive; in a reverie.

विचारवान् *(vicārvān)* वि. thoughtful; considerate.

विचार-विमर्श *(vicār-vimarś)* पु. deliberation .

विचारशील *(vicārsīl)* पु. considerate; deliberative; reflective; thoughtful.

विचारहीन *(vicārhin)* वि. thoughtless.

विचाराधीन *(vicārādhin)* वि. under-consideration.

विचारोत्तेजक *(vicārotejak)* वि. stimulating; thought-provoking.

विचित्र *(vi-citr)* वि. unusual; strange; peculiar; queer; curious; wonderful; surprising.

विचित्रता *(vi-citratā)* स्त्री. unusualness; strangeness; wonderfulness; peculiarity.

विच्छिन्न *(vi-cchinn)* वि. cut off or split; torn asunder; separated; ceased; ended; crooked.

विच्छेद *(vi-cched)* पु. cutting; splitting; amputation; brokenness; break; separation; cessation; end.

विछोह *(vi-choh)* पु. separation.

विजन *(vi-jan)* पु. lonely place; wilderness; lack of witness.

विजय *(vi-jay)* स्त्री. victory; conquest; success.

विजयचिन्ह *(vi-jay-cinha)* पु. trophy.

विजया *(vi-jayā)* स्त्री. goddess Durga; triumphal festivity.

विजयी *(vi-jayī)* वि. victorious; successful.

विजातीय *(vi-jātīya)* वि. of different caste; tribe or kind; heterogeneous.

विजित *(vi-jit)* वि. conquered; defeated; vanquished.

विजेता *(vi-jetā)* पु. conqueror; victor; winner.

विज्ञ *(vi-jña)* वि. conversant; expet; learned.

विज्ञप्ति *(vi-jñāpti)* स्त्री. notice; communique; act of informing; pamphlet; notification.

विज्ञान *(vi-jñān)* पु. science.

विज्ञापन *(vi-jñāpan)* पु. advertisement; handbill; announcement.

विज्ञापनदाता *(vi-jñāpandātā)* पु. advertiser.

विज्ञापित *(vi-jñāpit)* वि. advertised; informed; made known; notified.

विटप *(viṭap)* पु. tree.

विडंबना *(vi-ḍambanā)* स्त्री. mockery; scoff; irony; ridicule.

वितरण *(vi-taraṇ)* पु. distribution; disbursement; delivery.

वितरित *(vi-tarit)* वि. distributed; disbursed; delivered.

वित्त *(vitt)* पु. wealth; property; finance; authority; power.

वित्तीय *(vittīya)* वि. financial.

विदग्ध *(vi-dagdh)* वि. learned; skilled; burnt.

विदग्धता *(vi-dagdhatā)* स्त्री. learnedness; scholarship; skill; hedonism.

विदा *(vidā)* स्त्री. (अ.) parting; departure; permission to leave; knowledge; learning; wisdom.

विदारक *(vidārak)* वि. tearing; rending.

विदित *(vidit)* वि. known; learnt; renowned; informed; consentient; promised.

विदीर्ण *(vi-dīrṇ)* वि. torn; broken; killed; spread; opened.

विदुषी *(viduṣī)* स्त्री. wise or learned women.

विदूषक *(vi-dūṣak)* पु. jester; buffoon.

विदेश *(vi-deś)* पु. foreign country.

विदेशी *(vi-deśī)* पु. foreinger.

विद्यमान *(vidyamān)* वि. existent; present; prevalent; real; extant.

विद्यमानता *(vidyamānatā)* स्त्री. existence; presence.

विद्या *(vidyā)* स्त्री. knowledge; learning; education; science; skill.

विद्यार्थी *(vidyārathi)* पु. student; pupil.

विद्यालय *(vidyālaya)* पु. school.

विद्युतीकरण *(vidyutikaran)* पु. electrification.

विद्युत् *(vi-dyut)* स्त्री. lighting; electricity.

विद्युत्दर्शी *(vi-dyutdarśī)* पु. electroscope.

विद्युदणु *(vi-dyutdanu)* पु. electron; proton.

विद्रुम *(vi-drum)* पु. coral; young sprout or shoot.

विद्रुप[1] *(vidrūp)* वि. disfigured; ugly.

विद्रुप[2] *(vidrūp)* पु. the taunt; sarcasm.

विद्रोह *(vi-droh)* पु. rebell; revolt; sedition.

विद्रोही *(vi-drohī)* वि. relating to rebellion; rebellious; insurgent.

विद्वत्ता *(vidvattā)* स्त्री. scholarship; learning; knowledge; erudition.

विद्वत्तापूर्ण *(vidvattāpurn)* वि. scholarly; learned; erudite.

विद्वान्[1] *(vidvān)* पु. scholarly; learned; erudite.

विद्वान्[2] *(vidvān)* पु. scholar; learned person.

विद्वेष *(vidveṣ)* पु. hostily; spite;

illwill; enmity.

विधना *(vidhanā)* स्त्री. destiny.

विधर्म¹ *(vi-dharm)* पु. different religion; injustice; irreligion.

विधर्म² *(vi-dharm)* वि. unjust; unrighteous.

विधर्मी *(vi-dharmī)* वि. irreligious; belonging to different religion; converted.

विधवा *(vidhavā)* स्त्री. widow.

विधा *(vi-dhā)* स्त्री. mode; manner; style; kind; form; section; part.

विधाता *(vi-dhātā)* पु. creator; Hindu god Brahma; maker; legislator; law-maker.

विधान *(vi-dhān)* पु. law; regulation; arrangement; making; doing.

विधायक¹ *(vi-dhāyak)* वि. performing; disposing; doing; making; constructive; arranging; managing; establishing a rule or law.

विधायक² *(vi-dhāyak)* पु. member of legislative assembly (legislative council).

विधि *(vi-dhi)* स्त्री. manner; method; process; law; religious act or ceremony; rite.

विधिक *(vi-dhik)* वि. pertaining to law; applicable in the form of law; legal; in accordance with law.

विधिज्ञ *(vi-dhijna)* पु. legal expert; lawyer.

विधिपूर्वक *(vi-dhipuravak)* क्रि. वि. according to rule or law; duly; formally.

विधिवत् *(vi-dhivat)* क्रि. वि. according to law; in conformity to prescribed rules; in due form; duly; methodically; formally.

विधिवेत्ता *(vi-dhivetā)* पु. jurist; law expert.

विधिशास्त्र *(vi-dhi-śastra)* पु. jurisprudence; secience of law.

विधिशास्त्री *(vi-dhi-śastri)* पु. jurist.

विधुर *(vidhur)* पु. widower.

विधेयक *(vi-dheyak)* पु. legislation.

विध्वंस *(vi-dhvaṃs)* पु. devastation; ruin; destruction; animosity; rancour; hatred; humiliation; dishonour; enmity.

विध्वंसक¹ *(vi-dhvaṃsak)* पु. one who spells devastation; destroyer.

विध्वंसक² *(vi-dhvaṃsak)* पु. devastating; destructive; vile.

विध्वस्त *(vi-dhvast)* वि. ruined; destroyed; scattered.

विनत *(vi-nat)* वि. bent down; bowed; humble; modest; inclined; sunk down; curved; depressed.

विनती *(vi-natī)* स्त्री. request; entreaty.

विनम्र *(vi-namra)* वि. modest; humble; courteous; submissive.

विनम्रता *(vi-namratā)* स्त्री. humbleness; meekness; courtesy; modesty.

विनय *(vi-nay)* स्त्री. polite conduct; good breeding or manners; modesty; humility.

विनयशील *(vi-naysīl)* वि. modest; humble.

विनयी *(vi-nayī)* वि. humble; submissive.

विनष्ट *(vi-naṣṭ)* वि. utterly lost or ruined; perished.

विनाश *(vi-nāś)* पु. destruction; ruin; bad condition; utter loss; annihilation; clamity; breakdown.

विनाशकारी *(vi-nāśkārī)* वि. destructive.

विनिमय *(vi-ni-may)* पु. barter; exchange.

विनियम *(vi-ni-yam)* पु. regulation; prohibition; control; restraint.

विनियोग *(vi-ni-yog)* पु. investment; approtionment; distribution; division; use; application; employment; appropriation.

विनिवेश *(vi-niveś)* पु. entry; admission; settlement; impression.

विनीत *(vi-nīt)* वि. modest; humble; meek; decent; refined; plain; simple; carried away; removed; spread.

विनोद *(vi-nod)* पु. amusement; humour; removal; recreation; earnest desire.

विनोदपूर्ण *(vi-nod-purna)* वि. humorous; jolly.

विनोदप्रिय *(vi-nod-priya)* वि. jocular.

विनोदी *(vo-nodī)* वि. amusing; jovial; humorous; jolly.

विन्यास *(vi-ny-ās)* पु. putting down; placing; laying down; arrangement; adjustment.

विपक्ष *(vi-pakṣ)* पु. opposite party; opposition.

विपक्षी[1] *(vi-pakṣī)* वि. opponent.

विपक्षी[2] *(vi-pakṣī)* पु. enemy; member of the opposition party; rival.

विपत्ति *(vi-patti)* स्त्री. calamity; misfortune; hardship; disaster; oppression.

विपथ *(vi-path)* पु. different way or path; wrong course; indulgence in wrong deeds.

विपदा *(vi-padā)* स्त्री. calamity; grief.

विपद् *(vi-pad)* स्त्री. calamity; misfortune; distress.

विपन्न *(vi-pann)* वि. afflicted; distressed; poor; fallen into adversity; ruined; destroyed; decayed.

विपन्नता *(vi-pannatā)* स्त्री. misfortune; ruin; trouble.

विपरीत *(vi-parît)* वि. opposite; reverse; unfavourable; adverse; disagreeable.

विपरीतता *(vi-parîtatā)* स्त्री. opposition; contrariety.

विपर्यय *(vi-pary-ay)* पु. transposition; reversion.

विपिन *(vipin)* पु. forest; jungle; garden.

विपुल *(vi-pul)* वि. extensive; large; abundant.

विपुलता *(vi-pultā)* स्त्री. extensiveness; largeness; abundance.

विप्र *(vipr)* पु. Brahman; priest; man of knowledge; moon.

विप्रलंभ *(vi-pra-lambh)* पु. separation; feeling or sentiment of lovers in separation; disunion.

विप्लव *(vi-plav)* पु. tumult; affray; insurgency; insurrection; revolt.

विफल *(vi-phal)* वि. fruitless; unsuccessful; useless; worthles; ineffective.

विफलता *(vi-phalatā)* स्त्री. fruitlessness; unprofitableness; failure; uselessness.

विभक्त *(vi-bhakt)* वि. divided; separated; different; decorated; ornamented; measured.

विभक्ति *(vi-bhakti)* स्त्री. (gram.) inflection; division; partition; inherited share; separation.

विभा *(vi-bhā)* स्त्री. lustre; splendour; beauty.

विभाग *(vi-bhāg)* पु. department; division; section; part; portion or share in general; chapter;

management.

विभागाध्यक्ष *(vi-bhāgādhyaksha)* पु. head of the department.

विभागीय *(vi-bhāgīya)* वि. departmental.

विभाजक *(vi-bhājak)* पु. one who divides; divider; distributor.

विभाजन *(vi-bhājan)* पु. act of dividing into shares; division; partition.

विभाजित *(vi-bhājit)* वि. divided; distributed; broken; fragmented.

विभाज्य *(vi-bhājya)* वि. divisible.

विभिन्न *(vi-bhinn)* वि. various; different.

विभिन्नता *(vi-bhinnatā)* स्त्री. variation.

विभीषिका *(vi-bhīṣikā)* स्त्री. means of terrifying; terror; dread.

विभु *(vi-bhu)* वि. supreme; grand; pervasive.

विभूषित *(vi-bhūṣit)* वि. ornamented; adorned; decorated.

विभेद *(vi-bhed)* पु. difference; subdivision; distinction.

विभोर *(vibhor)* वि. engrossed; absorbed; overjoyed; overwhelmed.

विभ्रम *(vi-bhram)* पु. delusion; doubt; hallucination; misunderstanding.

विमर्श *(vi-mars̈)* पु. critical study; thorough review; deliberation; consultation; consideration.

विमल *(vi-mal)* वि. free from dirt; spotless; flawless; clean; transparent.

विमाता *(vi-mātā)* स्त्री. step mother.

विमान *(vi-mān)* पु. aeroplane; heavenly car (of gods moving; through the skies); bier of a Mahatma; decorated with garlands; open palanquin carried on men's shoulders.

विमान चालक *(vi-mān-cālak)* पु. pilot.

विमान-चालन *(vi-mān-cālan)* पु. aviation; pilotage.

विमानन *(vi-mānan)* पु. aviation.

विमानशाला *(vi-mānśālā)* स्त्री. hanger for aircraft repairs.

विमुक्त *(vi-mukt)* वि. set free; released; liberated; devoid; discharged.

विमुक्ति *(vi-mukti)* स्त्री. release; riddance; exemption.

विमुख *(vi-mukh)* वि. indifferent; adverse; devoid; with the face averted or turned away; disappointed.

विमूढ़ *(vi-muṛth)* वि. foolish; dull of understanding; stupid; tempted; seduced.

विमोचन *(vi-mocan)* पु. freedom; redeem; release.

वियुक्त *(vi-yukt)* वि. detached; dissociated; separated (from); deserted (by).

वियोग *(vi-yog)* पु. disjunction; separation (especially of lovers); bereavement; pangs of separation.

वियोगी *(vi-yogī)* वि. separated from the beloved one.

विरक्त *(vi-rakt)* वि. detached (from the world); indifferent; unconcerned; void of attachment to wordly objects.

विरक्ति *(vi-rakti)* स्त्री. detachment; feeling of renunciation; weariness from the world.

विरह *(vi-rah)* पु. separation; agony of separation; absence.

विरहानल *(virahānal)* पु. agony of

parted lovers.

विरहिणी *(vi-rahiṇī)* स्त्री. a woman in the pangs of separation from her husband or lover.

विरही *(vi-rāhī)* वि. separated from one's beloved.

विराजना *(vi-rājnā)* अ. क्रि. to look splendid; to shine; to be present; to grace an occasion or place; to be seated.

विराट *(vi-rāṭ)* वि. colossal; gigantic.

विराम *(vi-rām)* पु. cessation; discontinuance; pause in or at the end of the sentence; full stop; rest; repose; halt; interval; intermission.

विरासत *(virāsat)* स्त्री. (अ.) inheritance; legacy; heritage.

विरुद *(virud)* पु. eulogy; fame; glory.

विरुदावली *(virudāvali)* स्त्री. a collection of epithets; eulogy.

विरुद्ध *(vi-ruddh)* वि. opposed; contrary; adverse; inimical; hostile.

विरुप *(vi-rūp)* वि. deformed; defaced; ugly; of different types; changed; graceless.

विरुपता *(vi-rūpatā)* स्त्री. ugliness; deformity; variety.

विरेचक *(vi-recak)* वि. purgative.

विरचेन *(vi-recan)* पु. evacuation of the bowels; purgation; purgative.

विरोध *(vi-rodh)* पु. opposition; contradiction; enmity; discord; rift; restriction; repugnancy; conflict; protestation.

विरोधी *(vi-rodhī)* वि. adverse; hostile; contradictory; contrary; opposite.

विलंब *(vi-lamb)* पु. delay; lethargy.

विलंबित *(vi-lambit)* वि. delayed; suspended; dependent; of slow tempo (music).

विलक्षण *(vi-lakṣaṇ)* वि. peculiar; strange; unique; distinct; prodigious; quaint.

विलक्षणता *(vi-lakṣaṇatā)* स्त्री. peculiarity; uniqueness; distinctiveness; remarkability; oddity; prodigiousness.

विलग *(vi-lag)* वि. separate; detached.

विलय *(vi-lay)* पु. merger; annihilation; destruction; liquefaction; blend; absorption.

विलसित *(vi-lasit)* वि. sportive; manifested; overjoyed; elated; adorned.

विलाप *(vi-lāp)* पु. lamentation; wailing.

विलायत *(vilāyat)* स्त्री. (अ.) foreign country.

विलायती *(vilāyatī)* वि. European; foreign.

विलास *(vi-lās)* पु. enjoyment; luxury; amorous playfulness; wantonness.

विलासिता *(vi-lāsitā)* स्त्री. luxury.

विलासिनी *(vi-lasini)* स्त्री. fair damsel; lustful lady; prostitute.

विलासी *(vi-lāsī)* वि. lustful; debauched; shining; radiant; sportive.

विलीन *(vilina)* वि. dissolved; melted; merged; vanished; disappeared; dead.

विलुप्त *(vi-lupt)* वि. extinct; vanished; disappeared; destroyed ruined; kidnapped; abducted.

विलेय *(vi-leya)* वि. soluble.

विलेयता *(vi-leyatā)* वि. solubility.

विलोकन *(vi-lokan)* पु. observation; notice; consideration; contemplation

विलोकना *(vilokanā)* स. क्रि. to see; to observe; to search.

विलोकनीय *(vi-lokanīya)* वि. seeable; viewable; noticeable; worth seeing.

विलोप *(vi-lop)* पु. disappearance; extinction; destruction; damage; obstruction; injury; omission; cancellation.

विलोपित *(vi-lopit)* वि. effaced; omitted; eliminated; cancelled.

विलोम *(vi-lom)* पु. reverse; created by reverse order.

विवर, विविर *(vi-var)* पु. hole; burrow; slit; cave; cavity; gap.

विवरण *(vi-varan)* पु. description; narration; particulars; details; commentary.

विवरणिका *(vi-varaṇikā)* स्त्री. report; brochure.

विवश *(vi-vaś)* वि. obliged; helpless; compelled; weak; powerless.

विवशता *(vi-vaśatā)* स्त्री. absence of will; helplessness; compulsion; cause of compulsion.

विवाचक *(vi-vācak)* पु. arbitrator.

विवाचन *(vi-vācan)* पु. arbitration.

विवाद *(vi-vād)* पु. dispute; discussion; quarrel; controversy.

विवादग्रस्त *(vi-vādgrast)* वि. controversial; disputed.

विवादात्मक *(vi-vādātmak)* वि. disputable; controversial.

विवादास्पद *(vi-vādāsped)* वि. controversial; debatable.

विवादी[1] *(vi-vādī)* वि. disputant; discordant.

विवादी[2] *(vi-vādī)* पु. disputer.

विवाह *(vi-vāh)* पु. marriage; nuptials; marriage celebration.

विवाहिता *(vi-vāhitā)* स्त्री. married woman.

विविध *(vi-vidh)* वि. of various sorts or kinds; miscellaneous; variegated.

विविधता *(vi-vidhatā)* स्त्री. variety; miscellany.

विवेक *(vi-vek)* पु. power of discrimination; discretion; real knowledge.

विवेकरहित *(vi-vek-rahit)* वि. indiscreet; imprudent.

विवेकी *(vi-vakī)* वि. discreet; wise.

विवेचक *(vi-vecak)* पु. critic; discriminant.

विवेचन *(vi-vecan)* पु. critical study; review; evaluation; argumentation; expatiation; profound thought.

विशद *(vi-śad)* वि. elaborate; detailed; clear cut; lucid; clean; pure; free from anxiety; calm; stable; charming.

विशाल *(viśāl)* वि. large; big; grand; great.

विशालता *(vi-śaltā)* स्त्री. greatness; largeness; extension.

विशिष्ट *(vi-śiṣṭ)* वि. special; specific; prominent; typical .

विशिष्टतः *(vi-sishtatah)* क्रि. वि. paricularly; in particular.

विशिष्टता *(viśiṣṭatā)* स्त्री. speciality; peculiarity.

विशुद्ध *(viśudha)* वि. completely cleansed or purified; genuine real; pious; free from vice; faultless; without a blemish; pure.

विशुद्धता *(vi-śudhatā)* स्त्री. purity; genuineness.

विशुद्धि *(vi-śudhi)* स्त्री. complete purity; faultessness; genuineness; rectification.

विशुद्धिकरण *(vi-śudhikaran)* पु. purification.

विश्रंखल *(vi-śṛnkhal)* वि. disorderly; chainless; uncontrolled.

विश्रंखलता *(vi-śṛnkhalatā)* स्त्री. disorderliness; disarray.

विशेष *(vi-śeṣ)* वि. particular; special.

विशेषज्ञ *(vi-śeshagna)* पु. expert; specialist.

विशेषज्ञता *(vi-śeshagnatā)* स्त्री. specialisation

विशेषण *(vi-śeṣaṇ)* वि. attribute; epithet; *(gram.)* adjective.

विशेषतः *(vi-śeṣtah)* क्रि. वि. specially.

विशेषता *(vi-śeṣatā)* स्त्री. speciality; singularity; attribute; quality.

विशेषाधिकार *(vi-śeṣadhikār)* पु. privilege.

विश्रांत *(vi-śrānt)* वि. restful; abated; calmed; tired; exhausted.

विश्रांति *(vi-śrānti)* स्त्री. rest; repose; tiredness; interval; intermission; gap.

विश्राम *(vi-śram)* पु. relaxation; rest; interval; intermission; tranquility.

विश्लेषण *(vi-śleṣaṇ)* पु. analysis; separation; disintegration.

विश्लेषणात्मक *(vi-śleṣaṇātmak)* वि. analytical.

विश्लेषित *(vi-śleṣit)* वि. analysed; separated.

विश्व *(viśva)* पु. universe; the world.

विश्वकोष *(viśvakośa)* पु. encyclopaedia.

विश्वविद्यालय *(viśva-vidyālaya)* पु. university.

विश्वसनीय *(vi-śvasanīya)* वि. reliable; credible; trustworthy; confidential.

विश्वसनीयता *(vi-śvasanīyatā)* स्त्री. reliability; credibility; trustworthiness.

विश्वस्त *(vi-śvast)* वि. reliable; assured.

विश्वस्तता *(vi-śvastatā)* स्त्री. reliability; fidelity.

विश्वास *(vi-śvās)* पु. belief; faith; trust; assurance; confidence.

विश्वासघात *(vi-śvāsghat)* पु. breach of trust; disloyalty; infidelity; treachery; treason.

विश्वासघाती *(vi-śvāsghātī)* वि. treacherous; disloyal.

विश्वासी[1] *(vi-śvāsī)* वि. trustful.

विश्वासी[2] *(vi-śvāsī)* पु. believer.

विष *(viṣ)* पु. poison; venom; (fig.) destructive or harmful element.

विषण *(viṣaṃ)* वि. gloomy; melancholy; demoralised; disheartened.

विषनाशक *(viṣh-nāsak)* वि. alexipharmic; anti-poison.

विषम *(vi-sam)* वि. uneven; odd (number); hard; difficult; adverse; dangerous; fearful; intense.

विषमता *(vi-ṣamatā)* स्त्री. unevenness; dissimilarity; contrast; difference; hardship; difficulty; intensity.

विषय *(vi-ṣay)* पु. subject; topic; theme; matter; content; sexual intercourse; sensual pleasure; pleasures of senses; wordly pleasures.

विषयक *(vi-ṣayak)* वि. cocerning; related (to); pertaining (to).

विषविज्ञान *(viṣ-vijnan)* पु. toxicology.

विषविज्ञानी *(viṣ-vijnāni)* पु. toxicolosist.

विषाक्त *(vi-śakta)* वि. poisonous.

विषाणु *(viṣaṇu)* पु. virus.

विषाद *(vi-ṣad)* पु. gloominss; despondency; melancholia.

विषुवत् रेखा *(viṣuvat-rekhā)* स्त्री. equator.

विषैला *(viṣailā)* वि. poisonous.

विषैलापन *(viṣailāpan)* पु. poisonousness; venomousness; vituperativeness; toxicity.

विसंगत *(vi-saṁgat)* वि. incongruous; inconsistent.

विसंगति *(vi-saṁgati)* स्त्री. incongruity; inconsistency.

विसर्जन *(vi-sarjan)* पु. donation; end; finish; excretion; throwing; adjournment; disposal of an idol; abandoment; dispersal; dismissal.

विसर्जित *(vi-sarjit)* वि. remitted; disposed; dispersed.

विस्तार *(vi-stār)* पु. dimension; extent; extension; details.

विस्तीर्ण *(vi-stīrṇa)* वि. spread out; expanded; spacious.

विस्तृत *(vi-stṛt)* वि. spread; extended; detailed; elaborate; spacious.

विस्फोट *(vi-sphoṭ)* पु. explosion; blast (noise); noise of such explosion.

विस्फोटक *(vi-sphotak)* पु. explosive material.

विस्मय *(vi-smay)* पु. wonder; surprise; doubt; uncertainty.

विस्मयकारी *(vi-smaykārī)* वि. wonderful; surprising; amazing; sensational.

विस्मरण *(vi-smaraṇ)* पु. forgetting; oblivion.

विस्मित *(vi-smit)* वि. amazed; surprised; wonderstruck.

विस्मृत *(vi-smṛt)* वि. forgotten.

विस्मृति *(vi-smṛti)* स्त्री. forgetfulness; oblivion.

विहंग *(vi-haṅg)* पु. bird; arrow; cloud; sun; moon; a snake; planet.

विहंगम *(vi-haṅgam)* पु. bird.

विहान *(vihān)* पु. dawn; early morning.

विहार *(vi-hār)* पु. roaming or walking about for pleasure etc; monastery; consecration for a sacrifice; sexual enjoyment; pleasure; sport; play; playground; palace; extension; extent.

विहीन *(vi-hīn)* वि. wanting; lacking; completely abandoned; low; mean; devoid (of).

विह्वल *(vi-hval)* वि. perturbed; restless; confounded; bewildered; scared; distressed; disappointed.

विह्वलता *(vi-hvalatā)* स्त्री. perturbation; restlessness; bewilderment.

वीक्षा *(vîkshā)* स्त्री. observation; perception; inspection.

वीणा *(vīnā)* स्त्री. Indian flute; lyre; lightning.

वीणावादिनी *(vīnā-vādini)* स्त्री. goddess Saraswati.

विथि, वीथी *(vīthi)* स्त्री. way; road; gallery; row; runway; balcony.

वीर *(vīr)* वि. mighty; brave; adventurous; fearless.

वीरगति *(vīrgati)* स्त्री. heroic end; death in battle.

वीरता *(vīratā)* स्त्री. bravery; adventure; fearlessness; excellence; heroic deed.

वीरांगना *(virānganā)* स्त्री. heroine;

brave woman.

वीरान *(virān)* वि. (फ़ा.) desolate; uninhabited; (fig.) devoid of glamour or grace; devastated.

वीराना *(virānā)* पु. (फ़ा.) uninhabited place; desolate place; forest.

वीर्य *(virya)* पु. semen; virility; valour; heroism; vigour; strength.

वृंद *(vrnd)* पु. multitude; assemblage; bunch; chorus.

वृंदगान *(vrndgān)* पु. chorus; choral song.

वृंदवाद्य *(vṛnd-vādya)* पु. orchestra.

वृक्ष *(vṛks)* पु. tree; plant; vegetation.

वृत *(vṛt)* वि. wedded; selected; covered; hidden; encircled; surrounded; consented; accepted; requested; spoiled; served; round.

वृत्त *(vṛtt)* पु. report; account; metre; circle; circumference; history; news; vacation; profession; conduct; good deeds; prescribed rules; change.

वृतांत *(vitanta)* पु. report; account; opportunity; event; happening; news; description.

वृत्ति *(vrtti)* स्त्री. mental disposition; attitude; typical condition of mind in Yoga; work; business; profession; stipend; remuneration; commentary; nature.

वृथा *(vṛthā)* वि. improper; false; useless; purposeless.

वृद्ध *(vṛddh)* वि. old; grown up; elderly; wise; learned.

वृद्धता *(vṛddhatā)* स्त्री. old age; senility.

वृद्धा *(vṛddhā)* स्त्री. old woman.

वृद्धि *(vṛddhi)* स्त्री. growth; rise; enhancement; enlargement; addition; progress; increment; interest; profit.

वृहत् *(vṛhat)* वि. great; big; heavy.

वे *(ve)* सर्व. they; those.

वेग *(veg)* पु. impulse; passion; velocity; speed; quickness; haste; expulsion of the faeces.

वेणी *(veṇi)* स्त्री. braid of hair.

वेतन *(vetan)* पु. salary; pay; remuneration; wages; labour charges.

वेदना *(vedānā)* स्त्री. torture; pain; agony.

वेदी *(vedi)* स्त्री. a place prepared for wedding ceremony; altar.

वेध *(vedh)* पु. piercing; penetration; perforation; hole; depth of a pit; observation.

वेधशाला *(vedhśālā)* स्त्री. observatory.

वेला *(velā)* वि. time; occasion.

वेश *(veś)* पु. dress; costume; uniform; external appearance.

वेश्या *(veśyā)* स्त्री. prostitute; harlot; whore.

वेश्यालय *(veśyālya)* पु. brothel.

वेष्टन *(veṣṭan)* पु. anything that encloses or wraps; enclosure; cover; veil.

वैकुंठ *(vaikuṇṭh)* पु. heaven.

वैज्ञानिक *(vaijnānik)* पु. scientist.

वैदिक *(vaidik)* वि. relating to the Veda; Vedic; prescribed in the Vedas.

वैद्य *(vidya)* पु. an expert of Indian medical science Ayurveda; Ayurvedic physician.

वैद्यक *(vaidyak)* पु. the Indian science of Medicine; Ayurveda.

वैध *(vaidh)* वि. lawful; legal; in accordance with rule; legitimate; just; constitutional.

वैधता *(vaidhatā)* स्त्री. legality lawfulness; contitutionality.

वैधव्य *(vaidhavya)* पु. widowhood.

वैधानिक *(vaidhānik)* वि. constitutional.

वैभव *(vaibhav)* पु. wealth; glory; greatness; grandeur; splendour.

वैभवशाली *(vaibhavsāli)* वि. wealthy; rich; grand; glorious; magnificent.

वैमनस्य *(vaimanasya)* पु. discordancy; enmity.

वैमानिकी *(vaimāniki)* स्त्री. aeronotics.

वैयक्तिक *(vaiyaktik)* वि. personal; individual; private; pertaining to self; subjective.

वैयाकरण *(vaiyākaran)* वि. pertaining to grammar.

वैर *(vair)* पु. enmity; opposition.

वैरागी *(vaiarāgi)* पु. religious devotee; saint.

वैराग्य *(vairāgya)* पु. freedom from passions or from worldy attachments; detachment.

वैरी *(vairi)* पु. enemy; foe.

वैवाहिक *(vaivāhik)* वि. nuptial; matrimonial; relating to marriage.

वैषम्य *(vaiṣamya)* पु. dissimilarity; unevenness; roughness; difficulty; hardship.

व्यंग्य *(vy-aṅgya)* पु. suggestiveness of the words; sarcasm; ironical remarks; irony; suggested or implied sense; satire.

व्यंग्यचित्र *(vyangya-citra)* पु. cartoon.

व्यंजक *(vy-añjak)* पु. suggestive word; gesture; suggestion; (Maths.) expression.

व्यंजन *(vyanjan)* पु. food; cooking.

व्यंजना *(vy-añjanā)* स्त्री. implied meaning of a word; expression; suggested; learned.

व्यक्त *(vy-akt)* वि. manifested; expressed; displayed; articulated; suggested meaning.

व्यक्ति *(vy-akti)* पु. individual; person.

व्यक्तिगत *(vy-aktigat)* वि. individual; personal; subjective.

व्यक्तित्व *(vy-aktitva)* पु. personality; individuality.

व्यग्र *(vy-agra)* वि. perplexed; bewildered; agitated.

व्यग्रता *(vy-agratā)* स्त्री. perplexity; agitation.

व्यतिरेक *(vy-ati-rek)* पु. contrast; difference; paucity; encroachment.

व्यथा *(vyathā)* स्त्री. pain; agony; anguish.

व्यथित *(vyathit)* वि. afflicted; distressed.

व्यभिचार *(vy-abhi-cār)* पु. fornication; adultery; debauchery.

व्यभिचारिणी *(vy-abhi-cārini)* स्त्री. wanton woman; unchaste wife.

व्यभिचारी *(vy-abhi-cāri)* पु. debauched; immoral; adulterous; violative; unlawful.

व्यय *(vy-ay)* पु. expenditure; cost; consumption; decay; cutlay.

व्यर्थ *(vy-arth)* वि. useless; futile; unnecessary; unprofitable; vain; ineffective.

व्यवधान *(vy-av-dhān)* पु. hindrance; intervention; obstruction; interruption.

व्यवसाय *(vy-ava-sāy)* पु. profession; occupation; business; employment; effort; try; practice; industry.

व्यवसायी[1] *(vy-ava-sāyi)* वि. performing; doing; employed; professional; painstaking; industrious; diligent; laborious; employed in business or trade.

व्यवसायी[2] *(vy-ava-sāyī)* पु. businessman; trader; craftsman.

व्यवस्था *(vy-ava-sthā)* स्त्री. order; system; management; arrangement; ruling; provision; settlement.

व्यवस्थापक *(vy-ava-sthāpak)* पु. manager; one who gives legal opinion; one who arranges things systematically; member of ligislative assembly.

व्यवस्थित *(vy-ava-sthit)* वि. systematic; methodical; orderly.

व्यवहार *(vy-ava-hār)* पु. behaviour; conduct; utilization; consumption; implementation; compliance; mercantile transaction; customs; usage.

व्यष्टि *(vy-aṣṭi)* स्त्री. an independent part of the community; individuality.

व्यसन *(vy-asan)* पु. addication; evil habit; excessive indulgence; calamity; distress; disaster.

व्यसनी *(vy-asanī)* वि. addicted to some vice or evil practice; excessively devoted to something.

व्यस्त *(vy-ast)* वि. engaged; busy.

व्याकरण *(vy-ā-karaṇ)* स्त्री. grammar.

व्याकुल *(vy-ākul)* वि. agitated; perplexed; restless; troubled; confounded; impatient; perturbed; curious; eager; keenly desirous; distracted.

व्याकुलता *(vy-ākulatā)* स्त्री. restlessness; perturbation; impatience; distraction; eagerness; curiousity.

व्याख्या *(vy-ā-khyā)* स्त्री. explanation; exposition; critical appreciation; commentary; interpretation.

व्याख्याता *(vy-ā-khyātā)* पु. commentator; explainer; lecturer; interpreter.

व्याख्यान *(vy-ā-khyan)* पु. speech; lecture; explanation; interpretation; narration.

व्याघ्र *(vyāghra)* पु. tiger.

व्याज *(vy-āj)* पु. pretext; pretence; trick; fraud; wickedness; hindrance; delay.

श

श *(śa)* the first sibilant of the Devnagri alphabets.

शंका *(śaṅkā)* स्त्री. doubt; uncertainty; fear; apprehension; dread; suspicion; distrust; misgiving.

शंकालु, शंकाशील *(śaṅkālu, śaṅkāsil)* वि. suspicious; distrustful.

शंकित *(śankit)* वि. suspicious; suspecting; distrustful; filled with doubt; alarmed; frightened; apprehensive.

शंकु *(śaṅku)* पु. cone.

शंख *(śaṅkh)* पु. conchshell; shell; number equal to 10;00;000 crores or a thousand billion.

शऊर *(śaūr)* पु. (अ.) mannerliness; manners; decency; etiquette; sense; sensibility.

शक *(śak)* पु. (अ.) doubt; suspicion;

illusion; apprehension.

शकर *(śakar)* पु. (फ़ा.) sugar.

शकरकंद *(śakarkand)* पु. sweet potato.

शकुन *(śakun)* पु. omen.

शक्कर *(śakkar)* see शकर।

शक्ति *(śakti)* स्त्री. strength; power; force; ability; competency; capacity; energy; potency; control; influence; effect; powerful and resourceful nation or country.

शक्तिमान, शक्तिशाली *(śaktimān, śaktiśālī)* वि. strong; powerful; mighty;forceful.

शक्तिहीन *(śaktihin)* वि. powerless; weak; impotent.

शक्ल *(śakl)* स्त्री. (अ.) shape; figure; appearance; countenance; looks; (in Geom.) diagram; figure.

शख़्स *(śakhs)* पु. (अ.) person; individual.

शग़ल *(śagal)* पु. (अ.) occupation; work.

शठ *(śaṭh)* वि. wicked; crafty; cunning; dishonest; roguish; deceitful; fraudulent.

शठता *(śaṭhatā)* स्त्री. wickedness; cunningness; craftiness; roguery; knavery; deceitfulness; perfidiousness.

शतक *(śatak)* पु. collection of one hundred stanzas; century; one hundred.

शतरंज *(śatrañj)* पु., स्त्री. (फ़ा.) chess.

शताब्दी *(śatabdi)* स्त्री. century; span of hundred years; centenary.

शतायु *(śatū)* वि. of hundred years of age.

शती *(śatī)* स्त्री. collection of hundred; century.

शत्रु *(śatru)* पु. enemy; adversary; foe; malefactor.

शत्रुता *(śatrutā)* स्त्री. enmity; hostility; animosity.

शनाख़्त, शिनाख़्त *(śanakht, śinakht)* स्त्री. (फ़ा.) identification; discretion.

शनिवार *(śanivār)* पु. Saturday.

शनैः शनैः *(śanaih-śanih)* क्रि. वि. slowly; by slow degrees; gradually; in course of time.

शपथ *(śapath)* स्त्री. oath; swearing.

शब *(śab)* स्त्री. (फ़ा.) night.

शबनम *(śabnam)* स्त्री. (फ़ा.) dew; a very thin cloth of white colour.

शबाब *(śabāb)* पु. (अ.) youthfulness; beauty; the prime of an object.

शब्द *(śabd)* पु. sound; note; noise; word; term; verbal authority.

शब्दकोश *(śabdkośa)* पु. lexicon; dictionary.

शब्दशः *(śabdśah)* वि. verbatim; word for word.

शब्दाडंबर *(śabdāmdār)* पु. bombast; verbosity; high sounding or grandiloquent word; verbiage.

शब्दावली *(śabdāvali)* स्त्री. vocabulary; words used and their order followed in a sentence etc.; terminology; glossary.

शमन *(śaman)* वि. appeasement; allaying; pacification; alleviation; quenching; extinguishing; quelling; suppression; subdual.

शमा *(śamā)* स्त्री. (अ.) wax candle; candle; lamp.

शयन *(śayan)* पु. sleep; lying down; bed; couch; bedding; copulation; sexual union.

शयनागार *(śayanāgār)* पु. bed chamber; bedroom.

शय्या *(śayyā)* स्त्री. bed; bedstead; couch.

शोर *(śor)* पु. noise.

शरण *(śaraṇ)* स्त्री. refuge; shelter; place of refuge; resort; asylum; protection; defence.

शरणागत *(śaranāgat)* वि. seeking protection or shelter.

शरणार्थी *(śaranāthi)* पु. refugee.

शरबत *(śarbat)* पु. (अ.) sweet beverage; syrup.

शरमाना *(śarmānā)* अ. क्रि. to be bashful; to feel abashed; to blush; to feel embarrassed; to feel shame; to make (one) ashamed; to put to shame; to abash.

शराफ़त *(śarāfat)* स्त्री. (अ.) nobility; civility; gentlemanliness.

शराब *(śarāb)* स्त्री. (अ.) wine; liquore.

शराबख़ोर *(śarabkhor)* वि. (अ.) addicted to drinking.

शराबख़ोरी, शराबख़्वारी *(śarabkhorī, śarabkhvārī)* स्त्री. addiction to liquor; habitual drinking; drunkenness.

शराबी *(śarābī)* पु. drunkard; boozer.

शरारत *(śarārat)* स्त्री. (अ.) wickedness; mischief; vice; villainy.

शरीक *(śarīk)* वि. (अ.) included; participating; partaking.

शरीफ़[1] *(śarīf)* पु. (अ.) gentleman; nobleman; virtuous man; man of good family; a highborn.

शरीफ़[2] *(śarīf)* वि. (अ.) gentlemanly; noble; virtuous; of good family; high born.

शरीर[1] *(śarīr)* पु. body.

शरीर[2] *(śarīr)* पु. mischievous.

शरीर-रचनाविज्ञान *(śarīr-racnā-vijnān)* पु. anatomy.

शरीरविज्ञान *(śarīr-vijnān)* पु. physiology.

शर्करा *(śarkarā)* स्त्री. sugar.

शर्त *(śart)* स्त्री. (अ.) wager; bet; condition; term; provision.

शर्तिया[1] *(śartiyā)* वि. sure; unfailing; definite.

शर्तिया[2] *(śartiyā)* क्रि. वि. surely; without fail; definitely; certainly; positively.

शर्म *(śarm)* (फ़ा.) shame; honour; regard; shyness.

शर्मनाक *(śarmnak)* वि. (फ़ा.) shameful; disgraceful.

शर्मिंदा *(śarmindā)* वि. (फ़ा.) ashamed; abashed.

शर्मीला *(śarmila)* वि. shy; shamefaced; bashful.

शलग़म, शलजम *(śalgam)* पु. (फ़ा.) turnip.

शलभ *(śalabh)* पु. moth; locust.

शल्यक्रिया *(salyakriya)* स्त्री. surgical operation; surgery.

शल्यचिकित्सक *(śalyachiketsak)* पु. surgeon.

शल्यचिकित्सा *(śalyachiketsā)* स्त्री. surgery.

शव *(śav)* पु. dead body; corpse.

शवगृह *(śavgraha)* पु. mortuary.

शवपरीक्षा *(śavpariskā)* स्त्री. postmortem; autopsy.

शवयात्रा *(śavyātrā)* स्त्री. funeral procession.

शशक *(śaśak)* पु. hare.

शशि *(śaśi)* पु. moon.

शस्त्र *(śastra)* पु. weapon; arms; instrument.

शस्त्रशाला *(śastraśālā)* arsenal; armoury.

शह *(śah)* पु. (फ़ा.) instigation; incitement; support; help; check (in chess).

शहज़ादा *(śahzādā)* पु. (फ़ा.) prince.

शहज़ादी *(śahzādī)* स्त्री. (फ़ा.) princess.

शहतीर *(śahtir)* पु. (फ़ा.) beam; girder.

शहतूत *(śahtut)* पु. (फ़ा.) mulberry (tree and fruit).

शहद *(śahd)* पु. (अ.) honey.

शहनाई *(śahnāī)* स्त्री. (फ़ा.) a musical instrument; Indian clarinet (clarionet).

शहर *(śahr)* पु. (फ़ा.) city; town.

शहरी[1] *(śahrī)* पु. city-dweller; citizen.

शहरी[2] *(śahrī)* वि. urban.

शहादत *(śahādat)* स्त्री. (अ.) martyrdom; evidence; testimony; witness; proof.

शहीद *(śahīd)* पु. (अ.) martyr.

शांत *(śānt)* वि. abated; subsided; suppressed; allayed; pacified; ceased; stopped; calm; quiet; unperturbed; tarnquil; silent; quenched; extinguished; peaceful; still; undisturbed.

शांति *(śānti)* स्त्री. peace; comfort; rest; ease; repose; abatement; subsidence; suppression; allayment pacification; calmness; tranquillity; quietness; unperturbedness; absence of passion; silence; quietude.

शाक *(śak)* पु. vegetable; pot herb; any edible leaf etc. used as a vegetable; cooked vegetable.

शाकाहारी *(śākāhārī)* वि. vegetarian.

शाख़, शाख़ा *(śākhā)* स्त्री. (फ़ा.) offshoot; bough; twig (of a tree); branch; lateral extension or subdivision; part; section etc.; school of thought etc.

शागिर्द *(śāgird)* पु. (फ़ा.) pupil; disciple; student; apprentice.

शागिर्दी *(śāgirdī)* स्त्री. apprenticeship; discipleship.

शातिर *(śātir)* वि. (फ़ा.) cunning sly; mischievous; roguish; vicious.

शादी *(śādi)* स्त्री. (फ़ा.) marriage; wedding; festivity.

शान *(śān)* स्त्री. (फ़ा.) grandeur; pomp; splendour; honour; dignity; pride; glory; vastness; whetstone.

शानदार *(śāndār)* वि. (फ़ा.) pompous; splendid; glorious; praiseworthy; stately; grand.

शाप *(śāp)* पु. curse; imprecation; anathema.

शापित *(śāpit)* वि. imprecated; cursed; accursed.

शाबाश *(śābāś)* क्रि. वि. (फा.) well done! bravo! excellent!

शाबाशी *(śābāśī)* स्त्री. praise; applause; plaudit.

शाब्दिक *(śābdik)* वि. relation to sounds or words; literal; verbal; oral; verbatim.

शाम *(śām)* स्त्री. (फ़ा.) evening; dusk.

शामियाना *(śāmiyānā)* पु. (फ़ा.) canopy.

शामिल *(śāmil)* वि. (अ.) included; associated; united (to); connected (with).

शायद *(śāyad)* क्रि. वि. (फा.) perhaps; possible; probably.

शायर *(śāyar)* पु. (अ.) poet.

शायराना *(śāyrānā)* वि. worthy of poet; like a poet; poetic.

शायरी *(śāyarī)* स्त्री. the art or practice of poetry; poetry; poetic composition.

शारीरिक *(śārīrik)* वि. relating to the body; bodily; corporal; physical; material.

शालीन *(śālīn)* वि. modest; humble; gentle; well-behaved; cultured.

शालीनता *(śālinatā)* स्त्री. modesty; gentleness; humbleness; politeness.

शावक *(śāvak)* पु. young one (of an animal).

शाश्वत *(śāśvat)* वि. eternal; perpetual; immortal; everlasting.

शाश्वतता *(śāśvatatā)* स्त्री. perpetuity.

शासक *(śāsak)* पु. ruler; administrator.

शासकीय *(śāskīya)* वि. official.

शासन *(śāsan)* पु. government; administration; rule; control; check; restraint; order; command.

शासन-तंत्र *(śāsan-tantra)* पु. government.

शासित *(śāsit)* वि. ruled; governed; administered; restrained; controlled.

शास्त्र *(śāstra)* religious or sacred treatise; sacred book; scripture; systematic knowledge; science; philosophy; any department of knowledge; discipline.

शास्त्रकार *(śāstrakār)* पु. scripturist.

शास्त्रज्ञ *(śāstrajna)* वि. conversant with scriptures.

शास्त्रार्थ *(śāstrārth)* पु. discussion; contention; debate or discourse on the scriptures.

शास्त्री *(śāstrī)* पु. one who is well versed or skilled in the Shastras; a scholar or authority on the scriptures; one who has mastered the Shastras; a great Pandit.

शास्त्रीय *(śāstrīya)* वि. scriptural; classical; authorised by or conformable to Shastras; scientific; academic.

शाह *(śāh)* पु. (फ़ा.) king; monarch; king in chess or cards.

शाही *(śāhī)* वि. (फ़ा.) royal; imperial.

शिकंजा *(śikañjā)* पु. (फ़ा.) clamp; clasp; clutches.

शिकंजी *(śikañjī)* स्त्री. lemon squash; syrup prepared from fresh lemon.

शिकन *(śikan)* स्त्री. (फ़ा.) wrinkle; crease.

शिकस्त *(sikast)* स्त्री. (फ़ा.) defeat; failure; unsuccess.

शिकायत *(śikayat)* स्त्री. (अ.) accusation; complaint; grievance; defect.

शिकार *(śikār)* पु. (अ.) hunting; hunt; prey; game; victim.

शिकारा *(śikārā)* पु. small cosy boat (in Kashmir).

शिकारी *(śikārī)* पु. hunter; huntsman.

शिक्षक *(śikṣak)* पु. teacher; educator; instructor; tutor; trainer.

शिक्षण *(śikṣaṇ)* पु. teaching; instruction.

शिक्षा *(śikṣā)* स्त्री. learning; study; instruction; education; knowledge; moral; lesson; punishment (fig.); training.

शिक्षार्थी *(śikṣārthi)* पु. student; pupil.

शिक्षाविद् *(śikṣāvid)* पु. educationist.

शिक्षित *(śikṣit)* वि. educated; taught; instructed; trained; brilliant; intelligent; gentle; tamed; learned.

शिक्षु *(śikṣu)* पु. apprentice.

शिखंडी *(śikhaṇḍī)* पु. peacock; peacocktail; cock; arrow; Lord Vishnu; son of king Drupad of Mahabharat.

शिखर *(śikhar)* पु. top; peak; pinnacle; armpit.

शिखर-सम्मेलन *(śikhar-sammelan)* पु. summit conference.

शिथिल *(śithil)* वि. loose; slack; lax; slow; tardy; languid; weary; tired; loosely done; not strictly or rigidly performed; relaxed.

शिथिलता *(śithilatā)* स्त्री. looseness; slackness; laxity; slowness; tardiness; weariness; tiredness; relaxation; remission; unrigid or unstrict performance; laxity or looseness in the construction of a sentence.

शिनाख़्त *(śinākht)* identification

शिर *(śir)* पु. head; skull; peak; summit; top; chief; principal; forehead; front; forepart.

शिरा *(śirā)* स्त्री. vein; blood-vessel.

शिरोधार्य *(śirodhrāya)* वि. acceptable; greatly honourable.

शिरोमणि *(śiromani)* वि. most outstanding.

शिला *(śilā)* स्त्री. stone; rock.

शिल्प *(śilp)* पु. handicraft; skill (in any art); craft; art.

शिल्पकार *(śilpkār)* पु. artisan; craftsman; architect.

शिल्पी *(śilpī)* पु. craftsman; artisan; architect.

शिविर *(śivir)* पु. camp; military camp; tent; fort.

शिशिर *(śiśir)* पु. cold season; winter.

शिशु *(śiśu)* पु. child; infant; baby.

शिश्न *(śiśn)* पु. penis.

शिष्ट *(śiṣṭ)* वि. noble; civil; cultured; polite; intelligent.

शिष्टता *(śiṣṭatā)* स्त्री. politeness; civility; courteousness; gentleness; good behaviour; decency.

शिष्टाचार *(śiṣṭatācār)* पु. gentlemanly conduct; proper behaviour; good manners. politeness; civility; courtesy; formal conduct or manners; formal politeness; etiquette.

शिष्य *(śisya)* पु. student; pupil; disciple; follower.

शीघ्र *(śīghra)* क्रि. वि. quickly; immediately; urgently; speedily; rapidly; soon; in a short time.

शीघ्रता *(śīghratā)* स्त्री. quickness; swiftness; haste; hastiness; hurry.

शीत *(śīt)* पु. cold; coldness; cold season; winter.

शीतल *(śītal)* वि. cool; cold; chilly; frigid; not exciting; calm.

शीतलता *(śītalatā)* स्त्री. coldness; chilliness; calmness; unexicitedness; composure.

शीतला *(śītalā)* स्त्री. smallpox.

शीर्ष *(śīrṣ)* पु. head; forehead; upper part; tip; top; (geom.) vertex; head (of account); item.

शीर्षक *(śirṣak)* पु. title; heading; caption.

शीर्षस्थ *(śīrṣastha)* वि. highest; eminent.

शील *(śīl)* पु. moral conduct; morality; good conduct; virtue; piety; modesty; politeness; humbleness; courtesy; shyness; bashfulness.

शीश *(śīś)* पु. head.

शीशम *(śīśam)* पु. Indian rose-wood tree.

शीशमहल *(śīśmahal)* पु. apartment with walls inlaid with pieces of glass; glass house.

शीशा *(śīśā)* पु. glass; looking glass; mirror.

शीशी *(śīśī)* स्त्री. small bottle; phial; vial.

शुक्र¹ *(śukr)* पु. the planet Venus; semen; sperm; Friday.

शुक्र² *(śukr)* पु. (अ.) thanks; gratitude.

शुक्रगुज़ार *(śukrgujār)* वि. (अ.) thankful; grateful; obliged.

शुक्रिया *(śukriyā)* पु. (फा.) gratitude; thanks.

शुचि *(śuci)* वि. pure; sacred; clean; clear; free from fault; flawless; guiltless; honest; upright; true; virtuous.

शुचिता *(śucitā)* स्त्री.purity; sanctity; holiness;cleanliness;clearness; honesty; virtuousness; uprightness; faultlessness; flawlessness; guiltlessness.

शुतुरमुर्ग *(śtūrmurg)* पु. (फ़ा.) ostrich.

शुद्ध *(śūddh)* वि. pure; sacred; clean; clear; purified; unadulterated; genuine; faultless; flawless; guiltless; correct; rectified; defectless.

शुद्धता *(śuddhatā)* स्त्री. purity; holiness; cleanliness; clearness; faultlessness; flawlessness; unadulteratedness; genuineness.

शुद्धि *(suddhi)* स्त्री. purity; holiness; sanctity; cleanliness; clearness; faultlessness; guiltlessness; flawlessness; correction; rectification; unadulteratedness; genuineness; cleaning; clearing.

शुबहा *(śubahā)* पु. (अ.) doubt; apprehension.

शुभ¹ *(śubh)* वि. auspicious; lucky; happy; fortunate.

शुभ² *(śubh)* पु. auspiciousness; welfare; well-being; good fortune; happiness.

शुभ्र *(śubhrā)* वि. white; shining; bright; radiant; spotless; immaculate.

शुभ्रता *(śūbhrātā)* स्त्री. whiteness; radiance; brightness; spotlessness; immaculateness.

शुरूआत *(śūruāt)* स्त्री. beginning; initiative.

शुरू *(śurrū)* पु. (अ.) beginning; commencement; rise.

शुल्क *(śulk)* पु. duty; fee; subscription.

शुश्रूषा *(śuśrśā)* स्त्री. service; attendance; nursing; narration; desire to hear; flattery.

शुष्क *(śuṣk)* वि. dried up; dry; withered; aird; droughty; unfeeling; emotionless; prosaic; uninteresting; tedious.

शुष्कता *(śuṣkātā)* स्त्री. sryness; witheredness; unfeeling temperament; emotionlessness; hardness; prosaicness; aridity; drought.

शुहरत *(śuharat)* स्त्री. (अ.) fame; reputation.

शूद्र *(śūdrā)* पु. fourth of the four principal castes of Hindus; member of the above caste.

शून्य *(śūnya)* वि. empty; void; vacant; non-existent; desolate; deserted; (in comp.) devoid (of).

शून्यता *(śūnyata)* स्त्री. blankness; vacuum.

शूर *(śūr)* पु. brave or valiant man; warrior; eminent person; sun; lion; pig; dog; cock.

शूरता *(śūratā)* स्त्री. bravery; courage; valour; heroism; gallantry.

शूरवीर *(śūrvīr)* पु. warrior; man of valour.

शूल *(śūl)* पु. spear; lance; pointed big thorn; sharp pain in the stomach; colic pain; any sharp or acute pain; grief; sorrow.

शृंखला *(śṛṅkhalā)* स्त्री. series; succession; range; line; row; queue; order; sequence; chain or belt worn round the waist; chain; fetter in general; bond; tie.

शृग *(śṛṅg)* पु. horn; top or summit (or a mountain); top of a building; turnet; point of an arrow; supremacy; possession; reign.

शृंगार *(śṛṅgār)* पु. erotic sentiment; make-up; decoration; embellishment; ornament.

शृंगारिक *(śṛṅgārik)* वि. related to love; of erotic sentiment.

शृंगारी[1] *(śṛṅgārī)* see शृंगारिक।

शृंगारी[2] *(śṛṅgārī)* lustful man; voluptuary; elegantly dressed man; make-up; elephant.

शृगाल *(śṛgāl)* पु. jackal; (fig.) coward.

शेख़ी *(śekhī)* स्त्री. (फ़ा.) vanity; boast; brag.

शेख़ीबाज़ *(śekhībāz)* पु. boaster; braggart.

शेर[1] *(śer)* पु. (फ़ा.) couplet (Urdu poetry).

शेर[2] पु. (फ़ा.) (lion; fig). fearless; courageous and brave man.

शेष[1] *(śeṣ)* वि. remaining; rest; all the other; terminated; destroyed; outstanding; left out or omitted to be said; surplus.

शेष[2] *(śeṣ)* पु. remaining portion; rest; residue; remainder; end; termination; conclusion; surplus; balance; outstanding amount.

शै *(śai)* स्त्री (अ.) thing; object.

शैक्षिक *(śaikṣik)* वि. academic; educational.

शैतान[1] *(śaitān)* पु. (अ.) devil; Satan; an evil spiril; evil genius; tyrant; wicked person.

शैतान[2] *(śaitān)* वि. naughty; mischievous; guileful; wicked.

शैतानी[1] *(śaitānī)* वि. devilish; diabolical.

शैतानी[2] *(śaitānī)* स्त्री. naughtiness; wickedness; mischief.

शैथिल्य *(śaithilya)* स्त्री. lethargy; laziness; looseness.

शैल[1] *(śail)* पु. mountain; hill; rock.

शैल[2] *(śail)* वि. pertaining to mountain or rock; rocky; hard as stone.

शैली *(śailī)* स्त्री. way; manner; method; style; mode of expression.

शैशव *(saisav)* स्त्री. infancy; childhood.

शोक *(śok)* पु. mourning; lamentation; wailing; sorrow; grief; anguish; condolence.

शोकगीत *(śokgeet)* पु. elegy.

शोकाकुल, शोकातुर *(śokākūl)* वि. overwhelmed with grief; greatly distressed.

शोख़ी *(śokhī)* स्त्री. (फ़ा.) insolence; boldness; playfulness; sportiveness; mischievousness; brightness; gaudiness; coquetry.

शोचनीय *(śocānīya)* वि. causing concern or anxiety; lamentable; deplorable; pitiable.

शोणित *(śoṇit)* पु. blood; vermillion; copper; saffron.

शोध *(śodh)* पु. research; acquittance; paying off (as of debts); purification.

शोधक[1] *(śodhak)* वि. purificatory; purifying; cleansing.

शोधक[2] *(śodhak)* पु. rectifier; corrector; researcher.

शोधन *(śodhan)* पु. purification; cleansing; refinement; correction; rectification; payment; discharge; acquittance (of debt).

शोधपत्र *(śodhpatra)* पु. research paper.

शोध-प्रबंध *(śodh-praband)* पु. thesis; research work.

शोधित *(śodhit)* वि. purified; cleansed; refined; corrected; rectified; researched; discoverd.

शोभन *(śobhan)* वि. handsome; beautiful; lovely; graceful; adorning; beautifying; befitting; becoming; proper; good; auspicious; fortunate.

शोभनीय *(śobhanīya)* वि. befitting; becoming; proper; suitable; handsome; lovely; graceful.

शोभा *(śobhā)* स्त्री. natural beauty; grace; elegance; lustre; brilliance; radiance; beautifying element; embellishment.

शोभायमान *(śobhāyamān)* वि. beautiful; graceful; lustrous; adding to the beauty of gracing (the occasion or place) by one's presence; graciously seated.

शोभित *(śobhit)* वि. beautiful; lovely; graceful; adorned; graced; decorated; embellished; graciously seated; gracing (an occasion or place) by one's presence.

शोर *(śor)* पु. (फ़ा.) cry; noise; outcry; din; tumult.

शोरगुल *(śorgul)* पु. (फ़ा.) din and noise.

शोरबा *(śorbā)* पु. (फ़ा.) soup; broth.

शोषक[1] *(śoṣak)* वि. drying up; sucking up; absorbing; absorbent.

शोषक[2] *(śoṣak)* पु. exploiter; one who exploits; absorber; that which absorbs.

शोषण *(śoṣaṇ)* पु. drying up; sucking up; suction; absorption; soaking; desiccation; exploitation.

शोषित *(śoṣit)* वि. dried up; sucked up; absorbed; exploited.

शौक़ *(śauq)* पु. (अ.) desire; yearning; fondness; deep longing; inclination; predilection; liking; interest; fancy; addiction; compelling habituation; hobby.

शौक़िया *(śauqiyā)* क्रि. वि. as a hobby; fondly; fashionably.

शौक़ीन *(śauqin)* वि. fond of fine things; desirous; longing deeply; foppish; dandy; fashionable.

शौच *(śauc)* पु. purity; cleanness; purification; voiding of excrement; evacuation of bowels.

शौचालय *(śaucālaya)* पु. latrine; lavatory.

श्मशान *(śmaśān)* पु. burning ground; cremation ground; cemetery; grave-yard; a deserted place (fig.).

श्याम *(śyām)* वि. dark blue; slightly dark complexioned; dark coloured; black.

श्यामल *(śyāmal)* वि. dark-blue; blackish; dark-complexioned.

श्रद्धांजलि *(śraddhānjalī)* स्त्री. tribute; homage.

श्रद्धा *(śraddhā)* स्त्री. respect; reverence; veneration; trust; faith; belief; confidence.

श्रद्धालु *(śraddhālu)* वि. having veneration or reverence; respectful; reverent; having faith; faithful; trustful.

श्रद्धेय *(śraddheya)* वि. venerable; reverend.

श्रम *(śram)* पु. labour; exertion; toil; hard labour; weariness; fatigue; exhaustion; effort; exercise.

श्रमजीवी[1] *(śramjīvī)* वि. working; subsisting on labour.

श्रमजीवी[2] *(śramjīvī)* पु. labourer; one who lives by one's sweat.

श्रमदान *(śramdān)* पु. voluntary contribution of labour for a public cause.

श्रमिक *(śramik)* पु. labourer.

श्रवण *(śravaṇ)* पु. hearing; audition.

श्रांत *(śrant)* वि. wearied; tired; fatigued; exhausted.

श्राद्ध *(śrāddh)* पु. a funeral rite performed in honour of the spirits of dead relatives.

श्री *(śrī)* स्त्री. the goddess of wealth; Lakshmi; wealth; riches; affluence; prosperity; plenty; grandeur; glory; magnificence; beauty; grace; fame; renown; an honorific term prefixed to names of men (mister; Mr.).

श्रीमती *(śrimatī)* स्त्री. wife; an honorific term prefixed to the name of a married woman; Mrs.; Madam.

श्रुत *(śrut)* वि. heard; listened; wellknown; famous; celebrated; renowned.

श्रुति *(śruti)* स्त्री. hearing; ear; the organ of hearing.

श्रेणि, श्रेणी *(śreṇī)* स्त्री. line;row; queue; order; sequence; series; succession; range; category; class; grade; rank.

श्रेय *(śrey)* पु. goodness; merit; worth; welfare; good fortune; well being; fame; renown; credit.

श्रेष्ठ *(śreṣṭh)* वि. best; excellent; pre-eminent; superior; great; large-hearted; noble.

श्रेष्ठता *(śreṣṭhatā)* स्त्री. superiority; eminence; excellence.

श्रेष्ठी *(śreṣṭhī)* पु. wealthy merchant; moneyed man; very rich person; the head or chief of a mercantile guild; chief of the merchants.

श्रोता *(śrotā)* पु. hearer; listener; audience (in plural)

श्लाघनीय *(ślāghanīya)* वि. admirable; praise-worthy; laudable; commendable.

श्लाघा *(ślāghā)* स्त्री. praise; admiration; commendation; flattery.

श्लील *(ślīl)* वि. not obscence; decent; cultured; graceful; affluent.

श्लेष *(śleṣ)* पु. paronomasia; agnomination; adhesion; embrace.

श्लोक *(ślok)* पु. object of praise; a stanza in sanskrit poetics; stanza or verse in general (in Sanskrit).

श्वसुर *(śvaśur)* पु. father-in-law;

श्वश्रू *(śvaśrū)* स्त्री. mother-in-law.

श्वसन *(śvāsan)* पु. breathing.

श्वान *(śvān)* पु. dog.

श्वास *(śvās)* पु. breath; respiration; asthma.

श्वेत *(śvet)* वि. white; clean; flawless; blemishless.

ष

षट्कोण *(ṣaṭkon)* पु. hexagon; any six angle figure.

षट्पद *(ṣaṭpad)* पु. bee; big male black bee; type of verse having six feet.

षड्यंत्र *(ṣaḍyantra)* पु. underhand plotting; plot; intrigue; conspiracy.

षष्ठी *(ṣaṣṭhī)* स्त्री. sixth day of a lunar fortnight; sixth day from the day of childbirth; and the celebrations of that day; (in gram.) the sixth or genitive case; possessive case.

षाण्मासिक *(ṣaṇmāsik)* वि. six monthly.

षोडश *(ṣhodś)* पु. the number sixteen.

षोडशी *(ṣhodśī)* वि. (a girl) of sixteen years of age; young (girl or woman).

स

स *(sa)* last of the three sibilants of the Devnagri alphabets.

संकट *(saṅ-kaṭ)* पु. distress; crisis; emergency; trouble; danger.

संकटपूर्ण *(saṅ-kaṭ-purna)* वि. critical; adverse; distressing.

संकर *(saṅ-kar)* पु. hybrid; cross breed; mixture.

सँकरा *(saṅ-karā)* वि. narrow; strait.

संकलन *(san-kalan)* पु. the act of heaping together; collection; compilation; anthology.

संकलित *(saṅ-kalit)* वि. amassed; assembled; compiled; anthologised; added.

संकल्प *(saṅ-kalp)* पु. determination; resolve; solemn vow; resolution; pledge.

संकाय *(saṅ-kāy)* स्त्री. faculty.

संकीर्ण *(san-kīrn)* वि. narrow; parochial.

संकुचित *(san-kucit)* वि. contracted; adridged; narrow; parochial; illiberal.

संकुल *(saṅ-kul)* वि. thick; dense; congested; filled; full; narrow.

संकेंद्रण *(saṅ-kendran)* पु. concentration.

संकेंद्रित *(saṅ-kendrit)* वि. concentrated.

संकेत *(saṅ-ket)* पु. sign; gesture; hint; signal; mark; token.

संकोच *(saṅ-koc)* पु. shrinking up; contraction; hesitation; modesty; shyness; dilemma; fix.

संकोची *(saṅ-kocī)* वि. shrinking; contractive; hesitant; shy; bashful; modest.

संक्रमण *(saṅ-kraman)* पु. transition; infection; departure.

संक्रामक *(saṅ-krāmak)* वि. infectious; contagious.

संक्षिप्त *(saṅ-kṣipt)* वि. short; abridged; brief; concise; restrained.

संक्षिप्तीकरण *(san-kṣiptikaran)* पु.

abridgement; summarization.

संक्षेप *(saṅ-kṣep)* पु. abridgement; summary; epitome; precis; abridged form.

संखिया *(saṅkhiyā)* स्त्री. arsenic.

संख्या *(saṅ-khyā)* स्त्री. reckoning; calculation; number; figure.

संग[1] *(saṅg)* पु. association; company; contact; friendship.

संग[2] *(saṅg)* पु. (फ़ा.) stone.

संगठन *(saṅ-gathan)* see संघठन।

संगठित *(saṅ-gaṭhit)* see संघठित।

संगत[1] *(saṅ-gat)* स्त्री. company; accompaniment (in music).

संगत[2] *(saṅ-gat)* वि. relevant; proper; apt; logical; compatible; consistent.

संगति *(saṅ-gati)* स्त्री. company; society; association; fitness; appropriateness; salvation; copulation; sexual intercourse; harmony; consistency; relevancy; compatibility.

संगम *(saṅ-gam)* पु. confluence (of rivers); union; junction; conjunction; mating; suitability; combat.

संगिनी *(saṅ-ginī)* स्त्री. female companion; wife.

संगी[1] *(saṅgī)* पु. companion; associate; comrade.

संगी[2] *(saṅgi)* adhesive; associated; habituated; infatuated; libidinous; lustful.

संगीत *(saṅ-gīt)* पु. music.

संगीतकार *(saṅ-gitkār)* पु. composer; musician.

संगीतज्ञ *(san-gītya)* पु. musician.

संगीन[1] *(saṅgīn)* वि. (फ़ा.) made of stone; hard; firm solid; grave; serious.

संगीन[2] *(saṅgīn)* स्त्री. (फ़ा.) bayonet.

संगृहीत *(saṅ-grahīt)* वि. collected; compiled; controlled; acquired; abridged.

संग्रह *(saṅ-grah)* पु. collection; depository; storage.

संग्रहण *(saṅ-grahan)* पु. seisure; collection; sexual intercourse; kidnap.

संग्रहणी *(saṅ-grahaṇī)* स्त्री. dysentery.

संग्रहणीय *(saṅ-grahaṇīya)* वि. preservable; worthy of acqiring.

संग्रहालय *(saṅ-grahālaya)* पु. museum.

संग्राम *(saṅ-grām)* स्त्री. battle; war.

संग्रह्य *(saṅ-grahya)* वि. fit to be collected; preservable; inculcable; conceivable.

संघ *(saṅ-gh)* पु. assemblage; multitude; crowd; organization; association; federation; union.

संघटन *(saṅ-ghaṭan)* पु. union; organization; constitution.

संघटित *(saṅ-ghaṭit)* वि. organised; unified; united.

संघर्ष *(saṅ-gharṣ)* पु. competition; rivalry; contest for superiority; struggle.

संघीय *(saṅghīya)* वि. federal.

संचय *(saṅ-cay)* पु. collection; accumulation; heap; quantity; joint.

संचरण *(sañ-caraṇ)* पु. locomotion; movement; crossing.

संचार *(sañ-cār)* पु. movement; infusion; communication; mode; method; way of life; difficult voyage; trouble; difficulty; leadership; inducement.

संचारी *(sañ-cārī)* वि. dynamic; movable; mobile; roving; communicable; unstable; momentary.

संचालक *(sañ-cālak)* पु. conductor;

director; convener.

संचालन *(sañ-cālan)* पु. conduction; control; performance; execution.

संचालित *(sañ-cālīt)* वि. directed; conducted convened.

संचित *(sañ-cit)* वि. accumulated; collected; dense; counted.

संजीदगी *(sañjidaī)* स्त्री. (फ़ा.) seriousness; sincerity; discreetness.

संजीदा *(sañjīdā)* स्त्री. (फ़ा.) serious; wise; discreet; tolerant; calm; quiet; sedate.

संजीवनी[1] *(sañ-jīvanī)* (फ़ा.) a kind of elixir (said to restore the dead to life).

संजीवनी[2] *(sañ-jīvanī)* वि. vitalising.

सँजोना *(saṁjonā)* स. क्रि. to decorate; to embellish; to put together; to arrange; to cherish.

संज्ञा *(sañ-jñā)* स्त्री. consciousness; sense; name; designation; appellation; noun (gram).

संडास *(saṇḍās)* पु. cesspool; latrine.

संत *(sant)* पु. saint; hermit.

संतत[1] *(san-tat)* वि. continuous; uninterrupted; expanded; stretched.

संतत[2] *(san-tat)* क्रि. वि. always; eternally; continuously.

संतति *(san-tati)* स्त्री. offspring; posterity; extension; continuity.

संतप्त *(san-tapt)* वि. greatly heated or inflamed; red-hot; scorched; tormented; distressed; afflicted.

संतरण *(san-taraṇ)* पु. launching.

संतरा *(santrā)* पु. orange.

संतरी *(santrī)* पु. sentry; porter.

संतान *(san-tān)* स्त्री. progeny; offspring; issue.

संताप *(san-tāp)* पु. intense heat; burning heat; remorse; penitence; repentance; agony; grief.

संतापन *(san-tāpn)* पु. heating; burning; tormenting.

संतापित *(san-tāpit)* पु. heated; burnt; blazed; tormented.

संतुलन *(san-tulan)* पु. balance; equilibrium; equipose.

संतुलित *(san-tulit)* वि. balanced; equipoised; equal.

संतुष्ट *(san-tust)* वि. satisfied; gratified; contented; consoled; comforted.

संतुष्टि *(san-tuṣṭi)* स्त्री. satisfaction; gratification; delight; patience; consolation; contentment.

संतोष *(san-toś)* पु. gratification; satisfaction; contentment; delight.

संतोषप्रद *(san-tosprad)* वि. satisfactory.

संतोषी *(san-toṣī)* वि. contented; complacent.

संत्रास *(san-trās)* पु. fear; terror; panic; dismay.

संत्रासन *(san-trānsan)* पु. terrorisation.

संदर्भ *(san-darbh)* पु. reference; context; threading; stringing; tying together; weaving; compilation; arranging; ordering; systematisation.

संदल *(sandal)* पु. (अ.) sandal wood.

संदिग्ध *(san-digdh)* वि. dubious; doubtful; uncertain; ambiguous.

संदीपन *(san-dipan)* पु. excitation; provocation; stimulus.

संदीप्त *(san-dīpt)* वि. kindled; inflamed; excited; stimulated;

aroused.

संदूक *(sandūq)* पु. (अ.) box; coffin.

संदेश *(san-deś)* पु. news; tidings; report; message.

संदेह *(san-deh)* पु. doubt; uncertainty; suspicion; misgiving.

संदेहजनक *(san-deh-janak)* वि sus-picious.

संदेहात्मक *(san-dehātamak)* वि. doubtful.

संधान *(san-dhān)* पु. fixing (an arrow to a bow); act of placing or holding together; welding.

संधि *(san-dhi)* स्त्री. treaty; joint; breach; chasm; conjunction; period of transition (in a drama).

संध्या *(san-dhyā)* स्त्री. evening; twilight; evening prayer.

संन्यास *(saṃ-ny-ās)* पु. the fourth religious order (asram); relinquishment; resignation; abandonment; renunciation.

सन्यासी *(saṃ-nyāsī)* पु. one belonging to the fourth order or asram; one who abandons or renounces.

संपत्ति *(sam-patti)* स्त्री. opulence; wealth; prosperity.

संपदा *(sam-padā)* स्त्री. wealth; opulence; estate.

संपन्न *(sam-pann)* वि. accomplished; effected; completed; endowed (with); possessed (of); prosperous; thriving; rich; perfect; fully developed.

संपर्क *(sam-park)* पु. mixture; contact; association; touch; addition; sum; intercourse.

संपादक *(sam-pādak)* पु. editor.

संपादकीय *(sam-pādakiya)* पु. editorial.

संपादन *(sam-pādan)* पु. accomplishment; enforcement; fulfilment; editing.

संपादित *(sam-pādit)* वि. accomplished; edited.

संपूरक *(sam-purak)* वि. supplementary; complementary.

संपूर्ण *(sam-pūrṇ)* वि. all; whole; complete; entire; completed; finished.

संपूर्णता *(sam-pūrṇatā)* स्त्री. entirety; completness.

सँपेरा *(sampérā)* पु. snake-charmer.

सँपोला *(sampolā)* पु. young one of a snake.

संप्रदान *(sam-pra-dān)* पु. (gram.) dative case; gift; bestowal.

संप्रदाय *(sam-pra-dāy)* पु. traditional doctrine or faith; sect; community.

संप्रेक्षण *(sam-preṣaṇ)* पु. observation; inspection.

संप्रेषक *(sam-presak)* पु. transmitter.

संप्रेषण *(sam-prêṣaṇ)* पु. transmission

संबंध *(sam-bandh)* पु. relation; relationship; friendly connection; friendship; relation; as the meaning of the genitive case (in gram.); intimacy; marriage.

संबंधी *(sam-bandhī)* वि. connected with; belonging to; related (to).

संबद्ध *(sam-baddh)* वि. joined; bound; fastened together; attached; connected (with); related (to); belonging (to); affiliated (to).

संबल *(sam-bal)* पु. support; backing; stock of provisions for a journey; water.

संबोधन *(sam-bodhan)* पु. address; accost; an epithet (used in calling a person); (gram.) vocative case; awaking.

संबोधित *(sam-bodhit)* वि. addressed.

सँभलना *(saṁbhalnā)* अ. क्रि. to recoup; to be alert; to be cautious; to recuperate.

संभव[1] *(sam-bhav)* वि. possible; probable.

संभव[2] *(sam-bhav)* पु. birth; existence; happening; cause; meeting; union; copulation; capability; possibility; hint; sign; match.

संभवत *(sam-bhavta)* क्रि. वि. probably; perhaps; possibly.

सँभालना *(saṁbhālnā)* स. क्रि. to support; to sustain; to look after; to manage; to superintend; to hold up; to uphold; to prop; to reconcile; to amend.

संभावना *(sam-bhāvanā)* स्त्री. possibility; probability; likelihood.

संभावित *(sam-bhāvit)* वि. probable; likely.

संभाव्य *(sam-bhāvya)* वि. imaginable; probable; speculative; proper; fit.

संभाषण *(sam-bhāṣaṇ)* पु. conversation; discourse; debate; discussion.

संभोग *(sam-bhog)* पु. sexual union; coition; consumption; enjoyment.

संभोग्य *(sam-bhogya)* वि. consumable; enjoyable.

संभ्रांत *(sam-bhrānt)* वि. respectable; confused; deluded; perplexed; perturbed; agitated.

संभ्रांति *(sam-bhrānti)* स्त्री. uneasiness; eagerness; haste; confusion; astoundment.

संयंत्र *(saṃ-yantra)* पु. plant; machinery.

संयत *(saṃ-yat)* वि. controlled; disciplined; regulated; confined; limited.

संयम *(sam-yam)* पु. restraint; control; continence; sobriety; temperance; forbearance; moderation; discipline.

संयुक्त *(saṃ-yukt)* वि. connected; united; consisting of two or more partners; combined.

संयोग *(saṃ-yog)* पु. combination; communion; association; chance; coincidence; union conjunct consont; wedlock; copulation.

संयोजक[1] *(saṃ-yojak)* पु. joining together; connecting.

संयोजक[2] *(saṃ-yojak)* वि. convener; conjunction (gram.).

संयोजन *(saṃ-yojan)* पु. unification; combination; arrangement.

संरक्षक *(saṃ-rakṣak)* पु. custodian; protector; guardian; patron; warden.

संरक्षण *(saṃ-raksaṇ)* पु. protection; patronage; guardianship; supervision.

संरचना *(saṃ-racanā)* स्त्री. construction; structure; formation.

संलग्न *(saṃ-lagn)* वि. attached; appended; absorbed.

संलाप *(saṃ-lāp)* पु. conversation; discourse.

संलापी *(saṃ-lāpī)* वि. talkative.

संवतत् *(saṃ-vatat)* पु. year; era.

संवर्द्धन *(saṃ-vardhan)* संवर्धन पु. augmentation; increase; bringing up; rearing; raising; culture(of plants; birds etc.);

enrichment; promotion; growth; development.

संवाद *(saṃ-vād)* पु. conversation; dialogue; information; news.

संवाददाता *(saṃ-vād-dātā)* पु. correspondent; pressman.

सँवारना *(saṁvārnā)* स. क्रि. to dress; to decorate; to arrange; to methodize; to correct; to mend; to improve.

संवाहक *(saṁvāhak)* पु. carrier; conductor.

संविदा *(saṃvīdā)* स्त्री. contract.

संविधान *(saṁ-vidhān)* पु. constitution.

संवेग *(saṁvak)* पु. emotion; passion; momentum; impetus; impulse; intensity; force.

संवेदन *(sam-vedan)* पु. sensation; feeling; making own; communication.

संवेदनशील *(saṃ-vedanasil)* वि. sensitive; emotional.

संवेदना *(sam-vedanā)* स्त्री. sensitivity; sensation; sympathy; condolence.

संवैधानिक *(samvaidhānik)* वि. constitutional.

संशय *(saṃ-śay)* पु. uncertainty; risk; peril; danger; apprehension; suspicion; doubt.

संशयी *(saṃ-śayī)* पु. wavering or sceptic person.

संशोधक[1] *(saṃ-śodhak)* पु. mender; rectifier; purifier; refiner.

संशोधक[2] *(saṃ-śodhak)* वि. corrective; recftifying; reformative.

संशोधन *(sam-śodhan)* पु. purification; cleansing; correction; amendment.

संशोधित *(saṃ-śodhit)* वि. completely cleansed and purified; corrected; amended.

संश्लिष्ट *(saṃ-śliṣṭ)* वि. mixed up; synthesised; synthetic.

संश्लेषण *(saṃ-śleṣan)* पु. synthesis; mixture; blend.

संसक्त *(saṃ-sakt)* वि. adjoining; continuous; attached; mixed up.

संसद् *(saṃ-sad)* स्त्री. parliament.

संसदीय *(saṃsadīya)* वि. parliamentary.

संसर्ग *(saṃ-sarg)* पु. contact; company; association; copulation; intercourse; intimacy; closeness; contagion; connection; conjunction.

संसाधन *(saṃ-sādhan)* पु. accomplishment; prepartion; resources.

संसार *(saṃ-sār)* पु. mundane existence; the world.

संसिक्त *(sam-sikt)* वि. drenched; soaked; fertilized.

संसिद्धि *(saṃ-sīdhī)* स्त्री. accomplishment; success; salvation.

संसूचन *(saṃ-sūcan)* पु. exposure; intimation; reproof; condemnation; suggestion; hint.

संसृति *(saṃ-sṛti)* स्त्री. process of birth and rebirth; flow; continuity.

संसृष्टि *(saṃ-sṛsti)* being born together; association; union; accumulation; composition; creation.

संस्कार *(saṃ-skār)* पु. refinement; mental impression; ritual; sacrament; ceremony; culture.

संस्कृत *(saṃ-skṛt)* वि. cultured; refined; polished.

संस्कृति *(saṃ-skṛti)* स्त्री. civilization; culture; perfection; purification; decoration; determination; industry; tradition.

संस्तुत *(saṃ-stut)* वि. recommended.

संस्तुति *(saṃ-stutī)* स्त्री. recommendation; commendation.

संस्था *(saṃ-sthā)* स्त्री. institution; organisation; committee.

संस्थान *(saṃ-sthān)* पु. institute; institution; structure; configuration.

संस्थापक *(sam-sthāpak)* पु. founder; precusor; pioneer.

संस्थापन *(saṃ-sthāpan)* पु. act of establishing; founding; pioneering; introducing something; establishment.

संस्पर्शी *(saṃ-sparśī)* वि. touching; coming in contact.

संस्मरण *(saṃ-smaran)* पु. remembering; calling to mind; memoirs; reminiscences; recollection.

संहार *(saṁhār)* पु. annihilation; destruction; massacre.

सकना *(saknā)* अ. क्रि. can; may; to be able; to be competent.

सकपकाना *(sakpakānā)* अ. क्रि. to be started; to hesitate; to be shaky.

सकरकंद *(sakarkand)* पु. sweet potato.

सकर्मक *(sa-karmak)* वि. (in Gram.) having an object; transitive.

सकल *(sakal)* वि. all; entire; whole; gross.

सकाम *(sa-kām)* वि. desirous; lustful.

सकारना *(sakārnā)* स. क्रि. to accept or endorse as accepted (a bill); to accept; to agree.

सकुचाना *(sakucānā)* अ. क्रि. to hesitate; to blush; to wither; to contract; to put to shame.

सक़्क़ा *(saqqā)* पु. (फ़ा.) watercarrier.

सक्रिय *(sa-kriya)* वि. active.

सक्रियता *(sa-kriyatā)* स्त्री. activeness.

सक्षम *(sa-kṣam)* वि. capable; efficient; competent; authorised.

सखा *(sakhā)* पु. friend; associate; companion.

सखी *(sakhī)* स्त्री. a woman's female friend or confidant.

सख़्त *(sakht)* वि. hard; stiff; difficult; intense; vehement; violent; excessive.

सख़्ती *(sakhtī)* स्त्री. strictness; stiffiness; rigidity; atrocity; cruelty.

सगा *(sagā)* वि. real; born of the same parents; related in blood.

सगाई *(sagāī)* स्त्री. betrothal; engagement.

सगोत्र *(sa-gotra)* वि. being of the same family or kin; related.

सघन *(sa-ghan)* वि. thick;dense; solid; cloudy.

सच[1] *(sac)* वि. true; real.

सच[2] *(sac)* पु. truth; reality.

सचमुच *(sacmuc)* क्रि. वि. truly; verily; indeed.

सचाई *(sacāī)* स्त्री. truth; reality; sincerity; honesty.

सचित्र *(sa-citr)* वि. pictorial; picturesque; illustrated.

सचिव *(saciv)* पु. minister; counsellor; secretary.

सचिवालय *(sacivālaya)* पु. secretariat.

सचेत *(sa-cet)* वि. conscious; watchful.

सचेतक *(sa-cetak)* पु. one who is cautious.

सचेतन *(sa-cetan)* वि. conscious.

सचेष्ट *(sa-ceṣṭ)* वि. making efforts;

active.

सच्चा *(saccā)* वि. true; genuine; real; honest; sincere; pure; unalloyed; faithful.

सच्चाई *(saccāī)* स्त्री. truth; sincerity; faithfulness.

सजग *(sa-jag)* वि. alert; cautious; vigilant.

सजधज *(sa-jdaj)* स्त्री. ornamentation; adornment.

सजन *(sajan)* पु. husband; beloved; darling.

सजना *(sajnā)* अ. क्रि. to be adorned or decorated; to be well arranged or neatly dressed; to be ready for a battle etc.; to put on; to wear; to decorate; to arrange.

सजनी *(sajnī)* स्त्री. sweetheart; beloved; wife; friend.

सजल *(sa-jal)* वि. wet; moist;humid.

सज़ा *(sazā)* स्त्री. (फ़ा.) punishment; penalty; revenge; imprisonment.

सजाति, सजातीय *(sa-jāti)* वि. of one and the same species; of the same tribe or caste or race; homogeneous.

सजाना *(sajānā)* स. क्रि. to furnish; to arrange; to decorate; to beautify; to embellish; to dress neatly.

सजावट *(sajāvat)* स्त्री. decoration; ornamentation; make-up; display.

सजीला *(sajīlā)* वि. welस.dressed; graceful; handsome; stylish.

सजीव *(sa-jīv)* वि. animate; living; alive.

सज्जन *(sajjan)* पु. gentleman; nobleman.

सज्जा *(sajjā)* स्त्री. apparatus; equipment; dress; decoration.

सज्जित *(sajjit)* वि. dressed; decorated; embellished; equipped.

सटना *(saṭnā)* अ. क्रि. to stick; to adhere; to come close; to be in physical contact; to be adjacent.

सटपट *(saṭpat)* स्त्री. hesitation; dubiousness.

सटपटाना *(saṭpatānā)* अ. क्रि. to be amazed or confounded; to be unnerved; to hesitate.

सटीक *(sa-tīk)* वि. accompanied by a commentary; apt; befitting; correct and accurate; meaningful.

सट्टा *(saṭṭā)* पु. speculation.

सठियाना *(saṭhiyānā)* अ. क्रि. to be of sixty years; to become decrepit; to be in (one's) dotage; to be senile.

सड़क *(saṛak)* स्त्री. road; highway.

सड़न *(saṛan)* स्त्री. decay; decomposition; putrefaction; rottenness.

सड़ना *(saṛnā)* अ. क्रि. to decay; to rot; to be in misery.

सड़ांध *(saṛāṁdh)* स्त्री. putrefaction; stench; putrescence; putridity; stink.

सड़ियल *(saṛiyal)* वि. worthless; good for nothing; dirty; shabby.

सत *(sat)* पु. essence; juice; strength; vitality; truth; truthfulness.

सतत[1] *(satat)* वि. constant; lasting; incessant.

सतत[2] *(satat)* क्रि. वि. incessantly; uninterrruptedly.

सतर्क *(sa-tark)* वि. alert; cautious; careful; argumentative; reasoned; logical.

सतर्कता *(sa-taratā)* स्त्री. vigilance;

alertness.

सतह *(satah)* स्त्री. (अ.) surface; level.

सतही *(satahī)* वि. of or belonging to a surface; superficial.

सताना *(satānā)* स. क्रि. to harass; to torment; to trouble.

सती *(satī)* स्त्री. chaste woman; woman who immolates herself on her husband's funeral pyre.

सतीत्व, सतीपन *(satitva)* पु. virtuousness; chastity.

सत् *(satt)* वि. living; existing; existent; good; virtuous; honest; excellent; best.

सत्कार *(satkār)* पु. hospitality; reverence; respect; honour.

सत्त *(satt)* पु. essence; extract.

सत्ता *(sattā)* स्त्री. existence; entity; being; power; authority; sovereignty.

सत्ताधारी *(sattādhārī)* पु. man in power; man of authority.

सत्पथ *(satpath)* पु. path of virtue; noble course; good behaviour.

सत्पात्र *(satpātra)* पु. deserving person.

सत्त्व *(sattva)* पु. substance; strength; vitality; vigour; natural property or quality; extract; essence.

सत्य[1] *(satya)* वि. true; real; genuine.

सत्य[2] *(satya)* पु. truth; reality.

सत्यकाम *(satyakām)* वि. truth-loving.

सत्यता *(satyatā)* स्त्री. truth; veracity; reality; eternity.

सत्याग्रह *(satyāgraha)* पु. satyagraha (insistence on truth); passive resistance.

सत्याग्रही *(satyā-grahi)* पु. one who offers passive resistance.

सत्यानास *(satyānās)* पु. complete ruin; devastation; total destruction.

सत्यानासी *(satyā-nāsi)* वि. ruinous; devastating; destructive.

सत्वर[1] *(sa-tvar)* वि. speedy; swift; quick.

सत्वर[2] *(sa-tvar)* क्रि. वि. quickly; speedily.

सत्संग *(satsang)* पु. association with virtuous people; assembly of saints.

सदन *(sadan)* पु. residence; house; dwelling place; either house of legislature.

सदमा *(sadmā)* पु. (अ.) emotional stroke; shock.

सदय *(sa-day)* वि. kind; compassionate; merciful.

सदर[1] *(sadar)* वि. (अ.) head; chief.

सदर[2] *(sadar)* पु. (अ.) chairman; president; upper or uppermost part or end (of anything).

सदस्य *(sadasya)* पु. member.

सदस्यता *(sadasyata)* स्त्री. membership.

सदा[1] *(sadā)* क्रि. वि. always; perpetually; continually; ever.

सदा[2] *(sadā)* पु. (अ.) call; voice; prayer; entreaty.

सदाचार *(sadācār)* पु. virtuous conduct.

सदाबहार *(sadābahār)* वि. evergreen; perennial.

सदी *(sadī)* स्त्री. (फा) century; a hundred years.

सदुपयोग *(sadūpayog)* पु. good or proper use.

सदृश *(sa-dṛś)* वि. resembling; of the same rank; similar; semblant.

सदृशता *(sa-dṛśatā)* स्त्री. similarity; resemblance.

सदेह[1] *(sa-deh)* वि. with the body;

in a physical form; corporeal bodied.

सदेह² *(sa-deh)* क्रि. वि. bodily; physically.

सदैव *(sadaiv)* क्रि. वि. always; ever.

सद्गती *(sad-gatī)* स्त्री. salvation.

सद्गुण *(sad-gūn)* पु. virtue; merit.

सद्गुणी *(sad-gunī)* वि. virtuous; meritorious.

सद्गुरू *(sad-guru)* पु. worthy preceptor; teacher.

सद्भाव *(sad-bhāv)* पु. kindly feelling; amiability; understanding; goodwill.

सधना *(sadhnā)* अ. क्रि. to be accomplished; to be finished; to be familiarized; to be accustomed; to be trained.

सधवा *(sadhavā)* स्त्री. woman whose husband is alive.

सनक *(sanak)* स्त्री. craze; mania; caprice; eccentricity; whim.

सनकी *(sankī)* वि. whimsical; crazy; eccentric.

सनद *(sanad)* स्त्री. (अ.) testimonial; certificate.

सनम *(sanam)* पु. (अ.) idol; beloved.

सनसनाना *(sansanānā)* अ. क्रि. to produce a whizzing sound; to have a thrilling sensation.

सनसनी *(sansanī)* स्त्री. tingling or thrilling sensation; panic.

सनातन *(sanātan)* वि. perpetual; constant; eternal; primeval; ancient; orthodox.

सन् *(san)* पु. era; year.

सन्न *(sann)* वि. stunned; stupefid; contracted; shrunken; slow; inactive.

सन्नद्ध *(san-naddh)* वि. ready; prepared; tied together; bound; attached; appended.

सन्नाटा *(sannāṭā)* पु. silence; solitude; quietude.

सन्मार्ग *(sanmārg)* पु. right path; path of virtue.

सन्मुख *(sanmūkh)* see सम्मुख।

सपत्नीक *(sa-patnīk)* वि. accompanied by one's wife.

सपना *(sapnā)* पु. dream.

सपरिवार *(sa-pari-vār)* वि. with family.

सपाट *(sapāṭ)* वि. flat; smooth; even; plain.

सपूत *(sapūt)* पु. dutiful or worthy son.

सपेरा *(saperā)* पु. snake charmer.

सप्ताह *(saptâh)* पु. week.

सफ़र *(safar)* पु. (अ.) journey; travel.

सफ़रनामा *(safarnāmā)* पु. travelogue.

सफल *(sa-phal)* वि. fruitful; productive; accomplished; fulfilled· successful; materialised.

सफलता *(sa-phaltā)* स्त्री. success; fulfilment; purposiveness; achievement.

सफ़ाचट *(sa-fācat)* वि. perfectly clean; blank; tonsured; cleanshaven.

सफ़ाई *(safāī)* स्त्री. (अ.) cleanliness; purity; clarification; defence (in law suit); smoothness; simplicity; honesty; uprightness; amity; reconciliation; devastation.

सफ़ाया *(safāyā)* पु. clean sweep; ruinnation.

सफ़ेद *(safed)* वि. white; clean and bright.

सफ़ेदपोश *(safedpoś)* वि. white-collared; dressed in white.

सफ़ेदा *(safedā)* पु. white lead; a kind of mango; eucalyptus; morning light; a kind of melon.

सफ़ेदी *(safedī)* पु. whiteness; white-wash.

सब *(sab)* वि. all; entire; whole; total.

सबक़ *(sabaq)* पु. (अ.) lesson; moral.

सबब *(sabab)* पु. (अ.) cause; reason; basis; ground.

सबल *(sa-bal)* वि. strong; powerful; valid.

सबूत *(sabūt)* see सुबूत।

सबेरा *(saberā)* see सवेरा।

सब्ज़ *(sabz)* वि. (फ़ा.) green.

सब्ज़ी *(sabzī)* स्त्री. (फ़ा.) herbage; vegetables; verdure; greenery greenness.

सब्र *(sabr)* पु. (अ.) patience; selfrestraint; contentment; endurance; forbearance.

सभा *(sabhā)* स्त्री. assembly; meeting; association; society.

सभाकक्ष *(sabhā-kakś)* पु. assembly-hall; chamber; lobby.

सभासद *(sabhā-sad)* पु. member of an assembly.

सभ्य *(sabhya)* वि. refined; civilized; cultured; civil.

सभ्यता *(sabhyātā)* स्त्री. civilization; culture; courtesy; decency; good etiquette.

समंजन *(sam-añjan)* पु. co-ordination; adjustment; dovetailing; massage; anointment.

सम *(sam)* वि. plain; smooth; even; homogeneous; similar; equal; impartial; honest.

समकक्ष *(sam-kakś)* वि. equal; equivalent.

समकालीन *(sam-kālīn)* वि. contemporary; contemporaneous.

समकोण *(sam-koṇ)* पु. right angle.

समक्ष *(sam-akṣ)* क्रि. वि. before; in front.

समग्र *(sam-agra)* वि. all; entire; whole.

समझ *(samajh)* स्त्री. understanding grasp; perception; sense; wisdom.

समझदार *(samjhdār)* वि. intelligent; sensible; wise.

समझदारी *(samajhdari)* स्त्री. understanding; wisdom.

समझना *(samjhna)* स. क्रि. to understand; grasp; to think; consider; to suppose; deem.

समझाना *(samjhānā)* स. क्रि. to explain; to advise; to persuade.

समझौता *(samjhautā)* पु. compromise; reconciliation; agreement; pact.

समतल[1] *(sam-tal)* वि. level; even; plain.

समतल[2] *(sam-tal)* पु. plain surface.

समता *(samatā)* स्त्री. similarity; equality; parity; evenness; impartiality.

समतुल्य *(samtulya)* वि. equivalent; similar.

समदर्शी *(sam-darśī)* वि. looking at both sides; impartial.

समधी *(samdhī)* पु. son's or daughter's father-in-law.

समन्वय *(sam-anv-ay)* पु. coordination; harmony.

समन्वित *(sam-anv-it)* वि. coordinated; harmonized.

समय *(sam-ay)* पु. time; hour; period; opportunity; occasion; last time; end; tradition.

समर *(sam-ar)* पु. war; battle.

समरनीति *(sam-ar-nītī)* स्त्री. strategy.

समरभूमि *(sam-ar-bhumi)* स्त्री. battlefield.

समरस *(sam-ras)* *वि.* harmonious; equanimous.

समरसता *(sam-rastā)* *स्त्री.* equanimity; harmony.

समर्थ *(sam-arth)* *वि.* powerful; strong; capable; competent; made suitable;prepared; having same aim.

समर्थक[1] *(sam-arthak)* *पु.* supporter; vindicator.

समर्थक[2] *(sam-arthak)* *वि.* capable; competent; supporting; confirmative; corroborative.

समर्थन *(sam-arthan)* *पु.* support; corroboration; vindication.

समर्थित *(sam-arthit)* *वि.* supported; vindicated.

समर्पक *(sam-arpak)* *वि.* surrendering (person).

समर्पण *(sam-arpan)* *पु.* surrender; dedication; presentation.

समर्पित *(sam-arpit)* *वि.* surrendered; dedicated.

समवाय *(sam-āvây)* *पु.* collection; multitude; company; intimacy; inseparable relationship; concourse; concomitance.

समवायी *(sam-āvâyi)* *वि.* inseparable; concomitant; substantial.

समवेत *(sam-avêt)* *वि.* collective; enternally related; permeated.

समवेतगान *(sam-avêtgān)* *पु.*chorus; choral song.

समवेदना *(sam-vedanā)* *स्त्री.* condolence; sympathy.

समशीतोष्ण *(sam-śetosaṇ)* *वि.* temperate; moderate.

समष्टि *(sam-asṭi)* *स्त्री.* collectivenes; totality; aggregate.

समसामयिक *(sam-sāmayik)* *वि.* contemporary.

समस्त *(sam-ast)* *वि.* all; whole entire; complete.

समस्या *(sam-asyā)* *स्त्री.* problem; last portion or line of a metrical composition which is meant for completion in the same metre by a competitor.

समाँ *(samāṁ)* *पु.* (*अ.*) time; occasion; weather; season; scene; landscape; view; spectacle.

समागत *(sam-ā-gat)* *वि.* arrived; returned.

समाचार *(sam-ā-cār)* *पु.* news; report; message; behaviour; conduct; convention; tradition; discourse; conversation.

समाचार-पत्र *(sam-ā-cār-patra)* *पु.* newspaper.

समाज *(sam-āj)* *पु.* community; society; congregation; club; association.

समाजवाद *(sam-āj-vād)* *पु.* socialism.

समाजवादी *(sam-āj-vādī)* *पु.* socialist.

समाजशास्त्र *(sam-āj-sastra)* *पु.* sociology.

समाजशास्त्री *(sam-āj-sastrī)* *पु.* sociologist.

समाजशास्त्रीय *(sam-āj-sastrīya)* *वि.* sociological.

समाजीकरण *(samājīkaran)* *वि.* socialisation.

समादरणीय *(sam-ā-daraṇīya)* *वि.* honourable; esteemed.

समादृत *(sam-ā-dṛt)* *वि.* respected; honoured.

समाधान *(sam-ā-dhān)* *पु.* solution; unification; matching; curiosity; meditation; removal of doubt; abrogation; closeness; stability; exposition; acceptance.

समाधि *(sam-ā-dhi)* स्त्री. meditation; tranee; grave; tomb; memorial.

समान *(samān)* वि. equal; equivalent; alike; identical; tantmount.

समानता *(samānatā)* स्त्री. parity; equality; similarity; likeness.

समानांतर *(samānāntar)* वि. parallel.

समाना *(samānā)* अ. क्रि. to be contained (in); to permeate; to pervade; to be assimilated.

समानार्थक *(samānārthak)* वि. having the same meaning; synonymous.

समापक *(sam-āpak)* वि. concluding; closing; slaughterous.

समापन *(sam-āpan)* पु. completion; conclusion; slaughtering; killing; winding up; closure; trance.

समाप्त *(sam-āpt)* वि. completed; concluded; exhausted; finished; terminated.

समाप्तप्राय *(sam-āpt-prāya)* वि. almost finished; nearing completion.

समाप्ति *(sam-āptī)* स्त्री. completion; end; termination; expirty; expiration; extinction.

समायोजक *(sam-ā-yojak)* पु. one who adjusts; adjuster; compere.

समायोजन *(sam-ā-yojan)* पु. comparing; adjustment.

समारंभ *(sam-rambh)* पु. commencement; inauguration.

समारोह *(sam-ā-roh)* पु. function; celebration; festivity.

समालोचक *(sam-ā-locak)* पु. critic.

समालोचना *(sam-ā-locanā)* स्त्री. criticism.

समाविष्ट *(sam-ā-viṣṭ)* वि. entered; included; incorported.

समावेश *(sam-ā-veś)* पु. inclusion; entry; incorporation; pervasion; permeation.

समास *(sam-ās)* पु. conjunction; combination; union; contraction; abbreviation; compound word.

समाहार *(sam-a-hār)* पु. collection; accumulation; concentration; heap; pile; procuration; sum; total; aggregate; conjunction; connection (of words or sentences); compounding of words.

समाहित *(sam-ā-hit)* वि. brought together; assembled; concentrated; composed; collected; calm (as mind).

समिति *(sam-iti)* स्त्री. committee; union; association.

समीकरण *(samīkaraṇ)* पु. the act of making even or equal; equalization; equation.

समीक्षक *(sam-īkṣak)* पु. reviewer. critic.

समीक्षा *(sam-īkṣā)* स्त्री. review; criticism; critique; commentary.

समीक्षाकार *(sam-īkṣākār)* see समीक्षक।

समीचीन *(samīcīn)* वि. fit; proper; right; equitable.

समीचीनता *(samicinatā)* स्त्री. propriety; fitness; equitability.

समीप *(samīp)* वि. near; adjacent.

समीपता *(samīpatā)* स्त्री. nearness; proximity.

समीपवर्ती *(samīpvartī)* वि. adjacent; neighbouring.

समीर, समीरण *(sam-īr)* पु. wind; air; breeze.

समुचित *(sam-ucit)* वि. fit; right; proper; appropriate.

समुच्चय *(sam-uc-cay)* पु. collection; accumulation; (in gram.) conjunction of words.

समुदाय *(sam-ud-āy)* पु. group; assembly; community.

समुद्र *(sam-udra)* sea; ocean.

समुद्री, समुद्रीय *(sam-udrī)* वि. marine; oceanic; pertaining to the sea.

समुद्री डाकू *(sam-udrī-dāku)* पु. pirate.

समुद्री तार *(sam-udrī-tār)* पु. cable.

समूचा *(samūcā)* वि. whole; entire; complete.

समूह *(sam-ūh)* पु. quantity; heap; group; multitude; assemblage; community.

समृद्ध *(sam-raddh)* वि. very prosperous; flourishing; wealthy.

समृद्धि *(sam-ṛddhi)* स्त्री. prosperity; affluence; richness.

समेटना *(sametṇā)* स. क्रि. to collect together; to amass; to wind up.

समेत[1] *(sam-êt)* वि. united together; associated (with).

समेत[2] *(sam-êt)* क्रि. वि. with; together with; along with.

सम्मत *(sam-mat)* वि. of one mind; of the same opinion; unanimous; supported; approved; acknowledged; authenticated.

सम्मति *(sam-mati)* स्त्री. advice; opinion; consent; agreement.

सम्मान *(sam-mān)* पु. honour; respect; homage; distinction.

सम्माननीय *(sam-mānanīya)* see सम्मान्य।

सम्मानित *(sam-mānit)* स्त्री. honoured; respected.

सम्मान्य *(sam-mānya)* वि. honour; respect; homage.

सम्मिलित *(sam-milit)* वि. included; collective.

सम्मिश्रण *(sam-miśraṇ)* पु. mixture; composition; compound; adulteration.

सम्मुख *(sam-mukh)* वि. in front (of) in the presence (of); before; opposite.

सम्मेलन *(sam-melan)* पु. gathering conference; mixture; combination.

सम्मोह *(sam-moh)* पु. hypnosis; infatuation; fascination; ignorance; folly; uneasiness; unconsciousness.

सम्मोहक *(sam-mohak)* वि. hypnotic; hypnotising; fascinating.

सम्मोहन *(sam-mohan)* पु. fascination; hypnosis; beguilement.

सम्मोहित *(sam-mohit)* वि. hypnotised; fascinated; charmed; made unconscious; flabbergasted.

सम्यक् *(samyak)* वि. right; fit; appropriate; correct; accurate.

सम्राज्ञी *(samrājñī)* स्त्री. empress.

सम्राट् *(samrāt)* पु. emperor.

सयाना *(sayānā)* वि. grown up; adolescent; sagacious; wise; clever; shrewd; cunning.

सरकना *(saraknā)* अ. क्रि. to slide; to slip; to crawl; to move slowly.

सरकार *(sarkār)* स्त्री. (फ़ा.) government.

सरकारी *(sarkārī)* वि. (फ़ा.) official; governmental.

सरग़ना *(sarganā)* पु. (फ़ा.) ringleader.

सरगर्मी *(sargarmī)* स्त्री. hectic activity.

सरज़मीन *(sarzamiṇ)* स्त्री. native country.

सरपंच *(sarpanch)* पु. (फ़ा.) head of a panchayat.

सरपट *(sarpaṭ)* *वि.* quick; galloping.

सरफ़रोशी *(sarforśī)* *स्त्री.* (*फ़ा.*) sacrifice of life.

सरमाया *(sarmāyā)* *पु.* (*फ़ा.*) capital.

सरमायेदार *(sarmāyedār)* *पु.* (*फ़ा.*) capitalist.

सरमायेदारी *(sarmāyedāri)* *स्त्री.* (*फ़ा.*) capitalism.

सरल *(saral)* *वि.* straight; not crooked; straightforward; upright; honest; sincere; artless; simple; easy; ingenuous.

सरलता *(saralatā)* *स्त्री.* artlessness; simplicity; easiness.

सरस *(sa-ras)* *वि.* juicy; sapid; fresh; new; blooming; beautiful; elegant; interesting; humorous.

सरसों *(sarsoṁ)* *स्त्री.* mustard seed or plant.

सरहद *(sarhad)* *स्त्री.* (*फ़ा.*) boundary; frontiers; border.

सराफ़ *(sarāf)* *पु.* (*अ.*) person who deals in gold; jeweller; a money changer.

सराबोर *(sarābor)* *वि.* completely drenched; soaked.

सराय *(sarāy)* *स्त्री.* (*फ़ा.*) inn; tavern; hostelry.

सरासर *(sarāsar)* *क्रि. वि.* wholly; entirely; out and out.

सराहना[1] *(sarāhnā)* *स्त्री.* praise; eulogy.

सराहना[2] *(sarāhnā)* *स. क्रि.* to praise; commend; applaud.

सराहनीय *(sarāhniya)* *वि.* praise worthy; laudable.

सरिता *(saritā)* *स्त्री.* river; stream; flow; current.

सरीखा *(sarīkhā)* *वि.* similar; resembling.

सरोज *(saroj)* *पु.* lotus.

सरोवर *(sarovar)* *पु.* large lake or pond.

सर्ग *(sarg)* *पु.* section; chapter; canto.

सर्द *(sard)* *वि.* (*फ़ा.*) cold; cool; insipid; tasteless; lifeless.

सर्दी *(sardī)* *स्त्री.* cold; winter; chill.

सर्प *(sarp)* *पु.* serpent; snake.

सर्पण *(sarpan)* *पु.* crawling; slipping away stealthily; moving crookedly.

सर्पिणी *(sarpinī)* *स्त्री.* female snake.

सर्पिल *(sarpil)* *वि.* serpentine.

सर्राफ़ *(sarrāf)* see सराफ़।

सर्व *(sarv)* *वि.* all; whole; entire; complete.

सर्वज्ञ *(sarvajna)* *वि.* all knowing; omniscient.

सर्वथा *(sarvathā)* *क्रि. वि.* in every respect; by all means; completely; absolutely.

सर्वदा *(sarvadā)* *क्रि. वि.* at all times; always.

सर्वनाम *(sarvnām)* *पु.* pronoun.

सर्वनाश *(sarvnāś)* *पु.* complete ruin; holocaust; total devastation.

सर्वप्रिय *(sarvpriya)* *वि.* popular; dear to all.

सर्वव्यापक *(sarv-vyapak)* *वि.* omnipresent; all pervasive.

सर्वव्यापी *(sarv-vyapi)* see सर्वव्यापक।

सर्वशक्तिमान *(sarv-saktiamān)* *वि.* omnipotent; almighty.

सर्वश्रेष्ठ *(sarv-śreṣt)* *वि.* the best; best of the lot.

सर्वसम्मत *(sarv-sammat)* *वि.* unanimous.

सर्वसम्मति *(sarv-sammati)* *स्त्री.* unanimity.

सर्वसाधारण *(sarv-sadharān)* *पु.* people at large; populace.

सर्वस्व *(sarv-asva)* पु. the whole of a person's property or possessions; one's all.

सर्वहारा *(sarv-hārā)* पु. proletariat.

सर्वेक्षण *(sarve-kśhaṇ)* पु. survey.

सर्वोच्च *(sarvoccā)* वि. supreme; uppermost; paramount.

सर्वोच्चता *(sarvoccata)* स्त्री. supremacy.

सर्वोच्च-न्यायालय *(sarvoccā-nyāyālaya)* पु. Supreme Court.

सर्वोत्कृष्ट *(sarvotkrśt)* वि. superiormost; the best.

सर्वोत्तम *(sarvottam)* वि. best of all; most excellent.

सर्वोदय *(sarvoday)* पु. uplift of all; universal progress.

सर्वोपरि *(sarvoparī)* वि. supreme; topmost; highest.

सलज्ज *(sa-lajj)* वि. bashful; shy; modest.

सलाई *(salāī)* स्त्री. knitting needle; thin wire; stick.

सलाख़ *(salākh)* स्त्री. thin iron rod; bar.

सलाम *(salām)* पु. (अ.) salutation (among Muslims); adieu; goodbye.

सलामत *(salamat)* वि. (अ.) safe; sound.

सलामती *(salamati)* स्त्री. safety; welfare; well-being.

सलामी *(salami)* स्त्री. (फ़ा.) salutation; salutation in honour of a respected guest or officer; guard of honour; salute by the booming of guns.

सलाह *(salāh)* स्त्री. (अ.) advice; counsel; consultation.

सलाहकार *(salāhkār)* पु. (अ.) advisor; counsellor.

सलिल *(salil)* पु. water.

सलीक़ा *(salīqā)* पु. (अ.) manners; etiquette; quality; ability.

सलीब *(salib)* स्त्री. (अ.) cross.

सलूक *(salūk)* see सुलूक।

सलोना *(salonā)* वि. salted; tasteful; beautiful; charming.

सल्तनत *(saltnat)* स्त्री. (अ.) empire; kingdom.

सवर्ण *(sa-varṇ)* वि. of the same colour; of the same caste or tribe.

सवार *(savār)* पु. (फ़ा.) rider; horseman; person boarding a carriage.

सवारी *(savārī)* स्त्री. riding; vehicle; conveyance; procession; passenger.

सवाल *(savāl)* पु. (अ.) problem (Arith.). begging; asking; question.

सविनय *(savinay)* वि. modest; humble; mannerly; civil.

सवेरा *(saverā)* पु. morning; daybreak.

सशंक *(sa-śaṅk)* वि. suspicious; doubtful; cowardly.

सशक्त *(sa-śakt)* वि. powerful; strong; forceful.

सशस्त्र *(sa-śastra)* वि. having arms; armed.

ससुर *(sasur)* पु. father-in-law.

ससुराल *(sasurāl)* स्त्री. father-in-law's house.

सस्ता *(sastā)* वि. (स्त्री सस्ती) cheap; lowpriced; inferior.

सस्य *(sasa)* पु. crop; fruit of a tree.

सस्यविज्ञान *(sa-sasya-vijnan)* पु. agronomy.

सह *(sah)* क्रि. वि. along with; with; simultaneously

सहकार *(sah-kār)* पु. cooperation; cooperative enterprise; collaboration.

सहकारिता *(sah-kāritā)* स्त्री. cooperation; collaboration.

सहकारी *(sah-kārī)* वि. cooperative; collaborative.

सहगान *(sahgān)* पु. collective singing; chorus.

सहचर *(sah-car)* पु. associate; companion; friend; associate element.

सहज *(saha-j)* वि. innate; inherent; easy; simple; facile; congenital; straight forward; normal.

सहजता *(saha-jatā)* स्त्री. spontaneity.

सहधर्म *(sah-dharm)* पु. common religion or law; common duty.

सहधर्मिणी *(sah-dharmini)* स्त्री. wife.

सहन[1] *(sahn)* वि. forbearing; patient; given to forgiveness; powerful.

सहन[2] *(sahn)* पु. forbearance; tolerance; forgiveness.

सहनशक्ति *(sahn-sakti)* स्त्री. endurance.

सहनशील *(sahn-sil)* वि. patient; tolerant; forbearing.

सहनशीलता *(sahn-siltā)* स्त्री. tolerance.

सहनीय *(sahnīya)* वि. tolerable; pardonable.

सहपाठी *(sah-pāṭhī)* पु. class-fellow; class mate.

सहभोज *(sah-bhoj)* पु. collective feasting; community dinner.

सहमत *(sah-mat)* वि. agreed; consented.

सहमति *(sah-mati)* स्त्री. agreement; consent; concurrence.

सहयोग *(sah-yog)* पु. cooperation; collaboration; assistance.

सहयोगी *(sah-yogī)* पु. collague; co-worker; cooperator.

सहर *(sahr)* पु. (अ.) day-break; dawn.

सहल *(sahl)* वि. (अ.) easy; simple.

सहलाना *(sahlānā)* स. क्रि. to rub gently; to caress.

सहशिक्षा *(sahśiska)* स्त्री. co-education.

सहसा *(sahasā)* क्रि. वि. suddenly; at once; unawares; abruptly.

सहानुभूति *(sahânu-bhūti)* स्त्री. sympathy.

सहानुभूतिपूर्ण *(sahânu-bhūti-puran)* वि. sympathetic.

सहानुभूतिपूर्वक *(sahânu-bhūti-purvak)* क्रि. वि. sympathetically.

सहायक[1] *(sahâyak)* वि. helpful; assistant; auxiliary; ancillary; conducive; subsidiary.

सहायक[2] *(sahâyak)* पु. helper; assistant.

सहायता *(sahâyatā)* स्त्री. help; assistance; support; aid; relief.

सहारा *(sahārā)* पु. help; assistance; dependence; reliance; support; prop.

सहित *(sahit)* क्रि. वि. along with.

सहिष्णु *(sahiṣṇu)* वि. tolerant; forbearing.

सही *(sahī)* वि. real; factual; true; faultless; accurate; correct; right; proper; suitable.

सही-सलामत *(sahī-salāmat)* वि. safe and sound; safe and well.

सहूलियत *(sahūliyat)* स्त्री. (अ.) ease; facility; convenience.

सहृदय *(sa-hṛday)* वि. kind; compassionate; tender-hearted; considerate.

सहृदयता *(sa-hṛdayatā)* स्त्री. kindness; compassion; tender-heartedness; considerateness.

सहेजना *(sahejnā)* स. क्रि. to put in order; to manage; to handle; to examine; to hand over with care.

सहेली *(sahelī)* स्त्री. a woman's female companion or friend.

सहोदर *(sahôdar)* पु. real brother.

सह्य *(sahya)* वि. edurable; tolerable.

सांकेतिक *(sānketik)* वि. symbolic; indicative.

साँठ-गाँठ *(sāṁṭh-gāṁṭh)* स्त्री. intrigue; collusion.

साँड *(sāṁr)* पु. bull or stallion brought up for the purpose of mating.

साँड़नी *(sāṁṛnī)* स्त्री. she-camel.

सांत्वना *(sāntvanā)* स्त्री. consolation; means of consolation.

साँप *(sāṁp)* पु. snake; serpent; viper.

सांप्रदायिक *(sāmpradāyik)* वि. communal; setarian.

सांप्रदायिकता *(sāmpradāyikatā)* स्त्री. communalism; sectarianism.

सांयोगिक *(sāmyogik)* वि. accidental; fortuitous.

साँवला *(sāṁvalā)* वि. of a dark or sallow complexion; darkish; swarthy.

साँवलापन *(sāṁvlāpan)* पु. slight darkness of complexion.

साँस *(sāṁs)* स्त्री. breath; respiration.

साँसत *(sīṁsat)* स्त्री. physical pain; trouble; distress; affliction; suffocation.

सांसद *(sāṁsad)* पु. member of parliament.

सांसारिक *(sāṃsārik)* वि. belonging to the world; worldly; material; mundance.

सांसारिकता *(sāṁsāriktā)* स्त्री. worldiness.

सांस्कृतिक *(sāṁskṛtik)* वि. cultural.

साईस *(sāīs)* पु. (अ.) groom; horse keeper.

साकार *(sâkār)* वि. possessed of form or shape; physical; implemented (scheme; etc.).

साकिन *(sākin)* पु. (अ.) resident.

साक़ी *(sāqī)* पु. (अ.) cup-bearer barmaid; water-server.

साक्षर *(sâkṣar)* वि. literate.

साक्षरता *(sâkṣaratā)* स्त्री. literacy.

साक्षात् *(sâkṣāt)* क्रि. वि. before the eyes; in sight (of); visibly; apparently.

साक्षात्कार *(sâkṣātkār)* पु. being face to face; interview; meeting.

साक्षी *(sâkṣī)* स्त्री. evidence; eyewitness.

साक्ष्य *(sâksya)* पु. testimony; evidence.

साख *(sākh)* स्त्री. credit; good will; over-bearing influence; sway.

साग *(sāg)* स्त्री. vegetable; greens.

सागर *(sāgar)* पु. ocean; sea.

सागूदाना *(sāgūdānā)* पु. sago.

साज़ *(sāz)* पु. (फ़ा.) embellishment; appurtenance; orchestra; harness; equipment.

साजन *(sājan)* पु. husband; lover; paramour.

साज़िश *(sāziś)* स्त्री. (अ.) conspiracy; intrigue.

साझा *(sājhā)* पु. partnership; share (in a company etc.).

साझी, साझेदार *(sājhī)* पु. partner; shareholder.

साझेदारी *(sājhīdār)* स्त्री. partnership.

साड़ी *(sārī)* स्त्री. a kind of female dress; sari.

साढ़ू *(sāṛhū)* पु. husband of wife's

sister.

सात्त्विक *(sāttvik)* वि. noble; pure; upight; honest; chaste; puritan.

साथ[1] *(sāth)* पु. company; association; support.

साथ[2] *(sāth)* क्रि. वि. with; together; along with.

साथी *(sāthī)* पु. companion; comrade; friend.

सादगी *(sādagī)* स्त्री. (फ़ा.) openness; simplicity; innocence.

सादर[1] *(sâdar)* वि. respectful; regardful.

सादर[2] *(sâdar)* क्रि. वि. respectfully; with respect.

सादा *(sādā)* वि. (फ़ा.) (स्त्री. सादी) pure; unmixed; plain; simple; guileless; artless; unadorned.

साधन *(sādhan)* accomplishment; completion; means; instrument; agency; gratification.

साधना *(sādhanā)* स्त्री. penance; worship; gratification; devotion; practice; mental training.

साधारण *(sādhāraṇ)* वि. ordinary; general; common; commonplace; simple; plain; moderte; medium; average; mediocre.

साधु *(sādhu)* वि. good; excellent; complete; proper; religious; compassionate.

साधुवाद *(sādhuvād)* पु. approbation; applause; acclamation.

साध्य *(sādhya)* वि. accomplishable; attainable; provable; curable; feasible; practicable.

साध्यता *(sādhyatā)* स्त्री. curability; attainability.

साध्वी *(sādhvī)* स्त्री. good and virtuous woman; faithful wife; chaste wife.

सानंद *(sānand)* क्रि. वि. happily; joyfully; dilightfully.

सान *(sān)* पु. whetstone.

सानना *(sānanā)* स. क्रि. to knead; to wet up; to implicate; to involve; to smear.

सानी[1] *(sānī)* वि. matching equal; equally competent or excellent.

सानी[2] *(sānī)* स्त्री. cattle food.

सान्निध्य *(sānnidhya)* पु. nearness; proximity; affinity.

सापेक्ष *(sâpekṣ)* वि. relative; conditional; qualified.

सापेक्षता *(sâpekṣatā)* वि. relativity.

साप्ताहिक *(sāptâhik)* स्त्री. relating to a week; continuing for a week; weekly.

साफ़ *(sāf)* वि. (अ.) clean; innocent; sincere; clear; ligible; smooth; level; plaine; frank; processed; refined; distinct.

साफ़गो *(sāfgo)* वि. (अ.) frank; plain-spoken.

साफ़गोई *(sāfgoī)* स्त्री. (अ.) frankness.

साफ़ा *(sāfā)* पु. (अ.) turban.

साबित *(sābit)* वि. (अ.) proved; unbroken; entire; steady; unwavering.

साबुन *(sābun)* पु. soap.

साबूदाना *(sābudānā)* पु. sago.

साभार *(sābhār)* क्रि. वि. gratefully; withgratitude.

सामंजस्य *(sāmañjasya)* पु. adjustment; consistency; harmony.

सामंत *(sāmant)* पु. feudatory prince; chieftain; feudal lord.

सामंतवाद *(samantvād)* पु. feudalism.

सामंती *(sāmantī)* वि. feudal; feudalistic.

सामग्री *(sāmagrī)* स्त्री. material; baggage; articles; implements or opparatus.

सामना (*sāmnā*) *पु.* face; front; meeting; confrontation; encounter.

सामने *(sāmne) क्रि. वि.* in front; opposite; before.

सामयिक *(sāmayik) वि.* seasonable; timely; opportune; punctual; contemporary; corrent; periodical; topical; casual.

सामरिक *(sāmarik) वि.* belonging to war or battle; martial; strategic.

सामर्थ्य *(samarthya) स्त्री.* capability; capacity; competence; force of words; power; strength.

सामर्थ्यवान *(sāmarthyavān) वि.* competent; capable; powerful; strong.

सामाजिक *(sāmājik) वि.* social; kindhearted; sociable.

सामान *(sāmān) पु.* material; accessories; luggage; baggage.

सामान्य *(sāmānya) वि.* ordinary; common; normal; insignificant.

सामान्यतः, सामान्यता *(sāmānyatā) क्रि. वि.* normally; generally; usually; as a matter of routine.

सामिष *(sâmiṣ) वि.* non-vegetarian (food).

सामीप्य *(sāmipya) पु.* nearness; proximity; vicinity.

सामुदायिक *(sāmudāyik) वि.* belonging to a community; collective.

सामूहिक *(sāmuhik) वि.* collective.

साम्य *(sāmya) पु.* equality; likeness; similarity; resemblance; analogy.

साम्यवाद *(sāmyavād) पु.* communism.

साम्यवादी *(samyavadi) पु.* communist.

साम्राज्य *(sāmrājya) पु.* empire.

साम्राज्यवाद *(sāmrājyavād) पु.* imperialism.

सायंकाल *(sāyaṁkāl) पु.* evening.

साया *(sāyā) पु.* (फ़ा.) shade; shadow.

सारंग[1] *(sāraṅg) पु.* variegated colour; large bee; cuckoo; deer.

सारंग[2] *(sāraṅg) वि.* multi-coloured; spotted; dyed; coloured.

सारंगी *(sāraṅgī) स्त्री.* kind or stringed instrument like violin.

सार *(sār) पु.* substance; essence; abstract; summary; gist; epitome.

सारगर्भित *(sārgarbhit) वि.* substantial; sententious.

सारतत्व *(sārtatva) पु.* extract; substance.

सारथी *(sārathī) पु.* charioteer.

सारभूत *(sārbhut) वि.* essential; substantial.

सारस *(sāras) पु.* crane.

सारा *(sārā) वि.* all; whole; complete; entire.

सारिका *(sārikā) स्त्री.* a kind of bird (Gracula religiosa); procuress; bard.

सार्थक *(sārthak) वि.* meaningful; significant; useful.

सार्थकता *(sārthakatā) स्त्री.* utility; usefulness; importance.

सार्वकालिक *(sārvakālik) वि.* perennial; everlasting; enternal; pertaining to all times.

सार्वजनिक, सार्वजनीन *(sārvajanik) वि.* public; universal; suitable for all; common.

सार्वदेशिक *(sārvadeśik) वि.* universal; belonging to all lands or territories.

सार्वभौमिक *(sārvabhaumik)* वि. universal; belonging or pertaining to all beings and all places; cosmopolitan.

सार्वलौकिक *(sārvlokik)* वि. universal; cosmopolitan.

साल[1] *(sāl)* पु. (फ़ा.) year.

साल[2] *(sāl)* पु. name of a tree and its wood.

सालगिरह *(sālgirah)* स्त्री. (फ़ा.) anniversary; birthday.

सालना *(sālnā)* स. क्रि. to cause pain; to pierce; to prick; to torment; to torture.

साला *(sala)* पु. wife's brother; brother-in-law.

सालाना[1] *(sālanā)* वि. (फ़ा.) yearly; annual.

सालाना[2] *(sālanā)* क्रि. वि. (फ़ा.) every year; yearly.

साली *(sālī)* स्त्री. remuneration paid to carpenters; barbers etc. in villages; wife' sister.

सावधान *(sâvadhān)* वि. cautious; alert; attentive; watchful.

सावधानी *(sâvadhānī)* स्त्री. alertness; cautiousness; attention; carefulness; watchfulness.

सावन *(sāvan)* पु. fifth Hindu month.

साष्टांग *(sāṣtaṅg)* वि. with eight parts of the body.

सास *(sās)* स्त्री. mother-in-law.

साहचर्य *(sāhacarya)* पु. association; company.

साहब *(sāhab)* पु. (अ.) master; lord; title of courtesy; Mr.; Sir; European; boss; gentleman; white-collared person.

साहबज़ादा *(sāhabjādā)* पु. (अ.) son; son of a great man.

साहबज़ादी *(sāhabjādī)* स्त्री. (अ.) daughter; daughter of a great man.

साहबी *(sāhabī)* स्त्री. officialdom; lordliness; bossism.

साहस *(sāhas)* पु. boldness; daring; courage; nerve; guts; enterprise.

साहसिक *(sāhasik)* वि. daring courageous; bold.

साहसी *(sāhasī)* वि. bold; courageous; enterprising.

साहित्य *(sāhitya)* पु. literary composition; literature; poetics.

साहित्यकार *(sāhityakār)* पु. one who composes literature; writer; author.

साहित्यिक *(sāhityik)* वि. literary.

साहूकार *(sāhukār)* पु. wealthy trader or banker; money lender.

सिंकना *(siṁknā)* अ. क्रि. to be formented or heated; to be roasted.

सिंगार *(siṅgār)* पु. make-up; ornamentation; embellishment.

सिंघाड़ा *(siṁghāṛā)* पु. water-chestnut; a kind of pastry; a kind of fire-work.

सिंचन *(simcan)* पु. irrigation; sprinking of water.

सिंचाई *(siṁcāi)* स्त्री. irrigation; wages paid for irrigation.

सिंचित *(siñcit)* वि. irrigated.

सिंदूर *(sindūr)* पु. red lead; vermillion.

सिंदूरी *(sindūrī)* वि. of vermillion colour; of or pertaining to vermillion.

सिंधु *(sindhu)* पु. ocean; sea.

सिंह *(siṃh)* पु. lion; the sign of Leo of the Zodiac.

सिंहद्वार *(siṃhdvār)* पु. main entrance to a place.

सिंहनाद *(simhnād)* पु. lion's roar; challenging cry; war whoop; confident assertion.

सिंहावलोकन *(simhālokan)* पु. retrospection; round up; conspectus.

सिंहासन *(simhāsan)* पु. throne.

सिकता *(siktā)* स्त्री. sand; sandy soil.

सिकुड़न *(sikuṛan)* अ. क्रि. contraction; shrinkage; wrinkle; fold.

सिकुड़ना *(sikuṛnā)* अ. क्रि. to contract; to shrink; to wrinkle.

सिकोड़ना *(sikoṛnā)* स. क्रि. to contract; to compress; to brace up.

सिक्का *(sikkā)* पु. (अ.) coin; coinage; influence; awe.

सिक्त *(sikt)* वि. soaked; wet; moistured.

सिखाना *(sikhānā)* स. क्रि. to teach; to instruct; to train; to tutor.

सिटपिटाना *(siṭpiṭānā)* अ. क्रि. to be confounded; to be stupefied.

सिट्टी *(siṭṭī)* स्त्री. talkativeness; bragging.

सिड़ *(siṛ)* स्त्री. craziness; whim; eccentricity.

सिड़ी *(siṛī)* वि. crazy; whimsical; eccentric.

सित *(sit)* वि. white; clear; bright.

सितम *(sitam)* पु. (फ़ा.) oppression; tyranny.

सितमगर *(sitamgar)* वि. (फ़ा.) tyrannical.

सितार *(sitār)* पु. a kind of guitar.

सितारा *(sitārā)* पु. star; planet; fortune; fate; destiny; popular actor; starlets of gold or solver sewn on cloth for decoration.

सिद्ध¹ *(siddh)* वि. accomplished; religious; pious; successful; expert; validated; substantiated; cooked on fire; endowed with supernatural powers.

सिद्ध² *(siddh)* पु. saint who is indowed with supernatural powers; ascetic; magician.

सिद्धहस्त *(siddh-hast)* वि. skilled; proficient.

सिद्धांत *(siddhānt)* पु. established truth; principle; theory; doctrine; treatise on a system of some science of art.

सिद्धांततः *(siddhāntatah)* क्रि. वि. theoretically; as a matter of principle.

सिद्धांती *(siddhāntī)* पु. man of principles; theoriest; theoretician.

सिद्धि *(siddhi)* स्त्री. accomplishment; fulfilment; complete mastery or knowledge of some subject; the acquisition of supernatural powers by magical means or through the performance of certain mystical processes.

सिधारना *(sidhārnā)* अ. क्रि. to set out; to go; to depart; to die; to expire.

सिनकना *(sinakanā)* स. क्रि. to blow (the nose).

सिपहसालार *(sipahsālār)* पु. (फ़ा.) commander-in-chief.

सिपाही *(sipāhī)* पु. (फ़ा.) soldier; police-man.

सिपुर्द, सुपुर्द *(sūpurd)* वि. (फ़ा.) entrusted; committed.

सिफ़र *(sifr)* पु. (अ.) zero; cipher; blank.

सिफारिश *(sifāriś)* स्त्री. (फ़ा.) recommendation; flattery; approach.

सिफ़ारिशी *(sifāriśī)* वि. (फ़ा.) recommendatory; of recommendation.

सिमटना *(simaṭnā)* अ. क्रि. to be collected; to be wound up; to be contracted; to be abashed.

सिम्त *(simt)* स्त्री. (अ.) direction.

सियापा *(siyāpā)* पु. mourning; weeping and wailing over a death by women.

सियार *(siyār)* पु. jackal.

सियासत *(siyāsat)* स्त्री. (अ.) polities.

सियासी *(siyāsī)* वि. (अ.) political.

सिर *(sir)* पु. head; skull; top; highest part or point.

सिरका *(sirkā)* पु. (फ़ा.) vinegar.

सिरताज *(sirtāj)* पु. crown; lord; diadem; husband.

सिरफिरा *(sirfirā)* वि. crankish; crazy.

सिरमौर *(sirmor)* see सिरताज।

सिरा *(sirā)* पु. top or head of a thing; end; edge.

सिर्फ़ *(sirf)* वि. (अ.) only; mere.

सिलना *(silnā)* (अ.) क्रि. to be sewn; स. क्रि. to sew; to stitch.

सिलवाना *(silvānā)* स. क्रि. to cause to be sewn or stitched.

सिलसिला *(silsilā)* पु. (अ.) succession; chain; series; arrangement.

सिलसिलेवार *(silsilavār)* पु. (अ.) in line or series; systematic.

सिलाई *(silāī)* स्त्री. sewing; seam; sewing-charges.

सिलाना *(silānā)* see सिलवाना।

सिल्ली *(sillī)* स्त्री. whetstone; ingot; big piece of ice.

सिवाय *(sivāy)* क्रि. वि. (फ़ा.) except.

सिसकना *(sisaknā)* अ. क्रि. to sob; to weep within; to breathe backwards; to be on the varge of death; to be uneasy.

सिसकारना *(siskārnā)* अ. क्रि. to hiss; to stir (dogs etc.) to attack.

सिसकारी *(siskārī)* स्त्री. to hissing sound.

सिसकी *(siskī)* स्त्री. sob; hissing sound.

सिहरन *(sihran)* स्त्री. trembling; shuddering; thrill.

सिहरना *(sihrānā)* अ. क्रि. to shiver; to quake or to tremble (with fear).

सींक *(sīṁk)* स्त्री. shoot of grass; an ornament for nose.

सींकचा *(sīṁkcā)* पु. window-bar.

सींग *(sīṁg)* पु. horn; musical instrument made of horn.

सींचना *(sīṁcnā)* स. क्रि. to irrigate. to water; to moisture.

सीकर *(sīkar)* पु. drop of water; drop of sweat.

सीख *(sīkh)* स्त्री. instruction; advice; counsel.

सीखना *(sīkhnā)* स. क्रि. learn.

सीझना *(sījhnā)* अ. क्रि. to boil; to become soft; to bear physical pain.

सीटी *(sītī)* स्त्री. whistling sound through mouth; whistle.

सीठा *(sīṭhā)* वि. tasteless; insipid.

सीठी *(sīṭhī)* स्त्री. dregs.

सीढ़ी *(sīṛhī)* स्त्री. ladder.

सीताफल *(sītāfal)* पु. a kind of vegetable; the custard apple.

सीध *(sīdh)* स्त्री. alignment; straightness; directness.

सीधा[1] *(sīdhā)* वि. (स्त्री.) straight; simple. easy; right (hand); gentle; innocent.

सीना *(sīnā)* पु. (फ़ा.) breast; chest.

सीपी *(sīpī)* स्त्री. oyster-shell.

सीमंत *(sīmant)* पु. the parting line of the locks of hair on the head; limit; boundary-line; joint of bones.

सीमा *(sīmā)* स्त्री. boundary; frontier; border; limit; extremity; range; extent; verge; landmark; edge.

सीमित *(sīmit)* वि. limited; bounded; restricted; qualified.

सील, सीलन *(sīl)* स्त्री. dampness; moisture (of land).

सीवन *(sīvan)* स्त्री. sewing; stitching; seam.

सीस, सीसा *(sīs)* पु. lead; black lead.

सुँघनी *(suṁghnī)* स्त्री. snuff prepared of tobacco leaves.

सुँघाना *(suṁghānā)* स. क्रि. to cause to smell; to make one smell.

सुंदर *(sundar)* वि. handsome; beautiful; charming; lovely.

सुंदरता *(sundaratā)* स्त्री. beauty; handsomeness.

सुंदरी *(sundarī)* स्त्री. beautiful woman.

सुअर *(suar)* see सूअर।

सुई, सुई *(suī)* स्त्री. needle; hand (of a watch); syrings.

सुकर *(su-kar)* वि. simple; easy; easily controllable.

सुकुमार *(su-kumār)* वि. very soft or tender; tender bodied; smooth.

सुकुमारी *(su-kumārī)* वि. (स्त्री.) having delicate body.

सुकृत *(su-kṛt)* welस.done; fortunate; lucky; well constructed; righteous.

सुकोमल *(su-komal)* वि. extremely soft; very delicate.

सुख *(sukh)* पु. pleasure; happiness; comfort; contentment; bliss.

सुखद *(sukhad)* वि. pleasant; comfortable.

सुखदायक *(sukhdāyak)* see सुखद।

सुखपूर्वक *(sukh-purvak)* क्रि. वि. happily; comfortably.

सुखाना *(sukhānā)* स. क्रि. to dry; to dry up.

सुखी *(sukhī)* वि. pleased; happy; comfortable; full of happiness; satisfied.

सुगंध, सुगंधि *(su-gandh)* स्त्री. pleasant smell; perfume; fragrance.

सुगंधित *(su-gandhit)* वि. perfumed; sweet smelling; fragrant.

सुगठित *(su-gathit)* वि. well-built; shapely; muscular; well-organised.

सुगति *(su-gati)* स्त्री. salvation; welfare; comfort.

सुगम *(su-gam)* वि. easy of access or approach; easy; intelligible.

सुघड़ *(su-ghaṛ)* वि. well-formed; well-made; skilled; efficient.

सुघड़ता *(su-ghaṛtā)* स्त्री. (पु. सुघड़पन) beauty; grace; skilfulness; competence.

सुघड़ाई *(su-ghaāī)* स्त्री. state of being welस.formed; prettiness; beauty; skilfulness.

सुचारू *(su-cāru)* वि. very lovely or beautiful; charming.

सुचालक *(su-cālak)* पु. good conductor.

सुजान *(su-jān)* वि. intelligent; clever; skilful; accomplished.

सुझाना *(sujhānā)* स. क्रि. to cause; to perceive; to suggest; to propose.

सुझाव *(sujhāv)* पु. suggestion; proposal.

सुड़कना *(suṛaknā)* स. क्रि. to drink through nose; to gulp.

सुडौल *(su-ḍaul)* वि. well-formed; well-shaped; hefty.

सुत *(sut)* पु. son.

सुतली *(sutlī)* स्त्री. thin rope of jute.

सुता *(sutā)* स्त्री. daughter.

सुथरा *(suthrā)* वि. tidy; clean; neat.

सुदि, सुदी *(sudi)* स्त्री. light half of the lunar month.

सुदूर *(sudūr)* क्रि. वि. gery far; far away.

सुदृढ़ *(su-dṛṛh)* क्रि very firm or strong; very rigid.

सुध *(sudh)* स्त्री. consciousness; memory; remembrance.

सुध-बुध *(sudh-budh)* स्त्री. consciousness; senses; memory.

सुधरना *(sudharnā)* अ. क्रि. to be rectified; to be corrected; to be set right; to be mended; to be repaired; to be reformed.

सुधाकर *(su-dhākar)* पु. moon.

सुधार *(su-dhār)* पु. reform; improvement; repair; modification; amendment.

सुधारक *(sudhārak)* पु. one who corrects or ammends; repairer; reformer.

सुधारना *(sudhārnā)* स. क्रि. to reform; to improve; to mend; to repair.

सुनना *(sunnā)* स. क्रि. to hear; to listen; to heed; to attend to.

सुनवाई *(sunvāī)* स्त्री. hearing; hearing of a case.

सुनसान *(sun-sān)* वि. lonely; deserted; desolate.

सुनहरा *(sunahrā)* वि. gold-coloured; golden; opportune.

सुनाना *(sunānā)* स. क्रि. to cause to hear; to relate; to recite; to pronounce; to rebuke; to chide.

सुनाम *(su-nām)* पु. celebrity; reputation; fame; goodwill.

सुनार *(sunār)* पु. goldsmith.

सुनीति *(su-nīti)* स्त्री. good manner; equity.

सुन्न *(sunn)* वि. benumbed; etherised; insensitive; stilled; stupefied.

सुपथ्य *(su-pathya)* पु. salubrious diet.

सुपात्र *(su-pātr)* वि. fit or worthy; deserving.

सुपारी *(supārī)* स्त्री. areca catech; arecanut; betel-nut; glands of penis.

सुपुर्द *(supurd)* see सिपुर्द।

सुप्त *(supt)* वि. sleeping; closed (as a flower); latent; dormant; insensitive (organs).

सुप्रतिष्ठित *(su-prati-ṣṭhit)* वि. well-established; reputed; celebrated.

सुप्रसिद्ध *(su-prasidh)* वि. well-known; renowned; famous; eminent.

सुबह *(subah)* स्त्री. dawn; day-break; morning.

सुबुद्धि *(su-buddhi)* वि. of good understanding; intelligent.

सुबोध *(su-bodh)* वि. intelligible; easy.

सुभग *(su-bhag)* वि. beautiful; lovely; charming; possessing good fortune.

सुभगता *(su-bhagatā)* स्त्री. state or quality of being charming; symptoms of good fortune; affection; love.

सुभाषित *(su-bhāṣit)* पु. maxim; quotable saying.

सुभीता *(subhītā)* पु. convenience; comfort; ease.

सुमति *(su-mati)* वि. very clever.

सुमन[1] *(su-man)* पु. flower.

सुमन[2] *(su-man)* वि. happy; favourably disposed.

सुमरना *(sumarnā)* स. क्रि. to remember; to adore; to worship.

सुमार्ग *(su-mārg)* पु. moral course; just course.

सुमुखी *(su-mukhī)* वि. prettily-faced; beautiful.

सुयोग *(su-yog)* पु. favourable juncture; good opportunity; coincidence.

सुयोग्य *(su-yogya)* वि. worthy; very able; well-qualified.

सुरंग *(suraṅg)* स्त्री. tunnel; mine.

सुर *(sur)* पु. tone; note (in music); vowel; god.

सुरक्षा *(su-rakṣā)* स्त्री. security; protection.

सुरभि *(su-rabhi)* स्त्री. fragrance; perfume; cow of plenty.

सुरक्षित *(su-rakṣit)* वि. perfumed; scented; odorous.

सुरमा *(surmā)* पु. (फ़ा.) antimony; collyrium.

सुरलोक *(surlok)* पु. abode of gods.

सुरसुरी *(sursurī)* स्त्री. see सुरसुराहट a kind of firework; weevil.

सुरा *(surā)* स्त्री. liquor; wine.

सुराख़ *(surākh)* see सूराख़।

सुराग़ *(surāg)* पु. (अ.) trace; clue.

सुरीला *(surīlā)* वि. melodious; sweet; mellifluous.

सुरुचि *(su-ruci)* स्त्री. refined taste; good taste.

सुरूप *(su-rūp)* वि. beautiful; goodlooking shapely.

सुरूर *(surūr)* पु. (अ.) pleasant after-effect of intoxication.

सुर्ख़ *(surkh)* वि. (फ़ा.) red; ruddy.

सुर्ख़रू *(surkhru)* वि. (फ़ा.) reputed; honourable.

सुर्ख़ी *(surkhī)* स्त्री. (फ़ा.) redness; headline; brick-dust; lipstick.

सुलक्षण *(su-lakṣaṇ)* वि. having charming features or characteristics; lucky; fortunate; gifted with laudable ways.

सुलक्षणा *(su-lakṣaṇā)* स्त्री. lady having good characteristics.

सुलगना *(sulagnā)* अ. क्रि. to smoulder; to begin to burn; to be ignited.

सुलगाना *(sulgānā)* स. क्रि. to kindle; to ignite; to burn; to incite; to rouse.

सुलझना *(sulajhnā)* अ. क्रि. to be disentangled; to be solved; to be resolved.

सुलझाना *(suljhānā)* स. क्रि. to solve; to set right; to disentane.

सुलझाव *(suljhāv)* पु.disentanglement; solution.

सुलतान *(sultān)* पु. (अ.) king; Sultan.

सुलताना *(sultānā)* स्त्री. (अ.) queen; wife or mother of a Sultan.

सुलभ *(su-labh)* वि. easily available; handy; accessible; easy; natural; useful.

सुलह *(sulh)* स्त्री. (अ.) treaty; reconciliation; compromise; agreement.

सुलाना *(sulānā)* स. क्रि. to cause to sleep; to lull; to kill; to murder.

सुलूक *(sulūk)* पु. (अ.) treatment; behaviour; unity.

सुलेख *(sulekh)* पु. good handwriting; calligraphy.

सुवर्ण *(su-varṇ)* वि. of good colour; yellow; golden; bright; belonging to higher caste.

सुवास *(su-vās)* स्त्री. sweet smell; fragrance.

सुवासित *(su-vāsit)* वि. well-scented or perfumed; fragrant; aromatic.

सुविचारित *(su-vi-cārit)* वि. well-considered.

सुविधा *(suvidhā)* see सुभीता।

सुविधाजनक *(suvidhājanak)* वि. convenient.

सुव्यवस्था *(su-vyavastha)* स्त्री. orderliness; good administration; fine organisation.

सुव्यवस्थित *(su-vyavasthit)* वि. orderly; regular; well-administered; well-organised.

सुशिक्षित *(su-siksit)* वि. well-educated; highly educated.

सुशील *(su-śīl)* वि. good tempered; modest; courteous; pious; righteous; simple.

सुशोभित *(su-śobhit)* वि. graceful; adorned.

सुश्री[1] *(su-śrī)* वि. elegant; graceful; wealthy.

सुश्री[2] *(su-śrī)* स्त्री. an honorific word prefixed to the name of a woman.

सुषमा *(su-ṣamā)* स्त्री. exquisite beauty; splendour; charm.

सुषुप्त *(su-ṣupt)* वि. fast asleep; in deep slumber; dormant.

सुषुप्ति *(su-ṣupti)* स्त्री. deep or profound sleep; spiritual ignorance.

सुष्ठु *(su-ṣṭhu)* वि. elegant; appropriate; in a proper manner.

सुसंगति *(su-san-gati)* स्त्री. good company; companionship of the good validity; concord; relevance.

सुसंस्कृत *(su-saṁskrit)* वि. well-cultured; refined.

सुसाध्य *(su-sādhya)* वि. easily achievable; easily controllable; curable.

सुस्त *(susṭ)* वि. (फ़ा.) slow; languid; dull; lazy; slack; idle; depressed; spiritless.

सुस्ताना *(sustānā)* अ. क्रि. to take repose; to relax; to rest.

सुस्ती *(sustī)* स्त्री. dulling; indolence; idleness; laziness; slowness.

सुस्वाद *(su-svād)* वि. delicious; tasteful.

सुहबत *(su-habat)* स्त्री. (अ.) company; association; cohabitation; coition.

सुहागा *(suhāgā)* पु. borax.

सुहागिन *(suhāgin)* स्त्री. a woman whose husband is alive.

सुहाना *(suhānā)* अ. क्रि. to be pleasing; to be agreeable; to appeal; to look charming.

सुहावना *(suhāvnā)* वि. pleasant; beautiful; charming.

सुहृदय *(su-hṛday)* पु. friend.

सूँघना *(sūṁghnā)* स. क्रि. to sniff; to smell; to eat in small quantity.

सूँड *(sūṁṛ)* स्त्री. trunk of an elephant; proboscis.

सूँस *(sūṁs)* स्त्री. porpoise.

सुअर *(sūar)* पु. boar; pig; a word of abuse; swine; a dirty or thick skinned person.

सुई *(sūī)* स्त्री. needle; hand of a clock or watch.

सुक्ति *(sûkti)* स्त्री. mixim; epigram.

सुक्ष्म *(sūkṣma)* वि. subtle; minute; fine; thin.

सूक्ष्मता *(sūkṣmatā)* स्त्री. minuteness; subtlety; fineness; thinness; precision.

सूक्ष्मदर्शक *(sūkṣmdarshak)* पु. microscope.

सूक्ष्मदर्शी *(sūkṣmdarshī)* वि. keen-eyed; having the quality of minute observation.

सूखना *(sūkhna)* अ. क्रि. to dry up; to evaporate; to get lean and thin; to wither; to dwindle.

सूखा *(sūkhā)* वि. dry; sapless; not given to emotion; unenergetic; gloomy.

सूचक *(sūcak)* पु. indicator; informer; pointer; needle; tailor; backbiter.

सूचकांक *(sūcakaṇk)* पु. index number.

सूचना *(sūcanā)* पु. information; intimation; notice; notification; announcement.

सूचि *(sūci)* स्त्री. needle; any sharp pointed instrument; index; table of contents (of a book); list.

सूचिका *(sūcikā)* स्त्री. needle.

सूचित *(sūcit)* वि. informed; notified; suggested; hinted; indicated.

सूची *(sūcī)* स्त्री. needle; list; catalogue.

सूचीपत्र *(sūcīpatra)* पु. catalogue.

सूजन *(sūjan)* स्त्री. swelling; inflammation.

सूजना *(sūjnā)* अ. क्रि. to swell; to be or become inflamed.

सूझ *(sūjh)* स्त्री. idea; concept; imagination; insight; vision; perception; understanding; intelligence.

सूझना *(sūjhnā)* अ. क्रि. to oçcur to one's mind; to be visible.

सूत *(sūt)* पु. thread; yarn; a measure of length; a charioteer; bard.

सूतिका *(sūtikā)* स्त्री. a woman who has recently given birth to a child.

सूतिकागृह *(sūtikagraha)* पु. confinement chamber.

सूत्र *(sūtr)* पु. thread; string; sacred thread; precept; axiom; clue; formula.

सूत्रधार *(sūtrdhār)* पु. stage-manager; principal actor in a dramatic performance.

सूत्रपात *(sūtrpāt)* पु. beginning; commencement.

सूत्रात्मक *(sūtratmak)* वि. terse; pithy; in the nature of a formula.

सूद *(sūd)* पु. (फ़ा.) interest.

सूदख़ोर *(sūdkhor)* पु. (फ़ा.) usurer.

सूदख़ोरी *(sūdkhori)* स्त्री. (फ़ा.) usury.

सूना *(sūnā)* वि. lonely; desolate; empty; solitary.

सूनापन *(sūnāpan)* पु. loneliness; desolateness; solitude.

सूप *(sūp)* पु. winnowing basket; soup; broth; cook; arrow.

सूफ़ी *(sūfi)* वि. (फ़ा.) saintly; pious.

सूबा *(sūbā)* पु. (अ.) province.

सूबेदार *(sūbedār)* पु. (अ.) governor of a province; a military rank.

सूरज *(sūraj)* पु. the sun.

सूरजमुखी *(sūrajmukhi)* पु. sunflower.

सूरत *(sūrat)* स्त्री. (अ.) figure; shape; face; state; condition; idea; manner; way out.

सूरमा *(sūrmā)* पु. warrior; brave or valiant person.

सूराख़ *(sūrākh)* पु. (फ़ा.) hole; opening; bore; orifice.

सूर्य *(sūrya)* पु. the sun.

सूर्यकांत *(sūryakant)* पु. sun stone.

सूर्यग्रहण *(sūryagrahan)* पु. solar eclipse.

सूर्यमुखी *(sūryamukhī)* पु. sunflower.

सूर्यास्त *(sūryāst)* पु. sun-set; time of sun-set.

सूर्योदय *(sūryoday)* पु. sunrise; time of sun-rise.

सूली *(sūlī)* स्त्री. gallows; gibbet; state of deep agony.

सृष्टि *(sṛṣṭi)* स्त्री. world; universe; creation.

सेंक *(seṁk)* स्त्री. fomentation; baking; heat; warmth.

सेंकना *(seṁkna)* स. क्रि. to roast; parch; to warm; to heat; to foment.

सेंतना *(seṁtña)* स. क्रि. to preserve carefully; to take care of; to collect; to accumulate.

सेंध *(seṁdh)* स्त्री. hole in a wall made by the burglars; burglary.

सेंधा *(seṁdhā)* पु. rock-salt.

से *(se)* क्रि. वि. from; out of; with; by; than; since; for.

सेठ *(seṭh)* पु. moneyed man; wealthy merchant.

सेठानी *(seṭhānī)* स्त्री. rich woman; wife of a wealthy merchant.

सेतु *(setu)* पु. bridge; ridge between two fields; barrage; limit; blockade; fixed rule; causeway.

सेना[1] *(senā)* स. क्रि. to hatch; to serve; to lie idle(on); to worship.

सेना[2] *(senā)* स्त्री. army; military; body of troops.

सेनापति *(senāpati)* पु. military chief; commander.

सेनानी *(senānī)* पु. commander of the army.

सेब *(seb)* पु. apple.

सेम *(sem)* स्त्री. bean.

सेमल *(semal)* पु. silk-cotton tree and its flower.

सेर *(ser)* पु. seer; weight equivalent to sixteen chhataks or a little over two lbs.

सेलखड़ी *(selkharī)* स्त्री. soap stone.

सेव *(sev)* पु. a kind of sweet or saltish preparation of gram flour.

सेवक *(sevak)* पु. servant; attendant; worshipper; devotee; dependent.

सेवन *(sevan)* पु. regular use; consumption; service; attendance; worship; practice.

सेवा *(sevā)* स्त्री. service; attendance; worship; homage.

सेवानिवृत्ति *(sevānivrit)* स्त्री. retirement.

सेवायोजक *(sevāyojak)* पु. employer.

सेविका *(sevikā)* स्त्री. female servant; attendant; maid servant; midwife.

सेहत *(sehat)* स्त्री. (अ.) health; soundness of body.

सेहरा *(sehrā)* पु. head-dress worn at the time of marriage; eulogy composed for such occasion.

सैद्धांतिक *(saidhāntik)* वि. theoretical; pertaining to some theory or doctrine.

सैनिक[1] *(sainik)* पु. soldier; guard; sentry.

सैनिक[2] *(sainik)* पु. relating to army; martial.

सैनिकीकरण *(saịnikikaran)* पु. militarisation.

सैन्य[1] *(sainya)* वि. pertaining to army.

सैन्य[2] *(sainya)* पु. body of troops; army; soldier; sentry; guard; camp.

सैन्यनायक *(sainyanāyak)* पु. military commander.

सैयाँ *(saiyā)* पु. husband; master; lord.

सैयाद *(saiyād)* पु. (अ.) fowler; hunter; fisherman.

सैर *(sair)* स्त्री. (अ.) excursion; outing; picnic; walk.

सैलानी[1] *(sailānī)* पु. (अ.) tourist; wanderer.

सैलानी[2] *(sailānī)* वि. (अ.) pertaining to flow of water; fond of touring or wandering.

सैलाब *(sailāb)* पु. (फ़ा.) flood.

सोंठ *(soṁṭh)* स्त्री. dry ginger.

सोख़ता *(sokhtā)* पु. blotting paper.

सोच *(soc)* स्त्री. musing; brooding; anxiety; concern; regret; repentance; consideration; reflection.

सोचना *(socnā)* स. क्रि. to think; to ponder; to consider; to imagine; to conceive; to worry; to be sad; to repent.

सोना *(sonā)* अ. क्रि. to sleep; to lie down; to be numbed; gold.

सोमवार *(somvār)* पु. Monday.

सोयम *(soyam)* पु. (फ़ा.) third.

सोहना *(sohnā)* अ. क्रि. to look attractive or beautiful.

सोहबत *(sohbat)* स्त्री. (अ.) association; company; copulation; sexual intercourse.

सौंदर्य *(saundarya)* पु. beauty; loveliness; gracefulness; elegance.

सौंदर्यशास्त्र *(saundarya-sastra)* पु. aesthetics.

सौंदर्यशास्त्री *(saundarya-sastrī)* पु. aesthetician.

सौंपना *(saumpnā)* स. क्रि. to delegate; to hand over; to entrust.

सौंफ़ *(saumph)* स्त्री. aniseed; feneel.

सौंगंध *(saugand)* स्त्री. oath; swearing; vow.

सौग़ात *(saugāt)* स्त्री. (फ़ा.) present; gift.

सौजन्य *(saujanya)* पु. goodness; courtesy; gentlemanliness.

सौत[1] *(saut)* स्त्री. co-wife.

सौत[2] *(saut)* पु. whip.

सौतेला *(sautelā)* वि. of or belonging to a co-wife; born of a co-wife.

सौदा *(saudā)* पु. (फ़ा.) goods; transaction; bargain; trade; commerce.

सौदागर *(saudāgar)* पु. (फ़ा.) trader; merchant.

सौदागरी *(saudāgarī)* स्त्री. (फ़ा.) calling of trader or merchant; trade; commerce.

सौभाग्य *(saubhāgya)* पु. good fortune; good luck; prosperity; welfare; the auspicious state of wifehood.

सौभाग्यवती *(saubhāgyavati)* स्त्री. married woman whose husband is alive.

सौम्य *(saumya)* वि. mild; placid; gentle lovely; charming; pleasing.

सौम्यता *(saumyatā)* स्त्री. gentleness; placidity; beauty.

सौरभ *(saurabh)* पु. fragrance; odour; aroma.

सौष्ठव *(sauṣṭhav)* पु. beauty; elegance; charm; excellence; skilfulness; swiftness; a posture of body or dance; self confidence.

स्खलन *(skhalan)* पु. falling down; slipping; moral lapse; blunder; error; mistake; discharge; emission.

स्सखलित *(skhalit)* वि. fallen; dropped down; slipped; deviated from the right course; erring; blundering.

स्तंभ *(stambh)* पु. pillar; post; stem; trunk (of a tree); column; part of a newspaper devoted to special subject.

स्तंभित *(stambhit)* वि. benumbed; paralysed; flabbergasted; amazed; repressed; restrained.

स्तन *(stan)* पु. breast of a woman; mammary glands; udder.

स्तब्ध *(stabdh)* वि. motionless; numbed; paralysed; wonderstruck; stupefied.

स्तब्धता *(stabdhtā)* स्त्री. motionless; hardness; stupefaction.

स्तर *(star)* पु. fold; level; stratum; standard; grade.

स्तवन *(stavan)* पु. praise; eulogy; hymn; song of praise; panegyric.

स्तुति *(stuti)* स्त्री. praise; eulogy; commendation; laudation; hymn of praise; panegyric; adulation; flattery; prayer; invocation.

स्तूप *(stup)* पु. heap; pile; mound; a Buddhistic monument.

स्तोत्र *(strotra)* पु. hymn of praise; panegyric; panegyrical composition or work (especially in verse).

स्त्री *(stri)* स्त्री. woman; wife.

स्त्रैण *(strain)* वि. henpecked; effeminate; suited or belonging to woman; feminine; womanish; womanly.

स्थगन *(sthagan)* पु. adjournment; postponement; suspension.

स्थगित *(sthagit)* वि. postponed; adjourned.

स्थल *(sthal)* पु. ground; land; firm or dry ground; dry land; place; spot; venue; site; location; field; tract; topic; subject point under discussion; part; portion.

स्थलसेना *(sthal-senā)* पु. land forces; army.

स्थान *(sthān)* पु. open land; ground; field; place; site; spot; location; locality; abode; house; dwelling place; residence; post; office; rank; place of sitting; seat; organ of utterance of letter; character or part of an actor; space; room; accommodation.

स्थानांतर *(sthānāntar)* पु. transfer.

स्थानांतरण *(sthānāntaran)* पु. transfer; transferrence.

स्थानांतरित *(sthānāntarit)* वि. transferred; removed from one place to another.

स्थानापन्न *(sthānāpann)* वि. substituted in place of another; acting; officiating.

स्थानीय *(sthānīya)* वि. local; endemic.

स्थापत्य *(sthāpatya)* पु. architecture; science of architecture; guard of harem.

स्थापन *(sthāpan)* पु. erection; installation; establishment; setting up; enunciation.

स्थापना *(sthāpanā)* स्त्री. installation; foundation.

स्थापित *(sthāpit)* वि. founded; instituted; established; propounded; enunciated; set up; raised; erected; placed; fixed located; installed.

स्थायित्व *(sthāyitva)* पु. permanency; stability.

स्थायी *(sthāyī)* वि. permanent; stable; durable; lasting; steady; firm; regular; invariable.

स्थायीकरण *(sthayikaran)* पु. prepetuation; confirmation.

स्थित *(sthit)* वि. situated; existing steady; firm; determined resolved; established; set; stable; immovable; stationary; present.

स्थिति *(sthiti)* स्त्री. situation; location; site; continuance in one state; state; condition; natural state; rank; dignity; position; status.

स्थिर *(sthir)* वि. constant; steady; firm; stable; enduring; lasting permanent. established; fixed; stationary; calm; pacific; placed; located.

स्थिरता *(sthiratā)* स्त्री. constancy; steadiness; firmness; stability; permanence; poise; calmness; fixity.

स्थूल *(sthūl)* वि. fat; corpulent; massive; plain; rough; gross; coarse; thick.

स्थूलता *(sthūlatā)* स्त्री. concreteness; fatness; corpulence; bulkiness; largeness; coarseness; thickness.

स्थैतिकी *(sthaitiki)* वि. static.

स्नातक *(snātak)* पु. graduate.

स्नातकोत्तर *(snātkottar)* वि. post-graduate.

स्नान *(snān)* पु. bath; abution; basking.

स्नायु *(snāyu)* स्त्री. nerve; tendon; ligament; string of bow.

स्निग्ध *(sngdh)* वि. oily; greasy; smooth; not rough; glossy; loving; affectionate; friendly; tender.

स्नेह *(sneh)* पु. affection; love; kindness; fat; lubricant; oil; oiliness; viscidity; unctuousness; lubricity.

स्नेही *(snehī)* वि. affectionate; tender; loving.

स्पंदन *(spandan)* पु. vibration; tremor; quivering; trembling; beat; pulsation; movement; motion.

स्पर्द्धा, स्पर्धा *(spardha)* स्त्री. rivalry; competition; emulation; jealousy; envy.

स्पर्श *(spars)* पु. tangibility; touch; feel; contact; encounter; donation; gift; air; sky; spy.

स्पष्ट *(spaṣṭ)* वि. distinct; clear; apparent; evident; obvious; manifest; intelligible; easy; plain; straightforward; honest positive; unambiguous; conspicuous.

स्पष्टता *(spaṣṭatā)* स्त्री. distinctness; clearness; plainness; obviousness; straight-forwardness; explicit-ness.

स्पष्टवादी *(spaṣṭvādī)* वि. outspoken; straightforward; plain-spoken.

स्पष्टीकरण *(spaṣṭikaraṇ)* पु. explanation; elucidation; clarification.

स्पृहणीय *(spṛhaṇīya)* वि. desirable; worth yearning for; worth envy; charming; fascinating; praise-worthy.

स्पृहा *(spṛhā)* स्त्री. desire; eagerness; ardent wish; longing; envy.

स्फटिक *(sphaṭik)* पु. crystal; quartz; pebble.

स्फीति *(sphīti)* स्त्री. puff; swelling; inflation; progress.

स्फूर्त *(sphūrt)* वि. vibrated throbbed; skaken; flashed (on the mind).

स्फूर्ति *(sphūrti)* स्त्री. agility; smartness; quickness; vibration; flash on the mind.

स्फोट *(sphoṭ)* पु. breaking forth; splitting open; eruption; burst; explosion; boil; eternal sound.

स्मरण *(smaraṇ)* पु. remembrance; recollection; memory.

स्मरणपत्र *(smaraṇpatra)* पु. reminder; memorandum.

स्मरणशक्ति *(smaraṇ-shakti)* स्त्री. memory.

स्मारक *(smārak)* पु. memorial; monument.

स्मित *(smit)* पु. smile; gentle laugh.

स्मृति *(smṛti)* स्त्री. memory; remembrance; recollection; book of traditional code of Hindu Law; reflection.

स्याना *(syānā)* वि. clever; crooked; mature; adult.

स्याही *(syāhī)* स्त्री. (फ़ा.) ink; blackness;darkness; soot.

स्रष्टा *(sraṣṭā)* पु. maker; creator; God.

स्राव *(srāv)* पु. flow or course of water; ooze; stream; current; miscarriage; premature abortion; secretion.

स्रोत *(srot)* पु. stream; current; flow or course of water; spring; source; resource.

स्वकीय *(svakīya)* वि. one's own; personal.

स्वकीया *(svakīyā)* स्त्री. loyal heroine (in Indian poetics); wife.

स्वगत *(sva-gat)* वि. belonging to own self; own; personal; passing in one's own mind; speaking to oneself.

स्वचालित *(svacālit)* वि. automatic.

स्वच्छंद *(sva-cchand)* वि. capricious; selfwilled; unrestrained; arbitrary.

स्वच्छंदता *(sva-cchandatā)* स्त्री. arbitrariness; absence of restaint.

स्वच्छ *(svacch)* वि. clean; neat; clear; pure; straightforward; honest; frank; readable; fair.

स्वच्छता *(svacchatā)* स्त्री. cleanliness; neatness; clearness; sanitation; purity; frankness; sincerity; straight-forwardness.

स्वजन *(sva-jan)* पु. kinsmen; relative; kith and kin; one's own people or kindred.

स्वजातीय *(sva-jātīya)* वि. co-racial; belonging to one's own caste or race.

स्वतंत्र *(sva-tantra)* वि. independent; free; unrestrained; uncontrolled; self-dependent; separate.

स्वतंत्रता *(sva-tantratā)* स्त्री. independence; freedom; latitude; liberty.

स्वत *(svata)* क्रि. वि. voluntarily; spontaneously.

स्वत्व *(svatva)* पु. ego; claim; one's due; ownership; interest.

स्वत्वाधिकार *(svatvadhikār)* पु. copyright.

स्वदेश *(sva-deś)* पु. native country; motherland; homeland.

स्वदेशी, *(sva-deśī)* **स्वदेशीय** वि. belonging to one's own country; made or produced in one's own country; indigenous.

स्वन *(svan)* पु. sound; phone; a kind of fire.

स्वनिम *(svanīm)* पु. phoneme.

स्वप्न *(svapn)* पु. dream; conscious indulgence of fancy; reverie.

स्वप्नदर्शी *(svapndarsi)* वि. dreamy.

स्वभाव *(sva-bhāv)* पु. nature; character; disposition; temperament; habit; essential or inherent property.

स्वभावतः *(sva-bhāvatah)* क्रि. वि. from natural disposition; by nature; naturally.

स्वयं *(svayaṁ)* क्रि. वि. of one's own accord; by oneself; personally; automatically.

स्वयंभू *(svayaṁbhu)* वि. selfborn; self-existent; self-begotten; self-styled.

स्वयंवर *(svayaṁvar)* पु. self-choice; self-selection; ancient custom wherein a bride chose her husband of her own accord; the ceremony or celebration of choosing a husband by the bride.

स्वयंसिद्ध *(svayaṁsidh)* वि. self-evident; axiomatic.

स्वर *(svar)* पु. vowel; sound; noise; voice; a note of musical scale or gamut; tone; tune; air breathed through the nostrils.

स्वराज्य *(sva-rājya)* पु. independence; autonomy; home-rule; self-government.

स्वराष्ट्र *(sva-rāṣṭra)* पु. homeland; native country.

स्वरूप *(sva-rūp)* पु. shape; form; countenance; appearance; system; order; plan; nature; character.

स्वर्ग *(svarg)* पु. heaven; abode of gods; paradise.

स्वर्गवास *(svargvās)* पु. residence in heaven; death.

स्वर्गवासी *(svargvāsī)* वि. belonging or relating to heaven; dead; late.

स्वर्गीय *(svargiya)* वि. belonging or relating to heaven; divine; late; dead; super-natural; extra-worldly; divine.

स्वर्ण *(svarṇ)* पु. gold.

स्वर्णकार *(svarṇkār)* पु. goldsmith.

स्वर्णिम *(svarṇim)* वि. golden.

स्वस्थ *(sv-asṭh)* वि. healthy; hale; free from defect; sound; conducive to social and mental health; refined; good; robust.

स्वस्थता *(sv-asthatā)* स्त्री. health; healthiness.

स्वागत *(svâgat)* पु. reception; welcome; acceptance.

स्वागतक *(svâgatak)* पु. receptionist.

स्वातंत्र्ययुद्ध *(svātantrya-yudh)* पु. war of independence.

स्वाद *(svād)* पु. taste; flavour; relish; savour; enjoyment; pleasure; habit.

स्वादिष्ट, स्वादिष्ठ *(svādiṣṭ)* वि. tasteful; delicious; dainty.

स्वाधीन *(svâdhīn)* वि. in one's own power or control; at one's own disposal; dependent on oneself; self dependent; independent; free; uncontrolled.

स्वाधीनता *(svâdhīnatā)* स्त्री. self-dependence; independence; liberty; freedom.

स्वाभाविक *(svābhāvik)* वि. natural; consistent with one's disposition or nature; innate; inborn; inherent.

स्वाभिमान *(svābhīman)* पु. self-respect.

स्वामित्व *(svāmitva)* पु. ownership; proprietorship.

स्वामिनी *(svāmini)* स्त्री. female proprietor; proprietoress; wife of the master; mistress.

स्वामिभक्त *(svāmībhakt)* वि. loyal;

faithful.

स्वामिभक्ति *(svāmībhaktī)* स्त्री. loyalty; faithfulness.

स्वामित्व *(svāmīsva)* पु. royalty.

स्वामी *(svāmī)* पु. proprietor; owner; master; husband; king; monarch; sovereign; title prefixed to names of saints and ascetics.

स्वायत्त *(svâyatt)* वि. within one's control or subjection; autonomous.

स्वार्थ *(svârth)* वि. selfishness; one's own advantage or interest; self-interest.

स्वार्थी *(svârthī)* वि. selfish; self-seeking.

स्वावलंबन *(svâlamban)* पु. self-sufficiency; self-reliance; self-dependence.

स्वावलंबी *(svâlambi)* वि. self-sufficient; self-reliant; self-dependent.

स्वास्थ्य *(svāsthya)* वि. health; physical fitness.

स्वास्थ्यकर *(svāsthyakar)* वि.congenial to health; wholesome; healthy.

स्वास्थ्यलाभ *(svāsthyalabh)* पु. convalescence.

स्वास्थ्य विज्ञान *(svāsthya-vijnan)* पु. hygiene.

स्वीकार *(isvīkār)* पु. making one's own; adoption; acceptance; assent; consent; confession.

स्वीकार्य *(svīkārya)* वि. acceptable; admissible.

स्वीकृत *(svīkṛt)* वि. sanctioned; granted; accepted; assented; admitted.

स्वीकृति *(svīkṛtī)* वि. consent; assent; acceptance; sanction.

स्वेच्छा *(svêcchā)* स्त्री. one's own wish or will; free will.

स्वेच्छाचार *(svêcchācār)* पु. bacting as one likes; arbitrariness; acting without restrain.

स्वैर *(svair)* वि. self willed; licentious.

ह

ह *(ha)* the thirty third consonant of Devnagri alphabets.

हँकार *(haṁkār)* स्त्री. loud shout; roar.

हंगामा *(haṅgāmā)* पु. (फा.) noise; tumult; commotion; confusion; uproar; riot; disturbance.

हंगामी *(haṅgāmī)* वि. (फा.) uproarious; tumultuous; noisy; emergent.

हँडिया *(haṁḍiyā)* स्त्री. small earthen boiler or pot; glass pot used as decoration piece in rich drawing rooms.

हंता *(hantā)* पु. murderer; slayer.

हंस *(haṁs)* पु. swan; goose; the individual soul.

हँसना *(haṁsnā)* अ. क्रि. to laugh; to smile; to be merry; to jest; to joke; to fun.

हँसमुख *(haṁsmukh)* वि. of a smiling countenace; gay; cheerful; facetious; jocular; funny.

हँसाना *(haṁsānā)* स. क्रि. to cause to laugh; to make (one) laugh; to amuse.

हँसिया *(haṁsiyā)* पु. sickle; scythe.

हँसी *(haṁsī)* स्त्री. laughter; laugh; fun; joke; ridicule; derision; mockery.

हँसोड़[1] *(haṁsoṛ)* वि. laughing loudly; facetious; humorous; jocular; jolly.

हँसोड़[2] *(haṁsoṛ)* पु. jester.

हक़दार *(haqdār)* वि. (अ.) having a claim; right or title; rightful; entitled.

हकला[1] *(haklā)* वि. stuttering; stammering.

हकला[2] *(haklā)* पु. stammerer.

हकलाना *(haklānā)* अ. क्रि. to stammer; to stutter.

हकलाहट *(haklāhaṭ)* स्त्री. stammer; stammering.

हक़ीक़त *(haqīqat)* स्त्री. (अ.) truth; reality; fact.

हक़ीक़ी *(haqīqī)* वि. (अ.) real; true.

हक़ीम *(hakīm)* पु. (अ.) physician or medical practitioner trained in the Yunani system of medicine.

हक़ीर *(haqīr)* वि. (अ.) mean; detestable.

हक्का-बक्का *(hakkā-bakkā)* वि. confounded; confused; struck-dumb; stunned; amazed; stupefied; flabbergasted.

हज, हज्ज *(hajj)* पु. (अ.) pilgrimage to Mecca.

हज़म[1] *(hazm)* वि. digested; usurped.

हज़म[2] *(hazm)* पु. (अ.) digestion; embezzlement.

हजामत *(hajāmat)* स्त्री. (अ.) shaving; hair-cutting.

हजूम *(hajūm)* पु. (अ.) crowd; multitude.

हज्जाम *(hajjām)* पु. (अ.) barber.

हटना *(hatna)* अ. क्रि. to move away; to go away; to abstain; to be averse; to withdraw; to recede; to be put off; to be postponed; to be removed; to be ended; to be terminated; to resign.

हटवाना *(haṭvānā)* स. क्रि. to cause to remove or terminate etc.

हटाना *(haṭānā)* स. क्रि. to take away; to remove; to move out; to set aside.

हट्टा-कट्टा *(haṭṭā-kaṭṭā)* वि. stout and active; strong and sturdy; welस.built; robust; healthy and hefty.

हठ *(haṭh)* पु. stubbornness; obstinacy; firm pledge; resolve; adamancy.

हठात् *(haṭhāt)* क्रि. वि. forcibly; per force; suddenly; all of a sudden.

हठी *(haṭhī)* वि. obstinate; stubborn; adamant.

हठीला *(haṭhīlā)* वि. of obstinate disposition; of firm pledge; determined; resolved.

हड़कंप *(haṛakamp)* पु. turmoil; panic; terror.

हड़ताल *(haṛtāl)* स्त्री. strike.

हड़पना *(haṛapanā)* स. क्रि. to usurp; to purloin; to grab; to swallow; to gulp; to eat hastily.

हड़बड़ाना *(haṛbaṛānā)* अ. क्रि. to be in a hurry; to act hastily; to be impatient; to be confused; to be agitated; to be non-plussed; to flurry; to confuse; to perplex.

हड़बड़ाहट, हड़बड़ी *(haṛbaṛī)* स्त्री. haste; hastiness; rashness; impetuosity; confusion.

हड्डी *(haḍḍī)* स्त्री. bone.

हत *(hat)* वि. killed; slain; hurt;

struck; injured.

हतप्रभ *(hatprabh)* वि. dimmed in lustre; out of wits; nonplussed.

हताश *(hatāsh)* वि. dejected; frustrated; despondent.

हताशा *(hatāshā)* स्त्री. frustration; despondency; dejection.

हताहत *(hattāhat)* वि. killed and wounded.

हतोत्साह *(hatotsāh)* वि. demoralised; disheartened.

हत्था *(hatthā)* पु. handle; butt; batten; imprint or impression by hand; arm (of a chair); a large bunch of bananas.

हत्या *(hatyā)* स्त्री. slaughter; murder; assassination.

हत्याकांड *(hatyākand)* पु. murder; assassination.

हत्यारा *(hatyārā)* पु. murderer; assassin.

हथकंडा *(hathkandā)* पु. trick; intrigue; tactics.

हथकड़ी *(hatkarī)* स्त्री. handcuffs.

हथगोला *(hathgolā)* पु. hand grenade.

हथियाना *(hathiyānā)* स. क्रि. to grab; to usurp; to seize; to acquire by force; to take in hand.

हथियार *(hathiyār)* पु. weapon; arms.

हथेली *(hathelī)* स्त्री. palm of the hand.

हथौड़ा *(hathaurā)* स्त्री. large hammer.

हथौड़ी *(hathaurī)* स्त्री. small hammer.

हद *(had)* स्त्री. limit; extent; extreme; extremity; boundary; limit of propriety.

हदबंदी *(hadbandī)* स्त्री. demarcation; delimitation.

हफ़्ता *(haftā)* पु. (फ़ा.) week.

हम *(ham)* सर्व. we.

हमउम्र *(ham-umr)* वि. of equal age.

हमख़याल *(hamkhyāl)* वि. (फ़ा.) having similar views.

हमजोली *(hamjolī)* पु. associate; companion; friend.

हमदर्द *(hamdard)* वि. (फ़ा.) sympathetic; tenderhearted.

हमदर्दी *(hamdardī)* स्त्री. (फ़ा.) sympathy.

हमराह *(hamrāha)* वि. travelling together.

हमराही *(hamrāhī)* पु. (फ़ा.) traveller; co-traveller.

हमल *(haml)* पु. (अ.) pregnancy; conception.

हमला *(hamlā)* पु. (अ.) attack; invasion; assault; blow; stroke.

हमलावर *(hamlāvar)* पु. (अ.) assailant; invader; aggressor.

हमवतन *(hamvatan)* पु. (फ़ा.) compatriot.

हमवार *(hamvār)* वि. (फ़ा.) even; plain; level.

हमशक्ल *(hamśakal)* वि. (फ़ा.) having similar appearance.

हमसफ़र *(hamsafar)* see हमराही।

हमाम *(hamām)* see हम्माम।

हमारा *(hamārā)* सर्व. our; ours.

हमें *(hamem)* सर्व. us; to us; for us.

हमेशा *(hameśā)* क्रि. वि. (फ़ा.) always; ever; continually; perpetually; incessantly.

हम्माम *(hammām)* पु. (अ.) bathroom.

हया *(hayā)* स्त्री. (अ.) shame; sense of shame; modesty.

हयात *(hayāt)* स्त्री. (अ.) life; soul.

हर *(har)* वि. (फ़ा.) every; each.

हरएक *(harek)* वि. every; each.

हरकहीं *(harkahin)* क्रि. वि. everywhere.

हरकत *(harkat)* स्त्री. (अ.) motion; movement; action; activity; vibration; pulsation; throbbing; improper or bad action; misdemeanour; mischief.

हरकारा *(harkārā)* पु. (फ़ा.) courier; messenger.

हरण *(haraṇ)* पु. seizure; kidnapping; abduction; removal; destruction; deprivation.

हरना *(harnā)* स. क्रि. to take away; to seize; to remove; to destroy; to captivate; to charm; to attract; to kidnap; to abduct.

हरफ़नमौला *(harfanmaulā)* वि. (फ़ा.) expert in all trades.

हरम *(haram)* पु. (अ.) harem; women's appartment in a royal household.

हरषाना *(harśanā)* अ. क्रि. to rejoice; to fill with joy.

हरा *(harā)* वि. green; verdant; verdurous; half raw; unripe; fresh; gay; delighted; unhealed (wound).

हरापन *(harāpan)* पु. greenness; greenery.

हराना *(harānā)* स. क्रि. to defeat; overcome; overthrow; conquer; to weary; tire out.

हरा-भरा *(harā-bharā)* वि. verdurous covered with green; verdant.

हराम *(harām)* वि. (अ.) forbidden; prohibited; unlawful; abandonable; renounceable; unacceptable; troublesome; painful; distressing; unpleasant; improper.

हरामी *(harāmī)* वि. illegitimate; unscrupulous; utterly indolent.

हरिजन *(harijan)* पु. an untouchable; a devotee of God.

हरिण *(hariṇ)* पु. a dear; antelope.

हरित *(harit)* वि. green; fresh; verdurous; covered with green; verdant; grassy; delighted; gay.

हरियाली *(hariyālī)* स्त्री. devotion to God.

हरीतिमा *(harītimā)* स्त्री. greenery; verdure; verdancy.

हर्ज, हर्जा *(harjā)* पु. (फ़ा.) loss; harm; damage; interruption; obstacle; delay.

हर्फ़ *(harf)* पु. (अ.) letter (of the alphabet).

हर्ष *(harṣ)* पु. joy; delight; pleasure jubilation; gladness; rapture; glee.

हर्षध्वनि *(harṣ-dhvanī)* स्त्री. jubilation; cry of joy.

हर्षविह्वल *(harṣ-vihal)* वि. overwhelmed with joy.

हर्षाना *(harsānā)* अ. क्रि. to be delighted; to be jubilant.

हर्षित *(harṣit)* वि. delighted; happy; cheerful.

हल *(hal)* पु. plough; solution; working out; answer.

हलक़ *(halaq)* पु. (अ.) throat; windpipe.

हलक़ा *(halqā)* पु. (अ.) zone; area; region.

हलका *(halkā)* वि. light; mild; soft; gentle; faint; dim; easy; free from burden or responsibility; easy to digest; digestible; inferior.

हलकापन *(halkāpan)* पु. lightness; mildness; shallowness; easiness; cheapness; freshness; inferiority; thinness.

हलचल *(halcal)* वि. commotion; hustle; tumult; agitation; movement; perturbation.

हलदी *(haldī)* स्त्री. turmeric; curcuma.

हलफ़ *(half)* पु. (अ.) oath.

हलफ़नामा *(halfnāmā)* पु. (अ.) declaration on oath; affidavit.

हलवा *(halvā)* पु. typical Indian pudding.

हलवाई *(halvāī)* पु. confectioner; sweet-seller.

हलवाहा *(halvāhā)* पु. ploughman; tiller.

हलाल *(halāl)* वि. (अ.) legitimate; lawful; having religious sanction; hard-earned.

हलाहल *(halāhal)* पु. poison.

हल्ला *(hallā)* पु. uproar; tumult; attack; assault.

हवन *(havan)* स्त्री. offering an oblation with fire; a fire sacrifice.

हवस *(havas)* पु. lust; concupiscence; zeal; gusto; greed; false love.

हवा *(havā)* स्त्री. air; wind; breeze; breath; undesirable effect or impact; evil spirit; ghost; fame; credit; remour.

हवाई *(havāī)* वि. of or pertaining to air; airy; aerial.

हवाई अड्डा *(havāī-addā)* पु. aerodrome; airport.

हवाई छतरी *(havāī-cātri)* स्त्री. parachute.

हवाईजहाज़ *(havāī-jahaz)* पु. aeroplane; aircraft.

हवादार *(havādār)* वि. airy; well-ventilated.

हवाबाज़ *(havābāz)* पु. aeronaut; pilot.

हवाला *(havālā)* पु. reference; allusion; citation; quotation.

हवालात *(havālāt)* स्त्री. (अ.) custody-room; custody; lock-up.

हश्र *(haśr)* पु. (अ.) catastrophe; doom's day; disturbance; calamity.

हसरत *(hasrat)* स्त्री. (अ.) sorrow; regret for an unaccomplished thing; wish; aspiration; longing.

हसीन *(hasīn)* वि. (अ.) beautiful; charming; attractive

हसीना *(hasīnā)* स्त्री. beautiful woman.

हस्त *(hast)* पु. hand; cubit.

हस्तक्षेप *(hastśep)* पु. interference; meddling.

हस्तगत *(hastgat)* वि. fallen into one's possession; obtained; secured; received.

हस्तरेखा *(hastrekhā)* स्त्री. the lines of one's palm (studied in palmistry).

हस्तलिखित *(hastlikhit)* वि. handwritten; in manuscript form.

हस्तलिपि *(hastlipi)* स्त्री. handwriting; manuscript.

हस्तशिल्प *(hastsilp)* पु. handicraft.

हस्तांतरण *(hastāṇtaran)* पु. transfer; transference.

हस्तांतरित *(hastāṇtrit)* वि. transfered.

हस्ताक्षर *(hastākśer)* पु. signature.

हस्ताक्षरकर्ता *(hastākśerkartā)* पु. signatory.

हस्ताक्षरित *(hastākśrīt)* वि. signed.

हस्ती *(hastī)* स्त्री. (फ़ा.) existence; being; life; worth; value; significance.

हहरना *(haharna)* अ. क्रि. to tremble; to shiver; to quiver; to be wonderstruck; to be astonished; to be agitated with jealousy.

हहराना *(haharānā)* स. क्रि. to terrrify; to frighten.

हाँ¹ *(hāṁ)* स्त्री. affirmative; consent.

हाँ² *(hāṁ)* क्रि. वि. yes.

हाँक *(hāṁk)* स्त्री. loud call; outcry or entreaty for help; halloo; cry of challenge.

हाँकना *(hāṁknā)* स. क्रि. to call aloud; to halloo; to challenge loudly; to urge on; to goad (animal); to drive (animal-driven vehicle); to drive away (fly etc.) by fan air.

हाँपना, हाँफना *(hāṁphnā)* अ. क्रि. to pant; to be out of breath; to breathe heavily.

हाकिम *(hākim)* पु. (अ.) ruler; boss; officer.

हाज़मा *(hāzmā)* पु. (अ.) digestion; digestive function; digestive power.

हाज़िर *(hāzir)* वि. (अ.) present; in attendance; ready; prepared.

हाज़िर-जवाब *(hāzir-javāb)* वि. (अ.) quick witted; ready witted; witty.

हाज़िर-जवाबी *(hāzir-javābī)* स्त्री. (अ.) quick wittedness; ready wit.

हाज़िरी *(hāzirī)* स्त्री. presence; attendance; rolस.call.

हाट *(hāṭ)* स्त्री. a temporary and periodic market; market; bazar.

हाटक¹ *(hāṭak)* पु. gold; stramonium; thorn-apple (dhatura); rent of shop.

हाटक² *(hāṭak)* वि. made of gold.

हाथ *(hāth)* पु. arm; fore-arm; cubit; inspiration; cooperation; contribution; share; involvement; manual skill; turn in a game of cards; etc.; handle.

हाथापाई *(hāthāpaī)* स्त्री. scuffie; struggle; tussle; exchange of blows.

हाथी *(hāthi)* पु. elephant; (at chess) the castle or rook.

हाथीदाँत *(hāthīdāmt)* पु. elephant's tusk; ivory.

हाथीपाँव *(hāthipamv)* पु. elephantiasis.

हाथों-हाथ *(hāthon-hāth)* क्रि. वि. in no time; immediately; quickly; expeditiously; on the spot; at the spur of the moment; then and there.

हानि *(hāni)* स्त्री. loss; damage; harm; destruction; relinquishement.

हानिक *(hānik)* वि. causing loss or injury etc.; injurious; harmful; damaging; detrimental.

हामी *(hāmī)* स्त्री. acceptance.

हाय *(hāy)* स्त्री. ah! alas!; oh!;

हार¹ *(har)* स्त्री. defeat; loss.

हार² *(har)* पु. garland; necklace.

हारना *(hārnā)* अ. क्रि. to be defeated; to lose (in battle; play etc.); to be unsuccessful; to fail; to be fatigued; to be tired out; to be wearied; to lose; to let go; to give up; to hand over.

हारीत *(hārīt)* पु. thief; rogue; theft; cheating; a kind of pigeon.

हार्दिक *(hārdik)* वि. hearty; cordial.

हाल¹ *(hāl)* पु. present time; recent time; condition; state; account; news; statement; trance; ecastasy.

हाल² *(hāl)* स्त्री. hoop or metallic tyre over wooden wheel; movement; jerk.

हाल-चाल *(hāस.cāl)* पु. general welfare; state of affairs; news.

हालत *(hālat)* स्त्री. (अ.) state; condition.

हाला *(hālā)* स्त्री. wine; liquor.

हावी *(hāvī)* वि. (अ.) dominant.

हाशिया *(hāśiyā)* पु. (अ.) margin; border; fringe.

हास *(hās)* पु. laughter; fun; joke; derisive laughter; derision; ridicule; mockery; happiness.

हासिल *(hāsil)* वि. (अ.) acquired. obtained; carried; forward; remaining.

हास्य¹ *(hāsya)* पु. laughter; smile; derisive laughter; derision; ridicule; mockery; the sentiment of mirth or humour (one of the nine sentiments in poetry).

हास्य² *(hāsya)* वि. laughable; ridiculous.

हास्यास्पद *(hāsyaspad)* वि. ridiculous; funny.

हास्योत्पादक *(hāsyotpādak)* वि. provoking laughter; funny; humorous; ridiculous.

हाहाकार *(hāhākār)* पु. lamentation; loud wailing.

हिंडोला *(hiṇḍolā)* पु. swing; cradle.

हिंदी¹ *(hindī)* पु. Indian.

हिंदी² *(hindī)* स्त्री. Hindi language.

हिंदुत्व *(hindutva)* पु. Hinduism.

हिंदुस्तान *(hindustān)* पु. (फ़ा.) India.

हिंदुस्तानी *(hindustani)* वि. (फ़ा.) Indian.

हिंसक *(hiṃsak)* वि. murderous; fierce; ferocious; hurtful; injurious; fatal; violent.

हिंसा *(hiṁsā)* स्त्री. killing; murder; injury; mischief; wrong; harm; hurt; violence.

हिंसात्मक *(hiṃsātmak)* वि. injuriour; violent.

हिंस्त्र¹ *(hiṃsra)* वि. murderous; fierce; ferocious; savage; evil; cruel.

हिंस्त्र² *(hiṃsra)* पु. person rejoicing in the distress of others; cruelty; beast.

हिकमत *(hikmat)* स्त्री. (अ.) contrivance; manoeuvre; device; medical practice (under the Yunani system); intelligence; wisdom.

हिक़ारत *(hiqārat)* स्त्री. contempt; scorn; derision.

हिचक *(hicak)* स्त्री. hitch; hesitation.

हिचकना *(hicaknā)* अ. क्रि. to hesitate; to shilly-shally; to hiccup; to hiccough.

हिचकिचाना *(hickicānā)* अ. क्रि. to hesitate; to shilly-shally.

हिचकी *(hicki)* स्त्री. hiccough; hiccup.

हिचकोला *(hickolā)* पु. jerk; jolt.

हिजड़ा¹ *(hijṛā)* पु. eunuch.

हिजड़ा² *(hijṛā)* वि. impotent; cowardly.

हिज्जे *(hijje)* पु. (अ.) spelling.

हित *(hit)* पु. welfare; welस.being; good; benefit; gain; advantage; interest.

हितकर *(hitkar)* वि. beneficial; useful; advantageous.

हितकारी *(hitkārī)* पु. benefactor.

हितैषी *(hitaiśi)* वि. desiring others welfare; benevolent.

हिदायत *(hidāyat)* स्त्री. (अ.) instruction; guidance.

हिफ़ाज़त *(hifāzat)* स्त्री. (अ.) protection; security; safety.

हिम *(him)* पु. frost; hoar-frost.

हिमगिरि *(himgirī)* पु. the Himalayas.

हिमपात *(himpāt)* पु. snow-fall.

हिमांशु *(himānśu)* पु. moon.

हिमाक़त *(himāqat)* *स्त्री.* (*अ.*) foolishness; folly; stupidity.

हिमाच्छन्न *(himācānn)* *वि.* icecovered; snow-covered.

हिमायत *(himāyat)* *स्त्री.* (*अ.*) support; backing; protection; defence.

हिमायती *(himāyatī)* *पु.* (*अ.*) supporter; protector; defender.

हिमालय *(himālaya)* *पु.* the Himalayas.

हिम्मत *(himmat)* *स्त्री.* (*अ.*) spirit; courage; boldness; firmness; resoluteness.

हिम्मती *(himmatī)* *वि.* (*अ.*) courageous; bold.

हिया *(hiyā)* *पु.* heart; bosom; courage.

हिरन *(hiran)* *पु.* deer; antelope.

हिरासत *(hirāsat)* *स्त्री.* (*फ़ा.*) custody; charge; lock-up; custodyroom.

हिलकोर *(hilkor)* *स्त्री.* surge; billow; wave.

हिलकोरना *(hilkornā)* *स. क्रि.* to stir (water).

हिलकोरा *(hilkorā)* *पु.* see हिलकोर।

हिलगना *(hilagnā)* *अ. क्रि.* to be associated; to be attached; to hold fast.

हिलगाना *(hilagānā)* *स. क्रि.* to cause to adhere; to attach; to fix.

हिलना *(hilna)* *अ. क्रि.* to move; to stir; to shake; to tremble; to undulte; to wave; to swing in a gay mood or intoxication; to sway to and fro; to get loose; to slacken; to be flickering; to be unsteady (to mind); to be familiar; to slip; to slide.

हिलाना *(hilana)* *स. क्रि.* to shake or rock; to move; to stir; to cause to slip or slide; to cause to tremble; to familiarize; to cause to get intimate; to cause to be fickle or unsteady; to swing; to move to and fro.

हिलोर *(hilor)* *स्त्री.* wave; billow; surge.

हिसाब *(hisāb)* *पु.* (*अ.*) arithmetic; calculation; account; rate; manner.

हिस्सा *(hissā)* *पु.* (*अ.*) component; constituent; part; portion; division; fragment; portion (of partition); share (of capital); divident.

हिस्सेदार *(hissedār)* *पु.* (*अ.*) shareholder; co-sharer; party; partner.

हीन *(hīn)* *वि.* destitute or deprived; bereft; causing concern or anxiety; worthless; insignificant; trivial; inferior; lower; low; base; mean; vile.

हीनता *(hīntā)* *स्त्री.* destitution; deprivation (in comp); worthlessness; insignificance; inferiority; low-liness; meanness; baseness; vileness.

हीनबुद्धि *(hīnbudhī)* *वि.* stupid; nitwitted.

हीरा *(hīrā)* *पु.* diamond.

हुंकार *(huṁkār)* *पु.* call of challenge or halloing; voice of defiance; roaring; bellowing in general; shouting; cry.

हुंकारना *(huṁkārnā)* *अ. क्रि.* to challenge loudly (of a fight); to shout; to cry; to roar; to bellow.

हुंडी *(huṇḍī)* *स्त्री.* bill of exchange; bill; draft; bond; debenture.

हुकूमत *(hukūmat)* *स्त्री.* (*अ.*) sway; rule; control; government; reign.

हुक़्क़ा *(huqqā)* *पु.* (*अ.*) hubble-bubble.

हुक्म *(hukm)* पु. (अ.) order; command; judgement; verdict; ordinance; statute; regulation; one of the suits in playing cards; the spade; control.

हुक्म उदूली *(hukm-uduli)* स्त्री. (अ.) disobedience; insubordination.

हुक्मनामा *(hukmnāmā)* पु. (अ.) edict; written order.

हुजूम *(hujūm)* पु. (अ.) crowd; gathering.

हुजूर *(huzūr)* पु. (अ.) gracious presence; royal presence; court (of a king or superior authority); your honour; your majesty; your lordship; sir.

हुज्जत *(hujjat)* स्त्री. (अ.) wrangling; disputation; altercation; contention; obstinacy; objection.

हुड़दंग *(hurdang)* पु. noise; tumult; commotion; uproar; rowdyism; hooliganism.

हुतात्मा *(hutātmā)* पु. martyr.

हुनर *(hunar)* पु. (फ़ा.) art; craft; skill; competence; ability.

हुलसना *(hulasnā)* अ. क्रि. to be gladdened; to be rejoiced; to be pleased; to be delighted.

हुलसाना *(hulsānā)* स. क्रि. to gladden; to delight; to exhilarate; to cheer.

हुलिया *(huliyā)* स्त्री. appearance; form physical feature; description of the face or countenance; description of physical features.

हुल्लड़ *(hullar)* पु. noise; uproar; tumult; commotion; disturbance; riot.

हूक *(hūk)* स्त्री. shooting pain (in heart); ache; smarting agony; (mental) affliction; lingering agony.

हुकना *(hūknā)* अ. क्रि. to ache; to feel pain.

हूबहू *(hū-ba-hū)* वि. exactly similar.

हूर *(hūr)* स्त्री. (अ.) virgin of paradise; nymph; fairy.

हृत *(hṛt)* पु. part; portion.

हृदय *(hṛday)* पु. heart; conscience; bosom; chest; breast; the interior or essence of any thing; core.

हृदयगत *(hṛdaygat)* वि. hearty; dwelling in the heart; mentally assimilated.

हृदयग्राही *(hṛdayagrāhi)* वि. heart-captivating; charming; interesting.

हृदयविदारक *(hṛdayavidārak)* वि. heart-rending; producing pathos; pathetic; pitiful; touching; poignant.

हृदयस्पर्शी *(hrday-sparśī)* वि. pathetic; heart-touching; poignant.

हृदयहारी *(hrday-hārī)* वि. charming; attractive

हर्षित *(hṛṣit)* वि. happy; joyful; thrilled; fresh; astonished.

हृष्टा *(hṛṣṭā)* वि. happy; thrilled; astonished; hard; inelastic; blunt.

हृष्ट-पुष्ट *(hṛṣṭ-pūst)* वि. stout; robust.

हेकड़ी *(hekṛī)* स्त्री. hubris; arrogance; bullysm; show of force or strength; stubbornness.

हेठा *(heṭhā)* वि. low; inferior; mean.

हेठी *(heṭhī)* स्त्री. insult; abasement; disgrace; dishonour; indignity; humiliation.

हेतु *(hetu)* पु. object; motive; purpose; cause; reason.

हेय *(hey)* वि. fit to be left or

abadoned; abominable; heinous; trifling; trivial.

हेरना *(hernā)* स. क्रि. to search (for); to see; to observe.

हेर-फेर *(her-pher)* पु. change; alteration; exchange; interchange; rotation (crops); manipulation.

हेरा-फेरी *(herā-pherī)* स्त्री. manipulation; unscrupulous activity; tempering; exchange; interchange.

हैरत *(hairat)* स्त्री. (अ.) amazement; consternation; astonishment.

हैरतअंगेज़ *(hairataṇgez)* वि. (अ.) astonishing; amazing.

हैरान *(hairān)* वि. (अ.) astonished; amazed; perplexed; disturbed; worried; troubled.

हैरानी *(hairānī)* स्त्री. (अ.) astonishment; amazement; confusion; perplexity; perturbation; distraction.

हैवान *(haivān)* पु. (अ.) animal; beast; brute; uncivil; person; savage.

हैवानियत *(haivāniyat)* स्त्री. (अ.) brutality; beastliness; cruelty; inhumanity.

हैसियत *(haisiyat)* स्त्री. (अ.) status; position; capacity; capability; property; wealth; prestige; importance.

होंठ, ओंठ *(homṭh)* पु. lip.

होड़ *(hoṛ)* स्त्री. rivalry; competition; wager; bet.

होनहार[1] *(honhār)* वि. inevitable; certain; sure; promising.

होनहार[2] *(honhār)* स्त्री. the inevitable; destiny.

होना *(honā)* अ. क्रि. to be; to exist; to continue; to last; to attain (to); to become; to carry in a particular state or position; to take place; to occur; happen; to be born; to result; to be effected; to pass; to be over; to come to an end; to belong;to be related to.

होनी *(honī)* स्त्री. destiny; fate; the inevitable.

होम *(hom)* पु. offering an oblation to fire.

होलिका *(holikā)* स्त्री. the Holi festival; heap of wood; straw etc. accumulated for holi.

होली *(holi)* स्त्री. the Holi festival; the pile of fuel prepared for bonfire in the night preceding the Holi festival; a class of songs sung during the months of Magh and phalgun in different modes; bonfire.

होश *(hoś)* पु. (फ़ा.) sense; consciousness; memory; recollection; reminiscence; understanding; judgement; intellect.

होशियार *(hośiyār)* पु. (फ़ा.) cautious; alert; careful; vigilant; clever; wise; intelligent; skilful; skilled; proficient; dexterous.

होशियारी *(hośiyārī)* स्त्री. (फ़ा.) caution; vigilance; watchfulness alertness; carefulness; cleverness; wisdom; intelligence; skilfulness; dexterity; proficiency.

हौआ *(hauā)* पु. an imaginary demon intended to terrorise children; bogey; bug-bear; scare crow.

हौज़ *(hauz)* पु. (अ.) tank; reservoir of water; sink; small pond; manger.

हौल *(haul)* पु. (अ.) horror; shock.

हौवा *(hauvā)* पु. (अ.) Eve; the first woman on earth regarded as the mother of mankind; bugaboo; bugbear; bogey; scare crow.

हौसला *(hauslā)* पु. (अ.) courage. spirit; morale; enthusiasm; zest; gusto; aspiration; longing; ambition; desire.

ह्रस्व[1] *(hrasva)* वि. short; small little (in size etc.); unstressed; unaccented.

ह्रस्व[2] *(hrasva)* पु. short vowel; unaccented syllable.

ह्रास *(hrās)* पु. decay; waste; decline; fall; dawn-fall; diminution decrease.

ह्रासोन्मुख *(hrāsonṁukh)* वि. decaying; diminishing; decadent.